LET'S GO

■ THE RESOURCE FOR THE INDEPENDENT TRAVELER

"The guides are aimed not only at young budget travelers but at the independent traveler; a sort of streetwise cookbook for traveling alone."

—The New York Times

"Unbeatable; good sight-seeing advice; up-to-date info on restaurants, hotels, and inns; a commitment to money-saving travel; and a wry style that brightens nearly every page."

—The Washington Post

"Lighthearted and sophisticated, informative and fun to read. [Let's Go] helps the novice traveler navigate like a knowledgeable old hand."

—Atlanta Journal-Constitution

"A world-wise traveling companion—always ready with friendly advice and helpful hints, all sprinkled with a bit of wit."

—The Philadelphia Inquirer

■ THE BEST TRAVEL BARGAINS IN YOUR PRICE RANGE

"All the dirt, dirt cheap."

—People

"Anything you need to know about budget traveling is detailed in this book."

—The Chicago Sun-Times

"Let's Go follows the creed that you don't have to toss your life's savings to the wind to travel—unless you want to."

—The Salt Lake Tribune

■ REAL ADVICE FOR REAL EXPERIENCES

"The writers seem to have experienced every rooster-packed bus and lunar-surfaced mattress about which they write."

—The New York Times

"A guide should tell you what to expect from a destination. Here Let's Go shines."

—The Chicago Tribune

LET'S GO PUBLICATIONS

TRAVEL GUIDES

Alaska & the Pacific Northwest 2003
Australia 2003
Austria & Switzerland 2003
Britain & Ireland 2003
California 2003
Central America 8th edition
Chile 1st edition **NEW TITLE**
China 4th edition
Costa Rica 1st edition **NEW TITLE**
Eastern Europe 2003
Egypt 2nd edition
Europe 2003
France 2003
Germany 2003
Greece 2003
Hawaii 2003 **NEW TITLE**
India & Nepal 7th edition
Ireland 2003
Israel 4th edition
Italy 2003
Mexico 19th edition
Middle East 4th edition
New Zealand 6th edition
Peru, Ecuador & Bolivia 3rd edition
South Africa 5th edition
Southeast Asia 8th edition
Southwest USA 2003
Spain & Portugal 2003
Thailand 1st edition **NEW TITLE**
Turkey 5th edition
USA 2003
Western Europe 2003

CITY GUIDES

Amsterdam 2003
Barcelona 2003
Boston 2003
London 2003
New York City 2003
Paris 2003
Rome 2003
San Francisco 2003
Washington, D.C. 2003

MAP GUIDES

Amsterdam
Berlin
Boston
Chicago
Dublin
Florence
Hong Kong
London
Los Angeles
Madrid
New Orleans
New York City
Paris
Prague
Rome
San Francisco
Seattle
Sydney
Venice
Washington, D.C.

EUROPE
2003

JEFFREY DUBNER EDITOR

JENNIFER MAY-ANNE CHEN ASSOCIATE EDITOR
TABATHA L. GEORGE ASSOCIATE EDITOR
MATTHEW K. HUDSON ASSOCIATE EDITOR
KALEN J.S. INGRAM ASSOCIATE EDITOR
HANNAH J. TRIERWEILER ASSOCIATE EDITOR

RESEARCHER-WRITERS
JANE CAFLISCH
NICK TOPJIAN

JULIE STEPHENS MAP EDITOR
CELESTE NG MANAGING EDITOR
JOHN ATA BACHMAN TYPESETTER

ST. MARTIN'S PRESS ☙ NEW YORK

HELPING LET'S GO If you want to share your discoveries, suggestions, or corrections, please drop us a line. We read every piece of correspondence, whether a postcard, a 10-page email, or a coconut. Please note that mail received after May 2003 may be too late for the 2004 book, but will be kept for future editions. **Address mail to:**

> Let's Go: Europe
> 67 Mount Auburn Street
> Cambridge, MA 02138
> USA

Visit Let's Go at **http://www.letsgo.com,** or send email to:

> **feedback@letsgo.com**
> **Subject: "Let's Go: Europe"**

In addition to the invaluable travel advice our readers share with us, many are kind enough to offer their services as researchers or editors. Unfortunately, our charter enables us to employ only currently enrolled Harvard students.

WHO WE ARE

A NEW LET'S GO FOR 2003

With a sleeker look and innovative new content, we have revamped the entire series to reflect more than ever the needs and interests of the independent traveler. Here are just some of the improvements you will notice when traveling with the new *Let's Go*.

MORE PRICE OPTIONS

Still the best resource for budget travelers, *Let's Go* recognizes that everyone needs the occassional indulgence. Our "Big Splurges" indicate establishments that are actually worth those extra pennies (pulas, pesos, or pounds), and price-level symbols (❶ ❷ ❸ ❹ ❺) allow you to quickly determine whether an accommodation or restaurant will break the bank. We may have diversified, but we'll never lose our budget focus—"Hidden Deals" reveal the best-kept travel secrets.

BEYOND THE TOURIST EXPERIENCE

Our Alternatives to Tourism chapter offers ideas on immersing yourself in a new community through study, work, or volunteering.

AN INSIDER'S PERSPECTIVE

As always, every item is written and researched by our on-site writers. This year we have highlighted more viewpoints to help you gain an even more thorough understanding of the places you are visiting.

IN RECENT NEWS. *Let's Go* correspondents around the globe report back on current regional issues that may affect you as a traveler.

CONTRIBUTING WRITERS. Respected scholars and former *Let's Go* writers discuss topics on society and culture, going into greater depth than the usual guidebook summary.

THE LOCAL STORY. From the Parisian monk toting a cell phone to the Russian *babushka* confronting capitalism, *Let's Go* shares its revealing conversations with local personalities—a unique glimpse of what matters to real people.

FROM THE ROAD. Always helpful and sometimes downright hilarious, our researchers share useful insights on the typical (and atypical) travel experience.

SLIMMER SIZE

Don't be fooled by our new, smaller size. *Let's Go* is still packed with invaluable travel advice, but now it's easier to carry with a more compact design.

FORTY-THREE YEARS OF WISDOM

For over four decades *Let's Go* has provided the most up-to-date information on the hippest cafes, the most pristine beaches, and the best routes from border to border. It all started in 1960 when a few well-traveled students at Harvard University handed out a 20-page mimeographed pamphlet of their tips on budget travel to passengers on student charter flights to Europe. From humble beginnings, *Let's Go* has grown to cover six continents and *Let's Go: Europe* still reigns as the world's best-selling travel guide. This year we've beefed up our coverage of Latin America with *Let's Go: Costa Rica* and *Let's Go: Chile;* on the other side of the globe, we've added *Let's Go: Thailand* and *Let's Go: Hawaii.* Our new guides bring the total number of titles to 61, each infused with the spirit of adventure that travelers around the world have come to count on.

HOW TO USE THIS BOOK

If you're reading this, you're probably about to embark on a grand tour of Europe—maybe your first, maybe your seventeenth. For the 43rd year in a row, *Let's Go: Europe* is here to guide you to the grandest cathedrals, the cleanest hostels, and the finest €1.20 wines. Things are changing in Europe: you can now travel between half the countries on the continent without so much as pulling out your passport, and you're more likely to come across an Internet terminal than a phone that takes a simple little coin. It's a pretty different place than you may remember—but we've been keeping up. Whether you're a globetrotter from way back or an international newbie, the freshly reformatted and always updated *Let's Go: Europe 2003* will tell you everything you need to know. Just sit back and let go.

ORGANIZATION. *Let's Go: Europe* is arranged to make the information you need easy to find. The **Discover** chapter offers highlights of the region, tips on when to travel (including a calendar of festivals), and suggested itineraries. **Essentials** details the nitty-gritty of passports, money, communications, and more—everything you'll need to plan your trip and stay safe on the road. The **Transportation** section will get you to and around Europe, while **Alternatives to Tourism** gives advice on how to work or volunteer your way across the continent. Next come 38 jam-packed **country chapters**, from Andorra to Ukraine; each begins with essential information on traveling in that specific country. At the back is a **language appendix** (p. 1051), a crash course in 24 local dialects to help you navigate along your way.

PRICE RANGES AND RANKINGS. Our researchers list establishments in order of value from best to worst. Our absolute favorites are denoted by the Let's Go thumbs-up (🖑). Since the best value does not always mean the cheapest price, we have incorporated a system of **price ranges** (❶❷❸❹❺) into our coverage of accommodations and restaurants. At a glance, you can compare the cost of a night's stay in towns a mile apart or halfway across the country. The price ranges for each country can be found in the introductory sections of each chapter.

NEW FEATURES. Long-time readers will notice a number of other changes in *Europe 2003*, most notably the sidebars that accompany much of our coverage. The **Your Own Way** boxes, for instance, highlight lesser-known destinations where you can chart your own path and spend days or months discovering hidden gems. We've listed only the bare-bones details—enough description to whet your appetite and enough transportation and contact information to get your journey off the ground; the rest is up to you. You should also take a look at the **Scholarly Articles** (p. 1067), found just after the language tables, which offer a more penetrating look at some of the important issues dominating European society at the moment.

ENJOY YOUR TRIP. Need we say more?

A NOTE TO OUR READERS The information for this book was gathered by *Let's Go* researchers from May through August of 2002. Each listing is based on one researcher's opinion, formed during his or her visit at a particular time. Those traveling at other times may have different experiences since prices, dates, hours, and conditions are always subject to change. You are urged to check the facts presented in this book beforehand to avoid inconvenience and surprises.

CONTENTS

ACKNOWLEDGMENTS IX

DISCOVER EUROPE 1
What to Do 2
Suggested Itineraries 6

ESSENTIALS 12
Documents and Formalities 12
Money 15
Safety and Security 18
Health and Insurance 20
Packing 24
Accommodations 25
Communication 32
Specific Concerns 35
Other Resources 40

TRANSPORTATION 43
Getting to Europe 43
Getting around Europe 52

ALTERNATIVES
TO TOURISM 68
Studying Abroad 68
Working 70
Volunteering 72

ANDORRA 74

AUSTRIA 76
Carinthia (Kärnten) 93
Salzburger Land and Upper Austria 94
Tyrol (Tirol) 102

BELARUS 107

BELGIUM 111
Flanders (Vlaanderen) 121
Wallonie 127

BOSNIA AND
HERZEGOVINA 129

BRITAIN 135
ENGLAND 140
London 140
Southern England 168
East Anglia and the Midlands 174
Northern England 183
WALES 191
SCOTLAND 196

BULGARIA 214

CROATIA 227
Northern Coast 232
Dalmatian Coast 234

CYPRUS 240

CZECH REPUBLIC 243
West and South Bohemia 261
Moravia 265

DENMARK 268
Jutland (Jylland) 286

ESTONIA 291

FINLAND 300

FRANCE 317
Normandy (Normandie) 352
Loire Valley (Val de Loire) 359
Périgord and Aquitaine 363
The Pays Basque and Gascony 366
Languedoc-Roussillon 368
Provence 370
French Riviera (Côte d'Azur) 376
Corsica (La Corse) 386
The Alps (Les Alpes) 389
Lyon 392
Berry-Limousin 397
Burgundy (Bourgogne) 397
Alsace-Lorraine and Franche-Comté 398
Champagne and the North 402

GERMANY 407
Eastern Germany 432
Northern Germany 440
Central and West Germany 447
Southwest Germany 457
Bavaria (Bayern) 464

GREECE 481
The Peloponnese 493
Northern and Central Greece 498
Ionian Islands 503
The Sporades 505
The Cyclades 507
Crete 510
Eastern Aegean Islands 512

HUNGARY 516

ICELAND 538

REPUBLIC OF IRELAND AND
NORTHERN IRELAND 550
Southeast Ireland 564
Southwest Ireland 566
Western Ireland 572
Northwest Ireland 577
NORTHERN IRELAND 579

ITALY 587
The Veneto 618
Friuli-Venezia Giulia 631
Piedmont (Piemonte) 632
The Lake Country 633

The Dolomites (Dolomiti) 634
Lombardy (Lombardia) 635
Italian Riviera (Liguria) 642
Emilia-Romagna 646
Tuscany (Toscana) 650
Umbria 662
The Marches (Le Marche) 663
Southern Italy 664
Amalfi Coast 668
Sicily (Sicilia) 671
Sardinia (Sardegna) 673

LATVIA **675**

LIECHTENSTEIN **683**

LITHUANIA **685**

LUXEMBOURG **695**

MOROCCO **704**

THE NETHERLANDS **716**

NORWAY **744**
The Fjords and West Country 759
Southern Norway 767
Farther North 770

POLAND **772**

PORTUGAL **801**
Central Portugal 813
Algarve 815
Northern Portugal 817

ROMANIA **822**
Transylvania (Transilvania) 830
Moldavia and Bukovina 833

RUSSIA **836**

SLOVAK REPUBLIC **863**
The Tatra Mountains (Tatry) 871

SLOVENIA **873**

SPAIN **881**
CENTRAL SPAIN 899
Castilla la Mancha 899
Castilla y León 902
Extremadura 905
SOUTHERN SPAIN 905
EASTERN SPAIN 924
NORTHEAST SPAIN 927
Cataluña 927
The Pyrenees 946
Navarra 947
Basque Country (País Vasco) 950
Balearic Islands 955
NORTHWESTERN SPAIN 957
Galicia (Galiza) 957
Asturias 958

SWEDEN **960**
Southern Sweden 975
Dalarna 980
Lapland (Sápmi) 983

SWITZERLAND **985**
GERMAN SWITZERLAND 989
Jungfrau Region 998
Valais 1000
FRENCH SWITZERLAND 1001
ITALIAN SWITZERLAND 1009

TURKEY **1011**
Aegean Coast 1028
Mediterranean Coast 1034
Central Turkey 1037
Cappadocia 1038

UKRAINE **1040**

LANGUAGE BASICS **1051**

ARTICLES **1067**

INDEX **1070**

ACKNOWLEDGMENTS

TEAM EUROPE WORSHIPS: Mama Celeste and Marla Mia. Julie, whose presence we always felt above our heads. The Fount of all that is Good and Wealthy: Noah. Eastern Europe, who dreamt of a society of brotherhood (only to be ground beneath the relentless heel of Capitalism). See Nick and Jane run. Prod for solving the unsolvable. Country guides too numerous to list. And many, many others.

JEFF THANKS: My AEs, whose work and care meant more to me and this book than anything else. To Kalen, who always beat us to work; to Tabby, who never failed to surprise us; to Jen, who was the baby in her own eyes only; to Hannah, who smiled the whole way through; and to Matt, who fears rivers. Nick and Jane, for making RW calls the highlights of each week. Celeste, whose efficiency helped us run like clockwork. Julie, whose path I hope to cross again. My family, for whose love I can never say enough thanks. Jenn, the best podmate this side of Vladivostok. Sarah, for stability (for starters). Pickles and Hatchet. Noah, for Doves and Wagner. Matt and Brian, for running the whole shebang. Alex and Michelle, for the bang that they missed. Aaron, Aarti, Matt, and Armando. Jon, Shawn, Taylor... and Alex? And, most importantly, all whose devotion to this company encouraged me to return for another year.

MATT THANKS: Team Europe: Tabby, for her warmth, Southern gentility, and graceful, if belated, Bow; Hannah, for her constant dilligence, incredible assistance, and easy laugh; Kalen, for her impressive dedication and some of the best stick-handling I've never seen; Jen, for re-introducing me to the simple joys of *Major League Baseball*; Bri, for showing us the way to Waterloo (see p.73), and Jeff, for making sure we weren't Napoleon.

HANNAH THANKS: Tabby for Santa Ana, Matt for conspiratorial confusion, Kalen for a.m. inspiration, Jen for "awww...," Bri for pats on the back, and Jeff for Kings of Convenience. Julie, Marla, Celeste, David, Kathleen, Sonja, Teresa, Jonelle, Andrew, and Eustace for wisdom. Lowell girls, H-West, Tess, Bennett, and Natalie for love. Sarah for keeping my chin up until it's done and done. Mom, Gordon, Dad, Deanna, John, Megan, and David—I love you.

TABBY THANKS: Hannah for always being on my page (re: boys), Matt for eloquence under fire and for making me laugh (Boom.), Kalen for knowing good beer, Jen for late-night company, Celeste for being amazing. Jeff for a truly outstanding job, and for keeping things light. Mom and Dad for love, and for being so smart. Maggie and Elvis for love and speaking their mind. Christy, forever my best friend. Justin for constant support. Erik for being there when I fell in love with Europe.

JEN THANKS: Jeff for hiring me, and for being hilarious and always patient—congratulations and good luck next year! Celeste, thanks for all the help and smiles. My dearest Hannah, Kalen, Matt, and Tabby get my love and awe (Noah: "awww") for being such wonderful co-AEs and keeping me sane. I owe many extra hugs to Mulky, Andy Poon, and Dave Bright. Special thanks to EEUR (The Motherland) for taking me under its wing. Incredible EEUR RWs: I love you! Mommy, Daddy, Ian, Pete, Julianne, and Abi, I love you too.

KALEN THANKS: The AEs—Tabby, Matt, Hannah, and Jen—we make a great team. Jeff, whose dedication to the job was inspiring. All the best next year as EIC. I have no doubt you will bring *Let's Go* to new heights. Celeste for keeping us calm and well fed. The fat camp crew—❆Sean, ❆Jody, Haigher, Space, Jim, Kat, Cull, and Ang—for keeping me energized. The McAuliffe family for your generosity. For a lifetime of love, Mom, Dad, David, and Kelsey—I've missed you this summer.

JULIE THANKS: Team Europe for super map edits. Jeff—my future partner in crime. Mapland for map raves and late night camaraderie. The MEs for a year of fun. 7 Story St. for good times. Michelle and Marla for good food and gossip. Kuba for reminding me that there is more to life than work. Mom, Dad, David, and Sarah for their patience, love, and support.

RESEARCHER-WRITERS

Jane Caflisch   *Finland and Sweden*

A demure student of religion, Jane was the perfect pair of eyes to take in every *kirkko* and cafe in the eastern half of Scandinavia. Not far removed from working on a trail crew in the Pacific Northwest, Jane scouted out some of the purest landscapes of northern Europe, from the exquisite island of Gotland up to remote Abisko. Quick to adapt and even quicker to befriend those along her way, Jane and her contributions to the book were simply invaluable.

Nick Topjian   *Iceland and Norway*

A veteran researcher who previously crossed the Czech Republic for the glorious *Let's Go: Eastern Europe 2001*, Nick sailed through Iceland and Norway without a moment's setback. Whether earning his way by playing guitar on the streets of Kristiansand or discovering the wonders that lie beyond from Tromsø, Nick forged his own itinerary and added a wealth of new nightlife listings and routes through the countryside and up the coast.

REGIONAL STAFF

LET'S GO: AMSTERDAM 2003
Sarah E. Kramer   *Editor*
Stefan Atkinson, Catherine Burch, Ian MacKenzie   *Amsterdam and the Netherlands*

LET'S GO: AUSTRIA & SWITZERLAND 2003
Joanna Shawn Brigid O'Leary   *Editor*
Deborah Harrison   *Associate Editor*
Jocelyn Beh   *Bernese Oberland, Italian Switzerland, Lucerne*
Alinna Chung   *Zurich, Basel, Bern, Geneva, Northern Switzerland*
Tom Miller   *Carinthia, Hohe Tauern Region, Tyrol, Vorarlberg*
Christine Peterson   *Niederösterreich, Salzburgerland, and Styria*
Lora Sweeney   *Vienna, Burgenland, Oberösterreich*

LET'S GO: BARCELONA 2003
Anna Elizabeth Byrne   *Editor*
Colleen Gargan, Rei Onishi, Adam Weiss   *Barcelona and Catalunya*

LET'S GO: BRITAIN & IRELAND 2003
Sonja Nikkila   *Editor*
Teresa Elsey   *Associate Editor*
Jenny Pegg   *Wales, Isle of Man, Midlands, Northwest England*
Angie Sun   *Midlands, Southwest, Heart of, and Northern England*
Sarah A. Tucker   *South and Heart of England, Midlands, East Anglia, Yorkshire*
John T. Witherspoon   *Glasgow, Central Scotland, Highlands, & Islands*
Daniel Zweifach   *Northern England, Southern and Central Scotland*

LET'S GO: EASTERN EUROPE 2003

Jennifer Anne O'Brien	Editor
Susan E. Bell, Rochelle Lundy, Mahmoud Youssef	Associate Editor
Charles L. Black	Russia
Dunia Dickey	Estonia, Latvia, Lithuania
Nicholas Gossen	Bosnia-Herzegovina, Croatia
Clay Kaminsky	Moldova, Romania
Sandra Nagy	Eastern Slovak Republic, Hungary
Matej Sapak	Bratislava
Werner Schäfer	Belarus, Ukraine
Stefanie Videka Sherman	Bulgaria, Romanian Black Sea Coast
Dalibor Eric Snyder	Czech Republic
Barbara Urbańcyzk	Poland
Vik Vaz	Slovenia, Western Slovak Republic

LET'S GO: FRANCE 2003

Annalise Nelson	Editor
Paul Eisenstein, Sarah Levine-Gronningsater	Associate Editors
Emily Buck	Loire Valley, Poitou-Charentes, Berry-Limousin, Périgord
Edward B. Colby	Provence, Lyon and the Auvergne, Burgundy
Laure "Voop" de Vulpillières	Champagne, Alsace-Lorraine, Flanders, Languedoc
Robert Madison	Côte d'Azure, Corsica, the Alps
Genevieve Sheehan	Brittany and Normandy
Julia Steele	Languedoc-Roussillon, Aquitane, Pays Basque

LET'S GO: GERMANY 2003

Jesse Reid Andrews	Editor
Karoun Demirjian	Associate Editor
Charlotte Douglas	North Rhine-Westphalia, Lower Saxony, and Bremen
Deidre Foley-Mendelssohn	Berlin, Potsdam, and Mecklenburg-Upper Pomerania
Paul G. Kofoed	Schleswig-Holstein, Hamburg, and Mecklenburg-Upper Pomerania
Patrick Morrissey	Saxony-Anhalt, Lower Saxony, Hessen, and Bavaria
Andrew Price	Saxony, Thuringia, Brandenburg, and Saxony-Anhalt
Matej Sapak	Hessen (Frankfurt), Baden Württemberg, Bavaria, and Rhineland-Palatine
Becky Windt	Bavaria

LET'S GO: GREECE 2003

Jonelle Lonergan	Editor
Andrew Zaroulis	Associate Editor
Kevin Connor	Central Greece, the Sporades, Saronic Gulf, and Northeast Aegean Islands
Gary Cooney	Central and Northern Greece
Emily Ogden	Cyprus and the Dodecanese
Geoffrey Reed	Crete, the Cyclades, and Northeast Aegean Islands
Jen Taylor	Peloponnese and Ionian Islands
Scottie Thompson	Athens and the Cyclades

CONTRIBUTING WRITERS

LET'S GO

Charles Ehrlich   *Reclaiming the Past*

Charles Ehrlich was a Researcher-Writer for *Let's Go: Spain, Portugal & Morocco.* He is a former Senior Staff Attorney at the Claims Resolution Tribunal that adjudicates claims to Swiss bank accounts from the Nazi era.

Jeremy Faro   *With or Without EU*

Jeremy Faro is a former Senior Consultant at Interbrand and has worked in the past on *Let's Go: Britain & Ireland.* He is currently a master's student in European Studies at Cambridge University.

Kathleen Holbrook   *Europe in Black & White*

Kate Holbrook is pursuing graduate work in Religion and Literature with a focus on globalization and human values. She was voted Harvard University's best teaching fellow in 2002.

Caitlin Hurley   *When in Rome*

Caitlin Hurley, a teacher at Marymount International School in Rome, was a Researcher-Writer for *Let's Go: USA 1994.*

Matthew Lazen   *Many Cultures, One Race*

Matthew Lazen spent two years in Brittany and Alsace on a Chateaubriand Fellowship for dissertation research on regional cultures in post-modern France. He is currently a lecturer in History & Literature at Harvard University.

Brian C.W. Palmer   *Europe in Black & White*
        Women and Children First

Brian Palmer, Ph.D., lectures on globalization at Harvard University and in Sweden. For a course which the New York Times nicknamed "Idealism 101," he was voted Harvard's best young faculty member.

Tobie Whitman   *Got Change for a Euro?*

Tobie Whitman was a Researcher-Writer for *Let's Go: London 1999* and *2000,* as well as *Let's Go: Britain and Ireland 1998.* After an internship with the EU, she entered Cambridge University to pursue a Master's Degree in European Studies.

Europe

Reykjavík **ICELAND**

0 ———— 400 miles
0 ———— 400 kilometers

Faroe Islands

Shetland Islands

Orkney Islands

SCOTLAND

NORTHERN IRELAND

Glasgow
Edinburgh

Belfast

IRELAND

Dublin

GREAT BRITAIN

North Sea

DEN

Berg

Hambur

WALES
Cardiff

ENGLAND

London

THE NETHERLANDS

Amsterdam

ATLANTIC OCEAN

Brussels

BELGIUM

GER

Fr

LUXEMBOUR

Paris

LIECHTENSTEIN

Nantes

Zurich

SWITZERLAND

Bern

Bay of Biscay

Bordeaux

Lyon

Milan

Ve

Santiago de Campostela

FRANCE

Marseille

Nice

Florenc

PORTUGAL

ANDORRA

MONACO

Corsica (Fr.)

Ror

Lisbon

Madrid

Barcelona

SPAIN

Valencia

Sevilla

Granada

Balearic Islands (Sp.)

Sardinia (It.)

Tyr

Mediterranean Sea

Tangier

GIBRALTAR

Fez

Rabat

MOROCCO

ALGERIA

Algiers

Tunis

TUNI

XIV

PDAs

&

Travel

LET'S GO

(it's not what you're thinking)

Let's Go City Guides
are now available for
Palm OS™ PDAs.
Download a free trial at
http://**mobile.letsgo.com**

AMSTERDAM BARCELONA BOSTON LONDON PARIS ROME NEW YORK CITY SAN FRANCISCO WASHINGTON D.C.

Palm OS is a registered trademark of Palm, Inc. Let's Go is a registered trademark of Let's Go Publications, Inc. Guidewalk is a registered trademark of Guidewalk LLC.

DISCOVER EUROPE

To many travelers, thoughts of Europe conjure images of ruins and relics, soaring architectural triumphs, and a world steeped in the past yet driving the present. A patchwork continent, built upon the foundations of empires past, Europe stands as a living history of countries and cultures still wet behind the ears. Not all of the memories are fond—the specter of colonialism lingers still in the hearts and minds of those who suffered, and a century of devastating warfare scarred the earth and its inhabitants. That was then....

This is now. Economic rebirth, spurred by a sentiment of interdependent unity, has brought a diverse array of nations closer together than ever before. The results are impressive: emerging cities like Kraków and Stockholm challenge the elder statesmen of Rome, Prague, and Vienna for international prominence and travelers' attentions. New cultural showpieces like Bilbao's Guggenheim and London's Tate Modern complement timeless galleries and architectural shrines like the Louvre and the Hermitage, and fashion-forward locals and a constant influx of students keep the nightlife as hot as the innumerable beaches. Whether it's the pubs of Dublin, the upscale bistros of Lyon, or the calm hills of Switzerland that call to you, *Let's Go: Europe 2003* has the answer.

Average Temp. and Precipitation	January			April			July			October		
	°C	°F	in	°C	°F	in	°C	°F	in	°C	°F	in
Amsterdam	5/1	41/34	3.1	11/4	53/40	1.5	20/12	69/55	2.9	13/7	57/46	4.1
Athens	12/6	55/44	1.9	18/11	66/52	0.9	31/22	89/73	0.2	22/15	73/60	2.1
Berlin	1/-3	35/26	1.6	12/2	54/37	1.6	22/13	73/56	2.0	13/5	56/42	1.0
Budapest	2/-3	36/25	1.2	15/5	60/41	1.5	26/15	79/59	2.3	15/6	59/43	1.4
Copenhagen	2/-1	37/30	1.7	9/2	49/36	1.6	20/12	69/55	2.6	11/6	53/44	2.1
Dublin	7/2	46/37	2.5	11/5	52/41	1.9	18/12	66/54	2.6	12/7	55/46	2.9
İstanbul	7/2	46/37	3.7	15/8	60/47	1.7	27/18	82/66	0.7	19/12	67/55	2.1
Kraków	0/-5	33/22	1.3	12/3	54/38	1.9	21/12	71/55	3.5	12/4	55/40	1.7
London	7/2	45/36	2.4	12/5	55/41	1.7	22/13	72/56	1.8	14/7	58/46	2.9
Madrid	10/0	51/32	1.8	17/5	63/42	1.8	32/16	90/61	0.4	20/8	68/47	1.8
Moscow	-6/-11	21/11	1.4	9/1	49/34	1.5	21/12	71/55	3.2	7/0	45/33	2.0
Paris	6/1	43/34	0.2	13/5	57/42	0.2	23/14	75/58	0.2	15/7	59/46	0.2
Prague	1/-4	34/24	0.8	12/2	54/36	1.4	22/12	72/54	2.6	12/3	54/39	1.2
Rome	12/3	55/39	3.2	17/8	63/47	2.6	28/18	83/66	0.6	21/13	71/56	4.5
Stockholm	0/-5	31/22	1.2	8/0	47/31	1.1	21/12	70/54	2.5	8/3	48/38	2.0
Vienna	2/-2	36/27	1.5	13/5	57/41	2.0	25/15	77/59	2.9	13/6	57/43	1.9

WHAT TO DO

Let's be honest—we've never met you, we don't know where we'd take you on our first date, and we certainly don't know what'll make your dream vacation. So we've compiled a few launching pads from which you can start drawing up a custom itinerary: **themed categories** to let you know where to find your museums, your mountains, your madhouses; **Let's Go Picks** to point you toward some of the quirkiest gems you could uncover; and **suggested itineraries** to outline the common paths across Europe. Turn to the country-specific **Discover** sections at the beginning of each chapter to flesh out your self-directed, nobody-but-you itinerary.

MUSEUM MANIA

Europe's most precious artifacts reside in her museums; nearly every city houses a sculpture, a painting, or a relic recognized the world over. **London** (p. 140) is packed with artistic gems, not least of which are the imperialist booty at the British Museum and the striking Tate Modern Gallery. On the other side of the Channel, **Paris** (p. 323) is equally well-stocked—although you could spend half your life at the Louvre, you'd have to take some breaks to visit the Musée d'Orsay, the Musée Rodin, and the endearingly garish Pompidou Centre. For museums designed with as much artistic inspiration as their collections, try Spain's Guggenheim Museum in **Bilbao** (p. 953), and the Dalí Museum in **Figueres** (p. 945). **Madrid** (p. 886) preserves the world's largest collection of paintings in the Prado, while the Reina Sofía shelters Picasso's overpowering *Guernica*.

Florence (p. 650) was the home of the Renaissance and still retains many of its masterworks in the Uffizi and the Accademia. The Vatican Museum in **Rome** (p. 592) houses the Sistine Chapel and other priceless works of sculpture and art. Celebrate Germany's reunification at the East Side Gallery in **Berlin** (p. 412), built around the longest remaining stretch of the Wall. **Munich** boasts the technological Deutsches Museum and the twin Pinakotheks (p. 465); if those don't raise your spirits, try **Hamburg**'s Erotic Art Museum (p. 441). The biggest sin you could commit in **Amsterdam** (p. 720) would be to overlook the Rijksmuseum and the van Gogh Museum. **Moscow**'s Kremlin once contained the secrets to an empire; it still holds the legendary Fabergé eggs (p. 840). The Hermitage, in **St. Petersburg,** has the world's largest art collection (p. 853). **Budapest**'s Museum of Fine Arts houses little-seen but nonetheless spectacular works by Raphael, Rembrandt, and the rest of the usual suspects (p. 520). And lastly, the finest museum in the Baltics is the Occupation Museum in **Rīga** (p. 677), detailing the lengthy Soviet occupation.

■ LET'S GO PICKS: AIR-CONDITIONED & FULL OF ART

LEAST CHILD-FRIENDLY MUSEUMS: Your impressionable babe will be sure to learn a great deal from Amsterdam's kinky **Sex Museum** (p. 730) or Rome's **Museo Criminologico** (p. 613), which displays the tools of Italy's terrorists, spies, and druggies.

BEST-HUNG WALL HANGINGS: Reykjavik's **Phallalogical Museum** (p. 546) preserves the manhoods of over 100 Icelandic mammals and will soon be acquiring its first human specimen. (Applicants no longer desired.)

BEST WAY TO MULTI-TASK: You're learning *and* killing brain cells at Dublin's **Old Jameson Distillery** (p. 562), and Moscow's **Russian Vodka Museum** (p. 860).

RUINS & RELICS

For those who prefer to meet history outside of a museum case, Europe's castles, churches, and ruins are a dream come true. In **London** (p. 140), royals wander around Buckingham Palace, while choirboys croon at Westminster Abbey. Venture away from the city to ponder the mysteries of **Stonehenge** (p. 172). Nobody could miss **Paris**'s breathtaking Cathédrale de Notre-Dame (p. 336). Elsewhere in France, the *châteaux* of the **Loire Valley** (p. 359) and Normandy's fortified abbey of **Mont-St-Michel** (p. 355) are must-sees, as is the fortress of **Carcassonne** (p. 369). Manmade treasures are strewn throughout Spain, including the largest Gothic cathedral in the world in **Sevilla** (p. 914) and the luxurious Palacio Real in **Madrid** (p. 895). **Barcelona** (p. 927) sports fanciful Modernism, headlined by Antoni Gaudí's La Sagrada Família. Muslim-infused Andalucía offers the mosque in **Córdoba** (p. 906) and the Alhambra in **Granada** (p. 919). And although Morocco is not *technically* in Europe, **Fez**'s Bou Inania Madrasa (p. 710) competes with any attraction north of Gibraltar.

Germany's marvels include the cathedral at **Cologne** (p. 449) and the pure gold tea house at **Potsdam**'s breathtaking Schloß Sans Souci (p. 431). Go a little crazy in Mad King Ludwig's castles (p. 479), or try to figure out Denmark's **Kvaerndrup** (p. 284) and the optical illusion that makes the castle of Egeskov Slot float on water. **Rome** (p. 592) practically invented architecture as we know it, beginning with the Pantheon, Colosseum, and Forum. In Greece, the crumbling Acropolis—the foundation of Western civilization—towers above **Athens** (p. 486). Journey to the navel of the ancient world to learn your fate from the oracle at **Delphi** (p. 493) or the temple of Apollo on **Delos** (p. 507). Across the Aegean, in **İstanbul** (p. 1022), Topkapi Palace, Hagia Sophia, and the Blue Mosque all stand within sight of one other. **Prague** Castle (p. 247) has been the seat of the Bohemian government for 1000 years, but the kaleidoscopic onion domes of St. Basil's Cathedral in **Moscow** (p. 840) are the true emblem of Eastern Europe.

◪ LET'S GO PICKS: PEOPLE MAKE THE DARNDEST THINGS

MOST LIKELY TO STAND FOREVER: Ireland's **Newgrange** tomb (and the bones inside it) has been around since the 4th millenium BC (p. 564).

MOST LIKELY TO BE GONE BY JULY: Sweden's **IceHotel** melts away each April, only to be built anew by the craftiest team of ice sculptors in the world (p. 984).

HOLIEST DOODIE: The **Cathedral of the Assumption of the Virgin Mary** in Dubrovnik houses Baby Jesus's diapers among its religious relics (p. 238).

MOST THRILLING WAY TO JUST EAT IT: Head to the Szabó Marzipan Museum and Confectionary in Budapest, where it doesn't matter if you're black or a **white chocolate statue of Michael Jackson** (p. 531).

THE GREAT OUTDOORS

You've seen the Eiffel Tower. You've been to the British Museum. Now it's time to heed the call of the wild. Britain brims with national parks; our favorite is the **Lake District** (p. 190). For jagged peaks and crashing waves, head north to Scotland; the **Outer Hebrides** (p. 212) are particularly breathtaking. Ireland's **Ring of Kerry** (p. 570) is home to secluded Irish villages, and **Killarney National Park** (p. 569) features spectacular mountains. The majestic Pyrenees are the setting for Spain's **Parque Nacio-**

nal de Ordesa (p. 946). **Grenoble** (p. 390), in the French Alps, brims with hiking opportunities and tempts skiers with some of the world's steepest slopes. North of Sicily, the **Aeolian Islands** (p. 672) boast pristine beaches, dramatic volcanoes, and bubbling thermal springs. Watch for endangered griffin vultures while trekking in Crete's **Samaria Gorge** (p. 511), and keep your eyes peeled in Turkey's **Butterfly Valley** (p. 1035). The dramatic **Tatra** mountain range stretches across Eastern Europe; the trails from the Slovak Republic's **Starý Smokovec** (p. 871) are especially rewarding. **Kitzbühel** (p. 106), in Austria, provides the challenges of world-class hiking and skiing. For fresh Swiss Alpine air, conquer the **Matterhorn** (p. 1000) or take up adventure sports in **Interlaken** (p. 999). Soak up the scenery of Germany's **Saxon Switzerland** (p. 435), then hike through the eerie **Black Forest** (p. 463), which inspired the Brothers Grimm. Western **Norway** (p. 759) is splintered by dramatic fjords and glaciers, all open for exploration. At the end of your trip, soak your weary feet in the warm mineral mud of Iceland's **Blue Lagoon** (p. 547)

▨ LET'S GO PICKS: MOUNTAIN MEN & VALLEY GIRLS

BONNIEST PLACE TO KISS: On the bonny, bonny banks of Loch Lomond (p. 209).

BEST WAYS TO HANG OUT: Cliff-diving is so much more fun when you're naked, according to Corfu's **Pink Palace** (p. 503). And be sure to stop and smell the roses, albeit very, very carefully, in **Lokrum**'s nudist botanical garden (p. 238).

BIGGEST REASONS TO DOUBT OUR SANITY: Our researchers will try anything, from running in Liechtenstein's **LGT-Alpin Marathon** (p. 684) to scrambling with the *toros* at **San Fermines** (Running of the Bulls; p. 948) in Pamplona.

WILD LIFE

When the museums close and the sun sets over the mountains, Europe's wildest parties are just beginning. **Edinburgh** (p. 197) has the highest concentration of pubs in Europe, but it's often overlooked for the pub crawls of **Dublin** (p. 555). There's nowhere sunnier and sexier than **Lagos** (p. 815), on the Algarve coast of Portugal. Along Spain's **Costa del Sol,** hip clubs line the beaches of **Marbella** (p. 919), but it's the **Balearic Islands** that are an absolute must; **Ibiza** (p. 956) in particular is frenzied all hours of the day. Once you've eliminated each and every tan line, head inland to the festive cities of **Madrid** (p. 886) and **Barcelona** (p. 927) or flaunt your way to the one and only **Côte d'Azur** (p. 376). Dynamic **Milan** (p. 635) will introduce you to Italian style in a hurry. Bop down to the Greek islands for the beautiful beaches of **Corfu** (p. 503) and for **Ios** (p. 509), a frat party run amok. Things only get wilder as you head farther east to **Bodrum,** the Turkish "Bedroom of the Mediterranean" (p. 1033). Don't just focus on the Mediterranean, though—the best beaches in Europe lie just north, along Croatia's **Dalmation Coast** (p. 234). **Prague** (p. 247) and **Munich** (p. 465) know that discriminating drinkers don't need a beach to get sloshed, and **Amsterdam** (p. 720)... trust us, it knows everything it needs to.

▨ LET'S GO PICKS: ALL THE NEWS THAT'S FIT TO DRINK

BEST REASON TO MISS SATURDAY MORNING CARTOONS: The ragers at **Space** (p. 956) in Ibiza, Spain, feature more go-go than an episode of Inspector Gadget.

MEAT TO MAKE YOU MEET YOUR MAKER: Wash down the Icelandic dish *hâkarl* (rotten shark meat that has been buried underground) with the national drink, *Brennivín,* also known as "the Black Death."

MOST EXCESSIVE HOUSE SPECIAL: Le Bar Des Deux Frères (p. 383) knows that after a hard day of sunning on the Riviera, you don't need a tequila shot—you need 10.

SHORTEST DISTANCE BETWEEN KEG AND BED: The bungalow city of **Na Vlachovce** in Prague, replete with bedding in romantic two-person *Budvar* barrels.

FÊTES! FESTAS! FESTIVALS!

COUNTRIES	APR. – JUNE	JULY – AUG.	SEPT. – MAR.
AUSTRIA AND SWITZERLAND	Vienna Festival (May 9-June 15)	Salzburger Festspiele (late July to late Aug.) Open-Air St. Gallen (late June)	Fasnacht (Basel; Mar. 10-12) Escalade (Geneva; early Dec.)
BRITAIN AND IRELAND	Bloomsday (Dublin; June 16) Wimbledon (London; late June)	Edinburgh Int'l Festival (Aug. 11-31) Fringe Festival (Aug. 4-26)	Matchmaking Festival (Lisdoonvarna; Sept.) St. Patrick's Day (Mar. 17)
CROATIA	World Festival of Animated Film (Zagreb; May)	Int'l Folklore Festival (July 17-21) Dubrovnik Summer Fest. (July 10-Aug. 25)	Int'l Puppet Festival (Sept.) Zagreb Fest (Nov.)
CZECH REPUBLIC	Prague Spring Festival (May)	Český Krumlov Int'l Music Fest (Aug.)	Int'l Organ Fest (Olomouc; Sept.)
FRANCE	Cannes Film Festival (May14-24)	Festival d'Avignon (July) Bastille Day (July 14) Tour de France (July)	Carnevale (Nice, Nantes; Feb. 21-Mar. 5)
GERMANY	May Day (Berlin; May 1) Christopher St. Day (late June)	Love Parade (Berlin; late July) Rhine in Flames Festival (Rhine Valley; Aug. 9)	Fasching (Munich; Jan. 7-Mar. 4) Oktoberfest (Munich; Sept. 20-Oct. 5)
HUNGARY	Golden Shell Folklore (Siófok; June)	Sziget Rock Fest (Budapest; July) Baroque Festival (Eger; July)	Eger Vintage Days (Sept.) Festival of Wine Songs (Pécs; Sept.)
ITALY	Maggio Musicale (Florence; May 11-Aug. 1) Scoppio del Carro (Florence; Easter Su)	Il Palio (Siena; Aug. 16) Umbria Jazz Festival (July 12-21)	Carnevale (Feb. 21-Mar. 5) Festa di San Gennaro (Naples; Dec. 16, Sept. 19, May 7) Dante Festival (Ravenna; mid-Sept.)
THE NETHERLANDS	Queen's Day (Apr. 30) Holland Festival (June)	Gay Pride Parade (Aug.)	Flower Parade (Aalsmeer; Sept.) Cannabis Cup (Nov.)
POLAND	Int'l Short Film (Kraków; May) Festival of Jewish Culture (Kraków; June)	Street Theater (Kraków; July) Highlander Folklore (Zakopane; Aug.)	Kraków Jazz Fest (Oct.) Nat'l Blues Music (Toruń; Nov.)
PORTUGAL	Burning of the Ribbons (Coimbra; May 6-7)	Feira Internacional de Lisboa (June) Feira Popular (mid-July)	Carnival (mid-Mar.) Semana Santa (Mar. 24-31)
SCANDINAVIA	Midsummer (June 21-23) Bergen Festival (May 21-June 1) Norwegian Wood (Oslo; early June)	Quart Music Festival (Kristiansand; early July) Savonlinna Opera Fest. (July 3-Aug. 3)	Helsinki Festival (Aug. 22-Sept. 7)
SPAIN	Feria de Abril (Sevilla; Apr. 29-May 4)	San Fermines (Pamplona; July 6-14)	Semana Santa (Apr. 13-20) Las Fallas (Valencia; Mar. 15-18) Carnival (Feb. 21-Mar. 5)

DISCOVER

SUGGESTED ITINERARIES

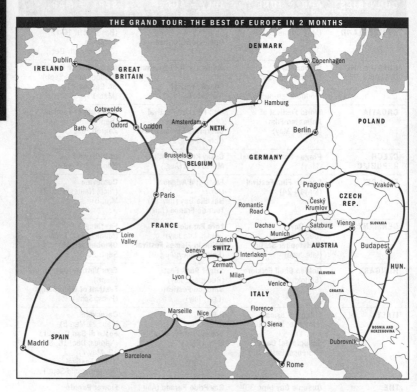

THE GRAND TOUR: THE BEST OF EUROPE IN 2 MONTHS

THE GRAND TOUR

THE BEST OF EUROPE IN 2 MONTHS

From **London** (4 days; p. 140), catch a cheap flight to energetic **Dublin** (2 days; p. 555). Get studious in **Oxford** (1 day; p. 175), then take in the natural beauty of the **Cotswolds** (1 day; p. 179) en route to elegant **Bath** (2 days; p. 172). Meet the continent in the museums and cafes of **Paris** (4 days; p. 323), and the gorgeous châteaux of the **Loire Valley** (1 day; p. 359). Venture south to worldly **Madrid** (2 days; p. 886) and then hook around to otherworldly **Barcelona** (3 days; p. 927). After a night in **Marseille** (1 day; p. 374), soak in the Riviera's rays at **Nice** (1 day; p. 379). Continue on to the orange roofs of **Florence** (2 days; p. 650) and pause at stunning **Siena** (1 day; p. 659) en route to **Rome** (3 days;

p. 592). Wind through **Venice** (2 days; p. 618) on your way to posh **Milan** (1 day; p. 635). Stop in **Lyon** (1 day; p. 392) for your trip's best meal before heading to international **Geneva** (1 day; p. 1001). Scale the Swiss Alps around **Zermatt** (1 day; p. 1000) and **Interlaken** (1 day; p. 999). Move on to cultured **Zürich** (1 day; p. 992) and classical **Salzburg** (1 day; p. 95) before taking in an opera in **Vienna** (2 days; p. 80). Go south toward Croatia's beautiful **Dalmatian Coast** and up-and-coming **Dubrovnik** (2 days; p. 234). Soak in the baths of **Budapest** (2 days; p. 520), then turn back westward to historical **Kraków** (2 days; p. 784). **Prague** (3 days; p. 247) and gorgeous **Český Krumlov** (1 day; p. 264) may convince you never to leave Central Europe, but it's onward for a beer in **Munich** (2 days; p. 465) and a sobering daytrip to nearby **Dachau** (1 day; p. 473). The **Romantic Road** (2 days; p. 478) will steer you to **Berlin** (3 days; p. 412). Head north to cosmopolitan **Copenhagen** (2 days; p. 273) and restless **Hamburg** (2 days; p. 441). Take a last wild breath in **Amsterdam** (3 days; p. 720), then top off your trip in peaceful **Brussels** (1 day; p. 115).

BUILDING BLOCKS

THE BEST OF EUROPE IN 1 MONTH
Start in **London** (3 days; p. 140), spinning from theater to museum to club, then chunnel to rejuvenating **Paris** (3 days; p. 323). Sample the cuisine of **Lyon** (1 day; p. 392) en route to animated **Barcelona** (2 days; p. 927). Graze the Mediterranean shoreline, hitting the French Riviera in **Nice** (1 day; p. 379) and strolling by the Renaissance art of **Florence** (2 days; p.

650). Discover the one and only **Rome** (3 days; p. 592) before gliding through **Venice** (2 days; p. 618). Break out the clubbing clothes in **Milan** (1 day; p. 635), then don your banker's suit in **Geneva** (1 day; p. 1001). Continue north for a frothy pint in **Munich** (2 days; p. 465) and a cup of coffee in **Vienna** (2 days; p. 80), before following the crowds to enrapturing **Prague** (2 days; p. 247) and hip **Kraków** (2 days; p. 784). Overwhelm yourself in sprawling **Berlin** (2 days; p. 412). Indulge in the goods of **Amsterdam** (2 days; p. 720), then recuperate with a final day in **Brussels** (p. 115).

THE MEDITERRANEAN (37 DAYS)
From **Madrid,** take the high-speed train to flower-filled **Sevilla** (2 days; p. 910) before partying in the Costa del Sol resort town of **Marbella** (1 day; p. 919). Skip inland to **Granada** (2 days; p. 919), where you'll wind your way through the Moorish Albaicín to the Alhambra. From **Valencia** (2 days; p. 925), island hop in the **Balearic Islands** between the foam parties at **Ibiza** and **Formentera** (2 days; p. 956). Ferry to vibrant **Barcelona** (3 days; p. 927), saving time for a daytrip out to **Costa Brava** and the Dalí museum in **Figueres** (1 day; p. 945). Head to France, stopping first in fortified **Carcassonne** (1 day; p. 369) and then Roman **Arles** (1 day; p. 372). Papal riches await in **Avignon** (1 day; p. 371), culinary delights in **Marseille** (1 day; p. 374). Move on to the glittery Côte d'Azur, soaking in the celebrity of flashy **Cannes** (1

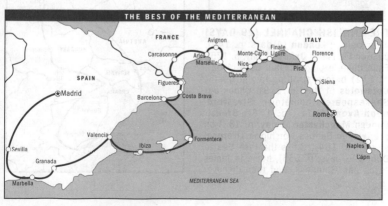

day; p. 377) and the Riviera's capital, **Nice** (2 days; p. 379). If you have any money left, blow it at the world-famous **Monte-Carlo** casino (1 day; p. 385). Take a break from your vacation in Italy's restful **Finale Ligure** (2 days; p. 644) and snap photos in **Pisa** (1 day; p. 661) before David-hopping through **Florence**'s magnificent art collections (3 days; p. 650). Check out the two-tone *duomo* of **Siena** (2 days; p. 659) and find a forum for all things ancient in **Rome** (4 days; p. 592). From **Naples** (2 days; p. 664), home of pizza and pickpockets, finish off your trip in sundrenched **Capri** (2 days; p. 670). Or, continue your journey using the Greece and Turkey itinerary.

the charming villages of rural Ireland in the **Ring of Kerry** (2 days; p. 570). From **Galway** (1 days; p. 574), a center of Irish culture, continue on to neighborly **Belfast** (2 days; p. 579). From there, it's back across the Irish Sea to Stranraer, train-bound for historic **Edinburgh** (2 days; p. 197) and the sublime **Lake District** (2 days; p. 190). Head back to London and hop a train for carefree **Paris** (4 days; p. 323). Use **Tours** (2 days; p. 361) as a hub for exploring the fertile **Loire Valley** before pressing on to **Rennes** (1 day; p. 355). The fortified island of **Mont-St-Michel** (1 day; p. 355) gives you a chance to stretch your legs and imagination before you settle into the seaside paradise of **St-Malo** (2 days; p. 357). A train will whisk you back to Paris and your homebound airline of choice. But should your craving *française* persist, a train to **Marseille** (p. 374) leaves you at the heart of the Mediterranean itinerary.

THE ENGLISH CHANNEL (29 DAYS)

NORTH SEA

NORTHERN IRELAND   SCOTLAND

Edinburgh
Belfast   Lake District   GREAT BRITAIN
Galway
Dublin
IRELAND
Ring of Kerry   Manchester
Liverpool
WALES   ENGLAND
Stratford-upon-Avon
Cotswolds
Bath   Oxford
London

St-Malo   Mont-St-Michel
Rennes   Paris
ATLANTIC OCEAN   Tours
Loire Valley
FRANCE

THE ENGLISH CHANNEL (29 DAYS)
After visiting **London** (4 days; p. 140), punt on the Isis in **Oxford** (1 day; p. 175). From there, explore elegant **Bath** (1 day; p. 172) before strolling in the quaint **Cotswolds** (1 day; p. 179). Check out Shakespeare's hometown, **Stratford-upon-Avon** (1 day; p. 178). Breeze through **Manchester** (1 day; p. 183) on your way to Beatles worship in **Liverpool** (1 day; p. 184). Cross the Irish Sea to **Dublin** (2 days; p. 555), home to James Joyce and Guinness, and then discover

BEST OF CENTRAL EUROPE

Gdańsk
POLAND   Warsaw
Wrocław
Prague   Kraków
CZECH REPUBLIC   Zakopane
Stary
SLOVAKIA   Smokovec
Vienna   Bratislava
AUSTRIA
HUNGARY   Budapest
Ljubljana   SLOVENIA   Lake Balaton
Zagreb
CROATIA
BOSNIA
Split   Sarajevo
Dalmatian Coast
Dubrovnik

CENTRAL EUROPE (31 DAYS). Begin in glamorous, Bohemian **Prague** (3 days; p. 247), then stop in stately **Wrocław** (1 day; p. 792) on the way to the seaport of **Gdańsk** (1 day; p. 796). Continue to no-nonsense **Warsaw** (2 days; p. 776), then to trendy **Kraków** (2 days; p. 784). Hike in the Tatra Mountains surrounding **Zakopane** (2 days; p. 791) and **Starý Smokovec** (1 day; p. 871). Next, visit vibrant **Budapest** (3 days; p. 520), followed by the warm, shallow waters of **Lake Balaton** (2 days; p. 536). Wander the streets of **Zagreb** (2 days; p. 231), then stop over in **Sarajevo** (2 days; p. 131) before returning to Croatia to explore the heavenly islands of the **Dalmatian Coast** (3 days; p. 234), between Dubrovnik and Split. Continue on to lovely **Ljubljana** (2 days; p. 876), then experience the grandeur of **Vienna** (3 days; p. 80), ending up in blossoming **Bratislava** (2 days; p. 867).

Rhodes (2 days; p. 514) and partying in **Kos** (1 day; p. 514). Cross over to **Bodrum,** Turkey, the "Bedroom of the Mediterranean" (2 days; p. 1033). From there, two routes diverge; they both meet up in **Cappadocia.** If you've come to see ruins, head up to **Kuşadasi** to check out the crumbling magnificence at **Ephesus** (2 days; p. 1032), and move on to the thermal springs of **Pamukkale** and **Aphrodisias** (2 days; p. 1033). Or, if you're more into beaches, head from Bodrum to **Fethiye** and serene **Ölüdeniz** (1 day; p. 1035) and the eternal flame of **Olimpos** (2 days; p. 1036). Either way, experience the surreal world of **Göreme** (2 days; p. 1038) in Cappadocia, and then get wild in **İstanbul** (3 days; p. 1016).

BEST OF GREECE AND TURKEY

GREECE & TURKEY (28 DAYS). Get off the ferry at **Corfu** (1 day; p. 503), beloved by literary luminaries and partiers alike, then continue on to **Patras** (1 day; p. 493). Discover the mysteries of love in the ruins of **Corinth** (1 day; p. 497), and a jumble of things ancient and modern in chaotic **Athens** (2 days; p. 486). Party all night long in the **Cyclades**—fast-paced **Mykonos** (p. 507), sacred **Delos** (p. 507), and the earthly paradise of **Santorini** (4 days; p. 510). Catch the ferry to **Crete**, where chic **Iraklion** and **Knossos,** home to the Minotaur, await (2 days; p. 510). Base yourself in **Rethymno** or **Hania** and hike the spectacular **Samaria Gorge** (2 days; p. 511). Backtrack to Iraklion to catch the ferry to the Dodecanese, hitting historical

THE BEST OF BALTIC EUROPE

THE BALTIC SEA (22 DAYS). Begin in the bustling, medieval streets of **Tallinn** (2 days; p. 294), then relax on the tranquil and secluded **Estonian Islands** (4 days; p. 299). Move on to lively **Tartu,** the oldest city in the Baltics (2 days; p. 298), before immersing yourself in glitzy **Rīga** (2 days; p. 677). Head down the coast of Lithuania to **Palanga, Klaipėda,** and dreamy **Nida** (3 days; p. 693). Continue to up-and-coming **Vilnius** (2 days; p. 688), one of the many "New Pragues," then wake up from the night train in **Moscow's** historic Red Square (4 days; p. 840). Cap it off spending some time in **St. Petersburg,** home of the ornate delights of the Hermitage (3 days; p. 853). You can connect to the Scandinavian route (see below) via Helsinki.

DISCOVER

THE BEST OF SCANDINAVIA

SCANDINAVIA (21 DAYS). From modern **Copenhagen** (4 days; p. 273), daytrip to the glorious Elsinore castle in **Helsingør** (1 day; p. 282). Head to Sweden through **Malmö** (1 day; p. 976) to reach luxurious **Gothenburg** (2 days; p. 978). Zip to Norway's bustling capital, **Oslo** (2 days; p. 749), and take the Oslo-Bergen railway to inspiring **Bergen** (2 days; p. 759) before plunging into the natural wonders that are **Sognefjord** (1 day; p. 757) and **Geirange fjord** (1 day; p. 765). Head back to Oslo to catch the night train to Sweden's **Stockholm** (2 days; p. 964), the jewel of Scandinavia's cities. Take a daytrip to **Uppsala** (1 day; p. 973), home of Sweden's oldest university. Hop on the ferry to Finland's **Helsinki** (2 days; p. 304), where east meets west, and end your travels gazing at the scenic marvels surrounding **Savonlinna** (2 days; p. 314). Ferry to Estonia's Tallinn (p. 294) to link with the Baltic Sea itinerary.

ESSENTIALS

ENTRANCE REQUIREMENTS.
Passport (p. 12): Required to visit any European country.
Visa (p. 13): Western European countries require visas for citizens of South Africa, but not for citizens of Australia, Canada, Ireland, New Zealand, the UK, or the US (for stays shorter than 90 days). Eastern European countries are more likely to require visas. Belarus, Russia, and Ukraine require invitations.
Immunizations (p. 20): Travelers to Europe should be up to date on vaccines for measles, mumps, rubella, diptheria, tetanus, pertussis, polio, haemophilus influenza B, hepatitis A, and hepatitis B.
Work Permit (p. 14): Required for all foreigners planning to work in Europe, except for citizens of EU member countries.
Driving Permit (p. 62): An International Driving Permit is required for those planning to drive.

DOCUMENTS AND FORMALITIES

Information on European **consular services** at home, foreign consular services in Europe, and specific entry requirements is located in individual country chapters.

PASSPORTS

REQUIREMENTS. Citizens of Australia, Canada, Ireland, New Zealand, South Africa, the UK, and the US need valid passports to enter European countries and to reenter their own country. Most countries do not allow entrance if the holder's passport expires in under six months. Returning home with an expired passport is illegal and may result in a fine.

NEW PASSPORTS. Citizens of Australia, Canada, Ireland, New Zealand, the UK, and the US can apply for a passport at most post offices, passport offices, or courts of law. Citizens of South Africa can apply for a passport at any Home Affairs office. Any new passport or renewal application must be filed well in advance of the departure date, although most passport offices offer rush services for a very steep fee.

PASSPORT MAINTENANCE. Be sure to photocopy the page of your passport with your photo, as well as your visas, traveler's checks' serial numbers, and any other important documents. Carry one set of copies in a safe place, apart from the originals, and leave another set at home. Consulates also recommend that you carry an expired passport or an official copy of your birth certificate in a part of your baggage separate from other documents.

If you lose your passport, immediately notify the local police and the nearest embassy or consulate of your home government. To expedite its replacement, you will need to know all information previously recorded and show ID and proof of citizenship. US passports must be printed within the US, so processing and delivery of your passport may take several weeks. Any visas stamped in your

ONE EUROPE. The idea of European unity has come a long way since 1958, when the European Economic Community (EEC) was created in order to promote solidarity and cooperation. Since then, the EEC has become the European Union (EU), with political, legal, and economic institutions spanning 15 member states: Austria, Belgium, Denmark, Finland, France, Germany, Greece, Ireland, Italy, Luxembourg, the Netherlands, Portugal, Spain, Sweden, and the UK.

What does this have to do with the average non-EU tourist? In 1999, the EU established **freedom of movement** across 15 European countries–the "Schengen Zone," made up of the entire EU minus Ireland and the UK, but plus Iceland and Norway. This means that border controls between participating countries have been abolished and visa policies harmonized. While you're still required to carry a passport (or government-issued ID card for EU citizens) when crossing an internal border, you're free to travel to all participating states once you've been admitted into any of the 15 countries. Britain and Ireland have also formed a **common travel area,** abolishing passport controls between the UK and the Republic of Ireland. This means that the only times you'll see a border guard within the EU are traveling between the British Isles and the Continent.

For other important consequences of the EU for travelers, see **Customs in the EU** (p. 15) and **The Euro** (p. 16). For an in-depth look at the imminent expansion of the EU, see **With or Without EU** (p. 1068).

old passport will be irretrievably lost. In the case of "emergency travel"—lost or stolen passports that need to be replaced—consulates can issue temporary passports, which cannot be extended. More detailed info regarding lost and stolen passports is available at www.usembassy.it/cons/acs/passport-lost.htm.

VISAS, INVITATIONS, WORK PERMITS

VISAS. Some countries require a visa—a stamp, sticker, or insert in your passport specifying the purpose of your travel and the permitted duration of your stay—in addition to a valid passport for entrance. Most standard visas cost US$10-70, are valid for one to three months, and must be validated within six months to one year from the date of issue. Many countries grant double-entry visas for a premium. The **Center for International Business and Travel** (**CIBT;** US ☎ 800-925-2428; www.cibt.com) secures visas for travel to almost any country for a service charge.

The requirements in the chart below apply only to tourist stays shorter than 90 days. If you plan to stay longer than 90 days, or if you plan to **work or study abroad** (see p. 68), your requirements will differ. In any case, check with the nearest embassy or consulate of your desired destination for up-to-date information. US citizens can also consult www.travel.state.gov/foreignentryreqs.html.

Note that the following countries are not listed in this chart: **Austria, Belgium, Croatia, Denmark, Finland, France, Germany, Greece, Iceland, Italy, Luxembourg, The Netherlands, Norway, Portugal, Slovenia, Spain,** and **Sweden.** These require visas of South Africans, but not for nationals of Australia, Canada, Ireland, New Zealand, the UK, or the US (for stays shorter than 90 days). Also not listed are the **UK, Ireland, Malta,** and **Switzerland,** which do not require visas for any of the seven nationalities listed above (including South Africans) for stays shorter than 90 days. Travelers to **Andorra** should contact a French or Spanish embassy with any inquiries, while those going to **Liechtenstein** should contact a Swiss embassy.

DO I NEED A VISA? — FOR STAYS OF 90 DAYS OR LESS IN:

	AUS	CAN	IRE	NZ	SA	UK	US
BELARUS	Y^I	Y^I	Y^I	Y^I	Y^I	Y^I	Y^I
BOSNIA	Y	N	N^{30}	Y	Y	N	N^{30}
BULGARIA	N^{30}	N^{30}	N^{30}	N^{30}	Y	N^{30}	N^{30}
CROATIA	N	N	N	N	Y	N	N
CZECH REP.	Y	Y	N	N	Y	N	N^{30}
ESTONIA	N	Y	N	N	Y	N	N
HUNGARY	Y	N	N	N	N^{30}	N	N
LATVIA	N^{10}	Y	N	Y	Y	N	N
LITHUANIA	N	N	N	N	Y	N	N
MACEDONIA	Y	Y	N	N	Y	N	N
POLAND	Y	Y	N	Y	Y	N	N
ROMANIA	Y	Y	N^{30}	Y	Y	N^{30}	N^{30}
RUSSIA	Y^I	Y^I	Y^I	Y^I	Y^I	Y^I	Y^I
SLOVAK REP.	Y	N	N	Y	N^{30}	N	N^{30}
UKRAINE	Y^I	Y^I	Y^I	Y^I	Y^I	Y^I	Y^I
TURKEY	Y^B	Y^B	Y^B	N	N^{30}	Y^B	Y^B

KEY: Y tourist visa required; **N** tourist visa not required; N^{30} tourists can stay up to 30 days without visa; N^{10} tourists can stay up to 10 days without visa; Y^I invitation required; Y^B tourist visa available on arrival/at border

INVITATIONS. In addition to a visa, **Belarus, Russia,** and **Ukraine** require that visitors from any country obtain an invitation from a sponsoring individual or organization. See country chapters to learn how to acquire invitations. Requirements can change rapidly, so double-check with the appropriate consulate in your home country.

IDENTIFICATION

When you travel, always carry two or more forms of identification on your person, including at least one photo ID; a passport combined with a driver's license or birth certificate is usually adequate. Never carry all your forms of ID together, split them up in case of theft or loss, and keep photocopies in your luggage and at home.

TEACHER, STUDENT, AND YOUTH IDENTIFICATION. The **International Student Identity Card (ISIC),** the most widely accepted form of student ID, provides discounts on sights, accommodations, food, and transport; access to a 24hr. emergency helpline (call US collect ☎715-345-0505); and insurance benefits for US cardholders (see **Insurance,** p. 24). The ISIC is preferable to an institution-specific card (such as a university ID) because it is more likely to be recognized and honored abroad. Applicants must be degree-seeking students of a secondary or postsecondary school and must be at least 12 years of age. Because of the proliferation of fake ISICs, some services (particularly airlines) require additional proof of student identity, such as a school ID or a letter attesting to your student status, signed by your registrar and stamped with your school seal.

The **International Teacher Identity Card (ITIC)** offers teachers the same insurance coverage as the ISIC with similar but limited discounts. For travelers who are 25 years old or younger but are not students, the **International Youth Travel Card** (**IYTC;** formerly the **GO 25** Card) also offers many of the same benefits as the ISIC.

Each of these identity cards costs US$22. ISIC and ITIC cards are valid for roughly one and a half academic years; IYTC cards are valid for one year from the date of issue. For a list of issuing agencies, or for more information, contact the **International Student Travel Confederation (ISTC),** Herengracht 479, 1017 BS Amsterdam, Netherlands (☎20 421 28 00; www.istc.org).

CUSTOMS

Upon entering a country, you must declare certain items from abroad and pay a duty on the value of those articles. Note that goods and gifts purchased at **duty-free** shops are not exempt from duty or sales tax upon return and must be declared; "duty-free" only means tax-free in the country of purchase. In order to expedite your return, make a list of any valuables brought from home and register them with customs before traveling abroad. Also, be sure to keep receipts for all goods acquired abroad.

TAXES. The European Union imposes a **value-added tax (VAT)** on goods and services, usually included in the sticker price. Non-EU citizens may obtain a **refund** for taxes paid on retail goods, but not for taxes paid on services. As the VAT is 15-25%, it might be worthwhile to file for a refund. To do so, you must obtain **Tax-free Shopping Cheques,** available from shops sporting the Europe Tax-free Shopping logo, and save your receipts. Upon leaving the EU, present your goods, invoices, and passport to customs and have your checks stamped. Then go to an ETS cash refund office or file for a refund once back home. Keep in mind that goods must be taken out of the country within three months of the end of the month of purchase, and that some stores require minimum purchase amounts to become eligible for refund. For more information on tax-free shopping, visit www.globalrefund.com.

CUSTOMS IN THE EU. As well as freedom of movement of people within the EU (see p. 13), travelers in the EU (Austria, Belgium, Denmark, Finland, France, Germany, Greece, Ireland, Italy, Luxembourg, The Netherlands, Portugal, Spain, Sweden, and the UK) can also take advantage of the freedom of movement of goods. This means that there are no customs controls at internal EU borders (i.e., you can take the blue customs channel at the airport), and travelers are free to transport whatever legal substances they like as long as it is for their own personal (non-commercial) use—up to 800 cigarettes, 10L of spirits, 90L of wine (60L of sparkling wine), and 110L of beer. You should also be aware that duty-free was abolished on June 30, 1999 for travel between EU member states; however, travelers between the EU and the rest of the world still get a duty-free allowance when passing through customs.

MONEY

CURRENCY AND EXCHANGE

As a general rule, it's cheaper to convert money in Europe than at home. However, you should bring enough foreign currency for the first 24 to 72 hours of a trip to avoid being cashless if you arrive after bank hours or on a holiday. Travelers from the US can call **International Currency Express** (☎ 888-278-6628), which delivers foreign currency or traveler's checks 2nd-day (US$12) at competitive exchange rates.

When changing money abroad, try to go only to banks or change bureaus that have at most a 5% margin between their buy and sell prices. Since you lose money with every transaction, convert large sums, but no more than you'll need.

If you use traveler's checks or bills, carry some in small denominations (the equivalent of US$50 or less) in case you must exchange money at disadvantageous rates, but bring a range of denominations since charges may be levied per check cashed. Store your money in a variety of forms; carry cash, traveler's checks, and an ATM and/or credit card. All travelers should also consider carrying about $50 worth of US dollars, which are preferred by local tellers in some countries.

THE EURO. The official currency of 12 members of the European Union (Austria, Belgium, Finland, France, Germany, Greece, Ireland, Italy, Luxembourg, the Netherlands, Portugal, and Spain) is now the euro. The new currency has some important—and positive—consequences for travelers hitting more than one euro-zone country. For one thing, money-changers across the euro-zone are obliged to exchange money at the official, fixed rate (see below), and at no commission (though they may still charge a small service fee). Second, euro-denominated traveler's checks allow you to pay for goods and services across the entire euro-zone, again at the official rate and commission-free. To read more about the transition to the euro at the beginning of 2002, see **Got Change for a Euro** (p. 1068).

At the time of printing, **1€=US$0.99=CAD$1.55=AUD$1.82.** For the latest exchange rates, check a currency converter, such as www.xe.com or www.europa.eu.int.

TRAVELER'S CHECKS

Traveler's checks are one of the safest and least troublesome means of carrying funds. American Express and Visa are the most widely recognized brands. Many banks and agencies sell them for a small commission. Check issuers provide refunds if the checks are lost or stolen, and many provide additional services such as toll-free refund hotlines abroad, emergency message services, and stolen credit card assistance. They are readily accepted across Europe. Ask about toll-free refund hotlines and the location of refund centers when purchasing checks, and always carry emergency cash.

American Express: Checks available with commission at select banks and all AmEx offices. **AAA** (www.aaa.com) offers AmEx Traveler's Cheques to its members at no fee. US residents can also purchase checks by phone (☎888-887-8986) or online (www.aexp.com). Checks are available in US, Australian, British, Canadian, Euro, and Japanese currencies. *Cheques for Two* can be signed by either of 2 people traveling together. For purchase locations or more information, contact AmEx's service centers: in the US and Canada ☎800-221-7282; in the UK ☎0800 521 313; in Australia ☎800 25 19 02; in New Zealand ☎0800 441 068; elsewhere US collect ☎801-964-6665.

Visa: Checks available (generally with commission) at banks worldwide. Checks available in US, British, Canadian, Euro, and Japanese currencies. For the location of the nearest office, call Visa's service centers: in the US ☎800-227-6811; in the UK ☎0800 89 50 78; elsewhere UK collect ☎020 7937 8091.

Travelex/Thomas Cook: In the US and Canada call ☎800-287-7362; in the UK call ☎0800 62 21 01; elsewhere call UK collect ☎1733 31 89 50.

CREDIT, DEBIT, AND ATM CARDS

Where they are accepted, **credit cards** often offer superior exchange rates—up to 5% better than the retail rate used by banks and other currency exchange establishments. Credit cards may also offer services such as insurance or emergency help and are sometimes required to reserve hotel rooms or rental cars. Master-Card and Visa are the most welcomed; American Express cards work at some ATMs and at AmEx offices and major airports.

Automatic Teller Machine (ATM) cards are widespread in Europe, and you can probably access your personal bank account from abroad. ATMs get the same wholesale exchange rate as credit cards, but there is often a limit on the amount of money you can withdraw per day (around US$500), and the computer networks occasionally fail. While there is typically an international withdrawal surcharge of US$1-5, a growing number of banks waive this fee for the first few transactions each month.

Debit cards are a relatively new form of purchasing power that are as convenient as credit cards but have a more immediate impact on your funds. A debit card can be used wherever its associated credit card company (usually MasterCard or Visa) is accepted, yet the money is withdrawn directly from the holder's checking account. Debit cards often also function as ATM cards and can be used to withdraw cash from associated banks and ATMs throughout Europe. Ask your local bank about obtaining one.

The two major international money networks are **Cirrus** (to locate ATMs US ☎800-424-7787 or www.mastercard.com) and **Visa/PLUS** (to locate ATMs US ☎800-843-7587 or www.visa.com). Most ATMs charge a transaction fee that is paid to the bank that owns the ATM.

PIN NUMBERS AND ATMS. To use a cash or credit card to withdraw money from an ATM in Europe, you must have a four-digit **Personal Identification Number (PIN).** If your PIN is longer than four digits, ask your bank whether you can just use the first four, or whether you'll need a new one. **Credit cards** don't usually come with PINs, so if you intend to use a credit card to get cash advances at an ATM, call your credit card company to request one before leaving.

People with alphabetic (rather than numerical) PINs may also be thrown off by the lack of letters on European cash machines. The following handy chart gives the corresponding numbers to use: 1=QZ; 2=ABC; 3=DEF; 4=GHI; 5=JKL; 6=MNO; 7=PRS; 8=TUV; and 9=WXY. Note that if you mistakenly punch the wrong code into the machine three times, it will swallow your card for good.

GETTING MONEY FROM HOME

If you run out of money while traveling, the easiest and cheapest solution is to have someone back home make a deposit to your credit card or cash (ATM) card. Failing that, consider one of the following options.

WIRING MONEY. It is possible to arrange a **bank money transfer,** which means asking a bank back home to wire money to a bank in Europe. This is the cheapest way to transfer cash, but it's also the slowest, usually taking several days or more. Note that some banks may only release your funds in local currency, potentially sticking you with a poor exchange rate; inquire about this in advance. Money transfer services like **Western Union** are faster and more convenient than bank transfers—but also much pricier. Western Union has many locations worldwide. To find one, visit www.westernunion.com, or call: US ☎800-325-6000, Canada ☎800-235-0000, UK ☎0800 83 38 33, Australia ☎800 501 500, New Zealand ☎800 27 0000, or South Africa ☎0860 100031. Money transfer services are also available at **American Express** and **Thomas Cook** offices (p. 16).

US STATE DEPARTMENT (US CITIZENS ONLY). In dire emergencies only, the US State Department will forward money within hours to the nearest consular office, which will then disburse it according to instructions for a US$15 fee. If you wish to use this service, you must contact the Overseas Citizens Service division of the US State Department (☎202-647-5225; nights, Sundays, and holidays ☎202-647-4000).

COSTS

With so many options, the cost of your trip can be difficult to estimate. Your single biggest purchase will probably be your round-trip **airfare** to Europe (p. 43); a **railpass** can be another major pre-departure expense (p. 53). Before you go, calculate a reasonable per-day budget that will cover your needs without breaking the bank. To give you a general idea, the typical first-time, under-26 traveler planning to spend most of his or her time in Western Europe and then tack on a quick jaunt into Eastern Europe, sleeping in hostels and traveling on a two-month unlimited Eurail pass, can probably expect to spend about US$2000, plus cost of plane fare (US$300-800), railpass (US$882), and backpack (US$150-400). Also, don't forget emergency reserve funds (at least US$200).

TIPS FOR STAYING ON A BUDGET. Saving just a few dollars a day over the course of your trip might pay for days or weeks of additional travel, so learn to take advantage of freebies; for example, many museums are free once a week, and cities often host open-air concerts and cultural events. Bring a sleepsack (p. 25) to save on sheet charges in hostels, and do your **laundry** in the sink (unless you're explicitly prohibited from doing so). Multi-bed rooms are almost always cheaper per person than singles, so sharing **accommodations** can save you a bundle. Also, buying **food** in supermarkets provides an inexpensive and creative alternative to dining out.

SAFETY AND SECURITY

While tourists may be more vulnerable than the average individual, a few simple precautions will help you avoid problems.

PERSONAL SAFETY

EXPLORING. Respecting local customs (in many cases, dressing more conservatively) may placate would-be hecklers. Familiarize yourself with your surroundings before setting out. Never admit that you are traveling alone, and be sure someone at home knows your itinerary. When walking at night, stick to busy, well-lit streets and avoid dark alleyways. If you feel uncomfortable, leave as quickly and directly as you can.

SELF-DEFENSE. There is no sure-fire way to avoid all the threatening situations you might encounter when you travel, but a good self-defense course will give you concrete ways to react to unwanted advances. **Impact, Prepare, and Model Mugging** can refer you to local self-defense courses in the US (☎800-345-5425). Visit the website at www.impactsafety.org for a list of nearby chapters. Workshops (2-3hr.) start at US$50; full courses run US$350-500.

TERRORISM AND CIVIL UNREST. Use vigilance and caution to protect your security while traveling. Keep an eye on the news, heed travel warnings, steer clear of big crowds and demonstrations, and comply with security measures.

Overall, risks of civil unrest tend to be localized and rarely directed towards tourists. Though the peace process in Northern Ireland is progressing, tension tends to surround the July "marching season." Notoriously violent separatist movements include the ETA (a Basque group), which operates in France and Spain, and FLNC (Corsican separatists) in France. The November 17 group in Greece is known for anti-Western acts, though they do not target tourists; while

TRAVEL ADVISORIES. The following government offices provide travel information and advisories by telephone, by fax, or via the web:

Australian Department of Foreign Affairs and Trade: ☎13 0055 5135; faxback service 02 6261 1299; www.dfat.gov.au.

Canadian Department of Foreign Affairs and International Trade (DFAIT): In Canada and the US call ☎800-267-6788; www.dfait-maeci.gc.ca. Call for their free booklet, *Bon Voyage...But.*

New Zealand Ministry of Foreign Affairs: ☎04 494 8500; fax 04 494 8506; www.mft.govt.nz/trav.html.

United Kingdom Foreign and Commonwealth Office: ☎020 7008 0232; fax 020 7008 0155; www.fco.gov.uk.

US Department of State: ☎202-647-5225, faxback service 202-647-3000; travel.state.gov. For the booklet *A Safe Trip Abroad,* call 202-512-1800.

ESSENTIALS

guerilla conflict has subsided in Southeast Turkey, Chechen sympathizers have been known to target Western travelers. For now, it is safest to avoid conflict-ridden Macedonia, Serbia, Montenegro, and Bosnia-Herzegovina. The box below will help you find an up-to-date list of your government's travel advisories.

FINANCIAL SECURITY

PROTECTING YOUR VALUABLES. There are a few steps you can take to minimize the financial risk associated with traveling. First, bring as little with you as possible. Second, buy a combination padlock to secure your belongings either in your pack or in a hostel or train station locker. Third, carry as little cash as possible. Keep your traveler's checks and ATM/credit cards in a money belt—not a "fanny pack"—along with your passport and ID cards. Fourth, keep a small cash reserve separate from your primary stash. This should be about US$50 sewn into or stored in the depths of your pack, along with your traveler's check numbers and important photocopies.

CON ARTISTS & PICKPOCKETS. In large cities **con artists** often work in groups and employ small children. Beware of certain classic scams, including sob stories that require money, rolls of bills "found" on the street, and mustard spilled (or saliva spit) onto your shoulder to distract you while they snatch your bag. Don't ever let your passport and your bags out of your sight. Beware of **pickpockets** in city crowds, especially on public transportation. Also, be alert in public telephone booths: if you must say your calling card number, do so very quietly; if you punch it in, make sure no one can look over your shoulder. Cities such as Rome, Paris, London, Moscow, and Amsterdam have higher rates of petty crime.

ACCOMMODATIONS AND TRANSPORTATION. Never leave your belongings unattended; crime occurs in even the most demure-looking hostel or hotel. Be particularly careful on **buses** and **trains,** as sleeping travelers are easy prey for thieves. Carry your backpack in front of you where you can see it. When traveling with others, sleep in shifts. When alone, use good judgement in selecting a train compartment: Never stay in an empty one, and use a lock to secure your pack to the luggage rack. Try to sleep on top bunks with your luggage stored above you (if not in bed with you), and keep important documents and other valuables on your person. If traveling by **car,** don't leave valuables (such as radios or luggage) in sight while you are away.

DRUGS AND ALCOHOL

Drug and alcohol laws vary widely throughout Europe. In the Netherlands you can buy "soft" drugs on the open market; in Turkey and much of Eastern Europe drug possession may lead to a heavy prison sentence. If you carry **prescription drugs**, you must carry both a copy of the prescriptions themselves and a note from a doctor, especially at border crossings. **Public drunkenness** is culturally unacceptable and against the law in many countries, and it can also jeopardize your safety.

TROUBLE WITH THE LAW. Travelers who run into trouble with the law, both accidentally and knowingly, do not retain the rights of their home country; instead, they have the same rights as a citizen of the country they are visiting. The law mandates that police notify the embassy of a traveler's home country if he or she is arrested. In custody, a traveler is entitled to a visit from a consular officer. US citizens should check the Department of State's website (www.state.gov) for more information.

HEALTH AND INSURANCE

BEFORE YOU GO

In your **passport,** list any allergies or medical conditions, and write the names of any people you wish to be contacted in case of a medical emergency. While most prescription and over-the-counter **drugs** are available throughout Europe, matching a prescription to a foreign equivalent is not always easy, safe, or possible, so carry up-to-date, legible prescriptions or a statement from your doctor stating the medication's trade name, manufacturer, chemical name, and dosage. See www.rxlist.com to figure out what to ask for at the pharmacy counter. While traveling, be sure to keep all medication with you in your carry-on luggage. For tips on packing a basic **first-aid kit** and other health essentials, see p. 25.

IMMUNIZATIONS AND PRECAUTIONS. Travelers over two years old should be sure that the following vaccines are up to date: MMR (for measles, mumps, and rubella); DTaP or Td (for diptheria, tetanus, and pertussis); OPV (for polio); HbCV (for haemophilus influenza B); and HBV (for hepatitis B). For travelers going to Western Europe, Hepatitis A vaccine and/or immune globulin (IG) is recommended. Those headed to Eastern or Southern Europe should also consider the typhoid vaccine. Some countries may deny entrance to travelers arriving from parts of South America and sub-Saharan Africa without a certificate of vaccination for yellow fever. For more **region-specific information** on vaccination requirements, as well as recommendations on immunizations and prophylaxis, consult the CDC (see below) in the US or the equivalent in your home country.

USEFUL ORGANIZATIONS AND PUBLICATIONS. The US **Centers for Disease Control and Prevention** (CDC; ☎877-FYI-TRIP; www.cdc.gov/travel) maintains an international travelers' hotline and an informative website. The CDC's comprehensive booklet *Health Information for International Travel,* an annual rundown of disease, immunization, and general health advice, is free online or US$25 via the Public Health Foundation (☎877-252-1200). Consult the appropriate government agency of your home country for consular information sheets on health, entry requirements, and other issues for various countries (see the listings in the box on **Travel Advisories,** p. 19).

For information on medical evacuation services and travel insurance firms, see the US government's website (travel.state.gov/medical.html) or the **British Foreign and Commonwealth Office** (www.fco.gov.uk). For detailed information on travel health, including a country-by-country overview of diseases, try the **International Travel Health Guide**, by Stuart Rose, MD (US$19.95; www.travmed.com). For general health info, contact the **American Red Cross** (☎ 800-564-1234; www.redcross.org).

MEDICAL ASSISTANCE ON THE ROAD. While health care systems in Western Europe tend to be quite accessible and of high quality, medical care varies greatly across Eastern and Southern Europe. Major cities such as Prague and Budapest will have English-speaking medical centers or hospitals for foreigners, whereas English-speaking facilities are nearly non-existent in relatively untouristed countries like Belarus or Latvia. Tourist offices may have names of local doctors who speak English. In general, medical service in these regions is not up to Western standards; though basic supplies are always there, specialized treatment is not. If available, private hospitals tend to have better facilities than state-operated ones. All EU citizens can receive free first-aid and emergency services by presenting an **E11 form** (available at post offices).

If you are concerned about being able to access medical support while traveling, contact one of these two services: *MedPass*, from **GlobalCare, Inc.** (US ☎ 800-860-1111; www.globalems.com), which provides 24hr. international medical assistance, support, and medical evacuation resources; or the **International Association for Medical Assistance to Travelers** (IAMAT; US ☎ 716-754-4883, Canada ☎ 416-652-0137; www.iamat.org), which has free membership, lists English-speaking doctors worldwide, and offers detailed information on immunization requirements and sanitation. If your regular insurance policy does not cover travel abroad, you may wish to purchase additional coverage (p. 24).

Those with medical conditions (diabetes, allergies to antibiotics, epilepsy, heart conditions) may want to get a stainless-steel **Medic Alert** ID tag (first year US$35, US$20 thereafter), which identifies the condition and gives a 24hr. collect-call number. Contact the Medic Alert Foundation (US ☎ 888-633-4298; www.medicalert.org).

For emergencies and quick information on health and other travel warnings, contact a passport agency, embassy, or consulate abroad; U.S. citizens can also call the **Overseas Citizens Services** (☎ 202-647-5225; after-hours 202-647-4000).

ONCE IN EUROPE

ENVIRONMENTAL HAZARDS

Heat exhaustion and dehydration: Heat exhaustion can lead to fatigue, headaches, and wooziness. Avoid it by drinking plenty of fluids, eating salty foods (e.g. crackers), and avoiding dehydrating beverages (e.g. alcohol and caffeinated beverages). Continuous heat stress can eventually lead to heatstroke, characterized by a rising temperature, severe headache, and cessation of sweating. Victims should be cooled off with wet towels and taken to a doctor.

High altitude: Allow your body a couple of days to adjust to less oxygen before exerting yourself. Note that alcohol is more potent and UV rays are stronger at high elevations.

Hypothermia and frostbite: A rapid drop in body temperature is the clearest sign of overexposure to cold. Victims may also shiver, feel exhausted, have poor coordination or slurred speech, hallucinate, or suffer amnesia. Do not let hypothermia victims fall asleep. To avoid hypothermia, keep dry, wear layers, and stay out of the wind. When the temperature is below freezing, watch out for frostbite. If skin turns white, waxy, and cold, do not rub the area. Drink warm beverages, get dry, and slowly warm the area with dry fabric or steady body contact until a doctor can be found.

INSECT-BORNE DISEASES

Many diseases are transmitted by insects—mainly mosquitoes, fleas, ticks, and lice—especially when hiking and camping in wet or forested areas. **Mosquitoes** are most active from dusk to dawn. Wear pants and long sleeves, tuck pants into socks, and sleep in a mosquito net. Use insect repellents such as DEET and soak or spray gear with permethrin (approved for use on clothing). **Ticks** can give you **Lyme disease,** which is marked by a two-inch bull's-eye on the skin. If you find a tick attached to your skin, grasp the head with tweezers as close to the skin as possible and apply slow, steady traction. Later symptoms include fever, headache, fatigue, and aches and pains. Left untreated, Lyme disease can cause problems in joints, the heart, and the nervous system. Antibiotics are effective if administered early. Ticks can also give you **encephalitis,** a viral infection. Symptoms can range from headaches and flu-like symptoms to swelling of the brain, but the risk of contracting the disease is relatively low, especially if precautions are taken against tick bites. **Leishmaniasis,** a parasite transmitted by **sand flies,** can also occur in Europe. Common symptoms are fever, weakness, and swelling of the spleen. There is a treatment, but no vaccine.

FOOD- AND WATER-BORNE DISEASES

Unpeeled fruit and vegetables and tap water should be safe throughout most of Europe, particularly Western Europe. In Turkey, Southern Europe, and Eastern Europe, however, be cautious of ice cubes and anything washed in tap water, like salad. Other sources of illness are raw shellfish, unpasteurized milk, and sauces containing raw eggs. Buy bottled water, or purify your own water by bringing it to a rolling boil or treating it with **iodine tablets,** especially in Morocco and parts of Turkey, where food- and water-borne diseases are a common cause of illness.

Cholera: An intestinal disease caused by bacteria found in contaminated food. A danger in Russia and Ukraine. Symptoms include diarrhea, dehydration, vomiting, and muscle cramps. See a doctor immediately; if left untreated, it may be fatal. Antibiotics are available, but rehydration is most important. Consider getting a vaccine (50% effective) if you have stomach problems or will be living where the water is not reliable.

Hepatitis A: A viral liver infection acquired primarily through contaminated water. An intermediate risk in Eastern Europe, most prevalent in rural areas. Symptoms include fatigue, fever, loss of appetite, nausea, dark urine, jaundice, vomiting, aches and pains, and light stools. Ask your doctor about the vaccine (Havrix or Vaqta) or an injection of immune globulin (IG; formerly called gamma globulin).

Mad Cow Disease: The human variant is called Cruetzfeldt-Jakob disease (nvCJD), and involves invariably fatal brain diseases. Incidents in the UK have been tentatively linked to consuming infected beef, but the risk is calculated to be around 1 per 10 billion servings of meat. Information on nvCJD is not conclusive, but it is believed that milk and milk products do not pose a risk.

Parasites: Microbes, tapeworms, etc. that hide in unsafe water and food. **Giardiasis,** for example, is acquired by drinking untreated water from streams or lakes. Symptoms include swollen glands or lymph nodes, fever, rashes or itchiness, and digestive problems. Boil water, wear shoes, and eat only cooked food.

Traveler's diarrhea: Results from drinking untreated water or eating uncooked foods. Symptoms include nausea, bloating, and urgency. Try quick-energy, non-sugary foods with protein and carbohydrates to keep your strength up. Over-the-counter anti-diarrheals (e.g. Imodium) may counteract the problems. The most dangerous side effect is dehydration; drink uncaffeinated soft drinks or 8oz. of water with ½ tsp. of sugar or honey and a pinch of salt, and eat salted crackers. If you develop a fever or your symptoms don't go away after 4-5 days, consult a doctor. Consult a doctor immediately for treatment of diarrhea in children.

OTHER INFECTIOUS DISEASES

Foot and Mouth Disease (FMD): FMD experienced one of its worst outbreaks in 2001, largely in the United Kingdom and other Western European countries. FMD does not pose a health threat to humans but is devastating to animals. It can be transmitted by human as well as animal contact, and in the event of an outbreak, travel to farms and other rural areas may be restricted.

Hepatitis B: A viral infection of the liver transmitted via bodily fluids or needle-sharing. Symptoms may not surface until years after infection. A three-shot vaccination sequence is recommended for health-care workers, sexually-active travelers, and anyone planning to seek medical treatment abroad; it must begin six months before traveling.

Hepatitis C: Like Hepatitis B, but the mode of transmission differs. IV drug users, those with occupational exposure to blood, hemodialysis patients, and recipients of blood transfusions are at the highest risk, but the disease can also be spread through sexual contact or sharing items like razors and toothbrushes that may have traces of blood.

Rabies: Transmitted through the saliva of infected animals; fatal if untreated. By the time symptoms (thirst and muscle spasms) appear, the disease is in its terminal stage. If you are bitten, wash the wound thoroughly, seek immediate medical care, and try to have the animal located. A rabies vaccine, which consists of 3 shots given over a 21-day period, is available but is only semi-effective.

AIDS, HIV, AND STDS

For detailed information on **Acquired Immune Deficiency Syndrome (AIDS)** in Europe, call the CDC's 24hr. hotline at US ☎ 800-342-2437, or contact the **Joint United Nations Programme on HIV/AIDS (UNAIDS)** (☎ (+41) 22 791 3666; www.unaids.org). Belarus, Bulgaria, Cyprus, Hungary, Russia, and Ukraine screen incoming travelers for HIV, primarily those planning extended visits for work or study, and deny entrance to those who test HIV-positive. Contact the country's consulate or the CDC in the US for information.

Sexually transmitted diseases (STDs) such as **gonorrhea, chlamydia, genital warts, syphilis,** and **herpes** are easier to catch than HIV and can be just as deadly. Hepatitis B and C can also be transmitted sexually (see p. 23). Though condoms may protect you from some STDs, oral or even tactile contact can lead to transmission. If you think you may have contracted an STD, see a doctor immediately.

WOMEN'S HEALTH

Women traveling in unsanitary conditions are vulnerable to **urinary tract and bladder infections,** common and very uncomfortable bacterial conditions that cause a burning sensation and painful (sometimes frequent) urination. Over-the-counter medicines can sometimes alleviate symptoms, but if they persist, see a doctor.

Vaginal yeast infections may flare up in hot and humid climates. Wearing loosely fitting trousers or a skirt and cotton underwear will help, as will over-the-counter remedies like Monistat or Gynelotrimin. Bring supplies from home if you are prone to infection, as they may be difficult to find on the road.

Since **tampons, pads,** and reliable **contraceptive devices** are sometimes hard to find when traveling, bring supplies with you.

ESSENTIALS

INSURANCE

Travel insurance generally covers four basic areas: medical/health problems, property loss, trip cancellation/interruption, and emergency evacuation. Although your regular insurance policies may well extend to travel-related accidents, you should consider purchasing travel insurance if the cost of potential trip cancellation/interruption or emergency medical evacuation is greater than you can absorb. Prices for travel insurance purchased separately generally run about US$50 per week for full coverage, while trip cancellation/interruption may be purchased separately at a rate of about US$5.50 per US$100 of coverage.

Medical insurance (especially university policies) often covers costs incurred abroad; check with your provider. **US Medicare** does not cover foreign travel. Canadians are protected by their home province's health insurance plan for up to 90 days after leaving the country; check with the provincial Ministry of Health or Health Plan Headquarters for details. Australians traveling in the UK, the Netherlands, Sweden, Finland, Italy, or Malta are entitled to many of the services that they would receive at home as part of the Reciprocal Health Care Agreement. **Homeowners' Insurance** (or your family's coverage) often covers theft during travel and loss of travel documents (passport, plane ticket, railpass, etc.) up to US$500.

ISIC and **ITIC** (see p. 14) provide basic insurance benefits, including US$100 per day of in-hospital sickness for up to 60 days, US$3000 of accident-related medical reimbursement, and US$25,000 for emergency medical transport. Cardholders have access to a toll-free 24hr. helpline (run by the insurance provider **TravelGuard**) for medical, legal, and financial emergencies overseas (US and Canada ☎ 877-370-4742, elsewhere call US collect ☎ 715-345-0505). **American Express** (US ☎ 800-528-4800) grants most cardholders automatic car rental insurance (collision and theft, but not liability) and ground travel accident coverage of US$100,000 on flight purchases made with the card.

INSURANCE PROVIDERS. Council and **STA** (see p. 43) offer a range of plans that can supplement your basic coverage. Other US and Canadian providers include **Access America** (☎ 800-284-8300) and **Berkely Group/Carefree Travel Insurance** (☎ 800-323-3149; www.berkely.com). The UK has **Columbus Direct** (☎ 020 7375 0011; www.columbusdirect.net), and Australia **AFTA** (☎ 02 9375 4955; www.afta.com.au).

PACKING

Pack light: lay out only what you absolutely need, then take half as many clothes and twice as much money. If you plan to do a lot of hiking, also see **Camping and the Outdoors**, p. 29.

LUGGAGE. If you plan to cover most of your itinerary by foot, a sturdy **frame backpack** is unbeatable. (For the basics on buying a pack, see p. 31.) Toting a **suitcase** or **trunk** is fine if you plan to live in one or two cities and explore from there, but a very bad idea if you're going to be moving around a lot. In addition to your main piece of luggage, a **daypack** (a small backpack or courier bag) is a must.

CLOTHING. No matter when you're traveling, it's always a good idea to bring a **warm jacket** or wool sweater, a **rain jacket** (Gore-Tex® is both waterproof and breathable), sturdy shoes or **hiking boots,** and **thick socks. Flip-flops** or waterproof sandals are must-haves for grubby hostel showers. You may also want to add one outfit beyond the jeans and t-shirt uniform, and maybe a nicer pair of shoes if you have the room. If you plan to visit any religious or cultural sites, remember that you'll need something besides tank tops and shorts to be respectful.

SLEEPSACK. Some hostels require that you either provide your own linen or rent sheets from them. Save cash by making your own sleepsack: Fold a full-size sheet in half the long way, then sew it closed along the long side and one short side.

CONVERTERS AND ADAPTERS. In Europe, electricity is 220V AC, enough to fry any 110V North American appliance. Americans and Canadians should buy an **adapter** (which changes the shape of the plug) and a **converter** (which changes the voltage; US$20). Don't make the mistake of using only an adapter (unless appliance instructions state otherwise). New Zealanders, South Africans, and Australians won't need a converter, but will require an adapter. The website www.kropla.com/electric.htm has comprehensive info on what you'll need.

FIRST-AID KIT. For a basic first-aid kit, pack: bandages, pain reliever, antibiotic cream, a thermometer, a Swiss Army knife, tweezers, moleskin, decongestant, motion-sickness remedy, upset-stomach or diarrhea medication (Pepto Bismol or Imodium), an antihistamine, **sunscreen,** insect repellent, and burn ointment.

FILM. Film and developing in Europe are expensive, so consider bringing along enough film for your entire trip and developing it at home. Less serious photographers may want to bring a **disposable camera** or two rather than an expensive permanent one. Despite disclaimers, airport security X-rays *can* fog film, so buy a lead-lined pouch at a camera store or ask security to hand-inspect it. Always pack film in your carry-on luggage, since higher-intensity X-rays are used on checked luggage.

OTHER USEFUL ITEMS. For safety purposes, you should bring a **money belt** and small **padlock**. Basic **outdoors equipment** (plastic water bottle, compass, waterproof matches, pocketknife, sunglasses, sunscreen, hat) may also prove useful. Quick repairs of torn garments can be done on the road with a needle and thread; also consider bringing electrical tape for patching tears. Other things you're liable to forget: an **umbrella,** sealable **plastic bags** (for damp clothes, soap, food, shampoo, etc.), an **alarm clock,** safety pins, rubber bands, a flashlight, **earplugs,** and garbage bags.

IMPORTANT DOCUMENTS. Don't forget your passport, traveler's checks, ATM and/or credit cards, and adequate ID (see p. 14). Also check that you have any of the following that might apply to you: a hosteling membership card (see p. 26); driver's license; travel insurance forms; and/or rail or bus pass (see p. 52).

ACCOMMODATIONS

HOSTELS

In the summer Europe is overrun by young budget travelers. Hostels are the hub of this subculture, allowing young people from around the world to meet, find travel partners, and learn about places to visit. Hostels are generally laid out dorm-style, often with large single-sex rooms and bunk beds, with a common bathroom and a lounge down the hall. Some offer private rooms for families and couples. Other amenities may include kitchens and utensils, bike or moped rentals, storage areas, Internet access, and laundry facilities. There can be drawbacks: some hostels close during certain daytime "lockout" hours, have a curfew, don't accept reservations, impose a maximum stay, or, less frequently, require chores. A bed in a hostel averages around US$10-25 in Western Europe and US$5-10 in Eastern Europe.

ESSENTIALS

HOSTELLING INTERNATIONAL

Joining the youth hostel association in your own country (listed below) automatically grants you membership privileges in **Hostelling International (HI)**, a federation of national hostelling associations. HI hostels are scattered throughout Europe and are typically less expensive than private hostels. Many accept reservations via the **International Booking Network** (US ☎202-783-6161; www.hostelbooking.com). HI's umbrella organization's web page (www.iyhf.org), which lists the web addresses and phone numbers of all national associations, is a great place to begin researching hostelling in a specific region. Other comprehensive hostelling websites include www.hostels.com and www.hostelplanet.com.

Most HI hostels also honor **guest memberships.** You'll get a blank card with space for six validation stamps; each night you'll pay a nonmember supplement (one-sixth the membership fee) and earn one guest stamp. Six stamps grants you full membership. This system works well in most of Western Europe, but in some countries you may need to remind the hostel reception. Most student travel agencies (see p. 43) sell HI cards, as do the national hostelling organizations listed below. All prices listed below are valid for **one-year memberships.**

Australian Youth Hostels Association (AYHA), Level 3, 10 Mallett St., Camperdown NSW 2050 (☎02 9565 1699; www.yha.org.au). AUS$52, under 18 AUS$16.

Hostelling International-Canada (HI-C), 400-205 Catherine St., Ottawa, ON K2P 1C3 (☎800-663-5777 or 613-237-7884; www.hihostels.ca). CDN$35, under 18 free.

Hostelling International Northern Ireland (HINI), 22-32 Donegall Rd., Belfast BT12 5JN, Northern Ireland (☎02890 31 54 35; www.hini.org.uk). UK£10, under 18 UK£6.

Youth Hostels Association of New Zealand (YHANZ), P.O. Box 436, 193 Cashel St., 3rd Fl. Union House, Christchurch 1 (☎03 379 9970; yha.org.nz). NZ$40, under-17 free.

Hostels Association of South Africa, 3rd fl. 73 St. George's House, P.O. Box 4402, Cape Town 8000 (☎021 424 2511; www.hisa.org.za). SAR55; under 18 SAR30.

Youth Hostels Association (England and Wales) Ltd., Trevelyan House, Dimple Rd., Matlock, Devonshire DE4 3YH, UK (☎01629 59 26 00; www.yha.org.uk). UK£13, under 18 UK£6.50, families UK£26.

An Óige (Irish Youth Hostel Association), 61 Mountjoy St., Dublin 7 (☎01 830 4555; www.irelandyha.org). IR£10, under 18 IR£4.

Scottish Youth Hostels Association (SYHA), 7 Glebe Crescent, Stirling FK8 2JA (☎01786 89 14 00; www.syha.org.uk). UK£6.

Hostelling International-American Youth Hostels (HI-AYH), 733 15th St. NW, #840, Washington, D.C. 20005 (☎202-783-6161; www.hiayh.org). US$25, under 18 free.

OTHER TYPES OF ACCOMMODATIONS

HOTELS, GUESTHOUSES, AND PENSIONS. In Britain, Switzerland, Austria, and northern Europe, **hotels** generally start at a hefty US$35 per person. Elsewhere, couples and larger groups can get by fairly well. You'll typically share a hall bathroom; a private bathroom or hot shower will cost extra. Some hotels offer "full pension" (all meals) and "half pension" (no lunch). Smaller **guesthouses** and **pensions** are often cheaper than hotels. For written reservations, indicate your night of arrival and number of nights you plan to stay. The manager will send a confirmation and may request payment for the first night. Not all establishments take reservations, and few accept checks in foreign currency. Enclosing two **International Reply Coupons** will ensure a prompt reply (each US$1.05; available at any post office).

BED AND BREAKFASTS (B&BS). For a cozy alternative to impersonal hotel rooms, B&Bs (private homes with rooms available to travelers) range from the acceptable to the sublime. B&Bs are particularly popular in Britain and Ireland, where rooms average UK£20/€30 per person. For more info on B&Bs, see **InnFinder** (www.inncrawler.com) or **InnSite** (www.innsite.com).

YMCAS & YWCAS. **Young Men's Christian Association (YMCA), and Young Women's Christian Association (YWCA)** lodgings are usually cheaper than a hotel but more expensive than a hostel. Not all locations offer lodging; those that do are often located in urban downtowns. Many YMCAs accept women and families; some will not lodge those under 18 without parental permission. Book online at **Travel-Y's International** (www.travel-ys.com) for free. For a small fee ($3 in North America, $5 elsewhere), **Y's Way International** makes reservations between June and September for the YMCAs throughout Europe (224 E. 47th St., New York, NY 10017, USA; ☎212-308-2899; fax 212-308-3161).

UNIVERSITY DORMS. Many **colleges and universities** open their residence halls to travelers when school is not in session; some do so even during term-time. Getting a room may take a couple of phone calls and require advanced planning, but rates tend to be low, and many offer free local calls.

HOME EXCHANGES. **Home exchange** offers the traveler various types of homes (houses, apartments, condominiums, villas, even castles in some cases), plus the opportunity to live like a native and to cut costs. For more information, contact **HomeExchange.Com** (☎800-877-8723; www.homeexchange.com), **Intervac International Home Exchange** (☎800-756-4663; www.intervac.com), or **The Invented City: International Home Exchange** (US ☎800-788-CITY, elsewhere US collect ☎415-252-1141; www.invented-city.com).

CAMPING AND THE OUTDOORS

Organized campgrounds exist just outside most European cities. Showers, bathrooms, and a small restaurant or store are common; some have more elaborate facilities. Prices are low, US$5-15 per person plus additional charges for tents and/or cars. While camping is cheaper than hostelling, the cost of transportation to the campsites can add up. Some parks or public land allow **free camping,** but check local regulations before you set up camp.

USEFUL PUBLICATIONS AND RESOURCES. An excellent resource for travelers planning on camping or spending time in the outdoors is the **Great Outdoor Recreation Pages** (www.gorp.com). Campers heading to Europe should consider buying an **International Camping Carnet.** Similar to a hostel membership card, it's required at a few campgrounds and provides discounts at others. It is available in North America from the **Family Campers and RVers Association** and in the UK from **The Caravan Club** (see below). For information about camping, hiking, and biking, contact the publishers listed below to receive a **free catalog.**

> **Automobile Association,** A. A. Publishing. Orders and enquiries to TBS Frating Distribution Centre, Colchester, Essex CO7 7DW, UK (☎01206 255 800, www.theaa.co.uk). Publishes *Caravan and Camping: Europe* and *Britain and Ireland* (UK£8) as well as *Big Road Atlases* for most European countries.

> **The Caravan Club,** East Grinstead House, East Grinstead, West Sussex RH19 1UA, UK (☎01342 326 944; www.caravanclub.co.uk). For UK£27.50, members receive equipment discounts, a 700-page directory and handbook, and a monthly magazine.

The European Federation of Campingsite Organizations, EFCO Secretariat, 6 Pullman Court, Great Western Rd., Gloucester GL 1 3 ND (UK ☎01452 526 911; efco@bhpa.org.uk; www.campingeurope.com). The website has a comprehensive list of links to campsites in most European countries.

The Mountaineers Books, 1001 SW Klickitat Way, #201, Seattle, WA 98134, USA (☎800-553-4453 or 206-223-6303; www.mountaineersbooks.org). Over 400 titles on hiking, biking, mountaineering, natural history, and conservation.

CAMPING AND HIKING EQUIPMENT

WHAT TO BUY... Good camping equipment is both sturdy and light. It is generally more expensive in Australia, New Zealand, and the UK than in North America.

Sleeping Bag: Most sleeping bags are rated by season ("summer" means 30-40°F at night; "four-season" or "winter" often means below 0°F). They are made either of **down** (warmer and lighter, but more expensive and miserable when wet) or of **synthetic** material (heavier, more durable, and warmer when wet). Prices range US$80-210 for a summer synthetic to US$250-300 for a good down winter bag. **Sleeping bag pads** include foam pads (US$10-20), air mattresses (US$15-50), and Therm-A-Rest self-inflating pads (US$45-80). Bring a **stuff sack** to store your bag and keep it dry.

Tent: The best tents are free-standing (with their own frames and suspension systems), set up quickly, and require staking only in high winds. Low-profile dome tents are the best all-around. Good 2-person tents start at US$90, 4-person at US$300. Seal the seams of your tent with waterproofer, and make sure it has a rain fly. Other tent accessories include a **battery-operated lantern**, a **plastic groundcloth**, and a **nylon tarp.**

Backpack: Internal-frame packs mold better to your back, keep a lower center of gravity, and flex adequately to allow you to hike difficult trails. **External-frame packs** are more comfortable for long hikes over even terrain, as they keep weight higher and distribute it more evenly. Make sure your pack has a strong, padded hip-belt to transfer weight to your legs. Any serious backpacking requires a pack of at least 4000 cubic inches, plus 500 cubic inches for sleeping bags in internal-frame packs. Sturdy backpacks cost anywhere from US$125-420. This is one area in which it doesn't pay to economize. Fill up any pack with something heavy and walk around the store with it to get a sense of how it distributes weight before buying it. Either buy a **waterproof backpack cover,** or store all of your belongings in plastic bags inside your pack.

Boots: Be sure to wear hiking boots with good **ankle support.** They should fit snugly and comfortably over one or two pairs of wool socks and thin liner socks. Break in boots over several weeks first in order to spare yourself painful and debilitating blisters.

Other Necessities: Synthetic layers, like those made of polypropylene, and a **pile jacket** will keep you warm even when wet. A **"space blanket"** will help you to retain your body heat and doubles as a groundcloth (US$5-15). Plastic **water bottles** are virtually shatter- and leak-proof. Bring **water-purification tablets** for when you can't boil water. For those places that forbid fires or the gathering of firewood (virtually every organized campground in Europe), you'll need a **camp stove** (the classic Coleman starts at US$40) and a propane-filled **fuel bottle** to operate it. Also don't forget a **first-aid kit, pocketknife, insect repellent, calamine lotion,** and **waterproof matches** or a **lighter.**

...AND WHERE TO BUY IT. The mail-order/online companies listed below offer lower prices than many retail stores, but a visit to a local camping or outdoors store will give you a good sense of the look and weight of certain items.

Campmor, 28 Parkway, P.O. Box 700, Upper Saddle River, NJ 07458, USA (US ☎ 888-226-7667; elsewhere US ☎ 201-825-8300; www.campmor.com).

Discount Camping, 880 Main North Rd., Pooraka, South Australia 5095, Australia (☎ 08 8262 3399; www.discountcamping.com.au).

Eastern Mountain Sports (EMS), 1 Vose Farm Rd., Peterborough, NH 03458, USA (☎ 888-463-6367 or 603-924-7231; www.shopems.com).

L.L. Bean, Freeport, ME 04033 (US and Canada ☎ 800-441-5713; UK ☎ 0800 891 297; elsewhere, call US ☎ 207-552-3028; www.llbean.com).

Mountain Designs, 51 Bishop St., Kelvin Grove, Queensland 4059, Australia (☎ 07 3856 2344; info@mountaindesigns.com; www.mountaindesigns.com).

Recreational Equipment, Inc. (REI), Sumner, WA 98352, USA (☎ 800-426-4840 or 253-891-2500; www.rei.com).

YHA Adventure Shop, 152-160 Wardour St., London WIF 8YA, UK (☎ 020 7025 1900; www.yhaadventure.com).

CAMPERS AND RVS

Renting an RV will always be more expensive than tenting or hosteling, but it's cheaper than staying in hotels and renting a car (see **Renting,** p. 62), and the convenience of bringing along your own bedroom, bathroom, and kitchen makes it an attractive option, especially for older travelers and families with children. Rates vary widely by region, season (July and August are the most expensive months), and type of RV. **Motorhome.com** (www.motorhome.com/rentals.html) lists rental companies for several European countries. **Auto Europe** (US ☎ 800-223-5555; UK ☎ 0800 899 893; www.autoeurope.com) rents RVs in Britain, France, and Germany.

ORGANIZED ADVENTURE TRIPS

Organized **adventure tours** offer another way of exploring the wild. Activities include hiking, biking, skiing, canoeing, kayaking, rafting, climbing, photo safaris, and archaeological digs. Tourism bureaus can suggest parks, trails, and outfitters; stores and organizations that specialize in camping and outdoor equipment like REI and EMS are also good resources (see above). The **Specialty Travel Index** (☎ 800-442-4922 or 415-459-4900; www.specialtytravel.com) compiles tours worldwide.

 ENVIRONMENTALLY RESPONSIBLE TOURISM. The idea behind responsible tourism is to leave no trace of human presence behind. A campstove is a safer and more efficient way to cook than using vegetation, but if you must make a fire, keep it small and use only dead branches or brush rather than cutting vegetation. Make sure your campsite is at least 150 ft. (50m) from water supplies or bodies of water. If there are no toilet facilities, bury human waste (but not paper) at least four inches (10cm) deep and above the high-water line, and 150 ft. or more from any water supplies and campsites. Always pack your trash in a plastic bag and carry it with you until you reach the next trash receptacle. For more information on these issues, contact one of the organizations listed below.

Earthwatch, 3 Clock Tower Pl. #100, Box 75, Maynard, MA 01754, USA (☎ 800-776-0188 or 978-461-0081; info@earthwatch.org; www.earthwatch.org).

International Ecotourism Society, 28 Pine St., Burlington, VT 05402, USA (☎ 802-651-9818; ecomail@ecotourism.org; www.ecotourism.org).

National Audubon Society, Nature Odysseys, 700 Broadway, New York, NY 10003, USA (☎ 212-979-3000; www.audubon.org).

Tourism Concern, Stapleton House, 277-281 Holloway Rd., London N7 8HN, UK (☎ 020 7753 3330; info@tourismconcern.org.uk; www.tourismconcern.org.uk).

COMMUNICATION

BY MAIL

SENDING MAIL HOME FROM EUROPE. Airmail is the best way to send mail home from Europe. From Western Europe to North America, airmail averages seven days; from Central or Eastern Europe, allow anywhere from seven days to three weeks. In Russia, Ukraine, and Belarus, your mail will probably be opened and may not be sent. **Aerogrammes,** printed sheets that fold into envelopes and travel via airmail, are available at post offices. Write "par avion" (or *por avion, mit Luftpost, via aerea,* etc.) on the front. Most post offices will charge exorbitant fees or simply refuse to send aerogrammes with enclosures. **Surface mail** is by far the cheapest and slowest way to send mail. It takes one to three months to cross the Atlantic and two to four to cross the Pacific—good for items you won't need to see for a while, such as souvenirs or other articles you've acquired along the way that are weighing down your pack.

SENDING MAIL TO EUROPE. Mark envelopes "par avion" or "airmail" in your country's language; otherwise, your letter or postcard will not arrive. In addition to the standard postage system, **Federal Express** (Australia ☎ 13 26 10; New Zealand ☎ 0800 733 339; US and Canada ☎ 800-247-4747; UK ☎ 0800 123 800; www.fedex.com) handles express mail services from most home countries to Europe.

Australia: www.auspost.com.au/pac. Allow 5-7 days for regular **airmail** to Europe. Post-cards and letters up to 20g cost AUS$1; packages up to 0.5kg AUS$13, up to 2kg AUS$46. **EMS** can get a letter there in 2-3 days for AUS$32.

Canada: www.canadapost.ca/CPC2/common/rates/ratesgen.html#international. Allow 4-7 days for regular airmail to Europe. Postcards and letters up to 20g cost CDN$1.05; packages up to 0.5kg CDN$10.20, up to 2kg CDN$34.00.

Ireland: www.letterpost.ie. Allow 2-3 days for regular airmail to the UK and Western Europe. Postcards and letters up to 25g cost €0.40 to the UK, €0.60 to the continent. **International Swiftpost** zips letters to some major European countries for an additional €3.30 on top of priority postage.

New Zealand: www.nzpost.net.nz/nzpost/control/ratefinder. Allow 6-12 days for airmail to Europe. Postcards cost NZ$1.50; letters up to 200g NZ$2-5; small parcels up to 0.5kg NZ$16.50, up to 2kg NZ$52.61.

UK: www.royalmail.com/international/calculator. Allow 2-3 days for airmail to Europe. Letters up to 20g cost UK£0.36; packages up to 0.5kg UK£2.67, up to 2kg UK£9.42. **UK Swiftair** delivers letters a day faster for an extra UK£2.85.

US: http://ircalc.usps.gov. Allow 4-7 days for regular airmail to Europe. Postcards/aero-grammes cost US$0.70; letters under 1oz. US$0.80; packages under 1lb. US$14; larger packages up to 5lb. $22.75. **Global Express Mail** takes 2-3 days; ½lb. costs US$20, 1lb. US$24.75. **US Global Priority Mail** delivers flat-rate envelopes to Europe in 3-5 days for US$5-9.

RECEIVING MAIL IN EUROPE. There are several ways to pick-up letters sent to you by friends and relatives while you are abroad. Mail can be sent via **Poste Restante** (General Delivery; *Lista de Correos, Fermo Posta, Postlagernde Briefe*, etc.) to almost any city or town in Europe with a post office. See individual country chapters to see how to address *Poste Restante* letters. The mail will go to a special desk in the central post office, unless you specify a post office by street address or postal code. It's best to use the largest post office, since mail may be sent there regardless. It is usually safer and quicker, though more expensive, to send mail express or registered. Bring your passport (or other photo ID) for pick-up; there may be a small fee. If the clerks insist that there is nothing for you, check under your first name as well. *Let's Go* lists post offices in the **Practical Information** section for each city and most towns.

American Express travel offices offer a free **Client Letter Service** (mail held up to 30 days and forwarded upon request) for cardholders who contact them in advance. Address the letter as you would for Poste Restante. Some offices offer these services to non-cardholders (especially AmEx Traveler's Cheque holders), but call ahead. *Let's Go* lists AmEx office locations for most large cities in **Practical Information** sections; for a complete, free list, call US ☎ 800-528-4800.

BY TELEPHONE

TIME DIFFERENCES. All of Europe falls within three hours of **Greenwich Mean Time (GMT)**. Consult the **time zone chart** on the inside back cover. GMT is five hours ahead of New York time, eight hours ahead of Vancouver and San Francisco time, two hours behind Johannesburg time, 10 hours behind Sydney time, and 12 hours behind Auckland time. Some countries ignore **daylight savings time;** fall and spring switchover times vary.

PLACING INTERNATIONAL CALLS. To call Europe from home or to call home from Europe, dial:

1. The **international dialing prefix.** To dial out of **Australia,** dial 0011; **Canada** or the **US,** 011; the **Republic of Ireland, New Zealand,** or the **UK,** 00; **South Africa,** 09. See the inside back cover for a full list of dialing prefixes.

2. The **country code** of the country you want to call. To call **Australia,** dial 61; **Canada** or the **US,** 1; the **Republic of Ireland,** 353; **New Zealand,** 64; **South Africa,** 27; the **UK,** 44. See the back cover for a full list of country codes.

3. The **city/area code.** *Let's Go* lists the city/area codes for cities and towns opposite the city or town name within each country's chapter, next to a ☎. If the first digit is a zero (e.g., 020 for London), omit the zero when calling from abroad (e.g., dial 20 from Canada to reach London).

4. The **local number.**

CALLING HOME FROM EUROPE. A **calling card** is probably cheapest. Calls are billed collect or to your account. Let's Go has recently partnered with **ekit.com** to provide a calling card that offers a number of services, including email and voice messaging. Before purchasing any calling card, always be sure to compare rates with other cards, and to make sure it serves your needs; for instance, a local phonecard is generally better for local calls. For more information, visit www.letsgo.ekit.com. You can also purchase cards from your national telecommunications companies:

AT&T (US): ☎ 800-361-4470.

British Telecom: ☎ 0800 345 144.

Canada Direct: ☎ 800-668-6878.

Ireland Direct: ☎ 0800 400 000.

MCI (US): ☎ 800-444-3333.

Telecom New Zealand: ☎ 0800 000 000.

Sprint (US): ☎ 800-877-4646.

Telkom South Africa: ☎ 10 219.

Telstra Australia: ☎ 132 200.

To call home with a calling card, contact the operator for your service provider in the country of your travel by dialing the appropriate toll-free access number (listed in the Essentials section of each country under Communications). Keep in mind that phone cards can be problematic in Russia, Ukraine, Belarus, and Slovenia—double-check with your provider before setting out. You can usually make **direct international calls** from pay phones, but if you aren't using a calling card, you may need to continually add more change. Where available, **prepaid phone cards** and occasionally major credit cards can be used for direct international calls, but they are still less cost-efficient. (See the box on **Placing International Calls,** p. 34, for directions on how to place a direct international call.) Placing a **collect call** through an international operator is a more expensive alternative. You can typically place collect calls through the service providers listed above, even if you don't possess one of their phone cards; **direct dial** numbers are listed for major providers in most country chapters.

CALLING WITHIN EUROPE. The simplest way to call within the country is to use a coin-operated phone. However, much of Europe has switched to a **prepaid phone card** system, and in some countries you may have a hard time finding any coin-operated phones at all. Prepaid phone cards (available at newspaper kiosks and tobacco stores), which carry a certain amount of phone time depending on the card's denomination, usually save time and money in the long run. The computerized phone will tell you how much time, in units, you have left on your card. Another kind of prepaid telephone card comes with a Personal Identification Number (PIN) and a toll-free access number. Instead of inserting the card into the phone, you call the access number and follow the directions on the card. These cards can be used to make international as well as domestic calls. Phone rates tend to be highest in the morning, lower in the evening, and lowest on Sunday and late at night.

BY EMAIL AND INTERNET

Email is popular and easily accessible in most of Europe. Take advantage of free **web-based email accounts** (e.g., www.hotmail.com and www.yahoo.com); while it's sometimes possible to forge a remote link with your home server, in most cases this is a much slower and more expensive option. Travelers with laptops can call an Internet service provider via a **modem.** Long-distance phone cards specifically intended for such calls can defray normally high phone charges; check with your long-distance phone provider to see if it offers this option. **Internet cafes** and the occasional free Internet terminal at a public library or university are listed in the **Practical Information** sections of major cities. For lists of additional cybercafes in Europe, check out cybercaptive.com or netcafeguide.com.

SPECIFIC CONCERNS

WOMEN TRAVELERS

Women travelling on their own inevitably face some additional safety concerns, but you can still be adventurous without taking undue risks. If you are concerned, consider staying in hostels with **single rooms** that lock from the inside or in religious organizations with rooms for women only. Communal **showers** in some hostels are safer than others; check them before settling in. Stick to centrally located accommodations and avoid solitary late-night treks or public transportation rides. Always carry extra money for a phone call, bus, or taxi. **Hitchhiking** is never safe for women, or even for two women traveling together. Choose **train compartments** occupied by women or couples; ask the conductor to put together a women-only compartment if he or she doesn't offer to do so first. Look as if you know where you're going and approach older women or couples for directions if you're lost or uncomfortable.

In general, the less you look like a tourist, the better off you'll be. Try to dress conservatively, especially in rural areas. Wearing a conspicuous **wedding band** may help prevent unwanted overtures; some travelers report that carrying pictures of a "husband" or "children" is extremely useful to help document marriage status. Even a mention of a husband waiting back at the hotel may be enough in some places to discount your potentially vulnerable, unattached appearance. Solo women travelers are a phenomenon in Eastern Europe, as Eastern European women never eat out by themselves, so you might get a few surprised stares. Consider wearing skirts rather than shorts to blend in; avoid baggy jeans, T-shirts, and sneakers, since they may make it obvious that you're a foreigner.

Your best answer to verbal harassment is no answer at all; feigning deafness, sitting motionless, and staring straight ahead will do a world of good that reactions usually don't achieve. The extremely persistent can often be dissuaded by a firm, loud, and very public "Go away!" in the appropriate language (see Language Basics). Don't hesitate to seek out a police officer or passersby if you are being harassed. Memorize the emergency numbers in places you visit, and consider carrying a whistle or airhorn on your keychain. A **self-defense course** will both prepare you for a potential attack and raise your level of awareness of your surroundings and your confidence (p. 18). Also be aware of the health concerns that women face when traveling (p. 23). *Journeywoman* (www.journeywoman.com) posts an online newsletter and other resources providing female-specific travel tips. *Women Traveling Together* (www.women-traveling.com) places women in small groups to explore the world.

FURTHER READING: WOMEN TRAVELERS.

Active Women Vacation Guide, Evelyn Kaye. Blue Panda Publications (US$18).

A Foxy Old Woman's Guide to Traveling Alone: Around Town and Around the World, Jay Ben-Lesser. Crossing Press (US$11).

A Journey of One's Own: Uncommon Advice for the Independent Woman Traveler, Thalia Zepatos. Eighth Mountain Press (US$17).

Safety and Security for Women Who Travel, Sheila Swan. Travelers' Tales Guides, Inc. (US$13).

SOLO TRAVELERS

There are many benefits to traveling alone, among them greater independence and more opportunities to interact with the residents of the region you're visiting. On the other hand, a solo traveler is more vulnerable to harassment and street theft. Lone travelers need to be well-organized and look confident at all times. Try not to stand out as a tourist, and be especially careful in deserted or very crowded areas. If questioned, never admit that you are traveling alone. Maintain regular contact with someone at home who knows your itinerary. The **Travel Companion Exchange,** P.O. Box 833, Amityville, NY 11701 (US ☎631-454-0880 or 800-392-1256; www.whytravelalone.com) links solo travelers with companions who have similar travel habits; subscribe to their bi-monthly newsletter for more information (US$48). **Contiki Holidays** (888-CONTIKI; www.contiki.com) offers a variety of European vacation packages designed exclusively for 18- to 35-year-olds. For an average cost of $60 per day, tours include accommodations, transportation, guided sightseeing and some meals. The books and organizations listed below provide information and services for the lone wanderer.

FURTHER RESOURCES: SOLO TRAVELERS.

American International Homestays, P.O. Box 1754, Nederland, CO 80466, (US ☎303-258-3234; www.aihtravel.com). Arranges lodgings with host families across the world.

Connecting: Solo Travel Network, 689 Park Road, Unit 6, Gibsons, BC V0N 1V7 (☎604-886-9099; www.cstn.org; membership US$28), offers solo travel tips, host information, and individuals looking for travel companions.

Traveling Solo, Eleanor Berman. Globe Pequot Press (US$17).

Travel Alone & Love It: A Flight Attendant's Guide to Solo Travel, Sharon B. Wingler. Chicago Spectrum Press (US$15).

OLDER TRAVELERS

Senior citizens are eligible for discounts on transportation, museums, movies, theaters, concerts, restaurants, and accommodations. If you don't see a senior citizen price listed, ask, and you might be surprised. However, keep in mind that some hostels, particularly in Germany, do not allow guests over age 26; call ahead to check. The books *No Problem! Worldwise Tips for Mature Adventurers*, by Janice Kenyon (Orca Book Publishers; US$16) and *Unbelievably Good Deals and Great Adventures That You Absolutely Can't Get Unless You're Over 50*, by Joan Rattner Heilman (NTC/Contemporary Publishing; US$13) are both excellent resources. For more information, contact one of the following organizations:

ElderTreks, 597 Markham St., Toronto, ON M6G 2L7 (Canada ☎800-741-7956; www.eldertreks.com). Adventure travel programs for ages 50+ in Finland and Iceland.

Elderhostel, 11 Ave. de Lafayette, Boston, MA 02111 (US ☎877-426-8056; www.elderhostel.org). Organizes one- to four-week "educational adventures" throughout Europe on varied subjects for those 55+.

The Mature Traveler, P.O. Box 15791, Sacramento, CA 95852 (US ☎800-460-6676). Deals, discounts, and travel packages for the 50+ traveler. Subscription US$30.

Walking the World, P.O. Box 1186, Fort Collins, CO 80522 (US ☎800-340-9255; www.walkingtheworld.com). Organizes trips for 50+ travelers to Britain, the Czech Republic, France, Ireland, Italy, Norway, Portugal, Scotland, the Slovak Republic, and Switzerland.

BI-GAY-LESBIAN TRAVELERS

Attitudes toward bisexual, gay, and lesbian travelers are particular to each region in Europe. Acceptance is generally highest in large cities and The Netherlands, and generally lower in eastern nations, particularly Turkey. Listed below are contact organizations, mail-order bookstores, and publishers that offer materials addressing some specific concerns. **Out and About** (www.planetout.com) offers a biweekly newsletter addressing travel concerns as well as a comprehensive site.

Gay's the Word, 66 Marchmont St., London WC1N 1AB (UK ☎020 7278 7654; www.gaystheword.co.uk). The largest gay and lesbian bookshop in the UK, with both fiction and non-fiction titles. Mail-order service available.

FURTHER READING: BI-GAY-LESBIAN TRAVELERS.
Damron Men's Travel Guide, Damron Women's Traveler, Damron's Accommodations, and *Damron Amsterdam Guide.* Damron Travel Guides (US$10-19). For more info, call US ☎800-462-6654 or visit www.damron.com.
Ferrari Guides' Gay Travel A to Z, Ferrari Guides' Men's Travel in Your Pocket, and *Ferrari Guides' Inn Places.* Ferrari Publications (US$16-20). Purchase the guides online at www.ferrariguides.com.
The Gay Vacation Guide: The Best Trips and How to Plan Them, Mark Chesnut. Citadel Press (US$15).
Odysseus International Gay Travel Planner, Eli Angelo and Joseph Bain. Odysseus Enterprises Ltd. (US$31).
Spartacus International Gay Guide 2001-2002, Bruno Gmunder Verlag (US$33).

ESSENTIALS

Giovanni's Room, 1145 Pine St., Philadelphia, PA 19107 (US ☎215-923-2960; www.queerbooks.com). An international lesbian/feminist and gay bookstore with mail-order service (carries many of the publications listed below).

International Gay and Lesbian Travel Association, International Lesbian and Gay Association (ILGA), 81 rue Marché-au-Charbon, B-1000 Brussels, Belgium (☎02 502 2471; www.ilga.org). Provides political info, such as homosexuality laws of specific countries.

TRAVELERS WITH DISABILITIES

Countries vary in accessibility to travelers with disabilities. Some national and regional tourist boards provide directories on the accessibility of various accommodations and transportation services. If these services are not available, contact institutions of interest directly. Those with disabilities should inform airlines and hotels of their disabilities when making reservations; some time may be needed to prepare special accommodations. Call ahead to restaurants, museums, and other facilities to find out about the existence of ramps, the widths of doors, or the dimensions of elevators. **Guide dog owners** should inquire as to the quarantine policies of each destination country. At the very least, they will need to provide a certificate of immunization against rabies.

Rail is probably the most convenient form of travel for disabled travelers in Europe: Many stations have ramps, and some trains have wheelchair lifts, special seating areas, and specially equipped toilets. Large stations in Britain are equipped with wheelchair facilities, and the French national railroad offers wheelchair compartments on all TGV (high-speed) and Conrail trains. All Eurostar, some InterCity (IC), and some EuroCity (EC) trains are wheelchair-accessible and CityNightLine trains, French TGV, and Conrail trains feature special compartments. In general, the countries with the most **wheelchair-accessible rail networks** are: Denmark (IC and Lyn trains), France (TGVs and other long-distance trains), Germany (ICE, EC, IC, and IR trains), Ireland (most major trains), Italy (all Pendolino and many EC and IC trains), The Netherlands (most trains), Sweden (X2000s, most IC and IR trains), and Switzerland (all IC, most EC, and some regional trains). Austria, Poland, and Great Britain offer accessibility on selected routes. Greece and Spain's rail systems have limited resources for wheelchair accessibility. For those who wish to rent cars, some major **car rental** agencies (Hertz, Avis, and National) offer hand-controlled vehicles.

USEFUL ORGANIZATIONS

Mobility International USA (MIUSA), P.O. Box 10767, Eugene, OR 97440 (US ☎541-343-1284, voice and TDD; www.miusa.org). Sells *A World of Options: A Guide to International Educational Exchange, Community Service, and Travel for Persons with Disabilities* (US$35).

Moss Rehab ResourceNet (www.mossresourcenet.org). An Internet information resource center on international travel accessibility and other travel-related concerns for those with disabilities.

Society for the Advancement of Travel for the Handicapped (SATH), 347 Fifth Ave., #610, New York, NY 10016 (US ☎212-447-7284; www.sath.org). An advocacy group that publishes free online travel information and the travel magazine *OPEN WORLD* (US$18, free for members). Annual membership US$45; students and seniors US$30.

TOUR AGENCIES

Directions Unlimited, 123 Green Ln., Bedford Hills, NY 10507 (US ☎800-533-5343 or 914-241-1700; www.travel-cruises.com). Specializes in arranging individual and group vacations, tours, and cruises for the physically disabled.

The Guided Tour Inc., 7900 Old York Rd., #114B, Elkins Park, PA 19027 (US ☎800-783-5841 or 215-782-1370; www.guidedtour.com). Organizes travel programs for persons with developmental and physical challenges around Ireland, London, and Rome.

FURTHER READING: DISABILITIES.
Access in London, Gordon Couch. Cimino Publishing Group (US$12).
Around the World Resource Guide, Patricia Smither. Access for Disabled American Publishing (US$15).
Resource Directory for the Disabled, Richard Neil Shrout. Facts on file (US$45).
Wheelchair Around the World, Patrick D. Simpson. Pentland Press, Inc. (US$25).
Wheelchair Through Europe, Annie Mackin. Graphic Language Press (US$13).

MINORITY TRAVELERS

In general, minority travelers will find a high level of tolerance in large cities; the small towns and the countryside are more unpredictable. *Romany* (Gypsies) encounter the most hostility throughout Eastern Europe, and travelers with darker skin of any nationality might be mistaken for *Romany* and face unpleasant consequences. Other minority travelers, especially those of African or Asian descent, will usually meet with more curiosity than hostility; travelers of Arab ethnicity may also be treated more suspiciously. Anti-Semitism is still a problem in many countries and anti-Muslim sentiment has increased in many places after the September 11th attacks on the United States; sad to say, it is generally best to be discreet about your religion. Skinheads are on the rise in Europe, and minority travelers, especially Jews and blacks, should regard them with caution. Still, attitudes will vary from country to country and town to town; travelers should use common sense—consult **Safety and Security** (p. 18) for tips on how to avoid unwanted attention. To read more about xenophobia in Europe, see p. 1069.

TRAVELERS WITH CHILDREN

Family vacations often require that you slow your pace and always require that you plan ahead. When deciding where to stay, remember the special needs of young children; if you pick a B&B or a small hotel, call ahead and make sure it's child-friendly. If you rent a car, make sure the rental company provides a car seat for younger children. **Be sure that your child carries some sort of ID** in case of an emergency or in case he or she gets lost.

FURTHER READING: TRAVELERS WITH CHILDREN.
Backpacking with Babies and Small Children, Goldie Silverman. Wilderness Press (US$10).
Take Your Kids to Europe, Cynthia W. Harriman. Globe Pequot Press (US$18).
How to take Great Trips with Your Kids, Sanford and Jane Portnoy. Harvard Common Press (US $10).
Have Kid, Will Travel: 101 Survival Strategies for Vacationing With Babies and Young Children, Claire and Lucille Tristram. Andrews McMeel Publishing (US$9).
Adventuring with Children: An Inspirational Guide to World Travel and the Outdoors, Nan Jeffrey. Menasha Ridge Press (US$15).
Trouble Free Travel with Children, Vicki Lansky. Book Peddlers (US$9).

Museums, tourist attractions, accommodations, and restaurants often offer discounts for children. Children under two generally fly for 10% of the adult airfare on international flights (this does not necessarily include a seat). International fares are usually discounted 25% for children from two to 11.

DIETARY CONCERNS

Vegetarians should have no problem finding suitable cuisine in most of Western Europe. Particularly in city listings, *Let's Go* notes many restaurants that cater to vegetarians or that offer good vegetarian selections. The North American Vegetarian Society (see box below) publishes information about vegetarian travel, including *Transformative Adventures: A Guide to Vacations and Retreats* (US$15).

Travelers who keep **kosher** should contact synagogues in larger cities for information on food options. Your own synagogue or college Hillel should have access to lists of Jewish institutions across the globe. If you are strict in your observance, you may have to prepare your own food on the road. The website www.kashrut.com/travel provides contact information and further resources, while www.shamash.org/kosher catalogues kosher restaurants worldwide.

FURTHER RESOURCES: DIETARY CONCERNS.
North American Vegetarian Society, P.O. Box 72, Dolgeville, NY 13329 (US ☎518-568-7970, www.navs-online.org).
The Vegetarian Society of the UK (VSUK), Parkdale, Dunham Rd, Altringham, Cheshire WA14 4QG (UK ☎0161 925 2000; www.vegsoc.org).
The Vegan Travel Guide: UK and Southern Ireland. Book Publishing Co. (US$15).
The Vegetarian Traveler: Where to Stay if You're Vegetarian, Vegan, Environmentally Sensitive, Jed and Susan Civic. Larson Publications (US$16).

OTHER RESOURCES

Let's Go tries to cover all aspects of budget travel, but we can't include *everything*. Listed below are books, organizations, and websites for your own research.

TRAVEL PUBLISHERS AND BOOKSTORES

Adventurous Traveler Bookstore, 245 S. Champlain St., Burlington, VT 05401, USA (☎800-282-3963 or 802-860-6776; www.adventuroustraveler.com), offers information and gear for outdoor and adventure travel.

Bon Voyage!, 2069 W. Bullard Ave., Fresno, CA 93711, USA (☎800-995-9716, elsewhere call US ☎559-447-8441; www.bon-voyage-travel.com), specializes in Europe and sells videos, travel gear, books, maps, and railpasses. Free newsletter.

Hippocrene Books, Inc., 171 Madison Ave., New York, NY 10016, USA (☎212-685-4371; orders 718-454-2366; www.hippocrenebooks.com). Publishes travel guides, as well as foreign language dictionaries and learning guides. Free catalog.

Hunter Publishing, 130 Campus Dr., Edison, NJ 08818, USA (☎800-255-0343; www.hunterpublishing.com). Has an extensive catalog of travel guides and diving and adventure travel books.

Rand McNally, 8255 N. Central Park Ave., Skokie, IL 60076, USA (☎800-275-7263; elsewhere call US ☎847-329-6656; www.randmcnally.com), publishes a number of comprehensive road atlases (from US$10).

Travel Books & Language Center, Inc., 4437 Wisconsin Ave. NW, Washington, D.C. 20016, USA (☎800-220-2665; www.bookweb.org/bookstore/travelbks). Sells travel aids, language cassettes, dictionaries, travel books, atlases, and maps. No web orders, but ships worldwide.

THE WORLD WIDE WEB

Almost every aspect of budget travel is accessible via the web. With 10 minutes at the keyboard, you can make a reservation at a hostel, get advice on travel hotspots from other travelers who have just returned from Europe, or find out exactly how much a train from Paris to Munich costs.

Listed here are some budget travel sites to start off your surfing; other relevant web sites are listed throughout the book. Because web-site turnover is high, use search engines (such as www.google.com) to strike out on your own.

LEARNING THE ART OF BUDGET TRAVEL

Backpacker's Ultimate Guide: www.bugeurope.com. Tips on packing, transportation, and where to go. Also tons of country-specific travel information.

Backpack Europe: www.backpackeurope.com. Helpful tips, a bulletin board, and links.

How to See the World: www.artoftravel.com. A compendium of great travel tips, from cheap flights to self-defense to interacting with local culture.

Rec. Travel Library: www.travel-library.com. A fantastic set of links for general information and personal travelogues.

TripSpot: www.tripspot.com/europefeature.htm. An outline of links to help plan trips, transportation, sleeping accommodations, and packing.

COUNTRY-SPECIFIC INFORMATION

CIA World Factbook: www.odci.gov/cia/publications/factbook/index.html. Tons of vital statistics on European geography, governments, economics, and politics.

Foreign Language for Travelers: www.travlang.com. Provides free online translating dictionaries and lists of phrases in European languages from Albanian to Yiddish.

DESTINATION GUIDES

Atevo Travel: www.atevo.com/guides/destinations. Detailed introductions, transportation tips, and suggested itineraries. Free travel newsletter.

CNN: europe.cnn.com/TRAVEL. Detailed information about services, sites, shopping, dining, nightlife, and recreation in the major cities of Europe.

Columbus Travel Guides: www.travel-guides.com/navigate/region/eur.asp. Well-organized site with practical information on geography, government, communication, health precautions, economy, and useful addresses.

Geographia: www.geographia.com. Describes highlights and attractions of the various European countries.

In Your Pocket: www.inyourpocket.com. Extensive virtual guides to select Baltic and Eastern European cities.

ESSENTIALS

MyTravelGuide: www.mytravelguide.com. Country overviews, with everything from history to transportation to local newspapers and weather.

LINKS TO EUROPEAN TOURISM PAGES

TravelPage: www.travelpage.com. Links to official tourist office sites throughout Europe.

Lycos: cityguide.lycos.com/europe. General introductions to cities and regions throughout Europe, accompanied by links to applicable histories, news, and local tourism sites.

PlanetRider: www.planetrider.com/travel-guide.cfm/Destinations/Europe.htm. A subjective list of links to the "best" websites covering the culture and tourist attractions of major European cities.

 WWW.LETSGO.COM Our newly designed website now features the full online content of all of our guides. In addition, trial versions of all nine City Guides are available for download on Palm OS™ PDAs. Our website also contains our newsletter, links for photos and streaming video, online ordering of our titles, info about our books, and a travel forum buzzing with stories and tips.

TRANSPORTATION

GETTING TO EUROPE

BY PLANE

When it comes to airfare, a little effort can save you a bundle. If your plans are flexible enough to deal with the restrictions, courier fares are the cheapest. Standby seats and tickets bought from consolidators are also good deals, but last-minute specials, charter flights, and airfare wars often generate even lower rates. The key is to hunt around, be flexible, and ask persistently about discounts. Students, seniors, and those under 26 should never pay full price for a ticket.

AIRFARES

Airfares to Europe peak between mid-June and early September; holidays are also expensive. The cheapest times to travel are November to mid-December and early January to March. Midweek (Monday to Thursday morning) return flights run US$40-50 cheaper than weekend flights, but they are generally more crowded and less likely to permit frequent-flier upgrades. Flights without a fixed return date ("open return") or those that arrive and depart from different cities ("open jaw") can be pricier. Patching one-way flights together is the most expensive way to travel. Flights between Europe's capitals or regional hubs—London, Paris, Amsterdam, and Frankfurt—tend to be cheaper.

If Europe is only one stop on a more extensive globe-hop, consider a round-the-world (RTW) ticket. Tickets usually include at least five stops and are valid for about a year; prices range US$1200-5000. Try **Northwest Airlines/KLM** (US ☎ 800-447-4747; www.nwa.com) or **Star Alliance,** a consortium of 22 airlines including United Airlines (US ☎ 800-241-6522; www.star-alliance.com).

BUDGET AND STUDENT TRAVEL AGENCIES

While knowledgeable agents specializing in flights to Europe can make your life easier and help you save, they get paid on commission, so they may not spend the time to find you the lowest possible fare. Travelers holding **ISIC and IYTC cards** (p. 14) qualify for big discounts from student travel agencies. Most flights from budget agencies are on major airlines, but in peak season some may sell seats on less reliable chartered aircraft.

Council Travel (www.counciltravel.com). Countless US offices, including branches in Atlanta, Boston, Chicago, L.A., New York, San Francisco, Seattle, and Washington, D.C. Check the website or call US ☎ 800-2-COUNCIL (226-8624) for the office nearest you. Also an office at 28A Poland St. (Oxford Circus), **London** W1V 3DB (UK ☎ 020 7437 7767). *As of May, Council had declared bankruptcy and was subsumed under STA (see below). However, their offices are still in existence and transacting business.*

CTS Travel (www.ctstravelusa.com). Offices across Italy as well as in Paris, London, and New York. Call toll free US ☎ 877-287-6665. In UK, 44 Goodge St., **London** W1T 2AD (☎ 020 7636 0031; ctsinfo@ctstravel.co.uk).

STA Travel (www.sta-travel.com). A student and youth travel organization with over 300 offices worldwide, including over 100 US offices. Check their website for the nearest location. Ticket booking, travel insurance, railpasses, and more. For 24hr. reservations and info, call US ☎800-781-4040. In the UK, walk-in office 11 Goodge St., **London** W1T 2PF (☎020 7436 7779). In New Zealand, Shop 2B, 182 Queen St., **Auckland** (☎09 309 0458). In Australia, 366 Lygon St., **Carlton** Vic 3053 (☎03 9349 4344).

Travel CUTS (Canadian Universities Travel Services Limited; www.travelcuts.com). 60 offices across Canada, including 187 College St., **Toronto,** ON M5T 1P7 (☎416-979-2406). Also 295-A Regent St., **London** W1R 7YA (UK ☎020 7255 1944).

usit world (www.usitworld.com). Over 50 **usit campus** branches in the UK, including 52 Grosvenor Gardens, **London** SW1W 0AG (☎0870 240 10 10); and **Edinburgh** (☎0131 668 3303). Nearly 20 **usit NOW** offices in Ireland, including 19-21 Aston Quay, O'Connell Bridge, **Dublin** 2 (☎01 602 1600; www.usitnow.ie); and **Belfast** (☎02 890 327 111; www.usitnow.com).

Wasteels, Skoubogade 6, 1158 **Copenhagen,** Denmark (☎3314 4633; www.wasteels.dk/uk). A huge chain; 165 locations across Europe. BIJ (Billets Internationals de Jeunesse; see p. 61) tickets discounted 30-45%. 2nd-class international train tickets with unlimited stopovers for those under 26. Sold only in Europe.

 FLIGHT PLANNING ON THE INTERNET. The Internet is a great place to look for travel bargains—it's fast and convenient, and you can spend as long as you like exploring options without driving your travel agent insane.

Many airline companies offer special last-minute deals on the Web. Some require email addresses, so be aware of each site's privacy policy before you submit. Airlines like Continental (www.continental.com/cool) and United (www.united.com, click on "Special Deals") require membership logins or email subscriptions before allowing access to special prices.

Other sites do the legwork and compile the deals for you; try www.bestfares.com, www.flights.com, www.hotdeals.com, www.onetravel.com, and www.travelzoo.com. ■ **Student Universe** (www.studentuniverse.com), **STA** (www.sta-travel.com), and **Orbitz.com** provide quotes on student tickets, while **Expedia** (www.expedia.com) and **Travelocity** (www.travelocity.com) offer full travel services. **Priceline** (www.priceline.com) allows you to specify a price but obligates you to buy any ticket that meets or beats it; be prepared for antisocial hours and odd routes. **Skyauction** (www.skyauction.com) allows you to bid on both last-minute and advance-purchase tickets.

An indispensable resource on the Internet is the *Air Traveler's Handbook* (www.cs.cmu.edu/afs/cs/user/mkant/public/travel/airfare.html), a comprehensive listing of links to everything you need to know before you board a plane.

One last note: To protect yourself, make sure that the site you use has a secure server before handing over any credit card details.

COMMERCIAL AIRLINES

The commercial airlines' lowest regular offer is the **APEX** (Advance Purchase Excursion) fare, which provides confirmed reservations and allows "open-jaw" tickets. Generally, reservations must be made seven to 21 days ahead of departure, with seven- to 14-day minimum-stay and up to 90-day maximum-stay restrictions. These fares carry hefty cancellation and change penalties. Book peak-season APEX fares early or you'll have a hard time getting your desired departure date. Use **Microsoft Expedia** (www.expedia.com) or **Travelocity** (www.travelocity.com) to get an idea of the lowest published fares, then use the resources outlined here to try and beat those fares. Low-season fares should be appreciably cheaper than the high-season (mid-June to August) ones listed here.

TRAVELING FROM NORTH AMERICA

Basic return fares to Europe are roughly US$200-750: to Frankfurt, US$300-750; London, US$200-600; Paris, US$250-700. Standard commercial carriers like American (☎800-433-7300; www.aa.com) and United (☎800-241-6522; www.ual.com) will probably offer the most convenient flights, but they may not be the cheapest unless you grab a special promotion ticket. You might find flying one of the following airlines a better deal, even with their limited departure points.

Icelandair: US ☎800-223-5500; www.icelandair.com. Stopovers in Iceland for no extra cost on most transatlantic flights. New York to Frankfurt May-Sept. US$500-780; Oct.-May US$390-$450.

Finnair: US ☎800-950-5000; www.us.finnair.com. Cheap return fares from San Francisco, New York, and Toronto to Helsinki. Connections throughout Europe.

Martinair: US ☎800-627-8462; www.martinairusa.com. Fly from California or Florida to Amsterdam mid-June to mid-Aug. US$880; mid-Aug. to mid-June US$730.

TRAVELING FROM THE UK AND IRELAND

Because many carriers fly from the British Isles to the continent, we only include discount airlines or those with cheap specials here. The **Air Travel Advisory Bureau** in London (☎020 7636 5000; www.atab.co.uk) provides referrals to travel agencies and consolidators that offer discounted airfares out of the UK.

Aer Lingus: Ireland ☎0818 365 000; UK ☎0845 084 4444; www.flyaerlingus.com. Return tickets from Dublin, Shannon, and Cork to Amsterdam, Brussels, Düsseldorf, Frankfurt, Madrid, Milan, Munich, Paris, Rome, Stockholm, and Zurich (€40-135).

British Midland Airways: UK ☎0870 60 70 555; www.flybmi.com. Departures from throughout the UK. Discounted online fares including London to Brussels (UK£83), Madrid (UK£118), Milan (£126), and Paris (UK£84).

buzz: UK ☎0870 240 70 70; www.buzzaway.com. From London to Berlin, Frankfurt, and Paris (UK£30-35). Tickets cannot be refunded and flight changes cost UK£15.

easyJet: UK ☎0870 600 00 00; www.easyjet.com. London to Amsterdam, Athens, Barcelona, Geneva, Madrid, Nice, and Zurich (from UK£30). Online ticketing.

Go-Fly Limited: UK ☎09063 020 150, from elsewhere call UK ☎41279 666 388; www.go-fly.com. A subsidiary of British Airways. From London to Barcelona, Copenhagen, Edinburgh, Naples, Prague, Rome, and Venice (return UK£50-180).

KLM: UK ☎08705 074 074; www.klmuk.com. Cheap return tickets from London and elsewhere direct to Amsterdam, Brussels, Frankfurt, and Zurich; via Amsterdam Schiphol Airport to Düsseldorf, Milan, Paris, Rome, and elsewhere.

Ryanair: Ireland ☎0818 30 30 30, UK ☎08701 569 569; www.ryanair.ie. From Dublin, London, and Glasgow to destinations in France, Germany, Ireland, Italy, Scandinavia, and elsewhere. Deals from as low as UK£9 on limited weekend specials.

TRAVELING FROM AUSTRALIA AND NEW ZEALAND

Air New Zealand: New Zealand ☎0800 737 000; www.airnz.co.nz. From Melbourne, Auckland, and elsewhere to London, Paris, Rome, Frankfurt, and beyond.

Qantas Air: Australia ☎13 13 13; New Zealand ☎0800 808 767; www.qantas.com.au. Flights from Australia and New Zealand to London AUS$2400-3000.

Singapore Air: Australia ☎13 10 11; New Zealand ☎0800 808 909; www.singaporeair.com. Flies from Auckland, Sydney, Melbourne, and Perth to Amsterdam, Brussels, Frankfurt, London, Manila, and more.

Thai Airways: Australia ☎1300 65 19 60; New Zealand ☎09 377 02 68; www.thaiair.com. Auckland, Sydney, and Melbourne to Rome, Frankfurt, London, and more.

TRANSPORTATION

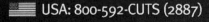

TRAVELING FROM SOUTH AFRICA

Air France: South Africa ☎0860 340 340; www.airfrance.com/za. Johannesburg to Paris; connections throughout Europe.

British Airways: South Africa ☎0860 011 747; www.british-airways.com/regional/sa. Johannesburg to London; connections to the rest of Western Europe from SAR3400.

Lufthansa: South Africa ☎0861 842 538; www.lufthansa.co.za. From Cape Town, Durban, and Johannesburg to Germany and elsewhere.

Virgin Atlantic: South Africa ☎011 340 3400; www.virgin-atlantic.co.za. Flies to London from both Cape Town and Johannesburg.

AIR COURIER FLIGHTS

Those who travel light should consider courier flights. Couriers help transport cargo on international flights by using their checked luggage space for freight. Generally, couriers must travel with carry-ons only and must deal with complex flight restrictions. Most flights are return with short fixed-length stays (usually one week) and a limit of one ticket per issue. Most flights also operate only out of gateway cities, mostly in North America. Generally, you must be over 21.

In summer, popular destinations require advance reservation of about two weeks, and you can usually book up to two months ahead. Super-discounted fares may be available for "last-minute" flights (three to 14 days ahead).

TRAVELING FROM NORTH AMERICA. Return courier fares from the US to Europe run about US$200-500. Most flights leave from New York, Los Angeles, San Francisco, or Miami in the US; and from Montreal, Toronto, or Vancouver in Canada. The organizations below provide their members with lists of opportunities and courier brokers worldwide for an annual fee (typically US$50-60). Alternatively, you can contact a courier broker directly; most charge registration fees, but a few don't. Prices quoted below are return.

Air Courier Association, 350 Indiana St., Suite 300, Golden, CO 80401 (US ☎800-282-1202, elsewhere call US ☎303-279-3600; www.aircourier.org). Ten departure cities throughout the US and Canada to London, Madrid, Paris, Rome, and throughout Western Europe (high-season US$150-360). One-year membership US$39.

International Association of Air Travel Couriers (IAATC), P.O. Box 980, Keystone Heights, FL 32656 (☎352-475-1584; www.courier.org). From nine North American cities to Western European cities, including London, Madrid, Paris, and Rome. One-year membership US$45-50.

Global Courier Travel, P.O. Box 3051, Nederland, CO 80466 (☎866-470-3061; www.globalcouriertravel.com). Searchable on-line database. Departures from the US and Canada to Amsterdam, Athens, Brussels, Copenhagen, Frankfurt, London, Madrid, Milan, Paris, and Rome. Lifetime membership US$40, 2 people US$55.

FROM THE UK, IRELAND, AUSTRALIA, AND NEW ZEALAND. The minimum age for couriers from the **UK** is usually 18. **Brave New World Enterprises,** P.O. Box 22212, London SE5 8WB (www.courierflights.com) publishes a directory of all the companies offering courier flights in the UK (UK£10, in electronic form UK£8). **Global Courier Travel** (see above) also offers flights from London and Dublin to continental Europe. **British Airways Travel Shop** (☎0870 240 0747; www.batravelshops.com) arranges some flights from London to destinations in continental Europe (specials may be as low as UK£60; no registration fee). From **Australia** and **New Zealand, Global Courier Travel** (see above) often has listings from Sydney and Auckland to London and occasionally Frankfurt.

STANDBY FLIGHTS

Traveling standby requires considerable flexibility in arrival and departure dates and cities. Companies dealing in standby flights sell vouchers rather than tickets, along with the promise to get to your destination (or near your destination) within a certain window of time (typically 1-5 days). You call in before your specific window of time to hear your flight options and the probability that you will be able to board each flight. You can then decide which flights you want to try to make, show up at the appropriate airport at the appropriate time, present your voucher, and board if space is available. Vouchers can usually be bought for both one-way and return travel. You may receive a monetary refund only if every available flight within your date range is full; if you opt not to take an available (but perhaps less convenient) flight, you can only get credit toward future travel. Carefully read agreements with any company offering standby flights, as tricky fine print can leave you in a lurch. To check on a company's service record in the US, call the Better Business Bureau (☎212-533-6200). It is difficult to receive refunds, and vouchers will not be honored when an airline fails to receive payment in time.

TICKET CONSOLIDATORS

Ticket consolidators, or "bucket shops," buy unsold tickets in bulk from commercial airlines and sell them at discounted rates. The best place to look is in the Sunday travel section of any major newspaper (such as *The New York Times*), where many bucket shops place tiny ads. Call quickly, as availability is typically extremely limited. Not all bucket shops are reliable, so insist on a receipt that gives full details of restrictions, refunds, and tickets, and pay by credit card (in spite of the 2-5% fee) so you can stop payment if you never receive your tickets. For more information, see www.travel-library.com/air-travel/consolidators.html.

TRAVELING FROM NORTH AMERICA. Travel Avenue (☎800-333-3335; www.travelavenue.com) searches for the best available published fares and then uses several consolidators to attempt to beat that fare. Other consolidators worth trying are **Interworld** (☎305-443-4929; fax 443-0351); **Pennsylvania Travel** (☎800-331-0947); **Rebel** (☎800-227-3235; www.rebeltours.com); **Cheap Tickets** (☎800-377-1000; www.cheaptickets.com); and **Travac** (☎800-872-8800; www.travac.com). Consolidators on the web include the **Internet Travel Network** (www.itn.com); **Travel Information Services** (www.tiss.com); **TravelHUB** (www.travelhub.com); and **The Travel Site** (www.thetravelsite.com). Keep in mind that these are just suggestions; *Let's Go* does not endorse any of these agencies. As always, be cautious and research companies before you hand over your credit card number.

TRAVELING FROM THE UK, AUSTRALIA, & NEW ZEALAND. In UK, the **Air Travel Advisory Bureau** (☎0207-636-5000; www.atab.co.uk) can provide names of reliable consolidators and discount flight specialists. From Australia and New Zealand, look for consolidator ads in the travel section of the *Sydney Morning Herald*.

CHARTER FLIGHTS

Charters are flights a tour operator contracts with an airline to fly extra loads of passengers during peak season. Charter flights fly less frequently than major airlines, make refunds particularly difficult, and are almost always fully booked. Schedules and itineraries may also change or be cancelled at the last moment (as late as 48 hours before the trip, and without a full refund), and check-in, boarding, and baggage claim are often pretty slow. However, they can also be cheaper.

Discount clubs and **fare brokers** offer members savings on last-minute charter and tour deals. Study contracts closely; you don't want to end up with an unwanted overnight layover. **Travelers Advantage,** Trumbull, CT, USA (☎ 203-365-2000; www.travelersadvantage.com; US$60 annual fee includes discounts and cheap flight directories) specializes in European travel and tour packages.

BY CHUNNEL FROM THE UK

Traversing 27 mi. under the sea, the Chunnel is undoubtedly the fastest, most convenient, and least scenic route from England to France.

BY TRAIN. Eurostar, Eurostar House, Waterloo Station, London SE1 8SE (UK ☎ 0990 186 186; US ☎ 800-387-6782; elsewhere call UK ☎ 020 7928 5163; www.eurostar.com; www.raileurope.com) runs frequent trains between London and the continent. Ten to 28 trains per day run to Paris (3hr., US$75-159 2nd-class), Brussels (3hr. 50min., US$75-159 2nd-class), and Eurodisney. Routes include stops at Ashford in England, and Calais and Lille in France. Book at major rail stations in the UK, at the office above, by phone, or on the web.

BY BUS. Both **Eurolines** and **Eurobus** provide bus-ferry combinations (see p. 62).

BY CAR. Eurotunnel, Customer Relations, P.O. Box 2000, Folkestone, Kent CT18 8XY (UK ☎ 08000 969 992; www.eurotunnel.co.uk) shuttles cars and passengers between Kent and Nord-Pas-de-Calais. Return fares for vehicle and all passengers range from UK£100-210 with car, UK£259-636 with campervan. Same-day return costs UK£110-150, five-day return UK£139-195. Book online or via phone. Travelers with cars can also look into sea crossings by ferry (see below).

BY BOAT FROM THE UK AND IRELAND

The fares below are **one-way** for **adult foot passengers** unless otherwise noted. Though standard return fares are usually just twice the one-way fare, **fixed-period returns** (usually within five days) are almost invariably cheaper. Ferries run **year-round** unless otherwise noted. **Bikes** are usually free, although you may have to pay up to UK£10 in high season. For a **camper/trailer** supplement, you will have to add UK£20-140 to the "with car" fare. If more than one price is quoted, the quote in UK£ is valid for departures from the UK, etc. A directory of ferries in this region can be found at www.seaview.co.uk/ferries.html.

P&O Stena Line: UK ☎087 0600 0611; from Europe, call UK ☎44 1304 864 003; www.posl.com. **Dover** to **Calais** (1¼hr., 30 per day, UK£24).

Hoverspeed: UK ☎0870 240 8070; www.hoverspeed.co.uk. **Dover** to **Calais** (35-55min., every hr., UK£24) and **Ostend, Belgium** (2hr., 5-7 per day, UK£28). **Newhaven** to **Dieppe, France** (2¼-4¼hr., 1-3 per day, UK£28).

DFDS Seaways: UK ☎08705 33 30 00; www.dfdsseaways.co.uk. **Harwich** to **Hamburg** (20hr.) and **Esbjerg, Denmark** (19hr.). **Newcastle** to **Amsterdam** (14hr.); **Kristiansand, Norway** (19hr.); and **Gothenburg, Sweden** (22hr.).

Brittany Ferries: UK ☎08703 665 333; France ☎08 25 82 88 28; www.brittany-ferries.com. **Plymouth** to **Roscoff, France** (6hr.; in summer 1-3 per day, off-season 1 per week; UK£20-58 or €21-46) and **Santander, Spain** (24-30hr., 1-2 per week, return UK£80-145). **Portsmouth** to **St-Malo** (8¾hr., 1-2 per day, €23-49) and **Caen, France** (6hr, 1-3 per day, €21-44). **Poole** to **Cherbourg** (4¼hr., 1-2 per day, €21-44). **Cork** to **Roscoff, France** (13½hr., Apr.-Sept. 1 per week, €52-99).

P&O North Sea Ferries: UK ☎0870 129 6002; www.ponsf.com. Daily ferries from **Hull** to **Rotterdam, Netherlands** (13½hr.) and **Zeebrugge, Belgium** (14hr.). Both UK£38-48, students UK£24-31, cars UK£63-78. Online bookings.

Fjord Line: www.fjordline.no. Norway ☎55 54 88 00; UK ☎0191 296 1313; booking@fjordline.com. **Newcastle** to **Stavanger** (19hr.) and **Bergen** (26hr.), **Norway** (UK£50-110, students £25-110). Also between **Bergen** and **Egersund, Norway**, and **Hanstholm, Denmark**.

Irish Ferries: Ireland ☎1890 31 31 31; France ☎01 44 88 54 50; UK ☎08705 17 17 17; www.irishferries.ie. **Rosslare, Ireland** to **Cherbourg** and **Roscoff, France** (17-18hr., Apr.-Sept. 1-9 per week, €60-120, students €48) and **Pembroke, UK** (3¾hr., €25-39/€19). **Holyhead, UK** to **Dublin** (2-3hr., return £20-31/£15).

Stena Line: UK ☎4123 364 68 26; www.stenaline.co.uk. **Harwich** to **Hook of Holland** (5hr., UK£26). **Fishguard** to **Rosslare** (1-3½hr., UK£18-21, students £14-17). **Holyhead** to **Dublin** (4hr., UK£23-27/£19-23) and **Dún Laoghaire, Ireland** (1-3½hr., £23-27/£19-23). **Stranraer** to **Belfast** (1¾-3¼hr., UK£14-36/£10).

GETTING AROUND EUROPE

Fares on all modes of transportation are either **single** (one-way) or **return** (round-trip). "Period returns" require that you return within a specific number of days. "Day returns" require you to return on the same day. Unless stated otherwise, *Let's Go* always lists single fares for trains and buses. Return fares on trains and buses in Europe are simply double the single fare.

BY PLANE

Although flying is almost invariably more expensive than traveling by train, if you are short on time (or flush with cash) you might consider it. Student travel agencies sell cheap tickets, and budget fares are frequently available in the spring and summer on high-volume routes between northern Europe and areas of Greece, Italy, and Spain; consult budget travel agents and local newspapers. For information on cheap flights from Britain to the continent, see **Traveling from the UK, p. 46.**

The **Star Alliance European Airpass** offers low Economy Class fares for travel within Europe to more than 200 destinations in 43 countries. The pass is available to transatlantic passengers on Star Alliance carriers, including Air Canada, Austrian Airlines, BMI British Midland, Lufthansa, Mexicana, Scandinavian Airlines System, Thai Airways, United Airlines, and Varig, as well as on certain partner airlines. Prices are based on mileage between destinations.

In addition, a number of European airlines offer coupon packets that considerably discount the cost of each flight leg. Most are available only as tack-ons to their transatlantic passengers, but some are available as stand-alone offers. Most must be purchased before departure, so research in advance.

Austrian Airlines: US ☎ 800-843-0002; www.austrianair.com/greatdeals/ europe_airpass.html. "European Airpass" available in the US to Austrian Airlines transatlantic passengers (min. 3 cities; max. 10). Prices based on mi. between destinations.

Europe by Air: US ☎ 888-387-2479; www.europebyair.com. Coupons good on 30 partner airlines to 150 European cities in 30 countries. Must be purchased prior to arrival in Europe. US$99 each, excluding airport tax. Also offers 15- and 21-day unlimited passes; US$699-$899.

Iberia: US ☎ 800-772-4642; www.iberia.com. "EuroPass" allows Iberia passengers flying from the US to Spain to tack on additional destinations in Europe.

KLM/Northwest: US ☎ 800-800-1504; www.nwavacations.com. "Passport to Europe," available to US transatlantic passengers, connects 90 European cities (3-city min., 12-city max.). US$100 each.

Lufthansa: US ☎ 800-399-5838; www.lufthansa.com. "Discover Europe" available to US travelers on transatlantic Lufthansa flights (3 cities min., 9 max.). US$119 each for the first three cities, US$99 each for additional cities.

Scandinavian Airlines: US ☎ 800-221-2350; www.scandinavian.net. One-way coupons for travel within Scandinavia, the Baltics, or all of Europe. US$75-155, 8 coupons max. Most are available only to transatlantic Scandinavian Airlines passengers, but some United and Lufthansa passengers also qualify.

BY TRAIN

Trains in Europe are generally comfortable, convenient, and reasonably swift. Second-class compartments, which seat two to six, are great places to meet fellow travelers. For long trips, make sure you are on the correct car, as trains sometimes split at crossroads. Towns listed in parentheses on European train schedules require a train switch at the town listed immediately before the parenthesis. For safety tips on train travel, see p. 19.

You can either buy a **railpass,** which allows you unlimited travel within a particular region for a given period of time, or rely on buying individual **point-to-point** tickets as you go. Almost all countries give students or youths (usually defined as anyone under 26) direct discounts on regular domestic rail tickets, and many also sell a student or youth card that provides 20-50% off all fares for up to a year.

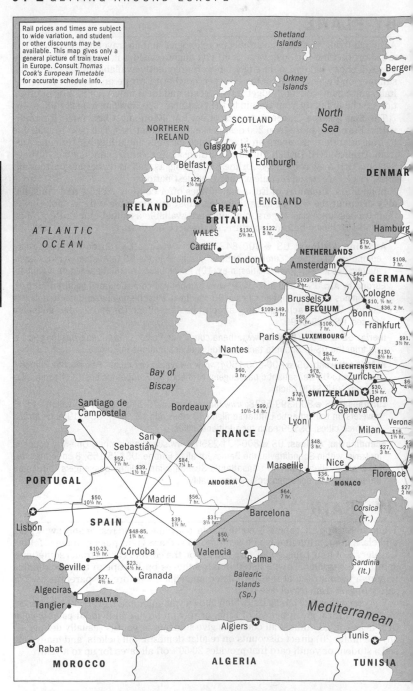

Rail prices and times are subject to wide variation, and student or other discounts may be available. This map gives only a general picture of train travel in Europe. Consult *Thomas Cook's European Timetable* for accurate schedule info.

TRANSPORTATION

Shetland Islands

Orkney Islands

Berger

SCOTLAND

NORTHERN
IRELAND

Glasgow $47,
3½ hr.

Edinburgh

Belfast

*North
Sea*

DENMAR

$22,
2½ hr.

Dublin

IRELAND

GREAT
BRITAIN

ENGLAND

Hamburg

*ATLANTIC
OCEAN*

WALES

Cardiff

London

$130,
5¾ hr.

$122,
5 hr.

NETHERLANDS

Amsterdam

$79,
6 hr.

$108,
7 hr.

$46,
3 hr.

GERMAN

$109-149,
3 hr.

Cologne

$10, ½ hr.

$36, 2 hr.

Brussels

BELGIUM

Bonn

$109-149,
3 hr.

Frankfurt

$68,
1¾ hr.

$108,
7 hr.

Paris

LUXEMBOURG

$91,
3½ hr.

Nantes

$84,
4½ hr.

$130,
8½ hr.

LIECHTENSTEIN

Zurich

$60,
3 hr.

$78,
3¾ hr.

$6
4

*Bay of
Biscay*

Bordeaux

$99,
10½-14 hr.

$78,
2¼ hr.

SWITZERLAND

Bern

$30,
1¼ hr.

Santiago de
Compostela

Geneva

Verona

Lyon

Milan

$16,
1½ hr.

San
Sebastián

FRANCE

$48,
3 hr.

$27,
3 hr.

2¼

$52,
7½ hr.

$84,
7¼ hr.

Nice

Florence

$39,
1½ hr.

Marseille

$36,
2¾ hr.

MONACO

$27
2 hr

PORTUGAL

Madrid

$56,
7 hr.

ANDORRA

$64,
7 hr.

*Corsica
(Fr.)*

$50,
10½ hr.

Barcelona

Lisbon

SPAIN

$39,
1½ hr.

$31,
3½ hr.

$10-23,
1½ hr.

Córdoba

$48-85,
1¾ hr.

Valencia

$50,
4 hr.

Palma

*Sardinia
(It.)*

Seville

$23,
4½ hr.

Granada

*Balearic
Islands
(Sp.)*

$27,
4½ hr.

Algeciras

GIBRALTAR

Tangier

Mediterranean

Algiers

Tunis

Rabat

MOROCCO

ALGERIA

TUNISIA

Rail Planner

TRANSPORTATION

RESERVATIONS. While seat reservations (usually US$3-10) are required only for selected trains, you are not guaranteed a seat without one. You should strongly consider reserving in advance during peak holiday and tourist seasons (at the very latest, a few hours ahead). You will have to purchase a **supplement** (US$10-50) or special fare for high-speed or high-quality trains such as Spain's AVE, Cisalpino, Finland's Pendolino S220, Italy's ETR500 and Pendolino, Germany's ICE, and certain French TGVs. InterRail holders must also purchase supplements (US$10-25) for trains like EuroCity, InterCity, Sweden's X2000, and many French TGVs; supplements are unnecessary for Eurailpass and Europass holders.

OVERNIGHT TRAINS. On night trains, you won't waste valuable daylight hours traveling, and you can avoid the hassle and expense of staying at a hotel. However, the main drawbacks include discomfort, sleepless nights, and the lack of scenery. **Sleeping accommodations** on trains differ from country to country, but typically you can either sleep upright in your seat (for free) or pay for a separate space. **Couchettes** (berths) typically have four to six seats per compartment (about US$20 per person); **sleepers** (beds) in private sleeping cars offer more privacy and comfort, but are considerably more expensive (US$40-150). If you are using a railpass valid only for a restricted number of days, inspect train schedules to maximize the use of your pass: an overnight train or boat journey uses up only one of your travel days if it departs after 7pm.

SHOULD YOU BUY A RAILPASS? Railpasses were conceived to allow you to jump on any train in Europe, go wherever you want whenever you want, and change your plans at will. In practice, it's not so simple. You still must stand in line to validate your pass, pay for supplements, and fork over cash for seat and couchette reservations. More importantly, railpasses don't always pay off. Consult our railmap (pp. 52-53) to estimate the point-to-point cost of each leg of your journey; add them up and compare the total with the cost of a railpass. If you are planning to spend extensive time on trains, hopping between big cities, a railpass will probably be worth it. But in many cases, especially if you are under 26, point-to-point tickets may prove a cheaper option.

You may find it tough to make your railpass pay for itself in Belgium, Greece, Ireland, Italy, Luxembourg, The Netherlands, Portugal, Spain, Eastern Europe, or the Balkans, where train fares are reasonable, distances short, or buses preferable. If, however, the total cost of your trips nears the price of the pass, the convenience of avoiding ticket lines may be worth the difference.

MULTINATIONAL RAILPASSES

EURAILPASS. Eurail is valid in most of Western Europe: Austria, Belgium, Denmark, Finland, France, Germany, Greece, Hungary, Ireland, Italy, Luxembourg, The Netherlands, Norway, Portugal, Spain, Sweden, and Switzerland. It is not valid in the UK. Standard **Eurailpasses,** valid for a consecutive given number of days, are best for those planning to spend extensive time on trains every few days. **Flexipasses,** valid for any 10 or 15 days within a two-month period, are more cost-effective for those traveling longer distances less frequently. **Saverpasses** provide first-class travel for travelers in groups of two to five (prices are per person). **Youthpasses** and **Youth Flexipasses** provide parallel second-class perks for those under 26. As of January 1, 2003, the Europass will be replaced by the **Selectpass,** which allows five to 15 travel days within a two-month period, in three to five pre-selected, contiguous countries. (For the purpose of the Selectpass, Belgium, The Netherlands, and Luxembourg are considered one country.) Youth and Saver Selectpasses are also available.

Take advantage of the specialty and high-speed trains of Europe!

FREE Thomas Cook timetable with Eurail/Europass orders over $1,000   We offer most European railpasses

catalog and rail brochure

EURAILPASSES	15 DAYS	21 DAYS	1 MONTH	2 MONTHS	3 MONTHS
Eurailpass	US$588	US$762	US$946	US$1338	US$1654
Eurailpass Saver	US$498	US$648	US$804	US$1138	US$1408
Eurailpass Youth	US$414	US$534	US$664	US$938	US$1160

SELECTPASSES		5 DAYS	6 DAYS	8 DAYS	10 DAYS	15 DAYS
Selectpass:	3-country	US$356	US$394	US$470	US$542	N/A
	4-country	US$398	US$436	US$512	US$584	N/A
	5-country	US$438	US$476	US$552	US$624	US$794
Saver:	3-country	US$304	US$336	US$400	US$460	N/A
	4-country	US$340	US$372	US$436	US$496	N/A
	5-country	US$374	US$406	US$470	US$560	US$674
Youth:	3-country	US$249	US$276	US$329	US$379	N/A
	4-country	US$279	US$306	US$359	US$409	N/A
	5-country	US$307	US$334	US$387	US$437	US$556

FLEXIPASS	10 DAYS IN 2 MONTHS	15 DAYS IN 2 MONTHS
Flexipass	US$694	US$914
Flexipass Saver	US$592	US$778
Flexipass Youth	US$488	US$642

Passholders receive a timetable for major routes and a map with details on ferry, steamer, bus, car rental, hotel, and Eurostar (see p. 51) discounts. Passholders often also receive reduced fares or free passage on many bus and boat lines.

SHOPPING AROUND FOR A EURAIL PASS. Eurail passes are designed by the EU itself and can be bought only by non-Europeans, almost exclusively from non-European distributors. These passes must be sold at uniform prices determined by the EU. However, some travel agents tack on a US$10 handling fee, and others offer certain bonuses with purchase, so shop around. Also, keep in mind that pass prices usually go up each year, so if you're planning to travel early in the year, you can save by purchasing before January 1 (you have three months from the purchase date to validate your pass in Europe).

It is best to buy your Eurail or Europass before leaving; only a few places in major European cities sell them, and at a marked-up price. You can get a replacement for a lost pass only if you have purchased insurance on it under the Pass Protection Plan (US$14). Passes are available through travel agents and student travel agencies like STA and Council (see p. 43). Several companies specialize in selecting and distributing appropriate railpasses; two to try are **Rail Europe** (US ☎ 888-382-7245; UK ☎ 0990 84 88 48; www.raileurope.com) and **Railpass.com** (US ☎ 877-724-5727; www.railpass.com/new).

OTHER MULTINATIONAL PASSES. If your travels will be limited to one area, regional passes are often good values. The new **France'n Italy Pass** lets you travel in France and Italy for four days in a two-month period (standard US$239, under 26 US$199). The **ScanRail Pass,** which covers rail travel in Denmark, Finland, Norway, and Sweden, is available both in the UK and the US (standard/under 26 passes for five days of 2nd-class travel in a one month period US$214/161; 10 days in two months US$288/216; 21 consecutive days US$332/249). The **Benelux Tourrail Pass** for Belgium, The Netherlands, and Luxembourg is available in the UK, in the US, and at train stations in Belgium and Luxembourg, but not in The Netherlands. (Standard/under 26 passes for five days of 2nd-class travel in a one month period US$155/104. Discount for companion traveler.) The **Balkan Flexipass** is valid for travel in Bulgaria, Greece, Macedonia, Montenegro, Romania, Serbia, Turkey, and Yugoslavia (five days of travel in a one month period US$152, under 26 US$90). The **European East Pass** covers Austria, the Czech Republic, Hungary, Poland, and the Slovak Republic (five days of travel in a one month period US$154).

INTERRAIL PASS. If you have lived for at least six months in any European country, **InterRail Passes** prove an economical option. There are eight InterRail zones. The **Under 26 InterRail Card** allows either 21 consecutive days or one month of unlimited travel within one, two, three, or all of the eight zones; the cost is determined by the number of zones the pass covers (UK£119-249). A card can also be purchased for 12 days of travel in one zone (UK£119). The **Over 26 InterRail Card** (UK£169-355) provides the same services as the Under 26 InterRail Card, as does the new **Child Pass** (ages 4-11;UK£85-178). Passholders receive **discounts** on rail travel, Eurostar journeys, and most ferries to Ireland, Scandinavia, and the rest of Europe. Most exclude **supplements** for high-speed trains. For info and ticket sales in Europe, contact **Student Travel Centre**, 24 Rupert St., 1st fl., London W1V 7FN (☎020 7437 8101; www.student-travel-centre.com). Tickets are also available from travel agents, at major train stations throughout Europe, or through on-line vendors (www.railpassdirect.co.uk).

DOMESTIC RAILPASSES

If you are planning to spend a significant amount of time within one country or region, a national pass—valid on all rail lines of a country's rail company—will probably be more cost-effective than a multinational pass. Several national and regional passes offer companion fares, allowing two adults traveling together to save about 50% on the price of one pass. However, many national passes are limited and don't provide the free or discounted travel on many private railways and ferries that Eurail does. Some of these passes can be bought only in Europe, some only outside of Europe; check with a railpass agent or with national tourist offices.

NATIONAL RAILPASSES. The domestic analogs of the Eurailpass, national railpasses (called "flexipasses" in some countries) are valid either for a given number of consecutive days or for a specific number of days within a given period. Usually, they must be purchased before you leave your home country. Though national passes will usually save frequent travelers money, in some cases (particularly in Eastern Europe) you may find that they are actually more expensive than point-to-point tickets. Regional passes are also available for areas where the main pass is not valid. For more information, contact Rail Europe (p. 59).

EURO DOMINO. Like the InterRail Pass, the Euro Domino Pass is available to anyone who has lived in Europe for at least six months; however, it is only valid within the country that you designate upon buying the pass, which cannot be your country of residence. The Euro Domino Pass is available for first- and second-class travel for 28 European countries plus Morocco, with a special rate for those under 26. It can be used for three to eight days of unlimited travel within a one-month period, but is not valid on Eurostar or Thalys trains. **Supplements** for many high-speed (e.g., French TGV, German ICE, and Swedish X2000) trains are included, though you must still pay for **reservations** where they are compulsory. The pass must be bought within your country of residence; each destination has a different price. Inquire with your national rail company for more information.

RAIL-AND-DRIVE PASSES

In addition to simple railpasses, many countries (as well as Europass and Eurail) offer rail-and-drive passes, which combine car rental with rail travel—a good option for travelers who wish both to visit cities accessible by rail and to make side trips into the surrounding areas.

DISCOUNTED RAIL TICKETS

For travelers under 26, **BIJ** tickets (Billets Internationals de Jeunesse; i.e. **Wasteels, Eurotrain,** and **Route 26**) are great alternatives to railpasses. Available for international trips within Europe, travel within France, and most ferry services, they knock 20-40% off regular second-class fares. Issued for a specific international route between two points, they must be used in the direction and order of the designated route and must be bought in Europe. However, tickets are good for 60 days after purchase and allow a number of stopovers along the normal direct route of the train journey. The equivalent for those over 26, **BIGT** tickets provide a 20-30% discount on 1st- and 2nd-class international tickets for business travelers, temporary residents of Europe, and their families. Both types of tickets are available from European travel agents, at Wasteels or Eurotrain offices (usually in or near train stations), or directly at the ticket counter in some nations. For more information, see www.wasteels.com.

FURTHER RESOURCES ON TRAIN TRAVEL.
Point-to-Point Fares and Schedules: www.raileurope.com/us/rail/ fares_schedules/index.htm. Allows you to calculate whether buying a railpass would save you money. See also our **railmap** (pp. 52-53)
European Railway Servers: mercurio.iet.unipi.it/misc/timetabl.html. Links to rail servers throughout Europe.
Info on Rail Travel and Railpasses: www.eurorail.com; www.raileuro.com.
Thomas Cook European Timetable, updated monthly, covers all major and most minor train routes in Europe. In the US, order it from Forsyth Travel Library (US$27.95; ☎800-367-7984; www.forsyth.com). In Europe, find it at any Thomas Cook Money Exchange Center. Alternatively, buy directly from Thomas Cook (www.thomascookpublishing.com).
Guide to European Railpasses, Rick Steves. Free online at www.ricksteves.com /subscribe/home.htm (US ☎425-771-8303).
On the Rails Around Europe: A Comprehensive Guide to Travel by Train, Melissa Shales. Thomas Cook Ltd. (US$18.95).
Europe By Eurail 2002, Laverne Ferguson-Kosinski. Globe Pequot Press (US$17.95).

BY BUS

Though European trains and railpasses are extremely popular, buses may prove a better option. In Spain, Hungary, and the Baltics, the bus and train systems are on par with trains; in Britain, Greece, Ireland, Portugal, and Turkey, bus networks are more extensive, more efficient, and often more comfortable than trains; and in Iceland and parts of northern Scandinavia, bus service is the only ground transportation available. In the rest of Europe, scattered offerings from private companies can be inexpensive but sometimes unreliable. Often cheaper than railpasses, **international bus passes** typically allow unlimited travel on a hop-on, hop-off basis between major European cities. In general these services tend to be more popular among non-American backpackers.

Eurolines, 52 Grosvenor Gardens, London SW1W 0AU (UK ☎ 1582 404 511; www.eurolines.co.uk). The largest operator of Europe-wide coach services, Eurolines offers unlimited peak-season 30-day (UK£229, under 26 UK£186) or 60-day (UK£279/205) travel between 30 major European cities in 16 countries; off-season prices are lower. Euroexplorers mini-passes offer stops at select cities across Europe (UK£55-69).

Busabout, 258 Vauxhall Bridge Rd., London SW1V 1BS (UK ☎ 207 950 1661; www.busabout.com) covers 60 cities and towns in Europe. Consecutive-Day standard/student passes range from US$269/239 for 2 weeks to US$1069/959 for a season pass. Flexipass standard/student passes range from US$259/229 for 6 days out of 1 month to US$839/759 for 25 days out of 4 months.

BY CAR

RENTING

While a single traveler won't save cash by renting a car, four typically will. Rail Europe and other railpass vendors offer **rail-and-drive packages** both for individual countries and for all of Europe. **Fly-and-drive packages** are often available from travel agents or airline/rental agency partnerships.

RENTAL AGENCIES. It is usually less expensive to reserve a car from the US in advance than when already in Europe, so make reservations before you leave by calling a US-based firm with European offices (Avis, Budget, or Hertz), a European-based company with local representatives (Europcar), or a tour operator that will arrange a rental for you from a European company at its own rates (Auto Europe or Europe By Car). Multinationals offer greater flexibility, but tour operators often strike better deals. Occasionally their price and availability information is not consistent with what local offices in your country will tell you; check with both numbers to get the best price. Local branches are included in town listings; for offices in your home country, call your local directory.

Minimum age to rent a car varies from country to country but is usually 21-25; some companies charge those aged 21-24 an additional insurance fee. Policies and prices vary from agency to agency; be sure to ask about the insurance coverage and deductible, and read the fine print. Rental agencies in Europe include:

Auto Europe, US ☎ 888-223- 5555; www.autoeurope.com.

Avis, US ☎ 800-230-4898; Canada ☎ 800-272-5871; UK ☎ 0870 60 60 100; Australia ☎ 136 333; www.avis.com.

Budget, US ☎ 800-527-0700; elsewhere call US ☎ 800-472-3325; www.budget.com.

Europe by Car, US ☎ 800-223-1516; www.europebycar.com.

Europcar, France ☎ 03 31 30 44 90 00; US ☎ 877-506-0070; www.europcar.com.

Hertz, US ☎ 800-654-3131; Canada ☎ 800-263-0600; UK ☎ 870 844 8844; Australia ☎ 613 9698 2555; www.hertz.com.

Kemwel Holiday Autos, US ☎ 877-820-0668; www.kemwel.com.

INTERNATIONAL DRIVING PERMIT (IDP). If you plan to drive a car while in Europe, you must be over 18 and have an International Driving Permit (IDP), although certain countries (such as the UK) allow travelers to drive with a valid American or Canadian license for a limited number of months. It may be a good idea to get one anyway, in case you're in an accident or stranded in a smaller town where the police do not know English; information on the IDP is also printed in French, Spanish, Russian, German, Arabic, Italian, Scandinavian, and Portuguese.

Your IDP, valid for one year, must be issued in your own country before you depart. An application for an IDP usually requires one or two passport photos, a valid local license, and a fee (about US$10). To apply, contact the national or local branch of your home country's automobile association.

COSTS AND INSURANCE. Rates vary widely by country; expect to pay anywhere from US$100-450 per week, plus tax. Some chains allow you to choose a drop-off location different from your pick-up city, but there is often a minimum hire period and an extra charge. Particularly during the summer, rental in parts of Eastern Europe and Scandinavia, as well as in Denmark, Ireland, Italy, and Turkey, might be more expensive; some companies charge extra fees for traveling into Eastern Europe. Reserve ahead and pay in advance if possible. Expect to pay more for larger cars and for 4WD. Cars with **automatic transmission** are far more expensive than manuals (stick shift), and are more difficult to find in most of Europe. It is virtually impossible to obtain an automatic 4WD. Many rental packages offer unlimited kilometers, while others offer 200km per day with a surcharge of around US$0.15 per kilometer after that. Return the car with a full tank of **petrol (gasoline)** to avoid high fuel charges in the end. Petrol is generally most expensive in Scandinavia; in any country, fuel tends to be cheaper in cities than in outlying areas.

If you rent, lease, or borrow a car, you will need a **green card,** or **International Insurance Certificate,** to certify that you have liability insurance and that it applies abroad. Green cards can be obtained at car rental agencies, car dealers (for those leasing cars), some travel agents, and some border crossings. Rental agencies may require you to purchase theft insurance in countries that they consider to have a high risk of auto theft. Remember that if you are driving a conventional vehicle on an **unpaved road** in a rental car, you are almost never covered by insurance; ask about this before leaving the rental agency. Always check if prices quoted include tax and **insurance** against theft and collision; some credit card companies cover the deductible on collision insurance, allowing their customers to decline the collision damage waiver. Be aware that cars rented on **American Express** or **Visa/Mastercard Gold or Platinum** credit cards in Europe might *not* carry the automatic insurance that they would in some other countries; check with your credit card company. Ask about discounts and check the terms of insurance, particularly the deductible.

DRIVING PRECAUTIONS. When traveling in the summer or in the desert, bring substantial amounts of water (5L of **water** per person per day) for drinking and for the radiator. For long drives to unpopulated areas, register with police before beginning your trek, and again upon arrival at the destination. Check with the local automobile club for details. When traveling long distances, make sure tires are in good repair and have enough air, and get good maps. A **compass** and a **car manual** can also be very useful. You should always carry a **spare tire** and **jack, jumper cables, extra oil, flares,** a **torch (flashlight),** and **heavy blankets** (in case your car breaks down at night or in the winter). If you don't know how to **change a tire,** learn before heading out, especially if you are planning on traveling in deserted areas. Blowouts on dirt roads are exceedingly common. If you do have a breakdown, **stay with your car;** if you wander off, there's less likelihood that trackers will find you.

ON THE ROAD

Before setting off, know the laws of the countries in which you'll be driving (e.g., headlights and seatbelts must be on at all times in Sweden, and vehicles drive on the left in Ireland and the UK). For an informal primer on European road signs, driving conventions, and driving guidelines, check out www.travlang.com/signs.

DANGERS. Cheaper rental cars tend to be less reliable and harder to handle on difficult terrain. Less expensive 4WD vehicles in particular tend to be more top-heavy and are more dangerous when navigating bumpy roads. Road conditions in Eastern Europe are often poor, and many travelers prefer public transportation. Western European roads are generally excellent, but keep in mind that each area has its own hazards. In Scandinavia, for example, you'll need to watch for moose and elk (particularly in low light), while on the Autobahn, cars driving 150kph will probably pose more of a threat. Road conditions fluctuate with seasons; winter weather will make driving difficult in some countries, while in others, spring thaws cause flooding due to melted ice in others. Roads in mountainous areas are unpredictably steep and curvy, and may be closed in the winter. The **Association for Safe International Road Travel (ASIRT),** 11769 Gainsborough Rd., Potomac, MD 20854 (US ☎301-983-5252; www.asirt.org) can provide specific information about road conditions. ASIRT considers road travel to be relatively safe in most of Western Europe and slightly less safe in developing nations due to poorly maintained roads and inadequately enforced traffic laws. Carry emergency equipment with you (see Driving Precautions, above) and know what to do in case of a breakdown.

CAR ASSISTANCE. Each country has its own national automobile association; consult the introduction to a specific country for the location and phone number of the appropriate group.

BY FERRY

Most European ferries are slow but inexpensive and quite comfortable; even the cheapest ticket typically includes a reclining chair or couchette. However, ferries may dock in remote parts of the country, forcing you to arrange connections to larger cities at additional cost. Plan ahead and reserve tickets in advance, or you may spend days waiting in port for the next sailing. Fares jump sharply in July and August but can be reduced—ISIC holders can often get student fares, and Eurail-pass holders get many discounts and free trips. Occasional port taxes should be less than US$10. For more information, consult the *Official Steamship Guide International* (available at travel agents), or www.youra.com/ferry.

ENGLISH CHANNEL AND IRISH SEA FERRIES. Ferries are frequent and dependable. The main route across the **English Channel,** from England to France, is Dover-Calais. The main ferry port on the southern coast of England is Portsmouth, which has connections to France and Spain. Ferries also cross the **Irish Sea,** connecting Northern Ireland with Scotland and England, and the Republic of Ireland with Wales. For more information on sailing (also called hovering) in this region, see **By Ferry from the UK and Ireland,** p. 52, or www.ferrybooker.com.

NORTH AND BALTIC SEA FERRIES. Ferries in the **North Sea** are reliable and cheap. For information on ferries heading across the North Sea to and from the UK, see p. 52. **Baltic Sea** ferries service routes between Poland and Scandinavia.

> **Polferries:** Sweden ☎84 11 49 80; www.polferries.com.pl/ieen. Ferries run from Poland to Sweden and Denmark.

> **Color Line:** Norway ☎22 94 44 00; www.colorline.com. Offers ferries from Norway to Denmark, Sweden, and Germany.

> **Silja Line:** US sales ☎800-323-7436, Finland ☎09 18041; www.silja.com. Helsinki to Stockholm (16hr.); Tallinn, Estonia (3hr., June to mid-Sept.); and Rostock, Germany (23-25hr., June to mid-Sept.). Also Turku to Stockholm (10hr.).

> **DFDS Seaways:** US ☎800-533-3755; www.seaeurope.com. Offers routes within Scandinavia and between Scandinavia and England, Germany, Holland, and Poland.

TRANSPORTATION

MEDITERRANEAN AND AEGEAN FERRIES. Mediterranean ferries run from France and Spain to Morocco. Reservations are recommended, especially in the summer. Shop around—many companies operate on erratic schedules, with similar routes and varying prices. Beware of lines that don't take reservations.

Companies such as **Superfast Ferries** (US ☎ 954 771-9200; www.superfast.com) offer routes across the **Adriatic and Ionian Seas** from Ancona and Bari, Italy to Patras and Igoumenitsa, Greece, as well as to Split and Dubrovnik, Croatia. **Eurail** is valid on certain ferries between Brindisi, Italy and Corfu, Igoumenitsa, and Patras, Greece. Countless ferry companies operate these routes simultaneously; websites such as www.ferries.gr list various schedules. See specific country chapters for more information.

BY BICYCLE

Biking is one of the key elements of the classic budget Eurovoyage. Many airlines will count your bike as your second free piece of luggage; a few charge extra (up to US$110 one-way). Bikes must be packed in a cardboard box with the pedals and front wheel detached; airlines often sell **bike boxes** at the airport (US$10). Most ferries let you take your bike for free or for a nominal fee, and you can always ship your bike on trains. If your touring will be confined to one or two regions, renting a bike beats bringing your own. Some youth hostels rent bicycles for low prices. In Switzerland, train stations rent bikes and often allow you to drop them off elsewhere; check train stations throughout Europe for similar deals.

EQUIPMENT. In addition to **panniers** to hold your luggage, you'll need a good **helmet** (from US$25) and a U-shaped **Citadel** or **Kryptonite lock** (from US$20). For equipment, **Bike Nashbar,** 6103 State Rte. 446, Canfield, OH 44406 (US ☎ 800-627-4227; www.nashbar.com), beats all competitors' offers and ships anywhere in the US or Canada. For more information, purchase *Europe by Bike,* by Karen and Terry Whitehill (US$14.95), from Mountaineers Books (US ☎ 800-553-4453; www.mountaineersbooks.org).

BIKE TOURS. If you feel nervous about striking out on your own, several companies lead European bike tours.

> **Bike Tours Ltd. of Bath** (UK ☎ 1225 310 859; www.biketours.co.uk) offers various 1- to 2-week tours throughout Europe.

> **Blue Marble Travel** (US ☎ 215-923-3788; www.bluemarble.org) leads dozens of trips through Western Europe and Scandinavia that range from 6 days to 5 weeks.

> **CBT Tours** (US ☎ 800-736-2453; www.cbttours.com) offers full-package 9- to 13-day biking, mountain biking, and hiking tours (around US$190 per day) in Western and Central Europe and The Netherlands.

> **EURO Bike and Walking Tours** (☎ 800-321-6060; www.eurobike.com) gives dozens of 6-day to 5-week bike tours across Central and Western Europe, and The Netherlands.

BY MOPED AND MOTORCYCLE

Motorized bikes (mopeds) use little gas, can be put on trains and ferries, and are a good compromise between the cost of car travel and the limited range of bicycles. However, they're uncomfortable for long distances, dangerous in the rain, and unpredictable on rough roads and gravel. Always wear a helmet and never ride with a backpack. If you've never been on a moped before, a twisting Alpine road is not the place to start. Expect to pay about US$20-35 per day; try auto repair shops,

and remember to bargain. **Motorcycles** can be much more expensive and normally require a license, but are better for long distances. Before renting, ask if the quoted price includes tax and insurance to avoid unexpected additional fees. Avoid offering your passport as a deposit; if you have an accident or mechanical failure you may not get it back until you cover all repairs. Pay ahead of time instead. For more information, try *Motorcycle Journeys through the Alps and Corsica*, by John Hermann (US$24.95), *Motorcycle Touring and Travel*, by Bill Stermer (US$19.95), both Whitehorse Press, or *Europe by Motorcycle*, by Gregory W. Frazier (Arrowstar Publishing, US$19.95).

BY FOOT

Europe's grandest scenery can often be seen only by foot. *Let's Go* describes many daytrips in town listings for those who want to hoof it, but native inhabitants, hostel proprietors, and fellow travelers are the best source for tips. Many European countries have hiking and mountaineering organizations; alpine clubs in Germany, Austria, Switzerland, and Italy, as well as tourist organizations in Scandinavia, provide accommodations in splendid settings.

BY THUMB

> *Let's Go* strongly urges you to consider the risks before you choose to hitch. We do not recommend hitching as a safe means of transportation, and none of the information presented here is intended to do so.

Never hitch before carefully considering the risks involved. Hitching means entrusting your life to a random person that happens to stop beside you on the road, and risking theft, assault, sexual harassment, and unsafe driving. In spite of this, there are advantages to hitching when it is safe: It allows you to meet local people and get where you're going, especially in northern Europe and Ireland, where public transportation is spotty. The choice, however, remains yours.

BY REGION. Getting a lift in Britain and Ireland is easy. In Scandinavia, hitching is slow but steady. Hitching in Southern Europe is generally mediocre; France is the worst. In parts of Central and Eastern Europe, drivers may expect to be paid.

SAFETY TIPS. Safety-minded hitchers avoid getting in the back of two-door cars (or any car they wouldn't be able to get out of in a hurry) and never let go of their backpacks. If you ever feel threatened, insist on being let off immediately. Acting as if you are going to open the car door or vomit will usually get a driver to stop. Hitchhiking at night can be particularly dangerous; experienced hitchers stand in well-lit places and expect drivers to be leery of nocturnal thumbers.

SUCCESSFUL HITCHING. Long-distance hitching in the developed countries of northwestern Europe demands close attention to expressway junctions, rest stop locations, and destination signs. For women traveling alone, hitching is just too dangerous. A man and a woman are a safer combination, but men traveling together may have a harder time getting a ride. Experienced hitchers pick spots where drivers will have time to look over potential passengers as they approach; rest stops or entrance ramps to highways are common pick-up spots. Hitching on super-highways is usually illegal. In the **Practical Information** section

of many cities, *Let's Go* lists the tram or bus lines that take travelers to strategic hitching points. Success depends on appearance: travel light and stack belongings in a compact but visible cluster. Most Europeans signal with an open hand rather than a thumb; many write their destination on a sign in large, bold letters and draw a smiley-face under it. Drivers prefer hitchers who are neat and wholesome, and no one stops for people wearing sunglasses.

RIDE SERVICES. Most Western European countries offer a ride service (listed in the Practical Information for major cities), a cross between hitchhiking and the ride boards common at many universities, which pairs drivers with riders; the fee varies according to destination. **Eurostop International** (Verband der Deutschen Mitfahrzentralen in Germany and Allostop in France) is the largest in Europe. Riders and drivers can register online at www.taxistop.be.

ALTERNATIVES TO TOURISM

Traveling from place to place around the world may be a memorable experience. But if you are looking for a more rewarding and complete way to see the world, you may want to consider alternatives to tourism. Working, volunteering, or studying for an extended period of time can be a better way to understand life in a foreign country. This chapter outlines some of the different ways to get to know a new place, whether you want to fund your trip or just get the personal satisfaction that comes from studying and volunteering. In most cases, you will feel that you partook in a more meaningful and educational experience—something that the average budget traveler often misses out on.

There is a limitless range of opportunities for non-tourism travel in Europe—far more than we could sensibly list in this guide. We've compiled a list of some of the most useful organizations to contact: education umbrellas, international work-placement firms, and volunteer companies. For specific short-term work listings and extensive national information, pick up any of our European city or country guides, such as *Let's Go: Barcelona* or *Let's Go: Italy*.

> **WORK AND STUDY VISA INFORMATION.** Work and study visas for most countries can be acquired only with the help of a sponsoring organization in that country; non-EU nationals looking for transient work will have a hard time getting permission. The organizations listed under **Long-Term Work** (see p. 70) may be able to find sponsors, while the **Center for International Business and Travel** (**CIBT;** see p. 13) can help expedite the visa process. Study-abroad programs or universities should have no problems sponsoring study visas; check before applying to any institution. Citizens of the EU are free to work in any EU member country, but they may need special permits. Contact the consulates of specific countries in which you may seek work for further information.

STUDYING ABROAD

Study-abroad programs range from basic language and culture courses to college-level classes, and may count for credit at your university. In order to choose a program that best fits your needs, you will want to find out what kind of students participate in the program and what sort of accommodations are provided. You may feel more comfortable in programs with large groups of students who speak the same language, but you will not have the same opportunities to practice a foreign language or to befriend other international students. Dorm accommodations provide good opportunities to mingle with fellow students, but there is less of a chance to experience the local scene. If you live with a family, there is a potential to build lifelong friendships with natives and to experience day-to-day life in more depth, but conditions can vary greatly from family to family.

Those relatively fluent in the local language may find it cheaper to enroll directly in a university abroad, although getting college credit may be more difficult. Some American schools require students to pay them for credits obtained elsewhere. Most university-level study-abroad programs are meant as language and culture enrichment opportunities and are therefore conducted in the local language. Still, many programs do offer classes in English and lower-level or beginner language courses.

STUDY ABROAD DIRECTORIES

The following websites are good resources for finding programs that cater to your particular interests. Each has links to various study-abroad programs broken down by a variety of criteria, including desired location and focus of study.

www.studyabroad.com. A great starting point for finding college- or high-school-level programs in foreign languages or specific academic subjects. Also maintains a page of links to several other useful websites.

www.petersons.com/stdyabrd/sasector.html. Lists summer and full-year study-abroad programs at accredited institutions that usually offer cross-credit.

www.westudyabroad.com/europe.htm. Lists language and college-level programs in a number of European countries.

AMERICAN PROGRAMS

The following organizations help place students in university programs abroad or have their own branches throughout Europe.

American Institute for Foreign Study, College Division, River Plaza, 9 W. Broad St., Stamford, CT 06902, USA (☎800-727-2437, ext. 5163; www.aifsabroad.com). Organizes programs for high-school and college study at universities in Austria, Britain, the Czech Republic, France, Italy, The Netherlands, Poland, Russia, and Spain.

Arcadia University for Education Abroad, 450 S. Easton Rd., Glenside, PA 19038, USA (☎866-927-2234; www.arcadia.edu/cea). Operates programs in Britain, Greece, Ireland, Italy, and Spain. Costs range from $2200 (summer) to $29,000 (full-year).

Central College Abroad, Office of International Education, 812 University, Pella, IA 50219, USA (☎800-831-3629 or 641-628-5284; www.central.edu/abroad). Offers internships, as well as summer, semester, and year-long programs in Austria, Britain, France, The Netherlands, and Spain. US$25 application fee.

Council on International Educational Exchange (CIEE), 633 3rd Ave., 20th fl., New York, NY 10017, USA (☎800-407-8839; www.ciee.org/index/cfm). Sponsors work, volunteer, academic, and internship programs in Belgium, Britain, the Czech Republic, France, Hungary, Italy, The Netherlands, Poland, Russia, Spain, and Turkey.

International Association for the Exchange of Students for Technical Experience (IAESTE), 10400 Little Patuxent Pkwy. Suite 250, Columbia, MD 21044, USA (☎410-997-2200; www.aipt.org). 8- to 12-week programs in Britain, Finland, France, Germany, Ireland, Sweden, and Switzerland for college students who have completed 2 years of technical study. US$25 application fee.

School for International Training, College Semester Abroad, Admissions, Kipling Rd., P.O. Box 676, Brattleboro, VT 05302, USA (☎800-336-1616 or 802-257-7751; www.sit.edu). Semester- and year-long programs in the Balkans, the Czech Republic, France, Germany, Ireland, The Netherlands, Russia, Spain, and Switzerland run US$10,600-13,700. Also runs the **Experiment in International Living** (☎800-345-2929; www.usexperiment.org), 3- to 5-week summer programs that offer high-school students cross-cultural homestays, community service, ecological adventure, and language training in Britain, France, Germany, Ireland, Italy, Poland, Spain, Switzerland, and Turkey (US$1900-5000).

LANGUAGE SCHOOLS

Unlike American-affiliated universities, language schools are frequently independently-run international or local organizations or divisions of foreign universities that rarely offer college credit. Language schools are a good alternative to university study if you desire a deeper focus on the language or a slightly less rigorous courseload. These programs are also good for younger high school students that might not feel comfortable with older students in a university program. Some good programs include:

Eurocentres, 101 N. Union St. Suite 300, Alexandria, VA 22314, USA (☎703-684-1494; www.eurocentres.com) or Head Office, Seestr. 247, CH-8038 Zurich, Switzerland (☎1 485 50 40; fax 1 481 61 24). Language programs for beginning to advanced students with homestays in Britain, France, Germany, Italy, Russia, Spain, and Switzerland.

Language Immersion Institute, 75 South Manheim Blvd., SUNY-New Paltz, New Paltz, NY 12561, USA (☎845-257-3500; www.newpaltz.edu/lii). 2-week summer language courses and some overseas courses in France, Italy, and Spain. Program fees are around US$1000.

LanguagesPLUS, 413 Ontario St., Toronto, Ontario M5A 2V9, Canada (US ☎888-526-4758; international 416-925-7117; www.languagesplus.com), runs 1- to 36-week programs in Britain, France, Germany, Ireland, Italy, and Spain. US$350-3000; includes tuition and accommodations with host families or apartments. Must be 18+.

WORKING

Most travelers look for one of two kinds of work. Some travelers want long-term jobs that allow them to get to know another part of the world in depth (e.g. teaching English, working in the tourist industry). Other travelers seek out short-term jobs to finance their travel. They usually seek employment in the service sector or in agriculture, working for a few weeks at a time to finance the next leg of their journey. This section discusses both short-term and long-term opportunities for working throughout Europe. Make sure you understand the relevant **visa requirements** for the country in which you are working (See p. 68 for more information).

LONG-TERM WORK

If you're planning on spending a substantial amount of time (more than three months) working abroad, search for a job well in advance. International placement agencies are often the easiest way to find employment abroad, especially for teaching English. **Internships,** usually for college students, are a good way to segue into working abroad, although they are often unpaid or poorly paid. Be wary of advertisements or companies that claim the ability to get you a job abroad for a fee—often their listings will have gone out of date or are easily available online or in newspapers. Some reputable organizations include:

Council Exchanges, 52 Poland St., London W1F 7AB, UK (☎020 7478 2000; US ☎888-268-6245; www.councilexchanges.org). Charges a US$300-475 fee for arranging three- to six-month working authorizations. They also provide extensive information on different job opportunities throughout Europe.

Escapeartist.com, 832-1245 World Trade Center, Panama, 832 (jobs.escapeartist.com). International employers post directly to this web site; various European jobs advertised. No fee.

International Co-operative Education, 15 Spiros Way, Menlo Park, CA, 94025, USA (☎650-323-4944; www.icemenlo.com). Finds summer jobs for students in Belgium, Finland, Germany, and Switzerland. Costs include a $200 application fee and a $600 fee for placement.

International Employment Gazette, 423 Townes Street, Greenville, SC, 29601, USA (☎ 800-882-9188; www.intemployment.com). A biweekly publication that lists jobs in all sectors, including education, health care, social services, and agriculture. Six-month internet subscription US$45.

TEACHING ENGLISH

Teaching jobs abroad are rarely well-paid, although some elite private American schools pay competitive salaries. Volunteering as a teacher in lieu of getting paid is a popular option; in those cases, teachers often get some sort of a daily stipend to help with living expenses.

In almost all cases, you must have at least a bachelor's degree to be a full-fledged teacher, although college undergraduates can often get summer positions teaching or tutoring. Some schools prefer applicants from within the EU, to simplify the work permit process; for this reason, non-EU citizens may have a harder time finding teaching jobs. Many schools require teachers to have a **Teaching English as a Foreign Language (TEFL)** certificate. This does not necessarily exclude you from finding a teaching job, but certified teachers often find higher paying jobs. Native English speakers working in private schools are most often hired for English-immersion classrooms where the native language is not spoken. Those volunteering or teaching in public or poorer schools are more likely to be working in both English and the local dialect.

Placement agencies or university fellowship programs are the best resources for finding teaching jobs. The alternative is to make contacts directly with schools or just to try your luck once you get there. If you are going to try the latter, the best time of the year is several weeks before the start of the school year. The following organizations are extremely helpful in placing teachers.

Teaching English as a Foreign Language (TEFL), TEFL Professional Network Ltd., 72 Pentyla Baglan Rd., Port Talbot SA12 8AD, UK (www.tefl.com). Maintains the most extensive database of openings throughout Europe; offers job training and certification.

Central European Teaching Program (CETP), Beloit College, 700 College St., Beloit, WI 53511, USA (☎ 608-363-2619; www.beloit.edu/~cetp). Half- or full-year periods in Hungary, Latvia, Lithuania, Poland, Romania, and Slovakia. $3500 full-year placement fee ($1700 half-year) includes airfare. college graduates only.

International Schools Services (ISS), 15 Roszel Rd., Box 5910, Princeton, NJ 08543, USA (☎ 609-452-0990; www.iss.edu). Hires teachers for more than 200 schools worldwide; candidates should have experience teaching or with international affairs. Two-year commitment expected.

AU PAIR WORK

Au pairs are typically women, aged 18-27, who work as live-in nannies, caring for children and doing light housework in foreign countries in exchange for room, board, and a small spending allowance or stipend. Most former au pairs speak favorably of their experience, saying it allowed them to get to know the country well without the high expenses of traveling. Drawbacks, however, often include long hours of constantly being on-duty, and the sometimes mediocre pay. The agencies below are a good starting point for employment as an au pair.

Accord Cultural Exchange, 750 La Playa, San Francisco, CA 94121, USA (☎ 415-386-6203; www.cognitext.com/accord).

Au Pair Homestay, World Learning, Inc., 1015 15th St. NW, Suite 750, Washington, DC 20005, USA (☎ 800 287-2477; fax 202-408-5397).

Au Pair in Europe, P.O. Box 68056, Blakely Postal Outlet, Hamilton, Ontario L8M 3M7, Canada (☎905-545-6305; fax 905-544-4121; www.princeent.com).

Childcare International, Ltd., Trafalgar House, Grenville Pl., London NW7 3SA, UK (☎020 8906 3116; fax 020 8906 3461; www.childint.co.uk).

InterExchange, 161 Sixth Ave., New York, NY 10013, USA (☎212-924-0446; fax 212-924-0575; www.interexchange.org).

SHORT-TERM WORK

Traveling for long periods of time can get expensive, so many travelers look for short-term jobs to fund the next leg of their journey. Hotels, resorts, and restaurants often have temporary work available, which can be found by word of mouth or simply by talking to the owner. Many places, especially due to the high turnover in the tourism industry, are always eager for even temporary help. Jobs can usually be found quickly, but be aware that during busy times you may have to work long hours, and the pay can be low.

It is also possible to find unofficial temporary work—such as agricultural work in the summer or fall—which means you can avoid the usual paperwork and hassle of getting employment in Europe. Such jobs may be advertised locally, but inquiring directly with farmers may uncover more opportunities. **World-Wide Opportunities on Organic Farms (WWOOF;** www.wwoof.org) also maintains an international database of farms that need immediate or seasonal help. Agricultural work, however, is often physically strenuous, and you won't be protected by the government's labor regulations. Another popular option is to work several hours a day at a hostel in exchange for free or discounted room and/or board; you'll have more luck calling ahead and asking about specific dates than showing up to see about immediately available opportunities.

If you are interested in working your way through Europe, we recommend picking up *Let's Go* city and country guides such as *Let's Go: Paris* and *Let's Go: Ireland*. These guides contain thorough information on local work opportunities at specific hostels, restaurants, and the like, all updated yearly.

VOLUNTEERING

Volunteering can be one of the most fulfilling experiences in life, especially if you combine it with the wonder of travel in a foreign land. Many volunteer services charge you a fee to participate in the program and to do work. These fees can be surprisingly hefty (although they frequently cover airfare and most, if not all, living expenses). Try to research a program before committing—talk to people who have previously participated and find out exactly what you're getting into, as living and working conditions can vary greatly. Different programs are geared toward different ages and levels of experience, so make sure you're not taking on too much or too little.

Most people choose to go through a parent organization that takes care of logistical details and provides a group environment and support system. There are two main types of organizations—religious (often Catholic), and non-sectarian—although there are rarely restrictions on participation for either.

Opportunities for volunteer work are more abundant in Eastern Europe than in Western. Habitat for Humanity and Peace Corps placements, for example, are not available in Western Europe.

Archaeological Institute of America, 656 Beacon St., Boston, MA 02215, USA (☎617-353-9361; www.archaeological.org). The *Archaeological Fieldwork Opportunities Bulletin,* available on the organization's website, lists field sites throughout Europe.

Business Enterprises for Sustainable Travel supports travel that helps communities preserve natural and cultural resources and create sustainable livelihoods. Their web site (www.sustainabletravel.org) has listings of local programs, innovative travel opportunities, and internships.

Earthwatch Institute, 57 Woodstock Rd., Oxford OX2 6HJ, UK (☎01865 318 838; www.earthwatch.org). Arranges 1- to 3-week programs to promote conservation of natural resources. Fees vary based on program location and duration, costs average $1700 plus airfare.

Habitat for Humanity International, 121 Habitat St., Americus, GA 31709, USA (☎229-924-6935 ext. 2551; www.habitat.org). Volunteers build houses in over 83 countries for anywhere from 2 weeks to 3 years. Short-term programs in Europe, including airfare, room, board, and insurance costs range from US$1800-2600.

Oxfam International, 266 Banbury Road, Suite 20, Oxford, OX2 7DL, UK (☎18 65 31 39 39; www.oxfam.org). Runs poverty relief campaigns.

Peace Corps, Office of Volunteer Recruitment and Selection, 1111 20th St., NW, Washington, D.C., 20526 USA (☎800-424-8580; www.peacecorps.gov). Various opportunities throughout the developing world, including Morocco and parts of Eastern Europe.

Service Civil International Voluntary Service (SCI-IVS), SCI USA, 3213 W. Wheeler St., Seattle, WA 98199, USA (☎/fax 206-350-6585; www.sci-ivs.org). Arranges placement in work camps throughout Europe for those aged 18+. Registration fee US$125.

UNICEF, (www.unicef.org). Volunteers recruited through the US Fund for UNICEF, 333 E. 38th St., 6th fl., New York, NY 10016, USA (☎800-367-5437). Offices in Belarus, Bosnia, Croatia, Macedonia, Moldova, Montenegro, Romania, Russia, Ukraine, and Serbia.

UNHCR (United Nations High Commission for Refugees), Case Postale 2500, CH-1211 Genève 2 Dépôt, SWI (☎22 739 8111; www.unhcr.org), will gladly provide advice on how and where to help.

Volunteers for Peace, 1034 Tiffany Rd., Belmont, VT 05730, USA (☎802-259-2759; www.vfp.org). Arranges placement in work camps throughout Europe. Membership required for registration. Programs average US$200-500 for 2-3 weeks. Annual *International Workcamp Directory* US$20.

Global Volunteers, 375 E. Little Canada Rd., St. Paul, MN 55117, USA (☎800-487-1074). A variety of one- to three-week volunteer programs throughout Europe. Fees range from US$1295-2395 including room and board, but not airfare.

FOR FURTHER READING ON ALTERNATIVES TO TOURISM

Alternatives to the Peace Corps: A Directory of Third World and U.S. Volunteer Opportunities, by Joan Powell. Food First Books, 2000 (US$10).

How to Get a Job in Europe, by Sanborn and Matherly. Surrey Books, 1999 (US$22).

How to Live Your Dream of Volunteering Overseas, by Collins, DeZerega, and Heckscher. Penguin Books, 2002 (US$17).

International Directory of Voluntary Work, by Whetter and Pybus. Peterson's Guides and Vacation Work, 2000 (US$16).

International Jobs, by Kocher and Segal. Perseus Books, 1999 (US$18).

Overseas Summer Jobs 2002, by Collier and Woodworth. Peterson's Guides and Vacation Work, 2002 (US$18).

Work Abroad: The Complete Guide to Finding a Job Overseas, by Hubbs, Griffith, and Nolting. Transitions Abroad Publishing, 2000 (US$16).

Work Your Way Around the World, by Susan Griffith. Worldview Publishing Services, 2001 (US$18).

ANDORRA

The forgotten country sandwiched between France and Spain, Andorra (pop. 65,000; 464 sq. km), has had its democratic constitution for only ten years; it spent its first 12 centuries caught in a tug-of-war between the Spanish Counts of Urgell, the Church of Urgell, and the French King. Catalán is the official language, but French and Spanish are widely spoken. All establishments were once required to accept *pesetas* and *francs*, but the country's now on the euro system. Because of Andorra's diminutive size, one day can include sniffing aisles of duty-free perfume, hiking through a pine-scented valley, and relaxing in a luxury spa.

▐ TRANSPORTATION AND PRACTICAL INFORMATION

The only way to get to Andorra is by car or bus. All traffic from Spain enters through the town of La Seu d'Urgell; the gateway to France is Pas de la Casa. **Andor-Inter/Samar** buses (in Madrid ☎914 68 41 90; in Toulouse ☎561 58 14 53; in Andorra ☎82 62 89) run from Andorra la Vella to **Madrid** (9hr.; Tu and F-Su 11am; W-Th and Su 10pm; €33), as does **Eurolines** (Andorra ☎80 51 51; Madrid ☎915 06 33 60; Tu-Th and Su 11:30am; F and Su 10pm; €33). **Alsina Graells** (Andorra ☎82 65 67) runs to **Barcelona** (4hr., 5 per day, €17), as does **Eurolines** (3¼hr., 5 per day, €18.50). To go anywhere in Spain other than Madrid or Barcelona, you must first go to the town of La Seu d'Urgell on a **La Hispano-Andorra** bus (☎82 13 72; 30min., 5-7 per day, €2.50), departing from Av. Meritxell 11. From La Seu, Alsina Graells buses continue into Spain via Puigcerdà (1hr., 2 per day, €3.50) and Lérida (2½hr., 2 per day, €10). **Driving** in Andorra la Vella is an adventure for some, a nightmare for others. Motorcycles curve through the avenues with ease; larger vehicles must squeeze their way around tight, confusing streets. It's best to simply follow signs and desert the car as soon as possible in one of the city's many parking lots. Efficient intercity buses connect the villages along the three major highways that converge in Andorra la Vella. Since most towns are only 10min. apart, the country's cities can be seen in a single day via public transportation. **Bus** stops are easy to find; rides cost €0.60. All buses make every stop in the city. Making an international **telephone call** in Andorra is a chore; you'll have to buy a STA *teletarjeta* (telecard) at the tourist office or the post office (€3 minimum). For directory assistance dial ☎111 or 119 (international). The **country code** is ☎**376.** Andorra's **price diversity** is the same as the range in Spain, see p. 885.

ANDORRA LA VELLA

Andorra la Vella (pop. 23,000) is little more than Spain and France's shopping mall. Effectively a single cluttered road flanked by shop after duty-free shop, this city is anything but *vella* (old); most of the old buildings have been upstaged by shiny new stores. After shopping, you're best off escaping to the countryside.

▐ PRACTICAL INFORMATION. The **tourist office** is on Av. Doctor Villanova and offers the free *Sports Activities* and *Hotels i Restaurants* guides. (☎82 02 14. Open July-Aug. daily M-F 9am-1:30pm and 3-7pm; Sept.-June 10am-1pm and 3-7pm, Su 9am-1pm.) In a **medical emergency** call ☎116 or the **police**, Prat de la Creu 16 (☎87 20 00). For **weather and ski conditions,** call Ski Andorra (☎86 43 89).

⌐ ⊏ ACCOMMODATIONS AND FOOD. Try **Hotel Viena ❸**, C. de la Vall 3. Its sunny doubles are a steal. (Doubles €30. MC/V.) To reach the inviting, spacious rooms of **Hostal del Sol ❶**, Pl. Guillemó, take a left onto C. Les Canals after the Pyrenees department store on the main road, then follow the signs for Spain until you reach the plaza with a water fountain. (☎ 82 37 01. €12 per person. MC/V.) You don't exactly rough it at shaded **Camping Valira ❶**, Av. Salou, behind the Estadi Comunal d'Andorra la Vella, which has video games, hot showers, and an indoor pool. (☎ 82 23 84. €4 per person, per tent, and per car.) Check out one of the three-story supermarket monstrosities in nearby Santa Coloma or the **Grans Magatzems Pyrénées**, Av. Meritxell 11, the country's biggest department store. (Open Sept.-July M-F 9:30am-8pm, Sa 9:30am-9pm, Su 9:30am-7pm.)

▌⃟ EXCURSIONS. The best thing to do in Andorra la Vella is drop your bags in a hostel and get out. The **Caldea-Spa**, in nearby **Escaldes-Engordany**, is the largest in Europe, with luxurious treatments and prices to match. (☎ 80 09 95. €23 for 3hr., plus fees for each service. Open daily 10am-11pm.) The parish of **Ordino** bucks the Andorran trend of "bigger is better" with its quirky ▧**Microminiature Museum**, Edifici Margada. Using yogic breathing to steady his hand, Nikolai Siadristy has created amazingly small, often microscopic objects, including the tiniest inscription ever made. A grain of rice has never been so enthralling. (☎ 83 83 38. Open Tu-Sa 9:30am-1:30pm and 3:30-7pm, Su 9:30am-1:30pm. €2.) If you have no patience for the miniscule, visit **Canillo** for some fun in the colossal **Palau de Gel D'Andorra**, a recreational complex complete with swimming pool, ice-skating rink ("ice disco" by night), and squash courts. (☎ 80 08 40. Palace open daily 10am-11:30pm; each facility has its own hours. Each €5; full palace €10. Equipment rental €2.50.)

▨ HIKING AND THE OUTDOORS. The tourist office brochure *Sports Activities* has 52 suggested hiking itineraries, as well as cabin and *refugios* listings. La Massana is home to Andorra's tallest peak, **Pic Alt de la Coma Pedrosa** (2946m). For organized hiking trips, try the **La Rabassa Sports and Nature Center** (☎ 32 38 68), in southwest Andorra. In addition to *refugio*-style accommodations, the center has mountain biking, guided hikes, horseback riding, archery, and other field sports.

◂ SKIING. With five outstanding resorts, Andorra offers skiing opportunities galore (Nov.-Apr.; €30-40). **Pal** (☎ 73 70 00), 10km from La Massana, is accessible by bus from La Massana (5 per day, last returning at 5pm; €1.50). Seven buses run daily from La Massana to nearby **Arinsal**, the last returning at 6:45pm (€1). On the French border, **Pas de la Casa Grau Roig** (☎ 80 10 60) offers 600 hectares of skiable land, lessons, two medical centers, night skiing, and 27 lifts serving 48 trails for all levels of ability. **Soldeu-El Tarter** (☎ 89 05 00) occupies 840 hectares of skiable area between Andorra la Vella and Pas de la Casa. **Free buses** pick up skiers from their hotels in Canillo. The more horizontal **La Rabassa** (☎ 32 38 68) is Andorra's only cross-country ski resort, offering sleighing, skiing, and horse rides. Call **SKI Andorra** (☎ 86 43 89; www.skiandorra.ad) or the tourist office with any questions.

ANDORRA

AUSTRIA
(ÖSTERREICH)

At the peak of Habsburg megalomania, the Austrian Empire was one of the largest in history, encompassing much of Europe from Poland and Hungary in the east to The Netherlands in the west. Although the mighty empire crumbled during World War I, Austria remains a complex, multiethnic country with a unique political and cultural history. Drawing on centuries of Habsburg political maneuvering, Austria has become a skillful mediator between Eastern and Western Europe, connecting its seven bordering countries. Today, Austria owes much of its glory to the overpowering Alpine landscape that hovers over the remnants of its tumultuous past. The mention of Austria evokes images of onion-domed churches set against snow-capped alpine peaks, castles rising from lush meadows of golden flowers, and 10th-century monasteries towering over the majestic Danube.

DISCOVER AUSTRIA

In Austria's capital, **Vienna** (p. 80), soak up cafe culture, stare down works by Klimt and other Secessionist artists and listen to a world-famous opera or orchestra for a mere pittance. An easy stopover between Vienna and Munich, **Salzburg** (p. 94) was home to both Mozart and the von Trapp family—some travelers find the overabundance of kitsch a tad overwhelming. Hike around historic **Hallstatt** (p. 100) in the nearby **Salzkammergut** region, or explore the natural pleasures of the **Hohe Tauern National Park** (p. 101), including the Krimml Waterfalls (p. 102). Farther west, **Innsbruck** (p. 102) is a great jumping-off point for skiers and hikers into the snow-capped peaks of the Tyrolean Alps. For superior skiing, head to **Kitzbühel** (p. 105).

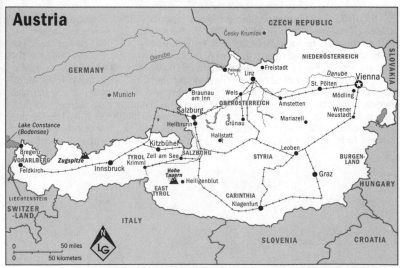

AUSTRIA

FACTS AND FIGURES

Official Name: Republic of Austria.	**Land Area:** 83,857 sq. km.
Capital: Vienna.	**Time Zone:** GMT + 1.
Major Cities: Salzburg, Innsbruck, Graz.	**Language:** German.
Population: 8,151,000.	**Religions:** Roman Catholic (78%), Protestant (5%), Muslim and other (3%).

ESSENTIALS

WHEN TO GO

November to March is peak ski season; prices in western Austria double and travelers need reservations months in advance. The situation reverses in the summer, when the flatter, eastern half fills with vacationers. Sights and accommodations are cheaper and less crowded in the shoulder season (May-June and Sept.-Oct.). But some Alpine resorts close in May and June—call ahead. The Vienna State Opera, the Vienna Boys' Choir, and many major theaters throughout Austria don't have any performances during July and August.

In August 2002, extreme weather conditions caused massive flooding in the area surrounding **Salzburg.** As of press time, the ultimate extent of the damage was not known. Many establishments we list may have been forced to shut down or may have altered opening times; additionally, train routes may be disrupted or changed. Make sure to check ahead thoroughly: call hostels and hotels in advance, and confirm the feasibility of your itinerary with Austria's National Tourist Office (www.austria-tourism.at).

DOCUMENTS AND FORMALITIES

VISAS. Citizens of Australia, Canada, New Zealand, South Africa, and the US need valid passports to enter Austria and can stay three months without a visa.

EMBASSIES. All foreign embassies in Austria are in Vienna (p. 84). Austrian embassies at home include: **Australia,** 12 Talbot St., Forrest, Canberra ACT 2603 (☎(00) 62 95 15 33; austria@dynamite.com.au); **Canada,** 445 Wilbrod St., Ottawa, ON K1N 6M7 (☎613-789-1444; www.austro.org); **Ireland,** 15 Ailesbury Court, 93 Ailesbury Rd., Dublin 4 (☎(01) 269 45 77; dublin-ob@bmaa.gv.at); **New Zealand,** Level 2, Willbank House, 57 Willis St., Wellington (☎(04) 499 63 93); **South Africa,** 1109 Duncan St., Momentum Office Park, Brooklyn, Pretoria 0011 (☎(012) 45 29 155; autemb@mweb.co.az); **UK,** 18 Belgrave Mews West, London SW1 X 8HU (☎(020) 72 35 37 31; www.austria.org.uk); **US,** 3524 International Ct. NW, Washington, D.C. 20008-3035 (☎202-895-6700).

TRANSPORTATION

BY PLANE. The only major international airport is Vienna's Schwechat Flughafen (VIE). European flights also land in Salzburg, Graz, and Innsbruck. From the UK, **buzz** flies to Vienna (☎(0870) 240 70 70; www.buzzaway.com).

BY TRAIN. The **Österreichische Bundesbahn (ÖBB),** Austria's federal railroad, operates an efficient system with fast and comfortable trains. **Eurail, InterRail,** and **Europe East** passes are valid in Austria; however, they do not guarantee a

AUSTRIA

seat without a reservation (US$11). The **Austrian Railpass** allows three days of travel within any 15-day period on all rail lines; it also entitles holders to 40% off on bike rental at train stations (2nd-class US$107, each additional day US$15).

BY BUS. The efficient Austrian bus system consists mainly of orange **Bundes-Buses,** which cover areas inaccessible by train. They usually cost about as much as trains, but railpasses are not valid. Buy tickets at the station or from the driver. For bus information, dial ☎ (0222) 711 01 (7am-8pm).

BY CAR. Driving is a convenient way to see more isolated parts of Austria, but some small towns prohibit cars. The roads are generally good and well-marked, and Austrian drivers are quite careful. **Mitfahrzentrale** (ride-sharing services) in larger cities, pair drivers with riders for a small fee. Riders then negotiate fares with the drivers. Be aware that not all organizations screen their drivers and riders; ask in advance.

BY BIKE. Bikes are a great way to get around Austria; roads are generally level and safe. Many train stations rent bikes and allow you to return them to any participating station. Consult local tourist offices for bike routes and maps.

TOURIST SERVICES AND MONEY

EMERGENCY	**Police: ☎ 133. Ambulance: ☎ 144. Fire: ☎ 122.**

TOURIST OFFICES. Virtually every town has a tourist office marked by a green "i" sign. Most brochures are available in English. Visit www.austria-tourism.at for more Austrian tourist information.

MONEY. Austria formerly used the *Schilling* as its unit of currency; now as a member of the European Union, it has almost completely switched over to the **euro** (see p. 15). In Austria, railroad stations, airports, hotels, and most travel agencies offer exchange services, as do banks and currency exchanges. If you stay in hostels and prepare most of your own food, expect to spend anywhere from €30-65 per person per day. Accommodations start at about €12, while a basic sit-down meal usually costs around €14. Menus will say whether service is included (*Preise inclusive* or *Bedienung inclusiv*); if it is, you don't have to tip. If it's not, leave a tip up to 10%. Austrian restaurants expect you to seat yourself, and servers will not bring the bill until you ask them to do so. Say *Zahlen bitte* (TSAHL-en BIT-uh) to settle your accounts, and don't leave tips on the table. Be aware that some restaurants charge for each piece of bread that you eat during your meal. Don't expect to bargain except at flea markets and the Naschmarkt in Vienna. Austria has a 10-20% **value-added tax** (VAT), which is applied to purchased goods. You can get refunds for purchases of at least €75 at one store.

COMMUNICATION

TELEPHONES. Wherever possible, use a calling card for international phone calls, as the long-distance rates for national phone services are often exorbitant. Prepaid phone cards and major credit cards can be used for direct international calls, but they are still less cost-efficient. Direct dial access numbers include: **AT&T,** ☎ (0800) 20 02 88; **British Telecom,** ☎ (0800) 20 02 09; **Canada Direct,** ☎ (0800) 20 02 17; **Ireland Direct,** ☎ (0800) 40 00 00; **MCI,** ☎ (0800) 20 02 35; **Sprint,** ☎ (0800) 20 02 36; **Telecom New Zealand,** ☎ (0800) 20 02 22; **Telkom South Africa,** ☎ (0800) 20 02 30.

PHONE CODES	Country code: 43. International dialing prefix: 00 (from Vienna, 900). From outside Austria, dial int'l dialing prefix (see inside back cover) + 43 + city code + local number. To call Vienna from outside Austria, dial int'l dialing prefix + 43 + 1 + local number.

MAIL. Letters take 1-2 days within Austria. Airmail to North America takes 4-7 days, up to 9 days to Australia and New Zealand. Mark all letters and packages "mit Flugpost." Aerogrammes are the cheapest option. *Let's Go* lists the addresses for mail to be held (*Postlagernde Briefe*) in the practical information of big cities.

LANGUAGE. German is the official language. English is the most common second language; outside of cities and among older residents, English is less common. For basic German words and phrases, see p. 1057.

ACCOMMODATIONS AND CAMPING

AUSTRIA	❶	❷	❸	❹	❺
ACCOMMODATIONS	under €9	€9-15	€16-30	€31-70	over €70

Always ask if your lodging provides a **guest card** (*Gästekarte*), which grants discounts on activities, museums, and public transportation. In Austria, the *Österreiches Jugendherbergsverband-Hauptverband* **(OJH)** runs the over 80 **hostels** in the country. Because of the rigorous standards of the national organizations, hostels are usually as clean as any hotel. Most hostels charge €13-22 per night for dorms; non-HI members are usually charged a surcharge. **Hotels** are expensive (singles €40-100; doubles €80-150). The cheapest have *Gasthof*, *Gästehaus*, or *Pension-Garni* in the name. Renting a **Privatzimmer** (room in a family home) is an inexpensive and friendly way to house yourself. Rooms range from €35-70 a night; contact the local tourist office for a list. Slightly more expensive, **Pensionen** are similar to American and British bed-and-breakfasts. **Camping** in Austria is less about getting out into nature and more about having a cheap place to sleep; most sites are large plots with many vans and cars and are open in summer only. Prices run €4-6 per person and €4-8 per tent.

FOOD AND DRINK

AUSTRIA	❶	❷	❸	❹	❺
FOOD	under €5	€5-10	€11-16	€17-25	over €26

Loaded with fat, salt, and cholesterol, traditional Austrian cuisine is a cardiologist's nightmare but a delight to the palate. Staple foods include pork, veal, sausage, eggs, cheese, bread, and potatoes. Austria's best known dish, *Wienerschnitzel*, is a breaded meat cutlet (usually veal or pork) fried in butter. Vegetarians should look for *Spätzle* (noodles), *Eierschwammerl* (yellow mushrooms), or anything with the word "Vegi" in it. The best supermarkets are Billa and Hofer, where you can buy cheap rolls, fruits, and veggies. Natives nurse their sweet tooths with *Kaffee und Kuchen* (coffee and cake). Try *Sacher Torte*, a rich chocolate cake layered with marmalade; *Linzer Torte*, a light yellow cake with currant jam; *Apfelstrudel*; or just about any pastry. Austrian beers are outstanding—try *Stiegl Bier*, a Salzburg brew; *Zipfer Bier* from upper Austria; and Styrian *Gösser Bier*.

HIKING AND SKIING. Nearly every town has **hiking** trails in its vicinity; consult the local tourist office. Trails are usually marked with either a red-white-red marker (only sturdy boots and hiking poles necessary) or a blue-white-blue marker (mountaineering equipment needed). Most mountain hiking trails and mountain huts are open only from late June to early September because of snow in the higher passes. Western Austria is one of the world's best **skiing** regions; the areas around Innsbruck and Kitzbühel are saturated with lifts and runs. High season normally runs from mid-December to mid-January and from February to March. Tourist offices provide information on regional skiing and can suggest budget travel agencies that offer ski packages.

HOLIDAYS AND FESTIVALS

Holidays: Just about everything closes down on public holidays, so plan accordingly. New Year's Day (Jan. 1); Epiphany (Jan. 6); Good Friday (Apr. 18); Easter Monday (Apr. 21); Labor Day (May 1); Ascension (May 29); Whitmonday (June 9); Corpus Christi (June 19); Assumption Day (Aug. 15); Austrian National Day (Oct. 26); All Saints' Day (Nov. 1); Immaculate Conception (Dec. 8); Christmas (Dec. 25); Boxing Day (Dec. 26).

Festivals: Vienna celebrates **Fasching** (Carneval) during the first two weeks of February. Austria's most famous summer music festivals are the **Wiener Festwochen** (mid-May to mid-June) and the **Salzburger Festspiele** (late July to late Aug.).

VIENNA (WIEN) ☎ 0222

From its humble origins as a Roman camp along the Danube, Vienna became the cultural heart of Europe for centuries, the setting for fledgling musicians, writers, artists, philosophers, and politicians to achieve greatness—or infamy. At the height of its artistic ferment at the turn of the century, during the smoky days of its great cafe culture, the Viennese self-mockingly referred to their city as the "merry apocalypse." Its smooth veneer of waltzes and *Gemütlichkeit* (good nature) concealed a darker side expressed in Freud's theories, Kafka's dark fantasies, and Mahler's deathly beautiful music. The city has a reputation for living absent-mindedly in this grand past, but as the last fringes of the Iron Curtain have been drawn back, Vienna has tried to reestablish itself as the gateway to Eastern Europe and as a place where experimentalism thrives.

✈ INTERCITY TRANSPORTATION

Flights: The **Wien-Schwechat Flughafen** (VIE; ☎ 700 72 22 33) is home to **Austrian Airlines** (☎ 517 89). The **airport** is 18km from the city center; the cheapest way to reach the city is S7 Flughafen/Wolfsthal, which stops at **Wien Mitte** (30min., every 30min. 5am-9:30pm, €3; Eurail not valid). The heart of the city, **Stephansplatz**, is a short Metro ride from Wien Mitte on the U3 line. The **Vienna Airport Lines Shuttle Bus,** which runs between the airport and the City Air Terminal, at the Hilton opposite Wien Mitte, is more convenient, but also more expensive. (☎ 93 00 00 23 00. Every 20min. 6:30am-11:10pm, every 30min. midnight-6am; €5.80.) **Buses** connect the airport to the *Südbahnhof* and *Westbahnhof* (see below) every 30min. 8:55am-7:25pm and every hr. from 8:20pm-8:25am.

Trains: Vienna has two main train stations with international connections. For general train information, dial ☎ 17 17 (24hr.) or check www.bahn.at.

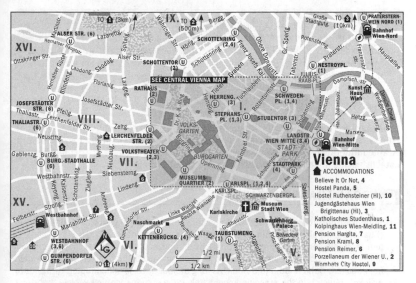

Vienna

🔺 ACCOMMODATIONS

Believe It Or Not, 4
Hostel Panda, 5
Hostel Ruthensteiner (HI), 10
Jugendgästehaus Wien
Brigittenau (HI), 3
Katholisches Studenthaus, 1
Kolpinghaus Wien-Meidling, 11
Pension Hargita, 7
Pension Kraml, 8
Pension Reimer, 6
Porzellaneum der Wiener U., 2
Wombats City Hostel, 9

Westbahnhof, XV, Mariahilferstr. 132. Most trains head west, but a few go east and north. To: **Amsterdam** (14½hr., 1 per day, €166); **Berlin Zoo** (11hr., 1 per day, €123); **Bregenz** (8hr., 9 per day, €58); **Hamburg** (9½hr., 2 per day, €176); **Innsbruck** (5-6hr., every 2hr., €48); **Munich** (4½hr., 5 per day, €60); **Paris** (14hr., 2 per day, €156); **Salzburg** (3½hr., every hr., €34); **Zurich** (9¼hr., 3 per day, €81). **Info counter** open daily 7:30am-8:40pm.

Südbahnhof, X, Wiedner Gürtel 1a, on the D tram. To get to the city take the tram (dir.: Nußdorf) to Opera/Karlspl. Trains generally leave for destinations south and east. To: **Budapest** (3-4hr., 6 per day, €32); **Graz** (2¾hr., every hr., €23); **Kraków** (7-8hr., €37); **Prague** (4½hr., 3 per day, €39); **Rome** (14hr., 1 per day, €99); **Venice** (9-10hr., 3 per day, €64). **Info counter** open daily 6:30am-9:20pm.

Buses: Buses in Austria are seldom cheaper than trains; compare prices before buying a ticket. **City bus terminals** at Wien Mitte/Landstr., Hütteldorf, Heiligenstadt, Floridsdorf, Kagran, Erdberg, and Reumannpl. **BundesBuses** run from these stations. Ticket counter open M-F 6am-5:50pm, Sa-Su 6am-3:50pm. Many international bus lines also have agencies in the stations. For info, call BundesBus (☎ 711 01; 7am-7pm).

Hitchhiking and Ride Sharing: Hitchhikers headed for Salzburg take U4 to Hütteldorf; the highway is 10km farther. Hitchers traveling south often ride tram #67 to the last stop and wait at the rotary near Laaerberg. *Let's Go* does not recommend hitching. A safer alternative is ride sharing; **Mitfahrzentrale Wien** pairs drivers and riders. Call to see what's available. (☎408 22 10. Open M-F 8am-noon and 2-7pm, Sa-Su 1-3pm.) A ride to **Salzburg** costs €16, to **Prague** €33. Reserve 2 days in advance.

⚡ ORIENTATION

Vienna is divided into 23 **districts** *(Bezirke)*. The first is the *Innenstadt* (city center), defined by the **Ringstraße** on three sides and the Danube Canal on the fourth. The Ringstraße (or "Ring") consists of many different segments, each with its own name, such as Opernring or Kärntner Ring. Many of Vienna's major attractions are in District I and immediately around the Ringstraße. Districts II-IX spread out from the city center following the clockwise traffic of the Ring. The remaining districts expand from yet another ring, the **Gürtel** ("belt"). Like the Ring, this major

> **LITTLE PIECES OF REVOLUTION** Travelers may be perplexed by the little paper strips taped around columns in train stations, subway stops, and crowded streets. The slips, known as *Pflücktexte* (from *pflücken*, to pluck), contain short poems with vaguely anti-establishment messages and are meant to be "plucked" from the columns, whereupon they are mysteriously replaced. *Let's Go* sleuths have determined that the poems are composed by one Helmut Seethaler, Wasnerg. 43/8, 1200 Wien, who offers more insurgent poems via mail "for a small bill."

thoroughfare has numerous segments, including Margaretengürtel, Währinger Gürtel, and Neubaugürtel. Street signs indicate the district number in Roman or Arabic numerals *before* the street and number. **Let's Go includes district numbers for establishments in Roman numerals before the street address.**

⌐ LOCAL TRANSPORTATION

Public transportation: call ☎580 00 for general information. The **subway** (U-Bahn), **tram** (Straßenbahn), **elevated train** (S-Bahn), and **bus** systems operate under one ticket system. A **single fare** (€1.80 on board, €1.50 in advance from a ticket machine, ticket office, or tobacco shop), lets you travel to any single destination in the city and switch from bus to U-Bahn to tram to S-Bahn, as long as your travel is uninterrupted. To **validate a ticket,** punch it in the machine immediately upon entering the first vehicle, but don't stamp it again when you switch trains. Otherwise, plainclothes inspectors may fine you €40. Other ticket options (available at the same places as pre-purchased single tickets) are a **24hr. pass** (€5), a **3-day "rover" ticket** (€12), a **7-day pass** (€11.20; valid M 9am to M 9am), or an **8-day pass** (€24; valid any 8 days, not necessarily consecutive; valid also for several people traveling together). The **Vienna Card** (€16.90) offers free travel for 72hr. as well as discounts at sights and events. Regular trams and subway cars stop running between midnight and 5am. **Nightbuses** run every 30min. along most routes; "N" signs designate night bus stops. (€1.10; €3.30 for 4; day transport passes not valid.) A complete night bus schedule is available at bus information counters in U-Bahn stations. **Information stands** (marked with an "i") in many stations help with tickets and give out an indispensable pocket map of the U- and S-Bahn systems. Stands in the U-Bahn at Karlspl., Stephanspl., and the *Westbahnhof* are the most likely to have information in English. (Open M-F 6:30am-6:30pm, Sa-Su and holidays 8:30am-4pm.)

Taxis: (☎313 00, 401 00, 601 60, or 814 00). Stands at *Westbahnhof, Südbahnhof,* Karlspl. in the city center, and by the Bermuda Dreieck for late-night revelers. Accredited taxis have yellow-and-black signs on the roof. Rates generally run €2.20 per km; slightly more expensive Su, holidays, and 11pm-6am.

Car Rental: Avis, I, Opernring 3-5 (☎587 62 41). Open M-F 7am-8pm, Sa 8am-2pm, Su 8am-1pm. **Hertz** (☎700 73 26 61), at the airport. Open M-F 7:15am-11pm, Sa 8am-8pm, Su 8am-11pm.

Bike Rental: Pedal Power, II, Ausstellungsstr. 3 (☎729 72 34), rents bikes (€5 per hr., €32 for 24hr. with delivery) and offers bike tours (€19-23). Student and Vienna Card discounts. Open May-Sept. daily 8am-8pm. Pick up *Vienna By Bike,* at the tourist office.

Central Vienna

♠ ACCOMMODATIONS
Hotel Zur Wiener
  Staatsoper, **14**
Studentenwohnheim der
  Hochschule für Musik, **12**

♦ FOOD
DO&CO, **8**
Levante, **5**
Margaritaville, **7**
Maschu Maschu, **3**
Trzesniewski, **6**
University Mensa, **1**

☕ COFFEEHOUSES
Café Central, **4**
Café Sperl, **15**
Hotel Sacher, **13**
Kleines Café, **9**

▣ NIGHTLIFE
Das Möbel, **11**
Mapitom der
  Bierlokal, **2**
Objektiv, **10**

Central Vienna

AUSTRIA

VIII.

VII.

1.

Donaukanal

Franz Josefs Kai

ÖDSG Ferry Docks

Museum of Applied Art

City Air Terminal

STADTPARK

Schubertring

Kärntner Ring

Parkring

Stubenring

Schwedenpl.

Stephansdom

St. Peter

Kirche am Hof

AM HOF

Minoriten Kirche

Rathaus

Parlament

Burgtheater

Universität

Natur-historisches Museum

Kunst-historisches Museum

MUSEUMS-QUARTIER

Volkstheater

Neue Hofburg

Alte Hofburg

National Bibliothek

Spanish Riding School

Augustiner Kirche

Albertina Museum

Staatsoper

Kapuziner Kirche

Schottenstift

Altes Rathaus

Franziskaner Kirche

Messe Palast

Theseus Tempel

VOLKSGARTEN

BURGGARTEN

HELDENPL.

MARIA THERESIENPL.

Dr. Karl Lueger Ring

Dr. K. Renner Ring

Dr. Karl Renner Ring

RATHAUSPL.

STEPHANSPL.

HOHER MARKT

JUDENPL.

PETERSPL.

Graben

Kärntner Str.

MICHAELERPL.

HERRENG.

NEUER MARKT

ALBERTINAPL.

FRANZISKANERPL.

STUBENTOR

DR. KARL LUEGERPL.

JULIUS-RAAB-PL.

SCHWEDENPL.

SCHOTTENRING

BEETHOVENPL.

Am Heumarkt

United States

Canada

Postsparkasse

Regierungs-gebäude

TO ↑ (200m)

TO ↑ (100m)

250 yards

250 meters

0

Staatsoper

CRIME IN THE CITY. Vienna is a metropolis with crime like any other; use common sense, especially after dark. Karlspl. is home to many pushers and junkies. Avoid areas in districts V, X and XIV, as well as Landstraßer Hauptstr. and Prater Park, after dark. Vienna's Red Light District covers sections of the Gürtel.

⁊ PRACTICAL INFORMATION

Main Tourist Office: I, Albertinapl. (www.info.wien.at). Follow Operng. up 1 block from the Opera House. The staff gives a free map of the city and the pamphlet *Youth Scene*, and books rooms for a €3 fee plus a 1-night deposit. Open daily 9am-7pm.

Embassies and Consulates: Australia, IV, Mattiellistr. 2 (☎506 74). **Canada,** I, Laurenzerberg 2 (☎531 38 30 00). **Ireland,** I, Rotenturmstr. 16-18 5th fl. (☎71 54 24 60). **New Zealand,** Consulate, XIX, Karl-Tomay-g. 34 (☎318 85 05). **South Africa,** XIX, Sandg. 33 (☎320 64 93). **UK,** III, Jauresg. 12 (☎716 13 51 51). **US,** IX, Boltzmanng. 16 (☎313 39).

Currency Exchange: ATMs are your best bet. The 24hr. exchange at the **main post office** has excellent rates and an €8 fee for up to US$1100 in travelers' checks.

American Express: I, Kärntnerstr. 21-23, P.O. Box 28, A-1015 (☎515 40), down the street from Stephanspl. Cashes AmEx and Thomas Cook (min. €5 commission) checks, sells theater tickets, and holds mail for 4 weeks. Open M-F 9am-5:30pm, Sa 9am-noon.

Bi-Gay-Lesbian Resources: Pick up either the monthly magazine (in German) called *Extra Connect;* the free monthly publication *Bussi* at any gay bar, cafe, or club; or the straight *Falter* newspaper, which lists gay events under a special heading. **Rosa Lila Villa,** VI, Linke Wienzeile 102 (☎586 81 50), is a favored resource and social center for homosexual Viennese and visitors alike. Friendly staff speaks English and provides information, a library, and nightclub listings. Open M-F 5-8pm.

Laundromat: Schnell und Sauber, VII, Westbahnhofstr. 60. U6: Burgg./Stadthalle. Wash €4.40; dry €0.75 per 15min. Soap included. Open 24hr.

EMERGENCY AND COMMUNICATION

Police: ☎33. **Ambulance:** ☎144. **Fire:** ☎122.

Crisis Hotlines: All have English speakers. **24hr. immediate help:** ☎717 19. **Rape Crisis Hotline:** ☎523 22 22. M 10am-6pm, Tu 2-6pm, W 10am-2pm, Th 5-9pm.

Medical Assistance: Allgemeines Krankenhaus (hospital), IX, Währinger Gürtel 18-20 (☎404 00 19 64). **Emergency care:** ☎141.

Pharmacy: 24hr. pharmacy: ☎15 50. Consulates have lists of English-speaking doctors, or call **Fachärzte Zugeck** (☎512 18 18; 24hr.).

Internet Access: bigNET.internet.cafe, I, Karntnerstr. 61 (☎503 98 44) or I, Hoher markt 8-9 (☎533 29 39). Hip English-speaking crew. €3.65 per 30min. **Libro,** XXII, Donauzentrum (☎202 52 55), provides free access at 6 terminals. Open M-F 7am-7pm, Sa 9am-5pm. **Jugend-Info des Bundesministeriums,** I, Franz-Josefs-Kai 51 (☎533 70 30), has free access at 2 PCs. Open M-F 11am-6pm.

Post Offices: Hauptpostamt, I, Fleischmarkt 19. Open 24hr. Address mail to be held: SURNAME, Firstname; Postlagernde Briefe; Hauptpostamt; Fleischmarkt 19; A-1010 Wien. Branches throughout the city and at the train stations; look for the yellow signs with the trumpet logo. **Postal Codes:** A-1XX0, where XX is the number of the district in Arabic numerals (ex.: District I: A-1010, District II: A-1020, District XVII: A-1170.)

ACCOMMODATIONS AND CAMPING

Hunting for cheap rooms in Vienna during peak tourist season (June-Sept.) can be unpleasant; call for reservations at least five days in advance. Otherwise, plan on calling between 6 and 9am to put your name down for a reservation. If full, ask to be put on a waiting list. The summer crunch for budget rooms is slightly alleviated in July, when university dorms convert into makeshift hostels.

HOSTELS

Hostel Ruthensteiner (HI), XV, Robert-Hamerlingg. 24 (☎ 893 42 02). Exit *Westbahnhof* at the main entrance, turn right onto Mariahilferstr., and continue until Haidmannsg. Turn left, then take the first right on Robert-Hamerlingg. Knowledgeable, English-speaking staff, spotless rooms, and a snack bar. Relax in their rose-filled courtyard. Internet €2. Breakfast €2.50. Lockers and kitchen available. Sheets (except for 10-bed dorms) included. 4-night max. stay. Reception 24hr. Reservations recommended. "The Outback" summer dorm €10.50; 3- to 10-bed dorms €12-13.50; singles €20-22; doubles €40-44. AmEx/MC/V. ❷

Wombats City Hostel, XIV, Grang. 6 (☎ 897 23 36). Exit *Westbahnhof* at the main exit, turn right onto Mariahilferstr., right onto Rosinag., and continue until Grang. While near train tracks and a number of auto-body shops, this modern hostel compensates with a pub and various perks. Internet €1 per 12min. Bike or in-line skate rental €7.30 per day. Breakfast €3. Laundry €4.50. 2-, 4-, and 6-bed dorms €14-36 per person. ❷

Believe It Or Not, VII, Myrtheng. 10, Apt. #14 (☎ 526 46 58). From *Westbahnhof,* take U6 (dir.: Floridsdorf) to Burgg./Stadthalle, then bus #48A (dir.: Ring) to Neubaug. Walk back on Burgg. 1 block and take the 1st right on Myrtheng. Ring the bell. A converted apartment, with kitchen and 2 bedrooms. Reception 8am until early afternoon—call early. Lockout 10:30am-12:30pm. Easter-Oct. €11.65; Nov.-Easter €8. ❶

Hostel Panda, VII, Kaiserstr. 77, 3rd fl. (☎ 522 53 53). From *Westbahnhof,* U6 (dir.: Floridsdorf) to Burgg./Stadthalle. Take 2nd left on Kaiserstr. Housed in an old-fashioned Austrian apartment building, this eclectic hostel has 2 co-ed dorms. Kitchen and TV. Bring lock for lockers. Dorms €12.50; Nov.-Easter €9. 1-night stays add €3.50. ❷

Kolpinghaus Wien-Meidling, XIII, Bendlg. 10-12 (☎ 813 54 87). U6 to Niederhofstr. Head right on Niederhofstr., and take the 4th right onto Bendlg. Breakfast €3.80. Institutional hostel with 202 beds. Showers in all rooms. Reception 24hr. Check-out 9am. 8- and 10-bed dorms €11.30; 4- and 6- bed dorms €13.50-14.50. AmEx/MC/V. ❷

IN RECENT NEWS

THE TEURO

If everything seems more expensive in Austria, it may not be unfavorable exchange rates or faulty memories of the good old days when a schilling could buy a horse and a tankard of ale. The euro, (termed the "Teuro" by many Austrians, punning on *teurer,* German for "expensive"), may be, at least, partly to blame.

Effective July 1, 2002, the schilling officially ceased to exist as currency and all transactions were carried out in euros. Though the transition went off without a major incident, it hasn't stopped people from grumbling. "It was bloody easy for the shopkeepers to make the switch," complains an Austrian expatriate. "They just rounded everything up."

While most people were content to pay a few extra cents here and there, some increases were harder to swallow. "In many places, they simply divided all the prices by 10 and called that the price in euros," explains a retired school teacher in Voralberg. What may seem like a reasonable solution is outrageous considering that the actual conversion rate was 13.7 schillings to the euro. Merchants who divided by 10 quietly upped prices 37% literally overnight.

Now that the logistical nightmare of refitting every vending machine, automat, and price tag is over, prices have finally stabilized. This means that while your money won't go quite as far as it used to, the runaway inflation of the first few months has come to a halt.

Jugendgästehaus Wien Brigittenau (HI), XX, Friedrich-Engels-Pl. 24 (☎332 82 94 or 330 05 98). U1 or 4 to Schwedenpl., then Tram N to Floridsdorferbrücke/Friedrich-Engels-Pl.; follow the signs. This roomy hostel has excellent facilities for the disabled, but it's 25min. from the city center. Breakfast and lockers included. Internet access. 5-night max. stay. Reception 24hr. Lockout 9am-1pm. 24-bed dorms (men only) €12.15; 4-bed dorms €15-17; doubles with bath €30-34. Nonmembers add €3.50. ❷

HOTELS AND PENSIONS

Pension Kraml, VI, Brauerg. 5 (☎587 85 88). U3 to Zierierg. Exit onto Otto-Bauerg., take 1st left, then 1st right. From *Südbahnhof*, take bus #13A to Esterhazyg. and walk up Brauerg. Near the *Innenstadt* with large rooms, a lounge, cable TV, and a kind staff. Breakfast €2.50. Singles €26; doubles €43, with shower €55, with bath €65; triples €65, with shower €70. Apartment with bath €100-115 for 3-5 people. MC/V. ❸

Pension Hargita, VII, Andreasg. (☎526 19 28). U3 to Zieglerg. Use the Andreasg. exit. A quiet pension that offers amicable service and a prime location. Breakfast €3. Reception daily 8am-10pm. Singles €31, with shower €50; doubles €45/€52. ❹

Pension Reimer, IV, Kircheng. 18 (☎523 61 62). Centrally located with huge, comfortable rooms that are always clean. Breakfast included. Singles €31-38; doubles €50-56, with bath €60-64. MC/V. ❹

Hotel Zur Wiener Staatsoper, I, Krugerstr. 11 (☎513 12 74 75). From Karlspl., exit Oper and follow Kärtnerstr. towards the city center; turn right on Krugerstr. This luxurious hotel offers simple elegance and a prime location. Breakfast included. Singles €76-88; doubles €109-124; triples €131-146. AmEx/MC/V. ❺

UNIVERSITY DORMITORIES

From July through September, many university dorms become hotels, usually with singles, doubles, and a few triples and quads. These rooms don't have much in the way of character, but showers and sheets are standard, and their cleanliness and relatively low cost make them particularly suited to longer stays.

Porzellaneum der Wiener Universität, IX, Porzellang. 30 (☎317 728 20). From *Südbahnhof*, take tram D (dir.: Nußdorf) to Fürsteng. From *Westbahnhof*, take tram #5 to Franz-Josefs *Bahnhof*, then tram D (dir.: Südbahnhof) to Fürsteng. Great location in the student district. Reception 24hr. Singles €16-18; doubles €30-35; quads €56-64. ❸

Katholisches Studentenhaus, XIX, Peter-Jordanstr. 29 (☎369 55 85). From *Westbahnhof*, take U6 (dir.: Heiligenstadt) to Nußdorferstr., then bus #35A or tram #38 to Hardtg. and turn left. From *Südbahnhof*, take tram D to Schottentor, then tram #38 to Hardtg. Reception daily until 10pm. Singles €18; doubles €30. ❸

Studentenwohnheim der Hochschule für Musik, I, Johannesg. 8 (☎514 84 48). Walk 3 blocks down Kärntnerstr. away from Stephansdom and turn left onto Johannesg. Unbeatable location and cheap meals. Breakfast included. Reception 24hr. Reserve well in advance. Singles €33-36; doubles €58-70; triples €66; quads €80; quints €100. Apartment with 2 double rooms, bathroom, kitchen, and living room €28.50 per person, €90 for entire apartment. ❹

CAMPING

Wien-West, Hüttelbergstr. 80 (☎914 23 14). Take U4 to Hütteldorf, then bus #14B or 152 (dir.: Campingpl.) to Wien West. This campground, 8km from the city center, is crowded but grassy and pleasant. Laundry, grocery stores, wheelchair access, and cooking facilities. Reception daily 7:30am-9:30pm. Closed Feb. Electricity €3. July-Aug. €6 per person, Sept.-June €5; €3 per tent. ❶

Aktiv Camping Neue Donau, XXII, Am Kleehäufel 119 (☎ 202 40 10), is 4km from the city center and adjacent to Neue Donau beaches. Take U1 to Kaisermühlen, then bus #91a to Kleehäufel. Laundry, supermarket, and kitchen. Showers included. Open mid-May to mid-Sept. Electricity €3. July to mid-Aug. €5.50 per person; May-June and Sept. €3.50 per person. €3 per tent. ❶

✂ FOOD

Vienna's restaurants are as varied as its cuisine. The restaurants near Kärntnerstr. are generally expensive—a cheaper area is the neighborhood north of the university, near the *Votivkirche* (U2 to Schottentor), where Universitätsstr. and Währingerstr. meet. Cafes with cheap meals also line **Burggasse** in district VI. The area radiating from the Rechte and Linke Wienzeile near Naschmarkt (U4 to Kettenbrückeg.) houses cheap restaurants. The **Naschmarkt** itself contains stands where you can purchase a variety of ethnic foods. Almost all year long, **Rathausplatz** hosts food stands tied into the current festival. The open-air **Brunnenmarkt** (U6 to Josefstädterstr.; walk up Veronikag. one block and turn right) is cheap and cheerful. Supermarkets chains include **Zielpunkt, Hofer,** and **Spar.** Kosher groceries are available at the **Kosher Supermarket,** II, Hollandstr. 10 (☎ 216 96 75).

INSIDE THE RING

▩ **DO&CO,** I, Stephanspl. 12. Set above the Stephanspl. cathedral, this modern gourmet restaurant offers both traditional Austrian dishes and other international specialties like Thai noodles and Uruguay beef (€18.50-21.50). Prices are high, but so is the quality and location. Open daily noon-3pm and 6pm-midnight. ❹

▩ **Trzesniewski,** I, Dorotheerg. 1, 3 blocks down the Graben from the Stephansdom. This unpronounceable but famous establishment has been serving petite open-faced sandwiches for over 80 years. A filling lunch—6 sandwiches and a mini-beer—costs about €5. This was Kafka's favorite place to eat. Open M-F 8:30am-7:30pm, Sa 9am-5pm. ❷

Levante, I, Wallnerstr. 2. Walk down Graben away from the Stephansdom, turn left on Kohlmarkt, and right onto Wallnerstr. Greek-Turkish franchise features street-side dining with some vegetarian dishes. Entrees €7-12. Open daily 11am-11pm. ❸

Margaritaville, I, Bartensteing. 3. Take U2 to Lerchenfelderstr., exit onto Museumstr., and cut across the triangular green to Bartensteing. Offers authentic Tex-Mex food among Spanish-speakers. Open M-Sa 4pm-2am, Su 4pm-midnight. MC/V. ❸

Maschu Maschu, I, Rabensteig 8. In the Bermuda Dreieck; serves filling and super-cheap Israeli *falafel* (€3). Open M-W 11:30am-midnight, Th-Sa 11:30am-3am. ❶

OUTSIDE THE RING

▩ **Centimeter,** IX, Liechtensteinstr. 42. Tram D to Bauernfeldpl. This chain offers huge portions of greasy Austrian fare and an unbelievable selection of beers. You pay by the centimeter. Open M-F 10am-2am, Sa 11am-2am, Su 11am-midnight. AmEx/MC/V. ❷

Elsäßer Bistro, IX, Währingerstr. 32. U2 to Schottentor. In the palace that houses the French Cultural Institute—walk into the garden and follow your nose for an extravagant meal. Wonderful food, with prices hovering around €14, and exquisite French wines. Open M-F 11am-3pm and 6:30-11pm. ❹

Café Nil, VII, Siebensterng. 39. Enjoy vegetarian dishes (€6-11) with tortured writers and philosophers. Breakfast until 3pm. Open daily 10am-midnight. ❷

AUSTRIA

VIENNA COFFEE CULTURE. The 19th-century coffeehouse was a haven for artists, writers, and thinkers, who stayed long into the night composing operettas, writing books, and cutting into each other's work. The bourgeoisie followed suit, and the coffeehouse became the living room of the city. The original literary cafes were Café Griensteidl, Café Central, and Café Herrenhof. Cafes still exist under all these names, but only Café Central looks like it used to. Most cafes also serve hot food, but don't order anything but pastries with your *Melange* (Viennese coffee) unless you want to be really gauche. The most serious dictate of coffeehouse etiquette is that you linger; the waiter (*Herr Ober*) will serve you when you sit down, then leave you to sip, read, and brood. When you're ready to leave, just ask to pay: *"Zahlen bitte!"* Vienna has many coffeehouses; the best are listed below. ❷

Kleines Café, I, Franziskanerpl. 3. Turn off Kärtnerstr. onto Weihburg. and follow it to the *Franziskanerkirche*. This tiny, cozy cafe features courtyard tables and salads that are minor works of art (€6.50). Open M-Sa 10am-2am, Su 1pm-2am.

Café Sperl, VI, Gumpendorferstr. 11. U2 to Museumsquartier; exit to Mariahilferstr., walk 1 block on Getreidemarkt, and turn right on Gumpendorferstr. One of Vienna's oldest and most beautiful cafes. Coffee €2-4.50; cake €2.50-3.85. Open M-Sa 7am-11pm, Su 11am-8pm; July-Aug. closed Su.

Café Central, I, at the corner of Herreng. and Strauchg. inside Palais Fers. Cafe Central has become touristy because of its fame, but this mecca of the cafe world is still worth a visit. Open M-Sa 8am-8pm, Su 10am-6pm. AmEx/MC/V.

Hotel Sacher, I, Philharmonikerstr. 4, behind the opera house. This historic sight has served world-famous *Sacher Torte* in red velvet opulence for years. Cafe open daily 11am-11:30pm. Bakery open daily 9am-11:30pm. AmEx/MC/V.

OH Pot, OH Pot, IX, Währingerstr. 22. U2 to Schottentor. This adorable joint serves filling "pots," stew-like veggie or meat concoctions. (€7-€10). Open M-F, Su 11:30am-midnight, Sa noon-midnight. AmEx/MC/V. ❸

Blue Box, VII, Richterg. 8. U3 to Neubaug., turn onto Neubaug., and take the 1st left onto Richterg. Blue Box is a restaurant by day and a club by night. Dishes are fresh and original (€3.50-7), and DJs spin the latest trance and trip-hop. Open M 6pm-2am, Tu-Su 10am-2am. V. ❸

University Mensa, IX, Universitätsstr. 7, on the 7th fl. of the university building, between U2 stops Rathaus and Schottentor. Ride the old-fashioned *Pater Noster* elevator (no doors and never stops, so jump in and out and say your prayers) to the 6th fl. and take the stairs up. Not much atmosphere, but the food is cheap. Typical cafeteria meals €3.85. Open M-F 11am-2pm, but snack bar open 8am-3pm; closed July-Aug. ❶

🜛 SIGHTS

Vienna's streets are by turns startling, cozy, scuzzy, and grandiose; expect contrasts around every corner. To wander on your own, grab the brochure *Vienna from A to Z* (with Vienna Card €4; available at the tourist office). The range of available **tours** is overwhelming—there are 42 themed walking tours alone, detailed in the tourist office's brochure *Walks in Vienna*. Contact **Vienna-Bike**, IX, Wasag. (☎319 12 58), for **bike rental** (€5) or a 2-3hr. **cycling tour** (€20). **Bus tours** are given by **Vienna Sight Seeing Tours,** III, Stelzhamerg. 4/11 (☎712 46 83), and **Cityrama,** I, Börgeg. 1. (☎534 13. Bus tours from €30.) The sights below are arranged for a do-it-yourself walking tour.

AUSTRIA

INSIDE THE RING
District I is Vienna's social and geographical epicenter, as well as a gallery of the history of aesthetics from Romanesque to *Jugendstil* (Art Nouveau).

STEPHANSPLATZ, GRABEN, AND PETERSPLATZ. Right at the heart of Vienna, this square is home to the massive **Stephansdom** (St. Stephen's Cathedral), Vienna's most treasured symbol. The elevator in the North Tower (€3.50) leads to a view of the city; the 343 steps of the South Tower climb to a 360° view. *(Open daily 9am-5:30pm. South Tower €2.50.)* Downstairs, skeletons of thousands of plague victims fill the **catacombs**. The **Gruft** (vault) stores all of the Habsburg innards. *(Cathedral tours M-Sa every 30min. 10-11:30am and 1-4:30pm, Su and holidays 1:30-4:30pm; €3.)* From Stephanspl., follow **Graben** for a landscape of *Jugendstil* architecture, including the **Ankerhaus** (#10), Otto Wagner's red-marble **Grabenhof,** and the underground public toilet complex designed by Adolf Loos. Graben leads to **Petersplatz** and the 1663 **Pestsäule** (Plague Column), which was built in celebration of the passing of the Black Death. *(U1 or U3: Stephanspl.)*

HOHER MARKT AND STADTTEMPEL. Once both a market and an execution site, **Hoher Markt** was the heart of the Roman encampment, Vindobona. Roman ruins lie beneath the shopping arcade on its south side. *(Open Tu-Su 9am-12:15pm and 1pm-4:40pm. €1.85, students €0.75.)* The biggest draw is the 1914 *Jugendstil* **Ankeruhr** (clock), whose 3m historical figures—from Marcus Aurelius to Maria Theresia—rotate past the old Viennese coat of arms accompanied by music of their time period. *(1 figure per hr. At noon all figures appear. Follow Judeng. from Hoher Markt to Ruprechtspl.)* Hidden at Seitenstetteng. 2-4, the **Stadttempel** (City Temple) is the only synagogue in Vienna to escape Nazi destruction during *Kristallnacht.* *(Bring passport. Open Su-F. Free. Take Milchg. out of Peterspl., turn right, and go 3 blocks on Tuchlauben; Hoher Markt is on the right.)*

ALTES RATHAUS, AM HOF, AND FREYUNG. The **Altes Rathaus** (Old Town Hall), Wipplingerstr. 8, was occupied from 1316 to 1885. It's also home to the **Austrian Resistance Museum,** which chronicles anti-Nazi activity during World War II. *(Open M and W-Th 9am-5pm. Free.)* Follow Drahtg. to Am Hof, a grand courtyard which was once a medieval jousting square and now houses the **Kirche am Hof** (Church of the Nine Choirs of Angels). Just west of Am Hof is **Freyung,** an uneven square with the **Austriabrunnen** (Austria fountain) in the center. Freyung ("sanctuary") took its name from the **Schottenstift** (Monastery of the Scots) just behind the fountain, where fugitives could claim asylum in medieval times. It was once used for public executions, but the annual **Christkindl markt** held here blots out such unpleasant memories. *(From Hoher Markt, follow Wipplingerstr.)*

HOFBURG. The sprawling **Hofburg** was the winter residence of the Habsburgs. Construction began in 1279, and hodge-podge additions and renovations continued until the end of the family's reign in 1918. When you come through the

AUSTRIA

AUSTRIAN GRAFFITI Scratched into the stones near the entrance of the Stephansdom is the abbreviation "O5." It's not a sign of hoodlums up to no good but rather a reminder of a different kind of subversive activity. During World War II, "O5" was the secret symbol of Austria's resistance movement against the Nazis. The capital letter "O" and the number "5," for the fifth letter of the alphabet, form the first two letters of "Oesterreich"—meaning Austria. Recently the monogram has received new life. Every time alleged Nazi collaborator and ex-president of Austria Kurt Waldheim attends mass, the symbol is highlighted in chalk. Throughout the city, "O5" has also been appearing on buildings and flyers in protest of the anti-immigrant policies of Jörg Haider and the Freedom Party.

Michaelertor, you'll first enter the courtyard called **In der Burg** (within the fortress). On your left is the red-and-black-striped **Schweizertor** (Swiss Gate), erected in 1552. On the right side of the Michaelertor is the entrance to the **Kaiserappartements** (Imperial Apartments). They were once the private quarters of Emperor Franz Josef and Empress Elisabeth, but the rooms are disappointingly lifeless. The **Hofsilber und Tafelkammer** (Court Silver and Porcelain Collection), on the ground floor opposite the ticket office, displays examples of Imperial cutlery. *(Both open 9am-4:30pm. Combined admission €6.90, students €5.45.)*

Behind the Schweizertor lies the **Schweizerhof**, the inner courtyard of the **Alte Burg** (Old Fortress), which stands on the same site as the original 13th-century palace. The stairs to the right of the Schweiztor lead to the Gothic **Burgkapelle** (chapel), where the members of the **Wiener Sängerknaben (Vienna Boys' Choir)** raise their heavenly voices every Sunday (see p. 92). Beneath the stairs is the entrance to the **Weltliche und Geistliche Schatzkammer** (Worldly and Spiritual Treasury), containing Habsburg jewels, and an assortment of other treasures. *(Open W-M 10am-6pm. €7, students €5. Free audio guide available in English.)*

Built between 1881 and 1926, the **Neue Burg** is the youngest wing of the palace. The double-headed golden eagle crowning the roof symbolizes the double empire of Austria-Hungary. Today, the Neue Burg houses Austria's largest library, the **Österreichische Nationalbibliothek.** *(Open Oct.-June M-F 9am-7pm, Sa 9am-12:45pm; July-Aug. and Sept. 23-30 M-F 9am-3:45pm, Sa 9am-12:45pm; closed Sept. 1-22.)*

High masses are still held in the 14th-century **Augustinerkirche** (St. Augustine's Church). The hearts of the Habsburgs are stored in the **Herzgrüftel** (Little Heart Crypt). *(Open M-Sa 10am-6pm, Su 11am-6pm. Mass 11am. To reach Hofburg, head through the half-moon-shaped Michaelertor in Michaelerpl.)*

OUTSIDE THE RING

Some of Vienna's most famous modern architecture is outside the Ring, where 20th-century designers found more space to build. This area is also home to a number of Baroque palaces and parks that were once beyond the city limits.

KARLSPLATZ AND NASCHMARKT. Karlspl. is home to Vienna's most beautiful Baroque church, the **Karlskirche**, an eclectic masterpiece combining a Neoclassical portico with a Baroque dome and towers on either side. *(U1, 2, or 4 to Karlspl. Or, from the Hofburg, walk down Tegetthoffstr. to Neuer Markt and follow Kärntnerstr. to Karlspl. Open M-F 7:30am-7pm, Sa 8:30am-7pm, Su 9am-7pm. Free.)* West of Karlspl., along Linke Wienzeile, is the **Naschmarkt**, a colorful food bazaar. On Saturdays, the Naschmarkt becomes a massive flea market. *(Open M-F 7am-6pm, Sa 7am-5pm.)*

SCHLOß BELVEDERE. The **Schloß Belvedere** was originally the summer residence of Prince Eugène of Savoy, Austria's greatest military hero. The grounds, stretching from Schwarzenberg Palace to the *Südbahnhof*, contain three excellent museums (see p. 91) and an equal number of spectacular sphinx-filled gardens. *(Take tram D or #71 one stop past Schwarzenbergpl.)*

SCHLOß SCHÖNBRUNN. From its humble beginnings as a hunting lodge, **Schönbrunn** ("beautiful brook") was Maria Theresia's favorite residence. Tours of some of the palace's 1500 rooms reveal the elaborate taste of her era, giving you access to the **Great Gallery,** where the Congress of Vienna met, and the **Hall of Mirrors,** where 6-year-old Mozart played. *(U4: Schönbrunn. Palace open July-Aug. daily 8:30am-7pm; Apr.-June and Sept.-Oct. 8:30am-5pm; Nov.-Mar. 8:30am-4:30pm. 22-room tour €7.50, students €7. 44-room tour €10/€8. Audio-guides included.)* Even more impressive than the palace itself are the classical **gardens** behind it, which extend nearly four times the length of the palace and contain a hodgepodge of attractions, including the **Schmetterlinghaus** (Butterfly House). *(Park open 6am-dusk. Free.)*

ZENTRALFRIEDHOF (CENTRAL CEMETERY). Tor I (Gate 1) leads to the old **Jewish Cemetery.** Many of the headstones are cracked and neglected because the families of most of the dead have left Austria. Behind **Tor II** (Gate 2) are Beethoven, Strauss, and an honorary monument to Mozart, whose true resting place is an unmarked paupers' grave in the **Cemetery of St. Mark,** III, Leberstr. 6-8. **Tor III** (Gate 3) leads to the Protestant section and the new Jewish cemetery. *(XI, Simmeringer Hauptstr. 234. Take tram #71 from Schwarzenbergpl. or tram #72 from Schlachthaus. Open May-Aug. daily 7am-7pm; Mar.-Apr. and Sept.-Oct. 7am-6pm; Nov.-Feb. 8am-5pm.)*

🏛 MUSEUMS

Vienna owes its vast selection of masterpieces to the acquisitive Habsburgs and to the city's own crop of art schools and world-class artists. An exhaustive list is impossible to include here, but the tourist office's free *Museums* brochure lists all opening hours and admission prices. All museums run by the city of Vienna are **free on Friday** before noon (except on public holidays). If you're going to be in town for a while, invest in the **Museum Card** (ask at any museum ticket window).

■ ÖSTERREICHISCHE GALERIE (AUSTRIAN GALLERY). The Upper Belvedere houses European art of the 19th and 20th centuries, including Klimt's *The Kiss.* The Lower Belvedere contains an extensive collection of sculptures, David's portrait of Napoleon on horseback, and the Museum of Medieval Austrian Art. *(III, Prinz-Eugen-Str. 27, in the Belvedere Palace behind Schwarzenbergpl. (see p. 90). Walk up from the Südbahnhof, then take tram D to Schloß Belvedere or tram #71 to Unteres Belvedere. Both Belvederes open Tu-Su 10am-6pm; Upper open Th until 9pm. €7.50, students €5.)*

■ KUNSTHISTORISCHES MUSEUM (MUSEUM OF FINE ARTS). The world's 4th-largest art collection, featuring Venetian and Flemish paintings, Classical art, and an Egyptian burial chamber. *(U2 to Museumsquartier, U3 or tram 1, 2, D, or J to Volkstheater. Across from the Burgring and Heldenpl. on Maria Theresia's right. Open Tu-Su 10am-6pm. €9, students €6.50. Audio guides €2.)*

■ MUSEUM FÜR VÖLKERKUNDE (ETHNOLOGY MUSEUM). Houses an impressive collection including Benin bronzes, Chinese paper kites, and West African Dan heads. The focal point, however, is undoubtedly the crown of Montezuma, which still draws a crowd of protesters demanding its return to Mexico. *(I, in the Neue Burg on Heldenpl. U2 or 3, or tram 1, 2, D, or J to Volkstheater. Open Apr.-Dec. W-M 10am-6pm. €7.50, students €5.50. Free May 16, Oct. 26, Dec. 10 and 24.)*

MUSEUMSQUARTIER. A huge conglomeration of museums. **Kunsthalle Wien** features thematic exhibitions of international contemporary artists. *(U2 to Museumsquartier, U2 or 3 or tram 1, 2, D, or J to Volkstheater. Open daily 10am-7pm, Th until 10pm. Hall 1 €6.50, students €5; Hall 2 €5/€3.50; both €8/€6.50.)* **Museum Moderner Kunst** (Museum of Modern Art) holds Central Europe's largest collection of modern art. *(Open Tu-Su 10am-7pm, Th until 9pm. €8, students €6.50.)*

HISTORISCHES MUSEUM DER STADT WIEN (HISTORICAL MUSEUM OF THE CITY OF VIENNA). This amazing collection of historical artifacts and paintings documents Vienna's evolution from a Roman encampment, through the Turkish siege of Vienna, to the subsequent 640 years of Habsburg rule. *(IV, Karlspl., to the left of the Karlskirche. Open Tu-Su 9am-6pm. €3.50, students €1.50.)*

SIGMUND FREUD HAUS. The famed couch is not here, but Freud's former home provides lots of photos and documents, including his report cards and circumcision certificate. *(IX, Bergg. 19. U2 to Schottentor; walk up Währingerstr. to Bergg. or take tram D to Schlickg. Open July-Sept. daily 9am-6pm; Oct.-June 9am-4pm. €5, students €3.)*

KUNST HAUS WIEN. Artist Friedenreich Hundertwasser built this museum without straight lines—even the floor bends. In addition to Hundertwasser's work, it hosts contemporary art from around the world. *(III, Untere Weißgerberstr. 13. U1 or 4 to Schwedenpl., then tram N to Hetzg. Open daily 10am-7pm. €8, students €6; M half-price.)*

🎵 🔊 ENTERTAINMENT AND FESTIVALS

While Vienna offers all the standard entertainments in the way of theater, film, and festivals, the heart of the city beats to music. All but a few of classical music's marquee names lived, composed, and performed in Vienna. Mozart, Beethoven, and Haydn wrote their greatest masterpieces in Vienna, creating the **First Viennese School;** a century later, Schönberg, Webern, and Berg teamed up to form the **Second Viennese School.** Every Austrian child must learn to play an instrument during schooling, and the Vienna **Konservatorium** and **Hochschule** are world-renowned conservatories. All year, Vienna has performances ranging from the above-average to the sublime, with many accessible to the budget traveler. Note that the venues below have **no performances in July and August.**

Vienna hosts an array of important annual festivals, mostly musical. The **Vienna Festival** (mid-May to mid-June) has a diverse program of exhibitions, plays, and concerts. (☎58 92 20; www.festwochen.or.at.) The Staatsoper and Volkstheater host the annual **Jazzfest Wien** during the first weeks of July, featuring many famous acts. (☎503 5647; www.viennajazz.org.) From mid-July to mid-August, the **Im-Puls Dance Festival** (☎523 55 58; www.impuls-tanz.com) attracts some of the world's greatest dance troupes and offers seminars to enthusiasts. In mid-October, the annual city-wide international film festival, the **Viennale,** kicks off.

Staatsoper, I, Opernring 2 (www.wiener-staatsoper.at), is Vienna's premier opera, performing nearly every night Sept.-June. Standing-room tickets are available right before the performance (1 per person, €2-3.50). The box office (Bundestheaterkasse), I, Hanuschg. 3, around the corner from the opera, sells tickets in advance. (☎514 44 78 80. Open M-F 8am-6pm, Sa-Su 9am-noon, 1st Sa of each month 9am-5pm.) Tickets are available at www.bundestheater.at, with a 20% commission.

Wiener Philharmoniker (Vienna Philharmonic Orchestra) plays in the **Musikverein,** Austria's premiere concert hall. Write or visit the box office of the Musikverein for tickets, including standing-room tickets, well in advance (Gesellschaft der Musikfreunde, Bösendorferstr. 12, A-1010 Wien) or stop by the Bundestheaterkasse (see Staatsoper, above). Tickets are available at www.wienerphilharmoniker.at.

Wiener Sängerknaben (Vienna Boys' Choir) sings during mass every Su at 9:15am (mid-Sept. to May only) in the **Hofburgkapelle** (U3 to Herreng.). For more information, contact hofmusikkapelle@asn-wien.ac.at.

🔲 NIGHTLIFE

With one of the highest bar-to-cobblestone ratios in the world, Vienna is a great place to party, whether you're looking for a quiet evening with a glass of wine or a wild night in a disco full of black-clad musclemen and drag queens. Take U1 or 4 to Schwedenpl., which will drop you within blocks of the **Bermuda Dreieck** (Triangle), an area packed with lively, crowded clubs. If your vision isn't foggy yet, head down **Rotenturmstraße** toward Stephansdom or walk around the areas bounded by the Jewish synagogue and Ruprechtskirche. Slightly outside the Ring, the streets off **Burggasse** and **Stiftgasse** in the 7th district and the **university quarter** (Districts XIII and IX) have tables in outdoor courtyards and loud, hip bars.

Viennese nightlife starts late, often after 11pm. For the scoop, pick up a copy of the indispensable **Falter** (€2), which prints listings of everything from opera and theater to punk concerts and updates on the gay and lesbian scene.

▨ **Objektiv**, VII, Kirchbergg. 26. U2 or 3 to Volkstheater. An eclectic bar with a mellow atmosphere and cheap drinks. Happy Hour daily 11pm-1am. Open M-Sa 6pm-2am.

▨ **U-4**, XII, Schönbrunnerstr. 222. U4 to Meidling Hauptstr. In the late 80s, U-4 hosted Nirvana and Hole before they were famous. Two dance areas and multiple bars. Check in advance for theme nights. Cover €8. Open daily 10pm-5am.

Das Möbel, VII, Burgg. 10. U2 or 3 to Volkstheater. Metal couches, car-seat chairs, and Swiss-army tables are filled by a trendy crowd. Open M-F noon-1am, Sa-Su 10am-1am.

Mapitom der Bierlokal, I, Seitenstetteng. 1. Located in the center of the Bermuda Triangle, this bar has large tables clustered in a warehouse-style interior. Beer and drinks about €3. Open Su-Th 5pm-3am, F-Sa 5pm-4am.

CARINTHIA (KÄRNTEN)

Carinthia covers the southernmost part of Austria. The sunny climate and laid-back atmosphere give the province a Mediterranean feel. Though foreigners take little notice of this part of the country, natives consider it a vacation paradise.

GRAZ ☎ 0316

Wonderfully under-touristed, Graz's *Altstadt* rewards the rare traveler with an unhurried Mediterranean feel, picturesque red-tiled roofs, and Baroque domes. The second largest of Austria's cities, Graz offers a sweaty, energetic nightlife thanks to the 45,000 students at Karl-Franzens-Universität.

☐ TRANSPORTATION. Trains run from the **Hauptbahnhof**, Europapl. (open daily 7am-8:45pm), for: Innsbruck (6hr., 4 per day, €42); Munich (6½hr., 4 per day, €57); Salzburg (4¼hr., €34); Vienna *Südbahnhof* (2½hr., 9 per day, €25); and Zurich (8½hr., daily at 10pm, €108).

⊠ PRACTICAL INFORMATION. From the train station, go down Annenstr. and cross the Hauptbrücke (bridge) to reach **Hauptplatz**, the center of town. Five minutes away is **Jakominiplatz**, the hub of the public transportation system; **Herrengasse**, a pedestrian street lined with cafes and boutiques, connects the two squares. The **tourist office**, Herreng. 16, has free city maps and a guide to walking the city. The staff offers English-language **tours** of the *Altstadt* (2hr.; Apr.-Oct. Tu-W and F-Su 2:30pm; €7.50) and makes free room reservations. (☎807 50. Open June-Sept. M-F 9am-7pm, Sa 9am-6pm, Su 10am-4pm; Oct.-May M-F 9am-6pm, Sa 9am-3pm, Su 10am-3pm.) **Café Zentral**, Andreas-Hofer-Pl. 9, has **Internet access**. (€4.50 per hr. Open M-F 6am-midnight, Sa 6am-noon.) **Postal code:** A-8010.

☐☐ ACCOMMODATIONS AND FOOD. In Graz, most hotels, guest houses, and pensions are pricey and far from the city center. Luckily, the web of local transport provides a reliable and easy commute to and from the outlying neighborhoods. To reach **Jugendgästehaus Graz (HI)** ❷, Idlhofg. 74, from the train station, cross the street, head right on Eggenberger Gürtel, turn left on Josef-Huber-G., then take the first right; the hostel is through the parking lot on your right. Buses #31 and 32 run here from Jakominipl. (☎71 48 76. Internet €1.50 for 20min. Breakfast included.

Laundry €3. All rooms with bath. Reception daily 7am-10pm. Doors open every 30min. 10pm-2am. 4-bed dorms €17; singles €24; doubles €40. €2.50 surcharge for stays of less than 3 nights. MC/V.) **Hotel zur Stadthalle "Johannes"** ❹, Munzgrabenstr. 48, has pleasant rooms close to the *Altstadt*. Take streetcar #6 to Neue Technik. The hotel is the pale yellow building close to the stop. (☎83 77 66. Breakfast, TV, and bath included. Singles €45; doubles €67.)

Find an inexpensive meal on **Hauptplatz,** where concession stands sell sandwiches, *Wurst* (€1.50-3), and other fast food. Cheap student hangouts line **Zinzendorfgasse** near the university. **China Restaurant Mond** ❷, Harrachg. 12a, serves an all-you-can-eat lunch buffet (M-F 11:30am-2:30pm) for €5.10 and a daily menu for €3.80. (Open daily 11:30am-3pm and 5:30-10pm.) **Gasthaus "Alte Münze"** ❸, Schloßbergpl. 8, serves scrumptious Styrian specialties in a traditional setting. (Open Tu-Sa 8am-midnight, Su-M 10am-7pm.) A grocery store, **Merkur,** is to your left as you exit the train station. (Open M-Th 8am-7pm, F 7:30am-7:30pm.)

◙ ▧ **SIGHTS AND NIGHTLIFE.** The **Landhaus,** which houses the tourist office, is a sight itself; the building was remodeled by architect Domenico dell'Allio in 1557 in Lombard style. The **Landeszeughaus** (Provincial Arsenal), Herreng. 16, details the history of Ottoman attacks on the arsenal and has enough spears, muskets, and armor to outfit 28,000 burly mercenaries. (Open Mar.-Oct. Tu-Su 9am-5pm; Nov.-Dec. Tu-Su 10am-3pm. €1.50.) North of Hauptpl., the wooded **Schloßberg** (Castle Mountain) rises 123m above Graz. The hill is named for the castle that stood there from 1125 until 1809, when it was destroyed by Napoleon's troops. Though the castle is mostly gone, the Schloßberg remains a beautiful city park. Climb the zigzagging stone steps of the **Schloßbergstiege,** built by Russian prisoners during WWI, for sweeping views of the vast Styrian plain.

The hub of after-hours activity is the so-called **Bermuda Triangle,** an area of the old city behind Hauptpl. and bordered by Mehlpl., Färberg., and Prokopig. At **Kulturhauskeller,** Elisabethstr. 30, a young crowd demands ever louder and more throbbing dance music, but the partying doesn't get started until 11pm on weekends. (No sports or military clothing. 19+. Cover €2. Open Tu-Sa from 9pm.) **Triangle,** Burgg. 15, is a low-key bar with vaulted brick ceilings, mirrored arches, and a clientele of trendy 20-somethings. (No cover. Open Tu-Sa 9:30pm-4am.)

SALZBURGER LAND AND UPPER AUSTRIA

Salzburger Land derives its name from the German *Salz* (salt), and it was this white gold that first drew visitors to the region. Combined with Upper Austria, this region encompasses the shining lakes and rolling hills of the Salzkammergut, where Hallstatt is among the more enticing destinations.

SALZBURG ☎0662

Wedged between mountains and graced with Baroque wonders, Salzburg offers both spectacular sights and a rich musical culture. Laying claim to Mozart's birthplace and *The Sound of Music*, Salzburg's streets resonate with plenty of melodies. The city's adulation for classical music and the arts reaches a dizzying climax every summer during the **Salzburger Festspiele,** a five-week music festival featuring hundreds of operas, concerts, plays, and open-air performances.

⌐ TRANSPORTATION

Trains: Hauptbahnhof, in Südtirolerpl. To: **Graz** (4hr., every 2hr., €33.40); **Innsbruck** (2hr., every 2hr., €27.60); **Munich** (2hr., 27 per day, €21.60); **Vienna** (3½hr., 29 per day, €33.40); **Zurich** (6hr., 3 per day, €63.40). For reservations, call ☎05 17 17; regular ticket office open 24hr.

Public Transportation: Lokalbahnhof (☎44 80 61 66), next to the train station. Single tickets (€1.60) available at automatic machines or from the bus drivers. Books of **five tickets** (€6.50), **daypasses** (€2.90), and **week passes** (€9) available at machines, the ticket office, or *Tabak* shops (newsstand/tobacco shops). Punch your ticket when you board in order to validate it or risk a €36 fine. Buses usually make their last run at 10:30-11:30pm, but **BusTaxi** fills in when the public buses stop. Get on at Hanuschpl. or Theaterg. and tell the driver where you need to go (every 30min. Su-Th 11:30pm-1:30am, F-Sa 11:30pm-3am; €2.55 for anywhere within the city limits).

◼◤ 🔲 ORIENTATION AND PRACTICAL INFORMATION

Just a few kilometers from the German border, Salzburg covers both banks of the **Salzach River.** Two hills loom up in the skyline: the **Mönchesberg** over the **Altstadt** (old city) on the south side and the **Kapuzinerberg** by the **Neustadt** (new city) on the north side. The *Hauptbahnhof* is on the northern side of town beyond the *Neustadt;* buses #1, 5, 6, 51, and 55 connect it to downtown. On foot, turn left out of the station onto Rainerstr. and follow it straight under the tunnel and on to Mirabellpl.

Tourist Office, Mozartpl. 5 (☎88 98 73 30), in the *Altstadt*. From the station, take bus #5, 6, 51, or 55 to Mozartsteg, head away from the river and curve right around the building into Mozartpl. The office gives free hotel maps, guided tours of the city (daily 12:15pm, €8), and sells the **Salzburg Card,** which grants admission to all museums and sights as well as unlimited public transportation (24hr. card €18; 48hr. €26; 72hr. €32). Room reservation service €2.20. Open daily 9am-6pm.

Currency Exchange: ReiseBank, Alter Markt 15, has extended exchange hours. Open daily 10am-2:30pm and 3-8pm.

American Express: Mozartpl. 5 (☎80 80), near the tourist office. Provides all banking services; no commission on AmEx checks. Holds mail and books tours. Open M-F 9am-5:30pm, Sa 9am-noon.

Luggage Storage: At the train station. 24hr. lockers €2-3.50.

Bi-Gay-Lesbian Resources: Homosexual Initiative of Salzburg (HOSI), Müllner Hauptstr. 11 (☎43 59 27), hosts regular workshops and meetings, including a **cafe-bar** open W from 7pm, F and Sa from 8pm.

Emergencies: Police: ☎133. **Ambulance:** ☎144. **Fire:** ☎122.

Pharmacies: Elisabeth-Apotheke, Elisabethstr. 1a (☎87 14 84). Pharmacies in the city center open M-F 8am-6pm, Sa 8am-noon. There are always 3 pharmacies open for emergencies; check the list on the door of any closed pharmacy.

Internet Access: Internet Café, Mozartpl. 5 (☎84 48 22). €0.15 per minute. Open Sept.-May daily 9am-11pm; July-Aug. 9am-midnight.

Post Office: At the *Hauptbahnhof* (☎88 30 30). Address *Poste Restante*: Firstname SURNAME, *Postlagernde Briefe,* Bahnhofspostamt, **A-5020** Salzburg, AUSTRIA. Open M-F 7am-8:30pm, Sa 8am-2pm, Su 1-6pm.

AUSTRIA

Salzburg

🏠 **ACCOMMODATIONS**
Haunspergstraße (HI), **1**
Institut St. Sebastian, **3**
Pension Sandwirt, **2**

🍎 **FOOD**
Café Tomaselli, **9**
Zum Fidelen Affen, **5**
Zweitler's, **10**

🍺 **PUBS**
Augustiner
Bräustübl-Mülln, **4**
Shamrock, **7**
Vis á Vis, **8**
Zweistein, **6**

⌐ ACCOMMODATIONS AND CAMPING

Housing in Salzburg is expensive; most affordable options lie on the outskirts of town. Be wary of hotel hustlers at the station. Instead, ask for the tourist office's list of **private rooms** or the *Hotel Plan* (which has information on hostels). From mid-May to mid-September, hostels fill by mid-afternoon; call ahead, and be sure to make reservations during the *Festspiele* (see p. 99).

HOSTELS, DORMS, AND CAMPING

Stadtalm, Mönchsberg 19c (☎/fax 84 17 29). Take bus #1 (dir.: Maxglan) to Mönchsbergaufzug, go down the street and through the stone arch on the left to the Mönchsberglift (elevator), and ride up (9am-11pm, round-trip €2.40). At the top, turn right, climb the steps, and follow signs for Stadtalm. Breakfast included. Shower €0.80 per 4min. Reception 9am-9pm. Curfew 1am. Open Apr.-Sept. Dorms €12.50. AmEx/MC/V. ❷

Institut St. Sebastian, Linzerg. 41 (☎87 13 86). From the station, bus #1, 5, 6, 51, or 55 to Mirabellpl.; continue in the same direction as the bus, turn left onto Bergstr., and left again onto Linzerg.; the hostel is through the arch. Breakfast included. Sheets €2 for dorms. Laundry €2.90. Reception 8am-noon and 4-9pm. Dorms €15; singles €21, with shower €33; doubles €40/€54; triples €60/€69; quads €72/€84. ❷

Pension Sandwirt, Lastenstr. 6a (☎/fax 87 43 51). Exit the main train station from the platform #13 staircase, turn right on the footbridge, right again onto Lastenstr., and go behind the building with the Post sign. The down-to-earth hosts of this bed-and-breakfast speak excellent English. All rooms have TVs. Laundry included. Singles €21; doubles €35, with shower €42; triples €50; quads €64. ❸

Haunspergstraße (HI), Haunspergstr. 27 (☎87 50 30), near the train station. Walk straight out onto Kaiserschützenstr., which becomes Jahnstr., then take the 3rd left onto Haunspergstr. Spacious rooms in a convenient location. Breakfast included. Key deposit €10. Reception 7am-2pm and 5pm-midnight. Check-out 9am. Open July-Aug. 3- to 4-bed dorms €14.50; singles €19. ❷

Panorama Camping Stadtblick, Rauchenbichlerstr. 21 (☎45 06 52). Take bus #51 to Itzling-Pflanzmann, walk back 50m, then turn right onto Rauchenbichlerstr., cross the footbridge, and continue along the gravel path. On-site store. Laundry €5. Open Mar. 20-Nov. 11. €5.90 per person; €1.50 per tent. *Let's Go* discount available. ❶

PRIVATZIMMER

The rooms on **Kasern Berg** are officially out of Salzburg, which means the tourist office can't recommend them, but the personable hosts and bargain prices make these *Privatzimmer* (rooms in a family home) a terrific housing option. All northbound trains run to Kasern Berg (4min., every 30min. 6:15am-11:15pm, €1.60; Eurail valid). Get off at Salzburg-Maria Plain and take the only road uphill. All the Kasern Berg pensions are along this road. **Haus Lindner ❷,** Panoramaweg 5, offers homey rooms, some with mountain views. (☎45 66 81. Breakfast included. Call for pickup from the station. €14-15 per person.) To reach **Haus Moser ❷,** Turnerbühel 1, climb up the steep hidden stairs on the right side of Kasern Berg road across from German Kapeller. A charming couple offers comfortable rooms in their cozy, dark-timbered home. (☎45 66 76. Breakfast and laundry included. €14 per person. Cheaper after 1st night.) **Germana Kapeller ❷,** Kasern Bergstr. 64, maintains traditional rooms. (☎45 66 71. Breakfast included. €15 per person.)

◖ FOOD

Countless beer gardens and pastry-shop patios make Salzburg a great place to eat outdoors. Local specialties include *Salzburger Nockerl* (egg whites, sugar, and raspberry filling baked into three mounds that represent the three hills of

Salzburg), *Knoblauchsuppe* (a rich cream soup loaded with croutons and pungent garlic), and the world-famous *Mozartkugeln* (hazelnut coated in marzipan, nougat, and chocolate). **Supermarkets** cluster on the Mirabellpl. side of the river, and **open-air markets** are held on Universitätpl. (Open M-F 6am-7pm, Sa 6am-1pm.) **Zweitler's ❸,** Kaig. 3, in the *Altstadt,* cooks up tasty *Spinatnockerl,* spinach baked into a pan with cheese and parsley for €6.50. (Open daily 6pm-1am, during the *Festspiele* 11am-2pm and 6pm-1am.) **Zum Fidelen Affen ❸,** Priesterhausg. 8, serves hearty, honest Austrian food that keeps everyone coming back "To the Faithful Ape." (Open M-Sa 5-11pm.) The delectable desserts of **Café Toma-selli ❷,** Alter Markt 9, have been a favorite with wealthier Salzburgers since 1705. (Open M-Sa 7am-9pm, Su 8am-9pm.)

🅖 SIGHTS

THE NEUSTADT

MIRABELL PALACE AND GARDENS. Mirabellpl. holds the marvelous **Schloß Mirabell,** which the supposedly celibate Archbishop Wolf Dietrich built for his mistress and their 10 children in 1606. Behind the palace, the delicately cultivated **Mirabellgarten** is a maze of seasonal flower beds and groomed shrubs. The Mirabellgarten contains a wooden, moss-covered shack called the **Zauberflöten-häuschen,** allegedly where Mozart spent five months composing *The Magic Flute.*

MOZARTS WOHNHAUS. Mozart moved here at age 17 with his family, staying from 1773-1780. See some Mozart memorabilia and hear lots of excerpts from his music. The audio guides, unfortunately, tend to confuse more than enlighten. *(Makartpl. 8. Open July-Aug. daily 9am-7pm; Sept.-June 9am-6pm. €5.50, students €4.50.)*

SEBASTIANSKIRCHE AND MAUSOLEUM. A little way down Linzerg. from the river stands the 18th-century **Sebastianskirche,** and its Italian-style graveyard, containing the impressive **mausoleum** of Prince Archbishop Wolf Dietrich. The tombs of Mozart's wife and father are along the main path. *(Linzerg. 41. Open Apr.-Oct. daily 9am-7pm; Nov.-Mar. 9am-4pm.)*

THE ALTSTADT

MOZARTS GEBURTSHAUS. Mozart's birthplace, on the 2nd floor of Getreideg. 9, holds an impressive collection of the child genius' belongings, including his first viola and violin and a pair of keyboardish instruments. Several rooms recreate his young years as a traveling virtuoso. Come before 11am to avoid the crowd. *(Open July-Aug. daily 9am-6:30pm; Sept.-June 9am-5:30pm. €5.50, students and seniors €4.50.)*

TOSCANINIHOF, CATACOMBS, AND THE DOM. Steps lead from **Toscaninihof,** the courtyard of **St. Peter's Monastery,** up the Mönchesberg cliffs. **Stiftskirche St. Peter,** within the monastery, features a marble portal from 1244. In the 18th century, the building was remodeled in Rococo style. *(Open daily 9am-12:15pm and 2:30-6:30pm.)* Near the far end of the cemetery, against the Mönchsberg, is the entrance to the **Catacombs.** In the lower room (St. Gertrude's Chapel), a fresco commemorates the martyrdom of Thomas á Beckett. *(Open May-Sept. Tu–Su 10:30am-5pm; Oct.-Apr. W-Su 10:30am-4pm. €1, students €0.60.)* The exit at the other end of the cemetery leads to the immense Baroque **Dom** (cathedral), where Mozart was christened in 1756 and later worked as *Konzertmeister* and court organist. The square leading out of the cathedral, **Domplatz,** features a statue of the Virgin Mary and figures representing Wisdom, Faith, the Church, and the Devil. *(Free, but donation requested.)*

RESIDENZ. Salzburg's ecclesiastical elite have resided in the magnificent Residenz for the last 700 years. Stunning Baroque **Prunkräume** (state rooms) house gigantic ceiling frescoes, gilded furniture, Flemish tapestries from the 1600s, and ornate stucco work. A **gallery** exhibits 16th- to 19th-century art. *(Open daily 10am-5pm. €7.25, students €5.50; audio guide included.)*

FESTUNG HOHENSALZBURG. Built between 1077 and 1681, Festung Hohensalzburg (Hohensalzburg Fortress), which looms over Salzburg from atop Mönchesberg, is the largest completely preserved castle in Europe—partly because it was never successfully attacked. The castle contains formidable Gothic state rooms, the fortress organ (nicknamed the "Bull of Salzburg" for its off-key snorting), and a watchtower that affords an unmatched view of the city and mountains. The **Burgmuseum** inside the fortress displays medieval instruments of torture and has side-by-side histories of Salzburg, the Festung, and the world. *(Take the trail or the Festungsbahn funicular up to the fortress from Festungsg. May-Sept. every 10min. 9am-9pm; Oct.-Apr. 9am-5pm. Ascent €5.55, return €6.35; includes entrance to fortress. Grounds open mid-June to mid-Sept. 8:30am-8pm; mid-Sept. to mid-Mar. 9am-5pm; mid-Mar. to mid-June 9am-6pm. Interior open mid-June to mid-Sept. 9am-6pm; mid-Sept. to mid-Mar. 9:30am-5pm; mid-Mar. to mid-June 9:30am-5:30pm. If you make the steep 20min. walk up, entrance to fortress €3.55; combo ticket including fortress, castle interiors, and museum €7.10.)*

🎭 ENTERTAINMENT

Max Reinhardt, Richard Strauss, and Hugo von Hofmannsthal founded the renowned **Salzburger Festspiele** in 1920. Ever since, Salzburg has become a musical mecca from late July to the end of August. On the eve of the festival's opening, over 100 dancers don regional costumes and perform a *Fackeltanz* (torchdance) on Residenzpl. Operas, plays, films, concerts, and tourists overrun every available public space. Information and tickets for *Festspiele* events are available through the *Festspiele* Kartenbüro (ticket office) and Tageskasse (daily box office) in Karajanpl., against the mountain and next to the tunnel. (Open M-F 9:30am-3pm; July 1-July 22 M-Sa until 5pm; July 23-end of festival daily until 6:30pm.)

Even when the *Festspiele* are not on, many other concerts and events occur around the city. The **Salzburg Academy of Music and Performing Arts** performs a number of concerts on a rotating schedule in the **Mozarteum** (next to the Mirabell gardens), and the **Dom** has a concert program in July and August. (Th-F 11:15am. €8.75, students €7.30.) In addition, from May through August there are **outdoor performances,** including concerts, folk-singing, and dancing, around the Mirabellgarten. The tourist office has leaflets on scheduled events, but an evening stroll through the park might answer your questions just as well. **Mozartpl.** and **Kapitelpl.** are also popular stops for talented street musicians and touring school bands.

🍺 PUBS AND BEER GARDENS

Munich may be known as the world's beer capital, but a lot of that liquid gold flows south to Austria's pubs and **Biergärten** (beer gardens). These lager oases cluster in the city center by the Salzach River. *Altstadt* nightclubs (especially along Gstätteng. and near Chiemseeg.) attract a younger crowd and tourists; the other side of the river has a less juvenile atmosphere. ❖**Augustiner Bräustübl-Mülln,** Augustinerg. 4, has been serving home-brewed beer since 1621. (Open M-F 3-11pm, Sa-Su 2:30-11pm.) Settle into an armchair at **Vis à Vis,** Rudolfskai 24. (Open daily from 8pm.) **Shamrock,** Rudolfskai 24, a relaxed and friendly Irish pub, has plenty of room and nightly live music. (Open Th-Sa 3pm-4am, Su-M 3pm-2am, Tu-W 3pm-3am.) **Zweistein,** Giselakai 9, is the leader of Salzburg's gay and lesbian scene. (Open M-W 8pm-4am, Th 6pm-4am, F-Su 6pm-5am.)

AUSTRIA

▓ DAYTRIPS FROM SALZBURG

HELLBRUNN AND UNTERSBERG PEAK. Just south of Salzburg lies the unforgettable **Lustschloß Hellbrunn**, a sprawling estate with a large palace, fish ponds, flower gardens, and the **Wasserspiele**, elaborate water-powered figurines and a booby-trapped table that could spout water on drunken guests. Pictures of you getting sprayed are available at the end of the tour. *(To reach Lustschloß Hellbrunn and the Wasserspiele, take bus #55 (dir.: Anif) to Hellbrunn from the train station, Mirabellpl., or Mozartsteg. Open July-Aug. 9am-10pm; May-June and Sept. 9am-5:30pm; Apr. and Oct. 9am-4:30pm. Mandatory castle tour €2.95, students €2.20. Wasserspiele tour €5.85, students €4.40. Combined tour €7.30, students €5.85.)* Continue on bus #55 to St. Leonhard, where Charlemagne supposedly rests under **Untersberg Peak**, prepared to return and reign over Europe when needed. A cable car glides over the rocky cliffs to the summit, and from there hikes lead off into the distance. On top is a memorial cross and unbelievable mountain scenery. Don't leave your camera behind. *(Open July-Sept. Th-Tu 8:30am-5pm; Mar.-June and Oct. 9am-5pm; Dec.-Feb. 10am-4pm. Round-trip €7.)*

HOHE TAUERN NATIONAL PARK. Conquer Europe's largest national park, boasting the **Krimml Waterfalls** and the spectacular **Großglocknerstraße** (p. 101).

HALLSTATT   ☎ 06134

Tiny Hallstatt seems to defy gravity by clinging to the face of a stony slope at the southern tip of the Salzkammergut. It's easily the most beautiful lakeside village in the Salzkammergut, if not all of Austria. The 2500-year-old **Salzbergwerke**, the oldest salt mine in the world, can be visited on a fascinating guided tour that zips you down a wooden mining slide on a burlap sack to an eerie lake deep inside the mountain. (☎ (06132) 200 24 00. English and German tours 1hr. Open May-Sept. daily 9:30am-4:30pm; Oct. 9:30am-3pm. €14; students and seniors €9.20.) In the 19th century, Hallstatt was also the site of an immense and incredibly well-preserved Iron Age archaeological find. The **Prähistorisches Museum**, across from the tourist office, and the smaller **Heimatmuseum** around the corner, exhibit some of these treasures. (Open July-Aug. daily 10am-7pm; Sept.-June 9am-6pm. €6.) The **charnel house** next to St. Michael's Chapel is a bizarre repository filled with the remains of over 610 villagers dating from the 16th century on; the latest were added in 1995. The dead were previously buried in the mountains, but villagers soon ran out of space and transferred older bones to the charnel house to make room for more corpses. From the ferry dock, follow the signs marked K. Kirche. (Open June-Sept. daily 10am-6pm; May-Oct. 10am-4pm. €1.)

Buses are the cheapest way to get to Hallstatt from Salzburg (€10.30) but require layovers in both Bad Ischl and Gosaumühle. The **train station** is on the other side of the lake, but there is no staffed office to help travelers. All trains come from Attnang-Puchheim in the north or Stainach-Irdning in the south. **Trains** run hourly to Bad Ischl (30min., €2.75) and Salzburg via Attnang-Puchheim (€17). The **tourist office**, Seestr. 169, finds rooms and offers help with the town's confusing system of street numbers. (☎82 08. Open July-Aug. M-F 9am-5pm, Sa 10am-4pm, Su 10am-2pm; Sept.-June M-Tu, Th-F 9am-noon and 2-5pm, W 9am-noon.) To reach **Gästehaus Zur Mühle ❷**, Kirchenweg 36, from the tourist office, walk uphill, heading for a short tunnel at the upper right corner of the square; it's at the end of the tunnel by the waterfall. (☎83 18. Breakfast €2.50. Reception daily 10am-2pm and 4-10pm. Closed Nov. Dorms €10.) **Frühstückspension Sarstein ❸**, Gosamühlstr. 83, offers glorious views as well as a beachside lawn. From the ferry landing, turn right on Seestr. and walk 10min. (☎82 17.

Breakfast included. Showers €1 per 10min. Singles €18; doubles €38.) The cheapest eats are at the **Konsum** supermarket across from the bus stop; the butcher's counter prepares sandwiches on request. (Open M-Tu, Th-F 7:30am-noon and 3-6pm, W 7:30am-12:30pm, Sa 7:30am-noon.) **Postal code:** A-4830.

⊠ DAYTRIP FROM HALLSTATT: DACHSTEIN ICE CAVES. In nearby Obertraun, the magnificent Dachstein Ice Caves are proof of the region's geological hyperactivity. From Hallstatt, catch the bus to Obertraun (10min., every hr. 8:35am-4:50pm, €1.70), stop at Dachstein, and ride up to Schönbergalm to reach the ice and mammoth caves (every 15min. 8:40am-5:30pm, round-trip €13). The Koppenbrüller cave is a 15min. walk from the Dachstein bus stop in Obertraun. Wear good footwear and something warm. Mandatory tours are offered in English and German. (☎ (06131) 84 00. Open May to mid-Oct. daily 9am-5pm. Admission to each cave €8; children €4.80.)

HOHE TAUERN NATIONAL PARK

The enormous Hohe Tauern range, part of the Austrian Central Alps, boasts 246 glaciers and 304 mountains over 3000m. One of the park's goals is preservation, so there are no large campgrounds or recreation areas; most of it is pristine. The best way to explore this rare preserve is to hike one of the park's numerous trails, which range from pleasant ambles to difficult mountain ascents. *An Experience in Nature*, available at park offices and most area tourist offices, plots and briefly describes 84 different hikes. The center of the park is Franz-Josefs-Höhe and the Pasterze glacier, which sits right above the town of Heiligenblut. Aside from the skiing and hiking, the main tourist attractions are the Krimml Waterfalls, in the northwestern corner near Zell am See, and the Großglocknerstraße, a high mountain road that runs south from Zell am See through Franz-Josefs-Höhe.

⊡ TRANSPORTATION. Trains arrive in **Zell am See** from: Innsbruck (1½-2hr., 3:45am-9:25pm, €20); Kitzbühel (45min., 7:15am-11:30pm, €8.10); and Salzburg (1½hr., 1-2 per hr. 3am-10pm, €11). From Zell am See, a rail line runs west along the northern border of the park, terminating in Krimml (1½hr., 6am-10:55pm, €6.80); a bus also runs directly to the Höhe (2hr., 2 per day, €10). The park itself is crisscrossed by **bus** lines that operate on a complicated timetable; ask for specific connections at local tourist offices.

FRANZ-JOSEFS-HÖHE. This tourist center, stationed above the Pasterze glacier, has an amazing view of the Großglockner (3797m). The Höhe has its own **park office** and information center at the beginning of the parking area. (☎ (04824) 27 27. Open July-Aug. daily 9am-6pm; mid-May to June and Sept. to mid-Oct. 10am-4pm.) The free elevator next to the information center leads to the **Swarovski Observation Center,** a crystal-shaped building with binoculars for viewing the surrounding terrain. (Open daily 10am-4pm. Free.)

HEILIGENBLUT. The closest town to the highest mountain in Austria and a great starting point for hikes, Heiligenblut also has convenient accommodations for those wishing to explore Franz-Josefs-Höhe and the Hohe Tauern Region. Heiligenblut can be reached by **bus** from Franz-Josefs-Höhe (30min.; July-Sept. 8:40am-4pm, May-Oct. daily at 4pm; €3.60) and Zell am See (2½hr., 3 per day 9:20am-12:20pm, €11.60; connect in Franz-Josefs-Höhe). The **tourist office,** Hof 4, up the street from the bus stop, dispenses information about accommodations, hiking, and park transportation. (☎20 01 21. Open July-Aug. M-F 8:30am-6pm, Sa 9am-noon and 4-6pm; Sept.-June M-F 8:30am-noon and

AUSTRIA

2:30-6pm, Sa 9am-noon and 4-6pm.) To reach the **Jugendgästehaus Heiligenblut (HI) ❸**, Hof 36, take the path down from the wall behind the bus stop parking lot. (☎22 59. Breakfast included. Reception July-Aug. daily 7-10am and 5-10pm; Sept.-June 7-10am and 5-9pm. Dorms €20; singles €27.25; doubles €47.25. Ages 19-27 €5 less, under 19 €10 less.) ☎04824.

KRIMML. Over 400,000 visitors per year arrive here to see the extraordinary **Krimml Waterfalls**, a set of three cascades spanning 380m. (8am-6pm €1.50; free after 6pm.) These waterfalls are usually enjoyed as a daytrip from Zell am See; **buses** run from Zell am See (1½ hr., 5:45am-8:55pm, €7.50) to Maustelle Ort, the start of the path to the falls. The trail, called the **Wasserfallweg** (4km), maintains a constant upward pitch. The first set of falls are accessible almost directly from the entrance; it's about 30min. from the first to the second set of falls, and an additional 30min. to the third set. To reach the **tourist office**, Oberkrimml 37, follow the road from the Krimml Ort bus stop and turn right down the hill in front of the church. (☎72 39. Open M-F 8am-noon and 2:30-5:30pm, Sa 8:30-10:30am.)

TYROL (TIROL)

Tyrol's mountains overwhelm the average mortal with their superhuman scale and beauty. Although this topography has made it impossible for Tyrol to avoid becoming one of the primary mountain playgrounds for the world, this region has more to offer than just inclines. The urbane city of Innsbruck shows why it was a Habsburg favorite with a seamless blend of gilded houses and snowy mountains.

INNSBRUCK   ☎0512

The 1964 and 1976 winter Olympics were held in Innsbruck, bringing international recognition to this beautiful mountain city. The nearby Tyrolean Alps await skiers and hikers, and the tiny cobblestone streets of the *Altstadt* are peppered with fancy facades and remnants of the Habsburg Empire.

▄▄ TRANSPORTATION AND PRACTICAL INFORMATION

Trains: Hauptbahnhof, Südtirolerpl. (☎05 17 17). To: **Munich** (2hr., 13 per day, €30); **Rome** (8½-9½hr., 2 per day, €59.20); **Salzburg** (2-2½hr., 13 per day, €27); **Vienna Westbahnhof** (5½-7hr., 10 per day, €48); **Zurich** (4hr., 4 per day, €43.50).

Public Transportation: For schedules and information on transportation in Innsbruck, head to the **IVB** Office, Stainerstr. 2 (☎530 17 99), near Maria-Theresien-Str. Open M-F 7:30am-6pm. The main bus station is in front of the main entrance to the train station. Buses stop running at 10:30 or 11:30pm; 3 *Nachtbus* lines run after hours.

Tourist Office: Innsbruck Tourist Office, Burggraben 3, 3rd fl. (☎598 50). Off the end of Museumstr. Sells maps (€1) and the **Innsbruck Card**, which provides free access to public transportation and many sights (24hr. €19, 48hr. €24, 72hr. €29). Open M-F 8am-6pm, Sa 8am-noon.

Police: ☎133. **Ambulance:** ☎144 or 142. **Fire:** ☎122.

Internet Access: International Telephone Discount, Bruneckstr. 12 (☎59 42 72 61). Turn right from the *Hauptbahnhof*; it's on the left, just past the end of Südtirolerpl. €0.10 per min. Open daily 9am-11pm.

Post Office: Maximilianstr. 2 (☎500 79 00). Open M-F 7am-11pm, Sa 7am-9pm, Su 8am-9pm. Address mail to be held: Postlagernde Briefe für Firstname SURNAME, Hauptpostamt, Maximilianstr. 2, **A-6020** Innsbruck AUSTRIA.

Innsbruck

🏠 ACCOMMODATIONS

Gasthof Innbrücke, **2**
Haus Wolf, **5**
Hostel Fritz Prior-
 Schwedenhaus, **1**
Jugendherberge Innsbruck, **6**

🍴 FOOD

Gasthof Weißes Lamm, **3**
Salute Pizzeria, **4**

Walderpark
Herreng.
Dom St. Jakob
Alpenzoo
Weyerburgg.
Inn
Herzog Otto-Str.
Badg.
Pfarrg.
Rennweg
Höblinghaus
Hofburg
Goldenes
Dachl
Maxilianeum
Hofg.
Herzog-Friedrich-Str.
Hotel
Goldener
Adler
Stadtturm
Kiebachg.
Seilerg.
Rieseng.
Hofkirche
Schlosserg.
Stiftg.
Burggraben
Markgraben
Hoher Weg
Rennweg
Innstr.
Innsteg
Elisabethstr.
Kaiserjägerstr.
Falkstr.
Claudiastr.
Schillerstr.
TO 6
(1.5km)
Blenerstr.
Karl-Kapferer-Str.
Sieberestr.
Kochstr.
St-Nikolaus-G.
Waltherpark
Herzog-Otto-Str.
Hofgarten
Kapuzinerkirche
HÖTTING
Höttingerg.
Congress
SEE INSET ABOVE
Landestheater
U.K.
Etzel Str.
Jahnstr.
BRÜCKEN-
PLATZ
Köntnerstr.
Mariahilfstr.
Inn-
Brücke
Hofburg
Universitätsstr.
Alpferzeilg.
Sillg.
Meinhardstr.
Ingenieur
Weinhartstr.
Dreiheiligenstr.
König Laurin Str.
Sill
PRADL
Stadt
Park
Höttinger Au
Inn
Herzog Sigmund Ufer
Volksgarten
Burgstr.
Maria-Theresien-Str.
Tiroler
Landesmuseum
Ferdinandeum
(reopens Spring 2003)
Erlerstr.
Museumstr.
Bruneckstr.
Defreggerstr.
Amraserstr.
Blasius-Hueber-Str.
Innrain
Meranerstr.
BOZNERPL.
Brixnerstr.
Adamg.
Landhaus
SÜDTI-
ROLERPL.
Haupt-
bahnhof
Hunoldstr.
Sill
Sillufer
Anzengruberstr.
Anichstr.
Kaiser Josef Str.
Stainerstr.
Maximilianstr.
Salurnerstr.
Triumphpforte
Heiliggeiststr.
Südbahnstr.
Peter-Mayr-Str.
Müllerstr.
Andreas- Hofer- Str.
Templstr.
Michael-Gaismayr-Str.
WILTEN
Leopoldstr.
Schopfstr.
Fritz-Pregl-Str.
Speckbacherstr.
Franz-Fischer-Str.
Stafflerstr.
Neuhauserstr.
Tschamlerstr.
Anton Melzer Str.
Fritz Konzert-Str.
Olympiastr.
Olympiabrücke
Olympic Ice
Stadium
Westfriedhof
Egger-Lienz-Str.
Grassmayr
Bell-Foundry
Karwendel str.
Westbahnhof
Basilika
Wilten
Feldstr.
Stiftskirche
Wilten
0   200 yards
0   200 meters
Pastorstr.
Autobahn A12
TO 5 IN MUTTERS (2.3km)
TO SCHLOß
AMBROS (2km)

FROM THE ROAD

LOVE THE STICK

As a veteran runner and former Boy Scout, I have, at times, felt entitled to break the common-sense rules of Alpine hiking. I've hiked alone (and gotten lonely), I've hiked on glaciers in the afternoon (and sank, getting snow in my underwear), and I've hiked in sneakers (and nearly broken my ankles). I have, to be honest, done only two things right: I always carry a map, and I finally broke down and bought a walking stick.

I first saw them being used by an older couple, one in each hand, in the rolling hills of Bregenz. I thought they were primarily for older people who needed an extra boost. Then I saw people in their teens and 20s using them and figured walking sticks were cool accessories for weekend wanderers. Then I nearly fell off the Rotmoosferer glacier in Obergurgl, near Innsbruck, and decided I needed one.

I bought a half-price walking stick for €15 and couldn't tell the difference between mine and the €50 model. Like most models, the height is adjustable. The correct height for a stick when hiking uphill or over level ground is high enough such that your elbow forms a 90° angle when you hold the stick in front of you. When descending, add an extra couple of inches, since you'll be reaching down.

Does it work? It won't turn you into an *übermensch*, but it will improve your balance. If nothing else, it comes in handy fending off love-struck goats and bus drivers.

—Tom Miller

ACCOMMODATIONS AND FOOD

Inexpensive accommodations are scarce in June when only two hostels are open. The opening of student dorms to backpackers in July and August somewhat alleviates the crush. Visitors should join the free **Club Innsbruck** by registering at any Innsbruck accommodation. Membership gives discounts on skiing, bike tours, and the club's hiking program

From the *Altstadt*, cross the Inn River to Innstr., in the university district, for ethnic restaurants and cheap pizzerias. There are **M-Preis Supermarkets** at Museumstr. 34 and across from the train station. (Open M-F 7:30am-6:30pm, Sa 7:30am-5pm.) **Salute Pizzeria ❷**, Innrain 35, is a popular student hangout. (Open daily 11am-midnight.) **Gasthof Weißes Lamm ❸**, Mariahilfstr. 12, on the 2nd floor, serves Austrian fare to a mostly local crowd. (Open F-W noon-2pm and 6pm-midnight.)

Haus Wolf, Dorfstr. 48 (☎54 86 73). Exit the train station through the main exit and walk straight to the traffic island. Take the streetcar (STB) to Mutters, then walk toward the church and turn right onto Dorfstr. Call ahead—the friendly owners are thinking of closing up shop after 30 years of true *gemütlichkeit*. €12-13 per person. ❷

Gasthof Innbrücke, Instr. 1 (☎28 19 34). From the *Altstadt*, cross the Innbrücke; the *gasthof* is at the corner of the intersection. The 575-year-old inn has a riverside and mountain view. Breakfast included. Singles €26-33; doubles €44-49; quads €109. ❸

Gasthof zur Stern, Schulstr. 17 (☎54 65 00). Take the Stubaitalbahn to Natters, then head uphill on Bahnhofstr. and turn left onto Schulstr. in front of the SPAR market. In the suburban village of Natters, for those looking to get away from the crowds. Breakfast included. All rooms with shower and toilet. €17-20 per person. ❸

Jugendherberge Innsbruck (HI), Reichenauer Str. 147 (☎34 61 79). From the train station, take tram 3 to Sillpark and bus O to Jugendherberge. Breakfast included. Laundry €3.30. Reception July-Aug. daily 3-10pm; Sept.-June 5-10pm. Curfew 11pm. 6-bed dorms €12, after 1st night €9.50; 4-bed dorms €14.80/€12.25; singles with shower €28; doubles with shower €41. Nonmembers add €3. ❷

Hostel Fritz Prior-Schwedenhaus (HI), Rennweg 17b (☎58 58 14). From the station, take bus A or tram 4 to Handelsakademie, continue to the end and across Rennweg to the river. Spacious, clean rooms with private shower and bath. No door locks, but closet keys available. Sheets €3.10. Laundry €5.50. Reception daily 7-9:30am and 5-10:30pm. Check-in before 6pm. Lockout 9:30am-5pm. Curfew 10:30pm. Open July-Aug. and Dec. 27-Jan. 5. Dorms €10; doubles €28; triples €41.25. ❷

🔍 SIGHTS

Inside the **Goldenes Dachl** (Golden Roof) on Herzog-Friedrich-Str., the tiny **Maximilianeum** commemorates emperor Maximilian I. (Open May-Sept. Tu-Su 10am-6pm; Oct.-Apr. 10am-12:30pm and 2-5pm. €3.65, students €1.45.) A block behind the *Goldenes Dachl* rise the twin towers of the **Dom St. Jakob,** which displays *trompe l'oeil* ceiling murals. (Open Apr.-Sept. daily 7:30am-7:30pm; Oct.-Mar. 8am-6:30pm. Free.) The entrance to the grand **Hofburg** is behind and to the right of the *Dom*. (Open daily 9am-5pm. €5.45, students €3.65.) Across Rennweg sits the **Hofkirche** which holds larger-than-life bronze statues of saints and Roman emperors, including some by Dürer. (Open M-Sa 9am-5pm, Su noon-5pm. €2.20, students €1.45.) The **Tiroler Volkskunstmuseum** (Tyrolean Folk Art Museum), in the same building, details the everyday life of the Tyrolean people. (Open M-Sa 9am-5pm, Su 9am-noon. €4.35, students €2.25.) Up Rennweg past the *Dom*, the **Hofgarten** is a beautiful park complete with ponds, a concert pavilion, and an oversized chess set.

🥾 ⛷ HIKING AND SKIING

A **Club Innsbruck** membership (see **Accommodations,** above) grants access to a **hiking** program with guides, transportation, and equipment (including boots) at no additional cost. Participants meet in front of the Congress Center (June-Sept. daily 8:45am), board a bus, and return after a moderate hike around 4 or 5pm. To hike on your own, take the J-line bus to Patscherkofel Seilbahnen (20min.) The lift provides access to moderate 1½-5hr. hikes near the bald summit of the Patscherkofel. (Open 9am-noon and 12:45-4:30pm; round-trip €15.) For Club-Innsbruck-led **ski excursions,** take the complimentary ski shuttle (schedules at the tourist office) to any cable car. The **Innsbruck Gletscher Ski Pass** (available at all cable cars and at Innsbruck-Information offices) is valid for all 59 lifts in the region (with Club Innsbruck card: 3-day €80, 6-day €141). The tourist office also rents **ski equipment** (€19-23 per day).

📍 DAYTRIPS FROM INNSBRUCK

SCHLOß AMBRAS. In the late 16th century, Ferdinand II transformed a royal hunting lodge into one of Austria's most beautiful castles, **Schloß Ambras,** and filled it with vast collections of art, armor, weapons, and trinkets. Don't miss the famous **Spanischer Saal** (Spanish Hall) and the impressive **Portrait Gallery** (open in summer only). The **gardens** outside vary from manicured shrubs with modern sculptures to shady, forested hillsides. (Schloßstr. 20. Open Apr.-Oct. daily 10am-5pm; Dec.-Mar. closed Tu. Apr.-Oct. €7.50, students €5.50; Dec.-Mar. €4.50/€3.) The castle is accessible by tram #6 (dir.: Igls) to Tummelplatz/Schloß Ambras (20min., €1.60); follow the signs from the stop.

KITZBÜHEL ☎ 05356

Kitzbühel welcomes tourists with glitzy casinos and countless pubs, yet few visitors remain at ground level long enough to enjoy them. The town's **ski area,** the **Ski Circus,** is regarded as one of the best in the world. A one-day **ski pass** (€33) or a 3- or 6-day summer **vacation pass** (€35/€48) grants passage on all lifts and the shuttle buses that connect them; purchase either at any lift. For summer visitors, more than 70 **hiking trails** snake up the mountains surrounding Kitzbühel. Pick up a free Hiking Trail Map at the tourist office.

Trains leave from the *Hauptbahnhof*, Bahnhofpl. 1, for: Innsbruck (1hr., every 2hr., €13.40); Salzburg (2½hr., 9 per day, €18.90); and Vienna (6hr., 6:25am-

12:45am, €41.45). To reach the *Fußgängerzone* (pedestrian zone) from the *Hauptbahnhof*, head straight down Bahnhofstr.; turn left at the main road, turn right at the traffic light, and follow the road uphill. The **tourist office,** Hinterstadt 18, is near the *Rathaus* in the *Fußgängerzone*. (☎621 550. Open July-Aug. and Christmas to mid-Mar. M-F 8:30am-6:30pm, Sa 8:30am-noon and 4-6pm, Su 10am-noon and 4-6pm; Nov. to Christmas and mid-Mar. to June M-F 8:30am-12:30pm and 2:30-6pm, Sa 8:30am-noon.) Make sure to pick up a free **guest card,** which provides guided hikes (Jun.-Oct. M-F 8:45 am) and informative tours (M 10am). The well-equipped rooms of **Hotel Haselberger ❹,** Maurachfeld 4, is one minute from the bottom station of the *Hahmennkammerbahn* ski lift. (☎628 66. Breakfast included. In summer €31-35 per person; in winter €37-44. AmEx/MC/V.) Although many of Kitzbühel's restaurants prepare gourmet delights at astronomical prices, cheaper locales pepper the area surrounding the *Fußgängerzone*. **SPAR supermarket,** Bichlstr. 22, is at the intersection with Ehrenbachg. (Open M-F 8am-7pm, Sa 7:30am-1pm.) **Postal Code:** A-6370.

BELARUS (БЕЛАРУСЬ)

Flattened by the Germans during WWII, then exploited by the Soviets until 1990, Belarus has become the unwanted stepchild of Mother Russia. While Minsk evokes the glory days of the USSR, the unspoiled countryside harkens back to an earlier era of agricultural beauty. For those willing to endure the difficulties of travel in Belarus, the country presents a unique look at a people in transition.

FACTS AND FIGURES

Official Name: Republic of Belarus.

Capital: Minsk.

Major Cities: Brest, Gomel, Hrodna.

Population: 10,400,000.

Land Area: 207,600 sq. km.

Time Zone: GMT +2.

Language: Belarussian, Russian.

Religions: Eastern Orthodox (80%).

ESSENTIALS

DOCUMENTS AND FORMALITIES. To visit Belarus, you must secure a visa, an invitation, and medical insurance. If you have an acquaintance in Belarus who can provide you with an **official invitation**, you may obtain a 90-day single-entry (5-day processing €50; next-day €100) or multiple-entry (5-day processing €170; next-day €340) **visa** at an embassy or consulate. Those without contacts can consult **Russia House** (see Russia, p. 836), which will get you both an invitation and a visa (5-day processing €225; 3-day €275; next-day €325). **Host Families Association (HOFA)** provides invitations for its guests (see Russia, p. 836). Transit visas (€40), valid for 48 hours, are issued at consulates and sometimes at the border. All foreign nationals are required to purchase **medical insurance** at the port of entry, regardless of any other insurance they might already have. Insurance currently costs €1 for a one-day stay, €15 for a 60-day stay, and up to €85 for one year.

Foreign embassies are in Minsk (see p. 109). Embassies at home include: **Canada**, 130 Albert St., Suite 600, Ottawa, ON K1P 5G4 (☎613-233-9994; fax 233-8500); **UK**, 6 Kensington Ct., London, W8 5DL (☎020 7937 3288; www.belemb.freeservc.co.uk); **US**, 1619 New Hampshire Ave. NW, Washington, D.C. 20009 (☎202-986-1606; www.belarusembassy.org).

TRANSPORTATION. The national airline, **Belavia** (www.belavia.net), flies into Minsk from many European capitals; **Lufthansa** also offers daily flights from Frankfurt. However, Minsk's airports (MHP and MSQ) often fail to meet Western safety standards; entering by train or bus is better. Some international train tickets must be paid partly in euros and partly in Belarussian rubles; **Eurail** is not valid. All immigration and customs formalities are done on the trains. For **city buses,** buy tickets at a kiosk and punch them on board.

| EMERGENCY | Police: ☎01. Ambulance: ☎02. Fire: ☎03. |

TOURIST SERVICES AND MONEY. The only tourist resource is **Belintourist** (Белінтурíст; see p. 109), though Hotel Belarus and Hotel Yubilyenaya in Minsk have **private agencies.** There are few ATMs outside Minsk, and traveler's checks are rarely accepted. Some hotels take credit cards, mostly AmEx and Visa. Be sure to carry plenty of **hard cash;** Russian rubles (which cannot be exchanged abroad) and euros are preferred. In Belarus, posted prices often omit the final three zeros;

<table>
<tr><td rowspan="7">**BELARUSSIAN RUBLES**</td></tr>
</table>

BELARUSSIAN RUBLES		
AUS$1 = 1017BR	1000BR = AUS$0.98
CDN$1 = 1186BR	1000BR = CDN$0.85
EUR€1 = 1808BR	1000BR = EUR€0.55
NZ$1 = 869BR	1000BR = NZ$1.15
ZAR1 = 175BR	1000BR = ZAR5.71
UK£1 = 2821BR	1000BR = UK£0.36
US$ = 1842BR	1000BR = US$0.55

Let's Go prices follow that convention, and because **inflation** is rampant, many prices are listed in euros. Bills printed since 2000 also lack the zeros, but are difficult to differentiate from the old bills that remain in circulation.

COMMUNICATION. Avoid the mail system at all costs. Local calls require **tokens** sold at kiosks or **magnetic cards** available at the post office, train station, and some hotels (200-500BR). International calls must be placed at the telephone office and paid for in advance, in cash. Write down the number you're calling and say *"Ya hatchoo po-ZVAH-neet"* ("I'd like to call...") followed by the name of the country; pay with exact change. Calls to the US and Western Europe cost €1-3 per minute. International direct access numbers include: **AT&T, ☎**8 80 01 01; **British Telecom, ☎**8 800 44; **Canada Direct, ☎**8 108 001 11; **MCI, ☎**8 80 01 03 from Hrodna, Brest, Minsk, and Vitebsk, **☎**8 108 001 03 from Gomel and Mogilev.

PHONE CODE	**Country code: 375. International dialing prefix: 810.** From outside Belarus, dial int'l dialing prefix (see inside back cover) + 375 + city code + local number.

ACCOMMODATIONS. Keep all receipts from hotels; when exiting the country, you may have to show them to the authorities to avoid fines. **Hotels** are very cheap for Belarussians and reasonable for citizens of CIS member countries, but outrageous for foreigners; desk clerks will request your passport, making it impossible to pass as a native. To find a **private room,** look for postings at train stations, or ask taxi drivers, who may know of a lead. The *babushki* at train stations are usually willing to feed and house you for €10 or less.

BELARUS	❶	❷	❸	❹	❺
ACCOMMODATIONS	under €10	€10-15	€16-25	€26-55	over €55
FOOD	under €2	€2-5	€6-10	€11-20	over €20

HEALTH AND SAFETY. Although Belarus was greatly affected by the 1986 Chernobyl accident, it is now possible to travel through formerly contaminated areas. *Let's Go* does not cover any affected regions, but it is important to be aware of certain safety considerations: stay away from mushrooms and berries, which collect radioactivity, and avoid cheap dairy products, which likely come from contaminated areas (opt instead for something German or Dutch). Drink only bottled water; tap water, especially in the southeast, may be contaminated.

MAJOR HOLIDAYS. Orthodox Christmas (Jan. 7); International Women's Day (Mar. 8); Constitution Day (Mar. 15); Catholic Easter (Mar. 31-Apr. 1); Victory Day and Mother's Day (May 9); Independence Day (July 3); Remembrance Day (Nov. 2); October Revolution Day (Nov. 7); Catholic Christmas (Dec. 25).

MINSK (МІНСК) ☎ 8017

For the supreme Soviet city, skip Moscow and head to Minsk (pop. 1.7 million). Hurry, though—there are already two McDonald's, and construction sites everywhere attest to the government's effort to give the city a face-lift. However, Lenin's statue still presides over Independence Square, and the Soviet past breathes in Minsk's uniform residences, transportation system, and omnipresent police.

█◪ TRANSPORTATION AND PRACTICAL INFORMATION. Trains depart from **Chigunachni Vakzal** (Чыгуначны Вакзал; ☎225 54 10, international 225 67 05), on Privakzalnaya pl., for: Kyiv (14hr.; 1 per day; 29,000BR); Moscow (14hr.; 7 per day; 59,000BR); St. Petersburg (2 per day; 63,000BR); and Vilnius (4½hr.; 1 per day; 9000BR); trains also run to Berlin, Prague, and Warsaw. Buy tickets at Belintourist (see below). **Buses** go from **Avtovakzal Tsentralni** (Автовакзал Цэнтральны), vul. Babruyskaya 6 (Бабруйская; ☎227 41 89), to the right of the train station, to Prague (1 per day, 90,500BR) and Vilnius (4hr., 3 per day, 7895BR). From the train station, go up vul. Leningradskaya and left on Svyardlova (Свярдлова) to **ploschad Nezalezhnastsi** (Незалежнасці), connected by pr. Frantsishka Skoriny (Францішка Скарыны) to pl. Peramohi (Перамогі). English-speaking staff at **Belintourist** (Белінтурíст), pr. Masherava 19 (Машэрава), next to Hotel Yubileyny, can give information; pr. Masherava is perpendicular to pr. F. Skoriny. (☎226 90 56; www.belintourist.by. M-red: Nyamíha. Open M-F 10am-6pm.) **Embassies: Russia,** vul. Staravilenskaya 48 (Старавіленская; ☎222 49 85; open M-F 9am-1pm); **UK,** vul. Karla Marksa 37 (Карла Маркса; ☎210 59 20; open M-F 9am-5:30pm); **Ukraine,** vul. Staravilenskaya 51 (☎283 19 58; open M-F 9am-1pm); **US,** vul. Staravilenskaya 46 (☎210 12 83; open M-F 8:30am-5:30pm). A **pharmacy,** Apteka #13, is at pr. Skoriny 16. (Open M-F 8am-8pm, Sa-Su 11am-6pm.) **City Hospital #2** is at vul. Maksima Bogdanovicha 2 (☎234 01 40). All **phone numbers** have seven digits and start with a "2"; add an initial "2" to any six-digit numbers. Check email at **Internet Klass** (Интернет Класс), vul. Karla Marksa 10. (M-blue: Ploshcha nezalazhnasti. 1400BR per hr. Open daily 10am-10pm.)

█◻ ACCOMMODATIONS AND FOOD. To get to hotel **Gastsinitsa Sputnik ❸** (Спутник), vul. Brilevskaya 2 (Брилевская), from pl. Nezalezhnasti, cross the street to the red cathedral and take trolleybus #2 (5min.) just past the bridge. (☎229 36 19. Basic rooms with bath, fridge, TV. Singles 45,000BR; doubles 64,000BR.) From M-blue: Park Chelyuskintsev (Парк Челюскинцев), take the left staircase, then make a right on the street in front of you, which runs perpendicular to the main road, to reach **Gastsinitsa Druzhba ❸** (Дружба), vul. Tolbukhina 3, which has renovated bathrooms. (☎266 24 81. Singles 59,000BR; doubles 86,000BR.) **Vulitsa Karla Marksa** and **Prospekt Skoriny** are lined with restaurants, cafes, and bars.

◙▣ SIGHTS AND ENTERTAINMENT. After most of Minsk's buildings were obliterated in World War II, the city was rebuilt in grand Stalinist style. A block north of the train stations, **ploschad Nezalezhnastsi** (Незалежнасці; Independence Sq.) formerly pl. Lenina, stands as the symbol of Belarussian independence. (M-blue: pl. Nezalezhnastsi; пл. Незалежнасці.) After much controversy, a department store is now being built on part of the square. The crimson **Church of St. Simon,** Savetskaya 15, stands behind a statue of the saint slaying a dragon. The **Jewish memorial,** vul. Melnikaite (Мельникайте), commemorates the more than 5000 Jews who were shot and buried here by the Nazis in 1942. (M-red: Frunzenskaya; фрунзенская.) The **National Arts Museum** (Нацыянальны Мастацкі Музей Распублікі Беларусь; Natsyanalny Mastatski Muzey Raspubliki Belarus), pr. Len-

BELARUS

THE NYAMIHA TRAGEDY On May, 1999, thousands of people were attending an outdoor concert when the weather suddenly soured. Concert-goers rushed into the nearby Nyamiha Metro for cover, and 53 people died in the stampede. A permanent memorial to the victims is outside the north entrance of the station. Fifty-three sculpted roses, one for each of the victims, are scattered on a small staircase. Another makeshift memorial lies just inside the entrance. Passers-by solemnly pause at the memorial as they enter and exit the station.

ina 20 (Леніна), brims with fantastic Russian and Belarussian art. (M-red/blue: Kastrytchnitskaya. Open W-M 11am-7pm. 5000BR.) The grim **Museum of the Great Patriotic War** (Музей Велікой Отечественной Войны; Muzey Velikoy Otechestvennoy Voyny) is at pr. Skoriny 25a. (M-red/blue: Kastrytchnitskaya. Open Tu-Su 10am-5pm. 3000BR.) Vul. F. Skoriny is interrupted by the monument of **Victory Square** before continuing to the **Opera and Ballet Theater**, vul. Paryzhskai Kamuny 1 (Парыжскай Камуны•, one of the best ballets in the former USSR. The season is from September to May; purchase tickets at pr. Skoriny 13. (M-blue: Nyamiha; Няміra. ☎234 01 41. Tickets under €5.) For nightlife listings, check *What and Where in Minsk* (www.wwminsk.com), available at hotels and tourist centers.

⚐ DAYTRIP FROM MINSK: MIR CASTLE. Deep in the Belarussian countryside, where horses are still used in agriculture and cows amble along village roads, stands the 16th-century **Mir Castle**, a prime example of the country's Gothic architecture. In 2000, the castle became the first Belarussian monument to appear on the UNESCO World Cultural Heritage list. (Castle free. Museum 5,000BR.) To reach Mir, take a **bus** from Minsk (3hr., 3400BR) and ask to be let off at Mirski Zamak, or ride to the Mir bus station and backtrack about 1km to the castle.

BELGIUM

(BELGIQUE, BELGIË)

Situated between France and Germany, little Belgium rubs shoulders with some of Western Europe's most powerful cultural and intellectual traditions. Travelers too often mistake Belgium's subtlety for dullness, but its cities offer some of Europe's finest art and architecture, and its castle-dotted countryside provides a beautiful escape for hikers and bikers. While Brussels, the nation's capital and home to the head offices of NATO and the European Union, buzzes with international decision-makers, regional tension persists within Belgium's borders between Flemish-speaking Flanders and French-speaking Wallonie. But some things transcend politics: from the deep caves of the Ardennes to the white sands of the North Sea coast, Belgium's diverse beauty is even richer than its chocolate.

FACTS AND FIGURES

Official Name: Kingdom of Belgium.

Capital: Brussels.

Major Cities: Antwerp, Ghent, Charleroi, Liège.

Population: 10,250,000.

Land Area: 30,230 sq. km.

Time Zone: GMT +1.

Language: Dutch, French, German.

Religions: Roman Catholic (75%); Protestant, Muslim, Jewish, other (25%).

DISCOVER BELGIUM

Starting out in the northern region of Flanders, take in the old city and diverse museums of **Brussels** (p. 115), then spend at least two days in **Bruges** (p. 121), a majestic town with Gothic beauty unparalleled elsewhere in Europe. Spend a day in bustling **Antwerp** (p. 125) and a day (and definitely a night) with the students in **Ghent** (p. 126), then head south to the Wallonie region for a day or two of biking and exploring in and around **Namur** (p. 127) and **Dinant** (p. 127).

ESSENTIALS

WHEN TO GO

Belgium, temperate and rainy, is best visited May to Sept., when temperatures average 13-21°C (54-72°F) and precipitation is the lowest. Winter temperatures average 0-5°C (32-43°F). Bring a sweater and umbrella whenever you go.

DOCUMENTS AND FORMALITIES

VISAS. EU citizens may stay in Belgium for as long as they like. Citizens of Australia, Canada, New Zealand, South Africa, and the US do not need a visa for stays of up to 90 days.

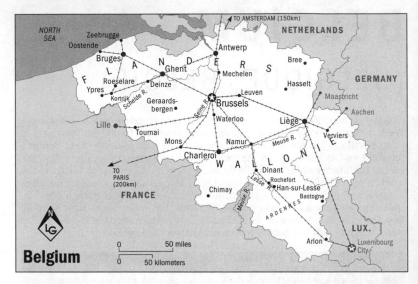

Belgium

EMBASSIES. All foreign embassies are in Brussels (p. 115). For Belgian embassies at home: **Australia,** 19 Arkana St., Yarralumla, Canberra, ACT 2600 (☎02 62 73 25 01; fax 62 73 33 92); **Canada,** 80 Elgin St., 4th fl., Ottawa, ON K1P 1B7 (☎613-236-7267; fax 613-236-7882); **Ireland,** 2 Shrewsbury Rd., Ballsbridge, Dublin 4 (☎353 269 15 58, fax 283 84 88); **New Zealand,** Willis Corroon House, 12th fl., Willeston St. 1-3, PB 3379, Wellington (☎04 472 95 58; fax 471 27 64); **South Africa,** 625 Leyds St., Muckleneuk, Pretoria 0002 (☎2712 44 32 01; fax 44 32 16); **UK,** 103-105 Eaton Sq., London SW1W 9AB (☎020 470 37 00; www.belgium-embassy.co.uk); **US,** 3330 Garfield St NW, Washington, D.C. 20008 (☎202-333-6900; www.diplobel.org/us).

TRANSPORTATION

BY PLANE. Several major airlines fly into **Brussels** from Europe, North America, and Africa. **SN Brussels Airlines** (Belgium ☎070 35 11 11, UK ☎0870 735 23 45; www.brussels-airlines.com) has taken over the service of Sabena airlines.

BY TRAIN AND BUS. The extensive and reliable **Belgian Rail** (www.b-rail.be) network traverses the country. **Eurail** is valid in Belgium. A **Benelux Tourrail Pass** allows five days of unlimited **train** travel in a one-month period in Belgium, The Netherlands, and Luxembourg (€159, 50% companion discount; under 26 €106). The best deal for travelers under 26 may be the **Go Pass,** which allows 10 trips over one year in Belgium and may be used by more than one person (€39); the equivalent for travelers over 26 is the **Rail Pass** (€58). Because the train network is so extensive, **buses** are used primarily for municipal transport (€1-1.25).

BY FERRY. **P&O European Ferries** (UK ☎01482 795 141, Belgium ☎(050) 54 34 30; www.ponsf.com) cross the Channel from **Zeebrugge,** north of Bruges, to **Hull, England** (14hr.; departures at 6:15pm; £38-48, under 26 £24-31). **Ostend Lines** also crosses from Ostend to **Ramsgate, England,** 2hr. from London's Victoria Station (☎(059) 55 99 55; 6 per day, round-trip €39.70).

BY CAR, BIKE, AND THUMB. Belgium honors most foreign driver's licenses, including those from Australia, Canada, the EU, and the US. **Speed limits** are 120kph on motorways, 90kph on main roads, and 50kph elsewhere. **Fuel** costs about €1 per liter. **Biking** is popular, and many roads have bike lanes (which you are required to use). In addition to being illegal, **hitchhiking** is not common in Belgium, nor does Let's Go recommend it as a safe means of transport.

TOURIST SERVICES AND MONEY

EMERGENCY	Police: ☎ 101. Ambulance: ☎ 105. Fire: ☎ 100.

TOURIST OFFICES. Bureaux de Tourisme, marked by green-and-white or blue signs labelled "i," are supplemented by **Infor-Jeunes/Info-Jeugd,** a service that helps young people secure accommodations. For info, contact the main office of the **Belgian Tourist Board,** 63 r. de Marché aux Herbes, B-1000 Brussels (☎ (02) 504 03 90; www.tourism-belgium.net; see p. 115). The weekly English-language *Bulletin* (€2.15 at newsstands) lists everything from movies to job openings.

MONEY. The official currency of Belgium is the **euro.** The Belgian franc can still be exchanged at a rate of 44.34BF to €1. For exchange rates and more information on the euro, see p. 15. Expect to pay €12.50-16 for a hostel bed, €22-30 for a hotel room, €5-13 for a cheap restaurant meal, and €7-13 for a day's groceries. A barebones day in Belgium might cost €19-30; a slightly more comfortable day might cost €32-45. The European Union imposes a **value-added tax (VAT)** on goods and services purchased within the EU, which is included in the price (see p. 15).

BUSINESS HOURS. Banks are generally open Monday through Friday 9am-4pm, but some take a lunch break noon-2pm. **Stores** are open Monday to Saturday 10am to 6 or 7pm; during summer some shops are open Sunday. Most **sights** are open Sundays but closed Mondays except in Bruges and Tournai, where museums are closed Tuesday or Wednesday. Most stores close on holidays; museums stay open during all except for Christmas, New Year's, and Armistice Day.

COMMUNICATION

PHONE CODES	Country code: 32. International dialing prefix: 00.

TELEPHONES. Most phones require a phone card (€5), available at post offices, supermarkets, and magazine stands. Coin-operated phones are rare and more expensive. Calls are cheapest from 6:30pm to 8am and on weekends. For **operator assistance** within Belgium, dial ☎ 12 07 or 13 07; for **international assistance,** ☎ 12 04 or 13 04 (€0.25). **International direct dial** numbers include: **AT&T,** ☎ 0800 100 10; **British Telecom,** ☎ 0800 100 24; **Canada Direct,** ☎ 0800 100 19 or 0800 700 19; **Ireland Direct,** ☎ 0800 10 353; **MCI,** ☎ 0800 100 12; **Sprint,** ☎ 0800 100 14; **Telecom New Zealand,** ☎ 0800 100 64; **Telkom South Africa,** ☎ 0800 100 27; **Telstra Australia,** ☎ 0800 100 61.

MAIL. A postcard or letter (up to 20g) sent to a destination within Belgium costs €0.42, within the EU €0.47-0.52, and to the rest of the world €0.74-0.84. Most post offices open Monday to Friday 9am to 4 or 5pm (sometimes with a midday break) and sometimes on Saturdays 9 or 10am to noon or 1pm.

INTERNET ACCESS. There are cybercafes in the larger towns and cities in Belgium. For access to the web, expect to pay €2.50-3.25 per 30min. Many hostels have Internet access for around €0.07-0.10 per min.

LANGUAGES. Belgium is a multilingual nation, with several official languages. Flemish (a variation of Dutch) is spoken in Flanders, the northern half of the country; French is spoken in Wallonie, the southern region; and German is spoken in a small enclave in the west. Both Flemish and French are spoken in Brussels. Most people, especially in Flanders, speak English. For basic French words and phrases, see p. 1056; for German, see p. 1057.

ACCOMMODATIONS AND CAMPING

BELGIUM	❶	❷	❸	❹	❺
ACCOMMODATIONS	under €9	€9-16	€17-25	€26-32	over €32

There is a wide range of accommodations throughout Belgium; however, **hotels** are fairly expensive, with "trench-bottom" singles from €22 and doubles around €30-35. Belgium's 31 **HI youth hostels,** which charge about €12.50 per night, are generally modern and many boast cheap bars. **Private hostels,** however, often cost about the same but are much nicer. Most receptionists speak at least some English, and reservations are a good idea, particularly in the summer and on weekends. Pick up a free copy of *Camping* at any tourist office for complete listings of hostels and campsites. **Campgrounds** charge about €3.25 per night. An **international camping card** is not required in Belgium.

FOOD AND DRINK

BELGIUM	❶	❷	❸	❹	❺
FOOD	under €5	€5-7.50	€8-9.50	€10-15	over €15

Belgian cuisine, a combination of French and German traditions, is praised throughout Western Europe, but a native meal may cost as much as a night in a decent hotel. Seafood, fresh from the coast, is served in a variety of dishes. **Moules** (steamed mussels), regarded as the national dish, are usually tasty and reasonably affordable (€14 is the cheapest, usually €17-20). Belgians claim that they invented **frites** (potato fries), which they drown in mayonnaise and consume in abundance. Belgian **beer** is both a national pride and a national pastime; more varieties—over 300, ranging from ordinary **Pilsners** to religiously brewed **Trappist** ales—are produced here than in any other country. Prices range from as little as €1 for regular or quirky blonde up to €3 for other varieties. Leave room for Belgian **waffles** (*gaufres*)—soft, warm, glazed ones on the street (€1.50) and bigger, crispier ones piled high with toppings at cafes (€2-5)—and for the many famous brands of delectable **chocolates,** from Leonidas to Godiva.

HOLIDAYS & FESTIVALS

Holidays: New Year's Day (Jan. 1); Easter (Apr. 20); Easter Monday (Apr. 21); Labor Day (May 1); Ascension Day (May 29); Whit Sunday and Monday (June 8-9); Independence Day (July 21); Assumption Day (Aug. 15); All Saints Day (Nov. 1); Armistice Day (Nov. 11); Christmas (Dec. 25).

Festivals: Ghent hosts the **Gentse Feesten,** also know as 10 Days Off (July 19-28). Wallonie hosts a slew of quirky and creative carnivals, including the **Festival of Fairground Arts** (late May), **Les Jeux Nautiques** (early Aug.), the **International French-language Film Festival** (early Sept.), and the **International Bathtub Regatta** (mid-Aug.).

BRUSSELS (BRUXELLES, BRUSSEL) ☎02

Beyond the international traffic resulting from the city's association with NATO and the EU, Brussels (pop. 1,100,000) has a relaxed and witty local character best embodied in its two boy heroes, Tintin and the Mannekin Pis. The museums of Brussels are rich with collections of Flemish masters, modern art, and antique sculptures, but you don't need to go inside for a visual feast—many of the city's restaurants, lounges, and movie theaters were built in the style of Art Nouveau architect Victor Horta.

⊟ TRANSPORTATION

Flights: Brussels International Airport (BRU; ☎753 42 21 or 723 31 11; www.brusselsairport.be) is 14km from the city. See p. 112 for information on **Sabena,** the Belgian national carrier. Trains run to the airport from Gare du Midi (25min., every 20min., €2.50), stopping at Gare Centraal and Gare du Nord.

Trains: Info ☎555 25 55. All international trains stop at **Gare du Midi;** most also stop at **Gare Centraal** (near Grand Place) or **Gare du Nord** (near the Botanical Gardens). To: **Amsterdam** (2½hr.; €32.50, under 26 €16); **Antwerp** (30min., €5); **Bruges** (45min., €9.70); **Cologne** (2¾hr.; €31.25, under 26 €22.35); **Luxembourg City** (1¾hr., €23); **Paris** (1½hr.; €54, under 26 €24.80). **Eurostar** goes to **London** (2¾hr.; from €140, discount for Eurail and Benelux rail pass holders; under 26 from €81).

Public Transportation: The **Métro (M),** buses, and **trams** run daily 6am-midnight. 1hr. ticket €1.40, day pass €3.60, 5 trips €6.20, 10 trips €9. All three are run by the **Société des Transports Intercommunaux Bruxellois (STIB),** Gare du Midi (☎515 20 00; www.stib.irisnet.be). Open M-F 7:30am-5pm, first and last Su of each month 8am-2pm. **Branches** at M: Porte de Namur and M: Rogier. Open M-F 8:30am-5:15pm.

Hitchhiking: Hitchhiking is illegal on highways and slip-roads in Belgium. *Let's Go* does not recommend hitchhiking.

◼🛈 ORIENTATION AND PRACTICAL INFORMATION

Most major attractions are clustered around the **Grand-Place,** between the **Bourse** (Stock Market) to the west and the **Parc de Bruxelles** to the east. Two **Métro** lines circle the city, while efficient trams run north to south. A **tourist passport** (*Carte d'un Jour;* €7.45), which includes two days of public transit, a map, and discounted museum admissions, is sold at the TIB and bookshops.

Tourist Offices: National, 63 r. du Marché aux Herbes (☎504 03 90; www.belgium-tourism.net), one block from Grand Place. Books rooms all over Belgium and offers the free weekly *What's On.* Open July-Aug. M-F 9am-7pm, Sa-Su 9am-1pm and 2-7pm; Sept.-June M-F 9am-6pm, Sa-Su 9am-1pm and 2-6pm; Nov.-Apr. closed Su afternoon. **Brussels International-Tourism and Congress** (TIB; ☎513 89 40; www.tib.be), on Grand Place, in the Town Hall, offers bus tours (3hr.; Apr.-Oct. 10, 11am, 2pm; Nov.-Mar. 10am, 2pm; €19.90, students €17), which leave from 8 r. de la Colline. Open Apr.-Oct. daily 9am-6pm; Nov.-Mar. M-Sa 9am-6pm, Su 10am-2pm.

Budget Travel: Infor-Jeunes Bruxelles, 155 r. Van Arteveld (☎514 41 11; bruxelles@inforjeunes.be). Budget travel info for young travelers. Open M-F 10am-5pm.

Embassies: Australia, 6-8 r. Guimard, 1040 (☎286 05 00; fax 230 68 02). **Canada,** 2 av. Tervueren, 1040 (☎741 06 11; fax 448 00 00). **Ireland,** 89 r. Froissart, 1040 (☎230 53 37; fax 230 53 12). **New Zealand,** 1 de Meeussquare, 1000 (☎512 10 40).

BELGIUM

Brussels

ACCOMMODATIONS
Auberge de Jeunesse
"Jacques Brel" (HI), **3**
Hotel Des Eperonniers, **11**
Hôtel Pacific, **5**
Jeugdherberg Bruegel (HI), **13**
Sleep Well, **1**

FOOD
Arcadi Cafe, **9**
Hemispheres, **7**
Le Perroquet, **14**
Super GB, **4**
Ultième Hallutinatie, **2**
Zebra, **10**

NIGHTLIFE
À La Bécasse, **8**
L'Archiduc, **6**

ENTERTAINMENT
Poechenellekelder, **12**

South Africa, 26 r. de la Loi (☎285 44 00). Generally open M-F 9am-5pm. **UK,** 85 r. d'Arlon, 1040 (☎287 62 11; fax 287 63 55). **US,** 27 bd. du Régent, 1000 (☎508 21 11; www.usinfo.be). Open M-F 9am-noon.

Currency Exchange: Many exchange booths near Grand Place stay open until 11pm. Most banks and booths charge a commission (€2.50-3.75) to cash checks. **CBC-Automatic Change,** 7 Grand-Place (☎547 12 11). Open 24hr. Exchange booths are also available in the train stations.

Bi-Gay-Lesbian Resources: Call ☎733 10 24 for info on local events. Staffed Tu 8-10pm, W 8-11pm, F 8-11pm. The tourist office offers a guide on gay establishments.

Laundromat: Salon Lavoir, 62 r. Blaes, around the corner from the Jeugdherberg Bruegel (see below). M: Gare Centrale. Wash and dry €3.25. Open daily 7am-10pm.

Emergencies: Medical: ☎100. **Police:** ☎101.

Pharmacies: Neos-Bourse Pharmacie (☎218 06 40), bd. Anspach at r. du Marché-aux-Polets. M: Bourse. Open M-Sa 8:30am-6:30pm.

Medical Assistance: Free Clinic, 154a Chaussée de Wavre (☎512 13 14). Misleading name—you'll have to pay. Open M-F 9am-6pm. **Medical Services,** (☎479 18 18.) Open 24hr.

Internet Access: easyEverything, (www.easyeverything.com), Place de Brouckère. Approx. €1.25 per hr., rate varies according to the time of day. Open 24hr.

Post Office: Pl. de la Monnaie, Centre Monnale, 2nd fl. (☎226 21 11). M: de Brouckère. Open M-F 8am-7pm, Sa 9:30am-3pm. Address mail to be held: Firstname SURNAME, Poste Restante, pl. de la Monnaie, **1000** Bruxelles, Belgium.

ACCOMMODATIONS

Lodgings can be difficult to find in Brussels, especially on weekends in June and July. In general, accommodations are well-kept and centrally located. If booked, staffs will usually call other establishments on behalf of prospective guests.

Hotel Des Eperonniers, 1 r. des Eperonniers (☎513 53 66). Follow r. Inf. Isabelle from Gare Centraal into pl. Agora. Great location close to Grand Place. Well-kept rooms. Breakfast €3.75. Reception daily 7am-midnight. Singles €25-42; doubles €42-47. ❸

Hôtel Pacific, 57 r. Antoine Dansaert (☎511 84 59). M: Bourse. Follow the street in front of the Bourse, which becomes r. A. Dansaert after the intersection; it's on the right. Basic rooms in an excellent location. Breakfast included. Showers €5. Reception daily 7am-midnight. Curfew midnight. Singles €30; doubles €50; triples €70. ❹

Sleep Well, 23 r. du Damier (☎218 50 50; www.sleepwell.be), near Gare du Nord. M: Rogier. Exit onto r. Jardin Botanique, facing the pyramid, and go right; take the 1st right on r. des Cendres, then go slightly to the right at the intersection and continue onto r. du Damier. Breakfast included. Internet access. Curfew 3am. Lockout 10am-4pm. Dorms €16; singles €23.50; doubles €36. Reduced price after 1st night. ❷

Auberge de Jeunesse "Jacques Brel" (HI), 30 r. de la Sablonnière (☎218 01 87), on pl. des Barricades. M: Botanique; then take r. Royale, with the botanical gardens to your right, and take the 1st left onto r. de la Sablonnière. Clean, spacious rooms. Breakfast included. Sheets €3.25. Reception daily 8am-1am. HI members only. Dorms €12.50; singles €22.50; doubles €35; triples €43.50. ❷

Centre Vincent Van Gogh-CHAB, 8 r. Traversière (☎217 01 58; www.ping.be/chab). M: Botanique. Exit on r. Royale, head right, and turn right again. Newly renovated rooms. Internet €1.50 per 15min. Breakfast included. Sheets €3.50. Laundry €4.50. Reception daily 7am-2am. Dorms €9-12; singles €21; doubles €31. ❷

Jeugdherberg Bruegel (HI), 2 r. de St-Esprit (☎511 04 36; jeugdherberg.bruegel@ping.be). From the back exit of Gare Centraal, go right on bd. de l'Empereur, then left on r. de St-Esprit. Breakfast and sheets included. Reception daily 7am-1am. Lockout 10am-2pm. Curfew 1am. Dorms €12.50; singles €22.50; doubles €35; quads €58. Nonmembers add €2.50. ❷

🍴 FOOD

Cheap restaurants cluster around **Grand Place,** and **Rue du Marché aux Fromages,** to the south of Grand Place, has cheap Middle Eastern food. Just to the north of Grand Place, shellfish and *paella* are served up on **Rue des Bouchers,** but cheaper seafood can be found at the small restaurants on **Quai aux Briques,** in the Ste-Catherine area behind pl. St-Géry. **Belgaufras,** a waffle vendor chain, is everywhere (€1.40). The two-level **Super GB** grocery store is on the corner of r. du Marché aux Poulets and r. des Halles. (M: Bourse. Open M-Sa 9am-8pm, F until 9pm.)

Zebra, 33-35 pl. St-Géry. This inexpensive but chic cafe is centrally located and serves light, tasty sandwiches and pastas (€2-6). Open daily 10am-1am. ❶

Arcadi Cafe, 1b r. d'Arenberg. Huge selection of quiches, sandwiches, and pastries (€3-6). Lots of vegetarian choices. Open daily 7:30am-11pm. ❶

Le Perroquet, 31 r. Watteau. Sit down for lunch, an afternoon beer, or a late-night pastry. Wide selection of salads and sandwiches from €5. Open daily noon-1am. ❷

Hemispheres, 65 r. de l'Ecuver. Libyan, Turkish, Chinese, and Indian cuisine. Vegetarian meals €7-10. Open M-F noon-3pm and 6:30-10:30pm, Sa 6:30pm-midnight. ❸

Ultième Hallutinatie, 316 r. Royale. Housed in a splendid Art Nouveau house with stained glass and a garden. Restaurant in the front and a cheaper tavern with an outdoor patio in back. Salads, pastas, and omelettes in the tavern from €6.20. Open M-F 11-2:30pm and 7:30-10:30pm, Sa 4-10:30pm. ❷

Maison Antione, 1 pl. Jourdan. M: Schuman. The brown kiosk in the middle of the *place.* Serves the best *frites* in town. A delicious cone of fries is €1.60-1.80; a huge selection of sauces an additional €0.50. Open Su-F 11:30am-1am, Sa 11:30am-2am. ❶

👁 SIGHTS

GRAND PLACE AND ENVIRONS. Victor Hugo once called the gold-trimmed **Grand-Place** "the most beautiful square in the world." There is a flower market each morning, and at night the **Town Hall** is illuminated by 800 multi-colored floodlights while classical music plays. *(Apr.-Aug. and Dec. daily around 10 or 11pm. Tours available. Inquire at the Town Hall for info. ☎279 43 65.)* Three blocks behind the Town Hall, on the corner of r. de l'Etuve and r. du Chêne, is Brussels's most giggled-at sight, the **Mannekin Pis,** a statue of an impudent boy (with an apparently gargantuan bladder) steadily urinating. The most commonly told story claims that it commemorates a boy who ingeniously defused a bomb destined for Grand Place. In reality, the fountain was installed to supply the neighborhood with drinking water during the reign of Archduke Albert and Archduchess Isabelle. Locals have created hundreds of outfits for him, competitively dressing him with the ritual coats of their organization or region, each with a little hole for his you-know-what. His wardrobe is on display across from the Town Hall on the third floor of the **Museum of the City of Brussels (Maison de Roi),** which also gives the history of Brussels. *(Open Tu-F 10am-5pm, Sa-Su 10am-1pm. €2.50, students €2.)* In the glorious **Galerie Saint Hubert** arcade, one block behind Grand Place, you can window-shop for everything from square umbrellas to marzipan frogs. Built over the course of six centuries, the magnificent **Cathédral Saint Michel** is an excellent example of the Gothic style but mixes in a little Romanesque and modern architecture for good measure. *(Pl. St-Gudule, just north of Gare Centraal. Open M-F 7am-7pm, Sa-Su 8:30am-7pm. Free.)*

MONT DES ARTS. The ◩**Musées Royaux des Beaux-Arts** houses the **Musée d'Art Ancien,** the **Musée d'Art Moderne,** a sculpture gallery, and temporary exhibitions. Together the museums house a huge collection of Belgian art spanning the centuries, including Bruegel the Elder's *Landscape with the Fall of Icarus* and pieces by Salle de Rubens and Brussels native Magritte. Other masterpieces not to be missed are David's *Death of Marat* and paintings by Ingres, Delacroix, Seurat, Gauguin, and Van Gogh. The panoramic view of Brussels's cityscape from the 4th floor of the 19th-century wing is alone worth the admission fee. *(R. de la Régence 3. M: Parc. ☎508 32 11. Open Tu-Su 10am-5pm. Some wings close noon-2pm. €5, students €3.50; 1st W of each month 1-5pm free.)* The **Musical Instrument Museum (MIM),** located in an Art Nouveau building in the beautifully restored Old England retail complex, houses over 1500 instruments. Headphones automatically play music from the instrument you are standing in front of. There is a fabulous panoramic view of the city from a corner turret on the third floor. *(R. Montagne de la Cour 2. One block from the Musées des Beaux-Arts. ☎545 01 30. Open Tu, W, F 9:30am-5pm; Th 9:30am-8pm; Sa-Su 10am-5pm. €5, students €3.50; headphones included.)*

BELGIAN COMIC STRIP CENTRE. This museum in the "Comic Strip Capital of the World" pays homage to *les bandes dessineés* with hundreds of Belgian comics. The **museum library,** in a renovated Art Noveau warehouse, features a reproduction of Tintin's rocket ship and works by over 700 artists. For Tintin souvenirs, check out the museum store or the Tintin Boutique near Grand Place. *(20 r. des Sables. M: Rogier. From Gare Centraal, take bd. de l'Impératrice until it becomes bd. de Berlaimont, and turn left onto r. des Sables. ☎219 19 80. Open Tu-Su 10am-6pm. €6.20, students €5.)*

PARKS AND SQUARES. The charming hills around the **Place du Grand Sablon** are home to antique markets, art galleries, and cafes. Hidden behind the church lies the pastoral **Place du Petit Sablon.** Around **Place au Jeu de Balle,** you can practice the fine art of bargaining at the morning **flea market.** The **Botanical Gardens** on r. Royale are beautiful in summer. The **Parc de Bruxelles,** just behind Gare Centraal, and the **Parc Leopold,** amidst the EU buildings, are pleasantly green sanctuaries in otherwise urban surroundings.

OTHER SIGHTS. The enormous **Musée du Cinquantenaire (Musées Royaux d'Art et d'Histoire)** covers a wide variety of periods and parts—Roman torsos without heads, Syrian heads without torsos, and Egyptian caskets with feet. The eerily illuminated *Salle au Tresor* is one of the museum's main attractions. *(10 Parc du Cinquantenaire. M: Mérode. From the station, walk through the arch, turn left, go past the doors*

INTERNATIONAL MAN OF MYSTERY Tintin (pronounced "tan-tan") is the greatest comic-strip hero in the French-speaking world. From Nice to Quebec City, he remains perpetually young to fans who play hardball at auctions for Tintin memorabilia. His creator, Georges Rémi (whose pen-name "Hergé," are his initials pronounced backwards) sent him to the Kremlin, Shanghai, the Congo, outer space, and the wilderness of... Chicago. Countless dissertations and novels have been written about Tintin's possible androgyny; many also say that Indiana Jones was Tintin made into a man. When former French president Charles de Gaulle was asked whom he feared the most, he replied, "Tintin is my only international competitor."

that appear to be the entrance, and turn left again for the real entrance. ☎ *741 72 11. Open Tu-F 9:30am-5pm, Sa-Su 10am-5pm. €4, students €3.)* Master architect Baron Victor Horta's graceful home, now the **Musée Horta**, is a skillful application of his Art Nouveau style to a domestic setting. *(25 r. Américaine. M: Horta. Take a right from the stop, walking uphill on ch. de Waterloo (7min.), then turn right on ch. de Charleroi and right on r. Américaine.* ☎ *543 04 90. Open Tu-Su 2-5:30pm. €5.)* The **European Parliament** has been called *Caprice des Dieux* ("Whim of the Gods"), perhaps because of its exorbitant cost. *(43 r. Wiertz. M: Schuman.* ☎ *284 34 53; www.europarl.eu.int. Visits M-Th 10am and 3pm, F 10am; Apr. 14-Oct. 13 also open Sa 10, 11:30am, and 2:30pm.)* The **Atomium,** a shining 102m monument of aluminum and steel built for the 1958 World's Fair, represents an iron crystal molecule magnified 165 billion times. An elevator takes visitors to the very top for a view of the city. *(Bd. du Centenaire. M: Huysel.* ☎ *475 47 77; www.atomium.be. Open Apr.-Aug. daily 9am-8pm; Sept.-Mar. 10am-6pm. €6.)* Nearby is the **Bruparck entertainment complex,** home of the **Kinepolis cinema,** Europe's largest movie theater, as well as **Mini-Europe** (a collection of European landmarks in miniature) and the **Oceade** water park. *(*☎ *474 83 77; www.bruparck.com. Hours vary.)*

🎵 🍷 ENTERTAINMENT AND NIGHTLIFE

For information on events, check the weekly *What's On*, available from the tourist office. The flagship of Brussels's theater network is the beautiful **Théâtre Royal de la Monnaie,** on pl. de la Monnaie. (M: de Brouckère. Info ☎ 229 13 72, tickets 229 12 00; www.lamonnaie.be. Tickets €7.50-75.) The theater is renowned worldwide for its opera and ballet. Its performance of the opera *Muette de Portici* in August 1830 inspired the audience to take to the streets and begin the revolt that led to Belgium's independence. The **Théâtre Royal de Toone VII,** 21 petite r. des Bouchers, is a 170-year-old puppet theater that stages marionette performances, a distinctly Belgian art form. (☎ 513 54 86. Shows regularly in French; German, Flemish, and English on request. Usually Tu-Sa 8:30pm. €10, students €6.20.) In summer, **concerts** are held on **Grand Place,** on **Place de la Monnaie,** and in the **Parc de Bruxelles.**

On summer nights, **Grand Place** and the **Bourse** come to life with street performers and live concerts. Students crowd in bars around **Place Saint Géry.** The 19th-century puppet theater **Poechenellekelder,** 5 r. de Chêne, across from the Mannekin Pis, is today filled with lavishly costumed marionettes and a selection of Belgian beers. (Beer from €1.25. Open Su-Th noon-midnight, F-Sa noon to 1 or 2am.) **À La Bécasse,** 11 r. de Tabora, one of Brussels's oldest and best-known cafes, specializes in the local wheat beer. (Beer €1.25-2.25. Open daily 10am-midnight.) **L'Archiduc,** 6 r. A. Dansaert, is a pricey but casual Art Deco jazz bar. (Open daily 4pm-late.) **Le Fuse,** 208 r. Blaes, one of Belgium's trendiest clubs, plays techno. (Open daily 10pm-late.)

🏛 DAYTRIPS FROM BRUSSELS

WATERLOO. At Waterloo, site of the famous Napoleonic battle, the Allied troops, commanded by the Duke of Wellington, and the Prussians, led by Marshal Blucher, encountered the French army on June 18th, 1815. It took only nine hours to defeat Napoleon, but 50,000 men were killed in the process. **The Lion's Mound,** 5km outside of town, is a huge hill overlooking the battlefield; the nearby visitors' center houses a panoramic painting of the battle and a brief movie about Waterloo. (Open Apr.-Sept. daily 9:30am-6:30pm; Oct. 9:30am-5:30pm; Nov.-Feb. 10:30am-4pm; Mar. 10am-5pm. Lion's Mound €1; with movie and panorama €7.60, students €6.20.) In the center of Waterloo, **Musée Wellington,** 147 ch. de Bruxelles, served as Wellington's headquarters and has artifacts from the battle. (Open daily Apr.-Sept. 9:30am-6:30pm;

Oct.-Mar. 10:30am-5pm. €5, students €4.) **Bus W** leaves pl. Rouppe near Brussels's Gare Midi (1¼hr., every hr., €2.70); exit at the train station in Braine L'Alleud. Belgian Railways offers a **B-excursion ticket,** which gives round-trip transit between Brussels Midi and Braine L'Alleud (45min., every hr.), a bus pass from Braine L'Alleud to Waterloo, and entrance to all sights (€17.60, students €16.40). The **tourist office** is next to the Musée Wellington, at 149 ch. de Bruxelles. (☎354 99 10. Open Apr.-Sept. daily 9:30am-6:30pm; Oct.-Mar. 10:30am-5pm.) ☎**02.**

MECHELEN (MALINES). Mechelen, historically the ecclesiastic capital of Belgium, is best known today for its abundance of treasure-filled churches and its grim role in the Holocaust. The stately **St. Rumbold's Cathedral,** down Consciencestr. from the station, features gorgeous stained-glass windows and the Gothic **St. Rumbold's Tower,** which rises 97m over **Grote Markt** and houses two 49-bell carillons. (Tours daily 2:15pm, M also 7:15pm; €2.50. Carillon recitals M and Sa 11:30am, Su 3pm; June-Sept. also M 8:30pm.) Early Renaissance buildings, including the **Stadhuis,** line the Grote Markt. (Open M-Sa 8:30am-5:30pm, Su 2-5:30pm.) The ▨**Jewish Museum of Deportation and Resistance,** 153 Goswin de Stassartstr., is housed in the 18th-century military barracks used as a temporary camp for Jews en route to Auschwitz during the Holocaust. From the Grote Markt, take Wollemarkt, which becomes Goswin de Stassartstr. (☎29 06 60. Open Su-Th 10am-5pm, F 10am-1pm. Free.) The **botanical gardens** along the Dilje River are a great place for a picnic. **Trains** arrive from Brussels (15min., €3.20) and Antwerp (15min., €2.80). The **tourist office** in the Stadhuis finds rooms for free. (☎29 76 55; www.mechelen.be. Open Easter-Oct. M-F 8am-6pm, Sa-Su 9:30am-12:30pm and 1:30-5pm; Nov.-Easter reduced hours.) There are several places to eat around the **Grote Markt.** *Asperges* (asparagus) appears on most menus, as Mechelen is in the center of the growing region; white asparagus is a regional specialty. **Postal Code:** 2800. ☎**015.**

FLANDERS (VLAANDEREN)

In Flanders, the Flemish-speaking part of Belgium, you can party in Antwerp, bask in Bruges, and sate your castle cravings with Ghent's Gravensteen. The three major cities offer a taste of Flanders' 16th-century Golden Age, when its commercial centers were among the largest in Europe and its innovative artists motivated the Northern Renaissance. The well-preserved cities are rich in art as well as friendly, multilingual people who pride their region more than their country.

BRUGES (BRUGGE) ☎050

Famed for its lace and native Jan van Eyck, Bruges is considered one of the most beautiful cities in Europe; it is also the most touristed city in Belgium. Canals carve their way through rows of stone houses and lead to the breathtaking Gothic Markt. The city remains one of the best-preserved examples of Northern Renaissance architecture. Its beauty, however, belies the destruction sustained in World War I; eight decades after the war, farmers still uncover 200 tons of artillery every year as they plough their fields.

⬛❷ TRANSPORTATION AND PRACTICAL INFORMATION

Bruges is enclosed by a circular canal, with the train station just beyond its southern extreme. Its historic district is entirely accessible on foot. The dizzying **Belfort** (belfry) towers above the center of town, presiding over the handsome Markt.

BELGIUM

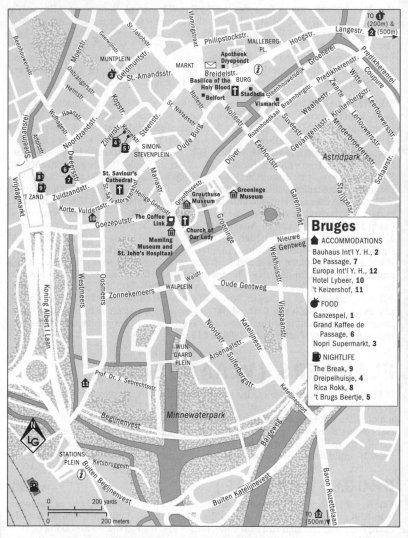

Bruges

🏠 ACCOMMODATIONS

Bauhaus Int'l Y. H., **2**
De Passage, **7**
Europa Int'l Y. H., **12**
Hotel Lybeer, **10**
't Keizershof, **11**

🍎 FOOD

Ganzespel, **1**
Grand Kaffee de
  Passage, **6**
Nopri Supermarkt, **3**

🍷 NIGHTLIFE

The Break, **9**
Dreipelhuisje, **4**
Rica Rokk, **8**
't Brugs Beertje, **5**

Trains: Leave from **Stationsplein** (☎ 38 23 82; open daily 7am-9pm), a 15min. walk
south of the city, for: **Brussels** (1hr., €9.45); **Antwerp** (1hr., €9.80); **Ghent** (25min.,
€4.70); **Ostend** (17min., €2.90); **Zeebrugge** (10min., €2.10).

Bike Rental: At the train station (☎ 30 23 29). €6.30 per half-day, €8.80 per day. **'t
Koffieboontje,** Hallestr. 4 (☎ 33 80 27), off the Markt by the belfry. €5.60 per half-day,
€8.10 per day; student discount. Open daily 9am-10pm. Many hostels and hotels also
rent bikes for around €7.50 per day.

Tourist Office: Burg 11 (☎ 44 86 86; www.brugge.be), in Burg Square. From the station,
head left to 't Zand Square, right on Zuidzandstr., and right on Breidelstr. through the
Markt (15min.). Books rooms (€12.50 deposit and service fee) and sells maps

(€0.65). Open Apr.-Sept. M-F 9:30am-6:30pm, Sa-Su 10am-noon and 2-6:30pm; Oct.-Mar. M-F 9:30am-5pm, Sa-Su 9:30am-1pm and 2-5:30pm. **Branch** office at the train station. Open M-Sa 10am-6pm.

Currency Exchange: Currency exchanges fill the streets around the Markt, but there is no place to change money at the train station.

Luggage Storage: At the train station; €1.50-3.30. **Lockers** at the tourist office; €1.

Emergencies: ☎100. **Police:** ☎101. Police station at Hauwerstr. 7 (☎44 88 44).

Pharmacies: Apotheek Dryepondt, Markt 7, and **Apotheek K.Dewolf,** Zuidzandstr. 1. Both open M-F 9am-12:30pm and 2-6:30pm, Sa until 6pm.

Internet Access: The Coffee Link, Mariastr. 38 (☎34 99 73), in the Oud Sint-Jan Historic Hospital. €1.25 for first 15min., €0.07 per min. thereafter. Open M-Sa 10am-9:30pm, Su 10am-7:30pm. **KSI Online,** Katelijnestr. 67. €1.50 per 15min. Open Tu-F 9am-12:30pm and 2-6:30pm, Sa 2-6:30pm.

Post Office: Markt 5. Open M-F 9am-7pm, Sa 9:20am-12:30pm. Address mail to be held: Firstname SURNAME, Poste Restante, Hoedenmakerstr. 2, **8000** Brugge, Belgium.

▌ ACCOMMODATIONS

Reasonably priced accommodations are available just blocks away from the city center, but rooms can be hard to come by on weekends.

De Passage, Dweersstr. 26 (☎34 02 32). From the station, cross the street and go left along the path; at the end, bear left on 't Zand, turn right on Zuidzandstr., and take the 1st left onto Dweersstr. Recently remodeled and ideally located. Offers guests a free beer at the lively restaurant downstairs. Breakfast €2. Reception daily 8:30am-11pm. Dorms €12; singles €22; doubles €35. ❷

Hotel Lybeer, Korte Vuldersstr. 31 (☎33 43 55; hotel.lybeer@pandora.be). Follow the directions for De Passage to Zuidzandstr.; take the 1st right onto Hoogste van Brugge, followed by an immediate left. Great location. Old-fashioned charm with modern comforts. Backpacker-friendly. Free Internet access. Breakfast included. Reception daily 7:30am-midnight. Singles €25; doubles €43; triples €57; quads €89. ❸

't Keizershof, Oostmeers 126 (☎33 87 28; hotel.keizershof@12move.be). From the station, walk to the traffic lights on the left, cross the street, and follow signs pointing to the Memling Museum and Oud St-Jan. The hotel is 80m up on the left. Pretty, comfortable rooms on a quiet street. Breakfast included. Laundry €7.55. Singles €24.50; doubles €36; triples €54; quads €64.50. ❸

Charlie Rockets, Hoogstr. 19 (☎33 06 60; info@charlierockets.com). From Markt, follow Breidelstr., which becomes Hoogstr. Central location. Packed restaurant-bar. Breakfast included. Reception daily 8am-4am. Dorms €13-16; doubles €46. ❷

Bauhaus International Youth Hotel, Langestr. 133-137 (☎34 10 93; info@bauhaus.be). Take bus #6 or 16 to Gerechtshof and go right about 50m; it's on the left. Cybercafe and popular bar. Nearby laundromat. Breakfast €2. Reception daily 8am-2am. Dorms €13.50-22.50; doubles €25-35. ❷

Europa International Youth Hostel (HI), Baron Ruzettelaan 143 (☎35 26 79; brugge@vjh.be). Quiet, away from the Markt and the nightlife. Turn right from the station and follow Buiten Katelijnevest to Baron Ruzettelaan (15min.). Or, take bus #2 to Wantestraat. Breakfast included. Sheets €3.10. Key deposit €2.50. Reception daily 7:30-10am and 1-11pm. Dorms €12.50; nonmembers add €2. ❸

Camping: St-Michiel, Tillegemstr. 55 (☎38 08 19). From the station, take bus #7 to Jagerstr. Go left on Jagerstr. and bear left at the 1st intersection, staying on Jagerstr. and going around the rotary to Tillegemstr. €2.85 per person, €3.35 per tent. ❶

⊡ FOOD

Inexpensive food can be hard to find in Bruges, but it is worth splurging at least once on Belgium's famous *mosselen* (mussels; usually €15-22). From the Burg, cross the river and turn left to buy fresh (raw) seafood at the **Vismarkt.** (Open Tu-Sa 8am-1pm.) **Ganzespel ❹,** Ganzestr. 37, serves hearty portions of simple food. (Meals €6-15, quiche €6. Open W-F noon-2:30pm and 6-10pm, Su noon-10pm.) **Grand Kaffee de Passage ❸,** Dweerstr. 26-28, is a good spot for traditional Belgian cuisine. (€4.50-14. Open daily 5pm-1am.) For cheaper fare, head to **Nopri Supermarket,** Noordzandstr. 4, just off 't Zand. (Open M-Sa 9:30am-6:30pm.)

⊡ SIGHTS

Small enough to be explored on short walks and lined with gorgeous canals, Bruges is best seen on foot. The tourist office leads **walking tours** (July-Aug. daily 3pm; €3.75), and **boat tours** traverse Bruges's canals (every 30min., €5); ask at the tourist office or pick up tickets at the booth on the bridge between Wollestr. and Dijver. The combination ticket (€15) covers five sights of your choice, including the Gruuthuse, the Groeninge Museum, the Memling, the Belfort, and the Stadhuis.

MARKT AND BURG. Over the **Markt** looms the 88m medieval bell tower of the **Belfort.** During the day, climb its dizzying 366 steps for a great view; return at night, when the tower serves as the city's torch. *(Open daily 9:30am-5pm. Tickets sold until 4:15pm. Bell concerts M, W, Sa 9pm; Su 2:15pm. €5, students €3.)* Behind the Markt, the **Burg** is dominated by the flamboyant Gothic facade of the medieval **Stadhuis** (City Hall), filled with paintings and wood carvings. Upstairs is a gilded hall where many Bruges residents still get married. *(Open daily 9:30am-5pm. €2.50, students €1.50. Audioguide included.)* Hidden in the corner of the Burg next to the Stadhuis, the **Basilica of the Holy Blood** houses a relic that allegedly holds the blood of Christ. *(Open Apr.-Sept. daily 9:30am-noon and 2-6pm; Oct.-Mar. 10am-noon and 2-4pm; closed W afternoon. Free. Worship of relic F 8:30-10am (ground floor), 10-11am, and 3-4pm (upstairs). €1.)*

MUSEUMS. From the Burg, follow Wollestr. left and then head right on Dijver to reach the **Groeninge Museum,** which has a comprehensive collection of Belgian and Dutch paintings from the last six centuries, featuring works by Bruges-based Jan Van Eyck, Bruges-born Hans Memling, and the master of medieval macabre Hieronymous Bosch. *(Dijver 12. Open daily 9:30am-5pm; off-season closed Tu. €5, students €3.)* Next door, the **Gruuthuse Museum** houses an amazing collection of weapons, tapestries, musical instruments, and coins that date back to the 6th century. The small chapel, which protrudes into the Church of Our Lady (see below), was built so that the Palace residents could attend church services from the comfort of their own home. *(Dijver 17. Open daily 9:30am-5pm; Oct.-Mar. closed Tu. €5, students €3.)* Continue on Dijver as it becomes Gruuthusestr. and walk under the stone archway to enter the **Memling Museum,** housed in **St-Janshospitaal,** one of the oldest surviving medieval hospitals in Europe. The museum reconstructs everyday life in the hospital and has several paintings by Hans Memling. *(Mariastr. 38. Open Apr.-Sept. daily 9:30am-5pm; Oct.-Mar. Th-Tu 9:30am-12:30pm and 2-5pm. €7, students €3.)*

OTHER SIGHTS. The 13th- to 16th-century **Church of Our Lady,** at Mariastr. and Gruuthusestr., near the Groeninge Museum, contains Michelangelo's *Madonna and Child* as well as medieval frescoed tomb fragments and the 16th-century mausoleums of Mary of Burgundy and Charles the Bold. *(Open daily 9:30am-12:30pm and 1:30-5pm. Church free. Tomb fragment viewing €2.50, students €1.50.)* From the church, turn left, follow Mariastr., and turn right onto Stoofstr., where you will come to Walplein. Cross the footbridge to enter the Beguinage, a grassy cove encircled by picturesque medieval cloisters inhabited today by Benedictine nuns. *(Open Mar.-Nov. daily 10am-noon and 1:45-5:30pm; July-Aug. until 6pm. Gate closes at sunset. €1.50.)* The 230-year-old windmill **Sint-Janshuismolen** is still used to grind flour in the summer months. From the Burg, follow Hoogstr., which becomes Langestr., and turn left at the end onto Kruisvest. *(Open May-Sept. daily 9:30am-12:30pm and 1:30-5pm. €1, students €0.50.)* The **Minnewater** (Lake of Love), on the southern end of the city, has a less-than-idyllic history as the site of an ammunition dump, but you'd never know it from the picnickers lounging happily in the beautiful park.

NIGHTLIFE

The best nighttime entertainment in Bruges is wandering through the city's romantic streets and over its cobblestoned bridges. Other options include the popular bar at the Bauhaus Hostel (see above) or the 300 varieties of beer at **'t Brugs Beertje**, Kemelstr. 5, off Steenstr. (Open M-Tu and Th 4pm-1am, F-Sa 4pm-2am, Su 4pm-1am.) Next door, the **Dreipelhuisje** serves tantalizingly fruity *jenever*, a flavored Dutch gin, but be careful—the flavors mask a very high alcohol content. (Open Tu-F 6pm-midnight, Sa-Su 6pm-2am.) **Rica Rokk**, 't Zand 6, is popular with local 20-somethings. (Beer from €1.80. Open daily 8am-5am.) **The Break**, 't Zand 9, has pulsing music. (Beer from €1.80. Open M-Sa 10am-late, Su 1pm-late.)

ANTWERP (ANTWERPEN, ANVERS) ☎03

Home to the Golden Age master painter Rubens, Antwerp today is distinctly cosmopolitan. Its main street, the Meir, showcases trendy clothing, diamond jewelry, and delectable chocolate. At the end of the Meir, beer flows so cheaply that crowds pass another round in lieu of breakfast.

TRANSPORTATION AND PRACTICAL INFORMATION. Trains go from Berchem Station to: Amsterdam (2hr., €24); Brussels (1hr., €5); and Rotterdam (1½hr., €17.35). To get from the station to the **tourist office**, Grote Markt 15, take tram #8 to Groenplaats. (☎232 01 03; fax 231 19 37. Open M-Sa 9am-6pm, Su 9am-5pm). **Postal code:** 2000.

ACCOMMODATIONS AND FOOD. The **New International Youth Hotel and Hostel ❷**, Provinciestr. 256, is centrally located. To get there, take tram #2, 11, or 15 to Plantin, go under the bridge onto Baron Joostensstr., take a right onto Van Den Nestlei, head left onto Kruikstr., and take an immediate right onto Provinciestr. (☎230 05 22; niyh@pandora.be. Breakfast included. Sheets €3. Reception daily 8am-11pm. No lockout. 8-bed dorms €13; singles €26; doubles €40-50; quads €65-77.) To reach the modern **Jeugdherberg Op-Sinjoorke (HI) ❷**, Eric Sasselaan 2, take tram #8 or 11 to Groenplaats, then take tram #2 (dir.: Hoboken) to Bouwcentrum. From the tram stop, walk toward the fountain, take a left, and follow the yellow signs. (☎238 02 73. Breakfast included. Sheets €3.35. Lockout 10am-4pm. Dorms €12.50, nonmembers €15; doubles €17/€20.) You can **camp** near the Jeugdherberg Op-Sinjoorke at **Sted. Kamp Vogelzangan ❶**. (☎238 57 17. Open Apr.-Sept. €1.60 per person, €0.90 per car; €0.90 per tent, €2.10 per tent with electricity.) There are loads of cheap Middle Eastern restaurants and seafood places around **Grote Markt** and **Groenplaats**.

SIGHTS AND NIGHTLIFE. Many of Antwerp's best sights are free. Fanciful mansions built in the city's Golden Age line the **Cogels Osylei**. A stroll down the promenade by the Schelde River leads to the 13th-century **Steen Castle**, which houses the **National Maritime Museum**. (Open Tu-Su 10am-5pm. €4; F free.)

The **Cathedral of our Lady,** Groenpl. 21, boasts a magnificent Gothic tower and Rubens's *Descent from the Cross.* (Open M-F 10am-5pm, Sa 10am-3pm, Su 1-4pm. €2.) Nearby, the dignified **Stadhuis** stands in Grote Markt. (Info ☎203 95 33. €30.75.) The **Mayer van den Bergh Museum,** Lange Gasthuisstr. 19, features a formerly private collection and showcases Bruegel's *Mad Meg.* (Open Tu-Su 10am-5pm. €3; F free.) The **Rubens Huis,** Wapper 9-11, off Meir, was built by Antwerp's favorite son and is filled with his masterful art. (Open Tu-Su 10am-5pm. €5; F free.) The **Royal Museum of Fine Arts,** Leopold De Waelpl. 1-9, has one of the world's finest collections of Old Flemish Master paintings. (Open Tu-Su 10am-5pm. €5; F free.)

Get a copy of *Week Up* from the tourist office for information on Antwerp's nightlife. The streets behind the cathedral are crowded at night; **Bierland,** Korte Nieuwstr. 28, is a popular student hangout. (Open Su-Th 9am-noon, F-Sa 8am-2am.) Next to the cathedral, over 600 Flemish religious figurines eye the drinkers at **Elfde Gebod,** Torfburg 10. (Beer €1.75-3. Open M-F noon-1am, Sa-Su noon-2am.) Sample local *elixir d'Anvers* in the candle-lit, 15th-century **Pelgrom,** Pelgrimstr. 15. (Open daily noon-late.) Gay nightlife clusters on **Van Schoonhovenstraat,** just north of Centrale Station.

GHENT (GENT) ☎09

Once the heart of the Flemish textile industry, Ghent lives and breathes industrial pride, with many of its grand buildings and monuments testifying to its former grandeur. During the **Gentse Feesten** ("10 Days Off" celebration; July 20-29, 2002; ☎269 09 45), which commemorates the first vacation granted to sweatshop workers in 1860, the streets come to life with performers, live music, and carnival rides.

⌨️ TRANSPORTATION AND PRACTICAL INFORMATION. Trains run from St-Pietersstation (take tram #1 or 12): to Antwerp (40min., €6.80); Brussels (40min., €6.10); and Bruges (20min., €4.70). The **tourist office** is in the belfry's crypt, Botermarkt 17a. (☎266 52 32. Open Apr.-Oct. daily 9:30am-6:30pm; Nov.-Mar. 9:30am-4:30pm.) **Postal Code:** 9000.

🏠 ACCOMMODATIONS AND FOOD. Modern **De Draeke (HI) ❷,** St-Widostr. 11, blends into the shadows of a castle in downtown Ghent. From the station, take tram #1, 10, or 11 to Gravensteen (15min.). Facing the castle, head left, then head right on Gewad and right again on St-Widostr. (☎233 70 50; youthhostel.gent@skynet.be. Breakfast and sheets included. Internet €0.07 per min. Reception daily 7:30am-11pm. Dorms €15; singles €22.50; doubles €36. Nonmembers add €2.50.) **The Hotel Flandria ❺,** Barrestr. 3, is on a quiet road near Saint Bavo's Cathedral. (☎223 06 26; www.flandria-centrum.be. Breakfast included. Reception daily 7am-9pm. Singles €33, with bath €41; doubles €38/€48.) To get to **Camping Blaarmeersen ❶,** Zuiderlaan 12, take bus #9 from St-Pietersstation and ask the driver to connect you to bus #38 to Blaarmeersen. When you get off, take the first street on your left to the end. (☎221 53 99; blaarmeersen@gent.be. Open Mar. to mid-Oct. only. €3.25-4 per person and tent.) **Korenmarkt** and **Vrijdagmarkt** are surrounded by restaurants and pubs, and **Oudburg,** near Patershol, has many inexpensive Turkish restaurants.

👁️ SIGHTS AND NIGHTLIFE. The **Leie canal** runs through the center of the city, wrapping around the sprawling medieval fortress of **Gravensteen,** St-Veerleplein 11, which holds a crypt, dungeon, and torture chamber. (Open Apr.-Aug. daily 9am-5:15pm; Sept.-Mar. 9am-4:15pm. €6.20, students €1.20.) The castle is near the historic **Partershol** quarter, a network of well-preserved 16th- to 18th-century houses. Wind your way up the towering **Belfort** for some serious vertigo.

(Open mid-Mar. to Nov. daily 10am-12:30pm and 2-5:30pm. €2.50, students €1.50.) The **Stadhuis** is a mix of Gothic and Renaissance architecture. A block away on Limburgstr., the 14th- to 16th-century **Saint Bavo's Cathedral** boasts van Eyck's *Adoration of the Mystic Lamb* and Rubens's *St. Bavo's Entrance into the Monastery of Ghent.* (Cathedral open Apr.-Oct. daily 8:30am-6pm; Nov.-Mar. M-Sa 8:30am-5pm, Su 2-7pm. Free. Crypt and *Mystic Lamb* open M-Sa 9:30am-5pm, Su 1-5pm. €2.50, audioguide included.) Citadel Park, near the center, has a 14th- to 16th-century Flemish collection at the **Museum voor Schone Kunsten** (open Tu-Su 10am-6pm; €2.50, students €1.20) and great contemporary art at the **Stedelijk Museum voor Actuele Kunst** (**SMAK;** open Tu-Su 10am-6pm; €5, students €2.50).

During the school year, cafes and discos light up **Overpoortstraat.** The Art Deco bar **Vooruit,** on St-Pietersnieuwstr., was once the meeting place of the Socialist Party and was later occupied by Nazis. (Open M-Th 11:30am-2am, F-Sa 11:30am-3am, Su 4pm-2am.) **Dulle Grief,** on the Vrijdagmarkt, stocks over 250 types of beer. (Open M 4:30pm-12:30am, Tu-Sa noon-12:30am, Su noon-7:30pm.)

WALLONIE

The towns in the Ardennes offer a relaxing hideaway, with hiking trails that lead through deep forests to impressive citadels and cool caves. The most exceptional portion of the Belgian Ardennes lies in the southeast corner, where gorgeous train rides sweep through peaceful farmland.

NAMUR   ☎ 081

The quiet and friendly city of **Namur,** in the heart of Wallonie, is the last sizable outpost before the wilderness of the Ardennes. Given the proximity of opportunities for **hiking, biking, caving,** and **kayaking,** it is the best base for exploring the area. The foreboding **citadel,** on top of a rocky hill to the south, was built by the Spanish in the Middle Ages, expanded by the Dutch in the 19th century, the site of a bloody battle in WWI, and occupied until 1978. Climb up or take a mini-bus from the tourist office at sq. Leopold and r. de Grognon; the bus will let you off at the Citadel, where you can join a tour of the fortress. (Mini-bus mid-June to mid-Sept. daily, Apr.-June Sa-Su; every hr.; €1. Citadel open daily 11am-5pm. €6, students €5.25.)

Trains link Namur to Brussels (1hr., €6.40). Two **tourist offices,** one a few blocks left of the train station at sq. Leopold (☎ 22 28 49; open daily 9:30am-6pm), and the other in **Hôtel de Ville** (☎ 24 64 44; www.ville.namur.be; open M-F 8:30am-4:30pm), help plan excursions. To reach the friendly **Auberge Félicien Rops (HI) ❷,** 8 av. Félicien Rops, take bus #3 directly to the door or take bus #4 and ask the driver to let you off. (☎ 22 36 88; namur@laj.be. **Bikes** €12.40 per day. Breakfast included. Sheets €2.75. Laundry €6.45. Reception daily 7:30am-1am. Lockout 11am-3pm. Dorms €11; singles €20; doubles €30. Nonmembers add €2.50.) To **camp** at **Les Trieux ❶,** 99 r. des Tris, 6km away in Malonne, take bus #6. (☎ 44 55 83. Open Apr.-Oct. €2.15 per person or per tent.) Restaurants cluster on the small streets around **Place Chanoine Deschamps** and **Rue Saint Jean. Brasserie Henry ❹,** 3 pl. St-Aubain, has a long menu of French food and stays open late. (Main dishes €7.50-12.50. Open daily noon-midnight.) For Italian food, try the 15th-century cellar of **La Cava ❷,** 20 r. de la Monnaie. (Entrees €5-10. Open daily noon-11pm.) Try the regional **Ardennes ham** (from €1.75) at one of the sandwich stands throughout the city.

▓ **DAYTRIP FROM NAMUR: DINANT.** The tiny town of Dinant boasts wonders out of proportion to its size. The imposing **citadel** towers over the Meuse River. Ride the cable car up or brave the steep steps along the fortress. (☎ 22 36 70. Citadel open daily 10am-6pm. Mandatory tours in French and Dutch every 20min. €5.20.)

Bring a sweater to the tour of the cascade-filled caves of **La Grotte Merveilleuse,** 142 rte. de Phillippeville. To reach the Grotte from the citadel, cross the bridge and take the second left onto rte. de Phillippeville. (Open July-Aug. daily 10am-6pm; Apr.-June and Sept.-Oct. daily 10am-5pm; Nov.-Mar. Sa-Su 1-4pm. Mandatory tours in French, Dutch, and English every hr. €5, students €4.50.) Dinant is also a good base for **climbing** and **kayaking** excursions. **Dakota Raid Adventure,** r. Saint Roch 17, leads rock-climbing daytrips in the area. (☎22 32 43. **Bikes** €12.40 per half-day, €20 per day. Open daily 9am-6:30pm.) Dinant is accessible by **train** from Brussels (1hr., €9:30) or by **bike** from Namur; on summer weekends, take a river cruise from Namur (3hr.). The **tourist office,** Quai Cadoux 8 (☎22 28 70), helps plan outdoor activities and books rooms. With your back to the train station, turn right, take the first left, and then the very next left. ☎ **082.**

BOSNIA AND HERZEGOVINA

 In June 2002, the US State Department reiterated its **Travel Warning** against unnecessary travel to certain regions in Bosnia, particularly the Republika Srpska. For updates, consult http://travel.state.gov/travel_warnings.html.

The mountainous heart of the former Yugoslavia, Bosnia and Herzegovina's distinctiveness—and troubles—springs from a history as a melting pot for Muslim Bosniaks, Catholic Croats, and Orthodox Serbs. In Sarajevo, harmony is at least verbally maintained, but ethnic tensions continue in the countryside. Bosnia's last decade has been brutal, with much of its population displaced due to the bloody war broadcast nightly to the world from 1991 to 1995. The landscape, though full of rolling hills, sparkling rivers, and lush valleys, is now dotted with abandoned houses and gaping rooftops. Though the future of the now-independent country is uncertain, reconstruction has begun, and its resilient citizens are optimistic.

FACTS AND FIGURES

Official Name: Bosnia and Herzegovina.

Capital: Sarajevo.

Major Cities: Mostar.

Population: 3,500,000 (40% Serbs, 38% Bosnian Muslims, 22% Croats).

Land Area: 51,233 sq. km.

Languages: Bosnian, Serbian, Croatian.

Time Zone: GMT +1.

Religions: Muslim (40%), Orthodox (31%), Catholic (15%), Protestant (4%).

Administrative Division: Muslim/Croat Federation (51%), Serb-led Republika Srpska (49%).

ESSENTIALS

DOCUMENTS AND FORMALITIES

VISAS. Citizens of Canada, South Africa, the UK, and the US may visit Bosnia visa-free for up to 90 days; visas are required for citizens of Australia, Ireland, and New Zealand. (Transit or 30-day single-entry €35; 90-day multiple-entry €65; long-term multiple-entry €85.) There are occasional police checkpoints within the country; register with your embassy upon arrival, and keep your papers with you at all times. Visitors are required to register with the police upon arrival; accommodations will often register guests automatically.

EMBASSIES. Foreign embassies in Bosnia-Herzogovina are in Sarajevo (p. 131). Bosnian embassies at home include: **Australia,** 5 Beale Crescent, Deakin, ACT 2600 (☎616 232 4646; www.bosnia.webone.com.au); **Canada,** 130 Albert St., Suite 805, Ottawa, Ontario K1P 5G4 (☎613-236-0028); **South Africa,** 25 Stella St., Brooklyn 0181, Pretoria (☎012 346 5546; fax 346 2295); **UK,** Morley House, 4th fl. 320 Regent St., London W1R 3BF (☎020 7255 3758; bosnia@embassy_london.ision.co.uk); **US,** 2109 E St. NW, Washington, D.C. 20037 (☎202-337-1500; consular ☎212-593-0264; www.bosnianembassy.org).

TRANSPORTATION

Buses are reliable, clean, and uncrowded, but Balkan driving can be nervewracking. Buses run daily from Sarajevo to Dubrovnik, and to Split and Zagreb. Commercial **plane** service into Sarajevo (SJJ) is limited and expensive; **Croatia Airlines** (☎385 148 727 27; www.croatiaairlines.hr) has regular service to Sarajevo from Zagreb. **Railways** are not functional and should not be considered an option. In addition, avoid driving, biking, and hitchhiking.

Bosnia and Herzegovina

TOURIST SERVICES AND MONEY

EMERGENCY . **Police:** ☎92. **Ambulance:** ☎94. **Fire:** ☎93.

The Bosnian **convertible mark** (KM), introduced in 1998, is fixed to the euro at a rate of 1KM to €0.51. The Croatian **kuna** was named an official Bosnian currency in 1997; while not legal tender in Sarajevo, it is accepted in the western (Croatian) area of divided Mostar. The old Bosnian *dinar* is no longer valid currency. Change your money back to euros when you leave, as the convertible mark is inconvertible outside Bosnia. Banks are the best places to exchange money; some in Sarajevo cash traveler's checks. Western Union in Sarajevo has a very helpful English-speaking staff. **ATMs** are available in Sarajevo, Banja Luka, and Međugorje. Most post offices give MasterCard cash advances. If you travel outside of Sarajevo, bring both convertible marks and euros with you. Accommodations are around €15-30 per night, while meals run €2-5. Tip waitstaff only for excellent service.

CONVERTIBLE MARKS		
AUS$1 = 1.10KM	1KM = AUS$0.91	
CDN$1 = 1.30KM	1KM = CDN$0.78	
HRV KUNA1 = 0.27KM	1KM = HRV KUNA3.75	
EUR€1 = 1.96KM	1KM = EUR€0.51	
NZ$1 = 0.93KM	1KM = NZ$1.07	
ZAR1 = 0.19KM	1KM = ZAR5.31	
UK£1 = 3.06KM	1KM = UK£0.33	
US$1 = 1.99KM	1KM = US$0.50	

COMMUNICATION

MAIL. Yellow-and-white "PTT" signs indicate post offices; service is becoming increasingly efficient. Mail to Europe takes 3-5 days, to North America 7-10 days. *Poste Restante* is now available; address mail to be held: Firstname SURNAME, *Poste Restante*, Zmaja od Bosne, Sarajevo 71000, BOSNIA.

TELEPHONES AND INTERNET. Phones are troublesome and expensive; the best option is to call collect from the Sarajevo post office. Calls to the UK are roughly 3.50KM per minute, the US 5KM; prices vary. The **AT&T** direct access number is ☎ 00 800 0010. **Internet access** (2-4KM per hr.) is becoming widely available.

PHONE CODE	**Country code: 387. International dialing prefix:** 00. From outside Bosnia-Herzegovina, dial int'l dialing prefix (see inside back cover) + 387 + city code + local number.

ACCOMMODATIONS AND CAMPING

BOSNIA	❶	❷	❸	❹	❺
ACCOMMODATIONS	under 35KM	35-40KM	41-50KM	51-60KM	over 61KM
FOOD	under 4KM	4-6KM	7-10KM	11-14KM	over 14KM

Accommodations options are very limited in Bosnia—**hotels** are usually the only choice. **Private rooms** exist only in Sarajevo, and usually cost the same as cheaper hotels (30-40KM). **Camping** should be avoided except through special organizations such as Green Visions (see p. 133).

HEALTH AND SAFETY

Hundreds of thousands of **landmines** and **unexploded ordnance (UXO)** cover the country, many on road shoulders and in abandoned houses. Outside Sarajevo, **NEVER set foot off the pavement;** even in Sarajevo, stay on paved roads and hard-covered surfaces. Do not pick up any objects on the ground. The **Mine Action Center (MAC),** Zmaja od Bosne 8 (☎ 66 73 10 and 20 12 99), has more information. In Sarajevo, finding medical help and supplies is not difficult; your embassy is your best resource. Peacekeeping operations have brought English-speaking doctors, but not insurance; cash is the only method of payment. All drugs are sold at pharmacies, while basic hygiene products are sold at many drugstores.

HOLIDAYS

Holidays: New Year's (Jan. 1); Orthodox Christmas (Jan. 7); Republic Day (Jan. 9); Orthodox New Year's (Jan. 14); Independence Day (Mar. 1); Catholic Easter (Apr. 20-21); Orthodox Easter (Apr. 25 27); Labor Day (May 1); St. George's Day (May 6); Vidovdan (June 28); Petrovdan (July 12); Ilindan (Aug. 2); Velika gospa (Aug. 15); Assumption (Aug. 28); Ramadan (roughly Oct. 27-Nov. 25); 'Id al-Fitr (Nov. 26); National Day (Nov. 25); Catholic Christmas (Dec. 25).

SARAJEVO ☎ 033

Once the proud host of the 1984 Olympic Games, Sarajevo is now best known for the siege it underwent during the recent war (1991-1995). Emotional and physical scars have been slow to fade; visitors will still rub shoulders with uniformed SFOR officers, camera-wielding journalists, and foreign aid workers. However, the burgeoning arts scene and revived nightlife are inspiring signs for the future.

 The following outlying areas of Sarajevo were battlegrounds during the war and still contain landmines: Grbavica, Lukavica, Illidža, and Dobrinja.

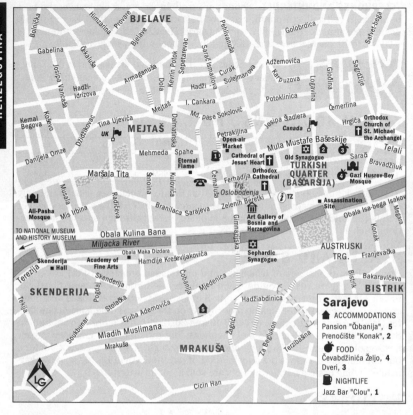

Sarajevo

▲ ACCOMMODATIONS
Pansion "Čobanija", **5**
Prenoćište "Konak", **2**

🍴 FOOD
Čevabdžinića Željo, **4**
Dveri, **3**

🍸 NIGHTLIFE
Jazz Bar "Clou", **1**

📠📶 **TRANSPORTATION AND PRACTICAL INFORMATION.** Buses (☎ 53 28 74)
run from Kranjćevića 9, behind the Holiday Inn at the corner with Halida Kajtaza,
to: Dubrovnik (7hr., 2 per day, 40KM); Frankfurt (15hr., 1 per day, 196KM); Split
(8hr., 4 per day, 36KM); Vienna (12hr., 1 per day, 81KM); and Zagreb (9hr., 3 per
day, 51KM). Turn left from the station and walk on Kranjčevića for 20min. to reach
the city's main street, **Maršala Tita**, or take a cab (7-8KM). To reach the tourist
bureau, **Turistička Zajednica**, Zelenih Beretki 22a, bear right past the Eternal Flame
on Maršala Tita; when you see the Catholic church on your left, take a right down
Strossmajerova, then turn left onto Zelenih Beretki. (☎ 22 07 24. Open M-Sa 9am-

WATCH YOUR TONGUE Croatian, Serbian, and Bosnian indi-
cate nationality, while Croat, Serb, and Bosnian refer to ethnicity. Thus, a Bosnian Serb
denotes a Serb living in Bosnia (most often in the Republika Srpska (RS), the Serb-
dominated area in northeast Bosnia). Likewise, a Bosnian Croat is a Croat living in Bos-
nia. Bosnian Muslims usually go by the term "Bosniak." Bosnians often refer to their
Bosnian Serb enemies as "Četnik," or "Chetnik," a revived World War II ethnic slur. In
other words, a Serb is different from a Chetnik—do not make this mistake. Also note
that the Bosnian Army is precisely that, *not* the "Muslim Army."

8pm, Su 10am-6pm.) Many organizations welcome volunteers and donations to help the country rebuild (see p. 72). **Embassies: Australians** should contact the embassy in Vienna (p. 84); **Canada,** Logavina 7 (☎44 79 00; open M-F 8:30am-noon and 1-5pm); citizens of **New Zealand** should contact the embassy in Rome (p. 594); **UK,** Tina Ujevića 8 (☎44 44 29; open M-F 8:30am-5pm); and **US,** Alipašina 43 (☎44 57 00; www.usis.com.ba; open M-F 9am-1pm). **Central Profit Banka,** Zelenih Beretki 24, changes money. (Open M-F 8am-7pm, Sa 8am-1pm.) There are 24hr. **ATMs** through the door to the right of the main entrance; more machines are along Maršala Tita, a few blocks before the Flame. There are several **Internet** cafes along Ferhadija (2-3KM per hr.). **Postal code:** 71000.

⌐⌐ ACCOMMODATIONS AND FOOD. Relatively cheap **private rooms** (30-50KM) are all over; ask a taxi driver at the station for help if you arrive late. From Maršala Tita, go left at the Eternal Flame and walk past the market to get to **Prenoćište "Konak" ❷,** Mula Mustafe Bašeskije 48, on the right. (☎53 35 06. Singles 40KM; doubles 60KM.) To reach modern **Pansion "Čobanija" ❺,** Čobanija 29, from the Eternal Flame, take the first left onto Kulovića, which crosses the river to become Čobanija. (☎44 17 49; fax 20 39 37. Reserve ahead by fax. Singles 80KM; doubles 120KM.) Hidden in a small alley, **⧉Dveri ❸,** Prote Bakovice 12, serves delicious, authentic Bosnian food, and has vegetarian options. Walk up Ferhadija from the Baščaršija end and turn right at the first sidestreet; the alley is on your immediate left. (Main dishes 7-15KM. Open M-Sa 11am-4pm and 5-11pm.) Scour the Turkish Quarter for **ćevabdžinića** (kebab) shops; **Ćevabdžinića Željo ❷,** Kundurdžiluk 19, is the most popular. (Ćevap 4KM. Open daily 8am-10pm.)

◪ SIGHTS. The **Eternal Flame,** where Maršala Tita splits into Ferhadija and Mula Mustafe Bašeskije, was lit in 1945 as a memorial to all Sarajevans who died in WWII; its homage to South Slav unity now seems painfully ironic. Within the city center, reconstruction has hidden most signs of the recent siege, but the glaring **treeline** in the hills still marks the front lines; Bosnians trapped in Sarajevo cut down all the safely available wood for winter heat. From Maršala Tita, walk toward the river to Obala Kulina Bana and turn left to find the **National Library,** at the tip of the Turkish Quarter. Once Sarajevo's most beautiful building, the library was firebombed on August 25, 1992, the centennial of its construction. As the building burned, citizens risked their lives to salvage the library's treasures, but most of the collection was destroyed. Walk toward the center to the

THE BIG SPLURGE

GREEN VISIONS

Foreign visitors to Bosnia are often amazed by the beauty of the countryside, whose towering mountains and blue-green rivers are a far cry from the gray, dreary images of Bosnia's civil war. With miles of untouched wilderness, the country should be an outdoorsman's paradise. There's just one enormous problem: during the war, fighting covered the country, and wherever there was a front line, there are now landmines.

Green Visions, an eco-tourism company founded in 2000, is dedicated to determining safe locations in Bosnia for outdoor exploration. It provides trips throughout the country, ranging from three-hour walks in the mountains around Sarajevo (65KM) to week-long treks in some of the most inaccessible parts of the country (700KM, including equipment and food). Before planning trips, the Green Visions staff consults the **Mine Action Center** (see p. 131) as well as the armies of both the Muslim-Croat Federation and the Serb Republic to determine if there are any mines. If there is any possibility of danger, the excursion is cancelled; any trip that does proceed is thoroughly scouted beforehand.

Green Visions also organizes rafting expeditions in Bosnia and Montenegro, rock-climbing trips for climbers of all levels, homestays in remote mountain villages, and paragliding courses.

(☎/fax 33 20 71 69; www.greenvisions.ba.)

SARAJEVO ROSES All along Sarajevo's main thoroughfare, Maršala Tita, the pavement is littered with splash-shaped indentations. These distinctive marks were created by exploding shells during the city's Serbian siege. Those marks filled in with red concrete are called "Sarajevo Roses" and commemorate civilians killed on those spots. Even in the most normalized and seamless of Sarajevo's neighborhoods, they are a constant reminder of the war and the thousands of Bosnians lost.

second bridge on Obala Kulina Bana, where Serbian terrorist Gavrilo Princip shot the Austrian Archduke Franz Ferdinand on June 28, 1914, triggering WWI.

The places of worship for various religions huddle together in the city center. Walk left at the Flame on Ferhadija, which becomes Sarači, to find the 16th-century **Gazi Husrev-Bey mosque,** Sarači 12, perhaps Sarajevo's most famous building. The interior is closed for repairs, but prayer continues in the beautiful courtyard. The low, red-roofed buildings surrounding the mosque make up **Baščaršija,** the Turkish Quarter, whose centerpiece is its traditional bazaar. The **National Museum** and the **History Museum** are at Zmaja od Bosne 3 and 5, respectively. The former is among the Balkans' most famous museums, but will be under construction for much of 2003; the latter houses contemporary art, much of which pertains to the civil war. (National Museum open Tu, Th, F, and Su 10am-2pm, W 11am-7pm. 5KM, students 1KM. History Museum open M-F 9am-2pm, Sa-Su 9am-1pm. Free.) Next to the National Museum, the shattered tower of the **Parliament Building** is a shocking reminder of what most of Sarajevo looked like following the recent war. In 1992, a peace rally began from Parliament and marched on ul. Vrbanja across the bridge; Serb snipers opened fire, causing the first casualties of the war. A small monument to the victims can be now found at the side of the bridge.

🎵 🎬 **ENTERTAINMENT AND NIGHTLIFE.** Every summer in July, the Turkish Quarter hosts the **Turkish Nights** (Baščaršija Noci) featuring open-air music, theater, and film. In late August, the **Sarajevo Film Festival** rolls into theaters throughout the city. (☎/fax 66 45 47; www.sff.ba. Box office open in summer M-F 9am-6pm. 4-5KM per film.) Sarajevo also holds the annual **Sarajevan Winter** (Sarajevska Zima; ☎ 20 79 48) from late December to early January; this celebration of art and culture persisted even through the siege. **Futura 2003** in mid- to late July will feature techno and house raves. There are always underground events going on; the best way to find out about them is to befriend some young Sarajevans. Cafes along **Ferhadija** and **Maršala Tita** are flourishing, but the best nightlife is found in basement bars and side street cafes. At Mula Mustafe Bašeskije 5, through an unmarked door near the Eternal Flame, 🎵**Jazz Bar "Clou"** plays the best music in town and hosts local bands Friday and Saturday. (Beer 5KM. Open nightly 8:30pm-5am.)

BRITAIN

Having spearheaded the Industrial Revolution, colonized two-fifths of the globe, and won every foreign war in its history but two, Britain seems intent on making the world forget its tiny size. But this small island nation is just that: small. The rolling farms of the south and the rugged cliffs of the north are only a day's train ride apart, and peoples as diverse as London clubbers, Cornish miners, Welsh students, and Gaelic monks all occupy a land area half the size of Spain. Beyond the stereotypical snapshots of Merry Olde England—gabled cottages with flowery borders, tweed-clad farmers shepherding their flocks— Britain today is a cosmopolitan destination driven by international energy. Though the British Empire may have petered out, its legacy survives in multi-cultural urban centers and a dynamic arts and theater scene—the most accessible in the world, as long as English remains the planet's most widespread language. Brits eat kebab as often as they do lemon curd and scones, and five-story dance clubs in post-industrial settings draw as much attention as fairy-tale country homes with picturesque views.

Travelers should be aware that names hold political force. "Great Britain" refers to England, Scotland, and Wales; the term "United Kingdom" refers to these nations as well as Northern Ireland. *Let's Go* uses the term "Britain" to refer to England, Scotland, and Wales because of legal and currency distinctions.

FACTS AND FIGURES

Official Name: United Kingdom of Great Britain and Northern Ireland.

Capital: London.

Major Cities: Manchester, Liverpool, Cardiff, Glasgow, Edinburgh.

Population: 57,100,000.

Land Area: 244,110 sq. km.

Time Zone: GMT.

Language: English; also Welsh, Scottish, and Gaelic.

Religions: Anglican (68%), Roman Catholic (28%), other (4%).

DISCOVER BRITAIN

London (p. 140) brims with cultural wonders. Don't miss a trip to Tate Modern, which mixes the work of Andy Warhol with that of Monet. Southwest of London, the lovely **Winchester** (p. 170) celebrates Jane Austen; prehistoric **Stonehenge** (p. 172) and the massive cathedral at **Salisbury** (p. 171) sit close by. **Newquay** (p. 173), Britain's take on surfer culture, is farther west on the Cornish Coast. The rich and famous of Georgian England once flocked to **Bath** (p. 172) for Roman-style healing; visitors head there today for both the ruins and the elegantly preserved mansions. *Let's Go* can't promise that a visit to **Oxford** (p. 175), **Cambridge** (p. 181), and the Shakespeare-crazy **Stratford-Upon-Avon** (p. 178) will make you smarter, but the fascinating history of the three towns makes it worth a try. All you need is love in **Liverpool** (p. 184), which basks in Beatlesmania, and all you'll need is a camera in the dramatic **Lake District National Park** (p. 190), filled with rugged hills and windswept fells. In Wales, cavort with sheep and commune with nature in **Snowdonia National Park** (p. 194) and enjoy the theaters of **Cardiff** (p. 192). Farther north in Scotland, enjoy the cultural capitals of **Edinburgh** (p. 197) and **Glasgow** (p. 205), then head to the beautiful **Isle of Skye** (p. 211) and the famed **Loch Ness** (p. 210), where Nessie awaits.

ESSENTIALS

WHEN TO GO

It may be wise to plan around the high season (June-Aug.). Spring or autumn (Apr.-May and Sept.-Oct.) are more appealing times to visit; the weather is still reasonable and flights are cheaper, though there may be fewer services in rural areas. If you intend to visit the large cities and linger indoors at museums and theaters, the off season (Nov.-Mar.) is most economical. Keep in mind, however, that sights and accommodations often close or run reduced hours, especially in rural regions. Another factor to consider is hours of daylight—in Scotland, summer light lasts almost to midnight, but in winter the sun may set as early as 3:45pm. Regardless of when you go, it will rain; have warm, waterproof clothing on hand.

DOCUMENTS AND FORMALITIES

VISAS. EU citizens do not need a visa. Citizens of Australia, Canada, New Zealand, South Africa, and the US do not need a visa for stays up to six months.

EMBASSIES. Foreign embassies for Britain are in London (p. 140). For British embassies and high commissions at home, contact: **Australia,** British High Commission, Commonwealth Ave., Yarralumla, Canberra, ACT 2606 (☎02 6270 6666; www.uk.emb.gov.au); **Canada,** British High Commission, 80 Elgin St., Ottawa, ON K1P 5K7 (☎613-237-1530; www.britain-in-canada.org); **Ireland,** British Embassy, 29 Merrion Rd., Ballsbridge, Dublin 4 (☎01 205 3700; www.britishembassy.ie); **New Zealand,** British High Commission, 44 Hill St., Thorndon, Wellington 1 (☎04 924 2888; www.britain.org.nz); **South Africa,** British High Commission, 91 Parliament St., Cape Town 8001 (☎021 405 2400); **US,** British Embassy, 3100 Massachusetts Ave. NW, Washington, D.C. 20008 (☎202-588-6500; www.britainusa.com).

TRANSPORTATION

BY PLANE. Most flights into Britain that originate outside Europe land at London's Heathrow and Gatwick airports (p. 140). Some fly directly to regional airports such as Manchester or Edinburgh (p. 197).

BY TRAIN. For info on getting to Britain from the Continent, see p. 51. Britain's train network is extensive. Prices and schedules often change; find up-to-date information from **National Rail Inquiries** (☎08457 484 950) or online at **Railtrack** (www.railtrack.co.uk; schedules only). The **BritRail Pass,** only sold outside Britain, allows unlimited travel in England, Wales, and Scotland (8-day US$270, under 26 US$220; 22-day US$500, under 26 US$360); in Canada and the US, contact **Rail Europe** (Canada ☎800-361-7245; US ☎800-456-7245; www.raileurope.com). Rail discount cards, available at rail stations and through travel agents, grant 33% off most fares and are available to those ages 16-25 and full-time students (£18), seniors (£18), and families (£20). **Eurail** is not valid in Britain.

BY BUS. The British distinguish between **buses,** which cover short local routes, and **coaches,** which cover long distances; *Let's Go* uses the term "buses" to refer to both. **National Express** (☎08705 808 080; www.gobycoach.co.uk) is the principal long-distance coach service operator in Britain, although **Scottish Citylink** (☎08705 505 050) has coverage in Scotland. **Discount Coachcards** (£9) are available for seniors over 50, students, and young persons ages 16-25; they reduce fares on National Express by about 30%. The **Tourist Trail Pass** offers unlimited travel for a number of days within a given period (2 days out of 3 £49, students, seniors, and children £39; 5 of 30 £85/£69; 8 of 30 £135/£99; 15 of 30 £190/£145).

BY FERRY. Several ferry lines provide service between Britain and the Continent. Ask for discounts; ISIC holders can sometimes get student fares, and Eurail passholders can get reductions and free trips. Book ahead June through August. For information on boats from Wales to Dublin and Rosslare, Ireland, see p. 192; from Scotland to Belfast, see p. 197; from England to the Continent, see p. 52.

BY CAR. To drive, you must be 17 and have a valid license from your home country. Britain is covered by a high-speed system of **motorways** ("M-roads") that connect London with other major cities. Visitors may not be accustomed to driving on the left, and automatic transmission is rare in rental cars. Roads are generally well-maintained, but parking in London is impossible and traffic is slow.

BY BIKE AND BY THUMB. Much of Britain's countryside is well suited for **biking**. Many cities and villages have bike rental shops and maps of local cycle routes. Large-scale Ordnance Survey maps, often available at tourist offices, detail the extensive system of long-distance **hiking** paths. Tourist offices and National Park Information Centres can provide extra information about routes. Hitchhiking is illegal on M-roads; *Let's Go* does not recommend hitchhiking.

TOURIST SERVICES AND MONEY

EMERGENCY	Police: ☎999. Ambulance: ☎999. Fire: ☎999.

TOURIST OFFICES. The **British Tourist Authority** (BTA; www.visitbritain.com) is an umbrella organization for the separate tourist boards outside the UK. **Tourist offices** within Britain usually stock maps and information on sights and accommodations.

MONEY. The **pound sterling** is the main unit of currency in the United Kingdom. It is divided into 100 pence, issued in standard denominations of 1p, 2p, 5p, 10p, 20p, 50p, and £1 in coins, and £5, £10, £20, and £50 in notes. Scotland has its own bank notes, which can be used interchangeably with English currency, though you may have difficulty using Scottish £1 notes outside Scotland. Expect to spend anywhere from £25-50 per day. London in particular is a budget-buster, with the bare minimum for accommodations, food, and transport costing £30-40. **Tips** in restaurants are often included in the bill, sometimes as a "service charge." If gratuity is not included, you should tip 10-15%. Tipping the barman in pubs is not at all expected, though a waiter should be tipped. Taxi drivers should receive a 10-15% tip, and bellhops and chambermaids usually expect somewhere between £1 and £3. Aside from open-air markets, don't expect to **bargain**. The European Union imposes a **value-added tax (VAT)** on goods and services purchased within the EU, which is included in the price (see p. 15).

BRITISH POUNDS		
AUS$1 = UK£0.36		UK£1 = AUS$2.77
CDN$1 = UK£0.42		UK£1 = CDN$2.38
EUR€1 = UK£0.64		UK£1 = EUR€1.56
NZ$1 = UK£0.31		UK£1 = NZ$3.24
ZAR1 = UK£0.06		UK£1 = ZAR16.15
US$1 = UK£0.65		UK£1 = US$1.53

COMMUNICATION

PHONE CODES	**Country code: 44. International dialing prefix: 00.** From outside Britain, dial int'l dialing prefix (see inside back cover) + 44 + city code + local number.

TELEPHONES. Most public pay phones in Britain are run by **British Telecom (BT)**. The BT phonecard, available in denominations from £2-20, is a useful purchase, as BT phones are everywhere. Public phones charge a minimum of 10p and don't accept 1p, 2p, or 5p coins. For directory inquiries, which are free from pay phones, call ☎192. International direct dial numbers include: **AT&T,** ☎0800 013 0011; **British Telecom,** ☎0800 345 144; **Canada Direct,** ☎0800 890 016; **MCI,** ☎0800 890 222; **Sprint,** ☎0800 890 877; and **Telkom South Africa,** ☎0800 890 027.

MAIL. To send a postcard or letter within Europe costs £0.37; a postcard to any other international destination costs £0.40, while a letter costs £0.65. Address mail to be held according to the following example: Firstname SURNAME, *Poste Restante*, New Bond St. Post Office, Bath BA1 1A5, UK.

INTERNET ACCESS. Britain is one of the world's most wired countries. Cybercafes can be found in larger cities. They cost £4-6 per hour, but you often pay for only the time used, not for the whole hour. Online guides to cybercafes in Britain and Ireland, updated daily, include the **Cybercafe Search Engine** (http://cybercaptive.com) and **Cybercafes.com** (www.cybercafes.com).

ACCOMMODATIONS AND CAMPING

BRITAIN	❶	❷	❸	❹	❺
ACCOMMODATIONS	under £10	£10-19	£20-30	£31-59	over £60

Hostels are run by the **Youth Hostels Association (YHA) of England and Wales** (www.yha.org.uk) and the **Scottish Youth Hostels Association** (SYHA; www.syha.org.uk). Unless noted as "self-catering," the YHA hostels listed in *Let's Go* offer cooked meals at standard rates (breakfast £3.20, small/standard packed lunch £2.80/£3.65, evening meal £4.15, and children's meals £1.75-2.70). Hostel dorms will cost around £9 in rural areas, £13 in larger cities, and £15-20 in London. You can book **B&Bs** by calling directly, or by asking the local tourist office to help you find accommodations. Tourist offices usually charge a 10% deposit on the first night's or the entire stay's price, deductible from the amount you pay the B&B proprietor; often a flat fee of £1-3 is added on. **Campsites** tend to be privately owned and cost £3-10 per person per night. It is illegal to camp in national parks, since much of their land is privately owned.

FOOD AND DRINK

BRITAIN	❶	❷	❸	❹	❺
FOOD	under £5	£5-9	£10-14	£15-20	over £21

Britons like to start their day off heartily with the famous, cholesterol-filled, meat-anchored English breakfast, served in most B&Bs across the country. The best native dishes for lunch or dinner are roasts—beef, lamb, and Wiltshire hams—and puddings, including the standard Yorkshire. The ploughman's lunch, served in pubs, consists of cheese, bread, and pickles. Fish and chips (french fries) are traditionally drowned in vinegar and salt. To escape English food, try Chinese, Greek, or Indian cuisine. British "tea" refers to both a drink and a social ritual. The refreshment is served strong and milky. The ceremony might include cooked meats, salad, sandwiches, and pastries. Cream tea, a specialty of Cornwall and Devon, includes toast, shortbread, crumpets, scones, jam, and clotted cream.

HOLIDAYS AND FESTIVALS

Holidays: New Year's Day (Jan. 1); Good Friday (Apr. 18); Easter Sunday and Monday (Apr. 20 and 21); May Day (May 5); Bank Holiday (May 26); and Christmas (Dec. 25).

Festivals: One of the largest festivals in the world is the **Edinburgh International Festival** (Aug. 10-30); also highly recommended is the **Fringe Festival** (Aug. 3-25). Manchester's Gay Village hosts **Mardi Gras** (late Aug.). Muddy fun abounds at the **Glastonbury Festival,** Britain's biggest homage to rocks (June 27-29).

ENGLAND

In a land where the stately once prevailed, conservatism has been booted in two successive elections and a wild profusion of the avant-garde has emerged from hallowed academic halls. The country that once determined the meaning of "civilised" now takes many of its cultural cues from former fledgling colonies. The vanguard of art, music, film, and eclecticism, England is a youthful, hip nation looking forward. But traditionalists can rest easy; for all the moving and shaking in the large cities, around the corner there are handfuls of quaint towns, dozens of picturesque castles, and scores of comforting cups of tea.

LONDON ☎020

London defies easy categorization. Those expecting tea-drinking, Royal-loving, Kensington-bred green-thumbs will quickly find equal numbers of black-clad youth lounging in Soho bars, Indian takeaway owners in the East End, and pin-striped bankers in the City. While London abounds with remnants of Britain's long history, a trip to one of many futuristic boutiques will eclipse any impression that this city is chained to bygone days. Pubs may close early, but London roars on, full throttle, around the clock. One of the world's greatest centers for the arts, London dazzles with concert halls, theaters, museums, and bookshops. Despite the dismal reputation of British food, London has steadily gained status as a culinary center, in no small measure due to a diverse and ever-growing international population that infuses the metropolis with energy and optimism.

✈ INTERCITY TRANSPORTATION

Flights: Heathrow (LON; ☎(0870) 000 0123) is London's main airport. The **Piccadilly Line** heads from the airport to central London (45min.-1hr.; every 4-5min.; £3.60, under 16 £1.50). The **Heathrow Express** train shuttles to Paddington (15min.; every 15min.; £11, round-trip £20). From **Gatwick Airport** (LGW; ☎(0870) 000 2468), the **Gatwick Express** heads to Victoria (30-35min.; 6am-8pm every 15min., 8pm-6am every 30min.; £11, round-trip £21), as do cheaper **Connex** commuter trains (35-45min.; £8.20, round-trip £16.40).

Trains: London has 8 major stations: **Charing Cross** (serves south England); **Euston** (the northwest); **King's Cross** (the northeast); **Liverpool St.** (East Anglia); **Paddington** (the west and south Wales); **St. Pancras** (the Midlands and the northwest); **Victoria** (the south); and **Waterloo** (the south, the southwest and the Continent). All stations are linked by the Underground (Tube). Itineraries involving a change of stations in London usually include a cross-town transfer by Tube. Get info at the station ticket office or from the **National Rail Inquiries Line** (☎(08457) 484 950; www.britrail.com).

Buses: Long-distance buses (known as **coaches** in the UK) arrive in London at **Victoria Coach Station,** 164 Buckingham Palace Rd. (☎7730 3466; Tube: Victoria). Some services stop at nearby **Eccleston Bridge,** behind Victoria train station.

✴ ORIENTATION

The heart of London is the vaguely defined **West End,** which stretches east from Park Lane to Kingsway and south from Oxford St. to the River Thames; within this area you'll find aristocratic **Mayfair,** the shopping streets around **Oxford Circus,** the bars and clubs of **Soho,** and the street performers and boutiques of **Covent Garden.**

Heading east of the West End, you'll pass legalist **Holborn** before hitting the ancient **City of London** (a.k.a. "the City"), the site of the original Roman settlement and home to St. Paul's Cathedral and the Tower of London. The City's eastern border jostles the ethnically diverse, working-class **East End.**

Westminster encompasses the grandeur of **Trafalgar Square,** extending south along the Thames; this is the heart of royal and political London, with the Houses of Parliament, Buckingham Palace, and Westminster Abbey. Farther west lies artsy, prosperous **Chelsea.** Across the river from Westminster and the West End, the **South Bank** has an incredible variety of entertainment and museums, from Shakespeare's Globe Theatre to the Tate Modern. The enormous expanse of **Hyde Park** lies to the west of the West End; along its southern border lies chic **Knightsbridge,** home to Harrods and Harvey Nicks, and posh **Kensington.** North of Hyde Park is the media-infested **Notting Hill** and the B&B-filled **Bayswater.** Bayswater, Mayfair, and **Marylebone** meet at Marble Arch, on Hyde Park's northeast corner; from there, Marylebone stretches west to meet academic **Bloomsbury,** north of Soho and Holborn. **Camden Town, Islington, Hampstead,** and **Highgate** lie to the north of Bloomsbury and the City. A good street atlas is essential for efficient navigation; the best is *London A to Z* (£5), available at bookstores and newsstands.

▣ LOCAL TRANSPORTATION

Public Transportation: Run by Transport for London (TfL; 24hr. info ☎ 7222 1234; www.transportforlondon.gov.uk). Pick up maps at all Tube stations; TfL **Information Centres** at Euston, Heathrow Terminals 1, 2, and 3, Liverpool St., Oxford Circus, Paddington, Piccadilly Circus, St. James's Park, and Victoria also offer guides.

Underground: The Underground (a.k.a. the Tube) network is divided into 6 concentric zones, and fares depend on the number of zones crossed. Buy your ticket before you board and pass it through automatic gates at both ends of your journey. A one-way trip in Zone 1 costs £1.60. The Tube runs approx. 5:30am-12:30am, depending on the line; always check last train times. See the color maps section at the front or back of this book.

Buses: Divided into 4 zones. Zones 1-3 are identical to the Tube zones. Fares £0.70-1. Buses run 6am-midnight, after which a limited network of **Night Buses,** prefixed by an "N," take over.

Passes: The **Travelcard** is valid for travel on all TfL services. Daily, weekend, weekly, monthly, and annual cards. 1-day Travelcard from £5.30 (Zones 1-2). Passes expire at 4:30am the morning after their printed expiration date.

Licensed Taxicabs: An illuminated "taxi" sign on the roof of a black cab signals availability. Expensive, but drivers know their stuff. Tip 10%. For pick-up (min. £2 extra charge), call **Computer Cabs** (☎ 7286 0286), **Dial-a-Cab** (☎ 7253 5000), or **Radio Taxis** (☎ 7272 0272).

Minicabs: Private cars. Cheaper than black cabs, but less reliable—stick to a reputable company. **Teksi** (☎ 7267 0267) offers 24hr. pick-up anywhere in London.

▨ PRACTICAL INFORMATION

TOURIST, FINANCIAL, AND LOCAL SERVICES

Tourist Offices: Britain Visitor Centre, 1 Lower Regent St. (www.visitbritain.com). Tube: Oxford Circus. Open M 9:30am-6:30pm, Tu-F 9am-6:30pm, Sa-Su 10am-4pm; June-Sept. extended hours Sa. **London Visitor Centres** (www.londontouristboard.com). Tube branches at: **Heathrow Terminals 1, 2,** and 3 (open Oct.-Aug. daily 8am-6pm; Sept. M-Sa 9am-7pm and Su 8am-6pm); **Liverpool St.** (open June-Sept M-Sa 8am-7pm, Su 8am-6pm; Oct.-May daily 8am-6pm); **Victoria** (open Easter-Sept. M-Sa 8am-8pm, Su 8am-6pm; Oct.-Easter daily 8am-6pm); **Waterloo** (open daily 8:30am-10:30pm).

BRITAIN

Central London

● SIGHTS

Albert Memorial, 74	B4	
All Souls Langham Place, 17	C3	
Apsley House, 64	C4	
Bank of England, 26	F3	
Banqueting House, 69	D4	
The Barbican, 14	E3	
British Library, 1	D2	
British Museum, 10	D3	
Buckingham Palace, 76	C4	
Cabinet War Rooms, 79	D4	
Chelsea Physic Garden, 96	C5	

Chinatown, 47	D3	
Design Museum, 59	F4	
The Gilbert Collection, 40	D3	
Gray's Inn, 11	E3	
Hayward Gallery, 71	D4	
HMS Belfast, 57	F4	
The Houses of Parliament, 81	D4	
ICA, 67	D4	
Imperial War Museum, 84	E5	
Jewel Tower, 83	D4	
Kensington Palace, 62	B4	
Lincoln's Inn, 20	E3	
London Eye, 70	D4	
London Planetarium, 5	C3	

Madame Tussaud's, 6	C3	
Millennium Bridge, 52	E4	
Museum of London, 15	E3	
National Gallery, 49	D4	
National History Museum, 85	B5	
National Portrait Gallery, 48	D4	
Old Bailey, 23	E3	
Queen's Gallery, 77	C4	
Royal Academy, 45	D4	
Royal Albert Hall, 75	B4	
Royal Courts of Justice, 21	E3	
The Royal Hospital, 97	C5	
The Royal Mews, 78	C4	

Royal Opera House, **33** — D3
Samuel Johnson's
House, **22** — E3
Savile Row, **44** — D3
Science Museum, **86** — B5
Serpentine Gallery, **63** — B4
Shakespeare's Globe Theatre, **54** — E4
Sherlock Holmes Museum, **4** — C3
Sir John Soane's Museum, **19** — E3
Smithfield Market, **12** — E3
South Bank Centre, **72** — D4
Southwark Cathedral, **55** — E3
St. Bartholomew the Great, **13** — E3

St. Bride's, **39** — E3
St. James's Church, **47** — D4
St. James's Palace, **66** — D4
St. John's Square, **9** — E3
St. Margaret's Westminster, **80** — D4
St. Martin-in-the-Fields, **51** — D4
St. Mary-le-Bow, **25** — E3
St. Mary-le-Strand, **37** — D3
St. Paul's Cathedral, **24** — E3
St. Paul's Church, **34** — D3
Tate Britain, **92** — D5
Tate Modern, **53** — E4

The Temple, **38** — E3
Theatre Royal, Dury Lane, **35** — D3
Tower Bridge, **56** — F4
The Tower of London, **58** — F4
Trafalgar Sq. , **50** — D4
Transport Museum, **36** — D3
University College London, **8** — D3
Victoria and Albert Museum, **87** — B5
The Wallace Collection, **16** — C3
The Wellington Arch, **65** — C4
Westminster Abbey, **82** — D4
Westminster Cathedral, **90** — D5
Whitehall, **68** — D4

BRITAIN

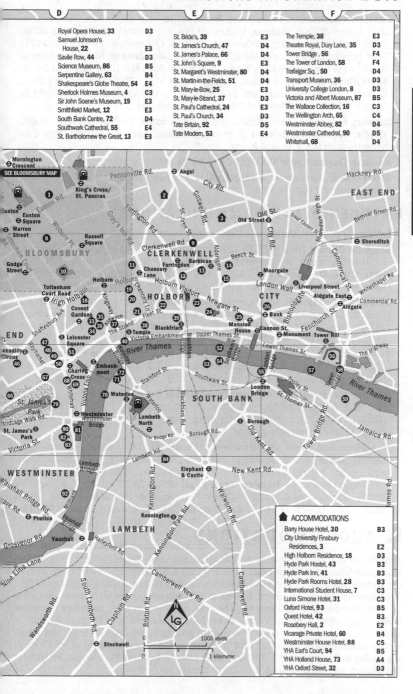

ACCOMMODATIONS
Barry House Hotel, **30** — B3
City University Finsbury
Residences, **3** — E2
High Holbom Residence, **18** — D3
Hyde Park Hostel, **43** — B3
Hyde Park Inn, **41** — B3
Hyde Park Rooms Hotel, **28** — B3
International Student House, **7** — C3
Luna Simone Hotel, **31** — C3
Oxford Hotel, **93** — B5
Quest Hotel, **42** — B3
Rosebery Hall, **2** — E2
Vicarage Private Hotel, **60** — B4
Westminster House Hotel, **88** — C5
YHA Earl's Court, **94** — B5
YHA Holland House, **73** — A4
YHA Oxford Street, **32** — D3

Embassies: Australia, Australia House, The Strand (☎ 7379 4334). Tube: Temple. Open daily 9:30am-3:30pm. **Canada,** MacDonald House, 1 Grosvenor Sq. (☎ 7258 6600). Tube: Bond St. Open daily 8:30am-5pm. **Ireland,** 17 Grosvenor Pl. (☎ 7235 2171). Tube: Hyde Park Corner. Open M-F 9:30am-4:30pm. **New Zealand,** New Zealand House, 80 Haymarket (☎ 7930 8422). Tube: Leicester Sq. Open M-F 10am-noon and 2-4pm. **South Africa,** South Africa House, Trafalgar Sq. (☎ 7451 7299). Tube: Charing Cross. Open M-F 8:45am-12:45pm. **US,** 24 Grosvenor Sq. (☎ 7499 9000). Tube: Bond St. Open M-F 8:30am-12:30pm and 2-5pm. Phones answered 24hr.

Currency Exchange: The best rates are found at banks, such as **Barclays, HSBC, Lloyd's, National Westminster** (NatWest), and **Royal Bank of Scotland.** Most bank branches open M-F 9:30am-4:30pm.

American Express: Call ☎ (0800) 521 313 for the nearest location.

Bi-Gay-Lesbian Resources: London Lesbian and Gay Switchboard (☎ 7837 7324). 24hr. advice and support service.

EMERGENCY AND COMMUNICATIONS

Emergency (Medical, Police, and Fire): ☎ 999; no coins required.

Hospitals: Charing Cross (☎ 8846 1234), on Fulham Palace Rd.; enter on St. Dunstan's Rd. Tube: Baron's Ct. or Hammersmith. **Royal Free** (☎ 7794 0500), on Pond St. Tube: Belsize Park. **St. Thomas's** (☎ 7928 9292), on Lambeth Palace Rd. Tube: Waterloo. **University College Hospital** (☎ 7387 9300), on Grafton Way. Tube: Warren St.

Chemists (Pharmacies): Most chemists keep standard hours (usually M-Sa 9:30am-5:30pm). Late-night and 24hr. chemists are rare; one 24hr. option is **Zafash Pharmacy,** 233 Old Brompton Rd. (☎ 7373 2798). Tube: Earl's Ct. **Bliss Chemists,** 5-6 Marble Arch (☎ 7723 6116). Tube: Marble Arch. Open daily 9am-midnight.

Police: London is covered by two police forces: the **City of London Police** (☎ 7601 2222) for the City, and the **Metropolitan Police** (☎ 7230 1212) for the rest. There is at least one police station in each borough open 24hr. Call to locate the nearest one.

Internet Access: Try the ubiquitous **easyInternet Cafe** (☎ 7241 9000). Locations include 9-16 Tottenham Court Rd. (Tube: Tottenham Court Rd.); 456-459 The Strand (Tube: Charing Cross); and 9-13 Wilson Rd. (Tube: Victoria). From £1 per hr.; min. charge £2. Prices vary with demand. All open 24hr.

Post Office: Post offices are everywhere; call ☎ (08457) 740 740 for locations. When sending mail to London, be sure to include the full postal code, since London has 7 King's Roads, 8 Queen's Roads, and many other opportunities for misdirected mailings. The largest office is the **Trafalgar Square Post Office,** 24-28 William IV St. (☎ 7484 9304). Tube: Charing Cross. All mail sent *Poste Restante* to unspecified post offices ends up here. Open M-Th and Sa 8am-8pm, F 8:30am-8pm. **Postal Code:** WC2N 4DL.

▟ ACCOMMODATIONS

Hostels are not always able to accommodate every written request for reservations, much less on-the-spot inquiries, but they frequently hold a few beds. Sheets are included at all YHA hostels, but towels are not; buy one from reception (£3.50). YHA hostels also sell discount tickets to theaters and major attractions. No YHA hostels have lockouts or curfews. The best deals in town are **university residence halls,** which often rent out rooms over the summer and, less frequently, Easter vacations. Rooms are rarely luxurious, although generally clean and well-equipped. In London, the term **"B&B"** encompasses accommodations of wildly varying quality and personality, often with little relation to price. Plan ahead, especially in summer; accommodations are almost always booked solid.

WESTMINSTER

Pimlico, south of Victoria station, is full of budget hotels; **Belgrave Road** has the highest number. Quality improves the farther you go from the station.

▨ **Westminster House Hotel,** 96 Ebury St. (☎ 7730 7850). Tube: Victoria. The welcoming proprietors keep the 10 rooms spotless. All rooms with TV and almost all with private bath. English breakfast included. Singles £50, with bath £55; doubles £70/£80; triples with bath £90; quads with bath £100. AmEx/MC/V. ❹

▨ **Luna Simone Hotel,** 47-49 Belgrave Rd. (☎ 7834 5897). Tube: Victoria. Modern rooms with TV and phone are concealed by a Victorian facade. English breakfast included. Singles £40, with bath £60; doubles £60/£80; triples with bath £110. Off-season discounts for longer stays. MC/V. ❹

THE WEST END

▨ **High Holborn Residence,** 178 High Holborn (☎ 7379 5589). Tube: Holborn. Comfortable, modern student residence. Suites of 4-5 rooms share phone, kitchen, and bath. Continental breakfast included. Laundry. Open mid-June to late Sept. Singles £29-36; doubles £48-58, with bath £58-68; triples with bath £68-78. MC/V. ❸

YHA Oxford Street, 14-18 Noel St. (☎ 7734 1618). Tube: Oxford Circus. Limited facilities, but an unbeatable location for Soho nightlife. Continental breakfast £3.40. Reserve at least 1 month ahead. Dorms £22, under 18 £17.75; doubles £24. ❷

BAYSWATER

The streets between **Queensway** and **Paddington** station house London's highest concentration of cheap accommodations.

HOSTELS

Hyde Park Hostel, 2-6 Inverness Terr. (☎ 7229 5101). Tube: Queensway or Bayswater. Crowded women's and coed dorms. Private rooms are more spacious and the bathrooms are a cut above average. Continental breakfast included. Internet and kitchen access, bar, cafeteria, laundry, lounge, luggage room. Ages 16-35 only. Reserve at least 2 weeks ahead. Dorms £11-17.50; doubles £42-45. MC/V. ❷

Quest Hotel, 45 Queensborough Terr. (☎ 7229 7782). Tube: Queensway or Bayswater. Better beds and a more personal size than at Hyde Park Hostel, but dorms without bath could be 2 fl. from a shower. Continental breakfast and sheets included. Kitchen access and laundry. Reserve 2-3 weeks ahead. Dorms £14-17; doubles £42. MC/V. ❷

Hyde Park Inn, 48-50 Inverness Terr. (☎ 7229 0000). Tube: Queensway or Bayswater. Cheap and cheerful. Continental breakfast included. Internet and kitchen access. Laundry. Lockers £1. Luggage storage £1.50. Sheets and key deposit £10. Dorms £9-19; singles £29-32; doubles £36-42. MC/V (2.5% surcharge). ❶

B&BS AND HOTELS

▨ **Hyde Park Rooms Hotel,** 137 Sussex Gdns. (☎ 7723 0225). Tube: Paddington. All rooms with sink and TV. June-Aug. reserve ahead. Singles £30, with bath £40; doubles £40-45/£50-55; triples £60/£72; quads £80/£96. AmEx/MC/V (5% surcharge). ❸

Barry House Hotel, 12 Sussex Pl. (☎ 7723 7340). Tube: Paddington. Bright, small rooms with phone, TV, kettle, and hair dryer; most with bath. Singles £38, with bath £52; doubles £75; triples £90; quads £105; quints £120. AmEx/MC/V. ❹

BLOOMSBURY AND MARYLEBONE

Bloomsbury's proximity to Soho makes it well suited for those who want to stay near nightlife. Many B&Bs are on busy roads, so be wary of noise levels. The area becomes seedier closer to King's Cross.

HOSTELS AND STUDENT RESIDENCES

The Generator, Compton Pl. (☎7388 7655), off 37 Tavistock Pl. Tube: Russell Sq. or King's Cross/St. Pancras. In a former police station, this hostel features cell-like units with metal bunks. Basement dorms have lockers and military-style bathrooms. Bar and cafeteria. Internet access. No noise after 9pm. Reserve ahead for weekends. Dorms £15-17; singles £42; doubles £53; triples £68; quads £90. MC/V. ❷

Ashlee House, 261-265 Gray's Inn Rd. (☎7833 9400; www.ashleehouse.co.uk). Tube: King's Cross/St. Pancras. Not the best neighborhood, but convenient to nightlife. Quiet and friendly. Steel bunks crammed into clean, bright rooms. Continental breakfast included. Sightseeing tours Th-Sa. TV room, Internet and kitchen access. Towels £1. Laundry. Dorms £15-£19; singles £36; doubles £48. ❷

International Student House, 229 Great Portland St. (☎7631 8300). Tube: Great Portland St. A thriving international metropolis. Continental breakfast included with private rooms; with dorms £2. 3 bars, cafeteria, fitness center. Internet access. Laundry. Key deposit £10. Reserve at least 1 month ahead. Dorms £10; singles £31, with bath £33; doubles £50/£52; triples £60; quads £70. MC/V. ❷

Carr-Saunders Hall, 18-24 Fitzroy St. (☎7580 6338). Tube: Warren St. Larger rooms than most student halls, with sink and phone. English breakfast included; served on a beautiful terrace. July-Aug. reserve 6-8 weeks ahead. Open Easter vacation and mid-June to mid-Sept. Singles in summer £27, Easter £23.50; doubles £45/£37, with bath £50/£42. MC/V. ❸

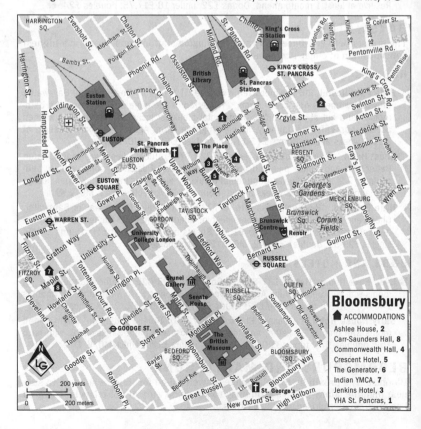

Bloomsbury

🏠 ACCOMMODATIONS

Ashlee House, **2**
Carr-Saunders Hall, **8**
Commonwealth Hall, **4**
Crescent Hotel, **5**
The Generator, **6**
Indian YMCA, **7**
Jenkins Hotel, **3**
YHA St. Pancras, **1**

Commonwealth Hall, 1-11 Cartwright Gdns. (☎ 7685 3500). Tube: Russell Sq. Basic student-residence singles. Unbeatable value. English breakfast included. July-Aug. reserve at least 2 months ahead; no walk-ins. Open Easter vacation and mid-June to mid-Sept. Dorms £22, with dinner £26; UK students £19 (dinner included). MC/V. ❸

YHA St. Pancras International, 79-81 Euston Rd. (☎ 7388 9998). Tube: King's Cross/ St. Pancras. Opposite the British Library. Comfortable dorms, most with bath and A/C. English breakfast included. Dinner (£5) served 6-9pm. Internet and kitchen access. Lockers. Laundry. Reserve at least 2-4 weeks ahead. Dorms £24, under 18 £20; doubles £52, with bath £58; quads with bath £104. AmEx/MC/V. ❸

Indian YMCA, 41 Fitzroy Sq. (☎ 7387 0411). Tube: Warren St. Great location by a Georgian square. Standard rooms with institutional shared bathrooms. Continental breakfast and Indian dinner included. Reservations essential. Dorms £20; singles £34; doubles £46, with bath £52. AmEx/MC/V. ❸

B&BS AND HOTELS

🏨 **Jenkins Hotel,** 45 Cartwright Gdns. (☎ 7387 2067); enter on Barton Pl. Tube: Euston. Bright, non-smoking rooms with antique-style furniture, TV, phone, fridge, hair dryer, and safe. Some baths are very small. Guests can use tennis courts. English breakfast included. Reserve at least 1-2 months ahead. Singles £52, with bath £72; doubles with bath £85; triples with bath £105. MC/V. ❹

🏨 **Crescent Hotel,** 49-50 Cartwright Gdns. (☎ 7387 1515). Tube: Russell Sq. Artistic rooms in a family-run atmosphere. All rooms with TV, tea kettle, wash stand, and phone. Singles £45, with shower £50, with bath £72; doubles with bath £87; triples with bath £97; quads with bath £106. Discounts for longer stays. MC/V. ❹

HOLBORN AND CLERKENWELL

City University Finsbury Residences, 15 Bastwick St. (☎ 7040 8811). Tube: Barbican. Student residence with a grim tower-block facade but renovated interior. Short walk to City sights, Islington restaurants, and Clerkenwell nightlife. English breakfast included. Dinner £4.70. Open late June to mid-Sept. £21 per person, students £19. MC/V. ❸

Rosebery Hall, 90 Rosebery Ave. (☎ 7278 3251). Tube: Angel. Exit left from the Tube, cross the street, and take the second right onto Rosebery Ave. (10min.). Modern student residence by a sunken garden. English breakfast included. Reserve at least 6 weeks ahead; cancellation fee £10. Open Easter vacation and mid-June to mid-Sept. Singles £26-31; doubles £35-46, with bath £58; triples £55. MC/V. ❸

KENSINGTON AND EARL'S COURT

Earl's Court feeds on budget tourism; the area is especially popular with Australian travelers, once earning the nickname "Kangaroo Valley." Be careful at night, and be cautious of guides trying to lead you from the station to a hostel. Some B&Bs conceal grimy rooms behind fancy lobbies and well-dressed staff; always ask to see a room.

🏨 **Vicarage Private Hotel,** 10 Vicarage Gate (☎ 7229 4030). Tube: High St. Kensington. Beautifully kept house with TV lounge and superb rooms. English breakfast included. Singles £46; doubles £76, with bath £100; triples £93; quads £100. ❹

🏨 **Oxford Hotel,** 24 Penywern Rd. (☎ 7370 1161). 3min. from the Connex train to Heathrow or Gatwick. Large rooms with enormous windows afford grand views of the gardens. Continental breakfast included. Reserve at least 3-4 weeks ahead. Singles with shower £36, with bath £50; doubles £57/£67; triples £69/£79; quads £87/£93; quints £105/£115. Discounts for longer stays. AmEx/MC/V. ❹

YHA Holland House, Holland Walk (☎ 7937 0748). Tube: High St. Kensington or Holland Park. On the edge of Holland Park, this hostel has dorms in both a 17th-century mansion and a 1970s unit. Breakfast included. In summer reserve at least 1 month ahead. Dorms £21, under 18 £18.75. AmEx/MC/V. ❸

YHA Earl's Court, 38 Bolton Gdns. (☎ 7373 7083). Tube: Earl's Court. Rambling Victorian townhouse, more casual than most YHAs. Garden. Single-sex dorms. Breakfast included for doubles. Sheets included. Reserve at least 1 month ahead. Dorms £16-19; doubles £52; quads £76. AmEx/MC/V. ❷

◖ FOOD

Forget stale stereotypes: in terms of quality and choice, London's restaurants offer a gastronomic experience as diverse, stylish, and satisfying as you'll find, albeit an expensive one. An entree under £10 is regarded as "cheap"; add drinks and service and you're nudging £15. The trick to eating cheaply and well is knowing where and when to eat. Special offers at lunchtime and in the early evening make it possible to dine in style and stay on budget. While pubs offer hearty staples, many of the best budget meals are found in the variety of ethnic restaurants. For the best ethnic food, head to the source: Whitechapel for Bengali *baltis*, Islington for Turkish *meze*, Marylebone for Lebanese *schwarma*, and Soho for Cantonese *dim sum*.

WESTMINSTER

Jenny Lo's Teahouse, 14 Eccleston St. (☎ 7259 0399). Tube: Victoria. Stripped-down Chinese fare at communal tables. *Cha shao* (pork noodle soup) £5. Teas, from £0.85, are blended in-house and served in hand-turned stoneware. £5 min. Open M-F 11:30am-3pm and 6-10pm, Sa noon-3pm and 6-10pm. ❷

Red Lion, 48 Parliament St. (☎ 7930 5826). Tube: Westminster. The MPs' hangout, where the Chancellor's press secretary was infamously overhead leaking information in 1998. A "division bell" alerts MPs to drink up when a vote is about to be taken. Entrees £3-6. Open M-Sa 11am-11pm, Su noon-7pm; food served daily noon-3pm. MC/V. ❷

THE WEST END

▨ **Mô,** 23 Heddon St. (☎ 7434 3999). Tube: Piccadilly Circus. A "salad bar, tea room, and bazaar," Mô is functionally and aesthetically Marrakesh. Mix and match *tapas*-style dishes £6-7.50. Wash it down with sweet mint tea (£2). No reservations, but very popular—arrive early or late. Open M-W 11am-11pm, Th-Sa noon-midnight. AmEx/MC/V. ❷

▨ **Mr. Kong,** 21 Lisle St. (☎ 7437 7341). You can't go wrong at Mr. Kong. Deep-fried Mongolian lamb £6.50, shark fin soup £6. £7 min. Open daily noon-3am. AmEx/MC/V. ❷

Pâtisserie Valerie, 44 Old Compton St. (☎ 7437 3466). Renowned goodies at this continental patisserie. Delicious croissants £0.90, cakes and pastries £1-3, sandwiches £3-6. Open M-F 7:30am-8pm, Sa 8am-8pm, Su 9:30am-7pm. AmEx/MC/V. ❶

Bar Italia, 22 Frith St. (☎ 7437 4520). Tube: Tottenham Court Rd. A fixture of the late-night Soho scene. Nothing stronger than an espresso here (£1.80), but it's *the* place for a post-club panini (£4-6). £10 min. Open 24hr. except M 3-7am. AmEx/MC/V. ❸

THE CITY OF LONDON

▨ **Futures,** 8 Botolph Alley (☎ 7623 4529), off Botolph Ln. Tube: Monument. Suits besiege this tiny takeaway for breakfast (pastries £0.80, porridge £1) and later for a variety of vegetarian dishes (£2-4). Open M-F 7:30-10am and 11:30am-3pm. ❶

Cafe Spice Namaste, 16 Prescot St. (☎ 7488 9242). Tube: Tower Hill. The standard-bearer for a new breed of Indian restaurants. Carnivalesque decoration brings an exotic feel to this old Victorian warehouse, as does the menu of Goan and Parsee specialities. Meat dishes are on the pricey side (£11-13), but vegetarian meals are a bargain (£7-8). Open M-F noon-3pm and 6:15-10:30pm, Sa 6:30-10pm. AmEx/MC/V. ❸

THE SOUTH BANK

■ **Cantina del Ponte,** 36c Shad Thames (☎ 7403 5403), Butler's Wharf. Tube: Tower Hill or London Bridge. Amazing riverside location and high-quality Italian food. Bargain fixed menu £10 for 2 courses, £12.50 for 3 (available M-F noon-3pm and 6-7:30pm). Pizzas £7-8, entrees £12-15. Live Italian music Tu and Th evenings. Open M-Sa noon-3pm and 6-10:45pm, Su noon-3pm and 6-9:45pm. MC/V. ❸

BAYSWATER

■ **Royal China,** 13 Queensway (☎ 7221 2535). Tube: Bayswater. Renowned for London's best *dim sum* (£2-3 per dish; count on 3-4 dishes per person), served M-Sa noon-5pm, Su 11am-5pm. On weekends arrive early or expect to wait 30-45min. Open M-Th noon-11pm, F-Sa noon-11:30pm, Su 11am-10pm. AmEx/MC/V. ❷

BLOOMSBURY AND MARYLEBONE

■ **Diwana Bhel Poori House,** 121-123 Drummond St. (☎ 7387 5556). Tube: Euston Square. No frippery here—just great, cheap south-Indian vegetarian food. Filling *Paneer Dosa* (rice pancake stuffed with potato and cheese) £5. *Thali* fixed meals (£4-6) offer great value. Open daily noon-11:30pm. AmEx/MC/V. ❷

ICCo (Italiano Coffee Co.), 46 Goodge St. (☎ 7580 9250). 11-inch thin-crust pizzas, made to order, cost an incredible £3.50. Sandwiches and baguettes from £1.50, rolls from £0.50. Buy any hot drink before noon and get a fresh-baked croissant for free. Pizzas available after noon. Open M-Sa 7am-11pm, Su 9am-11pm. ❶

HOLBORN AND CLERKENWELL

■ **Bleeding Heart Tavern** (☎ 7404 0333), on the corner of Greville St. and Bleeding Heart Yard. Tube: Farringdon. Light, laid-back upstairs pub and cozy restaurant below. Restaurant decor provides a romantic backdrop to the hearty English fare, which includes spit-roasted pork with crackling. Entrees £8-10. Open M-F noon-10:30pm. AmEx/MC/V. ❷

Ye Olde Cheshire Cheese, 145 Fleet St. (☎ 7353 6170), in Wine Office Ct. Tube: Black-friars. Dark labyrinth of oak-panelled rooms on 3 fl., dating from 1667; a one-time haunt of Johnson, Dickens, Twain, and Teddy Roosevelt. Multiple bars and restaurants dish out traditional English food at many price ranges. Food served M-F noon-9:30pm, Sa noon-2:30pm and 6-9:30pm, Su noon-2:30pm. Open M-F 11:30am-11pm, Sa 11:30am-3pm and 5:30-11pm, Su noon-3pm. AmEx/MC/V. ❸

Tinseltown 24-Hour Diner, 44-46 St. John St. (☎ 7689 2424). Tube: Farringdon. Cavernous underground haven for pre- and post-clubbers. Burgers (£5.50) and shakes (£3.50). Open 24hr. ❶

KENSINGTON AND EARL'S COURT

■ **Zaika,** 1 Kensington High St. (☎ 7795 6533). Tube: High St. Kensington. Arguably London's best Indian restaurant: elegant decor, attentive service, and sophisticated food. Appetizers £6-8, entrees £13-18, desserts £4-5. 2-course min. for dinner. Lunch fixed menu £12 for 2 courses, £14 for 3. 5-course dinner menu £33.50, with wine £40. Dinner reservations recommended. Lunch M-F noon-2:30pm, Su noon-2:45pm; dinner M-Sa 6:30-10:45pm, Su 6:30-9:45pm. MC/V. ❺

Raison d'Être, 18 Bute St. (☎ 7584 5008). Tube: South Kensington. Caters to the local French community with a bewildering range of filled *baguettes* (£2-5) and *salades* (£3.50-4.70). Open M-F 8am-6pm, Sa 9:30am-4pm. ❶

NOTTING HILL

■ **George's Portobello Fish Bar,** 329 Portobello Rd. (☎8969 7895). Tube: Ladbroke Grove. Choose from the fillets on display or ask them to fry up a new one (£4-5), add a generous helping of chunky chips (£1), and wolf it down outside (no inside seating). Open M-F 11am-midnight, Sa 11am-9pm, Su noon-9pm. ❶

■ **The Grain Shop,** 269a Portobello Rd. (☎7229 5571). Tube: Ladbroke Grove. It's hard to ignore the aromatic invitation of this mini-bakery. The generous homemade pastries and salads are phenomenal; mix as many dishes as you like to make a small (£2.25), medium (£3.45), or gut-busting large (£4.60) takeaway box. The line is long but fast-moving. Organic breads baked on-site (£1-2). Open M-Sa 9:30am-6pm. MC/V. ❶

AFTERNOON TEA

Afternoon tea provides a great chance to lounge in sumptuous surroundings that at any other time would be beyond all but a Sultan's budget.

The Lanesborough, Hyde Park Corner (☎7259 5599). Tube: Hyde Park Corner. For sheer opulence, the interior of The Lanesborough out-ritzes The Ritz. Set tea £23, champagne tea £27. A la carte, including scones with jam and clotted cream, £6.50. Dress code: smart casual. £9.50 per person min. ❸

The Ritz, on Piccadilly (☎7493 8181). Tube: Green Park. The world's most famous tea (£27). Reserve at least 1 month ahead for the weekday sittings, 3 months for weekends; alternatively, skip lunch and arrive at noon for an early tea. No jeans or sneakers; jacket and tie preferred for men. Sittings at 3:30 and 5pm daily. AmEx/MC/V. ❺

◉ SIGHTS

ORGANIZED TOURS

The classic London **bus tour** is on an open-top double-decker; in good weather, it's undoubtedly the best way to get a good overview of the city. Tickets for the **Big Bus Company,** 48 Buckingham Palace Rd., are valid for 24hr. on three hop-on, hop-off routes, with 1hr. walking tours and a short Thames cruise included. (☎7233 9533; www.bigbus.co.uk. Tube: Victoria. £16, children £6.) For a more in-depth account, you can't beat a **walking tour** led by a knowledgeable guide. **Original London Walks** is the biggest walking-tour company, running 12-16 walks per day, from the "Magical Mystery Tour" to the nighttime "Jack the Ripper's Haunts" and guided visits to larger museums. Most walks last 2hr. and start from Tube stations. (☎7624 3978; www.walks.com. £5, students and seniors £4, under 16 free.)

WESTMINSTER

The City of Westminster has been the seat of British power for over a thousand years.

BUCKINGHAM PALACE

The Mall; entrance to State Rooms on Buckingham Palace Rd. Tube: Victoria, Green Park, or St. James's Park. ☎7839 1377. State Rooms open early Aug. to Sept. daily 9:30am-4:30pm. Tickets ☎7321 2233. Ticket Office in Green Park open late July to Sept. £11.

Originally built for the Dukes of Buckingham, Buckingham House was acquired by George III in 1762 and converted into a full-scale palace by George IV. During the summer opening of the **State Rooms,** visitors have access to the **Throne Room,** the **Galleries,** and the **Music Room,** where Mendelssohn played for Queen Victoria, among others. In the opulent **White Room,** the large mirrored fireplace hides a door used by the Royal Family at formal dinners. Since 2001, Queen Elizabeth has also allowed visitors to take a brief excursion into the **gardens.**

CHANGING OF THE GUARD. The Palace is protected by a detachment of Foot Guards in full dress uniform. Accompanied by a band, the "New Guard" starts marching down Birdcage Walk from Wellington Barracks around 10:30am, while the "Old Guard" leaves St. James's Palace around 11:10am. When they meet at the gates of the palace, the officers touch hands, symbolically exchanging keys, *et voilà*, the guard is changed. Show up well before 11:30am and stand directly in front of the palace; for a less-crowded close-up of the marching guards, stand along the Mall between the Victoria Memorial and St. James's Palace or along Birdcage Walk. *(Daily Apr.-Oct., every other day Nov.-Mar. Dependent on whether the Queen is in residence, the weather, and state functions. Free.)*

WESTMINSTER ABBEY

Parliament Sq.; enter the Old Monastery, Cloister, and Garden from Dean's Yard, behind the Abbey. Abbey ☎ 7222 7110; Old Monastery ☎ 7222 5897. Tube: Westminster. Abbey open M-Tu and Th-F 9:30am-3:45pm, W 9:30am-7pm, Sa 9:30am-1:45pm, Su for services only. Museum open daily 10:30am-4pm. Chapter House open Apr.-Oct. daily 9:30am-4:45pm; Nov.-Mar. 10am-4pm. Cloisters open daily 8am-6pm. Abbey £6, students £3; services free. Chapter House £1. Cloisters and Garden free.

On December 28, 1065, Edward the Confessor, the last Saxon King of England, was buried in the church of the West Monastery; a year later, the Abbey saw the coronation of William the Conqueror, thus establishing the Abbey's twin traditions as the figurative birthplace and literal resting place of royalty. It was this connection that allowed Westminster, uniquely among England's great monasteries, to escape wholesale destruction during Henry VIII's campaign against the Pope.

The **north transept** contains memorials to Victorian statesmen, including Prime Ministers Disraeli and Gladstone. Early English kings are buried around the Confessor's tomb in the **Shrine of St. Edward,** behind which the **Coronation Chair** stands at the entry to the Tudor **Lady Chapel.** Henry VII and his wife Elizabeth lie at the end of the chapel. Queen Elizabeth I and the cousin she beheaded, Mary Queen of Scots, are buried on opposite sides of the chapel. **Poet's Corner** begins with Geoffrey Chaucer, buried in 1400; plaques at his feet commemorate both poets and prose writers, as does the stained-glass window above. At the center of the Abbey, the **Sanctuary** holds the altar, where coronations and royal weddings are held. After a detour through the **Cloisters,** visitors re-enter the nave. At the western end is the **Tomb of the Unknown Warrior,** whose epitaph is

inscribed in molten bullets; just beyond is the simple grave of **Winston Churchill.** The north aisle holds **Scientists' Corners,** with physicists and biologists resting around the tombs of Isaac Newton and Charles Darwin respectively. The **Old Monastery** houses the **Great Cloister,** festooned with monuments and plaques, from which passages lead to the **Chapter House,** the original meeting place of Parliament, the **Pyx Chamber,** formerly the Abbey treasury, and the **Abbey Museum,** which features an array of royal funeral effigies. The pleasant **Gardens** are reached from the Cloisters; concerts are occasionally held here in summer.

THE HOUSES OF PARLIAMENT

Parliament Sq. Tube: Westminster. ☎ 7219 4272. Debates open to all while Parliament is in session (Oct.-July). Advance tickets required for Prime Minister's Question Time (W 3-3:30pm). M-Th after 6pm and F are least busy. Lords usually sits M-W from 2:30pm, Th 3pm, occasionally F 11:30am; closing times vary. Commons sits M-W 2:30-10:30pm, Th 11:30am-7:30pm, F 9:30am-3pm. Free. Tours Aug.-Sept. M-Sa 9:15am-4:30pm; reserve through Firstcall (☎ 0870 906 3773). £7, students £3.50.

The Palace of Westminster, as the building in which Parliament sits is officially known, has been at the heart of English government since the 11th century, when Edward the Confessor established his court here. William the Conqueror found the site to his liking, and under the Normans the palace was greatly extended. Westminster Hall aside, little of the Norman palace remained after the massive fire of October 16, 1834; the rebuilding started in 1835 under the joint command of Charles Barry and Augustus Pugin.

OUTSIDE THE HOUSES. A statue of Oliver Cromwell, the sole survivor of the 1834 fire, stands in front of the midpoint of the complex, **Westminster Hall.** Unremarkable from the outside, the Hall's chief feature is a magnificent hammer-beam roof, constructed in 1394 and considered the finest timber roof ever made. During its centuries as a court of law, famous defendants included Thomas More and Charles I. Today, it is used for public ceremonies and occasional exhibitions. The **Clock Tower** is universally miscalled **Big Ben,** which actually refers only to the bell within; it's named after the robustly proportioned Sir Benjamin Hall, who served as Commissioner of Works when the bell was cast in 1858.

DEBATING CHAMBERS. Visitors to the debating chambers first pass through **St. Stephen's Hall.** Formerly the king's private chapel, in 1550 St. Stephen's became the meeting place of the House of Commons. At the end of the hall, the **Central Lobby** marks the separation between the two houses, with the Commons to the north and the Lords to the south. The ostentatious **House of Lords** is dominated by the **Throne of State,** under a gilt canopy. The Lord Chancellor presides over the Peers from the giant red **Woolsack.** In contrast is the restrained **House of Commons,** with simple green-backed benches under a plain wooden roof. The **Speaker** sits at the rear of the chamber, with government MPs to his right and the opposition to his left. With seating for only 437 out of 635 MPs, things get hectic when all are present.

TRAFALGAR SQUARE AND THE STRAND

John Nash suggested the design of **Trafalgar Square** in 1820 to commemorate Nelson's 1805 victory over Napoleon's navy at the Battle of Trafalgar. Nelson stands atop his fluted pillar with four bronze lions below. The reliefs at the column's base are cast from captured French and Spanish cannons. Every December the square hosts a giant **Christmas Tree,** donated by Norway to thank the British for assistance against the Nazis. (Tube: Charing Cross)

ST. MARTIN-IN-THE-FIELDS. James Gibbs's 1720s creation was the model for countless Georgian churches in Britain and America. It's still the Queen's parish church; look for the royal box to the left of the altar. The **crypt** downstairs has a life of its own, home to a cafe, bookshop, art gallery, and the **London Brass Rubbing Centre.** *(St. Martin's Lane, in the northeast corner of Trafalgar Sq. Tube: Leicester Sq. Brass Rubbing Centre open daily 10am-7pm. Rubbings £3-15.)*

SOMERSET HOUSE. A magnificent Palladian structure completed in 1790, Somerset House was London's first intended office block. Originally home to the Royal Academy and the Royal Society, the building now harbors the magnificent **Courtauld Institute** (see p. 162). From mid-December to mid-January the central **Fountain Courtyard** is iced over to make an open-air rink. *(On the Strand. Tube: Charing Cross. Courtyard open daily 7:30am-11pm. Free. Tours Sa 1:30 and 3:45pm. £2.75.)*

OTHER WESTMINSTER SIGHTS

WHITEHALL. A long stretch of imposing facades housing government ministries, Whitehall is synonymous with the British civil service. From 1532 until a fire in 1698, Whitehall was the main royal palace. All that remains is Inigo Jones's **Banqueting House,** which features magnificent ceiling paintings by Rubens. Charles I was executed on a scaffold outside the house in 1649. *(Whitehall. Tube: Westminster. Open M-Sa 10am-5pm; last admission 4:30pm. £4, students and seniors £3.)* Opposite Banqueting House, tourists line up to be photographed with the Household Cavalry at **Horseguards;** the guard is changed Monday to Friday at 11am and Saturday at 10am. Just off Whitehall, King James St. leads to the **Cabinet War Rooms** (see p. 162). Current Prime Minister Tony Blair lives on **Downing Street,** separated from Whitehall by steel gates. The Prime Minister traditionally lives at #10, but Tony's family is so big that he's had to swap with the Chancellor, Gordon Brown, at #11.

WESTMINSTER CATHEDRAL. Westminster, London's first Catholic cathedral after Henry VIII espoused Protestantism, was started in 1887; in 1903, money ran out, leaving the interior only partially completed. The blackened brick domes contrast dramatically with the swirling marble of the lower walls and the magnificence of the side chapels. An elevator carries visitors up the striped 90m **bell tower.** *(Cathedral Piazza, off Victoria St. Tube: Victoria. Cathedral open daily 7am-7pm. Suggested donation £2. Bell tower open Apr.-Nov. daily 9am-5pm; Dec.-Mar. Th-Su 9am-5pm. £2, students £1.)*

THE WEST END

MAYFAIR AND ST. JAMES'S

Home to Prince Charles, the Ritz, and exclusive gentlemen's clubs, this is London's aristocratic quarter. On **Jermyn St.,** one block south of Piccadilly, stores cater to the tastes of the traditional English squire with hand-cut suits and hunting gear. The only one of Piccadilly's aristocratic mansions that stands today, **Burlington House** was built in 1665. Today, it houses numerous regal societies, including the **Royal Academy,** heart of the British artistic establishment and home to some excellent exhibitions (see p. 162). Prince Charles lives in **St. James's Palace,** between the Mall and Pall Mall, built in 1536. The only part of the palace open to the public is the **Chapel Royal,** open for Sunday services from October to Easter at 8:30 and 11am. (Tube: Green Park.) From Easter to September, services are held in **Queen's Chapel,** across Marlborough Rd.

SOHO

Soho has a history of welcoming all colors and creeds to its streets. The first settlers were French Huguenots fleeing religious persecution in the 17th century. These days, a concentration of gay-owned restaurants and bars has turned **Old Compton Street** into the heart of gay London.

PICCADILLY CIRCUS. In the glow of lurid neon signs, five of the West End's major arteries merge and swirl round the **statue of Eros,** dedicated to the Victorian philanthropist, Lord Shaftesbury. Eros originally pointed down Shaftesbury Ave., but recent restoration work has put his aim significantly off. *(Tube: Piccadilly Circus.)*

LEICESTER SQUARE. Amusements at this entertainment nexus range from London's largest cinema to the **Swiss Centre** glockenspiel, whose atonal renditions of Beethoven's *Moonlight Sonata* are enough to make even the tone-deaf weep. Be true to your inner tourist by having your name engraved on a grain of rice and sitting for a caricature. *(Tube: Leicester Sq. or Piccadilly Circus.)*

CHINATOWN. The pedestrian, tourist-ridden **Gerrard Street,** with dragon gates and pagoda-capped phone booths, is the heart of London's tiny slice of Canton, but gritty **Lisle Street,** one block to the south, has a more authentic feel. Chinatown is most vibrant during the raucous Chinese New Year in February. *(Between Leicester Sq., Shaftesbury Ave., and Charing Cross Rd.)*

COVENT GARDEN

The Covent Garden piazza, designed by Inigo Jones in the 17th century, is one of the few parts of London popular with locals and tourists alike. On the very spot where England's first Punch and Judy show was performed, street entertainers delight the thousands who flock here year round. (Tube: Covent Garden.)

THE ROYAL OPERA HOUSE. The Royal Opera House reopened in 2000 after a major expansion. After wandering the ornate lobby of the original 1858 theater, head up to the enormous **Floral Hall.** From there, take the escalator to reach the **terrace,** which has great views of London. *(Bow St. Open daily 10am-3:30pm. 1¼hr. backstage tours M-Sa 10:30am, 12:30 and 2:30pm; reservations essential. £8, students £7.)*

THEATRE ROYAL DRURY LANE. Founded in 1663, this is the oldest of London's surviving theaters. Pieces of Drury Lane lore are brought back to life in the backstage tours. *(Entrance on Catherine St. Tours M-Tu and Th-F 2:15 and 4:45pm, W and Sa 10:15am and noon. £8.50, children £6.50.)*

THE CITY OF LONDON

Until the 18th century, the City *was* London; the was rest merely outlying villages. Yet its modern appearance belies a 2000-year history; what few buildings survived the Great Fire of 1666 and WWII bombings are now overshadowed by giant temples of commerce. The second half of the 20th century has had an even more profound effect on the City than the cosmetic rearrangement of the Blitz: as its power in international finance grew, the City's relevance to ordinary Londoners diminished. Nowadays, of the 300,000 who work here, only 8000 people call the City home. The **City of London Information Centre,** in St. Paul's Churchyard, offers acres of leaflets and maps, sells tickets to sights and shows, and provides info on a host of traditional municipal events. (☎ 7332 1456. Tube: St. Paul's. Open Apr.-Sept. daily 9:30am-5pm; Oct.-Mar. M-F 9:30am-5pm, Sa 9:30am-12:30pm.)

ST. PAUL'S CATHEDRAL

St. Paul's Churchyard. ☎ 7246 8348; www.stpauls.co.uk. Tube: St. Paul's. Open M-Sa 8:30am-4pm; open for worship daily 7:15am-6pm. £6, students £5; worshippers free. Audio tours £3.50, students £3. 1½hr. tours M-F 4 per day; £2.50, students £2.

Sir Christopher Wren's masterpiece is the fifth cathedral to occupy the site; the original was built in AD 604. With space to seat 2500 worshippers, the **nave** is festooned with monuments to great Britons. The tombs, including those of Nelson, Wellington, and Florence Nightingale, are all downstairs in the **crypt.** Surrounded by Blake, Turner, and Henry Moore, Christopher Wren lies beneath the epitaph

Lector, si monumentum requiris circumspice ("Reader, if you seek his monument, look around"). To see the inside of the second-tallest freestanding **dome** in Europe (after St. Peter's in the Vatican), climb the 259 steps to the **Whispering Gallery.** The gallery is a perfect resounding chamber: whisper into the wall, and your friend on the opposite side should be able to hear you. From here, 119 more steps lead to **Stone Gallery,** on the outer base of the dome, and it's another 152 to the summit's **Golden Gallery.** Back inside, the mosaic of *Christ Seated in Majesty* overlooks the marble **High Altar.** The statue of **John Donne** in the south quire aisle is one of the few monuments to survive from Old St. Paul's.

THE TOWER OF LONDON

Tower Hill. ☎ 7709 0765; www.hrp.org.uk. Tube: Tower Hill. Open Mar.-Oct. M-Sa 9am-5:30pm, Su 10am-5:30pm; Nov.-Feb. M 10am-4:30pm, Tu-Sa 9am-5:30pm. £11.50, students £8.75. Tickets also sold at Tube stations; buy them in advance to avoid horrendous lines. Audio tours £3. 1hr. tours M-Sa 9:30am-3:30pm, Su 10am-3:30pm; free.

The Tower of London, palace and prison of English monarchs for over 900 years, is steeped in blood and history. Conceived by William the Conqueror in 1067 to provide protection *from* rather than *to* his new subjects, the original wooden palisade was replaced by a stone structure in 1078 that over the next 20 years would grow into the **White Tower.** Colorfully dressed Yeomen Warders, or "Beefeaters" (a reference to their former daily allowance of meat), serve as guards and tourist guides; to be eligible for Beefeaterhood, candidates must have 20 years of distinguished service in the armed forces.

From the western entrance near the **Middle Tower,** you pass over the old moat, now a garden, entering the **Outer Ward** though **Byward Tower.** Just beyond Byward Tower is a massive **Bell Tower,** dating from 1190; the curfew bell has been rung nightly for over 500 years. The stretch of the Outer Ward along the Thames is **Water Lane,** which until the 16th century was adjacent to the river. **Traitor's Gate** is associated with the prisoners who passed through it on their way to execution at **Tower Green.** Some of the victims are buried in the **Chapel Royal of St. Peter and Vincula,** including Catholic martyr Sir Thomas More and Henry VIII's wives Catherine Howard and Anne Boleyn. The green abuts the White Tower, now home to a fearsome display of arms and armor from the Royal Armory. Across the green is the **Bloody Tower,** so named because Richard III allegedly imprisoned and then murdered his nephews here before usurping the throne in 1483.

The most famous sights in the Tower are the **Crown Jewels;** moving walkways ensure no awestruck gazers hold up the queue. While the eye is naturally drawn to the **Imperial State Crown,** don't miss the **Sceptre with the Cross,** topped with the First Star of Africa, the largest quality-cut diamond in the world. Other famous gems include the **Koh-i-Noor,** set into the **Queen Mother's Crown;** legend claims the stone will bring luck only to women. These jewels, along with retired crowns and other treasures, are displayed in the **Martin Tower,** at the end of **Wall Walk.**

OTHER CITY OF LONDON SIGHTS

BANK OF ENGLAND AND ENVIRONS. Government financial difficulties led to the founding of the **Bank of England** (a.k.a. "The Old Lady of Threadneedle St.") in 1694—the bank's creditors supplied £1.2 million, and the national debt was born. Other hallowed institutions stand on the streets nearby: the **Stock Exchange,** on Throgmorton St.; the **Royal Exchange,** between Cornhill and Threadneedle St., founded in 1566; and the 18th-century **Mansion House,** on Walbrook, the official residence of the Lord Mayor. The most famous modern structure in the City is **Lloyd's of London,** on Leadenhall, designed by Richard Rogers. With metal ducts, lifts, and chutes on the outside, it wears its heart on its sleeve. *(Tube: Bank.)*

MONUMENT. Raised in 1677, Christopher Wren's 202 ft. column stands exactly that distance from the bakery on Pudding Lane where the Great Fire started in 1666. *(Monument St. Tube: Monument. Open daily 9:30am-5pm. £1.50.)*

TOWER BRIDGE. This iconic symbol of London is often mistaken for its plain upriver sibling, London Bridge—the story goes that when an Arizona millionaire bought the previous London Bridge and shifted it stone-by-stone to the US, he thought he was getting Tower Bridge. The **Tower Bridge Experience** offers a cutesy introduction to the history and technology of the unique lifting mechanism, though the view isn't all it's cracked up to be. *(Tube: Tower Hill. Open daily 9:30am-6pm; last admission 5pm. £4.50, students £3.)*

WREN CHURCHES. Aside from St. Paul's Cathedral, the City's greatest architectural treasures are the 22 surviving churches designed by Christopher Wren to replace those lost in the Great Fire of 1666. The most famous is **St. Mary-le-Bow;** traditionally, the term "cockney" is reserved for those born within range of its bells. For the past 800 years, the Archbishop of Canterbury has sworn in bishops in the 11th-century crypt, whose "bows" (arches) gave the church its epithet. *(On Cheapside, near Bow Ln. Tube: St. Paul's. Open M-F 6:30am-6pm. Free.)*

THE SOUTH BANK

From the Middle Ages until Cromwell's arrival, the South Bank was London's center of amusement; banished from the strictly regulated City, all manner of illicit attractions sprouted in "the Borough" at the southern end of London Bridge. Today, the South Bank is once again at the heart of London entertainment, with some of the city's top concert halls, theaters, cinemas, and galleries.

LONDON EYE. At 135m, the London Eye, also known as the Millennium Wheel, is the world's biggest observational wheel. The ellipsoid glass "pods" give uninterrupted views at the top of each 30min. revolution; on clear days, Windsor is visible to the west. *(Jubilee Gardens, between County Hall and the Festival Hall. Tube: Waterloo. Open late May to early Sept. daily 9:30am-10pm; Apr. to late May and late Sept. 10:30am-8pm; Oct.-Mar. 10:30am-7pm; the ticket office, in the corner of County Hall, opens 30min. earlier; advance booking recommended. May-Sept. £10.50; Oct.-June £9.50.)*

THE SOUTH BANK CENTRE. Sprawling on either side of Waterloo Bridge, this concrete complex is Britain's premier cultural center. Its nucleus is the **Royal Festival Hall,** a classic piece of white 1950s architecture. Nearby, the **Purcell Room** and **Queen Elizabeth Hall** host smaller concerts, while just behind, the **Hayward Gallery** shelters excellent modern art exhibitions. The **National Film Theatre,** on the embankment beneath the bridge, offers London's most varied cinematic fare, while the **National Theatre** (see p. 163) looms past the bridge. To find out how one of the world's largest, most modern theaters operates, join a backstage tour. *(On the riverbank between Hungerford and Waterloo Bridges. Tube: Waterloo. Tours M-Sa 10:15am, 12:15 and 5:15pm. £5, students £4.25.)*

TATE MODERN AND THE MILLENNIUM BRIDGE. Squarely opposite each other on Bankside are the biggest success and most abject failure of London's millennial celebrations. **Tate Modern** (see p. 161), created from the shell of the Bankside power station, is as visually arresting as its contents are thought-provoking. The **Millennium Bridge,** built to link the Tate to the City, was completed six months too late for the Y2K festivities and, following a literally shaky debut, has only recently been stabilized. *(Queen's Walk, Bankside. Tube: Southwark.)*

SHAKESPEARE'S GLOBE THEATRE. In the shadow of Tate Modern, the half-timbered Globe, opened in 1997, sits just 200m from where the original burned down in 1613. Try to arrive in time for a tour of the theater itself, given on mornings during the performance season. *(Bankside. Tube: Southwark. Open May-Sept. daily 9am-noon and 1-4pm; Oct.-Apr. 10am-5pm. £8, students £6.50. See also p. 163.)* Nearby lie the ruins of the 1587 **Rose Theatre,** where both Shakespeare and Marlowe performed. The site was rediscovered in 1989; not much is left, though the outline is clearly visible. *(56 Park St. Open daily 11am-5pm. £4, students £3; £1 discount with same-day Globe ticket.)*

BLOOMSBURY AND MARYLEBONE

Marylebone's most famous resident (and address) never existed: 221b Baker St. was the fictional lodging house of Sherlock Holmes. The **Sherlock Holmes Museum** gives its address as 221b, although a little sleuthing will reveal that it in fact stands at #239. Bloomsbury's intellectual reputation was bolstered in the early 20th century when Gordon Sq., east of Marylebone, resounded with the philosophizing of the **Bloomsbury Group,** an early 20th-century coterie of intellectuals that included Virginia Woolf, John Maynard Keynes, and Bertrand Russell.

▓ BRITISH LIBRARY. Since its 1998 opening, the new British Library has won acclamation from visitors and users alike. The 325km of underground shelving can hold up to 12 million books. The library also houses a dramatic glass cube containing the 65,000 volumes of George III's King's Library, and a stunning display of books, manuscripts, and artifacts, from the 2nd-century *Unknown Gospel* to Joyce's handwritten draft of *Finnegan's Wake*. *(96 Euston Rd. ☎ 7412 7332. Tube: King's Cross. Open M and W-F 9:30am-6pm, Tu 9:30am-8pm, Sa 9:30am-5pm, Su 11am-5pm. Free. Tours M, W, F-Sa 3pm, also Sa 10:30am. £5, students £3.50. Tours including one reading room Tu 6:30pm, Su 11:30am and 3pm. £6, £4.50. Reservations recommended for all tours.)*

ACADEMIA. The strip of land along **Gower Street** and immediately to its west is London's academic heartland. Established in 1828, **University College London** was the first in Britain to admit Catholics, Jews, and women. The embalmed body of founder **Jeremy Bentham** has occupied the South Cloister since 1850. *(Main entrance on Gower St. South Cloister entrance through the courtyard. Tube: Warren St.)* Now the administrative headquarters of the University of London, **Senate House** was the model for the Ministry of Truth in *1984;* George Orwell worked there as part of the BBC propaganda unit in WWII. *(At the southern end of Malet St. Tube: Goodge St.)*

HOLBORN AND CLERKENWELL

Squeezed between the capitalism of the City and the commercialism of the West End, Holborn is historically the home of two of the world's least-loved professions—lawyers and journalists.

INNS OF COURT. These venerable institutions house the chambers of practicing barristers and provide apprenticeships for law students. Most impressive of the four Inns are those of the **Middle** and **Inner Temple,** south of Fleet St. *(Between Fleet St., Essex St., Victoria Embankment, and Temple Ave./Bouvier St. Numerous passages lead from these streets into the Temple. Tube: Temple.)* The 12th-century **Temple Church** is the finest surviving round church in England. *(Open W-Th 11am-4pm, Sa 10am-2:30pm, Su 12:45-4pm. Free.)* Shakespeare premiered *Twelfth Night* in front of Elizabeth I in **Middle Temple Hall,** whose large wooden dining table is made from the hatch of Sir Francis Drake's *Golden Hinde*. According to Shakespeare's *Henry VI*, the red-and-white flowers of the War of the Roses were plucked in **Middle Temple Garden,** south of the hall. *(Garden open May-Sept. M-F noon-3pm. Free.)*

FLEET STREET. Named for the river (now underground) that flows from Hampstead to the Thames, Fleet Street's association with publishing goes back to the days when Wyken de Worde relocated from Westminster to the precincts of **St. Bride's** church, ever since known as "the printer's cathedral." Christopher Wren's odd steeple is the original inspiration for the tiered wedding cake, invented by a local baker. *(On St. Bride's Ave., just off Fleet St. Tube: Temple. Open daily 8am-4:45pm. Free.)*

ROYAL COURTS OF JUSTICE. This elaborate neo-Gothic structure—easily mistaken for a cathedral—straddles the official division between Westminster and the City of London; the courtrooms are open to the public during cases. *(Where the Strand becomes Fleet St. Tube: Temple. Open M-F 9am-6pm. Cases start 10am.)*

KENSINGTON

Nobody took much notice of Kensington before 1689, when the newly crowned William III and Mary II moved into Kensington Palace. Then, in 1851, the Great Exhibition brought in enough money to finance the museums and colleges of South Kensington. Now the neighborhood is home to London's most expensive stores, including Harrods and Harvey Nichols, and it's hard to imagine the days when the area was known for its taverns and its highwaymen.

KENSINGTON PALACE. Remodelled by Wren for William III and Mary II, parts of the palace are still in use today as a royal residence. Princess Diana lived here until her death. The **Royal Ceremonial Dress Collection** features 19th-century court costumes along with the Queen's demure evening gowns and some of Diana's sexier numbers. *(On the eastern edge of Kensington Gardens; enter through the park. Tube: High St. Kensington. Open Mar.-Oct. daily 10am-6pm; Nov.-Feb. 10am-5pm. £10, students £7.50.)*

HYDE PARK AND KENSINGTON GARDENS. Surrounded by London's wealthiest neighborhoods, giant Hyde Park has served as the model for city parks around the world, including Central Park in New York and Bois de Boulogne in Paris. **Kensington Gardens,** to the west, is contiguous with Hyde Park. The 41-acre **Serpentine** was created in 1730; innumerable people pay to row and swim here. At the northeastern corner of the park, near Marble Arch, proselytizers, politicos, and flat-out crazies dispense their knowledge to bemused tourists at **Speaker's Corner** on Sundays. *(Tube: Queensway, Lancaster Gate, Marble Arch, Hyde Park Corner, or High St. Kensington. Hyde Park open daily 5am-midnight. Kensington Gardens open dawn-dusk. Both free.)*

NORTH LONDON

CAMDEN TOWN. An island of good, honest tawdriness in an increasingly affluent sea, Camden Town has effortlessly thrown off attempts at gentrification thanks to the ever-growing **Camden Markets** (see p. 165).

HAMPSTEAD HEATH. Hampstead Heath is one of the last remaining commons in England, open to all since 1312. **Parliament Hill** is the highest open space in London, with excellent views of the city. Farther north, ■**Kenwood** is an 18th-century country estate, designed by Robert Adams for the first Earl of Mansfield and home to the impressive **Iveagh Bequest** of Old Masters, including works by Rembrandt, Vermeer, Turner, and Botticelli. *(Tube: Hampstead. Rail: Hampstead Heath. A 20min. walk from the station. Kenwood open Apr.-Sept. daily 8am-8pm; Oct.-Mar. 8am-4pm.)*

EAST LONDON

THE EAST END AND DOCKLANDS. Whitechapel is the oldest part of the East End. In the 19th century it was thronged with Jewish refugees from Eastern Europe; today it's the heart of London's Bangladeshi community, which centers around the restaurants, spice shops, and markets of **Brick Lane.** The most recent wave of immigrants is made up of artists. *(Tube: Aldgate East or Liverpool St.)* The area of the East End along the river is known as the **Docklands.** This man-made archipelago of docks and wharves was for centuries the commercial heart of the British Empire. In 1981, the Thatcher government decided to redevelop the area; the showpiece of the regeneration is **Canary Wharf,** with Britain's highest skyscraper, the 244m pyramid-topped **One Canada Square.** Under the tower, the vast **Canada Place** and **Cabot Square** malls suck in shoppers from all over London, while the plaza is lined with pricey corporate drinking and eating haunts. *(Tube: Canary Wharf.)*

GREENWICH. Greenwich's position as the "home of time" is intimately connected to its maritime heritage—the **Royal Observatory,** in Greenwich Park and the site of the **Prime Meridian,** was founded in 1675 to produce star-charts once essential to navigation. Wren's **Flamstead House** is next to the Meridian; the long windows in its **Octagon Room** were designed to accommodate telescopes. *(Rail: Cutty Sark. Open daily 10am-5pm. Free.)* The **Cutty Sark,** on King William Walk, was launched in 1869; she was the fastest ship of her time, making the trip to and from China in only 120 days. *(Rail: Cutty Sark. Open daily 10am-5pm; last admission 4:30pm. £3.90, students £2.90.)* For information on other sights and on how to get to Greenwich, contact the **Greenwich Tourist Information Centre,** Pepys House, 2 Cutty Sark Gdns. *(☎(0870) 608 2000. Open daily 10am-5pm.)*

WEST LONDON

KEW GARDENS. The Kew Gardens (a.k.a. the Royal Botanic Gardens) feature thousands of flowers, fruits, trees, and vegetables from around the globe. The three **conservatories,** housing a staggering variety of plants ill-suited to the English climate, are the highlight of the gardens. *(Main entrance at Victoria Gate. Tube: Kew Gardens. Open Apr.-Aug. M-F 9:30am-6:30pm, Sa-Su 9:30am-7:30pm; Sept.-Oct. daily 9:30am-6pm; Nov.-Jan. daily 9:30am-4:15pm; Feb.-Mar. daily 9:30am-5:30pm. Glasshouses close Feb.-Oct. 5:30pm, Nov.-Mar 3:45pm. £6.50, "late entry" (45min. before closing) £4.50; students £4.50.)*

▨ **HAMPTON COURT PALACE.** Although a monarch hasn't lived here for 250 years, Hampton Court still exudes regal charm. In addition to touring the sumptuous rooms of the palace, including Henry's **State Apartments** and William's **King's Apartments,** be sure to leave time for the gardens, including the devilish **maze.** Take the train from Waterloo (35min., every 30min., round-trip £4) or a boat from

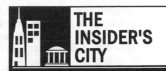

THE INSIDER'S CITY

THE JUBILEE LINE

While subway stations might not seem like worthy tourist destinations, London Underground's Jubilee Line is certainly an exception. The line was begun in 1977 to honor Queen Elizabeth's 25 years on the throne. In 2002, more stations were added to celebrate Liz's 50th anniversary as monarch. The phenomenal architecture of the stations combines with their proximity to London's aboveground sights for a fascinating tour.

Westminster Underground: Lots of glass and massive pillars, pipes, and escalators. **Overground:** State-of-the-art gives way to the stately British brilliance of Big Ben and Parliament.

Southwark Underground: Steep walls, high skylit ceilings, and daylight at the rotunda exit. **Overground:** Gleaming beams (the now-sturdy Millennium Bridge) and the big brick block Tate Modern.

Canary Wharf Underground: Precipitous escalator, arching overhang, and a sloping concrete ceiling. **Overground:** A financial mecca of glass skyscrapers and thriving urbanity.

North Greenwich Underground: Bold purple floods the walls, then yields to a cool breezeway. **Overground:** The Millennium Dome—an eye-catching, albeit hollow, testament to modern architecture.

Westminster Pier (4hr.; 4 per day; £10, round-trip £14); to leave time to see the palace, take the boat one way and return by train. *(Open mid-Mar. to late Oct. M 10:15am-6pm, Tu-Su 9:30am-6pm; late Oct. to mid-Mar. closes 4:30pm. £11, students £8.25. Maze only £3. Gardens only free.)*

🏛 MUSEUMS

Centuries spent as the capital of an empire, together with a decidedly English penchant for collecting, have given London a spectacular set of museums. Art lovers, history buffs, and amateur ethnologists won't know which way to turn when they arrive. And there's even better news for museum lovers: the government now plans to return all major collections—once some of the capital's most expensive attractions—to free admission.

◪ BRITISH MUSEUM

Great Russell St., Bloomsbury. Rear entrance on Montague St. ☎ 7323 8000; www.thebritishmuseum.ac.uk. Tube: Tottenham Court Rd., Russell Sq., or Holborn. Great Court open M 9am-6pm, Tu-W and Su 9am-9pm, Th-Sa 9am-11pm. Galleries open Sa-W 10am-5:30pm, Th-F 10am-8:30pm. Suggested donation £2. Temporary exhibitions £7, students £3.50. Audio tours £2.50. 1½hr. highlights tour M-Sa 10:30am and 1pm, Su 11am, 12:30, 1:30, 2:30, and 4pm. £7, students £4.

The funny thing about the British Museum is that there's almost nothing British in it. The December 2000 opening of the **Great Court,** the largest covered square in Europe, finally restored to the museum its focal point; for the past 150 years the area was used as the book stacks of the British Library. The courtyard remains dominated by the enormous rotunda of the **Reading Room,** whose desks have shouldered the weight of research by Marx, Lenin, and Trotsky as well as almost every major British writer and intellectual. The **Western Galleries** house the most famous items in the collection. Room 4 harbors Egyptian sculpture, including the **Rosetta Stone,** and Room 18 is entirely devoted to the Athenian **Elgin Marbles.** The **Northern Galleries** feature eight rooms of mummies and sarcophagi and nine of artifacts from the ancient Near East, including the **Oxus Treasure** from Iran. The northern wing also houses the excellent African and Islamic galleries, the giant Asian collections, and the Americas collection. The upper level of the **South** and **East Galleries** is dedicated to ancient and medieval Europe, some of which is actually British.

◪ NATIONAL GALLERY

Main entrance on north side of Trafalgar Sq., Westminster. ☎ 7747 2885; www.nationalgallery.org.uk. Tube: Charing Cross or Leicester Sq. Open Th-Tu 10am-6pm; W 10am-9pm, Sainsbury Wing exhibitions until 10pm. Free; some temporary exhibitions £5-7, students £2-3. Audio tours free; suggested donation £4. 1hr. gallery tours start at Sainsbury Wing info desk daily 11:30am and 2:30pm, W also 6:30pm. Free.

The National Gallery was founded by an Act of Parliament in 1824, with 38 paintings displayed in a townhouse; it grew so rapidly in size and popularity that a new gallery was constructed in 1838. The new **Sainsbury Wing** houses the oldest, most fragile paintings, including the 14th-century English *Wilton Diptych*, Botticelli's *Venus and Mars*, and the *Leonardo Cartoon*. The **West Wing** displays paintings from 1510-1600 and is dominated by Italian High Renaissance and early Flemish art. The **North Wing** spans the 17th century, with an exceptional array of Flemish work. Room 23 boasts no fewer than 17 Rembrandts; the famous *Self Portrait at 63* gazes knowingly at his *Self Portrait at 34.* The **East Wing** is the most popular in the gallery, thanks to an array of Impressionist works including van Gogh's *Sunflowers*, Cézanne's *Bathers*, and two of Monet's *Waterlilies*.

TATE MODERN

Bankside, The South Bank. Main entrance on Holland St. ☎ 7887 8006; www.tate.org.uk. Tube: Blackfriars. Open Su-Th 10am-6pm, F-Sa 10am-10pm. Free. Special exhibitions £5-7; students £4-6. Audio tours £1. Free tours meet on the gallery concourses: Landscape/ Matter/Environment 11am, level 3; Still Life/Object/Real Life noon, level 3; Nude/Body/ Action 2pm, level 5; History/Memory/Society 3pm, level 5.

Since opening in May 2000, Tate Modern has been credited with single-handedly reversing the long-term decline in museum attendance in Britain. The largest modern art museum in the world, its most striking aspect is the building, formerly the Bankside power station. A conversion by Swiss firm Herzog and de Meuron added a seventh floor with wraparound views of north and south London, and turned the old **Turbine Hall** into an immense atrium that often overpowers the installations commissioned for it. For all its popularity, the Tate has been criticized for its controversial curatorial method, which groups works according to themes rather than period or artist: the four divisions are **Landscape/Matter/Environment, Still Life/ Object/Real Life, Nude/Body/Action,** and **History/Memory/Society.** Even skeptics admit that this arrangement throws up some interesting contrasts, such as the nascent geometry of Cézanne's *Still Life with Water Jug* overlooking the checkerboard tiles of Carl André's *Steel Zinc Plain.* It's now impossible to see the Tate's more famous pieces, which include Marcel Duchamp's *Large Glass* and Picasso's *Weeping Woman,* without also confronting challenging and invigorating works by little-known contemporary artists.

TATE BRITAIN

Millbank, near Vauxhall Bridge, Westminster. Wheelchair access via Clore Wing. ☎ 7887 8008; www.tate.org.uk. Tube: Pimlico. Open daily 10am-5pm. Free. Special exhibitions £3-9. Audio tours £1. Highlights tour M-F 11:30am, Sa 3pm. Free.

The original Tate opened in 1897 as a showcase for modern British art. Before long, it had expanded to include contemporary art from all over the world, as well as British art from the Middle Ages on. Despite many expansions, it was clear that the dual role was too much for one building; the problem was resolved with the relocation of almost all the contemporary art to Tate Modern (see above). At the same time, the original Tate was rechristened and rededicated to British art. The **Clore Gallery** continues to display the Turner Bequest of 282 oils and 19,000 watercolors; other painters featured heavily are William Blake, John Constable, Dante Gabriel Rossetti, Lucien Freud, and David Hockney. The annual **Turner Prize** for contemporary art is still held here. The short-listed works go on display from early November to mid-January every year.

VICTORIA AND ALBERT MUSEUM

Main entrance on Cromwell Rd., Kensington. ☎ 7942 2000; www.vam.ac.uk. Tube: South Kensington. Open Th-Tu 10am-5:45pm, W and last F of month 10am-10pm. Free; additional charge for some exhibitions. Free introductory tours daily 10:30, 11:30am, 1:30, 2:30pm; W also 4:30pm. Gallery talks daily 1pm. Free. Talks, tours, and live music W from 6:30pm; last F of month also fashion shows, debates, and DJs.

Founded in 1852 to encourage excellence in art and design, the V&A is the largest museum of the decorative arts in the world. The subject of a £31 million renovation, the vast **British Galleries** hold a series of recreated rooms from every period between 1500 and 1900. The **Raphael Gallery** is not to be missed, hung with paintings commissioned by Leo X in 1515. The V&A's **Asian** collections are particularly formidable—if the choice of objects occasionally seems to rely on national cliches (Indian carvings, Persian carpets, Chinese porcelain, Japanese ceramics), it says more about how the V&A has formed opinion than followed it. In contrast to the geographically themed ground floor, the **upper levels** are mostly arranged in specialist galleries devoted to everything from jewelry to musical instruments to stained glass. An exception to the materially themed arrangements is the large **20th-century** collections, featuring design classics from Salvador Dalí's 1936 "Mae West" sofa lips to a pair of 1990s rubber hot pants. The six-level **Henry Cole wing** is home to the V&A's collection of British paintings, including some 350 works by Constable and numerous Turners. The **Frank Lloyd Wright gallery** contains a full-size recreation of the office commissioned by Edgar J. Kauffmann for his Pittsburgh department store in 1935.

OTHER MUSEUMS AND GALLERIES

■ **Courtauld Institute,** Somerset House, The Strand, Westminster (☎ 7848 2526). Tube: Charing Cross. Small, outstanding collection. 14th- to 20th-century abstractions, focusing on Impressionism. Open M-Sa 10am-6pm. £5, students £4; M 10am-2pm free.

■ **Natural History Museum,** on Cromwell Rd., Kensington (☎ 7942 5000). Tube: South Kensington. Cathedral-like building home to an array of minerals and stuffed animals. Open M-Sa 10am-5:50pm, Su 11am-5:50pm. Free.

■ **Royal Academy,** Burlington House, Piccadilly, The West End (☎ 7300 8000). Tube: Piccadilly Circus. Founded in 1768 as both an art school and meeting place for Britain's foremost artists. Outstanding exhibitions on all manner of art. Open Sa-Th 10am-6pm, F 10am-10pm. Around £7; £1-4 student discounts.

■ **Cabinet War Rooms,** Clive Steps, Westminster (☎ 7930 6961). Tube: Westminster. The rooms where Churchill and his ministers and generals lived and worked from 1939 to 1945. Open Apr.-Sept. daily 9:30am-6pm; Oct.-Mar. 10am-6pm. £5.80, students £4.20.

■ **London's Transport Museum,** Covent Garden Piazza, The West End (☎ 7565 7299). Tube: Covent Garden or Charing Cross. Informative *and* fun. Kids and adults will find themselves engrossed in the history of London's public transportation system. Open Sa-Th 10am-6pm, F 11am-6pm. £6, students £4, under 16 free with adult.

■ **Wallace Collection,** Manchester Sq., Marylebone (☎ 7563 9500). Tube: Bond St. Palatial Hertford House holds a stunning array of porcelain, medieval armor, and weaponry. Open M-Sa 10am-5pm, Su noon-5pm. Free.

Imperial War Museum, Lambeth Rd., South London (☎ 7416 5320). Tube: Lambeth North. The commendably un-jingoistic exhibits follow every aspect of war from 1914 on, covering conflicts large and small. The largest and most publicized display, the Holocaust Exhibition, graphically documents Nazi atrocities. Open daily 10am-6pm. Free.

Institute of Contemporary Arts (ICA), Nash House, The West End (☎ 7930 3647). Tube: Charing Cross. Down the road from Buckingham Palace—convenient for questioning the establishment. Open M noon-11pm, Tu-Sa noon-1am, Su noon-10:30pm; galleries close 7:30pm. M-F £1.50, Sa-Su £2.50.

Sir John Soane's Museum, 13 Lincoln's Inn Fields, Holborn. Tube: Holborn. Architect John Soane built this intriguing museum for his own art collection. Open Tu-Sa 10am-5pm; first Tu of month also 6-9pm. Suggested donation £1.

Science Museum, Exhibition Rd., Kensington (☎ (0870) 870 4868). Tube: South Kensington. A mix of state-of-the-art interactive displays and priceless historical artifacts, encompassing all forms of technology. Open daily 10am-6pm. Free.

Museum of London, London Wall, The City of London (☎ 7600 3699). Tube: Barbican. Enter through the Barbican. Engrossing collection traces the history of London. Open M-Sa 10am-6pm, Su noon-6pm; last admission 5:30pm. Free.

National Portrait Gallery, St. Martin's Pl., Westminster (☎ 7312 2463). Tube: Charing Cross. The artistic *Who's Who* of Britain. Began in 1856 as "the fulfillment of a patriotic and moral ideal." Open Sa-W 10am-6pm, Th-F 10am-9pm. Free.

🎭 ENTERTAINMENT

On any given day or night in London, you can choose from the widest range of entertainment a city can offer. *Time Out* (£2.20), which comes out every Wednesday and is available from newsstands, has indispensable listings.

THEATER

At a **West End** theater (referring to all the major stages, whether or not they're actually in the West End), you can expect a mainstream production and top-quality performers. **Off-West End** theaters usually present more challenging work but are as professional as their West End brethren. The **Fringe** refers to smaller, less commercial theaters, often just a room in a pub basement with a few benches and a team of dedicated amateurs. **tkts,** on the south side of Leicester Sq., releases half-price tickets on the day of the show. You have to buy them in person, with cash and no choice in seating (most expensive tickets sold first); there's no way to know in advance what shows will have tickets available that day. Be prepared to wait, especially on Saturday. (Tube: Leicester Sq. £2.50 booking fee per ticket. Open M-Sa 10am-7pm, Su noon-3pm.)

Barbican Theatre, on Barbican (☎ 7638 8891), main entrance on Silk St. Tube: Barbican. A futuristic auditorium that hosts touring companies and short-run shows. Tickets £6-30; cheapest M-F evening and Sa matinee. Student standbys from 9am day of performance. In the same complex, **The Pit** is an intimate 200-seat theater used primarily for new and experimental productions. Tickets £10-15.

National Theatre, just down river of Waterloo Bridge (info ☎ 7452 3400; box office ☎ 7452 3000). Tube: Waterloo. Since opening in 1963, the National has been at the forefront of British theater. The **Olivier** stage seats 10,800 in a fan-shaped open-stage layout. The **Lyttelton** is a proscenium theater with 890 seats. The 300-seat **Cottesloe** stages experimental dramas. Box office open M-Sa 10am-8pm. Tickets £10-33, students £8-15; same-day £10 from 10am, standby £15 2hr. before curtain.

Royal Court Theatre, Sloane Sq. (☎ 7565 5000). Dedicated to challenging new writing and innovative interpretations of classics. Experimental work runs in the intimate upstairs auditorium. Main stage £7-26, students £9; standing places £0.10 1hr. before curtain. Upstairs £12-15, students £9; M all seats £7.50.

Shakespeare's Globe Theatre, 21 New Globe Walk (☎ 7401 9919). Tube: London Bridge. A faithful reproduction of the original 16th-century playhouse. For tours of the Globe, see **Sights,** p. 157. Performances mid-May to late Sept. Tu-Sa 7:30pm, Su 6:30pm; June to late Sept. also Tu-Sa 2pm, Su 1pm. Box office open M-Sa 10am-6pm, until 8pm on performance days. Seats £12-27, students £10-24; yard (standing) £5.

CINEMA

London's film scene offers everything. The heart of the celluloid monster is **Leicester Square** (p. 154), where the latest releases premiere a day before hitting the chains. **The Empire** (☎ (0870) 010 2030) is the most famous first-run theater.

BFI London IMAX Cinema (☎ 7902 1234), at the south end of Waterloo Bridge, accessed via underground walkways. Tube: Waterloo. Stunning glass drum houses UK's biggest screen. £7.10, students and seniors £6, under 17 £5; additional film £4.20.

National Film Theatre (NFT) (☎ 7928 3232), on the south bank, right underneath Waterloo Bridge. Tube: Waterloo, Embankment, or Temple. One of the world's leading cinemas. 6 different movies daily, starting around 6pm. £7.20, students £5.50.

BRITAIN

MUSIC

ROCK AND POP

Birthplace of the Rolling Stones, the Sex Pistols, and the Chemical Brothers, home to Madonna and Paul McCartney, London is a town steeped in rock 'n' roll history.

Borderline, Orange Yard (☎ 7395 0777), off Manette St. Tube: Tottenham Court Rd. Basement hosted secret REM gig years ago, now stages up-and-coming groups with a strong folk-rock flavor. Music M-Sa from 8pm. Box office open M-F 1-7:30pm. Tickets £5-10 in advance.

The Water Rats, 328 Grays Inn Rd. (☎ 7837 7269). Tube: King's Cross/St. Pancras. Pub-cafe by day, stomping venue for top new talent by night. Oasis was signed here after their first London gig. Cover £5, £4 with band's flyer. Open for coffee M-F 8am-noon, surprisingly good lunch (£5-6) served M-F noon-3pm, music M-Sa 8pm-11pm.

CLASSICAL

Home to four world-class orchestras, three major concert halls, two opera houses, two ballet companies, and scores of chamber ensembles, London is center stage for serious music. To hear some of the world's top choirs for free, head to Westminster Abbey (p. 151) or St. Paul's Cathedral (p. 154) for Evensong.

▨ English National Opera (☎ 7632 8300), at the Coliseum, St. Martin's Lane. Tube: Charing Cross or Leicester Sq. All the classics, plus contemporary and avant-garde work, sung in English. £6-60; under 18 half-price with adult. Same-day seats for the dress-circle (£31) and balcony (£3) released M-F 10am (12:30pm by phone). Standbys 3hr. before curtain; students £12.50, seniors £18.

Barbican Hall, same details as for Barbican Theatre (p. 163). One of Europe's leading concert halls. The resident **London Symphony Orchestra** plays throughout the year. Also hosts jazz, world musicians, and international orchestras. Tickets £6-35.

The Proms, at the Royal Albert Hall, Kensington Gore (www.bbc.co.uk/proms). Tube: Knightsbridge. Concerts every night from mid-July to mid-Sept. Tickets go on sale in mid-May (£5-30); standing places sold from 1½hr. before the concert (£4).

Royal Opera House, Bow St. (☎ 7304 4000). Tube: Covent Garden. Also home to the **Royal Ballet.** Standing room and restricted-view seating under £5. Same-day seats £10-40 from 10am on performance day. Standby £12-15 4hr. before curtain.

Royal Festival Hall (☎ 7960 4242), on the south bank of the Thames between Hungerford and Waterloo Bridges. Tube: Waterloo or Embankment. The two resident orchestras, the **Philharmonia** and the **London Philharmonic,** predominate, but big-name jazz, Latin, and world-music groups also visit. Classical concerts £6-33; others £10-30.

JAZZ, FOLK, AND WORLD

London's jazz scene is small but serious; top clubs pull in big-name performers from around the world. Folk and world music keep an even lower profile, mostly restricted to pubs and community centers.

Ronnie Scott's, 47 Frith St. (☎ 7439 0747). Tube: Tottenham Court Rd. London's oldest and most famous jazz club. Music M-Sa 9:30pm-3am, Su 7:30-11:30pm. M-Th cover £15, F-Sa £25, Su £8-12; M-W students £10. Reservations recommended; if it's sold out, try coming back at midnight to catch the second set.

606 Club, 90 Lot's Rd. (☎ 7352 5953). Hard to find, but the intrepid will be rewarded with some of the best British and European jazz in a classic, smoky venue. M-W music 8-1:30am; Th doors open 8pm, music 9:30pm-1:30am; F-Sa doors open 8pm, music 10pm-2am; Su doors open 8pm, music 9pm-midnight.

SPECTATOR SPORTS

FOOTBALL. From late August to May, over 500,000 people attend professional football (soccer) matches every Saturday. The three major London teams are: **Arsenal,** Highbury Stadium, Avenell Rd. (☎ 7713 3366; Tube: Arsenal); **Chelsea,** Stamford Bridge, Fulham Rd. (☎ 7386 7799; Tube: Fulham Broadway); and **Tottenham Hotspur,** White Hart Lane (☎ 8365 5000; Tube: Seven Sisters).

RUGBY. The rugby season is from August to May; games are on weekend afternoons. The four major teams are: **London Wasps** (☎ 8740 2545); **NEC Harlequins** (☎ 8410 6000); **Saracens** (☎ (01923) 496 200); and **London Broncos** (☎ 8853 8800). International competitions, including the springtime **Six Nations Championship,** are played at **Twickenham** (☎ 8831 6666; Rail: Twickenham); tickets are nearly impossible to get.

TENNIS. Every year for two weeks in late June and early July, tennis buffs the world over focus their attention on **Wimbledon.** Reserve months ahead or arrive by 6am (gates open 10:30am) to secure one of the 500 Centre and #1 court tickets sold every morning; otherwise, settle for a "grounds" ticket for the outer courts. (All England Lawn Tennis Club. ☎ 8971 2473. Tube: Southfields. Rail: Wimbledon. Grounds £9-11; after 5pm £5-7. Show courts £17-50.)

◪ SHOPPING

From its earliest days, London has been a trading city, its power built upon almost two millennia of commerce. From Harrods's proud boast to supply "all things to all people" to outrageous club wear in Camden, you could shop for a lifetime.

DEPARTMENT STORES

Harrods, 87-135 Old Brompton Rd. (☎ 7730 1234). Tube: Knightsbridge. The only thing bigger than the store itself is the mark-up. No wonder only tourists and oil sheikhs actually shop here. Bewildering. Open M-Sa 10am-7pm. AmEx/MC/V.

Harvey Nichols, 109-125 Knightsbridge (☎ 7235 5000). Tube: Knightsbridge. Imagine Bond St., rue St-Honoré, and Fifth Avenue all rolled up into 5 fl. of the biggest names in fashion and the hippest contemporary unknowns. Open M-Tu and Sa 10am-7pm, W-F 10am-8pm, Su noon-6pm. AmEx/MC/V.

CLOTHING AND FOOTWEAR

▨ **Cyberdog/Cybercity,** Stables Market (☎ 7482 2842). Tube: Camden Town. Unbelievable club clothes for superior life forms. Alien goddesses will want to try on steel corsets with rubber breast hoses. Open M-F 11am-6pm, Sa-Su 10am-7pm. AmEx/MC/V.

Dr. Marten's Dept. Store, 1-4 King St. (☎ 7497 1460). Tube: Covent Garden. Tourist-packed 5-tiered megastore. Baby Docs, papa Docs, and the classic yellow-stitched boots. Open M-W and F-Sa 10am-7pm, Th 10:30am-8pm, Su noon-6pm. AmEx/MC/V.

BOOKSTORES

Bookshops line **Charing Cross Road** between Tottenham Court Rd. and Leicester Sq.; many sell used paperbacks. Establishments along **Great Russell Street,** by the British Museum, and in **Cecil Court,** near Leicester Sq., stock esoteric titles.

Waterstone's, 203-206 Piccadilly (☎ 7851 2400). Tube: Piccadilly Circus. Europe's largest bookstore. The 8 fl. house a cafe, Internet station, and posh basement restaurant. Open M-Sa 10am-11pm, Su noon-6pm. AmEx/MC/V.

STREET MARKETS

Camden Markets, off Camden High St. and Chalk Farm Rd. Tube: Camden Town. London's 4th-biggest tourist attraction. On Su the market fills with hordes looking for the latest mainstream, vintage, and off-beat fashions.

Stables Market, farthest from the station and the best of the bunch. The railway arches hold club wear and a good selection of vintage clothes. Open F-Sa, a few shops open M-Th.

Camden Lock Market, from the railway bridge to the canal. Arranged around food-filled courtyard. Indoor shops sell pricier items (carpets, household goods). Most stalls operate F or Sa-Su only.

Camden Canal Market, down tunnel opposite the Lock, starts promisingly (jewelry, watches), but degenerates (sub-par club wear, tourist trinkets). Good spot for a bite to eat, though. Open F-Su.

Portobello Market, Portobello Rd. and north. Similar to Camden. Sa is the best day.

Antiques Market Chepstow Villas to Elgin Crescent. Tube: Notting Hill Gate. Cheapish bric-a-brac outside. Numerous indoor market halls. Sa 7am-5pm.

General Market, Elgin Crescent to Lancaster Rd. Tube: Westbourne Park or Ladbroke Grove. Food, flowers, and household essentials. M-W 8am-6pm, Th 9am-1pm, F-Sa 7am-7pm.

Clothes Market, north of Lancaster Rd., stretching along the Westway. Tube: Ladbroke Grove. Second-hand clothes, cheap club wear, electronics. F-Sa 8am-3pm.

▨ NIGHTLIFE

The **West End**—especially **Soho**—is the scene of most of London's after-dark action, from the glitzy Leicester Sq. tourist traps, like the Hippodrome and Equinox, to semi-secret underground clubs. The other major axis of London nightlife is East London's **Shoreditch** and **Hoxton** (known as Shoho).

THE WEST END

PUBS

Dog and Duck, 18 Bateman St., Soho (☎ 7494 0697). The oldest and smallest pub in Soho. The name and decor serve as a reminder of the area's hunting past. Open M-F noon-11pm, Sa 2-11pm, Su 6-10:30pm.

Lamb and Flag, 33 Rose St., Covent Garden (☎ 7497 9504). Tube: Leicester Sq. Traditional dark-wood interior. Food daily noon-3pm. Live jazz upstairs Su 7:30pm. Open M-Th 11am-11pm, F-Sa 11am-10:45pm, Su noon-10:30pm.

BARS

▨ **Freud,** 198 Shaftesbury Ave., Covent Garden (☎ 7240 9933). Invigorate your psyche in this off-beat underground hipster hangout. Occasional live music. Cheap cocktails (from £3.40). Light meals noon-4:30pm (£3.50-6). No cover. Open M-Sa 11am-11pm, Su noon-10:30pm. MC/V.

Point 101, 101 New Oxford St. (☎ 7379 3112), underneath the Centrepoint office tower. Tube: Tottenham Court Rd. 1970s decor. Long vinyl booths line the balcony bar (accessed via a separate door). Nightly DJs tend toward jazz, Latin, and soul. Big crowds, but enough space for all. Open M-Th 8am-2am, F-Sa 8am-2:30am, Su 8am-11:30pm. AmEx/MC/V.

NIGHTCLUBS

Sound, 10 Wardour St., Soho (☎ 7287 1010). Tube: Leicester Sq. Different rooms hidden over 4 fl. Cover £8, before 11pm £6. Open daily 10pm-3am.

Velvet Room, 143 Charing Cross Rd., Soho (☎ 7734 4687). Tube: Tottenham Court Rd. Small, and showing its age, but packed even mid-week. Come here for the music, not the posing scene. Cover £5-10. M gay night, with R&B and hip-hop (10pm-3am). W ▨ *Swerve* with Brazilian-flavored drum and bass (10pm-2:30am). House and garage dominate the weekend (F-Sa 10pm-4am, Su 7pm-midnight).

BLOOMSBURY

PUBS

The Lamb, 94 Lamb's Conduit St. (☎7405 0713). Tube: Russell Sq. This old-fashioned pub is an actors' hangout. Peter O'Toole is a regular, and fading daguerreotypes of past thespian tipplers line the walls. The "snob screens" around the bar originally provided privacy for "respectable" men meeting with ladies of ill-repute. Food served M-Sa noon-2:30pm and daily 6-9pm. Open M-Sa 11am-11pm, Su noon-10:30pm. MC/V.

CLERKENWELL

NIGHTCLUBS

Fabric, 77a Charterhouse St. (☎7336 8898). Tube: Farringdon. Bigger than a B52 and 100 times as loud. When they power up the underfoot subwoofer, lights dim across London. 3 dance fl., chill-out beds, multiple bars, and unisex toilets, all crammed with up to 2500 dance-crazed Londoners. Yow. F *Fabric Live* (hip-hop, break-beat; 9:30pm-5am), Sa mega dance fest *Fabric* (house, techno; 9:30pm-7am). Cover £10-15.

EAST LONDON

BARS

Soshomatch, 2 Tabernacle St. (☎7920 0701). Tube: Moorgate. A 2-floor bar/restaurant that converts into a stylish club Th-Sa. DJ-driven atmosphere with acres of comfy leather couches. F-Sa cover £5. Open M-W 11am-midnight, Th-Sa 11am-2am. AmEx/MC/V.

Vibe Bar, 91-95 Brick Ln. (☎7247 3479). Tube: Aldgate East. Young, fun, clubby bar, with an interior straight out of a magazine. M-Sa DJs from 7:30pm, Su from 6:30pm. In summer, a second DJ works the shady courtyard. Tends towards soul/jazz/funk. Occasional cover £2. Open Su-Th noon-11pm, F-Sa noon-1am.

NIGHTCLUBS

93 Feet East, 150 Brick Ln. (☎7247 3293). Tube: Aldgate East. One of the hottest new clubs in East London. Barn-like main dance floor, sofa-strewn room upstairs. W salsa with a live Latin band (7-11pm); Th world-dance mixes (9pm-3am); F techno and house (9pm-3am); Sa anything from house to ska (9pm-2am). Cover £3-10.

Cargo, 83 Rivington St., Kingsland Viaduct (☎7739 3440). Tube: Old Street. Despite the superclub trimmings—two enormous arched rooms, fab acoustics, movie projectors, and an intimate candle-lit lounge—Cargo is crippled by a 1am license. On the plus side, the place is kicking by 9:30pm. Strong Latin lineup with mixing DJs and live music. Cover £3-7. Open M-F noon-1am, Sa 6pm-1am, Su noon-midnight.

SOUTH LONDON

BARS

The Dogstar, 389 Coldharbour Ln. (☎7733 7515). Tube: Brixton. At 9pm, the tables are cleared from the dance floor and the projectors turned on. House, hip hop, and dance music. Su-Th no cover; F before 10pm free, 10-11pm £4, after 11pm £5; Sa before 10pm free, 10-11pm £5, after 11 pm £7. Open Su-Th noon-2am, F-Sa noon-4am.

NIGHTCLUBS

The Fridge, Town Hall Parade, Brixton Hill (☎7326 5100). Tube: Brixton. Turn left from the station and bear right at the fork onto Brixton Hill; it's opposite the church. Giant split-level dance floor. F trance glo-stick madness; Sa usually gay night. Cover £10-17; sometimes less before 10:30pm. Open F-Sa 10pm-6am. After-parties start Sa-Su 5:30am at the neighboring **Fridge Bar;** cover £6.

Ministry of Sound, 103 Gaunt St. (☎ 7378 6528). Tube: Elephant and Castle. Take the exit for South Bank University. The granddaddy of serious clubbing. Arrive early or wait in line all night. Dress code generally casual, but famously unsmiling door staff makes it sensible to err on the side of dressy (no sneakers). F garage and R&B (10:30pm-5am); Sa US and vocal house (11pm-8am). Cover £12-15.

GAY AND LESBIAN NIGHTLIFE

London has a very visible gay scene, ranging from flamboyant to mainstream. Gay newspapers include *Capital Gay*, *Pink Paper*, and *Shebang* (for women). *Boyz* magazine and the *Ginger Beer* web site (www.gingerbeer.co.uk) track the gay and lesbian nightlife scene. Soho—especially **Old Compton Street**—is the heart of gay London, with much smaller scenes in Islington, Earl's Court, and Brixton.

The Box, 32-34 Monmouth St. (☎ 7240 5828). Recently renovated, this spacious gay/mixed bar-brasserie is popular with a stylish media/fashion crowd. Daily food specials (entrees around £9). Also sells club tickets. Food served until 5pm. Open M-Sa 11am-11pm, Su 7-10:30pm. MC/V.

Comptons of Soho, 53 Old Compton St. (☎ 7479 7461). Tube: Leicester Sq. or Piccadilly Circus. Soho's "official" gay pub is always busy. Horseshoe bar encourages the exchange of meaningful glances, while upstairs (opens 6pm) offers a more mellow scene and a pool table. Open M-Sa 11am-11pm, Su noon-10:30pm. MC/V.

G-A-Y (☎ 7434 9592; www.g-a-y.co.uk). M and Th at the Mean Fiddler, 165 Charing Cross Rd.; F-Sa at the London Astoria, 157 Charing Cross Rd. Tube: Tottenham Court Rd. London's biggest gay and lesbian night, 4 nights a week. M *Pink Pounder* 90s classics with 70s-80s faves in the bar; F *Camp Attack* 70s and 80s cheese; Sa *G-A-Y* big night out, rocking the capacity crowd with commercial-dance DJs and live pop performances. Cover free-£10. Open M, Th, F until 4am, Sa until 5am.

Vespa Lounge, St. Giles Circus (☎ 7836 8956). Tube: Tottenham Court Rd. Relaxed lesbian lounge bar. Thai food from downstairs restaurant. First Su of month "Laughing Cows" comedy night (£4-6), plus occasional theme nights. Gay men welcome as guests. Open M-Sa 6-11pm.

◪ DAYTRIPS FROM LONDON

OXBRIDGE. Don your academic regalia for a day in the intellectual meccas of **Oxford** (p. 175) and **Cambridge** (p. 181), both 1hr. from London by train.

BRIGHTON. Indulge in a "dirty weekend" in Brighton (p. 169), 1hr. from London.

SALISBURY AND CANTERBURY. Make like a pilgrim and head to Canterbury (p. 169), or ponder the powers that be at **Salisbury Cathedral** and **Stonehenge** (p. 171), all less than 2hr. from London by train.

SOUTHERN ENGLAND

Southern England's history has deep continental roots. Early Britons settled the pastoral counties of Kent, Sussex, and Hampshire after crossing the Channel. Later, William the Conqueror left his mark in the form of awe-inspiring cathedrals, many built around settlements begun by Romans. During WWII, German bombings uncovered long-buried evidence of an invasion by Caesar. This historied landscape, so intertwined with that of continental Europe, has in turn had a profound influence on the country's national identity, inspiring such distinctly British literati as Geoffrey Chaucer, Jane Austen, and E.M. Forster. For detailed info on over- and underwater transport options to the Continent, see p. 51.

CANTERBURY   ☎01227

Archbishop Thomas à Becket was beheaded at ▨**Canterbury Cathedral** in 1170 after an irate Henry II asked, "Will no one rid me of this troublesome priest?" Later, in his famed *Canterbury Tales*, Chaucer captured the irony of tourists visiting England's most famous execution site. (☎762 862. Open M-Sa 9am-5pm, Su 12:30-2:30pm and 4:30-5:30pm. ₤3, students ₤2. Audio tour ₤2.50.) **The Canterbury Tales,** on St. Margaret's St., is a museum that simulates the journey of Chaucer's pilgrims. (☎479 227. Open July-Aug. daily 9am-5:30pm; Mar.-June and Sept.-Oct. daily 9:30am-5:30pm; Nov.-Feb. Su-F 10am-4:30pm, Sa 9:30am-5:30pm. ₤6, students ₤5.50.) On Stour St., the **Canterbury Heritage Museum** tells the history of Canterbury from medieval times to WWII. (☎452 747. Open June-Oct. M-Sa 10:30am-5pm, Su 1:30-5pm; Nov.-May M-Sa 10:30am-5pm. ₤2.60, students ₤1.70.) For a quiet break, walk to the riverside gardens of England's first Franciscan friary, **Greyfriars,** Stour St. (Open in summer M-F 2-4pm. Free.)

Trains from London Victoria arrive at Canterbury's **East Station** (1½hr., 2 per hr., ₤15.90), while trains from London Charing Cross and Waterloo arrive at **West Station** (1½hr., every hr., ₤15.90). National Express **buses** (☎(08705) 808 080) arrive from London at St. George's Ln. (2hr., every hr., ₤9.50). The **tourist office** is in The Buttermarket, 12-13 Sun St. (☎378 100. Open M-Sa 9:30am-5:30pm, Su 10am-4pm.) **B&Bs** cluster near West Station, around **High Street,** and on **New Dover Road.** The front rooms of **The Tudor House ❷,** 6 Best Ln., off High St., have incredible views of the cathedral. (☎765 650. Singles ₤18-22; doubles ₤36-38, with bath ₤44-45.) The **YHA Canterbury ❷,** 54 New Dover Rd., is in a beautiful old house. (☎462 911. Kitchen. Internet ₤2.50 per 30min. Reception 7:30-10am and 1-11pm. Dorms ₤11.25, under 18 ₤8.) **The Camping and Caravaning Club Site ❶,** on Bekesbourne Ln., has good facilities. (☎463 216. ₤5 per tent, plus ₤4-5.50 per person.) ▨**Marlowe's ❷,** 55 St. Peter's St., serves an eclectic mix of English and Mexican food. (Entrees €7-10. Open daily 11:30am-10:30pm.) For groceries, head to **Safeway** supermarket, on St. George's Pl. (☎769 335. Open M-F 8am-8pm, Su 10am-4pm.) **Postal Code:** CT1 2BA.

BRIGHTON   ☎01273

According to legend, the future King George IV scuttled into Brighton (pop. 250,000) for some decidedly common hanky-panky around 1784. Today, Brighton is still the unrivaled home of the "dirty weekend"—it sparkles with a tawdry luster all its own. Before indulging, check out England's long-time obsession with the Far East at the excessively ornate **Royal Pavilion,** on Pavilion Parade, next to Old Steine. (Open June-Sept. daily 10am-6pm, Oct.-May 10am-5pm. ₤5.20, students ₤3.75. Guided tours at 11:30am and 2:30pm, ₤1.25. Audio tour ₤1.) Around the corner on Church St. stands the **Brighton Museum and Art Gallery,** with paintings, English pottery, and a wild collection of Art Deco and Art Nouveau pieces—leer at Salvador Dalí's sexy red sofa, *Mae West's Lips.* (Open Tu 10am-7pm, W-Sa 10am-5pm, Su 2-5pm. Free.) Before heading out to the rocky **beach,** stroll the **Lanes,** a jumble of 17th-century streets forming the heart of Old Brighton.

Brighton has plenty of nightlife options; for tips, pick up *The Punter* or *What's On* at music stores, news agents, and pubs. Sample the hot chocolate and dark rum concoction at the trendy pub **Mash Tun,** 1 Church St., which attracts an eclectic student crowd. (Open M-Sa noon-11pm, Su noon-10:30pm.) Relax with a drink on the sand at **Fortune of War,** 157 King's Rd., the place to be at sunset. (Open M-Sa 10:30am-11pm, Su 11am-10:30pm.) Most clubs are open M-Sa 9pm-2am. Brighton native Fatboy Slim still mixes occasionally at **The Beach,** 171-181 King's Rd., a popular shore-side club. **Casablanca,** on Middle St., plays live jazz to a predominantly student crowd. **Event II,** on West St., is crammed with the down-from-London crowd looking for thrills. Gay clubbers flock to the zany **Zanzibar,** 129 James St., for drinks and nightly entertainment.

Trains (☎ (0345) 484 950) leave from the station at the northern end of Queen's Rd. for London (1¼hr., 6 per hr., £11.90) and Portsmouth (1½hr., every hr., £11.70). National Express **buses** (☎ (08705) 808 080) arrive at Pool Valley from London (2hr., 15 per day, round-trip £8). The **tourist office** is at 10 Bartholomew Sq. (☎ (0906) 711 2255. Open M-F 9am-5pm, Sa 10am-5pm; Mar.-Oct. also Su 10am-4pm.) Rest at **Baggies Backpackers** ❷, 33 Oriental Pl., which has exquisite murals and frequent live music. Head west of West Pier along King's Rd., and Oriental Pl. is on the right. (☎ 733 740. Dorms £11; doubles £27.) The rowdy **Brighton Backpackers Hostel** ❷, 75-76 Middle St., features a downstairs lounge that functions as an all-night party spot. (☎ 777 717. Dorms £11-12; doubles £25-30.) Crowds pack **Food for Friends** ❶, 17a-18a Prince Albert St., a delicious vegetarian cafe. (Entrees £2-6. Open M-Sa 8am-10pm, Su 9:15am-10pm.) **Postal Code:** BN1 1BA.

PORTSMOUTH   ☎023

Set Victorian seaside holidays against prostitutes, drunkards, and a lot of bloody cursing sailors, and the 900-year history of Portsmouth (pop. 190,500) will emerge. On the **seafront**, visitors relive D-Day, explore warships, and learn of the days when Britannia truly ruled the waves. War buffs and historians will want to plunge head first into the unrivaled ⚅**Portsmouth Historic Dockyard,** in the Naval Base, which houses a fleet of Britain's most storied ships, including Henry VIII's *Mary Rose*, the HMS *Victory*, and the HMS *Warrior*. The entrance is next to the tourist office on The Hard. (Ships open Mar.-Oct. daily 10am-5:30pm; Nov.-Feb. 10am-5pm. Individual site tickets £6. All-inclusive ticket £18, seniors and children £14.50.) The ⚅**D-Day Museum,** on Clarence Esplanade, leads visitors through life-size dioramas of the 1944 invasion. (Open Apr.-Sept. daily 10am-5:30pm; Oct.-Mar. 10am-5pm. £5, students £3, seniors £3.75, families £13.)

Trains (☎ (0345) 484 950) run to Southsea Station, on Commercial Rd., from Chichester (40min., 2 per hr., £4) and London Waterloo (1½hr., 3 per hr., £20). National Express **buses** (☎ (08705) 808 080) arrive from London (2½hr., every hr., £10.50) and Salisbury (2hr., every hr., £8.25). The **tourist office** is on The Hard, next to the dockyard. (☎ 9282 6722. Open daily 9:30am-5:45pm.) Moderately priced **B&Bs** (around £20) clutter **Southsea**, 2½km east of The Hard along the coast. Take any Southsea bus and get off at The Strand to reach the energetic ⚅**Portsmouth and Southsea Backpackers Lodge** ❷, 4 Florence Rd. (☎ 9283 2495. Internet £1 per 15min. Dorms £10; doubles £22.) **Birchwood Guest House** ❷, 44 Waverly Rd., offers bright, spacious rooms and an ample breakfast. (☎ 9281 1337. Singles £18; doubles £40.) The owner of the **Brittania Guest House** ❸, 48 Granada Rd., loves to share his maritime interests with guests. (☎ 814 234. Full breakfast included. Singles £20; doubles £40-45.) **Country Kitchen** ❶, 59a Marmion Rd., serves savory vegetarian and vegan entrees. (£4-6. Open daily 9:30am-5pm.) **Pubs** near The Hard provide weary sailors with galley fare and jars of gin. **Postal Code:** PO1 1AA.

WINCHESTER   ☎01962

The glory of Winchester (pop. 32,000) stretches back to Roman times, when William the Conqueror deemed it the center of his kingdom. Duck under the archway, pass through the square, and behold the 900-year-old **Winchester Cathedral,** 5 The Close. Famed for the small stone figure in its nave, the 169m long cathedral is the longest medieval building in Europe; the interior holds magnificent tiles and Jane Austen's tomb. The **Norman crypt,** supposedly the oldest in England, can be viewed only in the summer by guided tour. The 12th-century Winchester Bible resides in the library. (Open daily 7:15am-5:30pm; East End closes 5pm. Free tours 10am-3pm. Suggested donation £3.50, students £2.30.) About 25km north of Winchester is the meek village of **Chawton**, where Jane Austen lived. It was in her cottage that she penned *Pride and Prejudice, Emma, Northanger Abbey*, and *Persuasion*, among others. Many of her manuscripts are on display. Take Hampshire **bus** #X64 (M-Sa 11 per day, round-trip £5.30), or the London and Country bus #65 from the bus station (Su); ask to be let off at the Chawton roundabout and follow the signs. (☎ (01420) 83 262. Open Mar.-Dec. daily 11am-4:30pm; Jan.-Feb. Sa-Su 11am-4:30pm. £4, students £3, under 18 £0.50.)

Trains (☎ (08547) 484 950) arrive at Winchester's Station Hill, at City Rd. and Sussex St., from London Waterloo (1hr., 2 per hr., £16.60) and Portsmouth (1hr., every hr., £7). National Express **buses** (☎ (08705) 808 080) go to London (1½hr., 7 per day, £12); Hampshire Stagecoach (☎ (01256) 464 501) goes to Salisbury (#68; 45min., 7 per day, round-trip £4.45) and Portsmouth (#69; 1½hr., 12 per day, round-trip £4.45). The **TIC**, The Guildhall, Broadway, is across from the bus station. (☎ 840 500; fax 850 348. Open May-Sept. M-Sa 9:30am-5:30pm, Su 11am-4pm; Oct.-Apr. M-Sa 10am-5pm.) The lovely home of **Mrs. P. Patton ❸**, 12 Christchurch Rd., between St. James Ln. and Beaufort Rd., is near the cathedral. (☎ 854 272. Singles £25-28; doubles £33-40.) Go past the Alfred statue and across the bridge to reach the **YHA Winchester ❶**, 1 Water Ln. (☎ 853 723. Lockout 10am-5pm. Curfew 11pm. Open from late Mar. to early Nov. daily; late Nov. to early Mar. weekends only. Dorms £9.50, students £8.25, under 18 £7.) **Royal Oak ❶**, on Royal Oak Passage, next to Godbegot House off High St., is yet another pub touting itself as the UK's oldest. The locally brewed hogshead cask ale (£1.75) is delicious. (Open daily 11am-11pm.) A **Sainsbury's** supermarket is on Middle Brook St., off High St. (Open M-Sa 7am-8pm, Su 11am-5pm.) **Postal Code:** SO23 8WA.

SALISBURY   ☎ 01722

Salisbury (pop. 36,890) centers around ▧**Salisbury Cathedral** and its astounding 123m spire. The bases of the pillars literally bend inward under the strain of 6400 tons of limestone; if a pillar rings when you knock on it, you should probably move away. (☎ 555 120. Open June-Aug. M-Sa 7:15am-8:15pm, Su 7:15am-6:15pm; Sept.-May daily 7:15am-6:15pm. Free tours May-Oct. M-Sa 9:30am-4:45pm, May-Sept. until 6:15pm; Nov.-Feb. M-Sa 10am-4pm. Donation £3.50, students and seniors £2.50.) The 1½hr. roof and tower tours are also worthwhile. (May-Sept. M-Sa 11am, 2, 3pm, Su 4:30pm; June-Aug. also M-Sa 6:30pm; winter hours vary. £3, students £2. Call ahead.) One of four surviving copies of the **Magna Carta** rests in the **Chapter House**. (Open June-Aug. M-Sa 9:30am-5:30pm, Su noon-5:30pm; Sept.-May M-Sa 9:30am-5:30pm, Su 1-3:15pm. Free.)

Trains arrive at South Western Rd. from London (1½hr., every hr., £22-30) and Winchester (1½hr., every hr., £11.50). National Express **buses** (☎ 08705 808 080) pull into 8 Endless St. from London Victoria (2¾hr., 4 per day, £12.20); Wilts & Dorset buses (☎ 336 855) arrive from Bath (#X4; every hour from 7am-6pm, £3.95). The **Tourist Information Centre** is on Fish Row in the Guildhall; from the train station, turn left on South Western Rd., bear right on Fisherton St., continue on Bridge St., cross the bridge onto High St., and walk straight down Silver St., which becomes Butcher Row, then Fish Row (10-15min.). From the bus station, head left on Endless St., which becomes Queen St. Turn right at the first old building on the right to enter Fish Row. (☎ 334 956. Open June-Sept. M-Tu 9:30am-5pm, W-Sa 9:30am-6pm, Su 10:30am-4:30pm; Oct.-Apr. M-Sa 9:30am-5pm; May M-Sa 9:30am-5pm, Su 10:30am-4:30pm.) From the TIC, head left on Fish Row, right on Queen St., left on Milford St., and under the overpass to find the **YHA Salisbury ❷**, in Milford Hill House, on Milford Hill. (☎ 327 572. Lockout 10am-1pm. Dorms £11.25.) **Matt and Tiggy's ❸**, 51 Salt Ln., a welcoming 450-year-old house with warped floors and exposed ceiling beams, is just up from the bus station. (☎327 443. Dorms ₤11-12.) At ▩**Harper's "Upstairs Restaurant" ❷**, 6-7 Ox Rd., inventive international and English dishes (₤6-10) make hearty meals and the "8B48" (2 courses for ₤8 before 8pm) buys a heap of food. (☎333 118. Open M-F noon-2pm and 6-9:30pm, Sa noon-2pm and 6-10pm, Su 6-9pm.) **Sainsbury's** supermarket is at The Maltings. (Open M-Th 8am-8pm, F 8am-9pm, Sa 7:30am-7pm, Su 10am-4pm.) **Postal Code:** SP1 1AB.

⚑ DAYTRIP FROM SALISBURY: STONEHENGE. A sunken colossus amid swaying grass and indifferent sheep, Stonehenge stands unperturbed by winds whipping at 80km per hour and legions of people who have visited for over 5000 years. The monument has retained its present shape since about 1500 BC; before it was a complete circle of 7m-high stones weighing up to 45 tons. Though fantastical attributions of Stonehenge ranging from Merlin to helpful extraterrestrials have helped build an attractive mythology around the site, the more plausible source—Neolithic builders—is perhaps the most astonishing of all. The laborers' technological capabilities were extremely advanced; their unknown methods continue to elude archaeologists. You may admire Stonehenge for free from nearby Amesbury Hill, 2½km up A303, or pay admission at the site. (☎01980 624 715. Open June-Aug. daily 9am-7pm; mid-Mar. to May and Sept. to mid-Oct. 9:30am-6pm; mid-Oct. to mid-Mar. 9:30am-4pm. ₤4.20, students ₤3.20.) Wilts & Dorset **buses** (☎336 855) connect from Salisbury's center and train station (40min., round-trip ₤5.25).

BATH   ☎01225

A visit to the elegant Georgian city of Bath (pop. 83,000) remains *de rigueur*, even though today it's more of a museum (or a museum gift shop) than a resort. But expensive trinkets can't conceal the fact that Bath, immortalized by Austen and Dickens, once stood second only to London as the social capital of England.

▣⚶ TRANSPORTATION AND PRACTICAL INFORMATION. Trains leave from Bath for: Bristol (15min., 4 per hr., ₤4.60); Exeter (1¼hr., every hr., ₤22); and London Paddington (1½hr., 2 per hr., ₤32). National Express **buses** (☎(08705) 808 080) run to London (3hr., every hr., ₤13) and Oxford (2hr., daily, ₤10.25). The train and bus stations are near the south end of Manvers St.; walk towards the town center and turn left on York St. to reach the **tourist office**, in Abbey Chambers. (☎477 221. Open May-Sept. M-Sa 9:30am-6pm, Su 10am-4pm; Oct.-Apr. M-Sa 9:30am-5pm, Su 10am-4pm.) **Postal Code:** BA1 1AJ.

⚶⚶ ACCOMMODATIONS AND FOOD. Many **B&Bs** cluster on Pulteney Rd., Pulteney Gdns., and Crescent Gdns. The **International Backpackers Hostel ❷**, 13 Pierrepont St., which has whimsical, musically themed rooms, is up the street from the stations. (☎446 787. Internet. Laundry ₤2.50. Dorms ₤12.) To get to the friendly, well-priced **Toad Hall Guest House ❸**, 6 Lime Grove, go across Pulteney Bridge and through Pulteney Gardens. (☎423 254. Singles ₤22-25; doubles ₤42-45.) **The White Hart ❷**, Widcombe Hill, has a friendly staff and simple rooms. (☎313 985. Dorms ₤12.50; singles ₤20; doubles ₤40.) To reach **Newton Mill Camping ❶**, 4km west on Newton Rd., take bus #5 from the station to Twerton and ask to be let off at the campsite. (☎333 909. Tents ₤4.25-12.) **Demuths Restaurant ❸**, 2 North Parade Passage, has creative vegetarian and vegan dishes. (Entrees ₤8-11. Open daily 10am-10pm.) Fantastic pan-Asian noodles at **f.east ❷**, 27 High St., range from ₤5-8. (Open M-Sa noon-11pm, Su noon-5pm.) **Guildhall Market** has fresh fruit and vegetables and is between High St. and Grand Parade. (Open daily 9am-5:30pm.)

◙ SIGHTS. For 400 years, Bath flourished as a Roman city, its bubbling hot springs making the city a pilgrimage site for those seeking religious miracles and physical healing. The ▨**Roman Baths Museum** showcases the complexity of Roman architecture and engineering, which included central heating and internal plumbing. (Open Apr.-June and Sept. daily 9am-6pm; July-Aug. 9am-10pm; Oct.-Mar. 9:30am-5pm; last admission 1hr. before closing. Audio tour included. ₤8, seniors and students ₤7, children ₤4.) Next to the baths, the towering 15th-century **Bath Abbey** has a whimsical west facade with several angels climbing ladders up to heaven, and curiously enough, two climbing down. (Open Apr.-Oct. M-Sa 10am-6pm, Su 8am-8pm; Nov.-Mar. M-Sa 10am-4pm, Su 8am-8pm. ₤2.) Head north up Stall St., turn left on Westgate St., and turn right on Saw Close to reach Queen Sq.; Jane Austen lived at #13. Continue up Gay St. to **The Circus,** where Thomas Gainsborough, William Pitt, and David Livingstone lived. To the left down Brock St. is the **Royal Crescent,** a half-moon of Gregorian townhouses bordering **Royal Victoria Park.** The **botanical gardens** nurture 5000 species of plants. (Open M-Sa 9am-dusk, Su 10am-dusk. Free.) Backtrack down Brock St. and bear left at The Circus to reach Bennett St. and the dazzling **Museum of Costume,** which will satisfy any fashion fetish. (Open daily 10am-5pm. ₤5; joint ticket with Roman Baths ₤10.)

GLASTONBURY   ☎ 01458

The reputed birthplace of Christianity in England and the seat of Arthurian myth, Glastonbury (pop. 6900) is an intersection of mysticism and religion. Present-day pagan pilgrimage destination **Glastonbury Tor** is supposedly the site of the mystical Isle of Avalon, where King Arthur is predicted to return. To reach the Tor, turn right at the top of High St. onto Lambrook, which becomes Chilkwell St.; turn left onto Wellhouse Ln. and follow the path up the hill (summer buses ₤1). On your way down, visit the **Chalice Well,** on Chilkwell St., the purported resting place of the Holy Grail. (Open Apr.-Oct. daily 10am-6pm; Nov. 11am-5pm; Dec.-Jan. 11am-4pm; Feb.-Mar. 11am-5pm. ₤1.60.) The annual summertime **Glastonbury Festival** is Britain's largest music event. (Tickets ☎ (0115) 912 9129; www.glastonburyfestivals.co.uk.) No trains serve Glastonbury, but First **buses** (☎ (0870) 608 2608) run from Bath (1¼hr., ₤4; change at Wells). From the bus stop, turn right on High St. to reach the **tourist office,** The Tribunal, 9 High St. (☎ 832 954. Open Apr.-Sept. Su-Th 10am-5pm, F-Sa 10am-5:30pm; Oct.-Mar. Su-Th 10am-4pm, F-Sa 10am-4:30pm.) ▨**Glastonbury Backpackers ❷,** at the corner of Magdalene St. and High St., has a fantastic location and an attached sandwich shop. (☎ 833 353. Free Internet access. Dorms ₤10; doubles ₤26-30.) **Postal Code:** BA6 9HG.

THE CORNISH COAST

With lush cliffsides stretching out into the Atlantic, Cornwall's terrain doesn't feel quite like England. Indeed, Cornwall's isolation made it a favored place for Celtic migration in the face of Saxon conquest; though the Cornish language is no longer spoken, the area remains protective of its distinctive past. England's southwest tip has some of the broadest, sandiest beaches in northern Europe, and the surf is up year-round, whether or not the sun decides to break through.

NEWQUAY. An outpost of surfer subculture, Newquay lures the bald, the bleach-blond, and even the blue-haired to its waves and pubs. Winds descend on **Fistral Beach** with a vengeance, creating what some consider the best surfing conditions in Europe. The enticing **Lusty Glaze Beach** beckons from the bay side. Drink up at **The Red Lion,** on North Quay Hill, at Tower Rd. (open M-Sa 11am-11pm, Su 11am-10:30pm), then dance at **Bertie's,** on East St. (Cover ₤5-7. Open daily 9:30pm-2am.) All **trains** (☎ (08457) 484 950) to Newquay come from **Par** (50min., 4-5 per day, ₤4.30).

From Par, trains connect to Plymouth (1hr., 15 per day, £8.10) and Penzance (1¾hr., every hr., £10.30). First (☎ (0870) 608 2608) runs **buses** to St. Ives (2hr., June-Sept. 1 per day, £5). National Express (☎ (08705) 808 080) runs to London (6hr., 1-3 per day, £30.50). The **tourist office** is on Marcus Hill, a block from the bus station. (☎ 854 020. Open Easter-Oct. M-Sa 9:30am-5:30pm, Su 9:30am-4:30pm; Nov.-Easter M-F 9:30am-4:30pm, Sa 9:30am-12:30pm.) **Original Backpackers ❷**, 16 Beachfield Ave., has a fantastic location off Bank St. and near Central Sq., facing the beach. (☎ 874 668. £12 per person, £50 per week.) ☎ **01637.**

PENZANCE. Penzance is the very model of an ancient English pirate town. A Benedictine monastery, **St. Michael's Mount,** was built on the spot where St. Michael appeared in AD 495. The interior is unspectacular, but the grounds are lovely and the 30-story views are captivating. (Open Apr.-Oct. M-F 10:30am-5:30pm; July-Aug. also most weekends; Nov.-Mar. M, W, F by guided tours only. £4.60.) During low tide, visitors can walk to the mount; during high tide, take ferry bus #2 or 2A to Marazion Sq. and catch a ferry (£1). Penzance boasts an impressive number of art galleries; pick up the *Cornwall Gallery Guide* (£1) at the tourist office. **Trains** (☎ (08457) 484 950) go to London (5½hr., every hr., £56) and Plymouth (2hr., every hr., £10.30). National Express (☎ (08705) 808 080) **buses** also run to London (8hr., 8 per day, £28.50) and Plymouth (3hr., 2 per hr., £6). The **tourist office** is between the train and bus stations on Station Rd. (☎ 362 207. Open May-Sept. M-Sa 9am-6pm, Su 10am-1pm; Oct.-Apr. M-F 9am-5pm, Sa 10am-1pm.) ▨**Blue Dolphin Penzance Backpackers ❷**, on Alexandra Rd., is relaxed and well-kept. (☎ 363 836. Dorms £10; doubles £24.) The 13th-century **The Turk's Head,** 49 Chapel St., is a pub once sacked by Spanish pirates. ☎ **01736.**

ST. IVES. St. Ives is 15km north of Penzance, on a spit of land edged by pastel beaches and azure waters. The town drew a colony of painters and sculptors in the 1920s; Virginia Woolf's *To the Lighthouse* is thought to refer to the Godrevy Lighthouse in the distance. The *Cornwall Gallery Guide* (£1) will help you navigate the dozens of galleries here, but St. Ives's real attractions are its beaches. ▨**Porthminster Beach,** downhill from the train station, is a magnificent stretch of white sand and tame waves. **Trains** (☎ (08457) 484950) arrive from Penzance (25min., 2 per hr., £3). National Express (☎ (08705) 808 080) **buses** go to Plymouth (3hr., 4 per day) and Penzance (20min., 4 per day). First (☎ (0870) 608 2608) buses #16, 16B, and 17 go to Penzance (30-40min., 2 per hr., £2.50); buses #57 and 57D run to Newquay (2¼hr., 3 per day, £2.50). The **tourist office** is in the Guildhall on Street-an-Pol. From the stations, walk down to the foot of Tregenna Hill and turn right. (☎ 796 297. Open Easter-Sept. M-Sa 9:30am-6pm, Su 10am-1pm; Oct.-Easter M-F 9am-5pm.) **St. Ives International Backpackers ❶**, The Stenmack, is in a 19th-century Methodist church. (☎ 799 444. Dorms £8-12.) ☎ **01736.**

EAST ANGLIA AND THE MIDLANDS

The rich farmland and watery flats of East Anglia stretch northeast from London, cloaking the counties of Cambridgeshire, Norfolk, and Suffolk, as well as parts of Essex. Literally England's newest landscape, the vast plains of the fens were drained as late as the 1820s. Mention of The Midlands inevitably evokes grim urban images, but there is a unique heritage and quiet grandeur to this smoke-stacked pocket. Even Birmingham, the region's much-maligned center, has its saving graces, among them a lively nightlife and the Cadbury chocolate empire.

OXFORD
☎ 01865

A near millennium of scholarship at Oxford has seen the education of 22 British prime ministers as well as numerous other world leaders. Academic pilgrims can delve into the basement room of Blackwell's Bookstore, explore the impeccable galleries of the Ashmolean Museum, or stroll through the perfectly maintained quadrangles of Oxford's 39 colleges. Secluded from the touring crowds, these quiet destinations reveal Oxford's history and irrepressible grandeur.

🔃 TRANSPORTATION AND PRACTICAL INFORMATION

Trains (☎ 794 422) run from Botley Rd., which is down Park End, to London Paddington (1hr., 2-4 per hr., round-trip £14.80). **Buses** depart from Gloucester Green. **Oxford CityLink** (☎ 785 400) goes to and from London Victoria (1¾hr.; 3 per hr.; round-trip £9, students £7), Gatwick (2hr.; every hr. daytime, every 2 hr. at night; round-trip £22, children £11), and Heathrow (1½hr.; 2 per hr.; round-trip £12, children £6). Most local buses board on the streets around Carfax and have fares around 80p. The **tourist office**, 15-16 Broad St., books rooms for a £3 fee. (☎ 726 871. 2hr. walking tours £6-7. Open M-Sa 9:30am-5pm, Su 10am-3:30pm.) You can access the **Internet** at **Pickwick Papers**, 90 Gloucester Green, near the bus station. (£1 for 30min. Open M-Sa 5am-9pm, Su 8am-8pm.) **Postal Code:** OX1.

🛏 ACCOMMODATIONS

In summer, book at least one week ahead. **B&Bs** line the main roads out of town. On Banbury Rd. (bus #2A, 2C, or 2D), B&Bs are located in the 300s; cheaper ones lie in the 200s and 300s on Iffley Rd. (bus #4), and on Abingdon Rd. in South Oxford (bus #16). Expect to pay £25 per person. **Oxford Backpacker's Hotel ❷**, 9a Hythe Bridge St., has a lively backpacker atmosphere. (☎ 721 761. Internet £1 for 15min. £12.) The **YHA Youth Hostel ❷**, 2a Botley Rd., immediately to the right of the train station, is in a superb location with bright surroundings. Most rooms have 4-6 bunks. (☎ 727 275. Breakfast included. Dorms £18.50, under 18 £13.50, £1 off for students.) Walk 20 minutes or take the "Rose Hill" bus from the bus station, train station, or Carfax Tower to reach **Heather House ❹**, 192 Iffley Rd. (☎ 249 757. Singles £33; doubles £66. Cheaper for longer stays.) **Falcon Private Hotel ❶**, 88-90 Abingdon Rd., is a great place to nest while exploring Oxford. (☎ 511 122. Singles £36; doubles £56.) The lovely prices at **The Acorn ❸**, 260 Iffley Rd., about ¼ mile east of Heather House, make up for its relative lack of amenities. (☎ 247 998. Singles £29 with wash bin; doubles £52.)

🍴 FOOD

Oxford students tired of cafeteria food keep cheap restaurants in business. **Kebab vans** roam Broad St., High St., Queen St., and St. Aldate's St. Across Magdalen Bridge, try restaurants along the first four blocks of Cowley Rd. **Kazbar ❷**, 25-27 Cowley Rd., is a favorite *tapas* bar among locals. (£5 lunch special includes two *tapas* and a drink, M-F noon-4pm.) **The Nosebag ❷**, 6-8 St. Michael's St., has a gourmet-grade menu served cafeteria-style. (Lunch under £6.50; dinner under £8. Open M-Th 9:30am-10pm, F-Sa 9:30am-10:30pm, Su until 9pm.) The chic **Chiang Mai ❷**, 130a High St., tucked down an alley, is a popular Thai restaurant; try the jungle curry with wild rabbit (£7). Reservations recommended. (Open M-Sa noon-2pm and 6-11pm, Su noon-1pm and 6-10pm.) **Heroes ❶**, 8 Ship St., is filled with students feeding on sandwiches and freshly baked breads.

BRITAIN

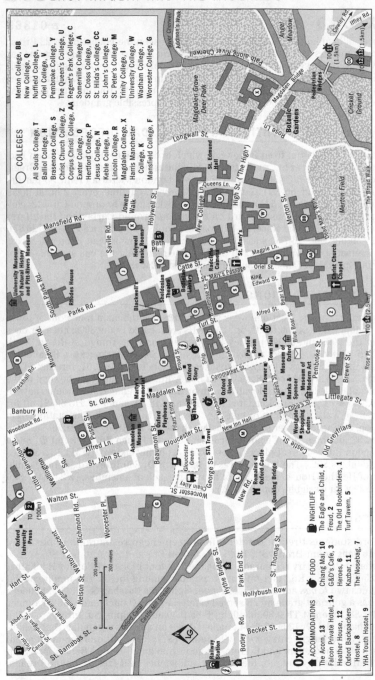

COLLEGES

All Souls College, **T**
Balliol College, **H**
Brasenose College, **S**
Christ Church College, **Z**
Corpus Christi College, **AA**
Exeter College, **O**
Hertford College, **P**
Jesus College, **N**
Keble College, **B**
Lincoln College, **R**
Magdalen College, **X**
Harris Manchester College, **K**
Mansfield College, **F**
Merton College, **BB**
New College, **Q**
Nuffield College, **L**
Oriel College, **V**
Pembroke College, **Y**
The Queen's College, **U**
Regent's Park College, **C**
Somerville College, **A**
St. Cross College, **D**
St. Hilda's College, **CC**
St. John's College, **E**
St. Peter's College, **M**
Trinity College, **I**
University College, **W**
Wadham College, **J**
Worcester College, **G**

Oxford

ACCOMMODATIONS
The Acorn, **13**
Falcon Private Hotel, **14**
Heather House, **12**
Oxford Backpackers Hostel, **8**
YHA Youth Hostel, **9**

FOOD
Chiang Mai, **10**
G&D's Cafe, **3**
Heroes, **6**
Kazbar, **11**
The Nosebag, **7**

NIGHTLIFE
The Eagle and Child, **4**
Freud, **2**
The Old Bookbinders, **1**
Turf Tavern, **5**

(£1.90-£3.65. Open M-F 8am-9pm, Sa 8:30am-6pm, Su 10am-5pm.) **G&D's Cafe ❶**, 55 Little Clarendon St., serves up superb ice cream and sorbet. (£1.65-£3.45. Open daily 8am-midnight.) The **Covered Market,** between Market St. and Carfax, sells produce, deli goods, and breads. (Open M-Sa 8am-5:30pm.)

👁 SIGHTS

The tourist office's *Welcome to Oxford* guide (£1) lists the colleges' public visiting hours. Start by hiking up the 99 steps of **Carfax Tower** for a great view of the city. (Open Apr.-Oct. M-F 10am-5pm, Su 11am-5pm. £1.20.) Just down St. Aldate's St. from Carfax, **Christ Church College** has Oxford's grandest quad and its most socially distinguished students. The **Christ Church Chapel** also serves as the university's cathedral. It was here where the Reverend Charles Dodgson (better known as Lewis Carroll) first met Alice Liddell, the dean's daughter, and the White Rabbit can also be spotted fretting in the hall's stained glass. (☎286 573. Open M-Sa 9:30am-5:30pm, Su noon-5:30pm. Services Su 8, 10, 11:15am, 6pm; weekdays 7:35am, 6pm. £4, students £3.) Plants have flourished for three centuries at the High St. **Botanic Garden.** The path connecting the Botanic Garden to the Christ Church Meadow provides a beautiful view of the Thames. (☎286 690. Open daily Apr.-Sept. 9am-5pm; Oct.-Mar. 9am-4:30pm. Apr.-Aug. £2, children free; Sept.-Mar. free.) The imposing 🎨**Ashmolean Museum,** Beaumont St., houses works by da Vinci, Monet, Manet, van Gogh, Michelangelo, Rodin, and Matisse. From Carfax, head up Cornmarket St., which becomes Magdalen St.; Beaumont St. is on the left. (Open Tu-Sa 10am-5pm, Su 2-5pm. Free.) **Bodleian Library,** Catte St., is Oxford's principal reading and research library with over five million books; no one has ever been permitted to check one out. Take High St. and turn left on Catte. (Open M-F 9am-6pm, Sa 9am-1pm. Tours £3.50.) Next to the Bodleian is the **Sheldonian Theatre,** a Romanesque auditorium where graduation ceremonies are conducted in Latin. The cupola affords a picturesque view of Oxford's spires. (Open M-Sa 10am-12:30pm and 2-4:30pm. £1.50, children £1.) You could browse for days at **Blackwell's Bookstore,** 53 Broad St., which according to the *Guinness Book of Records* is the world's largest room devoted to bookselling. (☎333 606. Open M and W-Sa 9am-6pm, Tu 9:30am-6pm, Su 11am-5pm.)

🎵 🎭 ENTERTAINMENT AND NIGHTLIFE

Punting on the river Thames (known in Oxford as the Isis) or on the River Cherwell (CHAR-wul) is a traditional Oxford pastime. Punters receive a tall pole, a small oar, and an advisory against falling into the water. **Magdalen Bridge Boat Co.,** just under Magdalen Bridge, rents boats. (☎202 643. M-F £9 per hr., Sa-Su £10 per hr.; deposit £20 plus ID. Open Mar.-Nov. daily 10am-9pm.) Music and drama at Oxford are cherished arts. Attend a concert or Evensong service at one of the colleges— the **New College Choir** is one of the best boy choirs around. The **Oxford Playhouse,** 11-12 Beaumont St., is a venue for bands, dance troupes, and both amateur and professional plays. (☎798 600. Standby tickets available for seniors and students.) The **City of Oxford Orchestra,** the city's professional orchestra, gives monthly concerts in the Sheldonian Theatre. (☎744 457. Tickets £10-12; 25% student discount.)

Pubs far outnumber colleges in Oxford. The 13th-century 🍺**Turf Tavern** on Bath Pl., off Holywell St., is a popular student bar. (Open M-Sa 11am-11pm, Su noon-10:30pm. Kitchen open noon-8pm.) Walk up Walton St. and take a left at Jericho St. to reach 🍺**The Old Bookbinders,** 17-18 Victor St., a crowded little pub featuring low ceilings and a young crowd. (Open M-Sa until 11pm) **The Eagle and Child,** 49 St. Giles, moistened the tongues of C.S. Lewis and J.R.R. Tolkien for 25 years; *The Chronicles of Narnia* and *The Hobbit* were first read aloud here. (Open M-Sa

BRITAIN

11am-11pm, Su 11am-10:30pm.) Although pubs in Oxford tend to close down by 11pm, nightlife can last until 3am; grab *This Month in Oxford* at the tourist office. **Walton Street** and **Cowley Road** host late-night clubs, as well as a jumble of ethnic restaurants and offbeat shops. **Freud,** 119 Walton St., in the former St. Paul's Parish Church, is a cafe by day and collegiate cocktail bar by night. (Open until midnight M-Tu, 1am W-Th, 2am F-Sa, 10:30pm Su.)

STRATFORD-UPON-AVON   ☎01789

Former native William Shakespeare is now the area's industry; you'll find even the most vague connections to the Bard exploited to their full potential. Of course, all the perfumes of Arabia will not sweeten the exhaust from tour buses, but beyond the "Will Power" t-shirts, the aura of Shakespeare does remain: in the grace of the weeping Avon and for the pin-drop silence before a soliloquy in the Royal Shakespeare Theatre.

☐ TRANSPORTATION. Thames **trains** (☎ (08457) 484 950) arrive from: London Paddington (2¼hr., 7 per day, £22.50); Birmingham (1hr., every hr., £3.80); and Warwick (25min., 7 per day, £2.80). National Express (☎ (08705) 808 080) runs **buses** from London Victoria (3hr., 3 per day, £12).

⚡ PRACTICAL INFORMATION. The **tourist office,** Bridgefoot, across Warwick Rd. toward the waterside park, offers maps and a free accommodations guide. (☎ 293 127. Open Apr.-Oct. M-Sa 9am-6pm, Su 10:30am-4:30pm; Nov.-Mar. M-Sa 9am-5pm.) Surf the **Internet** at **Cyber Junction,** 28 Greenhill St. (£3 per 30min., £5 per hr.; students £2.50, £4.) **Postal Code:** CV37 6PU.

⚐ ACCOMMODATIONS. To B&B or not to B&B? B&Bs line **Evesham Place, Evesham Road, Grove Road,** and **Shipston Road,** but 'tis nobler in summer to make advance reservations. The **Stratford Backpackers Hotel ❷,** 33 Greenhill St., is conveniently located just across the bridge from the train station and has clean rooms, a common lounge, and a kitchen. (☎ 263 838. Dorms £12.) The friendly proprietress makes **Clodagh's ❷,** 34 Banbury Rd., difficult to leave. (☎ 269 714. Free internet access. Book early; only two rooms available. Singles £17; doubles £34.) A 10min. walk down Evesham, **Penhurst Guest House ❸,** 34 Evesham Pl., has clean and spacious rooms beneath a drab exterior. (☎ 205 259. Singles £18-24; doubles £30-46.) Warm and attentive proprietors consider **The Hollies ❹,** 16 Evesham Pl., their labor of love. (☎ 266 857. Doubles £35, with bath £45.) **Riverside Caravan Park ❶,** Tiddington Rd., 1½km east of Stratford on B4086, has **camping** with beautiful but crowded views of the Avon. (☎ 292 312. Open Easter-Oct. Tent and 2 people £8, each additional person £1.)

❏ FOOD. Opposition ❸, 13 Sheep St., is a bistro that receives rave reviews from locals. (Entrees £8-12. Open M-Sa noon-2pm and 5-10pm, Su noon-2pm and 6-9 pm.) **Hussain's Indian Cuisine ❷,** 6a Chapel St., has fantastic chicken *tikka masala;* keep an eye out for regular Ben Kingsley. (Lunch £6, main dishes from £6.50. Open daily 5pm-midnight, also Th-Su 12:30-2:30pm.) A great place for breakfast or lunch is **Le Petit Croissant ❶,** 17 Wood St. (Baguettes from 80p. Open M-Sa 8am-6pm.) A **Safeway** supermarket is on Alcester Rd., just across the bridge past the train station. (Open M-W and Sa 8am-9pm, Th-F 8am-10pm, Su 10am-4pm.)

◼ SIGHTS. Traffic at the Shakespeare sights peaks around 2pm, so try to hit them before 11am or after 4pm. Die-hard fans can buy a ticket for admission to all five official Shakespeare properties: Anne Hathaway's cottage, Mary Arden's

House and Countryside Museum, Shakespeare's Birthplace, New Place and Nash's House, and Hall's Croft (£12, students and seniors £11). You can also buy a ticket that covers only the latter three sights (£8.50, students and seniors £7.50). **Shakespeare's Birthplace**, on Henley St., is part period re-creation and part exhibition of Shakespeare's life and works. (Open summer M-Sa 9am-5pm and Su 9:30am-5pm; mid-season M-Sa 10am-5pm and Su 10:30am-5pm; winter M-Sa 10am-4pm and Su 10:30am-4pm.) **New Place**, on High St., was Stratford's finest address when Shakespeare bought it in 1597. Only the foundation remains—it can be viewed from **Nash's House**, which belonged to the husband of Shakespeare's granddaughter. **Hall's Croft** and **Mary Arden's House** also capitalize on connections to Shakespeare's extended family, but provide exhibits of what life was like in Elizabethan times. Pay homage to Shakespeare's grave in the **Holy Trinity Church**, on Trinity St. (£1).

🎭 **ENTERTAINMENT.** Get thee to a performance at the world-famous **Royal Shakespeare Company;** recent sons include Kenneth Branagh and Ralph Fiennes. Tickets for all three theaters—the Royal Shakespeare Theatre, the Swan Theatre, and The Other Place—are sold through the box office in the foyer of the Royal Shakespeare Theatre, on Waterside. (☎403 403. 24hr. ticket hotline ☎ (0870) 609 1110. £5-40. Highly demanded student standbys £8-12. Open M-Sa 9:30am-8pm. Tours M-Sa 1:30, 5:30pm, Su noon, 1, 2, 3, 5:30pm. £4, students and seniors £3.)

CHELTENHAM ☎01242

The spa town of Cheltenham (pop. 107,000) is a pleasant break from heavily touristed Bath and Stratford, as well as a useful starting point for visiting the Cotswolds. Residents sunbathe at the exquisite **Imperial Gardens**, five minutes north of the center of town. **Trains** (☎(08457) 484 950) arrive at the station on Queen's Rd. from: Bath (1½hr., every hr., £11); Exeter (2hr., every 2hr., £32.50); and London (2hr., every hr., £36.30). To reach the **tourist office**, 77 The Promenade, walk down Queen's Rd. and bear left onto Lansdown Rd.; head left again at the Rotunda onto Montpellier Walk, which leads to The Promenade. The staff posts accommodations vacancies after hours. (☎522 878. Open M-Tu and Th-Sa 9:30am-5:15pm, W 10am-5:15pm.) **Benton's Guest House ❸**, 71 Bath Rd., has towel warmers, generous hospitality, and breakfasts that barely fit on the plates. (☎517 417. £25 per person.) The well-situated **YMCA ❷**, on Vittoria Walk, houses both men and women. At Town Hall, turn left onto The Promenade and walk three blocks; Vittoria Walk is on the right. (☎524 024. Breakfast included. Reception 24hr. £16 per person.) **Postal Code:** GL50 1AA.

THE COTSWOLDS

Stretching across western England—bounded by Cheltenham in the north, Banbury in the northeast, Malmesbury in the south, and Bradford-on-Avon in the southwest—the Cotswolds' verdant, vivid hills hide tiny towns barely touched by modern life. These old Roman settlements and tiny Saxon villages, hewn from the famed Cotswold stone, demand a place on any itinerary, although their relative inaccessibility via public transportation will necessitate extra effort to get there.

🚍 **TRANSPORTATION.** Useful gateway cities are Cheltenham, Oxford, and Bath. **Moreton-in-Marsh** is one of the bigger villages and has **trains** to Oxford (30min., every hr., £7.80) and London (1½hr., every hr., £23.90). It's much easier to reach by **bus.** *Getting There*, a pamphlet that details bus information in The Cotswolds, is available free from the Cheltenham tourist office. **Pulham's Coaches** (☎(01451) 820 369) run from Cheltenham to Moreton-in-Marsh (1hr.; M-Sa 7 per day, Su 1 per day; £2) via Stow-on-the-Wold (50min., £1.55).

Local roads are perfect for biking. **The Toy Shop,** on High St. in Moreton-in-Marsh, rents bikes. (☎(01608) 650 756. Open M, W-Sa 9am-1pm and 2-5pm. ₤12 per day.) Visitors can also experience the Cotswolds as the English have for centuries by treading footpaths from village to village. **Cotswold Way,** spanning 160km from Bath to Chipping Camden, gives hikers glorious vistas of hills and dales. The *Cotswold Events* booklet lists anything from music festivals and antique markets to cheese-rolling and woolsack races along the Cotswold Way. A newer way of seeing the region, the **Cotswold Experience** is a full-day bus tour that starts in Bath and visits five of the most scenic villages. (☎(01225) 325 900. ₤23.50, students ₤19.50.)

WINCHCOMBE, MORETON-IN-MARSH, STOW-ON-THE-WOLD. 10km north of Cheltenham on the A46, **Sudeley Castle,** once the manor of King Ethelred the Unready, crowns the town of **Winchcombe.** (Open Mar.-Oct. daily 11am-5pm. ₤6.50.) The Winchcombe **tourist office** is in Town Hall. (☎(01242) 602 925. Open Apr.-Oct. M-Sa 10am-1pm and 2-5pm, Su 10am-1pm and 2-4pm.) With a train station, relatively frequent bus service, and bike shop, **Moreton-in-Marsh** is a convenient base for exploring the Cotswolds. Three miles east of Moreton on the A24, visitors to the **Longborough Farm Shop** can pick fruit on 10 acres of farmland. (☎(01451) 830 413. Open M-Sa 9am-6pm, Su 10am-6pm. Self-picking June-Sept. ₤1-3 per basket.) The **tourist office** is in the District Council Building. (☎(01208) 650 881. Open Easter-Oct. M-F 9am-5pm.) **Warwick House B&B ❸,** on London Rd., offers many small luxuries, including access to a nearby gym. Book in advance. (☎(01608) 650 733. www.snoozeandsizzle.com. ₤25 per person, two nights or more ₤20.) **Stow-on-the-Wold,** the self-proclaimed "Heart of the Cotswolds," quietly sleeps atop a hill, offering visitors fine views and a sense of the Cotswold pace of life. The **tourist office** is in Hollis House on The Square. (☎(01451) 831 082. Open Easter-Oct. M-Sa 9:30am-5:30pm, Su 10:30am-4pm; Nov.-Easter M-Sa 9:30am-4:30pm.) The **YHA youth hostel ❷** is near the tourist office on The Square. (☎(01451) 830 497. Open Apr.-Sept. Dorms ₤12.75, students ₤11.75.)

BIRMINGHAM ☎0121

As the industrial heart of the Midlands, Birmingham (pop. 1,200,000) is resolutely modern, its center packed with convention-goers in three-piece suits. Twelve minutes south of town by rail lies ▧**Cadbury World,** an unabashed celebration of the chocolate company. Take a train from New St. to Bournville, or bus #83, 84, or 85 from the city center. (☎451 4159. Open daily 10am-3pm; closed certain days Nov.-Feb. ₤8.25, students and seniors ₤6.75, children ₤6.25. Includes free chocolate.)

Birmingham is the center of a web of train and bus lines between London, central Wales, southwest England, and all destinations north. **Trains** arrive in New St. Station (☎(08457) 484 950) from: Liverpool Lime St. (1½hr., 1-2 per hr., ₤18.50); London Euston (2hr., 2 per hr., ₤29.60); Manchester Piccadilly (2½hr., every hr., ₤16.50); and Oxford (1¼hr., 1-2 per hr., ₤16.50). National Express **buses** (☎(08705) 808 080) arrive in Digbeth Station from: Cardiff (3hr., 3 per day, round-trip ₤17.80); Liverpool (2½hr., every hr., round-trip ₤11.75); London (3hr., every hr., round-trip ₤11.50); and Manchester (2½hr., every 2hr., round-trip ₤13). The **tourist office,** 2 City Arcade, makes room reservations. (☎643 2514. Open M-Sa 9:30am-5:30pm.) Despite its size, Birmingham has no hostels, and inexpensive B&Bs are rare; **Hagley Road** is your best bet. To reach **Grasmere Guest House ❷,** 37 Serpentine Rd., take bus #22, 23, or 103 from Colmore Row to the Harbourne swimming bath (20min.); turn right off Harborne Rd. onto Serpentine Rd. (☎/fax 427 4546. Singles ₤15, with bath ₤25; doubles ₤30.) **Postal Code:** B2 4AA.

CAMBRIDGE ☎01223

In contrast to museum-oriented, metropolitan Oxford, Cambridge is determined to retain its pastoral academic robes. As the tourist office will tell you, the city manages—rather than encourages—visitors. No longer the exclusive preserve of upper-class sons, the university has finally opened its doors to women and state-school pupils; during May Week, which marks the end of exams, Cambridge shakes off its reserve with gin-soaked glee.

▐▀▐ TRANSPORTATION AND PRACTICAL INFORMATION. Trains (☎(08457) 484 950) run from Station Rd. to London King's Cross (45min., 2 per hr., £15.10) and London Liverpool St. (1¼hr., 2 per hr., £15.10). **Buses** run from Drummer St.; **National Express** (☎(08705) 808 080) goes to London Victoria (2hr., 17 per day, from £8), and **Stagecoach Express** runs to Oxford (2¾hr., 10-12 per day, from £6). The **tourist office,** on Wheeler St., is just south of Market Sq. (☎322 640. Open Apr.-Oct. M-F 10am-5:30pm, Sa 10am-5pm, Su 11am-4pm; Nov.-Mar. closed Su.) **Postal Code:** CB2 3AA.

▐▛▐ ACCOMMODATIONS AND FOOD. Many of the **B&Bs** around **Portugal Street** and **Tenison Road** are open only in summer. Check the list at the tourist office or pick up their guide to lodgings (£0.50). Two blocks from the train station, **▓Tenison Towers Guest House ❸,** 148 Tenison Rd., is impeccable. (☎566 511. Singles £20-25; doubles £40-50.) **YHA Cambridge ❷,** 97 Tenison Rd., has a welcoming atmosphere. (☎354 601. Kitchen. Laundry. Dorms £15.10; under 18 £11.40.) **Netley Lodge ❸,** 112 Chesterton Rd., has a conservatory lush with greenery. (☎363 845. Singles £28; doubles £45-55.) **Warkworth Guest House ❹,** Warkworth Terr., near the bus station, offers sunny rooms and lunches on request. (☎363 682. Singles £35; doubles £55-60.) Take Cambus #118 from Drummer St. to reach **Highfield Farm Camping Park ❶,** Long Rd., Comberton. (☎262 308. £7 per tent; £8.75 with car.)

Market Square has fruits and vegetables. (Open M-Sa 9:30am-4:30pm.) **Groceries** are available at **Sainsbury's,** 44 Sidney St. (Open M-F 8am-9pm, Sa 7:30am-9pm, Su 11am-5pm.) **▓Dojo's Noodle Bar ❶,** 1-2 Miller's Yard, Mill Ln., whips out enormous plates of noodles for less than £6. (Open M-Th noon-2:30pm and 5:30-11pm, F-Su noon-4pm and 5:30-11pm.) **Rainbow's Vegetarian Bistro ❷,** 9a King's Parade, is a tiny, creative burrow featuring delicious international vegan and vegetarian fare. (All entrees £6.95. Open M-Sa 11am-11pm.)

▐▛▐ SIGHTS AND ENTERTAINMENT. Cambridge is an architect's dream—it packs some of the most breathtaking examples of English architecture into less than 3 square kilometers. It's most exciting during the university's three eight-week terms: Michaelmas (Oct.-Dec.), Lent (Jan.-Mar.), and Easter (Apr.-June). **Trinity College** houses the stunning **Wren Library,** on Trinity St., home to A.A. Milne's handwritten manuscript of *Winnie the Pooh*. (Chapel and courtyard open daily 10am-5pm; library open M-F noon-2pm, Sa 10:30am-12:30pm. Easter-Oct. £1.75.; Nov.-Easter free.) **King's College,** south of Trinity on King's Parade, is E.M. Forster's alma mater. Rubens's magnificent *Adoration of the Magi* hangs behind the altar of the college's spectacular Gothic chapel. (Open M-Sa 9:30am-4:30pm, Su 9:30am-2:30pm. Tours arranged through the tourist office. £3.50, students £2.50.) A welcome break from academia, the **▓Fitzwilliam Museum,** on Trumpington St., displays Egyptian, Greek, and Asian treasures. (Open Tu-Sa 10am-5pm, Su 2:15-5pm. Suggested donation £3. Guided tours Sa 2:30pm; £3.)

The best source of information on student activities is the newspaper *Varsity;* the tourist office also has useful information. **Punts** (gondola like boats) are a favorite form of entertainment in Cambridge. Beware that punt-bombing—jumping from bridges into the river alongside a punt, thereby tipping its occupants into

BRITAIN

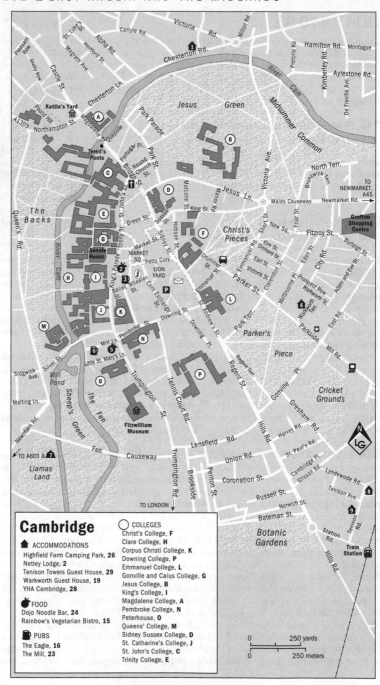

Cambridge

ACCOMMODATIONS
Highfield Farm Camping Park, **26**
Netley Lodge, **2**
Tenison Towers Guest House, **29**
Warkworth Guest House, **19**
YHA Cambridge, **28**

FOOD
Dojo Noodle Bar, **24**
Rainbow's Vegetarian Bistro, **15**

PUBS
The Eagle, **16**
The Mill, **23**

○ **COLLEGES**
Christ's College, **F**
Clare College, **H**
Corpus Christi College, **K**
Downing College, **P**
Emmanuel College, **L**
Gonville and Caius College, **G**
Jesus College, **B**
King's College, **I**
Magdalene College, **A**
Pembroke College, **N**
Peterhouse, **O**
Queens' College, **M**
Sidney Sussex College, **D**
St. Catharine's College, **J**
St. John's College, **C**
Trinity College, **E**

0   250 yards
0   250 meters

the Cam—has evolved into an art form. **Tyrell's**, at Magdalene Bridge, rents boats. (☎ (01480) 413 517. £10 per hr. plus a £40 deposit.) Even more traditional than punting is **pub-crawling;** most pubs are open from 11am-11pm. The oldest pub in Cambridge is **The Eagle**, 8 Benet St. **The Mill**, 14 Mill Ln., off Silver St. Bridge, claims a riverside park as its own for punt- and people-watching.

NORTHERN ENGLAND

BRITAIN

The north's innovative music and arts scenes are world-famous: Liverpool and Manchester alone produced four of *Q* magazine's ten biggest rock stars of the century. Its principal urban areas may have grown out of the wool and coal industries, bearing 19th-century scars to prove it, but their newly refurbished city centers have redirected their energies toward accommodating visitors. Find respite from city life in the Peak District to the east or the Lake District to the north.

MANCHESTER   ☎ 0161

The Industrial Revolution transformed the once unremarkable village of Manchester into Britain's second-largest urban area. With few attractive areas and fewer budget accommodations in the city center, Manchester proves that you don't have to be pretty to be popular, attracting thousands with its pulsing nightlife and vibrant arts scene.

▐ TRANSPORTATION. Trains leave **Piccadilly Station,** on London Rd., and **Victoria Station,** on Victoria St., for: London Euston (2½hr., 1 per hr., £49); Birmingham (1¾hr., 2 per hr., £16.50); Chester (1hr., every hr., £8.95); Edinburgh (4hr., every hr., £45.90); Liverpool (50min., 2 per hr., £7.40); and York (40min., 2 per hr., £17.90). National Express **buses** (☎ (08705) 808 080) go from Chorlton St. to London (4-5hr., 7 per day, £17) and Liverpool (50min., every hr., £4.75). **Piccadilly Gardens** is home to about 50 local bus stops; pick up a route map at the tourist office.

▐ PRACTICAL INFORMATION. Manchester Visitor Centre, in the Town Hall Extension on Lloyd St., provides maps and books accommodations for £2.50. (☎ 234 3157; info (0891) 715 533. Open M-Sa 10am-5pm, Su 10:30am-4:30pm.) Check **email** at **Internet Exchange,** 1-3 Piccadilly Sq., on the 2nd fl. of Coffee Republic. (£1 per hr. with £2 membership, otherwise £1 per 15min. Open M-F 7:30am-6:30pm, Sa 8am-6:30pm, Su 9:30am-5:30pm.) **Postal Code:** M2 1BB.

▐▐ ACCOMMODATIONS AND FOOD. The elegant **Jury's Inn Manchester ❺,** 56 Bridgewater St., offers enormous, economic triples, luxurious baths, and professional service. (☎ 953 8888. A double and single bed in each room; £65 per room. £45 weekend special subject to availability.) Take bus #33 from Piccadilly Gardens toward Wigan to reach the swanky **YHA Manchester ❷,** Potato Wharf, Castlefield. (☎ 839 9960. Lockers £1-2. Laundry £1.50. Internet £0.50 per 6min. Reception 7am-11pm. Dorms £18.50, under 18 £13.50.) **◼Tampopo Noodle House ❷,** 16 Albert Sq., is a chic Manchester favorite (Entrees £3-8. Open M-Sa noon-11pm, Su noon-10pm.) At **Gaia ❸,** 46 Sackville St., skilled chefs fuse British and Mediterranean cuisines. (Entrees £8-13. Open Su-Th noon-midnight, F-Sa noon-2am.)

◨ ◪ SIGHTS AND ENTERTAINMENT. The exception to Manchester's unspectacular buildings is the neo-Gothic **Manchester Town Hall,** behind the tourist office in St. Peter's Sq. Nearby is the domed **Central Library,** one of the largest municipal libraries in Europe. (Open M-Th 10am-8pm, F-Sa 10am-5pm.) In the **Museum of**

THE LOCAL STORY

Science and Industry, on Liverpool Rd. in Castlefield, working steam engines provide a dramatic vision of Britain's industrialization. (Open daily 10am-5pm. Free. Special exhibit £3-5.) The **Manchester United Museum and Tour Centre,** on Sir Matt Busby Way at the Old Trafford football stadium, revels in everything that is the football team Manchester United. Follow the signs up Warwick Rd. from the Old Trafford Metrolink stop. (Open daily 9:30am-5pm. Museum £5.50, seniors and children £3.75. Tours every 10min. 9:40am-4:30pm. £3, seniors and children £2.) One of Manchester's biggest draws is its artistic offerings, most notably its theater and music scenes; the **Royal Exchange Theatre,** on St. Ann's Sq., regularly puts on Shakespeare and original works. (☎833 9333. Box office open M-Sa 9:30am-7:30pm. £7-24. Student discounts in advance.)

Come nightfall, try the lively ◼**The Lass O'Gowrie,** 36 Charles St., for good food at even better prices. (Food served 9am-7pm, £2-5. Open M-Sa 11am-11pm, Su noon-10:30pm.) ◼**Musicbox,** on Oxford Rd., is a popular underground warehouse club that hosts weekly events. (Cover £5-8. Open Th-Sa from 10pm.) Manchester's gay nightlife is centered around the vibrant **Gay Village,** northeast of Princess St.; bars line **Canal Street,** the center of the village. Enthusiastic crowds pack **Cruz 101,** 101 Princess St., the champion of Manchester's nightlife. (M, F, Sa cover £2-5, Tu-Th free. Open M-Sa 10:30pm-2:30am.)

LIVERPOOL ☎0151

Free museums, a raucous nightlife, and restaurants on every block make Liverpool, hometown of the Beatles, a great destination for travelers. Scousers—as Liverpudlians are colloquially known—are usually happy to introduce you to their dialect and to discuss the relative merits of Liverpool's two football teams.

◼◼ **TRANSPORTATION AND PRACTICAL INFORMATION. Trains** (☎(08457) 484 950) leave Lime St. for: Birmingham (1¾hr., 2-5 per day, £18.50); Chester (45min., 2 per hr., £3.20); London Euston (3hr., every hr., £48.40); and Manchester Piccadilly (1½hr., 2-3 per hr., £7.40). National Express **buses** (☎(08705) 808 080) go from Norton St. Coach Station to: Birmingham (2½hr., 5 per day); London (4½hr., 5 per day, £16.50); and Manchester (1hr., 1-2 per hr.). The Isle of Man Steam Packet Company (☎(08705) 523 523) runs **ferries** from Princess Dock to Dublin.

The main **tourist office,** in the Queen Square Centre, sells the handy *Visitor Guide to Liverpool and Merseyside* (£1) and books beds for a 10% deposit. (☎ (0906) 680 6886; £0.25 per min. Open M and W-Sa 9am-5:30pm, Tu 10am-5:30pm, Su 10:30am-4:30pm.) Expert guide Phil Hughes runs personalized **Beatles tours** (☎ 228 4565) for the lucky eight that fit in his van. Check **email** at the **Central Library,** on William Brown St. (Free. Open M-Sa 9am-5pm, Su noon-5pm.) **Postal Code:** L1 1AA.

⌨ ▤ ACCOMMODATIONS AND FOOD. Budget hotels are mostly on **Lord Nelson Street,** next to the train station, and **Mount Pleasant,** one block from Brownlow Hill. Clean rooms and a relaxing bar await at **Aachen Hotel ❸,** 89-91 Mt. Pleasant, the winner of numerous awards. (☎ 709 3477. Singles £28-38; doubles £46-54.) **YHA Liverpool ❷,** 24 Tabley St., off The Wapping, is in an ideal location. (☎ 709 8888. Breakfast included. Dorms £19, under 18 £14.50.) The **International Inn ❷,** 4 South Hunter St., off Hardman St., is clean *and* fun, a rare hostel combo. (☎ 709 8135. Dorms £15; doubles £36.) The pleasant **Thistle Hotel ❹,** on Chapel St., is a short walk from downtown Liverpool. (☎ 227 4444. Singles £50-100. Call ahead for discounts.)

Trendy cafes and well-priced Indian restaurants line **Bold Street** and **Hardman Street,** while fast-food joints crowd **Hardnon Street** and **Berry Street.** Many eateries stay open until 3am. **Simply Heathcotes ❹,** 25 The Strand, Beetham Plaza, is simply elegant. Try the breaded veal escalope or seared fillet of salmon. (Entrees average £15. Open M-Sa noon-2:30pm and 6-10pm.) **Tavern Co. ❷,** in Queen Sq., near the tourist office, serves burritos and taco salads (£5-7) in a popular wine-bar atmosphere. (Open M-Sa noon-11pm, Su 10:30am-10:30pm; food served until 10pm.)

◪ SIGHTS. The tourist office's **Beatles Map** (£2.50) leads visitors through Beatles-themed sights, including **Strawberry Fields** and **Penny Lane.** At Albert Dock, **The Beatles Story** pays tribute to the group's work with a recreation of the Cavern Club and a yellow submarine. (Open Apr.-Oct. daily 10am-6pm; Nov.-Mar. 10am-5pm. £8, students £5.50.) The intimate Liverpool branch of the **Tate Gallery,** also on Albert Dock, contains a select range of 20th-century artwork. (Open Tu-Su 10am-6pm. Free; some special exhibits £4.) The Anglican **Liverpool Cathedral,** on Upper Duke St., boasts the highest Gothic arches ever built and the heaviest bells in the world. Climb to the top of the 100m tower for a

LG: Sort of Pollock-style...

AW: Heh. Yeah...

LG: And how did you become their manager?

AW: I put this big rock 'n' roll show on. They came and saw me the next day and said, "Hey Al? When are you going to do something for us like?" And I said to them, "Look, there's no more painting to be done." And they said, "No, we've got a *group.*" I said, "I didn't know that." And they said, "Well, will you manage us?" By then I had got to know them, and they were quite nice personalities—very witty. And I go, "Oh yeah, this could be fun." And then I managed them.

Williams felt that it was their stint in Hamburg, and not Liverpool, that made the Beatles. He describes his falling out with the group as a disagreement over—what else?—contract disputes and general rock-star ingratitude.

AW: I wrote them a letter saying that they appeared to be getting more than a little swell-headed and "Remember, I managed you when nobody else wanted to know you. But I'll fix it now so that you'll never ever work again."

LG: Uh-oh.

AW: So that's my big mistake, yeah. Heh. And on that note, we'll finish.

view stretching to Wales. (Cathedral open daily 8am-6pm. Suggested donation £2.50. Tower open M-Sa 11am-4pm, weather permitting. £2.) Neon-blue stained glass casts a glow over the interior of the **Metropolitan Cathedral of Christ the King,** on Mt. Pleasant, and modern sculptures fill the chapels. (Open in summer M-F 8am-6pm, Sa-Su 8:30am-6pm; off-season M-F 8am-6pm, Sa 8:30am-6pm, Su 8:30am-5pm. Free.) The **Liverpool** and **Everton football clubs**—intense rivals—both offer tours of their grounds. Bus #26 runs from the city center to both stadiums. (Book in advance. Everton ☎330 2277; £5.50. Liverpool ☎260 6677; £8.50.)

🎵 **NIGHTLIFE.** Consult the *Liverpool Echo*, an evening paper sold by street vendors, for up-to-date information on nightlife. **Slater Street** in particular brims with £1 pints, while on weekend nights, the downtown area—especially **Mathew Street, Church Street,** and **Bold Street**—overflows with young clubbers. John Lennon once said that the worst thing about fame was "not being able to get a quiet pint at the Phil." Fortunately, the rest of us can sip in solitude at **The Philharmonic,** 36 Hope St. (Open M-Sa noon-11pm, Su noon-10:30pm.) **The Jacaranda,** on Slater St., the site of the Beatles' first paid gig, has live bands and a dance floor. (Open M-Sa noon-2am, Su noon-10:30pm.) **Medication,** in Wolstonholme Sq., offers the wildest student night in town. (Students only; bring ID. Open W 10am-2am. Cover £5.) **The Cavern Club,** 10 Mathew St., is on the site where the Fab Four gained prominence; today it draws locals for live bands. (No cover until 10pm, 10-11pm £2, 11pm-2am £4. Live music Th-F 8pm-2am, Sa 2-11pm. Open Th-F 6pm-2am, Sa 6pm-3am; pub open M-Sa from noon, Su noon-11:30pm.)

PEAK DISTRICT NATIONAL PARK

A green cushion between England's industrial giants of Manchester, Sheffield, and Nottingham, Britain's first national park sprawls across 1400 sq. km of rolling hills and windswept moors, offering a playground for its 22 million urban neighbors.

🎫 **TRANSPORTATION AND PRACTICAL INFORMATION.** The invaluable *Peak District Timetable* (£0.60), available at tourist offices, has transport routes and a map. Two **train** lines originate in Manchester and enter the park from the west: one stops at Buxton, near the park's edge (1hr., every hr., £5.70), and the other crosses the park (1½hr., 9-17 per day) via Edale (£6.70), Hope (near Castleton), and Hathersage, terminating in Sheffield (£11). Trent (☎01773 712 2765) **bus** TP, the "Transpeak," goes from Manchester to Nottingham (3hr.), stopping at Buxton, Bakewell, Matlock, Derby, and other towns in between. First PMT (☎01782 207 999) #X18 runs from Sheffield to Bakewell (45min., M-Sa 5 per day). First Mainline (☎01709 515 151) #272 and Stagecoach East Midland (☎01246 211 007) #273 and 274 run from Sheffield to Castleton (40-55min., 12-15 per day). The **Derbyshire Wayfarer,** available at tourist offices, allows one day of train and bus travel through the Peak District north to Sheffield and south to Derby (£7.25).

The **National Park Information Centres** (NPICs) at Bakewell, Castleton, and Edale offer walking guides. Info is also available at **tourist offices** in Buxton (☎01298 25 106) and Matlock Bath (☎01629 55 082). There are 20 **YHA youth hostels** ❷ in the park (£8-15); for Bakewell, Castleton, and Edale, see below, or try Buxton (☎01298 22 287) or Matlock (☎01629 582 983). To stay at the 13 **YHA Camping Barns** ❶ throughout the park (£3.60 per person), book ahead at the **Camping Barns Reservation Office,** 6 King St., Clitheroe, Lancashire BB7 2EP (☎01200 420 102). The park operates six **Cycle Hire Centres** (£12 per day); a free brochure, *Peak Cycle Hire,* available at NPICs, includes phone numbers, hours, and locations.

CASTLETON. The main attraction in **Castleton** (pop. 705) is ▨**Treak Cliff Cavern,** which hides seams of Blue John, a mineral found only in these hills. (40min. mandatory tours every 15-30min. Open Easter-Oct. daily 10am-4:45pm; Nov.-Feb. 10am-3:20pm; Mar.-Easter 10am-4:20pm. £5.50, students £4.50.) Castleton lies 3.2km west of **Hope.** The Castleton **NPIC** is on Buxton Rd. (☎620 679. Open Apr.-Oct. daily 10am-5:30pm; Nov.-Mar. Sa-Su 10am-5pm.) **YHA Castleton ❷** is in Castleton Hall, a pretty country house in the heart of town. (☎620 235. Internet access. Open Feb. to late Dec. Dorms £11-14, under 18 £8-10.) ☎**01433.**

BAKEWELL AND EDALE. The town of **Bakewell,** 50km southeast of Manchester, is the best spot from which to explore the region; several scenic walks through the **White Peaks** leave from nearby. Bakewell's **NPIC** is in Old Market Hall, at Bridge St. (☎813 227. Open Mar.-Oct. daily 9:30am-5:30pm; Nov.-Feb. 10am-5pm.) The cozy **YHA Bakewell ❷,** on Fly Hill, is 5min. from the town center. (☎812 313. Open Mar.-Oct. M-Sa; Nov.-Feb. daily. Dorms £10.25, under 18 £7.) ☎**01629.**

The northern Dark Peak area contains some of the wildest and most rugged hill country in England. The area around **Edale** is spectacular, and the National Park Authority's *8 Walks Around Edale* (£1.20) details nearby trails. The town offers little other than a church, cafe, pub, school, and the nearby **YHA youth hostel ❷.** (☎670 302; dorms £11.25, under 18 £8.) ☎**01433.**

YORK ☎**01904**

Although its well-preserved city walls have foiled many, York fails to impede its present-day hordes of visitors. Today's marauders brandish cameras instead of swords and are after York's compact collection of rich historical sights, including Britain's largest Gothic cathedral.

◧▨ TRANSPORTATION AND PRACTICAL INFORMATION. Trains run from Station Rd. to: Edinburgh (2-3hr., 2 per hr., £52.50); London King's Cross (2hr., 2 per hr., £65); Manchester Piccadilly (1½hr., 2 per hr., £16.10); and Newcastle (1hr., 2 per hr., £15.50). National Express **buses** (☎(08705) 808 080) depart from Rougier St. for: Edinburgh (5hr., 2 per day, £26.50); London (4½hr., 6 per day, £19.50); and Manchester (3hr., 6 per day, £7.25). To reach the **tourist office,** in De Grey Rooms, Exhibition Sq., follow Station Rd., which turns into Museum St., go over the bridge, and turn left on St. Leonards Pl. (Open June-Oct. daily 9am-6pm; Nov.-May 9am-5pm.) **Cafe of the Evil Eye,** 42 Stonegate, has **Internet** access (£2 per hr.). **Postal Code:** YO1 8DA.

▨◨ACCOMMODATIONS AND FOOD. B&Bs are concentrated on the side streets along **Bootham** and **Clifton,** in the **Mount** area down **Blossom Street,** and on **Bishopsthorpe Road,** south of town. Book ahead in summer, when competition for all types of accommodations can be fierce. ▨**York Backpackers Hostel ❶,** 88-90 Micklegate has a fun atmosphere in an 18th-century mansion. Their "Dungeon Bar" is open three nights per week, long after the pubs close. (☎627 720. Dorms £9-14; doubles £30.) ▨**Avenue Guest House ❷,** 6 The Avenue, off Clifton, is immaculate and comfortable. (☎620 575. Singles £18-20; doubles £34-44.) **Alexander House ❹,** 94 Bishopsthorpe Rd., 5min. from the train station, has luxurious rooms with flowers and king-sized beds. (☎625 016. Singles £55-60; doubles £64-70.) **Cornmill Lodge ❸,** 120 Haxby Rd. is a quiet, vegetarian B&B. From Exhibition Sq. go up Gillygate to Clarence St., which becomes Haxby Rd., or take bus #A1 from the station. (☎620 566. Singles £20-30; doubles £40-60.)

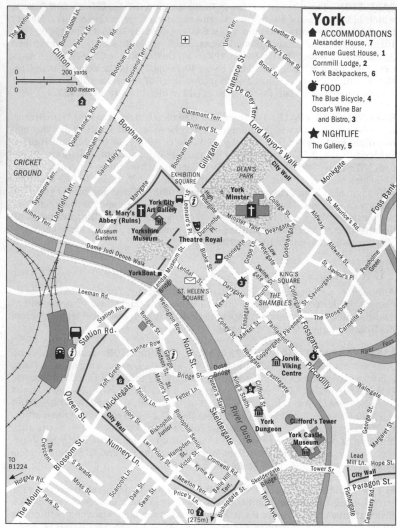

York

♠ ACCOMMODATIONS
Alexander House, 7
Avenue Guest House, 1
Cornmill Lodge, 2
York Backpackers, 6

🍎 FOOD
The Blue Bicycle, 4
Oscar's Wine Bar
and Bistro, 3

★ NIGHTLIFE
The Gallery, 5

The Blue Bicycle ❹, 34 Fossgate, serves light and delicious French food. (Entrees £11-18. Open daily noon-2:30pm and 6-10pm.) **Oscar's Wine Bar and Bistro ❷,** 8 Little Stonegate, stuffs patrons with massive portions of pub grub for £6-8. (Open daily 11am-11pm.) Fruits and vegetables are available at **Newgate market,** between Parliament St. and Shambles. (Open Apr.-Dec. M-Sa 9am-5pm, Su 9am-4:30pm; Jan.-Mar. M-Sa 9am-5pm.)

🌀 📷 **SIGHTS AND NIGHTLIFE.** The best introduction to York is the 4km walk along its **medieval walls.** Beware of the tourist stampede, which slows only in the early morning and just before the walls and gates close at dusk. A free 2hr. **walking** tour is offered daily by the **Association of Voluntary Guides** (☎630 284); tours leave from the York City Art Gallery, across from the tourist office. Everyone and everything in York converges at the enormous ▨**York Minster.** Half of all the medieval stained glass in England glitters here; the **Great East Window** depicts the beginning and end of the world in over 100 scenes. (Cathedral open in summer daily 7am-8:30pm; off-season 7am-6pm. Suggested donation £3. Tours 9:30am-3:30pm.) The ▨**York Castle Museum,** at the Eye of York, between Tower St. and Piccadilly St. in a former debtor's prison, is arguably Britain's premier museum dedicated to everyday life. (Open Apr.-Oct. daily 9:30am-5pm; Nov.-Mar. 9:30am-4:30pm. £6.75, students £4.) The **Jorvik Viking Centre,** on Coppergate, is one of the busiest places in York; visit early or late to avoid lines, or call at least 24hr. in advance. Visitors pass through the York of AD 948, with authentic artifacts and painfully accurate smells. (☎643 211. For advance booking, call ☎543 403 M-F 9am-5pm. Open Apr.-Oct. daily 9am-5:30pm; Nov.-Dec. daily 10am-4:30pm; Jan.-Mar. Su-F 9am-3:30pm, Sa 9am-4:30pm. £9, students £7.50.) The **Yorkshire Museum** presents Roman, Anglo-Saxon, and Viking artifacts, as well as the £2.5 million **Middleham Jewel** from circa 1450. (Enter from Museum St. or Marygate. Open daily 10am-5pm. £4, students £3, families £11.50. Gardens and abbey free.)

The monthly *What's On* and *Artscene* guides, available at the tourist office, publish info on live music, theater, cinema, and exhibitions. **The Gallery,** 12 Clifford St., has two dance floors and six bars. (Cover £1.50-4. Open F-W 9:30pm-2am, Th 10pm-2am.)

NEWCASTLE-UPON-TYNE   ☎0191

Hardworking Newcastle is legendary for its pub and club scene, but ambitious building efforts have lent the city genuine daytime energy. Explore the masterful **Tyne Bridge** and neighboring **Castle Keep,** erected in the 12th century. (Open Apr.-Sept. daily 9:30am-5:30pm; Oct.-Mar. 9:30am-4:30pm. £1.50.) **LIFE Interactive World,** Times Sq., on Scotswood Rd., is an enjoyable hands-on science museum. (Open daily 10am-6pm. £6.95, seniors and students £5.50, children £4.50.) The ▨**Laing Art Gallery,** on New Bridge St., showcases an excellent collection of local art. (Open M-Sa 10am-5pm, Su 2-5pm. Free.) Rowdy **Bigg Market** features the highest concentration of pubs in England, while **Quayside** (KEY-side) is slightly more relaxed and attracts local students. **Chase,** 10-15 Sandhill, is a flashy pub, while nearby **Offshore 44,** 40 Sandhill, has a tropical theme. (Both open M-Sa 11am-11pm and Su noon-6pm.) The hottest dance club is **The Tuxedo Princess,** on a cruise ship under the Tyne Bridge. (Open M and W-Sa 7:30pm-2am.) Gays and lesbians flock to Waterloo St. to drink and dance at **The Powerhouse.** (Open M and Th 10pm-2am, Tu-W 11pm-1am, F-Sa 10pm-3am.)

Trains leave from Neville St. for London (3hr., every hr., £83) and Edinburgh (1½hr.; M-Sa 23 per day, Su 16 per day; £33.50). National Express **buses** (☎08705 808 080) leave Percy St. for London (6hr., 6 per day, round-trip £23) and Edinburgh (3hr., 3 per day, round-trip £13). The **tourist office** is on 132 Grainger St., facing Grey's Monument. (☎277 8000. Open M-W and F-Sa 9:30am-5:30pm, Th 9:30am-7:30pm; June-Sept. also Su 10am-4pm.) To get to the friendly **YHA youth hostel ❷,** 107 Jesmond Rd., take the Metro to Jesmond, turn left onto Jesmond Rd., and walk past the traffic lights. (☎281 2570. Lockout 10am-5pm. Open Feb.-Dec. Dorms £11.25, under 18 £8.) **Portland Guest House ❸,** 134 Sandyford Rd., is cheap and convenient. From the Jesmond metro stop, turn left onto Jesmond Rd., then right onto Portland Terr.; the guest house is at the end. (☎232 7868. Breakfast included. Singles £18-30; doubles £36-40.) **Don Vito's ❶,** 82 Pilgrim St., stands out among the many Italian eateries. (☎232 8923. Entrees £4-6. Open M-F 11:45am-2pm and 5-10pm, Sa 11:45am-10:30pm.) **Postal Code:** NE1 7AB.

LAKE DISTRICT NATIONAL PARK

The Lake District was gouged by glaciers during the last ice age, creating the most dramatic landscape in all England. Jagged peaks and windswept fells stand in desolate splendor and water wends its way in every direction. Use Windermere, Ambleside, Grasmere, and Keswick as bases from which to ascend into the hills—the farther west you go from the **A591**, which connects these towns, the more countryside you'll have to yourself.

The **National Park Visitor Centre** is in **Brockhole**, halfway between Windermere and Ambleside. (☎ 015394 46 601. Open Easter-Oct. daily 10am-5pm; Nov.-Easter most weekends.) **National Park Information Centres** book accommodations and dispense free information and town maps. While B&Bs line every street in every town and there's a hostel around every bend, lodgings do fill up in summer; book ahead.

☰ TRANSPORTATION. Trains (☎ 08457 484 950) run to Oxenholme from: Birmingham (2½hr., 1-2 per hr., ₤41.50); Edinburgh (2½hr., 6 per day, ₤41.50); London Euston (4-5hr., 11-16 per day, ₤101); and Manchester Piccadilly (1½hr., 5-7 per day, ₤17). A short line covers the 16km between Windermere and Oxenholme (20min., every hr., ₤3.10). There is also direct service to Windermere from Manchester Piccadilly (2hr., 3-4 per day, ₤19.80). National Express **buses** (☎ 08705 808 080) arrive in Windermere from Birmingham (4½hr., 1 per day, ₤24.50) and London (7½hr., 1 per day, ₤26), and continue north through Ambleside and Grasmere to Keswick. **Stagecoach in Cumbria** (☎ 0870 608 2608) is the primary operator of bus service in the region; a complete timetable, *The Lakeland Explorer*, is available at tourist offices. An **Explorer** ticket offers unlimited travel on all area Stagecoach buses (1-day ₤7, children ₤5; 4-day ₤16/₤12). The Ambleside YHA Youth Hostel offers a convenient **minibus** service (☎ 015394 32 304) between hostels (₤2.50) as well as free service from the Windermere train station to the Windermere and Ambleside hostels. Cyclists can get **bike rental** information at tourist offices; the *Ordnance Survey Cycle Tours* (₤10) has route maps.

WINDERMERE AND BOWNESS. Windermere and its sidekick **Bowness-on-Windermere** fill to the gills with vacationers in summer, when sailboats and waterskiers criss cross incessantly over Lake Windermere. At **Windermere Lake Cruises** (☎ 433 60), at the north end of Bowness Pier, boats are more frequent in summer and sail north to Waterhead Pier in Ambleside (30min., round-trip ₤6.20) and south to Lakeside (40min., round-trip ₤6.40). Lakeland Experience **buses** to Bowness (#599; 3 per hr., ₤1) leave from the train station. The **tourist office** is next door. (☎ 46 499. Open July-Aug. daily 9am-7:30pm; Easter-June and Sept.-Oct. 9am-6pm; Nov.-Easter 9am-5pm.) The local **National Park Information Centre**, on Glebe Rd., is beside Bowness Pier. (☎ 42 895. Open July-Aug. daily 9:30am-6pm; Apr.-June and Sept.-Oct. daily 9am-5:30pm; Nov.-Mar. F-Su 10am-4pm.) To get to the spacious **YHA Windermere ❷**, on High Cross in Troutbeck, 1.5km north of Windermere off A591, take the Ambleside bus to Troutbeck Bridge and walk 1.25km uphill, or catch the YHA shuttle from the train station. (☎ 43 543. Bike rental. Open mid-Feb. to Oct. daily; Nov. to mid-Feb. F-Sa only. Dorms ₤11.25, under 18 ₤8.) **Camp at Park Cliffe ❷**, Birks Rd., 5km south of Bowness. Take bus #618 from Windermere station. (☎ (015295) 31 344. ₤10-₤13 per tent.) ☎**015394.**

AMBLESIDE. About 2km north of Lake Windermere, Ambleside is an attractive village with convenient access to the southern lakes. It's popular with hikers, who are drawn by its location—or perhaps by its absurd number of outdoors shops. Splendid views of higher fells can be had from the top of **Loughrigg** (a moderately difficult 11km round-trip hike); 1km from town is the lovely waterfall **Stockghyll Force**. The tourist office has guides to these and other walks. Lakeslink **bus** #555

(☎ 32 231) leaves from Kelsick Rd. for Grasmere, Keswick, and Windermere (every hr., £2-6.50). The **tourist office** is located in the Central Building on Market Cross. (☎ 31 576. Open daily 9am-5:30pm.) To reach the **National Park Information Centre**, on Waterhead, walk south on Lake Rd. or Borrans Rd. from town to the pier. (☎ 32 729. Open Easter-Oct. daily 9:30am-6pm.) Bus #555 also stops at the superb ◙**YHA Ambleside ❷,** 1.5km south of Ambleside and 5km north of Windermere, on the north shore of Lake Windermere. (☎ 32 304. Bike rental. Mar.-Oct. no curfew; Nov.-Feb. midnight. Dorms £13.50, under 18 £9.50.) ☎ **015394.**

GRASMERE. The peace that Wordsworth enjoyed in the village of Grasmere is still apparent on quiet mornings. The 17th-century ◙**Dove Cottage,** 10 minutes from the center of town, was Wordsworth's home from 1799 to 1808 and remains almost exactly as he left it; next door is the outstanding **Wordsworth Museum.** (Both open mid-Feb. to mid-Jan. daily 9:30am-5pm. £5.50, students £4.70.) The **Wordsworth Walk** (9.5km) circumnavigates the two lakes of the Rothay River, passing the cottage, the poet's grave in St. Oswald's churchyard, and ◙**Rydal Mount,** where Wordsworth lived until his death. (Rydal open Mar.-Oct. daily 9:30am-5pm; Nov.-Feb. W-M 10am-4pm. £3.75, students £3.25.) **Bus** #555 stops in Grasmere every hour on its way south to Ambleside or north to Keswick. The **National Park Information Centre** is on Redbank Rd. (☎ 35 245. Open Easter-Oct. daily 9:30am-5:30pm; Nov.-Easter Sa-Su 10am-4pm.) **The Hardwood ❸,** on Red Lion Sq., has eight comfortable rooms right in the center of town. (☎ 35 248. 2 night min. stay on weekends. £24.50-32.50 per person.) Sarah Nelson's famed Grasmere Gingerbread, a staple since 1854, is a bargain at £0.22 in **Church Cottage,** outside St. Oswald's Church. (Open Easter-Nov. M-Sa 9:15am-5:30pm, Su 12:30-5:30pm; Dec.-Easter M-Sa 9:15am-5pm, Su 12:30-5pm.) ☎ **015394.**

KESWICK. Between towering Skiddaw peak and the north edge of Lake Derwentwater, Keswick (KEZ-ick) rivals Windermere as the Lake District's tourist capital but surpasses it in charm. A standout 6.5km day-hike from Keswick visits the **Castlerigg Stone Circle,** a 5000-year-old neolithic henge. Another short walk hits the beautiful **Friar's Crag,** on the shore of Derwentwater, and **Castlehead,** a viewpoint encompassing the town, the lakes, and the peaks beyond. Both of these walks are fairly easy, although they do have their more strenuous moments. Maps and information on these and a wide selection of other walks are available at the **National Park Information Centre,** in Moot Hall, Market Sq. (☎ 72 645. Open Aug. daily 9:30am-6pm; Sept.-July 9:30am-5:30pm.) ◙**YHA Derwentwater ❷,** in Barrow House, Borrowdale, is in a 200-year-old house with its own waterfall. Take bus #79 (every hr.) 3km south out of Keswick. (☎ 77 246. Open Feb. to early Oct. daily; Dec.-Jan. F-Sa only. Dorms £11.25, under 18 £8.) ☎ **017687.**

WALES

Wales may border England, but if many of the 2.9 million Welsh people had their way, it would be floating oceans away. Ever since England solidified its control over the country with the murder of Prince Llywelyn ap Gruffydd in 1282, relations between the two have been marked by a powerful unease. Wales clings steadfastly to its Celtic heritage, continuing a centuries-old struggle for independence, and the Welsh language endures in conversation, commerce, and literature. As coal, steel, and slate mines fell victim to Britain's faltering economy in the mid-20th century, Wales turned its economic eye from heavy industry to tourism. Travelers come for the sandy beaches, grassy cliffs, brooding castles, and dramatic mountains that typify the rich landscape of this corner of Britain.

■ **FERRIES TO IRELAND**

Irish Ferries (☎08705 171 717; www.irishferries.ie) run to Dublin, Ireland, from Holyhead (2-3hr., round-trip £20-31) and to Rosslare, Ireland, from Pembroke (4hr., round-trip £25-39). **Stena Line** (☎01233 646 826; www.stenaline.co.uk) runs from Holyhead to Dublin, Ireland (4hr., £23-27), and Dún Laoghaire, Ireland (1-3½hr., £23-27). **Swansea Cork Ferries** (☎(01792) 456 116) run from Swansea to Cork, Ireland (10hr., £24-34).

CARDIFF (CAERDYDD)   ☎029

Formerly the main port of call for Welsh coal, Cardiff (pop. 325,000) is now the port of arrival for a colorful international population—you're as likely to hear Urdu on a street corner as you are to hear Welsh. Climb the Norman keep of the flamboyant **Cardiff Castle** for a sweeping view of the city, then tour its restored medieval interior. (Open Mar.-Oct. daily 9:30am-6pm; Nov.-Feb. 9:30am-4:30pm. £5.50, students £4.20.) At the **National Museum and Gallery**, in the Civic Centre across North Rd. from the castle, a dazzling audio-visual exhibit on the evolution of Wales speeds you through millennia of geological transformation. (Open Tu-Su 10am-5pm. Free.) ▓**The Prince of Wales**, at the corner of St. Mary St. and Wood St., is a sprawling, boisterous pub. (Open M-Sa 11am-11pm, Su noon-10:30pm.) A colorful live-music venue, **The Toucan**, 95-97 St. Mary's St., features a wide variety of sounds, from hip-hop to salsa. (Open Tu-Su noon-2am.) **Clwb Ifor Bach** (the Welsh Club), 11 Womanby St., is a manic, three-tiered club with everything from Motown tunes to video games. (Cover £2-8. Open M-Th until 2am, F-Sa until 3am.)

Trains (☎(08457) 484 950) arrive at **Central Station,** Central Sq., from: Bath (1-1½hr., 1-3 per hr., £12.20); Edinburgh (7hr., 7 per day, £105); and London Paddington (2hr., every hr., £46.80). National Express **buses** (☎(08705) 808 080) leave from Wood St. for London Victoria (3½hr., 6 per day, £12.50) and Manchester (5½hr., 4 per day, £19.50). The **tourist office** is at 16 Wood St., across from the bus station. (☎2022 7281. Open July-Aug. M-Sa 9am-6pm, Su 10am-4pm; Sept.-June M-Sa 9am-5pm, Su 10am-4pm.) **Internet Exchange** is located at 8 Church St., by St. John's Church. (£4 per hr. Open M-Th 9am-9pm, F-Sa 9am-8pm, Su 11am-7pm.) The best **B&Bs** are on Cathedral Rd. (take bus #32 or walk 15min. from the castle). To get to the colorful **Cardiff International Backpacker ❷**, 98 Neville St., from the train station, go west on Wood St., turn right on Fitzham Embankment, and turn left onto Despenser St. (☎2034 5577. Kitchen access. Internet £1 per 15min. Dorms £14.50; doubles £35; triples £43.) **Anned Lon ❸**, 157-159 Cathedral Rd., provides a peaceful respite from the city. (☎2022 3349. No smoking. Singles £20-25; doubles £40-45.) For quick food and a wide variety of options, head to the Victorian **Central Market,** in the arcade between St. Mary St. and Trinity St. ▓**Europa Cafe ❶**, 25 Castle St., across from the castle, is a comfortable coffeehouse. (Beverages £1-3. Open Su-Tu 11am-6pm, W-Sa 11am-11pm.) **Postal Code:** CF10 2ST.

WYE VALLEY   ☎01291

Crossing and recrossing the oft-troubled Welsh-English border, the Wye River (Afon Gwy) cuts through a tranquil valley, its banks riddled with trails, abbeys, and castles rich in legend. The past is palpable in the towns and clusters of homes and farms, from Tintern Abbey to the George Inn Pub.

▐ TRANSPORTATION. The valley is best entered from the south, at Chepstow. **Trains** go to Chepstow from Cardiff and Newport (40min., 7-8 per day). National Express **buses** (☎(08705) 808 080) arrive from Cardiff (50min., 7 per day) and London (2¼hr., 10 per day). There is little Sunday bus service in the valley. For schedules, pick up *Discover the Wye Valley on Foot and by Bus* in tourist offices.

Hiking grants the most stunning vistas of the valley. The 124km **Wye Valley Walk** treks north from Chepstow, through Hay-on-Wye, and on to Prestatyn along wooded cliffs and farmland. **Offa's Dyke Path** consists of more than 285km of hiking and biking paths along the length of the Welsh-English border. For information, consult the **Offa's Dyke Association** (☎ (01547) 528 753).

CHEPSTOW AND TINTERN. Chepstow's strategic position at the mouth of the river and the base of the English border made it an important fortification in Norman times. **Trains** arrive on Station Rd.; **buses** stop in front of Somerfield supermarket. Purchase tickets at **The Travel House,** 9 Moor St. (☎ 623 031. Open M-Sa 9am-5:30pm.) The **tourist office** is on Bridge St. (☎ 623 772. Open Apr.-Oct. daily 10am-5:30pm; Nov.-Mar. 10am-4:30pm.) Stay with the lovely proprietress of **Langcroft** ❸, 71 Kingsmark Ave. (☎ 625 569. £20 per person.) **Postal Code:** NP16 5DA.

Eight kilometers north of Chepstow on A466, the haunting arches of ▨**Tintern Abbey** "connect the landscape with the quiet of the sky"—as described in Wordsworth's famous poem, written just a few kilometers away. (☎ 689 251. Open June-Sept. daily 9:30am-6pm; Apr.-May and Oct. 9:30am-5pm; Nov.-Mar. M-Sa 9:30am-4pm, Su 11am-4pm. £2.50; students £2.) A 1½hr. hike will get you to **Devil's Pulpit,** from which Satan is said to have tempted the monks as they worked in the fields. A couple kilometers to the north on the A466, the **tourist office** is housed in a train carriage at the **Old Station.** (☎ 689 566. Open Apr.-Oct. daily 10:30am-5:30pm.) **YHA St. Briavel's Castle** ❷, 6.5km northeast of Tintern across the English Border, occupies a 12th-century fortress. From the A466 (bus #69 from Chepstow) or Offa's Dyke, follow signs for 3.25km from Bigsweir Bridge. (☎ (01594) 530 272. Dorms £11.25, under 18 £8.) The cozy **Holmleigh House** ❷ is near the Sixpence and Moon pub on the A466. (☎ 689 521. £16.50 per person.)

HAY-ON-WYE. More than 40 bookshops and numerous cafes spill from alleyways onto the narrow lanes of Hay. The 1961 appearance of **Booth's Books,** the world's biggest secondhand bookstore, sparked the development of this bibliophile's nirvana. In June, this smallest of towns hosts the largest of literary festivals, attracting literati such as Toni Morrison. The **tourist office,** on Oxford Rd., books beds for a £2 fee. (☎ (01497) 820 144. Open Apr.-Oct. daily 10am-1pm and 2-5pm; Nov.-Mar. 11am-1pm and 2-4pm.) ▨**The Bear** ❸, Bear St., has cozy rooms and warm hospitality. (☎ (01497) 821 302. Singles from £24.) **Postal Code:** HR3 5AE.

BRECON BEACONS NATIONAL PARK

The *Parc Cenedlaethol Bannau Brycheiniog* encompasses 1344 dramatic square kilometers of barren peaks, well-watered forests, and windswept moors. The park is divided into four regions: **Brecon Beacon,** where King Arthur's fortress is thought to have stood; **Fforest Fawr,** with the spectacular waterfalls of Ystradfellte; the eastern **Black Mountains;** and the remote western **Black Mountain** (singular). Brecon, on the fringe of the park, makes a pleasant touring base.

▣ TRANSPORTATION. Trains (☎ 08457 484 950) run from London Paddington to Abergavenny at the park's southeastern corner and to Merthyr Tydfil on the southern edge. National Express (☎ 08705 808 080) **bus** #509 runs once a day from Brecon, on the northern side of the park, to London and Cardiff. Stagecoach Red and White (☎ 01685 388 216) crosses the park en route to Brecon from: Abergavenny (#21; 1hr., M-Sa 5 per day, £3-4.10); Cardiff via Merthyr Tydfil (#X4 or X40, changing to #43; 1½hr., M-Sa 6 per day, £5-7); and Hay-on-Wye (#39; 45min., M-Sa 6 per day, £2.80-4.10).

BRECON (ADERHONDDU). Just north of the mountains, Brecon is the park's best hiking base. **Buses** arrive at the **Bulwark** in the central square. The **tourist office** is in the Cattle Market parking lot; walk through Bethel Square off Lion St. (☎622 485. Open daily 9:30am-5pm.) The **National Park Information Centre** (☎623 156) is in the same building. **Mulberry House ❷,** 3 Priory Hill, across from the cathedral, is in a former monks' habitation. (☎624 461. ₤18 per person.) Camp at **Brynich Caravan Park ❶,** 2.5km east on the A40, signposted from the A40-A470 roundabout. (☎623 325. Open Easter-Oct. ₤4.50 per person, ₤9.50 with car.) ☎01874.

FFOREST FAWR. Rivers tumble through rapids, gorges, and spectacular falls near Ystradfellte, about 11km southwest of the Beacons. The **YHA Ystradfellte ❶** is a perfect launching pad. (☎01639 720 301. Open mid-July to Aug. daily; Apr. to mid-July and Sept.-Oct. F-Tu. only. Dorms ₤8.50, under 18 ₤5.75.) From the hostel, 16km of trails pass **Fforest Fawr,** the headlands of the Waterfall District, on their way to the **Dan-yr-Ogof Showcaves.** (Open Apr.-Oct. daily 10:30am-5pm. ₤7.80, children ₤4.80.) Stagecoach Red and White **bus** #63 (1½hr.; 2-3 per day) stops at the hostel and caves en route to Brecon.

THE BLACK MOUNTAINS. Located in the easternmost section of the park, the Black Mountains are a group of long, lofty ridges offering 130 square kilometers of solitude, linked by unsurpassed ridge-walks. Begin forays from **Crickhowell,** or travel the eastern boundary along **Offa's Dyke Path,** which is dotted with a handful of impressive ruins. The **YHA Capel-y-ffin ❶** (kap-EL-uh-fin), along Offa's Dyke Path, is 13km from Hay-on-Wye. Take Stagecoach Red and White **bus** #39 from Hereford to Brecon, stop before Hay, and walk uphill. (☎01873 890 650. Lockout 10am-5pm. Open July-Sept. daily; Oct.-Dec. and Mar.-June F-Tu. Dorms ₤8.75, students ₤7.75.)

THE BRECON BEACONS. These peaks at the center of the park lure hikers with pastoral slopes. A pleasant hiking route starts in **Llanfaes,** Brecon's western suburb, and passes **Llyn Cwm Llwch** (HLIN koom hlooch), a 600m deep glacial pool. Walk 5km from Llanfaes down Ffrwdgrech Rd. to the car park, taking the middle fork after the first bridge, where the trail begins.

ST. DAVID'S (TYDDEWI)   ☎01437

An evening walk in St. David's (pop. 1700), medieval Wales's largest and richest diocese, inevitably leads to ▓**St. David's Cathedral,** where visitors and locals gather to watch the sunset. (Cathedral open daily 6am-5:30pm. Suggested donation ₤2.) The **Bishop's Palace,** across a bridged brook, was built from 1328 to 1347 by Bishop Henry Gower. (☎720 517. Open June-Sept. daily 9:30am-6pm; Oct. and Apr.-May daily 9:30am-5pm; Nov.-Mar. M-Sa 9:30am-4pm, Su noon-2pm. ₤2.) To reach St. David's from Cardiff, take a **train** to Haverfordwest (2½hr., 2 per day), and then take Richards Bros. **bus** #411 (50min., 2-5 per day). The **tourist office** is on The Grove. (☎720 392. Open Easter-Oct. daily 9:30am-5:30pm; Nov.-Easter M-Sa 10am-4pm.) Beautiful **Alandale ❸,** 43 Nun St., has friendly proprietors whose warmth and filling breakfasts will make your stay worthwhile. (☎720 404. ₤25 per person.) For excellent Welsh food, head to **Cartref ❷,** in Cross Sq. (Lunch ₤3-4, dinner from ₤8. Open Mar.-May daily 11am-2:30pm and 6:30-8:30pm; June-Aug. 11am-3pm and 6-8:30pm.) **Postal Code:** SA62 6SW.

SNOWDONIA NATIONAL PARK

Rough and handsome, misty purple and mossy green, the highest mountains of England and Wales stretch across 2175 square kilometers, from forested Machynlleth to sand-strewn Conwy. Although these lands lie largely in private hands, endless public footpaths accommodate droves of visitors.

📠 TRANSPORTATION AND PRACTICAL INFORMATION. Trains (☎08457 484 950) stop at several large towns on the park's outskirts, including Conwy (see p. 196). The **Conwy Valley Line** runs through the park from **Llandudno** through **Betws-y-Coed** to **Blaenau Ffestiniog** (1hr., 2-7 per day). At Blaneau Ffestiniog the Conwy Valley Line connects with the narrow-gauge Ffestiniog Railway (see p. 196), which runs through the mountains to Porthmadog, meeting the Cambrian Coaster to Llanberis and Aberystwyth. **Buses** run to the interior of the park from Conwy and Caernarfon; consult the *Gwynedd Public Transport Maps and Timetables*, available in all regional tourist offices. The **Snowdonia National Park Information Headquarters**, Penrhyndeudraeth, Gwynedd, Wales (☎01766 770 274), provides hiking info and Ordnance Survey Maps (£5-7), and can best direct you to the eight quality **YHA hostels** in the park as well as the region's other **tourist offices** (www.gwynedd.gov.uk).

🥾 HIKING. The park's most popular destination and the highest peak in England and Wales is **Mount Snowdon** (*Yr Wyddfa*; "the burial place"), measuring 1085m. Six paths of varying difficulties wind their way up Snowdon; tourist offices and National Park Information Centres can provide guides on these ascents. Weather on Snowdonia's exposed mountains shifts unpredictably. No matter how beautiful the weather is below, it will be cold and wet in the high mountains. Pick up the Ordnance Survey Landranger Map #115 (£6) and Outdoor Leisure Map #17 (£7), as well as individual path guides at tourist offices, park centers, and bookstores. Contact **Mountaincall Snowdonia** (☎0891 500 449; £0.35-0.50 per min.) for the local forecast and ground conditions. Weather forecasts are also tacked outside Park Information Centres.

LLANBERIS. Llanberis owes its outdoorsy bustle to the popularity of Mt. Snowdon, whose ridges and peaks unfold just south of town. The immensely popular **Snowdon Mountain Railway** whisks visitors to Snowdon's summit. (☎01286 870 223. Open mid-Mar. to Oct. only. Round-trip £18.) KMP (☎01286 870 880) **bus** #88 runs from Caernarfon (25min., 1-2 per hr.). The **tourist office** is at 41b High St. (☎01286 870 765. Open Easter-Oct. daily 10am-6pm; Nov.-Easter W and F-Su 11am-4pm.) Plenty of sheep keep hostelers company at the **YHA Llanberis ❷**. (☎0870 770 5990. Curfew 11:30pm. Open Apr.-Oct. daily; Nov.-Mar. Su-Th. only. Dorms £10.25, under 18 £7.) **☎01286.**

HARLECH ☎01766

This tiny coastal town just south of the Llyn Peninsula commands panoramic views of sea, sand, and Snowdonian summits. High above the sea and sand dunes is ▨**Harlech Castle,** another of Edward I's Welsh castles; this one served as the insurrection headquarters of Welsh rebel Owain Glyndŵr. (Open June-Sept. M-Sa 9:30am-6pm, Su 9:30am-5pm; May and Oct. daily 9:30am-5pm; Nov.-Mar. M-Sa 9:30am-4pm, Su 11am-4pm. £3, students £2.) Harlech lies midway on the Cambrian Coaster line; **trains** arrive from Machynlleth (1¼-1¾hr., 3-6 per day, £8.20) and connect to Pwllheli and other spots on the Llyn Peninsula. The **Day Ranger** pass allows unlimited travel on the Coaster line for one day (£4-7). The **tourist office**, 1 Stryd Fawr, doubles as a **Snowdonia National Park Information Centre**. (☎780 658. Open daily 10am-6pm.) Enjoy spacious rooms and Harlech's best views at **Arundel ❷**, Stryd Fawr. Call ahead for pick-up. (☎780 637. £15 per person.) At the **Plâs Cafe ❷**, Stryd Fawr, guests linger over afternoon tea (£1-4) and sunset dinners (from £7) while enjoying sweeping ocean views from the grassy patio. (Open Mar.-Oct. daily 9:30am-8pm; Nov.-Feb. 9:30am-5:30pm.) **Postal Code:** LL46 2YA.

BRITAIN

LLYN PENINSULA   ☎ 01766

The Llyn has been a hotbed of tourism since the Middle Ages, when crowds of religious pilgrims tramped through on their way to Bardsey Island, just off the western tip of the peninsula. Today, sun worshippers make the pilgrimage to the endless beaches that line the southern coast. **Porthmadog,** on the southeastern part of the peninsula, is the main gateway. This travel hub's principal attraction is the charming ▓**Ffestiniog Railway** (☎ 516 073), which runs from Harbour Station on High St. into the hills of Snowdonia (1¼hr., 2-10 per day, round-trip £14). **Trains** run from Aberystwyth (1½-2hr., 3-6 per day). TrawsCambria **bus** #701 travels once a day to Aberystwyth (2hr.) and Cardiff (7hr.). Express Motors bus #1 stops in Porthmadog on its way from Blaenau Ffestiniog to Caernarfon (M-Sa every hr.). The **tourist office** is on High St. by the harbor. (☎ 512 981. Open Easter-Oct. daily 10am-6pm; Nov.-Easter 10am-5pm.) The birthplace of Lawrence of Arabia is now the huge and comfortable **Snowdon Backpackers Hostel ❷.** (☎ 515 354. Dorms £11-13; doubles £29-33.) **Postal Code:** LL49 9AD.

CAERNARFON   ☎ 01286

Majestic and fervently Welsh, the walled city of Caernarfon (car-NAR-von) has a world-famous castle at its prow and mountains in its wake. Built by Edward I beginning in 1283, the ▓**Caernarfon Castle** was left unfinished when Eddie ran out of money and became distracted by unruly Scots. (☎ 677 617. Open June-Sept. daily 9:30am-6pm; Apr.-May and Oct. daily 9:30am-5pm; Nov.-Mar. M-Sa 9:30am-4pm, Su 11am-4pm. £4.50, students £3.50.) Arriva Cymru (☎ (08706) 082 608) **buses** #5 and 5x arrive from Conwy (1¼hr., 1-2 per hr.). TrawsCambria bus #701 arrives daily from Cardiff (7½hr.). National Express (☎ (08705) 808 080) bus #545 arrives daily from London (9hr.). The **tourist office** is on Castle St. (☎ 672 232. Open Apr.-Oct. daily 10am-6pm; Nov.-Mar. Th-Tu 9:30am-4:30pm.) ▓**Totter's Hostel ❷,** 2 High St., has huge rooms and a comfortable living room. (☎ 672 963. Dorms £12.) Try the Welsh lamb (£11) at **Stones Bistro ❸,** 4 Hole-in-the-Wall St., a crowded, candle-lit eatery near Eastgate. **Postal Code:** LL55 2ND.

CONWY   ☎ 01492

The central attraction of this tourist mecca is the 13th-century ▓**Conwy Castle,** another link in Edward I's chain of impressive North Wales fortresses. (Open June-Sept. daily 9:30am-6pm; Apr.-May and Oct. 9:30am-5pm; Nov.-Mar. M-Sa 9:30am-4pm, Su 11am-4pm. £3.50, students £3. Tours £1.) Arriva Cymru (☎ (08706) 082 608) **buses** #5 and 5X stop in Conwy on their way to Caernarfon from Bangor (1-2 per hr.). National Express (☎ (08705) 808 080) buses arrive from: Liverpool (2¾hr., 1 per day); Manchester (4hr., 1 per day); and Newcastle (10hr., 1 per day). The **tourist office** is at the castle entrance. (☎ 592 248. Open Easter-Oct. daily 9:30am-6pm; Nov.-Easter Th-Sa 10am-4pm.) **Bryn Guest House ❸,** below the town wall's highest point, has big bedrooms and hearty breakfasts. (☎ 592 449. All rooms with bath. Singles £23; doubles £40.) A **Spar** supermarket is on High St. (Open daily 8am-10pm.) **Postal Code:** LL32 8DA.

SCOTLAND

A little over half the size of England but with just a tenth of the population, Scotland possesses open spaces and wild natural splendor its southern neighbor cannot hope to rival. The craggy, heathered Highlands, the silver beaches of the west coast, and the luminescent mists of the Hebrides elicit any traveler's awe, while farmlands to the south and peaceful fishing villages on the east coast harbor a gentler beauty. Scotland at its best is a world apart from the rest of the UK. Before reluctantly joining with England in 1707, the Scots defended their independence, bitterly and heroically, for hundreds of years. Since the union, they have nurtured a separate identity, retaining control of schools, churches, and the judicial system. In 1999, the Scots finally regained a separate parliament, which gave them more power over domestic tax laws and strengthened their national identity.

TRANSPORTATION

Bus travel from London is generally cheaper than **train** fares. **British Airways** (☎08457 773 3377) sells a limited number of APEX round-trip tickets from £70. **British Midland** (☎(08706) 070 555) also offers a round-trip Saver fare from London to Glasgow (from £70). Scotland is also linked by **ferry** to Northern Ireland. From **Stranraer,** Stena Line (☎(08705) 707 070) sails to Belfast (1¾hr.-3¼hr; 9 per day; £14-24, students and seniors £10-19, children £7-12).

In the **Lowlands** (south of Stirling and north of the Borders), train and bus connections are frequent. In the **Highlands,** trains snake slowly on a few restricted routes, bypassing the northwest almost entirely, and many stations are unstaffed or nonexistent—buy tickets on board. A great money-saver is the **Freedom of Scotland Travelpass.** It allows unlimited train travel as well as transportation on most Caledonian MacBrayne ferries, with discounts on some other ferry lines. Purchase the pass *before* traveling to Britain, at any BritRail distributor (see By Train, (p. 137)). Buses tend to be the best way to travel; **Scottish Citylink** (☎08705 505 050) provides most intercity service. **MacBackpackers** (☎0131 558 9900; www.macbackpackers.com) and **HAGGiS** (☎0131 557 9393; www.radicaltravel.com) run hop-on/hop-off tours that let you travel Scotland at your own pace.

EDINBURGH   ☎0131

A city of elegant stone amid rolling hills and ancient volcanoes, Edinburgh (ED-in-bur-ra; pop. 500,000) is the jewel of Scotland. Since David I granted it burgh (town) status in 1130, Edinburgh has been a site of cultural significance—the seeds of the Scottish Reformation were sown here, as well as the philosophies of the Scottish Enlightenment. The tradition lives on during the festivals each August, when the city becomes a theatrical, musical, and literary magnet, drawing international talent and enthusiastic crowds. Of late, tourism has motivated a flurry of construction, from hostels and museums to government buildings.

TRANSPORTATION

Flights: Edinburgh International Airport (EDI; ☎333 1000), 11.25km west of the city center. **Lothian Buses' Airlink** (☎555 6363) shuttles to the airport (25min., £3.30) from Waverley Bridge. **Airsaver** gives you 1 trip on Airlink plus 1 day unlimited travel on local Lothian Buses (£4.20, children £2.50).

Trains: Waverley Station straddles Princes St., Market St., and Waverley Bridge. Trains (☎(08457) 484 950) to: **Aberdeen** (2½hr.; M-Sa every hr., Su 8 per day; £31); **Glasgow** (1hr., 2 per hr., £7.40-8.40); **Inverness** (3½hr., every 2hr., £31); **London King's Cross** (4¾hr., 2 per hr., £90); **Stirling** (50min., 2 per hr., £5.30).

Buses: The **bus station** is on the east side of St. Andrew's Sq. **National Express** (☎(08705) 808 080) from **London** (10hr., 5 per day, £27). **Scottish Citylink** (☎(08705) 505 050) from: **Aberdeen** (4hr., every hr., £15); **Glasgow** (1hr.; M-Sa 4 per hr., Su 2 per hr.; £3.80); **Inverness** (4½hr., 8-10 per day, £14.70). A bus-ferry route via Stranraer goes to **Belfast** (2 per day, £29-33) and **Dublin** (1 per day, £41).

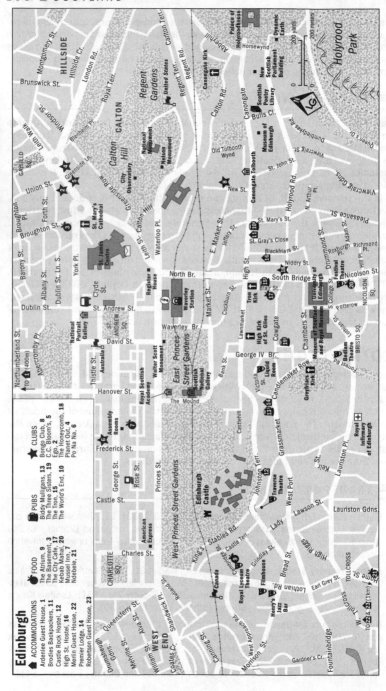

Edinburgh

▲ ACCOMMODATIONS
Ardenlee Guest House, **1**
Brodies Backpackers, **11**
Castle Rock Hostel, **12**
High St. Hostel, **16**
Merlin Guest House, **22**
Premier Lodge, **14**
Robertson Guest House, **23**

● FOOD
The Atrium, **9**
The Basement, **3**
The City Cafe, **17**
The Tron, **15**
Kebab Mahal, **20**
Mussel Inn, **7**
Ndebele, **21**

🍺 PUBS
Biddy Mulligans, **13**
The Three Sisters, **19**
The Tron, **15**
The World's End, **10**

★ CLUBS
Bongo Club, **8**
C.C. Bloom's, **5**
Ego, **2**
The Honeycomb, **18**
Planet Out, **4**
Po Na Na, **6**

Public Transportation: Lothian Buses (☎555 6363; www.lothianbuses.co.uk) provide most services. Exact change required (£0.50-£1). Buy a 1-day **Daysaver** ticket (all day M-F £2.20; after 9:30pm M-F and all day Sa or Su £1.50) from any driver or from the **Travelshops** on Hanover St. and Waverley Bridge. **Night buses** cover selected routes after midnight (£2). **First Edinburgh** also operates locally. **Traveline,** 2 Cockburn St. (☎(0800) 232 323) has info on all public transport.

Bike Rental: Biketrax, 11 Lochrin Pl. (☎228 6633). Mountain bikes £15 per day. Open M-F 9:30am-6pm, Sa 9:30am-5pm, Su noon-5pm.

▚ ⁊ ORIENTATION AND PRACTICAL INFORMATION

Edinburgh is a glorious city for walking. **Princes Street** is the main thoroughfare in **New Town,** the northern section of Edinburgh. From there you can view the impressive stone facade of the towering **Old Town,** the southern half of the city. **The Royal Mile** (Castle Hill, Lawnmarket, High St., and Canongate) is the major road in the Old Town and connects **Edinburgh Castle** in the west to the **Palace of Holyroodhouse** in the east. **North Bridge, Waverley Bridge,** and **The Mound** connect Old and New Town. Greater Edinburgh stretches well beyond Old and New Town; **Leith,** 3.2km northeast, is the city's seaport on the Firth of Forth.

Tourist Office: 3 Princes St. (☎473 3800), Waverley Market, on the north side of the Waverley Station complex. **Currency exchange.** Books rooms (£4) and has excellent free maps and pamphlets. Open July-Aug. M-Sa 9am-8pm, Su 10am-8pm; May-June and Sept. M-Sa 9am-7pm, Su 10am-7pm; Oct.-Apr. M-W 9am-5pm, Th-Sa 9am-6pm, Su 10am-5pm. In summer, look for **City Centre Representatives,** wearing yellow, who can answer questions in several languages.

Budget Travel: STA Travel, 27 Forrest Rd. (☎226 7747). Open M-Th 9:30am-6pm, F 10am-5:30pm, Sa 11am-5pm.

American Express: 139 Princes St. (☎718 2503 or (08706) 001 600). Open M-F 9am-5:30pm, Sa 9am-4pm.

Bi-Gay-Lesbian Resources: Pick up *Gay Information* at the tourist office or drop by the **Centre for Lesbians, Gays, and Bisexuals,** 58a Broughton St. (☎557 2625).

Emergency: ☎999 or 112; no coins required. **Police:** 5 Fettes Ave. (☎311 3131).

Hospital: Royal Infirmary of Edinburgh, 1 Lauriston Pl. (emergencies ☎536 4000, otherwise 536 1000).

Internet Access: easyInternet Cafe, 58 Rose St. (☎220 3577). £1 per 30min.-3hr., price varies with demand. Open M-Sa 7am-11pm, Su 8am-11pm. **e-corner,** Platform 1, Waverley Station. £1 per 20min. Open M-F 7:30am-9:30pm, Sa-Su 8am-9pm.

Post Office: (☎556 9546), in the St. James Shopping Centre, New Town. Open M 9am-5:30pm, Tu-F 8:30am-5:30pm, Sa 8:30am-6pm. **Postal Code:** EH1.

⋔ ACCOMMODATIONS

Hostels and hotels are the only options in the city center. B&Bs and guest houses begin on the outer edges; try **Pilrig,** northeast of eastern Princes St. (bus #11 east/northbound), or the neighborhoods south of Princes St., **Bruntsfield** (bus #11, 16, or 17 west/southbound) and **Newington** (bus #37, 7, or 31). It's absolutely essential to book ahead around festivals (late July to early Sept.) and New Year's.

▨ **High St. Hostel,** 8 Blackfriars St. (☎557 3984). Good facilities, party atmosphere, and convenient Royal Mile location. Continental breakfast £1.60. Dorms £10.50-13. ❷

■ **Merlin Guest House,** 14 Hartington Pl., Bruntsfield (☎229 3864), southwest of the Royal Mile. Comfortable, well-priced rooms in a leafy-green neighborhood. £15-22.50 per person; student discounts off-season. ❷

Ardenlee Guest House, 9 Eyre Pl. (☎556 2838), at the northern edge of New Town. Walk or take northbound bus #23 or 27 from Hanover St. to the corner of Dundas St. and Eyre Pl. This friendly guest house offers large, comfortable rooms. No smoking. £26-35 per person. ❸

Castle Rock Hostel, 15 Johnston Terr. (☎225 9666), just steps from the castle. Regal views and top-notch common areas. Internet £0.80 per 30min. Continental breakfast £1.60. Dorms £10.50-13. ❷

Brodies Backpackers, 12 High St. (☎/fax 556 6770; www.brodieshostels.co.uk). Relaxed, fun environment at this relatively small Royal Mile hostel. Internet access. Dorms £10-17; weekly £59-89. ❷

Robertson Guest House, 5 Hartington Gdns., Bruntsfield (☎229 2652). Quiet and welcoming, with top-notch breakfasts. No smoking. Singles £22-50; doubles £44-74. ❸

Premier Lodge, 94 Grassmarket (☎(0870) 700 1370). A chain hotel lacking in character but comfortable and well-located. £50 per room. ❹

Edinburgh Caravan Club Site, Marine Dr. (☎312 6874), by the Forth. Take bus #8A from North Bridge. Electricity, showers, hot water, and laundry facilities. £3.75-4.75 per person, £2-3 per tent. ❶

◖ FOOD

Edinburgh boasts an increasingly wide range of cuisines and restaurants. If it's traditional food you're after, the capital won't disappoint, with everything from haggis at the neighborhood pub to "modern Scottish" at the city's top restaurants. If you're looking for cheap eats, many pubs offer student discounts in the early evening, takeaway shops on **South Clerk Street, Leith Street,** and **Lothian Road** have well-priced Chinese and Indian fare, and there's always **Sainsbury's** supermarket, 9-10 St. Andrews Sq. (☎225 8400; open M-Sa 7am-10pm, Su 10am-8pm).

■ **The City Cafe,** 19 Blair St. (☎220 0125). Right off the Royal Mile behind the Tron Kirk, this Edinburgh institution is popular with the young and stylish. Relaxed by day, a flashy pre-club spot by night. Incredible shakes immortalized in *Trainspotting*. Burgers £4-6. Food served M-Th 11am-11pm, F-Su 11am-10pm; drinks until 1am. ❷

■ **The Basement,** 10a-12a Broughton St. (☎557 0097). Draws a lively mix of locals to its candlelit cavern. Menu changes daily, well-known for Mexican fare Sa-Su and Thai cuisine on W nights. Vegetarian options. Make reservations F-Sa. Food served daily noon-10pm; drinks until 1am. ❷

Ndebele, 57 Home St. (☎221 1141), in Tolcross, 800m south of western Princes St. Named for a tribe from Swaziland, this atmospheric restaurant serves generous portions of African food for under £5. Open daily 10am-10pm. ❶

The Atrium, 10 Cambridge St. (☎228 8882). One of Edinburgh's hottest eateries, serving modern Scottish cuisine. Two courses about £28. Reservations essential. Open M-F noon-2pm and 6-10pm; Sa 6-10pm. ❹

Kebab Mahal, 7 Nicolson Sq. (☎667 5214). This hole-in-the-wall will stuff you with Indian food for under £5. Open Su-Th noon-midnight, F-Sa noon-2am. ❶

Mussel Inn, 61-65 Rose St. (☎225 5979). Fresh, expertly prepared seafood. Lunch under £10, dinner under £15. Open M-Sa noon-10pm, Su 1:30-10pm. ❸

☞ SIGHTS

A boggling array of tour companies tout themselves as "the original" or "the scariest," but the most worthwhile is the ⬛Edinburgh Literary Pub Tour. Led by professional actors, this alcohol-sodden 2hr. crash course in Scottish literature meets outside the Beehive Inn in the Grassmarket. (☎226 6665. July-Aug. daily 6 and 7:30pm; June and Sept. daily 7:30pm; Apr.-May and Oct. Th-Su 7:30pm; Nov.-Mar. F 7:30pm. £7, students £5.) Alternatively, consider a one-on-one encounter with the MacKenzie Poltergeist on the **City of the Dead Tour,** 40 Candlemaker Row. (☎225 9044. Daily 8:30 and 10pm. £5, children £4.)

THE OLD TOWN AND THE ROYAL MILE

Edinburgh's medieval center, the fascinating Royal Mile defines Old Town and passes many classic houses and attractions. The Old Town once packed thousands of inhabitants into a scant few square miles, with narrow shop fronts and slum buildings towering to a dozen stories.

⬛**EDINBURGH CASTLE.** Perched atop an extinct volcano and dominating the city center, the castle is a testament to Edinburgh's past strategic importance. The castle is the result of centuries of renovation and rebuilding; the most recent additions date to the 1920s. The **One O'Clock Gun** fires daily (except Su) at 1pm. *(Open Apr.-Sept. daily 9:30am-6pm; Oct.-Mar. 9:30am-5pm. Last admission 45min. before closing. £8, seniors £6.50, children £2, under 5 free. Audio tours £3.)*

ALONG THE ROYAL MILE. Near the Castle, through Mylne's Close, the **Scottish Parliament** convenes in the **Church of Scotland Assembly Hall;** visitors are welcome to watch the MPs debate. *(☎348 5411. Sept.-June. Tickets must be reserved in advance. Free.)* The **Visitors Centre** is nearby, at the corner of the Royal Mile and the George IV Bridge. *(Open M-F 10am-5pm. Free.)* The 17th-century **Lady Stair's House** contains the **Writer's Museum,** featuring memorabilia and manuscripts belonging to three of Scotland's greatest literary figures: Robert Burns, Sir Walter Scott, and Robert Louis Stevenson. *(Through the passage at 477 Lawnmarket St. Open M-Sa 10am-5pm; during festival season also Su 2-5pm. Free.)* At the beautiful ⬛ **High Kirk of St. Giles** (St. Giles Cathedral), Scotland's principal church, John Knox delivered the fiery Presbyterian sermons that drove Mary, Queen of Scots, into exile. Now it offers free concerts year-round. *(Where Lawnmarket becomes High St. Open Easter to mid-Sept. M-F 9am-7pm, Sa 9am-5pm, Su 1-5pm; mid-Sept. to Easter M-Sa 9am-5pm, Su 1-5pm. Suggested donation £1.)* The 17th-century **Canongate Kirk,** on the steep hill at the end of the Mile, is the resting place of Adam Smith; royals also worship here when in residence. *(Same hours as the High Kirk. Free.)*

THE PALACE OF HOLYROODHOUSE. This Stewart palace abuts Holyrood Park and the peak of Arthur's Seat and dates from the 16th century. It remains Queen Elizabeth II's official Scottish residence. Once home to Mary, Queen of Scots, it was the site of the brutal murder of her secretary, David Rizzio. *(Open Apr.-Oct. daily 9:30am-6pm; Nov.-Mar. M-Sa 9:30am-4:30pm; last admission 45min. before closing. Closed during official residences. £6.50.)*

OTHER SIGHTS IN THE OLD TOWN. The ⬛**Museum of Scotland** and the connected **Royal Museum,** on Chambers St., just south of the George IV Bridge, are not to be missed. The former houses a definitive collection of Scottish artifacts in a stunning contemporary building; the latter contains a varied mix of art and natural history. *(Open M and W-Sa 10am-5pm, Tu 10am-8pm, Su noon-5pm. Free.)* Just across the street stands the statue of Greyfriar's loyal pooch, Bobby, marking the entrance to **Greyfriar's Kirk,** built in 1620 and surrounded by a beautiful and supposedly haunted churchyard. *(Off Candlemaker Row. Gaelic services Su 12:30pm, English 11am. Open Easter-Oct. M-F 10:30am-4:30pm, Sa until 2:30pm. Free.)*

BRITAIN

THE NEW TOWN

Edinburgh's New Town is a masterpiece of Georgian design. James Craig, a 23-year-old architect, won the city-planning contest in 1767; his rectangular grid of three parallel streets (Queen, George, and Princes) linking two large squares (Charlotte and St. Andrew) reflects the Scottish Enlightenment's belief in order.

THE GEORGIAN HOUSE AND THE WALTER SCOTT MONUMENT. The elegantly restored **Georgian House** gives a picture of life 200 years ago. *(7 Charlotte Sq. From Princes St., turn right on Charlotte St. and take the second left. Open Apr.-Oct. daily 10am-6pm; Nov.-Mar. 11am-4pm. £5, students £3.75.)* The **Walter Scott Monument** is a Gothic "steeple without a church"; climb the 287-step staircase for far views stretching out to Princes St. Gardens, the castle, and Old Town's Market St. *(On Princes St., between The Mound and Waverley Bridge. Open June-Sept. M-Sa 9am-8pm, Su 10am-6pm; Mar.-May and Oct. M-Sa 9am-6pm, Su 10am-6pm; Nov.-Feb. M-Sa 9am-4pm, Su 10am-6pm. £2.50.)*

THE NATIONAL GALLERIES

Edinburgh's National Galleries of Scotland form an elite group, with excellent collections housed in stately buildings and connected by a free shuttle every hr. The flagship is the ▓**National Gallery of Scotland,** on the Mound, which houses a superb collection of works by Renaissance, Romantic, and Impressionist masters and a fine spread of Scottish art. The **Scottish National Portrait Gallery,** 1 Queen St., north of St. Andrew Sq., features the faces of famous Scots. Take the free shuttle, bus #13 from George St., or walk to the **Scottish National Gallery of Modern Art,** 75 Belford Rd., west of town, and the new **Dean Gallery,** 73 Belford Rd., specializing in Surrealist and Dadaist art. *(All open M-Sa 10am-5pm, Su noon-5pm; longer hours during festival season. Free.)*

GARDENS AND PARKS

Just off the eastern end of the Royal Mile, **Holyrood Park** is a true city oasis, a natural wilderness replete with hills, moorland, and lochs. ▓**Arthur's Seat,** the park's highest point, affords stunning views of the city and countryside. The walk to the summit takes about 45min. The lovely **Royal Botanic Gardens** are north of the city center. Take bus #23 or 27 from Hanover St. *(Open Apr.-Aug. daily 9:30am-7pm; Mar. and Sept. 9:30am-6pm; Feb. and Oct. 9:30am-5pm; Nov.-Jan. 9:30am-4pm. Free.)*

🎵 ENTERTAINMENT

The summer sees an especially joyful string of events—music in the gardens, plays and films, and *ceilidhs*—even before the Festival comes to town. In winter, shorter days and the crush of students promote a flourishing nightlife. For the most up-to-date info on what's going on, check out *The List* (£2.20), a comprehensive biweekly guide to events, available from any local newsstand.

THEATER, FILM, AND MUSIC. The **Festival Theatre,** 13-29 Nicholson St., stages ballet and opera, while the affiliated **King's Theatre,** 2 Leven St., hosts comedy, drama, musicals, and opera. Same-day seats (£5.50) for the Festival Theatre go on sale daily at 10am. (☎529 6000. Box office open M-Sa 10am-6pm.) The **Stand Comedy Club,** 5 York Pl., has nightly acts. (☎558 7272. Tickets £1-7.) The **Filmhouse,** 88 Lothian Rd., offers quality European, arthouse, and Hollywood cinema. (☎228 2688. Tickets £3.20-5.20.) Thanks to an abundance of students, Edinburgh's live music scene is alive and well. For a run-down of upcoming acts, look to *The List* or *The Gig Guide.* Free live jazz can be found at **Henry's Jazz Bar,** 8 Morrison St. (Open W-Sa; performances around 8pm, doors open around 6pm.) **The Venue,** 15

Calton Rd., and **The Liquid Room,** 9c Victoria St., often host rock and progressive shows. **Whistle Binkie's,** 4 Niddry St., off High St., is a subterranean pub with live music most nights. (Open daily until 3am.)

📷 NIGHTLIFE

PUBS

Edinburgh claims to have the highest density of pubs anywhere in Europe. Pubs directly on the Royal Mile usually attract an older crowd, while students tend to loiter in the Old Town just to the south.

The Tron, 9 Hunter Sq., behind the Tron Kirk. Wildly popular for its incredible deals. Frequent live music on 3 hopping fl. All pints under £2. June-Sept. students and hostelers get £1 drinks on W nights. Open daily 11:30am-1am.

The Three Sisters, 139 Cowgate. Copious space for dancing, drinking, and socializing. Three themed bars and an outdoor beer garden. Open daily 9am-1am.

Biddy Mulligans, 96 Grassmarket. An Irish-themed pub. Open daily 9am-1am, food until 9pm.

The World's End, 4 High St. A locals spot. On open-mic night (Su 10pm-midnight), performers get a free pint.

CLUBS

Club venues are constantly closing down and reopening under new management; consult *The List* for updated info. Clubs cluster around the historically disreputable **Cowgate,** just downhill from and parallel to the Royal Mile; most close at 3am.

The Honeycomb, 15-17 Niddry St. Monthly theme nights and frequent guest DJs. Cover free-£10.

Bongo Club, 14 New St. Noted for hip-hop. Cover £4-6.

Le Belle Angele, 11 Hasties Close. Showcases hip-hop, trance, and progressive house. Cover £2-10.

Po Na Na, 26 Frederick St. Moroccan-themed and glamorous. Su-Th no cover, F-Sa £3.

GAY AND LESBIAN

The Broughton St. area of the New Town (better known as the **Broughton Triangle**) is the center of Edinburgh's gay community.

Planet Out, 6 Baxter's Pl. Start off the night at this mellow club. Open M-F 4pm-1am, Sa-Su 2pm-1am.

C.C. Bloom's, 23-24 Greenside Pl., on Leith St. A friendly gay club with no cover. M-Sa dancing, Su karaoke. Open M-Sa 6pm-3am, Su 8pm-3am.

Ego, 14 Picardy Pl. Hosts several gay nights, including the long-established **Joy** (1 Sa per month). Cover £10.

BRITAIN

🔘 FESTIVALS

Edinburgh has special events year-round, but the real show is in August. What's commonly referred to as "the Festival" actually encompasses a number of independently organized events. For more information on all the festivals, check out www.edinburghfestivals.co.uk. The **Edinburgh International Festival** (Aug. 10-30 in 2003), the largest of them all, features a kaleidoscopic program of music, drama, dance, and art. Tickets (£5-80) are sold beginning in April, but you can usually get tickets at the door; look for half-price tickets starting at 9am on performance days at **The HUB,** Edinburgh's Festival Centre, Castlehill. (☎473 2000. Open M-Sa.) Around the established festival has grown a less formal ⬛**Fringe Festival** (Aug. 3-25 in 2003), which now includes over 600 amateur and professional companies presenting theater, comedy, children's shows, folk and classical music, poetry, dance, and opera events that budget travelers may find more suitable for their wallets (usually free-£11). Contact the **Fringe Festival Office,** 180 High St. (☎226 0000; www.edfringe.com. Open mid-June to mid-July M-F; mid-July to Aug. daily.) Another August festival is the **Military Tattoo**—a spectacle of military bands, bagpipes, and drums. For tickets (£9-28), contact the **Tattoo Ticket Sale Office,** 32 Market St. (☎225 1188; www.edintattoo.co.uk). The excellent **Edinburgh International Film Festival** is also in August at The Filmhouse (☎229 2550; tickets on sale starting late July), while the **Edinburgh Jazz and Blues Festival** is from late July to early August (☎467 5200; tickets on sale in June). The fun doesn't stop for the long, dark winter: **Hogmanay,** Edinburgh's traditional New Year's Eve festival, is a serious street party with a week of associated events (www.edinburghshogmanay.org).

🔳 DAYTRIP FROM EDINBURGH

ST. ANDREWS

Stagecoach Express Fife buses (☎01334 474 238) pull in from Edinburgh (bus #X59 or X60; 2hr.; M-Sa 2 per hr. until 6:45pm, fewer on Su; £5.70) and Glasgow (#X24, change at Glenrothes to #X59; 2½hr.; M-Sa every hr., fewer on Su; £5.50). Trains (☎08457 484 590) from Edinburgh stop 11km away at Leuchars (1hr., every hr., £8.10), where buses #94 and 96 (£1.60) depart for St. Andrews.

Golf overruns the small city of St. Andrews, where the rules of the sport were formally established. The **Old Course** is a frequent site of the British Open. (☎01334 466 666 for reservations or enter a same-day lottery for starting times. Apr.-Oct. £90 per round; Nov.-Mar. £56.) The budget option, still lovely, is the nine-hole **Balgove Course** for £7. If you're more interested in watching than playing, the **British Golf Museum,** next to the Old Course, details the ancient origins of golf. (Open Easter-Oct. daily 9:30am-5:30pm; Nov.-Easter Th-M 11am-3pm. £4, students £3.) **St. Andrews Cathedral** was the center of Scottish religion before and during the Middle Ages. The nearby **St. Andrews Castle** hides secret tunnels and bottle-shaped dungeons. (Cathedral and castle open Apr.-Sept. daily 9:30am-6:30pm; Oct.-Mar. 9:30am-4:30pm. Joint ticket £3.75.)

To get from the bus station to the **tourist office,** 70 Market St., turn right on City Rd. and take the first left. (☎01334 472 021. Open Apr.-June M-Sa 9:30am-5:30pm, Su 11am-4pm; July-Aug. M-Sa 9:30am-7pm, Su 10:30am-5pm; Sept. M-Sa 9:30am-6pm, Su 11am-4pm; Oct.-Mar. M-Sa 9:30am-5pm.) **Internet access** is across the street at **Costa Coffee,** 83 Market St. (£1 per 20min. Open M-Sa 8am-6pm, Su 10am-5:30pm.) B&Bs line **Murray Place** and **Murray Park** near the bus station. **St. Andrews Tourist Hostel** ❷, St. Mary's Pl., is in a great location and has sparkling facilities. (☎01334 479 911. Dorms £12; 4-bed family room £40-48.)

GLASGOW ☎ 0141

Scotland's largest metropolitan area, Glasgow (pop. 700,000) rose to prominence during the reign of Queen Victoria, exploiting heavy industry to become the world's leading center of shipbuilding and steel production, as evidenced by the cranes that litter the river Clyde. Across the river, however, the daring curves of a new multi-million pound Science Centre shimmer brilliantly, a bright spot southwest of the city center. Furthermore, dozens of free museums, excellent international cuisine, and shopping add cosmopolitan flair and separate the city from its industrial past. But the glamour wears off in Glasgow's bustling clubs and pubs, popular with the largest student population in Scotland and football-mad locals, which lie behind the city's national reputation for nighttime fun.

TRANSPORTATION

Flights: Glasgow Airport (☎ 887 1111), 15km west in Abbotsinch. Citylink buses connect to **Buchanan Station** (25min., 6 per hr., £3.30).

Trains: Trains leave from **Central Station,** on Gordon St. (U: St. Enoch), for **London-King's Cross** (5-6hr., every hr., £82) and **Stranraer** (2½hr., 3-8 per day, £15.50). From **Queen St. Station,** on George Sq. (U: Buchanan St.), trains go to: **Aberdeen** (2½hr., 11-24 per day, £31); **Edinburgh** (50min., 2 per hr., £7.40); **Inverness** (3¼hr., 5 per day, £31). Bus #88 runs between the two stations (4 per hr., £0.50).

Buses: Buchanan Station (☎ (0870) 608 2608), on Hanover St., 2 blocks north of Queen St. Station. **Scottish Citylink** (☎ (08705) 505 050) to: **Aberdeen** (4hr., every hr., £25.50); **Edinburgh** (1¼hr., 2-3 per hr., £5.50); **Inverness** (3½-4½hr., every hr., £25); **Oban** (3hr., 2-3 per day, £10.70). **National Express** (☎ (08705) 808 080) buses arrive daily from **London** (8hr.; every hr.; £21.50, round-trip £28).

Public Transportation: The circular **Underground (U)** subway line, a.k.a. the "Clockwork Orange," runs M-Sa 6:30am-11pm, Su 11am-5:30pm. £0.90. **The Discovery Ticket** is good for one day of unlimited travel. M-F after 9:30am, Su all day. £1.60.

ORIENTATION AND PRACTICAL INFORMATION

George Square is the center of town. Sections of Sauchiehall St., Argyle St., and Buchanan St. are pedestrian areas. **Charing Cross,** where Bath St. crosses M8 in the northwest, is a useful landmark. The vibrant **West End** revolves around **Byres Road** and **Glasgow University,** 1½km northwest of the city center.

Tourist Office: 11 George Sq. (☎ 204 4400), south of Queen St. Station, northeast of Central Station. U: Buchanan St. Books rooms for £2 fee plus 10% deposit. **Walking tours** depart M, Tu, Th, and F 2:30 and 6pm, Su 10:30am. (1½hr., £5.) Open July-Aug. M-Sa 9am-8pm, Su 10am-6pm; Sept.-June M-Sa 9am-7pm, Su 10am-6pm.

American Express: 115 Hope St. (☎ (08706) 001 060). Open July-Aug. M-F 8:30am-5:30pm, Sa 9am-5pm; Sept.-June M-F 8:30am-5:30pm, Sa 9am-noon.

Laundromat: Coin-Op Laundromat, 39-41 Bank St. (☎ 339 8953). U: Kelvin Bridge. Wash £3, dry £1. Open M-F 9am-7:30pm, Sa-Su 9am-5pm.

Emergency: ☎ 999; no coins required.

Police: 173 Pitt St. (☎ 532 2000).

Hospital: Glasgow Royal Infirmary, 84-106 Castle St. (☎ 211 4000).

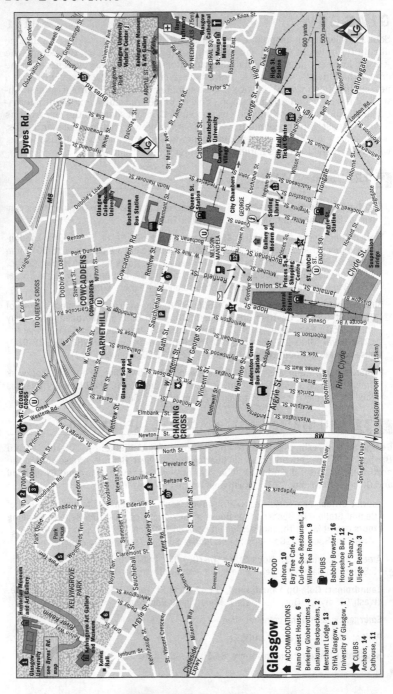

Byres Rd.

Botanical Gardens
Great George St.
Cresswell St.
Ashton Ln.
Observatory Rd.
University Ave.
Kelvingrove Park
University Gardens
Glasgow University Visitor's Center
Kelvingrove Museum & Art Gallery
15
Byres Rd.
TO ARGYLE ST. & ART GALLERY
Elie St.
Dowanhill St.
White St.
St. James's Rd.
Dalcross St.
Hyndland St.
Crown Rd.

Royal Infirmary
Glasgow Cathedral
John Knox St.
TO NECROPOLIS (75m)
CATHEDRAL SQ.
St. Mungo Ave.
St. Mungo Museum
Stirling Rd.
Rottenrow East
Duke St.
High St. Station

Glasgow

500 yards
500 meters
0

Gallowgate
Mohntlour St.
London Rd.
Morrison St.
Saltmarket

Cathedral St.
Strathclyde University
Campus Village
George St.
Taylor St.
John St.
Cochrane St.
Ingram St.
Glassford St.
Virginia St.
Miller St.
Princes Sq.
Hutcheson St.
Wilson St.
Blackfriars St.
Albion St.
Osborne St.
Bridgegate
Bell St.

City Chambers
GEORGE SQ.
City Hall Ticket Centre
Stirling Library
Gallery of Modern Art
ST. ENOCH SQ.
ST. ENOCH Shopping Centre
Argyle St. Station
Stockwell St.
Howard St.
Suspension Bridge
Clyde St.
Glasgow Br.
George V Br.
River Clyde

M8
Dobbie's Loan
Craighall Rd.
Corn St.
TO QUEEN'S CROSS
Port Dundas
Renton
Milton St.
Dobbie's Loan
Glasgow Caledonian University
Buchanan Bus Station
Killermont St.
Queen St. Station
NELSON MANDELA PL.
W. Nile St.
Renfield St.
Union St.
Central Station
Hope St.
Gordon St.
Buchanan St.
Mitchell St.
Jamaica St.

COWCADDENS
Cowcaddens Rd.
Stewart St.
Cambridge St.
Garscube Rd.
Maryhill Rd.
GARNETHILL
Rose St.
Dalhousie St.
Bath St.
Sauchiehall St.
Renfrew St.
W. George St.
Campbell St.
Blythswood St.
W. Regent St.
St. Vincent St.
Wellington St.
Douglas St.
Waterloo St.
Bothwell St.
Anderston Cross Bus Station
Cadogan St.

9

Glasgow School of Art
7
Garnet St.
Scott St.
Hill St.
Buccleuch St.
W. Graham St.
Maryhill Rd.
Graham Sq.
TO ST. GEORGE'S CROSS
Great Western Rd.
W. Prince's
Grant St.
Renfrew St.
Elmbank St.
Holland St.
Pitt St.
Douglas St.
CHARING CROSS
Newton St.
Elmbank St.
St. Vincent St.
McAlpine St.
Carrick St.
Brown St.
James Watt St.
York St.
Robertson St.
Oswald St.
Broomielaw
Washington St.
Anderston St.
Argyle St.
M8
TO GLASGOW AIRPORT

North St.
Cleveland St.
Granville St.
Beltane St.
Elderslie St.
8
10
Berkeley St.
Newton Pl.
Woodlands Rd.
Lynedoch Pl.
Lynedoch Terr.
Sandyford Pl.
Elderslie St.
Anderston Quay
Hydepark St.
Springfield Quay
TO 2 (700m) & 3 (100m)

Woodside Pl.
Woodside Terr.
Somerset Pl.
Claremont Terr.
Lynedoch St.
Park Circus
Park Terr.
Park Quad.
Woodlands Rd.
St. Vincent Cres.
Clifton St.
Minerva St.
Finnieston St.
Greenhill Pl.
TO GLASGOW AIRPORT (15km)

Hunterian Museum and Art Gallery
Glasgow University
see Byres Rd. map
KELVINGROVE PARK
Kelvingrove Art Gallery and Museum
Kelvin Hall
River Kelvin
6
Gray St.
Derby St.
Argyle St.
Kelvinhaugh St.
Kelvin Way
Sauchiehall St.
Minerva Way
Clydeside Expwy.

Glasgow

■ **ACCOMMODATIONS**
Alamo Guest House, **6**
Berkeley Globetrotters, **8**
Bunkum Backpackers, **2**
Merchant Lodge, **13**
SYHA Glasgow, **5**
University of Glasgow, **1**

● **FOOD**
Ashora, **10**
Bay Tree Cafe, **4**
Cul-de-Sac Restaurant, **15**
Willow Tea Rooms, **9**

🍺 **PUBS**
Babbity Bowster, **16**
Horseshoe Bar, **12**
Nice 'n' Sleazy, **7**
Uisge Beatha, **3**

★ **CLUBS**
Archaos, **14**
Cathouse, **11**

Internet Access: easyEverything Internet Cafe, 57-61 St. Vincent St. (☎222 2365). £1 buys 40min.-3hr. depending on time of day. Open daily 7am-10:45pm.

Post Office: 47 St. Vincent St. (☎204 3688). Open M-F 8:30am-5:45pm, Sa 9am-5:30pm. Postal Code: G2 5QX.

ACCOMMODATIONS

Reserve B&Bs and hostels in advance, especially in August. If rooms are booked in Glasgow, consider staying at the SYHA Loch Lomond (p. 209). Most B&Bs cluster on Argyle St. in the university area or near Westercraigs Road, east of the Necropolis.

Bunkum Backpackers, 26 Hillhead St. (☎581 4481). Though located away from the city center, Bunkum is minutes away from the vibrant West End. Spacious dorms with comfortable beds. Lockers. Laundry (£1.50 wash). Dorms £10 per day, £50 per week. ❷

Berkeley Globetrotters Hostel, 56 Berkeley St. (☎221 7880), about two blocks west of Charing Cross, just south of Sauchiehall St. Clean, basic rooms at rock bottom prices. Free breakfast. Dorms £9.50; £8.50 per night for longer stays. ❶

Merchant Lodge, 52 Virginia St. (☎552 2424). Originally a tobacco store, this upscale B&B is convenient and fairly priced. Singles £35; doubles £55; triples £70. ❸

University of Glasgow, No. 3 The Square, Conference & Visitor Services (☎330 5385). Enter the University of Glasgow from University St. and turn immediately right into the square. Summer housing at several dorms. Office open M-F 9am-5pm. Student dorms £14; B&B £17.50. ❷

Alamo Guest House, 46 Gray St. (☎339 2395), across from Kelvingrove Park at its southern exit. Beautiful location in the West End. Family-run and on a quiet street. Singles £20-22; doubles from £34. ❸

SYHA Glasgow, 7-8 Park Terr. (☎332 3004). U: St. George's Cross. From Central Station, take bus #44 from Hope St.; ask for the first stop on Woodlands Rd., then follow the signs. This hostel maintains an air of luxury. All rooms with bath. TV and game rooms. Breakfast included. Laundry (£1 wash and dry). Dorms July-Aug. £12, under 18 £9.50; Sept.-Oct. £11/£9.50; Nov.-Feb. £10/£8.50; Apr.-June £11/£9.50. ❷

FOOD

The area bordered by Otago St. in the west, St. George's Rd. in the east, and along Great Western Rd., Woodlands Rd., and Eldon St. brims with cheap kebab-and-curry joints. Byres Road and Ashton Lane, a tiny cobblestoned alley parallel to Byres Rd., thrive with cheap, trendy cafes.

Ashora, 108 Elderslie St. Just west of several hostels on Berkeley St., this award-winning restaurant features cheap, delicious Indian food. Lunch buffet £2.95, dinner buffet £5.95. Lunch served 11am-2pm. Open daily 11am-midnight. ❶

Willow Tea Rooms, 217 Sauchiehall St. Upstairs from Henderson the Jewellers. A Glasgow landmark. Sip one of 31 kinds of tea. £1.60-1.70 per pot. High tea £8.75. Open M-Sa 9am-4:30pm, Su noon-4:15pm. ❷

Cul-de-Sac Restaurant, 44-46 Ashton Ln. Turn from Byres Rd. onto Ashton Ln., and bear right. Three-course dinners include vegetable dishes, meat *cassoulet,* and the Scottish delicacy haggis (£13-20). Lunch M-Sa noon-5pm; brunch Su 12:30-4pm; dinner everyday until 10:30 pm. ❸

The Bay Tree Café, 403 Great Western Rd., at Park Rd. in the West End. Hummus with pita bread and salad £5.25. Open daily 10:30am-10pm. ❷

BRITAIN

🎯 SIGHTS

Follow George St. from George Square and take a left on High St., which turns into Castle St., to reach the Gothic **Glasgow Cathedral**, the only full-scale cathedral spared the fury of the 16th-century Scottish Reformation. (Open Apr.-Sept. M-Sa 9:30am-6pm, Su 2-5pm; Oct.-Mar. M-Sa 9:30am-4pm, Su 2-4pm. Free.) On the same street is the **St. Mungo Museum of Religious Life and Art,** 2 Castle St., which surveys every religion from Islam to Yoruba. (Open M-Sa 10am-5pm, Su 11am-5pm. Free.) Behind the cathedral is the spectacular **Necropolis,** a terrifying hilltop cemetery filled with broken tombstones. (Open 24hr. Free.)

In the West End, **Kelvingrove Park** lies on the banks of the River Kelvin. In the southwest corner of the park, at Argyle and Sauchiehall St., sits the magnificent **Kelvingrove Art Gallery and Museum,** which shelters works by van Gogh, Monet, and Rembrandt. (U: Kelvin Hall. Open M-Th and Sa 10am-5pm, F and Su 11am-5pm. Free.) Farther west rise the Gothic edifices of the **University of Glasgow.** The main building is on University Ave., which runs into Byres Rd. While walking through the campus, stop by the **Hunterian Museum,** home to the death mask of Bonnie Prince Charlie, or see 19th-century Scottish art at the **Hunterian Art Gallery,** across the street. (U: Hillhead. Open M-Sa 9:30am-5pm. Free.) Several buildings designed by Charles Rennie Mackintosh, Scotland's most famous architect, are open to the public; the **Glasgow School of Art,** 167 Renfrew St., south of the river, reflects a uniquely Glaswegian Modernist style. (Tours M-F 11am and 2pm, Sa 10:30am; July-Aug. also Sa 11:30am and 1pm, Su 10:30, 11:30am, and 1pm. £5, students £3.)

🎵 🏠 ENTERTAINMENT AND NIGHTLIFE

Glaswegians have a reputation for partying hard. *The List* (£2.20 from news-agents) has detailed nightlife and entertainment listings for both Glasgow and Edinburgh. The infamous **Byres Road** pub crawl slithers past the Glasgow University area, starting at Tennant's Bar and proceeding toward the River Clyde. ⚅**Uisge Beatha,** 232 Woodlands Rd., serves over 100 kinds of malt whiskey. (£1.30-1.60. Open M-Th 11am-11pm, F-Sa 11am-midnight, Su 12:30-11pm.) Go to ⚅**Babbity Bow-ster,** 16-18 Blackfriar St., for football talk and good drinks. (Open M-Sa 10am-midnight, Su 11am-midnight.) At **Nice 'n' Sleazy,** 421 Sauchiehall St., enjoy eclectic live music downstairs and cheap food and drink upstairs. (Open M-Sa 11:30am-midnight, Su 12:30pm-midnight.) **Horseshoe Bar,** 17-21 Drury St., boasts the longest continuous bar in the UK, as well as karaoke. (Open M-Sa 11am-midnight, Su 12:30pm-midnight.) At the club **Archaos,** 25 Queen St., students drink two-for-one whiskeys. (Cover £3-7. Open Tu, Th-Su 11pm-3am.) Grunge and indie music pleases mostly younger crowds at **Cathouse,** 15 Union St., a three-story club. (Cover £3-5, £1-2 student discount. Open W-Su 11pm-3am.)

STIRLING   ☎ 01786

The third point of a strategic triangle completed by Glasgow and Edinburgh, Stirling has historically presided over north-south movement in the region; it was once said that "he who controlled Stirling controlled Scotland." At the 1297 Battle of Stirling Bridge, **William Wallace** (of *Braveheart* fame) overpowered the English army; this enabled Robert the Bruce to finally overthrow the English at **Bannockburn,** 3.25km south of town. To reach Bannockburn, take bus #51 or 52 from Murray Pl. in Stirling. (Visitors center open Apr.-Oct. daily 10am-5:30pm; Mar. and Nov.-Dec. 10:30am-4:30pm. £2.50, children £1.70. Battlefield open year-round.) The ⚅**Stirling Castle** has prim gardens, superb views of the Forth Valley, and a militant history. (Open Apr.-Oct. daily 9:30am-6pm; Nov.-Mar. 9:30am-5pm. £6.50, children £2.) **Argyll's Lodging,** a

17th-century mansion on the castle's esplanade, has been impressively restored. (Open Apr.-Sept. daily 9:30am-6pm; Oct.-Mar. 9:30am-5pm. £3, children £1.40; free with castle admission.) The 19th-century **Wallace Monument Tower,** on Hillfouts Rd., 2.5km from town, offers incredible views. You can also admire the 1.5m sword William Wallace wielded against King Edward I. Take bus #62 or 63 from Murray Pl. (Open July-Aug. daily 9:30am-6:30pm; June and Sept. 10am-6pm; Mar.-May and Oct. 10am-5pm; Nov.-Feb. 10:30am-4pm. £4, students £3, seniors and children £2.75.)

Trains run from Goosecroft Rd. (☎(08457) 484 950) to: Aberdeen (2hr.; M-Sa every hr., Su 6 per day; £31); Edinburgh (50min., 2 per hr., £5.30); Glasgow (30min., 1-3 per hr., £5.40); Inverness (3hr., 3-4 per day, £31); and London King's Cross (5½hr., every hr., £44-84). **Buses** also run from Goosecroft Rd. to: Edinburgh (1¼hr., every hr., £4); Fort William (2¾hr., 1 per day, £13); Glasgow (40min., 2-3 per hr., £3.80); and Inverness (3¾hr., every hr., £11.80). The **tourist office** is at 41 Dumbarton Rd. (☎475 019. Open July-Aug. M-Sa 9am-7:30pm, Su 9:30am-6:30pm; June and Sept. M-Sa 9am-6pm, Su 10am-4pm; Oct.-May M-Sa 10am-5pm.) At the well-equipped **Willy Wallace Hostel ❷,** 77 Murray Pl., a delightful staff fosters a fun atmosphere. (☎446 773. Dorms £10-14.) The comfortable **Forth Guest House ❸,** 23 Forth Pl., is near the train station. (☎471 020. All rooms with bath. Singles £20-35; doubles £39-45.) **Postal Code:** FK8 2BP.

LOCH LOMOND ☎01389

With Britain's largest lake as its base, the landscape surrounding Loch Lomond is filled with the lush bays, wooded islands, and bare hills immortalized in the famous ballad. Hikers adore the **West Highland Way,** which snakes along the entire eastern side of the Loch and stretches north 152km from Milngavie to Fort William. At the southern tip of Loch Lomond is **Balloch,** the area's largest tourism center. Attractions and services at the new **Loch Lomond Shores** in Balloch include a giant-screen film about the loch, a **National Park Gateway Centre,** a tourist office, and bike and canoe rentals. A shuttle runs from the train station every 30min. during the summer. (☎721 500. Open Apr.-Sept. daily 7am-7pm, Oct.-Mar. 10am-5pm. £6, students £3.75.) One of the best introductions to the area is a **Sweeney's Cruises** boat tour, which leaves from the tourist office's side of the River Leven in Balloch (1hr.; every hr. 10am-4pm; £4.80, children £2.50).

Trains arrive on Balloch Rd. from Glasgow Queen St. (45min., 2 per hr., £3.20). Scottish Citylink **buses** (☎(08705) 808 080) arrive from Glasgow (40min., 3-5 per day, £3.60). First (☎(01324) 613 777) buses arrive from Stirling (1½hr., 1-3 per day, £4.80). **Tourist offices** are at Loch Lomond Shores (see above) and in the Old Station Building. (☎753 533. Open June-Sept. daily 9:30am-6pm; Apr.-May and Oct. 10am-5pm.) The ⚑**SYHA Loch Lomond ❷,** 3km north of town, is one of Scotland's largest hostels. From the train station, follow the main road for 800m; at the roundabout, turn right, continue 2.5km, turn left at the sign for the hostel, and it's a short way up the hill. (☎850 226. Book ahead in summer. Dorms £10-12.50, under 18 £8.50-11.) Camp at the luxurious **Lomond Woods Holiday Park ❶,** on Old Luss Rd., up Balloch Rd. from the tourist office. (☎759 475. Spa facilities. Bikes £7.50 per 4hr., £10 per 8hr.; deposit £100. Reception 8:30am-10pm. Tent and two people £6-9, with car £8-13; additional guests £2, free off-season.)

THE TROSSACHS ☎01877

The gentle mountains and lochs of the Trossachs form the northern boundary of central Scotland, and together with Loch Lomond, they have been designated Scotland's first national park. The A821 winds through the heart of the area between **Aberfoyle** and **Callander,** the region's main towns. It passes near **Loch Katrine,** the Trossachs' original lure and the setting of Scott's "The Lady of the Lake." A pedes-

YOUR OWN WAY

CAIRNGORM MOUNTAINS

The towering Cairngorms, scheduled to become a national park in 2003, are real Scottish wilderness: misty, mighty, and arctic year-round.

SEE THE SCENERY. Outdoor enthusiasts converge at **Cairngorm Mountain** for hikes on the **Windy Ridge Trail** and a trip on the newly unveiled funicular railway. Info ☎01479 861 261. Experienced hikers should consider taking the **Northern Corries Path** to the summit of Britain's second highest peak, **Ben MacDui.** Consult the **Cairngorm Rangers** (☎01479 861 703) for info.

SEE THE ANIMALS. The **Cairngorm Reindeer Centre** (☎01479 861 228) is home to dozens of sled-pullers, while the **Highland Wildlife Park** (☎01540 651 270) in Kincraig is dedicated to preserving native critters.

GET SOME SLEEP. The town of **Aviemore** is a concrete roadstrip with several places to stay. Info ☎01479 810 363.

TRANSPORTATION. Trains arrive in Aviemore from Inverness (45min., 7-8 per day, £7.20) and Edinburgh and Glasgow (2¼hr., 7 per day, £32). **Buses** run from: Inverness (40min., 15 per day, £4.70); Edinburgh (3hr., 12 per day, £12.50); and Glasgow (3½hr., 15 per day, £12.50). The **Cairngorm Service Station,** on Main St., rents cars. (☎01479 810 596. £34-42 per day.)

trian road traces the loch's shoreline, while the popular **Steamship Sir Walter Scott** cruises from the Trossachs Pier (2-3 per day; round-trip £5.50-6.50, children £3.60). Nearby hulks **Ben A'an'** (1207 ft.); the rocky 1hr. hike up begins a mile from the pier, along the A821. The Trossachs are known as "Rob Roy Country"; the **Rob Roy and Trossachs Visitor Centre** in Callander is a combined tourist office and exhibit on the 17th-century hero. (☎330 342. Open July-Aug. daily 9:30am-8pm; June daily 9:30am-6pm; Sept. daily 10am-6pm; Mar.-May and Oct.-Dec. daily 10am-5pm; Jan.-Feb. Sa-Su 11am-4:30pm. £3.25, children £2.25.)

From Callander, First (☎(01324) 613 777) **buses** run to Stirling (45min., 11 per day, £2.90) and Aberfoyle (45min., 4 per day, £3.40). **Postbuses** reach some remoter areas of the region; find timetables at tourist offices or call the **Stirling Council Public Transport Helpline** (☎(01786) 442 707). About 2km south of Callander on Invertrossachs Rd. is **Trossachs Backpackers ❷**, a comfortable hostel with an attractive setting. (☎331 200. Dorms £10-15.) Camp at **Trossachs Holiday Park ❶**, outside of Aberfoyle's town center. (☎382 614. Open Mar-Oct. £9 per person.)

INVERNESS AND LOCH NESS ☎01463

In AD 565, St. Columba repelled a savage sea beast as it attacked a monk; whether a prehistoric leftover or cosmic wanderer, the monster has captivated the world's imagination ever since. The **Loch Ness** guards its secrets 7.5km south of Inverness. Tour agencies are the most convenient ways to see the loch; **Guide Friday** offers a 3hr. bus and boat tour. (☎224 000. May-Sept. daily 10:30am and 2:30pm. £14.50, students and seniors £11.50, children £6.50.) Or, let **Kenny's Tours** take you around the entire loch and back to Inverness on a minibus. (☎252 411. Tours 10:30am-5pm. £12, students £10.) Three miles south on the A82, ▓**Urquhart Castle** (URK-hart) was one of the largest in Scotland before it was blown up in 1692 to prevent Jacobite occupation; alleged photos of Nessie have since been taken from the ruins. (☎(01456) 450 551. Open June-Aug. daily 9:30am-6:30pm; Apr.-May and Sept. daily 9:30am-5:45pm; Oct.-Mar. M-Sa 9:30am-3:45pm. £5.) The Jacobite cause died in 1746 on **Culloden Battlefield,** east of Inverness; take **Highland County bus** #12 from the post office at Queensgate (round-trip £2). Just 2.5km south of Culloden, the stone circles and chambered cairns (mounds of rough stones) of the **Cairns of Clava** recall civilizations of the Bronze Age. Bus #12 will also take you to the **Cawdor Castle,** home of the Cawdors since the 15th century; don't miss the maze. (Open May-Sept. daily 10am-5pm. £6.10, students and seniors £5.10, children £3.30.)

Trains (☎(08457) 484 950) run from Academy St. in Inverness's Station Sq. to: Aberdeen (2¼hr., 7-10 per day, £18.80); Edinburgh (3½-4hr., 5-7 per day, £31); Glasgow (3½hr., 5-7 per day, £31); and London (8hr., 3 per day, £84-110). Scottish Citylink **buses** (☎(08705) 505 050) run from Farraline Park, off Academy St., to Edinburgh and Glasgow (both 4½hr., 10-12 per day, £14.70). To reach the **tourist office,** Castle Wynd, from the stations, turn left on Academy St. and then right onto Union St. (☎234 353. Open mid-June to Aug. M-Sa 9am-7pm, Su 9:30am-5pm; Sept. to mid-June M-Sa 9am-5pm, Su 10am-4pm.) **Bazpackers Backpackers Hotel ❶,** 4 Culduthel Rd., has a homey atmosphere and great views of the city. (☎717 663. Reception 7:30am-midnight. Dorms £8.50-10; doubles £12-14.) A minute's walk from the city center, **Felstead ❸,** 18 Ness Bank, is a spacious B&B with comfortable beds. (☎321 634. £28-36 per person.)

FORT WILLIAM AND BEN NEVIS   ☎01397

With a slew of beautiful lochs and valleys, **Fort William** makes an excellent base camp for mountain excursions to **Ben Nevis** (1342m), the highest peak in Britain. The walk up Ben Nevis (round-trip 15km) starts in **Glen Nevis,** a gorgeous glacial valley 2.5km from town. The **Glen Nevis Visitor Centre,** at the trailhead, provides info on Ben Nevis and other nearby hikes. (Open June-Sept. daily 9am-6pm; Apr.-May and Oct. 9am-5pm.) **Trains** arrive on High St. in Fort William from Glasgow Queen St. (3¾hr., 2-3 per day, £18) and London Euston (12hr., 1 per day, £70-97). Scottish Citylink (☎(08705) 505 050) **buses** go from High St. to: Edinburgh (3¾hr., 2 per day, £15.20); Glasgow (3hr., 4 per day, £11.90); Inverness (2hr., 5-6 per day, £7.20); and Kyle of Lochalsh (2hr., 3 per day, £10.70). The **tourist office** is in Cameron Sq., just off High St. (☎703 781. Open mid-July to Aug. M-Sa 9am-8:30pm, Su 9am-6pm; mid-June to mid-July M-Sa 9am-7pm, Su 10am-6pm; Mar. to mid-June M-Sa 9am-6pm, Su 10am-4pm; Sept.-Oct. M-Sa 9am-6pm, Su 10am-5:30pm; Nov.-Feb. M-Sa 9am-5pm, Su 10am-4pm.) At the comfortable ☒**Farr Cottage Accommodation and Activity Centre ❷** in Corpach, the owners give Scottish history lessons and whiskey talks. Take Highland County bus #45 from Ft. William. (☎772 315. Laundry and kitchen. Dorms £11.) The **Glen Nevis Caravan & Camping Park ❶** is 5.5km east of town on Glen Nevis Rd. (☎702 191. Open mid-Mar. to Oct. Tent and two people £7.10, with car £12.) **Postal Code:** PH33 6AR.

THE INNER HEBRIDES

ISLE OF SKYE

Often described as the shining jewel in the Hebridean crown, Skye radiates natural beauty, from the serrated peaks of the Cuillin Hills to the rugged northern tip of the Trotternish Peninsula.

▦ **TRANSPORTATION.** The tradition of ferries carrying passengers "over the sea to Skye" ended with the **Skye Bridge,** which links **Kyle of Lochalsh,** on the mainland, to **Kyleakin,** on the Isle of Skye. **Trains** (☎08457 484 950) arrive at Kyle of Lochalsh from Inverness (2½hr., 2-4 per day, £15). Skye-Ways (☎01599 534 328) runs **buses** from: Fort William (2hr., 3 per day, £11); Glasgow (5½hr., 3 per day, £19); and Inverness (2½hr., 2 per day, £10.90). **Pedestrians** can traverse the Skye Bridge's 2.5km footpath or take the **shuttle bus** (2 per hr., £1.70). Buses on the island are infrequent and expensive; pick up the handy *Public Transport Guide to Skye and the Western Isles* (£1) at a tourist office.

KYLE OF LOCHALSH AND KYLEAKIN. Kyle of Lochalsh and Kyleakin (Ky-LAACK-in) bookend the Skye Bridge. The former, on the mainland, has an ATM, tourist office, and train station, making it of practical value to travelers. Kyleakin

BRITAIN

is a backpackers' hub with three hostels and countless tours. ◧MacBackpackers **Skye Trekker Tour,** departing from Kyleakin, offers one- or two-day historical and eco-conscious tours, with all necessary gear provided. (☎01599 534 510. Call ahead. 1-day £15, 2-day £45.) The picturesque **Eilean Donan Castle** is between Kyle of Lochalsh and Inverness; take a Scottish Citylink bus and get off at Dornie. (☎555 202. Open Apr.-Oct. daily 10am-5:30pm; Mar. and Nov. 10am-3pm. £4, students £3.20.) To enjoy the incredible sunset views from the quiet Kyleakin harbor, climb to the memorial on the hill behind the SYHA hostel. A slippery scramble to the west takes you to the small ruins of **Castle Moil.** Cross the little bridge behind the hostel, turn left, follow the road to the pier, and take the gravel path. The Kyle of Lochalsh **tourist office** is on the hill right above the train station. (☎534 276. Open May-Oct. M-Sa 9am-5:30pm.) The friendly owners of ◧Dun Caan Hostel ❷, in Kyleakin, have masterfully renovated a 200-year-old cottage. (☎534 087. **Bikes** £10 per day. Book ahead. Dorms £10.) ☎01599.

SLIGACHAN. The **Cuillin Hills** (COO-leen), the highest peaks in the Hebrides, are renowned for their cloud and mist formations and for hiking. *Walks from Sligachan and Glen Brittle* (£1), available at tourist offices, hotels, and campsites, suggests routes. West of Kyleakin, the smooth, conical Red Cuillin and the rough, craggy Black Cuillin Hills meet in Sligachan, a hiker's hub in a jaw-dropping setting. Your best bet is the **Sligachan Hotel ❹,** a classic hill-walker's and climber's haunt. (☎650 204. Breakfast included. £30-50 per person.) Campers should head to **Glenbrittle Campsite ❶,** in Glenbrittle at the foot of the Black Cuillins. Take bus #53 (M-Sa 2 per day) from Portree and Sligachan to Glenbrittle. (☎640 404. Open Apr.-Sept. £4 per person, children £2.) ☎01478.

PORTREE. The island's capital, **Portree,** has busy shops and an attractive harbor. Buses (1-3 per day) run from Portree to **Dunvegan Castle,** the seat of the clan MacLeod. The castle holds the **Fairy Flag,** a 1500-year-old silk. (☎521 206. Open Apr.-Oct. daily 10am-5:30pm; Nov.-Mar. 11am-4pm. £6. Gardens only £4.) **Buses** to Portree from Kyle of Lochalsh (5 per day, £7.80) stop at Somerled Sq. The **tourist office** is on Bayfield Rd. (☎612 137. Open July-Aug. M-Sa 9am-7pm, Su 10am-4pm; Sept.-Oct. and Apr.-June M-F 9am-5pm, Su 10am-4pm; Nov.-Mar. M-Sa 9am-4pm.) The **Portree Independent Hostel ❷,** The Green, has a multitude of amenities. (☎613 737. Internet £1 per 20min. Dorms £10.50; doubles £23.) ☎01478.

THE OUTER HEBRIDES

The landscape of the Outer Hebrides is extraordinarily beautiful and astoundingly ancient. Much of its rock is more than half as old as the Earth itself, and long-gone inhabitants have left a collection of tombs, standing stones, and other antiquities. While television and tourism have diluted old ways of life, you're still more likely to get an earful of Gaelic here than anywhere else in Scotland. The Western Isles remain one of Scotland's most undisturbed and unforgettable realms.

▣ **TRANSPORTATION.** Caledonian MacBrayne (☎(01475) 650 100) **ferries** serve the Western Isles, from Ullapool to Lewis and from Skye to Harris and North Uist. Find schedules in *Discover Scotland's Islands with Caledonian MacBrayne,* free from tourist offices. You'll also want to pick up the *Lewis and Harris Bus Timetables* (£0.40). Inexpensive **car rental** (from £20 per day) is possible throughout the isles. The terrain is hilly but excellent for **cycling.**

LEWIS AND HARRIS. The island of **Lewis** is relentlessly desolate, the landscape flat, treeless, and speckled with lochs. Mists shroud miles of moorland and fields of peat, nearly hiding Lewis's many archaeological sites, most notably the ◧Callanish

Stones, an extraordinary and isolated Bronze Age circle. Buses on the W2 route from Stornoway (M-Sa 5 per day) stop at the stones. (☎621 422. Visitors center open Apr.-Sept. M-Sa 10am-7pm; Oct.-Mar. 10am-4pm. £1.75, students £1.25.) CalMac **ferries** sail from Ullapool, on the mainland, to **Stornoway** (pop. 8000), the largest town in northwestern Scotland (M-Sa 2 per day; £13.35, round-trip £22.85). To get to the Stornoway **tourist office,** 26 Cromwell St., turn left from the ferry terminal, then right onto Cromwell St. (☎703 088. Open Apr.-Oct. M-Sa 9am-6pm and to meet late ferries; Nov.-Mar. M-F 9am-5pm.) The best place to lay your head is **Fair Haven Hostel ❷,** over the surf shop at the intersection of Francis St. and Keith St. From the pier, turn left onto Shell St., which becomes South Beach, then turn right on Kenneth St. and right again onto Francis St. The meals here are better than in town. (☎705 862. Dorms £10, with three meals £20.) ☎**01851.**

Harris is technically the same island as Lewis, but they're entirely different worlds. The deserted flatlands of Lewis, in the north, give way to another, more rugged and spectacular kind of desolation—that of Harris's steely gray peaks. Toward the west coast, the **Forest of Harris** (ironically, a treeless, heathersplotched mountain range) descends to yellow beaches bordered by indigo waters and *machair*—sea meadows of soft grass and summertime flowers. Essential *Ordnance Survey* hiking maps can be found at the tourist office in **Tarbert,** the biggest town on Harris. **Ferries** arrive in Tarbert from Uig on Skye (M-Sa 2 per day; £8.70, round-trip £14.90). The **tourist office** is on Pier Rd. (☎502 011. Open Apr. to mid-Oct. M-Sa 9am-5pm and for late ferry arrivals; mid-Oct. to Mar. for arrivals only.) **Rockview Bunkhouse ❶,** on Main St., is less than 5min. west of the pier, on the north side of the street. (☎502 211. Dorms £9.) ☎**01859.**

BULGARIA (БЪЛГАРИЯ)

The history of Bulgaria's people is not as serene as its landscape. Once the most powerful state in the Balkans, Bulgaria fell to the Turks in the late 14th century. During its 500 years under Ottoman rule, Bulgaria's nobles were obliterated and its peasants were enserfed. At the same time, however, underground monasteries were preserving the nation's culture. This paved the way for the National Revival of the 1870s, when education spread and much of the majestic architecture now gracing Bulgaria's cities was built. Today, the country struggles with a flagging economy and a lack of full European recognition, problems heightened by the recent Balkan wars. Nonetheless, travelers should not pass over Bulgaria's beautiful coastline, lush countryside, and lovely monasteries.

FACTS AND FIGURES

Official Name: Republic of Bulgaria.
Capital: Sofia.
Major Cities: Varna, Burgas, Ruse.
Population: 7,700,000.
Land Area: 110,910 sq. km.

Time Zone: GMT +2.
Language: Bulgarian.
Religions: Bulgarian Orthodox (85%), Muslim (13%), other (2%).

DISCOVER BULGARIA

Bulgaria is a convenient stop between Western Europe and Greece or Turkey. In **Sofia** (p. 218), admire Orthodox Churches and wander cobblestone alleyways. **Rila Monastery** (p. 222), in the highest mountains on the Balkan Peninsula, is the masterpiece of Bulgarian religious art. **Plovdiv** (p. 223) shelters Roman ruins and art museums, and is only 30min. from the splendid **Bachkovo Monastery** (p. 223). The **Black Sea Coast** (p. 224) is full of raucous discos and deserted beaches. On your way to the coast from western Bulgaria, stop in **Veliko Turnovo** (p. 224), the most beautiful town in the country.

ESSENTIALS

WHEN TO GO

Year-round, Bulgaria is milder than other Balkan countries due to the proximity of the Mediterranean and Black Seas. Spring and fall weather is generally ideal, as winter can be quite cold. For the Black Sea Coast, summer is the best time to visit.

DOCUMENTS AND FORMALITIES

VISAS. Citizens of Australia, Canada, the EU, New Zealand, and the US may stay without visas for up to 30 days. Citizens of South Africa and all travelers staying more than 30 days must obtain a 90-day visa from their local embassy or consulate.

EMBASSIES. Foreign embassies in Bulgaria are all in Sofia (see p. 220). Bulgarian embassies at home include: **Australia** (consular), 14 Carlotta Rd., Double Bay, Sydney, NSW 2028; P.O. Box 1000, Double Bay, NSW 1360 (☎02 9327 7592; bgconsul@ihug.com.au); **Canada,** 325 Stewart St., Ottawa, ON K1N 6K5 (☎613-789-3215; fax 613-789-3524); **Ireland,** 22 Bulington Rd. Dublin 4 (☎01 660 3293; fax 660 3915); **South Africa,** 1071 Church St., Hatfield, Pretoria 0083; P.O. Box 32569, Arcadia (☎012 342 37 20; embulgsa@iafrica.com); **UK,** 186-188 Queensgate, Lon-

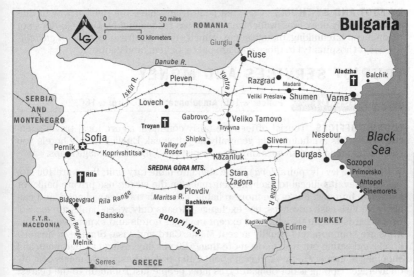

don SW7 5HL (☎020 7584 9400; fax 7584 4948); **US**, 1621 22nd St. NW, Washington, D.C. 20008 (☎202-387-0174 or 387-7969; www.bulgaria-embassy.org).

TRANSPORTATION

BY PLANE. Air France, British Airways, and Lufthansa fly into Sofia (SOF). There are no direct flights from the US; budget travelers can fly into a nearby capital such as Athens, İstanbul, or Bucharest and then take a bus to Sofia.

BY TRAIN. Bulgarian trains run to Hungary, Romania, and Turkey and are most useful for travel in the north; **Rila** is the main international train company. The train system is comprehensive but slow, crowded, and old. There are three types of trains: express (експрес; ekspres); fast (бърз; burz); and slow (пътнически; putnicheski). Avoid *putnicheski* like the plague—they stop at anything that looks inhabited, even if only by goats. *Purva klasa* (първа класа; first-class seating) is very similar to *vtora klasa* (втора класа; second-class) and not worth the extra money. Some **useful words:** *vlak* (влак; train); *avtobus* (автобус; bus); *gara* (гара; station); *peron* (перон; platform); *kolovoz* (коловоз; track); *bilet* (билет; ticket); *zaminavashti* (заминаващи; departure); *pristigashti* (пристигащи; arrival); and *ne/pushachi* (не/пушачи; non-/smoking).

BY BUS. Buses are better for travel in eastern and western Bulgaria; routes head north from Ruse and to İstanbul from anywhere on the Black Sea Coast. Traveling by bus is quicker, but less comfortable, than by train. For long distances, **Group Travel** and **Etap** offer modern buses at prices 50% higher than trains. Some buses have set departure times, but others may leave when they reach capacity. Grueling local buses stop everywhere. Due to the political situation in the former Yugoslavia, *Let's Go* does not recommend taking direct buses from Bulgaria to Central and Western Europe; instead, travel to Bucharest before turning westward.

BY TAXI. Yellow taxis are everywhere; some Black Sea towns can be reached only by cab. Refuse to pay in euros or US dollars and insist on a metered ride *("sus apparata")*; ask the distance and price per kilometer to do your own calculations.

BY FOOT AND BY THUMB. Cars, not pedestrians, have the right of way in Bulgaria; faithfully obey crosswalk signs, and cross roads quickly. *Let's Go* does not recommend hitchhiking, though some claim it yields a refreshing taste of *gostely-ubivnost* (hospitality) to those who are polite, patient, and cautious.

TOURIST SERVICES AND MONEY

EMERGENCY	Police: ☎ 166. Ambulance: ☎ 150. Fire: ☎ 160.

TOURIST OFFICES. Tourist offices are fairly common, as are local travel agencies. The staffs are helpful but generally do not speak English. In big hotels you can often find an English-speaking receptionist and English-language maps.

MONEY. The **lev** (lv; plural *leva*) is the standard monetary unit; there are 100 stotinki in a lev. It's illegal to exchange currency on the street; use private banks or exchange bureaus. **Banks** are more reliable, can cash traveler's checks, and can also give Visa cash advances; use exchange bureaus only when banks are closed. Credit cards are rarely accepted except in larger hotels and expensive resorts. **ATMs** are common, and usually accept MasterCard and Visa. Staying in hostels/hotels and eating out won't cost more than €20 per day; using campgrounds and shopping at grocery stores will cost about €10 per day. Restaurant meals cost 6lv on average. Tipping is not obligatory, as most people just round up to the nearest lev, but 10% doesn't hurt, especially in Sofia. A 7-10% service charge will occasionally be added for you; always check the bill or the menu. Tipping taxi drivers usually means rounding up to the nearest half-lev. Bargaining for fares is not done, but make sure there is a meter or agree on a price.

BUSINESS HOURS. Businesses open at 8 or 9am and take a one-hour lunch break between 11am and 2pm. Train and bus cashiers and post office attendants take occasional 15min. coffee breaks—be patient in lines. Banks are usually open 8:30am to 4pm, but some close at 2pm. *Vseki den* (всеки ден; every day) usually means Monday through Friday, and "non-stop" doesn't always mean open 24hr.

LEVA		
AUS$1 = 1.09LV	1LV = AUS$0.89
CDN$1 = 1.27LV	1LV = CDN$0.79
EUR€1 = 1.94LV	1LV = EUR€0.52
NZ$1 = 0.93LV	1LV = NZ$0.92
ZAR1 = 0.19LV	1LV = ZAR5.32
UK£1 = 3.04LV	1LV = UK£0.33
US$1 = 1.98LV	1LV = US$0.51

COMMUNICATION

PHONE CODE	**Country code: 359. International dialing prefix: 00.** From outside Bulgaria, dial int'l dialing prefix (see inside back cover) + 359 + city code + local number.

MAIL. Overseas mail requires a Bulgarian return address, and costs: 0.60lv for any European destination; 0.80lv for the US; 0.80-1.00lv for Australia, New Zealand, or South Africa. Write "С въздушна поща" for airmail. *Poste Restante* is unreliable at best; address mail to be held: Firstname SURNAME, *Poste Restante*, Gen. Gurko 6, Sofia 1000, BULGARIA.

TELEPHONES AND INTERNET. For local calls, it's best to buy a phone card. There are two brands, which are equally common: Bulfon (orange) and Mobika (blue), which work only at telephones of the same brand. Cards are sold at kiosks and bookstores. (400 units=20lv; 200 units=12lv; 100 units=7.50lv; 50 units=4.90lv.) Making international telephone calls from Bulgaria can be a challenge. Payphones are ludicrously expensive; opt for the phones in a telephone office. If you must make an international call from a pay phone, purchase a 400 unit card—units run out very quickly. To call collect, dial ☎01 23 for an international operator. The Bulgarian phrase for collect call is *za tyahna smetka* (за тяхна сметка). International direct access numbers include: **AT&T,** ☎00 800 0010; **British Telecom,** ☎00 800 99 44; **Bell Canada,** ☎00 800 1359; and **MCI,** ☎00 800 001. **Internet access** is widespread and cheap, around 1-2lv per hr., and Internet cafes are often open 24hr.

LANGUAGES. Bulgarian is a South Slavic language similar to Russian; learning the Cyrillic alphabet is advised. English is spoken mostly by young people and in tourist areas. German is understood in many places. For the Cyrillic alphabet, see p. 1051; for some Bulgarian words and phrases, see p. 1052.

 YES AND NO. To indicate "yes" and "no," Bulgarians shake their heads in the opposite directions from Brits and Yanks. If you are uncoordinated, it's easier to just hold your head still and say *dah* or *neh*.

ACCOMMODATIONS AND CAMPING

BULGARIA	❶	❷	❸	❹	❺
ACCOMMODATIONS	under 20lv	20-40lv	41-60lv	61-80lv	over 80lv

Upon crossing the border, citizens of South Africa may receive a statistical card to document where they stay. If you are not given a card, ask hotels or private room bureaus to stamp your passport or a receipt-like paper that you can show upon border re-crossing, or you will be fined. If you are staying with friends, you'll have to register with the Bulgarian Registration Office. See the consular section of your embassy (p. 214) for details.

Private rooms are indicated by частни квартири *(tschastnee kvartiri)* signs. Rooms can be arranged through Balkantourist (www.balkantourist.bg) or other tourist offices for €5-15 per night (be sure to ask for a central location), or from individuals in train and bus stations. Be careful if alone, and don't hand over any money until you've checked the place out. *Babushki* are the best; try to bargain them down. Bulgarian **hotels** are classed on a star system and licensed by the Government Committee on Tourism; rooms in one-star hotels are almost identical to those in two- and three-star hotels, but have no private bathrooms. Hotels are usually €8-40 per night, although foreigners are often charged even more. The majority of Bulgarian **youth hostels** are in the countryside. Outside major towns, most **campgrounds** provide tent space or spartan bungalows.

FOOD AND DRINK

BULGARIA	❶	❷	❸	❹	❺
FOOD	under 4lv	4-10lv	11-14lv	15-18lv	over 18lv

Tap water is generally safe for drinking. Bulgaria is known for cheese and yogurt; try *shopska salata* (шопска салата), a mix of tomatoes, peppers, and cucumbers with feta cheese, or *tarator* (таратор), a cold soup made with yogurt, cucumber, garlic, and sometimes walnuts. Baklava and *sladoled* (сладолед; ice cream) are sold in *sladkarnitsy* (сладкарници). Fruit and vegetables are sold in a *plod-zelenchuk* (плод-зеленчук; fruit store), *pazar* (пазар; market), or on the street. Kiosks sell *kebabcheta* (кебабчета; sausage burgers), sandwiches, pizzas, and *banitsa sus sirene* (баница със сирене; cheese-filled pastries). *Skara* (скара; grill restaurants) serve *kavarma* (каварма), meat dishes with onions, spices, and egg. In restaurants, seat yourself and ask for the bill when you are finished.

HEALTH AND SAFETY

Public bathrooms (Ж for women, M for men) are often holes in the ground; pack a small bar of soap and toilet paper, and expect to pay 0.05-0.20lv. The sign "Аптека" (apteka) denotes a **pharmacy.** There is always a night-duty pharmacy in larger towns; its address is posted on the doors of the others. **Emergency care** is far better in Sofia than in the rest of the country; services at the Pirogov State Hospital are free, some doctors speak English, and the tourist office will send someone along to interpret for you. Don't buy **alcohol** from street vendors, and watch out for homemade liquor—there have been cases of poisoning and contamination. Locals generally don't trust the police, and stories circulate of people being terrorized by the local mafia. While incidents of hate crimes are rare, persons of a foreign ethnicity might receive stares and suspicious looks. The Bulgarian government recently recognized **homosexuality,** but acceptance is slow in coming.

HOLIDAYS AND FESTIVALS

New Year's (Jan. 1); 1878 Liberation Day (Mar. 3); Good Friday (Apr. 18); Easter (Apr. 20-21); Labor Day (May 1); St. George's Day and Bulgarian Army Day (May 6); Education and Culture Day and Day of Slavic Heritage (May 24); Festival of the Roses (June 1); Day of Union (Sept. 6); Independence Day (Sept. 22); Christmas (Dec. 24-26).

SOFIA (СОФИЯ) ☎02

A history of cultural submission has left Bulgaria unsure of itself. In Sofia, spray-painted skateboarding ramps front the iron Soviet Army monument, while *babushkas* tote their bread loaves home in Harry Potter shopping bags. Although the McDonald's arches keep surfacing, the golden dome of St. Alexander Nevsky Cathedral is still Sofia's most prominent landmark, and there are plenty of places to find traditional Bulgarian food, folk music, and handmade souvenirs.

▐▀ TRANSPORTATION

Flights: Airport Sofia (SOF; ☎79 80 35). Bus #84 goes to Eagle Bridge, a 10min. walk from the city center (to the right as you exit international arrivals). Calling a cab (see below) is cheaper than hailing one; a ride to the city center costs no more than 5lv.

Trains: Tsentralna Gara (Централна Гара; Central Train Station), Knyaginya Maria Luiza St. (Мария Луиза). Trams #1 and 7 run to pl. Sv. Nedelya (Неделя); #9 and 12 head down Hristo Botev (Христо Ботев) and Vitosha bul. (Витоша). The **ticket office** (☎931 11 11) is open M-F 7am-7pm. To: **Burgas** (7 per day, 8.20-12lv); **Plovdiv** (13 per day, 3.80lv). Left of the main entrance, **Rila Travel Bureau** (Рила; ☎932 33 46) sells tickets to: **Athens** (1 per day, 65-90lv); **Budapest** (1 per day, 110-135lv).

Buses: Private buses, which leave from the parking lot across from the train station, are usually cheap and fast. **Group Travel** (☎32 01 22) has a kiosks labeled "Биллетн Център" (Billeten Tsentur). To: **Burgas** (2 per day, 16lv); **Varna** (3 per day, 16lv); **Veliko Tarnovo** (4 per day, 9lv). Arrive 30-45min. early to get a seat.

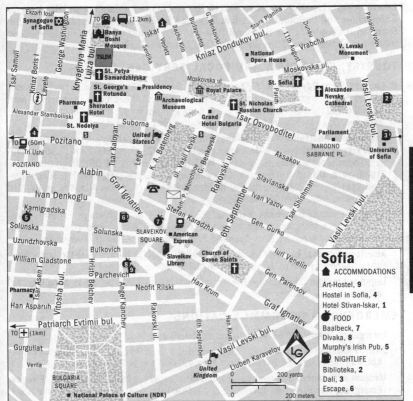

Sofia

▲ ACCOMMODATIONS

Art-Hostel, 9
Hostel in Sofia, 4
Hotel Stivan-Iskar, 1

🍎 FOOD

Baalbeck, 7
Divaka, 8
Murphy's Irish Pub, 5

🍸 NIGHTLIFE

Biblioteka, 2
Dali, 3
Escape, 6

BULGARIA

Local Transportation: Trams, trolleybuses, and **buses** cost 0.40lv per ride. Day-pass 2lv; 5-day pass 9lv. Buy tickets at kiosks with signs reading "Билети" (tickets; *bileti*), or from the driver. Punch them in the machines between the bus windows to avoid a 10lv fine. If you put your backpack on a seat, you might be required to buy a second ticket. Officially runs 5am-11:30pm, but rides are scarce after 9pm.

Taxis: Taxi S-Express (☎912 80), **OK Taxi** (☎973 21 21), and **INEX** (☎919 19) are reliable. At night, take cabs. Fares are 0.30-0.40lv per km, and upwards of 0.35-0.40lv per km after 10pm. Drivers don't speak English. Rather than bargaining, make sure the meter is on.

📧🔋 ORIENTATION AND PRACTICAL INFORMATION

The city center, **ploshad Sveta Nedelya** (Света Неделя), is bounded by Tsurkva Sv. Nedelya, the Sheraton Hotel, and the department store Tsentralen Universalen Magazin (TSUM). **Knyaginya Maria Luiza bulevard** (Княгиня Мария Луиза) connects pl. Sv. Nedelya to the train station. Trams #1 and 7 run from the station through pl. Sveta Nedelya and down **Vitosha bulevard** (Витоша), a main shopping and nightlife thoroughfare. Vitosha links pl. Sveta Nedelya to pl. Bulgaria and the huge, concrete **National Palace of Culture** (Национален Дворец Култура; Natsionalen Dvorets Kultura; NDK). Historical **Tsar Osvoboditel bulevard** (Цар Освободител; Tsar the

Liberator) heads to the university and the hottest spots for dancing and drinking in Sofia. Maps and the monthly English-language *Sofia City Guide* (2.40lv) can be found in the lobby of the Sheraton Hotel, tourist centers, and the outdoor book market at pl. Slaveikov (Славйков) on Graf Ignatiev (Граф Игнатиев).

TOURIST, FINANCIAL, AND LOCAL SERVICES

Tourist Office: Odysseia-In/Zig-Zag Holidays, Stamboliiski bul. 20-B (Стамболийски; ☎980 51 02; zigzag@omega.bg). From pl. Sv. Nedelya, head down Stamboliiski and take the 2nd right on Lavele; Odysseia is halfway down on the left, 2 floors up. A great resource. Open M-Sa 9am-6:30pm. Consultation 5lv per session.

Embassies: Australians, Canadians, and **New Zealanders** should contact the **UK embassy,** ul. Moshovsha 9 (Московска; ☎933 92 22). Open M-F 8am-12:30pm and 1:30-5pm. **South Africa,** ul. Gendov, bl. 1 (Гендов; ☎971 21 38). Open M and Th 10am-noon. **US,** ul. Suborna 1a (Съборна; ☎937 51 004). Open M-F 8:30am-1pm and 2pm-5pm. Consular section at Kapitan Andreev 1 (Капитан Андреев; ☎963 20 22), behind NDK. Open M-F 9am-5pm.

Currency Exchange: Bulbank (Булбанк; ☎923 21 11), pl. Sv. Nedelya 7, cashes traveler's checks for 1.4% commission and a minimum €3 fee and gives Visa cash advances for 4% commission. Open M-F 8:30am-6:30pm. **ATMs** are everywhere.

American Express: Ul. Vasil Levski 21 (☎988 49 43). On the left past the post office when heading toward pl. Slaveikov. Open M-F 9am-6pm, Sa 9am-noon.

Luggage Storage: Downstairs at the central train station. 0.80lv per piece; hand luggage only. Open daily 5:30am-midnight.

EMERGENCY AND COMMUNICATIONS

Emergency: Police: ☎166. **Ambulance:** ☎150. **Fire:** ☎160.

24hr. Pharmacies: Apteka #7, pl. Sv. Nedelya 5 (☎987 50 89). **Purva Chastna Apteka** (Първа Частна Аптека), Tsar Asen 42, near Neofit Rilski (☎952 26 22).

Medical Assistance: State-owned hospitals offer foreigners free emergency aid. **Pirogov Emergency Hospital,** Gen. Totleben bul. 21 (Ген. Тотлебен; ☎515 31), opposite Hotel Rodina. Take trolley #5 or 19 from city center. Open 24hr.

Telephones: Ul. Gurko 4. Turn right from the post office onto Vasil Levski then left onto Gurko; large, white building one block down. Phone, fax, email, Internet. Open 24hr.

Internet Access: Club Cyberia, Stephan Karadzha 18B (☎986 27 91; www.cyberi-anet.net). 1lv per hr.; noon-9pm 1.50lv per hr., students 1lv per hr. Open M-F 8am-1am, Sa-Su 10am-midnight. **Stargate,** Pozitano 20 (Позитано), 30m left when facing Hostel Sofia. 0.8lv per hr. Open 24hr.

Post Office: Gen. Gurko 6 (Гурко). Send international mail at windows #6-8 in the first hall; receive at window #12. Open M-F 8am-8pm, Sa 8am-noon. Address mail to be held: Firstname SURNAME, *Poste Restante*, Gen. Gurko 6, Sofia **1000,** BULGARIA.

🏠 🍴 ACCOMMODATIONS AND FOOD

Big hotels are rarely worth the exorbitant price; if hostels are full, **private rooms** may be the best option. A friendly staff awaits at **Hostel in Sofia ❶,** Pozitano 16 (Позитано). From pl. Sv. Nedelya, walk down Vitosha, and go right on Pozitano. (☎/fax 989 85 82; hostelsofia@yahoo.com. Breakfast included. Kitchen. 24hr. reception. US$8, first night US$9.) The spacious new **Art-Hostel ❶,** ul. Angel Kunchev (Ангел Кънчев) 21A, is part hostel, part art gallery. From pl. Sv. Nedelya, take Vitosha to William Gladstone (Уилям Гладстон), turn left, and after two blocks turn right onto Angel Kunchev. (☎987 05 45 or 980 91 30; www.art-hostel.com. Kitchen, bar, tea room, and garden. Internet access. 24hr. reception. US$9.) To get to **Hotel Stivan-Iskar ❸**, ul. Iskar 11B, walk up Maria Luiza bul. and turn right on ul. Ekzah Iosif (Екзарх Йосиф), then walk two blocks and go right on Bacho Kiro, and then left. (☎986 67 50; www.hoteliskar.com. Breakfast US$2. Check-out noon. Doubles US$25-37. Apartment with fridge US$50-55.)

Cheap meals are easy to find. The large **markets** Hali (Хали) and the Women's Bazaar (Жени Пазар) lie across bul. Maria Luiza from TSUM. **Divaka ❶**, ul. William Gladstone 54, serves huge salads (1.50-3.50lv) and sizzling veggie and meat *sacheta* (4.50lv). Facing McDonalds in pl. Slaveikov, take the left sidestreet and continue right at the fork; Divaka is on the left. (☎989 95 43. Open 24hr.) **Murphy's Irish Pub ❷**, Karnigradska 6 (Кърниградска), is a friendly haven for homesick English-speakers. (☎980 28 70. Main dishes 6.50-10.50lv. Open daily noon-1am.) **Baalbeck ❶**, ul. Vasil Levsky 4, has both Middle Eastern and Bulgarian offerings; you can grab a falafel sandwich (1lv) to go at the counter or eat in. (☎987 09 07. 1-3lv. Open M-Sa 10am-11pm.)

SIGHTS

PLOSHAD ALEXANDER NEVSKY. In the city center stands Sofia's pride and joy, the gold-domed **Cathedral of St. Alexander Nevsky** (Александър Невски; Aleksandr Nevsky), which was erected in memory of the 200,000 Russians who died in the 1877-78 Russo-Turkish War. Through a separate entrance left of the main church, the **crypt** contains a spectacular array of painted icons and religious artifacts, the richest collection of its kind in Bulgaria. *(Cathedral open daily 7:30am-7pm; free. Crypt open W-M 10:30am-6:30pm. 3lv, students 1.5lv.)*

AROUND PLOSHAD SVETA NEDELYA. The focal point of pl. Sveta Nedelya, the **Cathedral of St. Nedelya** (Катедрален Храм Св. Неделя; Katedralen Hram Sv. Nedelya) is filled with frescoes blackened by soot from candles lit by visitors. The church is a reconstruction of a 14th-century original destroyed by a bomb in an attempt on Tsar Boris III's life in 1925. Sunday liturgy shows off the church's great acoustics. *(Open daily 7am-6pm.)* In the courtyard behind the Sheraton Hotel stands the 4th-century **St. George's Rotunda** (Св. Георги; Sv. Georgi), which is adorned with beautiful 11th- to 14th-century murals. *(Open daily 8am-6pm.)* Walk up bul. Maria Luiza and take a left on Ekzarh Iosif to reach the **Synagogue of Sofia** (Софийска Синагога; Sofiiska sinagoga), Sofia's only synagogue, where a museum upstairs outlines the history of Jews in Bulgaria. *(Open M-F 9:30am-2pm. Weekly services F 7pm, Sa 10am. Donations welcome.)*

ALONG TSAR OSVOBODITEL BULEVARD. Historical Tsar Osvoboditel bul. stretches between the **House of Parliament** and the **Royal Palace.** Midway sits the exquisitely ornamented **St. Nicholas Russian Church** (Sv. Nikolai; Св. Николай), which is topped with Russian Orthodox onion domes. *(Open daily 9am-10:30pm.)*

MUSEUMS. The Royal Palace houses the **National Museum of Ethnography** (Национален Етнографски Музей; Natsionalen Etnografski Muzey), which is devoted to folk history, art, and crafts. *(Open Tu-Su 10am-5:30pm. 3lv, students 1.50lv.)* It also houses the **National Art Gallery** (Национална Художествена Галериа; Natsionalna Hudozhestvena Galeriya). *(Open Tu-Su 10:30am-6:30pm. 3lv, students 1.50lv.)* To reach the **National History Museum,** Residence Boyana, Palace 1 (Национален Исторически Музей; Natsionalen Istoricheski Muzey), take trolley #2 or bus #63 or 111 to Boyana. The museum traces the evolution of Bulgarian culture and holds archaeological treasures. *(Open daily 9:30am-6pm. 10lv, students 5lv.)*

BULGARIA

FROM THE ROAD

BULGARIAN WITHOUT VERBS

No offense, but you are probably not going to master the Bulgarian language. If you know the Cyrillic alphabet (created by the Bulgarian monks Cyril and Methodius) and are familiar with another Slavic language, you might stand some chance.

However, many foreigners' verbal skills remain at a rudimentary (think: caveman) level, even after spending considerable time in the country. A fellow traveler's greatest linguistic feat—after living in Bulgaria for six months—was a triumphant exchange with a hotel maid letting her know it was okay to clean the room; his phrase translates to "Now...good."

I quickly learned that a simple, functional form of the language—Bulgarian Without Verbs—is enough to get by. Just consult a phrase book, point, add a clause like *kolka* (how much?) for flair, and smile. You will find, as I did, that the effort is appreciated; a shopkeeper once exclaimed "Bravo" when I pointed to a yogurt and said, "Strawberry."

A potential snag, of course, is that the response to your question will be in Bulgarian; still, you might get lucky and meet an anglophone of the younger generation. In any case, German, Russian, and French can also come in handy, so be sure to brush up on those as well.

—*Stephanie Sherman*

🎵 🎸 ENTERTAINMENT AND NIGHTLIFE

Half a dozen theaters lie on **Rakovski** (Раковски), Bulgaria's theater hub. A left on Rakovski leads to the columns of the **National Opera House,** Rakovski 59. (☎981 15 49. Shows Tu-Sa 6pm. Box office open M-Tu 9:30am-2pm and 2:30pm-6:30pm, W-F 8:30am-7:30pm, Sa 10:30am-6:30pm, Su 10am-6pm.)

At night, smartly dressed Sofians roam the main streets, filling the outdoor bars along **Vitosha bulevard** and the cafes around the **NDK.** For the younger set, nightlife centers around the **University of Sofia** at the intersection of Vasil Levski and Tsar Osvoboditel. **Biblioteka** (Библиотека) has live bands and karaoke. Located in St. Cyril and Methodius Library; enter from Obhorishte. (Cover Sa 4lv, Su-F 3lv. Open daily 8pm-6am.) Most people stick to the bars, not the dance floor at the popular **Escape,** Angel Kunchev 1. (Men 4lv, women 3lv. Open W-Sa 10:30pm-4am.) **Dali,** behind the University on Hristo Georgiev, is the best Latin club in Sofia. (☎46 51 29. Men 3lv, women free. Call ahead to reserve a table, 10lv per person. Open daily 8pm-5am.) The mafia becomes bolder at night, so don't draw attention to yourself.

🏛 DAYTRIPS FROM SOFIA

RILA MONASTERY. Holy Ivan of Rila built the 10th-century Rila Monastery (Рилски Манастир; Rilski Manastir), Bulgaria's largest and most famous monastery, as a refuge from worldly temptation. The monastery sheltered the arts of icon painting and manuscript copying during the Byzantine and Ottoman occupations, and remained an oasis of Bulgarian culture for five centuries. Today's monastery, decorated with 1200 brilliantly-colored **frescoes,** was built between 1834 and 1837; little remains from the earlier structure. Maps and suggested hiking routes through **Rila National Park** are on signs outside the monastery. To get to Rila Town, take tram #5 from Hostel Sofia to Ovcha Kupel Station (Овча Къпел) and take a **bus** to Rila Town (2hr., 2 per day, 4.50lv). From Rila Town, catch the bus to the monastery (30min., 3 per day, 1.10lv). **Hotel Tsarev Vruh ❷** (Царев Връх) has private baths and phones. (☎/fax 22 80. Breakfast US$2. US$15.) The hotel is 100m down the path that follows the river from behind the monastery. Inquire at room #170 in the monastery about staying in a spartan, but heated, **monastic cell ❷.** (☎22 08. Curfew midnight. US$10-15 per person.) Behind the monastery is a cluster of restaurants, cafes, snack bars, and a mini-market. ☎07054.

KOPRIVSHTITSA. Todor Kableshkov's movement for rebellion against Ottoman rule started in this little town in the Sredna Gora mountains. Today, Koprivshtitsa (Копривища) is a historical center and home to Bulgaria's popular **folk festival** (held every five years), which attracts international throngs. The well-preserved **National Revival houses** were the homes of the town's first settlers; many have enclosed verandas and delicate woodwork. Many homes of the leaders of the 1876 Uprising have become **museums;** buy tickets (5lv, students 3lv) and maps at the tourist office. **Trains** come from Sofia (2hr., 6 per day, 2.70lv) and Plovdiv via Karlovo (3½hr., 3 per day, 2.30lv). A bus (1lv) runs from the train station to the **bus station** in town. (Open daily 9am-8pm.) Backtrack along the river bisecting town to reach the main square, where the **tourist office** sells an invaluable 2lv map (☎21 91; koprivshtitza@hotmail.com. Open daily 10:30am-6pm.) The office also arranges **private rooms ❶,** which are US$7-10 in the center. Small **hotels ❶,** often with "Kushta" (Къща) in the name, are also easy to find (US$3-10). ☎07184.

PLOVDIV (ПЛОВДИВ)　　　　☎032

BULGARIA

Although Plovdiv is smaller than Sofia, it is widely hailed as the cultural capital of Bulgaria. Most of Plovdiv's historical and cultural treasures are concentrated in the three hills (the **Trimondium**) of **Stari Grad** (Стари Град; Old Town). Stari Grad is filled with churches and National Revival houses, which protrude from the cobblestones with windows staring at crazy angles. To reach the 2nd-century Roman ▨**amphitheater** (Античен Театр; Antichen Teatr) from pl. Tsentralen (Централен), take a right off Knyaz Aleksandr (Княз Александр) onto Suborna (Съборна), then go right up the steps along Mitropolit Paicii to the steps next to the music academy. This marble masterpiece from the early Roman occupation of the Balkans currently serves as a popular venue for concerts and shows, hosting the **Festival of the Arts** in the summer and early fall, and the **Opera Festival** in June. (Amphitheater open daily 9am-9pm. 3lv.) Return to Knyaz Aleksandr and follow it to the end to pl. Dzhumaya (Джумая), home to the **Dzhumaya Mosque** and the ancient **Philipopolis Stadium,** which still has an intact gladiator's entrance. At the end of Suborna, the **Museum of Ethnography** (Етнографски Музей; Etnografski Muzey) has *kukerski maski* (masks used to scare away evil spirits) and other Bulgarian artifacts. (Open Tu-Th, Sa-Su 9am-noon and 2-5pm. 3lv, students 0.50lv.) At night, head to the fountainside cafe in **Tsentralni Park** (Централни Парк), by pl. Tsentralen.

Trains arrive from: Sofia (2½hr., 14 per day, 3.80-5.40lv); Burgas (5hr., 7 per day, 6-8.20lv); and Varna (5½hr., 3 per day, 7.80-10.80lv). Buy tickets at **Rila,** Hristo Botev bul. 31a (Христо Ботев). (☎44 61 20. Open M-F 8am-6:30pm, Sa 8am-2pm.) **Buses** from Sofia (2hr., 15 per day, 7lv) arrive at **Yug** (Юг) station, Hristo Botev bul. 47, diagonally across from the train station (☎62 69 37). An up-to-date map is absolutely essential; street vendors sell good **Cyrillic maps** for 3lv. Check **email** at **Speed,** Knyaz Aleksandr 12, on the left before the mosque. (1.20lv per hr. Open 24hr.) It is important to make reservations for rooms in Plovdiv in the summer. **Hotel Turisticheski Dom ❷** (Туристически Дом), P.R. Slaveykov 5 (П.Р. Славейков), is in Stari Grad. From Knyaz Aleksandr, take Patriarch Evtimii (Патриарх Евтимий) into town, pass under Tsar Boris III Obendinitel bul., and go left uphill on Slaveykov. (☎63 32 11. No English spoken. Curfew 11pm. 22lv.) **Hotel Bulgaria ❺,** Patriarch Evtimii 13, has private baths, TV, A/C, and a fitness center. (☎63 35 99. www.hotelbulgaria.net. Reception 24hr. Singles US$50.) **Postal code:** 4000.

▶ **DAYTRIP FROM PLOVDIV: BACHKOVO MONASTERY.** About 28km south of Plovdiv, in the plush green slopes of the Rodopi mountains, is Bulgaria's second-largest monastery, **Bachkovo Monastery** (Бачковски Манастир; Bachkovski Manastir), built in 1083. The main church holds the **icon of the Virgin Mary and Child** (икона Света Богородица; ikona Sveta Bogoroditsa), which is said to have miraculous healing power. (Open daily 7am-8pm.) Well-maintained hiking paths lie uphill from the monastery. **Buses** run from Plovdiv's Yug station to Asenovgrad (25min., every 30min., 0.70lv), as do **trains** (25min., 17 per day, 0.80lv). From Asenovgrad, take a bus headed to Luki (Лъки); the monastery is the 3rd stop (4 per day, 0.60lv).

VELIKO TARNOVO (ВЕЛИКО ТЪРНОВО)   ☎062

Picturesque Veliko Tarnovo, on the steep hills above the Yantra River, has been watching over Bulgaria for 5000 years. For centuries, the city has been the center of Bulgarian politics; its residents led the national uprising against Byzantine rule in 1185, and revolutionaries wrote the country's first constitution here in 1879. The remains of the ◼Tsarevets (Царевец), a fortress that once housed a cathedral and the Bulgarian king's castle, stretch across a hilltop above the city. (Open daily 8am-7pm. 4lv.) The beautiful **Church of the Ascension** (Църква Възнесениегосподне; Tsurkva Vuzneseniegospodne), restored for the 1300th anniversary of Bulgaria in 1981, is at the top of the hill. (Open daily 8am-6pm.) From the center, go down Nezavisimost, which becomes Nikola Pikolo, and turn right at ul. Ivan Vazov (Иван Вазов). The **National Revival Museum** (Музей на Възраждането; Muzey na Vuzrazhdaneto) documents Bulgaria's 19th-century cultural and religious revival. (Open W-M 8am-noon and 1-6pm. 4lv. English tours 8lv.) On summer evenings, there is often a ◼sound-and-light show above Tsarevets Hill. (30min. show starts between 9:45 and 10pm.)

All **trains** stop at nearby **Gorna Oryahovitsa** (Горна Оряховица; 20min., 10 per day, 0.80lv), where they then leave for Burgas (6hr., 1 per day, 7lv), Sofia (5hr., 11 per day, 7.50lv), and Varna (4hr., 5 per day, 6.80lv). Minibuses and city bus #10 go from the station to **ploshad Maika Bulgaria** (Майка Българиа), the town center. Just off the square is the **tourist office,** Hristo Botev 5. (Maps 2.50lv. Open M-F 9am-6pm.) Check **email** nearby at **Bezanata** (Безаната), Otets Paisii 10. (0.90lv per hr. Open 24hr.) ◼**Hotel Comfort** ❶ (Комфорт), Panayot Tipografov 5 (Панайот Типографов), has an amazing view of Tsarevets. From Stambolov, walk left on Rakovski (Раковски), turn left onto the small square, and look for the signs. (☎287 28. US$10 per person.) **Hotel Trapezitsa (HI)** ❷ (Хотел Трапезица), Stefan Stambolov 79, has private bathrooms. From the town center, walk down Nezavisimost toward the post office and follow the street to the right. (☎220 61. Singles 28lv; doubles 38lv.) **Postal code:** 5000.

BLACK SEA COAST

The Black Sea, the most popular vacation spot in Bulgaria, is covered with tiny fishing villages and secluded bays, as well as pricey resorts. Along the coast, you will run into more tourists than in any other part of Bulgaria, along with higher (but still reasonable) prices.

VARNA (ВАРНА)   ☎052

Varna's draws are its expansive beaches, Mediterranean-like climate, and summer festivals. Go right on bul. Primorski (Приморски) from the train station to reach the **beaches** and **seaside gardens.** Despite Varna's sprawl, its sights are within a 30min. walk of one another. In the city's old quarter, **Grutska Makhala** (Гръцка Махала), the well-preserved ruins of the ◼Roman Thermal Baths (Римски Терми; Rimski Termi) sit on San Stefano. (Open Tu-Su 10am-5pm. 3lv, students 2lv.) The **Archaeological Museum** (Археологически Музей; Arkheologicheski Muzey), in the park behind Maria Luiza, has world's oldest gold treasure. (Open in summer Tu-Su 10am-5pm, off-season closed Su. 4lv, students 2lv.) Varna's cultural events include the **International Jazz Festival** in late August and **Varna Summer,** a chamber music festival from June to July. For schedules and tickets, check the **Festivalen Complex,** on bul. Primorski, which also has cafes and a cinema; the international film festival "Love is Folly" takes place there from August to September.

Trains, near the commercial port, go to Plovdiv (7hr., 3 per day, 7.80-10.80lv) and Sofia (8hr., 6 per day, 10.20-13.20lv). **Buses,** at Ul. Vladislav Varenchik (Владислав Варенчик), go to Burgas (2½hr., 5 per day, 6lv) and Sofia (6hr., 16 per day, 18lv). **Megatours,** in the Hotel Cherno More, Slivnitsa 33, has tourist information. (Open June-Sept. M-F 9am-7pm, Sa 9am-3pm; Oct.-May M-F 9am-7pm, Sa 9am-2pm.) **Astra Tour,** near track #6 at the train station, finds private rooms for US$6-10 per person. (☎60 58 61; atratur@mail.vega.bg. Open in summer daily 6am-10pm.) **Hotel Trite Delfina ❷** (Трите Делфина; Three Dolphins), ul. Gabrovo 27, is close to the train station. Go up Simeon from the station and take a right on Gabrovo. (☎60 09 11. Singles US$15-20; doubles US$20-25. Call ahead.)

DAYTRIP FROM VARNA: BALCHIK. In the quiet fishing village of Balchik (Балчик), houses are carved into chalky cliffs. Sit on a marble throne at Romanian Queen Marie's ❧**Summer Palace,** then explore her botanical garden. (Open daily 8am-8pm. 4lv.) Take a taxi (4lv) to the **Tuzlata sanatorium,** 7km north, for a *grazni banya* (грязни баия; grand bath)—cover yourself in mud, then bask in the sun while it dries. (Open in summer daily 8:30am-7pm. 2lv.) **Minibuses** run to Mladost station in Varna (40min., every hr. 6:30am-7:30pm, 2.50lv).

BURGAS (БУРГАС)   ☎056

Though mostly used as a transport hub for the Southern Black Sea Coast, Burgas also has its own pleasant beaches and seaside gardens. The bus and train stations are near the port at pl. Garov (Гаров). **Trains** go to Sofia (6-8hr., 6 per day, 8-11lv) via Plovdiv and Varna (5hr., 6 per day, 4.80-7lv) via Karnobat. **Minibuses** run to the coastal resorts from the side of the bus station facing away from the train station. Many smaller resorts don't have places to change money. **Bulbank,** across the street from Hotel Bulgaria on Aleksandrovska, cashes traveler's checks and has an **ATM.** (Open M-F 8:30am-4pm.) If you stay overnight, **Febtours Bourgas** (Фебтурс), 20 Lermontov (Лермонтов) helps find private rooms. (☎84 20 30; febtours@abv.bg. Open M-F 10am-5pm. Singles 12lv; doubles 20lv.) Or, go up Aleksandrovska from the station, take a right on Bogoridi (Богориди), pass the Hotel Bulgaria, and take the second left on Lermontov to **Hotel Mirage ❶** (Мираж), Lermontov 18. (☎84 56 57. Doubles US$20; triples US$28.) **Postal code:** 8000.

DAYTRIPS FROM BURGAS: NESEBUR AND SOZOPOL. Nesebur (Несебър) is a charming, popular resort atop the peninsula at the south end of Sunny Beach. A walk through the ancient **Stari Grad** begins along the 3rd-century stone **fortress walls.** The Byzantine gate and port date from the 5th century. The **Archaeological Museum** (Археологически Музей; Arkheologicheski Muzey), to the right of the town gate, displays ancient ceramics and relics. (Open May-Oct. M-F 9am-12:30pm and 1-7pm, Sa-Su 9am-1pm and 2-5pm; Nov.-Apr. M-F 9am-5pm. 2.50lv.) From the center, take Mitropolitska to reach the 10th-century **Temple of John the Baptist** (Йоан Кръстител; Yoan Krustitel), a UNESCO-protected site that is now an art gallery. (Open daily 10am-10pm. Free.) The 13th-century **Church of Christ the Almighty** (Христос Пантократор; Hristos Pantokrator) in the main square also doubles as an art gallery in summer. (Open daily 9am-9pm.) Along the harbor, street kiosks sell fruit, nuts, and small meals. **Buses** go to Burgas (40min., every 40min. 6am-9pm, 2lv). ☎0554.

Sozopol (Созопол), settled in 610 BC, was once the resort of choice for Bulgaria's artistic community, and is still a haven for the creative set. Take a **boat cruise** (7 and 8:15pm; 5lv per person) from the seaport behind the bus station to get a closer look at the two nearby islands, **St. Peter** and **St. Ivan.** To explore some less-crowded beaches, rent a motorbike near the bus station and cruise along the shoreline (10lv per hr.). **Minibuses** arrive from Burgas (45min., every 30min. 5am-10pm, 1.90lv). Turn left on Apolonia (Аполония) to reach the Old Town. To get to the New Town, go right from the station and bear left at the fork onto Republikan-ska (Републиканска). **Excursion Travel Agency,** 31 Republikanska, arranges **private rooms ❶.** (☎43 30. Open daily 8am-8pm. July-Aug. call 2 weeks ahead. July-Aug. US$9 per person; June and Sept. US$7 per person.) Popular ⊠**Vyaturna Melnitsa ❶** (Вятърна Мелница; Windmill), Morski Skali 27a (Морски Скали), has an extensive menu and offers an incredible view of the sea and islands. Morski Skali runs along the tip of the Old Town peninsula; look for a little windmill. (Entrees 3-8lv. Open daily 10am-11:30pm. Summer folk shows daily 9pm.) ☎05514.

CROATIA (HRVATSKA)

Croatia is a land of unearthly beauty, blessed with thick forests, barren mountains, and crystal-clear waters. Positioned at the convergence of the Mediterranean, the Alps, and the Pannonian Plain, the country has been historically situated on dangerous political divides—between the Frankish and Byzantine empires in the 9th century, the Catholic and Orthodox churches since the 11th century, Christian Europe and Islamic Turkey from the 15th to the 19th centuries, and between its own fractious ethnic groups in the past decade. Although economic recovery from the recent war has been difficult, it is easy to forget the political tensions of Croatia's past; now that the country is independent for the first time in 800 years, Croatians and visitors can enjoy the extraordinary landscape in peace.

FACTS AND FIGURES

Official Name: Republic of Croatia.

Capital: Zagreb.

Major Cities: Split, Dubrovnik.

Population: 4,300,000 (78% Croat, 12% Serb, 1% Bosniak, 9% other).

Land Area: 56,414 sq. km.

Time Zone: GMT +1.

Languages: Croatian.

Religions: Catholic (77%), Orthodox (11%), Muslim (1%), other (11%).

DISCOVER CROATIA

Croatia's lively capital, **Zagreb** (p. 231), boasts relaxing Mediterranean breezes, Habsburg splendor, and the hippest cafe scene in the Balkans. **Pula** (p. 232), the 2000-year-old heart of the Istrian Peninsula, has impressive Roman ruins. The true highlight of Croatia, however, is the dazzling **Dalmatian Coast** (p. 234), where pristine beaches and azure waters meet. Bask on the sands of **Split** (p. 234) on the central coast, then visit **Dubrovnik** (p. 236), which George Bernard Shaw called "paradise on earth" for its stunning seascapes and walled city center.

ESSENTIALS

WHEN TO GO

Croatia's mild Mediterranean climate means that there is no wrong time to visit. The high season (July-Aug.) brings crowds to the coast; travelers will find lower prices and more breathing room in June or September.

DOCUMENTS AND FORMALITIES

VISAS. Citizens of Australia, Canada, Ireland, New Zealand, the UK, and the US do not need visas for stays of up to 90 days. Visas are required of South African citizens. All visitors must **register** with the police within two days of arrival, regardless of the length of their stay. Hotels, campsites, and accommodations agencies should automatically register you, but those staying with friends or in private rooms must register themselves to avoid fines or expulsion. Police may check passports anywhere. Note that is no required entry fee at the border.

EMBASSIES. Foreign embassies in Croatia are all in Zagreb (p. 231). Croatian embassies at home include: **Australia,** 14 Jindalee Crescent, O'Malley, Canberra ACT 2606 (☎ 06 286 69 88; croemb@dynamite.com.au); **Canada,** 29 Chapel Street,

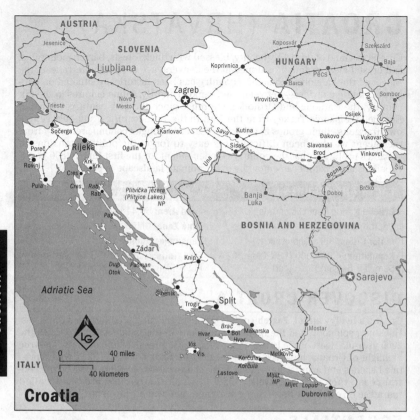

Croatia

Ottawa, ON K1N 7Y6 (☎ 613-562-7820; www.croatiaemb.net); **New Zealand** (consulate), 131 Lincoln Rd., Henderson, Auckland (☎ 09 836 5581; fax 09 836 5481); **South Africa,** 1160 Church St., Colbyn, Pretoria; P.O. Box 11335, Hatfield 0028 (☎ 012 342 1206; fax 342 1819); **UK,** 21 Conway St., London W1P 5HL (☎ 020 7387 2022; fax 020 7387 0310); **US,** 2343 Massachusetts Ave. NW, Washington, D.C. 20008 (☎ 202-588-5899; www.croatiaemb.org).

TRANSPORTATION

BY PLANE. Zagreb (ZAG) is the main entry point; **Croatia Airlines** often continues to Dubrovnik and Split. Rijeka, Zadar, and Pula also have international airports.

BY TRAIN AND BY BUS. Trains are very slow, and nonexistent south of Split. **Eurail** is not valid. *Odlazak* means departures, *dolazak* arrivals. For domestic travel, **buses** work best. Tickets are cheaper if you buy them on board.

BY FERRY. If you're on the coast, take one of the ferries run by **Jadrolinija** (www.jadrolinija.hr), which sail the Rijeka-Split-Dubrovnik route with island stops. Ferries also run from Split (p. 234) to Ancona, Italy (p. 663), and from Dubrovnik (p. 236) to Bari, Italy.

BY CAR AND BY THUMB. You can rent a car (350-400kn per day) in larger cities, but parking and gas can be expensive. Rural roads are in poor condition; in the Krajina region and other conflict areas, drivers should be wary of off-road land mines. Hitchhiking in Croatia is highly discouraged.

TOURIST SERVICES AND MONEY

EMERGENCY	Police: ☎092. Ambulance: ☎094. Fire: ☎093.

TOURIST OFFICES AND MONEY. Even the smallest towns have a branch of the excellent, English-speaking, state-run tourist board **turistička zajednica** (www.htz.hr). Accommodations are handled by private tourist agencies *(turistička/putnička agencija)*, the largest of which is the ubiquitous **Atlas**. Croatia's monetary unit is the **kuna** (kn), which is divided into 100 *lipa;* the *kuna* is virtually impossible to exchange abroad, except in Hungary and Slovenia. The South African rand is not exchangeable in Croatia. Most banks, tourist offices, hotels, and transportation stations exchange currency and traveler's checks. Banks usually have the best rates. **ATMs** *(bankomat)* are common. Most banks give MasterCard or Visa cash advances, and credit cards are widely accepted. A basic day in Croatia runs about 220kn. Tipping is not expected, but you may round up to the nearest whole *kuna.* In some cases, the establishment will do it for you—check your change. Bargaining is acceptable only for informal transactions.

KUNA		
AUS$1 = 4.15KN	10KN = AUS$2.41	
CDN$1 = 4.84KN	10KN = CDN$2.07	
EUR€1 = 7.38KN	10KN = EUR€1.36	
NZ$1 = 3.55KN	10KN = NZ$2.83	
ZAR1 = 0.71KN	10KN = ZAR14	
UK£1 = 11.52KN	10KN = UK£0.87	
US$1 = 7.52KN	10KN = US$1.33	

COMMUNICATION

PHONE CODE	Country code: 385. International dialing prefix: 00. From outside Croatia, dial int'l dialing prefix (see inside back cover) + 385 + city code + local number.

MAIL. *Avionski* and *zrakoplovom* both indicate airmail. Mail from the US should arrive in seven days or less; *Poste Restante* mail will be held for 90 days at the main post office. Address mail to be held: Firstname SURNAME, *Poste Restante*, Pt. Republike bb, Dubrovnik 200 00, CROATIA.

TELEPHONES. Post offices usually have public phones; pay after you talk. All payphones require phone cards *(telekarta)*, sold at all newsstands and post offices. A 23kn card lasts 150min. for domestic calls and 30min. for international calls (50% discount 10pm-7am, Su, and holidays). Calls to the US and Europe are expensive (20kn per min.). International direct dial numbers include: **AT&T,** ☎0800 22 01 11; **British Telecom,** ☎0800 22 00 44; **Canada Direct,** ☎0800 22 01 01; and **MCI,** ☎0800 22 01 12. Although operator assistance is free, some phones require a *telekarta*.

LANGUAGE. Croatian is written in Roman characters. Street designations on maps often differ from those on signs by "-va" or "-a" because of grammatical declensions. Young Croatians often know some English, but the most common second language among adults is German. For Croatian words and phrases, see p. 1052.

ACCOMMODATIONS AND CAMPING

CROATIA	❶	❷	❸	❹	❺
ACCOMMODATIONS	under 90kn	91-140kn	141-200kn	201-300kn	over 300kn

Croatia has only five youth hostels (in Zagreb, Pula, Zadar, Dubrovnik, and Punat); for information, contact the **Croatian Youth Hostel Association** in Zagreb (☎482 92 94; hfhs@alf.tel.hr). Camping is usually a good, cheap option; for information, contact the **Croatian Camping Union** in Poreč (☎52 45 13 24; www.camping.hr). **Private rooms** are also affordable; look for *sobe* signs, especially near transportation stations. Agencies generally charge 30-50% more if you stay less than three nights. All accommodations are subject to a tourist tax of 5-10kn. If you opt for a hotel, call a few days in advance, especially during the summer.

FOOD AND DRINK

CROATIA	❶	❷	❸	❹	❺
FOOD	under 30kn	31-60kn	61-120kn	121-200kn	over 200kn

In continental Croatia east of Zagreb, typically heavy Slavic meals predominate, while on the coast, seafood blends with Italian pasta dishes. *Purica s mlincima* (turkey with pasta) is the regional dish near Zagreb, and spicy *Slavonian kulen* is considered one of the world's best sausages by the panel of fat German men who decide such things. Along the coast, try *lignje* (squid) or *Dalmatinski pršut* (Dalmatian smoked ham). Ston Bay's oysters have received international awards; *slane sardele* (salted sardines) are a tasty (and cheaper) substitute. *Grešak varivo* (green bean stew), *tikvice va lešo* (steamed zucchini in olive oil), and *grah salata* (beans and onion salad) are meatless favorites. Croatia also produces excellent wines; mix red wine with tap water to make the popular *bevanda*, and white with carbonated water for *gemišt*. *Karlovačko* and *Ožujsko* are the most popular beers, especially with fishermen. Tap water is relatively safe, but may cause upset stomachs; bottled water is readily available.

HEALTH AND SAFETY

Although Croatia is no longer at war, travel to the Slavonia and Krajina regions remains dangerous due to **unexploded mines.** Croatians are friendly toward foreigners and sometimes a little too friendly to female travelers; going out in public with a companion will help ward off unwanted advances. Croatians are just beginning to accept homosexuality; discretion may be wise. Pharmacies are generally well stocked with Western products.

HOLIDAYS AND FESTIVALS

Holidays: New Year's Day (Jan. 1); Epiphany (Jan. 6); Easter (Apr. 20-21); Independence Day (May 30); Anti-Fascist Struggle Day (June 22); National Thanksgiving Day (Aug. 5); Assumption (Aug. 15); All Saints' Day (Nov. 1); Christmas (Dec. 25-26).

Festivals: Zagreb hosts many festivals: the **International Folklore Festival** in July, is the premier gathering of European folk dancers and singing groups; street performers swarm in for **Cest is D'best** in the 2nd week of June. On Korčula, the **Festival of Sword Dances** (Festival Viteških Igara) takes place from July-August. Both the **Split** and **Dubrovnik Summer Festivals** (July-Aug.) feature theater, ballet, opera, classical music, and jazz.

ZAGREB   ☎ 01

Despite its spacious boulevards, sprawling public parks, and stern Habsburg architecture, Croatia's capital maintains a distinctive small-town charm. Mediterranean breezes blow past magnificent churches and lively outdoor cafes, and the external scars of recent civil wars have all but vanished.

⌐ TRANSPORTATION. Trains leave the **Glavni kolodvor station**, Trg kralja Tomislava 12 (☎ 060 33 34 44), for: Budapest (7hr., 4 per day, 140kn); Ljubljana (2½hr., 4 per day, 81kn); Venice (7hr., 2 per day, 260kn); Vienna (6½hr., 2 per day, 320kn); and Zurich (8hr., 1 per day, 625kn). To reach the main square, **Trg bana Josipa Jelačića,** from the train station, cross the street, walk along the left side of the park until it ends, then follow Praška. **Buses** (☎ 060 31 33 33) head from **Autobusni kolodvor,** Držićeva bb, to: Ljubljana (2hr., 2 per day, 115kn); Sarajevo (9hr., 3 per day, 500kn); and Vienna (8hr., 2 per day, 200kn). To reach Trg b. Jelačića, exit on Držićeva, turn left, continue past Trg Žrtava Fašizma, and turn left onto Jurišićeva.

⚐ PRACTICAL INFORMATION. The **tourist office** is at Trg b. Jelačića 11. (☎ 481 40 51; info@zagreb-touristinfo.hr; www.zagreb-touristinfo.hr. Open M-F 8:30am-8pm, Sa 9am-5pm, Su 10am-2pm.) All foreigners staying in private accommodations must register within two days of arrival. In Zagreb, register at the **Department for Foreign Visitors,** room 103 at the central police station, Petrinjska 30. Use Form 14. (☎ 456 31 11. Open M-F 8am-4pm.) Hotels and hostels register guests automatically, bypassing this frustrating process. Find Internet access at **Art Net Club,** Preradovićeva 25. (☎ 455 84 71. Open M-Su 9am-9pm. 16kn per hr.) **Postal code:** 10000.

🏠🍴 ACCOMMODATIONS AND FOOD. Few rooms in Zagreb are cheap. **Omladinski Turistićki Centar (HI) ❶,** Petrinjska 77, is well-located; from the train station, walk right on Branimirova, and Petrinjska is on the left. (☎ 484 12 61; fax 484 12 69. Reception 24hr. Dorms 67kn, nonmembers 72kn; singles 149kn, 202kn with bath; doubles 204kn/274kn. Cash only.) **Hotel Astoria ❷,** just a few steps past Omladinski at Petrinjska 71, has small, clean rooms. (☎ 484 12 22; fax 484 12 12. Breakfast included. Singles 330kn; doubles 500kn; triples 600kn.) For traditional Croatian meat dishes, feast at 🍴**Baltazar ❶,** Nova Ves 4. (Main dishes 35-80kn. Open daily noon-midnight.) **Groceries** are available throughout the city, including at **Konzum** on the corner of Preradovićeva and Hebrangova. (Open M-F 7am-8pm, Sa 7am-3pm.)

◙ SIGHTS. The best way to see Zagreb is on foot. From Trg b. Jelačica, take Ilica, then turn right on Tomiceva. The funicular (2.50kn) allows easy access to many sights on the hills of Gornji Grad (Upper Town). **Lotršćak Tower** provides a spectacular view of the city. The elegant **St. Catherine's Church** is right of the tower. Follow ul. Cirilometodska to Markov Trg; the colorful roof tiles of Gothic **St. Mark's Church** (Crkva Sv. Marka) depict the coats of arms of Croatia, Dalmatia, and Slavonia on the left and of Zagreb on the right. Visible from anywhere in Zagreb, the striking neo-Gothic bell towers of the 11th-century **Cathedral of the Assumption of the Virgin Mary** loom over Kaptol Hill. (Open M-Sa 10am-5pm. Free.) Take an 8min. bus ride from Kaptol to **Mirogoj,** the country's largest and most beautiful cemetery; Croatia's first President, Franjo Tudjman, is buried beyond the grand mausoleum at the entrance. (Open M-F 6am-8pm, Su 7:30am-6pm. Free.)

Zagreb's museums focus on the best Croatian artwork. The **Museum of Arts and Crafts**, Trg Maršala Tita 10, has an eclectic mix of periods and media. (Open Tu-F 10am-6pm, Sa-Su 10am-1pm. 20kn, students 10kn.) The **Gallery of Modern Art**, Herbrangova 1, displays modern art. (Hours and prices depend on the exhibition.) The **Ivan Meštrovic Foundation**, Mletačka 8, shows off the work of the master sculptor. (Open Tu-F 9am-2pm, Sa 10am-6pm. 10kn, students 5kn.)

■ ■ **FESTIVALS AND NIGHTLIFE.** Zagreb fills the year with an impressive collection of festivals. The biannual **International Music Festival** takes place April 4-11. **Cest is d'Best**, in the second week of June, brings all kinds of street performers to Zagreb. The **International Folklore Festival**, July 16-20, is the premier gathering of European folk dancers and singing groups. There is also a huge **International Puppet Festival** at the beginning of each September. For up-to-date, detailed information and schedules, consult www.zagreb-touristinfo.hr.

Dance and swim at the lakeside club ⬛**Aquarius**, on Lake Jarun (☎364 02 31). Take tram #17 to Srednjaci, the third unmarked stop (15min.). Turn around, cross the street, follow any dirt path to the lake, and walk left along the boardwalk. Aquarius is the last building. (Cover 30kn. Club open W-Su 10pm-4am. Cafe open daily 9am-9pm.) The best and cheapest beer is chugged at **Pivnica Medvedgrad**, Savska 56. (Beer 15kn per liter. Open M-Sa 10am-midnight, Su noon-midnight.)

> **!** Plitvice Lakes National Park lies in the Krajina region, where Croatia's bloody war of independence began; over a million **landmines** remain in the surrounding area. **Under no circumstances should you leave marked roads or paths.** Please be intelligent about where you walk when exploring the natural wonders of the park.

🔁 **DAYTRIP FROM ZAGREB: PLITVICE LAKES NATIONAL PARK.** (Nacionalni park Plitvička jezera.) The park, made up of forested hills, lakes, and hundreds of waterfalls, is worth the long trip from Zagreb. Wooden pathways hovering just above the iridescent blue surface of the lakes lead up to the waterfalls. Most tourists circulate around the four lower lakes (Donja Jezera) to snap pictures of Plitvice's famous 78m waterfall, **Veliki Slap** (2-3hr.), but hidden falls reward visitors to the 12 upper lakes, **Gornja Jezera** (4hr.). Two bus routes (every 20min.) and a boat that runs on the largest lake (every 30min.) help visitors explore the park.

Buses run to Zagreb (2½hr., every 30min., 39kn); ask the driver to drop you at one of the park entrances. Tourist centers at each of the three entrances provide maps and a comprehensive guide. (Park open daily 7am-7pm. July-Aug. 60kn, students 40kn; May-June and Sept.-Oct. 50kn/30kn; Jan.-Apr. and Nov.-Dec. 40kn/20kn.)

NORTHERN COAST

As you approach the coast from Zagreb, you'll first encounter the islands of the **Gulf of Kvarner,** which are blessed by long summers and gentle breezes; Rab Island also boasts rare sand beaches. The Roman ruins at Pula sit farther north along the coast on the **Istrian Peninsula,** where the Mediterranean laps at the foot of the Alps.

PULA   ☎ 052

If you get to visit only one city in Istria, it should be Pula—not only for its cool, clear water, but also for its winding medieval corridors, outdoor cafes, and breathtaking Roman ⬛**amphitheater.** The amphitheater, the second largest in the world, is often used as a concert venue. (Open daily 8am-9pm. 16kn, students 8kn.) To get there from the bus station, take a left on Istarska. Following Istarska in the opposite direction will bring you to the **Arch of the Sergians** (Slavoluk obitelji Sergii), dating from 29 BC; go through the gates and down bustling **ulica Sergijevaca** to the **Forum,** which holds the remarkably well-preserved **Temple of Augustus** (Augustov hram.), built between 2 BC and AD 14. To reach the private coves of Pula's **beaches,** buy a bus ticket from any newsstand (8kn) and take bus #1 to the Stója campground or bus #2 toward the hostel. ▓**Fort Bourguignon,** Zlatne Stijene 6c, is a cafe, nightclub, and art gallery located in an old stone fortress. Take bus #2 or 7 from Giardini to the last stop; walk toward the sea, curving left. (Open M-F 8am-midnight, Sa 11am-4am, Su 6am-noon.)

Trains (☎54 19 82) run from Kolodvorska 5 to Ljubljana (7½hr., 3 per day, 120kn) and Zagreb (7hr., 4 per day, 97-120kn). **Buses** (☎21 89 28) go from Matta Balotta 6 to Trieste, Italy (3¾hr., 4 per day, 98kn) and Zagreb (5-6hr., 15 per day, 137kn). The **tourist office,** Forum 3, can help find private rooms (☎21 29 87; www.pulainfo.hr; open M-Sa 9am-8pm, Su 10am-6pm), as can travel agencies such as **Arenaturist,** Giardini 4 (☎21 86 96; www.arenaturist.hr). To get to the **Omladinski Hostel (HI) ❶,** Zaljev Valsaline 4, walk right from the bus station on Istarska to the small park on Giardini; take bus #2 (dir.: Veruda) and ask the driver where to get off, then follow the signs. (☎39 11 33; www.nncomp.com/hfhs. 63-97kn.) **Postal code:** 52100.

⚡ DAYTRIP FROM PULA: BRIJUNI ARCHIPELAGO. Scenic Brijuni Archipelago is one of Croatia's most fascinating and beautiful regions. The largest island in the archipelago, **Veli Brijun** has been the site of a Roman resort, a Venetian colony, the opulent residence of former Yugoslav president Josip Brož Tito, and the discovery of a prevention for malaria. A guided tour is the best way to see the island. The **Brijuni Agency,** Brijunska 10, in Fazana, has the lowest rates. (☎52 58 83; np-brijuni@pu.tel.hr. Round-trip ferry and 4hr. tour 160kn. Tours daily 11:30am; call at least one day in advance. Open daily 8am-7pm.)

RAB ☎051

Beautiful Rab Town on Rab Island is filled with old churches, whitewashed stone houses, and the scent of rosemary from backyard gardens. The best way to experience Rab Town is to stroll along **Gornja Ulica.** The street runs from the remains of **St. John's Church** (Crkva sv. Jvana), a Roman basilica, to **St. Justine's Church** (Crkva sv. Justine), which houses a museum of Christian art. (Open daily 9am-noon and 7:30-10pm. 7kn.) The top of the bell tower at **St. Mary's Church** (Crkva sv. Marije) is a great place for viewing sunsets, or for peering into the garden that the nuns maintain. (Open daily 7:30-10pm. 5kn.) **Beaches** are scattered all over Rab Island; ask at the tourist office for transportation information. Most sand beaches (some of the few in Croatia) are on the north end of the island, while rocky beaches lie on the west side and pebble beaches on the east.

Transportation to and from the island is difficult; be prepared for some frustrations. **Buses** arrive from Zagreb (5½hr., 3 per day, 127kn). The friendly **tourist office** is on the other side of the bus station. (☎77 11 11. Open daily 8am-10pm.) **Katurbo,** M. de Dominisa, between the bus station and the town center, arranges private rooms. (☎/fax 72 44 95; katurbo-tourist-agency@ri.tel.hr. Open Sept.-June daily 8am-1pm and 4-9pm; July-Aug. 8am-9pm. Singles 57-97kn. 30% surcharge on stays less than 3 nights.) **Hotel Istra ❸** has clean, modern rooms. (☎72 41 34. 160-289kn per person.) Walk east along the bay 2km from the bus station to reach **Camping Padova ❶.** (☎72 43 55. 29kn per person, 27kn per tent. Registration 4kn.) Restaurant **St. Maria ❷,** Dinka Dokule 6, serves Hungarian specialties in a medieval courtyard. (Main dishes 45-85kn. Open daily 11am-2pm and 4pm-midnight.) There's a **supermarket** in the basement of Merkur, Palit 71, across from the tourist office. (Open daily 7am-9pm.) **Postal code:** 51280.

DALMATIAN COAST

Stretching from the Rijeka harbor to Dubrovnik in the south, Croatia's coast is a stunning seascape set against dramatic mountains. With more than 1100 islands—only 66 of which are inhabited—Dalmatia boasts the Mediterranean's largest archipelago and cleanest waters, as well as bronze beaches and Roman ruins.

TROGIR
☎ 021

In Trogir, made up of tiny Trogir Island and Čiovo Island, medieval buildings crowd into winding streets and palmed promenades open onto well-maintained parks and the calm, blue sea. On Trogir Island, the beautiful Renaissance **North Gate** forms the entrance to **Stari Grad** (Old Town), which earned a coveted place on the UNESCO World Heritage List in 1997. Most sights, including the **Cathedral of St. Lawrence** (Crkva sv. Lovre), are in **Trg Ivana Pavla**, the central square. The **City Museum of Trogir,** which is housed in two buildings, contains many examples of Trogir's storied stone-carving tradition. One collection is at Gradska 45, near the cathedral. (Open M-Sa 9am-12pm and 6pm-9pm. 10kn, students 5kn, for both parts of the museum.) The other is in the convent of St. Nicholas off Kohl-Genscher past Trg Ivana Pavla. (Open M-Sa 9am-12:30pm and 4-6:30pm.) At the tip of the island lie the remains of the **Fortress of Kamerlengo,** which now serves as an open-air cinema. (Open M-Sa 9am-6pm. 10kn, students free. Movies 20kn.) Trogir's best beaches lie on **Čiovo Island,** accessible from Trogir Island by the Čiovski bridge, past Trg Ivana Pavla.

Buses from Zagreb stop in front of the station on the mainland on their way south to Split (30min., 22kn). **Local bus #37** also runs from Trogir to Split (30min., 3 per hr., 15kn). Across Čiovski bridge, **Atlas,** Obala kralja Zvonimira 10, has bus schedules. (☎ 88 42 79; fax 88 47 44. Open M-Sa 8am-9pm, Su 6-9pm.) The **tourist office,** Obala b. Berislavica 12, is at the end of Kohl-Genscher. (☎/fax 88 14 12. Open M-F 8am-2pm and 4-7:30pm, Sa 8-11am.) **Čipko,** Kohl-Genscher 41, across from the cathedral and through an archway, arranges private rooms. (☎/fax 88 15 54. Open daily 8am-8pm. July-Aug. singles 102-118kn; doubles 198-234kn. May-June and Sept. 85-101kn/165-197kn.) To reach beachside **Prenocište Saldun ❶,** Sv. Andrije 1, cross Čiovski bridge and take Put Balana up the hill, keeping right; Saldun is at the top. (☎ 80 60 53. Call ahead. 70kn. Tax 6kn.) Luxurious waterfront **Vila Sikaa ❺,** Obala Kralja Zvonimira 13, is across Čiovski Bridge. (☎ 88 12 23; stjepan.runtic@st.tel.hr. Reserve ahead. Singles 420kn; doubles 450-550kn.) **Čiovka Supermarket,** is next to Atlas. (Open M-Sa 5:30am-9pm, Su 6:30am-8pm.) **Bistro Lučica ❷,** Kralja Tomislava, across Čiovski bridge and to the right, grills delightful meat and seafood. (35-120kn. Open M-F 9am-midnight, Sa-Su 4pm-midnight.) Cafes and bars line Kohl-Genscher and the waterfront. **Postal code:** 21220.

SPLIT
☎ 021

This palatial city by the sea is more of a cultural center than a beach resort; Split boasts a wider variety of activities and nightlife than its neighbors. The **Stari Grad** (Old Town), wedged between a high mountain range and palm-lined waterfront, sprawls around a luxurious **palace** where Roman Emperor Diocletian, known for his violent persecution of Christians, spent his summers. The **cellars** of the city are near the entrance to the palace, across from the taxis on **Obala hrvatskog narodnog preporoda;** turn in either direction to wander around this haunting labyrinth. (Open daily 10am-7pm. 6kn, students 3kn.) Through the cellars and up the stairs is the open-air **peristyle,** a colonnaded square. The Catholic **cathedral** on the right side of the peristyle is the oldest in the world; ironically, it was once Diocletian's mausoleum. The view from atop the adjoining **Bell Tower of St. Dominus** (Zvonik sv. Duje) is incredible. (Cathedral and tower open daily 8:30am-9:30pm. Tower 5kn.)

A 25min. walk away along the waterfront, the **Meštrović Gallery** (Galerija Ivana Meštrovića), Šetaliste Ivana Meštrovića 46, features a collection by Croatia's most famous modern sculptor. (Open June-Aug. Tu-Sa 10am-6pm, Su 10am-3pm; Sept.-May Tu-Sa 10am-4pm, Su 10am-2pm. 15kn, students 10kn.)

Buses (☎33 84 83; schedules ☎(050) 32 73 27) go to: Dubrovnik (4½hr., 17 per day, 110kn); Ljubljana (11hr., 1 per day, 233kn); Sarajevo (7½hr., 6 per day, 171kn); and Zagreb (8hr., every 30min., 114-134kn). **Ferries** (☎33 83 33) head from the terminal across from the train and bus stations to Dubrovnik (8hr., 5 per week, 72kn) and Ancona, Italy (10hr., 4 per week, 256kn). From the bus station, follow Obala kneza Domagoja (also called Riva) until it runs into Obala hrvatskog narodnog preporoda, which is roughly east-west. The **tourist office** is at Obala hrv. 12. (☎/fax 34 21 42. Open M-F 7:30am-8:30pm, Sa 8am-2pm.) The **Daluma Travel Agency**, Obala kneza domagoja 1, near the bus and train stations, helps find private rooms. (☎33 84 84; daluma-st@st.tel.hr. May-Oct. singles 120kn, doubles 240kn; Nov.-Apr. 90/190kn. Open M-F 8am-8pm, Sa 8am-12:30pm.) To get from the stations to a bed at **Prenoćište Slavija ❸**, Buvinova 2, follow Obala hrv., turn right on Trg Braće Radića, then go right on Mihovilova širina; signs lead up the stairs. (☎34 70 53; fax 59 15 58. Breakfast included. Singles 180kn, with shower 220kn; doubles 210kn/260kn.) There is a **supermarket** at Svačićeva 4. (Open daily 7am-10pm.) To reach ✚**Jugo Restoran ❷**, Uvala Baluni bb, face the water on Obala hrv. and walk right along the waterfront for 10min., following the curves onto Branimirova Obala. (Main dishes 26-65kn. Open daily 9am-midnight.) The closest beach to downtown Split is sandy **Bačvice**, a nighttime favorite for local skinny dippers and the starting point of a great strip of waterfront bars. **Postal code:** 21000.

BRAČ ISLAND: BOL ☎021

Central Dalmatia's largest island, Brač is an ocean-lover's paradise. Most visitors come here for **Zlatni rat**, a peninsula with white pebble beach and emerald waters, just a short walk from the town center of Bol. The 1475 **Dominican Monastery,** on the eastern tip of Bol, displays Tintoretto's altar painting of the Madonna with Child. (Open daily 10am-noon and 5-7pm. 10kn.) The **ferry** from Split docks at Supetar (1hr., 7-13 per day, 23kn). From there, take a **bus** to Bol (1hr., 5 per day, 13kn). The last bus back to the ferry leaves at 5:50pm. From the bus station, walk left for 5min. to reach the **tourist office,** Porad bolskich pomorca bb, on the far side of the small marina. (☎63 56 38; tzo-bol@st.tel.hr.) **Adria Tours,**

YOUR OWN WAY

THE DALMATIAN COAST

The gorgeous Adriatic Coast of Croatia boasts more than a thousand spectacular islands, but these destinations are especially worth exploring:

KRK. Croatia's largest island is full of opportunities for scuba diving (148-320kn) and hiking, but maintains a wild, undiscovered feel. Krk is a good starting point for cruises down the alluring coast. Info: ☎051 22 26 61.

VIS. Vis Island's relative isolation has preserved its natural beauty and traditions, and its residents fish, grow olives, and make wine as they have for centuries. Info: ☎021 71 34 55.

HVAR. In 1997, *Traveler* magazine named Hvar one of the ten most beautiful islands in the world. The long, thin island offers breathtaking views of the mainland's mountains from its high, rugged hills. Info: ☎021 74 10 59; www.hvar.hr.

MLJET. Mljet National Park is located on this isolated, sparsely populated island, whose mystique has earned it a place in literature since the *Odyssey* and the writings of St. Paul.

TRANSPORTATION. Ferries run from from Split to Vis (2½hr., June-Sept. 1-2 per day, 22kn) and Hvar (2hr.; June-Aug. 3-5 per day; 28kn). Boats also run between Rab Island and Krk (1hr., 4 per day, 22.30kn), and between Dubrovnik and Mljet (1½hr., 1 per day, 35kn).

FROM THE ROAD

NO PLACE LIKE *SOBE*

Any budget traveler in Croatia will inevitably spend some nights in private rooms *(sobe)*, which are often the only affordable lodgings. While some hosts will invite you into their living room for coffee and whiskey at 10am, others demand payment with an outstretched hand, toss you the key, slam the door, and are never seen again. Some rooms are so cavernous you could play tennis in them, and others are so small you are more likely to giggle than complain when you see them.

Certain commonalities, however, are equally striking. First are the hideous, battleship-sized armoires that take up half of every Croatian bedroom, large or small. Second is the overbearing presence of Catholic kitsch art in nearly every home. In any given room, odds are that there will be a massive, life-size portrait of the Holy Family, usually in pastel colors and featuring cuddly animals.

Then, there's the mysterious, ubiquitous Weeping Child, a maudlin Balkan tradition that extends throughout the Former Yugoslavia and Albania. The portrait usually features a young girl with an enormous, glistening tear tumbling down one rosy cheek. It's not entirely clear what, exactly, the Weeping Child is supposed to signify, and no one seems to know the answer. They're sort of the equivalent of the Norman Rockwell posters in the United States; everyone has one, but no one's quite sure why.

— *Nick Gossen*

Obala Vladimira Nazora 28, to the right facing the sea from the bus station, rents small motorcycles (150kn per half-day, 250kn per day) and cars (400kn per day including mileage), and also books rooms. (66-142kn per person. ☎63 59 66; www.tel.hr/adria-tours-bol. Open daily 8am-9pm.) There are five **campsites** around Bol; the largest is **Kito ❶**, Bračka cesta bb, on the road into town. (☎63 54 24. Open May 1-Sept. 30. 38kn per person; tent included.) **Postal code:** 21420.

KORČULA   ☎020

Within sight of the mainland are the macchia thickets, and slender cypress trees of Korčula. Marco Polo was born here, among sacred monuments and churches dating from the time of the Apostles. The **Festival of Sword Dances** clangs into town July-Aug. (40kn; tickets available at tourist office.) **Buses** from Korčula board a ferry to the mainland and head to: Dubrovnik (3½hr., 1 per day, 62kn); Sarajevo (6½hr., 4 per week, 145kn); Split (5hr., 1 per day, 90kn); and Zagreb (11-13hr., 1 per day, 190kn). **Ferries** run to Dubrovnik (3½hr., 5 per week, 64kn) and Split (4½hr., 1 per day, 74kn). To reach the **tourist office**, face the water and walk left around the peninsula to Hotel Korčula; the office is next door. (Open M-Sa 8am-3pm and 4-9pm, Su 9am-1pm.) **Private rooms ❶** are the only budget lodgings available; shopping around is a good idea. **Marko Polo,** Biline 5, can also arrange rooms. (☎71 54 00; marko-polo-tours@du.tel.hr. Singles 81-167kn; doubles 105-219kn. Open daily 8am-10pm.) 🖩**Adio Mare ❸,** Marka Pola bb, serves authentic local specialties. (Entrees 40-70kn. Open M-Sa 1-11pm, Su 6-11pm.) **Postal code:** 20260.

DUBROVNIK   ☎020

George Bernard Shaw once wrote: "Those who seek Paradise on earth should come to Dubrovnik." Nearly scarless despite recent wars, the city continues to draw visitors with azure waters and golden sunsets over its 14th-century marble walls. If you make it as far south as Dubrovnik, you might never leave.

⌘🔃 TRANSPORTATION AND PRACTICAL INFORMATION. Jadrolinija **ferries** (☎41 80 00) depart from opposite Obala S. Radica 40 for Bari, Italy (9hr., 5 per week, 257kn) and Split (8hr., 1 per day, 72kn). **Buses** (☎35 70 88) run to: Sarajevo (6hr., 2 per day, 156kn); Split (4½hr., 17 per day, 103kn); Trieste (15hr., 1 per day, 210kn); and Zagreb (11hr., 7 per day, 190kn). To reach Stari Grad, walk around the bus station, turn left on Ante Starčevića, and follow it uphill to the Old Town's western gate (25min.). Or, to reach the ferry terminal, head left from the sta-

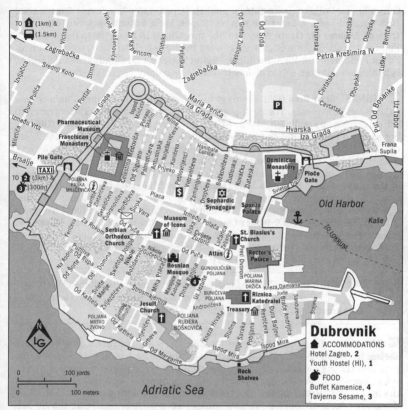

Dubrovnik

🔺 ACCOMMODATIONS
Hotel Zagreb, **2**
Youth Hostel (HI), **1**

🍴 FOOD
Buffet Kamenice, **4**
Tavjerna Sesame, **3**

Adriatic Sea

tion and then bear right. All local buses except #5, 7, and 8 go to Stari Grad's Pile Gate. (Tickets 7kn at kiosks, 10kn from driver.) From the bus stop at Pile Gate, walk up Ante Starčevića away from Stari Grad to reach the **Tourist Board,** Ante Starčevića 7, which has free maps and pamphlets. (☎41 69 99. Open in summer M-Sa 8am-7pm; off-season 8am-3pm.) **Turistička Zajednica Grada Dubrovnika,** Cvijete Zuzoric 1/2, gives out the free, invaluable *City Guide.* (☎32 38 87. Open M-F 8am-3pm, Sa 9am-1pm, Su 9am-noon.) **Postal code:** 20 000.

📱🍴 **ACCOMMODATIONS AND FOOD.** For two people, a **private room** is cheapest; arrange one through the Tourist Board (80-120kn) or **Atlas,** Lučarica 1, next to St. Blasius's Church. (☎44 25 28; www.atlas-croatia.com. Open June-Aug. M-Sa 8am-8pm, Su 9am-1pm; Sept.-May M-Sa 8am-7pm. Singles 100-150kn; doubles 120-180kn.) For cheaper rooms, try haggling with the women around the ferry and bus terminals. The ▨**HI youth hostel ❶,** b. Josipa Jelačića 15/17 is one of the best in Croatia. From the bus station, walk up Ante Starčevića, turn right at the lights (10min.), take a right on b. Josipa Jelačića, and look for the hidden HI sign on your left. (☎42 32 41; hfhs-du@du.hinet.hr. Open May-Dec. 65-87kn.) **Hotel Zagreb ❸,** near the beach at Šetalište Kralja Zvonimira 31, has a wonderful veranda. Take bus #6 (dir.: Dubrava) and ask to be let off at post office Lapad. (☎43 61 46. Reception 24hr. Singles 170-300kn; doubles 265-500kn.) Behind St. Blasius's Church, on

Gundulićeva Poljana, is an **outdoor market.** (Open daily 7am-8pm.) **Supermarket Mediator,** Od puča 4, faces the market. (Open M-Sa 6:30am-9pm, Su 7am-9pm.) **Tavjerna Sesame ❹,** Dante Alighiera bb, specializes in fresh pasta dishes. From Pile Gate, walk on Ante Starčevića toward the hostel. (Entrees 60-95kn. Open M-Sa 8am-midnight, Su 10am-midnight.) **Buffet Kamenice ❶,** Gundulićeva Poljana 8, is behind the market. (Main dishes 15-45kn. Open daily 7am-midnight.)

🖸 **SIGHTS.** Stari Grad (Old Town) is full of churches, museums, monasteries, palaces, and fortresses. The most popular sights are along **Placa.** The entrance to the staggering city walls *(gradske zidine)* lies just inside the **Pile Gate,** on the left. Set aside an hour for the 2km walk along the top. (Open daily 9am-7:30pm. 15kn, children 5kn.) The 14th-century **Franciscan Monastery** (Franjevački samostan), next to the city wall entrance on Placa, houses the oldest working pharmacy in Europe and a pharmaceutical museum. (Open daily 9am-6pm. 5kn.) The **Cathedral of the Assumption of the Virgin Mary** (Riznica Katedrale) dominates Buničeva Poljana. Its treasury holds religious relics, including the "Diapers of Jesus." (Cathedral open daily 6:30am-8pm; free. Treasury open daily 9am-7pm; 5kn.) To reach the 19th-century **Serbian Orthodox Church** (Pravoslavna Crkva) and its **Museum of Icons** (Muzej Ikona), Od Puča 8, walk from Pile Gate down Placa, go right on Široka, and then turn left on Od Puča. (Church open daily 8am-noon and 5-7pm; free. Museum open M-Sa 9am-1pm; 10kn.)

 WATCH YOUR STEP. As tempting as it may be to stroll in the hills above Dubrovnik or wander the unpaved paths on Lopud, both may still be laced with **landmines.** Stick to the paved paths and beach.

🄲 **BEACHES.** Right outside the fortifications of Stari Grad are a number of **rock shelves** for sunning and swimming. To the left of the cathedral entrance on Pobijana and through a small door into the wall is a great place to watch sunsets. (Open 9am-8pm.) For a truly surreal seaside experience, take a swim in the cove at the foot of the old **Hotel Libertas.** The hotel was damaged during the war, then abandoned for lack of tourists; it now looks like a post-apocalyptic movie set. Dubrovnik's youth gather to swim in the pristine water and to play soccer in the old swimming pool. For sand, palms, and crowds, follow the directions for Hotel Zagreb and then follow the pedestrian boulevard to the beach. The nearby island of **Lokrum** features a nude beach. Ferries shuttle to and from the Old Port every day (15min.; every hr. 9am-8pm; round-trip 25kn). Once there, stroll through the botanical garden and look back on Dubrovnik from the fortress.

🄽 🄵 **FESTIVALS AND NIGHTLIFE.** Dubrovnik becomes a cultural mecca and crazy party from mid-July to mid-August during the **Dubrovnik Summer Festival** (Dubrovački Ijetni Festival). The **festival office** on Placa has schedules and tickets. (☎42 88 64; www.dubrovnik-festival.hr. Open daily for info 8:30am-9pm, tickets 9am-2pm and 3-7pm. 50-300kn.) In the off-season, contact the head office (☎41 22 88) for information and ticket reservations.

Dubrovnik is lively by night, but the scene is often based in Old Town bars rather than in disco clubs. There are usually live bands playing in summer, and many bars stay open until 4 or 5am. Crowds gravitate to **Stari Grad** and the cafes on **Buničeva Poljana.** Another great center of nightlife is outside the city walls on **B. Josipa Jelačica** by the youth hostel, otherwise known as Bourbon St. 🄳**Divinae Follie,** Put Vatroslava Lisinskog 56, Babin Kuk, has two bars, a techno tent, and lots of outdoor seating. (☎43 56 77. Beer 15kn. Cover 70kn. Open Aug. daily 11pm-5am, call ahead to verify; June-July and Sept. Sa only.) **Be Bop Caffe Bar,** Kneza Damjana Jude 6, is a shrine to rock 'n' roll that plays a great selection of rock and blues. (Open daily 9am-2pm and 6pm-4am.)

⨀ DAYTRIP FROM DUBROVNIK: LOPUD ISLAND. Less than an hour from Dubrovnik is Lopud, an enchanting island of the Elafiti Archipelago. The tiny village, dotted with white buildings, chapels, and parks, stretches along the island's waterfront *(obala).* A short walk along the shore leads to an abandoned **monastery,** great for exploring—just be careful of crumbling floors. The island's highlight is its **beach,** Plaža Šunj. Arguably the best beach in Croatia, this cove has one thing that most of the Dalmatian Coast lacks—sand.

Ferries run from Dubrovnik to the Elafiti islands (50min.; in summer M-Sa 4 per day, Su 1 per day; round-trip 25kn). The beach is on the opposite side of the island from the village. Facing the water, walk left for 5min. and turn left onto the road between the high wall and the palm park; look for the "Konoba Barbara" sign and continue over the hill for 15min., keeping right when the path forks.

CYPRUS (Κυπρος)

Aphrodite blessed Cyprus with an abundance of natural beauty, from the sandy beaches of Agia Napa to the serene Troodos Mountains. After long-standing territorial disputes and a Turkish invasion, the island was partitioned in 1975 with Greeks in the south and Turks in the north, divided by the UN-manned Green Line. Restrictions prohibit travel from north to south except for tourists making short daytrips across the Green Line in Nicosia. *Let's Go: Europe 2003* only covers southern Cyprus. Journeys to northern Cyprus require careful planning and must begin in Turkey. For information on northern Cyprus, see *Let's Go: Turkey 2003*.

ESSENTIALS

CYPRUS POUNDS		
AUS$1 = £0.32	£1 = AUS$3.10
CDN$1 = £0.38	£1 = CDN$2.63
EUR€1 = £0.58	£1 = EUR€1.74
NZ$1 = £0.28	£1 = NZ$3.61
ZAR1 = £0.05	£1 = ZAR18.25
UK£1 = £0.90	£1 = UK£1.11
US$1 = £0.59	£1 = US$1.69

DOCUMENTS AND FORMALITIES

VISAS. Citizens of Australia, Canada, Ireland, New Zealand, the UK and the US do not need a visa to enter southern Cyprus for stays of up to 90 days; South Africans can stay without visas for up to 30 days.

EMBASSIES. Foreign embassies are in Lefkosia. For Cypriot embassies at home: **Australia,** 30 Beale Cr., Deakin, Canberra, ACT 2600 (☎6281 0832); **Canada,** 365 Bloor St. E., Suite 1010, Box #43, Toronto, ON M4W 3L4 (☎416-944-0998); **Greece,** 16 Herodotou, Athens (☎723 2727); **UK,** 93 Park St., London W1Y 4ET (☎0171 499 82 72); and **US,** 2211 R St. NW, Washington, D.C. 20008 (☎202-462-5772).

EMERGENCY	Police, Ambulance, and Fire: ☎199.

TRANSPORTATION

Cyprus is served by **Olympic Airlines** (US ☎800-223-1226; Cyprus ☎24 627 950; www.olympic-airways.gr), **Cyprus Airways** (US ☎212-714-2190; Cyprus ☎22 443 054; www.cyprusair.com.cy), and other major airlines. Round-trip fares from Athens to Larnaka cost about €140. An island-wide **bus** schedule is available at tourist offices. **Service taxis** are the most reliable form of transportation on Cyprus and are quite affordable; each taxi seats 4-7 passengers.

PHONE CODES	**Country code: 357.** The city code always must be dialed, even when calling from within the city. **International dialing prefix: 080.** From outside Cyprus, dial int'l dialing prefix (see inside back cover) + 357 + city code + local number.

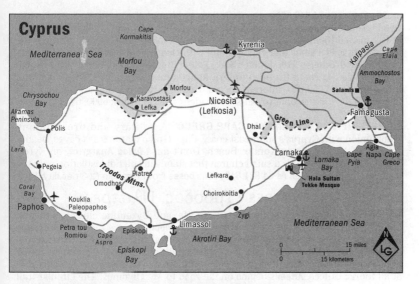

Cyprus

TOURIST SERVICES AND COMMUNICATION

Tourist offices in Cyprus (in Limassol, Lefkosia, Larnaka, Paphos, Polis, and Platres) are extremely helpful and efficient. **Cyprus Tourism Organization** (CTO; ☎ 22 674 264; cto@cyta.com.cy) provides free maps and information on buses, museums, and events. Officials generally speak English, Greek, German, and French.

In southern Cyprus, direct overseas calls can be made from all public phones, but you need a phone card to activate them even if you plan to use your own service provider. Cards are sold at banks and kiosks.

CYPRUS	❶	❷	❸	❹	❺
ACCOMMODATIONS	£1-6	£6-14	£14-24	£24-40	£40-60
FOOD	£1-3	£3-5	£5-10	£10-15	£15-20

LARNAKA (Λαρνακα)   ☎ 24

Tropical Larnaka (pop. 69,000) is one of the oldest continually inhabited cities in the world. The beautifully adorned 9th-century ▓**Church of Agios Lazarus,** north of Larnaka Fort, rests on the tomb of Lazarus, whom legend holds journeyed to Cyprus after rising from the dead. (Dress modestly. Open 8am-12:30pm and 3:30-6:30pm. £0.50.) The **Pierides Foundation Museum,** Zinonos Kitieos 4, showcases artifacts spanning 3000 years of Cypriot history. (Open M-Th 9am-4pm, F-Sa 9am-1pm, Su 11am-3pm. £1.) Outside of town, the **Hala Sultan Tekke Mosque** houses the tomb of Umm Haram, Muhammad's maternal aunt. Take bus #6 or 7 from Ag. Lazarus (15min., every hr., £0.50). Ask the driver to be let off at Tekke. After you're dropped off, walk along the paved road for 1km. (Open in summer daily 7:30am-7:30pm. Free.) Nearby **Agia Napa** (Αγια Ναπα) is a resort with white, sandy beaches and raucous nightlife; take a **bus** (2 per hr., £1.20) from Larnaka. At night, check out the beachfront pubs and eateries on **Athinon.**

Most **flights** to Cyprus land at the Larnaka airport; take bus #22 or 24 (£0.50) or a taxi (£5) to the town center. **Buses** leave from Leforos Athinon, by the marina, for Lefkosia (4-5 per day, £1.50) and Limassol (3-4 per day, £1.70). One **tourist office** is at the airport (☎24 643 575; open daily 8am-11pm), another at Pl. Vasileos Pavlou. (☎24 654 322. Open in summer Th-M 8:15am-6:30pm, Sa until 1:30pm; off-season M-F 8:15am-6:15pm, Sa 8:15am-1:30pm.) ◪Harry's Inn ❷, Thermopylon 2, near the tourist office, is a small and cheery hotel with clean rooms. (☎24 654 453. Breakfast included. Singles £10; doubles £16.) Petrou Bros. Hotel Apartments ❹, Armenikis Ekklisias 1, rents bright, modern apartments with baths, kitchens, and balconies. (☎24 650 600. Internet access. Laundry. Reception 24hr. Doubles £25; quads £35. 10-15% discount to Let's Go readers.) Postal Codes: 6900, 6902.

▣ DAYTRIP FROM LARNAKA: CAPE GRECO. A solitary and breathtaking communion with Cyprus's southeast coast, Cape Greco features sea caves, beautiful hikes, and the sandy Konnoi Beach. Don't miss Agiou Anargyroi, on Kyrou Nerou, the main road. It's a small church that stands in splendid isolation over the sea. Paralimni-Dherynia (☎24 821 318) runs buses from Larnaka (2-3 per day, £1).

TROODOS AND PLATRES (Τροοδος, Πλατρες) ☎25

With crisp mountain air, authentic village life, and Byzantine churches tucked among its pine-covered mountains, the Troodos Mountains are the perfect escape for hikers who wish to avoid Cyprus's summer heat. In winter, Mt. Olympus, the highest point in Cyprus (1951m), is host to hundreds of skiers. Four spectacular hikes originate near Troodos, 10km north of Platres (taxi £5); maps are available at all tourist offices. Artemis begins on the road to Mt. Olympus. The circular trail wraps around the mountain for 7km (2½hr.), providing majestic views of Cyprus. From the Troodos post office, the Atalanta trail mimics the Artemis trail at a lower altitude (12km, 5hr.); a fresh mountain spring 3km into the hike sustains hikers. The 3km Persephone trail leaves across from the police station in Pl. Troodos and gradually descends to a divine lookout point among huge slabs of limestone (2hr.). The Kaledonia trail, the shortest of the four (2km), begins to the left of To Psilo Dendro in Platres and heads to the 10m high Kaledonia Falls.

Platres is an inexpensive base for exploring the Troodos Mountains. Buses (☎25 354 119) arrive from Limassol (2 per day, £2). The tourist office is in the plateia, to the left of the parking lot. (☎25 421 316. Open M-F 9am-3:30pm.) From the post office, go down the hill and bear left to find the rooms at the Kallithea Hotel ❸. (☎25 421 746. Breakfast included. Singles £12-15.)

PAPHOS (Παφος) ☎26

Travelers flock to Paphos to enjoy the beauty of the limestone remnants and crystal waters brushing the sandy shores. The upper section of town, Ktima Paphos (referred to simply as Paphos), centers around Pl. Kennedy and is where you'll find the shops, budget hotels, and services; the lower Kato Paphos hosts the city's nightlife. Kato Paphos features over 2000 square meters of mosaic floors, depicting scenes from Greek mythology and daily life, in the House of Dionysus, the House of Theseus, and the House of Aion. (Open daily 8am-7:30pm. £1.50.) Ag. Pavlou holds the musty Catacombs, including a chapel with deteriorating Byzantine frescoes dedicated to St. Solomoni. (Open 24hr. Free.) The Tomb of the Kings is on Ag. Pavlou, about 2km before Kato Paphos. Local aristocracy, not kings, were interred in the tombs. (Open in summer daily 8:30am-7:30pm; off-season 8am-5pm. £0.75.)

Nea Amoroza Co. buses, Pallikaridi 79 (☎26 236 822), in Pl. Kennedy, go to Polis (6-11 per day, £1). The tourist office is at Gladstone 3. (☎26 932 841. Open in summer M-Tu and Th-F 8:15am-7pm, W and Sa 8:15am-1:30pm; off-season M-Tu and Th-F 8:15am-6:15pm, W and Sa 8:15am-1:30pm.) The convenient ◪Triaron Hotel Guest House ❶ is at Makarios 99. (☎232 193. Singles £5; doubles £8-12.)

CZECH REPUBLIC
(ČESKÁ REPUBLIKA)

From the Holy Roman Empire through the Nazi and Soviet eras, the Czechs have long stood at the crossroads of international affairs. In November 1989, following the demise of the Communist governments in Hungary and Poland and the fall of the Berlin Wall, the Czechs peacefully threw off the Communists and chose dissident playwright Václav Havel to guide them westward. President Havel attempted to preserve the Czech-Slovak union, but on New Year's Day, 1993, after more than 75 years of relatively calm coexistence, the two nations split bloodlessly. Because the Czechs have rarely fought back physically as countries have marched through their borders, their towns and cities are among the best-preserved in Europe.

DISCOVER THE CZECH REPUBLIC

From the medieval alleys of Staré Město and its fabulous Baroque and Art Nouveau architecture to the world's best beer value, **Prague** (p. 247) is truly the starlet of Central Europe. At nearby **Kutná Hora** (p. 261), human femurs and crania hang from the ceilings and chandeliers. In Western Bohemia, international crowds flock to **Karlovy Vary** (p. 262) for its summer film festival and for its *Becherovka*, a local herb liqueur with "curative powers" rivaled only by those of the many local hot springs. In Southern Bohemia, **Český Krumlov** (p. 264) charms visitors with its 13th-century castle, a summer medieval festival, and great nightlife.

FACTS AND FIGURES

Official Name: Czech Republic.

Capital: Prague.

Major Cities: Brno, Ostrava.

Population: 10,300,000.

Land Area: 78,866 sq. km.

Time Zone: GMT +1.

Language: Czech.

Religions: Atheist (40%), Roman Catholic (39%), Protestant (5%), other (16%).

ESSENTIALS

WHEN TO GO

Since the country is mobbed in summer, spring and fall are the best times to visit, although spring can be rainy. Winters are very cold, damp, and snowy.

In August 2002, extreme weather conditions caused massive flooding along the Vltava River. As of press time, the ultimate extent of the damage was not known. Many establishments we list may have been forced to shut down or may have altered opening times; additionally, train routes may be disrupted or changed. Make sure to check ahead thoroughly: call hostels and hotels in advance, and confirm the feasibility of your itinerary with CKM (www.ckm-praha.cz).

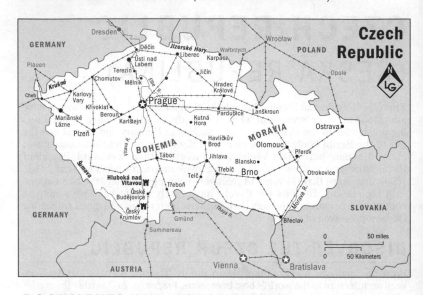

DOCUMENTS AND FORMALITIES

VISAS. Citizens of Ireland, New Zealand, and the US may visit the Czech Republic without a visa for up to 90 days, UK citizens for up to 180 days. Australians, Canadians, and South Africans must obtain 30-day tourist visas. Visas are available at embassies or consulates, but not at the border. Single-entry visas cost €41 for Australians, €53 for Canadians, and €24 for citizens of most other countries. Travelers on a visa must **register** with the Czech Immigration Police within three days of arrival; hotels register their guests automatically.

EMBASSIES. All foreign embassies are in Prague (p. 247). Czech embassies at home include: **Australia,** 8 Culgoa Circuit, O'Malley, Canberra, ACT 2606 (☎02 6290 1386; canberra@embassy.mzv.cz); **Canada,** 251 Cooper St., Ottawa, ON K2P OGZ (☎613-562-3875; www.czechembassy.org); **Ireland,** 57 Northumberland Rd., Ballsbridge, Dublin 4 (☎01 668 1135; dublin@embassy.mzv.cz); **New Zealand,** 48 Hair St., Wainuiomata, Wellington (☎04 939 1610; fax 04 564 9022); **South Africa,** 936 Pretorius St., Arcadia 0083, Pretoria; P.O. Box 3326, Pretoria 0001 (☎012 342 3477; www.icon.co.za/~czmzv); **UK,** 26 Kensington Palace Gardens, London W8 4QY (☎020 7243 1115; london@embassy.mzv.cz); and **US,** 3900 Spring of Freedom St. NW, Washington, D.C. 20008 (☎202-274-9103; www.mzv.cz/washington).

TRANSPORTATION

BY PLANE AND BY TRAIN. Many major carriers fly into Prague's Ruzyně airport (PRG), but the best way to enter and travel through the Czech Republic is by train. **Eastrail** is accepted, but **Eurail** is valid only with the **Prague Excursion Pass** supplement, which covers travel from any Czech border to Prague and back out of the country (return trip must be completed within 7 days; 2nd-class €35, under 26 €30). The fastest trains are *EuroCity* and *InterCity* (*expresní,* marked in blue on schedules). *Rychlík,* also known as *zrychlený vlak,* are fast domestic trains, marked in red on schedules. Avoid slow *osobní* trains, marked in white. Seat reservations (*místenka;* 10Kč) are recommended on *expresní* and international trains and for all first-class seating. *Odjezdy* (departures) are printed in stations on yellow posters, *příjezdy* (arrivals) on white posters.

BY BUS. Buses are the most efficient means of domestic travel, but schedules are often confusing. **ČSAD** runs national and international bus lines. Consult the timetables posted at stations or buy your own schedule (25Kč) from kiosks.

BY THUMB. Although it is a common way for young people to travel in the Czech Republic, *Let's Go* does not recommend hitchhiking.

TOURIST SERVICES AND MONEY

EMERGENCY	Police: ☎ 158. Ambulance: ☎ 155. Fire: ☎ 150.

TOURIST OFFICES. CKM (www.ckm-praha.cz), a national student tourist agency, books hostel beds and issues ISICs and HI cards. Municipal tourist offices in major cities provide lists of hostels and hotels and information on sights and cultural events; they sometimes also arrange rooms.

MONEY. The Czech unit of currency is the **koruna** (crown; Kč), plural *koruny*. Because inflation is only around 4.5%, prices and exchange rates should be relatively stable. Banks offer good exchange rates; **Komerční banka** and **Česká spořitelna** are common chains. **ATMs,** which have the best exchange rates, are everywhere; look for the red and black *"Bankomat"* signs. Traveler's checks can be exchanged almost everywhere, though rarely without commission. MasterCard and Visa are accepted at most high-priced establishments, but rarely at hostels. A day sleeping in a campground and shopping at grocery stores will run €15; sleeping in a hostel or hotel and eating in restaurants costs no more than €35. To **tip,** add 10-20% to the cost of your meal and tell the waiter the new amount; simply leaving *koruny* on the table is considered rude.

BUSINESS HOURS. Banks are usually open Monday to Friday 8am to 4pm, shops Monday to Friday 9am-5pm and Saturday 9am-noon. Almost all museums and galleries close on Mondays.

CZECH KORUNY			
AUS$1 = 17.3KČ		10KČ = AUS$0.58	
CDN$1 = 20.1KČ		10KČ = CDN$0.50	
EUR€1 = 30.7KČ		10KČ = EUR€0.33	
NZ$1 = 14.7KČ		10KČ = NZ$0.68	
ZAR1 = 3KČ		10KČ = ZAR3.37	
UK£1 = 31.3KČ		10KČ = UK£0.21	
US$1 = 31.3KČ		10KČ = US$0.32	

COMMUNICATION

PHONE CODE	Country code: 420. **International dialing prefix:** 00. From outside the Czech Republic, dial int'l dialing prefix (see inside back cover) + 420 + city code + local number.

MAIL. The Czech Republic has an efficient postal system; letters reach the US in less than 10 days. A postcard to the US costs 9Kč, to Europe 7Kč. When sending by airmail, stress that you want it to go on a *letecky* (plane). Go to the customs office

> **UNPRONOUNCEABLE** Not quite a Spanish "r" and simply not the Polish "rz," the Czech letter "ř" lies excruciatingly in between. Most foreigners substitute the "ž" in its place, but that subtle difference often changes the word entirely. A tip for attempting the elusive sound is to roll your tongue and quickly follow with a "ž."

to send international packages heavier than 2kg. Mail can be received general delivery through *Poste Restante*. Address mail to be held: Firstname SURNAME, *Poste Restante*, Jindřišská 14, Praha 1 110 00, CZECH REPUBLIC.

TELEPHONES AND INTERNET. Card-operated phones (175Kč per 50 units; 320Kč per 100 units) are simpler to use than coin phones. **Phone cards** are sold at most *Tábaks* and *Trafika* (convenience stores). Calls run 31Kč per min. to the UK; 63Kč per min. to Australia, Canada, or the US; and 94Kč per min. to New Zealand. Dial ☎ 1181 for English information, ☎ 0800 12 34 56 for the international operator. International direct access numbers include: **AT&T,** ☎ 00 42 00 01 01; **British Telecom,** ☎ 00 42 00 44 01; **Canada Direct,** ☎ 00 42 00 01 51; and **MCI,** ☎ 00 42 00 01 12. **Internet access** is readily available throughout the Czech Republic. Internet cafes offer computers that are fast and cheap, with rates around 2Kč per min.

LANGUAGES. Czech is a Western Slavic language, most closely related to Slovak and Polish. English is widely understood, and German phrases may be useful, especially in the western spas. Russian is also commonly understood but is not always welcome. For Czech words and phrases, see p. 1053.

ACCOMMODATIONS AND CAMPING

CZECH REPUBLIC	❶	❷	❸	❹	❺
ACCOMMODATIONS	under 300Kč	301-500Kč	501-800Kč	801-1200Kč	over 1200Kč

Hostels are consistently clean and safe; **university dorms** are the cheapest lodgings in July and August, with two- to four-bed rooms running 200-300Kč per person. **Pensions** are the next most affordable option; expect to pay 600Kč, including breakfast. Reserve at least one week ahead from June to September in Prague, Český Krumlov, and Brno. If you can't keep a reservation, always call to cancel. **Private homes,** indicated by *Zimmer frei* signs at train stations, are not nearly as popular (or as cheap) as in the rest of Eastern Europe. **Campgrounds** are strewn throughout the countryside, though most are open only mid-May to September.

FOOD AND DRINK

CZECH REPUBLIC	❶	❷	❸	❹	❺
FOOD	under 80Kč	81-100Kč	101-140Kč	141-200Kč	over 200Kč

Thick, pasty *knedlíky* dough is a staple of Czech meals. The national meal, known as *vepřo-knedlo-zelo*, consists of *vepřové* (roast pork), *knedlíky*, and *zelí* (sauerkraut). If you're in a hurry, try *párky* (frankfurters) or *sýr* (cheese) from food stands. Vegetarian restaurants serving *bez masa* (meatless) dishes are uncommon; at most restaurants, vegetarian options will be limited to *smažený sýr* (fried cheese) or *saláty* (salad). Ask for *káva espresso* rather than *káva* to avoid the mud that Czechs call coffee. The most beloved dessert is *koláč*—a tart with poppy-seed jam or sweet cheese. *Plzeňský Prazdroj* (Pilsner Urquell) is the most prominent beer, but many Czechs are loyal to *Budvar* or *Krušovice*.

HOLIDAYS AND FESTIVALS

Holidays: New Year's Day (Jan. 1); Catholic Easter (Apr. 20-21); May Day (May 1); Liberation Day (May 8); Cyril and Methodius Day (July 5); Jan Hus Day (July 6); St. Wenceslas Day (Sept. 28); Independence Day (Oct. 28); Day of Student Struggle for Freedom and Democracy (Nov. 17); Catholic Christmas (Dec. 24-25).

Festivals: The **Prague Spring Festival** (mid-May to early June) attracts international classical music lovers. Music also fills Český Krumlov for the **International Music Fest** (early August). Film fans flock to the **Karlovy Vary International Film Festival** (early July).

PRAGUE (PRAHA)   ☎02

According to legend, Countess Libuše stood above the Vltava and declared, "I see a grand city whose glory will touch the stars." Medieval kings, benefactors, and architects fulfilled the prophecy, building soaring cathedrals and lavish palaces that reflected Prague's status as capital of the Holy Roman Empire. Prague's maze of alleys spawned legends of demons and occult forces and imbued this "city of dreams" with a dark mystique that inspired Franz Kafka's tales of paranoia. Yet since the fall of the Iron Curtain, hordes of foreigners have flooded the city; in summer, tourists pack streets so tightly that crowd-surfing seems a viable way to travel. Walk a few blocks away from the major sights, though, and you'll be lost among cobblestone alleys and looming churches; at outlying Metro stops you'll find haggling *babičky* and sublime natives, without a backpack in sight.

PHONE MAYHEM. Prague is continuously updating its phone system, often giving businesses extremely short notice. Be aware that numbers change quickly, and some of the four- to eight-digit numbers provided in these listings may unfortunately be obsolete by the time you read this. Information ☎14111.

▐▀ TRANSPORTATION

Flights: Ruzyně Airport (PRG; ☎20 11 32 59), 20km northwest of the city. Take bus #119 to Metro A: Dejvická (daily 5am-midnight; 12Kč, luggage 6Kč); buy tickets from kiosks or machines. **Airport buses** (☎20 11 42 96) leave every 30min. from outside Metro stops at Nám. Republiky (90Kč) and Dejvická (60Kč). Taxis to the airport are extremely expensive (400-600Kč); try to settle a price before starting out.

Trains: ☎24 22 42 00; international ☎24 61 52 49; www.cdrail.cz.

Hlavní station (☎24 22 42 00; Metro C: Hlavní nádraží) is the largest. **BIJ Wasteels** (☎24 61 74 54; www.wasteels.cz), 2nd fl., to the right of the stairs, sells general bus tickets and discount international tickets to those under 26. Open summer M-F 7:30am-8pm, Sa 8-11:30am and 12:30-3pm; off season M-F 8:30am-6pm.

Holešovice station (☎24 61 32 49; Metro C: Nádraží Holešovice) serves international routes. BIJ Wasteels and regular train tickets sold at the **Czech Railways Travel Agency** (☎24 23 94 64; fax 24 22 36 00). Open M-F 9am-5pm, Sa-Su 8am-4pm. To: **Berlin** (5hr., 5 per day, 1400Kč); **Bratislava** (5½hr., 7 per day, 400Kč); **Budapest** (10hr., 5 per day, 1300Kč); **Kraków** (8½hr., 1 per day, 730Kč); **Moscow** (30hr., 1 per day, 2500Kč); **Munich** (6hr., 3 per day, 1700Kč); **Vienna** (4½hr., 3 per day, 750Kč); **Warsaw** (9½hr., 3 per day, 870Kč).

Masarykovo station at the corner of Hybernská and Havlíčkova (☎24 61 51 54; Metro B: Nám. Republiky) has domestic trains.

Smíchovské station opposite Vyšehrad (☎24 61 72 55; Metro B: Smíchovské nádraží) also has domestic service.

Central Prague

▲ ACCOMMODATIONS
Dům krále Jiřího, **14**
Pension Týn, **5**
Ritchie's Hostel, **10**
Traveller's Hostel Dlouhá 33, **2**
Traveller's Hostel Husova 3, **18**
U Lilie, **12**

◆ FOOD
Cafe Bambus, **4**
Klub architektů, **16**
Roma Due, **11**
U Špirků, **9**

🍺 PUBS, CAFES, AND NIGHTLIFE
Cafe Marquis de Sade, **7**
Dobrá Čajovna, **17**
Jazz Club Železná, **8**
Karlovy Lázně, **13**
Kavárna Imperial, **6**
Kozička, **3**
Roxy, **1**
U staré paní, **15**

Havličkova

200 yards
200 meters

Na poříčí

Truhlářská

Na Obecního domu

NÁM. REPUBLIKY

NÁMĚSTÍ REPUBLIKY

Senovážna

Revoluční

Benediktská

Kralovodvorská

Municipal House (Obecní dům)

American Express

Powder Tower (Prašná brána)

Kotva Department Store

Rybná

Nekázanka

Mucha Museum

Rybná

Masná

Templova

Rámová

TO 1 & 2

Dlouhá

Kozí

Masná

Dušní

Malá Štupartská

St. James (sv. Jakub)

Jakubská

House of the Golden Ring

Týnská

Tyn Church (Panna Marie před Týnem)

TÝN

Celetná

Czech Museum of Fine Arts

Panská

Na příkopě

Museum of Communism

Golz-Kinský Palace

Kamzíková

Estates Theatre (Stavovské divadlo)

Havířská

OVOCNÝ TRH

MŮSTEK

VÁCLAVSKÉ NÁM.

Vkolkovné

Dlouhá

Museum of Torture Instruments

Železná

St. Gall (sv. Havel)

Haveslká Ulica

Havelská

28. října

Spanish (Španělská)

Dušní

Věženská

Kostečná

St. Salvator (sv. Salvátor)

Pařížská

Jan Hus monument

STAROMĚSTSKÉ NÁM.

Karolinum (Charles University)

Kožná

Melantrichova

Michalská

Rytířská

V. kotcích

UHELNÝ TRH

El. Krásnohorské

Image Theater

Jáchymova

Maiselova

American Express

Kafka Museum

Cathedral of St. Nicholas (sv. Mikuláš)

Maisel (Maiselova)

Old Town Hall (Staroměstská radnice)

MALÉ NÁM.

Hlavsova

Michalská

Skořepka

Pařížská

Old-New (Staronová)

Vězeňská

Červená

High (Vysoká)

Jewish Town Hall (Židovská radnice)

Široká

Maiselova

Jilská

St. Gilles (sv. Jiljí)

Zlatá

Husova

Bílkova

Jewish Ceremonial Hall

Klaus (Klausova)

Rtuě Loutek Theater

Platnéřská

Linhartská

MARIÁNSKÉ NÁM.

Husova

Karlova

Jalovcova

Valentinská

Žatecká

Pinkas (Pinkasova)

Seminářská

Retězová

Bethlehem Chapel (Betlémská kaple)

BETLÉMSKÉ NÁM.

Na reidišti

Decorative Arts Museum (Umělecko-průmyslové)

Cemetery

Kaprova

17. listopadu

Thomas Cook

Liliová

Zlatá

Rudolfinum (Dům umělců)

NÁM. JANA PALACHA

STAROMĚSTSKÁ

Široká

Valentinská

Klementinum and sv Kliment (St. Clement Church)

Veleslavínova

Křižovnická

Museum of Medieval Torture Instruments

Anenská

ANENSKÉ NÁM.

Stříbrná

Náprstek Museum

Náprstkova

Dvořákovo náb.

Alšovo náb.

Mánesův most

Karlův most (Charles Bridge)

St. Francis (sv. František)

Smetana Museum

Theater of the Balustrade (Divadlo na zábradlí)

Karolíny Světlé

Betlova

River Vltava

Karlův most (Charles Bridge)

Jindřišská

Růžová

Provaznická

Na můstku

Jilská

Buses: Schedules ☎ 1034 (daily 6am-9pm; www.jiznirday.cz). Timetables are confusing; first look up the bus stop number for your destination. **ČSAD** has several terminals. The biggest is **Florenc**, Křižíkova 4 (☎ 24 21 49 90; Metro B, C: Florenc). Office open daily 6am-9pm. Buy tickets in advance. To: **Berlin** (8hr., 1 per day, 850Kč); **Budapest** (8hr., 1 per day, 1050Kč); **Paris** (18hr., 1 per day, 2200Kč); **Sofia** (26hr., 4 per day, 1600Kč); **Vienna** (8½hr., 1 per day, 800Kč). Students may get 10% discount. The **Tourbus** office upstairs (☎ 24 21 02 21; www.eurolines.cz) sells tickets for Eurolines and airport buses. Open M-F 7am-7pm, Sa 8am-7pm, Su 9am-7pm.

Public Transportation: Buy tickets for the **Metro, tram,** or **bus** from newsstands and *tabák* kiosks, machines in stations, or **DP** (*Dopravní Podnik;* transport authority) kiosks. The basic 8Kč ticket is good for 15min. on a tram (or 4 stops on the Metro); 12Kč is valid for 1hr. during the day, with unlimited connections between bus, tram, and Metro in any one direction. Large bags and bikes require extra 6Kč ticket. Validate tickets in machines above escalators or face a 400Kč fine. Before paying a fine, look for the officer's badge and get a receipt. The three **Metro** lines run daily 5am-midnight: A is green on maps, B is yellow, C is red. **Night trams** #51-58 and **buses** run all night after the last Metro; look for dark blue signs with white lettering at bus stops. The tourist office in Old Town Hall sells **multi-day passes** valid for the entire network (24hr. 70Kč, 3-day 200Kč, 7-day 250Kč; student 30-day pass 210Kč).

Taxis: RadioTaxi (☎ 24 91 66 66) or **AAA** (☎ 140 14). Both open 24hr. Prague's set rates are a 30Kč flat rate plus 22Kč per km, but taxi drivers are notorious scam artists. Check that the meter is set to zero, and ask the driver to start it (*"Zapněte taximetr"*). Always ask for a receipt (*"Prosím, dejte mi paragon"*) with distance traveled and price paid. If the driver doesn't comply, you aren't obligated to pay.

◢ ORIENTATION

Straddling the river **Vltava,** Prague is a mess of labyrinthine medieval streets and suburbs. Fortunately, most sights lie within the compact, walkable downtown. The Vltava runs south-northeast through central Prague and separates the **Staré Město** (Old Town) and the **Nové Město** (New Town) from **Malá Strana** (Lesser Side). On the right bank of the river, the Old Town's **Staroměstské náměstí** (Old Town Square) is the focal point of the city. From the square, the elegant Pařížská ulice (Paris Street) leads north into **Josefov,** the old Jewish ghetto. In the opposite direction from Josefov, Nové Město houses **Václavské náměstí** (Wenceslas Square), the administrative and commercial heart of the city. West of Staroměstské nám., **Karlův most** (Charles Bridge) spans the Vltava and connects the Old Town with **Malostranské náměstí** (Lesser Town Square). **Pražský Hrad** (Prague Castle) sits on the Hradčany hilltop above Malostranské nám.

All train and bus terminals are on or near the excellent Metro system. To get to Staroměstské nám., take the Metro A line to Staroměstská and walk down Kaprova away from the river. *Tabák* stands and bookstores sell the essential *plán města* (map), along with the English-language weekly *The Prague Post.*

◤ PRACTICAL INFORMATION

TOURIST AND FINANCIAL SERVICES

Tourist Offices: Green "i"s mark tourist agencies, which book rooms and sell maps, bus tickets, and guides. **Pražská Informační Služba** (Prague Info Service) is in the Old Town Hall (☎ 24 48 20 18; English ☎ 54 44 44). Branches at Na příkopě 20, Hlavní nádraží, and in the tower on the Malá Strana side of the Charles Bridge. All open in summer M-F 9am-7pm, Sa-Su 9am-6pm; off-season M-F 9am-6pm, Sa-Su 9am-5pm.

CZECH REPUBLIC

Budget Travel: CKM, Manesove 77 (☎22 72 15 95; www.ckm-praha.cz). Metro A: Jiřího z Poděbrad. Budget air tickets for those under 26. Also books lodgings in Prague from 250Kč. Open M-Th 10am-6pm, F 10am-4pm.

Passport Office: Foreigner police headquarters at Olšanská 2 (☎683 17 39). Take tram #9 from Václavské nám. toward Spojovací and get off at Olšanská. For a **visa extension,** get a 90Kč stamp inside, line up in front of doors #2-12, and prepare to wait up to 2hr. Little English spoken. Open M-Tu and Th 7:30-11:30am and 12:15-3pm, W 8am-12:15pm and 1-5pm, F 7:30-11:30am.

Embassies: Australia (☎51 01 83 50) and **New Zealand** (☎22 51 46 72) have consuls, but citizens should contact the UK embassy in an emergency. **Canada,** Mickiewiczova 6 (☎72 10 18 00; http://217.11.254.44/ca/). Metro A: Hradčanská. Open M-F 8:30am-12:30pm. **Ireland,** Tržiště 13 (☎57 53 00 61). Metro A: Malostranská. Open M-F 9:30am-12:30pm and 2:30-4:30pm. **South Africa,** Ruská 65 (☎67 31 11 14). Metro A: Flora. Open M-F 9am-noon. **UK,** Thunovská 14 (☎57 53 02 78; www.britain.cz). Metro A: Malostranská. Open M-F 9am-noon. **US,** Tržiště 15 (☎57 53 06 63; emergency ☎53 12 00; www.usis.cz). Metro A: Malostranská. Open M-F 9am-4pm.

Currency Exchange: Exchange counters are everywhere with wildly varying rates. Never change money on the street. **Chequepoints** may be the only ones open when you need cash, but usually charge commission. **Komerční banka,** Na příkopě 33 (☎24 43 21 11), buys notes and checks for 2% commission. Open M-F 8am-5pm. ATMs ("Bankomats") abound and offer the best rates, but sometimes charge large fees.

American Express: Václavské nám. 56 (☎22 80 02 37; fax 22 21 11 31). Metro A, C: Muzeum. The **ATM** outside takes AmEx cards. Grants MC/V cash advances for 3% commission. Open daily 9am-7pm. **Branches** on Mostecká 12 (☎57 31 36 38; open daily 9:30am-7:30pm), Celetná 17 (☎/fax 24 81 82 74; open daily 8:30am-7:15pm), and Staroměstské nám. 5 (☎24 81 83 88; open daily 9am-8:30pm).

LOCAL SERVICES

Luggage Storage: Lockers in all train and bus stations take two 5Kč coins. If these are full, or if you need to store your cargo longer than 24hr., use the luggage offices to the left in the basement of **Hlavní station** (15-30Kč per day; open 24hr.) or halfway up the stairs at **Florenc** (10-25Kč per day; open daily 5am-11pm).

Laundromat: Laundry Kings, Dejvická 16 (☎33 34 37 43), one block from Metro A: Hradčanská. Cross the tram and railroad tracks, and turn left. Very social. Wash 60Kč per 6kg; dry 15Kč per 8min. Open M-F 6am-10pm, Sa-Su 8am-10pm.

EMERGENCY AND COMMUNICATION

Medical Assistance: Na Homolce (Hospital for Foreigners), Roentgenova 2 (☎57 27 11 11; after-hours ☎57 77 20 25). Open M-F 8am-4pm. 24hr. emergency service. **American Medical Center,** Janovského 48 (☎87 79 73). Major foreign insurance accepted. On call 24hr. Appointments M-F 9am-4pm. Average consultation 50-200Kč.

24hr. Pharmacy: U Anděla, Štefánikova 6 (☎57 32 09 18). Metro B: Anděl.

Internet Access: Prague is an Internet nirvana. **Bohemia Bagel,** Masna 2 (www.bohemiabagel.cz). 1.5Kč per min. Open M-F 7am-midnight, Sa-Su 8am-midnight. **Cafe Electra,** Rašínovo nábřeží 62 (☎24 92 28 87). Metro B: Karlovo nám. Exit on the Palackého nám. side. 80Kč per hr. Open M-F 9am-midnight, Sa-Su 11am-midnight.

Telephones: Phone cards sell for 175Kč per 50 units and 320Kč per 100 units at kiosks, post offices, and some exchange places; don't let kiosks rip you off.

Post Office: Jindřišská 14. Metro A, B: Můstek (☎21 13 14 45). Airmail to the US takes 7-10 days. Open daily 2am-midnight. For *Poste Restante,* address mail to be held: Firstname SURNAME, *Poste Restante,* Jindřišská 14, Praha 1 **110 00,** CZECH REPUBLIC.

WINDOW OF INOPPORTUNITY At decisive points in European history, unlucky men tend to fall from Prague's window ledges. The Hussite wars began in 1419 after Catholic councillors were thrown to the mob from the New Town Hall on Karlovo nám. The Thirty Years' War devastated Europe after Habsburg officials were tossed from the windows of Prague Castle into a heap of manure in 1618. Two more falls this century have continued the tradition. In 1948, liberal foreign minister Jan Masaryk fell to his death from the top floor of his ministry just two weeks after the Communist takeover; murder was always suspected, but never proven. In 1997, Bohumil Hrabal, popular author of *Closely-Observed Trains*, fell from the fifth floor of his hospital window and died in his pajamas. Nothing unusual here, except that two of his books describe people killing themselves—by jumping out of fifth-floor windows.

⌐ ACCOMMODATIONS AND CAMPING

Although hotel prices are through the roof, rates in the glutted hostel market have stabilized at around 300-500Kč per night. Reservations are a must at hotels, which can be booked solid months in advance, and a good idea at the few hostels that accept them. Most accommodations have 24hr. reception and require check-out by 10am. A growing number of Prague residents rent out affordable rooms.

ACCOMMODATIONS AGENCIES
Many room hawkers at the train station offer legitimate deals, but some will rip you off. Apartments go for around 600-1200Kč per day, depending on proximity to the city center. Haggling is possible. If you don't want to bargain on the street, try a **private agency**. Ask where the nearest tram, bus, or Metro stop is, and don't pay until you know what you're getting; ask for details in writing. You can often pay in euros or US dollars, but prices are lower if you pay in Czech crowns. Some travel agencies book lodgings as well. **Ave.**, Hlavní nádraží, on the 2nd floor of the train station, books rooms starting at 800Kč per person and hostels from 290Kč. (☎ 24 22 352 26; ave@avetravel.cz. Open daily 6am-11pm. (Also see p. 250.).

HOSTELS
If you tote a backpack in Hlavní nádraží or Holešovice, expect to be bombarded by hostel runners. Many hostels are university dorms that free up from June to August, and often you'll be offered free transportation to the hostel. These rooms are convenient options for those arriving in the middle of the night without reservations. If you prefer more than just a place to sleep, smaller places are better alternatives. It's a good idea to call as soon as you know your plans, even if only the night before you arrive or at 10am when they know who's checking out. In Prague, the staff typically speaks English, and hostels have no curfews.

■ **Hostel Boathouse,** Lodnická 1 (☎41 77 00 57; www.aa.cz/boathouse), south of the city center. Take tram #21 from Národni south toward Sídliště. Get off at Černý Kůň (20min.) and follow the signs. As Věra the owner says, "This isn't a hostel, it's a crazyhouse." Summer camp vibe. Hot breakfast or dinner 70Kč. Dorms 300-320Kč. ❶

■ **Penzion v podzámčí,** V podzámčí 27 (☎ 41 44 46 09; evacib@yahoo.com), south of the city center. From Metro C: Budějovická, take bus #192 to the 3rd stop (Nad Rybníky). Homey, with kitchen and laundry. Dorms 280Kč; doubles 640Kč; triples 900Kč. ❶

Ritchie's Hostel, Karlova 9 (☎22 22 12 29; www.mujweb.cz/www/praguehostel.) in Staré Město. Metro A: Staroměstská, down Karlova from the Charles Bridge. Enter through souvenir shop. Great facilities and location; reduced rates for stays longer than 4 nights. Dorms 380-555Kč; doubles 1330-1480Kč; triples 1780-1960Kč. ❷

Hostel U Melounu, Ke Karlovu 7 (☎/fax 24 91 83 22; pus.praha@worldline.cz.), in Nové Město. Metro C: I.P. Pavlova; follow Sokolská to Na Bojišti; continue and turn left onto Ke Karlovu. A historic building with great facilities. Breakfast included. Reservations accepted. Dorms 380Kč; singles 500Kč; doubles 840Kč. 30Kč ISIC discount. ❷

Pension Týn, Týnská 19 (☎/fax 24 80 83 33; backpacker@razdva.cz), in Staré Město. Metro A: Staroměstská. From Old Town Square, head down Dlouhá, bear right at Masná then right onto Týnská. A quiet getaway located in the center of Staré Město. Immaculate facilities. Dorms 400Kč; doubles 1100Kč. 30Kč ISIC discount on doubles. ❷

Traveler's Hostels, in Staré Město (☎24 82 66 62; www.travellers.cz). These summertime big-dorm specialists round up travelers at bus and train stations and shuttle herds to one of their central hostels for lots of beds and beer. Breakfast included.

Dlouhá 33 (☎24 82 66 62). Metro B: Nám. Republiky. Follow Revoluční toward the river, turn left on Dlouhá. Unbeatable location; in the same building as the Roxy (see p. 259), but soundproof. Open year-round. Dorms 370-430Kč; doubles 1240Kč; triples 1440Kč. ❷

Husova 3 (☎22 22 00 78). Metro B: Národní třída; turn right on Spálená (which becomes Na Perštýně after Národní), and again on Husova. Open July-Aug. Classy dorms 400Kč. ❷

Střelecký ostrov (☎24 91 01 88), on an island off Most Legií bridge. Metro B: Národní třída. Open mid-June to mid-Sept. Spacious dorms 300Kč. ❶

Ujezd (☎57 31 24 03), across Most Legií bridge. Metro B: Národní třída. Sports facilities and park. Open June-Sept. Dorms 220Kč. ❶

Welcome Hostel, Zíkova 13 (☎24 32 02 02; www.bed.cz), outside the center. Metro A: Dejvická. Cheap, tidy, spacious, and convenient university dorm. Breakfast included. Singles 400Kč; doubles 540Kč. ISIC 10% discount. ❷

Welcome Hostel at Strahov Complex, Vaníčkova 5 (☎33 35 92 75), outside the center. Take bus #217 or 143 from Metro A: Dejvická to Koleje Strahov. Newly renovated highrise dorms next to the stadium. A little far, but there's always space, not to mention free beer at check-in. Singles 300Kč; doubles 480Kč. ISIC 10% discount. ❶

HOTELS AND PENSIONS

With so much tourist traffic in Prague, budget hotels have become scarce. Many of the cheaper places require reservations up to a month in advance, though some don't accept them. You may want to call several months ahead if you plan to visit during the summer (call first, then confirm by fax with a credit card). If you can't book a room, try an agency or a hostel (above). Make sure the hotel doesn't bill you for a more expensive room than the one you stayed in.

Dům krále Jiřího, Liliová 10 (☎22 22 09 25; www.kinggeorge.cz), in Staré Město. Metro A: Staroměstská. Exit onto Nám. Jana Palacha, walk down Křížovnická toward the Charles Bridge, turn left onto Karlova; Liliová is the first right. Gorgeous rooms with private baths. Breakfast included. Singles 1500-2000Kč; doubles 2700-3350Kč. ❺

U Lilie, Liliová 15 (☎22 22 04 32; fax 22 22 06 41; pensionulilie@centrum.cz), in Staré Město. Metro A: Staroměstská. See directions for Dům krále Jiřího (above). Lovely courtyard. Breakfast included. Singles with shower 1850Kč; doubles 2150-2800Kč. ❺

Hotel Kafka, Cimburkova 24 (☎22 78 13 33; fax 22 78 04 31), outside the center. From Metro C: Hlavní nádraží, take tram #5 (dir.: Harfa), #9 (dir.: Spojovací), or #26 (dir.: Nádraží Hostivař); get off at Husinecká. Head uphill along Seifertova then go left on Cimburkova. Brand-new hotel amid 19th-century buildings. Breakfast included. Apr.-Oct. singles 1700Kč; doubles 2200Kč. Nov.-Mar. singles 1200Kč; doubles 1600Kč. ❺

Pension Unitas/Cloister Inn, Bartolomějská 9 (☎232 77 00; fax 232 77 09; cloister@cloister-inn.cz), in Staré Město. Metro B: Národní třída. Cross Národní, head up Na Perštýně away from Tesco, and turn left on Bartolomějská. Renovated rooms in the cells of the former Communist prison where Václav Havel was incarcerated. Breakfast included. Singles 1100Kč; doubles 1400Kč; triples 1750Kč. ❹

CAMPING

Campsites can be found in both the outskirts and the centrally located Vltava islands. Bungalows must be reserved in advance, but tent space is generally available without prior notice. Tourist offices sell a guide to sites near the city (15Kč).

Sokol Troja, Trojská 171 (☎/fax 33 54 29 08), north of the center in the Troja district. Metro C: Nádraží Holešovice. Take bus #112 to Kazanka. Similar places line the road. 130Kč per person, 90-180Kč per tent. Dorms 270Kč; bungalow 230Kč per person. ❶

Na Vlachovce, Zenklova 217 (☎/fax 688 02 14). Take bus #102 or 175 from Nádraží Holešovice toward Okrouhlická, then walk up the hill. Reserve a week ahead. Beds in romantic 2-person beer barrels 400Kč; doubles with bath 975Kč. ❶

🍴 FOOD

The nearer you are to the center, the more you'll pay. Away from the center, you can get pork, cabbage, dumplings, and a half-liter of beer for 50Kč. You will be charged for everything the waiter brings to the table; check your bill carefully. Most restaurants accept only cash. Outlying Metro stops become markets in the summer. **Tesco,** Národní 26, has **groceries** right next to Metro B: Národní třída. (Open M-F 7am-10pm, Sa 8am-8pm, Su 9am-9pm.) Look for the **daily market** in Staré Město where Havelská and Melantrichova intersect. After a night out, grab a *párek v rohlíku* (hot dog) or a *smažený sýr* (fried cheese sandwich) from a Václavské nám. vendor, or a gyro from a stand on Spálená or Vodíčkova.

RESTAURANTS

🍴 **U Sádlů,** Klimentskà 2 (☎24 81 38 74). Metro B: Nám. Republiky. From the square, walk down Revoluční toward the river, then go right on Klimentskà. Medieval theme restaurant with bountiful portions; call ahead. Czech-only menu lists traditional meals (115-230Kč). Open daily 11am-midnight and 1-2am. ❸

🍴 **Klub architektů,** Betlémské nám. 52, in Staré Město. Metro B: Národní třída. A 12th-century cellar thrust into the 20th century. Veggie options 90-100Kč; meat dishes 140-150Kč. Open daily 11:30am-midnight. ❸

🍴 **Radost FX,** Bělehradská 120, is a both a dance club (see p. 259) and a late-night cafe with an imaginative menu. Metro C: I.P. Pavlova. Entrees 150Kč. Brunch Sa-Su 95-140Kč. Open daily 11am late. See also Clubs and Discos, p. 259. ❹

U Švejků, Újezd 22, in Malá Strana. Metro A: Malostranská. Head down Klárov and go right onto Letenská. Bear left through Malostranské nám. and follow Karmelitská until it becomes Újezd. Named after the lovable Czech cartoon hero from Hasek's novel, *The Good Soldier Svejk,* and decorated with scenes from the book. Nightly accordion music after 7pm. Main dishes 98-158Kč. Open daily 11am-midnight. ❸

Velryba (The Whale), Opatovická 24, in Nové Město. Metro B: Národní třída. Cross the tram tracks and follow Ostrovní, then go left onto Opatovická. Relaxed cafe-restaurant with a gallery downstairs. Main dishes 80-140Kč. Open M-Th 11am-midnight, F 11am-2am. Cafe and gallery open M-F noon-midnight, Sa 5pm-midnight, Su 3-10pm. ❷

Kajetanka, Hradcanské nám., in Malá Strana. Metro A: Malostranská. Walk down Letenská through Malostranské nám.; climb Nerudova until it curves to Ke Hradu, continue up the hill. Terrace cafe with a spectacular view. Meat dishes 129-289Kč, salads 49-69Kč. Open winter daily 10am-6pm, spring and summer daily 10am-9pm. ❹

Cafe Bambus, Benediktska 12, in Staré Město. Metro B: Nám. Republiky. An African oasis with an international menu. Main dishes 80-140Kč; sandwiches 45Kč. Open M-F 9am-midnight, Sa-Su 11am-midnight. ❷

CZECH REPUBLIC

U Špirků, ul. Kožná 12, in Staré Město. Metro A: Staroměstská. Authentic Czech decor and some of the city's best and cheapest food. Main dishes about 100Kč. Open daily 11am-midnight. ❶

El Centro Bar y Bodega, Maltezska nám. 9, in Malá Strana. Metro A: Malostranská. Walk towards Charles Bridge and take a right onto Mostecka then left on Lazenska. Spanish-themed restaurant with international cuisine (85-245Kč) and veggie options (95-140Kč). Open daily 11am-midnight. ❸

Roma Due, Liliová 18. Metro A: Staroměstská. Perfect to cap off a night out. Pasta (119-179Kč) until 11pm; pizza (99-150Kč) until 5am. Open 24hr. ❸

CAFES AND TEAHOUSES

▧ **Dobrá Čajovna U Čajovníka** (Good Tearoom), Boršov 2. Metro A: Staroměstská. Mysterious tea house and Moroccan saloon, with over 90 kinds of international tea (12-150Kč). Open M-Sa 10am-midnight, Su noon-midnight.

▧ **Kavarná Imperial,** Na Poříčí 15. Metro B: Nám. Republiky. Pillared cafe with a courtly air. Live jazz F-Sa 9pm. Open M-Th 9am-midnight, F-Sa 9am-1am, Su 9am-11pm.

Kavárna Medúza, Belgická 17. Metro A: Nám. Míru. Walk down Rumunská and turn left at Belgická. Cafe masquerading as an antique shop. Fluffed-up Victorian seats and lots of coffee (19-30Kč). Open M-F 11am-1am, Sa-Su noon-1am.

U Malého Glena, Karmelitská 23. Metro A: Malostranská. Take tram #12 to Malostranské nám. Their motto is: "Eat, Drink, Drink Some More." Killer margaritas 90Kč. Nightly jazz or blues 9pm. Cover 100-150Kč. Open daily 10am-2am.

The Globe Coffeehouse, Pštrossova 6. Metro B: Národní třída. At the Globe Bookstore. Exit Metro left on Spálená, turn right on Ostrovní, then left to Pštrossova. Tasty, strong black coffee (20Kč), gazpacho (35Kč), and English speakers trying to make a love connection (priceless). Open daily 10am-midnight.

U zeleného čaje, Nerudova 19. Metro A: Malostranská. Follow Letenská to Malostranské nám.; stay right of the church. Over 60 varieties of fragrant tea (28-62Kč) to please the senses and calm the mind. Sandwiches 25Kč. Open daily 11am-10pm.

Propaganda, Pštrossova 29. Metro B: Národní třída. See directions to The Globe (above). Comfy, low-slung chairs and sunny yellow interior. Serves cheap *Budvar* (25Kč) and espresso (19Kč). Open M-F 3pm-2am, Sa-Su 5pm-2am.

◉ SIGHTS

The only city in Central Europe left unscathed by World War II, Prague at its center is a blend of labyrinthine alleys and Baroque architecture. You can easily escape the packs by venturing away from **Staroměstské náměstí, Karlův Most** (Charles Bridge), and **Václavské náměstí.** Compact central Prague is best explored on foot. There are plenty of opportunities for exploration in the back alleys of **Josefov,** the hills of **Vyšehrad,** and the maze of streets in **Malá Strana.**

NOVÉ MĚSTO (NEW TOWN)
Established in 1348 by Charles IV, Nové Město has become the commercial center of Prague, complete with American chain stores.

WENCESLAS SQUARE. Not so much a square as a broad boulevard running through the center of Nové Město, Wenceslas Square (Václavské náměstí) owes its name to the Czech ruler and saint **Wenceslas** (Václav), whose statue sits in front of the National Museum (Národní muzeum). Wenceslas has presided over a century of turmoil and triumph, witnessing no fewer than five revolutions from his pedestal: the declaration of the new Czechoslovak state in 1918, the invasion by Hitler's troops in 1939, the arrival of Soviet tanks in 1968, Jan Palach setting himself on fire to protest the Soviet invasion, and the 1989 Velvet Revolution. The square stretches from the statue past department stores, discos, posh hotels, sausage stands, and trashy casinos. **Radio Free Europe,** which gives global news updates, and advocates peace, has been broadcasting from its glass building behind the National Museum since World War II. *(Metro A, C: Muzeum.)*

FRANCISCAN GARDEN AND VELVET REVOLUTION MEMORIAL. Monks somehow manage to preserve the immaculate and serene **rose garden** (Františkánská zahrada) in the heart of Prague's bustling commercial district. *(Metro A, B: Můstek. Enter through the arch to the left of Jungmannova and Národní, behind the statue. Open daily mid-Apr. to mid-Sept. 7am-10pm; mid-Sept. to mid-Oct. 8am-8pm; mid-Oct. to mid-Apr. 8am-7pm. Free.)* A plaque under the arcades halfway down Národní, across from the Black Theatre, memorializes the hundreds of citizens beaten by police on November 17, 1989. A subsequent wave of mass protests led to the total collapse of communism in Czechoslovakia during the Velvet Revolution.

THE DANCING HOUSE. American architect Frank Gehry (of Guggenheim-Bilbao fame; see p. 954) built the undulating "Dancing House" (Tanečni dům) at the corner of Resslova and Rašínovo nábřeží. Since its 1996 unveiling, it has been called an eyesore by some, and a shining example of postmodern design by others. *(Metro B: Karlovo nám. As you walk down Resslova toward the river, the building is on the left.)*

STARÉ MĚSTO (OLD TOWN)

Losing yourself among the narrow roads and Old-World alleys of Staré Město is the best way to appreciate the 1000-year-old neighborhood's charm.

CHARLES BRIDGE. Thronged with tourists and the hawkers who feed on them, the Charles Bridge (Karlův Most) is Prague's most recognizable landmark. On each side of the bridge, defense towers offer splendid views of the city and of the river. *(30Kč, students 20Kč. Open daily 10am-10pm.)* Five stars and a cross mark the spot where the saint Jan Nepomucký was tossed over the side of the bridge for guarding the queen's extramarital secrets from a suspicious King Wenceslas IV.

OLD TOWN SQUARE. The heart of Staré Město is Staroměstské náměstí (Old Town Square), surrounded by eight magnificent towers. Next to the grassy knoll stands **Old Town Hall** (Staroměstské radnice). The multi-facaded building has a bit blown off the front where the building was partially demolished

THE LOCAL STORY

LIFE ON THE CHARLES

Prague's Charles Bridge (Karlův Most) is filled with portrait artists who set up shop every day, contributing to the bridge's lively atmosphere. Many, such as Ivan, who has worked on the bridge for over a decade, occupy the same spot for years.

LG: Where did you get your start?
I: Oh, I went to a school of drawing, so I made drawings all the time. I started on the bridge after the Revolution. I came here just for weekends and was selling pictures of Prague. Then I saw people painting portraits here and I tried to make portraits too.

LG: Do you need a permit?
I: Yes, we have to have a permit, and every year we have to go through an exam. Last year it was a practical exam. You have to show your work and make portraits in a certain time. And then if you pass, you pay for one square meter here. Those two men in black uniforms are our agency; we pay, and they patrol the bridge every day to make sure no other portraitists are here without permission. The rules must be followed.

LG: Have you ever drawn a portrait for someone famous?
I: Not much, but I do caricatures of Ozzy Osbourne and sometimes I sell them, and ones of Ozzy Osbourne's band. Ozzy Osbourne was in Prague three or four times, and he has bought some of my pieces.

by the Nazis in the final week of World War II. Crowds gather on the hour to watch the **astronomical clock** chime, releasing a procession of apostles accompanied by a skeleton symbolizing Death. *(Metro A: Staroměstská; Metro A, B: Můstek. Town hall open summer M 11am-5:30pm, Tu-Su 9am-5:30pm. Clock tower open daily 10am-6pm. 30Kč, students 20Kč. Last chime 9pm.)* Opposite the Old Town Hall, the spires of **Týn Church** (Matka Boží před Týnem) rise above a mass of medieval homes. The famous astronomer Tycho Brahe is buried inside. Brahe died when he overindulged at one of Emperor Rudolf's lavish dinner parties, where it was unacceptable to leave the table unless the Emperor himself did so. Because he was forced to stay seated, his bladder burst. The bronze statue of theologian **Jan Hus,** the country's most famous martyr, stands in the middle of the square. In front of the Jan Hus statue sits the flowery **Goltz-Kinský Palace,** the finest of Prague's Rococo buildings. *(Open Tu-F 10am-6pm; closes early in summer for daily concerts.)*

POWDER TOWER AND MUNICIPAL HOUSE. One of the original eight city gates, the Gothic **Powder Tower** (Prašná Brána) looms at the edge of Nám. Republiky as the entrance to Staré Město. A steep climb to the top rewards you with expansive views. Next door, on the site of a former royal court, is the **Municipal House** (Obecnídům), where the Czechoslovak state declared independence on October 28, 1918. *(Nám. Republiky 5. Metro B: Nám. Republiky. Tower open Apr.-Oct. daily 10am-6pm. House open 10am-6pm. Guided tours Sa noon and 2pm. 150Kč.)*

JOSEFOV

Metro A: Staroměstská. Synagogues and museum open Su-F 9am-6pm. Closed for Jewish holidays. Admission to all six synagogues except Starnová 300Kč, students 200Kč. Starnová Synagogue 200Kč, students 140Kč. Museum only 300Kč, students 200Kč.

Josefov, the oldest Jewish settlement in Central Europe, lies north of Staroměstské nám., along Maiselova. In 1180, Prague's citizens built a 12ft. wall around the area. The closed neighborhood bred exotic tales, many of which centered around Rabbi Loew ben Bezalel (1512-1609) and his legendary *golem*—a mud creature that supposedly came to life to protect Prague's Jews. The city's Jews remained clustered in Josefov until WWII, when the ghetto was vacated as the residents were deported to death camps. Ironically, Hitler's wish to create a "museum of an extinct race" sparked the preservation of Josefov's cemetery and synagogues. Although it is only a fraction of its former size, there is still a Jewish community living in Prague today.

THE SYNAGOGUES. The **Maisel Synagogue** (Maiselova synagoga) displays artifacts from the Jewish Museum's collections. *(On Maiselova, between Široká and Jáchymova.)* Turn left down Široká to reach the 16th-century **Pinkas Synagogue** (Pinkasova), a sobering memorial to the 80,000 Czech Jews killed in the Holocaust. Upstairs is an exhibit of drawings made by children in the Terezín camp. Backtrack up Široká and go left on Maiselova to visit the oldest operating synagogue in Europe, the 700-year-old **Old-New Synagogue** (Staronová). Further up Široká on Dušní is the **Spanish Synagogue** (Španělská), which has an ornate Moorish interior.

OLD JEWISH CEMETERY. The Old Jewish Cemetery (Starý židovský hřbitov) remains Josefov's most-visited site. Between the 14th and 18th centuries, 20,000 graves were laid in 12 layers. The striking clusters of tombstones result from a process in which the older stones rose from underneath. Rabbi Loew is buried by the wall directly opposite the entrance. *(At the corner of Široká and Žatecká.)*

MALÁ STRANA

A seedy hangout for criminals and counter-revolutionaries for nearly a century, the cobblestone streets of Malá Strana have become prized real estate. The Malá Strana is centered around **Malostranské náměstí** and its centerpiece, the Baroque

St. Nicholas's Cathedral (Chrám sv. Mikuláše), whose towering dome is one of Prague's most prominent landmarks. *(Metro A: Malostranská; follow Letenská to Malostranské nám. Open daily 9am-4pm. 50Kč, students 25Kč.)* Along Letenská, a wooden gate opens through a 10m wall into the beautiful **Wallenstein Garden** (Valdštejnská zahrada), one of Prague's best-kept secrets. *(Letenská 10. Metro A: Malostranská. Open Apr.-Oct. daily 10am-6pm.)* **Church of Our Lady Victorious** (Kostel Panna Marie Vítězné) is known for the famous wax statue of the **Infant Jesus of Prague,** said to bestow miracles on the faithful. *(Metro A: Malostranská. Follow Letecká through Malostranské nám. and continue onto Karmelitská. Open M-F 9:30am-5:30pm, Sa 9:45am-8pm, Su open for mass.)*

PRAGUE CASTLE (PRAŽSKÝ HRAD)

Metro A: Malostranská. Take trams #22 or 23 to Pražský Hrad and go down U Prašného Mostu. Open Apr.-Oct. daily 9am-5pm; Nov.-Mar. 9am-4pm. Buy tickets opposite St. Vitus's Cathedral, inside the castle walls. 3-day ticket valid at Royal Crypt, Cathedral and Powder Tower, Old Royal Palace, and the Basilica. 220Kč, students 110Kč.

Prague Castle has been the seat of the Bohemian government for over 1000 years. From Metro A: Hradčanská, cross the tram tracks and turn left onto Tychonova, which leads to the newly renovated **Royal Summer Palace.** The main castle entrance is at the other end of the lush **Royal Garden** (Královská zahrada), where the Singing Fountain spouts and chimes. Before exploring, pass the main gate to see the **Šternberský Palace,** which houses art from the National Gallery.

ST. VITUS'S CATHEDRAL. Inside the castle walls stands the colossal St. Vitus's Cathedral (Katedrála sv. Víta), which looks Gothic but was in fact finished in 1929, 600 years after construction began. To the right of the high altar stands the **tomb of St. Jan Nepomuc,** 3m of solid, glistening silver weighing 1800kg. In the main church, the walls of **St. Wenceslas's Chapel** (Svatováclavská kaple) are lined with precious stones and a painting cycle depicting the legend of Wenceslas. Climb the 287 steps of the **Cathedral Tower** for the best view of the city, or descend underground to the **Royal Crypt,** which holds the tomb of Charles IV.

OLD ROYAL PALACE. The Old Royal Palace (Starý Královský Palác) is to the right of the cathedral, behind the Old Provost's House and the statue of St. George. The lengthy **Vladislav Hall** once hosted jousting competitions. Upstairs is the **Chancellery of Bohemia,** where the Second Defenestration of Prague took place (see p. 251).

ST. GEORGE'S BASILICA AND ENVIRONS. Behind the cathedral and across the courtyard from the Old Royal Palace stands St. George's Basilica (Bazilika sv. Jiří). The **National Gallery of Bohemian Art,** which has art ranging from Gothic to Baroque, is in the adjacent convent. *(Open Tu-Su 9am-5pm. 40Kč, students 20Kč.)* **Jiřská** street begins to the right of the basilica. Halfway down, tiny **Golden Lane** (Zlatá ulička) heads off to the right; alchemists once worked here, and Kafka later lived at #22.

OUTER PRAGUE

The city's outskirts are packed with greenery, churches, and panoramic vistas, all peacefully tucked away from tourist hordes. **Vyšehrad** is the former haunt of Prague's 19th-century Romantics; quiet walkways wind between crumbling stone walls to one of the Czech Republic's most celebrated sites, **Vyšehrad Cemetery,** home to the remains of composer Antonín Dvořák. The oldest monastery in Bohemia, **Břevnov Monastery,** was founded in 993 by King Boleslav II and St. Adalbert, each of whom was guided by a divine dream to build a monastery atop a bubbling stream. The stream leads to a pond to the right of **St. Margaret's Church** (Kostel sv. Markéty) within the complex. *(From Metro A: Malostranská, take tram #22 uphill to Břevnovsky klášter. Church open daily 7am-6pm.)* The traditional **Prague Market** (Pražskátrznice) has acres of stalls selling all kinds of wares. *(Take tram #3 or 14 from Nám. Republiky to Vozovna Kobylisy and get off at Pražskátrznice.)*

🏛 MUSEUMS

The city's museums often have striking facades but mediocre collections. Still, a few quirky museums are worth mentioning.

▨MUCHA MUSEUM. The museum is devoted entirely to the work of Alfons Mucha, the Czech Republic's most celebrated artist, who composed some of the pioneering strokes of the Art Nouveau Movement. *(Panská 7. Metro A, B: Můstek. Walk up Václavské nám. toward the St. Wenceslas statue. Go left onto Jindřišská and again onto Panská.* ☎ *62 84 162; www.mucha.cz. Open daily 10am-6pm. 120Kč, students 60Kč.)*

MUSEUM OF MEDIEVAL TORTURE INSTRUMENTS. The collection and highly detailed explanations are guaranteed to nauseate. *(Staroměstské nám. 20, in Old Town Square. Metro A: Staroměstská. Open daily 10am-10pm. 140Kč.)* Across the hall, the **Exhibition of Spiders and Scorpions** shows live venomous spiders and scorpions in their natural habitats. *(Open daily 10am-10pm. 100Kč, children 80Kč.)*

NATIONAL GALLERY. The massive collection of the National Gallery (Národní Galerie) is spread around nine different locations; the notable Šternberský palác and Klášter sv. Jiří are in the **Prague Castle** (see p. 257). The other major branch is at St. Agnes's Cloister (Klášter sv. Anežky), which is undergoing renovation. The cloister's collection of 19th-century Czech art has been moved to the **Trade Fair Palace and the Gallery of Modern Art** (Veletržní palác a Galerie moderního umwní), which also exhibits 20th-century Czech art. *(Dukelských hrinů 47. Metro C: Vltavská. All open Tu-Su 10am-6pm. 150Kč, students 70Kč.)*

COMMUNISM MUSEUM. This new gallery is committed to exposing the flaws of the Communist system that suppressed the Czech people from 1948-1989. It features 3-D objects, a model factory, and an interrogation office. *(Na Příkopě 10. Metro A: Můstek. Open daily 9am-9pm. 180Kč, students 90Kč.)*

🎵 ENTERTAINMENT

For concerts and performances, consult *Threshold* or *Do města-Downtown*, both free at many cafes and restaurants, or *The Prague Post*. Most performances start at 7pm and offer stand-by tickets 30min. beforehand. Between mid-May and early June, the **Prague Spring Festival** draws classical musicians from around the world. For tickets, try **Bohemia Ticket International,** Malé nám. 13, next to Čedok. (☎ 24 22 78 32; www.ticketsbti.cz. Open M-F 9am-5pm, Sa 9am-2pm.) The **National Theater** (Národní divadlo), Národní 2/4, stages drama, opera, and ballet. (☎ 24 92 15 28. Metro B: Národní třída. Box office open M-F 10am-6pm, Sa-Su 10am-12:30pm and 3-6pm.) **Estates Theater** (Stavovské divadlo), Ovocný trh 1, is to the left of the pedestrian Na Příkopě. (Metro A, B: Můstek.) Mozart's *Don Giovanni* premiered here; shows today are mostly classic theater. Use the National Theater box office, or show up 30min. before showtime. The **Marionette Theater** (Říše loutek), Žatecká 1, stages a hilarious marionette version of *Don Giovanni*. (Metro A: Staromwstská. Performances June-July Th-Tu 8pm. Box office open daily 10am-8pm. 490Kč, students 390Kč.)

🍺 NIGHTLIFE

With some of the best beers in the world on tap, it's no surprise that pubs and beer halls are Prague's most popular nighttime hangouts. Tourists have overrun the city center, so authentic pub experiences are now largely restricted to the suburbs and outlying Metro stops. Although dance clubs abound, Prague is not a clubbing city—locals prefer the many jazz and rock clubs.

ABSINTHE-MINDED Shrouded in Bohemian mystique, this translucent turquoise fire-water is a force to be reckoned with. Although absinthe has been banned in all except three countries due to allegations of opium-lacing and fatal hallucinations, Czechs have an attachment to the liquor. It has been the mainstay spirit of the Prague intelligentsia since Kafka's days, and during World War II every Czech adult was rationed a half-liter per month. Today's backpackers (who will apparently drink anything) have discovered the liquor, which at its strongest can be 160 proof. The bravest and most seasoned ex-pats sip it on the rocks, but you can douse a spoonful of sugar in the alcohol, torch it with a match until the sugar caramelizes and the alcohol burns off, and dump the residue into your glass.

BARS

■ **Vinárna U Sudu,** Vodičkova 10. Metro A: Můstek. Cross Václavské nám. to Vodičkova and follow the curve left. Infinite labyrinth of cavernous cellars. Red wine 120Kč per 1L. Open M-F noon-midnight, Sa-Su 2pm-midnight.

U Fleků, Křemencova 11. Metro B: Národní třída. Turn right on Spálená away from Národní, right on Myslíkova, and then right again on Křemencova. The oldest brewhouse in Prague. Home-brewed beer 49Kč. Open daily 9am-11pm.

Kozička (The Little Goat), Kozí 1. Metro A: Staroměstská. This giant cellar bar is always packed; you'll know why after your first 0.5L of *Krušovice* (18Kč). Czech 20-somethings stay all night. Open M-F noon-4am, Sa-Su 6pm-4am.

Molly Malone's, U obecního dvora 4. Metro A: Staroměstská. Overturned sewing machines serve as tables in this pub. Small groups can head to the loft. Guinness 80Kč—cheaper than in Ireland. Open Su-Th 11am-1am, F-Sa 11am-2am.

Cafe Marquis de Sade, Melnicka 5. Metro B: Nám. Republiky. Spacious bar decorated in rich red velvet. Happy Hour M-F 4-6pm. Velvet beer 27-35Kč. Open daily noon-2am.

Pivnice u Sv. Tomáše, Letenská 12. Metro A: Malostranská. Walk downhill on Letenská. While meat roasts on a spit, the mighty dungeons echo with boisterous revelry and gushing toasts. Order meats a day in advance. Beer 40Kč. Live brass band nightly 7-11pm. Open daily 11:30am-midnight.

Jo's Bar and Garáž, Malostranské nám. 7. Metro A: Malostranská. All-Anglophone with foosball, darts, cards, and a DJ. Beer 20Kč and under during Happy Hour (daily 6pm-10pm). Open daily 11am-2am.

Újezd, Újezd 18. Metro B: Národní třída. Exit onto Národní, turn left toward the river, cross the Legií bridge, continue straight on Vítězná, and turn right on Újezd. Decorated with gremlins and filled with hidden corners. Beer just 25Kč. Open daily 11am-4am.

Zanzibar, Saská 6. Metro A: Malostranská. Head down Mostecká toward the Charles Bridge, turn right on Lázeňská, and turn left on Saská. The classiest place to see and be seen. Cocktails 110-150Kč. Open daily 5pm-3am.

CLUBS AND DISCOS

■ **Radost FX,** Bělehradská 120 (www.radostfx.cz). Metro C: I.P. Pavlova. Plays intense techno, jungle, and house. Creative drinks. Cover 80-150Kč. Open M-Sa 10pm-late.

■ **Jazz Club Železná,** Železná 16. Metro A, B: Staroměstská. Vaulted cellar bar showcases live jazz nightly. Beer 30Kč. Cover 80-150Kč. Shows 9-11:30pm. Open daily 3pm-1am.

Roxy, Dlouhá 33. Metro B: Nám. Republiky. In the same building as the Dlouhá 33 Traveler's Hostel (see p. 252). Experimental DJs and theme nights. Crowds hang out on the huge staircases. Cover 100-350Kč. Open M-Tu and Th-Sa 9pm-late.

CZECH REPUBLIC

Palác Akropolis, Kubelíkova 27 (www.palacakropolis.cz). Metro A: Jiřího z Poděbrad. Head down Slavíkova and turn right onto Kubelíkova. Live bands several times a week. Top Czech act *Psí vojáci* is an occasional visitor. Open daily 10pm-5am.

Karlovy Láznkě, Novotného lávka 1. Four floors of themed dance floors under the Charles Bridge. Cover 100Kč, 50Kč before 10pm. Open nightly 9pm-late.

Ungelt, Tyn 2. Metro A, B: Staroměstská. Subterranean vault with live jazz daily from 9pm-midnight. Cover 150Kč. Or, listen from the pub for free. Open daily noon-midnight.

U staré paní, Michalská 9. Metro A, B: Můstek. Some of Prague's finest jazz vocalists in a tiny yet classy venue. Shows nightly W-Sa 9pm-midnight. Cover 160Kč, includes one drink. Open for shows 7pm-1am.

GAY NIGHTLIFE

At any of the places below, you can pick up a copy of *Amigo* (40Kč), the most thorough guide to gay life in the Czech Republic and Slovakia, with a lot in English, or *Gayčko* (59Kč), a glossier piece of work, written mostly in Czech.

U střelce, Karolíny Světlé 12. Metro B: Národní třída. Under the archway on the right, this gay club draws a diverse crowd for its cabarets. Cover 80Kč. Open W-Sa 9:30pm-5am, with shows after midnight.

A Club, Milíčova 25. Metro C: Hlavní nádraží. Take tram #3, 5, 9, 26, or 55 uphill and get off at Lipsanká. Prague's only lesbian nightspot. Men are free to enter, but expect funny looks. Beer 20Kč. Open nightly 7pm-dawn.

Tom's Bar, Pernerova 4. Metro B, C: Florenc. Walk down Křižíkova past the Karlin Theater, pass under the tracks, and go right on Prvního pluků. Follow the tracks as they veer left to become Pernerova. Dance floor and video screening rooms. Men only. Clothing optional Th. Open Tu-Th 8pm-4am, F-Sa 8pm-late.

▶ DAYTRIPS FROM PRAGUE

TEREZÍN (THERESIENSTADT). In 1941, when Terezín became a concentration camp, Nazi propaganda films touted the area as a resort where Jews would live a normal life. In reality, over 30,000 died here, some of starvation and disease, others in death chambers; another 85,000 Jews were transported to death camps further east. The **Ghetto Museum,** on Komenského in town, sets Terezín in the wider context of WWII. (Open Apr.-Sept. daily 9am-6pm; Oct.-Mar. 9am-5:30pm. Tickets to museum, barracks, and small fortress 160Kč, students 120Kč.) Across the river is the **Small Fortress** (Malá Peunost), which was used as a Gestapo prison. (Open Apr.-Sept. daily 8am-6pm; Oct.-Mar. 8am-4:30pm.) The **cemetery** and the furnaces of the **crematorium** are as they were 50 years ago, with the addition of tributes left by the victims' descendants. Men should cover their heads. (Open Mar.-Nov. Su-F 10am-5pm.) Terezín has been repopulated to about half of its former size; families now live in the barracks and supermarkets occupy former Nazi offices. A **bus** runs to Prague-Florenc station (45min., 9 per day, 59Kč); get off at the second Terezín stop, where the **tourist office** sells a 25Kč map. (Open Tu-Su 9am-4pm.) ☎0416.

KARLŠTEJN. A gem of the Bohemian countryside, Karlštejn is a turreted fortress built by Charles IV to store his crown jewels and holy relics. (Open July-Aug. Tu-Su 9am-6pm; May-June and Sept. 9am-5pm; Apr. and Oct. 9am-4pm; Nov.-Mar. 9am-3pm. English tours 200Kč, students 100Kč; 7-8 per day.) The **Chapel of the Holy Cross** is inlaid with precious stones and 129 apocalyptic paintings by medieval artist Master Theodorik. (☎ (02) 74 00 81 54; reservace@spusc.cz. Open Tu-Su 9am-5pm. Tours by reservation only; 600Kč, students 200Kč.) The area also has beautiful **hiking** and **biking** trails. A **train** runs to Praha-Smíchov (45min., every hr., roundtrip 50Kč). To reach the castle, turn right out of the station and go left over the modern bridge; turn right, then walk through the village. ☎ **0311.**

MĚLNÍK. Fertile Mělník is known for its **wine-making,** supposedly perfected about 1000 years ago when St. Wenceslas, the patron saint of Bohemian wine-makers, was initiated in its vineyards. In one day, you can tour the stately Renaissance **castle,** sample its homemade wines, and lunch in the old schoolhouse overlooking the Říp Valley. Wine tasting (110Kč) with Martin, the wine master, is available by reservation. (☎ 62 21 08; www.lobkowicz-melnik.cz. Open daily 10am-6pm. Tours 60Kč, students 40Kč.) **Buses** run from Prague-Holešovice (45min., every 30min., 32Kč). From the station, make a right onto Bezručova and head up the left fork onto Kpt. Jaroše, to the town center. Enter the Old Town Square (Nàm Míru); the castle is down Svatovaclvska to your left. ☎ **0206.**

KUTNÁ HORA. East of Prague, the former mining town of Kutná Hora (Mining Mountain) has a history as morbid as the **bone church** that has made the city famous. In the 13th century, the town's 100,000 silver-crazed diggers were hit by the Black Plague. When the graveyard became overcrowded, the Cistercian Order built a chapel to hold bodies. In a fit of whimsy (or insanity), one monk began designing floral shapes out of pelvises and crania; he never finished, but the artist František Rint eventually completed the project in 1870 with the bones of over 400,000 people, including femur crosses and a grotesque chandelier made from every kind of bone in the human body. (Open Apr.-Oct. daily 8am-6pm; Nov.-Mar. 9am-noon and 1-4pm. 30Kč, students 20Kč.) Take a **bus** (1½hr., 6 per day, 60Kč) from Prague-Florenc station. Exit left onto Benešova, continue through the rotary until it becomes Vítězná, then go left on Zámecká (2km).

ČESKÝ RÁJ NATIONAL PRESERVE. The narrow pillars and deep gorges of **Prachovské skály** (Prachovské Rocks) make for climbs and hikes with stunning views. Prachovské skály also boasts the ruins of the 14th-century rock castle **Pařez** and the rock pond **Pelíšek.** (Open Apr.-Oct. daily 8am-5pm; swimming May-Aug. 25Kč, students 10Kč.) The 588 acres of the park are interwoven by a dense network of **trails;** both green and yellow signs guide hikers to additional sights, while triangles indicate vistas off the main trails. Red signs mark the extremely long "Golden Trail," which connects Prachovské skály to **Hrubá Skála** (Rough Rock), a rock town surrounding a hilltop castle from which hikers enjoy the best view of the sandstone rocks. From the Hrubá Skála castle, the red trail leads up to what remains of **Wallenstein Castle** (Valdštejnský hrad). **Buses** run from Prague-Florenc station to **Jičín** (1½hr., 7 per day, 85Kč), where other buses go to Prachovské skály and Český Ráj (15min., several times daily, 9Kč). Buses to Český Ráj sometimes run less frequently than scheduled; you can also walk from Jičín along a relatively easy 6km trail beginning at Motel Rumcajs, Koněva 331. ☎ **0433.**

WEST AND SOUTH BOHEMIA

West Bohemia overflows with curative springs; over the centuries, emperors and intellectuals alike have soaked in the waters of Karlovy Vary (also known as Carlsbad). Those seeking good beer visit the *Pilsner Urquell* brewery in Plzeň or the *Budvar* brewery in South Bohemian České Budějovice. More rustic than West Bohemia, South Bohemia is filled with brooks, virgin forests, and castle ruins.

KARLOVY VARY (CARLSBAD) ☎035

A stroll into Karlovy Vary's hills or through its spa district reveals why this lovely town developed into one of the great "salons" of Europe, frequented by Johann Sebastian Bach, Peter the Great, Sigmund Freud, and Karl Marx. Although older Germans and Russians seeking the therapeutic powers of the springs are now the main visitors, film stars from around the world and fans from around the country also fill the town for the International Film Festival each July.

🖅🖬 TRANSPORTATION AND PRACTICAL INFORMATION. **Buses,** much more convenient than trains, run from Dolní nádraží, on Západní, to Plzeň (1½hr., 12 per day, 80Kč) and Prague (2½hr., 25 per day, 100-130Kč); buy tickets on board. To reach the town center from the bus station, turn left on Západní, continue past the Becher building, and bear right on T. G. Masaryka, which runs parallel to the other main thoroughfare, Dr. Davida Bechera. For a Centrum **taxi,** call ☎322 30 00. **Infocentrum,** Lazenska 1, next to the Mill Colonnade, (☎322 40 97) sells maps (30-169Kč) and theater tickets (60-400Kč), and also books rooms (from 400Kč). (Open Jan.-Oct. M-F 8am-6pm, Sa-Su 10am-4pm; Nov.-Dec. M-F 7am-5pm.) *Promenáda,* a part-English monthly booklet with event schedules and other information, is available here and at kiosks throughout town. The **post office** is at T. G. Masaryka 1. (Open M-F 7:30am-7pm, Sa 8am-1pm, Su 8am-noon.) **Postal code:** 36001.

🖥🖸 ACCOMMODATIONS AND FOOD. City Info, T. G. Masaryka 9, which has an English-speaking staff, offers pension singles from 600Kč and hotel doubles from 860Kč. (☎322 33 51. Open daily 9am-6pm.) From the main stop on Západní, take bus #6 (dir.: Stará Kysibelská) to the fourth stop, Blahoslavova, to reach **Pension Hestia ❷,** Stará Kysibelská 45. The spacious rooms are worth the trip. (☎322 59 85; hestiakv@volny.cz. Reception 24hr. Singles 320Kč; doubles 640Kč. Discount for multiple-night stays.) Follow the directions from the bus station to T.G. Masaryka and bear right at the post office to reach **Hotel Kosmos ❸,** Zahradní 39, in the center of the spa district. (☎322 54 76. Singles 700Kč, with bath 890Kč; doubles 1150Kč/1450Kč. Oct.-Apr. 100Kč less.) Karlovy Vary is known for its sweet *oplatky* (spa wafers); try them at a street vendor (5Kč). The **supermarket,** Horova 1, is in the large building with the "Městská tržnice" sign, near the local bus station. (Open M-F 6am-7pm, Sa 7am-5pm, Su 9am-5pm.) Trendy **E&T ❸,** Zeyerova 3, has a diverse menu. (Main dishes 70-235Kč. Open M-F 9:30am-2am, Sa-Su 11am-2am.)

🖾 🖪 SIGHTS AND ENTERTAINMENT. The **spa district,** which overflows with springs, baths, and colonnades, starts at the Victorian **Bath 5** (Lázně 5), Smetanovy Sady 1, across the street from the post office. (☎322 25 36; www.spa5.cz. Thermal baths 340Kč. Underwater massages 475Kč. Reserve ahead. Pool and sauna open M-F 8am-9pm, Sa 8am-6pm, Su 10am-6pm. 90Kč.) Mlýnské nábř. follows the Teplá River to **Bath 3,** which offers full-body massages for 714Kč. (Treatments daily 7am-2:30pm.) Next door, the imposing **Mill Colonnade** (Mlýnská kolonáda) shelters five different springs. Farther down is the **Zawojski House,** Trižiště 9, a cream-and-gold Art Nouveau building that now the houses Živnostenská Banka. Inside the **Strudel Colonnade** (Vřídelní kolonáda), the **Strudel Spring** (Vřídlo pramen), Karlovy Vary's hottest and highest-shooting spring, spouts 30L of 72°C (162°F) water each second. (Open daily 6am-7pm.)

Follow Stará Louka to find signs pointing you to the funicular (every 15min. 9am-7pm; 25Kč, round-trip 40Kč), which leads to the 555m **Diana Observatory** (Rozhledna) and a magnificent panorama of the city. (Tower open daily 9am-7pm. 10Kč.) Above the Ohře river, 12km west of Karlovy Vary, is the 12th-century **Loket Castle.** The castle's bleak dungeons contrast with the bright local porcelain also displayed there. (Open Apr.-Oct. daily 9am-4:30pm; Nov.-Mar. 9am-3:30pm. 70Kč, students 50Kč.) *Promenáda* (see above) lists each month's concerts and performances, including information about the **International Film Festival,** which screens independent films in early July. Tickets sell out quickly—go to the box office early. **Propaganda,** Jaltská 5, off Bechera, attracts a hip young crowd with live music and a trendy blue-steel interior. (Mixed drinks 40-100Kč. Open daily 5pm-late.)

⚡ DAYTRIP FROM KARLOVY VARY: PLZEŇ. A beer lover's perfect day begins at Plzeň's legendary ■**Pilsner Urquell Brewery** (Měšťanský Pivovar Plzeňský Prazdroj), where knowledgeable guides lead visitors to the fermentation cellars for samples. After the tour, take a lunch break at the on-site beerhouse **Na spilce,** which pours *Pilsner* for 20Kč per pint. The entrance to the complex is across the Radbuza River from Staré Město, where Pražská becomes U Prazdroje. (1hr. tour June-Aug. daily 10:30am and 12:30, 2, and 3pm; Sept.-May 12:30pm. 120Kč, students 60Kč.) From the square, go down Pražská and turn left on Perlová to visit the **Brewery Museum,** Veleslavínova 6, which traces the history of brewing from ancient times. (Open daily 10am-6pm. 60Kč, students 30Kč.) Stroll through the town center and the **Kopecký gardens** (Kopeckého sady) at the end of Františkánská, then cap off the day with dinner at **U Salzmannů ❸,** Pražská 8, the city's oldest beerhouse. (Entrees 62-163Kč. Beer 20Kč. Open M-Sa 11am-11pm, Su 11am-10pm.) **Buses** leave from Husova 58 for Karlovy Vary (1¾hr., 17 per day, 76Kč) and Prague (2hr., every hr., 66Kč). To reach the main square, Nám. Republiky, turn left on Husova, which becomes Smetanovy sady, then turn left on Bedřicha Smetany (15min.).

ČESKÉ BUDĚJOVICE   ☎038

České Budějovice is a great base for exploring the surrounding region's many wonders. The town was known as Budweis in the 19th century, inspiring the name of popular but pale North American Budweiser, which bears little relation to the malty local *Budvar.* Today, rivalry still lingers between Anheuser-Busch and the **Budvar Brewery,** Karoliny Světlé 4, which can be reached from the center by buses #2 and 4. (Tours 9am-4pm. English tours 120Kč, in Czech and for students 70Kč; includes tasting.) Cobblestone **Náměstí Přemysla Otakara II,** surrounded by colorful Renaissance and Baroque buildings, is the largest square in the country. More than 100 motorcycles dating from the early 1900s to today are displayed at the **Museum of Motorcycles** in

IN RECENT NEWS

THE ROMA DILEMMA

In nearly every city, hostel owners will warn you to watch your wallet around the gypsies. The Roma dilemma stares Czech society in the face everyday; many situations and stereotypes serve as constant reminders that something needs to be done. Around 75-90% of Roma in the Czech Republic are unemployed, giving them a standard of living far below that of the average citizen.

Illiteracy rates are also high and unlikely to improve, as schooling for Roma children is poor. Many never attend school, and those who do are often relegated to schools for the mentally challenged. The situation worsens as Roma families are pushed out of city centers into run-down homes where they are separated from the rest of society.

The European Union has urged the Czech Republic to provide better services for the Roma and to halt the blatant discrimination they face. The EU has, in fact, gone so far as to warn the Czech Republic that they will not be offered membership until they have addressed the Roma question. As the Czech Republic is eagerly hoping to join the EU by 2004, the government has begun to make a serious effort to improve Roma living conditions; among most members of Czech society, however, the perception that the Roma are second-class citizens has diminished little.

Piaristicke nám. The impressive exhibit takes less than 45min. to explore. (Open daily 10am-1:30pm and 2-6pm. 40Kč, students 20Kč.) **Buses** run to: Brno (4½hr., 6 per day, 180-220Kč); Český Krumlov (45min., 15 per day, 30Kč); and Prague (2½hr., 10 per day, 120-144Kč). **Trains** leave from opposite the bus station. The TIC **tourist office**, Nám. Otakara II 2, books private rooms from 250Kč. (☎/fax 635 94 80; infocb@c-budejovice.cz. Open May-Sept. M-F 8:30am-6pm, Sa 8:30am-5pm, Su 10am-4pm; Oct.-Apr. M-F 9am-5pm, Sa 9am-3pm.) To reach the center of town from the train station, turn right on Nádražní, take a left at the first crosswalk, and follow the pedestrian street Lannova třída, which becomes Kanovnická and leads into the square. To reach the friendly **Penzion U Výstaviště ❶**, U Výstaviště 17, from the bus station, take bus #1 five stops to U parku and walk 200m along the street that branches off to the right. (☎724 01 48. Call ahead. First night 250Kč, 200Kč thereafter.) **Večerka grocery** is at Palachého 10; enter on Hroznova. (Open M-F 7am-8pm, Sa 7am-1pm, Su 8am-8pm.) **Restaurance Ameno ❷**, Riegrova 8, serves huge portions of Italian and Mexican fare. From the center of town, take Černé věže and cross the moat onto Jírocova. (Pasta 65-110Kč. Open M-Sa 11am-midnight.) The brewhouse **Česká Rychta ❹**, Nám. Otakara II 30, under Grand Hotel Zvon, has a patio overlooking the square. (Entrees 104-252Kč. Open M-Sa 10am-midnight, Su 10am-11pm.) **Postal code:** 37001.

⌖ DAYTRIP FROM ČESKÉ BUDĚJOVICE: HLUBOKÁ NAD VLTAVOU.
Hluboká's extraordinary **castle** owes its appearance to Eleonora Schwarzenberg, who, after visiting fashionable England, turned the castle into a Windsor-style fairy-tale stronghold in the mid-19th century. A 45min. tour winds through 20 of the castle's 141 ornate rooms. (Open July-Aug. daily 9am-5pm; Apr. and Sept.-Oct. Tu-Su 9am-4:30pm; May-June Tu-Su 9am-5pm. English tours 150Kč, students 80Kč. Czech tours 80Kč/40Kč.) **Buses** run from České Budějovice (25min., 14Kč) frequently during the week but less often on weekends; look for buses with Týn nad Vltavou as their final destination, and get off at Pod Kostolem. Head left on Nad parkovištěm, take a right onto Zborovskám, and then turn right onto Bezručova and head uphill, bearing right at the fork. ☎038.

ČESKÝ KRUMLOV ☎0380

Curving medieval streets, an enormous 13th-century castle, and outdoor activities in the surrounding hills have made UNESCO-protected Český Krumlov one of the most popular spots in Central Europe.

▐▊ TRANSPORTATION AND PRACTICAL INFORMATION. Frequent **buses** arrive from České Budějovice (30-45min., 8-24 per day, 25Kč). To get to the main square, **Náměstí Svornosti,** head up the path from the back of the terminal, near stops #20-25. Go downhill at its intersection with Kaplická, then cross the highway and head onto Horní, which leads into the square. The **tourist office**, Nám. Svornosti 1, books pension rooms (from 600Kč) as well as cheaper private rooms. (☎70 46 22; www.ckrumlov.cz/infocentrum. Open July-Aug. daily 9am-8pm; May-June and Sept. 9am-7pm; Oct.-Apr. 9am-6pm.) **Postal code:** 38101.

▐▐ ACCOMMODATIONS AND FOOD. To reach ▨**Krumlov House ❶**, Rooseveltova 68, which is run by an American expat couple, follow the directions to the square from the station; turn left from Horní onto Rooseveltova after the light, just before the bridge, then follow the signs. (☎71 19 35; krumlovhostels@sendme.cz. Dorms 250Kč; doubles 600Kč; suites 750Kč.) The comfy beds at **Hostel 99 ❷**, Věžní 99, were acquired from a 4-star hotel. From Nám. Svornosti, head down Radniční, which becomes Latran; at the red-and-yellow gate, turn right onto Věžní. (☎71 28

12; www.hostel99.com. Bike rental. Dorms 300Kč; doubles 600Kč.) **Hostel Merlin** ❶, Kájovská 59, is the quietest in town. (☎ (0606) 25 61 45; www.ckrumlov.cz/nahradbach. Dorms 250Kč; doubles 500Kč; triples 750Kč.) From the right-hand corner of Nám. Svornosti, across from the tourist office, angle left onto Kájovská. Just down the street is **Na louži** ❸, Kájovská 66, which serves generous portions of Czech dishes. (85-135Kč. Open daily 10am-10pm.) **Krcma v Šatlavské** ❹, Horní 157, just off the square on the corner of Šatlavská and Masná, features big hunks of meat on a roaring wooden fire. (Meat 95-210Kč. Open daily noon-midnight.) Get groceries at **SPAR**, Linecká 49. (Open M-Sa 7am-6pm, Su 9am-6pm.)

◙◙ **SIGHTS AND NIGHTLIFE.** From Nám. Svornosti, take Radniční across the Vltava as it becomes Latrán to reach the main entrance of the **castle,** whose stone courtyards are free to the public. Two tours cover different parts of the lavish interior, including a frescoed ballroom, a splendid Baroque theater, and Renaissance-style rooms. The eerie galleries of the **crypts** showcase distorted sculptures. Climb the 162 steps of the tower for a fabulous view. (Castle open June-Aug. Tu-Su 9am-6pm; May and Sept. 9am-5pm; Apr. and Oct. 9am-4pm. 1hr. English tour 140Kč, students 70Kč. Crypts open June-Aug. daily 10am-5pm; 20Kč, students 10Kč. Tower open June-Aug. daily 9am-5:30pm; May and Sept. 9am-6pm; Apr. and Oct. 9:30am-4:30pm. 30Kč, students 20Kč.) The castle gardens also host the outdoor **Revolving South Bohemia Theater,** where operas and plays are performed in Czech during the summer. (Open June to early Sept. Shows at 9pm. Tickets at tourist office; 260-390Kč.) The Austrian painter Egon Schiele (1890-1918) lived in Český Krumlov—until residents ran him out for painting burghers' daughters in the nude. The ◙**Egon Schiele International Cultural Center,** Široká 70-72, displays his work, along with paintings by other 20th-century Central European artists. (Open daily 10am-6pm. 150Kč, students 75Kč.)

Rybárská is lined with lively bars and cafes, including **U Hada** (Snake Bar), Rybárská 37 (open M-Th 7pm-3am, F-Sa 7pm-4am, Su 7pm-2am) and **Babylon,** Rybárská 6 (open daily noon-late).

🏃 **OUTDOORS.** Rent a kayak or canoe from **Maleček Boat Rental,** Roosevltova 28, or an inner tube from any hostel to float down the Vltava. Hike into the hills to go horseback riding at **Jezdecký klub Slupenec,** Slupenec 1; from the town center, follow Horní to the highway, take the second left on Křížová, and follow the red trail up to Slupenec. (☎71 10 52; www.jk-slupenec.cz. 250Kč per hr. Call ahead. Open Tu-Sa 9am-6pm.) Rent a bike (300Kč per day) from **Vltava,** Kájovská 62, to cruise the Bohemian countryside or to pedal to **Zlatá Koruna,** a monastery built in 1263.

MORAVIA

The wine-making region of Moravia makes up the eastern third of the Czech Republic. Home to the country's finest folk-singing and two of its leading universities, Moravia is also the birthplace of Sigmund Freud, Johann Gregor Mendel, and Tomáš G. Masaryk, the founder and first president of Czechoslovakia.

BRNO   ☎05

The country's second-largest city, Brno has been an international marketplace since the 13th century. Today, global corporations compete with family-owned produce stands, while historic churches soften the glare of casinos and erotic clubs. The result is a dynamic city that epitomizes the modern Czech Republic.

▣❼ TRANSPORTATION AND PRACTICAL INFORMATION. Trains (☎ 42 21 48 03) go to: Bratislava (2hr., 9 per day, 203Kč); Budapest (4½hr., 2 per day, 864Kč); Prague (3hr., 16 per day, 257Kč); and Vienna (2hr., 1 per day, 543Kč). From the main exit, cross the tram lines on Nádražní, walk left, and then go right on Masarykova to reach **náměstí Svobody,** the main square. **Buses** (☎ 43 21 77 33) leave from Zvonařka, down Plotní from the train station, for Prague (3hr., several per day, 112-167Kč) and Vienna (2½hr., 3 per day, 250Kč). The **tourist office** (Kulturní a informační centrum města Brna), Radnická 8, inside the town hall, books rooms (from 400Kč) and hostels (200Kč). From Nám. Svobody, head down Masarykova and turn right onto Průchodní. (☎ 42 21 10 90; fax 42 21 07 58. Open M-F 8am-6pm, Sa-Su 9am-5pm.) **Internet Center Cafe,** Masarykova 2/24, has speedy computers in the center of town. (40Kč per hr. Open daily 8am-midnight.) **Postal code:** 601 00.

▐ ◖ ACCOMMODATIONS AND FOOD. From the train station, take Masarykova and turn right on Josefská; at the fork, veer right onto Novobranská to reach the clean, new **Hotel Astorka ❶,** at #3. (☎ 42 51 03 70; astorka@jamu.cz. Open July-Aug. Doubles 420Kč per person, students 210Kč; triples 315Kč/158Kč.) The beautifully furnished rooms in **Pension U Leopolda ❸,** Jeneweinova 49, have private baths. Take tram #12 or bus #a12 to Komarov, go left on Studnici, and then turn right on Jeneweinova. (☎ 45 23 30 36. Singles 578Kč; doubles 751Kč; triples 982Kč.) Enjoy a Czech feast amidst medieval paraphernalia at **Dávné Časy ❸,** Starobrněnská 20, up Starobrněnská from Zelny trh. (Main dishes 99-189Kč. Open daily 11am-11pm.) Students chill at **Livingstone ❶,** Dominikánske nám. 5, a tribal-themed pub. From Nám. Svobody, take Zámečnická and go left on Dominikánske nám. (Main dishes 50-110Kč; beer 20Kč. Open M-F 10am-2am, Sa-Su 5pm-2am.) A **Tesco** supermarket is behind the train station. (Open M-F 7am-8pm, Sa 7am-7pm, Su 8am-6pm.)

▣ ▐ SIGHTS AND NIGHTLIFE. In the 18th century, monks at the **Capuchin Monastery Crypt** (Hrobka Kapucínského kláštera), just left of Masarykova from the train station, developed an embalming technique that preserved more than 100 bodies. (Open May-Sept. M-F 9am-noon and 2-4:30pm, Sa 11-11:45am and 2-4:30pm. 40Kč, students 20Kč.) From Nám. Svobody, take Zámečnická and go right on Panenská; after Husova, head uphill to reach **Špilberk Castle** (Hrad Špilberk), which was used as a prison through several eras. (Open May-Sept. Tu-Su 9am-6pm; Oct. and Apr. 9am-5pm; Nov.-Mar. W-Su 9am-5pm. 90Kč, students 45Kč.) The newly expanded **Mendelianum,** Mendlovo nám. 1a, documents the life and work of Johann Gregor Mendel, who founded modern genetics in a Brno monastery. (Open Tu-Su 10am-6pm. 80Kč, students 40Kč.) On Petrov Hill, up Petrska from Zelný trh., is **Peter and Paul Cathedral** (Biskupská katedrála sv. Petra a Pavla). Brno was allegedly saved from a Swedish siege in 1645 when the attacking general told his army he would withdraw if they hadn't captured the town by noon. The folks of Brno rang the cathedral's bells early, and the Swedes slunk away; ever since, the bells have struck noon at 11am. (Cathedral open M-Sa 6:15am-6:15pm, Su 7am-6pm. Free.) In summer, **techno raves** are common; look for posters. Students frequent the dance club **Mersey,** Minská 14. Take tram #3 or 11 from Česká to Tábor. (Beer 19Kč. Open M-Sa 8pm-late.) After performances in the attached Merry Goose Theater, artsy crowds gather at **Divadelní hospoda Veselá husa,** Zelný trh. 9. (Open M-F 11am-1am, Sa-Su 3pm-1am.)

▐ DAYTRIPS FROM BRNO

TELČ. In enchanting Telč, local children perform traditional folk songs and dances each Sunday. The town's Italian aura results from the crew of artists and craftsmen that the town's ruler brought from Genoa in 1546. As you cross the cobblestone footbridge to the main square—flanked by long arcades of peach gables and time-worn terra-cotta roofs—it's easy to see why UNESCO designated the gingerbread town a World Heritage Monument. Two 45min. tours of Telč's **castle** are available. The more interesting *trasa A* leads you through Renaissance hallways, through the old chapel, and under extravagant ceilings; *trasa B* goes through rooms decorated in later styles. (Open May-Aug. Tu-Su 9am-noon and 1-5pm; Mar.-Apr. and Sept.-Oct. closes 1hr. earlier. Tours 60Kč, students 30Kč; English tour 120Kč.) Rent a **rowboat** from Půjčovná lodí to view the castle and town from the swan-filled lake. (Open June 20-Aug. daily 10am-8pm. 20Kč per 30min.) **Buses** running between Brno and České Budějovice stop at Telč (2hr., 8 per day, 80-85Kč). From the station, follow the walkway and turn right on Tyršova, left on Masarykovo, and pass under the archway on the right to reach **náměstí Zachariáše Hradce,** the main square. The **tourist office,** Nám. Zachariáše Hradce 10, is in the town hall. (☎724 31 45; www.telc-etc.cz. Open M-F 8am-6pm, Sa-Su 9am-6pm.) ☎**066.**

MORAVSKÝ KRAS. The Moravský Kras cave network lies in the forested hills of Southern Moravia. The tour of ◨**Punkevní** passes magnificent stalactites and stalagmites to emerge at **Stepmother Abyss** (Propast Macocha), then finishes with a boat ride down the eerily calm underground **Punkva River.** (Tours Apr.-Sept. 8:20am-3:50pm; Oct.-Mar. 8:20am-2pm. Buy tickets at the Skalní Mlýn bus stop or at the entrance; arrive early, as tours sell out quickly. 80Kč, students 40Kč.) BVV in Brno, Starobrněnská 20, organizes **afternoon tours** of Punkevní. (☎42 21 77 45. 640Kč per person, 4 person minimum.) Other caves in the area are also open to visitors, and the Moravský Kras Reserve has many leisurely **hiking trails.** For a great view of Stepmother Abyss, take a **cable car** (60Kč, students 40Kč) to the top. To reach the crystal-clear **swimming hole,** follow the tracks from the Blansko train station 200m toward Brno. A **train** runs from Brno to Blansko (30min., 7 per day, round-trip 43Kč). The Blansko bus station is up the road from the trains; take the bus (15min., 5 per day, 8Kč) to Skalní Mlýn or hike the 8km green trail. At Skalní Mlýn, there is a ticket and info **office** (☎41 35 75; www.cavemk.cz). To reach the caves from Skalní Mlýn, take a shuttle (round-trip 40Kč, students 30Kč) or walk 1.5km along the road. ☎**0506.**

DENMARK
(DANMARK)

Like Thumbelina, the heroine of native son Hans Christian Andersen's fairy tales, Denmark has a tremendous personality crammed into a tiny body. Danes delight in their eccentric traditions, such as burning witches in effigy on Midsummer's Eve and eating pickled herring on New Year's Day. Although the Danes are justifiably proud of their fertile farmlands and pristine beaches, their sense of self-criticism is reflected in the Danish literary canon: the more famous voices are Andersen, Søren Kierkegaard, and Karen Blixen. Located between Sweden and Germany, the country is the geographic and cultural bridge between Scandinavia and continental Europe, made up of the Jutland peninsula and the islands of Zealand, Funen, Lolland, Falster, and Bornholm, as well as some 400 smaller islands, some of which are not inhabited. With its Viking past behind it, Denmark now has one of the most comprehensive social welfare structures in the world, and liberal immigration policies have diversified the erstwhile homogeneous population. Today, Denmark has a progressive youth culture that beckons travelers to the hip pub scene in Copenhagen. Contrary to the suggestion of a certain English playwright, very little seems to be rotten in the state of Denmark.

FACTS AND FIGURES

Official Name: Kingdom of Denmark.
Capital: Copenhagen.
Major Cities: Aalborg, Århus, Odense.
Population: 5,360,000.
Land Area: 42,394 sq. km.

Time Zone: GMT +1.
Languages: Danish, Faroese, Greenlandic.
Religions: Evangelical Lutheran (91%), other Protestant/Roman Catholic (2%).

DISCOVER DENMARK

Begin in chic, progressive **Copenhagen** (p. 273), where you can cruise the canals, party until dawn, and ponder Kierkegaard. Daytrip north to the fabulous **Louisiana** museum (p. 280) and **Elsinore** (p. 282), Hamlet's castle, or shoot south to **Roskilde** (p. 281) and the fascinating Viking Ship Museum (p. 281). If you time it right, you'll hit the massive **Roskilde Festival,** when rock takes over the city. For the best beaches in Denmark, ferry to the island of **Bornholm** (p. 283). Move west over the Storebæltsbro bridge to the island of **Funen** (p. 284), including **Odense** (p. 284), the hometown of Hans Christian Andersen, then head south to the stunning 16th-century castle **Egeskov Slot** (p. 284). From the southern end of Funen, hop on a ferry to the idyllic island of **Ærø** (p. 285), a throwback to the Denmark of several centuries ago. Cross the Lillebælt to Jutland, where laid-back **Århus** (p. 286) delights with students and culture, then play with blocks at nearby **Legoland** (p. 288). On your way back down south, stop in historic **Ribe** (p. 289).

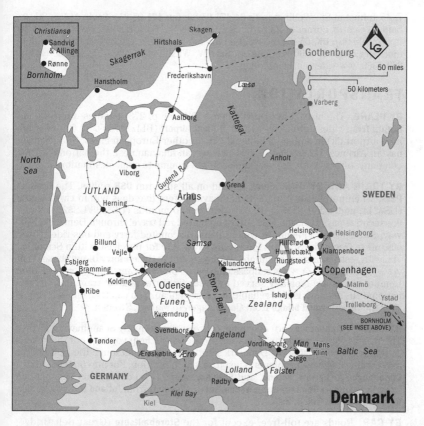

ESSENTIALS

WHEN TO GO

Considering its northern location, Denmark's climate is more solar than polar and more dry than wet. The four seasons are distinct, winters are relatively mild, and even summers aren't very warm.

DOCUMENTS AND FORMALITIES

VISAS. South Africans need a visa for stays of any length. Citizens of Australia, Canada, New Zealand, and the US do not need a visa for stays of up to 90 days. Citizens of the EU may stay for as long as they like.

EMBASSIES. Foreign embassies are in Copenhagen (see p. 273). Danish embassies at home include: **Australia,** 19 Arkana St., Yarralumla, Canberra, ACT 2600 (☎ 02 62 73 25 01; fax 62 73 33 92); **Canada,** 47 Clarence St., Suite 450, Ottawa, ON K1N 9K1 (☎ 613-562-1811; www.tradecomm.com/danish); **Ireland,** 121 St. Stephen's Green, Dublin 2 (☎ 01 475 64 04; www.denmark.ie); **New Zealand** (consulate), Level

7, 45 Johnston St., Wellington (☎04 471 05 20; fax 471 05 21); **South Africa,** 8th fl., Sanlam Centre, corner of Pretorius and Andries St., Pretoria 0002 (☎012 322 05 95; fax 322 05 96); **UK,** 55 Sloane St., London SW1X 9SR (☎020 333 02 00; www.denmark.org.uk); **US,** 3200 Whitehaven St. NW, Washington, D.C. 20008-3683 (☎202-234-4300; www.denmarkemb.org).

TRANSPORTATION

BY PLANE. The airport in Copenhagen (CPH; see p. 273) handles international flights from cities around the world. **Billund Airport** (BLL; ☎76 50 50 50; www.billund-airport.dk) in Jutland handles flights to other European cities. SAS (Scandinavian Airlines; US ☎800-437-5804; www.scandinavian.net), the national airline company, offers youth, spouse, and senior discounts to some destinations.

BY TRAIN AND BY BUS. Eurail is valid on all state-run **DSB** routes. The **Scanrail Pass,** when purchased outside Scandinavia, offers five days within two months (US$214, under 26 US$161), 10 days within two months (US$288/US$216), or 21 consecutive days (US$332/US$249) of unlimited rail travel through Denmark, Norway, Sweden, and Finland, as well as many discounted ferry and bus rides (from 50% off to free). The Scanrail Pass is also available for purchase within Scandinavia, with restrictions on the number of days spent in the country of purchase. Visit www.scanrail.com or www.railpass.com/eurail/passes/scanrail.htm for more info. Remote towns are typically served by **buses** from the nearest train station. The national **bus** network is also reliable and fairly cheap. You can take buses or trains over the new **Øresund bridge** from Copenhagen to Malmö, Sweden.

BY FERRY. Railpasses earn discounts or free rides on many Scandinavian ferries. The free *Vi Rejser* newspaper, at tourist offices, can help you sort out the dozens of smaller ferries that serve Denmark's outlying islands, although the best bet for overcoming language problems is just to ask at the station. For info on ferries from **Copenhagen** to **Norway, Poland,** and **Sweden,** see p. 273. For more on connections from **Bornholm** to **Germany** and **Sweden,** see p. 283, and from **Jutland** to **England, Norway,** and **Sweden,** see p. 286

BY CAR. Roads are toll-free, except for the **Storebæltsbro** (Great Belt Bridge; 210kr) and the **Øresund bridge** (around 220kr). **Car rental** is generally around US$75 per day, plus insurance and a per-kilometer fee; to rent a car, you must be at least 21 years old (in some cases even 25). Speed limits are 50kph (30mph) in urban areas, 80kph (50mph) on highways, and 110kph (68mph) on motorways. **Service centers** for motorists, called Info-terias, are spaced along Danish highways. **Gas** averages 6.50kr per liter. Watch out for bikes, which have the right-of-way. Driving in cities is discouraged by high parking prices and numerous one-way streets. For more info on driving in Denmark, contact the **Forenede Danske Motorejere (FDM),** Firskovvej 32, Box 500, 2800 Kgs. Lyngby (☎70 13 30 40; fax 45 27 09 33; www.fdm.dk).

BY BIKE AND BY THUMB. Flat terrain, well-marked bike routes, bike paths in the countryside, and raised bike lanes on most streets in towns and cities make Denmark a cyclist's dream. You can **rent bikes** (55-65kr per day) from some tourist offices, rental shops, and a few train stations. The **Dansk Cyklist Forbund** (Danish Cycle Federation), Rømersg. 7, 1362 Copenhagen K (☎33 32 31 21; fax 33 32 76 83; www.dcf.dk), can hook you up with longer-term rentals. For info on bringing your bike on a train (which costs 50kr or less), pick up *Bikes and Trains* at any train station. **Hitchhiking** is illegal on motorways and uncommon. *Let's Go* does not recommend hitchhiking.

TOURIST SERVICES AND MONEY

EMERGENCY **Police, Ambulance,** and **Fire: ☎ 112.**

TOURIST OFFICES. Contact the main tourist board in Denmark at Vesterbrog. 6D, 1620 Copenhagen V (☎ 33 11 14 15; dt@dt.dk; www.visitdenmark.dt.dk).

MONEY. The Danish unit of currency is the **krone (kr),** divided into 100 *øre.* The easiest way to get cash is from **ATMs; Cirrus** and **PLUS** cash cards are widely accepted, and many machines give advances on credit cards. Denmark has a high cost of living; expect to spend from 226kr (hostels and supermarkets) to 490kr-566kr (cheap hotels and restaurants) per day. The European Union imposes a **value-added tax (VAT)** on goods and services purchased within the EU, which is included in the price (see p. 15). Denmark's **value-added tax (VAT)** is one of the highest in Europe (25%). You can get a VAT refund upon leaving the country for purchases in any one store that total over 300kr.

DANISH KRONE		
AUS$1 = 4.08KR		10KR = AUS$2.45
CDN$1 = 4.80KR		10KR = CDN$2.08
EUR€1 = 7.43KR		10KR = EUR€1.35
NZ$1 = 3.49KR		10KR = NZ$2.87
ZAR1 = 0.70KR		10KR = ZAR14.44
UK£ = 11.66KR		10KR = UK£0.86
US$1 = 7.45KR		10KR = US$1.34

BUSINESS HOURS. Shops are normally open M-Th from about 9 or 10am to 6pm and F until 7 or 8pm; they are always open Sa mornings. Shops in Copenhagen stay open all day Sa). Regular **banking** hours are M-F 9:30am-4pm, Th until 6pm.

COMMUNICATION

PHONE CODES **Country code: 45. International dialing prefix: 00.**

TELEPHONES. There are no separate city codes; include all digits for local and international calls. Buy phone cards at post offices or kiosks (30 units 30kr; 53 units 50kr; 110 units 100kr). For **domestic directory info,** call ☎ 118; **international info,** ☎ 113; collect calls, ☎ 141. International direct dial numbers include: **AT&T,** ☎ 8001 0010; **British Telecom,** ☎ 8001 0290; **Canada Direct,** ☎ 8001 00 11; **Ireland Direct,** ☎ 8001 03 53; **MCI,** ☎ 8001 0022; **Sprint,** ☎ 8001 0877; **Telecom New Zealand,** ☎ 8001 0064; **Telkom South Africa,** ☎ 8001 0027; **Telstra Australia,** ☎ 8088 0543.

MAIL. Mailing a postcard/letter to Australia, Canada, New Zealand, the US, or South Africa costs 5.50kr; to elsewhere in Europe 4.50kr. Domestic mail costs 4kr.

LANGUAGES. Danish. The Danish add *æ* (like the "e" in "egg"), *ø* (like the "i" in "first"), and *å* (sometimes written as *aa;* like the "o" in "lord") to the end of the alphabet; thus Århus would follow Viborg in an alphabetical listing of cities. Knowing *ikke* ("not") will help you figure out such signs as "No smoking" *(ikke-ryger); aben/lukket* (O-ben/loock-et) means open/closed. Nearly all Danes speak flawless English, but a few Danish words might help break the ice: try *skal* (skoal), or "cheers." Danish has a distinctive glottal stop known as a *stød.*

ACCOMMODATIONS AND CAMPING

DENMARK	❶	❷	❸	❹	❺
ACCOMMODATIONS	under 76kr	76-95kr	96-130kr	131-200kr	over 200kr

While Denmark's **hotels** are generally expensive (300-850kr per night), the country's more than 100 **HI youth hostels** *(vandrehjem)* are cheap (dorms less than 100kr per night; nonmembers add 25kr), are well-run, and have no age limit. They are also given an official ranking of one to five stars, based on facilities and service. Sheets cost about 45-50kr. Breakfasts usually run 45kr and dinners 65kr. Reception desks normally close for the day around 8 or 9pm, although some are open 24hr. Reservations are highly recommended, especially in summer and near beaches. Make sure to arrive before check-in to confirm your reservation. For more info, contact the **Danish Youth Hostel Association,** Vesterbrog. 39, in Copenhagen. (☎31 31 36 12; www.danhostel.dk. Open M-Th 9am-4pm, F 9am-3pm.) Tourist offices offer the *Danhostel* booklet, which also has more information, and many book rooms in private homes (125-175kr).

Denmark's 525 official **campgrounds** (about 60kr per person) rank from one-star (toilets and drinking water) to three-star (showers and laundry) to five-star (swimming, restaurants, and stoves). You'll need either a **Camping Card Scandinavia,** available at campgrounds (1-year 80kr), or a **Camping Card International.** Campsites affiliated with hostels generally do not require this card. If you only plan to camp for a night, you can buy a 24hr. pass (20kr). The **Danish Camping Council** *(Campingradet;* ☎39 27 80 44) sells the campground handbook, *Camping Denmark,* and passes. Sleeping in train stations, in parks, or on public property is illegal.

FOOD AND DRINK

DENMARK	❶	❷	❸	❹	❺
FOOD	under 40kr	40-70kr	71-100kr	101-130kr	over 130kr

A "Danish" in Denmark is a *wienerbrød* ("Viennese bread"), found in bakeries alongside other flaky treats. For more substantial fare, Danes favor open-faced sandwiches called *smørrebrød.* Herring is served in various forms, though usually pickled or raw with onions or a curry mayonnaise. For cheap eats, look for lunch specials *(dagens ret)* and all-you-can-eat buffets *(spis alt du kan* or *tag selv buffet).* National beers are Carlsberg and Tuborg; bottled brew tends to be cheaper. A popular alcohol alternative is *snaps* (or *aquavit),* a clear distilled liquor flavored with fiery spices, usually served chilled and unmixed. Many vegetarian *(vegetarret)* options are the result of Indian and Mediterranean influences, but salads and veggies *(grønsager)* can be found on most menus.

HOLIDAYS & FESTIVALS

Holidays: New Year's (Jan. 1); Queen's Birthday (Apr. 16); Easter Holidays (Apr. 17-21); Worker's Day (May 1); Great Prayer Day (May 16); Ascension Day (May 29); Constitution Day (June 5); Whit Sunday and Monday (June 8-9); Midsummer Eve (June 24); Christmas (Dec. 24-26).

Festivals: Danes celebrate **Fastelavn** (Carneval) in Feb. and Mar. In early July, the **Copenhagen Jazz Festival** hosts a week of concerts, many free. The **Roskilde Festival** is an immense open-air music festival held in Roskilde in late June.

COPENHAGEN (KØBENHAVN)

Despite the swan ponds and cobblestone clichés that Hans Christian Andersen's fairy-tale imagery brings to mind, Denmark's capital is a fast-paced, modern city that offers cafes, nightlife, and style to rival those of the great European cities. But if you're still craving Andersen's Copenhagen, the *Lille Havfrue* (Little Mermaid), Tivoli, and Nyhavn's Hanseatic gingerbread houses are also yours to discover.

⌐ TRANSPORTATION

Flights: Kastrup Airport (CPH; ☎32 47 47 47). S-trains connect the airport to Central Station (12min., every 20min., 21kr).

Trains: Trains stop at **Central Station** (also called Hovedbanegården and København H). Domestic travel ☎70 13 14 15; international ☎70 13 14 16. To: **Berlin** (9hr.; 1 per day; 895kr, under 26 580kr); **Hamburg** (4½hr., 5 per day, 485kr/320kr); **Oslo** (9hr., 3 per day, 740kr/530kr); **Stockholm** (5½hr., 4-5 per day, 700kr/540kr). Reservations mandatory (20kr). For cheaper travel to **Oslo**, Norway, and **Gothenburg, Östersund,** and **Stockholm**, Sweden, buy a **Scanrabat** ticket a week ahead; you must reserve.

Ferries: Scandinavian Seaways (☎33 42 33 42) departs for **Oslo** (16hr.; 5pm; 480-735kr, under 26 315-570kr; Eurail and ScanRail 50% off). Trains to **Sweden** cross over on the **Helsingør-Helsingborg** ferry at no extra charge. **Hydrofoils** (☎33 12 80 88) go to **Malmö**, Sweden from Havneg., at the end of Nyhavn (every hr., 40min., 19-49kr). Both **Flyvebådene** and **Pilen** run hydrofoils to Malmö (every hr. 9am-11pm, 45min., 50kr). **Polferries** (☎33 11 46 45) set out from Ndr. Toldbod, 12A (off Esplanaden) for **Świnoujście,** Poland (10hr.; Su-M and W 8am, Th-F 7:30pm; 340kr, with ISIC 285kr).

Public Transportation: Bus info ☎36 13 14 15 (daily 7am-9:30pm); **train** info ☎33 14 17 01 (daily 6:30am-11pm). **Buses** and **S-trains** (subways and suburban trains; M-Sa 5am-12:30am, Su 6am-12:30am) operate on a zone system; 2-zone **tickets** run 14kr, additional zones 7kr each. The cheaper **rabatkort** (rebate card), available from kiosks and bus drivers, gets you 10 "clips," each good for 1 journey within a specified number of zones. The blue 2-zone *rabatkort* (90kr) can be clipped more than once for longer trips. Tickets and clips allow 1hr. of transfers. The **24hr. pass** (85kr), available at the Tivoli tourist office or any train station, grants unlimited bus and train transport in greater Copenhagen. **Railpasses,** including Eurail, are good on S-trains but not buses. **Night buses,** marked with an "N," run 12:30-5:30am on limited routes and charge double fare; they also accept the 24hr. pass. Copenhagen's newly renovated **Metro** system, opening in three stages in 2002, 2003, and 2006, should make public transportation even more efficient.

Taxis: ☎35 35 35 35; 38 77 77 77; or 38 10 10 10. Base fare 22kr; add 9.50-12.50kr per km. Central Station to airport 150kr.

Bike Rental: City Bike lends bikes for free within a designated area of the city. Deposit 20kr at any of 120 bike racks citywide; retrieve the coin upon return. **Københavns Cykler,** Reventlowsg. 11 (☎33 33 86 13; www.rentabike.dk), in Central Station. 50kr per day, 90kr for 2 days, 125kr for 3 days, 225kr per week; 300kr deposit. Open July-Aug. M-F 8am-5:30pm, Sa 9am-1pm, Su 10am-1pm; Sept.-June closed Su. Bikes are allowed on **trains** for an additional 10kr.

Hitchhiking and Ridesharing: Hitchhiking is illegal on motorways and is not common in Denmark. For info on ridesharing, check out www.nice.person.dk or links at the Use It website, www.useit.dk. *Let's Go* does not recommend hitchhiking.

DENMARK

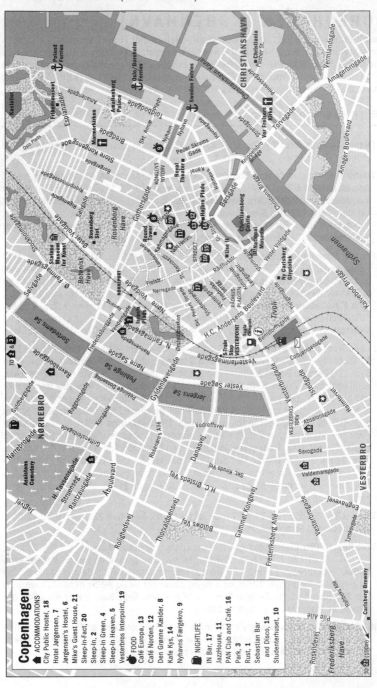

Copenhagen

⬆ ACCOMMODATIONS
City Public Hostel, **18**
Hotel Jørgensen, **7**
Jørgensen's Hostel, **6**
Mike's Guest House, **21**
Sleep-In-Fact, **20**
Sleep-In, **2**
Sleep-In Green, **4**
Sleep-In Heaven, **5**
Vesterbros Interpoint, **19**

🍴 FOOD
Café Europa, **13**
Café Norden, **12**
Den Grønne Kælder, **8**
Kafe Kys, **14**
Nyhavns Færgekro, **9**

🎵 NIGHTLIFE
IN Bar, **17**
JazzHouse, **11**
PAN Club and Café, **16**
Park, **3**
Rust, **1**
Sebastian Bar
and Disco, **15**
Studenterhuset, **10**

DENMARK

✈ ⁊ ORIENTATION AND PRACTICAL INFORMATION

Copenhagen lies on the east coast of the island of **Zealand** (Sjælland), across the Øresund sound from Malmö, Sweden. The 28km **Øresund bridge and tunnel,** which opened July 1, 2000, established the first "fixed link" between the two countries. Copenhagen's **Central Station** lies near the city's heart. North of the station, **Vesterbrogade** passes **Tivoli** and **Rådhuspladsen,** the central square and terminus of most bus lines, then cuts through the city center as **Strøget** (STROY-yet), which is the world's longest pedestrian thoroughfare and goes through a series of names: **Frederiksberggade, Nygade, Vimmelskaftet, Amagertorv,** and **Østergade.** The main pedestrian areas are **Orstedsparken, Botanisk Have,** and **Rosenborg Have.**

TOURIST, FINANCIAL, AND LOCAL SERVICES

Tourist Offices: Wonderful Copenhagen, Bernstorffsg. 1 (☎70 22 24 42; www.visit-copenhagen.dk). Head out the main exit of Central Station and go left, past the back entrance to Tivoli. Open May-Aug. M-Sa 9am-8pm, Su 10am-6pm; Sept.-Apr. M-F 9am-4:30pm, Sa 9am-1:30pm. Consult website for separate accommodations service and info-line hours. **Use It,** Rådhusstr. 13 (☎33 73 06 20; www.useit.dk). From the station, follow Vesterbrog., cross Rådhuspladsen onto Frederiksbergg., and turn right on Rådhusstr. Indispensable and geared toward budget travelers. Pick up a copy of *Play Time,* a comprehensive budget guide to the city. Provides daytime luggage storage, has free Internet access, finds lodgings, and holds mail. Open mid-June to mid-Sept. daily 9am-7pm; mid-Sept. to mid-June M-W 11am-4pm, Th 11am-6pm, F 11am-2pm. The **Copenhagen Card,** sold in hotels, tourist offices, and train stations, grants unlimited travel in North Zealand, discounts on ferries to Sweden, and admission to most sights (24hr. 215kr; 48hr. 375kr; 72hr. 495kr), but may not be worth it unless you plan to ride the bus frequently and see several museums per day. Also check out **www.aok.dk,** a helpful English-language website.

Budget Travel: Wasteels Rejser, Skoubog. 6 (☎33 14 46 33). Open M-F 9am-7pm, Sa 10am-3pm. **Kilroy Travels,** Skinderg. 28 (☎33 11 00 44). Open M-F 10am-5:30pm, Sa 10am-2pm.

Embassies: Australia (consulate), Dampfaergevej 26, 2nd fl. (☎70 26 36 76). **Canada,** Kristen Bernikowsg. 1 (☎33 48 32 00; fax 33 48 32 21). **Ireland,** Østerbaneg. 21 (☎35 42 32 33; fax 35 43 18 58). **New Zealanders** should contact their embassy in Brussels (see p. 115). **South Africa,** Gammel Vartovvej 8 (☎39 18 01 55; www.southafrica.dk). **UK,** Kastelsvej 36-40 (☎35 44 52 00; fax 35 44 52 93). **US,** Dag Hammarskjölds Allé 24 (☎35 55 31 44; www.usembassy.dk).

Currency Exchange: Numerous locations, especially on Strøget. 25kr commission standard. **Forex,** in Central Station. 25kr commission on cash, 15kr per traveler's check. Open daily 8am-9pm. **The Change Group,** Østerg. 61. 25kr commission minimum. Open May-Sept. M-Sa 9am-10pm, Su 10am-8pm; Oct.-Apr. daily 10am-6pm.

Luggage Storage: Free at **Use It** (see tourist offices, above) and most hostels. At **Central Station,** 25-35kr per 24hr. Open M-Sa 5:30am-1am, Su 6am-1am.

Laundromats: Look for **Vascomat** and **Møntvask** chains. At Borgerg. 2, Nansensg. 39, and Istedg. 45. Wash and dry 40-50kr. Most open daily 7am-9pm.

Bi-Gay-Lesbian Resources: Landsforeningen for Bøsser and Lesbiske (National Assoc. for Gay Men and Women), Teglgårdsstr. 13 (☎33 13 19 48; www.lbl.dk). Open M-F 11am-4pm. The monthly *Gay and Lesbian Guide to Copenhagen,* which lists clubs, cafes, and organizations, is available at several gay clubs (see p. 280). Also check out www.copenhagen-gay-life.dk, www.gayonline.dk., or www.panbladet.dk. The city is home to the annual **Mermaid Pride Parade** (www.mermaidpride.dk) each August.

EMERGENCY AND COMMUNICATIONS

Emergencies: ☎112. **Police:** ☎33 14 14 48. Headquarters are at Polititorvet.
Pharmacy: Steno Apotek, Vesterbrog. 6c (☎33 14 82 66). Open 24hr.; ring the bell.
Medical Assistance: Doctors on Call (☎33 93 63 00). Open M-F 8am-4pm; after hours, call ☎38 88 60 41. Visits 120-350kr, cash only. **Emergency rooms** at **Amager Hospital,** Kastrup 63 (☎32 34 32 34), and **Bispebjerg Hospital,** Bispebjerg Bakke 23 (☎35 31 35 31).
Internet Access: Free at **Use It** (see tourist offices, above). **Copenhagen Hovedbibliotek** (Central Library), Krystalg. 15 (☎33 73 60 60). Free. Open M-F 10am-7pm, Sa 10am-2pm. **Boomtown,** Axeltorv 1 (☎33 32 10 32), opposite Tivoli's main entrance. 20kr per first 30min., 30kr per hr. Open 24hr.
Post Office: In Central Station. Address mail to be held: SURNAME Firstname, Post Denmark, Hovedbanegårdens Posthus, Hovedbanegården, **1570** Kobenhavn V. **Use It** (see tourist offices, above) also holds mail. Address mail to: Firstname SURNAME, *Poste Restante,* Use It, 13 Rådhusstræde, **1466** Copenhagen K, DENMARK.

⋒ ⊮ ACCOMMODATIONS AND CAMPING

Comfortable and inexpensive accommodations can be hard to find in the city center, where most hostels are styled like warehouses and packed with 50 or more beds. On the upside, many hostels feature a lively social scene. The price jump between hostels and hotels is significant; for better accommodations, try the **Danhostels** outside the city center. During holidays (such as the national vacation in early August) and the largest festivals—especially Karneval (mid-May), Roskilde (late June), and Copenhagen Jazz (late July)—reserve rooms in advance.

HOSTELS

▧ **Jørgensen's Hostel,** Rømersg. 11 (☎33 13 81 86). 25min. from Central Station, 5min. from Strøget, next to Israels Plads. S-train: Nørreport. Go right along Vendersg.; it's on the left. Very popular; the most centrally located hostel. Breakfast included. Sheets 30kr. Internet 1kr per min. No reservations. Under 35 only. Dorms 125kr. ❸

Sleep-In Fact, Valdemarsg. 14 (☎33 79 67 79; info@sleep-in-fact.dk). From the main exit of Central Station, turn left on Vesterbrog., then left again on Valdemarstr. (10min.). Comfortable rooms in a new factory-turned-hostel. Bikes 50kr per day. Internet 20kr per 30min. Breakfast included. Free luggage storage. Sheets 30kr. Reception daily 6am-3am. Lockout 10am-4pm. Curfew 3am. Open mid-June to Sept. Dorms 120kr. ❸

Sleep-In Heaven, Struenseg. 7 (☎35 35 46 48; sleepinheaven@get2net.dk), in Nørrebro. Take bus #8 (dir.: Tingbjerg) five stops to Rantzausg.; continue in the same direction as the bus, then turn right on Kapelvej, left on Tavsensg., and left on Struenseg. Lively social atmosphere. Close to the hip Skt. Hans Torv nightlife. Internet 20kr per 30min. Breakfast 40kr. Free lockers. Sheets 30kr. Reception daily 7:30am-2am. Dorms 110kr; doubles 450kr. ❸

Sleep-In, Blegdamsvej 132 (☎35 26 50 59). Bus #1, 6, or 14: Trianglen. S-train: Østerport. Facing the station, go left and walk 10min. up Hammerskjölds. Near the city center and Østerbro nightlife. This popular (and noisy) warehouse of a hostel favors quantity over privacy. Kitchen. Internet 6kr per 15min. Sheets 30kr. Reception 24hr. Lockout noon-4pm. Open June 28-Aug. No reservations. Dorms 90kr. ❷

Sleep-In Green, Ravnsborgg. 18, Baghuset (☎35 37 77 77). Take bus #16 from the station to Nørrebrog., and then walk down Ravnsborgg. Cozy, eco-friendly hostel outside the city center. Ragged on the outside, but clean inside. Internet 20kr per 30min. Bikes 30kr per day. Organic breakfast 30kr. Sheets 30kr. Reception 24hr. Check-out noon. Lockout noon-4pm. Open mid-May to mid-Oct. Dorms 95kr. ❷

Vesterbros Interpoint, Vesterbros KFUM (YMCA), Valdemarsg. 15 (☎33 31 15 74). Across the street from Sleep-In Fact (see above). Super-friendly staff, homey atmosphere, and fewer beds per room than other area hostels. Breakfast 25kr. Sheets 15kr. Kitchen. Reception daily 8:30-11:30am, 3:30-5:30pm, and 8pm-12:30am. Curfew 12:30am. Open late June to early Aug. Dorms 85kr. ❷

City Public Hostel, Absalonsg. 8 (☎33 31 20 70; www.city-public-hostel.dk), in the Vesterbro Youth Center. From the station, walk away from the Rådhuspladsen on Vesterbrog. and turn left on Absalonsg. Breakfast 20kr. Lounge, BBQ, and kitchen. Sheets 30kr. Reception 24hr. Open early May to late Aug. Dorms 130kr. ❸

København Vandrerhjem Bellahøj (HI), Herbergvejen 8 (☎38 28 97 15; bellahoj@danhostel.dk), in Bellahøj. Take bus #11 (dir.: Bellahøj/Bronshøj Torv) from the station to Primulavej. Large, clean, and modern, but far from the city center. Bikes 60kr per day. Internet 1kr per min. Breakfast 40kr. Sheets 35kr. Laundry 30kr. Reception 24hr. Lockout 10am-2pm. Dorms 95kr; doubles 275kr. Nonmembers add 30kr. ❷

HOTELS

▩ **Hotel Jørgensen,** Rømersg. 11 (☎33 13 81 86; www.hoteljorgensen.dk). Same ownership as Jørgensen's Hostel (see above) and in the same location. Friendly staff. Breakfast included. Reception 24hr. Singles 475kr; doubles 575kr; triples 725kr. ❺

Mike's Guest House, Kirkevænget 13 (☎36 45 65 40). Bus #6 from Central Station toward Valby Langg. (10min.). Call ahead. Four clean, spacious rooms, some with private balconies, in Mike's own home. Quiet neighborhood near the Carlsberg brewery. Singles 200kr; doubles 290kr; triples 400kr. ❹

CAMPING

Bellahøj Camping, Hvidkildevej 66 (☎38 10 11 50), 5km from the city center. Take bus #11 to "Bellahøj." Shower included. Kitchen, cafe and market. Reception 24hr. Open June-Aug. 58kr per person; tents available for extra charge. ❶

Absalon Camping, Korsdalsvej 132, Rødovre (☎36 41 06 00), 9km from the city center. From Central Station, take bus #550S to "Korsdalsvej/Roskildevej" and ask the driver to let you off at the campsite. Kitchen, laundry (30kr), and store. Reception daily 8am-10pm. 62kr per person, 20kr per tent; cabins 195kr plus 54kr per person. ❷

◘ FOOD

The Vikings left many legacies, pickled herring among them. Around **Kongens Nytorv,** elegant cafes serve *smørrebrød* (open-faced sandwiches) for about 40kr. All-you-can-eat buffets (40-70kr) are popular, especially at Turkish, Indian, and Italian restaurants. **Fakta** and **Netto supermarkets** are budget fantasies; there are several around the Nørreport area (S-train: Nørreport). Open-air **markets** provide fresh fruits and veggies; try the one at **Israels Plads** near Nørreport Station. (Open M-Th 9am-5:30pm, F 9am-6:30pm, Sa 9am-3pm.) **Fruit stalls** line Strøget and the side streets to the north.

Nyhavns Færgekro, Nyhavn 5. Upscale fisherman's cottage atmosphere along the canal. Lunch on 10 varieties of all-you-can-eat herring (89kr). Lunch served 11:30am-5pm. Dinner around 165kr. Open daily 9:30am-11:30pm. ❹

Café Norden, Østerg. 61, on Strøget and Nicolaj Plads, in sight of the fountain. A French-style cafe with the best vantage point on Strøget. Great for people-watching. Lots of good food for a good price. Nachos 45-79kr, sandwiches 62-69kr, salads 82-98kr, pastries 15-40kr, brunch 89kr. Open daily 9am-midnight. ❸

Café Europa, Amagertorv 1, on Nicolaj Plads opposite Café Norden. If Norden is the place to see, then trendy Europa is the place to be seen. Smaller and somewhat pricier. Sandwiches 45-65kr, gourmet salads 89-119kr. Beer 45kr per pint. Great coffee. Open M-W 9am-midnight, F-Sa 9am-1am, Su 10am-7pm. ❸

Kafe Kys, Læderstr. 7, on a quiet street running south of and parallel to Strøget. Vegetarian options, sandwiches, and salads 48-75kr. Beer 24kr. Open M-Th 11am-1am, F-Sa 11am-2am, Su noon-10pm. Kitchen closes daily at 10pm. ❷

Den Grønne Kælder, Pilestr. 48. Popular, classy vegetarian and vegan dining in a casual atmosphere. Hummus 35-45kr, veggie burgers 35kr, salad combo meals 35-80kr. Open M-Sa 11am-10pm. ❷

🄶 SIGHTS

Compact Copenhagen is best seen by foot or bike. Various **tours** are detailed in Use It's *Play Time* and tourist office brochures. The squares along the lively pedestrian Strøget, which divides the city center, are Nytorv, Nicolaj Plads, and Kongens Nytorv. Opposite Kongens Nytorv is Nyhavn, the "new port" where Hans Christian Andersen wrote his first fairy tale. There are several canal tours, but **Netto Boats** offers the best value and covers a lot of sights. (Every 20min. Apr. to mid-Sept. 10am-5pm. 20kr.) Bus #6 travels through Vesterbro and Rådhuspladsen, alongside Strøget, and on to Østerbro, acting as a sight-seeing guide to the city. Wednesday is a great day to visit museums, as most are free.

CITY CENTER. The first sight you'll see as you exit the train station is **Tivoli,** the famed 19th-century **amusement park,** which has botanical gardens, marching toy soldiers, and, of course, rides. Saturday nights and some Sunday and Wednesday nights culminate with music and fireworks. An increasingly popular Christmas market is open mid-November through mid-December. *(Vesterbrog. 3. www.tivoligardens.com. Open mid-June to mid-Aug. Su-Th 11am-midnight, F-Sa 11am-1am; Mid-Aug. to Sept. Su-Tu 11am-11pm, W-Th and Sa 11am-midnight, F 11am-1am. Rides open at 11:30am, children's rides open noon. Admission 55kr; ride tickets 10kr, 1-5 tickets per ride; 1-day admission and unlimited rides 180kr.)* From Central Station, turn right on Bernstorffsg. and left on Tietgensg. to get to the beautiful ▨**Ny Carlsberg Glyptotek** with its collection of ancient and Impressionist art and sculpture and an enclosed Mediterranean garden. *(Dantes Plads 7. Open Tu-Su 10am-4pm. 30kr; free W and Su or with ISIC.)* Continue along Tietgensg., which becomes Stormg., to see Denmark's Viking treasures and other tidbits of cultural history at the **National Museum.** *(Ny Vesterg. 10. ☎33 13 44 11. Open Tu-Su 10am-5pm. 40kr, students 30kr; W free.)* **Christiansborg Castle,** Prins Jørgens Gård, features subterranean ruins, still-in-use royal reception rooms, and the *Folketing* (Parliament) chambers. To get there, continue down Tietgensg. from the city center and cross the canal. *(☎33 92 64 94. Tours of royal reception rooms June-Aug. daily 11am, 1, 3pm; May and Sept. 11am and 3pm; Oct.-Apr. Tu, Th, Sa-Su 11am and 3pm. 40kr, students 30kr. Palace ruins open May-Sept. daily 9:30am-3:30pm; Oct.-Apr. Tu-Th and Sa-Su 9:30am-3:30pm. 20kr. Ask for free Parliament tours.)*

CHRISTIANSHAVN. Climb the golden spire of **Vor Frelsers Kirke** (Our Savior's Church) for a great view of both the city and the water. *(Sankt Annæg. 29. Turn left off Prinsesseg.; or, take bus #8 from Central Station. Church open Mar.-Nov. daily 11am-4:30pm; Dec.-Feb. 10am-2pm. Free. Tower open Mar.-Nov. M-Sa 11am-4:30pm, Su noon-4:30pm. 20kr.)* In the southern section of Christianshavn, the "free city" of **Christiania,** which was founded in 1971 by youthful squatters in abandoned military barracks, is inhabited by a thriving group of artists and alterna-thinkers carrying 70s activism and free love into the new millennium. At Christmas, there is a fabulous **market** with curiosities from all over the world. Exercise caution in the aptly named **Pusher Street** area, the site of *many* hash and marijuana sales. Possession of even small amounts can get you arrested. Always ask before taking pictures, never take pictures on Pusher St. itself, and exercise caution in the area at night.

FREDERIKSTADEN. Edvard Eriksen's **den Lille Havfrue (The Little Mermaid)**, the tiny but touristed statue at the opening of the harbor, honors Hans Christian Andersen. *(S-train: Østerport; turn left out of the station, left on Folke Bernadottes Allé, right on the path bordering the canal, left up the stairs, and then right along the street. Open daily 6am-dusk.)* Head back along the canal and turn left to cross the moat to **Kastellet**, a 17th-century fortress, now with a park. Cross through Kastellet to the **Frihedsmuseet** (Museum of Danish Resistance), a fascinating museum documenting Denmark's efforts to rescue its Jews during the Nazi occupation, as well as its earlier period of acceptance of German "protection." *(At Churchillparken. ☎33 13 77 14. Open May to mid-Sept. Tu-Sa 10am-4pm, Su 10am-5pm; mid-Sept. to Apr. Tu-Sa 11am-3pm, Su 11am-4pm. 30kr; W free.)* From the museum, walk south down Amalieng. to reach the lovely ▩ **Amalienborg Palace**, residence of Queen Margarethe II and the royal family; most of the interior is closed to the public, but the apartments of Christian VII are open. The changing of the palace guard takes place at noon on the brick plaza. *(☎33 12 21 86; www.ses.dk. Open May-Oct. daily 10am-4pm; Nov.-Apr. Tu-Su 11am-4pm. 40kr, students 25kr; combined ticket with Rosenborg Slot (see below) 70kr.)* The 19th-century **Marmokirken** (Marble Church), opposite the palace, features an ornate interior and Europe's third-largest dome, which has a spectacular view of the city and neighboring sound. *(Fredriksg. 4. www.marmorkirken.dk. Open M-Tu and Th 10am-5pm, W 10am-6pm, F-Su noon-5pm. Free. Dome open mid-June to Aug. daily 1 and 3pm; Sept. to mid-June Sa-Su 1 and 3pm. 20kr.)* A few blocks north, **Statens Museum for Kunst** (State Museum of Fine Arts) displays an eclectic collection of Danish and Modern art in a beautifully designed building. From the church, head away from Amalienborg, go left on Store Kongensg., right on Dronningens Tværg., right on Borgerg., and left onto Sølvg. *(Sølvg. 48-50. S-train: Nørreport; walk up Øster Voldg. ☎33 74 84 94; www.smk.dk. Open Tu and Th-Su 10am-5pm, W 10am-8pm. 50kr, under 25 35kr; W free.)* Opposite the museum, **Rosenborg Slot** (Rosenborg Palace and Gardens) hoards royal treasures, including the ▩**crown jewels.** *(Øster Voldg. 4A. S-train: Nørreport; walk up Øster Voldg.; it's on the left past the intersection. ☎33 15 32 86. Open June-Aug. daily 10am-5pm; May and Sept. 10am-4pm; Oct. 11am-3pm; Nov.-Apr. Tu-Su 11am-2pm. 60kr, students 30kr.)*

OTHER SIGHTS. A trip to the **Carlsberg Brewery** will reward you with a wealth of ale-related knowledge and, more importantly, free samples. *(Ny Carlsbergvej 140. Take bus #6 west from Rådhuspladsen to Valby Langg. ☎33 27 13 14; www.carlsberg.com. Open Tu-Su 10am-4pm. Free.)* If the breweries haven't completely confused your senses, go play at the hands-on **Experimentarium** (Danish Science Center). It's geared toward kids but is fun for everyone. *(Tuborg Havnevej 7. Take bus #6 north from Rådhuspladsen. ☎39 27 33 33; www.experimentarium.dk. Open late June to mid-Aug. daily 10am-5pm; late Aug. to early June M and W-F 9am-5pm, Tu 9am-9pm, Sa-Su 11am-5pm. 89kr, children 62kr.)*

🎵🔘 ENTERTAINMENT AND FESTIVALS

For events, consult *Copenhagen This Week* (free at hostels and tourist offices), or pick up *Use It News* from Use It (see above). The **Royal Theater** is home to the world-famous Royal Danish Ballet; the box office is located at Tordenskjoldsg. 7. (Open M-Sa 10am-6pm.) For same-day half-price tickets, head to the **Tivoli ticket office,** Vesterbrog. 3. (☎33 15 10 12. Open mid-Apr. to mid-Sept. daily 10am-8pm; mid-Sept. to mid-Apr. 9am-7pm. Royal Theater tickets available at 4 or 5pm, others at noon.) Call **Arte,** Hvidkildevej 64 (☎38 88 22 22), to ask about student discounts.

Tickets for a variety of events are sold online at www.billetnet.dk. The relaxed **Kul-Kaféen**, Teglgårdsstr. 5, is a great place to see live performers, get info on music, dance, and theater, and grab some food. (Sandwiches 51kr. Open M-Sa 11am-midnight.) During the world-class **Copenhagen Jazz Festival** (☎33 93 20 13; www.cjf.dk) in mid-July, the city teems with free outdoor concerts as well as indoor shows. Other festivals include the **Swingin' Copenhagen** festival in late May (www.swinging-copenhagen.dk) and the **Copenhagen Autumn Jazz** festival in early November.

🎵 NIGHTLIFE

In Copenhagen, weekends often begin on Wednesday, nights rock until 5am, and "morning pubs" open when the clubs close so you can party around the clock. On Thursday, most bars and clubs have reduced covers and cheap drinks. The central **pedestrian district** reverberates with crowded bars and discos. **Kongens Nytorv** has fancier options, but many Danes just buy beer at a supermarket and head for the boats, cafes, and salty charisma of nearby **Nyhavn**. The **Scala** complex, opposite Tivoli, has many bars and restaurants, and students fill the cheaper bars in the **Nørrebro** area. Copenhagen's gay and lesbian scene is one of Europe's best.

▧ Park, Østerbrog. 79, in the Østerbro. Buses #6 and 14. An enormous (and enormously popular) club with 2 packed dance floors, live music hall, and rooftop patio. Pints 40kr. Cover Th-Sa 60kr. Open Th-Sa 11am-5am, Su-M 11am-midnight, Tu-W 11am-2am.

Rust, Guldbergsg. 8, in the Nørrebro. Buses #3, 5, and 16. 20-somethings pack this lively disco. Has places to dance and to chill. Long lines by 1am. Cover 50kr; free before 11pm. Open W-Sa 10pm-5am.

Café Pavillionen, Borgmester Jensens Allé 45, in Fælleaparken. This summer-only outdoor cafe has local bands 8-10pm, plus a disco W-Sa 10pm-5am. On Mondays, enjoy a concert (2:30-5pm), tango lessons (7-8:15pm; 50kr), and dancing until midnight.

IN Bar, Nørreg. 1. Drink cheaply and then dance on the speakers. Th-Sa 20+. F-Sa cover 150kr, includes open bar. Open Su-Th 10pm-5am, F-Sa 10pm-10am.

JazzHouse, Niels Hemmingsens Gade 10 (www.jazzhouse.dk). Turn left off Strøget from Gammeltorv (closer to Råhuspladsen) and Nytorv. Copenhagen's premier jazz venue makes for a sophisticated and potentially expensive evening. Cover depends on performer. Concerts Su-Th 8:30pm, F-Sa 9:30pm. Dance club open daily midnight-5am.

PAN Club and Café, Knabrostr. 3. Gay cafe, bar, and disco. Homoguide available. Cover W 30kr, F-Sa 50kr; Th no cover. Cafe opens daily 8pm; disco opens 11pm, and gets going around 1am. Both open late.

Sebastian Bar and Disco, Hyskenstr. 10, off Strøget. The city's best-known gay and lesbian bar. Relaxed, welcoming atmosphere. Homoguide available. Happy Hour 5-9pm. Open daily noon-2am.

Studenterhuset, Købmagerg. 52. Laid-back environment, popular with Copenhagen's students. Cheap bar with student discounts. W international, Th live jazz, F rock. Open M and Th noon-midnight, Tu noon-6pm, W noon-1am, F noon to 2 or 5am.

🎒 DAYTRIPS FROM COPENHAGEN

Stunning castles and white sand beaches hide in North and Central Zealand. Trains offer easy access to many attractive daytrips within an hour of Copenhagen.

HUMLEBÆK AND RUNGSTED. Humlebæk distinguishes itself with the spectacular ▧**Louisiana Museum of Modern Art,** 13 Gl. Strandvej, which contains works by Picasso, Warhol, Lichtenstein, Calder, and other 20th-century masters; the building and its beautifully landscaped, sculpture-studded grounds overlooking the sea are themselves worth the trip. Follow signs 1.5km north from the Humlebæk station or take bus #388. (☎49 19 07 19. Open Th-Tu 10am-5pm, W 10am-10pm. 68kr, students 60kr.) The quiet harbor town of **Rungsted** is where Karen Blixen (pseudonym Isak Dinesen) wrote *Out of Africa*. The **Karen Blixen Museum,** Rungsted Strandvej 111, houses her abode, personal belongings, and grave. Follow the street leading out of the train station and turn right on Rungstedsvej, then right again on Rungsted Strandvej; or, take bus #388 (2 per hr.) and tell the driver your destination. (☎45 57 10 57. Open May-Sept. Tu-Su 10am-5pm; Oct.-Apr. W-F 1-4pm, Sa-Su 11am-4pm. 35kr.) Both Humlebæk (45min., 38.50kr or 4 clips) and Rungsted (30min., 40kr or 4 clips on the blue *rabatkort*) are on the Copenhagen-Helsingør northern **train** line.

HILLERØD AND FREDENSBORG. Hillerød is home of the moated ◙**Frederiksborg Slot,** arguably the most impressive of North Zealand's castles. Free concerts are given Thursdays at 1:30pm on the famous 1610 **Esaias Compenius organ.** From the station, cross the street onto Vibekeg. and follow the signs. (Castle open Apr.-Oct. daily 10am-5pm; Nov.-Mar. 11am-3pm. 50kr, students 40kr. Gardens open May-Aug. daily 10am-9pm; Sept. and Apr. 10am-7pm; Oct. and Mar. 10am-5pm; Nov.-Feb. 10am-4pm. Free.) A final stop on the northern castle tour is **Fredensborg Palace.** Built in 1722, the castle still serves as the spring and fall royal residence. Follow the signs from the station. (☎33 40 31 87. Palace open July daily 1-4:30pm; mandatory tours every 15-30min.; call ahead about tours in English (2 per day). 30kr. Outlying gardens always open. Private gardens open July daily 9am-5pm. Free.) Hillerød is at the end of **S-train** lines A and E (40min., 42kr). Fredensborg is on the Lille Nord rail line connecting Hillerød and Helsingør. The **tourist office,** located in a kiosk down the hill from the palace, has information about seasonal boating on Lake Esrum. (☎48 48 21 00. Open June-Aug. M-F 10am-5pm, Sa 10am-3pm, Su 11am-3pm; Sept.-May M-F 10am-4pm, Sa 10am-1pm.)

ROSKILDE. Roskilde, in Central Zealand, served as Denmark's first capital when King Harald Bluetooth built the country's first Christian church here in AD 980. The ornate sarcophagi of the red-brick ◙**Roskilde Domkirke** in Domkirkepladsen hold most of the Danish monarchs since the Reformation. (☎46 35 27 00. Open Apr.-Sept. M-Sa 9am-4:45pm, Su 12:30-4:45pm; Oct.-Mar. Tu-Sa 10am-3:45pm, Su 12:30-3:45pm. 15kr, students 10kr. Free organ concerts June-Aug. Th 8pm.) The **Viking Ship Museum,** Vindeboder 12, near Strandengen along the harbor, houses remnants of five trade ships and warships sunk circa 1060 and salvaged in the late 1960s. From the tourist office, it is a pleasant walk to the cathedral and downhill through the park, or take bus #605 (dir.: Boserup). In summer, book a ride on a Viking longboat, but be prepared to take an oar— Viking conquest is no spectator sport. (☎46 30 02 00; www.vikingeskibsmuseet.dk. Museum open May-Sept. daily 9am-5pm; Oct.-Apr. 10am-4pm. May-Sept. 60kr; Oct.-Apr. 45kr. Boat trip 40kr, without museum ticket 80kr; book ahead.) Roskilde hosts one of Europe's largest **music festivals** (June 26-29 2003; ☎46 36 66 13; www.roskilde-festival.dk), drawing over 90,000 fans with such big-name bands as REM, U2, Radiohead, Smashing Pumpkins, and Metallica. Roskilde is accessible by **train** from Copenhagen (25-30min., 38.50kr or 4 clips). The **tourist office,** Gullandsstr. 15, sells festival tickets and books rooms for a 25kr fee and a 10-15% deposit. From the train station, turn left on Jernbaneg., right on Allehelgansg., and left again on Barchog.; it's on the left. (☎46 35 27 00. Open July-Aug. M-F 9am-6pm, Sa 10am-2pm; Apr.-June M-F 9am-5pm, Sa 10am-1pm; Sept.-Mar. M-Th 9am-5pm, F 9am-4pm, Sa 10am-1pm.) Although close enough to Copenhagen to be an easy daytrip, Roskilde's accommodations are nice enough to make staying the night a tempting option. The **HI Youth Hostel ❸**, Vindeboder 7, is on the harbor next to the Viking Museum shipyard. The gorgeous, modern facility is always booked during the festival. (☎46 35 21 84; www.danhostel.dk/roskilde. Reception 8am-noon and 4-10pm. Open Feb.-Dec. Dorms 100kr, nonmembers 115kr.) **Roskilde Camping ❶**, Baunehøjvej 7, is on the beach, 4km north of town; take bus #603 toward Veddelev to Veddelev Byg. (☎46 75 79 96. Reception 8am-9pm. Open Apr. to mid-Sept. 62kr per person.)

CHARLOTTENLUND AND KLAMPENBORG. Charlottenlund and Klampenborg, on the coastal line, feature topless **beaches.** Although less ornate than Tivoli, **Bakken,** the world's oldest amusement park, delivers more thrills. From the Klampenborg train station, turn left, cross the overpass, and head through the park. (☎39 63 73 00. Open July to early Sept. daily noon-midnight; mid-Sept. to Apr. M-F 2pm-midnight, Sa 1pm-midnight, Su noon-midnight. Entrance free. Rides open 2pm; 30-35kr each.) Bakken borders the **Jægersborg Deer Park,** the royal family's former hunting grounds. Still home to wooded paths, their **Eremitage** summer chateau, and over 2000 Red and Japanese sika deer, it is perfect for picnics and strolling. Charlottenlund and Klampenborg are both at the end of the **S-train** line C.

HELSINGØR AND HORNBÆK. Helsingør is evidence of the Danish monarchy's fondness for lavish architecture. The 15th-century **Kronborg Slot,** also known as **Elsinore,** is the setting for Shakespeare's *Hamlet* (although neither the historical "Amled" nor the Bard ever visited Kronborg). A statue of Viking chief Holger Danske sleeps in the castle's spooky casemates; according to legend, he will awake to face any threat to Denmark's safety. The castle also houses the **Danish Maritime Museum,** which contains a sea biscuit (the world's oldest, in fact) from 1852. From the train station, turn left and follow the signs along the waterfront to the castle. (☎49 21 30 78. Open May-Sept. daily 10:30am-5pm; Apr. and Oct. Tu-Su 11am-4pm; Nov.-Mar. Tu-Su 11am-3pm. 60kr.) Helsingør is at the end of the northern line (1hr.). The **tourist office,** Havnepladsen 3, is in the Kulturhuset, the large brick building across the street to the left of the station; the entrance is around the corner. (☎49 21 13 33. Open mid-June to Aug. M-Th 9am-5pm, F 9am-6pm, Sa 10am-3pm; Sept. to mid-June M-F 9am-4pm, Sa 10am-1pm.) **Hornbæk,** a small, untouristed fishing town near Helsingør, offers beautiful beaches. The town hosts a wild **harbor festival** on the fourth weekend in July. Bus #340 runs from Helsingør to Hornbæk (20min., 20kr).

◪ NEAR COPENHAGEN

MØN. To see what H.C. Andersen called one of the most beautiful spots in Denmark, head south of Copenhagen to the isle of Møn. Locals travel to Møn to explore the gorgeous chalk cliffs and the pastoral landscape. **Liselund Slot,** the only thatched castle in the world, is surrounded by a lush park with many hiking trails. Take the train from Copenhagen to Vordingborg (1½hr.), then bus #62 or 64 from **Stege** (45min., 33kr). From Stege, take bus #632 (30min., 3 per day), to **Liselund Slot,** the only thatched castle in the world, which is surrounded by a lush park with many hiking trails, or continue on to the cliffs of **Møns Klint.** The **Møns Turistbureau,** Storeg. 2, is next to the bus stop in Stege. (☎55 86 04 00; www.moentouristbureau.dk. Open June 15-Aug. M-F 10am-5pm, Sa 9am-6pm, Su 11am-1pm; Sept.-June 14 M-F 10am-5pm, Sa 9am-noon.) Stay at the lakeside **youth hostel (HI) ❸**, Langebjergvej 1. (☎55 81 20 30. Breakfast 45kr. Sheets 30-45kr. Reception 8am-noon and 4-8pm. Dorms 100kr; singles 225-280kr; doubles 270-280kr.)

BORNHOLM

In an area ideal for bikers and nature-lovers, Bornholm's red-roofed cliffside villas may seem Mediterranean, but the flowers and half-timbered houses are undeniably Danish. The unique round churches were both places of worship and fortresses for waiting out pirate attacks. The sandiest and longest **beaches** are at **Dueodde**, on the island's southern tip. For more info, check out www.bornholminfo.dk.

☎ TRANSPORTATION. Trains from Copenhagen to **Ystad, Sweden** are timed to meet the ferry to **Rønne**, Bornholm's capital (train ☎70 13 14 15; 1¾hr., 5-6 per day; ferry 1½hr.; total trip 205kr, under 26 180kr.) A cheaper option is the combo bus/ferry trip (bus ☎56 95 18 66; 1½hr., 4-6 per day; ferry 1½hr.; total trip 195kr, under 26 145kr.) Overnight ferries from Copenhagen to Rønne leave at 11:30pm and arrive in Rønne at 6:30am (224kr). **Bornholmstrafikken** (Rønne ☎56 95 18 66, M-F 9am-5pm; Copenhagen ☎33 13 18 66; Ystad ☎+46 (411) 558 700; www.bornholm-ferries.dk) offers the combo train/ferry and bus/ferry route and also operates ferries from **Fährhafen Sassnitz** in **Germany** (☎+49 38392 64420; 3½hr., 1-2 per day, 90-130kr). Bornholm has an efficient local BAT **bus** service. (☎56 95 21 21; 34kr to Gudhjem or Sandvig-Allinge, 42.50kr to Svaneke; 24hr. pass 110kr.) There are numerous well-marked cycling paths between all the major towns; pick up a guide at the tourist office in Rønne (40kr). **Biking** from Rønne to Sandvig is about 28km.

RØNNE. Tiny but charming Rønne, on the southwest coast, is Bornholm's principal port of entry. The town serves mainly as an outpost for biking trips through the surrounding fields, forests, and beaches. Rent a **bike** from **Bornholms Cykeludlejning,** Ndr. Kystvej 5. (☎56 95 13 59. Reserve ahead. 60kr per day. Open May-Sept. daily 7am-4pm and 8:30-9pm.) The **tourist office,** Ndr. Kystvej 3, a mirrored-glass building behind the gas station by the Bornholmstrafikken terminal, books private rooms for free. (☎56 95 95 00. Open June-Aug. M-Sa 9:30am-5:30pm, Su 10am-4pm; Sept.-May M-F 9am-4pm, Sa 10am-1pm.) The **HI youth hostel ❸**, Arsenalvej 12, is in a quiet, wooded area near the coastline. From the ferry terminal, take the bus directly or walk 15min. along Munch Petersens Vej; when the road forks, go left up the hill, then turn left on Zahrtmannsvej, right at the roundabout on Søndre Allé, and right on Arsenalvej, then follow the signs. (☎56 95 13 40. Breakfast 45kr. Sheets 55kr. Kitchen facilities. Reception 8am-noon and 4-5pm. Open mid-June to mid-Aug. Dorms 100kr, nonmembers add 30kr.) **Galløkken Camping ❶**, Strandvejen 4, is centrally located and near the beach. (☎56 95 23 20. **Bikes** 55kr per day. Reception daily 7:30am-noon and 2-9pm. Open mid-May to Aug. 56kr per person.) Get groceries at **Kvickly**, in the Snellemark Centret opposite the tourist office. (Open mid-June to Aug. daily 9am-8pm; Sept. to early June M-F 9am-8pm, Sa 8am-5pm, Su 10am-4pm.)

SANDVIG AND ALLINGE. On the tip of the spectacular northern coast, these little towns are home to white-sand and rock beaches. A few kilometers from central Allinge down Hammershusvej, **Hammershus** is northern Europe's largest castle ruin. **Østerlars Rundkirke** is the largest of the island's four uniquely fortified round churches. Take bus #3 or 9 to Østerlars. The **Nordbornholms Turistbureau,** Kirkeg. 4, is in Allinge. (☎56 48 00 01. Open mid-June to mid-Aug. M-F 10am-5pm, Sa 10am-3pm; mid-Aug. to mid-June 10am-5pm, Sa 10am-noon.) Rent **bikes** at the **Sandvig Cyke-ludlejning,** Strandvejen 121. (☎56 48 00 60. 55kr per day. Open June-Aug. M-F 9am-4pm, Sa 9am-2pm, Su 10am-1pm.) Just outside Sandvig is the lakeside **Sandvig Van-drerhjem (HI) ❸**, Hammershusvej 94. (☎56 48 03 62. Breakfast 45kr. Sheets 60kr. Reception daily 9-10am and 4-6pm. Open Apr.-Oct. Dorms 100kr; singles 250kr; doubles 350kr.) **Sandvig Familie Camping ❶**, Sandlinien 5, has sites on the sea. (☎56 48 04 47. **Bikes** 50kr per day, 200kr per week. Reception daily 8am-11pm. Open Apr.-Oct. 50kr per person, 15kr per tent.)

DENMARK

FUNEN (FYN)

Situated between Zealand to the east and the Jutland Peninsula to the west, the island of Funen is Denmark's garden. This remote breadbasket is no longer isolated from the rest of Denmark—a bridge and tunnel now connect it to Zealand. Pick up maps of the bike paths covering the island at Funen tourist offices (75kr).

ODENSE

Though most tourists are drawn by the legacy of Hans Christian Andersen and his fairytales, modern Odense (OH-n-sa) has a network of lively pedestrian streets and a noteworthy venue for contemporary art and photography. The town can easily be covered on foot. At **H. C. Andersens Hus,** Hans Jensens Stræde 37-45, you can learn about the author's eccentricities and see free performances of his work. From the tourist office, walk right on Vesterg., then turn left on Torveg. and right on Hans Jensens Str. (☎66 14 88 14. Performances June 19-July 30 11am, 1, 3pm. Museum open mid-June to Aug. daily 9am-7pm; Sept. to mid-June Tu-Su 10am-4pm. 35kr.) A few scraps of Andersen's own ugly-duckling childhood are on display at **H. C. Andersens Barndomshjem** (Childhood Home), Munkemøllestr. 3-5. (☎66 14 88 14. Open mid-June to Aug. daily 10am-4pm; Sept. to mid-June Tu-Su 11am-3pm. 10kr.) At the **Carl Nielsen Museum,** Claus Bergs Gade 11, near the main H. C. Andersens Hus, don headphones and listen to the work of another great Dane. (☎66 14 88 14. Open Jan.-Aug. Tu-Su noon-4pm; Sept.-Dec. Th-F 4-8pm, Su noon-4pm. 15kr.) Walk back to the tourist office and all the way down Vesterg. to the outstanding ▓**Brandts Klædefabrik,** Brandts Passage 37 and 43, a former cloth mill that houses the **Museum of Photographic Art,** the **Danish Press/Graphic Arts Museum,** and a **contemporary art** gallery with changing exhibitions. (☎66 13 78 97. All open July-Aug. daily 10am-5pm; Sept.-June Tu-Su 10am-5pm. 25-30kr each, joint ticket 50kr.) The **Fyns Kunstmuseum** (Funen Art Gallery), Jernbaneg. 13, features Danish art. (☎66 14 88 14, ext. 4601. Open Tu-Su 10am-4pm. 25kr.)

Trains arrive from Copenhagen via Fredericia (2¼hr.) and from Svendborg via Kværndrup (1¼hr.). **Buses** depart from behind the train station (18kr). The **tourist office,** on Rådhuspladsen, books rooms for a 35kr fee and sells the **Odense Adventure Pass,** good for admission to museums, discounts on plays, and unlimited public transport (24hr. 100kr; 48hr. 140kr). From the train station, take Nørreg., which becomes Asylg., and turn left at the end on Vesterg.; it's on the right. (☎66 12 75 20; www.visitodense.com. Open June 15-Aug. M-F 9:30am-7pm, Sa 10am-5pm, Su 10am-4pm; Sept.-June 14 M-F 9:30am-4:30pm, Sa 10am-1pm.) The brand-new **Danhostel Odense City (HI) ❹** is attached to the station. (☎63 11 04 25. **Internet** access. Sheets 50kr. Laundry 40kr. Reception daily 8am-noon and 4-8pm. Call ahead. Dorms 145kr; singles 405kr; doubles 490kr; triples 535kr. Nonmembers add 30kr.) To camp next to the Fruens Boge park at **DCU Camping ❷,** Odensevej 102, take bus #41 or 81. (☎66 11 47 02. Pool. Reception 7am-10pm. Open late Mar. to Sept. 58kr per person, 20kr per tent.) Get groceries at **Aktiv Super,** at Nørreg. and Skulkenborgg. (Open M-F 9am-7pm, Sa 9am-4pm.)

▓ **DAYTRIP FROM ODENSE: KVÆRNDRUP.** Just 30min. south of Odense on the Svendborg rail line is the town of Kværndrup, home to ▓**Egeskov Slot,** a stunning 16th-century castle that appears to float on the surrounding lake but is actually supported by 12,000 oak pilings. Spend at least two hours in the magnificent Renaissance interior and the equally splendid grounds, which include a large bamboo labyrinth as well as a car and motorcycle museum. On summer Sundays at 5pm, classical concerts resound in the **Knight Hall.** (Castle open July daily 10am-7pm; Apr.-June and Aug.-Sept. 10am-5pm. Grounds open July daily 10am-8pm;

June and Aug. 10am-6pm; Apr.-May and Sept. 10am-5pm. Grounds, maze, and museums 75kr, with castle 130kr. Ticket window closes 1hr. before castle.) Take the Svendborg-bound train to Kværndrup; from the station, go right and continue until you reach Bøjdenvej, the main road. Wait for bus #920 (every hr., 18kr), or turn right and walk 2km through wheat fields to the castle.

SVENDBORG AND TÅSINGE

On Funen's south coast, an hour from Odense by train, Svendborg is a beautiful harbor town and a departure point for ferries to the south Funen islands. On the adjacent island of Tåsinge, the 17th-century estate of **Valdemars Slot**, built by Christian IV for his son, holds a yachting museum, a hunting museum, a toy museum, and a beach. (☎ 62 22 61 06. Open May-Aug. daily 10am-5pm; Sept. Tu-Su 10am-5pm; Apr. and Oct. Sa-Su 10am-5pm. Castle 55kr, castle and all museums 105kr.) Cruise there on the antique passenger steamer **M/S Helge**, which leaves from Jensens Mole, behind the Svendborg train station (55min., May-Aug. 5 per day, round-trip 65kr).

Ferries from Ærø (see below) arrive behind the train station. The **tourist office**, on the Centrum Pladsen, books ferries and accommodations. From the train station, go left on Jernbaneg., then right on Brog., and right on Kyseborgstr.; it's in the plaza on the right. (☎ 62 21 09 80. Open late June to Aug. M-F 9:30am-6pm, Sa 9:30am-3pm; Sept. to mid-June M-F 9:30am-5pm, Sa 9:30am-1pm.) The **HI youth hostel ❸**, Vesterg. 45, is a five-star on the Danhostel scale. From the station, turn left on Jernbaneg. and walk with the coast to your left, then go right onto Valdemarsg., which becomes Vesterg. (☎ 62 21 66 99; dk@danhostel-svenborg.dk. Bikes 50kr per day. Kitchen. Breakfast 45kr. Sheets 50kr. Laundry 30kr. Reception M-F 8am-6pm, Su 8am-noon and 4-6pm. Dorms 100kr; singles and doubles 330kr; overflow mattresses 50kr. Nonmembers add 30kr.) To get to **Carlsberg Camping ❶**, Sundbrovej 19, across the sound on the top of Tåsinge, take bus #800, 801, or 910 from the ferry terminal to Bregninge Tåsinge and walk up the street. (☎ 62 22 53 84; www.carlsbergcamping.dk. Reception daily 8am-10pm. Open Apr.-Sept. 57kr per person.) **Jette's Diner ❷**, Kullingg. 1, between the train station and the docks, puts a Danish spin on diner fare. (☎ 62 22 16 97. Open daily noon-9:30pm.) **Postal code:** 5700.

ÆRØ

The wheat fields, harbors, and hamlets of Ærø (EH-ruh), a small island off the south coast of Funen, quietly preserve an earlier era in Danish history. Cows, rather than real estate developers, lay claim to the beautiful land, and bikes are the ideal way to explore the three towns, Ærøskøbing, Marstal, and Søby.

⌐ TRANSPORTATION. Several **trains** from Odense to Svendborg are timed to meet the **ferry** (☎ 62 52 40 00) to Ærøskøbing (1¼hr.; 6 per day; one-way 77kr, round-trip 128kr; buy tickets on board). From Mommark, on Jutland, **Ærø-Als** (☎ 62 58 17 17) sails to Søby (1hr.; 2-5 per day, Oct.-Mar. Sa-Su only; 80kr), on Ærø's northwestern shore. **Bus** #990 travels between Ærøskøbing, Marstal, and Søby (16kr).

ÆRØSKØBING. Due to economic stagnation followed by conservation efforts, the town of Ærøskøbing appears today almost as it did 200 years ago. Rosebushes and half-timbered houses attract tourists from Sweden and Germany as well as vacationing Danes. The **tourist office,** Vesterg. 1, opposite the ferry landing, arranges rooms (170kr) in private homes. (☎ 62 52 13 00; www.aeroe-turistbureau.dk. Open mid-June to Aug. M-F 9am-5pm, Sa 9am-2pm, Su 9:30am-12:30pm; Sept. to mid June M-F 9am-4pm, Sa 9.30am-12:30pm.) To get from the landing to the **HI youth hostel ❸**, Smedevejen 15, turn left on Smedeg., which becomes Nørreg., Østerg., and finally Smedevejen. The hostel's tree-lined lane leads to a small beach. (☎62 52 10 44. Breakfast 40kr. Sheets 35kr. Reception daily 8am-noon and 4-8pm. Check-in by 5pm or call ahead. Reserve far in advance. Open Apr. to mid-Oct. Dorms 100kr; nonmembers 130kr.) **Ærøskøbing Camping ❶**, Sygehusvejen 40b, is 10min. to the right along Sygehusvejen, off Vestre Allé as you leave the ferry. (☎62 52 18 54. Reception daily 8am-1pm and 3-9pm. Open May-Sept. 52kr per person, 20kr per tent.) To get to **Emerko supermarket**, Statene 3, walk uphill from the ferry on Vesterg., then turn right on Sluttergyden, which becomes Statene. (Open M-Th 9am-5pm, F 9am-6pm, Sa 9am-4pm, Su 10am-4pm.) **Postal Code:** 5970

JUTLAND (JYLLAND)

The Jutland peninsula, homeland of the Jutes who joined the Anglos and Saxons in the conquest of England, is Denmark's largest landmass. Beaches and campgrounds mark the area as prime summer vacation territory, while rolling hills, marshland, and sparse forests add color and variety.

◀ FERRIES TO ENGLAND, NORWAY, AND SWEDEN

From **Esbjerg**, on Jutland's west coast, **DFDF** sails to Harwich, England (18hr., 3-4 per week). From **Frederikshavn** (see p. 288), on the northern tip of Jutland, **Stena Line** ferries (☎96 20 02 00; www.stenaline.com) leave for Gothenburg, Sweden (2-3¼hr.; price varies, 50% off with Scanrail) and Oslo, Norway (8½hr.; 180kr, with Scanrail 90kr). **Color Line** (☎99 56 19 77; www.colorline.com) sails to Larvik, Norway (6¼hr.; 160-340kr, students and seniors 50% off). Color Line boats also go from Hirtshals, on the northern tip of Jutland, to Oslo (8-8½hr., 160-350kr) and Kristiansand, Norway (2½-4½hr., 160-350kr).

ÅRHUS

Århus (ORE-hoos), Denmark's second-largest city, bills itself as "the world's smallest big city." Studded with impressive museums and architectural gems, the city is a visual treat. Many travelers find this laid-back student and cultural center manageably sized.

◨⑦ TRANSPORTATION AND PRACTICAL INFORMATION. Trains run to Århus from: Aalborg (1¾hr.); Copenhagen (3hr.); Fredericia (2hr.); and Frederikshavn (2½hr.). Trains runs every 1-2hr. from Frederikshavn to Århus. Most public **buses** leave from the train station or from outside the tourist office. **Tourist passes** (see below) include unlimited bus transportation. The tourist office, in the city hall, books private rooms (125-175kr; no fee) and sells the Århus Pass, which includes unlimited public transit and admission to most museums and sights (1-day 88kr, 2-day 110kr). If you're not going to many museums, consider instead the **24hr. Tourist Ticket** (50kr), which provides unlimited bus transportation. To get to the office, exit the train station and go left across Banegardspladsen, then take the first right on Park Allé. (☎89 40 67 00; www.visitaarhus.com. Open late June to early Sept. M-F 9:30am-6pm, Sa 9:30am-5pm, Su 9:30am-1pm; May to mid-June M-F 9:30am-5pm, Sa 10am-1pm; early Sept. to Apr. M-F 9:30am-4:30pm, Sa 10am-1pm.) **Postal Code:** 8000.

◨◪ ACCOMMODATIONS AND FOOD. Popular with backpackers, **Århus City Sleep-In ❸**, Havneg. 20, is 10min. from the train station and in the middle of the city's nightlife. From the train station, follow Ryesg. (off of Banegardspladsen), which becomes Sønderg., all the way to the canal. Take the steps or elevator

down to Aboulevarden, cross the canal, and turn right; at the end of the canal, turn left on Mindebrog., then left again on Havneg. (☎86 19 20 55; www.citysleep-in.dk. Kitchen. **Internet.** Bikes 50kr per day; deposit 200kr. Breakfast 35kr. Sheets 35kr; deposit 30kr. Laundry 25kr. Key deposit 50kr. Reception 24hr. Check-out noon. Dorms 100kr; doubles 240-280kr.) **Hotel Guldsmeden ❺,** Guldsmedg. 40, is a small hotel with comfortable rooms in the center of town. The annex in the back has the cheapest rooms. From the tourist office, continue along Park Allé, which becomes Immervad, and veer left onto Guldsmedg. at the intersection of Vesterg. (☎86 13 45 50; www.hotelguldmeden.dk. Breakfast 60kr. Reception daily 7am-midnight. Singles 500-725kr; doubles 700-875kr.) **Pavillonen (HI) ❷,** Marienlundsvej 10, is in the Risskov forest, 3km north of the city center and 5min. from the beach. Take bus #1, 6, 9, 16, or 56 to Marienlund, then walk 300m into the park. (☎86 16 72 98; www.hostel-aarhus.dk. Breakfast 45kr. Sheets 30kr. Laundry. Reception daily 7:30-10am and 4-11pm. Dorms 95kr, nonmembers add 30kr; singles, doubles, and triples 285-400kr.) **Blommehavenn Camping ❶,** Ørneredevej 35, in the Marselisborg forest south of the city, is near the beach and the royal family's summer residence. In summer, take bus #19 from the station to the grounds; off-season, take bus #6 to Hørhavevej. (☎86 27 02 07; info@blommehaven.dk. Reception daily 7:30am-10pm. Open Apr.-Sept. 55kr per person.) The popular **Den Grønne Hjørne ❸,** Frederiksg. 60, has an all-you-can-eat Danish buffet (lunch 59kr, dinner 99kr). From the tourist office, turn left on Radhuspl. and then take an immediate right. (☎86 13 52 47. Open daily 11am-10pm.) Get groceries at **Fakta,** Østerg. 8-12. (Open M-F 9am-7pm, Sa 9am-4pm.)

🅖🅙 **SIGHTS AND ENTERTAINMENT.** In the town center, the 13th-century **Århus Domkirke** (cathedral) dominates Bispetorv and the pedestrian streets. (☎86 12 38 45. Open May-Sept. M-Sa 9:30am-4pm; Oct.-Apr. 10am-3pm. Free.) Next door, the **Women's Museum,** Domkirkeplads 5, has thoughtful exhibits on women throughout time. (☎86 13 61 44; www.kvindemuseet.dk. Open June-Aug. daily 10am-5pm; Sept.-May Tu-Su 10am-4pm. 30kr.) Just west of the town center lies **Den Gamle By,** Viborgvej 2, an open-air museum displaying a collection of Danish buildings from the Renaissance through the 20th century. From the center, take bus #3, 14, 25, or 55. (☎86 12 31 88. Open June-Aug. daily 9am-6pm; Apr.-May and Sept.-Oct. 10am-5pm; Feb.-Mar. and Nov.-Dec. 10am-4pm; Jan. 11am-3pm. Apr.-Dec. 70kr; Jan.-Mar. 45kr. Grounds free after hours.) The **Århus Kunstmuseum,** on Vennelystparken, has a fine collection of Danish Golden Age paintings. (☎86 13 52 55. Open Tu-Su 10am-5pm, W until 8pm. 40kr, students 30kr.) Just outside town is the spectacular **Moesgård Museum of Prehistory,** Moesgård Allé 20, which chronicles Århus's history from 4000 BC through the Viking age. Two millennia ago, the casualties of infighting were entombed in a nearby bog and mummified by its acidity. Today the ▨**Grauballe Man,** the only perfectly preserved bog person, is on display at the museum. Take bus #6 from the train station to the end. (Open Apr.-Sept. daily 10am-5pm; Oct.-Mar. Tu-Su 10am-4pm. 35kr, students 25kr.) The **Prehistoric Trail** is a beautiful walk that leads from behind the museum to a sandy **beach** (3km). In summer, bus #19 (last bus 10:18pm) returns from the beach to the Århus station. The exquisite rose garden of **Marselisborg Slot,** Kongevejen 100, Queen Margarethe II's summer getaway, is open to the public. From the train station, take bus #1, 18, or 19. (Palace and rose gardens closed in July and whenever the Queen is in residence. Changing of the guard daily at noon when the Queen is in residence.)

Aboulevarden, lined with trendy cafes and bars, is the heart of the town. Århus hosts an acclaimed **jazz festival** in late July (www.jazzfest.dk). The **Århus Festuge** (☎89 31 82 70; www.aarhusfestuge.dk), from late August to early September, is a rollicking celebration of theater, dance, and music. To get to **Tivoli Friheden,**

DENMARK

Skovbrynet 1, a smaller version of Tivoli, take bus #1, 4, 6, 8, 18, or 19. (☎86 14 73 00. Open late June to mid-Aug. daily 1-11pm; early to mid-June F-Sa 2-11pm, Su-Th 1-10pm; late Apr.-May F-Sa 2-10pm, Su-M 1-9pm. 35kr.) Chill at the jazz club **Bent J,** Nørre Allé 66 (☎86 12 04 92), on every Monday evening and occasional other weekday evenings. The **Pan Club,** Jægergårdsg. 42, has a cafe, bar, and mainly gay and lesbian dance club. (☎86 13 43 80. Cafe open Tu-Th 7pm-6am, F-Sa 8pm-5am. Club cover F-Sa 50kr. Open Th-Sa 11pm-5am.)

▶ DAYTRIP FROM ÅRHUS: BILLUND. Billund is renowned as the home of ▓**Legoland,** an amusement park built constructed out of 40 million Lego pieces. Don't skip the impressive indoor exhibitions. To get there, take the train from Århus to **Vejle** (45min., every hr.), then bus #912 or 244 (dir.: Grindsted). (☎75 33 13 33; www.legoland.dk. Open July to mid-Aug. daily 10am-9pm; June and late Aug. daily 10am-8pm; Apr.-May and Sept.-Oct. M-F 10am-6pm, Sa-Su 10am-8pm. Rides close 2hr. before park. 1 day 160kr, under 13 140kr; 2 days 220kr.)

AALBORG

Aalborg (OLE-borg) is the site of the earliest known Viking settlement. **Lindholm Høje,** Vendilavej 11, has 700 Viking graves and a museum of Viking life; take bus #6 or 25 (13kr) from outside the tourist office. (☎96 31 04 28. Site open daily dawn-dusk. Museum open Apr. to mid-Oct. daily 10am-5pm; mid-Oct. to mid-Mar. Tu and Su 10am-4pm. 30kr.) The frescoed 15th-century **Monastery of the Holy Ghost,** on C.W. Obelsplads, is Denmark's oldest social institution. From the tourist office, cross the street and head down Adelg.; the monastery is on the right. (English tours late June to mid-Aug. Tu and Th-F 1:30pm. 40kr.) The **Budolfi Church,** on Alg., has a brilliantly colored interior. From the tourist office, turn left onto Østeråg. and right on Alg. (Open May-Sept. M-F 9am-4pm, Sa 9am-2pm; Oct.-Apr. M-F 9am-3pm, Sa 9am-noon.) At the corner of Alg. and Molleg., in front of the Sallig department store, an elevator goes down to the medieval ruins of the **Franciscan Friary.** (Open in summer daily 10am-5pm; in winter Tu-Su 10am-5pm. 20kr.) For serious rollercoasters, visit **Tivoliland,** on Karolinelundsvej. From the tourist office, turn right on Østeråg., right on Nytorv, and right on Kjellerupsg. (Open Apr.-Sept. daily noon-8pm. Entrance 40kr, rides 10-40kr.)

Trains arrive from Århus (1¾hr.) and Copenhagen. From the station, cross J.F.K. Plads and turn left on Boulevarden, which becomes Østeråg., to find the **tourist office,** Østeråg. 8. (☎98 12 60 22; www.visitaalborg.com. Open July M-F 9am-5:30pm, Sa 10am-4pm; mid-June and Aug. M-F 9am-5:30pm, Sa 10am-1pm; Sept. to mid-June M-F 9am-4:30pm, Sa 10am-1pm.) **Aalborg Vandrerhjem and Camping (HI) ❷,** Skydebanevej 50, has cabins with modern facilities next to a fjord. Take bus #2, 8, or 9 (dir.: Fjordparken) to the very end. (☎98 11 60 44. Laundry. Reception daily mid-June to mid-Aug. 7:30am-11pm; mid-Jan. to mid-June and mid-Aug. to mid-Dec. 8am-noon and 4-9pm. Dorms 85-100kr; singles 250-398kr; doubles 325-398kr. Camping 49kr.) Bars and restaurants line **Jomfru Ane Gade;** from the tourist office, turn right on Østeråg. and then left on Bispensg. Jomfru Ane G. will be on the right. **Postal code:** 9000.

FREDERIKSHAVN

Despite noble efforts to showcase its endearing streets and hospitality, Frederikshavn is best known for its **ferry** links (see p. 64). The **tourist office,** Skandia Torv 1, inside the Stena Line terminal south of the rail station, reserves rooms (125kr fee). (☎98 42 32 66; www.frederikshavn.dk. Open mid-June to mid-Aug. M-Sa 8:30am-7pm, Su 8:30am-5pm; mid-Aug. to mid-June M-Sa 9am-4pm.) From the tourist office, walk left 10min. to reach the bus and train stations. To get from the station to the **youth hostel (HI) ❶,** Buhlsvej 6, walk right on Skipperg. for 10min., then turn left onto Norreg., and follow the signs. (☎98 42 14 75; www.danhostel.dk/frederik-shavn. Reception in summer daily 8am-noon and 4-9pm. Always call ahead. Open Feb.-Dec. Dorms 70-90kr; singles 150-200kr; doubles 210-270kr.) Take bus #4 from the station to Sinddallundvej/Campingpl. to get to **Nordstrand Camping ❸**, Aphol-menvej 40. (☎98 42 93 50. Open Apr. to mid-Oct. 60kr per person, 40kr per tent; off-season 47kr/28kr.) **Postal code:** 9900.

SKAGEN

Perched on Denmark's northernmost tip, sunny Skagen (SKAY-en) is a beautiful summer retreat amid long stretches of sea and white sand dunes. The houses are all painted in deep "Skagen yellow" and the roofs are covered in red tiles with white edges—supposedly decorated to welcome local fisherman home from sea. The powerful currents of the North and Baltic Seas colliding is visible at **Grenen.** Stand with one foot in each ocean, but don't try to swim in these dangerous waters; every year people are carried out to sea. To get to Grenen, take bus #99 or 79 from the Skagen station to Gammel (11kr) or walk 3km down Fyrvej; turn left out of the train station and bear left when the road forks. In summer, you can climb the **lighthouse** tower for an amazing view of the rough seas at Grenen (5kr). The spectacular **Råberg Mile** sand dunes, formed by a 16th-century storm, migrate 15m east each year. Take bus #79 or the train from Skagen to Hulsig, then walk along Kandestedvej. From here, you can swim along 60km of **beaches,** where the endless summer light attracted Denmark's most famous late-19th-century paint-ers. Their works are displayed in the wonderful **Skagen Museum,** Brøndumsvej 4. (☎98 44 64 44. Open June-Aug. daily 10am-6pm; May and Sept. 10am-5pm; Apr. and Oct. Tu-Su 11am-4pm; Nov.-Mar. W-F 1-4pm, Sa 11am-4pm, Su 11am-3pm. 50kr.) **Michael og Anna Archers Hus,** Markvej 2-4, is filled with the artists' works and set up as it was when they lived there. (☎98 44 30 09. Open mid-June to mid-Aug. daily 10am-6pm; May to mid-June and mid-Aug. to Sept. 10am-5pm; Apr. and Oct. 11am-3pm; Nov.-Mar. Sa-Su 11am-3pm. 40kr.) Equally impressive is **Holger Drachmanns Hus,** Hans Baghsvej 21. (☎98 44 51 88. Open July daily 10am-5pm; June and Aug. to mid-Sept. 11am-3pm; mid-Sept. to mid-Oct. and May Sa-Su 11am-3pm. 25kr.) Skagen has a large annual **Dixieland music festival** in late June (up to 150kr); contact the tourist office for more info.

Nordjyllands Trafikselskab (☎98 44 21 33) runs **buses** and **trains** from Frederik-shavn to Skagen (1hr.; 39kr, with ScanRail 20kr). Biking is the perfect way to see Skagen, including Grenen; rent **bikes** at **Skagen CykelUdlejning,** Banegardspladsen, right next to the bus station. (☎98 44 10 70. 70kr per day.) The **tourist office** is in the train station. (☎98 44 13 77; www.skagen.dk. Open June-Aug. M-Sa 9am-7pm, Su 10am-2pm; Sept.-May reduced hours.) The **Skagen Ny Vandrerhjem ❸**, Rolighedsvej 2, has a friendly and helpful staff and is wildly popular among vacationing Danish families. From the station, turn right on Chr. X's Vej, which becomes Frederik-shavnvej, then left on Rolighedsvej. (☎98 44 22 00; www.danhostelnord.dk/skagen. Breakfast 45kr. Kitchen. Reception daily 9am-noon and 4-6pm. Open Mar.-Nov. Dorms 100kr; singles 250-400kr; doubles 300-500kr.) **Campgrounds** abound in the area, but most are open only early May to early September. Bus #79 passes by sev-eral sites. Try **Grenen ❶,** Fyrvej 16 (☎98 44 25 46; open May to mid-Sept.; 65kr) to the north, or **Øster Klit ❶,** Flagbakkevej 53 (☎98 44 31 23; open late Mar. to mid-Oct.; 65kr), to the south; both are near the city center and the beach.

RIBE

Well aware of their town's historic value, the town government of Ribe forged preservation laws forcing residents to maintain the character of their houses and to live in them year-round. The result is a magnificently preserved medieval town, situated beautifully on the salt plains near Jutland's west coast. Ribe is particularly proud of the arrival of migratory storks who always roost on the roof of the town hall. For a great view of the birds and the surrounding landscape, climb the 248 steps through the clockwork and huge bells of the 12th-century **cathedral** tower. (☎ 75 42 06 19. Open July to mid-Aug. M-Sa 10am-5:30pm, Su noon-5:30pm; May-June and mid-Aug. to Sept. M-Sa 10am-5pm, Su noon-5pm; Apr. and Oct. M-Sa 11am-6pm, Su noon-4pm; Nov.-Mar. daily 11am-3pm. 12kr.) Next to the **Det Gamle Rådhus** (Old Town Hall), Von Støckens Plads, a former debtor's prison houses a small museum on medieval torture. (☎ 76 88 11 22. Open June-Aug. daily 1-3pm. May and Sept. M-F 1-3pm. 15kr.) Follow the **night watchman** on his rounds for an English or Danish tour of town beginning in Torvet, the main square. (35min.; June-Aug. 8 and 10pm; May and Sept. 10pm. Free.) Across from the train station, **Museet Ribes Vikinger,** Odin Plads 1, houses artifacts recovered from an excavation of the town, once an important Viking trading post. (☎ 76 88 11 22. Open July-Aug. Th-Tu 10am-6pm, W 10am-9pm; Apr.-June and Sept.-Oct. daily 10am-4pm; Nov.-Mar. Tu-Su 10am-4pm. 50kr.) Next door, the **Ribe Kunst Museum,** Sct. Nikolaig. 10, presents Danish paintings from the Golden Age through the present in a house built in the Dutch Renaissance style. (☎ 75 42 03 62. Open mid-June to Aug. daily 11am-5pm; Sept. to mid-June Tu-Sa 1-4pm, Su 11am-4pm. 30kr, students 20kr.) South of town, the open-air **Ribe Vikingcenter,** Lustrupvej 4, recreates a Viking town, complete with farm and marketplace. (☎ 75 41 16 11. Open July-Aug. daily 11am-4:30pm; May-June and Sept. M-F 11am-4pm. 50kr.) Take bus #711 to the **Vadehavscentret** (Wadden Sea Center), Okholmvej 5 in Vestervedsted, which gives tours of the local marshes on the Mandobus (☎ 75 44 51 07; 50kr). Tours start from the Sea Center and cross to Mandø, an island, at low tide. (☎ 75 44 61 61. Open Apr.-Oct. daily 10am-5pm; Feb.-Mar. and Nov. 10am-4pm. 45kr. Mandobus runs May-Sept.; times depend on tides. Consult the tourist office. Bus and center 80kr.)

Trains to Ribe run from nearby Bramming (25min., 4-5 per day, 28kr) and Esbjerg (40min., every hr., 46kr). The **tourist office,** Torvet 3, has free maps and arranges accommodations for a 20kr fee. From the train station, walk down Dagmarsg. to the left of the Viking museum; it's on the right in the main square. (☎ 75 42 15 030; www.ribe.dk. Open July-Aug. M-F 9:30am-5:30pm, Sa 10am-5pm, Su 10am-2pm; Apr.-June and Sept.-Oct. M-F 9am-5pm, Sa 10am-1pm; Nov.-Mar. M-F 9am-4:30pm, Sa 10am-1pm.) The centrally located **Ribe Vandrerhjem (HI) ❸,** Sct. Pedersg. 16, has a gorgeous view. From the station, cross the Viking Museum parking lot, bear right, walk down Sct. Nicolajg., then turn right on Saltg. and immediately left on Sct. Petersg. (☎ 75 42 06 20. **Bikes** 50kr per day. Breakfast 45kr. Sheets 38kr. Reception daily 8am-noon and 4-8pm; extended hours May-Sept. Open Feb.-Nov. Dorms 100kr; singles 250kr; doubles 295kr.) **Ribe Camping ❶,** Farupvej 2, is 1.5km from the town center. From the station, turn to face the Vikings Museum and go right on Rosen Allé until it becomes Norremarksvej. After the traffic light, go left along the bike path (Gronnestien) and cross onto Farupvej; it's on the second street on the right. Or, take bus #715 (every 1½hr.) from the station to Gredstedbro. (☎ 75 41 07 77. 50kr per person; 2-person cabins 175kr.) **Seminarievej,** near the hostel, is home to a cluster of **supermarkets.** Restaurants cluster around the Cathedral.

ESTONIA (EESTI)

Happy to discard its Soviet past, Estonia has quickly revived its ties with its Nordic neighbors as Finnish wealth revitalizes the nation. Material trappings mask the declining living standards common outside big cities, but having overcome successive centuries of domination by Danes, Swedes, and Russians, the Estonians are now ready to take their place in modern Europe. They currently are looking to cement these ties by joining the EU, a coupling that could come as soon as 2004.

FACTS AND FIGURES

Official Name: Republic of Estonia.

Capital: Tallinn.

Major Cities: Tartu, Pärnu.

Population: 1,400,000 (68% Estonian, 28% Russian, 6% other).

Land Area: 45,226 sq. km.

Time Zone: GMT +2.

Languages: Estonian (official); some Russian, Ukrainian, English, and Finnish.

Religions: Evangelical Lutheran, Russian Orthodox, Estonian Orthodox, and others.

ESSENTIALS

WHEN TO GO

The best time to visit is between May and September. Although it's quite far north, Estonia's climate is generally mild due to its proximity to the Baltic Sea. Winters, on the other hand, can be very severe.

DOCUMENTS AND FORMALITIES

VISAS. Citizens of Australia, Ireland, New Zealand, and the US do not need a visa for up to 90 days in a six-month period, UK citizens for 180 days in a year. Canadians and South Africans must obtain a visa, but may use a Latvian or Lithuanian visa to enter the country. (30-day single-entry visa €13, 90-day multiple-entry €65.) Visa extensions are not granted, and visas cannot be purchased at the border. For visa info, consult the **Estonian Ministry of Foreign Affairs** (www.vm.ee).

EMBASSIES. Foreign embassies are all in Tallinn (see p. 296). Estonian embassies at home include: **Australia,** 86 Louisa Rd., Birchgrove NSW, 2041 (☎ 02 9810 7468; eestikon@ozemail.com.au); **Canada,** 958 Broadview Ave., Toronto, ON M4K 2R6 (☎ 416-461-0764; estconsu@inforamp.net); **South Africa,** 16 Hofmeyer St., Welgemoed, 7530 (☎ 021 913 38 50; fax 913 2579); **UK,** 16 Hyde Park Gate, London SW7 5DG (☎ 020 7589 3428; www.estonia.gov.uk); and **US,** 2131 Massachusetts Ave. NW, Washington, D.C. 20008 (☎ 202-588-0101; www.estemb.org).

TRANSPORTATION

BY PLANE, TRAIN, BUS, AND FERRY. Estonian Air, Finnair, Lufthansa, and SAS have flights to Tallinn (TLL). If you're coming from Russia or a Baltic state, **trains** may be even cheaper than ferries, but expect more red tape during border crossings. Domestic **buses** are cheaper and more efficient than trains. From September to June, student bus tickets are half-price. Several **ferry lines** (☎ 631 85 50) connect Tallinn's harbor (see p. 294) to Finland and Sweden.

BY BIKE AND BY TAXI. On the islands, bike rentals (from 100EEK per day) are an excellent means of exploration. Taxis are safe; the average rate is 7EEK per km.

BY THUMB. *Let's Go* does not recommend hitchhiking. Those who choose to do so should stretch out an open hand. Or, call the **Vismutar** (☎ (8290) 010 50) agency, which will match you with a driver going in your direction 24hr. before you leave.

TOURIST SERVICES AND MONEY

EMERGENCY	Police, Ambulance, Fire: ☎ 112. In **Tallinn:** ☎ 0112.

TOURIST OFFICES. Unlike most of the former Soviet Union, Estonia is grasping the importance of tourist services; most towns have well-equipped tourist offices with literature and English-speaking staff. Smaller information booths, marked with a green "i," sell maps and give away brochures.

KROON		
	AUS$1 = 8.79EEK	10EEK = AUS$1.14
	CDN$1 = 10.26EEK	10EEK = CDN$0.98
	EUR€1 = 15.65EEK	10EEK = EUR€0.64
	NZ$1 = 7.50EEK	10EEK = NZ$1.33
	ZAR1 = 1.52EEK	10EEK = ZAR6.60
	UK£1 = 24.42EEK	10EEK = UK£0.41
	US$1 = 15.94EEK	10EEK = US$0.63

MONEY. The unit of currency is the **kroon** (EEK), divided into 100 *senti*. Inflation is around 3%, making prices and exchange rates relatively stable. **Hansapank** and **Eesti Ühispank,** the largest Estonian banks, cash traveler's checks. Many establishments accept credit cards, and ATMs are common. When making a purchase, cash is not passed between hands, but is placed in a small tray on the counter. Tipping is uncommon in Estonia, but a service charge may be included in the bill.

BUSINESS HOURS. Most businesses are open Monday to Friday from 9 or 10am to 6 or 7pm and Saturday from 10am to 2 or 3pm. Some food shops stay open until 10pm or later and are also open on Sunday. Businesses take hour-long breaks around 1pm. Banks are generally open Monday to Friday 9am-4pm.

COMMUNICATION

PHONE CODE	Country code: 372. **International dialing prefix:** 800. From outside Estonia, dial int'l dialing prefix (see inside back cover) + 372 + city code + local number.

MAIL. To Europe, an airmail letter is 6.50EEK and a postcard is 6EEK; to the rest of the world, 7.50EEK/8EEK. For *Poste Restante*, address envelope: First-name SURNAME, *Poste Restante*, Narva mnt. 1, Tallinn 10101, ESTONIA.

TELEPHONES AND INTERNET. Internet access is common, and usually costs 30-60EEK per hr. The phone system in Estonia is a little chaotic. Tallinn numbers all begin with the number 6 and have 7 digits, while numbers in smaller

Estonia

TO HELSINKI (82km)

Gulf of Finland

Baltic Sea

Tallinn

Lahemaa National Park

Ivangorod

Keila

Tapa

Rakvere

Jõhvi

Narva

Kärdla

Hiiumaa Heltermaa

Muhu

Kuivastu Virtsu

Saaremaa

Kuressaare

Gulf of Rīga

Kihnu

Häapsalu

Türi

Jõgeva

Mustvee

Lake Peipsi

Pärnu

Tartu

Viljandi

Elva

Otepää

Põlva

Räpina

RUSSIA

Rūjiena

Valga

Võru

Pskov

0 40 miles
0 40 kilometers

Valmiera
Limbaži

LATVIA

towns often have only 5 digits. Tallinn, unlike other Estonian cities, has no city code. The 0 listed in parentheses before each city code need only be dialed when placing calls within Estonia. The information number for **Eesti Telefon** is ☎07. For help, call the English-speaking **Ekspress Hotline** (☎011 88). Payphones require **digital cards,** available at any bank or newspaper kiosk. Cards come in denominations of 30, 50, and 100EEK. International calls can be made at post offices. Calls to the Baltic states cost 5EEK per min., to Russia 10EEK. Phoning the US costs US$1-4 per min. International direct dial numbers include: **AT&T,** ☎800 800 1001; **British Telecom,** ☎800 8001 0441; **Canada Direct,** ☎0 800 1011; and **MCI,** ☎0 800 800 1122.

LANGUAGES. Estonians speak the best English in the Baltic states; most young people also know Finnish or Swedish, but German is more common among the older set. Russian used to be mandatory, but many Estonians resist its use, except along the eastern border. For Estonian basics, see p. 1055.

ACCOMMODATIONS AND CAMPING

ESTONIA	❶	❷	❸	❹	❺
ACCOMMODATIONS	under 200EEK	200-400EEK	401-550EEK	551-600EEK	over 600EEK

Tourist offices have accommodation listings and can often arrange beds. There is little distinction between hotels, hostels, and guesthouses. For information on HI hostels, contact the **Estonian Youth Hostel Association,** Tatari (☎646 14 57; eyha.jg.ee). Some **hostels** are part of larger hotels, so ask for the cheaper rooms. Note that even some upscale **hotels** have hall toilets and showers. **Homestays** are common and cheap, but the cheapest hostels can be a better deal. The word *võõrastemaja* (guest house) in a place's name often implies that it is less expensive. **Camping** is a good way to experience the islands, but camping outside designated areas is illegal and a threat to the wildlife.

ESTONIA

FOOD AND DRINK

ESTONIA	❶	❷	❸	❹	❺
FOOD	under 40EEK	40-80EEK	81-100EEK	101-140EEK	over 140EEK

Much to the dismay of vegetarians and those trying to keep kosher, *schnitzel* (a breaded and fried pork fillet) appears on nearly every menu, and most cheap Estonian cuisine is fried and doused with sour cream. Estonian specialties include the typical Baltic *seljanka* (meat stew) and *pelmenid* (dumplings), as well as smoked salmon and trout. Bread is usually dark and dense. A delicious common dessert is pancakes with cheese curd and berries. The national brew *Saku*, and the darker *Saku Tume* are excellent, but local beers, like Kuressaare's *Saaremaa*, are less consistent. Carbonated *Värska* mineral water is particularly salty.

HOLIDAYS AND FESTIVALS

Holidays: New Year's Day (Jan. 1); Independence Day (Feb. 24); Good Friday (Apr. 18); Easter (Apr. 20); May Day (May 1); Victory Day (Battle of Võnnu; June 23); Jaanipäev (Midsummer; June 24); Restoration of Independence (Aug. 20); Christmas (Dec. 25).

Festivals: Open-air concerts take place throughout Vanalinn during Tallinn's **Old Town Days** (late May to early June). **Beersummer,** the 1st week of July, is one more excuse to loose the taps in Tallinn's bars. The **National Song festival** (July 2004), Estonia's biggest event, occurs only once every five years. The Tallinn festival honors Estonian folk music, culminating in a gigantic celebration featuring Estonians in native dress swilling local brews while singing their hearts out. Conductors and musical groups from around the world are drawn to **Pärnu** for its summer film and music festivals.

TALLINN   ☎ 0

In the heart of Tallinn, cosmopolitan shops contrast with the serene Old Town, where German spires, Danish towers, and Russian domes rise above the sea. For better or worse, tourists from all over Europe are quickly falling in love with the city's ethnic restaurants, vibrant nightlife, and low prices.

▄ TRANSPORTATION

Trains: Toompuiestee 35 (☎615 68 51; www.evrekspress.ee). Trams #1 and 5 connect the station to Hotel Viru. English spoken at the info desk. To **Moscow** (16½hr., 1 per day, 718EEK) and **St. Petersburg** (10hr., 1 every 2 days, 225-387EEK).

Buses: Lastekodu 46 (☎680 09 00), 1.5km southeast of Vanalinn. Take tram #2 or 4 or bus #2 to the city center. Buy tickets at the station or from the driver. **Eurolines** (☎680 09 09; www.eurolines.ee) runs to: **Rīga** (5½-6hr., 4 per day, 200EEK); **St. Petersburg** (9hr., 7 per day, 180-260EEK); and **Vilnius** (10½hr., 2 per day, 400EEK).

Ferries: (☎631 85 50; www.ts.ee). At the end of Sadama, 15min. from the city center. The following companies sail or hydrofoil to **Helsinki: Silja Line,** Terminal D (☎611 66 61; www.silja.ee. 1½hr.; 4 per day; 230-590EEK, students 180-540EEK). **Tallink Express,** Terminal D (☎640 98 08; www.tallink.ee. 1½hr.; 7 per day; 235-425EEK, students 212-384EEK). **Eckerö Line,** Terminal B (☎631 86 06; www.eckeroline.ee. 3½hr.; 1 per day; 220EEK/180EEK). **Nordic Jet Line,** Terminal C (☎613 70 00; www.njl.info. 1½hr., 6 per day, 280-580EEK).

Public Transportation: Buses, trams, and **trolleybuses** cover the entire metropolitan area 6am-midnight. Buy tickets (*talong*; 10EEK) from kiosks around town and validate them in the metal boxes on board or risk a 600EEK fine.

Tallinn (Vanalinn)

🍎 FOOD
Elevant, 5
Olde Hansa, 7
Troika, 4

🛏 ACCOMMODATIO)NS
Hostel Vana Tom, 8
Oldhouse Guesthouse, 1
Poska Villa, 3
Rasastra, 2

🍸 NIGHTLIFE
Café V.S., 10
Nimeta Baar, 9
Venus Club, 6

Taxis: Silver Takso (☎ 648 23 00 or 81 52 22). 5EEK per km. **Tulika Takso** (☎ 12 00) 7EEK per km. Call ahead to avoid the 8-50EEK "waiting fee."

🔆 🛈 ORIENTATION AND PRACTICAL INFORMATION

Tallinn's **Vanalinn** (Old Town) is surrounded the major streets Rannamäe tee, Mere pst., Pärnu mnt., Kaarli pst., and Toompuiestee. Vanalinn is divided into the larger, busier **All-linn** (Lower Town) and **Toompea**, a fortified rocky hill. Enter Vanalinn through the 15th-century **Viru ärarad,** the main gates in the city wall, 500m from **Hotel Viru,** Tallinn's central landmark. To reach Vanalinn from the ferry terminal, walk 15min. along Sadama, which becomes Põhja pst., and turn left on Pikk through **Paks Margareeta** (Fat Margaret) gate. To get to **Raekoja plats** (Town Hall Square), the center of All-linn, from the train station, cross under Toompuiestee and continue straight on Nunne; turn left on Pikk and then take a right on Kinga.

Tourist Office: Raekoja pl. 10 (☎ 645 77 77; http://tourism.tallinn.ee). Sells indispensable *Tallinn in Your Pocket* (35EEK). Open June-Aug. M-F 9am-8pm, Sa-Su 10am-6pm; Sept.-May M-F 9am-5pm, Sa-Su 10am-4pm. The **Tallinn Card** covers transportation, a city tour, and entry to most museums (1-day 205EEK, 2-day 275EEK, 3-day 325EEK).

ESTONIA

Embassies: For more information, contact the Estonian Foreign Ministry (www.vm.ee). **Australia,** Kopli 25 (☎650 93 08; fax 667 84 44). Open M-F 9am-5pm. **Canada,** Toom-Kooli 13 (☎627 33 11; canembt@zzz.ee). Open M, W, and F 9am-noon. **Russia,** Pikk 19 (☎646 41 75; visa ☎646 41 66; fax 646 41 78). Open M-F 9am-5pm. **UK,** Wismari 6 (☎667 47 00; www.britishembassy.ee). Open Tu-Th 2:30-4:30pm. **US,** Kentmanni 20 (☎668 81 00; www.usemb.ee). Open M-F 9am-noon and 2-5pm.

Currency Exchange: Throughout the city. **ATMs** are on nearly every street in Vanalinn.

American Express: Estravel, Suur-Karja 15 (☎626 62 11; www.estravel.ee). Books hotels and tours. Sells airline, ferry, and rail tickets. Arranges visas. Open June-Aug. M-F 9am-6pm, Sa 10am-5pm; Sept.-May M-F 9am-6pm, Sa 10am-3pm.

Emergencies: Police, Ambulance, Fire: ☎0112.

Pharmacy: Raeapteek, Raekoja pl. 11 (☎631 48 00), 2 doors from tourist office. In business since 1422. Open M-F 9am-7pm, Sa 9am-5pm, Su 9am-4pm.

Internet Access: Hallo, Narva mnt. 1, next to the post office. 20EEK per hr. Open M-F 9am-6pm, Sa 9am-3pm. **Kohvik@Grill,** Aia 3; entrance on Vana-Viru. 25EEK per hr. Open daily 10am-11pm.

Post Office: Narva mnt. 1, 2nd fl. (☎661 66 16), opposite Hotel Viru. Open M-F 7:30am-8pm, Sa 8am-6pm. Address mail to be held: Firstname SURNAME, *Poste Restante,* Narva mnt. 1, Tallinn **10101,** ESTONIA.

⚡🖪 ACCOMMODATIONS AND FOOD

Hostels fill fast, so book ahead. **Rasastra,** Mere pst. 4, 2nd fl., finds private rooms in many cities. (☎/fax 661 62 91; www.bedbreakfast.ee. Singles 260EEK; doubles 460EEK; triples 639EEK. Apartments from 800EEK. Open daily 9:30am-6pm.) 🏠**Hostel Vana Tom (HI) ❷,** Väike-Karja 1, 2nd fl., in Vanalinn, is unbeatable in cleanliness and location. (☎631 32 52; www.hostel.ee. Reception 24hr. Dorms 210EEK, nonmembers 225EEK; doubles 590EEK.) **Oldhouse Guesthouse Bed & Breakfast ❷,** Uus 22/1, has small, immaculate rooms. From Raekoja pl., follow Viru and turn left on Uus. (☎/fax 641 14 64; www.oldhouse.ee. Dorm 290EEK; single 450EEK; double 650EEK; quad 1300EEK. Apartments 950-2000EEK. 10% ISIC discount.) The residential guesthouse **Poska Villa ❺,** J. Poska 15, has small rooms with private baths. From Vanalinn, follow Gonsiori and turn left on J. Poska. (☎601 36 01; www.hot.ee/poskavilla. Singles 650EEK; doubles 760-980EEK.)

Extravagant 🏠**Troika ❹,** Raekoja pl. 15, has a different Russian menu each day. (Entrees 106-168EEK. Live music daily 6-10pm. Open daily 10am-11pm.) **Elevant ❸,** Vene 5, serves tasty, creative Indian fare. (Main dishes 84-278EEK. Open daily noon-11pm.) **Olde Hansa ❺,** Vana turg 1, is a popular medieval-themed restaurant near Raekoja pl. (Entrees 188-540EEK. Open daily 11am-midnight.) Buy groceries at **Kaubahall** on Aia and Inseneri, left off Viru coming from Vanalinn. Head toward the bus station on Lastekodu to reach the **central market** *(turg),* Keldrimaë 9.

👁 SIGHTS

VANALINN (OLD TOWN)

ALL-LINN. Enter Vanalinn through the Viru gate and head up Viru to reach **Raekoja plats** (Town Hall Square), where beer flows in outdoor cafes and local troupes perform throughout the summer. In July, classical music concerts are held each weekend in the town hall, Europe's oldest; buy tickets at the tourist office. *(Museum and interior open July M-F 10am-2pm. 30EEK, students 20EEK. Tower open June-Aug. Tu-Su 11am-6pm. 25EEK/15EEK.)* Take Mündi out of the square, turn right on Pühavaimu, and then left on Vene to reach the **Tallinn City Museum** (Tallinna Linnamuuseum), Vene 17. The visitor-friendly museum charts the city's history from its founding in 1219. *(Open May-Sept. W-M 10:30am-5:30pm; Oct.-Apr. 11am-4:20pm. 25EEK, students 10EEK.)* Continue up Vene, turn left on Olevimägi, and turn right on Pikk for a view of the medieval city's north towers. Head to the other end of Pikk and turn left on Rataskaevu to see **St. Nicholas Church** (Niguliste kirik) and its mighty spire. The church also houses an exquisite silver treasury. *(Open W-Su 10am-5pm. Organ music Sa-Su 4-4:30pm. Silver treasury 35 EEK, students 20EEK.)*

TOOMPEA. Toompea's **Lossi plats** (Castle Square) is dominated by the onion domes of golden **Aleksander Nevsky Cathedral**. *(From Raekoja pl., head down Kullassepa, right on Niguliste, and uphill on Lühike jalg. Open daily 8am-7pm. Services 9am and 6pm.)* Directly behind **Toompea Castle**, the current seat of the Estonian Parliament (closed to the public), an Estonian flag tops **Tall Hermann** (Pikk Hermann), Tallinn's tallest tower and most impressive medieval fortification. The spires of 13th-century **Toomkirik** tower over Toompea; to reach the cathedral, take either Piiskopi or Toom-Kooli to Kiriku pl. *(Open Tu-Su 9am-5pm. Services Su 10am.)* Next door is the **Art Museum of Estonia** (Eesti Kunstimuuseum), Kiriku pl. 1, which features 19th- to 20th-century Estonian art. *(Open W-Su 11am-6pm. 20EEK, students 5EEK.)*

KADRIORG. Among the quiet paths, shady trees, and fountains of Kadriorg Park is Peter the Great's ■**Kadriorg Palace**, whose sumptuous grand hall is considered to be one of the best Baroque rooms in Northern Europe. *(www.ekm.ee. Open May-Sept. Tu-Su 10am-5pm; Oct.-Apr. W-Su 10am-5pm. 35EEK, students 20EEK.)* The grounds also have two superb art museums, as well as the **Peter the Great Museum** in Peter's temporary residence. The museum holds many of the tsar's original furnishings, as well as an imprint of his extremely large hand. *(Mäekalda 2. From Vanalinn, follow Narva mnt. and at the fork veer right on Weizenbergi (20-30min.); or, take tram #1 or 3 to Kadriorg. Open W-Su 10:30am-5:30pm. 10EEK, students 5EEK.)*

ROCCA-AL-MARE. On the peninsula of Rocca-al-Mare, 10km west of the city center, is the **Estonian Open-Air Museum** (Eesti Vabaõhumuuseum). The park is filled with 17th- to 20th-century wooden mills and homesteads collected from all over the country. Estonian folk troupes perform here regularly. *(Vabaõhumuuseumi 12. From Tallinn's train station, take bus #21 or tram #7 (25min.). Open May-Aug. daily 10am-6pm; Sept. and Nov.-Apr. 10am-5pm; Oct. 10am-4pm. 25EEK, students 9EEK.)*

🎵 🎭 ENTERTAINMENT AND NIGHTLIFE

Pick up *Tallinn This Week* at the tourist office (free). The **Estonia Concert Hall** and the **Estonian National Opera** are both at Estonia pst. 4. (Concert Hall ☎614 77 60; www.concert.ee. Box office open M-F noon-7pm, Sa noon-5pm. Tickets 30-150EEK. Opera ☎626 02 60; www.opera.ee. Box office open daily noon-7pm. Tickets up to 200EEK.) On summer Sundays, all of Tallinn converges on the beach of **Pirita** on the outskirts of the city. (Take bus #1, 1a, 8, 34, or 38 from the post office to Pirita.) During **Old Town Days** (usually from late May to early June), the city fills with open-air concerts. The first week of July brings **Beersummer**, a celebration of all that foams. Vanalinn is packed with bars; a boisterous crowd gathers at **Nimeta Baar**, Suur-Karja 4/6. (Beer 32EEK. Happy Hour 6pm. Open Su-Th 11am-2am, F-Sa 11am-4am.) **Café V.S.** (Võitlev Sõna), Pärnu mnt. 28, decorated like a submarine, is a local favorite. (Beer 30EEK. Open M-Th 10am-1am, F-Sa 10am-3am, Su 1pm-1am.) The female-oriented **Venus Club**, Vana-Viru 14, at the corner with Mere pst., is decorated with statues of Venus and other goddesses. (Cover 100EEK, women free W-Th and 10-11pm F-Sa. Open W-Th 10pm-4am, F-Sa 10pm-5am.)

ESTONIA

⚡ DAYTRIP FROM TALLINN: PÄRNU

Breezy Pärnu, famous for its mud baths, beaches, and festivals, is the summer capital of Estonia. At the **Mudaravila** health resort, Ranna pst. 1, you can get hosed with mud or covered with mud compresses for 90-130EEK. (www.mudaravila.ee. Open M-F 8am-3pm.) Take a break from relaxing to visit Pärnu's **Museum of Modern Art,** Esplanaadi 10, which exhibits unorthodox contemporary art. (Open daily 9am-9pm. 15EEK, students 10EEK.) The clean water of the white-sand **beach** warms up in July and August. At night, crowds dance on the beach at **Sunset Club,** Ranna pst. 3. (Open W-Th and Su 10am-4am, F-Sa 10pm-6am.)

Buses (☎720 02; Eurolines ☎278 41) go from Ringi 3 to: Rīga (3½hr., 4 per day, 110-150EEK); Tallinn (2hr., 46 per day, 30-80EEK); and Tartu (2½hr., 24 per day, 45-180EEK). Tattapood, Riia 95 (☎324 40), rents **bikes** for 75EEK per day. (Open M-F 10am-6pm, Sa 10am-2pm.) The **tourist office,** Rüütli 16, gives out the invaluable *Pärnu In Your Pocket* for free. (☎730 00; www.parnu.ee. Open May 15-Sept. 15 M-F 9am-6pm, Sa 9am-4pm, Su 10am-3pm; Sept. 16-May 14 M-F 9am-5pm.) **Tanni-Vakoma Majutusbüroo,** Hommiku 5, behind the bus station, arranges **private rooms ❶.** (☎310 70. Open May-Aug. M-F 10am-8pm, Sa-Su 10am-3pm. 130-330EEK per person.) **Trahter Postipoiss ❷,** Vee 12, serves small, delicious portions of Russian delicacies, as well as fish and meat dishes. (☎648 64. Main dishes 45-175EEK. Call ahead on F-Sa; live music and dancing 9pm. Open Su-Th noon-midnight, F-Sa noon-2am.) Cafeteria-style **Georg ❶,** Rüütli 43, is packed with locals. (Main dishes under 35EEK. Open M-F 7:30am-10pm, Sa-Su 9am-10pm.) ☎044.

TARTU   ☎07

Tartu, the oldest city in the Baltics, is home to prestigious **Tartu University** (Tartu Ülikool). Tartu's social center is **Raekoja plats** (Town Hall Square), built in 1775. From there, follow Ülikooli behind the town hall to the university's main building at Ülikooli 18. In the attic is the ◪**student lock-up** *(kartser),* which until 1892 was used to detain rule-breaking students; their drawings and inscriptions are still visible. (Open M-F 11am-5pm. 5EEK, students 2EEK.) The **Tartu City Museum** (Tartu Linnamuuseum), Narva mnt. 23, details Tartu's history and hosts concerts. (Open Tu-Su 11am-6pm. 20EEK, students 5EEK.) **Cathedral Hill** (Toomemägi) features statues, an observatory, and the ruins of the **Cathedral of St. Peter and Paul** (Toomkirik).

Buses (☎47 72 27) leave from Turu 2, on the corner with Riia, 300m southeast of Raekoja pl. along Vabaduse, for: Pärnu (4hr., 20 per day, 50-95EEK); Rīga (5hr., 1 per day, 190EEK); St. Petersburg (10hr., 1 per day, 160EEK); and Tallinn (2-5hr., 46 per day, 50-80EEK). Some routes offer 30-50% ISIC discounts. **Trains** (☎615 68 51), generally less reliable than buses, go from the intersection of Kuperjanovi and Vaksali, 1.5km from the center, to Tallinn (3½hr., 2 per day, 70EEK). Public buses #5 and 6 run from the train stop to the city center and then to the bus station. From the bus station, follow Riia mnt. and turn right on Ülikooli to reach Raekoja pl. Pick up the helpful *Tartu Today* (15EEK) at the **tourist office,** Raekoja pl. 14. (☎/fax 44 21 11; www.tartu.ee. Open M-F 9am-5pm, Sa 10am-3pm; June-Aug. also Su 10am-2pm.) ◪**Üliôpilaselamu Hostel ❷,** Pepleri 14, has cheerful, modern rooms with private baths. From the bus station, take Vadabuse toward town, turn left on Vanemuise, then take a left on Pepleri. (☎842 76 08; janikah@ut.ee. Singles 250EEK; doubles 400EEK.) The tavern **Püssirohu Kelder ❸,** Lossi 28, has an international menu. (Live music Tu-Sa 9 or 10pm. Open M-Th noon-2am, F-Sa noon-3am, Su noon-midnight.) ◪**Wilde Irish Pub ❸,** Vallikraavi 4, serves Irish and Estonian dishes. (Main dishes 45-170EEK. Live music M-Sa 9 or 10pm. Open M-Tu 11am-midnight, W-Th 11am-1am, F-Sa 11am-3am, Su noon-midnight.) **Postal code:** 51001.

ESTONIAN ISLANDS

Afraid that Estonia's 1500 islands would serve as an escape route to the West, the Soviets cordoned them off from foreign and mainland influence; the islands now remain a preserve for all that is distinctive about Estonia.

SAAREMAA. Kuressaare, the largest town of the island of Saaremaa, is making a comeback with summer tourists but remains quiet and tranquil. Head south from Raekoja pl. (Town Hall Square) along Lossi, through the park, and across the moat to reach the 1260 ◪**Bishopric Castle** (Piiskopilinnus). Inside, the eclectic **Saaremaa Museum** chronicles the island's history. (Open May-Aug. daily 10am-6pm; Sept.-Apr. W-Su 11am-6pm. 30EEK, students 15EEK.) Rent a **bike** (135EEK per day) at **Oü Bivarix,** Tallinna 26, near the bus station, to pedal to the beaches of Southwest Saaremaa (8-12km from Kuressaare), to **Karujärve Lake** in West Saaremaa (23km), or to the striking 13th-century **Kaarma Church** in East Saaremaa (15km).

Direct **buses** (☎316 61) leave from Pihtla tee 2, at the corner with Tallinna, for Tallinn (3-4hr., 10 per day, 100-160EEK) and Pärnu (3½hr., 5 per day, 99-120EEK). The **tourist office,** Tallinna 2, in the town hall, has maps (10EEK) and arranges private rooms (200-250EEK) for no fee. (☎/fax 331 20; www.visitestonia.com. Open May-Sept. 15 M-F 9am-7pm, Sa 9am-5pm, Su 10am-3pm; Sept. 16-Apr. M-F 9am-5pm.) **Transvaali 28 B&B ❷,** Transvaali 28, has renovated rooms with private baths. (☎333 34; rand@tt.ee. 250EEK per person.) ☎045.

HIIUMAA. By restricting access to Hiiumaa for 50 years, the Soviets unwittingly preserved the island's rare plant and animal species. Creek-laced **Kärdla** is the island's biggest town. To explore the interesting sights along the coast, rent a **bike** (100EEK per day) from **Kerttu Sport,** Sadama 15, across the bridge from the bus station. (☎321 30. Open M-F 10am-6pm, Sa 10am-3pm.) Bike west from Kärdla toward Kõrgessaare to the spooky **Hill of Crosses** (Ristimägi; 6km) and turn right to reach the **Tahkuna Lighthouse** (11km, mostly unpaved), brought from Paris in 1874. Return to the main road and turn right again toward Kõrgessaare; continue 20km past the town to reach the impressive 16th-century **Kõpu Lighthouse,** which offers a panoramic view of the Baltic Sea. (15EEK, students 5EEK.) The whole trip is 38km; buses travel the same route. The tiny island of **Kassari** is attached to Hiiumaa by a land bridge from Käina, which can be reached from Kärdla by local buses or a 22km bike ride. The island's most beautiful sight is the 1.3m-wide ◪**Sääretirp** peninsula, covered in wild strawberry and juniper bushes and jutting 3km into the sea.

Ferries run between Saaremaa's Triigi port and Hiiumaa's Sõru port (1hr.; 3 per day; 50EEK, students 30EEK). Direct **buses** run from Sadama 13 (☎320 77), north of Kärdla's main square, Keskväljak, to Tallinn (4½hr., 3 per day, 140EEK). The **tourist office,** Hiiu 1, in Keskväljak, sells maps (15-40EEK) and *The Lighthouse Tour* (25EEK), an indispensable guide. (☎222 32; www.hiiumaa.ee. Open May-Sept. M-F 9am-6pm, Sa-Su 10am-2pm; Oct.-Apr. M-F 10am-4pm.) ◪**Eesti Posti Puh-kekeskus ❶,** Posti 13, has modern rooms and clean shared baths. From Keskväljak, turn onto Uus to reach Posti; look for the pink building on the left. (☎918 71. Bike rental 40EEK. Call ahead. Singles 150EEK; doubles 300EEK.) Käina boasts Hiiu-maa's best restaurant, ◪**Lilia Restoran ❸,** Hiiu mnt. 22, which serves high-society dishes at budget prices. (Main dishes 50-120EEK. Open daily noon-11pm.) ☎046.

COPS VS. PUNKS In Kuressaare, someone had the bright idea to put these epic rivals together on the pitch to let out their aggressions. Since that day, every June, the blue uniforms and the rainbow mohawks have had at each other with slide tackles and flurries of obscenities. The quality of the soccer is usually poor—the keg of beer on the sideline doesn't help—but the game is a town spectacle that draws crowds of fans, most of whom side with the underdog punks.

ESTONIA

FINLAND (SUOMI)

After seven centuries in the crossfire of warring Sweden and Russia, Finland gained autonomy in 1917 and never looked back. Hearty nationalism is expressed in typical Finnish fashion—with a heavy dose of modesty and prudence. But though politically and socially neutral, Finland is a country with dramatic natural extremes and cutting-edge architecture and design. Endless summer nights contrast with dark winter days, and provincial seaside towns stand against bustling, modern Helsinki. Even Finnish culture varies, with Swedish influences in the west and Russian characteristics in the east.

FACTS AND FIGURES

Official Name: Republic of Finland.

Capital: Helsinki.

Major Cities: Tampere, Turku, Oulu.

Population: 5,175,000.

Land Area: 305,000 sq. km.

Time Zone: GMT +2.

Languages: Finnish, Swedish.

Religions: Evangelical Lutheran (89%).

DISCOVER FINLAND

Vibrant **Helsinki** (p. 304) hugs the Russian border, mixing Orthodox cathedrals, Lutheran churches, sleek 20th-century architecture, and grand 19th-century avenues. Stroll along the river in **Turku** (p. 310), Finland's oldest city, before ferrying to the lovely **Åland Islands** (p. 310), best explored by bike and boat. For even more stunning scenery, head to the Lake District's **Savonlinna** (p. 314) and the **Punkaharju Ridge** (p. 314). Check out quirky **Tampere** (p. 313) before traveling north into **Lapland** (p. 316), Europe's last great wilderness.

ESSENTIALS

WHEN TO GO

The long days of Finnish summers make for a tourist's dream, although the situation reverses in winter. After coming out of the two-month *kaamos* (polar night) without any sunlight, winter fanatics start hitting the slopes in early February; the skiing continues into March and April. The temperature averages about 15-25°C (60-77°F) in the summer and dips as low as -20°C (-5°F) in the winter.

DOCUMENTS AND FORMALITIES

VISAS. South Africans need a visa for stays of any length. EU citizens may stay for as long as they like. Citizens of Australia, Canada, New Zealand, and the US do not need a visa for stays of up to 90 days, but this three-month period begins upon entry into any Nordic country; for more than 90 days in any combination of Denmark, Finland, Iceland, Norway, and/or Sweden, you will need a visa.

EMBASSIES. Foreign embassies are in Helsinki (p. 304). Finnish embassies at home include: **Australia,** 12 Darwin Ave., Yarralumla, ACT 2600 (☎26 273 38 00; www.finland.org.au); **Canada,** 55 Metcalfe St., Suite 850, Ottawa, ON K1P 6L5 (☎613-236-2389; www.finemb.com); **Ireland,** Russell House, Stokes Pl., St. Stephen's Green, Dublin 2 (☎01 478 1344; fax 01 478 3727); **South Africa,** P.O. Box

443, Pretoria 0001 (☎012 343 0275; fax 012 343 3095); **UK,** 38 Chesham Pl., London SW1X 8HW (☎020 7838 6200; www.finemb.org.uk); **US,** 3301 Massachusetts Ave. NW, Washington, D.C. 20008 (☎202-298-5800; www.finland.org).

TRANSPORTATION

BY PLANE. Finnair (Finland ☎(09) 818 83 83; US ☎800-950-5000; UK ☎020 7514 2400; www.finnair.com) flies from 50 international cities and also covers the domestic market. Finnair gives a domestic discount of up to 50% for ages 17-24, and has summer and snow rates that reduce fares by up to 60%.

BY TRAIN. Eurail is valid in Finland. The national rail company is **VR Ltd., Finnish Railways** (☎30 72 09 00; www.vr.fi). Efficient trains run at typically high Nordic prices; seat reservations (€2.20-8.40) are not required except on the faster *Inter-City* and *pendolino* trains. A **Finnrail Pass** gives three days (€114), five days (€154), or 10 days (208) of travel in a one month period. The *buy-in-Scandinavia* **Scanrail Pass** allows unlimited rail travel through Denmark, Norway, Sweden, and Finland, and many free or discounted ferry rides. (5 days within 15 days €270; 21 consecutive days €418.) Only three of those days can be used in the country of purchase, however, so the *buy-outside-Scandinavia* **Scanrail Pass** (see p. 59) is more economical for those not visiting Denmark, Norway, or Sweden.

BY BUS. Buses cost the same as or more than trains, but they are the only way to reach some smaller towns or to travel past the Arctic Circle. **Expressbus** covers most of Finland (☎0200 4000; www.expressbus.com). **Onni Vilkas Ltd.** (www.onnivilkas.fi) runs a daily bus between Helsinki and St. Petersburg, as well as domestic service. ISIC cardholders can buy a **student card** (€5.40 plus passport-sized photo), which discounts tickets by 50%, from bus stations. Most drivers will give the student discount to those with student ID. **Railpasses** are valid on VR Ltd. buses when trains are not in service.

BY FERRY. Viking Line (Helsinki ☎(09) 123 51; Stockholm ☎08 452 40 00) runs from Stockholm to: Helsinki; Mariehamn on Åland; and Turku. Scanrail holders get 50% off on Viking; Eurailers ride free. **Silja Line** (Helsinki ☎(09) 180 41; Stockholm ☎08 452 50 00; www.silja.com/english) sails from Stockholm to Helsinki, Mariehamn, and Turku. **Birka Lines** (Mariehamn ☎(018) 270 27; Stockholm ☎08 702 72 30; www.birkacruises.com) sails daily from Mariehamn to Stockholm.

BY CAR. A valid driver's license from your country of residence is needed to operate a car. Driving conditions are good, but be wary of reindeer crossings and winter hazards. Drive on the right side of the road. For car rentals, contact **Europcar** (☎ (0800) 121 54; www.europcar.com), **Budget** (☎ (0800) 12 44 24; www.budget.fi), or **Hertz** (☎ (0800) 11 22 33 or (020) 555 24 00; www.hertz.com); most companies charge about €320-480 per week.

BY BIKE AND BY THUMB. Finland has 10,000km of **cycling** paths. Rental rates average €5-15 per day or €35-50 per week. **Hitchhikers** find more rides in Finland than elsewhere in Scandinavia, but the language barrier is more likely to be a problem. *Let's Go* does not recommend hitchhiking.

TOURIST SERVICES AND MONEY

EMERGENCY	**Police:** ☎ 122. **Ambulance:** ☎ 123. **Fire:** ☎ 124.

TOURIST OFFICES. The helpful **Finnish tourist boards** offer a comprehensive website (www.mek.fi). Contact the tourist office of the region you plan to visit.

MONEY. The official currency of Finland is the **euro.** The *markka* can still be exchanged at a rate of 5.95mk to €1. For exchange rates and more information on the euro, see p. 16. Banks exchange currency and accept ATM cards. **Forex** offices and **ATMs** offer the best exchange rates. Orange "Otto" bank machines accept Cirrus, MC, Visa, and ATM cards. Food runs €10-17 per day if you're shopping in grocery stores; meals generally cost at least €6 for lunch and €10 for dinner. Restaurants include a 15% gratuity in the meal price, although an extra 10% tip is not uncommon for good service. Round the fare up to the nearest euro for cab drivers. A normal tip for bellhops, train porters, and sauna and coatroom attendants is €1-2. The European Union imposes a **value-added tax (VAT)** on goods and services purchased within the EU, which is included in the price (see p. 15).

BUSINESS HOURS. Most shops are open Monday to Friday from 9am until 8 or 9pm, and Saturday from 9am until 3 or 6pm. Some shops are open on Sundays from noon until 9pm. Banks are typically open Monday to Friday 9am-4:30pm.

COMMUNICATION

PHONE CODES	**Country code: 358. International dialing prefix: 00.** From outside Finland, dial the int'l dialing prefix (see inside back cover) + 358 + city code + local number.

TELEPHONES. To make a long-distance call within Finland, dial 0 and the number. Local and long-distance calls within Finland usually cost €0.55; **Finncards** are available from R-kiosks and post offices in €5, €6, and €10 denominations. Cell phones are the main mode of Finnish conversation; prepaid cellphone cards are widely available and can be used to make international calls, although rates are high. For domestic information, call ☎ 118. For international information, call ☎ 020 208. International direct dial numbers include: **AT&T**, ☎ 0800 1100 15; **British Telecom,** ☎ 0800 11 04 40; **Canada Direct,** ☎ 0800 1100 11; **Ireland Direct,** ☎ 0800 11 03 53; **MCI,** ☎ 08001 102 80; **Sprint,** ☎ 0800 11 02 84; **Telecom New Zealand,** ☎ 0800 11 06 40; **Telkom South Africa,** ☎ 0800 11 02 70; and **Telstra Australia,** ☎ 0800 11 00 610.

MAIL. Mail service is fast and efficient. Postcards and letters under 50g cost €0.60 within Finland, €0.80 within the EU, and €1.10 for outside Europe. Letters under 20g going outside Finland cost €0.60. *Poste Restante* can be sent to any town's main post office.

LANGUAGES. Finnish is spoken by most of the population. In Helsinki, about 90% of the city speaks English, and Swedish is officially spoken as well. Sami (Lappish) is the tongue of about 1700 people in northern Finland. There are fewer English speakers in smaller towns, but the language barrier shouldn't pose a problem. Some town names modify form on train and bus schedules. For example, "To Helsinki" is *"Helsinkiin,"* while "From Helsinki" is *"Helsingistä."* For Finnish words and phrases, see p. 1055.

ACCOMMODATIONS AND CAMPING

FINLAND	❶	❷	❸	❹	❺
ACCOMMODATIONS	under €12	€12-25	€25-50	€50-75	over €75

Finland has over 100 **youth hostels** (*retkeilymaja*; RET-kay-loo-MAH-yah), although only 50 are open all year. Prices average €10-50 per person; non-HI-members add €2.50. Most have laundry facilities and a kitchen; some have saunas and rent bicycles, boats, or ski equipment. The **Finnish Youth Hostel Association** (Suomen Retkeilymaja-järjestö; **SRM;** ☎ (09) 565 71 50; www.srmnet.org) is Finland's HI affiliate. **Hotels** are often exorbitant (over €50); *kesähotelli* (summer hotels) operate from June to August, and cost about €18.50 per person. The **Finland Tourism Board** (www.mek.fi) keeps a database of booking agencies for year-round and summer hotels. **Private room** rental is not particularly common. Local tourist offices can help you find the cheapest accommodations. About 350 **campgrounds** dapple the country, 70 open year-round (tent sites €7-20 per night; *mökit* (small cottages) from €26). Finnish or International Camping Cards (FICC; €5 at campsites) earn discounts at most campgrounds. For a campground guide, contact the **Finnish Campingsite Association** (☎ (09) 622 628 23; www.camping.fi). You may camp for free for one or two nights anywhere as long as you respect the flora, fauna, and the owner's privacy, and pick up all garbage.

FOOD AND DRINK

FINLAND	❶	❷	❸	❹	❺
FOOD	under €8	€8-15	€15-20	€20-30	over €30

A *kahvila* serves food, coffee, and beer; a *grilli* is a fast-food stand. A *ravintola* (restaurant) may be anything from a cafeteria to a pub. The best budget dining is at all-you-can-eat lunch buffets (€6-10), often found at otherwise pricey restaurants. Kebab and pizza joints are cheap (from €4), but their quality varies. The cheapest supermarkets are Alepa, Euromarket, Valintatalo, and K markets. The Finns are proud of their fish, including *taimen* (trout), *silakka* (Baltic herring), and *lohi* (salmon). Finnish dietary staples include rye bread, potatoes, sour milk, Karelian pastries, and *viili* (yogurt). Reindeer meat, roasted or in a stew, is on some menus. In summer, blueberries, cranberries, lingonberries, and Arctic cloudberries are picked for desserts, wines, vodka, and other liquors. You must be 18 to purchase beer and wine, 20 for hard liquor; the age limit in bars is usually 18 but can be as high as 25. Outside bars and restaurants, all alcohol stronger than light beer must be purchased at state-run Alko liquor stores.

HOLIDAYS AND FESTIVALS

Holidays: New Year's Day (Jan. 1); Epiphany (Jan. 6); Good Friday (Apr. 18); Easter (Apr. 20-21); May Day (May 1); Ascension Day (May 29); Midsummer (June 21-23); All Saints' Day (Nov. 1); Independence Day (Dec. 6); Christmas Day (Dec. 25); Boxing Day (Dec. 26). Virtually the entire country shuts down during Midsummer, when Finns party all night to the light of *kokko* (bonfires) and the midnight sun.

Festivals: The **Helsinki Festival** (Aug. 22-Sept. 7) fills the city with concerts, dance, theater, and opera. Savonlinna's **Opera Festival** (early July to early Aug.), in Olavinlinna Castle, is Finland's largest cultural event. The **Pori Jazz Festival** draws huge crowds and top musicians (July 12-20). Each Midsummer, thousands of Finns head for the beaches of Rauma for its annual **Rock Festival.** Finland's biggest rock festival, **Ruisrock,** takes place in Turku each July. Naantali hosts a well-known **Chamber Music Festival** (June).

HELSINKI (HELSINGFORS)   ☎09

With all the appeal of a big city but none of the grime, Helsinki's broad avenues, grand architecture, and green parks make it a model of 19th-century city planning. The city also distinguishes itself with a decidedly multicultural flair: Lutheran and Russian Orthodox cathedrals stand almost face-to-face, and youthful energy mingles with old-world charm. Baltic Sea produce fills the marketplaces and restaurants, while St. Petersburg and Tallinn are only a short cruise away.

▐ TRANSPORTATION

Flights: Helsinki-Vantaa Airport (HEL; ☎(020) 046 36). **Buses** #615 and 616 (less direct) run frequently between the airport and the train station square (€3). A **Finnair bus** shuttles between the airport and the Finnair building at Asemaaukio 3, next to the train station (35min., every 15min. 5am-midnight, €4.90).

Trains: ☎(030) 072 09 00. Reserve for all routes. To: **Moscow** (15hr., 5:40pm, €83); **Rovaniemi** (10-13hr., 5-8 per day, €68-70); **St. Petersburg** (7hr., 2 per day, €50); **Tampere** (2hr., 6am-10pm, €22-26); **Turku** (2hr., 12 per day, €22-26).

Buses: ☎020 040 00; for Espoo and Vantaa buses, ☎010 01 11. The station is between Salomonkatu and Simonkatu; from the Mannerheimintie side of the train station, take Postikatu past the statue of Mannerheim. Cross Mannerheimintie onto Salomonkatu; the station will be to your left. To: **Lahti** (1½hr., 2 per hr., €17); **Tampere** (2½hr., every hr., €18); **Turku** (2½hr., 2 per hr., €20.90).

Ferries: For route options, see p. 301. **Silja Line,** Mannerheimintie 2 (☎980 07 45 52 or 091 80 41). Take tram #3B or 3T from the city center to the Olympic terminal. **Viking Line,** Mannerheimintie 14 (☎12 35 77). **Tallink,** Erottajankatu 19 (☎22 82 12 77).

Local Transportation: ☎010 01 11. **Metro, trams,** and **buses** run roughly 5:30am-11pm; major tram and bus lines, including tram #3T, run until 1:30am. There is one Metro line (running approximately east to west), 10 tram lines, and many more bus lines. **Night buses,** marked with an N, run after 1:30am. Single-fare tickets are €2 on buses and trams or from machines at the Metro station; cheaper advance tickets (€1.40) and 10-trip tickets (€12.80) are available at R-kiosks and at the **City Transport** office in the Rautatientori Metro station (open in summer M-Th 7:30am-6pm, F 7:30am-4pm; off-season M-Th 7:30am-7pm, F 7:30am-5pm, Sa 10am-3pm). Tickets are valid for 1hr. (transfers free); punch your ticket on board. The **Tourist Ticket,** a convenient bargain for a 5-day stay, is available at City Transport and tourist offices and provides unlimited bus, tram, Metro, and local train transit (1-day €4.20, 3-day €8.40, 5-day €12.60; children 50% discount).

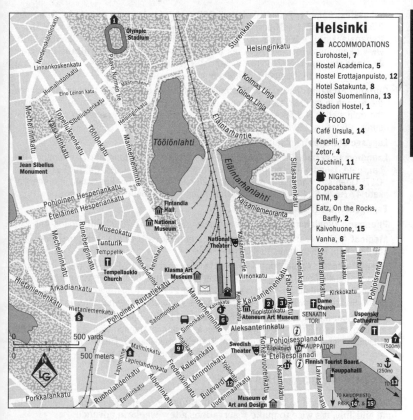

Helsinki

♦ ACCOMMODATIONS
Eurohostel, 7
Hostel Academica, 5
Hostel Erottajanpuisto, 12
Hotel Satakunta, 8
Hostel Suomenlinna, 13
Stadion Hostel, 1

● FOOD
Café Ursula, 14
Kapeli, 10
Zetor, 4
Zucchini, 11

■ NIGHTLIFE
Copacabana, 3
DTM, 9
Eatz, On the Rocks,
  Barfly, 2
Kaivohuone, 15
Vanha, 6

FINLAND

◤◪ ORIENTATION AND PRACTICAL INFORMATION

Sea surrounds Helsinki on the east and west, and the city center is bisected by two lakes. Water shapes everything in the Finnish capital, from relaxing city beaches to gorgeous parks around the lakes. Helsinki's main street, **Mannerheimintie,** passes between the bus and train stations on its way to the city center, eventually crossing **Esplanadi.** This tree-lined promenade leads east to **Kauppatori** (Market Square) and the beautiful South Harbor. Both Finnish and Swedish are used on all street signs and maps; *Let's Go* uses the Finnish names in all listings and maps.

Tourist Offices: City Tourist Office, Pohjoisesplanadi 19 (☎169 37 57; www.hel.fi). From the train station, walk two blocks down Keskuskatu and turn left on Pohjoisesplanadi. Open May-Sept. M-F 9am-8pm, Sa-Su 9am-6pm; Oct.-Apr. M-F 9am-6pm, Sa-Su 10am-4pm. The **Finnish Tourist Board,** Eteläesplanadi 4 (☎41 76 93 00; www.mek.fi), has information on all of Finland. Open May-Sept. M-F 9am-5pm, Sa-Su 11am-3pm; Oct.-Apr. M-F 9am-5pm. **Hotellikeskus** (Hotel Booking Center; ☎22 88 14 00), in the train station, books rooms for a fee of €5.05 in person and for free by phone or email. Open June-Aug. M-F 9am-7pm, Sa-Su 10am-6pm; Sept.-May M-F 9am-6pm, Sa 9am-5pm. The **Helsinki Card,** sold at the tourist office, Hotellikeskus, central R-kiosks, and most hotels, provides unlimited local transportation and free or discounted admission to most museums (24hr. €24; 48hr. €32; 72hr. €38).

FINLAND

Embassies: Canada, Pohjoisesplanadi 25B (☎17 11 41; www.canada.fi). Open M-F 8:30am-noon and 1-4:30pm. **Ireland,** Erottajankatu 7A (☎64 60 06). **South Africa** Rahapajankatu 1A 5 (☎68 60 31 00). **UK,** Itäinen Puistotie 17 (☎22 86 51 00; www.ukembassy.fi). Also handles diplomatic matters for **Australians** and **New Zealanders.** Open M-F 8:30am-5pm. **US,** Itäinen Puistotie 14A (☎17 19 31; www.usembassy.fi). Open M-F 8:30am-5pm.

Currency Exchange: Forex, with 5 locations in Helsinki. Best rates in the city. Hours vary; the **branch** in the train station is open 8am-9pm. **Exchange,** Kaivokatu 6, across from the train station. €3.50 fee to convert foreign money to euros, no fee to convert from euros. €6 fee per traveler's check.

Luggage Storage: Train station lockers €3 per day.

Laundromat: ▧ **Cafe Tin Tin Tango** (☎27 09 09 72), Töölöntorinkatu 7, a combination bar, cafe, laundromat, and sauna. Laundry €3.40. Sandwiches €4.50-5.30. Sauna €17. Open M-F 7am-2am, Sa-Su 10am-2am. More typical is **Easywash,** Runeberginkatu 47 (☎40 69 82). Open M-Th 10am-9pm, F 10am-6pm, Sa 10am-4pm.

Emergency: ☎112. **Police:** ☎100 22.

Pharmacy: Yliopiston Apteekki, Mannerheimintie 96 (☎41 78 03 00). Open 24hr.

Medical Assistance: 24hr. medical advice **hotline** (☎100 23). 24hr. medical clinic **Mehilainen,** Runeberginkatu 47A (☎431 44 44).

Internet Access: Cable Book Library, Mannerheimintie 22-24, in the Lasipalatsi mall directly across from the bus station. Free; 30min. limit. Open M-Th 10am-8pm, Sa-Su noon-6pm. **Academic Bookstore,** Keskuskatu 2. Free; 15min. limit. Open M-F 9am-9pm, Sa 9am-6pm. The tourist office can give you a list of Internet cafes in the city.

Post Office: Mannerheiminaukio 1A (☎98 00 71 00). Open M-F 9am-6pm. Address mail to be held: Firstname SURNAME, *Poste Restante,* Mannerheiminaukio 1A, **00100** Helsinki, Finland. Open M-F 9am-6pm. **Branch** at Helsinki 10, Elielinaukio 2F (☎04 51 49 48), also handles *Poste Restante.* Open M-F 9am-9pm, Sa-Su 10am-6pm.

▐▌ ACCOMMODATIONS

Helsinki hotels tend to be expensive, but budget hostels are often quite nice. In June and July, it's wise to make reservations a few weeks in advance.

▧ **Hostel Erottanjanpuisto (HI),** Uudenmaankatu 9 (☎64 21 69). Head right from the train station, turn left on Mannerheimintie, bear right onto Erottajankatu, and turn right on Uudenmaankatu. On the 3rd fl. of a 19th-century building in the heart of the city. Well-kept rooms, friendly staff, and an unbeatable location. Reserve in advance. Kitchen. Breakfast €2. Lockers €2. Reception 24hr. In summer, dorms €19.50; singles €43.50; doubles €55. Off-season €1.70-6 less. Nonmembers add €2.50. ❷

Eurohostel (HI), Linnankatu 9, Katajanokka (☎622 04 70; www.eurohostel.fi). 200m from Viking Line/Finnjet ferry terminal. From the train station, head right to Mannerheimintie and take tram #2 or 4 to Katajanokka. From Uspensky Cathedral, head down Kanavankatu, turn left on Pikku Satamankatu, and bear right on Linnankatu. The largest hostel in Finland, with bright rooms, non-smoking floors, and a sauna. Kitchen and cafe. Breakfast €5. Sheets included. Lockers. Internet €1 per 10min. Reception 24hr. Dorms €19.50; singles €34; doubles €19.50. Nonmembers add €2.50. ❷

Hotel Satakunta (HI), Lapinrinne 1A (☎69 58 52 31; ravintola.satakunta@sodexho.fi). Take the Metro to Kampi and walk downhill, or take bus #55 or 55a and tell the driver your destination. Spacious, well-equipped rooms, most with balconies. Breakfast and sheets €5 each, included in private rooms. Laundry €5.50. Reception 24hr. Check-in 2pm. Check-out noon. Open June-Aug. Dorms €11; singles €32.50; doubles €47.50; triples €57.50; quads €67.50. Nonmembers add €2.50. ❶

FINLAND

Stadion Hostel (HI), Pohj. Stadiontie 3B (☎49 60 71; fax 49 64 66). Take tram #7A or 3 to the Auroran Sairaala stop. Walk to the right of the stop about 250m, following the signs; it's inside the fence. The hostel, on the far side of the stadium, is a converted athletic space popular with school groups. Kitchen. Breakfast and sheets €5. Laundry €2.50. Lockers €1 per day. Reception June to early Sept. daily 7am-3am; mid-Sept. to May 8-10am and 4pm-2am. Lockout noon-4pm. Dorms €12-17; singles €24; doubles €34; nonmembers add €2.50. ❶

Hostel Academica (HI), Hietaniemenkatu 14A (☎13 11 43 34; hostel.academica@hyy.fi). Take tram #3T to Kauppakorkeakoulu, go left to the end of Lapuankatu, and turn right on Hietaniemenkatu. Reception 24hr. Check-in 2pm. Check-out noon. Breakfast €5, sheets €4.50; both included in private rooms. Open in summer only. Dorms €16-21; singles €41; doubles €58; triples €71; quads €84. ❷

Hostel Suomenlinna (HI), Iso Mustasaari (☎684 74 71; fax 79 44 81), right by the main quay on Suomenlinna. In an old brick building on Suomenlinna's western island. Comfortable, tasteful rooms in a peaceful setting. 15min. by boat from Kauppatori. Breakfast €3. Sheets included. Reception 4-11pm; call ahead to arrive at another time. Dorms €17.50; doubles and triples €24.50. Nonmembers add €2.50. ❷

Rastila Camping, 12km east of the city center (☎321 65 51). Take the metro east to Rastila; the campsite is 100m to the right. Beach access, toilets, showers, and cooking facilities. Reception mid-May to mid-Sept. 24hr; mid-Sept. to mid-May daily 8am-10pm. 1 person and tent €9, 2 and tent €14; 2-person cabins €40; 4-person cabins €62. Summer **hostel:** dorms €17; singles €26; doubles €23; triples €63. ❶

🛒 FOOD

Restaurants and cafes are easy to find on **Esplanadi** and the streets branching off from **Mannerheimintie** and **Uudenmaankatu.** Cheaper options surround the **Hietalahti** flea market. An **Alepa supermarket** is under the train station. (Open M-F 7:30am-10pm, Sa 9am-10pm, Su 10am-10pm.) **Open-air markets** line **Kauppatori,** by the port. (Open June-Aug. M-Sa 6:30am-2pm and 3:30pm-8pm; Sept.-May M-F 7am-2pm.) **Vanha Kauppahalli** (Old Market Hall) is nearby. (Open M-F 8am-7pm, Sa 8am-4pm.)

Kapelli, Eteläesplanadi 1, at the Unionkatu end of Esplanadi park. Frequented by well-heeled bohemians since 1837. Outdoor cafe is perfect for the Esplanadi jazz concerts (see Entertainment, below). In the cafe, salads and sandwiches €5-8. In the restaurant: entrees €12-18. Open daily 9am-2am; kitchen closed at 1am. ❶

Zetor, Kaivokatu 10, in Kaivopiha, the mall directly opposite the train station. The name translates to tractor, explaining the farm decor. (Homemade beer €4. Entrees €7-21. 22+ after 9pm. Open Su-M 3pm-1am, Tu-Th 3pm-3am, F 3pm-4am, Sa 1pm-4am. ❷

Café Ursula, Kaivopuisto Park. Delicious meals in an idyllic setting on the edge of the Baltic Sea. Sandwiches €4-6, salads €8-9. Open daily 9am-midnight. ❶

Zucchini, Fabianinkatu 4, near the tourist office. A casual *kasvisravintola* (vegetarian restaurant). Daily lunch special €7.20. Open M-F 11am-4pm; closed July. ❶

👁 SIGHTS

Home to bold new designs and polished Neoclassical works, Helsinki echoes famed Finnish architect Alvar Aalto's statement, "Architecture is our form of expression because our language is so impossible." Much of the layout and architecture of the old center, however, is the brainchild of a German. After Helsinki became the capital of the Grand Duchy of Finland in 1812, Carl Engel designed a grand city modeled after St. Petersburg. **Tram #3T** circles past the major attractions in an hour, offering the cheapest city tour. Better yet, walk—

most sights are packed within 2km of the train station. Pick up *See Helsinki on Foot* from the tourist office. Helsinki's beautiful parks are must-sees, especially the promenade along **Töölönlahti,** which blooms with lilacs in the summer; seaside **Kaivopuisto Park** (see Entertainment, below); and **Tahtitorninvuori** (Observatory Park), overlooking Uspensky Cathedral.

SENAATIN TORI (SENATE SQUARE). The square and its gleaming white **Tuomiokirkko** (Dome Church) showcase Engel's work and exemplify the splendor of Finland's Russian period. *(At Aleksanterinkatu and Unioninkatu in the city center. Church open June-Aug. M-Sa 9am-midnight, Su noon-midnight; Sept.-May M-Sa 9am-6pm, Su noon-6pm.)*

USPENSKINKATEDRAADI (USPENSKY ORTHODOX CATHEDRAL). Mainly known for its red-and-gold cupolas and great spires, which jut prominently out of the city skyline, the Cathedral also has an ornate interior. *(Follow Esplanadi down to Kauppatori. Interior open M and W-Sa 9:30am-4pm, Tu 9:30am-6pm, Su 9:30am-3pm.)*

SUOMEN KANSALLISMUSEO (NATIONAL MUSEUM OF FINLAND). The museum displays intriguing bits of Finnish culture, from Gypsy and Sami costumes to *ryijyt* (rugs), as well as a magnificent roof mural by Akseli Gallen-Kallela. *(Up the street from the Finnish Parliament House. Open Tu-W 11am-8pm and Th-Su 11am-6pm. €4.)*

ART MUSEUMS. Ateneum Taidemuseo, Finland's largest art museum, features a comprehensive look at Finnish art from the 1700s to the 1960s. *(Kaivokatu 2, opposite the train station. Open Tu and F 9am-6pm, W-Th 9am-8pm, Sa-Su 11am-5pm. €5.50; special exhibits €7.50.)* **Kiasma** picks up where Ateneum leaves off, showcasing great modern art in a funky silver building. *(Mannerheiminaukio 2. Open Tu 9am-5pm, W-Su 10am-10:30pm. €5.50, special exhibits €7.50.)* The **Museum of Art and Design** presents the work of well-established Finnish designers alongside exciting creations by young artists. *(Korkeavuorenkatu 3. Open June-Aug. daily 11am-6pm; Sept.-May Tu and Th-Su 11am-6pm, W 11am-8pm. €6.50.)*

FINLANDIA TALO. Home to the Helsinki Philharmonic and the Radio Symphony Orchestra, this magnificent white-marble concert hall stands testament to the skill of the Finnish architect Alvar Aalto, who also designed the interior and furnishings. *(Mannerheimintie 13E. Info ☎ 402 41; finlandia.hel.fi. Tours in summer daily at 1:30pm. Concerts in winter only.)*

TEMPPELIAUKIO KIRKKO. Designed in 1969 by Tuomo and Timo Suomalainen, this inspiring church is built into a hill of rock, with only the roof visible from the outside. Inside, its huge domed ceiling appears to be supported by rays of sunshine. *(Lutherinkatu 3. Walk away from the main post office on Paasikivenaudio, which becomes Arkadiagatan, then turn right on Fredrikinatu and follow it to the end. Open M-F 10am-8pm, Sa 10am-6pm, Su noon-1:45pm and 3:15-5:45pm. Services in English Su 2pm.)*

JEAN SIBELIUS MONUMENT. Dedicated in 1967 by sculptor Eila Hiltunen to one of the 20th-century's greatest composers, the Sibelius monument looks like a stormcloud of organ pipes ascending to heaven. A well-touristed spot in a scenic area, the monument and its surrounding park make a great place for an afternoon picnic. *(On Mechelininkatu in Sibelius Park. Catch bus #24 (dir.: Seurasaari) from Mannerheimintie; get off at Rasjasaarentie and the monument will be behind you and to the left.)*

SUOMENLINNA. This 18th-century Swedish military fortification consists of five beautiful interconnected islands used by the Swedes to repel attacks on Helsinki. The old fortress's dark passageways are great to explore, and a number of the islands' six museums are worth a visit. *(www.suomenlinna.fi. Most museums open May-Aug. daily 11am-5pm; Sept.-Apr. hours vary. €5.50, students €2.50; some museums have additional admission. Ferries depart from Market Square every 20min. 8am-11pm; round-trip €4.)*

SEURASAARI. A quick walk across the beautiful white bridge from the mainland brings you to the many paths of the island of Seurasaari, repository of old churches and farmsteads transplanted from all over the country. An open-air museum allows entrance into many of the island's historical buildings. Visit during Midsummer to witness the *kokko* (bonfires) and Finnish revelry in its full splendor. *(Take bus #24 from Erottaja, outside the Swedish Theater, to the last stop. The island is always open for hiking. Museum open M-F 9am-3pm, Sa-Su 11am-5pm. €3.40, children free.)*

🎵 🎭 ENTERTAINMENT AND NIGHTLIFE

Helsinki's parks are always animated, with afternoon jazz all July in the **Esplanadi park** near the Kauppatori (www.kultturi.hel.fi/espanlava) and occasional pop/rock events at **Kaivopuisto park** (on the corner of Puistokatu and Ehrenstromintie, in the southern part of town) and **Hietaniemi beach** (down Hesperiankatu on the western shore). The free English-language papers *Helsinki This Week, Helsinki Happens,* and *City* list popular cafes, bars, nightclubs, and events; pick up copies at the tourist office.

You must be at least 22 years old to enter many clubs. With the exception of licensed restaurants and bars, only the state-run liquor store **Alko** can sell alcohol more potent than light beer. (Branch at Mannerheimintie 1, in Kaivopiha across from the train station. Open M-F 9am-8pm, Sa 9am-6pm.) Bars and clubs, ranging from laid-back neighborhood pubs to sleek discos, line **Mannerheiminkatu, Uudenmaankatu,** and nearby streets. East of the train station, the scene flourishes around **Yliopistonkatu** and **Kaisaniemenkatu.** The current hottest spot is on Mikonkatu, where three popular bar/clubs share a terrace: international **Eatz** (no cover), edgy **On the Rocks** (cover €6-7), and chic **Barfly** (F-Sa cover €7). **Copacabana,** Yliopistonkatu 5, has a salsa night each Sunday (F-Sa cover €7-8.50). A student crowd gathers at **Vanha,** Mannerheimintie 3, in the Old Students' House (F-Sa cover €2). **DTM** (Don't Tell Mama), Annankatu 32, is a popular gay club with a mixed following (F-Sa cover €4.50-5.50). Wednesday night turns **Kaivohuone,** in Kaivopuisto park, into a swimming pool (cover €4-10). Finland's best DJs play legendary six-hour sets at the roving **Club Unity,** Finland's longest-running club night (www.clubunity.org).

🏃 DAYTRIPS FROM HELSINKI

PORVOO. Porvoo, the nation's most photographed town (pop. 44,000) hugs the Porvoo River and follows Old King Rd., which passes from Helsinki to Russia. In 1809, Tsar Alexander I granted Finland autonomy at the Porvoo **cathedral** in the old town. (Open May-Sept. M-F 10am-6pm, Sa 10am-2pm, Su 2pm-5pm; Oct.-Apr. Tu-Sa 10am-2pm, Su 2-4pm. Free.) The former home of **Johan Ludvig Runeberg,** Aleksanterinkatu 3, is unfortunately closed for renovations until 2004; its sculpture exhibition, however, will remain open. (Open May-Aug. M-Sa 10am-4pm, Su 11am-5pm; Sept.-Apr. W-Su 11am-3pm. €4.) Try the poet's favorite dessert, the Runeberg tart (€2.70), at the delightful **Tea and Coffee Shop Helmi,** Välikatu 7, which captures Porvoo's 19th-century appeal. (Open June-Aug. daily 10am-7pm; Sept.-May M-Sa 10am-5pm, Su 11am-6pm.) **Buses** roll into Porvoo from Helsinki (1hr., every 15min., €7.90). The helpful **tourist office,** Rihkamakatu 4, gives out maps and finds accommodations for no fee. (☎520 23 16; www.porvoo.fi. Open mid-June to Aug. M-F 9am-6pm, Sa-Su 10am-4pm; Sept. to mid-June reduced hours.) ☎**019.**

HANKO. The seaside resort of Hanko juts out into a beautiful archipelago. Great villas lining the coastline reflect the decadence of the vanished Russian nobility. Choose from over 30km of **beaches;** those along Appelgrenintie are the most popular. **Trains** arrive from Helsinki (2hr., 6 per day, €13.50), as do **buses** (2¼hr., 5 per

YOUR OWN WAY

ÅLAND ISLANDS (AHVENANMAA)

The 6500 tiny islands of the autonomous Ålands have their own flag, parliament, and postal system, but they retain strong ties to both Sweden and Finland. Miles of beaches and flower-covered bike paths make the islands an extremely restful stepping stone between the two countries.

MARIEHAMN. On the south coast of the main island, the only actual town in Åland. Info: ☎ (018) 280 40.

SUND. Northeast of Mariehamn lie a number of historical sites in the midst of gorgeous countryside. Along the bike path to Godby is the **Kastelholms Slot,** a castle whose idyllic grounds contain an open-air museum. A tsarist Russian fortress is 10km down the road in **Bomarsund.**

ELSEWHERE. West of Åland is **Eckerö,** which has some of the islands' best beaches. Northern **Geta's** trails lead to a sweeping view of the entire island chain from **Geta bergen.** The true Åland, according to locals, can only be found in the diverse, untouristed **eastern archipelago.**

TRANSPORTATION. For information on traveling to Mariehamn from Helsinki, see p. 301. Birka Lines's *Princess* sails daily from Stockholm to Mariehamn (8hr., €6.60). Inter-island **ferries** are free for foot passengers and cyclists. The main island, Åland, is best explored by bike; **RoNo Rent,** facing the ferry terminal in the eastern harbor of Mariehamn, rents **bikes.**

day, €13.50). The **tourist office,** Raatihuoneentori 5, helps find rooms. (☎ 220 34 11; www.hanko.fi. Open June-July M-F 9am-5pm, Sa 10am-4pm; Apr.-Aug. M-F 9am-5pm; Sept.-Mar. M-F 8am-4pm.) Many **guesthouses ❹** are in former villas along Appelgrenintie. (Singles €53-60; doubles €65-85; triples €86-100.) On Långsanda, a dirt path off Appelgrenintie, is **Neljän Tuulen Tupa ❶** (The House of the Four Winds), a cafe that was once owned by a Finnish war hero and is a peaceful place to watch the ocean. (Sandwiches from €2.50. Open in summer only.) ☎ **019.**

LAHTI. World-class winter sports facilities, beautiful parks, and a vibrant harbor make Lahti a pleasant afternoon away from fast-paced Helsinki. The **Ski Museum** has ski-jump and biathalon simulators (open M-F 10am-5pm, Sa-Su 11am-5pm; €3.40, students €2.55) and stands at the starting point of an extensive network of cross-country **ski trails** (100km). A trail winds up from the waterfront **Kanniemi Park** to the **Lanu Sculpture Park,** which holds an evocative series of sculptures that blend seamlessly into the wooded landscape. Lahti also serves as a transportation hub, with **buses** to Jyväskylä (3hr., €16.15) and Savonlinna (4hr., €20.30). **Trains** go to: Helsinki (1½-2hr., every hr., €11.80-16.80); Savonlinna (3-3½hr., 5 per day, €34.20); St. Petersburg, Russia (4hr., 5 per day, €37.50); and Tampere (2hr., 15 per day, €22). The **tourist office** is at Aleksanterinkatu 16. (☎ 814 45 66; www.lahtitravel.fi. Open in summer M-F 9am-6pm, Sa 10am-2pm; off-season M-F 9am-5pm.) **Lahden Kansanopisto Hostel (HI) ❷,** Harjukatu 46, has airy rooms in a 19th-century building. Walk away from the train station on Vesijärvenkatu one block and turn right on Harjukatu. (☎ 878 11 81; www.lahdenkansopuisto.fi. Breakfast included. Reception M-F 8am-9pm, Sa-Su 8am-noon and 4-9pm. Open June to mid-Aug. Dorms €18; singles €29-35; doubles €40-50. Nonmembers add €3-6.) ☎ **03.**

TURKU (ÅBO)   ☎ 02

Turku (pop. 163,000), Finland's oldest city, became the capital in 1809 when Tsar Alexander I snatched the country from Sweden and granted it autonomy. After the capital moved to Helsinki in 1812, the worst fire in Scandinavian history devoured Turku's wooden buildings. Today, rebuilt Turku flourishes as a cultural and academic center.

⌘ ☎ TRANSPORTATION AND PRACTICAL INFORMATION. Trains arrive from Helsinki (2hr., 12 per day, €21.50-25.50) and Tampere (2hr., 11 per day, €19-24). Viking and Silja Line **ferries** depart for

Åland and Stockholm (see p. 301); to get to the terminal at the southwestern end of Linnankatu, hop on the train (3 per day) to the *satama* (harbor) or catch bus #1 from Kauppatori (€1.80). The **tourist office**, Aurakatu 2, has accommodations info and allows 15 minutes of free **Internet** access. (☎262 74 44; www.turkutouring.fi. Open June-Aug. M-F 8:30am-6pm, Sa-Su 9am-4pm; Sept.-May M-F 8:30am-6pm, Sa 10am-3pm.)

Åland and Stockholm (see p. 301)

⌂◻ ACCOMMODATIONS AND FOOD. The spacious **Hostel Turku (HI) ❶**, Linnankatu 39, is on the river between the ferry terminals and the train station. From the station, walk west four blocks on Ratapihankatu, turn left on Puistokatu, and make a right on Linnankatu at the river. From the ferry, walk 20min. up Linnankatu. (☎262 76 80; fax 262 76 75. Breakfast €4.50. Sheets €4.50. Laundry €1. Kitchen. Lockers. Reception 3pm-10am. Dorms €11; doubles €32; quads €46. Nonmembers add €2.50.) For well-kept, well-equipped rooms in a peaceful setting, try nun-run **Bridgettine Sisters' Guesthouse ❸**, Ursininkatu 15A, near the corner of Puutarhakatu. (☎250 19 10; birgitta.turku@kolubus.fi. All rooms with bath. Reception 8am-9pm. Singles €42; doubles €61; triples €80.) **Ruissalo Camping ❶** is near a beach on Ruissalo Island. Hop on bus #8 from Eerikinkatu. (☎262 51 00. Reception 7am-11pm. Open June-Aug. One person and tent €8.45, extra person €7.55. Electricity €3.50.) **Blanko ❷**, Aurakatu 1, serves beautifully prepared international dishes and hosts a club on Friday and Saturday nights. (Entrees €7-14. Open M-Tu 11am-1am, W-Th 11am-2am, F 11am-4am, Sa noon-4am, Su noon-1am. Club open F-Sa 10pm-4am.) Produce fills **Kauppatori** (open M-Sa 7am-2pm) and **Kauppahalli**, on Eerikinkatu (open M-Th 8am-5pm, F 8am-2pm, Sa 8am-2pm).

◙❶ SIGHTS AND ENTERTAINMENT. Turku surrounds the river Aura, and most of the sights are within meters of its banks. The **Turku Cathedral** towers above Tuomiokirkkotori (Cathedral Square). (Open mid-Apr. to mid-Sept. daily 9am-8pm; mid-Sept. to mid-Apr. 9am-7pm.) The 700-year-old **Turun Linna** (Turku Castle), about 3km from the town center, contains a **historical museum** with dark passageways, medieval artifacts, and Iron-Age dioramas. Catch the #1 bus (€1.80) from Market Square. (Open mid-Apr. to mid-Sept. daily 10am-6pm; mid-Sept. to mid-Apr. Tu-Su 10am-3pm. €6.50, children €4.50.) **Luostarinmäki**, the only neighborhood to survive the 1827 fire, now houses an open-air **handicrafts museum** with over 30 workshops. (Open mid-Apr. to mid-Sept. daily 10am-6pm; mid-Sept. to mid-Apr. Tu-Su 10am-3pm. €3.40, children €2.60.) The collections of the **Turun Taidemuseo** (Art Museum), which include vibrant *Kalevala* paintings by Akseli Gallen-Kallela, are temporarily being housed on Vartiovuorenmaki. (Open Tu-Th 11am-7pm, F-Su 10am-4pm. €3.50-5.50, special exhibitions €7.) **Aboa Vetus Ars Nova**, built on an excavated medieval site, houses a modern art museum above ground and an archaeological museum below ground. (Open May-Sept. 15 daily 11am-7pm; Sept. 15-Dec. 1 and Jan 2-May Th-Su 11am-7pm. €7, students €6.)

Turku is known throughout Finland for its pubs and breweries, many of which are housed in unusual spaces: an old apothecary (**Pub Uusi Apteeki**, Kaskenkatu 1), a 19th-century girls' school (**Brewery Restaurant Koulu**, Eerikinkatu 18), and a public restroom (**Restaurant Puutorin Vessa**, Puutori), to name a few. In summer, the boat restaurants docked on either bank of the river are popular spots for drinking and dancing. Posh **Prima**, Aurakatu 16, is the best place for late-night clubbing; it features two sleek clubs, a bar, and a basement Indian restaurant. (Cover for club F-Sa €3-5. Club open W-Th and Su 11pm-4am; F-Sa 10pm-4am. Bar open M-Tu 10am-1am, W-Sa 10am-4am, Su noon-4am. Restaurant open daily 5-10pm.) In mid-June, Turku hosts **Down by the Laituri,** a music and cultural festival (☎250 44 20; www.dbtl.fi). Ruissalo Island hosts **Ruisrock,** Finland's largest rock festival, in mid-July (☎(0600) 07 08 09; www.ruisrock.fi).

☒ DAYTRIP FROM TURKU: NAANTALI. Naantali, an enclave of old wooden houses 15km west of Turku, is awakened each summer by vacationing Finns. Mannerheiminkatu leads to the **Old Town,** whose buildings date to the late 18th century. Across the harbor is the Finnish president's fortress-like summer home, **Kultaranta;** if the flag's up, keep an eye out for her. The tourist office gives daily tours of the park around the home from late June to mid-August (☎435 98 00). A bus leaves from the tourist office daily at 10am and 2pm (€8, children €4.50) and from the park's main gate at 3pm (€5/€2.50). Naantali's main attraction is **Moomin World,** a harborside fantasy theme park. (☎511 11 11. Open June to mid-Aug. daily 10am-7pm. €13-17.) The **Naantali Music Festival** (☎434 53 63; www.naantalinmusiikkijuhlat.fi) brings classical music and opera in early June. The most traditional Naantali summer event is **Sleepyhead Day** (July 27), when the residents of Naantali get up at 6am, wake anyone still sleeping, and, dressed in carnival costumes, proceed to crown the year's Sleepyhead and throw him or her into the harbor. **Buses** #11, 110, and 111 run to Naantali from the marketplace in Turku (30-45min., €3.50). The **tourist office,** Kaivotori 2, books accommodations for no fee. From the bus station, walk southwest on Tullikatu to Kaivokatu and go right 300m; it will be on the left. (☎435 98 00; www.naantalinmatkailu.fi. Open June to mid-Aug. M-F 9am-6pm, Sa-Su 10am-3pm; mid-Aug. to May M-F 9am-4:30pm.) ☎02.

RAUMA   ☎02

Farther up the Baltic Coast lies the culturally bustling town of Rauma, known for its distinct lace and dialect. Old Rauma, a Nordic wooden town located in Rauma's center, is a UNESCO World Heritage site. Visit the **Old Town Hall Museum** to learn more about Rauma's past. (Open mid-May to Aug. daily 10am-5pm. €4.) The town also neighbors great **beaches,** where Rauma's hugely popular **Finnish Rock Festival** takes place each Midsummer (www.raumanmerenjuhannus.com). **Buses** arrive every hour from Pori (1hr.; €10.10, students €5.20) and Turku (2hr.; €14.60/€7.30). To reach the **tourist office,** Valtakatu 2, from the bus terminal, walk down Nortamonkatu and turn right. (☎834 45 51; www.rauma.fi. Open June-Aug. M-F 8am-6pm, Sa 10am-3pm, Su 11am-2pm; Sept.-May M-F 8am-4pm.) **Kesahotelli Rauma ❶,** Satamakatu 20, is a well-equipped summer hotel and hostel. (☎824 01 30. Breakfast and sheets €3 each; included for singles and doubles. Reception 7am-10pm. Dorms €9.50; singles €33; doubles €52.)

PORI   ☎02

Each July the coastal town of Pori overflows with tourists attending the **Pori Jazz Festival,** which attracts varied acts ranging from Herbie Hancock to Paul Simon. (July 12-20. Info ☎626 22 00; tickets ☎626 22 15; www.porijazz.fi. Tickets €7-60; some events free.) Head to the **Pori Art Museum,** on the corner of Etelärantakatu and Raatihuoneenkatu behind the tourist office, for Finnish and international modern art. (Open Tu-Su 11am-6pm, W 11am-8pm. In summer €5, students €2.50; off-season €3.50/€1.) Walk by the river to view beautiful architecture and spectacular greenery, or take bus #2 to **Reposaari** fishing village and the gorgeous **Yteri beach,** a 6km stretch considered one of Finland's best. **Trains** run to Helsinki (3½-4hr.; 5-8 per day; €27-30, students €14-15), some via Tampere (1½hr.; 5-7 per day; €13.60/€6.80). **Buses** go to Tampere (2hr., 4 per day, €15) and Turku (2hr., 6-7 per day, €20). The **tourist office,** Hallituskatu 9A, was attractively designed by Carl Engel. (☎621 12 73; www.pori.fi. Open June-Aug. M-F 8am-6pm; Sept.-May 8am-4pm.)

TAMPERE ☎ 03

Once Finland's industrial leader, Tampere is a compact city full of quirky museums, expansive beaches, energetic nightlife, and frequent cultural festivals.

▣⚄ TRANSPORTATION AND PRACTICAL INFORMATION. Trains head to: Helsinki (2hr., 2 per hr., €18-25); Oulu (4-5hr., 8 per day, €48-53); and Turku (2hr., 11 per day, €19-24). **Boats** (☎212 48 04) sail to smaller towns in the surrounding Lake Region. The **tourist office**, Verkatehtaankatu 2, and its army zipping around town on green scooters, offers incredible service and free **Internet**. From the train station, walk up Hämeenkatu, turn left before the bridge, and look for the sign. (☎31 46 68 00; www.tampere.fi. Open June-Aug. M-F 8:30am-8pm, Sa-Su 10am-5pm; Sept.-May M-F 8:30am-5pm.)

⌐◻ ACCOMMODATIONS AND FOOD. Tampeeren NNKY (HI) ❶, Tuomiokirkonkatu 12, offers rooms near the cathedral. From the train station, walk down Hämeenkatu and make a right on Tuomiokirkonkatu. (☎254 40 20. Breakfast €5. Sheets €4.50. Reception 8-10am and 4-11pm. Dorms €11-12.50; singles €28.50; doubles €39. Nonmembers add €2.50.) Bus #1 (€2) goes to **Camping Härmälä ❷,** which overlooks Lake Pyhäjärvi. (☎265 13 55. Open early May to late Aug. Tents €13.50-15; cabins €27-60.) Cafes and restaurants cluster on **Hämeenkatu.** Tampere's **Kauppahalli,** Hämeenkatu 19, is the largest market hall in Scandinavia. (Open M-F 8am-6pm, Sa 8am-4pm.) The city's oldest pizzeria, **Napoli ❶,** Aleksanterinkatu 31, serves 100 different kinds of pies. (€6.30-11. Open M-Th 11am-10pm, F 11am-11pm, Sa noon-11pm, Su 1-11pm.) Laid-back brewery **Plevna Panimoravintola ❷,** Itäinenkatu 8, in an old spinning mill by the Tammerkoski Rapids, serves local specialties. (Open M-Th 11am-1am, F-Sa 11am-2am, Su noon-11pm.)

◙ SIGHTS. Tampere has some of the wackiest museums in Europe. The **Spy Museum,** Hatanpäänvaltatie 42, exhibits a variety of sneaky devices. (Open M-F noon-6pm, Sa-Su 10am-4pm. €6, students €4.) A defiant proletarian spirit burns at the last existing **Lenin Museum,** Hämeenpuisto 28, 3rd fl. The museum and its founders, the Finnish-Soviet Friendship Society, share the building where the first conference of Lenin's revolutionary party was held and where Lenin and Stalin first met. (Open M-F 9am-6pm, Sa-Su 11am-4pm. €4, students €2.) The **Amuri Museum of Workers' Housing,** Makasiininkatu 12, thought-provokingly presents the cramped living quarters of 25 workers and their families between 1882 and 1973. (Open early May to mid-Sept. Tu-Su 10am-6pm. €4, students €1.)

Bus #27 goes to **Pyynikki beach;** for a more Finnish beach experience—which involves jumping from a hot sauna into chilly water—take bus #2 to **Rauhaniemi beach.** (Sauna open M and W 6-10pm, F 3-9pm, Sa 2-10pm. €4.50.) Bus #27 will also take you to **Pyynikki forest park,** which offers walking trails through the wooded hills and shorelines of the Näsijärvi and Pyhäjärvi lakes. Take the stairs or ride an elevator to the top of the observation tower for a panoramic view. (Open daily 9am-8pm. €1.) For an even more spectacular sight, take the elevator up the 124m **Näsinuela** in the **Särkänniemi** amusement complex. (www.sarkanniemi.fi. Tower open daily 11am-midnight. €4.) A 30min. cruise away from the city, **Viikinsaari Island** has beautiful beaches, picnic spots, and walking trails through the Luonnonsuojelualue Nature Reserve. The island comes alive on summer evenings with live music at its dance pavilion. (Island open June to mid-Aug. Tu-F 10am-10:30pm, Sa 10am-12:30am, Su 10am-7:30pm; late Aug. M-F 4-10pm, Sa 10am-12:30pm, Su 10am-7:30pm. Dancing in summer Th 12:30pm-3:30am, Sa 6-10pm, Su 3-7pm.) Tammerlines boats sail from Laukontori quay every hour (round-trip €5).

☑ ⓕ FESTIVALS AND NIGHTLIFE. The quirky **Short Film Festival** features works from 30 countries. (Mar. 5-9 in 2003. ☎223 51 88; www.tampere.fi/festival/film.) August brings the **International Theater Festival,** transforming parks and streets into stages. (Aug. 12-16 in 2003. ☎223 10 66; tampere.fi/festival/theatre.) **Hämeenkatu** and its surrounding streets are energetic at night, and many hotels host discos. **Cafe Europa,** Aleksanterinkatu 29, serves meals and drinks in a bohemian setting with old couches and wine-bottle candlelight. (Beer €4, meals €5-10. 20+ after 6pm. Dancing upstairs W-Sa from 9pm. Open Su-Th noon-2am, F-Sa noon-3am.) **Telakka,** Tullikamarinaukio 3, houses a bar, restaurant, club, and theater in an old warehouse near the train station. (Live music F-Sa. Open M-Th 11am-2am, F 11am-3am, Sa noon-3am, Su noon-2am.)

SAVONLINNA   ☎015

Savonlinna rests atop a bridged chain of islands in the heart of Finland's lake country. The tsarist aristocracy was the first to discover Savonlinna's potential as a vacation spot, turning it into a fashionable spa town; the elegant **Olavinlinna Castle,** built to reinforce the Swedish-Finnish border against those tsars in 1475, has impressively towering spires and high-vaulted ceilings. From Kauppatori (Market Square), follow the docks along the water and hug Linnankatu as it winds between old wooden houses en route to the castle. (Open June to mid-Aug. daily 10am-5pm; mid-Aug. to May 10am-3pm. Tours every hr. €5.) Each July, the world-class **Savonlinna Opera Festival** is held in the castle, while smaller concerts are spread throughout the town. (July 3-Aug. 3. ☎47 67 50; www.operafestival.fi.) The secluded **Sulosaari Island** is a peaceful retreat two footbridges past Kauppatori.

Trains run to Savonlinna from Helsinki (5hr., 3 per day, €42.40); hop off at Savonlinna-Kauppatori in the center of town rather than at the distant Savonlinna stop. The **tourist office,** Puistokatu 1, across the bridge from the market, books rooms for free and has extensive information about the region's many parks and nature reserves, as well as other daytrips within easy reach of the town. (☎51 75 10; www.travel.fi/fin/savonlinna. Open June-Aug. daily 8am-8pm; Sept.-May M-F 9am-5pm.) **Vuorilinna Hostel (HI) ❷,** on Kylpylaitoksentie, offers well-equipped student apartments on the island of Kasinosaari, next to the spa and casino area. (☎739 54 30; fax 27 25 24. Breakfast €6. Sheets €5 for dorms, included in private rooms. Kitchen. Reception 7am-11pm. Open June-Aug. only. Dorms €19.50, nonmembers €22; singles €45-59, with bath €54-69; doubles €57-76/€71-86.) **Malakias Hostel (HI) ❷,** Pihlajavedenkuja 6, offers similar rooms 2km from the city center. Go right on Olavinkatu from the tourist office and bear left on Tulliportinkatu, or take bus #3. (☎53 32 83. Breakfast €6. Sheets €5 for dorms, included with private rooms. Reception 7am-11pm. Open June to mid-Aug. only. Dorms €19.50, nonmembers €22; singles €42-54, with bath €54-71; doubles €57-71/€71-81.) Bars and cafes line **Olavinkatu** and the marketplace area, and summer terraces off **Linnankatu** look out over the castle. The atmospheric **Panimoravintola Huvila ❷,** Puistokatu 4, serves thoughtfully prepared meals in a lakeside setting. From Kauppatori, cross the bridge, turn left on Puistokatu, and follow the road to the end. (Entrees from €12.50. Open daily 11am-3am, kitchen closes at 1am.)

ⓓ DAYTRIPS FROM SAVONLINNA: PUNKAHARJU AND THE RETRETTI.

About 30min. from Savonlinna by bus (7 per day, €4.50), the **Retretti Art Center** is a surreal exhibition space whose huge caves hold beautiful glassworks, dream-like installations, and fabulous rotating exhibits. (Open July daily 10am-6pm; June and Aug. 10am-5pm; exhibitions close 1hr. later. €15, students €9.) In the nearby Punkaharju Nature Conservation Area, an old road and pedestrian trails trace the breathtaking ⓘ**Punkaharju Ridge,** a narrow stretch of forests and eskers flanked on both sides by water. The road leads from Punkaharju town to the **METLA research park,** home to an arboretum and the insightful Lusto Finnish Forest Museum. (Open June-Aug. daily 10am-7pm; May and Sept. daily 10am-5pm; Oct.-Dec. and Feb.-Apr. Tu-Su 10am-5pm. €7, students €6.) The Punkaharju **tourist office,** Kauppatie 20, has more information on the Conservation Area and on nearby camping and accommodations. (☎ 734 12 33; www.punkaharju.fi.)

OULU   ☎ 08

Flower-lined avenues and warm winds give Oulu a relaxing feel that suits its location on the Gulf of Bothnia. The crystal-clear waters of **Nallikari** can be reached by bus #5 from Otto Karhin Park (€2.05). Closer to the city center is the island of **Pikisaari,** whose multi-colored cottages and azure seaside make an ideal setting for picnics; take the footbridge at the end of Kaarlenväylä. Across from Pikisaari, at the corner of Rantakatu and Kaarlenväylä, is the boisterous marketplace. Five-meter cactuses, gigantic banana plants, and other exotic flora flourish in the glass pyramids of the University of Oulu's **Botanical Gardens,** Kaitoväylä 5, a 15min. ride away on buses #4, 6, or 19 (€2.20). (Pyramids open June-Aug. Tu-F 8am-3pm, Sa-Su 11am-3pm; Sept.-May. Tu-F 8am-3pm, Sa-Su noon-3pm. €1.70. Open-air gardens open in summer daily 8am-8pm; off-season 7am-5pm, weather permitting. Free.) The **Tietomaa,** Nahkatehtaankatu 6, has interactive science exhibits, a huge IMAX theater, and the pants of the world's heaviest man. (Open July daily 10am-8pm; Aug.-June M-F 10am-6pm. €10.10, students €8.40.)

All **trains** between northern and southern Finland pass through Oulu, heading south to Helsinki (6-7hr., 5-6 per day, €58.50-63) and north to Rovaniemi (2½hr., 4 per day, €25.40). The **tourist office,** Torikatu 10, provides information on the entire Ostrobothnia region. Take Hallituskatu, the broad avenue perpendicular to the train station, up to the second left after passing through the park. (☎ 55 84 13 30; www.oulutourism.fi. Open mid-June to mid-Aug. M-F 9am-6pm, Sa 10am-3pm; mid-Aug. to mid-June M-F 9am-4pm.) The friendly **Oppimestari Summer Hostel ❸,** Nahkatehtaankatu 3, has bright student dorms for rent in the summer. From the train station, cross Rautatienkatu straight onto Asemakatu. After four blocks, turn right on Isokatu, which becomes Kasarmintie, and turn right onto Nahkatehtaankatu. (☎ 884 85 27; www.merikoski.fi/hotel. Breakfast and sheets included. Laundry €3. Singles €35; doubles €50.) Bus #5 (€2.05) goes to **Nallikari Camping ❶,** which has colorful bungalows. (☎ 55 86 13 50; fax 55 86 17 13. €11-15.50 per person; 4-person cabins €29.) Nightlife spills out of the pavilion on **Kirkkokatu,** the terraces lining **Otto Karhin Park** on Hallituskatu, and the club-lined **Asemakatu.**

KUOPIO   ☎ 017

Eastern Finland's largest city, Kuopio (pop. 87,000) is a center of religion and culture in the midst of a region known for its natural beauty. The archbishop of the Finnish Orthodox Church resides here, and the **Orthodox Church Museum,** Karjalankatu 1, houses a striking collection of textiles and icons, by turns lavish and austere. (Open May-Aug. Tu-Su 10am-4pm; Sept.-Apr. M-F noon-3pm, Sa-Su noon-5pm. €5.05, students €2.55.) The international **Kuopio Dance Festival** (www.kuopiodancefestival.fi) draws crowds in mid-June, while connoisseurs toast early July's **Wine Festival.** A 2km hike leads from the city center to the **Puijo Tower,** which has a lovely view of the forest- and lake-covered region. From Kauppatori, walk away from the water on Puijonkatu and continue up the hill. (Tower open May-Sept. daily 9am-5pm. €3.) Inquire about **cruises** at the guest harbor; Kuopio Roll Cruises (☎ 266 24 66) and Koski Laiva Oy (☎ 262 19 55) set sail every hour to view nearby islands (1½-3hr., €8.40-10.10).

Trains travel to Helsinki (5½hr.; 9 per day; €44.60, students €22.40) and Oulu (4½hr.; 6 per day; €37.20/€18.60). The **tourist office,** Haapaniemenkatu 17, has a stand at the train station that provides information about accommodations and the town. (Open June-Aug. for train arrivals.) To get to the main office from the station, go right on Asemakatu, turn left on Haapaniemenkatu, and walk for three blocks. (☎18 25 84; www.kuopioinfo.fi. Open June to mid-Aug. M-F 9:30am-5pm, July also Sa 10am-3pm; mid-Aug. to May 9:30am-3:30pm.) Close to the train station, **Retkeilymaja Virkkula ❷,** Asemakatu 3, offers bare-bones schoolhouse accommodations. (☎263 18 39. Breakfast €5. Sheets €5. Open mid-June to July. Reception 6pm-9am. Dorms €14.) **Rauhalahti Hostel ❹,** Katiskaniementie 8, at a spa 5km from the city center, is near walking trails, a beach, and the **Jatkaukamppa sauna.** (☎473 473, fax 473 470. Breakfast, sheets, and sauna included. Reception 24hr. Singles €57; doubles €66. Sauna open June-Aug. Tu and F, Sept.-May Tu only; €10 for non-guests.) Fresh produce and fish are available at **Kauppatori,** the market square in the center of town. (Open daily 7am-3pm.)

ROVANIEMI ☎016

Just south of the Arctic Circle, the modern capital of Finnish Lapland is a gateway to the northern wilderness and a popular spot for tourists during the summer and December. The **Arktikum** center, Pohjoisranta 4, is a wonderland of information on Arctic peoples, culture, landscapes, and wildlife. (Open mid-June to mid-Aug. daily 9am-7pm; early June and late Aug. daily 9am-6pm; Sept.-May Tu-Su 9am-6pm. €10, students €8.50.) The Arctic Circle itself passes through **Santa Claus's Village,** home to the world's favorite fat man. Take bus #8 from the train station. (€2.70). (Open June-Aug. and Dec. to mid-Jan. daily 9am-7pm; Sept. 9am-5pm; Oct.-Nov. and Jan.-June 10am-5pm.) The **Ranua Wildlife Park,** 80km south of Rovaniemi, has 3km of paths through the fenced-in territory of Arctic elk, bears, and wolves. (Open May and mid-Aug. to Sept. daily 10am-6pm; June to mid-Aug. 9am-8pm; Oct.-Apr. 10am-4pm. €10, children €8.50.) **Lapland Safaris,** Koskikatu 1 (☎331 12 00), offers longboat river cruises in summer and husky or snowmobile safaris in winter (€59-153).

Trains go south to Helsinki (10hr.; 4 per day; €84.10, students €42.10) via Oulu (2½hr.; €24.70/€12.40) and to Kuopio (8hr.; 3-4 per day; €53.20/€26.60). **Buses** run to destinations throughout northern Finland. The staff of the **tourist office,** Rovakatu 21, combs the town on yellow mopeds. If you don't spot them at the train station, head right on Ratakatu, pass the post office, go under the bridge onto Hallituskatu, and turn left on Rovakatu. The tourist office provides **Internet** access (€2 for 30min.) and books accommodations for free. (☎34 62 70; www.rovaniemi.fi. Open June-Aug. M-F 8am-6pm, Sa-Su 10am-4pm; Sept.-May M-F 8am-4pm.) Straight uphill from the station is the most affordable lodging in town, **Matka Borealis ❸,** Asemieskatu 1, a sunny guesthouse with comfortable rooms. (☎342 01 30; personal.inet.fi/business/matkaborealis. Breakfast, Sheets, and sauna included. Kitchen. Singles €40; doubles €52; triples €70; apartments from €110. Off-season prices slightly lower; more expensive around Christmas.) Restaurants, cafes, and bars can be found on **Koskikatu,** and many of the street's large hotels host discos.

FRANCE

PHONE CODES	Country code: 33. **International dialing prefix:** 00. France has no city codes. From outside France, dial int'l dialing prefix + 33 + local number (drop the leading zero).

The French celebrate the senses like no one else: the vineyards of Bordeaux, the savory dishes of Dijon, the sandy expanses of the Riviera, and the crisp air of the Alps combine for an exhilarating experience. France welcomes over 70 million visitors to its cities, chateaux, mountains, and beaches each year, making it the most popular tourist destination in the world. Yet to the French, it is only natural that outsiders should flock to their beloved homeland, so steeped in history, rich in art and architecture, and magnificently endowed with diverse landscapes. The fruits of France include the rich literature of Hugo, Proust, and Camus; the visionary art of Rodin, Monet, and Degas; and the philosophical rationalism of Voltaire, Sartre, and Derrida. From the ambition of Napoleon to the birth of existentialism and postmodernism, the French for many centuries occupied the driver's seat of history. While France no longer controls the course of world events, it nonetheless retains a spot among the most influential forces in Western history.

FACTS AND FIGURES

Official Name: French Republic.

Capital: Paris.

Major Cities: Lyon, Nice, Marseilles.

Population: 60 million.

Land Area: 547,030 sq. km.

Climate: Mild summers and cool winters.

Language: French.

Religions: Roman Catholic (90%).

DISCOVER FRANCE

Paris—ah, Paris. Aside from the requisite croissant-munching, tower-climbing activities, don't miss the less heralded sights. A stroll down the **Champs-Elysées** (p. 339), through the youthful **Latin Quarter** (p. 337), or into medieval **Montmartre** (p. 336) will reveal the unique facets of the city. When you've had your fill, be sure to squeeze in daytrips to ornate **Versailles** (p. 350) and the Gothic cathedral in **Chartres** (p. 351). Northwest of Paris lies **Rouen** (p. 352), home to a cathedral that caught Claude Monet in its spell of light. The story of William the Conqueror is depicted in the tapestry at nearby **Bayeux** (p. 354), which serves as a good base for exploring the **D-Day beaches** (p. 354) of Normandy. The majestic abbey of **Mont-St-Michel** (p. 355) rises from the sea above shifting sands between Normandy and Brittany, while the chateau-studded **Loire Valley** (p. 359) brings visitors back to the days of royal intrigue and opulence. Sweep down to wine-filled **Bordeaux** (p. 365) before exploring the *vieille ville* of **Carcassonne** (p. 369) with its spectacular medieval ramparts. To see Provence's **Camargue** (p. 372), an untamed flatland of bulls, wild horses, and flamingoes, stay in **Arles** (p. 372), whose picturesque streets once enchanted van Gogh. Arles also has the largest Roman amphitheater in France, but its sister in **Nimes** (p. 370) is even more well-preserved. Seven popes who called nearby **Avignon** (p. 371) home in the 15th century left behind an impressive palace. **Marseilles** (p. 374) and its wild nightlife are the gateway to the famously decadent

French Riviera (p. 376). **Nice** (p. 379), with its excellent museums and nightlife, is the first stop on most itineraries, but its rocky beaches will send you to better sand strips in more secluded towns. The star-studded beach enclaves of **Cannes** (p. 377) and **St-Tropez** (p. 376) are also worth a look. In the shadow of Mont Blanc lies **Chamonix** (p. 391), which features fantastic skiing and mountain climbing. Then stop over in the bustling Métropolis of **Lyon** (p. 392) before exploring the mix of French and German culture in **Strasbourg** (p. 398), home to an amazing Gothic cathedral and the beginning of **La Route du Vin** (p. 399).

ESSENTIALS

WHEN TO GO

In July, Paris starts to shrink; by August it is devoid of Parisians, animated only by tourists and the pickpockets who love them. The Côte d'Azur fills with Anglophones from June to September. On the other hand, the rest of France teems with Frenchmen during these months, especially along the Atlantic coast. Early summer and autumn are the best times to visit Paris—the city has warmed up but not completely emptied out. The north and west have cool winters and mild summers, while the less-crowded center and east have a more continental climate. From December to February, the Alps provide some of the best skiing in the world, while the Pyrenees offer a calmer, if less climatically dependable, alternative.

DOCUMENTS AND FORMALITIES

VISAS. For stays shorter than 90 days, only citizens of South Africa need a short-stay visa (30-day visas ZAR216.79; 90-day ZAR260.21-303.53). For stays longer than 90 days, all non-EU citizens require long-stay visas (€95.16).

EMBASSIES. Foreign embassies in France are in Paris (p. 325). For **French embassies** at home, contact: **Australia,** Consulate General, Level 26, St. Martins Tower, 31 Market St., Sydney NSW 2000 (☎02 92 61 57 79; www.france.net.au/consulat/index.htm); **Canada,** Consulate General, 1 pl. Ville Marie, 26th fl., Montréal, QC H3B 4SE (☎514-878-4385; www.consulfrance-montreal.org); **Ireland,** Consulate Section, 36 Ailesbury Rd., Ballsbridge, Dublin 4 (☎01 260 16 66; www.ambafrance.ie); **New Zealand,** 34-42 Manners St., P.O. Box 11-343, Wellington (☎04 384 25 55; www.ambafrance.net.nz); **South Africa,** Consulate General at Johannesburg, 191 Smuts Ave., Rosebank; mailing address P.O. Box 1027, Parklands 2121 (☎011 778 5600, visas 778 56005; www.france.co.za); **UK,** Consulate General, 21 Cromwell Rd., London SW7 2EN (☎020 7838 2000; www.ambafrance.org.uk); **US,** Consulate General, 4101 Reservoir Rd. NW, Washington, D.C. 20007 (☎202-944-6000; www.consulfrance-washington.org).

TRANSPORTATION

BY PLANE. The two major international airports in Paris are **Roissy-Charles de Gaulle** (CDG; to the north) and **Orly** (ORY; to the south). For information on cheap flights from the UK, see p. 46.

BY TRAIN. The French national railway company, **SNCF** (☎08 36 35 35 35; www.sncf.fr), manages one of Europe's most efficient rail networks. **TGV** (*train à grande vitesse*, or high-speed) trains, the fastest in the world, run from Paris to major cities in France, as well as to Geneva and Lausanne, Switzerland. **Rapide** trains are slower; local **Express** trains are, oddly, the slowest option. **Eurostar** pro-

France

BRITAIN · BELGIUM · GERMANY · LUX. · SWITZ. · ITALY · MONACO · SPAIN · ANDORRA

English Channel (La Manche) · ATLANTIC OCEAN · Bay of Biscay · Mediterranean Sea · Golfe du Lion

NORMANDY · ILE-DE-FRANCE · BRITTANY · MAINE · TOURAINE · ANJOU · POITOU · MARCHE · LIMOUSIN · AQUITAINE · GASCONY · LANGUEDOC · ROUSSILLON · PYRENEES · AUVERGNE · MASSIF CENTRAL · CEVENNES MTS. · PROVENCE · COTE D'AZUR · DAUPHINE · SAVOIE · THE ALPS · BURGUNDY · FRANCHE COMTE · ALSACE · LORRAINE · CHAMPAGNE · PICARDIE · FLANDERS · ORLEANAIS · CORSICA

— TGV Line
--- Chunnel

Plymouth · Portsmouth · Dover · Folkestone · Calais · Dunkerque · Lille · Brussels · Cologne · Boulogne · Arras · Douai · Channel Islands · Cherbourg · Fécamp · Dieppe · Amiens · Reims · Epernay · Metz · Le Havre · Rouen · Roscoff · Paimpol · St-Malo · Avranches · Paris · Chartres · Troyes · Nancy · Strasbourg · Brest · St-Brieuc · Dinan · St-Michel · le Mont · Epinal · Mulhouse · Crozon · Quimper · Rennes · Le Mans · Orléans · Fontainebleau · Semur-en-Auxois · Dijon · Besançon · Bern · Quiberon · Angers · Tours · Blois · Amboise · Bourges · Nevers · Beaune · Dole · Belle Ile · Nantes · Saumur · Poitiers · Vichy · Cluny · Tournus · Geneva · Lake Geneva · Ile d'Yeu · Les Sables-d'Olonne · La Rochelle · Rochefort · Limoges · Clermont-Ferrand · Lyon · Annecy · Mont Blanc · Chamonix · Saintes · Cognac · Angoulême · Périgueux · Les Eyzies · Brive · Grenoble · Turin · Bordeaux · Sarlat · Cahors · Montauban · Albi · Avignon · Nîmes · Aix-en-Provence · Menton · Nice · Cannes · Bayonne · Biarritz · Anglet · Pau · St-Jean-Pied-de-Port · Lourdes · Cauterets · Toulouse · Carcassonne · Montpellier · Béziers · Arles · Marseille · Toulon · St-Tropez · Perpignan · Bastia · Calvi · Corte · Ajaccio · Porto-Vecchio · Bonifacio · SARDINIA (ITALY) · Cap Corse

Somme R. · Seine R. · Marne R. · Rhine · Loire R. · Indre R. · Vienne R. · Gironde R. · Dordogne R. · Rhone R. · Adour R. · Aude R.

0 · 120 miles · 0 · 120 kilometers

vides rapid connections to London and Brussels (see p. 51). SNCF offers a wide range of discounted round-trip tickets called *tarifs Découvertes*. Get a calendar from a train station detailing *période bleue* (blue period), *période blanche* (white period), and *période rouge* (red period) times and days; blue gets the most discounts, while red gets none. Those under age 25 have two great options: the **Découverte 12-25** (€41.20) gives a 25% discount for any blue-period travel; and the **Carte 12-25** (€41.20), valid for a year, is good for 25-50% off all TGV trains, 50% off all non-TGV trips that started during a blue period, and 25% off non-TGV starting in a white period. Tickets must be validated in the orange machine at the entrance to the platforms at the *gare* (train station) and revalidated at any connections on your trip. Seat reservations, recommended for international trips, are mandatory on EuroCity (EC), InterCity (IC), and TGV trains. All three require a ticket supplement and reservation fee.

Eurail is valid in France. The SNCF's **France Railpass** grants three days of unlimited rail travel in France in any 30-day period (US$175; companion travelers US$141 each; up to 6 extra days US$30 each); the parallel **Youthpass** provides those under 26 with four days of unlimited travel within a two-month period (US$130; up to 6 extra days US$20 each). The **France Rail 'n' Drive pass** combines three days of rail travel with two days of car rental (US$240; companion travelers US$170 each; extra rail days US$30 each, extra car days US$49).

BY BUS. Within France, long-distance buses are a secondary transportation choice, as service is relatively infrequent. However, in some regions buses are indispensable for reaching out-of-the-way towns. Bus services operated by the SNCF accept railpasses. *Gare routière* is French for "bus station."

BY FERRY. Ferries across the English Channel *(La Manche)* link France to England and Ireland. The shortest and most popular route is between **Dover** (p. 52) and **Calais**, and is run by **P&O Stena Line, SeaFrance,** and **Hoverspeed** (p. 52). Hoverspeed also travels from **Dieppe** to **Newhaven**, England. **Brittany Ferries** (☎ 08 25 82 88 28; www.brittanyferries.co.uk) travels from **Cherbourg** (p. 355) to **Poole**, from **Caen** (p. 353) to **Portsmouth**, and from **St-Malo** (p. 357) to **Portsmouth**. **Irish Ferries** (☎ 01 44 88 54 50; www.irishferries.ie) has overnight ferries from **Cherbourg** and **Roscoff** to **Rosslare**, Ireland (p. 564). **Eurail** is valid on boats to Ireland (excluding port tax). For schedules and prices on English Channel ferries, see p. 52. For information on ferries from **Nice** and **Marseilles** to **Corsica**, see p. 386.

BY CHUNNEL. Traversing 27 miles under the sea, the Chunnel is undoubtedly the fastest, most convenient, and least scenic route from England to France. There are two types of passenger service. **Eurostar** runs a frequent train service from London to Paris and Brussels, with stops at Ashford in England and Calais and Lille in France. Book reservations in UK, by phone, or over the web. (UK ☎ 0990 18 61 86, US ☎ 800-387-6782; elsewhere ☎ 1233 61 75 75; www.eurostar.com, www.raileurope.com.) Eurostar tickets can also be bought at most major travel agents. **Eurotunnel** shuttles cars and passengers between Kent and Nord-Pas-de-Calais. (UK ☎ 0800 096 99 92, France ☎ 03 21 00 61 00; www.eurotunnel.co.uk.)

BY CAR. Unless you are traveling in a group of three or more, you won't save money traveling long distance by car rather than train, thanks to highway tolls, high gasoline cost, and rental charges. If you can't decide between train and car travel, get a **Rail 'n' Drive pass** from railpass vendors (see above). The French drive on the right-hand side of the road; France maintains its roads well, but the landscape itself often makes the roads a menace, especially in twisting Corsica.

BY BIKE AND BY THUMB. Of all Europeans, the French may be alone in loving cycling more than football. Drivers usually accommodate bikers on the wide country roads, and many cities banish cars from select streets each Sunday. Renting a bike (€7.65-18.30 per day) beats bringing your own if your touring will be confined to one or two regions. Many consider France the hardest country in Europe to get a lift. *Let's Go* does not recommend hitchhiking. In major cities, ride-sharing organizations such as **Eurostop International,** or **Allostop** in France (www.ecritel.fr/allostop), pair drivers and riders, though not all of them screen.

TOURIST SERVICES

EMERGENCY Police: ☎ 122. Ambulance: ☎ 123. Fire: ☎ 124.

TOURIST OFFICES. The extensive French tourism support network revolves around **syndicats d'initiative** and **offices de tourisme** (in the smallest towns, the **Mairie**, the mayor's office, deals with tourist concerns), all of which *Let's Go* labels "tourist office." All three distribute maps and pamphlets, help you find accommodations, and suggest excursions to the countryside. For up-to-date events and regional information, see www.francetourism.com.

MANY CULTURES, ONE RACE France was forged pell-mell by annexation of ethnically diverse territories: parts of Catalonia and the Basque Country in the South, the ever-volatile island of Corsica in the Mediterranean, the rest of Southern France (which goes by the name of Occitania), the Germanic regions of Alsace and part of Lorraine, Celtic Brittany, and the Flemish northern tip. Until the last century, these regions were like foreign countries on French soil. The project of unifying French language and culture was not given much practical support until the institution of free and obligatory public schooling in the 1880s. In many schools, children caught speaking their local tongues anywhere on the school grounds were punished. As compensation, however, schools assigned readings on rural France like the enduring *Le Tour de la France par deux enfants*, a picaresque journey around France by two Alsatian orphans from which today's ultimate bike race derives its name.

COMMUNICATION

MAIL. Mail can be held for pickup through *Poste Restante* (General Delivery) to almost any city or town with a post office. Address letters to: SURNAME Firstname; *Poste Restante: Recette Principale*; [5-digit postal code] town; FRANCE. Mark the envelope HOLD.

TELEPHONES. When calling from abroad, drop the leading zero of the local number. French payphones only accept stylish *Télécartes* (phonecards), available in 50-unit (€7.50) and 120-unit (€15) denominations at train stations, post offices, and *tabacs*. *Décrochez* means pick up; you'll then be asked to *patientez* (wait) to insert your card; at *numérotez* or *composez* you can dial. Use only public France Télécom payphones, as privately owned ones charge more. An expensive alternative is to call collect *(faire un appel en PCV)*; an English-speaking operator can be reached by dialing the appropriate service provider listed below. The information number is ☎12; for an international operator, call ☎00 33 11. International direct dial numbers include: **AT&T,** ☎0 800 99 00 11; **British Telecom,** ☎0 800 99 02 44; **Canada Direct,** ☎0 800 99 00 16 or 99 02 16; **Ireland Direct,** ☎0 800 99 03 53; **MCI,** ☎0 800 99 00 19; **Sprint,** ☎0 800 99 00 87; **Telecom New Zealand,** ☎0 800 99 00 64; **Telkom South Africa,** ☎0 800 99 00 27; **Telstra Australia,** ☎0 800 99 00 61.

INTERNET ACCESS. Most major **post offices** and some branches now offer Internet access at special "cyberposte" terminals; you can buy a rechargeable card that gives you 50 minutes of access at any post office for €8. Note that *Let's Go* does not list "cyberposte" locations. Most large towns in France have a cybercafe. Rates and speed of connection vary widely; occasionally there are free terminals in technologically-oriented museums or exhibition spaces. **Cybercafé Guide** (www.cyberiacafe.net/cyberia/guide/ccafe.htm#working_france) lists cybercafes in France.

LANGUAGE. Contrary to popular opinion, even flailing efforts to speak French will be appreciated, especially in the countryside. Be lavish with your *Monsieurs*, *Madames*, and *Mademoiselles*, and greet people with a friendly *bonjour* (*bonsoir* in the evening). For basic French vocabulary and pronunciation, see p. 1056.

ACCOMMODATIONS AND CAMPING

Hostels generally offer dormitory accommodations in large, single-sex rooms with four to 10 beds, though some have as m\any as 60. At the other end of the scale, many offer private singles and doubles. In France, a bed in a hostel averages around €7.65-15.25. The French **Hostelling International (HI)** (p. 26) affiliate, **Fédération Unie**

SYMBOL	❶	❷	❸	❹	❺
ACCOMMODATIONS	under €15	€16-25	€26-35	€36-55	over €55

des Auberges de Jeunesse (FUAJ), operates 178 hostels within France. Some hostels accept reservations through the **International Booking Network** (p. 26). Two or more people traveling together will often save money by staying in cheap **hotels** rather than hostels. The French government employs a four-star hotel ratings system. **Gîtes d'étapes** are rural accommodations for cyclists, hikers, and other ramblers in less-populated areas. Expect *gîtes* to provide beds, a kitchen facility, and a resident caretaker. After 3000 years of settled history, true wilderness in France is hard to find. It's **illegal to camp** in most public spaces, including national parks. Instead, look forward to organized *campings* (campsites), where you'll share your splendid isolation with vacationing families and all manner of programmed fun. Most campsites have toilets, showers, and electrical outlets, though you may have to pay extra for such luxuries (€2-6); you'll often need to pay a supplement for your car, too (€3-8). Otherwise, expect to pay €8-15 per site.

FOOD AND DRINK

SYMBOL	❶	❷	❸	❹	❺
FOOD	under €5	€6-10	€11-15	€16-25	over €25

French chefs cook for one of the most finicky clienteles in the world. The largest meal of the day is *le déjeuner* (lunch). A complete French meal includes an *apéritif* (drink), an *entrée* (appetizer), a *plat* (main course), salad, cheese, dessert, fruit, coffee, and a *digestif* (after-dinner drink). The French drink wine with virtually every meal; *boisson comprise* entitles you to a free drink (usually wine) with your meal. Most restaurants offer a *menu à prix fixe* (fixed-price meal) that costs less than ordering *à la carte*. The *formule* is a cheaper, two-course version for the hurried luncher. Odd-hour cravings between lunch and dinner can be satisfied at *brasseries*, the middle ground between casual cafes and structured restaurants. *Service compris* means the tip is included in *l'addition* (check). It's easy to get satisfying dinner for under €10 with staples such as cheese, pâté, wine, bread, and chocolate; for a picnic, get fresh produce at a *marché* (outdoor market) and then hop between specialty shops. Start with a *boulangerie* (bakery) for bread, proceed to a *charcuterie* (butcher) for meats, and then *pâtisseries* and *confiseries* (pastry and candy shops) to satisfy a sweet tooth. When choosing a cafe, remember that you pay for its location—those on a major boulevard are more expensive than smaller places a few steps down a side street. Prices are cheaper at the *comptoir* (counter) than in the *salle* (seating area). For supermarket shopping, look for the chains Carrefour, Casino, Monoprix, and Prisunic.

HOLIDAYS AND FESTIVALS

Holidays: Le Jour de l'an St-Sébastian (New Year's; Jan. 1); Le lundi de Pâques (Easter Monday; May. 11); La Fête du Travail (Labor Day; May 1); L'Anniversaire de la Liberation (celebrates the Liberation in 1944; May 8); L'Ascension (Ascension Day; June 1); Le lundi de Pentecôte (Whitmonday; June 12); La Fête Nationale (Bastille Day; July 14); L'Assomption (Feast of the Assumption; Aug. 15); La Toussaint (All Saints' Day; Nov. 1); L'Armistice 1918 (Armistice Day; Nov. 11); and Le Noël (Christmas; Dec. 25).

Festivals: Most festivals, like **fête du cinema** and **fête de la musique** (late June, when musicians rule the streets), are in summer. The **Cannes Film Festival** (May; www.festival-cannes.com) is mostly for directors and stars, but provides good people watching. The **Festival d'Avignon** (July-Aug.; www.festival-avignon.com/gbindex3.html) is famous for its theater. **Bastille Day** (July 14) is marked by military parades and fireworks nationwide. Although you may not be competing in the **Tour de France** (3rd or 4th Su in July; www.letour.fr), you'll enjoy all the hype. A **Vineyard Festival** (Sept., in Nice; www.nice-coteazur.org/americain/tourisme/vigne/index.html) celebrates the grape harvest with music, parades, and wine tastings. Nice and Nantes celebrate **Carnaval** in the last week or two before Ash Wednesday (culminating with Mardi Gras celebrations).

PARIS

City of light, of majestic panoramas and showy store windows, of the dark, and of the invisible—Paris somehow manages to be it all. From twisting alleys that shelter the world's best bistros to broad avenues flaunting the latest in *haute couture*, from the ancient gargoyles of Notre Dame to the vibrant, modern Centre Georges-Pompidou, Paris is at once a bastion of tradition and a leader of the cutting edge. You can never conquer this city, but you can get acquainted in just a few days; after a week, you may find you're old friends.

✈ INTERCITY TRANSPORTATION

Flights: Aéroport Roissy-Charles de Gaulle (CDG; ☎01 48 62 22 80; www.parisairports.com), 23km northeast of Paris, services most transatlantic flights. For flight info, call the 24hr. English-speaking information center. **Aéroport d'Orly** (ORY; English recording ☎01 49 75 15 15), 18km south of Paris, is used by charters and many continental flights. The cheapest and fastest ways to get into the city are by **RER** or **bus**.

Trains: There are 6 train stations in Paris. Each part of the Métro system services a different geographic region.

Gare du Nord: M: Gare du Nord. Serves Belgium, Britain, northern France, northern Germany, The Netherlands, and Scandinavia. To: **Amsterdam** (4-5hr., €73.30); **Brussels** (1½hr., €52); **Cologne** (4hr., €63). **Eurostar** departs for **London** (3hr., up to €255).

Gare de l'Est: M: Gare de l'Est. To Austria, eastern France, southern Germany, Luxembourg, and Switzerland. To: **Munich** (9hr., €99); **Vienna** (13hr., €161); **Zürich** (6-7hr., €70).

Gare de Lyon: M: Gare de Lyon. Serves southeastern France, Greece, Italy, and parts of Switzerland. To: **Geneva** (4hr., €65.40); **Nice** (6hr., €66); **Rome** (15hr., €160).

Gare d'Austerlitz: M: Gare d'Austerlitz. Serves southwestern France, the Loire Valley, Portugal, and Spain. To **Barcelona** (9hr., €94) and **Madrid** (12-13hr., €97).

Gare St-Lazare: M: Gare St-Lazare. Serves Normandy. To **Caen** (2hr., €26) and **Rouen** (2hr., €18).

Gare de Montparnasse: M: Montparnasse-Bienvenüe. Serves Brittany; also the departure point for **TGVs** to southwestern France. To **Rennes** (2-2½hr., €39).

Buses: Gare Routière Internationale du Paris-Gallieni, 28 av. du Général de Gaulle, just outside Paris in Bagnolet. M: Gallieni. **Eurolines** (☎01 43 54 11 99; www.eurolines.fr) sells tickets to most destinations in France and neighboring countries.

🧭 ORIENTATION

The **Ile de la Cité** and **Ile St-Louis** sit at the geographical center of the city, while the **Seine,** flowing east to west, splits Paris into two large expanses: the **Rive Gauche (Left Bank)** to the south and the **Rive Droite (Right Bank)** to the north. The Left Bank, with its older architecture and narrow streets, has traditionally been considered bohemian and intellectual, while the Right Bank, with grand avenues and designer shops, is more ritzy. Administratively, Paris is divided into 20 **arrondissements** (districts; e.g. 1*er*, 6*ème*) that spiral clockwise around the Louvre. Areas of interest are compact and central, and sketchier neighborhoods tend to lie on the outskirts of town. Refer also to this book's **color maps** of the city.

RIVE GAUCHE (LEFT BANK). The **Latin Quarter,** encompassing the 5ème and parts of the 6ème around the **Sorbonne** and the **Ecole des Beaux-Arts** (School of Fine Arts), has been home to students for centuries; the animated **boulevard St-Michel** is the boundary between the two *arrondissements*. The lively **rue Mouffetard** in the 5ème is quintessential Latin Quarter. The area around east-west **boulevard St-Germain,** which crosses bd. St-Michel just south of pl. St-Michel in the 6ème, is known as **St-Germain des Prés.** To the west, the gold-domed **Invalides** and the stern Neoclassical **Ecole Militaire,** which faces the **Eiffel Tower** across the **Champ-de-Mars,** recall the military past of the 7ème and northern 15ème, now full of traveling businesspeople. South of the Latin Quarter, **Montparnasse,** in the 14ème, eastern 15ème, and southwestern 6ème, lolls in the shadow of its tower. The glamorous **boulevard du Montparnasse** belies the surrounding residential districts. The eastern Left Bank, the 13ème, is Paris's new hot spot, centered on **place d'Italie.**

RIVE DROITE (RIGHT BANK). The **Louvre** and **rue de Rivoli** occupy the sight- and tourist-packed 1er and the more business-oriented 2ème. The crooked streets of the **Marais,** in the 3ème and 4ème, escaped Baron Haussmann's redesign of Paris and now support many diverse communities. From **Place de la Concorde,** at the western end of the 1er, **avenue des Champs-Elysées** bisects the 8ème as it sweeps up toward the **Arc de Triomphe** at **Charles de Gaulle-Etoile.** South of the Etoile, old and new money fills the exclusive 16ème, bordered to the west by the **Bois de Boulogne** park and to the east by the Seine and the **Trocadéro,** which faces the Eiffel Tower across the river. Back toward central Paris, the 9ème, just north of the 2ème, is defined by the sumptuous **Opéra.** East of the 9ème, the 10ème hosts cheap lodgings and the **Gare du Nord** and **Gare de l'Est.** The 10ème, 3ème, and the 11ème, which claims the newest hip nightlife in Paris (in **Bastille**), meet at **Place de la République.** South of Bastille, the 12ème surrounds the **Gare de Lyon,** petering out at the **Bois de Vincennes.** East of Bastille, the party atmosphere gives way to the quieter, more residential 20ème and 19ème, while the 18ème is home to the quaint and heavily touristed **Montmartre,** which is capped by the **Sacré-Cœur.** To the east, the 17ème begins in the red-light district of **Pigalle** and bd. de Clichy, and grows more elegant toward the Etoile, the **Opéra Garnier,** and the 16ème. Continuing west along the *grande axe* defined by the Champs-Elysées, the skyscrapers of **La Défense,** Paris's newest quarter, looms across the Seine from Bois de Boulogne.

▐ LOCAL TRANSPORTATION

Public Transportation: The efficient **Métropolitain,** or **Métro (M),** runs 5:30am-12:30am. Lines are numbered and are generally referred to by their number and final destinations; connections are called *correspondances.* **Single-fare tickets** within the city €1.30; **carnet** (packet) of 10 €9.30. Buy extras for when ticket booths are closed (after 10pm) and hold on to your ticket until you exit. The **RER** *(Réseau Express Régional),* the commuter train to the suburbs, serves as an express subway within central Paris; changing to and getting off the RER requires sticking your validated ticket into a turnstile. Watch the signboards next to the RER tracks and check that your stop is lit up before riding. **Buses** use the same €1.30 tickets (bought on the bus; validate in the machine by the driver), but transfer requires a new ticket. Buses run 6:30am-8:30pm, *Autobus de Nuit* until 1am, and *Noctambus* (3-4 tickets) every hr. 1:30-5:30am at stops marked with the bug-eyed moon between the Châtelet stop and the *portes* (city exits). The **Mobilis** pass covers the Métro, RER, and buses only (€5 for a 1-day pass in Zones 1 and 2). A weekly pass *(carte orange hebdomadaire)* costs €13.75 and expires every Su; photo ID required. Refer to this book's **color maps** of Paris's transit network.

Taxis: Alpha Taxis (☎01 45 85 85 85); **Taxis 7000** (☎01 42 70 00 42). Cabs are expensive and take 3 passengers (there is a €2.45 surcharge for a 4th). The meter starts running when you phone. Cab stands are near train stations and major bus stops.

Car Rental: Rent-a-Car, 79 r. de Bercy (☎01 43 45 98 99). Open M-Sa 8:30am-6pm.

Bike Rental: Paris à velo, 37 bd. Bourdon, 4ème (☎01 48 87 60 01; www.parisvelosympa.com). M: Bastille. Rentals available with a €305 or credit-card deposit. 24hr. rental €16; 9am-7pm €12.50; half day €9.15.

⚡ PRACTICAL INFORMATION

TOURIST AND FINANCIAL SERVICES

Tourist Offices: Bureau d'Accueil Central, 127 av. des Champs-Elysées, 8ème (☎08 36 68 31 12; www.paris-touristoffice.com). M: Georges V. English-speaking and enormous. Open daily 9am-8pm; off-season M-Sa 9am-8pm, Su 11am-6pm.

Embassies: Australia, 4 r. Jean-Rey, 15ème (☎01 40 59 33 00). M: Bir-Hakeim. Open M-F 9am-6pm. **Canada,** 35 av. Montaigne, 8ème (☎01 44 43 29 00). M: Franklin-Roosevelt or Alma-Marceau. Open M-F 9am-5pm. **Ireland,** 4 r. Rude, 16ème (☎01 44 17 67 00). M: Trocadéro. Open M-F 9:30am-1pm and 2:30-5:30pm. **New Zealand,** 7ter r. Leonardo de Vinci, 16ème (☎01 45 01 43 43). M: Victor-Hugo. Open July-Aug. M-Th 8:30am-1pm and 2-5:30pm, F 8:30am-2pm; Sept.-June M-F 9am-1pm and 2-5:30pm. **South Africa,** 59 quai d'Orsay, 7ème (☎01 53 59 23 23). M: Invalides. Open M-F 8:30am-5:15pm. **UK,** 18bis r. d'Anjou, 8ème (☎01 44 51 31 00). M: St-Augustin. Open M-F 9:30am-12:30pm and 2:30-5pm. **US,** 2 r. St-Forentin, 1er (☎01 43 12 22 22). M: Concorde. Open M-F 9am-12:30pm and 1-6pm.

Currency Exchange: Hotels, train stations, and airports offer poor rates but have extended hours; Gare de Lyon, Gare du Nord, and both airports have booths open 6:30am-10:30pm. Most **ATMs** accept **Visa** ("CB/VISA") and **MasterCard** ("EC"). Crédit Lyonnais ATMs take **AmEx;** Crédit Mutuel and Crédit Agricole ATMs are on the **Cirrus** network; and most Visa ATMs accept **PLUS**-network cards.

American Express: 11 r. Scribe, 9ème (☎01 47 14 50 00), opposite rear of the Opéra. M: Opéra or Auber. Mail held for cardholders and AmEx Travelers Cheque holders. Open M-Sa 9am-6:30pm, exchange counters open Su 10am-5pm.

LOCAL SERVICES

English-Language Bookstore: Shakespeare and Co., 37 r. de la Bûcherie, 5ème, across the Seine from Notre-Dame. M: St-Michel. A Paris fixture for anglophones, with a quirky, wide selection of new and used books. Open daily noon-midnight.

Gay and Lesbian Services: Centre Gai et Lesbien, 3 r. Keller, 11ème (☎01 43 57 21 47). M: Ledru Rollin or Bastille. Info hub for all gay services and associations in Paris. English spoken. Open M-Sa 2-8pm, Su 2-7pm. **Les Mots à la Bouche,** 6 r. Ste-Croix de la Bretonnerie, 4ème (☎01 42 78 88 30; www.motsbouche.com), is Paris's largest gay and lesbian bookstore and serves as an unofficial information center for queer life. M: Hôtel-de-Ville. Open M-Sa 11am-11pm, Su 2-8pm.

Laundromats: Laundromats are everywhere, especially in the 5ème and 6ème. **Arc en Ciel,** 62 r. Arbre Sec, 1er (☎01 42 41 39 39), does dry cleaning. M: Louvre. Open M-F 8am-1:15pm and 2:30-7pm, Sa 8:30am-1:15pm.

EMERGENCY AND COMMUNICATIONS

Emergencies: Ambulance: ☎ 15. **Fire:** ☎18. **Police:** ☎17. For non-emergencies, head to the local *gendarmerie* (police force) in each *arrondissement.*

FRANCE

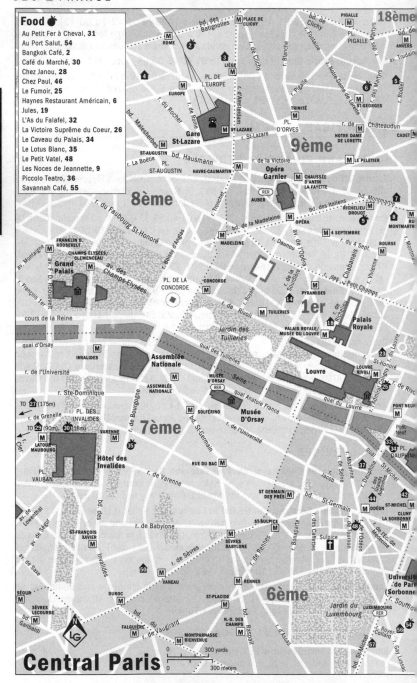

Food 🍎

Au Petit Fer à Cheval, **31**
Au Port Salut, **54**
Bangkok Café, **2**
Café du Marché, **30**
Chez Janou, **28**
Chez Paul, **46**
Le Fumoir, **25**
Haynes Restaurant Américain, **6**
Jules, **19**
L'As du Falafel, **32**
La Victoire Suprême du Coeur, **26**
Le Caveau du Palais, **34**
Le Lotus Blanc, **35**
Le Petit Vatel, **48**
Les Noces de Jeannette, **9**
Piccolo Teatro, **36**
Savannah Café, **55**

Central Paris

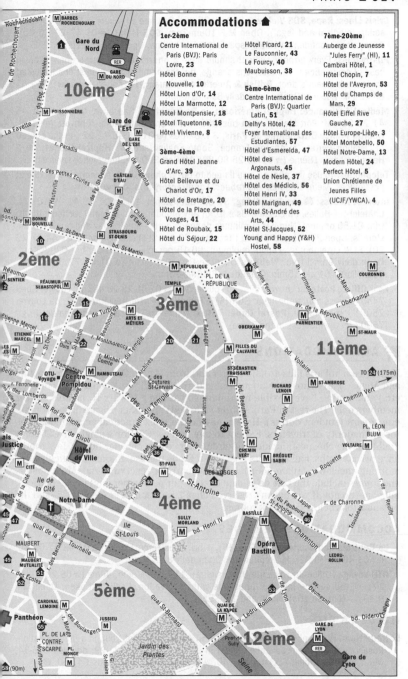

Accommodations ⌂

1er–2ème
Centre International de Paris (BVJ): Paris Lovre, **23**
Hôtel Bonne Nouvelle, **10**
Hôtel Lion d'Or, **14**
Hôtel La Marmotte, **12**
Hôtel Montpensier, **18**
Hôtel Tiquetonne, **16**
Hôtel Vivienne, **8**

3ème–4ème
Grand Hôtel Jeanne d'Arc, **39**
Hôtel Bellevue et du Chariot d'Or, **17**
Hôtel de Bretagne, **20**
Hôtel de la Place des Vosges, **41**
Hôtel de Roubaix, **15**
Hôtel du Séjour, **22**

Hôtel Picard, **21**
Le Fauconnier, **43**
Le Fourcy, **40**
Maubuisson, **38**

5ème–6ème
Centre International de Paris (BVJ): Quartier Latin, **51**
Delhy's Hôtel, **42**
Foyer International des Estudiantes, **57**
Hôtel d'Esmeralda, **47**
Hôtel des Argonauts, **45**
Hôtel de Nesle, **37**
Hôtel des Médicis, **56**
Hôtel Henri IV, **33**
Hôtel Marignan, **49**
Hôtel St-André des Arts, **44**
Hôtel St-Jacques, **52**
Young and Happy (Y&H) Hostel, **58**

7ème–20ème
Auberge de Jeunesse "Jules Ferry" (HI), **11**
Cambrai Hôtel, **1**
Hôtel Chopin, **7**
Hôtel de l'Aveyron, **53**
Hôtel du Champs de Mars, **29**
Hôtel Eiffel Rive Gauche, **27**
Hôtel Europe-Liège, **3**
Hôtel Montebello, **50**
Hôtel Notre-Dame, **13**
Modern Hôtel, **24**
Perfect Hôtel, **5**
Union Chrétienne de Jeunes Filles (UCJF/YWCA), **4**

Crisis Lines: Rape, SOS Viol (☎0 800 05 95 95). Call free anywhere in France for counseling (medical and legal). Open M-F 10am-7pm. **SOS Help!** (☎01 47 23 80 80). Anonymous, confidential English-speaking crisis hotline. Open daily 3-11pm.

Pharmacies: Every *arrondissement* should have a **pharmacie de garde** open 24hr. in case of emergencies. The locations change, but the name of the nearest one is posted on each pharmacy's door. **British & American Pharmacy,** 1 r. Auber, 9ème (☎01 42 65 88 29). M: Auber or Opéra. Open daily 8am-8:30pm.

Medical Assistance: Hôpital Américain de Paris, 84 bd. Saussaye, Neuilly (☎01 46 41 25 25). M: Port Maillot, then bus #82 to the end of the line. A private hospital. **Hôpital Franco-Britannique de Paris,** 3 r. Barbès (☎01 46 39 22 22), in the suburb of Levallois-Perret. M: Anatole-France. Some English spoken. **Hôpital Bichat,** 46 r. Henri Buchard, 18ème (☎01 40 25 80 80). M: Port St-Ouen. Emergency services.

Telephones: To use the phones, you'll need to buy a **phone card** *(télécarte),* available at post offices, Métro stations, and *tabacs.* For **directory info,** call ☎12.

Internet Access: ▨ **easyEverything,** 37 bd. Sébastopol, 1èr (☎01 40 41 09 10). M: Châtelet-Les-Halles. Purchase a User ID for any amount (min. €3) and recharge the ID with €1.50 or more. Number of minutes depends on the time of day and how busy the store is. Open 24hr. **Le Jardin de l'Internet,** 79 bd. St-Michel, 5ème (☎01 44 07 22 20). RER: Luxembourg. 15min. minimum. €0.15 per min., €6.10 per hr., €29 for 5hr. Open daily 9am-11pm. **WebBar,** 32 r. de Picardie, 3ème (☎01 42 72 66 55). M: République. €1 per 15min. Open daily 8:30am-2am.

Post Office: Poste du Louvre, 52 r. du Louvre, 1èr (☎01 40 28 20 40). M: Louvre. Open 24hr. Address mail to be held: SURNAME Firstname, *Poste Restante,* 52 r. du Louvre, 75001 Paris, France. **Postal Code:** 750xx, where "xx" is the *arrondissement* (e.g., 75003 for any address in the 3ème).

▗ ACCOMMODATIONS

High season in Paris falls around Easter and from May to October, peaking in July and August. Paris's hostels skip many standard restrictions (sleep sheets, curfews, etc.) and tend to have flexible maximum stays. The city's six HI hostels are for members only. The rest of Paris's dorm-style beds are either private hostels or quieter *foyers* (student dorms). Hotels may be the most practical accommodations for the majority of travelers. Expect to pay at least €25 for a single or €35 for a double in the cheapest, luckiest of circumstances. In cheaper hotels, few rooms have private baths; hall showers cost about €2.50 per use. Rooms fill quickly after morning check-out (10am-noon), so arrive early or reserve ahead. Most hostels and *foyers* include the **taxe de séjour** (€1-1.50 per person per day) in listed prices, but some do not. If you haven't reserved ahead, tourist offices (see p. 325) and the organizations below can book rooms.

ACCOMMODATIONS SERVICES

La Centrale de Réservations (FUAJ-HI), 4 bd. Jules Ferry, 11ème (☎01 43 57 02 60; fax 01 40 21 79 92). M: République. Open daily 8am-10pm.

OTU-Voyage (Office du Tourisme Universitaire), 119 r. St-Martin, 4ème (☎08 20 81 78 17). €1.55 service fee. Full price due with reservation. English spoken. Open M-F 9:30am-7pm, Sa 10am-noon and 1:30-5pm.

ILE DE LA CITÉ

▨ **Hôtel Henri IV,** 25 pl. Dauphine (☎01 43 54 44 53). M: Pont Neuf. In a prime location. Reserve one month in advance, earlier in summer. Singles €21-29; doubles €25-34; with shower and toilet €53; triples €40, with shower €47.50; quads €47.50. ❷

1ER AND 2ÈME: LOUVRE-PALAIS ROYAL

Central to the **Louvre**, the **Tuileries**, the **Seine**, and the ritzy **pl. Vendôme**, this area still has a few budget hotels. Avoid r. St-Denis.

▨ **Hôtel Montpensier,** 12 r. de Richelieu, 1er (☎01 42 96 28 50; fax 01 42 86 02 70). M: Palais-Royal. Clean rooms, English-speaking staff. Elevator. Shower €4. Reserve 2 months in advance in high season. Singles and doubles with toilet €53; with toilet and shower €74; with toilet, bath, and sink €87. Extra bed €12. AmEx/MC/V. ❹

▨ **Hôtel Tiquetonne,** 6 r. Tiquetonne, 2ème (☎01 42 36 94 58; fax 01 42 36 02 94). M: Etienne-Marcel. Near Marché Montorgueil and r. St-Denis. Elevator. Hall showers €5. Closed Aug. and 1 week at Christmas. Reserve 2 weeks ahead. Singles with shower €24-36; doubles with shower and toilet €41. AmEx/MC/V. ❷

▨ **Centre International de Paris (BVJ): Paris Louvre,** 20 r. Jean-Jacques Rousseau, 1er (☎01 53 00 90 90; fax 01 53 00 90 91). M: Louvre or Palais-Royal. Large hostel that draws a very international crowd. 4-10 beds per room. English spoken. Breakfast and showers included. Lockers €2. Reserve 1 week in advance by phone. Rooms held for only 10-30min. after your expected check-in time. Dorms €24. ❷

Hôtel Vivienne, 40 r. Vivienne, 2ème (☎01 42 33 13 26; paris@hotel-vivienne.com). M: Grands Boulevards. Elegant, with spacious rooms. Some rooms with balconies. Elevator. Breakfast €6. Singles with shower €48, with shower and toilet €78; doubles €63/€78; extra person 30%. MC/V. ❹

Hôtel Lion d'Or, 5 r. de la Sourdière, 1er (☎01 42 60 79 04; fax 01 42 60 09 14). M: Tuileries or Pyramides. Clean and quiet. English-speaking staff. Reserve 1 month ahead in high season. Singles with shower, toilet, and double bed €58-74, with bath €68-80; doubles €74-85/€80-95; triples €84-95/€90-105. Extra bed €10. AmEx/MC/V. ❺

Hôtel La Marmotte, 6 r. Léopold Bellan, 2ème (☎01 40 26 26 51; fax 01 42 42 96 20). M: Sentier. Reception in cheerful ground-floor bar. Quiet rooms with TVs, phones, and free safe-boxes. Breakfast €4. Shower €3. Reserve 1 month in advance. Singles and 1-bed doubles €28-35, with shower €42-53; 2-bed doubles €59; extra bed €12. ❷

Hôtel Bonne Nouvelle, 17 r. Beauregard, 2ème (☎01 45 08 42 42; www.hotel-bonne-nouvelle.com). M: Bonne Nouvelle. In a less-than-elegant neighborhood. Part Swiss chalet, part 70s motel. All rooms have bathrooms with toilet, shower, or bath. Elevator. Reserve 1 month in advance. Singles €46; singles and doubles with bath €54-77; triples with bath €85-100; quads €100-115. MC/V. ❸

3ÈME AND 4ÈME: THE MARAIS

The Marais's 17th-century mansions now house budget hotels close to the **Centre Pompidou** and the **Ile St-Louis;** the area is also convenient for sampling nightlife, as Paris's night buses converge in the 4ème at M: Châtelet.

▨ **Hôtel du Séjour,** 36 r. du Grenier St-Lazare, 3ème (☎/fax 01 48 87 40 36). M: Etienne-Marcel. One block from Les Halles and the Centre Pompidou. Clean, bright rooms and a warm welcome. Reserve a week in advance. Showers €4. Reception 7am-10:30pm. Singles €30; doubles €43, with shower and toilet €54; extra person €23. ❷

▨ **Hôtel des Jeunes (MIJE),** 4ème (☎01 42 74 23 45; www.mije.com). Books beds in Le Fourcy, Le Fauconnier, and Maubuisson (see below), 3 small hostels located on cobblestone streets in beautiful old Marais residences. English spoken. Breakfast, shower, sheets included. 7-day max. stay. Reception 7am-1am. Lockout noon-3pm. Curfew 1am. Dorms €22 per person; singles €38; doubles €27; triples €24; quads €23. ❶

Le Fourcy, 6 r. de Fourcy. M: St-Paul or Pont Marie. Hostel surrounds a social courtyard. Elevator.

Le Fauconnier, 11 r. du Fauconnier. M: St-Paul or Pont Marie. Ivy-covered building steps away from the Seine and Île St-Louis.

Maubuisson, 12 r. des Barres. M: Hôtel-de-Ville or Pont Marie. A half-timbered former girls' convent on a silent street by the St-Gervais monastery. Elevator.

FRANCE

Grand Hôtel Jeanne d'Arc, 3 r. de Jarente, 4ème (☎01 48 87 62 11; www.hoteljeanne-darc.com). M: St-Paul or Bastille. Rooms have showers and toilets. 2 wheelchair-accessible rooms. Elevator. Reserve 2 months in advance. Singles €53-64; doubles €67-92; triples €107; quads €122. Extra bed €12. MC/V. ❹

Hôtel de Roubaix, 6 r. Greneta, 3ème (☎01 42 72 89 91; fax 01 42 72 58 79). M: Réaumur-Sébastopol or Arts et Métiers. Helpful staff, clean rooms. All rooms have shower, toilet, telephone, locker, and TV. Reserve one week in advance. Singles €52-58; doubles €64-68; triples €78-81; quads €87; quints €92. MC/V. ❹

Hôtel Picard, 26 r. de Picardie, 3ème (☎01 48 87 53 82; fax 01 48 87 02 56). M: Temple. In a good location. Elevator. Hall shower €3. Reserve two weeks ahead. Singles €33, with shower €41, with shower and toilet €51; doubles €40-43, with shower €52, with bath €63; triples €59-82. 5% discount with Let's Go. MC/V. ❸

Hôtel de la Place des Vosges, 12 r. de Birague, 4ème (☎01 42 72 60 46; fax 01 42 72 02 64). M: Bastille. Beautiful interior with exposed beams and stone walls. Full bath in each room. Elevator. Reserve 2 months ahead with 1 night's deposit. Singles €76; doubles €101, with twin beds €106; triples €120; quads €140. AmEx/MC/V. ❺

Hôtel Bellevue et du Chariot d'Or, 39 r. de Turbigo, 3ème (☎01 48 87 45 60; fax 01 48 87 95 04). M: Etienne-Marcel. Clean rooms with toilets and baths. Reserve 2 weeks in advance. Singles €51; doubles €57; triples €74; quads €91. AmEx/MC/V. ❹

Hôtel de Bretagne, 87 r. des Archives, 3ème (☎01 48 87 83 14). M: Temple. Friendly staff, well-kept rooms. Reserve 1 week ahead. Singles €29, with shower and toilet €55; doubles €35-38, with full bath and toilet €61; triples €84; quads €92. ❸

5ÈME AND 6ÈME: LATIN QUARTER AND ST-GERMAIN-DES-PRÉS

The lively *quartier latin* and St-Germain-des-Prés offer proximity to the **Notre-Dame,** the **Panthéon,** the **Jardin du Luxembourg,** and the bustling student cafe culture.

🏨 **Young and Happy (Y&H) Hostel,** 80 r. Mouffetard, 5ème (☎01 45 35 09 53; fax 01 47 07 22 24). M: Monge. A lively hostel with laid-back staff, clean rooms. 2am curfew. Doubles €50; triples €66; quads €88. ❷

🏨 **Hôtel St-Jacques,** 35 r. des Ecoles, 5ème (☎01 44 07 45 45; fax 01 43 25 65 50). M: Maubert-Mutualité; RER: Cluny-La Sorbonne. Spacious rooms at reasonable rates, with balconies, TVs, and bathrooms. English spoken. Elevator. Singles €44, with toilet and shower €68; doubles €77/€102. AmEx/MC/V. ❹

🏨 **Hôtel de Nesle,** 7 r. du Nesle, 6ème (☎01 43 54 62 41; www.hotelnesle.com). M: Odéon. Absolutely sparkling, the Nesle is a stand-out among budget hotels. Singles €50-70; doubles €70-100; extra bed €12. AmEx/MC/V. ❹

Hôtel Marignan, 13 r. du Sommerard, 5ème (☎01 43 54 63 81; www.hotel-marignan.com). M: Maubert-Mutualité. Decent rooms; nice owner. Reserve 2 months ahead. Singles €42-45; doubles €60, with shower and toilet €86-92; triples €100-110; quads €120-130. Mid-Sept. to Mar. 15% discount. AmEx/MC/V for more than 5 nights. ❹

Hôtel St-André des Arts, 66 r. St-André-des-Arts, 6ème (☎01 43 26 96 16; fax 01 43 29 73 34). M: Odéon. In the heart of St-Germain, with the feel of a country inn. New bathrooms, free breakfast, and friendly owner. Reservations recommended. Singles €52-62; doubles €76-80; triples €93; quads €104. MC/V. ❹

Delhy's Hôtel, 22 r. de l'Hirondelle, 6ème (☎01 43 26 58 25; fax 01 43 26 51 06). M: St-Michel. Just steps from pl. St-Michel and the Seine. Modern facilities and quiet location. Hall showers €4. Reserve 2 weeks ahead. Singles €39-58, with shower €65-73; doubles €57-63/€71-79; triples €79-92/€92-115; extra bed €15.25. MC/V. ❹

Hôtel d'Esmerelda, 4 r. St-Julien-le-Pauvre, 5ème (☎01 43 54 19 20; fax 01 40 51 00 68). M: St-Michel. Clean but creaky rooms. By a small park with views of the Seine. Singles €30, with shower and toilet €60; doubles €60-85; triples €95; quads €105. ❸

Hôtel des Argonauts, 12 r. de la Huchette, 5ème (☎01 43 54 09 82; fax 01 44 07 18 84). M: St-Michel. Ideally located in a bustling, Old Paris pedestrian quarter (very close to the Seine). Clean rooms. Breakfast €4. Reserve 3-4 weeks in advance in high season. Singles with shower €44; doubles with bath and toilet €63-71. AmEx/MC/V. ❹

Centre International de Paris (BVJ): Paris Quartier Latin, 44 r. des Bernardins, 5ème (☎01 43 29 34 80; fax 01 53 00 90 91). M: Maubert-Mutualité. Boisterous, generic, slightly dingy hostel. English spoken. Showers in rooms. Reception 24hr. 97 beds. 5- and 6-person dorms €25; singles €30; doubles €54; triples €81. ❸

Foyer International des Etudiantes, 93 bd. St-Michel, 6ème (☎01 43 54 49 63). RER: Luxembourg. Across from the Jardin du Luxembourg. Library, laundry facilities, and TV lounge. Kitchenettes, showers, and toilets on hallways. July-Sept. hotel is co-ed. Reserve as early as January for summer. 2-bed dorms €39; singles €27. Oct.-June women only, and rooms are for rent by the month—call for prices and availability. ❷

Hôtel des Médicis, 214 r. St-Jacques, 5ème (☎01 43 54 14 66). M: Luxembourg. Rickety old place; Jim Morrison slummed here (room #4) for 3 weeks in 1971. 1 shower and toilet per floor. English spoken. Singles €16; doubles €31; triples €45. ❷

7ÈME: THE EIFFEL TOWER AND LES INVALIDES

■ **Hôtel du Champs de Mars,** 7 r. du Champ de Mars (☎01 45 51 52 30; www.hotel-du-champs-de-mars.com). M: Ecole Militaire. Elegant rooms. Reserve 1 month in advance. Elevator. Singles and doubles with shower €66-72; triples with bath €92. MC/V. ❺

Hôtel Montebello, 18 r. Pierre Leroux (☎01 47 34 41 18; fax 01 47 34 46 71). A bit far from the 7ème's sights, but great prices for the neighborhood. Clean, cheery rooms with full baths. Reserve at least 2 weeks in advance. Singles person €37; doubles people €42-45. ❹

Hôtel Eiffel Rive Gauche, 6 r. du Gros Caillou (☎01 45 51 24 56; eiffel@easynet.fr). M: Ecole Militaire. A favorite of Anglophone travelers. Rooms have cable TV, phone, and full baths. Dogs allowed. Breakfast €7. Rooms with double bed €76-85, with twin beds €80-92; triples €96-110. Extra bed €14. MC/V. ❺

8ÈME: CHAMPS-ELYSÉES

■ **Hôtel Europe-Liège,** 8 r. de Moscou (☎01 42 94 01 51; fax 01 43 87 42 18). M: Liège. Pleasant, quiet, and low-priced (for the 8ème). Friendly staff. Reserve 15 days in advance. Rooms have TV, hair dryer, phone, and shower or bath. 2 wheelchair-accessible rooms. Breakfast €6. Singles €65; doubles €80. AmEx/MC/V. ❹

Union Chrétienne de Jeunes Filles (UCJF/YWCA), 22 r. Naples (☎01 53 04 37 47; fax 01 53 04 37 54). M: Europe. Spacious and quiet. June-Aug. 3-day minimum stay; Sept.-May longer stays for women ages 18-26. (Men should contact the YMCA Foyer **Union Chrétienne de Jeunes Gens,** 14, r. de Trévise, 9ème, ☎01 47 70 90 94.) €4.58 YWCA membership fee, €8 (for 1-week stays) or €15.25 (for stays of 1 month or more) processing fee. Kitchen, laundry. Singles €25.93, weekly €155, monthly €497; doubles €46/€250/€793; triples €23/€375/€1189. ❷

9ÈME AND 10ÈME: OPÉRA AND GARE DE NORD

The northern part of the 9ème mixes pumping nightlife with a red-light district; avoid M: Pigalle, M: Barbès-Rochechouart, bd. de Clichy, the Gare de Nord, r. Faubourg St-Denis, bd. de Magneta, and near M: Barbés.

■ **Hôtel Chopin,** 46 passage Jouffroy, 9ème (☎01 47 70 58 10; fax 01 42 47 00 70). M: Grands Boulevards. Very clean, new rooms; a cut above most budget hotels. Elevator. Breakfast €7. Singles with shower €55, with shower and toilet €62-70; doubles with shower and toilet €69-80; triples with shower and toilet €91. AmEx/MC/V. ❺

FRANCE

Perfect Hôtel, 39 r. Rodier, 9ème (☎01 42 81 18 86 or 01 42 81 26 19; perfecthotel@hotmail.com). Phones, kitchen access, free coffee, and a concerned staff. Elevator. Breakfast free for *Let's Go* readers. English-speaking staff. Singles €30, with shower and toilet €48; doubles €36/€48; triples €45/€60. MC/V. ❸

Cambrai Hôtel, 129bis bd. de Magenta, 10ème (☎01 48 78 32 13; www.hotel-cambrai.com). M: Gare du Nord. Clean rooms. Showers €3. Singles €30, with toilet €35, with shower €41, with full bath €46; doubles €41/€46/€52, with twin beds and full bath €58; triples €76; family suite €84. MC/V. ❸

11ÈME AND 12ÈME: BASTILLE AND RÉPUBLIQUE

These hotels are conveniently close to hopping nightlife, but be careful at night.

🔣 **Hôtel de l'Aveyron,** 5 r. d'Austerlitz, 12ème (☎01 43 07 86 86; fax 01 43 07 85 20). M: Gare de Lyon. On a quiet street. Clean, unpretentious rooms. Downstairs lounge with TV. Helpful English-speaking staff. 26 rooms. Breakfast €4. Reserve 1 month in advance. Singles and doubles €30, with shower €42; triples €39/€49. MC/V. ❸

Centre International du Séjour de Paris: CISP "Ravel," 6 av. Maurice Ravel, 12ème (☎01 44 75 60 00; cisp@csi.com). M: Porte de Vincennes. Large rooms, cafeteria, and pool. Breakfast, sheets, towels included. Reserve a few days ahead. 8-bed dorm with shower and toilet in hall €15; 2-to 4-bed dorm €19; singles with shower and toilet €30; doubles with shower and toilet €24. AmEx/MC/V. ❶

Modern Hôtel, 121 r. de Chemin-Vert, 11ème (☎01 47 00 54 05; www.modern-hotel.fr). M: Père Lachaise. Modern furnishings and spotless marble bathrooms. All rooms have a hair dryer, modem connection, and safe-deposit box. Rooms are on the 6th fl.; no elevator. Breakfast €5. Singles €60; doubles €70; quads €95; extra bed €15. MC/V. ❺

Hôtel Notre-Dame, 51 r. de Malte, 11ème (☎01 47 00 78 76). M: République. Basic rooms. Elevator. Showers €3.50. Breakfast €6. Reserve 10 days ahead. Singles and doubles €35, with shower €42-55, with shower and toilet €56-67. AmEx/MC/V. ❸

Auberge de Jeunesse "Jules Ferry" (HI), 8 bd. Jules Ferry, 11ème (☎01 43 57 55 60; auberge@easynet.fr). M: République. Wonderful location next to pl. de la République. 100 beds. Clean rooms with sinks. Party atmosphere. 1-week max. stay. No reservations; arrive by 8am. 4- to 6-bed dorms €18.50; doubles €37. MC/V. ❷

13ÈME TO 15ÈME: MONTPARNASSE

Just south of the Latin Quarter, Montparnasse mixes intellectual charm with thriving commercial centers and cafes.

🔣 **Hôtel de Blois,** 5 r. des Plantes, 14ème (☎01 45 40 99 48; fax 01 45 40 45 62). M: Mouton-Duvernet. One of the best deals in Paris. Rooms have TVs, phones, hair dryers, and big, clean baths. Laundromat across the street. Reserve 10 days ahead. Singles €39, with shower €43, with shower and toilet €45, with bath and toilet €51; doubles €41/€45/€47/€56; triples €61; extra bed €12. Free hall showers. AmEx/MC/V. ❹

🔣 **Ouest Hôtel,** 27 r. de Gergovie, 14ème (☎01 45 42 64 99; fax 01 45 42 46 65). M: Pernety. Clean hotel with modest furnishings, great rates, and friendly staff. Breakfast €5. Hall shower €5. Singles €28, with shower €37; 2-bed doubles €34/€39. MC/V. ❷

🔣 **Hôtel Printemps,** 31 r. du Commerce, 15ème (☎01 45 79 83 36; fax 01 45 79 84 88). M: La Motte-Picquet-Grenelle. Clean rooms. Reserve 3-4 weeks ahead. Singles and doubles with sink €30, with shower €36, with shower and toilet €38. MC/V. ❸

FIAP Jean-Monnet, 30 r. Cabanis, 14ème (☎01 43 13 17 17; www.fiap.asso.fr). M: Glacière. 500-bed international student center; spotless rooms with phone, toilet, and shower. Has a game room, TV rooms, laundry, piano bar, restaurant, terrace, and disco. Curfew 2am. Reserve 2-4 weeks in advance. Wheelchair-accessible. Singles €49; doubles €62; triples €84; quads €112. MC/V. ❹

Centre International du Séjour de Paris: CISP "Kellerman," 17 bd. Kellerman, 13*ème* (☎01 44 16 37 38; www.cisp.asso.fr). M: Porte d'Italie. 396-bed hostel with clean rooms. In a boring area close to Cité Universitaire and the Métro. TV room, laundry, and cafeteria. Wheelchair-accessible. Reserve 2-3 weeks in advance. Free showers on floors with dorms. 8-bed dorms €15; 2- to 4-bed dorms €19; singles with shower and toilet €30; doubles with shower and toilet €24. AmEx/MC/V. ❶

■ **Three Ducks Hostel,** 6 pl. Etienne Pernet, 15*ème* (☎01 48 42 04 05; www.3ducks.fr). M: Félix Faure. 15min. from the Eiffel Tower. Shower, breakfast included. 1 week max. stay. Reserve with credit card a week ahead. Mar.-Oct. dorms €21; doubles €48; triples €67.50. Nov.-Feb. dorms €19; doubles €22.50. MC/V. ❷

❒ FOOD

In Paris, life is about eating. Establishments range from the famous repositories of *haute cuisine* to corner *brasseries*. Inexpensive bistros and *crêperies* offer the breads, cheeses, wines, pâtés, *pôtages*, and pastries central to French cuisine. *Gauche* or gourmet, French or foreign, you'll find it in Paris. **CROUS (Centre Regional des Oeuvres Universitaires et Scolaires),** 39 av. Georges Bernanos, 5*ème*, has information on university restaurants, which are a cheap way to get a great meal. (M: Port-Royal. Open M-F 9am-5pm.) To assemble a picnic, visit the specialty shops of the **Marché Montorgeuil,** 2*ème*, **rue Mouffetard,** 5*ème*, or the **Marché Bastille** on bd. Richard-Lenoir. (M: Bastille. Open Th and Su 7am-1:30pm.)

ILE DE LA CITE AND ILE ST-LOUIS

■ **Le Caveau du Palais,** 19 pl. Dauphine (☎01 43 26 04 28). M: Cité. A chic, intimate restaurant serving traditional, hearty French food. Basque specialties, which include lots of steak (€15-24) and fish (€19.50-24.40). A favorite with the locals. MC/V. ❸

Brasserie de l'Île St-Louis, 55 quai de Bourbon (☎01 43 54 02 59). M: Pont Marie. Known for its great cafe fare and for Alsatian specialities such as *choucroute garnie* (a mixture of sausages and pork on a bed of sauerkraut; €16). Open F-Tu noon-1am, Th 5pm-1am. AmEx/MC/V. ❸

1ER AND 2ÈME: LOUVRE-PALAIS ROYAL

Cheap options surround **Les Halles,** 1*er* and 2*ème*. Near the **Louvre,** the small streets of the 2*ème* teem with traditional bistros.

■ **Jules,** 62 r. Jean-Jacques Rousseau, 1*er* (☎ 01 40 28 99 04). M: Les Halles. Feels like home. Blend of modern and traditional French cooking from an award-winning chef. 4-course *menu* €21-28.50. Open M-F noon-2:30pm and 7-10:30pm. AmEx/MC/V. ❺

■ **La Victoire Suprême du Coeur,** 41 r. des Bourdonnais, 1*er* (☎01 40 41 93 95). M: Châtelet. All vegetarian, all very tasty. 3-course *formule* €16. Entrees €4-9. Open M-F 11:45am-2:45pm and 7-10pm, Sa noon-4pm and 7-10pm. MC/V. ❹

■ **Le Fumoir,** 6 r. de l'Amiral Coligny, 1*er* (☎01 42 92 05 05). M: Louvre. Close to the Louvre. Part bar, part tea house; feels decidedly untouristy. Serves the best brunch in Paris (€19); coffee €2.40. Open daily 11am-2am. AmEx/MC/V. ❹

■ **Les Noces de Jeannette,** 14 r. Favart, and 9 r. d'Amboise, 2*ème* (☎01 42 96 36 89). M: Richelieu-Drouot. *Menu* (€27.50) with large salad entrees, roasted fish, duck, and grilled meat *plats*. Reserve ahead. Open daily noon-1:30pm and 7-9:30pm. ❺

■ **Il Buco,** 18 r. Léopold Bellan, 2*ème* (☎01 45 08 50 10). M: Sentier. Serves fresh, flavorful Italian food to a hip local crowd. Entrees €9-10.50, *plats* €10-13. Reservations recommended. Open M-F noon-2:30pm and 8-11pm, Sa 8-11pm. MC/V. ❸

FRANCE

3ÈME AND 4ÈME: THE MARAIS

The Marais offers chic bistros, kosher delis, and couple-friendly cafes.

▨ **Chez Janou,** 2 r. Roger Verlomme, 3*ème* (☎01 42 72 28 41). M: Chemin-Vert. This hip and friendly restaurant is lauded for its reasonably priced gourmet food. The *ratatouille* entree (€7) is delicious. Main courses like *thon à la provençale* (€9.50-14). Open M-F noon-3pm and 7:45pm-midnight, Sa-Su noon-5pm and 7:45pm-midnight. ❸

▨ **Au Petit Fer à Cheval,** 30 r. Vieille-du-Temple, 4*ème* (☎01 42 72 47 47). M: Hôtel-de-Ville or St-Paul. An oasis of *chèvre, kir,* and *Gauloises,* and a loyal local crowd. *Filet mignon de veau* €15; excellent salads (€3.50-10). Open daily noon-1:15am. MC/V. ❸

▨ **Piccolo Teatro,** 6 r. des Ecouffes, 4*ème* (☎01 42 72 17 79). M: St-Paul. A romantic vegetarian eatery. Weekday lunch *menus* at €8.20, €10, or €13.30. *Entrées* €3-7, *plats* €8-13. Open Tu-Sa noon-3pm and 7-11:30pm. AmEx/MC/V. ❷

▨ **L'As du Falafel,** 34 r. des Rosiers, 4*ème* (☎01 48 87 63 60). M: St-Paul. A kosher falafel stand and restaurant with arguably the best falafel in Paris (€4). Thimble-sized (but damn good) lemonade €2.50. Open Su-F 11:30am-11:30pm. MC/V. ❶

404, 69 r. des Gravilliers, 3*ème* (☎ 01 42 74 57 81). M: Arts et Métiers. Classy, comfortable North African restaurant. Mouth-watering couscous (€13-23) and *tajines* (€13-19). Open daily noon-2:30pm and 8pm-midnight. AmEx/MC/V. ❹

Georges, on the 6th fl. of the Centre Pompidou, 3*ème* (☎01 44 78 47 99). M: Rambuteau. Ultra-sleek, Zen-cool, in-the-spotlight cafe; don't miss the terrace. Wine €8, champagne €10, gazpacho €8, fresh fruit salad €9.50. Open W-M noon-2am. ❸

Sacha Finkelsztajn, 27 r. des Rosiers, 4*ème* (☎01 42 72 78 91). M: St-Paul. Sandwiches €5. Go with an open mind and come away with combos like smoked salmon and green olive paste. Open M and W-Th 10am-2pm and 3-7pm, F-Su 10am-7pm. ❶

5ÈME AND 6ÈME: LATIN QUARTER AND ST-GERMAIN-DES-PRÉS

The way to the Latin Quarter's heart is through its cafes. Tiny low-priced restaurants and cafes pack the quadrangle bounded by boulevard St-Germain, boulevard St-Michel, rue de Seine, and the Seine. **Rue de Buci** harbors Greek restaurants and a street market, and **rue Gregoire de Tours** has cheap, greasy spoons for a quick bite.

▨ **Savannah Café,** 27 r. Descartes, 5*ème* (☎01 43 29 45 77). M: Cardinal Lemoine. Lebanese food. *Entrées* €6-11.50, *menu* €21.65. Open M-Sa 7-11pm. MC/V. ❹ Savannah's little sister is the **Comptoir Méditerranée,** 42 r. du Cardinal Lemoine, 5*ème* (☎01 43 25 29 08), with takeout and much lower prices. Open M-Sa 11am-10pm. ❶

▨ **Au Port Salut,** 163bis r. St-Jacques, 5*ème* (☎01 46 33 63 21). M: Luxembourg. This former cabaret now houses 3 floors of traditional French gastronomic joy. 3-course *menus* €12 and €21. Open Tu-Sa noon-2:30pm and 7-11:30pm. MC/V. ❸

▨ **Le Petit Vatel,** 5 r. Lobineau, 6*ème* (☎01 43 54 28 49). M: Mabillon. This charming little home-run bistro serves Mediterranean French specialties, all €10. €11 lunch *menu* usually has a vegetarian option. Open Tu-Sa noon-2pm and 8-10:30pm. ❸

Les Editeurs, 4 carrefour d'Odéon, 6*ème* (☎01 43 26 67 76). The newest classy café on the block. Jazz music and a piano upstairs. *Café* €2.50, *croque monsieur* €9.50. Happy Hour daily 6-8pm (cocktails €6-8). Open daily 8am-2am. AmEx/MC/V. ❷

Café de Flore, 172 bd. St-Germain, 6*ème* (☎01 45 48 55 26). M: St-Germain-des-Prés. Sartre composed *Being and Nothingness* here; Apollinaire, Picasso, and Thurber sipped brew. Espresso €4, pastries €6-11. Open daily 7:30am-1:30am. AmEx/MC/V. ❹

Les Deux Magots, 6 pl. St-Germain-des-Prés, 6*ème* (☎01 45 48 55 25). M: St-Germain-des-Prés. The other biggie (with Café de Flore), frequented by Mallarmé and Hemingway. Coffee €3.80, sandwiches €6.10-7.60. Open daily 7:30am-1:30am. AmEx/V. ❷

Le Sélect, 99 bd. du Montparnasse, 6ème (☎01 45 48 38 24). M: Vavin. Trotsky, Satie, Breton, Cocteau, and Picasso all frequented this huge Art Deco café. Today, this "American Bar" draws a local crowd. *Café* €2.15-2.60. Open daily 7am-3am. MC/V. ❷

7ÈME: THE EIFFEL TOWER AND LES INVALIDES

◪ **Café du Marché,** 38 r. Cler (☎01 47 05 51 27). M: Ecole Militaire. Good American-style food (caesar salad €8) along with customary French dishes (duck confit €9.50). Charming terrace. Open M-Sa 7am-1am (food served until 11pm), Su 7am-3pm. MC/V. ❷

◪ **Le Lotus Blanc,** 45 r. de Bourgogne (☎01 45 55 18 89). M: Varenne. Vietnamese specialties. Lunch *menu* €9-29. Veggie *menu* €6.50-10.50. Reservations encouraged. Open M-Sa noon-2:30pm and 7-10:30pm. Closed two weeks in August. AmEx/MC/V. ❸

8ÈME: CHAMPS-ELYSÉES

The 8ème is as glamorous and expensive as it gets. If your tastes are somewhat less extravagant, there are some affordable restaurants around **rue La Boétie.**

◪ **Bangkok Café,** 28 r. de Moscou (☎01 43 87 62 56). M: Rome. Inventive Thai food, including seafood salads (€8-10) and meat cooked in coconut milk (€12-18). Vegetarian options. Open M-F noon-2:30pm and 7-11:30pm, Sa 7-11:30pm. AmEx/MC/V. ❸

Bagel & Co., 31 r. de Ponthieu (☎01 42 89 44 20). M: FDR. One of the only cheap options in the 8ème. A New York-inspired deli; bagel and specialty sandwiches €3-5. Vegetarian, kosher options. Open M-F 7:30am-9pm, Sa 10am-8pm. AmEx/MC/V. ❶

9ÈME: OPÉRA

Meals close to the Opéra cater to the after-theater and movie crowd and can be quite expensive. **Rue Faubourg-Montmartre** is packed with cheap eateries.

◪ **Haynes Restaurant Américain,** 3 r. Clauzel (☎01 48 78 40 63). M: St-Georges. The first African-American-owned restaurant in Paris (1949), a center for expatriates, and a former hangout of Louis Armstrong and friends. Ma Sutton's fried chicken €14. Regular jazz and funk concerts. Open Tu-Sa 7pm-12:30am. AmEx/MC/V. ❸

◪ **Au Bon Café,** 2 bd. St-Marti (☎01 42 00 21 45). M: République. A haven from the frenzy of the pl. de la République, and a nice alternative to the *place's* pizza chain stores. Superb salads €9-10, quiches €6-8. AmEx/MC/V. ❷

Chartier, 7 r. du Faubourg-Montmartre, 9ème (☎01 47 70 86 29). M: Grands Boulevards. This Parisian fixture has been French cuisine since 1896. Main dishes €7-9.50. Side dishes of vegetables €2.20. Open daily 11:30am-3pm and 7-10pm. MC/V. ❷

11ÈME: BASTILLE AND RÉPUBLIQUE

◪ **Chez Paul,** 13 r. de Charonne (☎01 47 00 34 57). M: Bastille. A worn exterior hides a kicking bistro. Peppercorn steak €12.50. Reservations a must. Open daily noon-2:30pm and 7pm-2am; food served until 12:30am. AmEx/MC/V. ❸

Café de l'Industrie, 16 r. St-Sabin (☎01 47 00 13 53). M: Breguet-Sabin. This hip café pays tribute to France's colonialist past with palm trees and weapons on the walls. Coffee €2, salads €7-7.50. Open Su-F 10am-2am; lunch served noon-1pm. ❷

13ÈME AND 14ÈME: MONTPARNASSE

Scores of Asian restaurants pack Paris's **Chinatown,** south of pl. d'Italie on av. de Choisy. The 14ème is bordered at the top by the busy **boulevard du Montparnasse,** which is lined with a diverse array of restaurants. Rue du Montparnasse, which intersects with the boulevard, teems with reasonably priced *crêperies*. **Rue Daguerre** is lined with vegetarian-friendly restaurants. Inexpensive restaurants cluster on **rue Didot, rue du Commerce, rue de Vaugirard,** and **boulevard de Grenelle.**

THE INSIDER'S CITY

CHINATOWN'S BEST

While the edges of 13ème are pursuing a trendy rebirth, in its middle a pocket of tradition remains. Paris's take on Chinatown is actually multinational and largely culinary, with Thai, Vietnamese, and Chinese Restaurants. Here are some other reasons to stop by:

1 **Dong Nam A.** You'll be amazed by this store's selection of exotic produce.

2 **L'Empire des Thés** (☎01 45 85 66 33). A delightful tea shop—eat in on sesame eclairs, or take home a pot.

3 **Ka Sun Sas** (☎01 56 61 98 89). You may just find a priceless Ming vase here.

4 **Lycée Gabriel Faure.** Brilliant orange and blue tilings and swirling statues decorate this neighborhood school.

5 **Ho A Ly** (☎01 45 83 96 63). Beautiful Mandarin dresses, jackets, and blouses.

Café du Commerce, 39 r. des Cinq Diamants, 13ème (☎01 53 62 91 04). M: Place d'Italie. Traditional food with a funky twist. *Menus* €10.50-15.50. Open daily noon-3pm and 7pm-2am. Sa and Su brunch until 4pm. Reserve ahead for dinner. AmEx/MC/V. ❸

Phinéas, 99 r. de l'Ouest, 14ème (☎01 45 41 33 50). M: Pernety. A restaurant/comic book shrine. *Tartes salées* and *tartes sucrées* (€6-8) made before your eyes. Open Tu-Sa noon-11:30pm, 9am-noon for takeout. Su brunch 11am-3pm. AmEx/MC/V. ❸

Aquarius Café, 40 r. de Gergovie, 14ème (☎01 45 41 36 88). M: Pernety. A vegetarian oasis and local favorite. Tofu sausages, wheat pancakes, brown rice, and vegetables in a mushroom sauce €10. Open M-Sa noon-2:15pm and 7-10:30pm. AmEx/MC/V. ❸

18ÈME: MONTMARTRE

Bistros cluster in **place du Tertre** and **place St-Pierre.** Be cautious in the area, particularly at night. Charming bistros and cafes lie near **rue des Abbesses** and **rue Lepic.**

Le Soleil Gourmand, 10 r. Ravignan (☎01 42 51 00 50). M: Abbesses. A local favorite serving inventive *Provençale.* Try the specialty *bricks* (fried stuffed filo dough; €11), 5-cheese *tartes* with salad (€10), and house-baked cakes (€4.50-7). Vegetarian options available. Dinner reservations a must. Open daily 12:30-2:30pm and 8:30-11pm. ❸

🇬 SIGHTS

For its modest size, Paris is amazingly diverse. In a few hours, you can walk from the heart of the Marais in the east to the Eiffel Tower in the west, passing most major monuments along the way. A solid day of wandering will show you how close the medieval Notre Dame is to the modern Centre Pompidou and the funky *Quartier Latin* to the Louvre, and why you came here in the first place.

ÎLE DE LA CITÉ AND ÎLE ST-LOUIS

ÎLE DE LA CITÉ. If any one place is the heart of Paris, it is this small island. In the 3rd century BC, when it was inhabited by the *Parisii,* a Gallic tribe of hunters, sailors, and fishermen, the Île was all there was to Paris. Today, all distance-points in France are measured from *kilomètre zéro,* a sundial in front of Notre-Dame.

CATHÉDRALE DE NOTRE DAME DE PARIS. This 12th- to 14th-century cathedral, begun under Bishop Maurice Sully, is one of the world's most famous and beautiful examples of medieval architecture. After the Revolution, the building fell into disrepair and was even used to shelter livestock until Victor Hugo's 1831 novel *Notre Dame de Paris* (a.k.a. *The Hunchback of Notre Dame*) inspired citizens to lobby for restoration. The intricately carved, apocalyptic facade and soaring, apparently weightless walls, effects produced by brilliant Gothic engineering and optical illusions, are inspiring even for the most church-weary. The cathedral's biggest draws are its enormous stained-glass **rose windows** that dominate the north and south ends of the transept. A staircase inside the towers leads to a perch from which gargoyles survey the city. *M: Cité. ☎ 01 42 34 56 10; crypt ☎ 01 43 29 83 51. Open daily 8am-6:45pm. Towers open daily 10am-5pm. €5.50, ages 18-25 €3.50. Treasury open M-Sa 9:30am-12:30pm and 1:30-5:30pm, Su 1:30-5:30pm; last entrance 5:00pm. €2.50, students and ages 12-17 €2, 6-12 €1. Crypt open daily 10am-5:30pm; last ticket sold 30min. before closing. €3.30, over-60 €2.20, under 27 €1.60. Tours leave from the right of the entrance. In English W-Th noon, Sa 2:30pm; in French M-F noon, Sa 2:30pm.*

■ **STE-CHAPELLE AND CONCIERGERIE.** Within the courtyard of the **Palais de Justice,** which has housed Paris's district courts since the 13th century, the opulent, Gothic **Ste-Chapelle** was built by Saint Louis (Louis IX) to house his most precious possession, Christ's crown of thorns, now in Notre Dame. No mastery of the lower chapel's dim gilt can prepare the visitor for the **Upper Chapel,** where thin walls of stained glass glow and frescoes of saints and martyrs shine. *(4 bd. du Palais. M: Cité. ☎ 01 53 73 58 51 or 01 53 73 78 50. Open daily Apr.-Sept. 9:30am-5:30pm. Last admission 30min. before closing. €5.50, seniors and ages 18-25 €3.50, under 18 free. Twin ticket with Conciergerie €8, seniors and ages 18-25 €5, under 18 free.)* Around the corner is the **Conciergerie,** one of Paris's most famous prisons; Marie-Antoinette and Robespierre were imprisoned here during the Revolution. *(Entrance on bd. du Palais. M: Cité. ☎ 01 53 73 78 50. Open daily Apr.-Sept. 9:30am-6:30pm; Oct.-Mar. 10am-5pm. Last ticket 30min. before closing. €5.50, students €3.50. Tours in French, 11am and 3pm. For English tours, call ahead.)*

ÎLE ST-LOUIS. The Île St-Louis is home to some of Paris's most privileged elite, like the Rothschilds and Pompidou's widow, and formerly Voltaire, Baudelaire, and Marie Curie. Paris's best ice cream is at ■**Berthillon,** 31 r. St-Louis-en-Île. *(M: Pont Marie. Open Sept. to mid-July; take-out W-Su 10am-8pm; eat-in W-F 1-8pm, Sa-Su 2-8pm.)*

THE LATIN QUARTER AND ST-GERMAIN-DES-PRÉS: 5ÈME AND 6ÈME ARRONDISSEMENTS

The student population is the soul of the *Quartier Latin,* so named because prestigious *lycées* and universities taught in Latin until 1798. Since the violent student riots in May 1968, many artists and intellectuals have migrated to the cheaper outer *arrondissements,* and the *haute bourgeoisie* have moved in. The *5ème* still presents the most diverse array of bookstores, cinemas, bars, and jazz clubs in the city. Designer shops and cutting edge are galleries lie near **St-Germain-des-Prés.**

BOULEVARD ST-MICHEL AND ENVIRONS. At the center of the Latin Quarter, bd. St-Michel, which divides the *5ème* and *6ème,* is filled with cafes, restaurants, bookstores, and clothing boutiques. **Place St-Michel,** to the north, is filled with students, often engaged in a protest of some sort, and lots of tourists. *(M: St-Michel.)*

RUE MOUFFETARD. South of pl. de la Contrescarpe, **rue Mouffetard** plays host to one of the liveliest street markets in Paris, and, along with **rue Monge,** binds much of the Latin Quarter's tourist and student social life. *(M: Cardinal Lemoine or Place Monge.)*

JARDIN DU LUXEMBOURG. South along bd. St-Michel, the formal French gardens of the Jardin du Luxembourg are perfect for strolling and reading; it's also the home of the most famous *guignol* puppet theater. *(RER: Luxembourg; main entrance is on bd. St-Michel. Open Apr.-Oct. daily 7:30am-9:30pm; Nov.-Mar. 8:15am-5pm.)*

FRANCE

PANTHÉON. The **crypt** of the Panthéon, which occupies the highest point on the Left Bank, houses the tombs of Louis Braille, Victor Hugo, Jean Jaurès, Rousseau, Voltaire, and Emile Zola; you can spy each tomb from behind locked gates. The Panthéon also houses **Foucault's Pendulum,** which proves the rotation of the earth. *(Pl. du Panthéon. M: Cardinal Lemoine. From the métro, walk down r. Cardinal Lemoine and turn right on r. Clovis. ☎01 44 32 18 00. Open daily 10am-6:30pm; off-season 10am-6:15pm. Last admission 5:45pm. Admission €7, students €4.50, under 18 free. Free entrance first Su of every month from Oct.-Mar. Guided tours in French leave from inside the main door daily at 2:30 and 4pm.)*

EGLISE ST-GERMAIN-DES-PRÉS. Scarred by centuries of weather, revolution, and war, the Eglise St-Germain-des-Prés, begun in 1163, is the oldest standing church in Paris. *(3 pl. St-Germain-des-Prés. M: St-Germain-des-Prés. From the Métro, walk into pl. St-Germain-des-Prés to enter the church from the front. ☎01 55 42 81 33. Open daily 8am-8pm. Info office open Tu-Sa 10:30am-noon and 2:30-6:45pm, M 2:30-6:45pm.)*

JARDIN DES PLANTES. Opened in 1640 to grow medicinal plants for King Louis XIII, the garden now features science museums, rosarie, and a zoo, which Parisians raided for food during the Prussian siege of 1871. *(M: Gare d'Austerlitz or Jussieu. ☎01 40 79 37 94. Open daily 7:30am-8pm; off-season 7:30am-5:30pm.)*

7ÈME ARRONDISSEMENT

EIFFEL TOWER. Built in 1889 as the centerpiece of the World's Fair, the *Tour Eiffel* has come to symbolize the city. Despite criticism, tacky souvenirs, and Gustave Eiffel's own sentiment that "France is the only country in the world with a 300m flagpole," the tower is unfailingly elegant and commands an excellent view of the city. At night, when the lights are turned on, it will win over even the most jaded tourist. *(M: Bir-Hakeim or Trocadéro. ☎01 44 11 23 23; www.tour-eiffel.fr. Open mid-June through Aug. daily 9am-midnight; Sept.-Dec. 9:30am-11pm; Jan. through mid-June 9:30am-11pm. Elevator to 1st fl. €3.70, under 12 € 2.10; 2nd fl. €6.90/€3.80; 3rd fl. €9.90/€5.30. Stairs to 1st and 2nd fl. €3. Last access to top 30min. before closing.)*

INVALIDES. The tree-lined **Esplanade des Invalides** runs from the impressive **Pont Alexandre III** to the gold-leaf domed **Hôtel des Invalides.** The Hôtel, built for veterans under Louis XIV, now houses the **Musée de l'Armée** and **Napoleon's Tomb.** The **Musée Rodin** (see p. 342) is nearby on r. Varenne. *(M: Invalides, Latour Maubourg, or Varenne.)*

LOUVRE AND OPÉRA: 1ER, 2ÈME, AND 9ÈME ARRONDISSEMENTS

AROUND THE LOUVRE. World-famous art museum and former residence of kings, the **Louvre** (see p. 341) occupies about one-seventh of the 1*èr arrondissement.* **Le Jardin des Tuileries,** at the western foot of the Louvre, was commissioned by Catherine de Médicis in 1564 and improved by André Le Nôtre (designer of the gardens at Versailles) in 1649. *(M: Tuileries. Open Apr.-Sept. daily 7am-9pm; Oct.-Mar. 7:30am-7:30pm. Free tours in English from the Arc de Triomphe du Carrousel.)* Three blocks north along r. de Castiglione, **place Vendôme** hides 20th-century offices and luxury shops behind 17th-century façades. Look out for Napoleon on top of the column in the center of the *place*—he's the one in the toga. *(M: Tuileries or Concorde.)* The **Palais-Royal** was commissioned in 1632 by Cardinal Richelieu, who gave it to Louis XIII. In 1784, the buildings enclosing the palace's formal garden became *galeries,* the prototype of a shopping mall. The revolutions of 1789, 1830, and 1848 all began with angry crowds in the same garden. *(M: Palais-Royal/Musée du Louvre or Louvre-Rivoli.)*

OPÉRA. Located north of the Louvre in the 9*ème* arrondissement, Charles Garnier's grandiose **Opéra Garnier** was built under Napoleon III in the eclectic style of the Second Empire. Gobelin tapestries, gilded mosaics, a 1964 Marc Chagall ceiling, and a six-ton chandelier adorn the magnificent interior. *(M: Opéra. ☎08 36 69 78*

68. Open Sept. to mid-July daily 10am-5pm, last entry 4:30pm; mid-July to Aug. 10am-6pm, last entry 5:30pm. €4.60; ages 10-16, students, and over-60 €3. English tours daily at noon and 2pm in summer; €10; students, ages 10-16 and over-60 €8; under 10 €4.)

MARAIS: 3ÈME AND 4ÈME ARRONDISSEMENTS

The Marais became the most chic place to live with Henri IV's construction of the elegant **Place des Vosges** at the beginning of the 17th century; several remaining mansions, including Victor Hugo's former home, now house museums. Today, the streets of the Marais house the city's Jewish and gay communities as well as fun, hip restaurants and shops. The **rue des Rosiers** (M: St-Paul) is packed with kosher delis and falafel counters. At the confluence of the 1*èr*, 2*ème*, 3*ème*, and 4*ème*, the **Centre Pompidou** (see p. 342), a museum and cultural center, looms like a colorful factory over the vast place, where artists, musicians, and pickpockets gather. Be cautious at night. *(M: Rambuteau; take r. Rambuteau to pl. Georges Pompidou. Or, from M: Chatelet-Les Halles, take r. Rambuteau or r. Aubry le Boucher.)*

BASTILLE: 11ÈME AND 12ÈME ARRONDISSEMENTS

Further east, Charles V built the **Bastille** prison to guard the eastern entrance to his capital. When it became a state prison under Louis XIII, it housed religious heretics and political undesirables. On July 14, 1789, revolutionaries stormed the Bastille, searching for gunpowder and political prisoners. By 1792, nothing was left of the prison but its outline on the *place*. Today, the **July Column** stands at one corner of the *place* to commemorate those who died in the Revolution. On July 14, 1989, François Mitterrand inaugurated the glittering (and, some say, hideous) **Opéra Bastille** to preside over the *place. (130 r. de Lyon. M: Bastille. ☎ 01 40 01 19 70. Daily 1hr. tours usually at 1 or 5pm. €10, over-60 €8, students and under 26 €5.)*

CHAMPS-ELYSÉES AND NEARBY: 8ÈME AND 16ÈME ARRONDISSEMENTS

PLACE DE LA CONCORDE. Paris's most famous public square lies at the eastern end of the Champs-Elysées. Built between 1757 and 1777 for a monument to Louis X, the area soon became the **place de la Révolution,** site of the guillotine that severed 1343 necks from their blue-blooded bodies. After the Reign of Terror, the square was renamed *concorde* ("peace"). The huge, rose-granite, 13th-century BC **Obélisque de Luxor** depicts the deeds of Egyptian pharaoh Ramses II. Given to Charles X by the Viceroy of Egypt, it is Paris's oldest monument. *(M: Concorde.)*

IN RECENT NEWS

BEACH BUMMING

As the saying goes, if you can't stand the heat, then get the hell out of town. Among those who heed this mantra are the citizens of Paris, who, come August, flee their beloved city for the shores of Normandy and Côte d'Azur. But in the summer of 2002, the city figured out how to bring the beach to Paris. Bertrand Delanoe, the city's major, decided to transform 2km of Seine riverfront into "Paris Plage." The result was five patches of "beach"—one of sand, two of grass, and two of pebbles—that stretched from quai Tuileries to quai Henri IV. Equipped with lounge chairs, parasols, palm trees, and even a volleyball court, the beach drew hordes of sun-hungry citizens.

True, the *plage,* for which the city shelled out €1.5 million, fell short of paradise. Pollution by Parisians past, who failed to foresee the city's beach potential, makes the Seine unfit for swimming. More tragically, perhaps, the city discourages one of Europe's age-old customs, nude sunbathing.

Despite these setbacks, the *plage* was a resounding success. With any luck, this year it will again draw crowds eager to, if not beat the summer heat, then at least get a tan for their trouble. Just not a seamless one.

PARIS IS(N'T) BURNING As the Allied troops made their way to Paris after their successful landing on the beaches of Normandy, Hitler and the occupying Nazi forces prepared for a scorched-earth retreat. By August 23, 1944, following direct orders from Adolf Hitler, *Wehrmacht* engineers had placed mines at the base of every bridge in Paris. Despite Hitler's admiration of Napoleon's monumental tomb in the Invalides (see p. 338) during his smug visit in 1940, explosives were crammed into the basement of the Invalides, the Assemblée Nationale, and Notre Dame. The Opéra and Madeleine were to be destroyed, and the Eiffel Tower was rigged so that it would topple and prevent the approaching Allies from crossing the Seine. A brief order from German commander **Dietrich von Cholitz** would reduce every major monument in Paris—10 centuries of history—to heaps of rubble and twisted iron. Although in all other ways loyal to the Nazi party, von Cholitz simply couldn't oversee the destruction of a city such as Paris. Pestered by Hitler's incessant question, "Is Paris burning?" von Cholitz managed to stall until the Allies arrived. In 1968, he was awarded the French *Légion d'Honneur* for his bravery in the face of an irate Hitler.

CHAMPS-ELYSÉES. Stretching west and anchored by the Arc de Triomphe on one end and the pl. de Concorde on the other, the **avenue des Champs-Elysées** is lined with luxury shops, *haute couture* boutiques, cafes, and cinemas. The avenue is the work of Baron Haussmann, who was commissioned by Napoleon III to convert Paris into a grand capital with broad avenues, wide sidewalks, new parks, elegant housing, and sanitary sewers.

ARC DE TRIOMPHE. Napoleon commissioned the Arc de Triomphe, at the western terminus of the Champs-Elysées, in 1806 in honor of his Grande Armée. In 1940, Parisians were brought to tears as Nazis goose-stepped through the Arc; on August 26, 1944, British, American, and French troops liberating the city from Nazi occupation marched through to the roaring cheers of thousands. The terrace at the top has a fabulous view. The **Tomb of the Unknown Soldier** has been under the Arc since November 11, 1920. It bears the inscription, "Here lies a French soldier who died for his country, 1914-1918," but represents the 1,500,000 men who died during WWI. *(On pl. Charles de Gaulle. M: Charles-de-Gaulle-Etoile. Open Apr.-Sept. daily 10am-11pm; Oct.-Mar. 10am-10:30pm. €7, ages 18-25 €4.50, under 17 free.)*

THE MADELEINE. Mirrored by the Assemblée Nationale across the Seine, the Madeleine—formally called **Eglise Ste-Marie-Madeleine** (Mary Magdalene)—was begun in 1764 by Louis XV and modeled after a Greek temple. Construction was halted during the Revolution, when the Cult of Reason proposed transforming the building into a bank, a theater, or a courthouse. Characteristically, Napoleon decreed that it should become a temple to the greatness of his army, but Louis XVIII shouted, "It shall be a church!" Completed in 1842, the structure stands alone in the medley of Parisian churches, distinguished by four ceiling domes that light the interior, 52 exterior Corinthian columns, and a curious altarpiece. *(Pl. de la Madeleine. M: Madeleine. ☎ 01 44 51 69 00. Open daily 7:30am-7pm.)*

MONTMARTRE AND PERE-LACHAISE: 18ÈME AND 20ÈME ARRONDISSEMENTS

MOUNTING MONTMARTRE. Montmartre, comprised mostly of one very large hill, is one of the few Parisian neighborhoods Baron Haussmann left intact when he redesigned the city and its environs. During its Belle Epoque heyday from 1875 to 1905, it attracted bohemians like Toulouse-Lautrec and Erik Satie as well as performers and impresarios like Aristide Bruant. Later, Picasso, Modigliani, Utrillo, and Apollinaire came into its artistic circle. Nowadays, Montmartre is a mix of upscale bohemia (above r. des Abbesses) and sleaze (along bd. de Clichy). The northwestern part of the area retains some village charm, with breezy streets speckled with interesting shops and cafés. *(Funicular runs cars up and down the hill every 2min. Open 6am-12:30am. €1.30 or Métro ticket. M: Anvers or Abbesses.)*

BASILIQUE DU SACRÉ-COEUR. The Basilique du Sacré-Coeur crowns the butte Montmartre like an enormous white meringue. Its onion dome is visible from almost anywhere in the city, and its 112m bell tower is the highest point in Paris, offering a view that stretches up to 50km. *(35 r. du Chevalier de la Barre. M: Abbesses, Anvers, or Château-Rouge. From Anvers, take r. de Steinkerque off bd. de Rochechouart and climb the steps. Open daily 7am-11pm. Free. Dome and crypt open daily 9am-6pm. €5.)* Nearby, **place du Tertre** features outdoor cafes and sketch artists.

CIMETIÈRE PÈRE LACHAISE. The Cimetière Père Lachaise, located in the 20*ème*, holds the remains of Balzac, Sarah Bernhardt, Colette, Danton, David, Delacroix, La Fontaine, Haussmann, Molière, Proust, and Seurat within its peaceful, winding paths and elaborate sarcophagi. Foreigners buried here include Modigliani, Gertrude Stein, and Oscar Wilde, but the most visited grave is that of Jim Morrison. French Leftists make ceremonious pilgrimage to the **Mur des Fédérés** (Wall of the Federals), where 147 revolutionaries were executed and buried. *(16 r. du Repos. M: Père-Lachaise. Open Mar.-Oct. M-F 8am-6pm, Sa 8:30am-6pm, Su and holidays 9am-6pm; Nov.-Feb. M-F 8am-5:30pm, Sa 8:30am-5:30pm, Su and holidays 9am-5:30pm. Free.)*

PERIMETER SIGHTS: LA DÉFENSE AND BOIS DE BOULOGNE

LA DÉFENSE. Outside the city limits, west of the 16*ème*, the skyscrapers and modern architecture of La Défense make up Paris's newest (unofficial) *arrondissement*, home to the headquarters of 14 of France's top 20 corporations. The **Grande Arche**, inaugurated in 1989, completes the *axe historique* running through the Louvre, pl. de la Concorde, and the Arc de Triomphe. There's yet another stunning view from the top. Trees, shops, and sculptures by Miró and Calder line the esplanade. *(M/RER: La Défense; M, zone 2; RER, zone 3. Arch open daily 10am-8pm. €7; under 18, students, and seniors €5.50.)*

BOIS DE BOULOGNE. Popular by day for picnics, this 846-hectare (roughly 2,000-acre) park was until recently home to many drug dealers and prostitutes at night and is not the best bet for nighttime entertainment. *(On the western edge of the 16ème. M: Porte Maillot, Sablons, Pont de Neuilly, or Porte Dauphine.)*

🏛 MUSEUMS

The **Carte Musées et Monuments** grants immediate entry to 70 Paris museums (no waiting in line) and will save you money if you plan to visit three or more museums and major sights per day. It's available at major museums and Métro stations. (1-day €15, 3-day €30, 5-day €45.)

MUSÉE DU LOUVRE

1èr. M: Palais-Royal/Musée du Louvre. ☎01 40 20 51 51. Open M and W 9am-9:30pm, Th-Su 9am-6pm. Last entry 45min. before closing. M and W-Sa 9am-3pm €7.50; Su-M and W-Sa 3pm-close and Su €5.30, under 18 and first Su of the month free. English tours M and W-Sa at 11am, 2, 3:45pm. €3.

A short list of its masterpieces includes the *Code of Hammurabi*, Jacques-Louis David's *The Oath of the Horatii*, Vermeer's *Lacemaker*, and Delacroix's *Liberty Leading the People*. Oh, yeah, and there's that lady with the mysterious smile, too—the *Mona Lisa*. Enter through I.M. Pei's controversial glass **Pyramid** in the

Cour Napoléon, or skip lines by entering directly from the Métro. When visiting the Louvre, strategy is everything. The Louvre is organized into three different wings: Sully, Richelieu, and Denon. Each is divided into different sections according to the artwork's date, national origin, and medium. The color-coding and room numbers on the free maps correspond to the colors and numbers on the plaques at the entrances to every room within the wing.

The Italian Renaissance collection, on the 1st floor of the Denon wing, is rivaled only by that of the Uffizi in Florence. Look for Raphael's *Portrait of Balthazar Castiglione* and Titian's *Man with a Glove*. Bought by François I during the artist's visit to Paris, Leonardo da Vinci's *Mona Lisa* (or *La Joconde*, the Smiling One), smiles mysteriously at millions each year. Don't overlook her remarkable neighbors—da Vinci's *Virgin of the Rocks* displays his famous *sfumato* (smoky) technique. *Venus de Milo* and the *Winged Victory of Samothrace* are the tip of the Greek, Etruscan, and Roman antiquities iceberg.

MUSÉE D'ORSAY

> *62 r. de Lille, 7ème. M: Solférino; RER: Musée d'Orsay. ☎ 01 40 49 48 14. Open mid-June to mid-Sept. Tu-W and F-Su 9am-6pm, Th 9am-9:45pm; mid-Sept. to mid-June Tu-W and F-Su 10am-6pm, Th 10am-9:45pm. Last tickets 45min. before closing. €7, ages 18-25 and Su €5, under 18 free. Tours in English Tu-Sa 11:30am and 2:30pm, 1½hr., €5.50.*

While it's considered the premier Impressionist museum, the museum is dedicated to presenting all major artistic movements between 1848 and World War I. On the ground floor, works from Classicism and Proto-Impressionism are on display, including Manet's *Olympia*, a painting that caused a scandal when it was unveiled in 1865. The 1st room of the upper level features Manet's *Déjeuner sur l'Herbe (Luncheon in the Grass)*. Other highlights include: Monet's *La Gare St-Lazare (St-Lazare Train Station)* and *Cathédrale de Rouen (Rouen Cathedral)* series, Renoir's *Le bal du Moulin de la Galette (The dance at the Moulin de la Galette)*, Edgar Dégas's *La classe de danse (The Dance Class)*, Whistler's *Portrait of the Artist's Mother*, and paintings by Sisley, Pissaro, and Morisot. Over a dozen diverse works by Van Gogh follow, including his tormented *Portrait de l'Artiste (Portrait of an Artist)*. Cézanne's works experiment with the soft colors and geometric planes that would open the door to Cubism.

OTHER MUSEUMS

CENTRE NATIONAL D'ART ET DE CULTURE GEORGES-POMPIDOU. This inside-out building has inspired debate since its opening in 1977. The exterior is a sight, with chaotic colored piping and ventilation ducts. But it's an appropriate shell for the Fauves, Cubists, and Pop and Conceptual works inside. *(Pl. Georges-Pompidou, 4ème. M: Rambuteau or Hôtel-de-Ville. ☎ 01 44 78 12 33. Centre open W-M 11am-10pm; museum open W-M 11am-9pm, last tickets 8pm. Permanent collection €5.50, students and over-60 €3.50, under 13 free, 1st Su of month free.)*

MUSÉE RODIN. The 18th-century Hôtel Biron holds hundreds of sculptures by Auguste Rodin (and by his student and lover, Camille Claudel), including the *Gates of Hell*, *The Thinker*, *Burghers of Calais*, and *The Kiss*. *(77 r. de Varenne, 7ème. M: Varenne. ☎ 01 44 18 61 10. Open Apr.-Sept. Tu-Su 9:30am-5:45pm; Oct.-Mar. 9:30am-4:45pm. Last tickets 30min. before closing. €5; seniors, ages 18-25, and all on Su €3. Park open Apr.-Sept. Tu-Su 9:30am-6:45pm; Oct.-Mar. 9:30am-5pm. €1. Audio tour €4. MC/V.)*

MUSÉE PICASSO. This museum follows Picasso's career from his early work in Barcelona to his Cubist and Surrealist years in Paris and Neoclassical work on the Riviera. *(5, r. de Thorigny, 3ème. M: Chemin Vert. ☎ 01 42 71 63 15, 01 42 71 70 84, or 01 42 71 25 21. Open Apr.-Sept. W-M 9:30am-6pm; Oct.-Mar. 9:30am-5:30pm; last entrance 30min. before closing. €5.50, Su and ages 18-25 €4, under 18 free.)*

MUSÉE DE CLUNY. One of the world's finest collections of medieval art, the Musée de Cluny is housed in a medieval monastery built on top of Roman baths. Works include ■**La Dame et La Licorne** (The Lady and the Unicorn), one of the world's most beautiful extant medieval tapestry series. *(6 pl. Paul Painlevé, 5ème. M: Cluny-Sorbonne. ☎ 01 53 73 78 00. Open W-M 9:15am-5:45pm, last tickets 5:15pm. €6.70; students, under 25, over 60, and all on Su €5.20; under 18 free.)*

MUSÉE MARMOTTAN MONET. This hunting-lodge-turned-mansion features an eclectic collection of Empire furniture, Impressionist Monet and Renoir canvases, and medieval illuminations. *(2 r. Louis-Boilly, 16ème. M: La Muette. Follow Chaussée de la Muette (which becomes av. Ranelagh) through the Jardin du Ranelagh. ☎ 01 44 96 50 33. Open Tu-Su 10am-6pm. €6.50, students €4, under 8 free.)*

LA VILLETTE. This vast urban renewal project encloses a landscaped park, a science museum, a planetarium, a conservatory, a concert/theater space, a high-tech music museum, and more. *(19ème. M: Porte de la Villette or Porte de Pantin. Music museum open Tu-Sa noon-6pm, Su 10am-6pm; €6.10, students €4.60, children 6-18 €2.30, under 6 free. Science museum open Tu-Sa 10am-6pm, Su 10am-7pm; €7.50, students €5.50, under 7 free.)*

INVALIDES MUSEUMS. The resting place of Napoleon also hosts the **Musée de l'Armée**, which celebrates French military history, and the **Musée de l'Ordre de la Libération**, on bd. de Latour-Maubourg, which tells the story of the Resistance fighters. *(Esplanade des Invalides, 7ème. M: Invalides. ☎ 01 47 05 04 10. Open Apr.-Sept. daily 10am-6pm; Oct.-Mar. 10am-5pm. €6.10, students under 26 and 12-18 €4.50, under 18 free.)*

MUSEE D'ART MODERNE DE LA VILLE DE PARIS. In the magnificent Palais de Tokyo, this museum contains one of the world's foremost collections of 20th-century art. Two stand out: Matisse's *La Danse Inachevée* and Dufy's fauvist epic of electricity, *La Fée Electricité. (11 av. du Président Wilson, 16ème. M: Iéna. From Iéna, follow av. du Président Wilson with the Seine on your right. ☎ 01 53 67 40 00. Open Tu-F 10am-5:30pm, Sa-Su 10am-6:45pm. Permanent exhibits free, special exhibits €5, students €2.20-3.)*

INSTITUT DU MONDE ARABE. Featuring art from the Maghreb and the Near and Middle East, the riverside facade is shaped like a boat, representing the migration of Arabs to France. *(1 r. des Fossés St-Bernard 5ème. M: Jussieu. From the Métro, walk down r. Jussieu away from the Jardin des Plantes. ☎ 01 40 51 38 38. M: Jussieu. Open Tu-Su 10am-7pm; €3.80, ages 12-18 €3.05, under 12 free.)*

MUSÉE DE L'ORANGERIE. L'Orangerie houses Renoirs, Cézannes, Rousseaus, Matisses, and Picassos, but is most famous for Monet's eight gigantic *Water Lilies.* Unfortunately, the museum is closed until 2004. *(1èr. M: Concorde.)*

MUSÉE DE LA MODE ET DU COSTUME. With 30,000 outfits and 70,000 accessories, the museum has no choice but to showcase fashions of the past three centuries. A fabulous place to see the history of Parisian fashion, society, and *haute couture. (10 av. Pierre I-de-Serbie, 16ème, in the Palais Galliera. M: Iéna. ☎ 01 56 52 86 00. Open Tu-Su 10am-6pm; last entry 5:30pm. €7, students and seniors €5.50, children €3.50.)*

🎵 ENTERTAINMENT

Paris's cabarets, cinemas, theaters, and concert halls can satisfy all tastes and desires. The bibles of Paris entertainment, the weekly *Pariscope* and the *Officiel des Spectacles* (both €0.40), on sale at any kiosk or *tabac*, have every conceivable listing. *Pariscope* includes an English-language section. Some popular nightlife areas, such as Pigalle, Gare St-Lazare, and Beaubourg, are not always safe.

FREE CONCERTS. For listings of free concerts, check *Paris Selection*, free at tourist offices. Free concerts are often held in churches and parks, especially during summer festivals, and are extremely popular. The **American Church in Paris**, 65 quai d'Orsay, *7ème* (☎01 40 62 05 00; M: Invalides or Alma Marceau), sponsors free concerts (Sept.-May Su at 6pm). **Eglise St-Germain-des-Prés** (see p. 338) also has free concerts; check the information booth just inside the door for times. **Eglise St-Merri**, 78 r. St-Martin, *4ème* (M: Hôtel-de-Ville), is also known for its free concerts (Sept.-July Sa at 9pm, Su at 4pm); contact Accueil Musical St-Merri, 76 r. de la Verrerie, *4ème* (☎01 42 71 40 75 or 01 42 71 93 93; M: Châtelet). Concerts take place W-Su in the **Jardin du Luxembourg's** band shell, *6ème* (☎01 42 34 20 23); show up early for a seat or prepare to stand. Concerts in the **Musée d'Orsay**, 1 r. Bellechasse, *7ème* (☎01 40 49 49 66; M: Solférino), are sometimes free.

OPERA AND THEATER

Opéra de la Bastille, pl. de la Bastille, 12*ème* (☎08 92 69 78 68; www.opera-de-paris.fr). M: Bastille. Opera and ballet with a modern spin. Because of acoustical problems, it's not the place to splurge on front row seats. Subtitles in French. Tickets €57-105. Rush tickets for students under 25 and anyone over 65. MC/V.

Opéra Garnier, pl. de l'Opéra, 9*ème* (☎08 92 69 78 68; www.opera-de-paris.fr). M: Opéra. Hosts operas, symphonies, chamber music, and the Ballet de l'Opéra de Paris. Tickets available 2 weeks before shows. Box office open M-Sa 11am-6pm. Tickets usually €19-64. Last-minute discount tickets available 1hr. before showtime. AmEx/MC/V.

La Comédie Française, 2 r. de Richelieu, 1*er* (☎01 44 58 15 15; www.comedie-francaise.fr). M: Palais-Royal. Founded by Molière; now the granddaddy of all French theaters. Expect wildly gesticulated slapstick farce; you don't need to speak French to understand the jokes. Canonized plays by French greats Molière, Racine, and Corneille. Box office open daily 11am-6pm. Tickets €4.50-30, under 27 €4.50-7.50. Student rush tickets (€9) available 1hr. before showtime.

Odéon Théâtre de l'Europe, 1 pl. Odéon, 6*ème* (☎01 44 41 36 36; www.theatre-odeon.fr). M: Odéon. Programs in this elegant Neoclassical building range from classics to avant-garde. 1042 seats. Also **Petit Odéon,** an affiliate with 82 seats, which in the past has presented *Medea* by Euripedes and the poetry of Lou Reed. Box office open daily 11am-7pm. Tickets €5-28 for most shows; under 27 rush tickets €7.50, available 1½hr. before showtime. Petit Odéon €10. MC/V.

JAZZ AND CABARET

▨ **Au Duc des Lombards,** 42 r. des Lombards, 1*er* (☎01 42 33 22 88; www.jazzvalley.com/duc). M: Châtelet. The best in French jazz, with occasional American soloists. Cover €12-23, music students €7.40-18.60. Beer €5-8, cocktails €9. Music 9:30pm-1:30am. Open M-Sa 8pm-2am. MC/V.

Le Caveau de la Huchette, 5 r. de la Huchette, 5*ème* (☎01 43 26 65 05). M: St-Michel. Come prepared to listen, watch, and dance the jitterbug, swing, and jive in this extremely popular club. Bebop dance lessons at 9:30pm; call ☎01 42 71 09 09. Cover Su-Th €10.50, F-Sa €13. Students €9 during the week. Dance School €8. Drinks €5.50-8.50. Open daily 9:30pm-2:30am, F till 3:30am, Sa till 4am. AmEx/MC/V.

Au Lapin Agile, 22 r. des Saules, 18*ème* (☎01 46 06 85 87). M: Lamarck-Coulaincourt. Turn right on r. Lamarck, then right up r. des Saules. Picasso, Verlaine, Renoir, and Apollinaire hung out here; now audiences crowd in for comical poems and songs. Shows Tu-Su 9pm-2am. Admission €24, Su-F students €17. Drinks €6-7.

CINEMA

There are scores of cinemas throughout Paris, particularly in the *Quartier Latin* and on the Champs-Elysées. The two big theater chains—**Gaumont** and **UGC**—offer *cartes privilèges* discounts for five visits or more. Most cinemas offer student, senior, and family discounts. On Monday and Wednesday, prices drop by about €1.50 for everyone. Check *Pariscope* or *l'Officiel des Spectacles* (available at any newsstand, €0.40) for weekly film schedules, prices, and reviews.

▨ **Cinémathèque Française,** pl. du Trocadéro, 16ème (☎01 45 53 21 86, schedule ☎01 47 04 24 24; www.cinemathequefrancaise.com). M: Trocadéro. At the Musée du Cinéma in the Palais de Chaillot. **Branch:** 18 r. du Faubourg-du-Temple, 11ème. M: République. Two to three classics, near-classics, or soon-to-be classics per day. Usually in original language. €4.70, students €3. Open W-Su 5-9:45pm.

Musée du Louvre, 1er (info ☎01 40 20 53 17; schedules and reservations ☎01 40 20 52 99; www.louvre.fr). M: Louvre. Mainly art and silent films. Open Sept.-June. Free.

Les Trois Luxembourg, 67 r. Monsieur-le-Prince, 6ème (☎01 46 33 97 77). M: Cluny. Independent and classic films in original language. €6.40, students and seniors €5.

La Pagode, 57bis r. de Babylone, 7ème (☎01 45 55 48 48). M: St-François-Xavier. A Japanese pagoda built in 1895 and reopened as a cinema in 2000. Foreign and independent films, and the occasional American film. Stop in at the cafe in between shows. Tickets €7; over-60, under 21, students, and M and W €5.50. MC/V.

📷 SHOPPING

Like its food, nightlife, and conversation, Paris's fashion is an art. From the wild wear near r. Etienne-Marcel to the boutiques of the Marais to the upscale shops of St-Germain-des-Prés, everything Paris touches turns to gold (or, if we're talking about this year's runway looks, basic black). The great *soldes* (sales) of the year begin after New Year's and at the very end of June, with the best prices at the beginning of February and the end of July. And if at any time of year you see the word *braderie* (clearance sale) in a store window, march in without hesitation.

BY NEIGHBORHOOD

ETIENNE-MARCEL AND LES HALLES (1ER AND 2EME). Fabrics here are a little cheaper, and the style is younger. The stores on r. Etienne-Marcel and r. Tiquetonne are best for clubwear and outrageously sexy outfits. *(M: Etienne-Marcel.)*

MARAIS (4EME AND THE LOWER 3EME). The Marais has a line-up of affordable, trendy boutiques, mostly mid-priced clothing chains, independent designer shops, and vintage stores that line **rue Vieille-du-Temple, rue de Sévigné,** r. Roi de Sicile and r. des Rosiers. Lifestyle shops line r. de Bourg-Tibourg and r. des Francs-Bourgeois. The best selection of affordable-chic menswear in Paris can be found along r. Ste-Croix-de-la-Bretonnerie. *(M: St-Paul or Hôtel de Ville.)*

ST-GERMAIN-DES-PRES (6EME AND EASTERN BORDER OF 7EME). St-Germain-des-Prés, particularly the triangle bordered by **boulevard St-Germain, rue St-Sulpice,** and **rue des Sts-Pères,** is saturated with high-budget names. **Paul and Joe** (men's; no. 40; ☎01 45 44 97 70; open daily 11am-7:30pm) and **Sinéquanone** (women's; no. 16; ☎01 56 24 27 74; open M-Sa 10am-7:30pm). Closer to the Jardin du Luxembourg, calm **rue de Fleurus** hosts **A.P.C.** as well as the interesting designs of **t***** at no. 7 (M: St-Placide). In the *7ème,* visit **rue de Pré-aux-Clercs** and check out the avant-garde jewelry at Stella Cadente, **no. 22, rue de Grenelle.** In general, the 7ème is very expensive, but there are some impressive little boutiques around the Bon Marché department store on r. de Sèvres, and r. du Cherche-Midi. *(M: Vaneau, Duroc, Sèvres-Babylone, r. du Bac.)*

DEPARTMENT STORES

Au Bon Marché, 22 r. de Sèvres, 7ème. M: Sèvres-Babylone. Paris's oldest department store, with everything from scarves to smoking accessories to home furnishings. Across the street is *La Grande Epicerie de Paris*, Bon Marché's celebrated gourmet food annex. Open M-W and F 9:30am-7pm, Th 10am-9pm, Sa 9:30am-8pm. AmEx/MC/V.

Au Printemps, 64 bd. Haussmann, 9ème M: Chaussée d'Antin-Lafayette or Havre-Caumartin. Also at 30 pl. d'Italie, 13ème, M: Place d'Italie; and 21-25, cours de Vincennes, 20ème, M: Porte de Vincennes. One of the two biggies in the Parisian department store scene. Haussmann open M-W and F-Sa 9:30am-7pm, Th 9:30am-10pm. Other locations open M-Sa 10am-8pm. AmEx/MC/V.

Galeries Lafayette, 40 bd. Haussmann, 9ème (☎01 42 82 34 56). M: Chaussée d'Antin. Also at 22 r. du Départ, 14ème (☎01 45 38 52 87), M: Montparnasse. Chaotic and crowded, with mini-boutiques of Kookaï, agnès b., French Connection, and Cacharel. *Lafayette Gourmet*, on the first floor, has everything from a sushi counter to a mini-*boulangerie*. Haussmann open M-W, F, Sa 9:30am-7:30pm, Th 9:30-9pm; Montparnasse open M-Sa 9:45am-7:30pm. AmEx/MC/V.

Samaritaine, 67 r. de Rivoli, 1er (☎01 40 41 20 20). M: Pont Neuf, Châtelet-Les Halles, or Louvre-Rivoli. Not as chic as the bigger names—it dares to sell merchandise at reasonable prices. Open M-W and F-Sa 9:30am-7pm, Th 9:30am-10pm. AmEx/MC/V.

🎵 NIGHTLIFE

Though historically Parisians' nightlife involved provoking revolution and burning buildings, today nighttime pleasures tend more toward drinking, relaxing, and people-watching. The jazz is superb, and the club scene (when you finally make it past the door) is supremely fun. If you left your dancing shoes at home or are looking for some down time, the city's bars won't disappoint. Bisexual, lesbian, and gay entertainment is centered around the Marais in the fourth *arrondissement*, with most establishments clustered around r. du Temple, r. Ste-Croix de la Bretonnerie, r. des Archives, and r. Vieille du Temple.

A word on safety: in the 18ème, the streets are lined with aggressive peep-show hawkers and prowling drug-dealers; avoid making eye contact with strangers and stay near well-lit, heavily trafficked areas. Tourists, especially women, should avoid the areas around M: Pigalle, M: Anvers and M: Barbès-Rochechouart at night.

3ÈME, 4ÈME, 11ÈME: MARAIS AND RÉPUBLIQUE

🏛 **L'Apparemment Café,** 18 r. des Coutures St-Gervais, 3ème. M: St-Paul. Beautiful wood-and-red lounge complete with games and a calm, young crowd. Late-night meals €10-13, served until closing.

🏛 **Chez Richard,** 37 r. Vieille-du-Temple, 4ème. M: Hôtel-de-Ville. An atmosphere reminiscent of Casablanca. Jumping on weekends but chill during the week. Beer €4-5, cocktails €8-9. Open daily 6pm-2am. AmEx/MC/V.

🏛 **Lizard Lounge,** 18 r. du Bourg-Tibourg, 4ème. M: Hôtel-de-Ville. A hot, split-level space for Anglo/Franco late-20-somethings. Cellar has DJ every night. Happy Hour 6-10pm (cocktails €4.60). Pint of lager €5.20. MC/V.

▓ **Café Charbon,** 109 r. Oberkampf, 11ème. M: Parmentier or Ménilmontant. A spacious bar that bears traces of its dance-hall days but still manages to pack in a crowd of young locals and artists. Beer €3. Happy Hour 5-7pm. Open daily 9am-2am. MC/V.

Villa Keops, 58 bd. Sébastopol, 3ème. M: Etienne-Marcel. Stylish, candlelit couch bar decorated with beautiful people. Everyone comes here before heading to Les Bains. Open M-Th noon-2am, F-Sa noon-4am, Su 4pm-3am. AmEx/MC/V.

Les Etages, 35 r. Vieille-du-Temple, 4ème. M: St-Paul. Set in an 18th-century hotel-turned-bar. Its 3 floors are filled with chill kids basking in dim lighting. Sangria €4.50. Brunch buffet €15, Su 11am-4pm. Open daily 3:30pm-2am. MC/V.

Amnésia Café, 42 r. Vieille-du-Temple, 4ème. M: Hôtel-de-Ville. A largely gay crowd comes to lounge on plush sofas. This is one of the top spots in the Marais, especially on Sa nights. Espresso €2; kir €4. Open daily noon-2am. MC/V.

Mixer Bar, 23 r. Ste-Croix de la Brettonerie, 4ème. M: St-Paul. A mostly male crowd, though women are welcome. Always packed. DJs stationed above the doorway. Happy Hour 6-8pm. Beer €2.80-4.30; mixed drinks €7. Open daily 5pm-2am. AmEx/MC/V.

DANCE CLUBS

Les Bains, 7 r. du Bourg l'Abbé, 3ème. M: Etienne-Marcel or Réaumur-Sébastopol. Ultra-selective and super-crowded. Madonna and Mick Jagger have been spotted here. House and garage grunge; W hip-hop. Cover includes first drink Su-Th €16; F-Sa €19. Clubbing daily 11pm-6am; open for dinner until 9pm; reservations a must. AmEx/MC/V.

Le Dépôt, 10 r. aux Ours, 3ème. A veritable pleasure complex for gay men. Women welcome upstairs after 11pm, and W is lesbian night. Disco M, house/techno W, Latin Th, visiting DJ F, house Sa (called "Putas at Work"). Cover includes first drink; M-Th €7.50, F €10, Sa €12, Su €10; W free for ladies. Open daily 2pm-8am. V.

5ÈME, 6ÈME, 7ÈME, 13ÈME: LEFT BANK

▓ **Le Reflet,** 6 r. Champollion, 5ème. M: Cluny-La Sorbonne. Small and low-key; crowded with students and younger Frenchies. Beer €1.90-2.70 at the bar, kir €2. Open M-Sa 10am-2am, Su noon-2am. MC/V.

▓ **Le Caveau des Oubliettes,** 52 r. Galande, 5ème. M: St-Michel. Bar upstairs, an outstanding jazz club downstairs. Attracts a mostly local set. Jazz concerts every night; free jam session Su-Th from 10:30pm-1:30am; F-Sa concerts €7.50. Beer €3.70-4.10. Rum cocktail €3.80. Happy Hour 5-9pm. Open daily 5pm-2am.

▓ **Le Bar Dix (Bar 10),** 10 r. de l'Odéon, 6ème. M: Odéon. A classic student hangout with a tiny cellar for packing into; roomier upstairs. Sangria (€3) makes their great jukebox (everything from Edith Piaf to Aretha Franklin) even better. Open daily 5:30pm-2am.

Le Crocodile, 6 r. Royer-Collard, 6ème. M: Cluny-La Sorbonne. This unassuming bar lurks behind boarded-up windows on a quiet side street, but it packs in a lively crowd. Ring to be let in. 238 tasty cocktails (€8) to choose from. Pick a number from the menu or at random, write it down, and hand it across the bar. Open M-Sa 10:30pm-4am.

O'Brien's, 77 r. St-Dominique, 7ème. M: Latour-Maubourg. A lively Irish pub drawing a mix of locals and tourists. Happy Hour M-F from opening time until 8pm, pints €5. Otherwise, beer €4-7, cocktails €7. Open M-Th 6pm-2am, F-Su 4pm-2am. MC/V.

DANCE CLUBS

Batofar, facing 11 quai François-Mauriac, 13ème. M: Quai de la Gare. This barge/bar/club on the Seine has made it big with the electronic music crowd but maintains a friendly vibe. Open Tu-Th 9pm-3am, F-Sa until 4am; hours change for film and DJ events. Cover €6.50-9.50; usually includes first drink. MC/V.

FRANCE

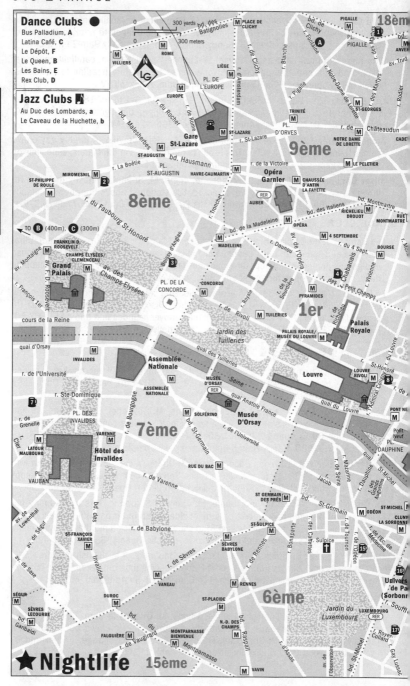

Dance Clubs ●
Bus Palladium, **A**
Latina Café, **C**
Le Dépôt, **F**
Le Queen, **B**
Les Bains, **E**
Rex Club, **D**

Jazz Clubs 🎵
Au Duc des Lombards, **a**
Le Caveau de la Huchette, **b**

★ **Nightlife**   **15ème**

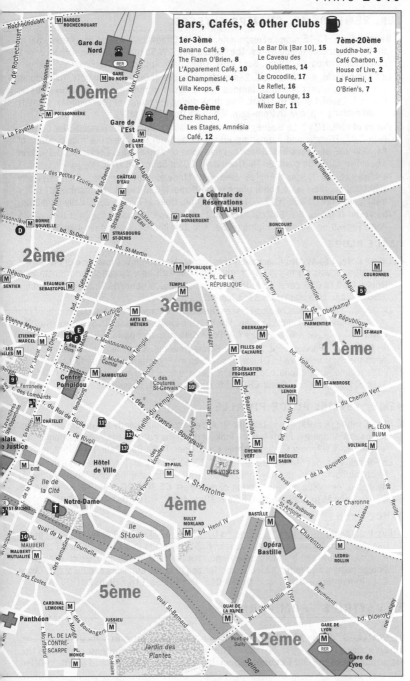

FRANCE

Bars, Cafés, & Other Clubs 🍺

1er–3ème
Banana Café, **9**
The Flann O'Brien, **8**
L'Apparement Café, **10**
Le Champmeslé, **4**
Villa Keops, **6**

4ème–6ème
Chez Richard,
    Les Etages, Amnésia
    Café, **12**

Le Bar Dix [Bar 10], **15**
Le Caveau des
    Oubliettes, **14**
Le Crocodile, **17**
Le Reflet, **16**
Lizard Lounge, **13**
Mixer Bar, **11**

7ème–20ème
buddha-bar, **3**
Café Charbon, **5**
House of Live, **2**
La Fourmi, **1**
O'Brien's, **7**

1ER, 2ÈME, 8ÈME: CHAMPS-ELYSÉES

▓ **Banana Café,** 13-15 r. de la Ferronnerie, 1er. M: Châtelet. The most popular gay bar in the 1er. Legendary theme nights. The "Go-Go Boys" W-Sa midnight-dawn. Drinks 2 for 1 during Happy Hour (4-10pm). Beer €5-7. Open daily 4pm-dawn. AmEx/MC/V.

▓ **Le Champmeslé,** 4 r. Chabanais, 2ème. M: Pyramides or Quatre Septembre. This lesbian bar is Paris's oldest and most famous. Mixed crowd in the front, women-only in back. Beer €4. Cabaret show Th 10pm. Free drink during the month of your birthday. Monthly photo exhibits. Open M-Th 2pm-2am, F and Sa 2pm-5am. MC/V.

▓ **House of Live,** 124 r. La Boétie, 8ème. M: Franklin D. Roosevelt. Formerly the Chesterfield Café. Friendly and happening American bar with first-class live music. A mix of Anglophones and Parisians. Snack bar has good ol' Yankee fare. Cocktails €8.10, beer €6, coffee €2-4. No cover Su-Th. Open daily 10am-5am. AmEx/MC/V.

buddha-bar, 8 r. Boissy d'Anglas, 8ème. M: Madeleine or Concorde. Stereotypically snobbish, but there is no hotter place in the 8ème. Mixed drinks and martinis €11. The mysterious Pure Delight (€12.20) is indeed that. Open M-F noon-3pm, daily 6pm-2am.

The Flann O'Brien, 6 r. Bailleul, 1er. M: Louvre-Rivoli. Arguably the best Irish bar in Paris. Packed on live music nights (F, Sa, and Su). Pint €6. Open daily 4pm-2am.

DANCE CLUBS

▓ **Latina Café,** 114 av. des Champs-Elysées, 8ème. M: George V. Draws one of the largest nightclub crowds on the glitzy Champs-Elysées with an energetic world music mix. Drinks €9-11. €16 cover includes first 2 drinks. Live concerts Th. Café open daily 7:30pm-2am, club open daily 11:30am-6:30am.

Le Queen, 102 av. des Champs-Elysées, 8ème. M: George V. Her majesty is one of the most fashionable gay clubs in town. Mostly male crowd. M disco; Th-Sa house; Su 80s. Cover Su-Th €9, F-Sa €18. Drinks €9. Open daily midnight-dawn. AmEx/MC/V.

Rex Club, 5 bd. Poissonnière, 2ème. M: Bonne-Nouvelle. A non-selective club which presents the most selective of DJ line-ups. A casual, subterranean venue to hear cutting-edge techno, jungle, and house fusion. Large dance floor and lots of seats as well. Shots €4-5, beer €5-7. Cover €8-12.50. Open Th-Sa 11:30pm-6am.

9ÈME, 18ÈME: PLACE PIGALLE

▓ **Chez Camille,** 8 r. Ravignan, 18ème. M: Abbesses. Small, trendy bar on the safe upper slopes of Montmartre. Pretty terrace looking down the *butte* to the Invalides dome. Coffee and tea €1-2, beer €2-3, cocktails €3-8. Open Tu-Sa 9am-2am, Su 9am-8pm.

La Fourmi, 74 r. des Martyrs, 18ème (☎01 42 64 70 35). M: Pigalle. A popular stop-off before clubbing. Has an artsy atmosphere, with a large zinc bar and industrial decor. Hyper-hip, energetic, scrappy young crowd. Beer €2.30-3.20, wine €2.50, cocktails €7-10. Open M-Th 8:30am-2am, F-Sa 8:30am-4am, Su 10:30am-2am. MC/V.

DANCE CLUBS

Bus Palladium, 6 r. Fontaine, 9ème (☎01 53 21 07 33). M: Pigalle, Blanche, or St-Georges. From Pigalle, walk down r. Jean-Baptiste Pigalle and turn right on r. Fontaine. A young, trendy, and beautiful crowd who rock this rock 'n' roll club, which still sports vintage posters and faded gilded decor. Getting past the bouncers can be tough. Cover €16. Tu free for ladies; Th rock. Drinks €13. Open Tu-Sa 11pm-6am. AmEx/V.

▐ DAYTRIPS FROM PARIS

VERSAILLES. Louis XIV, the Sun King, built and held court at Versailles' extraordinary palace, 12km west of Paris. The incredibly lavish chateau embodies the extravagance of the Old Regime, especially in the **Hall of Mirrors** and fountain-filled

gardens. (Chateau open May-Sept. Tu-Su 9am-6:30pm; Oct.-Apr. Tu-Su 9am-5:30pm. €7.50, over-60 and after 3:30pm €5.30 (entrance A). Audio (1hr., €4) and guided tours at entrances C and D (1-2hr., €4, under 18 €2.70), respectively. Gardens open dawn-dusk; €3, under 18 and after 6pm free.) A **shuttle** (round-trip €5, ages 3-12 €3) runs behind the palace to the **Grand** and **Petit Trianons,** and to Marie Antoinette's peasant fantasy, the **Hameau.** (Both Trianons Open Nov.-Mar. Tu-Sa noon-5:30pm, Apr.-Oct. noon-6pm. €5, under 18 free.)

Take any RER C5 train beginning with a "V" from M: Invalides to the Versailles Rive Gauche station (30-40min., every 15min., round-trip €4.90). Buy your RER ticket before getting to the platform; a Métro ticket will not get you through the RER turnstiles at Versailles.

CHÂTEAU DE FONTAINEBLEAU. The Château de Fontainebleau achieves the grandeur of Versailles with a unique charm. François I and Napoleon stand out among the parade of post-Renaissance kings who lived here; the former was responsible for the dazzling ballrooms lined with work from Michelangelo's school, the latter restored the post-Revolution dilapidation to a home befitting an emperor. In the long **Galerie de François I,** the most famous room at Fontainebleau, muscular figures by Il Rosso illustrate mythological tales of heroism. Since the 17th century, every queen and empress of France has slept in the gold-and-green **Queen's Bedchamber.** The **Musée Napoléon** features a collection of the Emperor's tiny toothbrush and tiny shoes, as well as his field tent and state gifts.

From the Gare de Lyon in Paris, **trains** run to Fontainebleau (45min., every hr., round-trip €14.60). The castle is a 30min. walk or a 10min. bus ride away. (Castle open W-M June-Aug. 9:30am-6pm; Sept-June 9:30am-12:30pm and 2-5pm. €5.50; ages 18-25 and Su €4, under 18 free.)

CHARTRES. Chartres's stunning **Cathédrale Notre-Dame** is one of the most beautiful surviving creations of the Middle Ages. Arguably the finest example of early Gothic architecture in Europe, the cathedral retains several of its original 12th-century stained-glass windows; the rest of the windows and the magnificent sculptures on the main portals date from the 13th century, as does the carved floor in the rear of the nave. You can enter the 9th-century **crypt** only from La Crypte, opposite the cathedral's south entrance. (Cathedral open Easter-Oct. daily 8am-8pm, Nov.-Easter daily 8:30am-7pm. Tower open May-Aug. M-Sa 9am-6pm, Su 1-6pm; Sept.-Oct. and Mar.-Apr. M-Sa 9:30-11:30am and 2-6:30pm, Su 2-5pm; Nov.-Feb M-Sa 10-11:30am and 2-4pm, Su 2-4pm. 1¼hr. tours in English Easter to early Nov. M-Sa noon and 2:45pm. €2.30, students €1.60, under 7 free.)

Trains run from Paris's Gare Montparnasse (1hr.; every hr.; return €22.70, under 26 €17.20, over 60 €11.50). From the station, walk straight, turn left into the pl. de Châtelet, turn right on r. Ste-Même, then turn left on r. Jean Moulin.

DISNEYLAND PARIS. It's a small, small world, and Disney is hell-bent on making it even smaller. When EuroDisney opened in 1992, it was met by jeers of French intellectuals and the popular press. However, resistance subsided once they renamed it Disneyland Paris and started serving wine. (www.disneyland-paris.com. Open Apr.-Sept. 9am-11pm; Oct.-Apr. M-F 10am-9pm, Sa-Su 10am-10pm; hours subject to change, especially in winter. Buy *passeports* (tickets) at Disneyland Hotel, at the Paris tourist office, or at RER stations on line A. Early Apr. to early Jan. €38, ages 3-11 €29; early Jan. to early Apr. €29/€25.)

From Paris, take the **RER A4** Marne-la-Vallée to the last stop, Marne-la-Vallée-Chessy (45min., every 30min., round-trip €11); the last train back leaves at 12:22am, but arrives after the Métro closes. Eurailers can take the **TGV** from Roissy/Charles de Gaulle Airport to the park (15min.).

GIVERNY. Today, Monet's house and gardens in Giverny are maintained by the **Fondation Claude Monet.** From April to July, Giverny overflows with roses, hollyhocks, poppies, and the heady scent of honeysuckle. The water lilies, the Japanese bridge, and the weeping willows seem to be plucked straight from Monet's paintings. Monet's thatched-roof house holds his collection of 18th- and 19th-century Japanese prints. The accompanying **Musée d'Art Américain** houses work by American impressionists Butler, Breck, and others. (Fondation Open Apr.-Oct. Tu-Su 10am-6pm. €5.50, students and ages 12-18 €4, ages 7-12 €3. Gardens €4.)

Trains (☎ 08 36 35 35 35; www.sncf.com) run infrequently from Paris-St-Lazare to Vernon, the station nearest Giverny (round-trip €21). When you purchase your ticket, check the timetables or ask for the **bus** schedules for travel from Vernon to Giverny. (Buses ☎ 02 32 71 06 39. 10min.; 4-6 per day; €2, round-trip €4.)

OTHER DAYTRIPS FROM PARIS

THE LOIRE VALLEY. Between Paris and Brittany stretches the Loire Valley, where renowned chateaux line the celebrated Loire river. Visit Blois, Chambord, or Cheverny (see p. 359).

ROUEN. Visit the city of a hundred spires, and party with the students in the largest city in Normandy (see p. 352).

RENNES. If Parisian students will travel out to Rennes for the nightlife, then you should too (see p. 355).

NORMANDY (NORMANDIE)

Fertile Normandy is a land of fields, fishing villages, and cathedrals. Vikings seized the region in the 9th century, and invasions have twice secured Normandy's place in military history: in 1066, William of Normandy conquered England; on D-Day, June 6, 1944, Allied armies began the liberation of France on Normandy's beaches.

ROUEN

However Gustave Flaubert may have criticized his home in *Madame Bovary*, Rouen (pop. 108,000) is no provincial town. The pathos of the Joan of Arc story and the Gothic splendor of Rouen's church have always entranced artists and writers, and today a younger crowd populates the *vieille ville*. The most famous of Rouen's "hundred spires" are those of the **Cathédrale de Notre-Dame,** in pl. de la Cathédrale, one of which is the tallest in France (151m). The facade incorporates nearly every style of Gothic architecture; don't miss the stained glass in the **Chapelle St-Jean de la Nef.** (Open M-Sa 8am-7pm, Su 8am-6pm.) Behind the cathedral, at the poorly marked 186 r. de Martainville, is the **Aître St-Maclou,** which served as the church's charnel house and cemetery through the later Middle Ages. Suspended behind a glass panel is the cadaver of a cat entombed alive to exorcise spirits. (Open daily 8am-8pm. Free.) A 6.5m cross commemorates the site where Joan of Arc died on **place du Vieux Marché,** to the left as you exit the station on r. du Donjon. Nearby is the unsightly **Eglise Ste-Jeanne d'Arc,** designed to resemble an overturned Viking boat. A block up r. Jeanne d'Arc, the **Musée des Beaux-Arts,** on pl. Verdrel, houses a worthwhile collection of European masters from the 16th to 20th centuries, including Monet and Renoir. (☎ 02 35 71 28 40. Open W-M 10am-6pm. €3, ages 18-25 and groups €2, under 18 free.)

Trains leave r. Jeanne d'Arc for **Lille** (3hr., 5 per day, €25.30) and **Paris** (1½hr., every hr., €16.50). From the station, walk down r. Jeanne d'Arc and turn left on r. du Gros Horloge to reach pl. de la Cathédrale and the **tourist office,** 25 pl. de la

Cathédrale. (☎02 32 08 32 40; fax 02 32 08 32 44. Open May-Sept. M-Sa 9am-7pm, Su 9:30am-12:30pm and 2-6pm; Oct.-Mar. M-Sa 9am-6pm, Su 9:30am-12:30pm and 2pm-6pm.) Check email at **Place Net,** 37 r. de la République, near the Eglise St-Maclou. (€4 per hr. Open M-Sa 11am-midnight, Su 2-10pm.) **Hôtel des Arcades ❸,** 52 r. de Carmes, is bright and clean. (☎02 35 70 10 30; www.hotel-des-arcades.fr. Singles and doubles €25, with shower €34-40. AmEx/MC/V.) Cheap eateries crowd **place du Vieux-Marché** and the **Gros Horloge** area. **Restaurant Punjab ❸,** 3 r. des Bons Enfants, just off r. Jeanne D'Arc, provides a taste of India in a more convenient location with a wide vegetarian selection and full bar and wine list. €8 and €10 lunch menus; dinner from €10, fixed menus €16-20. (☎02 35 88 63 48. Open M-Su 11:30am-3pm and 7pm-11:30pm. MC/V.) **Monoprix supermarket** is at 73-83 r. du Gros Horloge. (Open M-Sa 8:30am-9pm.) **Postal Code:** 76000.

NORMANDY COAST

LE HAVRE

An elegy to concrete, Le Havre (pop. 200,000) can brag of being France's largest transatlantic port and little else. For information on **ferries** to Portsmouth, see p. 64. **Trains** leave from cours de la République for: Fécamp (1hr., 9 per day, €6.70) via Etretat; Paris (2hr., 8 per day, €23.70); and Rouen (50min., 13 per day, €11.40). If you must stay in town, visit the spacious **Hôtel Le Monaco ❷,** 16 r. de Paris. (☎02 35 42 21 01. Reception daily 6:30am-11pm. Singles €22.90, with shower €28.30-33.55; doubles €26.70, with bath €33.10. AmEx/MC/V.) Get food for the ferry ride at **Super U,** bd. François 1er, near the tourist office. (Open M-Sa 8:30am-9pm.)

CAEN

Although Allied bombing leveled three-quarters of its buildings in World War II, Caen has skillfully rebuilt itself into a vibrant university town. Its biggest draw is the powerful ◪**Mémorial de Caen,** the best of Normandy's World War II museums, which features footage of the war, displays on pre-war Europe, a haunting testament to the victims of the Holocaust, and a new wing exploring the Cold War. Take bus #17 to Mémorial. (☎02 31 06 06 44. www.memorial-caen.fr. Open daily mid-July to Aug. 9am-8pm; Feb. to mid-July and Sept.-Oct. 9am-7pm; mid-Jan. to Feb. and Nov.-Dec. 9am-6pm. €16, students €14.) Flanking the ruined chateau of Caen's most famous denizen, the twin abbeys **Abbaye-aux-Hommes,** off r. Guillaume le Conquérant, and **Abbaye-aux-Dames,** off r. des Chanoines, hold the tombs of William the Conqueror and his wife. (Abbaye-aux-Hommes open 9:15am-noon and 2-6pm. €1.55, students €0.80. Abbaye-aux-Dames open M-Sa 8am-5:30pm, Su 9:30am-12:30pm. Free.)

Trains (☎08 29 35 35 35) run to: Paris (2½hr., 12 per day, €44.60); Rennes (3hr., 3 per day, €25.70); Rouen (2hr., 5 per day, €18.20); and Tours (3½hr., 2 per day, €26.70). **Bus Verts** (☎08 10 21 42 14) covers the beaches and the rest of Normandy. The **tourist office,** pl. St-Pierre, offers free maps. (☎02 31 27 14 14; www.ville-caen.fr. Open July-Aug. M-Sa 9:30am-7pm, Su 10am-1pm and 2-5pm; Sept.-June M-Sa 9:30am-1pm and 2-6pm, Su 10am-1pm.) The social **Auberge de Jeunesse (HI) ❶,** 68bis r. Eustache-Restout, is at Foyer Robert Reme. Take a right from the train station, take your second right on r. de Vaucelles, walk one block, and catch bus #5 or 17 (dir.: Fleury or Grâce de Dieu) from the stop on your left to Lycée Fresnel. (☎02 31 52 19 96; fax 02 31 84 29 49. Breakfast €2. Sheets €2.30. Reception 5-10pm. Dorms €9.45.) **Hôtel du Château ❹,** 5 av. du 6 Juin, has large, bright rooms. (☎31 86 15 37; fax 31 86 58 08. Reception 24hr. Singles and doubles €35-45. Prices €3.05 lower Oct.-Easter. MC/V.) Ethnic restaurants, *crêperies*, and *brasseries* line the

quartier Vaugueux near the chateau as well as the streets between **Eglise St-Pierre** and **Eglise St-Jean.** Get your groceries at **Monoprix supermarket,** 45 bd. du Maréchal Leclerc. (Open M-Sa 9am-8:30pm.) Caen's old streets pulsate by moonlight, especially around **rue de Bras, rue des Croisiers,** and **rue St-Pierre. Postal Code:** 14000.

BAYEUX

Relatively untouched by war, beautiful Bayeux (pop. 15,000) is an ideal base for exploring the nearby D-Day beaches. However, visitors should not miss its 900-year-old ☒**Tapisserie de Bayeux,** 70m of embroidery that relates the tale of William the Bastard's invasion of England and his earning of a more respectable name— "the Conqueror." The tapestry is displayed in the **Centre Guillaume le Conquérant,** on r. de Nesmond. (Open May-Aug. daily 9am-7pm; mid-Mar. to Apr. and Sept. to mid-Oct. 9am-6:30pm; mid-Oct. to mid-Mar. 9:30am-12:30pm and 2-6pm. €6.40, students €2.60.) Nearby is the original home of the tapestry, the extraordinary **Cathédrale Notre-Dame.** (Open July-Aug. M-Sa 8am-7pm, Su 9am-7pm; Sept.-June M-Sa 8:30am-noon and 2:30-7pm, Su 9am-12:15pm and 2:30-7pm. Free.) The amazing **Musée de la Bataille de Normandie,** bd. Fabian Ware, recounts the D-Day landing and subsequent 76-day battle. (Open May to mid-Sept. 9:30am-6:30pm; mid-Sept. to Apr. 10am-12:30pm and 2-6pm; closed early Jan. €5.70, students €2.50.) The **British Cemetery** across the street provides a strikingly simple yet moving wartime record. **Trains** (☎ 02 31 92 80 50) arrive at pl. de la Gare from: Caen (20min., 15 per day, €4.90); Cherbourg (1hr., 12 per day, €12.50); and Paris (2½hr., 12 per day, €26.55). To reach the **tourist office,** pont St-Jean, turn left on the highway (bd. Sadi-Carnot), bear right, follow the signs to the *centre ville,* and follow r. Larcher to r. St-Martin. (☎ 02 31 51 28 28; fax 02 31 51 28 29. Open mid-June to mid-Sept. M-Sa 9am-7pm, Su 9:30am-12:30pm and 2:30-6:30pm; mid-Sept. to mid-June M-Sa 9am-noon and 2-6pm.) From the tourist office, turn right onto r. St-Martin, follow through several name changes, and turn left onto r. General de Dais to reach the ☒**Family Home/ Auberge de Jeunesse (HI) ❶,** 39 r. General de Dais. (☎ 02 31 92 15 22; fax 02 31 92 55 72. Breakfast included. Dorms €16, nonmembers €18.) Follow r. Genas Duhomme to the right and continue straight on av. de la Vallée des Prés for **Camping Municipal ❶,** on bd. d'Eindhoven. (☎ 02 31 92 08 43. Open May-Sept. €3 per person, €3.55 per tent and car.) Get **groceries** at **Champion,** on bd. d'Eindhoven. **Postal Code:** 14400.

D-DAY BEACHES

On June 6, 1944, over one million Allied soldiers invaded the beaches of Normandy in the first of a chain of events that liberated France and led to the downfall of Nazi Europe. Today, reminders of that first devastating battle can be seen in somber gravestones, remnants of German bunkers, and the pockmarked landscape.

⬛ TRANSPORTATION. Most of the beaches and museums can be reached from Caen and Bayeux with **Bus Verts** (☎ 08 10 21 42 14); ask about the special "D-Day" line. You may want to buy a day pass (€17.50) if you plan to make many stops. **Utah Beach** is accessible only by car or foot from **Ste-Mère-Eglise.** Take a **train** from Bayeux to Caretan (30min., 10 per day, €6.60) and then a **bus** from Caretan to Ste-Mère-Eglise (15min.; 12:50pm, return 6:35pm; €2.90). English-language **Victory Tours** leave from behind the Bayeux tourist office. (☎ 02 31 51 98 14; www.victory-tours.com. 4hr. tour 12:30pm, €31; 8hr. tour 9am, €54. Reserve ahead.)

BEACHES NEAR BAYEUX. At **Utah Beach,** near Ste-Marie du Mont, the Americans headed the western flank of the invasion. The **Musée du Débarquement** here shows how 836,000 troops, 220,000 vehicles, and 725,000 tons of equipment came ashore. (☎ 02 33 71 53 35. Open June-Sept. daily 9:30am-7pm; Oct.-May reduced hours. €4.50.) The most difficult landing was that of the First US Infantry Division at **Pointe du Hoc.** The Pointe is considered a military cemetery because many who perished are still there, crushed beneath collapsed concrete bunkers. **Omaha Beach,** next to Colleville-sur-Mer and east of the Pointe du Hoc, is perhaps the most famous beach and the severe losses suffered there bestowed the moniker "bloody Omaha." Overlooking the beach, 9387 graves stretch over the **American Cemetery.** (Open mid-Apr. to Sept. daily 8am-6pm; Oct. to mid-Apr. 9am-5pm.) Ten kilometers north of Bayeux and just east of Omaha is Arromanches, a small town at the center of **Gold Beach,** where the British built the artificial Port Winston in a single day to provide shelter while the Allies unloaded their supplies. The Arromanches **360° Cinéma** combines images of modern Normandy with those of D-Day. Turn left on r. de la Batterie from the museum and climb the steps. (Open June-Aug. daily 9:40am-6:40pm; Sept.-May reduced hours; closed Jan. €3.65.)

CHERBOURG

On the northern tip of the Cotentin peninsula, Cherbourg (pop. 44,000) was the "Gateway to France," serving as the major supply port following the D-Day offensive of 1944. Today, the town's many ferry lines shuttle tourists from France to England and Ireland. **Ferries,** which leave from bd. Maritime, northeast of the *centre ville,* connect to Rosslare, Portsmouth, and Poole (see p. 52). Make sure to **reserve ahead** and check the up-to-date schedules. To get to the train station, go left at the roundabout onto av. A. Briand and follow it as it becomes av. Carnot; it's at the end of the canal right off av. Carnot on av. Millet (25min.). **Trains** go to: Bayeux (1hr., 8 per day, €12.80); Caen (1½hr., 10 per day, €15.70); Paris (3hr., 7 per day, €34.20); and Rouen (4½hr., 4 per day, €29.10). A **shuttle bus** connects the ferry terminal and train station. To reach the **tourist office,** 2 quai Alexandre III, turn right from the ferry terminal onto bd. Felix Amiot, go straight at the roundabout, and turn right across the canal; it will be on your left. (☎02 33 93 52 02; www.ot-cherbourg-cotentin.fr. Open 9am-12:30pm and 2pm-6pm.) **Postal Code:** 50100.

MONT-ST-MICHEL

Rising like a vision from the sea, the fortified island of Mont-St-Michel (pop. 42) is a dazzling labyrinth of stone arches, spires, and stairways that climb up to the **abbey.** Adjacent to the abbey church, **La Merveille,** a 13th-century Gothic monastery, encloses a seemingly endless web of passageways and chambers. (Open mid-July to Aug. daily 9am-7pm; Sept. to early July reduced hours. Admission €7, ages 18-25 €4.50.) The Mont is most stunning at night, but plan carefully—there is no late-night public transport off the island. Mont-St-Michel is best visited as a daytrip via Courriers Bretons **bus,** 104 r. Couesnon in Pontorson (☎02 33 60 11 43), from Rennes (1½hr., 3-6 per day, €11) or St-Malo (1½hr., 2-4 per day, €9). Hotels on Mont-St-Michel are expensive, starting at €45 a night. The **Pontorson tourist office,** pl. de l'Eglise, helps visitors find affordable accommodations (☎02 33 60 20 65; fax 33 60 85 67). The cheapest beds are at the **Centre Duguesclin (HI) ❶,** r. Général Patton. (☎/fax 02 33 60 18 65. Dorms €8.) **Postal Code:** 50116.

RENNES

Rennes (pop. 210,000) tempers its Parisian sophistication with traditional Breton spirit. Its half-timbered medieval houses rub elbows with hip cafes and bars; by dusk this youthful city—students comprise more than a quarter of its residents—invariably falls victim to the irresistible magnetism of its sizzling nightlife. A popular stopover between Paris and Mont-St-Michel, Rennes also makes for a packed weekend excursion of its own.

THE LOCAL STORY

BROTHER, CAN YOU SPARE A WEB DESIGN?

Frère Tobie, age 25, is a native Breton and monk at Mont St-Michel. He is a serious-looking young man, thin with closely cropped red hair, and he wears a monk's full-length dark blue robe and simple sandals. Attached to his belt, along with his prayer beads, is a mobile phone.

Q: What is life like on Mont St-Michel?

A: It's an exceptional place. The condition of life is particular to the location, because this is not just a monastery but also a tourist site, a place of pilgrimage, and an ancient monument. Life varies each day, but for us essentially this is a place of sanctuary, even though almost three thousand people visit each year. Living in the midst of the sea, we have to pay attention to the tides, because they dictate when we can venture off the island. At night and in the early morning the Mont is completely deserted. When you look out on the bay, with 500km of sand, it is a great desert.

Q: And the monastic community?

A: We have two communities, who live in parallel and have liturgies together. We have four monks and seven nuns. We hope to become more numerous over time, with more brothers and sisters from other communities.

Q: What is a normal day for you?

A: Our day begins at 6am. At 6:30 we have a half-hour of silent prayer and

🖅 TRANSPORTATION. Trains leave from pl. de la Gare (☎ 02 99 29 11 92) for: Brest (2¼hr., every hr. €26.90); Caen (3hr., 8 per day, €25.70); Nantes (1¼-2hr., 7 per day, €17.40); Paris (2hr., every hr., €44.80); and St-Malo (1hr., 15 per day, €10.70). **Buses** (☎ 02 99 30 87 80) leave the train station for Angers (2½-3hr., 3-4 per day, €14.95) and Mont-St-Michel (2½hr., 1-2 per day, €11).

🚺 PRACTICAL INFORMATION. To get from the train station to the **tourist office**, 11 r. Saint-Yves, take av. Jean Janvier to quai Chateaubriand, turn left, walk along the river until you reach r. George Dottin, then turn right onto r. Saint-Yves. (☎ 02 99 67 11 11; fax 02 99 67 11 10. Open Apr.-Sept. M-Sa 9am-7pm, Su and holidays 11am-6pm.) Access the **Internet** at **Cybernet Online**, 22 r. St. Georges (☎ 02 99 36 37 41. €6 per hr. Open M 2-8pm, Tu-Sa 10am-8pm; closed Aug. 1-20.) The **post office** (☎ 02 99 01 22 11) is at 27 bd. du Colombier, near the train station. **Postal Code:** 35032.

🏠🍴 ACCOMMODATIONS AND FOOD. The **Auberge de Jeunesse (HI) ❶**, 10-12 Canal St-Martin, provides cheap and decent lodging. From the train station, take av. Jean Janvier toward the canal (where it becomes r. Gambetta) for five blocks, turn left on r. des Fossés, take r. de la Visitation to pl. Ste-Anne, staying on the right; follow r. de St-Malo on your right until you cross the small canal. The hostel is on the right. (☎ 02 99 33 22 33; fax 02 99 59 06 21. Breakfast included. Reception 7am-11pm. Dorms €12.20; singles €21.20. MC/V.) **Hotel d'Angleterre ❷**, 19 r. Marechal Joffre, can't be beat for location. From the train station's north entrance, proceed along av. Jean Janvier to bd. de la Liberte; after three blocks, take a right on r. Marechal Joffre, and it's on the right. (☎ 02 99 79 38 61; fax 02 99 79 43 85. Breakfast €4.90. Reception 7am-10:30pm. Singles €22; doubles €31. MC/V.) **Camping Municipal des Gayeulles ❶**, deep within Parc les Gayeulles, is packed with activities. Take bus #3 (dir.: Gayeulles/St-Laurent) from pl. de la Mairie to the third stop after you reach the park. Follow the paths and the signs to the campgrounds. (☎ 99 36 91 22. Reception mid-June to mid-Sept. 7:30am-1pm and 2-8pm; mid-Sept. to mid-June 9am-12:30pm and 4:30-8pm. €3.05 per person. €1.55 per car. Electricity €2.60. MC/V.) Look for food on **rue St-Malo, rue St-Georges,** or **place St-Michel;** or, explore **place des Lices** and its Saturday market. The upscale **Café Breton ❷**, 14 r. Nantaise, serves Breton cuisine at reasonable prices. (☎ 02 99 30 74 95. Open M and Sa noon-4pm, Tu-F noon-3pm and 7-11pm.)

⊙ ♫ SIGHTS AND ENTERTAINMENT. Excellent examples of medieval architecture are near the tourist office on **rue de la Psalette** and **rue St-Guillaume.** At the end of St-Guillaume, turn left onto r. de la Monnaie to visit the imposing **Cathédrale St-Pierre,** which was begun in 1787. The center of attention is its carved and gilded altarpiece depicting the life of the Virgin. (Open daily 9:30am-noon and 3-6pm.) Across the street from the cathedral, the **Portes Mordelaises,** down an alley bearing the same name, are the former entrance to the city and the last vestiges of the medieval city walls. The **Musée des Beaux-Arts,** 20 quai Emile Zola, houses a collection that includes Pharoic Egyptian pieces, works by de la Tour and Picasso, and contemporary art. (☎02 99 28 55 85 40. Open W-M 10am-noon and 2-6pm. €4, students €2, under 18 free.) Across the river and up r. Gambetta is the lush **Jardin du Thabor,** considered to be among the most beautiful gardens in France. (Open June-Sept. 7:15am-9:30pm.) Next door is the magnificent 11th- to 19th-century **Eglise Notre Dame** where you can gaze at the remnants of a 15th-century fresco depicting the Baptism of Christ.

With enough bars for a city twice its size and a collection of clubs that draws students from Paris and beyond, Rennes is a partygoer's weekend mecca. Look for action in **place Ste-Anne, place St-Michel,** and the radiating streets. **Le Zing,** 5 pl. des Lices, packs the house with the young and beautiful. (☎02 99 79 64 60. Opens 2pm, active from midnight until 2am.) **L'Espace,** 45 bd. La Tour d'Auvergne, pounds all night with writhers of all sizes, styles, and sexual orientations. Upstairs, **L'Endroit** attracts a more relaxed mixed crowd. (☎02 99 30 21 95. Both open Th 11pm-4am, F-Sa 11pm-5am, Su-W midnight-4am. Cover €9.)

ST-MALO

St-Malo (pop. 52,000) is the ultimate oceanside getaway, combining miles of warm, sandy **beaches** and crystal blue waters with a historic *centre ville.* To the east of the city is the **Grand Plage,** the most popular beach. The best view of St-Malo is from its **ramparts**—enter the walled city through Porte St-Vincent and follow the stairs up on the right. **Trains** run from pl. de l'Hermine to: Dinan (1hr., 5 per day, €7.30); Paris (5hr., 3 per day, €49.60); and Rennes (1hr., 8-12 per day, €10.70). As you exit the station, cross bd. de la République and follow esplanade St-Vincent to the **tourist office,** near the entrance to the old city. (☎02 99 56 64 48; www.saint-malo-tourisme.com. Open July-Aug. M-Sa 8:30am-8pm, Su 10am-7pm; Sept.-June reduced hours.) The 247-bed **Auberge de Jeunesse (HI) ❶,** 37 av. du Révérend Père Umbricht, is

then *laudes,* the first services of the day. After breakfast we have *lectio divino,* a reading from the Bible, because the word of God is the basis of our life. At noon we have daily mass—in the abbey in summer, and the crypt in winter. We eat lunch in silence. In the afternoon we work. At 6:30pm, we have the adoration of the sacrement for an hour and then vespers, in which the public can participate. Later we eat dinner, also in silence, and celebrate *complies,* our final service.

Q: What kind of work do you do?
A: Our vocation is being monks in the town, among people. Here at Mont St-Michel, we divide up our daily tasks: we have one brother who cooks, one brother who cleans and gardens, and our superior who coordinates the masses. And I am the webmaster, so I develop Internet sites.

Q: What drew you to a monastic life?
A: The monastic life is chosen in response to a call from God. This is our answer. In the community, we have all possible routes: there is one brother who converted after spending 20 years as a communist, because he had such a strong personal experience. There are also those from devout families, who joined very young, just after finishing high school.

Q: How do you feel about all the tourists who come to the Mont?
A: For us, it's not difficult, because we need to interact with people. When people arrive at the top of the Mont, they are panting and out of breath; tired like this, they are perhaps more able to receive the message of Mont St-Michel, the calm of the environment. We have a mission here, and it allows this place to touch the hearts of those who come.

near the beach. From the train station, take bus #5 (dir.: Parame or Davier) or bus #1 (dir.: Rotheneuf) to Auberge de Jeunesse. (☎02 99 40 29 80; fax 02 99 40 29 02. Reception 24hr. Dorms €12.20.) To reach the simple-yet-spotless **Hôtel Avenir ❷**, 31 bd. de la Tour d'Auvergne, from the station, turn right onto bd. de la République and then right onto bd. de la Tour d'Auvergne; the hotel is on your left. (☎02 99 56 13 33. Breakfast €4. Singles €20; doubles €21.50.) **Champion supermarket,** on av. Pasteur, is near the hostel. (Open M-F 8:30am-1pm and 3-7:30pm, Sa 8:30am-7:30pm, Su 9:30am-noon.) **Postal Code:** 35400.

DINAN

Perhaps the best-preserved medieval town in Brittany, Dinan (pop. 10,000) sports cobblestone streets lined with 15th-century houses inhabited by traditional artisans. On the ramparts, the 13th-century **Porte du Guichet** is the entrance to the **Château de Dinan,** also known as the Tour de la Duchesse Anne. Climb to the terrace to look over the town or inspect the galleries of the 15th-century **Tour de Coëtquen,** which houses a collection of funerary ornaments. (Open June-Sept. daily 10am-6:30pm; Oct.-May reduced hours. €3.90, ages 12-18 €1.50.) On the other side of the ramparts from the chateau is the **Jardin du Val Cocherel,** which holds bird cages and a chessboard for life-sized pieces. (Open daily 8am-7:30pm.)

Trains run from the pl. du 11 novembre 1918 to Paris (3hr., 8 per day, €49.60) and Rennes (1hr., 8 per day, €11.20). To get from the station to the **tourist office,** r. du Château, bear left across pl. 11 novembre to r. Carnot, turn right on r. Thiers, turn left into the old city, and bear right onto r. du Marchix, which becomes r. de la Ferronnerie; it will be on your right. (☎02 96 87 69 76; www.dinan-tourisme.com. Open mid-June to mid-Sept. M-Sa 9am-7pm, Su 10am-12:30pm and 2:30-6pm; mid-Sept. to mid-June M-Sa 9am-12:30pm and 2-6:15pm.) To walk to the **Auberge de Jeunesse (HI) ❶,** in Vallée de la Fontaine-des-Eaux, turn left as you exit the station and cross the tracks; turn right, and follow the tracks and signs downhill for 1km before turning right again; it will be on your right. (☎02 96 39 10 83; fax 02 96 39 10 62. Reception 8am-noon and 5-8pm. Curfew 11pm. Dorms €8.50.) **Hôtel du Théâtre ❶,** 2 r. Ste-Claire, is in the heart of the *vieille ville.* (☎02 96 39 06 91. Singles €14.50; doubles €20.50; triples €36.) Get **groceries** at **Monoprix** on r. de la Ferronnerie. (Open M-Sa 9am-7:30pm.) Inexpensive *brasseries* lie on **rue de la Cordonnerie** and near **rue de la Ferronnerie** and **place des Merciers. Postal Code:** 22100.

ST-BRIEUC. Situated between the Côte d'Emeraude and the Côte de Granite Rose, St-Brieuc is a perfect base for daytrips to the scenic countryside. **Trains** arrive from Dinan (1hr., 2-3 per day, €8.60) and Rennes (1hr., 15 per day, €14.40). From the station, on bd. Charner, walk straight down r. de la Gare and bear right at the fork to reach pl. de la Résistance and the **tourist office,** 7 r. St-Guéno. (☎02 96 33 32 50; www.baiesaintbrieuc.com. Open July-Aug. M-Sa 9am-12:30pm and 2-7pm, Su 10am-1pm; Sept.-June M-Sa 9am-12:30pm and 2-6pm.) The **youth hostel ❶** is in a 15th-century house 3km from town; take bus #2 (dir.: Centre Commercial les Villages) and get off at the last stop. From the stop, turn right on bd. de l'Atlantique, take the 2nd left onto r. du Vau Meno, and turn right on r. de la Ville Guyomard; the hostel will be on the left. (☎02 96 78 70 70. Breakfast included. Reception 8am-noon, 2-4pm and 8-10pm. Dorms €12.20. MC/V.) **Postal Code:** 22000.

CAP FRÉHEL. The rust-hued cliffs of **Cap Fréhel** mark the northern point of the Côte d'Emeraude. Catch a CAT **bus** from St-Brieuc (1½hr.; 3-4 per day; €7.20, students €5.80) and follow the red- and-white-striped markers along the well-marked **GR34 trail** on the edge of the peninsula. There's also a scenic 1½ hr. walk to **Fort La Latte,** a 13th-century castle complete with drawbridges. To reach the **Auberge de**

Jeunesse Cap Fréhel (HI) ❶, in La Ville Hadrieux in Kerivet, get off the bus one stop after Cap Fréhel at Auberge de Jeunesse, take the only road that branches from the stop, and follow the fir-tree hostel signs. (☎96 41 48 98; mid-Sept. to Apr. ☎02 98 78 70 70. Breakfast €2.90. Open May-Sept. Dorms or camping €6.90.)

PAIMPOL. Paimpol, northwest of St-Brieuc at the end of the Côte de Granite Rose, offers easy access to nearby islands, beaches, and hiking. The **train** (1hr., 4-5 per day, €10) and CAT **buses** (1¼hr.; 8 per day; €7.20, students €5.80) leave av. Général de Gaulle for St-Brieuc. From the station, turn right onto av. de Général de Gaulle. Bear left at the roundabout; the **tourist office** will be on the left, and the port will be to the right. (☎02 96 20 83 16; fax 02 96 55 11 12. Open July-Aug. M-Sa 10am-7pm, Su 10am-1pm; Sept.-June Tu-Sa 10am-12:30pm and 2:30-6pm.) The blue "H" guides you to the comfortable rooms of the **Hôtel Berthelot ❷,** 1 r. du Port. (☎02 96 20 88 66. Singles and doubles €26. MC/V) **Postal Code:** 22500.

BREST

Brest (pop. 156,000) slowly rose from the ashes of WWII to become a metropolis that blends the prosperity of a major port with the youthful energy of a university town. Brest's **château** was the only building in the town to survive WWII, and is now the world's oldest active military institution, as well as home to the **Musée de la Marine,** off r. de Château, which highlights the local maritime history. (Open Apr.-Sept. daily 10am-6:30pm; Oct.-Mar. W-M 10am-noon and 2-6pm. €4.60, students €3.) The newly renovated **Océanopolis Brest,** at port de Plaisance, has tropical, temperate, and polar pavilions and a coral reef accessible by a glass elevator. From the Liberty terminal, take bus #7 (dir.: Port de Plaisance; M-Sa every 30min. until 7:30pm, €1) to Océanopolis. (☎02 98 34 40 40. Open Apr.-Aug. daily 9am-6pm; Sept.-Mar. Tu-Sa 10am-5pm and Su 10am-6pm. €13.50.)

Trains (☎02 98 31 51 72) leave pl. du 19*ème* Régiment d'Infanterie for Nantes (4hr., 6 per day, €33.80) and Rennes (1½hr., 15 per day, €25.30). From the station, av. Georges Clemenceau leads to the intersection of r. de Siam and r. Jean Jaurès, and the **tourist office,** at pl. de la Liberté. (☎02 98 44 24 96. Open July-Aug. M-Sa 9:30am-7pm, Su 2-4pm; Sept.-June M-Sa 10am-12:30pm and 2-6pm.) Access the **Internet** at **@cces.cibles,** 31 av. Clemenceau. (☎02 98 33 73 07. €3 per hr. Open M-Sa 11am-1am, Su 2-11pm.) For the luxurious ⚑**Auberge de Jeunesse (HI) ❶,** 5 r. de Kerbriant, 4km away near Océanopolis, take bus #7 (dir.: Port de Plaisance) from opposite the station to its final stop (M-Sa until 7:30pm, Su until 6pm; €1); with your back to the bus stop, go left toward the beach, take an immediate left, and follow the signs to the hostel. (☎02 98 41 90 41. Breakfast included. Reception M-F 7-9am and 5-8pm, Sa-Su 7-10am and 6-8pm. Curfew July-Aug. midnight; Sept.-June 11pm; ask for a key. Dorms €11.30.) To reach **Camping du Goulet ❶,** 7km from Brest, take bus #14 (dir.: Plouzane) to Le Cosquer. (☎02 98 45 86 84. Electricity €1.70-2.50. Shower included. €3.40 per person, €3.90 per tent.) For **groceries,** visit **Monoprix,** 49 r. de Siam. (Open M-Sa 8:30am-7:30pm.) **Postal Code:** 29200.

LOIRE VALLEY (VAL DE LOIRE)

The Loire, France's longest and most celebrated river, meanders to the Atlantic through a valley overflowing with gentle vineyards and majestic chateaux. Loire vineyards produce some of France's best wines, and the soil is among the country's most fertile. It is hardly surprising that a string of French (and English) kings chose to station themselves in opulent chateaux by these waters rather than in the dirt and noise of their capital cities.

▐▀ TRANSPORTATION

Faced with such widespread grandeur, many travelers plan over-ambitious itineraries—two chateaux a day is a reasonable limit. Bike is the best way to explore the region, since trains to chateaux are infrequent. The city of Tours is the region's best rail hub, although the chateaux Sully-sur-Loire, Chambord, and Cheverny aren't accessible by train. Many stations distribute the invaluable *Châteaux pour Train et Vélo* booklet with train schedules and bike and car rental information.

ORLÉANS

A pleasant gateway from Paris into the Loire, Orléans (pop. 117,000) clings tightly to its historical claim to Joan of Arc's fame. Most of Orléans's historical and architectural highlights are near **Place Ste-Croix.** Joan of Arc triumphantly marched down nearby **Rue de Bourgogne,** the city's oldest street, in 1429; the scene is vividly captured in *Jeanne d'Arc* at the **Musée des Beaux-Arts,** 1 r. Ferdinand Rabier. (☎38 79 21 55. Open M 1:30-6pm, Tu-Sa 10am-noon and 1:30-6pm. €3, students €1.50.) The **Église St-Paterne,** pl. Gambetta, is a massive showcase of modern stained glass. The stunning windows of **Cathédrale Ste-Croix,** pl. Ste-Croix, depict Joan's dramatic story. (Open July-Aug. daily 9:15am-6:45pm; Sept.-June reduced hours. Free.) Forty-two kilometers from Orléans, the imposing 14th-century fortress **Sully-sur-Loire** dominates the southern bank of the Loire. Catch the bus at 2 r. Marcel Proust (1hr., 5 per day, €7.30).

Trains arrive at the Gare d'Orléans on pl. Albert 1er from: Blois (30min., every hr. 7am-9pm, €8.30); Paris (1¼hr., 3 per hr., €14.60); Tours (1hr., 12 per day, €14.10). To get from the station to the **tourist office,** 6 pl. Albert 1er, go left under the tunnel to pl. Jeanne d'Arc; it's across the street. (☎02 38 24 05 05; www.tourismloiret.com. Open Apr.-Sept. M-Sa 10am-1pm and 2-7pm, Su 10am-noon. Oct.-Mar. reduced hours.) To get to the **Auberge de Jeunesse (HI) ❶,** 1 bd. de la Motte Sanguin, take bus RS (dir.: Rosette) or SY (dir.: Concyr/La Bolière) from pl. d'Arc to Pont Bourgogne; follow bd. de la Motte and it'll be up on the right. (☎02 38 53 60 06. Reception M-F 8am-7pm, Sa-Su 9-11am and 5-7pm. Spacious and clean dorms €8; singles €13.75.) Get **groceries** at **Carrefour** at pl. d'Arc. (Open M-Sa 8:30am-9pm.) **Rue de Bourgogne** has eateries. **Postal Code:** 45000.

BLOIS

Blois (pop. 50,000) welcomes visitors to the Loire Valley with pastoral charm. Home to monarchs Louis XII and François I, Blois's **château** was the Versailles of the late 15th and early 16th centuries; today it is decorated with François I's painted and carved salamanders and exemplifies the progression of French architecture from the 13th to the 17th century. Housed in the castle are excellent museums: the recently renovated **Musée de Beaux-Arts,** featuring a 16th-century portrait gallery; the **Musée d'Archéologie,** showcasing locally excavated glass and ceramics; and the **Musée Lapidaire,** preserving sculpted pieces from nearby chateaux. (☎54 78 06 62. Open July-Aug. daily 9am-7:30pm; Apr.-June and Sept. 9am-6pm; Oct.-Mar. 9am-12:30pm and 2-5:30pm. €6, students €4.) At night, move from the cafes of **Place de la Résistance** to ▨Z 64, r. Maréchal de Tassigny, for cocktails, dancing, and karaoke. (☎02 54 74 27 76. Open Tu-Su 8:30am-4am.)

Trains leave pl. de la Gare for: Orléans (30min., 14 per day, €8.30); Paris (1¾hr., 8 per day, €20) via Orléans; Tours (1hr., 10 per day, €8). **Transports Loir-et-Cher (TLC;** ☎02 54 58 55 44) sends buses from the station and pl. Victor Hugo to nearby chateaux (1¼hr., 4 per day, €5.35). Or, rent a **bike** from **Cycles Leblond,** 44 levée des Tuileries, for the hour-long ride to the valley. (☎02 54 74 30 13. €12.20 per day. Open daily 9am-9pm.) The **tourist office,** 3 av. Jean Laigret, can point the way.

(☎02 54 90 41 41; www.loiredeschateaux.com. Open Apr.-Oct. Tu-Sa 9am-7pm, Su-M and holidays 10am-7pm; Oct-Mar. M 10am-12:30pm and 2-6pm, Tu-Sa 9am-12:30pm and 2-6pm, Su 9:30am-12:30pm.) Five kilometers west is the **Auberge de Jeunesse (HI) ❶**, 18 r. de l'Hôtel Pasquier. To get there from the tourist office, follow r. Porte Côté, bear right along r. Denis Papin to the river, and take bus #4 (dir.: Les Grouets) to Auberge de Jeunesse. (☎/fax 02 54 78 27 21. Reception 6:45-10am and 6-10:30pm. Lockout 10am-6pm. Curfew 10:30pm. Open Mar. to mid-Nov. Dorms €7.) **Le Pavillon ❸**, 2 av. Wilson, has clean and bright rooms. (☎02 54 74 23 27; fax 02 54 74 03 36. Breakfast €5. Singles €20-36; quads €48. MC/V.) Fragrant *patisseries* entice from **Rue Denis Papin**, while **Rue Drussy, Rue St-Lubin,** and **Place Poids du Roi** have a wide variety of eateries. **Postal Code:** 41000.

▶️ DAYTRIPS FROM BLOIS: CHAMBORD AND CHEVERNY. Built between 1519 and 1545 to satisfy François I's egomania, **Chambord** is the largest and most extravagant of the Loire chateaux. With 440 rooms, 365 fireplaces, and 83 staircases, the chateau rivals Versailles in grandiosity. To cement his claim, François stamped 700 of his trademark stone salamanders throughout this "hunting lodge" and built a spectacular double-helix staircase in the center of the castle. (☎02 54 50 40 00. Open July-Aug. 9am-6:45pm; Sept.-June reduced hours. €7, ages 18-25 €4.50.) Take **TLC bus #2** from Blois (45min., €3.20) or **bike** south from Blois on D956 for 2 to 3km, and then turn left on D33 (1hr.).

    Cheverny and its manicured grounds are unique among the major chateaux. Its magnificent furnishings include elegant tapestries and delicate Delft vases. Fans of Hergé's *Tintin* books may recognize Cheverny's Renaissance facade as the inspiration for Marlinspike, Captain Haddock's mansion. The **kennels** hold 70 mixed English Poitevin hounds who stalk stags in hunting expeditions. (☎54 79 96 29. Open July-Aug. daily 9:15am-6:45pm. Hunting Oct.-Mar. Tu and Sa. Reduced hours off season. €5.80, students €2.60.) Cheverny is 45min. south of Blois by bike and on the route of TLC bus #2 (see above).

AMBOISE

The battlements of the 15th-century **château** at Amboise (pop. 11,000), that six paranoid French kings called home, stretch protectively above the town. In the **Logis de Roi,** the main part of the chateau, intricate 16th-century Gothic chairs stand over 2m high to prevent surprise attacks from behind. The jewel of the grounds is the 15th-century **Chapelle St-Hubert,** the final resting place of **Leonardo da Vinci.** (☎02 47 57 00 98. Open Apr.-Nov. daily 9am-6pm; Dec.-Mar. reduced hours. €6.50, students €5.50.) Four hundred meters away is **Clos Lucé** manor, where Leonardo da Vinci spent the last three years of his life. Check out the collection of 40 unrealized inventions. (☎02 47 57 62 88. Open Mar.-Oct. 9am-7pm; Nov.-Feb. reduced hours. €7, students €6.) **Trains** leave bd. Gambetta for: Blois (20min., 15 per day, €5); Orléans (1hr., 14 per day, €12); Paris (2hr., 5 per day, €22); and Tours (20min., 14 per day, €4). The **Centre International de Séjour (HI) Charles Péguy ❶,** on Ile d'Or, sits on an island in the middle of the Loire. (☎02 47 30 60 90; fax 02 47 30 60 91. Sheets €2.90. Reception M-F 3-7pm. Dorms €8.) **Postal Code:** 35400.

TOURS

Tours (pop. 250,000) works best as a base for nearby Loire chateaux, but its fabulous nightlife and collection of sights should not be missed. The **Cathédrale St-Gatien,** on r. Jules Simon, has dazzling stained glass. (Open daily 9am-7pm. Free.) At the **Musée du Gemmail,** 7 r. du Murier, works of *gemmail* (a fusion of enameled shards of brightly colored glass) by Picasso and Braque glow in rooms of dark velvet. (Open Apr. to mid-Nov. Tu-Su 10am-noon and 2-6:30pm; mid-Nov. to Mar. W-Su only. €4.60, students €3.05.)

Trains leave 3 r. Édouard Vaillant for Bordeaux (2½hr., 6 per day, €35.50) and Paris (2¼hr., 7 per day, €24.20). The **tourist office,** 78/82 r. Bernard Palissy, distributes free maps and books rooms. (☎02 47 70 37 37; www.ligeris.com. Open mid-Apr. to mid-Oct. M-Sa 8:30am-7pm, Su 10am-12:30pm and 2:30-5pm; mid-Oct. to mid-Apr. M-Sa 9am-12:30pm and 1:30-6pm, Su 10am-1pm.) ▨**Foyer des Jeunes Travailleurs ❷,** 24 r. Bernard Palissy, is centrally located. (☎02 47 60 51 51. Singles €15.25; doubles €24.40.) The owners of ▨**Hôtel Regina ❸,** 2 r. Pimbert, make you feel like family. It's near beautiful river strolls and good restaurants. (☎02 47 05 25 36; fax 02 47 66 08 72. Breakfast €4.15. Singles €20-26; doubles €26-30. MC/V.) Try **place Plumereau** for great restaurants, cafes, and bars. **La Souris Gourmande ❷,** 100 r. Colbert, is a friendly restaurant specializing in regional cheese dishes and fondues. (Open Tu-Sa noon-2pm and 7-10:30pm.) **Postal Code:** 37000.

▨ DAYTRIPS FROM TOURS

▨**CHENONCEAU.** Perhaps the most exquisite chateau in France, Chenonceau arches gracefully over the Cher river. A series of women created the beauty that is the chateau: first Catherine, the wife of a tax collector; then Diane de Poitiers, the lover of Henri II; and then Henri's widowed wife, Catherine de Médici. The part of the chateau bridging the Cher marked the border between occupied and Vichy France during WWII. (☎02 47 23 90 07; www.chenonceaux-sa.fr. Open mid-Mar. to mid-Sept. daily 9am-7pm; reduced hours off season. €7.65, students €5.) *Trains from Tours roll into the station 2km away from the castle (45min., 8 per day, €5.50). Fil Vert buses also connect Tours with Chenonceau (25min., 2 per day, €2).*

LOCHES. Surrounded by a walled medieval town that merits a visit in itself, the chateau of Loches consists of two distinct structures at opposite ends of a hill. To the north, the 11th-century keep and watchtowers changed roles from keeping enemies out to keeping them in when Charles VII turned it into a state prison, complete with suspended cages. The Logis Royal honors the famous ladies who held court here, including Agnès Sorel, the first Mistress of the King of France. (Open Apr.-Sept. daily 9am-7pm; Oct.-Mar. 9:30am-12:30pm and 2-5pm. Logis Royal €3.80.) *Trains and buses run from Tours to Loches (50min., 13 per day, €7.50; pay on board).*

ANGERS

From behind the massive stone walls of the **Château d'Angers,** on pl. Kennedy, the Dukes of Anjou ruled the surrounding area and a certain island across the Channel. The 13th-century chateau remains a well-preserved haven of medieval charm in a city filled with shops and sights. Inside the chateau is the 14th-century **Tapisserie de l'Apocalypse,** the world's largest tapestry. (Open May to mid-Sept. daily 9:30am-7pm; mid-Sept. to Apr. 10am-5:30pm. €5.50, students €3.50.) Angers's other woven masterpiece is the 1930 **Chant du Monde** ("Song of the World"), in the **Musée Jean Lurçat,** 4 bd. Arago. (☎02 41 24 18 45. Open mid-June to mid-Sept. daily 9:30am-6:30pm; late Sept. to mid-June Tu-Su 10am-noon and 2-6pm. €3.50.) In the *vieille ville* is the 12th-century **Cathédrale St-Maurice,** home to another impressive collection of tapestries. The tourist office sells a €4.50 admission to 5 museums and an €8 *billet jumelé,* which also includes the chateau.

From r. de la Gare, **trains** leave for: Nantes (1hr., 15 per day, €12); Paris (2-4hr., 3 per day, €39-49); and Tours (1hr., 7 per day, €13). **Buses** run from pl. de la République to Rennes (3hr., 2 per day, €15). To get from the station to the **tourist office,** at pl. du Président Kennedy, exit straight onto r. de la Gare, turn right at pl.

de la Visitation on r. Talot, and turn left on bd. du Roi-René; it's on the right, across from the chateau. (☎02 41 23 50 00; accueil@angers-tourisme.com. Open June-Sept. M-Sa 9am-7pm, Su 10am-6pm; Oct.-May M-Sa 9am-6pm.) Access the **Internet** at **Cyber Espace**, 25 r. de la Roë. (☎02 41 24 92 71. €3.85 per hr. Open M-Th 10am-10pm, F-Sa 10am-midnight.) To get to the **Centre d'Accueil du Lac de Maine (HI) ❷**, 49 av. du Maine, take bus #6 or 16 to Accueil Lac de Maine, cross the road, and follow the signs. (☎02 41 22 32 10; infos@lacdemaine.fr. Breakfast included. Singles and doubles with shower €24. HI members only.) Walk straight down r. de la Gare for the spacious **Royal Hôtel ❷**, 8bis pl. de la Visitation. (☎02 41 88 30 25; fax 02 41 81 05 75. Breakfast €4.60. Singles and doubles €24-41; quads €55. AmEx/MC/V.) Grab groceries in **Galeries Lafayette**, at r. d'Alsace and pl. du Ralliement. (Open M-Sa 9:30am-7:30pm.) **Postal Code: 49052.**

PÉRIGORD AND AQUITAINE

Périgord and Aquitaine present seductive images: green countryside splashed with yellow sunflowers, white chalk cliffs, golden white wine, plates of black truffles, and the smell of warm walnuts. First settled 150,000 years ago, the area around Les Eyzies-de-Tayac has produced more stone-age artifacts than anywhere on earth.

PÉRIGUEUX

The towering steeple and five massive cupolas of the **Cathédrale St-Front** dominate Périgueux (pop. 32,300) from above the Isle river. 1500 years of rebuilding, restoration, rethinking, and revision have produced the largest cathedral in southwestern France. (Open daily 8am-noon and 2:30-7pm.) Just down r. St-Front, the **Musée du Périgord**, 22 cours Tourny, houses one of France's most important collections of prehistoric artifacts, including 2m mammoth tusks and an Egyptian mummy whose toes peek out from crusty coverings, conspicuously mixed with works by local middle schoolers. (☎05 53 06 40 70. Open M and W-F 11am-6pm, Sa-Su 1-6pm. €3.50, students €1.75; Sept. 15-June 15 M-F noon-2pm free.)

Trains leave r. Denis Papin for: Bordeaux (1½hr., 7 per day, €15.40); Paris (4-6hr., 12 per day, €42.80); and Toulouse (4hr., 8 per day, €26.80). The **tourist office,** 26 pl. Francheville, has free maps. From the station, turn right on r. Denis Papin, bear left on r. des Mobiles-de-Coulmierts, which becomes r. du Président Wilson, and take the next right after passing r. Guillier; it will be on the left. (☎05 53 53 10 63; fax 05 53 09 02 50). Open July-Aug. M-Sa 9am-7pm, Su 10am-6pm; Sept.-June M-Sa 9am-6pm.) Across from the train station, **Hôtel des Voyageurs ❶**, 26 r. Denis Papin, has clean, bright rooms. (☎/fax 05 53 53 17 44. Breakfast €3.20. Singles €13; doubles €14, with shower €17.) If you're not completely cash-crunched, your stomach will thank you for visiting ⊠**Au Bien Bon ❸**, 15 r. Aubergerie, serving cuisine at the height of regional cooking with design-your-own lunch *formules*. (☎05 53 09 69 91. Open M 7:30-10pm, Tu-Sa noon-2pm and 7:30-10pm; €10-13.) **Monoprix** is on pl. de la République. (Open M-Sa 8:30am-8pm.) **Postal Code: 24070.**

SARLAT

The golden medieval *vieille ville* of Sarlat (pop. 11,000) has been the focus of tourist and movie cameras; Gérard Depardieu's *Cyrano de Bergerac* was filmed here. Today, its narrow 14th- and 15th-century streets fill with flea markets, dancing violinists, and purveyors of *gâteaux aux noix* (cakes with nuts) and golden Monbazillac wines. **Trains** go to Bordeaux (2½hr., 4 per day, €18.60) and Périgueux (3hr., 2 per day, €11.40). The **tourist office,** r. Tourny in the Ancien Eveche, can arrange accommodations (☎05 53 31 45 45. Open Apr.-Oct. M-Sa 9am-7pm, Su 10am-noon and 2-6pm; Nov.-Mar. M-Sa 9am-noon and 2-6pm). You can rent **bikes** at **Cycles Sarlandais,** 36 av. Thiers. (☎05 53 28 51 87. €10.70 for 24hr. Open Tu-Sa 9:30am-7pm. MC/V.) Sarlat's **Auberge de Jeunesse ❶,** 77 av. de Selves, is 40min. from the train station but only 10min. from the *vieille ville.* From the *vieille ville,* go straight on r. de la République, which becomes av. Gambetta, and bear left at the fork onto av. de Selves. (☎05 53 59 47 59. Reception 6-8:30pm. Open mid-Mar. to Nov. Reserve ahead. Dorms €10. **Camping** €6.) **Champion supermarket** is near the hostel on rte. de Montignac; continue following av. de Selves away from the *centre ville.* (Open M-Sa 9am-7:30pm, Su 9am-noon.) **Postal Code:** 24200.

▶ DAYTRIPS FROM SARLAT AND PÉRIGUEUX

CAVE PAINTINGS

CFTA (☎05 55 86 07 07) runs buses to the Caves of Lascaux, near Montignac, from Périgueux (1½hr., 1 per day, €5.35). Buses also run every morning from Sarlat (20min., 3 per day, €6.10). Trains run to Les Eyzies-de-Tayac from Périgueux (30min., 45 per day, €6.10) and Sarlat (1hr.; 3 per day, change at Le Buisson; €7.20).

The most spectacular cave paintings ever discovered line the **Caves of Lascaux,** near the town of **Montignac,** 25km north of Sarlat. They were discovered in 1940 by a couple of teenagers, but were closed in 1963—the oohs and aahs of tourists had fostered algae and micro-stalactites that ravaged the paintings. **Lascaux II** duplicates the original cave in the same pigments used 17,000 years ago. Although they may lack ancient awe and mystery, the new caves—filled with paintings of 5m tall bulls, horses, and bison—manage to inspire a wonder all their own. The **ticket office** (☎05 53 35 50 10) shares a building with Montignac's **tourist office** (☎53 51 82 60), on pl. Bertram-de-Born. (Ticket office open 9am until sold-out. €7.70.)

At the **Grotte de Font-de-Gaume,** 1km outside **Les Eyzies-de-Tayac** on D47 (10min. by foot), amazing 15,000-year-old paintings are still open for viewing. (☎05 53 06 86 00; www.leseyzies.com/grottes-ornees. Open Apr.-Sept. Th-Tu 9am-noon and 2-6pm; Mar. and Oct. Th-Tu 9:30am-noon and 2-5:30pm; Nov.-Feb. Th-Tu 10am-noon and 2-5pm. Reserve in advance. €5.50, ages 18-25 €3.50, under 18 free. Tours available in English.) Get more information at the **Point Accueil Prehistoire,** across from the post office, on the main street through town. (☎06 86 66 54 43. Open daily 9:15am-1:30pm and 3-7pm.) The **tourist office** is located at pl. de la Mairie, before the Point Accueil. (☎05 53 06 97 05; www.leseyzies.com. Open July-Aug. M-Sa 9am-8pm, Su 10am-noon and 2-6pm; Sept.-June reduced hours.)

THE DORDOGNE VALLEY

To get to and around the valley, you'll need to rent a car or be prepared for a good bike workout—the hills are steep but manageable. To paddle down the Dordogne River, rent canoes from Saga Team's Canoe. (☎55 28 84 84. Half-day €10, whole day €14.)

Steep, craggy cliffs and poplar tree thickets overlook the slow-moving turquoise waters of the Dordogne River, 15km south of Sarlat. The town of **Castelnaud-La Chapelle,** 10km southwest of Sarlat, snoozes in the shadow of its pale yellow **chateau.** (☎05 53 31 30 00. Open July-Aug. daily 9am-8pm; May-June and Sept. 10am-6pm; mid-Nov. to Feb. Su-F 2-5pm. €6.40.) **Domme** was built by King Philippe III (Philippe the Bold) in 1280 on a high dome of solid rock. Over 70 Templar Knights were imprisoned by King Philip IV in the **Porte des Tours.** The graffiti they scrawled upon the walls with their bare hands and teeth still remains. Consult the **tourist office,** pl. de la Halle (☎05 53 31 71 00), for tours (1hr.; 1 per day; €6, students €5).

BORDEAUX

Enveloped by emerald vineyards, Bordeaux (pop. 714,000) toasts the violet wine that made it famous. Not just a temple to wine connoisseurs, the city also has spirited nightclubs, a stunning opera house, and some of France's best food.

☐☑ TRANSPORTATION AND PRACTICAL INFORMATION. Trains leave Gare St-Jean, r. Charles Domercq (☎05 56 33 11 83), for: Nice (9-10hr., 5 per day, €66.90); Paris (TGV: 3-4hr., 15-25 per day, €55.10); and Toulouse (2-3hr., 11 per day, €27.30). From the train station, take bus #7 or 8 (dir.: Grand Théâtre) to pl. Gambetta and walk toward the Monument des Girondins for the **tourist office**, 12 cours du 30 juillet, which arranges winery tours. (☎05 56 00 66 00; www.bordeaux-tourisme.com. Open May-Oct. M-Sa 9am-7pm, Su 9:30am-6:30pm; Nov.-Apr. M-Sa 9am-6:30pm, Su 9:45am-4:30pm.) Walk away from the river up r. Judaique for **Internet** access at **France Telecom,** 2 r. Château d'Eau, near pl. Gambetta. (Open M-F noon-7pm. €4.50 per hr., students €3.) **Postal Code:** 33065.

☐☐ ACCOMMODATIONS AND FOOD. The newly renovated **Auberge de Jeunesse (HI) ❶,** 22 cours Barbey, is in a seedy area near the train station and 30min. from the *centre ville.* (☎05 56 33 00 70; fax 05 56 33 00 71. Breakfast €2.30. HI members only €12.20.) For the **Hôtel Boulan ❷,** 28 r. Boulan, take bus #7 or 8 from the station to cours d'Albret; it's around the corner from the museum. (☎05 56 52 23 62; fax 05 56 44 91 65. Breakfast €3.50. Singles €17, with shower €20-23; doubles €20/€25. MC/V.) **Hôtel Studio ❷,** 26 r. Huguerie, with sunny rooms and lots of amenities, is a backpacker fave for good reason. (☎05 56 48 00 14; fax 05 56 81 25 71. Singles and doubles €16-24; triples €30.50. MC/V.)

Bordelais take their food as seriously as their wine. Hunt around **rue St-Remi** and **place St-Pierre** for splendid regional specialties, including oysters, beef braised in wine sauce, and the cake *canelé de Bordeaux.* **La Casuccia,** 49 r. Saint Rémi, is perfect for an intimate dinner or a casual outing. (☎05 56 51 17 70. Open 11:30am-midnight. MC/V.) Stock up at **Auchan supermarket,** at the Centre Meriadeck on r. Claude Bonnier. (☎05 56 99 59 00. Open M-Sa 8:30am-10pm.)

☐☐ SIGHTS AND ENTERTAINMENT. Near the tourist office, on pl. de Quinconces, the elaborate fountains of the **Monument aux Girondins** commemorate revolutionary leaders from towns bordering the Gironde river. Retrace your steps to the breathtaking **Grand Théâtre,** on pl. de la Comédie, to see a performance or take a tour. (Tours €4.80, students €4.) Follow r. Ste-Catherine from the pl. de la Comédie, facing the theater, to reach the Gothic **Cathédrale St-André,** in pl. Pey-Berland. (Open Apr.-Oct. daily 7:30-11:30am and 2-6:30pm; Nov.-Mar. M-F only. €4, under 25 and seniors €2.50.) Walking toward the river along cours d'Alsace, turn left onto quai Richelieu for the **place de la Bourse,** whose pillars and fountains reflect Bordeaux's grandeur. On the left is the surprisingly interesting **Musée National des Douanes.** (Open Apr.-Sept. daily 10am-noon and 1-6pm; Oct.-Mar. M-Sa 10am-noon and 1-5pm. €3, students and seniors €1.50.) Near the river, just off quai des Chartrons, **Vinorama de Bourdeaux,** 12 cours du Médoc, features elaborate dioramas and wine samples. (Open June-Sept. Tu-Sa 10:30am-12:30pm and 2:30-6:30pm, Su 2-6:30pm; Oct.-May Tu-F 2-6:30pm, Sa 10:30am-12:30pm and 2:30-6:30pm. €5.50; students and seniors €2.50.)

For an overview of Bordeaux nightlife, pick up a copy of *Clubs and Concerts* at the tourist office, or purchase the magazine *Bordeaux Plus* (€0.30). **Place de la Victoire** and **place Gambetta** are year-round hot spots. **El Che,** 34 cours de l'Argonne, offers free Afro-Cuban salsa lessons. (W and F 8pm. Open Tu-Sa 7pm-2am.)

DAYTRIP FROM BORDEAUX: ST-ÉMILION. Just 35km northeast of Bordeaux, St-Émilion is home to viticulturists who have been refining their techniques since Roman times. Today, they gently crush hectares of grapes to produce 23 million liters of wine annually. Vineyards aside, the medieval-style village itself is a pleasure to visit, with its winding narrow streets and cafe-lined square. The **Eglise Monolithe** is the largest subterranean church is Europe. The **tourist office**, at pl. des Créneaux, near the church tower, rents **bikes** (€14 per day) and offers guided tours to the local chateaux. (☎ 05 57 55 28 28. Open July-Aug. daily 9:30am-8pm; Sept.-June approx. 9:30am-12:30pm and 1:45-6pm.) **Trains** run from Bordeaux to St-Émilion (30min., 2 per day, €10.10; the only return train leaves at 6:30pm).

THE PAYS BASQUE AND GASCONY

South of Aquitaine, the forests recede and the mountains of Gascony begin, shielded from the Atlantic by the Basque Country. Long renowned as fierce fighters, the Basques continue to struggle today, striving to win independence for their long-suffering homeland. Unlike the separatist Basques, Gascons have long considered themselves French. Today, people come to Gascony to be healed: millions of believers descend on Lourdes hoping for miracle cures, while thousands of others undergo barely more scientific treatments in the *thermes* of the Pyrenees.

BAYONNE

Bayonne (pop. 43,000) is a city where the pace of life has not changed for centuries. Here the word for walk is *flaner*, meaning "to stroll," rather than *marcher* or even *se promener*. Towering above it all, the grand Gothic 13th-century **Cathédrale Ste-Marie** marks the leisurely passing of time with the tolling of its bells. (Open M-Sa 7am-noon and 3-7pm, Su 3:30-10pm. Free.) The **Musée Bonnat,** 5 r. Jacques Laffitte, in Petit-Bayonne, contains works by Degas, El Greco, and Goya. (Open W-M 10am-6:15pm. €5.50, students €3.) The **Harmonie Bayonnaise** orchestra holds traditional Basque **concerts** in pl. de Gaulle. (July-Aug. Th at 9:30pm. Free.)

Trains depart from the station in pl. de la République, running to: Bordeaux (2hr., 9 per day, €20); Toulouse (4hr., 5 per day, €31); and San Sebastián, Spain (1½hr., 6 per day, €24). Trains run between Bayonne and Biarritz (10min., 11 per day, €2), but the local bus network is more extensive and cheaper than regional transit. Local STAB **buses** depart from the **Hôtel de Ville** for Anglet and Biarritz (every 30-40min., last bus M-Sa 8pm, Su 7pm; €1.15). The **tourist office,** on pl. des Basques, finds rooms. From the train station, take the middle fork onto pl. de la République, veer right over pont St-Esprit, pass through pl. Réduit, cross pont Mayou, turn right on r. Bernède and turn left for a 15min. walk down pl. des Basques. (☎ 05 59 46 01 46; www.bayonne-tourisme.com. Open July-Aug. M-Sa 9am-7pm, Su 10am-1pm; Sept.-June M-F 9am-6:30pm, Sa 10am-6pm.) Decent lodgings are near the train station and pl. Paul Bert, but the closest hostel is in Anglet. The **Hôtel Paris-Madrid ❷,** on pl. de la Gare, has cozy rooms. (☎ 05 59 55 13 98. Breakfast €4. Reception 6am-12:30am. Singles and doubles €15-20; triples and quads €39-42.) Get groceries at **Monoprix supermarket,** 8 r. Orbe. (Open M-Sa 8:30am-7:30pm.) **Postal Code:** 64100.

DAYTRIP FROM BAYONNE: ST-JEAN-DE-PORT. The Pyrenean village of St-Jean-Pied-de-Port (pop. 1600) epitomizes the spicy splendor of the Basque interior. The narrow streets ascend through the *haute ville* to the dilapidated fortress, which hovers over the calm Nive. This medieval capital of Basse-Navarre still hosts a procession of pilgrims on their way to Santiago de Compostela, Spain,

900km away. **Trains** arrive from Bayonne (1hr., 5 per day, €7.20) at the station on av. Renaud. Rent bikes at **Garazi Cycles,** 1 pl. St-Laurent. (☎ 05 59 37 21 79. Passport deposit. €18.50 per day, €23 per weekend. Open M-Sa 8:30am-noon and 3-6pm.) From the station, turn right on av. Renaud, follow it up to av. de Gaulle, and turn right to reach the **tourist office,** 14 av. de Gaulle. (☎ 05 59 37 03 57; fax 05 59 37 34 91. Open July-Aug. M-Sa 9am-12:30pm and 2-7pm, Su 10:30am-12:30pm and 3-6pm; Sept.-June M-F 9am-noon and 2-7pm, Sa 9am-noon and 2-6pm.) **Postal Code:** 64220.

BIARRITZ

Biarritz (pop. 29,000) is not a budget traveler's dream, but its free **beaches** make a daytrip *de luxe*. Surfers and bathers fill the **Grande Plage,** while bathers repose *au naturel* just to the north at the less-crowded **Plage Miramar.** A short **hike** to **Pointe St-Martin** affords a priceless view of the water. **BASC Subaquatique,** near Plateau de l'Atalaye (☎ 05 59 24 80 40), organizes **scuba** excursions in summer for €17-28.

Trains leave from **Biarritz-la-Négresse** (☎ 05 59 23 04 84), 3km from town, for Bordeaux (2hr., 7 per day, €20.30) and Paris (5hr., 5 TGVs per day, €61.10). STAB **bus** #1 and 2 run to the central Hôtel de Ville (1hr., €1.15). The **tourist office,** 1 sq. d'Ixelles, finds accommodations. (☎ 05 59 22 37 00. Open July-Aug. daily 8am-8pm; Sept.-June daily 9am-6pm.) The **Auberge de Jeunesse (HI) ❶,** 8 r. de Chiquito de Cambo, has a friendly staff and lakefront location. At the Bois de Boulogne stop on bus line #2. (☎ 05 59 41 76 00. Sheets €2.70. Dorms €12.20.) **Hôtel Barnetche ❷,** 5bis r. Charles-Floquet, is in *centre ville*. (☎ 05 59 24 22 25. Breakfast included. In Aug., obligatory half-*pension* €15.25. Reception 7:30am-10:30pm. Open May-Sept. Dorms €17; doubles €58.) **Shopi supermarket,** 2 r. du Centre, is just off r. Gambetta. (Open M-Sa 8:45am-12:30pm and 3-7pm.) **Postal Code:** 64200.

❷ DAYTRIP FROM BIARRITZ: ST-JEAN-DE-LUZ. The vibrant seaport of St-Jean-de-Luz lures visitors with the **Maison Louis XIV,** pl. Louis XIV, which temporarily housed the Sun King. (Tours every 30min. Open July-Aug. M-Sa 10:30am-noon and 2:30-6:30pm, Su 2:30-6:30pm; Sept.-June closes 5:30pm. €4.50) The village's earlier days of piracy funded its unique buildings, exemplified in the **Eglise St-Jean-Baptiste,** r. Gambetta, built to resemble a fishing boat. (Open daily 8:30am-noon and 2-6:30pm.) **Trains** roll in to bd. du Cdt. Passicot from Biarritz (15min., 10 per day, €2.40) and Bayonne (30min., 7 per day, €3.80). ATCRB **buses** (☎ 59 08 00 33), across from the train station, also run to Bayonne (7-13 per day, €3.60) and Biarritz (7-13 per day, €2.80). The **tourist office** is at pl. Foch. (☎ 05 59 26 03 16. Open July-Aug. M-Sa 9am-7pm, Su 10:30am-1pm and 3-7pm.) **Postal Code:** 64500.

LOURDES

In 1858, 14-year-old Bernadette Soubirous saw the first of 18 visions of the Virgin Mary in the Massabielle grotto in Lourdes (pop. 16,300). Today five million rosary-toting faithful annually make the pilgrimage. To get to **La Grotte de Massabielle** and the three **basilicas,** follow av. de la Gare, turn left on bd. de la Grotte, and follow it to the right and across the river Gave. Processions depart daily from the grotto at 5pm and 8:45pm. (No shorts or tank tops. Grotto open daily 5am-midnight. Basilicas open Easter to Oct. daily 6am-7pm; Nov.-Easter 8am-6pm.)

Trains leave the station, 33 av. de la Gare, for: Bayonne (2hr., 5 per day, €16.60); Bordeaux (3hr., 7 per day, €26.90); Paris (7-9hr., 5 per day, €79.80); and Toulouse (2½hr., 8 per day, €19.50). To get from the train station to the **tourist office,** on pl. Peyramale, turn right onto av. de la Gare, bear left onto av. Marasin, cross a bridge above bd. du Papacca, and climb uphill. The office is to the right. (☎ 05 62 42 77 40; lourdes@sudfr.com. Open May-Oct. M-Sa 9am-7pm; Nov.-Apr. 9am-noon and 2-

6pm.) The newly-renovated **Hotel du Commerce ❸**, 11 r. Basse, faces the tourist office. Bright, newly renovated rooms all have showers and toilets, while those in the back have a view of the chateau. (☎05 62 94 59 23; hotel-commerce-et-navarre@wanadoo.fr. Pizzeria on the first floor. Breakfast €3.80. July-Oct. singles €31.20; doubles €37.40; triples €44.60. MC/V.) **Camping de la Poste ❶**, 26 r. de Langelle, is 2min. from the post office. (☎05 62 94 40 35. Open Easter to mid-Oct. €2.50 per person, €3.60 per site. Electricity €2.45. Showers €1.30.) You can find groceries at **Prisunic supermarket**, 9 pl. du Champ-Commun. (Open M-Sa 8:30am-12:30pm and 2-7:30pm, Su 8am-noon.) **Postal Code:** 65100.

CAUTERETS

Nestled in a narrow, breathtaking valley on the edge of the **Parc National des Pyrenees Occidentales** is tiny, friendly Cauterets. Cauterets's hot sulfuric *thermes* have long been instruments of healing; for more information, contact **Thermes de Cesar**, av. Docteur Domer. (☎05 62 92 51 60. Open M-F 9am-12:30pm and 1:30-6pm, Sa 9am-12:30pm and 3-6pm.) Today, most visitors come for the skiing and hiking. The **tourist office**, on pl. Foch, has free maps of ski trails. (☎05 62 92 50 27; www.cauterets.com. Open daily 9:30am-12:30pm and 1:30-7pm.) For more **hiking** information and advice, head to **Parc National des Pyrenees** (see below). **Skilys**, rte. de Pierrefitte, on pl. de la Gare, rents **bikes** and **skates**. (☎05 62 92 52 10. Bikes €15.25 per day. Open daily 9am-7pm; off-season 8am-7:30pm.)

SNCF **buses** run from pl. de la Gare to Lourdes (1hr.; 6 per day; €5.90). The **Hôtel Bigorre ❷**, 15 r. de Belfort, has spacious rooms with views of the mountains. (☎65 92 52 81. Singles €20, with shower €28; doubles €31/€40; triples and quads €44-61.) The **Halles market**, on av. du Général Leclerc, has fresh produce. (Open daily 8:30am-12:30pm and 2:30-7:30pm.) **Postal Code:** 65110.

⚡ DAYTRIP FROM CAUTERETS: THE PYRENEES. The striking **Parc National des Pyrenees** shelters thousands of endangered animals in its snow-capped mountains and lush valleys. Touch base with the friendly and helpful **Parc National Office**, Maison du Parc, pl. de la Gare, before braving the wilderness. They have tons of information on the park and the 15 trails beginning and ending in Cauterets. The trails in the park are designed for a range of aptitudes, from rugged outdoorsman to novice hiker. From Cauterets, the **GR10** winds through **Luz-St-Saveur**, over the mountain, and then on to **Gavarnie**, another day's hike up the valley; this is also known as the **"circuit de Gavarnie."** One of the most spectacular trails follows the GR10 to the turquoise **Lac de Gaube** and then to the end of the glacial valley (2hr. past the lake) where you can spend the night at the **Refuges Des Oulettes ❶**, the first shelter past the lake. (☎05 62 92 62 97. Open June-Sept. €12.50.) Dipping into the Vallée Lutour, the **Refuge Estom ❷** rests near Lac d'Estom. (Summer ☎05 62 92 72 93, off-season ☎05 62 92 75 07. €8.50, demi-pension €26.)

LANGUEDOC-ROUSSILLON

An immense region called Occitania once stretched from the Rhône Valley to the foothills of the Pyrenees. The region was eventually integrated into the French kingdom, and its Cathar religion was severely persecuted by the Crown and Church. Their *langue d'oc* dialect of French faded, and in 1539, the northern *langue d'oïl* became official. Latent nationalism lingers, however, in vibrant cities like Toulouse and Pérpignan. Many speak Catalán, a relative of *langue d'oc*, and look to Barcelona, rather than Paris, for inspiration.

TOULOUSE

When all of France starts to look alike, rose-tinted Toulouse—*la ville en rose* (city in pink)—provides a breath of fresh air along with stately architecture and a vibrant twenty-something scene. A rebellious city during the Middle Ages, Toulouse has always retained an element of independence, pushing the frontiers of knowledge as a university town and the prosperous capital of the French aerospace industry.

TRANSPORTATION AND PRACTICAL INFORMATION. Trains leave **Gare Matabiau**, 64 bd. Pierre Sémard, for: Bordeaux (2-3hr., 14 per day, €26.10); Lyon (6½hr., 3-4 per day, €47.30); Marseilles (4½hr., 8 per day, €37.55); Paris (8-9hr., 4 per day, €68.65). To get from the station to the **tourist office**, r. Lafayette, in sq. Charles de Gaulle, turn left along the canal, turn right on allée Jean Jaurès, bear right around pl. Wilson, and turn right on r. Lafayette; it's in a park near r. d'Alsace-Lorraine. (☎05 61 11 02 22; www.mairie-toulouse.fr. Open Jun.-Sept. M-Sa 9am-7pm, Su 10am-1pm and 2-6pm; Oct.-May M-F 9am-6pm, Sa 9am-12:30pm and 2-6pm, Su 10am-12:30pm and 2-5pm.) Surf the **Internet** at **Espace Wilson Multimedia**, 7 allée du Président Roosevelt, at pl. Wilson. (€3.05 per hr. Open M-F 10am-7pm, Sa 10am-6pm.) **Postal Code:** 31000.

ACCOMMODATIONS AND FOOD. Antoine de St-Exupéry stayed in room #32 at the **Hôtel du Grand Balcon ❸**, 8 r. Romiguières, the official hotel of the French airborne postal service. (☎/fax 05 61 62 77 59. Breakfast €4. Singles and doubles €24.40, with bath €35.10; triples €41.20; quads without bath €35.10.) **Hôtel Beauséjour ❷**, 4 r. Caffarelli, sports bright, clean rooms and easy access to the station. (☎05 61 23 19 96; fax 05 61 21 47 66. Singles and doubles €20, with bath €25.) Take bus #59 (dir.: Camping) to **camp** at **Pont de Rupé ❶**, 21 chemin du Pont de Rupé. (☎05 61 70 07 35. €9, €3 per additional person.) **Markets** line **place des Carmes**, **place Victor Hugo**, and **boulevard de Strasbourg** (open Tu-Su 6am-1pm). Cheap eateries line **rue du Taur** and **place Wilson**.

SIGHTS AND ENTERTAINMENT. The brick palace next door to the tourist office is the city's most prominent monument, the **Capitole**. (Open M-F 8:30am-noon and 1:30-7pm, Sa-Su 10am-noon and 2-6pm. Free.) Rue du Taur leads to the **Basilique St-Sernin**, the longest Romanesque structure in the world; its **crypt** houses ecclesiastical relics gathered from Charlemagne's time. (☎05 61 20 70 18. Open July-Sept. M-Sa 8:30am-6:15pm, Su 8:30am-7:30pm; Oct.-June reduced hours. Free. Crypt open July-Sept. M-Sa 10am-6pm, Su 11:30-6pm; Oct.-June M-Sa reduced hours. €2.) Backtrack to the pl. du Capitole, take a right on r. Romiguières, and turn left on r. Lakanal to get to the 13th-century **Les Jacobins**, built in the Southern Gothic style. The ashes of St. Thomas Aquinas take center stage in this elevated, under-lit tomb. (69 r. Pargaminières. ☎05 61 22 21 92; www.jacobins.mairie-toulouse.fr. Open daily, 10am-7pm. €5.) Retracing your steps on r. de Metz takes you to the restored **Hôtel d'Assézat**, at pl. d'Assézat on r. de Metz, which houses the **Fondation Bemberg**, an impressive array of Bonnards, Pisarros, and Gauguins. (Open Tu and Th-Su 10am-12:30pm, 1:30-6pm. €2.75.) Toulouse has something to please almost any nocturnal whim, although nightlife is liveliest when students are in town. Numerous cafes flank **place St-Georges** and **place du Capitole**, and late-night bars line **rue St-Rome** and **rue des Filatiers**. The best dancing is at **Bodega-Bodega**, 1 r. Gabriel Péri, just off bd. Lazare Carnot. (Open Sa 7pm-6am, Su-F 7pm-2am.)

CARCASSONNE

When approaching breathtaking Carcassonne (pop. 45,000), you realize this is where Beauty may have fallen in love with the Beast. However, today the narrow streets of the *cité* are flooded with tourists. Built as a palace in the 12th century, the **Château Comtal,** 1 r. Viollet-le-Duc, became a citadel after a royal takeover in 1226. (☎04 68 25 01 66. Open June-Sept. daily 9am-7:30pm; Apr.-May and Oct. 9:30am-6pm; Nov.-Mar. 9:30am-5pm. €5.50, ages 18-25 €3.50.) Turned into a fortress after the Black Prince destroyed Carcassonne in 1355, the Gothic **Cathédrale St-Michel,** r. Voltaire, in bastide St-Louis, still has fortifications on its southern side. (☎04 68 25 14 48. Open M-Sa 7am-noon and 2-7pm, Su 9:30am-noon.) Although nightlife is limited, several bars and cafes along **Boulevard Omer Sarraut** and **Place Verdun** are open until midnight. Locals dance all night at **La Bulle,** 115 r. Barbacane. (☎04 68 72 47 70. Cover €9 includes 1 drink. Open F-Sa until dawn.)

   Trains (☎04 68 71 79 14) depart behind Jardin St-Chenier to: Marseilles (3hr., every 2hr., €31); Nice (6hr., 5 per day, €47); Nîmes (2½hr., 12 per day, €22); and Toulouse (50min., 24 per day, €11.60). Shops, hotels, and the train station are in the **bastide St-Louis,** once known as the *basse ville.* From the station, walk down av. de Maréchal Joffre, which becomes r. Clemenceau; after pl. Carnot, turn left on r. Verdun, which leads to pl. Gambetta and the **tourist office,** 15 bd. Camille Pelletan, pl. Gambetta. (☎04 68 10 24 30; www.carcassonne-tourisme.com. Open July-Aug. daily 9am-7pm; Sept.-June 9am-12:30pm and 1:30-6pm.) The **Auberge de Jeunesse (HI) ❶,** r. de Vicomte Trencavel, is in the *cité.* (☎04 68 25 23 16; carcassonne@fuaj.org. Breakfast included. Sheets €2.70. Internet €4.70 per hr. HI members only. Dorms €12.50. MC/V.) **Sidmum's Travelers' Retreat ❶,** 11 de la Croix d'Achille, will seem like paradise after the crowded castle walls with its beautiful countryside surroundings. Call for pickup from the station (€5) or take the Limoux bus for Preixan. (☎04 68 26 94 49; www.sidmums.com. Dorms €15; doubles €30.) The **Hôtel St-Joseph ❷,** 81 r. de la Liberté, has 37 rooms on a calm street 5min. from the train station. Take av. Maréchal Joffre across the canal, across bd. Omer Sarraut, and then continue for a block on r. G. Clemenceau before turning right. (☎04 68 71 96 89; fax 04 68 74 36 28. Breakfast €4.50. Singles €23, with shower €28; doubles €28. MC/V.) **Camping de la Cité ❶,** rte. de St-Hilaire, 2km from town across the Aude, has a pool and grocery store. A shuttle can take you there from the train station. (☎04 68 25 11 77. Reception 8am-9pm. Open Mar.-Oct. €12.20-16.80 per site.) The regional speciality is *cassoulet* (a stew of white beans, herbs, and meat). Restaurants on **Rue du Plo** have €8.40-9.15 *menus,* but save room for dessert at one of the *crêperies* in **Place Marcou.** Eat like a king at ▧**Les Fontaines du Soleil,** 32 r. du Plo. (☎04 68 47 87 06. Open daily 11:30am-3pm and 7-10:30pm.) **Postal Code:** 11000.

PROVENCE

Carpets of olive groves and vineyards unroll along hills dusted with lavender, sunflowers, and mimosas, while the fierce winds of the *mistral* carry the scent of sage, rosemary, and time well-spent. Generations of writers have rhapsodized about Provence's fragrant and varied landscape—from the Roman arena and cobblestoned elegance of Arles to Cézanne's lingering footsteps in Aix-en-Provence, life unfolds along Provence's shaded paths like a bottomless glass of *pastis.*

NÎMES

Southern France flocks to Nîmes (pop. 132,000) for the *férias,* celebrations featuring bullfights, flamenco dancing, and other hot-blooded fanfare. Yet Nîmes's star attractions are its incredible Roman structures. The magnificent **Les Arènes** is a well-preserved first-century Roman amphitheater that still holds bullfights and concerts. (☎04 66 76 72 77. Open daily 10am-6pm. €4.30, students €3.) North of the arena stands the exquisite **Maison Carrée,** a rectangular temple built in the first century BC. (☎04 66 36 26 76. Open June-Sept. daily 9am-7pm, Oct.-

May 10am-6pm. Free.) Across the square, the **Carrée d'Art** houses an excellent collection of contemporary art. (☎04 66 76 35 70. Open Tu-Su 10am-6pm. €4.30, students €3.) Along the canals to the left, off pl. Foch, the **Jardins de la Fontaine** hold the Roman ruins of the **Temple de Diane** and the **Tour Magne.** (Garden open Apr.-Sept. daily 7:30am-10pm; Oct.-Mar. 8am-6:30pm. Free. Tour Magne open July-Aug. daily 9am-7pm; Sept.-June 9am-5pm. €2.40, students €1.90.)

Trains chug from bd. Talabot to: Arles (25min., 8 per day, €6.30); Marseilles (1¼hr., 11 per day, €11.30); and Toulouse (3hr., 8 per day, €29.30). **Buses** (☎66 29 52 00) depart from behind the train station for Avignon (1½hr., 2-8 per day, €6.70). The **tourist office** is at 6 r. Auguste, just off pl. Comédie and near the Maison Carrée. (☎04 66 58 38 00; fax 04 66 58 38 01. Open July-Aug. M-F 8am-8pm, Sa 9am-7pm, Su 10am-6pm; May and Sept. reduced hours.) The newly renovated ▨**Auberge de Jeunesse (HI) ❶** is 4½km from quai de la Fontaine, at 257 chemin de l'Auberge de la Jeunesse, off chemin de la Cigale. Take bus #2 (dir.: Alès or Villeverte) to Stade, Route d'Alès and follow the signs uphill; after buses stop running, call for pick-up. (☎04 66 68 03 20; fax 04 66 68 03 21. Breakfast €3.20. Sheets €2.70 per week. Reception 24hr. Mar.-Sept. 4- to 6-bed dorms €8.65. **Camping** €4.95. MC/V.) Stock up at **Marché U supermarket,** 19 r. d'Alès, downhill from the hostel. (Open M-Sa 8am-12:45pm and 3:30-8pm.) **Postal Codes:** 30000 and 30900.

🔢 **DAYTRIP FROM NÎMES: PONT DU GARD.** In 19 BC, Augustus's close friend and advisor Agrippa built an aqueduct to channel water 50km to Nîmes from the Eure springs near Uzès. The architectural fruit of this 15-year project remains in the Pont du Gard, spanning the gorge of the Gardon River and towering over sunbathers and swimmers. A great way to see the Pont du Gard is to start from **Collias,** 6km toward Uzès. Here **Kayak Vert** rents two-person canoes, solo kayaks, and bikes. (☎66 22 80 76. Canoes and kayaks €14 per day; kayak/canoe rental and shuttle €16; bikes €17 per day. 15% discount for students or with stay at the hostel in Nîmes.) **STDG buses** (☎04 66 29 27 29) run to the Pont du Gard from Avignon (45min., 7 per day, €5) and Nîmes (30min., 2-5 per day, €4.75). **Camping le Barralet ❶,** r. des Aires in Collias, offers a pool and hot showers. (☎04 66 22 84 52; fax 04 66 22 89 17. Closed Oct.-Feb. 1 person €6-7.40; 2 people €11-13.50; 3 people €13.50-16.50. Lower prices Mar.-June and Sept. MC/V.)

AVIGNON

Avignon (pop. 100,000) is chiefly known for the Festival d'Avignon, a huge theatrical celebration. A reminder of Avignon's brief stint as the epicenter of the Catholic Church, the 14th-century golden ▨**Palais des Papes** launches gargoyles out over the city and the Rhône. Its walls are oddly cut with the tall, ecclesiastical windows of the **Grande Chapelle** and the dark cross of arrow-loops. In the **Grand Tinel,** a banquet hall 45m long, blue canvas flecked with gold stars deck the arched ceiling. (☎04 90 27 50 74. Open July-Sept. daily 9am-8pm; Apr.-June and Oct. 9am-7pm; Nov. to Mar. 9:30am-5:45pm. €7.50.) The riotous **Festival d'Avignon,** also known as the **IN,** goes from early July to early August, as Gregorian chanters rub shoulders with African dancers. (☎04 90 14 14 14. Tickets range from free to €30. Reservations accepted from mid-June. Standby tickets available 45min. before shows; 50% student discount.) **Place des Corps Saints** has a few lively bars.

Trains (☎04 90 27 81 89) run from porte de la République to: Arles (30min., 19 per day, €5.50); Marseilles (1¼hr., 8 per day, €14.60); Nîmes (30min., 12 per day, €7.10); and Paris (TGV 3½hr., 13 per day, €79.20). **Buses** leave from bd. St-Roch, to the right of the train station, for Arles (45min., 5 per day, €7.80) and Marseilles (2hr., 5 per day, €15.20). From the train station, walk through porte de la République to cours Jean Jaurès to reach the **tourist office,** 41 cours Jean

Jaurès (☎ 04 32 74 32 74; fax 04 90 82 95 03. Open M-Sa 9am-6pm, Su 10am-5pm.) Take an **Internet** break at **Webzone,** 3 r. St. Jean le Vieux, at pl. Pie (☎ 04 32 76 29 47. €4.50 per hr. Open M-F 9am-noon, Sa 11am-midnight, Su noon-8pm).

Avignon's hotels and *foyers* usually have room outside of festival season. The **Foyer YMCA/UCJG ❶,** 7bis chemin de la Justice, is across the river in Villeneuve. From the station, turn left and follow the city wall, cross pont Daladier and Ile Barthelasse, walk straight ahead, and turn left on chemin de la Justice; it will be up the hill on your left. (☎ 04 90 25 46 20; info@ymca-avignon.com. Reception 8:30am-noon and 1:30-6pm. *Demi-pension* obligatory in July. Dorms €15. AmEx/MC/V.) The **Hôtel Splendid ❸,** 17 r. Perdiguier, near the tourist office, lives up to its name. (☎ 04 90 82 71 55; fax 04 90 85 64 86. Breakfast €5. Reception 7am-11pm. Singles €30-34; doubles €40-46. MC/V.) **Camp** at **Pont d'Avignon ❶,** 300 Ile de la Barthelasse, 10min. past Foyer Bagatelle. (☎ 04 90 80 63 50; fax 04 90 85 22 12. Reception daily 8am-10pm. Open Mar. 27-Oct. 28. €13.45 per person with tent or car, extra person €4.20.) **Rue des Teinturiers** hosts a few lively restaurants. A **Petit Casino** supermarket is on r. St-Agricol. (Open M-F 8am-8pm, Sa-Su 9am-8pm.) **Postal Code:** 84000.

ARLES

The beauty and ancient history of Arles (pop. 35,000) have made it a Provence favorite. The streets of Arles all seem to lead to or from the great Roman arena, **Les Arènes,** which is still used for bullfights. (€4, students €3.) The city's Roman past comes back to life in the excellent **Musée d'Arles Antique,** on av. de la 1er D.F.L. (Open daily Mar.-Oct. 9am-7pm; Nov.-Feb. 10am-5pm. €5.35, students €3.85.) The **Fondation Van Gogh,** 26 Rond-Point des Arènes, houses tributes to the master painter by artists, poets, and composers. (Open daily 10am-7pm. €5, students €3.50.) The contemporary **Musée Réattu,** r. du Grand Prieuré, houses 57 drawings with which Picasso honored Arles in 1971. (Open daily May-Sept. 10am-noon and 2-6:30pm; Oct.-Mar. reduced hours. €4, students €3.) The city celebrates **Fête d'Arles** in costume the last weekend in June and the first in July.

Trains leave av. P. Talabot for: Avignon (30min., 17 per day, €5.50); Marseilles (1hr., 23 per day, €11.20); Montpellier (1hr., 6 per day, €11.80); and Nîmes (30min., 8 per day, €6.30). **Buses** (☎ 04 90 49 38 01) depart from next to the station for Avignon (45min., M-Sa 7 per day, €8.10) and Nîmes (1hr., M-Sa 4 per day, €5.20). To get to the **tourist office,** esplanade Charles de Gaulle on bd. des Lices, turn left from the station, walk to pl. Lamartine, turn left and follow bd. Emile Courbes to the big intersection, and then turn right on bd. des Lices. (☎ 04 90 18 41 20; fax 04 90 18 41 29. Open daily Apr.-Sept. 9am-6:45pm; Oct.-Mar. M-Sa 9am-5:45pm, Su 10am-2:30pm.) To get from the tourist office to the **Auberge de Jeunesse (HI) ❶,** on av. Maréchal Foch, cross bd. des Lices and follow the signs down av. des Alyscamps. (☎ 04 90 96 18 25; fax 04 90 96 31 26. Breakfast included. Reception 7-10am and 5-11pm. Lockout 10am-5pm. Curfew midnight; in winter 11pm. Reserve ahead Apr.-June. Bunks €13.50.) The friendly **Hôtel Mirador ❸,** 3 r. Voltaire, is centrally located. (☎ 90 96 28 05; fax 90 96 59 89. Breakfast €4.30. Reception 7am-11pm. Singles and doubles €30-38. AmEx/MC/ V.) Take the Starlette bus to Clemencau and then take bus #2 (dir.: Pont de Crau) to Hermite for **Camping-City ❶,** 67 rte. de Crau. (☎ 04 90 93 08 86. Reception 8am-8pm. Open Apr.-Sept. €6.20 per person.) **Monoprix** supermarket is on pl. Lamartine by the station. (Open M-Sa 8:30am-8pm.) **Place du Forum** and **place Voltaire** have many cafes. **Postal Code:** 13200.

▶ DAYTRIP FROM ARLES: THE CAMARGUE. Between Arles and the Mediterranean coast stretches the Camargue. Pink flamingos, black bulls, and the famous white Camargue horses roam freely across this flat expanse of protected wild marshland. Stop at the **Centre d'Information de Ginès**, along D570, for more information. (☎ 04 90 97 86 32. Open Apr.-Sept. daily 10am-6pm; Oct.-Mar. Sa-Th 9:30am-5pm.) Next door, the **Parc Ornithologique de Pont de Gau** offers views of birds and grazing bulls. (Open Apr.-Sept. daily 9am-dusk; Oct.-Mar. 10am-dusk. €5.50.) The best way to see the Camargue is on horseback; call the **Association Camarguaise de Tourisme Equestre** (☎ 04 90 97 58 45) for more information. Other options include jeep safaris (☎ 90 97 89 33; 2hr. trips €31, 4hr. trips €37) and boat trips (☎ 04 90 97 84 72; 1½hr., 3 per day, €10). Biking is another way to see the area, and informative trail maps are available from the Stes-Maries-de-la-Mer **tourist office**, 5 av. Van Gogh. (☎ 04 90 97 82 55. Open daily July-Aug. 9am-8pm; Apr.-June reduced hours.) Arles runs **buses** to Stes-Maries-de-la-Mer (1hr., 5 per day, €6), the region's largest town.

AIX-EN-PROVENCE

Famous for festivals, fountains, and former residents Paul Cézanne and Victor Vasarely, Aix (pop. 150,000) panders to tourists without being ruined by them. The **Chemin de Cézanne**, 9 av. Paul Cézanne, features a self-guided walking tour, including the artist's studio. (☎ 04 42 21 06 53. Open June-Sept. daily 10am-6:30pm; Oct.-May reduced hours. €5.50.) The **Fondation Vasarely**, av. Marcel-Pagnol, in Jas-de-Bouffan, designed by artist Victor Vasarely, is a must-see for modern art fans. (☎ 04 42 20 01 09. Open July-Sept. daily 10am-7pm; Oct.-June 10am-1pm and 2-6pm. €7.) **Cathédrale St-Sauveur**, r. Gaston de Saporta, on pl. de l'Université, is a dramatic mix of Romanesque, Gothic, and Baroque carvings and reliefs. (☎ 04 42 23 45 65. Open daily 9am-noon and 2-6pm.) In June and July, Aix's **International Music Festival** brings in operas and concerts. (☎ 04 42 17 34 34; www.aix-en-provence.com/festartlyrique. Tickets from €6.) Aix also hosts a two-week **dance festival** (☎ 04 42 23 41 24; tickets €7-38). The **Office des Fêtes et de la Culture**, Espace Forbin, 1 pl. John Rewald (☎ 04 42 63 06 75), has festival information. Bars and clubs line **Rue Verrerie**. House and club music pulsate at **Le Richelm**, 24 r. de la Verrerie. (☎ 04 42 23 49 29. Cover includes 1 drink. Tu-Th €9.15, women free; F €12.20; Sa €15.25. Open Tu-Sa 11:30pm-dawn.) **Bistro Aixois**, 37 cours Sextius, off La Rotonde, packs in students. (☎ 04 42 27 50 10. Open daily 6:30pm-4am.)

Trains, at the end of av. Victor Hugo, run almost exclusively through Marseilles (35min., 21 per day, €5.70). **Buses** (☎ 04 42 91 26 80), av. de l'Europe, run to Avignon (2hr., M-Sa 5 per day, €13.50) and Marseilles (30min., almost every 10min., €4). From the train station, follow av. Victor Hugo, bearing left at the fork, until it feeds into La Rotonde. On the left is the **tourist office**, 2 pl. du Général de Gaulle, which books rooms for free, sells a city museum pass (€6.10-9.15), and stocks maps and guides. (☎ 04 42 16 11 61; fax 04 42 16 11 62. Open July-Aug. daily 8:30am-8pm; Sept.-June M-Sa 8:30am-7pm, Su 8:30am-1pm and 2-6pm.) You can surf the **Internet** at **Millenium**, 6 r. Mazarine, off cours Mirabeau. (☎ 04 42 27 39 11. €3 per hr. Open daily 10am-midnight.) The excellent **Hôtel du Globe** ❸, 74 cours Sextius, is 5min. from *centre ville*. (☎ 04 42 26 03 58; fax 04 42 26 13 68. €8. Singles €32, with bath €35; doubles €48; triples €66; quads €77.) **Hôtel des Arts** ❸, 69 bd. Carnot, has compact modern rooms. (☎ 04 42 38 11 77; fax 04 42 26 77 31. Breakfast €4.30. Singles and doubles €30-35. MC/V.) To **camp** at **Arc-en-Ciel** ❶, on rte. de Nice, take bus #3 from La Rotonde to Trois Sautets or Val St-André. (☎ 04 42 26 14 28. €5.20 per person, €5.80 per tent.) The roads north of **cours Mirabeau** and **rue Verrerie**, off Cordiliers, are packed with reasonable restaurants. You can choose from three **Petit Casinos supermarkets** at: 3 cours d'Orbitelle (open M-Sa 8am-1pm and 4-7:30pm); 16 r. Italie (open M-Sa 8am-7:30pm, Su 8:30am-12:30pm); and 5 r. Sapora (open M and W-Sa 8:30am-7:30pm, Su 8:30am-12:30pm). **Postal Code:** 13100.

MARSEILLES (MARSEILLE)

France's third-largest city, Marseilles (pop. 900,000) is like the *bouillabaisse* dish for which it is famous: steaming hot and pungently spiced, with a little bit of everything mixed in. A blend of wild nightclubs, beaches, islands, gardens, and big-city adventure, Marseilles bites its thumb at the manicured nails of Monaco and struts a true, gritty urban intensity.

FRANCE

⌐ TRANSPORTATION

Flights: Aéroport Marseille-Provence (MRS; ☎04 42 14 14 14). Flights to **Lyon** and **Paris**. Buses connect airport to Gare St-Charles (3 per hr., 5:30am-9:50pm, €7.65).

Trains: Gare St-Charles, pl. Victor Hugo (☎08 36 35 35 35). To: **Lyon** (3½hr., 2-3 per day, €38.10); **Nice** (2¾hr., 13 per day, €23.50); **Paris** (4¾hr., 17 per day, €66.60).

Buses: Gare des Autocars, pl. Victor Hugo (☎04 91 08 16 40), half a block from the train station. Open M-Sa 6:30am-6:30pm, Su 7:30am-6:30pm. To: **Avignon** (2hr., 5 per day, €15); **Cannes** (2¼-3hr., 4 per day, €21); **Nice** (2¾hr., 1 per day, €22.50).

Ferries: SNCM, 61 bd. des Dames (☎08 91 70 18 01). Ferries to **Corsica** (€98) and **Sardinia** (€114).

Local Transportation: RTM, 6-8 r. des Fabres (☎04 91 91 92 10). Tickets sold at bus and Métro stations (day pass €3.85; 6- to 12-ride **Carte Liberté** €6.50-13). **Métro** runs M-Th 5am-9pm and F-Su 5am-12:30am.

Taxis: (☎04 91 02 20 20). 24hr. €20-30 from the train station to hostels.

⭑ 🔢 ORIENTATION AND PRACTICAL INFORMATION

Although the city is divided into 16 *arrondissements*, Marseilles is understood by neighborhood names and major streets. **La Canebière** divides the city into north and south, funneling into the **vieux port**, with its upscale restaurants and nightlife, to the east. North of the *vieux port*, working-class residents pile into the hilltop neighborhood of **Le Panier**, east of which lies **Quartier Belsunce**, the hub of the city's Arab and African communities. A few blocks to the southeast, **Cours Julien** has a younger, countercultural feel to it. Both **Métro** lines go to the train station; line #1 (blue) goes to the *vieux port*. The thorough **bus** system is essential to get to beaches, stretching along the coast southwest of the *vieux port*.

Tourist Office: 4 La Canebière (☎04 91 13 89 00; fax 04 91 13 89 20). Has brochures of walking tours, free maps, accommodations service, and RTM day pass. Offers city tours (€6.50) daily at 10am and 2pm, as well as frequent special excursions. Open July-Aug. M-Sa 9am-8pm, Su 10am-6pm; Oct.-June M-Sa 9am-7pm, Su and holidays 10am-5pm.

Currency exchange: La Bourse, 3 pl. Général de Gaulle (☎04 91 13 09 00). Good rates and no commission. Open M-F 8:30am-6:30pm, Sa 9am-5:30pm.

Police: 2 r. du Commissaire Becker (☎04 91 39 80 00). Also in the train station on esplanade St-Charles (☎04 91 14 29 97).

Internet: Info Café, 1 quai Rive Neuve (☎04 91 33 53 05). Open M-Sa 9am-10pm, Su 2:30-7:30pm. €4 per hr.

Post Office: 1 pl. Hôtel des Postes (☎04 91 15 47 20). Follow La Canebière toward the sea and turn right onto r. Reine Elisabeth as it becomes pl. Hôtel des Postes. Address mail to be held: Firstname SURNAME, *Poste Restante,* 1 pl. Hotel des Postes, **13001** Marseilles, France.

ACCOMMODATIONS

Marseilles has many cheap hotels but few reputable ones. Hotels listed here prioritize safety and location. Hostels are far from the town center, but there is frequent, if time-consuming, bus service.

Hôtel du Palais, 26 r. Breteuil (☎04 91 37 78 86; fax 04 91 37 91 19). Kind owner rents large, cheery rooms at a good value. Soundproofed rooms have A/C, TV, and showers. Breakfast €5. Singles €38; doubles €45; triples €53. Extra bed €8. MC/V. ●

Auberge de Jeunesse Bonneveine (HI), impasse Bonfils (☎04 91 17 63 30; fax 04 91 73 97 23), off av. J. Vidal. From the station, take Métro line #2 to Rond-Point du Prado, and transfer to bus #44 to pl. Bonnefon. At the bus stop, walk back toward the traffic circle and turn left at J. Vidal, then turn onto impasse Bonfils. A well-organized hostel for a young, international crowd. Breakfast included. Maximum stay 6 days July-Aug. Reception 7am-1am. No lockout. Curfew 1am. Reserve ahead in summer. Closed Dec. 22-Feb. Dorms Apr.-Aug. €13.60 first night, €11.90 thereafter; doubles €16.40/ €14.70. Sept.-Mar. prices lower. Members only. MC/V. ●

Auberge de Jeunesse Château de Bois-Luzy (HI), allée des Primevères (☎/fax 04 91 49 06 18). Take bus #8 (dir.: Saint-Julien) from La Canebière to Felibres Laurient, walk uphill and make the first left; the hostel will be on your left. The big yellow tower-topped hostel used to house a count and countess, or so they say. Mostly 3- to 6-bed dorms and a few doubles. Breakfast €3. Dinner €7.50. Luggage storage €2 per bag. Sheets €1.80. Reception 7:30am-noon and 5-10:30pm. Lockout noon-5pm. Dorms €7.65; singles €11.50; doubles €17. Members only. ●

Hôtel Béarn, 63 r. Sylvabelle (☎04 91 37 75 83; fax 04 91 81 54 98). Large rooms with airy ceilings. Internet access €4 per hr. Breakfast €4. Reception 7am-11pm. Singles and doubles with shower €23-34; triples with bath €41-42. AmEx/MC/V. ●

FOOD

For the city's famed seafood and North African fare, explore the *vieux port*, especially **place Thiers** and **cours d'Estienne d'Orves,** where one can eat *al fresco* for as little as €9. For a more artsy crowd and cheaper fare, head up to **cours Julien,** northeast of the harbor. **O'Provençal Pizzeria** ●, 7 r. de la Palud, off r. de Rome, serves up the best pizza in Marseilles. (☎91 54 03 10. Open M-Sa 11:30am-2:15pm and 7:30-11pm. AmEx/MC/V.) **Country Life** ●, 14 r. Venture, off r. Paradis, offers all-you-can-eat vegan food under a huge skylight. (☎96 11 28 00. Open M-F 11:30am-2:30pm.) You can pick up groceries at **Monoprix supermarket,** across from the AmEx office on La Canebière. (Open M-Sa 8:30am-8:30pm.)

SIGHTS

Marseilles in all its glory can be seen from the steps of the **Basilique de Notre Dame de la Garde.** Its golden statue of the Madonna, affectionately known as *"la bonne mère,"* towers 230m above the city. (☎04 91 13 40 80. Open in summer 7am-8pm; off-season 7am-7pm. Free.) The chilling catacombs of the fortified **Abbaye St-Victor,** on r. Sainte at the end of quai de Rive Neuve, contain an array of pagan and Christian relics, including the remains of 3rd-century martyrs. (☎04 96 11 22 60. Open daily 9am-7pm. Crypts €2.) Take a boat out to the **Château D'If,** the sun-blasted dungeon immortalized in Dumas's *Count of Monte Cristo,* or explore the wind-swept quarantine island of **Île Frioul.** (Boats ☎04 91 55 50 00. Depart from quai des Belges; 20min., both islands €13. Also worth a visit is **La Vieille Charite,** 2 r. de la

FRANCE

Charite, an old poorhouse and orphanage that now shelters Egyptian, prehistoric, and classical collections. (☎91 14 58 80. Open June-Sept. Tu-Sa 11am-6pm. Temporary exhibits €3, permanent €4.50; students with ID half-price.) Bus #83 (dir.: Rond-Point du Prado) takes you from the *vieux port* to Marseilles's **public beaches.** Catch it on the waterfront side of the street and get off just after it rounds the statue of David (20-30min.). Both **Plage du Prado** and **Plage de la Corniche** offer wide beaches, clear water, and plenty of grass for impromptu soccer matches.

■ NIGHTLIFE

People-watching and nightlife center around **place Thiers** and **cours Julien.** Local and international DJs spin at ■**Trolleybus,** 24 quai de Rive Neuve, a mega-club in an 18th-century warehouse. (☎04 91 54 30 45. Beer from €5, drinks €6.50. Sa cover €10, includes 1 drink. Open W-Sa 11pm-7am.) The vibrant **Le Scandale,** 16 quai de Rive Neuve, is packed with locals and travelers. (☎04 91 54 46 85. Pints for €4.60. Happy hour 6-10:30pm. Open daily 1pm-5am.) The friendly **L'Enigme,** 22 r. Beauvau, is one of the few gay/lesbian places around. (☎04 91 33 79 20. Open daily 7pm-5am.)

FRENCH RIVIERA (CÔTE D'AZUR)

Between Marseilles and the Italian border, the sun-drenched beaches and warm waters of the Mediterranean form the backdrop for this fabled playground of the rich and famous. F. Scott Fitzgerald, Cole Porter, Picasso, Renoir, and Matisse are among those who flocked to the coast in its heyday. Despite the Riviera's glorious past, this choice stretch of sun and sand is a curious combination of high-handed millionaires and low-budget tourists. High society steps out yearly for the Cannes Film Festival and the Monte-Carlo Grand Prix, both in May. Less exclusive are Nice's raucous *Carnaval* in February and various summer jazz festivals.

 Every woman who has traveled on the Riviera has a story to tell about men in the big beach towns. Unsolicited pick-up techniques range from subtle invitations to more, uh, bare displays of interest. Brush them off with a biting *"laissez-moi tranquille!"* ("leave me alone") or stony indifference, but don't be shy about enlisting the help of passersby or the police to fend off Mediterranean Don Juans.

ST-TROPEZ

Nowhere does the glitz and glamour of the Riviera shine more than in St-Tropez. The "Jewel of the Riviera" unfailingly attracts Hollywood stars and curious backpackers to its exclusive clubs and nude beaches. The free **shuttle** *(navette municipale)* leaves pl. des Lices four times a day to **Les Salins,** a secluded sunspot, and **plage Tahiti** (Capon-Pinet stop), the first of the famous **plages des Pampelonne.** Take a break from the sun at **La Musée de l'Annonciade,** pl. Grammont, which showcases Fauvist and neo-Impressionist paintings. (Open June-Sept. W-M 10am-noon and 3-7pm; Oct.-May 10am-noon and 2-6pm. Closed Nov. €5.35, students €2.30.)

Les Bateaux de St-Raphaël **ferries** (☎04 94 95 17 46), at the old port, sail to St-Tropez from St-Raphaël (1hr., 2-5 per day, €10). Sodetrav **buses** (☎04 94 97 88 51) leave av. Général Leclerc for St-Raphaël (2hr., 8-14 per day, €8.30). The **tourist office,** on quai Jean Jaurès, has schedules of the shuttle transport and a *Manifestations* guide that lists local events. (☎04 94 97 45 21; www.saint-tropez.st. Open July-Aug. daily 9:30am-8:30pm, reduced hours in off-season.) Budget hotels do not exist in St-Tropez, and the closest youth hostel is in Fréjus (see below). **Camping** is the cheapest option—a ferry to **Les Prairies de la Mer ❶**, Port Grimaud (€9 round-trip), leaves for St-Tropez every hour. (☎04 94 79 09 09; prairies@campazur.com. Open Apr.-Oct. Two people and tent €20.) The **vieux port** and the streets behind the waterfront are lined with charmingly expensive restaurants, so create your own meal at **Monoprix**, 9 av. du Général Leclerc. (July-Aug. 8am-10pm; Sept.-June 8am-7:50pm.) The restaurant-bar **Bodega de Papagayo**, on the old port, and nightclub **Le Papagayo** are magnets for tanned youth. (Open daily June-Sept. 11:30pm-5am; F-Su May and Oct. 11:30pm-5am. Cover €25. Free if you are attractive.)

ST-RAPHAËL AND FRÉJUS

The twin cities of St-Raphaël and Fréjus provide an excellent base for exploring the Riviera thanks to cheap accommodations, convenient transport, and proximity to the sea. In **St-Raphaël**, the boardwalk turns into a carnival and golden beaches stretch along the coast. The first weekend in July brings the **Compétition Internationale de Jazz New Orleans** (☎04 98 11 89 00). In Fréjus, the **Roman amphitheater**, on r. Henri Vadon, holds rock concerts and bullfights. (Open Apr.-Oct. M and W-Sa 10am-1pm and 2:30-6:30pm; Nov.-Mar. M and W-F 10am-noon and 1:30-5:30pm, Sa 9:30am-12:30pm and 1:30-5:30pm. Bullfights €22-61.) The **Musée Archeologique Municipal**, on pl. Calvini, houses Fréjus's city emblem, a stunning double-headed sculpture. (Open Apr.-Oct. M and W-Sa 10am-1pm and 2:30-6:30pm; Nov.-Mar. 10am-noon and 1:30-5:30pm. Free.)

St-Raphaël sends **trains** every 30 min. to Cannes (25min., €5.30) and Nice (1hr., €8.80). **Buses** leave from behind the train station in St-Raphaël for Cannes (1¼hr., 8 per day, €5.50) and Nice (2¼hr., 2 per day, €8.80). The **tourist office**, on r. Waldeck Rousseau, is opposite the train station. (☎04 94 19 52 52; www.saint-raphael.com. Open July-Aug. daily 9am-7pm; Sept.-June M-Sa 9am-12:30pm and 2-6:30pm.) Take bus #6 from St-Raphaël to pl. Paul Vernet to get to the tourist office in Fréjus, 325 r. Jean Jaurès. (☎04 94 51 83 83; www.ville-frejus.fr. Open M-Sa 9am-7pm, Su 10am-noon and 3pm-6pm; Sept.-June M-Sa 9am-noon and 3-6pm.) Take av. du 15ème Corps d'Armée from the tourist office and turn left on chemin de Councillier after the next roundabout to reach the 🏠**Auberge de Jeunesse de St-Raphaël-Fréjus (HI) ❶**. From St-Raphaël, a shuttle bus (€1.30) leaves quai #7 of the bus station for the hostel. (☎04 94 52 93 93; youth.hostel.frejus.st.raphael@wanadoo.fr. Breakfast included. Sheets €2.70. Reception 8-10am and 6-8pm. Closed Dec.-Jan. Dorms €12. Camping €8 per person with tent.) To reach the rooms at **Le Touring ❸**, in St-Raphaël at 1 quai Albert 1er, take your 3rd right after the train station. (☎04 94 95 01 72; fletouring@wanadoo.fr. Closed mid-Nov. to mid-Dec. Singles and doubles €32-58; triples €58-68. AmEx/MC/V.) St-Raphaël's **Monoprix** supermarket is on 14 bd. de Félix Martin, off av. Alphonse Karr near the train station. (Open M-Sa 8:30am-7:30pm.) **Postal Codes:** St-Raphaël: 83700; Fréjus: 83600.

CANNES

With its legendary film festival each May, the **Festival International du Film,** Cannes (pop. 78,000) has more associations with stardom than any other place on the coast. None of the festival's 350 screenings are open to the public, but the sidewalk show is free. For the other 11 months of the year, Cannes is among the most approachable of the Riviera's glam-towns. A palm-lined boardwalk, gorgeous sandy beaches, and innumerable boutiques ensure that anyone can sport the famous Cannes style. The best window-shopping along the Riviera lies along **rue d'Antibes** and **boulevard de la Croisette**. Farther west, the **Eglise de la Castre** and its courtyard stand on the hill on which *vieux Cannes* was built. Of Cannes's three **casinos,** the most accessible is **Le Casino Croisette**, 1 jetée Albert Edouard, next to

THE BIG SPLURGE

LA GROSSE TARTINE

Staring at celebrity handprints, you may get the urge to live it up in Cannes. For a wonderful meal, pass on the tourist-saturated rue du Suquet and head over to **La Grosse Tartine.** The friendly manager will greet and usher you to a table on the terrace or to a cozy yellow interior with tropical hints and old French posters.

Though the restaurant offers a budget-oriented selection of *tartines*, including lamb confit, chicken, goat cheese, and foie gras *poêlé* (€11-18.50), you should consider splurging on three courses from the main menu. To begin, try the house speciality: homemade, paté de foie gras, accompanied by grapes and figs (€17). For a main course, ask for the chef's recomendation; with an abundance of fish dishes (€16-30), from *saumon tartare* to royal king prawns, and a variety of meats (€18-30), including beef, lamb, steak tartare, and duck, don't be afraid to seek expert advice. For dessert (€8-9), do not miss the chocolate fondue.

Three courses and wine may force you to ration for a few days, but the generous portions and lingering pleasure are worth it. (9 rue du Batéguier. ☎93 68 59 28. Open M-Sa 7pm-midnight. AmEx/MC/V.)

the Palais des Festivals. (No shorts, jeans, or t-shirts. Jackets required for men. 18+ with ID. Cover €10. Gambling daily 8pm-4am; open for slots at 10am.) You can also lose your shirt dancing until sun-up at Cannes's favorite discothèque, **Jane's,** at 38 r. des Serbes. (Cover €10 before midnight; includes 1st drink. Open Th-Su 11pm-dawn.) The centrally located **Cat Corner,** 22 r. Macé, is a magnet for Cannes's coolest. DJs spin house, R&B, and funk. (Cover €16; includes 1st drink. Open daily 11:30pm-5am.)

Coastal **trains** depart from 1 r. Jean-Jaurès every 30min. for Antibes (15min., €2.10); Marseilles (2hr., €15.25); Monaco (1hr., €7.10); Nice (40min., €5); St-Raphaël (25min., €5.30). The **tourist office,** 1 bd. de la Croisette, helps find accommodations. (☎04 93 39 24 53; www.cannes-online.com. Open July-Aug. daily 9am-8pm; Sept.-June M-F 9am-7pm. **Branch** office at the train station. Open M-Sa 9am-7pm.) Access the **Internet** at **CyberCafé Institut Riviera Langue,** 26 r. de Mimont. (€4.60 per hr. Open daily 9am-10pm.)

Hostels are 10-20min. farther from the beach than other lodgings, but are the cheapest options in town. The **Hostel Les Iris ❷,** 77 bd. Carnot, thrives under the care of friendly English-speaking owners who have converted an old hotel into a clean, bright hostel with firm beds, a terrace for lounging and dining, and TV. (☎/fax 04 93 68 30 20; lesiris@hotmail.com. Breakfast €4.50. Dinner €7-8. No curfew. 2-6 bed dorms €16. MC/V.) **Hotel Mimont ❸,** 39 r. de Mimont, is two streets behind the train station, off bd. de la République. (☎04 93 39 51 64; fax 04 93 99 65 35. Singles €29; doubles €36.50; triples €51. AmEx/MC/V.) **Camp** at **Parc Bellevue ❶,** 67 av. M. Chevalier, in La Bocca. Take the #9 bus to the La Boissière stop (30min.) and walk for 100m; it's on the right. (☎04 93 47 28 97. With tent: €13, €17 per couple; €2 per car.) Save money at **Monoprix** supermarket, in Champion, 6 r. Meynadier. (Open M-Sa 8:30am-7:30pm.) Reasonably priced restaurants abound in the pedestrian zone around **Rue Meynadier. Postal Code:** 06400.

ANTIBES-JUAN-LES-PINS

Although officially one city, Antibes and Juan-Les-Pins are 2km apart and have separate train stations and tourist offices. Blessed with beautiful beaches and a charming *vieille ville*, Antibes remains less touristy than Nice and more relaxed than St-Tropez. The **Musée Picasso,** in the Château Grimaldi, on pl. Mariejol, displays works by the master and his contemporaries. (☎04 92 90 54 20. Open Tu-Su June-Sept. 10am-6pm; Oct.-May 10am-noon and 2pm-6pm. Audioguide €3. €4.60, students €2.30.) **Musée Peynet,** pl. Nationale, has over 300 colorful *naïf* drawings by local artist Raymond Peynet. (☎04 92 90 54 30. Open June-Sept. Tu-Su 10am-6pm; Oct.-May 10am-noon and 2-6pm. €3, students €1.50.) **Trains** leave av. Robert Soleau for: Cannes (15min., every hr., €2.10); Marseilles (2½hr., every hr., €21.80); Nice (30min., every hr., €3.30). **Buses** (station open M-F 8am-noon and 2-6pm, Sa 9am-noon and 2-5pm) leave from 200 pl. de Gaulle for Cannes (25min., every 20min., €2.40) and Nice (1hr., every 20min., €4.10). Exit the station, turn right on av. Robert Soleau, and follow the "Maison du Tourisme" signs to the **tourist office** at 11 pl. de Gaulle. (☎04 92 90 53 00; www.antibes-juanlespins.com. Open July-Aug. daily 9am-7pm; Sept.-June M-F 9am-12:30pm and 1:30-6pm, Sa 9am-noon and 2-6pm.) For the distant-but-beautiful **Relais International de la Jeunesse (Caravelle 60) ❶**, take bus #2A (every 40min., €1.15) from pl. Guynemer in Antibes. (☎04 93 61 34 40. Reception daily 5:30pm-10:30pm. No curfew. Dorms €14.)

Come summer, the young and hip **Juan-Les-Pins** is synonymous with wild night-life. Boutiques remain open until midnight, cafes until 2am, and nightclubs past dawn. **Discothèques** are generally open from 11pm to 5am. (Cover approx. €15, usually includes 1st drink.) **⬛Pulp**, at av. Gallice, fills with a spunky crowd. (Cover €15.25. F ladies free. Open July-Aug. daily midnight-5am; Sept.-June F-Sa only.) In psychedelic **Whisky à Gogo**, 5 r. Jacques Leonetti, a young crowd dances the night away to house, hiphop, and Latin beats amid water-filled columns. (Cover €15.25. Open July-Aug. daily midnight-6am; Sept.-June F-Sa only.)

Trains depart av. l'Esterel in Juan-les-Pins for: Antibes (5min., until 11:58pm, €1.20); Cannes (10min., €1.90); Nice (30min., €3.60). From the station, walk straight on av. du Maréchal Joffre and turn right onto av. Guy de Maupassant for the **tourist office** at 51 bd. Guillaumont. To get from Antibes's pl. du Général de Gaulle to Juan-Les-Pins on foot, follow bd. Wilson, which runs right into the center of town (about 1½km). Rather than make the trek back to Antibes, crash at **Hôtel Trianon,** 14 av. de L'Estérel. (☎/fax 04 93 61 18 11. Breakfast €4. Singles €24.50; doubles €30-37; triples €40-45. ❸) **Postal Codes:** Antibes: 06600; Juan-les-Pins: 06160.

NICE

Sun-drenched and spicy, Nice (pop. 380,000) is the unofficial capital of the Riviera. Its pumping nightlife, top-notch museums, and bustling beaches are unerring tour-ist magnets. During the annual three-week February **Carnaval,** visitors and *Niçois* alike ring in the spring with wild revelry, grotesque costumes, and raucous song and dance. Prepare to have more fun than you'll remember.

⌐ TRANSPORTATION

Flights: Aéroport Nice-Côte d'Azur (☎08 20 42 33 33). **Air France,** 10 av. Félix Faure (☎08 02 80 28 02), serves **Paris** (€283.15, under 25 €40.15).

Trains: Gare SNCF Nice-Ville (☎04 92 14 81 62), on av. Thiers. Open 5am-12:15am. To: **Cannes** (45min., every 15-45min., €5); **Marseilles** (2¾hr., every 30-90min., €24); **Monaco** (15min., every 10-30min., €2.90); **Paris** (5½hr., 6 per day, €75-91).

Buses: 5 bd. Jean Jaurès (☎04 93 85 61 81). Open M-Sa 8am-6:30pm. To: **Cannes** (1½hr., every 20min., €6) and **Monaco** (40min., every 15min., €3.40).

Ferries: SNCM, quai du Commerce (☎04 93 13 66 66; www.corsicaferries.com). Take bus #1 or 2 (dir.: Port) from pl. Masséna. To **Corsica:** €35-45. Dock open M-F 6am-7pm.

Public Transportation: Sunbus, 10 av. Félix Faure (☎04 93 16 52 10), near pl. Leclerc and pl. Masséna. Individual tickets €1.30. Long treks to museums, the beach, and hos-tels make the €4 day pass, €8.29 8-ticket *carnet,* €13 5-day pass, or €17 7-day pass a bargain. The tourist office provides **Sunplan** bus maps, schedules, and route info.

FRANCE

Nice

ACCOMMODATIONS
Hôtel Au Picardy, **13**
Hôtel Baccarat, **2**
Hôtel Belle Meunière, **5**
Hôtel des Flandres, **3**
Hôtel Les Orangiers, **6**
Hôtel Little Masséna, **11**
Hôtel Notre Dame, **7**
Hôtel Petit Trianon, **12**
Les Mimosas, **10**
Relais International de la
   Jeunesse "Clairvallon," **1**

FOOD
Acchiardo, **24**
La Merenda, **21**
Lou Pilha Leva, **15**
Speakeasy, **8**
J. Multari, **4**

CLUBS
Blue Boy, **9**
Saramanga, **22**
La Suite, **23**
Le Klub, **17**

■ **BARS**
De Klomp, **20**
Le Bar des Deux Frères, **19**
McMahon's, **16**
Nocy-Bé, **25**
Wayne's, **18**
Williams, **14**

TO ⛪ (3km), MUSÉE MATISSE,
MUSÉE ARCHEOLOGIE ET SITE GALLO-ROMAIN,
& MONASTÈRE DE CIMIEZ (1.5km)

Acropolis

Musée d'Art
Moderne et
Contemporain
Centre
Dramatique
National

Musée
Chagall

Urgence
Informatique

Basilique
Notre-Dame

Centre
Commercial
Nice Étoile

Organic
CyberCafe

Gare
Nice-Ville

Cambio

Change

Espace
Masséna

Sunbus

Hôtel de Ville

USIT
Budget Travel

American
Express

Musée
Masséna

Gare
Routière

Palais Lascaris

Théâtre du Cours

Palais de Préfecture

Palais de
Justice

Opéra de
Nice

St-Martin

TO GARE DU SUD

NICE

CHÂTEAU

Port

Baie des Anges

Promenade des Anglais

TO (4km)

400 yards
400 meters

Bike and Scooter Rental: JML Location, 34 av. Auber (☎04 93 16 07 00), opposite the train station. Bikes €11 per day, €42 per week; credit card deposit required. Open June-Sept. daily 8am-6:30pm; Oct.-May M-F 8am-1pm and 2-6:30pm, Sa 8am-1pm, Su 9am-1pm and 4-6:30pm.

✦ 🔃 ORIENTATION AND PRACTICAL INFORMATION

Avenue Jean-Médecin, on the left as you exit the train station, and **Boulevard Gambetta,** on the right, run directly to the beach. **Place Masséna** is 10min. down av. Jean-Médecin. Along the coast, **Promenade des Anglais** is a people-watching paradise. To the southeast, past av. Jean Médecin and toward the bus station, is **Vieux Nice.** Women should not walk alone after sundown, and everyone should **exercise caution** at night around the train station, *Vieux Nice,* and Promenade des Anglais.

Tourist Office: Av. Thiers (☎08 92 70 74 07; www.nicetourism.com.), by the train station. Makes same-day hotel reservations; best chances of getting a room are between 9 and 11am. Ask for *Nice: A Practical Guide; Museums and Churches of Nice;* and a map. Open June-Sept. M-Sa 8am-8pm, Su 9am-6pm; Oct.-May M-Sa 8am-7pm.

Consulates: Canada, 10 r. Lamartine (☎04 93 92 93 22). Open M-F 9am-noon. **UK,** 26 av. Notre Dame (☎04 93 62 13 56). Open M, W, and F 9:30-11:30am. **US,** 7 av. Gustave V (☎04 93 88 89 55). Open M-F 9-11:30am and 1:30-4:30pm.

American Express: 11 promenade des Anglais (☎04 93 16 53 53). Open 9am-8:30pm.

Laundromat: Laverie Niçoise, 7 r. d'Italie (☎04 93 87 56 50). Beside Basilique Notre-Dame. Open M-Sa 8:30am-12:30pm and 2:30-7:30pm.

Police: (☎04 93 17 22 22) At the opposite end of bd. M. Foch from bd. Jean Médecin.

Hospital: St-Roch, 5 r. Pierre Devoluy (☎04 92 03 33 75).

Internet Access: Organic CyberCafé, 16 r. Paganini. Mention *Let's Go* and pay €4.50 per hr. Open daily 9am-9pm. **Urgence Informatique,** 26 r. Pertinax (☎04 93 62 07 60), closes late. €5 per hr. Open Sept.-June M-Sa 9am-9pm, July-Aug. 9am-midnight.

Post Office: 21 av. Thiers (☎04 93 82 65 22), near the train station. Open M-F 8am-7pm, Sa 8am-noon. 24hr. **ATM.** Address mail to be held: Firstname SURNAME, *Poste Restante, Recette Principale,* Nice 06000, France. **Postal Code:** 06033 Nice Cedex 1.

🛏 ACCOMMODATIONS

To sleep easy, come to Nice with reservations. Affordable places surround the train station, but without reservations, made at least 2-3 weeks ahead in the summer, you'll be forced to risk a night on the beach or outside the train station. The city has two clusters of budget hotels: those by the station are newer but badly located; those nearer to *vieux Nice* are more convenient but less modern.

🏨 **Relais International de la Jeunesse "Clairvallon,"** 26 av. Scudéri (☎04 93 81 27 63; clajpaca@cote-dazur.com), in Cimiez, 4km out of town. Take bus #15 to Scudéri (dir.: Rimiez, 20min., every 10min.). It's you and 150 new friends in the luxurious villa of a deceased marquis. TV, swimming pool (open 5-7pm). In a pretty, residential neighborhood. Breakfast included. 5-course dinner €8.50. Laundry €4. Check-in 5pm. Lockout 9:30am-5pm. Curfew 11pm. 4- to 10-bed rooms. No reservations. Dorms €13. ❶

🏨 **Hôtel Baccarat,** 39 r. d'Angleterre (☎04 93 88 35 73), 2nd right off r. de Belgique. Large rooms in homey, secure atmosphere. 3- to 5-bed dorms €14; singles €29; doubles €36; triples €44. AmEx/MC/V. ❶

🏨 **Hôtel Little Masséna,** 22 r. Masséna (☎04 93 87 72 34). Small but functional rooms. Singles and doubles €28-48. Extra person €6.10. Oct.-May prices lower. MC/V. ❸

Hôtel des Flandres, 6 r. de Belgique (☎04 93 88 78 94). Large rooms with high ceilings and private bathrooms. Breakfast €5. Dorms €17; singles €35-45; doubles €45-51; triples €60; quads €67. Extra bed €12. MC/V. ❷

Hôtel Notre Dame, 22 r. de la Russie (☎04 93 88 70 44), 1 block west of av. Jean Médecin. Spotless, quiet rooms. Reception 24hr. Singles €31; doubles €42; triples €54; quads €67. Extra bed €9.15. MC/V. ❸

Hôtel Belle Meunière, 21 av. Durante (☎04 93 88 66 15), on a street facing the train station. Lively backpacker atmosphere in an elegant converted mansion. Breakfast included. Luggage storage €2. 4- to 5-bed co-ed dorms €13; doubles €45.50; triples €40-54. ❶

Hôtel Les Orangiers, 10bis av. Durante (☎04 93 87 51 41). Bright rooms, all with showers and fridges. Free luggage storage. Closed Nov. Dorms €14; singles €16-25; doubles €36-38; triples €46-48; quads €60. Off-season prices lower. MC/V. ❷

Les Mimosas, 26 r. de la Buffa (☎04 93 88 05 59). Close to the beach and r. Massena. Renovated, homey rooms. Singles €30.50; doubles €37-46; triples €46-53; quads €54-64. Oct.-Mar. prices €5 lower. ❸

Hôtel Petit Trianon, 11 r. Paradis (☎04 93 87 50 46), off r. Massena. Humble but elegant rooms. Singles €15.25; doubles €31; triples €50. Extra bed €8. MC/V. ❶

Hôtel Au Picardy, 10 bd. Jean-Jaurès (☎04 93 85 75 51), across from the bus station. Near *Vieux Nice.* Breakfast €3. Singles €19, with shower €27.30; doubles €24-27; triples €34-38; quads €38-48. Extra bed €5. ❷

🍴 FOOD

Nice is a city of restaurants, outdoor terraces, and tiny holes-in-the-wall. *Vieux Nice* is crowded and touristy, but good eats are easy to find. Stock up at the **Prisunic** supermarket, 42 av. Jean Médecin. (☎04 93 62 38 90. Open M-Sa 9am-8:30pm.)

🍲 **Lou Pilha Leva,** 13 r. du Collet (☎04 93 80 29 33). Get a lot of *niçois* food for little money. Pizza slices €3, *moules* (mussels) €5. Open daily 8am-11pm. ❶

🍲 **La Merenda,** 4 r. de la Terrasse. Those lucky enough to get a table can savor the work of a culinary master who abandoned a 4-star hotel to open this 12-table gem. Amazing value for the area (€7-12). Though the menu is always changing, expect more exotic dishes such as stuffed and fried sardines, fried zucchini flowers, oxtail, tripe, and veal head. Reserve in person. Open M-F noon-1:30pm and 7-9:30pm. ❷

Speakeasy, 7 r. Lamartine (☎04 93 85 59 50). Delectable and affordable vegetarian options. Open M-Sa for lunch noon-2:15pm. ❷

Acchiardo, 38 r. Droite (☎04 93 85 51 16), in *Vieux Nice.* Surprisingly reasonable pastas from €6. Open M-F noon-1:30pm and 7-10pm. ❶

J. Multari, 58bis av. Jean Médecin. This graceful *salon de thé,* bakery, and sandwich shop serves excellent fare at budget prices. Try a goat cheese, chicken, or ham sandwich on a freshly made baguette (€3.10), salad (€3), or pizza (€1.45). The wide selection of pastries should not be passed by (€1-2). Open M-Sa 6am-8:30pm. ❶

👁 SIGHTS

Many visitors to Nice head straight for the beaches and don't retreat from the sun and water until the day is done. Whatever dreams you've had about Nice's beach, though, the hard reality is an endless stretch of rocks; bring a beach mat if you plan to soak up the sun in comfort. Contrary to popular opinion, there are things in Nice more worthwhile than a long naked sunbath on a bunch of pebbles. Nice's **Promenade des Anglais,** named after the English expatriates who built it, is a sight in itself. At the **Négresco,** one of many luxury hotels lining the boulevard, the staff still don tophats and 19th-century uniforms. If you follow the Promenade east of bd. Jean Jaurès, you'll stumble upon **Vieux Nice**, a medieval *quartier* whose twisting streets and sprawling terraces draw massive crowds. *Vieux Nice* hosts a number of lively morning markets, including a fish frenzy at **Place St-François**. The **Eglise St-Martin**, pl. Augustine, is the city's oldest church and site of Italian revolutionary Garibaldi's baptism. Further down the Promenade is **Le Château**, a hillside park crowned with the remains of an 11th-century cathedral. (Open daily 7am-8pm.)

Even burn-hard sunbathers will have a hard time passing by Nice's first-class museums. Walk 15min. north of the train station onto av. du Dr. Ménard to find the concrete and glass ◪**Musée National Message Biblique Marc Chagall,** which showcases his 17 moving *Message Biblique* paintings. You can also take bus #15 (dir.: Rimiez) to Musée Chagall. (Open July-Sept. W-M 10am-6pm; Oct.-June 10am-5pm. €5.50, under 26 €4.) Higher up the hill is the ◪**Musée Matisse,** 164 av. des Arènes de Cimiez, in a 17th-century Genoese villa. Take bus #15, 17, 20, or 22 to Arènes. The museum's collection of paintings is disappointingly small, but the bronze reliefs and dozens of cut-and-paste *tableaux* are dazzling. (Open Apr.-Sept. W-M 10am-6pm; Oct.-Mar. 10am-5pm. €3.80, students €2.30.) Matisse, along with Raoul Dufy, is buried nearby in a cemetery beside the **Monastère Cimiez,** which contains a museum of Franciscan art and lovely gardens. (Museum open M-Sa 10am-noon and 3-6pm. Cemetery open daily 8am-6pm. Gardens open daily 8am-7pm; off-season 8am-7pm. Free.) Check out the onion-domed **Cathédrale Orthodoxe Russe St-Nicolas,** 17 bd. du Tzarevitch, west of bd. Gambetta near the train station, which was funded by Czar Nicolas II. (Open June-Aug. daily 9am-noon and 2:30-6pm, Sept.-May 9:30am-noon and 2:30-5pm. €2.30, students €1.85.)

Closer to *Vieux Nice*, the **Musée d'Art Moderne et d'Art Contemporain,** in Promenade des Arts, on av. St-Jean Baptiste near pl. Garibaldi, features avant-garde works by French and American provocateurs, including works by Lichtenstein, Warhol, and Klein. Take bus #5 (dir.: St-Charles) from the station to Garibaldi. (Open W-M 10am-6pm. €3.05, students €1.55.) Traditionalists will enjoy the **Musée de Beaux Arts,** 33 av. Baumettes, off bd. Francois Grosso. The museum's collection of French academic painting is overshadowed by rooms devoted to Van Dongen and Raoul Dufy. From the train station, take bus #38 to Chéret or bus #12 to Grosso. (Open Tu-Su 10am-noon and 2-6pm. €1.80.)

◪ NIGHTLIFE

FNAC, 24 av. Jean Médecin, in the Nice Etoile shopping center, sells tickets for performances around town (☎04 92 17 77 77; www.fnac.com). Nice's **Jazz Festival,** in mid-July at the Parc et Arènes de Cimiez near the Musée Matisse, attracts world-famous performers. (☎08 20 80 04 00; www.nicejazzfest.com. €30.) Nice's **Carnaval** in late February gives Rio a run for its money with three weeks of parades, outlandish costumes, fireworks, and parties.

The party crowd swings long after St-Tropez and Antibes have called it a night. The bars and nightclubs around r. Masséna and *Vieux Nice* pulsate with dance and jazz. The dress code at all bars and clubs is simple: look good. Most pubs will turn you away if they catch you wearing shorts, sandals, or a baseball cap.

BARS

De Klomp, 6 r. Mascoinat (☎04 93 92 42 85). 40 types of whiskey (from €6.50) and 18 beers on tap (pint €7). A variety of live music from salsa to jazz every night. Happy hour 5:30-9:30pm. Open M-Sa 5:30pm-2:30am, Su 8:30pm-2:30am.

Le Bar Des Deux Frères, 1 r. du Moulin (☎04 93 80 77 61). A young crowd tosses back tequila (10 for €22) and beer (€5). Open T-Sa 6pm-3:30am, Su-M 10pm-2:30am.

Wayne's, 15 r. de la Préfecture (☎04 93 13 46 99). Common denominators for this wild, crowded bar: young, Anglo, and on the prowl. Open noon-1am.

McMahon's, 50 bd. Jean Jaurès (☎04 93 13 84 07). Join the locals and expats who lap up Guinness at this low-key pub. Happy hour 4-9pm. Open daily 8am-2am.

Williams, 4 r. Centrale (☎04 93 62 99 63). When other bars close up, Williams keeps the kegs flowing. Karaoke nights M-Th. Live music F and Sa. Open 9pm-7am.

Nocy-Bé, 4-6 r. Jules Gilly (☎04 93 85 52 25). Get your mellow on at this Indian tea-room with one of 45 different teas or a heady fruit pipe. Open W-M 4pm-12:30am.

CLUBS

🖾 **Saramanga,** 45-47 Promenade des Anglais (☎04 93 96 68 00). A tropical theme reigns in Nice's hottest club, replete with exotic drinks, Hawaiian shirts, and fire-juggling show-girls. Cover €15. Open F-Sa 11pm-5am.

La Suite, 2 r. Brea (☎04 93 92 92 91). This *petite boite* attracts a funky, well-dressed, moneyed crowd. Cover €13. Open T-Su 11pm-2:30am.

Blue Boy, 9 r Jean-Baptiste Spinetta (☎04 93 44 68 24), in west Nice. Though far from town, Blue Boy's foam parties make it Nice's most popular gay club. Free Su-F; Sa cover €9. Foam parties on W, June-Sept. Open daily 11pm-6am.

Le Klub, 6 r. Halévy (☎04 60 55 26 61). Popular gay club caters to well-tanned crowd. Cover €11. Open T-Su 11:30pm-6am.

▶ DAYTRIPS FROM NICE

THE CORNICHES

Trains and buses between Nice and Monaco serve most of the Corniche towns frequently. Hourly **trains** *from Nice to Monaco stop at: Beaulieu-sur-Mer (7min., €1.30); Cap d'Ail (20min., €2.40); Eze-sur-Mer (16min., €2); Villefranche-sur-Mer (7min., €1.30). Also departing from the train station are numerous numbered* **RCA buses** *(☎04 93 85 64 44), which run between Nice and Monaco, making different stops along the way. Bus* **#111** *leaves Nice, stopping in Villefranche-sur-Mer (M-Sa 9 per day); 3 buses per day continue on to St-Jean-Cap-Ferrat. Bus* **#112** *travels from Nice to Monte-Carlo, stopping in Eze-le-Village (7 per day).* **RCA buses** *(☎04 93 85 61 81) run every hr. from Nice to: Ville-franche-sur-Mer (15min., €1.60); Beaulieu-sur-Mer (20min., €2); Eze-le-Village (25min., €2.40); Cap d'Ail (30min., €3); Monaco-Ville (40min., €4); Monte-Carlo (45min., €4).*

Rocky shores, pebble beaches, and luxurious villas glow along the Corniches, between hectic Nice and high-rolling Monaco. More relaxing than their glam-fab neighbors, these tiny towns have interesting museums, ancient finds, and breath-taking countryside. The train offers a glimpse of the coast up close, while bus rides on the high roads allow bird's-eye views of the steep cliffs and crashing sea below.

VILLEFRANCHE-SUR-MER. The town's narrow streets and pastel houses have enchanted Aldous Huxley, Katherine Mansfield, and many other artists. Strolling from the train station along quai Ponchardier, a sign to the *vieille ville* points to the spooky 13th-century **Rue Obscure**, the oldest street in Villefranche. At the end of the quai is the **Chapelle St-Pierre**, decorated by Jean Cocteau, former resident, film-maker, and jack-of-all-arts. (☎04 93 76 90 70. Call ahead for hours. €2.) To get to the **tourist office** from the train station, exit on quai 1 and head inland on av. G. Clemenceau, and continue straight when it becomes av. Sadi Carnot; it will be at the end of the street. (☎04 93 01 73 68. Open July-Aug. daily 9am-7pm; mid-Sept. to June M-Sa 9am-noon and 2-6pm.)

ST-JEAN-CAP-FERRAT. A lovely town with an even lovelier beach, St-Jean-Cap-Ferrat is the trump card of the Riviera. The **Fondation Ephrussi di Rothschild**, just off av. D. Semeria, is a stunning Italian villa that houses the collections of the Baroness de Rothschild, including Monet canvases, Gobelins tapestries, and Chinese vases. The seven lush gardens reflect different parts of the world. (Open July-Aug. daily 10am-7pm; Sept.-Nov. 1 and Feb. 15-June daily 10am-6pm; Nov. 2-Feb. 14 M-F 2-6pm, Sa-Su 10am-6pm. €8, students €6.) The town's beautiful **beaches** have earned the area the nickname *"presqu'île des rêves"* (peninsula of dreams).

EZE. Three-tiered Eze owes its fame to the pristine medieval town in the middle tier. It features the **Porte des Maures,** which served as a portal for a surprise attack by the Moors, and the **Eglise Paroissial,** containing sleek Phonecian crosses mixed with Catholic gilt. (Open daily 9am-7pm.) The best views are 40min. up the **Sentier Friedrich Nietzsche,** a windy trail where its namesake found inspiration; the path begins in Eze Bord-du-Mer, 100m east of the train station and tourist office, and ends near the base of the medieval city, by the **Fragonard parfumerie.**

CAP D'AIL. With 3km of cliff-framed foamy seashore, Cap d'Ail's **Les Pissarelles** draws hundreds of nudists, while **Plage Mala** is frequented by more modest folk. To get from the station to the **tourist office,** 87bis av. de 3 Septembre, turn right at the village, continue on av. de la Gare, and turn left on r. du 4 Septembre. (☎93 78 02 33; www.monte-carlo.mc/cap-d'ail. Open July-Aug. M-Sa 9am-noon and 2-6pm, Su 9am-noon; Sept.-June M-F 9am-noon and 2-6pm, Sa 9am-noon.) The **Relais International de la Jeunesse ❶,** on bd. F. de May, has a waterfront location. (☎04 93 78 18 58; clajpaca@cote-dazur.com. Breakfast included. Open Apr.-Oct. €13.)

MONACO AND MONTE-CARLO

Monaco (pop. 7,160) has money—lots of it—invested in ubiquitous surveillance cameras, high-speed luxury cars, and sleek yachts. At Monaco's spiritual heart is its famous casino in Monte-Carlo, a magnet for the wealthy and dissolute since 1885. The sheer spectacle of it all is worth a daytrip from Nice.

PHONING TO AND FROM MONACO	Monaco's country code is 377. To telephone Monaco from France, dial 00377, then the 8-digit Monaco number. To call France from Monaco, dial 0033, and drop the first zero of the French number.

TRANSPORTATION. Trains (☎08 36 35 35 35) run to: Antibes (1hr., every 30min., €6.40); Cannes (65min., every 30min., €7.10); and Nice (25min., every 30min., €2.90). **Buses** (☎93 85 61 81) leave pl. d'Armes or pl. du Casino for Nice (45min., every 15min., €3.70).

PRACTICAL INFORMATION. Follow the signs in the new train station for Le Rocher and Fontvieille to the **avenue Prince Pierre** exit; it's close to the **La Condamine** quarter, Monaco's port and nightlife hub. To the right of La Condamine rises the *vieille ville,* **Monaco-Ville.** Leaving the train station onto bd. Princess Charlotte or pl. St-Devote leads to **Monte-Carlo** and the casino. **Bus #4** links the train station to the casino in Monte-Carlo. (Buy tickets on board. €1.30, €3.30 for a *carte* of 4.) At the **tourist office,** 2a bd. des Moulins, a friendly, English-speaking staff provides city plans, a monthly events guide, and hotel reservations free of charge. (☎92 16 61 16; www.monacotourisme.com. Open M-Sa 9am-7pm, Su 10am-noon.) Stop by the lively **fruit and flower market** on pl. d'Armes, on av. Prince Pierre (open daily 6am-1pm) or the huge **Carrefour supermarket** in Fontvieille's plaza (open M-Sa 8:30am-10pm). Access the **Internet** at **Stars 'N' Bars,** 6 quai Antoine 1er. (Open daily 10am-midnight. €6 per 30min.) **Postal Code:** 06500.

FRANCE

⌐⌐ ACCOMMODATIONS AND FOOD. There's no need to stay in Monaco, since it is easily accessible from nearby coastal towns. 16- 31-year-old travelers can try the **Centre de Jeunesse Princesse Stéphanie ❶**, 24 av. Prince Pierre, 100m uphill from the station. The hostel is strict and a bit sterile. (☎93 50 83 20. Breakfast included. July-Aug. 5-day max. stay; Sept.-June 7-day max. stay. Check-out 9:30am. Closed mid-Nov. to mid-Dec. Dorms €14-16.) **L'Escale ❷**, 17 bd. Albert 1er, serves pizzas and pastas from €7. (Open daily noon-3pm and 7-11pm.)

⌐⌐ SIGHTS AND ENTERTAINMENT. The extravagant **Monte-Carlo Casino,** at pl. de Casino, is where Richard Burton wooed Elizabeth Taylor and Mata Hari shot a Russian spy. The slot machines open at 2pm, while blackjack, craps, and roulette open at noon (cover €10). The exclusive *salons privés*, where such French games as *chemin de fer* and *trente et quarante* begin at noon, will cost you an extra €10 cover. Next door, the more relaxed **Café de Paris** opens at 10am and has no cover. All casinos have **dress codes** (no shorts, sneakers, sandals, or jeans), and the *salons privés* require coat and tie. Guards are strict about the **21 age minimum;** bring a passport as proof. High above the casino is the **Palais Princier,** the occasional home of Prince Rainier and his tabloid-darling family. When the flag is down, the prince is away and visitors can tour the small but lavish palace, which includes Princess Grace's official state portrait and the chamber where England's King George III died. (☎93 25 18 31. Open June-Sept. 9:30am-6:20pm; Oct. 10am-5pm. €6, students and children 8-14 years old €3.) Next door, the **Cathédrale de Monaco,** at pl. St-Martin, is the burial site of the Grimaldi family and the site of Prince Rainer and Princess Grace's 1956 wedding; Princess Grace lies behind the altar in a tomb marked simply with her Latinized name, "Patritia Gracia." (Open Mar.-Oct. daily 7am-7pm; Nov.-Feb. 7am-6pm. Free.) The **Private Collection of Antique Cars of H.S.H. Prince Rainier III,** on les Terraces de Fontvielle, showcases 105 of the most glamorous cars ever made. (☎92 05 28 56. Open daily 10am-6pm. €6, students and ages 8-14 €3.) The **Musée Océanographique** on av. St-Martin, once directed by Jacques Cousteau, holds the most exotic and bizarre oceanic species. (☎93 15 36 00; www.oceano.mc. Open Apr.-Sept. daily 9am-7pm; Oct.-Mar. 10am-6pm. €11, students and ages 6-18 €6.) Monaco's nightlife centers in **La Condamine,** near the port. **Café Grand Prix,** at 1 quai Antoine 1er, serves up live music to a mixed crowd. (Open daily 10am-5am. No cover.)

CORSICA (LA CORSE)

An island of paradisiacal escape, Corsica thrives on tourism. From mid-June to August, flocks of mainland French and global comfort seekers retreat to the island's renowned beaches and pricey resorts. The summer climaxes in a nationalistic blast on August 15, when France celebrates the Fête de l'Assomption and Corsicans observe hometown-boy-made-good **Napoleon's birthday.** Tourists depart by September, when the weather is at its best and the waters their warmest. Winter visitors can explore sleepy coastal towns or head inland to ski.

⌐ TRANSPORTATION

Air France, 3 bd. du Roi Jérôme in Ajaccio (☎08 20 82 08 20), and its subsidiary **Compagnie Corse Méditerranée (CCM)** fly to Bastia and Ajaccio from Paris (€170, students €140), Nice (€120, students €98), Marseilles (€128, students €104), and Lyon (€142, students €114). There's also a direct link from Lille to Bastia (€196, students €178). **Air Liberté** services Calvi from Nice and Marseilles. Air

France/CCM offices are at the airports in Ajaccio (p. 387) and Bastia (p. 388). **Ferry** travel between the mainland and Corsica can be a rough trip and, in some circumstances, not much cheaper than a plane. High-speed ferries run between Nice and Corsica and take about 3½hr. Overnight ferries from Toulon and Marseilles take upwards of 10hr. The **Société National Maritime Corse Méditerranée (SNCM)**; (☎08 91 70 18 01; fax 04 91 56 35 86; www.sncm.fr) sends ferries from Marseilles (€43-60, under 25 €34-48) and Nice (€38-48, under 25 €23-33). SNCM schedules and fees are listed in a booklet available at travel agencies and ports. **SAREMAR** (☎04 95 73 00 96; fax 04 95 73 13 37) and **Moby Lines** (☎04 95 73 00 29; www.mobylines.de) run from Santa Teresa in Sardinia to Bonifacio. (3-10 per day depending on the season; €7-15.) **Corsica Ferries** (☎08 25 095 095; www.corsicaferries.com) crosses from Livorno and Savona in Italy to Bastia (€22.50-37.50). **Train** service in Corsica is slow and limited to the half of the island north of Ajaccio; **railpasses** are not valid. **Buses** aren't much better but provide more comprehensive service; call **Eurocorse Voyages** (☎04 95 21 06 30) for more info.

HIKING

Hiking is the best way to explore the island's mountainous interior. The **GR20** is an extremely difficult 14- to 15-day 200km trail that crosses the island. The popular **Mare e Monti** (10 days) and **Da Mare a Mare Sud** (4-6 days) trails are shorter and less challenging. The **Parc Naturel Régional de la Corse,** 2 Sargent Casalonga, in Ajaccio (☎04 95 51 79 10), publishes maps and a guide to *gîtes d'étapes*.

AJACCIO (AIACCIU)

Swinging Ajaccio (pop. 60,000) often trades in Corsican nationalism for the *français* flavor of life. Celebrating its diminutive native son is also a regular pastime, starting with the **Musée National de la Maison Bonaparte,** r. St-Charles, between r. Bonaparte and r. Roi-de-Rome. (☎04 95 21 43 89. Open Apr.-Sept. M 2-6pm, Tu-Su 9am-noon and 2-6pm; Oct.-Mar. Tu-Su 10am-noon and 2-4:45pm, M 2-4:45pm. €4, ages 18-25 €2.60, under 18 free.) Inside the **Musée Fesch,** 50-52 r. Cardinal Fesch, you'll find an impressive collection of 14th- to 19th-century Italian paintings gathered by Napoleon's uncle Fesch. Also within the complex is the **Chapelle Impériale,** the final resting place of most of the Bonaparte family—however, Napoleon himself is buried in a modest Parisian tomb. (☎04 95 21 48 17. Open July-Aug. M 1:30-6pm, Tu-Th 9am-6:30pm, F 9am-6:30pm and 9pm-midnight, Sa-Su 10:30am-6pm; Sept.-June reduced hours. Museum €5.35, students €3.85; chapel €1.55/€0.75.) Southwest of Ajaccio, the striking black cliffs of **Îles Sanguinaires** loom over the sea. Nave Va **ferries,** at a kiosk on the port, run to the largest island. (☎04 95 51 31 31. Apr.-Oct. daily. €20.)

Trains (☎04 95 23 11 03) leave pl. de la Gare, for Bastia (4hr., 4 per day, €23.10) and Calvi (4½hr., 2 per day, €26.90). Eurocorse Voyages **buses** (☎04 95 21 06 30) go to Bastia (3hr., 2 per day, €19) via Corte (1½hr., €10.50); Autocars SAIB (☎04 95 22 41 99) runs to Porto (2hr., 1-3 per day, €11). The **tourist office** is at 3 bd. du Roi Jérôme. (☎04 95 51 53 03; www.tourisme.fr/ajaccio. Open July-Aug. M-Sa 8am-8:30pm, Su 9am-1pm and 4-7pm; Apr.-June and Sept.-Oct. M-Sa 8am-7pm, Su 9am-1pm; Nov.-Mar. reduced hours.) The serene **Hôtel Kallisté** ❹ is at 51 cours Napoléon. (☎04 95 51 34 45; www.cyrnos.com. Singles €45; doubles €52; triples €69. AmEx/MC/V.) **Hôtel le Dauphin** ❹, 11 bd. Sampiero, is halfway between the station and port. (☎04 95 21 12 94; fax 04 95 21 88 69. May-Oct. Singles and doubles €49-60; triples €69; off-season reduced prices. AmEx/MC/V.) Get groceries at **Monoprix,** 31 cours Napoléon. (Open M-Sa 8am-7:40pm.) **Postal Code:** 20000.

IN RECENT NEWS

A POLITICAL OBSTACLE CORSE

Despite their politically volatile reputation, fully 80% of Corsicans subscribe to traditional French parties; a mere 20% support nationalist parties. Though there are 10 major nationalist parties, only one favors immediate independence: the *FLNC*, which is the political wing of *Indipendenza*, a clandestine organization that has been linked to terrorism. The other nationalist parties believe the island must experience political and economic autonomy before independence.

If the FLNC has any center of support, it is Corte, which served as capital to the short-lived independent Corsican state under Paoli. This maverick spirit has lingered in the Cortenais, but the political reality has changed. Since 1983, the mayor of Corte has always been affiliated with the RPR, not known for warmth towards the independence cause. This rather illogical status quo stems from the political division of local and national(ist) issues. Corte's current mayor, for instance, received overwhelming support from the right, the left, *and* the nationalists.

Regardless of individual relations and party affiliations, Corsicans are anxious to see how the new Interior Minister, Nicolas Sarkozy, will treat the island. Thus far, he seems more Corsica-friendly than his predecessor, but the question remains: in whose interests will he work when Corsica stands apart from the rest of France?

BONIFACIO (BONIFAZIU)

The fortified city of Bonifacio (pop. 3000) rises like a majestic sand castle atop jagged limestone cliffs; **Marina Croisères** offers **boat tours** of the hidden coves and grottoes. (☎ 04 95 73 09 77. €11-21.) All the companies by the port run frequent ferries (30min.) to the pristine sands of **Îles Levezzi**, a nature reserve with beautiful reefs just off its coast perfect for **scuba diving**. To explore the *haute ville*, head up the steep montée Rastello, the wide staircase halfway down the port, where excellent views of the ridged cliffs to the east await. Continue up montée St-Roch to the lookout at **Porte des Gênes**, a drawbridge built by invaders. Then walk to the **place du Marche** to see Bonifacio's famous cliffs and the **Grain de Sable.**

Eurocorse Voyages (☎ 04 95 21 06 30) runs **buses** to Ajaccio (3½hr., 2 per day, €20.50) as well as Porto Vecchio (30min., 1-4 per day, €6.50), where connections can be made to Bastia. To reach the **tourist office,** at the corner of av. de Gaulle and r. F. Scamaroni, walk along the port and then up the stairs before the *gare maritime*. (☎ 04 95 73 11 88; www.bonifacio.com. Open May to mid-Oct. daily 9am-8pm; mid-Oct. to Apr. M-F 9am-noon and 2-6pm, Sa 9am-noon.) Finding affordable rooms is difficult in summer; avoid visiting in August, when prices soar. Try **Hôtel des Étrangers ❹**, av. Sylvère Bohn. (☎ 04 95 73 01 09; fax 04 95 73 16 97. Singles and doubles €40-71; triples €62; quads €74. MC/V.) **Postal Code:** 20169.

BASTIA

Corsica's second largest city and a major transport hub, Bastia (pop. 40,000) is a good base from which to explore Cap Corse; with the frenetic new port encompassing the bulk of its coast, it may seem as if the entire city is waiting to move elsewhere. The 14th-century **Citadel**, also called Terra Nova, has beautiful views of the sea. The **Oratoire de St-Roch**, on r. Napoleon, is a jewel-box of a church with crystal chandeliers and meticulous *trompe l'oeil* decoration. The neoclassical towers of the **Eglise St-Jean Baptiste,** pl. de l'Hôtel de Ville, cover an immense interior with gilded domes. **Shuttle buses** leave pl. de la Gare for the **Bastia-Poretta airport** (30min., €8). **Trains** (☎ 04 95 32 80 61) also leave pl. de la Gare for Ajaccio (4hr., 4 per day, €23.10) and Calvi (3hr., 2 per day, €17.50). **Eurocorse buses** (☎ 95 21 06 30) leave r. Nouveau Port for Ajaccio (3hr., 2 per day, €17). The **tourist office** is on pl. St-Nicholas. (☎ 04 95 54 20 40; fax 04 95 31 81 34. Open July-Sept. daily 8am-8pm; Oct.-June M-Sa 8:30am-6pm.) **SPAR supermarket** is at 14 r. César Campinchini. (Open M-Sa 8:30am-12:30pm and 4-8:30pm.) The **Hôtel Central ❷**,

3 r. Miot, has large, well-kept rooms. (☎ 04 95 31 71 12; fax 04 95 31 82 40. Breakfast €5.50. Singles €35-50; doubles €40-68. AmEx/MC/V.) **Les Orangiers camping ❶** is 4km north in Miomo. (☎ 04 95 33 24 09. Open May. to mid-Oct. €4 per person, €2 per tent, €1.60 per car.) Inexpensive cafes crowd **place St-Nicolas.**

⊡ DAYTRIP FROM BASTIA: CAP CORSE. North of Bastia stretches the gorgeous Cap Corse peninsula, a necklace of tiny former fishing villages strung together by a narrow road of perilous curves and breathtaking views. The Cap is a dream for **hikers;** every jungle, forest, and cliff lays claim to some decaying Genoese tower or hilltop chapel. The cheapest and most convenient way to see Cap Corse is to take **bus #4** from pl. St-Nicolas in Bastia, which goes to: Erbalunga (20min., €2); Macinaggio (50min., €6.40); and Marina di Siscu (30min., €2.30). Ask the driver to drop you off wherever you feel the urge to explore. However, most buses serve only the coast; you'll have to hike or hitch to the inland villages.

CORTE

The most dynamic of Corsica's inland towns, Corte combines breathtaking natural scenery with a boisterous collegiate spirit. Sheer cliffs, snow-capped peaks, and magical gorges create a dramatic backdrop for the island's only university, whose students keep prices surprisingly low. The town's *vieille ville*, with its steep, barely accessible streets and stone **citadel**, has always been a bastion of Corsican patriotism. At the top of r. Scolisca is the engaging **La Musée de la Corse.** The museum also provides entrance to the higher fortifications of the citadel. (☎ 04 95 45 25 45; fax 04 95 45 25 36. Museum open June-Sept. daily 10am-8pm; off-season reduced hours. Citadel closes 1hr. earlier. Museum and citadel €3-5.30, students €2.30-3.) Corte's mountains and valleys feature numerous spectacular trails. Choose from **hiking** (call tourist office for maps and info; ☎ 08 92 68 02 20 for weather), **biking**, and **horseback riding.** Rent **horses** at **Ferme Equestre Albadu,** 1.5km from town on N193. (☎ 04 95 46 24 55. €14 per hr., €38 per half-day, €61 per day.)

Trains (☎ 04 95 46 00 97) leave from the rotary, where av. Jean Nicoli and N193 meet, for: Ajaccio (2hr., 4 per day, €12.30); Bastia (1½hr., 4 per day, €10.80); Calvi (2½hr., 2 per day, €14.60) via Ponte-Leccia. Eurocorse Voyages runs **buses** to Ajaccio (1¾hr., M-Sa 2 per day, €11.50) and Bastia (1¼hr., M-Sa 2 per day, €10). To reach the *centre ville* from the train station, turn right on D14 (av. Jean Nicoli), cross two bridges, and follow the road until it ends at **cours Paoli,** Corte's main drag. A left turn leads to **place Paoli,** the town center; at the *place's* top right corner, climb the stairs of r. Scolisca to reach the citadel and the **tourist office.** (☎ 04 95 46 26 70; fax 04 95 46 34 05; www.corte-tourisme.com. Open July-Aug. daily 9am-8pm; May-June and Sept. M-Sa 9am-1pm and 2-7pm; Oct.-Apr. M-F 9am-noon and 2-6pm.) The youthful **Hôtel-Residence Porette (H-R) ❷**, 6 allée du 9 Septembre, offers plenty of amenities. Bear left from the train station to the stadium and follow it around for another 100m. (☎ 04 95 45 11 11; fax 04 95 61 02 85. Breakfast €5. Reception 24hr. Singles €21, with bath €31; doubles €23-25, €27-35; triples €51; quads €54.) The huge **Casino supermarket** is near the train station, on allée du 9 Septembre. (Open mid-June to Aug. daily 8:30am-7:45pm; Sept. to mid-June M-F 8:30am-12:30pm and 3-7:30pm, Sa 8:30am-7:30pm.) **Postal Code:** 20250.

THE ALPS (LES ALPES)

Nature's architecture is the real attraction of the Alps. The curves of the Chartreuse Valley rise to rugged crags in the Vercors range and ultimately crescendo into Europe's highest peak, Mont Blanc. Winter **skiers** enjoy some of the world's most challenging slopes and then in the summer, **hikers** take over the mountains for endless vistas and clear air. Skiing arrangements should be made well in advance; Chamonix and Val d'Isère are the easiest bases. TGV **trains** whisk you from Paris to Grenoble or Annecy; scenic trains and slower **buses** service Alpine towns from there. The farther into the mountains you want to go, the harder it is to get there, although service is more frequent during ski season (Dec.-Apr.).

GRENOBLE

Grenoble (pop. 156,000) has the eccentric cafes and shaggy radicals of any university town, but it also boasts snow-capped peaks and sapphire-blue lakes cherished by athletes and aesthetes alike.

⌨️ TRANSPORTATION AND PRACTICAL INFORMATION. Trains arrive in Grenoble at pl. de la Gare from: Annecy (2hr., 18 per day, €14.10); Lyon (1½hr., 27 per day, €15.40); Marseilles (2½-4½hr., 15 per day, €32.30); Nice (5-6½hr., 5 per day, €47.20); and Paris (3hr., 6 per day, €58.80). **Buses** leave from the left of the station for Geneva (3hr., 1 per day, €25.50). From the station, turn right into pl. de la Gare, take the third left on av. Alsace-Lorraine, and follow the tram tracks on r. Félix Poulat and r. Blanchard to reach the **tourist office**, 14 r. de la République. (☎04 76 42 41 41; www.grenoble-isere.info. Open M-Sa 9am-6:30pm, Su 10am-1pm and 2-5pm.) **Postal Code:** 38000.

⌨️ ACCOMMODATIONS AND FOOD. To get from the station to the **Auberge de Jeunesse (HI) ❶**, 3 av. Victor Hugo, about 4km from Grenoble in Echirolles. Take bus #16 from Docteur Martin in the *centre ville* (dir.: Le Canton) to Monmousseau. From the stop, turn around and walk along av. Victor Hugo for about 50m. In a temporary location (a new hostel is being built for 2004), the two buildings bring an industrial feel to a quiet green space. (☎04 76 09 33 52; grenoble-echirolles@fuaj.org. Reception M-Sa 7:30am-11pm, Su 7:30-10am and 5:30-11pm. Lockout 10am-5:30pm. No curfew. Sheets €2.70. €9. MC/V.) **Hôtel de la Poste ❷**, 25 r. de la Poste, near the pedestrian zone, has amazing rooms. (☎/fax 04 76 46 67 25. Singles €22; doubles €28; triples €32; quads €37. MC/V.) To reach **Camping Les 3 Pucelles ❶**, 58 r. des Allobroges in Seyssins, take tram A (dir.: Fontaine-La Poya) to Louis Maisonnat, then take bus #51 (dir.: Les Nalettes) to Mas des Iles; it's on the left. (☎04 76 96 45 73; fax 04 76 21 43 73. €7.50 per person, tent, and car.) **University Restaurants (URs) ❶** sell meal tickets in *carnets* of 10 to those with a student ID. (☎04 76 57 44 00. Open during the school year. €2.40.) The two URs in Grenoble are **Restaurant d'Arsonval**, 5 r. d'Arsonval (open M-F 11:30am-1:30pm and 6:30-7:45pm) and **Restaurant du Rabot**, r. Maurice Gignoux (open daily noon-1:15pm and 6:30-7:50pm). **Monoprix**, opposite the tourist office, stocks groceries. (Open M-Sa 8:30am-7:30pm.)

⌨️ SIGHTS AND THE OUTDOORS. *Téléphériques* (lifts) depart from quai Stéphane-Jay every 10min. for the 16th-century **Bastille**, a fort that hovers above town. Enjoy the views from the top, then descend via the **Parc Guy Pape**, which crisscrosses through the fortress and deposits you just across the river from the train station. (Open July-Aug. M 11am-12:15am, Tu-Su 9:15am-12:15am; Sept.-June reduced hours.) Cross the Pont St-Laurent and go up Montée Chalemont for the **Musée Dauphinois**, 30 r. Maurice Gignoux, with its futuristic exhibits. (Open June-Sept. W-M 10am-7pm; Oct.-May 10am-6pm. €3.20, under 25 free.) Grenoble's major attraction is its proximity to the slopes. The biggest and most developed **ski areas** are to the east in **Oisans**; the **Alpe d'Huez** boasts 220km of trails. (Tourist office ☎04 76 11 44 44. €33 per day, €171 per week.) The **Belledonne** region, northeast of Grenoble, has lower elevation and prices. **Chamrousse**, its biggest and most popular ski area (lift tickets €23 per day, €79-113 per week), has a **youth hostel** (☎04 76 89 91 31; fax 04 76 89 96 96). Only 30min. from Grenoble by **bus** (€8.70), the resort also makes for a hiker's ideal daytrip in summer. Grenoble boasts plenty of funky cafes and bars; most nightspots are in the area between **Place St-André** and **Place Notre-Dame.**

CHAMONIX

The site of the first winter Olympics in 1924, Chamonix (pop. 10,000) is the ultimate ski town, with soaring mountains and the toughest slopes in the world. The town itself combines the dignity of Mont Blanc, Europe's highest peak (4807m), with the exuberant spirit of numerous Anglo travelers.

TRANSPORTATION AND PRACTICAL INFORMATION. Trains leave av. de la Gare (☎04 50 53 12 98) for: Annecy (2½hr., 7 per day, €16.80); Geneva (2½hr., 7 per day, €20.80); Lyon (4hr., 6 per day, €29.60); and Paris (6½hr., 9 per day, €50-70). Société Alpes Transports **buses** (☎04 50 53 01 15) leave the train station for Annecy (2¼hr., 1 per day, €15) and Geneva (1½hr., 2 per day, €29-32). **Local buses** connect to ski slopes and hiking trails (€1.50). From the station, follow av. Michel Croz, turn left on r. du Dr. Paccard, and take the 1st right to reach pl. de l'Eglise and the **tourist office,** 85 pl. du Triangle de l'Amitié. (☎04 50 53 00 24; fax 04 50 53 58 90. Open July-Aug. daily 8:30am-7:30pm; Dec.-Feb. 8:30am-7pm; Mar.-June and Sept.-Nov. 9am-noon and 2-6pm.) Facing the tourist office, **Compagnie des Guides,** in Maison de la Montagne, leads ski trips and summer hikes. (☎04 50 53 22 88; www.cieguides-chamonix.com. Open Jan.-Mar. and July-Aug. daily 8:30am-noon and 3:30-7:30pm; Sept.-Dec. and Apr.-June reduced hours.) **Postal Code:** 74400.

ACCOMMODATIONS AND FOOD. Chamonix's *gîtes* (mountain hostels) and dorms are cheap, but they fill up fast; call ahead. The **Auberge de Jeunesse (HI) ❶,** 127 montée Jacques Balmat, in Les Pèlerins at the base of the Glacier de Bossons, offers all-inclusive winter **ski packages** (€389-481 per week). Take the bus from the train station or pl. de l'Eglise (dir.: Les Houches) to Pèlerins Ecole (€0.60) and follow the signs uphill; by train, get off at Les Pèlerins and follow the signs. (☎04 50 53 14 52; www.aj-chamonix.fr.st. Breakfast included. Reception daily 8am-noon and 5-10pm. Dorms €13; singles €15.25; doubles €30.50. MC/V.) **Gîte le Vagabond ❶,** 365 av. Ravanel le Rouge, is near the center of town. (☎50 53 15 43; www.limelab.com/vagabond. Reception daily 8-10:30am and 4:30pm-1am. 4- to 8-bed dorms €12.50.) Turn left from the base of the Aiguille du Midi *téléphérique,* continue past the main roundabout, and look right to **camp** at **L'Ile des Barrats ❶,** on rte. des Pélerins. (☎/fax 04 50 53 51 44. Reception July-Aug. daily 8am-10:30pm; May-June and Sept. 8am-noon and 4-7pm. Open May-Sept. €5 per person, €3.60 per tent, €2 per car.) Get groceries at **Super U,** 117 r. Joseph Vallot. (Open M-Sa 8:15am-7:30pm, Su 8:30am-noon.)

HIKING AND SKIING. Whether you've come to climb up the mountains or ski down them, you're in for a challenge. But wherever you go, be cautious—on average, one person a day dies on the mountains. The **l'Aiguille du Midi** *téléphérique* offers a pricey, knuckle-whitening ascent over forests and snowy cliffs to a needlepoint peak at the top. A ride to the top reveals a fantastic panorama from 3842m. (☎04 50 53 40 00. €32.) Bring your passport to continue by gondola to **Helbronner, Italy** for views of three countries and the **Matterhorn** and **Mont Blanc peaks;** pack a picnic to eat on the glacier (round-trip €50). Hike or take a train to the **ice cave** carved afresh every year by **La Mer de Glace,** a glacier that slides 30m per year. Special trains (☎04 50 53 12 54) run from a small station next to the main one. (July-Aug. daily, every 20min. 8am-6pm; May-June and early Sept. Every 30min. 8:30am-5pm; mid-Sept. to Apr. 10am-4pm. Round-trip €13.) Sunken in a valley, Chamonix is surrounded by mountains ideal for skiing. To the south, **Le Tour-Col de Balme** (☎04 50 54 00 58), above the village of **Le Tour,** is ideal for beginner and intermediate skiers (day pass €24.60). On the northern side of the valley, **Les Grands Montets** is the *grande dame* of Chamonix skiing, with advanced terrain and remodeled **snowboarding** facilities. (☎04 50 53 13 18. €32 per day).

ANNECY

With narrow cobblestone streets, winding canals, and a turreted castle, Annecy appears more like a fairy-tale fabrication than a modern city. The **Palais de l'Isle** is a 13th-century fortress that served as a prison for Resistance fighters during World War II. (Open June-Sept. daily 10am-6pm; Oct.-May 10am-noon and 2-6pm. €3.10, students €0.80.) The shaded **Jardins de l'Europe** are Annecy's pride and joy. Although it may be hard to tear yourself away from the city's charming **vieille ville,** Annecy's Alpine forests boast excellent **hiking** and **biking trails.** One of the best hikes begins at the **Basilique de la Visitation,** near the hostel. An exquisite 16km scenic *piste cyclable* (bike route) hugs the lake shore along the eastern coast.

Trains (☎08 36 35 35 35) arrive at pl. de la Gare from: Chamonix (2½hr., 7 per day, €16.70); Grenoble (2hr., 12 per day, €14.10); Lyon (2hr., 9 per day, €18); Nice (7hr., 2 per day, €54.20); and Paris (4hr., 8 per day, €57.60). Autocars Frossard **buses** (☎04 50 45 73 90) leave from next to the station for Geneva (1¼hr., 6 per day, €9) and Lyon (3½hr., 2 per day, €16.40). From the train station, take the underground passage to r. Vaugelas, follow the street left for four blocks, and enter the Bonlieu shopping mall to reach the **tourist office,** 1 r. Jean Jaurès, in pl. de la Libération. (☎04 50 45 00 33; www.lac-annecy.com. Open July-Aug. M-Sa 9am-6:30pm, Su 9am-12:30pm and 1:45-6:30pm; Sept.-June daily 9am-12:30pm and 1:45-6pm.) In summer, you can reach the **Auberge de Jeunesse "La Grande Jeanne" (HI) ❶,** on rte. de Semnoz, via the *ligne d'été* (dir.: Semnoz) from the station (€1); otherwise, take bus #1 (dir.: Marquisats) from the station to Hôtel de Police, turn right on av. du Tresum, and follow signs pointing to Semnoz. (☎04 50 45 33 19; fax 04 50 52 77 52. Breakfast included. Sheets €2.70. Reception daily 8am-10pm. Dorms €12.70. AmEx/MC/V.) **Camping Bélvèdere ❶,** 8 rte. de Semnoz, is near the youth hostel. (☎04 50 45 48 30. Reception daily July-Aug. 8am-9pm; mid-Apr. to June and Sept. to mid-Oct. 8am-8pm. Open mid-Apr. to mid-Oct. €13 for 2 people, tent, and car.) A **Monoprix supermarket** fills the better part of pl. de Notre-Dame. (Open M-Sa 8:30am-7:30pm.) **Postal Code:** 74000.

LYON

World-renowned culinary capital, former center of the silk trade, and home to the French Resistance, Lyon (pop. 1.2 million) is a world-class city friendlier and more relaxed than Paris, with a few centuries' more history. While the narrow twisting streets of *vieux Lyon* are lined with elegant 16th-century townhouses, Lyon is a modern city with every urban comfort imaginable, from skyscrapers and cafes to speedy transport systems and lush parks to concert halls and *discothèques.*

▐▌ TRANSPORTATION

Flights: Aéroport Lyon-Saint-Exupéry (LYS) (☎04 72 22 72 21), 25km east of Lyon. 50 daily flights to Paris. The TGV stops at the airport, and is cheaper than flying. **Sato-buses/Navette Aéroport** (☎04 72 68 72 17) shuttle passengers to Gare de Perrache, Gare de la Part-Dieu, and subway stops Jean Mace, Grange-Blanche, and Mermoz Pinel (every 20min., €8.20). **Air France** is at 17 r. Victor Hugo, 2ème (☎04 20 82 08 20).

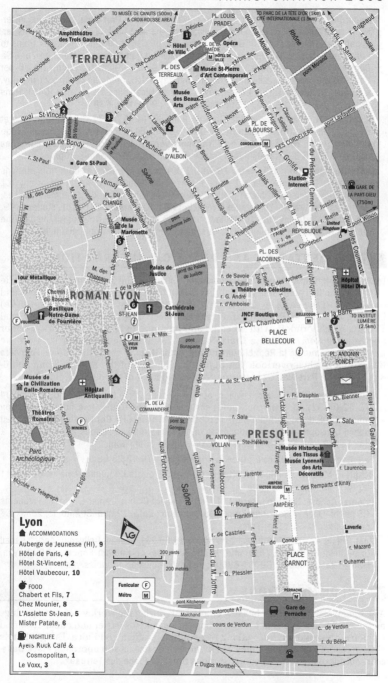

FRANCE

Lyon

🏠 **ACCOMMODATIONS**

Auberge de Jeunesse (HI), **9**
Hôtel de Paris, **4**
Hôtel St-Vincent, **2**
Hôtel Vaubecour, **10**

🍴 **FOOD**

Chabert et Fils, **7**
Chez Mounier, **8**
L'Assiette St-Jean, **5**
Mister Patate, **6**

🍸 **NIGHTLIFE**

Ayers Rock Café &
  Cosmopolitan, **1**
Le Voxx, **3**

FRANCE

Trains: Trains passing through Lyon stop only at **Gare de la Part-Dieu,** bd. Marius Vivier-Merle (M: Part-Dieu), in the business district on the east bank of the Rhône. Trains terminating at Lyon also stop at **Gare de Perrache,** pl. Carnot (M: Perrache). TGV trains to Paris stop at both. **SNCF** info and reservation desk at Part-Dieu open M-F 9am-7pm, Sa 9am-6:30pm; Perrache open M-F 9am-7pm, Sa 9am-6:30pm. To: Dijon (2hr., 6 per day, €21); Geneva, Switzerland (2hr., 13 per day, €19); Grenoble (1¼hr., 21 per day, €15.40); Marseilles (3hr., 17 per day, €32.90); Nice (6hr., 12 per day, €48); Paris (2hr., 26 TGVs per day, €53); Strasbourg (5½hr., 9 per day, €39).

Buses: On the lowest level of the Gare de Perrache (☎04 72 77 63 03), and also at Gare de Part-Dieu (**Allô Transports,** ☎04 72 61 72 61). Domestic companies include **Philibert** (☎04 78 98 56 00) and **Transport Verney** (☎04 78 70 21 01). **Eurolines** (☎04 72 56 95 30) travels out of France. Station open M-Sa 8am-8:30pm.

Local Transportation: TCL (☎04 78 71 70 00), has info offices at both train stations and major *Métro* stops. Pocket maps are available from the tourist office or any TCL branch. Tickets are valid for all methods of mass transport, including the Métro, buses, funiculars, and trams. 1hr. **single-fare tickets** €1.40; **carnet of 10** €11, students €9. The *Ticket Liberté* day pass (€4) allows unlimited use of all mass transit for the day. The efficient **Métro** runs 5am-midnight. **Buses** run 5am-9pm (a few until midnight).

■ *i* ORIENTATION AND PRACTICAL INFORMATION

Lyon is divided into nine **arrondissements** (districts). The 1*er*, 2*ème*, and 4*ème* lie on the **presqu'île** (peninsula), which juts south toward the **Saône** (to the west) and the **Rhône** (to the east) rivers. Starting in the south, the 2*ème* (the *centre ville*) includes the **Gare de Perrache** and **place Bellecour.** The 1*er* houses the nocturnal Terraux neighborhood, with its cafes and popular student-packed bars. Farther north is the 4*ème* and the **Croix-Rousse.** The main pedestrian roads on the *presqu'île* are **rue de la République** and **rue Victor Hugo.** West of the Saône, **Fourvière Hill** and its basilica overlook **Vieux Lyon** (5*ème*). East of the Rhône (3*ème* and 6-8*ème*) lies the **Part-Dieu** train station (3*ème*)and most of the city's population.

Tourist Office: In the Tourist Pavilion, at pl. Bellecour, 2*ème* (☎04 72 77 69 69; fax 04 78 42 04 32). M: Bellecour. Indispensable **Map and Guide,** free hotel reservation office, SNCF desk, and city tours (€6.50-9). The **Lyon City Card** authorizes unlimited public transport along with admission to 14 museums and various tours. Valid for: 1 day €15, 2 days €25, or 3 days €30. Open M-Sa 10am-6pm.

Emergency: ☎17. **Police:** 47 r. de la Charité (☎04 78 42 26 56).

Hospital/Medical Service: Hôpital Hôtel-Dieu, 1 pl. de l'Hôpital, 2*ème* (☎04 72 41 30 00), near quai du Rhône.

Internet Access: Station-Internet, 4 r. du President Carnot, 2*ème*. €7 per hr., students €5 per hr. Open M-Sa 10am-7pm. Also **Connectix Café,** 19 quai St-Antoine, 2*ème*. €7 per hr. Open M-Sa 11am-7pm.

Post Office: Pl. Antonin Poncet, 2 (☎04 72 40 65 22), near pl. Bellecour. Address mail to be held: SURNAME Firstname, *Poste Restante,* pl. Antonin Poncet, **69002** Lyon, France. **Postal Codes:** 69001-69009; last digit indicates *arrondissement.*

▗ ACCOMMODATIONS

As a financial center, Lyon has few empty beds during the work week but openings on the weekends. Fall is actually the busiest season; it's easier and cheaper to find a place in the summer, but making reservations is still a good idea. Budget hotels cluster east of **Place Carnot,** near Perrache. Prices rise as you approach **Place Bellecour,** but there are less expensive options north of **Place des Terreaux.**

▨ **Hôtel de Paris,** 16 rue de la Platière, 1er (04 78 28 00 95; fax 04 78 39 57 64). Bursting with color and character, with rooms ranging from the classic to the futuristic. Breakfast €7. Reception 24hr. Singles €42; doubles €49-75; triples €78. AmEx/MC/V. ❹

Hôtel St-Vincent, 9 r. Pareille, 1er (☎04 78 27 22 56; fax 04 78 30 92 87). Just off the Quai St-Vincent, north of passerelle St-Vincent. Simple, elegant rooms. Breakfast €6. Reception 24hr. Reserve ahead. Singles with shower €31; doubles €38. MC/V. ❸

Auberge de Jeunesse (HI), 41-45 montée du Chemin Neuf, 5ème (☎04 78 15 05 50; fax 04 78 15 05 51). Or take the funicular from Vieux Lyon to Minimes, walk down the stairs and go left down the hill for 5min. Breakfast included. Reception 24hr. HI members only. 4- to 8-bed dorms €12.20. ❶

Hôtel Vaubecour, 28 r. Vaubecour, 2ème (☎04 78 37 44 91; fax 04 78 42 90 17), on the east bank of the Saône. Elegantly furnished rooms. Breakfast included. Reception 24hr. Reserve ahead. Singles from €23; doubles from €26; triples and quads from €54. Extra bed €12.20. MC/V. ❷

Camping Dardilly, 10km from Lyon in a suburb (☎04 78 35 64 55). From the Hôtel de Ville, take bus #19 (dir.: Ecully-Dardilly) to Parc d'Affaires. Pool, TV, and restaurant. Reception 8am-10pm. €3 per person; €6 per tent; car free. Electricity €3. MC/V. ❶

◪ FOOD

The galaxy of *Michelin* stars adorning Lyon's restaurants confirms the city's reputation as the culinary capital of the Western world. But if *haute cuisine* doesn't suit your wallet, try one of Lyon's many **bouchons,** cozy restaurants serving local cuisine for low prices. *Bouchons* can be found in the **Terraux** district, along **Rue des Marronniers** and **Rue Mercière** (both in the 2ème), and on **Rue St-Jean** in Vieux Lyon. Ethnic restaurants are near **Rue de la République,** in the 2ème. A **Monoprix** is on r. de la République, at pl. des Cordeliers, 2ème. (Open M-Sa 8:30am-9:30pm.)

▨ **Chez Mounier,** 3 r. des Marronniers, 2ème (☎04 78 37 79 26). This tiny place satisfies a discriminating local clientele with generous traditional specialties. 4-course *menus* 61-€9.60-15.10. Open Tu-Sa noon-2pm and 7-10:30pm, Su noon-2pm. ❸

Chabert et Fils, 11 r. des Marronniers, 2ème (☎04 78 37 01 94). One of the better-known *bouchons* in Lyon. For dessert, try the delicious *Guignol.* Lunch *menus* start at €8-12.50. Open daily noon-2pm and 7-11pm. MC/V. ❷

L'Assiette St-Jean, 10 r. Saint Jean, 5ème (☎04 72 41 96 20). An excellent *bouchon,* with unusual, somewhat archaic decor. House speciality *gateau de foies de volaille* (chicken liver) €6.60; menus €13-27.50. Open in summer Tu-Su noon-2pm and 7-10:30pm; open in winter W-Su. AmEx/MC/V. ❸

Mister Patate, pl. St-Jean, 5ème (☎04 78 38 18 79). All potatoes, all the time, with plates from €6.80-8.10. Some vegetarian options. Open M-Sa 11:30am-3pm and 6-11:30pm, Su 11:30-3pm and 6-10pm. ❷

◪ SIGHTS

VIEUX LYON. Nestled along the Saône at the bottom of the Fourvière Hill, the cobblestone streets of *Vieux Lyon* wind between lively cafes and magnificent medieval and Renaissance **townhouses.** (M: Vieux Lyon.) The townhouses are graced with **traboules,** tunnels that lead from the street through a maze of courtyards. *(Tours in summer daily 2pm. €9, students €4.50.)* The southern end of *Vieux Lyon* is dominated by the 12th-century **Cathédrale St-Jean,** at pl. St-Jean, and its 14th-century astronomical clock. *(Open M-F 8am-noon and 2-7:30pm. Free.)*

FOURVIÈRE AND ROMAN LYON. From the corner of r. du Bœuf and r. de la Bombarde in *Vieux Lyon*, climb the stairs to reach the **Fourvière Hill**, the nucleus of Roman Lyon. (M: Fourvière.) Continue up via the rose-lined **chemin de la Rosarie,** through a garden to the **Esplanade Fourvière**, where a model of the cityscape points out local landmarks. Most prefer to take the funicular *(la ficelle)* from av. A. Max in *Vieux Lyon*, off pl. St-Jean, to the top of the hill. Behind the Esplanade is the **Basilique Notre-Dame de Fourvière,** with multicolored mosaics, gilded pillars, and elaborate carvings. *(Open daily 8am-7pm. Free.)* Set back into the hillside as you walk down from the church, you'll find the **Musée Gallo-Romain,** 17 r. Cléberg, *5ème*, and its huge collection of arms, pottery, statues, and jewelry. Check out the bronze tablet inscribed with a speech by Lyon's favorite son, Emperor Claudius. *(Open Mar.-Oct. Tu-Su 10am-6pm; Nov.-Feb. 10am-5pm. €3.80, students €2.30.)*

LE PRESQU'ÎLE AND LES TERREAUX. Monumental squares, statues, and fountains mark the **Presqu'île,** the lively area between the Rhône and the Saône. The heart is **place Bellecour,** a sea of red gravel lined with shops and flower stalls. The pedestrian **rue Victor Hugo** runs south from pl. Bellecour; to the north, the crowded **rue de la République** is the urban artery of Lyon. It terminates at **place Louis Pradel** in the 1*er*, at the tip of the **Terreaux** district. Across the square at pl. Louis Pradel is the spectacular 17th-century **Hôtel de Ville.** In pl. des Terreaux is the huge **Musée des Beaux-Arts,** second only to the Louvre with a comprehensive archaeological wing, works by Spanish and Dutch masters, and a sculpture garden. *(Open W-M 10:30am-6pm. €3.80, students €2.)*

EAST OF THE RHÔNE AND MODERN LYON. Lyon's newest train station and monstrous space-age mall form the core of the ultra-modern Part-Dieu district. The **Centre d'Histoire de la Résistance et de la Déportation,** 14 av. Bertholet, *7ème*, has documents, photos, and films of the Lyon-based resistance to the Nazis. *(M: Jean Mace. Open W-Su 9am-5:15pm. €3.80, students €2.)* The futuristic **Cité Internationale de Lyon,** quai Charles de Gaulle, *6ème,* houses a commercial complex housing offices, shops, theaters, Interpol's world headquarters, and the **Musée d'Art Contemporain.** *(Take bus #4 from M: Foch. Open W-Su noon-7pm. €3.80, students €2.)*

🎵 🎭 ENTERTAINMENT AND NIGHTLIFE

At the end of June is the two-week **Festival du Jazz à Vienne,** which welcomes jazz masters to Vienne, a medieval town south of Lyon, accessible by bus or train. (☎04 74 85 00 05. Tickets €26, students €24.) **Les Nuits de Fourvière** is a two-month summer music festival held in the ancient Théâtre Romain and Odéon. (☎04 72 32 00 00. Tickets and info at the Théâtre Romain and the FNAC shop on r. de la Republique.) The biennial **Festival de Musique du Vieux Lyon,** 5 pl. du Petit Collège, *5ème,* draws artists worldwide between mid-Nov. and mid-Dec. to perform in the churches of Vieux Lyon. (☎04 78 42 39 04. Tickets €10-35.)

Nightlife in Lyon is fast and furious. **Ayers Rock Café,** 2 r. Desirée, and **Cosmopolitan,** right next door, are packed with students. (Ayers open M-Sa 6pm-3am. Cosmopolitan open M-W 8pm-2am, Th-Sa 8pm-3am. No cover.) **Le Voxx,** 1 r. d'Algérie, is packed with stylish French and almost-stylish exchange students. (☎04 78 28 33 87. Open M-Sa 8pm-2am, Su 10pm-2am.) **Le Village Club,** 6 r. Violi, off r. Royale, features fabulous drag queens and attracts a thirty-something gay male crowd. (Open W-Th 9pm-3am, F-Sa 10pm-4am.) The city's best and most accessible late-night spots are a strip of **riverboat dance clubs** by the east bank of the Rhône.

BERRY-LIMOUSIN

Too often passed over for beaches and big cities, Berry-Limousin offers peaceful countryside, quaint villages, and fascinating towns. Bourges served as the capital of France and benefited from King Charles VII's financier, Jacques Coeur, who built a lavish string of chateaux. The region later became an artistic and literary breeding ground, home to Georges Sand, Auguste Renoir, and Jean Giraudoux.

BOURGES

In 1433, Jacques Coeur chose Bourges (pop. 80,000) as the site for one of his many chateaux. You'll see more of the unfurnished **Palais Jacques-Coeur** than he ever did, since he was imprisoned for embezzlement before its completion. (Open July-Aug. daily 9am-6pm; Apr.-June and Sept. 9am-noon and 2-6pm; Nov.-Mar. 9am-noon and 2-5pm. €5.50, ages 18-24 €3.50, under 18 free.) The **Cathédrale St-Etienne,** has stunning 13th-century handiwork in the **tower** and **crypt,** a dramatic Gothic facade, and stained-glass windows. (Open Apr.-Sept. daily 8:30am-7:15pm; Oct.-Mar. 9am-5:45pm. Closed Su morning. €5.50, students €3.50.) As you exit the cathedral, head right on r. des 3 Maillets and turn left on r. Molière for the **promenade des Remparts,** which offers a quiet stroll past ramparts and flowery gardens.

Trains leave from the station at pl. Général Leclerc (☎ 02 48 51 00 00) for: Paris (2½hr., 5-8 per day, €24) and Tours (1½hr., 10 per day, €17). From the station, follow av. H. Laudier, which turns into av. Jean Jaurès; bear left onto r. du Commerce, and continue down r. Moyenne to reach the **tourist office,** 21 r. Victor Hugo. (☎ 02 48 23 02 60; www.ville-bourges.fr. Open M-Sa 9am-7pm, Su 10am-7pm.) To get to the **Auberge de Jeunesse (HI) ❶,** 22 r. Henri Sellier, bear right from r. du Commerce on to r. des Arènes, which becomes r. Fernault, cross at the intersection to r. René Ménard, follow it to the right, and turn left at r. Henri Sellier. (☎ 02 48 24 58 09. Reception M-F 8am-noon and 2pm-1am, Sa-Su 8am-noon and 5-10pm. 3- to 8-bed dorms €8.) For the **Centre International de Séjour, "La Charmille" ❶,** 17 r. Félix-Chédin, cross the footbridge from the station over the tracks. (☎ 02 48 23 07 40. Singles €15; doubles €22; triples €33. MC/V.) **Place Gordaine, Rue des Beaux-Arts, Rue Moyenne,** and **Rue Mirabeau** are lined with eateries. The **Leclerc supermarket** is on r. Prado off bd. Juraville. (Open M-F 9:15am-7:20pm, Sa 8:30am-7:20pm.) **Le Phénicien ❷,** 13 r. Jean Girard, off pl. Gordaine, offers decent Middle Eastern cuisine. (Open M-Sa 11am-11pm.) **Postal Code:** 18000.

BURGUNDY (BOURGOGNE)

What the Loire Valley is to chateaux, Burgundy is to churches. During the Middle Ages, the duchy was the heart of the religious fever sweeping Europe: abbeys swelled in size and wealth, and towns eager for pilgrim traffic built magnificent cathedrals. Today, Burgundy's production of some of the world's finest wines and delectable dishes, like *coq au vin* and *bœuf bourguignon*, have made this region the homeland of Epicureans worldwide.

DIJON

Dijon (pop. 160,000) isn't just about the mustard. The capital of Burgundy is a charming city with gardens, a couple of good museums, and fine wines. The diverse **Musée des Beaux-Arts** occupies the east wing of the colossal **Palais des Ducs de Bourgogne,** in pl. de la Libération at the center of the *vieille ville.* (☎ 80 74 52 70. Open W-M 10am-6pm. €3.40, students €1.60.) The **Horloge à Jacquemart,** ticking above the tower of **Eglise Notre-Dame,** in pl. Notre-Dame, is worth the maneuevering to see. The brightly tiled **Cathédrale St-Bénigne,** in pl. St-Bénigne, has a spooky circular crypt. (☎80 30 14 90. Open 9am-6:30pm. Crypt €1.) Next door, the **Musée Archéologique,** 5 r. Dr. Maret, features Gallo-Roman sculpture and Neolithic house wares. (☎03 80 30 88 54. Open June-Sept. Tu-Su 9am-6pm; Oct.-May Tu-Su 9am-noon and 2-6pm. €2.20, students free, Su everyone free.) Get your **Grey Poupon** at the Maille Boutique 32 r. de la Liberté, where *moutarde au vin* has been made since 1747. (☎03 80 30 41 02. Open M-Sa 9am-7pm.)

From the train station at cours de la Gare, at the end of av. Maréchal Foch, **trains** chug to: Lyon (2hr., 7 per day, €21); Nice (7-8hr., 6 per day, €57); Paris (1½hr., 20 per day, €26). The **tourist office,** on pl. Darcy, is a straight shot down av. Maréchal Foch from the station. (☎03 80 44 11 44. Open July-Aug. daily 9am-8pm; Sept.-June 9am-7pm.) To get to the huge **Auberge de Jeunesse (HI), Centre de Rencontres Internationales ❶,** 1 av. Champollion, take bus #5 (or night bus A) from pl. Grangier to Epirey. (☎03 80 72 95 20; fax 03 80 70 00 61. Breakfast included. Dorms €15; singles €27.50. MC/V.) **Hôtel Montchapet ❸,** 26-28 r. Jacques Cellerier, north of av. Première Armée Française off pl. Darcy, is bright and comfortable. (☎03 80 53 95 00; fax 03 80 58 26 87. Breakfast €5. Reception 7am-10:30pm. Check-out 11am. Singles €24-39; doubles €36-46.) **Rue Berbisey** and **rue Monge** host a wide variety of low- to mid-priced restaurants. Fend for yourself at the supermarket in the **Galeries Lafayette,** 41 r. de la Liberté. (Open M-Sa 9am-7:15pm.) **Postal Code:** 21000.

▶ DAYTRIP FROM DIJON: BEAUNE. Wine has poured out of the well-touristed town of **Beaune,** just south of Dijon (25min., 37 trains per day, €5.70), for centuries. Surrounded by the famous Côte de Beaune vineyards, the town itself is packed with wineries offering free *dégustations* (tastings). The largest of the cellars belongs to **Patriarche Père et Fils,** 5-7 r. du Collège, a labyrinth of 5km of corridors packed with over four million bottles. (☎03 80 24 53 78. Open daily 9:30-11:30am and 2-5:30pm. €9.) The **tourist office,** 1 r. de l'Hôtel-Dieu, lists *caves* (cellars) in the region offering tours. (☎03 80 26 21 30; fax 03 80 26 21 39. Open mid-June to mid-Sept. M-Sa 9:30am-8pm, Su 9:30am-6pm; Oct.-June reduced hours.)

ALSACE-LORRAINE AND FRANCHE-COMTÉ

As first prize in the endless Franco-German border wars, France's northeastern frontier has had a long and bloody history. Heavily influenced by its tumultuous past, the entire region now maintains a fascinating blend of French and German in the local dialects, cuisine, and architecture. Alsace's well-preserved towns offer half-timbered Bavarian houses flanking tiny crooked streets and canals, while Lorraine's elegant cities spread to the west among wheat fields. In Franche-Comté, the Jura mountains have some of France's finest cross-country skiing.

STRASBOURG

Only a few kilometers from the Franco-German border, Strasbourg (pop. 260,000) has spent much of its history being annexed by one side or another. Today, German is often heard on its streets, and *winstubs* sit next door to *pâtisseries*. Strasbourg is also the joint center, along with Brussels, of the European Union. With half-timbered houses and flower-lined canals, the city makes a fantastic stopover.

⌐⊒ TRANSPORTATION AND PRACTICAL INFORMATION. Strasbourg is a major rail hub. **Trains** (☎03 88 22 50 50) go to: Luxembourg (2½hr., 14 per day, €25.20); Frankfurt, Germany (3hr., 18 per day, €36.60); Paris (4hr., 16 per day, €34.50); and Zürich, Switzerland (3hr., 18 per day, €39). The **tourist office,** 17 pl. de la Cathédrale, makes hotel reservations for €1.60 plus deposit. (☎03 88 52 28 28. Open June-Sept. M-Sa 9am-7pm, Su 9am-6pm; Oct.-May. daily 9am-6pm.) Rent **bikes** at **Vélocation,** at 4 r. du Maire Kuss, near the train station. (€4.50 per day. €45 deposit and copy of ID.) Get on the **Internet** at **Net computer,** 14 quai des Pêcheurs. (€3 per hr. Open M-F 9am-10pm, Sa and Su 11am-10pm.)

⌐⌐ ACCOMMODATIONS AND FOOD. Make reservations or arrive early to find reasonable accommodations. ▨**CIARUS (Centre International d'Accueil de Strasbourg) ❷,** 7 r. Finkmatt, has large, spotless facilities with an international atmosphere. From the train station, take r. du Maire-Kuss to the canal, turn left, and follow quais St-Jean, Kléber, and Finkmatt; turn left on r. Finkmatt, and it's on the left. (☎03 88 15 27 88; www.ciarus.com. Breakfast included. Reception 24hr. Check-in 3:30pm. Check-out 9am. Curfew 1am. Dorms €16; singles €38; doubles €42. MC/V.) **Hôtel de Bruxelles ❸,** 13 r. Kuhn, is up the street from the train station. Ask to see your room in advance. (☎03 88 32 45 31; fax 03 88 32 22 01. Breakfast €5.30. Singles and doubles €27-44; triples and quads €44-65. MC/ V.) **Auberge de Jeunesse, Centre International de Rencontres du parc du Rhin (HI) ❶,** r. des Cavaliers, is 7km from the station and 1km from Germany. From the station, take bus #2 (dir.: Pond du Rhin) to Parc du Rhin. Facing the tourist office, go to the left and look for the flashing red lights. (☎03 88 45 54 20; fax 03 88 45 54 21. Breakfast included. Reception daily 7am-12:30pm, 2-7:30pm, and 8:30pm-1am. Curfew 1am. Dorms €13. MC/V.)

Winstubs are informal places that serve Alsatian specialties such as *choucroute garnie* (spiced sauerkraut served with meats); try the **La Petite France** neighborhood, especially along r. des Dentelles and petite r. des Dentelles. Explore **place de la Cathédrale, rue Mercière,** or **rue du Vieil Hôpital** for restaurants, and **place Marché Gayot,** off r. des Frères, for lively cafes. For groceries, swing by the **ATAC,** 47 r. des Grandes Arcades, off pl. Kléber. (Open M-Sa 8:30am-8pm.)

◙ ⌐ SIGHTS AND ENTERTAINMENT. The ornate Gothic **Cathédrale de Strasbourg** sends its tower 142m skyward. Inside, the **Horloge Astronomique** demonstrates the wizardry of 16th-century Swiss clockmakers. While you wait for the clock to strut its stuff—daily at 12:30pm, apostles troop out of the clockface while a cock crows to greet Saint Peter—check out the **Pilier des Anges** (Angels' Pillar), a masterpiece of Gothic sculpture. You can climb the **tower** in front of the clock like the young Goethe, who scaled its 330 steps regularly to cure his fear of heights. (Cathedral open M-Sa 7-11:40am and 12:45-7pm, Su 12:45-6pm. Tickets for the clock on sale 8:30am in cathedral and 11:45am at south entrance; €0.80. Tower open daily 9am-6:30pm; €3, children €1.50.) **Palais Rohan,** 2 pl. du Château, houses three small but excellent museums: the **Musée des Beaux-Arts, Musée des Arts Décoratifs,** and **Musée Archéologique.** (Open Tu-Su 10am-6pm. €3 each; students €1.50 each.) Take bus #23, 30, or 72 for **L'Orangerie,** Strasbourg's most spectacular park; free concerts play in the summer at the Pavilion Joséphine (Th-Tu 8:30pm).

LA ROUTE DU VIN

Since the High Middle Ages, the wines of Alsace have been highly prized—and highly priced—across Europe. The vineyards of Alsace flourish along a 170km corridor known as La Route du Vin (Wine Route) that begins at **Strasbourg** (p. 398) and stretches south along the foothills of the Vosges, passing through 100 towns along the way to Mulhouse. Hordes of tourists are drawn each year to explore the beautifully preserved medieval villages along the route—and, of course, for the free *dégustations* (tastings) along the way.

Colmar (p. 400) and **Sélestat** (p. 400) offer excellent bases and fascinating sights of their own, but don't miss out on smaller, less-touristed villages. The most accessible towns from Strasbourg are **Molsheim**, a medieval university center, and **Barr**, with an intricate old town and a vineyard trail that leads up through the hills. The more famous towns lie to the south: the most visited sight in Alsace, the **Château de Haut Koenigsbourg**, towers over **Kintzheim**; and the 16th-century walled hamlet of **Riquewihr**, the Route's most popular village, houses many of Alsace's best-known wine firms. If you're in Strasbourg and are contemplating a detour along the Wine Route, pick up the ⊠*Alsace Wine Route* brochure from a tourist office.

⌐ TRANSPORTATION. Strasbourg, the northern terminus of the Wine Route, is a major rail hub, easily accessible from France, Germany, and Luxembourg. **Trains** from Strasbourg hit many of the towns along the northern half of the Route, including: **Barr** (50min., 13 per day, €6.10); **Sélestat** (30min., 20 per day, €6.40); and **Colmar** (40min., 43 per day, €9.10), although wine lovers are more likely to get there via **Sélestat** (15min., 20 per day, €3.60). **Bus** lines pepper the southern half of the Route, running from Colmar to **Kaysersberg** (20min., 9 per day, €2), **Riquewihr** (30min., 10 per day, €3), and many other small towns on the Route. From Mulhouse, leap into nearby **Basel**, Switzerland (20min., 7 per day €6); go to **Paris** (4½hr., 10 per day, €43), or return to **Strasbourg** (1hr., 16 per day, €13.60).

SÉLESTAT. Sélestat (pop. 17,200), between Colmar and Strasbourg, is a charming town often overlooked by tourists on their way to larger Route cities. The **Bibliothèque Humaniste**, 1 r. de la Bibliothèque, founded in 1452, contains a fascinating collection of ancient documents produced during Sélestat's 15th-century humanistic boom. (Open July-Aug. M and W-F 9am-noon and 2-6pm, Sa 9am-noon and 2-5pm, Su 2-5pm; Sept.-June closed Su. €3.50.) The **tourist office**, 10 bd. Gén. Leclerc, in the Commanderie St-Jean, rents **bikes**. (☎03 88 58 87 20; www.selestat-tourisme.com. €12.50 per day. Open May-Sept. M-F 9am-12:30pm and 1:30-7pm, Sa 9am-noon and 2-5pm, Su 9am-3pm; Oct.-Apr. M-F 8:30am-noon and 1:30-6pm, Sa 9am-noon and 2-5pm.) The ⊠**Hôtel de l'Ill ❷**, 13 r. des Bateliers, has bright rooms. (☎03 88 92 91 09. Breakfast €4.60. Reception daily 7am-3pm and 5-11pm. Singles €22.90; doubles €36.60; triples €53.40. MC/V.) **Camping Les Cigognes ❶** is on the south edge of the *vieille ville*. (☎03 88 92 03 98. Reception July-Aug. 8am-noon and 3-10pm; May-June and Sept.-Oct 8am-noon and 3-7pm. Open May-Oct. July-Aug. €9.15 per person, €12.20 per 2 or 3 people; reduced prices Sept.-June.) **Rue des Chevaliers** and **rue de l'Hôpital** hold a variety of restaurants. **Postal Code:** 67600.

COLMAR. The bubbling fountains, crooked lanes, and pastel houses of Colmar (pop. 65,000) evoke an intimate charm despite packs of tourists. The collection of **Musée Unterlinden**, 1 r. d'Unterlinden, ranges from Romanesque to Renaissance, with Grünewald's *Issenheim Altarpiece*. (Open daily Apr.-Oct. 9am-6pm; Nov.-Mar. W-M 10am-5pm. €7, students €5.) The **Eglise des Dominicains,** on pl. des Dominicains, has Colmar's other major masterpiece, Schongauer's *Virgin in the Rose Bower*. (Open Apr.-Dec. 10am-1pm and 3-6pm. €1.30, students €1.)

To get to the **tourist office**, 4 r. d'Unterlinden, from the train station, turn left on av. de la République (which becomes r. Kléber) and follow it to the right to pl. Unterlinden. (☎03 89 20 68 92; info@ot-colmar.fr. Open July-Aug. M-Sa 9am-7pm, Su 9:30am-2pm; Apr.-June and Sept.-Oct. M-Sa 9am-6pm, Su 10am-2pm; Nov.-Mar. M-Sa 9am-noon and 2-6pm, Su 10am-2pm.) To reach the **Auberge de Jeunesse (HI) ❶**, 2 r. Pasteur, take bus #4 (dir.: Logelbach) to Pont Rouge. (☎03 89 80 57 39.

Breakfast included. Sheets €3.50. Reception daily July-Aug. 7-10am and 5pm-midnight; Sept.-June 5-11pm. Lockout 10am-5pm. Curfew midnight. No reservations. Open mid-Jan. to mid-Dec. Dorms €12; singles €17; doubles €29. MC/V.) Take bus #1 (dir.: Horbourg-Wihr) to Plage d'Ill for **Camping de l'Ill ❶**, on rte. Horbourg-Wihr. (☎03 89 41 15 94. Reception daily July-Aug. 8am-10pm; Feb.-June and Sept.-Nov. 8am-8pm. Open Feb.-Nov. €2.90 per person, €1.70 per child, €3 per site. Electricity €2.40.) **Monoprix** is on pl. Unterlinden. (Open M-F 8am-8pm, Sa 8am-8pm.) **La Petite Venise** and the **Quartier des Tanneurs** have *brasseries*. **Postal Code:** 68000.

BESANÇON

As far back as 58 BC, when Julius Caesar founded a military post here, Besançon (pop. 120,000) has intrigued military strategists because of its prime geographic location. Today, Besançon boasts a smart, sexy student population and an impressive number of museums and discos. See the city's well-preserved Renaissance buildings from high up in the Vauban's **citadel**, at the end of r. des Fusillés de la Résistance. Within the citadel, the **Musée de la Résistance et de la Déportation** (☎03 81 65 07 55) chronicles the Nazi rise to power and the German occupation of France. Other sights include a natural history museum, a zoo, an aquarium, and a folk arts museum. (☎03 81 65 07 50. Grounds open July-Aug. daily 9am-7pm; Apr.-June and Sept.-Oct. 9am-6pm; Nov.-Mar. 10am-5pm. Exhibits open Apr.-Oct. daily 9am-6pm; Nov.-Mar. 10am-5pm. €7, students €6.) The **Cathédrale St-Jean,** beneath the citadel, holds two treasures: the white marble **Rose de St-Jean** and the intricate 19th-century **Horloge Astronomique.** (Open W-M 9am-7pm. Free.) The **Musée des Beaux-Arts et d'Archéologie,** on pl. de la Révolution, houses an exceptional collection ranging from ancient Egyptian mummies to works by Matisse. (☎03 81 87 80 49. Open W-M 9:30am-6pm. €4, students free; Su and holidays free.) The area between **rue C. Pouillet** and **rue Pont Battant** buzzes with nightlife. **Madigan's,** pl. 8 Septembre, is packed every night with a young crowd. (Open Su-Th 7am-1am, F-Sa until 2:30am.) Shoot pool at the surprisingly hip **Pop Hall,** 26 r. Proudhon. (Open Su-Th 6pm-1am, F-Sa until 2am.)

Trains pull up at the station on av. de la Paix (☎08 36 35 35 35) from: Dijon (1hr., 25 per day, €11.70); Paris Gare de Lyon (2hr., 8 per day, €42.50); and Strasbourg (3hr., 10 per day, €25.70). **Monts Jura buses,** 9 r. Proudhon (☎03 81 21 22 00), go to Pontarlier (1hr., 6 per day, €7.80). From the station, walk downhill; turn onto av. Maréchal Foch, and continue to the left as it becomes av. de l'Helvétie, until you reach pl. de la Première Armée Française. The *vieille ville* is across the pont de la République; the **tourist office,** 2 pl. de la Première Armée Française, is in the park to the right. (☎03 81 80 92 55; www.besancon.com. Open Apr.-Sept. M 10am-7pm, Tu-Sa 9:30am-7pm; mid-June to mid-Sept. also open Su 10am-noon and 3-5pm; Oct.-Mar. M 10am-6pm, Tu-Sa 9am-6pm.) Surf the **Internet** at **Centre Information Jeunesse (CIJ),** 27 r. de la République. (Open M and Sa 1:30-6pm, Tu-F 10am-noon and 1:30-6pm. Free.) Cheap beds can be found at the **Centre International de Séjour ❷,** 19 r. Martin-du-Gard. Take bus #8 (dir.: Campus) from the Foch stop near the station, in front of a gas station, to Intermarché. (☎03 81 50 07 54. Reception 7am-1pm. Singles €17.50; doubles €26.60; triples €30.) A variety of restaurants line **Rue Claude-Pouillet.** Buy groceries at **Monoprix,** 12 Grande Rue. (Open M-Sa 8:30am-8pm.) **La Boîte à Sandwiches ❶,** 21 r. du Lycée, off r. Pasteur, serves sandwiches and salads. (Open M-Sa 11:30am-2pm and 7pm-midnight.) **Postal Code:** 25000.

▶ **DAYTRIP FROM BESANÇON: PONTARLIER AND THE JURA.** The sedate town of **Pontarlier** is a good base from which to explore the oft-overlooked **Haut-Jura mountains.** The Jura are best known for cross-country **skiing**; eight trails cover every skill level. (Day pass €5, under 17 €2; available at the **Le Lar-**

mont and **Le Malmaison** trails.) Le Larmont is the closest Alpine ski area (☎ 03 81 46 55 20). **Sport et Neige,** 4 r. de la République (☎ 03 81 39 04 69), rents skis (€38 per week). In summer, **fishing, hiking,** and **mountain biking** are popular sports. Rent a **bike** from **Cycles Pernet,** 23 r. de la République. (☎ 03 81 46 48 00. €15 per day with passport deposit. Open Tu-Sa 9am-noon and 2-7pm.) Monts Jura **buses** (☎ 81 39 88 80) run to Besançon (1hr., 6 per day, €7.30). The **tourist office,** 14bis r. de la Gare, has regional guides and maps. (☎ 03 81 46 48 33; fax 03 81 46 83 32.) **L'Auberge de Pontarlier (HI) ❶,** 2 r. Jouffroy, is clean and central. (☎ 03 81 38 54 54. Breakfast €3.20. Sheets €2.70. Reception 8am-noon and 6-10pm. Dorms €8.) **Postal Code:** 25300.

NANCY

Nancy (pop. 100,000) has always been passionate about beauty: the town that spawned the art-nouveau "Nancy school" is today the artistic and intellectual heart of modern Lorraine. The elaborate ◪**Place Stanislas** houses three neoclassical pavilions, with *son-et-lumière* spectacles held nightly at 10pm in July and August. The collection in the **Musée des Beaux-Arts,** 3 pl. Stanislas, spans from the 14th century to today. (☎ 03 83 85 30 72. Open W-M 10am-6pm. €4.60, students €2.30; W and 1st Su of the month students free.) Pass through the five-arch **Arc de Triomphe** to the tree-lined **Place de la Carrière.** Portals of pink roses lead into the aromatic **Roseraie,** in the relaxing **Parc de la Pépinière,** just north of pl. de la Carrière. (Open May-Sept. 6:30am-11:30pm; Oct.-Apr. reduced hours. Free.)

Trains (☎ 03 83 22 12 46) depart from the station at pl. Thiers to: Metz (40min., 24 per day, €8); Paris (3hr., 14 per day, €35); and Strasbourg (1hr., 17 per day, €19). Head left from the station and turn right on r. Raymond Poincaré, which leads straight to pl. Stanislas, the center of the city, and the **tourist office.** Ask for the invaluable *Le Fil d'Ariane* guide. (☎ 03 83 35 22 41; www.ot-nancy.fr. Open Apr.-Sept. M-Sa 9am-7pm, Su 10am-5pm; Oct.-Mar. M-Sa 9am-6pm, Su 10am-1pm.) Access the Internet at **E-café,** on r. des Quatre Eglises. (☎ 03 83 35 47 34. €5.40 per hr. Open M-Sa 9am-9pm, Su 2-8pm.) **Centre d'Accueil de Remicourt (HI) ❶,** 149 r. de Vandoeuvre, is in Villiers-lès-Nancy, 4km away. From the station, take bus #122 to St-Fiacre (dir.: Villiers Clairlieu; 2 per hr., last bus 8pm; confirm direction with the driver); head downhill from the stop, turn right on r. de la Grange des Moines, which turns into r. de Vandoeuvre. Signs point to Château de Remicourt. (☎ 83 27 73 67. Breakfast included. Reception daily 9am-9pm. Dorms €12.50; doubles €29. MC/V.) **Hôtel Flore ❸,** 8 r. Raymond, is bright and homey. (☎ 03 83 37 63 28. Reception 7:30am-2am. Singles €26-32; doubles €37-40; triples €43. AmEx/MC/V.) Restaurants line **rue des Maréchaux, place Lafayette,** and **place St-Epvre.** A **SHOPI** market sits at 26 r. St-Georges. (Open M-Sa 9am-8pm.) **Postal Code:** 54000.

CHAMPAGNE AND THE NORTH

John Maynard Keynes once remarked that his major regret in life was not having consumed enough champagne; a trip through the rolling vineyards and fertile plains of Champagne promises many opportunities to avoid his mistake. The term "champagne" is fiercely guarded; the name can only be applied to wines made from regional grapes and produced according to a rigorous, time-honored method. To the north, Flanders, the coastal Pas de Calais, and Picardy remain the final frontiers of tourist-free France. As you flee the ferry ports, don't overlook the intriguing Flemish culture of Arras and the world-class art collections of Lille.

REIMS

Reims (pop. 185,000) delights in the bubbly champagne of its famed *caves* and the beauty of its architectural masterpieces. The **Cathédrale de Notre-Dame,** built with golden limestone quarried in the Champagne *caves*, features sea-blue stained-glass windows by Marc Chagall. (☎03 26 77 45 25. Open daily 7:30am-7:30pm. Tours daily 2:30pm; less frequently in Oct. and late Mar. to mid-June. €5.35, students €3.05.) Enter the adjacent **Palais du Tau,** at pl. du Cardinal Luçon, for dazzling 16th-century tapestries. (☎03 26 47 81 79. Open July-Aug. daily 9:30am-6:30pm; Sept. to mid-Nov and mid-Mar. to June daily 9:30am-12:30pm and 2-6pm; mid-Nov. to mid-Mar. M-F 10am-noon and 2-5pm, Sa-Su 10am-noon and 2-6pm. €5.50, students €3.50.) The firm of **Champagne Pommery,** 5 pl. du Général Gouraud, boasts the largest *tonneau* (vat) in the world. (☎03 26 61 62 56. Tours Apr.-Oct. daily 11am-7pm. €7, students €3.50.) For good deals on champagne, look for sales on local brands and check prices at Monoprix. Good bottles start at €9.15.

Trains (☎03 26 88 11 65) leave bd. Joffre for Paris (1½hr., 11 per day, €18.75). To get from the train station to the **tourist office,** 2 r. Guillaume de Machault, follow the right-hand curve of the rotary to pl. Drouet d'Erlon, turn left onto r. de Vesle, turn right on r. du Tresor, and it's on the left before the cathedral. (☎03 26 77 45 25; fax 03 26 77 45 27. Open mid-Apr. to mid-Oct. M-Sa 9am-7pm, Su 10am-6pm; mid-Oct. to mid-Apr. M-Sa 9am-6pm, Su 10am-5pm.) Inexpensive hotels cluster west of pl. Drouet d'Erlon, above the cathedral, and near the *mairie.* The sunny and spotless **Au Bon Accueil ❷,** 31 r. Thillois, is just off the central pl. d'Erlon. (☎03 26 88 55 74; fax 03 26 05 12 38. Breakfast €4.50. Reception 24hr. Reserve ahead. Singles €18-21; doubles €36-44. MC/V.) **Place Drouet d'Erlon** is crowded with cafes, restaurants, and bars. Relax at **Le Kraft ❸,** 5 r. Salin, which includes restaurant, bar, and lounge. (☎03 26 05 29 29. Open M-F 11am-3am, Sa 6pm-3am.) **Monoprix supermarket** is at r. de Vesle and r. de Talleyrand. (Open M-Sa 8:30am-9pm.) **Postal Code:** 51100.

⚑ DAYTRIP FROM REIMS: ÉPERNAY. Épernay, at the juncture of three wealthy grape-growing regions, is appropriately ritzy. **Avenue de Champagne** is distinguished by its palatial mansions, lush gardens, and swanky champagne firms. Both tours below offer a *petite dégustation* for those over 16. **Moët & Chandon,** 20 av. de Champagne, produces the king of all wines: **Dom Perignon.** (☎03 26 51 20 20. Open Apr. 1-Nov. 11 daily 9:30-11:30am and 2-4:30pm; Nov. 12-Mar. M-F only. 1hr. tour with one glass €6.) Ten minutes away is **Mercier,** 70 av. de Champagne, the self-proclaimed "most popular champagne in France," who gives tours in roller-coaster-like cars. (☎03 26 51 22 22. Open Mar.-Nov. M-F 9:30-11:30am and 2-4:30pm, Sa-Su 9:30-11:30am and 2-5pm; Dec. 1-19 and Jan. 13-Feb. Th-M only. 30min. tours €4.) **Trains** leave cour de la Gare for Paris (1¼hr., 18 per day, €16.60) and Reims (25min., 16 per day, €5.20). From the station, walk straight ahead through pl. Mendès France, go one block up r. Gambetta to the central **Place de la République,** and turn left on av. de Champagne to reach the **tourist office,** 7 av. de Champagne. (☎03 26 53 33 00. Open Easter-Oct. 15 M-Sa 9:30am-noon and 1:30-7pm, Su 11am-4pm; Oct. 16-Easter M-Sa 9:30am-5:30pm.) **Postal Code:** 51200.

TROYES

While the city plan of Troyes resembles a champagne cork, this city shares little with its grape-crazy northern neighbors. Gothic churches, 16th-century mansions, and an abundance of museums attest to the city's colorful role in French history, dating back to the Middle Ages. The **Musée d'Art Moderne,** on pl. St-Pierre, has over 2000 modern works by French artists, including Rodin, Degas, and Seurat. (Open Tu-Su 11am-6pm. €6, students €0.80; W free.) Cinemas and pool halls rub elbows with chic boutiques on **Rue Emile Zola**. On warm evenings, *Troyens* fill the cafes and taverns of **Rues Champeaux** and **Mole** near pl. Alexandre Israel.

Trains run from av. Maréchal Joffre to Paris (1½hr., 14 per day, €8.60) and Mulhouse (3hr., 9 per day, €31.80). The **tourist office**, 16 bd. Carnot, near the station, helps reserve rooms. (☎03 25 82 62 70; www.tourisme-troyes.fr. Open M-Sa 9am-12:30pm and 2-6:30pm.) ◼**Les Comtes de Champagne ❸**, 56 r. de la Monnaie, sports large and airy rooms. (☎25 73 11 70; fax 25 73 06 02. Reception 7am-10:30pm. Call ahead. Singles €25-31; doubles €28-34; triples €44-55; quads €49-58.) **Camping Municipal ❶**, 2km from Troyes, on N60, has showers and laundry. Take bus #1 (dir.: Pont St-Marie) and ask to be let off at the campground. (☎03 25 81 02 64. €4 per person, €4.60 per tent or car. Open Apr. to mid-Oct.) *Crêperies* and inexpensive eateries lie near **Rue Champeaux**, in *quartier* St-Jean, and on **Rue de la Cité**, near the cathedral. You can stock up at **Monoprix supermarket**, 78 r. Emile Zola. (Open M-Sa 8:30am-8pm.) **Postal Code:** 10000.

⚡ DAYTRIPS FROM TROYES: LES GRANDS LACS. About 30km from Troyes are the freshwater lakes of the **Forêt d'Orient. Lake Orient** welcomes sunbathers, swimmers, and windsurfers; **Lake Temple** is reserved for fishing and bird-watching; and **Lake Amance** roars with speedboats from **Port Dierville**. The **Comité Départmental du Tourisme de l'Aube,** 34 quai Dampierre, provides information on hotels and restaurants. (☎03 25 42 50 00; fax 03 25 42 50 88. Open M-F 8:45am-noon and 1:30-6pm.) The Troyes tourist office has bus schedules for routes to the Grands Lacs.

LILLE

A longtime international hub with a rich Flemish ancestry and exuberant nightlife, Lille (pop. 175,000) exudes big-city charm without the hassle. The impressive ◼**Musée des Beaux-Arts**, on pl. de la République (M: République), boasts a wide display of 15th- to 20th-century French and Flemish masters. (☎03 20 06 78 00. Open M 2-6pm, W-Th and Sa-Su 10am-6pm, F 10am-7pm. €4.60, students €3.05.) The **Musée d'Art Moderne**, 1 allée du Musée, in the suburb of Villeneuve d'Ascq, showcases Cubist and postmodern art, including works by Braque, Picasso, Léger, Miró, and Modigliani. Take the tram (dir.: 4 Cantons) to Pont du Bois, then take bus #41 (dir.: Villeneuve d'Ascq) to Parc Urbain-Musée. (☎03 20 19 68 68. Open W-M 10am-6pm; free 1st Su of every month 10am-2pm. €6.55, students €1.55.) The **Vieille Bourse** (Old Stock Exchange), on pl. Général de Gaulle, epitomizing the Flemish Renaissance, houses flower and book markets. (Markets Tu-Su 9:30am-7:30pm.) Head down r. de Paris for the 14th- to 19th-century **Eglise St-Maurice.** (M: Rihour. Open M-F 7:15am-7pm, Sa 8am-7pm.)

Trains leave from **Gare Lille Flandres,** on pl. de la Gare (M: Gare Lille Flandres), for Brussels, Belgium (1½hr., 20 per day, €21) and Paris (1hr., 21 per day, €32-46). **Gare Lille Europe,** on r. Le Corbusier (M: Gare Lille Europe; ☎03 36 35 35 35), sends **Eurostar** trains to London, Brussels, and Paris and all **TGVs** to the south of France and Paris. From Gare Lille Flandres, walk straight down r. Faidherbe and turn left through pl. du Théâtre and pl. de Gaulle; behind the huge war monument is the castle housing the **tourist office**, pl. Rihour (M: Rihour), which offers free maps and currency exchange. (☎03 20 21 94 21; fax 03 20 21 94 20. Open M-Sa 9:30am-6:30pm, Su 10am-noon and 2-5pm.) To reach the **Auberge de Jeunesse (HI) ❶**, 12 r. Malpart (M: Mairie de Lille), from Gare Lille Flandres, circle left around the station, turn right onto r. du Molinel, take the second left on r. de Paris, and take the 3rd right onto r. Malpart. (☎03 20 57 08 94; fax 03 20 63 98 93. Breakfast included. Sheets €2.75. Reception 7am-noon and 2pm-1am. Check-out 10:30am. Curfew 2am. Open Feb.-Dec. 17. 3- to 6-bed dorms €11.45; deposit of ID or €7.65 required.) The spotless **Hôtel Faidherbe ❸**, 42 pl. de la Gare (M: Gare Lille Flandres), is noise-proof. (☎03 20 06 27 93; fax 03 20 55 95 38. Reception 24hr. Singles and doubles €26-40. 10% discount with *Let's Go.* AmEx/MC/V.) Restaurants and markets line **rue de Béthune** and **rue Léon Gambetta.** Pubs and bars line **Rue Solférino** and **rue Masséna.** The intimate 🔳**Le Clave,** 31 r. Massena, serves tropical drinks (from €3.85) and Afro-Cuban jazz. (☎03 20 30 09 61.) A huge **Carrefour supermarket** is next to the Eurostar train station. (Open M-Sa 9am-10pm.) **Postal Code:** 59000.

🔼 DAYTRIPS FROM LILLE: ARRAS AND VIMY. The town hall of **Arras,** housed in the gorgeous **Hôtel de Ville,** is built over the eerie **Les Boves** tunnels, which have sheltered both medieval chalk miners and British WWI soldiers (€3.85, students €2.30). The lively **Place des Héros** has bars and cafes. **Trains** leave pl. Maréchal Foch for Lille (45min., 20 per day, €8.80). From the train station, walk across pl. Foch to r. Gambetta, turn left on r. Desire Delansorne, turn left, and walk two blocks to reach the **tourist office,** on pl. des Héros, in the Hôtel de Ville. (☎03 21 51 26 95. Open May-Sept. M-Sa 9am-6:30pm, Su 10am-1pm and 2:30-6:30pm; Oct.-Apr. M-Sa 9am-noon and 2-6pm, Su 10am-12:30pm and 3-6:30pm.) Stay at the central **Auberge de Jeunesse (HI) ❶,** 59 Grand'Place. (☎03 21 22 70 02; fax 03 21 07 46 15. Reception 8am-noon and 5-11pm. Curfew 11pm. Open Feb.-Nov. Dorms €8.)

The countryside surrounding Arras is dotted with war cemeteries and unmarked graves. The vast limestone **Vimy Memorial,** 12km from Arras, honors the more than 66,000 Canadians killed in WWI. The morbidly beautiful park, whose soil came from Canada, is dedicated to the crucial victory at Vimy Ridge in April 1917. The kiosk by the trenches is the starting point for an **underground tour** of the crumbling tunnels dug by British and Canadian soldiers. (☎03 21 59 19 34. Memorial open dawn-dusk. Free tunnel tours Apr. to mid-Nov. 10am-6pm.) The closest town, **Vimy,** is 3km away. **Buses** run from Arras to Vimy (20min., 8 per day, €2.40).

CALAIS

Calais (pop. 80,000) is the liveliest of the Channel ports, and with the Chunnel next door, English is spoken as often as French. Rodin's famous sculpture **The Burghers of Calais** stands in front of the **Hôtel de Ville,** at the juncture of bd. Jacquard and r. Royale. Follow r. Royale to the end of r. de Mer for Calais's wide, gorgeous **beaches.** For schedules and prices to **Dover,** England, see p. 52. During the day, free **buses** connect the ferry terminal and train station, **Gare Calais-Ville,** on bd. Jacquard, from which **trains** leave for: Boulogne (45min., 8 per day, €6.30); Lille (1¼hr., 8 per day, €13.40); Paris-Nord (3¼hr., 6 per day, €40). To reach the **tourist office,** 12 bd. Clemenceau, from the train station, turn left, cross the bridge, and it's on your right. (☎03 21 96 62 40; fax 03 21 96 01 92. Open M-Sa 9am-7pm, Su 10am-1pm.) **Morning markets** are held on pl. Crèvecoeur (Th and Sa) and on pl. d'Armes (W and Sa); or look for **Prisunic,** 17 bd. Jacquard. (Open M-Sa 8:30am-7:30pm, Su 10am-7pm.) The renovated **Centre Européen de Séjour/Auberge de Jeunesse (HI) ❶,** av. Maréchal Delattre de Tassigny, is near the beach. (☎21 34 70 20. Dorms €14.50.) The quiet **Hotel Bristol ❸,** 13-15 r. du Duc de Guise, is off the main road. (☎03 21 34 53 24. Singles and doubles €31-36. MC/V.) **Postal Code:** 62100.

BOULOGNE-SUR-MER

With its refreshing sea breeze and lavish floral displays, Boulogne is by far the most attractive Channel port. The huge **Château-Musée,** r. de Bernet, houses an eclectic art collection that includes Napoleon's second-oldest hat. (☎03 21 10 02 20. Open M and W-Sa 10am-12:30pm and 2-5pm, Su 10am-12:30pm and 2:30-5:30pm. €3.05.) Just down r. de Lille, the 19th-century **Basilique de Notre-Dame** sits above 12th-century labyrinthine crypts. (Open Apr. to mid-Sept. daily 9am-noon and 2-6pm; mid-Sept. to Mar. 10am-noon and 2-5pm. Crypt open M-Sa 2-5pm, Su

2:30-5pm. €1.55.) **Trains** leave **Gare Boulogne-Ville,** bd. Voltaire, for: Calais (30min., 18 per day, €6.40); Lille (2½hr., 11 per day, €16.50); Paris-Nord (2-3hr., 11 per day, €26-45). From the train station, turn right on bd. Voltaire, turn left on bd. Danou and follow it to pl. Angleterre; continue past pl. de France and pl. Frédéric Sauvage onto r. Gambetta and look right for the **tourist office,** 24 quai Gambetta. (☎03 21 10 88 10; fax 03 21 10 88 11. Open July-Aug. M-Sa 9am-7pm, Su 10am-1pm and 3-6pm; Sept.-June reduced hours.) The fantastic **Auberge de Jeunesse (HI) ❶,** 56 pl. Rouget de Lisle, is across from the station. (☎03 21 99 15 30; fax 03 21 80 45 62. Breakfast included. Internet €4.60 per 30min. Reception 8am-1am; in winter until midnight. Curfew 1am. Bunks €13; nonmembers €3 extra per night up to 6 nights. MC/V.) **Champion supermarket,** on r. Daunou, is in the Centre Commercial de la Liane mall. (Open M-Sa 8:30am-8pm.) **Postal Code:** 62200.

GERMANY (DEUTSCHLAND)

Germany is a nation saddled with an incredibly fractured past. Steeped deeply in Beethoven's fiery orchestration and Goethe's Faustian whirlwind, modern Germany must also contend with the legacy of xenophobia and genocide left by Hitler and the Third Reich. Even now, more than a decade after the fall of the Berlin Wall, Germans are still fashioning a new identity for themselves. After centuries of war and fragmentation, Germany finds itself a wealthy nation at the forefront of both European and global politics. Its medieval castles, snow-covered mountains, and funky metropolises make Germany well worth a visit.

FACTS AND FIGURES

Official Name: Federal Republic of Germany.

Capital: Berlin.

Major Cities: Munich, Frankfurt, Cologne, Hamburg.

Population: 83,030,000.

Land Area: 357,021 sq. km.

Time Zone: GMT + 1.

Language: German.

Religions: Protestant (38%), Roman Catholic (34%), Muslim (1.7%), unaffiliated or other (26.3%).

DISCOVER GERMANY

The myriad cultural and historical treasures of **Berlin** (p. 412), not to mention its chaotic nightlife, sprawl over an area eight times the size of Paris. **Dresden** (p. 432) is nearly as intense, with a jumping nightlife and exquisite palaces and museums. To the north, reckless **Hamburg** (p. 441), Germany's second-largest city, fuses the burliness of a port town with cosmopolitan flair, while **Cologne** (p. 449) is home to Germany's largest, most poignant cathedral and pounding nightlife. **Koblenz** (p. 457), to the south, is the gateway to the castles and wine towns of the **Rhine Valley.** Germany's oldest and most prestigious university sits below the ruins of a castle in **Heidelberg** (p. 459). From there, live out your favorite Grimms' fairy tales in the **Black Forest** (p. 463) or conquer the **Romantic Road** (p. 478), which snakes along the western edge of Bavaria. No trip to Germany would be complete without visiting the Bavarian capital of **Munich** (p. 465), which takes bucolic merriment to a frothy head with its excellent museums and jovial beer halls.

ESSENTIALS

WHEN TO GO

Germany's climate is temperate, with rain year-round (especially in summer). The cloudy, temperate months of May, June, and September are the best time to go, as there are fewer tourists and the weather is pleasant. Germans head to vacation spots en masse in early July with the onset of school vacations. Winter sports gear up November to April; skiing high-season is mid-December to March.

DOCUMENTS AND FORMALITIES

VISAS. Germany requires visas of South Africans, but not of nationals of Australia, Canada, the EU, New Zealand, or the US for stays of less than 90 days.

EMBASSIES. All foreign embassies are in Berlin (p. 412). German embassies at home include: **Australia,** 119 Empire Circuit, Yarralumla, Canberra, ACT 2600 (☎(02) 62 70 19 11); **Canada,** 1 Waverly St., Ottawa, ON K2P OT8 (☎(613) 232-1101); **Ireland,** 31 Trimleston Ave., Booterstown, Blackrock, Co. Dublin (☎(01) 269

In August 2002, extreme weather conditions caused massive flooding along the Elbe and Danube, especially in eastern Germany, surrounding **Dresden,** and its neighbors further east. As of press time, the ultimate extent of the damage was not known. Many establishments we list may have been forced to shut down or may have altered opening times; additionally, train routes may be disrupted or changed. Make sure to check ahead thoroughly: call hostels and hotels in advance, and confirm the feasibility of your itinerary with Germany's National Tourist Board (www.germany-tourism.de).

30 11); **New Zealand,** 90-92 Hobson St., Thorndon, Wellington (☎(04) 473 60 63); **South Africa,** 180 Blackwood St., Arcadia, Pretoria, 0083 (☎(012) 427 89 00); **UK,** 23 Belgrave Sq., London SW1X 8PZ (☎(020) 7824 1300); and **US,** 4645 Reservoir Rd., Washington, D.C. 20007 (☎202-298-4393).

TRANSPORTATION

BY PLANE. Most flights land in Frankfurt; Berlin, Munich, and Hamburg also have international airports. **Lufthansa,** the national airline, has the most flights in and out of the country, but they're not always the cheapest option. Flying within Germany is usually more expensive and less convenient than taking the train.

BY TRAIN. The **Deutsche Bahn (DB)** network (in Germany ☎(0180) 599 66 33; www.bahn.de) is Europe's best but also one of its most expensive. **RE** (Regional-Express) and the slightly slower **RB** (RegionalBahn) trains include a number of rail networks between neighboring cities. **IR** (InterRegio) trains, covering larger networks between cities, are speedy and comfortable. **D** trains are foreign trains that serve international routes. **EC** (EuroCity) and **IC** (InterCity) trains zoom along between major cities every hour from 6am-10pm. You must purchase a **Zuschlag** (supplement) for IC or EC trains (€3.60). **ICE** (InterCityExpress) trains approach the luxury and kinetics of an airplane, running at speeds up to 280km per hour. On all trains, second-class compartments are clean and comfortable.

Designed for tourists, the **German Railpass** allows unlimited travel for four to 10 days within a four-week period. Non-Europeans can purchase German Railpasses in their home countries and—with a passport—in major German train stations (2nd-class 5-day €202, 10-day €316). The **German Rail Youth Pass** is for those under 26 (5-day €156, 9-day €216). The **Twin Pass** is for two adults traveling together (2nd-class 5-day €303, 10-day €474). Travelers ages 12-25 can purchase **TwenTickets,** which knock 20% off fares. A **Schönes-Wochenende-Ticket** (€21) gives up to five people unlimited travel on any of the slower trains (*not* ICE, IC, EC, D, or IR) from 12:01am Saturday or Sunday until 3am the next day. The **Guten-Abend-Ticket** allows travel anywhere (*not* on InterCityNight or CityNightLines) in Germany between 7pm (2pm Saturdays) and 3am (2nd-class €30; F-Su €8.10 extra).

BY BUS. Bus service between cities and to outlying areas runs from the local **Zentralomnibusbahnhof (ZOB),** which is usually close to the main train station. Buses are often slightly more expensive than trains for comparable distances. Railpasses are not valid on any buses other than a few run by Deutsche Bahn.

BY CAR. German road conditions are generally excellent. It's true, there is no set speed limit on the *Autobahn,* only a recommendation of 130kph (80mph). Germans drive fast. Watch for signs indicating right-of-way (usually designated by a yellow triangle). The *Autobahn* is indicated by an intuitive "A" on signs; secondary highways, where the speed limit is usually 100kph, are accompanied by signs bearing a "B." Germans drive on the right side of the road. In cities and towns, speed limits hover around 30-60kph (20-35mph). Germans use mainly unleaded gas; prices run around €4.30 per gallon, or €1.10 per liter. **Mitfahrzentralen** are agencies that pair up drivers and riders for a small fee; riders then negotiate payment for the trip with the driver.

BY BIKE. Cities and towns usually have designated bike lanes and biking maps. *Germany by Bike*, by Nadine Slavinski (Mountaineers Books, 1994; US$15), details 20 tours throughout the country.

TOURIST SERVICES AND MONEY

EMERGENCY	Police: ☎110. Ambulance and Fire: ☎112.

TOURIST OFFICES. Every city in Germany has a tourist office, usually near the *Hauptbahnhof* (main train station) or *Marktplatz* (central square). All are marked by a thick lowercase "i" sign. Many offices book rooms for a small fee. The tourist information website for Germany is www.germany-tourism.de.

MONEY. On January 1, 2002, the **euro** (€) replaced the **deutsche Mark** or **Deutschmark** (abbreviated DM) as the unit of currency in Germany. For more information, see p. 16. As a general rule it's cheaper to exchange money in Germany than at home. If you stay in hostels and prepare your own food, expect to spend anywhere from €20-40 per person per day. Tipping is not practiced as liberally in Germany as elsewhere—most Germans just round up €1. Note that tips in Germany are not left lying on the table, but handed directly to the server when you pay. If you don't want any change, say *"Das stimmt so"* (das SHTIMMT zo). Germans rarely bargain except at flea markets. Most goods and services bought in Germany will automatically include a **Value Added Tax (VAT)**; see p. 15 for more information.

COMMUNICATION

PHONE CODES	Country code: 49. International dialing prefix: 00.

TELEPHONES. Most public phones accept only telephone cards. You can pick up a *Telefonkarte* (phone card) in post offices, at kiosks, or at selected Deutsche Bahn counters in major train stations. There is no standard length for telephone numbers. The smaller the city, the more digits in the city code, while individual phone numbers have between three and ten digits. International direct dial numbers include: **AT&T,** ☎800 22 55 288; **British Telecom,** ☎800 89 00 49; **Canada Direct,** ☎800 888 00 14; **Ireland Direct,** ☎08000 800 353; **MCI,** ☎800 88 88 000; **Sprint,** ☎800 888 00 13; **Telecom New Zealand,** ☎800 080 00 64; **Telkom South Africa,** ☎800 180 00 27; **Telstra Australia,** ☎800 08 00 061.

MAIL. Mail can be sent via Poste Restante *(Postlagernde Briefe)* to almost any German city or town with a post office. The mail will go to the main post office unless you specify a post office by street address or postal code. Air mail usually takes 3-7 days to North America, Europe, and Australia; 6-12 days to New Zealand.

INTERNET ACCESS. Most German cities (as well as a surprising number of smaller towns) have at least one Internet cafe with web access for about €1-5 per 30minutes. Some German universities have banks of computers hooked up to the Internet in their libraries, though ostensibly for student use.

LANGUAGE. Many people in Western Germany speak English; this is less common in the East. The letter ß is equivalent to a double *s*. For basic German words and phrases, see p. 1057.

ACCOMMODATIONS AND CAMPING

GERMANY	❶	❷	❸	❹	❺
ACCOMMODATIONS	under €14	€14-19	€20-35	€36-60	over €60

Germany currently has about 600 **hostels**—more than any other nation on Earth. Hostelling in Germany is overseen by **Deutsches Jugendherbergswerk (DJH)**, Bismarckstr. 8, 32756 Detmold, Germany (☎(05231) 740 10; www.djh.de). DJH has recently initiated a growing number of **Jugendgästehäuser**, youth guest houses that have more facilities and attract slightly older guests. DJH publishes *Jugendherbergen in Deutschland*, a guide to all federated German hostels. The cheapest **hotel-style** accommodations are places with *Pension, Gasthof, Gästehaus*, or *Hotel-Garni* in the name. Hotel rooms start at €20 for singles and €25 for doubles; in large cities, expect to pay nearly twice as much. *Frühstück* (breakfast) is almost always available and often included. The best bet for a cheap bed is often a **Privatzimmer** (a room in a family home). This option works best if you have a rudimentary knowledge of German. Prices generally run €15-30 per person. Travelers over 26 who would pay higher prices at youth hostels will find these rooms within budget range. Reservations are made through the local tourist office or through a private *Zimmervermittlung* (room-booking office) for free or a €1-4 fee. Germans love **camping;** over 2600 campsites dot the outskirts of even the most major cities. Facilities are well maintained and usually provide showers, bathrooms, and a restaurant or store. Camping costs €3-6 per person, with additional charges for tents and vehicles. Blue signs with a black tent on a white background indicate official sites. **Deutscher Camping-Club (DCC)**, Mandlstr. 28, 80802 München (☎(089) 380 14 20), has more information, and the National Tourist Office distributes a free map, *Camping in Germany*.

FOOD AND DRINK

GERMANY	❶	❷	❸	❹	❺
FOOD	under €4	€4-6	€7-12	€13-20	over €20

The typical German breakfast consists of coffee or tea with *Brötchen* (rolls), *Wurst* (cold sausage), and *Käse* (cheese). The main meal of the day, *Mittagessen* (lunch), includes soup, broiled sausage or roasted meat, potatoes or dumplings, and a salad or vegetable side dish. *Abendessen* or *Abendbrot* (dinner) is a reprise of breakfast, only beer replaces coffee and the selection of meats and cheese is wider. Many older Germans indulge in a daily ritual of *Kaffee und Kuchen* (coffee and cakes) at 3 or 4pm. To eat on the cheap, stick to the daily *Tagesmenü*, buy food in supermarkets, or, if you have a student ID, head to a university *Mensa* (cafeteria). Fast-food *Imbiß* stands also provide cheap fare; try the delicious Turkish *Döner*, something like a gyro. The average German beer is maltier and more "bread-like" than Czech, Dutch, or American beers; an affectionate German slang term for beer is *Flüßige Brot* ("liquid bread").

HOLIDAYS AND FESTIVALS

Holidays: Epiphany (Jan. 6); Good Friday (Apr. 18); Easter Sunday and Monday (Apr. 20-21); Labor Day (May 1); Ascension Day (May 29); Whit Sunday (June 8); Whit Monday (June 9); Corpus Christi (June 19); Assumption Day (Aug. 15); Day of German Unity (Oct. 3); All Saints' Day (Nov. 1); Christmas (Dec. 25-26).

Festivals: Check out **Fasching** in Munich (Jan. 7-Mar. 4; see p. 465), the **Berlinale Film Festival** (Feb. 5-16; see p. 428), **Karneval** in Cologne (Feb. 27-Mar. 3; see p. 452), **Christopher St. Day** in Berlin and other major cities (late June to early July), the **Love Parade** in Berlin (late July; see p. 429), **Oktoberfest** in Munich (Sept. 20-Oct. 5; see p. 465), and the **Christmas Market** in Nuremberg.

BERLIN   ☎030

Don't wait any longer to see Berlin. The city is nearing the end of a massive transitional phase, developing from a newly reunited metropolis reeling in the aftermath of the Cold War to an epicenter of the European Union—and the Berlin of five or even two years into the future will be radically different from Berlin of today. Germany is the industrial leader of the continent, and when the *Lehrter Stadtbahnhof* (Europe's largest train station) opens in 2004, the capital city will essentially become the capital of Europe. Berlin, itself, however, is not built around a single center but around many colorfully varied neighborhoods. As a result, the atmosphere is the most diverse and tolerant of any of Germany's cities, with a world-famous gay and lesbian scene and an almost-non-existent racial crime rate. Indeed the concept of a divided city is quite familiar to Berliners; the still-existing feelings of a division between East and West Germany is more prevalent here than anywhere else. Combined with the lasting effects of the Nazi regime, Germans question their own ability—and right—to govern. No other city is currently poised to attain such geopolitical importance, and the air is taut with hope and foreboding.

✖ INTERCITY TRANSPORTATION

Berlin is rapidly becoming the hub of the international rail network, with rail and air connections to most other European capitals. Almost all European airlines have service to one of Berlin's three airports.

Flights: For information on all 3 airports, call ☎(0180) 500 01 86. Currently, the city is making the transition from 3 airports to 1 (Flughafen Schönefeld), but for now, **Flughafen Tegel** (TXL) will remain western Berlin's main airport. Take express bus #X9 from Bahnhof Zoo, bus #109 from Jakob-Kaiser-Pl. on U7, bus #128 from Kurt-Schumacher-Pl. on U6, or bus TXL from Potsdamer Pl. **Flughafen Tempelhof** (THF), Berlin's smallest airport, has flights within Germany and Europe. U6 to Pl. der Luftbrücke. **Flughafen Schönefeld** (SXF), southeast of Berlin, has intercontinental flights. S45 or 9 to Flughafen Berlin Schönefeld.

Train Stations: Trains to and from Berlin are serviced by **Zoologischer Garten** (almost always called **Bahnhof Zoo**) in the West and **Ostbahnhof** (formerly the *Hauptbahnhof*) in the East. Most trains go to both stations, but some connections to cities in the former GDR only stop at *Ostbahnhof*. For **info,** call ☎(0180) 599 66 33 or visit www.bahn.de. Trains run to: **Cologne** (4¼hr., every hr., €98); **Dresden** (2¼hr., every 2hr., €22); **Frankfurt** (4hr., every hr., €106); **Hamburg** (2½hr., every hr., €45); **Leipzig** (2-2¾hr., every hr., €26-34); **Munich** (6½-7hr., every hr., €102). **International connections** to most major European cities. Times and prices change frequently—check at the train stations.

Buses: ZOB, the central bus station (☎301 03 80), is by the *Funkturm* near Kaiserdamm. U2 to Kaiserdamm or S4, 45, or 46 to Witzleben. Open daily 6:30am-9pm. Check *Zitty* and *Tip* for deals on long-distance buses, or call **Gulliver's** travel agency, Hardenbergpl. 14 (☎311 02 11 or 00800 4855 4837), at the far end of the bus parking lot in Bahnhof Zoo. Open M-F 8am-8pm, Sa-Su 10am-8pm. To **Paris** (14hr., €59) and **Vienna** (10½hr., €49).

Mitfahrzentralen (Ride Sharing): *Let's Go* does not recommend ride sharing as a safe mode of transportation. **City Netz,** Joachimstaler Str. 17 (☎ 194 44; fax 882 44 20) has a computerized ride-share database. U9 or 15 to Kurfürstendamm. To: **Frankfurt** or **Munich** (€18); **Hamburg** or **Hannover** (€16). Open M-F 9am-8pm, Sa-Su 9am-7pm. **Mitfahr2000,** Yorckstr. 52 (☎ 194 20 00; www.mitfahr.de) is a ride sharing service for gays and lesbians. Open daily 8am-8pm.

ORIENTATION

Berlin is an *immense* conglomeration of what were once two separate and unique cities. The former East contains most of Berlin's landmarks and historic sites, as well as an unfortunate number of concrete socialist architectural experiments. The former West functioned for decades as a small, isolated, Allied-occupied state and is still the commercial heart of united Berlin. The situation is rapidly changing, however, as businesses and embassies move their headquarters to Potsdamer Pl. and Mitte in the East.

The vast **Tiergarten,** Berlin's beloved park, lies in the center of the city; the grand, tree-lined **Straße des 17. Juni** runs through it from west to east and becomes **Unter den Linden** at the **Brandenburg Gate.** North of the Gate is the **Reichstag,** while south of the Gate **Ebertstraße** winds to glitzy **Potsdamer Platz.** Unter den Linden continues east through **Mitte,** location of countless historical sites. The street changes names once again, to **Karl-Liebknecht-Straße,** before emptying into **Alexanderplatz,** home to Berlin's most visible landmark, the **Fernsehturm** (TV tower). At the east end of Mitte is **Museumsinsel** (Museum Island). Cafe- and shop-lined **Oranienburgerstraße** cuts through the area of northeastern Mitte known as **Scheunenviertel,** historically the center of Berlin's Jewish life.

The commercial district of West Berlin lies at the southwest end of the Tiergarten, centered around **Bahnhof Zoo** and the **Kurfürstendamm** (**Ku'damm** for short). To the east is **Charlottenburg,** home to many cafes, restaurants, *Pensionen,* and pleasant squares including **Breitscheidplatz,** which is marked by the bombed-out **Kaiser-Wilhelm-Gedächtniskirche,** and **Savignyplatz.** Southeast of the Ku'damm, **Schöneberg** is a residential neighborhood and the traditional nexus of the city's gay and lesbian community. At the southeast periphery of Berlin lies **Kreuzberg,** a district home to an exciting mix of radical leftists and punks as well as a large Turkish population. Northeast of the city is **Prenzlauer Berg,** a former working-class area, and east of Mitte is **Friedrichshain,** the center of Berlin's counterculture and nightlife.

If you're planning to stay more than a few days, the **Falk Plan** (available at most kiosks and bookstores) is an indispensable city map that includes a street index and unfolds like a book (€6.50). Dozens of streets and subway stations in Eastern Berlin were named after Communist figures. Many, but not all, have been renamed in a process only recently completed; be sure that your map is up-to-date.

LOCAL TRANSPORTATION

Public Transportation: It is impossible to tour Berlin on foot, but the extensive **U-Bahn** (subway) and **S-Bahn** (surface rail) systems will take you anywhere. The city is divided into 3 transit zones. **Zone A** encompasses central Berlin, including Tempelhof Airport. Almost everything else falls into **Zone B,** while **Zone C** contains the outlying areas, including Potsdam. An **AB ticket** is the best deal, as you can buy regional Bahn tickets for the outlying areas. A single ticket for the combined network (Eizelfahrschein AB or BC, €2.10; or Eizelfahrschein ABC, €2.45) is good for 2hr. after validation and may be used on any S-Bahn, U-Bahn, bus or streetcar. However, it almost always makes sense to buy a pass. A **Tageskarte** (AB €6, ABC €6.50) is valid from validation until 3am the next day.

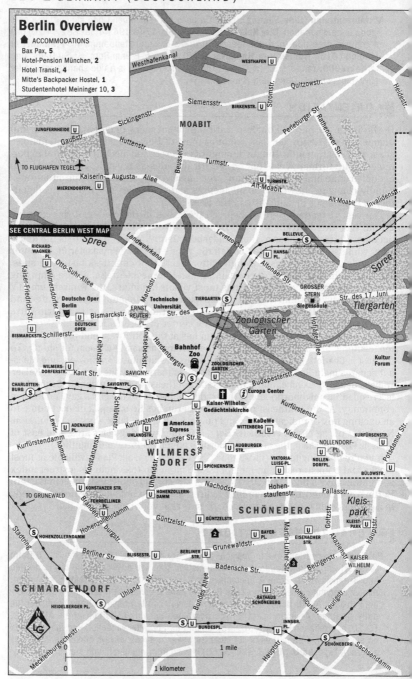

Berlin Overview

⌂ ACCOMMODATIONS

Bax Pax, **5**
Hotel-Pension München, **2**
Hotel Transit, **4**
Mitte's Backpacker Hostel, **1**
Studentenhotel Meininger 10, **3**

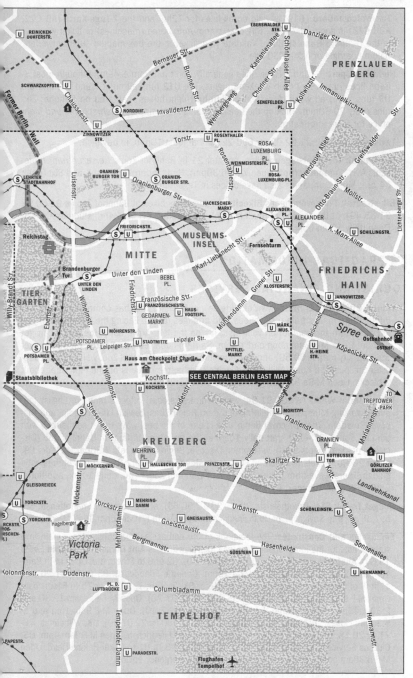

The **WelcomeCard** (€19) is valid on all lines for 72hr., and the **7-Tage-Karte** (AB €22, ABC €28) is good for 7 days. Buy tickets from *Automaten* (machines) or ticket windows in the U- and S-Bahn stations. Validate your ticket in the box marked "Hier entwerfen" before boarding or risk a €30 fine.

Night Transport: U- and S-Bahn lines generally don't run from 1-4am, although most S-Bahn lines run every hr. on weekend nights. The **U12** runs all night F and Sa, and the **U9** runs 24hr. all week. A system of **N-Bahn** (night buses) centered on Bahnhof Zoo runs every 20-30min.; pick up the free *Nachtliniennetz* map at a *Fahrscheine und Mehr* office for more information.

Taxis: ☎26 10 26, 21 02 02, or 690 22. Call at least 15min. in advance.

Car Rental: The **Mietwagenservice,** counter 21 in Bahnhof Zoo's *Reisezentrum,* represents Avis, Europacar (both open 7am-6:30pm), Hertz (open 7am-8pm), and Sixt (open 24 hr.). Most companies also have offices in Tegel Airport.

Bike Rental: The government's **Bikecity** program rents bikes at Bahnhof Zoo (☎01 60 98 21 35 49), at the far end of Hardenbergpl. €5 per 4hr., €8 per 24hr.; students €5/€3. Open daily 10am-6pm.

▓ PRACTICAL INFORMATION

TOURIST AND FINANCIAL SERVICES

Tourist Offices: ▓ **EurAide** (www.euraide.de), in Bahnhof Zoo, has comprehensive travel information, makes train reservations, and arranges rooms. Facing the Reisezentrum, go left and down the corridor on your right; it's on the left. Arrive early—the office can get packed. Open M-F 8am-noon and 1-4pm, Sa 8am-noon. **Europa-Center,** on Budapester Str., has city maps (€0.50) and free transit maps. From Bahnhof Zoo, walk along Budapester Str. past the Kaiser-Wilhelm-Gedächtniskirche; the office is on the right after about 2 blocks. Open M-Sa 8:30am-8:30pm, Su 10am-6:30pm.

Tours: Berlin Walks (☎301 91 94; www.berlinwalks.com) offers a range of English-language walking tours, including Infamous Third Reich Sites, Jewish Life in Berlin, and Discover Potsdam. Their Discover Berlin walk is one of the best ways to get acquainted with the city. Tours (2½-6hr.) start daily 10am at the taxi stand in front of Bahnhof Zoo (Discover Potsdam meets 9am); in summer, Discover Berlin also meets 2:30pm. All tours €9, under 26 €8. Tickets available at EurAide. **Insider Tour** (☎692 31 49) has enthusiastic guides. Tours leave from the McDonald's by Bahnhof Zoo. (4hr., daily 10am, additional 2:30pm tour in summer, €9.)

Budget Travel: STA, Dorotheenstr. 30, (☎20 16 50 63), at the corner of Charlottenstr. S3, 5, 7, 9, or 75 to Savignypl. or U6 to Friedrichstr. Open M, Th-F 10am-6pm, Tu-W 10am-8pm.

Embassies and Consulates: The locations of the embassies and consulates remain in a state of flux; for the latest information, call the **Auswärtiges Amt Dienststelle Berlin** (☎20 18 60). **Australia,** Friedrichstr. 200 (☎880 08 80). U2 or 6 to Stadtmitte. Open M-Th 8am-1pm and 2-5pm, F 8am-1pm and 2-4:15pm. **Canada,** Friedrichstr. 95 (☎20 31 20), on 12th fl. of the International Trade Center. U6 or S1, 2, 3, 5, 7, 9, 25, or 75 to Friedrichstr. Open M-F 9-11am. **Ireland,** Friedrichstr. 200 (☎22 07 20). Open M-F 9:30am-12:30 and 2:30-4:45pm. **New Zealand,** Friedrichstr. 60 (☎20 62 10). Open M-F 9am-1pm and 2-5:30pm; closes F 4:30pm. **South Africa,** Friedrichstr. 60 (☎22 07 30). Open M-F 9am-4pm. **UK,** Wilhelmstr. 70-71 (☎20 18 40). U6 or S1, 2, 3, 5, 7, 9, 25 or 75 to Friedrichstr. Open M-F 9am-4pm. **US,** Citizens Service/Consulate, Clayallee 170 (☎832 92 33). U1 to Oskar-Helene-Heim. Open M-F 8:30am-noon. After hours, call ☎830 50 for emergency advice.

GERMANY

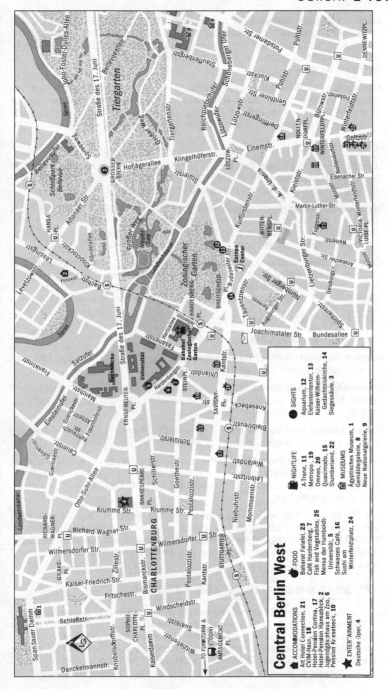

Central Berlin West

▲ ACCOMMODATIONS
Art Hotel Connection, **21**
CVJM-Haus, **18**
Hotel-Pension Cortina, **17**
Hotel-Pension Hansablick, **2**
Jugendgästehaus am Zoo, **6**
Pension Kresebeck, **10**

★ ENTERTAINMENT
Deutsche Oper, **4**

● FOOD
Baharat Falafel, **23**
Café Hardenberg, **7**
Fish and Vegetables, **25**
Mensa der Humboldt-
  Universität, **5**
Schwarzes Café, **16**
Sushi am
  Winterfeldtplatz, **24**

● NIGHTLIFE
A-Trane, **11**
Metropo, **19**
Omnes, **20**
Quasimodo, **15**
Slumberland, **22**

🏛 MUSEUMS
Ägyptisches Museum, **1**
Gemäldegalerie, **8**
Neue Nationalgalerie, **9**

● SIGHTS
Aquarium, **12**
Elefantentor, **13**
Kaiser-Wilhelm-
  Gedächtniskirche, **14**
Siegessäule, **3**

TO FUNKTURM &
(☐ ("00m))

Currency Exchange: Geldwechsel, Joachimstaler Str. 1-3 (☎882 63 71), has decent rates and no commission. Open M-F 9am-7pm, Sa 10am-3pm. **ReiseBank,** at Bahnhof Zoo (☎881 71 17; open daily 7:30am-10pm) and *Ostbahnhof* (☎296 43 93; open M-F 7am-10pm, Sa 8am-8pm, Su 8am-12pm and 12:30-4pm), is conveniently located but has worse rates.

American Express: Main Office, Bayreuther Str. 37 (☎21 49 83 63). U1, 2, or 15 to Wittenbergpl. Holds mail and cashes AmEx Traveler's Cheques with no commission. Long lines F-Sa. Open M-F 9am-7pm, Sa 10am-1pm. **Branch office,** Friedrichstr. 172 (☎20 17 40 12). U6 to Französischer Str. Offers the same services and same hours.

LOCAL SERVICES

Luggage Storage: In **Bahnhof Zoo.** Lockers €0.50-2 per day. 72hr. max. If all lockers are full, try **Gepäckaufbewahrung,** the next window over (€2 per piece per day). Open daily 6:15am-10:30pm. 24hr. lockers at **Ostbahnhof** and **Alexanderpl.**

Bi-Gay-Lesbian Resources: Lesbenberatung, Kulmer Str. 20a (☎215 20 00), offers counseling on lesbian issues. U7 to Kleistpark. Open M-Tu and Th 4-7pm, F 2-5pm. **Mann-o-Meter,** Motzstr. 5 (☎216 80 08), off Nollendorfpl., gives out info on gay nightlife and living arrangements. Open M-F 5-10pm, Sa-Su 4-10pm.

Laundromat: Waschcenter Schnell und Sauber, Leibnizstr. 72 in **Charlottenburg** (S3, 5, 7, 9, or 75 to Savignypl.); Wexstr. 34 in **Schöneberg** (U9 to Bundespl.); Mehringdamm 32 in **Kreuzberg** (U6 or 7 to Mehringdamm); Torstr. 115 in **Mitte** (U8 to Rosenthaler Pl.). Wash €2-4; dry €0.50 per 15min. All open daily 6am-11pm.

EMERGENCY AND COMMUNICATIONS

Police: ☎110. **Ambulance and Fire:** ☎112.

Disabled Resources: Berliner Behindertenverband, ☎20 43 847. Info and advice for the handicapped. Open M-F 8am-4pm.

Pharmacies: Europa-Apotheke, Tauentzienstr. 9-12 (☎261 41 42), near the Europa Center and Bahnhof Zoo. Open M-F 9am-8pm, Sa 9am-4pm. Closed pharmacies post signs directing you to the nearest open one.

Medical Assistance: American and British embassies have a list of English-speaking doctors. **Emergency Doctor,** ☎31 00 31. Open 24hr.

Internet Access: Easy Everything, on the corner of Kurfürstendamm and Meineckestr. €1 per 25min. Open 24hr. **ComLine,** Innsbrückerstr. 56, in Schöneberg. €1 per hr. Open 24hr. **Alpha,** Duncherstr. 72, in Prenzlauer Berg. U2 to Eberswalder Str. €4 per hr. Open daily 2pm-midnight.

Post Offices: Joachimstaler Str. 7, down the street from Bahnhof Zoo, near the intersection with Kantstr. Address mail to be held: Firstname, SURNAME, Postlagernde, Postamt in der Joachimstaler Str. 7, **10706** Berlin. Open M-Sa 8am-midnight, Su 10am-midnight. **Branch offices** at Tegel Airport open M-F 8am-6pm, Sa 8am-12pm; and *Ostbahnhof* open M-F 8am-8pm, Sa-Su 10am-6pm.

⌂ ⌂ ACCOMMODATIONS AND CAMPING

Thanks to the ever-growing hostel and hotel industry, same-day accommodations aren't impossible to find. Failing to make a reservation will, however, limit your options. For visits over four days, the various **Mitwohnzentralen** can arrange for you to housesit or sublet an apartment; for more information, contact **Home Company Mitwohnzentrale,** Joachimstaler Str. 17. (☎ 194 45. U9 or 15 to Kurfürstendamm. Open M-F 9am-6pm, Sa 11am-2pm.) For long stays or on weekends, reservations

Central Berlin East

🏠 ACCOMMODATIONS
Circus, **8**
Honigmond, **3**

🍽 FOOD
Assel, **10**
Beth Café, **5**
Mensa der Humboldt-U, **18**
Taba, **4**

🏛 MUSEUMS
Alte Nationalgalerie, **13**
Altes Museum, **17**
Deutsche Guggenheim Berlin, **23**
Deutsches Hist. Museum, **19**
Gemäldegalerie, **32**
Hamburger Bahnhof, **2**
Neue Nationalgalerie,**33**
Pergamonmuseum, **12**

● SIGHTS
Alte Bibliothek, **25**
Bertolt-Brecht-Haus, **1**
Brandenburger Tor, **21**

● SIGHTS (CONT.)
Deutsche Staatsoper, **24**
Fernsehturm, **14**
Führerbunker, **29**
Haus am Checkpoint Charlie, **34**
Hotel Adlon, **22**
Neue Synagogue, **9**
Neue Wache, **20**
Reichstag, **15**

🛏 NIGHTLIFE
Tresor, **30**
VEB-OZ, **6**
Zosch, **7**

⭐ ENTERTAINMENT
Ber. Philharmonisches
Orchester, **31**

✝ CHURCHES
Berliner Dom, **16**
Deutscher Dom, **28**
Französischer Dom, **27**
St.-Hedwigs-
Kathedrale, **26**

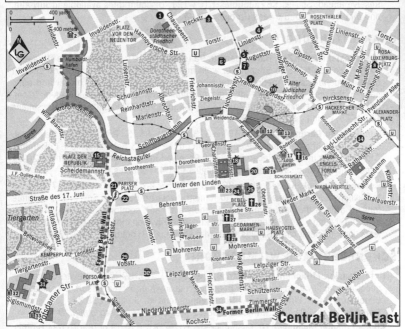

Central Berlin East

GERMANY

are essential. For visits during the **Love Parade** (see p. 429), call at least two months ahead for a choice of rooms and at least two weeks ahead for any bed at all. Some hostels increase prices that weekend by up to €10 per night.

MITTE

▨ Mitte's Backpacker Hostel, Chausseestr. 102 (☎262 51 40). U6 to Zinnowitzer Str. Friendly English-speaking staff, themed rooms, and a relaxed atmosphere. Bikes €5 per day. Internet access. Kitchen available. Sheets €2.50. Laundry €5. Reception 24hr. Dorms €13-15; doubles €44-46; triples €57-60; quads €68-72. ❶

Circus, Rosa-Luxemburg-Str. 39-41 (☎28 39 14 33). U2 to Rosa-Luxemburg-Pl. Bikes €6 per day. Sheets €2. Reception 24hr. Reservations should be reconfirmed 1 day before arrival. 6- to 8-bed dorms €14; 4- to 5-bed dorms €17; singles €30; doubles €46; triples €60. Apartment for 4 with kitchen and bath €92. ❶

Honigmond, Tieckstr. 12 (☎284 45 50). S1 or 2 to *Nordbahnhof* or U6 to Zinnowitzer Str. The romantic decor features canopy beds, iron grating, and bubbling fountains. Breakfast €3-9. Reception daily 9am-6pm. Check-in 3pm-1am; if checking in after 8pm, call beforehand. Singles €45-70; doubles €65-85, with bath €71-102. ❸

TIERGARTEN

Jugendgästehaus (HI), Kluckstr. 3 (☎25 79 98 08). From Bahnhof Zoo, take bus #129 (dir.: Hermannpl.) to Gedenkstätte or U1 to Kurfürstenstr., then walk up Potsdamer Str., turn left on Pohlstr., and right on Kluckstr. Bikes €8 per day, students €5. Breakfast included. Key deposit €5. Reception 24hr. Reservations strongly recommended. 6- to 10-bed dorms €14; 3- to 5-bed dorms €18.50. ❶

Hotel-Pension Hansablick, Flotowstr. 6 (☎390 48 00). S3, 5, 7, 9, or 75 to Tiergarten. All rooms have bath, minibar, phone, and cable TV. Breakfast included. Reception 24hr. Reserve ahead. Singles €82; doubles €101-121. Discount rates available in July-Aug. and mid-Nov. to Feb. 5% *Let's Go* discount. ❺

CHARLOTTENBURG

Jugendgästehaus am Zoo, Hardenbergstr. 9a (☎312 94 10), opposite Mensa TU (see p. 422). Take bus #145 to Steinpl., or walk from the back exit of Bahnhof Zoo straight down Hardenbergstr. A mellow hostel with spacious rooms. Use the buzzer and push hard on the front door; it's not locked. Reception daily 9am-midnight. Check-in 10am. Check-out 9am. Lockout 10am-2pm. 4- to 8-bed dorms €21, under 26 €18; singles €28/€25; doubles €49/€44. ❷

Hotel-Pension Cortina, Kantstr. 140 (☎313 90 59). S3, 5, 7, 9, or 75 to Savignypl. Spacious, bright rooms, and a great location off the main S-Bahn line, close to Bahnhof Zoo. Breakfast included. Reception 24hr. Reservations recommended. Dorms €20-31 depending on group size and season; singles €31-47; doubles €47-77. ❷

Pension Knesebeck, Knesebeckstr. 86 (☎312 72 55; fax 313 95 07). S3, 5, 7, 9, or 75 to Savignypl. Follow Knesebeckstr. to Kantstr., where it becomes Savignypl.; continue forward around the park semicircle. Friendly staff and comfortable rooms. Breakfast included. Laundry €4. Reception 24hr. Phone reservations must be confirmed by fax, letter, or with credit card. Singles €39, with shower €43; doubles €61/€72. ❸

SCHÖNEBERG AND WILMERSDORF

Hotel-Pension München, Güntzelstr. 62 (☎857 91 20). U9 to Güntzelstr. Gracefully-decorated white-walled rooms in a peaceful, relaxing part of Wilmersdorf. Breakfast €5. Check-out 11am. Written reservations recommended. Singles €33-36, with shower €48-57; doubles €40-47, with bath €58-72. Ask about *Mehrbettzimmer.* ❸

Studentenhotel Meininger 10, Meininger Str. 10 (☎78 71 74 14 or (0800) 634 64 64). U4, bus #146 or N46 to Rathaus Schöneberg. Walk toward the *Rathaus* on Freiherr-vom-Stein-Str., turn left onto Martin-Luther-Str. and then right on Meininger Str. Free shuttle pickup at Bahnhof Zoo. Run by students, for students. Breakfast included. Lockers €5 deposit. Reception 24hr. Large co-ed dorms €12.50; 3- to 4-bed dorms €21; singles €33; doubles €46. 5% *Let's Go* discount. ❶

CVJM-Haus, Einemstr. 10 (☎264 91 00). U1, 2, 4, or 15 to Nollendorfpl. Popular with school groups. Near gay nightlife of Nollendorfpl. Breakfast included. Sheets €4. Reception 24hr. Book in advance. €21 per person for dorms, singles, and doubles. ❷

Art Hotel Connection, Fuggerstr. 33 (☎217 70 28). U1, 2, or 15 to Wittenbergpl., on a side street off Martin-Luther-Str. For gays and lesbians only (mostly men). Artsy rooms come with phones, TVs, and alarm clocks. Breakfast included. Reservations required at least 1 month in advance. Singles €60-80; doubles €100; cheaper in off-season. ❹

Jugendhotel Berlin City, Crellestr. (☎78 70 21 30). U7 to Kleistpark. This hotel provides simple, clean rooms that are popular with school groups, so book ahead. Breakfast included. 6-bed dorms €26-28; singles €38-46; doubles €60-80. ❷

KREUZBERG

Bax Pax, Skalitzer Str. 104 (☎69 51 83 22). U1 or 15 to Görlitzer Bahnhof. Great location at the mouth of mighty Oranienstr. Fuzzy blue carpets and a room with a bed inside a VW Bug make this a unique hostelling experience. Sheets €2.50. Reception daily 7am-10pm. Dorms €15-18; singles €30; doubles €46; triples €60. ❷

Hotel Transit, Hagelberger Str. 53-54 (☎789 04 70). U6 or 7 or bus #N19 to Mehringdamm. Modern rooms; sleek lounge has a big-screen TV and a well-stocked bar. Breakfast included. Reception 24hr. Singles €52; doubles €60; triples €78; quads €104. The "Sleep-In" deal allows you to share a multi-bed room for €19. ❹

CAMPING

Deutscher Camping-Club runs the following campgrounds. Reservations are recommended. Call ☎218 60 71 or 218 60 72. All sites €5.10 per person, €3.80 per tent.

Dreilinden, Albrechts-Teerofen (☎805 12 01). S7 to Griebnitzsee, then turn right out of the station onto Rudolf-Breitschied-Str., take another right onto Bäkestr., and follow it to the campground (40min.). Isolated location, just off the river. Open Mar.-Oct. ❶

Kladow, Krampnitzer Weg 111-117 (☎365 27 97). U7 to Rathaus Spandau, then bus #135 (dir.: Alt-Kladow) to the end followed by bus #234 to Krampnitzer Weg/Selbitzerstr. Store, restaurant, and swimmable lake on premises. Open year-round. ❶

🍴 FOOD

Berlin defies all expectations with both tasty local options and terrific ethnic food from its Turkish, Indian, Italian, and Thai immigrants. Typical Berlin street food is Turkish; *Imbiße* (fast food stands) tend to stay open late. The *Döner Kebab*, a sandwich of lamb or chicken and salad, has cornered the fast food market, with *falafel* running a close second; either makes a small meal for €1.50-3. Berlin's numerous cafes, restaurants, and *Kneipen* (taverns) are budget-friendly and usually offer meals of many sizes.

Aldi, Plus, Edeka, and **Penny Markt** are the cheapest supermarket chains. Supermarkets are usually open Monday to Friday 9am-6pm and Saturday 9am-4pm. **Nimm's Mit,** near the Reisczentrum at Bahnhof Zoo, is open 24hr. The best **open-air market** occurs Saturday mornings on Winterfeldtpl.

MITTE

Mensa der Humboldt-Universität, Unter den Linden 6, behind the university's main building. The cheapest Mensa in Berlin, conveniently located amidst Mitte's many sights. Meals €1.80-3. Student ID required. Open M-F 11:30am-2:30pm. ❶

Assel, Oranienburgerstr. 21. S1, 2, or 25 to Oranienburgerstr. A rotating menu features everything from Tex-Mex to pastas (€5-8). Open daily 10pm-late. ❷

Taba, Torstr. 164. U6 to Rosenthaler Pl. Meals are pricey, but the vast buffet W-Th (€6.50) is a filling and tasty option at this festive Brazilian eatery. Buy your own Brazilian cigar or listen to the live music F-Su. Open Tu-Su from 7pm. ❸

Beth Café, Tucholskystr. 40, just off Auguststr. S1, 2, or 25 to Oranienburgerstr. Kosher restaurant in the heart of the Scheunenviertel. Open M-Th and Su 11am-10pm, F 11am-5pm; in off-season closes F 3pm. ❷

THE HIDDEN DEAL

BABEL

Schwarma, falafel, and thou. An Elysian field of eating, this crowded locale serves excellent Lebanese specialties on a pleasant Prenzlauer Berg boulevard.

The interior is a mish-mash of intensely orange walls, bundles of fresh flowers, eclectic chairs, and paintings of Mediterranean seascapes. Lush plants climb the walls, while the display reveals an awe-inspiring feast of rainbow-colored veggies, rotund pots of hummus, and delectable spinach-stuffed pastries.

The ingredients are superb—the fluffy falafel balls are stuffed with spices and the schwarma comes with mint and potatoes. A falafel or schwarma by itself makes a surprisingly filling meal (€3), while the plate option allows you to indulge in literally mountains of food without taking a bite out of your budget (most €5).

To avoid the temptation of ordering multiple meals, pick up your food at the counter and eat at the spacious sidewalk tables among salivating Prenzlauer Berg hipsters.

(☎440 313 18. Kastanienallee 33. U2 to Eberswalderstr. Open daily 11am-midnight.) ❷

CHARLOTTENBURG

Mensa TU, Hardenbergstr. 34. Bus #145 to Steinpl., or walk 10min. from Bahnhof Zoo. Meals, including good vegetarian dishes, €2-4. Cafeteria downstairs has longer hours and slightly higher prices. Open M-F 11am-2:30pm. Cafeteria open M-F 8am-5pm. ❶

Café Hardenberg, Hardenbergstr. 10. Opposite the *Mensa TU,* but more atmosphere. Breakfast (€3-6) served 24hr. along with salads and pasta dishes (€2-7). Open M-F 9am-1am, Sa-Su 9am-2am. ❶

Schwarzes Café, Kantstr. 148. S3, 5, 7, 9, or 75 to Savignypl. Always open, except for Tu 3-11am. Prices are a bit high, but cheaper breakfasts served all day. ❸

SCHÖNEBERG

Baharat Falafel, Winterfeldtstr. 37. U1, 2, 4, or 15 to Nollendorfpl. Falafel with veggies and hummus from €6. Open daily 11am-3am; closed last week in July. ❷

Fish and Vegetables, Goltzstr. 32. U1, 2, 4, or 15 to Nollendorfpl. A no-nonsense do-it-yourself Thai restaurant, bustling around lunchtime and during the evening. Dishes from €3. Open daily noon-midnight. Next door, **Rani** serves Indian food in a similar fashion. ❶

Sushi am Winterfeldtplatz, Goltzstr. 24. U1, 2, 4, or 15 to Nollendorfpl. Standing-room-only Japanese cuisine in the heart of Schöneberg. Sample the fresh sushi for €2-7. Open M-Sa noon-midnight, Su 3pm-midnight. Delivery until 1hr. before closing. ❷

KREUZBERG

Amrit, Oranienstr. 202-203. U1 or 15 to Görlitzer Bahnhof. Serves up generous, but pricey, dishes of colorful Indian food. Open Su-Th noon-1am, F-Sa noon-2am. ❹

Hannibal, at the corner of Wienerstr. and Skalitzerstr. Bus N29 or U1, 12, or 15 to Görlitzer Bahnhof. An eclectic spot for a leisurely breakfast or for scarfing down a massive Hannibal-burger (€6). Open M-Th 8am-3am, F-Sa 8am-4am, Su 9am-3am. ❷

Cafe V, Lausitzer Pl. U1 or 15 to Görlitzer Bahnhof. Berlin's oldest vegetarian restaurant. Top-of-the-line, bottom-of-the-food-chain. Open daily 10am-1am. ❸

PRENZLAUER BERG

■ **Osswald,** Göhrener Str. 5. U2 to Eberswalder Str. Popular with locals, this restaurant/bar produces simple but tasty German dishes. A staggering breakfast buffet (€7) packs the place until 5pm on Sunday. Open daily 9am-4am. ❸

Im Nu, Lychnerstr. 41. U2 to Eberswalderstr. Eclectic decor complements crunchy salads (€3-5) and sumptuous baguettes (€3). Open daily 8am-1am. ❷

SIGHTS

Berlin's sights stretch over an area eight times the size of Paris. For a guide to the city's major neighborhoods, see **Orientation**, p. 413. Below, the sights are organized by *Bezirk* (district), beginning with Mitte and spiralling outward. Many of central Berlin's major sights lie along the route of **bus #100**, from Bahnhof Zoo to Prenzlauer Berg; consider a day pass (€6) or a 7-day pass (€22).

MITTE

Formerly the heart of Imperial Berlin, Mitte contains some of Berlin's most magnificent sights and museums. Unter den Linden, the area between the Brandenburg Gate and Alexanderpl., is best reached by taking S1, 2, or 25 to Unter den Linden; alternatively, bus #100 runs the length of the boulevard every 4-6min.

■ **BRANDENBURGER TOR AND PARISER PLATZ.** For decades a barricaded gateway to nowhere, the **Brandenburg Gate** is the most powerful emblem of reunited Germany and Berlin. Standing right in the center of the city, it was in no-man's land during the time of the wall. All but a few of the venerable buildings near the gate were destroyed in WWII, but a massive reconstruction effort has already revived such pre-war staples as the **Hotel Adlon,** once the premiere address for all visiting dignitaries and celebrities.

NEUE WACHE. The "New Guardhouse" was designed in Neoclassical style. During the GDR era, it was known as the "Memorial to the Victims of Fascism and Militarism." After reunification, the building was reopened as a war memorial. The remains of an unknown soldier and an unknown concentration-camp victim are buried inside. *(Unter den Linden 4. Open daily 10am-6pm.)*

BEBELPLATZ. On May 10, 1933, Nazi students burned nearly 20,000 books here by "subversive" authors such as Heinrich Heine and Sigmund Freud. A plaque in the center of the square is engraved with Heine's eerily prescient 1820 quote: "Wherever books are burned, ultimately people are burned as well." The building with the curved facade is the **Alte Bibliothek,** which was once the royal library. On the other side of the square is the handsome **Deutsche Staatsoper** (opera house), fully rebuilt after the war from original sketches. The distinctive blue dome at the end of the square belongs to **St. Hedwigs-Kathedrale.** Built in 1773 as the first Catholic church erected in Berlin after the Reformation, it was burnt by American bombers in 1943 and rebuilt in the 1950s. *(Cathedral open M-Sa 10am-5pm, Su 1-5pm. Free.)*

POTSDAMER PLATZ AND FÜHRERBUNKER. Built under Friedrich Wilhelm I with the primary purpose of moving troops quickly, **Potsdamer Platz** was chosen to become the new commercial center of Berlin after reunification. Completion is now in sight, and many of the cutting-edge, wildly ambitious architectural designs make for spectacular sight-seeing. Near Potsdamer Pl., unmarked and inconspicuous, lies the site of the **Führerbunker** where Hitler married Eva Braun and then ended his life. Tourists looking for it often mistakenly head for the visible bunker at the southern edge of Potsdamer Pl.; it's actually on In den Ministergärten off Eberstr., behind a playground. *(U2 or S1, 2, 25 to Potsdamer Pl.)*

GENDARMENMARKT. Several blocks south of Bebelpl., this gorgeous plaza was known as the French Quarter in the 18th century when Protestant Huguenots settled there. During the last week of June and the first week of July, the square transforms into an outdoor stage for classical concerts. At either ends are **Deutscher Dom** and **Französischer Dom** (German and French Cathedrals).

BERLINER DOM. This multiple-domed cathedral, one of Berlin's most recognizable landmarks, was built during the reign of Kaiser Wilhelm II and recently emerged from 20 years of restoration after being damaged in a 1944 air raid. *(Open M-Sa 9am-7pm, Su noon-7pm. Dom and crypt €4, students €2. Free organ recitals W-F at 3pm.)*

ALEXANDERPLATZ AND FERNSEHTURM. Formerly the heart of Weimar Berlin, the plaza was transformed in East German times into an urban wasteland of fountains and pre-fab office buildings. The **Fernsehturm** (TV tower), the tallest structure in Berlin at 368m, is a bizarre building originally intended as proof of East Germany's technological capabilities. When the sun is out, the windows have a crucifix-shaped glint pattern known as the *Papsts Rache* (pope's revenge). *(Open daily Mar.-Oct. 9am-1am; Nov.-Feb. 10am-midnight. €6, under 16 €3.)*

NEUE SYNAGOGE. This huge building survived *Kristallnacht* when a local police chief, realizing that the building was a historic monument, ordered it spared. The synagogue was later destroyed by bombing but its restoration was completed in 1995. The interior, too big for Berlin's remaining Jewish community, now houses an exhibit chronicling the synagogue's history and temporary exhibits on the history of Berlin's Jews. *(Oranienburger Str. 30. Open Su-M 10am-8pm, Tu-Th 10am-6pm, F 10am-2pm. Museum €5, students €3. Entry to the dome €1.50, students €1.)*

TIERGARTEN. Once a hunting ground for Prussian monarchs, the **Tiergarten** is now a vast landscaped park in the center of Berlin, stretching from Bahnhof Zoo to the Brandenburg Gate. In early July, the Love Parade (see p. 429) brings unparalleled partying to the park. In the heart of the Tiergarten, the **Siegessäule**, a 70m "victory column" commemorates Prussia's humiliating defeat of France in 1870. *(Bus #100, 187, to Großer Stern. Open Apr.-Nov. M 1-6pm, Tu-Su 9am-6pm. €1.20, students €0.60.)*

■ **THE REICHSTAG.** Just north of the gate is the current home of Germany's governing body, the *Bundestag.* The glass dome on top is built around an upside-down solar cone that powers the building. A walkway spirals up the inside of the dome, leading visitors around a panoramic view to the top of the cone. *(Open daily 8am-midnight; last entrance 10pm. Free.)*

BERTOLT-BRECHT-HAUS. If any single man personifies the maelstrom of political and aesthetic contradictions that is Berlin, it is **Bertolt Brecht,** who lived and worked in this house from 1953 to 1956. *(Chausseestr. 125. U6 to Zinnowitzer Str. Mandatory German tours every 30min. Tu-F 10-11:30am, Th also 5-6:30pm, and Sa 9:30am-1:30pm; every hour Su 11am-6pm. €3, students €1.50.)* Brecht is buried in the attached **Dorotheenstädtischer Friedhof.** *(Open Apr.-Sept. daily 7am-7pm; Oct.-Mar. 8am-4pm.)*

CHARLOTTENBURG

ZOOLOGISCHER GARTEN AND AQUARIUM. Across from the Bahnhof Zoo station and through the maze of bus depots, the renowned **zoo** is one of the best in the world, with many animals displayed in open-air habitats instead of cages. The second entrance across from Europa-Center is the famous **Elefantentor,** Budapester Str. 34, a decorated pagoda of pachyderms. *(Open daily May-Sept. 9am-6:30pm; Oct.-Feb. 9am-5pm; Mar.-Apr. 9am-5:30pm. €8, students €6.)* Within the walls of the zoo is the excellent **aquarium,** with its broad collections of insects and reptiles as well as endless tanks of rainbow-colored fish. Its pride and joy is the 450kg Komodo dragon, the world's largest reptile. *(Budapester Str. 32. Open daily 9am-6pm. Aquarium €8, students €6.50. Combination ticket to zoo and aquarium €13, students €10.50, children €6.50.)*

KAISER-WILHELM-GEDÄCHTNISKIRCHE. Nicknamed "the rotten tooth" by Berliners, the jagged edges of this shattered church stand as a reminder of the destruction caused during World War II. Built in 1852 in a Romanesque-Byzantine style, the church has a striking interior with colorful mosaics covering the ceiling, floors, and walls. The ruins house an exhibit of unsettling photos of the entire city in ruins just after the war. *(Exhibit open M-Sa 10am-4pm. Church open daily 9am-7pm.)*

SCHLOß CHARLOTTENBURG. The broad Baroque palace commissioned by Friedrich I for his second wife, Sophie-Charlotte, sprawls over a park on the northern edge of Charlottenburg. The *Schloß*'s many buildings include the **Neringbau,** or *Altes Schloß*, the palace proper *(open Tu-F 9am-5pm, Sa-Su 10am-5pm; €8, students €5)*; the **Neuer-Pavillon,** a museum dedicated to Prussian architect Karl Friedrich Schinkel *(open Tu-Su 10am-5pm; €2, students €1.50)*; **Belvedere,** a small building housing the royal family's porcelain collection *(open Apr.-Oct. Tu-Su 10am-5pm, Nov.-Mar. Tu-F noon-4pm and Sa-Su noon-5pm; €2, students €1.50)*; and the **Mausoleum,** the final resting spot for most of the family *(open Apr.-Oct. Tu-Su 10am-noon and 1-5pm; €2, students €1.50)*. The **Schloßgarten** behind the main buildings is a paradise of small lakes, fountains, and carefully planted rows of trees *(open Tu-Su 6am-9pm; free).* (Bus #145 from Bahnhof Zoo to Luisenpl./Schloß Charlottenburg or U7 to Richard-Wagner-Pl. and walk 15min. down Otto-Suhr-Allee. **Entire complex €7,** students €5.)*

OLYMPIA-STADION. At the western edge of Charlottenburg, the Olympic Stadium was erected for the 1936 Olympic Games, in which Jesse Owens, an African-American, triumphed over Nazi racial theories by winning four golds. There is now a Jesse-Owens Allee to the south of the stadium. The stadium is currently under construction until 2004, but a great view of it can be had from the bell tower. *(U2 to Olympia-Stadion (Ost) or S5 or 75 to Olympiastadion.)*

FUNKTURM. Erected in 1926 to herald the radio age, the Funkturm offers a stunning view of the city from its 125m observation deck. The world's first television transmission was made here in 1931. *(S45 or 46 to Witzleben or U2 to Kaiserdamm. Panorama deck open M 11am-9pm, Tu-Su 11:30-11pm. €3.60, students €1.80.)*

GEDENKSTÄTTE PLÖTZENSEE. Housed in the terrifyingly well-preserved former execution chambers of the Third Reich, the memorial exhibits documented death sentences of "enemies of the people," including the officers who attempted to assassinate Hitler in 1944. More than 2500 people were murdered within this small, red brick complex. Still visible are the hooks from which victims were hanged. *(Hüttigpfad, off the main road where the bus stops, down Emmy-Zehden-Weg. Take U9 to Turmstr., then bus #123 (dir.: Saatwinkler Damm) to Gedenkstätte Plotzensee. English literature is available. Open daily Mar.-Oct. 9am-5pm; Nov.-Feb. 9am-4pm. Free.)*

SCHÖNEBERG AND KREUZBERG

South of the Ku'damm, Schöneberg is a pleasant, middle-class residential district noted for its shopping, lively cafes, and good restaurants. Schöneberg is also home to the more affluent segments of Berlin's gay and lesbian community (see **Gay and Lesbian Berlin,** p. 430). Kreuzberg, southeast of Mitte, is filled with diverse ethnic groups, revolutionary graffiti, punks galore, and a large, self-confident gay and lesbian community. It's also the site of the annual May 1st parades.

RATHAUS SCHÖNEBERG. West Berlin's city government convened here until the wall fell. On June 26, 1963, 15 years after the beginning of the Berlin Airlift, 1.5 million Berliners swarmed the streets beneath the tower to hear John F. Kennedy reassure them of the Allies' commitment to the city with the now-famous words "*Ich bin ein Berliner.*" Today, the fortress is home to Schöneberg's municipal government. *(John-F.-Kennedy-Pl. U4 to Rathaus Schöneberg. Open daily 9am-6pm.)*

■ **HAUS AM CHECKPOINT CHARLIE.** A fascinating museum at the location of the famous border-crossing point, Checkpoint Charlie is one of Berlin's most popular tourist attractions. A strange mix of eastern sincerity and western salesmanship, the collection contains all types of devices used to get over, under, or through the wall. *(Friedrichstr. 43-45. U6 to Kochstr. Open daily 9am-10pm. €7, students €4.)*

ORANIENSTRAßE. This was the site of frequent riots in the 1980s. Today, it is the starting point for the May Day parades. The rest of the year, neo-revolutionaries rub shoulders with traditional Turkish families, while an anarchist punk faction and a boisterous gay and lesbian population keep things lively after hours. Restaurants, clubs, and shops of all possible flavors make it a great place to wander. *(U1 or 15 to Kottbusser Tor or Görlitzer Bahnhof.)*

FRIEDRICHSHAIN AND LICHTENBERG

■ **EAST SIDE GALLERY.** The longest remaining portion of the Wall, the 1.3km stretch of cement and asbestos slabs also serves as the world's largest open-air art gallery. The murals are the efforts of an international group of artists who gathered here in 1989 to celebrate the end of the city's division. In 1999, the same artists came together to repaint their work and cover the scrawlings of later tourists; unfortunately, would-be artists are rapidly defacing the wall once again. *(Along Mühlenstr. U1 or 15 or S3, 5, 6, 7, 9, or 75 to Warschauer Str.; walk back toward the river.)*

FORSCHUNGS- UND GEDENKSTÄTTE NORMANNENSTRAßE. In the suburb of Lichtenberg stands perhaps the most feared building of the GDR regime: the headquarters of the East German secret police, the **Staatssicherheit,** or **Stasi.** Since a 1991 law opened the Stasi's records to the public, the "Horror-Files" have rocked Germany, exposing informants—and wrecking careers, marriages, and friendships—at all levels of society. Today, German-language exhibits display tiny microphones and hidden cameras used for surveillance, a GDR shrine full of Lenin busts, and countless other bits of bizarre memorabilia. *(Ruschestr. 103, Haus 1. U5 to Magdalenenstr. Open Tu-F 11am-6pm, Sa-Su 2-6pm. €3, students €1.50.)*

🏛 MUSEUMS

Berlin is one of the world's great museum cities, with collections of artifacts encompassing all subjects and eras. The **Staatliche Museen zu Berlin (SMB)** runs over 20 museums located in several regions—**Museumsinsel, Kulturforum, Mitte/Tiergarten, Charlottenburg,** and **Dahlem.** A single admission to these museums is €2, students €1; admission is free the first Sunday of every month. A *Tageskarte* (€4, students €2) is valid for all SMB museums on the day of purchase; the *Drei-Tage-Karte* (€8, students €4) is valid for three consecutive days. Either can be bought at any SMB museum. Non-SMB museums tend to be smaller and quirkier.

MUSEUMSINSEL (MUSEUM ISLAND)

Museumsinsel contains five separate museums, although several are undergoing extensive renovation. Take S3, 5, 7, 9, or 75 to Hackescher Markt or bus #100 to Lustgarten. All museums offer free audio tours in English.

■ **PERGAMONMUSEUM.** One of the world's great ancient history museums, it's named for Pergamon, the Turkish city from which the enormous Altar of Zeus (180 BC) in the main exhibit hall was taken. The museum features pieces of Mediterranean history from as far back as the 10th century BC. *(Kupfergraben. Open Tu-Su 10am-6pm. SMB prices.)*

ALTE NATIONALGALERIE. Attracts eager art-lovers, who come to see everything from German Realism to French Impressionism. Caspar Friedrich and Karl Schinkel are but two names in an all-star cast on display. *(Am Lustgarten. Open Tu-Su 10am-6pm. SMB prices.)*

ALTES MUSEUM. The museum contains the *Antikensammlung*, an excellent permanent collection of Greco-Roman art. *(Am Lustgarten. Open Tu-Su 10am-6pm. SMB prices.)*

TIERGARTEN-KULTURFORUM

The **Tiergarten-Kulturforum (TK)** is a complex of museums at the eastern end of the Tiergarten, near Potsdamer Pl. Take U2 or S1, 2, or 25 to Potsdamer Pl. and walk down Potsdamer Str.; the museums will be on your right on Mattäikirchpl. All museums are open Tu-W, F 10am-6pm, Th 10am-10pm, Sa-Su 11am-6pm.

■ **GEMÄLDEGALERIE.** One of Germany's most famous museums, and rightly so. It houses a stunning and enormous collection by Italian, German, Dutch, and Flemish masters, including Dürer and Rembrandt. *(SMB prices.)*

■ **HAMBURGER BAHNHOF/MUSEUM FÜR GEGENWARTKUNST.** Berlin's foremost collection of contemporary art features works by Warhol, Beuys, and Kiefer as well as in-your-face temporary exhibits. *Invalidenstr. 50-51. S3, 5, 7, 9, or 75 to Lehrter Stadtbahnhof or U6 to Zinnowitzer Str. €6, students €3. Tours Su at 4pm.*

NEUE NATIONALGALERIE. This sleek building contains both interesting temporary exhibits and a formidable permanent collection, including works by Warhol, Kirchner, and Ernst. Never has roadkill looked so cool. *(Potsdamer Str. 50. SMB prices for permanent collection; €6, students €3 for the whole museum.)*

CHARLOTTENBURG AND DAHLEM

■ **ÄGYPTISCHES MUSEUM.** This stern Neoclassical building contains a famous collection of ancient Egyptian art: animal mummies, elaborately painted coffins, a magnificent stone arch, original papyrus scrolls, and the famous bust of Queen Nefertiti. *(Schloßstr. 70. Take bus #145 to Luisenpl./Schloß Charlottenburg or U7 to Richard-Wagner-Pl. and walk down Otto-Suhr-Allee. Open Tu-Su 10am-6pm. €6, students €3.)*

■ **ETHNOLOGISCHES MUSEUM.** The Ethnological Museum alone makes the trek to Dahlem worthwhile. The exhibits range from ancient Central American stonework to ivory African statuettes to enormous boats from the South Pacific. The Museum für Indisches Kunst (Museum for Indian Art), and the Museum für Ostasiatisches Kunst (Museum for East Asian Art), housed in the same building, are smaller but no less fascinating. *(U1 to Dahlem-Dorf and follow the Museen signs. Open Tu-F 10am-6pm, Sa-Su 11am-6pm. SMB prices.)*

INDEPENDENT (NON-SMB) MUSEUMS

DEUTSCHE GUGGENHEIM BERLIN. Unter den Linden 13-15. Located in a newly renovated building across the street from the Deutsche Staatsbibliothek, the museum features changing exhibits of contemporary avant-garde art. *(Open daily 11am-8pm, Th until 10pm. €3, students €2; M free.)*

FILMMUSEUM BERLIN. This brand new museum traces the development of German film through history. The exhibits are fascinating, and the futuristic entrance is a mind-altering experience. *(Potsdamer Str. 2, 3rd and 4th fl. of the Sony Center. U2 or S1, 2, or 25 to Potsdamer Pl. Open Tu-Su 10am-6pm, Th until 8pm. €6, students €4.)*

DEUTSCHES HISTORISCHES MUSEUM. Traces German history up to the Nazis, while rotating exhibits examine the last 50 years. *(Unter den Linden 1, in the Kronprinzenpalais. S3, 5, 7, 9, or 75 to Hackescher Markt. Open Th-Tu 3-6pm. Free.)*

🎵 ENTERTAINMENT

CONCERTS AND MUSIC. Berlin reaches its musical zenith during the **Berliner Festwochen,** which lasts almost all of September and attracts the world's best orchestras and soloists. The **Berliner Jazztage** in November features top-notch jazz musicians. For information and tickets for both festivals, call or write in advance to Berliner Festspiele *(☎ 65 48 90; www.berlinerfestspiele.de).* In mid-July, the **Bachtage** offers an intense week of classical music, while every Saturday night in August, the **Sommer Festspiele** turns the Ku'damm into a multi-faceted concert hall with punk, steel-drum, and folk groups competing for attention. Look for concert listings in the monthly pamphlets *Konzerte und Theater in Berlin und Brandenburg* (free) and *Berlin Programm* (€1.50), as well as in the biweekly *Zitty* and *Tip.* The acoustically designed **Berliner Philharmonisches Orchester,** Matthäikirchstr. 1, is one of the world's finest, but it's almost impossible to get tickets. *(☎ 25 48 81 32. U2 or S1, 2, or 25 to Potsdamer Pl., then walk up Potsdamer Str.)* **Deutsche Oper Berlin,** Bismarckstr. 35, is Berlin's best and youngest opera. *(☎ 341 02 49; tickets ☎ (0800) 248 98 42. U2 to Deutsche Oper. Tickets €10-110. Tickets available 1hr. before performance. Student discounts available 1 week before performance. Box office open M-Sa from 11am until 1hr. before performance, Su 10am-2pm. Closed July-Aug.)*

THEATER AND FILM. Berlin has the best German-language theater in the world as well as a lively English-theater scene; look for listings in *Zitty* or *Tip* that say *in englischer Sprache* (in English) next to them. The **Deutsches Theater,** Schumannstr. 13a, has innovative productions of both classics and newer works. *(☎ 28 44 12 25. Box office open M-Sa 11am-6:30pm, Su 3-6:30pm. Tickets €4-36, students €8.)* **Hebbel-Theater,** Stresemannstr. 29, is the most avant of the avant-garde theaters in Berlin. *(☎ 25 90 04 27. Order tickets at the box office on Stresemannstr., by phone daily 4-7pm; or, show up 1hr. before performance.)* Berlin is also a movie-loving town; it hosts the international **Berlinale** film festival (Feb. 5-16, 2003), and on any night you can choose from over 150 different films, many in their original languages. *O.F.* next to a movie listing means original version (i.e., not dubbed); *O.m.U.* means original version with German subtitles. Check *Tip, Zitty,* or the ubiquitous blue *Kinoprogramm* posters plastered throughout the city. Mondays, Tuesdays, or Wednesdays are *Kinotage* at most movie theaters, with reduced prices. Bring a student ID for discounts. Potsdamer Pl., home to **Filmhaus** and **Cinemaxx,** has the most options for English films. **Freiluftkino Hasenheide,** at the Sputnik in Hasenheide Park, has open-air screenings of everything from silent films to last year's blockbusters. (U7 or 8 to Hermannpl.)

🎧 NIGHTLIFE

Berlin's nightlife is absolute madness. Bars typically open around 6pm and get going around 10pm, just as the clubs are opening their doors. As bar scenes wind down between midnight and 6am, club dance floors heat up around 1am and groove until dawn, when a variety of after-parties and 24hr. cafes keep up this seemingly perpetual motion. It's completely possible (if you can live without sleep) to party non-stop Friday night through Monday morning. The best sources of information about bands and dance venues are the biweekly magazines *Tip* and the superior *Zitty,* available at all newsstands, or the free and highly comprehensive *030,* distributed in several hostels, cafes, and bars.

THE LOVE PARADE During the third weekend of every July, the Love Parade brings Berlin to its knees—its trains run late, its streets fill with litter, and its otherwise patriotic populace scrambles to the countryside in the expectation of a wave of German teenagers dying their hair, dropping ecstasy, and getting down *en masse.* What started in 1988 as a DJ's birthday party has mutated into the world's only 1.5 million-person rave, dubbed *Die Größte Partei der Welt,* "the biggest party in the world." The city-wide party turns Str. des 17. Juni into a riotous dance floor and the Tiergarten into a garden of iniquity. The BVG offers a No-Limit-Ticket, useful for getting around from venue to venue during the weekend's 54 hours of nonstop partying (€5, condom included). Club prices skyrocket for the event as the best DJs from Europe are imported for a frantic weekend of beat-thumping madness.

Savignyplatz, near Zoologischer Garten, in west Berlin, has refined, laid back cafes and jazz clubs. Gay life in Berlin centers around **Nollendorfplatz,** where the crowds are usually mixed and establishments range from friendly to cruisey. **Gneisenaustraße,** on the western edge of **Kreuzberg,** offers a variety of ethnic restaurants and some good bars. Closer to the former Wall, a dizzying array of clubs and bars on and around **Oranienstraße** rage all night, every night, with a mixed crowd.

In East Berlin, Kreuzberg's reputation as dance capital of Germany is challenged as clubs sprout up in **Mitte, Prenzlauer Berg,** and near **Potsdamer Platz.** Berlin's largest bar scene sprawls down **Oranienburgerstraße** in Mitte; it's pricey, but never boring. **Prenzlauer Berg,** originally the edgy alternative to Mitte's trendier repertoire, has become a bit more classy and established, especially around **Kollwitzplatz.** South of it all, **Friedrichshain** has developed a reputation for lively, quirky nightlife, with a terrific group of bars along Simon-Dach-Str. and more on Gabriel-Max-Str.

If at all possible, try to hit (or, if you're prone to claustrophobia, avoid) Berlin during the **Love Parade,** usually held in the third weekend of July, when all of Berlin goes wild (see below). Prices hit astronomical heights during this weekend. It's also worth mentioning that Berlin has **de-criminalized marijuana possession** of up to eight grams, although police can arrest you for any amount if they feel the need; exercise discretion. Smoking in public is not yet accepted but is becoming common in some clubs—you'll know which ones.

MITTE

■ **Tresor,** Leipziger Str. 126a. U2, S1, 2, or 25 or bus #N5, N29, or N52 to Potsdamer Pl. One of the liveliest techno venues in Berlin. Cover W €3, F €7, Sa €7-11. Open W and F-Sa 11pm-6am.

VEB-OZ, Auguststr. 92 at the corner of Oranienburgerstr. S1, 2, or 25 to Oranienburger Str. Open until at least 2 or 3am every night, so it's a good weekday watering hole; most other area bars close by 1am. Open daily from 6pm.

Zosch, Tucholskystr. 30. U6 to Oranienburger Tor. Relaxed bar on the ground floor, live music in the basement. Open M-F from 4pm, Sa-Su from midnight.

CHARLOTTENBURG (SAVIGNYPLATZ)

A-Trane, Bleibtreustr. 1. S3, 5, 7, 9, or 75 to Savignypl. A mellow and intimate setting with excellent musicians and a crowd of jazz-loving locals. Cover €7-21 (usually €13 on weekends). Open M-F 10pm-2am, later on weekends.

Quasimodo, Kantstr. 12a. U2 or 12 or S3, 5, 7, 9, or 75 to Zoologischer Garten. This smoky basement jazz venue attracts a wide variety of artists, showcasing everything from disco to soul to swing. Cover Tu-W €5-6; on weekends, cover up to €27 depending on performance. Open Tu-W and F-Sa from 9pm, occasionally on Su-M.

SCHÖNEBERG

Slumberland, Winterfeldtpl. U1, 2, 4, 12, or 15 to Nollendorfpl. A cafe/bar with an African motif, R&B, and Bob Marley. Open Su-Th 6pm-2am, F 6pm-5am, Sa 11am-5am.

Mister Hu, Goltzstr. 39. U1, 2, 4, or 15 to Nollendorfpl. Happy Hour 5-8pm, Su all cocktails €5. Open daily 5pm-late, Sa 11am-late.

KREUZBERG

SO36, Oranienstr. 190. U1, 12, or 15 to Görlitzer Bahnhof or bus #N29 to Heinrichpl. Berlin's only truly mixed club (see p. 431), with all orientations grooving to a number of wild genres. Cover for parties €4-8, for concerts €7-18. Open daily from 11pm.

Bateau Ivre, Oranienstr. 18. Locals sit back and relax over coffee or beer at this friendly bistro-bar before shakin' that thing across the street at SO36. Open daily from 9am.

FRIEDRICHSHAIN

Euphoria, Grünbergerstr. 60, on the corner of Simon-Dach Str. U5 to Frankfurter Tor. Serves perhaps the best mixed drinks in Berlin. Happy Hour 6-8pm. Wide selection of Italian entrees and Sunday brunch (€8.50) also served. Open daily from 9am.

Dachkammer Bar (DK), Simon-Dach Str. 39. The friendly, rustic feel of the ground floor is complemented by the mellow music and lively crowd. Sip cocktails (€5-7) with appetizers (from €4). Open M-F from noon, Sa-Su from 10am.

Zehn Vorne, Simon-Dach Str. 9. A jam-packed little bar based mainly on Star Trek. Don't let the theme scare you off—this place is weird, but fun. Open daily from 3pm.

PRENZLAUER BERG

KulturBrauerei, Knaackstr. 97. U2 to Eberswalder Str. In a former brewery; houses everything from the highly popular clubs **Soda** and **Kesselhaus** to a Russian theater and an art school. Venues include disco, techno, and reggae; cover and opening times vary, so it's best to call ahead.

Pfefferberg, Schönhauser Allee 176. U2 or bus #N58 to Senefelderpl. Features a slightly younger crowd and a rooftop garden. Techno and world music rotate weekly. Cover free to €15. Garden open in summer M-F from 3pm, Sa-Su from noon.

▼ GAY AND LESBIAN NIGHTLIFE

Berlin is one of the most gay-friendly cities on the continent. All of **Nollendorfplatz** is a gay-friendly environment. The main streets, including **Goltzstraße, Akazienstraße,** and **Winterfeldtstraße,** tend to contain mixed bars and cafes. The **"Bermuda Triangle"** of Motzstr., Fuggerstr., and Eisenacherstr. is more exclusively gay. For up-to-date events listings, pick up a copy of the amazingly comprehensive *Siegessäule* (free).

SCHÖNEBERG

Metropol, Nollendorfpl. 5. U1, 2, 4, or 15 or bus #N5, 19, 26, 48, 52, or 75 to Nollendorfpl. Houses three dance venues: **Tanz Tempel, West-Side Club,** and **Love Lounge.** Every other F the Tanz Tempel and Love Lounge host the heterosexual *Fisch Sucht Fahrrad* party ("Fish Seeks Bicycle," for you Gloria Steinem fans). West-Side Club holds the infamous "Naked Sex Party," and other naked parties. Hours vary—check *Siegessäule* for details.

Omnes, Motzstr. 8. U1, 2, 4, or 15 to Nollendorfpl. A mainly male gay bar, it accommodates late-night revelers after a full night of partying. Open 24hr.

Anderes Ufer, Hauptstr. 157. U7 to Kleistpark. Featuring high ceilings, plush red chairs, and Frank Sinatra, Anderes Ufer is a quieter, more relaxed *Kneipe* away from the club scene. Open M-Th and Su 11am-1am, F-Sa 11am-2am.

KREUZBERG

Rose's, Oranienstr. 187. Gay and lesbian clientele packs this intense and claustrophobic party spot, marked only by "Bar" over the door. Open daily 10pm-6am.

SO36, while usually a mixed club (p. 430), sponsors three predominantly gay events: **Hungrige Herzen** (W from 10pm), a jam-packed gay and (somewhat) lesbian trance and drum 'n' bass party; **Café Fatal** (Su from 5pm) with ballroom dancing; and **Gayhane** (last Sa of the month), a self-described "HomOrientaldancefloor" for a mixed crowd of Turks and Germans.

FRIEDRICHSHAIN

Die Busche, Mühlenstr. 12. East Berlin's largest gay disco, with an incongruous rotation of techno and top 40. Open W and F-Su from 9:30pm. The party gets going around midnight and increases in intensity around 3am. Cover €4-5.

PRENZLAUER BERG

Schall und Rauch, Gleimstr. 23. U2 or S4, 8, or 85 to Schönhauser Allee. Sizable, popular spot, with a glossier classy feel. Ridiculously well-stocked bar, and friendly waitstaff ensure drinking bliss. Highly popular brunch Sa and Su for €7,50; reservations a must. Open daily 9am-late.

Café Amsterdam, Gleimstr. 24 (☎44 00 94 54). U2 or S4, 8, or 85 to Schönhauser Allee. Next to Schall und Rauch. Amidst silver curtains and glitzy paintings, Amsterdam's clientele downs cheap drinks and challenge each other to games of backgammon. Open daily 4pm-6am.

▶ DAYTRIPS FROM BERLIN

POTSDAM. Visitors disappointed by Berlin's unroyal demeanor can get their Kaiserly fix in nearby Potsdam, the glittering city of Friedrich II (the Great). The huge **Park Sanssouci** is a testament to Friedrich's wealth and the diversity of his aesthetic tastes. For information, stop by the **Visitor's Center** next to the windmill. (☎969 42 00. Open daily Mar.-Oct. 8:30am-5pm, Nov.-Feb. 9am-4pm.) **Schloß Sanssouci,** the park's main attraction, was built in 1747 to allow Friedrich to escape his wife. German-language tours are limited to 40 people and leave every 20min. (Open Apr.-Oct. Tu-Su 9am-5pm; Nov.-Mar. 9am-4pm. €8, students €5.) Don't miss the exotic gold-plated **Chinesisches Teehaus** (€1.05) and the **Sizilianischer Garten,** the park's most stunning garden. At the opposite end of the park is the largest of the castles, the 200-room **Neues Palais.** (Open Apr.-Oct. Sa-Th 9am-5pm; Nov.-Mar. 9am-4pm. €6, students €5; off-season €1 less.) To reach Potsdam's second park, **Neuer Garten,** take bus #692 to **Schloß Cecilienhof,** which was built in the style of an English Tudor manor; inside, exhibits document the **Potsdam Treaty,** which was signed here in 1945. It was supposed to be the "Berlin Treaty," but the capital was too devastated by bombings to house the Allies' head honchos. (Open Tu-Su 9am-12:30pm and 1-5pm. €3, students €2; tour €1.) Consider purchasing a **day ticket** (€15, students €10), valid and available at all castles in Potsdam. Berlin's **S7** runs from Bahnhof Zoo to Potsdam (30min., €2.50). ☎**0331.**

EASTERN GERMANY

Saxony *(Sachsen)* is known primarily for Dresden and Leipzig, the largest cities in Eastern Germany after Berlin. However, the entire region offers fascinating historical and cultural diversity. The castles around Dresden testify to the decadence of Saxony's Electors, while the boxy socialist monuments recall the former world of the GDR. Saxony is also home to the Sorbs, Germany's only national minority, which lends a Slavic feel to many of the region's eastern towns.

DRESDEN ☎ 0351

The stunning buildings of Dresden's *Altstadt* look ancient, but most are newly reconstructed—the Allied bombings of February 1945 claimed over 50,000 lives and destroyed 75% of the city center. Today, Dresden pulses with a historical intensity, engaging visitors with world-class museums and partially reconstructed palaces and churches (reconstruction is scheduled for completion by 2006, the city's 800-year anniversary). However, Dresden is not all nostalgic nods to the past; the city has entered the new millennium as a young, dynamic metropolis propelled by a history of cultural turbulence.

▄ TRANSPORTATION

Flights: Dresden's **airport** (DRS; ☎ 881 33 60) is 9km from town; the S2 makes the 20min. trip from both train stations (2 per hr., 4am-10:30pm, €1.50).

Trains: The **Dresden Hauptbahnhof,** in the *Altstadt,* and **Bahnhof Dresden Neustadt,** across the Elbe, both send trains to: **Berlin** (3hr., every hr., €30); **Budapest** (11hr., every 2 hr., €64); **Frankfurt** (7hr., 2 per hr., €70); **Leipzig** (1½hr., 1-2 per hr., €17); **Munich** (7hr., 24 per day, €27); **Prague** (2½hr., 12 per day, €20); **Warsaw** (8hr., 8 per day, €27). Buy tickets from the machines in the main halls of both stations, or from the staff at the *Reisezentrum* desk.

Public Transportation: Dresden's **streetcars** are efficient and cover the whole city. **Single-ride** €1.50; 4 or fewer stops €1. **Day pass** €4; **weekly pass** €13. Most major lines run every hr. after midnight. Tickets are available from *Fahrkarten* dispensers at major stops, on the streetcars themselves, and from **Verkehrs-Info** stands in front of the *Hauptbahnhof* or at Postpl. (Open M-F 7am-7pm, Sa 8am-6pm, Su 9am-6pm).

▄ ORIENTATION AND PRACTICAL INFORMATION

Dresden is bisected by the **Elbe.** The **Altstadt** lies on the same side as the *Hauptbahnhof;* **Neustadt,** to the north, escaped most of the bombing, paradoxically making it one of the oldest parts of the city. Many of Dresden's main attractions are centered between the **Altmarkt** and the **Elbe,** 5min. from the *Neustadt.*

Tourist Office: 2 locations: **Prager Straße 3,** near the *Hauptbahnhof* (open M-F 9am-7pm, Sa 9am-4pm); **Theaterplatz** in the *Schinkelwache,* in front of the Semper-Oper (☎ 49 19 20; open M-F 10am-6pm, Sa-Su 10am-4pm). Sells city maps (€2.50) and the **Dresden Card,** which includes 48hr. of public transit, free or reduced entry at many museums, and city tours (€14).

Currency Exchange: ReiseBank, in the *Hauptbahnhof.* 1-3% commission, depending on the amount; 1-1.5% for traveler's checks. Open M-F 8am-7:30pm, Sa 12:30pm-4pm, Su 9am-1pm. A self-service exchange machine is available, but rates are poor.

Luggage Storage: At both train stations. Lockers €1-2 for 24hr. storage.

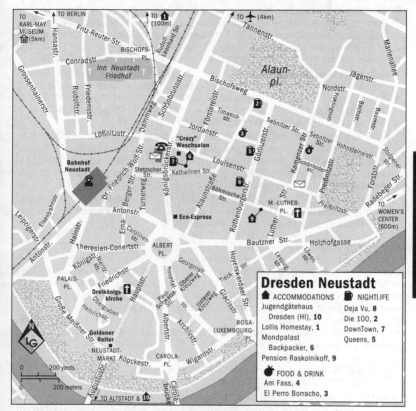

Dresden Neustadt

ACCOMMODATIONS	NIGHTLIFE
Jugendgätehaus	Deja Vu, **8**
Dresden (HI), **10**	Die 100, **2**
Lollis Homestay, **1**	DownTown, **7**
Mondpalast	Queens, **5**
Backpacker, **6**	
Pension Raskolnikoff, **9**	

FOOD & DRINK
Am Fass, **4**
El Perro Borracho, **3**

Bi-Gay-Lesbian Resources: Gerede-Dresdner Lesben, Schwule und alle Anderen, Prießnitzstr. 18 (☎802 22 51; 24hr. hotline ☎802 22 70). From Albertpl., walk up Bautzner Str. and turn left onto Prießnitzstr. Open M-F 3-5pm.

Laundromat: Groove Station, Katharinenstr. 11-13. Wash (€2.50) and dry (€1.50), while browsing the tattoo and piercing studio. Open daily 3pm-late.

Emergency: Police: ☎110. **Ambulance and Fire:** ☎112.

Pharmacy: Apotheke Prager Straße, Prager Str. 3 (☎490 30 14). Open M-F 8:30am-7pm, Sa 8:30am-4pm.

Internet Access: Internet Cafe Netzstatt, Schandauerstr. 64. €3 per hr. Open daily 1pm-midnight.

Post Office: Hauptpostamt, Königsbrücker Str. 21/29 (☎819 13 73), in *Neustadt.* Open M-F 8am-7pm, Sa 9am-1pm. Address mail to be held: *Postlagernde Briefe* für Firstname SURNAME, Hauptpostamt, **D-01099** Dresden, Germany.

🏠 ACCOMMODATIONS AND CAMPING

If there's one thing that attests to Dresden's status as a city on the rise, it's the state of its accommodations. New hotels and hostels are constantly being opened, although it's still hard to get a spot in a good location on weekends.

▨ **Mondpalast Backpacker,** Katharinenstr. 11-13 (☎/fax 804 60 61). From *Bahnhof Neustadt,* walk down Antonstr. toward Albertpl., turn left onto Königsbrücker Str., then turn right on Katharinenstr. Located in the heart of the *Neustadt* scene, it's the hippest place in town. Breakfast €4.50. Sheets €2.50. Key deposit €5. Reception 24hr. 8-bed dorms €13.50; 5- to 7-bed dorms €15; 3- to 4-bed dorms €16; doubles €34. ❷

Jugendgästehaus Dresden (HI), Maternistr. 22 (☎49 26 20). Take the Prager Str. exit from the *Hauptbahnhof* and turn left on Ammonstr., right on Rosen Str. and then left onto Maternistr. This sleek hostel has newly renovated rooms with more than 400 beds. Breakfast included. Reception 24hr. Check-in after 4pm. Check-out 9:30am. 2- to 4-bed dorms €17.50, with shower €21; singles €25/€28.50. ❷

Lollis Homestay, Seitenstr. 2A (☎819 84 58). From the *Neustadt* station, turn left on Dr.-Friedrich-Wolf-Str., follow it for 10min. to Bischofsweg, and turn left. After the tracks, take a right on Rudolf Leonardstr. and then a quick left and right after the park. Bear right; the hostel is directly ahead. A small and comfortably furnished hostel that feels like home. Breakfast €3. Laundry free. 6-bed dorms €13; singles €25; doubles €34. ❶

Pension Raskolnikoff, Böhmische Str. 34 (☎804 57 06). Located right in the middle of the *Neustadt,* this 6-room pension is the perfect way to escape the hostel scene. Singles €31; doubles €41; €8 for each extra person. ❸

◖ FOOD

Unfortunately, the surge in tourism has raised Dresden's food prices, particularly in the *Altstadt.* The cheapest eats in the *Altstadt* are at supermarkets or *Imbiß* stands along **Prager Straße.** The **Neustadt** rules the roost of quirky, ethnic, and student-friendly restaurants. **El Perro Borracho ❸,** Alaunstr. 70, serves traditional Spanish *tapas* and sangria. (Open M-F 11am-2am, Sa-Su 10am-1am.) **Am Fass ❷,** Kammenzerstr. 28, hidden behind a graffiti-covered sign in the *Neustadt,* provides a unique Hungarian eating experience. (Open M-F 11am-late.)

◗ SIGHTS

▨**ZWINGER.** The extravagant art collection of Friedrich August I (August the Strong), Prince Elector of Saxony and King of Poland, is housed in the magnificent **Zwinger** palace, a building championed as a triumph of Baroque design. The palace narrowly escaped destruction in the 1945 bombings; workers are busy restoring it to aesthetic perfection. In the Semper wing is the **Gemäldegalerie Alte Meister,** a world-class collection of paintings from 1400-1800. Across from the gallery is the **Rüstkammer,** a collection of courtly toys including silver- and gold-plated suits for both man and horse and a set of toddler-sized armor. *(Both open Tu-Su 10am-6pm. Joint admission €3.60, students €2.10. Tours F and Su 11am and 4pm. €0.50)*

SEMPER-OPER. This famed opera house, one of Dresden's major attractions, has been painstakingly restored to its original state. *(Theaterpl. 2. ☎491 14 96. Check the main entrance for tour times, usually M-F every 30min. 11am-3pm. €5, students €3.)*

KREUZKIRCHE. After being levelled four times (in 1669 by fire, in 1760 during the Seven Years War, in 1897 by fire, and finally in February 1945 by Allied bombing), the interior remains in a damaged state. The tower offers a bird's eye view of downtown Dresden. *(An der Kreuzkirche 6. Open in summer M-Tu and Th-F 10am-5:30pm, W and Sa 10am-4:30pm, Su noon-4:30pm; off-season M-Sa 10am-3:30pm, Su noon-4:30pm. Free. Tower closes 30min. before the church. €1.)*

DRESDENER SCHLOß. The proud home of August the Strong was ruined in the Allied firebombing of 1945, but its restoration is nearly complete. The 100m ▨**Hausmannsturm** hosts fascinating but sobering photographs and texts discussing the Allied bombings, and the top floor offers a 360° view of the city. *(Across from the Zwinger on Schloßpl. Open Tu-Su 10am-6pm. €3.50, students €2.)* Stop by the **Fürstenzug** (Procession of Electors) along Augustusstr., a 102m mural made of 24,000 tiles of Meißen china, for a history lesson on the rulers of Saxony from 1123 to 1904.

NEUSTADT. Across the magnificent **Augustusbrücke**, Hauptstr. is home to the **Goldener Reiter**, a gold-plated statue of August the Strong atop a steed in pompous glory. August's nickname was reputedly a homage to his remarkable virility; legend has it he fathered 365 children, though the official tally is 15. At the other end of Hauptstr. is **Albertplatz**, the gateway to the *Neustadt* scene.

SCHLACHTHOFRINGE. The **Schlachthofringe** (Slaughterhouse Circle) is a 1910 housing complex in a more dismal part of Dresden, used during WWII as a P.O.W. camp; its buildings have since been left to waste away. Novelist Kurt Vonnegut was imprisoned here during the bombing of Dresden, inspiring his masterpiece *Slaughterhouse Five. (Take bus #82 (dir.: Dresden Messe) to Ostragehege.)*

ALBERTINUM. The Albertinum holds the ◙**Gemälde-galerie der Neuen Meister,** which combines an ensemble of German and French Impressionists with a collection of Expressionists and Neue Sachlichkeit modernist works, including Otto Dix's renowned *War* triptych. *(Open F-W 10am-6pm. €4.50, students €2.50; includes admission to **Grünes Gewölbe**, a collection of Saxon figurines.)*

DEUTSCHES HYGIENEMUSEUM. This ill-named museum long celebrated the health and cleanliness of East Germans. Today, the rather bizarre, interactive, and playful collection includes optical illusions, a hallway of condom propaganda, and a glass cow whose innards light up. *(Lingnerpl. 1; enter from Blüherstr. Open Tu-F 9am-5pm, Sa-Su 10am-6pm. €2.50, students €1.50.)*

▣ NIGHTLIFE

Dresden's nightlife scene is young and dynamic; the **Neustadt,** roughly bounded by Königsbrückerstr., Bischofsweg, Kamenzerstr., and Albertpl., is its pulsing heart. At last count, over 50 bars packed the area; *Kneipen Surfer* (free at *Neustadt* hostels) lists all of them.

> **DownTown,** Katharinenstr. 11-13, below the Mondpalast hostel. The music is loud and seating is rare. Cover €3.50, students €2.50. Open Tu, Th-Sa 10pm-5am.

YOUR
OWN
WAY

SAXON SWITZERLAND

Saxon Switzerland—so dubbed because of its stunning, Swiss-like landscape—is one of Germany's favorite national parks.

RATHEN. Rathen's location on the edge of the park makes it a good starting point for hikes of any length. Info: ☎(035024) 704 22.

KÖNIGSTEIN. Above the town looms the impressive **Festung Königstein.** From the town, it's a 40min. uphill struggle, but the view is worth it. Info: ☎(035021) 682 21.

BAD SCHANDAU. The biggest town in the region, Bad Schandau offers plenty of hiking opportunities. Take the *Kirnitzschtalbahn* trolley car (Mar.-Oct. every 30min. 9:30am-5:30pm, €3) to the **Lichtenhain waterfall,** a favorite starting point for 3-4hr. hikes. The **tourist office,** Markt 12, finds rooms, suggests hikes, and offers city tours and trips to the Czech Republic. Info: ☎(030522) 900 30.

TRANSPORTATION. Dresden's S1 (dir.: Schöna) runs from the Dresden *Hauptbahnhof* to Rathen, Königstein, and Bad Schandau. The S-Bahn stops across the river from each of these towns; hop on the ferries to get to the sights. Since *Wanderwege* (footpaths) crisscross the area, you can also easily hike from town to town. From Bad Schandau, the end of the line, ride the S-Bahn back to Dresden (50min., every 30min., €4.50) or continue to Prague (2hr., every 2hr., €16).

Die 100, Alaunstr. 100. An unpolished and relaxed atmosphere in a dimly lit coal cellar. With over 300 wines, Die 100 is first and foremost a *Weinkeller.* Open daily 5pm-3am.

Deja Vu, Rothenburgerstr. 37. If you're tired of German beer and bar stools, head to this "milk bar" for a milkshake (alcoholic or non-) and a creamy, blue-lit decor. Open M-F 10am-3am, Sa-Su 10am-5am.

Queens, Görlitzer Str. 3. A popular gay bar with plenty of sparkle. Drinks (€2.50-7), music, and occasional special entertainment. Open daily from 8pm.

🔯 DAYTRIPS FROM DRESDEN

MEIßEN. Meißen, 30km from Dresden, is another testament to the frivolity of August the Strong. In 1710, the Saxon elector contracted severe *Porzellankrankheit* (the porcelain "bug," still afflicting tourists today) and turned the city's defunct castle into Europe's first porcelain factory. To prevent competitors from learning its techniques; the building was once more tightly guarded than KGB headquarters; today, anyone can tour the **Staatliche Porzellan-Manufaktur,** Talstr. 9. Finished products are showcased in the **Schauhalle** (€4.50, students €4), but the real fun lies in the high-tech tour of the **Schauwerkstatt** (show workshop), which demonstrates the manufacturing process. (Open May-Oct. daily 9am-6pm; Nov.-Apr. 9am-5pm. €3. English headsets available.) Romantic alleyways lead up to the **Albrechtsburg** castle and cathedral. (Open Mar.-Oct. daily 10am-6pm; Nov.-Feb. 10am-5pm. Last entry 30min. before closing. €3.50, students €2.50.) From the train station, walk straight onto Bahnhofstr. and follow it over the Elbbrücke. Cross the bridge, continue straight to the Markt, and turn right onto Burgstr. At the end of Burgstr., on Holweg, take the Schloßstufen (castle stairs) on your right, which lead up to Albrechtsburg. The **tourist office,** Markt 3, across from the church, finds private rooms for a €3 fee. (☎419 40. Open Apr.-Oct. M-F 10am-6pm, Sa-Su 10am-4pm; Nov.-Mar. M-F 10am-5pm, Sa 10am-3pm.) **Postal Code:** 01662.

LEIPZIG   ☎0341

Leipzig's *Innenstadt* is small in size, though anything but small in energy and style. Bursting with museums and monuments to Bach, cafes, and bars, Leipzig's appeal can be felt from almost any angle. As in much of former East Germany, unemployment still poses a problem, but Leipzig's fascinating historical role dating back to the time of Napoleon makes it well worth the visit.

▣🔢 TRANSPORTATION AND PRACTICAL INFORMATION. Leipzig lies on the Berlin-Munich line. **Trains** run to: Berlin (2-3hr., 3 per hr., €26); Dresden (1½hr., 3 per hr., €17); Frankfurt (5hr., 2 per hr., €62); and Munich (7hr., 3 per hr., €68). To find the **tourist office,** Richard-Wagner-Str. 1, cross Willy-Brandt-Pl. in front of the station and turn left at Richard-Wagner-Str. (☎710 42 60. Open M-F 9am-7pm, Sa 9am-4pm, Su 9am-2pm.) **Postal Code:** 04109.

🔳 ACCOMMODATIONS AND FOOD. To reach **Hostel Sleepy Lion ❷,** Käthe-Kollwitz-Str. 3, take streetcar #1 (dir.: Lausen) or #14 (dir.: S-Bahnhof Plagwitz) to Gottschedstr. Conveniently located next to the city's nightlife, the Sleepy Lion draws an international crowd. All rooms have shower and bathroom. (☎993 94 80. Internet €2 per hr. Breakfast €3. Sheets €2. Reception 24hr. 6- to 8-bed dorms €14; singles €24; doubles €36; quads €60.) **Kosmos Hotel ❸,** Gottschedstr. 1, is a 12min. walk from the train station. From the *Hauptbahnhof,* cross the street and turn right onto Richard-Wagner-Str.; when it ends, cut left through the parking lot and small park. At the end of the park, keep left on Dittrichring and it'll be ahead on the right. This funky hotel is part of a larger complex that includes a nightclub and restaurant. (☎233 44 20. Breakfast €5. Reception 8am-11pm. Singles from €30; doubles from €50.)

The *Innenstadt*, especially **Grimmaischestraße**, has *Imbiß* stands, bistros, and bakeries. Just outside the city center, **Karl-Liebknecht-Straße** (streetcar #10 or 11 to Kochstr.) is packed with cheap *Döner* stands and cafes that double as bars come nighttime. ⊠**Avocado** ❸, Karl-Liebknecht-Str. 79, has vegetarian and vegan options. (Open M-Th and Su 11:30am-1am, F 11:30am-2am and Sa 4pm-2am.) **Zur Pleißenburg** ❷, Schulstr. 2, just down Burgstr. from the Thomaskirche, is popular with locals and serves hearty fare. (Open daily 9am-5am.) A **market** on Richard-Wagner-Pl. at the end of the Brühl sells fresh goodies Tuesday and Friday (9am-5pm).

🖼🎦 **SIGHTS AND NIGHTLIFE.** The heart of Leipzig is the **Marktplatz**, a cobblestoned square guarded by the slanted 16th-century **Altes Rathaus.** Head down Grimmaischestr. to the **Nikolaikirche,** where massive weekly demonstrations led to the fall of the GDR. (Open M-Sa 10am-6pm, Su after services. Free.) Backtrack to the *Rathaus* and follow Thomasg. to the **Thomaskirche;** Bach's grave lies beneath the floor in front of the altar. (Open daily 9am-6pm. Free.) Just behind the church is the **Johann-Sebastian-Bach-Museum,** Thomaskirchof 16. (Open daily 10am-5pm. €3, students €2. Free English-language audio tours.) Head back to Thomasg., turn left, then turn right on Dittrichring to reach Leipzig's most fascinating museum, the **Museum in der "Runden Ecke,"** Dittrichring 24, which displays stunningly blunt exhibits on the history, doctrine, and tools of the *Stasi* (secret police). Ask for an English brochure in the office. (Open daily 10am-6pm. Free.) Outside the city ring, the ⊠**Völkerschlachtdenkmal** memorializes the 1813 Battle of Nations against Napoleon. Climb the 500 steps for a fabulous view. (Streetcar #15 from the train station to Völkerschlachtdenkmal. Open daily Apr.-Oct. 10am-6pm; Nov.-Mar. 10am-5pm. Free. To ascend €3, students €2.)

Free magazines *Fritz* and *Blitz* and the superior *Kreuzer* (€1.50 at newsstands) fill you in on nightlife. **Barfußgäßchen,** a street just off the Markt, serves as the see-and-be-seen nightlife area for everyone from students to *Schicki-mickis* (yuppies). Just across Dittrichring on **Gottschedstraße** and **Bosestraße** is a similar scene with a slightly younger crowd and slightly louder music. Leipzig university

THE BIG SPLURGE

AUERBACHS KELLER

It was in this 16th-century tavern that Mephistopheles, the most notorious of evil spirits, tricked some drunkards in Goethe's *Faust* before disappearing in a puff of smoke.

Since then, the Auerbachs Keller has become Leipzig's most famous restaurant and one of the most well-known eateries in all of Europe. Check out the scenes from *Faust* on the walls of the barrel cellar over a long lunch or dinner in this elegant and atmospheric, yet somehow unpretentious, restaurant.

The restaurant has several different eating areas, each with their own atmosphere and name. The Luther room reminds of one of the restaurant's early patrons. The old Leipzig room dates back to the "good times" of the late 19th century. The Goethe room keeps the legend of the restaurant's most famous guest alive with pictures and memorabilia on the wall. The barrel cellar, a more relaxed eating spot, is where the alleged disappearance took place.

The extensive menu includes duck, salmon, and steak entrees from €18-35. The dessert menu, featuring sorbet, crepes, and chocolate parfait, should also not be missed.

(Grimmaische Str. 2-4. Across from the Altes Rathaus, inside the Mädlerpassage. ☎21 61 00. Open daily 11:30am-midnight. MC/V.)

students spent eight years excavating a series of medieval tunnels so they could get their groove on in the ▨**Moritzbastei,** Universitätsstr. 9, which has multi-level dance floors and relaxed bars in cavernous rooms with vaulted brick ceilings. (Cover €4, students €2; higher for concerts. Open M 2pm-6am, Tu-F noon-2am.)

WITTENBERG ☎ 03491

The Protestant Reformation began here in 1517 when Martin Luther nailed his *95 Theses* to the door of the Schloßkirche; Wittenberg has been nuts about its heretical son ever since. All the major sights lie around **Collegienstraße.** The **Lutherhalle,** Collegienstr. 54, chronicles the history of the Reformation through letters, texts, art, and artifacts. (☎ 40 26 71. Call after Oct. 2002 for new hours. €5.) The **Schloßkirche** allegedly holds Luther's body and a copy of the *95 Theses.* The tower offers a sumptuous view of the countryside. (Down Schloßstr. Church open M-Sa 10am-5pm, Su 11:30am-5pm. Free. Tower open M-F noon-3:30pm, Sa-Su 10am-3:30pm. €1, students €0.50.)

Trains leave the *Hauptbahnhof* for Berlin (1½hr., every 2hr., €17) and Leipzig (1hr., every 2hr., €9). From the station, follow the street as it curves right and continue until Collegienstr., the beginning of the **pedestrian zone.** The **tourist office,** Schloßpl. 2, at the end of the pedestrian zone, provides maps, leads tours (€6), and books rooms. (☎ 49 86 10. Open Mar.-Oct. M-F 9am-6pm, Sa 10am-3pm, Su 11am-4pm; Nov.-Feb. M-F 10am-4pm, Sa 10am-2pm, Su 11am-3pm.) The **Jugendherberge (HI)** ❷ is in the castle; cross the street from the tourist office and head into the castle's enclosure, then trek up the stairs to the right. (☎ 40 32 55. Breakfast included. Sheets €3.50. Key deposit €5. Reception 3-10pm. Lockout 10pm. Dorms €15, under 26 €12.) Cheap eats lie along the Collegienstr.-Schloßstr. strip. There are plenty of supermarkets in this area as well. **Postal Code:** 06886.

WEIMAR ☎ 03643

While countless German towns leap at any excuse to build memorial *Goethehäuser* (proclaiming that Goethe slept here, Goethe ate here, Goethe once asked for directions here), Weimar features the real thing: the **Goethehaus** and **Goethe-Nationalmuseum,** Frauenplan 1, present the preserved private chambers where the poet entertained, wrote, and ultimately died after 50 years in Weimar. (Open mid-Mar. to mid-Oct. Tu-Su 9am-6pm; mid-Oct. to mid-Mar. 10am-4pm. Expect a wait of up to 2hr. on summer afternoons. €6, students €4.50.) The **Neuesmuseum,** Weimarpl. 4, hosts fascinating rotating exhibits of modern art, including an interactive "Terrororchestra," composed of knives, nails, and a hammer and sickle. (Open Apr.-Sept. Tu-Su 10am-6pm; Oct.-Mar. 10am-4:30pm. €3, students €2.) South of the town center in the **Historischer Friedhof,** Goethe and Schiller rest together in the basement of the **Fürstengruft.** Schiller, who died in an epidemic, was originally buried in a mass grave. Later, Goethe combed through the remains until he identified Schiller and had him interred in a tomb. Skeptics argued that Goethe was mistaken, but a team of Russian scientists verified his claim in the 1960s. (Cemetery open Mar.-Sept. daily 8am-9pm; Oct.-Feb. 8am-6pm. Tomb open mid-Mar. to mid-Oct. W-M 9am-1pm and 2-6pm; mid-Oct. to mid-Mar. W-M 10am-1pm and 2-4pm. €2, students €1.50.)

Trains run to: Dresden (3½hr., 2 per hr., €30); Frankfurt (3hr., every hr., €40); and Leipzig (1½hr., 2 per hr., €21.20). To reach **Goetheplatz** (the center of the *Altstadt*) from the station, follow Carl-August-Allee downhill to Karl-Liebknecht-Str., which leads into Goethepl. (15min.). The **tourist office,** Marktstr. 10, across from the *Rathaus,* hands out free maps, books rooms (€2.55 fee), and offers German-language **walking tours.** The Weimarer Wald desk has lots of info on **outdoor activities** in the area. (☎ 240 00. Open Apr.-Oct. M-F 9:30am-6pm, Sa 9:30am-4pm, Su

9:30am-3pm; Nov.-Mar. M-F 10am-6pm, Sa-Su 10am-2pm.) To get to the student-run ▨**Hababusch Hostel ❶**, Geleitstr. 4, follow Geleitstr. from Goethepl.; after it takes a sharp right, you'll come to a statue on your left. The entrance to the Hababusch is tucked in the ivied corner behind the statue. Conveniently in the heart of Weimar, the hostel has a laid-back atmosphere. (☎85 07 37. Reception 24hr. Dorms €10; singles €15; doubles €24.) **Gästehaus Appartements am Theater ❸**, Heinrich-Heine-Str. 16, has apartment-style rooms, each with a full kitchen and bathroom. From the station, walk down Carl-August-Allee, turn right at Rathenau-Pl., and keep heading south on Karl-Leibknecht-Str., which becomes Heinrich-Heine-Str. (☎50 41 66. Call ahead. Singles €28; doubles €38.) A combination cafe and gallery, **ACC ❸**, Burgpl. 1-2, is popular with students. (Open daily noon-1am.) The daily **produce market**, at Marktpl., has groceries. (Open M-Sa 7am-5pm.)

🖪 **DAYTRIP FROM WEIMAR: BUCHENWALD.** During World War II, 250,000 Jews, Gypsies, homosexuals, communists, and political prisoners were imprisoned at the labor camp of Buchenwald. Although it was not intended as an extermination camp, over 50,000 died here due to the harsh treatment by the SS. The **Nationale Mahnmal und Gedenkstätte Buchenwald** (National Monument and Memorial) has two principal sights. The **KZ-Lager** (*Konzentration-Lager;* concentration camp) refers to the remnants of the camps itself. The large storehouse building documents both the history of Buchenwald (1937-1945) and the general history of Nazism, including German anti-Semitism. The East German **Mahnmal** (monument) is on the other side of the hill; go straight up the main road that bisects the two large parking lots, or take the footpath uphill from the old Buchenwald *Bahnhof* and then continue on the main road. The camp **archives** are open to anyone searching for records of family and friends between 1937 and 1945. Schedule an appointment with the curator. (Archives ☎(03643) 43 01 54; library ☎(03643) 43 01 60. Outdoor camp area open daily until sundown.) Sadly, suffering in Buchenwald did not end with liberation—Soviet authorities used the site as an internment camp, **"Special Camp. No. 2,"** where more than 28,000 Germans—mostly Nazi war criminals and opponents of the communist regime, were held until 1950; an exhibit detailing this period opened in 1997.

The best way to reach the camp is by **bus** #6 from Weimar's train station or Goethepl. Check the schedule carefully; some #6 buses go to Ettersburg rather than Gedenkstätte Buchenwald. (20min.; M-F every hr., Sa-Su every 2hr.) Buses back to Weimar stop at the *KZ-Lager* parking lot and at the road by the *Glockenturm* (bell tower). There is an **information center** near the bus stop at Buchenwald, which offers a walking tour (€3) and shows an excellent video with English subtitles on the hour. (Open May-Sept. Tu-Su 9am-6pm; Oct.-Apr. 8:30am-4:30pm.)

EISENACH   ☎03691

Birthplace of Johann Sebastian Bach, Eisenach is also home to one of Germany's most treasured national symbols, ▨**Wartburg castle.** In 1521, the castle protected Martin Luther (disguised as a bearded noble named Junker Jörg) after his excommunication. Much of the castle's interior is not authentically medieval, but the Wartburg is still enchanting and the view from its south tower is spectacular. (Open Mar.-Oct. daily 8:30am-5pm; Nov.-Feb. 9am-3:30pm. Mandatory German tour €6, students and children €3.) According to local tradition, the actual location of Bach's birth in 1685 was the **Bachhaus**, Frauenplan 21. Every 40min., a guide gives a presentation on Bach's life in German and English, complete with musical interludes. (Open Apr.-Sept. M noon-5:45pm, Tu-Su 9am-5:45pm; Oct. Mar. M 1-4:45pm, Tu-Su 9am-4:45pm. €2.50, students €2.) Bach was baptized at the 800-year-old **Georgenkirche,** just off the Markt, where members of his family were organists for 132 years. (Open M-Sa 10am-12:30pm and 2-5pm, Su after services.) Just up the street sits the latticed **Lutherhaus,** Lutherpl. 8, Martin's home in his school days. (Open Apr.-Oct. daily 9am-5pm; Nov.-Mar. 10am-5pm. €2.50.)

Trains run frequently to **Weimar** (1hr., 2 per hr., €11). The **tourist office,** Markt 2, sells maps (€2), offers daily city tours (2pm, €3), and books rooms for free. From the train station, follow Bahnhofstr. through the tunnel and angle left until you turn right onto the pedestrian Karlstr. (☎194 33. Open M 10am-6pm, Tu-F 9am-6pm, Sa-Su 10am-2pm.) To reach the recently renovated **Jugendherberge Arthur Becker (HI) ❷,** Mariental 24, take Bahnhofstr. from the station to Wartburger Allee, which runs into Mariental. (☎74 32 59. Breakfast included. Sheets €3.30. Reception 8am-11pm. No curfew. Dorms €17, under 26 €14.) For groceries, head to **Edeka supermarket** on Johannispl. (Open M-F 8am-6:30pm, Sa 8am-12:30pm.) Near the train station, **Café Moritz ❷,** Bahnhofstr. 7, serves Thüringer specialities (€3-9) and sinful ice cream delicacies. (Open May-Oct. M-F 8am-9pm, Sa-Su 10am-9pm; Nov.-Apr. M-F 8am-7pm, Sa-Su 10am-7pm.) **Postal Code:** 99817.

NORTHERN GERMANY

Once a favored vacation spot for East Germans, Mecklenburg-Vorpommern, the northeasternmost portion of Germany, has suffered economic depression in recent years. To the west, Schleswig-Holstein, which borders Denmark, maintains close ties with Scandinavia. To the west, Bremen is Germany's smallest *Land.*

HANOVER (HANNOVER)   ☎0511

With a wealth of museums, and a tradition of festivals, Hanover reigns as the cultural capital of Lower Saxony. On the outskirts of the **Altstadt** stands the spectacular **Neues Rathaus;** take the elevator (€2, students €1.50) up the tower for a thrilling view of the city. (Open May-Sept. M-F 8am-10pm, Sa-Su 10am-10pm.) Right next door, the ▨**Kestner-Museum,** Trammpl. 3, features ancient, medieval, and Renaissance arts. (Open Tu and Th-Su 11am-6pm, W 11am-8pm. €2.60, students €1.55; F free.) The nearby ▨**Sprengel Museum,** Kurt-Schwitters-Pl., at the corner of the Maschsee and Maschpark, hosts the best of 20th-century art. (Open Tu 10am-8pm, W-Su 10am-6pm. Permanent collection €3.30, students €2; with special exhibits €6, students €3.50.) The gems of Hanover are the three bountiful **Herrenhausen gardens.** The largest, the geometrically trimmed **Großer Garten,** holds the **Große Fontäne,** Europe's highest-shooting fountain at 80m. (Fountain spurts M-F 11am-noon and 3-5pm, Sa-Su 11am-noon and 2-5pm. Garden open Apr.-Oct. 8am-8pm; Nov.-Mar. 8am-dusk. €2.50.)

Trains leave at least every hour for: Amsterdam (4½-5hr., €40); Berlin (2½hr., €40); Cologne (2hr., €50); Frankfurt (3hr., €80); Hamburg (1½hr., €25); and Munich (9hr., €130). To reach the **tourist office,** Ernst-August-Pl. 2, head out the main entrance of the train station; facing the large rear of the king's splendid steed, turn right. (☎16 84 97 00. Open M-F 9am-6pm, Sa 9am-2pm.) ▨**Jugendherberge Hannover (HI) ❷,** Ferdinand-Wilhelm-Fricke-Weg. 1, is far from the city center, but definitely worth the trek. U3 or 7 (dir.: Wettbergen) to Fischerhof/Fachhochschule. From the stop, backtrack 10m, turn right, cross the tracks, and walk on the path through the school's parking lot; follow the path as it curves, and cross the street. Go over the enormous red footbridge and turn right. The hostel is 50m down on the right. (☎131 76 74. Breakfast included. Reception daily 7:30am-11:30pm. Dorms €19-30, under 26 €16-28.) To reach **Hotel am Thielenplatz ❺,** Thielenpl. 2, take a left onto Joachimstr. from the station and go one block to Thielenpl. (☎32 76 91 93. Breakfast included. Check-out 11:30am. Singles with shower €66-76; doubles with shower €92-112. Weekends cheaper.) ▨**Jalda ❷,** Limmerstr. 97, serves Italian, Greek, and Arabic dishes for €4-8. (Open Su-Th 11:30am-midnight, F-Sa noon-1am.) **Uwe's Hannenfaß Hanover ❸,** Knochenhauerstr. 36, in the center of the *Altstadt,* serves traditional German fare for €5-7 and great brews for €3. (Open Su-F 4pm-2am, Sa noon-3am.) **Spar supermarkets** sit by the Lister Meile and Kröpcke U-Bahn stops. (Open M-F 7am-7pm, Sa 8am-2pm.) From the *Hauptbahnhof,* head to the **Markt-halle,** where a variety of snacks, meals, and booze awaits. (Open M-W 7am-6pm, Th-F 7am-8pm, Sa 7am-4pm.) **The Loft,** Georgstr. 50b, is packed with students on the weekends. (Disco night F and ladies night Sa have €3.50 covers. Open W-Sa from 8pm.) **Postal code: 30159.**

HAMBURG ☎040

The largest port city in Germany, Hamburg radiates an inimitable recklessness. The city proudly retains its autonomy as one of three German city-states. Restoration and riots determined the post-World War II landscape, but today's Hamburg has become a haven for contemporary artists, intellectuals, and party-goers in Germany's self-declared "capital of lust."

▐ TRANSPORTATION

Trains: The **Hauptbahnhof** handles most traffic: **Amsterdam** (5½hr., 3 per day, €68.60); **Berlin** (2½hr., every hr., €45); **Copenhagen** (4½hr., €67.20); **Frankfurt** (3¾hr., every hr., €98); **Hanover** (1¼hr., 3 per hr., €25.60); and **Munich** (5½hr., every hr., €133). Two other stations, **Dammtor** (near the university) and **Altona** (in the west) service the city; frequent trains and the S-Bahn connect the 3 stations. 24hr. **lockers** are available for €1-2 per day; just follow the overhead signs.

Buses: The **ZOB** is on Steintorpl. across from the *Hauptbahnhof,* between McDonald's and the Museum für Kunst und Gewerbe. To: **Berlin** (3¼hr., 8 per day, €22); **Copenhagen** (5½hr., 2 per day, €30); and **Paris** (12½hr., 1 per day, €56). Open M-F 9am-8pm, Sa 9:30am-1:30pm and 4-8pm, Su 4-8pm.

Public Transportation: HVV operates an efficient U-Bahn, S-Bahn, and bus network. Most single tickets within the downtown area cost €1, but can vary depending on where you go and what transport you take. 1-day (€5) and 3-day (€12.30) tickets are not as cost-effective as the **Hamburg Card** (see below). Buy tickets at the orange *Automaten.*

◣ ▐ ORIENTATION AND PRACTICAL INFORMATION

Hamburg's city center sits between the **Elbe River** and the two city lakes, **Außenalster** and **Binnenalster.** Most major sights lie between the **St. Pauli Landungsbrücken** port area in the west and the *Hauptbahnhof* in the east. Both the *Nordbahnhof* and *Südbahnhof* U-Bahn stations exit onto the *Hauptbahnhof.* The **Hanseviertel** is crammed with banks, shops, and art galleries. North of the downtown, the **university** dominates the **Dammtor** area and sustains a vibrant community of students and intellectuals. To the west of the university, the **Schanzenviertel** is a politically active community home to artists, squatters, and a sizeable Turkish population. At the south end of town, an entirely different atmosphere reigns in **St. Pauli,** where the raucous **Fischmarkt** (fish market) is juxtaposed with the equally wild (and no less smelly) **Reeperbahn,** home to Hamburg's infamous sex trade.

Tourist Offices: Hamburg's main tourist offices supply free English maps. All sell the **Hamburg Card,** which provides unlimited access to public transportation, reduced admission to most museums, and discounts on bus and boat tours. (€6.80 for 1 day;

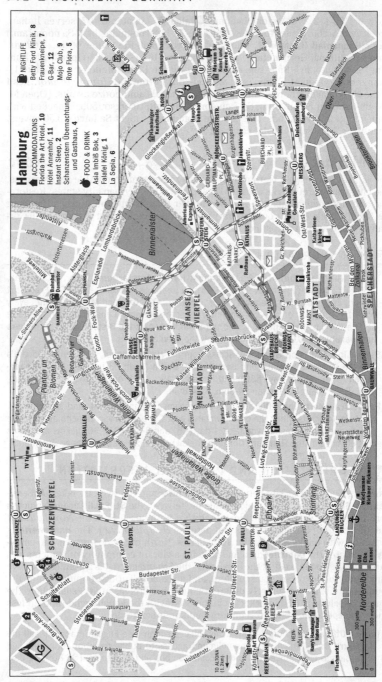

Hamburg

NIGHTLIFE
Betty Ford Klinik, **8**
Frauenkneipe, **7**
G-Bar, **12**
Mojo Club, **9**
Rote Flora, **5**

ACCOMMODATIONS
Florida the Art Hotel, **10**
Hotel Annenhof, **11**
Instant Sleep, **2**
Schanzenstern Übernachtungs-
und Gasthaus, **4**

FOOD & DRINK
Asia Imbiß Bok, **3**
Falafel König, **1**
La Sepia, **6**

€13 for 3 days.) The **Hauptbahnhof office,** in the Wandelhalle near the Kirchenallee exit (☎30 05 12 01), books rooms for €4. Open daily 7am-11pm. The **St. Pauli Landungsbrücken office,** between piers 4 and 5 (☎30 05 12 03), is less crowded.

Currency Exchange: ReiseBank, on the 2nd floor of the *Hauptbahnhof* near the Kirchenallee exit, provides Western Union, cashes traveler's checks, and exchanges money for a 4.5% commission. Open daily 7:30am-10pm.

American Express: Ballindamm 39, 20095 Hamburg (☎30 39 38 11 12). Take the S- or U-Bahn to Jungfernstieg. Letters held up to 5 weeks for members; all banking services. Open M-F 9am-6pm, Sa 10am-1pm.

Gay and Lesbian Resources: Hein und Fiete, Pulverteich 21 (☎24 03 33). Walk down Steindammstr. away from the *Hauptbahnhof* and turn right on Pulverteich; it's in the rainbow-striped building. Open M-F 4-9pm, Sa 4-7pm. **Magnus-Hirschfeld-Centrum,** Borgweg 8 (☎279 00 69), offers daily films and counseling sessions. U3 or bus #108 to Borgweg. Center open M and F 2-6pm, Tu-W 7-10pm.

Laundromat: Schnell und Sauber, Grindelallee 158, in the university district. Take S21 or 31 to Dammtor. Wash €3.50, dry €1 for 15min. Open daily 7am-10pm.

Emergency: Police: ☎110. **Fire** and **Ambulance:** ☎112.

Internet Access: Teletime, Schulterblatt 39, a call-shop and Internet cafe, has Internet for €3 per hr. Open daily 10am-midnight.

Post Office: At the Kirchenallee exit of the *Hauptbahnhof.* Open M-F 8am-10pm, Sa 9am-6pm, Su 10am-6pm. **Poste Restante:** Postlagernde Briefe für Firstname, SURNAME, Post Hamburg-Hauptbahnhof, **20099** Hamburg, Germany.

▐ ACCOMMODATIONS AND CAMPING

A slew of small, relatively cheap pensions (many rent by the hour) line **Steindamm, Steintorweg, Bremer Weg,** and **Bremer Reihe,** around the *Hauptbahnhof*. While the area is sketchy, the hotels are for the most part safe. The Sternschanze area has options a bit farther from both the good and the bad aspects of the *Hauptbahnhof* area. The tourist office's free *Hotelführer* aids in navigating past the filth.

▨ **Schanzenstern Übernachtungs-und Gasthaus,** Bartelsstr. 12 (☎439 84 41). S21 or U3 to Sternschanze, then turn left onto Schanzenstr., right on Susannenstr., and left onto Bartelsstr. In an electrifying neighborhood of students, working-class Turks, and left-wing dissenters. Clean, quiet, and bright. Wheelchair-accessible. Breakfast €3.60-5.65. Reception daily 6:30am-2am. Reservations a must in summer and at New Year's. Dorms €17; singles €35; doubles €50; triples €60; quads €73; quints €91. ❷

▨ **Instant Sleep,** Max-Brauer-Allee 277 (☎43 18 23 10). S21 or U3 to Sternschanze. From the station, go straight on Schanzenstr., turn left on Altonaer Str., and follow it until it becomes Max-Brauer-Allee. A family atmosphere; rooms are often left open while guests lounge together or cook their dinner. Sheets €3. Internet access €1 per 15min. Reception daily 9am-2pm. Call ahead. Dorms €15; singles €26; doubles €42; triples €57. ❷

Florida the Art Hotel, Spielbudenpl. 22 (☎31 43 93). U3 to St. Pauli, or S1 or 3 to Reeperbahn. Each room of this immaculate hotel reflects the work of a different artist. Breakfast included. Check-out 4pm. Call ahead. Singles €57; doubles €85. ❹

Hotel Annenhof, Lange Reihe 23 (☎24 34 26). From the train station's Kirchenallee exit, turn left onto Kirchenallee. Pass the *Schauspielhaus* on your right, then turn left on Lange Reihe. Simple rooms and soft beds. Breakfast €4. Singles €27; doubles €43. ❸

Camping: Campingplatz Rosemarie Buchholz, Kieler Str. 374 (☎540 45 32). From Altona train station, take bus #182 or 183 to Basselweg, then walk 100m in the same direction as traffic. Breakfast €4. Showers €1. Reception daily 8am-noon and 2-10pm. Check-out noon. Call ahead. €4 per person, €6 per tent. ❶

FOOD

Seafood abounds in Hamburg, as you'd expect in a port city. The most interesting part of town from a culinary standpoint is **Sternschanze,** where Turkish fruit stands, Asian *Imbiße,* and avant-garde cafes entice hungry passersby with good food and great atmosphere. **Schulterblatt, Susannenstraße,** and **Schanzenstraße** host funky cafes and restaurants, while slightly cheaper establishments abound in the **university** area, especially along **Rentzelstraße, Grindelhof,** and **Grindelallee.** In **Altona,** the pedestrian zone leading up to the train station is packed with ethnic food stands and produce shops. Check out the market inside Altona's massive **Mercado** mall, which includes everything from sushi bars to Portuguese fast food.

    🕍 **La Sepia,** Schulterblatt 36. A fine Portuguese restaurant with the city's best-prepared and most reasonably priced seafood. Dinner €8-14. Open daily 10am-3am. ❸

    Asia Imbiß Bok, Bartelstr. 28. To call this merely an *Imbiß* is misleading—this joint serves real restaurant food. Join the Bok's thrilled customers for spicy Thai noodles or roasted duck (€7-9). Open daily 11am-11:30pm. ❸

    Falafel König, Schanzenstr. 115. An excellent option for vegetarians. Made individually upon order, the falafel are fresh and sumptuous. Open Su-Th 9am-4am, F-Sa 24hr. ❶

🔍 SIGHTS

ALTSTADT. The gargantuan 18th-century **Michaelskirche** is the symbol of Hamburg. Its tower, accessible by foot or elevator, is the only one of the city's six spires that may be climbed. *(Organ music Apr.-Aug. daily noon and 5pm. Open May-Oct. M-Sa 9am-6pm, Su 11:30am-5:30pm; Nov.-Apr. M-Sa 10am-4:30pm, Su 11:30am-4:30pm. Tower €3, students €1.)* The **Rathaus** is a copper-spired neo-Renaissance monstrosity; inside are displays of the city's history. *(Tours in German every 30min. M-Th 10am-3pm, F-Su 10am-1pm. Tours in English every hr. M-Th 10:15am-3:15pm, F-Su 10:15am-1:15pm. Free.)* Blackened and ominous since its devastation by an Allied bomb in 1943, the spire of **Nikolaikirche** pierces the heavens as a dark reminder of war. *(Exhibition of its history open M-F 10am-5pm, Sa-Su 11am-6pm. €1.50.)* The buildings along nearby **Trostbrücke** sport huge copper models of clipper ships on their spires—a testament to Hamburg's sea-trade wealth. *(Just south of the Rathaus, off Ost-West-Str.)*

ST. PAULI LANDUNGSBRÜCKEN. Hamburg's harbor lights up at night with ships from all over the world. Take the elevator from the building behind Pier 6 to the old **Elbtunnel,** which was built 1907-1911 and runs 1200m under the Elbe—it's still used by commuters. At the **Fischmarkt,** charismatic vendors haul in and hawk huge amounts of fish, produce, and other goods. Don't shy away if you dislike fish—about 90% of the goods come in another variety. *(U- or S-Bahn to Landungsbrücken or S-Bahn to Königstr. Open Su 6-10am.)*

ASTER LAKES AND PLANTEN UN BLOMEN. To the west of the Alster lies **Planten und Blomen,** a huge expanse of manicured flower gardens and trees. *(Open 7am-11pm.)* Daily performances ranging from Irish step-dancing to Hamburg's police orchestra shake the outdoor **Musikpavillon** from May to September (3pm); there are also nightly **Wasserlichtkonzerte,** in which the fountains are bathed in rainbows of light. *(May-Aug. 10pm; Sept. 9pm.)* North of the *Altstadt,* the Alster Lakes, bordered by tree-lined paths and parks, provide further refuge from crowded Hamburg.

GEDENKSTÄTTE BULLENHUSER DAMM UND ROSENGARTEN. Surrounded by warehouses, this schoolhouse serves as a memorial to 20 Jewish children brought here from Auschwitz for "testing" and murdered by the S.S. only hours before

Allied troops arrived. Visitors are invited to plant a rose for the children in the garden behind the school, where plaques with the children's photographs line the fence. *(S21 to Rothenburgsort. Follow the signs to Bullenhuser Damm along Ausschläger Bildeich and across a bridge; the school is 200m down. Open Su 10am-5pm and Th 2-8pm. Free.)*

MUSEUMS. Hamburg has dozens of museums ranging from the Victorian to the erotic. The first-rate **Hamburger Kunsthalle** holds a dazzling collection spanning medieval through modern art. *(Turn left from the City exit of the Hauptbahnhof and cross the street. Open Tu-W and F-Su 10am-6pm, Th 10am-9pm. €7.50, students €5.)* Hamburg's contemporary art scene resides in the two buildings of the **Deichtorhallen Hamburg.** *(U1 to Steinstr., then follow signs (2 entwined iron circles) from the station. Open Tu-Su 11am-6pm. Each building €6.10, students €4.10.)* Follow the silver sperm painted on the floor through four floors of shocking iniquity at the **Erotic Art Museum.** *(S1 or 3 to Reeperbahn. Open Su-Th noon-midnight, F-Sa noon-2am. €8. Under 16 not admitted.)*

🎵 📷 ENTERTAINMENT AND NIGHTLIFE

MUSIC AND FESTIVALS
The **Staatsoper,** Große Theaterstr. 36, houses one of the best opera companies in Germany; the associated **ballet** company is the acknowledged dance powerhouse of the nation. (☎356 80. U1 to Stephanspl. Open M-F 10am-6:30pm, Sa 10am-2pm.) Orchestras abound—the Philharmonie, the Norddeutscher Rundfunk Symphony, and Hamburg Symphonia all perform at the **Musikhalle** on Johannes-Brahms-Pl. (Take U2 to Gänsemarkt or Messehallen. ☎34 69 20.) Live music prospers in Hamburg, satisfying all tastes. On Sunday mornings, musicians with a wide range of quality play at the **Fischmarkt.** The **West Port Jazz Festival,** Germany's largest, runs in mid-July; call the Koncertskasse (☎32 87 38 54) for information. The most anticipated festival is the **G-Move,** dubbed the "Love Parade of the North" (June 7, 2003).

NIGHTLIFE
The infamous **Reeperbahn,** a long boulevard lined with sex shops, strip joints, and peep shows, is the spinal cord of **St. Pauli;** although it's fairly safe, women should not wander onto adjacent streets. **Herbertstraße,** Hamburg's only remaining strip of legalized prostitution, runs parallel to the Reeperbahn and is open only to men over 18. The prostitutes flaunting their flesh on Herbertstr. are licensed professionals required to undergo health inspections, but others may be venereal roulette wheels. Those trying to avoid the hypersexed Reeperbahn should head north to the trendy streets of **Schanzenviertel.** Unlike St. Pauli, these areas are centered around cafes and weekend extravaganzas. Much of Hamburg's **gay scene** is in the **St. Georg** area of the city, near Berliner Tor. Gay and straight bars in this area are more welcoming and classier than those in the Reeperbahn. *Szene*, available at newsstands (€2.50), lists events and parties, while the magazine *hinnerk* (free at tourist offices) lists gay and lesbian events.

📷**Rote Flora,** Schulterblatt 71, is the nucleus of the Schanzenviertel scene. (Open from 8pm. Cover from €4.) **Mojo Club,** Reeperbahn 1, is adorned with artsy paper lamps and filled with stylish students. (Usually open 11pm-4am. Cover €5 on weekends.) At **Betty Ford Klinik,** Große Freiheit 6, rehab never hurt so good. Down apple sours (€2) in the atomic den of the most creative DJs and dancers in town. (Open Th 9pm-5am, F-Sa 11pm-6am. Cover €10.) **Fabrik,** Barnerstr. 36, a former weapons factory, has been put to better use as a venue for the likes of AC/DC. (Music daily from 9pm. Disco after shows F-Sa. Concerts €10-20.) **G-Bar,** Lange Reihe 81, is a comfortable gay bar with waiters in skin-tight shirts. (Open daily noon-2am.) **Frauenkneipe,** Stresemannstr. 60, is a club and meeting place for women only, gay or straight. (Open Su-M and W-F from 8pm, Sa from 9pm.)

LÜBECK
☎ 0451

Lübeck is easily Schleswig-Holstein's most beautiful city—you'd never guess that most of it was razed in World War II. In its heyday, it was the capital of the Hanseatic League, controlling trade across Northern Europe. Although no longer a center of political and commercial influence, Lübeck remains home to stunning churches and delicious marzipan.

⊡ ⁊ TRANSPORTATION AND PRACTICAL INFORMATION. Trains depart frequently for Berlin (3¼hr., 1 per hr., €38) and Hamburg (45min., 2 per hr., €10.80). A privately owned and expensive tourist office is in the train station. Head instead, for the **city tourist office** in the *Altstadt*, Breite Str. 62. (☎ 122 54 13. Open M-F 9:30am-7pm, Sa-Su 10am-3pm.) **Postal Code:** 23552.

⁊ ⓒ ACCOMMODATIONS AND FOOD. To reach **Rucksack Hotel ❶,** Kanalstr. 70, from the station walk past the Holstentor, turn left on An der Untertrave, and head right on Beckergrube; the hostel is on the corner of Kanalstr. (☎ 70 68 92. Breakfast €3. Sheets €3. Reception 10am-1pm and 4-9pm. 10-bed dorms €12; 6-bed dorms €13; double with bath €40; quads €60, with bath €68.) The **Baltic Hotel ❹,** Hansestr. 11, is across the street from the station and 5min. from the *Altstadt*. (☎ 855 75. Breakfast included. Reception 7am-10pm. Singles €35-45; doubles €58-65; triples from €80.) Lübeck's specialty is **marzipan,** a delectable candy made from almonds. Stop by the famous confectionery **◙I.G. Niederegger Marzipan Café ❶,** Breitestr. 89, for marzipan in the shape of pigs, jellyfish, and even the town gate. (Open M-F 9am-7pm, Sa 9am-6pm, Su 10am-4pm.) **Tipasa ❷,** Schlumacherstr. 12-14, serves pizza, pasta, and vegetarian dishes, and runs a *Biergarten* in back. (Open M-Th and Su noon-1am, F-Sa noon-2am.)

◻ SIGHTS. Between the station and the *Altstadt* stands the massive **Holstentor,** one of Lübeck's four 15th-century gates and the symbol of the city. The museum inside displays armor and torture implements. (Open Apr.-Sept. daily 10am-5pm; Oct.-Mar. closed M. €5, students €3.) The city skyline is dominated by the twin brick towers of the **Marienkirche,** a gigantic church housing the largest mechanical organ in the world. Photographs of the destroyed medieval masterpiece **Totentanzbild** ("Dance of the Dead") remind viewers that everything—even paintings—must die. (Open in summer daily 10am-6pm; in winter 10am-4pm. Short organ concerts daily at noon and Th at 6:30pm. €1 donation suggested.) The **Dom,** on Domkirchhof, shelters a majestic crucifix and is guarded by the trademark lion statue. (Open Apr.-Sept. 10am-6pm; Mar. and Oct. 10am-5pm; Nov. 10am-4pm; Dec.-Feb. 10am-3pm. Free.) The floor of the Gothic **Katharinenkirche,** Königstr. 27, is lined with gravestones. Formerly a Franciscan monastery, it was used as a stable by Napoleon. (Open Tu-Su 10am-1pm and 2-5pm. €0.50.) For a sweeping view of the spire-studded *Altstadt* take the elevator to the 50.5m steeple of the **Petrikirche.** (Church open daily 11am-4pm. Tower open Apr.-Oct. 9am-7pm. €2, students €1.) The **◙Museum für Puppentheater,** Kolk 16, is the largest private puppet collection in the world. (Open daily 10am-6pm. €3, students €2.50.)

SCHLESWIG
☎ 04621

With a harbor full of sailboats, and a shoreline sprinkled with cafes, Schleswig holds both the salty air of a seatown and the artistic flair of a big city. Scale the 237 steps of the **St. Petri Dom** for a striking view of town. (Open May-Sept. M-Sa 9am-5pm, Su 1:30-5pm; Oct.-Apr. M-Sa 10am-4pm, Su 1:30-5pm. €1) By the harbor, the 16th-century **Schloß Gottorf** houses the **Landesmuseen,** a treasure trove of Dutch and Danish pieces. On the other side of the *Schloß*, the **Kreuzstall** houses **Museum** des **20. Jahrhunderts,** devoted to artists of the Brücke school. The surrounding park holds an **outdoor sculpture museum.** (All museums open Apr.-Oct. daily 10am-6pm; Nov.-Mar. Tu-F 9:30am-4pm, Sa-Su 10am-5pm. €5, students €2.50.)

Schleswig centers around its **bus terminal** rather than its train station. Single rides on the bus network cost €2. The **train station** is 20min. south of the city center; take bus #1, 2, 4, or 5 from the stop outside the bus station. Consider buying a **Schleswig Card** (1-day €8, 3-day €11), valid for public transit and admission to most sights. The **tourist office,** Plessenstr. 7, is up the street from the harbor; from the ZOB, walk down Plessenstr. toward the water. The staff books rooms. (☎98 16 16; room reservations ☎98 16 17. Open May-Sept. M-F 9:30am-5:30pm, Sa 9:30am-12:30pm; Oct.-Apr. M-Th 10am-4pm, F 10am-1pm.) The **Jugendherberge (HI) ❶,** Spielkoppel 1, is close to the center of town. Take bus #2 (dir.: Hühnhauser Schwimmhalle) from either the train or bus station to Schwimmhalle; the hostel is across the street. (☎238 93. Breakfast included. Sheets €3.60. Reception daily 7am-1pm and 5-11pm. Curfew 11pm. Dorms €15, under 26 €12.30.) A windswept little **Hafen Pavilion ❷,** at the harbor, sells fresh seafood. (Open daily 9am-8pm.)

CENTRAL AND WEST GERMANY

Lower Saxony (*Niedersachsen*), which stretches from the North Sea to the hills of central Germany, has foggy marshland and broad agricultural plains inland. Just south of Lower Saxony, North Rhine-Westphalia is the most heavily populated and econo\mically powerful area in Germany. While the region's squalor may have inspired the philosophy of Karl Marx and Friedrich Engels, the area's natural beauty and the intellectual energy of Cologne and Düsseldorf inspired the muses of Goethe, Heine, and Böll.

DÜSSELDORF   ☎0211

As Germany's fashion hub and multinational corporation base, the rich city of Düsseldorf crawls with German patricians and would-be aristocrats. Set on the majestic Rhine, Düsseldorf's **Altstadt** hosts the best nightlife along the Rhine in authentic German style.

⌨️🔋 TRANSPORTATION AND PRACTICAL INFORMATION. Trains run to: Amsterdam (3hr., every hr., €39); Berlin (4½hr., 1-2 per hr., €93); Frankfurt (2½hr., 3 per hr., €32); Hamburg (3½hr., 2 per hr., €63); Munich (6hr., 2-3 per hr., €98); and Paris (4½hr., 7 per day, €87). The S-Bahn is the cheapest way to get to Aachen and Cologne. On the **public transportation system,** single tickets cost €1-7, depending on distance traveled. The *Tagesticket* (€6.35-17.50) lets up to five people travel for 24hr. on any line. Düsseldorf's S-Bahn is integrated into the mammoth regional **VRR** *(Verkehrsverbund Rhein-Ruhr)* system, which connects most surrounding cities. For **schedule information,** call ☎582 28. To reach the **tourist office,** Immermannstr. 65, head straight and to the right from the train station; look for the Immermanhof building. Books **rooms** (M-Sa 8am-8pm, Su 2-8pm) for a €3 fee. (☎172 02 22. Open M-F 8:30am-6pm, Sa 9am-12:30pm.) The **post office,** Konrad-Adenauer-Pl., **40210** Düsseldorf, is just to the right of the tourist office. (Open M-F 8am-6pm, Sa 9am-2pm.)

📷📇 ACCOMMODATIONS AND FOOD. It's not unusual for hotels in Düsseldorf to double their prices during a convention; call at least a month ahead if possible. **Jugendgästehaus Düsseldorf (HI) ❹,** Düsseldorfer Str. 1, is just over the Rheinkniebrücke from the *Altstadt.* Take U70, 74, 75, 76, or 77 to Luegpl., then walk 500m down Kaiser-Wilhelm-Ring. (☎55 73 10. Reception daily 7am-1am. Curfew 1am, doors open once every hr. 2-6am. Dorms €20.) To reach **Hotel Schaum ❸**, 63 Gustav-Poengsen-Str., exit left from the train station on Graf-Adolf-Str., take your first left, and follow the tracks to Gustav-Poengsen-Str. (☎311 65 10. Call for pickup from the station. Breakfast included. Singles from €30; doubles from €50.) **Hotel Komet ❹**, Bismarckstr. 93, is straight down Bismarckstr. from the train station and offers bright but snug rooms. (☎17 87 90. Singles with shower €48; doubles from €55.) To camp at **Kleiner Torfbruch ❶**, take any S-Bahn to Düsseldorf Geresheim, then bus #735 (dir.: Stamesberg) to Seeweg. (☎899 20 38. €4 per person, €5 per tent.) For a cheap meal, the endless eateries in the *Altstadt* can't be beat; rows of pizzerias, *Döner* stands, and Chinese restaurants reach from Heinrich-Heine-Allee to the banks of the Rhine. **Otto Mess** is a popular grocery chain; the most convenient location is at the eastern corner of Karlspl. in the *Altstadt*. (Open M-F 8am-8pm, Sa 8am-4pm.) **A Tavola ❸**, Wallstr. 11, has bottomless bread baskets and meticulously prepared pastas. (Open daily noon-3pm and 6-11pm.) **Pilsner Urquell ❷**, Gragenstr. 6, specializes in eastern European specialties. (Open M-Sa noon-1am, Su 4pm-midnight.)

◪ **SIGHTS.** The glitzy **Königsallee** (the **"Kö"**), just outside the *Altstadt*, embodies the vitality and glamor of wealthy Düsseldorf. Midway up is the awe-inspiring **Kö-Galerie**, a marble-and-copper shopping mall showcasing one haughty store after the other. (10min. down Graf-Adolf-Str. from the train station.) The Baroque **Schloß Benrath** in the suburbs of Düsseldorf was originally built as a pleasure palace and hunting grounds for Elector Karl Theodor. Strategically placed mirrors and false exterior windows make the castle appear larger than it is, but the enormous French gardens temper the effect. (S6 (dir.: Köln) to Schloß Benrath. Open Tu-Su 10am-6pm, W until 8pm. Tours every 30min. €4, students €1.75.) The **Heinrich-Heine-Institut** is the official shrine of Düsseldorf's melancholic son. (Bilker Str. 12-14. Open Tu-F and Su 11am-5pm, Sa 1-5pm. €2, students €1.) At the upper end of the Kö is the **Hofgarten park,** the oldest public park in Germany. At the east end of the park, the 18th-century **Schloß Jägerhof** houses the **Goethemuseum.** (Jakobistr. 2. Streetcar #707 or bus #752 to Schloß Jägerhof. Open Tu-F and Su 11am-5pm, Sa 1-5pm. €2, students and children €1.) The **Kunstsammlung Nordrhein-Westfalen** within the black glass edifice west of the Hofgarten, houses works by Picasso, Surrealists, Expressionists, and hometown boy Paul Klee. (Grabbepl. 5. U70, 75, 76, 78, or 79 to Heinrich-Heine-Allee; walk north two blocks. Open Tu-F 10am-6pm, Sa-Su 11am-6pm, first W of month until 10pm. €3, students €1.50.)

◪ **NIGHTLIFE.** Folklore says that Düsseldorf's 500 pubs make up *die längste Theke der Welt* (the longest bar in the world). Pubs in the *Altstadt* are standing-room-only by 6pm; by nightfall it's nearly impossible to see where one pub ends and the next begins. **Bolkerstraße** is jam-packed nightly with street performers. *Prinz* (€3) gives tips on happening scenes; it's often given out free at the youth hostel. *Facolte* (€2), a gay and lesbian nightlife magazine, is available at most newsstands. **Pam-Pam,** Bolkerstr 34, plays house, rock, pop, and plenty of American music. (Open F-Sa 10pm-dawn.) **Zur Uel,** Ratinger Str. 16, fills with a largely local crowd most nights. (Open M-F 9am-1am, Sa-Su 10am-3am.) **Unique,** Bolkerstr. 30, lives up to its name, drawing a younger, trendier crowd to its red-walled interior. (Open W-Sa 10pm-late. Cover €5.)

AACHEN ☎0241

Aachen, once the capital of Charlemagne's Frankish empire, possesses a trove of historical treasures and has become a thriving forum for up-and-coming European artists. The three-tiered dome and dazzling blue-gold mosaics of the **Dom** are in the center of the city; Charlemagne's remains lie in the reliquary behind the altar. (Open M-Sa 11am-7pm, Su 12:30-7pm, except during services.) Around the corner is the **Schatzkammer**, Klosterpl. 2, a treasury of reliquaries containing John the Baptist's hair and ribs, nails and splinters from the cross, and Christ's scourging robe. A silver bust of Charlemagne holds his skull. (Open M 10am-1pm, Tu-W and F-Su 10am-6pm, Th 10am-9pm. €2.50, students €2.) The **Ludwig-forum für Internationale Kunst**, Jülicherstr. 97-109, houses a rotating collection of cutting-edge art. (Open Tu and Th 10am-5pm, W and F 10am-8pm, Sa-Su 11am-5pm. Free tours Su 11:30am and 3pm. €3, students €1.50.)

Trains run to: Amsterdam (4hr., 1-2 per hr., €34); Brussels (2hr., every 2hr., €20); and Cologne (1hr., 2-3 per hr., €11). The **tourist office**, on Friedrich-Wilhelm-Pl. in the Atrium Elisenbrunnen, runs tours and finds rooms for free. From the train station, cross the street and head up Bahnhofstr.; turn left onto Theaterstr., which becomes Theaterpl., then right onto Kapuzinergraben, which becomes Friedrich-Wilhelm-Pl. (☎ 180 29 60. Open M-F 9am-6pm, Sa 9am-2pm.) The **Euroregionales Jugendgästehaus (HI) ❸**, Maria-Theresia-Allee 260, feels more like a hotel than a hostel. From the station, walk left on Lagerhausstr. until it intersects Karmeliterstr. and Mozartstr., then take bus #2 (dir.: Preusswald) to Ronheide. (☎ 71 10 10. Breakfast included. Curfew 1am. Dorms €21.) **Hotel Drei König ❸**, Büchel 5, on the corner of Marktpl., is just steps from the *Rathaus*. (☎ 483 93. Breakfast included. Reception daily 8am-11pm. Singles €34, with bath €65; doubles €54, with bath €75; triples €100.) **Pontstraße**, off Marktpl., and the pedestrian zone have a lot of great restaurants. **Van den Daele ❷**, Büchel 18-20, just off the *Markt*, serves Aachen delicacies. (Open M-Sa 9am-6:30pm, Su 11am-6:30pm.) **Postal code:** 52064.

COLOGNE (KÖLN) ☎ 0221

Although most of the inner city was destroyed in World War II, the magnificent Gothic *Dom* survived its 14 bombings and remains Cologne's main attraction. Today, the city is the largest in North Rhine-Westphalia and its most important cultural center, with a full range of world-class museums and theatrical offerings.

▛ TRANSPORTATION

Flights: Flights depart from **Köln-Bonn Flughafen** (CGN); a shuttle to **Berlin** leaves 24 times per day. Bus #170 to the airport leaves stop #3 at the train station. (20min; daily at 5:30, 6, 6:30am and then every 15min. until 8pm; every 30min. 8-11pm; €4.80.)

Trains: The trains in the northern part of the *Innenstadt* has trains departing for: **Amsterdam** (4hr., €44); **Berlin** (6½hr., 1-2 per hr., €98); **Brussels** (2½hr., €43); **Düsseldorf** (30min., 5 per hr., €6.50); **Frankfurt** (2hr., 3 per hr., €32); **Hamburg** (5hr., 3 per hr., €67); and **Munich** (6½hr., 3-4 per hr., €102).

Ferries: **Köln-Düsseldorfer** (☎ 208 83 18) begins its popular Rhine cruises here. Sail upstream to **Koblenz** (€33) or **Bonn** (€10.40). Eurail valid on most trips.

Public Transportation: VRS (Verkehrsverbund Rhein-Sieg) offices have free maps of the S- and U-Bahn, bus, and streetcar lines; one is downstairs in the train station.

◣✳ ❷ ORIENTATION AND PRACTICAL INFORMATION

Cologne stretches across the Rhine, but nearly all sights and the city center can be found on the western side. The *Altstadt* is split into **Altstadt-Nord**, near the **Hauptbahnhof**, and **Altstadt-Süd**, south of the **Severinsbrücke** (bridge).

Tourist Office: Verkehrsamt, Unter Fettenhennen 19 (☎ 194 33), across from the entrance to the *Dom*, provides free city maps and books rooms for €3. Open May-Oct. M-Sa 8am-10:30pm, Su 9am-10:30pm; Nov.-Apr. M-Sa 8am-9pm, Su 9:30am-7pm.

GERMANY

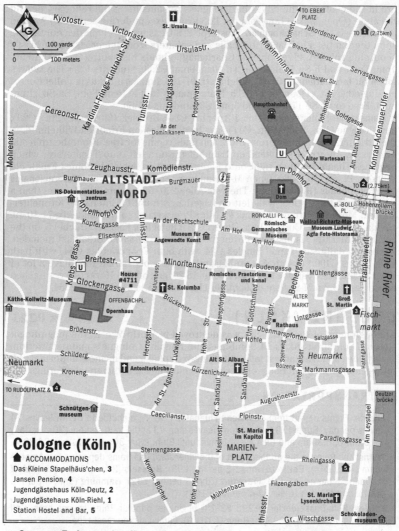

Cologne (Köln)

🏠 ACCOMMODATIONS

Das Kleine Stapelhäus'chen, **3**
Jansen Pension, **4**
Jugendgästehaus Köln-Deutz, **2**
Jugendgästehaus Köln-Riehl, **1**
Station Hostel and Bar, **5**

Currency Exchange: An office at the train station is open daily 7am-9pm.

Bi-Gay-Lesbian Resources: Schulz Schwulen-und Lesbenzentrum, Kartäuserwall 18 (☎93 18 80 80), near Chlodwigpl. Info, advice, and cafe. The tourist office also offers a "Gay City Map" with listings of gay-friendly hotels, bars, and clubs.

Police: ☎ 110. **Fire** and **ambulance:** ☎112.

Pharmacy: Apotheke im Hauptbahnhof, Gleisaufgang 10 (☎ 139 11 12), in the train station. Open M-F 6am-8pm, Sa 8am-4pm.

Internet access: FuturePoint, Richmodstr. 13 (☎206 72 06). €2 per 30min. ID required. Open daily 10:30am-11:30pm.

Post Office: at the corner of Breite Str. and Tunisstr. in the *WDR-Arkaden* shopping gallery. Address mail to be held: Postlagernde Briefe für Firstname SURNAME, Hauptpostamt, **50667** Köln, Germany. Open M-F 8am-8pm, Sa 8am-4pm.

ACCOMMODATIONS

Most hotels fill up in spring and fall when conventions come to town, and the two hostels are nearly always booked from June to September. Call ahead.

Jansen Pension, Richard-Wagner-Str. 18 (☎25 18 75). U1, 6, 7, 15, 17, or 19 to Rudolfpl. Owned by a welcoming English couple and featuring beautiful high-ceilinged rooms in Victorian style. Breakfast included. Singles €31-36; doubles €57-62. ❸

Station Hostel and Bar, Rheing. 34-36 (☎23 02 47). Clean rooms, a popular bar, and English-speaking staff. Free Internet. Reception 24hr. Reserved rooms held until 6pm. Singles €25; doubles €40; triples €54; quads €68. ❸

Jugendgästehaus Köln-Riehl (HI), An der Schanz 14 (☎76 70 81), on the Rhine north of the zoo. U16 (dir.: Ebertplatz/Mülheim) to Boltensternstr. Breakfast included. Reception 24hr. Call ahead. 4- to 6-bed dorms €21; singles €34. ❸

Jugendherberge Köln-Deutz (HI), Siegesstr. 5a (☎81 47 11), just over the *Hohenzollernbrücke.* S6, 11, or 12 to Köln-Deutz. Exit the station, walk down Neuhöfferstr., and take the 1st right; the hostel is in a courtyard. Newly renovated rooms. Breakfast included. Free laundry. Reception 11am-1am. Curfew 1am. Call ahead. Dorms €20. ❸

Das Kleine Stapelhäus'chen, Fischmarkt 1-3 (☎257 78 62). Cross the Altenmarkt from the back of the *Rathaus* and take Lintg. to the Fischmarkt. An old-fashioned, elegant inn overlooking the river. Breakfast included. Singles €39-41, with shower €52-64, with full bath €64-74; doubles €64-74/€90-97/€100-121. ❹

Campingplatz Poll, Weidenweg (☎83 19 66), on the Rhine, southeast of the *Altstadt.* U16 to Marenberg and cross the Rodenkirchener Brücke. Reception daily 8am-noon and 5-8pm. Open mid-Apr. to Oct. €4.50 per person, €2.50 per tent or car. ❶

FOOD

Cologne cuisine includes scrumptious *Rievekoochen* (slabs of fried potato dunked in applesauce) and smooth Kölsch beer. **Brauhaus Früh am Dom** ❸, Am Hof 12-14, serves some of Cologne's finest Kölsch as well as hearty regional specialties. (Open daily 8am-midnight.) Cheap restaurants line **Zülpicherstraße.** (U7 or 9 to Zülpicher Pl.). Mid-priced ethnic restaurants lie around the perimeter of the *Altstadt,* particularly from **Hohenzollernring** to **Hohenstaufenring;** the city's best cheap eats are on **Weideng** in the Turkish district. An open-air **market** on **Willhelmsplatz** takes over the neighborhood in the mornings. (Open M-Sa 8am-1pm.)

SIGHTS

DOM. Whether illuminated in a pool of eerie blue floodlighting or eclipsing the sun with its colossal spires, the *Dom,* Germany's greatest cathedral, is the first thing to greet travelers as they enter the city. Entering the choir, a chapel to the right houses a 15th-century **triptych,** depicting the city's five patron saints. Behind the altar, in the center of the choir is the **Shrine of the Magi,** which reportedly holds the remains of the Three Kings and is the most sacred element of the cathedral. Before exiting the choir, stop in the **Chapel of the Cross** to admire the 10th-century

Gero crucifix, which is the oldest intact sculpture of a crucified Christ with eyes shut. *(Cathedral open daily 6am-7pm. Free. Tours in English M-Sa 10:30am and 2:30pm, Su 2:30pm; €4, children €2.)* Fifteen minutes and 509 steps bring you to the top of the **Südturm** (south tower). *(Open Nov.-Feb. 9am-4pm; May-Sept. 9am-6pm; Mar.-Apr. and Oct. 9am-5pm. €2, students €1.)* Catch your breath at the **Glockenstube,** a chamber for the tower's nine bells, about three-quarters of the way up.

HOUSE #4711. The magic water **Eau de Cologne,** once prescribed as a drinkable curative, gave the town worldwide recognition. Today the house, labeled #4711 by a Napoleonic system that abolished street names, is a boutique where a corner fountain flows freely with the scented water. Visit the gallery upstairs for a full history of the famous fragrance. *(Glockeng., at the intersection with Tunisstr. From Hohe Str., turn right on Brückenstr., which becomes Glockeng. Open M-F 9:30am-8pm, Sa 9:30am-4pm.)*

RÖMISCHES PRAETORIUM UND KANAL. The excavated ruins of the former Roman military headquarters display remains of Roman gods and an array of rocks left by early inhabitants. *(From the Rathaus, take a right toward the swarm of hotels and then a left onto Kleine Budeng. Open Tu-F 10am-4pm, Sa-Su 11am-4pm. €1.50, students €0.75.)*

MUSEUMS. █**Heinrich-Böll-Platz** houses two complementary collections: the **Museum Ludwig,** which spans Impressionism through Dalí, Lichtenstein, and Warhol; and the **Agfa Foto-Historama,** which chronicles photography of the last 150 years, including a rotating display of Man Ray's works. *(Bischofsgartenstr. 1. Open Tu 10am-8pm, W-F 10am-6pm, Sa-Su 11am-6pm. €6.40, students €3.20.)* The galleries of the **Wallraf-Richartz Museum** are lined with masterpieces from the Middle Ages to Post-Impressionism. *(Martinstr. 39. From the Heumarkt, take Gürzenichtstr. 1 block to Martinstr. Open Tu 10am-8pm, W-F 10am-6pm, Sa-Su 11am-6pm. €5.10, students €2.60.)* The **Römisch-Germanisches Museum** displays a large array of artifacts documenting the daily lives of Romans both rich and poor. *(Roncallipl. 4. Open Tu-Su 10am-5pm. €3, students €2.)* The **Schokoladen Museum** (Chocolate Museum), presents every step of chocolate production from the rainforests to the gold fountain that spurts streams of silky chocolate. Resist the urge to drool and wait for the free samples. *(Rheinauhafen 1a, near the Severinsbrücke. From the train station, head for the river, walk along the Rhine heading right, go under the Deutzer Brücke, and take the 1st footbridge. Open M-F 10am-6pm, Sa-Su 11am-7pm. €5.50, students €3.)* The **Käthe-Kollwitz-Museum** houses the world's largest collection of sketches, sculptures, and prints by the brilliant 20th-century artist-activist. *(Neumarkt 18-24. On the top floor in the Neumarkt-Passage. U12, 14, 16, or 18 to Neumarkt. Open Tu-F 10am-6pm, Sa-Su 11am-6pm. €2.50, students €1.)*

🎵 🎭 ENTERTAINMENT AND NIGHTLIFE

Cologne explodes in celebration during **Karneval,** a week-long pre-Lent festival that begins on Ash Wednesday (Feb. 27, 2003) when the mayor abdicates leadership of the city to the women; the women then find their husbands at work and chop off their ties. The festivities build up to an out-of-control parade on **Rosenmontag** (Mar. 3, 2003). For more information, pick up the Karneval booklet at the tourist office.

Many bars and clubs change their music nightly; the best way to know what you'll get is to check the monthly magazine *Kölner* (€1). The closer to the Rhine or *Dom* you venture, the more quickly your wallet gets emptied. Students congregate in the **Bermuda-Dreieck** ("Bermuda Triangle"), bounded by Zülpicherstr., Zülpicherpl., Roonstr., and Luxemburgstr. The center of **gay nightlife** runs up Matthiasstr. to Mühlenbach, Hohe Pforte, Marienpl., and to the Heumarkt area by the *Deutzer Brücke.* █**Papa Joe's Jazzlokal,** Buttermarkt

37, is the oldest jazz club in Germany and has a worthy reputation for great music and good times. (Open M-Sa 7pm-2am, Su 3:30pm-midnight.) **Alter Wartesaal,** Johannisstr. 11, in the basement of the train station, has an enormous dance floor and an impressively hip crowd. (Opening hours vary; cover €6-12.) **M20,** Maastrichterstr. 20, plays some of the best drum 'n' bass in town to intimate crowds of locals. (Open M-Th 9pm-2am, F-Sa 9pm-3am.) **Vampire,** Rathenaupl. 5, is a gay and lesbian bar with a mellow atmosphere and delicious "holy water." (Open Tu-Th and Su 9pm-2am, F-Sa 9pm-3am.) **Hotel Timp,** Heumarkt 25, is an outrageous gay-friendly club with gaudy, glitter-filled cabarets. (Shows daily 1am-4am.)

BONN   ☎ 0228

Once an indistinct town, Bonn stumbled into the limelight by chance when it was named capital of West Germany because Konrad Adenauer, the first chancellor, resided in the suburbs. In 1999, the *Bundestag* packed up and moved back to Berlin, allowing Bonn to be itself again. Today, the streets of the *Altstadt* bustle with notable energy, and a thriving cultural scene resides in Bonn's well-respected university and excellent museums. Bonn is also fast becoming a center for Germany's computer-technology industry and hip cyber-culture.

█▐ TRANSPORTATION AND PRACTICAL INFORMATION. Trains run to: Cologne (20min., 5 per hr., €5); Frankfurt (1½hr., 2 per hr., €27); and Koblenz (1hr., 3 per hr., €8). The **tourist office** is at Windeckstr. 2, near the cathedral off Münsterpl. (☎ 194 33. Open M-F 9am-6:30pm, Sa 9am-4pm, Su 10am-2pm.) Consider buying the **Bonn Regio Welcome Card** (1-day €9; 2-day €14; 3-day €19), which covers transportation (M-F after 9am, Sa-Su 24hr.) and admission to more than 20 museums in Bonn and the surrounding area. Mail letters from the **post office,** Münsterpl. 17. (Open M-F 8:30am-8pm, Sa 8:30am-4pm.) **Postal code:** 53111.

▐▐ ACCOMMODATIONS AND FOOD. Take bus #621 (dir.: Ippendorf Altenheim) to Jugendgästehaus for the super-modern **Jugendgästehaus Bonn-Venusberg (HI) ❸,** Haager Weg 42. (☎28 99 70. Breakfast included. Laundry €5. Curfew 1am. Dorms €21; singles €34; doubles €48.) To reach **Campingplatz Genienaue ❶,** Im Frankenkeller 49, take U16 or 63 to Rheinallee, then bus #613 (dir.: Giselherstr.) to Guntherstr. Turn left on Guntherstr. and right on Frankenkeller. (☎34 49 49. Reception daily 9am-noon and 3-10pm. €5.20 per person, €3-5 per tent.)

The pedestrian zone in the city center and the area around the university are both packed with restaurants. Cheap eats are available at **Mensa ❶,** Nassestr. 11, a 15min. walk from the station along Kaiserstr. (Open M-F 11:30am-2:15pm and 5:30-7:30pm, Sa noon-1:45pm.) **Cafe Blau ❷,** Franziskanerstr. 5, across from the university, will sate your hunger without devouring your cash supply. (Chicken or pasta platters €3-5. Open daily 9am-1am.) The **market** on Münsterpl. teems with vendors selling meat, fruit, and vegetables. (Open M-F 9:30am-8pm, Sa 9am-4pm.) There's a **supermarket** in the basement of the Kaufhof department store on Münsterpl. (Open M-F 9:30am-8pm, Sa 9am-4pm.)

◎▐ SIGHTS AND NIGHTLIFE. Bonn's lively pedestrian zone is littered with historic niches. **Beethoven Geburtshaus** (Beethoven's birthplace) hosts a fantastic collection of his personal effects, from his primitive hearing aids to his first violin. (Bonng. 18-20. Open Apr.-Oct. M-Sa 10am-6pm, Su 11am-4pm; Nov.-Mar. M-Sa 10am-5pm, Su 11am-4pm. €4, students €3.) In its governmental heyday, the transparent walls of the **Bundestag** were meant to symbolize the government's responsibility to the public. (Take U16, 63, or 66 to Heussallee/Bundeshaus or bus #610 to Bundeshaus.) Students study within the **Kurfürstliches Schloß**, the huge 18th-century palace now serving as the center of Bonn's **Friedrich-Wilhelms-Universität**. To reach Bonn's other palace, follow Poppelsdorfer Allee to the 18th-century **Poppelsdorfer Schloß**, which boasts beautifully manicured **botanical gardens**. (Gardens open Apr.-Oct. M-F 9am-6pm, Su 10am-5pm; Nov.-Mar. M-F 9am-4pm. Free.) The Welcome card (see Practical Information, above) provides admission to most of Bonn's **"Museum Mile."** To start your museum-crawl, take U16, 63, or 66 to Heussallee or Museum König. ▧**Haus der Geschichte** (House of History), Adenauerallee 250/Willy-Brandt 4, examines post-World War II German history through interactive exhibits. (Open Tu-Su 9am-7pm. Free.) One block away, **Kunstmuseum Bonn**, Friedrich-Ebert-Allee 2, houses a superb selection of Expressionist and modern German art. (Open Tu and Th-Su 10am-6pm, W 10am-9pm. €5, students €2.50.)

For club and concert listings, pick up *Schnüss* (€1). The ▧**Jazz Galerie**, Oxfordstr. 24, hosts jazz and rock concerts as well as a jumping bar and disco. (Cover varies. Open daily Tu-Th and Su 9pm-3am, F-Sa 9pm-4am.) **Pantheon**, Bundeskanzlerpl., caters to eclectic tastes with a disco, concerts, and stand-up comedy; follow Adenauerallee out of the city to Bundeskanzlerpl. (Cover €6.50-8. Open M-Sa 11pm-4am.) **Boba's Bar**, Josephstr. 17, is one of Bonn's most popular gay and lesbian bars. (Open Tu-Su 8pm-3am.)

FRANKFURT AM MAIN   ☎069

Frankfurt's integral economic role as home to the central bank of the European Union lends it a glitzy vitality—international offices, shiny skyscrapers, and expensive cars lie at every intersection. Equally important is its role as a major transportation hub for all of Europe. Indeed, Frankfurt first made its appearance as a crossing point for the Main River—the Franks forded the river in early times, and the city's name literally means *ford of the Franks*. Today, the city spends more on cultural attractions and tourism than any other German city. Visitors are drawn by the selection of museums and exhibits—and, of course the highly trafficked transportation routes that make Frankfurt a likely stop on your itinerary.

▆ TRANSPORTATION

Flights: The airport, **Flughafen Rhein-Main** (☎ 69 00), is connected to the *Hauptbahnhof* by S8 and 9 (every 15min.; buy tickets for €3 from the green machines marked *Fahrkarten* before boarding).

Trains: Frequent trains leave the **Hauptbahnhof** for: **Amsterdam** (5hr.; 2 per hr.; €76, under 26 €61); **Berlin** (5-6hr.; 2 per hr.; €107/€86); **Cologne** (2½hr.; 3 per hr.; €39/€32); **Hamburg** (5hr.; 2 per hr.; €98/€79); **Munich** (3½-4½hr.; 2 per hr.; €76/€61); **Paris** (6-8hr.; 2 per hr.; €73/€59); **Rome** (15hr.; every hr.; €144/€111). Call ☎0180 599 66 33 for schedules, reservations, and information.

Public Transportation: Runs daily until about 1am. Single-ride tickets (€1.60, rush hour €1.90) are valid for 1hr. in one direction, transfers permitted. **Eurail** valid only on S-Bahn. The **Tageskarte** (day pass, valid until midnight of the day of purchase) provides unlimited transportation on the S-Bahn, U-Bahn, streetcars, and buses; buy from machines in any station (€4.45, children €2.70).

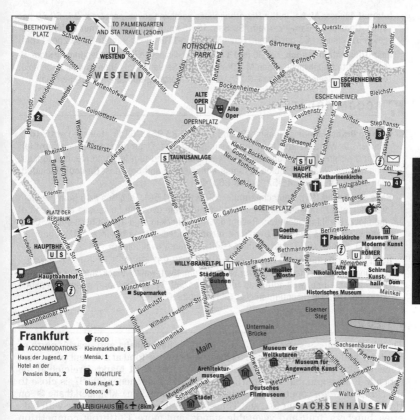

Frankfurt

ACCOMMODATIONS
Haus der Jugend, 7
Hotel an der
Pension Bruns, 2

FOOD
Kleinmarkthalle, 5
Mensa, 1

NIGHTLIFE
Blue Angel, 3
Odeon, 4

■ ■ ORIENTATION AND PRACTICAL INFORMATION

The train station lies at the end of Frankfurt's red light district; from the station, the **Altstadt** is a 20min. walk down Kaiserstr. or Münchener Str. To the north, the commercial heart of Frankfurt lies along **Zeil**. Cafes, stores, and services cluster in **Bockenheim** (U6 or 7 to Bockenheimer Warte). Across the Main, **Sachsenhausen** draws pub-crawlers and museum-goers (U1, 2, or 3 to Schweizer Pl.).

Tourist Office: (☎21 23 88 00), in the *Hauptbahnhof*. Open M-F 8am-9pm, Sa-Su and holidays 9am-6pm. Sells the **Frankfurt Card** (1-day €6.15, 2-day €9.75), which allows unlimited travel on all trains and buses and gives 50% off admission to many sights.

Laundromat: Schnell & Sauber, Wallstr. 8, near the hostel in Sachsenhausen. Wash €3, dry €0.50 per 15min. Soap included. Open daily 6am-11pm.

Emergency: Police: ☎110. **Fire** and **ambulance:** ☎112.

Disabled Resources: Frankfurt Forum, Römerberg 32 (☎21 24 00 00). Publishes a guide to handicapped-accessible locations in Frankfurt. Open M and W 10am-4:30pm, Tu 10am-6pm, and Th-F 10am-2pm.

Pharmacy: (☎23 30 47), in the Einkaufs passage of the train station. Open M-F 6:30am-9pm, Sa 8am-9pm, Su and holidays 9am-8pm. Emergencies ☎192 92.

Internet Access: Alpha, in the *Hauptbahnhof*'s gambling salon, past track 24. €0.50 per 5min. Open M-Sa 6am-12:45am, Su 8am-12:45am. **CybeRyder Internet Café,** Tönges-gasse 31, charges €3 per 30min. Open M-Th 9am-11pm, F-Sa 9am-1am, Su 2pm-11pm.

Post Office: Main branch, Zeil 90 (☎ 13 81 26 21), inside the *Karstadt* department store. U-or S-Bahn to Hauptwache. Open M-F 9:30am-8pm, Sa 9am-4pm. Address mail to be held: Postlagernde Briefe für Firstname SURNAME, Hauptpostamt, **60313** Frankfurt, Germany.

⌂ ACCOMMODATIONS

▓ **Pension Bruns,** Mendelssohnstr. 42, 2nd fl. (☎ 74 88 96). U6 (dir.: Heerstr.) or U7 (dir.: Hausen) to Westend and take the Siesmayerstr. exit. Once up the escalator, exit left under the sign Mendelssohnstr., then walk 1 block and turn left onto Mendelssohnstr. Ring the bell. Spacious Victorian rooms with cable TV and breakfast (in bed!) included. Call ahead. Doubles €46-52; triples €63. ❹

Haus der Jugend (HI), Deutschherrnufer 12 (☎ 610 01 50). Take bus #46 from the main train station to Frankensteiner Pl. Turn left along the river; the hostel sits at the end of the block. Breakfast included. Reception 24hr. Check-in after 1pm. Check-out 9:30am. Curfew 2am. Reservations by phone recommended. Dorms begin at €18, under 20 €14.50. Singles (€29) and doubles (€48) are rarely available. ❷

Hotel an der Galluswarte, Hufnagelstr. 4 (☎ 73 39 93). S3, 4, 5, or 6 to Galluswarte. Exit under the sign marked Mainzer Landstr., turn right, walk 1 block, and turn right onto Hufnagelstr. Large, well-equipped rooms each with TV, shower, and phone. Breakfast included. *Let's Go* discount: singles €41; doubles €52. ❹

🍴 FOOD

The cheapest meals surround the university in **Bockenheim** and nearby parts of Westend, and many of the pubs in **Sachsenhausen** serve food at a decent price. Just a few blocks from the youth hostel is a fully stocked **HL Markt,** Dreieichstr. 56 (open M-F 8am-8pm, Sa 8am-4pm); an **Alim Markt,** Münchener Str. 37, is close to the *Hauptbahnhof* (open M-F 8:30am-7:30pm, Su 8am-2pm). **Kleinmarkthalle ❶,** on Haseng. between Berliner Str. and Töngesg., is a three-story warehouse with bak-eries, butchers, fruit and vegetable stands, and more. Cutthroat competition between the many vendors pushes prices way down. (Open M-F 7:30am-6pm, Sa 7:30am-4pm.) **Mensa ❶,** has two floors of cheap cafeteria food. (U6 or 7 to Bocken-heimer Warte; open M-F 11:30am-3pm.)

👁 SIGHTS

Much of Frankfurt's historic splendor lives on only in memories and in recon-structed monuments, since Allied bombing left everything but the cathedral com-pletely destroyed. At the center of the *Altstadt* is **Römerberg Square** (U-Bahn to Römer), home to half-timbered architecture and a medieval fountain of justice that once spouted wine. At the west end of Römerberg Sq., the gables of **Römer** have marked the site of Frankfurt's city hall since 1405; upstairs, the **Kaisersaal,** a former imperial banquet hall, is adorned with portraits of the 52 German emperors from Charlemagne to Franz II. (Open daily 10am-1pm and 2-5pm. €1.50, students €0.50.) Next to the *Römer* stands the only building that survived the bombings, the red sandstone **Dom,** which contains several elaborate altarpieces. A new view-ing tower is scheduled to open sometime this year. (Open daily 9am-noon and 2:30-6pm.) Across Braubachstr. from the Römerberg, **Paulskirche** holds a confer-ence center and a political memorial to the trials and tribulations of German democracy. (Open daily 10am-5pm. Free.) A few blocks away is the **Museum für Moderne Kunst,** a triangular building (dubbed "the slice of cake") displaying an array of modern art. (Domstr. 10. Open Tu and Th-Su 10am-5pm, W 10am-8pm. €5, students €2.50; W free.) The **☒Städel,** Schaumainkai 63, has important paintings from nearly every period of the Western tradition. (Open Tu and F-Su 10am-5pm, W-Th 10am-8pm. €6, students €5, Tu free.) Only Goethe-fanatics will be awestruck by his reconstructed first house, the **Goethehaus.** (Großer Hirschgraben 23-25. Open Apr.-Sept. M-F 9am-6pm, Sa-Su 10am-4pm; Oct.-Mar. M-F 9am-4pm, Sa-Su 10am-4pm. €5, students €2.50.) A simpler and more peaceful afternoon can be spent at the **Palmengarten,** in the northwest part of town. (Siesmayerstr. 61-63. U6 or 7 to Bockenheimer Warte. Open Mar.-Oct. daily 9am-6pm; Nov.-Jan. 9am-4pm; Feb. 9am-5pm. €3.50, students €1.50.)

🎵 🎭 ENTERTAINMENT AND NIGHTLIFE

Frankfurt's theater and opera are first-rate. The **Alte Oper,** Opernpl. (☎ 134 04 00; U6 or 7 to Alte Oper), offers a full range of classical music. The **Städtische Bühne,** Untermainanlage 11 (☎ 21 23 71 33; U1, 2, 3, or 4 to Willy-Brandt-Pl.), hosts ballets and operas. The **English Theatre,** Kaiserstr. 52 (☎ 24 23 16 20) puts on comedies and musicals in English. Shows and schedules are listed in *Fritz* and *Strandgut* (free). For information on tickets at most venues, call **Frankfurt Ticket** (☎ 134 04 00).

Frankfurt has a number of thriving discos and prominent techno DJs, mostly in the commercial district between **Zeil** and **Bleichstraße.** Wear something dressier than jeans if you plan to get past the selective bouncers. **Odeon,** Seilerstr. 34, packs its two floors with students and house, soul, and hip hop. (Cover €5, students €3; Th drinks half-price until midnight and free buffet from 11:30pm. Open Tu-Sa from 10pm.) **Blue Angel,** Brönnerstr. 17, is a Frankfurt institution and one of the liveliest gay men's clubs around. Ring the bell to be let in. (Cover €5. Open daily 11pm-4am.) For more drinks and less dancing, head to the **Alt-Sachsenhausen** district between Brückenstr. and Dreieichstr., home to a huge number of rowdy pubs and taverns. The complex of cobblestoned streets centering on **Grosse** and **Kleine Rittergaße** teems with cafes, bars, restaurants, and Irish pubs.

SOUTHWEST GERMANY

The valleys and castles along the Rhine and Mosel Rivers are a feast for the eyes and mouth; the rich agricultural tradition keeps produce in abundance, and dozens of vineyards provide delights for the palate. Just a bit farther south, the hinterlands of the Black Forest contrast with the region's modern industrial cities.

RHINE VALLEY (RHEINTAL)

The Rhine River runs from Switzerland to the North Sea, but in the popular imagination it exists only in the 80km Rhine Valley—a region prominent in historical legends, sailors' nightmares, and poets' dreams. The river flows north from **Mainz** to **Bonn** passing through **Bacharach** and **Koblenz.**

📠 TRANSPORTATION. Two different **train** lines (one on each bank) traverse the *Rheintal;* the line on the west bank stays closer to the water and provides superior views. If you're willing to put up with lots of tourists, **boats** are probably the best way to see the sights; the **Köln-Düsseldorfer (KD) Line** covers the Mainz-Koblenz stretch four times per day in summer.

MAINZ. The colossal sandstone **Martinsdom** stands as a memorial to former ecclesiastic power with the extravagant tombstones of archbishops of Mainz lining the walls. (Open Mar.-Oct. M-F 9am-6:30pm, Sa 9am-4pm, Su 12:45-3pm and 4-6:30pm; Nov.-Feb. M-F 9am-5pm, Sa 9am-4pm, Su 12:45-3pm and 4-5pm. Free.) The Gothic **Stephanskirche,** south of the *Dom,* is simple on the outside but inside hides stunning stained-glass windows created by artist Marc Chagall. (Stephansberg. Open daily 10am-noon and 2-5pm.) Johannes Gutenberg, the father of movable type, is immortalized at the **Gutenberg-Museum,** which contains a replica of his original press. (Liebfrauenpl. 5, across from the *Dom.* Open Tu-Sa 9am-5pm, Su 11am-3pm. €3.10, students €1.55.)

Trains run to Frankfurt (30min., €6); Heidelberg (1hr., €17); and Koblenz (1hr., €17). **KD ferries** (☎23 28 00) depart from the wharves on the other side of the *Rathaus.* The **tourist office** arranges **tours** and gives free maps. (☎28 62 10. Open M-F 9am-6pm, Sa 9am-4pm.) To reach the **Jugendgästehaus (HI) ❷,** Otto-Brunfels-Schneise 4, take bus #62 (dir.: Weisenau), 63 (dir.: Laubenheim), or 92 (dir.: Ginsheim) to Viktorstift/Jugendherberge and follow the signs. Backpackers will be greeted with clean rooms, all with private bath. (☎853 32. Breakfast included. Reception daily 7am-10pm. Dorms €16.10; doubles €21.20.) For groceries, try **Supermarkt 2000,** Am Brand 41, under the Sinn-Leffers department store (open M-F 9:30am-8pm, Sa 9am-4pm). ☎06131.

BACHARACH. With many *Weinkeller* and *Weinstuben* (wine cellars and pubs), Bacharach lives up to its name ("Altar of Bacchus"). **Die Weinstube,** Oberstr. 63, is a family-owned business that makes its own wine on the premises. Nearby are the remains of the 14th-century **Wernerkapelle,** a red sandstone chapel that took 140 years to build but only a few hours to destroy in the Palatinate War of Succession in 1689. The **tourist office,** Oberstr. 45, and the *Rathaus* share a building at one end of the town center. (☎91 93 03. Open Apr.-Oct. M-F 9am-5pm, Sa 10am-4pm; Nov.-Mar. M-F 9am-noon.) Hostels get no better than ▨**Jugendherberge Stahleck (HI) ❷,** a gorgeous 12th-century castle that provides an unbeatable panoramic view of the Rhine Valley. The steep 15min. hike to the hostel is worth every step. Call ahead; they're usually full by 6pm. Make a right out of the station pathway, turn left at the Peterskirche, and take any of the marked paths up the hill. (☎12 66. Breakfast included. Curfew 10pm. Dorms €14.20; doubles €35.) At ▨**Café Restaurant Rusticana ❸,** Oberstr. 40, a lovely German couple serves up three-course meals (€6-11) and lively conversation. (Open May-Oct. daily 11:30am-9:30pm.) ☎06743.

KOBLENZ
☎0261

Koblenz has long been a strategic hotspot; in the 2000 years since its birth, the city has hosted every empire seeking to conquer Europe. The city centers around the **Deutsches Eck** (German Corner), a peninsula at the confluence of the Rhine and Mosel that purportedly witnessed the birth of the German nation in 1216. The **Mahnmal der Deutschen Einheit** (Monument to German Unity) to the right is a tribute to Kaiser Wilhelm I. The ▨**Museum Ludwig im Deutschherrenhaus,** behind the *Mahnmal,* features contemporary French art. (Danziger Freiheit 1. Open Tu-Sa 10:30am-5pm, Su 11am-6pm. €2.50, students €1.50.) Head across the river to the **Festung Ehrenbreitstein,** a fortress at the highest point in the city. Today, it's a youth hostel. (Non-hostel guests €1.05; students €0.60. Tours €2.10.)

Trains run to: Bonn (30min., 4 per hr, €8); Cologne (1hr., 2-4 per hr., €13.50); Frankfurt (2hr., 1-2 per hr., €18.20); Mainz (1hr., 3 per hr., €13.50); and Trier (2hr., 1-2 per hr., €15.60). Directly across from the station is the **tourist office,** Bahnhofpl. 7. (☎30 38 80; open May-Oct. M-F 9am-8pm, Sa-Su 10am-8pm; Nov.-Apr. M-F 9am-6pm, Sa-Su 10am-6pm.) **Jugendherberge Koblenz (HI) ❷,** within the fortress, offers breathtaking views of the Rhine and Mosel. Take bus #9 or 10 from the stop just left of the train station on Löhrstr. to Charlottenstr. Then take the chairlift up (Mar.-Sept. daily 9am-5:50pm; €4, round-trip €5.60), or continue along the Rhine side of the mountain on the main road, following the DJH signs, and take the footpath up. (☎97 28 70. Breakfast included. Reception daily 7:15am-10pm. Curfew 11:30pm. Dorms €15.10; doubles €36.80.) **Ferries** (€1) cross the Mosel to **Campingplatz Rhein-Mosel ❶**, Am Neuendorfer Eck. (☎827 19. Reception daily 8am-10pm. Open Apr.-Oct. 15. €4 per person; €2.50 per tent.) **Marktstübchen ❷**, Am Markt 220, serves authentic German food at budget prices. (Open Su-Tu, and Th, 11am-midnight, W 11am-2pm, F 4pm-1am, Sa 11am-1am.)

TRIER ☎0651

Trier, the oldest town in Germany, was founded by the Romans and reached its heyday in the 4th century as the capital of the Western Roman Empire and a center for Christianity in Europe. A one-day **combination ticket** provides access to all the city's Roman monuments. (€6.20, students €3.10.) The most impressive is the massive 2nd-century **Porta Nigra** (Black Gate), which once served as the strongest line of defense against attacks on the city. (Open Apr.-Sept. daily 9am-6pm; Oct.-Mar. 9am-5pm. €2.10, students €1.60.) The nearby **Dom** shelters the *Tunica Christi* (Holy Robe of Christ) and the tombs of archbishops. (Open Apr.-Oct. daily 6:30am-6pm; Nov.-Mar. 6:30am-5:30pm. Free.) The enormous **Basilika** was originally the location of Emperor Constantine's throne room. (Open M-Sa 10am-6pm, Su noon 6pm. Free.) Near the southeast corner of the city walls are the 4th-century **Kaiserthermen** (Emperor's baths), most memorable for the gloomy underground passages remaining from their ancient sewer network—avoid contact with the walls. (Open Apr.-Sept. daily 9am-6pm; Oct.-Mar. 9am-5pm. €2.15, students €1.60.) A 10min. walk uphill along Olewiger Str. brings you to the **amphitheater;** once the site for bloody gladiatorial games, it's now a stage for city productions. (Open Apr.-Sept. daily 9am-6pm; Oct.-Mar. 9am-5pm. €2.10, students €1.60.)

Trains run to Koblenz (1¾hr., 2 per hr., €16) and Luxembourg (45min., 1 per hr., €8). From the station, walk down Theodor-Haus-Allee or Christophstr. to reach the **tourist office,** under the shadow of the Porta Nigra. (☎97 80 80; open Apr.-Oct. M-Sa 9am-6pm, Su 10am-3pm; Nov.-Dec. and Mar. M-Sa 9am-6pm, Su 10am-1pm; Jan.-Feb. M-F 10am-5pm, Sa 10am-1pm. English tours daily 1:30pm; €6, students €5.) The staff at nearby **Vinothek,** Margaritengässchen 2a, can give information on **wine tasting** in the region. (☎978 08 34. Open M-Sa 10am-6pm.) The **Jugendhotel/Jugendgästehaus Kolpinghaus ❷**, Dietrichstr. 42, one block off the Hauptmarkt, has well-used rooms in an unbeatable location. (☎97 52 50. Breakfast included. Sheets €2.50 for dorms. Dorms €13.50; singles €22; doubles €44.) ◪**Astarix ❷**, Karl-Marx-Str. 11, serves excellent food at unbelievable prices (under €5). It's squeezed into a passageway next to Miss Marple's. (Open M-Th 11:30am-1am, F-Sa 11:30am-2am, Su 2pm-1am.) There's a **Plus supermarket,** Brotstr. 54, near the Hauptmarkt. (Open M-F 8:30am-7pm, Sa 8:30am-4pm.)

HEIDELBERG ☎06221

This sunlit town and its crumbling castle once lured writers and artists—including Twain, Goethe, and Hugo—today, roughly 32,000 tourists are drawn in each summer day. However, the incessant buzz of mass tourism is worth enduring to experience Heidelberg's beautiful hillside setting and famous university.

▐ TRANSPORTATION

Trains run to: Frankfurt (50min., 2 per hr., €12) and Stuttgart (40min., 1 per hr., €31); other trains run regularly to towns in the Neckar Valley. On Heidelberg's **public transportation** system, **single-ride tickets** cost €2; **day passes** (€5) are available

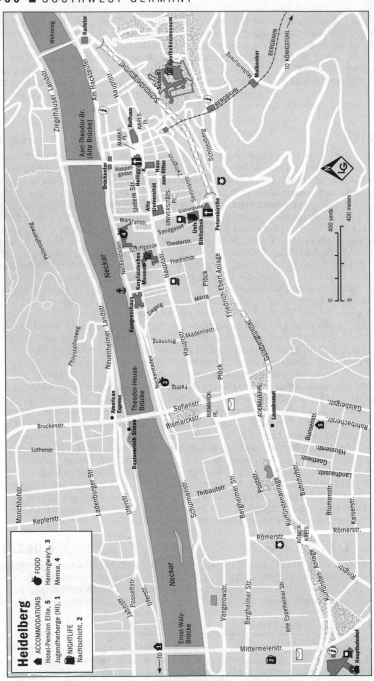

GERMANY

Heidelberg

▲ ACCOMMODATIONS
Hotel-Pension Elite, **5**
Jugendherberge (HI), **1**

◗ NIGHTLIFE
Nachtschicht, **2**

✦ FOOD
Hemingway's, **3**
Mensa, **4**

from the tourist office. The Rhein-Neckar-Fahrgastschifffahrt (☎201 81), in front of the *Kongresshaus*, runs **ferries** all over Germany and provides round-trip Neckar cruises to Neckarsteinach (1½hr., Easter-Oct. 9:30am-3:30pm, €9.50).

■✦🔢 ORIENTATION AND PRACTICAL INFORMATION

Most of Heidelberg's attractions are in the eastern part of the city, along the south bank of the Neckar. From the train station, take any bus or streetcar to Bismarckpl., then walk east down **Hauptstraße**, the city's spine, to the **Altstadt.** The **tourist office,** in front of the station, books rooms for a €2.50 fee and a small deposit. (☎13 88 121. Open Apr.-Oct. M-Sa 9am-7pm, Su 10am-6pm; Nov.-Mar. M-Sa 9am-6pm.) They also sell the 2-day **Heidelberg Card,** which includes unlimited public transit and admission to most sights (€12). In an **emergency,** call ☎110; for an **ambulance** or in case of **fire,** call ☎112. Check your email at **Mode Bredl,** Hauptstr. 90, near Bismarckpl. (Open M-F 9:30am-7:30pm, Sa 9:30am-4pm. €3 per 30min.) The **post office,** Sofienstr. 8-10, **69155** Heidelberg, is open M-F 9am-6:30pm, Sa 9:30am-1pm.

🔟🔵 ACCOMMODATIONS AND FOOD

In summer, reserve ahead or arrive early in the day to spare yourself a headache. To reach the **Jugendherberge (HI) ❶,** Tiergartenstr. 5, take bus #33 (dir.: Zoo-Sportzentrum) to Jugendherberge. You'll find large rooms and a basement pub in this, one of the biggest hostels in Europe. (☎41 20 66. Sheets €3. Reception daily until 11:30pm. Lockout 9am-1pm. Curfew 11:30pm; stragglers admitted every ½hr. until 2am. Reserve at least a week ahead. HI members only. Dorms €17.60, under 26 €14.90.) At **Hotel-Pension Elite ❹,** Bunsenstr. 15, all rooms have high ceilings, bath, and TV. From Bismarckpl., follow Rohrbacher Str. away from the river and turn right on Bunsenstr.; from the train station, take streetcar #1 to Poststr.—the hotel is on the 2nd street behind the Holiday Inn. (☎257 34. Breakfast included. *Let's Go* discounted rates: singles €51; doubles €61; triples €77; quads €87.)

Most of the restaurants on and around Hauptstr. are expensive but the *Imbiße* (fast food stands) are reasonably priced. Just outside this central area, historic student pubs offer good values as well. To reach **Mensa ❶,** in the *Marstall* on Marstallstr., take bus #35 to Marstallstr. You'll find cheap cafeteria fare. (€4, with student ID €2; €1.50 plate deposit; CampusCard required for lunch. Open M-F 11:30am-2pm, 6-10pm.) The mood of **Hemingway's Bar-Café-Meeting Point ❷,** Fahrtg. 1, is embodied in "Ernie" (€5)—a dessert consisting of a shot of brandy and a cigar. (Lunch menu €4.10. Open Su-Th 9am-1am, F-Sa 9am-3am.)

👁 SIGHTS

▧**HEIDELBERGER SCHLOß.** The jewel in the crown of an already striking city, the Schloß stands careful watch over the armies (of tourists) who dare approach Heidelberg. Its construction began in the 14th century and after 1329 it housed the Prince Electors, whose statues decorate the facade in front of the entrance. Over a period of almost 400 years, the castle's residents commissioned their own distinctive additions, resulting in the conglomeration of styles you see today. The castle **wine cellar** houses the **Großer Faß,** the largest wine barrel ever made, holding 221,726L. *(Grounds open daily 8am-5:30pm. €2, students €1. English tours every hr. 11:15am-4:15pm. €3, students €1.50.)* The *Schloß* is accessible by the **Bergbahn,** Germany's oldest cable car. *(Take bus #11 (dir.: Köpfel) or 33 (dir.: Karlstor) to Bergbahn/Rathaus. Trams leave the parking lot next to the bus stop every 10min. 9am-8:20pm; round-trip €3.)*

UNIVERSITÄT. Heidelberg is home to Germany's oldest and most prestigious university, established in 1368. More than 20 Nobel laureates have called the university home, and it was here that sociology became a legitimate academic subject. The **Museum der Universität Heidelberg** traces the university's long history in a building containing **Alte Aula,** Heidelberg's oldest auditorium. Before 1914, students were exempt from prosecution by civil authorities thanks to the principle of academic freedom; instead, the crimes of naughty youths were tried and punished by the faculty in the **Studentenkarzer.** *(Grabeng. 1. Open Apr.-Oct. M-Sa 10am-4pm; Nov.-Mar. Tu-F 10am-2pm. Museum and Studentenkarzer €2.50, students €2.)*

MARKTPLATZ. The *Altstadt*'s center is the cobblestoned **Marktplatz,** where accused witches and heretics were burned at the stake in the 15th century. Heidelberg's oldest structures border the square: the 14th-century **Heiliggeistkirche** (Church of the Holy Spirit) and the 16th-century **Haus Zum Ritter,** opposite the church. *(Church open M-Sa 11am-5pm, Su 1-5pm. Free. Church tower €0.50.)*

PHILOSOPHENWEG. A high path opposite the Neckar from the *Altstadt*, the Philosophenweg (Philosopher's Way) offers the best views of the city. On the top of Heiligenberg (Holy Mountain) lie the ruins of the 9th-century **St. Michael Basilika,** the 13th-century **Stefanskloster,** and an **amphitheater** built under Hitler in 1934 on the site of an ancient Celtic gathering place. *(Take streetcar #1 or 3 to Tiefburg, to begin the hike upwards, or use the footpath 10m west of the Karl-Theodor-Brücke.)*

▌ NIGHTLIFE

The **Marktplatz** is the hub of the city's action; most popular nightspots fan out from here. **Unter Straße,** on the Neckar side of the Heiliggeistkirche, boasts the most prolific—and often congested—collection of bars in the city. **Hauptstraße** also harbors a fair number of venues. University students pack **Nachtschicht,** in Landfried-Komplex, and jam to a variety of music. (From *Hauptbahnhof*, take Mittermaier-str. past the post office, take the first left onto Alte Eppenheimerstr. and enter the parking lot on the right. Open M 8pm-3am, W 10pm-3am, Th-Sa 10pm-4am. Cover €3.50, students €1.50 on W and F.)

STUTTGART   ☎ 0711

Forget about *Lederhosen*—Porsche, Daimler-Benz, and a host of other corporate thoroughbreds keep Stuttgart speeding along in the fast lane. After almost complete destruction in World War II, Stuttgart was rebuilt in a thoroughly modern and uninspiring style. The city does have amazing **mineral baths** *(Mineralbäder)*. **Mineralbad Leuze,** Am Leuzebad 2-6, has indoor, outdoor, and thermal therapy pools. Take U1 or 14, or streetcar #2 to Mineralbäder. (☎216 42 10. Open daily 6am-9pm. 2hr. soak €6.40, students €4.80.) The superb ▨**Staatsgallerie Stuttgart,** Konrad-Adenauer-Str. 30-32, houses an excellent collection of modern art in the new wing. (Open Tu-W and F-Su 10am-6pm, Th 10am-9pm. €4.50, students €2.50; W free.) The **Mercedes-Benz Museum,** Mercedesstr. 137, is a must for car-lovers. Take S1 to Daimlerstadion. (Open Tu-Su 9am-5pm. Free.)

Stuttgart has direct **trains** to most major German cities, including: Berlin (5½-12hr., 2 per hr., €98-132); Frankfurt (1½-4½hr., 2 per hr., €28-44); and Munich (2½-3½hr., 2-3 per hr., €33-45). The tourist office, **tips 'n' trips,** Lautenschlagerstr. 20, has **Internet** access (€3 per hr., W free) and resources on the Stuttgart scene. (☎222 27 30. Open M-F noon-7pm, Sa 10am-2pm.) The **post office** is in the station. (Open M-F 8:30am-6pm, Sa 8:30am-12:30pm.) **Postal code:** 70173. To reach the **Jugendherberge Stuttgart (HI) ❷,** Haußmannstr. 27, take streetcar #15 to Eugenspl.

and go downhill on Kernerstr.; the entrance is up the stairs with the red handrail. (☎24 15 83; jh-stuttgart@t-online.de. Breakfast included. Sheets €3.10. Reception 24hr. Lockout 9:30am-1pm. Reserve at least a week ahead by mail or email. Dorms €16, under 26 €14.) **Hotel Espenlaub** ❹, Charlottenstr. 27, has pricey but well-equipped rooms. Take streetcar #15 or U5, 6, or 7 to Olgaeck. (☎21 09 10. Breakfast included. Singles €44, with bath €59; doubles €59/€79; triples €74/€92. MC/V.) The pedestrian zone between Pfarrstr. and Charlottenstr. has many reasonably priced restaurants, while Rotebühlpl. is filled with *Imbiße* (fast food stands).

BLACK FOREST (SCHWARZWALD)

The Black Forest owes its name to the eerie gloom that prevails under its ever-green canopy. Once inspiration for the Grimm Brothers' "Hansel and Gretel," the region now attracts hikers and skiers with more than just gingerbread.

⌂ TRANSPORTATION. The main entry point to the Black Forest is **Freiburg**, which is accessible by **train** from Stuttgart and Basel, Switzerland. Most visitors use a bike to explore the area, as public transportation is sparse. Rail lines encircle the perimeter, with only two **train** lines cutting through the region. **Bus** service is more thorough, albeit slow and less frequent.

FREIBURG IM BREISGAU. Freiburg may be the metropolis of the Schwarzwald, but it has yet to succumb to the hectic pace of city life. Its pride and joy is the majestic **Münster**, a stone cathedral with a 116m spire and a tower whose bell is the oldest in Germany. (Open M-Sa 10am-6pm, Su 1-6pm. Tower closes 1hr. earlier. Tower €1, students €0.50.) The surrounding hills brim with fantastic **hiking** trails; maps are available in the tourist office or at most bookstores, and all trails are clearly marked. **Mountain biking** trails also traverse the hills; look for signs with bicycles to guide you. (Maps €3.50-6 at tourist office.)

Trains run to Basel (30min.-1hr., 1-2 per hr., €9-16) and Stuttgart (2-3hr., 2 per hr., €32-35). The **tourist office**, Rotteckring 14, two blocks down Eisenbahnstr. from the station, has maps and books **Privatenzimmer** (rooms in private homes); these are usually the most affordable accommodations in Freiburg itself, since most hotels and *Pensionen* are outside the city center. (Open June-Sept. M-F 9:30am-8pm, Sa 9:30am-5pm, Su 10am-noon; Oct.-May M-F 9:30am-6pm, Sa 9:30am-2pm, Su 10am-noon.) To reach the **Jugendherberge (HI) ❷**, Kartäuserstr. 151, take S1 to Römerhof, backtrack and take the next right down Fritz-Geiges-Str., cross the stream, and follow the footpath to the right for 5min. (☎676 56. Breakfast included. Sheets €3.10. Dorms €18, under 26 €15; doubles €25/€22.) The **Freiburger Markthalle ❷**, next to the Martinstor, is home to food-stands serving ethnic specialties for €3-8. The main entrance is on Grünwälderstr. (Open M-F 7am-7pm, Sa 7am-4pm.) ▧**Brennessel ❸**, Eschholzstr. 17, behind the train station, has reasonable prices for the amount and quality of their food. (Open M-Sa 8am-1am, Su 5pm-1am.)

ST. PETER AND ST. MÄRGEN. The twin villages of St. Peter and St. Märgen lie between cow-speckled hills, just north of Titisee and 17km east of Freiburg. **Bus** #7216 runs from **Freiburg** to **St. Peter** (25min.); get off at Zähriger Eck to reach St. Peter's **tourist office,** in the Klosterhof, which has a list of affordable rooms. (☎(07660) 91 02 24. Open M-F 9am-noon and 2-5pm, Sa 10am-noon.; Sept.-June closed Sa.) Many hiking paths—most well marked—begin at the tourist office. An easy and very scenic 8km path leads to **St. Märgen;** follow the blue diamonds of the **Panoramaweg.** Alternatively, **bus** #7216 continues on to St. Märgen about

YOUR OWN WAY

THE BODENSEE

Nearly landlocked, Germany has no white sand beaches like the Riviera and no sparkling waters like the Greek Islands—except for a strip of land on the Bodensee.

CONSTANCE. The town's **Münster** (cathedral), built over 600 years, has a 76m soaring Gothic spire. Constance is also home to a number of beaches, all free and open May-Sept. **Freibad Horn** (bus #5) is the most popular. Info: ☎(07531)13 30 30.

MEERSBURG. The medieval fortress of **Burg Meersburg** towers over the Bodensee and is the centerpiece of the town. Info: ☎(07532)43 11 10.

FRIEDRICHSHAFEN. A former construction base for Zeppelins, the main attraction is the **Zeppelinmuseum,** Seestr. 22. (Open Tu-Sa 10am-5pm. €6.50.) Info: ☎(07541)300 01.

LINDAU. Connected to the mainland only by a narrow causeway, the island of Lindau is a perfect tourist lure. There are 4 major beaches, the busiest of which is **Eichwald** (bus #1 or 2 to Anheggerstr./ZUP). Info: ☎(08382)26 00 30.

TRANSPORTATION. Constance and Friedrichshafen have direct connections to many cities in southern Germany. **Rail** transport within the region requires long, tricky connections. The **BSB** ferries are usually a quicker alternative. Ships leave hourly from Constance and Friedrichshafen. ☎(07531) 28 13 98.

half the time; check with the driver. With links to all major Black Forest trails and a number of gorgeous **day hikes,** St. Märgen rightfully calls itself a *Wanderparadies* (hiking paradise). Most of the trails are marked from Hotel Hirschen, uphill from the bus stop. The **tourist office,** in the *Rathaus,* 100m from the bus stop, provides good hiking and biking maps (€2.60-3.50) and finds **rooms** for free. (☎(07669) 91 18 17. Open M-Th 9am-4:30pm, F 9am-2pm; July-Sept. also Sa 10am-noon.)

TRIBERG. The residents of touristy Triberg brag about the **Gutacher Wasserfall,** the highest in Germany, a series of bright cascades tumbling over moss-covered rocks for 163m. It's more of a mountain stream than a waterfall, but the idyllic hike through the lush park makes up for the unimpressive trickle. (Park open 9am-7pm. €1.50, students €1.20.) The signs for **Wallfahrtskirche** lead to the small **Pilgrim Church,** where the pious have, according to legend, been miraculously cured since the 17th century. The area around town offers several beautiful hikes; ask at the tourist office for information and maps.

Trains run to Freiburg (2-2½hr., 1-2 per hr., €16-25). The **tourist office,** Luisenstr. 10, is on the ground floor of the *Kurhaus;* from the station, turn right and follow the signs, or take **bus** #7265, which runs every hour to Marktpl. The staff has a mammoth catalog of all hotels, *Pensionen,* and private rooms. (☎(07722) 95 32 30. Open M-F 9am-5pm; May-Sept. also Sa 10am-noon.) Grab groceries for a picnic at **Plus,** Schulstr. 5. (Open M-F 8:30am-6:30pm, Sa 8am-2pm.)

BAVARIA (BAYERN)

Bavaria is the Germany of Teutonic myth, Wagnerian opera, and the Brothers Grimm's fairy tales. From the Baroque cities along the Danube to Mad King Ludwig's castles high in the Alps, the region draws more tourists than any other part of the country. Most foreigners' notions of Germany are tied to this land of *Biergartens* and *Lederhosen.* Mostly rural, Catholic, and conservative, it contrasts sharply with the rest of the country. Local authorities still use Bavaria's proper name, *Freistaat Bayern,* and its traditions and dialect have been preserved. Residents have always been Bavarians first and Germans second.

 REMINDER. HI-affiliated hostels in Bavaria generally do not admit guests over age 26 except in families or groups of adults with young children.

MUNICH (MÜNCHEN) ☎089

The capital and cultural center of Bavaria, Munich is a sprawling, relatively liberal metropolis in the midst of conservative southern Germany. World-class museums, handsome parks and architecture, a rambunctious arts scene, and an urbane population combine to create a city of astonishing vitality. *Müncheners* party zealously during Fasching (Karneval; Jan. 7-Mar. 4, 2003), shop with abandon during the Christmas Market (Nov. 28-Dec. 24, 2003), and consume unbelievable quantities of beer during the legendary Oktoberfest (Sept. 20-Oct. 5, 2003).

⌐ TRANSPORTATION

Flights: Flughafen München (☎97 52 13 13). S8 runs between the airport and the *Hauptbahnhof* (40min., every 20min., €8 or 8 stripes on the *Streifenkarte*).

Trains: Munich's **Hauptbahnhof** (☎22 33 12 56) is the transportation hub of Southern Germany, with connections to: **Amsterdam** (9hr., 1 per hr., €143); **Berlin** (8hr., 1 per hr., €141, or €103 via Leipzig); **Cologne** (6hr., 1 per hr., €101); **Frankfurt** (3½hr., 1 per hr., €76); **Hamburg** (6hr., 1 per hr., €138); **Paris** (10hr., 3 per day, €105); **Prague** (7hr., 2 per day, €60); **Salzburg** (1¾hr., 1 per hr., €25); **Vienna** (5hr., 1 per hr., €59); **Zurich** (5hr., 4 per day, €61). For 24hr. schedules, fare information, and reservations (in German), call ☎(01805) 99 66 33. **EurAide,** in the station, provides free train information and sells train tickets. **Reisezentrum** information counters open daily 6am-10:30pm. As of Dec. 2002, the Deutsche Bahn will be instituting a *new price system;* expect changes to existing fares.

Public Transportation: MVV, Munich's public transport system, runs Su-Th 5am-12:30am, F-Sa 5am-2am. The S-Bahn to the airport starts running at 3:30am. Eurail, InterRail, and German railpasses are valid on the S-Bahn, but *not* on the U-Bahn, streetcars, or buses.

Tickets: Buy tickets at the blue vending machines and **validate them** in the blue boxes marked with an E before entering the platform. Disguised officials check for tickets sporadically; if you jump the fare (known as *schwarzfahren*), you risk a €30 fine.

Prices: Single ride tickets €2, valid for 3hr. **Kurzstrecke** (short trip) tickets are good for 2 stops on U or S, or 4 stops on a streetcar or bus (€1). A **Streifenkarte** (10-strip ticket, €9) can be used by more than 1 person. Cancel 2 strips per person for a normal ride, or 1 strip per person for a *Kurzstrecke;* beyond the city center, cancel 2 strips per additional zone. A **Single-Tageskarte** (single-day ticket) is valid for one day of unlimited travel until 6am the next day (€4.50). The **3-Day Pass** (€11) is also a great deal. Passes can be purchased at the **MVV office** behind tracks 31 and 32 in the *Hauptbahnhof,* or at any of the *Kartenautomats.* Ask at tourist offices about the **Munich Welcome Card** (1-day €6.50, 3-day €15.50), which gives public transportation and various other discounts.

Taxis: Taxi-Zentrale (☎216 11 or 194 10) has large stands in front of the train station and every 5-10 blocks in the city center. Women can request a female driver.

Bike Rental: Radius Bikes (☎59 61 13), at the far end of the *Hauptbahnhof,* behind the lockers opposite tracks 30-36. €3 per hr., €13 per day, €43 per week. Deposit €50, passport, or credit card. 10% student, Eurail, and Munich Welcome Card discount. Open May-Oct. M-F 10am-6pm; July-Aug. also Sa-Su 9am-8pm. **Aktiv-Rad,** Hans-Sachs-Str. 7 (☎26 65 06). U1 or 2 to Frauenhofer Str. €12-20 per day. Open M-F 10am-1pm and 2-6:30pm, Sa 10am-1pm.

▟ ORIENTATION

Munich's center is a circle split into four quarters by one horizontal and one vertical line. The circle is the main traffic **Ring,** which changes names frequently around its length. The east-west and north-south thoroughfares cross at Munich's epicenter, the **Marienplatz,** and connect the traffic rings at **Karlsplatz** (called **Stachus** by

GERMANY

Munich (München)

⚑ ACCOMMODATIONS
4 You München, 6
Campingplatz Thalkirchen, 24
Creatif Hotel, 7
Euro Youth Hotel, 16
Hotel Kurpfalz, 15
Hotel-Pension am Markt, 20
Jungendhotel Marienherberge, 17
Jungendlager Kapuzinerhözl, 5
Pension Frank, 4
Pension Locarno, 12

⬤ FOOD
Café Hag/Confiserie Retenhäfen, 13
Café Ignaz, 1
Gollier, 22
Marché, 18
Schwimmkrabbe, 25

▮ NIGHTLIFE
Augustinerkeller, 10
Ballhaus, 2
Bei Carla, 23
Hirschgarten, 11
Hofbräuhaus, 19
Kunstpark Ost, 26
Nachtcafé, 8
Nachtwerk, Club, and Tanzloki, 14
Reitschule, 3
Sausalitos, 21
Soul City, 9

locals) in the west, **Isatorplatz** in the east, **Odeonsplatz** in the north, and **Sendlinger Tor** in the south. In the east beyond the Isartor, the **Isar River** flows north-south past the city center. The **Hauptbahnhof** (main train station) is just beyond Karlspl. to the west of the Ring. To get to Marienpl. from the station, use the main exit and head across Bahnhofpl.; keep going east through Karlspl., and Marienpl. will be straight ahead. Or, take any S-Bahn to Marienpl.

The **University** is north of Munich's center, next to the budget restaurants of the **Schwabing** district. East of Schwabing is the **English Garden**; west of Schwabing is the **Olympiapark**. South of town is the **Glockenbachviertel**, filled with all sorts of night hotspots, including many gay bars. The area around the train station is rather seedy, dominated by hotels and sex shops. Oktoberfest is held on the large, open **Theresienwiese**, southeast of the train station on the U4 and 5 lines.

🔢 PRACTICAL INFORMATION

Several publications help visitors navigate Munich. The most comprehensive is the monthly English-language *Munich Found* (€3), available at newsstands and bookshops, which provides a list of services, events, and museums.

TOURIST, FINANCIAL, AND LOCAL SERVICES

Main Tourist Office: (☎ 23 39 65 00), on the front (east) side of the train station, next to the SB-Markt on Bahnhofpl. They do speak English, but for more in-depth questions, the two organizations listed below may better suit your needs. The office books rooms for free with a 10-15% deposit, sells English city maps (€0.30), and offers the **Munich Welcome Card.** Open M-Sa 9am-8pm, Su 10am-6pm. **Branch office** just inside the entrance to the Neues Rathaus on Marienpl. Open M-F 10am-8pm, Sa 10am-4pm.

🔳 **EurAide** (☎ 59 38 89), along track 11 (room 3) of the *Hauptbahnhof*, near the Bayerstr. exit. Books train tickets, explains the public transport, and sells maps (€1) and tickets for English tours of Munich. Pick up the free brochure *Inside Track*. Open June-Sept. daily 7:45am-12:45pm and 2-6pm; Oct. 7:45am-12:45pm and 2-4pm; Nov.-Apr. 8am-noon and 1-4pm; May 7:45am-12:45pm and 2-4:30pm.

🔳 **Discover Bavaria** (☎ 25 54 39 88), Hochorückenstr., near the rear entrance of the Hofbräuhaus. Helps find rooms for free, rents bikes, and dispenses coupons for a variety of activities. Also sells tickets for the hugely popular Mike's Bike Tours of Munich, Neuschwanstein, and Dachau. Open daily 8:30am-9pm; closed Oct.-Mar.

Consulates: Canada, Tal 29 (☎ 219 95 70). S-Bahn to Isartor. Open M-Th 9am-noon and 2-5pm, F 9am-noon and 2-3:30pm. **Ireland,** Dennigerstr. 15 (☎ 20 80 59 90). Open M-F 9am-noon. **South Africa,** Sendlinger-Tor-Pl. 5 (☎ 23 11 63 37). U1, 2, 3, or 6 to Sendlinger Tor. Open M-F 9am-noon. **UK,** Bürkleinstr. 10, 4th fl. (☎ 21 10 90). U4 or 5 to Lehel. Open M-Th 8:30am-noon and 1-5pm, F until 3:30pm. **US,** Königinstr. 5 (☎ 288 80). Open M-F 8-11am.

Bi-Gay-Lesbian Resources: Gay services Information (☎ 260 30 56). **Lesbian Information** and the **LeTra Lesbentraum,** Angertorstr. 3 (☎ 725 42 72). Telephone times M and W 2:30-5pm, Tu 10:30am-1pm, Th 7-9pm. See also **Gay and Lesbian Munich.**

Disabled Resources: Info Center für Behinderte, Schellingstr. 31 (☎ 211 70; www.vdk.de/bayern), has a list of Munich's resources for disabled persons. Open M-Th 9am-noon and 12:30-6pm, F 9am-5pm.

Laundromat: SB Waschcenter, Paul-Heyse-Str. 21, near the train station. Turn right on Bayerstr., then left on Paul-Heyse-Str. Wash €4; dry €0.60 per 10min. Open daily 7am-11pm. **Kingsgard Waschsalon,** Amalienstr. 61, near the university. Wash €3; dry €1.50. Open M-F 8am-6:30pm, Sa 9am-1pm.

EMERGENCY AND COMMUNICATIONS

Police: ☎ 110. **Ambulance** and **Fire:** ☎ 112. **Medical service:** ☎ 192 22.

Pharmacy: Bahnhofpl. 2 (☎ 59 41 19 or 59 81 19), on the corner outside the train station. Open M-F 8am-6:30pm, Sa 8am-2pm. 24hr. service rotates among the city's pharmacies—check the window of any pharmacy for a list.

Internet Access: EasyEverything, on Bahnhofspl. next to the post office. Prices depend on demand (max. €3 per hr.) Open 24hr. **Savic Internet Point,** Schillerstr. 15, is slightly more expensive per hour. (Open daily 10am-midnight.)

Post Office: Bahnhofpl., **80335** Munich. The yellow building across the street from the main train station exit. Open M-F 7am-8pm, Sa 9am-4pm, Su 10am-3pm.

▐ ACCOMMODATIONS AND CAMPING

Munich's accommodations usually fall into one of three categories: seedy, expensive, or booked solid. During times like Oktoberfest, when prices usually jump 10-15%, only the latter exists. In summer, book a few weeks in advance or start calling before noon. At most of Munich's hostels you can check in all day, but try to start your search before 5pm. Don't even think of sleeping in any public area, including the *Hauptbahnhof;* police patrol frequently all night long.

HOSTELS AND CAMPING

▨ Euro Youth Hotel, Senefelderstr. 5 (☎ 59 90 88 11, 59 90 88 71, or 59 90 88 72). From the Bayerstr. exit out of the *Hauptbahnhof,* make a left on Bayerstr. and a right on Senefelderstr. Friendly and well-informed English-speaking staff. Breakfast buffet €4.90. Wash €2.80; dry €1.30. Reception 24hr. Dorms €17.50; doubles €48, with private shower, telephone, and breakfast €72; triples €63; quads €84. Inquire about their new location, scheduled to open early in 2003. ❷

4 You München, Hirtenstr. 18 (☎ 552 16 60), 200m from the *Hauptbahnhof.* Exit at Arnulfstr., go left, quickly turn right onto Pfefferstr., then hang a left onto Hirtenstr. Ecological youth hostel with restaurant and bar. Wheelchair-accessible. Breakfast buffet €4.35. 12-bed dorms €17.50; 4-, 6-, or 8-bed dorms €20-22; singles €35, with bath €43.50; doubles €52/€68.50. 15% surcharge for ages over 27. ❷

Jugendhotel Marienherberge, Goethestr. 9 (☎ 55 58 05), less than a block from the train station. Take the Bayerstr. exit and walk down Goethestr. **Open only to women.** Reduced prices for those 25 and under. Staffed by merry nuns, the rooms are spacious, cheery, and spotless. Breakfast included. Laundry €1.50. Reception daily 8am-midnight. Curfew midnight. 6-bed dorms €25; singles €31; doubles €50; triples €75. ❸

Jugendlager Kapuzinerhölzl ("The Tent"), In den Kirschen 30 (☎ 141 43 00). Streetcar #17 from the *Hauptbahnhof* (dir.: Amalienburgstr.) to Botanischer Garten (15min.). Follow the signs straight on Franz-Schrank-Str. and turn left at In den Kirschen. Sleep with 250 fellow campers under a big tent on a wooden floor. Laundry €2. Lockers €4. Internet €1 for 15min. Kitchen facilities available. Reception 24hr. Reservations only for groups over 15, but rarely full. Open June-Aug. €8.50 gets you a foam pad, blankets (you can also use your sleeping bag), a shower, and breakfast. Actual beds €11. Camping available for €5.50 per campsite plus €5.50 per person. ❶

Campingplatz Thalkirchen, Zentralländstr. 49 (☎ 723 17 07). U1 or 2 to Sendlinger Tor, then U3 to Thalkirchen, and change to bus #57 (20min.). From the bus stop, cross the busy street on the left and take a right onto the footpath next to the road. The entrance is down the tree-lined path on the left. Well-run, crowded grounds with jogging and bike paths, TV lounge, groceries, and a restaurant. Showers €1. Wash €4; dry €0.25 per 11min. Open mid-Mar. to late Oct. €4.40 per person, €8 per tent. ❶

HOTELS AND PENSIONS

■ **Hotel Helvetia,** Schillerstr. 6 (☎590 68 50), at the corner of Bahnhofspl. Just beyond the Vereinsbank, to the right as you exit the station. A friendly hotel with newly renovated rooms. Free Internet. Breakfast included. Laundry €6. Reception 24hr. Singles €30-35; doubles €40-55, with shower €50-65; triples €55-69; quads €72-90. ❸

■ **Pension Locarno,** Bahnhofspl. 5 (☎55 51 64). Cozy rooms, all with cable TV and phone. Reception daily 7:30am-5pm. Singles €38; doubles €57; triples €69; quads €81. ❸

Creatif Hotel, Lammerstr. 6 (☎55 57 85). Take the Arnulfstr. exit out of the station, hang a quick right, turn left on Hirtenstr., then right on Lammerstr. Uniquely modern rooms, all with bath, telephones, and TVs. Internet €1 per 30min. Reception 24hr. Singles €30-40; doubles €40-65; extra bed €10. ❸

Hotel Kurfplaz, Schwanthaler Str. 121 (☎540 98 60). Exit on Bayerstr. from the station, turn right and walk 5-6 blocks down Bayerstr., veer left onto Holzapfelstr., and make a right onto Schwanthaler Str. Or, take streetcar #18 or 19 to Holzapfelstr. and walk from there. TVs, phones, and bath in all rooms. Breakfast included. Free email; Internet €3 per 30min. Reception 24hr. Singles from €50; doubles from €100. ❹

Hotel-Pension am Markt, Heiliggeiststr. 6 (☎22 50 14), smack dab in the city center, off the Viktualienmarkt. Take any S-Bahn to Marienpl., then walk past the Altes Rathaus and turn right down the little alley behind the Heiliggeist Church. Small but spotless rooms are wheelchair-accessible. Breakfast included. Reception (3rd fl.) daily 7am-9pm. Singles €38, with shower €66; doubles €68/€87-92; triples €100/€123. ❹

Pension Frank, Schellingstr. 24 (☎28 14 51). U3 or 6 to Universität. Take the Schellingstr. exit, then the 1st right onto Schellingstr. Rooms with balconies in a great location for cafe and bookstore aficionados. Breakfast included. Reception daily 7:30am-10pm. 3- to 6-bed dorms €25; singles €35-40; doubles €52-55. ❸

FOOD

For an authentic Bavarian lunch, grab a *Brez'n* (pretzel) and spread it with *Leberwurst* (liverwurst) or cheese. **Weißwürste** (white veal sausages) are another native bargain. Don't eat the skin of the sausage, just slice it open and eat the tender meat. **Leberkäs** is a slice of a pinkish, meatloaf-like compound of ground beef and bacon, usually served in soup. **Leberknödel** are liver dumplings, usually served in soup.

The vibrant **Viktualienmarkt,** 2min. south of Marienpl., is Munich's gastronomic center. It's fun to browse, but don't plan to do any budget grocery shop-

IN RECENT NEWS

GOLDEN GOAL, COPPER WIRING

It seems as though Germans have discovered yet another means of assuaging an insatiable appetite for football. This time, however, the game is unspoiled by poor conditions, unhindered by broken bones, and uninterrupted by a flash of red cards.

The key: teams of fine-tuned two-wheelers. Since its birth in the early 1990s, robot soccer has flourished into an international enterprise. The mechanized sport consists of five leagues, including a simulation league, a small-size league, a medium-size league, a four-legged league, and a humanoid league.

Typically, teams of up to five robots are coached by university specialists, trained in the art of artificial intelligence. As one might expect, Germany has quickly become a dominant participant; since the first RoboCup in 1997, the same German team has rolled away with three world championships in the middle-size division, which features a playing field the size of nine ping-pong tables.

While these machines can't match the spectacular saves of Oliver Kahn, newer models are not without superhuman qualities, including special lasers and a reflex speed that clearly surpasses human capabilities. At this rate, competition with humans is not far off. Indeed, by 2050, robot soccer advocates hope to organize a team of humanoid robots that can contend with the real-life football superstars. And with so long to wait before the next World Cup, this sport is due to gather a greater German following.

ping here. (Open M-F 10am-8pm, Sa 8am-4pm.) **Beer gardens** serve savory snacks along with booze. The university district off **Ludwigstraße** is Munich's best source of inexpensive and filling meals. Many reasonably priced restaurants and cafes cluster on **Schellingstraße, Amalienstraße,** and **Türkenstraße** (U3 or 6 to Universität.)

■ **Marché,** Neuhauser Str., between Karlspl. and Marienpl. The top floor offers cafeteria-style food; downstairs, chefs prepare every food imaginable, including great vegetarian selections. You'll get a food card that will be stamped for each item taken; pay at the end. Bottom floor open 11am-10pm; top floor 8am-11pm, until 10pm in off-season. ❷

■ **Café Hag/Confiserie Retenhäfen,** Residenzstr. 25-26, across from the Residenz. Specializes in a delectable array of cakes and sweets (€2-4). Serves breakfast (€4-8) and entrees (€5-8). Open M-F 8:45am-7pm, Sa 8am-6pm. ❷

Schwimmkrabbe, Ickstattstr. 13. U1 or 2 to Frauenhoferstr. This family-run Turkish restaurant is popular with locals. Appetizers €4-9; meals €8-18. Open daily 5pm-1am. ❹

Gollier, Gollierstr. 83. U4 or 5, S7 or 27 to Heimeranpl. Delicious vegetarian fare €6-11. Open Tu-F 11:30-3pm and 5pm-midnight, Sa 5pm-midnight, Su 10am-midnight. ❸

Café Ignaz, Georgenstr. 67. U2 to Josephspl. Take Adelheidstr. Nutritious, inexpensive vegetarian menu. Lunch buffet €7.50, brunch buffet Sa-Su 9am-1:30pm €8. Open M-F 8am-10pm, Sa-Su 9am-10pm. ❷

🄶 SIGHTS

MARIENPLATZ. The **Mariensäule,** an ornate 17th-century monument to the Virgin Mary, was built to commemorate the city's survival during the Thirty Years' War. At the neo-Gothic **Neues Rathaus,** the **Glockenspiel** chimes with a display of jousting knights and dancing coopers. *(Daily 11am and noon; in summer also 5pm.)* At 9pm, a mechanical watchman marches out and the Guardian Angel escorts the *Münchner Kindl* (Munich Child, the town's symbol) to bed. Be careful while admiring the Glockenspiel; this is a likely spot for pickpocketing. The Neues Rathaus tower offers a sweeping view. *(Tower open M-F 9am-7pm, Sa-Su 10am-7pm. €1.50.)* On the face of the **Altes Rathaus** tower, to the right of the Neues Rathaus, are all of Munich's coats of arms since its inception as a city but one—the local government refused to include the swastika-bearing arms from the Nazi era.

PETERSKIRCHE AND FRAUENKIRCHE. Across from the Neues Rathaus is the 12th-century **Peterskirche,** the city's oldest parish church. More than 300 steps scale the tower to a spectacular view of Munich. *(Open daily 10am-7pm. €1.50, students €1.)* From the Marienpl., take Kaufingerstr. one block toward the *Hauptbahnhof* to the onion-domed towers of the 15th-century **Frauenkirche**—one of Munich's most notable landmarks and now the symbol of the city. *(Towers open Apr.-Oct. M-Sa 10am-5pm. €3, students €1.50.)*

RESIDENZ. Down the pedestrian zone from Odeonspl., the richly decorated rooms of the **Residenz** (Palace), built from the 14th to 19th centuries, form the material vestiges of the Wittelsbach dynasty. Behind the Residenz, the beautifully landscaped **Hofgarten** shelters the lovely temple of Diana. The **Schatzkammer** (treasury) contains jeweled baubles, crowns, swords, china, ivory work, and other trinkets. *(Open Apr. to mid-Oct. daily 9am-6pm; mid-Oct. to Mar. 10am-4pm. €4, students €3.)* The **Residenzmuseum** comprises the former Wittelsbach apartments and State Rooms, a collection of European porcelain, and a 17th-century court chapel. The 120 portraits in the **Ahnengalerie** trace the royal lineage in an unusual manner back to Charlemagne. *(Max-Joseph-pl. 3. U3-6 to Odeonspl. Residenz museum open same hours as Schatzkammer. €4, students €3. Combination ticket €7, students €5.50.)*

ENGLISCHER GARTEN. Extending from the city center is the vast **Englischer Garten** (English Garden), Europe's largest metropolitan public park. On sunny days, all of Munich turns out to bike, play badminton, ride horseback, or swim in the Eisbach. The garden includes a Japanese tea house, a Chinese pagoda, a Greek temple, and good old German beer gardens. **Nude sunbathing** areas are designated FKK *(Frei-Körper-Kultur)* on signs and park maps. Daring Müncheners surf the rapids of the Eisbach, which flows artificially through the park.

SCHLOß NYMPHENBURG. After 10 years of trying for an heir, Ludwig I celebrated the birth of his son in 1662 by erecting an elaborate summer playground. **Schloß Nymphenburg,** in the northwest of town, hides a number of treasures. Check out Ludwig's "Gallery of Beauties"; whenever a woman caught his fancy, he would have her portrait painted—a scandalous hobby considering many of the women were commoners. Four manors and a few lakes also inhabit the grounds. Finally, learn about the means of 17th-century royal travel in the **Marstallmuseum.** *(Streetcar #17 to Schloß Nymphenburg. All attractions open Apr. to mid-Oct. daily 9am-8pm; late Oct. to Mar. 10am-4pm. Museum and Schloß open Tu-Su 9am-noon and 1-5pm. Schloß €3.50, students €2.50. Each manor €3/€2. Museum €2.50/€2. Entire complex €7.50/€6.)*

OLYMPIAPARK. Built for the 1972 Olympic Games in Munich, the **Olympiapark** contains the architecturally daring, tent-like **Olympia-Zentrum** and the **Olympia Turm** (tower), the highest building in Munich at 290m. Two **tours** in English are available: the "Adventure Tour" of the entire park (Apr.-Oct. daily 2pm, €7) or a tour of just the soccer stadium (Mar.-Oct. daily 11am, €5). The Olympiapark also hosts various events all summer, ranging from concerts to flea markets to bungee jumping. *(U3 to Olympiazentrum. Tower open daily 9am-midnight. €3, students €2. Info Pavilion (Besucherservice) open M-F 10am-6pm, Sa 10am-3pm.)*

▥ MUSEUMS

Munich is a supreme museum city—many of the city's offerings would require days for exhaustive perusal. The *Münchner Volkshochschule* (☎48 00 62 29 or 48 00 62 30) offers tours of many city museums for €6. A **day pass** to all of Munich's state-owned museums is sold at the tourist office and many larger museums (€15). All state-owned museums are **free on Sunday.**

DEUTSCHES MUSEUM. One of the largest and best museums of science and technology, with fascinating displays, including a mining exhibit that winds through a labyrinth of recreated subterranean tunnels. The museum has over 50 department ments covering 17km. Grab an English guidebook for €4. *(Museuminsel 1. S1 or 8 to Isartor or streetcar #18 to Deutsches Museum. Open daily 9am-5pm. €6, students €2.50.)*

ALTE PINAKOTHEK AND NEUE PINAKOTHEK. Commissioned in 1826 by King Ludwig I, the world-renowned **Alte Pinakothek** houses Munich's most precious art, including works by da Vinci, Rembrandt, and Rubens. The **Neue Pinakothek** next door displays paintings and sculptures of the 19th to 20th centuries, including van Gogh, Cézanne, and Manet. *(Alte: Barerstr. 27. U2 to Königspl. Open Tu-Su 10am-5pm, Th until 10pm. Neue: Barerstr. 29. Open W-M 10am-5pm and Th until 10pm. Each €5, students €3.50; combination ticket for Alte and Neue Pinakotheken €8, students €5.)* The **Pinakothek Der Moderne** was under construction at the time of publication; it will eventually house the **Staatsgalerie Moderner Kunst** and is scheduled to open late 2002.

BMW MUSEUM. The ultimate driving museum features a fetching display of past, present, and future BMW products. The English brochure *Horizons in Time* guides you through the spiral path to the top of the museum. *(Petuelring 130. U3 to Olympiazentrum. Take the Olympiaturm exit and walk a block up Lerchenauer Str.; the museum will be on your left. Open daily 9am-5pm. €3, students €2.)*

ZAM: ZENTRUM FÜR AUSSERGEWÖHNLICHE MUSEEN. Munich's Center for Unusual Museums brazenly corrals—under one roof—such treasures as the Peddle-Car Museum and the Museum of Easter Rabbits. *(Westenriederstr. 41. Any S-Bahn or streetcar #17 or 18 to Isartor. Open daily 10am-6pm. €4, students €3.)*

🎵 🎭 ENTERTAINMENT AND NIGHTLIFE

Munich's cultural cache rivals the world's best. Sixty theaters of various sizes are scattered throughout the city; styles range from dramatic classics at the **Residenztheater** and **Volkstheater** to comic opera at the **Staatstheater am Gärtnerplatz** to experimental works at the **Theater im Marstall** in Nymphenburg. Munich's **opera festival** (in July) is held in the ▧**Bayerische Staatsoper** (Bavarian National Theater), Max-Joseph-pl. 2. (Tickets ☎21 85 19 20; recorded info ☎21 85 19 19. Streetcar #19 to Nationaltheater or U3-6 to Odeonspl. Standing-room and student tickets €4-10, sold 1hr. before performance at the side entrance on Maximilianstr. Box office open M-F 10am-6pm, Sa 10am-1pm. No performances Aug. to mid-Sept.) *Monatsprogramm* (€1.50) and *Munich Found* (€3) both list schedules for Munich's stages, museums, and festivals. Munich reveals its bohemian face in scores of small fringe theaters, cabaret stages, and art cinemas in **Schwabing.**

Munich's nightlife is a curious collision of Bavarian *Gemütlichkeit* ("warmth") and trendy cliquishness. The odyssey begins at one of Munich's beer gardens or beer halls, which generally close before midnight and are most crowded in the early evening. The alcohol keeps flowing at cafes and bars, which, except for Friday and Saturday nights, close their taps at 1am. Discos and dance clubs, sedate before midnight, throb relentlessly until 4am. The trendy spots along **Leopoldstraße** in **Schwabing** attract tourists from all over Europe. Many of these venues require you to at least attempt the jaded hipster look, and the Munich fashion police generally frown on shorts, sandals, and t-shirts.

BEER GARDENS (BIERGÄRTEN)

The six great Munich labels are *Augustiner, Hacker-Pschorr, Hofbräu, Löwenbräu, Paulaner,* and *Spaten-Franziskaner;* but most restaurants and *Gaststätte* have picked a side and only serve one brewery's beer. There are four main types of beer served in Munich: **Helles** (light), **Dunkles** (dark), **Weißbier** (cloudy blond beer made from wheat instead of barley), and **Radler** ("cyclist's brew"; half beer and half lemon soda). Saying *"Ein Bier, bitte"* will get you a liter, known as a *Maß* (€4-6). Specify if you want only a *halb-Maß* (€3-4).

▧ **Augustinerkeller,** Arnulfstr. 52, at Zirkus-Krone-Str. Any S-Bahn to Hackerbrücke. Founded in 1824, *Augustiner* is viewed by most *Müncheners* as the finest beer garden in town. Lush grounds, 100-year-old chestnut trees, and the delicious, sharp *Augustiner* beer (*Maß* €5.70) support their assertion. Open daily 10:30am-1am.

Hirschgarten, Hirschgarten 1. Streetcar #17 (dir.: Amalienburgstr.) to Romanpl. The largest beer garden in Europe (seating 9000) is boisterous and pleasant but somewhat remote, near Schloß Nymphenburg. *Maß* €5.30. Open daily 9am-midnight.

Hofbräuhaus, Platzl 9, 2 blocks from Marienpl. Many tables are reserved for locals—some even keep their personal steins in the hall's safe. To avoid tourists, go in the early afternoon. *Maß* €6. *Weißwürste* with pretzel €3.70. Open daily 9am-midnight.

BARS

▧ **Nachtcafe,** Maximilianspl. 5. U4 or 5 or any S-Bahn to Karlspl. Live jazz, funk, soul, and blues until the wee hours. Very *schicki-micki* (yuppie). Things don't get rolling until midnight. No cover, but prices are outrageous; do your drinking beforehand. Very picky dress code on weekends. Open daily 9pm-6am; live music 11pm-4am.

Reitschule, Königinstr. 34. U3 or 6 to Giselastr. A sleek bar with marble tables, as well as a cafe with a beer garden out back. *Weißbier* €3. Open daily 9am-1am.

Sausalitos, Im Tal 16. Any U-Bahn to Marienpl. Mexican bar and restaurant hopping with a 20-something crowd. Drinks €6-9. Open daily 11am-late.

CLUBS

🖾 **Kunstpark Ost,** Grafinger Str. 6. U5 or any S-Bahn to *Ostbahnhof;* follow signs for the Kunstpark Ost exit. A huge complex containing 40 different venues swarming with parties. Try the standard **MilchBar** (open M, W-F); the psychedelic-trance **Natraj Temple** (open F-Sa); or the cocktail bar and disco **K41** (open every night; Th 80s night). Hours, cover, and themes vary—check *Kunstpark* for details on specific club nights and specials. The entire venue will be moving to Frottmaning, outside the city center, sometime in 2003. Check their website (www.kunstpark.de) for details about the move.

Nachtwerk, Club, and Tanzlokal, Landesberger Str. 185. Streetcar #18 or 19 or bus #83 to Lautensackstr. **Nachtwerk** spins mainstream dance tunes for sweaty crowds in a packed warehouse. **Club** offers a 2-level dance floor just as tight and swinging as its neighbor. **Tanzlokal** (open F-Sa) has hip-hop on F. Beer €2.50 at all venues. Cover €5.50. Open daily 10pm-4am.

Ballhaus, Domagkstr. 33, in the Alabamahalle. U6 to Heide. Free shuttle from there to the club. On a former military base in Schwabing with 3 other discos. Start out in the beer garden, which opens 8pm. **Alabama** serves free drinks all night Sa and until 1am F (open F 9pm-4am, Sa 10pm-5am). **Tempel Club** has typical pop music (open Sa 10pm-4am) and **Schwabinger Ballhouse** plays international jams. (F-Sa 10pm-5am. Cover €8, drinks €1.50-3.)

GAY AND LESBIAN MUNICH

Although Bavaria has the reputation of being less welcoming to homosexuality, Munich sustains a respectably vibrant gay nightlife. The center of the gay scene is in the **Glockenbachviertel,** stretching from the area south of the Sendlinger Tor through the Viktualienmarkt/Gärtnerpl. area to the Isartor. *Our Munich,* Munich's gay and lesbian leaflet, is available at the tourist office, while *Sergej* is available at **Max&Milian Bookstore,** Ickstattstr. 2 (open M-F 10:30am-2pm and 3:30-8pm, Sa 11am-4pm), or at any other gay locale.

🖾 **Bei Carla,** Buttermelcherstr. 9. Any S-Bahn to Isartor. Walk 1 block south on Zweibrückenstr., take a right on Rumfordstr., turn left on Klenzestr., then left again onto Buttermelcherstr. One of Munich's best-kept secrets. Open M-Sa 4pm-1am, Su 6pm-1am.

Soul City, Maximilianspl. 5, at the intersection with Max-Joseph-Str. Purportedly the biggest gay disco in Bavaria; music ranges from disco to Latin to techno. Straights always welcome. Cover €5-13. Open W-Sa 10pm-late.

▶ DAYTRIPS FROM MUNICH

DACHAU   ☎08131

From Munich, take S2 (dir.: Petershausen) to Dachau (20min., €4, or 4 stripes on the Streifenkarte), then bus #724 (dir.: Kraütgarten) or 726 (dir.: Kopernikusstr.) to KZ-Gedenkstätte (10min., €1 or one stripe on the Streifenkarte). Informative but lengthy (2hr.) tours in English leave from the museum July-Aug. daily 12:30pm; Sept.-June Sa-Su and holidays 12:30pm. Free, but donation requested. ☎08131 17 41. Camp open Tu-Su 9am-5pm.

"Arbeit Macht Frei" ("work will set you free") was the first thing prisoners saw as they entered Dachau; it's written over the gate of the **Jourhaus,** formerly the only entry to the camp. Dachau was primarily a work camp (rather than a death camp,

like Auschwitz). During the war, prisoners made armaments in Dachau because the SS knew that the Allies would not bomb a concentration camp. Although Dachau has a **gas chamber,** it was never actually used because the prisoners purposely made mistakes and worked slowly in order to delay completion. Once tightly packed **barracks** are now, for the most part, only foundations; however, survivors ensured that at least two barracks would be reconstructed to teach future generations about the 206,000 prisoners who were interned here from 1933 to 1945. The walls, gates, and crematorium have been restored since 1962 in a chillingly sparse memorial to the victims of Dachau. The **museum,** located in the former administrative buildings, examines pre-1930s anti-Semitism, the rise of Nazism, the establishment of the concentration camp system, and the lives of prisoners through photographs, documents, and artifacts. The thick guide (€26) translates the propaganda posters, SS files, documents, and letters. Most exhibits are accompanied by short captions in English. A short film (22min.) is screened in English at 11:30am, 2pm, and 3:30pm. A new display in the **Bunker,** the concentration camp's prison and torture chamber, chronicles the lives and experiences of the camp's special prisoners and the barbarism of SS guards. When you visit, it is important to remember that, while the concentration camp is treated as a tourist attraction by many, it is, first and foremost, a memorial.

GARMISCH-PARTENKIRCHEN ☎ 08821

The **Zugspitze** (2964m), Germany's tallest mountain, is the main attraction in town. There are two ways to conquer it, neither of which should be attempted in poor weather. You can take the **cog railway** from the *Zugspitzbahnhof* (50m behind the Garmisch main station) to the *Zugspitzplatt* outlook (1¼hr., every hr. 7:35am-2:35pm), then continue on the **Gletscherbahn** cable car to the top. (Round-trip with train and cable car €42.) You can also get off the cog railway at Eibsee and take the **Eibsee Seilbahn,** one of the steepest cable car runs in the world, all the way to the top (1½hr., every hr. 8am-4:15pm, round-trip with train and cable car €42).

Garmisch-Partenkirchen is accessible by **train** from Innsbruck (1½hr., 1 per hr., €10) or Munich (1½hr., 1 per hr., €14), and by **bus** #1084 and 9606 from Füssen (2hr., 6-7 per day, €7). To get to the **tourist office,** Richard-Strauss-Pl. 2, turn left on Bahnhofstr. from the train station and turn left again onto Von-Brug-Str.; the office faces the fountain on the square. The staff distributes maps and finds rooms for free. (☎ 18 07 00. Open M-Sa 8am-6pm, Su 10am-noon.) To reach ▧**Naturfreundehaus ❶,** Schalmeiweg 21, from the station, walk straight on Bahnhofstr. as it becomes Ludwigstr.; follow the bend to the right and turn left on Sonnenbergstr. Continue straight as this becomes Prof. Michael-Sachs-Str. and then Schalmeiweg (25min.). Sleep in attic lofts with up to 16 other backpackers. (☎43 22. Kitchen use €0.50. Reception daily 6-8pm. Loft dorm beds €8; 3- to 5-bed dorms €10.) **HL Markt,** at the intersection of Bahnhofstr. and Von-Brug-Str., sells groceries. (Open M-F 8am-8pm, Sa 7:30am-4pm.)

THE CHIEMSEE ☎ 08051

The region's dramatic crescent of mountains and its picturesque islands, forests, and marshland have lured visitors for 2000 years. Today, prices have risen and the area has been overrun by resorts for the German *nouveaux riches.*

PRIEN AM CHIEMSEE. On the southwestern corner of the Chiemsee, Prien is a good base for exploring the islands. **Trains** depart from the station, a few blocks from the city center, for Munich (1hr., every hr., €12.40) and Salzburg (50min., every hr., €9). **Ferries** run from Prien to Herreninsel and Fraueninsel (every 40min., 6:40am-7:30pm, €5.50-6.60). To get to the ferry port, turn right from the main entrance of the Prien train station and follow Seestr. for 20min., or hop on the green *Chiemseebahn* steam train from the station (9:40am-6:15pm, round-trip €8.50). The **tourist office**, Alte Rathausstr. 11, dispenses maps and books private rooms for free. (☎690 50. Open M-F 8:30am-6pm, Sa 8:30am-noon.) The **Jugendherberge (HI) ❷**, Carl-Braun-Str. 66, is a 15min. walk from the station; go right on Seestr. and turn left on Staudenstr., which becomes Carl-Braun-Str. (☎687 70. Breakfast, showers, and lockers included. Reception 8-9am, 5-7pm, and 9:30-10pm. Open early Feb. to Nov. 4- to 6-bed dorms €15.50.) To reach **Campingpl. Hofbauer ❶**, Bernauer Str. 110, from the station, turn left on Seestr., left again at the next intersection, and then walk 25min. along Bernauerstr. heading out of town. (☎41 36. Showers included. Reception 7:30-11am and 2-8pm. Open Apr.-Oct. €6 per person, €5.10 per campsite.) Grab a cheap meal at **Bäckerei/Cafe Müller ❷**, Marktpl. 8. (Open M-F 6:30am-6pm, Sa 6:30am-12:30pm, Su 7:30-10:30am.)

HERRENINSEL AND FRAUENINSEL. Ludwig's palace on **Herreninsel** (Gentlemen's Island), **Königsschloß Herrenchiemsee**, is a shameless attempt to be larger, better, and more extravagant than Louis XIV's Versailles. Ludwig bankrupted Bavaria building this place—a few unfinished rooms (abandoned after funds ran out) contrast greatly with the completed portion of the castle. (Open Apr.-Sept. daily 9am-6pm; Oct. 9:40am-5pm; Nov.-Mar. 9:40am-4pm. Mandatory tour €5.50, students €4.50.) **Fraueninsel** (Ladies' Island) is home to the **Klosterkirche** (Island Cloister), the nunnery that complemented the monastery on Herreninsel. The nuns make their own marzipan, beeswax candles, and five kinds of liqueur, all sold in the convent shop. The 8th-century **Cross of Bischofhofen** and other religious artifacts are displayed in the Michaelskapelle above the **Torhalle** (gate), the oldest surviving part of the cloister. (Open May-Oct. 11am-5pm. €2, students €1.50.)

BERCHTESGADEN ☎08652

The area's natural beauty and the sinister attraction of **Kehlsteinhaus** ("Eagle's Nest"), Hitler's mountaintop retreat, draw world travelers to the town. The stone resort house, now a restaurant, has a spectacular view from the 1834m peak. From the train station, take bus #38 to Obersalzburg/Hintereck (June-Oct. every 45min., round-trip €3); at Hintereck, catch bus #49 to Kehlstein Parkpl./Eagle's Nest (June-Oct. every 30min. 9:30am-4pm, €12). Be sure to reserve your spot for the return bus when you get off. (Open May-Oct. daily except heavy snow days.) **Trains** run every hr. to Munich (3hr., €24.80) and Salzburg (1hr., €6.60). The **tourist office**, Königsseerstr. 2, opposite the station, has tips on **hiking** trails in the Berchtesgaden National Park. (☎96 71 50. Open mid-June to Oct. M-F 8:30am-6pm, Sa 9am-5pm, Su 9am-3pm; Nov. to mid-June M-F 8:30am-5pm, Sa 9am-noon.) To get to the **Jugendherberge (HI) ❷**, Gebirgsjägerstr. 52, turn right from the station, left on Ramsauer Str., right on Gmündbrücke, and left up the steep gravel path. You can also take bus #39 (dir.: Strub Kaserne) to Jugendherberge. (☎943 70. Breakfast and sheets included. Reception 6:30-9am and 5-7pm. Check-in until 10pm. Curfew midnight. Closed Nov.-Dec. 26. 10-bed dorms €15.40.) For groceries, stop by the **Edeka Markt**, Königsseerstr. 22. (Open M-F 7:30am-6pm, Sa 7:30am-noon.) The nearby **Bäckerei-Konditorei Ernst**, Königseer Str. 10, has fresh bread and pastries. (Open M-F 6:30am-6pm, Sa 6:30am-noon.) **Postal Code:** 83471. ☎08652.

◪ HIKING NEAR BERCHTESGADEN. From Berchtesgaden, the 5½km path to the **Königssee**—which winds through fields of flowers, across bubbling brooks, and past several beer gardens—affords a heart-stopping view of the Alps. From the train station, cross the street, turn right, and take a quick left over the bridge. Walk to the right of and past the green-roofed building (but not up the hill) and take a left onto the gravel path near the stone wall, then follow the Königssee signs. Alternatively, take bus #41 from the bus station to Königssee (round-trip €3.40). Once you arrive in Königstein, walk down Seestr. and look for the Nationalpark Informationstelle to your left, which has hiking information. To explore the **Berchtesgaden National Park,** take bus #46 from Berchtesgaden (15min., 6:10am-7:25pm, €2.10). Get off at the Neuhausenbrücke stop in Ramsau, then visit the Ramsau tourist office, Im Tal 2, for trail maps and hiking information. (☎(08657) 98 89 20. Open Oct.-June M-F 8am-noon and 1:15-5pm; July-Sept. M-Sa 8am-noon and 1:15-5pm, Su 9am-noon and 2-5pm.)

PASSAU ☎0851

This beautiful 2000-year-old city embodies the ideal Old-World Europe. Passau's Baroque architecture is capped by the sublime **Stephansdom,** Dompl., where cherubs sprawl across the ceiling and the world's largest church organ looms above the choir. (Open in summer daily 6:30am-7pm, in off-season 6:30am-6pm. Free. Organ concerts May-Oct. M-F noon, Th 7:30pm. M-W and F €3, students €1; Th €5/€3.) Behind the cathedral is the **Residenz,** home to the **Domschatz,** an extravagant collection of gold and tapestries. (Enter through the back of the Stephansdom, to the right of the altar. Open Easter-Oct. M-Sa 10am-4pm. €1.50, students €0.50.) The heights of the river during various floods are marked on the outside wall of the 13th-century Gothic **Rathaus.** (Open Apr.-Oct. daily 10am-4pm. €1.50, students €1.) Over the Luitpoldbrücke is the former palace of the bishopric, now home to the **Cultural History Museum.** (Open early Apr. to Oct. M-F 9am-5pm, Sa-Su 10am-6pm; Nov.-Mar. Tu-Su 9am-5pm. €4, students €2.50.)

Trains depart the **Hauptbahnhof** for: Frankfurt (4½hr., every 2hr., €64.40); Munich (2hr., every 2hr., €27); Nuremberg (2hr., every 2hr., €30.80); and Vienna (3½hr., 1 per hr., €31). To get to the **tourist office,** Rathauspl. 3, follow Bahnhofstr. from the train station to Ludwigspl., and bear left downhill across Ludwigspl. to Ludwigstr., which becomes Rindermarkt, Steinweg, and finally Große Messerg.; continue straight on Schusterg. and turn left on Schrottg. (☎95 59 80. Open Easter to mid-Oct. M-F 9am-5pm, Sa-Su 9am-1pm.) To reach **Pension Rößner ❸,** Bräug. 19, from the *Rathaus,* walk downstream along the Danube. These homey rooms are the cheapest in the *Altstadt.* (☎93 13 50. Breakfast included. Singles €35; doubles €50-60.) The student district centering on **Innstraße,** parallel to the Inn River, is lined with good, cheap places to eat. Pick up groceries at **Edeka supermarket,** Ludwigstr. 2, at the intersection with Grabeng. (Open M-F 8am-8pm, Sa 8am-4pm.) Get meat, baked goods, sandwiches, and salad by weight at **Schmankerl Passage ❷,** Ludwigstr. 6. (Open M-F 7:30am-6pm, Sa 7:30am-2pm.) **Postal Code:** 94032.

REGENSBURG ☎0941

Regensburg is alive with students and the places that cater to their appetites for food, drink, and fun. The city is reputed to have more cafes and bars per square foot than any other city in Europe. The **Dom St. Peter** dazzles with richly colored stained glass. Inside, the **Domschatz** (Cathedral Treasury) displays gold and jewels purchased by the bishops as well as the preserved hand of Bishop Chrysostomus, who died in AD 407. (Open Apr.-Oct. daily 6:30am-6pm; Nov.-Mar. 6:30am-5pm. Free. Wheelchair-accessible.) A few blocks away, the **Rathaus** (town hall) served as capital of the Holy Roman Empire until 1803. It houses the **Reichstagsmuseum,** which documents the town's history. (English tours May-Sept. M-Sa at 3pm. €2.50, students and seniors €1.25.)

Trains head to: Munich (1½hr., every hr., €19.20); Nuremberg (1-1½hr., 1-2 per hr., €14); and Passau (1-1½hr., every hr., €16.60). The **tourist office** is in the *Altes Rathaus* on Rathauspl. From the station, walk down Maximilianstr., turn left on Grasg., turn right at the end onto Obere Bachg., and follow it for five blocks. (☎507

44 10. Open M-F 8:30am-6pm, Sa 9am-4pm, Su 9:30am-2:30pm; Apr.-Oct. also open Su until 4pm.) To get to the **Jugendherberge (HI) ❷**, Wöhrdstr. 60, from the station, walk to the end of Maximilianstr., turn right at the *Apotheke* onto Pflugg., and turn left immediately at the *Optik* sign onto tiny Erhardig.; at the end, take the steps down and walk left over the bridge, and veer right onto Wöhrdstr. The hostel is on the right. Or, take bus #3, 8, or 9 (€1.50) from the station to Eisstadion. (☎574 02. Breakfast included. Reception daily 6am-1am. Check-in until 1am. Dorms €17.) **Hinterhaus ❷**, Rote-Hahnen-Gasse 2, serves both vegetarian (from €4) and meat (from €5) dishes. (Open daily 6pm-1am.) ▧**Historische Wurstküche**, Thundorfer Str., an 850-year-old beer garden, is ideal for sipping brew while watching ships drift by on the Danube. There's a **supermarket** in the basement of Galeria Kaufhof, on Neupfarrpl. (Open M-F 9am-8pm, Sa 9am-4pm.) **Postal Code:** 93047.

NUREMBERG (NÜRNBERG)   ☎0911

Nuremberg served as the site of massive Nazi rallies; Allies later chose it as the site of the post-war tribunals. Today, the townspeople are working to forge a new image for their city as the *Stadt der Menschenrechte* (City of Human Rights). While physical remnants of Nazi rule remain, Nuremberg's cultural aspects outweigh the bitter memories; today, the city is known locally for its Christmas market and sausages as much as for its ties to Nazism.

▢⊞ TRANSPORTATION AND PRACTICAL INFORMATION. Trains go to: Berlin (6hr., every 2hr., €78-120); Frankfurt (3½hr., 2 per hr., €36-55); Munich (2½hr., 2 per hr., €38); and Stuttgart (2¾hr., 6 per day, €28). **DB Reisezentrum**, located in the central hall of the station, sells tickets. (Open daily 6am-9:30pm.) The **tourist office**, Königstr. 93, books rooms for free. Walk through the tunnel from the station to the *Altstadt* and take a right. (☎233 61 31. Open M-Sa 9am-7pm.) **Internet** access is available at **Flat-s**, on the second floor of the train station. (€1 for 15min. Open Su-Th 7am-11pm, F-Sa 24hr.) **Postal Code:** 90402.

▮▢ ACCOMMODATIONS AND FOOD. Jugendgästehaus (HI) ❷, Burg 2, is in a castle above the city. From the tourist office, follow Königstr. through Lorenzerpl. and over the bridge to the Hauptmarkt. Head toward the fountain on the left and bear right on Burgstr., then head up the hill. (☎230 93 60. Reception 7am-1am. Curfew 1am. 4- to 6-bed dorms €18.) To reach **Gasthof Schwänlein ❸**, Hintere Sterng. 11, take the underground passage from the station to Königstr. and immediately turn left on Frauentormauerstr.; follow the town wall and bear right onto Hintere Sterng. The rooms are small, but comfortable. (☎22 51 62; fax 241 90 08. Breakfast included. Reservations by fax or mail only. Singles €26-28, with bath €30-38; doubles €41-43/€46-57.) ▧**Sushi Glas ❸**, Kornmarkt 7, next to the Nationalmuseum, attracts a chic yuppie crowd with delicious Japanese specialties. (Open M-W noon-11pm, Th-Sa noon-midnight, Su 6-11pm.) **Edeka**, Hauptmarkt 12, near the Frauenkirche, sells groceries. (Open M-F 8:30am-7pm, Sa 8am-3pm.)

◙▟ SIGHTS AND ENTERTAINMENT. Allied bombing left little of Nuremberg for posterity; its churches, castle, and other buildings have all been reconstructed. The walled-in Handwerkerhof market near the station is a tourist trap masquerading as a historical attraction; head up Königstr. for the real sights. Take a detour to the left for the pillared **Straße der Menschenrechte** ("Avenue of Human Rights") as well as the **Germanisches Nationalmuseum**, Kartäuserg. 1, which chronicles German art from pre-history to the present. (Open Tu-Su 10am-5pm, W until 9pm. €4, students €3; free W 6-9pm.) Across the river is the **Hauptmarktplatz**, the site of the annual **Christmas market.** Hidden in the fence of the **Schöner Brunnen** (Beautiful Fountain), in the northwest corner of the Hauptmarkt, is a seamless gold-colored ring; spinning it will supposedly bring good luck. Walk uphill to the **Rathaus;** the **Lochgefängnisse** (dungeons) beneath contain medieval torture instruments. (Open Tu-Su 10am-4:30pm. Mandatory tours every 30min. €2, students €1.) Atop the hill, the **Kaiserburg** (emperor's fortress), Nuremberg's symbol, offers the best vantage point of the city. (Open Apr.-Sept. daily 9am-6pm; Oct.-Mar. 10am-4pm. Mandatory tours every 30min. €5, students €4.)

The ruins of **Dutzendteich Park,** site of the Nazi Party Congress rallies, remind visitors of Nuremberg's darker history. On the far side of the lake is the **Tribüne,** the marble platform where throngs gathered to hear Hitler. The "Fascination and Terror" exhibit, in the **Kongresshalle,** at the north end of the park, covers the rise of the Third Reich and the war crimes trials. (Open M-F 9am-6pm, Sa-Su 10am-6pm. €5, students €2.50.) To reach the park, take S2 (dir.: Freucht/Altdorf) to Dutzendteich, then take the middle of three exits, go down the stairs, and turn left. Walk past the lake on your left, turn left, then turn right to reach the Kongresshalle. On the other side of town, Nazi leaders faced Allied judges during the historic Nuremberg war crimes trials, held in room 600 of the **Justizgebäude.** (Fürtherstr. 110. U1 (dir.: Stadthalle) to Bärenschanze. Tours Sa-Su 1, 2, 3, and 4 pm. €2, students €1.)

Nuremberg's nightspots are clustered around the *Altstadt;* the most popular are in the west, near the river. **Cine Città,** Gewerbemuseumspl. 3, has 16 bars and cafes, 21 cinemas, an IMAX theater, and a disco. (Open Su-Th until 3am, F-Sa until 4am.) **Frizz,** Weißgerberg. 37, is a hip bar that swings to oldies and 80s rock. (Cover men €2, women free. Open M and Th 8pm-2am, F-Sa 8pm-4am.)

ROMANTIC ROAD

The landscape between Würzburg and Füssen is like a mammoth picnic: plates of circular cities, castles in tasty shades of lemon and mint, and dense forests of healthy greenery. The German tourist industry christened the area the Romantic Road (*Romantische Straße*) in 1950; it's now the most traveled road in Germany.

⌐ TRANSPORTATION. Europabus runs daily at 10am from bus platform #13 in Würzburg through Rothenburg ob der Tauber to Füssen. Students receive a 10% discount, Eurail and German Rail Pass holders 60%. For reservations or additional information, contact **EurAide.** (☎ (089) 59 38 89; www.euraide.de/romantic.) A more flexible and economical way to travel the Romantic Road is by the frequent **trains** that connect all the towns.

WÜRZBURG. The university town of Würzburg is surrounded by vineyard slopes and bisected by the Main River. In 1895, Wilhelm Conrad Röntgen discovered X-rays here and was awarded the first Nobel Prize. Inside the striking **Fortress Marienburg** are the 11th-century **Marienkirche,** the 40m **Bergfried watchtower,** under which lies the Hole of Fear (dungeon), and the **Fürstengarten,** built to resemble a ship. Outside the main fortress is the castle arsenal, which now houses the **Mainfränkisches Museum.** Take bus #9 from the station to Festung, or walk toward the castle on the hill. (40min.; tours depart from the main courtyard; Apr.-Oct. Tu-F 11am, 2, and 3pm, Sa-Su every hr. 10am-4pm. €2, students €1.50. Museum open Apr. to mid-Oct. Tu-Su 9am-6pm; mid-Oct. to Mar. 10am-4pm. €2.50/€2.) The **Residenz,** on Residenzpl., houses the largest ceiling fresco in the world, and the **Residenzhofkirche** inside is a Baroque fantasy of gilding and pink marble. (Open Apr. to mid-Oct. daily 9am-6pm, Th until 8pm; mid-Oct. to Mar. 10am-4pm. €4, students €3. English tours Sa-Su 11am and 3pm.) **Trains** head to: Frankfurt (2hr., 2 per hr.,

€19); Munich (3hr., every hr., €39); Nuremberg (1hr., 2 per hr., €15); and Rothenburg ob der Tauber (1hr., every hr., €9). The **tourist office**, in the yellow Haus zum Falken on the Marktpl., provides maps and helps find rooms. (☎37 23 98. Open M-F 10am-6pm, Sa 10am-2pm; Apr.-Oct. also Su 10am-2pm.) ☎**0931.**

ROTHENBURG OB DER TAUBER. After the Thirty Years' War, Rothenburg had no money to modernize; it remained unchanged for 250 years. When it became a tourist destination at the end of the 19th century, new laws protected the integrity of the medieval *Altstadt;* today, Rothenburg is probably your only chance to see a walled medieval city without a single modern building. After the war, the conquering general promised to spare the town from destruction if any local could chug a wine keg—3.25L of wine. The mayor successfully met the challenge, then passed out for several days. The **Meistertrunk** is reenacted each year, and the town clock performs a slow motion version every hour over the Marktpl. For many other fascinating tidbits of Rothenburg history, take the 1hr. English tour led by the ▓**night watchman,** which starts from the Rathaus. (Easter-Christmas daily 8pm. €3.) The 60m tower of the Renaissance **Rathaus,** on Marktpl., provides a panoramic view of the town. (Open Apr.-Oct. daily 9:30am-12:30pm and 1-5pm; Nov.-Mar. noon-3pm, Dec. closed M-F. €1.) The ▓**Medieval Crime Museum,** Burgg. 3, exhibits torture instruments for anyone who can stomach the truth of iron-maiden justice. (Open Apr.-Oct. daily 9:30am-6pm; Nov. and Jan.-Feb. 2-4pm; Dec. and Mar. 10am-4pm. €3, students €2.) Head to **Christkindlmarkt** (Christ Child Market), Herrng. 2, and **Weihnachtsdorf** (Christmas Village), Herrng. 1, which houses a **Christmas Museum** documenting the evolution of gift-giving. (Open Jan. to mid-May M-F 9am-6:30pm, Sa 9am-4pm; mid-May to Dec. also Su 11am-6pm.)

Trains run to and from Steinach (15min., €1.75), where you can transfer to trains for Würzburg and Munich. The **Europabus** leaves from the *Busbahnhof,* next to the train station. The **tourist office,** Marktpl. 2, books rooms. (☎404 92. Open May-Oct. M-F 9am-noon and 1-6pm, Sa 10am-3pm; Nov.-Apr. M-F 9am-noon and 1-5pm, Sa 10am-1pm.) Many other **private rooms** are not registered with the tourist office; look for Zimmer frei signs and knock on the door to inquire. ☎**09861.**

FÜSSEN. At the foot of the Romantic Road, in the foothills of the Bavarian Alps, the name Füssen (feet) is apt for this little town. The main attraction of Füssen is its easy access to Ludwig's famed **Königsschlösser** (see p. 479). Within the town, the inner walls of the **Hohes Schloß** (High Castle) courtyard feature arresting *trompe-l'oeil* windows and towers, and the **Staatsgalerie** in the castle shelters a collection of Gothic and Renaissance art. (Open Apr.-Oct. Tu-Su 11am-4pm; Nov.-Mar. 2-4pm. €2.50, students €2.) Inside the **Annenkapelle,** macabre paintings depict everyone from the Pope and Emperor to the smallest child engaged in the *Totentanz* (death dance), a public frenzy of despair that overtook Europe during the plague. (Open Apr.-Oct. Tu-Su 11am-4pm, Nov.-Mar. 2-4pm. €2.50, students €2.) **Trains** run to Munich (2hr., every 2hr., €18). Füssen can also be reached by **bus** #1084 or 9606 from Garmisch-Partenkirchen (2¼hr., €7). To get from the train station to the **tourist office,** Kaiser-Maximilian-Pl. 1, walk the length of Bahnhofstr. and head across the roundabout to the big yellow building on your left. The staff finds **rooms** for free. (☎938 50. Open Apr.-Sept. M-F 8:30am-6:30pm, Sa 9am-12:30pm, Su 10am-noon; Oct.-Mar. M-F 9am-5pm, Sa 10am-noon.) ☎**08362.**

KÖNIGSSCHLÖßER (ROYAL CASTLES). King Ludwig II, a zany visionary and fervent Wagner fan, used his cash to create fantastic castles. In 1886, a band of nobles and bureaucrats deposed Ludwig, had him declared insane, and imprisoned him. Three days later, the King and a loyal advisor were mysteriously discovered dead in a nearby lake. The fairy tale castles that framed Ludwig's life and the enigma of his death still captivate tourists today. The glitzy ⊠**Schloß Neuschwanstein** is now Germany's most clichéd tourist attraction and was the inspiration for Disney's Sleeping Beauty Castle. The completed chambers (63 remain unfinished) include a Byzantine throne room, a small artificial grotto, and an immense *Sängersaal* (singer's hall) built expressly for performances of Wagnerian operas. Ludwig grew up in the bright yellow, neo-Gothic **Schloß Hohenschwangau** across the way. (Both open Apr.-Sept. daily 9am-6pm, Th until 8pm; Oct.-Mar. 10am-4pm. Mandatory tours €7 per castle; combination ticket €13.) Tickets can be purchased at the **Ticket-Service Center,** Alpseestr. 12 (☎ (08362) 93 08 30), about 100m south of the Hohenschwangau bus stop.

From Füssen, hop on **bus** #73 or 78 marked Königsschlösser, which departs from the train station (10min., 2 per hr., €1.40). It will drop you in front of the information booth (open daily 9am-6pm); the Ticket-Service Center is a short walk uphill on Alpseestr. Separate paths lead up to both Hohenschwangau and Neuschwanstein. A *Tagesticket* (€5.60; from the bus driver) gives unlimited regional bus use.

GREECE (Ελλας)

A land where sacred monasteries are mountainside fixtures, three-hour seaside siestas are standard issue, and dancing on tables until daybreak is a summer rite—Greece's treasures are impossibly varied. Much of the history of the Western world owes its character to the philosophical, literary, artistic, and athletic mastery of the ancient Greeks, and schoolkids still dream of Hercules and Medusa, only to long later for Greece's island beaches and the gorgeous natural landscape, once the playground of a pantheon of gods. The all-encompassing Greek lifestyle is a mix of high speed and sun-inspired lounging: old men hold lively debates in town *plateias*, mopeds skid through the streets around the clock, and unpredictable schedules force a go-with-the-flow take on life.

FACTS AND FIGURES

Official Name: Hellenic Republic.
Capital: Athens.
Major Cities: Thessaloniki.
Population: 10,600,000.

Land Area: 131,940 sq. km.
Time: GMT.
Language: Greek.
Religion: Eastern Orthodox (98%).

DISCOVER GREECE

Make the sprawl of **Athens** (p. 486) more manageable by hitting the highlights: the Acropolis, the National Museum, a sunset atop Lycavittos, a night clubbing in Glyfada, and a trip to Cape Sounion. Greece's second-largest and less-touristed city, **Thessaloniki** (p. 498), home to both trendy shopping and some of Byzantium's most precious ruins, will give you a taste of authentic Greek life. Spend a few days on the lovely island of **Corfu** (p. 503), immortalized by Edward Lear, Oscar Wilde, and sun-hungry partiers, or indulge in hedonism for nights on end on **Mykonos** (p. 507) or **Ios** (p. 509). For a quieter trip, climb up to the cliffside monasteries of **Meteora** (p. 502), commune with the ancient gods at **Mount Olympus** (p. 501), and hike through Europe's longest gorge, **Samaria** (p. 511). Finally, reflect on your travels at the awe-inspiring Temple of Apollo on the sacred isle of **Delos** (p. 507).

ESSENTIALS

WHEN TO GO

June through August is high season in Greece; consider visiting during May or September, when the weather is equally beautiful but the crowds thinner. The off season, from mid-September through May, offers cheaper airfares and lodging, but many sights and accommodations have shorter hours or close altogether. Ferries and trains run considerably less frequently, although ski areas at Mt. Parnassos, Mt. Pelion, and Metsovo beckon winter visitors.

DOCUMENTS AND FORMALITIES

VISAS. South Africans need a visa for stays of any length. Citizens of Australia, Canada, the EU, New Zealand, and the US do not need a visa for stays of up to 90 days, though they are ineligible for employment.

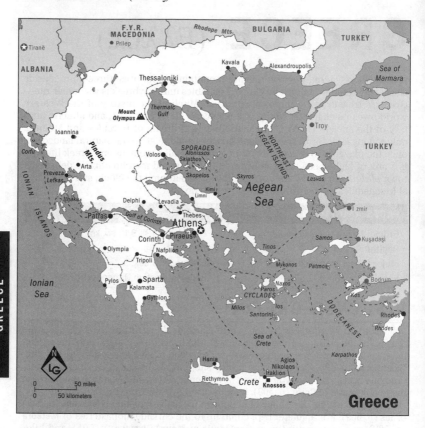

Greece

EMBASSIES. Foreign embassies for Greece are in Athens (p. 486). For Greek embassies at home: **Australia,** 9 Turrana St., Yarralumla, Canberra, ACT 26000 (☎ 02 6273 3011); **Canada,** 80 MacLaren St., Ottawa, ON K2P 0K6 (☎ 613-238-6271; www.greekembassy.ca); **Ireland,** 1 Upper Pembroke St., Dublin 2 (☎ 01 6767 2545); **South Africa,** 1003 Church St., Hatfield, Pretoria 0028 (☎ 12 437 351); **UK,** 1a Holland Park, London W11 3TP (☎ 0171 229 3850); and **US,** 2221 Massachusetts Ave. N.W., Washington, D.C. 20008 (☎ 202-939-5800; www.greekembassy.org).

TRANSPORTATION

BY PLANE. Basic round-trip fares from North America to Athens range from €600-1100. Flights from London average €320. The domestic service of **Olympic Airways,** Syngrou 96-100, Athens 11741 (☎ 2810 114 4444), has increased greatly. A 1hr. flight from Athens (€60-90) can get you to almost any island in Greece. Even in the off season, remote destinations are serviced several times per week, while developed areas may have several flights per day.

BY TRAIN. Greece is served by a number of international train routes that connect Athens, Thessaloniki, and Larissa to most European cities. Train service within Greece, however, is limited and sometimes uncomfortable, and no lines go to the western coast. The new express, air-conditioned intercity trains, while slightly more expensive and infrequent, are worth the price. **Eurail** passes are valid on all Greek trains. **Hellenic Railways Organization** (OSE; www.osenet.gr) connects Athens to major Greek cities; from Greece, call ☎145 or 147 for schedules and prices.

BY BUS. There are almost no buses running directly from any European city to Greece. **Busabout,** 258 Vauxhall Bridge Rd., London (☎0171 950 1661; www.busabout.com), is one of the few European bus companies that runs to Greece. Domestic bus service is extensive and fares are cheap. **KTEL** (www.ktel.org) runs most domestic buses; always check with an official source about scheduled departures, as posted schedules are often outdated. Smaller towns may use cafes as bus stops. Confirm your destination with the driver; signs may be wrong. If your stop is passed, yell *"Stasi!"* (STASH; "Stop!"). Intercity buses are usually blue.

BY FERRY. The most popular way of getting to Greece is by ferry from Italy. Boats travel from Brindisi, Italy, to Patras (p. 493), Corfu (p. 503), and Kephalonia (p. 504), and from Ancona, Italy (p. 663), to Patras and Corfu. Ferries also run from Greece to various points on the Turkish coast (p. 512). There is frequent ferry service to the Greek islands, but schedules are irregular and faulty information is common. Check schedules posted at the tourist office or the *limenarcheio* (port police), or at www.ferries.gr. Make reservations and arrive at least 1-2hr. before your departure time. **Flying Dolphins** (www.dolphins.gr) provides extensive hydrofoil service between the islands at twice the cost and speed as ferries; their routes are listed in the **Transportation** sections where appropriate.

BY CAR AND MOPED. Cars are a luxury in Greece, a country where public transportation is nonexistent after 7pm. Ferries charge a transport fee for cars. Rental agencies may quote low daily rates that exclude the 20% tax and **Collision Damage Waiver (CDW)** insurance; expect to pay €20-40 per day for a rental. Foreign drivers are required to have an **International Driving Permit** and an **International Insurance Certificate** to drive in Greece. The **Automobile and Touring Club of Greece (ELPA),** Messogion 395, Athens 11527, provides assistance and offers reciprocal membership to foreign auto club members. (☎01 606 8800. 24hr. emergency roadside assistance ☎104. Info line for Athens ☎174; elsewhere 01 606 8838. Open M-F 7am-3pm.) **Mopeds** can be great for exploring, but they also make you extremely vulnerable to the carelessness of other drivers; wear a helmet.

TOURIST SERVICES AND MONEY

EMERGENCY	Police: ☎100. Ambulance: ☎166. Hospital: ☎106.

TOURIST OFFICES. Tourism in Greece is overseen by two national organizations: the **Greek National Tourist Organization (GNTO)** and the **tourist police** *(touristiki astinomia)*. The GNTO, Amerikis 2, Athens (☎01 327 1300), known as the **EOT** in Greece, can supply general information about sights and accommodations throughout the country. The tourist police (24hr. info ☎171) deal with local and immediate problems: bus schedules, accommodations, lost passports, etc. They are open long hours and are willing to help, although their English is often limited.

MONEY. The official currency of Greece is the **euro.** The Greek drachma can still be exchanged at a rate of 340.75dr to €1. For exchange rates and more information on the euro, see p. 16. If you're carrying more than €1000 in cash when you enter Greece, you must declare it upon entry. A bare-bones day in

Greece, staying at hostels, campgrounds, or *domatia* (rooms to let), and buying food at supermarkets or outdoor food stands, costs about €35. A day with more comforts, like accommodation in a nicer *domatia* or budget hotel, and eating one meal per day in a restaurant, runs €50. There is no **tipping** anywhere except restaurants. Generally, **bargaining** is expected for street wares and in other informal venues, but shop owners whose goods are tagged will consider bargaining rude and disrespectful. The European Union imposes a **value-added tax (VAT)** on goods and services purchased within the EU, which is included in the price. For more info, see p. 15.

BUSINESS HOURS. Normal business hours in Greece include a break from about 2 until 6pm or so. Hours vary, but banks are normally open M-F 8am-1:30pm, and also 3:30-6pm in some larger cities.

COMMUNICATION

PHONE CODE	**Country code: 30. International dialing prefix: 00.** The city code must always be dialed, even when calling from within the city. From outside Greece, dial int'l dialing prefix (see inside back cover) + 30 + local number.

TELEPHONES. The only way to use the phone in Greece is with a prepaid phone card. You can buy the cards at *peripteros* (streetside kiosks) in denominations of €3, €12, and €25. Time is measured in minutes or talk units (100 units=30min. of domestic calling). A calling card is the cheapest way to make international phone calls. To place a call with a calling card, contact your service provider's Greek operator: **AT&T,** ☎00 800 1311; **British Telecom,** ☎00 800 4411; **Canada Direct,** ☎00 800 1611; **Ireland Direct,** ☎00 155 1174; **MCI,** ☎00 800 1211; **Sprint,** ☎00 900 1411.

Throughout 2002, Greece was changing its phone code system. In January, most numbers gained an additional "0" at the end of the local code; as of fall 2002, it was proposed that in November, the leading "0" of most phone numbers would become a "2." In addition, all local calls in Greece must now include the area code. Phone numbers in Let's Go: Greece reflect the proposed November changes, but as of press time further changes were still possible. Contact the Greek National Tourist Organization (see **Tourist Offices**) for further info.

MAIL. To send a letter weighing up to 50g within Europe costs €0.85; anywhere else in the world costs €0.90. Mail sent to Greece from the Continent generally takes at least 3 days to arrive; from the US, South Africa, and Australia airmail will take 5-10 days. Address *Poste Restante* according to the following example: Firstname SURNAME, Corfu Town Post Office, Corfu, Greece 8900, POSTE RESTANTE. The mail will go to a special desk in the central post office, unless you specify otherwise.

INTERNET ACCESS. The availability of the Internet in Greece is rapidly expanding. In all big cities, most small cities and large towns, and most of the touristed islands, you will able to find Internet access. Expect to pay €3-6 per hour.

LANGUAGE. Although many Greeks in Athens and other heavily touristed areas—particularly young people—speak English, rural Greeks rarely do. Greek body language will help you avoid misunderstandings. To say no, Greeks lift their heads back abruptly while raising their eyebrows; they emphatically nod once to say yes. A hand waving up and down that seems to say "stay there" actually means "come." For the Greek alphabet, see p. 1051; for basic words and phrases, see p. 1058.

ACCOMMODATIONS AND CAMPING

GREECE	❶	❷	❸	❹	❺
ACCOMMODATIONS	under €10	€10-24	€25-40	€40-70	over €70

Lodgings in Greece are a bargain. Tourist offices usually maintain lists of inexpensive accommodations. A bed in a **hostel** averages around €7. Those not currently endorsed by HI are in most cases still safe and reputable. In many areas, **domatia** (rooms to let) are an attractive and perfectly dependable option. Often you'll be approached by locals as you enter town or disembark from your boat, a practice that is theoretically illegal, but common. Prices are quite variable; expect to pay €12-20 for a single and €25-35 for a double. Always negotiate with *domatia* owners before settling a price, and never pay more than you would for a hotel in town. If in doubt, ask the tourist police; they may set you up with a room and conduct the negotiations themselves. **Hotel** prices are regulated, but proprietors may try to push you to take the most expensive room. Budget hotels start at €15 for singles and €25 for doubles. Check your bill carefully, and threaten to contact the tourist police if you think you are being cheated. Greece hosts plenty of official **campgrounds**, which run about €4.50 per person, plus €3 per tent. Discreet freelance camping on beaches—though illegal—is common in July and August but may not be the safest way to spend the night.

FOOD AND DRINK

GREECE	❶	❷	❸	❹	❺
FOOD	under €5	€5-9	€10-15	€16-24	over €25

Penny-pinching carnivores will thank Zeus for lamb, chicken, or beef *souvlaki*, stuffed into a pita to make *gyros* (yi-ROS). Vegetarians can also eat their fill on the cheap, with *horiatiki* (Greek salad) and savory pastries like *tiropita* (cheese pie) and *spanakopita* (spinach and feta pie). Frothy, iced coffee *frappés* take an edge off the heat in the summer. *Ouzo*, a powerful, licorice-flavored spirit, is served with *mezedes*, which are snacks of octopus, cheese, and sausage.

Breakfast, served only in the early morning, is generally very simple: a piece of toast with *marmelada* or a pastry. Lunch, a hearty and leisurely meal, can begin as early as noon but is more likely eaten sometime between 2 and 5pm. Dinner is a drawn-out, relaxed affair served late. A Greek restaurant is known as a *taverna* or *estiatorio;* a grill is a *psistaria.* Many restaurants don't offer printed menus.

HOLIDAYS AND FESTIVALS

Holidays: Feast of St. Basil/New Year's Day (Jan. 1); Epiphany (Jan. 6); 1st Monday in Lent (Mar. 10); Greek Independence Day (Mar. 25); St. George's Day (Apr. 23); Easter (Apr. 27); Labor Day (May 1); Ascension (June 5); Pentecost (June 15); Feast of the Assumption of the Virgin Mary (Aug. 15); The Virgin Mary's Birthday (Sept. 8); Feast of St. Demetrius (Oct. 26); Ohi Day (Oct. 28); Christmas (Dec. 25).

Festivals: Three weeks of **Carnival** feasting and dancing (Feb. 17-Mar. 10) precede Lenten fasting. April 23 is **St. George's Day,** when Greece honors the dragon-slaying knight with horse races, wrestling matches, and dances. The **Feast of St. Demetrius** (Oct. 26) is celebrated with particular enthusiasm in Thessaloniki.

ATHENS (Αθηνα) ☎ 210

Ancient ruins sit quietly amid hectic modern streets as tacit testaments to Athens's rich history, while the Acropolis looms larger than life, a perpetual reminder of ancient glory. Byzantine churches recall an era of foreign invaders, when the city was ruled from Macedonia, Rome, and Constantinople. But the packs of mopeds in Pl. Syndagma prove that Athens refuses to become a museum—over the past two centuries, democracy has revived the city in a wave of madcap construction.

☞ TRANSPORTATION

Flights: El. Venizelou (ATH; ☎ 210 353 0000), Greece's new international airport, is one massive, easily navigable terminal. Arrivals are on the ground floor, departures are on the 2nd fl. 4 bus lines run from the airport to Athens, Piraeus, and Rafina.

Trains: Hellenic Railways (OSE), Sina 6 (☎ 210 362 4402; www.ose.gr). **Larissis Train Station** (☎ 210 529 8837) serves northern Greece and Europe. Open 24hr. Take trolley #1 from El. Venizelou (also known as Panepistimiou) in Pl. Syndagma (every 10min. 5am-midnight, €0.45). Trains depart for **Thessaloniki** (7hr., 4 per day, €14.10) and **Prague, Czech Republic** (€128.60). **Peloponnese Train Station** (☎ 210 513 1601) serves **Patras** (4¼hr., €5.30) as well as major towns in the Peloponnese. From Larissis, exit to your right and go over the footbridge.

Buses: Terminal A: Kifissou 100 (☎ 210 512 4910). Take blue bus #051 from the corner of Zinonos and Menandrou near Pl. Omonia (every 15min., €0.45). Buses to: **Corinth** (1½hr., 1 per hr., €5.70); **Corfu** (10hr., 4 per day, €28); **Patras** (3hr., 30 per day, €12.25); **Thessaloniki** (6hr., 11 per day, €28). **Terminal B:** Liossion 260 (☎ 210 831 7153, M-F only). Take blue bus #024 from Amalias outside the National Gardens (45min., every 20min., €0.45). Buses to **Delphi** (3hr., 6 per day, €10.20).

Public Transportation: KTEL (ΚΤΕΛ) **buses** around Athens and its suburbs are blue or orange and designated by 3-digit numbers. Buy bus/trolley tickets at any street kiosk. Hold on to your ticket—you can be fined €18-30 by police if caught without one. **Trolleys** are yellow and crowded, sporting 1- or 2-digit numbers; they are distinguished from buses by their electrical antennae. **Subway:** The Athens **Metro** consists of 3 lines. **M1** runs from northern Kifissia to the port of Piraeus. **M2** runs from Ag. Antonios to Dafni. **M3** runs from Ethniki Amyna to Pl. Syndagma in central Athens. Trains run 5am-midnight. Buy tickets (€0.60) in any station.

Car Rental: Try the places on **Singrou.** €30-50 for a small car with 100km mileage (including tax and insurance). Student discounts up to 50%. Prices rise in summer.

Taxis: Meters start at €0.75, with an additional €0.25 per km; midnight-5am €0.45 per km. There's a €1.20 surcharge from the airport and a €0.60 surcharge for trips from bus and railway terminals, plus €0.30 for each piece of luggage over 10kg.

PIRAEUS PORT: FERRIES FROM ATHENS

The majority of ferries from Athens leave from the town of Piraeus Port. Ferries sail to nearly all Greek islands (except the Sporades and Ionian Islands). Ferries to Crete: **Hania** (9½hr., 1 per day, €17.60); **Iraklion,** (14hr., 3 per day, €21-26); and **Rethymno** (11hr., 1 per day, €21.40). Additional ferries to: **Chios** (9hr., 1 per day, €18.10); **Hydra** (3hr., every hr., €14.30); **Ios** (7½hr., 2-5 per day, €16.70); **Lesvos** (12hr., 1 per day, €22.40); **Milos** (7hr., 2-5 per day, €15.80); **Mykonos** (6hr., 2-5 per day, €16.30); **Naxos** (6hr., 2-5 per day, €16.10); **Paros** (6hr., 2-5 per day, €16.10); **Poros** (2½hr., every hr., €13.20); **Rhodes** (15hr., 2-5 per day, €26.80); **Santorini** (9hr., 2-5 per day, €18.70); and **Spetses** (4½hr., every hr., €20.50).

GREECE

Athens

🏠 ACCOMMODATIONS

Adonis Hotel, **5**
Hotel Dryades, **1**
Hotel Orion, **2**
Hotel Tempi, **4**
Pella Inn, **3**

Student's &
Traveler's Inn, **6**
Youth Hostel #5
Pangrati, **7**

⊁ 🚹 ORIENTATION AND PRACTICAL INFORMATION

Athenian geography mystifies newcomers and natives alike. If you lose your bearings, ask for directions back to well-lit **Syndagma** or look for a cab; the **Acropolis** serves as a reference point, as does **Mt. Lycavittos.** Athens's suburbs occupy seven hills in southwest Attica, near the coast. Syndagma, the central *plateia* containing the Parliament building, is encircled by the other major neighborhoods. Clockwise, they are **Plaka, Monastiraki, Psiri, Omonia, Exarhia, Kolonaki,** and **Pangrati.** Plaka, the center of the old city and home to many accommodations, is bounded by the city's two largest ancient monuments—the **Temple of Olympian Zeus** and the Acropolis. Omonia is the site of the city's central subway station. Two parallel avenues, **Panepistimiou** and **Stadiou,** connect Syndagma to Omonia. Omonia's neighbor to the east, progressive Exarhia, sports some of Athens's most exciting nightlife, while nearby Kolonaki, on the foothills of Mt. Lycavittos, has plenty of glitz and swanky shops. Pangrati, southeast of Kolonaki, is marked by several Byzantine churches, a park, the **Olympic Stadium,** and the **National Cemetery.**

Tourist Office: Amerikis 2 (☎210 331 0565), off Stadiou near Pl. Syndagma. Bus, train, and ferry schedules and prices; lists of museums, embassies, and banks; brochures on travel throughout Greece; and an indispensable Athens map. Open M-F 9am-4:30pm.

Banks: National Bank of Greece, Karageorgi Servias 2 (☎210 334 0015), in Pl. Syndagma. Open M-Th 8am-2pm, F 8am-1:30pm; open for **currency exchange** only M-Th 3:30-5:20pm, F 3-6:30pm, Sa 9am-3pm, Su 9am-1pm. Currency exchange available 24hr. at the **airport,** but exchange rates and commissions may be unfavorable.

American Express: Ermou 7 (☎210 322 3380), in Pl. Syndagma. Cashes traveler's checks commission-free, exchanges money, and provides travel services for cardholders. Open M-F 8:30am-4pm, Sa 8:30am-1:30pm.

Laundromats: Most *plintirios* have signs reading "Laundry." A grandmother who lives at **Angelou Geront 10,** in Plaka, provides full laundry service for €8. Open M-Sa 8am-7pm, Su 9am-2pm. **National,** Apollonos 17, in Syndagma. Wash and dry €4.50 per kg. Open M-Th 8am-5pm, F 8am-8pm.

Emergencies: Police, ☎100. **Doctor,** ☎105 from Athens, 101 elsewhere; line open daily 2pm-7am. **Ambulance,** ☎166. **Fire,** ☎199. **AIDS Help Line,** ☎210 722 2222. *Athens News* lists emergency hospitals. Free emergency health care for tourists.

Tourist Police: Dimitrakopoulou 77 (☎171). English spoken. Open 24hr.

Pharmacies: Identified by a **red** (signifying a doctor) or **green cross** hanging over the street. Many are open 24hr.; check *Athens News* or the chart in pharmacy windows for the day's emergency pharmacy.

Hospitals: Emergency hospitals on duty ☎106. **Geniko Kratiko Nosokomio** (Public State Hospital), Mesogion 154 (☎210 777 8901). **Ygeia,** Erithrou Stavrou 4 (☎210 682 7904), is a private hospital in Maroussi. "Hospital" is *nosokomio* in Greek.

Internet Access: Berval Internet Access, Voulis 44A (☎210 331 1294), in Plaka near Pl. Syndagma. €5 per hr. Open daily 9am-9pm.

Post Office: Syndagma (☎210 322 6253), on the corner of Mitropoleos. Open M-F 7:30am-8pm, Sa 7:30am-2pm. **Postal Code:** 10300. Branch offices in **Omonia,** at Aiolou 100, and **Exarhia,** at the corner of Zaimi and K. Deligiani.

🏠 ACCOMMODATIONS

The **Greek Youth Hostel Association,** Damareos 75, lists hostels in Greece. (☎210 751 9530. Open daily M-F 9am-3pm.) The **Hellenic Chamber of Hotels,** Karageorgi Servias 2, provides info and makes reservations for all types of hotels throughout Greece.

Reservations require a cash deposit; you must contact them at least one month in advance and know the length of your stay and the number of people. (☎210 323 7193. Open May-Nov. M-Th 8:30am-2pm, F 8:30am-1:30pm, Sa 9am-12:30pm.)

■ **Student's and Traveler's Inn,** Kydatheneon 16 (☎21 324 4808), in Plaka. Unrivaled location and lively atmosphere. Bring your own sheets and towel, and ask for toilet paper at the desk. Midnight curfew. Reserve ahead and arrive on time. Co-ed dorms €15-20; doubles €30-47; triples €45-60; quads €75-80. ❷

Adonis Hotel, Kodrou 3 (☎210 324 9737), in Plaka. From Syndagma, follow Filellinon; turn right on Nikodimou and left onto Kodrou. A family hotel with a delightful rooftop lounge. Reserve far in advance. All rooms with bath. Singles €27-39; doubles €56; triples €74. A/C €10 extra per person. Discounts for longer stays. ❸

Hotel Tempi, Aiolou 29 (☎210 321 3175), in Monastiraki. Simple rooms with fans. Front-facing rooms are brighter. Luggage storage. Laundry service. Check-out 11am. Singles €30; doubles €40, with bath €48; triples €55. Off-season 20% discount. ❸

Pella Inn, Karaiskaki 1 (☎210 325 0598), in Monastiraki. Walk 10min. down Ermou from Pl. Syndagma; it's two blocks from the Monastiraki subway station. Features a large terrace with impressive views of the Acropolis. Free luggage storage. Dorms €10-12; doubles €30-35; triples €36-55; quads €48-60. ❷

Hotel Dryades, Dryadon 4 (☎210 382 7116), in Exarhia. Elegant Dryades offers some of Athens's nicest budget accommodations, with large rooms and private baths. Internet €2 per 30min. Singles €35-40; doubles €44-53; triples €50-65. ❸

Hotel Orion, Em. Benaki 105 (☎210 382 7362), in Exarhia. From Pl. Omonia, walk up Em. Benaki or take bus #230 from Pl. Syndagma. Orion rents small rooms with shared baths. Sunbathers relax on the rooftop. Internet €2 per hr. Laundry €3. Singles €20-30; doubles €30-36; triples €36-40. Bargain for better prices. ❷

Youth Hostel #5 Pangrati, Damareos 75 (☎210 751 9530). From Omonia or Pl. Syndagma, take trolley #2 or 11 to Filolaou. There's no sign for this cheery hostel, just a green door. Owner speaks English. Hot showers €0.50 for 5min. Sheets €0.75; pillowcases €0.50. Laundry €3. Quiet hours 2-5pm and 11pm-7am. Dorms €7.50. Bring a sleeping bag to stay on the roof (€6). ❶

Hotel Omiros, Apollonos 15 (☎210 323 4486), near Pl. Syndagma. Relatively spacious rooms have A/C and private baths. Breakfast included. Call ahead. Singles €50; doubles €75; triples €93; quads €111. Bargain for student discounts. ❹

☐ FOOD

Athens offers a mix of fast-food stands, open-air cafes, side-street *tavernas*, and intriguing restaurants. Cheap food abounds in **Syndagma** and **Omonia**. Pick up groceries at the markets on **Nikis.**

■ **Pluto,** Plutarchou 38 (☎210 724 4713), in Kolonaki. Chic, warm ambience with an international menu. Try the grilled eggplant with feta and tomatoes (€8.50) or strawberry meringue (€9). Open daily 11am-3pm. ❸

■ **Eden Vegetarian Restaurant,** Lysiou 12 (☎210 324 8858), in Plaka. Fantastic dishes like *boureki* pie (zucchini with feta; €4.90), as well as flavorful mushroom *stifado* with onions and peppers (€8.80). Open W-M noon-midnight. ❷

Dragon Palace, Andinoros 1 (☎210 724 2795), in Pangrati. Delicious Chinese food €7-12. Open daily 6:30pm-midnight; also open noon-1pm in winter. ❷

Kallimarmaron, Eforionos 13 (☎210 701 9727), in Pangrati. Serves some of the best traditional Greek food in the city. Entrees €10-20. ❹

GREECE

IN RECENT NEWS

STARTING BLOCKS

Throughout 2002, extensive preparations were underway in Athens in anticipation of the 2004 Olympic Games. Cranes towered over the city, and scaffolding blanketed buildings everywhere. The seemingly endless projects gave the appearance that all was running smoothly—but the reality was that the clock was ticking and funds were quickly disappearing. In July 2002, Gianna Angelopoulos-Daskalaki, the president of the Organizing Committee (ATHOC), announced that budget cuts were being implemented in order to decrease construction time and costs.

When Athens won the bid for the Olympics in 1997, the city and the IOC allotted a budget of €2.5 billion; as of August 2002, the city expected their costs would total almost €4.4 billion. The remodeling of the Olympic Stadium alone had already exceeded the original estimate by €119 million. ATHOC decided to cut back on spending by cancelling the construction of facilities that would have the least pertinence in the aftermath of the games. Plans to build a new football stadium were all but dropped, and the committee scrambled for an alternative venue for this popular event. Despite the financial difficulties, ATHOC remains adamant that Athens would be prepared to host the 2004 Olympic Games, over a century since the city first welcomed international athletes in the world's inaugural modern games.

Yiantes, Valtetsiou 44 (☎210 330 1369), in Exarhia. A vine-covered oasis that serves a complete Greek meal for €15. Fresh fish €6. Open daily 1pm-1am. ❷

Jungle Juice, Aiolou 21, under the Acropolis (☎210 331 6739). A fresh-squeezed smoothie and sandwich stand. Snag a turkey sandwich (€1.50) and a "Leone Melone," a blend of cantaloupe, mango, and pineapple (€3). Open daily 8am-9pm. ❶

👁 SIGHTS

ACROPOLIS

☎210 321 0219. Open in summer daily 8am-7:30pm; off-season 8am-2:30pm. Admission includes access to all of the sights below the Acropolis (including Hadrian's Arch, the Olympian Temple of Zeus, and the Agora) within a 48hr. period; tickets can be purchased at any of the sights. €12, students €6.

Looming majestically over the city, the Acropolis complex has been the heart of Athens since the 5th century BC. Although each Greek *polis* had an *acropolis* ("high point of the city"), the buildings atop Athens's central peak outshone their imitators and continue to awe visitors today. Visit as early in the day as possible to avoid crowds and the broiling midday sun.

TEMPLE OF ATHENA NIKE. This tiny cliff-side temple was raised during the Peace of Nikias (421-415 BC), a respite from the Peloponnesian War. The temple, known as the "jewel of Greek architecture," is ringed by eight miniature Ionic columns and once housed a statue of the winged goddess of victory, Nike. One day, in a paranoid frenzy, the Athenians were seized by a fear that Nike would flee the city and take peace with her, so they clipped the statue's wings. The remains of the 5m-thick **Cyclopean wall,** predating the Classical Period, lie below the temple.

PARTHENON. The **Temple of Athena Parthenos** (Athena the virgin), more commonly known as the Parthenon, keeps vigil over Athens and the modern world. Ancient Athenians saw their city as the capital of civilization, and the **metopes** (scenes in the open spaces above the columns) on the sides of the Parthenon celebrate Athens's rise. On the far right of the south side—the only side that has not been defaced—the Lapiths battle the Centaurs; on the east side, the Olympian gods defeat the giants; the north depicts the victory of the Greeks over the Trojans; and the west depicts their triumph against the Amazons.

ERECHTHEION. The Erechtheion, to the left of the Parthenon, was completed in 406 BC, just before Sparta defeated Athens in the Peloponnesian War. The building takes its name from the snake-bodied Erechtheus; the eastern half is devoted to the goddess of wisdom, Athena, the western half to the god of the sea, Poseidon.

ACROPOLIS MUSEUM. The museum, which neighbors the Parthenon, houses a superb collection of sculptures, including five of the original Caryatids that supported the south side of the Erechtheion. The statues seem to be replicas, but a close look at the folds of their drapery reveals delicately individualized detail. *(Open in summer M 11am-7:30pm, Tu-Su 8am-7:30pm; off-season M 11am-2pm, Tu-Su 8am-2pm.)*

ELSEWHERE ON THE ACROPOLIS. The southwest corner of the Acropolis looks down over the reconstructed **Odeon of Herodes Atticus,** a functional theater dating from the Roman period (AD 160). See the *Athens News* for a schedule of concerts and plays. *(Entrance on Dionissiou Areopagitou. ☎ 210 322 1459. Purchase tickets at the door or by phone.)*

OTHER SIGHTS

AGORA. The Agora served as the city's marketplace, administrative center, and hub of daily life from the 6th century BC to AD 500. Here, the debates of Athenian democracy raged; Socrates, Aristotle, Demosthenes, Xenophon, and St. Paul all preached here. Today, visitors have free reign over what is now an archaeological site. The 415 BC ◪**Hephaesteion,** on a hill in the northwest corner of the Agora, is the best-preserved classical temple in Greece, flaunting **friezes** depicting Hercules's labors and Theseus's adventures. The **Stoa of Attalos** was a multi-purpose building filled with shops and home to informal gatherings of philosophers. Reconstructed in the 1950s, it now houses the **Agora Museum,** which contains relics from the site. According to Plato, Socrates's first trial was held at the recently excavated **Royal Stoa,** to the left of the Adrianou exit. *(Enter the Agora off Pl. Thission, from Adrianou, or as you descend from the Acropolis. Open Tu-Su 8:30am-3pm. €4, students and EU seniors €2, under 18 and EU students free.)*

KERAMEIKOS. The Kerameikos's rigidly geometric design becomes clearly visible from above, even before entering the grounds; the site includes a large-scale cemetery and a 40m-wide boulevard that ran through the Agora and the Diplyon Gate and ended at the sanctuary of **Akademos,** where Plato founded his academy. The **Oberlaender Museum** displays finds from the burial sites; it houses an excellent collection of highly detailed pottery and sculpture. *(Ermou 48, northwest of the Agora. From Syndagma, walk toward Monastiraki on Ermou for 25min. Open Tu-Su 8:30am-3pm. €2, students and EU seniors €1, under 18 and EU students free.)*

TEMPLE OF OLYMPIAN ZEUS AND HADRIAN'S ARCH. In the middle of downtown Athens, you'll spot the traces of the largest temple ever built in Greece. The 15 Corinthian columns of the Temple of Olympian Zeus mark where the temple once stood. Started in the 6th century BC, it was completed 600 years later by Roman emperor Hadrian, who attached his name to the effort by adding an arch to mark the boundary between the ancient city of Theseus and Hadrian's own new city. *(Vas. Olgas at Amalias, next to the National Garden. Open Tu-Su 8:30am-3pm. Temple €2, students and EU seniors €1, under 18 and EU students free. Arch free.)*

OLYMPIC STADIUM. The Panathenaic Olympic Stadium is wedged between the National Gardens and Pangrati, carved into a hill. The site of the first modern Olympic Games in 1896, the stadium is now being refurbished in preparation for the **2004 Summer Olympics.** A new Olympic stadium sits in the northern suburb of Irini; take the M1 Metro line right to it. *(On Vas. Konstantinou. From Syndagma, walk up Amalias 15min. to Vas Olgas, then follow it left. Alternatively, take trolley #2, 4, or 11 from Syndagma. Open daily 8am-8:30pm. Free.)*

AROUND SYNDAGMA. Be sure to catch the changing of the guard in front of the **Parliament** building. Every hour on the hour, two *evzones* (guards) wind up like toy soldiers, kick their tasselled heels in unison, and fall backward into symmetrical little guardhouses on either side of the **Tomb of the Unknown Soldier.** Athens's endangered species—greenery and shade—are preserved in the **National Gardens.** Women should avoid strolling here alone.

MT. LYCAVITTOS. Of Athens's seven hills, Lycavittos is the largest and most central. Ascend at sunset to catch a glimpse of Athens's densely packed rooftops in waning daylight and watch the city light up for the night. At the top is the **Chapel of St. George,** a popular spot for weddings. A leisurely stroll around the church provides a view of Athens's panoramic expanse.

■ **NATIONAL ARCHAEOLOGICAL MUSEUM.** This astounding collection deserves a spot on even the most packed itinerary. The museum's highlights include the archaeologist Heinrich Schliemann's treasure, the **Mask of Agamemnon,** a death mask of a king who lived at least three centuries earlier than Agamemnon himself. *(Patission 44. Take trolley #2, 4, 5, 9, 11, 15, or 18 from the uphill side of Syndagma, or trolley #3 or 13 from the north side of Vas. Sofias. Open Apr.-Oct. M 12:30-7pm, Tu-Su 8am-7pm; Nov.-Mar. 8am-5pm; holidays 8:30am-3pm. €6, students and EU seniors €3; Nov.-Mar. free Su and holidays.)*

NATIONAL GALLERY. The National Gallery (a.k.a. Alexander Soutzos Museum) exhibits the work of Greek artists, with periodic international displays. The permanent collection includes works by El Greco, as well as drawings, photographs, and sculpture gardens. *(Vas. Konstantinou 50. Set back from Vas. Sofias, by the Hilton. ☎ 210 723 5857. Open M and W-Sa 9am-3pm, Su 10am-2pm. €6.50, students and seniors €3.)*

🎵 🍸 ENTERTAINMENT AND NIGHTLIFE

The weekly *Athens News* (€1) gives locations, hours, and phone numbers for events, as well as news and ferry information. The **Athens Flea Market,** adjacent to Pl. Monastiraki, is a jumble of second-hand junk and valuable antiques. Sunday is the best day, when it is open from 8am-1pm. Summertime performances are staged in **Lycavittos Theater** as part of the **Athens Festival,** which has included acts from the Greek Orchestra to Pavarotti to the Talking Heads. The **Festival Office,** Stadiou 4, sells tickets. (☎ 210 322 1459. Open M-F 9:30am-4pm, Sa-Su 9:30am-2pm. Tickets €10-16. Student discounts.) The cafe/bar flourishes throughout Athens, especially in **Kolonaki.** In summertime, chic Athenians head to the seaside clubs of **Glyfada,** past the airport. **Privilege, Venue,** and **Prime,** all along Poseidonos, are perfect places to enjoy the breezy night air. (Dress well; no shorts. Drinks €4-10. Cover €10-15.) Take the A3 or the B3 bus from Vas. Amalias to Glyfada (€0.75), and then catch a cab from there to your club. Taxis to Glyfada run about €8, but the return trip typically costs more.

■ **Vibe,** Aristophanous 1 (☎ 210 324 4794), just beyond Plateia Iroön in Monastiraki. Unusual lighting makes a great atmosphere.

Bee (☎ 210 321 2624), at the corner of Miaoli and Themidos, off Ermou; a few blocks from the heart of Psiri in Monastiraki. DJs spin while the friendly staff keeps the booze flowing. Drinks €3-9. Open daily 9pm-late.

Cafe 48, Karneadou 48 (☎ 210 725 2434). Classicists and students exchange stories at the bar and practice their dart game in the back room. With a student ID, beer costs €3. Free shot with each drink on Tu and Th. Open M-Sa 9am-2am, Su 4pm-2am.

The Daily, Xenokratous 47 (☎ 210 722 3430). Kolonaki's chic student population converges here to imbibe, listen to Latin and reggae, and watch sports on TV. Fabulous outdoor seating and open-air bar. Drinks €3-6. Open daily 9am-2am.

▶ DAYTRIPS FROM ATHENS

TEMPLE OF POSEIDON. The **Temple of Poseidon** has been a dazzling white landmark for sailors at sea for centuries. The original temple was constructed around 600 BC, destroyed by the Persians in 480 BC, and rebuilt by Pericles in 440 BC; 16 Doric columns remain. The temple sits on a promontory at █**Cape Sounion,** 65km from Athens. (Open daily 10am-sunset. €4, students €2, EU students free.) Two **bus** routes run to Cape Sounion from Athens; the shorter and more scenic route begins at the Mavromateon 14 stop near Areos Park (2hr., every hr., €4.10).

DELPHI. Troubled denizens of the ancient world journeyed to the **Oracle of Delphi,** where the priestess of Apollo related the god's cryptic advice. Head east out of town to reach the site. (Open 7:30am-6:45pm. Museum and site €9, students and seniors €5, EU students free; museum or site only €6/3/free.) **Buses** leave Athens for Delphi from Terminal B, Liossion 260 (3hr., 6 per day, €10.20). Delphi's **tourist office,** Friderikis 12, is in the town hall. (☎ 22650 82 900. Open M-F 8am-2:30pm.) If you spend the night, stay at **Hotel Sibylla ❷,** Pavlou 9, which has rooms with wonderful views and private baths at the best prices in town. (☎ 22650 82 335. Singles €15; doubles €20; triples €27.)

THE PELOPONNESE (Πελοποννεσος)

A hand-shaped peninsula stretching its fingers into the Mediterranean, the Peloponnese is steeped in history and folklore that contribute to its otherworldly atmosphere. The majority of Greece's top archaeological sites are here, including Olympia, Mycenae, Messene, Corinth, Mystras, and Epidavros. A world apart from the islands, the serenely beautiful and sparsely populated Peloponnese has been continuously inhabited for 5000 years, making it a bastion of Greek village life.

■ FERRIES TO ITALY AND CRETE

Boats go from Patras to destinations in Italy, including Brindisi, Trieste, Bari, Ancona, and Venice. **Manolopoulous,** Othonos Amalias 35, in Patras, sells tickets. (☎ 2610 223 621. Open M-F 9am-8pm, Sa 10am-3pm, Su 5pm-8pm.) Questions about departures from Patras should be directed to the Port Authority (☎ 2610 341 002).

PATRAS (Πατρας)   ☎ 2610

Sprawling Patras, Greece's third-largest city, serves primarily as a transport hub for island-bound tourists; during **Carnival** (mid-Jan. to Ash Wednesday), however, the port becomes one gigantic dance floor consumed by pre-Lenten madness. Follow the water to the west end of town to reach **Agios Andreas,** the largest Orthodox cathedral in Greece, which holds magnificent frescoes and St. Andrew's holy head. (Dress modestly. Open daily 9am-dusk.) Sweet black grapes are transformed into *Mavrodaphne* wine at the █**Achaïa Clauss Winery,** the country's most famous vineyard. Take bus #7 (30min., €0.85) from the intersection of Kolokotroni and Kanakari. (Open May-Sept. daily 11am-8pm; Oct.-Apr. 9am-8pm. In summer free tours every hr. noon-5pm. Free samples.)

Trains (☎ 2610 639 110) leave from Othonos Amalias for: Athens (3½-5hr., 8 per day, €5.50-10); Kalamata (5½hr., 2 per day, €5); and Olympia (1½hr., 8 per day, €3-6) via Pyrgos. **KTEL buses** (☎ 2610 623 886) leave from Othonos Amalias for: Athens (3hr., 33 per day, €12.25); Ioannina (4hr., 4 per day, €14.55); Kalamata (4hr., 2 per day, €14); Thessaloniki (8hr., 3 per day, €28.25); and Tripoli (4hr., 2 per day,

FROM THE ROAD

DOMATIAN NATION

Getting a room in a *domatia* at a fair price can be quite an ordeal. Once, two men offered to drive me to the next village and "fix me up" with a room for the night. In Greece, "fix you up" often translates to "do my uncle a favor and pass you off to him." Sure enough, my "friends" delivered me to an older gentleman and then took off with hardly a farewell.

It's customary to try and bargain with *domatia* owners, but this man was a force to be reckoned with. He drew the same figure on the table in front of him again and again, refusing to budge. I was tired, hungry, and weighed down by my heavy pack—and the old man knew it. At a bus stop or ferry dock, multiple offers make bargaining much easier. But once you're in the *domatia,* owners know you just want to take a load off and settle down right there. I had walked right into a trap and we both knew it.

Luckily, I hadn't parted with any cash when the owner threw me out a few hours later for turning on the heat in my room. Another man who lived in the house walked me out, telling me the proprietor was "very difficult." This man then promised to "fix me up" at a place down the road. Alarms went off, but I decided to take a chance. I took one look at the beautiful room, heard the indecently low price, and immediately scrapped the hasty resolution I'd made moments ago to never trust the kindness of strangers.

—Kevin Connor

€10.45). **Ferries** go to: Corfu (6-8hr., 1 per day, €19-22); Ithaka (2½hr., 1 per day, €11) via Kephalonia (€10); and Italy (see above). The **tourist office** is on Othonos Amalias, between 28 Octovriou and Astingos. (☎2610 461 740. Open daily 7:30am-12:30am.) The **Youth Hostel ❶**, Iroon Polytechniou 62-68, occupies a creaky turn-of-the-century mansion. (☎2610 427 278. Dorms €9.) The friendly, cafeteria-style **Europa Center ❶**, on Othonos Amalias between the customs exit and the bus station, serves cheap, large portions. (Entrees €3-5.50.) **Postal Code:** 26001.

OLYMPIA (Ολυμπια) ☎26240

Set among meadows and shaded by cypress and olive trees, modern Olympia is a friendly town whose mega-attraction—the ancient **Olympic arena**—draws hordes of tourists. The gigantic **Temple of Zeus** dominates **Ancient Olympia**, although **Hera's Temple**, dating from the 7th century BC, is better preserved. The **Archaeological Museum** has an impressive sculpture collection that includes the **Nike of Paionios** and the **Hermes of Praxiteles**. Maps, available at the site (€2-4), are essential for navigation. (Site open in summer daily 8am-7pm. Museum open M noon-3pm, Tu-Su 8am-7pm. Site or museum €6, both €9; students and seniors €3/€5; under 18 and EU students free.)

Buses run to Tripoli (4hr., 3 per day, €7.80). The **tourist office**, on Kondili, is on the east side of town toward the ruins. (☎26240 23 100. Open M-F 8am-3pm, Sa reduced hours.) **Zounis Rooms ❷**, two blocks uphill from Kondili, between the National Bank and Pirgos, has pleasant rooms with balconies. (☎26240 22 644. No reception; ask for the proprietor at the Anesi Cafe-Tavern, 13 Avgerinou. Singles €15; doubles €25; triples €30.) **Camping Diana ❶** is uphill from Kondili, past the Sports Museum. (☎26240 22 314. €5 per person, children €3.50; €3.50 per car, €3.50-5 per tent. 10% student discount.) **Minimarkets** along **Kondili** sell picnic fixings. Restaurants on Kondili are overpriced, but a walk toward the railroad station or up the hill leads to inexpensive *tavernas*. **Postal Code:** 27065.

TRIPOLI (Τριπολη) ☎2710

The transportation hub of Arcadia, Tripoli is crowded and fast-paced; the *plateias* and huge city park are a break in the city's otherwise urban landscape. The **Archaeological Museum** on Evangelistrias, Pl. Ag. Vasiliou, has a large prehistoric collection, including pottery, jewelry, and weaponry from the Neolithic to the Mycenaean periods. **Trains** arrive from: Athens (4hr., 4 per day, €8); Corinth (2½hr., 3 per day, €4.50); and Kalamata (2½hr., 4 per day, €4.50). **Buses** arrive at Pl. Kolokotronis, east of the center of town, from Athens (3hr., 14 per day, €15.50) and Nafplion (1hr., 4 per day, €3.50). Buses arrive at the KTEL Messenia and Laconia depot, across from the train station, from Kalamata (1½hr., 12 per day, €5.20) and Sparta (1hr., 10 per day, €3.40). **Hotel Alex ❸**, Vas. Georgiou 26, between Pl. Kolokotronis and Pl. Agios Vasiliou, has spacious, spotless rooms. (☎2710 223 465. Singles €30; doubles €50; triples €60.) Try the goat with mushrooms in egg and lemon sauce (€8.20) at **Klimataria ❸**, on Eth. Antistasis, four blocks past the park as you walk from Pl. Petriou. (Entrees €10-12.) **Postal Code:** 22100.

DIMITSANA AND STEMNITSA ☎27950

The villages of Dimitsana (Δημητσανα) and Stemnitsa (Στεμνιτσα), west of Tripoli, are excellent bases for hiking excursions into the idyllic, rugged countryside. The quintessentially Arcadian **Dimitsana** clings to a steep, rocky mountainside covered with pines; every turn in the road reveals another spectacular vista. The **Lousios River** is popular for swimming and rafting in the summer and fall, but winter snows bring the most visitors to the village. **Bus** service is erratic, but buses are scheduled to leave each day for Olympia (1hr., 1 per day, €4.30) and Tripoli (1½hr., 2 per day, €3.60). *Domatia* are really the only lodging option; most establishments are beautifully furnished. Try above the **grocery store ❸**. (☎27950 31 084. Singles €30; doubles €38.)

A lengthy but beautiful 11km stroll (taxi €4) along the road from Dimitsana will bring you to **Stemnitsa**, whose narrow, irregular cobblestone streets recall the village's medieval roots. Many consider the town the most beautiful in Greece. **Buses** allegedly arrive daily from Tripoli and Dimitsana, but service is irregular. The splendid **Hotel Triokolonion ❸** is on the left side of the main road from Dimitsana. Its terrace offers a relaxing place to unwind after a day of hiking. (☎27950 81 297. Breakfast included. Reserve ahead. Singles €25-30; doubles €40; triples €53.)

KALAMATA (Καλαματα) ☎27210

Kalamata flourishes as a port and beach resort, and also serves as a useful transportation hub. Take a bus from Kalamata (1hr., M-Sa 2 per day, €1.50) to **Ancient Messene** in nearby **Mavromati**, one of Greece's most impressive archaeological sites. (Open daily 24hr. Free.) To reach the train station, walk toward the waterfront in Pl. Georgiou, turn right on Frantzi at the far end of the *plateia*, and walk a few blocks to Sideromikou Stathmou. **Trains** run to: Athens (6½hr., 4 per day, €7) via Tripoli (2½hr., €2.80); Corinth (5¼hr., €5.60); and Patras (5½hr., 4 per day, €5). **Buses** leave from the station on Artemidos to: Athens (4hr., 11 per day, €14); Patras (4hr., 2 per day, €13.50); Sparta (2hr., 2 per day, €3); and Tripoli (2hr., €4.50). **Tourist information** is available at **D.E.T.A.K.,** Polivou 6, just off Aristomenou near the Old Town. (☎27210 21 700. Open M-F 7am-2:30pm.) **Hotel George ❷,** on Dagre near the train station, is convenient, clean, and comfortable. (☎27210 27 225. Singles €20; doubles €26.) Good meals can be found along the waterfront. Before leaving town, sample the famous Kalamata olives and figs. The immense **New Market,** across the bridge from the bus station, has an assortment of meat, cheese, and fruit shops, as well as a daily farmer's market. **Postal Code:** 24100.

▶ DAYTRIPS FROM KALAMATA: PYLOS AND METHONI. Unspoiled **Pylos** (Πυλος) has wonderful beaches and two fortresses. Walk up the road towards Methoni to reach **Neocastro,** where well-preserved walls enclose a fast-decaying church along with a citadel and a collection of engravings. (☎27230 22 010. Open Tu-Su 8:30am-3pm. €3, students €2.) The beautiful, long **Yaialova Beach** is 6km north of town. **Buses** from Kalamata stop in Pylos (1½hr., 9 per day, €3) before going on to Methoni (15min., 7 per day, €0.80). **Methoni's** (Μεθωνη) hibiscus-lined streets wind around its **Venetian fortress,** a 13th-century mini-city. (Open M-Sa 8:30am-7pm, Su 9am-7pm. Free.)

KARDAMYLI (Καρδαμυλη)   ☎ 27210

Kardamyli's white pebble beach and views of the surrounding mountains captivate an increasing number of foreign visitors. One kilometer along the waterfront towards Kalamata is the magnificent **Ritsa Beach,** on an enormous natural bay encircled by barren mountains. Trail maps for the nearby **Taygetus Mountains** can be found in many of Kardamyli's tourist shops and bookstores. A popular 1½hr. hike begins in town; the trail has black and yellow markers. **Buses** leave from the *plateia* and go to: Athens (6hr., 1 per day, €19); Kalamata (1hr., 5 per day, €2.40); and Itilo (30min., 4 per day, €2.40), where you can switch to the Areopolis bus (20min., €0.80). *Domatia* are everywhere, but start with the excellent, cheap rooms let by **Olympia Domatia ❷.** To get there, turn right off the main road across from the post office. (☎ 27210 73 623. Singles €17; doubles €24; triples €30.)

SPARTA (Σπαρτη) AND MYSTRAS (Μυστρας)   ☎ 27310

Citizens of today's Sparta make olive oil, not war. Pleasant public gardens and broad, palm-lined boulevards make Sparta hospitable, and it is by far the best base for exploring the Byzantine ruins of Mystras. **Ancient Sparta** is only a 1km walk north down Paleolougou. **Buses** from Sparta go to: Areopolis (1½hr., 2 per day, €4.80); Athens (3½hr., 9 per day, €12.65) via Corinth (2½hr., €7.60) and Tripoli (1hr., €3.40); and Monemvasia (2hr., 3 per day, €6.15). To reach the town center from the bus station, walk about 10 blocks west on Lykourgou; the **tourist office** is in the *plateia*. (☎ 27310 24 852. Open daily 8am-2pm.) **Hotel Apollon ❸,** Thermopilion 84, across Paleolougou from Hotel Cecil, is wackily decorated but clean. (☎ 27310 22 491. Private baths. Breakfast €4.50. Singles €25-30; doubles €35-44.)

Mystras, 4km from Sparta, was once the religious center of all Byzantium and the locus of Constantinople's rule over the Peloponnese. Its extraordinary hillside ruins comprise a city of Byzantine churches, chapels, and monasteries. Modest dress is required at the functioning convent. (Open in summer daily 8am-7pm; in winter 8:30am-3pm. €5, children and EU students free.) **Buses** from Sparta to the top of the ruins leave from the station and from the corner of Lykourgou and Leonidou (20min., 9 per day, €0.80).

AREOPOLIS (Αρεοπολη)   ☎ 27330

Just 11km from Areopolis, the unusual **Vlihada Cave,** part of a subterranean river, is cool, quiet, and strung with tiny crystalline stalagmites. (Open daily 8am-3pm. Mandatory 30min. tour. €14; students €7. A bus runs from Areopolis at 11am and returns at 12:45pm; €0.80). **Buses** stop in Areopolis's main *plateia* and go to Athens (6hr., 4 per day, €20) and Sparta (2hr., €6.30). To reach **Tsimova ❷,** which rents narrow rooms with tiny doors and windows typical of tower houses, turn left at the end of Kapetan Matapan, the road leading to the Old Town. (☎ 27330 51 301. Singles €20; doubles €40.) **Postal Code:** 23062.

MONEMVASIA (Μονεμβασια) AND GEFYRA (Γεφυρα) ☎ 27320

The island of Monemvasia has an otherworldly quality, despite being a major tourist destination. No cars or bikes are allowed on the island, and pack horses bear residents' groceries into the city. Narrow streets hide tiny doorways and flowered courtyards. At the edge of the cliffs perches the 12th-century **Agia Sofia;** to get there, navigate through the maze of streets to the inland edge of town, where a path climbs the side of the cliff to the tip of the rock. Stay in more modern and less expensive **Gefyra,** a 15min. walk down the main road and across the causeway from Monemvasia. An **orange bus** runs between the causeway and Monemvasia's gate (every 15min., €0.29). Three **buses** per day leave for: Athens (6hr., €18.65);

Corinth (5hr., €14); Sparta (2½hr., €6.15); and Tripoli (4hr., €9.70). ◼Hotel Akrogi-ali ❷, across from Malvasia Travel at Iouliou 23, has glowing white rooms with private baths. (☎27320 61 360. Singles €20-23; doubles €26-33.) ◼To Limanaki ❶ in Gefyra serves exceptional Greek food, including excellent *pastitsio* (€4).

NAFPLION (Ναυπλιο)   ☎27520

Beautiful old Nafplion glories in its fortresses, Venetian architecture, and nearby pebble beaches. The town's crown jewel is the 18th-century **Palamidi Fortress,** which provides spectacular views of the town and harbor. To get there, walk or take a taxi (€3) up the 3km road; or climb the grueling 999 steps up from Polizoid-hou, across the park from the bus station. (Open in summer daily 8am-6:45pm; off-season 8:30am-5:45pm. €4, students €2.) To reach **Bouboulinas,** the waterfront promenade, from the station, go left and follow Singrou to the harbor and the **Old Town.** Nafplion's small, pebbly beach **Arvanitia** is away from town on Polizoidhou with Palamidi on your left; if it gets too crowded on a hot day, follow the footpath for lovely private coves. **Buses** leave from Singrou, off Pl. Kapodistrias, for Athens (3hr., every hr., €8.50) via Corinth (2hr., €3.80). The **tourist office** is on 25 Martiou across from the telephone office. (☎27520 24 444. Open daily 9am-1pm and 4-8pm.) For the Old Town rooftop views from **Dimitris Bekas' Domatia ❷,** turn up the stairs on Kokkinou, following the sign for rooms off Staikopoulou; climb to the top and go up another 50 steps. (☎27520 24 594. Singles €13-16; doubles €18-20.) ◼To **Fanaria ❷,** above the *plateia* on Staikopoulou in a trellised alleyway, serves tanta-lizing entrees in an intimate atmosphere. (Soups €2.50-3, fish dishes €6-8.)

▶ **DAYTRIPS FROM NAFPLION: MYCENAE AND EPIDAVROS.** The supreme city of Greece from 1600 to 1100 BC, **Mycenae** (Μυκηνες) was once ruled by Agamemnon, leader of the attacking forces in the Trojan War. Excavations of ancient Mycenae have persisted for 126 years, turning the area into one of the most visited sites in Greece. Backpackers and senior citizens stampede to the famed Lion's Gate and Tomb of Agamemnon. (Both sites open Apr.-Sept. daily 8am-7pm; Oct.-Mar. 8am-5pm. €6, students €3. Keep your ticket or pay twice for both sites.) Join the ranks of Virginia Woolf, Claude Debussy, William Faulkner, and Allen Ginsberg by staying at **Belle Helene Hotel ❸,** which doubles as a bus stop on the main road. (☎27510 76 225. Singles €25; doubles €40.) The only direct **bus** to Mycenae is from Nafplion (45min., 4 per day, €1.90) via Argos (20min., €0.80).

The grandest structure at the ancient site of **Epidavros** (Επιδαυρος) is the **Theater of Epidavros,** built in the early 2nd century BC. The incredible acoustics allow you to stand at the top row of seats—14,000 seats back—and hear a match lit on stage. Near the theater and on the road to the sanctuary's ruins is Epidavros's **museum.** (☎27520 22 009. Open daily 8am-7pm. Ticket office open daily 7:30am-7pm, during festival season also F-Sa 7:30am-9pm. €6, students €3.) From late June to mid-Aug., the **Epidavros Theater Festival** brings performances of classical Greek plays on F and Sa nights. Shows are at 9pm; purchase tickets at the site or in advance by calling the Athens Festival Box Office. (☎210 322 1459. Tickets €12, students €6.) **Buses** arrive in Epidavros from Nafplion (45min., 4 per day, €1.90).

CORINTH (Κορινθος)   ☎27410

Most visitors to the Peloponnese travel to the ruins of **Ancient Corinth,** at the base of the **Acrocorinth.** Columns lie majestically around the courtyard of the **Temple of Apollo,** down the stairs to the left of the excellent **archaeological museum.** The **fortress** at the top of Acrocorinth is a tough 2-3hr. hike, but there is always the option of a taxi to the summit (€6) and back down (€9). At the top, explore the surpris-

GREECE

ingly intact remains of the **Temple to Aphrodite,** where disciples were initiated into the "mysteries of love." (☎27410 31 207 for museum. Open in summer daily 8am-7pm, off-season 8am-5pm. Museum and site €6, students €3.)

In **New Corinth,** the logical base for viewing the ruins, **buses** leave from station B, on Koliatsou, halfway through the park, to Ancient Corinth (20min., 15 per day 7am-9pm, €0.80). Buses leave station A, behind the train station, for Athens (1½hr., 30 per day, €5.07). Buses leave station C, **Argolis Station** (☎27410 24 403), at the intersection of Eth. Antistasis and Aratou, every hour for: Argos (€3); Mycenae (€2.40); and Nafplion (€3.80). **Trains** go from the station on Demokratias to Athens (2hr., 14 per day, €2.60) and to Patras (2½hr., 8 per day, €3.20). The **tourist police,** Ermou 51, are located in the city's park and will provide tourists with maps, brochures, and other assistance. (☎27410 23 282. Open daily 8am-2pm.) **Hotel Akti ❷,** Eth. Antistasis 3 in New Corinth, is the best bet for accommodations, with simple, utilitarian bedrooms and a convenient location. (☎27410 23 337. Singles €12-15; doubles €25-30.) **AXINOS ❶,** Damaskinou 41, offers cheery *al fresco* dining by the waterfront. (☎27410 28 889. *Moussaka* €4.70, feta in olive oil €2.35.)

NORTHERN AND CENTRAL GREECE

Under 19th-century Ottoman rule, Macedonia, Thessaly, and Thrace acquired a Byzantine aura. It's still discernible along forgotten mountain-goat paths that lead to the treasures of the era, with glorious vistas overlooking silvery olive groves, fruit-laden trees, and patchwork farmland.

THESSALONIKI (Θεσσαλονικη) ☎2310

Thessaloniki, a jumble of ancient, Byzantine, European, Turkish, Balkan, and contemporary Greek culture and history, fans out from its hilltop fortress toward the Thermaic Gulf. From its peak, the fortress oversees the Old Town's placid streets stretching down to the city's long, congested avenues. Golden mosaics, frescoes, and floating domes still gleam in the industrial city's Byzantine churches. Most travelers spend a couple of days in Thessaloniki going to clubs, checking out the sights, and enjoying the tranquility of countryside hikes.

TRANSPORTATION

Trains: Main Terminal (☎2310 517 517), on Monastiriou in the western part of the city. Take any bus down Egnatia (€0.44). To: **Athens** (6-8hr., 10 per day, €15). The **Travel Office** (☎2310 598 112) can provide updated schedules.

Buses: Most **KTEL** buses leave from one central, dome-shaped bus station west of the city center. To: **Athens** (☎2310 595 495; 6hr., 11 per day, €28); **Corinth** (☎2310 595 405; 7½hr., 11:30am, €32); **Patras** (☎2310 595 419; 7hr., 3 per day, €32.55).

Ferries: Buy tickets at **Karacharisis Travel and Shipping Agency,** Koundouriotou 8 (☎2310 524 544). Open M-F 8:30am-8pm, Sa 8:30am-2:30pm. To **Chios** (20hr., Sa 1am, €27) via **Limnos** (8hr., €17) and **Lesvos** (14hr., €27), and to **Mykonos** (15hr., 1 per day, €31). **Crete Air Travel,** Dragoumi 1 (☎2310 534 376), operates daily ferries to **Skiathos** (4½hr., €31) and **Skopelos** (5½hr., €31). Open M-F 8am-9pm.

Public Transportation: Local buses cost €0.44 and run throughout the city. Buses #10, #11, and #31 run up and down Egnatia. Buy tickets at *periptera* or at major stations.

GREECE

Thessaloniki

▲ ACCOMMODATIONS
Hotel Augustos, 2
Hotel Emporikon, 4
Hotel Ilios, 3
Youth Hostel, 6

🍴 FOOD
Ouzeri Mithron, 5
Zithos K'Yvesis, 1

300 meters
300 yards

Gulf of Thessaloniki

ARISTOTLE UNIVERSITY

INTERNATIONAL TRADE FAIRGROUNDS

Museum of Byzantine Culture
Archaeological Museum
Garden Theater
Vassiliko Theatro
White Tower
OTE Tower
Museum of Contemporary Art

PLAGIA SOPHIAS
PUBLIC MARKET
LADADIKA
DIMOKRATIAS (VARDARI)

Agii Apostoli (Holy Apostles)
Agia Sophia
Agia Ekaterini
Agios Dimitrios
Profitis Ilias
Osios David
Agia Nikolaos Orphanos
Rotunda
Arch of Galerius
Palace
Museum of the Macedonian Struggle
United States

Train Station
TO DOMESTIC BUS TERMINAL (3km)
TO (15km) [airport]

City Bus Terminals
Aristotelous

⭐ 🔀 ORIENTATION AND PRACTICAL INFORMATION

Egnatia, an old Roman highway, runs down the middle of town and is home to the cheapest hotels. Running parallel to the water, the main streets are **Ermou, Tsimiski, Mitropoleos,** and **Nikis,** which runs along the waterfront. Inland from Egnatia is **Ag. Dimitriou** and the **Old Town** beyond. Intersecting these and leading into town are I. Dragoumi, El. Venizelou, Aristotelous, Ag. Sophias, and Eth. Aminis.

> **Tourist Office: EOT,** Pl. Aristotelous (☎2310 271 888). Open M-Sa 7:30am-3pm.
>
> **Banks:** Banks with currency exchange and 24hr. **ATMs** line Tsimiski, including **National Bank,** Tsimiski 11 (☎2310 230 783). Open M-Th 8am-2pm, F 8am-1:30pm.
>
> **Tourist Police:** Dodekanissou 4, 5th fl. (☎2310 554 870 or 871). Free maps and brochures. Open 24hr. For the **local police,** call ☎2310 553 800 or 100.
>
> **Telephones: OTE,** Karolou Diehl 27 (☎134), at the corner of Ermou, one block east of Aristotelous. Open M-F 7:10am-1pm.
>
> **Internet Access: E-Global,** Egnatia 105, one block east of Arch of Galerius, sports over 50 fast terminals. €2-3 per hr. Open 24hr.
>
> **Post Office:** On Aristotelous, just below Egnatia. Open M-F 7:30am-8pm, Sa 7:30am-2pm, Su 9am-1:30pm. A **branch** office (☎2310 229 324), on Eth. Aminis near the White Tower, is open M-F 7am-8pm. Both offer *Poste Restante.* **Postal Code:** 54101.

🔋 ACCOMMODATIONS

Most budget hotels cluster along the western end of Egnatia, between Pl. Dimokratias (500m east of the train station) and Pl. Dikastiriou. Egnatia can be noisy and gritty, but you'll have to pay more elsewhere.

> 🏨 **Hotel Augustos,** El. Svoronou 4 (☎2310 522 955). Walking down Egnatia, turn north at the Argo Hotel; Augustos is straight ahead. Cozy rooms. Singles with bath €18; doubles €25, with bath €38; triples with bath €48.15. ❷
>
> **Youth Hostel,** Alex. Svolou 44 (☎2310 225 946). Take any bus west down Egnatia and get off at the Arch of Galerius (the Kamara stop); or, walk toward the water and turn left after 2 blocks. Hot showers only available 9-11am and 7-11pm. €8 per person. ❶
>
> **Hotel Emporikon,** Singrou 14 (☎2310 525 560), at Egnatia. Simple, clean rooms with balconies overlooking leafy, tranquil Singrou. Quieter than most Egnatia accomodations. Singles €20; doubles €43; triples €40. ❷
>
> **Hotel Ilios,** Egnatia 27 (☎2310 512 620). Comfortable, modern rooms with big windows, A/C, and gleaming white baths. Singles €32; doubles €46; triples €55.20. ❸

🍴 FOOD

Ouzeri can be found in tiny streets off Aristotelous; the innovative places a block down from Egnatia between Dragoumi and El. Venizelou cater to a younger clientele. 🏨**Ouzeri Melathron ❷,** in an alleyway at El. Venizelou 23, has a humorous menu and delicious food. (Entrees €3.50-12.) Head up Tositsa and look for an alleyway entrance to find delicious meat and vegetarian dishes at **Zithos K Yvesis ❶,** near the intersection of El Venizelou and Filipou. (Entrees €2.50-€6.)

👁 🔀 SIGHTS AND ENTERTAINMENT

The streets of modern Thessaloniki are littered with the remnants of its significance during both the Byzantine and Ottoman empires. 🏛**Agios Dimitrios,** on Ag. Dimitriou north of Aristotelous, is the city's oldest and most famous church.

Although most of its interior was gutted in a 1917 fire, some lovely mosaics remain. (Open daily 8am-8pm.) South of Egnatia, on the square that bears its name, the magnificent domed **Agia Sophia** features a splendid ceiling mosaic of the Ascension. (Open daily 7am-1pm and 5-7pm.) Originally part of a palatial complex designed to honor the Roman Emperor, the **Rotunda** became a church under the Byzantines. Its walls were once plastered with some of the city's most brilliant mosaics; very few remain. (Open daily 7am-2:30pm.) A colonnaded processional once led south to the **Arch of Galerius,** on the eastern end of Egnatia, which was built in the 4th century AD by Emperor Galerius. Returning west down Egnatia, don't miss **Bey Hamami,** a perfectly preserved 15th-century bath house that served the Ottoman governor and his retinue. (Open daily 9am-9pm. Free.) The **Heptapyrgion,** a 5th-century Byzantine fortress, is the main attraction of the city's modest acropolis. (Open M 12:30-7pm, Tu-Su 8am-7pm. Museum open daily 10:30am-5pm.)

Thessaloniki's **Archaeological Museum,** at the western end of Tsimiski, across from the International Helexpo Fairgrounds, is full of discoveries gleaned from Neolithic tombs, mosaics from Roman houses, and a dazzling display of Macedonian gold. (Open M 12:30-7pm, Tu-Su 8am-7pm; reduced hours in winter. €4, students €2, EU students free.) Just across the street on 3 Septemvriou, the **Museum of Byzantine Culture** displays an impressive array of artifacts from both the Early and Middle Byzantine eras, from church mosaics and elaborate tombs to 1500-year-old personal effects. (Open M 12:30-7pm, Tu-Su 8am-7pm; reduced hours in winter. €4, students and seniors €2, EU students and under 18 free.) All that remains of a 15th-century Venetian seawall, the **White Tower** presides over the eastern edge of the waterfront like an overgrown chess piece. (Tower open M 12:30-7pm, Tu-Su 8am-3pm. Free.)

There are three main hubs for late-night fun: the bars and cafes of the **Ladadika** district, the waterfront, and the open-air discos that throb near the airport exit. (€8-9 by taxi). **Podon 2000,** 11km east of the city along the main highway, is a sophisticated hot spot that will introduce you to Greek music. (€10 cover includes 1 drink.) Nearby **Decadence** and **Mousis** are other popular discos. (Cover €10.)

▶ DAYTRIP FROM THESSALONIKI: VERGINA

The tombs of Vergina (Βεργινα), final home to ancient Macedonian royalty, lie only 30km from Thessaloniki. The principal sight is the **museum,** while the intricate gold work and brilliant frescoes of the tombs themselves are under the **Great Tumulus,** a huge, man-made mount 12m tall and 110m wide. Check out the bones of **Alexander IV,** son of Alexander the Great, as well as the magnificent **Tomb of Philip II,** Alexander's father. (Open M noon-7pm, Tu-Su 8am-7pm; in winter Tu-Su 8am-7pm. €8, students €4.) **Buses** run from Thessaloniki (55min., every hr., €4.40) to Veria. From Veria take the bus to Vergina (20min., 11 per day, €0.95). Buses drop passengers off in the Vergina *plateia;* follow the signs to the sights.

MOUNT OLYMPUS (Ολιμποσ)   ☎ 23520

The impressive height (nearly 3000m) and formidable slopes of the Thermaic Gulf's Mt. Olympus so awed the ancients that they proclaimed it the divine dwelling place of the gods. A network of well-maintained **hiking** trails now makes the summit accessible to just about anyone with sturdy legs and a taste for adventure. Two approaches to the peaks begin near **Litohoro** (280m); the first and most popular starts at **Prionia** (1100m), 18km from the village, and takes one full day roundtrip. The second, a longer and more picturesque route, begins at **Diastavrosi** (also called **Gortsia;** 1300m), 14km away. There is no bus to the trailheads from Litohoro, so you'll have to walk, drive, or take a taxi (Prionia €20; Diastavrosi €8). Unless you're handy with a crampon and an ice axe, make your ascent between May and October. **Mytikas,** the tallest peak, is inaccessible without special equipment before June. The EOS-run ◨**Spilos Agapitos** ❷ ("Refuge A") is about 800m below **Skala** and Mytikas peaks. The English-speaking staff dispenses hiking info over the phone to prospective hikers and can also help reserve spots in other refuges. (☎ 23520 81 800. Meals 6am-9pm. Lights out 10pm. Open mid-May to late-Oct. €10, €8 for members of mountain clubs. €4.20 to **camp** nearby and use facilities.)

Trains (☎ 23520 22 522) run to the Litohoro station from Athens (6hr., 4 per day, €15) and Thessaloniki (1½hr., 4 per day, €3); a **taxi** from the train station to the town center should cost around €6. KTEL **buses** (☎ 23520 81 271) run from Athens (5½hr., 3 per day, €24.70) and Thessaloniki (1½hr., 17 per day, €5.90). The **tourist office** is on Ag. Nikolaou by the park. (☎ 23520 83 100. Open July-Nov. 8:30am-2:30pm and 5-9pm.) If you're not bedding down in one of the refuges (see above), the most convenient place to stay is the **Hotel Park** ❷, Ag. Nikolaou 23, down from the *plateia* in Litohoro. (☎ 23520 812 52. Singles €20; doubles €30; triples €40.) **Camp** at **Olympus Zeus** ❶ (☎ 23520 22 115) or **Olympus Beach** ❶ (☎ 23520 22 112), both on the beach about 5km from town; expect to pay at least €8 for a site.

METEORA (Μετεωρα) ☎ 24230

The iron-gray pinnacles of the Meteora rock formations are stunning, offering astonishing views of fields, mountains, and monolithic stone. These wonders of nature are bedecked by 24 exquisite, gravity-defying Byzantine monasteries. Dress modestly: long skirts for women, long pants for men, and no bare shoulders. (Open Apr.-Sept. Sa-Su and W 10am-12:30pm and 3:30-5pm; hours vary during the rest of the week. €2 per monastery.) The **Grand Meteoron Monastery** is the oldest, largest, and most touristed of the monasteries. It houses a **folk museum** and the 16th-century **Church of the Transfiguration,** whose dome features a *Pantokrator* (a central image of Christ). To escape the hordes of tourists, venture to **Roussanou,** to the right after the fork in the road. Visible from most of the valley, it is one of the most spectacularly situated monasteries in the area. Buses leave for Meteora from the fountain in **Kalambaka,** the most popular base for exploring the sight (2 per day, €0.80). **Trains** leave Kalambaka for Athens (4hr., 3 per day, €19.10) and Thessaloniki (5hr., 3 per day, €10.50). **Buses** depart for Athens (5hr., 3 per day, €19.70) and Patras (6hr., Tu and Th 9am, €17.50). The rooms at **Koka Roka** ❷ offer awe-inspiring views of Meteora; from the central square, follow Vlachara until it ends, bear left, and follow the signs to Kanari. (☎ 24230 24 554. Singles €15; doubles €27, with bath €32; triples with bath €42.) Many of the **campsites** that line the roads out of town also rent cheap rooms. **Postal Code:** 42200.

IOANNINA (Ιωαννινα) ☎ 26510

The region's largest city, Ioannina, lies on the shores of Lake Pamvotis. Ioannina itself might not captivate you for long, but it is a useful transport hub if traveling between Greece and Italy. Aside from local finds, the highlights of the city's **Archaeological Museum,** off Averof, near the city center, are the lead tablets used by ancients to inscribe their questions to the oracle at Dodoni. (Open Tu-Su 8:30am-3pm. €2, students free.) Catch a boat from the waterfront (10min., €1) for **To Nisi** ("The Island") to explore Byzantine monasteries and the **Ali Pasha Museum.**

Buses run from the terminal at Zossimadon 4 to Athens (6½hr., 11 per day, €24.90) and Thessaloniki (7hr., 6 per day, €20.50). The **tourist office** is about 500m down Leoforis Dodoni on the left, immediately after the playground. (☎ 26510 46 662. Open July-Sept. M-F 7:30am-2:30pm and 5-8:30pm, Sa 9am-1pm; Oct.-June M-F 7:30am-2:30pm.) **Hotel Metropolis** ❷, Kristali 2, on the corner of Averof toward the waterfront, is conveniently located and has spacious rooms. (☎ 26510 26 207.

Singles €20; doubles €25.) **Hotel Olympic ❹**, Melandis 2, is beautifully decorated and fully equipped. Take the second left off Averof as you walk towards the waterfront. (☎26510 22 233. Singles €50; doubles €70; triples €80.) Several *souvlaki* stands are at the end of Averof near the Frourio, and seafood restaurants line the waterfront. ▨**Filippas ❷**, on the waterfront, has delicious specials; the chicken with honey and yogurt (€6.50) is a real treat. (Entrees €4.50-7.) **Postal Code:** 45110.

🄳 DAYTRIP FROM IOANNINA: DODONI. Ancient Dodoni (Δωδωνη), the site of mainland Greece's oldest oracle, is at the base of a mountain 22km southeast of Ioannina. According to myth, **Zeus** answered queries here from the roots of a giant oak tree. There is also a large 3rd-century **amphitheater** at the site. (Open daily 8am-5pm. €2, students €1, EU students free.) **Buses** to Dodoni run from Ioannina's smaller station at Bizaniou 21 (M, W, F 6:30am and 3:30pm; €1.35). Ask to be let off at the theater. The return bus passes by at about 4:45pm; alternatively, you can hire a **taxi** (at least €15 round-trip).

IONIAN ISLANDS (Νησια Του Ιουιου)

Just to the west of mainland Greece, the Ionian Islands are renowned for their medley of rugged mountains, rolling farmland, shimmering olive groves, and pristine beaches, all surrounded by a seemingly endless expanse of clear, blue water. The islands are a favorite among vacationing Brits, Italians, and Germans, as well as ferry-hopping backpackers heading to Italy.

🌙 FERRIES TO ITALY

To catch a ferry to Italy, buy your ticket at least a day ahead; be sure to find out if the port tax (€5-6) is included. **Corfu Mare** (☎26610 32 467), beneath the Ionian Hotel, sells tickets. Ferries go from Corfu to: Ancona (20hr., 1 per day, €56); Bari (9hr., 1 per day, €22); Brindisi (6-7hr., 3 per day, €30); Trieste (24hr., 4 per week, €38); and Venice (24hr., 1 per day, €42). Schedules vary; call ahead.

CORFU (KERKYRA; Κερκυρα) ☎26610

Ever since Homer's Odysseus washed ashore and praised its lush beauty, the seas have brought a multitude of conquerors, colonists, and tourists to verdant Corfu. Those who stray from the beaten path, however, will still encounter unspoiled, uncrowded beaches.

CORFU TOWN AND ENVIRONS. Corfu Town enchants with its two fortresses, various museums, and winding streets. The lovely **Paleokastritsa** beach, where Odysseus supposedly landed, lies west of town; take a KTEL bus to Paleokastritsa (45min., 9 per day, €1.50). A 90min. walk from there will bring you to the mountaintop monastery **Panagia Theotokos.** KTEL buses also run from Corfu Town to **Agios Gordios** (45min., 7 per day, €1.25), 10km south of Pelekas, home to impressive rock formations, a beach, and the **Pink Palace Hotel ❷**, which is immensely popular with American and Canadian backpackers. The Palace has an impressive list of amenities, including tennis courts, a nightclub, massages (€11), clothing-optional cliff-diving (€15), and other water sports. They also run buses to Athens (€38-47) that bypass Patras. (☎26610 53 024. Internet €3 per 30min. Breakfast, dinner, and ferry pick-up included. Dorms €19, with A/C and bath €25.)

Ferries run from Corfu Town to Italy (see above) and Patras (6-7hr., 1-2 per day, €20), and high-speed **catamarans** run to Kephalonia (3hr., W and Sa 9am, round-trip €62). KTEL runs **bus/ferry combos** to Athens (9hr., 3 per day, €27.90) and

Thessaloniki (9hr., 2 per day, €27). KTEL inter-city green buses depart from between I. Theotaki and the New Fortress; blue municipal buses leave from Pl. Sanrocco. The **EOT Tourist Office** is at the corner of Rizospaston Voulefton and I. Polila. (☎26610 37 520. Open M-F 8am-2pm.) **The Association of Owners of Private Rooms and Apartments,** I. Polila 24 (☎26610 26 133), has a complete list of rooms in Corfu. To get to **Hotel Europa ❸,** Giantsilio 10, from the port customs house, cross the main street and make a sharp right; Giantsilio is a tiny road on your left after the road turns sharply left and becomes Napoleonta. Rooms are white and airy, and the cheapest in Corfu Town. (☎26610 39 304. Singles €25, with bath €30; doubles €30/€35; triples €36.) **Restaurant Rex ❸,** Kapodistriou 66, one block back from the Spianada, has long been famed as one of Corfu's best. (Entrees €7.40-12.60.) The undisputed focus of Corfu Town's nightlife is the **Disco Strip,** on Eth. Antistaseos at the waterfront. **Postal Code:** 49100.

PELEKAS AND GLYFADA. The village of ▨**Pelekas** (bus #11 from Corfu Town; 30min., 7 per day, €0.75) has some of the best of Corfu's offerings: sandy beaches, great food, and fun bars. The long **beach** is a pleasant 30min. walk from town down a very steep road. The beaches at **Glyfada,** 5km from Pelekas Town, are more touristed; water spouts abound. Free shuttles run between Glyfada and Pelekas (10min., 6 per day). Glyfada is also accessible by green KTEL **buses** from Corfu Town (45min., 10 per day, €1.25). North of Glyfada, accessible by a dirt path off the main Pelekas road, lie the isolated beaches of **Moni Myrtidion** and **Myrtiotissa** (the unofficial nude beach). While lodging is available in Glyfada, Pelekas is your best bet for a cheap night's stay—try **Pension Tellis and Brigitte ❷,** down the hill from the bus stop. (☎26610 94 326. Singles €18; doubles €20-25.)

KEPHALONIA (Κεφαλονια) ☎26710

Mountains, subterranean lakes and rivers, caves, forests, and more than 250km of sand-and-pebble coastline make Kephalonia a nature lover's paradise. **Argostoli,** the capital of Kephalonia and Ithaka, is a lively city packed with pastel buildings that climb the hills from the calm waters of the harbor. Argostoli offers good shopping and nightlife, as well as easy access to other points on the island. **Buses** leave from the south end of the waterfront for Sami (4 per day, €2) and Fiskardo (2hr., 2 per day, €3.30). **Hotel Tourist ❷,** on the waterfront near the bus station, is a great deal. (☎26710 22 510. All rooms have balconies. Singles €24-36; doubles €37-52.)

Sami is 24km from Argostoli on the east coast. Amazing views stretch in every direction, from the waves crashing on the beach to the green hills cradling the town. Sami is close to the underground **Melissani Lake** and **Drogarati Cave,** a large cavern filled with stalactites and stalagmites. (Cave open daily until nightfall. €3, children €1.50.) **Fiskardo,** at the northern tip of the island, is the most beautiful of Kephalonia's towns; take a bus from either Sami (1hr., 2 per day, €2.70) or Argostoli (1½-2hr., 2 per day, €3.40). Buses from Fiskardo stop at the turn-off for ▨**Myrtos Beach,** one of Europe's best. (Beach 4km from turn-off.) **Ferries** run from Sami to: Ithaka (40min., 3 per day, €1.70); Patras (2½hr., 2 per day, €10.70); and Brindisi, Italy (July-Sept. 1 per day, €35). **Hotel Kyma ❷,** in Sami's main *plateia*, has spectacular views. (☎(26740) 22 064. Singles €17-26; doubles €30-46.)

ITHAKA (Ιθακη) ☎26740

The least-touristed of the Ionian Islands, Ithaka is all too often passed over for Lefkada and Kephalonia. Those who do discover the island delight in its pebbled beaches, rocky hillsides, and terraced olive groves. Ithaka was the kingdom that Odysseus left behind while he fought in the Trojan War. Its capital, **Vathy,** wraps around a bay skirted by steep, green hills. **Dexa** is the closest beach to Vathy, a

20min. walk along the main road out of town with the water on your right. The **Sarakiniko** and ☒**Filiatro** beaches, towards the mountain to the left of town as you are facing inland (about a 40min. walk), are more rewarding. Homer fans can climb (4km; about 1hr.) up to the **Cave of the Nymphs,** where Odysseus supposedly hid his treasure. (On the road out of town to Stavros; look for signs. Bring a flashlight.) In summer, the bus to Frikes (45min., €1.20) stops at the scenic village of **Stavros,** allegedly the former home of **Odysseus's Palace;** follow signs to a small museum filled with excavated items from the site. (Hours vary. A small tip is expected.)

Ferries connect Ithaka to Kephalonia (45min., 2-3 per day, €1.70) and to Patras, in the Peloponnese (4½hr., 2 per day, €11.50). Boats depart from Piso Aetos, near Vathy, and from Frikes. Schedules vary; check with **Delas Tours** (☎26740 32 104; open daily 9am-2pm and 3:30-9:30pm) or **Polyctor Tours** (☎26740 33 120; open daily 9:30am-1:30pm and 3:30-9pm), both in the main *plateia*. Private *domatia* are your best option for affordable accommodations; check with Delas Tours to see what they have available. **Andriana Domatia ❸,** on the far right of the waterfront as you are facing inland, has immaculate rooms with A/C. (☎26740 32 387. All rooms with bath. Singles €25-30; doubles €40-47.) **Taverna To Trexantiri ❷,** one block behind the post office off the *plateia*, is a favorite restaurant among locals. (Entrees under €6.) **Postal Code:** 28300.

THE SPORADES (Σποραδες)

Circling into the azure Aegean, the Sporades form a family of enchanting sea maidens. From wild Skiathos to sophisticated Skopelos to quiet Alonnisos, the islands have beckoned to visitors for millennia. Ancient Athenians and Romans, early Venetians, and modern-day tourists have all basked on their sunlit shores and trod their shaded forests.

▐ TRANSPORTATION

To get to most of the Sporades from Athens, take the bus to Agios Konstantinos (2½hr., every hr., €10.20), where **Hellas Lines** (☎22 209) operates **ferries** to: Alonnisos (5½hr., 2 per week, €13.40); Skiathos (2hr., 2 per day, €20.20); and Skopelos (3hr., 2 per day, €26.90). **Flying Dolphins** leave Agios Konstantinos for: Alonnisos (2¾hr., 1-5 per day, €26.90); Skiathos (1½hr., 1-5 per day, €20.30); and Skopelos (2½hr., 1-5 per day, €26.80). Ferries also shuttle between the islands (see below).

SKIATHOS (Σκιαθος)   ☎24270

Having grown up almost overnight from an innocent island daughter to a madcap dancing queen, Skiathos is the tourism hub of the Sporades. Buses leave the port in Skiathos Town for the southern beaches (every 30min., €1). The bus route ends in Koukounaries, near the lovely, pine-wooded ☒**Koukounaries Beach and Biotrope** and the nude **Banana Beach** and **Little Banana Beach.** Indulge at the countless bars in **Plateia Papadiamantis** or along **Polytechniou** or **Evangelista,** then dance all night long at the clubs on the eastern side of the waterfront. Hellas Lines (☎24270 22 209) runs **ferries** to Alonnisos (2hr., 1-2 per day, €6) and Skopelos (1½hr., 1-3 per day, €4.40). *Domatia* are the best deal in town. The **Rooms to Let Office,** in the wooden kiosk by the port, provides a list of available rooms. (☎24270 22 990. Open daily 9am-8pm.) The rooms at ☒**Australia Hotel ❷,** in an alley on Evangelistra off Papadiamantis, have A/C, private baths, fridges, and balconies. (Sept.-July singles €20; doubles €25-30; triples €36; Aug. prices increase.) **Primavera ❷** has delicious Italian food. (Entrees €5-10. Open daily 6:30pm-12:30am.) **Postal Code:** 37002.

THE BIG SPLURGE

TASIA'S

Good seafood restaurants aren't hard to come by in Greece, but **Tasia's** rises above the rest. This taverna, in the tiny village of Steni Vala on Alonnisos, is a family operation from start to finish.

Tasia Malamatenios, who inherited the business from her mother, prepares and serves the food with the help of her son and four daughters. Tasia's husband George, the family fisherman, is crucial to the taverna's distinctive appeal—instead of getting the fish from Volos, like most tavernas on Alonnisos, Tasia's is supplied exclusively by his rig. While the selection is not always as wide as that of other tavernas, the fish is as fresh as it gets. You can sit down to lunch here and eat fish that was caught hours (and never more than a day) before.

Seafood this fresh comes at a high price; the fish costs anywhere from €30-55 per kg. The delicious lobster (€51 per kg) with spaghetti, however, is worth every cent. Tasia's also has inexpensive options, such as fried fish (€5) and typical Greek fare, from stuffed tomatoes (€4) to *moussaka* (€5.50).

(The island's bus stops in Steni Vala; Tasia's is the first taverna you come to in the tiny harbor. Open daily noon-midnight.) ❹

SKOPELOS (Σκοπελος)   ☎24240

Skopelos sits between the whirlwind of Skiathos and the wilderness of Alonnisos and features the best elements of both. Hikes and moped rides lead to numerous monasteries, bright beaches, and white cliffs. Buses leave from the right of the waterfront (as you face the sea) for beaches near **Stafylos, Milia,** and **Loutraki.** At night, the waterfront strip closes to traffic and crowds swarm the streets in search of the tastiest *gyros* and the most authentic Greek *taverna.* Hellas Lines (☎24240 22 767) runs **ferries** to: Alonnisos (30min., 1-2 per day, €3.40); Skiathos (1hr., 3-4 per day, €3.10); and Thessaloniki (2 per week, €39). **Thalpos Travel Agency,** 5m to the right of Galanatsiou along the waterfront, provides tourist information. (☎24240 22 947. Open May-Oct. daily 10am-2pm and 6-10pm; Nov.-Apr. info available by phone.) The **Rooms and Apartments Association** can provide a list of current *domatia.* (☎24240 24 567. Open daily 10am-2pm and 6-10pm.) ▓**Pension Sotos ❷,** on the waterfront at the corner of Galanatsiou, has a fantastic location and unbeatable prices. (☎24240 22 549. Singles €17-35; doubles €24-35.) **Plateia Platanos** abounds with fast, cheap food. **Postal Code:** 37003.

ALONNISOS (Αλοννησος)   ☎24240

Of the 20-odd islands within Greece's new **National Marine Park,** only Alonnisos is inhabited. Hikers take to the highland trails in the north; pick up *Alonnisos on Foot* (€9) in **Patitiri** for walking routes. In the south, endless beaches satisfy less adventurous souls; many are accessible from the island's main road. A 1½hr. walk from Patitiri takes you to **Votsi;** locals dive off the 15-20m cliffs near **Votsi Beach.** Beautiful **Hora** (Χωρα; Old Town) is ideal for both hikers and beachgoers. The island's only **bus** runs between Hora and Patitiri (every hr., €1). **Ferries** run to Skiathos (2hr., 1-2 per day, €6) and Skopelos (30min., 1-2 per day, €5). **Alonissos Travel,** in the center of the waterfront, exchanges currency, finds rooms, books excursions, and sells ferry tickets. (☎24240 65 188. Open daily 8am-11pm.) **Panorama ❷,** down the first alley on the left from Ikion Dolophon, rents bright rooms and studios. (☎24240 65 240. All rooms with bath. Singles €15-30; doubles €25-45; triples €35-50.) Locals adore the *ouzeri* **To Kamaki ❶,** on the left side of Ikion Dolophon, past the National Bank. The warm octopus salad (€5) is delicious. (Open daily 11am-2am.) **Postal Code:** 37005.

THE CYCLADES (Κυκλαδες)

When people wax rhapsodic about the Greek islands, chances are they're talking about the Cyclades. Whatever your idea of Greece—cobblestone streets and whitewashed houses, breathtaking sunsets, scenic hikes, all-night revelry—you'll find it here. Although most islands are mobbed in the summer, each has quiet villages and untouched spots.

⌐ TRANSPORTATION

Ferries run from: Athens to Mykonos, Naxos, and Santorini; Crete to Naxos and Santorini; and Thessaloniki to Naxos and Ios. Frequent ferries also run between each of the islands in the Cyclades. See below for all ferry information. High-speed ferries and **hydrofoils** typically cover the same routes at twice the cost and speed.

MYKONOS (Μυκονος)   ☎ 22890

Coveted by pirates in the 18th century, Mykonos is still lusted after by those seeking revelry and excess. Nightlife, both gay and straight, abounds; the island is also the expensive playground of chic sophisticates. Ambling in colorful alleyways at dawn or dusk is the cheapest and most exhilarating way to experience the island, especially **Mykonos Town.** All of Mykonos's beaches are nudist, but the degree of bareness varies. **Plati Yialos, Paradise Beach,** and **Super Paradise Beach** are the most daring; **Elia** is a bit tamer. Buses run south from South Station to Plati Yialos (every 30min., €0.80), where *caïques* (little boats) go to the other beaches (around €1.50); direct buses also run to Paradise from South Station (every 30min., €0.80) and to Elia from North Station (30min., 8 per day, €1). After 11pm, wild dancing and irresistible hedonism are the norm at **Pierro's** on Matogianni (beer €5). The **Skandinavian Bar** on the waterfront has something for everyone in its two-building party complex. (Beer and shots €3-4. Open Su-F 8:30pm-3am, Sa 8:30pm-4am.)

Ferries run to: Athens (6hr., 2-3 per day, €17); Naxos (3hr., 1-2 per day, €6.30); Santorini (6hr., 3 per week, €11); and Tinos (45min., 3 per day, €3.50). The helpful **tourist police** are located at the ferry landing. (☎ 22890 22 482. Open daily 8am-11pm.) Most budget travelers bed down at Mykonos's several festive campsites, which offer a myriad of sleeping options beyond the standard plot of grass. There are **information offices** on the dock, one for **hotels** (☎ 22890 24 540; open daily 9am-midnight) and one for **camping** (☎ 22890 23 567; open daily 9am-midnight). **Hotel Apollon ❹,** on the waterfront, is an antique-laden house with a view of the harbor. (☎ 22890 22 223. Singles and doubles €42-50; doubles with bath €50-65.) The lively **Paradise Beach Camping ❶,** 6km from the village, is directly on the beach; the round-trip bus costs €0.80. (☎ 22890 22 852. €5-7 per person; €2.50-3 per tent; 2-person beach cabin €20-45.) Cheap creperies and *souvlaki* joints are on nearly all of Mykonos's streets. **Appaloosa ❸,** one block from Taxi Square on Mavrogeneous, has an eclectic mix of food; Mexican selections are its best. (Entrees €9-11. Open daily 8pm-1:30am.) **Postal Code:** 84600.

▶ DAYTRIP FROM MYKONOS: DELOS.

Delos (Δηλος) is the sacred center of the Cyclades. The **archaeological site,** which occupies much of the small island, takes several days to explore comp\letely, but the highlights can be seen in about three hours. From the dock, head straight to the **Agora of the Competaliasts;** continue in the same direction and go left onto the wide **Sacred Road** to reach the **Sanctuary of Apollo,** a collection of temples built from Mycenaean

GREECE

times onward. On the right is the biggest and most famous, the **Great Temple of Apollo.** Continue 50m past the end of the Sacred Road to the beautiful **Terrace of the Lions.** The **museum,** next to the cafeteria, contains an assortment of archaeological finds. (Open Tu-Su 8:30am-3pm. €5, students €2.) A path from the museum leads to the summit of **Mt. Kythnos** (112m), from which Zeus watched Apollo's birth. Excursion **boats** leave the dock near Mykonos Town for Delos (35min., 3 per day, round-trip €6).

TINOS (Τηνος) ☎ 22830

Beautiful Tinos spreads out from the summit of hulking **Mt. Exobourgo.** For the thousands of pilgrims who have flocked here each year since 1812, however, the island's allure lies not in its scenery but in the **Panagia Evangelistira Church,** home to the **Icon of the Annunciation,** one of the most sacred relics of the Greek Orthodox Church. The pilgrimage site is in **Tinos Town** (Hora), the island's capital. (Modest dress required. Open July-Aug. daily 7am-8pm; Sept.-June 7am-6pm. Free.) Beaches surround Tinos Town; **Kardiani** and **Agios Petros,** situated at the base of the mountains, are among the islands' most spectacular, while **Stavros** beach, a 2km walk out of town, is more touristy. For the best of the best, head east to **Agios Sostis** and **Porto;** take the KTEL bus from Tinos Town (3-5 per day, €0.60). Many hikes lead up **Mt. Exobourgo,** 14km north of Tinos Town, the site of the Venetian fortress **Xombourgo;** consult the agents at Windmills Travel (see below) for details.

Ferries (☎ 22830 22 348) run to Mykonos (30min., 4-5 per day, €3.50). **Windmills Travel,** opposite the park by the port, can help you find accommodations. (☎ 22830 23 398. Open daily 9am-3pm and 6-9pm.) **Vidalis,** Zanaki Alavanou 16, on the road inland from the right of the waterfront, rents **mopeds.** (☎ 22830 23 400. €10-13 per day. Open daily 8:30am-9pm.) ◪**Dimitris-Maria Thodosis ❸,** Evangelistrias 33, is midway up the road on the left, on the second floor. The comfortable rooms have flower-laced balconies. (☎ 22830 24 809. Open Mar.-Oct. Doubles €30.) **Tinos Camping ❶** is 10min. from the waterfront to the right; follow the signs. (☎ 22830 22 344. July-Aug. €6 per person; May-June and Sept.-Oct. €4 per person. €2-3 per tent. Bungalows for 1-5 people with kitchen and bath €30-45.) **Postal Code:** 84200.

PAROS (Παρος) ☎ 22840

Paros is famed for its slabs of pure white marble, used for many of the great statues and buildings of the ancient world. Today's visitors know the island for its tall mountains and long, golden beaches. Behind the commercial surface of **Paroikia,** Paros's port and largest city, flower-filled streets wind through archways and past one of the most treasured basilicas of the Orthodox faith, the **Panagia Ekatontapiliani** (Church of Our Lady of 100 Gates). Tradition holds that only 99 of the church's 100 doors are visible—when the 100th appears, Constantinople will again belong to the Greeks. (Dress modestly. Open daily 8:30am-10:30pm. Free.) Just 10km south of town is the cool, spring-fed ◪**Valley of the Butterflies** (a.k.a. **Petaloudes**), where rare *Panaxiaquadripunctaria* moths congregate during the mating season from June to late September. Take the bus from Paroikia to Aliki (10min., 8 per day, €0.80) and ask to be let off at Petaloudes. Follow the signs 2km up the road. (Open M-Sa 9am-8pm. €1.50.) At night, **Pirate Blues and Jazz** in the Old Town has eclectic music. (Beer €3, cocktails €7. Open daily 7pm-3am.)

Ferries sail to Ios (2½hr., 7-9 per day, €8) and Santorini (3½hr., 7-9 per day, €10.10). The **tourist police** are on the *plateia* behind the telephone office. (☎ 22840 21 673. Open daily 8am-2pm.) Turn left at the dock and take a right after the ancient cemetery ruins to reach the pleasant **Rena Rooms ❷.** (☎ 22840 22 220. Doubles €18-39; triples €27-45. 20% discount for *Let's Go* readers.) The psychedelic **Happy Green Cow ❸,** a block off the *plateia* behind the National Bank, serves tasty vegetarian fare. (Entrees €8-12. Open daily 7pm-midnight.) **Postal Code:** 84400.

NAXOS (Ναξος) ☎ 22850

The ancients believed Naxos, the largest of the Cyclades, was the home of Dionysus. Olive groves, wineries, small villages, and chalky white ruins fill its interior, while sandy beaches line its shores. **Naxos Town**, the capital, is crowned by the **Castro**, a Venetian castle now home to two museums. The **Venetian Museum** features evening concerts with traditional Greek music, dancing, and shadow theater. (Open daily 10am-4pm and 7-11pm. €5, students and seniors €3.) The **Archaeological Museum** occupies the former Collège Français, which educated Nikos Kazantzakis, author of *The Last Temptation of Christ* and *Zorba the Greek*. (Open Tu-Su 8:30am-2pm. €3, students €2.) The ■**Mitropolis Museum,** next to the Orthodox Church, is an architectural achievement in itself, built around the excavated site of a 13th-century BC civilization. (Open Tu-Su 8:30am-3pm. Free.) The 6th-century BC **Portara** archway, visible from the waterfront, is one of the few archaeological sites in Greece where you can actually climb all over the ruins. But to experience the island fully, it's essential to escape Naxos Town. A bus goes from the port to the beaches of **Agia Georgios, Agios Prokopios, Agia Anna,** and **Plaka** (every 30min., €1.10). Buses also run from Naxos Town to **Apollonas,** a fishing village on the northern tip of the island (2hr., €3.50). To get to the **Tragea** highland valley, an enormous, peaceful olive grove, take a bus from Naxos Town to Halki (15-20min.).

Ferries go from Naxos Town to: Athens (6½hr., 2 per day, €16.80); Crete (7hr., 3-5 per week, €16.30); Ios (1½hr., 2 per day, €6.90); Kos (7hr., 1 per week, €14.20); Mykonos (1½hr., 1 per day, €6.30); Paros (1hr., 2 per day, €4.50); Rhodes (13hr., 1 per week, €19.10); Santorini (3hr., 2 per day, €9.40); and Thessaloniki (14hr., 1-3 per week, €29). The **tourist office** is 300m up from the dock, by the bus station. (☎22850 24 358. Open daily 8am-11pm.) **Irene's Pension ❷,** about 100m from Ag. Giorgios, is near the center of the town. (☎22850 23 169. All rooms with A/C. Call ahead. Singles €15; doubles €20-30; triples €25-35.) **Panorama ❸,** in Old Naxos, has rooms with fans and fridges. (☎22850 22 330. Doubles from €25; triples from €30.) Naxos has three **camping ❶** options along the beach; see their representatives along the dock. (€4-6 per person, plus a small tent fee.) **Postal Code:** 84300.

IOS (Ιος) ☎ 22860

Ios has everything your mother warned you about—swimming less than 30 minutes after a meal, dancing in the streets, and drinking games all day long on the beach. The **port** (Yialos) is at one end of the island's sole paved road; the **village** (Hora) sits above it on a hill; but the beaches are the place to be. Most spend their days at **Mylopotas Beach,** a 20min. walk downhill from Ios town or a bus ride from the port or village (every 10-20min. 7am-midnight, €0.80). Sunning is typically followed by drinking; **Dubliner,** near the basketball courts, is a good place to start. On Thursday nights, €23.50 buys you pizza, a drink, and cover immunity at five bars that comprise the ultimate pub crawl. Head up from the *plateia* to reach the **Slammer Bar,** where you can get hammered on "tequila slammers" (€3), then run with the pack to **Red Bull** to get plastered on shots (€2.40). Then find techno at **Scorpion Disco,** the island's largest club, as you stumble your way back to the beach. (Cover after 1am.) After 2am, people dance on the tables at **Sweet Irish Dream,** near the "donkey steps." Take some aspirin in the morning and head down to the beach, where **Mylopotas Water Sports Center** offers rental and lessons for windsurfing, water-skiing, and snorkeling (€14-40).

Ferries go to: Mykonos (4hr., 1 per day, €11.64); Naxos (1¾hr., at least 3 per day, €7.32); and Santorini (1¼hr., 3 per day, €5.62). Once a week, ferries go to Thessaloniki (€31.06) and Tinos (€12.66). The main **tourist office** is next to the bus stop. (☎22860 91 343. Open daily 8am-midnight.) In the village, take the uphill steps to the left in the *plateia* and take the first left to reach ■**Francesco's ❷** for spectacular harbor views and a terrace bar. (☎22860 91 706. Dorms €7-15; doubles €10-25.) On the end of Mylopotas Beach, █Far Out Camping ❶ has a pool, plenty of tents, parties, and activities, including bungee jumping. (☎22860 92 301. Open Apr.-Sept. Tent rental €4-7.50; small cabins €5 and up; bungalows €7-18.) █Ali Baba's ❷, next to Ios Gym, offers delicious pad thai (€8.50) and burgers (€5.50). Around the corner from the church, **Lord Byron's** ❸ serves a unique blend of Greek and Smirniki food. (Entrees €12-15.) **Postal Code:** 84001.

SANTORINI (Σαντορινη)   ☎ 22860

Whitewashed towns balanced on cliffs, black-sand beaches, and deeply scarred hills make Santorini's landscape nearly as dramatic as the volcanic explosion that created it. Despite all the kitsch in touristy **Fira,** the island's capital, nothing can ruin the pleasure of wandering the town's cobblestoned streets, browsing its craft shops, and taking in the sunset from its western edge. On the southwestern part of the island, the excavations at **Akrotiri,** a late Minoan city, are preserved under layers of volcanic rock. (Open Tu-Su 8:30am-3pm. €5, students €3.) Buses run to Akrotiri from Fira (30min., 16 per day, €1.20). Frequent buses also leave Fira for the black-sand **beaches** of Perissa (15min., 30 per day, €1.40) and Kamari (20min., 2-3 per hr., €0.80) to the southeast. The bus stops before Perissa in Pyrgos; from there, you can hike to the **Profitias Ilias Monastery** (40min.; open daily 8am-1pm), and continue to the ruins of **Thira** (an extra 1½hr.; open Tu-Su 8am-2pm).

Ferries from Fira run to: Athens (9hr., 4-8 per day, €20.20); Ios (1½hr., 3-5 per day, €5.80); Iraklion (4hr., 1 per day, €12.60); Naxos (4hr., 4-8 per day, €10); Mykonos (7hr., 2 per week, €11.20); and Paros (4½hr., 3-5 per day, €10). Most ferries depart from Athinios harbor; frequent buses (30min., €1.50) connect to Fira. Head 300m north from the *plateia* in Fira to reach the **Thira Youth Hostel** ❶, in an old monastery. (☎22860 22 387. Open Apr.-Oct. Dorms €7.50-10; doubles €20-40.) Take a bus from Fira to **Oia** (25min., 30 per day, €0.85) for more options; the clean rooms at █**Youth Hotel Oia** ❷ are a good choice. (☎22860 71 465. Breakfast included. Open May-Oct. Dorms €14.) **Chelidonia** ❺, 100m to the left of Oia's church, rents traditional cave houses, with beds built into the wall. (☎22860 71 287. Kitchens and baths. Doubles €115; triples €147; quads €170.) **Mama's Cyclades Cafe** ❷, north of Fira on the road to Oia, serves up a big breakfast special. (☎22860 24 211. Entrees €5-8. Open daily 7am-midnight.) **Postal Code:** 84700.

CRETE (Κρητη)

According to a Greek saying, a Cretan's first loyalty is to his island, his second to his country. Since 3000 BC, Crete has maintained an identity distinct from the rest of Greece, first expressed in the language, script, and architecture of the ancient Minoans. Despite this insular mindset, residents are friendly to visitors who come to enjoy their island's inexhaustible trove of mosques, monasteries, mountain villages, gorges, grottoes, and beaches. Crete is divided into four main prefectures: Iraklion, Hania, Rethymno, and Lasithi.

▐ TRANSPORTATION

Olympic Airways and **Air Greece** connect Athens to: Sitia (2-3 per week, €83) in the east; Iraklion (45min., 13-15 per day, €84) in the center; and Hania (4 per day, €53) in the west. **Boats** run to Iraklion from: Athens (14hr., 3 per day, €27.50); Mykonos (8½hr., 5 per week, €20); Naxos (7hr., 3 per week, €17.10); Paros (9hr., 7 per week, €21); and Santorini (4hr., 2 per day, €12.60).

IRAKLION (Ηρακλιον)   ☎ 2810

Iraklion is Crete's capital and primary port. The chic locals live life in the fast lane, which translates into the most diverse nightlife on the island and an urban brusqueness unique among the cities of Crete. Iraklion's main attraction after Knossos (see below) is the superb ⊠**Archaeological Museum,** off Pl. Eleftherias. By appropriating major finds from all over the island, the museum has amassed a comprehensive record of the Neolithic and Minoan stages of Crete's history. (Open M 12:30-7pm, Tu-Su 8am-7pm. €6, students €3, EU students free.) A maze of streets between **Pl. Venizelou** and **Pl. Eleftherias** houses Iraklion's night spots.

At **Terminal A,** between the old city walls and the harbor, **buses** leave for Agios Nikolaos (1½hr., 20 per day, €4.70) and Malia (1hr., 2 per hr., €2.50). Buses leave opposite Terminal A for Hania (1½hr., 17 per day, €10.50) and Rethymno (1½hr., 18 per day, €5.90). The **tourist police** are at Dikeosinis 10. (☎ 2810 283 190. Open daily 8am-10pm.) **Gallery Games Net,** Korai 14, has **Internet** access. (☎ 2810 282 804. €3 per hr.) **Rent a Room Hellas ❶,** Handakos 24, two blocks from El Greco Park, has large dorm rooms and a garden bar. (☎ 2810 288 851. Dorms €8; doubles €24; triples €34.) **Ilaria Hotel ❸,** at Epimenidou and Ariandis, has basic rooms in an ideal location. Walking toward the water on 25 Augustou, make a right onto Epimendou and walk three blocks. (☎ 2810 227 103. Singles €35; doubles €50.) The **open-air market** near Pl. Venizelou has stalls piled high with fruits, vegetables, cheeses, and meats. (Open M-Sa 8am-2pm, Tu and Th-F 5-9pm.) **Prassein Aloga ❷,** Handakos 21, blends a variety of Mediterranean tastes. (Entrees €6-10. Open in summer M-Sa noon-midnight, Su 7pm-midnight; off-season M-Sa noon-4pm and 7pm-midnight.) **Postal Code:** 71001.

⚡ DAYTRIP FROM IRAKLION: KNOSSOS. At Knossos (Κνωσσος), the most famous archaeological site in Crete, excavations have revealed the remains of the largest and most complicated of Crete's **Minoan palaces.** Sir Arthur Evans, who financed and supervised the excavations, eventually restored large parts of the palace in Knossos; his work often crossed the line from preservation to artistic interpretation, but the site is nonetheless impressive. (Open in summer daily 8am-7pm; off-season 8am-5pm. €6, students €3; off-season Su free.) To reach Knossos from Iraklion, take **bus** #2 from 25 Augustou or Pl. Eleftherias (€0.85).

HANIA (Χανια)   ☎ 28210

The **Venetian lighthouse,** an odd tower of stone, guards the entrance to Hania's stunning architectural relic, the **Venetian Inner Harbor.** The inlet has retained its original breakwater and Venetian arsenal, and the Egyptians restored the lighthouse during their occupation of Crete in the late 1830s. Narrow Venetian buildings and Ottoman domes mingle in Hania's lively waterfront area, where a day is best spent sitting or meandering. **Ferries** arrive in the nearby port of Souda; buses connect from the port to Hania's supermarket on Zymvrakakidon (15min., €0.85). **Buses** (☎ 28210 93 306) leave from the station on the corner of Kydonias and Kelaidi for Rethymno (17 per day, €5.55). Turn right on Kidonias then turn left on Pl. 1866 to reach the **tourist office,** Kriairi 40. (☎ 28210 92 624. Open M-F 9am-2pm.) To get to ⊠**Hotel Fidias ❷,** Sarpaki 6, walk toward the harbor on Halidon and turn right onto Athinagora, which then becomes Sarpaki. (☎ 28210 52 494. Singles €12; doubles €12-18.) ⊠**Anaplous ❷** (☎ 28210 41 320), near the harbor on Sifaka, is an open-air bistro serving *pilino*, a pork and lamb creation enjoyed by locals (€23.50, serves three. Other dishes €6-8. Open daily 10am-1am.) **Postal Code:** 73100.

⚡ HIKING NEAR HANIA: SAMARIA GORGE. The most popular excursion from Hania and Iraklion is the 5-6hr. hike down Samaria Gorge (Φαραγγι τησ Σαμαριασ), a spectacular 16km ravine extending through the White Mountains.

GREECE

Sculpted by rainwater over 14 million years, the gorge—the longest in Europe—retains its allure despite having been trampled by thousands of visitors. Rare native plants peek out from sheer rock walls, wild *agrimi* goats clamber about the hills, and golden eagles and endangered griffin vultures circle overhead. (Open May to mid-Oct. daily 6am-6pm. €3, children under 15 and organized student groups free.) For more information, call **Hania Forest Service** (☎28210 92 287). The trail starts at **Xyloskalo;** take the 6:15am or 8:30am **bus** from Hania to Xyloskalo (1½hr., €5) for a day's worth of hiking. The 1:45pm bus from Hania will put you in **Omalos,** ready for the next morning. If you spend the night, rest up at **Gigilos Hotel** ❷ on the main road. (☎28210 67 181. Singles €12-15; doubles €20.) The trail ends in **Agia Roumeli,** on the southern coast, where you can hop on a **boat** to Hora Sfakion (1¼hr., 3-4 per day, €4.40) or take a return bus to Hania (€5.10).

SITIA (Σητεια)   ☎ 28430

Sitia makes a great base for exploring Crete's east coast. Skip the town's own beach and head to the beautiful **Vai Beach** and its palm tree forest, a one-hour bus ride away via Palaikastro (€2). Also near Sitia is the **Valley of Death,** a Minoan burial ground that's great for hiking. The **Minoan Palace** of Kato Zakros rests at the end of the valley. (Open daily 8am-5pm. €3, students and seniors €2.) To reach the valley, take a bus from Sitia via Palaikastro and Zakros (1hr., 2 per day, €3.75.) After midnight, everyone in Sitia heads to **Hot Summer,** 1km down the road to Palaikastro, where a swimming pool replaces the traditional dance floor. **Ferries** leave Sitia for: Athens (16-17hr., 5 per week, €23.50) via Agios Nikolaos (1½hr., €5.60); Karpathos (5hr., 3 per week, €11.20); and Rhodes (12hr., 3 per week, €18.80). From the center of town, head east along the water; the **tourist office** will be on your left. (☎28430 28 300. Open M-F 9:30am-2:30pm and 5:30-8:30pm.) **Venus Rooms to Let** ❷, Kondilaki 60, looks out on scenic views; walk up on Kapetan Sifi from the main *plateia* and turn right after the telephone office. (☎28430 24 307. Doubles €21; triples €25.) ▨**Cretan House** ❶, K. Karamanli 10, off the *plateia,* serves Cretan meals for €4-5. (Open daily 9am-1am.) **Postal Code:** 72300.

EASTERN AEGEAN ISLANDS

The intricate, rocky coastlines and unassuming port towns of the **Northeast Aegean Islands** enclose thickly wooded mountains and unspoiled villages and beaches. Despite their proximity to the Turkish coast and a noticeable military presence, the Northeast Aegean Islands dispense a taste of undiluted Greek culture. **The Dodecanese** are the farthest Greek island group from the mainland. Closer to Asia Minor than to Athens, these islands have experienced more invasions than the central parts of the country—eclectic architecture is the most visible legacy of these comings and goings.

◀ FERRIES TO TURKEY

Ferries run from Samos to Kuşadası (1¼hr., 5 per week, €30); from Chios to Çeşme (45min., 1 per day, €50); and from Kos to Bodrum (1 per day, round-trip €35-40). Citizens of Australia, Canada, Ireland, New Zealand, South Africa, the UK, and the US require a visa to enter Turkey (see p. 1012). Port taxes average €8-10.

SAMOS (Σαμος)   ☎ 22730

Visitors frequently stop in Samos en route to Kuşadası and the ruins of Ephesus on the Turkish coast. Palm trees shade quiet inland streets and red roofs speckle the hillsides of **Vathy (Samos Town),** one of the Aegean's most attractive port cities. The phenomenal ▨**Archaeological Museum** is behind the municipal gardens. (Open Tu-Su 8:30am-3pm. €3, seniors and students €2, EU students free.) The ancient city of **Pythagorion,** once the island's capital, is 14km south of Vathy. Near the town are the magnificent remains of Polykrates's 6th-century BC engineering project, the **Tunnel of Eupalinos,** which diverted water to the city from a natural spring 1.3km away. (Open Tu-Su 8:45am-2:45pm. €4, students €2, EU students free.) Buses go from Samos Town to Pythagorion (20min., €1.10). Polykrates's greatest feat was the **Temple of Hera,** in Heraion, a 30min. bus ride (€1.51) from Pythagorion. (Open Tu-Su 8:30am-3pm. €3, students €2.)

Ferries arrive in Vathy from: Athens (12hr., 1 per day, €22.10); Chios (5hr., 2 per week, €9.30); Mykonos (6hr., 6 per week, €16); Naxos (6hr., 3 per week, €16.70) via Paros (€14.10); and Rhodes (2 per week, €30). The **tourist office** is on a side street a block before Pl. Pythagoras. (☎22730 28 530. Open July-Aug. M-Sa 7am-2:30pm.) **Medousa Hotel ❷,** Sofouli 25, is on the waterfront between the port and Pl. Pythagoras. (☎22730 23 501. Doubles €15-30.) **Postal Code:** 83100.

CHIOS (Χιος) ☎22710

The lack of mass tourism on Chios (HEE-os) seems like an anomaly given its volcanic beaches, cypress-covered hills, and medieval villages. **Pyrgi,** 25km from Chios Town, is one of Greece's most striking villages, with fantastic black-and-white geometric designs covering its buildings. Farther south lies **Emborio** beach, where beige cliffs contrast with the black stones and blue water below. **Buses** run from Chios Town to Pyrgi (5-8 per day, €2.20) and Emborio (4 per day, €2.50). **Ferries** go from Chios Town to: Athens (8hr., 1-2 per day, €19); Mykonos (3 per week, €13); Rhodes (1 per week, €27); Samos (4hr., 3 per week, €10); and Tinos (3 per week, €13.50). To reach the **tourist office,** Kanari 18, turn off the waterfront onto Kanari and walk toward the *plateia.* (☎22710 44 344. Open May-Oct. daily 7am-10pm; Nov.-Mar. M-F 7am-2:30pm.) The hospitable owners at **Chios Rooms ❷,** Leofores 114, offer large rooms with hardwood floors. (☎22710 20 198. Singles €18-22; doubles €23-25, with bath €30; triples with bath €35.) **Postal Code:** 82100.

LESVOS (Λεσβος) ☎22510

Lesvos's cosmopolitan, off-beat culture incorporates horse breeding, ouzo, and leftist politics. Huge, geographically diverse, and far from the mainland, the island attracts visitors who spend weeks exploring its therapeutic hot springs, monasteries, petrified forest, sandy beaches, mountain villages, and seaside cliffs. Most travelers pass through the modern **Mytilini,** the capital and central port city. At the new ▨**Archaeological Museum,** on 8 Noemvriou, visitors can walk on preserved mosaic floors from ancient Mytilini. (Open daily 8am-7pm. €3, students €2, under 18 and EU students free.) Only 4km south of Mytilini along El. Venizelou, the village of **Varia** is home to two excellent museums. **Theophilos Museum** features the work of the neo-primitivist Greek painter Theophilos Hadzimichali. (Open May-Sept. Tu-Su 9am-2:30pm and 6-8pm. €2, students and under 18 free.) **Musée Tériade** displays Picasso, Miró, Chagall, and Matisse lithographs. (Open Tu-Su 9am-2pm and 5-8pm. €2, students and under 18 free.) The artist colonies of **Petra** and **Molyvos** have a quiet charm and more reasonable prices than the capital; take a bus from Mytilini (2hr., 4-5 per day, €4.50). **Eftalou** has beautiful pebble and black sand beaches, accessible by frequent buses from Molyvos.

Ferries go from Mytilini to: Athens (12hr., 1-2 per day, €24); Chios (3hr., 1-2 per day, €11.20); Limnos (5hr., 6 per week, €15); and Thessaloniki (13hr., 1 per week, €12). Book ferries at **NEL Lines,** Pavlou Koudourioti 67 (☎22510 22 220), on the east side of the waterfront. The **tourist police,** on Aristarchou near the ferry docks, offer maps and advice. (☎22510 22 776. Open daily 7:15am-10pm.) Mytilini *doma-*

tia are plentiful and well advertised. Be sure to negotiate; doubles should cost €20-23. ◼**Nassos Guest House ❷**, on the hill just into Molyvos, offers cheerful rooms with balconies. (☎ (22530) 71 432. Doubles €20-28; triples €24-34; discounts for longer stays.) **Postal Code:** 81100.

RHODES (Ροδος)   ☎22140

Although Rhodes is the undisputed tourism capital of the Dodecanese, it has retained a sense of serenity in the sandy beaches along its east coast, the jagged cliffs skirting its west coast, and the green mountains dotted with villages in the interior. The island's most famous sight is one that doesn't exist, the **Colossus of Rhodes**, a 35m bronze statue of Helios and one of the seven wonders of the ancient world. It supposedly straddled the island's harbor until it was destroyed by an earthquake in 237 BC. The **Old Town,** constructed by the Knights of St. John, lends **Rhodes Town** a medieval flair. At the top of the hill, a tall, square tower marks the entrance to the pride of the city, the **Palace of the Grand Master,** which features moats, drawbridges, battlements, and 300 rooms. (Open M 12:30-7pm, Tu-Su 8am-7pm. €6, students €3.) The beautiful halls and courtyards of the **Archaeological Museum,** dominating the **Plateia Argykastrou,** shelter small treasures, including the exquisite *Aphrodite Bathing* from the first-century BC. (Open Tu-Su 8:30am-7pm. €3, students €1.50.) Nightlife in Old Town focuses around **Militadou,** off Apellou. **Orfanidou,** in New Town, is popularly known as **Bar Street.** Fifteen kilometers south of the city, **Faliraki** is frequented by rowdy drinkers and beach bathers. Buses run to Faliraki from Rhodes Town (17 per day, €1.90).

Ferries leave Rhodes Town for: Athens (1-4 per day, €30); Karpathos (3 per week, €15); Kos (1-2 per day, €11); Patmos (1-2 per day, €17.10); Samos (1 per week, €21.10); and Sitia, Crete (3 per week, €19.40). There is a **Greek National Tourist Office (EOT)** up Papgou, a few blocks from Pl. Rimini, at Makariou. The ◼**Rhodes Youth Hostel ❶**, Ergiou 12, has a cool, quiet courtyard. Turn onto Fanouriou from Sokratous and follow the signs. (☎22410 30 491. Free luggage storage. Dorms €7; doubles and triples €20. Sleep on the roof for €5.) **Hotel Andreas ❸**, Omirou 28D, boasts spectacular views of the city. Ask for a room with a private balcony. (☎22410 34 156. Singles and doubles €30-52.) Fresh shellfish is the specialty at ◼**Nireas ❷**, Sophocleous 22, in Old Town. (Entrees €6-8. Open daily 7:30-11pm.)

KOS (Κως)   ☎22420

While the beaches of **Kos Town** draw a young party crowd, rural Kos attracts the traveler in search of serene mountain villages. At the sanctuary of ◼**Asclepion**, 3.5km northwest of Kos Town, Hippocrates opened the world's first medical school in the 5th century BC. In summer, buses (15min.) run there from Kos Town. (Open Tu-Su 8am-6:30pm. €3, students €2.) The island's best beaches stretch along Southern Kos to Kardamene and are all accessible by bus; stops are by request. **Agios Theologos,** south of Limionas, is a pebbly beach perfect for night swimming. Most bars are located in **Exarhia,** in the Old City past Pl. Platonos, or along **Porfirou,** between Averof and Zouroundi. Runway models loom on giant television screens at the **Fashion Club,** Kanari 2, the hottest spot in town. (Cover €8, includes 1 drink.) The **Hamam Club,** inland from the Pl. Diagoras taxi station, is a former bathhouse that is now a dance club. **Heaven,** on Zouroudi, opposite the beach, is a large, popular disco. (Open Su-Th 10am-4am, F-Sa 10am-dawn.)

Ferries run to: Athens (11-15hr., 2-3 per day, €15.30); Patmos (4hr., 1-2 per day, €9.45); and Rhodes (4hr., 2-3 per day, €12.35). The **Greek National Tourist Office (EOT)** is at Vas. Georgiou 1. (☎22420 24 460. Open M-F 8am-8pm, Sa 8am-3pm.) Take the first right off Megalou Alexandrou to get to ◼**Pension Alexis ❷**, Herodotou

9, where the hospitable owners offer their guests every service. (☎22420 28 798. Doubles €18-20; triples €25-30). **Studios Nitsa ❸**, Averof 47, has small rooms with baths and kitchenettes. Take Averof inland from Akit Koundourioti. (☎22420 25 810. Doubles €30; triples €35-45.) **Postal Code:** 85300.

PATMOS (Πατμος)   ☎22470

Given that it has lately become a favorite destination of the rich and famous and that it has also been declared the "Holy Island" by ministerial decree, Patmos has an interesting blend of visitors. The white houses of **Hora** and the majestic walls of the sprawling **Monastery of St. John the Theologian** are visible from all over the island. (Dress modestly. Monastery open daily 8am-1pm; also Tu, Th, Su 4-6pm. Free.) Buses from **Skala**, the port town, run to Hora (10min., 11 per day, €1); alternatively, take a taxi (€3) or tackle the steep hike. The **Apocalypsis Monastery**, between Skala and Hora, is built on the site where St. John stayed while on Patmos. Most visitors come to Patmos to see the **Sacred Grotto of the Revelation**, the cave where St. John dictated the Book of Revelation. (Dress modestly. Open daily 8am-1pm; also T, Th, Su 4-6pm. Free.)

Ferries arrive in Skala from: Athens (10-12hr., 6 per week, €20); Kos (4hr., 2-3 per day, €7.15); Rhodes (9hr., 1 per day, €21); Samos (3 per week, €11); and Thessaloniki (22hr., 1 per week, €37). The **tourist office** is opposite the dock. (☎22470 31 666. Open daily 7am-2:30pm and 4-9pm.) *Domatia* are offered by locals who meet the ferries; expect to pay €15-20 for singles and €20-30 for doubles. To reach **Flower Stefanos Camping at Meloi ❶**, 2km northeast of Skala, follow the waterfront road past Apollon Travel as it wraps along the port. The campground is on the left at the bottom of the hill. (☎22470 31 821. €5 per person.) **To Kyma ❸**, near the campground at Meloi Beach, serves freshly prepared fish. (Fish €20-40 per kg. Open daily noon-midnight.) **Postal Code:** 85500.

GREECE

HUNGARY
(MAGYARORSZÁG)

After 1100 years of repression and renewal, Hungary now appears at ease with its new-found capitalist identity. The country's social and economic keystone may still be Budapest, but travelers who skip the countryside for a whirlwind tour of the capital will miss hills rich with wine valleys to the north, a rough-and-tumble cowboy plain to the south, and a beach resort to the east.

FACTS AND FIGURES

Official Name: Republic of Hungary.

Capital: Budapest.

Major Cities: Eger, Szombathely, Debrecen, Pécs.

Population: 10,000,000 (90% Magyar, 4% Roma, 3% German, 2% Serb).

Land Area: 92,340 sq. km.

Time Zone: GMT +1.

Language: Hungarian (Magyar).

Religions: Roman Catholic (68%), Calvinist (20%), Lutheran (5%), other (7%).

DISCOVER HUNGARY

Budapest (p. 520), Hungary's capital, is quickly being discovered as Central Europe's most cosmopolitan city. Boat down the river to reach the relaxed villages of the **Danube Bend** (p. 531) nearby. In Southern Transdanubia, **Eger** (p. 533) is home to one of Hungary's most important castles, and the vibrant wine cellars of the Valley of the Beautiful Women are a stone's throw away. Don't miss charming **Győr** (p. 535), which overflows with cultural treasures, and the nearby **Archabbey of Pannonhalma** (p. 535). **Lake Balaton** (p. 536), the Hungarian summer capital, hosts a kitschy beach scene. **Keszthely** (p. 537), on the lake's western end, has a stunning palace and provides an escape from the thonged throngs of **Siófok** (p. 536).

ESSENTIALS

WHEN TO GO

Temperatures are most pleasant from May to September. Because Budapest never feels crowded, even in the high season, time your visit to coincide with some of the summer festivals. Fall and spring, though a bit chillier, can be quite nice as well. Avoid visiting in winter, as it tends to get very cold.

DOCUMENTS AND FORMALITIES

VISAS. Citizens of Canada, Ireland, South Africa, the UK, and the US can visit without visas for 90 days, provided their passport does not expire within six months of their journey's end. Australians and New Zealanders must obtain 90-day tourist visas from a Hungarian embassy or consulate. Visas cost: single-entry US$40, €65; double-entry US$75, €100; multiple-entry US$180, €200; and 48hr. transit US$38, €50. Border officials are generally quite efficient; there is no border fee. Visa extensions are rare; apply at a Hungarian police station.

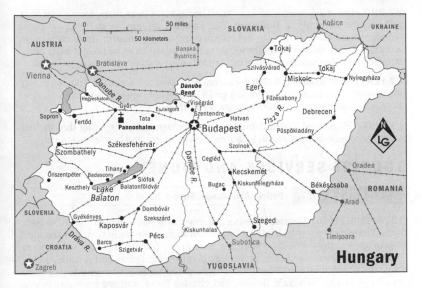

EMBASSIES. All foreign embassies in Hungary are in Budapest (see p. 520). Hungarian embassies at home include: **Australia,** 17 Beale Crescent, Deakin, ACT 2600 (☎02 6282 2226; www.matra.com.au/~hungemb); **Canada,** 299 Waverley St., Ottawa, ON K2P 0V9 (☎613-230-2717; www.docuweb.ca/Hungary); **Ireland,** 2 Fitzwilliam Pl., Dublin 2 (☎01 661 2903; fax 01 661 2880); **New Zealand,** 151 Orangi Kaupapa Rd., Wellington, 6005 (☎644 938 0427; www.geocities.com/hu-consul-nz); **South Africa,** 959 Arcadia St., Hatfield, Arcadia; P.O. Box 27077, Sunnyside 0132 (☎012 430 3020; hunem@cis.co.za); **UK,** 35B Eaton Pl., London SW1X 8BY (☎020 7235 5218; www.huemblon.org.uk); and **US,** 3910 Shoemaker St. NW, Washington, D.C. 20008 (☎202-362-6730; www.hungaryemb.org).

TRANSPORTATION

BY PLANE. Several international airlines fly into Budapest (BUD); the national airline, **Malév** (www.malev.hu), has daily direct flights from New York and London.

BY TRAIN. Most trains *(vonat)*, which are generally reliable and cheap, pass through Budapest; be cautious of theft on the Vienna-Budapest line. Book international tickets in advance. Consult www.elvira.hu for schedules and fares. **Eurail** is valid in Hungary. Students and those under 26 may be eligible for a 30% discount on train fares; ask ahead and be persistent. An **ISIC** card gets discounts at IBUSZ, Express, and station ticket counters. Flash your card and repeat *"diák"* (DEE-ahk; student). *Személyvonat* trains are slow; *gyorsvonat* (listed on schedules in red) cost the same and are twice as fast. Large towns are accessible by the blue *expressz* lines. Air-conditioned *InterCity* trains are fastest. A seat reservation *(potegy)* is required for trains labeled "R." While you can board an *InterCity* train without a reservation, the fine for doing so is 1000Ft, and purchasing the reservation on board will double the price of the ticket. Some basic vocabulary words are: *érkezés* (arrival), *indulás* (departure), *vágány* (track), *állomás* or *pályaudvar* (station, abbreviated *pu.*), and *peron* (platform).

BY BUS. The cheap, clean, and crowded bus system links many towns that have rail connections only to Budapest. The **Erzsébet tér** station in Budapest posts schedules and fares. *InterCity* tickets are purchased on board; arrive early to get a seat. In larger cities, tickets for local transportation must be bought from newsstands; punch the ticket on board or face a fine. In smaller cities, pay on board.

BY FERRY. The **Danube hydrofoil** goes from Budapest to Vienna via Bratislava; contact Interticket Hungary in the US (☎ 781-275-5724; www.interticket.com) or MAHART Tours International in Hungary (☎ (01) 318 92 61).

BY BIKE. IBUSZ and Tourinform provide brochures about cycling that include maps, accommodations, rental locations, repair shops, and border crossings.

TOURIST SERVICES AND MONEY

EMERGENCY	Police, Ambulance, Fire: ☎ 112.

TOURIST OFFICES. Tourist bureaus are generally open in summer M-Sa 8am-8pm. **Tourinform** (www.tourinform.hu) has branches everywhere and is the most useful agency; they should be your first stop in any town. They can't book rooms, but they will check on vacancies, usually in university dorms and private *panzió*. Most **IBUSZ** offices (www.ibusz.hu) throughout the country arrange private rooms, exchange money, sell train tickets, and charter tours, and are generally best at helping with travel plans. The pamphlet *Tourist Information: Hungary* and the monthly entertainment guides *Programme in Hungary* and *Budapest Panorama* are all free and in English. **Express** (www.expresstravel.hu) handles lodgings and changes money. In outlying areas, regional agencies are the most helpful.

MONEY. The **forint** (Ft) is divided into 100 *fillérs*, which are quickly disappearing from circulation. Inflation is currently around 15%, so expect prices to increase over the next year. The maximum legal commission for cash-to-cash exchange is 1%. Never change money on the street. Currency exchange machines have excellent rates, but tend to be slow. **OTP Bank** and **Postabank** offices have the best rates for exchanging traveler's checks. **Credit cards** are accepted at expensive hotels and shops. A basic day in Hungary will run about €25. Rounding up the bill as a **tip** is standard etiquette. In restaurants, hand the tip to the server when you pay; it's rude to leave it on the table. Foreigners are expected to tip 15%, although locals never give more than 10%. Bathroom attendants get 30Ft.

FORINTS		
AUS$1 = 138FT	100FT = AUS$0.73	
CDN$1 = 160FT	100FT = CDN$0.63	
EUR€1 = 245FT	100FT = EUR€0.41	
NZ$1 = 117FT	100FT = NZ$0.86	
ZAR1 = 24FT	100FT = ZAR4.27	
UK£1 = 386FT	100FT = UK£0.26	
US$1 = 249FT	100FT = US$0.40	

COMMUNICATION

MAIL. The Hungarian mail system is somewhat reliable; airmail *(légiposta)* takes 5-10 days to the US and the rest of Europe, and two weeks to Australia, New Zealand, and South Africa. Postage costs around 25-35Ft for domestic mail and

110-220Ft for international. If you're mailing to a Hungarian citizen, the family name precedes the given name. For *Poste Restante*, address mail to be held: SUR-NAME Firstname, *Poste Restante*, Városház u. 18, 1052 Budapest, HUNGARY.

TELEPHONES. For intercity calls, wait for the tone and dial slowly; enter ☎06 before the phone code. International calls require red phones or new, digital-display blue phones, which unfortunately tend to cut you off after three to nine minutes. Phones often require phone cards *(telefonkártya)*, available at kiosks, train stations, and post offices (800Ft or 1600Ft). Direct calls can also be made from Budapest's phone office. To call collect, dial ☎190 for the international operator. To reach international carriers, insert a 10Ft and a 20Ft coin, dial ☎06, wait for the second tone, then dial the international direct dialing number: **AT&T,** ☎ 800 011 11; **British Telecom,** ☎ 800 044 11; **Canada Direct,** ☎ 800 012 11; and **MCI,** ☎800 014 11.

PHONE CODE	**Country code: 36. International dialing prefix: 00.** From outside Hungary, dial int'l dialing prefix (see inside back cover) + 36 + city code + local number.

INTERNET. Internet is available throughout the country; access is usually 500-700Ft per hr. The Hungarian keyboard differs significantly from English-language keyboards. When you first log on, go to the lower right-hand corner of the screen and look for the *"Hu"* icon; click here to switch the keyboard setting to *"Angol."*

LANGUAGES. Hungarian, a Finno-Ugric language, is related distantly to Turkish, Estonian, and Finnish. After Hungarian and German, English is the most commonly spoken language. For Hungarian basics, see p. 1059.

ACCOMMODATIONS AND CAMPING

HUNGARY	❶	❷	❸	❹	❺
ACCOMMODATIONS	under 1000Ft	1001-3000Ft	3001-6000Ft	6001-10,000Ft	over 10,000Ft

Many travelers stay in **private homes** booked through tourist agencies, who may try to foist their most expensive rooms on you. Singles are scarce—it's worth finding a roommate, as solo travelers often pay for a double room. Outside Budapest, the best offices are region-specific (e.g. EgerTourist in Eger). After staying a few nights, you can make arrangements directly with the owner, thus saving yourself the agencies' 20-30% commissions. **Panzió** (pensions), run out of private homes, are also common, although not always cheapest. **Hotels** exist in some towns, but most have disappeared. **Hostelling** is becoming more attractive, although it is rare outside Budapest; HI cards are increasingly useful. Many hostels can be booked through Express, the student travel agency, or through a regional tourist office. From June to August, **university dorms** become hostels; inquire at Tourinform. More than 300 **campgrounds** throughout Hungary are open from May to September. Tourist offices offer the annual booklet *Camping Hungary* for free. For more information and maps, contact Tourinform in Budapest (see p. 521).

FOOD AND DRINK

HUNGARY	❶	❷	❸	❹	❺
FOOD	under 400Ft	401-800Ft	801-1300Ft	1301-2800Ft	over 2800Ft

Hungarian food is more flavorful and varied than standard Eastern European fare. Paprika, Hungary's chief agricultural export, colors most dishes red. In Hungarian restaurants *(vendéglő* or *étterem)*, begin you meal with *halászlé*, a deliciously spicy fish stew. Alternatively, try *gyümölcsleves*, a cold fruit soup topped with whipped cream. The Hungarian national dish is *bográcsgulyás* (goulash), a beef stew with dumplings and paprika. *Borjúpaprikás* is veal with paprika and potato-dumpling pasta. Vegetarians can find recourse in the tasty *rántott sajt* (fried cheese) and *gombapörkölt* (mushroom stew) on most menus. In a *cukrászda* (confectionery), you can satisfy your sweet tooth cheaply. *Túrós rétes* is a chewy pastry pocket filled with sweetened cottage cheese. *Somlói galuska* is a rich, rum-soaked sponge cake of chocolate, nuts, and cream. *Unicum*, advertised as the national drink, is a fine herbal liqueur that Habsburg kings used to cure digestive ailments. Hungary also produces a diverse array of fine wines.

HEALTH AND SAFETY

Medical assistance is most easily obtained in Budapest, where most hospitals have English-speaking doctors available; embassies carry a list of Anglophone doctors. Outside Budapest, try to bring a Hungarian speaker with you. **Tourist insurance** is valid—and often necessary—for many medical services. Tap water is usually clean and drinkable. Public toilets vary in cleanliness: pack toilet paper, soap, and a towel, and be prepared to pay the attendant 30Ft. Men's rooms are labeled *Férfi*, and women's *Női*. *Gyógyszertár* (pharmacies) are well-stocked with Western brands and always carry tampons and condoms. In bigger towns, there are usually 24hr. pharmacies. Violent crime in Hungary is low, but in larger cities, especially Budapest, foreign tourists are favorite targets of petty thieves and pickpockets. Although **homosexuality** is legal, travelers may experience serious discrimination, especially outside of Budapest—discretion is wise.

HOLIDAYS AND FESTIVALS

Holidays: National Day (Mar. 15); Easter (Apr. 20-21); Labor Day (May 1); Pentecost (June 8); Constitution Day (Aug. 20); Republic Day (Aug. 23); Christmas (Dec. 25-26).

Festivals: Hotels and tourist offices have English-language guides to Budapest's many summer festivals (see p. 529). Eger celebrates its local wine in the **Bull's Blood Festival** (early July) and fills with opera during the **Baroque Festival** (late July to mid-Aug).

BUDAPEST ☎ 1

Ten times larger than any other Hungarian city, Budapest is reassuming its place as a major European capital. Originally two separate cities, Budapest was created in 1872 with the joining of Buda and Pest, soon becoming the most important Habsburg city after Vienna. World War II ravaged the city, but the Hungarians rebuilt it from rubble with the same pride they retained while weathering the Soviet occupation. Neon lights and legions of tourists may draw attention away from the city's cultural and architectural gems—but beneath it all beats a truly Hungarian heart.

▐ TRANSPORTATION

Flights: Ferihegy Airport (BUD; ☎ 296 96 96). **Malév** (Hungarian Airlines) flight reservations ☎ 296 72 11 and 296 78 31. The cheapest way to reach the city center is to take the **BKV Plusz Reptér Busz** (20min.; every 15min. 4:55am-11:20pm; 106Ft), followed by the M3 at Kőbanya-Kispest (15min. to Deák tér in downtown Pest).

Trains: There are 3 main stations *(pályaudvar)*: Keleti pu., Nyugati pu., and Déli pu. (☎ 461 55 00; www.mav.hu). Most international trains arrive at **Keleti Pályaudvar,** but some from Prague go to Nyugati pu. Each station has schedules for the others. To: **Berlin** (12hr., 1 per day, 22,900Ft; night train 15hr., 1 per day, 36,400Ft); **Bucharest** (14hr., 7 per day, 17,400Ft); **Prague** (8hr., 4 per day, 14,000Ft; night train 9hr., 1 per day, 14,000Ft); **Vienna** (3hr., 17 per day, 7000Ft); **Warsaw** (11hr., 2 per day, 13,950Ft). Reservation fees 700-2000Ft. The daily **Orient Express** stops on its way from Paris to İstanbul. Prices vary widely. Purchase train tickets at the **International Ticket Office**, Keleti pu. (Open daily 8am-6pm); or **MÁV Hungarian Railways**, VI, Andrássy út 35 (☎/fax 322 84 05); and at all stations. Open M-F 9am-5pm. For student or under 26 discount on tickets, indicate *diák* (student).

Buses: ☎ 117 29 66. Most buses to Western Europe leave from **Volánbusz main station**, V, Erzsébet tér (international ticket office ☎ 485 21 00, ext. 211). M1-3: Deák tér. Open M-F 6am-6pm, Sa 6:30am-4pm. Buses to much of Eastern Europe depart from **Népstadion**, Hungária körút 48/52 (☎ 252 18 96). M2: Népstadion. To: **Berlin** (14½hr., 5 per week, 19,900Ft); **Prague** (8hr., 4 per week, 6990Ft); **Vienna** (3-3½hr., 5 per day, 5790Ft). **Domestic buses** are cheap but slower than trains.

Commuter Trains: The **HÉV commuter railway** station is at Batthyány tér. Trains head north through Óbuda to **Szentendre** (40min., every 15min. 5am-9pm, 268Ft). Purchase tickets at the station for transport beyond Budapest city limits.

Public Transportation: Subways, buses, and **trams** are cheap, convenient, and easy to navigate. The **Metro** has three lines: yellow (M1), red (M2), and blue (M3). Pick up free **route maps** from hostels, tourist offices, and train stations. Night transit ("É") runs midnight-5am along major routes; buses #7É and 78É follow the M2 route, #6É follows the 4/6 tram line, and #14É and 50É follow the M3 route. **Single-fare tickets** for all public transport (one-way on one line 106Ft) are sold in Metro stations, in *Trafik* shops, and by some sidewalk vendors. Punch them in the orange boxes at the gate of the Metro or on buses and trams; punch a new ticket when you change lines, or face a 1500-3000Ft fine. **Day pass** 850Ft; **3-day** 1750Ft; **1-week** 2100Ft.

Taxis: Beware of scams; check that the meter is on, and inquire about the rates. **Budataxi** (☎ 233 33 33) charges 135Ft per km if you call. **Főtaxi** (☎ 222 22 22), **6x6 Taxi** (☎ 266 66 66), and **Tele 5 Taxi** (☎ 355 55 55) are also reliable.

ORIENTATION

Originally Buda and Pest, two cities separated by the **Duna River** (Danube), modern Budapest preserves the distinctive character of each. On the west bank, **Buda** has winding streets, breathtaking vistas, a hilltop citadel, and the Castle District. On the east bank is the city's bustling commercial center, **Pest**, home to shopping boulevards, theaters, Parliament (Országház), and the Opera House. Three main bridges join the two halves: **Széchenyi Lánchíd**, slender **Erzsébet híd**, and green **Szabadság híd**. Just down the north slope of Várhegy (Castle Hill) is **Moszkva tér**, the tram and local bus hub. **Batthyány tér**, opposite Parliament in Buda, is the starting point of the HÉV commuter railway. They city's Metro lines converge at **Deák tér**, next to the main international bus terminal at **Erzsébet tér**. Two blocks west toward the river lies **Vörösmarty tér** and the main pedestrian shopping zone **Váci utca.**

Addresses in Budapest begin with a Roman numeral representing one of the city's 23 **districts**. Central Buda is I; central Pest is V. To navigate Budapest's often-confusing streets, an up-to-date **map** is essential. The American Express and Tourinform offices have good free tourist maps, as do most hostels and hotels.

PRACTICAL INFORMATION

TOURIST AND FINANCIAL SERVICES

Tourist Offices: All sell the **Budapest Card** (Budapest Kártya), which provides discounts, unlimited public transport, and museum admission (2-day 3700Ft, 3-day 4500Ft). Your first stop should be **Tourinform**, V, Vigadó u. 6 (☎ 235 44 81; www.hungarytourism.hu).

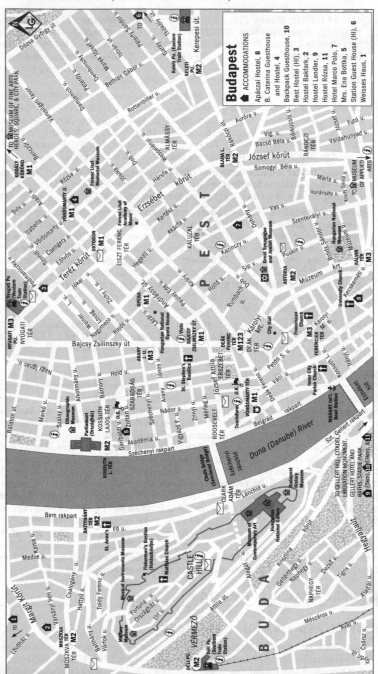

Budapest

ACCOMMODATIONS

Apáczai Hostel, **8**
B. Caterina Guesthouse
and Hostel, **4**
Backpack Guesthouse, **10**
Best Hostel (HI), **3**
Hostel Bakfark, **2**
Hostel Landler, **9**
Hostel Rózsa, **11**
Hotel Marco Polo, **7**
Mrs. Ena Bottka, **5**
Station Guest House (HI), **6**
Weisses Haus, **1**

M1: Vörösmarty tér. Walk toward the river from the Metro. Open 24hr. **Vista Travel Center**, Paulay Ede 7 (☎429 99 50; www.vista.hu). M1-3: Deák tér; exit on Bajcsy-Zsilinszky út. The multilingual staff arranges lodgings and books transportation tickets. Open M-F 9am-6:30pm, Sa 9am-2:30pm. ▓ **Budapest in Your Pocket** (www.inyourpocket.com; 750Ft) is a great resource, with maps and reviews.

Embassies: Australia, XII, Királyhágo tér 8/9 (☎457 97 77; www.ausembbp.hu). M2: Déli pu., then bus #21 or tram #59 to Királyhágo tér. Open M-F 9am-noon. **Canada,** XII, Budakeszi út 32 (☎392 33 60; www.canadaeuropa.gc.ca/hungary), entrance at Zugligeti út. 51-53. Take bus #158 from Moszkva tér to the last stop. Open M-F 8:30-11am and 2-3:30pm. **South Africa,** II, Gárdonyi Géza út 17 (☎392 09 99; emergency ☎(0620) 955 80 46; www.sa-embassy.hu). **UK,** V, Harmincad u. 6 (☎266 28 88), near the intersection with Vörösmarty tér. M1: Vörösmarty tér. Open M-F 9:30am-noon and 2:30-4pm. **US,** V, Szabadság tér 12 (☎475 44 00; emergency ☎475 47 03; www.usis.hu). M2: Kossuth tér. Walk 2 blocks down Akademia and turn on Zoltán. Open M-F 8:15am-5pm. **New Zealand** and **Irish** nationals should contact the UK embassy.

Currency Exchange: The best rates are in **ATMs** and banks. **Citibank,** V, Vörösmarty tér 4 (☎374 50 00). M1: Vörösmarty tér. Cashes traveler's checks for no commission and provides MC/V cash advances (passport required).

American Express: V, Deák Ferenc u. 10 (☎235 43 30; travel@amex.hu). M2, 3: Deák tér. Open M-F 9am-5:30pm, Sa 9am-2pm.

LOCAL SERVICES

Luggage storage: Lockers at all three train stations. 140-300Ft.

English-Language Bookstore: Bestsellers KFT, V, Október 6 u. 11 (☎312 12 95; www.bestsellers.hu), near the intersection with Arany János u. M1-3: Deák tér, or M3: Arany János u. Open M-F 9am-6:30pm, Sa 10am-5pm, Su 10am-4pm.

Bi-Gay-Lesbian Resources: GayGuide.net Budapest (☎(0630) 932 33 34; www.gayguide.net/europe/hungary/budapest), maintains a comprehensive website and runs a hotline (daily 4-8pm) with info for gay tourists and gay-friendly lodging lists.

EMERGENCY AND COMMUNICATIONS

Emergency: ☎112 connects to all. **Police:** ☎107. **Ambulance:** ☎04. **Fire:** ☎105.

Tourist Police: V, Vigadó u. 6 (☎235 44 79). M1: Vörösmarty tér. Walk toward the river from the Metro to reach the station, just inside Tourinform. Open 24hr.

24hr. Pharmacies: II, Frankel Leó út 22 (☎212 44 06); III, Szentendrei út 2/A (☎388 65 28); IV, Pozsonyi u. 19 (☎389 40 79); VI, Teréz krt. 41 (☎311 44 39); VII, Rákóczi út 39 (☎314 36 95). At night, call number on door or ring the bell.

Medical Assistance: Falck (SOS) KFT, II, Kapy út 49/B (☎200 01 00 and 275 15 35). Open 24hr. The US embassy (see Embassies, above) lists English-speaking doctors.

Telephones: Most phones require **phone cards,** available at newsstands, post offices, and Metro stations. 50-unit card 800Ft, 120-unit card 1800Ft. Use card phones for **international calls;** they cut you off after 20min., but are better than coin phones. Domestic operator ☎191; domestic information ☎198; international operator ☎190.

Internet Access: Cybercafes are everywhere, but access can get expensive and long waits are common. Try a wired hostel. **Ami Internet Coffee,** V, Váci u. 40 (☎267 16 44; www.amicoffee.hu). M3: Ferenciek tere. 200Ft for 10min., 400Ft for 30min., 700Ft per hr. Open daily 9am-10pm. **Eckermann,** VI, Andrássy út 24 (☎269 25 42). M1: Opera. Free. Call a week ahead in summer. Open M-F 8am-10pm, Sa 9am-10pm.

Post Office: V, Városház u. 18 (☎318 48 11). Open M-F 8am-8pm, Sa 8am-2pm. Address mail to be held: SURNAME First name, *Poste Restante,* V, Városház u. 18, **1052** Budapest, Hungary. **Branches** include: Nyugati pu.; VI, Teréz krt. 105/107 and Keleti pu.; and VIII, Baross tér 11/C. Open M-F 8am-9pm, Sa 8am-2pm.

HUNGARY

⚡ ACCOMMODATIONS AND CAMPING

Call ahead in summer, or save yourself blisters by storing your pack while you seek out a bed for the night. Travelers arriving at Keleti pu. will be swarmed with hawkers; be cautious and don't believe all promises of free rides or special discounts, but keep an open mind if you need a place to stay. For those who are willing to spend more, there are plenty of Western chain hotels.

ACCOMMODATION AGENCIES

Private rooms, slightly more expensive than hostels (3000-7500Ft per person, depending on location and bathroom quality), usually offer what hostels can't: peace, quiet, and private showers. Arrive early, bring cash, and haggle.

Budapest Tourist, I, Deli Pályaudvar (☎/fax 212 46 25). M2: Déli pu. Well-established. Singles in Central Pest 5000-7000Ft; doubles 6000-10,000Ft; triples 6000-12,000Ft. Off-season prices lower. Open M-F 9am-5pm. ❸

IBUSZ, V, Ferenciek tere (☎485 27 67 or 485 27 69; accomodations@ibusz.hu). M3: Ferenciek tere. Doubles 5000Ft; triples 5000-6000Ft. 1800Ft surcharge if staying fewer than 4 nights. Open M-Th 8:15am-4pm, F 8:15am-3pm. ❸

Non-Stop Hotel Service, V, Apáczai Csere J. u. 1 (☎266 80 42; tribus.hotel.service@mail.datanet.hu). M1-3: Deák tér. Singles, doubles, triples, and quads vary greatly in price, starting at 6000Ft. Open 24hr. ❹

YEAR-ROUND HOSTELS

Hostels act as social centers, with no curfews and beer- and music-filled common rooms that rival the city's bars and clubs. Most belong to the Hungarian Youth Hostels Association, whose representatives wear HI t-shirts. Although they are legitimate, don't rule out more convenient independent hostels or guesthouses. Unless otherwise noted, all hostels have luggage storage, kitchens, and TV.

⬛ Backpack Guesthouse, XI, Takács Menyhért u. 33 (☎/fax 385 89 46; www.backpackbudapest.hu), in Buda, 12min. from central Pest. From Keleti pu., take bus #7 or 7A toward Buda; get off at Tétenyi u. (5 stops past the river), walk back under the railway bridge, turn left at Hamzsabégi út., and go down the 3rd street on the right. Bathrooms are busy but clean. Superb CD and video collections. Internet 15Ft per min. Reception 24hr. Reserve ahead. Dorms 2300Ft; doubles 5600Ft. ❷

⬛ Hotel Marco Polo, VII, Nyár u. 6 (☎413 25 55; www.hotelmarcopolo.com), in Pest. M2: Astoria or M2: Blaha Lujza tér. Newly renovated, luxurious, and spotless. Internet 500Ft per 20min. Reception 24hr. Book 1-2 weeks in advance in summer. Dorms 4700Ft; singles 13,000Ft; doubles 17,000Ft. 10% HI and ISIC discount. ❸

Station Guest House (HI), XIV, Mexikói út 36/B (☎221 88 64; station@matavnet.hu; www.stationguesthouse.hu), in Pest. From Keleti pu., take bus #7 or night bus #78É 4 stops to Hungária Körút, walk under the railway pass, and take an immediate right on Mexikói út. Free billiards, live music, and a friendly staff. Internet 20Ft per min. Reserve ahead or end up in the attic. Attic 1700Ft; dorms 2200Ft; doubles 6000Ft; triples 9000Ft. All prices drop 100Ft with each night you stay, up to 5 nights. ❷

Best Hostel (HI), VI, Podmaniczky u. 27, 1st fl. (☎332 49 34; www.besthostel.hu), in Pest. Ring bell 33 in building across from Nyugati pu. Quiet, with spacious dorms. Common room and kitchen close nightly at 11pm. Breakfast included. Internet 10Ft per min. Dorms 2800Ft; doubles 8000Ft. 10% HI discount. ❷

SUMMER HOSTELS

Many university dorms, mostly near Móricz Zsigmond Körtér in District XI, act as hostels in July and August. They usually have kitchens, luggage storage, and a common room TV, and tend to be quieter than year-round hostels. Many summer hostels are run by the same companies, so they can easily find open beds.

Hostel Bakfark, I, Bakfark u. 1/3 (☎329 86 44), in Buda. M2: Moszkva tér. Comfortable dorms with lofts instead of bunks. Sparkling showers. Check-out 10am. Call ahead. Open mid-June to late-Aug. Dorms 3300Ft; 10% HI discount. ❸

Apáczai Hostel, V, Papnövelde 4/6 (☎267 03 11), in Pest. Great location, clean rooms, and a warm, friendly staff. Open late-June to mid-Aug. Dorms 3600Ft; doubles 4300Ft. 10% HI discount. ❸

Hostel Landler, XI, Bartók Béla út 17 (☎463 36 21), in Buda. Take bus #7 or 7A across the river and get off at Géllert; take Bartók Béla út away from the river. Comfy dorms. Free ride from the bus or train station. Check-out 9am. Open July 5-Sept. 5. Singles 5850Ft; doubles, triples, and quads 3900Ft per person. 10% HI discount. ❸

Hostel Rózsa, XI, Bercsényi u. 28/30 (☎463 42 50), in Buda. M2: Blaha Lujza tér or M3: Nyugati pu. Take tram #4 south toward Blaha Lujza tér to Buda; get off at the last stop, backtrack one block, then go left on Bercsényi ul. Clean (but curtainless) showers. Open July-Sept. Singles 5750Ft; doubles 7800Ft. 10% HI discount. ❸

GUESTHOUSES

Guesthouses and private rooms add a personal touch for about the same price as hostels. Owners will usually pick travelers up from the train station or airport.

Mrs. Ena Bottka, V, Garibaldi u. 5 (☎/fax 302 34 56; garibaldiguest@hotmail.com). M2: Kossuth tér. Charming Ena lets spacious rooms in her apartment and other suites in the building, some with kitchenette, TV, showers, and towels. Rooms from 3500Ft per person; apartments 6000-10,000Ft. All prices decrease with longer stays. ❸

B. Caterina Guesthouse and Hostel, VI, Andrássy út 47, 3rd fl., apt. #18, in Pest; ring bell #11. (☎342 08 04; caterina@mail.inext.hu). M1: Oktogon; or trams #4 and 6. Across from Burger King. Grandmother-style house—no curfew, but quiet after 10pm. Free Internet. Reception 24hr. Check-out 9am. Lockout 10am-2pm. Reserve by email. Dorms 2400Ft; doubles 2900Ft; triples 3500Ft. ❷

Weisses Haus, III, Erdőalja út 11 (☎/fax 387 82 36). M3: Árpád híd. Take tram #1 (dir.: Béci ut.) to Florian tér, then bus #137 to Iskola. A family-owned villa in a nice neighborhood 30min. from the city center. Some English spoken. No curfew, but bus #137 stops running at 11:30pm. Doubles US$30, off-season $20. ❹

CAMPING

For a full listing, pick up the pamphlet *Camping Hungary* at tourist offices.

Zugligeti "Niche" Camping, XII, Zugligeti út 101 (☎/fax 200 83 46; camping.niche@matavnet.hu). Take bus #158 from Moszkva tér to Laszállóhely, the last stop. Communal showers, a safe, and an on-site restaurant. Electricity 450Ft. 850Ft per person, 500-900Ft per tent, 700Ft per car. ❶

Római Camping, III, Szentendrei út 189 (☎368 62 60). M2: Batthyány tér. Take HÉV to Római fürdő; walk 100m toward river. Huge site with swimming pool (300Ft). Tents 1990Ft; bungalow 1690-15,000Ft. 3% tourist tax. 10% HI discount. ❷

▯ FOOD

Restaurants abound in Pest; the newest trendy area to dine is **Radáy út.** Food at family joints (*kifőzés* or *vendéglő*) is often tastier than in big restaurants. **Non-Stop** corner markets stock the basics. The ▨**Grand Market Hall,** IX, Fövam tér 1/3, next to Szabadság híd (M3: Kálvin Tér), is a tourist attraction in itself.

RESTAURANTS

▨ **Gandhi,** V, Vigyázó Ferenc u. 4, in Pest. New menu daily at this superior veggie eatery. Herbal teas and wheat beers. Main dishes 980-1680Ft. Open M-Sa noon-10:30pm. ❸

🍴 **Gundel,** XIV, Állatkerti út 2 (☎468 40 40), behind the Museum of Fine Arts. M1: Hősök tere. Hungary's most highly regarded restaurant. Seven-course dinners 13,000-17,500Ft; Su brunch buffet 3900Ft; cafe sandwiches 400-600Ft. Reservation only; jackets required in the evening. Open daily noon-4pm and 6:30pm-midnight. Bar open daily 9am-midnight. Su brunch 11:30am-3pm. ❺

Marquis de Salade, VI, Hajós u. 43, in Pest. M3: Arany János. Corner of Bajscy-Zsilinszky út. Subterranean dining rooms with huge international menu. Main dishes 1300-2300Ft. Open daily 11am-1am. ❹

Fatâl Restaurant, V, Váci u. 67 (☎266 26 07), in Pest. M3: Ferenciek tere or M3: Kálvin tér. Extremely popular. Large and hearty Hungarian meals. Giant, carefully garnished main courses 1070-2790Ft. Reservations only. Open daily 11am-2am. ❹

Robinson Mediterranean-Style Restaurant and Café, Városligeti tó. A spectacular, scenic view on City Park Lake. Veggie options. Main dishes 2300-6000Ft. Open daily noon-4pm and 6pm-midnight. ❹

Söröző a Szent Jupáthoz, II, Retek u. 16, in Buda. M2: Moszkva tér. Huge Hungarian menu and huge Hungarian portions. Main dishes 1090-2590Ft. Open 24hr. ❸

CAFES

Once the haunts of the literary, intellectual, and cultural elite—as well as political dissidents—the city's cafes boast histories as rich as the pastries they serve today.

Gerbeaud, V, Vörösmarty tér 7. M1: Vörösmarty tér. This cafe has been serving its signature layer cakes (520Ft) and homemade ice cream (95Ft) since 1858. The terrace dominates the northern end of Vörösmarty tér. Open daily 9am-9pm.

Művész Kávéház, VI, Andrássy út 29. M1: Opera. Across from the Opera. A crowd of mostly artsy people lounges around polished stone tables. Enjoy a cappuccino (260Ft) on the terrace. Open daily 9am-midnight.

Ruszwurm, I, Szentháromság u. 7, just off the square on Várhegy in the Castle District. This tiny cafe has been making sweets ever since it started catering to Habsburg tastes in 1827. Pastries and cake 120-220Ft. Open daily 10am-7pm.

🎯 SIGHTS

In 1896, Hungary's millennium celebration prompted the construction of what are today Budapest's most prominent sights. Among the works commissioned by the Habsburgs were **Heroes' Square** (Hősök tér), **Liberty Bridge** (Szbadság híd), **Vajdahunyad Castle** (Vajdahunyad vár), and continental Europe's first subway system. The domes of **Parliament** (Országház) and **St. Stephen's Basilica** (Szent István Bazilika) are both 96m high—vertical references to the historic date. Slightly grayer for wear, war, and Communist occupation, these monuments attest to the optimism of a capital at the peak of its Golden Age. **Absolute Walking & Biking Tours** (☎211 88 61; www.budapestours.com) meets on the steps of the yellow church in Deák tér (mid-May to Sept. daily 9:30am and 1:30pm; 3500Ft, under 26 3000Ft) and at Heroes' Square (daily 10am and 2pm).

BUDA

On the east bank of the Danube, **Buda** sprawls between the base of **Castle Hill** and southern **Gellért Hill,** rambling into Budapest's main residential areas. Older than Pest, Buda is filled with parks, lush hills, and islands.

CASTLE DISTRICT. Towering above the Danube on Castle Hill, the Castle District has been razed three times in its 800-year history, most recently in 1945. With its winding, statue-filled streets, breathtaking views, and hodge-podge of architectural styles, the UNESCO-protected district now appears much as it did in Habsburg times. Although the reconstructed **Buda Castle** *(vár)* now houses a number of fine museums (see p. 528), bullet holes in the palace facade still recall the 1956 Uprising. *(M2: Moszkva tér. Walk up to the hill on Várfok u. and enter at Vienna Gate (Becsi kapu). Alternatively, from Deák tér, take bus #16 across the Danube and get off at the base of the Széchenyi Chain Bridge. Take the funicular (sikló) up the hill. (Runs daily 9:30am-5:30pm; closed 2nd and 4th M of the month; 400Ft.) The upper lift station sits inside the castle walls near the National Gallery.)* Beneath Buda castle are the **Budvári Labirinths,** caverns that allow for spooky trips through the subterranean world of the city. *(Úri u. 9. ☎212 02 07. Open daily 9:30am-7:30pm. 900Ft, students 700Ft.)*

MATTHIAS CHURCH AND FISHERMAN'S BASTION. The multi-colored roof of Matthias Church (Mátyás templom) is one of Budapest's most popular sights. The church was converted into a mosque when Ottoman armies seized Buda in 1541, then reconverted 145 years later when the Habsburgs defeated the Turks. Ascend the spiral staircase to reach the gold-heavy exhibits of the **Museum of Ecclesiastical Art.** *(On Castle Hill. Open M-Sa 9am-5pm, Su 1pm-5pm. 600Ft, students 300Ft. High mass 7am, 8:30am, 6pm; Su also 10am and noon. Free. Concerts W and F 7:30pm. Free.)* Behind Matthias Church is the **Fisherman's Bastion** (Halászbástya), and an equestrian monument of King Stephen bearing his trademark double cross. The view across the Danube from the Bastion's fairy-tale **tower** is stunning. *(240Ft, students 120Ft.)*

GELLÉRT HILL. When King Stephen, the first Christian Hungarian monarch, was coronated, the Pope sent Bishop Gellért to convert the Magyars. The hill got its name (Gellért-hegy) when those unconvinced by his message hurled the good bishop to his death from the top. The **Liberation Monument** (Szabadság Szobor), created to honor Soviet soldiers who died "liberating" Hungary, looks over Budapest from atop the hill. The view from atop the adjoining **Citadel,** built as a symbol of Habsburg power after the foiled 1848 revolution, is especially spectacular at night. At the base of the hill sits the **Gellért Hotel and Baths,** Budapest's most famous Turkish bath (see p. 529). *(Take tram #18 or 19 to Hotel Gellért; follow Szabó Verjték u. to Jubileumi Park, continuing on the marked paths to the summit. Or, take bus #27 to the top; get off at Búsuló Juhász and walk 5min. to the peak.)*

PEST

Constructed in the 19th century, the winding streets of Pest now host cafes, corporations, and monuments. The crowded **Belváros** (Inner City) is based around the swarming pedestrian boulevards **Váci utca** and **Vörösmarty tér.**

▧ PARLIAMENT. Pest's riverbank sports a string of luxury hotels leading to its magnificent Gothic Parliament (Országház), modeled after Britain's. The massive palatial structure has always been too big for Hungary's government; today, the legislature uses only 12%. *(M2: Kossuth Lajos tér. English-language tours daily 10am and 2pm; come early. 1700Ft, students 800Ft. Purchase tickets at gate #10 and enter at gate #12.)*

ST. STEPHEN'S BASILICA. The city's largest church (Sz. István Bazilika) was decimated by Allied bombs in World War II. Its neo-Renaissance facade is still undergoing reconstruction, but the ornate interior attracts both tourists and worshippers. The **Panorama Tower** offers an amazing 360° view. The oddest attraction is St. Stephen's mummified right hand, one of Hungary's most revered religious relics; a 100Ft donation dropped in the box will light up the hand for two minutes. *(M1-3: Deák tér. Mass M-Sa 7, 8am, 6pm; Su 8:30, 10am, noon, 6pm. Basilica and museum open May-Oct. M-Sa 9am-6pm; Nov.-Apr. M-Sa 10am-4pm. Tower open June-Aug. daily 9:30am-6pm; Sept.-Oct. 10am-5:30pm; Apr.-May 10am-4:30pm. Tower 500Ft, students 400Ft.)*

GREAT SYNAGOGUE. The largest synagogue in Europe and the second-largest in the world after Temple Emmanuel in New York City, Pest's Great Synagogue (Zsinagóga) was designed to hold 3000 worshippers. The Moorish building has been under renovation since 1988, and much of its artwork is blocked from view. In the garden is a **Holocaust Memorial** that sits above a mass grave for thousands of Jews killed near the end of the war. The Hebrew inscription reads "Whose pain can be greater than mine?" with the Hungarian words "Let us Remember" beneath. Each leaf of this enormous metal tree bears the name of a family that perished, but the memorial represents only a fraction of those who suffered. Next door, the **Jewish Museum** (Zsidó Múzeum) documents Hungary's rich Jewish past. *(M2: Astoria. At the corner of Dohány u. and Wesselényi u. Open May-Oct. M-Th 10am-5pm, F 10am-3pm, Su 10am-2pm; Nov.-Apr. M-F 10am-3pm, Su 10am-1pm. Synagogue and museum 600Ft.)*

ANDRÁSSY ÚT AND HEROES' SQUARE. Hungary's grandest boulevard, Andrássy út, extends from Erzsébet tér in downtown Pest to **Heroes' Square** (Hősök tere) to the northeast. The **Hungarian State Opera House** (Magyar Állami Operaház), whose gilded interior glows on performance nights, is a vivid reminder of Budapest's Golden Age. If you can't see an opera, take a tour. *(Andrássy út 22. M1: Opera. Daily English-language tours 3 and 4pm; 1500Ft, students 600Ft. 20% Budapest card discount.)* At the Heroes' Square end of Andrássy út, the **Millenium Monument** (Millenniumi emlékmű) commemorates the nation's most prominent leaders. Right off Heroes' Square is the **Museum of Fine Arts** (see below).

CITY PARK. The City Park (Városliget) is home to a zoo, a circus, a run-down amusement park, and the lakeside **Vajdahunyad Castle**, whose collage of Romanesque, Gothic, Renaissance, and Baroque styles is intended to chronicle the history of Hungarian architecture. Outside the castle broods the hooded statue of King Béla IV's **anonymous scribe,** to whom we owe much of our knowledge of medieval Hungary. Rent a **rowboat** or **ice skates** on the lake next to the castle, or a **bike-trolley** to navigate the shaded paths. The main road through the park is closed to automobiles on weekends, making the park especially peaceful. *(M1: Széchenyi Fürdő. Park open Apr.-Aug. daily 9am-6pm; Sept.-Mar. 9am-3pm. Pedal boat rentals May-Aug. daily 10am-8pm; 980Ft per hr. Rowboat rental May-Aug. daily 10am-9:30pm; 500Ft per hr. Ice skate rental Oct.-Feb. daily 10am-2pm and 4-8pm; 500Ft per 4hr.)*

🏛 MUSEUMS

▓ MUSEUM OF FINE ARTS. (Szépművészeti Múzeum). A spectacular collection of European art is housed in the magnificent building. These are paintings you've never seen in books, but should not miss, especially those in the El Greco room. *(XIV, Dózsa György út 41. M1: Hősók tere. Open Tu-Su 10am-5:30pm. 500Ft, students 200Ft. Tours for up to five people 2000Ft.)*

▓ STATUE PARK. (Szoborpark Múzeum). After the collapse of Soviet rule, the open-air Statue Park Muzeum was created from a collection of communist statuary removed from Budapest's parks and squares. The indispensable English guidebook explains the statues' past and present positions. *(XXII, on the corner of Balatoni út and Szabadkai u. www.szoborpark.hu. Take the express red bus #7 from Keleti pu. to Étele tér, then take the yellow Volán bus from terminal #2 (dir.: Diósd.). Open in good weather Mar.-Nov. daily 10am-dusk; Dec.-Feb. weekends and holidays only. 300Ft, students 200Ft.)*

MUSEUM OF APPLIED ARTS. (Iparművészeti Múzeum). The Art Nouveau building of the Museum of Applied Arts was designed for Hungary's 1896 millenium celebration. Inside is an eclectic collection of impressive hand-crafted objects, including Tiffany glass and furniture, as well as excellent temporary exhibits highlighting specific crafts. *(IX, Üllői út 33-37. M3: Ferenc körút. Open Mar. 15-Oct. Tu-Su 10am-6pm; Nov.-Mar. Tu-Su 10am-4pm. 500Ft, students 250Ft.)*

BUDA CASTLE. Leveled by the Nazis and by the Soviets, the reconstructed Buda Castle (see Castle District, p. 526) now houses several museums. Wing A contains the **Museum of Contemporary Art** (Kortárs Művészeti Múzeum), as well as the smaller **Ludwig Museum** upstairs, which is devoted to Warhol, Lichtenstein, and other masters of modern art. Wings B-D hold the **Hungarian National Gallery** (Magyar Nemzeti Galéria), a definitive collection of the best in Hungarian painting and sculpture. *(Wings A-D open Tu-Su 10am-6pm. Wing A 400Ft, students 200Ft. Wings B-D 600Ft total, students 300Ft.)* Artifacts from the 1242 castle, unearthed by WWII bombings, lie in the **Budapest History Museum** (Budapesti Történeti Múzeum) in Wing E. *(I, Szent György tér 2. M1-3: Deák tér. Take bus #16 across the Danube to the top of Castle Hill. Wing E open mid-May to mid-Sept. daily 10am-6pm; mid-Sept. to Oct. and Mar. to mid-May W-M 10am-6pm; Nov.-Feb. W-M 10am-4pm. 600Ft, students 300Ft.)*

HUNGARIAN NATIONAL MUSEUM. (Magyar Nemzeti Múzeum). Two extensive exhibits chronicle Hungarian history; a cheery Stalin welcomes you to rooms devoted to Soviet propaganda. Room descriptions have English translations and helpful historical maps. *(VIII, Múzeum krt. 14/16. www.origo.hnm.hu. M3: Kálvin tér. Open Mar. 15-Oct. 15 Tu-Su 10am-6pm; Oct. 16-Mar. 14 Tu-Su 10am-5pm. 600Ft, students 300Ft.)*

🎭 ENTERTAINMENT

Budapest Program, Budapest Panorama, Pesti Est and the essential *Budapest in Your Pocket* (750Ft) are the best English-language entertainment guides, listing everything from festivals to cinemas to art showings. All are available at most tourist offices and hotels. The "Style" section of the *Budapest Sun* (www.budapestsun.com; 300Ft), has a comprehensive 10-day calendar and film reviews. (Tickets 550-1000Ft; cinema schedules change on Th.)

THEATER, MUSIC, AND DANCE. Ticket Express, VI, Andrássy út 15, next to the Opera House, and throughout the city, sells tickets to most shows for no commission. (☎312 00 00. Open M-F 10am-6pm.) For 3000-9800Ft you can enjoy an opera in the splendor of the gilded, neo-Renaissance ◪**Hungarian State Opera House** (see p. 528). The box office on the left side of the building sells cheaper stand-by tickets 30min. before showtime. (Box office ☎353 01 70. Open M-Sa 11am-5pm, Su 4-5pm; cashier open until 7pm on performance days.) The **Philharmonic Orchestra** has performances almost nightly Sept.-June. Buy tickets at V, Mérleg u. 10. (☎318 02 81. Open daily 9am-3pm. Tickets 2000-5000Ft, same-day discount available.) In late summer, the Philharmonic and Opera take a break, but performances continue at Budapest's acclaimed theaters. Buy tickets at the **Madách Theater Box Office,** VII, Madách tér 6. (☎322 20 15. Open M-Sa 2:30-7pm.) Many big musical acts pass through Budapest. **Music Mix 33 Ticket Service,** V, Váci ú. 33, has reasonably priced tickets. (☎317 77 36. Open M-F 10am-6pm, Sa 10am-1pm.)

THERMAL BATHS. To soak away the city grime, sink into a hot, relaxing thermal bath. First built in 1565, their services—from mud baths to massage—are quite cheap. Some baths are meeting spots for Budapest's gay community. **Széchenyi,** XIV, Állatkerti u. 11/14, is a welcoming bath with beautiful pools. (M1: Hősök tere. 1000Ft deposit on entry; keep your receipt. 15min. massage 1200Ft. Open May-Sept. daily 6am-7pm; Oct.-Apr. M-F 6am-7pm, Sa-Su 6am-5pm.) Famous **Gellért,** XI, Kelenhegyi út 4/6, one of the most elegant baths, has

THE HIDDEN DEAL

BUCK-NAKED IN BUDAPEST

The city's baths were first built in 1565 by a Turkish ruler who feared that a siege would prevent the population from bathing. Thanks to his anxiety, there's nothing to keep budget travelers from bathing, either: the range of services—from mud baths to massage—are cheap enough to warrant indulgence without guilt.

Although virgin bathers may be intimidated at first, guests at Budapest's baths always receive the royal treatment. Upon arrival, you will probably be handed a bizarre apron no bigger than a dish-rag (and no less dingy), which modesty requires that you tie around your waist. In general, women set the apron aside as a towel, while men keep theirs on; bring a bathing suit just in case. Customs vary greatly by establishment, so just do as the locals do—nothing is more conspicuous than a Speedo-clad tourist among naked natives.

Cycle through the sauna and thermal baths a couple times, then enter the massage area. For a good scrubbing, try the sanitary massage *(vízi);* if you're a traditionalist, stick to the medical massage *(orvosi).* Most baths provide a much-needed rest area once the process is complete. Refreshed, smiling, and somewhat sleepy, tip the attendant, lounge over mint tea, and savor your afternoon of guilt-free pampering.

(Baths and pools 700-2000Ft, massages 1000-7500Ft.)

a rooftop sundeck and an outdoor wave pool. Take bus #7 or tram #47 or 49 to Hotel Gellért, at the base of Gellért-hegy. (Bath and pool 2000Ft. 15min. massage 1100Ft. Open May-Sept. M-F 6am-6pm, Sa-Su 6am-4pm; Oct.-Apr. closes 1pm weekends.)

◪ NIGHTLIFE

All-night outdoor parties, elegant after-hours clubs, the nightly thump and grind—Budapest has it all. Pubs and bars bustle until 4am, but the streets themselves are empty and poorly lit. Upscale cafes and restaurants in **VI, Liszt Ferenc tér** (M1: Oktogon) attract Budapest's hip youth. In summer, the Buda side of the park **Peötlfi híd** becomes a nightly party. Gay life in Budapest is just becoming visible; it's still safer to be discreet. If you have concerns, call the **gay hotline** (see p. 523).

Undergrass, VI, Liszt Ferenc tér 10. M1: Oktogon. The hottest spot in Pest's trendiest area. A soundproof glass door divides a hip bar from a packed disco. Open daily 8pm-4am; disco Tu-Su 10pm-4am.

Piaf, VI, Nagymező u. 25. A much-loved lounge, and a good place to meet fellow travelers. Knock on the door to await the approval of the club's matron. Cover 500Ft, includes 1 beer. Open daily 11pm-6am, but don't come before 1am.

Capella, V, Belgrád rakpart 23 (www.extra.hu/capella-cafe). With glow-in-the-dark graffiti and an underground atmosphere, this spot draws a mixed gay and straight crowd. Cover 1000-1500Ft. Open Tu-Su 9pm-5am. The owners also run the three-level **Limo Cafe** down the street. Beer 350-700Ft. Open daily noon-5am.

Club Seven, Akácfa u. 7. M2: Blaha Lajos tér. This upscale underground music club is a local favorite. M-F no cover; Sa-Su 1000Ft, women free. Coffeehouse open daily 9pm-4am, restaurant 6pm-midnight, dance floor 10pm-5am.

Old Man's Music Pub, VII, Akácfa u. 13. M2: Blaha Lujza tér. Arrive early for nightly blues and jazz from 9-11pm, then relax in the restaurant (open 3pm-3am) or hit the dance floor (11pm-late). No cover. Open M-Sa 3pm to 4:30 or 5am.

Jazz Garden, V, Veres Páiné u. 44a. Although the "garden" is actually a vaulted cellar with Christmas lights, the effect works well. Live jazz nightly at 10:30pm. Beer 420-670Ft. Open Su-F noon-1am, Sa noon-2am.

Fat Mo's Speakeasy, V, Nyári Pal u. 11. M3: Kálvin tér. 14 varieties of draft beer (350-750Ft). Live jazz Su-M and Th 9-11pm. Th-Sa DJ from 11:30pm. Open M-F noon-2am, Sa noon-4am, Su 6pm-4am.

NIGHTLIFE SCAM. There have been reports of a mafia-organized scam involving English-speaking Hungarian women who approach foreign men, suggest meeting elsewhere, ask for a drink, then leave. The bill, accompanied by imposing men, can be US$1000 for a single drink. The U.S. Embassy (see Embassies, p. 523) has advised against patronizing a number of establishments in the Vci u. area. The names of these establishments change frequently. For the most current list of establishments about which complaints have been received, check with the embassy in Budapest or view their list on the web at www.usembassy.hu/conseng/announcements.html. If you are taken in, call the police. You'll probably still have to pay, but get a receipt to issue a complaint formally at the Consumer Bureau.

⚡ DAYTRIPS FROM BUDAPEST: THE DANUBE BEND

North of Budapest, the Danube sweeps in a dramatic arc called the Danube Bend (Dunakanyar), deservedly one of the most beloved tourist attractions in Hungary.

SZENTENDRE. Szentendre's narrow cobblestone streets brim with upscale art galleries and pricey restaurants. Head up **Church Hill** (Templomdomb) in Fő tér, above the town center, for an amazing view from the 13th-century Roman Catholic church. Just across Alkotmány u. is the **Serbian Orthodox Church** (Szerb Ortodox Templom); its ornate interior is an Orthodox take on Baroque. The church's museum displays the art of Szentendre's Serbian community. (Museum open Tu-Su 10am-6pm; church closes at 5pm. Together 200Ft.) The popular **Margit Kovács Museum**, Vastagh György u. 1, off Görög u., which branches from Fő tér, displays whimsical ceramic sculptures and tiles by the 20th-century Hungarian artist. (Open Mar.-Oct. daily 10am-6pm; Nov. daily 9am-5pm; Dec.-Feb. Tu-Su 10am-5pm. 400Ft.) The real thriller at the **Szabó Marzipan Museum and Confectionery**, Dumtsa Jenő u. 12, is the 80kg white chocolate statue of Michael Jackson. (Open daily 10am-6pm. 200Ft; desserts 120-240Ft.) Take the Skanzen bus (20-40min., 1 per hr.) from terminal #7 to the **Open-Air Village Museum** (Szabadtéri Néprajzi Múzeum), which has reconstructed settlements complete with basket-weaving and butter-making. (www.sznm.hu. Open Apr.-Oct. Tu-Su 9am-5pm. 500Ft, students 250Ft.)

HÉV commuter trains travel to Szentendre from Budapest's Batthyány tér (45min., every 10-15min., 286Ft). **Buses** run to Budapest's Árpád híd Metro station (30min., every 20-40min., 196Ft) and to Esztergom (1½hr., 476Ft) and Visegrád (45min., 246Ft). The HÉV and bus stations are 10min. from Fő tér; descend the stairs past the end of the HÉV tracks, go through the underpass, and head up Kossuth u. At the fork, bear right onto Dumtsa Jenő u., which leads to the town center. **MAHART boats** leave from a pier 20min. north of the town center (late-May to Aug. only). With the river on the right, walk along the water to the sign. Boats run to: Budapest (3 per day, 830Ft); Esztergom (1 per day, 870Ft); and Visegrád (3 per day, 830Ft). **Tourinform**, Dumtsa Jenő u. 22, between the town center and the station, has free maps. (☎/fax 31 79 65; www.szentendre.hu. Open Mar. 16-Oct. 15 M-F 9am-4:30pm, Sa-Su 10am-2pm; Oct. 16-Mar. 15 M-F 9:30am-4:30pm.) Restaurants are expensive; it's often better to dine in Budapest or Visegrád. Enjoy a pastry (from 350Ft) and cappuccino (from 350Ft) while being serenaded by the opera-singing owners of ▧**Nostalgia Cafe ❷**, Bogdányi u. 2. (Open Th-Su 10am-10pm). **Kedvenc Kifőzde ❶**, Bükköspart 21, is a tiny diner with incredible food. (Meals 300-460Ft. Open M-F noon-5pm; Sa noon-3pm.) There's also a **Kaiser supermarket** near the rail station. (Open M-W 7am-7pm, Th-F 7am-8pm, Sa-Su 7am-3pm.) ☎026.

VISEGRÁD. Host to the royal court in medieval times, Visegrád was devastated when the Habsburgs destroyed its 13th-century **citadel** in a struggle against free-dom fighters. This former Roman outpost gives a dramatic view of the Danube and surrounding hills. Hike a strenuous 30min. up Kalvária út, or take the local bus (2hr.; 9:30am, 12:30, and 3:30pm; 100Ft). Sprawling across the foothills above Fő út are the ruins of King Matthias's **Royal Palace** (Királyi Palota); impressive exhibits inside include a computerized reconstruction of the original castle. (Open Tu-Su 9am-5pm. 400Ft, students 200Ft.) The palace grounds relive their glory days of parades, jousting, and music during the **Viségrad Palace Games** (☎(01) 365 60 32) in the mid-July. At the end of Salamontorony u., the **King Matthias Museum,** inside Solomon's Tower (Alsóvár Salamon Torony), displays artifacts from the palace ruins. (Open Apr.-Oct. Tu-Su 9am-5pm. 400Ft, students 200Ft; Su students free.)

Buses run to Budapest's Árpád híd Metro station (1½hr., 30per day, 430Ft) and Esztergom (45min., every hr., 250Ft). **MAHART boats** run to: Budapest (2½-3hr., 5 per day, 870Ft); Esztergom (2hr., 3 per day, 830Ft); and Szentendre (1¼hr., 3 per day, 830Ft). From the bus stop, cross the parking lot; turn right on Fő út, which intersects with Rév út in the center (5min.). The tourist office, **Visegrád Tours,** Rév út 15, has 300Ft maps. (☎39 81 60. Open Apr.-Oct. daily 8am-7pm; Nov.-Mar. M-F 10am-4pm.) Across the road is **CBA Élelmiszer supermarket.** (Open M 7am-6pm, Tu-F 7am-7pm, Sa 7am-3pm, Su 7am-noon.) **Gulás Csárda ❸,** Nagy Lajos u. 4, is a cozy family restaurant. (Main dishes 950-1990Ft. Open daily noon-10pm.) ☎026.

ESZTERGOM. In Esztergom, a millennium of religious history revolves around a solemn hilltop **cathedral,** whose crypt holds the remains of Hungary's archbishops. The **cupola** (100Ft) offers the best view of the Danube Bend. The **Cathedral Treasury** (Kincstáv) to the right of the main altar has Hungary's most extensive collection of ecclesiastical treasures. To the left of the altar is the red marble **Bakócz Chapel,** a masterwork of Renaissance Tuscan craftsmanship. (Open Mar.-Oct. daily 9am-4pm; Nov.-Dec. M-F 11am-3:30pm, Sa-Su 10am-3:30pm. 300Ft. English-language guidebook 100Ft.) Beside the cathedral is the restored 12th-century **Esztergom Palace.** (Open May-Sept. Tu-Su 9am-4pm; Oct.-May Tu-Su 10am-3:30pm. 300Ft.) At the foot of the hill, the **Christian Museum** (Keresztény Múzeum), Berenyi Zsigmond u. 2, houses exceptional religious art. (Open Tu-Su 10am-5:30pm. 400Ft.)

Trains go to Budapest (1½hr., 22 per day, 804Ft). From the station, turn left on the main street, Baross Gábor út, and make a right onto Kiss János Altábornagy út, which becomes Kossuth Lajos u., to reach the square. **Buses** run to Szentendre (1½hr., every hr., 476Ft) and Visegrád (45min., every hr., 246Ft). From the bus station, walk up Simor János u. toward the street market to reach Rákóczi tér. **MAHART boats** depart from the pier at Gőzhajó u. on Primas Sziget Island for: Budapest (4hr., 3 per day, 890Ft); Szentendre (2¾hr., every hr., 870Ft); and Visegrád (1½hr., every hr., 830Ft). **Grantours,** Széchenyi tér 25, at the edge of Rákóczi tér, provides maps (200Ft-500Ft) and can arrange bike rentals. (☎41 70 52; grantour@net.hu. Open July-Aug. M-F 8am-6pm, Sa 9am-noon; Sept.-June M-F 8am-4pm, Sa 9am-noon.) A **Match supermarket** is just off of Rákóczi tér. (Open M-F 6:30am-6:30pm, Sa 6:30am-1pm.) ☎033.

SOUTHERN TRANSDANUBIA

Once the southernmost portion of the Roman province Pannonia, Southern Transdanubia is framed by the Danube to the west, the Dráva to the south, and Lake Balaton to the north. Known for its rolling hills, sunflower fields, mild climate, and red wine, the region is also filled with magnificent Habsburg architecture.

PÉCS   ☎072

Pécs (PAYCH), at the foot of the Mecsek mountains, is blessed with a pleasant climate and gorgeous vistas and architecture. Outdoor activities in the surrounding region and an intense nightlife fueled by university students make Pécs an attractive weekend spot. The ▧Csontváry Museum, Janus Pannonius u. 11, displays the works of Tivadar Csontváry Kosztka, known as the Hungarian van Gogh. (Open Tu-Sa 10am-6pm, Su 10am-4pm. 400Ft, students 300Ft.) In nearby Széchenyi tér stands the Mosque of Ghazi Kassim (Gázi Khasim Pasa dzsámija). Now a church once more, the building was once a Turkish mosque built on the site of an earlier church; this fusion of Christian and Muslim traditions has become an emblem of the city. (Open Apr. 16-Oct. 14 daily 10am-4pm; Oct. 15-Apr. 15 10am-noon. Free; donations requested.) Walk downhill from Széchenyi tér on Irgalmasok u. to Kossuth tér to reach the stunning 1869 synagogue, which serves the city's 140 remaining Jews. (Open Su-F 10-11:30am and noon-5pm. 200Ft, students 100Ft.)

To reach the train station, just south of the historic district, take bus #30, 32, or 33 from the town center. Trains run to Budapest (3½hr., 3 per day, 1996Ft), as do buses (4½hr., 7 per day, 2088Ft). Tourinform, Széchenyi tér 9, sells maps and phone cards. (☎21 26 32. Open June-Sept. M-F 9am-7pm, Sa-Su 10am-6pm; Oct.-May reduced hours.) Private rooms are the best budget option in the town center. Also in the center, off Kossuth tér, is well-kept Motel/Hotel Diana ❸, Timár u. 4a. (☎328 59; fax 33 33 73. Call ahead. Singles 5600Ft; doubles 8600Ft.) Szent Mór Kollégium ❷, 48-as tér 4, offers neat university dorm rooms. From the main terminal, take bus #21 to 48-as tér. (☎50 36 10. Curfew midnight. Call ahead. Open July-Aug. Triples only, 1000Ft.) Pécs's restaurants, cafes, and bars are among the city's biggest attractions. Afiúm ❸, Irgalmasok u. 2, has a delicious local Italian and Hungarian menu with many veggie options. (Entrees 830-1950Ft. Open M-Sa 11am-1am, Su 11am-midnight.) Caflisch Cukrászda Café ❶, Király u. 32, is the best cafe in town. (Pastries from 79Ft. Open daily 8am-10pm.) At night, chill with the artsy crowd at ▧Cafe Dante, Janus Pannonis u. 11, in the same building as the Csontváry Museum. (Beer 290-390Ft. Open daily 10am-1am, later on weekends.) Postal code: 7621.

EGER   ☎36

When an Ottoman army tried to seize Eger Castle (EGG-air) in 1552, locals fortified themselves with the region's wine, which stained their beards red. When the Hungarians didn't succumb to the overwhelming invading force, it was rumored among the Turks that the fierce Hungarians were quaffing the blood of bulls for strength. The wine thus earned the name bikavér, or Bull's Blood. This legend figures prominently in Hungarian lore and lives today in the vibrant wine cellars of the Valley of Beautiful Women and historical monuments throughout the city.

▣❼ TRANSPORTATION AND PRACTICAL INFORMATION. Budapest direct trains (2hr., 6 per day, 1036-1242Ft) split in Hatvan; make sure you're in the correct car. From the station, turn right on Deák Ferenc út., walk 10min., go right on Kossuth Lajos u., left on Széchenyi u., and right on Érsek u. to reach Dobó tér, the main square (20min.). Tourinform, Bajcsy-Zsilinszky u. 9, has maps and lodgings information. (☎51 77 15; www.ektf.hu/eger. Open June-Sept. M-F 9am-7pm, Sa-Su 10am-6pm; Sept.-June M-F 9am-5pm, Sa 9am-1pm.) OTP Bank, Széchenyi u. 2, grants AmEx/MC/V advances, cashes AmEx Traveler's Cheques without commission, and has a 24hr. ATM. (☎31 08 66. Open M-Tu and Th 7:45am-6pm.) Postal code: 3300.

▛▢ ACCOMMODATIONS AND FOOD. Private rooms are best (about 2000Ft); look for Zimmer frei or szòba eladò signs outside the main square, particularly on Almagyar u. and Mekcsey István u. near the castle. Eger Tourist ❸, Bajcsy-Zsilinszky u. 9, next to TourInform, arranges private rooms for about 3000Ft. (☎51 70 00. Open M-F 9am-5pm.) Take bus #5, 11, or 12 north to the Shell station (20min.) to reach Autós Caravan Camping ❶, Rákóczi u. 79. (Open Apr. 15 to Oct. 15. 900Ft, students 700Ft.) Széchenyi u is lined with restaurants. There is an ABC supermarket

FROM THE ROAD

between Sandor u. and Szt. Janos u. (Open M-F 6am-5pm, Sa 6am-1pm, Su 6-10am.) In the Valley of the Beautiful Women, crowds dine in the vine-draped courtyard of **Kulacs Csárda Borozó's** ❹. (Meals 950-1600Ft. Open Tu-Su noon-10pm.)

🎨🎭 **SIGHTS AND FESTIVALS.** Dobó István and his men repelled the attacking Ottoman army from medieval **Eger Castle,** which features subterranean barracks, catacombs, a crypt, and a wine cellar. One ticket covers the picture gallery, the **Dobó István Vármúzeum,** which displays artifacts and weapons, and the **dungeon exhibition.** (Castle open daily 8am-8pm. Wine cellars open daily 10am-7pm. Museums open Mar.-Oct. Tu-Su 9am-5pm; Nov.-Feb. 9am-3pm. Underground passages open daily 9am-5pm; 250Ft, students 120Ft. Castle 200Ft, students 100Ft. Museums Tu-Su 500Ft/250Ft. Wine cellars free; 140Ft per tasting. English tour 400Ft.) The **Lyceum,** at the corner of Kossuth Lajos u. and Eszterházy tér., houses an astronomical museum and a *camera obscura* that projects a live image of the surrounding town onto a table. (Open Apr.-Oct. Tu-Su 9:30am-1:30pm; Oct.-Dec. and Mar.-Apr. Th-F 9:30am-1pm, Sa-Su 9:30am-1:30pm. 200Ft, students 100Ft.)

After a morning exploring Eger's historical sights, spend the afternoon or evening in the wine cellars of the ◨**Valley of the Beautiful Women** (Szépass-zonyvölgy). To reach the wine cellars, start on Széchenyi u. with Eger Cathedral to your right. Turn right on Kossuth Lajos u., left on Deák Ferenc út. (ignore the sign directing you otherwise), and right on Telekessy u.; continue for about 10min. as Telekessy becomes Király u., then bear left onto Szépasszonyvölgy. The friendly proprietor of **Cellar #17** gives samples of delicious *bikavér*. **Cellar #20** becomes an after-hours bar with a DJ and live music. Samples are free, and bottles are available for purchase. Bring your own container for a discount at some cellars. (0.1L 50-80Ft; 1L 350Ft. Open from 9am, closing times vary.)

In summer, **open-air baths** offer a break from the sweltering city. (Open May-Sept. M-F 6am-7pm, Sa-Su 8:30am-7pm; Oct.-Apr. daily 9am-7pm. 500Ft, students and seniors 350Ft.) The city holds the **Eger Bull's Blood Festival** in the beginning of July and celebrates its heritage with nightly performances of opera and early court music during the **Baroque Festival** (late July to mid-August).

🚌 **DAYTRIP FROM EGER: SZILVÁSVÁRAD.** Perfect for an outing from Eger, Szilvásvárad (SEAL-vash-vah-rod) attracts both horse and nature lovers. **Horse shows** (800Ft) kick into action on most weekends in the arena on Szalajka u. **Lipicai Stables** is the stud farm for the town's famed Lipizzaner breed. From the park entrance on Egri út., turn left on Enyves u., then follow signs to the farm. (☎ 35 51 55. Open daily 8:30am-noon and 2-4pm. 80Ft.) Many farms offer **horseback riding,** especially in the summer. **Péter Kovács,** Egri út. 62 (☎ 35 53 43), rents horses (1500Ft per hr.) and two-horse carriages (4500Ft per hr.). For **hiking,** head to the nearby **Bükk mountains** and **Szalajka valley.** A 45min. walk along the green trail will lead you to the park's most popular attraction, the **Fátyol waterfall;** 30min. past the falls is the **Istálósk cave,** the Stone Age home to a bear-worshiping cult. **Bike rentals** and free cycling maps are available on Szalajka u. (600Ft 1st hour, 200Ft each additional hr. Open daily 10am-7pm.) Szilvásvárad can be reached by **train** (1hr., 7 per day, 262Ft) or **bus** (45min., every 30min-1hr., 294Ft) from Eger. From the train station (Szilvás-várad-Szalajkavölgy), follow Egri út. to Szalajka u. directly to the national park. There is no bus station in town; just get off at the second stop on Egri út. near Szalajka u. where the road bends sharply. Szilvásvárad has no tourist office; visit Eger's **TourInform** (see p. 533) before heading out.

GYŐR ☎ 096

In the unspoiled, far western region of Őrség, lively Győr (DYUR) overflows with religious monuments, well-kept museums, and 17th- and 18th-century architectu-rural gems. From the train station, go right until you come to the bridge; turn left just before the underpass, then cross the street to reach pedestrian **Baross Gabor utca.** Turn left on Kazinczy u. to reach Bécsi Kapu tér, the site of the 18th-century **Carmelite Church** (Karmelita-templom) and a **lapidarium** filled with fragments of Roman ruins. (Open Apr.-Oct. Tu-Su 10am-6pm; Nov.-Mar. 10am-2pm. 400Ft, students 200Ft.) Walking uphill on Czuczor Gergely u., one street to the right of Baross Gabor u., will lead you to the striking **Ark of the Covenant statue** (Frigylada szobor) and **Chapter Hill** (Káptalandomb). At the top of the hill is the **Episcopal Cathedral** (Székesegyház), which holds the **Weeping Madonna of Győr;** legends say that the icon wept blood for persecuted Irish Catholics on St. Patrick's Day in 1697. The **Diocesan Library and Treasury** (Egyházmegyei Kincstáv), Káptalandomb 26, hidden in an alley off the cathedral's square, displays priceless jewels and more religious art. (Open Tu-Su 10am-4pm. 300Ft, students 150Ft. English captions.) For contemporary art, head to the **Imre Patkó collection** at Széchenyi tér 4, down Czuczor Gergely u. from the statue; enter at Stelczera u. (Open Tu-Su 10am-6pm. 200Ft, students 100Ft.) Across the river from the town center is the huge and pop-ular **water park,** Cziráky tér 1, with thermal springs. From Bécsi Kapu tér, take the bridge over the small island and make the first right on the other side, then go right again onto Cziráky tér. (Open daily 8am-7pm. 500Ft, students 400Ft.)

Frequent **trains** go to Budapest (2½hr., 26 per day, 1130Ft) and Vienna (2hr., 13 per day, 4450Ft). **Buses** run to Budapest (2½hr., every hr., 1300Ft). The train station is 3min. from the city center; the underpass that links the rail platforms leads to the bus station. The **Tourinform kiosk,** Árpád u. 32, at the corner with Baross Gabor u., provides free maps and arranges lodgings. (☎/fax 31 17 71. Open June-Aug. M-F 8am-8pm, Sa-Su 9am-6pm.) ▓**Katalin's Kert ❸,** Sarkantyú köz 3, off Bécsi Kapu tér, has huge modern rooms with private baths. (☎/fax 45 20 88. Singles 5800Ft; doubles 7500Ft.) **Matróz Restaurant ❷,** Dunakapu tér 3, off Jedlik Ányos u. facing the river, fries up succulent fish. (Entrees 500-1100Ft. Open Su-Th 9am-10pm, F-Sa 9am-11pm.) **John Bull Pub ❸,** Aradi u., offers a break from the Hungarian diet. (Main dishes 810-1500Ft. Open daily 9am-midnight.) **Kaiser's supermarket** is at the corner of Arany János u. and Aradi vértanúk. (Open M 7:30am-7pm, Tu-F 6:30am-7pm, Sa 6:30am-2pm.) At night, music and young people spill from cellar bars onto Győr's streets. The fabulous patio at **Komédiás Biergarten,** Czuczor Gergely u., invites drinking and laughing crowds. (Beer 250-420Ft. Open M-Sa 11am-midnight.) **Postal code:** 9021.

DAYTRIP FROM GYŐR: ARCHABBEY OF PANNONHALMA. Visible at a distance from Győr, the hilltop Archabbey of Pannonhalma (Pannonhalmi Főapátság) has seen ten centuries of destruction and rebuilding since it was established in AD 996 by the Benedictine order. The UNESCO World Heritage site features an opulent, treasure-filled library, a 13th-century basilica, and frequent classical concerts. **Pax Tourist** (☎ 57 01 91; pax@osb.hu), to the left of the entrance, leads tours and has concert information. (Hungarian tour with English text every hr.; English tours in summer 11am and 1pm. Hungarian tour 1000Ft, students 300Ft; English tour 2000Ft/1000Ft.) To reach Pannonhalma from Győr, take the **bus** from stand #11 (45min.; 7 per day; 246Ft, round-trip 369Ft). Ask for Pannonhalma vár and look for the huge gates, or you may end up in the town 1km away.

LAKE BALATON

A retreat since Roman times, the warm Lake Balaton drew European elites in the 19th-century and is now a budget paradise for German and Austrian students. Be aware that storms can roll in quickly—when the yellow lights on tall harbor buildings speed up to one revolution per second, swimmers must get out of the water.

SIÓFOK. Tourist offices are more densely packed in Siófok than in any other Hungarian city, reflecting the influx of lake-bound vacationers who flock here every summer. Most attractions in Siófok pale in comparison with the **Strand**, a series of park-like lawns running to the concrete shoreline (some sections 200-400Ft per person). Bars and nightclubs of varying seediness line the lakefront, and **disco boats** push off at 9pm. Right in the center of the Strand is the ⓇRenegade Pub, Petőfi Sétány 3, a casual bar and dance club. (No cover. Open June-Sept. daily 8pm-5am.) **Palace Disco**, Deák Ferenc Sétány 2, is a party complex with discos, bars, and restaurants. (Cocktails 980-1750Ft. Cover 1500-3500Ft. Disco open May-Sept. 10pm-5am. Pizzeria open 11am-5am.)

Off Fő u., the town's main drag, **trains** go to Budapest (2½hr., every hr., 926Ft); **express buses** *(gyorsjárat)* also head to Budapest (1½hr., 9 per day, 1320Ft) and Pécs (3hr., 4 per day, 2456Ft). **Tourinform**, Fő u. at Szabadság tér, in the base of the water tower across from the train station, helps find rooms (6000-15,000Ft) and has free maps. (☎31 53 55; www.siofok.com. Open July-Aug. M-Sa 8am-8pm, Su 9am-6pm; Sept.-June M-F 9am-4pm.) ⓇHotel Park ❺, Batthány u. 7, has modern rooms right by the Strand. (☎/fax 31 05 39; www.programinfonet/parkhotel. Reception 24hr. July-Aug. doubles 10,000-15,000Ft; Sept.-June 8000-10,000Ft.) To get to the small **Balaton Panzio** ❹, Szent László u. 16, turn left from the train station, cross the tracks, take an immediate right onto Ady Endre u.; turn left on Tátra u., then take a right on Szent László. (☎31 05 71. Open July-Aug. only. Doubles 7500Ft.) **Hotel Viola** ❸, Bethlen Gabor u. 1, is popular with a younger crowd. From the train station, walk along Fő u. with the tracks on your right and cross at Bethlen Gabor u. (☎31 28 45; www.siofok.com/viola. Reception 24hr. Book well in advance. July-Aug. Doubles 4600Ft; May-June and Sept.-Oct. 3200Ft.) ☎084.

TIHANY. With its scenic hikes, charming cottages, and panoramic views, the Tihany peninsula is the pearl of Lake Balaton. The **Benedictine Abbey** (Bencés Apátság) draws over a million visitors annually to its luminous frescoes, gold-leaf Baroque altars, and a crypt housing one of Hungary's earliest kings. (Open Mar.-Oct. M-Sa 9am-5:30pm, Su 11am-5:30pm. 260Ft, students 130Ft; Su free.) The well-marked **hiking** trails across the peninsula take only an hour or two. The green-line trail runs past the **Hermit's Place** (Barátlakások), where the cells and chapel hollowed out by 11th-century Greek Orthodox hermits are still visible. **MAHART ferries**

go to Tihany from Siófok (1hr., every hr., 700Ft). To reach the town from the ferry pier and neighboring Strand, walk underneath the elevated road and follow the "Apátság" signs up the steep hill to the abbey. ☎087.

KESZTHELY. At the lake's west tip, the resort of Keszthely (KESS-tay), once the playground of the powerful Austro-Hungarian Festetics family, now hosts an agricultural college and year-round thermal springs. The ▩**Helikon Palace Museum** (Helikon Kastélymúzeum) in the **Festetics Palace** (Kastély) is a storybook Baroque palace with a 90,000-volume library, extravagantly furnished chambers, an exotic arms collection, and a porcelain exhibit. From Fő tér, follow Kossuth Lajos u. toward Tourinform until it becomes Kastély u. (Open Tu-Su 9am-6pm. 1500Ft, students 750Ft.) The **Strand,** on the coast to the right as you exit the train station, attracts crowds in spite of its rocky and swampy terrain. From the center, walk down Erzsébet u. as it curves right into Vörösmarty u.; after the train tracks, go through the park on the left to get to the beach. (Open 8:30am-7pm. 320-370Ft.).

   Express trains run between Keszthely and Budapest (3hr., 13 per day, 1956Ft). From the train station, take Mártirok u., which ends in Kossuth Lajos u., and turn left to reach the main square, Fő tér. **Tourinform,** Kossuth Lajos u. 28, on the palace side of Fő tér, arranges private rooms from 3000Ft. (☎/fax 31 41 44. Open July-Aug. M-F 9am-8pm, Sa-Su 9am-6pm; Oct.-June M-F 9am-5pm, Sa 9am-1pm.) **Admiral Panzio ❹,** Pázmány P. u. 1, has immaculate, spacious rooms and a helpful staff. (☎31 42 68; www.admiralpanzio.hu. Reception 24hr. Singles 5924-10,124Ft; doubles 7648-11,848Ft.) **Castrum Camping ❷,** Móra Ferenc u. 48, has large sites with amenities such as tennis courts. (☎31 21 20. 930Ft per person. July-Aug. 580-680Ft per tent; Sept.-June 450-680Ft per tent.) **Corso Restaurant ❸,** Erzsébet Királyné u. 23, in the Abbázia Club Hotel, serves fish from Balaton. (Main dishes 650-1600Ft. Open M-Sa 7am-11pm.) **Oázis-Reform Restaurant ❶,** Rákóczi tér 3, is a vegetarian's lunchtime heaven. (210Ft per 100g. Open M-F 11am-4pm, Sa 11am-2pm.) ☎083.

ICELAND (ÍSLAND)

Iceland's landscape is uniquely warped and contorted, having been forged by the tempers of still-active volcanoes and raked by the slow advance and retreat of timeless glaciers. Nature is the country's greatest attraction—few other places allow visitors to walk across lava-filled moonscapes, dodge warm water shooting from geysers, and sail across a glacial lagoon filled with icebergs. Civilization has made a powerful mark on Iceland; the geothermal energy that causes numerous earthquakes also provides hot water and electricity to Iceland's settlements, and a network of roads carved through seemingly inhospitable terrain connects even the smallest villages to larger cities. A booming tourist industry attests to the fact that physical isolation has not set the country behind the rest of Europe. However, Iceland's island status has allowed it to achieve a high standard of living without damaging its pristine natural surroundings and deeply rooted sense of community.

FACTS AND FIGURES

Official Name: Ísland.

Capital: Reykjavík.

Major Cities: Hafnarfjörður, Höfn, Ísafjörður, Vík.

Population: 275,000.

Land Area: 103,000 sq. km.

Time Zone: GMT

Language: Icelandic; English is widely spoken.

Religions: Evangelical Lutheran (93%).

DISCOVER ICELAND

Spend a day exploring the heart of **Reykjavík** (p. 542), then daytrip to the peerless wonders of **Gullfoss, Geysir,** and **Blue Lagoon** (p. 547). Return to the city as the sun attempts to set, enjoying an intimate cafe or the never-ending Icelandic nightlife.

ESSENTIALS

WHEN TO GO

High season hits in July, when the interior opens up, snow almost disappears, and all the bus lines are running. In summer, the sun dips below the horizon for a few hours each night, but the sky never truly gets dark and it's warm enough to camp and hike. With warm clothing you could travel as late as October, but in winter there is very little sun. The temperature rarely gets higher than 60°F (16°C) in summer or dips below 20°F (-6°C) in winter.

DOCUMENTS AND FORMALITIES

VISAS. South Africans need a visa for stays of any length. Citizens of Australia, Canada, the EU, New Zealand, and the US do not need a visa for stays of up to 90 days, but this three-month period begins upon entry into any Nordic country; for more than 90 days in any combination of Denmark, Finland, Iceland, Norway, and/or Sweden, you will need a visa.

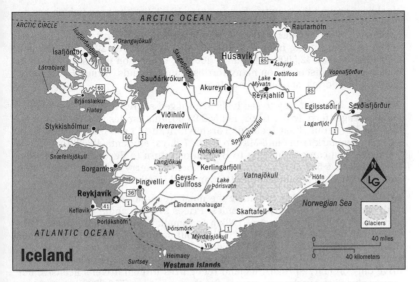

Iceland

EMBASSIES. Foreign embassies in Iceland are in Reykjavík (see p. 544). For Icelandic embassies at home: **Canada,** 360 Albert St., Suite 710, Ottawa, ON KIR 7X7 (☎613-482-1944; fax 613-482-1945); **UK,** 2A Hans St., London SW1X 0JE (☎020 7259 3999; www.iceland.org.uk); and **US,** 1156 15th St. NW, Suite 1200, Washington, D.C. 20005 (☎202-265-6653; www.iceland.org).

TRANSPORTATION

BY PLANE. Icelandair (US ☎800-223-5500; UK ☎020 7874 1000; www.icelandair.net) flies to Reykjavík year-round from the US and Europe. Icelandair provides free stopovers of up to three days on all transatlantic flights; it also offers some student discounts, including half-price standby flights. Domestic **Flugfélag Islands** (☎750 30 30; eyjaflug.is) flies between Reykjavík and Iceland's other major towns; tickets can be issued at BSÍ Travel (see p. 542). Another option is the **Air/Bus Rover** (fly one way, bus the other), offered jointly by the domestic air carriers and BSÍ Travel (June-Sept.; from 8000Ikr). Weather can ground flights; leave yourself time for delays.

BY BUS. Iceland has no trains; although flying is faster and more comfortable, buses are usually cheaper and provide a closer look at the terrain. One tour company, **Destination Iceland** (☎591 10 00; www.dice.is), which has offices in the Reykjavík bus terminal, coordinates all schedules and prices. Schedules are available at hostels and tourist offices. Their main brochure lists all bus schedules and is a must for anyone traveling the **Ring Road,** the loop that circles Iceland. Buses run daily on each segment from mid-June to August, but frequency drops dramatically in the off season. The going is slow, since some roads are unpaved. The circle can be rushed through in three days, but ten days is a much more adequate time frame.

The **Full Circle Passport** lets travelers circle the island at their own pace on the Ring Road (available mid-May to Sept.; 21,000Ikr). It allows travel only in a continuous direction, so travelers must move either clockwise or counterclockwise around the country. For an extra 10,000Ikr, the pass (which has no time limitation) provides access to the Westfjords in the island's extreme northwest. The **Omnibus Passport** gives a period of unlimited travel on all scheduled bus routes, including non-Ring roads (1-week 23,000Ikr, 2-week 33,000Ikr, 3-week 42,500Ikr, 4-week 47,000Ikr; off-season prices lower). Both passes give 5% discounts on many ferries, campgrounds, farms, *Hótel Edda* sleeping-bag dorms, and guided bus tours.

BY FERRY. The best way to see Iceland's rugged shores is on the **Norröna** car and passenger ferry (☎562 63 62; fax 552 94 50) that circles the North Atlantic via: Seyðisfjörður, East Iceland; Tórshavn in the Faroe Islands; and Hanstholm, Denmark (runs mid-May to Aug.; 7 days, students 42,500Ikr). From Tórshavn, you can continue on to Bergen or return to Seyðisfjörður. **Eimskip** (reservations ☎585 4070) offers more expensive ferry rides on cargo ships from Reykjavík to Immingham, Rotterdam, and Hamburg.

BY CAR. Travelers using cars have the most freedom. Iceland is overflowing with car rental *(bílaleiga)* companies. Prices average about 5000Ikr per day and 40Ikr per km after the first 100km for smaller cars, but are substantially higher for 4-wheel-drive vehicles (ask about special package deals). **Ragnar Bjarnason,** Staðarbakka 2 (☎557 42 66; fax 557 42 33), offers the lowest rates. You are required to keep your headlights on at all times, wear a seatbelt, and drive only on marked roads. Iceland recognizes foreign driver's licenses, but you may need to purchase insurance for the rented car (750-2000Ikr).

BY BIKE AND BY THUMB. Cycling is gaining popularity, but ferocious winds, driving rain, and nonexistent road shoulders make it difficult. Buses will carry bikes for a 5000-7000Ikr fee, depending on the distance covered. Trekking is extremely arduous; well-marked trails are rare, but several suitable areas await the truly ambitious. Ask the tourist office in Reykjavík for maps and more info. Determined hitchers try the roads in summer, but sparse traffic and harsh weather exacerbate the inherent risks. Nevertheless, for those who last, the ride usually does come (easily between Reykjavík and Akureyri; harder in the east and the south). *Let's Go* does not recommend hitchhiking.

TOURIST SERVICES AND MONEY

EMERGENCY	Police: ☎112. Ambulance: ☎112. Fire: ☎112.

TOURIST OFFICES. Tourist offices in large towns have schedules, maps, and brochures; check at hotel reception desks in smaller towns for local information. The free brochure *Around Iceland* (accommodation, restaurant, and museum listings for every town in the country), *The Complete Iceland Map*, and the BSÍ bus schedule are all must-haves. Reykjavík's tourist office maintains a helpful website (www.tourist.reykjavik.is), as does the US tourist board (www.goiceland.org).

MONEY. Iceland's monetary unit is the **króna,** which is divided into 100 *aurar.* There are 1Ikr, 5Ikr, 10Ikr, 50Ikr, and 100Ikr coins; notes are in denominations of 500Ikr, 1000Ikr, 2000Ikr, and 5000Ikr. Costs are high: on average, a night in a hostel might cost you 1750Ikr, a budget hotel 6500-8500Ikr, and a budget restaurant meal 1000-2000Ikr. Tipping is not customary in Iceland. **Value-added tax (VAT)** is included in all posted prices; refunds are available upon departure for purchases of 4000Ikr or more (see p. 15).

ICELANDIC KRÓNUR	AUS\$1 = 46.98IKR	100IKR = AUS\$2.12
	CDN\$1 = 55.39IKR	100IKR = AUS\$2.12
	EUR€1 = 83.89IKR	100IKR = EUR€1.20
	NZ\$1 = 40.32IKR	100IKR = NZ\$2.48
	ZAR1 = 7.97IKR	100IKR = ZAR12.54
	UK£1 = 131.16IKR	100IKR = UK£0.76
	US\$1 = 86.26IKR	100IKR = US\$1.15

BUSINESS HOURS. Stores are generally open Monday to Friday 9am-5pm (6pm in summer) and Saturday mornings.

COMMUNICATION

TELEPHONES. Telephone *(sími)* offices are often in the same building as post offices. Pay phones take phone cards or 10Ikr, 50Ikr, or 100Ikr pieces; local calls cost 20Ikr. For the best prices, make calls from telephone offices; next best is a prepaid phone card. To make an international call, insert a phone card or dial direct (see numbers below). To reach the operator, call ☎118 (59Ikr per minute). International direct dial numbers include: **AT&T,** ☎800 90 01; **British Telecom,** ☎800 90 44; **Canada Direct,** ☎800 90 10; **Ireland Direct,** ☎800 93 53; **MCI,** ☎800 90 02; **Sprint,** ☎800 90 03; **Telecom New Zealand Direct,** ☎800 199 64; **Telkom South Africa,** ☎800 199 27; and **Telstra Australia,** ☎800 199 61.

PHONE CODE	**Country code: 354. International dialing prefix: 00.** There are no city codes in Iceland. From outside Iceland, dial int'l dialing prefix (see inside back cover) + 354 + local number.

MAIL. Mailing a postcard or letter from Iceland costs 80Ikr to Australia, Canada, New Zealand, the US, or South Africa; to Europe, 55Ikr. Post offices *(póstur)* are generally open M-F 9am-4:30pm. See p. 545 for information on *Poste Restante*.

INTERNET ACCESS. Internet access is widespread in Iceland, although in small towns it may only be available in public libraries.

ACCOMMODATIONS AND CAMPING

ICELAND	❶	❷	❸	❹	❺
ACCOMMODATIONS	500-1500Ikr	1500-3000Ikr	3000-5000Ikr	5000-10000Ikr	over 10000Ikr

Iceland's 27 **HI youth hostels,** invariably clean and always with kitchens, are uniformly priced at 1500Ikr for members, 1850Ikr for nonmembers. Pick up the free *Hostelling in Iceland* brochure at tourist offices. **Sleeping-bag accommodations** *(svefnpokapláss)*—available on farms, at summer hotels, and in guesthouses *(gistiheimili)*—are relatively cheap (see p. 545). In early June, many schoolhouses become *Hótel Eddas,* which have sleeping-bag accommodations (no kitchens; 950-1500Ikr, 5% discount with bus pass). Most also offer breakfast and beds, both quite expensive. Staying in a tiny farm or hostel can be the highlight of a trip, but the nearest bus may stop 20km away and run once a week. Many remote lodgings will pick up tourists in the nearest town for a small fee. In cities and nature reserves, **camping** is permitted only at designated campsites. Outside

ICELAND

of official sites, camping is free but discouraged; watch out for *Tjaldstœði bönnuð* (No Camping) signs, and always ask at the nearest farm before you pitch a tent. Use gas burners; Iceland has no firewood, and it is illegal to burn the sparse vegetation. Official campsites (summer only) range from rocky fields with cold water taps to the sumptuous facilities in Reykjavík (around 700Ikr). Many offer discounts for students and bus-pass holders.

FOOD AND DRINK

ICELAND	❶	❷	❸	❹	❺
FOOD	under 800Ikr	800-1200Ikr	1200-2000Ikr	2000-3500Ikr	over 3500Ikr

Traditional foods include *lundi* (puffin) on the Westman Islands, *rjúpa* (ptarmigan) around Christmas, and *selshreifar* (seal flippers) during the Þorra *matur* (Thorri or Mid-Winter Feast). Fish, lamb, and chicken are the most common components of authentic dishes, although more adventurous diners can try *svið* (singed and boiled sheep's head), *hrútspungur* (ram's testicles), or *hákarl* (rotten shark meat that has been buried underground), all of which are traditional dishes consumed during the Thorri Feast. International cuisine also has a strong presence in Iceland, and Italian, American, and Asian fare can usually be found even in smaller towns. Food is very expensive in Iceland; a *cheap* restaurant meal will cost at least 800Ikr. Grocery stores are the way to go; virtually every town has a couple of them. Gas stations usually run a grill and sell snacks. Bonus and Netto are cheaper alternatives to the more ubiquitous Hagkaup and 10-11. Iceland has some of the purest water in Europe. Beer costs 500-600Ikr at most pubs, cafes, and restaurants. The national drink is *Brennivín*, a type of schnapps known as "the Black Death." The rarely enforced drinking age is 20.

HOLIDAYS

Holidays: New Year's (Jan. 1); Good Friday (Apr. 18); Easter (Apr. 20-21); Labor Day (May 1); Ascension Day (May 29); National Day (June 17); Whit Sunday and Monday (Seventh Sunday and Monday after Easter); Commerce Day (Aug. 5); Christmas Eve and Day (Dec. 24-25); Boxing Day (Dec. 26); New Year's Eve (Dec. 31).

REYKJAVÍK

Reykjavík's character more than makes up for its modest size. Bold, modern architecture complements a backdrop of snow-dusted purple mountains, and the city's refreshingly clear air is matched by its sparkling streets and gardens. Although quiet during the week, the world's smallest metropolitan capital comes alive on weekends. Inviting and virtually crime-free, Reykjavík's only weaknesses are its often-frigid weather and its high cost of living.

⊏ TRANSPORTATION

Flights: All international flights arrive at **Keflavík Airport** (KEF), 55km from Reykjavík. From the main exit, catch a **Flybus** (☎562 10 11, departs 30min. after every arrival, 900Ikr) to the domestic **Reykjavík Airport** (REK) or Hótel Loftleiðir; from the hotel, you can take Flybus minivans to your hostel or hotel (free of charge) or bus #7 (every 20min. until 7pm, every hr. after 7pm; 200Ikr) downtown to Lækjartorg. Flybuses back to the airport stop at Hótel Loftleiðir (2hr. before each departure), Grand Hótel Reykjavík (2½hr. before), and

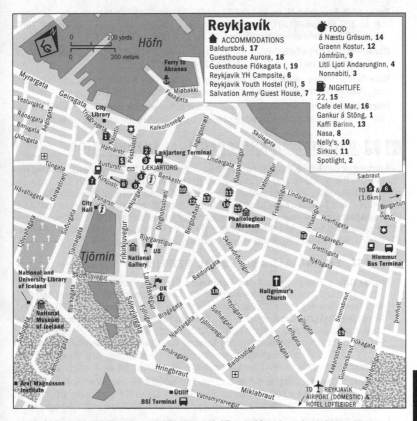

Reykjavík

🏠 ACCOMMODATIONS
Baldursbrá, 17
Guesthouse Aurora, 18
Guesthouse Flókagata I, 19
Reykjavik YH Campsite, 6
Reykjavik Youth Hostel (HI), 5
Salvation Army Guest House, 7

🍴 FOOD
á Næstu Grösum, 14
Graenn Kostur, 12
Jómfrúin, 9
Litli Ljoti Andarunginn, 4
Nonnabiti, 3

🍺 NIGHTLIFE
22, 15
Cafe del Mar, 16
Gankur á Stöng, 1
Kaffi Barinn, 13
Nasa, 8
Nelly's, 10
Sirkus, 11
Spotlight, 2

the youth hostel (June-Aug. 4:45am and 1:15pm). Most hostels and guesthouses can arrange for their guests to be picked up by Flybus at no extra charge. The **Omnibus Pass** (but not Full Circle Passport; see p. 539) covers Flybus; get a refund at Destination Iceland (see below) or Reykjavík Excursions (in the Hótel Loftleiðir; open 24hr.).

Buses: Umferðarmiðstöð (also known as **BSÍ Station**), Vatnsmýrarvegur 10 (☎552 23 00), off Hringbraut near Reykjavík Airport. Walk 15-20min. south along Tjörnin from the city center, or take bus #7 or 8 (every 20-30min., 200Ikr). Open daily 7am-midnight; tickets sold 7:30am-10pm. **Destination Iceland** (☎591 10 20; www.dice.is), inside the bus terminal, sells bus passes and tour packages. Open June-Aug. M-F 7:30am-7pm, Sa-Su 7:30am-5pm; Sept.-May M-F 9am-5pm.

Public Transportation: Strætisvagnar Reykjavíkur (SVR; ☎551 27 00) operates yellow city buses (200Ikr). Pick up SVR's helpful city map and bus schedule at its terminals. Tickets are sold at four terminals; the two major terminals are **Lækjartorg** in the center of town (open M-F 7am-11:30pm, Sa 8am-11:30pm, Su 10am-11:30pm) and **Hlemmur,** farther east on Hverfisg. (open M-Sa 8am-11:30pm, Su 10am-11:30pm). Either buy packages of 10 adult fares (1000Ikr) or 20 senior fares (1600Ikr) beforehand or buy tickets on the bus (exact change only). Ask the driver for a free transfer ticket (*skiptimiði*; valid for 45min.). Buses run M-Sa 7am-midnight, Su and holidays 10am-midnight. Night buses #125, 130, and 135 run limited routes F-Sa until 4:30am.

ICELAND

Taxis: BSR, Skolatröð 18 (☎561 00 00). 24hr. service. Tipping not customary. City center to: BSÍ Station 600-700lkr; Keflavík Airport 7200lkr; and Reykjavík Airport 700-800lkr. Other companies: **Hreyfill** (☎588 55 22); **BSH** (☎555 08 88).

Car Rental: Hertz (☎505 06 00), in the Reykjavík Airport. 3510-11440lkr per day. Also at the **youth hostel** (see p. 545). 4900-12500lkr per day.

Bike Rental: At the **youth hostel campsite** (see p. 545). 800lkr per 6hr., 1500lkr per day. Also at **Central Reykjavik Travel Service** (see Tourist Office). 1600lkr per day.

Hitchhiking: Hitchhiking is uncommon but not difficult in Iceland. Those looking for a ride generally head to the east edge of town. *Let's Go* does not recommend hitchhiking.

■◪ ◲ ORIENTATION AND PRACTICAL INFORMATION

Lækjartorg is Reykjavík's main square and a good base for navigation. **Lækjargata** leads from the southern end of Lækjartorg to **Tjörnin** (the pond), which lies halfway between the square and BSÍ Station. Reykjavík's main thoroughfare extends east and west from Lækjartorg, changing names from **Austurstræti** to **Bankastræti** and then **Laugavegur** as it moves west to east. City maps are available at the tourist office or around town, and the monthlies *What's On in Reykjavík* and *Reykjavík This Month* provide information about exploring the city (all free).

TOURIST, FINANCIAL, AND LOCAL SERVICES

Tourist Office: Upplýsingamiðstöð Ferðamála í Íslandi, Bankastr. 2 (☎562 30 45; www.tourist.reykjavik.is), at Lækjartorg and Bankastr. **Branches** at the airport and City Hall. Open June-Aug. daily 8:30am-6pm; Sept.-May M-F 9am-5pm, Sa-Su 10am-2pm. All sell the **Reykjavík Card,** which allows unlimited public transportation and free entry to several museums and sights. (1-day 1000lkr, 2-day 1500lkr, 3-day 2000lkr. See p. 546 for participating establishments.) **Central Reykjavík Travel Service,** Lækjarg. 2 (☎511 24 42; www.travelservice.is), provides personal attention, rents **bikes,** and has **Internet** access (250lkr per 30min.). Open M-F 8am-10pm, Sa-Su 10am-10pm.

Embassies: Canada, Túngata 14 (☎533 55 50; fax 568 08 99). Open M-F 8am-4pm. **UK,** Laufásvegur 31 (☎550 51 00; fax 550 51 05). Open M-F 9am-noon. **US,** Laufásvegur 21 (☎562 91 00; fax 562 91 10). Open M-F 8am-12:30pm and 1:30-5pm.

Luggage Storage: At BSÍ Station, next to ticket window. 300lkr per day. Open daily 7:30am-7pm.

Laundromat: Þvottahusið Drifa, Hringbraut 19. **Þvottahusið Emla,** Barónsstíg. 3, just south of Hverfisg. Full service. 1700lkr per load. Open M-F 8am-6pm.

EMERGENCY AND COMMUNICATIONS

Emergency: ☎112.

Police: Headquarters at Hverfisg. 113-115 (☎569 90 20). Downtown office at Tryggvag. 19 (☎569 90 25).

Pharmacies: Lyf og Heilsa, Haaleitisbraut 68 (☎581 21 01). Open daily 8am-midnight. **Lyfja Apótek,** Laugavegur 16 (☎552 40 45). Open M-F 9am-7pm, Sa 10am-4pm.

Medical Assistance: National Hospital at Fossvogur (☎525 17 00), on Hringbraut, has a 24hr. emergency ward. From the center of town, take bus #3 southeast.

Telephones: Phones require either coins or a phone card (500 or 1000lkr; available at the tourist office, post office, and most convenience stores). For local calls insert at least 20lkr. Phones accept 10, 50, or 100lkr coins. International assistance: ☎1811.

Internet Access: City Hall cafe, north of Tjörnin. Free 20min. slots. Open M-F 8am-7pm, Sa-Su 10-6pm. **Ground Zero,** Vallarstr. 4. 300lkr per 30min. Open daily 10am-1am. **K-Lanið,** Laugavegur 103. 250lkr per 30min., 1000lkr per day. Open daily 10am-11pm.

Post Office: Íslandspóstur, Pósthússtr. 5, at Austurstr. (☎580 11 01). Address mail to be held: Firstname SURNAME, Poste Restante, ÍSLANDSPÓSTUR, Pósthússtr. 5, 101 Reykjavík, ICELAND. Mail held for 56 days, packages 28 days. Open M-F 9am-4:30pm.

ACCOMMODATIONS AND CAMPING

Many *gistiheimili* (guesthouses) offer "sleeping-bag accommodations" (bed, mattress, and pillow in a dorm room; add 300-500Ikr for a blanket). **Útilíf**, located directly in front of BSÍ Station, sells and rents sleeping bags and tents. (Open June-Aug. M-F 9am-6pm, Sa 10am-4pm.) Cheap hotels cost at least 5500Ikr. Call ahead for reservations, especially between mid-June and August.

Hjálpræðisherinn Gisti-og Sjómannaheimili (Salvation Army Guest and Seamen's Home), Kirkjustr. 2 (☎561 32 03; www.guesthouse.is), in a pale yellow house one block north of Tjörnin, at the corner of Kirkjustr. and Tjarnarg. Bustles with backpackers enjoying the fantastic location and friendly staff. Kitchen. Breakfast 800Ikr. Laundry 700Ikr. May-Sept. sleeping-bag accommodations 1800Ikr; singles 4000Ikr; doubles 5500Ikr; triples 7000Ikr; quads 8500Ikr. Oct.-Apr. reduced prices. ❷

Guesthouse Flókagata 1, Flókag. 1 (☎552 11 55; guesthouse@eyjar.is). From Hallgrímur's Church, head down Egilsg. and turn left onto Snorrabraut. The guesthouse is on the corner on the right. Pristine rooms. Breakfast included. Reception 24hr. May-Sept. sleeping-bag accommodations 2500Ikr; singles 6900Ikr; doubles 9900Ikr. Extra bed 3200Ikr. Oct.-Apr. prices drop 10%. ❷

Reykjavík Youth Hostel (HI), Sundlaugavegur 34 (☎553 81 10; info@hostel.is). Take bus #5 from Lækjarg. to Sundlaugavegur. Far from the center of town, but next to Laugardalslaug (see p. 546). Kitchen. Laundry 300Ikr. Internet 200Ikr per 15min. Flybus pickup 900Ikr. Reception 8am-11pm; ring bell after hours. Sleeping bag accommodations 1500Ikr; singles 1500Ikr; doubles 2800Ikr. Nonmembers add 350Ikr. ❶

Guesthouse Aurora, Freyjug. 24 (☎552 55 15; fax 551 48 94). Head south on Njarðarg. from Hallgrímur's Church and turn right onto Freyjug.; Aurora is the purple house on the left-hand corner. In a quiet neighborhood 10min. from the city center. Rustically homey, perfect for couples. Kitchen. Breakfast included. Laundry 250Ikr. July-Aug. singles 5500Ikr; doubles 7000Ikr; triples 9500Ikr. Sept.-June reduced prices. ❹

Baldursbrá, Laufásvegur 41 (☎552 66 46; heijfis@centrum.is), 10min. north of BSÍ Station, 5-10min. south of city center. Family-run guesthouse in a quiet residential neighborhood. Reserve ahead. Kitchen and sauna 300Ikr. May-Sept. singles 6500Ikr; doubles 8500Ikr. Oct.-Apr. singles 4350Ikr; doubles 7000Ikr. 10% cash discount. ❷

Reykjavík Youth Hostel Campsite (☎568 69 44), next to the youth hostel. Take bus #5 from city center. Campsite in a huge field next to Laugardalslaug (see p. 546). Friendly staff. Free bus from the campsite to BSÍ Station at 7:30am. Laundry 300Ikr. Free showers. Open mid-May to mid-Sept. 700Ikr per person; 2-bed cabins 3800Ikr. ❶

FOOD

An authentic Icelandic meal featuring seafood, lamb, or puffin will cost at least 1000Ikr and is worth splurging on at least once. Otherwise, buy fresh food at a market and take advantage of the kitchen in your hostel or guesthouse. Many supermarkets are on **Austurstræti**, **Hverfisgata**, and **Laugavegur**. Cheap fast-food joints are easy to find in the area west of Lækjartorg, especially on **Hafnarstræti** and **Tryggvagata**. The best of them is **Nonnabiti ❶**, Hafnarstr. 18, an Icelandic-style sandwich shop. (550-640Ikr. Open Su-Th 10am-2am, F-Sa 10am-5:30am.)

á Næstu Grösum (One Woman Restaurant), Laugavegur 20B, at the intersection with Klapparstígur. Delicious vegetarian fare, soothing environment. Daily special 600-900Ikr. Open M-Sa 11:30am-2pm and 5-10pm, Su 5-10pm. ❶

ICELAND

Jómfrúin, Lækjarg. 4. Casual Danish restaurant serves delectable open sandwiches (530-1680Ikr) that are almost too pretty to eat. Outdoor seating available. Beer 200-500Ikr. Open Apr.-Sept. daily 11am-10pm; Oct.-Mar. 11am-6pm. ❷

Litli Ljoti Andarunginn, Lækjarg. 6B. Litli's fish buffet (1990Ikr, available after 6pm), is the most affordable way to sample the Arctic's delicacies. Catch of the day 1090Ikr. Wine 650Ikr, beer 350Ikr. Open Su-Th 11am-1am, F-Sa 11am-3am. ❷

Grænn Kostur, Skólavörðustígur 8B. Two daily vegetarian specials (800Ikr) and luscious dessert cakes (450Ikr). Open M-Sa 11:30am-9pm, Su 1pm-9pm. ❶

🚶 📷 SIGHTS AND HIKING

SIGHTS. Laugardalslaug is the largest of Reykjavík's geothermally heated pools. It boasts a giant slide and a series of jacuzzis, each one hotter than the last. (On Sundlaugavegur, next to the youth hostel campground. Bus #5. Open M-F 6:50am-9:30pm, Sa-Su 8am-8pm. 200Ikr.) A stunning domed gallery houses the **Ásmundur Sveinsson Sculpture Museum,** on Sigtún. (Bus #5. Open May-Sept. daily 10am-4pm; Oct.-Apr. 1-4pm. 500Ikr.) **Listasafn Íslands** (National Gallery of Iceland), Fríkirkjuvegur 7, on the east shore of Tjörnin, displays small exhibits of traditional Icelandic art, while the **Reykjavík Art Museum,** on Sigtún, focuses on more modern painting and sculpture. (Listasafn open Tu-Su 11am-5pm, Th until 10pm. 400Ikr, seniors 250; W free. Reykjavík Art open daily 11am-6pm, Th until 7pm. Free Internet in cafe. 500Ikr.) Laugardalslaug and these three museums are among the sights covered by the **Reykjavík Card** (see p. 544); ask for a list other participating institutions when you purchase the card.

Some of the city's must-sees are free or not covered by the Reykjavík Card. **City Hall,** on the north end of Tjörnin, is home to a raised relief map of Iceland as well as rotating exhibits. (Open M-F 8am-7pm, Sa-Su 10am-6pm. Free.) East of Lækjartorg is the world's only **Phallological Museum,** Laugavegur 24, a collection of Arctic and Icelandic mammal members sure to humble any man. Look for the sign and turn right through the yellow corridor. (Open Tu-Sa 2-5pm. 400kr.) Turn off Laugavegur onto Skólavörðustígur to reach **Hallgrímskirkja** (Hallgrímur's Church), whose soaring steeple is the highest point in the city. A trip to the top provides a spectacular view and a good sense of Reykjavík's layout. (Open daily 9am-6pm. Services Su 11am. Elevator to the top 200Ikr.)

HIKING. South of the city lies the **Heiðmörk Reserve,** a large park and sports complex. Heiðmörk has the best hiking trails and picnicking spots in the Reykjavík area; however, there is no public transportation directly to the park. Pleasant **Viðey Island,** home to Iceland's second-oldest church, has been inhabited since the 10th century. (Ferry schedules are available at tourist offices and BSÍ Station.) Across the bay from Reykjavík looms **Mt. Esja,** which you can ascend via a well-maintained trail (2-3hr.). While the trail is not difficult, hikers are often assaulted by rain, hail, and snow, even in summer. (Take bus #10 or #110 to Artún and transfer to bus #20, exiting at Mógilsá. Bus #20 runs only once every 1-2hr.; consult SVR city bus schedule before departing.)

📷 NIGHTLIFE

Although quiet on weeknights, Reykjavík reasserts its reputation as a wild party town each weekend; nowhere else on earth can you step out of a club at 3am to a sky that has barely dimmed to twilight. To avoid vicious drink prices and cover charges, most Icelanders pregame at home and then hit the clubs just before covers kick in. Only designated liquor stores can sell alcohol; **Nelly's,** Þingholtsstr. 2, sells the cheapest beer in town. (Open Su-Th noon-1am, F-Sa noon-6am.) Most cafes turn into boisterous bars on weekend nights, and crowds happily bar-hop along the vibrant streets **Austurstræti, Tryggvagata,** and **Laugavegur.**

CAFES

Kaffi Barinn, on Bergstaðastr. near Laugavegur. Cafe by day, bar by night, madhouse on weekends. Coffee 200-250Ikr, beer 550Ikr. Food served noon-6pm. Live DJ Th-Sa. Open M-Th 11am-1am, F 11am-4am, Sa noon-5am, Su 2pm-1am.

Sirkus, Klapparstígur 30. Outside patio and upstairs room make Sirkus the undisputed place to relax in Reykjavík. They've got the barbecue and basketball hoop if you've got beef or a ball. Beer 550Ikr. Open M-Th 5pm-1am, F-Sa 5pm-5:30am, Su 7pm-1am.

Cafe del Mar, Vitastígur 10A. One of the only cafes that keeps the coffeepot full after other cafes tap the keg. Live DJ Th. Pot of coffee 600Ikr. Open M-Sa 10:30am-1am, Su 2-11:30pm.

PUBS AND CLUBS

Gaukur á Stöng, Tryggvag. 22. Iceland's first pub and the most popular spot for live music. Schedules on www.gaukurinn.is. Open Su-Th 9pm-1am, F-Sa 9pm-5:30am.

22, Laugavegur 22. Upstairs disco, downstairs bar. A solid starter for your Laugavegur bar-hopping. 500Ikr cover after 1am. Open Su-Th 11:30am-1am, F-Sa noon-5:30am.

Nasa, Viðausturvöll 18. Reykjavík's most all-out dance club. Open F-Sa 11pm-4am.

Spotlight, Hafnarstr. 17, just down from the SVR Lækjartorg bus station. A self-proclaimed "straight-friendly" bar, Spotlight welcomes anyone and everyone to its all-night raves. Beer 600Ikr. Open Su-Th 9pm-1am, F-Sa 9pm-6am.

◪ DAYTRIPS FROM REYKJAVÍK

Reykjavík is nice and all, but Iceland's true attractions are its mesmerizing natural wonders. Renting a car may be the best approach for groups (see p. 540); the comprehensive **bus tours** are more economical for solo travelers. **Iceland Excursions** runs the popular **Golden Circle** guided tour, stopping at Hveragerði, Kerið, Skálholt, Geysir, Gullfoss, and Þingvellir National Park. (Departs from Hótel Loftleiðir daily at 8:30am. 8hr. 5200Ikr). Book ahead in the tourist office or by phone (☎ 562 10 11). Free pickup at a number of other hotels and hostels in Reykjavík is available.

BLUE LAGOON. Southwest of Reykjavík lies paradise: a vast pool of geothermally heated water in the middle of a lava field. The lagoon is alongside a natural power plant that provides Reykjavík with electricity and heat by harnessing geothermal steam. Though the lagoon attracts a few too many tourists, its unique concentrations of silica, minerals, and algae are soothing enough to rejuvenate any crowd-weary traveler. Once inside the misty blue waters, bathers may further indulge in a steam bath, a skin-soothing mud facial, or a massage (1200Ikr per 10min.). The lagoon rents towels (300Ikr) and bathing suits (250Ikr) if you've forgotten your own. (3hr. admission 880Ikr; locker included.) **Buses** run from BSÍ Station in Reykjavík to the Blue Lagoon. (Daily 10am, 1:30, 5:15, and 6pm; return 12:40, 4, 6, and 8pm. 850Ikr each way.) Most hostels and hotels can arrange for pickup if you call ahead.

◪ GULLFOSS AND GEYSIR. A glacial river plunging over 30m creates Gullfoss, the "Golden Falls." The greatest attraction of Gullfoss, besides the falls themselves, is the stunning view of the surrounding mountains, plains, and glaciers from atop the hill adjacent to the falls. Only 9km away is the **Geysir** area, a rocky, rugged tundra with steaming pools of hot water every few meters. The energetic **Strokkur** erupts every 5-10min., reaching heights of up to 25-35m. BSÍ runs a round-trip **bus** to both sites, stopping at Gullfoss for 1hr. and Geysir for 1-2hr. The ride is lengthy and roundabout, but the beautiful destinations are worth it. (Departs Reykjavík daily June-Aug. 8:30am and 12:30pm; Sept.-May M-Sa 9:30am, Su 12:30pm. 3800Ikr.)

ÞINGVELLIR NATIONAL PARK. Straddling the divide between the European and North American tectonic plates, Þingvellir National Park features impressive scenery. The **Öxará River,** slicing through lumpy lava fields and jagged fissures, leads to the **Drekkingarhylur** (Drowning Pool), where adulterous women were once drowned, and to **Lake Þingvallavatn,** the largest lake in Iceland. Not far from the Drekkingarhylur lies the site of **Alþing,** the ancient parliament of the first Icelandic democracy in AD 930. For almost nine centuries, Icelanders gathered once a year in the shadow of the Lögberg (Law Rock) to discuss matters of blood, money, and justice. A **bus** runs from Reykjavík to Þingvellir, dropping visitors off at an **information center.** (☎482 26 60. Open May-Sept. daily 8:30am-8pm. Bus May 20-Sept. 10 daily 1:30pm, return 4:50pm. 850Ikr, round-trip 1700Ikr.) Ask for directions for the 30-45min. walk along the road to reach the lake or the main historical sites. The **campground** by the information center has showers and laundry machines (500Ikr).

WESTMAN ISLANDS (VESTMANNAEYJAR)

Vaulting boldly from the depths of the North Atlantic, the black cliffs off the Westman Islands are the most recent products of the volcanic fury that created Iceland. Heimaey, the only inhabited island, is one of the most important fishing ports in the country. The three-day **Þjóðhátíð** (People's Feast) draws a hefty percentage of Reykjavík's livelier citizens to the island's shores for an annual festival of drinking and dancing (Aug. 1-3); the rest of the year, Heimaey is quiet and subdued.

⌨🔃 TRANSPORTATION AND PRACTICAL INFORMATION. Getting to and from the Westman Islands is relatively easy. Flugfélag Islands (Air Iceland) has daily **flights** from Reykjavík Airport. (☎570 30 30. One-way from 5865Ikr.) A slower but much cheaper option is the Herjólfur **ferry** (☎481 28 00) departing from Þorlákshöfn. (3hr. In summer, daily at noon, Su-F also 7:30pm; return M-Sa 8:15am, Su 2pm, F also 4pm. In winter, M-Sa noon, Su 6pm, F also 7:30pm; return daily 8:15am, Su-F also 4pm. 1500Ikr.) Buses go from BSÍ Station in Reykjavík to the dock in Þorlákshöfn 1hr. before departure (750Ikr). The **tourist office** is on Básaskersbryggin, right in the central harbor. (☎481 35 55; www.eyjar.is. Open May-Sept. M-F 8am-5pm, Sa 10am-4pm, Su 10am-4pm; Oct.-May M-F 8am-5pm.) Ask about island **bus tours** (daily 8am and noon, or upon request; 1800Ikr) and **boat tours** (daily 10:30am and 3:30pm, 2000Ikr).

🔲🔳 ACCOMMODATIONS AND FOOD. Guesthouse Hreiðreið and Bolið ❶, Faxastigur 33, is just past the Volcanic Show cinema on Heiðarvegur. (☎699 89 45. Sleeping-bag accommodations 1500Ikr; singles 3200Ikr; doubles 5200Ikr.) **Guesthouse Sunnoholl ❷,** Vestmannabraut 28, houses visitors in a white house behind Hótel Þorshamar. (☎481 29 00. Sleeping-bag accommodations 2700Ikr, 1800Ikr per person if two or more; singles 3900Ikr.) The **campground ❶,** 10min. west of town on Dalvegur, near the golf course, has showers and cooking facilities. (☎692 69 52. 500Ikr.) Get groceries at **Krónan** on Strandavegur. (Open daily 11am-7pm.)

◼ SIGHTS. In 1973, the fiery **Eldfell** volcano tore through the northern section of Heimaey island, spewing glowing lava and hot ash in a surprise eruption that forced the population to flee in a dramatic overnight evacuation. When the eruption finally ceased five months later, a third of the town's houses had been destroyed but the island itself had grown by the same amount. Nearly all of its former inhabitants returned, rebuilding a more modern Heimaey. Today, visitors can feel the heat of the still-cooling lava, hike among the black and green mountains that shelter its harbor, and observe the chilling remnants of buildings half-crushed by the lava. The **Volcanic Show** cinema runs a fascinating but slow documentary about the eruption's full effects on the Westman Islands. (Shows daily at 11am and 3:30pm. 400Ikr.)

Hiking in the area is encouraged; the tourist office distributes a free map outlining hiking trails. Spectacular spots include the cliff's edge at **Há** and the puffin colony at **Stórhöfði**. Há provides a stunning view of the town, the twin volcanic peaks, and the snow-covered mainland. Both volcanic peaks also await intrepid hikers, but strong winds often make for rough going over the summits. Head to the **aquarium** on Heiðarvegur, near the gas station, to see some of the island's strange and wonderful sea creatures. (Open May-Sept. daily 11am-5pm; Sept.-Apr. Sa-Su 3-5pm; also upon request. 300Ikr.)

ICELAND

REPUBLIC OF IRELAND AND NORTHERN IRELAND

Travelers who come to Ireland with their heads filled with poetic imagery will not be disappointed—this largely agricultural and sparsely populated island still looks as it did when Celtic bards roamed the land. Windswept scenery is found all along the coast, and untouched mountain chains stretch across the interior bogland. The landscape is punctuated with pockets of civilization, ranging in size from one-street villages to large cities: Dublin and Belfast are cosmopolitan centers whose international populations greatly influence their immediate surroundings. Some fear this threatens the native culture, but the survival of traditional music, dance, and storytelling proves otherwise. The Irish language lives on in small, secluded areas known as *gaeltachts*, as well as on road signs, in national publications, and in a growing body of modern literary works. While non-violence usually prevails in Northern Ireland, recent negotiations hope to ensure peace for future generations. Although the Republic and Northern Ireland are grouped together in this chapter for geographical reasons, no political statement is intended.

FACTS AND FIGURES: REPUBLIC OF IRELAND

Official Name: Éire.
Capital: Dublin.
Major Cities: Cork, Limerick.
Population: 3,800,000.

Land Area: 70,280 sq. km.
Time Zone: GMT.
Languages: English, Irish.
Religion: Roman Catholic (91.6%).

DISCOVER IRELAND

Above all, take time to explore the thousand-year-old **Dublin** (p. 555), a bastion of literary history and the stomping-ground of international hipsters. Wander the grounds of Trinity College, catch a film in Temple Bar, and down a pint or two at one of the city's seemingly infinite pubs. A walk through **Belfast** (p. 579) will give you a glimpse of Northern Ireland's rich, complicated history. **Giant's Causeway** (p. 586), also in the North, is a unique formation of rocks called the 8th natural wonder of the world. In **Donegal Town** (p. 577), visitors get a taste of traditional Irish music, commonly called *trad*, before clambering the **Slieve League** (p. 577), Europe's tallest seacliffs. Devotees of W.B. Yeats shouldn't miss the region surrounding **Sligo** (p. 577), the poet's home town, which inspired many of his more famous poems. **Galway** (p. 574) is an artsy student town that draws the island's best musicians. The legendary scenery of the **Ring of Kerry** (p. 570) and the exquisite mountains and lakes of **Killarney National Park** (p. 569) will satisfy any nature lover. Wherever you go, stay hydrated by visiting any of Ireland's historical **breweries.**

ESSENTIALS

WHEN TO GO

Irish weather is subject to frequent changes but relatively constant temperatures. The southeastern coast is the driest and sunniest, while western Ireland is considerably wetter and cloudier. May and June are the sunniest months, July and

Ireland: Republic of Ireland and Northern Ireland

August the warmest. December and January have the worst weather. Take heart when you wake to clouded, foggy mornings—the weather usually clears by noon.

DOCUMENTS AND FORMALITIES

VISAS. Citizens of Australia, Canada, the EU, New Zealand, South Africa, and the US do not need a visa for stays of up to 90 days.

EMBASSIES. All embassies for the Republic of Ireland are in Dublin (p. 555). For Irish embassies at home, contact: **Australia,** 20 Arkana St., Yarralumla, Canberra ACT 2600 (☎062 73 3022); **Canada,** Suite 1105, 130 Albert St., Ottawa, ON K1P 5G4 (☎613-233-6281); **New Zealand,** Honorary Consul General, 6th fl., 18 Shortland St.

1001, Auckland 1 (☎09 997 2252); **South Africa,** 1st fl., Southern Life Plaza, 1059 Shoeman St., Arcadia 0083, Pretoria (☎012 342 5062); **UK,** 17 Grosvenor Pl., London SW1X 7HR (☎020 7235 2171); and **US,** 2234 Massachusetts Ave. NW, Washington, D.C. 20008 (☎202-462-3939).

TRANSPORTATION

BY PLANE. Flying to London and connecting to Ireland is often easier and cheaper than flying direct. A popular carrier to Ireland is its national airline, **Aer Lingus** (☎01 886 8888; US ☎800-IRISHAIR; www.aerlingus.ie), which has direct flights to the US, London, and Paris. **Ryanair** (☎01 609 7900; www.ryanair.ie) is a smaller airline that offers a "lowest-fare guarantee." The web-based phenomenon **easyJet** (UK☎08706 000 000; www.easyjet.com) has recently begun flying from Britain to Belfast. **British Airways** (UK ☎0845 773 3377; Republic ☎800 626 747; US ☎800-AIRWAYS; www.british-airways.com) flies into most Irish airports daily.

BY TRAIN. Iarnród Éireann (Irish Rail; ☎01 836 3333; www.irishrail.ie) is useful only for travel to urban areas. The **Eurail** pass is accepted in the Republic but not in Northern Ireland. The BritRail Pass does not cover travel in Northern Ireland or the Republic, but the month-long **BritRail+Ireland** pass works in both the North and the Republic, with rail options and round-trip ferry service between Britain and Ireland (€400-570). **Northern Ireland Railways** (☎028 9066 6630; www.nirailways.co.uk) is not extensive but covers the northeastern coastal region well; the major line connects Dublin to Belfast. A valid **Northern Ireland Travelsave** stamp (UK£6), affixed to the back of an ISIC card, will get you up to 33% off all train fares and 15% off bus fares over UK£1.45 within Northern Ireland. The **Freedom of Northern Ireland** ticket allows unlimited travel by train and Ulsterbus (1-day UK£11, 3-day UK£27.50, 7-day UK£40).

BY BUS. Bus Éireann (☎01 836 6111; www.buseireann.ie), the national bus company, reaches Britain and the Continent by working in conjunction with ferry services and the bus company **Eurolines** (www.eurolines.com). Most buses leave from Victoria Station in London (to Belfast: 15hr., €49/UK£31, round-trip €79/UK£51; Dublin: 12hr., €42/UK£27, round-trip €69/UK£45); other major city stops include Birmingham, Bristol, Cardiff, Glasgow, and Liverpool. Services run to Cork, Derry, Galway, Limerick, Waterford, and Tralee, among others. Discounted fares are available in the off-season, as well as for people under 26 or over 60. Bus Éireann operates both long-distance Expressway buses, which link larger cities, and local buses, which serve the countryside and smaller towns.

Ulsterbus (☎028 9033 3000; Belfast ☎028 9032 0011; www.ulsterbus.co.uk) runs extensive routes throughout Northern Ireland. The **Irish Rover** pass covers both Bus Éireann and Ulsterbus services (3 of 8 consecutive days €60/UK£90, children €33/UK£50; 8 of 15 €135/UK£200, children €75/UK£113; 15 of 30 €195/UK£293, children €110/UK£165). The **Emerald Card** offers unlimited travel on Ulsterbus, Northern Ireland Railways, Bus Éireann Expressway, and many local services; for more info, see www.buseireann.ie (8 of 15 consecutive days €168/UK£108, children €84/UK£54; 15 of 30 €290/UK£187, children €145/UK£94).

BY FERRY. Ferries, more economical than air travel, journey between Britain and Ireland several times per day (€28-55/UK£18-35). Weeknight travel promises the cheapest fares. An Óige (HI) members receive up to a 20% discount on fares from Irish Ferries and Stena Sealink, while ISIC cardholders with the TravelSave stamp receive a 15-17% discount on Stena Line and Irish Ferries. Ferries run from Cork to South Wales and Roscoff, France (see p. 566), and from Rosslare Harbour to Pembroke, Wales, and Roscoff and Cherbourg, France (see p. 564).

BY CAR. Drivers in Ireland use the left side of the road, and their steering wheels are on the right side of the car. Petrol (gasoline) prices are high. Be particularly cautious at roundabouts—give way to traffic from the right. **Dan Dooley** (☎062 53103, UK ☎0181 995 4551, US ☎800-331-9301; dandooley.com) is the only company that will rent to drivers between 21 and 24, though such drivers incur an added surcharge. Prices are €150-370/UK£95-235 (plus VAT) per week, including insurance and unlimited mileage. If you plan to drive a car while in Ireland for longer than 90 days, you must have an **International Driving Permit (IDP)**. If you rent, lease, or borrow a car, you will need a **green card** or **International Insurance Certificate** to certify that you have liability insurance and that it applies abroad.

BY BIKE, FOOT, AND THUMB. Much of the Ireland's countryside is well suited for **biking,** as many roads are not heavily traveled. Single-digit N roads in the Republic and M roads in the North are more busily trafficked; try to avoid these. Ireland's mountains, fields, and heather-covered hills make **walking** and **hiking** an arduous joy. The **Wicklow Way** has hostels within a day's walk of each other. Locals do not recommend **hitchhiking** in Northern Ireland, where it is illegal along motorways; some caution against it in Co. Dublin, as well as the Midlands. *Let's Go* does not recommend hitchhiking.

TOURIST SERVICES AND MONEY

EMERGENCY	Police: ☎999. Ambulance: ☎999. Fire: ☎999.

TOURIST OFFICES. Bord Fáilte (the Irish Tourist Board; ☎01850 230 330; www.ireland.travel.ie) operates a nationwide network of offices. Most tourist offices book rooms for a small fee and a 10% deposit, but many fine hostels and B&Bs are not on the board's central list. The **Northern Ireland Tourist Board** (☎028 9023 1221; www.discovernorthernireland.com) offers similar services.

MONEY. The official currency of the Republic of Ireland is the **euro.** The Irish pound can still be exchanged at a rate of IR£0.79 to €1. For exchange rates and more information on the euro, see p. 16. Legal tender in Northern Ireland is the **British pound;** for more info, see p. 138. Northern Ireland has its own bank notes, identical in value to English and Scottish notes of the same denominations. Although all of these notes are accepted in Northern Ireland, Northern Ireland notes are not accepted in Britain.

If you stay in hostels and prepare your own food, expect to spend anywhere from €20-34/UK£12-22 per person per day. Some restaurants in Ireland figure a service charge into the bill; some even calculate it into the cost of the dishes themselves. The menu often indicates whether or not service is included. Most people working in restaurants, however, do not expect a tip, unless the restaurant is targeted exclusively toward tourists. In those incidences, consider leaving 10-15%, depending upon the quality of the service. Tipping is very uncommon for other services, such as taxis and hairdressers, especially in rural areas. In most cases, people are usually happy if you simply round up the bill to the nearest euro. The European Union imposes a **value-added tax (VAT)** on goods and services purchased within the EU, which is included in the price; for more info, see p. 15.

BUSINESS HOURS. Most banks are open Monday to Friday 9am-4:30pm, sometimes later on Thursdays. Pubs are usually open Monday to Saturday 10:30am to 11 or 11:30pm, Sundays 12:30 to 2pm and 4 to 11pm.

COMMUNICATION

PHONE CODES	**Country code:** 353 (Republic); 44 (Northern Ireland; dial 048 from the Republic). **International dialing prefix:** 00. From outside the Republic of Ireland, dial int'l dialing prefix (see inside back cover) + 353 + city code + local number.

TELEPHONES. Both the Irish Republic and Northern Ireland have public phones that accept coins (€0.20/UK£0.15 for about 4min.) and pre-paid phone cards. In the Republic, dial ☎ 114 for an international operator, 10 for a national operator, or 11850 for a directory. International direct dial numbers in the Republic include: **AT&T,** ☎ 800 550 000; **British Telecom,** ☎ 800 550 144; **Canada Direct,** ☎ 800 555 001; **MCI,** ☎ 800 551 001; **New Zealand Direct,** ☎ 800 550 064; **Telkom South Africa,** ☎ 800 550 027; and **Telstra Australia,** ☎ 800 550 061. In Northern Ireland, call ☎ 155 for an international operator, 100 for a national operator, or 192 for a directory. International direct dial numbers in Northern Ireland include: **AT&T,** ☎ 0800 013 0011; **Canada Direct,** ☎ 0800 890 016; **MCI,** ☎ 800 551 001; **New Zealand Direct,** ☎ 0800 890 064; **Telkom South Africa,** ☎ 0800 890 027; **Telstra Australia,** ☎ 0800 856 6161. For more info on making calls to and from Northern Ireland, see p. 579.

MAIL. In the Republic, postcards and letters up to 25g cost €0.40 domestically and to the UK, €0.45 to the Continent, and €0.60 to any other international destination. Airmail letters take about 6-9 days between Ireland and North America and cost €0.80. Dublin is the only place in the Republic with postal codes. Even-numbered codes are for areas south of the Liffey, odd-numbered are for those north. The North has the same postal system as the rest of the UK (p. 139). Address *Poste Restante* according to the following example: Firstname SURNAME, Poste Restante, Enniscorthy, Co. Wexford, Ireland. The mail will go to a special desk in the central post office, unless you specify otherwise.

INTERNET ACCESS. Internet access is available in cafes, hostels, and most libraries. One hour of web time costs about €4-6/UK£2.50-4; an ISIC card often earns you a discount. Look into a county library membership in the Republic (€2.50-3), which gives unlimited access to participating libraries and their Internet terminals.

ACCOMMODATIONS AND CAMPING

THE REPUBLIC	❶	❷	❸	❹	❺
ACCOMMODATIONS	under €15	€15-24	€25-39	€40-54	over €55

A **hostel** bed will average €12-18 in the Republic and UK£7-12 in the North. An **Óige** (an OYJ), the **HI** affiliate, operates 32 hostels countrywide. (☎ 01 830 4555; www.irelandyha.org. One-year membership €15, under 18 €7.50.) Many An Óige hostels are in remote areas or small villages and were designed primarily to serve hikers, long-distance bicyclists, anglers, and others seeking nature, and do not offer the social environment typical of other European hostels. The North's HI affiliate is **HINI** (Hostelling International Northern Ireland; formerly known as **YHANI**). It operates only eight hostels, all comfortable. (☎ 028 9031 5435; www.hini.org.uk. One-year membership UK£10, under 18 UK£6.) A number of hostels in Ireland belong to **Independent Holiday Hostels** (IHH; ☎ 01 836 4700; www.hostels-ireland.com). Most of the 140 IHH hostels have no lockout or curfew, accept all ages, require no membership card, and have a comfortable atmosphere that generally feels less institutional than that at An Óige hostels; all are Bord Fáilte-approved. Numerous **B&Bs**, in virtually every Irish town, can provide a luxurious break from hostelling; expect to pay €20-30/UK£12-20 for singles and €35-50/UK£22-32 for doubles. "Full Irish breakfasts" are often filling enough to get you through to dinner. **Camping** in Irish State Forests and National Parks is not allowed; camping on public land is permissible only if there is no official campsite nearby. Sites cost €5-13, depending on the level of luxury. Northern Ireland treats its campers royally; there are well-equipped campsites throughout (UK£3-8). For more info on price ranges in Northern Ireland, see p. 579.

FOOD AND DRINK

THE REPUBLIC	❶	❷	❸	❹	❺
FOOD	under €5	€5-9	€10-14	€15-19	over €20

Food in Ireland is expensive, but the basics are simple and filling. Find quick and greasy staples at chippers (fish 'n' chip shops) and takeaways (takeout joints). Most pubs serve food like Irish stew, burgers, soup, and sandwiches. Soda bread is delicious and keeps well, and Irish cheeses are addictive. Guinness, a rich, dark stout, is revered in Ireland with a zeal usually reserved for the Holy Trinity. Known as "the dark stuff" or "the blonde in the black skirt," it was once recommended as food for pregnant mothers, and its head is so thick its rumored that you can stand a match in it. Irish whiskey, which Queen Elizabeth once claimed was her only true Irish friend, is sweeter than its Scotch counterpart. Irish monks invented whiskey, calling it *uisce beatha*, meaning "water of life." For info on price ranges in Northern Ireland, see p. 579.

HOLIDAYS AND FESTIVALS

Holidays: Holidays for the Republic of Ireland include: New Year's Day (Jan. 1); St. Patrick's Day (Mar. 17); Good Friday; Easter Monday (Apr. 21); and Christmas (Dec. 25-26). There are Bank Holidays in the Republic and Northern Ireland during the summer months; check at tourist offices for dates. Northern Ireland has the same national holidays as the Republic; it also observes Orange Day (July 12).

Festivals: All of Ireland goes green for **St. Patrick's Day** (Mar. 17th). On **Bloomsday** (June 16), Dublin celebrates James Joyce's *Ulysses* (see p. 562).

DUBLIN   ☎01

In a country known for its relaxed pace and rural sanctity, Dublin stands out for its boundless energy and international flair. The city and its suburbs, home to one-third of Ireland's population, are at the vanguard of the country's rapid social change. In an effort to stem international and rural emigration, vast portions of the city have undergone renovation and redevelopment, funded by the deep pockets of the EU. Dublin may hardly look like the rustic "Emerald Isle" promoted on tourist brochures, but its people and history still embody the charm and warmth that have made the country famous.

▛ TRANSPORTATION

Flights: Dublin Airport (DUB; ☎844 4900). **Dublin buses** #41, 41B, and 41C run from the airport to Eden Quay in the city center with stops along the way (every 20min., €1.50). The **Airlink shuttle** (☎844 4265) runs non-stop to Busáras Central Bus Station and O'Connell St. (20-25min., every 10-15min., €3.85) and on to Heuston Station (50min., €4.50). A **taxi** to the city center costs roughly €15-20.

Trains: The **Iarnród Éireann** travel center, 35 Lower Abbey St. (☎836 6222), sells tickets for **Irish Rail.** Open M-F 9am-5pm, Sa 9am-1pm. **Connolly Station,** Amiens St. (☎702 2358), is north of the Liffey and close to Busáras Central Bus Station. Buses #20, 20A, and 90 go from the station to destinations south of the river, and the DART (see below) runs to Tara on the south quay. Trains to: **Belfast** (2hr., 5-8 per day, €27); **Sligo** (3½hr., 3-4 per day, €19); **Wexford** (3hr., 3 per day, €14). **Heuston Station** (☎703 2132) is south of Victoria Quay, west of the city center (25min. walk from Trinity College). Buses #26, 51, 90, and 79 go to the city center. Trains to: **Cork** (3½hr., 6-11 per day, €43); **Galway** (2½hr., 4-5 per day, €21); **Limerick** (2½hr., 9 per day, €34); **Tralee** (4hr., 4-7 per day, €44); **Waterford** (2½hr., 3-4 per day, €16.50).

Buses: Info available at the **Dublin Bus Office,** 59 O'Connell St. (☎872 0000); the Bus Éireann window is open M-F 9am-5:30pm, Sa 9am-1pm. Buses arrive at **Busáras Central Bus Station** (☎836 6111), on Store St., directly behind the Customs House and next to Connolly Station. Bus Éireann runs to: **Belfast** (3hr., 6-7 per day, €16.50); **Derry** (4¼hr., 4-5 per day, €16.50); **Donegal Town** (4¼hr., 5-6 per day, €13.50); **Galway** (3½hr., 13 per day, €13.30); **Limerick** (3½hr., 7-13 per day, €13.30); **Rosslare Harbour** (3hr., 7-10 per day, €12.70); **Sligo** (4hr., 4-5 per day, €12.10); **Waterford** (2¾hr., 5-7 per day, €8.90); **Wexford** (2¾hr., 7-10 per day, €10.10).

Ferries: Irish Ferries (☎638 3333) has an office off St. Stephen's Green at 2-4 Merrion Row. Open M-F 9am-5pm, Sa 9:15am-12:45pm. Ferries arrive from **Holyhead, UK** at the **Dublin Port** (☎607 5665), from which buses #53 and 53A run every hr. to Busáras (€1). **Norse Merchant Ferries** also dock at the Dublin Port and run a route to **Liverpool, UK** (7½hr.; 1-2 per day; from €63.50, car from €215); booking for Norse Merchant is only available from **Gerry Feeney,** 19 Eden Quay (☎819 2999). **Stena Line** ferries arrive from Holyhead at the **Dún Laoghaire** ferry terminal (☎204 7777); DART (see below) trains run from Dún Laoghaire to the Dublin city center. Dublin Bus also runs connection buses timed to fit the ferry schedules (€2.50-3.20).

Public Transportation: Dublin Bus, 59 O'Connell St. (☎873 4222). Open M 8:30am-5:30pm, Tu-F 9am-5:30pm, Sa 9am-1pm. The smaller **City Imp** buses run every 8-15min. Dublin Bus runs the **NiteLink** service to the suburbs (M, W at 12:30am and 2am; Th-Sa nights at 12:30, 1:30, 2:30, and 3:30am; €3.80). **Travel Wide** passes offer unlimited rides for a day (€4.50) or a week (€16.50). **DART** trains serve the suburbs and the coast (every 10-15min., 6:30am-11:30pm, €0.75-1.40).

Taxis: National Radio Cabs, 40 James St. (☎677 2222). €2.75 plus €1.35 per mi. before 10pm, €1.80 per mi. after 10pm.; €1.50 call-in charge.

Car Rental: Budget, 151 Lower Drumcondra Rd. (☎837 9611), and at the airport. In summer from €40 per day, €158 per week; off-season €38/€138. Min. age 23.

Bike Rental: Cycle Ways, 185-6 Parnell St. (☎873 4748). Open M-W and F-Sa 10am-6pm, Th 10am-8pm. €20 per day, €80 per week; deposit €80.

■ ⑦ ORIENTATION AND PRACTICAL INFORMATION

The **River Liffey** is the natural divide between Dublin's North and South Sides. Heuston Station and the more famous sights, posh stores, and upscale restaurants are on the **South Side.** Connolly Station and the majority of hostels and the bus station cling to the **North Side.** The streets running alongside the Liffey are called **quays** (KEYS); each bridge over the river has its own name, and streets change names as they cross. If a street running parallel to the river is split into "Upper" and "Lower," then the "Lower" is always the part of the street closer to the mouth of the Liffey. **O'Connell Street,** three blocks west of the Busáras Central Bus Station, is the primary link between north and south Dublin. **Fleet Street** becomes **Temple Bar** one block south of the Liffey. **Dame Street** runs parallel to Temple Bar until **Trinity College,** which defines the southern edge of the district. Trinity College is the nerve center of Dublin's cultural activity, with legions of bookshops and student-oriented pubs. The North Side hawks merchandise cheaper than in the more touristed South. **Henry Street** and **Mary Street** comprise a pedestrian shopping zone that intersects with O'Connell after the **General Post Office (GPO)**, two blocks from the Liffey. The North Side has the reputation of being rougher, especially after sunset.

TOURIST, FINANCIAL, AND LOCAL SERVICES

Tourist Information: Main Office, Suffolk St. (☎(1850) 230 330). From Connolly Station, turn left down Amiens St., take a right onto Lower Abbey St., and continue until O'Connell St. Turn left, cross the bridge, and walk past Trinity College; Suffolk St. is on the right. Books rooms for €4 plus a 10% non-refundable deposit. Open July-Aug. M-Sa 9am-8:30pm, Su 11am-5:30pm; Sept.-June M-Sa 9am-5:30pm. The **Northern Ireland Tourist Board,** 16 Nassau St. (☎679 1977 or (1850) 230 230), books accommodations in the North. Open M-F 9:15am-5:30pm, Sa 10am-5pm.

Embassies: Australia, 2nd fl., Fitzwilton House, Wilton Terr. (☎676 1517; www.australianembassy.ie); **Canada,** 65/68 St. Stephen's Green (☎478 1988); **South Africa,** 2nd fl., Alexandra House, Earlsfort Terr. (☎661 5553); **United Kingdom,** 29 Merrion Rd., Ballsbridge (☎205 3700; www.britishembassy.ie); **United States,** 42 Elgin Rd. (☎668 8777). **New Zealanders** should contact their embassy in London.

Banks: Bank of Ireland, AIB, and **TSB** branches with currency exchange and 24hr. **ATMs** cluster on Lower O'Connell St., Grafton St., and in the Suffolk and Dame St. areas. Most bank branches are open M-F 10am-4pm.

American Express: 43 Nassau St. (☎679 9000). Currency exchange; no commission for AmEx Traveler's Cheques. Mail held. Open M-F 9am-5pm.

Luggage Storage: Connolly Station. €2.50 per item per day. Open M-Sa 7:40am-9:20pm, Su 9:10am-9:45pm. **Heuston Station.** €1.90-5.10 per item, depending on size. Open daily 6:30am-10:30pm.

Laundry: The Laundry Shop, 191 Parnell St. (☎872 3541), near Busáras. Wash and dry €8-12. Open M-F 8am-7pm, Sa 9am-6pm, Su 11am-5pm.

EMERGENCY AND COMMUNICATIONS

Emergency: ☎999 or 112; no coins required.

Police *(Garda)*: Dublin Metro Headquarters, Harcourt Terr. (☎666 9500); Store St. Station (☎666 8000); Fitzgibbon St. Station (☎666 8400).

Pharmacy: O'Connell's, 55 Lower O'Connell St. (☎873 0427). Open M-Sa 7:30am-10pm, Su 10am-10pm. Branches throughout the city, including two on Grafton St.

Hospital: St. James's Hospital (☎453 7941), on James St. Served by bus #123. **Mater Misericordiae Hospital** (☎830 1122), on Eccles St., off Lower Dorset St. Served by buses #10, 11, 13, 16, 121, and 122.

Internet Access: The Internet Exchange, 146 Parnell St. (☎670 3000). €2.50 per hr. Open daily 9am-10:30pm.

Post Office: General Post Office (GPO, ☎705 7000), on O'Connell St. Even-numbered postal codes are for areas south of the Liffey, odd-numbered are for the north. *Poste Restante* pick-up at the currency exchange window. Open M-Sa 8am-8pm, Su 10am-6:30pm. **Postal Code:** Dublin 1.

▮ ACCOMMODATIONS

Reserve accommodations at least a week in advance, especially during Easter, other holidays, and summer. **Hostel** dorms range from €10 to €24 per night. Quality **B&Bs** blanket Dublin and the surrounding suburbs, although prices have risen with housing costs; most charge €20-40 per person.

IRELAND

HOSTELS

Dublin's hostels lean toward the institutional, especially in comparison to their more personable country cousins. The beds south of the river fill up fastest; they also tend to be more expensive than those to the north.

■ **Abbey Court Hostel,** 29 Bachelor's Walk, O'Connell Bridge (☎878 0700). Great location. Clean rooms, most with bath. Internet €1 per 8min. Laundry €8. Breakfast included. Dorms €17-28; doubles €76-88. ❷

■ **Four Courts Hostel,** 15-17 Merchants Quay (☎672 5839), south of the river, near O'Donovan Rossa Bridge. First-rate mega-hostel with clean rooms and parking. Internet access. Breakfast included. Dorms €15-21.50; doubles €27-32.50. ❷

Brown's Hostel, 89-90 Lower Gardiner St. (☎855 0034). Glistening rooms with TVs, wardrobes, and A/C. Internet €1 per 20min. Breakfast included. Dorms €12.50-25. Attached to **Brown's Hotel;** ask for the hotel's €75 backpacker special. ❶

Barnacle's Temple Bar House, 19 Temple Ln. (☎671 6277). In the heart of Dublin—expect noise. Breakfast included. Dorms €15-23; doubles €62-74. ❷

The Brewery Hostel, 22-23 Thomas St. (☎453 8600). Follow Dame St. past Christ Church and through name changes, or take bus #123. Close to the Guinness brewery and a 15min. walk from Temple Bar. Breakfast included. All rooms with bath. Dorms €16-28; doubles €65-78. ❷

Avalon House (IHH), 55 Aungier St. (☎475 0001). Top-notch security. Internet access. Breakfast included. Dorms €15-30; singles €30-37; doubles €28-35. ❷

BED AND BREAKFASTS

B&Bs with a green shamrock sign out front are registered and approved by Bord Fáilte. On the North Side, B&Bs cluster along **Upper** and **Lower Gardiner Street,** on **Sheriff Street,** and near **Parnell Square.**

Parkway Guest House, 5 Gardiner Pl. (☎874 0469), just off Gardiner St. Clean rooms in an excellent location. Singles €32; doubles €52-60, with bath €60-70. ❸

Mona's B&B, 148 Clonliffe Rd. (☎837 6723). Gorgeous house. Full Irish breakfasts. Open May-Oct only. Singles €35; doubles €66. ❸

Mrs. Bermingham, 8 Dromard Terr. (☎668 3861), on Dromard Ave. Take the #2 or 3 bus and get off at Tesco. Soft, comfortable beds. Open Feb.-Nov. only. Singles €28; doubles with bath €52. ❸

Mrs. Dolores Abbot-Murphy, 14 Castle Park (☎269 8413). Take the #3 bus to Sandymount Green. Continue past Browne's Deli and take the 1st left; it's on the right at the end of the road. A 5min. walk from Sandymount DART stop. Cheerful rooms in a charming cul-de-sac. Open May-Oct. only. Singles €28; doubles €56. ❸

CAMPING

Most campsites are far away from the city center, and while it may be convenient, camping in **Phoenix Park** is both illegal and unsafe.

Camac Valley Tourist Caravan & Camping Park (☎464 0644), Naas Rd., Clondalkin, near Corkagh Park. Accessible by bus #69 (35min. from city center, €1.50). Food shop and kitchen facilities. Laundry €4.50. Hikers/cyclists €7; 2 people with car €14. ❶

▸ FOOD

Dublin's **open-air markets** sell fresh and cheap fixings. On Saturdays, a gourmet open-air market takes place in Temple Bar in Meeting House Square. The cheapest **supermarkets** around Dublin are the **Dunnes Stores** chain, with branches at St. Stephen's Green (open M-W and F-Sa 8:30am-7pm; Th 8:30am-9pm; Su noon-6pm), the ILAC Centre off Henry St., and North Earl St. **Temple Bar** has creative eateries catering to every budget.

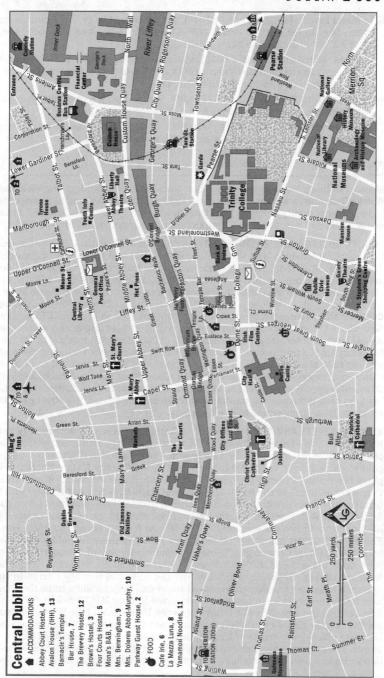

Central Dublin

▲ ACCOMMODATIONS

Abbey Court Hostel, 4
Avalon House (IHH), 13
Barnacle's Temple
Bar House, 7
The Brewery Hostel, 12
Brown's Hostel, 3
Four Courts Hostel, 5
Mona's B&B, 1
Mrs. Bermingham, 9
Mrs. Dolores Abbot-Murphy, 10
Parkway Guest House, 2

● FOOD

Cafe Irie, 6
La Mezza Luna, 8
Yamamoi Noodles, 11

IRELAND

▨ **La Mezza Luna,** 1 Temple Ln. (☎671 2840), on the corner of Dame St. Refined but not pretentious. Try the wok-fried chicken (€8.25). Entrees €5-10. Open M-Th 8am-11pm, F-Sa 9:30am-11:30pm, Su 9:30am-10:30pm. ❷

Cafe Irie, 11 Fownes St. (☎672 5090), above the clothing store Sé Sí Progressive. A small eatery with an impressive selection of sandwiches under €4. Great coffee. Vegan-friendly. Open M-Sa 9am-8pm, Su noon-6pm. ❶

Zaytoons, 14-15 Parliament St. (☎677 3595). Persian food served on big platters of warm bread. Excellent chicken kebab €6.50. Open M-Sa noon-4am. ❷

Yamamori Noodles, 71-72 S. Great Georges St. (☎475 5001). Exceptional Japanese cuisine. Entrees €12-14. Open Su-W and Su 12:30-11pm, Th-Sa 12:30-11:30pm. ❸

👁 SIGHTS

Most of Dublin's sights lie less than 2km from O'Connell Bridge. The **Historical Walking Tour** provides a 2hr. crash course in Irish history, stopping at a variety of sights. Meet at Trinity College's front gate. (☎878 0227. Tours May-Sept. M-F 11am and 3pm; Sa-Su 11am, noon, and 3pm. Oct.-Apr. F-Su noon. €10, students €8.)

TRINITY COLLEGE AND ENVIRONS. The British built Trinity in 1592 as a Protestant religious seminary that would "civilize the Irish and cure them of Popery." Jonathan Swift, Robert Emmett, Thomas Moore, Edmund Burke, Oscar Wilde, and Samuel Beckett are just a few of the famous Irishmen who studied here. *(Between Westmoreland and Grafton St. The main entrance is on College Green. Pearse St. runs along the north edge of the college, Nassau St. to its south. Grounds open 24hr. Free.)* **Trinity College Walking Tour** is run by students and concentrates on University lore. *(June-Sept. daily 10:15am–3:40pm; Mar.-May weekends only. Tours leave roughly every 45min. from the info booth inside the front gate. €7, students €6; includes admission to the Old Library.)* **The Old Library** holds a priceless collection of ancient manuscripts, including the magnificent **Book of Kells.** *(From Trinity's main gate, go straight; the library is on the south side of Library Sq. Open June-Sept. M-Sa 9:30am-5pm, Su noon-4:30pm; Oct.-May M-Sa 9:30am-5pm, Su noon-4:30pm. €6, students and seniors €4.)* The area south of College Green, off-limits to cars, is a haven for tourists and residents alike. Grafton's **street performers** range from string octets to jive limboists.

KILDARE STREET AND TEMPLE BAR. The **National Museum of Archaeology and History** is Dublin's largest museum and has extraordinary artifacts spanning the last two millennia, including the **Tara Brooch,** the **Ardagh Hoard,** and other Celtic gold work. *(Kildare St., adjacent to Leinster House.)* The ▨**Natural History Museum** displays fascinating examples of classic taxidermy. *(Upper Merrion St.)* The Collins Barracks are home to the **National Museum of Decorative Arts and History,** which features an impressive collection of furniture, textiles, costumes, and silver. *(On Benburb St., off Wolfe Tone Quay. Take the Museum Link, or bus #10 from O'Connell. General info line for all three National Museums ☎677 7444. All open Tu-Sa 10am-5pm, Su 2-5pm. Free.)* The **National Gallery** has a collection of over 2400 paintings, including canvases by Bruegel, Goya, Caravaggio, Vermeer, Rembrandt, and El Greco. *(Merrion Sq. West. Open M-W and F-Sa 9:30am-5:30pm, Th 10am-8:30pm, Su noon-5pm. Free.)* The **National Library** chronicles Irish history and exhibits literary curios in its entrance room. A genealogical research room can help families trace the thinnest tendrils of their Irish family tree. *(On Kildare St. Open M-W 10am-9pm, Th-F 10am-5pm, Sa 10am-1pm. Free.)* West of Trinity, between Dame St. and the Liffey, the **Temple Bar** neighborhood has rapidly become one of Europe's hottest night spots. Narrow cobblestone streets link cafes, theaters, rock venues, and used clothing stores. The government-sponsored Temple Bar Properties spent over IR£30 million to build a fleet of arts-related attractions. Among the most inviting are: **The**

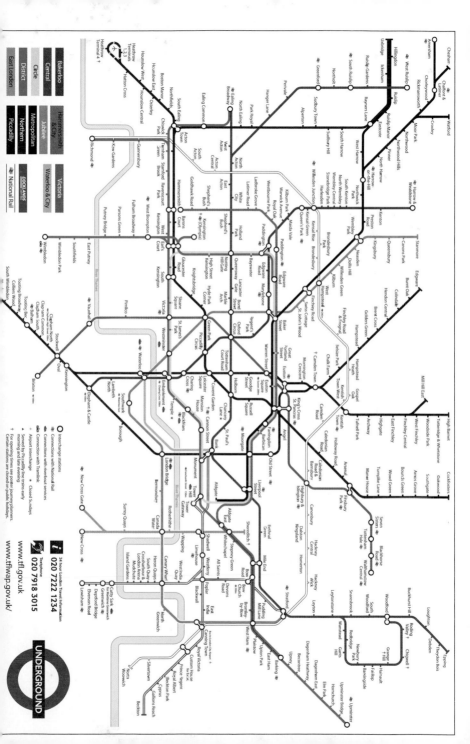

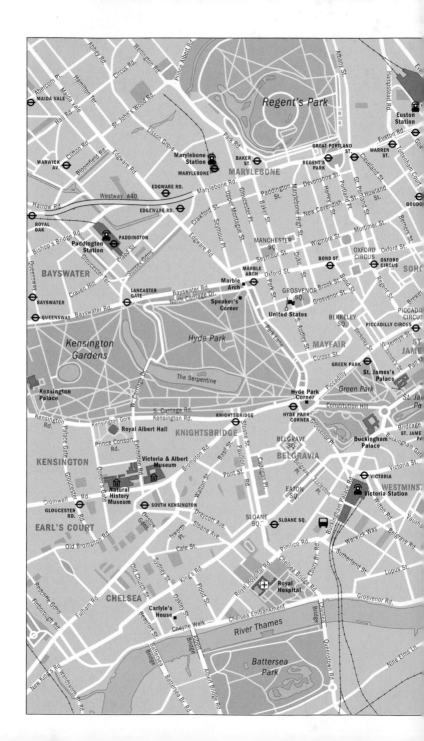

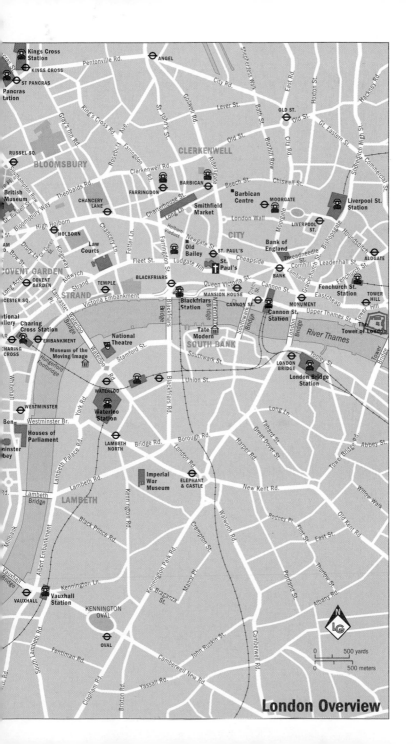

London Overview

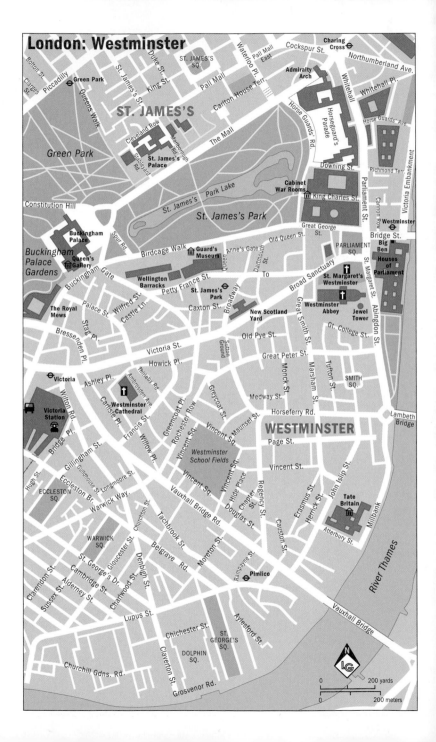

London: Westminster

ST. JAMES'S

Green Park

Piccadilly
Green Park
Bolton St.
Clarges St.
Queens Walk
Duke St.
King St.
St. James's St.
ST. JAMES'S SQ.
Waterloo Pl.
Pall Mall East
Pall Mall
Carlton House Terr.
Cockspur St.
Charing Cross
Admiralty Arch
Northumberland Ave.
Whitehall
Whitehall Pl.

Cleveland Row
Marlborough Rd.
The Mall
Horse Guards' Rd.
Horseguard's Parade
Horse Guards' Ave.
St. James's Palace
Stableyard Rd.

Constitution Hill
St. James's Park Lake
St. James's Park
Downing St.
Cabinet War Rooms
King Charles St.
Richmond Terr.
Victoria Embankment

Buckingham Palace
Buckingham Palace Gardens
Queen's Gallery
Spur Rd.
Birdcage Walk
Guard's Museum
Anne's Gate
Old Queen St.
Great George St.
PARLIAMENT SQ.
Westminster Bridge St.
Big Ben
Houses of Parliament
Parliament St.
Cannon Row

The Royal Mews
Buckingham Gate
Palace St.
Wilfred St.
Castle Ln.
Wellington Barracks
Petty France St.
St. James's Park
Caxton St.
Broadway
Queen
Dartmouth St.
To
Broad Sanctuary
St. Margaret's Westminster
Westminster Abbey
Jewel Tower
St. Margaret St.
Abingdon St.

Bressenden Pl.
Stag Pl.
New Scotland Yard
Old Pye St.
Great Smith St.
Gt. College St.

Victoria
Ashley Pl.
Victoria St.
Howick Pl.
Sutton Ground
Great Peter St.
Monck St.
Marsham St.
Tufton St.
SMITH SQ.
Medway St.

Victoria Station
Wilton Rd.
Bridge Pl.
Thirleby Rd.
Ambrosden Ave.
Carlisle Pl.
Westminster Cathedral
Francis St.
Willow Pl.
Greencoat Pl.
Rochester Row
Greycoat St.
Vincent Sq.
Maunsel St.
Horseferry Rd.
WESTMINSTER
Page St.
Lambeth Bridge

Gillingham St.
Guildhouse St.
Longmoore St.
Eccleston Br.
Warwick Way
High St.
ECCLESTON SQ.
Church St.
Westminster School Fields
Vincent St.
Hide Place
Chapter St.
Regency St.
Vincent St.
Erasmus St.
Herrick St.
John Islip St.
Tate Britain
Millbank

WARWICK SQ.
St. George's Dr.
Gloucester St.
Belgrave Rd.
Tachbrook St.
Vauxhall Bridge Rd.
Moreton St.
Douglas St.
Causton St.
Atterbury St.

Clarendon St.
Cambridge St.
Alderney St.
Sussex St.
Charlwood St.
Denbigh St.
Rampayne St.
Pimlico
River Thames

Lupus St.
Chichester St.
ST. GEORGE'S SQ.
Aylesford St.
Claverton St.
DOLPHIN SQ.
Vauxhall Bridge

Churchill Gdns. Rd.
Grosvenor Rd.

N

0   200 yards
0   200 meters

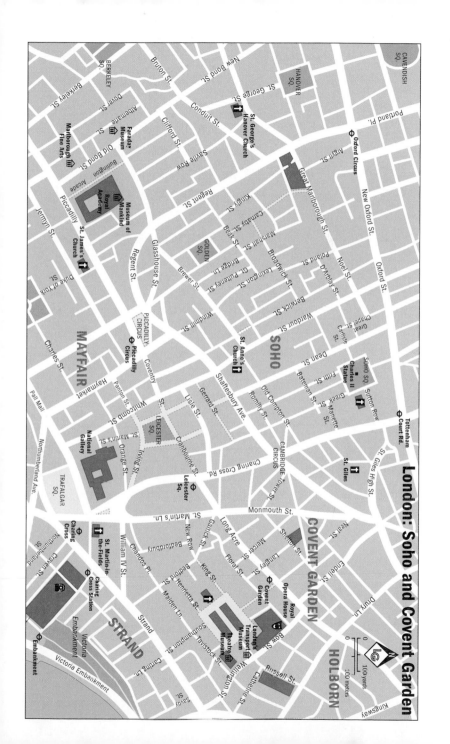

London: Soho and Covent Garden

CAVENDISH SQ.

BERKELEY SQ.

HANOVER SQ.

Bruton St.

New Bond St.

St. George St.

Conduit St.

Dover St.

Albemarle St.

Clifford St.

Savile Row

Regent St.

Portland Pl.

⊖ Oxford Circus

Argyll St.

New Oxford St.

Oxford St.

Great Marlborough St.

Poland St.

Noel St.

Marlborough Fine Arts

Faraday Museum 🏛

Burlington Arcade

Old Bond St.

Royal Academy 🏛 Museum of Mankind

Carnaby St.

Marshall St.

Broadwick St.

D'Arblay St.

Great Chapel St.

Carlisle St.

St. James's Church †

Piccadilly

GOLDEN SQ.

Beak St.

Gt. Pulteney St.

Lexington St.

Brewer St.

Berwick St.

Wardour St.

Dean St.

Frith St.

Greek St.

SOHO SQ.

Charles II Statue

Sutton Row

Glasshouse St.

Regent St.

Jermyn St.

Duke of York St.

Windmill St.

SOHO

Old Compton St.

Bateman St.

St. Anne's Church †

St. Manette St.

Tottenham ⊖ Court Rd.

⊖ Piccadilly Circus

PICCADILLY CIRCUS

Coventry

St.

Gerrard St.

Shaftesbury Ave.

Romilly St.

CAMBRIDGE CIRCUS

St. Giles †

St. Giles High St.

MAYFAIR

Haymarket

Panton St.

Whitcomb St.

Lisle St.

LEICESTER SQ.

Irving St.

Cranbourne St.

Charing Cross Rd.

Tower St.

Charles St.

National Gallery

St. Martin's St.

Orange St.

Leicester ⊖ Sq.

Monmouth St.

Neal St.

Endell St.

Drury Ln.

Pall Mall

TRAFALGAR SQ.

Northumberland Ave.

St. Martin's Ln.

Long Acre

Garrick St.

Mercer St.

Shelton St.

COVENT GARDEN

HOLBORN

New Row

Bedfordbury

Floral St.

Langley St.

⊖ Charing Cross

St. Martin-in-the-Fields †

William IV St.

Chandos Pl.

Bedford St.

King St.

⊖ Covent Garden

Royal Opera House

Bow St.

Russell St.

Kingsway

Craven St.

Northumberland St.

⊖ Charing Cross Station

Strand

Henrietta St.

Maiden Ln.

Southampton St.

Tavistock St.

Theatre Museum 🏛

London's Transport Museum 🏛 Wellington St.

Catherine St.

STRAND

Carting Ln.

Savoy St.

⊖ Embankment

Victoria Embankment

Victoria Embankment

0   100 yards
0   100 meters

N

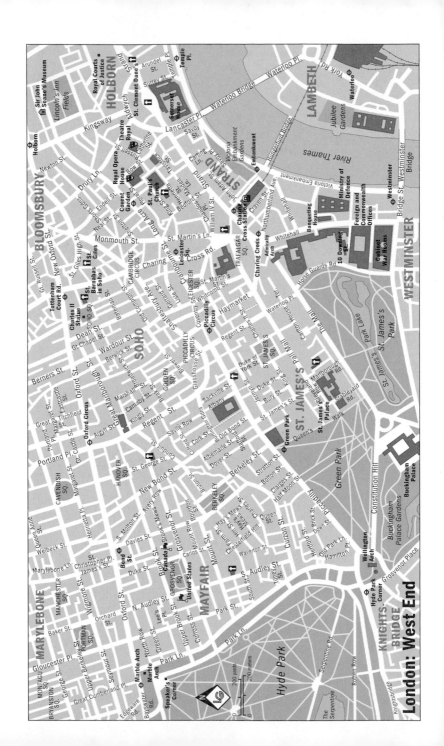

London: West End

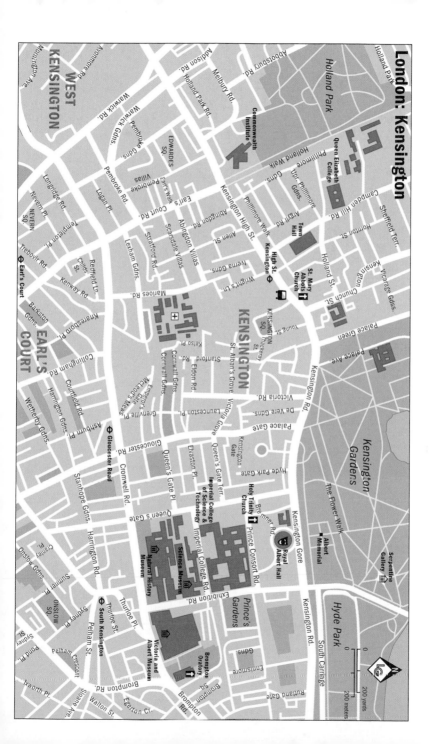

London: Kensington

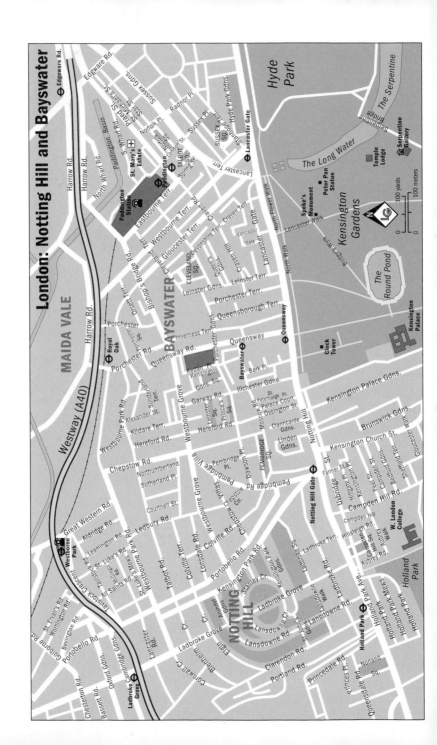

London: Notting Hill and Bayswater

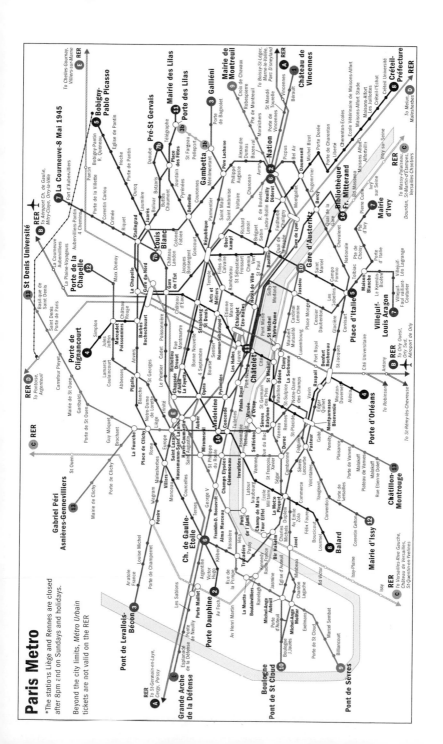

Paris Metro

*The stations Liège and Rennes are closed after 8pm and on Sundays and holidays.

Beyond the city limits, *Métro Urbain* tickets are not valid on the RER

Paris: Overview and Arrondissements

1 Cimetière de Montmartre
2 Sacré Coeur Basilica
3 Parc La Villette
4 Parc des Buttes Chaumont
5 Jardins du Trocadero
6 Palais Chaillot
7 Cimetière de Passy
8 American Embassy
9 British Embassy
10 Petit Palais
11 Grand Palais
12 Arc de Triomphe
13 Madeleine
14 Gare St-Lazare
15 Parc Monceau
16 Palais de la Découverte
17 Opéra Garnier
18 Galeries Lafayette
19 Printemps
20 Gare du Nord
21 Gare de l'Est
22 Opéra Bastille
23 Palais Omnisports de Bercy
24 Ministère des Finances
25 Gare de Lyon
26 Parc de Montsouris
27 Cité Universitaire
28 Cimetière Montparnasse
29 Gare Montparnasse

30 Bureau des Objets Trouvés (Lost and Found)
31 Louvre
32 Palais Royale
33 Forum des Halles
34 Musée de l'Orangerie
35 Central Post Office
36 Bourse
37 Bibliothèque Nationale
38 Ecole des Arts et Métiers
39 Archives Nationales
40 Musée Carnavalet
41 Musée Picasso
42 Centre George Pompidou
43 place des Vosges
44 Musée Victor Hugo
45 Notre Dame
46 Mémorial de la Déportation
47 Université de Paris (Sorbonne)

48 Ecole Normal Supérieure
49 Musée de Cluny
50 Museum Nationale d'Histoire Naturelle
51 Panthéon
52 Eglise St-Etienne du Mont
53 La Mosquée
54 Jardin des Plantes
55 Jardins du Luxembourg
56 Eglise St-Sulpice
57 Théâtre Nationale de l'Odéon
58 Eiffel Tower
59 Champs de Mars

60 Ecole Militaire
61 UNESCO
62 Hôtel des Invalides
63 Assemblée Nationale
64 Musée d'Orsay
65 Cimetière de l'Est du Pere Lachaise

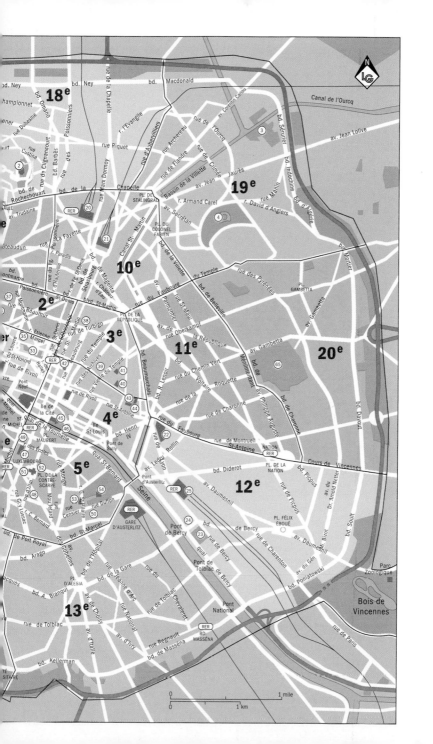

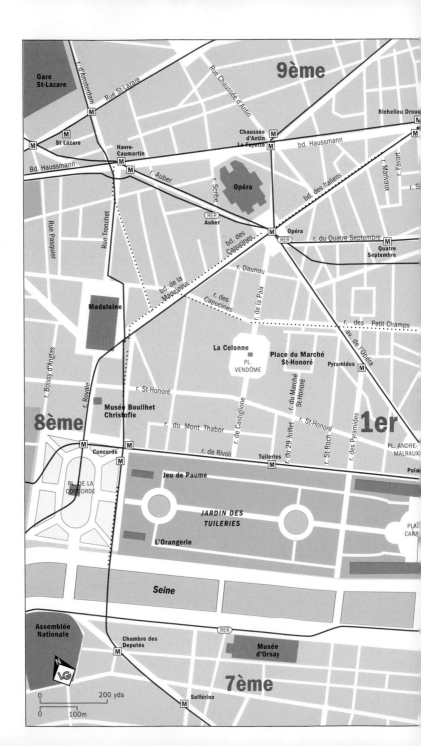

Paris: 1er & 2ème

Bonne
Nouvelle
bd. de Bonne Nouvelle

Strasbourg
St-Denis

bd. Poissonnière

Grands
Boulevards

r. Beauregard

r. Poissonnière

r. de Cléry

r. d'Aboukir

bd. de Sébastopol

3ème

r. St-Denis

r. Notre Dame des Victoires

Bourse
des Valeurs

urse

Sentier

r. Réaumur

Réamur-
Sébastopol

Arts et
Métiers

r. des Petits Carreaux

r. St. Sauveur

nèque
ale

2ème

r. Montmartre

r. Greneta

r. Monorgueil

r. de Turbigo

r. Tiquetonne

r. Etienne Marcel

Etienne
Marcel

r. Beaubourg

N DU
S

r. Jean Jacques
Rousseau

Eglise de
St-Eustache

r. St-Martin

r. Coquillere

Les
Halles

Les Halles

Rambuteau

r. du Louvre

r. Croix des Petits Champs

r. du Colonel Driant

r. Rambuteau

Forum

Centre
Pompidou

r. Jean Jacques Rousseau

Châtelet-
Les Halles

r. Berger

RER

Bd. de Sébastopol

r. St-Honoré

SQ.
DES INNOCENTS

4ème

r. de la Ferronnerie

r. des Halles

r. du Renard

r. des Bourdonnais

Louvre

Louvre

r. de Rivoli

Rue S.-Denis

Hôtel
de Ville

Châtelet

mide
UR
LEON

r. Amal.-de-Coligny

PLACE DU
CHÂTELET

r. du Pont Neuf

Pont Neuf

Châtelet

Châtelet

Quai de la Mégisserie

Pont
Neuf

Pont
au Change

Pont Notre Dame

Pont
d'Arcole

ne

Conciergerie

Pl. Lépine

Cité

**Palais
de Justice
Sainte-Chapell**

R. de
Lutèce

**Ile de
la Cité**

bd. du Palais

Notre
Dame

Nationale
eure des
Arts

Institut
de France

Hôtel
des
Monnaies

Quai des
Grands Augustins

Pont
St-Michel

Petit Pont

PLACE
DU
PARVIS

Pont au Double

6ème

RER

Pont
St-Michel

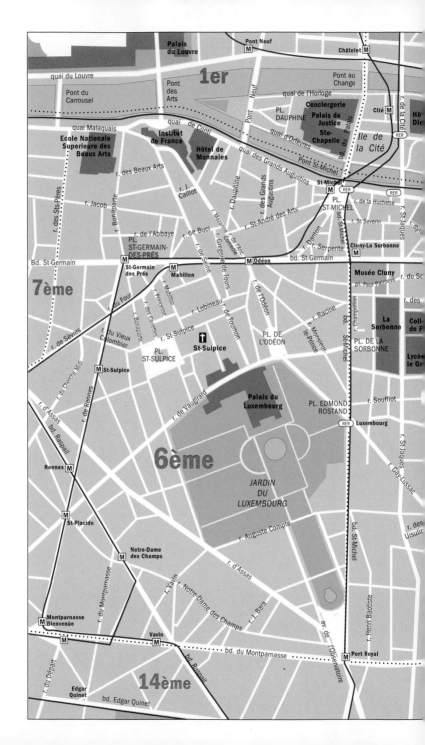

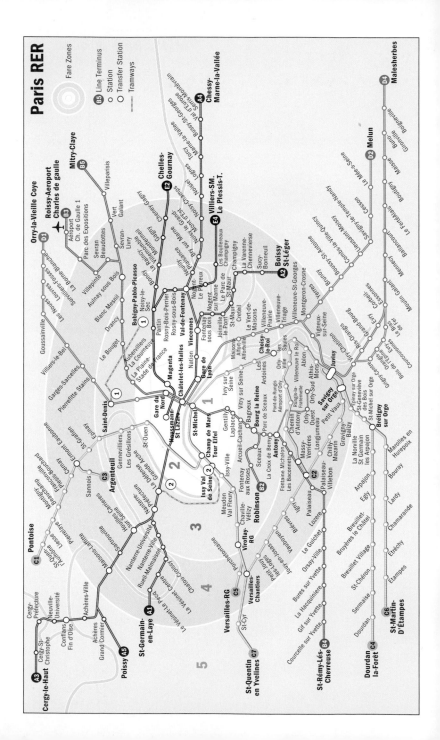

Paris RER

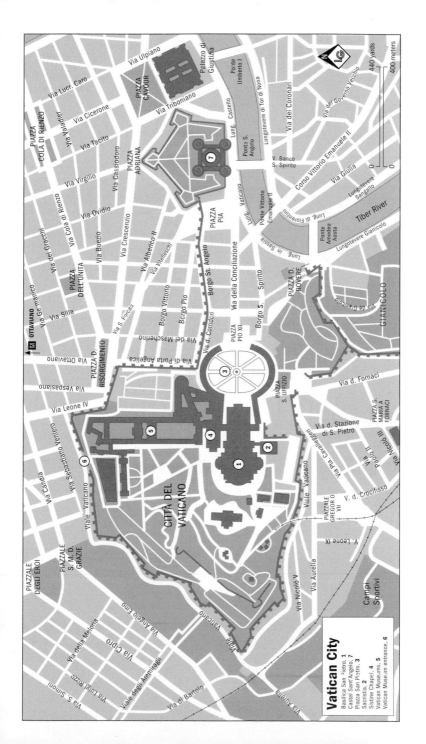

Vatican City

Basilica San Pietro, 1
Castel Sant'Angelo, 7
Piazza San Pietro, 3
Sacristia, 2
Sistine Chapel, 4
Vatican Museums, 5
Vatican Museum entrance, 6

440 yards
400 meters

M OTTAVIANO

Tiber River

GIANICOLO

CITTÀ DEL VATICANO

PIAZZA CAVOUR

PIAZZA COLA DI RIENZO

PIAZZA ADRIANA

PIAZZA DELL'UNITÀ

PIAZZA D. RISORGIMENTO

PIAZZALE DEGLI EROI

PIAZZALE S. M. D. GRAZIE

PIAZZA PIA

PIAZZA PIO XII

PIAZZA S. UFFIZIO

PIAZZA D. ROVERE

PIAZZA S. MARIA A FORNACI

PIAZZALE GREGOR O VII

Palazzo di Giustizia

Ponte Umberto I

Lungotevere di Tor di Nona

Via dei Coronari

Via del Governo Vecchio

Corso Vittorio Emanuele II

Via Giulia

Lungotevere Sangallo

Lungotevere Gianicolo

Lung. di Fiorentini

Ponte Amedeo Aosta

Lung. in Sassia

Ponte Vittorio Emanuele II

Lung. Vaticano

V. Banco S. Spirito

Ponte S. Angelo

Lung. Castello

Via Triboniano

Via Ulpiano

Via Lucr. Caro

Via Cicerone

Via Tacito

Via Virgilio

Via Ovidio

Via Cola di Rienzo

Via dei Gracchi

Via Germanico

Via Silla

Via Vespasiano

Via Leone IV

Via Sebastiano Veniero

Via Candia

Via della Meloria

Via S. Simoni

Via Luigi Rizzo

Via S. Cipro

Viale degli Ammiragli

Viale Angelo Emo

Viale Vaticano

Via di Bartolo

Via Aurelia

Via Nicoló V

Via Aurelia

V. Leone IX

Campi Sportivi

V. d. Crocifisso

Via Paolo II

Via Nicoló III

Via Gregorio VII

Via Cavalleggeri

Via d. Stazione di S. Pietro

Via d. Fornaci

Borgo S. Spirito

Borgo S.

Via della Conciliazione

Borgo St. Angelo

Via d. Corridori

Via di Porta Angelica

Via del Mascherino

Via S. Fornari

Borgo Pio

Borgo Vittorio

Via Vitelleschi

Via Alberto II

Via Crescenzio

Via Boezio

Via Cassiodoro

Via Valadier

Viale Vaticano

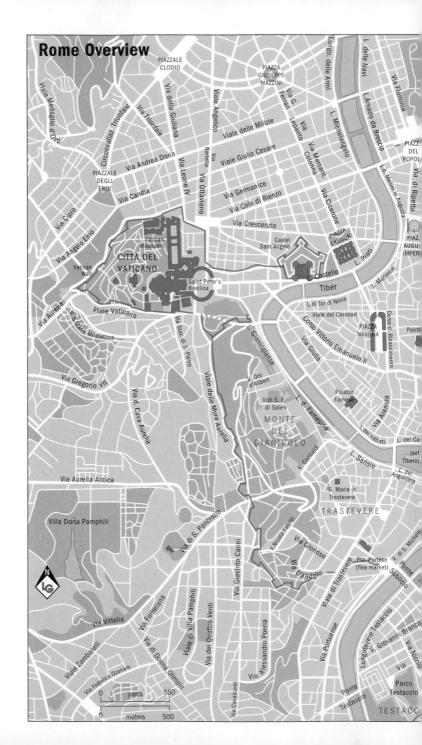

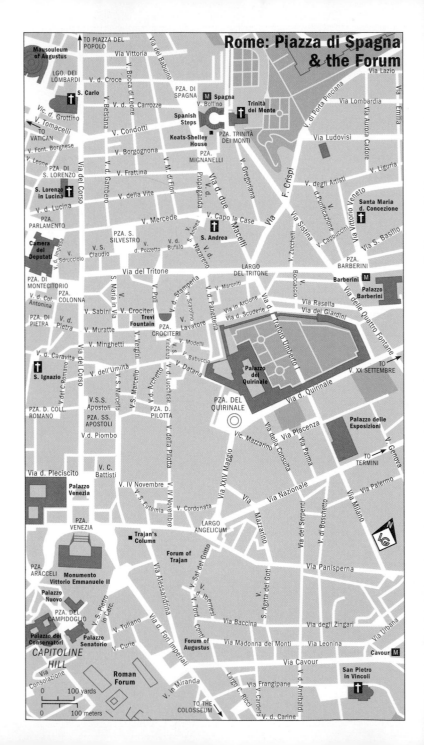

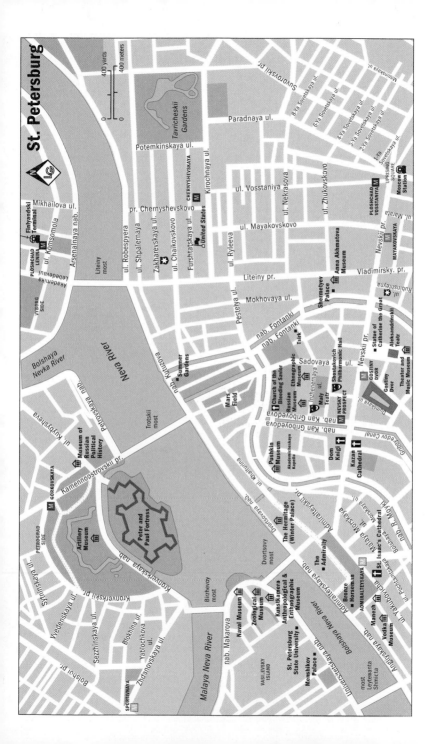

St. Petersburg

400 yards
400 meters

VYBORG Side

Finlyandski Terminal

PLOSHCHAD LENINA

ul. Komsomola

Akademika Lebedeva

Arsenalnaya nab.

Mikhailova ul.

Liteiny most

ul. Robespyera

ul. Shpalernaya

Zakharevskaya ul.

ul. Chaikovskovo

Furshtatskaya ul.

ul. Ryleeva

pr. Chernyshevskovo

CHERNYSHEVSKAYA

Kirochnaya ul.

ul. Vosstaniya

ul. Nekrasova

ul. Zhukovskovo

PLOSHCHAD VOSSTANIYA

ul. Marata

MAYAKOVSKAYA

United States

ul. Mayakovskovo

Liteiny pr.

Mokhovaya ul.

Pestelya ul.

Paradnaya ul.

Potemkinskaya ul.

Tavricheskii Gardens

8-ya Sovetskaya ul.

6-ya Sovetskaya ul.

4-ya Sovetskaya ul.

3-ya Sovetskaya ul.

2-ya Sovetskaya ul.

1-ya Sovetskaya ul.

UPRISING SQUARE
Moscow Station

Mininskaya ul.

Suvorovskii pr.

Nevskii pr.

Vladimirskiy. pr.

Statue of Catherine the Great

Aleksandrinskii Teatr

Theater and Music Museum

ul. Rubinsteina

Anna Akhmatova Museum

Shermetyev Palace

nab. Fontanki

nab. Fontanki

Tsirk

Sadovaya

Ethnographic Museum

Shostakovich Philharmonic Hall

GOSTINY DVOR

Gostiny Dvor

Inzhenernaya

Maly Teatr

Russian Museum

Church of the Bleeding Savior

NEVSKY PROSPECT

Sadovaya ul.

nab. Kan Griboyedova

nab. Kan Griboyedova

Dimitrovskaya

Summer Gardens

Mars Field

nab. Kutuzova

Neva River

Bolshaya Nevka River

Museum of Russian Political History

ul. Kuybysheva

Petrovskaya nab.

Trotskii most

Kamennoostrovskii pr.

GORKOVSKAYA

Artillery Museum

PETROGRAD SIDE

Kronverkskaya nab.

Peter and Paul Fortress

Kronverkskii pr.

Sytninskaya ul.

Vvedenskaya ul.

Sezzhinskaya ul.

Blokhina ul.

Yablochkova ul.

Zhdanovskaya ul.

Bolshoi pr.

SPORTIVNAYA

Malaya Neva River

nab. Makarova

Naval Museum

Zoological Museum

Kunstkamera Anthropological & Enthnographic Museum

St. Petersburg State University

Menshikov Palace

VASILEVSKY ISLAND

Universitetskaya nab.

Bolshaya Neva River

Birzhevoy most

Dvortsovy most

Dvortsovaya nab.

The Hermitage (Winter Palace)

The Admiralty

Admiralteyskiy pr.

Admiralteyskaya nab.

Bronze Horseman

St. Isaac's Cathedral

ADMIRALTEYSKAYA

Manezh

Vodka Museum

Malaya Morskaya

Bolshaya Morskaya ul.

Angliyskaya nab.

most Leytenanta Shmicta

ul. Yakubovicha

ul. Pochtamtskaya

nab. reki Moyki

Gribyedov Canal

Pushkin Museum

Akademicheskaya Kapella

Dom Knigi

Kazan Cathedral

ul. Khalturina

Nevskii pr.

Sadovaya ul.

Moskovskii pr.

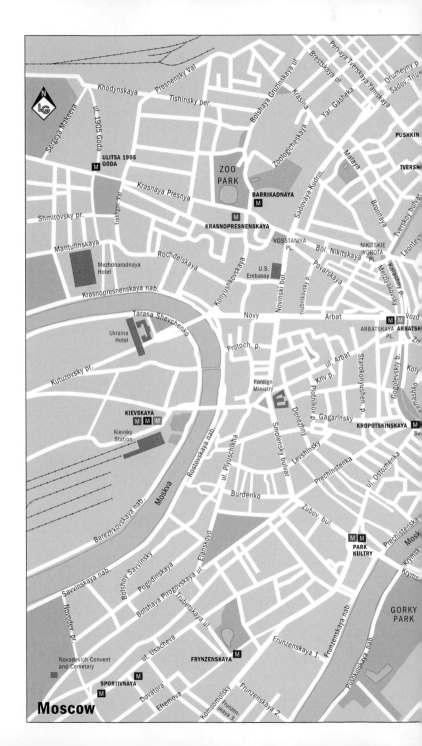

Moscow

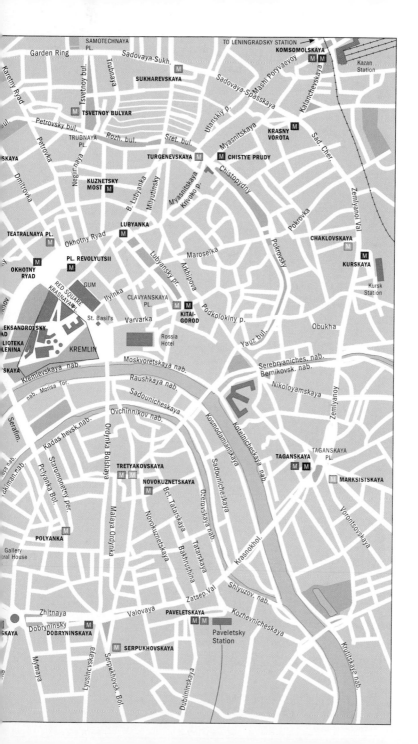

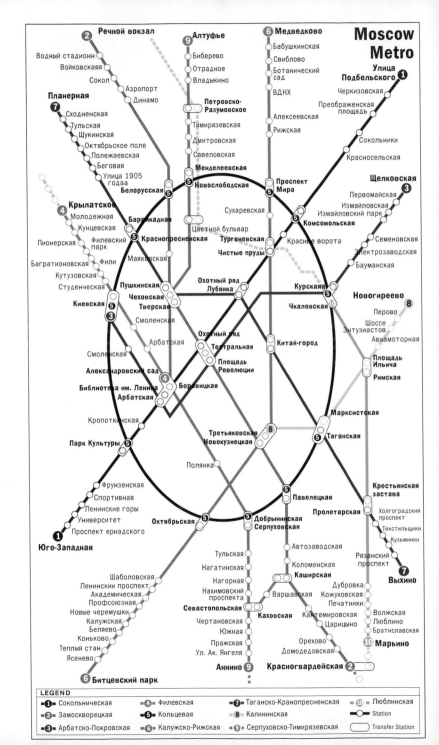

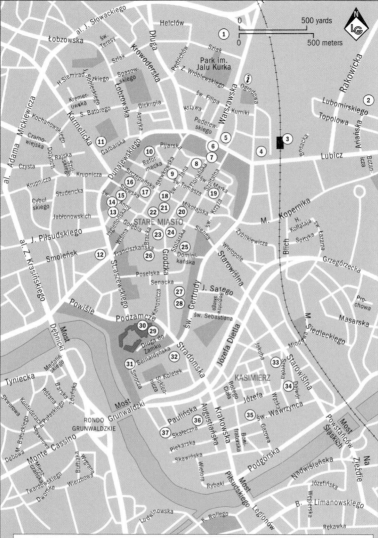

Central Kraków

Akademia Ekonomiczna, **2**
Almatur Office, **24**
Barbican, **6**
Bernardine Church, **32**
Bus Station, **4**
Carmelite Church, **11**
Cartoon Gallery, **9**
City Historical Museum, **17**
Collegium Maius, **14**
Corpus Christi Church, **35**
Czartoryski Art Museum, **8**
Dominican Church, **25**
Dragon Statue, **31**

Filharmonia, **12**
Franciscan Church, **26**
Grunwald Memorial, **5**
Jewish Cemetery, **33**
Jewish Museum, **34**
Kraków Glowny Station, **3**
Monastery of the
  Reformed Franciscans, **10**
Muzeum Historii Fotografii, **23**
Orbis Office, **19**
Pauline Church, **37**
Police Station, **18**
Politechnika Krakowska, **1**

St. Andrew's Church, **28**
St. Anne's Church, **15**
St. Catherine's Church, **36**
St. Florian's Gate, **7**
St. Mary's Church, **20**
St. Peter and Paul Church, **27**
Stary Teatr (Old Theater), **16**
Sukiennice (Cloth Hall), **21**
Town Hall, **22**
University Museum, **13**
Wawel Castle, **29**
Wawel Cathedral, **30**

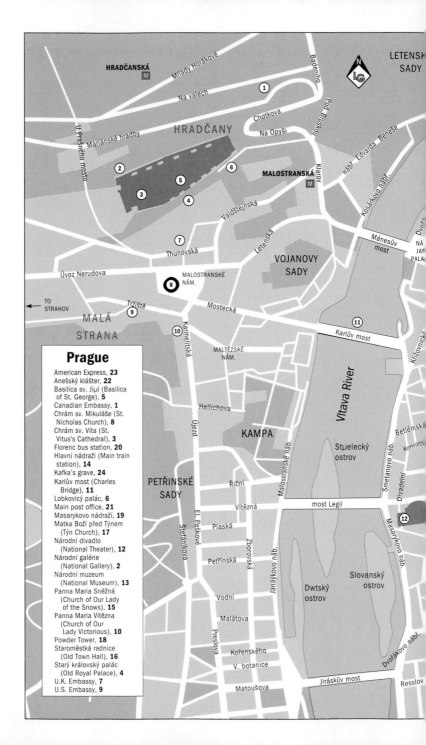

HRADČANSKÁ M

Milady Horákové

Na valech

Chotkova

LETENSK
SADY

N LG

HRADČANY

Na Opyši

Badeniho

Pod Bruskou

nábř. Edvarda Beneše

Kosárkovo nábř.

MALOSTRANSKÁ M

Klárov

Mariánské hradby

U Prašného mostu

② ① ⑥

⑤

③ ④

Valdštejnská

Letenská

Mánesův
most

NÁ
JAI
PALA

Dvoř

VOJANOVY
SADY

⑦

Thunovská

MALOSTRANSKÉ
NÁM.

Úvoz Nerudova

⑧

Mostecká

⑪

Karlův most

TO
STRAHOV

Tržiště
⑨

MALÁ
STRANA

⑩

Karmelitská

MALTÉZSKÉ
NÁM.

Vltava River

Křižovnick

Betlémská

Konvikts

Prague

American Express, **23**
Anežský klášter, **22**
Basilica sv. Jiří (Basilica
of St. George), **5**
Canadian Embassy, **1**
Chrám sv. Mikuláše (St.
Nicholas Church), **8**
Chrám sv. Víta (St.
Vitus's Cathedral), **3**
Florenc bus station, **20**
Hlavní nádraží (Main train
station), **14**
Kafka's grave, **24**
Karlův most (Charles
Bridge), **11**
Lobkovický palác, **6**
Main post office, **21**
Masarykovo nádraží, **19**
Matka Boží před Týnem
(Týn Church), **17**
Národní divadlo
(National Theater), **12**
Národní galérie
(National Gallery), **2**
Národní muzeum
(National Museum), **13**
Panna Maria Sněžná
(Church of Our Lady
of the Snows), **15**
Panna Maria Vítězna
(Church of Our
Lady Victorious), **10**
Powder Tower, **18**
Staroměstská radnice
(Old Town Hall), **16**
Starý královský palác
(Old Royal Palace), **4**
U.K. Embassy, **7**
U.S. Embassy, **9**

Hellichova

Újezd

KAMPA

Malostranské náb.

Střelecký
ostrov

Smetanovo náb.

Divadelní

PETŘÍNSKÉ
SADY

Říční

Štefánikova

Vítězná

El. Peškové

most Legií

⑫

Masarykovo náb.

Plaská

Zborovská

Janáčkovo náb.

Petřínská

Slovanský
ostrov

Vodní

Dwtský
ostrov

Malátova

Preslova

Kořenského

V. botanice

Jiráskův most

Dvořákovo nábř.

Matoušova

Resslov

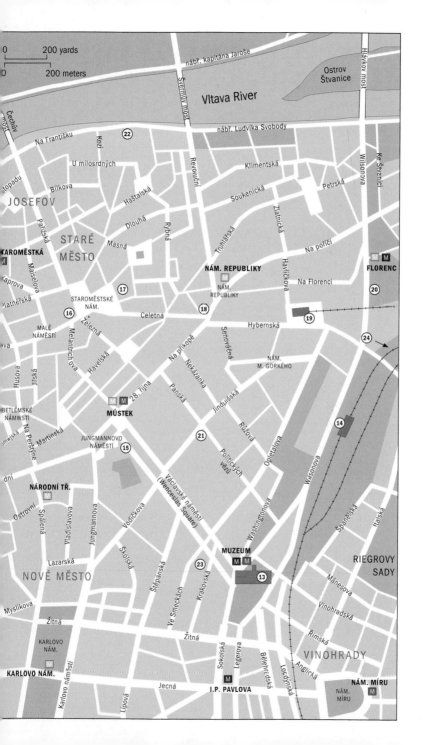

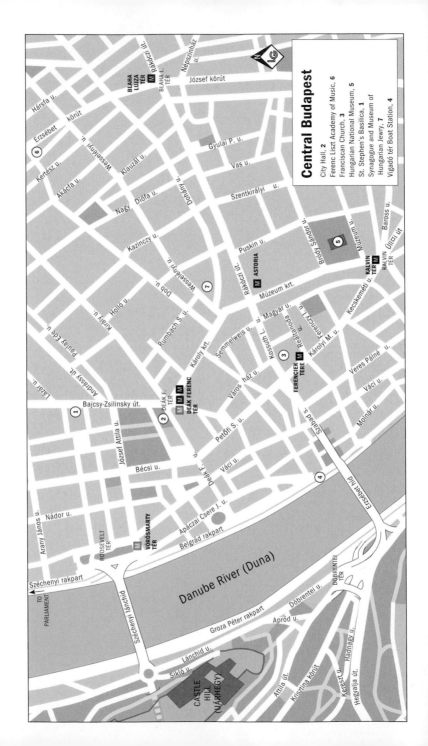

Central Budapest

City Hall, **2**
Ferenc Liszt Academy of Music, **6**
Franciscan Church, **3**
Hungarian National Museum, **5**
St. Stephen's Basilica, **1**
Synagogue and Museum of
Hungarian Jewry, **7**
Vigadó tér Boat Station, **4**

Danube River (Duna)

CASTLE HILL (VÁRHEGY)

TO PARLIAMENT

Berlin Transit

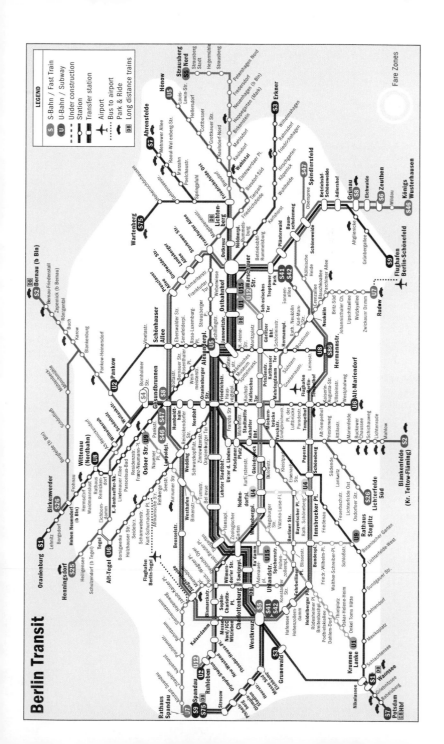

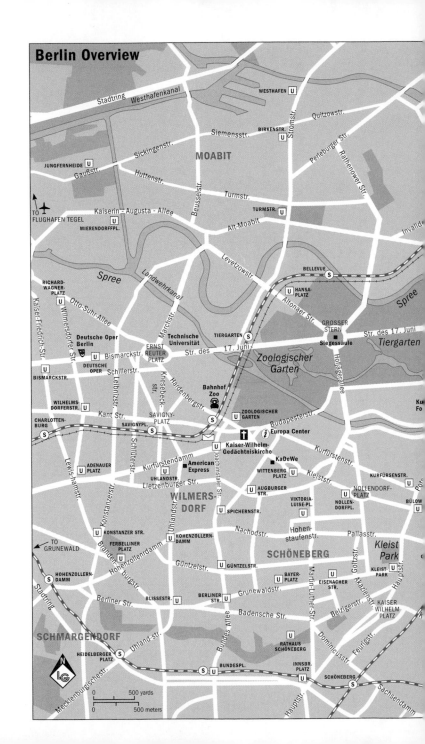

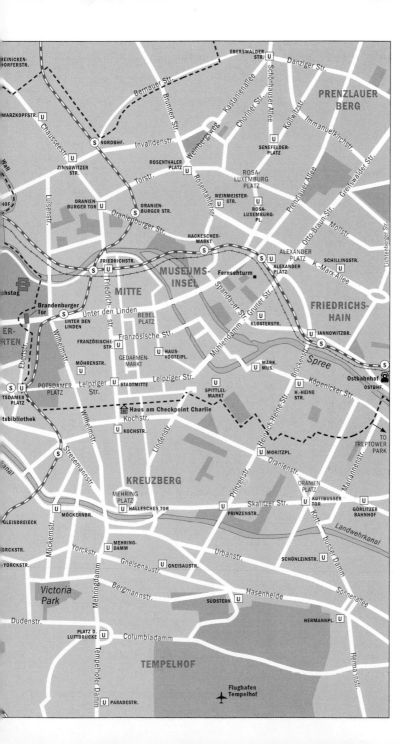

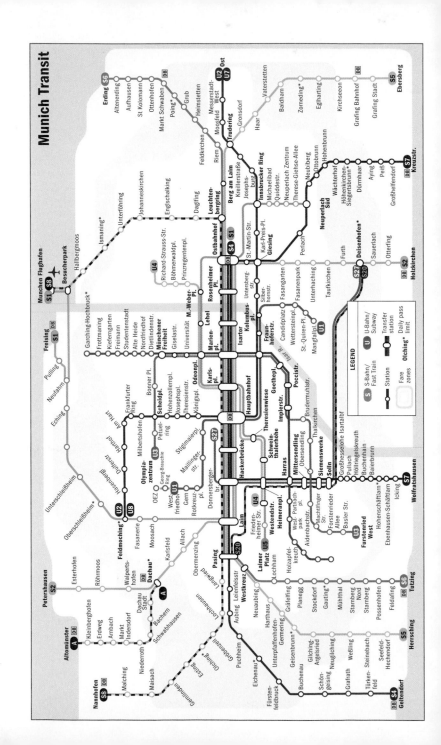

Munich Transit

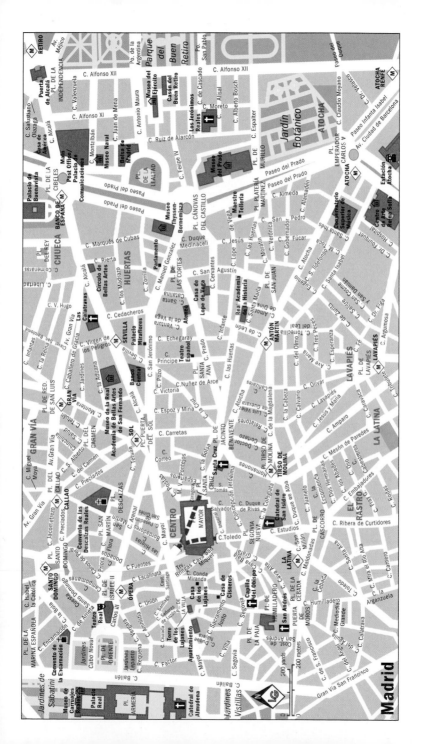

Madrid

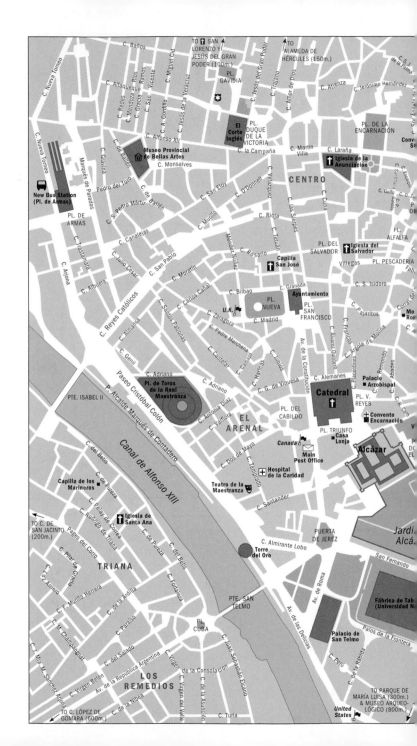

Sevilla

ACARENA

C. Peñuelas

C. del Sol

PL. PONCE
DE LEON

C. Azafrán

C. Santiago

C. Imperial

C. Caballerizas

guilas

**Casa de
Pilatos**

PL.
PILATOS

C. Lino

de Ibarra

PL. DE LAS
MERCENARIAS

C. Tevies

C. Céspedes

C. San Clemente

C. Acietuna

C. Cano y Cueto

C. Sta. María la Blanca

Crces. Mariscal

NTA
Z

Jardines
de
Murillo

C. General Ríos

C. A. Fernández

C. Demetrio de los Ríos

Av. Menéndez Pelayo

C. Capitán Vigueras

Av. de Cádiz

PL. DE
SAN
SEBASTIÁN

**Estación
Prado San
Sebastián**

ÓN
DE
RÍA

C. José María Osborne

C. Diego Riaño

Av. Carlos V

Infanta Luisa de Orleans

Infante Carlos de Borbón

Av. de Portugal

PL. DE
ESPAÑA

PUERTA OSARIO

C. de los Navarros

C. Conde Negro

C. Recaredo

C. Vir. de Gracia y Esperanza

C. Guadalupe

C. Fray Alonso

PL. CARMEN
BENÍTEZ

PL. SAN
AGUSTÍN

Av. Luis Montoto

C. la Florida

C. Menéndez Pelayo

SANTA
CRUZ

C. J. María
Moreno Galván

C. Juan de Matacarneza

C. San Bernardo

Av. Málaga

C. Saturno

C. Arroyo

C. María Auxiliadora

C. Salecianos

C. Arroyo

C. Pérez Hervás

C. Urquiza

C. Venecia

C. Dr. Delgado Ríos

C. San Juan Bosco

C. Esperanza de la Trinidad

C. Gonzalo Bilbao

C. Amador de los Ríos

C. Arroyo

C. Jupiter

C. La Vega

Lope de

C. Juan de Vera

C. Padre Méndez Casariego

C. Jose Laguillo

**Estación de
Santa Justa**

TO ✈

C. Juan Antonio Cavestany

C. Campo de los Mártires

C. Lictores

C. Beata Juana Jugan

C. Pablo Picasso

LA CALZADA

PL. DEL
SACRIFICIO

C. San Benito

C. Vía Crucis

S. Florencio

C. Averroes

■ **Ruinas
Acueducto**

C. Jiménez Aranda

C. José Cámara

C. Manuel Pérez

C. Fuentidueña

C. Trovador

Av. Eduardo Dato

C. Fernando Tirado

C. Virgen Valvaner

C. Eduardo Rivas

C. Maese Farfán

C. Pilar

C. Oscar Carvallo

C. Pirineos

C. Cofia

C. Gallinato

C. Tentudia

C. Portaceli Huestes

Av. De La Buhaira

C. Campamento

C. Virgen de
la Sierra

C. Ciudad Ronda

Dr. Pedro
Castro

C. Enramadilla

Dr. A. C. Ubato

C. Barrau

C. Enramadilla

0 ___ 200 yards
0 ___ 200 meters

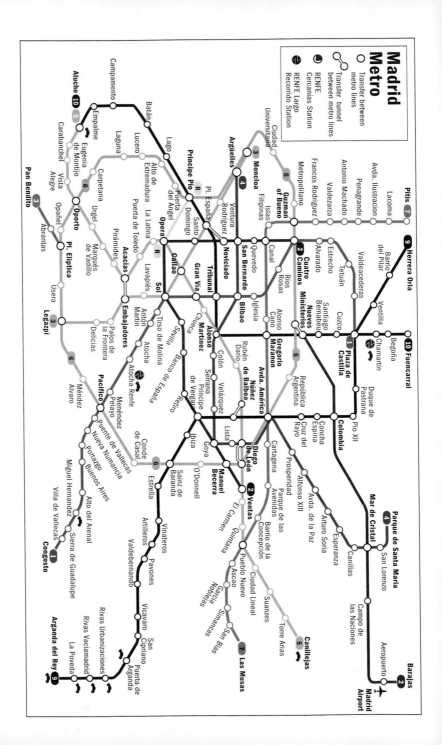

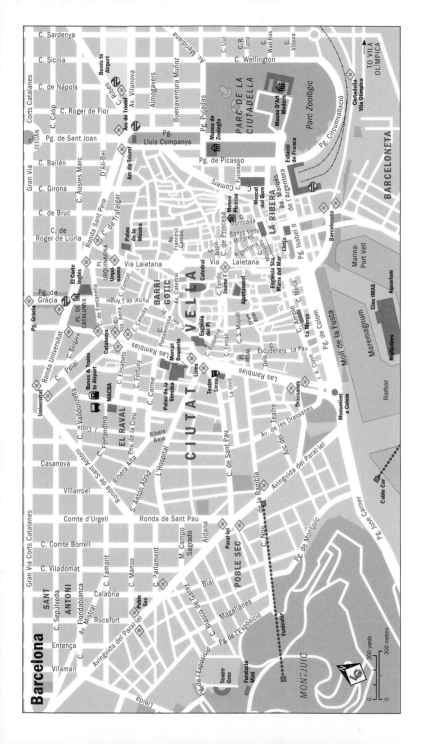

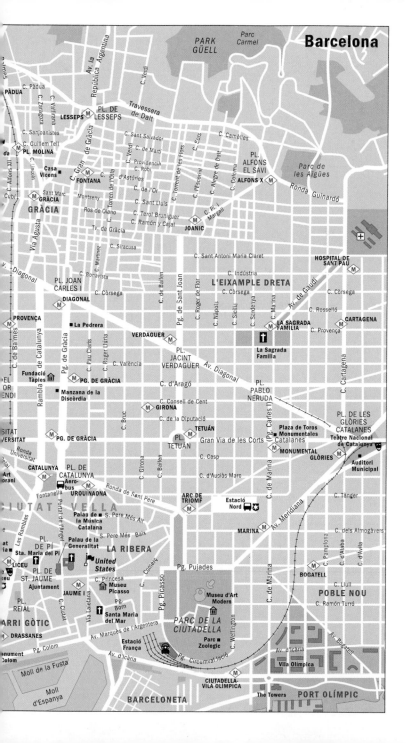

Barcelona Metro

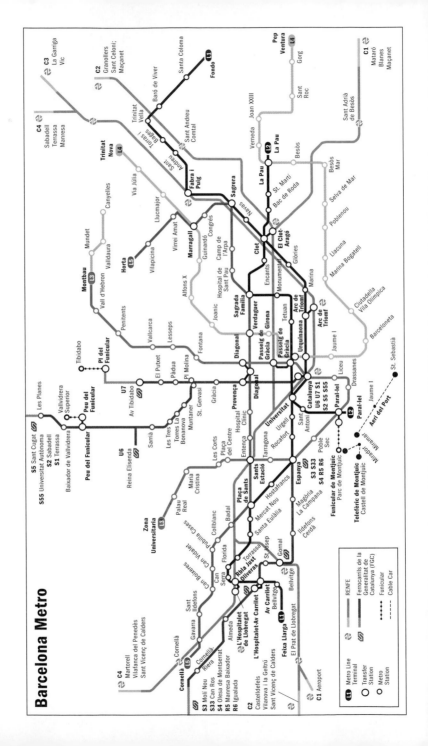

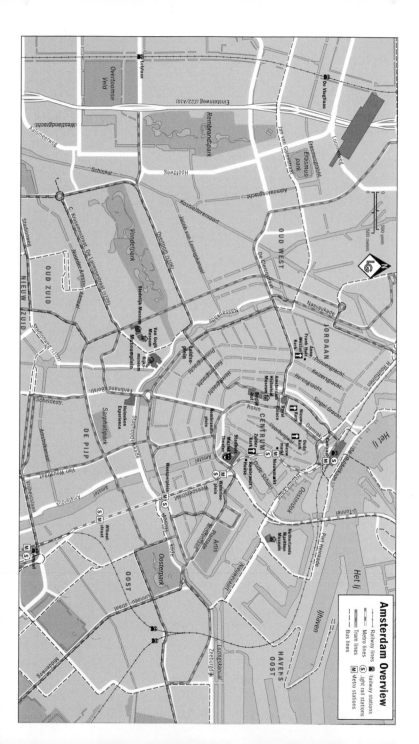

Amsterdam Overview

- Railway lines — Railway stations
- Metro lines — Ⓢ Light rail stations
- Tram lines — Ⓜ Metro stations
- Bus lines

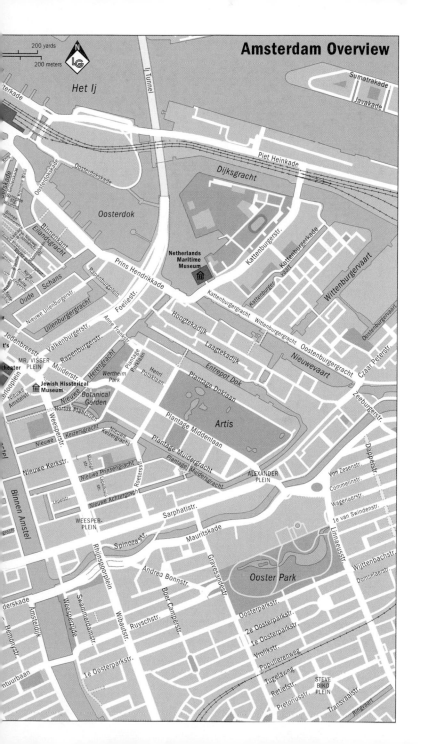

Amsterdam Overview

200 yards
200 meters

Het Ij

Ij Tunnel

Sumatrakade

Javakade

Piet Heinkade

Dijksgracht

Oosterdok

Oosterdokskade

Binnenkant
Eilandsgracht

Oude Schans

Prins Hendrikkade

Netherlands
Maritime
Museum

Kattenburgerstr.

Kattenburgerkade

Kattenburger
vaart

Wittenburgervaart

Oostenburgervaart

Rapenburgplein

Nieuwe Uilenburgerstr.

Uilenburgergracht

Foeliestr.

Hoogtekadijk

Kattenburgergracht

Wittenburgergracht

Anne Frankstr.

Laagtekadijk

Oostenburgergracht

Nieuwevaart

Czaar Peterstr.

Jodenbreestr.

Valkenburgerstr.

Rapenburgerstr.

Muiderstr.

Herengracht

Plantage
Parklaan

Entrepot Dok

MR. VISSER
PLEIN

Wertheim
Park

Henri
Polaklaan

Plantage Doklaan

Zeeburgerstr.

Jewish Hisstorical
Museum

Nieuwe
Amstelstr.

Nieuwe Botanical
Garden

Hortus Plantsoen

Plantage Doklaan

Artis

Weesperstr.

Nieuwe Keizersgracht

Nieuwe
Keizersgracht

Plantage Middenlaan

Nieuwe Prinsengracht

Roetersstr.

Plantage Muidergracht

ALEXANDER
PLEIN

Von Zesenstr.

Daniëlstr.

Nieuwe Kerkstr.

Nieuwe Achtergracht

Commelinstr.

Wagenaarstr.

1e van Swindenstr.

Binnen Amstel

Tepelstr.

Sarphatistr.

WEESPER-
PLEIN

Mauritskade

Linnaeusstr.

Spinoza str.

Rhijnspoorplein

Andrea Bonnstr.

Boer Campeslr.

Gravensandestr.

Ooster Park

Wijttenbachstr.

Domselaerstr.

Amsteldijk

Swammerdamstr.

Weesperzijde

Wibautstr.

Ruyschstr.

Oosterparkstr.

2e Oosterparkstr.

1e Oosterparkstr.

Vrolikstr.

Hemonystr.

tuurbaan

1e Oosterparkstr.

Populierenweg

Tugelaweg

Retiefstr.

STEVE
BIKO
PLEIN

Pretoriusstr.

Transvaalstr.

Ringvaart

Amsterdam Tram Lines

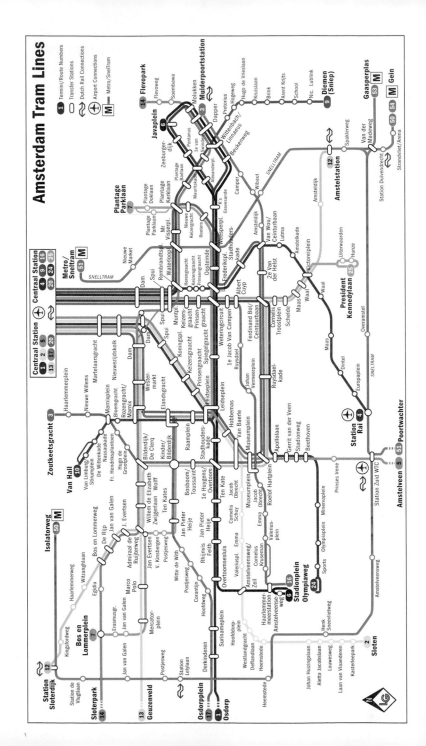

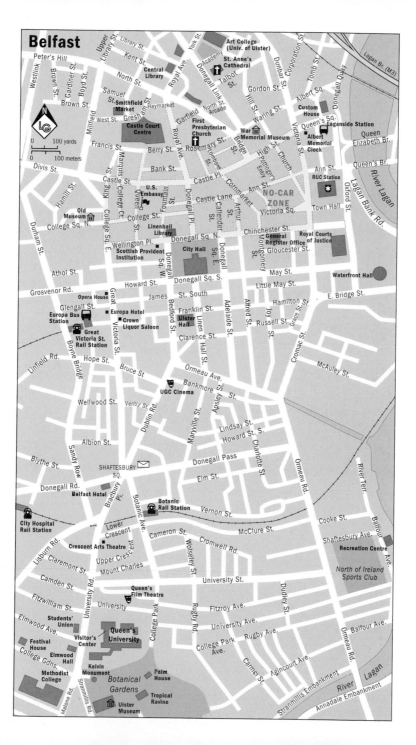

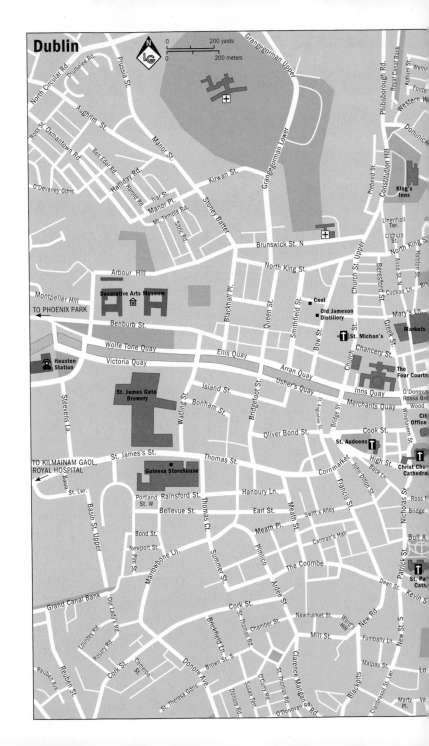

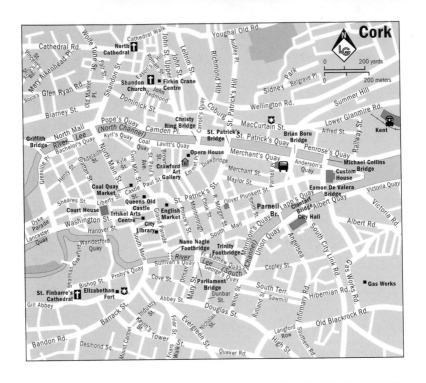

Cork

Cathedral Rd. · Cathedral Walk · St. Vincent's Rd. · St. Aikenhead Pl. · Wolfe Tone St. · Mary Aikenhead Pl. · North Cathedral · John St. Upper · John St. · Leitrim St. · Roman St. · Youghal Old Rd. · Richmond Hill · Audley Pl. · Sidney Park · Belgrave Pl. · LG · Cork · 0 · 200 yards · 0 · 200 meters

Glen Ryan Rd. · Boyce's St. · Old Market Pl. · Shandon St. · Eason Ave. · John Redmond · Shandon Church · Firkin Crane Centre · Dominick St. · St. Patrick's Hill · Coburg St. · Wellington Rd. · Summer Hill · Lower Glanmire Rd.

Blarney St. · Pope's Quay · (North Channel) · Camden Pl. · Christy Ring Bridge · Carroll's Quay · St. Patrick's Bridge · St. Patrick's Quay · Brian Boru Bridge · Alfred St. · Railway St. · Kent

Griffith Bridge · North Mall · Bachelor's Quay · Kyrl's Quay · River Lee · North Quay · Lavitt's Quay · Coal Quay · Opera House · Merchant's Quay · Penrose's Quay · Michael Collins Bridge

Grenville Pl. · Henry St. · Gratten St. · North Main St. · Kyle St. · Paul St. Ave. · Crawford Art Gallery · Emmet Pl. · Drawbridge · Merchant St. · Anderson's Quay · Custom House · Victoria Quay

Coal Quay Market · Com Mkt. St. · Castle Paul St. · Maylor St. · Eamon De Valera Bridge

Sheares St. · Liberty St. · Queens Old Castle · St. Patrick's St. · R. Morgan St. · Oliver Plunkett St. · Lapp's Quay · Clontarf Bridge · Albert Quay

Court House · Washington St. · Triskel Arts Centre · English Market · Grand Parade · Princes St. · Marlborough St. · Parnell Br. · City Hall · Albert Rd.

Dyke Parade · Lancaster Quay · Hanover St. · City Library · Nano Nagle Footbridge · South Mall · Morrison's Quay · Union Quay · South City Link Rd.

Wandesford Quay · South Main · Sullivan's Quay · River Lee (South Channel) · Trinity Footbridge · Fr. Mathew Quay · George's Quay · Copley St. · Angelsea · South Terr.

Sharman Crawford · Bishop St. · Cove St. · Mary St. · Parliament Bridge · Dunbar St. · White St. · Sawmill · Infirmary Rd. · Hibernian Rd. · Gas Works Rd. · Gas Works

St. Finbarre's Cathedral · Elizabethan Fort · Abbey St. · Douglas St. · Rutland St. · Old Blackrock Rd.

Gill Abbey · Barrack St. · Industry St. · Nicholas St. · Friar St. · Evergreen St. · Langford Row · Southern Rd. · High St.

Bandon Rd. · Kevin's Tower · Mount Carmel · St. Friars Walk · Quaker Rd. · Desmond Sq.

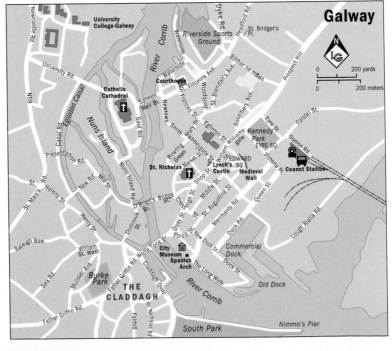

Galway

Newcastle Rd. · University Rd. · N59 · University College-Galway · River Corrib · Waterside · Dyke Rd. · Riverside Sports Ground · Headford Rd. · St. Bridget's Pl. · Bóthar na mBan · Prospect Hill · LG · Galway · 0 · 200 yards · 0 · 200 meters

Eglinton Canal · Canal Rd. · Salmon Weir Br. · Catholic Cathedral · Gaol Rd. · Courthouse · Waterside · St. Vincents Ave. · Woodquay · St. Brendan's Ave. · Rosemary Ave. · Forster St. · Eyre St. · Station Rd.

Nuns Island · Presentation Rd. · Newtown · Smith · Frances St. · Abbeygate St. · Eglinton St. · William St. · Kennedy Park · EYRE SQ. · Ceannt Station

St. Mary's Rd. · New Rd. · Mill St. · Nuns Island Rd. · Bowling Green · St. Nicholas · Market St. · Shop St. · Mary St. · William · EDWARD · Lynch's Castle · EDWARD SQ. · Medieval Wall · Victoria Pl. · Queen St.

St. Helens St. · Henry St. · Dominick St. · St. Brian's Bridge Br. · Cross High St. · Middle St. · St. Augustine St. · Merchants Rd. · Dock St.

Raleigh Row · William St. West · Sea Rd. · Munster Ave. · Burke Park · THE CLADDAGH · Father Griffin Rd. · Wolfe Tone Br. · Claddagh Quay · City Museum · Spanish Arch · The Long Walk · Commercial Dock · Dock St. · Old Dock · Lough Atalia Rd.

Father Griffin Rd. · Fairhill · St. Nicholas Rd. · River Corrib · South Park · Nimmo's Pier

Irish Film Centre, which screens specialty and art house film *(6 Eustace St.),* Ireland's only **Gallery of Photography** *(Meeting House Sq.),* and the **Temple Bar Gallery & Studios** *(5-9 Temple Bar).*

DAME STREET AND THE CATHEDRALS. King John built **Dublin Castle** in 1204 on top of the Viking settlement of Dubh Linn. For 700 years after its construction, it was the seat of British rule in Ireland. Since 1938, each president of Ireland has been inaugurated here. *(On Dame St., at the intersection of Parliament and Castle St. Open M-F 10am-5pm, Sa-Su 2-5pm. €4.50, students and seniors €3.50. Grounds free.)* **St. Patrick's Cathedral,** Ireland's largest, dates to the 12th century, although Sir Benjamin Guinness remodeled much of it in 1864. St. Patrick allegedly baptized converts in the park next door. *(On Patrick St. Take bus #49, 49A, 50, 54A, 56A, 65, 65B, 77, or 77A from Eden Quay. Open Mar.-Oct. daily 9am-6pm; Nov.-Feb. Sa 9am-5pm, Su 9am-3pm. €4, students, seniors, and children free.)* Sitric Silkenbeard, King of the Dublin Norsemen, built a wooden church on the site of the **Christ Church Cathedral** around 1038; Strongbow rebuilt it in stone in 1169. Further additions were made in the following century and again in the 1870s. Stained glass sparkles above the raised crypts, and fragments of ancient pillars are scattered about like bleached bones. *(At the end of Dame St., across from the castle. Take bus #50 from Eden Quay or 78A from Aston Quay. Open daily 9:45am-5:30pm except during services. Suggested donation €3.)*

GUINNESS BREWERY AND KILMAINHAM. Guinness brews its black magic at the St. James Gate Brewery, next door to the ▨**Guinness Storehouse.** In 1759, farsighted Arthur Guinness signed a 9000-year lease for the original 1759 brewery. The lease is displayed in the Storehouse's atrium, an architectural triumph that rises seven floors and has a center shaped like a pint glass. View the exhibit on Guinness's infamously clever advertising—and then drink, silly tourist, drink. *(On St. James's Gate. From Christ Church Cathedral, follow High St. west through its name changes: Cornmarket, Thomas, and James. Take bus #51B or 78A from Aston Quay or #123 from O'Connell St. Open Apr.-Sept. daily 9:30am-7pm; Oct.-Mar. 9:30am-5pm. €12, students €8, seniors and children €5.30.)* Almost all of the rebels who fought in Ireland's struggle for independence from 1792 to 1921 spent time at **Kilmainham Gaol.** Tours wind through the chilly limestone corridors of the prison and end in the haunting execution yard. *(On Inchicore Rd. Take bus #51 from Aston Quay, #51A from Lower Abbey St., or #79 from Aston Quay. Open Apr.-Sept. daily 9:30am-4:45pm; Oct.-Mar. M-F 9:30am-4pm, Su 10am-4:45pm. €4.40, seniors €3.10, students and children €1.90.)*

THE HIDDEN DEAL

THE EMERALD ISLE'S GOLDEN EGG

Many of Ireland's most touristed sights—its national parks, museums, monuments and gardens—are owned and operated by the Irish Department of Arts and Heritage. While the price of admission to these sights is typically quite low, the accumulated cost of visiting each may start to overwhelm the budget traveler.

Recently, the Department of Heritage began to offer the **Dúchas Heritage Discount Card,** perhaps Ireland's greatest hidden deal. The card grants access to all of the sights owned and operated by the Department of Heritage for one full year. At €19, the card is worthwhile even for those in Ireland for a short time; the savings start to accrue after visiting only three or four Heritage sights, whose individual admissions average €5-7.

The card will prove valuable for most Irish itineraries. It covers sights across the isle, including Kilmainham Gaol in Dublin, Kilkenny Castle, the Brú na Bóinne Visitors Centre in Newgrange, and Reginald's Tower in Waterford. The card can be purchased online and at Dúchas Heritage sights.

(Info ☎ 1850 600 601; international ☎ 01 647 2461; www.heritageireland.ie/en/HeritageCard. €19, students and children €7.60, seniors €12.70, families €45.75.)

O'CONNELL ST. AND PARNELL SQUARE. In the early 20th century, Dubliners refused to finance **The Hugh Lane Municipal Gallery of Modern Art** to hold American painter Lane's collection of French Impressionist paintings; although the gallery was eventually constructed, Yeats lamented his city's provincial attitude in a string of poems. *(Buses #3, 10, 11, 13, 16, and 19 all stop near the gallery, in Parnell Sq. Open Tu-Th 9:30am-6pm, F-Sa 9:30am-5pm, Su 11am-5pm. Free; occasional special exhibits may charge.)* The city's rich literary heritage comes to life at **The Dublin Writers' Museum,** which displays rare editions, manuscripts, and memorabilia of Swift, Shaw, Wilde, Yeats, Beckett, Brendan Behan, Patrick Kavanagh, and Sean O'Casey. *(18 Parnell Sq. North. Open June-Aug. M-F 10am-6pm, Sa 10am-5pm, Su 11am-5pm; Sept.-May M-Sa 10am-5pm. €5.50, students and seniors €5. Combined ticket with James Joyce Centre €9/€8.)* The **James Joyce Cultural Centre** features a wide range of Joyceana, including portraits of the individuals who inspired his characters. Call for info on lectures, walking tours, and Bloomsday events. *(35 N. Great Georges St., past Parnell St. ☎878 8547. Open July-Aug. M-Sa 9:30am-5pm, Su 11am-5pm; Sept.-June M-Sa 9:30am-5pm, Su 12:30-5pm. €4, students and seniors €3.)*

SMITHFIELD AND ELSEWHERE. At the **Old Jameson Distillery,** learn how science, grain, and tradition come together to create the golden fluid called **whiskey.** The experience ends with a glass of the Irish whiskey of your choice. *(On Bow St. From O'Connell St., turn onto Henry St. and continue straight as the street dwindles to Mary St., then Mary Ln., then May Ln.; the warehouse is on a cobblestone street on the left. Tours daily 9:30am-5:30pm. €6.50, students and seniors €3.80.)* **Phoenix Park,** Europe's largest enclosed public park, is most famous for the 1882 "Phoenix Park murders." The Invincibles, a nationalist splinter group, stabbed the Chief Secretary of Ireland, Lord Cavendish, and his under Secretary 180m from the **Phoenix Column.** The 712-hectare park incorporates the President's residence *(Áras an Uachtaraín)*, cricket pitches, polo grounds, and grazing deer. **Dublin Zoo,** Europe's largest, is in the park. It contains 700 animals and the world's biggest egg. *(Take bus #10 from O'Connell St. or #25 or 26 from Middle Abbey St. Park always open. Free. Zoo open June-Aug. M-Sa 9:30am-6pm, Su 10:30am-6pm. Closes at sunset in winter. €8, students €6.)*

🎵 🎭 ENTERTAINMENT AND NIGHTLIFE

Whether you fancy poetry or punk, Dublin is equipped to entertain you. The free *Event Guide* is available at the tourist office and Temple Bar restaurants. The **Abbey Theatre,** 26 Lower Abbey St., was founded in 1904 by Yeats and Lady Gregory to promote Irish culture and modernist theater. *(☎878 7222. Box office open M-Sa 10:30am-7pm. Tickets €12-25; M-Th student rate €10.)* **St. Patrick's Day** (Mar. 17) and the half-week leading up to it host a carnival of concerts, fireworks, street theater, and intoxicated madness. *(☎675 3205; www.paddyfest.ie.)* Dublin returns to 1904 on **Bloomsday** (June 16), the day of Leopold Bloom's journey in Joyce's *Ulysses.* The James Joyce Cultural Centre *(☎873 1984)* sponsors a reenactment of the funeral and wake, a lunch at Davy Byrne's, and a Guinness breakfast.

Trad (traditional music) is an important element of the Dublin music scene—some pubs in the city center have sessions nightly. The best pub for *trad* is ▨**Cobblestones** *(☎872 1799)*, on King St. North, in Smithfield. James Joyce once proposed that a "good puzzle would be to cross Dublin without passing a pub." A radio station once offered IR£100 to the first person to solve the puzzle. The winner explained that you could take any route—you'd just have to visit them all on the way. *Let's Go* recommends beginning your journey at the gates of Trinity College, moving onto Grafton St., stumbling onto Camden St., teetering down S. Great Georges St., and, finally, triumphantly crawling into the Temple Bar area.

PUBS

The Celts, 81-82 Talbots St. Step out of the city and into Olde Ireland. A welcoming pub with nightly *trad*. Open Su-W 10:30am-11:30pm, Th-Sa 10:30am-12:30am.

Zanzibar, at the Ha'Penny Bridge. A hot spot with both a bar and a dance floor. DJ M-Th from 10pm, F-Sa from 9pm. Open M-Th 5pm-2:30am, F-Sa 4pm-2:30am, Su 4pm-1am.

Whelan's, 25 Wexford St., down S. Great Georges St. The stage venue in back hosts big-name *trad* and rock, with live music every night at 9:30pm (doors open 8pm). Cover €7-12. Open for lunch daily 12:30-2:30pm; pub open W-Sa until late.

The Stag's Head, 1 Dame Ct. This beautiful Victorian pub has a largely student crowd. Excellent food. Entrees about €10. Food served M-F noon-3:30pm and 5-7pm, Sa 12:30-2:30pm. Open M-W 11:30am-11:30pm; Th-Sa 11:30am-12:30am.

The Long Stone, 10-11 Townsend St. Hand-carved banisters and old books give the place a rustic feel. Lots of interesting rooms; the largest has an enormous carving of a bearded man whose mouth serves as a fireplace. Lunch 12:30-2:30pm. Open M-W noon-11:30pm, Th-F 10am-12:30am, Sa 3pm-12:30am, Su 4-11pm.

Messrs. Maguire, on Burgh Quay. A classy multi-floor watering hole with homemade microbrews. *Trad* Su-Tu 9:30-11:30pm. Open Su-Tu 10:30am-12:30am, W-Th 10:30am-1:30am, F 10:30am-2am, Sa 12:30pm-2am.

CLUBS

The PoD, 35 Harcourt St. Spanish-style decor meets hard core dance music. The brave venture upstairs to **The Red Box** (☎478 0225), a separate, more intense club with a warehouse atmosphere. Often hosts big-name DJs, when cover charges skyrocket. Cover €10-20; Th and Sa €7 with ISIC; Th ladies free before midnight. Open until 3am.

Rí-Rá, 1 Exchequer St. Good music that steers clear of pop and house extremes. Two floors, several bars, lots of nooks and crannies. Cover €7-10. Open daily 11pm-2am.

Gaiety, S. King St., just off Grafton St. This elegant theater shows its wild side late night, with DJs and live music from salsa to soul. Cover from €10. Open F-Sa midnight-4am.

The George, 89 S. Great Georges St. Dublin's first and most prominent gay bar. All ages gather throughout the day to chat and drink. The attached nightclub is open W-Su until 2am. Frequent theme nights. Dress well—no effort, no entry. Cover €8-10 after 10pm.

▶ DAYTRIPS FROM DUBLIN

HOWTH. Howth (rhymes with "both") dangles from the mainland in Edenic isolation, less than 16km from Dublin. A 3hr. **cliff walk** circles the peninsula, passing heather and thousands of seabird nests. The best section of the walk is a 1hr. hike between the harbor and the lighthouse at the southeast tip. To get to the trailhead from town, turn left at the DART station and follow Harbour Rd. around the coast for about 20min. Just offshore is **Ireland's Eye,** a former sanctuary for monks that has become an avian refuge. **Ireland's Eye Boat Trips,** on the East Pier, jets passengers across the water. (☎01 831 4200. €8 round-trip, students and children €4.) To reach the private **Howth Castle,** which features a curiously charming patchwork of architectural styles, turn right as you exit the DART station and then left after 400m, at the entrance to the Deer Park Hotel. Turn left out of the station to get to the **tourist office,** in the Old Courthouse on Harbour Rd. (☎01 832 0405. Open May-Aug. M-F 11am-1pm, also Tu-F 1:30-5pm.) To get to Howth, take a northbound DART train to the end of the line (30min., 6 per hr., €1.50).

IRELAND

BOYNE VALLEY. The thinly populated Boyne Valley hides Ireland's greatest archaeological treasures. Along the curves of the river between Slane and Drogheda lie no fewer than 40 crypt-like passages constructed by the Neolithics around the 4th millenium BC. **Newgrange** is the most spectacular; a roof box over the entrance allows a solitary beam of sunlight to shine directly into the tomb for 17min. on the winter solstice, a breathtaking experience simulated on the tour. You may only enter Newgrange by admission at ▨**Brú na Bóinne Visitors Centre,** near Donore on the south side of the River Boyne, across from the tombs. (☎041 988 0300. Open June to mid-Sept. daily 9am-7pm; May and late Sept. 9am-6:30pm; Mar.-Apr. and Oct. 9:30am-5:30pm; Nov.-Feb. 9:30am-5pm. Center and 1hr. tour €5, students €2.50.) A group of enormous, well-preserved Norman castles—including **Trim Castle,** conquered by Mel Gibson in *Braveheart*—overlooks **Trim** proper on the River Boyne. (Open May-Oct. 10am-6pm. Tours every 45min. Limited to 15 people; sign up upon arrival in Trim. Grounds only €1.20. Tour and grounds €3.10, students €1.20.) The Trim **visitors center** is on Mill St. (☎046 37 227. Open M-W and F-Sa 10am-5pm; Su noon-5:30pm.) From Dublin, Bus Éireann shuttles to the Brú na Bóinne Visitors Centre (1½hr.; M-Sa every 15min., Su every hr.; €12.70 round-trip) and Trim Castle (1hr.; M-Sa every hr., Su 3 per day; €10.20).

SOUTHEAST IRELAND

A base first for the Vikings and then the Normans, the Southeast echoes a fainter Celtic influence than the rest of Ireland. Town and street names in this region reflect Norse, Norman, and Anglo-Saxon influences rather than Gaelic ones. The Southeast's busiest attractions are its beaches, which draw admirers to the coastline stretching from Kilmore Quay to tidy Ardmore.

◧ FERRIES TO FRANCE AND BRITAIN

Irish Ferries (☎053 33 158) sails from Rosslare Harbour to Pembroke, Wales (4hr., every day, €28-38) and Roscoff and Cherbourg, France (18hr., every other day). **Eurail** passes grant passage on ferries to France. **Stena Line** (☎053 61 567) runs from Rosslare Harbour to Fishguard, Wales (3½hr., €28-35).

THE WICKLOW MOUNTAINS   ☎0404

Over 600m high, carpeted in fragrant heather, and pleated by sparkling rivers, the Wicklow summits are home to grazing sheep and scattered villages. Smooth glacial valleys embrace the two lakes and the monastic ruins. Public transportation is severely limited, so driving is the easiest way to get around. The lush, blessed valley of **Glendalough** draws a steady summertime stream of coach tours filled with hikers and ruin-oglers. The **National Park Information Office,** between the two lakes, is the best source for hiking advice. (☎45 425. Open May-Aug. daily 10am-6pm; Apr. and Sept. Sa-Su 10am-6pm.) **St. Kevin's Bus Service** (☎(01) 281 8119) arrives in town from St. Stephen's Green in Dublin (2 per day, €13 round-trip). The **tourist office** is across from the Glendalough Hotel. (☎45 688. Open from mid-June to Sept. M-Sa 10am-1pm and 2-6pm.) Good beds are at ▨**The Glendaloch Hostel (An Óige/HI) ❷,** 5min. up the road from the tourist office. (☎45 342. Internet €2 per 20min. Bike rental. Laundry €5. Dorms €19.50; doubles €43; off-season €2 less.) For more affordable food, B&Bs, and groceries, head to **Laragh,** 1.5km up the road.

ROSSLARE HARBOUR   ☎053

Rosslare Harbour is a useful departure point for Wales or France. **Trains** run from the ferry port to Dublin (3hr., 3 per day, €14.50) and Limerick (2½hr., 1-2 per day, €13.50) via Waterford (1¼hr., €8.50). **Buses** run from the same office to: Dublin

(3hr., 10-12 per day, €12.70); Cork (3-5 per day, €17); Galway (4 per day, €22) via Waterford; Limerick (3-5 per day, €17); and Tralee (2-4 per day, €13). The Rosslare-Kilrane **tourist office** is 1.5km from the harbor on the Wexford road in Kilrane. (☎33 622. Open daily 10:15am-8pm.) If you need to stay overnight before catching a ferry, try the seaside ☒**Mrs. O'Leary's Farmhouse ❷**, off N25 in Kilrane, a 15min. drive from town. Call for pickup. (☎33 134. Singles €23, with bath €25.50.)

KILKENNY   ☎056

Ireland's best-preserved medieval town, Kilkenny (pop. 25,000), is also a center of great nightlife; nine churches share the streets with 80 pubs. **Tynan Walking Tours** provide the down-and-dirty on Kilkenny's folkloric tradition; hour-long tours depart from the tourist office. (☎65 929. €5, students €4.50.) The 13th-century **Kilkenny Castle** housed the Earls of Ormonde from the 1300s until 1932. The basement shelters the **Butler Gallery**'s modern art exhibitions. (☎21 450. Open June-Sept. daily 9:30am-7pm; Oct.-Mar. 10:30am-12:45pm and 2-5pm; Apr.-May 10:30am-5pm. Mandatory guided tour €4.40, students €1.90.) Climb the narrow 30m tower of **St. Canice's Cathedral**, up the hill off Dean St., for a panoramic view of town and its surroundings. (☎64 971. Open Easter-Sept. M-Sa 9am–6pm; Su 2-6pm; Oct.-Easter M-Sa 10am–4pm, Su 2-4pm. Donation requested.) Start your pub crawl at either the top of **John Street** or the end of **Parliament Street;** outstanding *trad* can be found at **Anna Conda**, on Parliament St.

Trains (☎22 024) arrive at Dublin Rd. from Dublin (2hr., €15.90) and Waterford (45min., €7). **Buses** (☎64 933) arrive at Dublin Rd. and the city center from: Cork (3hr., 2-3 per day, €15.20); Dublin (2hr., 5-6 per day, €9); Galway (5hr., 3-5 per day, €19); Limerick (2½hr., 1-5 per day, €13.30); Rosslare Harbour (2hr., 3-6 per day, €13.40); and Waterford (1½hr., 1-2 per day, €6.40). The **tourist office** is on Rose Inn St. (☎51 500. Open July-Aug. M-Sa 9am-7pm, Su 11am-5pm; Apr.-June and Sept. M-Sa 9am-6pm, Su 11am-5pm; Oct.-Mar. M-Sa 9am-5pm.) **B&Bs** are concentrated on **Waterford Road** and the more remote **Castlecomer Road.** Stay in former royal quarters at the 15th-century ☒**Foulksrath Castle (An Óige/HI) ❶**, in Jenkinstown, 12.5km north of town on the N77. Buggy's Buses run to the hostel from the Parade (20min., M-Sa 2 per day, €2) in Kilkenny. (☎67 674. Sheets €2. Dorms €12-14.) **Pordylo's ❹**, on Butterslip Ln. between Kieran St. and High St., has excellent world cuisine, including many vegetarian options. (Entrees €10-23. Open daily 6-11pm.) A **Dunnes** supermarket is on Kieran St. (☎61 655. Open M-Tu and Sa 8:30am-7pm, W-F 8:30am-10pm, Su 10am-6pm.)

WATERFORD   ☎051

The highlight of Waterford, Ireland's oldest city, is the ☒**Waterford Crystal Factory,** 3km away on the N25 (the Cork road). One-hour tours allow you to witness the transformation of molten glass into polished crystal. Catch the City Imp minibus outside Dunnes on Michael St. and request a stop at the factory (10-15min., every 15-20min., €1) or take city bus #1 (2 per hr., €1.10), which leaves across from the Clock Tower. (☎373 311. Gallery open Mar.-Dec. daily 8:30am-6pm; Jan. M-F 9am-5pm; Feb. daily 9am-5pm. Tours Mar.-Oct. daily 8:30am-4pm; Nov.-Dec. M-F 9am-3:15pm; Jan.-Feb. M-F 9am-5pm. Tours €6, students €3.50.) **Reginald's Tower**, at the end of The Quay, has guarded the city's entrance since the 12th century. (☎873 501. Open June-Sept. daily 9:30am-6:30pm; Oct.-May 10am-5pm. €1.90, students €0.70.) The Quays are crowded with pubs; try **T&H Doolan's,** on George's St., which has been serving crowds for 300 years.

Trains (☎876 243) leave across the bridge from The Quay for: Dublin (2½hr., 5-6 per day, €17-22); Kilkenny (40min., 3-5 per day, €7); Limerick (2½hr., M-Sa 2 per day, €13.40); and Rosslare Harbour (1hr., M-Sa 2 per day, €8.25). **Buses** depart from The Quay for: Cork (2½hr., 10-13 per day, €13.30); Dublin (2¾hr.,

6-12 per day, €9); Galway (4¾hr., 5-6 per day, €17.10); Kilkenny (1hr., 1 per day, €7); Limerick (2½hr., 6-7 per day, €13.30); and Rosslare Harbour (1¼hr., 3-5 per day, €11.60). The **tourist office** is on The Quay, across from the bus station. (☎875 823. Open July-Aug. M-Sa 9am-6pm; Su 11am-5pm; Sept.-Oct. and Apr.-June M-Sa 9am-6pm; Nov.-Mar. M-Sa 9am-5pm.) There are no hostels in town. **The Anchorage ❸,** 9 The Quay, is a conveniently located B&B. (☎854 302. Singles €35-40; doubles €65-75.) **▨Haricot's Wholefood Restaurant ❷,** 11 O'Connell St., serves healthy and innovative home-cooked meals. (Entrees €8-10. Open M-F 9am-8pm, Sa 9am-6pm.)

CASHEL ☎062

Cashel sits at the foot of the 90m ▨**Rock of Cashel** (a.k.a. **St. Patrick's Rock**), a huge limestone outcropping topped by medieval buildings. (Open mid-June to mid-Sept. daily 9am-7:30pm; mid-Sept. to mid-Mar. 9:30am-4:30pm; mid-Mar. to mid-June 9:30am-5:30pm. €4.40, students €1.90.) Down the cow path from the Rock lie the ruins of **Hore Abbey,** built by Cistercian monks and presently inhabited by sheep. The **GPA-Bolton Library,** on John St., houses ecclesiastical texts and rare manuscripts, including a 1550 edition of Machiavelli's *Il Principe* and the world's smallest book. The internationally acclaimed **Brú Ború Heritage Centre,** at the base of the Rock, stages traditional music and dance performances; participation is encouraged. (☎61 122. Performances mid-June to mid-Sept. Tu-Sa 9pm. €13, with dinner €35.) **Bus Éireann** (☎62 121) leaves from the Bake House on Main St. for: Cork (1½hr., 6 per day, €12); Dublin (3hr., 6 per day, €15.40); and Limerick (1hr., 5 per day, €12). The **tourist office** is in the City Hall on Main St. (☎61 333. Open M-Sa 9:15am-6pm.) Just out of town on Dundrum Rd. is the outstanding ▨**O'Brien's Farmhouse Hostel ❶.** (☎61 003. Laundry €8-10. Dorms €13-15; doubles €40-45. **Camping** €6, plus €15 for a car with two people.)

SOUTHWEST IRELAND

With a dramatic landscape that ranges from lakes and mountains to stark, ocean-battered cliffs, Southwest Ireland is a land rich in storytellers and history-makers. Outlaws and rebels once lurked in the hidden coves and glens now overrun by visitors. If the tourist mayhem is too much for you, you can always retreat to the placid stretches along the Ring of Kerry and Cork's southern coast.

◧ FERRIES TO FRANCE AND BRITAIN

Swansea-Cork Ferries (☎021 427 1166) go between Cork and Swansea, South Wales (10hr., 1 per day, €30-43). **Brittany Ferries** (☎021 427 7801) sail from Cork to Roscoff, France (14hr., €50-100).

CORK CITY ☎021

Cork (pop. 150,000), the country's second-largest city, serves as the center of the sports, music, and arts scenes in Ireland's southwest. Cork is a great place to eat and sleep for those who want to explore the surrounding countryside.

◧◪ TRANSPORTATION AND PRACTICAL INFORMATION

Cork is compact and pedestrian-friendly. **St. Patrick Street** becomes **Grand Parade** to the west; to the north it crosses **Merchant's Quay,** home of the bus station. North across **St. Patrick's Bridge, McCurtain Street** runs east to **Lower Glanmire Road** and the train station, before becoming the N8 to Dublin, Waterford, and Cobh. Downtown action concentrates on the vaguely parallel **Paul Street, Oliver Plunkett Street,** and St. Patrick Street. Their connecting north-south avenues are shop-lined and largely pedestrian.

Trains: Kent Station (☎450 6766), on Lower Glanmire Rd., across the river from the city center. Open M-Sa 6:35am-8:30pm, Su 7:50am-8pm. Connections to: **Dublin** (3hr., 5-7 per day, €45); **Killarney** (2hr., 4-7 per day, €18); **Limerick** (1½hr., 4-7 per day, €18); **Tralee** (2½hr., 3 per day, €23).

Buses: (☎450 8188), Parnell Pl., 2 blocks east of Patrick's Bridge on Merchants' Quay. Info desk open daily 9am-6pm. To: **Dublin** (4½hr., 5-6 per day, €19); **Galway** (4hr., 4-7 per day, €16); **Killarney** (2hr., 10-13 per day, €12); **Limerick** (2hr., 14 per day, €12.10); **Rosslare Harbour** (4hr., 3 per day, €17.10); **Sligo** (7hr., 5 per day, €21.40); **Tralee** (2½hr., 12 per day, €13); **Waterford** (2¼hr., 13 per day, €13.30).

Public Transportation: City buses criss cross the city and its suburbs every 10-30min. (M-Sa 7:30am-11:15pm, Su 10am-11:15pm; from €0.95). From downtown, catch buses along St. Patrick St., across from the Father Matthew statue.

Tourist Office: (☎427 3251), on Grand Parade, near the corner of South Mall, along the Lee's south channel. Open June-Aug. M-F 9am-6pm, Sa 9am-5:30pm; Sept.-May M-Sa 9:15am-5:30pm.

Banks: TSB, 40 Patrick St. (☎427 5221). Open M-W and F 9:30am-5pm, Th 9:30am-7pm. **Bank of Ireland,** 70 Patrick St. (☎427 7177). Open M 10am-5pm, Tu-F 10am-4pm. Patrick St. has plenty of **24hr. ATMs.**

Emergency: ☎999; no coins required. **Police** *(Garda)*: (☎522 000), on Anglesea St.

Pharmacies: Regional Late Night Pharmacy (☎434 4575), on Wilton Rd., opposite the Regional Hospital on bus #8. Open M-F 9am-10pm, Sa-Su 10am-10pm. **Phelan's Late Night,** 9 Patrick St. (☎427 2511). Open M-Sa 9am-10pm, Su 10am-10pm.

Hospital: Mercy Hospital (☎427 1971), on Grenville Pl. €25.40 fee for emergency room access. **Cork Regional Hospital** (☎454 6400), on Wilton St., on the #8 bus.

Internet Access: ▧**Web Workhouse** (☎434 3090), on Winthrop St., near the post office. €2.50-5 per hr. Open M-Th and Su 8am-3am, F and Sa 24hr.

Post Office: (☎427 2000), on Oliver Plunkett St., at the corner of Pembroke St. Open M-Sa 9am-5:30pm.

▛ ACCOMMODATIONS

B&Bs are clustered along **Patrick's Hill,** rising upward from St. Patrick's Bridge above Glanmire Rd., and on **Western Road** near University College.

▧ **Sheila's Budget Accommodation Centre (IHH),** 4 Belgrave Pl. (☎450 5562), at the intersection of Wellington St. and York St. Helpful, energetic staff. Internet €1 per 15min. Breakfast €3.20. 24hr. reception desk is also a general store. Check-out 10:30am. Key deposit €2. Dorms €13-16; singles €30; doubles €20-25. ❶

Kinlay House (IHH; ☎450 8966), on Bob and Joan Walk. Down the alley to the right of Shandon Church. Internet €1 per 15min. Breakfast included. Laundry €7. Dorms €14-16; singles €25-30; family rooms €70-80. ISIC discount 10%. ❷

Cork International Hostel (An Óige/HI), 1-2 Redclyffe, Western Rd. (☎454 3289), a 15min. walk from the Grand Parade. Bus #8 stops across the street. Immaculate and spacious bunk rooms in a stately brick Victorian townhouse. All rooms with bath. Breakfast €3.50. Check-in 8am-midnight. Open June-Sept. Dorms €14-17; doubles €41. ❷

Clare D'Arcy B&B, 7 Sidney Place, Wellington Rd. (☎450 4658). From St. Patrick's Bridge, start up St. Patrick's Hill, turning right onto Wellington Rd. A luxurious guesthouse with an elegant Parisian interior. Doubles €80, with bath €90. ❺

FOOD

Delicious restaurants and cafes abound on the lanes connecting St. Patrick St., Paul St., and Oliver Plunkett St. **Tesco** (☎427 0791), on Paul St., is the biggest grocery store in town. (Open M-W and Sa 8:30am-8pm, Th-F 8:30am-10pm.)

■ **Quay Co-op,** 24 Sullivan's Quay (☎431 7660). Delicious vegetarian and vegan meals. Soup €2.80. Entrees around €6.50. Open M-Sa 9am-9pm. ❷

The Farmgate Cafe (☎427 8134), above the English Market. Balcony seating overlooks the market. Baguette sandwiches, excellent soups, and the best desserts in Cork, all under €4. Open daily for breakfast 8:30-10:30am, lunch noon-4pm. ❶

SIGHTS AND NIGHTLIFE

Cork's sights are loosely divided into several districts, but all can be reached by foot. Pick up the *Cork Area City Guide* at the tourist office (€1.90). **St. Anne's Church** (a.k.a. **Shandon's Church**), across the river to the north, has earned the nickname "the four-faced liar," because the tower's four clocks are notoriously out of sync with one another. Walk up Shandon St. and take a right down the unmarked Church St. (Open June-Sept. M-Sa 9:30am-5:30pm. €4, students and seniors €3.50.) The **Crawford Art Gallery,** off Paul St., specializes in paintings by Irish masters, along with contemporary work. (Open M-Sa 10am-5pm. Free.) The **Cork City Gaol** offers multimedia tours of the former prison; cross the bridge at the western end of Fitzgerald Park, turn right on Sunday's Well Rd., and follow the signs. (Open Mar.-Oct. daily 9:30am-6pm; Nov.-Feb. 10am-5pm. €5, students €4; includes audio tour.) The grounds of the nearby **University College Cork,** on the riverbank along Western Rd., are good for strolling.

The lively streets of Cork make finding entertainment easy; try **Oliver Plunkett Street, Union Quay,** and **South Main Street** for pubs and live music. To keep on top of the scene, check out *List Cork*, free at local shops. Unless otherwise noted, establishments listed close M-Th 11:30pm, F-Sa 12:30am, and Su 11pm. ■**The Lobby,** 1 Union Quay, gave some of Ireland's most famous folk acts their big breaks; it features nightly live music with a view of the river. (Occasional cover €2.50-6.50.) At **An Spailpín Fanac,** 28 South Main St., live *trad* complements the decor. **The Old Oak,** on Oliver Plunkett St., wins one of the "Best Traditional Pub in Ireland" awards year after year. (Open F-Sa until 1:45am.) At classy **Bodega,** 46-49 Cornmarket St., off the northern end of Grand Parade in a striking converted warehouse, patrons relax with glasses of wine on velvet couches. ■**Half Moon,** on Academy Ln. to the left of the Opera House, is the most popular dance club in Cork City. (18+. Cover €9. Open daily until 2am. Purchase tickets from the box office across the street.)

DAYTRIP FROM CORK CITY: BLARNEY. Tourists eager for quintessential Irish scenery and a cold kiss head northwest of Cork to see **Blarney Castle** and its legendary **Blarney Stone,** which confers the gift of gab upon those who smooch it while leaning over backwards. The top of the castle provides an airy and stunning view of the countryside. Try to come early in the morning to avoid crowds. (☎438 5252. Open June-Aug. M-Sa 9am-7pm, Su 9:30am-5:30pm; Sept. M-Sa 9am-6:30pm, Su 9:30am-dusk; Oct.-Apr. M-Sa 9am-6pm or dusk, Su 9:30am-5pm or dusk; May M-Sa 9am-6:30pm, Su 9:30am-5:30pm. €4.50, students and seniors €3, children €1.50.) **Buses** run from Cork to Blarney (10-16 per day, round-trip €4.10).

SCHULL AND THE MIZEN HEAD PENINSULA ☎ 028

The seaside hamlet of **Schull** is an ideal base for exploring the craggy and beach-laden southwest tip of Ireland. A calm harbor and numerous shipwrecks make it a diving paradise; the **Watersports Centre** rents gear. (☎ 28 554. Open M-Sa 9:30am-6pm.) The coastal road winds past the **Barley Coast Beach** and continues on to **Mizen Head**. The Mizen becomes more scenic and less populated the farther west you go from Schull; **Betty Johnson's Bus Hire** offers tours of the area. (☎ 28 410. Call ahead. €12.) In summer, **ferries** (☎ 28 138) depart from Schull for Cape Clear Island (Jun.-Sept. 2-3 per day, round-trip €12). **Buses** arrive in Schull from Cork (1-3 per day, €12) and Goleen (1-3 per day, €3.10). There is no other public transportation on the peninsula. Confident **cyclists** can daytrip to Mizen Head (29km from Schull). The immaculate **Schull Backpackers' Lodge (IHH) ❶**, on Colla Rd., has **hiking** and **biking** maps and info. (☎ 28 681. Bike rental €11 per day, €50 per week. Dorms €10.50-11.50; doubles €32-33.) **The Courtyard ❶**, on Main St., has delicious options for breakfast and lunch; the fruit scones (€0.55) and the sandwiches on fresh ciabatta (€7-9.50) are both worth a try. (Open M-Sa 9:30am-6pm.)

CAPE CLEAR ISLAND ☎ 028

Although the scenery visible from the ferry landing at Cape Clear Island *(Oileán Chléire)* is desolate and foreboding, the main industry of this beautiful island is farming. Cape Clear provides asylum for gulls, petrels, cormorants, and their attendant flocks of ornithologists; the **Cape Clear Bird Observatory** (☎ 39 181), on North Harbour, has bird-watching and ecology courses. At **Cléire Goats** (☎ 39 126), on the steep hill between the harbor and the heritage center, sample rich goat's milk ice cream (€1.50). **Ferries** (☎ 28 138) go to Schull (45min., 1-3 per day, round-trip €11.50). There is an **information office** is in the pottery shop to the left of the pier. (☎ 39 100. Open July-Aug. 11am-1pm and 3-6pm; June and Sept. 3-6pm.) **Cléire Lasmuigh (An Óige/HI) ❶** is a 10min. walk from the pier; follow the main road and keep left. (☎ 39 198. June-Sept. dorms €11; Oct.-May €9.) To reach **Cuas an Uisce Campsite ❶**, on the south pier, walk 5min. uphill from the harbor and bear right before Ciarán Danny Mike's; it's 400m down on the left. (☎ 39 136. Open June-Sept. €5 per person, under 16 €2.50.) Groceries are available at **An Siopa Beag**, on the pier. (Open July-Aug. daily 11am-9pm; June 11am-6pm; Sept.-May 11am-4:30pm.)

KILLARNEY AND KILLARNEY NATIONAL PARK ☎ 064

The town of Killarney is just minutes from some of Ireland's most glorious natural scenery. The 95 square-kilometer national park outside town blends forested mountains with the famous **Lakes of Killarney**. Five kilometers south of Killarney on Kenmare Rd. is **Muckross House**, a massive 19th-century manor with a garden that blooms brilliantly each year. A path leads to the 20m high **Torc Waterfall**. (Open July-Aug. daily 9am-7pm; Sept.-Oct. and mid-Mar. to June 9am-6pm. €5.10, students €2.) Walk or drive to the 14th-century **Ross Castle** by taking a right on Ross Rd. off Muckross Rd., 3km from Killarney; the footpaths from Knockreer (out of town on New St.) are more scenic. (Open June-Aug. daily 9am-6:30pm; May and Sept. 10am-6pm; Oct. and mid-Mar. to Apr. 10am-5pm. €3.80, students €1.60.) Bike around the **Gap of Dunloe**, which borders **Macgillycuddy's Reeks**, Ireland's highest mountain range. Hop on a boat from Ross Castle to the head of the Gap (1½hr., €12; book at the tourist office). From **Lord Brandon's Cottage**, on the Gap, head left over the stone bridge, continue 3km to the church, and turn right onto a winding road. Huff the 2km to the top, and your reward is an 11km coast downhill through the park's most breathtaking scenery. The 13km ride back to Killarney (bear right after Kate Kearney's Cottage, turn left on the road to Fossa, and turn right on Killorglin Rd.) passes the ruins of **Dunloe Castle,** demolished by Cromwell's armies.

Trains (☎31 067) arrive at Killarney station, off East Avenue Rd., from: Cork (2hr., 4 per day, €17.80); Dublin (3½hr., 4 per day, €45); and Limerick (3hr., 4 per day, €19.70). **Buses** (☎30 011) leave from Park Rd. for Cork (2hr., 10-14 per day, €12) and Dublin (6hr., 5-6 per day, €19). **O'Sullivan's,** on Bishop's Ln., rents **bikes.** (☎31 282. Free locks and maps. Open daily 8:30am-6:30pm. €12 per day, €70 per week.) The **tourist office** is on Beech St., off New St. (☎31 633. Open July-Aug. M-Sa 9am-8pm, Su 10am-6pm; June and Sept. M-Sa 9am-6pm, Su 10am-6pm; Oct.-May M-Sa 9:15am-5:30pm.) The immense and immaculate **Neptune's (IHH) ❶,** on Bishop's Ln., is up the first walkway off New St. on the right. (☎35 255. Dorms €11-12; doubles €34.) **Orchard House B&B ❸,** on Fleming's Ln., is near the town center and an unbeatable bargain. (☎31 879. Singles €25-30; doubles €45-60.) A **Tesco** grocery store is in the arcade off New St. (Open M-W 8:30am-8pm, Th-F 8:30am-9pm, Sa 8:30am-7pm.) ▨**The Grand,** on High St., brings together locals and tourists for fantastic live music. (No cover before 11pm. Open daily 7pm-3am.)

RING OF KERRY   ☎066

The Southwest's most celebrated peninsula holds picturesque villages, fabled ancient forts, and rugged mountains. Although tour buses often hog the roads, rewards await those who take the time to explore the landscape on foot or by bike.

▣ **TRANSPORTATION.** The term "Ring of Kerry" usually describes the entire **Iveragh Peninsula,** though it technically refers to the ring of roads circumnavigating it. Hop on the circuit run by **Bus Éireann,** based in Killarney and stopping at the major towns on the Ring (mid-June to Aug. 2 per day), including Cahersiveen (from Killarney 2½hr., €11.50) and Caherdaniel (from Cahersiveen 1hr., €4.25).

CAHERSIVEEN. Although best known as the birthplace of patriot Daniel O'Connell, Cahersiveen (CAR-sah-veen) serves as an excellent base for jaunts to Valentia Island, the Skelligs, and local archeological sites. The ruins of **Ballycarbery Castle,** once held by O'Connell's ancestors, are past the barracks on Bridge St. and the bridge, off the main road to the left. About 200m past the castle turn-off stands a pair of Ireland's best-preserved stone forts, **Cahergall Fort** and **Leacanabuaile Fort.** The **tourist office** is directly across from the bus stop, next to the post office. (☎947 2589. Open June to mid-Sept. M-F 9:30am-1pm and 2-5:30pm.) The welcoming **Sive Hostel (IHH) ❶** is at 15 East End, Main St. (☎947 2717. Dorms €10.50; doubles €25-32; **camping** €5 per person.) **O'Shea's B&B ❸,** next to the post office on Main St., boasts comfortable rooms, some with impressive views. (☎947 2402. Singles €25-30; doubles €50.) **Main Street** has several pubs that harken back to the early 20th century, when establishments served as both watering holes and the proprietor's main business, be it general store, blacksmith, or leather shop.

The quiet ▨**Valentia Island** is a fantastic daytrip. The little roads of this unspoiled gem are perfect for biking or light hiking. Bridges on either end of the island connect it to the mainland; alternatively, a **ferry** runs during the summer (3min., May-Oct. 8:15am-10pm; €2, with bike €3) from **Reenard Point,** 5km west of Cahersiveen. A taxi to the ferry dock from Cahersiveen is about €7. Another recommended daytrip is to the **Skellig Rocks,** about 13km off the shore of the Iveragh Peninsula. From the boat, **Little Skellig** may appear snow-capped; it's actually covered with 24,000 pairs of crooning birds. Climb 630 steps to reach a **monastery** built by 6th-century Christian monks, whose beehive-like dwellings are still intact. The hostel and campground in Cahersiveen can arrange the **ferry** ride (about 1hr.) for €32-35, including a ride to the dock.

IRELAND

CAHERDANIEL. There's little in the village of **Caherdaniel** to attract the Ring's droves of buses. But nearby **Derrynane National Park,** 2.5km along the shore from the village, holds 3km of gorgeous beach ringed by picture-perfect dunes. Follow the signs for **Derrynane House,** once the residence of Daniel O'Connell. (Open May-Sept. M-Sa 9am-6pm, Su 11am-7pm; Apr. and Oct. Tu-Su 1-5pm; Nov.-Mar. Sa-Su 1-5pm. €3, students €1.50.) Guests are made to feel at home at **The Travellers' Rest Hostel ❶.** (☎947 5175. Breakfast €4. Dorms €12; singles €15.)

DINGLE PENINSULA ☎066

For decades, the Ring of Kerry's undertouristed counterpart has remained more congested with ancient sites than tour buses; the Ring's tourist blitz has only just begun to encroach upon the spectacular cliffs and sweeping beaches of the Irish-speaking Dingle peninsula. Many visitors explore the area by bike, an especially attractive option given the scarcity of public transportation.

▐ TRANSPORTATION. Dingle Town is most easily reached by **Bus Éireann** from Tralee (1¼hr., 4-6 per day, €7.90); other routes run from Dingle to Ballydavid (Tu and F 3 per day, €4 round-trip), Ballyferriter (M and Th 3 per day; €3.20), and Dunquin (1-5 per day, €3.15). In summer, additional buses tour the south of the peninsula beginning in Dingle (June-Sept. M-Sa 2 per day).

DINGLE TOWN. Lively Dingle Town, adopted home of **Fungi the Dolphin** (now a major focus of the tourist industry), is a good base for exploring the peninsula. **Sciúird Archaeology Tours** leave from the pier for 3hr. whirlwind bus tours of the area's ancient spots. (☎915 1606. 2 per day, €15; book ahead.) **Moran's Tours** runs great trips to Slea Head, passing through majestic scenery and stopping at historical sites. (☎915 1155. 2 per day, €10.20; book ahead.) The **tourist office** is on Strand St. (☎915 1188. Open July-Aug. M-Sa 9am-7pm, Su 10am-5pm; Sept.-Oct. and mid-Mar. to June M-Sa 9:30am-6pm, Su 9:30am-5pm.) The laid-back **Grapevine Hostel ❶** is on Dykegate St., off Main St. (☎915 1434. Dorms €10.80-13.35.) **Ballintaggart Hostel (IHH) ❶,** 25min. east on Tralee Rd., is supposedly haunted by the murdered wife of the Earl of Cork. (☎915 1454. Free shuttle to town. Dorms €12.50-15; doubles €43; off-season €1.30-2.50 less. **Camping** €11.)

SLEA HEAD AND DUNQUIN. By far the most rewarding way to see Slea Head and Dunquin's cliffs and crashing waves is to **bike** along the predominantly flat **Slea Head Drive.** Past Dingle Town toward Slea Head sits the village of **Ventry** (Ceann Trá), home to a sandy beach and the marvelous **Ballybeag Hostel ❷;** a regular shuttle runs from Dingle Town. (☎915 9876. Bike rental €7. Laundry €2. €20 per person.) The **▤Celtic and Prehistoric Museum,** 3km farther down the road, is a must-see—the collection ranges from sea worm fossils to Millie, a 50,000-year old woolly mammoth. (☎915 9931. Open from Mar. to mid-Nov. daily 10am-5pm; call ahead from mid-Nov. to Feb. €5, students €3.50.) North of Slea Head, the scattered settlement of Dunquin (Dún Chaoin) boasts **Kruger's ❸,** purportedly the westernmost pub in Europe. Come for the music sessions and superlative views. (☎915 6194. Entrees €7-13.) Past Dunquin on the road to Ballyferriter, the **▤Great Blasket Centre** has outstanding exhibits about the isolated Blasket Islands. (☎915 6444. Open July-Aug. daily 10am-7pm; Easter-June and Sept.-Nov. 10am-6pm. €3.10, students €1.20.) At **An Óige Hostel (HI) ❶,** on the Dingle Way across from the turnoff to the Blasket Centre, each bunk has its own ocean view. (☎915 6121. Reception 9-10am and 5-10pm. Lockout 10am-5pm. Dorms €9-12; doubles €26.)

TRALEE. Tralee (pop. 20,000), a good departure point for the Ring of Kerry or the Dingle Peninsula, has a hustle and bustle appropriate for the economic and residential capital of County Kerry. ▉**Kerry the Kingdom,** in Ashe Memorial Hall on Denny St., features a high-tech history of Ireland from 8000 BC to the present. (☎712 7777. Open mid-Mar. to Oct. daily 10am-6pm; Nov. noon-4:30pm. €8, students €6.50.) During the last week of August, the nationally-known **Rose of Tralee Festival** brings a horde of lovely Irish lasses to town to compete for the title "Rose of Tralee." **Trains** go from the station on Oakpark Rd. to: Cork (2½hr., 3-4 per day, €23); Galway (5-6hr., 3 per day, €45.10); and Killarney (40min., 4 per day, €7.50). **Buses** leave from the train station for: Cork (2½hr., 10-14 per day, €12.70); Galway (5-6hr., 9-11 per day, €17.10); Killarney (40min., 5-14 per day, €5.85); and Limerick (2¼hr., 7-8 per day, €12.20). To get from the station to the **tourist office** in Ashe Memorial Hall, head down Edward St., turn right on Castle St., and then left on Denny St. (☎712 1288. Open July-Aug. M-Sa 9am-7pm; Su 9am-6pm; May-June and Oct. M-Sa 9am-6pm; Nov.-Apr. M-F 9am-5pm.) **Courthouse Lodge (IHH) ❶,** 5 Church St., has a great location. (☎712 7199. Internet €1 per 10min. Dorms €14; doubles €32.) After a comfortable night's sleep at **Castle House ❹,** 27 Upper Castle St., don't miss the great pancakes. (☎712 5167. Singles €40; doubles €65.)

WESTERN IRELAND

Even Dubliners will tell you that the west is the "most Irish" part of Ireland. The potato famine that plagued the island was most devastating in the west—entire villages emigrated or died. The region still has less than half of its 1841 population. Though miserable for farming, the land from Connemara north to Ballina is great for hikers and cyclists who enjoy the isolation of mountainous landscapes.

LIMERICK   ☎061

What little attention Limerick received in the 20th century focused on its squalor—a tradition exemplified by Frank McCourt's celebrated memoir, *Angela's Ashes.* Despite the stigma, Limerick is a city on the rise and a fine place to stay en route to points west. The ▉**Hunt Museum,** in Custom House on Rutland St., has been recognized for its outstanding, diverse collection; visitors browse through drawers to find surprises like the world's smallest jade monkey. (Open M-Sa 10am-5pm, Su 2-5pm. €7, students and seniors €4.) Limerick's student population adds spice to the pub scene. **Dolan's ❷,** on Dock Rd., hosts nightly *trad* and rambunctious local patrons. **Trains** (☎315 555) leave Parnell St. for: Cork (2½hr., 5-6 per day, €18); Dublin (2hr., 9-10 per day, €33.10); Ennis (2 per day, €7); Killarney (2½hr., 3-4 per day, €20); and Waterford (2hr., 1-2 per day, €23). **Buses** (☎313 333) leave the train station for: Cork (2hr., 14 per day, €12.10); Derry (6½hr., 3 per day, €23); Donegal (6hr., 4 per day, €20.20); Dublin (3½hr., 13 per day, €13.30); Ennis (45min., 14 per day, €6.70); Galway (2hr., 14 per day, €12.10); Killarney (2½hr., 3-6 per day, €12.40); Rosslare Harbour (4hr., 3-4 per day, €15-16); Tralee (2hr., 7 per day, €12.10); and Waterford (2½hr., 6-7 per day, €13.30). The **tourist office** is on Arthurs Quay. From the station, walk down Davis St., turn right on O'Connell St., then left at Arthurs Quay Mall. (☎317 522. Open July-Aug. M-F 9am-6:30pm, Sa-Su 9am-6pm; May-June and Sept.-Oct. M-Sa 9:30am-5:30pm; Nov.-Apr. M-F 9:30am-5:30pm, Sa 9:30am-1pm.) **Summerville Holiday Hostel ❷,** past Dolan's on Dock Rd., is a brick complex of university dormitory singles. Take the Raheen bus (€0.95) from Williams St. (☎302 500. Continental breakfast included. Laundry €2. Check-out 10:30am. Open June-Aug. Dorms €16; singles €22; doubles €38; triples €50.) Close to the city center, **Alexandra House B&B ❸,** on O'Connell St. south of the Daniel O'Connell statue, is one of the better B&B values in Limerick. (☎318 472. Singles €26; doubles €48-64.) Dolan's (see above) is Limerick's best choice for evening meals. (Entrees €5-9.)

ENNIS AND DOOLIN ☎ 065

Ennis's proximity to Shannon Airport and The Burren make it a common stopover for tourists, who come for a day of shopping followed by a night of pub crawling. Sixty pubs line the streets of Ennis. At ▨**Cruises Pub,** on Abbey St., local musicians appear nightly for cozy *trad* sessions. **Glor** is a newly opened, state-of-the-art music center that features nightly performances of both *trad* and more contemporary music, along with film, theater, and dance. (☎684 3103. Box office open M-Sa 9:30am-5:30pm. Tickets €12-22.) **Trains** leave from Station Rd. for Dublin (1-2 per day, €26.60). **Buses** also leave from Station Rd. for: Cork (3hr., every hr., €13.90); Doolin (1hr., 2 per day, €4.70); Dublin (4hr., every hr., €13.30); Galway (1hr., 5 per day, €9.80); Limerick (40min., every hr., €6.70); and Shannon Airport (40min., every hr., €6.10). The **tourist office** is on Arthur's Row, off O'Connell Sq. (☎28 366. Open July-Sept. daily 9am-6pm; Apr.-June and Oct. M-Sa 9:30am-6pm; Nov.-Mar. M-F 9:30am-6pm.) The recently renovated **Abbey Tourist Hostel ❶** is on Harmony Row. (☎682 2620. Breakfast included. Internet €0.10 per 10min. Curfew Su-W 1:30am, Th 2:30am, F-Sa 3am. Dorms €13-15; singles €25; doubles €38.)

Something of a shrine to Irish music, the little village of **Doolin** draws thousands every year to its three pubs. The pubs are commonly known by the mnemonic **MOM:** ▨**McDermott's** (in the Upper Village), **O'Connor's** (in the Lower), and **McGann's** (Upper). All have *trad* sessions nightly at 9:30pm. The ▨**Cliffs of Moher,** 10km south of town, feature a 200m vertical drop into the sea. Take the bus from Doolin (#50; 15min., 1-3 per day). **Buses** leave from Doolin Hostel for Dublin via Ennis and Limerick (#15; 2 per day) and Galway (#50; 1½hr., 1-5 per day). Almost every house on the main road is a **B&B. Aille River Hostel (IHH) ❶,** between the Upper and Lower Villages, has a friendly atmosphere and a gorgeous location. (☎707 4260. Internet €6 per hr. Dorms €12; doubles €27. **Camping** €6.)

THE BURREN ☎ 065

Limestone, butterflies, ruined castles, and labyrinthine caves make The Burren, which covers 260 sq. km, a unique geological fairyland. ▨**Burren Exposure,** between Kinvara and Ballyvaughn on N67, gives a soaring introduction to the region through films shown on a wall-to-wall screen. (☎707 7277. €5, children €2.50.) The Burren town of **Lisdoonvarna** is synonymous with its **Matchmaking Festival,** a month-long *craic*-and-snogging celebration that attracts over 10,000 singles each September. The **Hydro Hotel ❹** has information on the festival and its own nightly music. (☎707 4005. Wheelchair-accessible.

THE LOCAL STORY

HELLO, DALY

Let's Go *interviews Willie Daly, the Lisdoonvarna "matchmaker."*

LG: So people fill out a form about themselves and then they receive phone numbers?

WD: Aye, they do. They give us the form and we give them the names of people we think would be suitable.

LG: Have any marriages resulted?

WD: Well, I get invited to some, but I don't attend in case it embarrasses them, since people know what I do.

(Mr. Daly takes a phone call.)

WD: ...I'll send you a form and you can put in a little bit about yourself. Write down the sorts of things that you desire... When did you get the last one, John? Was there not anything in it that was suitable for you, then? Hmmm. Have you got a pen with you, and I'll give you the name of a nice girl I have now.

(The phone cuts off.)

LG: So, what is the most important advice you have?

WD: A woman needs to be treated with respect. She needs be made to feel important and wanted. You can't take her for granted. That's the key.

(The phone rings again.)

WD: Sorry, okay John. So here's another number for you... You've got a good attitude, you'll be fine. You have the number now, so you have no excuse. Okay John, good luck. You're welcome. It's not a problem, I do this all the time. It's me job.

Open Mar.-Oct. €45 per person.) The Burren is difficult to get around; the surrounding tourist offices (at Kilfenora, Ennis, Corofin, and the Cliffs of Moher) have detailed maps of the region. Hikers can set out on the 40km **Burren Way**, a trail from Liscannor to Ballyvaughan marked by yellow arrows. **Bus Éireann** (☎ 682 4177) connects Galway to towns in and near the Burren a few times a day during summer but infrequently during winter. In **Kinvara**, stay at **Fallon's B&B ❹**, next to the market. (☎ (091) 637 483. €40 per person, all with bath.) **Cois Cuain B&B ❸**, also in Kinvara on the Quay, is quaint and good for couples. (☎ (091) 637 119. Open Apr.-Nov. €26.50 per person.)

GALWAY CITY   ☎091

Galway (pop. 70,000) has a mix of over 13,000 university students, a transient population of 20-something Europeans, and waves of international backpackers. Its main attractions are its nightlife and setting—it's a convenient starting point for trips to the Clare Coast or Connemara.

▤▨ TRANSPORTATION AND PRACTICAL INFORMATION. Trains (☎ 561 444) leave from Eyre Sq. for Dublin (3hr., 4-5 per day, €20-30) via Athlone (€10-15). Transfer at Athlone for lines to all other cities. **Bus Éireann** (☎ 562 000) leaves from Eyre Sq. for: Belfast (7hr., 2-3 per day, €27.50); Cork (4¼hr., 13 per day, €15.80); Donegal (4hr., 4 per day, €15.20); and Dublin (4hr., every hr., €12). The main **tourist office,** on Forster St., is a block south of Eyre Sq. (☎ 537 700. Open July-Aug. daily 9:30am-7:45pm; May-June and Sept. 9am-5:45pm; Oct.-Apr. Su-F 9am-5:45pm, Sa 9am-12:45pm.) Check email at **Neatsurf,** 7 St. Francis St. (☎ 533 976. €0.75 per 10min.)

▛▟ ACCOMMODATIONS AND FOOD. ▩Sleepzone ❷, Bóthar na mBán, northwest of Eyre Sq., takes the "s" out of "hostel." (☎ 566 999. Internet €4.50 per hr. Breakfast included. All rooms with bath. July-Aug. M-F dorms €16-20; singles €40; doubles €54. Weekend and off-season rates vary.) The conveniently located B&B **St. Martin's ❸**, 2 Nuns Island Rd., has a gorgeous garden. (☎ 568 286. All rooms with bath. Singles €32; doubles €60.) **Bananaphoblacht ❶**, on Dominick St., is an outstanding cafe. (Pastries €2-5; beverages €2-3. Open M-F 8:30am-2am, Sa 10:30am-2am, Su noon-2am.) **The River God Cafe ❸**, on High St., combines French and Asian flavors in seafood and tofu dishes. (Entrees €10-14. Open daily 5-10pm.) On Saturdays, an ▩**open-air market** sets up in front of St. Nicholas Church on Market St. (Open Sa 8am-1pm.)

◙▧ SIGHTS AND NIGHTLIFE. The **Nora Barnacle House,** 8 Bowling Green, was once the home of James Joyce's life-long companion. Today, a friendly staff happily discusses their favorite author while pointing out his original love letters to Ms. Barnacle. (Open mid-May to mid-Sept. W-F 10am-1pm and 2-5pm; off-season by appointment. €2.50.) The Lynch family ruled Galway from the 13th to the 18th century; their elegant 1320 mansion, **Lynch's Castle,** now houses the Allied Irish Bank. A small display recalls the story of an elder Lynch who hung his own son, thus giving his name to executions performed without legal authority. The castle is in front of the Church of St. Nicholas on Market St. (Exhibit open M-W and F 10am-4pm, Th 10am-5pm. Free.) Drift down the **Corrib** for great views of the city, the countryside, and nearby castles. Frank Dolan rents **rowboats** at 13 Riverside, Woodquay (€4 per hr.). In mid-July, the **Galway Arts Festival** (☎ 583 800) attracts scores of *trad* musicians, rock groups, theater troupes, and filmmakers.

The pubs along **Quay Street** tend to cater to tourists and students, while the pubs on **Dominick Street** (across the river from the Quay) are popular with locals. ◙**The King's Head**, on High St., has three floors and nightly rock. Galway's best live music is hidden at the back of ◙**Roisín Dubh** ("The Black Rose"), on Dominick St. (Occasional cover €5-20.) **The Crane**, 2 Sea Rd., is a great place to hear nightly *trad.*

ARAN ISLANDS (OILEÁIN ÁRANN)　　　　☎099

Twenty-four kilometers off the western edge of Co. Galway, the Aran Islands feel like the edge of the world. Their fields are hatched with a maze of limestone—the result of centuries of farmers piling stones into thousands of meters of walls. The tremendous cliff-top forts of the early islanders give the illusion of having sprung from the limestone itself. Of the dozens of ruins, forts, churches, and holy wells that rise from the stony terrain of **Inishmore** (Inis Mór; pop. 900), the most amazing is the **Dún Aengus** ring fort, where concentric stones circle a sheer 100m drop. The **Inis Mór Way** is a mostly paved route that passes the majority of the island's sights and is great for biking; pick up a map at the tourist office (€2). Windswept **Inishmaan** (Inis Meáin; pop. 300) and **Inisheer** (Inis Oírr; pop. 300), the smallest island, also both feature paths that pass by the islands' incomparable ruins.

　　Island Ferries (☎(091) 561 767) go from **Rossaveal,** west of Galway, to Inishmore (40min., 2-3 per day, round-trip €20) and Inisheer (40min., 2 per day, round-trip €20). **Queen of Aran II** (☎566 535), based in the islands, also leaves from Rossaveal for Inishmore (4 per day, round-trip €19). Both companies run **buses** to Rossaveal, departing from Kinlay House, on Merchant St. in Galway, 1½hr. before ferry departure (€6, students €5). Ferries to Inishmore arrive at **Kilronan**. The **tourist office** there stores luggage (€0.95), changes money, and finds accommodations. (☎61 263. Open July-Sept. daily 10am-6:45pm; Oct. 10am-5pm; Nov.-Mar. 10am-4pm.) ◙**Mainistir House (IHH) ❶**, less than 2km from town on the main road, is a sprawling hostel that was once a haven for musicians and writers. Don't miss the nightly vegetarian buffet (€12), an excellent place to meet other travelers. (☎61 169. Bike rental €10 per day. Laundry €6. Dorms €12; singles €20; doubles €32.) The **Spar Market** in Kilronan functions as an unofficial community center. (Open in summer M-Sa 9am-8pm, Su 10am-6pm; off-season M-Sa 9am-8pm, Su 10am-5pm.)

CONNEMARA

Connemara, a largely Irish-speaking region, is comprised of a lacy net of inlets and islands, a gang of inland mountains, and desolate stretches of bog. This thinly populated region of northwest County Galway harbors some of Ireland's most breathtaking scenery, from rocky offshore islands to the green slopes of the area's two major mountain ranges, the Twelve Bens and the Maamturks.

CLIFDEN (AN CLOCHÁN)　　　　☎095

Busy, English-speaking Clifden has more amenities than its old-world, Irish-speaking neighbors. Clifden's proximity to the scenic bogs and mountains of the region attracts crowds of tourists, who use it as a base for exploring the region. The **Connemara Walking Centre,** on Market St., runs tours of the bogs. (☎21 379. Open Mar.-Oct. M-Sa 10am-6pm. 1-2 tours per day; €20-32.) **Bus Éireann** goes from the library on Market St. to Galway via Oughterard (2hr., 1-6 per day, €9) and Westport via Leenane (1½hr., late June to Aug. 1-3 per day). Michael Nee runs a bus from the courthouse to Galway (June-Sept. 2 per day, €7.60). Rent a **bike** at **Mannion's,** on Bridge St. (☎21 160. €9 per day, €60 per week; deposit €20. Open M-Sa 9:30am-6:30pm, Su 10am-1pm and 5-7pm.) The **tourist office** is on Galway Rd. (☎21 163. Open July-Aug. M-Sa 9am-6pm, Su noon-4pm; Sept.-Oct. and Mar.-May M-Sa 10am-5pm; June M-Sa 10am-6pm.) **B&Bs** are everywhere and start at €25 per person.

Clifden Town Hostel (IHH) ❶, on Market St., has great facilities and spotless rooms. (☎21 076. Call ahead Dec.-Feb. Dorms €10.20; doubles €30.50; triples €38-42; quads €46.) Tranquil **Shanaheever Campsite ❶** is 1.5km outside Clifden on Westport Rd. (☎22 150. Hot showers. Laundry. €10.20 for 2 people and tent.) Most restaurants in Clifden are attached to pubs and serve the standard fare. **O'Connor's SuperValu** supermarket is on Market St. (Open M-F 9am-7pm, Su 10am-6pm.)

CONNEMARA NATIONAL PARK   ☎095

Connemara National Park occupies 12.5 square kilometers of mountainous countryside that thousands of birds call home. Bogs constitute much of the park's terrain, often thinly covered by a deceptive screen of grass and flowers—be prepared to get muddy. The **Snuffaunboy Nature** and **Ellis Wood Trails** are easy 20min. hikes. Trails lead from the back of the Ellis Wood Trail and along the Bog Road onto ▨**Diamond Hill,** a more strenuous 2hr. hike that rewards climbers with views of the bog, the harbor, and the forest. (Diamond Hill was closed in 2002 for erosion control; call the Visitors Centre to confirm opening.) Experienced hikers often head for the **Twelve Bens** (Na Benna Beola, a.k.a. the Twelve Pins), a rugged range that reaches 2200m heights (not recommended for solo or beginning hikers). A tour of all 12 Bens takes experienced hikers about 10hr. **Biking** the 65km circle through Clifden, Letterfrack, and the Inagh Valley is truly captivating, but only appropriate for fit bikers. A guidebook mapping out 30min. walks (€6.35) is available at the **Visitors Centre,** where the staff helps plan longer hikes. They'll also explain the differences between hummocks and tussocks. (☎41 054. Open June daily 10am-6:30pm; July-Aug. 9:30am-6:30pm; May and Sept. 10am-5:30pm. €2.60, students €1.25.) Hikers often base themselves at the **Ben Lettery Hostel (An Óige/HI) ❶**, in Ballinafad, 13km east of Clifden. (☎51 136. Dorms €10.20-11.45.)

Tiny **Letterfrack** is the gateway to the park. The Galway-Clifden **bus** (mid-June to Aug. 11 per week, Sept. to mid-June 4 per week; no buses on Su) and the summertime Clifden-Westport bus (1-2 per day) stop at Letterfrack. The ▨**Old Monastery Hostel ❶** is one of Ireland's finest. (☎41 132. Bike rental €9 per day. Internet €4 per hr. Breakfast included. Dorms €10.20-12.70. **Camping** €6.40.)

WESTPORT   ☎098

Palm trees and steep hills lead down to Westport's busy Georgian streets. Nearby, the conical **Croagh Patrick** rises 650m over Clew Bay. The summit has been revered as a holy site for thousands of years. St. Patrick worked here in AD 441, praying for 40 days and nights to banish snakes from Ireland. Climbers start their excursion from the 15th-century **Murrisk Abbey,** several kilometers west of Westport on R395 toward Louisburgh. Buses go to Murrisk (2-3 per day); for groups, cabs (☎27 171) are cheaper and more convenient. Sheep calmly rule **Clare Island,** a desolate but beautiful speck in the Atlantic. Take a bus to Roonah Pier, 29km from Westport, and then a ferry to the island. (Bus departs Westport's tourist office at 10am and returns by 6pm; €25 for bus and ferry combined.) **Matt Molloy's,** on Bridge St., is owned by a member of the Irish band the Chieftains and has nightly *trad.* (Open M-W 12:30-11:30pm, Th-Sa 12:30pm-12:30am, Su 12:30-11pm.)

Trains arrive at the **Altamont St. Station** (☎25 253), a 5min. walk up the North Mall, from Dublin (2-3 per day, €21-23) via Athlone. **Buses** leave Mill St. for Galway (2hr., 4-8 per day, €11.60). The **tourist office** is on James St. (☎25 711. Open July-Aug. M-Sa 9am-6:45pm, Su 10am-6pm; Apr.-June and Sept.-Oct. M-Sa 9am-5:45pm.) **B&Bs** cluster on **Altamont Road** and **The Quay.** A conservatory and garden grace ▨**The Granary Hostel ❶**, a 25min. walk from town, just at the bend in The Quay. (☎25 903. Open Apr.-Sept. Dorms €10.) Restaurants are concentrated on **Bridge Street.** The **SuperValu** supermarket is on Shop St. (Open M-Sa 8:30am-9pm, Su 10am-6pm.)

NORTHWEST IRELAND

The farmland of the upper Shannon stretches northward into Co. Sligo's mountains, lakes, and ancient monuments. A mere sliver of land connects Co. Sligo to Co. Donegal, the second-largest and most remote of the Republic's counties. Donegal's *gaeltacht* is a storehouse of genuine, unadulterated Irish tradition.

SLIGO   ☎071

Since the beginning of the 20th century, Sligo has seen a literary pilgrimage of William Butler Yeats devotees; the poet spent summers in town as a child and set many of his poems around Sligo Bay. **Sligo Town,** the commercial center, is an excellent base from which to explore Yeats's haunts. The well-preserved 13th-century **Sligo Abbey** is on Abbey St. (Open Apr.-Oct. daily 10am-6pm; Nov.-Mar. call for hours. €1.90, students €0.70.) **The Model Arts Centre and Niland Gallery,** on the Mall, houses one of the finest collections of modern Irish art. (Open Tu-Sa 10am-5:30pm. Free.) Yeats is buried in **Drumcliffe Churchyard,** on the N15, 6.5km northwest of Sligo. Buses from Sligo to Derry stop at Drumcliffe (10min., 3-7 per day, round-trip €4). Over 70 pubs crowd the main streets of Sligo. The trendy **Shoot the Crows,** on Grattan St., has fairies and skulls dangling from the ceiling.

   Trains (☎69 888) go from Lord Edward St. to Dublin via Carrick-on-Shannon and Mullingar (3 hr., 4 per day, €19). From the same station, **buses** (☎60 066) head to: Belfast (4hr., 2-3 per day, €22); Derry (3hr., 4-7 per day, €13.30); Dublin (3-4hr., 4-5 per day, €12.40); Galway (2½hr., 4-6 per day, €11.40); and Westport (2½hr., 1-4 per day, €12.70). Turn left on Lord Edward St., then follow the signs right onto Adelaid St. and around the corner to Temple St. to find the **tourist office.** (☎61 201. Open June-Aug. M-Sa 9am-7pm, Su 10am-6pm; Oct.-May M-F 9am-5pm.) **B&Bs** cluster on **Pearse Road,** on the south side. **Eden Hill Holiday Hostel (IHH) ❶,** off Pearse Rd., has Victorian decor and a friendly staff. From the town center, follow Pearse Rd., turn right at the Marymount sign, and take another right after one block. (☎43 204. Laundry. Dorms €11.) A **Tesco** supermarket is on O'Connell St. (☎62 788. Open M-Tu and Sa 8:30am-7pm, W-F 8:30am-9pm, Su 10am-6pm.)

COUNTY DONEGAL AND SLIEVE LEAGUE   ☎073

Tourists are a rarity in County Donegal. Its geographic isolation in the northwest has spared it from the widespread deforestation of Ireland: vast wooded areas engulf many of Donegal's mountain chains, while the coastline alternates between beaches and cliffs. Travelers use **Donegal Town** as the gateway to the county. **Buses** (☎21 101) stop outside the Abbey Hotel on The Diamond and run to Dublin (4hr., 5-6 per day, €13.40) and Galway (4hr., 3-5 per day, €13.40). With your back to Abbey Hotel, turn right; the **tourist office,** on Quay St., is just outside of The Diamond. (☎21 148. Open July-Aug. M-Sa 9am-6pm, Su noon-4pm; Sept.-Oct. and Easter-June M-F 9am-5pm, Sa 10am-2pm.) **Donegal Independent Town Hostel (IHH) ❶,** on Killybegs Rd., is family-run and has a homey atmosphere. (☎22 805. Call ahead. Dorms €10.50; doubles €24. **Camping** €6.)

   The **Slieve League Peninsula'**s rocky cliffs, Europe's highest, jut to the west of Donegal Town. The cliffs and mountains of this sparsely-populated area harbor coastal hamlets, untouched beaches, and dramatic scenery. **Glencolmcille** (glen-kaul-um-KEEL), on the western tip of the peninsula, is a parish of several tiny villages wedged between two monstrous cliffs. The villages are renowned for their handmade products, particularly sweaters. On sunny days, visitors to the **Silver Strand** are rewarded with stunning views of the gorgeous beach and rocky cliffs; the trek along the Slieve League coastline begins here. **Bus Éireann** runs from Donegal Town to Glencolmcille and Dungloe, stopping in tiny **Kilcar** (1-3 per day),

IRELAND

the gateway to Donegal's *gaeltacht* and a commercial base for many Donegal tweed weavers. Many Slieve League hikers stay in Kilcar, where they can comfortably drive, bike, or hike to the mountains. The fabulous **Derrylahan Hostel (IHH) ❶** is 3km from Kilcar on the coast road to Carrick; call for pickup. (☎38 079. Laundry €7. Dorms €10; singles €14; doubles €28. **Camping** €6.) In Glencolmcille, sleep at the hillside ▊**Dooey Hostel (IHO) ❶**, which has an ocean view and a beautiful garden. (☎30 130. Dorms €9.50; doubles €21. **Camping** €5.50.)

DERRYVEAGH MOUNTAINS ☎075

Beaches are separated by boglands in the eerie stillness of the Derryveagh Mountains. On the eastern side of the mountains is **Glenveagh National Park,** 60 sq. km of forest glens, bogs, and herds of red deer. (On the R251, east of Dunlewy. ☎(074) 37 090. Open Mar. to early Nov. daily 10am-5pm. Free.) **Crolly,** a village at the intersection of N56 and R259, and **Dunlewy,** off the R251, are excellent bases for exploring **Mount Errigal.** From Crolly, Feda O'Donnell (☎48 114) runs daily **buses** to Galway and Donegal Town via Letterkenny; Swilly (☎21 380) passes Crolly on its Dungloe-Derry route; John McGinley Coaches (☎(074) 35 201) goes to Dublin; and O'Donnell Trans-Ulster Express (☎48 356) goes to Belfast via Derry. Buses don't travel near Dunlewy; you'll need a car to get around. **Errigal Youth Hostel (An Óige/HI) ❶**, off the R251 in Dunlewy, is clean and basic. (☎31 180. Lockout 10am-5pm. Curfew 1am. Dorms €9-11.) **Screagan an Iolair Hill Hostel ❶** (SCRAG an UH-ler) is in Tor, 6.5km outside Crolly. It's close to many Derryveagh hikes, if you can bear to leave it; each room has its own decor and the common room is very cozy. (☎48 593. Dorms €12.50; singles €15.)

LETTERKENNY ☎074

Letterkenny, while difficult to navigate, is a lively place to make bus connections to the rest of Donegal, the Republic, and Northern Ireland. **Buses** leave from the junction of Port Rd. and Pearse Rd., in front of the shopping center. Bus Éireann (☎21 309) runs to: Derry (30min., 3-6 per day, €6.35); Dublin (4½hr., 5-6 per day, €12.70); Galway (4¾hr., 4 per day, €15.25) via Donegal Town (50min., €6.35); and Sligo (2hr., 3-5 per day, €11.50). Lough Swilly (☎22 863) runs to Derry (M-Sa 11 per day, €5.60) and the Inishowen Peninsula (3-4 per day, €5.70). The **Chamber of Commerce Visitors Information Centre** is at 40 Port Rd. (☎24 866. Open M-F 9am-5pm.) **The Port Hostel (IHO) ❶**, Orchard Crest, is convenient to the city center. (☎25 315. Dorms €12; singles €13-16.) There is a **Tesco** supermarket behind the bus station. (Open M-Tu and Sa 8:30am-7pm, W 8:30am-8pm, Th-F 8:30am-9pm, Su noon-6pm.)

INISHOWEN PENINSULA AND MALIN HEAD ☎077

Brochures trumpet the Inishowen Peninsula as the "crown of Ireland." It combines rocky grasslands and bogs with the barren beauty that pervades much of Donegal. The clearly marked **Inish Eoghain 100** road winds around the peninsula's perimeter. The peninsula's most popular attraction is **Malin Head,** remarkable for its rocky, wave-tattered coast and sky-high sand dunes, reputedly the highest in Europe (up to 30m). The raised beaches around Malin Head are covered with semi-precious stones; walkers sifting through the sands may find jasper, quartz, small opals, or amethyst. **Bamba's Crown** is the northernmost tip of Ireland, a tooth of dark rock rising up from the ocean spray. Lough Swilly **buses** (☎61 340) run from Derry, the nearest city to Inishowen, to points on the peninsula including Malin Head (1½hr., 2-3 per day). To reach the ▊**Sandrock Holiday Hostel (IHO/ IHH) ❶**, on Port Ronan Pier, take the left fork off the Inish Eoghain 100 at the Crossroads Inn (also a bus stop). The friendly owners provide maps and walking tours. (☎70 289. Sheets €1.25. Wash €4, dry €2. Dorms €10.)

NORTHERN IRELAND

FACTS AND FIGURES: NORTHERN IRELAND

Official Name: Northern Ireland.
Capital: Belfast.
Population: 1,700,000.
Land Area: 14,160 sq. km.

Time Zone: GMT.
Language: English.
Religions: Protestant (56%), Roman Catholic (44%).

The calm tenor of life in the North has been overshadowed internationally by concerns about riots and bombings. But acts of violence and extremist fringe groups are less prominent than the division in civil society that sends Protestants and Catholics to separate neighborhoods, separate stores, separate pubs, and often separate schools, with separate, though similar, traditional songs and slang. The 1998 Good Friday Agreement, which granted Home Rule to Northern Ireland with the hope of resolving some of the region's struggles, has been struggling itself. London briefly took the reins again in the summer of 2001, and both sides renewed their efforts to make their country as peaceful as it is beautiful. While everyday life in Northern Ireland may be divided, its landscape and society are for the most part quiet and peaceful.

N. IRELAND	❶	❷	❸	❹	❺
ACCOMMODATIONS	under £12	£12-19	£20-29	£30-44	over £45
FOOD	under £3	£3-5	£6-9	£10-14	over £15

PHONE CODES	The regional code for all of Northern Ireland is 028. From outside Northern Ireland, dial int'l dialing prefix (see inside back cover) + 44 (from the Republic, 048) + 28 + local number.

BELFAST ☎ 028

Belfast (pop. 330,000), the second-largest city on the island, is the focus of the North's cultural, commercial, and political activity. Acclaimed writers and the annual arts festival in November support Belfast's reputation as a thriving artistic center. West Belfast's famous sectarian murals are perhaps the most informative source on the effects of what the locals call "the Troubles." Despite the violent associations conjured by the name Belfast, the city feels more neighborly than most international—and even Irish—visitors expect.

⬛ TRANSPORTATION

Flights: Belfast International Airport (BFS; ☎ 9442 2888), in Aldergrove. **Airbus** (☎ 9033 3000) runs from the airport to the Europa and Laganside bus stations (M-Sa every 30min., Su about every hr.; £5). **Trains** connect the **Belfast City Airport** (Sydenham Halt), at the harbor, to Central Station (£1).

Trains: Central Station (☎ 9066 6630), on E. Bridge St. To **Derry** (2hr., 3-9 per day, £6.70) and **Dublin** (2hr., 5-8 per day, £20). **Centrelink** buses run from the station to the city center (free with rail tickets).

Buses: Europa Station (☎ 9066 6630), off Great Victoria St. Serves the north coast, the west, and the Republic. Buses to **Derry** (1¾hr., 6-19 per day, £7.50) and **Dublin** (3hr., 5-7 per day, £10.40). **Laganside Station** (☎ 9066 6630), Donegall Quay, serves Northern Ireland's east coast. **Centrelink** buses connect both stations with the city center.

IRELAND

Ferries: SeaCat (☎(08705) 523 523; www.seacat.co.uk) leaves for: **Heysham, England** (4hr., Apr.-Nov. 1-2 per day); the **Isle of Man** (2¾hr., Apr.-Nov. 1-2 per day); **Troon, Scotland** (2½hr., 2-3 per day). Fares £10-30 without car.

Local Transportation: The red **Citybus Network** (☎9024 6485) is supplemented by **Ulsterbus's** suburban "blue buses." Travel within the city center £1.10, students and children £0.50. **Centrelink** buses traverse the city (every 12min. M-F 7:25am-9:15pm, Sa 8:35am-9:15pm; £1.10, free with bus or rail ticket). Late **Nightlink** buses shuttle to small towns outside the city (F-Sa 1 and 2am; £3, payable on board).

Taxis: Value Cabs (☎9080 9080). Residents of West and North Belfast use the huge **black cabs;** some are metered, and some follow set routes.

✈ ❷ ORIENTATION AND PRACTICAL INFORMATION

Buses arrive at the Europa bus station on **Great Victoria Street.** To the northeast is the **City Hall** in **Donegall Square.** South of the bus station, Great Victoria St. meets **Dublin Road** at **Shaftesbury Square;** this stretch of Great Victoria St. between the bus station and Shaftesbury Sq. is known as the **Golden Mile** for its high-brow establishments and Victorian architecture. **Botanic Avenue** and **Bradbury Place** (which becomes **University Road**) extend south from Shaftesbury Sq. into the **Queen's University** area, where cafes, pubs, and budget lodgings await. To get to Donegall Sq. from Central Station, turn left, walk down East Bridge St., turn right on Oxford St., and make your first left on May St., which runs into Donegall Sq.; or, take the Centrelink bus. Divided from the rest of Belfast by the Westlink Motorway, working-class **West Belfast** is more politically volatile; the area is best seen by day. The Protestant neighborhood stretches along **Shankill Road,** just north of the Catholic neighborhood, which is centered around **Falls Road.** The two are separated by the **peace line.** During the week, the area north of City Hall is essentially deserted at night, and it's a good idea to use taxis after dark.

Tourist Office: The Belfast Welcome Centre, 47 Donegall Pl. (☎9024 6609). Has a great booklet on Belfast and info on surrounding areas. Open June-Sept. M-Sa 9am-7pm, Su noon-5pm; Oct.-May M-Sa 9am-5:30pm.

Banks: Banks and **ATMs** are on almost every corner. **Bank of Ireland,** 54 Donegall Pl. (☎9023 4334). Open M-F 9am-4:30pm.

Laundry: Globe Drycleaners & Launderers, 37-39 Botanic Ave. (☎9024 3956). About £3-4 per load. Open M-F 8am-9pm, Sa 8am-6pm, Su noon-6pm.

Emergency: ☎999; no coins required. **Police,** 65 Knock Rd. (☎9065 0222).

Hospitals: Belfast City Hospital, 9 Lisburn Rd. (☎9032 9241). From Shaftesbury Sq., follow Bradbury Pl. and take a right at the fork. **Royal Victoria Hospital,** 12 Grosvenor Rd. (☎9024 0503). From Donegall Sq., take Howard St. west to Grosvenor Rd.

Internet Access: Belfast Central Library, 122 Royal Ave. (☎9050 9150). £1.50 per 30min. Open M and Th 9am-8pm, Tu-W and F 9am-5:30pm, Sa 9:30am-1pm.

Post Office: Central Post Office, 25 Castle Pl. (☎9032 3740). *Poste Restante* mail comes here. Open M-Sa 9am-5:30pm. **Postal Code:** BT1 1NB. Branch offices: **Botanic Garden,** 95 University Rd., across from the university (☎9038 1309; **postal code:** BT7 1NG); **Botanic Avenue,** 1-5 Botanic Ave. (☎9032 6177; **postal code:** BT2 7DA). Branch offices open M-F 8:45am-5:30pm, Sa 10am-12:30pm.

⌂ ACCOMMODATIONS

Most budget accommodations are located near Queen's University, south of the city center, which is convenient to pubs and restaurants. Take **Citybus** #69, 70, 71, 83, 84, or 86 from Donegall Sq. to areas in the south. B&Bs occupy virtually every house between **Malone Road** and **Lisburn Road,** just south of Queen's University.

The Ark (IHH), 18 University St. (☎9032 9626). A 10min. walk from Europa Bus Station on Great Victoria St. Take a right and head away from the Europa Hotel; at Shaftesbury Sq., take the right fork on Bradbury Pl., then fork left onto University Rd. University St. is the fourth left. Community feel. Weekend luggage storage. Internet £1 per 20min. Laundry £4. Curfew 2am. Dorms Su-Th £8.50, F-Sa £9.50; doubles £32. ❶

Arnie's Backpackers (IHH), 63 Fitzwilliam St. (☎9024 2867). From Bradbury Pl. (see The Ark, above), fork left onto University Rd.; Fitzwilliam St. is on the right. Friendly atmosphere. Key deposit £2. Luggage storage. Dorms £7-8.50. ❶

Camera Guesthouse, 44 Wellington Park (☎9066 0026). A family-run guesthouse with fabulous breakfasts. Singles £25, with bath £37; doubles £50/£55. July discounts. ❸

Belfast Hostel (HINI), 22 Donegall Rd. (☎9031 5435), off Shaftesbury Sq. Clean and inviting interior despite concrete facade. Books tours of Belfast and Giant's Causeway. Breakfast £2. Laundry £3. Reception open 24hr. Dorms £8.50-10.50. ❶

Botanic Lodge, 87 Botanic Ave. (☎9032 7682), at the intersection with Mt. Charles Ave. A short walk to the city center. Singles £25, with bath £35; doubles £40/£45. ❸

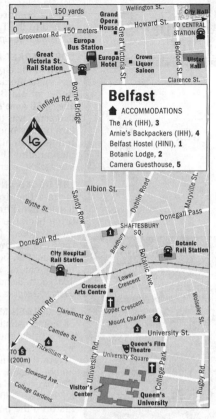

Belfast

⌂ ACCOMMODATIONS

The Ark (IHH), **3**
Arnie's Backpackers (IHH), **4**
Belfast Hostel (HINI), **1**
Botanic Lodge, **2**
Camera Guesthouse, **5**

🍴 FOOD

Dublin Road, Botanic Avenue, and the **Golden Mile** have a high concentration of restaurants. **▨Azzura ❷**, 8 Church Ln., has gourmet pizzas, pastas, and sandwiches. (Entrees under £4. Open M-Sa 9am-5pm.) **Maggie May's Belfast Cafe ❷**, 50 Botanic Ave., boasts some of the best breakfasts around. (Entrees £4-6. Open M-Sa 8am-10:30pm, Su 10am-10:30pm.) Mismatched dishes mingle with counter-culture paraphernalia at **Bookfinders ❶**, 47 University Rd. (Sandwiches £2-2.50. Open M-Sa 10am-5:30pm.) Find fruits and vegetables at **St. George's Market,** on East Bridge St., between May St. and Oxford St. (Open Th 3-9pm and F 6am-1pm.)

👁 SIGHTS

DONEGALL SQUARE. The **Belfast City Hall** is the administrative and geographic center of Belfast. Its green copper dome is visible from any point in the city. Check out the statues in the garden. *(1hr. tour June-Sept. M-F 10:30, 11:30am, 2:30pm; Sa 2:30pm.*

THE INSIDER'S CITY

THE CATHOLIC MURALS

The following is a tour of Catholic Belfast's more important murals, as well as other sights related to Northern Ireland's Troubles centered on Falls Rd.

1 A mural on the side of the library illustrating the **Hunger Strikes of 1981,** when several Catholic prisoners died in protest of the conditions of their detainment.

2 Murals on the walls opposite the old **Sein Féin Office,** once used as the North's national headquarters.

3 A portrait of **Bobby Sands,** on the Sevastopol St. side of the Sinn Féin Office. Sands, elected to British Parliament during the height of the Troubles, was one of the first hunger strikers to die. He is the North's most legendary martyr.

4 **Northern Ireland's National RUC Headquarters.** The most bombed police station in England, the Republic, and the North, with a fortified, barb-wired facade.

Oct.-May M-Sa 2:30pm. Free.) The **Linen Hall Library** contains a comprehensive collection of documents related to the Troubles in Northern Ireland. *(Enter via 52 Fountain St. Open M-F 9:30am-5:30pm, Sa 9:30am-4pm.)*

CORNMARKET AND ST. ANNE'S CATHEDRAL. North of the city center, this shopping district envelops eight blocks around Castle St. and Royal Ave. Relics of old Belfast remain in the **entries,** or tiny alleys. **St. Anne's Cathedral,** also known as the **Belfast Cathedral,** was begun in 1899. Each of its interior pillars names one of Belfast's professions: Science, Industry, Healing, Agriculture, Music, Theology, Shipbuilding, Freemasonry, Art, and Womanhood. *(Donegall St., near the city center. Open M-Sa 10am-4pm.)*

THE DOCKS AND EAST BELFAST. Belfast's newest mega-attraction, **Odyssey,** a gigantic center that houses five different science attractions, promises to bring back the hordes to this previously industrial area. *(2 Queen's Quay. ☎ 9045 1055.)* The best feature is the ■**W5 Discovery Centre,** a science and technology museum that beckons geeks of all ages to play with pulley chairs, laser harps, and robots. *(Open M-Sa 10am-6pm, Su noon-6pm; last admission 5pm. £5.50, students and seniors £4, children £3.50, families £15.)*

THE GOLDEN MILE. This strip along Great Victoria St. contains many of Belfast's jewels, including the city's pride and joy, the **Grand Opera House,** which was cyclically bombed by the IRA, restored to its original splendor at enormous cost, and then bombed again. *(Tours Sa 11am; £3, seniors and children £2. Office open M-W 8:30am-8pm, Th 8:30am-9pm, F 8:30am-6:30pm, Sa 8:30am-5:30pm.)* The National Trust has restored the popular **Crown Liquor Saloon,** 46 Great Victoria St., to a showcase of carved wood, gilded ceilings, and stained glass. Damaged by 32 blasts, the **Europa Hotel** has the dubious distinction of being "Europe's most bombed hotel."

WEST BELFAST AND THE MURALS. West Belfast is not a "sight" in the traditional sense. The streets display political **murals,** which you will come across quickly as you wander among the houses. Be discreet if photographing the murals. It is illegal to photograph military installations; do so and your film may be confiscated. The Protestant Orangemen's **marching season** (July 4-12) is a risky time to visit the area, since the parades are underscored by mutual antagonism. Cab tours provide a fascinating commentary detailing the murals, paraphernalia, and sights on both sides of the peace line. Michael Johnston of **Black Taxi Tours** has made a name for himself with his witty, objective presentations. *(☎ 0800 052 3914; www.belfasttours.com. £9 per person.)*

🎵🎭 ENTERTAINMENT AND NIGHTLIFE

Belfast's cultural events and performances are covered in the monthly *Arts Council Artslink* (free at the tourist office). The **Grand Opera House**, on Great Victoria St., stages a mix of opera, ballet, musicals, and drama. Buy tickets at the box office, 2-4 Great Victoria St. (☎9024 1919. Tickets from £12.50.) The **Queen's University Festival** (☎9066 7687) in November draws opera, film, and more. For more, consult *The List*, available in the tourist office and hostels.

Pubs close early; start crawling while the sun's still up. In Cornmarket, begin with an afternoon pint at Belfast's oldest pub, **White's Tavern**, Winecellar Entry, off High St. Then stumble along Dublin Rd. and the Golden Mile, where some of the best pubs lie. **Robinson's**, 38 Great Victoria St., hosts nightly *trad* sessions. **Lavery's**, 12 Bradbury Pl., offers three floors of unpretentious socializing. The bars near the university stay open the latest. **The Botanic Inn (the "Bot")**, 23 Malone Rd., and **The Eglantine Inn (the "Egg")**, 32 Malone Rd., are almost official extracurriculars. Explore the club scene at **The Manhattan**, 23-31 Bradbury Pl., packed with gyrating 20-somethings. Socialites head to **The Fly**, 5-6 Lower Crescent, a fun vodka lounge. **The Kremlin**, 96 Donegall St., is the newest gay hot spot.

🏃 DAYTRIP FROM BELFAST: ULSTER FOLK MUSEUM

The 🏛Ulster Folk Museum and **Transport Museum** stretch over 71 hectares in **Holywood**. Established by an Act of Parliament in the 1950s, the Folk Museum aims to preserve the way of life of Ulster's farmers, weavers, and craftspeople. The Transport and **Railway Museums** are across the road. (☎9042 8428. Open Mar.-June M-F 10am-5pm, Sa 10am-6pm, Su 11am-6pm; July-Sept. M-Sa 10am-6pm, Su 11am-6pm; Oct.-Feb. M-F 10am-4pm, Sa 10am-5pm, Su 11am-5pm. Each museum £4, students £2.50. Combined ticket £5/£3.) Buses and trains stop here on the way to Bangor.

DERRY (LONDONDERRY)   ☎028

Modern Derry is in the middle of a determined and largely successful effort to cast off the legacy of its political Troubles. Although the landscape was razed by years of bombings and violence still erupts occasionally during the marching season (July 4-12), recent years have been relatively peaceful, and today's rebuilt city looks sparklingly new. Derry's **city walls**, 5.5m high and 6m thick, erected between 1614 and 1619, have never been breached—hence Derry's nickname "the Maiden City." The raised por-

THE INSIDER'S CITY

THE PROTESTANT MURALS

Most Protestant murals are found in the Shankill area of West Belfast, which is to the north of Shankill Rd., near Hopewell St. and Hopewell Crescent, and down Shankill Parade.

1 A mural of a **Loyalist martyr,** killed in prison in 1997, remembers those who have died fighting for British-Ulster rule.

2 A depiction of the **Grim Reaper** with a gun and British flag. Beside him are crosses with the names of three IRA men who set off a bomb in the Shankill area in 1993.

3 A collage representing Northern Ireland's **Loyalist militant groups:** the UFF, the UDU, and the UDA.

4 The large black silhouette on this orange-and-yellow mural represents the **Scottish Brigade,** a symbol illustrative of the connection Protestant Loyalists feel to their brethren across the way.

tion of the wall past New Gate was built to protect **St. Columb's Cathedral,** off Bishop St., the symbolic focus of the city's Protestant defenders. (Open Easter-Oct. M-Sa 9am-5pm; Nov.-Easter M-Sa 9am-1pm and 2-4pm. Suggested donation £1.) At Union Hall Place, just inside Magazine Gate, the **Tower Museum**'s engaging exhibits recount Derry's long history. (Open July-Aug. M-Sa 10am-5pm, Su 2-5pm; Sept.-June Tu-Sa 10am-5pm. £4.20, students £1.60.) West of the city walls, Derry's residential neighborhoods—both the Protestant **Waterside** and **Fountain Estate** as well as the Catholic **Bogside**—display brilliant murals. After dark, roll by **Peadar O'Donnell's,** 53 Waterloo St., and the **Gweedore Bar,** 59-61 Waterloo St., which have been connected since Famine times.

Trains (☎7134 2228) arrive on Duke St., Waterside, from Belfast (2½hr., 4-7 per day, £7.80). A free Rail-Link bus connects the **train station** and the **bus station,** on Foyle St., between the walled city and the river. **Ulsterbus** (☎7126 2261) goes to Belfast (1½-3hr., 6-16 per day, £8) and Dublin (4¼hr., 4-6 per day, £10.40). The **tourist office** is at 44 Foyle St. (☎7126 7284. Open July-Sept. M-Sa 9am-7pm, Sa 10am-6pm; Su 10am-5pm; Oct.-Easter M-F 9am-5pm; Easter-June M-F 9am-5pm, Sa 10am-5pm.) Go down Strand Rd. and turn left on Asylum Rd. just before the RUC station to reach the friendly ▨**Derry Independent Hostel (Steve's Backpackers) ❶,** 4 Asylum Rd. (☎7137 7989. Breakfast and Internet access included. Laundry £3. Dorms £9; doubles £24.) At **The Saddler's House (No. 36) ❸,** 36 Great James St., the friendly owners welcome you into their lovely Victorian home. (☎7126 9691. Singles £20, with bath £25; doubles £40/£50.) **Fitzroy's ❸,** 2-4 Bridge St., next to Bishop's Gate, is an above average cafe, serving everything from chicken to mango lamb. (Entrees £4-12. Open M-Tu 9:30am-8pm, W-Sa 9:30am-10pm, Su noon-8pm.) **Postal Code:** BT48.

GLENS OF ANTRIM ☎028

Glaciers left nine deep scars in the mountainous coastline of northeastern County Antrim. Over the years, water collected in these glens, fostering lush flora not usually found in Ireland. The glens and their mountains and waterfalls are best visited as daytrips from the villages of Glenarm and Cushendall.

▣ TRANSPORTATION. Ulsterbus (☎9032 0011) #156 runs from Belfast to Glenarm (3-7 per day, £3-6) and sometimes continues to Waterfoot, Cushendall, and Cushendun (2-4 per day). Bus #150 runs from Ballymena to Glenariff (M-Sa 5 per day, £2.60), then to Waterfoot, Cushendall, and Cushendun (3-5 per day, £4.30).

GLENARM. Lovely Glenarm was once the chief dwelling place of the MacDonnell Clan. The village is comprised of centuries-old houses and is a starting point for several short walks. The huge arch at the top of Altmore St. marks the entrance to **Glenarm Forest,** where trails trace the river's path. (Open daily 9am-dusk.) The **tourist office** is in the town council building. (☎2884 1087. Internet £4 per hr. Open M 10am-4pm, Tu-F noon-7pm, Su 2-6pm.) **Margaret's B&B ❶,** 10 Altmore St., provides comfortable rooms with 1950s decor. (☎2884 1307. Tea and toast breakfast included. Full Irish breakfast £4. £10 per person.)

GLENARIFF. Antrim's broadest (and arguably most beautiful) glen, Glenariff, lies 6.5km south of **Waterfoot** along Glenariff Rd., in the large **Glenariff Forest Park.** Bus #150 stops at the park entrance; if you're walking from Waterfoot, you can enter the park 2.5km downhill of the entrance by taking the road that branches left toward the Manor Lodge Restaurant. The stunning 5km ▨**Waterfall Trail** follows the cascading, fern-lined Glenariff River from the park entrance to the Manor Lodge. (☎2175 8769 or 2177 1796. Open daily 10am-dusk. £1.50 per pedestrian, £3 per car.)

CUSHENDALL. Cushendall, nicknamed the capital of the Glens, houses a variety of goods, services, and pubs unavailable elsewhere in the region. The **tourist office**, 25 Mill St., is near the bus stop at the northern end of town. (☎2177 1180. Open July-Sept. M-F 10am-5:30pm, Sa 10am-4:30pm; Oct. to mid-Dec. and Feb.-June Tu-Sa 10am-1pm.) A warm welcome and huge rooms await at ▨**Glendale ❷**, 46 Coast Rd., south of town overlooking the sea. (☎2177 1495. £17 per person.)

CUSHENDUN. This minuscule, picturesque seaside village is 8km north of Cushendall on the A2. Its white-washed and black-shuttered buildings sit next to a vast beach with wonderful, murky **caves** carved within red sea cliffs. Visitors can choose between the immaculate **B&B ❸** and **camping barn ❶** at **Drumkeerin**, just west of town on the A2 at 201a Torr Rd. (☎2176 1554. B&B singles £20; doubles £35. Camping barn £8.) **Mary McBride's ❶**, 2 Main St., used to hold the *Guinness Book of World Records* title "smallest bar in Europe"—until it expanded. (☎2176 1511. Steak-and-Guinness pie £5. Food served daily noon-9pm.)

CAUSEWAY COAST ☎028

Past Cushendun, the northern coast becomes even more dramatic. Sea-battered cliffs tower 185m over white beaches before giving way to the spectacular geology of **Giant's Causeway,** for which the region is named. Thousands of visitors swarm to the site today, but few venture beyond the visitors center to the stunning and easily-accessible coastline that stretches beyond.

▤ TRANSPORTATION. Ulsterbus (☎7043 334) #172 runs between Ballycastle and Portrush along the coast (1hr., 4-6 per day, £3.70). The Antrim Coaster #252 runs from Belfast to Portstewart via most small towns along the coast (2 per day). The open-topped Bushmills Bus traces the coast between Coleraine, 8km south of Portrush, and the Causeway (July-Aug. 7 per day).

BALLYCASTLE AND ENVIRONS. The Causeway Coast leaves the sleepy glens behind when it hits **Ballycastle,** a bubbly seaside town that shelters tourists bound for Giant's Causeway. **Ulsterbus** #162A goes to Cushendall via Cushendun (50min., M-F 1 per day, £3), and #131 goes to Belfast (3hr., M-Sa 5-6 per day, £6.10). The **tourist office** is in Sheskburn House, 7 Mary St. (☎2076 2024. Open July-Aug. M-F 9:30am-7pm, Sa 10am-6pm, Su 2-6pm; Sept.-June M-F 9:30am-5pm.) Sleep at **Castle Hostel (IHH) ❶**, 62 Quay Rd. (☎2076 2337. Dorms £7.)

Just off the coast of Ballycastle, bumpy, boomerang-shaped **Rathlin Island** ("Fort of the Sea") is home to more puffins (pop. 20,000) than people (pop. 100). A minibus drives to the **Kebble Bird Sanctuary** at the western tip of the island, 7km from the harbor (20min., every 45min., £2.50). Caledonian MacBrayne (☎2076 9299) **ferries** run to the island from the pier at Ballycastle, up the hill from Quay Rd. (45min., 2-4 per day, round-trip £8.40).

Eight kilometers west of Ballycastle, the modest village of **Ballintoy** attracts the crowds on their way to the tiny **Carrick-a-rede Island.** From the mainland, cross the fishermen's rope bridge (about 2m wide) over the dizzying 30m drop to rocks and sea below; be extremely careful in windy weather. A sign marks the turn-off for the bridge from the coastal road east of Ballintoy. The island's **Larry-bane sea cliffs** are home to a variety of species of gulls. The **Sheep Island View Hostel (IHH) ❶** is at 42A Main St. in Ballintoy. (☎2076 9391. Continental breakfast £3. Laundry £2. Dorms £10. **Camping** £5 per person.)

GIANT'S CAUSEWAY. Geologists believe that the unique rock formations found at ◪Giant's Causeway were formed some 60 million years ago. Comprised of over 40,000 perfectly symmetrical hexagonal basalt columns, the site resembles a large descending staircase that leads out from the cliffs to the ocean's floor below. Ulsterbuses #172 to Portrush, the #252 Antrim Coaster, and the Bushmills Bus all drop off visitors at the **Giant's Causeway Visitors Centre.** A minibus (£1.20) runs from the center to the columns. (Causeway always open and free to pedestrians. Visitors Centre open July-Aug. daily 10am-6pm; June 10am-5pm; Sept.-May 10am-4:30pm. Parking £5.)

ITALY (ITALIA)

	Country code: 39. International dialing prefix: 00.
PHONE CODE	The city code always must be dialed, even when calling from within the city. From outside Italy, dial int'l dialing prefix + 39 + local number (drop the leading zero).

At the crossroads of the Mediterranean, Italy has served as the home of powerful empires, eccentric leaders, and great food. The country burst onstage as the base for the ambitious Roman empire; then it was persecutor and popularizer of an upstart religion called Christianity; next, Italy became the center of the artistic and philosophical Renaissance; and finally it emerged as a world power that has changed governments more than 50 times since World War II. Countless invasions have left the land rich with examples of nearly every artistic era; Egyptian obelisks, Etruscan huts, Greek temples, Augustan arches, Byzantine mosaics, Renaissance *palazzi*, Baroque fountains, and postmodern superstructures sprawl across the 20 regions. From perfect pasta to the creation of pizza, Italy knows that the quickest way to a country's happiness is through its stomach. Italy is also the champion of romance—passionate lovers shout their *amore* from the rooftops of southern Italy and Venice. Somewhere between the leisurely gondola rides and the frenetic nightclubs, you too will proclaim your love to Italy.

FACTS AND FIGURES

Official Name: Italian Republic.

Capital: Rome.

Major Cities: Florence, Venice, Milan, Naples.

Population: 57 million. Urban 67%, rural 33%.

Land Area: 301,230 sq. km.

Climate: Mediterranean; Alpine in the far north, hot and dry in the south.

Language: Italian; some German, French and Slovenian.

Religions: Roman Catholic (98%).

DISCOVER ITALY

The inevitable place to begin an Italian voyage is in **Rome** (p. 592), where you can view the rubble of the toga-clad empire, the cathedrals of high Christianity, and the art of the Renaissance. Shoot north to Umbria and shun worldly wealth à la Saint Francis in **Assisi** (p. 662) before checking out the black-and-white *duomo* of stunning **Siena** (p. 659) and the medieval towers of **San Gimignano** (p. 659). Continue the northward jaunt to be enchanted by **Florence** (p. 650), where burnt-orange roofs shelter incredible works by Renaissance masters. The not-so-Leaning Tower is in nearby **Pisa** (p. 661). Gritty **Genoa** (p. 642) is no postcard darling but has personality and palaces. Gawk at the mysterious shroud at **Turin** (p. 632) before exploring the five bright fishing villages of **Cinque Terre** (p. 645) on the Italian Riviera. Away from the coast, the nightlife in **Milan** (p. 635) is unrivaled, as is the beauty of **Lake Como** (p. 633). Dreamy **Verona** (p. 630) makes it easy to indulge your romantic, star-crossed side, while nearby **Trent,** (p. 634) in the Dolomites, offers year-round skiing. In **Venice** (p. 618), misty mornings give way to mystical *palazzi*. For a change of pace, head to fresco-filled **Padua** (p. 629) and glittering **Ravenna** (p. 648), a Byzantine treasure chest on the east coast. Move inland to sam-

ITALY

ple the culinary delights of **Bologna** (p. 646), then satisfy pizza cravings in **Naples** (p. 664). A daytrip to **Pompeii** (p. 668) reveals Roman remains buried in AD 79. Sail to captivating **Capri** (p. 670) and the **Amalfi Coast** (p. 668), framed by crystal-blue waters. Take the ferry from Naples to vibrant **Palermo** (p. 671), the perfect start to an exploration of Sicily. Round out your tour of Italy at the spectacular **Aeolian Islands** (p. 672), with Stromboli's simmering volcano and beaches of ebony sand.

ESSENTIALS

WHEN TO GO

Traveling to Italy in late May or early September, when the temperature drops to a comfortable 77°F (25°C), will assure a calmer and cooler vacation. Also keep weather patterns, festival schedules, and tourist congestion in mind. Tourism enters overdrive in June, July, and August: hotels are booked solid, with prices limited only by the stratosphere. During *Ferragosto*, a national holiday in August, all Italians take their vacations and flock to the coast like well-dressed lemmings; northern cities become ghost towns or tourist-infested infernos. Though many visitors find the larger cities enjoyable even during the holiday, most agree that June and July are better months for a trip to Italy.

DOCUMENTS AND FORMALITIES

VISAS. Citizens of Australia, Canada, the EU, New Zealand, South Africa, and the US do not need a visa for stays of up to 90 days. Those wishing to stay in Italy for more than three months must apply for a *permesso di soggiorno* (residence permit) at a police station *(questura)*.

EMBASSIES. Foreign embassies are in Rome (p. 592). For Italian embassies at home, contact: **Australia,** 12 Grey St., Deakin, Canberra ACT 2600 (☎02 6273 3333; www.ambitalia.org.au); **Canada,** 275 Slater St., 21st fl., Ottawa, ON K1P 5H9 (☎613-232-2401; www.italyincanada.com); **Ireland,** 63 Northumberland Rd., Dublin (☎01 660 1744; fax 668 2759; http://homepage.eircom.net/~italianembassy); **New Zealand,** 34 Grant Rd., Wellington (☎006 4473 5339; www.italyembassy.org.nz); **South Africa,** 796 George Ave., Arcadia 0083, Pretoria (☎012 43 55 41; www.ambital.org.za); **UK,** 14 Three Kings Yard, London W1Y 2EH (☎020 73 12 22 00; www.embitaly.org.uk); and **US,** 1601 Fuller St. NW, Washington, D.C. 20009 (☎202-328-5500; www.italyemb.org).

TRANSPORTATION

BY PLANE. Rome's international airport, known as both Fiumicino and Leonardo da Vinci, is served by most major airlines. You can also fly into Milan's Malpensa or Linate airports or Florence's Amerigo Vespucci airport. **Alitalia** (US ☎800-223-5730; UK 870 544 8259; www.alitalia.it/eng) is Italy's national airline and may offer off-season youth fares.

BY TRAIN. The Italian State Railway **Ferrovie dello Stato,** or **FS** (national information line ☎147 88 80 88; www.fs-on-line.com), offers inexpensive and efficient service. There are several types of trains: the *locale* stops at every station on a particular line; the *diretto* makes fewer stops than the *locale;* and the *espresso* stops only at major stations. The air-conditioned *rapido,* an **InterCity (IC)** train, zips along but costs a bit more. Tickets for the fast, pricey **Eurostar** trains require reservations. If you are under 26 and plan to travel extensively in Italy, the **Cartaverde** should be your *first* purchase. The card (€20.65) is valid for one year and

Italy

gives a 20% discount on state train fare. **Eurail** is valid without a supplement on all trains except Eurostar. For a couple or a family, an **Italian Kilometric Ticket** (€103.30-174.45; good for 20 trips or 3000km), can pay off. Otherwise, railpasses are seldom cost effective since regular fares are cheap. For more information, contact the **Italian State Railways** in the US (☎212-730-2121).

BY BUS. Intercity buses serve countryside points inaccessible by train and occasionally arrive in more convenient places in large towns. For city buses, buy tickets in *tabacchi* or kiosks and validate them on board to avoid a fine.

BY FERRY. Portside ferries in Bari, Brindisi, and Ancona (p. 663) connect Italy to Greece. Boats from Trieste (p. 631) serve the Istrian Peninsula down to Croatia's

Dalmatian Coast. Ferries also connect Italy's islands to the mainland. For Sardinia, boats go from Genoa (p. 642), La Spezia (p. 646), and Naples (p. 664). Travelers to Sicily (p. 671) take the ferry from Naples (p. 664) or Reggio di Calabria.

BY CAR. There are four kinds of roads: *Autostrada* (Superhighways; mostly toll-roads); *strade statali* (state roads); *strade provinciali* (provincial); and *strade communali* (local). Italian driving is frightening; congested traffic is common in large cities and in the north. On three-lane roads, be aware that the center lane is for passing. **Mopeds** (€20-31 per day) can be a great way to see the islands and the more scenic areas of Italy, but can be disastrous in the rain and on rough roads. Call the **Automobile Club Italiano (ACI)** at ☎116 if you break down.

BY BIKE AND BY THUMB. Bicycling is a popular national sport, but bike trails are rare, drivers often reckless, and, except in the Po Valley, the terrain challenging. *Let's Go* strongly urges you to consider the risks before choosing to hitchhike. Hitchhiking in Italy, especially in areas south of Rome or Naples, can be unsafe.

TOURIST SERVICES

TOURIST OFFICES. In provincial capitals, look for the **Ente Provinciale per il Turismo (EPT)** or **Azienda di Promozione Turistica (APT)** for information on the entire province and the town. Local tourist offices, **Informazione e Assistenza ai Turisti (IAT)** and **Azienda Autonoma di Soggiorno e Turismo (AAST)**, are generally the most useful. **Italian Government Tourist Board (ENIT)** includes: **Australia,** Level 26, 44 Market St., Sydney NSW 2000 (☎02 9262 1666; fax 9262 5745); **Canada,** 175 E. Bloor St., #907 South Tower, Toronto, ON M4W 3R9 (☎416-925-4887; fax 416-925-4799; initaly@ican.net); **UK,** 1 Princes St., London WIR 9AY (☎020 7355 1439; fax 7493 6695; www.enit.it); **US,** 630 Fifth Ave., #1565, New York, NY 10111 (☎212-245-5618; fax 212-586-9249; www.italiantourism.com).

BUSINESS HOURS. Nearly everything closes from around 1 to 3 or 4pm for siesta. Most museums are open 9am-1pm and 3-6pm; some are open through lunch, however. Monday is often their *giorno di chiusura* (day of closure).

COMMUNICATION

MAIL. Airmail letters sent from North America, the United Kingdom, or Australia to Italy take anywhere from three to seven days. Since Italian mail is notoriously unreliable, it is usually safer and quicker to send mail express *(espresso)* or registered *(raccomandata)*. *Fermo Posta* is Italian for *Poste Restante*.

TELEPHONES. Pre-paid phone cards, available from *tabacchi*, vending machines, and phone card vendors, carry a certain amount of time depending on the card's denomination (€2.60; €5.20; or €7.75). International calls start at €1.05 and vary depending on where you are calling. A collect call is a *contassa a carico del destinatario* or *chiamata collect*. International direct dial numbers: **AT&T,** ☎172 10 11; **British Telecom,** ☎172 00 44; **Canada Direct,** ☎172 10 01; **Ireland Direct,** ☎172 03 53; **MCI,** ☎172 10 22; **Sprint,** ☎172 18 77; **Telecom New Zealand,** ☎172 10 64; **Telkom South Africa,** ☎172 10 27; **Telstra Australia,** ☎172 10 61.

INTERNET ACCESS. Though Italy had initially lagged behind in building ramps and turnpikes on the information superhighway, it's now playing the game of catch-up like a pro. While Internet cafes are still rare in rural and industrial cities,

"Internet points" such as bars and even laundromats appear at an alarming rate in well-touristed areas. Rates range from €5-8 per hour. For free Internet access, try the local universities and libraries. For a list of Italian cyberspots, check www.ecs.net/cafe/#list and www.cybercaptive.com.

LANGUAGE. Any knowledge of Spanish, French, Portuguese, or Latin will help you understand Italian. The tourist office staff usually speaks some English. For a traveler's survival kit of basic Italian, see p. 1060.

ACCOMMODATIONS AND CAMPING

SYMBOL	❶	❷	❸	❹	❺
ACCOMMODATIONS	under €15	€16-25	€26-35	€36-60	over €60

Associazione Italiana Alberghi per la Gioventù (AIG), the Italian hostel federation is a Hosteling International (HI) affiliate, though not all Italian hostels *(ostelli per la gioventù)* are part of AIG. A full list is available from most **EPT** and **CTS** offices and from many hostels. Prices start at about €12.40 per night for dorms. Hostels are the best option for solo travelers (single rooms are relatively scarce in hotels), but curfews, lockouts, distant locations, and less-than-perfect security detract from their appeal. For more information, contact the **AIG office** in Rome, V. Cavour 44 (☎ 06 487 11 52; www.hostels-aig.org). Italian **hotel** rates are set by the state. Hotel owners will need your passport to register you; don't be afraid to hand it over for a while (usually overnight), but ask for it as soon as you think you will need it. Hotel singles *(camera singola)* usually start at around €25.85-31 per night, and doubles *(camera doppia)* start at €36.15-41.35. A room with a private bath *(con bagno)* usually costs 30-50% more. Smaller **pensioni** are often cheaper than hotels. Be sure to confirm the charges before checking in; Italian hotels are notorious for tacking on additional costs at check-out time. The **Azienda di Promozione Turismo (APT),** provides lists of hotels that have paid to be listed; some of the hotels we recommend may not be on the list. **Affittacamere** (rooms for rent in private houses) are another inexpensive option. For more information, inquire at local tourist offices. There are over 1700 **campsites** in Italy; the **Touring Club Italiano,** Corso Italia, 10-20122 Milano (☎ 02 852 61; fax 53 59 95 40) publishes numerous books and pamphlets on the outdoors. Rates average €4.15 per person or tent, and €3.65 per car.

FOOD AND DRINK

SYMBOL	❶	❷	❸	❹	❺
FOOD	under €5	€6-10	€11-15	€16-25	over €25

Breakfast in Italy often goes unnoticed; lunch is the main feast of the day. A *pranzo* (full meal) is a true event, consisting of an *antipasto* (appetizer), a *primo* (first course of pasta or soup), a *secondo* (meat or fish), a *contorno* (vegetable side dish), and then finally *dolce* (dessert or fruit), a *caffè*, and often an after-dinner liqueur. If you don't have a big appetite, you can buy authentic snacks for a picnic at *salumeria* or *alimentari* (meat and grocery shops). A bar is an excellent place to grab coffee or a quick snack. They usually offer *panini* (hot and cold sandwiches), drinks with or without alcohol, and *gelato*. Grab a lighter lunch at an inexpensive *tavola calda* (hot table), *Rosticceria* (grill), or *gastronomia* (serving hot prepared dishes). *Osterie, trattorie,* and *ristoranti* are, in ascending order, fancier and more expensive. Many restaurants offer a fixed-price tourist menu *(menù turistico)* that includes *primo, secondo,* bread, water, and wine. Italian dinner is a lighter meal, often a snack. In the north, butter and cream sauces dominate, while Rome and central Italy are notoriously spicy regions. Farther south, tomatoes play a significant role. Coffee is another rich and varied focus of Italian life; for a standard cup of *espresso*, request a *caffè; cappuccino* is the breakfast beverage. *Caffè macchiato* (spotted coffee) has a touch of milk, while *latte macchiato* is heavier on the milk and lighter on the coffee. Wines from the north of Italy, such as the Piedmont's *Asti Spumante* or Verona's *Soave*, tend to be heavy and full-bodied; stronger, fruitier wines come from southern Italy and the islands. Almost every Italian shop sells Italy's greatest contribution to civilization: *gelato* (ice cream).

HOLIDAYS AND FESTIVALS

Holidays: New Year's Day (Jan. 1); Epiphany (Jan. 6); Easter Sunday and Monday (Mar. 31 and Apr. 1); Liberation Day (Apr. 25); Labor Day (May 1); Assumption of the Virgin (Aug. 15); All Saints' Day (Nov. 1); Immaculate Conception (Dec. 8); Christmas Day (Dec. 25); and Santo Stefano (Dec. 26).

Festivals: The most common excuse for a local festival is the celebration of a religious event—a patron saint's day or the commemoration of a miracle. Most include parades, music, wine, obscene amounts of food, and boisterousness. **Carnevale,** held in February during the 10 days before Lent, energizes Italian towns; in Venice, costumed Carnevale revelers fill the streets and canals. During **Scoppio del Carro,** held in Florence's P. del Duomo on Easter Sunday, Florentines set off a cart of explosives, following a tradition dating back to medieval times. On July 2 and August 16, the **Palio** hits Siena (p. 659) with a bareback horse race around the central *piazza*.

ROME (ROMA)

Centuries of sporadic growth transformed Rome from a fledgling city-state to the capital of the Western world. At its zenith, the glory of Rome transcended human imagination and touched upon the divine; from legendary founding in the shadows (͡nre-history, to the demi-god emperors who reveled in human form, to the modern papacy's global political influence, earthly ideas have proved insufficient to capture the Eternal City. Looking at Rome today, the phrase "decline and fall" seems preposterous—though, perhaps, Rome no longer dictates the course of Western history, its claim upon the modes of culture remains firmly intact. Style. Art. Food. Passion. These are Rome's new empire, tying the city to the living moment, rather than relegating it to stagnate in a museum case.

Today, while the Colosseum crumbles from industrial pollution, Romans celebrate their city: concerts animate the ancient monuments, designer boutiques call the faithful to worship at the temples of capitalism, children play football around the Pantheon, and august *piazze* serve as movie houses for the latest Hollywood costume dramas. In a city that has stood for nearly three thousand years, Rome's glory is not dimmed, merely altered.

◪ INTERCITY TRANSPORTATION

Flights: da Vinci International Airport (FCO; ☎06 65 951) known as **Fiumicino,** handles most flights. The **Termini line** runs nonstop to Rome's main station, **Termini Station** (30min.; 2 per hr.; €20). After hours, take the blue **COTRAL bus** to Tiburtina from the ground floor outside the main exit doors after customs (€4.50). From Tiburtina, take bus #40N to Termini. Most charter flights arrive at **Ciampino** (CIA; ☎06 79 49 41). To get to Rome, take the COTRAL bus (every 30min.; €1) to Anagnina station.

Trains: From Termini Station to: **Bologna** (2¾-4¼hr., €19); **Florence** (2-3hr., €22); **Milan** (4½-8hr., €26); **Naples** (2-2½hr., €10); **Venice** (5hr., €34). Trains arriving in Rome between midnight and 5am arrive at **Stazione Tiburtina** or **Stazione Ostiense,** which are connected to Termini by the #40N and 20N-21N buses, respectively.

▟ ORIENTATION

From the **Termini** train station, **Via Nazionale** is the central artery connecting **Piazza della Repubblica** with Piazza Venezia, home to the immense wedding-cake-like Vittorio Emanuele II monument. West of P. Venezia, Largo Argentina marks the start of C.V. Emanuele, which leads to Centro Storico, the medieval and Renaissance tangle of sights around the Pantheon, Piazza Navona, **Campo dei Fiori,** and Piazza Farnese. From P. Venezia, V. dei Fori Imperiale leads southeast to the **Forum** and **Colosseum,** south of which are the ruins of the Baths of Caracalla and the **Appian Way,** and the neighborhoods of southern Rome: the Aventine, Testaccio, Ostiense, and EUR. **Via del Corso** stretches from P. Venezia north to **Piazza del Popolo.** East of the Corso, fashionable streets border the Piazza di Spagna and, to the northeast, the Villa Borghese. South and east are the Fontana di Trevi, Piazza Barberini, and the Quirinal Hill. Across the Tiber to the north is **Vatican City,** and to the south **Trastevere** is the best neighborhood for wandering. It's impossible to navigate Rome without a map. Pick up a free one from a tourist office. The invaluable **Roma Métro-Bus map** (€4) is available at newsstands.

▟ LOCAL TRANSPORTATION

Public Transportation: The 2 **Metropolitana** subway lines (A and B) meet at Termini and run 5:30am-11:30pm. **Buses** run 6am-midnight (with limited, unreliable late-night routes); board at the front or back and validate your ticket in the machine. Buy **tickets** (€0.80) at *tabacchi,* newsstands, and station machines; they're valid for 1 Métro ride or unlimited bus travel within 1¼hr. of validation. **BIG daily tickets** (€4.15) and **C.I.S. weekly tickets** (€16.35) allow unlimited public transport, including Ostia but not Fiumicino. **Pickpocketing is rampant on buses and trains.**

Taxis: Easily located at stands, or flag them down in the street. Ride only in yellow or white taxis, and make sure your taxi has a meter (if not, settle on a price before you get in the car). **Surcharges** at night (€2.55), on Su (€1), and when heading to or from Fiumicino (€7.25) or Ciampino (€5.20). Fares run about €9 from Termini to the Vatican; between city center and Fiumicino around €35.

Bike and Moped Rental: Bikes generally cost €2.50 per hr. or €8 per day, but the length of a "day" varies according to the shop's closing time. In summer, try the stands on V.d. Corso at P.d. San Lorenzo and V. di Pontifici. (Open daily 10am-7pm. 16+.)

▟ PRACTICAL INFORMATION

TOURIST, FINANCIAL, AND LOCAL SERVICES

▧ **Tourist Agency: Enjoy Rome,** V. Marghera 8a (☎ 06 445 18 43; www.enjoyrome.com). From middle concourse of Termini (between trains and ticket booths), exit right, with the trains behind you; cross V. Marsala and follow V. Marghera 3 blocks. Full-service travel agency, booking transportation worldwide and lodgings throughout Italy. Open M-F 8:30am-2pm and 3:30-6:30pm, Sa 8:30am-2pm.

ITALY

Termini & San Lorenzo

🏠 ACCOMMODATIONS

Hotel Adventure, **7**
Hotel Bolognese, **1**
Hotel Castelfidardo and
  Hotel Lazzari, **2**
Hotel Des Artistes, **6**
Hotel Dolomiti and Hotel Lachea, **5**
Hotel Kennedy, **13**
Hotel Magic, **8**
Hotel Papa Germano, **3**
Hotel San Paolo, **11**
Pensione Cortorillo, **12**
Pensione Fawlty Towers, **9**

🍴 FOOD

Africa, **4**
Trattoria da Bruno, **10**

Foreign Embassies: Australia, V. Alessandria 215 (☎06 85 27 21; fax 06 85 27 23 00). Consular and passport service around the corner at C. Trieste 25. Open M-F 8:30am-12:30pm and 1:30-5:30pm. **Canada,** V.G.B. De Rossi 27 (☎06 44 59 81). Open M-F 8:30am-4:30pm. **Ireland,** P. Campitelli 3 (☎06 697 91 21; fax 06 69 79 12). Open M-F 10am-12:30pm and 3-4:30pm. **New Zealand,** V. Zara 28 (☎06 441 71 71; fax 06 440 29 84). Open M-F 8:30am-12:45pm and 1:45-5pm. **South Africa,** V. Tanaro 14 (☎06 85 25 41; fax 06 85 25 43). Open M-F 8:30am-4:30pm. **UK,** V. XX Settembre 80/A (☎06 482 54 41; www.grbr.it). Open M-F 8:30am-4:30pm. **US,** V. Veneto 119/A (☎06 467 41; fax 06 488 26 72). Open M-F 8:30am-10:30am.

ITALY

American Express: P. di Spagna 38 (☎06 676 41; lost or stolen cards and/or checks ☎06 722 82; fax 06 67 64 24 99). Open Sept.-July M-F 9am-7:30pm, Sa 9am-3pm; Aug. M-F 9am-6pm, Sa 9am-12:30pm. **Holds mail:** P. di Spagna 38; 00187 Roma.

Luggage Storage: In train station Termini, by track 1.

Gay and Lesbian Resources: ARCI-GAY and **ARCI-Lesbica** share offices at V. Orvinio 2 (☎06 86 38 51 12) and V. Lariana 8 (☎06 855 55 22). ARCI-GAY membership (€10 per year) gives admission to all gay clubs. **Circolo di Cultura Omosessuale Mario Mieli,** V. Corinto 5 (☎06 541 39 85; www.mariomieli.it), provides information about gay life in Rome. M: B-San Paolo, walk 1 block to Largo Beato Placido Riccardi, turn left, and walk 1½ blocks to V. Corinto. Open M-F 9am-1pm and 2-6pm; closed Aug.

Laundromat: OndaBlu, V. La Mora 7 (☎800 86 13 46). Locations throughout Rome. Wash €3 per 6.5kg load; dry €3 per 6.5kg load; soap €0.75. Open daily 8am-10pm.

EMERGENCY AND COMMUNICATIONS

Police: ☎113. **Carabinieri:** ☎112. **Medical emergency:** ☎118. **Fire:** ☎115.

Pharmacies: Farmacia Internazionale, P. Barberini 49 (☎06 482 54 56). **Farmacia Piram,** V. Nazionale 228 (☎06 488 07 54). Both open 24hr.

Hospitals: International Medical Center, V.G. Amendola 7 (☎06 488 23 71; nights and Su ☎06 488 40 51). Call first. Prescriptions filled, paramedic crew on call, referral service to English-speaking doctors. General visit €68. Open M-Sa 8:30am-8pm. On-call 24hr. **Rome American Hospital,** V.E. Longoni 69 (☎06 225 51; www.rah.it). Private emergency and laboratory services, HIV and pregnancy tests. On-call 24hr.

Internet Service: ▓ **Marco's Bar,** V. Varese 54 (☎06 44 70 35 91). €2.50 per hr. with *Let's Go* or student ID, otherwise €4 per hr. Open daily 5:30am-2am. **Trevi Tourist Service: Trevi Internet,** V.d. Lucchesi 31-32 (☎/fax 06 69 20 07 99). €2.50 per hr., €4 for 2hr. Open daily 9:30am-10pm.

Post Office: Main Post Office (Posta Centrale), P. San Silvestro 19 (☎06 679 50 44; fax 06 678 66 18). Open M-F 9am-6:30pm, Sa 9am-2pm. **Branch,** V.d. Terme di Diocleziano 30 (☎06 481 82 98; fax 06 474 35 36). Same hours as San Silvestro branch.

▌ ACCOMMODATIONS

Rome swells with tourists around Easter, from May through July, and in September. Prices vary widely with the time of year, and a proprietor's willingness to negotiate increases with length of stay, number of vacancies, and group size. Termini is swarming with hotel scouts. Many are legitimate and have IDs issued by tourist offices; however, some imposters have fake badges and direct travelers to rundown locations with exorbitant rates, especially at night.

CENTRO STORICO

If being a bit closer to the sights is important to you, then choosing Rome's medieval center over the area near Termini may be worth the higher prices.

Albergo Pomezia, V.d. Chiavari 13 (☎/fax 06 686 13 71; hotelpomezia@libero.it). Off C.V. Emanuele II, behind Sant'Andrea della Valle. The rooms on all 3 floors have recently been renovated. Clean and quiet with phones, fans, and heat in the winter. Breakfast included (8-10:30am). Singles €50, with bath €60; doubles €77.50/€110; triples €120/€127.50; extra bed 35% surcharge. AmEx/MC/V. ❹

Albergo della Lunetta, P. del Paradiso 68 (☎06 686 10 80; fax 06 689 20 28). The 1st right off V. Chiavari from C.V. Emanuele II, behind Sant'Andrea della Valle. Clean, well-lit rooms with phones. Great location between Campo dei Fiori and P. Navona. Reservations recommended (with credit card or check). Singles €52, with bath €62; doubles €83/€109; triples €112/€147). MC/V. ❹

ITALY

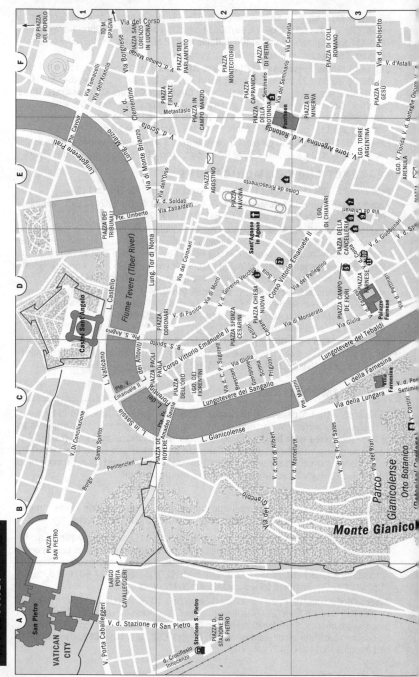

ITALY

V. d. San Fedoro

4

5

Emanuele II

Monte Palatino

PIAZZA S. ANASTASIA

6

Circo Massimo

F

PIAZZA BOCCA D. VERITÀ **Santa Maria in Cosmedin**

V. Petroselli

L. Pierleoni

Via della Greca

V. S. Maria in Cosmedin

V. d. Portico d'Ottavio

Teatro di Marcello

Via d. Tempio

Lungotevere dei Cenci

Isola Tiberina

Ponte Pte. Fabricio

Pte. Palatino

V. d. Anguillara & V. Lungarina & Albertesschi

Lungotevere Raffaello Sanzio

L. d. Vallati

V. d. Zoccolette

L. dei Vallati

PIAZZA G. G. BELLI

PIAZZA S.B. Vaccinari

Via Arenula

Lungo Tiberina

Pte. Garibaldi

V. d. Lungaretta

PIAZZA S. G. DE MATHA

V. del Salumi

Vic. del Genovesi

Santa Cecilia in Trastevere

PIAZZA SANTA CECILIA

E

Lungotevere Aventino

Lunte. Ripa

Lungotevere di Ripa Grande

Porto di Ripa Grande

PIAZZA DI EMPORIO

LG

Pte. Sublicio

200 yards

200 meters

0

0

D

PIAZZA S. APOLLONIA

Teatro Belli

V. della Cisterne

PIAZZA S. MARIA IN TRAST.

V. d. Frate di Trastevere

PIAZZA MASTAI

Via della Luce

Via d. Michele

V. d. Anicia

PIAZZA SAN FRANCESCO D'ASSISI

Viale di Trastevere

V. S. Cosimato

V. S. Francesco a Ripa

PIAZZA DI PORTA PORTESE

PIAZZA DI PORTA PORTESE

Via d. Porta Portese

Pte. Testaccio

Lungotevere Testaccio

Fiume Tevere (Tiber River)

Santa Maria in Trastevere

V. della Scala

PIAZZA S. EGIDIO

PIAZZA DELLA SCALA

V. d. Paglia

V. di Mattonato

V. Garibaldi

PIAZZA DE SAN PIETRO IN MONTORIO

V. Di Panieri

V. Luciano Manara

V. Natale del Grande

Via Bertani

PIAZZA DI COSIMATO

V. G. Santini

V. Roma Libera

V. E. Morosini

Ministero de Pubblica Istruzione

V. Ascianghi

V. G. Induno

V. di P. Porto

LGO BERNARDINO DA FELTRE

Lungotevere Portuense

Via Portuense

Via della Mura Portuensi

C

V. Gariibaldi

LGO. D. PORTA S. PANCRAZIO

V. G. Mameli

V. G. Bettani

Viale Giorioso

Villa Sciarra

Via Dandolo

Viale di Trastevere

PIAZZA IPPOLITO NIEVO

TO TRASTEVERE STATION

B

Via Giancarlo Canali

V. d. San Pancrazio

Centro Storico & Trastevere

▲ ACCOMMODATIONS

Albergo Abruzzi, **3** — F2
Albergo della Lunetta, **6** — E3
Albergo del Sole, **8** — E3
Albergo Pomezia, **7** — E3
Hotel Ca'mel, **17** — C5
Hotel Navona, **4** — E2
Hotel Piccolo, **9** — E3
Hotel Trastevere, **15** — C5

🍴 FOOD

L'Oasi della Pizza, **11** — D3
Pizzeria Baffetto, **1** — D2
Pizzeria San Calisto, **14** — D4
Ristorante a Casa di Alfredo, **16** — C5

🍸 NIGHTLIFE

Artu Cafe, **13** — C4
Bartaruga, **12** — E4
The Drunken Ship, **5** — D3
Groove, **2** — D2
Sloppy Sam's, **10** — D3

ITALY

FROM THE ROAD

WHEN IN ROME...

Here are a few tips to help travelers survive their first trip to Rome:

First, finding your *albergo* or *ostello* can be a harrowing experience, and many wily cabbies possess the innate ability to identify confused and weary travelers. Don't let your guard down, or you might find yourself on the receiving end of a €150 fare. Some will attempt to charge you for their return to wherever they picked you up, so make sure you agree upon the terms before you get taken for a ride.

If you are so foolhardy as to attempt to cross the *corso*, seize any break in traffic to edge into the street, staring the oncoming driver in the eye. He may accelerate for a perilous moment, but will, theoretically, not hit you. This tactic is helpful while trolling for souvenirs along one of Rome's impossibly narrow sidewalks; when a harried motorist attempts to park on you, hold your ground. If it's you vs. the car, however, let the car win.

Finally, lines and queues are decidedly *not* Italian. If and when you make your way across the street, you may want to grab a bite, yet a group of ravenous tourists will doubtlessly be waiting in what you (newcomer that you are) naively assume to be a line. As locals brush past, it will become clear that they are taking advantage of your patience. After a couple of such waits, you too will push your way in, past the unfortunates in "line."

—Caitlin Hurley

Albergo Abruzzi, P. della Rotonda 69 (☎06 679 20 21). A mere 200 ft. from the Pantheon, these are rooms with a view. The facilities are old-fashioned but clean. A/C €10. Singles €43-65; doubles €73-95; triples €125. ❹

Hotel Piccolo, V.d. Chiavari, 32 (☎06 689 23 30), off C.V. Emanuele II behind Sant'Andrea della Valle. Recently renovated. All rooms have fans and telephones. English spoken. Breakfast €4. Curfew 1am. Check-out noon. Singles €52, with bath €62; doubles €62/€82; triples with bath €88; quads with bath €90. AmEx/MC/V. ❹

Hotel Navona, V.d. Sediari 8, 1st fl. (☎06 686 42 03; www.hotelnavona.com). Take V.d. Canestrari from P. Navona, cross C.d. Rinascimento, and go straight. Recently refurbished 16th-century building that has been used as a *pensione* for over 150 years. Brand-new bathrooms equipped with the luxury of heated towel racks. A/C €15. Breakfast included. Check-out 10am. Singles €84; doubles €110; triples €150. Reservations with credit card and first night pre-payment. All other payments in cash (euros or US dollars). ❺

Albergo del Sole, V.d. Biscione 76 (☎06 68 80 68 73; fax 06 689 37 87). Off Campo dei Fiori. 61 comfortable modern rooms with phone, fan, TV, and fantastic antique furniture. Some rooms on the rowdy street; others overlook a pleasant courtyard garden. Parking garage €18-23. Singles €65, with bath €83; doubles €95/€110-125. ❺

NEAR PIAZZA DI SPAGNA

These accommodations might cost a few euros more, but can you really put a price tag on living just a few steps from Prada?

▨ Pensione Panda, V.d. Croce 35 (☎06 678 01 79; www.webeco.it/hotelpanda), between P.d. Spagna and V.d. Corso. Lovely, immaculate rooms and arched ceilings (some with frescoes). Centrally located but shielded from the noise. Always an English speaker on staff. Check-out 11am. Reservations recommended. Mar.-Dec. singles €42, with bath €62; doubles with bath €83; triples with bath €124; quads with bath €168. Jan.-Feb. singles €37, with bath €57; doubles with bath €83; triples with bath €109; quads with bath €145. Jan.-Feb. *Let's Go* discount 5%. AmEx/MC/V. ❹

Hotel Pensione Suisse S.A.S., V. Gregoriana 54 (☎06 678 36 49; info@HotelSuisseRome.com). Turn right at the top of the Spanish Steps. Impeccable service, sleek, old-fashioned furniture, comfortable beds, phone and fan in every room. Breakfast included. All rooms with bath. Singles €88; doubles €134; triples €184; quads €208. MC/V. ❺

Daphne B&B, V.d. Avignonesi 20 (☎/fax 06 47 82 35 29; www.daphne-rome.com). Off the P. Barberini. Friendly English-speaking owners and a substantial list of amenities just steps from P.d. Spagna and the Trevi Fountain make these rates exceptional for Rome. A/C, daily maid service, common bathrooms. Check-out 10am. Reservations strongly recommended. Singles €100; doubles €110; triples €165; quads €220. Jan.-Feb. and Nov.-Dec. 26 as much as 40% cheaper. MC/V. ❺

Hotel Boccaccio, V.d. Boccaccio 25 (☎/fax 06 488 59 62; www.hotelboccaccio.com). M: A-Barberini. Off V.d. Tritone. This quiet, well-situated hotel offers 8 elegantly furnished rooms near many sights. Reception 9am-11pm, late-night access via key. Singles €42; doubles €62, with bath €84; triples €84/€112. AmEx/MC/V. ❹

Pensione Jonella, V.d. Croce 41 (☎06 679 79 66), between P.d. Spagna and V.d. Corso. 4 beautiful rooms. Quiet, roomy, and cool in summer. No reception; call to arrange for someone to meet you when you arrive. 4th fl. location. No private bathrooms. Doubles €62. ❸

BORGO AND PRATI (NEAR VATICAN CITY)

Home to lots of priests and nuns, the Vatican and environs are pretty quiet at night.

▨ **Colors,** V. Boezio 31 (☎06 687 40 30; www.colorshotel.com). M: A-Ottaviano, or take a bus to P. Risorgimento. Take V. Cola di Rienzo to V. Terenzio. Located in the elegant Prati area, Colors offers rooms painted with a bravado that would put Caravaggio to shame. Kitchen. Internet €3 per hr., laundry €2.10 per load. Beautiful terrace and kitchen open 7:30am-11pm. Credit card for private room reservations (call 9pm night before). Dorms €20; doubles €68-83; triples €78-99. ❷

▨ **Pensione Ottaviano,** V. Ottaviano 6 (☎06 39 73 72 53; www.pensioneottaviano.com). 6- to 8-bed dorms; TV, fridge, a microwave, hot showers, sheets, and Internet access included. Lock-out 11:30am-2:30pm. Dorm-style rooms Oct.-June €15; July-Sept., winter holidays €18. Doubles €62/€50; one triple €70/€62. ❶

Hotel Lady, V. Germanico 198, 4th fl. (☎06 324 21 12; venneri@libero.it), between V. Fabbio Massimo and V. Paolo Emilio. The 8 rooms, some with beautiful loft-style open wood-work ceilings and tile floors, lack A/C but are cool in the middle of summer. Singles without bath €65; doubles €82, with bath €100; triples €106/€130. Prices quoted include a *Let's Go* discount, so mention it when you reserve. AmEx/MC/V. ❺

Hotel Florida, V. Cola di Rienzo 243 (☎06 324 18 72; www.hotelfloridaroma.it), on the 1st-3rd floors, reception on 2nd. TV, phone, and hair dryers in each of the 18 rooms. A/C €10. 1 single with sink €31, with bath €72; doubles €68/€103; triples with bath €134; quads with bath €155. Call ahead to reserve; ask about discounts. 5% discount if you pay in cash. AmEx/MC/V. ❸

TRASTEVERE

Hotels here are scattered, most of them too pricey for budget travelers, but the area does offer great nightlife and a location near the Vatican.

Hotel Carmel, V.G. Mameli 11 (☎06 580 99 21; hotelcarmel@hotmail.com). Take a right on V.E. Morosini (V.G. Mameli) off V.d. Trastevere. A short walk from the heart of Trastevere, this hotel offers 9 no-frills, smallish rooms, all with bath. Breakfast included. Singles €75; doubles €85; triples €110; quads €130. AmEx/MC/V. ❺

Hotel Trastevere, V. Luciano Manara 25 (☎06 581 47 13; fax 06 588 10 16). Take a right off V.d. Trastevere onto V.d. Fratte di Trastevere, which becomes V. Luciano Manara. 9 simple and airy rooms with bath, TV, and phone. English spoken. Breakfast included. Singles €77; doubles €98-103; triples €129; quads €154. Short-term apartments for 2- 6 persons with small kitchens and loft beds available. AmEx/MC/V. ❺

TERMINI AND SAN LORENZO

This is budget-traveler central. Rooms range from ultra-cheap to moderate, but beware of *pensioni* that agree to reserve you a room and, when you arrive, offer you accommodations in a "sister" hotel. The rates will usually be twice as high.

NORTH OF TERMINI

Although this region has its fair share of tourist traps, it's cheaper than the historical center and is considerably nicer than seedy Esquilino to the south.

Pensione Fawlty Towers, V. Magenta 39 (☎/fax 06 445 03 74; www.fawltytowers.org). Exit Termini to the right from the middle concourse, cross V. Marsala onto V. Marghera, and turn right onto V. Magenta. 15-room hotel/hostel with common room, satellite TV, library, refrigerator, microwave, and free Internet access. Frequently full. Check-out 9am for dorms, 10am for private rooms. Reservations possible a week in advance; confirm all reservations 48hr. before arrival. Dorms €23; singles €44, with shower €51; doubles €62, with shower €67, with bath €77. ❷

Hotel Des Artistes, V. Villafranca 20 (☎06 445 43 65; www.hoteldesartistes.com). From the middle concourse of Termini, exit right, then turn left onto V. Marsala, right onto V. Vicenza, and left onto the 5th cross-street. 3-star hotel with clean, elegant rooms. Free Internet access. Breakfast included with rooms with bath, otherwise €4.50. Reception 24hr. Check-out 11am. Singles €39-57, with bath €98-140; doubles €46-85/€103-150; triples €57-114/€103-150; quads €72-130/€146-195. €15 discount with cash payment. AmEx/MC/V. ❹

Hotel Papa Germano, V. Calatafimi 14a (☎06 48 69 19; www.hotelpapagermano.com). From the middle concourse of Termini, exit right, and turn left onto V. Marsala, which shortly becomes V. Volturno; V. Calatafimi is the 4th cross-street on your right. Clean rooms, all with TV and telephone. English spoken. Internet access €2.60 per hr. Check-out 11am. Dorms €18-25; Singles €23-40; doubles €42-70, with bath €52-93; triples €54-78/€72-105. Nov.-Mar. 10% discount. AmEx/MC/V. ❷

Hotel Dolomiti and **Hotel Lachea,** V.S. Martino della Battaglia 11 (☎06 495 72 56; www.hotel-dolomiti.it). From the middle concourse of Termini, exit right, turn left onto V. Marsala and right onto V. Solferino (V.S. Martino della Battaglia). 3-star hotels with the same reception (on 2nd fl.). Bar, breakfast room, and Internet access (€2.60 per 30min.). Breakfast €6. A/C €13 per night. Check-out 11am. Check-in 1pm. Singles €52-67; doubles €73-93; triples €83-108; quads €114-135; quints €145-155. ❹

Hotel Cathrine, V. Volturno 27 (☎06 48 36 34). From the middle concourse of Termini, exit right and turn left onto V. Marsala (V. Volturno). 2 common bathrooms serve the 8 singles and doubles with sinks. Breakfast €2. *Let's Go* discount available. Singles €35-45; doubles €47-62, with bath €52-72; €15 per extra bed. ❸

Hotel Adventure, V. Palestro 88 (☎06 446 90 26; www.hoteladventure.com). From the middle concourse of Termini, exit right, cross V. Marsala onto V. Marghera, and take the 4th right onto V. Palestro. Newly renovated rooms, all with bath, satellite TV, telephone, and fridge. Breakfast included. Check-out 11am. A/C €13. Singles €100; doubles €120; triples €140. AmEx/MC/V. ❺

Hotel Bolognese, V. Palestro 15 (☎/fax 06 49 00 45). From the middle concourse of Termini, exit right. Walk down V. Marghera and take your 4th left on V. Palestro. In a land of run-of-the-mill *pensioni*, this place is spruced up by the artist-owner, whose paintings decorate all the rooms. It won an award from the Knights of Malta for hospitality. Check-out 11am. Singles €31, with bath €43; doubles €47-60/€72; triples €62-77.50. ❸

Hotel Magic, V. Milazzo, 20 (☎06 495 98 80; fax 06 444 14 08). From the middle concourse of Termini, exit right. Take a right on V. Marsala and your first left on V. Milazzo. The owners of Hotel Magic will make a clean, modern room and a bar appear before your very eyes. All rooms include private baths, TVs, hair-dryers, and in-room safes. A/C €10. Singles €52; doubles €77; triples €103; quads €118. MC/V. ❹

Hotel Galli, V. Milazzo 20 (☎06 445 68 59; www.albergogalli.com). From the middle concourse of Termini, exit right. Take a right on V. Marsala and your first left on V. Milazzo. Offers clean, modern rooms with tile floors and wrought-iron beds. All 12 rooms have bath, TV, mini-bar, and safe. Breakfast, A/C included. Singles €50; doubles €80; triples €90; quads €120. Winter 10-15% lower. AmEx/MC/V. ❹

VIA XX SETTEMBRE
Dominated by government ministries and private apartments, this area is less noisy than nearby Termini.

■ **Pensione Tizi,** V. Collina 48 (☎06 482 01 28; fax 06 474 32 66). A 10min. walk from the station. Take V. Goito from P. dell'Indipendenza, cross V. XX Settembre onto V. Piave, then go left on V. Flavia and right on V. Collina. Or, take bus #319 or 270 from Termini. Marble floors adorn spacious, renovated rooms. Check-out 11am. Singles €42; doubles €52, with bath €62; triples €80/€90; quads €100/€110. AmEx/MC/V. ❹

Hotel Castelfidardo and **Hotel Lazzari,** V. Castelfidardo 31 (☎06 446 46 38; www.castelfidardo.com). Two blocks off V. XX Settembre. Both run by the same friendly family. Renovated rooms with sparkling clean floors. 3 floors of modern, shiny comfort and plenty of bathroom space. Hall bathrooms shared by 3 rooms at most. Check-out 10:30am. English spoken. Singles €42, with bath €52; doubles €60/€70; triples €77/€93; quads with bath €108. AmEx/MC/V. ❹

Hotel Baltic, V. XX Settembre 89 (☎06 481 47 75; fax 06 48 55 09). Sleek and well-maintained, quiet rooms more like those in a business hotel than the typical *pensione;* all have phone, TV, microfridge, and safe. Breakfast €5. Check-out 11am. A/C €10. Singles €45; doubles €62; triples €77; quads €100. AmEx/MC/V. ❹

Pensione Monaco, V. Flavia 84 (☎/fax 06 42 01 41 80). From V. XX Settembre, turn left onto V. Quinto Sellia and right onto V. Flavia. Friendly Italian woman and English-speaking children keep these 11 sunlit rooms, all with bathroom. Comfortable mattresses, bright courtyard. Check-out 9am. *Let's Go* discount prices: singles €35; doubles €56; triples €75; quads €100. Off-season prices about 10% lower. ❸

SOUTH OF TERMINI (ESQUILINO)
Women might feel uncomfortable walking in this area at night.

■ **Pensione di Rienzo,** V. Principe Amedeo 79a (☎06 446 71 31; fax 06 446 69 80). A tranquil, family-run retreat with spacious, newly-renovated rooms. Plain and cheap. 20 rooms with balconies, TVs. Breakfast €7. Check-out 10am. Singles €19-47; doubles €23-57, with bath €26-67. Prices vary by season. MC/V. ❷

■ **Pensione Cortorillo,** V. Principe Amedeo 79a, 5th fl. (☎06 446 69 34; fax 06 445 47 69). This small *pensione* has TVs and A/C in all 14 rooms, and a cheap lobby phone. English, French, and Spanish spoken. Breakfast included. Check-out 10am. Singles €30-70; doubles €40-100; triples €50-110; quads €60-120. AmEx/MC/V. ❸

■ **Hotel Kennedy,** V. Filippo Turati 62-64 (☎06 446 53 73; www.hotelkennedy.net). Ask not what you can do for Hotel Kennedy, ask what Hotel Kennedy can do for you. Classical music in the bar, leather couches, and a large color TV in the lounge. Private bath, satellite TV, phone, and A/C. Hearty all-you-can-eat breakfast included. English, French, Spanish, and Portuguese spoken. Check-out 11am. Singles €45-88; doubles €70-139; triples €80-159; quads €90-258. 10% *Let's Go* discount. AmEx/MC/V. ❹

Hotel Il Castello, V. Vittorio Amedeo II 9 (☎06 77 20 40 36; www.ilcastello.com). M: A-Manzoni. Beyond Termini, but well within the backpacker's budget. Walk down V. San Quintino and take the first left. Housed in a castle with smallish rooms and eager serving knaves (mostly native English speakers). Breakfast €3. Check-out 10:30am. Dorms €17; singles €42; doubles €57, with bath €68; triples €65-95. MC/V. ❷

WEST OF TERMINI
Close by the bustle of Termini, this area houses more restaurants and shops.

■ **Hotel San Paolo,** V. Panisperna 95 (☎06 474 52 13; www.hotelsanpaoloroma.com). Exiting from the front of the train station, turn left onto V. Cavour. After you pass Santa Maria Maggiore (on the left), bear right onto V.d. Santa Maria Maggiore (V. Panisperna). 10min. from Termini; housed in a bright little *palazzo* with whimsically decorated rooms. Hall baths are clean and private. English spoken. Breakfast €5. Check-out 11am. Singles €39; doubles €57, with bath €78; triples €78. Lovely, large 6- to 10-person suite €26 per person. AmEx/MC/V. ❹

ITALY

Pensione Sandy, V. Cavour 136 (☎06 488 45 85; www.sandyhostel.com). Just past the intersection with V. S. Maria Maggiore. No sign; Sandy is one door to the right of Hotel Valle. 4th fl. Under the same ownership as Pensione Ottaviano, but not quite as nice. Free Internet access and individual lockers (bring your own lock) in each room. No curfew, no lock-out. Simple 3- to 5-person dorms €18. ❷

RELIGIOUS ACCOMMODATIONS

Nuns and priests in Rome skin tourists to the tune of €30 a night, usually for rooms with a strict curfew and some light housework associated with them. The best ones provide quiet rooms, usually in lovely surroundings. Most are open to people of all religions.

▨ **Domus Nova Bethlehem,** V. Cavour 85/A (☎06 478 24 41; www.suorebambinogesu.it/DNB). Walk down V. Cavour from Termini and pass P.d. Esquilino on the right. A clean, modern, and centrally located hotel that happens to carry a religious name, decorations, and a 1am curfew along with it. Newly-renovated rooms come with A/C, baths with showers, TV, and phone. Singles €67; doubles €94; triples €123. AmEx/MC/V. ❺

Santa Maria Alle Fornaci, P.S. Maria alle Fornaci 27 (☎06 39 36 76 32; ciffornaci@tin.it). Facing St. Peter's Basilica, take a left (through the basilica walls) onto V. d. Fornace. Take your third right onto V. d. Gasperi, which leads to P. S. Maria alle Fornaci. Just south of the Vatican, this *casa per ferie*, in the Trinitarian tradition of hospitality, offers 54 rooms, each with a private bath and phone. Simple, small, and clean. No curfew. Breakfast included. Singles €47; doubles €78; triples €104. AmEx/MC/V. ❹

🍴 FOOD

Ancient Roman dinners were lavish, festive affairs lasting as long as 10 hours. Peacocks and flamingos were served with their full plumage, while acrobats and fire-eaters distracted guests between their courses of camels' feet and goats' ears. Food orgies went on *ad nauseam*, literally—after gorging themselves, guests would retreat to a special room called the *vomitorium*, throw it all up, and return to the party. Meals in Rome are still lengthy affairs. Restaurants tend to close between 3 and 7pm, so plan accordingly.

RESTAURANTS

ANCIENT CITY

Despite its past glory, this area has yet to discover the noble concept of "affordable food." But along **Via dei Fori Imperiali,** several restaurants offer decent prices.

▨ **I Buoni Amici,** V. Aleardo Aleardi 4 (☎06 70 49 19 93). The food is worth the walk. Choices include the *linguine all'astice* (linguine with lobster sauce; €6.50) and *penne alla vodka* (€5.50). Open M-Sa noon-3pm and 7-11:30pm. AmEx/MC/V. ❶

Taverna dei Quaranta, V. Claudia 24 (☎06 700 05 50), off P.d. Colosseo. Shaded by the trees of the Celian Park, outdoor dining at this corner *taverna* is a must. The menu changes weekly and often features the sinfully good *oliva ascolane* (olives stuffed with meat and fried; €3.87). Reservations suggested, especially for a table outside. Open daily 12:30-3:30pm and 7:45-11:30pm. AmEx/MC/V. ❷

CENTRO STORICO

The twisting streets of Rome's historic center offer many hidden gems, especially just off the main *piazze*.

▨ **Pizzeria Baffetto,** V.d. Governo Vecchio 114 (☎06 686 16 17). At the intersection of V.d. Governo Vecchio and V. Sora. Once a meeting place for 60s radicals, Baffetto now overflows with hungry Romans. Be prepared to wait a long time. Pizza €4.50-7.50. Open daily 8-10am and 6:30pm-1am. ❶

L'Oasi della Pizza, Via della Corda 3-5 (☎06 687 28 76). The *capricciosa* (tomato, moz-zarella, ham, eggs, and mushrooms; €8) is great; you'll get your vegetables with the leafy *margherita* (€6). Open Th-Tu noon-3pm and 7-11:30pm. ❶

CAMPO DEI FIORI AND THE JEWISH GHETTO

▨ **Trattoria da Sergio,** V.d. Grotte 27 (☎06 654 66 69). Take V.d. Giubbonari and your 1st right. Sergio offers Roman ambience and hearty portions. Try the *spaghetti Matriciana* (with bacon and spicy tomato sauce; €6) and the *Straccetti* (shredded beef with nocket salad; €8). Reservations suggested. Open M-Sa 12:30-3pm and 6pm-midnight. MC/V. ❷

▨ **Hostaria Grappolo d'Oro,** P. della Cancelleria 80-81 (☎06 689 70 80), between C.V. Emanuele II and the Campo. A Roman legend, it's running out of space in its front window to plaster all the awards it's won over the years. *Primi* €7-8; *secondi* €12-13. Open Tu-Sa noon-2:30pm and 7:30-11pm, M 7:30-11pm. AmEx/MC/V. ❸

Trattoria Da Luigi, P.S. Cesarini 24 (☎06 686 59 46), near Chiesa Nuova. Enjoy cuisine such as the delicate *carpaccio di salmone fresco con rughetta* (€8). Bread €1. Open Tu-Su noon-3pm and 7pm-midnight. AmEx/MC/V. ❷

PIAZZA DI SPAGNA

Although the upscale P. d. Spagna might appear to have little in common with Ter-mini, they both share one thing: tons of bad, bad food. The difference is that you'll pay €10 more for the atmosphere here. The best food is closer to the Ara Pacis, across V. d. Corso, away from the throngs of tourists.

▨ **Trattoria da Settimio all'Arancio,** V.d. Arancio 50-52 (☎06 687 61 19). Take V.d. Con-dotti from P.d. Spagna; take the 1st right after V.d. Corso, then the 1st left. Order the fried artichokes (€4.50), although the less inhibited might try the squid's ink risotto (€7.50). Bread €1. Open M-Sa 12:30-3pm and 7:30-11:30pm. AmEx/MC/V. ❷

▨ **Vini e Buffet,** P. Torretta 60 (☎06 687 14 45). From V.d. Corso, turn into P.S. Lorenzo in Lucina. Take a left on V. Campo Marzio, a quick right onto V. Toretta. Popular salads are creative and fresh—the *insalata con salmone* (€8.50/€10 gigante) is delightful. Reserva-tions recommended. Open M-Sa 12:30-3pm and 7-11pm. ❷

Il Brillo Parlante, V. Fontanella 12 (☎06 324 33 34; www.ilbrilloparlante.com), near P. del Popolo. The wood-burning oven, fresh ingredients, and excellent wine attract many lunching Italians. Pizza €5-7.75. Open Tu-Su noon-3pm and 7:30pm-1am. MC/V. ❷

BORGO AND PRATI (NEAR VATICAN CITY)

Establishments near the Vatican serve mediocre sandwiches at hiked-up prices, but just a few blocks northeast is better and much cheaper food.

▨ **Franchi,** V. Cola di Rienzo 204 (☎06 687 46 51; www.franchi.it). Delicacies include var-ious croquettes (€1.29), marinated munchies (anchovies, peppers, olives, and salmon, all sold by the kg), and pastas (vegetarian lasagna or *cannellini* stuffed with ricotta and beef €5). Open M-Sa 8:15am-9pm. AmEx/MC/V. ❷

Guido, V. Borgo Pio 13 (☎06 687 54 91). There's no sign, but you can recognize it by the men playing cards in the sun. Guido holds court behind a counter filled with all the mak-ings of a beautiful *tavola calda*. A full meal (*primi, secondi,* and all the wine you want) will run you less than €8. Open M-Sa 9am-8pm. ❷

TRASTEVERE

Perhaps one of the best places to enjoy a meal in Rome, Trastevere has fabulous, largely undiscovered restaurants.

▨ **Pizzeria San Calisto,** P.S. Calisto 9a (☎06 581 82 56). Right off P.S. Maria in Traste-vere. Simply the best damn pizza in Rome. Gorgeous thin crust pizzas so large they hang off the plates (€4.15-7.75). Open Tu-Su 7pm-midnight. MC/V. ❷

Ristorante a Casa di Alfredo, V. Roma Libera 5-7 (☎06 588 29 68). Try the *gnocchi tartufo e gamberi* (€9.30) to start and the grilled calamari (€10.40) or the *filetto a pepe verde* (€12.40) as a main dish. Open daily noon-3pm and 7:30-11:30pm. ❸

TERMINI
Tourist traps abound; avoid the torturous €8 "quick lunch" advertised in windows.

🍴 **Africa,** V. Gaeta 26-28 (☎06 494 10 77), near P. Independenza. Excellent Eritrean/Ethiopian food. The meat-filled *sambusas* (€2.50) are a flavorful starter; both the *zighini beghi* (roasted lamb in a spicy sauce; €7) and the *misto vegetariano* (mixed veggie dishes; €6) make fantastic entrees. Open M-Sa 8pm-midnight. AmEx/MC/V. ❷

Trattoria da Bruno, V. Varese 29 (☎06 49 04 03). From V. Marsala, next to the train station, walk three blocks down V. Milazzo and turn right onto V. Varese. Start with the *tortellini con panna e funghi* (with cream and mushrooms; €6.50) and continue with the delicious *ossobuco* (€7.80). Open daily noon-3:30pm and 7-10:15pm. Closed Aug. AmEx/MC/V. ❷

SAN LORENZO
Rome's funky university district, San Lorenzo, offers many good, cheap eateries. From Termini, walk south on V. Pretoriano to P. Tiburtino, or take bus #492. Women may find the walk a little uncomfortable at night.

🍴 **Il Pulcino Ballerino,** V. d. Equi 66-68 (☎06 494 12 55). Take a right off V. Tiburtina. Dishes like *conchiglione al "Moby Dick"* (shells with tuna, cream, and greens). Open M-Sa 1-3:30pm and 8pm-midnight. Closed mid-Aug. AmEx/MC/V. ❷

Arancia Blu, V. d. Latini 65 (☎06 445 41 05), off V. Tiburtina. *Tonnarelli con pecorino romano e tartufo* (pasta with sheep cheese and truffles; €6.20) or fried ravioli stuffed with eggplant and smoked *caciocavallo* with pesto sauce (€8.50) make excellent meals. Open daily 8:30pm-midnight. ❷

Il Capellaio Matto, V.d. Marsi 25. From V. Tiburtina, take the 4th right off V.d. Equi. Pasta and rice dishes like *risotto al pepe verde* (with green peppercorn; €5), imaginative salads like *insalata di rughetta, pere, e parmigiano* (arugula, pears, and parmesan; €3.75), and a variety of crepes (€3.65-4.65). Open W-M 8pm-midnight. ❶

TESTACCIO
This working-class southern neighborhood is the center of Roman nightlife, and eateries here offer food made of just about every animal part imaginable.

🍴 **La Cestia,** V. di Piramide Cestia 69. M: B-Piramide. Walk across P. di Porta San Paolo to V. di Piramide Cestia; restaurant is on the right. Pasta €4.20-7.20, *secondi* €6.20-11. Open Tu-Su 12:30-3pm and 7:30-11pm. D/MC/V. ❸

Trattoria da Bucatino, V. Luca della Robbia 84-86 (☎06 574 68 86). Take V. Luigi Vanvitelli off V. Marmorata, then the first left. The animal entrails you know and love, and plenty of gut-less dishes as well. Heaping mounds of *tripe alla romana* (€7). Pizza €4-7. Cover €1.50. Open Tu-Su 12:30-3:30pm and 6:30-11:30pm. Closed Aug. MC/V. ❷

DESSERT AND COFFEE
Cheap *gelato* is as plentiful on Roman streets as leather pants. Look for *gelato* with very muted (hence natural) colors. Coffee (*espresso*) is Italian for "wash away those early morning hostel lock-out blues" and "drink that goes well with pastry/*gelati*/wine/beer."

🍴 **San Crispino,** V.d. Panetteria 42 (☎06 679 39 24). Very near the Trevi Fountain. Crispino is almost universally acknowledged as the best *gelato* in Rome. Every flavor from scratch. Cups €1.70-6.30. Open Su-M and W-Th noon-12:30am, F-Sa noon-1:30am.

■ **The Old Bridge,** Vle. dei Bastioni di Michelangelo (☎06 39 72 30 26), off P. del Risorgimento, perpendicular to Vatican museum walls. Huge cups and cones (€1.50-3) filled with your choice of 20 homemade *gelato* flavors. Open M-Sa 9am-2am, Su 3pm-2am.

Pasticceria Ebraica Boccione, Portico d'Ottavia 1 (☎06 687 86 37). Little fanfare, just long queues of locals who line up for what they all acknowledge to be the best pastry in Rome. *Torta Riccotta Vicciole* and *Torta Ricotta Cioccolate* are the most in famous of their creations (€10.33/kg). Open Su-Th 8am-8pm, F 8am-5:30pm.

Bar Giulia (a.k.a. Caffe Peru), V. Giulia 84 (☎06 686 13 10), near P.V. Emmanuele II. Giulia serves what may be the cheapest (and most delicious) coffee in Rome (€0.75), and they'll add your favorite liqueur at no extra charge. Open M-Sa 4am-9:30pm.

ENOTECHE (WINE BARS)

Roman wine bars range from laid-back and local to chic and international. They often serve excellent food to accompany your bottle.

■ **Bar Da Benito,** V.d. Falegnami 14 (☎06 686 15 08), off P. Cairoli in the Jewish Ghetto. A *tavola calda* lined with bottles and hordes of hungry workmen. Glasses of wine from €1; bottles from €5.50. One hot pasta prepared daily (€4), along with fresh *secondi* like *prosciutto* with vegetables (€5). Closed Aug. Open M-Sa 6:30am-7pm; lunch noon-3:30pm.

■ **Cul de Sac,** P. Pasquino 73 (☎06 68 80 10 94). Off P. Navona. Specialty *pates* (such as pheasant and mushroom; €5) are exquisite, as are the scrumptious *escargot alla bourguigonne* (€4.50). Open M 7pm-12:30am, Tu-Sa noon-4pm and 6pm-12:30am.

Enoteca Cavour 313, V. Cavour 313 (☎06 678 54 96). A short walk from M: B-Cavour. Wonderful meats and cheeses (€8-9 for a mixed plate) listed by region or type, many fresh salads (€5-7), and rich desserts (€4-5). Massive wine list (€11-€260). M-Sa 12:30-2:30pm and 7:30pm-1am (kitchen closes 12:30am). Closed Aug.

◉ SIGHTS

Rome wasn't built in a day, and it's not likely that you'll see any substantial portion of it in 24 hours, either. Ancient temples and forums, Renaissance basilicas, 280 fountains, and 981 churches—there's a reason, according to Robert Browning, that "everyone sooner or later comes round by Rome."

ANCIENT CITY

What Rome lacks in a "downtown" it more than makes up for in ruins—the downtown Cicero and Catullus knew. The **Umbilicus Urbis,** literally "navel of the world," marked the center of the known universe. And who said Romans were egocentric?

ROMAN FORUM

M: B-Colosseo, or bus to P. Venezia. Main entrance is on V.d. Fori Imperiali (at Largo C. Ricci, between P. Venezia and the Colosseum). Open in summer daily 9am-6:30pm; in off-season daily 9am-3:30pm. Free. Guided tour €3.50; audioguide €4 in English, French, German, Italian, Japanese, or Spanish available at main entrance.

Here the pre-Romans founded a thatched-hut shantytown in 753 BC. The entrance ramp leads to V. Sacra, Rome's oldest street, near the **Basilica Aemilia,** built in 179 BC, and the area once known as the Civic Forum. Next to the Basilica stands the **Curia** (Senate House); it was converted to a church in AD 630 and restored by Mussolini. The broad space in front of the Curia was the Comitium, where male citizens came to vote and representatives of the people gathered for public discussion. Bordering the Comitium is the large brick Rostrum (speaker's platform) erected by Julius Caesar in 44 BC, just before his death. The hefty **Arch of Septimius Severus,** to the right of the Rostrum, was dedicated in AD 203 to celebrate Caesar's victories in

IN RECENT NEWS

FISHING IN THE TREVI

Roberto Cercelletta was no stranger to the Roman *carabinieri*, who affectionately called him by his nickname, D'Artagnan, and looked the other way as the otherwise unemployed, mentally unstable man looted about €1000 per day from the Trevi Fountain. Six mornings a week, clad in galoshes and armed with a large magnet on a pole, he carried away the coins tossed into the fountain by tourists hoping for a return visit to the Eternal City and intended for a number of Roman charities. On the seventh day, he rested, watching from afar the civic officials who came to collect the money, which, somehow, was always less than they expected.

For 34 years, it wasn't clear that Cercelletta was actually breaking any laws. The coins didn't belong to anyone, not even the city of Rome. An ordinance passed in 1999 to protect city monuments, however, hefted a fine upon anyone who waded in the fountain. Cercelletta was charged several times, but police found no indication, despite his staggering daily take, that he was able to pay. He owned a moped and a cell phone, but little else. In August 2002, after the Italian media made his crime public, he was arrested after one of his early morning wades and charged.

The loopholes of the legal system that allowed his morning swims to go on for so long has prompted a widespread reconsideration of the place of the homeless in society. Whatever the verdict for Cercelletta, Italian officials have taken steps to ensure that such behavior does not reoccur.

the Middle East. The **market square** holds a number of shrines and sacred precincts, including the *Lapis Niger* (Black Stone), where Romulus was supposedly murdered by Republican senators. Below the Lapis Niger are the underground ruins of a 6th-century BC altar and the oldest known Latin inscription in Rome. In the square, the **Three Sacred Trees** of Rome—olive, fig, and grape—have been replanted by the Italian state. The newest part of the Forum is the Column of Phocas, erected in AD 608. The three great temples of the **Lower Forum** have been closed off for excavations; however, the eight columns of the 5th-century BC **Temple of Saturn**, next to the Rostrum, have been restored. Around the corner, rows of column bases are all that remain of the **Basilica Julia**, a courthouse built by Julius Caesar in 54 BC. At the far end, three marble columns mark the massive podium of the recently restored **Temple of Castor and Pollux**, built to celebrate the Roman defeat of the Etruscans. The circular building is the **Temple of Vesta**, where Vestal Virgins tended the city's sacred fire, keeping it lit for more than a thousand years.

In the Upper Forum lies the **House of the Vestal Virgins.** For 30 years, the six virgins who officiated over Vesta's rites lived in seclusion here from the ripe old age of seven. Near here, V. Sacra runs over the Cloaca Maxima, the ancient sewer that still drains water from the otherwise marsh-like valley. V. Sacra continues out of the Forum proper to the Velia and the gargantuan Basilica of Maxentius. The middle apse of the basilica once contained a gigantic statue of Constantine with a bronze body and marble head, legs, and arms. The uncovered remains, including a 2m foot, are displayed at the Palazzo dei Conservatori on the Capitoline Hill (see p. 608). V. Sacra leads to an exit on the other side of the hill to the Colosseum; the path that crosses before the **Arch of Titus** heads to the Palatine Hill.

THE PALATINE HILL

The Palatine rises to the south of the Forum. Open in summer daily 9am-6:30pm; off-season hours vary. Last entrance 45min. before closing. Ticket to the Palatine Hill and the Colosseum €8; EU citizens ages 18-24 €4; EU citizens under 18, over 65 free. 7-day ticket book good for entrance to the 4 Musei Nazionali Romani, the Colosseum, the Palatine Hill, the Terme di Diocleziano, and the Crypti Balbi €20, EU citizens ages 18-24 €10.

The best way to attack the Palatine is from the stairs near the Forum's **Arch of Titus.** Throughout the garden complex, terraces provide breathtaking views. Farther down, excavations continue on the 9th-century BC village, the **Casa di Romulo.** To the right of the village is the podium of the 191 BC **Temple of**

Cybele. The stairs to the left lead to the **House of Livia**, which is connected to the **House of Augustus** next door. Around the corner, the long, spooky **Cryptoporticus** connected Tiberius's palace with the buildings nearby. The path around the House of Augustus leads to the vast ruins of a giant palace and is divided into two wings. The solemn **Domus Augustana** was the private space for the emperors; the adjacent wing, the sprawling **Domus Flavia,** once held a gigantic octagonal fountain. Between the Domus Augustana and the Domus Flavia stands the **Palatine Antiquarium,** the museum that houses the artifacts found during the excavations of the Palatine Hill. *(30 people admitted every 20min. starting at 9:10am. Free.)* Outside on the right, the palace's east wing contains the curious **Stadium of Domitian,** or *Hippodrome,* a sunken oval space once surrounded by a colonnade but now decorated with fragments of porticoes, statues, and fountains. The **Arch of Constantine** lies between the Colosseum and the Palatine Hill, marking the tail end of the V. Sacra. One of the best-preserved monuments in the area, it commemorates Constantine's victory over Maxentius at the Milvian Bridge in AD 315.

FORI IMPERIALI. Across the street from the Ancient Forum are the **Fori Imperiali,** a conglomeration of temples, basilicas, and public squares constructed in the first and second centuries. Excavations will proceed through 2003, so the area is closed off, but you can still get free views by peering over the railing from V.d. Fori Imperiali or V. Alessandrina. Built between AD 107 and 113, the **Forum of Trajan** included a colossal equestrian statue of Trajan and an immense triumphal arch. At one end of the now-decimated forum, 2500 carved legionnaires march their way up the almost perfectly preserved ■**Trajan's Column,** one of the greatest extant specimens of Roman relief-sculpture. The crowning statue is St. Peter, who replaced Trajan in 1588. The gray tufa wall of the **Forum of Augustus** commemorates Augustus's victory over Caesar's murderers in 42 BC. The aptly named **Forum Transitorium** (also called the **Forum of Nerva**) was a narrow, rectangular space connecting the Forum of Augustus with the Republican Roman Forum. The only remnant of **Vespatian's Forum** is the mosaic-filled **Church of Santi Cosma e Damiano** across V. Cavour, near the Roman Forum. *(Open daily 9am-1pm and 3-7pm.)*

THE COLOSSEUM. This enduring symbol of the Eternal City—a hollowed-out ghost of marble that dwarfs every other ruin in Rome—once held as many as 50,000 spectators. Within 100 days of its opening in AD 80, some 5000 wild beasts perished in the arena (from the Latin word for sand, *harena,* which was put on the floor to absorb blood). The floor (now partially restored) covers a labyrinth of brick cells, ramps, and elevators used to transport wild animals from cages up to arena level. Beware the men dressed as gladiators: they want to take a picture with you for €5. *(M: B-Colosseo. Open May-Oct. daily 9am-6:30pm; Nov.-Apr. 9am-3:30pm.)*

DOMUS AUREA. This park houses just a portion of Nero's "Golden House," which once covered a huge chunk of Rome. After deciding that he was a god, Nero had architects build a house worthy of his divinity. The Forum was reduced to a vestibule of the palace; Nero crowned it with the 35m Colossus, a huge statue of himself as the sun. *(On the Oppian Hill. From the Colosseum, walk up V.d. Domus Aurea and make the 1st left. Open daily 9am-6:45pm, closed Tu. Groups of 30 admitted every 20min. €5; EU citizens ages 18-24 €2.50.)*

VELABRUM. The **Velabrum** is a flat flood plain south of the Jewish Ghetto. At the bend of V. del Portico d'Ottavia, a shattered pediment and a few ivy-covered columns are all that remain of the once magnificent **Portico d'Ottavia.** The stocky, gray **Teatro di Marcello** next door is named for Augustus's nephew, whose early and sudden death remains a mystery. Farther down V. di Teatro di Marcello, **Chiesa di San Nicola in Carcere** incorporates three Roman temples originally dedicated to Juno, Janus, and Spes. *(☎06 686 99 72. Open Sept.-July M-Sa 7:30am-noon and 4-7pm.)* Across the street, the **Chiesa di Santa Maria in Cosmedin** harbors some of Rome's most beautiful medieval decorations. The Audrey Hepburn film *Roman Holiday* made the portico's relief, the ▧**Bocca della Verità,** famous; according to legend, the hoary face will chomp on the hand of a liar. *(Church open daily 10am-1pm and 3-7pm. Portico open daily 9am-7pm.)*

CAPITOLINE HILL. Home to the original capitol, the **Monte Capitolino** still serves as the seat of the city government. Michelangelo designed its crowning **Piazza di Campidoglio,** now home to the **Capitoline Museums** (see p. 613). Stairs lead up to the rear of the 7th-century **Chiesa di Santa Maria in Aracoeli.** The gloomy **Mamertine Prison,** consecrated the **Church of San Pietro in Carcere,** lies down the hill from the back stairs of the Aracoeli. Saint Peter, imprisoned here, baptized his captors with the waters that flooded his cell. *(Open daily 9am-noon and 2:30-6pm. Donation requested.)* At the far end of the *piazza,* opposite the stairs, lies the turreted **Palazzo dei Senatori,** the home of Rome's mayor. *(To get to the Campidoglio, take any bus that goes to P. Venezia. From P. Venezia, walk around to the right to P. d'Aracoeli, and take the stairs up the hill.)*

CENTRO STORICO

PIAZZA VENEZIA AND VIA DEL CORSO. The **Via del Corso** takes its name from its days as Rome's premier racecourse, running between P. del Popolo and the rumbling P. Venezia. **Palazzo Venezia** was one of the first Renaissance *palazzi* built in the city; Mussolini used it as an office and delivered his famous orations from its balcony, but today it's little more than a glorified traffic circle dominated by the **Vittorio Emanuele II monument.** Off V. del Corso, the picturesque **Piazza Colonna** was named for the colossal **Colonna di Marco Aurelio,** designed in imitation of Trajan's column. Off the northwest corner of the *piazza* is the **Piazza di Montecitorio,** dominated by Bernini's **Palazzo Montecitorio,** now the seat of the Chamber of Deputies. The opulent **Il Gesu,** mother church of the Jesuit order, makes few concessions towards poverty, chastity, or obedience. *(Take V.C. Battisti from P. Venezia, which becomes V.d. Plebiscito before entering P.d. Gesu. Open daily 6am-12:30pm and 4-7:15pm.)*

THE PANTHEON. Architects still wonder how this 2000-year-old temple was erected; its dome—a perfect half-sphere made of poured concrete without the support of vaults, arches, or ribs—is the largest of its kind. The light that enters the roof was used as a sundial to indicate the passing of the hours and the dates of equinoxes and solstices. In AD 606, it was consecrated as the **Church of Santa Maria ad Martyres.** *(In P. della Rotonda. Open M-Sa 8:30am-7:30pm, Su 9am-6pm. Free.)*

PIAZZA NAVONA. Originally a stadium built in AD 86, the *piazza* once hosted wrestling matches, track and field events, and mock naval battles (in which the stadium was flooded and filled with fleets skippered by convicts). Each of the river god statues in Bernini's **Fountain of the Four Rivers** represents one of the four continents of the globe (as known then): the Ganges for Asia, the Danube for Europe, the Nile for Africa (veiled, since the source of the river was unknown), and the Río de la Plata for the Americas. The **Church of Sant'Agnese in Agone** dominates the *piazza*'s western side. *(Open daily 9am-noon and 4-7pm.)*

OTHER SIGHTS. In front of the temple, the *piazza* centers on Giacomo della Porta's late-Renaissance fountain and an Egyptian obelisk added in the 18th century. Around the left side of the Pantheon, another obelisk marks the center of tiny **Piazza Minerva.** Behind the obelisk, the **Chiesa di Santa Maria sopra Minerva** hides some Renaissance masterpieces, including Michelangelo's **Christ Bearing the Cross, Annunciation** by Antoniazzo Romano, and a statue of St. Sebastian recently attributed to Michelangelo. The south transept houses the famous **Carafa Chapel,** home to a brilliant fresco cycle by Filippino Lippi. Catherine of Siena's body also rests here. *(Open M-Sa 7am-7pm, Su 7am-1pm and 3:30-7pm.)* From the upper left-hand corner of P. della Rotonda, V. Giustiniani goes north to intersect V. della Scrofa and V. della Dogana Vecchia at the **Church of San Luigi dei Francesi,** home to three of Caravaggio's most famous paintings: **The Calling of St. Matthew, St. Matthew and the Angel,** and **Crucifixion.** *(Open F-W 7:30am-12:30pm and 3:30-7pm, Th 7:30am-12:30pm.)*

CAMPO DEI FIORI

Campo dei Fiori lies across C.V. Emanuele II from P. Navona. During papal rule, the area was the site of countless executions; now the only carcasses that litter the *piazza* are the fish in the colorful produce **market** (M-Sa 6am to 2pm). South of the Campo lie P. Farnese and the huge, stately **Palazzo Farnese,** the greatest of Rome's Renaissance *palazzi*. To the east of the *palazzo* is the Baroque facade of the **Palazzo Spada** and the collection of the **Galleria Spada** (see p. 591).

THE JEWISH GHETTO. The Jewish community in Rome is the oldest in Europe—Israelites came in 161 BC as ambassadors from Judas Maccabei, asking for help against invaders. The Ghetto, the tiny area to which Pope Paul IV confined the Jews in 1555, was closed in 1870 but is still the center of Rome's vibrant Jewish population of 16,000. In the center of the ghetto are **Piazza Mattei** and the 16th-century **Fontana delle Tartarughe.** Nearby is the **Church of Sant'Angelo in Pescheria;** Jews were forced to attend mass here every Sunday and quietly resisted by stuffing their ears with wax. *(Toward the eastern end of V.d. Portico d'Ottavia. Prayer meetings W 5:30pm, Sa 5pm.)* The **Sinagoga Ashkenazita,** on the Tiber near the Theater of Marcellus, was bombed in 1982; guards now search all visitors. *(Open for services only.)*

PIAZZA DI SPAGNA AND ENVIRONS

▦ THE SPANISH STEPS. Designed by an Italian, funded by the French, named for the Spaniards, occupied by the British, and currently under the sway of American ambassador-at-large Ronald McDonald, the **Scalinata di Spagna** exude an international air. The pink house to the right of the Steps was the site of John Keats's 1821 death; it's now the **Keats-Shelley Memorial Museum.**

▦ FONTANA DI TREVI. The extravagant **Fontana di Trevi** emerges from the back wall of **Palazzo Poli.** Legend says that a traveler who throws a coin into the fountain is ensured a speedy return to Rome; a traveler who tosses two will fall in love there. Forget about funding your vacation with an early morning treasure hunt: several homeless men were arrested in the summer of 2002 and fined €500 (see sidebar). Opposite is the Baroque **Chiesa dei Santi Vincenzo e Anastasio,** rebuilt in 1630. The crypt preserves the hearts and lungs of popes from 1590-1903. *(Open daily 8am-7:30pm.)*

PIAZZA DEL POPOLO. P. del Popolo, once a favorite venue for public executions of heretics, is now the lively "people's square." In the center is the 3200-year-old **Obelisk of Pharaoh Ramses II,** which Augustus brought back as a souvenir from Egypt in the first century BC. Behind an early-Renaissance shell, the **Church of Santa Maria del Popolo** contains Renaissance and Baroque masterpieces. Two exquisite Caravaggios, *The Conversion of St. Paul* and *Crucifixion of St. Peter,* are found in the **Cappella Cerasi.** Raphael designed the **Cappella Chigi** for the great Renaissance financier Augustino Chigi. *(Open M-Sa 7am-noon and 4-7pm, Su 8am-1:30pm and 4:30-7:30pm.)*

VILLA BORGHESE. To celebrate his purchase of a cardinalship, Scipione Borghese built the **Villa Borghese** north of P.d. Spagna and V.V. Veneto. Its huge park houses three art museums: world-renowned **Galleria Borghese,** stark **Galleria Nazionale d'Arte Moderna,** and the intriguing **Museo Nazionale Etrusco di Villa Giulia.** North of the Borghese are the **Santa Priscilla catacombs.** *(M: A-Spagna and follow the signs. Open M-F 9:30am-5pm, Sa-Su 9:30am-6pm. €8.)*

VATICAN CITY

M: A-Ottaviano, A-Cipro/Musei Vaticani, bus #64, #492 from Termini or Largo Argentina #62 from P. Barberini, or #23 from Testaccio. ☎ *06 69 82.*

Vatican City—almost .5 sq. km of independent territory entirely within the boundaries of Rome—is the seat of the Catholic Church and was once the mightiest power in Europe. The nation preserves its independence by running a separate postal system and maintaining an army of Swiss Guards.

BASILICA DI SAN PIETRO (ST. PETER'S). A colonnade by Bernini leads from **Piazza San Pietro** to the church. The **obelisk** in the center is framed by two fountains; stand on the round discs set in the pavement and the quadruple rows of the colonnade will visually resolve into one perfectly aligned row, courtesy of the Reformation popes' battery of architects. Above the colonnade are 140 statues; those on the basilica represent Christ, John the Baptist, and the Apostles (except for Peter, naturally). The pope opens the **Porta Sancta** (Holy Door) every 25 years by knocking in the bricks with a silver hammer; the last opening was in 2000, so don't hold your breath. The basilica itself rests on the reputed site of St. Peter's tomb. To the right, Michelangelo's *Pietà* has been protected by bulletproof glass since 1972, when an axe-wielding fiend smashed Christ's nose and broke Mary's hand. Arnolfo di Cambio's *Peter*, in the central nave of the basilica, was not originally malformed, but centuries' worth of pilgrims rubbing his foot have crippled him. The climb to the top of the **Dome** might very well be worth the heart attack it will undoubtedly cause. An elevator will take you up about 300 of the 330 stairs. *(Dress modestly—no shorts, skirts above the knee, sleeveless shirts, or sundresses allowed. Multilingual confession available. Open daily 7am-7pm. Mass M-Sa 9, 10, 11am, noon, 5pm; Su 9, 10:30, 11:30am, 12:10, 1, 4, 5:30pm. Dome: From inside the basilica, exit the building, and re-enter the door to the far left with your back to the basilica. €4, by elevator €5. Open Apr.-Sept. daily 7am-5:45pm; Oct.-Mar. 7am-4:45pm.)*

■ **SISTINE CHAPEL.** Ever since its completion in the 16th century, the **Sistine Chapel** (named for its founder, Pope Sixtus IV) has served as the chamber in which the College of Cardinals elects new popes. The frescoes on the side walls predate Michelangelo's ceiling; on the right, scenes from the life of Moses complement parallel scenes of Christ's life on the left. Each section of the ceiling depicts a story from Genesis. It appears vaulted but is actually flat; contrary to legend, Michelangelo painted not flat on his back but standing up and craning backwards, and he never recovered from his strained neck and eyes. In his *Last Judgment*, on the altar, the figure of Christ as judge hovers in the upper center. *(Admission included with Vatican Museums.)*

CASTEL SANT'ANGELO. Built by **Hadrian** (AD 117-138) as a mausoleum for himself, this hulking mass of brick and stone has served the popes as a fortress, prison, and palace. When the city was wracked with plague in 590, Pope Gregory saw an angel sheathing his sword at the top of the complex; the plague abated soon after, and the edifice was rededicated to the angel. It now contains a **museum of arms and artillery** and offers an incomparable view of Rome and the Vatican. *(Walk along the river with St. Peter's behind you and the towering castle to your left; follow the signs the entrance. Open Tu-Su 9am-7pm. €5; EU citizens under 18 and over 65 free.)*

TRASTEVERE

Right off the **Ponte Garibaldi** stands the statue of the famous dialect poet G.G. Bellie. On V. di Santa Cecilia, behind the cars, through the gate, and beyond the courtyard full of roses is the **Basilica di Santa Cecilia in Trastevere;** Carlo Maderno's famous statue of Santa Cecilia lies under the altar. *(Open M-Sa 8am-12:30pm and 4:15-6:30pm, Su 9:30-10am, 11:15-noon, and 4:15-6:30pm.)* From P. Sonnino, V.

della Lungaretta leads west to P. di S. Maria in Trastevere, home to numerous stray dogs, expatriates, and the **Chiesa di Santa Maria in Trastevere,** built in the 4th century. *(Open M-Sa 9am-5:30pm, Su 8:30-10:30am and noon-5:30pm.)* North of the *piazza* are the Rococo **Galleria Corsini,** V. della Lungara 10, and, across the street, the **Villa Farnesina,** the jewel of Trastevere. Atop the Gianicolo hill is the **Chiesa di San Pietro in Montorio,** built on the spot once believed to be the site of St. Peter's upside-down crucifixion. Next door in a small courtyard is Bramante's tiny ■**Tempietto,** constructed to commemorate the site of Peter's martyrdom. *(Church and Tempietto open daily 9:30am-12:30pm and 4-6:30pm.)*

NEAR TERMINI

The sights in this urban part of town are concentrated northwest of the station and to the south, near P. Vittorio Emanuele II.

PIAZZA DEL QUIRINALE AND VIA XX SETTEMBRE. Several blocks south of P. Barberini and northeast of P. Venezia, the statues of Castor and Pollux, Rome's protectors, flank yet another obelisk that served as part of Sixtus V's redecoration plan for city. The **Church of Sant'Andrea al Quirinale,** full of Bernini's characteristic jolly cherubs, highlights the artist's ability to combine architecture and painting for a single, coherent effect—even if that effect is as overdone as most Baroque work. *(Open W-M 8am-noon and 4-7pm; Aug. W-M 8am-noon.)* A Counter-Reformation facade by Maderno marks **Santa Susanna,** the American parish in Rome. The Mannerist frecoes by Croce are worth a look. *(Open daily 9am-noon and 3:30-7pm.)*

BASILICA OF SANTA MARIA MAGGIORE. As one of the five churches in Rome granted extraterritoriality, this basilica, crowning the Esquiline Hill, is officially part of Vatican City. To the right of the altar, a marble slab marks the **tomb of Bernini.** The 14th-century mosaics in the **loggia** recount the story of the August snowfall that showed the pope where to build the church. *(Open daily 7am-7pm. Loggia open daily 9:30am-noon and 2-5:30pm. Tickets in souvenir shop €2.70. Dress code strictly enforced.)*

SOUTHERN ROME

The area south of the center is a great mix of wealthy and working-class neighborhoods and is home to the city's best nightlife and some of its grandest churches.

CAELIAN HILL. Southeast of the Colosseum, the Caelian, along with the Esquiline, is the biggest of Rome's seven original hills and home to some of the city's greatest chaos. Split into three levels, each from a different era, the **Church of San Clemente** is one of Rome's most intriguing churches. A fresco cycle by Masolino dating from the 1420s graces the **Chapel of Santa Caterina.** *(M: B-Colosseo. Turn left out of the station and walk east on V. Fori Imperiali. Open M-Sa 9am-12:30pm and 3-6pm, Su and holidays 10am-12:30pm and 3-6pm. €3.)* The immense **Chiesa di San Giovanni in Laterano** was the seat of the pope until the 14th century; founded by Constantine in AD 314, it's Rome's oldest Christian basilica. The two golden reliquaries over the altar contain the heads of St. Peter and St. Paul. Across the street is the **Scala Santa,** which houses what are believed to be the 28 steps used by Jesus outside Pontius Pilate's house. *(M: A-San Giovanni or bus #116 from Termini. Open daily 7am-7:30pm. €2; museum €1. Dress code enforced.)*

APPIAN WAY. Since burial inside the city walls was forbidden during ancient times, fashionable Romans made their final resting places along the Appian Way. At the same time, early Christians secretly dug maze-like catacombs under the ashes of their persecutors. *(M: A-San Giovanni. Take bus #218 from P. di S. Giovanni to the intersection of V. Ardeatina and V.d. Sette Chiese. €4.15.)* **San Callisto,** V. Appia Antica 110, is the largest catacomb in Rome, with nearly 22km of subterranean paths. Its four levels once held 16 popes, St. Cecilia, and 500,000 other Christians. *(Take the private* *road that runs northeast to the entrance to the catacombs. Open Th-Tu 8:30am-5:30pm; off-season Th-Su 8:30am-noon and 2:30-5pm; closed Feb.)* **Santa Domitilla** houses an intact 3rd-century portrait of Christ and the Apostles. *(Facing V. Ardeatina from the exit of S. Callisto, cross the street and walk up V.d. Sette Chiese. Open W-M 8:30am-5:30pm; off-season W-M 8:30am-5pm; closed Jan.)* **San Sebastiano,** V. Appia Antica 136, once held the bodies of Peter and Paul. *(Open Tu-Su 9am-7pm. €2.60, EU residents ages 18-24 €1.55.)*

AVENTINE HILL. The ◼**Roseto Comunale,** Rome's official rose garden, is host to the annual Premio Roma, the worldwide competition for the best blossom. Entries are sent in May. *(On both sides of V.d. Valle Murcia, across the Circus Maximus from the Palatine Hill. Open daily 8am-7:30pm.)* The **Giardini degli Aranci** nearby is also a pleasant place for an afternoon stroll. *(Open daily dawn to dusk.)* The **Church of Santa Sabina** and its accompanying monastery were home to St. Dominic, Pius V, and St. Thomas Aquinas, and dates from the 5th century. *(At the southern end of Parco Savello. Open daily 6:30am-12:45pm and 3:30-7pm.)*

EUR. EUR (AY-oor) is an Italian acronym for the 1942 Universal Exposition of Rome, which Mussolini planned as a showcase of Fascist achievement. The center of the area is **Piazza Guglielmo Marconi.** According to legend, when St. Paul was beheaded at the **Abbazia delle Tre Fontane (Abbey of the Three Fountains),** his head bounced three times, creating a fountain at each bounce. *(M: B-Laurentina. Walk north on V. Laurentina and turn right on V. di Acque Salve; the abbey is at the bottom of the hill. Open daily 9am-noon and 3-6pm.)*

🏛 MUSEUMS

Etruscans, emperors, popes, and *condottiere* have been busily stuffing Rome's belly full with artwork for several millennia, leaving behind a city teeming with galleries. Museums are generally closed holidays, Sunday afternoons, and all day Mondays.

VATICAN MUSEUMS. More or less the content of every art book you've ever seen. The four color-coded routes displayed at the entrance are the only way to see the museums, but route C is the most comprehensive. The **Egyptian Museum** contains a small, high-quality sample of Egyptian and pseudo-Egyptian statuary and paintings. The walk through the entire gallery comes out in the **Belvedere Courtyard,** with its gigantic bronze pinecone, and a view of the **Tower of the Winds,** where Queen Christina of Sweden lived briefly before insisting on more comfortable accommodations. The **Pio-Clementine Museum** is the western world's finest collection of antique sculpture, and features, among other wonders, the Apollo Belvedere. Minor galleries (Candelabra, Tapestries, Maps) abound, and a trip to the Vatican without a sojourn in the ◼**Raphael Rooms** is no trip at all. The **Stanza della Segnatura** and its companions hold the *School of Athens* and a number of famous frescoes. The **Pinacoteca,** the Vatican's painting collection, spans eight centuries. *(Walk north from the right hand side of P.S. Pietro along the wall of the Vatican City for about 10 blocks. ☎ 06 69 88 49 47. Open M-F 8:45am-3:30pm, Sa 8:45am-1:30pm. Last entrance 1hr. before closing. €10, with ISIC card €7. Free last Su of the month 8:45am-1:45pm. Plan to spend at least 4-5hr.)*

GALLERIA BORGHESE. One of the most important and enjoyable art collections in Rome, the collection attests to the buying power of Cardinal Scipione Borghese, nephew to Paul V. **Room 1** on the ground floor is home to Canova's seductive statue of Pauline Bonaparte Borghese, thought so luscious by contemporaries that it was hidden from view for years. In **Room 3,** see *Apollo and Daphne,* sculpted by Bernini when he was only 24. The Pinacoteca at the Galleria Borghese is accessible from the gardens in back of the gallery. It primarily contains Renaissance work, and a few genuinely famous paintings, like Raphael's *Deposition* in **Room 9.** If the face of Christ looks familiar, it's because it was modeled on Michelangelo's *Pieta. (M: A-Spagna. Take the exit labeled Villa Borghese, and walk to* *your right past the Mètro stop to V. Muro Torto and P. Porta Pinciana; Viale del Museo Borghese will be in front of you. Open daily 9am-7pm. Entrance on the hr., visits limited to 2hr.; last entrance 30min. before closing. €7, EU citizens under 18 and over 65 €4.25.)*

CAPITOLINE MUSEUMS. Founded in 1471 by Sixtus IV, the Capitoline Museums are the world's oldest public art collection. The Palazzo Nuovo is home to the 2nd-century copy of the equestrian statue of Marcus Aurelius, much imitated during the Renaissance. The Palazzo dei Conservatori, reached by underground passage from the Palazzo Nuovo, is a walk through the ancient myths about the founding of Rome. The Capitoline She-Wolf, a 6th-century BC Etruscan bronze, resides in Room 4. *(On top of the Capitoline Hill, behind the Vittorio Emanuele II monument. Open Tu-Su 9:30am-7pm. Ticket office closes 1hr. before. €7.75; with ISIC €5.68.)*

EUR MUSEUMS. All of the museums splayed around Mussolini's obelisk are small and manageable, and serve as a break from the usual decadent Classical and Renaissance offerings of Rome's more popular museums. The intimidating facade of the **Museo della Civilità Romana** gives way to a number of scale models of life in ancient Rome. See how the Longobards overran the remains of the Empire in the **Museo dell'Alto Medioevo,** a collection of weapons, jewelry, and household items from Late Antiquity. The **Museo Nazionale delle Arti e Tradizioni Popolari** contains such incongruent items as a Carnevale costume and a wine press. The skull of the famous Neanderthal Guattari Man, discovered near Circeo, is found at the **Museo Preistorico ed Etnografico Luigi Pigorini.** *(M: B-EUR-Palasport or B-EUR-Fermi. Walk north up V. Cristoforo Colombo. Civilita Romana: Open Tu-Sa 9am-6:45pm, Su and holidays 9am-1:30pm. €4.15. Alto Medioevo: Open Tu-Su 9am-8pm. €2. Nazionale delle Arti e Tradizioni Popolari: Open Tu-Su 9am-8pm. Closed holidays. €4. Preistorico ed Etnografico Luigi Pigorini: Open daily 9am-8pm. €4. All museums: under 18 and over 65 free.)*

OTHER RECOMMENDED COLLECTIONS. Montemartini, Rome's first power plant, was converted to hold displaced sculpture from the Capitoline Museums in the 1990s. *(V. Ostiense 106. M: B-Piramide. Open Tu-Su 9:30am-7pm. €4; EU citizens ages 18-24 €3.)* The **Doria Pamphilj** family, whose relations with Pope Innocent X coined the term "nepotism," still owns its stunning private collection. Titian's *Salome* and Velasquez's portrait of Innocent X alone are worth the visit. *(P. del Collegio Romana 2. Open F-W 10am-5pm. €7.30, students and seniors €5.70. Audioguide included.)* After overdosing on "artwork" and "culture," get your aesthetic stomach pumped at the one museum dedicated to crime and punishment, the **Museo Criminologico.** Etchings like *A Smith Has His Brains Beaten Out With a Hammer* hang on the walls along with terrorist, spy, and druggie paraphernalia. *(V. del Gonfalone 27. Open Tu-Th 9am-1pm and 2:30-6:30pm, F-Sa 9am-1pm. €2; under 18 and over 65 €1.)*

🎵 ENTERTAINMENT

Unfortunately, Roman entertainment just ain't what it used to be. Back in the day, you could swing by the Colosseum to watch a man get mauled by a bear; today, Romans seeking diversion are more likely to go to a nightclub than fight some hairy beast to the death. Check *Roma C'è* (which has an English-language section) or *Time Out*, available at newsstands, for club, movie, and events listings.

THEATER AND CINEMA. The **Festival Roma-Europa** in late summer brings a number of world-class acts to Rome (consult www.romace.it for more information), but for year-round performances of classic Italian theater, **Teatro Argentina,** Largo di Torre Argentina 52, is the grand matriarch of all Italian venues. (☎06 68 80 46 01. Box office open M-F 10am-2pm and 3-7pm, Sa 10am-2pm. Tickets around €20.60, depending on performance; students €15.50. AmEx/D/MC/V.) **Teatro Colosseo,** V. Capo d'Africa 5a, usually features work by foreign playwrights translated into Italian, but also hosts an English theater night. Call for details. (☎ 06 700 49 32. M: B-Colosseo. Box office open Tu-Sa 6-9:30pm. Tickets €5-15.50. Student discount €7.75. Closed in summer.)

Most English-language films are dubbed into Italian; check newspapers or *Roma C'è* for listings with a **v.o.** or **l.o.** These indicate that the film is in the original language. For a sure bet, pay a visit to **Il Pasquino**, P. Sant-Egidio 10, off P.S. Maria in Trastevere. Three different screens show English films, and the program changes daily. (☎ 06 58 33 33 10. €6.20, students €4.15.)

MUSIC. Founded by Palestrina in the 16th century, **Accademia Nazionale di Santa Cecilia** remains the best in classical music performances. Concerts are held at the **Auditorio Pio**, V.d. Conciliazione 4. (☎ 06 361 10 64; www.santacecilia.it. Box office at the Auditorio Pio open Th-Tu 11am-7pm, until showtime on concert days.)

Alexanderplatz Jazz Club, V. Ostia 9, is the current residence of that *je ne sais quoi* that was expatriate life in Italy during the 50s. Read messages on the wall from old jazz greats, and be prepared to move outside during the summer to the Villa Celimontana. (☎ 06 39 74 21 71. M: A-Ottaviano, near the Vatican City. Required *tessera* €6.20. Open Sept.-June daily 9pm-2am. Shows start at 10pm.) The **Cornetto Free Music Festival Roma Live** attracts acts like Pink Floyd, The Cure, and the Backstreet Boys at a number of venues throughout the city during the summer. (☎ 06 592 21 00; www.bbecom.it. Shows start at 9:30pm.)

SPECTATOR SPORTS. While other spectator sports may exist in Rome, it's *calcio* (football) that brings the scantily-clad fans and the large-scale riots that the world knows and loves. Rome has two teams in Italy's Serie A: **A.S. Roma** and **S.S. Lazio.** Games are played at the Stadio Olimpico in the Foro Italico (M: A-Ottaviano to bus #32). *Tifosi*, as hardcore fans are called, arrive hours or sometimes days ahead of time for big games, to drink, sing, and taunt rivals. Tickets can be bought at the stadium box office, but are easier to obtain at the **A.S. Roma Store**, P. Colonna 360. (☎ 06 678 65 14; www.asroma.it. Open daily 10am-10pm, tickets sold 10am-6:30pm. Tickets start at €15.50. AmEx/MC/V.)

▛▜ SHOPPING

Everything you need to know about Italian fashion is summed up in one simple phrase: *la bella figura.* It describes a beautiful, well-dressed, put-together woman, and it is very, very important in Rome. Think whole picture: tinted sunglasses, Ferragamo suit, Gucci pumps with six-inch heels, and, stuffed in your Prada bag, a *telefonino* with a signature ring. For men, a single gorgeous black suit will do the trick.

If you're not a Telecom heir or heiress, there are still ways to purchase grace and aplomb. Sales happen twice a year, in mid-January and mid-July, and a number of boutiques, while not as fashionable as their counterparts on the Via Condotti, won't require the sale of a major organ.

BOUTIQUES

No matter what anti-capitalist mantra you may espouse, you know you've secretly lusted after that Versace jacket. So indulge. If you spend over €155 at one store, you are eligible for a tax refund. (As if you needed another incentive to splurge.)

▨ **Dolce & Gabbana,** V.d. Condotti 52 (☎ 06 69 92 49 99). Open M-Sa 10am-7:30pm.

▨ **Prada,** V.d. Condotti 88-95 (☎ 06 679 08 97). Open M-Sa 10am-7pm, Su 2-8pm.

Salvatore Ferragamo, Men: V.d. Condotti 64-66 (☎ 06 678 11 30). Women: V.d. Condotti 72-74 (☎ 06 679 15 65). Open June-July M-F 10am-7pm, Sa 9am-1pm; Aug.-May M 3-7pm, Tu-Sa 10am-7pm.

Bruno Magli, V.d. Gambero 1 (☎ 06 679 38 02). Open M-Sa 10am-7:30pm.

Gucci, V.d. Condotti 8 (☎ 06 678 93 40). Open Tu-F 10am-7pm, Sa 9:30am-1:30pm.

CHEAP AND CHIC

Designer emporiums such as **David Cenci**, V. Campo Marzio 1-7 (☎06 699 06 81; open M 4-8pm, Tu-F 9:30am-1:30pm and 4-8pm, Sa 10am-8pm), **Antonelo & Fabrizio**, C.V. Emanuele 242-243 (☎06 68 80 27 49; open in summer daily 9:30am-1:30pm and 4-8pm; off-season 3:30-7:30pm), and **Discount dell'alta Moda**, V. Agostino Depretis 87 (☎06 47 82 56 72; open M 2:30-7:30pm, Tu-Sa 9:30am-7:30pm), stock many lines of designer clothes and shoes—sometimes at half their normal prices.

Diesel, V.d. Corso 186 (☎06 678 39 33). Off V.d. Condotti. Also at V.d. Babuino 95. *The* label in retro fashion is surprisingly high-octane. Prices are cheaper than elsewhere in the world, so it's worth the visit. Open M-Sa 10:30am-8pm, Su 3:30-8pm.

MISCELLANEOUS

Alcozer, V.d. Carozze 48 (☎06 679 13 88). Near P. di Spagna. Gorgeous old-world jewelry at decent prices. Earrings €22; a jeweled crucifix Lucrezia Borgia would've been proud of for €65. Open M 2-7:30pm, Tu-Sa 10am-7:30pm.

Materozzoli, P.S. Lorenzo in Lucina 5, off V.d. Corso (☎06 68 89 26 86). This old-world *profumeria* carries everything from the exclusive Aqua di Parma line to shaving brushes. Hard-to-find perfumes and colognes. Open M 3:30-7:30pm, Tu-Sa 10am-1:30pm and 3:30-7:30pm. Closed Aug. 10-28.

Campo Marzio Penne, V. Campo Marzio 41 (☎06 68 80 78 77). Fountain pens (€26+) and leather goods, in addition to brightly-colored journals and photo albums (€25+). The small address books (€6) make great presents. Open M-Su 10am-1pm and 2-7pm.

Disfunzioni Musicali, V. degli Etruschi 4 (☎06 446 19 84; fax 06 445 17 04), in San Lorenzo. CDs, cassettes, and LPs available, including excellent selections of rock, avant-garde classical, jazz, and ethnic. Open M-Sa 10:30am-8pm. Closed major holidays and Ferragosto. MC/V.

▚ NIGHTLIFE

PUBS

For organized, indoor drunkenness, stop into any of Rome's countless pubs, many of which have some sort of Irish theme. Drink prices often increase after 9pm.

Jonathan's Angels, V.d. Fossa 14-16. West of P. Navona. Not since Pope Julius II has there been a case of Roman megalomania as severe as that of Jonathan, whose face serves as the theme for the decor in this bar. Medium beer on tap €5; delicious cocktails/long drinks €8. Open daily 9:30am-2am.

Trinity College, V.d. Collegio Romano 6. Off V.d. Corso near P. Venezia. Offers degrees in such diverse curricula as Guinness, Harp, and Heineken. Tuition €3-4.50. Happy Hour noon-8pm. Classes held every day noon-3am. AmEx/MC/V.

Il Simposio, V. d. Latini 11. Off V. Tiburtina. Chances are good that on any given night a splattered painter will be hard at work beautifying a discarded refrigerator. With cocktails from €3.50 and a glass of *fragolino* for €2.75, even starving artists can afford the place. Open daily 9pm-2am. Closed late July-Aug.

The Nag's Head, V. IV Novembre 138b. Dance floor inside; live music twice a week. Guinness €5; cocktails €8. Cover €5; F and Sa men €7.75; no cover Su. Open in summer daily 8pm-2am; winter noon-2am. MC/V.

Nuvolari, V. degli Ombrellari 10. Off V. Vittorio. This cocktail bar (serving beer and tropical drinks) also functions as an *enoteca* with wine by the glass (€3.50), a diverse wine list, and the usual salads (choose from 30 at €6 each) and meat and cheese platters (€7.50). Open M-Sa 8pm-2am.

Artu Cafe, Largo Fumasoni Biondi 5. Good selection of drinks (beer €4.50; wine €3-5.50 per glass; cocktails €6.20-7.20). Enjoy specialty cocktails made with fresh juices. Free *apertivi* buffet 6:45-9pm. Open Tu-Su 6pm-2am. MC/V.

Pub Hallo'Ween, P. Tiburtino 31, at the corner of V. Tiburtina and V. Marsala. Plastic skulls and fake spiders and spiderwebs. Draft beer €3.70-4.20, bottles €3.70. Cocktails €4.20-5.20. Open daily 8:30pm-2:30am, Su 5pm-2:30am. Closed Aug.

Il Barone Rosso, V. Libetta 13. M: B-Garbatella. Plenty of room on the 2 floors and outdoor patio, plenty of snacks (€3-5.50), and plenty of beer (€4). Open Tu-Su 8pm-3am. Dinner served until 9:30pm. Closed Aug.

ketumbar, V. Galvani 24. A taste of New York decadence in the middle of Italy. It even doubles as a Japanese restaurant (sushi plates €18-36). Wear black; everyone else will. Open M-Sa 8pm-3am. Closed Aug. AmEx/MC/V.

Mount Gay Music Bar, V. Galvani 54. Named for the rum and not the crowd (although the W evening drag show attracts more diverse patrons). Open daily 11pm-6am. MC/V.

The Proud Lion Pub, Borgo Pio 36. The outside of the pub says "Rome, Borgo Pio," but the beer and scotch says "Hey, I don't forget my Highland roots." Beer and cocktails €4; single malts €4.50-5. Open M-Sa 8:30-late.

The Drunken Ship, Campo dei Fiori 20-21. Because you're tired of meeting Italians. Because you feel the need to have an emotion-free fling with a kindred spirit. Because you're proud to be an American, dammit. Happy Hour daily 5-8pm. W 9-10pm power hour (all you can drink; €6). Open daily 11am-2am. AmEx/MC/V.

Sloppy Sam's, Campo dei Fiori 9-10. The identical twin of the Drunken Ship. Note that once home, wistful stories about that "special someone" you "befriended" at Sloppy Sam's will probably be regarded somewhat cynically. Beer €3; shots €2.50. Ask about theme nights. Happy Hour 5-8pm. Open M-F 4pm-2am, Sa-Su 11am-2am. AmEx/MC/V.

Night and Day, V.d. Oca 50. Off V. di Ripetta near P. del Popolo. Don't even think of coming until the rest of the bars close. At 2am, Italians who don't let dawn stop their fun stream in. Buy a membership card (€5) for discounts on drinks. Beer €3-5, Guinness €4.50. Happy Hour until midnight. Open daily 7pm-6am. Closed part of Aug.

Bartaruga, P. Mattei 7/8, in the Jewish Ghetto. A surreal drinking experience in a myriad of Murano glass, light blue and pink sofas, and tasseled drapery. Wide variety of cocktails available; beer €4. Open M-Sa 3pm-2am.

CLUBS

Although Italian discos can be a flashy, sweaty good time, the scene changes as often as Roman phone numbers. Check *Roma C'è* or *Time Out*. Rome has fewer gay establishments than most cities its size, but those it has are solid and keep late hours. Many gay establishments require an **ARCI-GAY pass** (€10 yearly), available from **Circolo di Cultura Omosessuale Mario Mieli** (☎ 06 541 39 85).

Chic and Kitsch, V.S. Saba 11a. Uniting the elegant with the eclectic; music (often House or a variant) is selected by resident DJ Giuliano Marchili. Cover: men €13, women €10 includes 1st drink. Open Th-Sa 11:30pm-4am. Closed Aug.

Groove, V. Savelli 10. Look for the black door. Lose it to acid jazz, funk, soul, and disco. F-Sa 1-drink minimum (€5). Open W-Su 10pm-2am. Closed most of Aug.

Alien, V. Velletri 13-19. One of the biggest discos in Rome. As of this writing, the comfy chill-out room had not yet reached 1987. Cover varies (about €15, including a drink). Open Tu-Su 11pm-5:30am.

Piper, V. Tagliamento 9. A popular club that occasionally hosts gay nights. 70s, rock, and disco, as well as house and underground. Gay friendly all the time. Cover €10-18, includes 1st drink. Open F-Sa 11pm-4:30am; in summer Sa-Su 11pm-4:30am.

Il Giardini di Adone, V.d. Reti 38a. Off V.d. Sabelli. Though it fancies itself a "spaghetti-pub," the happy students who frequent this little place would remind you that tables are properly used for dancing, not for eating linguine. Cover €6, includes 1st drink. Open Tu-Su 8pm-3am. Closed late July-Aug.

Charro Cafe, V. di Monte Testaccio 73. So you wanted to go to Tijuana, but got stuck in Rome. Weep no more, *mis amigos:* make a run for Charro, home of the €2.60 tequila *bum bum.* Open daily midnight-3am.

Aquarela, V. di Monte Testaccio 64. You want pottery shards? You got pottery shards. A fine example of urban renewal, Roman-style. Entrance €10, includes 1st drink. Open Tu-Su 8:30pm-3am.

Caruso Caffe, V. di Monte Testaccio 36. 5 rooms of tropical decor and writhing Latino wannabes. Live music F. Cover €7-10, includes 1st drink. Open Tu-Sa 11:30pm-3am.

Radio Londra Caffè, V. di Monte Testaccio 65b. Packed with an energetic, good-looking, young crowd. Pint of Carlsberg €3.60. Pizza, *panini,* and hamburgers (€4-6). 1 yr. membership €5. Open M-Sa 9pm-3am.

Classico Village, V. Libetta 3. M: B-Garbatella. Exit onto V. Argonauti and take a left on V. Libetta. Women probably don't want to travel alone in this area at night. One of the best-known *centri sociali* in Rome—your one-stop shop for all things countercultural. Hosts live music, films, art exhibits, poetry readings, African cuisine tastings, and more. Hours and cover vary (€8-10).

🔀 DAYTRIPS FROM ROME

PONZA

From Rome, take the train from Termini to Anzio (1hr.; every hr. 6am-11pm, €2.90) and then the Linee Vetor hydrofoil from Anzio to Ponza (1hr.; 3-5 per day 8:10am-5:15pm, return 9:50am-7pm; M-F €20, Sa-Su and Aug. €23.) Ticket office in Anzio is on the quay (☎ 06 984 50 85; www.vetor.it.). Autolinee Isola di Ponza buses leave from V. Dante (every 15-20min. until 1am; buy tickets from driver for €1). Follow C. Pisacane until it become V. Dante, past the tunnel; stop is to your left. Buses stop by request; flag them down at stops. Pro Loco Tourist Office, V. Molo Musco, at the far right of the port, in the long red building next to the lighthouse. Offers tours of archaeological sights. (☎ 07 718 00 31; prolocoponza@liberto.it. Open in summer M-Sa 9am-1pm and 4-8:30pm, Su 9am-1pm and 5-8:10pm.)

As the largest of the Pontine Islands, Ponza was also the one most susceptible to pirate attacks, which were frequent until the arrival of the fierce and wealthy Bourbon monarchs in 1734. Pirates aside, *dunque, tutti siamo in vacanza:* we're all equal in the eyes of the sun gods. The laid-back island lifestyle has resulted in a happy disregard for signs, street names, or maps. The only streets you'll ever need to know are **Via Banchina Nuova,** which runs along the docks and changes into **Via Dante** on the other side of the **Sant'Antonio tunnel; Corso Pisacane,** which runs along the port above the docks; **Via Molo Muscolo,** jutting out along the pier to your right as you face the water; and **Piazza Carlo Pisacane,** where V. Molo Muscolo meets C. Pisacane. *Isole Pontine,* a comprehensive guide to the islands, is available at newsstands for €6.20.

Beaches are the reason for the season in Ponza. **Cala dello Schiavone** and **Cala Cecata** (on the bus line) are the best and most accessible spots. The most spectacular views on the island are available at **Chiaia di Luna,** an expansive, rocky beach set at the bottom of a 200-meter tufo cliffside. Another point of sunbathing interest is the **Piscine Naturale,** just a quick ride through Ponza's lovely hillside. *(Take the bus to Le Foma and ask to be let off at the Piscine. Cross the street and make your way down the long, steep path. Spiny sea urchins line the rocks, so take caution.)*

Hotel rooms in Ponza hover somewhere around the €100 mark, so *Let's Go* recommends forgoing hotels entirely and checking out one of the many *immobiliare vacanze* (vacation property) offices instead. The folks at **Isotur ❹,** Corso Pisacane

ITALY

18 can set you up with a double room with a bath, kitchen, terrace, and beautiful views of the port. (☎07 718 03 39; www.isotur.it. Open May M-F 9:30am-12:30pm and 4:30-8pm, Sa 9am-1pm and 4-8:30pm; June-Aug. daily 9:15am-8:30pm. €45-60.)

FRASCATI

A 15min. bus ride from Anagnina Station; the bus driver will let you off at the depot in P. Marconi, the town center. I.A.T. Tourist Office, P. Marconi 1 is across the street, next to the town hall. (Open M and W 9am-1pm; Tu, Th-Sa 9am-1pm and 4-7pm.)

Patrician villas dotting the hillside are a testament to the peculiar power of Frascati, and, possibly, of its superb dry white wines. The sculpture-filled gardens of the **Villa Aldobrandini** dominate the hills over P. Marconi, while a 1km walk up on F. Massaia leads to the tiny **Chiesa dei Cappuccini.** A sign above the door announces that you need reservations for marriages, but the **Ethiopian Museum** next door requires no such foresight. It houses a collection of weapons, handmade crafts, and the death mask of the cardinal who collected the artifacts while doing missionary work. *(Open daily 9am-noon and 4-6pm. Free.)*

The town of **Tusculum** was an ancient resort for the who's who of ancient Roman society, including Cicero and Cato. From the entrance of the Villa Aldobrandini, turn right onto V. Tusculo, which climbs 5km over winding country roads to reach the ruins of the collection of villas.

THE VENETO

From the rocky foothills of the Dolomites to the fertile valleys of the Po River, the Veneto region has a geography as diverse as its historical influences. Once loosely linked under the Venetian Empire, these towns retained their cultural independence, and visitors are more likely to hear regional dialects than standard Italian when neighbors gossip across their geranium-bedecked windows. The sense of local culture and custom that remains strong within each town may surprise visitors lured to the area by Venice, the *bella* of the north.

VENICE (VENEZIA)   ☎041

There is a mystical quality to Venice's decadence: her lavish palaces stand proudly on a steadily sinking network of wood, treading in the clouded waters of age-old canals lapping at the feet of her abandoned front doors. Venice's labyrinthine streets lead to a treasury of Renaissance art, housed in scores of palaces, churches, and museums that are themselves architectural delights. But the same streets that once earned the name *La Serenissima* (Most Serene) are now saturated with visitors, as Venice grapples with an economy reliant on the same tourism that forces more and more of the native population away every year. Still, Romanticism dies hard, and the sinking city persists beyond the summer crowds and polluted waters, united by winding canals and the memory of a glorious past.

▐▀ TRANSPORTATION

The **train station** is on the northwest edge of the city; be sure to get off at **Santa Lucia,** *not* Mestre on the mainland. Buses and boats arrive at **Piazzale Roma,** just across the Canal Grande from the train station. To get from either station to **Piazza San Marco** or the **Ponte di Rialto** (Rialto Bridge), take *vaporetto* #82 or follow the signs for the 40min. walk—from the train station, exit left on Lista di Spagna.

Flights: Aeroporto Marco Polo (VCE; ☎041 260 61 11; www.veniceairport.it), 10km north of the city. Ticket office open daily 5:30am-9:30pm. Take the **ATVO shuttlebus** (☎041 520 55 30) from the airport to Piazzale Roma (30min., 2 per hr., €2.70).

Trains: Stazione - Santa Lucia, northwest corner of the city. Open daily 3:45am-12:30am. **Info office** at the left as you exit the platforms, open daily 7am-9pm. To: **Bologna** (2hr., 1 per hr., €7.90-18.33); **Florence** (3hr., every 2hr., €26.60); **Milan** (3hr., 1-2 per hr., €12.40); and **Rome** (4½hr., 5 per day, €45).

Buses: ACTV, on Piazzale Roma (☎041 528 78 86). The local line for buses and boats. Long-distance carrier buses run to nearby cities. Ticket office open daily 6:30am-11pm. ACTV offers a 3-day **discount vaporetto pass** (€13) to Rolling Venice cardholders.

Public Transportation: The **Canal Grande** can be crossed on foot only at the Scalzi, Rialto, and Accademia *ponti* (bridges). Most **vaporetti** (water buses) run 5am-midnight, the *Notte* line 11:30pm-5:30am. Single-ride €3.10. 24hr. *biglietto turistico* pass €9.30, 3-day €18.10 (€12.95 with Rolling Venice Card), 7-day €31. Buy tickets from booths in front of *vaporetto* stops, self-serve dispensers at the ACTV office in Piazzale Roma and the Rialto stop, or from the conductor. Pick up extra *non timbrati* (non-validated) tickets for when the booths aren't open. Validate them yourself before boarding to avoid a fine. **Lines #82** (faster) and **#1** (slower) run from the station down Canale Grande and Canale della Giudecca; **line #52** goes from the station through Canale della Giudecca to Lido and along the city's northern edge, then back to the station; **line #12** runs from Fond. Nuove to Murano, Burano, and Torcello.

■ 🛈 ORIENTATION AND PRACTICAL INFORMATION

Venice spans 118 bodies of land in a lagoon and is connected to the mainland by a thin causeway. Venice is a veritable labyrinth and can confuse even its natives, most of whom simply set off in a general direction and then patiently weave their way through the city. If you follow their example by ungluing your eyes from your map and going with the flow, you'll discover some of the unexpected surprises that make Venice spectacular. A few tips will help you to orient yourself. Locate the following landmarks on a map: **Ponte di Rialto** (the bridge in the center), **Piazza San Marco** (central south), the **Ponte Accademia** (bridge in the southwest), **Ferrovia** (the train station, in the northwest), and **Piazzale Roma** (directly south of the station). The Canal Grande snakes through the city, creating six *sestieri* (sections): Cannaregio, Castello, Santa Croce, San Polo, San Marco, and Dorsoduro. Within each *sestiere*, there are no street numbers—door numbers in a section form one long, haphazard set, consisting of around 6000 numbers. While these boundaries are nebulous, they can give you a general sense of location. **Cannaregio** is in the north and includes the train station, Jewish ghetto, and Cà d'Oro; **Castello** extends east toward the Arsenale; **San Marco** fills in the area between the Ponte di Rialto and Ponte Accademia; **Dorsoduro,** across the bridge from S. Marco, stretches the length of Canale della Giudecca and up to Campo S. Pantalon; **San Polo** runs north from Chiesa S. Maria dei Frari to the Ponte di Rialto; and **San Croce** lies west of S. Polo, across the Canal Grande from the train station. If *sestiere* boundaries prove too vague, Venice's **parrochie** (parishes) provide a more defined idea of where you are; *parrochia* signs, like *sestiere* signs, are painted on the sides of buildings.

TOURIST, FINANCIAL, AND LOCAL SERVICES

Tourist Office: APT, Calle della Ascensione, P.S. Marco 71/F (☎/fax 041 529 87 40; www.tourismovenezia.it), directly opposite the Basilica. Open M-Sa 9:30am-3:30pm. The APT desk at the nearby **Venice Pavilion,** Giardini E Reali, S. Marco 2 (☎041 522 51 50) sells ACTV tickets. Open daily 9am-6pm.

ITALY

Venice

🏠 **ACCOMMODATIONS**

Allogi Gerotto Calderan, **3**
Domus Civica (ACISJF), **14**
Foresteria Valdesi, **15**
Hotel Galleria, **20**
Locanda Ca'San Marcuola, **7**
Ostello Santa Fosca, **2**

🍴 **FOOD**

Ae Oche, **10**
Antica Birraria La Carte, **13**
Cantinone del Vino, **21**
Cantina Do Mori, **11**
Due Colonne, **12**
Gelateria Nico, **22**
Pizza al Volo, **18**
Ristorante Brek, **6**
STANDA Supermarket, **8**
Trattoria da Bepi, **9**

🍺 **NIGHTLIFE**

Bar Santa Lucia, **4**
Café Blue, **16**
Casanova, **5**
Duchamp, **19**
Il Caffé, **17**
Paradiso Perduto, **1**

AVA (☎041 171 52 88), in the train station, to the right of the tourist office. Makes same-day room reservations for €0.55. Open in daily 9am-10pm. Offices also in Piazzale Roma (☎041 523 13 79) and the airport (☎541 51 33). Call for reservations.

Rolling Venice Card: Offers discounts at over 200 restaurants, cafes, hotels, museums, and shops. Ages 14-29 only. Tourist office provides list of participating vendors. Cards cost €2.60 and are valid for one year from date of purchase. The card is sponsored by ACTV and can be purchased at the **ACTV VeLa** office (☎041 274 7650) in the Piazzale Roma, open daily 8:30am-6pm. The card is also available at any APT tourist office, and ACTV VeLa kiosks next to the Ferrovia, Rialto, S. Marco, and Vallaresso *vaporetto* stops.

Budget Travel: CTS, Fondamenta Tagliapietra, Dorsoduro, 3252 (☎041 520 5660; www.cts.it). From Campo S. Barnaba, cross the bridge and follow the road through the piazza. Turn left at the foot of the large bridge. Sells discounted student plane tickets and issues ISIC cards. English spoken. Open M-F 9:30am-1:30pm and 2:30-6pm.

Currency Exchange: Money exchangers charge high prices for service. Use banks whenever possible and inquire about fees beforehand. The streets around S. Marco and S. Polo are full of banks and ATMs. Many 24hr. automatic change machines, outside banks and next to ATMs, offer low commissions and decent rates.

EMERGENCY AND COMMUNICATIONS

Emergency: ☎113. **First Aid:** ☎118.

Police: ☎113. **Carabinieri (civil corps):** Campo S. Zaccaria, Castello, 4693/A (☎112). **Questura,** V. Nicoladi 24 (☎041 271 55 11). Contact the Questura if you have a serious complaint about your hotel.

Pharmacy: Farmacia Italo Inglese, Calle della Mandola, S. Marco, 3717 (☎041 522 4837), Follow C. Cortesia out of Campo Manin. Open M-F 9am-12:30pm and 3:45-7:30pm, Sa 9am-12:30pm. Late-night and weekend pharmacies rotate; check the list posted in the window of any pharmacy.

Hospital: Ospedale Civile, Campo S.S. Giovanni e Paolo, Castello (☎041 529 4111).

Internet Access: The NetGate, Crosera S. Pantalon, Dorsoduro, 3812/A (☎041 244 0213). From Santa Frari, take C. Scalater to C. Pantalon and follow signs for C. Margherita. €4 for 1hr. Open M-F 10am-8pm, Sa 10am-10pm, Su 2-10pm. AmEx/MC/V.

Post Office: Poste Venezia Centrale, Salizzada Fontego dei Tedeschi, S. Marco, 5554 (☎041 271 71 11), off Campo S. Bartolomeo. Open M-Sa 8:30am-6:30pm.

Postal Codes: S. Marco: 30124; Castello: 30122; S. Polo, S. Croce, and Canareggio: 30121; Dorsoduro: 30123.

ACCOMMODATIONS

Religious institutions around the city offer both dorms and private rooms during the summer for about €25-70. Options include **Casa Murialdo,** Fondamenta Madonna dell'Orto, Cannaregio 3512 (☎041 719 933); **Casa Capitania,** S. Croce 561 (☎520 3099; open June-Sept.); **Patronato Salesiano Leone XIII,** Calle S. Domenico, Castello 1281 (☎240 3611); **Domus Cavanis,** Dorsoduro 896 (☎041 528 7374), near the Accademia Bridge; **Ostello Santa Fosoa,** Cannaregio 2372 (☎041 715 775); **Instituto Canossiano,** F. delle Romite, Dorsoduro 1323 (☎041 240 9711); and **Instituto Ciliota,** Calle Muneghe S. Stefano, S. Marco 2976 (☎041 520 4888).

CANNAREGIO AND SANTA CROCE

The station area, around the Lista di Spagna, has some of the best budget accommodations in Venice. At night the streets bustle with young travelers and students, even though the area is a 20 min. *vaporetto* ride from most major sights.

▨ **Alloggi Gerotto Calderan,** Campo S. Geremia, 283 (☎041 71 55 62; www.casagerottocalderan.com). Great bargains. 34 big, bright rooms. 4 clean common bathrooms per floor. Internet €3.10 per 30min. Check-out 10am. Curfew 12:30am for dorms, 1am for private rooms. Reserve at least 15 days in advance. Dorms €21; singles €31-41; doubles €46-72, with bath €78-108; triples €78-108/€120. ❷

▨ **Locanda Ca'San Marcuola,** Campo S. Marcuola, Cannaregio, 1763 (☎041 71 60 48; www.casanmarcuola.com). From the Lista di Spagna, follow signs for S. Marcuola. This homey 17th century Venetian house has clean, bright rooms, completely refurbished for

ITALY

Central Venice

FOOD
Harry's Bar, **9**
La Boutique Del Gelato, **3**
Rosticceria San Bartolomeo, **1**
Vino, Vino, **8**

ACCOMMODATIONS
Albergo Casa Petrarca, **6**
Albergo San Samuele, **7**
Hotel Bruno, **2**
Locanda Ca' Foscari, **5**

NIGHTLIFE
Inkshark Irish Pub, **4**
Piccolo Mondo, **10**

supreme comfort. For a real treat, the *doppia superiore* (€140-180; for 3, €180-200) has a soaring ceiling with a chandelier and balcony view of canal. All rooms with A/C, TV, and bath. Free Internet. Handicapped-accessible elevator. Breakfast included. Singles €51-80; doubles €100-130; triples €140-180. AmEx/MC/V. ❹

Ostello Santa Fosca, Fondamenta Canale, Cannaregio, 2372 (☎/fax 041 71 57 75; www.santafosca.it). From the Lista di Spagna left, turn into Campo S. Fosca. Cross 1st bridge and turn left onto Fondamenta Canale. Student-operated, quiet, and church-affiliated. July-Sept. 140 beds available; Oct.-June 31 beds. July-Sept. reception daily 7am-noon and 6-11pm. Oct.-June reception daily 8am-noon and 5-8pm; curfew 1am. Dorms €18; singles €21; doubles €42. €2 discount with ISIC or Rolling Venice. ❷

Instituto Cannosiano, Ponte Piccolo, Giudecca, 428 (☎/fax 041 522 2157). From the Palanca stop on *vaporetto* #82, walk left over the bridge. **Women only.** 35 beds. Lockout 12-3pm. Strict curfew 10:30pm; off-season 10pm. Large dorms €13. ❶

SAN MARCO AND SAN POLO

Surrounded by exclusive shops, souvenir stands, scores of *trattorie* and *pizzerie*, and many of Venice's most popular sights, these accommodations are the most expensive choices for those who seek Venice's showy, tourist-oriented side.

Albergo San Samuele, S. Marco, 3358 (☎/fax 041 522 8045). Follow Calle delle Botteghe from Campo S. Stefano and turn left on Salizzada S. Samuele. A crumbling stone courtyard leads to this charming, fabulously priced hotel. Colorful, clean rooms with sparkling bathrooms. 8 rooms with gorgeous balcony views of S. Marco's red rooftops; 2 rooms downstairs without view are more spacious. Reserve 1-2 months ahead. Singles €26-45; doubles €36-70, with bath €46-100; triples €62-135. ❸

Albergo Casa Petrarca, Calle Schiavine, S. Marco, 4386 (☎/fax 041 520 0430). From Campo St. Luca, follow C. Fuseri; take your second left and then a right. A tiny hotel with 7 small, clean rooms. Bright and cheery sitting room with rows of books in English overlooks an alley of salmon-colored houses. Fans in each room. Breakfast €7. 4 rooms with bath. Singles €44; doubles €88. Discounts for extended stays. ❹

Domus Civica (ACISJF), Campiello Chiovere Frari, S. Polo, 3082 (☎041 72 11 03; fax 041 522 7139). From the station, cross the Scalzi Bridge and turn right. Turn left on Fondamenta dei Tolentini, then left through the courtyard onto Corte Amai. The hostel is the building with the rounded facade on the right after the bridge. Simple student housing. Check-in 7:30am-2pm. Curfew 11:30pm. Open mid-June to Sept. Singles €29, with Rolling Venice or ISIC €23; doubles and triples €26/€21 per person. ❸

CASTELLO

A room with a view of red rooftops and breakhtaking sights is worth the inevitability of losing your way amongst the narrow, tightly clustered streets of Castello.

▨ **Foresteria Valdesi**, Castello, 5170 (☎041 528 6797; www.chiesavaldese.org/venezia). From Campo S. Maria Formosa, take Calle Lunga S. Maria. Housed in the Palazzo Cavagnis, immediately over the 1st bridge. Frescoed ceilings grace both the 33-bed dorms and the private rooms. Breakfast included. Reception daily 9am-1pm and 6-8pm. Lockout 10am-1pm. No curfew. Closed Nov. Dorms €20 first night, €19 each additional night; doubles €54-70; quads €98. Also has 2 apartments with bath and kitchen, €99-110. €1 Rolling Venice discount. MC/V. ❷

Hotel Bruno, Salizzada S. Lio, Castello, 5726/A (☎041 523 0452; www.hoteldabruno.it). From Campo S. Bartolomeo, take the Salizzada S. Lio and cross the bridge. High-ceilinged rooms decorated in elaborate Venetian style. All with bath and A/C. Breakfast included. Singles €60-155; doubles €80-210; triples €120-260. MC/V. ❺

DORSODURO

Spartan facades and peaceful canals trace the quieter, wider streets of Dorsoduro. Numerous art museums draw visitors to canal-front real estate, but the interior remains a little-visited residential quarter.

Hotel Galleria, Rio Terra Antonio Foscarini, Dorsoduro, 878/A (☎041 523 2489; www.hotelgalleria.it), on the left as you face the Accademia museum. Sumptuous oriental rugs and tasteful art prints lend the Galleria an elegance appropriate to its location on the Grand Canal. Stunning views from the 10 rooms compensate for their small size. Breakfast included. Singles €62; doubles €88-135. AmEx/MC/V. ❺

Locanda Ca' Foscari, Calle della Frescada, Dorsoduro, 3887b (☎041 71 04 01; altersc@tin.it), in a quiet neighborhood near the *vaporetto*. From *vaporetto*: San Tomà, turn left at the dead end, cross the bridge, turn right, and then take a left into the little alleyway. Chandeliers and Carnevale masks embellish this simple hotel. Breakfast included. Curfew 1am. Book 2-3 months in advance. Closed 1st week of Aug. and Nov.-Dec. Singles €60; doubles €70-90; triples €87-110; quads €108-130. MC/V. ❹

CAMPING

If camping, plan on a 20min. boat ride to Venice. In addition to these listings, the **Litorale del Cavallino,** on the Lido's Adriatic side, has endless beach campsites.

Camping Miramare, Lungomare Dante Alighieri 29 (☎041 96 61 50; www.camping-miramare.it). A 40min. boat ride (*vaporetto* #14) from P. S. Marco to Punta Sabbioni. Campground is 700m along the beach to your right. 3-night min. stay in high-season. Open mid-Mar. to Dec. €3.60-5.85 per person, €3.25-14.20 per tent. Bungalows €23.20-58.50. 15% Rolling Venice discount. ❶

Camping Fusina, V. Moranzani 79 (☎041 547 0055; www.camping-fusina.com), in Malcontenta. From Mestre, take bus #1. Call ahead. €6 per person, €8-13 per tent and car, €11 to sleep in car. ❶

🗋 FOOD

In Venice, dining well on a budget requires exploration. The best and most affordable restaurants are hidden in the less-traveled alleyways. For an inexpensive and informal option, visit any *osteria* or *bacario* in town and create a meal from the vast array of **cicchetti** (meat- and cheese-filled pastries; €1-3), tidbits of seafood, rice, meat, and *tramezzini* (triangular slices of soft white bread with any imaginable filling). The key ingredients of Venetian cuisine come fresh from the sea. *Spaghetti al vongole* (pasta with fresh clams and spicy vegetables) is served on nearly every menu. Good local wines include the sparkling *prosecco della Marca* white wine or the red *valpolicella*. **STANDA supermarket,** Strada Nuova, Cannaregio, 3650, near Campo S. Felice, has a large grocery store in the back, behind the clothing. (Open M-Sa 8:30am-7:20pm, Su 9am-7:20pm.)

RESTAURANTS

Trattoria da Bepi, Cannaregio, 4550. Traditional Venetian restaurant with copper pots dangling from the ceiling. Huge bread baskets and authentic cuisine. *Primi* €7-10.50, *secondi* €9.50-18. Open F-W noon-2:30pm, 7-10pm. MC/V. ❸

Ristorante Brek, Lista di Spagna, Cannaregio, 124a. Italian fast-food chain whips up fresh pasta and salad dishes from an extensive array of ingredients that you pick out. Perfect for a fast, cheap meal on the go. Menu and prices change daily. €2-8. 11:30am-10:30pm. ❷

Vino, Vino, Ponte delle Veste, S. Marco, 2007A. Dark, no-frills wine bar has over 350 varieties of wine. Seafood-focused menu changes daily. *Primi* €5, *secondi* €9. Open daily 10:30am-midnight. 15% Rolling Venice discount. ❸

Rosticceria San Bartomoleo, Calle della Bissa, S. Marco, 5424a. Offers a smorgasbord of sandwiches, pasta, and *cicchetti* to be enjoyed on the go or seated at a window booth. The full-service restaurant upstairs is open for lunch. Entrees start at €4.90. Open Tu-Su 9:30am-9:30pm. AmEx/MC/V. ❶

Harry's Bar, Calle Vallaresso, S. Marco 1323. This cafe pours pricey drinks to tourists and such notables as Ernest Hemingway, Katharine Hepburn, Robert DeNiro, and Tom Cruise. *Bellini* €13. Service 15%. Open daily 10:30am-11pm. MC/V. ❹

Pizza al Volo, Campo S. Margherita, Dorsoduro, 2944. Serves delicious, cheap pizza. The tasty house specialty is a sauceless pie topped with *mozzarella, grado,* and eggplant. Slices from €1.30. Large pizzas from €3.40. Take-out only. Open daily 11:30am-4pm and 5:30pm-1:30am. ❶

Cantinone del Vino, Fondamente Meraviglie, Dorsoduro, 992. A spectacular display of wines, featured in Gourmet Magazine, line the walls, ranging in price from €3-200 a bottle. Enjoy a glass at the bar with some *cicchetti* from €1. Open M-Sa 8am-2:30pm and 3:15-8:30pm. ❷

Ae Oche, Santa Croce, 1552a/b. Choose from 100 different types of huge pizzas (€4-7). Open daily noon-3pm, 7pm-midnight. MC/V. ❷

Antica Birraria La Carte, Campo S. Polo, S. Polo, 2168. Lively restaurant popular with Venetian students. Musicians play nightly on their accordions just outside. Beer €1.50-4.30; pizzas €4-8. Open Tu-Su noon-3pm and 6pm-midnight. AmEx/MC/V. ❷

Due Colonne, Campo S. Agostin, S. Polo, 2343. Students, families, and tourists crowd the large indoor booths and the *campo* seating to sample the variety of pizzas (€3.50-7.50). Cover €0.80. Service 10%. Closed Aug. Open M-Sa 8am-3pm and 7-11pm. Kitchen closes 10pm. ❶

Cantina Do Mori, Calle due Mori, S. Polo, 429. Venice's oldest wine bar may be a tourist attraction, but it is still an elegant place to grab a a few *cicchetti* (from €1.50) or a superb glass of local wine. No seating. Open M-Sa 9am-9pm. ❷

GELATERIE

 La Boutique del Gelato, Salizzada S. Lio, Castello, 5727. Large cones with the cheapest prices. Single scoop €0.80. Open daily 10am-8pm.

Gelateria Nico, Fondamenta Zattere, Dorsoduro, 922. Great view of the Giudecca Canal. Try the Venetian specialty *gianduiotto al passagetto* (a slice of dense chocolate-hazelnut ice cream dunked in whipped cream, €2.30). Gelato €0.80-6.50. Open daily 6:45am-11pm.

◎ SIGHTS

AROUND THE RIALTO BRIDGE

CANAL GRANDE. The Canal Grande loops through Venice, and the splendid facades of the *palazzi* that crown its banks testify to the city's history of immense wealth. Although their external decorations vary, the palaces share the same basic structure. A **nighttime tour** reveals the startling beauty of the *palazzi*. *(Vaporetto #82 or #1: P.S. Marco.)*

PONTE DI RIALTO. The Ponte di Rialto (1588-91) arches over the Canal Grande, symbolizing Venice's commercial past. Antonio da Ponte created this image that graces postcards throughout the city. *(Vaporetto: Rialto.)*

CHIESA DI SAN GIACOMO DI RIALTO. Between the Ponte di Rialto and the markets stands Venice's first church, diminutively called "San Giacometto." The bent stone statue was once the finish line for convicted thieves after they had run naked from P.S. Marco, lashed all the way by bystanders. *(Vaporetto: Rialto. Cross the bridge and head right. Open daily 10am-5pm. Free.)*

THE LOCAL STORY

THE AGE OF JANUARIUS

Dr. Luigi Garlaschelli is an organic chemist at the University of Pavia who, in his spare time, investigates the authenticity of blood relics.

Q: Can you explain the ubiquitousness of relics in Italian churches?
A: In the Middle Ages, it was believed that they would protect the city from its enemies. [Relics include] the last breath of St. Joseph, the feather of the Archangel Michael, the milk of the Virgin Mary, and the fingernails and blood of Christ.

Q: What was your first project?
A: My first work was on the blood of St. Januarius, which is contained in a small vial kept in the duomo in Naples. Januarius was beheaded in 305 AD. The relic appeared in the Middle Ages, 1000 years later. Normally blood taken from a living body will clot only once; the "miracle" of this blood is that it liquefies twice a year during religious ceremonies.

Q: How does that work?
A: Well, using an iron salt, which exists naturally near active volcanoes (like Vesuvius, near Naples, active at the time of the discovery of the blood), kitchen salt, and techniques available in the Middle Ages, we were able make a substance of the same color and properties as the reputed blood of St. Januarius. The matter would be closed were we to open the vial and take a sample. But, of course, the vial is sealed.

See http://chifis.unipv.it/garlaschelli for more information on Dr. Garlaschelli's research.

AROUND PIAZZA SAN MARCO

■ **BASILICA DI SAN MARCO.** The interior of this glittering church sparkles with both 13th-century Byzantine and 16th-century Renaissance mosaics. Behind the altar screen is the **Pala D'Oro,** a gem-encrusted relief covering the tomb of Saint Mark. To the right of the altar is the **tesoro** (treasury), a hoard of gold and relics from the Fourth Crusade. Steep stairs in the atrium lead to the **Galleria della Basilica,** which offers a staggering perspective on the interior mosaics, a tranquil vista of the exterior *piazza,* and an intimate view of the original bronze *Horses of St. Mark.* St. Mark's is worth the long lines; visit in the early morning for the shortest wait, or at dusk for the best natural illumination of the mosaics. *(Basilica open daily 9:30am-4:30pm. Dress code enforced. Free. Pala D'Oro open daily 9:45am-5pm. €1.50. Treasury open M-Sa 9:45am-5pm. €2. Galleria open daily 9:45am-5pm. €1.50.)*

■ **PALAZZO DUCALE.** (Doge's Palace.) Once the home of Venice's *doge* (mayor), the Palazzo Ducale now houses one of Venice's best museums. Within the palace lie the *doge's* private apartments and the magnificent state rooms of the Republic. Climb the richly decorated Scala d'Oro (Golden Staircase) to reach the Sala del Maggior Consiglio (Great Council Room), dominated by Tintoretto's *Paradise,* the largest oil painting in the world. Passages lead through the courtrooms of the much-feared Council of Ten and the even-more-feared Council of Three, crossing the Ponte dei Sospiri (Bridge of Sighs) and continuing into the prisons. *(☎041 520 9070; mkt.musei@comune.venezia.it. Wheelchair accessible. Open Nov.-Apr. daily 9am-3:30pm, Apr.-Oct. 9am-5:30pm. €9.50, students €5.50, ages 6-14 €3. Audio guides €5.50.)*

■ **PIAZZA SAN MARCO.** In contrast to the narrow, labyrinthine streets that wind through most of Venice, P.S. Marco (Venice's only official *piazza*) is a magnificent expanse of light and space. Enclosing the *piazza* are the unadorned 16th-century Renaissance **Procuratie Vecchie (Old Treasury Offices),** the more ornate 17th-century Baroque **Procuratie Nuove (New Treasury Offices),** and the smaller Neoclassical **Ala Napoleonica,** sometimes called the *Procuratie Nuovissime* (Really New Treasury Offices), which Napoleon constructed when he took the city in 1797. The brick **campanile** (96m) across the *piazza* stands on Roman foundations. *(Campanile open daily 9am-9pm. €6. Audioguide for 1 €3, for 2 €4.)*

CHIESA DI SAN ZACCARIA. Dedicated to the father of John the Baptist and designed by (among others) Coducci in the late 1400s, this Gothic-Renaissance church holds one of the masterpieces of Venetian Renaissance painting, **Giovanni Bellini**'s *Virgin and Child Enthroned with Four Saints*. *(☎041 522 1257. Vaporetto: S. Zaccaria. From P.S. Marco, turn left along the water, cross the bridge, and turn left on Calle Albanesi. Take a right and go straight. Open daily 10am-noon and 4-6pm. Free.)*

SAN POLO

▨ BASILICA DI SANTA MARIA GLORIOSA DEI FRARI. Within the cavernous brick walls of this church rest outstanding paintings by masters of the Renaissance. ▨**Titian's** *Assumption* (1516-18) on the high altar marks the height of the Venetian Renaissance. In the Florentine chapel to the right is Donatello's *St. John the Baptist* (1438), a wooden Renaissance sculpture. *(Vaporetto: S. Tomà. Follow signs back to Campo dei Frari. Open M-Sa 9am-6pm, Su 1-6pm. €2.)*

SCUOLA GRANDE DI SAN ROCCO. Venice's most illustrious *scuola*, or guild hall, stands as a monument to painter Jacopo Tintoretto. The *scuola* commissioned Tintoretto to complete all of the building's paintings, a task that took 23 years. *(Behind Basilica dei Frari in Campo S. Rocco. ☎523 4864. Open Nov.-Mar. M-F 10am-1pm, Sa-Su 10am-4pm. €5.50, students €3.75. Audioguides free.)*

DORSODURO

▨ GALLERIE DELL'ACCADEMIA. The Accademia houses the most extensive collection of Venetian art in the world. At the top of the double staircase, **Room I,** topped by a ceiling full of cherubim, houses Venetian Gothic art, with a luxurious use of color that influenced Venetian painting for centuries. Among the enormous altarpieces in **Room II,** Giovanni Bellini's *Madonna Enthroned with Child, Saints, and Angels* stands out for its lush serenity. **Rooms IV** and **V** display more Bellinis and **Giorgione's** enigmatic *La Tempesta*. On the opposite wall is Titian's last painting, a brooding *Pietà*. In **Room XX,** works by Gentile Bellini and Carpaccio display Venetian processions and cityscapes so accurately that scholars use them as "photos" of Venice's past. *(☎041 522 2247. Vaporetto: Accademia. Open M 8:15am-2pm, T-Su 9:15am-7:15pm. €6.50. Guided tours free for groups.)*

▨ COLLEZIONE PEGGY GUGGENHEIM. Guggenheim's Palazzo Venier dei Leoni now displays works by Brancusi, Marini, Kandinsky, Picasso, Magritte, Rothko, Ernst, Pollock, and Dalí. The Marini sculpture *Angel in the City*, in front of the *palazzo*, was designed with a detachable penis. Guggenheim occasionally modified this sculpture so as not to offend her more prudish guests. *(☎041 240 5411. Calle S. Cristoforo, Dorsoduro 710. Vaporetto: Accademia. Turn left and follow the yellow signs. Open Su-M and W-F 10am-6pm, Sa 10am-10pm. €8, under 12 free. Audioguides €4.)*

CHIESA DI SAN SEBASTIANO. The painter Veronese hid here when he fled Verona in 1555 after allegedly killing a man, and filled the church with some of his finest works. His breathtaking *Stories of Queen Esther* covers the ceiling. *(Vaporetto: S. Basilio. Open M-Sa 10am-5pm, Su 3-5pm. €2.)*

CASTELLO

CHIESA DI SANTISSIMI GIOVANNI E PAOLO. This immense church is the final resting place of 25 *doges*, its walls lined with monuments to them and other honored citizens. Outside stands the bronze **statue of Bartolomeo Colleoni,** a mercenary who left his inheritance to the city on the condition that a monument to him be erected in front of S. Marco. The city, unwilling to honor him in such a grand space, decided to pull a fast one and place the statue in front of the Scuola di San Marco. *(☎041 523 5913. Vaporetto: Fond. Nuove. Turn left, then right onto Fond. dei Mendicanti. Open M-Sa 7:30am-12:30pm and 3:30-7pm, Su 3-6pm. Free)*

CHIESA DI SANTA MARIA DEI MIRACOLI. Among the most stunning Venetian churches, this Renaissance jewel was designed by the Lombardos in the late 1400s. *(From S.S. Giovanni e Paolo, cross Ponte Rosse. Open M-Sa 10am-5pm, Su 1-5pm. €2.)*

GIARDINI PUBLICI AND SANT'ELENA. Those who long for trees and grass can stroll through the Public Gardens, installed by Napoleon, or bring a picnic lunch to the shady lawns of Sant'Elena. *(Vaporetto: Giardini or S. Elena. Free.)*

CANNAREGIO

JEWISH GHETTO. In 1516 the *doge* forced Venice's Jewish population into the old cannon-foundry area, creating the first Jewish ghetto in Europe; the word "ghetto" is the Venetian word for "foundry." The oldest *schola* (synagogue), **Schola Grande Tedesca (German Synagogue)**, shares a building with the **Museo Ebraica di Venezia (Hebrew Museum of Venice)** in the Campo del Ghetto Nuovo. *(Cannaregio, 2899b. ☎041 71 53 59. Vaporetto: S. Marcuola. Follow the signs straight ahead and then turn left into Campo del Ghetto Nuovo. Hebrew Museum: open June-Sept. Su-F 10am-7pm; €3, students €2. Entrance to synagogues by guided tour only (40min.). English tours leave from the museum every hr. from 10:30am-4:30pm. Museum and tour €8, students €6.50.)*

CÀ D'ORO AND GALLERIA GIORGIO FRANCHETTI. The most spectacular facade on the Canal Grande and the premiere example of Venetian Gothic, the Cà d'Oro, built between 1425 and 1440, now houses the Giorgio Franchetti collection. For the best view of the palace, take the *traghetto* across the canal to the Rialto Markets. *(Vaporetto: Ca' d'Oro. ☎041 523 8790. Open M-Su 9am-2pm. €3.50.)*

GIUDECCA AND SAN GIORGIO MAGGIORE

BASILICA DI SAN GIORGIO MAGGIORE. Standing on its own monastic island, S. Giorgio Maggiore contrasts sharply with most other Venetian churches. Palladio ignored the Venetian fondness for color and decorative excess, constructing an austere church of simple dignity. Ascend the elevator to the top of the **campanile** for a breathtaking view. *(Vaporetto: S. Giorgio Maggiore. ☎041 522 7827. Open M-Sa 10am-12:30pm and 2:30-4:30pm. Basilica free. Campanile €3. Pay the Brother in the elevator.)*

ISLANDS OF THE LAGOON

BURANO. In this traditional fishing village, fishermen haul in their catch every morning as their black-clad wives sit in the doorways of the fantastically colored houses, creating unique knots of Venetian lace. The small *Scuola di Merletti di Burano* (Lace Museum) displays their handiwork. *(A 40min. boat ride from Venice. Vaporetto #12: Burano from either S. Zaccaria or Fond. Nuove. Museum in P. Galuppi. ☎041 73 00 34. Open W-M 10am-5pm. €4. Included on Palazzo Ducale ticket or full museum pass.)*

MURANO. Famous for its glass since 1292, the island of Murano affords visitors the opportunity to witness the glass-blowing process. The **Museo Vetrario** (Glass Museum) houses a splendid collection that includes pieces from Roman times. Farther down the street is the 12th-century **Basilica di Santa Maria e San Donato.** *(Vaporetto #12 or 52: Faro from S. Zaccaria. Museo Vetrario: Fond. Giustian 8. ☎041 73 95 86. Open Th-Tu 10am-5pm. €5, students €3. Basilica open daily 8am-noon and 4-7pm. Free.)*

LIDO. The Lido is now mostly a summer beach town, complete with cars, blaring radios, and beach bums. Head for the **public beach,** which features an impressive shipwreck at the southern end. *(Vaporetto: Lido.)*

▓ NIGHTLIFE

The weekly booklet, **A Guest in Venice** (free at hotels and tourist offices or online at www.unospitedivenezia.it), lists current festivals, concerts, and gallery shows. The famed **Biennale di Venezia**, a world-wide contemporary art exhibition, covers the *Giardini Publici* and the Arsenal in provocative international art every odd-numbered year. (☎241 1058; www.labiennale.org.) Venice's famous **Carnevale** draws masked figures and camera-happy tourists during the 10 days before Ash Wednesday, doubling the city's population by Mardi Gras. Student nightlife is concentrated around **Campo Santa Margherita** in Dorsoduro and the areas around the **Lista di Spagna** in Cannaregio.

▓ **Paradiso Perduto,** Fondamenta della Misericordia 2540. Students and locals flood this unassuming bar with conversation and laughter, while the young waitstaff doles out large portions of *cicchetti* (mixed plate €11). Live jazz Su. Open Th-Su 7pm-2am.

Piccolo Mondo, Accademia, Dorsoduro 1056a. With your back to the canal, facing the Accademia, turn right and follow the street around. Join in with the dance-happy students, locals, and tourists at this small, pumping discoteca where such notables as Shaquille O'Neil and Prince Albert of Monaco have strutted their stuff. No cover. Drinks start €7. Open nightly 10pm-4am. AmEx/MC/V.

Duchamp, C. Santa Margherita 3019. Lively place with students and tourists noisily congregating. Outdoor seating. Beer €4.30 per pint. Wine €1.10. Open nightly 9pm-2am, Sa 5pm-2am.

Casanova, Lista di Spagna, Cannaregio 158/A (www.casanova.it). Perpetual strobe lights and house and techno beats. Open daily 10pm-4am. F-Sa Cover €10; includes 1 drink. AmEx/MC/V.

Inishark Irish Pub, Calle Mondo Novo, Castello 5787. Most creative Irish pub in Venice with themed decorations. Guinness €4.65; Harp €4.50. Open Tu-Su 6pm-1:30am.

Il Caffè, Campo S. Margherita, Dorsoduro 2963. Music pumps at the door and people are stuffed inside of this tiny, nondescript bar. Outdoor seating. Wine €0.80, beer €1.35. Open M-Sa 8am-2am.

Café Blue, S. Pantalon, Dorsoduro 5778. Bright, noisy, and crowded American bar with droves of expats and exchange students. Free email kiosk. Afternoon tea in winter 3:30-7:30pm. Bar open M-Sa 9:30pm-2am.

Bar Santa Lucia, Lista di Spagna, Cannareggio 282b. This tiny bar stays crowded and noisy long into the night with American travelers and the locals who want to meet them. Good selection of Irish beers. Guinness €5. Wine €2.10. Open M-Sa 6pm-2am.

PADUA (PADOVA) ☎049

Book-toting students walk through sculpture-lined *piazze* in Padua, epitomizing the city's unique blend of ancient and modern culture. The ▓**Cappella degli Scrovegni** (Arena Chapel), P. Eremitani 8, contains Giotto's breathtaking 38-panel fresco cycle, illustrating the lives of Mary and Jesus. Buy tickets at the adjoining **Musei Civici Eremitani,** which features a restored Giotto crucifix. (☎049 820 45 50. Open Feb.-Oct. Tu-Su 9am-7pm; Nov.-Jan. Tu-Su 9am-6pm. Chapel open Feb.-Dec. daily 9am-7pm. €9, students €4.) Thousands of pilgrims are drawn to Saint Anthony's jawbone and well-preserved tongue at the **Basilica di Sant'Antonio,** in P. del Santo, a medieval conglomeration of eight domes filled with beautiful frescoes. (Dress code enforced. Open Apr.-Sept. daily 6:30am-8pm; Nov.-Mar. 6:30am-7pm. €2.) From the basilica, follow signs to V. Orto Botanico 15, for **Orto Botanico,** which tempts visitors with water lilies, medicinal herbs, and a 417-year-old palm tree that still offers shade. (☎049 65 66 14. Open daily 9am-1pm and 3-6pm; in winter M-F 9am-1pm. €2.60, students €1.55.) Next to the **duomo**, in P. Duomo, lies the 12th-century **Battistero**, the jewel of Padua, with a dome of highly concentrated frescoes. (☎049 66 28 14. Open M-Sa 7:30am-noon and 3:45-7:45pm, Su 7:45am-1pm and 3:45-8:30pm. €2.50, students €1.50.) Ancient university buildings are scattered throughout the city, centered in **Palazzo Bó**. For nighttime action, **Lucifer Young,** V. Altinate 89, near the university, is a hip young bar. (☎049 66 55 31. Open Su-Tu and Th 7pm-2am, F-Sa 7pm-4am.)

Trains depart from P. Stazione for: Bologna (1½hr., 1-2 per hr., €6); Milan (2½hr., 1-2 per hr., €17); Venice (30min., 3-4 per hr., €2.30); Verona (1hr., 1-2 per hr., €7). **Buses** (☎049 820 68 11) leave from P. Boschetti for Venice (45min., 2 per hr., €3.25). The **tourist office,** in the train station, sells the one-year **Biglietto Unico,** valid at most of Padua's museums. The *biglietto* is also available at participating sights. (☎049 875 20 77. Open M-Sa 9:15am-7pm, Su 9:30am-12:15pm. Biglietto €7.75, students €5.20.) Take bus #18 from the station to the stop after Prato della Valle; then walk 2 blocks, turn right on V. Marin, turn left on V. Torresino, turn right on V. Aleardi, and **Ostello Città di Padova (HI) ❶**, V. Aleardi 30, will be on the left. (☎049 875 22 19. Breakfast and sheets included. Reception 7-9:30am and 2:30-11pm. Curfew 11pm. Reserve 1 week in advance. Dorms €13.) **Hotel Al Santo ❹**, V. del Santo, 147, near the basilica, rents airy, well-kept rooms. (☎049 875 21 31. Breakfast included. Open Feb. to mid-Dec. Singles €52; doubles €90; triples €130. MC/V.) Join a lively crowd at **Pizzeria Al Borgo ❷**, V.L. Belludi 56, near the Basilica di S. Antonio. (Pizzas from €3.50. Open W-Su noon-3pm and 7-11:30pm.) **Postal Code:** 35100.

VERONA ☎045

A glorious combination of majestic Roman ruins, colorful Venetian facades, and orange rooftops, Verona is one of the most beautiful cities in Northern Italy. Gazing at the town from one of its many bridges at sunset sets the tone for romantic evenings befitting the home of *Romeo and Juliet*. Meanwhile, its artistic and historical treasures fill days with rewarding sightseeing.

🖪🖪 **TRANSPORTATION AND PRACTICAL INFORMATION. Trains** (☎045 800 08 61) go from P. XXV Aprile to: Bologna (2hr., every hr., €5.75); Milan (2hr., every hr., €6.85); and Venice (1¾hr., every hr., €5.75). The **tourist office,** in P. Brà, is on the left of the *piazza*. (☎806 86 80. Open daily 10am-7pm.) **Postal Code:** 37100.

🖪🖪 **ACCOMMODATIONS AND FOOD.** Reserve lodgings ahead, especially in opera season (June-Sept.). The **🖪Ostello della Gioventù (HI) ❶**, Villa Francescatti, Salita Fontana del Ferro 15, is in a renovated 16th-century villa with gorgeous gardens; from the station, take bus #73 or night bus #90 to P. Isolo, turn right, and follow the yellow signs uphill. (☎045 59 03 60. Breakfast included. 5-night max. stay. Check-in 5pm. Check-out 7-9am. Lockout 9am-5pm. Curfew 11pm; flexible for opera-goers. No reservations. Dorms €12.50.) Women can also try the beautiful **Casa della Giovane (ACISJF) ❶**, V. Pigna 7. (☎045 59 68 80. Reception 9am-11pm. Curfew 11pm; flexible for opera-goers. Dorms €11.50; singles €16.50; doubles €26.) To get to **Locanda Catullo ❹**, Vco. Catullo 1, walk to V. Mazzini, turn onto V. Catullo, and turn left on Vco. Catullo. (☎045 800 27 86. July-Sept. 3-night min. stay. Singles €37; doubles €52-62; triples €78-93.) Verona is famous for its wines, such as the dry white *soave* and red *valpolicella*. Prices in **Piazza Isolo** are cheaper than those in P. delle Erbe. **🖪Cantore**, V. A. Mario 2, has cheap, delicious food, including pizzas from €4.30. (Open Th-Tu noon-3pm and 4pm-midnight.) **Pam supermarket** is at V. dei Mutilati 3. (Open M-Sa 8:30am-8pm and Su 9am-1pm.)

◙ **SIGHTS.** The physical and emotional heart of Verona is the majestic, pink-marble, first-century **Arena** in P. Brà. (Open Tu-Su 8:30am-7:30pm. €3.10, students €2.10.) From P. Brà, V. Mazzini leads to the markets and stunning medieval architecture of **Piazza delle Erbe,** the former Roman forum. The 83m ◙**Torre dei Lamberti,** in P. dei Signori, offers a stunning view of Verona. (Open Tu-Su 9:30am-6pm. Elevator €2.60, students €2.10. Stairs €2.60.) The **Giardino Giusti,** V. Giardino Giusti 2, is a magnificent 16th-century garden with a labyrinth of mythological statues. (Open Apr.-Sept. daily 9am-8pm; Oct.-Mar. 9am-dusk. €4.50, students €3.50.) The della Scala fortress, **Castelvecchio,** down V. Roma from P. Brà, is filled with walkways, parapets, and an art collection that includes Pisanello's *Madonna and Child.* (Open Tu-Su 8:30am-7:30pm. €4.20, students €3.10; first Su of each month free.) Thousands of tourists have immortalized **Casa di Giulietta** (Juliet's House), V. Cappello 23, where the Capulet family never really lived. Don't waste money just to stand on the balcony. (Open Tu-Su 8:30am-7:30pm. €3.10, students €2.10.) From late June to early September, tourists and singers from around the world descend on the Arena for the city's annual **Opera Festival.** (☎045 800 51 51. General admission Su-Th €19.50, F-Sa €21.50.)

FRIULI-VENEZIA GIULIA

Friuli-Venezia Giulia traditionally receives less than its fair share of recognition, but this region has served as inspiration to a number of prominent literary figures. James Joyce lived in Trieste for 12 years, during which he wrote most of *Ulysses;* Ernest Hemingway drew part of the plot for *A Farewell to Arms* from the region's role in WWI; and Freud and Rilke both worked and wrote here. The city of Trieste attracts large numbers of tourists to the cheapest beach resorts on the Adriatic.

TRIESTE (TRIEST)   ☎040

In the post-Napoleonic real estate grab, the Austrians snatched Trieste (pop. 230,000); after a little more ping-pong, the city became part of Italy in 1954, but it still remains divided between its Slavic and Italian origins. While Trieste's fast-paced center, with Gucci-clad locals and bustling quays, is undeniably urban, the colors of the surrounding Carsoian hillside and the tranquil Adriatic Sea temper the metropolis with stunning natural beauty. The **Città Nuova,** a grid-like pattern of streets lined with crumbling Neoclassical palaces, centers around the **Canale Grande.** Facing the canal from the south is the striking Serbian Orthodox **Chiesa di San Spiridione.** (Dress modestly. Open Tu-Sa 9am-noon and 5-8pm.) The ornate **Municipio** complements the **Piazza dell'Unità d'Italia,** the largest *piazza* in Italy. Take bus #24 to the last stop (€0.90) to reach the 15th-century Venetian **Castello di San Giusto,** which presides over **Capitoline Hill,** south of P. Unità, the city's historical center, and includes a museum. From P. Goldoni, you can ascend the hill by the daunting 265 Steps of the Giants, or **Scala dei Giganti.** (☎040 31 36 36. Castle open daily 9am-sunset. Museum €1.55.) **Piazza della Cattedrale** overlooks the sea and downtown Trieste. The archaeological **Museo di Storia e d'Arte,** V. Cattedrale 15, is down the hill past the *duomo.* (☎040 37 05 00. Open Tu-Su 9am-1pm. €1.55.)

    Trains (☎379 47 37) leave P. della Libertà 8, down Corso Cavour from the quays, for Budapest (12hr., 2 per day, €71) and Venice (2hr., 2 per hr., €8.15). The **APT tourist office** is at P. dell'Unità d'Italia 4/E. (☎040 347 83 12; fax 040 347 83 20. Open M-Sa 7:30am-8:30pm.) **Hotel Alabarda ❸,** V. Valdirivo 22, is near the city center. From P. Oberdan, head down V. XXX Ottobre, and turn right onto V. Valdirivo. (☎040 63 02 69; fax 040 63 92 84. Singles €31-33; doubles €43-48. AmEx/MC/V.) To get from the station to **Ostello Tegeste (HI) ❶,** V. Miramare 331, 6km away just south from Castle Miramare, take bus #36 (€0.90), which leaves from across V. Miramare, and ask for the Ostello stop. From there, walk along the Barcola, following the seaside road toward the castle. (☎/fax 040 22 41 02. Breakfast included. Reception daily 8am-11:30pm. HI members only. Dorms €12.) For cheap food, stop by **Euro Spesa** supermarket at V. Valdirivo 13/F, off Corso Cavour. (Open M-Sa 8am-8pm.) **Pizzeria Barattolo ❶**, P.S. Antonio 2, along the canal, has a delicious sweet pizza crust. (☎ 63 14 80. Pizza €4.30-9.20. Open daily 8:30am-midnight.) **Postal Code:** 34100.

PIEDMONT (PIEMONTE)

Piedmont has been a politically influential region for centuries, as well as a fountainhead of fine food, wine, and nobility. After native-born Vittorio Emanuele II and Camillo Cavour united Italy, Turin served as the capital from 1861 to 1865.

TURIN (TORINO)   ☎ 011

Turin's elegance is the direct result of centuries of urban planning–graceful, church-lined avenues lead to spacious *piazze*. At the same time, Turin vibrates with economic energy of the modern era as it continues to provide a reliable headquarters for the **Fiat Auto Company** and prepares to host the **2006 Winter Olympics**. The city is also home to one of the more famous relics of Christianity: the ▨**Holy Shroud of Turin** is housed in the **Cattedrale di San Giovanni**, behind the **Palazzo Reale**. The church is undergoing restoration, but remains open. (Open daily 7am-12:30pm and 3-7pm. Free.) The **Museo Egizio**, in the **Palazzo dell'Accademia delle Scienze**, V. dell'Accademia delle Scienze 6, boasts a collection of Egyptian artifacts second only to the British Museum, including several copies of the Egyptian Book of the Dead. (Open Tu-F and Su 8:30am-7:30pm, Sa 8:30am-11pm. €6.50, ages 18-25 €3, under 18 and over 65 free.) The **Museo dell'Automobile**, Corso Unita d'Italia, 40, documents the evolution of the automobile, including prototype models of the Ford, Benz, Peugeot, and the homegrown Fiat. From the station, head south along V. Nizza. (Open Tu-Su 10am-7pm. €2.70.) One of Guarini's great Baroque palaces, the **Palazzo Carignano**, V. dell'Accademia delle Scienze 5, houses the **Museo Nazionale del Risorgimento Italiano**, commemorating the 1706-1846 unification of Italy. (Open Tu-Su 9am-7pm. €4.25, students €2.50, under 10 and over 65 free.)

Trains leave **Porta Nuova** on Corso Vittorio Emanuele (☎ 011 531 327) for: Genoa (2hr., every hr., €7.90); Milan (2hr., every hr., €7.90); Rome (4½hr., 5 per day, €32.60); Venice (4½hr., 2 per day, €27.70). **Buses** leave Turin for Aosta (3½hr., 6 per day, €6.28) and Milan (2hr., every hr., €5.70). The **tourist office**, P. Castello 161, has free maps. (☎ 011 53 51 81. Open M-Sa 9:30am-7pm, Su 9:30am-3:30pm.) To get to the clean and comfortable **Ostello Torino (YHI) ❶**, V. Alby 1, take bus #52 (bus #64 on Su) from

SHROUD OF MYSTERY Called a hoax by some and a miracle by others, the Holy Shroud of Turin (a 1m by 4.5m piece of linen) was supposedly wrapped around Jesus' body in preparation for burial after his crucifixion. Visible on the cloth are outflows of blood: around the head (supposedly from the Crown of Thorns), all over the body (from scourging), and, most importantly, from the wrists and feet (where the body was nailed to the cross). Although radiocarbon dating places the piece in the 12th century AD, the shroud's uncanny resemblance to that of Christ precludes its immediate dismissal. Scientists agree that the shroud was wrapped around the body of a 5'7" man who died by crucifixion, but whether it was the body of Jesus remains a mystery. For Christian believers, however, the importance of this relic is best described by Pope Paul VI's words: "The Shroud is a document of Christ's love written in characters of blood."

Stazione Porto Nuova to the 2nd stop past the Po river. Turn right onto Corso Lanza and look for the Ostello sign on the corner. Follow the signs to V. Gatti and then climb up 200m up a winding road. (☎ 011 660 29 39; hostelto@tin.it. Reception 7-10am and 3:30-11pm. Curfew 11:30pm; ask for a key if you go out. Closed Dec. 20-Feb. 1. Dorms €12; doubles €13.) To **camp** at **Campeggio Villa Rey ❶**, Strada Superiore Val S. Martino 27, take bus #61 from Porta Nuova until P. Vittorio and then take bus #56 and follow the signs after the last stop. (☎ 011 819 01 17. €3 per person; €2.10 for 1 tent, €3.65 for 2 tents.) Cheap fruit, cheese, and bread shops are on **Via Mazzini** and at **Di Per Di,** V. Carlo Alberto at the corner of V. Maria Vittoria. (Open Th-Tu 8am-1pm and 3:30-7:30pm, W 8am-1pm.) **Postal Code:** 10100.

THE LAKE COUNTRY

When Italy's monuments and museums start to blur together, escape to the natural beauty of the northern Lake Country, where clear water laps at the foot of the encircling mountains. A youthful crowd descends upon Lake Garda, with its watersports by day and thriving club scene at night; palatial hotels line Lake Maggiore's sleepy shores; and Lake Como's urbane shore hosts three excellent hostels.

LAKE MAGGIORE (LAGO MAGGIORE)

Lake Maggiore cradles similar temperate mountain waters and idyllic shores, but without the frenzy of its eastern neighbors.

STRESA. The romantic resort town Stresa is only an hour from Milan by **train** (every hr., €5.10). The local **tourist office** is in the ferry building at the dock on P. Martini. (☎/fax 0323 30 150. Open daily 10am-12:30pm and 3-6:30pm.) To get to comfy beds at **Hotel Mon Toc ❹**, in Stresa at V. Duchessa di Genova 67/69, turn right from the station and then right again at the intersection under the tracks. (☎ 0323 302 82; info@hotelmontoc.com. Breakfast included. Singles €45; doubles €78.)

▣ DAYTRIP FROM LAKE MAGGIORE: BORROMEAN ISLANDS. Stresa is a perfect stepping-stone to the gorgeous Borromean Islands. Daily excursion tickets (€10) allow you to hop back and forth between Stresa and the three islands (**Isola Bella, Isola Superiore dei Pescatori,** and **Isola Madre**). The islands boast lush, manicured botanical gardens, elegant villas, and an opulent Baroque palace.

LAKE GARDA (LAGO DI GARDA)

Garda has staggering mountains and breezy summers. **Desenzano,** the lake's southern transport hub is only 30min. from Verona, 1hr. from Milan, and 2hr. from Venice. Sirmione and Gardone Riviera, easily accessible by bus and boat, are best explored as daytrips, as accommodations are scant and pricey.

SIRMIONE. Sirmione's beautiful 13th-century castle and Roman ruins make for a leisurely day or a busy afternoon. **Buses** run every hour from: Brescia (1hr., €3.10); Desenzano (20min., €1.45); and Verona (1hr., €2.65). **Battelli** (water steamers) run until 8pm to: Desenzano (20min., €3); Gardone (1¼hr., €6); and Riva (4hr., €8.50). The **tourist office,** V. Guglielmo Marconi 2, is in the disc-shaped building. (☎030 91 61 14. Open Apr.-Oct. daily 9am-9pm; Nov.-Mar. reduced hours.) The **Albergo Grifone ❸,** V. Bocchio 4, has a prime location. (☎030 91 60 14; fax 030 91 65 48. Reserve ahead. Singles €32; doubles €55.) **Postal Code:** 25019.

RIVA DEL GARDA. Riva's calm pebble beaches are Lake Garda's compromise for the budget traveler. Travelers **swim, windsurf, hike,** and **climb** near the most stunning portion of the lake, where cliffs crash into the water. Riva is accessible by **bus** (☎0464 55 23 23) from Trent (2hr., 6 per day, €3.20) and Verona (2hr., 11 per day, €5). **Ferries** (☎030 914 95 11) leave from P. Matteoti for Gardone (€6.60). The **tourist office,** Giardini di Porta Orientale 8, is near the water. (☎0464 55 44 44; fax 52 03 08. Open M-Sa 9am-noon and 3-6pm, Su 10am-noon and 4-6:30pm.) Snooze at the fabulous **Locanda La Montanara ❷,** V. Montanara 20, off V. Florida. (☎/fax 0464 55 48 57. Breakfast €5. Singles €16; doubles €32.) **Postal Code:** 38066.

THE DOLOMITES (DOLOMITI)

With their sunny skies and powdery, light snow, the Dolomites offer immensely popular downhill skiing. These amazing peaks, which start west of Trent and extend north and east to Austria, are also fantastic for hiking and rock climbing.

TRENT. Between the Dolomites and the Veneto, Trent offers an affordable sampling of northern Italian life with superb restaurants and hikes against dramatic scenery. The **Piazza del Duomo,** Trent's center and social heart, contains the city's best sights. The **Fontana del Nettuno** stands, trident in hand, in the center of the *piazza.* Nearby is the **Cattedrale di San Vigilio,** named for the patron saint of Trent. (Open daily 6:40am-12:15pm and 2:30-7:30pm. Free.) Walk down V. Belenzani and head right on V. Roma to reach the well-preserved **Castello del Buonconsiglio.** (Open daily 10am-6pm. €5, students and seniors €2.50.) **Monte Bondone** rises majestically over Trent, making a pleasant daytrip or overnight excursion. Catch the **cable car** (☎0461 38 10 00; every 30min., €0.80) to **Sardagna** on Mt. Bondone from V. Lung'Adige Monte Grappa, between the train tracks and the river.

Trains (☎0461 98 36 27) leave V. Dogana for: Bologna (3hr., 13 per day, €10.15); Bolzano (45min., 2 per hr., €2.90); Venice (3hr., 5 per day, €10.15); and Verona (1hr., every hr., €4.65). Atesina **buses** (☎0461 82 10 00) go from V. Pozzo, next to the train station, to Riva del Garda (1hr., every hr., €2.80). The **tourist office,** V. Alferi 4, offers advice on biking, skiing, and hiking. (☎0461 98 38 80; www.apt.trento.it. Open daily 9am-7pm.) The central **Hotel Venezia ❹** is at P. Duomo 45. (☎/fax 0461 23 41 14. Breakfast €5.20. Singles €40; doubles €59. MC/V.) From the station, turn right on V. Pozzo and left on V. Torre Vanga to get to **Ostello Giovane Europa (HI) ❶,** V. Torre Vanga 11. (☎0461 26 34 84; fax 22 25 17. Breakfast and sheets included. Reception 7:30am-11pm. Check-out 9:30am.

Curfew 11:30pm. Reserve ahead. Dorms €13; singles €21.) **Ristorante Al Vo ❸**, V. del Vo 11, gives new meaning to "family-run restaurant," with 650 years of classic Trentino cooking to back it up. (Open M-Sa 11:30am-3pm, Th-F also 7pm-9:30pm. AmEx/MC/V.) **Postal Code:** 38100.

BOLZANO. In the tug-of-war between Austrian and Italian cultural influences, Bolzano pulls on Austria's side. The town's prime location beneath vineyard-covered mountains makes it a splendid base for hiking or skiing in the Dolomites. Artwork and numerous frescoes fill the Gothic **duomo**, off P. Walther. (Open M-F 9:45am-noon and 2-5pm, Sa 9:45am-noon. Free.) The fascinating **South Tyrol Museum of Archaeology**, V. Museo 43, near Ponte Talvera, houses the actual 5000-year-old **Ice Man**. (☎0471 98 06 48. Open Tu-W and F-Su 10am-6pm, Th 10am-8pm. €6.70, students €3.60.) **Trains** (☎0471 97 42 92) leave P. Stazione for: Milan (3hr., 3 per day, €21); Trent (45min., 2 per hr., €3); and Verona (2hr., 1-2 per hr., €6.80). Walk up V. Stazione from the train station to reach the **tourist office**, P. Walther 8. (☎30 70 00; fax 98 01 28. Open M-F 9am-6:30pm, Sa 9am-12:30pm.) **Croce Bianca ❸**, P. del Grano 3, is around the corner from P. Walther. (☎0471 97 75 52. Singles €28; doubles €47.) **Casa al Torchio ❷**, V. Museo 2c, off P. Erbe, serves up great traditional food. (Open M-F noon-2pm and 7-11pm, Su 6:30-11pm.) **Postal Code:** 39100.

LOMBARDY (LOMBARDIA)

Over the centuries, Roman generals, German emperors, and French kings have vied for control of Lombardy's rich agricultural wealth and fertile soil. Lombardy has recently become an even sturdier cornerstone of Italy's economy with huge increases in employment and business. While Milan may bask in the cosmopolitan spotlight of glamour and wealth, equally important are the rich culture and beauty of Bergamo, Mantua, and the nearby foothills of the Alps.

MILAN (MILANO)   ☎02

Although it was the capital of the western Roman Empire from 286 to 402, Milan has embraced modern life more forcefully than any other major Italian city. The pace of life is quick, and *il dolce di far niente* (the sweetness of doing nothing) is an unfamiliar taste. Football unites all Milanese as the city's modern religion, and the bi-annual game between AC Milan and Inter Milan is more important than Christmas. Although Milan's growth has brought petty crime and drugs, the city remains vibrant and on the cutting edge of finance, fashion, and fun.

▣ TRANSPORTATION

Flights: Malpensa Airport (MXP; ☎02 74 85 22 00), 45km from town. Handles intercontinental flights. **Malpensa Express** leaves Cadorna Métro station for the airport (45min., €9). **Linate Airport** (LIN; ☎02 74 85 22 00), 7km away, covers Europe. Take bus #73 from MM1: P.S. Babila (€1).

Trains: Stazione Centrale (☎(01) 47 88 80 88), in P. Duca d'Aosta on MM2. Info office open daily 7am-9:30pm. Every hour to: **Florence** (2½hr., €22); **Genoa** (1½hr., €8); **Rome** (4½hr., €28); **Turin** (2hr., €8); and to **Venice** (3hr., 21 per day, €13).

Buses: Stazione Centrale. Intercity buses tend to be less convenient and more expensive than trains. **SAL, SIA, Autostradale,** and other carriers leave from P. Castello and nearby (MM1: Cairoli) for **Bergamo,** the **Lake Country,** and **Turin.**

ITALY

Public Transportation: The **subway** (Metropolitana Milanese, or **MM**) runs 6am-midnight. ATM **buses** handle local transportation. Info and ticket booths (toll-free ☎ 800 01 68 57) are open M-Sa 7:15am-7:15pm. Single-fare tickets (€1) are good for 75min. of surface transportation. Day passes €3, 2-day €5.50.

▚ ▞ ORIENTATION AND PRACTICAL INFORMATION

The layout of the city resembles a giant target, encircled by a series of ancient concentric city walls. In the outer rings lie suburbs built during the 1950s and 60s to house southern immigrants. Within the inner circle are four central squares: **Piazza Duomo**, at the end of V. Mercanti; **Piazza Cairoli**, near the Castello Sforzesco; **Piazza Cordusio**, connected to Largo Cairoli by V. Dante; and **Piazza San Babila**, the business and fashion district along Corso Vittorio Emanuele. The **duomo** and **Galleria Vittorio Emanuele** constitute the bull's-eye, roughly at the center of the downtown circle. Radiating from the center are two large parks, the Giardini Pubblici and the Parco Sempione. From the colossal **Stazione Centrale** train station, farther northeast, you can take a scenic ride on bus #60 or the more efficient commute on subway line #3 to the downtown hub. **Via Vito Pisani,** which leads to the mammoth **Piazza della Repubblica,** connects the station to the downtown area.

Tourist Office: APT, V. Marconi 1 (☎ 02 72 52 43 00; www.milanoinfotourist.com), in the Palazzo di Turismo in P. del Duomo. Pick up the comprehensive ▨ **Milano: Where, When, How** as well as *Milano Mese* for info on activities and clubs. Open M-F 8:30am-8pm, Sa 9am-1pm and 2-7pm, Su 9am-1pm and 2-5pm.

American Express: V. Brera 3 (☎ 02 72 00 36 93), on the corner of V. dell'Orso. Walk through the Galleria, across P. Scala, and up V. Verdi. Holds mail free for AmEx members for 1 month, otherwise €5 per month. Handles wire transfers for AmEx cardholders. Also **exchanges currency.** Open M-F 9am-5:30pm.

Emergencies: ☎ 118. **Toll-free Operator:** ☎ 12. **Medical Assistance:** ☎ 38 83.

Police: ☎ 113 or 027 72 71. **Carabinieri** (civil corps): ☎ 112.

Hospital: Ospedale Maggiore di Milano, V. Francesco Sforza 35 (☎ (025) 50 31).

Late-Night Pharmacy: *Galeria* at Stazione Centrale, open 24hrs (☎ (026) 69 07 35).

Internet Access: Manhattan Lab, in the Università Statale, formerly the Ospedale Maggiore on V. Festa del Perdono. Use the entrance opposite V. Bergamini. Take the stairs on the right to the 3rd fl. Turn left and walk to the end of the corridor. Take 2 lefts; it's the 3rd door on your left. Microsoft workstations are only for Easmus students, but at the far end are computers for the public. Free. Open M-F 8:15am-6pm.

Post Office: V. Cordusio 4 (☎ 02 72 48 22 23). Address mail to be held: First Name SURNAME, *In Fermo Posta,* Ufficio Postale Centrale di Piazza Cordusio 4, Milano **20100,** Italia. Open M-F 8:30am-7:30pm, Sa 8:30am-1pm. **Postal Code:** 20100.

⌂ ACCOMMODATIONS

Every season in Milan is high season. Except August. Go figure. A single room in a decent establishment for under €35 is a real find. For the best deals, try the city's southern periphery or areas south and east of the train station. When possible, make reservations well ahead of time.

▨ **Hotel Sara,** V. Sacchini 17 (☎ 02 20 17 73). MM1/2: Loreto. From Loreto take V. Porpora; the 3rd street on the right is V. Sacchini. Recently renovated on a peaceful street. Singles €42-48; doubles €65-72; triples €88-93. ❹

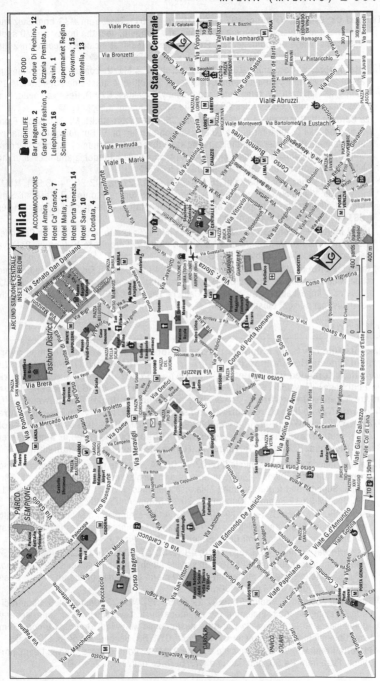

Milan

▲ ACCOMMODATIONS
Hotel Ambra, **9**
Hotel Ca' Grande, **7**
Hotel Malta, **11**
Hotel Porta Venezia, **14**
Hotel Sara, **10**
La Cordata, **4**

■ NIGHTLIFE
Bar Magenta, **2**
Girard Café Fashion, **3**
Lelephante, **16**
Scimmie, **6**

● FOOD
Fondue Di Pechino, **12**
Pizzeria Premiata, **5**
Savini, **1**
Supermarket Regina Giovanna, **15**
Tarantella, **13**

Around Stazione Centrale

Around Stazione Centrale INSET MAP BELOW

Hotel Ca' Grande, V. Porpora 87 (☎02 26 14 40 01). Take tram #33 from Stazione Centrale; it runs along V. Porpora and stops at V. Ampere, near the front door. 20 spotless rooms over a beautiful garden. Free Internet. Breakfast included. Reception 24hr. Singles €41, with bath €51; doubles €62/€72. AmEx/MC/V. ❹

Hotel Ambra, V. Caccianino 10 (☎02 26 65 465). MM1/2: Loreto. V. Caccianino is about a block up on the right from Ca' Grande. Set off on a quiet side street; offers 19 rooms, all with bath, TV, telephone, and balcony. Breakfast €2.50. Reserve ahead. Singles €42; doubles €68; triples €91. Inquire about student discounts. ❹

La Cordata, V. Burigozzo 11 (☎02 58 31 46 75; www.lacordata.it). MM3: Missori. From P. Missori take C. Italia for about 10 blocks then turn left on V. Burigozzo (the entrance is just around the corner from the camping store that shares its name). Surprisingly convenient hostel caters to younger crowd. Most rooms have bathrooms and access to the kitchen. Reception 9am-12:30am. Dorms €15.50. ❷

Hotel Porta Venezia, V.P. Castaldi 26 (☎02 29 41 42 27; fax 02 20 24 93 97). MM1: P. Venezia. Walk down C. Venezia for two blocks, then turn right onto V.P. Castaldi. Simple but clean rooms with phone and TV. Friendly staff speaks some English. Singles €31-47; doubles without bath €41-77. MC/V. ❸

Hotel Malta, V. Ricordi 20 (☎022 04 96 15). MM1/2: Loreto. From Stazione Centrale, take tram #33 to V. Ampere and backtrack along V. Porpora to V. Ricordi. Reserve ahead. Singles €47; doubles €73. ❹

Camping Citta di Milano, V. G. Airaghi 61 (☎02 48 20 01 34). From Stazione Centrale take Métro to MM1/3: Duomo or MM1/2: Cadorna; from either of these, take the #62 towards D'Angelli and get off at Vittoria Caldera. Laundry €4.50. €13 for plot, electricity and cost per person. Closed Dec.-Jan. ❶

⬛ FOOD

Like its fine *couture*, Milanese cuisine is sophisticated and sometimes overpriced. Specialties include *risotto giallo* (rice with saffron), *cotoletta alla milanese* (breaded veal cutlet with lemon), and *cazzouela* (a mixture of pork and cabbage). *Pasticcerie* and *gelaterie* crowd every block. Bakeries specialize in the Milanese sweet bread *panettone*, an Italian fruitcake. The newspaper *Il Giornale Nuovo* lists all restaurants and shops open in the city, and the brochure *Milano: Where, When, How*, available at the tourist office, has a detailed list of foreign restaurants. Pick up groceries near Corso Buenos Aires at **Supermarket Regina Giovanna,** V. Regina Giovanna 34. (Open M-F 8am-9pm, Sa 8am-8pm.)

Savini, Galleria Vittorio Emanuele II (☎02 72 00 34 33). One of few restaurants able to maintain an international reputation and its own high standards for more than a 100 years. Superb food features strong Milanese elements. (*Primi* €13-20. *Secondi* €21-29. Open M-Sa 12:30pm-2:30pm and 7:30-10:30pm. AmEx/MC/V) ❺

Tarantella, V. Abruzzi 35 (☎02 29 40 02 18). A fine example of a Milanese eatery with fresh produce filling and spilling over the restaurant. Emphasis on freshness and what the season has to offer. *Primi* €5-8. *Secondi* €12-20. Pizza €6-8. ❸

L'Osteria del Treno, V. S. Gregorio 46/48 (☎02 670 04 79). MM2/3 Centrale F.S. Hearty and reasonably priced food; self-service lunch and *primi* go for €4.20, *secondi* €6.50. In the evening the restaurant is sit-down and prices rise by a euro or two. Open Su-F noon-2:30pm and 7pm-10:30pm. ❶

Fondue di Pechino, V. Tadino 52 (☎02 29 40 58 38). MM1/3: Centrale F.S. Ultra-traditional Pekingese food, including the infamous duck. Give your waiter some general guidelines, and let them take you on a gastronomic whirlwind. Open M-Su noon-3pm and 6pm-midnight. Lunch menu €7.50. *Primi* €1-3.50. *Secondi* €3.50-8. MC/V. ❷

Pizzeria Premiata, V. Alzaia Naviglio Grande 2. MM2: Porto Genova. Serves hearty portions. Pizza from €4.50, *primi* around €7.75. Open daily noon-2am. ❶

◎ SIGHTS

🎨 DUOMO. The Gothic *duomo*, on P. del Duomo, is the geographical and spiritual center of Milan. More than 3400 statues, 135 spires, and 96 gargoyles grace the third-largest church in the world. *(MM1: Duomo. Open daily 9am-5:30pm. Modest dress strictly enforced. Free. Roof access €3.50, with elevator €5.)* To the right of the *duomo* in Palazzo Reale, the **Museo d'Arte Contemporanea** holds a fine permanent collection of 20th-century Italian art and a few Picassos. *(Open Tu-Su 9:30am-5:30pm. Free.)*

🎨 TEATRO ALLA SCALA. Known simply as La Scala, this is the world's most renowned opera house. Singer Maria Callas became a legend in this 18th-century Neoclassical building. Enter through the **Museo Teatrale alla Scala**, which includes such memorabilia as Verdi's famous top hat. *(P. della Scala, at the opposite end of the galleria from the duomo. Open daily 9am-noon and 2-5:30pm. €5.)*

PINACOTECA DI BRERA. The Brera Art Gallery presents one of Italy's most impressive collection of paintings, with works by Caravaggio, Bellini, and Raphael. *(V. Brera 28. Open daily 8:30am-7:30pm. €6.20.)*

GALLERIA VITTORIO EMANUELE II. On the left as you face the *duomo*, a glass barrel vault covers a five-story arcade of cafes and shops with mosaic floors and walls. *(Open M-Sa 10am-11pm, Su 10am-8pm.)*

🎨 CASTELLO SFORZESCO. Restored after heavy bomb damage in 1943, the enormous Castello Sforzesco is one of Milan's best-known monuments and a great place for a picnic. It houses the **Musei Civici**, which features Michelangelo's unfinished last work, *Pietà Rondanini. (MM1: Cairoli. Open Tu-Su 9:30am-7:30pm. Free.)*

CHIESA DI SANTA MARIA DELLE GRAZIE. Once a 15th-century convent, the church's Gothic nave is dark and elaborately patterned with frescoes. Next to the church entrance, in what was once the dining hall, is the **Cenacolo Vinciano (Vinciano Refectory),** one of Milan's most famous sites and home to one of the most important pieces of art in the world: **Leonardo da Vinci's Last Supper.** *(Church is at P. di S. Maria delle Grazie, 2, on Corso Magenta, off V. Carducci below MM1: Cadorna Cairoli. ☎ 02 89 42 11 46. Arrive early or late to avoid a long wait. Open Tu-Su 8am-7:30pm, Sa 8am-11pm. €6.50.)*

🎨 BASILICA DI SANT'AMBROGIO. A prototype for Lombard-Romanesque churches throughout Italy, Sant'Ambrogio is the most influential medieval building in Milan. The 4th-century **Cappella di San Vittore in Ciel D'Oro,** with exquisite 5th-century mosaics adorning its cupola, lies through the 7th chapel on the right; enter, walk a few paces, and then turn left. *(MM1: Sant'Ambrogio. Open M-Sa 7:30am-noon and 2:30-7pm, Su 3-7pm. Free.)*

🎨 NAVIGLI DISTRICT. The "Venice of Lombardy," the Navigli district comes alive at night. Complete with canals, footbridges, open-air markets, and cafes, this area once constituted part of a medieval canal system used to transport tons of marble for the *duomo* and linking Milan to various northern cities and lakes. *(Outside the MM2: Porta Genova station, through the Arco di Porta Ticinese.)*

BASILICA DI SANT'EUSTORGIO. Founded in the 4th century to house the bones of the Magi, the church lost its original function when the dead wise men were spirited off to Cologne in 1164. The triumph of the church is the **Portinari Chapel,** one of the great masterpieces of early Renaissance art. *(P.S. Eustorigio 3, down Corso Ticinese from S. Lorenzo Maggiore. Tram #3. Open W-M 9:30am-noon and 3:30-6pm. Free.)*

CHIESA DI SAN LORENZO MAGGIORE. The oldest church in Milan, San Lorenzo Maggiore testifies to the city's 4th-century greatness. To its right lies the **Cappella di Sant'Aquilino,** which contains a 5th-century mosaic of a beardless Christ among his apostles. *(On Corso Ticinese. MM2: Porta Genova, then tram #3 from V. Torino. Open daily 7:30am-6:45pm. Cappella €1.)*

PINACOTECA AMBROSIANA. The Ambrosiana's 23 rooms display exquisite works from the 14th through 19th centuries, including paintings by Botticelli, Leonardo, Raphael, Caravaggio, Titian, and Breugel. *(P. Pio XI 2. ☎ 02 86 46 29 81. Follow V. Spadari off V. Torino and make a left onto V. Cantù. Open Tu-Su 10am-5:30pm. €7.50.)*

['] 🅂 SHOPPING AND NIGHTLIFE

Ciak, V. Sangallo 33, near P. Gorini Argonne, southeast of the *duomo,* offers cabaret popular with young Milanese. Take tram #5 from Stazione Centrale to V. Beato Angelico Argonne. (☎ 02 76 11 00 93. Cover €12.95-20.70.) The **Teatri d'Italia di Porta Romana,** Corso di Porta Romana 124 (☎ 02 58 31 58 96), puts on experimental productions and first-rate plays (€14.50). **Milan Oltre** is a festival of drama, dance and music; call the **Ufficio Informazione del Comune** (☎ 02 86 46 40 94) for more details.

If Milan's status as a world-famous fashion capital has lured you here for shopping, don't despair about the prices. If you can tolerate the stigma of being an entire season behind, purchase your famous designer duds from *blochisti* (wholesale clothing outlets) such as **Monitor** on V. Monte Nero (MM3: Porta Romana, then tram #9 or 29) or the well-known **Il Salvagente,** V. Bronzetti 16, off Corso XXII Marzo (bus #60 from MM1: Lima or MM2/3: Stazione Centrale). The clothing sold along **Corso Buenos Aires** is more affordable—all the stores are open 10am-12:30pm and 2:30-7pm. Winter sales begin January 10. Shop in late July for end-of-the-summer sales (20-50% off) and a glimpse of the new fall lines. The brochure *Milano: Where, When, How,* available at the tourist office, has a great list of markets and second-hand stores. Hard-core window shoppers should head to the world-famous 🅂fashion district between **Corso Vittorio Emanuele** near the *duomo* and **Via Monte Napoleone** off P. San Babila. Take your credit card at your own risk. The dresses come straight from the designers and the selection is more up-to-date than anywhere else in the world, including New York and Tokyo. Expect to find high-class places to buy perfume, glasses, leather goods, shoes, and jewelry.

🅂 **Le Trottoir,** near V. Brera. From MM2: Lanza, take V. Tivoli to the Corso Garibaldi intersection. A lively atmosphere with live bands nightly. Open daily 7pm-2:30am.

🅂 **Scimmie,** V. Sforza 49. A legendary, energetic bar. Different theme every night and frequent concerts; fusion, jazz, soul, and reggae dominate. Open daily 8pm-1:30am.

Bar Magenta, V. Carducci 13. A traditional Guinness bar with an overflowing crowd. Open M-Su 8am-2am, sometimes until 5am.

Artdeco Cafe, V. Lombro 7. MM1: Porta Venezia. Walk 3 blocks up Corso Buenos Aires, turn right on V. Melzi, and walk 3 blocks on the left. This discobar defines Milan's elegance. Dancing after midnight. Open daily 6am-2am.

Loolapaloosa, Corso Como 15. A wild crowd will have you dancing on the tables. €6 cover includes 1st drink. Open Su-Th 6pm-3am.

Grand Café Fashion, Corso Porta Ticinese, near V. Vetere. A bar/restaurant/dance club with a stunningly beautiful crowd and velour leopard-print couches. €7.75 cover includes 1st drink. Open Tu-Su 6pm-4am.

Lelephante, V. Melzo 22. MM2: Porta Venezia; then walk up Corso Buenos Aires and turn right on V. Melzo. Vaguely 60s gay club with lava lamps. Open Tu-Su 6:30pm-2am.

🔲 DAYTRIPS FROM MILAN

BERGAMO. Bergamo's medieval palaces, fabulous art museum, and 12th-century basilica are only a one-hour train ride from Milan (p. 641).

LAKE COUNTRY. The magnificence of Lakes Como, Maggiore, and Garda awaits one hour from Milan by train (p. 633).

MANTUA (MANTOVA)   ☎ 0376

Mantua owes its literary fame to its most famous son, the poet Virgil. Its grand *palazzi* and graceful churches come thanks to the Gonzaga family who, after ascending to power in 1328, imported well-known artists to change Mantua's small-town image. Today, Mantua is a bustling city with easy passage to the surrounding lakes. Once the largest palace in Europe, the opulent 🔲**Palazzo Ducale** towers over **Piazza Sordello,** sheltering the Gothic **Magna Domus** *(duomo)* and **Palazzo del Capitano.** Inside, check out a breathtaking array of frescoes, gardens, and facades. Outside the *palazzo*, signs point to the **Castello di San Giorgio** (1390-1406), once a formidable fortress before its absorption into the *palazzo* complex. (Open Tu-Su 8:45am-6:30pm. €6.50, students €3.25, children and seniors free.) In the far south of the city, down V.P. Amedeo, through P. Veneto, and down Largo Parri, lies the opulent **Palazzo di Te,** built by Giulio Romano in 1534 as a suburban retreat for Federico II Gonzaga. It is widely considered the finest building in the Mannerist style. (☎ 0376 32 32 66. Open Tu-Su 9am-6pm, M 1-6pm. €8, students €2.50, under 11 free.) Just south of P. Sordello is the 11th-century Romanesque **Piazza delle Erbe;** opposite the *piazza* is Leon Alberti's **Chiesa di Sant'Andrea,** Mantua's greatest contribution to the Italian Renaissance. (*Piazza* open daily 10am-12:30pm and 2:30-6:30pm. Free.) Walk from P. dell'Erbe to P. Broletto and then take V. Accademia to the end to reach the lovely **Teatro Bibiena,** one of Italy's few theaters *not* modeled on Milan's La Scala. (☎ 0376 32 76 53. Open Tu-Su 9:30am-12:30pm and 3-6:30pm. €2.10, students €1.05.)

Trains (☎ 0376 84 88 88 088) go from P. Don E. Leoni to Milan (2hr., 9 per day, €7.90) and Verona (40min., every hr., €2.30). From the train station, head left on V. Solferino, through P.S. Francesco d'Assisi to V. Fratelli Bandiera, and right on V. Verdi to reach the **tourist office,** P. Mantegna 6, next to Chiesa Sant'Andrea. (☎ 32 82 53; fax 36 32 92. Open M-Sa 8:30am-12:30pm and 3-6pm.) Charming **Hotel ABC ❸,** P. Don E. Leoni 25, is opposite the station. (☎ 0376 32 33 47; fax 0376 32 23 29. Breakfast included. Singles €40-67; doubles €65-88; triples €90-118.) **Antica Osteria ai Ranari ❷,** V. Trieste 11, down V. Pomponazzo near Porta Catena, specializes in regional dishes. (☎ 0376 32 84 31. *Primi* €4.50-6, *secondi* €4.50-9. Closed for 3 weeks in July and Aug. Open Tu-Su noon-2pm and 7-11:30pm.) **Postal Code:** 46100.

BERGAMO   ☎ 035

Bergamo's two sections reflect its colorful history: while the *città alta* (upper city) reveals its origins as a Venetian outpost, the *città bassa* (lower city) is a modern metropolis packed with Neoclassical buildings. **Via Pignolo,** in the *città bassa,* winds past a succession of handsome 16th- to 18th-century palaces. Turning left onto V.S. Tomaso and then right brings you to the astounding 🔲**Galleria dell'Accademia Carrara,** which holds works by Titian, Rubens, Breughel, and van Dyck. (Open W-M 9:30am-12:30pm and 2:30-5:30pm. €2.60, under 18 and over-60 free.) From the Galleria, the terraced **Via Noca** ascends to the medieval *città alta* through the 16th-century **Porta S. Agostino.** Stroll down V. Porta Dipinta to V.

Gambito, which ends in **Piazza Vecchia,** an ensemble of medieval and Renaissance buildings flanked by restaurants and cafes at the heart of the *città alta.* Head through the archway flanking P. Vecchia to P. del Duomo, and see the fresco-laden **Cappella Colleoni.** (Open daily Mar.-Oct. 9am-12:30pm and 2-6:30pm; Nov.-Feb. 9am-12:30pm and 2:30-4:30pm. Free.) Immediately left of the Cappella Colleoni is the ▨**Basilica di Santa Maria Maggiore,** a 12th-century basilica with an ornate Baroque interior and tapestries depicting biblical scenes. (Open daily Apr.-Oct. 9am-12:30pm and 2:30-6pm; Nov.-Mar. reduced hours. Free.) Climb the **Torre Civica** (Civic Tower) for a marvelous view of Bergamo and the hills (€1).

The train station, bus station, and many budget hotels are in the *città bassa.* **Trains** (1hr., every hr., €3.65) and **buses** (every 30min. €4.10) pull into P. Marconi from Milan. To get to the **tourist office,** V. Aquila Nera 2, in the *città alta,* take bus #1a to the top of the *città alta.* (☎035 24 22 26; www.apt.bergamo.it. Open daily 9am-12:30pm and 2-5:30pm.) To get from the train station to **Ostello della Gioventù di Bergamo (HI) ❶,** V.G. Ferraris 1, take bus #9 to Comozzi, then take bus #14 to Leonardo da Vinci and walk up the hill. (☎/fax 035 36 17 24. Breakfast included. HI members only. Dorms €13.50. MC/V.) **Locanda Caironi ❷,** V. Torretta 6B, off V. Gorgo Palazzo, is in a quiet residential neighborhood. Take bus #5 or 7 from V. Angelo Maj. (☎035 24 30 83. Singles €15.50; doubles €28.50. MC/V.) **Trattoria Casa Mia ❸,** V.S. Bernardino 20A, provides full meals from €11. (☎035 22 06 76. Open M-Sa noon-2pm and 7-10pm.) **Postal Code:** 24122.

ITALIAN RIVIERA (LIGURIA)

The Italian Riviera stretches 350km along the Mediterranean between France and Tuscany, forming the most famous and touristed area of the Italian coastline. Genoa divides the crescent-shaped strip into the **Riviera di Levante** ("rising sun") to the east and the **Riviera di Ponente** ("setting sun") to the west. The elegant coast beckons with lemon trees, almond blossoms, and turquoise seas. Especially lovely is the **Cinque Terre** area, just to the west of **La Spezia.**

▐ TRANSPORTATION

The coastal towns are linked by the main **rail** line, which runs west to Ventimiglia (near the French border) and east to La Spezia (near Tuscany), but slow local trains can make short trips take hours. Frequent intercity **buses** pass through all major towns, and local buses run to inland hill-towns. **Boats** connect most resort towns. **Ferries** go from Genoa to Olbia, Sardinia and Palermo, Sicily.

GENOA (GENOVA)   ☎010

Genoa, city of grit and grandeur, has little in common with its resort neighbors. A Ligurian will tell you, *"Si deve conosceria per amaria"*—"you have to know her to love her." If lacking in the laid-back intimacy and friendliness of a small-town resort, Genoa more than makes up for it in its rich cultural history and bewitching sights. Since falling into decline in the 18th century, modern Genoa has turned its attention from industry and trade to the restoration of its bygone splendor.

▐ **TRANSPORTATION.** The **C. Columbo Internazionale** airport (GOA), in Sesti Ponente, services European destinations. Take **Volabus #100** from Stazione Brignole to the airport (every 30min., €2) and get off at Aeroporto. Most visitors arrive at one of Genoa's two **train stations: Stazione Principe,** in P. Acquaverde, or **Stazione Brignole,** in P. Verdi. **Trains** go to Rome (5hr., 14 per day, €23.50) and Turin

(2hr., 19 per day, €8.70). **AMT buses** (☎558 24 14) run throughout the city. One-way tickets (€0.80) are valid for 1½hr.; all-day passes cost €3. **Ferries** depart from the Ponte Assereto arm of the port; buy tickets at **Stazione Marittima** in the port.

■ ▤ **ORIENTATION AND PRACTICAL INFORMATION.** To get to the center of town, **Piazza de Ferrari**, from Stazione Principe, take **Via Balbi** to **Via Cairoli**, which becomes **Via Garibaldi**, and turn right on **Via XXV Aprile** at P. delle Fontane Marose. From Stazione Brignole, turn right onto **Via Fiume**, and right onto **Via XX Settembre.** Or, take bus #19, 20, 30, 32, 35, or 41 from Stazione Principe or bus #19 or 40 from Stazione Brignole to Piazza de Ferrari in the center of town. The **centro storico** (historic center) contains many of Genoa's monuments. The **tourist office** is on Porto Antico, in Palazzina S. Maria. From the aquarium, walk toward the complex of buildings to the left. (☎010 24 87 11. Open daily 9am-1pm and 2-6pm.) Log on at **Internet Village**, at V. Brigata Bisagno and C. Buenos Aires, across from P. Vittoria. (€7.75 per hr. Open M-Sa 9am-1pm and 3-7pm.) **Postal Code:** 16121.

▛▟ **ACCOMMODATIONS AND FOOD. Ostello per la Gioventù (HI) ❶,** V. Costanzi 120, has a cafeteria, TV, and a view of the city far below. From Stazione Principe, take bus #35 to V. Napoli and #40 to the hostel. From Stazione Brignole, pick up bus #40 (every 15min.) and ask to be let off at the *ostello*. (☎/fax 010 242 24 57. Breakfast included. Reception 7-11am and 3:30pm-12:30am. No curfew. HI card available at hostel. Dorms €13.) **Albergo Carola ❸,** V. Gropallo 4/12, has elegant rooms overlooking a garden. From Stazione Brignole, turn right on V. de Amicis and continue into P. Brignole; turn right when facing Albergo Astoria, and walk 15m. Albergo is 2 flights up from Albergo Argentina. (☎010 839 13 40. Singles €26; doubles €42.) **Hotel Balbi ❸,** V. Balbi 21/3, offers large, ornate rooms. (☎/fax 010 25 23 62. Breakfast €4. With *Let's Go:* singles €25-32; doubles €45-55. AmEx/MC/V.) **Camping** is popular; check the tourist office for availability, or try **Genova Est ❶** on V. Marcon Loc Cassa. Take the train from Stazione Brignole to the suburb of Bogliasco (10min., 6 per day, €1); a free bus (5min., every 2hr. 8:10am-6pm) will take you from Bogliasco to the campsite. (☎010 347 20 53. Electricity €1.60 per day; laundry €3.50 per load. €4.65 per person, €9.30 per large tent.) ▨**Trattoria da Maria ❷,** V. Testa d'Oro 14r, off V. XXV Aprile, has a new menu every day, with the *pranzo turistico* (set-price lunch) for €6.75. (☎010 58 10 80. Open Su-F noon-2:30pm and 7-9:30pm.)

◑ ▛ **SIGHTS.** Genoa boasts a multitude of *palazzi* built by its famous merchant families. These are best seen along **Via Garibaldi**, on the edge of *centro storico*, and **Via Balbi,** in the heart of the university quarter. The 17th-century **Palazzo Reale,** V. Balbi 10, 10min. west of V. Garibaldi, is filled with Rococo rooms bathed in gold and upholstered in red velvet. (Open M-Tu 9am-3:30pm, W-Su 8:15am-7:15pm. €4, ages 18-25 €2, under under 18 and seniors free.) Follow V. Balbi through P. della Nunziata and continue to L. Zecca, where V. Cairoli leads to **Via Garibaldi,** the most impressive street in Genoa, bedecked with elegant *palazzi* that once earned it the names "Golden Street" and "Street of Kings." The **Galleria di Palazzo Bianco,** V. Garibaldi 11, exhibits Ligurian, Dutch, and Flemish paintings. Across the street, the 17th-century **Galleria Palazzo Rosso,** V. Garibaldi 18, has magnificent furnishings in a lavishly frescoed interior. (Both open Tu-Sa 9am-7pm, Su 10am-6pm. €3.10 each, €5.20 together. Su free.) The **Villetta Di Negro,** on the hill further down V. Garibaldi, contains waterfalls, grottoes, and terraced gardens. From P. de Ferrari, take V. Boetto to P. Matteotti for the ornate **Chiesa di Gesù.** (Open daily 7:15am-12:30pm and 4-7:30pm. Free.) Head past the Chiesa di Gesù down V. di Porta Soprana to V. Ravecca to reach the medieval twin-towered **Porta Soprana,** the supposed boyhood home of **Christopher Columbus.** Off V.S.

ITALY

Lorenzo lies the **San Lorenzo Duomo,** a church in existence since the 9th century, which boasts a striped Gothic facade with a copiously decorated main entrance and 9th-century carved lions. (Open M-Sa 8am-7pm, Su 7am-7pm. Free.) The **centro storico,** the eerie and beautiful historical center, is a mass of winding and confusing streets bordered by the port, V. Garibaldi, and P. Ferrari. Due to an extremely dangerous night scene, the center is only safe during weekdays when stores are open. It is, however, home to some of Genoa's most memorable monuments, including the **duomo** and the medieval **Torre Embraici.** Once you're back on P. Matteotti, go down V.S. Lorenzo toward the water, turn left on V. Chiabrera and left on V. di Mascherona to reach the ◪**Chiesa S. Maria di Castello,** a labyrinth of chapels, courtyards, cloisters, and cruxifices. (Open daily 9am-noon and 3-6pm. Free.) Kids and ocean-lovers will adore the massive **aquarium,** on Porto Antico to the right of the APT tourist office. (Open M-F 9:30am-7:30pm, Sa-Su 9:30am-8:30pm; in summer Th until 11pm. €12.)

🎇 **DAYTRIP FROM GENOA: THE RIVIERA.** Several idyllic Riviera towns are accessible from Genoa by train, including **Finale Ligure** (1hr.; p. 644), **Santa Margherita Ligure** (40min.; p. 645), and **Cinque Terre** (1½hr.; p. 645).

RIVIERA DI PONENTE

FINALE LIGURE
☎019

A beachside plaque proclaims the town of Finale Ligure the place for "*Il riposo del popolo*" (the people's rest). Whether your idea of *riposo* involves bodysurfing in the choppy waves near Torrente Porra, browsing through Finalmarina's chic boutiques, or scaling Finalborgo's looming 15th-century Castello di San Giovanni, the *popolo* have many options. The city is divided into three sections: **Finalpia** to the east, **Finalmarina** in the center, and **Finalborgo** further inland. The train station and most sights are in Finalmarina. Skip the packed beaches in town and walk east along V. Aurelia through the first tunnel, turning right for a less populated **free beach.** Climb the tough trail to the ruins of **Castel Govone** for a spectacular view of Finale. Enclosed within ancient walls, **Finalborgo,** the historic quarter of Finale Ligure proper, is a 1km walk or short bus ride up V. Bruneghi from the station. **Pilade,** V. Garibaldi 67, features live jazz on Friday nights. (☎019 69 22 20. Open daily 10am-2am.) The towns near Finale Ligure are also worth exploring. SAR **buses** run from the train station to **Borgo Verezzi** (10min., 8 per day, €0.80).

Trains leave from P. Vittorio Veneto for Genoa (1hr., every hr., €3.70). The IAT **tourist office,** V.S. Pietro 14, gives out free maps. (☎019 68 10 19; fax 019 68 18 04. Open M-Sa 9am-12:30pm and 3:30-6:30pm, Su 9am-noon.) ◪**Castello Wuillerman (HI)** ❶, on V. Generale Caviglia, is well worth the hike. From the station, take a left onto V. Mazzini, which becomes the narrow V. Torino, turn left on V. degli Ulivi, and trudge up the daunting steps. (☎019 69 05 15; hostelfinaaleligure@libero.it. Breakfast and sheets included. Reception daily 7-10am and 5-10pm. Curfew 11:30pm. Email reservations. €11.) **Albergo Carla** ❷, V. Colombo 44, offers a bar and a restaurant. (☎019 69 22 85; fax 019 68 19 65. Breakfast €3.70. Singles €23-29; doubles €44-49. AmEx/MC/V.) **Camping Del Mulino** ❶, on V. Castelli, has a restaurant and mini-market on the premises. Take the Calvisio bus from the station to the Boncardo Hotel and follow the brown and yellow signs to the campsite entrance. (☎019 60 16 69. Reception Apr.-Sept. 8am-8pm. €7 per person, €7 per tent.) Cheap restaurants lie along **Via Rossi** and **Via Roma. Ferinata e Vino** ❷, V. Roma 25, serves up homestyle cooking. (☎019 692 562. *Primi* €4.65-7.25; *secondi* €6.20-9.30. Open daily 12:30-2pm and 7:30-9pm.) **Coop supermarket** is at V. Dante Alighieri 7. (Open M-Sa 8:30am-7:30pm, Su 9am-1pm. MC/V.) **Postal Code:** 17024.

RIVIERA DI LEVANTE

CAMOGLI. Postcard-perfect Camogli shimmers with color. Sun-faded peach houses crowd the hilltop, red and turquoise boats bob in the water, piles of fishing nets cover the docks, and bright umbrellas dot the dark stone beaches. **Trains** run on the Genoa-La Spezia line to Genoa (20min., 32 per day, €1.50) and La Spezia (1½hr., 21 per day, €3.50). Golfo Paradiso **ferries**, V. Scalo 3 (☎0185 77 20 91; www.golfoparadiso.it), near P. Colombo, go to Portofino (€8) and Cinque Terre (€12). Buy tickets on the dock. Head right from the station to find the **tourist office**, V. XX Settembre 33, which can help find rooms. (☎0185 77 10 66. Open M-Sa 9am-12:30pm and 3:30-7pm, Su 9am-1pm.) Exit the train station, walk down the stairway to the right, and look for the large blue sign for the ▨**Albergo La Camogliese ❹**, V. Garibaldi 55. (☎0185 77 14 02; fax 77 40 24. Reserve ahead. Singles €51-59; doubles €69-75. 10% *Let's Go* discount with cash. AmEx/MC/V.) **Postal Code:** 16032.

SANTA MARGHERITA LIGURE. Santa Margherita Ligure led a calm existence as a fishing village until the early 20th century, when it fell into favor with Hollywood stars. Today, grace and glitz paint the shore, but the serenity of the town's early days still lingers. If ocean waves don't invigorate your spirit, try the holy water in seashell basins at the **Basilica di Santa Margherita**, at P. Caprera. **Trains** along the Pisa-Genoa line go from P. Federico Raoul Nobili, at the top of V. Roma, to Genoa (40min., 2-3 per hr., €2) and La Spezia (2 per hr., €3.80). Tigullio **buses** (☎0185 28 88 34) go from P.V. Veneto to Camogli (30min., every hr., €1.20) and Portofino (20min., 3 per hr., €1.50). Tigullio **ferries**, V. Palestro 8/1b (☎0185 28 46 70), have tours to Cinque Terre (July-Sept. W and Sa-Su 1 per day; €20) and Portofino (every hr., €3.20). Turn right from the train station on V. Roma, left on Corso Rainusso, turn left and take a hard right onto V. XXV Aprile from Largo Giusti to find the **tourist office**, V. XXV Aprile 2b, which arranges lodging. (☎0185 28 74 85; fax 28 30 34. Open M-Sa 9am-12:30pm and 3-7:30pm, Su 9:30am-12:30pm and 4:30-7:30pm.) ▨**Hotel Nuova Riviera ❹**, V. Belvedere 10, has spacious rooms. (☎/fax 0185 28 74 03. Breakfast included. Singles €55-75; doubles €62-92; triples €90-120. MC/V.) ▨**La Piadineria and Creperia ❷**, V. Giuncheto 5, off P. Martiri della Libertà, serves large portions. (Sandwiches from €5. Open daily 5pm-3am.) **Postal Code:** 16038.

PORTOFINO. As long as you don't buy anything, princes and paupers alike can enjoy the curved shores and tiny bay of Portofino. A 1hr. walk along the ocean road offers the chance to scout out small rocky **beaches**. **Njasca** offers boat rental in the summer months (€6-13 per hr.); **Paraggi** (where the bus stops) is the area's only sandy beach, but only a small strip is free. In town, follow the signs uphill from the bay to escape to the cool interior of the **Chiesa di San Giorgio**. A few minutes up the road toward the **castle** is a serene garden with sea views. (Open daily 10am-5pm. €2.50.) To get to town, take the bus to Portofino Mare (*not* Portofino Vetta). From P. Martiri della Libertà, Tigullio **buses** go to Santa Margherita (3 per hr., €1); buy tickets at the green kiosk. **Ferries** also go to Camogli (2 per day, €7) and Santa Margherita (every hr. 9am-7pm, €3.50). The **tourist office**, V. Roma 35, is on the way to the waterfront from the bus stop. (☎0185 26 90 24. Open daily 10:30am-1:30pm and 2:30-7pm.)

CINQUE TERRE. The five bright fishing villages of Cinque Terre cling to a stretch of terraced hillsides and steep crumbling cliffs, with the dazzling turquoise sea lapping against their shores. You can hike through all five—Monterosso, Vernazza, Corniglia, Manarola, and Riomaggiore—in a few hours. **Monterosso** is the most developed, with sandy beaches and exciting nightlife; **Vernazza** has a seaside *piazza* with colorful buildings and a busy harbor; **Corniglia** hovers high above the sea in peaceful solitude; **Manarola** has quiet streets and a spectacular swimming cove; and **Riomaggiore** has a tiny harbor and lots of rooms for rent. The best views are from the narrow goat paths that link the towns, winding through vineyards, streams, and dense foliage. The best hike lies between Monterosso and Vernazza (1½hr.); the trail between Vernazza and Corniglia (2hr.) also winds through spectacular scenery. The largest **free beach** lies directly below the train station; get there early to reserve a space. Alternatively, follow V. Fegina through the tunnel to get to another free beach. **Guvano Beach,** a pebbly strip frequented by nudists, is through the tunnel at the base of the steps leading up to Corniglia (€2.60). Tiny trails off the road to Vernazza lead to popular hidden coves.

The Genoa-La Spezia rail line connects the five towns; Monterosso is the most accessible. From V. Fegina, at the north end of town, **trains** run to: Pisa (2½hr., every hr.); Genoa (1½hr., every hr.); La Spezia (20min., every 30min.); and Rome (7hr., every 2hr.). Trains also connect the five towns (5-20min., every 50min., €1). Reserve rooms several weeks in advance. Private rooms *(affittacamere)* are the most plentiful and economical options. To find Manarola's hostel, **Albergo Della Gioventù-Ostello "Cinque Terre" ❷,** V.B. Riccobaldi 21, turn right from the train station and go uphill 300m to discover more fabulous amenities than can be believed. (☎0187 92 02 15; www.cinqueterre.net. Breakfast €3.50. Reception daily 2am-1pm and 5pm-1am. Reserve 1 month ahead. Dorms €16-19; quads €64-76. AmEx/MC/V.) In Vernazza, ask in Trattoria Capitano about **Albergo Barbara ❸,** P. Marconi 30, top floor, at the port. (☎/fax 0187 81 23 98. 2-night min. stay. Doubles €43-55; triples €65; quads €70.) In Monterosso, try the **tourist office** (☎0187 81 75 06) or **Hotel Souvenir ❸,** V. Gioberti 24, the best deal in town. (☎0187 81 75 95. Breakfast €5. Singles €35, students €30.) For private rooms in Riomaggiore, call **Robert Fazioli ❸,** V. Colombo 94. (☎0187 92 09 04. Rooms €20-50.) Get supplies for a romantic picnic at **Cantina di Sciacchetrà,** V. Roma 7, in Monterosso. (Open Mar.-Oct. daily 9am-11pm; Dec.-Feb. Sa-Su 9am-11pm; closed Nov.)

LA SPEZIA. A departure point for Corsica and an unavoidable transport hub for Cinque Terre, La Spezia is among Italy's most beautiful ports, with regal palms lining the promenade and citrus trees growing throughout the parks. La Spezia lies on the Genoa-Pisa **train** line. Happy Lines, with a ticket kiosk on V. Italia, sends **ferries** to Corsica (round-trip €44-64). Navigazione Golfo dei Poeti, V. Mazzoni 21, run ferries to: each village in Cinque Terre and Portovenereo (€11); Capraia (5hr., €41); and Elba (3½hr., €41). The **tourist office,** V. Mazzini 45, is at the port. (☎0187 77 09 00. Open M-Sa 9:30am-12:30pm and 3:30-7:30pm.) **Albergo Ilsole ❹,** V. Cavalloti, off V. Prione, offers rooms with couches and high ceilings. (☎0187 73 51 64. Doubles €39-47; triples €52-62. MC/V.) **Postal Code:** 19100.

EMILIA-ROMAGNA

Go to Florence, Venice, and Rome to sightsee, come to Emilia-Romagna to eat. Italy's wealthy wheat- and dairy-producing region covers the fertile plains of the Po River Valley, and celebrates the finest culinary traditions on the peninsula. The Romans originally settled here, but the towns later fell under the rule of great Renaissance families whose names adorn every *palazzo* and *piazza* in the region.

BOLOGNA   ☎051

Bright facades line the cobblestone roads that twist by churches, but the city's appeal extends far beyond aesthetics. Blessed with prosperity and Europe's oldest university, which counts Dante, Petrarch, and Copernicus among its graduates, Bologna has developed an open-minded atmosphere with strong minority and gay political activism. The city also prides itself on a great culinary heritage.

⧆⧆ TRANSPORTATION AND PRACTICAL INFORMATION. Bologna is a rail hub for all major Italian cities and the Adriatic coast. **Trains** leave the northern tip of the walled city for: Florence (1½hr., every 2hr., €5); Milan (3hr., 2 per hr., €10); Rome (4hr., every hr., €21); and Venice (2hr., every hr., €10). **Buses** #25 and 30 run between the train station and the historic center at **Piazza Maggiore** (€1). The **tourist office,** P. Maggiore 1, is next to the Palazzo Comunale. (☎051 648 76 07; www.prenotabologna.it. Open M-Sa 10am-2pm and 3-7pm.) **Postal Code:** 40100.

⧆⧆ ACCOMMODATIONS AND FOOD. The sparklingly clean **Albergo Panorama ❹,** V. Livraghi 1, 4th fl., has a prime location. Follow V. Ugo Bassi from P. Maggiore and take the third left. (☎051 22 18 02; fax 051 26 63 60. Singles €47; doubles €62; triples €78. AmEx/MC/V.) **Ostello due Torre San Sisto (HI) ❶,** V. Viadagola 5, is off V. San Donato, in the Località di San Sisto, 6km from the center of town. Walk down V. dell'Indipendenza from the station, turn right on V. della Mille, and take bus #93 from across the street to San Sisto. (☎/fax 051 50 18 10. Breakfast included. Reception 7am-midnight. Lockout 10am-3:30pm. Curfew midnight. Dorms €12. Family rooms €13-14 per person.) For the clean **Pensione Marconi ❸,** V. Marconi 22, turn right from the train station and turn left on V. Amendola, which becomes V. Marconi. (☎051 26 28 32. Singles €34-43; doubles €53-68; triples €90.)

Don't leave without sampling Bologna's signature *spaghetti alla bolognese.* Scout **Via Augusto Righi, Via Piella,** and **Via Saragozza** for traditional *trattorie.* A **PAM** supermarket, V. Marconi 26, is by the intersection with V. Riva di Reno. (Open M-W and F-Sa 7:45am-7:45pm, Th 7:45am-1pm.) Locals chat over regional dishes like *tagliatelle* at **Trattoria Da Maro ❸,** V. Broccaindosso 71b, between Strada Maggiore and V.S. Vitale. (☎051 22 73 04. *Primi* €5-6, *secondi* €5-7. Open M 8-10:15pm, Tu-Sa noon-2:30pm and 8-10:15pm.) Savor hearty food in **Antica Trattoria Roberto Spiga ❸,** V. Broccaindosso, 21a. (☎051 23 00 63. *Primi* €6-8, *secondi* €8-10. Open Sept.-July M-Sa noon-3pm and 7:30-10pm.) **Il Gelatauro,** V.S. Vitale 82/b, uses only fresh fruit to create delicious sorbets. (Cones from €2. Open June-Aug. daily 11am-11pm; Sept.-May Tu-Su 11am-11pm.)

⧆⧆ SIGHTS AND ENTERTAINMENT. Forty kilometers of porticoed buildings line the streets of Bologna in a mix of Gothic, Renaissance, and Baroque styles. The tranquil **Piazza Maggiore** flaunts both Bologna's historical and modern wealth. The cavernous Gothic interior of the city's *duomo,* **Basilica di San Petronio,** was meant to be larger than Rome's St. Peter's, but the jealous Church ordered that the funds be used instead to build the nearby Palazzo Archiginnasio. It hosted both the Council of Trent (when it wasn't meeting in Trent) and the 1530 ceremony in which Pope Clement VII gave Italy to the German king Charles V. The pomp and pageantry of the exercises at the church allegedly inspired a disgusted Martin Luther to reform religion in Germany. (Open M-Sa 7:15am-1pm and 2-6pm, Su 7:30am-1pm and 2-6:30pm. Sacristy open daily 8am-noon and 4-6pm.) The **Palazzo Archiginnasio,** behind S. Petronio, was once a university building; the upstairs theater was built in 1637 to teach anatomy to students. (☎051 23 64 88. Open M-F 9am-7pm, Sa 9am-2pm. Theater open M-Sa 9am-1pm. Both closed 2 weeks in Aug. Free.) On the northern side of P. Maggiore is the **Palazzo de Podestà,** remodeled by Fioravanti's son Aristotle, who later designed Moscow's Kremlin. Next to P. Maggiore, **Piazza del Nettuno** contains Giambologna's famous 16th-century fountain, *Neptune and Attendants.* From P. Nettuno, go down V. Rizzoli to **Piazza Porta Ravegana,** where seven streets converge to form Bologna's medieval quarter. Two towers that constitute the city's emblem rise magnificently from the *piazza;* you can climb the **Torre degli Asinelli.** (Open daily May-Aug. 9am-6pm; Sept.-Apr. 9am-5pm. €3.) From V. Rizzoli, follow V.S. Stefano to Piazza Santo Stefano, where four of the original seven churches of the Romanesque **Piazza Santo Stefano Church Complex** remain. Bologna's patron saint, San Petronio, lies buried under the pulpit of the **Chiesa di San Sepolcro.** (Open daily 9am-noon and 3:30-6pm.) Take Strada Maggiore to P. Aldrovandi to reach the remarkably intact **Chiesa di Santa Mari dei Seru,** whose columns support an unusual combination of arches and ribbed vaulting. The **Pinacoteca Nazionale,** V. delle Belle Arti, 56, off V. Zamboni, traces the history of Bolognese artists. (☎ 051 24 32 22. Open Tu-Su 9am-6:30pm. €7.)

Bologna's hip student population ensures raucous nighttime fun. **Cluricaune,** V. Zamboni 18/b, is an Irish bar packed with students who flock to its pool table and dart boards. (Pints €4.20. Happy Hour 5-8:30pm; drinks €3.10. Open Su-F 11pm-3am, Sa 4pm-3am.) **Cassero,** in the Porta Saragozza, is a lively gay bar packed with men and women. (Open daily 10pm-2am.)

PARMA ☎0521

Parma maintains an artistic and culinary elegance from its rich past, while vibrating with youthful energy from the nearby university. From P. Garibaldi, follow Strada Cavour toward the train station and take the third right on Strada al Duomo to reach the 11th-century Romanesque **duomo,** in P. del Duomo, which is filled with masterpieces. Most spectacular is the dome, where Correggio's *Virgin* ascends to a golden heaven in a spiral of white robes, pink *putti,* and blue sky. The pink-and-white marble **baptistery** was built between the Romanesque and Gothic periods. (*Duomo* open daily 9am-noon and 3-7pm. Baptistery open daily 9am-12:30pm and 3-7pm. €2.70, students €1.50.) Behind the *duomo* is the frescoed dome of the **Chiesa di San Giovanni Evangelista,** P.S. Giovanni, designed by Correggio. (Open daily 9am-noon and 3-7pm.) From P. del Duomo, follow Strada al Duomo across Strada Cavour, walk one block down Strada Piscane, and cross P. della Pace to reach the 17th-century **Palazzo della Pilotta,** Parma's artistic treasure chest, which houses the **Galleria Nazionale.** (Open daily 9am-2pm. €6.)

Parma is on the Bologna-Milan rail line. **Trains** go from P. Carlo Alberto della Chiesa to: Bologna (1hr., 2 per hr., €4); Florence (3hr., 7 per day, €14.20); and Milan (1½hr., every hr., €7). Walk left from the station, turn right on V. Garibaldi, and turn left on V. Melloni to reach the **tourist office,** V. Melloni 1a. (☎0521 21 88 89; fax 0521 23 47 35. Open M-Sa 9am-7pm, Su 9am-1pm.) **Supermarket 2B** is at V. XXII Luglio 27c. (Open M-W and F-Sa 8:30am-1pm and 4:30-8pm, Th 8:30am-1pm.) From the station, take bus #9 (€0.75) and get off when the bus turns left on V. Martiri della Libertà for the **Ostello Cittadella (HI) ❶,** on V. Passo Buole, in a corner of a 15th-century fortress. (☎96 14 34. 3-night max. stay. Lockout 9:30am-5pm. Curfew 11pm. Open Apr.-Oct. HI members only. Dorms €9. €6 per person, €11 per site.) **Albergo Leon d'Oro ❸,** V. Fratti 4, off V. Garibaldi, is 2 blocks from the train station. (☎0521 77 31 82. Singles €30; doubles €47. AmEx/MC/V.) Look for **Via Garibaldi** is home to fragrant Parma cuisine. **Le Sorelle Picchi,** Strada Farini 27, near P. Garibaldi, is a traditional *trattoria* and *salumeria.* (☎0521 23 35 28. *Primi* €5-6, *secondi* €7-8. *Trattoria* open M-Sa noon-3pm; *salumeria* open 8:30am-7pm.) **K2,** Borgo Cairoli 23, next to the Chiesa di San Giovanni Evangelista, has great *gelato.* (Cones from €1.50. Open Th-Tu 11am-midnight.) **Postal Code:** 43100.

RAVENNA ☎0544

Ravenna's 15min. of historical superstardom came and went 14 centuries ago when Justinian and Theodora, rulers of the Byzantine Empire, headquartered their campaign here to restore order in the anarchic west. Take V. Argentario from V. Cavour to reach the 6th-century ◼Basilica di San Vitale, V.S. Vitale 17. An open courtyard overgrown with greenery leads to the brilliant, glowing mosaics inside; those of the Emperor and Empress adorn the lower left and right panels of the apse. Behind S. Vitale, the city's oldest and most intriguing mosaics cover the glittering interior of the **Mausoleo di Galla Placidia.** (☎ 0544 21 62 92. Open Apr.-Sept. daily 9am-7pm; Oct.-Mar. 9:30am-4:30pm. Joint ticket €3.10.) Take bus #4 or 44 across from the train station (€0.70) to Classe, south of the city, to see the astounding mosaics at the ⬛**Chiesa di Sant'Apollinare in Classe.** (Open M-Sa 8:30am-7:30pm, Su 9am-1pm. €2.10, Su free.) Much to Florence's dismay, Ravenna is also home to the **Tomb of Dante Alighieri,** its most popular sight. In the adjoining **Dante Museum,** his heaven and hell come alive in etchings, paintings, and sculptures. From P. del Popolo, cut through P. Garibaldi to V. Alighieri. (☎ 0544 302 52. Tomb open daily 9am-7pm. Free. Open Apr.-Sept. Tu-Su 9am-noon and 3:30-6pm. €2.)

  Trains (☎ 0544 21 78 84) leave P. Farini for Ferrara, Florence, and Venice (1hr., every 2hr., €4.50) via Bologna (1hr., every 1-2hr., €4). Follow V. Farini from the station to V. Diaz, which runs to the central P. del Popolo and the **tourist office,** V. Salara 8. (☎ 0544 354 04; fax 0544 48 26 70. Open M-Sa 8:30am-7pm, Su 10am-4pm.) Take bus #1 or 70 from V. Pallavicini at the station (1-4 per hr., €0.70) to reach **Ostello Dante (HI) ❶,** V. Nicolodi, 12. (☎/fax 0544 42 11 64. Breakfast included. Reception 7-10am and 5-11:30pm. Lockout 10am-5pm. Curfew 11:30pm. 4- to 6-bed dorms €12.50. MC/V.) Walk down V. Farini and go right at P. Mameli for the renovated **Albergo Al Giaciglio ❸,** V. Rocca Brancaleone 42. (☎ 0544 394 03. Breakfast €2-5. Singles €28-32; doubles €35-45; triples €45-60. MC/V.)

FERRARA ☎ 0532

Rome has its mopeds, Venice its boats, and Ferrara its bicycles. Old folks, young folks, and babies perched precariously on handlebars whirl through Ferrara's jumble of major thoroughfares and twisting medieval roads. Take a deep breath of fresh air, hop on a bike, and head for the giant castle.

🔁 TRANSPORTATION AND PRACTICAL INFORMATION. Ferrara **trains,** on the Bologna-Venice line, go to: Bologna (30min., 1-2 per hr., €2.75); Padua (1hr., every hr., €4); Ravenna (1hr., 1-3 per hr., €4); Rome (3-4hr., 7 per day, €31); and Venice (2hr., 1-2 per hr., €6). ACFT (☎ 0532 59 94 92) and GGFP **buses** leave V. Rampari S. Paolo or the train station for Bologna (1½hr., 15 per day, €3.30) and Ferrara's beaches (1hr., 12 per day, €4-5). To get to the center of town, turn left out of the train station and then veer right on **Viale Costituzione.** This road becomes Viale Cavour and runs to the **Castello Estense** at the center of town (1km). Or, take bus #2 to the Castello stop or bus #1 or 9 to the post office (every 15-20min., €0.85). The **tourist office** is in Castello Estense. (☎ 0532 20 93 70. Open daily 9am-1pm and 2-6pm.) Rent cheap **bikes** at P. le Stazione 2. (€7 per day. Open daily 6:30am-1pm and 3:30-7pm.) **Postal Code:** 44100.

🔂 ACCOMMODATIONS AND FOOD. Walk down Corso Ercole I d'Este from the *castello,* or take bus #4c from the station and ask for the *castello* stop to reach the central ⬛**Ostello della Gioventu Estense (HI) ❶,** Corso B. Rossetti 24, with simple bunk bed rooms. (☎/fax 0532 20 42 27. Reception 7-10am and 5-11:30pm. Lockout 10am-3:30pm. Curfew 11:40pm. Dorms €13.) **Casa degli Artisti ❷,** V. Vittoria 66, near P. Lampronti, is in the historic center of Ferrara. (☎ 0532 76 10 38. Singles €21; doubles €38.) The **Albergo Nazionale ❹,** Calle Porta Reno 32, is on a busy street right off the *duomo.* (☎/fax 0532 20 96 04. Curfew 12:30am. Singles €40; doubles with bath €65; triples €78. AmEx/MC/V.) Gorge on delicious triangular meat ravioli served in a broth or the traditional *Ferrarese* dessert of luscious *pampepato,* chocolate-covered almond and fruit cake. Try delicious *panini* with one of 600 varieties of wine at the oldest *osteria* in Italy, **Osteria Al Brindisi 11 ❷,** V.G. degli Adelardi 9b. (☎ 0532 20 91 42. Open Tu-Su 8:30am-1am.) For picnic supplies, stop by the **Mercato Comunale,** on V. Mercato, next to the *duomo.* (Open M-W 7am-1:30pm and 4:30-7:30pm, F 4:30-7:30pm, Th and Sa 7am-1:30pm.)

ITALY

🔲 ♫ **SIGHTS AND ENTERTAINMENT. Bike** the tranquil, wooded concourse along the city's well-preserved 9km **medieval wall,** which begins at the far end of Corso Giovecca. The imposing **Castello Estense** stands precisely in the center of town. Corso della Giovecca lies along the former route of the moat's feeder canal, separating the medieval section from the part planned by the d'Este's architect. (☎0532 29 92 33. Open Tu-Su 9:30am-5pm. €4.10, students €3.) From the *castello,* take Corso Martiri della Libertà to P. Cattedrale and the **Duomo San Romano,** which contains the **Museo della Cattedrale.** (Cathedral open M-Sa 7:30am-noon and 3-6:30pm, Su 7:30am-12:30pm and 4-7:30pm. Museum ☎0532 20 74 49. Open Tu-Sa 10am-noon and 3-5pm, Su 10am-noon and 4-6pm.) From the *castello,* cross Largo Castello to Corso Ercole I d'Este and walk to the corner of Corso Rossetti to reach the gorgeous **Palazzo Diamanti,** built in 1493. Inside, the **Pinacoteca Nazionale** holds many of the best works of the Ferrarese school. (Open Tu-W and F-Sa 9am-2pm, Th 9am-7pm, Su and holidays 9am-1pm. €4.) Follow Corso Ercole I d'Este behind the *castello* and go right on Corso Porta Mare to find the **Palazzo Massari,** Corso Porta Mare 9, which houses both the **Museo d'Arte Moderna e Contemporanea "Filippo de Pisis,"** and, upstairs, the spectacular **Museo Ferrarese dell'Ottocento/Museo Giovanni Boldini.** (Both open daily 9am-1pm and 3-6pm. Joint ticket €6.70.) In July and August, a free **Discobus** (☎0532 59 94 11) runs every Saturday night between Ferrara and the hottest clubs; pick up flyers in the train station. **Postal code:** 44100.

TUSCANY (TOSCANA)

The vision that is Tuscany has inspired countless artists, poets, and hordes of tourists. Its rolling hills, prodigious olive groves, and cobblestone streets beg visitors to slow their frenetic pace, sip some wine, and relax in fields of brilliant sunflowers. Tuscany fostered some of Italy's, and the world's, greatest cultural achievements under the tender care—and devious machinations—of the powerful Medici family, gaining eternal eminence in the arts for its staggering accomplishments during a scant half-century. Today, tourists flock to Tuscany to witness the glory that was, and the wonder that still is, *Toscana.*

FLORENCE (FIRENZE)   ☎ 055

The rays of the setting sun shimmer over a sea of burnt-orange roofs and towering domes to reveal the breathtaking concentration of beauty in Florence. Once a busy 13th-century wool- and silk-trading town, Florence took a decidedly different path under Medici rule. By the mid-15th century, the city was the undisputed European capital of art, architecture, commerce, and political thought. Present-day Florence is a vibrant mix of young and old: street graffiti quotes Marx and Malcolm X, businessmen whiz by on Vespas, and children play soccer against the *duomo.*

▐ TRANSPORTATION

Flights: Amerigo Vespucci Airport (FLR; ☎31 58 74), in Peretola. The **ATAF** bus #62 connects the train station to the airport (€1). **Galileo Galilei Airport** (PSA) (☎(050) 50 07 07), in Pisa. Take airport express from the train station (1¼hr., €4.85).

Trains: Santa Maria Novella Station, across from S. Maria Novella. Trains depart every hr. for **Bologna** (1hr., €7.75), **Milan** (3½hr., €22), and **Rome** (3½hr., €15-22); and less frequently to **Siena** (1½hr., 10 per day, €5.30) and **Venice** (3hr., 4 per day, €19).

Buses: SITA, V.S. Caterina da Siena 15r (☎28 46 61). Runs to: **Arezzo** (2½hr., 3 per day, €4.10); **San Gimignano** (1½hr., 14 per day; €5.70); and **Siena** (1½hr., 2 per day, €6.50). **LAZZI,** P. Adua, 1-4r (☎35 10 61) sends buses to **Pisa** (every hr., €5.80).

Public Transportation: ATAF (☎055 565 02 22), outside the train station, runs orange city buses (6am-1am). 1hr. tickets €1; 3hr. €1.80; 24hr. €4; 3-day €7.20. Buy tickets at any newsstand, *tabacchi,* or automated ticket dispenser before boarding. Validate your ticket using the orange machine on board or risk a €50 fine.

Taxis: ☎055 43 90, 055 47 98, or 055 42 42. Outside the train station.

Bike/Moped Rental: Alinari Noleggi, V. Guelfa 85r (☎055 28 05 00). Bikes €12-18 per day, mopeds €28-55 per day.

 ## ORIENTATION AND PRACTICAL INFORMATION

From the train station, a short walk on V. de' Panzani and a left on V. de' Cerretani leads to the **duomo,** the center of Florence. Major arteries radiate from the duomo and its two *piazze.* A bustling walkway, **Via de' Calzaiuoli** runs south from the duomo to **Piazza Signoria.** V. Roma leads from P.S. Giovanni through **Piazza della Repubblica** to the **Ponte Vecchio** (Old Bridge), which spans the Arno River to the **Oltrarno** district. Note that most streets change names unpredictably. For guidance through Florence's tangled center, grab a **free map** from the tourist office. Sights are scattered throughout Florence, but few lie beyond walking distance.

> **! AND YOU THOUGHT THE AIRPORT WAS CONFUSING.** Florence is comprised of streets numbered in red and black sequences. Red numbers indicate commercial establishments and black numbers denote residential addresses (including most sights and hotels). Black addresses appear in *Let's Go* as a numeral only, while red addresses are indicated by a number followed by an "r." If you reach an address and it's not what you're looking for, you've probably got the wrong color sequence.

TOURIST, FINANCIAL, AND LOCAL SERVICES

Tourist Office: Informazione Turistica, P. della Stazione 4 (☎055 21 22 45), across the *piazza* from the main exit. Info on entertainment and cultural events. Be sure to ask for a free map with a street index. Open daily 8:30am-7pm.

Consulates: UK, Lungarno Corsini 2 (☎055 28 41 33). Open M-F 9:30am-12:30pm and 2:30-4:30pm. **US,** Lungarno Amerigo Vespucci 38 (☎055 239 82 76), at V. Palestro, near the station. Open M-F 9am-12:30pm. Others are in Rome or Milan.

Currency Exchange: Local banks offer the best rates. Most are open M-F 8:20am-1:20pm and 2:45-3:45pm, some also Sa morning. 24hr. **ATMs** abound.

American Express: V. Dante Alighieri 20-22r (☎055 509 81). From the *duomo,* walk down V. dei Calzaiuoli and turn left on V. dei Tavolini. Mail held free for AmEx customers, otherwise €1.55. Open M-F 9am-5:30pm, Sa 9am-12:30pm.

EMERGENCY AND COMMUNICATIONS

Emergency: ☎113. **Fire:** ☎115. **Police:** V. Zara 2 (☎055 497 71).

24-Hour Pharmacies: Farmacia Comunale (☎055 28 94 35), at the train station by track #16. **Molteni,** V. dei Calzaiuoli, 7r (☎055 28 94 90).

Medical Emergency: ☎118.

Florence

▲ ACCOMMODATIONS
Albergo Bellavista, **10**
Albergo Brunetta, **16**
Ausonia and Kursaal, **3**
Camping Michelangelo, **30**
Camping Villa Camerata, **31**
Hotel Elite, **12**
Hotel il Perseo, **15**
Hotel La Scaletta, **29**
Hotel Montreal, **11**
Hotel San Marco, **6**
Hotel Tina, **2**
Hotel Visconti, **17**
Istituto Gould, **27**
Ostello Archi Rossi, **4**
Ostello Santa Monaca, **26**
Tourist House, **14**
Via Faenza 56, **5**
Via Faenza 69, **8**

● **FOOD**
Acqua al Due, **19**
Gelateria Triangolo delle
  Bermuda, **7**
Le Colonnine, **25**
Oltrarno Trattoria Casalinga, **28**
Ristorante Il Vegetariano, **1**
Trattoria Anita, **23**
Trattoria da Benvenuto, **24**
Trattoria da Giorgio, **13**
Trattoria Mario, **9**
Vivoli, **20**

● **NIGHTLIFE**
Blob, **22**
May Day Lounge, **18**
Montecarla, **21**
Tabasco, **21**

Internet Access: Walk down almost any busy street and you'll find an Internet cafe. Try **Internet Train.** 15 locations listed on www.internettrain.it/citta.isp. Adults €4 per hr., students €3 per hr. Most open M-F 9am-midnight, Sa 10am-8pm, Su noon-9pm.

Post Office: V. Pellicceria (☎055 21 61 22), off P. della Repubblica. Address mail to be held: Firstname SURNAME, *In Fermo Posta*, L'Ufficio Postale, V. Pellicceria, Firenze, **50100** ITALY. Open M-F 8am-7pm, Sa 8:15am-noon.

▌ ACCOMMODATIONS AND CAMPING

As the astute reader will discern from the abundance of ❹s and ❺s, Florence don't come cheap. **Consorzio ITA,** in the train station by track #16, can find cheap rooms for a €2.50-7.75 commission. (☎28 28 93. Open daily 8:45am-8pm.) Because of the constant stream of tourists in Florence, it is best to make reservations *(prenotazioni)* in advance, especially if you plan to visit during Easter or summer.

HOSTELS

▓ **Ostello Archi Rossi,** V. Faenza 94r (☎055 29 08 04; fax 055 230 26 01). Exit left from the station on V. Nazionale and take the 2nd left on V. Faenza. Has patio brimming with young travelers. Wheelchair accessible. Breakfast €1.60. Laundry €5.20. Lockout 11:30am-2pm. Curfew 1am. No reservations; in summer, arrive before 8am. 4- to 9-bed dorms €17-23; rooms for handicapped €26. ❷

▓ **Istituto Gould,** V. dei Serragli 49 (☎055 21 25 76), in the Oltrarno. Exit the station by track #16, head right to P. della Stazione, walk to the left of the church, and continue through the P.S. Marla Novella and down V. dei Fossi (15min.). Spotless rooms. Reception M-F 9am-1pm and 3-7pm, Sa 9am-1pm. No check-in or check-out Sa afternoons or Su. Singles €30; doubles €44; triples €56. ❸

Ostello Santa Monaca, V.S. Monaca 6 (☎055 26 83 38). Exit the station by track #16, head right to P. della Stazione, walk to the left of the church, continue through P.S. Maria Novella and down V. dei Fossi, and turn right onto V.S. Monaca off V. dei Serragli. 7-night max. stay. Reception 6am-1pm and 2pm-1am. Curfew 1am. Reserve in writing 3 days in advance. Dorms €16. AmEx/MC/V. ❷

HOTELS

OLD CITY (NEAR THE DUOMO)

▓ **Hotel Il Perseo,** V. de Cerretani 1 (☎055 21 25 04), en route to the *duomo* from the station, opposite the Feltrinelli bookstore. Immaculate rooms with fans. Bar and TV lounge. Breakfast included. Singles €50; doubles €70; triples €93. MC/V. ❹

Albergo Brunetta, Borgo Pinti 5 (☎055 247 81 34). Exit P. del Duomo on V. dell' Oriuolo behind the *duomo.* After 2 long blocks, turn left on Borgo Pinti. Central location and rooftop terrace with superb view. Singles €51; doubles €82; triples €103. ❹

AROUND PIAZZA SANTA MARIA NOVELLA

▓ **Hotel Elite,** V. della Scala 12 (☎055 21 53 95). Exit to the right from the train station onto V. degli orti Oricellari and turn left on V. della Scala. Brass glows in this 2-star hotel's lovely rooms. Breakfast €6. Singles €52; doubles €70; triples €95. ❹

Hotel Visconti, P. Ottaviani 1 (☎/fax 055 21 38 77). Exit the train station from the left and cross behind S. Maria church into P.S. Maria Novella, and walk to the left until you reach tiny P. Ottaviani. Look for huge Grecian nudes. Breakfast included. Singles €40; doubles €60; triples €80; quads €90. ❹

Hotel Montreal, V. della Scala 43 (☎055 238 23 31), near Hotel Elite (see above). Clean, modern rooms. Curfew 1:30am. Singles €40; doubles €65; triples €85. ❹

Albergo Bellavista, Largo F. Alinari 15 (☎055 28 45 28; fax 055 28 48 74), steps from the train station, in an old *palazzo*. Exit from the train station and cross the *piazza* diagonally left. Simple, comfortable rooms. Doubles €98; triples €139. AmEx/MC/V. ❺

Tourist House, V. della Scala 1 (☎055 26 86 75). All rooms with bath. Singles €67; doubles €83; quads €124. MC/V. ❺

AROUND PIAZZA SAN MARCO

▨ **Hotel Tina,** V.S. Gallo 31 (☎055 48 35 19). From P.S. Marco, follow V. XXII Aprile and turn right on V.S. Gallo. *Pensione* with high ceilings, new furniture, and amicable owners. Singles €44; doubles €62; triples €77.50. ❹

Hotel San Marco, V. Cavou 50 (☎055 28 42 35), off P.S. Marco. Modern, airy rooms. Breakfast included. Curfew 1:30am; ask for a key. Singles €41.50; doubles €56.85; triples €103.30; quads €134.30. MC/V. ❹

AROUND VIA NAZIONALE

Via Faenza 56 houses six separate *pensioni,* some of the best deals in the city. From the train station, exit left onto V. Nazionale, walk 1 block, and turn left on V. Faenza. The prices and amenities for Azzi, Anna, and Paola are listed under Azzi.

Pensione Azzi (☎055 1 38 06) has large rooms and a terrace. Breakfast included. Singles €41; doubles €62; triples €77.50. AmEx/MC/V. ❹

Albergo Anna (☎055 239 83 22) has lovely singles and doubles with frescoes and fans. ❹

Locanda Paola (☎055 21 36 82) has spartan doubles with views of the surrounding hills. ❹

Albergo Merlini (☎055 21 28 48; www.hotelmerlini.it) has some rooms with views of the *duomo*. Curfew 1am. Doubles €69; triples €80. AmEx/MC/V. ❺

Albergo Marini (☎055 28 48 24) boasts spotless rooms. Breakfast €5.15. Singles €47; doubles €62; triples €82.65; quads €103.30; quints €123.95. ❹

Albergo Armonia (☎055 21 11 46) decorates its rooms with film posters. Singles €42; doubles €65; triples €90; quads €100. ❹

Via Faenza 69 houses no-frills hotels. Same directions as for Via Faenza 56.

Locanda Giovanna (☎055 238 13 53) has basic, well-kept rooms with garden views. Singles €37.40; doubles €57. ❹

Hotel Nella/Pina (☎055 265 43 46) has 14 basic rooms and Internet. Singles €47; doubles €62. AmEx/MC/V. ❹

Ausonia and Kursaal, V. Nazionale 24 (☎055 49 65 47). Exit the train station to the left and turn left on V. Nazionale. Lots of amenities. Wheelchair-accessible. Breakfast included. No curfew. Doubles €82-116; triples €109-143; quads €170. MC/V. ❺

OLTRARNO

▨ **Hotel La Scaletta,** V. Guicciardini 13b (☎055 28 30 28). Turn right onto V. Roma from the *duomo*, cross Ponte Vecchio and walk on V. Guicciardini. Has views of Boboli gardens. Breakfast included. Reception open until midnight. Singles €40; doubles €100; triples €154; quads €170. 10% *Let's Go* discount when you pay cash. MC/V. ❹

CAMPING

Campeggio Michelangelo, V. Michelangelo 80 (☎055 681 19 77), beneath Piazzale Michelangelo. Take bus #13 from the bus station (15min.; last bus 11:25pm). Crowded, but a great view of Florence. Open Apr.-Nov. €8 per person, €5 per tent. ❶

Villa Camerata, V.A. Righi 2-4 (☎055 60 03 15), on the #17 bus route. Breakfast €1. Reception daily 1pm-midnight. Check-out 7-10am. €6 per person, €5 per tent. ❶

🔲 FOOD

Florence's hearty cuisine originated in the peasant fare of the surrounding countryside. Specialties include *bruschetta* (grilled bread soaked with olive oil and garlic and topped with tomatoes and basil, anchovy, or liver paste) and *bistecca alla Fiorentina* (thick sirloin steak). Wine is a Florentine staple, and genuine *chianti classico* commands a premium price; a liter costs €3.65-5.20 in Florence's *trattorie*, while stores sell bottles for as little as €2.60. The local dessert is *cantuccini di prato* (almond cookies made with egg yolks) dipped in *vinsanto* (a rich dessert wine made from raisins). Florence's own Buontalenti family supposedly invented *gelato* centuries ago; true or not, you must sample it. For lunch, visit a *rosticceria gastronomia*, peruse the city's pushcarts, or pick up fresh produce or meat at the **Mercato Centrale,** between V. Nazionale and S. Lorenzo. (Open June-Sept. M-Sa 7am-2pm; Oct.-May M-F 7am-2pm, Sa 7am-2pm and 4-8pm.) To get to **STANDA supermarket,** V. Pietrapiana 1r, turn right on V. del Proconsolo, take the 1st left on Borgo degli Albizi, and continue straight through P.G. Salvemini; it will be on the left. (Open M 2-9pm, Tu-Su 8:30am-9pm.)

OLD CITY (THE CENTER)

🔳 **Trattoria Anita,** V. del Parlascio 2r (☎055 21 86 98), just behind the Bargello. Dine by candlelight, surrounded by expensive wine bottles on wooden shelves. Traditional Tuscan fare—filling pastas and an array of meat dishes from roast chicken to beefsteak Florentine. *Primi* €4.70-5.20; *secondi* from €5.20. Fantastic lunch *menu* €5.50. Cover €1. Open M-Sa noon-2:30pm and 7-10pm. AmEx/MC/V. ❷

🔳 **Acqua al Due,** V. Vigna Vecchia 40r, behind the Bargello. Popular with young Italians. Serves Florentine specialties, including an excellent *assaggio* (€7.50). *Primi* €6.70; *secondi* from €7-19. Cover €1. Reserve ahead. Open daily 7:30pm-1am. ❸

Le Colonnine, V. dei Benci 6r, north of the Ponte alle Grazie. Delicious traditional fare. Pizza €4.70; pasta *secondi* from €7. Famous *paella* could feed a small army (€18). Open daily noon-3:30pm and 6:30pm-midnight. ❷

Trattoria da Benvenuto, V. della Mosca 16r, on the corner of V. de' Neri. Wonderfully fresh *spaghetti alle vongole* (with clams) for €5.50. Cover €1.50. Open M-Sa 11am-3pm and 7pm-midnight. ❸

PIAZZE SANTA MARIA NOVELLA AND DEL MERCATO CENTRALE

🔳 **Trattoria da Giorgio,** V. Palazzuolo 100r. Generous portions. *Menù* €8-9. Expect a wait. Open M-Sa noon-3:30pm and 7pm-12:30am. ❷

🔳 **Trattoria Mario,** V. Rosina 2r, around the corner from P. del Mercato Centrale. Incredible pasta and meat dishes. *Primi* €3.50; *secondi* €3-10. Open M-Sa noon-3:30pm. ❷

Ristorante Il Vegetariano, V. delle Ruote 30r, off V.S. Gallo. Fresh, inventive meat-free dishes. Smoke-free. *Primi* from €4.65; *secondi* from €5.70. Open Tu-F 12:30-3pm and 7:30pm-midnight, Sa-Su 8pm-midnight. ❸

OLTRARNO

🔳 **Oltrarno Trattoria Casalinga,** V. Michelozzi 9r. Delicious Tuscan specialties. *Primi* €4-6; *secondi* €5-9. Cover €1.50. Open M-Sa noon-2:30pm and 7-10pm. ❸

GELATERIE

🔳 **Vivoli,** V. della Stinche 7, behind the Bargello. A renowned Florentine *gelateria* with a huge selection of the self-proclaimed "best ice cream in the world." Cups from €1.50. Open T-Sa 7:30am-1am; Su 9:30-1am.

🔳 **Gelateria Triangolo delle Bermuda,** V. Nazionale 61r. Blissful *crema venusiana* has hazelnut, caramel, and meringue. Cones €1.60. Open daily 11am-midnight.

ITALY

⊙ SIGHTS

Florence's museums run €3.10-6.20 per venue, and no longer offer student discounts. In summer, watch for **Sere al Museo**, evenings when certain museums are free from 8:30-11pm. Also, many of Florence's churches are treasuries of great art.

PIAZZA DEL DUOMO

DUOMO. The red brick of Florence's *duomo*, the **Cattedrale di Santa Maria del Fiore,** at the center of P. del Duomo, is visible from virtually every part of the city. Filippo Brunelleschi drew from long-neglected classical methods to come up with his revolutionary double-shelled construction that utilized self-supporting interlocking bricks. The *duomo* claims the world's third longest nave. *(Open M-Sa 10am-4:45pm, Su 1:30-4:45pm. Mass daily 7am-12:30pm and 5-7pm.)* Climb the 463 steps inside the dome to **Michelangelo's lantern,** which offers an unparalleled view of the city. *(Open M-F 8:30am-7pm, Sa 8:30am-5:40pm. €6.)* The top of the 82m high ▓**campanile** next to the *duomo* has beautiful views. *(Open daily 8:30am-7:30pm. €6.)*

BATTISTERO. The *battistero* (baptistery) next to the *duomo*, built between the 5th and 9th centuries, was the site of Dante's christening; its Byzantine-style mosaics inspired the details of his *Inferno*. The famous **bronze doors** were a product of intense competition among Florentine artists; Ghiberti was commissioned to forge the last set of doors. The products, reportedly dubbed the ▓**Gates of Paradise** by Michelangelo, exchanged his earlier 28-panel design for 10 large, gilded squares, each of which employs mathematical perspective to create the illusion of deep space. Under restoration since a 1966 flood, they will soon be housed in the Museo dell' Opera del Duomo. *(Open M-Sa noon-7pm, Su 8:30am-2pm. €3.)*

MUSEO DELL'OPERA DEL DUOMO. Most of the *duomo*'s art resides behind the cathedral in the Museo dell'Opera del Duomo. Up the first flight of stairs is a late *Pietà* by Michelangelo, who, according to legend, destroyed Christ's left arm with a hammer in a fit of frustration; soon after, a diligent pupil touched up the work, leaving visible scars on parts of Mary Magdalene's head. The museum also houses four frames from the baptistery's *Gates of Paradise*. *(P. del Duomo 9, behind the duomo. ☎ 055 264 7287 Open M-Sa 9am-6:30pm, Su 9am-1pm. €6.)*

PIAZZA DELLA SIGNORIA AND ENVIRONS

From P. del Duomo, the bustling **Via dei Calzaiuoli,** one of the city's oldest streets, runs south through crowds and chic shops to P. della Signoria.

PIAZZA DELLA SIGNORIA. The destruction of powerful Florentine families' homes in the 13th century created a empty space that cried out *"piazza!"* With the construction of the Palazzo Vecchio in 1299, the square became Florence's civic and political center. In 1497, religious leader and social critic Savonarola convinced Florentines to light the **Bonfire of the Vanities,** a grand roast in the square that consumed some of Florence's best art. A year later, disillusioned citizens sent Savonarola up in smoke on the same spot, marked today by a granite disc. Monumental sculptures cluster in front of the *palazzo*, including a copy of Michelangelo's *David*. The awkward *Neptune* to the left of the Palazzo Vecchio so revolted Michelangelo that he insulted the artist: "Oh Ammannato, Ammannato, what lovely marble you have ruined!" The graceful 14th-century **Loggia dei Lanzi,** built as a stage for civic orators, contains world-class sculpture free of charge.

PALAZZO VECCHIO. Arnolfo del Cambio designed this fortress-like *palazzo* in the late-13th century as the governmental seat. It later became the Medici family home; in 1470, Michelozzo decorated the ▓**courtyard** in Renaissance style. Inside are works by Michelangelo, da Vinci, and Bronzino. *(Open June-Aug. M and F 9am-11pm, Tu-W and Sa 9am-7pm, Th and Su 9am-2pm; Sept.-May M-W and F-Sa 9am-7pm, Th 9am-2pm, Su 9am-2pm. €9.20.)*

◙**THE UFFIZI.** Vasari designed this palace in 1554 for the offices *(uffizi)* of Duke Cosimo's administration; today, it houses more first-class art per square inch than any other museum in the world. Botticelli, da Vinci, Michelangelo, Raphael, Titian, Giotto, Fra Angelico, Caravaggio, Bronzino, Cimabue, della Francesca, Bellini, even Dürer, Rubens, and Rembrandt—you name it, they have it. *(Extends from P. della Signoria to the Arno River. ☎ 055 21 83 41. Open Tu-Su 8am-7pm. €8.50.)*

PONTE VECCHIO. From the Uffizi, follow V. Georgofili left and turn right along the river to reach the nearby **Ponte Vecchio** (Old Bridge). The oldest bridge in Florence, it replaced an older Roman version in 1345. In the 1500s, the Medici kicked out the butcheries and tanneries that lined the bridge and installed goldsmiths and diamond-carvers instead. The view of the bridge from the neighboring Ponte alle Grazie at sunset is breathtaking, and the bridge itself buzzes with pedestrians and street performers, particularly at night.

BARGELLO. The heart of medieval Florence lies in this 13th-century fortress between the *duomo* and P. della Signoria. Once the residence of the chief magistrate and later a brutal prison with public executions in the courtyard, it was restored in the 19th century and now houses the sculpture-filled **Museo Nazionale.** Donatello's bronze *David*, the first freestanding nude since antiquity, stands opposite the two bronze panels of the *Sacrifice of Isaac*, submitted by Ghiberti and Brunelleschi in the baptistery door competition. Michelangelo's early works, including *Bacchus*, *Brutus*, and *Apollo*, are on the ground floor. *(V. del Proconsolo, 4, between duomo and P. della Signoria. ☎ 055 238 86 06. Open daily typically 8:15am-1:50pm; closed 2nd and 4th M of each month, though hours and off days vary by month. €4.)*

SAN LORENZO AND FARTHER NORTH

BASILICA DI SAN LORENZO. The Medici, who lent the city the funds to build the church (designed in 1419 by Brunelleschi), retained artistic control over its construction. The family cunningly placed Cosimo Medici's grave in front of the high altar, making the entire church his personal mausoleum. Michelangelo designed the exterior but, disgusted by Florentine politics, he abandoned the project to study architecture in Rome. *(☎ 055 21 66 34. Open daily M-Sa 10am-5pm. €2.50.)*

To reach the ◙**Cappelle dei Medici** (Medici Chapels), walk around to the back entrance on P. Madonna degli Aldobrandini. The **Cappella dei Principi** (Princes' Chapel) is a rare Baroque moment in Florence, while the **Sacrestia Nuova** (New Sacristy) shows Michelangelo's work and holds two Medici tombs. *(Open daily 8:15am-5pm; closed the 2nd and 4th Su and the 1st, 3rd, and 5th M of every month. €6.)*

◙**ACCADEMIA.** Michelangelo's triumphant **David** stands in self-assured perfection in a rotunda designed specifically for it. In the hallway stand Michelangelo's four *Prisoners*; the master left these intriguing statues intentionally unfinished, chipping away just enough to liberate the "living stone." *(V. Ricasoli 60, between churches of S. Marco and S.S. Annunziata. Wheelchair accessible. Open Tu-Su 8:15am-6:50pm. €6.50.)*

PIAZZA SANTA CROCE AND ENVIRONS

◙**CHIESA DI SANTA CROCE.** The thrifty Franciscans ironically built the city's most splendid church. Among the luminaries buried here are Machiavelli, Galileo, Michelangelo (who rests at in the right aisle in a tomb designed by Vasari), and humanist Leonardo Bruni, shown holding his precious *History of Florence*. Note also Donatello's gilded *Annunciation*. *(Open M-Sa 9:30am-5:30pm, Su and holidays 3-5:30pm.)* Intricate *pietra serena* pilasters and statues of the evangelists by Donatello grace Brunelleschi's small **Cappella Pazzi**, at the end of the cloister next to the church. *(Enter through the Museo dell' Opera. Open Th-Tu 10am-7pm. €2.60.)*

THE OLTRARNO

Historically disdained by downtown Florentines, the far side of the Arno remains a lively and unpretentious quarter, even in high season.

PALAZZO PITTI. Luca Pitti, a nouveau-riche banker of the 15th century, built his *palazzo* east of Santo Spirito against the Boboli hill. The Medici acquired the *palazzo* and the hill in 1550 and enlarged everything possible. Today, it houses six museums, including the **ØGalleria Palatina.** The Galleria was one of only a few public galleries when it opened in 1833 and today houses Florence's most important art collection after the Uffizi. Works by Raphael, Titian, Andrea del Sarto, Caravaggio, and Rubens line the walls. Other museums display Medici family treasures, costumes, porcelain, carriages, and *Apartamenti Reale* (royal apartments)—lavish reminders of the time when the *palazzo* was the royal House of Savoy's living quarters. *(Open Tu-Su 8:30am-6.50pm. €6.50)*

BOBOLI GARDENS. With geometrically sculpted hedges, contrasting groves of holly and cypress trees, and bubbling fountains, the elaborate gardens are an exquisite example of stylized Renaissance landscaping. A large oval lawn is just up the hill from the back of the palace, with an Egyptian obelisk in the middle and marble statues in freestanding niches dotting the hedge-lined perimeter. *(Open daily Nov.-Feb. 9am-4:30pm; Mar.-May and Sept.-Oct. 9am-5:30pm, June-Aug. 9am-7:30pm.*

CHIESA DI SANTA MARIA DEL CARMINE. Inside, the **Brancacci Chapel** holds Masaccio's 15th-century frescoes, declared masterpieces even in their time. With such monumental works as *The Tribute Money*, this chapel drew many artists, including Michelangelo. *(Open M and W-Sa 10am-5pm, Su 1-5pm. €3.10.)*

🎵 ENTERTAINMENT

In June, the *quartieri* of Florence turn out in costume to play their own medieval version of soccer, known as **calcio storico,** in which two teams of 27 players face off over a wooden ball in one of the city's *piazze*. These games often blur between athletic contest and riot. Tickets (from €12.40) are sold at the box office. The **Festival of San Giovanni Battista,** on June 24, features a tremendous fireworks display in P. le Michelangelo (easily visible from the Arno) starting around 10pm. May starts the summer music festivals with the classical **Maggio Musicale.** The **Estate Fiesolana** (June-Aug.) fills the Roman theater in nearby Fiesole with concerts, opera, theater, ballet, and film. September brings the **Festa dell'Unità,** a concert series at Campi Bisenzia (take bus #30). On the first Sunday after Ascension Day is the **Festa del Grillo** (Festival of the Cricket), when crickets in tiny wooden cages are sold in the Cascine park and then released into the grass.

🎵 NIGHTLIFE

For information on what's hot in the nightlife scene, consult the monthly *Firenze Spettacolo* (€2). Begin your nighttime *passeggiata* along V. dei Calzaiuoli and end it with coffee or *gelato* in a ritzy cafe on P. della Repubblica, where singers prance about the stage in front of **Bar Concerto.** In the Oltrarno, **Piazza San Spirito** has plenty of bars and restaurants, and live music in summer.

Montecarla, V. dei Bardi 2, in the Oltrarno, off P. de' Mozzi. A 3-tiered wonderland of cougar-print upholstery. This plush club is laid-back in the summer and packed in the winter. Mixed drinks €7. Open Su-Th 9pm-3:30am, F-Sa 9pm-5:30am.

May Day Lounge, V. Dante Alighieri 16r. Aspiring artists display their work on the walls of this eclectic lounge. Play Pong on the early 80s gaming system or sip mixed drinks (€4) to the beat of the background funk. Happy Hour 8-10pm. Open daily 8pm-2am.

Rio Grande, V. degli Olmi 1, near Parco delle Cascinè. Among locals and tourists alike, this is the most popular of Florence's discos. Cover €16; includes 1 drink. Special nights include soul, hip-hop, house, and reggae. Open Tu-Sa 11pm-4am. AmEx/MC/V.

Central Park, in Parco della Cascinè. Open-air dance floor pulses with hip-hop, jungle, reggae, and "dance rock." Mixed drinks €8. Open M-Sa 11pm-late. AmEx/MC/V.

Blob, V. Vinegia 21r, behind the Palazzo Vecchio. DJs, movies, foosball, and an evening bar buffet. Mixed drinks €6. Open 6pm-3:30am.

Yab, V. Sassetti 5. Another dance club seething with American students and locals. With classic R&B and Reggae on Mondays. A very large dance floor, mercifully free of strobe lights, is packed come midnight. Mixed drinks €5.20. Open daily 9pm-1am.

Tabasco Gay Club, P.S. Cecilia 3r from Palazzo Vecchio. Smoke machines and strobe lights on dance floor. Florence's popular gay disco. Caters primarily to men. 18+. Cover €13, includes first drink. Open Tu-Su 10pm-4am. AmEx/MC/V.

SIENA ☎ 0577

Many travelers rush from Rome to Florence, ignoring gorgeous, medieval Siena. The Sienese have a rich history in arts, politics, and trade; one of their proudest celebrations is the semiannual **Palio,** a wild horse race among the city's 17 competing *contrade* (districts).

◨ ⊞ TRANSPORTATION AND PRACTICAL INFORMATION. Trains (☎ 0577 28 01 15) leave P. Rosselli hourly for Florence (1½hr., 12 per day, €5.30) and Rome (3hr., 16 per day, €16.25) via Chiusi. **TRA-IN/SITA buses** (☎ 0577 20 42 45) depart from P. Gramsci and the train station for Florence (every hr., €6.50) and San Gimignano (8 per day, €5). From the train station, cross the street and take **TRA-IN/SITA buses** #3, 4, 7-10, 14, 17, or 77 into the center of town at **Piazza del Sale** or **Piazza Gramsci** (€0.80). The central **APT tourist office** is at Il Campo 56. (☎ 0577 28 05 51; fax 27 06 76. Open daily mid-Mar. to mid-Nov. 8:30am-7:30pm; mid-Nov. to mid-Mar. 8:30am-1pm and 3-7pm.) **Prenotazioni Alberghiere,** in P.S. Domenico, finds rooms for €2. (☎ 0577 28 80 84. M-Sa 9am-7pm.) Check email at **Internet Train,** V. di Citta 121. (€5.20 per hr. Open M-Sa 10am-8pm, Su noon-8pm.) **Postal Code:** 53100.

▐ ⊟ ACCOMMODATIONS AND FOOD. Finding a room in Siena can be difficult from Easter to October. Book months ahead if coming during *Il Palio*. The tastefully furnished **Albergo Tre Donzelle ❸** is at V. Donzelle 5. (☎ 0577 28 03 58; fax 0577 22 39 38. Curfew 1am. Singles €31; doubles €44-57. MC/V.) Take bus #15 from P. Gramsci to reach the **Ostello della Gioventù "Guidoriccio" (HI) ❶,** V. Fiorentina 89, in Località Lo Stellino. (☎ 0577 522 12. Curfew midnight. Reserve ahead. Dorms €13. MC/V.) **Santvario S. Caterina Alma Domus ❹,** V. Camporegio 37, behind S. Domenico, has spotless rooms with views of the *duomo*. (☎ 0577 441 77; fax 0577 476 01. Curfew 11:30pm. Singles €42; doubles €55; triples €70; quads €85.) To **camp** at **Colleverde ❶,** Strada di Scacciapensieri 47, take bus #3 or 8 from P. del Sale. (☎ 0577 28 00 44. Open mid-Mar. to mid-Nov. €8 per adult, including tent; €4.15 per child.)

Siena specializes in rich pastries, of which the most famous is *panforte*, a confection of honey, almonds, and citron; indulge in this serious pastry at **Bar/Pasticceria Nannini**, V. Banchi di Sopra 22-24, the oldest *pasticceria* in Siena. Next to Santuario di S. Caterina is the divine **Osteria La Chiacchera ❷**, Costa di S. Antonio 4. (☎ 0577 28 06 31. *Secondi* €4.65-6.75. Open W-M 12:30-3pm and 7-10:30pm.) **Consortio Agrario supermarket**, V. Pianigiani 5, is off P. Salimberi. (Open M-F 8am-7:30pm.)

⑥ ♫ SIGHTS AND ENTERTAINMENT. Siena offers two **biglietto cumulativi** (cumulative tickets)—the first is good for five days (€7.50) and allows entry into the Museo dell'Opera Metropolitana, baptistery, and Piccolomini library; the second is valid for seven days (€16) and covers four more sights, including the Museo Civico. Both may be purchased at any of the included sights. Siena radiates from **Piazza del Campo (Il Campo)**, a shell-shaped brick square designed for civic events. At the top of Il Campo is the **Fonte Gaia**, still fed by the same aqueduct used in the 1300s. At the bottom, the **Torre del Mangia** clock tower looms over the graceful Gothic ▧**Palazzo Pubblico.** Inside the *palazzo*, the **Museo Civico** contains excellent Gothic and early Renaissance paintings; also check out the **Sala del Mappamondo** and the **Sala della Pace.** (*Palazzo*, museum, and tower open Mar.-Oct. daily 10am-7pm; Nov.-Feb. 10am-4pm. Tower €5.50; museum €6.50, students €4; combined ticket with tower €9.50.) From the *palazzo*, take the right-side stairs and cross V. di Città for Siena's Gothic ▧**duomo.** The apse would have been left hanging in mid-air save for the construction of the lavishly decorated **baptistery** below. (Open mid-Mar. to Oct. daily 9am-7:30pm; Nov. to mid-Mar. 10am-1pm and 2:30-5pm. Free except when floor is uncovered in Sept. €4-5.50.) The **Libreria Piccolomini**, off the left aisle, holds frescoes and 15th-century scores. (Same hours as *duomo*. €1.50.) The **Museo dell'Opera della Metropolitana**, to the right of the *duomo*, houses overflow art. (Open Apr.-Oct. daily 9am-7:30pm; Nov.-Mar. 9am-1:30pm. €5.50.)

Siena's ▧**Il Palio**, July 2 and Aug. 16, is a traditional bareback horse race around the packed P. del Campo. Arrive three days earlier to watch the five trial runs and to pick a *contrada* to root for. At *Il Palio*, the jockeys take about 90 seconds to tear around Il Campo three times. To stay in Siena during the Palio, book rooms at least four months in advance, especially budget accommodations—write the APT in March or April for a list of rented rooms.

↗ DAYTRIP FROM SIENA: SAN GIMIGNANO. The hilltop village of San Gimignano looks like an illumination from a medieval manuscript. The city's famous 14 towers, which are all that survive of its original 72, earned San Gimignano its nickname as the *Città delle Belle Torri* (City of Beautiful Towers). Not for the faint of heart, ▧**Museo Della Tortura**, V. del Castello 1, just off P. Cisterna, offers a morbidly fascinating history of torture from Medieval Europe to the present. (Open Apr.-Oct. 10am-8pm; Nov.-Mar. 10am-6pm. Entrance €8, students €5.50.) The **Museo Civico**, on the 2nd floor of **Palazzo del Popolo**, houses an amazing collection of Sienese and Florentine artwork. Within the museum is the entrance to the **Torre Grossa**, the tallest remaining tower; climb its 218 steps for a panorama of Tuscany. (Palazzo open Tu-Su 9am-7:30pm. Museum and tower open Mar.-Oct. daily 9:30am-7:20pm; Nov.-Feb. Sa-Th 10:30am-4:20pm. Museum €5, students €4; tower €5/€4. Combined ticket €7.50/€5.50.)

TRA-IN buses leave P. Montemaggio for Siena (1hr., every hr., €5) and Florence (1½hr., every hr., €5.70) via Poggibonsi (20min., every hr., €1.35). From the bus station, pass through the *porta*, climb the hill, following V.S. Giovanni to the city center **Piazza della Cisterna**, which runs into P. del Duomo and the **tourist office**, P. del Duomo 1. (☎ 0577 94 00 08; fax 0577 94 09 03. Open Mar.-Oct. daily 9am-1pm and 3-7pm; Nov.-Feb. 9am-1pm and 2-6pm.) Accommodations are pricey in San Gimignano—*affitte camere* (private rooms) are a good alternative at about

€40. The **Associazione Strutture Extralberghiere**, P. della Cisterna 6, finds private rooms. (☎94 08 09. Open Mar.-Nov. daily 9:30am-7:30pm.) From the bus stop, enter through Porta S. Giovanni for the quaint **Camere Cennini Gianni ❺**, V.S. Giovanni 21. The reception is at the *passticceria* at V.S. Giovanni 88. (☎94 10 51; www.sangiapartments.com. Reserve ahead. Doubles €55; triples €65; quads €75.) **Camp** at **Il Boschetto ❶**, at Santa Lucia, a 2.5km bus ride (€0.80) from Porta S. Giovanni. (☎94 03 52. Reception daily 8am-1pm, 3-10pm. Open Apr.-Oct. €5 per person, €5 per tent. Showers included.) **La Bettola del Grillo ❸**, V. Quercecchio 33, off V.S. Giovanni, opposite P. della Cisterna, serves traditional Tuscan delights. The *menù* (€13) includes wine and dessert. (*Primi* €5-7, *secondi* €7.50. Open Tu-Su 12:30-3pm and 7:30-11pm.)

PISA   ☎050

Tourism hasn't always been Pisa's prime industry: during the Middle Ages, the city was a major port with its own Mediterranean empire. But when the Arno River silted up and the tower started leaning, the city's power and wealth declined accordingly. Today the city seems resigned to welcoming tourists and myriad t-shirt and ice cream vendors to the **Piazza del Duomo,** also known as the **Campo dei Miracoli** (Field of Miracles), a grassy expanse enclosing the tower, *duomo,* baptistery, Camposanto, Museo delle Sinopie, and Museo del Duomo. An **all-inclusive ticket** to the Campo's sights–other than the tower–costs €10.50. Begun in 1173, the famous **Leaning Tower** began to tilt when the soil beneath suddenly shifted. In June of 2001, a multi-year stabilization effort was completed; the tower is considered stable at its present inclination. Guided tours of 40 visitors are permitted to ascend the 300 steps once every 40 minutes. The dazzling **duomo,** also on the Campo, is a treasury of art, and considered one of the finest Romanesque cathedrals in the world. (Open daily 10am-7:30pm. €2.) Next door is the **baptistry,** whose precise acoustics allow an unamplified choir to be heard 2km away. (Open late Apr. to late Sept. daily 8am-7:30pm; Oct.-Mar. 9am-6pm. €6 includes 1 other museum or monument.) The adjoining **Camposanto,** a cloistered cemetery, has Roman sarcophagi and a series of haunting frescoes by an unidentified 14th-century artist known only as the "Master of the Triumph of Death." (Open late Apr. to late Sept. daily 8am-7:30pm; Mar. and Oct. 9am-5:40pm; Nov.-Feb. 9am-4:40pm. €6 includes 1 other museum or monument.) The **Museo delle Sinopie,** across the *piazza* from the Camposanto, displays preliminary fresco sketches discovered during post-WWII restoration. Behind the tower is the **Museo dell'Opera del Duomo.** (Both open late Apr. to late Sept. daily 8am-7:20pm; Mar. and Oct. 9am-5:20pm; Nov.-Feb. 9am-4:20pm. €6.20 includes 1 other museum or monument.) From the Campo, walk down V.S. Maria and over the bridge to the Gothic **Chiesa di Santa Maria della Spina,** whose tower allegedly holds a thorn from Christ's crown.

Trains (☎050 147 808 88) leave **Piazza della Stazione,** in the southern part of town, for: Florence (1hr., every hr., €4.85); Genoa (2½hr., €7.90); Rome (3hr., €23.50). To reach the Campo from the train station, take **bus** #3 (€0.75). The **tourist office** is to the left as you exit the station. (☎422 91; www.turismo.toscana.it. Open M-Sa 9am-7pm, Su 9:30am-3:30pm.) The **Albergo Helvetia ❸**, V. Don G. Boschi 31, 2min. from the *duomo,* off P. Archivescovado, has large, clean rooms. (☎050 55 30 84. Singles €32; doubles €42.) The **Hotel Galileo ❹**, V.S. Maria 12, has spacious simple rooms. (☎050 406 21. Singles and doubles €42; triples €57.) Try the heavenly *risotto* at the lively **❀Il Paiolo ❶**, V. Curtatone e Montanara 9. (*Menù* with *primi* and *secondi* €4-6. Open M-F noon-10pm, Sa 5-10pm.) **Trattoria da Matteo ❷**, V. l'Aroncio 46, serves authentic cuisine and 40 types of pizza. (*Menù* €12. Cover €1. ☎410 57. Open Su-F 9am-3pm and 6-11pm.) Get **groceries** at **Superal,** V. Pascoli 6, just off C. Italia. (Open M-Sa 8am-8pm.) **Postal Code:** 56100.

UMBRIA

Umbria is known as the "Green Heart of Italy," a land rich in natural beauty, encompassing wild woods, fertile plains, craggy gorges, and tiny villages. Christianity transformed Umbria's architecture and regional identity, turning it into a breeding ground for saints and religious movements; it was here that St. Francis of Assisi shamed the extravagant church with his humility.

PERUGIA ☎ 075

Between Perugia's art and architecture and its big-city vitality and gorgeous countryside, there's no reason not to visit this gem of a city. The city's most popular sights frame **Piazza IV Novembre**. In the center of the *piazza*, the **Fontana Maggiore** is adorned with sculptures and bas-reliefs by Nicolà and Giovanni Pisano. At the end of the *piazza*, the imposing Gothic **duomo** houses the purported wedding ring of the Virgin Mary. (Open daily 8am-noon and 4pm-dusk.) The 13th-century **Palazzo dei Priori** presides over the *piazza* and houses the impressive ⊠**Galleria Nazionale dell'Umbria**, Corso Vannucci 19. (Open daily 8:30am-7:30pm; closed 1st M each month. €6.50.) At the end of town past the Porta S. Pietro, the **Basilica di San Pietro**, on Corso Cavour, has a beautiful garden. (Open daily 8am-noon and 3:30pm-dusk.)

Trains leave P.V. Veneto, Fontiveggio, for: Assisi (25min., every hr., €1.60); Florence (2½hr., 7 per day, €7.90); and Rome (2½hr., €10.15; via Terontola or Foligno). From the station, take bus #6, 7, 9, 13d, or 15 to the central P. Italia (€0.80), then walk down Corso Vannucci to P. IV Novembre and the **tourist office**, P. IV Novembre 3. (☎075 572 33 27; fax 075 573 93 86. Open M-Sa 8:30am-1:30pm and 3:30-6:30pm, Su 9am-1pm.) To get from the tourist office to ⊠**Ostello della Gioventù/Centro Internazionale di Accoglienza per la Gioventù ❶**, V. Bontempi 13, walk down Corso Vannucci past the *duomo* and P. Danti, take the farthest street right through P. Piccinino, and turn right on V. Bontempi. (☎075 572 28 80; www.perugia.it. Sheets €1.50. Lockout 9:30am-4pm. Curfew midnight. Open mid-Jan. to mid-Dec. Dorms €12.) ⊠**Albergo Anna ❹**, V. dei Priori 48, off Corso Vannucci, has cozy 17th-century rooms with great views. (☎/fax 573 63 04. Singles €40, with bath €45; doubles €46/€60; triples €70/€85. AmEx/MC/V.) **Ristorante da Gianocarlo ❸**, V. dei Priori 36, off Corso Vannucci, is full of locals dining on delicious food. (*Primi* €6-14; *secondi* from €9-21. Open Sa-Th noon-3pm and 6-10pm.) The **COOP**, P. Matteotti 15, has groceries. (Open M-Sa 9am-8pm.) **Postal code:** 06100.

ASSISI ☎ 079

The undeniable jewel of Assisi is the 13th-century ⊠**Basilica di San Francesco.** Giotto's renowned *Life of St. Francis* fresco cycle decorates the walls of the upper church, paying tribute to his sainthood and consecration. From P. del Commune, take V. Portica. (Dress code strictly enforced. Lower basilica open daily 6:30am-7pm. Upper basilica open daily 8:30am-7pm.) The dramatic fortress **Rocca Maggiore** towers above town, offering panoramic views. (Open daily 10am-dusk. €1.70, students €1.) The pink and white **Basilica of Santa Chiara** houses St. Francis's tunic, sandals, and crucifix. (Open daily 9am-noon and 2-7pm.)

From the station near the Basilica Santa Maria degli Angeli, **trains** go to: Ancona (8 per day, €6.85); Florence (7 per day, €9); and Rome (5 per day, €9); more frequent trains go to Rome via Foligno and to Florence via Ternotola. **Buses** run from P. Unita D'Italia to Florence (2½hr., 1 per day, €6.40) and Perugia (1hr., 11 per day, €2.70). From P. Matteotti, follow V. del Torrione, bear left in P.S. Rufino, and take V.S. Rufino to **Piazza del Comune,** the town center, and the **tourist office,** in P. del Comune. (☎079 81 25 34; www.umbria2000.it. Open M-F 8am-2pm and 3:30-6:30pm, Sa 9am-1pm and 3:30-6:30pm, Su 9am-1pm.) Perhaps the cleanest hostel you'll find,

ITALY

the lovely **Camere Annalisa Martini ❷**, V.S. Gregorio 6, has lots of amenities and a friendly atmosphere. (Singles €22; doubles €32; triples €48-52; quads €57.) For **Ostello della Pace (HI) ❶**, V. di Valecchi 177, turn right out of the station, then left on V. di Valecchi. (☎/fax 079 81 67 67. Breakfast included. Reception daily 7-9am and 3:30-11:30pm. Check-out 9:30am. Dorms €14. MC/V.) **Postal code: 06081.**

THE MARCHES (LE MARCHE)

In the Marches, green foothills separate the gray shores of the Adriatic from the Apennine peaks and the traditional hill towns from the umbrella-laden beaches. Inland towns, easily accessible by train, rely on agriculture and preserve the region's historical legacy in the architectural remains of Gauls and Romans.

URBINO ☎0722

Urbino's fairy-tale skyline, scattered with humble stone dwellings and an immense turreted palace, has changed little over the past 500 years. The city's most remarkable monument is the imposing Renaissance **Palazzo Ducale** (Ducal Palace), in P. Rinascimento, though its facade is more thrilling than its interior. The central courtyard is the essence of Renaissance balance and proportion; to the left, stairs lead to the former private apartments of the Duke, which now house the **National Gallery of the Marches.** (Open M 8:30am-2pm, Tu-F 8:30am-7:15pm, Sa 8:30am-10:30pm, Su 8:30am-7:15pm. €4.) Walk back across P. della Repubblica and continue onto V. Raffaello to Raphael's birthplace, the **Casa di Rafaele**, V. Raffaello 57, now a museum that contains a reproduction of his earliest work, *Madonna e Bambino.* (Open M-Sa 9am-1pm and 3-6pm, Su 10am-1pm. €3.)

Bucci **buses** (☎0722 13 24 01) go from Borgo Mercatale to Rome (5hr., 1 per day, €18.50). Blue SOBET **buses** (☎0722 223 33) run to P. Matteotti and the train station in Pesaro (1hr., 4-10 per day, €2.10; buy tickets on the bus). From there, a short walk uphill on V.G. Mazzini leads to **P. della Repubblica,** the city center. The **tourist office,** P. Rinascimento 1, is opposite the palace. (☎0722 328 568; fax 0722 309 457. Open mid-June to mid-Sept. M-Sa 9am-1pm and 3-7pm, Su 9am-1pm; in winter 9am-1pm and 3-6pm.) **Hotel San Giovanni ❷,** V. Barocci 13, has simple, clean rooms. (☎0722 28 27. Open Aug.-June. Singles €22, with bath €27; doubles €38/€48; triples €57.) **Camping Pineta ❶,** on V.S. Donato, is 2km away in Cesane; take bus #4 or 7 from Borgo Mercatale to Camping. (☎0722 47 10. Reception daily 9-11am and 3-10pm. Open Apr. to mid-Sept. €6 per person, €13 per tent.) **Margherita supermarket** is at V. Raffaello 37. (Open M-Sa 7:30am-2pm and 3-8pm.) **Postal Code:** 61029.

ANCONA ☎071

Ancona is the epicenter of Italy's Adriatic Coast—a major port in a small, whimsical, largely unexplored city. **Piazza Roma** is dotted with yellow and pink buildings, and **Piazza Cavour** is the heart of the town. Ancona has **ferry service** to Greece, Croatia, and northern Italy. **Adriatica** (☎071 20 49 15; www.adriatica.it), **Jadrolinija** (☎20 43 05; www.jadrolinija.tel.hr/jadrolinija), and **SEM Maritime Co.** (☎071 20 40 90; www.sem.hr) run to Croatia (from €45). **ANEK** (☎071 207 23 46; www.anek.gr) and **Blue Star (Strintzis)** (☎071 207 10 68; www.strinzis.gr) ferries go to Greece (from €50). Schedules and tickets are available at the Stazione Marittima; reserve ahead in July or August. **Trains** arrive at P. Rosselli from: Bologna (2½hr., 1-2 per hr., €12); Milan (5hr., 24 per day, €21); Rome (3-4hr., 9 per day, €15); and Venice (5hr., 3 per day, from €15). Take bus #1/4 (€0.80) along the port past **Stazione Marittima** and up Corso Stamira to reach P. Cavour. A branch of the **tourist office** is located in Stazione Marittima and provides ferry information. (☎071 20 11 83.

ITALY

Open June-Sept. Tu-Sa 8am-8pm, Su-M 8am-2pm.) From the train station, cross the *piazza*, turn left, then take the first right and make a sharp right behind the newsstand to reach the new **Ostella della Gioventù ❶**, V. Lamaticci 7. (☎/fax 071 422 57. Reception daily 6:30-11am and 4:30pm-midnight. Dorms €13.) **CONAD supermarket** is at V. Matteotti 115. (Open M-Sa 8-1:30pm and 5-7:30pm.) **Postal Code:** 60100.

SOUTHERN ITALY

South of Rome, the sun gets brighter, the meals longer, and the passion more intense. The introduction to the *mezzogiorno* (Italian South) begins in Campania, the fertile cradle of the Bay of Naples and the Gulf of Salerno. The shadow of Mt. Vesuvius hides the famous ruins of Pompeii, lost to time and a river of molten lava, while the Amalfi Coast cuts a dramatic course down the lush Tyrrhenian shore. The region remains justly proud of its open-hearted populace, strong traditions, classical ruins, and relatively untouristed beaches.

NAPLES (NAPOLI)   ☎ 081

Italy's third-largest city is also its most chaotic—shouting merchants flood markets and summer traffic jams clog the broiling city. The city's color and vitality, evident in the street markets and the world's best pizza, have gradually overcome its traditionally rough-edged image. In recent years, aggressive restoration has reopened monuments, revealing exquisite architectural works of art.

▐ TRANSPORTATION

Flights: Aeroporto Capodichino, V. Umberto Maddalena (☎081 789 61 11), northwest of the city. Connects to all major Italian and European cities. A CLP **bus** (☎081 531 16 46) leaves from P. Municipio (20min., 6am-10:30pm, €1.55).

Trains: Ferrovie dello Stato goes from Stazione Centrale to: **Brindisi** (5hr., 5 per day, €18.85); **Milan** (8hr., 13 per day, €50); **Rome** (2hr., 34 per day, €9.60). **Circumvesuviana** (☎081 772 24 44), heads for **Herculaneum** (€1.55) and **Pompeii** (€1.90).

Ferries: Depart from **Molo Angioino** and **Molo Beverello,** at the base of P. Municipio. From P. Garibaldi, take tram #1; from P. Municipio, take the R2 bus. **Caremar,** Molo Beverello (☎081 551 38 82), goes frequently to **Capri** and **Ischia** (both 1½hr., €5). **Tirrenia Lines,** Molo Angioino (☎081 720 11 11), goes to **Palermo, Sicily,** and **Cagliari, Sardinia.** Schedules and prices change frequently, so check *Qui Napoli.*

Public Transportation: Giranapoli tickets (1½hr.; €0.80, full-day €2.35) are valid on **buses, Métro** (subway), **trams,** and **funiculars.**

Taxis: Cotana (☎081 570 70 70) or **Napoli** (☎081 556 44 44). Take metered taxis.

◢✳❼ ORIENTATION AND PRACTICAL INFORMATION

The main train and bus terminals are in the immense **Piazza Garibaldi** on the east side of Naples. From P. Garibaldi, broad **Corso Umberto I** leads southwest to P. Bovi, from which V. Depretis leads left to **Piazza Municipio,** the city center, and **Piazza Trieste e Trento** and **Piazza Plebiscito.** Below P. Municipio lie the **Stazione Marittima** ferry ports. From P. Trieste e Trento, **Via Toledo** (also known as **Via Roma**) leads through the Spanish quarter to **Piazza Dante.** Make a right into the historic **Spaccanapoli** neighborhood, which follows **Via dei Tribunali** through the middle of town. While violence is rare in Naples, theft is relatively common. Always be careful.

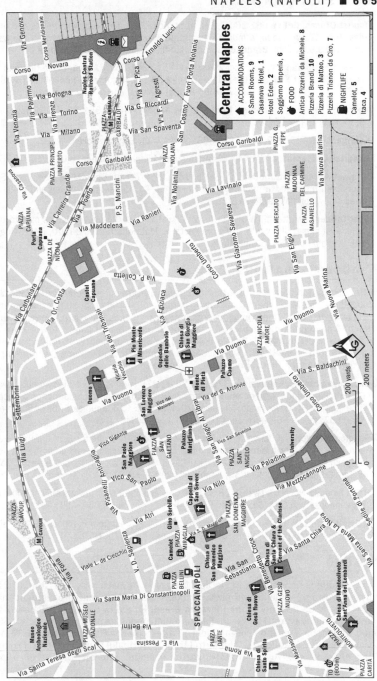

Central Naples

▲ ACCOMMODATIONS
6 Small Rooms, 9
Casanova Hotel, 1
Hotel Eden, 2
Soggiorno Imperia, 6

✦ FOOD
Antica Pizzeria da Michele, 8
Pizzeria Brandi, 10
Pizzeria di Matteo, 3
Pizzeria Trianon da Ciro, 7

■ NIGHTLIFE
Camelot, 5
Itaca, 4

Tourist Offices: EPT (☎081 26 87 79), at Stazione Centrale. Helps with hotels and ferries. Grab ▨ *Qui Napoli,* a monthly tourist publication full of schedules and listings. Open M-Sa 9am-7pm. **Branches** at P. dei Martiri 58 and Stazione Mergellina.

Consulates: Canada, V. Carducci 29 (☎081 40 13 38). **South Africa,** Corso Umberto 1 (☎551 75 19). **UK,** V. dei Mille 40 (☎081 423 89 11). **US,** P. della Repubblica (☎081 583 81 11, emergency ☎03 37 94 50 83), at the west end of Villa Comunale.

Currency Exchange: Thomas Cook, at the airport (☎081 551 83 99). Open M-F 9:30am-1pm and 3-6:30pm.

Emergency: ☎113. **Police:** ☎113 or 081 794 11 11. English spoken.

Hospital: Cardarelli (☎081 747 28 59), on the R4 line. **Ambulance:** ☎081 752 06 96.

Internet Access: Internetbar, P. Bellini 74. €2.50 per hr. Open M-Sa 9am-2am, Su 8am-2am. **Internet Multimedia,** V. Sapienza 43. €1.55 per hr. Scanning and printing available. Open daily 9:30am-9:30pm.

Post Office: P. Matteotti (☎081 552 42 33), at V. Diaz (R2 line). Address mail to be held: First name, SURNAME, *In Fermo Posta,* P. Matteotti, Naples **80100,** ITALY. Open M-F 8:15am-6pm, Sa 8:15am-noon.

▐ ACCOMMODATIONS

Although Naples has some fantastic bargain lodgings, especially near **Piazza Garibaldi,** be cautious when choosing a room. Avoid hotels that solicit customers at the station, never give your passport until you've seen the room, agree on the price *before* unpacking, be alert for unexpected costs, and gauge how secure a lodging seems. The **ACISJF/Centro D'Ascolto,** at Stazione Centrale, helps women find safe rooms. (☎081 28 19 93. Open M-Tu and Th 3:30-6:30pm.) Rooms are scarce in the historic district between P. Dante and the *duomo.*

▨ **Casanova Hotel,** C. Garibaldi 333 (☎081 26 82 87). From P. Garibaldi, continue down C. Garibaldi and turn right before V. Casanova. Clean, airy rooms, and a rooftop terrace. Breakfast €4. Reserve ahead. Singles €20, with bath €26; doubles €36/€46; triples €49/€57; quads €69. 10% *Let's Go* discount. AmEx/MC/V. ❷

▨ **Soggiorno Imperia,** P. Miraglia 386 (☎081 45 93 47). Take the R2 from the train station, walk up V. Mezzocannone through P.S. Domenico Maggiore, and enter the 1st set of green doors to the left on P. Miraglia. Clean rooms in a 16th-century *palazzo.* Call ahead. Dorms €16; singles €30; doubles €42; triples €60. ❶

Hotel Eden, C. Novara 9 (☎081 28 53 44). Convenient for backpackers arriving without reservations. With *Let's Go:* singles €30; doubles €40; triples €60. AmEx/MC/V. ❸

6 Small Rooms, V. Diodato Lioy 18 (☎081 790 13 78), up from P. Monteolivieto. Big rooms in a friendly atmosphere. Dorms €16; singles €20.70. ❶

▐ FOOD

Pizza-making is an art born in Naples. ▨**Pizzeria Di Matteo ❷,** V. Tribunali 94, draws a crowd of students and pizza connoisseurs to this small, pre-eminent eatery. (Open M-Sa 9am-midnight.) **Pizzeria Brandi ❷,** Salita S. Anna di Palazzo 1, counts Luciano Pavarotti and Isabella Rossellini among its patrons. (Cover €1.55. Open M-Su noon-3pm and 7pm-midnight.) To get to **Antica Pizzeria da Michele ❷,** V. Cesare Sersale 1-3, walk up C. Umberto I from P. Garibaldi and take the first right. Get a slice of *marinara* (tomato, garlic, oregano, and oil) or *margherita* (tomato, mozzarella, and basil) and a beer for €4.15. (Open M-Sa 8am-11pm.) Some of the best pizza in Naples is at **Pizzeria Trianon da Ciro ❶**, V. Pietro Colletta 44, a block off C. Umberto I. (Pizza €3-7. Open daily 10am-3:30pm and 6:30-11pm.) For excellent waterfront seafood, take the C25 bus to P. Amedeo.)

⊙ SIGHTS

▨ MUSEO ARCHEOLOGICO NAZIONALE. This world-class collection houses exquisite treasures from Pompeii and Herculaneum, including the outstanding "Alexander Mosaic." The sculpture collection is also quite impressive. *(From M: P. Cavour, turn right and walk 2 blocks. Open W-M 9am-7:30pm. €6.50.)*

SPACCANAPOLI. This east-west neighborhood overflows with gorgeous architecture, meriting at least a 30min. meander. From P. Dante, walk through Porta Alba and P. Bellini before turning on V. dei Tribunali, where the churches of **San Lorenzo Maggiore** and **San Paolo Maggiore** lie. Turn right on V. Duomo and turn right again on V.S. Biago to stroll past the **University of Naples** and the **Chiesa di San Domenico Maggiore,** where, according to legend, a painting once spoke to St. Thomas Aquinas. *(In P.S. Domenico Maggiore. Open daily 7:15am-12:15pm and 4:15-7:15pm. Free.)*

DUOMO. The main attraction of the 14th-century *duomo* is the **Cappella del Tesoro di San Gennaro.** A beautiful 17th-century bronze grille protects the high altar, which holds a gruesome display of relics like the saint's head and two vials of his coagulated blood. Supposedly, disaster will strike if the blood does not liquefy on the celebration of his *festa* (three times a year); miraculously, it always does. *(3 blocks up V. Duomo from Corso Umberto I. Open M-F 8am-12:30 and 4:30-7pm, Sa-Su 9am-noon. Free.)*

MUSEO AND GALLERIE DI CAPODIMONTE. This museum, in a royal *palazzo*, is surrounded by a pastoral park and sprawling lawns. The true gem is the amazing **Farnese Collection,** which displays works by Bellini and Caravaggio. *(Take bus #110 from P. Garibaldi to Parco Capodimonte; enter by Portas Piccola or Grande. Open Tu-F and Su 8:30am-7:30pm. €7.50, after 2pm €6.50.)*

PALAZZO REALE AND CASTEL NUOVO. The 17th-century **Palazzo Reale** contains opulent royal apartments, the **Museo di Palazzo Reale,** and a fantastic view from the terrace of the **Royal Chapel.** The **Biblioteca Nazionale** stores 1½ million volumes, including the scrolls from the **Villa dei Papiri** in Herculaneum. The **Teatro San Carlo** is reputed to top the acoustics in Milan's La Scala. *(Take the R2 bus from P. Garibaldi to P. Trieste e Trento and go around to the P. Plebiscito entrance. Open M-Tu and Th-F 9am-8pm. €4.15.)* From P. Trieste e Trento, walk up V. Vittorio Emanuele III to P. Municipio for the five-turreted **Castel Nuovo,** built in 1286 by Charles II of Anjou. The double-arched entrance commemorates the arrival of Alphonse I of Aragon in Naples. Inside, admire the **Museo Civico.** *(Open M-Sa 9am-7pm. €5.20.)*

♫ ▣ ENTERTAINMENT AND NIGHTLIFE

Piazza Vanvitelli in Vomero is where the cool kids go to relax and socialize. Take the funicular from V. Toledo or the C28 bus from P. Vittoria. Outdoor bars and cafes are a popular choice in **Piazza Bellini,** near P. Dante. **Itaca,** P. Bellini 71, mixes eerie trance music with dark decor. (Cocktails from €6. Open daily 10am-3am.) **Camelot,** V.S. Pietro A Majella 8, just off P. Bellini in the historic district, plays mostly pop and house. (Open Sept.-June Tu-Su 10:30pm-5am.) **ARCI-Gay/Lesbica** (☎ 551 82 93) has information on gay and lesbian club nights.

◨ DAYTRIPS FROM NAPLES

Mount Vesuvius, the only active volcano on the European continent, looms over the area east of Naples. Its infamous eruption in AD 79 buried the nearby Roman city of **Ercolano** (Herculaneum) in mud and neighboring **Pompei** (Pompeii) in ashes.

POMPEII. Since 1748, excavations have unearthed a stunningly well-preserved picture of Roman daily life. The site hasn't changed much since then, and neither have the victims, whose ghastly remains were partially preserved by plaster casts in the hardened ash. Take the Circumvesuviana **train** (☎772 24 44) from Naples's Stazione Centrale to Pompeii (dir.: Sorrento; 2 per hr., €1.90). To reach the site, head downhill and take your first left to the west (Porta Marina) entrance. Walk down V.D. Marina to reach the colonnaded ▧**Forum,** which was once the commercial, civic, and religious center of the city. Exit the Forum through the upper end by the cafeteria, and head right on V. della Fortuna to reach the ▧**House of the Faun,** where a bronze dancing faun and the spectacular Alexander Mosaic (today in the Museo Archeologico Nazionale) were found. Continue on V. della Fortuna and turn left on V. dei Vettii to reach the **House of the Vettii,** on the left, and the most vivid frescoes in Pompeii. Back down V. dei Vettii, cross V. della Fortuna to V. Storto, turn left on V. degli Augustali, and take a quick right to reach a small **brothel** (the Lupenar). After 2000 years, it's still the most popular place in town. V. dei Teatri, across the street, leads to the oldest standing **amphitheater** in the world (80 BC), which once held up to 12,000 spectators. To get to the ▧**Villa of the Mysteries,** the complex's best-preserved villa, head west on V. della Fortuna, right on V. Consolare, and all the way up Porta Ercolano. (Archaeological site open daily 8:30am-7:30pm. €10.) To get to the **tourist office,** V. Sacra 1, walk right from the station and continue to the bottom of the hill. (Open M-F 8am-3:30pm, Sa 8am-2pm.) Food at the on-site cafeteria is expensive, so bring lunch.

HERCULANEUM. Herculaneum is 500m downhill from the Ercolano stop on the Circumvesuviana train from Naples (dir.: Sorrento; 20min., €1.90). Stop at the **tourist office,** V. IV Novembre 84 (☎081 88 12 43), to pick up a free **map.** The city is less excavated than Pompeii; highlights include the **House of Deer.** (Open daily 8:30am-7:30pm. €10.)

MT. VESUVIUS. You can peer into the only active volcano on mainland Europe at Mt. Vesuvius. Trasporti Vesuviani **buses** (buy ticket on board; roundtrip €3.10) run from the Ercolano Circumvesuviana station to the crater. Although Vesuvius hasn't erupted since March 31, 1944 (and scientists say volcanoes should erupt every 30 years), experts deem the trip safe.

AMALFI COAST. The dramatic scenery and pulsing nightlife of the towns on the Amalfi Coast are easily accessible from Naples by train, ferry, and bus (p. 668).

BAY OF NAPLES. Only an hour away from Naples by ferry, the isles of Capri and Ischia tempt travelers with luscious beaches and enchanting grottos. (p. 670).

AMALFI COAST

The beauty of the Amalfi coast rests in immense, rugged cliffs plunging downward into calm azure waters and coastal towns climbing the sides of narrow ravines. The picturesque villages provide stunning natural panoramas, delicious food, and throbbing nightlife.

☎ TRANSPORTATION. The coast is accessible from Naples, Sorrento, Salerno, and the islands by ferry and blue SITA buses. **Trains** run directly to Salerno from Naples (45min., 29 per day, €5-10); Rome (2½-3hr., 19 per day, €20-30); and Venice (9hr., 1am, €35). **Buses** also link Paestrum and Salerno (1hr., every hr. 7am-7pm, L4700/€2.50). From Salerno, Travelmar (☎ 089 87 31 90) runs **ferries** to Amalfi (35min., 6 per day, €3.50) and Positano (1¼hr., €5). From Sorrento, Linee Maritime Partenopee **ferries** (☎ 081 807 18 12) run to Capri (40min., 5 ferries per day 8:30am-4:50pm, €6.50; 20min., 17 hydrofoils per day 7:20am-5:40pm, €8.50.).

AMALFI AND ATRANI. Breathtaking natural beauty surrounds the narrow streets and historic monuments of **Amalfi.** Visitors crowd the P. del Duomo to admire the elegant 9th-century **Duomo di Sant'Andrea** and the nearby **Fontana di Sant'Andrea,** a marble nude with water spouting from her breasts. **A'Scalinatella ❶,** P. Umberto 12, has hostel beds and regular rooms all over Amalfi and Atrani. (☎ 089 87 19 30. Dorms €10.25; doubles €26.45. **Camping** €7.75 per person.) The tiny beachside village of **Atrani** is a 10min. walk around the bend from Amalfi. **Path of the Gods,** a spectacular 3hr. hike, runs the coast from Bomerano to Positano.

RAVELLO. Perched atop 330m cliffs, Ravello has provided a haven for many celebrity artists over the years. The Moorish cloister and gardens of **Villa Rufolo,** off P. Duomo, inspired Boccaccio's *Decameron* and Wagner's *Parsifal.* (Open daily 9am-8pm. €4.) The small road to the right leads to the impressive **Villa Cimbrone,** whose floral walkways and gardens hide temples and statue-filled grottoes. (Open daily 9am-7:30pm. €4.50.) **Classical music concerts** are performed in the gardens of the Villa Rufolo; call the *Società di Concerti di Ravello* (☎ 089 85 81 49) for more info. All 10 rooms at the **Albergo Garden,** V.G. Boccaccio 4, have a great view of the cliffs. (☎ 089 85 72 26; www.starnet.it/hgarden. Breakfast included. Reserve ahead. Doubles €77-88. Closed Nov. 15-Feb. 15. AmEx/MC/V.)

POSITANO. Today, Positano's most frequent visitors are the wealthy few who can afford pricey *Positanese* culture, yet the town has its picturesque charms. To see the large *pertusione* (hole) in **Montepertuso,** one of three perforated mountains in the world, hike 45 min. uphill or take the bus from P. dei Mulini. Positano's **beaches** are also popular, and although boutiques may be a bit pricey, no one charges for window-shopping. The **tourist office,** V. del Saraceno 4 (☎ 089 87 50 67), is below the *duomo.* **Ostello Brikette ❷,** V.G. Marconi 358, 100m up the main coastal road to Sorrento from Viale Pasitea, has incredible views from two large terraces. (☎ 089 87 58 57. Breakfast and sheets included. Dorms €20; doubles €65.) **Casa Guadagno ❸,** V. Fornillo 22, has 15 spotless rooms. (☎ 089 87 50 42; fax 81 14 07. Breakfast included. Reserve ahead. With *Let's Go:* doubles €85; triples €95. MC/V.) Prices in the town's restaurants reflect the high quality of the food. For a sit-down dinner, thrifty travelers head toward the beach at **Fornillo.**

SORRENTO. The most heavily touristed town on the peninsula, lively Sorrento makes a convenient base for daytrips around the Bay of Naples. Caremar **ferries** (☎ 081 807 30 77) go to Capri (20min., €5.70). The **tourist office,** L. de Maio 35, is off P. Tasso. (☎ 081 807 40 33. Open Apr.-Sept. M-Sa 8:45am-7:45pm; Oct.-Mar. M-Sa 8:30am-2pm and 4-6:15pm.) Halfway to the free **beach** at **Punta del Capo** (bus A), **⬛Hotel Elios ❷,** V. Capo 33, has comfy rooms. (☎ 081 878 18 12. Singles €25-30; doubles €40-50.) For extensive amenities, stay at **Hotel City ❸,** C. Italia 221; turn left on C. Italia from the station. (☎ 081 877 22 10. Singles €37-46; doubles €40-50.) It's easy to find good, affordable food in Sorrento. **⬛Davide ❶,** V. Giuliani 39, off Corso Italia, two blocks from P. Tasso, has divine *gelato* and masterful *mousse* (60 flavors. Open daily 10am-midnight.) After 10:30pm, a crowd gathers in the rooftop lemon grove above **The English Inn,** C. Italia 56. (Open daily 9am-1am.)

SALERNO AND PAESTUM. Industrial **Salerno** is best used as a base for daytrips to nearby **Paestum,** the site of three spectacularly preserved ▨**Doric buildings,** including the **Temple of Ceres,** the **Temple of Poseidon,** and the **basilica.** (Temples open daily 9am-6:30pm. Closed 1st and 3rd M each month. €4.) To sleep at **Ostello della Gioventù "Irno" (HI) ❶,** in Salerno at V. Luigi Guercio 112, go left from the station on V. Torrione, then left under the bridge on V. Mobilio. (☎ 089 79 02 51. Breakfast included. Curfew 1:30am. Dorms €10.)

BAY OF NAPLES ISLANDS ☎ 081

CAPRI. Visitors flock to the renowned ▨**Blue Grotto,** a sea cave whose waters shimmer with neon-blue light. (Open daily 9am-5pm. Boat tour €8.10.) In the summer months crowds and prices increase, so the best times to visit are in the late spring and early fall. Capri proper sits above the port, and buses departing from V. Roma make the trip up the mountain to Anacapri every 15 min. until 1:40am. Away from the throngs flitting among Capri's expensive boutiques, Anacapri is home to budget hotels, spectacular vistas, and empty mountain paths. Upstairs from P. Vittoria in Anacapri, **Villa San Michele** sports lush gardens, ancient sculptures, and a remarkable view of the island. (Open daily 9:30am-6pm. €5.) To appreciate Capri's Mediterranean beauty from higher ground, take the chairlift up **Monte Solaro** from P. Vittoria. (Open Mar.-Oct. daily 9:30am-4:45pm. Round-trip €5.50.) For those who prefer cliff to coastline, Capri's hiking trails lead to some stunning panoramas; take a short but very uphill hike to the magnificent ruins of Emperor Tiberius's **Villa Jovis,** the largest of his 12 Capri villas. Always the gracious host, Tiberius tossed those who displeased him over the precipice. The view from the **Cappella di Santa Maria del Soccorso,** built onto the villa, is unrivaled.

Caremar (☎ 081 837 07 00) **ferries** run from Marina Grande to Naples (1¼hr., 6 per day) and Sorrento (50min., 3 per day, €5.70). LineaJet (☎ 081 837 08 19) runs hydrofoils to **Naples** (40min., 10 per day 8:30am-6:25pm, €11) and **Sorrento** (20min., €7.25). Ferries and hydrofoils to **Ischia** and **Amalfi** run with much less frequency and regularity; check with the lines at Marina Grande for details. The Capri **tourist office** (☎ 081 837 06 34) sits at the end of Marina Grande; in Anacapri, it's at V. Orlandi 59 (☎ 081 837 15 24), to the right of the P. Vittoria bus stop. (Both open June-Sept. M-Sa 8:30am-8:30pm; Oct.-May M-Sa 9am-1:30pm and 3:30-6:45pm.) For quick access to the beach and center of Capri, stay at the **Bed and Breakfast Tirrenia Roberts ❹,** V. Mulo 27. Walk away from P. Umberto on V. Roma and take the stairs on your right just before the fork. (☎ 081 837 61 19; bbtirreniaroberts@iol.it. 3 rooms, all doubles. €80-105. Reserve well in advance.) Also try **Pensione 4 Stagioni ❸,** V. Marina Piccola 1. From P. Umberto, walk 5min. down V. Roma. Turn left at the triple fork, and look for the green gate on the left. (☎ 081 837 00 41; www.hotel4stagionicapri.com. Breakfast included. Doubles €110; in winter €90. AmEx/MC/V.) Bear right at the fork to reach **Dimeglio supermarket.** (Open M-Sa 8:30am-1:30pm and 5-9pm.) At night, dressed-to-kill Italians come out for Capri's *passegiatta;* bars around **Piazza Umberto** keep the music pumping late, but Anacapri is cheaper and more fun. **Postal codes:** Capri: 80073; Anacapri: 80021.

ISCHIA. Augustus fell in love with Capri's fantastic beauty in 29 BC, but swapped it for its more fertile neighbor, Ischia; just across the bay, edenic Ischia offers sandy beaches, natural hot springs, ruins, forests, vineyards, and lemon groves. Orange SEPSA **buses** #1, CD, and CS (every 20 min., €1, day pass €2.75) depart from the ferry landing and follow the coast in a circular route, stopping at: **Ischia Porto,** a port formed by the crater of an extinct volcano; **Casamicciola Terme,** with a crowded beach and legendary thermal waters; **Lacco Ameno,** the oldest Greek settlement in the western Mediterranean; and popular **Forio,** home to lively bars. Caremar **ferries** (☎98 48 18) arrive from **Naples** (1½hr., 14 per day, €5) and Alilauro (☎99 18 88, www.alilauro.it) runs hydrofoils to **Sorrento** (6 per day).

Stay in Ischia Porto only if you want to be close to the ferries and nightlife—most *pensioni* are in Forio. **Pensione Di Lustro ❹**, V. Filippo di Lustro 9, is near the beach. (☎99 71 63. Breakfast included. Doubles €45-62.) The **Ostello "Il Gabbiano" (HI) ❷**, Strada Statale Forio-Panza, 162, is accessible by buses #1, CS, and CD, and is near the beach. (☎90 94 22. Breakfast included. Lockout 10am-1pm. Curfew 12:30am. Open Apr.-Sept. Dorms €16.) **Camping Internazionale ❶** is at V. Foschini 22, 15 min. from the port. Take V. Alfredo de Luca from V. del Porto; bear right on V. Michele Mazzella at P. degi Eroi. (☎081 99 14 49; fax 99 14 72. Open May-Sept. €6-9 per person, €3-10 per tent. 2-person bungalows €26-39.)

SICILY (SICILIA)

With a history steeped in chaos, catastrophe, and conquest, it's no wonder that the island of Sicily possesses such passionate volatility. The tempestuousness of Sicilian history and political life is matched only by the island's dramatic landscapes, which are dominated by craggy slopes. Entire cities have been destroyed in seismic and volcanic events, but those that have survived have lived up to the cliché and grown stronger; Sicilian pride is a testament to resilience during centuries of occupation and destruction.

▐ TRANSPORTATION

Tirrenia Ferries (☎(091) 33 33 00) offers extensive service. From southern Italy, take a **train** to **Reggio di Calabria,** then a NGI or Meridiano **ferry** (40min.; NGI: 10-12 per day, €0.55; Meridiano: 11-15 per day, €1.55) or Ferrovie Statale **hydrofoil** (☎(096) 586 35 40) to Messina, Sicily's transport hub (25min., 12 per day, €2.60). Ferries also go to Palermo from Sardinia (14hr., €42) and Naples (10hr., 2 per day, €38). **SAIS Trasporti** (☎(091) 617 11 41) and SAIS **buses** (☎(091) 616 60 28) serve destinations throughout the island. **Trains** head to Messina directly from Naples (4½hr., 7 per day, €22) and Rome (9hr., 7 per day, €30). Trains continue west to Palermo (3½hr., 15 per day, €10.10) via Milazzo (45min., €2.35) and south to Syracuse (3hr., 14 per day, €6.75) via Taormina (1hr., €2.85).

PALERMO   ☎091

From twisting streets lined by ancient ruins to the symbolic marionette strings of Italian organized crime, gritty Palermo is a city whose recent history provides shade and texture to a rich cultural heritage. To get to the magnificent **Teatro Massimo,** where the climactic opera scene of *The Godfather: Part III* was filmed, walk up V. Maqueda past the intersection of Quattro Canti and Corso Vittorio

LA FAMIGLIA Pin-striped suits, machine guns, and *The Godfather* are a far cry from the reality of the **Sicilian Mafia.** The system has its roots in the *latifondi* (agricultural estates) of rural Sicily, where land managers and salaried militiamen (a.k.a. landlords and bouncers) protected their turf and people. Powerful because people owed them favors, strong because they supported one another, and feared because they did not hesitate to kill offenders, they founded a tradition that has dominated Sicilian life since the late 19th century. Since the mid-1980s, the Italian government has worked to curtail Mafia influence. Today Sicilians shy away from any Mafia discussion, referring to the system as *Cosa Nostra* (our thing).

Emanuele. (Open Tu-Su 10am-5:30pm for 20min. tours.) Up Corso Vittorio Eman-uele, the **Palazzo dei Normanni** contains the ⌧**Cappella Palatina,** full of incredible golden mosaics. (Open M-Sa 9am-noon and 3-4:45pm, Su 9-10am and noon-1pm.) The morbid **Cappuchin Catacombs,** in P. Cappuccini, are only for the strong of stom-ach. Eight thousand corpses and twisted skeletons line the underground labyrinth. To get there, take buses #109 or 318 from Stazione Centrale to P. Indipendenza and then transfer to bus #327. (Open M-Su 9am-noon and 3-5pm. €1.50.)

Trains leave Stazione Centrale, in P. Giulio Cesare, at V. Roma and V. Maqueda, for Milan (19½hr., 2 per day, €50) and Rome (11hr., 7 per day, €53). All four **bus** lines run from V. Balsamo, next to the train station. After purchasing tickets, ask exactly where your bus will arrive and its logo. Ask an **AMAT** or **Métro** information booth for a combined Métro and bus map. The **tourist office,** P. Castelnuovo 34, is opposite Teatro Politeama; from the train station, take a bus to P. Politeama, at the end of V. Maqueda. (☎ 091 605 83 51; fax 091 58 63 38. Open daily 8am-5pm.) Homey **Hotel Regina ❷,** Corso Vittorio Emanuele 316, is off V. Maqueda. (☎ 091 611 42 16; fax 091 612 21 69. Kitchen. Singles €18; doubles €34.) Grab a bite at **Pizzeria Bellini ❶,** P. Bellini 6. (Pizza from €3. Open W-M 6am-1am.) **Postal Code:** 90100.

AEOLIAN ISLANDS (ISOLE EOLIE)   ☎ 090

Homer thought the **Aeolian Islands** to be the second home of the gods, and indeed, these last few stretches of unspoiled seashore border on the divine. Sparkling seas, smooth beaches, and fiery volcanoes testify to the area's stunning beauty.

◧ TRANSPORTATION

The archipelago lies off the Sicilian coast, north of **Milazzo,** the principal and least expensive departure point. Hop off a **train** from Messina (30min., €2.35) or Pal-ermo (2½hr., €9) and onto an orange AST **bus** for the port (10min., every hr., €0.75). Siremar (☎ 090 98 60 11) and Navigazione Generale Italiana (NGI; ☎ 090 98 30 03) **ferries** depart for Lipari (2hr., €5.45-5.95); Stromboli (5hr., €8.55-9.85); Vul-cano (1½hr., €5.20-5.70). **Hydrofoils** *(aliscafi)* make the trip in half the time, but cost twice as much. All three have ticket offices on V. Dei Mille facing the port in Milazzo. **Ferries** visit the islands less frequently from Molo Beverello port in **Naples.** Ferries from Lipari to Vulcano cost €2.35; from Lipari to Stromboli, €13.20.

LIPARI

Lipari, the largest and most developed of the islands, is renowned for its amazing beaches and stunning hillside views. To reach the popular beaches of **Spiaggia Bianca** and **Porticello,** take the Lipari-Cavedi bus a few kilometers north to Can-neto; Spiaggia Bianca is *the* spot for topless (and sometimes bottomless) sunbath-ing. Lipari's other offerings include a splendidly rebuilt medieval **castello,** the site of an ancient Greek acropolis. The fortress shares its hill with an **archaeological park,** the **San Bartolo church,** and the superb ⌧**Museo Archeologico Eoliano,** up the stone steps off V. Garibaldi. (☎ 090 988 01 74. Open May-Oct. M-Su 9am-1:30pm and 4-7pm; Nov.-Apr. M-Su 9am-1:30pm and 3-6pm. €4.32.)

The **tourist office,** Corso Vittorio Emanuele 202, is near the ferry dock. (☎ 090 988 00 95; www.net-net.it/aasteolie. Open July-Aug. M-Sa 8am-2pm and 4-10pm, Su 8am-2pm; Sept.-June M-F 8am-2pm and 4:30-7:30pm, Sa 8am-2pm.) **Casa Vit-torio ❶,** Vico Sparviero 15, is on a quiet side street in the center of town. Rooms range from intimate singles to a five-person penthouse. (☎ 090 981 15 23. €16-37 per person.) The elegant **Pensione Enso il Negro ❷,** V. Garibaldi 29, is 20m up V. Garibaldi. (☎ 090 981 31 63. Singles €30-47; doubles €50-80.) **Hotel Europeo ❸,** Corso Vittorio Emanuele 98, has small, spare rooms in a great location. (☎ 090 981 15 89. July-Aug. €30 per person.) **Camp** at **Baia Unci ❶,** V. Marina Garibaldi 2,

2km from Lipari at the entrance to the hamlet of Canneto. (☎090 981 19 09. www.campeggitalia.it/sicilia/baiaunci. Reserve for Aug. Open mid-Mar. to mid-Oct. €6.20-11 per person, with tent.) Stock up at **UPIM supermarket,** Corso Vittorio Emanuele 212. (Open M-Sa 8:30am-1:30pm and 4-9:30pm.) ▓**Da Gilberto ❶,** V. Garibaldi 22-24, is known for delicious sandwiches. (☎090 981 27 56. Sandwiches from €2.60. Open 7pm-midnight; closing time varies.)

VULCANO

Black beaches, bubbling seas, and natural mud spas attract visitors worldwide to this island. A steep 1hr. **hike** to the inactive **Gran Cratere** (Grand Crater) snakes between the volcano's noxious yellow fumaroles. On a clear day, you can see all the other islands from the top. The therapeutic **Laghetto di Fanghi** (Mud Pool) is just up V. Provinciale to the right from the port. If you would prefer not to bathe in sulfuric radioactive mud, you can step gingerly into the scalding waters of the **acquacalda,** where underwater volcanic outlets make the sea percolate like a jacuzzi, or visit the nearby black sands and clear waters of **Sabbie Nere.** (Follow the signs off V. Ponente.) To get to Vulcano, take the 30min. **ferry** from the port at nearby Lipari (30min., 2 per day, €1.30). For more info, see the **tourist office** at V. Provinciale 41. (☎090 985 20 28. Open May-Aug. daily 8am-1:30pm and 3-5pm.) For **rented rooms** *(affittacamere),* call ☎090 985 21 42.

STROMBOLI

If you find luscious beaches and hot springs a bit tame, a visit to Stromboli's active **volcano,** which spews orange cascades of lava and molten rock about every 10min. each night, will quench your thirst for adventure. A guided hike to the crater rewards diligent climbers with a view of the nightly eruptions. **Hiking** the *vulcano* on your own is **illegal** and **dangerous,** but **Magmatrek** offers tours. (☎/fax 986 57 68. Tours depart from V. Vittorio Emanuele. €21-34.) Bring sturdy shoes, a flashlight, snacks, water, and warm clothes; don't wear contact lenses, as the wind sweeps ash and dust everywhere. **Siremar** (☎090 986 011) runs an infrequent **ferry** from Milazzo to Stromboli, and boat rentals are readily available. From July to September, you won't find a room without a reservation; your best bet may be one of the non-reservable *affittacamere.* Expect to pay €15-25 for a room. The best value is ▓**Casa del Sole ❷,** on V. Giuseppe Cincotta, off V. Regina at the end of town. At the church of St-Bartholomew, take a right down the stairs and go straight down the alley. Large rooms face a shared terrace. (☎090 986 017. June €18; July-Aug. €20.)

SARDINIA (SARDEGNA)

When the boyish vanity of over-cultivated mainland Italians starts to wear thin, when one more church interior will send you into the path of the nearest speeding Fiat, Sardinia's savage coastline and rugged people will be a reality check for your soul. D. H. Lawrence sought respite from the "deadly net of European civilization," and he found his escape among the wild horses, wind-carved rock formations, and pink flamingos of this remote island. The ancient feudal civilizations that settled in Sardinia some 3500 years ago left about 8000 *nuraghe* ruins, cone-shaped stone tower-houses assembled without mortar.

▐ TRANSPORTATION

Tirrenia **ferries** (☎1678 240 79) run to **Olbia,** on the northern tip of Sardinia, from Civitavecchia, just north of Rome (6hr., 4 per day, from €17), and Genoa (9hr., 6 per week, from €28). They also chug to southern **Cagliari** from Civitavecchia (15-18hr.,

2 per day, from €26); Genoa (20hr., July-Sept. 2 per week, from €45); Naples (16hr., Jan.-Sept. 1 per week, €26); and Palermo (13½hr., 1 per week, from €24). **Trains** run from Cagliari to Olbia (4hr., €13) via Oristano (1½hr., €4.55) and Sassari (4hr., 2 per day, from €12.10). From Sassari, trains run to **Alghero** (40min., 11 per day, €3.10). PANI **buses** connect Cagliari to Oristano (1½hr., €5.85).

CAGLIARI   ☎ 070

Cagliari combines the bustle and energy of a modern Italian city with the endearing rural atmosphere of the rest of the island. Its Roman ruins, medieval towers, and cobblestone streets contrast with the regal tree-lined streets and sweeping beaches downtown. Climb Largo Carlo Felice to reach the city's impressive **duomo**, P. Palazzo 3, with dazzling gold mosaics topping each of its entryways. (☎ 070 66 38 37. Open daily 8am-12:30pm and 4-8pm.) The 2nd-century **Roman ampitheater** comes alive with concerts, operas, and classic plays during the summer **arts festival.** If you prefer to worship the sun, take city **bus** P, PQ, or PF to **Il Poetto** beach (20min., €0.80), which has pure white sand and turquoise water. The **tourist office** is on P. Matteotti. (☎ 070 66 92 55; fax 070 66 49 23. Open in summer M-Sa 8:30am-1:30pm and 2:30-7:30pm.) The elegant **Hotel Aer Bundes Jack Vittoria ❹** is at V. Roma 75. (☎ 070 65 79 70. Singles €36-43; doubles €60-65.) **Postal Code:** 09100.

ALGHERO   ☎ 079

Vineyards, ruins, and horseback rides are all a short trip away from Alghero's palm-lined parks and twisting medieval streets. The nearby ▨**Grotte di Nettuno,** an eerie stalactite-filled 60- to 70-million-year-old cavern complex, in Capo Caccia, can be reached by **bus** (1hr., 3 per day, round-trip €1.75). Visitors descend 632 steps between massive white cliffs. (Open Apr.-Sept. daily 9am-7pm; Oct. 10am-5pm; Nov.-Mar. 9am-2pm. €10.) The **tourist office,** P. Porta Terra 9, is to the right from the bus stop. (☎ 079 97 90 54. Open Apr.-Oct. M-Sa 8am-8pm, Su 9am-1pm; Nov.-Mar. M-Sa 9am-1pm.) To get to **Hotel San Francisco ❹**, V. Machin 2, walk straight from the tourist office and take the 3rd right. (☎ 079 98 03 30; hotsfran@tin.it. Singles €36-43; doubles €62-77. MC/V.) **Postal Code:** 07041.

ORISTANO AND THE SINIS PENINSULA   ☎ 0783

The town of **Oristano** is an excellent base for excursions to the nearby Sinis Peninsula. From the train station, follow V. Vittorio Veneto straight to P. Mariano, then take V. Mazzini to P. Roma to reach the town center (25min.). Rent a moped or car to explore the tranquil beaches, stark white cliffs, and ancient ruins on the mystical **Sinis Peninsula.** At the tip, 17km west of Oristano, lie the ruins of the ancient Phoenician port of **Tharros.** Take the ARST bus to San Giovanni di Sinis (dir.: Is Arutas; 40min., 5 per day, €1.45). Slightly to the north off the road to Cuglieri is **S'Archittu,** where youths leap from a 15m limestone arch into the waters of a rocky inlet. ARST **buses** go to S'Archittu (30min., 7 per day, €1.45). The secluded white quartz sands of **Is Arutas** are well worth the trip. The ARST bus to Is Arutas runs only during July and August (50min., 5 per day, €1.45). The **tourist office,** V. Vittorio Emanuele 8, provides maps. (☎/fax 0783 30 32 12. Open M-F 9am-12:30pm and 4:30-8pm, Sa 9am-12:30pm.) To get some rest at **ISA ❹**, P. Mariano 50, exit from the back of the ARST station, turn left, turn right on V. Vittorio Emanuele, walk through P. D'Aborea and P. Martini, and follow V. Lamarmora to its end. Turn right, turn left, and take the first right down V. Mazzini to P. Mariano. (☎/fax 0783 36 01 01. Singles €50; doubles €83. AmEx/MC/V.) **Postal Code:** 09170.

LATVIA (LATVIJA)

At the Baltic crossroads, Latvia has been caught for hundreds of years in international political struggles. The country has been conquered and reconquered so many times that the year 2003 will only be Latvia's 34th year of independence— ever. National pride, however, abounds, from patriotically renamed streets bleeding with crimson-and-white flags to a rediscovery of native holidays predating even the Christian invasions. Rīga, Latvia's only large city, is a westernized capital luring more and more international companies, while the rest of the country is mostly a provincial expanse of green hills dominated by tall birches and pines, dairy pastures, and quiet towns.

FACTS AND FIGURES

Official Name: Republic of Latvia.

Capital: Rīga.

Population: 2,400,000 (57% Latvian, 30% Russian, 13% other).

Land Area: 64,589 sq. km.

Time Zone: GMT +2.

Languages: Lettish, Lithuanian, Russian.

Religions: Lutheran, Roman Catholic, Russian Orthodox.

ESSENTIALS

DOCUMENTS AND FORMALITIES

VISAS. Irish, UK, and US citizens can visit Latvia for up to 90 days without a visa. Citizens of Australia, Canada, New Zealand, and South Africa require 90-day visas, obtainable at a Latvian consulate. Single-entry visas cost €15; multiple-entry €31-77. Apply for extensions at the Department of Immigration and Citizenship in Rīga, Raiņa bulv. 5 (☎721 91 81).

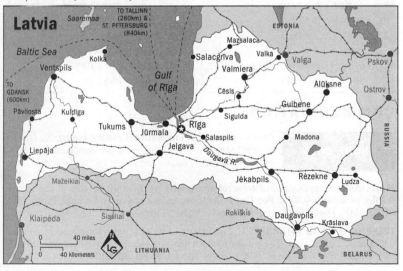

LATVIA

EMBASSIES. All foreign embassies are in Rīga (see p. 677). For Latvian embassies at home, contact: **Australia** (consulate), 38 Longstaff Street, East Ivanhoe, Victoria 3079 (☎03 9499 6920; fax 03 9499 7088); **Canada**, 280 Albert St., Suite 300, Ottawa, ON K1P 5G8 (☎613-238-6014; www.magmacom.com/~latemb); **UK**, 45 Nottingham Pl., London W1M 3FE (☎0171 312 00 40); and **US**, 4325 17th St. NW, Washington, D.C. 20011 (☎202-726-8213; www.latvia-usa.org).

TRANSPORTATION

Air Baltic, SAS, Finnair, and Lufthansa, among others, fly into Rīga (RIX). **Trains** link Latvia to Berlin, Lviv, Moscow, Odessa, St. Petersburg, Tallinn, and Vilnius. **Eurail** is not valid. Trains are cheap and efficient, but stations aren't well marked—always carry a map. The **suburban rail** system renders the entire country a suburb of Rīga, and is a better choice than buses for daytrips from the capital. Latvia's quicker **bus** network reaches Prague, Tallinn, Vilnius, and Warsaw. **Ferries** run to Rīga from Stockholm, Sweden and Kiel, Germany. **Hitchhiking** is common, but hitchers may be expected to pay. *Let's Go* does not recommend hitchhiking.

TOURIST SERVICES AND MONEY

EMERGENCY	Police: ☎02. Ambulance: ☎03. Fire: ☎01.

Tourist offices are scarce; look for a green "i." Private offices such as **Patricia** (see p. 679) are more helpful. The Latvian **Lat** (abbreviated "Ls"), is divided into 100 *santims*. Inflation is around 3%. It's often hard to exchange currencies other than US dollars and euros. There are many **ATMs** in Rīga and in large towns, most linked to Cirrus, MasterCard, and Visa. Larger businesses, restaurants, and hotels accept MasterCard and Visa. Traveler's checks are harder to use; both AmEx and Thomas Cook can be converted in Rīga, but elsewhere, Thomas Cook is a safer bet.

LATS		
AUS$1 = 0.33 LVL		1LVL = AUS$3.01
CDN$1 = 0.39 LVL		1LVL = CDN$2.58
EUR€1 = 0.59 LVL		1LVL = EUR€1.69
NZ$1 = 0.28 LVL		1LVL = NZ$3.53
ZAR1 = 0.057 LVL		1LVL = ZAR17.47
UK£1 = 0.92 LVL		1LVL = UK£1.08
US$1 = 0.60 LVL		1LVL = US$1.66

COMMUNICATION

PHONE CODE	**Country code: 371. International dialing prefix: 00.** From outside Latvia, dial int'l dialing prefix (see inside back cover) + 371 + city code + local number.

MAIL. Ask for *gaisa pastu* to send something by airmail. Letters abroad cost 0.40Ls, postcards 0.30Ls. For *Poste Restante*, address mail to be held: Firstname SURNAME, *Poste Restante*, Stacijas laukums 1, Rīga, LV-1050 LATVIA.

TELEPHONES AND INTERNET. If a number is only six digits long, you must dial a 2 before the number. The phone system has been undergoing changes; phone offices and *Rīga in Your Pocket* have the latest information. Latvia is by far the most difficult of the Baltic states from which to call the US; there's no way to make a free call on a Latvian phone to an international operator. **International calls** can be made from telephone offices or booths. Access numbers include: **AT&T,** ☎700 70 07 in Rīga, ☎82 700 70 07 everywhere else; **British Telecom,** ☎800 1044; and **MCI,** ☎800 88 88. To call abroad from an analog phone, dial ☎1, then 00, then the country code. From a digital phone, simply dial ☎00, then the country code. Most telephones take **cards** (available in 2, 3, 5, or 10Ls denominations) from post offices, telephone offices, and large state stores. **Internet** is available only in Rīga.

LANGUAGES. Heavily influenced by German, Russian, Estonian, and Swedish, Lettish is one of two languages (the other is Lithuanian) in the Baltic language group. Russian is in disfavor in the countryside but is more acceptable and widespread in Rīga. Many young Latvians study English, but don't rely upon it. Older Latvians know some German. For Lettish basics, see p. 1061.

ACCOMMODATIONS AND FOOD

LATVIA	❶	❷	❸	❹	❺
ACCOMMODATIONS	under 10Ls	10-14Ls	15-19Ls	20-24Ls	over 24Ls
FOOD	under 2Ls	2-3Ls	4-5Ls	6-7Ls	over 7Ls

ACCOMMODATIONS. College **dormitories,** which open to travelers in the summer, are often the cheapest places to sleep. In Rīga, Patricia (see p. 679) arranges **homestays** and **apartment** rentals for around 10Ls per night. There are very few budget-range (3-15Ls) hotels.

FOOD. Latvian food is heavy and starchy, but tasty. Rīga is one of the easiest places to find vegetarian options in all the Baltics. Tasty national specialties include the holiday dish *zirņi* (gray peas with onions and smoked fat), *maizes zupa* (bread soup usually made from corn bread and full of currants, cream, and other goodies), and the warming *Rīgas* (or *Melnais*) *balzams* (a black liquor great with ice cream, Coke, or coffee). Dark rye bread is a staple. Try *speķa rauši,* a warm pastry, or *biezpienmaize,* bread with sweet curds. Latvian beer is stellar, especially *Porteris* and other offerings from the Aldaris brewery.

HOLIDAYS

Holidays: New Year's Day (Jan. 1); Good Friday (Mar. 29); Catholic Easter (Mar. 31); Labor Day (May 1); Ligo (Midsummer Festival; June 23); Independence Day (Nov. 18); Ziemsvetki (Christmas; Dec. 25-26); New Year's Eve (Dec. 31).

RĪGA   ☎2

More Westernized and cosmopolitan than the rest of Latvia, sprawling Rīga feels strangely out of place as the capital of a small, struggling country. Despite its abundance of casinos, Rīga envisions itself as the "Paris of the East." Striving to become a major European cultural and social center, the self-proclaimed capital of the Baltics has been working hard to rebuild since the fall of the USSR.

The phone code in Rīga is 2 for all 6-digit numbers; there is no phone code for 7-digit numbers. Information: ☎800 80 08. Latvian operator: ☎116. International operator: ☎115. Directory services: ☎118, 722 22 22, or 777 07 77.

LATVIA

⌐ TRANSPORTATION

Flights: Lidosta Rīga (RIX; ☎720 70 09), 8km southwest of Vecrīga. Take bus #22 from Gogol iela.

Trains: Centrālā Stacija (Central Station), Stacijas laukums (☎583 30 95), down the street from the bus station. Long-distance trains depart from the larger building to the left; destinations include: **Moscow** (16hr., 2 per day, 12.78Ls); **St. Petersburg** (13hr., 1 per day, 10.69Ls); and **Vilnius** (8hr., 3 every other day, 6Ls).

Buses: Autoosta, Prāgas 1 (☎900 00 09), 200m toward the Daugava River from the train station, across the canal from the central market. To: **Kaunas** (4-5hr., 2 per day, 5.20Ls); **Minsk** (10-12hr., 3 per day, 6.20-6.90Ls); **Tallinn** (4-6hr., 9 per day, 7-8.50Ls); **Vilnius** (5hr., 6 per day, 3.80-6Ls). **Eurolines** (☎721 40 80; www.eurolines.lv), in the bus station, sends buses to **Prague** (25½hr.; 2 per week; 28Ls, students 24Ls) and **Warsaw** (12hr., 1 per day, 16-18Ls).

◼◼ ❼ ORIENTATION AND PRACTICAL INFORMATION

The city is divided in half by **Brīvības bulvāris,** which leads from the outskirts to the **Freedom Monument** in the center, becoming **Kaļķu iela** and passing through **Vecrīga** (Old Rīga). To reach Vecrīga from the train station, turn left on Marijas iela and then right on any of the small streets beyond the canal. For good maps and information, pick up *Rīga in Your Pocket* (1.20Ls) at kiosks, hotels, or travel agencies.

Tourist Office: Tourist Information Center, Rātslaukums 6 (☎703 79 00; www.rigatourism.com), in the town square, next to the House of Blackheads. Sells maps and provides advice and brochures. Open daily 10am-7pm.

Embassies: Australia, Alberta iela 13 (☎733 63 83; acr@latnet.lv). Open M-F 10am-noon and 3-5pm. **Canada,** Doma laukums 4, 3rd and 4th fl. (☎722 63 15; canembr@bkc.lv). Open Tu and Th 10am-1pm. **Ireland,** Brīvības bulv. 54 (☎702 52 59; fax 702 52 60). Open M-Tu and Th-F 9:30am-noon. **Russia,** Antonijas iela 2 (☎721 01 23). Open M-F 9am-5:30pm. **UK,** Alunāna iela 5 (☎777 47 00; www.britain.lv). Open M-F 9am-1pm and 2-5pm. **US,** Raiņa bulv. 7 (☎703 62 00; www.usembassy.lv). Open M-Tu and Th 9-11:30am.

Currency Exchange: At any of the *Valutos Maiņa* kiosks or shops in the city. **Unibanka,** Pils iela 23, gives MC/V cash advances and cashes AmEx and Thomas Cook traveler's checks, both without commission. Open M-F 9am-5pm. **ATMs** are common.

24hr. Pharmacies: Mēness aptieka, Brīvības bulv. 121 (☎737 78 89). **Rudens aptieka,** Ģertrūdes iela 105/1 (☎724 43 22).

Internet Access: Elik, Kaļķu iela 11 (☎722 70 70), in the center of Vecrīga; **branch** at Čaka iela 26 (☎728 45 06). 0.50Ls per hr. Open 24hr. **Delat,** Baznicas iela 4a (☎722 05 10), also serves tea and beer. 0.40Ls per hr. Open 24hr.

Telephone Office: Brīvības bulv. 19 (☎701 87 38). Open M-F 7am-11pm, Sa-Su 8am-10pm. **Branch** at the post office by the train station. Open 24hr.

Post Office: Stacijas laukums 1 (☎701 88 04; www.riga.post.lv), near the train station. *Poste Restante* at window #3. Open M-F 8am-8pm, Sa 8am-6pm, Su 8am-4pm. **Branch** at Brīvības bulv. 19 (see Telephone Office, above). Address mail to be held: Firstname SURNAME, *Poste Restante,* Stacijas laukums 1, Rīga, **LV-1050** LATVIA.

ACCOMMODATIONS

For private rooms, contact **Patricia,** Elizabetes iela 22, which arranges home-stays from US$25 and apartments from US$40. (☎728 48 68; www.rigalatvia.net. Open M-F 9:15am-6pm, Sa-Su 11am-1pm.)

Laine, Skolas iela 11 (☎728 88 16; www.laine.lv). From Vecrīga, take Brīvības bulv., turn left on Dzirnava iela, then right on Skolas iela. Comfortable modern hotel. Some rooms have private baths. Call ahead. Singles 15-60Ls; doubles 25-70Ls. ❸

Valdemārs, Kr. Valdemāra iela 23 (☎733 44 62; www.valdemars.lv). From Vecrīga, take Kr. Valdemāra iela past Elizabetes iela. Ask for a room with a balcony. Private baths. Singles 18-28Ls; doubles 28-38Ls. ❸

LU Dienesta Viesnicas, Basteja bulv. 10 (☎782 03 60; fax 721 62 21). From the bus station, cross under the tracks, take the foot tunnel under the highway, and bear right on Aspazijei bul. Great location. Singles 10Ls, with bath 20Ls; doubles 16Ls/30Ls. ❷

FOOD

Look for 24-hour food and liquor stores along **Elizabetes iela, Marijas iela,** and **Ģertrūdes iela.** The **Centrālais Tirgus** (Central Market) is one of the largest in Europe; prices are low, but remember to haggle. (Open daily 8am-6pm.)

Terra Incognita, Blaumaņa iela 27. Restaurant, art gallery, and venue for spirited African drumming. Live music W-Sa 8pm. Main dishes 2.30-3.70Ls. Open M noon-11pm, Tu Sa 11am-11pm. Cover 1Ls some nights. ❷

Velvets, Skārņu iela 9, just off Kaļķu iela in Vecrīga. A stylish French restaurant with out-side seating and a dance floor in the back. Main dishes 1-6.65Ls. Open Su-Th 10am-2am, F-Sa 10am-4am. ❶

Kamāla, Jauniela iela 14, around the corner from the Dome Cathedral. Serves Indian vegetarian cuisine in a decadent setting. Main dishes 2-3.95Ls. Open M-Sa noon-11pm, Su 2-10pm. ❷

SIGHTS

FREEDOM MONUMENT AND ENVIRONS. Take time to savor the winding streets and unusual architecture of Vecrīga (Old Rīga). In the center stands the beloved **Freedom Monument** (Brīvības Piemineklis), affectionately known as "Milda." *(At the corner of Raiņa bulv. and Brīvības bulv.)* Continuing along Kaļķu iela from the Freedom Monument toward the river, you'll see one of the few Soviet monuments not torn down: the **Latvian Riflemen Monument** (Latviešu Strēlnieku Laukums), which honors Lenin's famous bodyguards. Rising behind the stat-ues are the black walls of the ▨**Occupation Museum** (Okupācijas muzejs), Strēlnieku laukums 1, where the initial Soviet occupation is depicted so vividly that you can almost hear the Red Army marching through the streets of Rīga. *(Open May-Sept. daily 11am-6pm; Oct.-Apr. Tu-Su 11am-5pm. Free; donations accepted.)* Just beyond the museum stands the **House of Blackheads** (Melngalvju nams) Rātslaukums 7. Built in 1344 and completely destroyed by the Nazis and the Soviets, the unusual and magnificent building was reconstructed in 1999 in honor of Rīga's 800th birthday, and is now used for meetings and concerts. *(Open Tu-Su 10am-5pm. 1Ls.)*

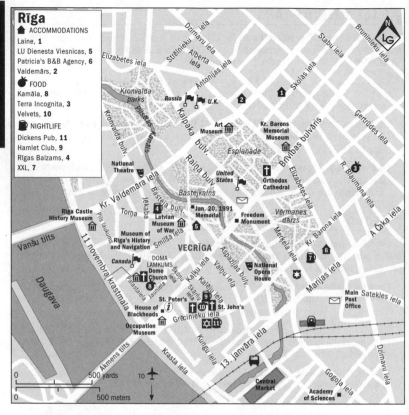

Rīga

⌂ ACCOMMODATIONS
Laine, **1**
LU Dienesta Viesnicas, **5**
Patricia's B&B Agency, **6**
Valdemārs, **2**

⏷ FOOD
Kamāla, **8**
Terra Incognita, **3**
Velvets, **10**

◼ NIGHTLIFE
Dickens Pub, **11**
Hamlet Club, **9**
Rīgas Balzams, **4**
XXL, **7**

ELSEWHERE IN VECRĪGA. Follow Kaļķu iela from the Freedom Monument and turn right on Šķūņu iela to reach the cobblestone **Doma laukums** (Dome Square), home of the 13th-century **Dome Cathedral** (Doma baznīca), the largest cathedral in the Baltics. *(Open Tu 11am-6pm, W-F 1-6pm, Sa 10am-2pm. 0.50Ls, students 0.10Ls.)* Behind the cathedral is the **Museum of Rīga's History and Navigation** (Rīgas Vēstures un Kugnie-cības Muzejs), Palasta iela 4. Housed in a 13th-century monastery, the permanent collection traces the history of the city. *(Open May-Sept. W-Su 10am-5pm; Oct.-Apr. 11am-5pm. 1.20Ls, students 0.40Ls. English tours 3Ls/2Ls.)* From the top of the dark 123m spire of **St. Peter's Church** (Sv. Pētera baznīca), you can see the entire city and the Baltic Sea. *(On Skāmu iela, off Kaļķu iela. Open in summer Tu-Su 10am-7pm; off-season 10am-5pm. Church free. Tower 1.60Ls, students 1Ls.)* The magnificent neoclassical **Art Museum** (Valsts mākslas muzejs), Kr. Valdemāra iela 10a, displays 18th- to 20th-century Latvian art and hosts occasional concerts. *(Near the intersection of Elizabetes iela and Kr. Valdemāra iela. Open Apr.-Oct. W–M 11am-5pm, Th until 7pm; Oct.-Apr. W-M 11am-5pm. 0.50Ls, students 0.40Ls. English tours 3Ls.)* The newer areas of Rīga feature some fantastic **Art Nouveau** (Jugendstil) architecture. Elaborately adorned buildings dot the city; the largest grouping is on Alberta iela, and others are on Elizabetes iela and Strēlnieku laukums.

BASTEJKALNS. The ruins of the old city walls lie in Bastejkalns, a central park near the old city moat (Pīlsētas kanāls). Across and around the canal, five red stone slabs stand as memorials to those killed on January 20, 1991, when Soviet special forces stormed the Interior Ministry on Raiņa bulv. At the north end of Bastejkalns, on Kr. Valdemāra iela, sits the **National Theatre,** where Latvia first declared its independence on November 18, 1918. *(Open daily 10am-7pm.)*

SALASPILS MEMORIAL. Just outside of the city, the **Salaspils Memorial** marks the remains of the Kurtenhof concentration camp, which was primarily a transit point to larger death camps from 1941-1944. Four clusters of massive sculptures watch over the Way of Suffering, the circular path that connects the barracks foundations. A black box covered in wreaths emits a low ticking sound, like the pulse of a beating heart. *(Green electric trains run to Dārziņi; 20min., 14 per day, 0.30Ls. Make sure the train will be stopping at Dārziņi, not "Salaspils." Facing the Dārziņi station, cross the tracks and turn right on the paved road, then go left after the soccer fields.)*

🎵 📻 ENTERTAINMENT AND NIGHTLIFE

In May, 2003, Rīga's Skonto Hall will host the **Eurovision Song Contest,** one of the most widely-watched events in the world. The city also eagerly anticipates the **Festival of Song and Dance** (June 29-July 6, 2003), which takes place only once every four years; check the tourist office for a schedule. Summer is the off-season for theater, but the Opera House and the Dome Cathedral hold summer performances. The **Rīga Ballet** carries on the proud tradition of native star Mikhail Baryshnikov. Tickets for most performances can be purchased at Teātra 10/12. (☎722 57 47. Open daily 10am-7pm.) The night scene is centered in **Vecrīga;** for a mellow alternative to its many 24hr. casinos and *diskotekas,* relax with locals at a beer garden. The classy **Hamlet Club,** Jāņa Sēta 5, in the heart of Vecrīga, has live jazz most nights from 9:30 or 10pm. (Open M-Sa 7pm-2am. Jazz cover 2.50Ls.) Also in Vecrīga, **Rīgas Balzams,** Torņa iela 4 (☎721 44 94), serves Black Balza, the Latvian national drink. (Open daily noon-midnight.) The **Dickens Pub,** Grēcinieku 9/1, has great Latvian pork dishes, traditional steaks, and sandwiches. (Entrees 3.45-6.15Ls. Open Su-Th 11am-1am, F-Sa 11am-2am.) The gay bar and club **XXL,** A Kalniņa iela 4, is off K. Barona iela; buzz to be let in. (www.xxl.lv. Open 4pm-6am.)

🔗 DAYTRIPS FROM RĪGA

JŪRMALA. Boardwalks and sun-bleached, powder-fine sand cover the narrow spit Jūrmala. Visitors, including the Soviet elite, have been drawn to its warm waters since the 19th century. The coastal towns between **Bulduri** and **Dubulti** are popular for sunning and swimming, but Jūrmala's social center is **Majori,** where masses file to the crowded beach or wander along **Jomas iela,** a pedestrian street lined with cafes, restaurants, and shops. The **commuter rail** runs from Rīga to Jūrmala (every 30min. 5am-11:30pm, 0.51Ls). **Public buses** (0.18Ls) and **microbuses** (0.20-0.30Ls) string together Jūrmala's towns. From the train station in Majori, cross the road, walk through the cluster of trees in the small park, and turn right. The **tourist office** is at Jomas iela 42. (☎642 76; www.jurmala.lv. Open in summer daily 10am-9pm; off-season 10am-5pm.) After a long day at the beach, sip a cocktail at **De La Presse ❸,** Jomas iela 57; the upstairs lounge is a disco after 9pm. (Main dishes 2.30-11.85Ls. Open daily 10am-4am.) ☎77.

SIGULDA. Situated in **Gaujas Valley National Park,** Sigulda feels refreshingly distant from hectic Rīga. For English tours of the park, visit the **Gaujas National Park Center,** Baznicas iela 3. (☎713 45. Open M 9:30am-6pm. Tours 20Lt per group. Call ahead.) The area offers great biking, bungee jumping, horseback riding, hot-air ballooning, and bobsledding, as well as skiing in winter; **Makars Tourism Agency,** Peldu 1, can arrange all kinds of outdoor excursions. (☎924 49 48; www.makars.lv.) The restored brick fortifications of ▨**Turaida Castle** (Turaidas Pils), Turaidas iela 10, across the river from Sigulda and 2km down the road, are visible throughout the Gauja valley and surrounding hilltops. Climb the steep staircase of the main tower for a scenic view of the region. (Tower open daily 8am-9pm.) Take Turaidas iela 10-15min. back down the hill to reach the legendary **caves** of Sigulda. Inscriptions and coats of arms from as early as the 16th century cover the chiseled mouth of **Gutman's Cave** (Gūtmaṇa ala). On a ridge to the right of Gaujas iela, on the near side of the gorge, is the **Sigulda Dome** palace, behind which lie the remains of 13th-century **Sigulda Castle** (Siguldas pilsdrupas). The immense ruins form the backdrop for the renowned **Sigulda Opera Festival** in late July.

Trains run from Rīga on the Rīga-Lugaži commuter rail line (1hr., 15 per day, 0.85Ls). From the station, walk up Raiņa iela to the center. Continue as it turns into Gaujas iela, which, after the Gaujas Bridge, becomes the steep Turaidas iela and passes Turaida Castle. **Bus #12** runs directly to Turaida Castle (0.20Ls). The **Sigulda Tourist Information Center,** Pils iela 6, in Hotel Sigulda, gives out free maps and brochures and arranges B&B rooms in Sigulda. (7Ls, with breakfast 8Ls. ☎/fax 713 35; www.sigulda.lv. Open May-Oct. daily 10am-7pm; Nov.-Apr. 10am-5pm.) The ▨**Krimulda Rehabilitation Center ❶,** Menieku iela 3, offers rooms in neoclassical Krimulda Castle. (☎797 22 32; krimulda@lis.lv. Dorms 5Ls; singles 5-7Ls; doubles 10-15Ls.) ▨**Pilsmuižas Restorāns ❷,** Pils iela 16, inside Sigulda Dome, serves delicious and generous portions. For a great view, ask to go to the roof. (Main dishes 2.50-5Ls. Open daily noon-midnight.) For a huge, inexpensive meal, try **Trīs Draugi ❶,** Pils iela 9. (Open daily 8am-10pm.) ☎79.

LIECHTENSTEIN

PHONE CODES Country code: 0423. International dialing prefix: 00.

A tourist brochure for Liechtenstein amusingly mislabeled the already tiny 160 sq. km country as an even tinier 160 sq. m; that's about how much most tourists see of the world's only German-speaking monarchy. Enter Liechtenstein by **bus** from **Sargans** or **Buchs** in Switzerland, or from **Feldkirch**, Austria (20min., 4SFr). A cheap, efficient **Post Bus** system links all 11 villages (short trips 3SFr, long trips 4SFr; students half-price; SwissPass valid). Remember to carry your passport when traveling. The **official language** is German (see p. 1057); the **currency** is the Swiss franc (SFr; see p. 987). **Police:** ☎ 117. **Medical emergencies:** ☎ 144. **Postal code:** FL-9490.

SYMBOL	❶	❷	❸	❹	❺
ACCOMMODATIONS	under 16SFr	16-35SFr	36-60SFr	61-120SFr	over 120SFr
FOOD	under 9SFr	9-15SFr	16-24SFr	25-34SFr	over 34SFr

VADUZ AND LOWER LIECHTENSTEIN. As the national capital, Vaduz attracts the most visitors of any village in Lichtenstein. Above town, the 12th-century **Schloß Vaduz (Vaduz Castle)** is home to Hans Adam II, Prince of Liechtenstein. The interior is off-limits to the masses; however, you can hike up to the castle for a closer look and a phenomenal view of the whole country. The 15min. trail begins down the street from the tourist office, heading away from the post office. Across the street from the tourist office is the **Kunstmuseum Liechtenstein,** Städtle 32. Mainly focusing on modern art, the museum boasts paintings by Dalí, Kandinsky, and Klee, as well as rotating special exhibits and installations. (Open Tu-W and F-Su 10am-5pm, Th until 8pm. 8SFr, students and seniors 5SFr.) Liechtenstein's national **tourist office,** Städtle 37, one block up the hill from the Vaduz Post Bus stop, stamps passports (2SFr), sells **hiking maps** (15.50SFr), locates rooms, and has free maps and hiking advice. (☎ 232 14 43. Open July-Sept. M-F 8am-5:30pm, Sa-Su 9am-5pm; Oct.-June M-F 8am-noon and 1:30-5:30pm; Apr. and Oct. also Sa 9am-noon and 1:30-5pm;

Liechtenstein

THE LOCAL STORY

A SIX-HOUR TOUR

Though we joke about being able to see all of Liechtenstein in a day, it's actually possible to see the entire nation in a little under six hours. The LGT-Alpin Marathon runs 42km from just outside of Schaan to Malbun.

The course began in relatively flat farmland near the Rhine. The smell of cow manure was overwhelming at times as we ran past farmers harvesting hay. When we hit Vaduz, the next 11km were entirely uphill, rising over 1000m. Most of us slowed to a walk, but the enthusiastic Liechtensteiners were out in force chanting, "Haub! Haub! Bravo!" as we lumbered past.

Coming around a corner, I heard dozens of ringing bells and wondered if a local church had decided to ring its bells for us. As I came around the hairpin turn, I found 400 cows, all wearing bells. To my left, I had a perfect view of the yellow and green rolling hills in the Rhine valley below and of the snow-covered peaks of the Alps straight ahead. A paraglider chose this moment to fly overhead and I wondered if I hadn't stumbled into a picture postcard by mistake.

The final 8km were all downhill as we circled Malbun's valley at reckless speeds. I finished in 5 hours and 40 minutes, almost 2½ hours behind the winner, having crossed the entire country and ascended 1800m in the process. The mountain goats didn't seem too impressed, though—they've been doing the same thing for years.

—Tom Miller

May also Sa-Su 9am-noon and 1:30-5pm.) Budget lodgings in Vaduz are few and far between, but nearby **Schaan** is more inviting. Liechtenstein's sole **Jugendherberge ❷**, Untere Rüttig. 6, is in Schaan. From Vaduz, take bus #1 to Mühleholz, walk toward the intersection with traffic lights, and turn left down Marianumstr. Walk 4-5min. and follow the signs to this spotless pink hostel on the edge of a farm. (☎232 50 22. Breakfast included. Laundry 8SFr. Reception daily 5-10pm. Check-out 10am. Curfew 10pm. Key code available. Open Feb.-Oct. Dorms 28.60SFr; doubles 37.10SFr. HI members only.) Your best bet for a cheap meal is **Migros supermarket**, Aulestr. 20, across from the tour bus parking lot in Vaduz. (Open M-F 8am-1pm and 1:30-6:30pm, Sa 8am-4pm.)

UPPER LIECHTENSTEIN. Just when it seems that the roads cannot possibly become any narrower or steeper, they do—welcome to Upper Liechtenstein. These heights are where the real character and beauty of Liechtenstein lie. Even if you're in the country for one day, take the short bus trip to **Triesenberg** or **Malbun** (30min. from Vaduz) for spectacular views of the Rhine Valley below. **Triesenberg** (take bus #10), the principal town, is spanned by a series of switchbacks and foothills 800m above the Rhine. The **tourist office** (☎262 19 26) shares a building with the **Walser Heimatmuseum,** which chronicles the history of the region. (Both open Tu-F 1:30-5:30pm, Sa 1:30-5pm, Su 2-5pm; Sept.-May closed Su. Museum 2SFr.) The tourist office is an essential checkpoint for anyone planning on hiking in the area; the friendly English-speaking staff will talk to you at length about the many trails in the area and can provide maps. **Malbun** sits in an alpine valley in the southeastern corner of Liechtenstein. It is undoubtedly the hippest place in the principality, harboring approachable people, plenty of hiking, and affordable ski slopes (ski day-pass 33SFr). Contact the **tourist office** for more information. (☎263 65 77. Open June-Oct. and mid-Dec. to mid-Apr. M-Sa 9am-noon and 1:30-5pm.) The best place to stay for hiking and skiing access is **Hotel Alpen ❸**, which is close to the bus stop and tourist office. (☎263 11 81. Reception daily 8am-10pm. Open mid-May to Oct. and mid-Dec. to Apr. In summer 45-65SFr per person; in winter 20SFr more.)

LITHUANIA (LIETUVA)

Lithuania shrank continuously as it faced oppression from Tsarist Russia, Nazi Germany, and the Soviet Union, but it also became the first Baltic nation to declare its independence from the USSR in 1990. The spectacular capital, Vilnius, welcomes hordes of tourists into the largest old town in Europe. In the opposite corner of the country, the mighty Baltic Sea washes up against Palanga and the towering dunes of the Curonian Spit.

FACTS AND FIGURES

Official Name: Republic of Lithuania.
Capital: Vilnius.
Major cities: Šiauliai, Klaipėda.
Population: 3,600,000.
Land Area: 65,200 sq. km.

Time Zone: GMT +2.
Languages: Lithuanian, Polish, Russian.
Religions: Roman Catholic (80%), Lutheran, Russian Orthodox, and others.

DISCOVER LITHUANIA

Vilnius (p. 688) is touted as the "New Prague" for its thriving art scene and sprawling Old Town; fairy-tale **Trakai Castle** (p. 692) is nearby. Sun, fun, and sea lions welcome visitors to **Klaipėda** (p. 693), the Curonian Spit's premier beach town.

ESSENTIALS

DOCUMENTS AND FORMALITIES

VISAS. Citizens of Australia, Canada, Ireland, New Zealand, the UK, and the US do not need a visa for visits up to 90 days. Citizens of South Africa who have visas from Estonia or Latvia can enter Lithuania; otherwise, 90-day visas are required. Obtain visas from embassies or consulates: single-entry visas cost €10; multiple-entry visas €20; 48-hr. transit visas €5. Obtaining a visa extension is tricky; try the **Immigration Service** in Vilnius, Virkių 3, #3 (☎75 64 53).

EMBASSIES. Foreign embassies are all in Vilnius (p. 688). Lithuanian embassies at home include: **Australia** (consulate), 40B Fiddens Wharf Rd., Killara, NSW 2071 (☎02 949 825 71); **Canada** (consulate), 130 Albert St. #204, Ottawa, ON K1P 5G4 (☎613-567-5458; ltemb@storm.ca); **New Zealand** (consulate), 28 Heather St., Parnell Auckland (☎09 336 7711; saul@f1rst.co.nz); **South Africa** (consulate), Killarney Mall, 1st fl., Riviera Rd., Killarney Johannesburg; P.O. Box 1737, Houghton, 2041 (☎011 486 36 60; lietuvos@iafrica.com); **UK,** 84 Gloucester Pl., London W1H 3HN (☎20 74 86 64 01; www.users.globalnet.co.uk/~lralon); and **US,** 2622 16th St. NW, Washington, D.C. 20009-4202 (☎202-234-5860; www.ltembassyus.org).

TRANSPORTATION

Ferries (☎31 42 57; info ☎31 11 17) connect Klaipėda with German cities Kiel (34hr.) and Muhkran (18hr.). Vilnius, Kaunas, and Klaipėda are easily reached by train or bus from Belarus, Estonia, Latvia, Poland, and Russia. Domestically, **buses** are faster, more common, and only a bit more expensive than the often-crowded **trains.** If you do ride the rails, two major lines cross Lithuania: one runs north-south from Latvia through Kaunas to Poland, and the other runs east-west from Belarus through Kaunas and Vilnius to Kaliningrad.

TOURIST SERVICES AND MONEY

EMERGENCY	**Police:** ☎02. **Ambulance:** ☎03. **Fire:** ☎01.

Tourist offices are generally knowledgeable. The most helpful is **Litinterp,** which will reserve accommodations, usually without a surcharge. Vilnius, Kaunas, and Klaipėda each have an edition of the *In Your Pocket* series. The unit of **currency** is the **Litas** (plural *Litai;* 1Lt=100 *centas*). In February 2002 the Litas was fixed to the euro at €1=3.4528Lt. It's difficult to exchange currencies other than US dollars and euros. Traveler's checks, especially AmEx and Thomas Cook, can be cashed at most banks (usually for a 2-3% commission). Cash advances are available on Visa cards. **Vilniaus Bankas** accepts major credit cards and traveler's checks for a small commission. **ATMs,** especially Cirrus, are readily available in most cities. Hostel beds run €6-8, hotels €15-20, and meals €4-6. Tipping is not expected, but some Lithuanians leave 10% for excellent service.

AUS$1 = 1.94LT	1LT = AUS$0.52
CDN$1 = 2.26LT	1LT = CDN$0.44
EUR€1 = 3.45LT	1LT = EUR€0.29
NZ$1 = 1.66LT	1LT = NZ$0.61
ZAR1 = 0.34LT	1LT = ZAR2.99
UK£1 = 5.39LT	1LT = UK£0.19
US$1 = 3.52LT	1LT = US$0.29

COMMUNICATION

PHONE CODES	**Country code:** 370. **International dialing prefix:** 810. From outside Lithuania, dial int'l dialing prefix (see inside back cover) + 370 + city code + local number.

MAIL AND TELEPHONES. Airmail *(oro pastu)* letters abroad cost 1.70Lt, postcards 1.20Lt; each takes about seven days to reach the US. International Express Mail Service takes 3-5 days. For *Poste Restante*, address mail to be held: Firstname SURNAME, Centrinis Paštas, Gedimino pr. 7, Vilnius LT-2000, LIETUVA. There are two kinds of public phones: rectangular ones that accept **magnetic strip cards** and rounded ones that accept **chip cards.** Both are sold at phone offices and many kiosks in denominations of 3.54Lt, 7.08Lt, and 28.32Lt. Calls to Estonia and Latvia cost 1.65Lt per minute, to Europe 5.80Lt, and to the US 7.32Lt. Most countries can be dialed directly. Dial ☎8, wait for the 2nd tone, dial ☎10, then enter the country code and number. International direct dialing numbers include: **AT&T,** ☎8 80 09 28 00; **British Telecom,** ☎8 80 09 00 44; and **Canada Direct,** ☎8 80 09 10 04. For countries without direct dialing, dial ☎8, wait for the 2nd tone, and dial ☎194 or 195 for an English-speaking operator.

LANGUAGES. Lithuanian, like Lettish, is a Baltic language. Russian is often useful; Polish is helpful in the south and German on the coast. For some Lithuanian phrases, see p. 1061.

LITHUANIA

ACCOMMODATIONS

LITHUANIA	❶	❷	❸	❹	❺
ACCOMMODATIONS	under 30Lt	31-80Lt	81-130Lt	131-180Lt	over 181Lt

Lithuania has several **youth hostels** and plans to open more. HI membership is nominally required, but an LJNN guest card (€3 at any of the hostels) will suffice. The head office in Vilnius has *Hostel Guide*, a handy booklet with info on bike and car rentals, reservations, and maps showing how to reach various hostels.

FOOD AND DRINK

LITHUANIA	❶	❷	❸	❹	❺
FOOD	under 10Lt	11-20Lt	21-30Lt	31-40Lt	over 41Lt

Lithuanian cuisine tends to be heavy and very greasy. Keeping a vegetarian or kosher diet will prove difficult, if not impossible. Restaurants serve various types of *blynai* (pancakes) with *mėsa* (meat) or *varske* (cheese). *Cepelinai* are heavy, potato-dough missiles of meat, cheese, and mushrooms, launched from street stands throughout Western Lithuania. *Šaltibarščiai,* a beet and cucumber soup, is prevalent in the east. *Karbonadas* is breaded pork fillet, and *koldunai* are meat dumplings. Lithuanian beer is very good; *Kalnapis* is popular in Vilnius and most of Lithuania, *Baltijos* reigns supreme around Klaipėda, and the award-winning *Utenos* is widely available. Lithuanian vodka *(degtinė)* is also very popular.

HEALTH AND SAFETY

A triangle pointing downward indicates men's restrooms, an upward-pointing triangle indicates women's facilities; be aware that many restrooms are nothing but holes in the ground. Well-stocked pharmacies are everywhere. Drink bottled water, and boil tap water for 10 minutes first if you must drink it.

HOLIDAYS

Holidays: New Year's Day (Jan. 1); Independence Day (Feb. 16); Restoration of Lithuanian Statehood (Mar. 11); Easter (Apr. 20-21); May Day (May 1); Day of Statehood (July 6); All Saints' Day (Nov. 1); All Souls' Day (Nov. 2); and Christmas (Dec. 24-25).

VILNIUS ☎ 5

Deluged by new businesses and foreign investment, Vilnius maintains its strong Lithuanian pride. Founded in 1321 after a prophetic dream by Grand Duke Gediminas, Vilnius grew and flourished throughout the centuries despite numerous foreign occupations. Scarred but not destroyed by WWII, the Holocaust, and the iron grip of the Soviet Union, Vilnius remains a rich cultural and commercial center today, with a classic 19th-century atmosphere.

⌐ TRANSPORTATION

Flights: The airport (*oro uostas;* VNO), Rodūnės Kelias 2 (info ☎30 66 66, booking ☎75 26 00), is 5km south. Take bus #1 or 2 to the Old Town (15-20min.). To: **Berlin** (2hr.); **Moscow** (2hr.); **Stockholm** (2hr.); and **Warsaw** (1¼hr.).

Trains: Geležinkelio Stotis, Geležinkelio 16 (☎33 00 86; www.litrail.lt). Domestic tickets are sold to the left of the entrance, and international tickets (☎62 69 47, Western Europe ☎69 37 22) to the right. Open daily 6-11am and noon-6pm. All international trains (except those heading north) pass through Belarus (see p. 107). To: **Minsk** (5½hr., 2 per day, 57Lt); **Moscow** (17hr., 1 per day, 128Lt); **Rīga** (7½hr., 5 per day, 72Lt); **St. Petersburg** (18hr., 3 per day, 110Lt); and **Warsaw** (8hr., 4 per day, 115Lt).

Buses: Autobusų Stotis, Sodų 22 (☎900 016 61; reservations ☎16 29 77), opposite the train station. **Tarpmiestinė Salė** covers long-distance buses; windows #13-15 serve destinations outside the former Soviet Union. Open daily 7am-8pm. To: **Minsk** (5hr., 8 and 9am, 22Lt); **Rīga** (6hr., 5 per day, 30-40Lt); **Tallinn** (11hr., 6am and 8:45pm, 90Lt); and **Warsaw** (8hr., 9am and 9:30pm, 80Lt).

Public Transportation: Buses and **trolleys** run daily 6am-midnight. Buy tickets at any kiosk (0.80Lt) or from the driver (1Lt). Tickets are checked frequently; always punch them on board to avoid the hefty fine. Monthly passes available for students (5Lt).

Taxis: Autvela (☎215 05 05), **Fiakvas** (☎70 57 05), and **Kortesa** (☎73 73 73) are 0.65Lt per km. **Private taxis** show a green light in the windshield; agree on the fare before getting in.

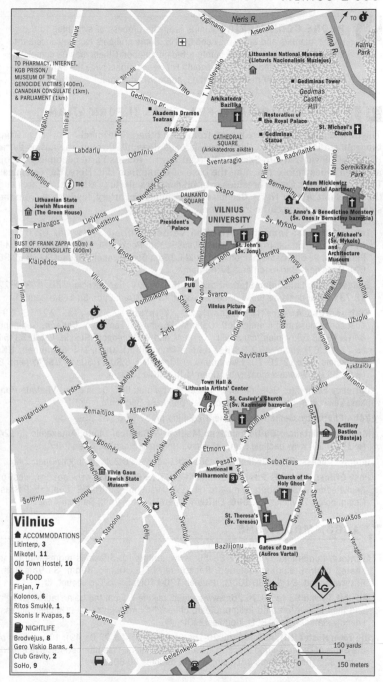

LITHUANIA

Vilnius

🏠 ACCOMMODATIONS
Litinterp, **3**
Mikotel, **11**
Old Town Hostel, **10**

🍴 FOOD
Finjan, **7**
Kolonos, **6**
Ritos Smuklė, **1**
Skonis Ir Kvapas, **5**

🍺 NIGHTLIFE
Brodvėjus, **8**
Gero Viskio Baras, **4**
Club Gravity, **2**
SoHo, **9**

> **PHONE CODE MANIA.** Vilnius is in the process of switching to 7-digit phone numbers and a new city code, (8)5. Some numbers can be converted to the new system by dialing 2 before a 6-digit number. Others may be completely changed; automated messages should list new numbers once the switch is completed in 2003. For more information, see www.telecom.lt.

■✴🛈 ORIENTATION AND PRACTICAL INFORMATION

The **train** and **bus stations** are across from each other. Geležinkelio runs right from the train station to Aušros Vartų, which leads downhill through the **Aušros Vartai** (Gates of Dawn) and into **Senamiestis** (Old Town). Aušros Vartų becomes Didžioji and then Pilies before reaching the base of Gediminas Hill. Here, the **Gediminas Tower** of the Higer Castle presides over **Arkikatedros aikštė** (Cathedral Square) and the banks of the river Neris. **Gedimino,** the commercial artery, leads west from the square in front of the cathedral's doors.

Tourist Offices: Tourist Information Center, Didžioji 31 (☎/fax 62 07 62; www.vilnius.lt), in the Town Hall, sells *Vilnius in Your Pocket* (8Lt). Open in summer M-F 9am-7pm, Sa-Su 10am-4pm; off-season M-F 10am-6pm. **Branch,** Vilniaus 22 (☎62 96 60). Open daily 9am-noon and 12:45-6pm.

Budget Travel: Lithuanian Student and Youth Travel, V. Basanavičiaus 30, #13 (☎22 13 73). Great deals for those under 27. Open M-F 8:30am-6pm, Sa 10am-2pm.

Embassies: Australia (consulate), Vilniaus 23 (☎/fax 22 33 69; aust.con.vilnius@post.omnitel.net). Open M, W, and F 11am-2pm. **Canada,** Gedimino 64 (☎49 68 53; vilnius@canada.lt). Open M and W 9am-noon. **Russia,** Latvių 53/54 (☎72 17 63; visas ☎72 38 93; rusemb@rusemb.lt). Open M-F 8am-noon. **UK,** Antakalnio 2 (☎12 20 70; www.britain.lt). Open M-F 8:30-11:30am. **US,** Akmenų 6 (☎66 55 00; www.usembassy.lt). Open M-Th 8:30-11:30am.

Currency Exchange: Geležinkelio 6, left of the train station. Open 24hr. **Vilniaus Bankas,** Vokiečių 9, cashes traveler's checks. Open M-F 8am-6pm.

24hr. Pharmacy: Gedimino Vaistinė, Gedimino pr. 27 (☎61 01 35).

Medical Assistance: Baltic-American Medical & Surgical Clinic, Antakalnio g. 124 (☎34 20 20; www.baclinic.com), at Vilnius University Hospital. Open 24hr.

Internet Access: Bazė, Gedimino pr. 50. 3-6Lt per hr., 20-25Lt per night. Open 24hr.

Post Office: Centrinis Paštas, Gedimino pr. 7 (☎62 54 68; www.post.lt), west of Arkikatedros aikštė. Address mail to be held: Firstname SURNAME, Centrinis Paštas, Gedimino pr. 7, Vilnius LT-2000, LIETUVA. Open M-F 7am-7pm, Sa 9am-4pm.

🛈 ACCOMMODATIONS

▨ **Litinterp,** Bernardinų 7/2 (☎12 38 50; www.litinterp.lt). Spacious rooms with clean shared bath. Breakfast included. Reception M-F 8:30am-5:30pm, Sa 9am-2pm. Reserve ahead. Singles 80-100Lt; doubles 120-140Lt. 5% ISIC discount. ❸

Mikotel, Pylimo 63 (☎60 96 26; www.travel.lt/mikotel). From the train station, go right and then take a left onto Pylimo. Clean, cheerful rooms with shower. Kitchen access. Friendly staff. Singles 180Lt; doubles 240Lt. ❹

Old Town Hostel (HI), Aušros vartų 20-15a (☎62 53 57; fax 22 01 49), 100m south of the Gates of Dawn. A good place to meet fellow travelers. Free Internet. Reserve ahead. Dorms 32Lt, nonmembers 34Lt; singles and doubles 40-60Lt. ❷

FOOD

IKI supermarkets, which stock foreign brands, are all over Vilnius. The IKI at the bus station is the closest branch to the Old Town. (Open daily 8am-10pm.) Locals and students linger at ▨**Kolonos ❶,** Dailamtp Sq. 2, for great soup, crêpes, dessert, and beer, all for less than 15Lt. (Open daily 11am-11pm.) **Finjan ❸,** Vokiečių 18, offers a mix of Lebanese, Israeli, and Egyptian cuisine. (Entrees 24-45Lt. Belly dancer Th-Sa nights. Open daily 11am-midnight.) **Ritos Smuklė ❷** (Rita's Tavern), Žirmūnų 68, is a traditional Lithuanian tavern with live folk music W-Sa 8-10pm. Take tram #12, 13, or 17. (Main dishes 15-30Lt. Open daily 10am-midnight.) The cafe **Skonis Ir Kvapas ❶,** Trakų 8, has exotic teas (2.50-10Lt) and all-day breakfasts, desserts, and light meals. (Open M-F 8:30am-11pm, Sa-Su 9:30am-11pm.)

SIGHTS

SENAMIESTIS. (Old Town.) The 16th-century **Aušros Vartai** (Gates of Dawn) guard Vilnius's Old Town, the largest in Eastern Europe. After the gates, enter the first door on the right to ascend to the 17th-century **Chapel of the Gates of Dawn** (Aušros Vartų Koplyčia), packed with locals praying to the gilded Virgin Mary icon. Around the corner is **St. Theresa's Church** (Šv. Teresės bažnyčia), known for its Baroque sculptures, multicolored arches, and frescoed ceiling. A few steps farther down, a gateway leads to the bright 17th-century **Church of the Holy Spirit** (Šv. Dvasios bažnyčia), the seat of Lithuania's Russian Orthodox Archbishop. The street merges with the pedestrian Pilies and leads to the main entrance of **Vilnius University** (Vilniaus Universitetas), at Pilies and Šv. Jono. Founded in 1570, the university is the oldest in Eastern Europe. Further north on Pilies is **Arkikatedros aikštė** (Cathedral Square); its **cathedral,** built on a pagan worship site, resembles a Greek temple. From behind the cathedral, walk up the Castle Hill path to **Gediminas Tower** for a great view of Vilnius' spires. Behind the tower sits the **Lithuanian National Museum** (Lietuvis Nacionalinis Muziejus), Arsenalo 1, which chronicles the history of the Lithuanian people. *(Open W-Su 10am-5pm. 4Lt, students 2Lt.)* Off Pylimo, between Kalinausko 1 and 3, is the continent's most random monument: a 4-meter steel shaft topped with a bust of the late freak-rock legend **Frank Zappa.**

THE OLD JEWISH QUARTER AND GENOCIDE MEMORIAL. Vilnius was once a center of Jewish life comparable to Warsaw and New York, with a Jewish population of 100,000 (in a city of 230,000) at the start of WWII. Nazi persecution left only 6000 survivors and only one of pre-war Vilnius's 105 **synagogues,** at Pylimo 39. The **Genocide Memorial,** Agrastų 15, is in **Paneriai,** 10min. away by train (0.90Lt). Head right from the train station and follow Agrastų to the memorial. Between 1941 and 1944, 100,000 people, including 70,000 Jews, were shot, burned, and buried here. The memorials, at pits that served as mass graves, are connected by paved paths. Return by bus #8, on the other side of the tracks. *(Open M and W-Sa 11am-6pm. Free.)* The **Holocaust Museum,** locally called "The Green House," tracks the destruction of Vilnius's Jewish community. *(Pamėnkalnio 12. Open M-Th 9am-5pm, F 9am-4pm. Donations requested.)* For information on the Jewish Quarter or on locating ancestors, visit the **Jewish Cultural Centre.** *(Šaltinių 12. ☎ 41 88 09. Open daily 9am-6pm.)*

▨ **MUSEUM OF GENOCIDE VICTIMS.** (Genocido Aukų Muziejus.) Built in 1899, the Nazis turned the building into a Gestapo headquarters during World War II. When the Soviets came to town, the building became Vilnius's KGB headquarters. One of the guides, G. Radžius, was once a prisoner here; finding a translator is worth the effort. *(Aukų 2a, at the intersection with Gedimino. Open May 15.-Sept. 15 Tu-Su 10am-6pm; Sept. 16-May 14. Tu-Su 10am-4pm. 2Lt.)*

LITHUANIA

🎵🎸 ENTERTAINMENT AND NIGHTLIFE

Summer is full of festivals, including the National Philharmonic's **Vilniaus Festivalis** in June (www.filharmonija.lt); check *Vilnius in Your Pocket* or the Lithuanian morning paper *Lietuvos Rytas* for more performances. Vilnius has a vibrant night scene, whether you prefer a mellow pub or a raging dance floor. For information on gay nightlife, check the **Lithuanian Gay and Lesbian Homepage** (www.gayline.lt). ◙**Club Gravity,** Jasinkio 16, is an ultra-modern techno club. (Cover 25Lt. Open Th-Sa 10pm-6am.) **Brodvėjus,** Mėsinių 4, is a popular bar and dance club that has live classical music Su. (Open M noon-3am, W-Sa noon-5am, Su noon-2am.) In the center of town, **Gero Viskio Baras,** Pilies 34, is a three-floor bar. (Basement cover men 5Lt, women free. Open Su-Th 10am-3am, F-Sa 10am-5am.) **SoHo,** Aušros Vartų 7, is a brand-new bar with a different activity each night of the week. (M 15% student discount, Tu finger painting, W cocktail night, Th live jazz, F 4-6pm All-You-Can-Eat (15Lt) and live music 8pm, Sa-Su live jazz 1-3pm, Su live classical music 3-10pm. M-F Happy Hour 4-6pm. Open Su-Th 10am-2am, F-Sa 10am-3am.)

🔳 DAYTRIPS FROM VILNIUS

TRAKAI CASTLE. Trakai's fairy-tale castle has inspired legends since its construction in the 15th century. In 1665, the Tsar of Russia accomplished what 15th-century Germans could not—plundering the town and razing the castle. Following a lengthy restoration under the Soviets from 1955 to 1980, five stories of red bricks now tower over beautiful lakes and woods. Climb the spiral staircase in the watchtower to the third floor for a magnificent view of the medieval courtyard below. Across from the tower, the **City and Castle History Museum** chronicles the history of Trakai and Lithuania. (Museum open daily 10am-7pm. 8Lt, students 3.50Lt. Tours 40Lt, students 20Lt.) The castle also forms a dramatic backdrop for a summer concert series (www.trakaifestival.lt). Paddleboats and waterbikes are available for rent by the footbridge to the castle. Trakai, 28km west of Vilnius, is accessible by **bus** (30min., every hr. 6:45am-9:30pm, 2.60Lt; buy tickets on the bus). The last return is usually at 8:30pm, but the bus leaves early when it reaches capacity.

KAUNAS. Kaunas, easily accessible from Vilnius, is considered the cradle of Lithuanian culture. At the end of **Laisvės,** the main pedestrian boulevard, is the sumptuous, domed **St. Michael the Archangel Church.** (Open M-F 9am-3pm, Sa-Su 8:30am-2pm.) Nearby is the **Museum of Exiles and Political Prisoners** (Tremties ir rezistencijos Muziejus), Vytauto 46. The curator was once an exile herself; find someone to translate her tours. (Open W-Sa 10am-4pm. Donation requested.) Also at this end of Laisvės is the **Devil Museum** (Velnių Muziejus), V. Putvinskio 64, which displays more than 2000 depictions of devils in various media. (Open Tu-Su 10am-5pm. 5Lt, students 2.50Lt.) Take microbus #46 across the Neris River to IX Fortas (2-5 per hr. 2am-9pm) to reach the **Ninth Fort,** which was used as a Nazi death camp; 64 men escaped on Christmas Day, 1943, but most were later caught. (Open W-M 10am-6pm. Museum 2Lt, students 1Lt.) To reach Kaunas from Vilnius, take a **train** (2hr., 11 per day, 9.80Lt) or **bus** (1½hr., every 30min., 12.40Lt). The **Tourist Information Center** is at Laisvės 36. (☎32 34 36; www.kaunas.lt. Open M-F 9am-6pm, Sa-Su 9am-1pm and 1-6pm). ◙**Litinterp,** Gedimino 28, arranges **private rooms ❸.** (☎/fax 22 87 18; www.litinterp.lt. Reserve ahead. Open M-F 8:30am-5:30pm, Sa 9am-3pm. Singles 80-140Lt; doubles 140-260Lt.) **Žalias Ratas ❷,** Laisvės 36b, is an excellent traditional tavern. (Entrees 5-28Lt. Open daily 11am-midnight.)

KLAIPÉDA ☎846

Guarding the Curonian Spit is Klaipéda, Lithuania's third-largest city. Strategically located on the tip of the Neringa peninsula, it was briefly the Prussian capital in the 19th century, and was later handed to France in the 1919 Treaty of Versailles. In WWII, the city served as a German U-boat base before being industrialized by the Soviets after the war. On mainland Klaipéda, the **Clock Museum** (Laikrodživ Muziejus), Liepų g. 12, displays every conceivable kind of timekeeping device. From S. Daukanto g., turn right on H. Manto and left on Liepų g. (Open Tu-Su noon-5:30pm. 4Lt, students 2Lt. English tour 40Lt.) **Klaipéda Drama Theater** (Klaipédos Dramos Teatras), Teatro aikštė, on the other side of H. Manto g., was one of Wagner's favorite haunts. (Tickets ☎31 44 53. Open Tu-Su 11am-2pm and 4-7pm.) The main attraction in **Smiltynė**, across the lagoon, is the ⊠**Maritime Museum, Aquarium, and Dolphinarium** (Lietuvos Jūrų Muziejus), Smiltynė 3, in an 1860s fortress. (www.juru.muziejus.lt. Open June-Aug. Tu-Su 10:30am-6:30pm; off-season closes earlier. 8Lt, students 4Lt.) Forest paths lead west 500m to the **beaches**. The best bars line H. Manto g. **Kurpai,** an excellent jazz club, is at Kurpių g. 1a. (Live jazz 9:30pm. Cover 5-10Lt. Open daily 12pm-3am.) **Paradox,** Minijos 2, has a pulsing disco, a mellow pool room, and a relaxed bar. From the rotary at the end of Tiltų g., turn right on Gallnio Pylimo g. and cross another rotary onto Minijos. (Bar open M-Tu noon-3am, W-Su noon-6am. Disco open W-Su 9pm-6am.)

Buses (☎41 15 47; reservations ☎41 15 40) go from Butkų Juzés 9 to: Kaunas (3hr., 14 per day, 28Lt); Palanga (30-40min., 23 per day, 2.50-3LT); and Vilnius (4-5hr., 12 per day, 35-38Lt). **Ferries** (☎31 42 57; info ☎31 11 17) run from Old Castle Port, Žveju 8, to Smiltynė (10min., every 30min., free) and connect with microbuses to Nida (1hr., 7Lt). The staff at the **tourist office,** Tomo g. 2, speaks fluent English, sells maps, and arranges tours. (☎41 21 86; www.klaipeda.lt Open M-F 8am-6pm; Sa 9am-4pm.) **Litinterp,** S. Šimkaus g. 21/4, arranges rooms. (☎31 14 90. Singles 90-120Lt; doubles 140-180. Off-season 20-40Lt less. Call ahead. Open M-F 8:30am-5:30pm, Sa 9:30am-3:30pm.) ⊠**Klaipéda Traveler's Guesthouse (HI) ❷,** Butkų Juzés 7-4, 50m from the bus station, has spacious dorms and free Internet. (☎21 18 79; oldtown@takas.lt. Free beer with email reservation. Dorms 32Lt; nonmembers 34Lt.) Heading away from the Danė River on Tiltų, make a left on Kulių Vartų g., then turn left onto Bangų g. to reach **Aribé Hotel ❹,** Bangų g. 17a, a modern hotel with private bathrooms. (☎49 09 40; vitetur@klaipeda.omnitel.net. Singles 140Lt; doubles 180Lt; luxury suite 260Lt. Off-season 20Lt less.) Romantic ⊠**Luja ❸,** H. Manto g. 20, serves Lithuanian and international dishes. (☎41 24 44. Call ahead. Main dishes 7-62Lt. Open daily noon-midnight.) **IKI supermarket** is at M. Mažvyado 7/11. (Open daily 8am-10pm.) **Postal code:** LT-5800.

▶ DAYTRIPS FROM KLAIPÉDA: NIDA AND PALANGA. Windswept white sand dunes have long drawn summer vacationers to **Nida,** only 3km north of the Kaliningrad region on the Curonian Spit. From the remains of the immense sundial on the highest of the ⊠**Drifting Dunes of Parnidis,** you can look down on the glorious dunes, the Curonian Lagoon, and the Baltic. A walk along the beach or through forest paths leads to surreal mountains and sheets of white sand blowing gracefully into the sea from 100m above. From the center of town, follow the promenade by the water and bear right on Skruzdynés g. to reach the **Thomas Mann House** (Thomo Manno Namelis) at #17. Mann built the cottage in 1930 and wrote *Joseph and His Brothers* here, but had to give the house up when Hitler invaded. (Open June-Aug. Tu-Su 10am-6pm; Sept.-May Tu-Sa 11am-5pm. 2Lt.) From Naglių 18e, **microbuses** (☎524 72) run to Smiltynė (1hr., every 30min., 7Lt; buy tickets on board); the last bus should get you there in time for the 11:15pm ferry back to mainland Klaipéda. The **Tourist Info Center,** Taikos g. 4, opposite the bus station, arranges private

LITHUANIA

rooms for a 5Lt fee. (☎523 45. Open July 15-Sept. 1 M-F 9am-1pm and 2-8pm, Sa 10am-8pm, Su 10am-3pm; June 1-July 14 M-F 9am-1pm and 2-6pm, Sa 10am-6pm, Su 10am-3pm; Sept.-May M-F 9am-1pm and 2-6pm, Sa-Su 10am-3pm.) ☎**8469**.

The largest park in the country, over 20km of shoreline, and an exuberant nightlife make **Palanga** the hottest summer spot in Lithuania. While the beach is the main attraction, Palanga's pride and joy is the **Amber Museum** (Gintaro muziejus) in a mansion in the Botanical Gardens. The collection consists of 15,000 pieces of amber that have primeval flora and fauna trapped inside. (Open June-Aug. Tu-Sa 10am-8pm, Su 10am-7pm; Sept.-May daily 11am-4:30pm. 5Lt, students 2.50Lt.) Palanga's main streets are **Vytauto gatrė,** which runs parallel to the beach and passes the bus station, and **J. Basanavičiaus,** which runs perpendicular to Vytauto g., ending at the boardwalk. **Meilės alėja** runs south of the pier along the beach, becoming **Birutės alėja** in the Palanga Park and Botanical Garden. **Buses** (☎533 33) from Klaipėda (30min., every 30min., 2.50Lt) arrive at Kretinjos 1; **tourist info** is available to the right of the station entrance (☎488 11; www.palangatic.lt). **Litinterp** in Klaipėda (see p. 693) arranges **private rooms** ❸ in Palanga (singles 90-120Lt; doubles 140-180Lt). Vytauto g. and J. Basanavičiaus g. are lined with cafes and restaurants that have outdoor seating. ☎**8460**.

LUXEMBOURG

Too often overlooked by budget travelers, the tiny Grand Duchy of Luxembourg boasts impressive fortresses and castles as well as beautiful hiking trails. Established in 963, the original territory was called *Lucilinburhuc*, named for the "little fortresses" that saturated the countryside after successive waves of Burgundians, Spaniards, French, Austrians, and Germans had receded. Today, Luxembourg has become a notable European Union member and a prominent international financial center. Judging by their national motto, *"Mir welle bleiwe wat mir sinn"* ("We want to remain what we are"), it seems that the Luxembourgians are pleased with their accomplishments.

FACTS AND FIGURES

Official Name: Grand Duchy of Luxembourg.
Capital: Luxembourg City.
Population: 415,000.
Land Area: 2586 sq. km.

Time Zone: GMT +1.
Languages: French, German, Luxembourgian.
Religions: Roman Catholic (90%).

DISCOVER LUXEMBOURG

Luxembourg is a charming stopover between France or Belgium and Germany. **Luxembourg City** (p. 697) is arguably one of Europe's most beautiful capitals. Your next stop should be **Vianden** (p. 701), whose gorgeous chateau and outdoor opportunities make it well worth an overnight stay. If you have extra time, consider daytripping to **Diekirch** (p. 702), or hiking and biking around **Echternach** (**p. 703**).

ESSENTIALS

WHEN TO GO

Luxembourg has a temperate climate with less moisture than Belgium. Anytime between May and mid-Oct. is a good time to visit.

DOCUMENTS AND FORMALITIES

VISAS. South Africans need a visa for stays of any length. Citizens of Australia, Canada, the EU, New Zealand, and the US do not need a visa for stays of up to 30 days. Contact your embassy for more information.

EMBASSIES. All foreign embassies are in Luxembourg City (p. 697). Foreign embassies in Brussels also have jurisdiction over Luxembourg. Luxembourg embassies at home include: **Australia** (consulate), Level 18, Royal Exchange Building, 56 Pitt St., Sydney NSW 2000 (☎02 92 41 43 22; fax 92 51 11 13); **Canada** (consulate), 3706 St. Hubert St., Montréal, PQ H2L 4A3 (☎514-849-2101); **South Africa** (consulate), P.O. Box 357, Lanseria 1748 (☎011 659 09 61); **UK**, 27 Wilton Crescent, London SW1X 8SD (☎020 7235 6961; fax 7235 9734); **US**, 2200 Massachusetts Ave. NW, Washington, D.C. 20008 (☎202-265-4171; fax 202-328-8270).

TRANSPORTATION

The Luxembourg City airport (LUX) is serviced by **Luxair** (☎479 81, reservations ☎4798 42 42; www.luxair.lu) and by flights from the UK and throughout the continent. A **Benelux Tourrail Pass** allows five days of unlimited **train** travel in a one-month period in Belgium, The Netherlands, and Luxembourg (€159, 50% companion discount; under 26 €106). The **Billet Réseau** (€4.50, book of 5 €17.50) is good for one day of unlimited bus and train travel. The **Luxembourg Card** (see below) also includes unlimited transportation. **Hiking** and **biking trails** run between Luxembourg City and Echternach, from Diekirch to Echternach and Vianden, and elsewhere. **Bikes** aren't permitted on buses, but are allowed on many trains for free.

TOURIST SERVICES AND MONEY

TOURIST OFFICES. For general information, contact the **Luxembourg National Tourist Office**, P.O. Box 1001, L-1010 Luxembourg (☎(352) 42 82 82 10; www.etat.lu/tourism). The **Luxembourg Card,** available from Easter to October at tourist offices, hostels, and many hotels and public transportation offices, provides unlimited transportation on national trains and buses and includes admission to 32 tourist sites (1-day €9, 2-day €16, 3-day €22).

MONEY. The official currency of Luxembourg is the **euro.** The Luxembourg franc can still be exchanged at a rate of 40LF to €1. For exchange rates and more information on the euro, see p. 16. The European Union imposes a **value-added tax (VAT)** on goods and services purchased within the EU (see p. 15). Luxembourg's VAT (15%) is already included in most prices. Luxembourg's refund threshold (US$85) is lower than most other EU countries; refunds are usually 13% of the purchase price. The cost of living in Luxembourg is moderate to high. Expect to pay €13.60-15.50 for a hostel bed, €30-45 for a hotel room, and €8-11 for a restaurant meal.

EMERGENCY	Police: ☎112. Ambulance: ☎112. Fire: ☎112.

COMMUNICATION

TELEPHONES. There are no city codes; just dial 352 plus the local number. Most public phones accept phone cards, which are sold at post offices and newspaper stands. International direct dial numbers include: **AT&T,** ☎8002 0111; **British Telecom,** ☎8002 0044; **Canada Direct,** ☎8002 0119; **Ireland Direct,** ☎0800 353; **MCI,** ☎8002 0112; **Sprint,** ☎8002 0115; **Telecom New Zealand,** ☎8002 0064.

Luxembourg (map)

TO LIÈGE (88km) & BRUSSELS (186km)

BELGIUM

Troisvierges

Clervaux

THE ARDENNES

Esch-sur-Sûre

Clerf R.

Our R.

GERMANY

Vianden

Sûre R.

Ettelbrück

Sûre R.

Diekirch

Echternach

TO TRIER (13km)

TO BRUSSELS (196km)

Hollenfells

Alzette R.

Bourglinster

Wasserbillig

Arlon

LA MOSELLE

Mosel R.

Luxembourg City

Remich

Longwy

FRANCE

TO METZ (46km) & PARIS (330km)

0 — 10 miles

0 — 10 kilometers

PHONE CODES	Country code: 352. **International dialing prefix:** 00. Luxembourg has no city codes.

MAIL. Mailing a postcard or a letter (up to 20g) from Luxembourg costs €0.55 to the UK and Europe and €0.75 anywhere else.

LANGUAGES. French and German are the administrative languages, and, since a referendum in 1984, *Letzebuergesch*, a mixture of the other two that sounds a bit like Dutch, is the national language. French is most common in the city, while German is more common in smaller towns. For basic phrases in French and German, see p. 895. English is also commonly spoken.

ACCOMMODATIONS AND CAMPING

LUXEMBOURG	❶	❷	❸	❹	❺
ACCOMMODATIONS	under €12	€13-16	€17-30	€31-40	over €40

Luxembourg's 12 **HI youth hostels** *(Auberges de Jeunesse)* are often filled with school groups. Check the sign posted in any hostel to find out which hostels are full or closed each day. Prices range from €13.60-15.50; nonmembers pay €2.75 extra. Breakfast and sheets are included, a packed lunch costs €3.80, and dinner €7.10. Half of the hostels close from mid-November to mid-December, and the other half close from mid-January to mid-February. Contact **Centrale des Auberges de Jeunesse Luxembourgeoises** (☎26 29 35 00; www.youthhostels.lu) for information. **Hotels** advertise €25-50 per night, depending on amenities; make sure you clarify the price you will pay. Luxembourg is a **camping** paradise; most towns have campsites close by. Two people with a tent will typically pay €5-9 per night.

FOOD AND DRINK

COUNTRY NAME	❶	❷	❸	❹	❺
FOOD	under €5	€6-9	€10-14	€15-20	over €21

HOLIDAYS & FESTIVALS

Holidays: New Year's Day (Jan. 1); Carnival (Mar. 3); Easter (Apr. 20); Easter Monday (Apr. 21); May Day (May 1); Ascension Day (May 29); Whit Sunday and Monday (June 8-9); National Holiday (June 23); Assumption Day (Aug. 15); All Saints' Holiday (Nov. 1); Christmas (Dec. 25); and Saint Stephen's Day (Dec. 26).

Festivals: Luxembourg City hosts the **Luxembourg City Fete** (Sept. 1).

LUXEMBOURG CITY

With a medieval fortress perched on a cliff that overlooks lush green river valleys, and high bridges stretching all over the downtown area, Luxembourg City (pop. 81,800) is one of the most attractive and dramatic capitals in Europe. As an international banking capital, it is home to thousands of frenzied foreign business executives; even so, most visitors find it surprisingly relaxed and idyllic.

▣ TRANSPORTATION

Flights: Findel International Airport (LUX), 6km from the city. **Bus #9** (€1.10) is cheaper than the Luxair bus (€3.75) and runs the same route every 10-20min.

Trains: Gare CFL, av. de la Gare (toll-free info ☎49 90 49 90; www.cfl.lu), near the foot of av. de la Liberté, 10min. south of the city center. To: **Amsterdam** (5¾hr., €42, under 26 €34.20); **Brussels** (2¾hr., round-trip €39/€13.30); **Frankfurt** (5hr., €43.20/ €38.20); **Paris** (3½-4hr., €39.20/€31.30).

Buses: Buy a **billet courte distance** (short-distance ticket) from the driver (single-fare €1.10, full-day €4.40), or pick up a package of 10 (€7.95) at the train station. Tickets also valid on **local trains.** Buses run until midnight; night buses offer limited service.

Taxis: ☎48 22 33. €0.87 per km. 10% extra 10pm-6am; 25% extra on Su. €17-20 from the city center to the airport.

Bikes: Rent from **Velo en Ville,** 8 r. Bisserwé (☎47 96 23 83). Open daily 10am-noon and 1-8pm. €12.50 per half-day, €20 per day, €37.50 per weekend, €75 per week; under 26 20% discount.

✱? ORIENTATION AND PRACTICAL INFORMATION

Five minutes by bus and 15min. by foot from the train station, Luxembourg City's historic center revolves around the **Place d'Armes.** Facing the municipal tourist office, located in the commemorative Town Hall, turn right down r. Chimay to reach **Boulevard Roosevelt.**

Tourist Offices: Grand Duchy National Tourist Office (☎42 82 82 20; www.etat.lu/ tourism), in the train station, has tons of info and lacks the long lines of the office in town. Open July-Sept. 9am-7pm; Oct.-June 9:15am-12:30pm and 1:45-6pm. **Municipal Tourist Office,** pl. d'Armes (☎22 28 09; www.luxembourg-city.lu/touristinfo). Open Apr.-Sept. M-Sa 9am-7pm, Su 10am-6pm; Oct.-Mar. M-Sa 9am-6pm, Su 10am-6pm. Also, look for the helpful, yellow-shirted **"Ask Me"** representatives all over the city; they give out free tourist info. **Center Information Jeunes,** 26 pl. de la Gare (☎26 29 32 00), inside Galerie Kons across from the train station, is a great service for young travelers, offering information on everything from hostels to finding jobs as well as free **Internet** access for students (max. 1hr.). Open M-F 10am-6pm.

Budget Travel: SOTOUR, 15 pl. du Théâtre (☎46 15 14). Sells BIJ and other discount tickets for international flights; makes train reservations that begin or end in Luxembourg. Open M-F 9am-6pm, Sa 9am-noon.

Embassies: Ireland, 28 r. d'Arlon (☎45 06 10; fax 45 88 20). Open M-F 10am-12:30pm and 2:30-5pm. **UK,** 14 bd. Roosevelt (☎22 98 64; fax 22 98 67). Open M-F 9am-12:30pm. **US,** 22 bd. Emmanuel Servais (☎46 01 23; www.amembassy.lu). Open M-F 8:30am-12:30pm. **Australians, Canadians, New Zealanders,** and **South Africans** should contact their embassies in France or Belgium.

Currency Exchange: Banks are the only option for changing money or cashing traveler's checks. Most are open M-F from 8:30am until 4 or 4:30pm. All are closed on weekends. Expect to pay a commission of €5 for cash and €8.30 for traveler's checks.

Luggage Storage: In train station. €2.50 per day (1-month max.); 2-day lockers €2-4.

Laundromat: Quick Wash, 31 r. de Strasbourg, near the station. Wash and dry €10. Open M-F 8:30am-6:30pm, Sa until 6pm. Cheaper at the HI hostel (see below).

Emergency: Police: ☎113. **Ambulance:** ☎112.

Pharmacy: Pharmacie Goedert, 5 pl. d'Armes (☎22 39 91). Open M 1-6:15pm, Tu-F 8am-6:15pm, Sa 8am-12:30pm. Check any pharmacy window for night info.

Medical Services: Doctors and pharmacies on call: ☎112. **Clinique Ste-Therese** (☎49 77 61 or 49 78 81), r. Ste-Zithe.

Internet Access: Center Information Jeunes (see above) has free Internet for students. **Sparky's,** 11a av. Monterey, at pl. d'Armes (☎620 12 23). €0.10 per min. Open M-F 8am-8pm, Sa 11am-8pm.

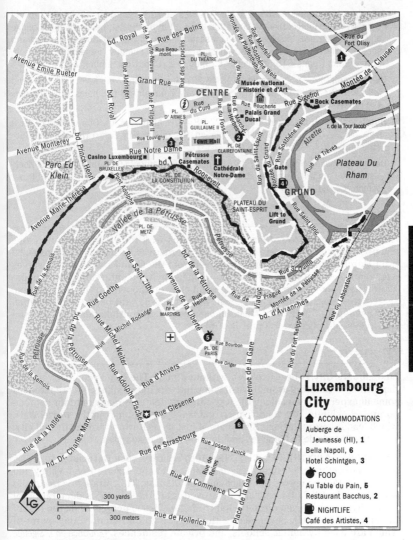

Post Office: 38 pl. de la Gare, across the street and left of the train station. Open M-F 6am-7pm, Sa 6am-noon. Address mail to be held: Firstname SURNAME, *Poste Restante,* Recette Principale, **L-1009** Luxembourg City, Luxembourg. **Branch office,** 25 r. Aldringen, near the pl. d'Armes. Open M-F 7am-7pm, Sa 7am-5pm.

ACCOMMODATIONS

Budget travelers have two options: the city's hostel, often filled with school and tour groups in the summer, or the inexpensive accommodations near the train station, where a night's stay costs about €50 less than in the city center.

Auberge de Jeunesse (HI), 2 r. du Fort Olisy (☎22 19 20 or 22 68 89; luxembourg@youth.hostels.lu). Take bus #9 and get off at the hostel; head under the bridge and turn right down the steep path. Low security; lock up your valuables. Breakfast and sheets included. Laundry €7.50. 6-night max. stay in summer. Reception 7am-1am. Curfew 2am. Dorms €15.50; singles €23; doubles €36. Nonmembers add €2.75. ❷

Bella Napoli, 4 r. de Strasbourg (☎48 46 29). Simple rooms with hardwood floors and full bath. Breakfast included. Reception daily 7am-midnight. Singles €38; doubles €45; triples €60. ❹

Hotel Schintgen, 6 r. Notre Dame (☎22 28 44; schintgn@pt.lu). One of the cheapest hotels in the Old Center. Breakfast included. Reception daily 7am-11pm. Singles €50-65; doubles €75-85; triples €87. ❺

Camping: Kockelscheuer (☎47 18 15), outside Luxembourg City. Take bus #5 to Kockelscheuer-Camping from the station. Showers included. Open Easter-Oct. €3.50 per person, €4 per tent. ❶

◪ FOOD

Although the area around **Place d'Armes** teems with touristy fast-food options and pricey restaurants, there are desirable alternatives. **Restaurant Bacchus ❷**, 32 r. du Marché-aux-Herbes, down the street from the Grand Ducal palace, serves excellent pizza and pasta (€7-12) in a homey environment. (Open Tu-Su noon-10pm.) **Au Table du Pain ❷,** 37 av. de la Liberté, on the way to the train station, serves up soups, salads (€8-11), sandwiches (€4-8), and baked goods. (Open daily 8am-6pm.) Stock up at **Alima supermarket,** on r. Bourbon near the train station. (Open M-F 8:30am-6:30pm, Sa until 6pm.)

◉ SIGHTS

Luxembourg City is best explored without a map. The city is compact enough that just by wandering around you'll bump into the major sights. Be prepared for some unexpected treats along the way—the city features many outdoor contemporary art exhibits. If you crave more guidance, signs point out the **Wenzel Walk,** which leads visitors through 1000 years of history as it winds around the old city, along the **Chemin de la Corniche,** and down into the casemates.

FORTRESSES AND THE OLD CITY. The 10th-century **Bock Casemates** fortress, part of Luxembourg's original castle, looms over the Alzette River Valley and offers a fantastic view of the **Grund** and the **Clausen.** This strategic stronghold was closed in 1867 and partially destroyed after the country's declaration of neutrality, but was used during WWII to shelter 35,000 people while the rest of the city was ravaged. Seventeen of the original 23km remain today, parts of which are used by banks, schools, and private residences. *(Entrance on r. Sigefroi, just past the bridge leading to the hostel. Open Mar.-Oct. daily 10am-5pm. €1.75.)* The **Pétrusse Casemates** were built by the Spanish in the 1600s to reinforce the medieval structures and were later improved by the Austrians. In the 19th century, a second ring was extended and a third began around the city, giving Luxembourg the nickname "Gibraltar of the North." *(Pl. de la Constitution. Open July-Sept. €1.75, students €1.50. Tours every hr. 11am-4pm.)* The view from the nearby **place de la Constitution** is incredible. Stroll down into the lush green valley, or catch one of the little tourist trains that run down from pl. de la Constitution into the valley and back up to the **Plateau du Rham.** *(Trains ☎651 16 51. Mid-Mar. to Oct. 10am-6pm every 30min. except 1pm. €6.50.)*

MUSEUMS. The **Luxembourg Card** (see p. 696) covers entrance to all museums in the city. The **All-in-One Ticket** covers five museums over two days *(€8.70 at the Municipal Tourist Office).* The eclectic collection at the **Musée National d'Histoire et d'Art** chronicles the influences of the various European empires, from ancient to contemporary, that controlled Luxembourg. *(Marché-aux-Poissons, at r. Boucherie and Sigefroi. ☎479 33 01; www.mnha.lu. Open Tu-Su 10am-5pm. €5, students €3.)* The **Musée d'Histoire de la Ville de Luxembourg** features quirky exhibits that allow you to view the history of the city through photographs, films, and music clips. *(14 r. du St-Esprit. ☎47 96 30 61. Open Tu-Su 10am-6pm, Th until 8pm. €5, students €3.70.)*

OTHER SIGHTS. Built in 1574, the Renaissance **Palais Grand Ducal** became the official city residence of the Grand Duke in 1890. *(Mandatory tours mid-July to Aug. M-F afternoons and Sa mornings; tickets sold at the Municipal Tourist Office. Reservations ☎22 28 09; English-language tours available. €5.45.)* Nearby, the 7th-century **Cathédrale Notre Dame,** which incorporates features of the Dutch Renaissance and early Baroque styles, houses the tomb of John the Blind, the 14th-century King of Bohemia and Count of Luxembourg. *(Entrance at bd. Roosevelt. Open daily 10am-noon and 2-5:30pm. Free.)*

🎵 🎭 ENTERTAINMENT AND NIGHTLIFE

At night, the **place d'Armes** comes to life with free concerts and stand-up comedy. Pick up *La Semaine à Luxembourg* at the tourist office for a list of events. On the **Grand Duke's birthday** (June 23), the city shuts down for a large procession. Nightlife centers on the valley in the **Grund** (by the bottom of the elevator lift on pl. du St-Esprit) and the **Clausen** area. Check the monthly *Nightlife.lu*, available at most cafes and newsstands. For a more relaxed and slightly older crowd, warm up in the Grund at the candle-lit piano bar ▨**Café des Artistes,** 22 Montée du Grund. (☎52 34 46. Beer €2.50. Piano W-Su 10:30pm-2am. Open daily 2:30pm-late.)

THE ARDENNES

Almost six decades ago, the Battle of the Bulge (1944) mashed Luxembourg into slime and mud. Today, the forest is verdant again, and the quiet towns, looming castles, and pleasant hiking trails are powerful draws.

ETTELBRÜCK. Ettelbrück's position on the main railway line between Liège, Belgium, and Luxembourg City makes it a transportation hub of the Ardennes. To get to the city center from the train station, go left on r. du Prince Henri, continue right on the same street, then turn left on Grand Rue and follow it to pl. de l'Église. The **General Patton Memorial Museum,** 5 r. Dr. Klein, commemorates the liberation of Luxembourg during WWII. To get there, walk back along the Grand Rue, away from pl. de l'Église, and go left onto r. Dr. Klein. (☎81 03 22. Open July to mid-Sept. daily 10am-5pm; mid-Sept. to June Su 2-5pm. €2.50.) The **tourist office** at the train station has information about excursions to the surrounding Ardennes towns. (☎81 20 68; site@pt.lu. Open M-F 9am-noon and 1:30-5pm, July-Aug. also Sa 10am-noon and 2-4pm.) To get to the **Ettelbrück Hostel (HI) ❷,** r. G.D. Josephine-Charlotte, follow signs from the station. (☎81 22 69; ettelbruck@youthhostels.lu. Lockout 10am-5pm. Breakfast and sheets included. Dorms €13.60.) **Camping Kalkesdelt ❶** is located at 22 r. du Camping. (☎81 21 85. Open Apr.-Oct. Reception daily 7:30am-noon and 2-10pm. €3.80 per person, €4 per tent.)

VIANDEN. The village of Vianden, in the dense Ardennes woods along the Our River, is home to one of the most impressive castles in Western Europe. Backpackers **hike** and **kayak** along the Sûre River, just south of Vianden, or **bike** to Diekirch (15-20min.) and Echternach (30min.). The **château,** a mix of Carolingian, Gothic, and Renaissance architecture, is filled with medieval armor, 16th-century furniture, and 17th-century tapestries. From March to October, the château hosts classical concerts each weekend. Walk uphill from the town or downhill from the *télésiège* (chairlift) to get to the château. (☎83 41 08. Open Apr.-Sept. daily 10am-6pm.; Mar. and Oct. M-F 10am-5pm, Sa 10am-5:30pm, Su 10am-6pm; Nov.-Feb. daily 10am-4pm. €4.50, students €3.50. Concerts €7.45-12.40.) For a stellar view of the château, ride the *télésiège*, 39 r. de Sanatorium. From the tourist office, cross the river, go left on r. Victor Hugo, then left again on r. de Sanitorium. (☎83 43 23. Open July-Aug. daily 10am-6pm; Easter-June and Sept.-Oct. 10am-5pm. €2.75; round-trip €4.25.) The **Maison Victor Hugo,** 37 r. de la Gare, is the former home of the famous French writer. (☎26 87 40 88; www.victorhugo.lu. Open Apr.-Nov. Tu-Su 11am-5pm; Dec.-Mar. Sa 11am-5pm.)

Buses arrive from Ettelbrück (#570; 2 per hr., €2.25) via Diekirch. The **tourist office,** 1 r. du Vieux Marché, next to the main bus stop, sells trail maps (€2.30) and has info on kayaking and private rooms. (☎83 42 57; www.tourist-info-vianden.lu. Open M-F 8am-noon and 1-6pm, Sa 10am-2pm, Su 2-4pm.) To reach the **HI youth hostel ❷,** 3 Montée du Château, from the bus stop or tourist office, follow Grande Rue away from the river and head up the hill; bear onto Montée du Château and follow the signs. (☎83 41 77; vianden@youthhostels.lu. Sheets €3.10. Reception daily 8-10am and 5-9pm. Lockout 10am-5pm. Curfew 11pm. Open mid-Mar. to mid-Nov. Call ahead. Dorms €13.60; nonmembers add €2.75.) **Camp op dem Deich ❶,** r. Neugarten, alongside the Our river, is 5min. downstream from the tourist office. (☎83 43 75. Open Easter-Oct. €4 per person, €3.50 per tent.)

DIEKIRCH. Diekirch is a convenient outpost for biking and canoeing. The **National Museum of Military History,** 10 Bamertal, presents a comprehensive exhibit of relics from WWII's Battle of the Bulge. (☎80 89 08. Open Apr.-Oct. daily 10am-6pm; Nov.-Mar. 2-6pm. €5, students €3.) The 15th-century **Église Saint-Laurent,** in the *Zone Pietone* (pedestrian area), is built upon Roman ruins. (Open Easter-Oct. Tu-Su 10am-noon and 2-6pm.) **Trains** arrive from Ettelbrück hourly, while the more scenic **bus** rolls in every 15min. Buses run from Echternach hourly and drop you off on the Esplanade in front of the Municipal Museum. Buses headed for Vianden stop in the center of Diekirch, just off the Esplanade at the end of the *Zone Pietone* (#570; every 30min.). To get to the **tourist office,** 3 pl. de la Liberation, from the station, take the underground stairs to r. St. Antione and walk to the end; it's directly across the Place. (☎80 30 23; www.diekirch.lu. Hiking maps €2.30, mountain-biking maps €5. Open July-Aug. M-F 9am-5pm, Sa-Su 10am-noon and 2-4pm; M-F 9am-noon and 2-5pm, Sa 2-4pm. Free guided tours daily 3pm.) Rent **bikes** at **Speicher Sport,** 56 r. Clairefontaine (☎80 84 38; speibike@pt.lu; €10 per half-day, €15 per day), or **canoes** at **Outdoor Center,** 10 r. de la Sure (☎86 91 39). Stay at the conveniently located **Au Beau-Sejour ❺,** 12 Esplanade. (☎80 34 03; hotelbeausejour@hotmail.com. All rooms have shower and TV. Reception daily 8am-midnight. Singles €52; doubles €72.) Pitch your tent at **Camping de la Sûre ❶,** 34 rte. de Gilsdorf. (☎80 94 25; tourisme@diekirch.lu. Open Apr.-Sept. €3.50 per person, €3.75 per tent. Showers €0.75.) Restaurants line **Grand Rue.** The **Match** grocery store is just off r. Alexis Heck. (Open M-Th 8:30am-7:30pm, F 8:30am-8pm, Sa 8am-6pm.)

CLERVAUX. Little Clervaux's **château** houses the striking ▨**Family of Man** exhibition, compiled in 1955 by Luxembourgian photographer Edward Steichen. (☎92 96 57. Open Mar.-Dec. Tu-Su 10am-6pm. €3.75, students €2.) To get to the château and the **Benedictine Abbey,** turn left from the train station and walk straight. (Abbey open daily 9am-7pm. Free.) Clervaux lies right on the main **railway** line that connects Luxembourg City, Ettelbrück, and Liège, Belgium. The **tourist office,**

in the castle, books private rooms at Clervaux's B&Bs. (☎92 00 72; www.tour-isme-clervaux.lu. Open July-Oct. daily 9:45am-11:45am and 2-6pm, Sept.-Oct. closed Su; Apr.-June M-Sa 2-5pm.) **Camping Officiel ❶**, 33 Klatzewe, is situated alongside the river. (☎92 00 42. Open Apr.-Nov. €4.30 per person, €4.30 per tent.)

LITTLE SWITZERLAND (LE MULLERTHAL)

In the eastern corner of Luxembourg, the region known as Little Switzerland, provides the ideal setting for hiking and rock-climbing. The unusual sandstone rock formations and numerous paths are the main attraction for visitors to the area.

ECHTERNACH. A favorite vacation spot of European families, the Lower-Sûre village of **Echternach** is known for its millennial rock formations and 7th-century monastic center. In the Middle Ages, the monastic center was known for its ▓**illu-minated manuscripts;** several are at the 18th-century **Benedictine Abbey.** From the bus station, go left at the marketplace on r. de la Gare, take the last left, and walk past the basilica. (☎72 74 72. Open July-Aug. daily 10am-6pm; Sept.-June 10am-noon and 2-5pm. €2, students €1.) Echternach is accessible by **bus** from Ettel-brück and Luxembourg City. The **tourist office** is next to the abbey on Porte St-Will-ibrord. (☎72 02 30. Open in summer daily 9am-5pm; off-season M-F 9am-5pm.) To get from the bus station to the centrally located **youth hostel (HI) ❷**, 9 r. André Drechscher, turn left on av. de la Gare and take the last right. (☎72 01 58; echter-nach@youthhostels.lu. Breakfast and sheets included. Reception daily 5-11pm. Lockout 10am-5pm. Open Feb.-Dec. Dorms €13.60; nonmembers add €2.75.)

MOROCCO المغرب

Morocco has carved its identity out of a host of influences. At the crossroads of Africa, Europe, and the Middle East, it combines Arab culture and Islamic religion, African history and landscape, European influences and ties, and languages of all three. At the same time, the country teeters between the past and present as both an ancient civilization descended from nomadic tribes and as a modern nation that has struggled against imperial powers for its sovereignty. For travelers weary of another visit to a Spanish cathedral, a short excursion into Morocco can unexpectedly become the highlight of their trip. Excitement and adventure do not need to be planned or paid for lavishly: just step outside your hotel door and wander down an ancient medina street for an introduction to the Islamic and African city. While Morocco is only a few hours from Europe, it's an entirely different world.

FACTS AND FIGURES

Official Name: Kingdom of Morocco.

Capital: Rabat.

Major Cities: Agadir, Casablanca, Fez, Marrakesh, Tangier.

Population: 30 million.

Land Area: 446,500 sq. km.

Time Zone: GMT.

Languages: Arabic, French, Berber Dialects.

Religion: Islam (98.7%).

DISCOVER MOROCCO

Spend as little time as possible in Tangier; instead, discover the charm of the brilliant white medina and beaches of **Asilah** (p. 709). **Fez** (p. 710) is easily accessible and best epitomizes traditional Morocco. Jimi Hendrix and Cat Stevens discovered the enchantment of **Essaouira** (p. 712) three decades ago, and while hippie expats have mostly gone home, the city's easy-going charm remains. For those seeking a little more action, **Marrakesh** (p. 713) never disappoints; a visit to the city's main square will unveil mystics, acrobats, snake-charmers, and storytellers.

ESSENTIALS

DOCUMENTS AND FORMALITIES

VISAS. Citizens of Canada, Ireland, Australia, New Zealand, South Africa, the UK, and the US need only a valid passport for stays of up to 90 days.

EMBASSIES. Foreign embassies in Morocco are all in Rabat. Moroccan embassies at home include: **Australia,** 11 West St., #2, North Sydney, NSW 2060 (☎299 57 67 17; maroc@magna.com.au); **Canada,** 38 Range Rd., Ottawa, ON K1N 8J4 (☎613-236-7391; www.ambassade-maroc.ottawa.on.ca); **South Africa,** 799 Shoeman St., Pretoria (☎12 343 0230; fax 343 0613); **UK,** 49 Queens Gate Gardens, London SW7 5NE (☎20 7581 5001; fax 7225 3862); and **US,** 1601 21st St. NW, Washington, D.C. 20009 (☎202-462-7979; fax 265-0161).

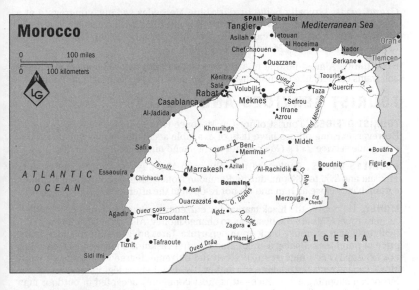

Morocco

0   100 miles

0   100 kilometers

SPAIN • Gibraltar

Mediterranean Sea

Tangier •

Asilah •   • Tetouan

Chefchaouen •   Al Hoceima   Nador   Oran

• Ouazzane   Berkane •   Tlemcen

Kènitra   Taourirt •

Salé   Oued S   Guercif

Volubilis •   • Fez   Taza

Rabat   Meknes   • Sefrou   Oued Moulouya

Casablanca   • Ifrane

Al-Jadida   Azrou

Khouribga   • Midelt   • Bouâfra

Safi   Oum er B   • Beni-   Boudnib   Figuig •

Essaouira   O. Tensift   Memmal   Al-Rachidia   O. Rhé

ATLANTIC   Chichaoua   Marrakesh • Azilal

OCEAN   Boumaine

• Asni   Merzouga • Erg   Cherbi

Ouarzazaté   O. Dadès

Agadir   Oued Sous   Agdz •   O. Drâa

• Taroudannt   Zagora •

Tiznit   • Tafraoute   M'Hamid   ALGERIA

Sidi Ifni •   Oued Drâa

TRANSPORTATION

BY PLANE. Royal Air Maroc (in Casablanca ☎ 022 31 41 41 or airport 022 33 90 00; in US ☎ 800-344-6726; in UK ☎ 07439 43 61), Morocco's national airline, flies to and from most major cities in Europe, including Madrid and Lisbon.

BY FERRY. For travel from Spain to Morocco, the most budget-minded mode is by sea. Spanish-based **Trasmediterranea** (in Spain ☎ (+34) 902 45 46 45; www.tras-mediterranea.es/homei.htm) runs ferries on a shuttle schedule from **Algeciras** (☎ (+34) 956 65 62 44) to **Ceuta,** known within Morocco as Sebta (☎ (+34) 956 50 94 11), and **Tangier.** "Fast" ferries run from Algeciras to Ceuta. **Comarit** (☎ 956 66 84 62, www.comarit.com) runs from Algeciras to Tangier and offers **vehicle transport.** Check online for Comarit's unpredictable weekly schedule.

BY TRAIN. Where possible, trains are the best way to travel. Second-class train tickets are slightly more expensive than corresponding CTM bus fares; first-class tickets cost around 20% more than second-class. The main line runs from Tangier to Marrakesh via Rabat and Casablanca. A spur with the main line at Sidi Kasem connects Fez, Meknes, and points east. There is one nightly *couchette* train between Fez and Marrakesh. **Interrail** is valid in Morocco, but **Eurail** is not. Fares are so low, however, that Interrail is not worth it.

BY BUS. Bus travel is less frequent and less reliable than in Spain or Portugal. Plan well ahead if you are thinking of using buses as your method of transport. They're not all that fast and they're not very comfortable, but they're extremely cheap and travel to nearly every corner of the country. **Compagnie de Transports du Maroc (CTM),** the state-owned line, has the best buses. In many cities, CTM has a station separate from other lines; reservations are usually not necessary.

BY CAR AND BY TAXI. Taxis are dirt-cheap by European standards. Make sure the driver turns the meter on. There is a 50% surcharge after 8pm. Drivers may stop for other passengers or pick you up with other passengers in the car; if you are picked up after the meter has been started, note the initial price.

Grand taxis, typically beige or dark-blue Mercedes sedans, congregate at a central area in town and won't go until they are filled with passengers going in the same direction. Rent a car in Morocco only for large group travel or travel to areas not reached by Morocco's bus lines.

BY THUMB. Almost no one in Morocco **hitches,** although flagging down buses and trains can feel like hitchhiking. *Let's Go* does not recommend hitchhiking.

TOURIST SERVICES AND MONEY

TOURIST OFFICES. Tourist offices in Morocco tend to be few and far between. However, existing offices have lists of available accommodations and an official tour-guide service. *Let's Go* does not recommend hiring unofficial guides.

BUSINESS HOURS. Banks are usually open Monday through Friday 8:30 to 11:30am and 2:30 to 4:30pm, during Ramadan from 9:30am to 2pm. In the summer, certain banks close at 1pm and do not re-open in the afternoon.

MONEY. Do not try the **black market** for currency exchange—you'll be swindled. As in Europe, **ATMs** are the best way to change money. Also know that it is very difficult to change currency back upon departure. **Taxes** are generally included in the price of purchases. **Tipping** a small amount after restaurant meals, while certainly not necessary, is a nice gesture given the extreme degree of poverty of many Moroccan citizens. **Bargaining** (see below) is definitely a legitimate part of the Moroccan shopping experience—it is most commonly accepted in outdoor markets. Do not try to bargain in supermarkets or established stores.

DIRHAM (DH)		
US $1= 10.70DH		1DH=US $0.09
CDN $1= 6.91DH		1DH=CDN $0.15
EUR €1= 10.52DH		1DH=EUR €0.09
UK £1= 16.40DH		1DH=UK £0.06
AUS $1= 5.82DH		1DH=AUS $0.17
NZ $1= 4.97DH		1DH=NZ $0.20
SAR 1= 0.98DH		1DH=ZAR 1.02

COMMUNICATION

PHONE CODES	**Country code: 212. International dialing prefix:** 00. From outside Morocco, dial int'l dialing prefix (see inside back cover) + 212 + city code + local number.

Morocco has recently invested hundreds of millions of dollars into modernizing its telephone system, resulting in markedly improved services. **Pay phones** accept only phone cards, which are available at post offices, but are usually in denominations too large to be practical. Entrepreneurial Moroccans hang around phone banks and let you use their phone cards. You pay for the units used—typically 2dh per unit, a rate not much worse than doing it yourself. To use the card, insert and dial 00. Once the dial tone turns into a tune, dial the number. **Air mail** *(par avion)* can take anywhere from a week to a month to reach the US or Canada (about 10dh for a slim letter, postcards 4-7dh). Less reliable **surface mail** *(par terre)* takes up to 2 months. **Express mail** *(recommandé* or *exprès postaux),* is slightly faster than regular air mail and more reliable. Post offices and some *tabacs* sell **stamps.** For very fast service (2 days to the US), your best bet is DHL (www.dhl.com), which has drop-off locations in most major cities, or FedEx (www.fedex.com).

ACCOMMODATIONS AND CAMPING

SYMBOL	❶	❷	❸	❹	❺
ACCOMMODATIONS	under 60dh	60-100dh	100-150dh	150-200dh	over 200dh

The **Federation Royale des Auberges de Jeunesse (FRMAJ)** is the Moroccan Hosteling International (HI) affiliate. Beds cost 30-40dh per night, and there is a surcharge for nonmembers. **Camping** is popular and cheap (about 15dh per person), especially in the desert, mountains, and beaches. Like hotels, conditions vary widely. You can usually expect to find restrooms, but electricity is not as readily available. Use caution if camping unofficially, especially on beaches, as theft is a problem.

FOOD AND DRINK

SYMBOL	❶	❷	❸	❹	❺
FOOD	under 40dh	40-60dh	60-80dh	80-110dh	over 110dh

Moroccan chefs lavish aromatic and colorful spices on their dishes—pepper, ginger, cumin, saffron, honey, and sugar are culinary staples. The distinctive Moroccan flavor comes from a unique blend of spices, known as *ras al-hanut*. However, no matter how delicious everything may seem, be prepared to get sick at least once, as Morocco is full of things to which tourists are not immune. Taking extra precautions may help. Bottled mineral water is the way to go, as is peeling all fruits and vegetables. The truly cautious may avoid salads as well, or ensure that their vegetables are washed in purified water. Most food sold on the street, especially meat, can be quite risky and should be regarded as such.

SAFETY AND SECURITY

EMERGENCY	Police: ☎ 19. Highway services: ☎ 177.

Visitors should be suspicious of people offering free food, drinks, or cigarettes, as they have been known to be drugged. Avoid unofficial tour guides in large cities like Tangier and Fez. Women should always dress conservatively and never travel alone. Travelers should drink only bottled or boiled water, and should avoid tap water, fountain drinks, and ice cubes. It's also advisable to only eat fruit and vegetables that are cooked and that you have peeled yourself. Stay away from food sold by street vendors, and check to make sure that dairy products have been pasteurized. There is only a slight malaria risk in Morocco, but it would still be wise to take extra precaution against insect bites and consider getting a vaccine before leaving.

HOLIDAYS

Holidays include: New Year's (Jan. 1); Independence Manifesto (Jan. 11); 'Eid al-Adha (Feb. 12); Islamic New Year (Mar. 5); Labor Day (May 1); Reunification Day (Aug. 14); Anniversary of the King's and the People's Revolution (Aug. 20); Young People's Day (Aug. 21); Anniversary of the Green March (Nov. 6); Ramadan (begins Oct. 26); Independence Day (Nov. 18); 'Eid al-Fitr (Nov. 24-27).

TANGIER طنجة ☎ 039

For travelers venturing out of Europe for the first time, disembarking in Tangier (pop. 500,000), Morocco's main port of entry, can be a distressing experience. Many visitors' stories make the city out to be a living nightmare, but for the determined traveler, it can be surprisingly pleasant. If you have a few extra hours, learn

MOROCCO

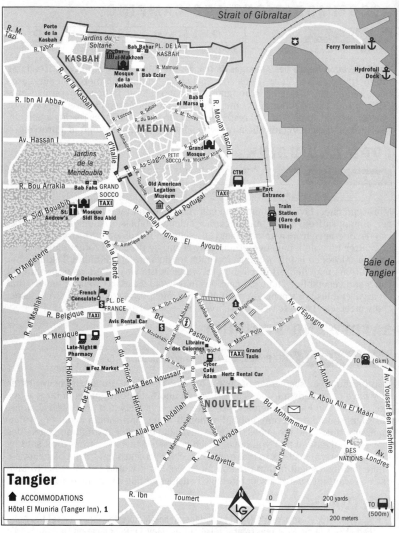

Tangier

⌂ ACCOMMODATIONS
Hôtel El Muniria (Tanger Inn), **1**

about Tangier's international past at the ■**Old American Legation,** 8 r. d'America. (Open M-F 10am-1pm and 3-5pm. Free; donation suggested.) Or, visit the opulent palace-turned-museum **Dar al-Makhzen** (open W-M 9am-12:30pm and 3-5:30pm; 10dh) and the hectic **markets** in the **Grand Socco.** In the evening, sip mint tea in front of the **Café de Paris,** 1 pl. de France, which hosted countless rendezvous between secret agents during World War II. Coming from the Grand Socco, look to the left. (Open daily 7am-11:30pm.)

Flights arrive at the Royal Air Maroc, pl. France (☎37 95 08), from Barcelona, London, Madrid, Marrakesh, and New York. **Trains** leave from Mghagha Station (☎95 25 55), 6km from the port, for Asilah (1hr., 4 per day, 13dh). **Buses** leave from av. Yacoub al-Mansour, 2km from the port entrance at pl. Jamia al-Arabia, for Fez (6hr., 11 per day, 63dh) and Marrakesh (10hr., 3 per day, 115dh). The CTM Station (☎93 11 72) near the port entrance offers posher (and pricier) bus service to the same destinations. **Ferries,** 46 av. d'Espagne (☎94 26 12), head to Algeciras (2½hr., every hr. 7am-9pm, 210dh) and Tarifa (35min., 3-5 per day, 200dh). You'll need a boarding pass, available at any ticket desk, and a customs form (ask uniformed agents). The **tourist office,** 29 bd. Pasteur, has a list of accommodations. (☎94 80 50. Open M-F 8:30am-7:30pm.) Expect to pay around 50-60dh for a single and 80-100dh for a double. The most convenient hostels cluster near **rue Mokhtar Ahardan** (formerly r. des Postes), off the Petit Socco; from the Grand Socco, take the first right down r. al-Siaghin. **Pension Amal ❶,** 5 r. Mokhtar Ahardan, at the bottom of the Petit Socco, has rooms that are clean and plain, if a bit run-down. (☎93 36 00. Free cold showers. Singles 50dh; doubles 100dh.) **Hôtel El Muniria (Tanger Inn) ❸,** r. Magellan, has spacious rooms and hot showers. From the port, walk south along the pedestrian walkway, take the first right after Hôtel Biarritz, and follow r. Magellan as it winds uphill. (☎93 53 37. Singles 100dh; doubles 130dh.) Grab lunch for less than 15dh at the **Brahim Abdelmalek ❶,** 14 rue de Mexique. (See **The Local Story,** right. Open daily 10:30am-3am.)

ASILAH   ☎039

Just a short trip from Tangier, Asilah has sandy shores, a laid-back atmosphere, and a brilliant white medina. Except for the first two weeks in August when an international art festival is held, Asilah remains a peaceful spot for kicking back and soaking up the sun on Atlantic beaches. The stunning █**medina** is bound by heavily fortified 15th-century Portuguese walls. Bab Kasaba, the gate off r. Zallakah, leads past the **Grand Mosque.** Across from the mosque is the modern and spacious **Centre Hassan II des Rencontres Internationales,** which houses an excellent collection of art created during the international art festival. (Open daily 9am-12:30pm and 3:30-7:30pm. Free.) There are two popular coastal stretches of beach: the closest is toward the train station, along the Tangier-Asilah highway (about 15min. from the medina), but the nicest is the enclosed █**Paradise Beach,** an hour's walk from the medina in the opposite direction. If you'd rather not go by foot, you can take a horse-drawn wagon (round-trip 150-200dh).

Trains (☎41 73 27) run to Marrakesh (9hr., 3 per day, 101-150dh) and Tangier (40min., 4 per day, 14-20dh). The train station is a 25min. walk from town

THE LOCAL STORY

THE ROYAL TREATMENT

Ahmed Soussi Tamli is the proprietor of Brahim Abdelmalek in Morocco.

"The idea of making sandwiches came only accidentally to my father. In 1960, the Casino players, mostly European, would come in hungry late at night, asking my father for a piece of bread with tuna. They loved it. They started calling my father the King of the Sandwiches.

"King Hassan II visited Tangier around 1964, walking the streets at night to see how the people lived. He came to the shop at about 3am, asking for a sandwich. My father didn't recognize him because he was wearing dark sunglasses. He took a piece of bread to make him a sandwich. But the King didn't eat anything but salami and olives; he just wanted to talk. At this time, my father started thinking, 'Who is this person who doesn't want to eat?'

"They were talking about life in Tangier when a Jew came in asking for a sandwich. When he'd left, the King said, 'Why do you speak to the other man very gently, and not to me?' My father said, 'I don't know you. That is my customer, I see him everyday.' The King gave my father a 20dh bill and said to keep the change. That was a lot of money back then. My father said, 'Take your change and come tomorrow.' They laughed, and the King gave him 10dh instead. Then he saw the King's limousine with the flag. The King took off the dark sunglasses and started laughing. This is the story of the sandwich."

on the Asilah-Tangier highway, past a strip of campgrounds; a taxi to or from town costs about 10dh. **Buses** go to: Fez (4hr., 3:45 and 7:45pm, 55dh); Marrakesh (9hr., 5pm, 130dh); and Tangier (1hr., 12:15 and 4:15pm, 10dh). Grand **taxis** bound for Tangier pick up passengers in pl. Mohammed V (12dh). The bulk of Asilah's restaurants, accommodations, and cafes are on **rue Zallakah,** off pl. Mohammed V. **Hôtel Sahara ❷,** 9 r. Tarfaya, a block inland from av. Mohammed V and two blocks before pl. Mohammed V, has immaculate rooms maintained by a Spanish-speaking staff. (☎41 71 85. Hot showers 5dh. Singles 98dh; doubles 126dh; triples 186dh; quads 252dh.) Av. Hassan II holds the town **market.**

CHEFCHAOUEN شفشوان ☎039

High in the Rif Mountains, but easily accessible from Tangier or Fez, Chefchaouen (pop. 30,000) refreshes weary travelers with its cool mountain air. Its steep ▉**medina** is one of Morocco's best. Enter through Bab al-Ain and walk uphill toward pl. Uta al-Hammam, the center of the medina. In the *place* stands the 16th-century **Grand Mosque** and its red-and-gold minaret, as well as a 17th-century *kasbah.* (Open daily 9am-1pm and 3-6:30pm. 10dh.) Chefchaouen's **souq** operates Mondays and Thursdays outside the medina and below both av. Hassan II and av. Allal ben Abdalallah. The town makes a spectacular base for **hiking;** follow the Ras al-Ma river upstream into the hills for a few kilometers. For a quick view of the city from the hills, hike following signs for the *ville nouvelle.* Highlights of the trail include the **Spanish mosque** and the rocky arch **Pont de Dieu.**

Buses (☎98 95 73) run to Fez (5hr., 1:15 and 3pm, 45-55dh) and Tangier via Tetouan (28-33dh). From the bus station, head up the steep hill and turn right after several blocks onto the large road, which leads to the circular pl. Mohammed V; it's about a 20min. walk to the center of town. Cross the *place* and continue east on **avenue Hassan II,** the main road of the *ville nouvelle.* Chefchaouen has no tourist office. A slew of budget hotels are on **Bab al-Ain** and **place Uta al-Hammam,** uphill in the medina. The best of the lot is ▉**Hotel Andalus ❶,** 1 r. Sidi Salem, directly behind Credit Agricola on pl. Uta al-Hammam. (☎98 60 34. Singles 30dh; doubles 60dh; triples 90dh; quads 120dh; terrace 20dh.)

FEZ فاس ☎055

Fez's bustling, colorful medina epitomizes Morocco—no visit to the country is complete without seeing it. Artisans bang out sheets of brass, donkeys strain under crates of Coca-Cola, children balance trays of dough on their heads, and tourists struggle to stay together. Founded in the 8th century, Fez rose to prominence with the construction of the Qairaouine, a university-mosque complex. Post-independence Fez has been somewhat eclipsed by Rabat (the political capital), Casablanca (the economic capital), and Marrakesh (the tourist capital), yet it remains at the artistic, intellectual, and spiritual helm of the country.

▉ TRANSPORTATION. Flights arrive at **Aérodrome de Fès-Saïs** (☎62 47 12), 12km out of town on the road to Immouzzèr. **Royal Air Maroc (RAM),** 54 av. Hassan II (☎62 55 16), flies daily to Casablanca. RAM also services Marrakesh, Marseilles, Paris, and Tangier. **Trains** (☎93 03 33) leave from the intersection of av. Almohades and r. Chenguit for Marrakesh (9hr., 7 per day, 171-255dh) and Tangier (5hr., 4 per day, 96-141dh). CTM **buses** (☎73 29 92) run to: Chefchaouen (4hr., 11am and 11:45pm, 50dh); Marrakesh (8hr., 2 per day, 130dh); Meknes (1hr., 7 per day, 18dh); and Tangier (6hr., 3 per day, 85dh). Buses stop near pl. d'Atlas, at the far end of the *ville nouvelle.* From pl. Florence, walk 15min. down bd. Mohammed V, turn left onto av. Youssef ben Tachfine, and take the first right at pl. d'Atlas.

BARGAINING 101 You'll have to do it for everything from taxi rides to camel treks, carpets to ice cream cones, so you might as well do it right. You'll get the best deals if you bargain in Arabic; key phrases include *sh-HAL ta-MAN* (how much does it cost) and *GHEH-lee bez-ZAF* (too expensive). You'll have to make a counter-offer to the initial asking price. Decide what you ultimately want to pay (probably half to one-third of the initial price) then offer one-third to half of *that*. The shopkeeper may respond harshly, at which point you may choose to politely but firmly walk out. Invariably, you will be dragged back in. You can gauge the seller's willingness to negotiate by how quickly (and by how much) he drops his price. If you're at a standstill, tell the shopkeeper that you have made your final offer: *A-khir TA-man d-YA-li HU-wa HA-da.*

ORIENTATION AND PRACTICAL INFORMATION. Fez is large and spread out but still manageable. Essentially three cities in one, the main areas of Fez are: the fashionable **ville nouvelle,** a couple kilometers from the medina; Arab **Fez al-Jdid** (New Fez), which sits next to the medina and contains both the Jewish cemetery and the palace of Hassan II; and the enormous medina area of **Fez al-Bali** (Old Fez). Hire an official local guide at the Syndicat d'Initiative **tourist office,** pl. Mohammed V. (☎62 34 60. Half-day with guide 150dh, full-day 250dh. Open M-F 8:30am-noon and 2:30-6:30pm, Sa 8:30am-noon.) Access the **Internet** at **Soprocon,** off pl. Florence. (10dh per hr. Open daily 9am-11pm.)

ACCOMMODATIONS AND FOOD. Rooms in the *ville nouvelle* are close to local services and more comfortable than those in the medina. The cheapest lodgings and eateries surround **boulevard Mohammed V,** between av. Mohammed al-Slaoui near the bus station and av. Hassan II near the post office. **Hôtel du Commerce ❶,** pl. Alaouites, by the Royal Palace in Fez al-Jdid, has friendly owners and comfortable rooms. (☎62 22 31. Cold showers. Singles 50dh; doubles 90dh.) **Hôtel Central ❶,** 50 r. Brahim Roudani, off pl. Mohammed V, has clean rooms with nice furnishings. (☎62 23 33. Singles 59dh, with shower 89dh; doubles 89dh/119dh; triples 150dh/180dh.) Budget rooms fill the **Bab Boujeloud** area. **Hôtel Cascade ❶,** 26 Serrajine Boujeloud, is popular with both backpackers and families. (☎63 84 42. 50dh per person; terrace 20dh.)

Cheap sandwich dives, cafes, and juice shops line both sides of bd. Mohammed V. For those in search of local eats, sort through stalls of fresh food at the **central market** on bd. Mohammed V, two blocks up from pl. Mohammed V. (Open daily 7am-1pm.) Food stalls line Tala'a Kebira and Tala'a Seghira, near the Bab Boujeloud entrance to Fez al-Bali. **Restaurant des Jeunes ❶,** 16 r. Serrajine, next to Hôtel Cascade by Bab Boujeloud, serves inexpensive Moroccan specialties. (Entrees 25-30dh. Open daily 6am-midnight.)

SIGHTS AND ENTERTAINMENT. Hiring an official guide at the Syndicat d'Initiative (see tourist office, above) will save you time, discourage hustlers, and provide detailed explanations; make sure to nail down an itinerary and price beforehand. Fez's **medina** is the handicraft capital of the country and exports goods around the world. With over 9000 streets and nearly 500,000 residents, the crowded medina is also possibly the most difficult to navigate in all Morocco. Its narrow, frenzied streets contain fabulous mosques, *madrassas*, and *souqs*. At the head of the main thoroughfare, Tala'a Kebira, is the spectacular **Bou Inania Madrasa,** a school built in 1326 for teaching the Qur'an and other Islamic sciences. *(Undergoing renovation; reopening date uncertain. Normally open daily 9am-5:30pm. 10dh.)* Down Tala'a Kebira, the otherwise-mundane **Nejjarine Museum of Art** holds a tranquil rooftop **salon de thé** (tea room) and Morocco's finest bathrooms. *(Open daily*

MOROCCO

10am-5pm. 10dh.) Back on Tala'a Kebira is the **Attarine ("Spice") Souq,** perhaps the most exotic market. Walking through the market leads to **Zaouia Moulay Idriss II,** the resting place of the Islamic saint credited with founding Fez. Non-Muslims are not allowed to enter but can peer through the doors. The Tala'a Kebira ends at Madrasa al-Attarine, which dates from 1324. Exiting the *madrasa,* turn left, and then left again; a few meters down is a little opening into the **Qairaouine mosque,** which can hold up to 20,000 worshippers (second only to Hassan II in Casablanca). Non-Muslims may not enter through the portal. Keeping the mosque on the right, you'll eventually come to pl. Seffarine, known for its fascinating **metal souq,** which deafens travelers with incessant cauldron-pounding. In Fez al-Jdid, the gaudy **Dar al-Makhzen,** former palace of Hassan II, borders pl. Alaouites. Tourists may enter the grounds but not the palace. Nearby is the **mellah** (Jewish ghetto). The **jewelers' souq** glitters at the top of Grande Rue des Merinides. Cackling chickens, salty fish, and dried okra are sold at the **covered market,** inside Bab Smarine at the entrance to Fez al-Jdid proper.

ESSAOUIRA الصويرة ☎044

Sultan Muhammad ben Abdallah and his band of pirates leveled the Portuguese city of Mogador and constructed Essaouira's fortifications to protect themselves. In the late 1960s, the arrival of Jimi Hendrix and Cat Stevens triggered a mass hippie migration, and over the next decade, the city achieved international fame as an expat enclave. Though most of the hash smoke has cleared, Essaouira remains one of Morocco's most enchanting communities.

TRANSPORTATION AND PRACTICAL INFORMATION. Supratours **buses** (☎47 53 17) run from the Bab Marrakesh to **Marrakesh** (2½hr., 6:10am and 4pm, 55dh) and various other destinations. The **tourist office,** Syndicat d'Initiative du Tourism, is on r. de Caire. (☎47 50 80. Open M-F 9am-noon and 2:30-6:30pm.) **Internet** access is available at **Mogador Informatique,** av. Oqba ben Nafil, 3rd fl. (10dh per hr. Vague hours; usually daily 9am-midnight.)

ACCOMMODATIONS AND FOOD. Though it was once Morocco's best-kept secret, Essaouira has lost its anonymity; reservations may be necessary in summer. From pl. Moulay Hassam, facing Credit du Maroc, make a left on r. Skala, take the right just before the archway, and follow the street around to **Hôtel Cap Sim ❹,** 11 Ib Rochd. It's a beautiful new hotel decorated with local art. (☎78 58 34. Singles or doubles 158dh, with shower 258dh.) **Hôtel Smara ❷** is at 26 r. Skala, next to Banque Populaire. The rooms are a little damp, what with ocean waves crashing only 100m away. (☎47 56 55. Singles 62dh; doubles 94dh, with ocean view 124dh; triples 156dh; quads 196dh.) **Hôtel Souiri ❷,** 37 r. Attarine, off r. Sidi Mohammed Ben Abdallah, is comfortable and worth the extra dirhams. (☎47 53 39. Singles 95dh, with shower 220dh; doubles 150dh/310dh; triples 225dh/375dh. MC/V.)

Informal dining, mostly geared toward tourists, is common near the port and **place Moulay Hassan.** At the many **port fish grilles,** fried sardines (with fish, bread, and tomatoes; 20dh) and grilled shrimp (25dh) are sure bets. The so-called **Berber cafes,** near Porte Portugaise and off av. l'Istiqlal, have low tables, straw mats, and fresh fish *tajine* and couscous (20dh). Establish prices before eating. For outstanding Moroccan food at reasonable prices, try **Restaurant Laayoune ❷.** (4 set *menús* 45-72dh. Open daily noon-4pm and 7-11pm.)

SIGHTS AND OUTDOORS. Essaouira has two *skalas* (forts) that sit high atop fortifications. Buttressed by formidable ramparts, dramatic, sea-sprayed **Skala de la Kasbah,** up the street from Hôtel Smara and away from the main square, is the nicer of the two. Visitors can go up the large turret- and artillery-lined wall to see cannons facing the sea. Follow the sound of pounding hammers and the scent of *thuya* wood to the **carpenters' district,** comprised of cell-like niches set in the **Skala Stata de la Ville.** On sale are unique masks and statues, as well as the more typical drums, chess sets, dice, and desk tools. For a quality overview of Essaouira's goods and prices, go to the cooperative **Afalkai Art,** 9 pl. Moulay Hassan (open daily 9am-8pm), and browse the many shops lining **rue Abd al-Aziz al-Fechtaly,** off r. Sidi ben Abdallah. For silver jewelry, head to the *souq* located just outside the medina walls on av. Oqba ben Nafil. **Museum Mohammed ben Abdallah,** near the Hôtel Majestic on r. Derb Laalouj, is in the former residence of a *pasha*. It features antique woodwork and important manuscripts, including a 13th-century Qur'an. (☎47 53 00. Open W-M 9am-noon and 3-6:30pm. 10dh.)

Though infamous for its winds, the wide beach of Essaouira is still one of Morocco's finest. To get to the sand, head to the port and veer left; you can't miss it. Windsurfing clubs lining the beach rent boards. Try **Fanatic Fun Center** for good rental deals. (☎34 70 13. Windsurfing boards with harness and wetsuit 300dh for a half-day; bodyboards 150dh per day; windsurfing lessons 180-230dh per hr.) Just off-shore from Essaouira are the famed Purple Isles. Dominated by the **Isle of Mogador,** the Isles are now a nature reserve for the rare Eleanora's falcons. A Berber king from Mauritania, Juba II, set up dye factories on the islands around 100 BC to produce the purple dye used to color Julius Caesar's cape (among other things), giving the Isles their name. Visiting the Isles requires permission from the tourist office, which can take a couple of days; a tip may expedite the process.

MARRAKESH مراكش ☎044

Founded in 1062, the imperial city of Marrakesh has been exerting an unshakable grip on visitors for centuries. Djema'a al-Fna, the centrally-located main square, is home to boxers, musicians, snake-charmers, acrobats, storytellers, dentists, and mystics. Marrakesh's *souqs* and craftwork are some of Morocco's best, and the bustling city is generally more tourist-friendly than the rest of the country.

⌐⌐ TRANSPORTATION AND PRACTICAL INFORMATION

Flights arrive at Aéroport de Marrakesh Menara (RAK; ☎44 79 10), 5km south of town. Bus #11 runs from the airport to the Koutoubia Mosque (7am-10pm, 3dh). **Trains** run from av. Hassan II (☎44 65 69) to Fez (8hr., 6 per day, 225dh) and Tangier (8hr., 3 per day, 188dh). **Buses** (☎43 39 33) run from outside the medina walls by Bab Doukkala to Essaouira (8 per day 4am-5pm) and other destinations. Most of the excitement, as well as budget food and accommodations, centers around the **Djema'a al-Fna** and the **medina** streets directly off it. The **bus** and **train stations** are in **Guéliz** *(ville nouvelle)* down av. Mohammed V; from the Djema'a al-Fna, walk to the towering Koutoubia Minaret and turn right. Bus #1 runs between the minaret and the heart of the Guéliz (1.50dh). Or, take one of the many *petits taxis* (10dh) or horse-drawn carriages (15dh, sometimes more at night). The **tourist office,** av. Mohammed V (☎43 61 79), is at pl. Abdel Moumen ben Ali. Walk 35min. from the Djema'a al-Fna or take a *petit taxi* (15dh). Many tobacco shops sell better maps (15dh), although **official guides** (full day 150dh), a worthwhile option in Marrakesh, can be booked here. (Open in summer daily 7:30am-3pm; off-season 8:30am-noon and 2:30-6:30pm.) Many good **Internet** cafes are on Bab Agnaou, the pedestrian mall off the Djema'a al-Fna. **Cyber Bab Agnaou, Cyber Mohammed Yassine,** and **Hanan Internet Cyber Cafe** each charge 10dh per hr. (Open daily 8am-11pm.)

 Marrakesh's **petit taxi** drivers are notorious for taking scenic routes. Make sure the meter's on and have a clear sense of how to get to your destination.

ACCOMMODATIONS AND FOOD

Most of Marrakesh's inexpensive accommodations are near the Djema'a al-Fna. Many places allow you to sleep on the rooftop terrace for about 20dh, a good option in the summer when rooms get hot and a nice way to meet other travelers. The self-contained tourist compound **Hôtel Ali ❶**, r. Moulay Ismail, is past the post office near the Djema'a al-Fna. Enjoy good suites with soap, towels, and toilet paper, as well as a restaurant and an Internet cafe. (☎44 49 79; fax 44 05 22. Breakfast included. Dorms or terrace 40dh; singles 100dh; doubles 150dh; triples 200dh.) To reach **Hôtel Essaouira ❶**, 3 Derb Sidi Bouloukat, from the Djema'a al-Fna, walk just beyond Café de France, take the first right after the Hôtel de France, and look for signs. (☎44 38 05. Hot showers 5dh. Singles 40dh; doubles 80dh; terrace 25dh.) **Hôtel Sindi Sud ❶**, 109 Riad Zitoun El Quduim, is just off the intersection with Derb Sidi Bouloukat, across from Hôtel Essaouira. Popular with American Peace Corps workers, it has clean, well-furnished rooms and a nice indoor courtyard. (☎44 33 37. Hot shower and breakfast included. 40dh per person; terrace 25dh.)

For delicious dinner bargains, head for the **food stalls** in the Djema'a al-Fna. Follow locals to the best *harira* (spicy bean soup; 2dh), *kebab* (skewered meat; 2dh), and fresh-squeezed orange juice (2.50dh). On the other end of the price spectrum, Marrakesh also has many **"palace restaurants"** where music, liquor, and outrageous portions combine for a memorable, if expensive, evening (300-600dh per person). Two **markets** peddle fresh produce along the fortifications surrounding the city. **Star Foods ❶**, off pl. Abdel Boumem Ben Ali, in Gueliz, makes a double cheeseburger (28dh) that would make any American proud, but also serves Moroccan dishes. (Open daily 8:30am-11pm.)

SIGHTS

DJEMA'A AL-FNA. The Djema'a al-Fna (Assembly of the Dead) is one of the world's most frantically exotic squares, where sultans once beheaded criminals and displayed the remains. While snake-charmers and monkey-handlers entice tourists, the vast majority of the audience are townspeople from outlying villages. Villagers consult potion dealers and fortune tellers; crowds encircle preachers, storytellers, and musicians; women have their children blessed by mystics; and promoters encourage bets on boxing matches between young boys (and girls). Come here for wonderful food and the chance to watch the spectacular.

MEDINA AND SOUQS. The best place in Morocco to buy spices, Marrakesh's medina is also where you'll find the most colorful iron and sheepskin lampshades. A worthwhile survey of the medina begins at the *souqs*. If you get lost, ask a merchant for directions. Enter the medina from the Djema'a al-Fna, directly across from the Café de France. This runs to the medina's main thoroughfare; turn toward the **smarine souq** (textiles) by taking a quick left after the **pottery souq.** Berber blankets and yarn pile the alleyways of the **fabric souq.** Head through the first major orange gateway and make a quick right to the Zahba Qedima, a small plaza containing the **spice souq,** complete with massive sacks of saffron and cumin as well as the apothecaries' more unusual remedies—goat hoof for hair loss, ground-up ferrets for depression, and live chameleons for sexual frustration. Farther on are the bubbling vats of the **dye souq,** as well as the **carpentry souq.** Try **Chateau des Souks** for Berber rugs and carpets. *(44 Souk Semmarine.)* At **Herboristerie Avenzoar,** you can hear fascinating explications of the healing qualities of herbs and spices in fluent English. *(78 Derb N'Khel, off the Rahba Kedima.)*

AL-BAHIA PALACE. The ruthless late-19th-century vizier Si Ahmad Ibn Musa, also known as Ba Ahmad, constructed this palace and named it al-Bahia (The Brilliance). Its impressive ceilings are beautifully preserved. *(Open Sa-Th 8:30-11:45am and 2:30-5:45pm, F 8:30-11:30am and 3-5:45pm. 10dh.)*

MADRASA BEN YOUSSEF. In 1565, Sultan Moulay Abdallah al-Ghalib raised the Madrasa ben Youssef in the medina center. It reigned as the largest Qur'anic school in the Maghreb until closing in 1960. *(Open June-Aug. Tu-Su 9am-1pm and 2:30-6pm; Sept.-May Tu-Su 9am-6:30pm. 20dh, under 18 10dh.)*

OTHER SIGHTS. The 19th-century palace **Dar Si Said** was built by Si Said, brother of Grand Vizier Ba Ahmed, and houses the **Museum of Moroccan Art,** which features splendid Berber carpets, pottery, jewelry, Essaouiran ebony, and Saadian woodcarving. (Open W-Th and Sa-M 9-11:45am and 2:30-5:45pm, F 9-11:30am and 3-5:45pm. 10dh.) One of Morocco's best museums, the **Museum of Marrakesh** features both thematic exhibits on Moroccan culture and private collections. (Open daily 9am-6pm. 30dh, students 10dh.) The unpainted cupola of the 12th-century **Koubba al-Ba'adiyn,** the oldest monument in town, is the only relic of the Almoravid dynasty and the original from which all other Moroccan buildings have borrowed their unique style. (Open daily 9am-5:30pm. 10dh, plus 5-10dh tip for the custodian-guide.)

■ NIGHTLIFE

Most travelers hang around the Djema'a al-Fna, or in one of the terrace cafes that overlooks it, for most of the night. Try the bars at the **Tazi** (☎ 44 27 87) and **Foucauld** (☎ 44 54 99) hotels, where locals and tourists mix with the help of 15dh *Spéciale Flag.* (Both bars open at 9pm. Cover 50dh.) For international karaoke, visit **Safran et Cannelle,** av. Hassan II. The **Diamant Noir** is a nightclub in Hôtel Marrakesh in Guéliz; the city's largest club is **Paradise,** at the far end of Guéliz.

■ DAYTRIP FROM MARRAKESH

CASCADES D'OUZOUD
Buses for Azilal (window #18) run from the main station in Marrakesh (3½hr., 2 per day, 40dh). Ask to be dropped off at the turn-off for the Cascades and then grab a grand taxi (10dh) the rest of the way. The return trip may be difficult; if you miss one of the two evening buses running from Azilal to Marrakesh (2:30 and 7:30pm), organize a group to share a grand taxi back to Marrakesh from either Azilal or, if you're lucky, the falls themselves (400dh). A round trip grand taxi from the Djema'a al-Fna is about 550dh.

Picturesque and enchanting, the Cascades D'Ouzoud adorn posters in hotel rooms across Morocco for good reason. The Cascades are dotted with refreshing pools and waterfalls, while the surrounding valley trees are home to Barbary apes. Once you get beyond the unnecessary guides at the top of the waterfall, you can find relative tranquility by the river below the base of the falls. From the top of the falls, take the path to the left and descend the stairs. You are better off crossing the river (water taxi 2dh) and hiking down to the many secluded pools below. Spending the night at the Cascades can be highly enjoyable, as there are plenty of excellent **campgrounds** (10-20dh per person; 5dh per tent, although no tent is necessary as thin mattresses and blankets are provided). If you prefer a roof above your head, the clean, well-furnished rooms at **Hôtel Challal D'ouzoud ❷** are the best option. (☎ 023 45 96 60. Singles 65dh; doubles 120dh; triples 180dh; terrace 25dh.)

MOROCCO

THE NETHERLANDS

(NEDERLAND)

The Dutch say that although God created the rest of the world, *they* created The Netherlands (pop. 15.9 million; 41,532 sq. km). The country is a masterful feat of engineering; since most of it is below sea level, vigorous pumping and many dikes were used to create dry land. What was once the domain of seaweed is now packed with windmills, bicycles, tulips, and wooden shoes. The Netherlands' wealth of art and its canal-lined towns draw as many travelers as do the unique hedonism and perpetual, indulgent partying of Amsterdam.

FACTS AND FIGURES

Official Name: The Kingdom of The Netherlands.

Capital: Amsterdam.

Major Cities: Amsterdam, Maastricht, Rotterdam, Utrecht.

Population: 16 million.

Land Area: 41,526 sq. km.

Time Zone: 1hr. ahead of GMT.

Language: Dutch.

Religions: Catholic (34%), Protestant (25%), Muslim (3%).

DISCOVER THE NETHERLANDS

Roll it, light it, then smoke it in **Amsterdam** (p. 720), a hedonist's dream, with chill coffeeshops and peerless museums. Clear your head in the rustic Dutch countryside; the amazing **Hoge Veluwe National Park** (p. 741), southeast of Amsterdam, shelters within its 30,000 wooded acres one of the finest modern art museums in Europe. Beautifully preserved **Leiden** (p. 737) and **Utrecht** (p. 740), less than 30 minutes away, delight with picturesque canals. Dutch politics and museums abound in **The Hague** (p. 738); for more innovative art and architecture, step into futuristic **Rotterdam** (p. 739). An afternoon in **Delft** (p. 739) provides a dose of small-town Dutch charm. Visit the sand dunes and isolated beaches of the tiny **Wadden Islands** (p. 743), a biker's paradise.

ESSENTIALS

WHEN TO GO

The ideal time to visit is between mid-May and early October, when day temperatures are generally 20-31°C (70-80°F), with nights around 10-20°C (50-60°F). It can be quite rainy; bring an umbrella. The tulip season runs from April to mid-May.

DOCUMENTS AND FORMALITIES

VISAS. South Africans need a visa for stays of any length. Citizens of Australia, Canada, the EU, New Zealand, and the US do not need a visa for stays of up to 90 days.

EMBASSIES. All foreign embassies and most consulates are in The Hague (p. 738). The US has a consulate in Amsterdam (p. 720). For Dutch embassies at home: **Australia,** 120 Empire Circuit, Yarralumla Canberra, ACT 2600 (☎02 62 73 31

The Netherlands

11; www.netherlandsembassy.org.au); **Canada,** 350 Albert St., Ste. 2020, Ottawa ON K1R 1A4 (☎6130-237-5030; www.netherlandsembassy.ca); **Ireland,** 160 Merrion Rd., Dublin 4 (☎012 69 34 44; www.netherlandsembassy.ie); **New Zealand,** P.O. Box 840, at Ballance and Featherston St., Wellington (☎04 471 63 90; netherlandsembassy.co.nz); **South Africa,** 825 Arcadia St., Pretoria, P.O. Box 117, Pretoria (☎012 344 3910; www.dutchembassy.co.za). **UK,** 38 Hyde Park Gate, London SW7 5DP (☎020 75 90 32 00; www.netherlands-embassy.org.uk); and **US,** 4200 Linnean Ave., NW, Washington, D.C. 20008 (☎202-244-5300; www.netherlands-embassy.org).

TRANSPORTATION

BY PLANE. KLM/Northwest, Martinair, Continental, Delta, United, and **Singapore Airlines** serve Amsterdam's sleek, glassy Schiphol Airport.

BY TRAIN. The national rail company is the efficient **Nederlandse Spoorwegen** (**NS;** Netherlands Railways; www.ns.nl). Train service tends to be faster than bus service. *Sneltreins* are the fastest; *stoptreins* make the most stops. One-way tickets are called *enkele reis;* normal round-trip tickets, *retour;* and same-day return tickets (valid only on day of purchase, but cheaper than normal round-trip tickets), *dagretour.* **Eurail** and **InterRail** are valid in The Netherlands. The **Holland Railpass**

(US$52-98) is good for three or five travel days in any one-month period. Although available in the US, the Holland Railpass is cheaper in The Netherlands at DER Travel Service or RailEurope offices. **One-day train passes** cost €35, which is about the equivalent of the most expensive one-way fare across the country. The fine for a missing ticket on one of The Netherlands' trains is a whopping €90.

BY BUS. A nationalized fare system covers city buses, trams, and long-distance buses. The country is divided into zones; the number of strips on a **strippenkaart** (strip card) required depends on the number of zones through which you travel. A trip between destinations in the same zone costs one strip; a trip that traverses two zones requires two strips. On buses, tell the driver your destination and he or she will cancel the correct number of strips; on trams and subways, stamp your own *strippenkaart* in either a yellow box at the back of the tram or in the subway station. Train and bus drivers sell tickets, but it's cheaper to buy in bulk at public transit counters, tourist offices, post offices, and some tobacco shops and newsstands. *Dagkarten* (day passes) are valid for unlimited use in any zone (€5.20, children and seniors €3.60). Unlimited-use passes are valid for one week in the same zone (€21, seniors and children €13; requires a passport photo and picture ID). Riding without a ticket can result in a €30 fine.

BY CAR. The Netherlands have well-maintained roadways. North Americans and Australians need an International Driver's License; if your insurance doesn't cover you abroad, you'll also need a green insurance card. Fuel comes in two types; some cars use benzene (€1.50 per liter), while others use gasoline (€0.50 per liter). The **Royal Dutch Touring Association** (ANWB) offers roadside assistance to members. (☎0800 08 88.) For more information, contact the ANWB at Wassenaarseweg 220, 2596 EC The Hague (☎070 314 71 47), or Museumsplein 5, 1071 DJ Amsterdam (☎0800 05 03).

BY BIKE AND BY THUMB. Cycling is the way to go in The Netherlands—distances between cities are short, the countryside is absolutely flat, and most streets have separate bike lanes. Bikes run about €7 per day or €30 per week. Bikes are sometimes available at train stations and hostels, and *Let's Go* also lists bike rental shops in many towns. For more information, try www.visitholland.com. Hitchhiking is somewhat effective, but there is cutthroat competition on the roads out of Amsterdam. For more information on hitching, visit www.hitchhikers.org. *Let's Go* does not recommend hitchhiking.

TOURIST SERVICES AND MONEY

EMERGENCY	**Police, Ambulance,** and **Fire:** ☎112.

TOURIST OFFICES. VVV (vay-vay-vay) tourist offices are marked by triangular blue signs. The website www.goholland.com is also a useful resource.

MONEY. A bare-bones day traveling in The Netherlands will cost €30-35; a slightly more comfortable day will run €50-60. Service charges are always included in bills for hotels, shopping, and restaurants. Tips for services are accepted and appreciated but not necessary. Taxi drivers are generally tipped 10% of the fare.

BUSINESS HOURS. Most stores are open Monday to Friday 9am-6pm, and generally open late at night on the weekends. During holidays and the tourist season, hours are extended into the night and stores open their doors on Sundays. Banks are typically open the same hours as shops but remain closed on Sundays. Post offices close at noon on Saturdays and remain closed on Sundays.

COMMUNICATION

PHONE CODES	Country code: 31. **International dialing prefix:** 00. From outside The Netherlands, dial int'l dialing prefix (see inside back cover) + 31 + city code + local number.

MAIL. Post offices are generally open Monday to Friday 9am-6pm, and some are also open Saturday 10am-1:30pm; larger branches may stay open later. Mailing a postcard or letter (up to 20g) in the EU or a postcard outside of Europe costs €0.54; letters to outside of Europe cost €0.75. Mail takes 2-3 days to the UK, 4-6 to North America, 6-8 to Australia and New Zealand, and 8-10 to South Africa.

TELEPHONES. **Pay phones** require a **Chipknip** card, which can be bought at hostels, train stations, and tobacconists, for as little as €4.50. Even when using a calling card, a chipknip card is necessary to gain access to the phone system. For directory assistance, dial 09 00 80 08; for collect calls, dial 06 04 10. International dial direct numbers include: **AT&T** ☎0800 022 91 11; **Sprint** ☎0800 022 91 19; **Australia Direct** ☎0800 022 20 61; **BT Direct** ☎0800 022 00 44; **Canada Direct** ☎0800 022 91 16; **Ireland Direct** ☎0800 02 20 353; **MCI WorldPhone Direct,** ☎0800 022 91 22; **NZ Direct** ☎0800 022 44 64; Telekom South Africa Direct ☎0800 022 02 27.

INTERNET ACCESS. Email is easily accessible within The Netherlands. In small towns, if Internet access is not listed, try the library or even your hostel.

LANGUAGE. Dutch is the official language of The Netherlands; however, most natives speak English fluently. Dutch uses a gutteral "g" sound for both "g" and "ch." "J" is usually pronounced as the English "y"; e.g., *hofje* is "hof-YUH." "Ui" is pronounced "ow," and the dipthong "ij" is best approximated in English as "ah" followed by a long "e." For basic Dutch words and phrases, see p. 1054.

ACCOMMODATIONS AND CAMPING

SYMBOL	❶	❷	❸	❹	❺
ACCOMMODATIONS	under €20	€20-34	€35-49	€50-64	over €65

VVV offices supply accommodation lists and can nearly always reserve rooms in both local and other areas (fee around €2). **Private rooms** cost about two-thirds as much as hotels, but they are hard to find; check with the VVV. During July and August, many cities add a tourist tax of €1.15 to the price of all rooms. The country's best values are the 34 **HI youth hostels**, run by the **NJHC (Dutch Youth Hostel Federation).** Hostels are divided into four price categories based on quality. Most are exceedingly clean and modern. The VVV has a hostel list, and the useful *Jeugdherbergen* brochure describes each one (both free). For more information, contact the NJHC at P. O. Box 9191, 1006 AD, Amsterdam (☎010 264 60 64; www.njhc.org). **Camping** is available across the country, but many sites are crowded and trailer-ridden in summer.

FOOD AND DRINK

SYMBOL	❶	❷	❸	❹	❺
FOOD	under €10	€10-14	€15-19	€20-30	over €30

Traditional Dutch cuisine is hearty, heavy, meaty, and wholesome. Expect a lot of bread and cheese for breakfasts and lunch, and generous portions of meats and fishes for dinner. Popular seafood choices include all sorts of grilled fishes and shellfish, fish stews, and raw herring. To round out a truly authentic Dutch meal, ask (especially in May and June) for white asparagus, which can be a main dish on its own, served with potatoes, ham, and eggs. Early on, the Dutch appropriated dishes from their nearby neighbors, the Swiss, including fondue, a delicious, though not health-conscious option. Fill up on *dagschotel* (dinner special), *broodje* (bread or sandwich), *bier* (beer), and *kaas* (cheese). The Dutch conception of a light snack often includes *tostjes*, piping hot grilled cheese or ham and cheese sandwiches, *broodjes* (sandwiches), *oliebollen* (doughnuts), or *poffertjes* (small pancakes). Colonial history has brought Surinamese and Indonesian cuisine to The Netherlands, followed closely by near-relatives from other South American and Asian countries. Indonesian cuisine is probably one of the safest bets for vegetarians and vegans. Wash it all down with a small, foamy glass of domestic beer: Heineken or Amstel.

HOLIDAYS AND FESTIVALS

Holidays: New Year's Day (Jan. 1); Good Friday (Apr. 18); Easter Monday (Apr. 20); Liberation Day (May 5); Ascension Day (May 9), Whitsunday and Whitmonday (June 3-4); Christmas Day (Dec. 25); Boxing Day (Dec. 26; also called Second Christmas Day).

Festivals: Koninginnedag (Queen's Day; Apr. 30) turns the country into a huge carnival. The **Holland Festival** (in June) features more than 30 productions in a massive celebration of the arts. **Bloemen Corso** (Flower Parade; first Sa in Sept.) runs from Aalsmeer to Amsterdam. Many historical canal houses and windmills are open to the public for **National Monument Day** (2nd Sa in Sept.). The **Cannabis Cup** (November) celebrates the magical mystery weed that brings millions of visitors to Amsterdam every year.

AMSTERDAM ☎ 020

Some say the best vacation to Amsterdam is one you can't remember. The city lives up to its reputation as a never-never land of bacchanalian excess: the aroma of cannabis wafts through public parks, and the city's infamous sex scene swathes itself in red lights. But a large array of coffeeshops isn't the only thing that will take your breath away—the Golden Age of art flourished here, and troves of Rembrandts, Vermeers, and van Goghs remain as a result. Moreover, a walk down the city's endless cobblestone streets or a stroll along its sparkling canals will prove that the beauty of the city isn't limited to its museums. A land of substance in more ways than one, any visit to Amsterdam makes for quite a trip.

▎ TRANSPORTATION

Flights: Schiphol Airport (AMS; ☎0800 7244 74 65). **Trains** connect the airport to Centraal Station (20min., every 10min., €3).

Trains: Centraal Station, Stationspl. 1, at the end of the Damrak (☎0900 92 92, €0.30 per min.; www.ns.nl). International reservations daily 6:30am-11:30pm. To: **Brussels** (3-4hr., 10-28 per day, €120-250); **Groningen** (2-3hr., every 30min., €24); **Haarlem** (20min., €3); **Leiden** (20min., every 30min. until 2:45am, €11); **Paris** (8hr., 10-28 per day, €120-250); **Rotterdam** (1hr., €11); **The Hague** (50min., €8); **Utrecht** (30min., 3-6 per hr., same day round-trip €10).

Buses: Trains are quicker, but the **GVB** (see below) will direct you to a bus stop for domestic destinations not on a rail line. **Muiderpoort** (2 blocks east of Oosterpark) sends buses east; **Marnixstation** (at the corner of Marnixstr. and Kinkerstr.) west; and the **Stationsplein depot** north and south.

Public Transportation: GVB (☎09 00 92 92, €0.30 per min.) Stationspl. In front of Centraal Station. Open M-F 7am-9pm, Sa-Su 8am-9pm. **Tram, Metro,** and **bus** lines radiate from Centraal Station. Trams are most convenient for inner-city travel; the Metro leads to farther-out neighborhoods. The last trams leave Centraal Station M-F at midnight, Sa-Su at 12:25am. Pick up a *nachtbussen* (night bus) schedule from the GVB office. Single bus or train ticket €1.40. The 45-strip *strippenkaart* can be used on trams and buses throughout The Netherlands and is available at the VVV and newsstands.

Bike Rental: Bikes run about €5-12 per day, plus a €30-100 deposit. Try **Frederic Rent a Bike,** Brouwersgracht 78 (☎624 55 09; www.frederic.nl), in the Shipping Quarter. Bikes €10 per day, which includes lock and theft insurance. Reserve online. AmEx/MC/V.

ORIENTATION

A series of roughly concentric canals ripple out around the **Centrum** (city center), resembling a giant horseshoe opening to the northeast. Emerging from Centraal Station, at the top of the horseshoe, you'll hit **Damrak,** a key thoroughfare leading to **Dam Square.** Just east of Damrak in the Centrum is Amsterdam's infamous **Red Light District,** bounded by Warmoestr., Zeedijk, Damstr., and Klovenniersburgwal. Don't head into the area until you've locked up your bags at the train station or a hostel. South of the Red Light District but still within the horseshoe lies the **Rembrandtplein.** The canals radiating around the Centrum (lined by streets of the same names) are **Singel, Herengracht, Keizergracht,** and **Prinsengracht.** West of the Centrum, beyond Prinsengracht, lies the **Jordaan,** an attractive residential neighborhood. Moving counterclockwise around Prinsengracht, you'll hit the **Leidseplein,** which lies just across the canal from **Vondelpark** and the **Museumplein,** followed by **De Pijp,** another less crowded residential neighborhood.

PRACTICAL INFORMATION

TOURIST, FINANCIAL, AND LOCAL SERVICES

Tourist Office: Stationsplein 10 (☎0900 400 40 40; €0.55 per min.), to the left and in front of Centraal Station. Room booking €2.75. Open M-F 9am-5pm. **Branches** at Centraal Station, Leidsepl. 1, and the airport. Open M-Sa 8am-8pm, Su 9am-5pm.

Budget Travel: Eurolines, Rokin 10 (☎560 87 88; www.eurolines.nl). Books coach travel throughout Europe. Open M-F 9:30am-5:30pm, Sa 10am-4pm.

Consulates: All foreign embassies are in **The Hague** (p. 738). **US** consulate, Museumpl. 19 (☎575 53 09; www.usemb.nl). Open M-F 8:30am-noon.

American Express: Damrak 66 (☎504 87 70). Excellent rates and no commission on their own Traveler's Cheques, 3% commission for others'. Exchange €2.25 plus 2.25% commission. Mail held. Students with ISIC card get 25% discount. Open M-F 9am-5pm, Sa 9am-noon. **Branch** at Schiphol open 24hr.

English-Language Bookstores: Spui, near the Amsterdam University, is lined with bookstores. **Oudemanhuispoort,** in the Oude Zijd, is a book market. Open daily; times vary.

Bi-Gay-Lesbian Resources: COC, Rozenstr. 14 (☎626 30 87; www.cocamsterdam.nl), is a social network and main source of info. M-Tu and Th-F 10am-5pm, W 10am-8pm. **Gay and Lesbian Switchboard** (☎623 65 65) takes calls daily 10am-10pm.

Laundry: Wasserette-Stomerij "De Eland," Elandsgr. 59 (☎625 07 31), has self-service. €4 per 4kg, €6 per 6kg. Open M-Tu and Th-F 8am-8pm, W 8am-6pm, Sa 9am-5pm.

EMERGENCY AND COMMUNICATIONS

Emergency: ☎112 (Police, Ambulance, and Fire Brigade).

Police: Headquarters, Elandsgr. 117 (☎0800 88 44), at the intersection with Marnixstr.

Crisis Lines: General counseling at **Telephone Helpline** (☎675 75 75). Open 24hr. **Rape crisis hotline** (☎612 02 45) staffed M-F 10:30am-11pm, Sa-Su 3:30-11pm. **Drug counseling, Jellinek Clinic** (☎570 23 55). Open M-F 9am-5pm.

Medical Assistance: Tourist Medical Service (☎592 33 55). Take tram #9 or bus #22 to Tropenmuseum, cross the canal to the north, and turn left on Sarphatistr. Call 24hr for assistance. Open M-F 9am-5pm. For hospital care, call **Academisch Medisch Centrum,** Meibergdreef 9 (☎566 91 11), near the Holendrecht Metro stop. **Kruispost,** Oudezijds Voorburgwal 129 (☎624 90 31), a walk-in clinic, offers first aid daily 7am-9:30pm. From Centraal Station, turn left at the Victoria Hotel, then turn right on Oudezijds Voorburgwal. **STD Line** (hotline ☎555 58 22). Free testing at Groenburgwal 44. Open M-F 8am-noon and 1-4pm.

Late-Night Pharmacy: Rotates; check list posted at any pharmacy.

Internet Access: Internet access in Amsterdam leaves much to be desired—the best bet may be a cozy coffeeshop with a single computer in the back. **easyEverything,** Reguliersbreestr. 22 and Damrak 34. Base price €1 buys differing amounts of time depending on computer availability. Open 24hr. **Free World,** Nieuwendijk 30. €1 per 30min. Open Su-Th 9am-1am, F-Sa 9am-3am. **Cyber Cafe Amsterdam,** Nieuwendijk 17. €1.50 per 30min. Open Su-Th 10am-1am, F-Sa 10am-2am. **Internet Cafe,** Martelaarsgr. 11. 20min. free with a drink. Otherwise, €1 for 30min. Open Su-Th 9am-1am, F-Sa 9am-2am.

Post Office: Singel 250 (☎556 33 11), at Raadhuisstr. Address mail to be held: First-name, SURNAME, *Poste Restante,* Singel 250, Amsterdam 1016 AB, The Netherlands. Open M-W and F 9am-6pm, Th 9am-9pm, Sa 10am-1:30pm. **Postal code: 1016.**

ACCOMMODATIONS

Accommodations near **Centraal Station** often take good security measures due to the chaos of the nearby Red Light District. Hostels and hotels in **Vondelpark** and the **Jordaan** are quieter (by Amsterdam's standards) and safer; they're also close to bars, coffeeshops, museums, and the busy Leidsepl. and are only 15min. by foot or 2min. by train from the city center. The hotels and hostels in the **Red Light District** (in the Oude Zijd) are often bars with beds over them. Consider just how much pot and smoke you want to inhale, and how much noise you can sleep with, before booking a bed there. Accommodations are listed by neighborhoods.

OUDE ZIJD, NIEUWE ZIJD, AND THE RED LIGHT DISTRICT

Flying Pig Downtown, Nieuwendijk 100 (☎420 68 22; www.flyingpig.nl). Helpful staff, spacious dorms, and a knockout location make this hostel a perennial favorite. Internet and kitchen available. Breakfast and sheets included. Key deposit €10. 7-day max. stay. Ages 18-35 only. Dorms €19-25; singles €72; doubles €72. AmEx/MC/V. ❷

Hotel Winston, Warmoesstr. 125 (☎623 13 80; www.winston.nl). Rooms painted by local artists make for a colorful, unique atmosphere. Club downstairs. Singles €57-61, with bath €69; doubles €71-80, with bath €90. ❹

De Oranje Tulp, Damrak 32 (☎428 16 18; people.a2000.nl/oranje00). Slick, well-appointed rooms and a restaurant downstairs. Breakfast included. Singles €45-60; doubles €75-110; triples €80-110; quads €80-120; quints €80-140. AmEx/MC/V. ❹

Hotel Groenendael, Nieuwendijk 15 (☎624 48 22; www.hotelgroenendael.com). Located right by Centraal Station, this is one of the best deals in the city. Rooms are well-lit and decorated with bright, cheerful colors; some have balconies. Free lockers. Key deposit €5. Singles €32; doubles €50, with shower €55; triples €75. ❷

Anna Youth Hostel, Spuistr. 6 (☎620 11 55). By far the most beautiful hostel in the city. The quiet ambience is surprising given its central location in the Nieuwe Zijd. Sheets and lockers included. 2-night min. stay on weekends. Open Mar.-Dec. only. Dorms €16-17; doubles with bath €75-80. ❶

Hotel Brouwer, Singel 83 (☎ 624 63 58; www.hotelbrouwer.nl). 8 gorgeous, restored rooms, each with private bathroom and canal view. Breakfast included. Singles €45; doubles €80. ❸

City Hostel Stadsdoelen (HI), Kloveniersburgwal 97 (☎ 624 68 32; www.njhc.org). Take tram #4, 9, 16, 20, 24, or 25 to Muntplein. From Muntplein, proceed down Nieuwe Doelenstr. (which is just off of Muntplein); Kloveniersburgwal will be over the bridge on your right. Sleeps 170 and provides clean, drug-free lodgings for very reasonable prices. Plain dorms get the job done. Internet (€1 per 12min.) and kitchen facilities. Breakfast, lockers, and sheets included. Reception 7am-1am. Book through website. Dorms €18.50; nonmembers add €2.50. MC/V. ❶

Bob's Youth Hostel, Nieuwezijds Voorburgwal 92 (☎ 623 00 63). Well-known among European backpackers, Bob's provides the bare necessities. Young clientele relaxes in the underground reception area, the only place where drugs are permitted. Breakfast and sheets included. Locker deposit €10. Key deposit €10. 2-night min. stay on weekends, 7-day max. stay. Reception 8am-3am. No reservations; arrive before 10am. Dorms €17; doubles €70, additional person €10. ❶

Old Quarter, Warmoesstr. 20-22 (☎ 626 64 29; info@oldquarter.a2000.nl). Modern rooms; some with canal view. Downstairs *bruine cafe* a great place to watch a football game (kitchen open noon-10pm). Th night jazz jam sessions, F-Sa rock and funk acts. Reception 24hr. Breakfast included. Singles from €35; doubles from €60. ❸

Nelly's Hostel, Warmoesstr. 115/117 (☎ 638 01 25; nellys@xs4all.nl). Cozy hostel above an Irish pub. Clean, mixed-sex dorms. Guests drink after hours in the bar. Breakfast and sheets included. Locker deposit €10. Reception 24hr. Dorms €20-25. ❷

Hotel Rokin, Rokin 73 (☎ 626 74 56; www.rokinhotel.com), well-located just a few blocks south of Dam Sq. A tad upscale, but well worth the extra cash for rooms with TV and VCR. Continental breakfast included. Singles €50-60; doubles €60-75; triples €110-145; quads €140-185; 6-person rooms €195-255. AmEx/MC/V. ❹

Hotel Brian, Singel 69 (☎ 624 46 61). From Centraal Station, turn right at the Victoria Hotel, then turn left onto Singel. Basic communal digs in a friendly, low-key atmosphere. Liberal drug policy. Clean rooms with an effort made at decoration. Picturesque canalside location puts you near the action in Nieuwendijk, the Shipping Quarter, and Spui. Breakfast included. Key deposit €10. Reception 8am-11pm. Dorms €27. ❷

The Shelter, Barndesteeg 21 (☎ 625 32 30; www.shelter.nl), off the Nieuwmarkt. Finding virtue amid red lights, with clean rooms and a friendly staff. Religious slogans abound, but all are welcome. Breakfast included. No drugs. Locker deposit €5. Sheets included. Curfew Su-Th midnight, F-Sa 1am. Dorms €13-17. MC/V with 5% surcharge. ❶

Young Budget Hotel Kabul, Warmoesstraat 38-42 (☎ 623 71 58; kabulhotel@hotmail.com). 4-16 person dorms have comfortable beds in carpeted, spacious rooms. Breakfast and sheets included. Internet €1 per 17min. No curfew. Max. stay 1 week. €5 key deposit. Dorms €21-29. AmEx/MC/V. ❷

SHIPPING QUARTER, CANAL RING WEST, AND THE JORDAAN

▨ **Hotel Clemens,** Raadhuisstr. 39 (☎ 624 60 89; www.clemenshotel.nl). Take tram 13, 17, or 20 to Westermarkt. Fridge, TV, Internet connection, safe, and hairdryer in all rooms. Deluxe rooms have private bath and more space than budget rooms. Breakfast €7. Key deposit €20. Book well in advance. 3-night min. stay during weekend. Singles €55; budget doubles €70-75; deluxe €110; budget triples with bath €125, deluxe €150. ❹

Ramenas Hotel, Haarlemmerdijk 61 (☎ 624 69 60 30; www.amsterdamhotels.com). Walk from Centraal Station along Nieuwendijk as it turns into Haarlemmerstr. and then Haarlemmerdijk. Ascetic rooms get the job done. Breakfast included. Doubles, triples, and quints €28 per person; with bath €34. Cash only. ❷

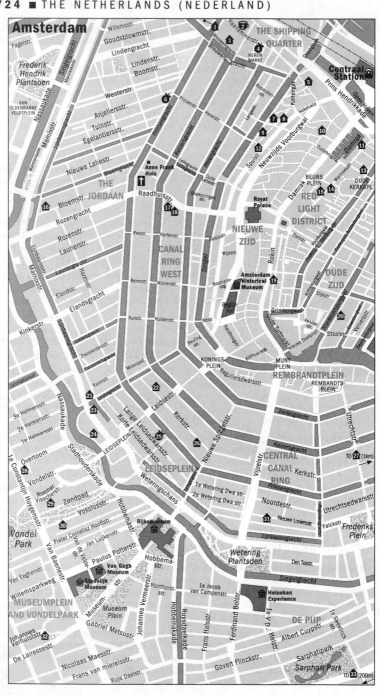

Amsterdam

THE NETHERLANDS

The Shelter Jordan, Bloemstr. 179 (☎624 47 17; www.shelter.nl). Take tram #13 or 17 to Marnixstr., then follow Lijnbaansgr. (off Rozengr.) for 5min., and turn right on Bloemstr.; the shelter is on your right. Hostel has an English-speaking, friendly staff in a quiet corner of the Jordaan. Nightly Bible study groups. Internet access €1 per 40min. Breakfast included. Locker deposit €5. Curfew 2am. Single-sex dorms. No smoking, no alcohol. Age limit 35. Arrive by 11am to get a room. Dorms €14-17. Cash only. ❶

Frederic Rent a Bike, Brouwersgr. 78 (☎624 55 09; www.frederic.nl). In addition to bikes, Frederic also rents rooms, some of which you'll find in the back of his rental shop, others located throughout the city in varying places and in all different price ranges. Amenities vary with the rooms. Singles €50-60; doubles €60-70; apartments available for short-term stays as well. Cash only, credit card required for reservation. ❹

Wiechmann Hotel, Prinsengr. 328-332 (☎626 33 21; www.hotelwiechmann.nl). Take tram #1, 2, or 5 to Prinsengr.; turn right and walk along the left side of the canal. Three restored canal houses. Sizeable rooms, many with canal views. All rooms with bath. Breakfast included. Key deposit €20. 2-night min. stay on weekends. Singles €70-90; doubles €125 135; triples and quads €170-230. ❺

LEIDSEPLEIN AND MUSEUMPLEIN

▨ **NJHC City Hostel Vondelpark (HI),** Zandpad 5 (☎589 89 96; www.njhc.org/vondelpark). Take tram #1, 2, or 5 to Leidseplein, walk to the Marriott, and take a left. Walk a block and turn right onto Zandpad just before the park; the hostel will be on the right. Exceptionally clean, 10- to 20-person single-sex rooms. Smaller, mixed rooms with bath also available. Bike rental €5.50 per day. Breakfast and sheets included. Lockers €2.50. Reception 7:30am-midnight. Dorms €19-23; doubles €54-71; quads €96-108. IYHF members €2.50 less. ❷

▨ **Quentin Hotel,** Leidsekade 89 (☎626 21 87; fax 622 01 21). You don't have to sacrifice style to get budget accommodations. Hallway walls are plastered with vintage music posters, and each room has its own distinct motif and cable TV. Singles €35, with bath €75; doubles €90; triples €133. AmEx/MC/V with 5% surcharge. ❸

The Flying Pig Palace, Vossiusstr. 46-47 (☎400 41 87; www.flyingpig.nl). Take tram #1, 2, or 5 from Centraal Station to Leidsepl., walk to the Marriott and turn left; go past the entrance to the park and take the first right onto Vossuistr. Fun and friendly hostel geared toward the backpacker. All rooms mixed gender. Free Internet and kitchen. Breakfast included. Key deposit €10. Reception 8am-9pm. Ages 18-35 only. Call or stop by at 8am to reserve a room. Dorms €16-23; doubles €54-58, with bath €58-62. For long stays, ask about the option of doing work in exchange for rent. AmEx/MC/V. ❷

Hotel Bema, Concertgebouw 19b (☎679 13 96; www.bemahotel.com). Take tram #16 to Museumplein. Facing the Concertgebouw, take a left and cross the street; it's on the left. Seven-room hotel with more style than most. Free breakfast delivered to the room. Reception 8am-midnight. Singles €45-55; doubles €55-85; triples €85, with shower €95; quads €115. ❹

Amsterdam

♠ ACCOMMODATIONS
Anna Youth Hostel, **8**
Bicycle Hotel, **33**
Bob's Youth Hostel, **12**
City Hostel Stadsdoelen (HI), **20**
De Oranje Tulp, **13**
Euphemia Budget Hotel, **31**
Flying Pig Downtown, **10**
The Flying Pig Palace, **30**
Frederic Rent a Bike, **3**
The Golden Bear, **22**
Hans Brinker Hotel, **26**
Hotel Bema, **24**
Hotel Brian, **9**
Hotel Brouwer, **7**
Hotel Clemens, **17**
Hotel de la Haye, **21**
Hotel de Lantaerne, **23**
Hotel Europa 92, **28**
Hotel Groenendael, **5**
Hotel Pension Kitty, **27**
Hotel Rokin, **19**
Hotel Winston, **15**
Nelly's Hostel, **14**
NJHC City Hostel Vondelpark (HI), **29**
Old Quarter, **11**
Quentin Hotel, **32**
Ramenas Hotel, **1**
The Shelter Jordan, **16**
Weichmann Hotel, **18**

● FOOD
Bojo, **25**
Bolhoed, **6**
Harlem: Drinks and Soulfood, **4**

● COFFEESHOP
Barney's Coffeeshop, **2**

THE NETHERLANDS

Hotel Europa 92, 1e Constantijn Huygenstr. 103-105 (☎618 88 08; www.europa92.nl), between. Vondelstr. and Overtoom. Take tram #1 or 6 to 1e Constantijn Huygenstr. Converted from 2 adjacent houses into 1 labyrinthine hotel. All rooms with bath. Breakfast included. Singles €65-90; doubles €100-125; triples €115-150; quads €135-170. ❺

Hotel de Lantaerne, Leidsekade 111 (☎623 22 21; www.hotellantaerne.com), right by Leidseplein. Lovely accommodations in two converted houses. Stylish rooms have TV, phone, and hairdryer. Breakfast included. Singles €65, with bath €75; doubles €80/€110; triples €105/€140. ❺

Hotel de la Haye, Leidsegr. 114 (☎624 40 44; www.hoteldelahaye.com). Take tram #1, 2, or 5 to Leidseplein. Walk up Marnixstr. 1 block and turn right. Conveniently located hotel combines the activity of Leidseplein with the serenity of a canal view. Breakfast included. Reception 8am-10pm. Singles €35-59; doubles €65-82, with bath €75-95; triples €100-130; quads €120-168; quints €150-185. ❹

Hans Brinker Hotel, Kerkstr. 136 (☎622 06 87; www.hansbrinker.com). Take tram #1, 2, or 5 from Centraal Station and get off at Kerkstr.; it's one block down on the left. All-you-can-eat breakfast buffet included. Key deposit €5. Safe €0.50. Reception 24hr. Dorms €21; singles €52; doubles €58-75; triples €90; quads €96. AmEx/MC/V. ❷

CENTRAL CANAL RING

Euphemia Budget Hotel, Fokke Simonszstr. 1-9 (☎622 90 45; www.euphemiahotel.com), 10min. from Rembrandtplein or Leidseplein. Take tram #16, 24, or 25 to Weteringcircuit, backtrack on Vijzelstr. for about 200m, and turn right on Fokke Simonszstr. Quiet hotel in a former monastery. Rooms are basic but clean, and recent renovations lend a colorful feel. Internet €1. Excellent breakfast €5. Reception 8am-11pm. Dorms, doubles and triples €23-55 per person. Discounts for reservations made on their website. AmEx/MC/V with 5% surcharge. ❸

The Golden Bear, Kerkstr. 37 (☎624 47 85; www.goldenbear.nl). Take tram #1, 2, or 5 to Prinsengr., backtrack one block to Kerkstr. Open since 1948, the Golden Bear is the oldest gay hostel in Amsterdam. Mainly male couples frequent these digs, though lesbians are welcome as well. All rooms include phone, safe, and cable TV. Breakfast included. Singles from €50; doubles from €61, with bath €102. ❹

DE PIJP, JODENBUURT, AND THE PLANTAGE

Bicycle Hotel, Van Ostadestr. 123 (☎679 34 52; www.bicyclehotel.com). From Centraal Station, take tram #24 or 25 to Ceintuurbaan, continue south along Ferdinand Bolstr. for one block, then turn left on Van Ostadestr.; the hotel will be half a block down on the left. Clean rooms. Bike rental €5 per day; maps of recommended bike trips outside Amsterdam available. All rooms have TV. Breakfast included. Doubles €68-70, with bath €99; triples €90/€120; quads with bath €130. ❺

Hotel Pension Kitty, Plantage Middenlaan 40 (☎622 68 19). Take tram #9 or 14 to Plantage Kerklaan. From there, take Plantage Middenlaan southeast and the unmarked Hotel Pension Kitty will be on your right. Laid-back and comfortable, and the staff asks guests to maintain the quiet atmosphere. Singles €50; doubles €60-70. ❹

 FOOD

Many cheap restaurants cluster around **Leidseplein, Rembrandtplein,** and the **Spui.** Cafes, especially in the Jordaan, serve inexpensive sandwiches (€1.50-4) and good meat-and-potatoes fare (€5.50-9). Bakeries line **Utrechtsestraat,** south of Prinsengr. Fruit, cheese, flowers, and even live chickens fill the **markets** on **Albert Cuypstraat,** behind the Heineken brewery. (Open M-Sa 9am-6pm.)

NIEUWE ZIJD AND OUDE ZIJD

In de Waag, Nieuwmarkt 4 (☎452 77 72; www.indewaag.nl.) In the late 1400s, this castle served as the eastern entrance to the city. Today, sandwiches and salads (€4-6) are served on the patio for lunch. At night, the restaurant lights 250 candles and patrons pack the medieval space to enjoy some of the city's tastiest Italian fare. Entrees €17-22. Open Su-Th 10am-midnight, F-Sa 10am-1am. ❸

Pannenkoekenhuis Upstairs, Grimburgwal 2 (☎626 56 03). A tiny nook with the best pancakes (€4-9) in the city. Open M-F noon-7pm, Sa noon-6pm, Su noon-5pm. ❶

Ristorante Caprese, Spuistr. 259-261 (☎620 00 59). Enjoy excellent Italian food while listening to jazz in a candlelit setting. Open daily 5-10:45pm. ❷

Stereo Sushi, Jonge Roelensteeg 4 (☎777 30 10), between Kalverstr. and Nieuwezijds Voorburgwal, south of Dam Sq. One of the city's most unique hot spots. Sushi (€4-9) and big noodle soups (€10-12). Open Su and Tu-Th 6pm-1am, F-Sa 6pm-3am. ❷

Aneka Rasa, Warmoesstr. 25-29 (☎626 15 60). Find elegance amid the seediness of the Red Light District. Indonesian *rijsttafel* (rice table) €16-27 per person. Open daily 5-10:30pm. AmEx/MC/V. ❸

Foodism, Oude Leliestr. 8 (☎427 51 03). Cool and casual, on one of the city's finest side-streets. Sandwiches from €5, soups and salads from €4, pasta dishes from €8. Open Su-Th 11am-10pm, F-Sa 11am-11pm. ❶

CANAL RING WEST, JORDAAN, AND THE SHIPPING QUARTER

Harlem: Drinks and Soulfood, Haarlemmerstr. 77 (☎330 14 98), at the Herenmarkt. Soul food, mixed with Amsterdam's finest nouvelle cuisine. Relax to cool jazz inside, or grab some fresh air on the patio. Dinner €11-16. Open M-Th 10am-1am, F-Sa 10am-3am, Su 11am-1am. ❷

Bolhoed, Prinsengr. 60-62 (☎626 18 03). Serves the city's best vegetarian and vegan fare in a bright, funky setting. Dinner menu includes a vegan special for €13. Mexican dishes, pasta, and casserole for €12-15. Reserve in advance for dinner. Open daily 4-11:30pm; kitchen closes at 10:45pm. ❷

hein, Berenstr. 20 (☎623 10 48). It's a one-woman-show at this refined and relaxed lunchery. Everything is homemade by Hein herself with the freshest of ingredients. Lunch menu includes crepes and *croques monsieurs*. Snacks and sandwiches €2-10. Open W-M 9:30am-6pm. ❶

Padi, Harlemmerdijk 50 (☎625 12 80). Locals rave about this Indonesian *eethuis*. *Lontong opor* (coconut-simmered chicken; €8). Open daily 5-10pm. ❶

Wolvenstraat 23, Wolvenstr. 23 (☎320 08 43). At this trendy spot, lunch is sandwiches, while dinner is strictly Chinese cuisine. Open M-Th 8am-1am, F 8am-2am, Sa 9am-2am, Su 10am-1am. ❷

Manzano, Rozengr. 106 (☎624 57 52). A nice retreat from the hectic Rozengr., this restaurant serves reasonably-priced *tapas* with a wide variety of meat, fish, and vegetable selections. Dips and veggie *tapas* from €4-8. Entrees €9-27. Restaurant open Tu-Su 5:30pm-midnight; shop open noon-10pm. AmEx/MC/V. ❸

LEIDSEPLEIN AND THE CENTRAL CANAL RING

Bojo, Lange Leidsedwarsstr. 51 (☎622 74 34). Bamboo walls, a sassy waitstaff, and excellent Javanese cuisine make for an unforgettable experience. Mini *rijsttafel* €10. **Bojo Speciaal,** just around the corner to the left on Leidsekruisstraat, offers the same menu, plus mixed drinks and a larger *rijsttafel* dish (€15). Open M-Th 4pm-2am, F 4pm-4am, Sa noon-4am, Su noon-2am. ❷

Santa Lucia, Leidsekruisstr. 20-22 (☎623 46 39). Great location puts you in the middle of the action. Pizza €4. Open daily noon-11pm. MC/V. ❶

THE NETHERLANDS

👁 🏛 SIGHTS AND MUSEUMS

Amsterdam is fairly compact, so tourists can easily explore the area from the Rijksmuseum to the Red Light District on foot. **Circle Tram 20**, geared toward tourists, stops at 30 attractions throughout the city (every 10min. 9am-7pm; day-pass €5, buy on the tram or at VVV offices). The more peaceful **Museumboot Canal Cruise** allows you to hop on and off along its loop from the VVV to the Anne Frank Huis, the Rijksmuseum, the Bloemenmarkt, Waterloopl., and the old shipyard. (Every 30min. 10am-5pm, day-pass €14, after 1pm €11. Buy tickets at any stop. Pass also gives 20% off some museums.) Rent a canal bike to power your own way through the canals. (Deposit €50. 1-2 people €7 per person per hr., 3 or more people €6; pick-up and drop-off points at Rijksmuseum, Leidsepl., Keizergr. at Leidsestr., and Anne Frank Huis. Open daily 10am-10pm.)

MUSEUMPLEIN

▧ VAN GOGH MUSEUM. This architecturally breathtaking museum houses the largest collection of van Goghs in the world (mostly from his family's private collection) and a diverse group of 19th-century paintings by his contemporaries and personal influences. *(Paulus Potterstr. 7. Take tram #2, 5, or 20 from the station. ☎ 570 52 52. Open daily 10am-6pm. €7, ages 13-17 €2.50, under 12 free.)*

▧ STEDELIJK MUSEUM OF MODERN ART. The outstanding collection includes Picasso, Pollock, de Kooning, Malevich, and up-and-coming contemporary work. Unfortunately, the museum will close for renovations and expansion on Dec. 31, 2002, and remain closed for three years. During this time, the museum will show some of its collection at the **COBRA** museum and the **Nieuwe Kerk.** See its website for more information. *(☎ 573 27 45; www.stedelijk.nl. Open daily 11am-5pm. €5.)*

RIJKSMUSEUM AMSTERDAM (NATIONAL MUSEUM). If you've made it to Amsterdam, it would be sinful to leave without seeing the Rijksmuseum's impressive collection of works by Rembrandt, Vermeer, Hals, and Steen. With thousands of Dutch Old Master paintings, it can be an overwhelming place—a good approach is to follow the crowds to Rembrandt's famed militia portrait *The Night Watch*, in the Gallery of Honor, and then proceed into **Aria,** the interactive computer room, which can create a personalized map of the museum. Don't miss the dollhouse exhibits, chronicling the boredom of rich married women in 18th-century Holland. In October 2003, the main building of the museum will close for renovations until 2008. The Phillips Wing will remain open to show masterpieces of 17th-century painting. *(On Stadhouderskade. Take tram #2 or 5 from the station. ☎ 674 70 00; www.rijksmuseum.nl. Open daily 10am-5pm. €8.50, under 18 free.)*

HEINEKEN EXPERIENCE. Every day, busloads of tourists discover that no beer is made in the Heineken Brewery. Plenty is served, however. Your visit includes three beers and a souvenir glass, all of which are well worth the price of admission. The brewery itself has been transformed and renamed the "Heineken Experience," an alcohol-themed amusement park. Highlights include the "bottle ride," which replicates the experience of becoming a Heineken beer. Guide yourself past holograms, virtual reality machines, and other multimedia treats. *(Stadhouderskade 78, at the corner of Ferdinand Bolstr. ☎ 523 96 66; www.heinekenexperince.com. Open Tu-Su 10am-6pm, last entry at 5pm. Those under 18 must be accompanied by a parent. €7.50.)*

JODENBUURT AND THE PLANTAGE

VERSETZMUSEUM AND HOLLANDSCHE SCHOUWBERG. Despite the fact that the Dutch military fell to the crushing power of the Nazis in 1940, The Netherlands maintained an underground, active resistance throughout the war. **The Versetzmuseum**

(Resistance Museum) focuses on the members of a secret resistance army, providing visitors with the details of their lives and struggles. It's housed in the Plancius Build ing, originally built in 1876 as the social club for a Jewish choir. **The Hollandsche Schouwberg** was originally one of the city's most popular theaters. After Nazi invasion, however, it became the only place that Jews were allowed to congregate. Not long after that, the building was changed into an assembly point for Dutch Jews who were to be deported to Westerbork, the transit camp to the north. The majority of these people eventually ended up in Auschwitz, Bergen-Belsen, or Sobibor. Today, the Hollandsche Schouwberg is a monument to the 104,000 Dutch Jews who were deported and killed during WWII. *(Versetzmuseum: Plantage Kerklaan 61. Tram #9 or 20 to Plantage Kerklaan; #6 or 14 to Plantage Middenlaan/Kerklaan. ☎ 620 25 35; www.verzetsmu seum.org. Open Tu-F 10am-5pm, Sa-M noon-5pm. €4.50, ages 7-15 €2.50, under 7 free. Hollandsche Schouwberg: Plantage Middenlaan 24. ☎ 626 99 45. Open daily 11am-4pm. Free.)*

MUSEUM HET REMBRANDT. Recently restored in 17th-century fashion, this museum was the home of Rembrandt until the city confiscated the house for taxes. It holds 250 of his etchings and dry points as well as many of his tools and palettes. *(Jodenbreestr. 4-6, at the corner of the Oudeschans Canal. Take tram #9, 14, or 20. Open M-Sa 10am-5pm, Su 1-5pm. €7, ISIC holders €5.)*

JOODS-PORTUGUESE SYNAGOGUE AND JOODS HISTORISCH MUSEUM. After being expelled from their countries in the 15th century, a sizable number of Spanish and Portuguese Jews established a community in Amsterdam and built the handsome **Joods-Portuguese Synagogue.** The Dutch government protected the building from Nazi torches by declaring it a national historic site. Across the street, the **Joods Historisch Museum** (Jewish Historical Museum), housed in three connected former synagogues, traces the history of Dutch Jews. *(Museum: Jonas Daniel Meijerpl., at Waterloopl. Take tram #9, 14, or 20. www.jhm.nl. Open daily 11am-5pm. €4.50, ISIC holders €3. Synagogue: Mr. Visserplein 1-3. Open Apr.-Oct. Su-F 10am-4pm; Nov.-Mar. Su-Th 10am-4pm, F 10am-3pm. €4.50.)*

OTHER SIGHTS. Thanks to the Dutch East India company, the **Museum of the Tropics (Tropenmuseum)** has artifacts from Asia, Africa, and Latin America (especially fine Indonesian art) and an engaging children's wing. *(Linnaeusstr. 2. Tram #9 and bus #22 stop right outside the museum. Open daily 10am-5pm. €6.80, students €4.50.)* Take a respite from the city in the **Hortus Botanicus**. Founded in 1638, this former medical garden is the oldest of its kind in the world. Once home to Europe's first coffee plant, the garden now holds over 6000 species of plants. *(Plantage Middenlaan 2A. Take tram #7, 9, or 14 to the Waterlooplein/Plantage Parklaan. Open Apr.-Oct. M-F 9am-5pm, Sa-Su 11am-5pm; Nov.-Mar. M-F 9am-4pm, Sa-Su 11am-4pm. €5.)* The **Artis Zoo,** the largest zoo in the country, houses a zoological museum, a museum of geology, an aquarium, and a planetarium. *(Plantage Kerklaan 38-40. Tram #9 or 20 to Waterlooplein. Open daily 9am-5pm. €13.50.)*

NIEUWE ZIJD, OUDE ZIJD, AND THE RED-LIGHT DISTRICT

BEGIJNHOF. This stunning courtyard full of little gardens and surrounded by handsome gabled houses provides a quiet escape from the excesses of the city. Begijnhof was founded in 1346 as a convent for Beguines, free-thinking religious women who did not take vows but still lived dedicated to religious contemplation, charity, and manual work. Make sure to visit **Het Houten Huys (the Wooden House),** the oldest house in Amsterdam; the **Engelsekerk;** and the **Begijnhofkapel.** *(Begijnhof: Open daily 10am-5pm. Free. Het Houten Huys: Open M-F 10am-4pm. Engelsekerk: Begijnhof 48. Open for public prayer Su 10:30am. Begijnhofkapel: Begijnhof 30. Open M-F 9am-5pm, Sa 9am-7pm, services Sunday.)*

DAM SQUARE AND KONINKLIJK PALACE. Completed as the town hall in 1655, the palace's indisputable highlight is the beautiful Citizen's Hall, designed to replicate the universe in a single room. Across from Dam Sq. is the Dutch **Nationaal Mon-**

ument, unveiled in 1956 to honor Dutch victims of World War II. Inside the 21m white stone obelisk is soil from all twelve of Holland's provinces as well as the Dutch East Indies. *(Palace open June-Aug. daily 12:30-5pm; Sept.-May hours vary. €4.50.)*

NIEUWE KERK. The Nieuwe Kerk, which has been rebuilt after several fires, is still used for coronations and royal weddings. It also hosts modern and contemporary art. In early 2003, it will open its doors to rotating exhibits from the Stedelijk collection while that museum is being renovated. *(Adjacent to Dam Sq., beside Koninklijk Palace. Open daily 10am-6pm. Organ recitals July-Sept. Su 8pm; €8.)*

THE RED LIGHT DISTRICT. The Red Light District is surprisingly liveable. Pushers, porn shops, and live sex theaters do run a brisk business, but a surprising number of people there have nothing to do with the debauchery; in many ways the area is less outrageous and seedy than you might have expected. During the day, the Red Light District is comparatively flaccid, with tourists milling about and consulting their maps. As the sun goes down, people get braver and the area comes to life. Cops from the police station on Warmoestr. patrol the district until midnight, but women may feel uncomfortable walking through this area, and all tourists are prime targets for pickpockets.

OUR LORD IN THE ATTIC. A secret enclave of virtue and piety hides in the 17th-century **Museum Amstelkring, Ons' Lieve Heer op Solder** ("Our Lord in the Attic"), where a Catholic priest, forbidden to practice his faith in public during the Reformation, established a surprisingly grand chapel in his attic. *(Oudezijds Voorburgwal 40, at the corner of Oudezijds Armstr., 5min. from Centraal Station. Open M-Sa 10am-5pm, Su and holidays 1-5pm. €4.50, students €3.40.)*

THE VICES. If it's weed that interests you, far and away your best bet is the staggeringly informative **Cannabis College,** Oudezijds Achterburgwal 124. The center for "higher" education offers info on everything from the uses of medicinal marijuana to facts about the War on Drugs to the creative applications of industrial hemp. For a curated taste of the seaminess that runs down Amsterdam's underbelly, your best bet is to get your jollies right off the train at the **Amsterdam Sex Museum,** Damrak 18, less than a five-minute walk from Centraal Station. The low admission fee won't leave you feeling burned if you find that walls plastered with pictures of bestiality and S&M are not your thing. *(Cannabis College open daily 11am-7pm. Free. Sex Museum open daily 10am-11:30pm. €2.50.)*

CANAL RING AND THE JORDAAN

You haven't seen Amsterdam until you've spent some time wandering in the Canal Ring. It's the city's highest rent district and, arguably, its most beautiful. Four main waterways encircle the western and southern sides of the old city. Inside the crescent is most of the tourist traffic of the city center, while the ring itself is a quieter, more picturesque place. Collectively, **Prinsengracht** (Prince's canal), **Keizersgracht** (Emperor's canal), and **Herengracht** (Gentlemen's canal) are known as the *grachtengordel* (literally "canal girdle"). The Ring is home to some of Amsterdam's most important and beautiful architecture. **The Jordaan** is the neighborhood next door—it's less touristed, but still filled with galleries, markets, and great nightlife.

ANNE FRANK HUIS. A visit to the Anne Frank House is a must for everyone, whether or not you've read the famous diary. The museum chronicles the two years the Frank family and four other Jews spent hiding in the annex of this warehouse on the Prinsengr. The rooms are no longer furnished, but personal objects in display cases and text panels with excerpts from the diary bring the story of the eight inhabitants to life, and the magazine clippings and photos that Anne used to decorate her room still hang on the wall. Footage of interviews with Otto Frank,

Miep Gies (who supplied the family with food and other necessities), and childhood friends of Anne provide further information and details. *(Prinsengr. 267. Trams #13, 14, 17, or 20 to Westermarkt. Open Apr.-Aug. daily 9am-9pm; Sept.-Mar. 9am-7pm. Last admission 30min. before closing. €6.50, ages 10-17 €3.)*

OTHER SIGHTS. The stately Herengr. leads to the **Museum Willet-Holthuysen,** a richly decorated 18th-century canal house with a peaceful, pristine garden. *(Herengr. 605, between Reguliersgr. and Vijzelstr., 3min. from Rembrandtpl. Open M-F 10am-5pm, Sa-Su 11am-5pm. €3.40.)* Near the Anne Frank Huis is the city's stately **Westerkerk,** a Protestant church built in 1631. Climb the church's tower for the best view in the city. *(Raadhuisstr. between Keizersgr. and Prinsengr. Trams #13, 17, or 20 to Westermarkt. Open Apr.-Sept. M-F 11am-3pm; July-Aug. also Sa. Tours every hr. €3.)*

⛏ ENTERTAINMENT

The **Amsterdams Uit Buro (AUB),** Leidsepl. 26, is stuffed with fliers, pamphlets, and guides to help you sift through current events; pick up the free monthly *UITKRANT* at any AUB office to see what's on. The AUB also sells tickets and makes reservations for just about any cultural event. (☎621 13 11; www.uitlijn.nl. Open F-W 10am-6pm, Th 10am-9pm.) The VVV **tourist office,** Stationspl. 10, has a theater desk that can also make reservations. (Open M-Sa 10am-5pm.) If you're thirsty for more info on bars, coffeeshops, and the latest events, pick up *Shark* (www.underwateramsterdam.com; print versions available throughout the city).

CONCERTS. In the summer, the Vondelpark Openluchttheater hosts free performances of all sorts every Wednesday through Sunday. (☎673 14 99; www.openluchttheater.nl.) The **Royal Concertgebouw Orchestra,** one of the world's finest orchestras, plays in the **Concertgebouw,** Concertgebouwplein 2-6. Take tram #316 to Museumplein. (☎671 83 45; www.concertegebouw.nl. Tickets from €7. Guided tours Su at 9:30am; €7. Sept.-June, those under 27 can get last minute tickets for anything that isn't sold out for €7. Free lunchtime concert W 12:30pm, no tickets necessary. Ticket office open daily 10am-7pm.)

FILM. Check out www.movieguide.nl for movie listings. In the Vondelpark, head left from the main entrance on Stadhouderskade to see what's on at the stately **Filmmuseum** independent movie theater. (☎589 14 00. Info center open M-F from 10am; Sa-Su box office opens 1hr. prior to first showing. €6.25, students €3.50.) **The Movies,** Harlemmerstr. 159, is the city's oldest movie theater. (☎624 57 90. Open M-Tu and Th 4:15-10:15pm, W 2-10:15pm, F 4:15pm-12:30am, Sa 2pm-12:30am, Su 11:30am-10:15pm. €7.50, students €6.50)

▣ COFFEESHOPS AND SMART SHOPS

COFFEESHOPS
Marijuana and hashish are tolerated in The Netherlands. Coffeeshops sell pot or hash or will let you buy a drink and smoke your own stuff. Look for the green-and-white "Coffeeshop BCD" sticker that means that the shop is reputable. Although Amsterdam is known as the **hash** capital of the world, **marijuana** is increasingly popular. You can legally possess up to 5g of marijuana or hash. Pick up a free copy of the *BCD Official Coffeeshop Guide* for the pot-smoker's map of Amsterdam. For info on legal ins and outs, call the **Jellinek clinic** (☎570 23 55). **Never buy drugs from street dealers.** Don't get too caught up in Amsterdam's narcotic quirk; use common sense, and remember that any experimentation with drugs can be dangerous. If you choose to indulge, you will find that coffeeshops carry a range of products, described below.

THE LOCAL STORY

POT QUIZ

Mark has owned The Rookies coffeeshop in Leidseplein for over 10 years. He's a "second-generation cannabis retailer" and on the board of two cannabis unions.

LG: What do you like about working in a coffeeshop?
M: It's not aggressive, it's a very tolerant atmosphere and people from all over the world come in.
LG: What do you think it is about Dutch culture that makes cannabis permissible here and nowhere else?
M: Well, it originally started because they needed to separate the soft and hard drugs markets. If a young person wants to get high, then he goes to a coffeeshop and he doesn't get involved with other stuff. In other countries, the same person who sells cannabis will sell ecstasy, pills, cocaine, and other drugs. The coffeeshops are very clean; there are no hard drugs here. Coffeeshops are still here because it's really working. Neighboring countries are beginning to follow our system. The Christian Democrats Party wants to get rid of everything, but it's unrealistic to think you can get rid of drugs in general; there's always going to be people who use them. It's much better to leave it in the open instead of shoving it under the carpet, because then if it's still in the open you have more social control on it.

Cont. next page.

Spacecakes, Spaceshakes, and **Space Sweets** are cakes and sweets made with hash or weed; hash chocolate, popsicles, and bonbons are also available. Because they need to be digested, they take longer to affect you and longer to rinse out; they produce a body stone that can take up to an hour to start, so don't gobble down another brownie just because you don't feel effects immediately. Be very careful who you buy from; hard drugs may be mixed in, which have been known to cause permanent side effects such as paralysis and impotence. **Hash** comes in two varieties, black (like Afghani and Nepali) and blonde (like Moroccan). Black tends to be heavier and hits harder. It's grown at high elevations in the mountains; the higher the elevation, the better the hash. Any **marijuana** with white in its name, such as white widow, white butterfly, or white ice, is guaranteed to be strong. It's not a good idea to drink very much while smoking, since getting high can disarm the body's ability to regulate the amount of alcohol consumed, and alcohol poisoning can be much more severe if your gag reflex is hindered. The Dutch tend to mix tobacco with their pot, so joints are harsher on your lungs; ask at coffeeshops if pre-rolled joints are rolled with tobacco or pure cannabis. Dutch marijuana costs €5-22 per gram. Staff at coffeeshops can explain the different kinds of pot on the menu to tourists. Most places will supply rolling papers and filter tips. Almost no one smokes out of pipes; while some places provide bongs, usually only tourists use them. When you move from one coffeeshop to another, it is courteous to buy a drink in the next coffeeshop even if you already have weed.

SMART SHOPS

Smart shops, which peddle a variety of **"herbal enhancers"** and **hallucinogens** that walk the line between soft and hard drugs, are also legal. Some shops are alcohol-free. **All hard drugs are illegal** and possession is treated as a serious crime.

Magic mushrooms start to work thirty minutes to an hour after consumption and act on your system for four to eight hours, often causing panic or a faster heartbeat. Never look for mushrooms in the wild and never buy from a street dealer; it's extremely difficult to tell the difference between poisonous mushrooms and hallucinogenic mushrooms. Don't mix hallucinogens such as shrooms with alcohol; if you have a bad trip, call ☎ 122 to go to the hospital or ask someone for help—you won't be arrested, and they've seen it all before.

WHERE TO GO...

Barney's Coffeeshop, Haarlemmerstr. 102. Eat a greasy breakfast with your big fat joint. Open daily 7am-8pm.

Kadinsky, Rosmarijnsteeg 9. Stylish spot hidden off an alley near Spui is one of the city's friendliest stoneries. 20min. free Internet with purchase. Open daily 10am-1am.

Grey Area, Oude Leliestr. 2. Where coffeeshop owners go for the best. One of the only owner-operated spots left in the city. The Yankee expat behind the counter will be happy to lend you one of the coffeeshop's bongs. Open Tu-Su noon-8pm.

The Rookies, Korte Leidsedwarsstr. 145-147. One of the few remaining places outside of the Red Light District that serves both liquor and marijuana. Open Su-Th 10am-1am, F-Sa 10am-3am.

Abraxas, J. Roelensteeg 12-14. Swanky, casual, no-pressure atmosphere. 12min. free Internet access with drink. Open daily 10am-1am.

Siberie, Brouwersgr. 11. Snacks (*tosti* €1.60) and Internet (€1.15 per 30min.) also available. Open Su-Th 11am-11pm, F-Sa 11am-midnight.

Hill Street Blues, Warmoesstr. 52. A rock 'n' roll vibe permeates this coffeeshop and bar. Open 9am-1am, F-Sa 9am-3am.

Rusland, Ruslandstr. 16. One of the city's oldest coffeeshops. An intimate, comfy nook with an extensive menu. Open Su-Th 10am-midnight, F-Sa 10am-1am.

The Magic Mushroom, Spuistr. 249. At this museum of a smartshop, procure all the mushrooms, herbal XTC, energy and smart drinks, smart drugs, and stoner art you've ever dreamed existed. Open daily 11am-10pm.

Dutch Flowers, Singel 387. The long line is evidence of the quality hash. Outside seating on the beautiful Singel canal. Open Su-Th 10am-1am, F-Sa 10am-2am.

Paradox, 1e Bloemdwarsstr. 2. The owners match the feel of this place: colorful, free-spirited, and ready to have a good time. Weed, hash, and awesome veggie burgers (€3.50). Open daily 10am-8pm, kitchen closes at 4pm.

NIGHTLIFE

CAFES AND BARS

Amsterdam's finest cafes are the old, dark, wood-paneled *bruine cafes* (brown cafes) of the **Jordaan,** so named because of the years of cigarette smoke accumulated on the ceilings. Many have outdoor seating lining the canal on **Prinsengracht.** The **Leidseplein** and **Rembrandtplein** are the liveliest nightspots, with crazy coffeeshops, loud bars, and tacky clubs galore. Gay bars line **Reguliersdwarsstraat,** which connects Muntpl. and Rembrandtspl., and **Kerkstraat,** five blocks north of Leidsepl.

LG: When the laws on marijuana were first relaxed in the early 1970s, were there any groups that protested the new legislation?

M: Of course; it's only 10% of the Dutch population that smokes. Even now if you want to open a coffeeshop a lot of people are against it. It's still somehow a conservative country.

LG: 10%?

M: More youngsters smoke in England than in The Netherlands. Maybe 1.5% of users have a problem with cannabis but with alcohol it's as high as 20%. A lot of people are pointing at the 1.5%—I think it's ridiculous.

LG: Since cannabis isn't legal here, just tolerated, how socially accepted is it? Would employers ever hesitate to hire someone who had worked in a coffeeshop?

M: Not really, but it depends on the person. I had a manager who worked here for four years and is now a policeman.

LG: How do you think membership in the EU will affect the status of coffeeshops?

M: It's a minor thing, I think. They just made a law that allows a French policeman to arrest someone here if he committed a felony. But there are two exceptions that they can't hurt somebody: one is for coffeeshops selling soft drugs and the other is euthanasia. Only France and Sweden are giving us problems about it, France especially. But their alcoholism rate is so high; it's really ridiculous that they're complaining about the drug issue. They complain that drugs come from Holland, but so many drugs come from Morocco. And if it comes from Morocco, then it has to come through France.

Café de Engelbewaarder, Kloveniersburgwal 59. A great atmosphere any time of the week, especially on Su when the cafe hosts live jazz (4:40-7pm). Beer €2. Open M-Th noon-1am, F-Sa noon-3am, Su 2pm-1am. Kitchen open 5:30-10pm.

Absinthe, Nieuwezijds Voorburgwal 171, just south of Dam Sq. Draws a young, hip crowd with a mellow vibe. The bar is known for its house drink, a variant called "smart absinthe" with 10% wormwood (€10). Open Su-Th 8pm-3am, F-Sa 8pm-4am.

Lux, Marnixstr. 403. More a lounge than a bar, Lux has a distinctive retro design that sets it apart from its peers. There's not much dancing, but the candles, wave lamps, and DJ (W-Su) will get you pumped to hit the clubs. Beer €2; hard liquor €4. Open Su-Th 8pm-3am, F-Sa 8pm-4am.

M Bar, Reguliersdwarsstr. 13-15, just off Leidsestr. Tram #1, 2, or 5 to Koningspl. Sleek, slippery minimalist bar, located on a famously gay street but drawing a mainly straight crowd. DJs spin house, club, and techno Th-Su. Beer €2; wine €3; mixed drinks €6. Open W-Th and Su 6pm-3am, F-Sa 6pm-4am.

Montmartre, Halvemaarsteg 17. Rococo interior bedecked with flowers and rich draperies houses some of the wildest parties in the city. Voted best gay bar in Amsterdam by local gay magazine *Gay Krant*. Open Su-Th 5pm-1am, F-Sa 5pm-3am.

The Tara, Rokin 85-89, a few blocks south of Dam Sq. Irish-themed watering hole with a maze-like interior. Three bars where they know how to pull a real pint of Guiness. DJs or bands usually F-Sa. Beer €2; pints €4. Open Su-Th 11am-1am, F-Sa 11am-3am.

Maximiliaan, Kloveniersburgwal 6-8. Stop in for the fabulous home-brews. Alcohol content can get to a heady 7%. Open Tu-Th and Su 3pm-1am, F-Sa 3pm-3am.

Arc Bar, Reguliersdwarsstr. 44. Lounge in a beige leather chair and watch discreet projections of clouds on the wall. On weekends, the black table-tops in the front are lowered to become platforms for dancing. Open Su-M 10am-1am, F-Sa 10am-3am.

LIVE MUSIC

Paradiso, Weteringschans 6-8 (☎626 45 21; www.paradiso.nl). When big-name rock, punk, new-wave, hip-hop, and reggae bands come to Amsterdam, they almost invariably play at this converted church. Grace the place where Lenny Kravitz got his big break and the Stones taped their latest live album. Tickets €5-25.

Bourbon Street Jazz & Blues Club, Leidsekruisstr. 6-8 (☎623 34 40; www.bourbonstreet.nl). Blues, soul, funk, and rock bands keep the crowds coming every night. Mostly smaller bands play this intimate venue, although in the past they have drawn the Stones and Sting. Cover Su and Th €3, F-Sa free if you enter 10-10:30pm. Open Su-Th 10pm-4am, F-Sa 10pm-5am.

Melkweg, Lijnbaansgr. 234a (☎624 17 77; www.melweg.nl), off Leidsepl. Legendary nightspot where bands, theater, films, shows, an art gallery, and a discotheque make for sensory overload. Concerts €10-22. Box office open M-F 1-5pm, Sa-Su 4-6pm.

Casablanca, Zeedijk 24-26 (☎625 56 85; www.casablanca-amsterdam.nl), between Oudezijds Kolk and Vredenburgersteeg. Casablanca has been around since 1946, and it's still one of the best spots to hear live jazz. Jazz Su-W nights; DJ-hosted dance parties Th-Sa. Open Su-Th 8pm-3am, F-Sa 8pm-4am.

CLUBS AND DISCOS

Many clubs charge a membership fee in addition to normal cover, so the tab can get high. Be prepared for cocky doormen who love to turn away tourists; show up early or hope the bouncer thinks you're cute. It's customary to tip bouncers €1-2 on the way out. There are pricey discos aplenty on **Prinsengracht,** near

Leidsestraat, and on **Lange Leidsedwarsstraat.** Gay discos almost exclusively for men line **Amstelstraat** and **Reguliersdwarsstraat.** Pick up a wallet-sized *Clu* guide, free at cafes and coffeeshops, for a club map of the city, and *Gay and Night,* a free monthly magazine, for info on gay parties.

Escape, Rembrandtpl. 11. People pour into this massive venue for a night at one of Amsterdam's hottest clubs. 2 floors with 6 bars and an enormous dance floor. Scenesters groove to house, trance, disco, and dance classics. Be sober, well-dressed, and female to increase your chances of entry. Open Th-Su 11pm-4am, F-Sa 11pm-5am.

Arena, Gravesandestr. 51-53, in the Oost. Former chapel throws wild parties. Open F-Sa 11pm-4am, Su 6pm-3am.

Dansen Bij Jansen, Handboogstr. 11-13, near Konigsplein. The hottest student dance club in Amsterdam, popular with backpackers and local students. Show student ID to enter or be accompanied by a student. Open Su-Th 11pm-4am, F-Sa 11pm-5am.

Cockring, Warmoestr. 90. Somewhere between a sex club and a disco. Dark room in the back where anything goes. Men only. No cover, except for special parties, when it runs around €5. Open Su-Th 11pm-4am, F-Sa 11pm-5am.

Item, Nieuwezijds Voorburgwal 163-165, just south of Dam Sq. Young, trendy, and tourist-oriented. In an area with few late-night discos, Item stands out. Cover €10-15. Open Su-Th 11pm-4am, F-Sa 11pm-5am.

De Beetles, Lange Leidsedwarsstr. 81. Find an ideal mix of cool and crazy at this hip drink house. F-Sa 9pm-12:30am 6 beers for €2. Open Su-Th 9pm-4am, F-Sa 9pm-5am.

The Ministry, Reguliersdwarsstr. 12. The very popular Ministry is upscale enough to be classy and hip, but without any attitude. Cover €5-12; look for fliers for free admittance. Open Su-Th 11pm-4am, F-Sa 11pm-5am.

🔋 DAYTRIPS FROM AMSTERDAM

TULIP COUNTRY: AALSMEER AND LISSE. Easily accessible by bus or bike, old-fashioned **Aalsmeer** is home to the world's largest flower auction. The **Bloemenveiling Aalsmeer,** Legmeerdijk 313, is the world's largest trade building with 878,000 square meters of floor space; the worldwide price of flowers is largely determined here. (☎297 39 21 85; www.vba-aalsmeer.nl. Open M-F 7:30-11am. €4.) From Amsterdam's Centraal Station, take **bus** #172 (45min., every 15min., 5 strips). For the best action, get there early; buses begin leaving Amsterdam at 6:10am.

To see even more flowers, check out the town of **Lisse** in late spring. The **Keukenhof Gardens** become a kaleidoscope of color as over 5 million bulbs come to life. (www.keukenhof.nl. In 2003, open Mar. 21-May 18 daily 8am-7:30pm; tickets on sale until 6pm. €11.) **The Zwarte Tulip Museum** details the history and science of "bulbiculture," or tulip raising. Many call the ongoing quest for the *zwarte* (black) tulip impossible, since the color does not exist naturally. (☎025 241 79 00. Open Tu-Su 1-5pm. €3.) Take a **train** from Amsterdam's Centraal Station to Leiden (20min., every 30min. until 2:45am, €11), then catch **bus** #50 or 51 to Lisse (5 strips).

ZAANSE SCHANS. Duck-filled canals, working windmills, and restored houses make Zaanse Schans feel like a museum village, although a handful of people actually live and work here. The **De Kat Windmill** has been grinding plants into artists' pigments since 1782. (Open Apr.-Oct. daily 9am-5pm; Nov.-Mar. Sa-Su 9am-5pm. €2.) The oldest oil mill in the world is the **De Zoeker Windmill.** (Open Mar.-Oct. daily 9:30am-4:30pm. €2.) The **Cheesefarm Catharina Hoeve** offers free samples of its homemade wares as well as a tour of its workshop. (Open daily 8am-6pm.) Watch craftsmen mold blocks of wood into comfy clogs at **Klompenmakerij de Zaanse Schans,** or see where the ubiquitous Albert Heijn supermarket craze started at the original shop, now the **Albert Heijn Museumwinkel.** Next door you can stop by the **Museum van het Nederlandse Uurwerk (Museum of the Dutch Clock),** Kalverringdijk 3, to view the oldest working pendulum clock in the world. (Open Apr.-Oct. daily 10am-5pm. €2.30.) The pint-sized **Museum Het Noorderhuis** features original costumes from the Zaan region. (Open July-Aug. daily 10am-5pm; Mar.-June and Sept.-Oct. Tu-Su 10am-5pm; Nov.-Feb. Sa-Su 10am-5pm. €1.)

From Amsterdam, take the *stoptrein* heading to Alkmaar and get off at Koog Zandijk (20min., €2.25). From there, follow the signs across a bridge to Zaanse Schans (12min.). An **information center** is at Schansend 1. (☎616 82 18; www.zaanseschans.nl. Open daily 8:30am-5pm.)

HAARLEM ☎023

With narrow cobblestone streets, calm canals, and fields of tulips, it's clear how Haarlem inspired native Frans Hals and other Golden Age Dutch artists. Most visitors come to take in the city's amazing artistic and historic sights.

■▼ **TRANSPORTATION AND PRACTICAL INFORMATION.** Reach Haarlem from Amsterdam by **train** (20min.; €2.90, same-day round-trip €5.20) from Centraal Station or by **bus** #80 from Marnixstr., near Leidsepl. (every 30min., 2 strips). The VVV **tourist office,** Stationspl. 1, just to your right when you walk out of the train station, finds private rooms (from €18.50) for a €5 fee. (☎090 06 16 16 00; www.vvvzk.nl. Open in summer M-F 9:30am-5:30pm, Sa 10am-4pm; off-season Sa 10am-2pm.)

▐▐ **ACCOMMODATIONS AND FOOD.** Walk to Grote Markt and take a right to reach **Joops Intercity Apartments ❹,** Oude Groenmarkt 20. (☎532 20 08; joops@easynet.nl. Reception 7:30am-9pm. Singles €28-65; doubles €55-100. AmEx/MC/V.) **Hotel Carillon ❷,** Grote Markt 27, is ideally located right on the town square, to the left of the Grote Kerk. (☎531 05 91; www.hotelcarillon.com. Breakfast included. Reception 7:30am-midnight. Singles €29, with bath €55; doubles €55/€71; triples €92. MC/V.) Take bus #2 (dir.: Haarlem-Noord; every 10min. until 6pm, then every 15min. until 12:30am), then a cab from Haarlem station (for about €12) to Jeugdherberg to stay at the **NJHC-Hostel Haarlem (HI) ❷,** Jan Gijzenpad 3. (☎537 37 93; www.njhc.org/haarlem. Breakfast included. Dorms €19-25. AmEx/MC/V.) To **camp** at **De Liede ❶,** Lie Over 68, take bus #2 (dir.: Zuiderpolder) and walk 10min. (☎535 86 66. €3.50 per person plus €2.75 per tent or car. For cheap meals, try cafes in the **Grote Markt** or **Botermarkt;** many offer outdoor patios.

▣▥ **SIGHTS AND MUSEUMS.** The action centers on the **Grote Markt,** Haarlem's vibrant main square. To get there from the train station, head south along Kruisweg, which becomes Kruisstraat and then Barteljorisstraat. The ▦**Grote Kerk,** at the opposite end of Grote Markt, houses a mammoth Müller organ once played by an 11-year-old Mozart. (Open M-Sa 10am-4pm. €1.50.) From the front of the church, take a right on to Warmoestraat and walk three blocks to the ▦**Frans Hals Museum,** Groot Heiligland 62, which houses a collection of Golden Age paintings by several masters, including work by Haarlem resident Frans Hals. (Open Tu-Sa 11am-5pm, Su noon-5pm. €5.40, under 19 free.) A two-minute walk toward the train station from Grote Markt is the moving ▦**Corrie Ten Boomhuis,** Barteljorisstraat 19, which served as the headquarters of Corrie Ten Boom's movement to protect Jews during World War II. The savior of an estimated 800 lives, Corrie was caught and sent to a concentration camp but survived to write *The Hiding Place*, which was later made into a film. The **Teyler's Museum,** Spaarne 16, is The Netherlands' oldest museum, and contains an eclectic assortment of scientific instruments, fossils, paintings, and drawings, including works by Raphael, Michelangelo, and Rembrandt; from the church, turn left onto Damstr. and follow it until Spaarne. (Open Tu-Sa 10am-5pm, Su noon-5pm. €4.50.) The **De Hallen Museum,** Grote Markt 16, displays rotating exhibits of modern art and is housed in the 17th-century Dutch Renaissance indoor meat market. (Open M-Sa 11am-5pm, Su 1-5pm. €4, under 19 free.) Dedicated to the many uses of hemp, the **Global Hemp Museum,** Spaarne 94, has everything from hemp denim to a hemp snowboard. (www.globalhempmuseum.com. Open daily 11am-8pm, Su noon-8pm. €2.50.)

⚑ DAYTRIPS FROM HAARLEM: ZANDVOORT AND BLOEMENDAAL. A mere seven miles from Haarlem, the seaside town of **Zandvoort** draws sun-starved Nederlanders to its miles of sandy beaches. To find the shore from the train station, follow the signs to the Raadhuis, then head west along Kerkstraat. For a different feel, walk 30min. to hip **Bloemendaal,** which has been transformed from a quiet, family-oriented beach town to one of the best beach parties in Holland. The hippie-style club ⚑**Woodstock 69** hosts **Beach Bop** the last Sunday of every month (www.beachbop.info), although lower-profile parties go on other nights of the week. The town's clubs, including **Republic, De Zomer,** and **Solaris,** are open only in summer, generally from April to September.

Trains arrive in Zandvoort from Haarlem (10min., round-trip €2.75). The VVV **tourist office,** Schoolplein 1, is just east of the town square, off Louisdavidstraat. (☎ 571 79 47; www.vvvzk.nl. Open M-Sa 9am-5pm.) The **Hotel Noordzee ❹,** Hogeweg 15, has cheerful rooms just 100m from the beach. (☎ 571 31 27; www.hotel-nordzee.nl. Breakfast included. Doubles €47-60.)

LEIDEN
☎ 071

Home to one of the oldest and most prestigious universities in Europe, Leiden brims with bookstores, bicycles, windmills, gated gardens, hidden walkways, and some truly outstanding museums. Rembrandt's birthplace and the site of the first **tulips,** The Netherlands' third-largest city offers visitors a gateway to flower country. Follow signs from the train station to the spacious and modern ⚑**Museum Naturalis,** which explores the history of our earth and its inhabitants, providing scientific and anthropological explanations of fossils, minerals, animals, evolution, and even astronomy. (www.naturalis.nl. Open July-Aug. daily 10am-6pm; Sept.-June Tu-Su 10am-6pm. €6.) The ⚑**Rijksmuseum voor Volkenkunde** (National Museum of Ethnology), Steenstr. 1, is one of the world's oldest anthropological museums, with a fantastic collection from the Dutch East Indies. (www.rmv.nl. Open Tu-Su 10am-5pm. €6.50.) The **Rijksmuseum van Oudheden** (National Antiquities Museum), Rapenburg 28, holds the restored Egyptian Temple of Taffeh, a gift removed from the reservoir basin of the Aswan Dam. (www.rmo.nl. Open Tu-F 10am-5pm, Sa-Su noon-5pm. €6.50.) Sharing a main gate with the Academy building is the university's 400-year-old garden, the **Hortus Botanicus,** Rapenburg 73, where the first Dutch tulips were grown. Its grassy knolls alongside the **Witte Singel** canal make it an ideal picnic spot. (www.hortusleiden.nl. Open Mar.-Nov. daily 10am-6pm; Dec.-Feb. Su-F 10am-4pm. €4.) Scale steep staircases to inspect the inside of a functioning windmill at the **Molenmuseum ("De Valk"),** 2e Binnenvestgracht 1. (Open Tu-Sa 10am-5pm, Su 1pm-5pm. €2.50.) The **Museum De Lakenhal,** Oude Singel 32, exhibits works by Rembrandt and Jan Steen. (Open Tu-Sa 10am-5pm, Su noon-5pm. €4.)

Leiden is easily reached by **train** from Amsterdam's Centraal Station (20min., every 30min until 2:45am, €11) or The Hague (20min., every 30min. until 3:15am, €4.50). The VVV **tourist office,** Stationsweg 2d, a 5min. walk from the train station, sells maps (€1.15) and walking tour brochures (€2) and helps find hotel rooms (€2.50 fee). (☎ 090 02 22 23 33; www.leiden.nl. Open M-F 10am-6:30pm, Sa 10am-4:30pm; Apr.-May and July-Aug. also open Su 11am-3pm.) The **Hotel Pension Witte Singel ❷**, Witte Singel 80, 5min. from Hortus Botanicus, has immaculate rooms. Take bus #43 to Merenwijk and tell the driver your destination. (☎ 512 45 92; wvanvriel@pensione-ws.demon.nl. Singles from €31; doubles from €47.) Locals and students pack the popular **de Oude Harmonie ❷**, Breestr. 16, just off Rapenburg. (Entrees €6-13. Open M-Th noon-1am, F-Sa 3pm-3am, Su 3pm-1am.) The **Super de Boer supermarket**, Stationsweg 40, is opposite the train station. (Open M-F 7am-9pm, Sa 9am-8pm, Su noon-7pm.)

THE HAGUE (DEN HAAG) ☎ 070

William II moved the royal residence to The Hague in 1248, prompting the creation of Parliament buildings, museums, and sprawling parks. Today, countless diplomats fill designer stores, merging rich history with a bustling metropolis.

▐▐ TRANSPORTATION AND PRACTICAL INFORMATION. Trains roll in from Amsterdam (50min., €8) and Rotterdam (25min., €3.50) to both of The Hague's major stations, Centraal Station and Holland Spoor. Trams #1, 9, and 12 connect the two stations. The VVV **tourist office**, Kon. Julianapl. 30, just outside the north entrance to Centraal Station and right next to the Hotel Sofitel, books rooms for a €2 fee and sells detailed city maps. A hotel booking by computer is available 24 hours a day. (☎ 090 03 40 35 05; www.denhaag.com. Open M and Sa 10am-5pm, Tu-F 9am-5:30pm, Su 11am-5pm.) Most foreign **embassies** are in The Hague: **Australia**, Carnegielaan 4, 2517 KH (☎ 310 82 00; open M-F 8:45am-4:30pm); **Canada**, Sophialaan 7, 2514 JP (☎ 311 16 00; open M-F 9am-1pm and 2-5:30pm); **Ireland**, 9 Dr. Kuyperstr., 2514 BA (☎ 363 09 93; call for hours); **New Zealand**, Carnegielaan 10, 2517 KH (☎ 346 93 24; open M-F 9am-12:30pm and 1:30-5:30pm); **South Africa**, Wassenaarseweg 40, 2596 CJ (☎ 392 45 01; open daily 9am-noon); **UK**, Lange Voorhout 10, 2514 ED (☎ 427 04 27; call for hours); **US**, Lange Voorhout 102, 2514 EJ (☎ 310 92 09; open M-F 8am-4:30pm).

▐▐ ACCOMMODATIONS AND FOOD. The **NJHC City Hostel ❷**, Scheepmakerstr. 27, is near Holland Spoor; turn right from the station, follow the tram tracks, turn right at the big intersection, and Scheepmakerstr. is 3min. down on your right. From Centraal Station, take tram #1 (dir.: Delft), 9 (dir.: Vrederust), or 12 (dir.: Duindrop) to Rijswijkseplein (2 strips); cross to the left in front of the tram, cross the big intersection, and Scheepmakerstr. is straight ahead. (☎ 315 78 88; www.njhc.org/denhaag. In-house restaurant/bar. Breakfast included. Dorms €23; singles €47; doubles €61. Nonmembers add €2.50.) Budget takeaway places line **Lage Poten** and **Korte Poten** near the Binnenhof.

▐▐ SIGHTS AND ENTERTAINMENT. The Hague has served as the seat of Dutch government for 800 years; lately, it has also become headquarters for the international criminal justice system. Andrew Carnegie donated the **Peace Palace** (Het Vredespaleis) at Carnegiepl. to be the opulent home of the International Court of Justice. (www.vredespaleis.nl. Train #7 or 8 north from the Binnenhof. Tours M-F 10, 11am, 2, 3pm. Book through the tourist office. €3.50, under 13 €2.30.) For snippets of Dutch politics, visit the **Binnenhof**, The Hague's Parliament complex. Just outside the north entrance of the Binnenhof, the 17th-century **Mauritshuis**, Korte Vijverberg 8, features an impressive collection of Dutch paintings, including works by Rembrandt and Vermeer. (www.mauritshuis.nl. Open Tu-Sa 10am-5pm, Su 11am-5pm. €7, under 18 free.) Guided tours leave from Binnenhof

8a and visit the 13th-century **Ridderzaal** (Hall of Knights) as well as the chambers of the States General. (Open M-Sa 10am-4pm, last tour leaves at 3:45pm. Entrance to courtyard free, tour €5.) The impressive modern art collection at the **Gemeentemuseum**, Stadhouderslaan 41, displays Piet Mondrian's *Victory Boogie Woogie*. Take tram #7 from Holland Spoor or bus #4 from Centraal Station. (Open Tu-Su 11am-5pm. €7.) For vibrant nightlife, prowl the Strandweg in nearby **Scheveningen**.

DELFT   ☎015

Delft's lily-lined canals and stone footbridges offer the same images that native Johannes Vermeer immortalized in paint over 300 years ago. It's best to visit on Thursdays and Saturdays, when townspeople flood the marketplace. The town is renowned for **Delftware**, blue-on-white china developed in the 16th century. Watch Delftware made from scratch at **De Candelaer**, Kerkstraat 13a-14, located in the center of town. (Open 9am-6pm.) To see a larger factory, take Tram #1 to Vrijenbanselaan and enjoy a free demonstration at **De Delftse Pauw**, Delftweg 133. (Open Apr.-Oct. daily 9am-4:30pm; Nov.-Mar. M-F 9am-4:40, Sa-Su 11am-1pm.)

Built in 1381, the **Nieuwe Kerk** hosts the restored mausoleum of Dutch liberator Willem of Orange. Climb the tower, which holds a 48-bell carillon, for a view of old Delft. (Church open Apr.-Oct. M-Sa 9am-6pm; Nov.-Mar. M-F 11am-4pm, Sa 11am-5pm. €2. Tower closes 1hr. earlier. €1.60.) Founded in 1200, the **Oude Kerk**, a Dutch Reformed church, has a rich history and a 75m tower that leans 2m out of line. (Open Apr.-Oct. M-Sa 9am-6pm; Nov.-Mar. 11am-4pm, Sa 11am-5pm. €2. Tours every hr.) **Rondvaart Delft**, Koormarkt 113, offers canal rides and rents water bikes. (☎212 63 85. Open Mar.-Oct. daily 10am-6pm.)

The easiest way into Delft is the 15min. ride on **tram** #1 from The Hague (2 strips) to Delft station. **Trains** also arrive from Amsterdam (1hr., €9). The **VVV tourist office**, Markt 85, has hiking and cycling maps. From the station, cross the bridge, turn left, turn right at the first light, and follow signs to the Markt. (☎213 01 00; www.vvvdelft.nl. Open M-Sa 9am-5:30pm; Apr.-Sept. also open Su 11am-3pm.) While the tourist office will help with room booking, your best bet is to sleep in The Hague; it's 15min. away and has much better deals. **Delftse Hout Recreation Area ❷** has campsites and cabins. (☎213 00 40; www.tours.nl/delftsehout. Reception May to mid-Sept. 9am-10pm; mid-Sept. to Apr. 9am-6pm. 2-person tent €22; 4-person camping hut €30.) Restaurants line **Volderstraat** and **Oude Delft**.

ROTTERDAM   ☎010

The second-largest city in The Netherlands and the busiest port city in the world, Rotterdam lacks the quaint, classic feel that characterizes much of The Netherlands. After it was bombed in 1940, experimental architects replaced the rubble with striking (some say strikingly ugly) buildings, creating an urban, industrial conglomerate. Artsy and innovative, yet almost decrepit in its hyper-modernity, the Rotterdam that arose from the ashes—rife with museums, parks, and groundbreaking architecture—is today one of the centers of cultural activity in Europe.

📑 TRANSPORTATION AND PRACTICAL INFORMATION. Trains run from: Amsterdam (1¼hr., €11); The Hague (25min., €3.40); and Utrecht (45min., €7). The VVV **tourist office**, Coolsingel 67, opposite the *Stadhuis*, books rooms for a €2 fee. (Open M-Th 9:30am-6pm, F 9:30am-9pm, Sa 9:30am-5pm.) **Postal code:** 3016.

🏠 ACCOMMODATIONS AND FOOD. To reach the **NJHC City-Hostel Rotterdam (HI) ❷**, Rochussenstr. 107-109, take the Metro to Dijkzigt; at the top of the Metro escalator, exit onto Rochussenstr. and turn left. (☎436 57 63. Breakfast and sheets included. Reception 7am-midnight. Dorms €22; singles €31; doubles €52.) To get from the station to the **Hotel Bienvenue ❸**, Spoorsingel 24, exit through the back and walk straight along the canal for 5min.; it'll be on the right. (☎466 93 94. Breakfast included. Reception M-F 7:30am-9pm, Sa-Su 8am-9pm. Singles €43; doubles €70; triples €90.) Chinese food and schwarma await along **Witte de Withstraat,** where you can easily grab a meal for under €5, or try **Lijbaan** for its array of pubs, bars, and all their accompanying culinary charm.

🅖 🅙 **SIGHTS AND ENTERTAINMENT.** For a dramatic example of Rotterdam's eccentric designs, check out the **Kijk-Kubus** (Cube Houses) by Piet Blom. Take tram #1 or the Metro to Blaak, turn left, and look up. (Open Mar.-Dec. daily 11am-5pm; Jan.-Feb. F-Su only. €1.75.) Try to decipher the architectural madness at the **Netherlands Architecture Institute,** Museumpark 25. (Open Tu-Sa 10am-5pm. €5, under 17 €3.) Then, refresh yourself with Rubens, van Gogh, Rembrandt, Rubinstein, Rothko, and Magritte across the street at the **Museum Boijmans van Beuningen,** Museumpark 18-20. (M: Eendractspl. or tram #5. Open Tu-Sa 10am-5pm, Su 11am-5pm. €6.) Restored to its medieval splendor after the bombing, **St. Laurenskerk,** Grote Kerkplein 15, is one of the most remarkable churches in the country and home to the largest mechanical organ in Europe. (Open Tu-Sa 10am-4pm. Su services free.) Step aboard the *De Buffel*, a restored 19th-century turret ship, at the **Maritiem Museum,** Leeuvehaven 1, or peruse hundreds of intricately detailed model ships. (Open July-Aug. M-Sa 10am-5pm, Su 11am-5pm; Sept.-June closed M. €3.50.) Make sure to swing by the powerful **Zadkine Monument,** to the left of the museum. Known as the Monument for the Destroyed City and erected only 11 years after the bombing, it depicts a man with a hole in his heart writhing in agony. **Museumpark** features sculptures, mosaics, and monuments designed by some of the world's foremost artists and architects; take tram #5 to reach the outdoor exhibit.

Coffeeshop-hop along **Oude Binnenweg** and **Nieuwe Binnenweg,** or dance the night away at **Night Town,** West Kruiskade 26-28. (Cover for dancing €8, bands €11-25. Open F-Sa 11pm-5am.)

UTRECHT   ☎030

Utrecht (pop. 250,000) has something for everyone: a Gothic cathedral, a prestigious university, gorgeous canals, numerous museums, and a crazy nightlife. The awe-inspiring **Domkerk** was started in 1254 and finished 250 years later. Initially a Roman Catholic cathedral, the Domkerk has held Protestant services since 1580. (Open M-Sa 10am-5pm, Su 2-4pm. Free.) The **Domtoren,** blown off the cathedral during a medieval tornado, is the highest tower in The Netherlands. (Tickets for tours sold at RonDom. Daily July-Aug. every 30min. 10am-4-30pm; Sept.-Jun. every hr. 10am-4pm. €6, children €3.60.) Get information on churches and museums at **RonDom,** Domplein 9, the Utrecht visitor's center for cultural history.

Trains from Amsterdam (30min., 3-6 per hr., day return €9.50.) arrive in the Hoog Catharijne. To get to the VVV **tourist office,** Vinkenbrugstraat 19, follow the signs to Vredenberg, which heads to the town center. (☎0900 128 87 32; info@vvvutrecht.nl. Open M-W and F 9:30am-6:30pm, Th 9:30am-9pm, Sa 9:30am-5pm, Su 10am-2pm.) Near the corner of Lucasbolwerk and Nobelstraat, **B&B Utrecht City Centre ❶**, Lucasbolwerk 4, offers a kitchen, sauna, piano, and home video system. (☎0650 434 884; www.hostelutrecht.nl. Free Internet. 24hr. breakfast. Dorms €16; singles from €55; doubles from €65; triples from €85; quads from €100.) Slightly farther from the city, the same owners run **B&B Utrecht ❶,** Egelantierstraat 25. Take bus #3 to Watertoren (€1), cross the street and head to Anemoonstraat, then go two blocks to the end and turn left. The street turns into Egelantierstraat and the hostel is on your left. (☎0650 434 884; www.hotelinfo.nl. Free Internet. 24hr. breakfast. Dorm €12; singles from €40; doubles from €45; triples from €70; quads from

€85.) For a pastoral setting perfect for recharging, try **NJHC Ridderhofstad Rhijnau-wen (HI) ❷**, Rhijnauwenselaan 14, in nearby Bunnik. Take bus #40, 41, or 43 from Centraal Station (10-15min., €2.10 each way) and tell the driver to let you off at Bunnik. From the stop, cross the street, backtrack, turn right on Rhijnauwense-laan, and it's 0.5km down the road. The hostel offers bike rental and a small bar. (☎656 12 77; www.njhc.org/bunnik. Breakfast included. Dorms July-Aug. week-nights €21.25, weekends €22.50; Sept.-June €2 less. Doubles €51.50; triples €63.50-€76.50; quads €77.50-€93.50.) Look for cheap meals along **Nobelstraat.**

Nightlife in Utrecht thrives seven days a week. **'t Oude Pothuys,** Oudegracht 279, has live music every night until 3am. **Kafe Belgie,** Oudegracht 196, has 196 different beers for €1.60 each (open F-Sa until 5am, Th 4am, Su-W 3am). Students party at **Woolloo Moollo** on Janskerkhof 14 (student ID required; cover varies; open W-Sa 11pm-late) and **De Beurs,** Neude 35-37, near the post office (open daily 10am-late).

DE HOGE VELUWE NATIONAL PARK   ☎0318

The impressive **Hoge Veluwe National Park** (HO-geh VEY-loo-wuh) is a 13,565-acre preserve of woods, heath, dunes, red deer, and wild boars. (☎59 16 27, www.hogeveluwe.nl. Park open June-July daily 8am-10pm; May and Aug. 8am-9pm; Sept. 9am-8pm; Apr. 8am-8pm; Oct. 9am-7pm; Nov.-Mar. daily 9am-5:30pm. €5, children 6-12 €2.50; 50% discount May-Sept. after 5pm.) Deep in the park, the **Rijksmuseum Kröller-Müller** has troves of van Goghs from the Kroller-Muller family's outstanding collection, as well as key works by Seurat, Mondrian, Picasso, and Brancusi. The museum's striking **sculpture garden,** one of the largest in Europe, has exceptional works by Rodin, Bourdelle, and Hepworth. (www.kmm.nl. Open Tu-Su 10am 5pm, sculpture garden closes at 4:30pm. €5, children €2.75.) Take one of the free **bikes** in the park and get a map (€2) at the **visitor's center** to explore over 33km of paths. (☎055 378 81 19. Visitor's center open daily 10am-5pm.)

Arnhem and **Apeldoorn** (both 15km from the park) are good bases for exploration. Bus #12 comes from Arnhem to the park entrance and the museum, while bus #110 runs from Apeldoorn (25min.). Contact the park or either **tourist office** for more information. (Arnhem ☎0900 202 40 75; www.vvvarnhem.nl. Apeldoorn ☎0 900 168 16 36.) In Arnhem, stay at the **NJHC Herberg Alteveer (HI) ❷**, Diepenbrocklaan 27. Take bus #3 from the station to Rijnstate Hospital; as you face the hospital turn right, then left on Cattepoelseweg and about 150 meters ahead turn right up the brick steps, and at the top turn right. (☎026 442 01 14; arnhem@njhc.org. Breakfast included. Reception 8am-11pm. Dorms €20-22; singles €28-30; doubles €50-53; tri-ples €69-73; quads €87-93. Nonmembers add €2.50.) To get to Apeldoorn's lively **De Grote Beer (HI) ❷**, Asselsestr. 330, take bus #4 or 7 (dir.: Orden) from the sta-tion, get off at Chamavenlaan, cross the street, turn left, walk past the intersection, and the hostel will be on your right. (☎055 355 31 18; fax 355 38 11; apel-doorn@njhc.org. Breakfast and sheets included. Reception 8am-10pm. Dorms €20-22; nonmembers add €2.50.)

MAASTRICHT   ☎043

Situated on a narrow strip of land between Belgium and Germany, Maastricht (pop. 120,000) is one of the oldest cities in The Netherlands. It has been a symbol of Euro-pean unity since the 1991 Maastricht Treaty, which established the European Union. Home of the prestigious **Jan van Eyck Academie of Art,** Maastricht is also known for its abundance of art galleries and antique stores. The striking **Bonnefan-tenmuseum,** Ave. Ceramique 250, contrasts Maastricht's traditional Dutch brickwork with its futuristic rocketship design. The museum houses permanent collections of archaeological artifacts, medieval sculpture, Northern Renaissance painting, and contemporary art. (www.bonnefanten.nl. Open Tu-Su 11am-5pm. €7; students €6.)

Despite its contemporary status as the birthplace of modern European unity, Maastricht has seen its share of interstate rivalries; centuries of foreign threats culminated in an innovative subterranean defense system. The **Mount Saint Peter Caves'** 20,000 underground passages were used as a siege shelter as late as WWII and contain inscriptions and artwork by generations of inhabitants. Access to the caves is possible only with a tour guide at two locations: the **Northern System** (Grotten Noord), Luikerweg 71 (tours in Dutch, English available depending on guide; €3); and the **Zonneberg Caves**, Slavante 1 (tours in English July-Aug. daily 2:45pm; €3).

The train station is on the eastern side of town, across the river from most of the action. **Trains** arrive from Amsterdam (2½hr., €24). To get from the train station to the VVV **tourist office**, Kleine Staat 1, walk straight on Station Str., cross the bridge, go one more block, take a right, and walk down a block; the office will be on the right. (☎ 325 21 21. Open May-Oct. M-Sa 9am-6pm, Su 11am-3pm; Nov.-Apr. M-F 9am-6pm, Sa 9am-5pm.) Spend the night on the centrally located ⬛**Botel ❷**, Maasboulevard 95, a boat with tiny cabins and a cozy deckroom lounge. (☎ 321 90 23. 24hr. reception. Singles €27- 30; doubles €41-43; triples €60.) To get from the train station to **City-Hostel de Dousberg (HI) ❷**, Dousbergweg 4, take bus #11 on weekdays, bus #33 on weeknights after 6pm, and bus #8 or 18 on weekends. (☎ 346 67 77; www.dousberg.nl. Breakfast included with HI membership. Dorms €20; triples €75.) Cheap food can be found around the central **Vrijthof** area. For entertainment info, check out the free *Uit in Maastricht*. **Night Live,** Kesselkade 43, is a church converted to a disco. (Cover €4-6. Open Th-Sa 11pm-6am.)

GRONINGEN   ☎ 050

With 35,000 students and the nightlife to prove it, Groningen (pop. 175,000) ranks as perhaps the most happening city in the northern region of The Netherlands. The town's spectacular ⬛**Groninger Museum,** a unique pastel assemblage of squares, cylinders, and metal, forms a bridge between the station and the city center. The multicolored galleries create a futuristic laboratory atmosphere for their contemporary art exhibits. (www.groninger-museum.nl. Open Tu-Su 10am-5pm; July and Aug. also open M 1-5pm. €6, seniors €5, ages 5-15 €3, under 5 free.) Admire the city from atop the Grote Markt's **Martinitoren Tower,** which weathered the German attacks during World War II. (Open Apr.-Oct. daily 11am-5pm; Nov.-Mar. noon-4pm. €2.20, under 13 €1.20.) Relax in the serene 16th-century **Prinsenhoftuin** (Princes' Court Gardens); the entrance is on the canal 10min. away from the Martinitorin. (Open Apr. to mid-Oct. 10am-dusk.) Inside the gardens, the tiny **Theeschenkerij Tea Hut** offers 130 kinds of tea (€0.80). Cool off at **Noorderplantsoen,** a fountain-filled park that serves as host space for the huge **Noorderzon (Northern Sun) Festival** of art in late August, Groningen's annual cultural climax.

Trains roll in from Amsterdam (2½hr.; every 30min.; €23.80). To reach the VVV **tourist office,** Grote Markt 25, turn right as you exit the station, walk along the canal, turn left at the first bridge, head straight through the Hereplein on Herestr., cross Gedempte Zuiderdiep, and keep on Herestr. until it hits the Grote Markt. (☎ (0900) 202 30 50; info@vvvgroningen.nl; www.vvvgroningen.nl. Open M-W, F 9am-6pm, Th 9am-8pm, Sa 10am-5pm; July-Aug. also Su 11am-3pm.) Hang out with a fun crowd at **Simplon Youthhotel ❶**, Boterdiep 73-2. Take bus #1 from the station (dir.: Korrewegwijk) to Boterdiep; the hostel is through the yellow- and white-striped entranceway. (☎ 313 52 21; www.xs4all.nl/~simplon. Breakfast €3.40. Free lockers. Sheets €2.50, included in private rooms. Lockout noon-3pm. All-female dorm available. Dorms €10.90; singles €28.35; doubles €41.30; triples €59; quads €76.) For cheap pitchers of beer and shoulder-to-shoulder packed bars, head to the southeastern corner of Grote Markt on Poelestraat and Peperstraat. The intimate, candlelit **de Spieghel Jazz Café,** Peperstr. 11, has two floors of live jazz, funk, or blues every night. (Wine €2 per glass. Open daily 8pm-4am.) **Postal code:** 9725.

WADDEN ISLANDS (WADDENEILANDEN)

Wadden means "mudflat" in Dutch, but sand is the defining characteristic of these islands: gorgeous beaches hide behind ridges covered in golden grass. Deserted, tulip-lined bike trails carve through vast, flat stretches of grazing land to the sea. Sleepy and isolated, the islands are truly Holland's best-kept secret.

⌐ TRANSPORTATION. The islands arch clockwise around the northwestern coast of Holland: Texel (closest to Amsterdam), Vlieland, Terschelling, Ameland, and Schiermonnikoog. To reach **Texel,** take the train from Amsterdam to **Den Helder** (1½hr., €11), bus #33 (2 strips), and a ferry to 't Hoorntje, the southernmost town on Texel (20min., every hr. 6:30am-9:30pm, round-trip €4). **Buses** depart from the ferry dock to various locales throughout the island, though the best way to travel is to rent a **bike** from **Verhuurbedrijf Heijne,** opposite the ferry dock. (From €4.50 per day. Open Apr.-Oct. daily 9am-8pm; Nov.-Mar. 9am-6pm.)

TEXEL. The largest of the Wadden Islands, Texel boasts stunning beaches and museums. **Beaches** lie near De Koog, on the western side of the island. **Nude beaches** beckon the uninhibited; you can bare it all near paal 9 (2km southwest of Den Hoorn) or paal 27 (5km west of De Cocksdorp). Say hi to the playful *zee-honden* (seals) at the **Museum and Aquarium,** Ruijslaan 92, in De Koog. (www.eco-mare.nl. €7; under 13 €3.50. Open daily 9am-5pm.) The staff can also arrange a tour of the surrounding **nature reserves;** ask for an English-speaking guide.
  A **Texel Ticket** (€3.50) allows one day of unlimited travel on the island's bus system. (Runs mid-June to mid-Sept.). The VVV **tourist office,** Emmaln 66, is located just outside Den Burg, about 300m south of the main bus stop; look for the blue signs. (☎02 22 31 47 41; www.texel.net. Open M-Th 9am-6pm, F 9am-9pm, Sa 9am-5:30pm; July-Aug. also Su 10am-1:30pm.) Take bus #29 and tell the driver you're going to **Panorama (HI) ❶,** Schansweg 7, which is snuggled amid sheep pastures, 7km from the dock at 't Hoorntje and 3km from Den Burg's center. (☎02 22 31 54 41. Bikes from €4 per day. Breakfast and sheets included. Reception 8:30am-10:30pm. Dorms €15-19, nonmembers add €2.50.) **Campgrounds** cluster south of De Koog and near De Cocksdorp; ask at the tourist office.

THE NETHERLANDS

NORWAY (NORGE)

Norway is blessed with an abundance of natural beauty, from its renowned fjords to turquoise rivers and glacier-capped mountain ranges. The long Nordic history manifests itself in an intimate relationship with the sea. The country's original seafarers, the Vikings, dominated a realm that spanned from the British Isles to southern Europe. The late 19th century saw Norway's artistic reputation rise with luminaries like Edvard Munch and Henrik Ibsen. In the years since World War II, Norway has developed into a modern welfare state. Although prices and taxes are among the world's highest, they translate into unparalleled social services, little class stratification, and a high standard of living. As a result of Norway's prosperity and low crime rate, visitors encounter a safe and easy place to travel and can focus their attention on the country's main attraction—the breathtaking scenery.

FACTS AND FIGURES

Official Name: Kingdom of Norway.

Capital: Oslo.

Major Cities: Bergen, Stavanger, Trondheim, Tromsø.

Population: 4,500,000.

Land Area: 307,000 sq. km.

Time Zone: GMT +1.

Language: Norwegian; Swedish and English widely spoken.

Religions: Evangelical Lutheran (86%).

DISCOVER NORWAY

Cosmopolitan **Oslo** (p. 749), the first stop on most travelers' itineraries, swarms with lively cafes and museums. After you've exhausted the capital, hop on the gorgeous **Oslo-Bergen rail line** (p. 756) to fjord country. At the other end lies cultural **Bergen,** a relaxed, seaside city with pointed gables lining its wharf (p. 759). If you only have one day to see the fjords, spend it exploring the **Sognefjord** (p. 757); the popular **"Norway in a Nutshell"** tour (p. 756), a daytrip from Bergen, gives a glorious glimpse of fjord country's scenery. With more time, continue a fjord circuit with the **Geirangerfjord** (p. 765) and **Jostedalsbreen Glacier** (p. 764), or explore the mountains of **Jotunheimen National Park** (p. 758). If you have substantially more time in Norway, go north to the isolated **Lofoten Islands** (p. 770) or head to the southern coast and explore the lively cities of **Kristiansand** (p. 767) and **Stavanger** (p. 769).

ESSENTIALS

WHEN TO GO

The majority of hostels are crowded with tourists in July and August; June or September may be a better time to go. Climate can also serve as a good guide for when to travel. Oslo averages 18°C (63°F) in July and -4°C (24°F) in January. In the north, average temperatures drop and it is wetter than the south and east; Bergen and the surrounding mountains, in particular, see more than their share of rain. For a few weeks around the summer solstice (June 21), the area north of Bodø basks in the midnight sun. You stand the best chance of seeing the Northern Lights from above the Arctic Circle (Nov.-Feb.). Skiing is best just before Easter.

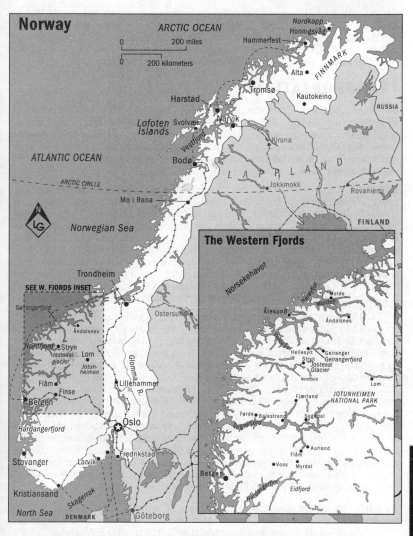

Norway

ARCTIC OCEAN

ATLANTIC OCEAN

The Western Fjords

NORWAY

DOCUMENTS AND FORMALITIES

VISAS. South Africans need a visa for stays of any length. Citizens of Australia, Canada, the EU, New Zealand, and the US do not need a visa for stays of up to 90 days, but this period begins upon entry into any Nordic country; for more than 90 days in any combination of Denmark, Finland, Iceland, Norway, and Sweden, you will need a visa.

EMBASSIES. Foreign embassies are in Oslo (see p. 750). Norwegian embassies at home include: **Australia** and **New Zealand,** 17 Hunter St., Yarralumla, Canberra ACT 2600 (☎ 26 273 34 44; emb.canberra@mfa.no); **Canada,** Suite 532, 90 Sparks St.,

Ottawa, ON K1P 5B4 (☎613-238-6571; emb.ottawa@mfa.no); **Ireland,** 34 Moles-worth St., Dublin 2 (☎01 662 18 00; emb.dublin@mfa.no); **South Africa,** 1166 Park St., Hatfield, 0083 (☎12 342 61 00; embpta@noramb.co.za); **UK,** 25 Belgrave Sq., London SW1X 8QD (☎020 7591 5500; emb.london@mfa.no); and **US,** 2720 34th St. NW, Washington, D.C. 20008 (☎202-333-6000; www.norway.org).

TRANSPORTATION

BY PLANE. The main international airport is in Oslo, though a few flights land at Trondheim and Bergen. **SAS** (US ☎800-221-2350; UK ☎845 6072 7727; Norway ☎815 20 400; www.scandinavian.net) flies to Norway, as do **Finnair** and **Icelandair** (see p. 50). Those under 25 and students under 32 qualify for special youth fares that make flying an option for domestic travel (from 100kr). **SAS** (☎81 00 33 00) offers domestic standby tickets *(sjanse billetter).*

BY FERRY. Car ferries *(ferjer)* are usually much cheaper (and slower) than the many passenger express boats *(hurtigbat* or *ekspressbat)* cruising the coasts and fjords; both often have student, Scanrail, and InterRail discounts. The **Hurtigruten** (www.hurtigruten.com) takes six days for the incredible voyage from Bergen to Kirkenes on the Russian border; there is one northbound and one southbound departure daily from each of its 34 stops. There are no railpass discounts, but students get 50% off. Buses and trains are usually more affordable, but the savings on accommodations can make up the difference for overnight trips. The most common ports for international ferries are Oslo, Bergen, Kristiansand, and Stavanger; destinations include: Hanstholm, Denmark; Newcastle, England; and Iceland.

BY TRAIN. Norway's train system includes an extensive commuter train network around Oslo and long-distance lines running from Oslo to Bergen, to Stavanger via Kristiansand, and to Trondheim. Overnight trains may be your best option for travel as far north as Trondheim and Bodø; from there, you'll need buses or ferries to get farther north. Trains do run southeast from Narvik, going through Kiruna, Sweden (p. 983). All stations have an information desk that can provide regional schedules. Seat reservations (30kr) are compulsory on many trains, including the high-speed Signatur trains, which cover some of the long-distance lines.

Eurail is valid on all trains run by the Norwegian State Railway. The **Norway Rail-pass** and *buy-in-Scandinavia* **Scanrail Pass** both allow five days within 15 days (1620kr, 25% under 26 discount) or 21 consecutive days (2510kr, 25% under 26 discount) of unlimited rail travel, as well as heavily discounted fares on many ferries and buses. Only three of those days can be used in the country of purchase, however, so the *buy-outside-Scandinavia* **Scanrail Pass** (p. 59) is more economical for those not visiting Denmark, Finland, or Sweden.

BY BUS. Buses are quite expensive, but are the only land option north of Bodø and in the fjords. **Norway Bussekspress** (☎23 00 24 40; www.nor-way.no) operates 75% of the domestic bus routes and publishes a free timetable *(Rutehefte)* containing schedules and prices, available at bus stations and on buses. Scanrail and InterRail pass holders are entitled to a 50% discount on most bus routes, and students get a 35% discount—be insistent, and follow the rules listed in the Norway Bussekspress booklet. Bus passes, valid for one (1375kr) or two (2200kr) weeks, are good deals for those exploring the fjords or the north.

BY CAR. Citizens of Canada, the EU, or the US need only a valid driver's license in their home country to drive in Norway. Insurance is required and is usually included in the price of rental. Roads in Norway are in good condition, although blind curves are common and roads are frighteningly narrow in some places. Drivers should remember to be cautious, especially on mountain roads and tunnels. Driving around the fjords can be frustrating, as only Nordfjord has a road completely circumnavigating it; there are numerous car ferries, but check timetables in advance to connect with the boats. RVs are common. Rental cars are expensive, but for groups they can be more affordable than trains and buses. Gas is prohibitively expensive (10-11kr per liter); plan carefully, since distances between stations can be substantial. Vehicles are required to keep headlights on at all times.

BY BIKE AND BY THUMB. Biking is becoming increasingly common. The beautiful scenery is rewarding for cyclists, although the hilly terrain can be rough on bikes. Contact **Syklistenes Landsforening** (☎22 41 50 80) for maps, suggested routes, and other information. Hitching is notoriously difficult in Norway. Some Norwegians hitch beyond the rail lines in northern Norway and the fjord areas of the west, but many others try for six hours and end up exactly where they started. Hitchers should bring several layers of clothing, rain gear, and a warm sleeping bag. *Let's Go* does not recommend hitchhiking.

TOURIST SERVICES AND MONEY

EMERGENCY	Police: ☎110. Ambulance: ☎113. Fire: ☎112.

TOURIST OFFICES. Virtually every town and village has a **Turistinformasjon** office; look for a white lower-case "i" on a square green sign. In July and the first half of August, all tourist offices are open daily; most have reduced hours the rest of the year. For more information, contact the **Norwegian Tourist Board,** P.O. Box 722 Sentrum, NO-0105, Oslo; street address: Stortorvet 10 (☎24 14 46 00; www.ntr.no).

MONEY. The Norwegian **kroner (kr)** is divided into 100 rarely used øre. Coins come in 50 øre, as well as 1kr, 5kr, 10kr, and 20kr denominations; bills are in 50kr, 100kr, 200kr, 500kr, and 1000kr denominations. Banks and large post offices change money, usually for a commission but at good rates. Prices are sky-high throughout all of Norway. As a general rule, more isolated areas have even higher prices; the Lofoten Islands are especially pricey. Tipping is not essential, but it is customary to tip 5-15% for restaurant service. A 15% service charge is often included in hotel bills. **Value-added tax (VAT;** 10-17%) refunds are available for single-item purchases of more than 300kr in a single store in a single visit (p. 15).

NORWEGIAN KRONER		
AUS$1 = 4.15KR	1KR = AUS$0.24	
CDN$1 = 4.90KR	1KR = CDN$0.20	
EUR€1 = 7.42KR	1KR = EUR€0.13	
NZ$1 = 3.56KR	1KR = NZ$0.28	
ZAR1 = 1.42KR	1KR = ZAR0.70	
UK£1 = 11.59KR	1KR = UK£0.09	
US$1 = 7.62KR	1KR = US$0.13	

BUSINESS HOURS. Business hours are short in summer, especially on Friday and in August, when Norwegians vacation. Shop hours are Monday to Friday 10am-5pm, Saturday 10am-2pm; hours may be extended on Thursday. Banks are generally open Monday to Wednesday and Friday 8:15am-3pm, Thursday 8:15am-5pm.

COMMUNICATION

PHONE CODE	Country code: 47. International dialing prefix: 095. There are no city codes in Norway. From outside Norway, dial int'l dialing prefix (see inside back cover) + 47 + local number.

TELEPHONES. Phone calls are expensive. There are three types of public phones; the black and gray phones accept 1kr, 5kr, 10kr, and 20kr coins; green phones accept only phone cards; and red phones accept coins, phone cards, and major credit cards. All calls, including international direct dial calls, usually require at least 5kr. Buying a phone card (*telekort;* 40kr, 90kr, or 140kr at Narvesen Kiosks and post offices) is more economical. Pay phones cost twice as much as calls from private lines; prices drop between 5pm and 8am. To make domestic collect calls, dial ☎117; international collect calls, ☎115. **International direct dial** numbers include: **AT&T,** ☎800 190 11; **British Telecom,** ☎800 190 44; **Canada Direct,** ☎800 191 11; **Ireland Direct,** ☎800 193 53; **MCI,** ☎800 199 12; **Sprint,** ☎800 198 77; **Telecom New Zealand,** ☎800 140 58; **Telkom South Africa Direct,** ☎800 199 27; **Telstra Australia,** ☎800 199 61. **MAIL.** Mailing a postcard or letter within Norway costs 5.50kr; to Sweden or Finland 7kr; within Europe 9kr; to regions outside Europe 10kr.

INTERNET ACCESS. There are a good number of Internet cafes in Oslo and Bergen. Smaller cities might have one or two Internet cafes, but most have a public library open on weekdays that offers free Internet access in 15-30min. time slots.

LANGUAGE. Norwegian is fairly similar to the Nordic languages of Swedish and Icelandic. Sami is spoken by the indigenous people of northern Norway. Most Norwegians speak flawless English. For Norwegian phrases, see p. 1062.

ACCOMMODATIONS AND CAMPING

NORWAY	❶	❷	❸	❹	❺
ACCOMMODATIONS	under 200kr	200-350kr	350-500kr	500-650kr	over 650kr

HI youth hostels (*vandrerhjem*) are run by **Norske Vandrerhjem,** Dronninggensgt. 26, in Oslo (☎23 13 93 00; fax 23 13 93 50). Beds run 85-180kr; another 40-60kr usually covers breakfast. Sheets typically cost 40-60kr per stay. Usually only rural or smaller hostels have curfews, and only a few are open year-round. Most open in mid- to late June and close after the third week in August. Most tourist offices book **private rooms** and last-minute hotel rooms for a fee (25-35kr).

Norwegian law allows free **camping** anywhere on public land for up to two nights, provided that you keep 150m from all buildings and fences and leave no trace behind. **Den Norske Turistforening (DNT;** Norwegian Mountain Touring Association) sells excellent maps (60-70kr), offers guided hiking trips, and maintains about 350 **mountain huts** (*hytter*) throughout the country. (☎22 82 28 00; www.turistforeningen.no. Membership cards available at DNT offices, huts, and tourist offices; 365kr, under 25 175kr. 65-170kr per night; nonmembers add 50kr.) Staffed huts, open around Easter and from late June to early September, serve meals. Unstaffed huts are open from late February until mid-October; if you're a member, you can pick up entrance keys (100kr deposit) from DNT and tourist offices. Official campgrounds charge about 110-125kr for one or two people in a tent. Some also have cabins (450-800kr). Hot showers almost always cost extra.

FOOD AND DRINK

NORWAY	❶	❷	❸	❹	❺
FOOD	under 60kr	60-135kr	136-200kr	200-300kr	over 300kr

Eating in Norway is pricey; markets and bakeries are the way to go. The supermarket chains Rema 1000 and Rimi generally have the best prices (usually open M-F 9am-8pm, Sa 9am-6pm). You can also join Norwegians at outdoor markets for cheap seafood and fruit. Many restaurants have inexpensive *dagens ret* (dish of the day; full meal 70-80kr); otherwise, you'll rarely spend less than 100kr. Taking meals at cafes (45-85kr) can also save you money without compromising quality; all-you-can-eat buffets and self-service *kafeterias* are other inexpensive options. Fish in Norway—cod, salmon, and herring—is fresh and relatively inexpensive. National specialties include *ost* (cheese); *kjøttkaker* (pork and veal meatballs) with boiled potatoes; and, for more adventurous carnivores, reindeer, ptarmigan (a type of bird), and *hval* (whale meat). Around Christmas, you can also delight in a special meal of *lutefisk* (dried fish soaked in water). Norway grows divine berries. Beer is very expensive (45-60kr for 0.5L in a bar). Beer is cheapest in supermarkets, and alcohol is almost exclusively available in bars and government-run liquor stores. You must be 18 to buy beer, 20 to buy wine and alcohol.

HOLIDAYS AND FESTIVALS

Holidays: New Year's Day (Jan. 1); Easter Sunday and Monday (Apr. 20-21); May Day (May 1); National Independence Day (May 17); Ascension Day (May 29); Christmas Eve and Day (Dec. 24-25); Boxing Day (Dec. 26); New Year's Eve (Dec. 31).

Festivals: The **Bergen Festival** in May offers world-class performances in music, dance, and theater. The **Norwegian Wood** rock festival (www.norwegianwood.no) in early June in Oslo features big-name rock bands, while Kristiansand's week-long **Quart** music festival (www.quart.no; see p. 768) in early July attracts acts from Moby to Beck to Ben Harper. **Midsummer Night** (St. Hansaften), June 23, the longest day of the year, is celebrated with bonfires and huge parties. For more information about Norway's festivals, check out the website www.norwayfestivals.com.

OSLO

The Viking capital of Oslo has grown into a comfortable city of 500,000 blond Norwegians. Its urban edge is typified by classy cafes, cool boutiques, and tight, trendy clothing, while its natural charm lies in the pine-covered hills to the north and the blue waters of the Oslofjord in the south. In winter, the short days and blue dusks may remind you of the gloomier works of natives Edvard Munch and Henrik Ibsen; come summer, though, Oslo's only drawback is its rooftop prices.

▐▀ TRANSPORTATION

Flights: The high-speed **FlyToget** train runs between **Gardermoen Airport** (GEN) and various stops in downtown Oslo (20min., every 20min. 4:15am-12:15am, 100-170kr). White **Flybussen** make the same trip (1hr.; every 15-20min.; 100kr, students 50kr, round-trip 150kr), with pickup and drop-off at bus and train stations and the Radisson SAS Scandinavia. To airport daily 4:15am-10pm; from airport daily 5:15am-midnight.

Trains: Oslo Sentralstasjon (Oslo S; ☎81 50 08 88). Trains run by **NSB** (www.nsb.no). *Minipriser* (40% discount) available M-Th and Sa to major cities if you book 5 days ahead. Trains run to: **Bergen** (6-7hr., 6-7 per day, 600kr); **Copenhagen**

(8hr.; 2 per day; 1140kr, under 26 820kr); **Stockholm** (6hr.; 4 per day; 750-900kr, under 26 579kr); **Trondheim** (6-7hr., 8-10 per day, 750kr). Mandatory reservations (40kr) for regular trains and for 2nd-class on *Signatur* Oslo-Kristiansand and Oslo-Trondheim trains; 60kr for 1st-class.

Buses: Norway Bussekspress, Schweigårdsgt. 8 (☎815 44 444). Follow the signs from the train station through the Oslo Galleri Mall to the Bussterminalen Galleriet. Schedules at the terminal's info office. Students usually receive a 25% discount.

Ferries: Color Line (☎22 94 44 00; fax 22 83 07 76). To **Hirtshals, Denmark** (12hr., 7:30pm, from 580kr) and **Kiel, Germany** (20hr., 1:30pm, from 1430kr). 50% student discount mid-Aug. to mid-June. **DFDS Seaways** (☎22 41 90 90; fax 22 41 38 38) goes to **Helsingborg, Sweden** (14hr.) and **Copenhagen, Denmark** (16hr.) daily at 5pm (from 750kr). Color Line departs 20min. west of train station, DFDS from 10min. south.

Public Transportation: Trafikanten (☎177), in front of train station. Tourist office also has comprehensive schedules. Bus, tram, subway, and ferry 22kr per ride; 750kr fine for traveling without valid ticket. **Dagskort** (day pass) 50kr; **Flexicard** (8 trips) 135kr; **7-day Card** 160kr. The **Oslo Card** (see Tourist Office, below) grants unlimited public transport. Late-night service midnight-5am, 44kr.

Bikes: For information on cycling, contact **Syklistenes Landsforening** (☎22 41 50 80). They have maps and can suggest routes. Also, see www.bike-norway.com.

Hitchhiking: Those heading south (E-18 to **Kristiansand** and **Stavanger**) take bus #31 or 32 to Maritim. Hitchers to **Bergen** take bus #161 to the last stop; to **Trondheim,** Metro #5 or bus #32 or 321 to Grorud; to **Sweden,** local train (dir.: Ski) to Nordstrand or bus #81, 83, or 85 to Bekkelaget. *Let's Go* does not recommend hitchhiking.

■★🔒 ORIENTATION AND PRACTICAL INFORMATION

At Oslo's center is the **Nationaltheatret,** which lies just beside **Oslo University** and the **Royal Palace.** The city's main street, **Karl Johans gate,** runs through the heart of town to **Oslo Sentralstasjon ("Oslo S")** at the eastern end. Don't be confused by reading "gate," the Norwegian word for "street." The harbor is south of the city, the peninsula **Bygdøy** farther southwest. Parks are scattered throughout Oslo, especially north of the Nationaltheatret. An excellent network of public trams, buses, and subways makes transportation through the outskirts quick and simple.

Tourist Offices: Main Tourist Office, Brynjulf Bullsplass 1 (☎23 11 78 80; www.oslo-pro.no), in a yellow building on the corner between City Hall and the harbor. Sells the **Oslo Card,** which covers public transit and admission to nearly all sights (1-day 180kr; 2-day 270kr; 3-day 360kr), and books hotels and private rooms (☎23 10 62 62; 35kr fee). Open daily June-Aug. 9am-7pm; Sept. and Apr.-May M-Sa 9am-5pm; Oct.-Mar. M-F 9am-4pm. Branch at **Oslo S** open May-Aug. daily 8am-11pm; Sept. M-Sa 8am-11pm; Oct.-Apr. M-Sa 8am-5pm. ◪**Use It,** Møllergata 3 (☎22 41 51 32; unginfo.oslo.no/useit) is an info center for backpackers. They book accommodations for free, help plan travel elsewhere in Norway, and put out the invaluable **Streetwise Budget Guide to Oslo.** Go up Karl Johans gt. from Oslo S and turn right onto Møllergata; it's on the left. Open July-Aug. M-F 9am-6pm; Sept.-June M-F 11am-5pm, Th until 6pm.

Budget Travel: STA Travel, Karl Johans gt. 8 (☎81 55 99 05; www.statravel.no), a few blocks up from Oslo S. Books student airfares. Open M-F 10am-5pm, Sa 11am-3pm.

Embassies: Australia (consulate), Jermbanetorget 2 (☎22 47 91 70; fax 22 42 26 83). Open M-F 9am-noon and 2-4pm. **Canada,** Wergelandsveien 7 (☎22 99 53 00; www.canada.no). Open M-F 8:30am-4:45pm. **Ireland,** P.O. Box 5683, Briskeby, N-0209 (☎22 36 11 57; fax 22 12 20 71). **South Africa,** Drammensveien 88c (☎23 27 32 20; fax 22 44

Oslo

▲ ACCOMMODATIONS
Albertine Hostel, **6**
Cochs Pensjonat, **3**
Ekeberg Camping, **14**
Ellingsens Pensjonant, **2**
MS Inrvik, **15**
Oslo Vandrerhjem
Haraldsheim (HI), **5**
Perminalen, **13**

⬤ FOOD
Kaffistova, **9**
Lofotstua, **1**
Sult, **4**
Vegeta Vertshus, **7**

🎵 NIGHTLIFE
Living Room, **12**
Mono, **11**
So What!, **10**
Studenten, **8**

NORWAY

39 75). Open M-F 8am-12:30pm and 1-4pm. **UK,** Thomas Heftyes gt. 8 (☎23 13 27 00; www.britain.no). Open M-F 8:30am-4pm. **US,** Drammensveien 18 (☎22 44 85 50; www.usembassy.no). Open M-F 8:30am-5pm. Hours may be shortened in summer.

Currency Exchange: Available at AmEx office, the main post office, and the banks along Karl Johans gt. On weekends, try hotels along Karl Johans gt. or the branch of K Bank in the Oslo S train station. Open M-F 7am-7pm, Sa-Su 8am-5pm.

American Express: Fridtjof Nansens plass 6 (☎22 98 37 35), across from City Hall. Open M-F 9am-4:30pm, Sa 10am-3pm; July to late Aug. also Su 11am-3pm.

Luggage Storage: Lockers at the train station. 7-day max. From 20kr per 24hr. Office open M-F 9am-3pm. Some hostels offer luggage storage; bags can be left in the Use It office (see Tourist Offices) for an afternoon or night.

Laundromat: Look for the word *Myntvaskeri.* **Selvbetjent Vask,** Ullevålsveien 15. Wash 30-60kr; dry 30kr. Open daily 8am-8pm. *The Streetwise Budget Guide* lists others.

Gay and Lesbian Services: The **Landsforeningen for Lesbisk og Homofil fri gjøring (LLH),** St. Olavs plass 2 (☎23 32 73 73; fax 22 11 47 45). Open M-F 9am-4pm. Sells *Blikk* (50kr), a monthly newspaper with attractions and nightlife listings.

Emergency: Police: ☎112. **Ambulance:** ☎113. **Fire:** ☎110.

Pharmacy: Jernbanetorvets Apotek (☎22 41 24 82), opposite the train station, is Oslo's only 24hr. pharmacy.

24hr. Medical Assistance: Oslo Kommunale Legevakt, Storgata 40 (☎22 11 80 80).

Internet Access: Free terminals in **Oslo S** and **Use It,** as well as public libraries. **Deichmanske Library,** Henrik Ibsensgt. 1. Sign up for free 15min. slots. Open June-Aug. M-F 10am-6pm, Sa 9am-2pm; Sept.-May M-F 10am-8pm, Sa 9am-3pm. The most conveniently located is **Studenten,** corner of Karl Johans gt. and Universitetsgata. 20kr per 15min., 30kr per 30min., 55kr per hr. Open Tu-Sa noon-8pm, Su-M noon-10pm.

Post Office: Main post office at Dronningens gt. 15 (☎23 14 78 02); enter at Prinsens gt. Address mail to be held: Firstname SURNAME, *Poste Restante,* Dronningens Gate 15, N-0101 Oslo 1, NORWAY. Open M-F 9am-5pm. Other branches near the city center.

▛ ACCOMMODATIONS

Hostels in Oslo fill up quickly in the summer—make reservations, especially if traveling in a group. The **private rooms** arranged by **Use It** (see above), Møllergata 3, are a good deal (from 125kr). **Pensions** *(pensjonater)* are usually cheaper and more central than the city's hostels. Check with the tourist office for last-minute deals on accommodations. You can **camp** for free in the forest north of town as long as you avoid public areas; try the end of the Sognsvann line. Fires are not allowed.

Albertine Hostel, Storgata 55 (☎22 99 72 00; www.albertine.no). Take Karl Johans gt. away from the train station, around the cathedral, and up Storgata. Or, take tram #11, 12, 15, or 17 to Hausmanns gt.; it's 100m up Storgata on the left, behind the Anker Hotel. 15min. walk to city center. Breakfast 55kr. Sheets 40kr. Laundry 100kr. Internet 30kr per 30min. Reception 24hr. Open June-Aug. Dorms 135-155kr; doubles 370kr. ❶

Perminalen, Øvre Slottsgt. 2 (☎23 09 30 81; perminalen@statenskantiner.no). From Oslo S, head up Karl Johans gt. and turn left onto Øvre Slottsgt. Clean and convenient. Less than 5min. from the heart of Oslo. Breakfast included. Internet 15kr per 15min. Reception 24hr. Dorms 275kr; singles 495kr; doubles 650kr. ❷

Ellingsens Pensjonat, Holtegata 25 (☎22 60 03 59; fax 22 60 99 21). Take tram #19 to Briskeby. From the intersection of Holtegata and Uranienborgveien, walk away from the church; it's an unmarked off-white house on the right. Popular with backpackers due to its central location, pleasant surroundings, and friendly management. Reception M-F 7:30am-10:30pm, Sa-Su 8am-10:30pm. Singles 300kr, with bath 430kr; doubles 490kr/570kr. ❷

Cochs Pensjonat, Parkveien 25 (☎23 33 24 00; fax 23 33 24 10), at Hegdehaugs-veien. From the train station, walk 25min. along Karl Johans gt. through Slottsparken; or, take tram #11 or 19 to the end of the park. Quiet rooms on the upper floors of a building next to the royal park. Reception on 3rd fl. Singles 350kr, with bath 500kr; doubles 500kr/650kr; triples 615kr/735kr; quads 860kr/1010kr. ❸

Oslo Vandrerhjem Haraldsheim (HI), Haraldsheimveien 4 (☎22 15 50 43; www.harald-sheim.oslo.no). Flybus or tram #15 or 17 to Sinsenkrysset. Follow the dirt path across the field and up hill; it's on the far right side of the field. Breakfast included. Internet 10kr per 15min. Reception 24hr. No singles or doubles in summer. Dorms 170kr, with bath 155kr; singles 290kr; doubles 425kr/505kr. Nonmembers add 25kr. ❶

MS Innvik, Langkaia 49 (☎22 41 95 00; www.msinnvik.no), a botel just south of Oslo S. Cross the large white overpass and head right along the harbor. Small but well-kept rooms. Live music on Sa in summer. Breakfast included. Free laundry. Reception 24hr. Singles 300kr; doubles 600kr. Extra bed 200kr. ❷

Ekeberg Camping, Ekebergveien 65 (☎22 19 85 68), 3km from town. Take bus 34B from the Oslo S (10min.). Cooking facilities, grocery store (open daily 8am-9pm), and laundry. Free showers. Reception daily 7:30am-11pm. Open May 25-Aug. 2 people with tent 130kr, with car 170kr. Extra person 40kr. 20kr Interrail or Scanrail discount. ❶

◘ FOOD

Visitors should have no problem finding authentic Norwegian meals or dishes from any part of the globe, but they may have trouble affording them. **Grocery stores** may be the best option; look for **Rema 1000** or **Kiwi,** two chains that dot the city. **Lunch buffets,** offered by most restaurants in the city center, are the cheapest way to eat out; lower-budget fast food is common in the **Grønland** district east of the train station and near **Oslo S.**

Kaffistova, at the intersection of Rosenkrantz gt. and Kristian IV gt. Beautiful, quiet cafe-teria-style eatery with traditional Norwegian meat, fish, porridges, and desserts. Vege-tarian options. Entrees 70-120kr. Open M-F 9:30am-8pm, Sa-Su 10:30am-5pm. ❷

Lofotstua, Kirkeveien 40. Oslo's best bargain fish restaurant. The only place in town serving whale and seal. Entrees from 75kr. Open M-F 3-10pm. ❷

Vegeta Vertshus, Munkedamsveien 3b, off Stortings gt. near the National Theater. Cafe-teria-style vegetarian buffet and salad bar. Full buffet 135kr; single serving 85-95kr. Open daily noon-10pm; buffet closes at 9pm. ❷

Sult, Thorvald Meyersgt. 26, in trendy Grüner Løkka. Artfully presented food; speedy ser-vice. Dinner 100-170kr, appetizers 70kr. Beer 42kr. Outdoor seating. Open Tu-F 2pm-12:30am, Sa-Su 1pm-12:30am. Kitchen closes 10pm. Closed July 1-Aug. 5. ❸

◎ SIGHTS

Exploring Oslo's museums, castles, and halls can be both tiring and expensive; any sightseeing itinerary should mix in time enjoying Oslo's greatest resources—its free parks and tree-lined streets. Small parks dot the city, and even central areas like the grounds of Akershus Fortress can be great for an afternoon picnic.

VIGELANDSPARKEN. Inside the larger **Frognerparken,** the 80-acre **Vigeland-sparken** is home to over 200 of Gustav Vigeland's creative sculptures depicting each stage of the human life cycle. More than one million visitors come annually, making the park Norway's most visited attraction. Highlights include a towering monolith created using a single piece of granite. *(Entrance on Kirkeveien. Take bus #20 or tram #12 or 15 to Vigelandsparken. Open 24hr. Free.)*

EDVARD MUNCH. The **Munch Museum** (Munch-museet) displays rotating exhibits of over 20,000 paintings, prints, drawings, and watercolors that Munch bequeathed to the city of Oslo before his death in 1944. *(Tøyengata 53. Take bus #20 to Munch-museet or the subway to Tøyen, or walk 10min. northeast from the train station. Open June to mid-Sept. daily 10am-6pm; mid-Sept. to May M-F 10am-4pm, Sa-Su 11am-5pm. 60kr; students 30kr; free with Oslo Card.)* The **National Art Museum** (Nasjonalgalleriet) houses a large collection of Scandinavian artwork and also has several rooms dedicated to the works of Impressionists. *(Universitetsgata 13. Open M, W, and F 10am-6pm, Th 10am-8pm, Sa 10am-4pm, Su 11am-4pm. Free.)* Next door at **Oslo University,** several gigantic murals by Munch grace the walls of a concert hall. *(Enter through the door by the columns off Karl Johans gt. Open mid-June to mid-Aug. M-F 10am-2:45pm. Free.)*

AKERSHUS CASTLE AND FORTRESS. Built in 1299, this waterfront complex was transformed into a Renaissance palace by Christian IV between 1637 and 1648. Explore dungeons, underground passages, and vast halls. *(Take bus #60 to Bankplassen or tram #10 or 15 to Christiania torv. Fortress complex open daily 6am-9pm. Free. Castle open May to mid-Sept. M-Sa 10am-4pm, Su 12:30-4pm. 30kr; students, seniors, children 10kr; free with Oslo Card. Tours of the castle M-Sa 11am, 1, 3pm; Su 1 and 3pm.)* The castle grounds also house the powerful **Hjemmefrontmuseet** (Resistance Museum), which documents Norway's efforts to subvert Nazi occupation. *(Open mid-June to Aug. M, W, and F 10am-5pm, Tu and Th 10am-6pm, Sa 10am-5pm, Su 11am-5pm; Sept. to mid-June closes 1-2hr. earlier. 25kr; students, seniors, and children 10kr; free with Oslo Card.)*

BYGDØY. The peninsula of Bygdøy is right across the inlet from downtown Oslo; although mainly residential, it boasts some of the city's best museums and a few beaches. *(All museums free with Oslo Card.)* In summer, a public ferry leaves from pier 3 in front of City Hall for Bygdøy. *(10min.; late-May to mid-Aug. every 20-40min. M-F 7:45am-9pm, Sa-Su 9am-9pm; 22kr, seniors and children 11kr. Ferry information ☎ 177. Or, take bus #30 from the National Theater or Oslo S to Folkemuseet or Bygdøynes.)* Uphill from the ferry port are the **Norsk Folkmuseum,** one of Europe's largest open-air museums, and the **Viking Ship Museum,** which showcases three wooden vessels promoted as the best-preserved of their kind. *(Walk up the hill leading away from the dock and follow signs to the right (10min.), or take bus #30 to Folkemuseet or Vikingskipshuset. Folkmuseum: Open mid-May to mid-Sept. daily 10am-6pm; mid-Sept. to mid-May M-F 11am-3pm, Sa-Su 11am-4pm. 70kr, students and seniors 50kr. Viking Ship: Open May-Sept. daily 9am-6pm; Oct.-Apr. 11am-4pm. 40kr, students and children 20kr.)* Additional oceanographically important artifacts can be found at the **Fram Museum,** home to the enormous polar ship "Fram," and the **Kon-Tiki Museum,** which details Norwegian Thor Heyerdahl's daring 1947 ocean crossing from South America to Polynesia. *(10min. walk toward Bygdøynes, or bus #30b. Fram: Open mid-June to Aug. daily 9am-7pm; Sept. to early June reduced hours. 30kr, students and children 15kr. Kon-Tiki: June-Aug. daily 9:30am-5:45pm; Apr.-May and Sept. 10:30am-5pm; Oct.-Mar. 10:30am-4pm. 30kr, students 20kr.)* On the southwestern side of Bygdøy, there are two popular beaches, **Huk** and **Paradisbukta.** Huk appeals to a younger crowd, while Paradisbukta is more family-oriented. The stretch of shore between them is a nude beach. *(Take bus #30 or walk south for 25min. from the Bygdøynes ferry stop.)*

OTHER SIGHTS. The annual Nobel Peace Prize ceremony takes place each December 10 in the huge main ballroom of **Rådhus** (city hall). Upstairs there are several exhibits, including an evocative Per Krohg mural that covers every inch of wall and ceiling in a long, narrow room. *(South of the National Theater and Karl Johans gt. on Fridtjof Nansens plass, near the harbor. Open daily 9am-5pm. 25kr; students, seniors, and children 15kr; free with Oslo Card. Tours daily 10am, noon, and 2pm.)* The **Royal Palace,** on a hill at the western end of Karl Johans gt., is open to the public via guided tours, but tickets sell out well in advance. *(Open late-June to mid-Aug. Tours in English daily 2pm. Purchase tickets at any post office. 65kr.)* You can watch the changing of the guard daily at

1:30pm in front of the palace. *(Tram #12, 15, or 19, or bus #30-32 or 45 to Slottsparken. Free.)* For a great panorama of the Oslofjord and the city, head to the mighty ski jump Holmenkollen at the world's oldest **Ski Museum**. A simulator recreates the adrenaline rush of a leap off a ski jump and a 4min., 130kpm downhill ski run. *(Take subway #1 on the Frognerseteren line to Holmenkollen. It's a 10min. walk uphill from the subway stop. Open June-Aug. daily 9am-8pm; May and Sept. 10am-5pm; Oct.-Apr. 10am-4pm. Museum 70kr, students 40kr, children 35kr; free with Oslo Card. Simulator 45kr.)*

🎭 🎷 ENTERTAINMENT AND NIGHTLIFE

The monthly *What's On in Oslo* (free at tourist offices), chronicles the current opera, symphony, and theater. **Filmenshus**, Dronningens gt. 16 (☎ 22 47 45 00), is the center of Oslo's indie film scene. In addition to the countless bars along **Karl Johans gate** and in the **Aker Brygge** harbor complex, Oslo boasts a number of nightclubs and cafes featuring DJs and live music.

Mono, Pløens gt. 4, is the core of the live music scene, while **So What!**, Grensen 9, delivers a heavier vibe to a younger crowd. (Beer 40kr. 2-3 concerts per week. Cover 60-150kr. Open daily 2pm-3am. Dance floor opens daily 10pm, 9pm for concerts.) Both are a 5min. walk from Karl Johans gt. Top-40 hits attract backpackers to the bar and dance floor of **Studenten**, on the corner of Karl Johans gt. and Universitetsgata. (Beer 50kr. 50kr cover F-Sa after 9:30pm. Open M-Sa 11am-3am, Su noon-3am.) **Living Room**, Olav V's gt. 1, stays busy seven days a week. (Beer 50kr. Open daily 10pm-3:30am. 24+.)

🧭 DAYTRIPS FROM OSLO

The nearby islands of inner **Oslofjord** offer cheap, delightful daytrips. The ruins of a **Cistercian Abbey** lie on the landscaped island of **Hovedøya**, while **Langøyene** has Oslo's best **beach**. Take bus #60 (22kr) from the City Hall to **Vippetangen** to catch a ferry to either island. About an hour from Oslo by ferry, **Drøbak** has traditional wooden houses. The **ferry** (☎ 22 08 40 00 or 177) to Drøbak leaves from in front of the Rådhus. Ask the tourist office about cross-country ski rental. **The Wilderness House** *(Villmarkshuset)*, Christian Krohgs gt. 16 (☎ 22 05 05 22), rents canoes and kayaks on the Akerselva river.

LILLEHAMMER

Lillehammer, a small city set in a valley at the edge of a lake, retains an unmistakable air of former glory from its days as host of the 1994 Winter Olympics. The **Norwegian Olympic Museum** traces the history of the modern Olympic Games from their inception in 1896. From the train station, it's a 15-20min. walk; head two blocks uphill, turn left on Storgata, turn right on Tomtegata, go up the stairs, and follow the road uphill to the left. The museum is in the farther dome. (Open late May to mid-Aug. daily 10am-6pm; late Aug. to mid-May Tu-Su 11am-4pm. 60kr, students 50kr.) You can climb up the endless steps of an Olympic **ski jump** in sight of the museum spire (open daily mid-June to mid-Aug. 9am-8pm; early June and late Aug. 9am-5pm; Sept.-Oct. and Feb.-May 11am-4pm; 15kr) or give your spine a jolt on a **bobsled simulator** (40kr) at the bottom of the hills. Combo tickets for both of these and a round-trip chairlift ride are also available (60kr).

Trains run to Lillehammer from Oslo (2½hr., every 2hr., 257kr). From Lillehammer, you could also catch the north-bound train to Trondheim (4½hr., 6 per day, 526kr). The **tourist office**, Elvegata 19, one block uphill from Storgata, has good information on hiking and attractions and lends **bikes** for a refundable 100kr deposit. (☎ 61 25 92 99. Open mid-June to Aug. M-Sa 10am-8pm, Su 11am-6pm; Sept.-May M-F 9am-4pm, Sa 10am-2pm.) The comfy **Lillehammer Youth Hostel (HI) ❷** is on the top floor of the train station. (☎61 24 87 00. Breakfast included. Sheets 60kr. **Internet** 20kr per 15min. Reception daily 8am-10pm. Dorms 180kr; singles 450kr; doubles 460kr.) Most restaurants and fast-food kiosks are around the pedestrian section of **Storgata,** two blocks uphill from the station.

ALONG THE OSLO-BERGEN RAIL LINE

The 7hr. rail journey from Oslo to Bergen is one of the most famous scenic rides in the world. From Oslo, there are stops at Finse, Myrdal (the transfer point for the Flåm railway), and Voss, before the train finally pulls into Bergen.

■**FLÅM AND THE FLÅM RAILWAY.** The spectacular railway connecting Myrdal, a stop on the Oslo-Bergen line, to the tiny fjord town of Flåm is one of Norway's most celebrated attractions. The railway is an incredible feat of engineering, descending almost 864m in 55min. as it winds through tunnels and past rushing waterfalls. The centerpiece of the ride is the magnificent **Kjosfossen falls,** where the train stops for an incomparable view. Alternatively, a 20km **hike** (4-5hr.) on well-tended paths from Myrdal to Flåm allows for extended lingering and free camping amid the rainbow-capped waterfalls and snowy mountain vistas. Taking the train in the opposite direction, uphill to Myrdal, opens up a wonderful bike ride back to Flåm. For bike rental and more detailed info inquire at the tourist office (see below). Flåm sits at the edge of the **Aurlandsfjord,** an inlet off the Sognefjord. During the day, the tiny town is heavily touristed; when Flåm empties out in the off-season, the stunning surroundings make this a terrific place to spend a night or two.

Eight to 10 trains cover the railway in each direction daily (55min.; 125kr one-way, round-trip 205kr). The **tourist office** is in the large building beside the train station. (☎57 63 21 06. Open June-Aug. daily 8:30am-8pm; May and Sept. 8:45am-5pm.) The rest of the year, the main tourist office in Aurland handles all Flåm questions. (Open M-F 8am-4pm. **Bikes** 30kr per hr., 175kr per day.) From Flåm, there are daily express boats to Aurland, Balestrand, and Bergen, and ferries to Gudvangen (inquire at the tourist office for up-to-date schedules).

NORWAY IN A NUTSHELL. The immensely popular "Norway in a Nutshell" tour combines a ride along the stunning rail line between **Myrdal** and **Flåm** (55min.; 8-10 per day; 125kr, round-trip 205kr), a cruise through the narrowest branches of the **Sognefjord** between Gudvangen and Flåm (2hr.; 1-4 per day; 170kr, round-trip 210kr; 50% student and Interrail discount), and a twisting bus ride over the mountains from **Gudvangen** to **Voss** (1¼hr., 8-10 per day, 70kr).

The tour is unguided and extremely flexible, allowing "nutshellers" to complete the trip in one day or take stopovers at transfer points. The three-part excursion can be done as a round-trip from Oslo or Bergen or as a side-trip while going from one city to the other. Each version starts with a train to Myrdal and continues to Flåm, Gudvangen, and possibly Voss. At the end, you have the choice of returning to Oslo or Bergen, or further exploring the heart of the country. **Tickets** can be bought separately for each leg of the journey while traveling, or purchased in advance as a package from tourist offices or train stations in Oslo and Bergen. The cheapest route is a round-trip loop from Bergen; round-trip from Oslo is the most expensive (630-1440kr). Railpass holders and students may be able to get a better deal by purchasing individual tickets along the way.

FINSE. Outdoor enthusiasts hop off at Finse and hike north for several days down the Aurlandsdal Valley to **Aurland,** 10km from Flåm. Be sure to ask about trail conditions at the Finse rail station or the DNT in Oslo or Bergen before you set off. You can sleep in DNT *hytte*, all spaced a day's walk apart along the trail to Aurland. For maps, prices, and reservations, inquire at **DNT** in Oslo (☎22 82 28 22) or Bergen (☎55 32 22 30).

VOSS. Stretched along a glassy lake that reflects snow-capped mountains, Voss is an adventurer's dream. In winter, skiing is plentiful; in summer, Voss accommodates kayaking, paragliding, horseback riding, and white-water rafting. Book through **Nordic Ventures** (☎56 51 00 17; www.nordicventures.com) or the next-door **Voss Rafting Center** (☎56 51 05 25; www.bbb.no), both located behind the Park Hotel in the corner of a mini-mall. (Nordic Ventures: Open late Apr. to early Oct. daily 10am-7pm; Nov.-Mar. 10am-5:30pm; late May to late Apr. daily 10am-6pm; closed late Oct. Voss Rafting: Open May-Oct. M-F 9am-5pm, Sa 9am-7pm; Nov.-Apr. by phone only, M-F 9am-4pm.)

Trains leave for Oslo (5½-6hr., 5 per day, 550kr) and Bergen (1¼hr., 16 per day, 134-174kr). The central train station is a few minutes west of downtown. To get to the **tourist office**, Hestavangen 10, turn left as you exit the station and bear right at the fork by the church. (☎56 52 08 00. Open June-Aug. M-Sa 9am-7pm, Su 2-7pm; Sept.-May M-F 9am-4pm.) Turn right as you exit the station and walk along the lakeside road to reach Voss's modern, well-equipped **HI youth hostel ❷**, home to a sauna and a terrific view. (☎56 51 20 17. Canoe, rowboat, bike, and kayak rental. Reception 24hr. Dorms 200kr; nonmembers 220kr.) Those set on camping should head left from the station, stick to the lake shore, and turn right onto the gravel path at the church. **Voss Camping ❶** is at the end. (☎56 51 15 97. Reception mid-June to mid-Aug. daily 8am-6pm. 2 people with tent 80kr; additional person 40kr; 5-person cabin 400kr.) Pick up groceries at **Kiwi** supermarket, on the main street just past the post office. (Open M-F 9am-9pm, Sa 9am-6pm.)

SOGNEFJORD

The slender fingers of Sognefjord, the longest and deepest fjord in Europe, reach all the way to the foot of the Jotunheimen Mountains in central Norway. Sognefjord is a short, stunning ride north of the rail line running west from Oslo, or a quick boat trip from Bergen. **Fylkesbaatane** (☎55 90 70 70) sends boats on day-trips to towns on the Sognefjord and back to Bergen, and offers day tours of the Sognefjord and the Flåm valley. The boats depart from Strandkaiterminalen; buy tickets there or at Bergen's tourist office. Transportation on the northern coast of the Sognefjord and up to the Geirangerfjord can be confusing and frustrating due to the limited number of bus routes, especially on weekends; plan ahead and consult tourist offices for help in navigating the area.

SOGNDAL (NIGARDSBREEN). Sogndal is a cozy town on the northern coast of Sognefjord that serves as a useful base for trips deeper into the fjord. In particular, it offers access to glacier-walking routes on the icy expanse of the nearby Nigardsbreen arm of Jostedalsbreen. **Jostedalen Breførarlag** (☎57 68 32 50) runs everything from 1hr. outings to full-day jaunts (140-600kr). **Buses** leave Sogndal for the glacier every day at 8:25am, returning at 5pm (100kr).

Fylkesbaatane **express boats** run to: Bergen (4½hr., daily 7am, 7430kr) via Balestrand (1hr., 110kr); and Flåm (2hr., 1 per day, 82kr). Get ticket information at the tourist office and harbor; students receive a 50% discount. Norway Bussekspress **buses** leave for Fjaerland (30min.; M-F 7-8 per day, Sa-Su 3-4 per day; 54kr) and Førde (2hr., 8 per day, 150kr), where they connect with all major bus routes (25% student discount, 50% with railpass). The **tourist office** is in the Sogndal Kulturhus at the corner of Gravensteingata and Hovevegen. (☎57 67 30 83. Open June to mid-

YOUR OWN WAY

JOTUNHEIMEN NATIONAL PARK

In Norse mythology, Jotunheimen was ruled over by the king of frost giants; the physical truth is not far from the legend. In addition to Galdøpiggen, northern Europe's highest peak (2469m), Jotunheimen's glacier-topped mountains spread far beyond the horizon, encircling majestic lakes and natural expanses inhabited only by wild animals and the occasional solitary hermit.

LOM. The tiny town of Lom serves as the information center of Jotunheimen; its **tourist office** (☎61 21 29 90) sells trail maps (45kr) and can help choose hikes appropriate to any skill level. Lom's well-preserved wooden **stave church** is an unexpected must-see sight; its markets and prehistoric museums help push it beyond the lifeless ranks of the average tourist base.

HIKING. The most beloved hike suited to in-and-out daytrippers is the 6hr. **Memurubu-Gjendesheim** trail made famous in native writer Henrik Ibsen's *Peer Gynt*. More challenging hikes can be tackled farther west, in the harsh peaks of the **Hurrungane.**

TRANSPORTATION. Jotunheimen lies in the heart of Norway, just northeast of Sognefjord. Lom can be reached by **bus** from: Oslo (7hr.; 2-3 per day; 460kr, students 345kr); Sogndal (3½hr., 2 per day, 195kr); and Stryn (2hr.; 2 per day; 170kr, students 130kr).

Sept. M-F 9-8pm, Sa 9am-4pm, Su 3pm-8pm.) The Sogndal library, also in the Kulturhus, provides free **Internet access.** (Up to 30min. Open late June to mid-Aug. M-F 10am-3pm, Th until 6pm; late Aug. to mid-June Tu-W and F 10am-4pm, M and Th 1pm-7pm, Sa 10am-2pm.) The Sogndal **youth hostel (HI)** ❶ has clean rooms and a fjord-side spot east of the town center. From the bus station, turn left on Dalavegen, then left on Gravensteinsgata; go past the roundabout until it becomes Helgheimsvegen, then follow the signs (10-13min). (☎57 67 20 33. Kitchen. Open mid-June to mid-Aug. Dorms 100kr; singles 165kr; doubles 230kr. Nonmembers add 25kr.) The best **campground** ❶ in the area is about 1½hr. outside of town at Nigardsbreen. (☎57 68 31 35. 90kr for 2-3 people with tent; 4-person cabin 285kr.)

BALESTRAND. Balestrand is a beautifully situated town on the north side of the Sognefjord, quieter than Sogndal and an equally ideal base for the fjord. The **Sognefjord Akvarium** gives a view of the rarely seen marine life of the fjords, displaying numerous Norwegian species. (In front of the ferry docks. English guidebooks available. Open July to mid-Aug. daily 9am-10pm; May-June and late Aug. to early Nov. 9:30am-6pm. 60kr.) **Hiking** in the area immediately around Balestrand is also excellent. On a clear day, the 972m peak **Raudmelen** towers over an expansive 360° panorama of the landscape surrounding Balestrand. For trail maps and other information, stop by the **tourist office** near the quay. (☎57 69 12 55. Open late June to Aug. M-F 7:30am-1pm and 3:30-9pm, Sa-Su until 6:30pm; Sept. to late June M-Sa 7:30am-1pm and 3:30-6pm, Su 8am-12:30pm and 3:30-5:30pm. **Internet** 20kr per 15min.) **Express boats** connect Bergen and Balestrand (4hr., 2 per day, 355kr; 50% student and railpass discount). The **Kringsjå Hotel and Youth Hostel (HI)** ❶ is 100m up the hill behind town. (☎57 69 13 03. Breakfast included. Kitchen. Laundry 15kr. Open mid-June to mid-Aug. Dorms 180kr; doubles 520kr. Nonmembers add 20kr per person.) **Sjøtun Camping** ❶, 1km past the brown church on the coastal road, has tent sites and huts. (☎57 69 12 23. Open June-Sept. 20kr per person; 40kr per tent; cabins 220-300kr.)

◪ DAYTRIP FROM SOGNEFJORD: FJÆRLAND AND FJÆRLANDSFJORD. With Balestrand perched at its mouth, Fjærlandsfjord branches off from Sognefjord in a thin northward line to the tiny town of **Fjærland,** resting beneath the looming Jostedalsbreen at the end of the fjord. The town is known throughout Norway for its 13 multilingual book stores as well as its annual book celebration on the Saturday closest to Midsummer. The ▨**Glacier Museum** (Norsk Bremuseum), 3km outside town, is Fjærland's other point of interest and screens a beautiful panoramic film about Jostedalsbreen and the surrounding national park. (Open daily June-Aug. 9am-7pm; Apr.-May and Sept.-Oct. 10am-4pm. 75kr, students 35kr.)

Ferries run between Balestrand and Fjærland (1¼hr., 2 per day, 140kr; 50% student and railpass discount). **Buses** line up with boat arrivals to shuttle passengers to the Glacier Museum and, after a stopover, whisk them to view two offshoots of Jostedalsbreen, then return them to Fjærland's harbor to catch the boat back to Balestrand. Tickets (90-115kr) can be purchased on the boat or at the Balestrand tourist office. Travelers just passing through Fjaerland should take the bus to the Glacier Museum (20kr) to connect to: Ålesund (6hr., 4-5 per day, 358kr); Førde (1¼hr., 7 per day, 105kr); Sogndal (30min., 6-7 per day, 81kr); or Stryn (2½hr., 3-4 per day, 155kr). All routes offer a 25% student discount. Ask bus drivers for assistance in navigating bus connections. The **tourist office** helps solve transportation woes and provides hiking maps. (☎ 57 69 32 33. Open daily 9:30am-5:30pm.)

THE FJORDS AND WEST COUNTRY

Spectacular views and long summer days make fjord country irresistible to all types of travelers. Buses and ferries wind through this unique coastal region; although transportation can be complicated, the scenery through the window is half the fun. Call ☎**177** for regional transportation information; tourist offices, boat terminals, and bus stations can also help plan routes through the fjords. Plan your route ahead of time, as lines and times vary from day to day. **Bergen** is the major port for boats serving the region; **HSD express boats** (☎55 23 87 80; ticket office at Strandkaiterminalen) run to Hardangerfjord, Stavanger, and points south of the city, while **Fylkesbaatane** (☎55 90 70 71; tickets also at Strandkaiterminalen) takes care of boats north into the Sognefjord and surrounding areas. Almost all fjord towns connect via **bus** to Bergen (see p. 759) or Sogndal (see p. 757).

BERGEN

Situated between steep, forested mountains and the waters of the Puddefjorden, Bergen bills itself as the "Gateway to the Fjords." Despite being Norway's second-largest metropolis, the city has a compact downtown and a host of attractions which are easily accessible on foot. Many prefer Bergen's friendly west-coast feel to that of Oslo and the east.

▗ TRANSPORTATION

Trains: ☎81 50 08 88. The station is a 7-10min. walk south of the harbor. Daily to: **Myrdal** (2½hr., 5-8 per day, 197-237kr); **Oslo** (6½hr.; 4-5 per day; 633kr, 356kr if booked 5 days in advance); and **Voss** (1¼hr., 15 per day, 134kr).

Buses: Busstasjon, Strømgaten 8. Look for the "Bergen Storsenter" sign (☎ 177, outside Bergen ☎55 55 90 70). Serves: **Ålesund** (10hr., 1-2 per day, 544kr); **Oslo** (11hr., daily, 620kr); and **Trondheim** (14hr., daily, 785kr). 25% student discount and 50% Interrail and Scanrail discount. Buy tickets on board. An **info center** is to the left of the bus terminal entrance. Open M-F 7am-6pm, Sa 7am-2pm.

Ferries: The **Hurtigruten,** or Coastal Steamer (☎81 03 00 00; www.hurtigruten.com) begins its journey up the coast from **Bergen** and stops in **Ålesund,** the **Lofoten Islands, Tromsø,** and **Trondheim,** as well as other places (Apr.-Sept. daily 8pm, 400-2965kr; Oct.-Apr. daily 10:30pm, 400-2616kr; 50% student discount). **Flaggruten** (☎51 86 87

80) boats head southward to Stavanger (4hr.; 1-2 per day; 620kr, students 360kr; 50% Interrail and Scanrail discounts, 25% Bergen Card discount). **Fjord Line**, on Skolte-grunnskaien (☎ 55 54 88 00; www.fjordline.com), sends ships to **Hanstholm, Denmark** (16hr., 3-5 per week, from 340kr) and **Newcastle, England** (25hr., 2-3 per week, from 400kr). **Smyril Line**, Slottsgaten 1, 5th fl. (☎ 55 59 65 20; fax 55 59 65 30), departs Tuesdays at 3pm for: the **Faroe Islands** (24hr., from 880kr); **Iceland** (45hr., from 1560kr.); and the **Shetland Islands** (12hr., June-Aug. only, from 620kr; 25% student discount). All international ferries, except the Hurtigruten, depart from **Skoltegrunns-kaien**, a 10-15min. walk past Bryggen along the right side of the harbor.

Public Transportation: Yellow and red buses chauffeur you around the city. 10kr in city center, 22kr outside. Free bus #100 goes from the bus station to the Galleriet shopping mall on Torgalmenningen by the harbor.

■◢ ▐ ORIENTATION AND PRACTICAL INFORMATION

Central Bergen is small enough for visitors to walk everywhere. Using the **Torget** (fish market) in front of the harbor as a basis for navigation, the city can be broken down into a few basic areas. North of the **Torget**, where the main street **Bryggen** curves around the harbor, is the touristy old city; southwest of the Torget is **Torgal-menningen**, the city's main shopping street. More authentic parts of Bergen lie down Torgalmenningen, past **Håkons gaten** and **Nygårdsgaten**. The train and bus stations are about 10min. south of the Torget.

Tourist Office: Vågsalmenningen 1 (☎ 55 55 20 00; fax 55 55 20 01), just past the Tor-get. Books private rooms (30kr fee) and has free copies of the useful *Bergen Guide*. A special section in the office helps visitors plan travel through the fjords. The **Bergen Card** grants free museum admissions and unlimited public transportation as well as various discounts (1-day 165kr, 2-day 245kr). Open June-Aug. daily 8:30am-10pm; May and Sept. daily 9am-8pm; Oct.-Apr. M-Sa 9am-4pm.

Hiking Information: DNT, Tverrgt. 4-6 (☎ 55 33 58 12), off Marken, sells detailed topo-logical maps (80kr) for all of Norway and provides comprehensive hiking information. Open M-W and F 10am-4pm, Th 10am-6pm.

Currency Exchange: At banks near the harbor (generally open M-W and F 9am-3pm, Th 9am-5:30pm) and the post office. After hours, the tourist office will change currency at a rate less favorable than the bank rate, but without commission.

Luggage storage: At train and bus stations. 20-40kr per day. Open daily 7am-10:50pm.

Budget Travel: STA Travel, Vaskerelven 32 (☎ 81 55 99 05; bergen@statravel.no), sells discounted tickets for international flights and books accommodations. Take Torgal-menningen southwest from the Torget; turn right on Vaskerelven. Open M-F 10am-5pm.

Laundry: Jarlens Vaskoteque, Lille Øvregt. 17. Wash 45kr; dry 5kr per 15min. Detergent 5kr. Open M-Tu and F 10am-6pm, W-Th 10am-8pm, Sa 10am-3pm.

Emergency: Police: ☎ 112. **Ambulance:** ☎ 113. **Fire:** ☎ 110.

Pharmacy: Apoteket Nordstjernen (☎ 55 21 83 84), on 2nd fl. of the bus station. Open M-Sa 8am-midnight, Su 9:30am-midnight.

Medical Assistance: 24-hour Accident Clinic, Vestre Strømkai 19 (☎ 55 32 11 20).

Internet Access: Bibliotek (public library), at the intersection of Stromgt. and Vestre Strømkaien. Free 15min. slots. **CyberHouse**, Vetrlidsalm. 13, between the Torget and the funicular. 20kr per 30min. Open Sa-Th 9am-midnight, F 24hr.

Post Office: Småstrandgt. (☎ 55 54 15 00). Open M-F 8am-6pm, Sa 9am-3pm. Address mail to be held: Firstname SURNAME, *Poste Restante*/P.O. Box 1372, 5811 Bergen, NORWAY. *Poste Restante* office open M-F 8am-3pm, Sa 9am-3pm.

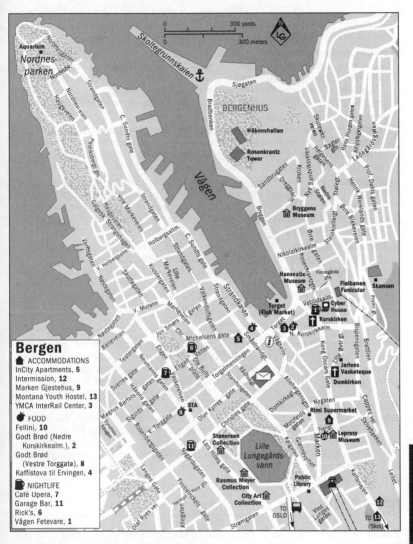

Bergen

🏠 ACCOMMODATIONS
InCity Apartments, **5**
Intermission, **12**
Marken Gjestehus, **9**
Montana Youth Hostel, **13**
YMCA InterRail Center, **3**

🍎 FOOD
Fellini, **10**
Godt Brød (Nedre
  Korskirkealm.), **2**
Godt Brød
  (Vestre Torggate), **8**
Kaffistova til Ervingen, **4**

🍷 NIGHTLIFE
Café Opera, **7**
Garage Bar, **11**
Rick's, **6**
Vågen Fetevare, **1**

🏠 ACCOMMODATIONS

In the summer, it's best to reserve ahead. The tourist office books **private rooms** for a 30kr fee (singles 200-300kr; doubles 375-600kr). You can **camp** for free on the far side of the hills above town.

    Intermission, Kalfarveien 8 (☎55 30 04 00). Head right from the train or bus station and right down Kong Oscars gt., which becomes Kalfarveien, and look for the white house on the left (5-10min.). Friendly staff and communal atmosphere. Free laundry.

Internet 15kr per 30min. Kitchen. Reception Su-Th 7-11am and 5pm-midnight, F-Sa until 1am. Lockout 11am-5pm. Curfew Su-Th midnight, F-Sa 1am. Open mid-June to mid-Aug. 100kr. **Camping** in backyard 100kr. ●

YMCA InterRail Center, Nedre Korskirkealm. 4 (☎55 31 72 52; fax 55 31 35 77). Exit the train or bus station, turn right, and head up the hill; turn left onto Kong Oscars gt. and left again at Nedre Korskirkealm. (7-10min.). Newly renovated in an ideal location. Supermarket next door. Kitchen. Reception 7am-midnight. Lockout 11am-3:30pm. Dorms 100kr; 4- to 6-person room 160kr per person. Nonmembers add 25kr. ●

Marken Gjestehus, Kong Oscars gt. 45 (☎55 31 44 04; markengjestehus@smisi.no). Entrance around corner on Tverrgt. Reception on 4th fl. Small, centrally located guesthouse. Immaculate rooms, some with nice views of the nearby mountains. Breakfast 55kr. Kitchen. Laundry 15kr. Sheets 45kr. Reception May-Sept. 9am-11pm; Oct.-Apr. 9am-7pm. Dorms 165-190kr; singles 340kr; doubles 440kr. ●

InCity Apartments, Chr. Michelsens gt. (☎55 23 16 13; www.incity.no). From the Torget, turn right onto Strandgt. and then right again onto Chr. Michelsens gt.; it'll be a few doors down on the left (3-5min.). Brand new, spacious rooms; apartments available for short- or long-term rent. All rooms have bath and cooking facilities. Laundry 20kr. Single 490kr; double 690kr; 2-person apartments 890kr. ❸

Montana Youth Hostel (HI), Johan Blyttsvei 30 (☎55 20 80 70; montvh@online.no), 5km from the city center. Take bus #31 (dir.: Lægdene; 22kr) from behind the post office to Montana (10min.). Don't miss the commanding views from the lookout point. Breakfast included. Kitchen. Sheets 55kr. Laundry 25kr. Internet 1kr per min. Reception 24hr. Lockout 10am-1pm. Dorms 130kr; 4-bed room 185kr per person; doubles 540kr, with bath 580kr. Nonmembers add 25kr per person. ●

🍴 FOOD

Bergen's culinary centerpiece is the **fish market** that springs up on the Torget; it's sometimes unclear, however, whether fish or tourists are the main haul. (Open year-round M-F 7am-4pm, Th 7am-7pm, Sa 7am-3pm.) **Godt Brød ❶**, Vestre Torggt. 6 and Nedre Korskirkealm. 12, prepares the best sandwiches in town (25-49kr). The N. Korskirkealm. location has outdoor seating. (V. Torggt. open M-F 8am-6pm, Sa 8am-4:30pm. N. Korskirkealm. open M-F 7:15am-6pm, Sa 7:15am-3:30pm.) **Fellini ❷**, Tverrgt., just off Marken, serves Italian specialties and great pizza from 59kr. (Lunch special 49kr. Open M-Th 2pm-midnight, F-Sa 2pm-3am, Su 2pm-11pm.) Enjoy Norwegian cuisine with the older set at cafeteria-style **Kaffistova til Ervingen ❷**, Strandkaien 2B, 2nd fl. (Daily special 88kr, soup 46kr. Open M-F 8am-7pm, Sa 8am-5pm, Su noon-7pm.)

👁 🏔 SIGHTS AND THE OUTDOORS

BRYGGEN AND BERGENHUS. Gazing down the right side of the harbor from the Torget yields a view of **Bryggen**'s pointed gables. This row of medieval buildings has weathered numerous fires and the explosion of a Nazi munitions ship, surviving well enough to be listed by UNESCO as one of the world's most significant examples of the history and culture of the Middle Ages. The **Hanseatic Museum,** at the bottom of Bryggen, displays secret compartments, mummified hanging fish, and other relics from the life of 18th-century Hanseatic merchants. *(Open June-Aug. daily 9am-5pm; Sept.-May 11am-2pm. May-Sept. 40kr; Oct.-Apr. 25kr.)* At the other end of the street, the **Bryggens Museum** reenacts scenes of medieval Norway. *(Dreggsalm. 3, behind a small park at the end of the Bryggen houses. Open May-Aug. daily 10am-5pm; Sept.-Apr. M-F 11am-3pm, Sa noon-3pm, Su noon-4pm. 30kr, students 15kr.)*

English-language walking tours of Bryggen begin at the Bryggens Museum and travel down to the Hanseatic Museum. *(1½hr., June-Aug. daily 11am and 1pm, 70kr.)* Not included in the tour is the former city fortress, **Bergenhus.** On its grounds stand **Rosenkrantz Tower,** in late medieval splendor, and the cavernous 13th-century **Håkonshallen,** which is all that remains of the royal residence. *(At the north end of Bryggen; walk along the harbor away from the Torget. Mid-May to Aug. hall and tower open daily 10am-4pm; Sept. to mid-May tower open Su noon-3pm, hall open F-W noon-3pm and Th 3-6pm. Guided tours every hr. in summer. 20kr for each building, students and children 10kr.)* Stray just east of Bryggen to the steep streets between the **Korskirken** church and **Skansen** tower for a glimpse of authentic, untouristed Bergen neighborhoods.

MUSEUMS. There are three branches of the **Bergen Art Museum** lining the west side of the Lille Lungegårdsvann pond near the city center. The best of the three is the **Stenersen Collection,** which features works by Picasso, Miró, and Munch; the Norwegian **City Art Collection** and the **Rasmus Meyers Collection** are just down the road. *(Rasmus Meyers allé 3 and 7, and Lars Hilles gt. 10, respectively. All 3 open mid-May to mid-Sept. daily 11am-5pm; mid-Sept. to mid-May Tu-Su 11am-5pm. 35kr for all 3 museums, temporary exhibits additional 15kr.)* The University of Bergen has tastefully documented the history of one disease in an 18th-century hospital at the **Leprosy Museum.** *(Kong Oscars gt. 59. Open late May to Aug. daily 11am-3pm. 30kr, students 15kr.)*

HIKING. A vast archipelago spreads westward from Bergen, the only side of town not bordered by towering mountains. Trails surrounding the city are well kept and easily accessible. The **Fløibanen funicular** runs up **Mt. Fløyen** to a spectacular lookout point. *(From the Torget, follow Vetrlidsalm. east and up a small hill. Runs June-Aug. M-F 7:30am-midnight, Sa 8am-midnight, Su 9am-midnight; Sept.-May closes 11pm. Round-trip 50kr, children 25kr.)* At the summit, you'll find terrific views and plenty of tourists, as well as several **trailheads** that lead through an equally striking, less-crowded landscape dotted by mammoth boulders, springy moss, pristine waterfalls, and quiet pools. Classical music concerts are held indoors at the top of Mt. Fløyen (1hr., mid-June to mid-Aug. M-F 8pm, 160kr). A 4hr. trail from Fløyen leads to the top of **Mt. Ulriken,** the highest peak above Bergen, and a panoramic view over the city, fjords, mountains, and nearby islands. A **cable car** also runs to the top of Mt. Ulriken; the best option is to ride to the top and follow the trails downward. *(Car runs May-Sept. daily every 7min. 9am-10pm; Oct.-Apr. 10am-5pm. Round-trip 70kr.)* Pick up **maps** of the hills above Bergen at the DNT office (simple maps free; more detailed ones 80-95kr).

🔊 🎵 NIGHTLIFE AND ENTERTAINMENT

Bergen doesn't pick up until late on weekend nights; many locals pre-game at home before heading to the bars and clubs. To get away from the touristy harborside bars, take Torgallm. to **Nygårdsgaten,** home to an array of pubs and cafes. The **Garage Bar,** at the corner of Nygårdsgt. and Christies gt., is Bergen's most popular alt-rock pub and club. (Cover after 12:30am, Su-Th 20kr, F-Sa 30kr. Open M-Th 1pm-3am, F-Sa 1pm-3:30am, Su 3pm-3am.) **Rick's,** Veiten 3, is a huge club with several packed venues. (Occasionally 26+. Cover 60kr F-Sa after 10:30pm. Open Su-Th 10pm-3am, F-Sa 10pm-3:30am.) Bergen's cafes are a more relaxing nightlife alternative. 🌊**Vågen Fetevare,** Kong Oscars gt. 10, is the best of them, plying locals with board games, quality coffee (15-33kr), and inexpensive food. (Open M-F 8am-11pm, Sa 9am-6pm, Su 11am-11pm.) **Café Opera,** Engen 18, is another mellow cafe serving light meals and drinks; a DJ steps it up after 11pm on weekends. (Open Su-M noon-1:30am, Tu-Th noon-3am, F-Sa noon-3:30am.)

The city pulls out all the stops in late May for two simultaneous festivals: the annual **Bergen International Festival,** a 12-day program of music, ballet, folklore, and drama, and the **Night Jazz Festival.**

NORWAY

🔃 DAYTRIP FROM BERGEN: HARDANGERFJORD

Slicing through one of Norway's fruit-growing regions, the steep banks of the Hardangerfjord, south of Bergen, are lined with orchards and waterfalls. Local tourist offices distribute the free *Hardanger Guide*, which provides detailed information about transportation and accommodations. At Bergen's tourist office, find more information on **Hardanger Sunnhordlandske Dampskipsselskap** (**HSD;** ☎ 55 23 87 80), which offers day cruises through the Hardangerfjord, with stops at larger towns. Most tours depart from platforms #4 or 21 at Bergen's bus station. **Bergen Fjord Sightseeing** offers tours of all the area's fjords. (☎ 55 25 90 00. From 290kr.)

EIDFJORD. Stampeding hikers can be heard in beautiful Eidfjord, 45km southeast of Voss on RV13, as they pass through this gateway to **Hardangervidda,** Norway's largest national park. A scenic 1½hr. walk from the harbor allows for visits to the **Eidfjord Old Church** and **Viking Burial Place** in Hereid (open July-Aug. M-F 9am-3:30pm). Pick up a free map of the walking trail from the tourist office (see below) and then head out along Simadalvegen. After passing the bridge, turn right and walk along the river. Also popular is a **mini-tour** that starts with a trolley ride 20km up through the mountains to **Vøringstossen,** one of Norway's most famous waterfalls. (Mid-June to mid-Aug. Su-F daily, departs after ferry arrival. 165kr.)

The simplest way to get to the Eidfjord from Bergen is a **bus/ferry** combo (4¼hr., Su-F at 7:30am, 540kr; individual tickets to Voss and then Ulvik may be cheaper). The trip can also be done in the opposite direction as a **train/bus/boat** combo. (3hr., Su-F 8:40am, 540kr; transfer at Norheimsund). Either way, reservations are mandatory. Ask at the **tourist office** for information about the area's fantastic hikes. (☎ 53 67 34 00. Open July to mid-Aug. M-F 9am-8pm, Sa 9am-6pm, Su 11am-8pm; late June and late Aug. M-Sa 9am-6pm; Sept. to mid-June M-F 8:30am-4pm.) Ask the tourist office to find you a hut (from 200kr), or try 🏠**Saebø Camping ❶,** which has a spectacular location on the fjord 7km away from town. (☎ 53 66 59 27. 55kr per person and tent; 40kr per car; extra person 15kr; cabins 230-600kr.)

NORDFJORD AND JOSTEDALSBREEN

Although the Nordfjord itself places a distant third compared to the Geirangerfjord and the Sognefjord, its icy 800km cocoon of Jostedalsbreen (Jostedal glacier) is becoming an increasingly popular destination for guided excursions. The glacier is difficult to miss as it winds through mountain passes in frozen cascades of luminous blue. Adventurous travelers should note that it is dangerous to venture onto glaciers without a guide, as all glaciers have hidden soft spots and crevices.

STRYN (BRIKSDALSBREEN). Stryn is wedged between the mountains near the inner end of the Nordfjord, just northwest of the glacier. It's not an attraction in and of itself, but it provides a good base for glacier walks and other outdoor excursions. **Briksdal Breføring** (☎ 57 87 68 00) and the especially good **Olden Aktiv** (☎ 57 87 38 88) run a variety of tours for different fitness and skill levels on the nearby Briksdalsbreen arm of Jostedalsbreen (230-400kr; reserve ahead). The former meets at the Briksdalsbre Fjellstove lodge, the latter 30min. away at Melkevoll Bretun (see below). A daily bus departs from the Stryn bus station at 10am; the last return from Briksdal is at 2pm, however, so you will only have an hour on the ice unless you are staying in one of the lodges. 🏠**Melkevoll Bretun ❶** is a particularly good glacier-side lodge with nice rooms and an unreal cave-dorm. (☎ 57 87 38 64; fax 57 87 38 90. Cave-dorm 100kr; 4- to 6-person cabins 370-690kr.) Also popular is the nearby summer **ski center.** (☎ 92 25 83 33. Open May-Sept. daily 10am-

4pm, weather-dependent. Call ahead in July. Day pass 260kr, ages 13-18 220kr. Rentals from 250kr. Bus leaves Stryn station daily at 9am, returns 4:15pm; 65kr.) **Bus/train** combos connect Stryn to Trondheim, Lillehammer, and Oslo via Otta (3hr., 3 per day, 255kr); buses come and go from Ålesund (5½-6hr., 2 per day, 214kr; 50% Interrail and Scanrail discount.) To get to the **tourist office,** Perhusveien 19, walk past the Esso station and follow the signs. They can book rooms (30kr deposit) and recommend some of Stryn's great walks. (☎57 87 40 54; rooms ☎57 87 40 53; www.nordfjord.no. Internet 15kr per 15min. Open July daily 8:30am-8pm; June and Aug. 8:30am-6pm; Sept.-May M-F 8:30am-3:30pm.) The **youth hostel (HI) ❶** overlooks the whole of Stryn; from the tourist office, turn left onto Tonningsgt. and then right onto Setrevegen. Head up the hill and look for the hostel's signs. (☎57 87 11 06. Breakfast included. Laundry 20kr. Reception 8-11am and 4-11pm. Lockout 11am-4pm. Open June-Aug. only. Dorms 170kr; singles 250kr; doubles 400kr, with bath 500kr. Nonmembers add 25kr.) **Stryn Camping ❶** is in the center of town. (☎57 87 11 36. Reception 8am-11pm. Showers 15kr. 90kr per person and tent. 4- to 6-person cabins 350kr-850kr.)

GEIRANGERFJORD

Only 16km long, the narrow cliffs and waterfalls of the Geirangerfjord make it one of the prettiest places in Norway. While cruising through the green-blue water, watch for the Seven Sisters waterfalls and the Suitor geyser opposite them. The Geirangerfjord can be reached from the north via the famous Trollstigen road from Åndalsnes, or by the bus from Ålesund that stops in Hellesylt.

GEIRANGER. Geiranger is situated at Geirangerfjord's glorious eastern end. An endpoint of the famous **Trollstigen** road splintered by sheer inclines, the town is one of Norway's most visited destinations. Even the tourists don't overwhelm the picture-perfect area. **Hiking** abounds in this charmed country; some of the highlights include **Storseter Waterfall** (3hr.), **Flydalsjuvet Cliff** (1½hr.), **Skageflå Farm** (5hr.), and **Dalsnibba Mountain** (10-12hr. walk; 3hr. by bus, round-trip 100kr). All estimated hiking times are round-trip. Each hike has its own starting point, which may require a short bus ride. For hiking maps and more details, head to the **tourist office,** up from the ferry landing. They can also help find private rooms. (☎70 26 30 99; www.geiranger.no. Open mid-May to Aug. daily 9:15am-8pm.) One kilometer uphill to the right of the tourist office is the brand-new **Fjord Center,** whose staff knows all there is to know about the fjords. (Open mid-May to Aug. daily 10am-10pm; Sept. 10am-6pm. 75kr.) **Vinjebakken Hostel ❶** is up on the main road behind town; head to the church and look for the sign. (☎70 26 32 05. Laundry. Reception 24hr. Reserve ahead. Open June-Sept. only. Dorms 130kr.) **Geiranger Camping ❶** is by the water, 100m from the town center. (☎70 26 31 20. Open mid-May to early Sept. only. 13kr per person; 60kr per tent; 90kr with car. Shower 10kr.) **Buses** run directly to Ålesund (3hr.; departs 8am and 4pm from Union Hotel), but getting to Trondheim, Oslo, or Lillehammer requires connecting through Åndalsnes (3hr., departs 1 and 6:10pm, 144kr; 50% Interrail and Scanrail discount).

ÅLESUND

The largest city between Bergen and Trondheim, Ålesund (OH-les-oond) is renowned for its Art Nouveau architecture and oceanside location. The best view of the city and the distant mountains is 418 steps up from the park near the city center, at the ▧**Aksla** viewpoint. Immerse yourself in Ålesund's marine life at the **Atlantic Sea Park;** the innovative tanks are submerged in the ocean and illuminated by natural daylight. Stop by at 1pm to see the daily diver. To reach the park, take bus #13 or #18 (10min., 6-7 per day, 21kr) from St. Olavs Pass or in front of the tourist office to Atlanterhavsparken. (Open mid-June to mid-Aug. Su-F 10am-7pm, Sa 10am-4pm; mid-Aug. to mid-June M-Sa 11am-4pm, Su noon-5pm. 85kr, students and seniors 70kr.) Buses #13, 14, 18, and 24 (15min., every 15min., 19kr) run to the **Sunnmøre Museum,** Borgundgavlen, an outdoor exhibit of traditional Norwegian life and old sea vessels. (Open June-Aug. M-Sa 11am-5pm, Su noon to 4 or 5pm; Sept. to May M-F 11am-3pm, Su noon to 4 or 5pm. 55kr, students 40kr.) There's an old Viking site and an 11th-century marble church on the nearby island of **Giske,** a popular spot for "kite-surfing." Bus #64 travels through the tunnel connecting Ålesund and Giske (20min.; M-F 8 per day, Sa 5 per day; 45kr, students 30kr).

Buses go to Stryn (3½hr., 1-2 per day, 191kr; 25% Interrail and Scanrail discount) via Hellesylt (2½hr., 3 per day, 168kr) and to Trondheim (8hr.; 2 per day; 474kr, students 272kr). There is also a bus/train combo to Trondheim; a bus runs to Åndalsnes (2½hr., 3 per day, 168kr) and connects with a waiting train (4hr., 4 per day, 476kr; ask about seasonal discounts). The luxurious **Hurtigruten** also heads to Trondheim; considering that it may save a night's accommodation, it can be an affordable alternative. (Departs 10min. north of the tourist office and bus station; daily at 6:45pm, arrives in Trondheim at 8:15am the next morning; 800kr, students 400kr.) The **tourist office,** on Keiser Wilhelms gt., is opposite the bus station in the city hall; it books accommodations for a 30kr fee. (☎70 15 76 00. Open June-Aug. M-F 8:30am-7pm, Sa 9am-5pm, Su 11am-5pm; Sept.-May M-F 9am-4pm.) It's a 5-7min. walk from the bus station to the enjoyable **Ålesund Vandrerhjem ❶,** Parkgata 14; head uphill on Keiser Wilhelms gt. until it becomes Kipervik gt., turn left onto Rådstugt. and right onto Parkgt., and the hostel will be on the right. (☎70 11 58 30; eaaa@online.no. Breakfast included. Kitchen. Laundry. Open May-Sept. only. Reception 8:30-11am and 3:30pm-midnight. Lockout 11am-3:30pm. Dorms 145kr; singles 370; doubles 470kr. Nonmembers add 25kr.) **Volsdalen Camping ❶** is 2km along the main highway, next to a beach. Take bus #13, 14, 18, or 24 (19kr) to Hellandbakken, turn right off the highway, follow the road downhill, turn left across the overpass, and turn right; it'll be 200m down on the left. (☎70 12 58 90. Reception daily 8am-10pm. Open May to mid-Sept. 110kr per tent; cabins 300-420kr.)

TRONDHEIM

A thousand years ago, Viking kings turned Trondheim (then Nidaros) into Norway's seat of power. Today, the city is a leading technological center whose vivacity stems from its 25,000 university students. Characterized by wide boulevards and a low-key attitude, Trondheim is an enjoyable place to stop for a day or two while heading north to the Arctic Circle.

🖰🖿 TRANSPORTATION AND PRACTICAL INFORMATION. Trains go to: Bodø (11hr., 3 per day, 813kr); Oslo (6½hr., M-F 2-5 per day, 707kr); and Stockholm (11hr., 2 per day, 437-659kr). **Long-distance buses** leave the train station for: Ålesund (7¼hr., 2-3 per day, 502kr); Oslo (9¾hr., 4 per week, 620kr); and Bergen (14hr., 2 per day, 785kr). **City buses** run along Munkeg., Dronningensg., and Olav Tryggvasong. (15kr within city center, 22kr to outlying regions). Trondheim is a bike-friendly city; the city keeps 270 serviceable bicycles parked at stations in town (20kr deposit). Maps showing the locations of the various bike stations in town are available at the **tourist office,** Munkegt. 19, which also books accommodations (20kr fee). To get there from the train station, cross the bridge, walk six blocks down Søndreg., go right on Kongensg., and look to your left as you approach the roundabout. (☎73 80 76 60; www.trondheim.com. Open mid-May to mid-Aug. M-F 8:30am-4pm, Sa-Su 10am-4pm; mid-Aug. to mid-May M-F 8am-4pm.) **DNT,** Sandgata 30, has hiking maps (69-95kr) and information on huts and trails. (☎73 92 42 00. Open M-F 8am-4pm, Th until 6pm.)

🏠🍴 ACCOMMODATIONS AND FOOD. To get from the station to the lively **InterRail Centre ❶**, Elgeseterg. 1, in the Studentersamfundet, take bus #41, 44, 46, 48, 49, 52, or 63 (22kr) to Samfundet. (☎73 89 95 38; tirc@stud.ntnu.no. Free **Internet**. Breakfast included. Dinner 45kr. Sheets 30kr. Open late June to mid-Aug. only. Sleeping-bag dorms 115kr.) For more peaceful lodging, take Lillegårdsbakken (off Øvre Bakklandet, near the Old Town Bridge) up to the student-run **Singsaker Sommerhotell ❶**, Rogertsg. 1, near the Kristiansten Fortress. (☎73 89 31 00. Open June to mid-Aug. Sleeping-bag dorms 135kr, sheets 30kr; singles 365-465kr; doubles 560-660kr; triples 765-865kr.)

There's a cluster of enjoyable cafes on the far end of the Old Town Bridge. Get groceries at **Rema 1000** on the main square (open M-F 9am-9pm, Sa 9am-6pm); in summer, look for strawberry stands in front of the tourist office (baskets 20-25kr).

🏛 SIGHTS. Most sights are concentrated in the south end of town around the gigantic **Nidaros Cathedral,** easily the main attraction. The cathedral is the site of all Norwegian coronations and the repository of the crown jewels, which are on display in summer. (Open June 20-Aug. 20 M-F 9am-6pm, Sa 9am-2pm, Su 1-4pm; Aug. 21-June 19 reduced hours. 35kr. Crown jewels on display June 20-Aug. 20 M-Th and Sa 9am-12:30pm, Su 1-4pm; Apr.-May and Aug. 21-Oct. F 2pm.) In the complex next door is **Erkebispegården** (Archbishop's Palace; open June 20-Aug. 20 M-F 10am-5pm, Sa 10am-3pm, Su noon-5pm; Aug. 21-June 19 reduced hours), as well as the **Rustkammeret** (Army Museum) and **Hjemmefrontmuseet** (Resistance Museum). (Both open June-Aug. M-F 9am-3pm, Sa-Su 11am-4pm; Mar.-May and Oct.-Nov. Sa-Su 11am-4pm. Free.) Just down Bispegata from the cathedral is the **Trondheim Kunstmuseum**, Bispegata 7B, whose collection features good Danish artwork and a hallway of Edvard Munch prints. (Open June-Aug. Tu-Su 10am-5pm; Sept.-May 11am-5pm. 40kr, students 20kr.) The image of Olav Tryggvason, who founded Trondheim in AD 997, lords over the town from a pillar in the main market square, **Torget**. Across the **Gamle Bybro** (Old Town Bridge), you'll find the **old district,** where former fishing houses have been transformed into galleries and cafes. To reach the bridge from Torget, head toward the spires of Nidaros Cathedral, then turn left onto Bispegata and follow it around to the bridge. On the hill above the old district, the **Kristiansten Fortress** yields a splendid view; take the bike lift up from the base of the Old Town Bridge (pick up key-card at tourist office or adjacent cafes; 100kr deposit). **Munkholmen** (Monk's Island), is 10min. by boat from the end of Munkegaten, near the train station (in summer daily every hr. 10am-6pm, return trip at 10:15, 11:15, etc.; 45kr). Originally an execution site, Munkholmen later served as home to an 11th-century monastery which burnt down in 1531 after a severe storm swept through. The standing fortress dates back to 1680. (10min. English-language tour upon request; tours start 5min. after boat arrivals. 25kr.)

SOUTHERN NORWAY

Norway's southern coast substitutes serenity for drama, creating the premier summer holiday destination for Norwegian couples and families. *Skjærgard*, archipelagos of water-worn rock, hug the shore, stretching southward from Oslo to the pleasant beaches past Kristiansand. Fishing, hiking, rafting, and canoeing are popular in summer, while cross-country skiing reigns in winter.

KRISTIANSAND

Kristiansand's summery beaches attract winter-weary Norwegian tourists. The city center's grid layout is easy to navigate: the harbor, train station, and bus station sit at the bottom of the grid; **Markensgata**, the main street, is a block from the water; and **Posebyen**, the well-preserved old town, begins two blocks farther away at **Festningsgata**.

THE BIG SPLURGE

QUART FESTIVAL

Kristiansand is normally a quiet town of about 60,000 people; the first week of each July, however, another 20,000 Norwegians flood in for the five-day **Quart Festival**, a time of world-class concerts, movie premieres, and endless partying. Unlike similar European rock festivals, Quart possesses a neighborly, down-to-earth quality thanks to the fact that it is relatively undiscovered outside of Northern Europe. The crowds that pack the harborside venues are almost entirely Scandinavian, despite the festival's widespread appeal.

The Quart Festival was started by a group of Kristiansand residents in 1992, growing to its present size by 1996. Each year, about 100 groups perform on the various stages; past headliners have included Moby, Nine Inch Nails, and the Beastie Boys. The 2002 line-up featured established artists such as David Bowie and No Doubt as well as breakout groups like Doves and Travis. The 2003 program can be found online at **www.quart.no**, along with more information on tickets and accommodations.

Plan far in advance if you're hoping to attend the festival; book transportation and sleeping arrangements at least two months in advance. The two official **Quart Camps** are the best option for a few hours' sleep each night; one is 2km away, another 8km. (200kr per tent, 60kr per person.) A **5-day pass** is pricey (1500kr), but individual **day passes** (400kr) allow you to catch your favorite bands and take in the rest of southern Norway on off days.

☐ ☑ TRANSPORTATION AND PRACTICAL INFORMATION. Trains run to Oslo (4½-5½hr., 6 per day, 502kr) and Stavanger (3hr., 8 per day, 366kr). Color Line **ferries** (☎81 00 08 11) sail to Hirsthals, Denmark (2½-4hr.; 2-6 per day; from 390kr, off-season reduced prices). The **tourist office** is opposite the train station at Henrik Wegerlandsgt. and Vestre Strandsgt. They book accommodations (30kr fee) and can arrange elk safaris in local forests. (☎38 12 13 14. **Internet** 15kr per 15min. Open mid-June to mid-Aug. M-F 8am-6pm, Sa 9am-6pm, Su noon-6pm; mid-Aug. to mid-June M-F 8am-3:30pm.) The tourist office also has a **branch** in the town center, at the intersection of Markensgt. and Rådhusgt.

☐ ☐ ACCOMMODATIONS AND FOOD. The Kristiansand Youth Hostel (HI) ❶, Skansen 8, is 25min. from the harbor and train station. Walk away from the water until you reach Elvegata, turn right, then turn left onto Skansen and follow the signs. (☎38 02 83 10. Breakfast included. Kitchen. Laundry. Lockers. Reception mid-June to mid-Aug. 24hr.; mid-Aug. to mid-June 5-11pm. Dorms 190kr; singles 380kr; doubles 420kr. Nonmembers add 25kr.) The former hostel **Centrum Motel ❸**, Vestre Strandgt. 49, is next door to the train station. (☎38 02 79 69; fax 38 09 48 96. Reception 24hr. Breakfast included. Kitchen. Free laundry. All rooms with bath. Singles 490kr; doubles 650kr; triples 750kr; off-season reduced prices.) The noisy **Roligheden campground ❶** is a 35min. walk from town; or, take bus #15 or 16 and ask the driver to let you off at the campground turnoff. (☎38 09 67 22. Laundry 30kr. Reception 7am-midnight. Open June-Aug. 30kr per person, 80kr per tent. Showers 10kr per 5min.)

Few restaurants in Kristiansand are cheap, even by Norwegian standards; that said, look around **Markensgata** for reasonable options. **Frk. Larsen ❷**, Markensgata 5, serves a full crowd of locals day and night. (Sandwiches 69-74kr. Open M-Th 10am-midnight, F-Sa 10am-3am, Su noon-midnight.)

☐ ☐ SIGHTS AND ENTERTAINMENT. The city's best-known attraction is **◼Dyreparken,** "the living park," which contains a zoo, an amusement park, and a circus. The zoo is one of Europe's best; its newly acquired Siberian tigers are not to be missed. Take bus #1 or #8 (dir.: Sørlandsparken) from the stop on H. Wergelandsgt. in front of the tourist office. (Open mid-May to Sept. daily 10am-7pm; Sept. to mid-May M-F 10am-3:30pm, Sa-Su 10am-5pm. 215kr, children 180kr, seniors 120kr;

Sept.-June reduced prices.) Bus #1 also stops at the **Kristiansand Kanonenmuseum,** which displays the remains of a Nazi bunker and the world's second-largest cannon. (Open mid-June to Aug. daily 11am-6pm; May to mid-June and Sept. M-W 11am-3pm, Th-Su 11am-6pm. 50kr, seniors 30kr, children 20kr.) The solitary 17th-century **Christiansholm Fortress** has a view of the beach and islands near the city. (Open mid-May to Sept. daily 9am-9pm. Free.) **Posebyen,** the pleasant old town just two blocks from Markensgata, is worth meandering through. Ferries head to the scenic **Skerries,** a well-loved group of tiny islands and fjords. (3½hr.; departs 11am from Nupen Park in East Harbor, returns 5pm; round-trip 180kr. Inquire at the tourist office.)

STAVANGER

A delightful port town with colorful wooden pier-houses and a lively fish market, Stavanger is known for its cultural history and its proximity to great hikes. On the eastern side of the harbor is **Gamle Stavanger,** a neighborhood maintained at its prosperous 19th-century state. The 1125 **Stavanger Domkirke** solemnly dominates the modern town center. (Open mid-May to mid-Sept. M-Tu 11am-6pm, W-Sa 10am-6pm, Su 1-6pm; mid-Sept. to mid-May W-Sa 10am-3pm. Free.) The **Norsk Oljemuseum** (Norwegian Petroleum Museum) explains the driving force of Norway's powerful oil industry. Walk along Kirkegata from the cathedral; the museum is by the water on Havneringen. (Open June-Aug. daily 10am-7pm; Sept.-May M-F 10am-4pm, Su 10am-6pm. 75kr; students, seniors, and children 35kr.) **Pulpit Rock** (Preikestolen), in nearby **Lysefjord,** is one of Norway's postcard darlings. To get there, take the ferry to Tau (June 16-Sept. 1 only; 40min.; 8:20 and 9:05am, return 2:30 and 4:15pm; 30kr), catch the waiting bus (45kr), and hike up the marked trail (1½hr.). Ask at the tourist office (see below) for information on other adventurous options, including some of the world's best base-jumping at **Kjerag.**

Trains pull in from Oslo (8½-9hr., 2 per day, 740kr) directly or via Kristiansand (3hr., 8 per day, 340kr; 50% advance-purchase discount). Trains and buses arrive at Stavanger's central station; from the front entrance, walk around the pond and down the stairs to reach the harbor. Flaggruten (☎51 86 87 80) **boats** speed to Bergen (see p. 759), docking at a terminal on the eastern side of the city; exit the terminal through the main door and walk straight along Kirkegata to reach the town center. Fjordline **ferries** (☎55 54 88 00; booking@fjordline.com) go to Newcastle, England (17-20hr., 2-3 per week, from 400kr), departing and arriving at a terminal on the western side of the harbor; the city center is a short walk along the water. (Ferry terminal open Tu 9pm-midnight, F 2:30-5:30pm, Su 8-11pm.) The **tourist office,** Rosenkildetorget 1, is across from the fish market on the harbor. (☎51 85 92 00. Open June-Aug. daily 9am-8pm; Sept.-May M-F 9am-4pm, Sa 9am-2pm.)

Tone's Bed and Breakfast ❷, Peder Claussøns gt. 22, is one of the cheaper bed and breakfasts in town, providing cozy rooms and generous hospitality. (☎/fax 51 52 42 07. Breakfast included. Free laundry upon request. Singles 250kr; doubles 420kr.) If Tone's is full, ask at the tourist office for more recommendations or take bus #97 from the cathedral to **Mosvangen Vandrerhjem (HI) ❶,** Ibsensgt. 21. (☎51 87 29 00; fax 51 87 06 30. Reception daily 8-11am and 3-10pm. Open June-Aug. Dorms 145kr; nonmembers 170kr.) The **market** opposite the cathedral sells fresh Norwegian strawberries and other delights. (Open M-F 8am-5pm, Sa varying hours.) Inexpensive restaurants can be found throughout the small streets behind the cathedral. **Postal code:** 4001.

NORWAY

FARTHER NORTH

LOFOTEN ISLANDS

An amalgam of emerald mountains and rustic fishing villages, the Lofotens prove that there is more to Norwegian beauty than fjords. As late as the 1950s, isolated fishermen lived in small *rorbuer*, wooden shacks along the coast, yet Lofoten residents gladly greet the occasional traveler coming to fish under the midnight sun.

⌐ TRANSPORTATION. To get to the Lofoten Islands from Trondheim, you will probably need to take a **train** to Bodø (11hr., 2-3 per day including a night train, 848kr; mandatory seat reservations). From **Bodø,** you have four options: a car ferry to Moskenes (3-4hr., 4-7 per day, 122kr), an express boat to Svolvær (3½hr., Su-F 1 per day, 251kr; 50% student discount), a bus to Svolvær (7-8hr., daily 7:10am and 4:25pm, 414kr; 50% Interrail discount), or the Hurtigruten to Stamsund (4½hr., 306kr) or Svolvær (6hr., 328kr). If you want to go directly to the islands, you can take the **Hurtigruten** all the way from Trondheim to Stamsund (31½hr.; departs daily at noon, arrives in Stamsund 7:30pm the next day; 770-793kr; 50% student discount). Within the islands, **buses** are the main form of transport; pick up the invaluable *Lofoten Trafikklag* bus timetable at a tourist office in Bodø or the Lofotens. Dial ☎ 177 to reach a regional **transport information** desk. An **Interrail** pass allows you to pay children's prices on all routes within the islands; **Scanrail** discounts are available only if your destination is on a rail line.

MOSKENES AND FLAKSTAD. Travelers are drawn to Moskenes and Flakstad by their jagged mountains and quaint fishing communities. **Ferries** from Bodø to the islands dock in Moskenes, the southernmost of the large Lofotens. The **tourist office,** by the ferry landing, has tours (5hr., 590kr) that take you through the **Maelstrom,** one of the most dangerous ocean currents in the world, to see the ancient **Refsvika caves** and their 3000-year-old drawings. (☎ 76 09 15 99; www.lofoten-info.no. Internet access 15kr per 15min. Open early June M-F 9am-5pm; mid-June to mid-Aug. daily 10am-7pm.)

Incoming ferry passengers usually head 5km south to **Å** (OH), a tiny but well-known fishing village at the end of the E10 highway. **Buses** depart from the backside of the tourist office 5-15min. after boat landings (5-10min., 4-5 per day). Once you get to Å, pick up a free map of the town at the bus station's **service center,** then head down the hill and into town. Six unconnected buildings comprise the exceptional ▧**Norsk Fiskeværsmuseum,** which depicts life in an old-fashioned fishing village. (Open mid-June to mid-Aug. daily 10am-5:30pm; mid-Aug. to mid-June M-F 10am-3pm. 40kr, students 30kr.) The **Å Vandrerhjem and Rorbuer ❶** has bunks in 19th-century buildings. (☎ 76 09 11 21. Rowboats and bikes 150kr per day. Laundry 50kr. Reserve ahead. Dorms 125-200kr. Nonmembers add 25kr. *Rorbuer* cabins 600-1500kr. Off-season reduced prices.) An even cheaper bet is the privately run **Å Hamna Rorbuer As ❶,** right in the town center (☎ 76 09 11 21. Free laundry. June-Sept. reception 24hr. Reserve ahead. 2- to 4-person rooms 100kr.) Or, **camp** for free on the shores of the lake behind town.

VESTVÅGØY. Farther north is Vestvågøy, an island that some travelers visit just so they can stay at the seaside ▧**Justad youth hostel (HI) ❶.** A 15min. walk from the ferry dock, in the hamlet of **Stamsund,** the bustling hostel is great for those looking to fish and hike; long-time owner Roar, however, is the biggest draw of all. (☎ 76 08 93 34; fax 76 08 97 39. Fishing gear and rowboats 100kr deposit. Bikes 100kr per day. Laundry 30kr. Showers 5kr per 5min. Open mid-Dec. to mid-Oct.

Dorms 90kr; doubles 250kr; *rorbuer* 450-650kr.) Hiking in the area is great, most notably the trek up **Stein Tinden,** from where the midnight sun can be seen all through June (500m peak; round-trip 6hr.). Another good option is the peak at **Justad Tinden** (732m; round-trip 6-7hr.), which provides a panoramic view of the Lofoten Islands and northern Scandinavia. Talk to Roar, the hostel owner, for directions and advice on weather conditions; he also stocks free hiking maps. Between June 14 and 27, borrow a hostel rowboat and paddle out about 300m for the best lowland chance at seeing the **midnight sun.** On clear nights between late August and March, Stamsund is a good place to see the **Northern Lights.**

Thirty kilometers north of Stamsund, on the road between Leknes and Svolvær, is the site of the largest extant Viking building, in the town of **Borg;** the longhouse holds the **Lofotr Viking Museum,** staffed by costumed Norse folk who do full-scale reenactments. (Open late May to early Sept. daily 10am-7pm. 80kr, students 65kr.) Take a bus from Stamsund to Leknes (25min., 6-9 per day, 27kr), and then another bus from Leknes to Borg (15min., 4-8 per day, 27kr). The nocturnal **tourist office,** at the ferry dock, is better for transportation info than outdoors suggestions. (☎ 76 08 97 92. Open mid-June to mid-Aug. daily 6-9:30pm.)

TROMSØ

Norway's so-called "northern capital," Tromsø has always been recognized for its sophisticated culture and hospitable residents. Enjoyable and easy to walk around, Tromsø provides those heading to Nordkapp a final dose of Norwegian city-life. **Polaria,** Hjarlmar Johansens gt. 12, is a sleek, hands-on museum exploring the surrounding Arctic region. From the tourist office, exit left and walk down Storgt. until you reach Mack's Brewery; the museum is the next left. (Open mid-May to mid-Aug. daily 10am-7pm; mid-Aug. to mid-May noon-5pm. 75kr, seniors 60kr, students 55kr.) Just over the city's main bridge lies the hard-to-miss **Arctic Cathedral,** which contains one of the largest stained-glass windows in Europe. Walk across the bridge (15min.) or take bus #26 or #28 (21kr) from in front of Peppes Pizza. (Open June to mid-Aug. M-Sa 10am-8pm, Su 1-8pm. 20kr. Services Su 11am.) **Fjellheisen Tromsø,** the city's cable cars (75kr, including fare on bus #26), yield the best view of the greater Tromsø area and the best chance to see the **Northern Lights** (Aug.-Feb., especially Dec.-Feb.).

The **Hurtigruten** comes to Tromsø from Stamsund, in the Lofoten Islands (departs 7:30pm, arrives 2:30pm the next day; 854kr; 50% student discount), and other coastal destinations. **Buses** go to Narvik (4½hr., 1-3 per day, 308kr; 50% student and railpass discount), which has transportation links to Finland and Sweden. The **tourist office,** Storgata 63, books rooms in private homes. (☎ 77 61 00 00; www.destinasjontromso.no. Open June to mid-Aug. M-F 8:30am-6pm, Sa 10am-5pm, Su 10:30am-5pm; mid-Aug. to May reduced hours.) **Tromsø Vandrerhjem (HI)** ❶ is changing its location for 2003; ask at the tourist office for its contact number. Affordable food, killer cappucino (28kr), and free **Internet** access are available at **Amtmandens Datter,** Grønne gt. 81. (Open June-Aug. Su-Th 3pm-1:30am, F 3pm-3am, Sa noon-3am; Sept.-May M-Sa noon-3am, Su 3pm-3am.)

NORWAY

POLAND (POLSKA)

Caught at the threshold of East and West, Poland's moments of freedom have always been brief. From 1795 to 1918, the country simply did not exist on any map of Europe. Ravaged in World War II and then suppressed by Stalin and the USSR, Poland has at long last been given room to breathe, and its residents are not letting the opportunity slip by. The most prosperous of the "Baltic tigers," Poland now has a rapidly increasing GDP and a new membership in NATO. Although capitalism has brought with it Western problems such as rising crime and unemployment, the Poles are also using their new wealth to explore their cultural roots and to repair buildings destroyed in the wars.

FACTS AND FIGURES

Official Name: Republic of Poland.

Capital: Warsaw.

Major Cities: Łódź, Kraków, Lublin, Poznań, Katowice, Gdańsk, Wrocław.

Population: 39,000,000.

Land Area: 312,685 sq. km.

Time Zone: GMT +1.

Language: Polish.

Religions: Roman Catholic (95%); Eastern Orthodox, Protestant, and other (5%).

DISCOVER POLAND

Over 19 million visitors flock annually to Poland's spectacular castles, Old Towns, and museums, as well as to its as villages, forests, and beaches. The vibrant, glamorous capital, **Warsaw** (p. 776), gives living testimony to Poland's resiliency. Much-adored **Kraków** (p. 784), the only Polish city to make it through the 20th century unscathed by natural disaster or war, has a magnificent castle and perfectly preserved Old Town. To the south, in the heart of the High Tatras, **Zakopane** (p. 791) boasts ear-popping hikes, music festivals, and Tatran folk culture. **Gdańsk** (p. 796), where World War II began, was also the base of Poland's anti-Communist Solidarity movement in the 1980s. On the Baltic Coast, **Sopot** (p. 799) shelters Poland's best beaches, while **Malbork** (p. 799) has the biggest brick castle in the world.

ESSENTIALS

WHEN TO GO

Visit the Tatras between November and February to ski, or in August to hike. Elsewhere, summer and autumn are the best times to visit, as winters can be dreary.

DOCUMENTS AND FORMALITIES

VISAS. Citizens of Ireland and the US can travel to Poland without a visa for up to 90 days, UK citizens for up to 180 days. Australians, Canadians, New Zealanders, and South Africans need visas (180-day single-entry €60, students €45; multiple-entry €100/€75; 48hr. transit €20/€15). To extend your stay, apply to the regional government branch *(voi vodine)* of the city you are staying in, or at the **Ministry of Internal Affairs** at ul. Stefana Batorego 5 in Warsaw (☎022 621 02 51).

EMBASSIES. All foreign embassies are in Warsaw (see p. 776) and Kraków (see p. 784). Polish embassies at home include: **Australia,** 7 Turrana St., Yarralumla ACT 2600 Canberra (☎06 273 1208 or 06 273 1211; ambpol@clover.com.au); **Can-**

Poland

ada, 443 Daly St., Ottawa, ON K1N 6H3 (☎613-789-0468; polamb@hookup.com);
Ireland, 5 Ailesbury Rd., Ballsbridge, Dublin 4 (☎01 283 0855; fax 01 269 8309);
New Zealand, 17 Upland Rd., Kelburn, Wellington (☎04 712 456;
polishembassy@xtra.co.nz); **South Africa,** 14 Amos St., Colbyn, Pretoria 0083
(☎012 432 631; amb.pol@pixie.co.za). **UK,** 47 Portland Pl., London W1N 4JH
(☎020 7580 4324; http://home.btclick.com/polishembassy); and **US,** 2640 16th St.
NW, Washington, D.C. 20009 (☎202-234-3800; www.polandembassy.org).

TRANSPORTATION

BY PLANE. LOT (www.lot.com) flies into Warsaw's modern Okęcie Airport
(WAW) from London, New York, Chicago, and Toronto, among other cities.

BY TRAIN. Trains are generally faster and more convenient than buses. Be alert—
stations are not announced and can be poorly marked. Stations have boards that
list towns alphabetically and posters that list trains chronologically. *Odjazdy*
(departures) are in yellow, *przyjazdy* (arrivals) in white. **InterCity** and **ekspresowy**
(express) trains are listed in red with an "IC" or "Ex" before the train number.
Pośpieszny (direct; also in red) are almost as fast. *Osobowy* (in black) are the
slowest but are 35% cheaper than *pośpieszny*. All InterCity, *ekspresowy*, and

some *pośpieszny* trains require seat reservations (indicated by a boxed R on the schedule); ask the clerk for a *miejscówka* (myay-TSOOF-kah; reservation). Allot time for long, slow lines or buy your ticket in advance at the station or an Orbis office. On board, the *konduktor* sells surcharged tickets. Tickets are valid only for the day they are issued. **Eurail** passes are not valid in Poland. While Polish students and seniors can buy *ulgowy* (half-price) tickets, foreign travelers are not eligible for discounts; there is a hefty fine for traveling with an *ulgowy* ticket without Polish ID. Tickets cost 20% less on Sundays. **BIJ-Wasteels** tickets and **Eurotrain** passes, sold at Almatur and Orbis, give under-26 travelers 40% off international tickets.

BY BUS AND BY FERRY. PKS buses are cheapest and fastest for short trips. Like trains, there are *pośpieszny* (direct; marked in red) and *osobowy* (slow; in black) buses. Purchase advance tickets at the station and expect long lines. Tickets for many routes can be bought only from the driver. In the countryside, PKS markers (steering wheels that look like upside-down, yellow Mercedes-Benz symbols) indicate bus stops; drivers will also often stop if you flag them down. Traveling with a backpack can be a problem if the bus is full, since there are no storage compartments. The private **Polski Express** has more luxurious buses, but service is limited. **Ferries** run from Sweden and Denmark to Gdańsk (see p. 64).

BY TAXI AND BY THUMB. Arrange cabs by phone rather than hailing one on the street. Taxi drivers generally try to gouge foreigners; arrange the price before getting in or be sure the meter's on. The going rate is 1.50-2zł per km. Hand-waving is the accepted sign for hitchhiking. Although it is legal in Poland, *Let's Go* does not recommend hitchhiking.

TOURIST SERVICES AND MONEY

EMERGENCY	Police: ☎997. Ambulance: ☎999. Fire: ☎998.

TOURIST OFFICES. City-specific offices are generally more helpful than the larger chains. All offices provide free information in English and should be of some help with accommodations. **Orbis** (www.orbis-use.com), the state-sponsored travel bureau staffed by English speakers, operates luxury hotels and sells transportation tickets. **Almatur** (www.almatur.com.pl), the Polish student travel organization, sells ISICs, arranges dorm rooms in summer, and sells student tickets. Both provide maps and brochures, as do **PTTK** and **IT** *(Informacji Turystycznej)* bureaus.

MONEY. The Polish **złoty** (plural *złote)* is composed of 100 *grosze.* Private **kantor** offices (except for those at the airport and train stations) usually offer better exchange rates than banks. **Bank PKO S.A.** also has fairly good exchange rates; they cash traveler's checks and give MasterCard and Visa cash advances. **ATMs** *(banko-mat)* are everywhere except the smallest villages; MasterCard and Visa are the most widely accepted networks. Budget accommodations rarely, if ever, accept credit cards, although some restaurants and upscale hotels will. A 10% tip is customary in restaurants; if you're paying with a credit card, give the tip in cash.

BUSINESS HOURS. Business hours tend to be Monday to Friday 10am-6pm and Saturday 9am-2pm. Saturday hours vary, as some shops distinguish "working" *(pracująca)* Saturdays, when hours are extended, from "free" *(wolna)* ones, when hours are shorter. Very few stores or businesses are open on Sunday. Museums are generally open Tuesday to Sunday 10am-4pm and banks Monday to Friday 9am to 3 or 6pm.

ZŁOTE		
AUS$1 = 2.30ZŁ	1ZŁ = AUS$0.44	
CDN$1 = 2.68ZŁ	1ZŁ = CDN$0.37	
EUR€1 = 4.09ZŁ	1ZŁ = EUR€0.25	
NZ$1 = 1.96ZŁ	1ZŁ = NZ$0.51	
ZAR1 = 0.40ZŁ	1ZŁ = ZAR 2.53	
UK£1 = 6.38ZŁ	1ZŁ = UK£0.16	
US$1 = 4.17ZŁ	1ZŁ = US$0.24	

COMMUNICATION

MAIL. Mail is generally efficient; airmail *(lotnicza)* reaches the US in about 2 weeks. Letters abroad cost about 2.20zł, depending on weight. When picking up *Poste Restante*, you may have to pay a small fee (1.10zł) or show your passport. Address mail to be held: Firstname SURNAME, *Poste Restante*, ul. Swiętokrzyska 31/33, Warsaw 1, 00-001 POLAND.

TELEPHONES AND INTERNET. Card phones have become the standard for public phones. Cards, which come in several denominations, are sold at post offices, *Telokomunikacja Polska* offices, and most kiosks. To make a collect call, write the name of the city or country, the number, and *"Rozmowa 'R'"* on a slip of paper and hand it to a post office clerk. Most mid-sized towns have at least one **Internet club or cafe** and larger cities have several. Access costs around 5-10zł per hour.

PHONE CODES	**Country code: 48. International dialing prefix: 00.** From outside Poland, dial int'l dialing prefix (see inside back cover) + 48 + city code + local number.

LANGUAGES. Polish varies little across the country; the exceptions are Kaszuby, which has a Germanized dialect, and Karpaty, where the highlanders' accent is extremely thick. In western Poland and Mazury, German is the most commonly known foreign language, although many Poles in big cities, especially students, can speak English. Try English and German before Russian, which many Poles show an aversion to speaking. Most Poles can understand Czech or Slovak. For basic phrases, see p. 1062.

ACCOMMODATIONS AND CAMPING

POLAND	❶	❷	❸	❹	❺
ACCOMMODATIONS	under 35zł	35-60zł	61-80zł	81-100zł	over 100zł

Private rooms (around €5-15 per night) are available in most towns but are not regulated; tourist offices can usually help you find reputable renters. **PTSM** is the national organization of **youth hostels** *(schroniska młodzieżowe)*, which average 15-40zł per night. As they are often booked solid, call at least a week in advance. **University dorms** transform into spartan budget housing in July and August; these are an especially good option in Kraków. The Warsaw office of **Almatur** (see p. 778) can arrange dorm stays in all major cities. **PTTK** runs a number of hotels called **Dom Turysty**, which have multi-bed rooms as well as budget singles and doubles. **Hotels** generally cost 80-120zł per night. **Campsites** average €3 per person; **bungalows** are also often available (about €5). *Polska Mapa Campingów* lists all campsites.

POLAND

FOOD AND DRINK

POLAND	❶	❷	❸	❹	❺
FOOD	under 8zł	8-15zł	16-25zł	26-35zł	over 35zł

Polish staples include meat, potatoes, cabbage, and butter. Meals always begin with soup, often *barszcz* (clear broth), *chłodnik* (a cold beet soup with buttermilk and hard-boiled eggs), *kapuśniak* (cabbage soup), or *żurek* (barley-flour soup loaded with eggs and sausage). Hearty main courses include *gołąbki* (cabbage rolls stuffed with meat and rice), *kotlet schabowy* (pork cutlets), *naleśniki* (cream-topped crepes filled with cottage cheese or jam), and *pierogi* (stuffed dumplings). Poland bathes in beer, vodka, and spiced liquor. *Żywiec* is the most popular strong beer; *EB* is its excellent, gentler brother. Other available beers include *EB Czerwone, Okocim*, and *Piast*. The *Wyborowa, Żytnia*, and *Polonez* brands of *Wódka* usually decorate private bars, while *Belweder* (Belvedere) is Poland's most prized alcoholic export.

HEALTH AND SAFETY

Public restrooms (up to 0.70zł) are marked with an upward-pointing triangle for men and a circle for women. Pharmacies are well-stocked, and at least one in each large city stays open 24hr. Avoid state hospitals. There are usually clinics in major cities with private, English-speaking doctors; expect to pay 50zł per visit. Tap water is theoretically drinkable, but bottled mineral water, available carbonated *(gazowana)* or flat *(nie gazowana)*, will spare you from some unpleasant metals and chemicals. Always be on your guard against pickpockets, especially when at big train stations, while finding a train compartment, and when aboard crowded public buses and trams.

HOLIDAYS AND FESTIVALS

Holidays: New Year's Day (Jan. 1); Catholic Easter (Apr. 20-21); Labor Day (May 1); Constitution Day (May 3); Corpus Christi (June 19); Assumption Day (Aug. 15); Independence Day (Nov. 11); Christmas (Dec. 25-26).

Festivals: Kraków is Poland's festival capital, especially in summer. The most notable include the **International Short Film Festival** (late May), the **Festival of Jewish Culture** (early July), and the **Jazz Festival** (Oct.-Nov.).

WARSAW (WARSZAWA) ☎022

According to legend, Warsaw was created when a fisherman netted and released a mermaid *(syrena)* who promised that if he founded a city, she would protect it forever. In World War II alone, however, two-thirds of the population was killed and 83% of the city destroyed. Although it has taken decades to rebuild, Warsaw is once again a beautiful, glamorous capital and is quickly throwing off its Soviet legacy to emerge as an important international business center.

▐ TRANSPORTATION

Flights: Port Lotniczy Warszawa-Okęcie (Terminal 1; WAW), ul. Żwirki i Wigury. (☎650 41 00, reservations (0)801 300 952). Take bus #174, 175, or 192 (bus #611 after 11pm) to the city center. Buy tickets at the *Ruch* kiosk in the departure hall or at the *kantor* outside. Open M-F 8am-8pm.

Trains: Warszawa Centralna, al. Jerozolimskie 54 (☎94 36), is the most convenient of Warsaw's 4 train stations. English is rare; write down where and when you want to go, then ask *Który peron?* ("Which platform?"). The **IT office** inside can help with schedules and translations. Yellow signs list departures *(odjazdy)*, white signs list arrivals *(przyjazdy)*. To: **Berlin** (6hr., 10 per day, 129zł); **Bratislava** (8-15hr., 2 per day, 163zł); **Budapest** (13hr., 2 per day, 216zł); **Gdańsk** (3½-4½hr., 12 per day, 57-106zł); **Kyiv** (23hr., 3 per day, 149zł); **Kraków** (2½-5hr., 10 per day, 55-101zł); **Minsk** (11hr., 3 per day, 111zł); **Prague** (10hr., 4 per day, 185zł); and **Vilnius** (10hr., 2 per day, 147zł).

Buses: Both PKS and Polski Express buses serve Warsaw.

PKS Warszawa Zachodnia, al. Jerozolimskie 144 (☎822 48 11; international ☎823 55 70; domestic ☎94 33), in same building as Warszawa Zachodnia train station. For international bus tickets, check **Centrum Podróży AURA** at the Zachodnia station. (☎823 68 58. Open M-F 9am-6pm, Sa 9am-2pm.) Buses depart for: **Prague** (12hr., 129zł); and **Venice** (20hr., 2-3 per day, 370-660zł). **PKS Warszawa Stadion,** on the other side of the river, sends buses east and south.

Polski Express, al. Jana Pawła II (☎630 03 20), in a kiosk near Warszawa Centralna train station, offers fast, comfortable domestic bus service to: **Gdańsk** (6hr., 2 per day, 37zł); **Kraków** (6hr., 2 per day, 33zł); and **Łódź** (2½hr., 7 per day, 17zł).

Public Transportation: (☎94 84; www.ztm.waw.pl) **Trams, buses,** and **Metro** run 5am-11pm. 2.40zł, with ISIC 1.25zł; extra ticket required for large baggage. **Day pass** 7.20zł, with ISIC 3.70zł. Buy tickets at kiosks; at night buy from the driver. Punch the end marked by the arrow *"tu kasować"* in the machines on board. Bus #175 runs from the airport to Stare Miasto via Warszawa Centralna and ul. Nowy Świat. Buses #127, 130, and 517 connect Warszawa Zachodnia with the city center. Warsaw's single **Metro** line runs north-south through the center. Two new **sightseeing bus routes,** #100 and 180, have been added for tourists.

Taxis: MPT Radio Taxi (☎919), **Euro Taxi** (☎96 62), or **Halo Taxi** (☎96 23). Call for pickup to avoid overcharging. State-run cabs with a mermaid sign tend to be safe. Fares from 4zł, plus 1.60zł per km. Legal maximum fare: daytime 2zł per km, night 2.40zł.

◆ ORIENTATION

The main part of Warsaw lies west of the **Vistula River.** Although the city is huge, its grid layout and efficient public transportation system make it easy to navigate. The main east-west thoroughfare, **Aleja Jerozolimskie,** is intersected by several north-south avenues, including **ulica Marszałkowska,** a major tram route. At that intersection, the enormous **Palace of Culture and Science** (Pałac Kultury i Nauki) hulks over **plac Defilad** (Parade Square); its clock tower, visible from most places near the city center, is useful for orientation. To the west lies **Warszawa Centralna,** the main train station, at the intersection of Al. Jerozolimskie with **Aleja Jana Pawła II.** To the east is **Rondo Charles de Gaulle,** the traffic circle where **ulica Nowy Świat** (New World Street) intersects al. Jerozolimskie and becomes **ulica Krakowskie Przedmieście** as it leads into **Stare Miasto** (Old Town). Going south, the road becomes **Aleja Ujazdowskie** as it runs past the embassy sector toward palaces and gardens.

◆ PRACTICAL INFORMATION

TOURIST, FINANCIAL, AND LOCAL SERVICES

Tourist Offices: Informacji Turystyczna (IT), al. Jerozolimskie 54 (☎94 31; www.warsawtour.pl), in Warszawa Centralna. Very helpful staff provides maps, currency exchange, and hotel reservations. English-language *Warsaw Insider* (7zł) sold in kiosks outside the office. Open May-Sept. daily 8am-8pm; Oct.-Apr. 8am-6pm. **Branch** at ul.

Krakowskie Przedmieście 89, across from Pl. Zamkowy. Open May-Sept. daily 8am-8pm; Oct.-Apr. 9am-6pm. **City Information System,** Pl. Defilad 1 (☎656 68 54; msitur@msi-warszawa.com.pl), in Pałac Kultury, also has information on travel and cultural events.

Budget Travel: Almatur, ul. Kopernika 23 (☎826 35 12; fax 826 45 92), off ul. Nowy Świat. International bus and plane tickets at student discounts. English spoken. Open M-F 9am-7pm, Sa 10am-3pm. **Orbis,** ul. Bracka 16 (☎827 07 30; fax 827 76 05). Entrance is on al. Jerozolimskie near ul. Nowy Świat. Sells plane, train, ferry, and international bus tickets. Open M-F 8am-6pm, Sa 9am-3pm.

Embassies: Most are near ul. Ujazdowskie. **Australia,** ul. Nowogrodska 11 (☎521 34 44). Open M-F 9am-1pm and 2-4pm. **Canada,** al. Matejki 1/5 (☎584 31 00). Open M-F 8:30am-4:30pm. **South Africa,** ul. Koszykowa 54 (☎625 62 28). Open M-Th 8:30am-5pm, F 9am-3pm. **UK,** al. Róż 1 (☎628 10 01). Open M-F 10:30am-4:30pm. **US,** al. Ujazdowskie 29/31 (☎628 30 41; www.usinfo.pl). Open M-F 8:30am-5pm.

Currency Exchange: *Kantory* have the best rates. **24hr. exchange** is available at Warszawa Centralna. **Bank PKO S.A.,** pl. Bankowy 2 (☎531 10 00), and ul. Grójecka 1/3 (☎658 82 17), in Hotel Sobieski, cash AmEx/Visa **traveler's checks.** Open M-F 8am-6pm, Sa 10am-2pm.

AmEx: al. Jerozolimskie 65/79 (☎630 69 52), in the Marriott. Open M-F 9am-7pm, Sa 10am-6pm. **Branch** at ul. Sienna 39 (☎581 51 53). Open M-F 9am-6pm.

Luggage Storage: At Warszawa Centralna train station, below the main hall. 4zł per day per item, plus 2.25zł per 50zł of declared value. Open 24hr. In Zachodnia Station, 4zł for a large pack. Open daily 7am-7pm.

Laundromat: ul. Karmelicka 17 (☎831 73 17). Take bus #180 or 516 from ul. Marszałkowska toward Żoliborz, get off at ul. Anielewicza, and go back one block. Wash and dry 26.60zł. Detergent 3zł. Open M-F 9am-5pm, Sa 9am-1pm. Call ahead.

EMERGENCY AND COMMUNICATIONS

Emergency: Police: ☎997. **Ambulance:** ☎999. **Fire:** ☎998.

24hr. Pharmacy: Apteka Grabowskiego (☎825 69 86), at the main train station.

Medical Assistance: CM Medical Center, al. Jerozolimskie 65/70 (24hr. emergency ☎458 70 00, ambulance ☎630 30 30), at the Marriott. English-speaking doctors and staff. 80zł for an appointment. **Branch** at ul. Domaniewski 41.

Telephones: At the post office; sells tokens and cards. **Directory assistance:** ☎913.

Internet Access: e-cafe, ul. Marszałkowska, across from Galeria Centrum, inside the Kino Relax complex. 8zł per hr. Open daily 10am-9pm. **Klub Podróżników Internetowych,** al. Jana Pawła II 57. 10zł per hr. Open 24hr.

Post Office: ul. Świętokrzyska 31/33 (☎827 00 52). Take a ticket at the entrance and wait in line. For stamps and letters, push "D"; for packages, push "F"; for *Poste Restante,* inquire at window #42 in the room to the left. Open 24hr. **Photocopy** and **fax** bureau (fax 30 00 21) open daily 7am-10pm. Address mail to be held: Firstname SUR-NAME, *Poste Restante,* ul. Świętokrzyska 31/33, Warsaw 1, **00-001** POLAND.

▸ ACCOMMODATIONS AND CAMPING

In summer, rooms become scarce and prices rise; call ahead, particularly for hostels. For help finding **private rooms ❸,** consult the **Office of Private Quarters** (Biuro Kwater Prywatnych), ul. Krucza 17, off al. Jerozolimskie, near Hotel Syrena. (☎628 75 40. Open M-Sa 9am-7pm, Su 2-7pm. Singles 79zł, 68zł after 3 nights; doubles 109zł/96zł.) **Almatur** and **IT** (p. 777) can arrange stays in **university dorms** July-Aug.

Warsaw

🏠 **ACCOMMODATIONS**
Camping "123", **18**
Dom Przy Rynku, **1**
Hotel Mazowiecki, **10**
Hotel Metalowcy, **8**
Portos/Aramis/Atos, **20**
Schronisko Mlodziezowe
  (HI), **16**
Schronisko Mlodziezowe
  "Agrykola", **19**
Szkolne Schronikso
  Mlodziezowe #6 (HI), **9**

🍴 **FOOD**
Bar Mleczny Familyjny, **14**
Bistrot, **13**
Gospoda Pod Kogutem, **7**
Mata Hari, **11**
Pod Gołebiami, **6**
Pod Samsonem, **3**

🍸 **NIGHTLIFE**
Morgan's, **12**
Pasieka, **2**
Piekarnia, **15**

☕ **CAFES**
Antykwariat Cafe, **17**
Pożegnanie z Afryką, **4**
Same Fusy Herbaciarnia, **5**

POLAND

Szkolne Schronisko Młodzieżowe #6 (HI), ul. Karolkowa 53a (☎632 88 29; www.ptsm.com.pl/ssmnr6). Take tram #12, 22, or 24 west from al. Jerozolimskie or the train station to D. T. Wola. Turn right at the underpass and follow the IYH signs. Great bathrooms and a cafe. Sheets 4zł. Lockout 10am-5pm. Curfew 11pm. Dorms 32zł, nonmembers 35zł, students 16zł; singles with bath 160zł; doubles with bath 260zł. ❷

Schronisko Młodzieżowe "Agrykola," ul. Myśliwiecka 9 (☎622 91 10; www.hotelagrykola.pl). Near Łazienki Park. Take bus #151 from the train station, or bus #107, 420, or 520 from Marszałkowska to Rozbrat. Continue as it turns into Myśliwiecka, then turn right at the path that leads to Ujazdowski Castle. Part hostel, part sports complex. Dorms 40zł; singles 274zł; doubles 329zł. 10% discount with "Euro<26" youth card. ❷

Schronisko Młodzieżowe (HI), ul. Smolna 30, top fl. (☎827 89 52), across from the National Museum. From the train station, take any eastbound tram to the 3rd stop, Muzeum Narodowe. Great location, but strict 11pm curfew. Sheets 5zł, towels 2zł. Lockout 10am-4pm. 3-day max. stay. Call 2 weeks ahead in summer, 2 days before otherwise. Dorms 30-33zł; singles 60zł; doubles 110zł; triples 150zł. ❷

Dom Przy Rynku, Rynek Nowego Miasta 4 (☎/fax 831 50 33). Take bus #175 from the center to Franciszkańska; turn right on Franciszkańska, then right into the *rynek*. Cozy rooms with clean baths. Open July-Aug. only. Lockout 10am-5pm. Dorms 45zł. ❷

Hotel Mazowiecki, ul. Mazowiecka 10 (☎/fax 827 23 65; www.mazowiecki.com.pl), off ul. Świętokrzyska. Next to the Stare Miasto; newly renovated bathrooms. Singles 150zł, with bath 210zł; doubles 200zł/270zł; triples 255zł. ❺

Hotel Metalowcy, ul. Długa 29 (☎831 40 21, ext. 29; www.inhotel.pl). Take any tram north along ul. Marszałkowska to Plac Bankowy, backtrack a bit, and turn right on Długa. Great location. Singles 56zł; doubles 88zł; quads with bath 155zł. ❷

Portos, Aramis, and **Atos,** ul. Mangalia 1/3a/3b (☎/fax 842 68 51, ☎842 09 74, and ☎841 43 95). From ul. Marszałkowska, take bus #410 or 519 (dir.: Wilanów) to Mangalia; turn right on ul. Mangalia. Rooms with bath in 3 side-by-side hotels. Singles 120-150zł; doubles 150-196zł; triples 174zł. ❹

Camping "123," ul. Bitwy Warszawskiej 15/17 (☎822 91 21), by Warszawa Zachodnia, across from the Hotel Vera. Take bus #127, 130, or 517 to Zachodnia, cross the street at the traffic circle, and turn left to Bitwy Warszawskiej. Open May-Sept. Guarded 24hr. English spoken. 10zł per person, 10zł per tent. Electricity 10zł. ❷

🖰 FOOD

Food stands are all over the city center. Cafeteria-like **milk bars** *(bar mleczny)* are satisfactory and inexpensive. There are **24hr. supermarkets,** often called *delikatesy*, at Warszawa Centralna and at ul. Nowy Świat 53. (☎826 03 22. Open daily 7am-5am.) Upscale restaurants can be found along ul. Foksal.

RESTAURANTS

🍴 **Gospoda Pod Kogutem,** ul. Freta 48 in Stare Miasto. Devour local food in the rustic interior or, during the summer, in the relaxed garden outside. Beer 5zł. Main dishes 10-20zł. Open daily 11am-midnight. ❷

🍴 **Bistrot,** ul. Foksal 2 (☎827 87 07). Specializes in delicious international gourmet cuisine. Romantic stone terrace, classy atmosphere, and formal waitstaff make it worth the splurge. Entrees 35-80zł. Open M-Sa 11am-midnight, Su noon-10pm. ❺

Pod Samsonem, ul. Freta 3/5, between Stare Miasto and Nowe Miasto. Hearty Polish-Jewish food. Decorated with pre-war photos. Meals 8-30zł. Open daily 10am-11pm. ❷

Pod Gołębiami, ul. Piwna 4a. The best *naleśniki* (Polish crepes; 4-8zł) in town, made before your eyes. Main dishes 9-30zł. Open daily 10am-11pm. ❶

Bar Mleczny Familijny, ul. Nowy Świat 39. A cozy dining room and tasty, cheap meals. Soups 1zł. Meals 2-6zł. Open M-F 7am-8pm, Sa-Su 9am-5pm. ❶

Mata Hari, ul. Nowy Świat 52. Incredibly cheap vegetarian Indian dishes. Soups and samosas 2.50-5.50zł. Open M-F 11am-7pm, Sa noon-6 pm. ❶

CAFES

🎔 **Pożegnanie z Afryka,** ul. Freta 4/6 and ul. Dobra 56/66. Terrific coffee (8-15zł). Tables are worth the wait. Open July-Aug. daily 11am-10pm; Sept.-June 11am-9pm.

Antykwariat Cafe, ul. Żurawia 45, 2 blocks south of Rondo Charles de Gaulle. Comfy; plush chairs welcome lingerers. Coffee 5-10zł. Open M-F 11am-11pm, Sa-Su 1-11pm.

Same Fusy Herbaciarnia, ul. Nowomiejska 10. Earthy teahouse in a forest-themed cellar. 150 varieties of tea (10-35zł per pot). Open M-F 1-11pm, Sa-Su 1pm-late.

ⓒ SIGHTS

Razed beyond recognition during World War II, Warsaw was almost entirely rebuilt from the rubble. Thanks to impressive renovations, buildings have been nearly restored to their pre-war state. Because sights are so spread out, the new tourist buses are a blessing: **Route #100** begins at Plac Zamkowy and runs along Plac Teatralny, ul. Marszalkowska, al. Ujazdowskie, Łazienki Park, and back up the Royal Way, then loops through Praga before returning to Plac Zamkowy. **Route #180** runs south from Wilanów past Łazienki and up the Royal Way before turning west to the Jewish Cemetery and then doubling back. In museums, *"Kwierunek Zwiedzania"* arrows aren't mere suggestions; follow these routes to avoid being accosted by flustered museum employees.

STARE MIASTO. Warsaw's postwar reconstruction shows its finest face in the cobblestone streets and colorful facades of the **Stare Miasto** (Old Town), at the very end of ul. Krakowskie Przedmieście in pl. Zamkowy. *(Take bus #175 or E3 from the city center to Miodowa.)* The landmark **Statue of King Zygmunt III Waza,** constructed in 1644 to honor the king who transferred the capital from Kraków to Warsaw, towers over the entrance to Stare Miasto. To the right stands the impressive **Royal Castle** (Zamek Królewski), the royal residence since the late 16th century. When it was plundered and burned down by the Nazis in September 1939, many Varsovians risked their lives hiding priceless works in the hope they might one day be returned. Today the palace houses the 🎔**Royal Castle Museum,** which has paintings, artifacts, and the stunning Royal Apartments. *(Pl. Zamkowy 4. Route 1 open M 11am-4pm, Tu-Sa 10am-4pm; Route 2 (Royal Apartments) closes 2hr. later; last entry 1hr. before closing. Route 1 8zł, students 3zł; Route 2 14zł/7zł. Su "highlights" tour 11am-6pm; free.)* Across ul. Świętojańska sits Warsaw's oldest church, **St. John's Cathedral** (Anrchi-Katedra św. Jana), decimated in the 1944 Uprising but rebuilt after the war. (Open daily 10am-1pm and 3-5:30pm. Crypts 2zł, students 1zł.) Ul. Świętojańska leads to the restored Renaissance and Baroque **Rynek Starego Miasta** (Old Town Square); the mermaid statue sits in the center. Ul. Krzywe Koło (Crooked Wheel) starts in the northeast corner of the *rynek* and leads to the restored **Barbican** *(barbakan)*, a rare example of 16th-century Polish fortification and a popular spot to relax. The *barbakan* opens onto ul. Freta, the edge of **Nowe Miasto** (New Town). Nobel prizewinning physicist and chemist **Marie Curie** was born at ul. Freta 16.

TRAKT KRÓLEWSKI. The attractive Trakt Królewski (Royal Way) thoroughfare starts at the entrance to the Stare Miasto on pl. Zamkowy and stretches 4km south toward Kraków, Poland's former capital. On the left as you leave pl. Zamkowy looms the 15th-century **St. Anne's Church** (Kościół św. Anny). Rebuilt in Baroque style, its most striking feature is a gilded altar. *(Open daily dawn-dusk.)*

Frederick Chopin spent his childhood in the neighborhood near ul. Krakówskie Przedmieście. He gave his first public concert in **Pałac Radziwiłłów**, ul. Krakówskie Przedmieście 46/48, the building guarded by four stone lions; it is now known as Pałac Namiestnikowski, the Polish presidential mansion. **Pałac Czapskich,** where Chopin wrote some of his best-known works, was his last home before he left for France in 1830; today, the palace houses his preserved Drawing Room (Salonik Chopinów) and the Academy of Fine Arts. *(Ul. Krakówskie Przedmieście 5. Open M-F 10am-2pm. 3zł, students 2zł.)* Chopin died abroad at the age of 39 and was buried in Paris, but his heart belongs to Poland; it now rests in an urn in **Holy Cross Church** (Kościół św. Krzyża), next to the Academy. For more Chopin relics, visit the **Frederick Chopin Museum** (Muzeum Fryderyka Chopina), which has a collection of original letters, scores, paintings, and keepsakes, including the great composer's last piano and a section of his first polonaise, penned when he was seven years old. *(Ul. Okólnik 1; enter from ul. Tamka. Open May-Sept. M, W, F 10am-5pm, Th noon-6pm, Sa-Su 10am-2pm; Oct.-Apr. M-W and F-Sa 10am-2pm, Th noon-6pm. 8zł, students 4zł. Audio guides 4zł.)*

The Royal Way continues down fashionable **ulica Nowy Świat.** Turn left just after Rondo Charles de Gaulle to reach Poland's largest museum, the **National Museum** (Muzeum Narodowe), which has an impressive art collection. *(Al. Jerozolimskie 3. Open Tu-W and F 10am-4pm, Th noon-5pm, Sa-Su 10am-5pm. 15zł, students 8zł; Sa free.)* Farther down, the Royal Way turns into al. Ujazdowskie and runs alongside sprawling **Łazienki Park** (on your left). Farther into the park is the striking Neoclassical **Palace on Water** (Pałac na Wodzie or Pałac na Wyspie), which houses rotating art exhibits. *(Take bus #116, 180, or 195 from ul. Nowy Świat or #119 from the city center south to Bagatela. Park open daily dawn-dusk. Palace open Tu-Su 9:30am-4pm. 11zł, students 8zł.)* Just north of the park, off ul. Agrykola, the exhibitions in the **Center of Contemporary Art** (Centrum Sztuki Współczesnej), al. Ujazdowskie 6, break all aesthetic barriers. *(Open Sa-Th 11am-5pm, F 11am-9pm. 10zł, students 5zł.)*

THE FORMER WARSAW GHETTO AND SYNAGOGUE. Still referred to as the Ghetto, the modern **Muranów** ("walled") neighborhood north of the city center holds few traces of the nearly 400,000 Jews who made up one-third of the city's population prior to World War II. The **Umschlagplatz**, at the corner of ul. Dzika and ul. Stawki, was the railway platform where the Nazis gathered 300,000 Jews for transport to death camps. *(Take tram #35 from ul. Marszałkowska to Dzika.)* With the Umschlagpl. monument to your left, continue down Stawki and turn right on ul. DuBois, which becomes ul. Zamenhofa; you will pass a stone monument marking the location of the command bunker of the 1943 ghetto uprising. Farther on, in a large park to your right, the large **Monument of the Ghetto Heroes** (Pomnik Bohaterów) pays homage to the leaders of the uprising. Continue along ul. Zamenhofa for two blocks and then take a right on Dzielna. On the corner of Dzielna and al. Jana Pawall, the **Museum of Pawiak Prison** (Muzeum Więzienia Pawiaka) exhibits photographs and artifacts, including the artwork and poetry of many former prisoners. Over 100,000 Polish Jews were imprisoned here from 1939-1944; 37,000 were executed and 60,000 were transferred to concentration camps. *(Ul. Dzielna 24/26. Open W 9am-5pm, Th and Sa 9am-4pm, F 10am-5pm, Su 10am-4pm. English captions. Free; donation requested.)* Follow al. Jana Pawall, take a left on ul. Anielewicza, and continue for five blocks to reach the **Jewish Cemetery** (Cmentarz Żydowski), in the western corner of Muranów. The extensive, thickly wooded cemetery is the final resting place of 250,000 Varsovian Jews. *(Tram #22 runs from the city center to Cm. Żydowski. Open Apr.-Oct. Su-Th 9am-4pm; Nov.-Mar. 9am-3pm. 4zł.)* The beautifully reconstructed **Nożyk Synagogue** (Synagoga Nożyka) is a living remnant of Warsaw's Jewish life. The only synagogue to survive the war, today it serves as the spiritual home for the few hundred observant Jews who remain in Warsaw. *(Ul. Twarda 6, north of the Pałac Kultury. From the city center, take any tram north along ul. Jana Pawla II to Rondo ONZ. Turn right on Twarda and left at the Jewish Theater (Teatr Żydowski). Daily service schedules ☎ 620 43 24. Open Su-F 7am-8pm. 5zł.)*

WILANÓW. After his coronation in 1677, King Jan III Sobieski bought the sleepy village of Milanowo, had its existing mansion rebuilt into a Baroque palace, and named the new residence Villa Nova (Wilanów). Since 1805, **Pałac Wilanowski** has functioned both as a public museum and as a residence for the highest-ranking guests of the Polish state. Surrounded by elegant, formal gardens, the palace is filled with lovely frescoed rooms, portraits, and extravagant royal apartments. Multilingual signs along the way allow you to break off from the slow-moving Polish-language tour to explore on your own. *(☎ 842 81 01. Take bus #180, 410, or 414 from ul. Marszałkowska, or bus #519 from the train station south to Wilanów; the road leading to the palace is across the street to the right. Palace open mid-June to mid-Sept. M, W-Sa 9:30am-2:30pm; Su 9:30am-4:40pm; mid-Sept. to mid-June W-M 9:30am-4pm. 15zł, students 8zł. English tours 120zł; groups of 6-35 24zł per person. Gardens open M and W-F 9:30am-dusk. 3zł, students 2zł.)* On the way out, take a left to see ads, art, and everything in between at the **Poster Museum.** *(Open Tu-F 10am-4pm, Sa-Su 10am-5pm. 8zł, students 5zł. W free.)*

ELSEWHERE IN CENTRAL WARSAW. The center of Warsaw's commercial district, southwest of Stare Miasto near Warszawa Centralna, is dominated by the 70-story Stalinist **Palace of Culture and Science** (Pałac Kultury i Nauki) on ul. Marszałkowska. Locals claim the view from the top is the best in Warsaw—partly because it's the only place from which you can't see the building, which is reviled more as a symbol of Soviet domination than as an eyesore. Below is **plac Defilad** (Parade Square), Europe's largest square—bigger than even Moscow's Red Square. Adjacent to **Saxon Garden** (Ogród Saski) is the **John Paul II Collection,** with works by Dalí, Rembrandt, van Gogh, Goya, Renoir, and others. *(Pl. Bankowy 1. Open May-Oct. Tu-Su 10am-5pm; Nov.-Apr. 10am-4pm. 8zł, students 4zł.)*

🎭 🎵 ENTERTAINMENT AND NIGHTLIFE

PERFORMING ARTS. For the latest schedule of performances, call the tourist information line (☎ 94 31). Inquire about classical concerts at the **Warsaw Music Society** (Warszawskie Towarzystwo Muzyczne), ul. Morskie Oko 2. (☎ 849 56 51. Take tram #4, 18, 19, 35, or 36 to Morskie Oko from ul. Marsza-

THE LOCAL STORY

AN IRISHMAN IN WARSAW

Thomas Morgan is the owner of the popular Morgan's Pub in Warsaw.

LG: This is a unique space for a pub—in a castle, under a Chopin museum.
TM: Yeah, it's a great place. Upstairs, people don't even know there's a pub down here, which is good, you know, since we don't bother them.

LG: So, why Poland?
TM: Well, it wasn't planned. I was working in another pub and I got bored with that, so I opened up this place a couple years ago.
LG: Do you speak Polish?

(Mr. Morgan laughs)

TM: Very badly! Most of the time I have no idea what customers are saying or singing, but as long as they're happy and having a good time, that's all I care about.

LG: Morgan's has become something of a legend here in Warsaw. Do you expect to stay here long?
TM: Oh yeah, as long as we're doing well, I'll stick around. Poles are great—love to sing, always telling stories. But too impatient—just like the Irish!

LG: Does the Guinness sell well, or do the Poles stick to local brews?
TM: Yeah, it sells really well. To be honest, I don't really like the stuff. But I don't want to disappoint them, so I play along.

(Imitates drinking and grimaces, but then smiles and gives a thumbs up.)

łkowska.) The **Warsaw Chamber Opera** (Warszawska Opera Kameralna), al. Solidarności 76B (☎831 22 40), hosts a Mozart festival each year in early summer. Łazienki Park hosts free performances at the **Chopin Monument** (Pomnik Chopina) on Sundays. (May-Oct. noon and 4pm.) **Teatr Wielki,** pl. Teatralny 1 (☎692 07 58; www.teatrwielki.pl), Warsaw's main opera and ballet hall, offers performances almost daily. **Sala Kongresowa** (☎620 49 80), on the train station side of the Pałac Kultury, hosts jazz and rock concerts with famous international bands; enter from ul. Emilii Plater. **Warsaw Summer Jazz Days** takes place annually in June.

BARS AND CLUBS. In the evening, Warsaw is full of energy. Cafes *(kawiarnie)* around Stare Miasto and ul. Nowy Świat continue serving until late into the night, and a large variety of pubs attract crowds with live music. In summer, large outdoor beer gardens complement the pub scene. Gay life is a bit underground; call ☎628 52 22 for information. (Open Tu-W 6-9pm, F 4-10pm.) *Inaczej* and *Filo,* sold in kiosks, list gay establishments. **▓Morgan's,** ul. Okólnik 1, is a friendly Irish joint with raucous karaoke on Tuesdays. (Guinness 15zł. Open M-F 3pm-midnight, Sa-Su 2pm-midnight.) **Pasieka,** ul. Freta 7/9, specializes in mead, an alcoholic honey brew that singes your throat but leaves a sweet, soothing aftertaste. (Open daily 10am-10pm.) Ultra-hip **Piekarnia,** ul. Młocinska 11, has a packed dance floor and expert DJs. (Cover F 20zł, Sa 25zł. Open F-Sa 10am-late.)

▓ DAYTRIPS FROM WARSAW

ŻELAZOWA WOLA. Twisting paths wind through the expansive, well-maintained gardens of **Frederick Chopin's birthplace.** (Cottage and park 10zł, students 5zł. Park only 4zł, students 2zł. Open May-Sept. Tu-Su 9:30am-5:30pm; Oct.-Apr. Tu-Su 9:30am-4pm.) From May to September, Polish musicians perform free **concerts** of Chopin's works. (Su at 11am and 3pm.) Concert schedules are posted throughout Warsaw and are also available at Warsaw's Chopin Museum (see p. 781). The **Wyszogród bus** runs from Warsaw (1hr., 3 per day, 7.80zł). Take one of the first two buses since no direct buses return after 4:30pm.

CZĘSTOCHOWA. Since 1382, Częstochowa (chen-sto-HO-va) has housed Poland's most sacred icon, the **Black Madonna** (Czarna Madonna). Each year, millions of Catholics visit the fortress-like **Paulite Monastery** (Klasztor Paulinów) on **Jasna Góra** (Bright Mountain) to see the Madonna. The reportedly miraculous icon is veiled and revealed several times a day in a solemn ceremony. (Chapel open daily 5am-9:30pm. Icon revealed June-Aug. M-F 6am-noon and 1-9:15pm, Sa-Su and holidays 2-9:15pm; Sept.-May M-F 6am-noon, 3-7 and 9-9:15pm, Sa-Su and holidays 6am-1pm, 3-7 and 9-9:15pm. Free, but donations encouraged.) The monastery also houses several other noteworthy museums. Take a **train** (2½hr.; 11 per day; 33.20zł, express 58.10zł) or **bus** (3½hr., 3 per day, 30-30zł) from Warsaw.

KRAKÓW   ☎012

Home to 100,000 students and scores of museums, galleries, and underground pubs, Kraków (KRAH-koof) is the highlight of Poland. Although it emerged only recently as a trendy international hot spot, the city has always figured prominently in Polish history. Wedged between the notorious Stalinist-era Nowa Huta steelworks to the east and the Auschwitz-Birkenau death camp 70km to the west, Kraków endured much darkness in the 20th century. Earlier, the city protected centuries of Central European kings and astounding architectural achievements, many of which still stand in the colorful Old Town.

POLAND

TRANSPORTATION

Flights: Balice Airport (KRK; ☎411 19 55; tickets 411 67 00; airport@lotnisko-balice.pl), 15km west of the center. Connected to the main train station by northbound bus #192 or 208 (40min.). A taxi to the center costs 30-50zł.

Trains: Kraków Główny, pl. Kolejowy 1 (☎624 54 39; info 624 15 35). To: **Berlin** (11hr., 2 per day, 120-160zł); **Bratislava** (8hr., 1 per day, 95-135zł); **Budapest** (11hr., 1 per day, 114-163zł); **Gdańsk** (dir.: Gdynia; 6½hr., 6 per day, 44-77zł); **Kyiv** (22hr., 1 per day, 200zł); **Lviv** (dir.: Odessa; 12½hr., 2 per day, 101zł); **Prague** (9hr., 1 per day, 100-160zł); **Vienna** (8½hr., 2 per day, 116-164zł); **Warsaw** (3hr., 34 per day, 51zł); and **Zakopane** (5hr., 5 per day, 17-27zł).

Buses: On ul. Worcella, directly across from Kraków Główny (☎93 16). To: **Warsaw** (5hr. 3 per day, 40zł) and **Zakopane** (2hr., 33 per day, 10zł). **Sindbad**, in the main hall, sells international tickets (☎421 02 40). To: **Berlin** (12hr., 3 per week, 142zł); **Budapest** (11hr., 2 per week, 116zł); **Lviv** (10hr., 1 per day, 50zł); **Prague** (11hr., 3 per week, 139zł). Comfortable **Polski Express** (☎022 620 03 30) buses depart from outside the PKS bus station to **Warsaw** (8hr., 2 per day, 45zł).

Public Transportation: Buy tickets at kiosks near **bus** and **tram** stops (2.20zł, after 11pm 4zł); punch them on board or face a fine. Large backpacks need their own tickets. Day pass 9zł; weekly 22zł. Student fares do not apply to foreigners.

Taxis: Barbakan Taxi (☎96 61, toll-free 0800 400 400); **Euro Taxi** (☎96 64); **Express Taxi** (☎96 29); **Radio Taxi** (☎919); **Wawel Taxi** (☎96 66).

ORIENTATION

The true heart of the city is the huge **Rynek Główny** (Main Market), in the center of **Stare Miasto** (Old Town). Circling Stare Miasto are the **Planty gardens** and a ring of roads including Basztowa, Dunajewskiego, Podwale, and Westerplatte. The gigantic **Wawel Castle** looms South of the *rynek*. The **Wisła** (Vistula, VEE-swa) river snakes past the castle and borders the old Jewish village of **Kazimierz,** which is accessible from the market by ul. Starowiślna (called ul. Sienna near the *rynek*). The **bus** and **train** stations are located just to the northeast of the Planty ring. To reach the *rynek* from either, follow the "*do centrum*" signs through the underpass to the Planty gardens. A number of streets lead from there to the square.

PRACTICAL INFORMATION

Tourist Offices: MCI, Rynek Główny 1/3 (☎421 77 06; info@mcit.pl). Sells maps and the handy *Kraków in Your Pocket* guide (5zł, English 10zł). Open May-Sept. M-F 9am-8pm, Sa 9am-3pm; Oct.-Apr. M-F 9am-6pm.

Budget Travel: Orbis, Rynek Główny 41 (☎422 40 35; www.orbis.krakow.pl). Sells train tickets, arranges trips to Wieliczka and Auschwitz, and exchanges currency. English spoken. Open M-F 9am-6pm, Sa 10:30am-2pm.

Consulates: UK, św. Anny 9, 4th fl. (☎421 70 30; fax 422 42 64; ukconsul@bci.krakow.pl). Open M-F 9am-2pm. **US,** ul. Stolarska 9 (☎429 66 55; emergency ☎429 66 58; www.usconsulate.krakow.pl). Open M-F 8:30am-5pm.

Currency Exchange: *Kantory*, except those around the train station, have the best rates. 24hr. exchange at the **Forum Hotel,** ul. M. Konopnickiej 28. **ATMs** all over the city.

American Express: Rynek Główny 41 (☎422 91 80), in the Orbis office (see above).

Luggage Storage: Kraków Główny. 1% of luggage value plus 3.90zł per day. Open 24hr.

POLAND

English Bookstore: Szawal, ul. Krupnicza 3. Open M-F 10am-6pm, Sa 10am-2pm.

Laundromat: Ul. Piastowska 47, in the basement of Hotel Piast. Wash and dry 9zł each. Open Tu, Th, Sa noon-6pm.

Pharmacy: Apteka Pod Żółtym Tygrysem, Szczepańska 1 (☎422 92 93). Open M-F 8am-8pm, Sa 8am-3pm. Lists 24hr. pharmacies in window.

Medical Assistance: Medicover, ul. Krótka 1 (☎422 76 33; emergency ☎430 00 34; www.medicover.pl). English spoken. Open M-F 8am-8pm, Sa 9am-2pm.

Telephones: At the post office and opposite the train station, ul. Lubicz 4. Open 24hr. Fax and phone cards at **Telekomunikacja Polska,** Rynek Głowny 19 (☎429 17 11).

Internet Access: Enter Internet Cafe, ul. Basztowa 23/1 (☎429 42 25. 8-11am 1.5zł per hr., 11am-10pm 3zł per hr. Open daily 8am-10pm.). **Cafe Internet,** ul. Sienna 14 (☎431 23 94. 5zł per hr. Open Su-Th 9am-2am, F-Sa 24hr.).

Post Office: Ul. Lubicz 4. *Poste Restante* at counter #5. Open M-F 7am-8pm, Sa open 8am, services stop at different times. Address mail to be held: Firstname SURNAME, Poste Restante, Kraków 1, **31-075,** Poland.

▐ ACCOMMODATIONS

Call ahead in summer. **Waweltur ❸**, ul. Pawia 8, arranges **private rooms.** (☎422 16 40. Open M-F 8am-8pm, Sa 8am-2pm. Singles 75zł; doubles 118zł.). The student dorms Żaczek, Bydgoska, and Piast offer rooms year-round.

▓ **Hostel Express,** ul. Wrocławska 91 (☎/fax 633 88 62; express.91@rodan.net). From the train station, take bus #130 five stops and then turn right uphill. Spacious bungalows with baths, TV, and kitchens. No curfew. Dorms 29zł; doubles 70zł; triples 99zł. ❶

Dom Wycieczkowy Pod Sokołem, ul. Sokolska 17 (☎292 01 99; sokoldw@inetia.pl). Take tram #8 or 10 from the train station (dir.: Łagiewniki) and get off at Korona, the 1st stop after the bridge. Backtrack toward the river, then turn left on ul. Sokolska, using the stairs just before the bridge. No curfew. Doubles 80zł; triples 110zł. ❷

Schronisko Młodzieżowe (HI), ul. Oleandry 4 (☎633 88 22). Take tram #15 from the train station (dir.: Cichy Kącik); get off at Cracovia, just after the National Museum. Take the right fork up 3-go Maja, then turn right on Oleandry. Excellent location. Flexible lockout 10am-5pm. Curfew midnight. Dorms 20-33zł. ❶

Dom Studencki Żaczek, ul. 3-go Maja 5 (☎622 11 42; www.zaczek.com.pl), just on the *rynek* side of Schronisko Młodzieżowe (above). Superb location, but has a noisy basement disco. Singles 75zł, with bath 95zł; doubles 85zł/150zł; triples 105zł/165zł. ❸

Hotel Studencki Piast, ul. Piastowska 47 (☎637 33 00; http://piast.bratniak.krakow.pl). Take tram #4 or 13 from the train station (dir.: Os. Bronowice Nowe) or #14 toward "Bronowice" and get off at WKS Wawel. Walk toward the tram and turn left on ul. Piatowska. Tidy rooms. Cafe and store on ground floor. Singles 65zł, with bath 125zł; doubles 88zł/120zł; triples with bath 168zł. ❸

Hotel Bydgoska 19, ul. Bydgoska 19c (☎636 80 00; http://bydgoska.krakow.pl). Take tram #4 or 13 from the train station (dir.: Os. Bronowice Nowe) or #14 (dir.: Bronowice) and get off at Biprostal. Take

Kraków: Stare Miasto

SEE ALSO COLOR INSERT

🏠 ACCOMMODATIONS
Dom Studencki Żaczek, 17
Dom Wycieczkowy Pod Sokołem, 20
Hotel Bydgoska 19, 2
Hostel Express, 1
Hotel Polonia, 5
Hotel Studencki Piast, 4
Schronisko Młodzieżowe, 18
Strawberry Youth Hostel, 3

🍴 FOOD
Ariel, 21
Cafe Zakątek, 16
Camelot, 6
Chimera, 8
Jadłodajnia "Anna Kwaśniewska," 15
Jadłodajnia u Stasi, 11
Nietoperz, 19

🍺 NIGHTLIFE
Bastylia, 14
Jazz Club "U Muniaka", 9
Klub Kulturalny, 7
Kredens, 13
Pod Jaszczurami, 12
Pod Papugami, 10

the 1st left on al. Kijowska, the 1st right on ul. Lea, and then a left on ul. Skarbińskiego, which ends in ul. Bydgoska. Grocery store, cafe, and post office downstairs. Dorms 25zł; singles 50zł, with bath 98-106zł; doubles 70-124zł; triples 90-134zł. ❶

Strawberry Youth Hostel, ul. Raclawicka 9 (☎636 15 00; www.strawberryhostel.com). Student dorm open July-Aug. No curfew. Singles US$8, doubles US$12. ❶

Hotel Royal, ul. św. Gertrudy 26-29 (☎421 58 57; www.royal.com.pl). From train station, take tram #10 (dir.: Łagiewniki) and get off at Wawel. Excellent location, spotless rooms. Singles 180-210zł; doubles 220-375zł; triples 360zł; quads 400zł. Single apartment 400zł; double 450zł. ❺

Hotel Polonia, ul. Basztowa 25 (☎422 12 33; www.hotel-polonia.com.pl). Across from the train station. Great location, elegant rooms. Singles 99zł, with bath 251zł; doubles 119zł/285zł; triples 139zł/329zł. ❹

⚫ FOOD

Many restaurants, cafes, and grocery stores are located on and around the *rynek*. More grocery stores surround the bus and train stations.

▨ **Cafe Zakątek,** ul. Grodzka 2. Fresh sandwiches (3-4.5zł), salads (3zł), and a stack of sentimental albums in this tiny *zakątek* niche. Open M-Sa 8:30am-8pm. ❶

Kraków

Camelot, ul. św. Tomasza 17. An Old Town legend. Cafe/gallery serves sandwiches (3-6zł), salads (19-21zł). Music or cabaret W and F 8pm. Open daily 9am-midnight. ❷

Chimera, ul. św. Anny 3. Cellar and romantic ivy garden. The oldest and most famous salad joint in town. Salad 7-10zł. Open M-Sa 9am-11pm, Su 9am-10pm. ❷

Nietoperz (The Bat), ul. Senacka 7. Intimate, woodsy cafe near Wawel. Desserts 3.50-5zł, żywiec 6zł. Open M-Th 9am-midnight, F-Sa 10am-1am, Su 10am-midnight. ❶

Jadłodajnia u Stasi, ul. Mikołajska 16. One-man operation serving old-fashioned budget dinners. *Pierogi* 2-4zł. Open M-F 12:30pm until food is gone, around 3 or 4pm. ❶

Jadłodajnia "Anna Kwaśniewska," ul. Sienna 11. Elegant lace curtains and antique photos. Traditional main dishes 4.60-9zł. Open M-F 9am-5pm, Sa 10am-3pm. ❶

Ariel, ul. Szeroka 18, in Kazimierz. Antique interior. Creative, non-kosher Polish-Jewish fare (8-35zł). Jewish music nightly 8pm (cover 20zł). Open daily 9am-midnight. ❷

Krew i Roza, ul. Grodzka 9. Cellar restaurant and garden serves regional cuisine. Main dishes 20-70zł. Live minstrel music F-Su. Open daily noon-midnight. ❹

◙ SIGHTS

OLD TOWN. Europe's biggest square, **Rynek Główny,** stretches across the center of the Stare Miasto. The *rynek* is a sea of cafes and bars, surrounded by multi-colored row houses. A trumpet call blares from the towers of **St. Mary's Church** (Kościół Mariacki) once in each direction every hour; its abrupt ending recalls the destruction of Kraków in 1241, when the invading Tartars are said to have shot down the trumpeter in the middle of his song. The church, which has a stunning blue-and-gold interior, encases the world's oldest Gothic altarpiece, a 500-year-old treasure once dismantled by the Nazis. *(At the corner of the rynek closest to the train station. Open daily 11:30am-6pm. Altar 4zł, students 2zł.)* In the middle of the *rynek*, the yellow Italianate **Cloth Hall** (Sukiennice) houses vendors hawking souvenirs and a gallery of the **National Museum** that displays Polish paintings and sculptures. *(Open Tu-W and F-Su 10am-3:30pm, Th 10am-6pm. 7zł, students 4zł.)* Ul. Floriańska runs from the **Barbakan** and **Floriańska Gate,** the old entrance to the city, to the *rynek*. The Barbakan and the Gate are the only remnants of the city's medieval fortifications. From the *rynek*, walk down Grodzka and turn right one block to reach the vibrantly colored **Franciscan Church,** an active church which houses Stanisław Wyspiański's amazing stained-glass window, *God the Father. (Open daily to 7:30pm.)*

AROUND WAWEL CASTLE. ◙**Wawel Castle** (Zamek Wawelski) is one of Poland's finest architectural works. Begun in the 10th century but remodeled during the 1500s, the castle contains 71 chambers, including a magnificent sequence of 16th-century tapestries commissioned by the royal family. *(Open Tu and F 9:30am-4:30pm, W-Th and Sa 9:30am-3pm, Su 10am-3pm. Royal chambers 15zł, students 12zł; armory and treasury 12zł, students 7zł; M free.)* Next door is **Wawel Cathedral** (Katedra Wawelska), where Kraków native Karol Wojtyła was archbishop before he became Pope. Earlier ages saw Poland's monarchs crowned and buried here. The steep wooden stairs from the church lead to **Sigismund's Bell** (Dwon Zygmunta). The climb affords a great view of the city. *(Open Apr.-Oct. M-Sa 9am-5:15pm, Su 12:15-5:15pm; Oct.-Apr. daily 9am-3:15pm. Tombs and bell 6zł, students 3zł.)* The entrance to **Dragon's Den** (Smocza Jama) is in the southwest corner of the complex. Legends say that a shepherd left a poisoned sheep outside the cave; the dragon took the bait and got so thirsty it drank itself to death at the Wisła river. *(Open May-Oct. daily 10am-5pm. 3zł.)*

KAZIMIERZ. South of the Stare Miasto lies 600-year-old Kazimierz, Kraków's old **Jewish quarter.** On the eve of World War II, 68,000 Jews lived in the Kraków area, many of them in Kazimierz, but occupying Nazis forced most out. All were deported by March 1943, many to the nearby Płaszów (where parts of *Schindler's List* were filmed) and Auschwitz-Birkenau concentration camps. Kazimierz today is a focal point for the 5000 Jews remaining in Poland and serves as a starting place for those seeking their roots. *(The walk from the rynek leads down ul. Sienna by St. Mary's Church; ul. Sienna turns into Starowislna. After 1km, turn right onto Miodowa, then take the 1st left onto Szeroka. Or, take tram #3, 13, or 24 toward Bieżanow Nowy from the train station.)* The tiny **Remuh Synagogue** is surrounded by **Remuh's Cemetery,** one of Poland's oldest Jewish cemeteries, with graves dating back to the plague of 1551-52 and a wall constructed from tombstones recovered after the Nazi occupation. *(Ul. Szeroka 40. Open M-F 9am-4pm. 5zł, students 2zł. Services F dusk and Sa morning.)* Back on Szeroka is the **Old Synagogue,** Poland's oldest synagogue, which houses a museum of sacred art. *(Ul. Szeroka 24. Open Apr. 8-Oct. 13 Tu-Su 9am-5pm; Oct. 14-Apr. 7 W-Th 9am-3pm, F 11am-6pm, Sa-Su 9am-3pm. Closed the 1st Sa-Su and open the 1st M of every month. 6zł, students 4zł. M free.)* **The Center for Jewish Culture,** in the former Bene Emenu prayer house, organizes cultural events and arranges heritage tours. *(Rabina Meiselsa 17, just off Plac Nowy. Open M-F 10am-6pm, Sa-Su 10am-2pm.)*

🎵 🎭 ENTERTAINMENT AND NIGHTLIFE

The **Cultural Information Center,** ul. św. Jana 2, sells the comprehensive monthly guide *Karnet* (3zł; www.karnet.krakow2000.pl) and tickets for upcoming events. (☎421 77 87. Open M-F 10am-6pm, Sa 10am-4pm.) Summer festivals are especially abundant, including the **International Short Film Festival** (late May), the **Festival of Jewish Culture** (early July), the **Street Theater Festival** (early July), and the **Jazz Festival** (Oct.-Nov.). The opera performs at the **J. Słowacki Theater,** Pl. św. Ducha 1. (☎422 40 22. Box office open M-Sa 11am-2pm and 3-7pm, Su 2hr. before performance.) The **Stary Teatr** has several stages in the city. (Tickets at Pl. Szczepański 1. ☎422 40 40. Open Tu-F 8am-4pm, Sa 8am-1pm.)

At night, cozy pubs come alive in the brick basements of 14th-century buildings near the *rynek*. 🅑**Pod Papugami,** ul. Mikolajska 2, is a laid-back disco with many nooks to schmooze in. (Beer 5zł. 18+. Cover F 8zł, Sa 12zł. Ladies free F. Open 7pm-3am.) 🅑**Kredens,** Rynek Główny 20, is a casual club packed with multinational party-goers. (21+. Cover 5zł. Open Su-W 4pm-2am, Th-Sa 4pm-4am.) **Klub Kulturalny,** ul. Szewska 25, is extremely hip and hidden below ground. (Beer 5.50zł. Open M-F noon-2am.) **Bastylia,** ul. Stolarska 3, is a friendly five-floor pub; look into any of the peepholes in the walls for a surprise. (Open daily 3pm-3am.) **Jazz Club "U Muniaka,"** ul. Floriańska 3, is the home of Kraków's jazz scene. (Shows M-Sa 9:30pm. M-W 10zł, Th-Sa 20zł. 50% student discount. Open Su-W 3pm-midnight, F-Sa 3pm-1am. At **Pod Jaszczurami,** Rynek Główny 8, students dance the night away amid Gothic arches. (Open daily 10am to 3 or 4am.)

🔼 DAYTRIPS FROM KRAKÓW

AUSCHWITZ-BIRKENAU. An estimated 1½ million people, mostly Jews, were murdered—and thousands more suffered unthinkable horrors—in the Nazi concentration camps at **Auschwitz** (in Oświęcim) and **Birkenau** (in Brzezinka). The gates over the smaller **Konzentrationslager Auschwitz I** are inscribed with the ironic dictum *"Arbeit Macht Frei"* ("Work Makes You Free"). Tours begin at the **museum** at Auschwitz; as you walk past the remnants of thousands of lives—suitcases, shoes, glasses, and more than 100,000lb. of women's hair—the sheer enormity of the evil committed comes into focus. A 15min. English-language **film,** with footage shot by the Soviet Army that liberated the camp on January 27,

KEEPING THE FAITH Visitors to Auschwitz and Birkenau will hear the name of Maksymilian Kolbe, a priest who sacrificed his own life while imprisoned at Auschwitz. When another man was sentenced to death by starvation, Kolbe willingly took his place, submitting himself to even more ghastly torture than he was already enduring. He was able to keep up his strength and stave off death for two weeks, but his efforts proved to be in vain—frustrated by how long it was taking to kill Kolbe, the Nazis shot him. After his death, Kolbe became a strong symbol of faith in the face of persecution: in 1971 he became the first Nazi victim to be proclaimed blessed by the Catholic Church, and in 1982 he was canonized by Pope John Paul II. The man whom Kolbe replaced survived, living to see not only the liberation of the camp, but also old age. Kolbe's starvation cell (#18), located in barrack II of Auschwitz I, can be seen by visitors. A tribute to the priest has been set up inside.

1945, is shown at 11am and 1pm. (Open June-Aug. daily 8am-7pm; closes earlier Sept.-May. Free. 3½hr. tour in English daily at 11:30am. 25zł, film included.)

The larger, starker **Konzentrationslager Auschwitz II-Birkenau** is located in the countryside 3km from the original camp. A 30min. walk along a well-marked route or a quick **shuttle** ride from the parking lot of the Auschwitz museum (mid-Apr. to Oct. every hr. 11:30am-5:30pm, 2zł) will get you there. Birkenau was built later in the war, when the Nazis developed a more brutally efficient means of exterminating the massive numbers of people brought to Auschwitz. Little is left of the camp today; most was destroyed by retreating Nazis who tried to conceal the genocide. The train tracks, reconstructed after the liberation, lead to the ruins of the crematoria and gas chambers, where a memorial pays tribute to all those who died in the Auschwitz system. Near the monument lies a pond, still gray from the ashes deposited there half a century ago.

The **Auschwitz Jewish Center and Synagogue** features exhibits on pre-war Jewish life in the town of Oświęcim, films based on survivors' testimonies, genealogy resources, and a reading room. Tours of Auschwitz are available. (*Pl. Ks. Jana Skarbka 5. ☎ 33 844 70 02; www.ajcf.org. Take bus #1, 3, 4, 5, 6, or 8 from the train station to the town center, get off at the 1st stop after the bridge, and backtrack to Pl. Ks. Jana Skarbka. Or take a taxi (about 15zł). Open Apr.-Sept. Su-F 8:30am-6pm; Oct.-Mar. Su-F 8:30am-8pm.*)

Buses from Kraków's central bus station go to **Oświęcim** (1½hr., 10 per day, 7zł). The bus back to Kraków leaves from the stop on the other side of the parking lot—turn right out of the museum to reach it. Less convenient **trains** leave from Kraków Główny (1¾hr., 3 per day, 8.70zł) and from Kraków Płaszów, south of the town center. Buses #2-5, 8, 9, and 24-29 connect the Oświęcim train station to the Muzeum Oświęcim stop; or, walk right as you exit the station, walk a block, turn left onto ul. Więźniów Oświęcimia, and walk 1.6km to Auschwitz.

WIELICZKA. A 1000-year-old ▓**salt mine** sits at ul. Daniłowicza 10 in the tiny town of Wieliczka, 13km southeast of Kraków. Pious Poles carved the immense underground complex of chambers out of salt; in 1978, UNESCO declared the mine one of the 12 most priceless monuments in the world. The most spectacular cavern is **St. Kinga's Chapel,** complete with salt chandeliers, an altar, and relief works. (☎278 73 66; www.kopalnia.pl. Open Apr.-Oct. daily 7:30am-7:30pm; Nov.-Mar. 8am-4pm. Tours 35zł, students 25zł.) Most travel companies, including **Orbis** (p. 778), organize trips to the mines, but the cheapest way to go is on the private **minibuses,** such as "Lux-Bus," which depart from between the train and bus stations (30min., every 15min., 2zł). Look for *"Wieliczka"* marked on the door. In Wieliczka, follow the path of the former tracks, then the *"do kopalni"* signs.

LUBLIN ☎081

Unlike most cities in Poland, Lublin's cobblestones and medieval buildings survived WWII. The 14th-century **Lublin Castle** (Zamek Lubelski), in the *rynek* of the **Stare Miasto** (Old Town), was used as a Gestapo jail during the Nazi occupation. Adjacent **Holy Trinity Chapel** contains stunning Russo-Byzantine frescoes. (Castle museum open W-Sa 9am-4pm, Su 9am-5pm. 5zł, students 3zł. Chapel open M-Sa 9am-3:30pm, Su 9am-4:30pm. 6zł, students 4zł. Entry to both 9zł/5zł) Take eastbound bus #28 from the train station, trollies #153 or 156 from al. Racławickie, or walk 30min. on Droga Męczenników Majdanka (Road of the Martyrs of Majdanek) to Zamość in order to reach **Majdanek,** the second largest concentration camp during WWII. Nazis did not have time to destroy the camp, so the original structures still stand. (☎744 26 48; www.majdanek.pl. Open May-Sept. Tu-Su 8am-6pm; Mar.-Apr. and Oct.-Nov. Tu-Su 8am-3pm. Free; children under 14 not permitted. Tours 100zł per group; call ahead. English guidebooks 7zł; maps free.) **Trains** (☎94 36) run from pl. Dworcowy 1 to: Kraków (4hr.; 6 per day; 38zł, express 45zł); Warsaw Central Station (3hr., 8 per day, 29-57zł); and Wrocław (8½hr., 8 per day, 41zł). The **tourist office**, ul. Jezuica 1/3, is near the Kraków Gate, next to the Hotel Victoria. Walk or take bus #8, 9, or 11 south on Narutowicza from the city center. (☎532 44 12; loit@inetia.pl. Open May-Aug. M-Sa 9am-6pm; Sept.-Apr. M-F 9am-5pm, Sa 10am-3pm.) From Zamkowy Square, walk past the castle and through the gate to reach ▓**Domu Rekolekcyjnym ❶,** ul. Podwale 15, an old abbcy with comfortable rooms. (☎532 41 38; j.halasa@kuria.lublin.pl. No curfew. Dorms 20-40zł.) Lublin's eateries cluster near **ulica Krakówskie Przedmieście,** and a dozen beer gardens are spread throughout Stare Miasto. **Café Szeroka 28 ❸,** ul. Grodza 21, serves regional and international cuisine on a terrace with a great view of the castle. (Entrees 20zł. Open Su-Th 11am-11pm, F-Sa 11am-midnight.) The *naleśniki* (Polish crepes; 4-12zł) at **Naleśnikarnia/Kawiarnia "Zadora" ❶,** Rynek 8, are excellent. (Open daily 10am-11pm.) **Postal code:** 20-950.

ZAKOPANE ☎018

Poland's premier year-round resort is set in a valley surrounded by jagged Tatran peaks and alpine meadows. During peak seasons (Jan.-Feb. and June-Sept.), Zakopane swells with hikers and skiers who come for the magnificent **Tatra National Park** (Tatrzański Park Narodowy); entrances lie at the trailheads. (2zł, students 1zł. Keep your ticket.) The bus station is on the corner of ul. Kościuszki and ul. Jagiellońska, across from the train station. **Buses** (☎201 46 03) go to: Kraków (2hr., 22 per day, 11zł); Warsaw (8½hr., 1 per day, 49zł); and Poprad, Slovakia (2¼hr., 2 per day, 15zł). A private **express line** runs between Zakopane and Kraków (2hr., 15 per day, 10zł); buses leave from a stop on ul. Kościuszki, 50m toward the center from the station. **Trains** (☎201 45 04) go to Kraków (2¾hr., 8 per day, 27-40zł) and Warsaw (8½hr., 3 per day, 63zł). Walk down ul. Kościuszki, which intersects the central ul. Krupówki (15min.). **Tourist Agency Redykołka,** ul. Kościeliska 1, gives information on private rooms (30-50zł) and runs English-language tours. (☎/fax 201 32 53; info@tatratours.pl. Open M-Sa 9am-5pm, Su 10am-5pm.) *Pokój, noclegi,* or *Zimmer* signs indicate private rooms (25-30zł). **Schronisko Morskie Oko ❶,** by the Morskie Oko lake, is a gorgeous hostel in an ideal hiking location. Take a bus (45min., 11 per day, 4zł) from the station to Palenice Białczańska or a direct minibus (20min., 6-10zł) from opposite the bus station. (☎207 76 09. Reserve well in advance. Dorms 30-40zł.) **PTTK Dom Turysty ❶,** ul. M. Zaruskiego 5, is a large chalet in the center of town. From the bus station, walk down ul. Kościuszki, which turns into ul. M. Zaruskiego. (☎206 32 07. Curfew midnight. Dorms 23 41zł.) Most restaurants are expensive; use the **Delikatesy** grocery store on ul. Krupówki 41, however, is cheap. (Open M-Sa 7am-10pm, Su 8am-10pm.) **Postal code:** 34-500.

◪ **HIKING NEAR ZAKOPANE.** The best place to start hiking is **Kuźnice,** south of central Zakopane. Walk from the train station along ul. Jagiellońska, which becomes ul. Chałubińskiego, then continue down ul. Przewodników Tatrzańskich to the trailheads (45min.). Alternatively, catch the Kasprowy Wierch **cable car,** (1987m) which runs between Zakopane and Kuźnice. (July-Aug. daily 7:30am-6:30pm; June and Sept. 7:30am-5pm; Oct. 7:30am-3pm. Round-trip 28zł, students 18zł.) The trails are well-marked, but pick up the tourist map *Tatrzański Park Narodowy* (7zł) at a kiosk or bookstore before hiking.

> **Mt. Giewont** (1894m; 6½hr.) has a silhouette that looks like a man lying down. It's crowded and the final ascent is steep, so be careful. From Kuźnice, take the moderately difficult blue trail (7km) to the peak for a view of Zakopane, the Tatras, and Slovakia.
>
> **Valley of the Five Polish Tarns** (Dolina Pięciu Stawów Polskich; full-day) is an intense, beautiful hike. It starts at Kuźnice and follows the blue trail to Hala Gąsienicowa. After several steep ups and downs, the blue trail ends at Morskie Oko. From here, it's 2km farther down to a parking lot in Palenica Białczańska, where buses return to Zakopane.
>
> **Sea Eye** (Morskie Oko; 1406m; 5-6hr.) is a dazzling glacial lake. Take a bus from the Zakopane station (45min., 11 per day, 4zł), or a private minibus (6-10zł) from opposite the station to Palenica Białczańska. Hike the popular 18km round-trip on a paved road, or take a horse and carriage (round-trip 2½hr.; 30zł up, 15zł down).
>
> **Dolina Kościeliska** (full-day) offers an easy and lovely hike crossing the valley of Potok Kościeliski. A bus shuttles from Zakopane to Kiry (every 30min., 2zł) and the trailhead.

WROCŁAW   ☎ 071

Thanks to Wrocław's elaborate post-war and post-communist reconstructions, the city shows little evidence of the its destruction in World War II. Now, Wrocław captivates visitors with the antique grace of its 19th-century buildings and lush parks. The gothic **Town Hall** *(ratusz)* towers over the *rynek* (Main Square) the heart of the city. The beautiful central street **Ulica Świdnicka** runs by the *rynek*. Entering the rotunda that contains the ◪**Racławice Panorama,** ul. Purkyniego 11, is like stepping right onto a battlefield; the painting depicts the 18th-century peasant insurrection led by Tadeusz Kosiuśzko against the Russian occupation. To reach the exhibit, face away from the *ratusz*, bear left onto Kuźnicza, and turn right onto Kotlarska, which becomes ul. Purkyniego. (Open Tu-Su 9am-4pm. 19zł, students 15zł.) Just across the street is the massive **National Museum** (Muzeum Narodowe), pl. Powstancow Warszawy 5, which has permanent modern art exhibits. (Open Tu-W and F-Su 10am-4pm; Th 9am-4pm. 10zł, students 7zł; Sa free.) The center of Wrocław's cultural life, the **University** (Uniwersytet Wrocławski), houses many architectural gems. Climb the **Mathematical Tower** at pl. Uniwersytecki 1 for a sweeping view of the city. (4zł, students 2zł.) Across the Oder river lies the serene **Cathedral Square** (Plac Katedralny). With your back to the *ratusz*, take any street forward until you hit ul. Piaskowy; take a left over Piakowsky bridge to **Cathedral Island,** then a right onto Tumski bridge to pl. Katedralny to reach the 13th-century **Cathedral of St. John the Baptist** (Katedra św. Jana Chrzciciela), whose spires dominate the skyline. (Open daily 10am-5:30pm. 4zł, students 3zł.)

Trains, ul. Piłsudskiego 105 (☎368 83 33), go from Wrocław Głowny to: Berlin (6hr., 2 per day, 141zł); Budapest (5hr., 1 per day, 209zł); Dresden (5½hr., 4 per day, 119zł); Kraków (4½hr., 8 per day, 35zł); Moscow (36hr., 1 per day, 290zł); Poznań (2hr., 21 per day, 29zł); Prague (7hr., 3 per day, 117zł); and Warsaw (5hr., 11 per day, 40zł). **Buses,** generally slower than trains, leave from behind the train station. From the train station, turn left on ul. Piłsudskiego, take a right on ul. Świdnicka, and go past Kościuszki pl. over the Fosa river to reach the *rynek*. **IT,**

Rynek 14, can help find rooms in student dorms. (☎343 71 19; fax 344 29 62. Open M-F 9am-5pm, Sa 10am-3pm.) Surf the Internet at **Internet Klub Navig@tor Podziemia,** ul. Kuźnicza 11/13. (7zł per 2hr. Open daily 9am-10pm.) The cheerful ■**Youth Hostel "Mlodziezowy Dom Kultury im. Kopernika" (HI) ❶,** ul. Kołłątaja 20, is directly opposite the train station on the road perpendicular to ul. Piłsudskiego. (☎343 88 56. Lockout 10am-5pm. Curfew 10pm. Call ahead. Dorms 22zł; doubles 28zł. Discount after two nights.) A 24hr. **Delikatesy grocery store,** pl. Solny 8/9 is near the *rynek.* Students crowd into ■**REJS Pub,** ul. Kotlarska 32a. (Beer 3.50zł. Open M-Sa 9:30am-late, Su 11am-late.) **Postal code:** 50-900.

KARPACZ   ☎075

Karpacz is a beautiful gateway to **Karkonosze National Park** (Karkonoski Park Narodowy; 3zł, students 1.50zł; 3-day pass 6zł, 3zł), where several 2¼-3hr. trails lead to **Pod Śnieżka** (1394m) on **Śnieżka** (Mt. Snow; 1602m), the highest peak in the Czech Republic; the Polish-Czech border runs across the summit. The Kopa chair lift also runs to Pod Śnieżka. (Follow the black trail from Hotel Biały Jar to the lift, on the left. Runs June-Aug. daily 8:30am-5:30pm; Sept.-May 8am-4pm. 2-3hr. Before 1pm 17zł, students 14zł; round-trip 22zł/18zł. After 1pm 13zł/9zł; round-trip 16zł/12zł.) **PKS buses** from Jelenia Góra (45min., every 30min.-1hr., 5.20zł) stop at eight points throughout Karpacz (3-20min., 2.20zł). **Buses** from Jelenia Góra run to Kraków (3hr., 2 per day, 42zł); Póznan (5hr., 2 per day, 38zł); and Wrocław (3hr., 8 per day, 19zł). Get off the PKS bus at Karpacz Bachus and head uphill to the Karpacz **tourist office,** ul. 3-go Maja 52, for information about various outdoor activities. (☎761 95 47. Open M-F 9am-5pm, Sa 9am-4pm; July-Aug. also Su 10am-4pm.) The office also makes reservations for **D.W. Szczyt ❶,** ul. Na Śniezkę 6, at the Karpacz Wang stop. (25zł per person.) Near the tourist office at ul. 3-go Maja 29 is the grocery store **Delikatesy.** (Open M-Sa 8:30am-9pm, Su 10am-8pm.) **Postal code:** 58-540.

POZNAŃ   ☎061

International trade fairs every March, June, and October fill Poznań, the capital of Wielkopolska (Greater Poland), with tourists and businessmen. Opulent 15th-century merchant homes surround the Renaissance **Town Hall** *(ratusz),* a multicolored gem with an ornately painted ceiling. (Open M-Tu and F 10am-4pm, W noon-6pm, Th and Sa 9am-4pm, Su 10am-3pm. Museum 5.50zł, students 3.50zł. Sa free.) The **National Museum** (Muzeum Narodowe), ul. Marcinkowskiego 9, contains a marvelous collection of 13th- to 19th-century paintings. (Open Tu 10am-6pm, W 9am-5pm, Th and Su 10am-4pm, F-Sa 10am-5pm. 10zł, students 6zł; Sa free.) The **Museum of Musical Instruments** (Muzeum Instrumentów Muzycznych), Stary Rynek 45/47, holds a fascinating display of antique and foreign instruments, including one of Chopin's pianos. (Open Tu-Sa 11am-5pm, Su 11am-3pm. 5.50zł, students 3.50zł. Sa free.) Sculpted ceilings and columns spiral heavenward in the **Parish Church of the City of Poznań,** at the end of ul. Świętosławska off Stary Rynek. (Free concerts M-Sa 12:15pm.) On the outskirts of town stands the first Polish cathedral, the **Cathedral of St. Peter and St. Paul** (Katedra Piotra i Pawła). In the **Golden Chapel** (Kaplica Złota) are the tombs of Prince Mieszko I and his son Bolesław Chrobry (the Brave), the first king of Poland. (Open daily 9am-4pm, except during mass. Entrance to crypt 2.50zł, students 1.50zł.)

Trains (☎866 12 12) go from Poznań Główny to: Berlin (3hr.; 8 per day; 95zł, students 85zł); Kraków (5½hr., 10 per day, 44zł); and Warsaw (3hr., 19 per day, 73.30zł). To reach the **Stary Rynek** (Old Market), take any tram heading down Św. Marcin (to the right) from the end of ul. Dworcowa, and get off at ul. Marcinkowskiego. **Centrum Informacji Turystycznej (CIT),** Stary Rynek 59/60 (☎852 98 05), sells 6zł maps. (Open June-Aug. M-F 9am-5pm, Sa 10am-2pm; Sept.-May

POLAND

M-F 9am-5pm.) ⬛**Przemysław,** ul. Głogowska 16, arranges **private rooms** ❷ near the city center. (☎866 35 60; przemyslaw@przemyslaw.com.pl. Singles 42zł; doubles 64zł. During fairs 26-32zł more. Open M-F 8am-6pm, Sa 10am-2pm; closed some Sa July-Aug.) **Bar Mleczny "Przysmak"** ❶, ul. Podgorna 2, has salads and pasta downstairs and heartier meals upstairs. (Open M-F 9am-9pm, Sa 11am-7pm.) For tickets and information on cultural events contact **Centrum Informacji Miejskiej,** ul. Ratajczka 44, next to the Empik Megastore. (☎94 31 or 851 96 45. Open M-F 10am-7pm, Sa-Su 10am-5pm.) **Postal code:** 61-890.

TORUŃ
☎**056**

Toruń bills itself as the birthplace and childhood home of Mikołaj Kopernik, also known as Copernicus; even before the local genius came to fame, his hometown was known far and wide as "beautiful red Toruń" for its impressive brick and stone structures. **Stare Miasto** (Old Town), on the right bank of the Wisła River, was constructed by the Teutonic Knights in the 13th century. The 14th-century **Town Hall** *(ratusz)* that dominates **Rynek Stromiejski** (Old Town Square) is one of the finest examples of monumental burgher architecture in Europe. (Town Hall museum and tower open Tu-Sa 10am-6pm, Su 10am-4pm. Each 6zł, students 4zł.) The birthplace of Copernicus, the man who "stopped the sun and moved the earth," is at ul. Kopernika 15/17; the meticulously restored **Dom Kopernika** features historical artifacts and an interesting sound-and-light show. (Open Tu-Sa 10am-6pm, Su 10am-4pm. Show every 30min. House 6zł, students 4zł. Show 8zł/5zł. Both 12zł/7zł. House free Su.) A city-wide burghers' revolt in 1454 led to the destruction of the **Teutonic Knights' Castle,** but the ruins on ul. Przedzamcze are still impressive. (Open daily 10am-6pm. 0.50zł.) The 15m **Leaning Tower** (Krzywa Wieża), ul. Krzywa Wieża 17, was built in 1271 by a Teutonic knight being punished for breaking the Order's rule of celibacy. The **Cathedral of St. John the Baptist and St. John the Evangelist** (Bazylika Katedralna pw. Św. Janów), at the corner of ul. Żeglarska and Św. Jana, is the most impressive of the many Gothic churches in the area. From there, it's a short walk across the *rynek* to the slender stained glass windows of the **Church of the Virgin Mary** (Kościół Św. Marii) on ul. Panny Marii.

The **train station,** across the Wisła River from the city center at ul. Kujawska 1, serves: Gdańsk (3hr., 6 per day, 36zł); Kraków (8hr., 3 per day, 46zł); Poznań (2½hr., 6 per day, 29zł); Warsaw (3hr., 5 per day, 33.20zł); and Wrocław (4hr., 2 per day, 49zł). **Polski Express buses** leave from pl. Teatralny for Kołobrzeg (7hr., 1 per day, 60zł) and Warsaw (3½hr., 16 per day, 20-37zł). **Dworzec PKS buses,** ul. Dąbrowskiego 26, leave for Gdańsk (3½hr., 3 per day, 32zł) and Warsaw (4hr., 5 per day, 36zł). The **IT tourist office,** Rynek Staromiejski 1, offers helpful advice in English and helps find lodgings. From the train station, take city bus #22 or 27 to Plac Rapackiego, the first stop across the river, and head through the little park; the office is on your left. (☎621 09 31; www.it.torun.pl. Open May-Dec. M and Sa 9am-4pm, Tu-F 9am-6pm, Su 9am-1pm; Sept.-Apr. closed Su.) Check email at **Internet Club Jeremi,** Rynek Staromiejski 33. (5zł per hr. Open 24hr.)

⬛**Hotel Trzy Korony** ❸, Rynek Staromiejski 21, has an amazing location. (☎/fax 622 60 31. Reception 24hr. Singles 90zł, with bath 150zł; doubles 110zł/190zł; triples 140zł/230zł, apartments 250zł.) **Hotel "Gotyk"** ❺, ul. Piekary 20, has beautiful rooms with Internet access. (☎658 40 00; gotyk@ic.torun.pl. Reception 24hr. Singles 150zł; doubles 250zł; apartments 300-350zł.) To reach the student-filled **PTTK Dom Turystycyny** ❷, ul. Legionów 24, from the *rynek,* follow ul. Chelmińska past pl. Teatralny; take the second right after the park and turn left onto ul Legionów. (☎/fax 622 38 55. Dorms 30zł; singles 70zł; doubles 80zł; triples 99zł.) There's a 24hr. **grocery store** at ul. Chelmińska 22. ⬛**U Sołtysa** ❶, ul. Mostowa 17, serves hearty Polish food. (Pierogi 7.50-13zł. Open M-Sa 11:30am-midnight, Su 1pm-midnight.) The pub **Miś**, in the basement at Św. Ducha 6, has an artsy reputation, but patrons gather here for laid-back pinball and darts. (Beer 4zł. Live music daily, DJ F-Sa. Open daily 6pm-late.) **Postal code:** 87-100.

ŁÓDŹ   ☎042

Łódź (WOODGE) once held the largest Jewish ghetto in Europe, which doubled as a Nazi textile factory during World War II. Because the ghetto had become a valuable source of labor, its 70,000 residents were not deported to death camps until 1944. Of those, 20,000 survived, and the Red Army saved another 800 from mass execution. The **Jewish cemetery** (Cmentarz Żydowski) is the largest in Europe, with over 200,000 graves. Near the entrance is a memorial to the Jews killed in the Łódź ghetto; signs lead the way to the **Ghetto Fields** (Pole Ghettowe), which are lined with the faintly marked graves of those who died there. (Take tram #1 from ul. Kilinskiego north to Strykowska Inflancka at the end of the line. Continue up the street, take a left on ul. Zmienna, and enter by the small gate in the wall on your right. Open May-Sept. M-F and Su 9am-5pm; Oct.-Apr. M-F and Su 9am-3pm. 4zł; free for those visiting relatives' graves.) The **Jewish Community Center** (Gmina Wyznaniowa Żydowska), ul. Pomorska 18, in the center of town, has information about those buried in the cemetery. (Open M-F 10am-2pm. Services daily.) Łódź is historically significant because of the Jewish ghetto, but it also happens to be the second-largest city in Poland. Its main thoroughfare, **ulica Piotrkowska**, is a bustling pedestrian shopping drag by day and a lively publand by night.

Trains run to Kraków (3hr., 2 per day, 33.50zł) and Toruń (2½hr., 6 per day, 29.30zł) from the Łódź Kaliska station, and to Warsaw (2hr., 18 per day, 25zł) from Łódź Fabryczna station. Polski Express **buses** depart from the front of the PKS station to Kraków (5hr., 3 per day, 42.40zł) and Warsaw (2½hr., 7 per day, 28zł). **IT**, ul. Piotrkowska 153, has tourist and lodging information. (☎/fax 638 59 55; it@uml.lodz.pl. Open M-F 8:30am-4:30pm, Sa 9am-1pm.)

KOŁOBRZEG   ☎094

Long known as the "Pearl of the Baltic," Kołobrzeg (koh-WOH-bzheg), with its excellent beaches and healing **salt springs,** was voted Poland's most popular holiday resort in 2001. The glamour of the modern city belies its history; in March, 1945, the Poles battled fiercely with the Nazis over the port, and although most of the city was destroyed, the Poles ultimately triumphed. They threw a wedding ring into the Baltic to symbolize Poland's claims on Kołobrzeg, and a **monument** near the beach now commemorates the event—"Poland's marriage to the sea" (Zaślubiny z Morzem). The 1745 **lighthouse** nearby offers an expansive view of the Baltic. (Open July-Aug. daily 10am-sunset; Sept.-June 10am-5pm. 3zł, students 2zł.) The **Gallery of Modern Art** (Galeria Sztuki Współczesnej), in the town hall, ul. Armii Krajowej 12, displays an exquisite collection of Polish crafts and artwork. (Open Tu-Su 10am-5pm. 4zł, students 2zł.) The **Museum Oręza Polskiego,** ul. Emilii Gierczak 5, features an impressive array of military paraphernalia. (Open Th-Tu 9:30am-5pm, W 9:30am-6pm. 6zł, students 3zł. Free W noon-6pm.)

Dworzec PKP trains (☎352 35 76) run from ul. Kolejowa to: Gdynia (6hr., 7 per day, 37zł); Kraków (12hr., 1 per day, 51zł); Poznań (4hr., 6 per day, 40zł); Warsaw (10hr., 7 per day, 49zł); and Wrocław (7hr., 2 per day, 45zł). **Dworzec PKS buses** (☎352 39 28) depart from next door to: Gdańsk (6hr., 1 per day, 37zł); Gdynia (5hr., 2 per day, 33zł); Poznań (5hr., 4 per day, 40zł); and Warsaw (11hr., 3 per day, 60zł). To reach the city center from the stations, take ul. Dworcowa, turn left onto ul. Armii Krajowej, the main thoroughfare, and continue to the town hall (15min.). Reaching the beach can be tricky; free English information and maps are available

POLAND

at the **CIT tourist office**, ul. Dworcowa 1, opposite the stations. (☎/fax 352 79 39; www.kolobrzeg.turystyka.pl. Open July-Aug. daily 8am-6pm; Sept.-May M-F 8am-4pm.) **Private rooms ❶** are the best lodging options; look for locals with *"wolne pokoje"* signs at the stations. **PTTK**, in the tower at ul. Dubois 20, can also help. (☎/fax 352 32 87. 20-50zł. Open M-Sa 9am-4pm.) **Jadłodajnia Całoroczna ❷**, ul. Budowlana 28, is a delightful milk bar hidden off the main square. From the town hall, turn left on ul. Armii Krajowej, turn right on Budowlana, and pass under the arch; enter through the back. (Meals 15zł. Open daily 10am-7pm.) **Postal code:** 78-100.

GDAŃSK ☎ 058

The strategic location of Gdańsk on the Baltic Coast and at the mouth of the Wisła has put it at the forefront of Polish history for more than a millennium. As the free city of Danzig, it was treasured by Poles as the "gateway to the sea" during long years of occupation in the 18th and 19th centuries. During WWII, it was the site of the first casualties and of the Germans' last stand; by the early 1980s, it was back in the spotlight as the birthplace of Lech Wałęsa's Solidarity trade union. Efficient transport makes it the perfect starting point to explore Malbork, as well as Sopot and Gdynia, with which Gdańsk forms the Tri-City area (Trójmiasto).

▐ TRANSPORTATION

Trains: Gdańsk Główny, ul. Podwale Grodzkie 1 (☎94 36). To: **Berlin** (8hr., 1 per day, 205zł); **Kraków** (7hr., 11 per day, 43zł); **Poznań** (4½hr., 7 per day, 41zł); **Prague** (14hr., June-Aug. 1 per day, 218zł); **Toruń** (3hr., 7 per day, 36zł); **Warsaw** (5hr., 18 per day, 73-83zł); and **Wrocław** (5½hr., 5 per day, 46zł). **SKM trains** (☎628 57 78) run to **Gdynia** (35min.; 4zł, students 2zł) and **Sopot** (20min.; 2.80zł/1.40zł) every 10min. during the day and less frequently at night.

Buses: ul. 3-go Maja 12 (☎302 15 32), behind the train station, connected by an underground passage. To **Kołobrzeg** (5hr., 8 per day, 36zł) and **Warsaw** (4½hr., 6 per day, 50-57zł). Nice **Polski Express** buses also run to Warsaw (4½hr., 2 per day, 45zł).

Ferries: (☎301 49 26; www.zegluga.gda.pl). Depart from under the Green Gate. May-Sept. to **Gdynia** (1½hr.; 2 per day; round-trip 54zł, students 37zł; one-way 39zł/28zł) and **Sopot** (1½hr.; 4 per day; round-trip 42zł/30zł; one-way 30zł/21zł). Apr.-Oct. to **Westerplatte** (50min.; every hr. 10am-6pm; 31zł/17zł).

Local Transportation: Buses and **trams** cost 1.10-3.30zł; day pass 6.20zł. Night buses 3.30zł; night pass 5.50zł. Large baggage needs a ticket.

Taxis: Super Hallo Taxi: ☎301 91 91. **Hallo Taxi:** ☎91 97. Both 1.80zł per km.

◢✚▐ ORIENTATION AND PRACTICAL INFORMATION

The city center is southeast of the train station, bordered on the west by **Wały Jagiellońskie** and on the east by the **Motława**. Take the underpass in front of the train station, turn right, exit the shopping center, then take a left on ul. Heweliusza. Turn right on ul. Rajska and follow the signs to **Główne Miasto** (Main Town), turning left on ul. Długa, which becomes **Długi Targ** as it widens near Motława. The suburbs are north of Główne Miasto.

Tourist Offices: IT Gdańsk, ul. Długa 45 (☎301 91 51; www.pttk-gdansk.com.pl), in Główne Miasto. Open June-Aug. daily 10am-8pm; Sept.-May 10am-6pm. **Branch** on the top floor of the train station (☎328 52 89). Open daily 10am-6pm.

Budget Travel: Adamar (☎/fax 301 68 99; www.adamar.pl), in the basement of the train station. Sells international tickets. Open July Sept. M-F 9am-5pm, Sa 10am-1pm; Oct.-June M-F 9am-5pm. **Orbis**, ul. Podwale Staromiejskie 96/97 (☎301 45 44; orbis.gdanskpod@pdp.com.pl). International and domestic tickets. Open M-F 9am-6pm, Sa 10am-3pm.

Currency Exchange: The train station has a 24hr. *kantor* with decent rates. **PKO SA**, ul. Garncarska (☎801 365 365), cashes traveler's checks for a 1% commission and provides cash advances for no commission. Open M-F 9am-5pm, 1st and last Sa of the month 10am-2pm. **24hr. ATMs** are on most street corners.

24hr. Pharmacy: Aptekus, at the train station (☎763 10 74). Ring the bell at night.

Internet Access: Rudy Kot Internet Music Café, ul. Garncarska 18/20 (☎301 86 49). Off Podwale Staromiejskie. 2.50zł per 30min. Open daily 10am-midnight.

Post Office: ul. Długa 23/28 (☎301 88 53). For *Poste Restante* use the back entrance on ul. Pocztowa. Open M-F 8am-8pm, Sa 9am-3pm. Address mail to be held: Firstname SURNAME, *Poste Restante*, Gdańsk 1, **80-801**, POLAND.

ACCOMMODATIONS

Reserve ahead, especially in summer. Or, get a **private room ❷** through **Grand-Tourist** (Biuro Zakwaterowania), ul. Podwale Grodzkie 8, downstairs in the City Forum shopping complex, connected to the train station by an underground passage. (Singles 43-55zł; doubles 73-90zł. ☎301 26 34; tourist@gt.com.pl. Open July-Aug. daily 8am-8pm; Sept.-June M-Sa 9am-6pm.)

Schronisko Młodzieżowe (HI), ul. Wałowa 21 (☎301 23 13). Cross the street in front of the train station, head up ul. Heweliusza, turn left at ul. Łagiewniki, then right after the church onto Wałowa. Popular and in a convenient location. Luggage storage 1zł. Sheets 4.28zł. Lockout 10am-5pm. Curfew midnight. Dorms 14.40zł, nonmembers 16zł; singles 27zł/30zł; doubles 54zł/60zł. ❶

Dom Aktora, ul. Stragarniarska 55/56. European luxury and a home-style feel just a stone's throw away from Długi Targ. Reception 24hr. Singles 200zł; doubles 250zl. ❺

Dom Studencki Angielski, ul. Chlebnicka 13/16 (☎301 28 16), 1 block off Długi Targ. Amazing location. Curfew midnight. Bring a sleeping bag and toilet paper. Open July-Aug. Dorms 28zł, students 25zł. ❶

Schronisko Młodzieżowe (HI), ul. Grunwaldzka 244 (☎/fax 341 16 60). From the train station, take tram #6 or 12 north (to your left facing away from the station) and ride 14 stops to Abrahama; you will see a complex of tram garages on the left (20-25min.). Turn right on ul. Abrahama, then right again on Grunwaldzka; the entrance is by the track. Immaculate rooms and bathrooms. Lockout 10am-5pm. Curfew 10pm. Dorms 18zł; doubles 30zł, with bath 41zł. ❶

Dom Wycieczkowy Zaułek, ul. Ogarna 107/108 (☎301 41 69). Ul. Ogarna is 1 block before Długi Targ when coming from the train station. Well-priced for the location, but noisy. Dorms 22-27.50zł; singles 50zł; doubles 70zł; triples 90zł. ❷

FOOD

La BoMba ❷, ul. Rybackie Pobrzeże 5/7, is a tiny creperie with a creative menu. (Crepes 4.50-15zł. Open June-Aug. daily 10:30am-10:30pm; Sept.-May 11am-9pm. Try the *szarlotka* (apple pie; 5zł) at **Cafe Kamienica ❷**, ul. Mariacka 37/39, in the shadow of St. Mary's Church. (Tea 4zł. Coffee 5zł. Entrees 12-19zł.) **Bar Pod Ryba ❶,** Długi Targ 35/38, has huge stuffed baked potatoes as well as good fish and chips. (Entrees 6-15zł. Open July-Aug. daily 11am-10pm; Sept.-June 11am-7pm.) **Bar Mleczny Neptun ❶**, ul. Długa 33/34, is a traditional cafeteria with some veggie dishes. (Entrees 5-10zł. Open M-F 7am-6pm, Sa-Su 9am-5pm.) For fresh produce, try **Hala Targowa** on ul. Pańska, just off Podwale Staromiejskie. (Open M-F 9am-6pm, 1st and last Sa of the month 9am-3pm.)

👁 SIGHTS

DŁUGI TARG. The heart of **Główne Miasto** (Main Town) is the handsome square Długi Targ (Long Market), where the 16th-century facade of **Arthur's Court** (Dwór Artusa) faces out onto **Neptune Fountain** (Fontanna Neptuna). The court features a magnificent Renaissance interior and spiraling carved wood staircase. Next to the fountain, where ul. Długa and Długi Targ meet, is the 14th-century **Town Hall** *(ratusz)*, which houses a branch of the **Gdańsk History Museum** (Muzeum Historii Gdańska) and its amazing collection of amber. *(Court and museum open Tu and Th 11am-6pm, W 10am-4pm, F-Sa 10am-5pm, Su 11am-5pm. 5zł, students 2.50zł.)* A block toward the train station is the **Church of the Blessed Virgin Mary** (Kościół Najświętszej Marii Panny), which has an intricate 15th-century astronomical clock. Climb the 405 steps to the top of the steeple for a fantastic vista. *(Open June-Aug. M-Sa 9am-5:30pm; off-season hours vary. 3zł, students 1.50zł.)*

ELSEWHERE IN GŁÓWNE MIASTO. The **National Museum** (Muzeum Narodowe Gdańsku) has a large collection of 16th- to 20th-century art and furniture. *(Signs lead from opposite the Town Hall, down Lawnicza and Żabi Kruk, under Podwale Przedmiejskie, and right on Toruńska. Open June to mid-Sept. Tu-F 9am-4pm, Sa-Su 10am-5pm; mid-Sept. to May Tu-Su 9am-4pm.)* The **Memorial to the Defenders of the Post Office Square** (Obroń ców Poczty) honors the postal workers who bravely defended themselves on September 1, 1939, at the start of WWII. *(From Podwale Staromiejskie, take Olejarna and turn right at the sign for Urzad Poctowy Gdańsk 1. Open M and W-F 10am-4pm, Sa-Su 10:30am-2pm. 3zl, students 2zl.)* Cobblestone ul. Mariacka, with Gdańsk's famous stone porch steps and gaping dragon's-head gutter-spouts, leads to riverside ul. Długie Pobrzeże. The huge **Gothic Harbor Crane** (Żuraw), part of **Central Maritime Museum** (Centralne Muzeum Morskie), is along the left. The other two branches lie across the river: one on land, the other on board the ship *Sołdek*. *(All branches open June-Aug. daily 10am-6pm; Sept.-May. Tu-Su 9:30am-4pm. Museums and ferry 12zł, students 7zł.)* The flags of Lech Wałęsa's trade union *Solidarność* (Solidarity) fly high once again at the **Gdańsk Shipyard** (Stocznia Gdańska) and at the **Solidarity Monument**, on pl. Solidarności, north of the city center at the end of ul. Wały Piastowskie.

GDAŃSK-OLIWA. The most beautiful of Gdańsk's many suburbs, Oliwa provides a respite from the big city. From the city center, take the commuter rail (dir.: Wejherowo; 15min.; 2.80zł, students 1.40zł). Trams #6 and 12 get there more slowly (30-35min.). From the Oliwa train station, go up ul. Poczty Gdańskiej, take a right on ul. Grundwaldzka, and turn left at the signs for the cathedral on ul. Rybińskiego. To the right you'll find the shady ponds of lush **Park Oliwski.** *(Open May-Sept. daily 5am-11pm; Mar.-Apr. and Oct. 5am-8pm; Nov.-Feb. 5am-6pm.)* Within the park's gates is the oldest church in the Gdańsk area, the 13th-century **Oliwska Cathedral** (Katedra), which houses a magnificent 18th-century organ. *(The tourist office has a complete schedule of daily concerts.)*

WESTERPLATTE. When Germany attacked on September 1, 1939, the little island fort guarding Gdańsk's harbor gained the unfortunate distinction of being the first target of World War II. Its defenders held out bravely for a week until lack of food and munitions forced them out. **Guardhouse #1** has been converted into a museum. *(Take bus #106 or 158 south from the train station to the last stop*

(20-25min.). Open May-Sept. daily 9am-6pm. 2zł, students 1.50zł.) The path beyond the museum passes the bunker ruins and, farther up, the massive **Memorial to the Defenders of the Coast** (Pomnik Obrońców Wybrzeża). Giant letters below spell out "Nigdy Więcej Wojny" ("No More War"). On March 31, 1945, Westerplatte also became the site of the Germans' last resistance.

BRZEŹNO. Brzeźno is perfect for a day at the beach. Though not as trendy as Sopot (see below), Brzeźno has **Park Brzeźnieński,** a wonderful haven full of tall pine trees. *(Take tram #13, 15, or 63 north from the train station to the last stop, Brzeźno. Follow the footpath in the wooded area ahead to reach the beach.)*

◪ NIGHTLIFE

Długi Targ hums at night as crowds of all ages pack its pubs, clubs, and beer gardens. Local magazines like *City* list events and venues in the Tri-City area. Eclectically decorated ▨**Latający Holender Pub,** ul. Waly Jagiełłońskie 2/4, is toward the end of ul. Dluga in the basement of the LOT building. (Beer 6zł. Coffee 4zł. Open daily noon-midnight.) The new **Blue Cafe,** ul. Chmielna 103/104, just across the first bridge at the end of Długi Targ, has occasional live music and an illuminated dance floor. (Beer 7zł. Open daily 11am-late.)

◪ DAYTRIPS FROM GDAŃSK

MALBORK. Malbork is home to the largest brick **castle** in the world, built by the Teutonic Knights. The castle's treasures include spectacular collections of amber and weapons. The best point from which to see the entire castle is across the river, on the other side of the complex from the train and bus stations. Buy the red English booklet sold in the kiosks (7zł) or call ahead for an English guide (126zł). Both **trains** (40-60min., 37 per day, 9zł) and **buses** (1hr., 8 per day, 7.20zł) run from Gdańsk to Malbork. Facing away from the station, walk right on ul. Dworcowa and turn left at the fork, following the signs to Elbląg. Turn the corner to the roundabout and cross to ul. Kościuszki, then veer right on ul. Piasłowska and follow signs for the castle. (☎ 647 09 76; www.zamek.malbork.com.pl. Castle open May-Sept. Tu-Su 9am-8pm; Oct.-Apr. 9am-3pm. 19.50zł, students 11.50zł. Mandatory 3hr. tour in Polish. Courtyards, terraces, and moats open May-Sept. daily 9am-6pm; Oct.-Apr. 9am-4pm. 6zł, students 4zł.) ☎ **055.**

SOPOT. Sopot is Poland's premier seaside spa town. The most popular golden sands lie at the end of **ulica Bohaterów Monte Cassino,** which is lined with cafes, pubs, and discos. (Beach M-F 2.50zł, Sa-Su 3.30zł.) The **SKM commuter rail** connects Sopot to Gdańsk (20min.; 2.80zł, students 1.40zł). Ul. Dworcowa begins at the train station and leads to the pedestrian ul. Bohaterów Monte Cassino, which runs along the sea to the 512m pier *(molo).* **Ferries** (☎ 551 12 93) go from the end of the pier to: Gdańsk (1hr.; 1 per day; round-trip 46zł, students 32zł); Gdynia (35min.; 4 per day; 45zł/34zł); and Westerplatte (35min.; 2 per day; 34zł/22zł). The **IT tourist office,** ul. Dworcowa 4, by the train station, arranges rooms. (Singles 39-46zł; doubles 62-78zł; triples 90zł. ☎ 550 37 83. Accommodations bureau open June-Aug. M-F 8:30am-5pm, Sa-Su 9am-2pm; Sept.-May M-F 9am-2pm.) ☎ **058.**

GDYNIA. Prosperous Gdynia is Poland's major port. The highlight of the massive pier off Skwer Kościuzki is the destroyer **Błyskawica** (Lightning), where sailors lead tours. (Open Tu-Su 10am-12:30pm and 2-4pm. 4zł, students 2zł.) The 1909 sailboat **Dar Pomorza** (Gift of Pomerania), once known as the "fastest and most beautiful ship of the seas," has taken first honors at the Cutty Sark Tall Ships. (Open June-Aug. daily 10am-6pm; Sept.-May 10am-4pm. 5zł, students 3zł; June-Aug. Sa free.)

The gargantuan **Museum of Oceanography and Aquarium** (Muzeum Oceanograficzne i Akwarium Morskie) sits at the end of the pier. (www.mir.gdynia.pl/akw. 8.50zł, students 5zł. Open daily 9am-7pm.) The beach stretches to the right of the pier.

   SKM Commuter trains run every 10min. from platform #1 at Gdynia Główna (☎94 36) to Gdańsk (35min.; 4zł, students 2zł) and Sopot (15min.; 2.80zł/1.40zł). The **IT tourist office,** pl. Konstytuciji 1, in the train station, has free maps and accommodation lists. (☎628 54 66. Open May-Sept. M-F 8am-6pm, Sa 9am-4pm, Su 9am-3pm; Oct.-Apr. M-F 10am-5pm, Sa 10am-4pm.) Any of the roads running away from the train station on your right will take you toward the waterfront. Gdynia's most intimate pub is ▓**Cafe Strych,** pl. Kaszubski 76, at the end of ul. Jana z Kolna. (Live piano music Th-F and Su 6:30-10:30pm. Open June-Aug. daily 4pm-1am; Sept.-May Tu-Su noon-midnight.) ☎058.

PORTUGAL

In the era of Christopher Columbus, Vasco da Gama, and Magellan, Portugal was one of the world's most powerful nations, ruling a wealthy empire that stretched from America to Asia. Today, it is often overshadowed by its larger neighbor Spain. But while it shares the beaches, nightlife, and strong architectural heritage of the Iberian Peninsula, Portugal is culturally and geographically quite unique. It contains the most pristine wilderness areas in all of Europe, and some villages in the northeast have not changed in over 800 years. Despite ongoing modernization, Portugal's rich, age-old traditions seem destined to stay—rows of olive trees give way to ancient castles, and Porto's wines are as fine as ever.

FACTS AND FIGURES

Official Name: Portuguese Republic.

Capital: Lisbon.

Major Cities: Coimbra, Lisbon, Porto.

Population: 10 million.

Land Area: 91,951 sq. km.

Time Zone: GMT.

Language: Portuguese.

Religion: Roman Catholic (94%).

DISCOVER PORTUGAL

Most tours start in charmingly sophisticated **Porto** (p. 819), home to its namesake dessert wine, and continue on to the thriving university town of **Coimbra** (p. 817). The rich history and constant action of **Lisbon** (p. 804) are not to be missed, nor is a climb to the nearby castles of **Sintra** (p. 812). **Lagos** (p. 815) has a wild nightlife and a spectacular coast that may be impossible to leave, but those who escape are rewarded by the glorious beach **Praia da Rocha** (p. 817).

ESSENTIALS

WHEN TO GO

Summer is high season, but the southern coast draws tourists March through November. In the off-season, many hostels cut their prices by 50% or more, and reservations are seldom necessary. But while Lisbon and some of the larger towns (especially Coimbra, with its university) burst with vitality year-round, many smaller towns virtually shut down, and sights cut their hours nearly everywhere.

DOCUMENTS AND FORMALITIES

VISAS. Citizens of the US, Canada, the UK, and New Zealand can travel without visas for up to 90 days. Australian and South African citizens need visas for stays of any length.

EMBASSIES. Most foreign embassies are in Lisbon (p. 805). For Portuguese embassies at home, contact: **Australia,** 23 Culgoa Circuit, O'Malley, ACT 2603; mailing address P.O. Box 9092, Deakin, ACT 2600 (☎62 90 17 33; embport@mail2me.com.au); **Canada,** 645 Island Park Dr., Ottawa, ON K1Y OB8 (☎613 729 0883); **South Africa,** 599 Leyds St., Muckleneuk, Pretoria (☎12 341 2340; portemb@satis.co.ca); **UK,** 11 Belgrave Sq., London SW1X 8PP (☎020 7581 8722); and **US,** 2125 Kalorama Rd. NW, Washington, D.C. 20008 (☎202-328-8610). **New Zealanders** should refer to the Australian embassy.

TRANSPORTATION

BY PLANE. Most international airlines serve Lisbon; some serve Porto, Faro, and the Madeiras. **TAP Air Portugal** (in Lisbon ☎218 43 11 00; in US and Canada ☎800-221-7370; in UK ☎0845 601 09 32; www.tap.pt) is Portugal's national airline, serving all domestic locations and many major international cities. **Portugália** (www.pga.pt) is a smaller Portuguese airline that flies between Porto, Faro, Lisbon, all major Spanish cities, and other Western European destinations.

BY TRAIN. Caminhos de Ferro Portugueses (www.cp.pt) is Portugal's national railway, but for long-distance travel outside of the Braga-Porto-Coimbra-Lisbon line, buses are much better. The exception is around Lisbon, where local trains are fast and efficient. Trains often leave at irregular hours, and posted schedules *(horarios)* aren't always accurate; check station ticket booths upon arrival. Unless you own a Eurail, **round-trip tickets** must be used before 3am the following day. Don't ride without a ticket; if you're caught *sem bilhete* you'll be fined exorbitantly. Though there is a Portugal Flexipass, it is not worth buying.

BY BUS. Buses are cheap, frequent, and connect just about every town in Portugal. **Rodoviária** (national info ☎213 54 57 75), the national bus company, has recently been privatized. Each company name corresponds to a particular region of the country, such as Rodoviária Alentejo or Minho e Douro, with notable exceptions such as EVA in the Algarve. Be wary of non-express buses in small regions like Estremadura and Alentejo, which stop every few minutes. Express coach service *(expressos)* between major cities is especially good; inexpensive city buses often run to nearby villages.

BY CAR. Portugal has the highest rate of automobile accidents per capita in Western Europe. The new highway system (IP) is quite good, but off the main arteries, the narrow, twisting roads are difficult to negotiate. Speed limits are ignored, recklessness is common, and lighting and road surfaces are often inadequate. Buses are safer options. Moreover, parking space in cities borders on nonexistent. **Gas** prices are high by North American standards—€0.60-0.90 per liter. Portugal's national automobile association, the **Automóvel Clube de Portugal (ACP)**, R. Rosa Araújo 42, 1250 Lisbon (☎123 18 01 00), provides breakdown and towing service (M-F 9am-5pm) and first aid (24hr.).

BY THUMB. Hitchers are rare in Portugal. Rides are easiest to come by at gas stations near highways and rest stops. *Let's Go* does not recommend hitchhiking.

TOURIST SERVICES AND MONEY

EMERGENCY	Dial ☎ **112** for police, medical, or fire.

TOURIST OFFICES. The official tourism website is www.portugalinsite.pt. When in Portugal, stop by municipal and provincial tourist offices for maps and advice.

BUSINESS HOURS. Official banking hours are Monday through Friday 8:30am to 3pm, but play it safe by giving yourself extra time.

MONEY. Taxes are included in all prices in Portugal and are not redeemable like those in Spain, even for EU citizens. **Tips** are customary only in fancy restaurants or hotels. Some cheaper restaurants include a 10% service charge; if they don't and you'd like to leave a tip, round up and leave the change. Taxi drivers do not expect a tip unless the trip was especially long. **Bargaining** is not customary in shops.

COMMUNICATION

PHONE CODES	**Country code: 351. International dialing prefix: 00.** From outside Portugal, dial int'l dialing prefix (see inside back cover) + 351 + local number.

MAIL. Air mail *(via aerea)* can take from one to two weeks (or longer) to reach the US or Canada. It is slightly quicker for destinations in Europe and longer for Australia, New Zealand, and South Africa. **Surface mail** *(superficie)*, for packages only, takes up to two months. **Registered** or **blue mail** takes five to eight business days but is for roughly three times the price of air mail. **EMS** or **Express Mail** will probably get there in three to four days for more than double the blue mail price.

TELEPHONES. Pay phones are either coin-operated or require a phone card. The basic unit for all calls is €0.10. Telecom phone cards are most common in Lisbon and Porto. Credifone cards are sold at drugstores, post offices, and locations posted on phone booths, and are most useful outside these two big cities. City codes all begin with a 2, and local calls do not require dialing the city code. **Calling cards** probably remain the best method of making international calls.

INTERNET. Cybercafes are common in cities and most smaller towns. When in doubt, try the library; they often have at least one computer with Internet access.

LANGUAGE. Portuguese is a Romance language similar to Spanish. English, Spanish, and French are fairly widely spoken. For basic Portuguese words and phrases, see p. 1063.

ACCOMMODATIONS AND CAMPING

SYMBOL	❶	❷	❸	❹	❺
ACCOMMODATIONS	under €15	€15-24	€25-34	€35-50	over €50

Movijovem, Av. Duque de Ávila 137, 1069 Lisbon (☎ 707 20 30 30; www.pousadasjuventude.pt), the Portuguese Hostelling International affiliate, oversees the country's HI hostels. All bookings can be made through them. A bed in a *pousada da juventude* (not to be confused with plush *pousadas*) costs €10-15 per night; slightly less in the off-season. To reserve a bed in the high season, obtain an **Inter-**

national **Booking Voucher** from Movijovem (or your country's HI affiliate) and send it from home to the desired hostel four to eight weeks in advance. In the off-season (Oct.-Apr.), double-check to see if the hostel is open. **Hotels** tend to be pricey. When business is weak, try bargaining down in advance. **Quartos** are rooms in private residences, similar to Spain's *casas particulares*. These rooms may the only option in smaller towns (particularly in the south) or the cheapest one in bigger cities; tourist offices can usually help you. There are over 150 official **campgrounds** (*parques de campismo*) with lots of amenities. Police are strict about illegal camping—especially near official campgrounds. Tourist offices stock the free *Portugal: Camping and Caravan Sites*, an official campgrounds guide. Or, write the **Federação Portuguesa de Campismo e Caravanismo**, Av. Coronel Eduardo Galhardo 24D, 1199-007 Lisbon (☎218 12 68 90; www.fpcampismo.pt).

FOOD AND DRINK

SYMBOL	❶	❷	❸	❹	❺
FOOD	under €6	€6-10	€11-15	€16-25	over €25

Dishes are seasoned with olive oil, garlic, herbs, and sea salt, but few spices. The fish selection includes *chocos grelhados* (grilled cuttlefish), *linguado grelhado* (grilled sole), and *peixe espada* (swordfish). *Sandes* (cheese sandwiches) come on delectable bread. For dessert, try *pudim* or *flan* (caramel custard). The hearty *almoço* (lunch) is eaten between noon and 2pm; *jantar* (dinner) between 8pm and midnight. *Meia dose* (half-portions) are often adequate; full portions may satisfy two. The *prato do dia* (special of the day) or *ementa* (menu) of appetizer, bread, entree, and dessert is filling. *Vinho do porto* (port) is a dessert in itself. *Madeira* wines have a unique "cooked" flavor. Coffees are *bica* (black espresso), *galão* (with milk, served in a glass), and *café com leite* (with milk, in a cup).

HOLIDAYS AND FESTIVALS

Holidays: New Year's Day (Jan. 1); Good Friday (Apr. 18); Easter (Apr. 20); Liberation Day (Apr. 25); Labor Day (May 1); Feast of the Assumption (Aug. 15); Republic Day (Oct. 5); All Saints' Day (Nov. 1); Feast of the Immaculate Conception (Dec. 8); Christmas (Dec. 25).

Festivals: All of Portugal celebrates **Carnival** March 4 and the **Holy Week** Apr. 13-20. Coimbra holds the **Burning of the Ribbons** festival in early May, and Lisbon hosts the **Feira Internacional de Lisboa** in June. Coimbra's **Feira Popular** takes place the 2nd week of July. For more information on Portuguese festivals, see www.portugal.org.

LISBON (LISBOA)   ☎21

Once the center of the world's richest and farthest-reaching empire, Lisbon hit its peak at the end of the 15th century when Portuguese navigators pioneered explorations of Asia, Africa, and South America. The city works to preserve its rich history, continually renovating its monuments and meticulously maintaining its black-and-white mosaic sidewalks, pastel facades, and cobbled medieval alleys. In 1998, Lisbon hosted the World Expo, sparking a citywide face-lift and beginning a movement to reclaim its place as one of Europe's grandest cities.

▐ TRANSPORTATION

Flights: Aeroporto de Lisboa (LIS; ☎218 41 35 00), on the city's northern edge. **Buses** #44 and 45 (15-20min., every 12-15min., €0.90) and the express **AeroBus** #91 (15min., every 20min., €2.30) go to Pr. dos Restauradores from outside the terminal. A **taxi** to downtown costs about €11, plus a €1.50 luggage fee.

Trains: Caminhos de Ferro Portuguêses (☎800 20 09 04; www.cp.pt). Four main stations, each serving different destinations. Portuguese trains are usually quite slow; buses are often a better choice.

Estação Barreiro, across the Rio Tejo, goes south. Station accessible by ferry from the Terreiro do Paço dock off Pr. Comércio (30min., every 30min., price included in train ticket). Trains to **Évora** (2½hr., 7 per day, €6) and **Lagos** (5½hr., 5 per day, €14).

Estação Cais do Sodré (☎213 47 01 81), to the right of Pr. Comércio when walking from Baixa. M: Cais do Sodré. To **Estoril** and **Cascais** (30min., every 20min., €1.10).

Estação Rossio (☎213 46 50 22), serves points west. M: Rossio or Restauradores. To **Sintra** (45min., every 15-30min., €1.10) via **Queluz** (€0.70).

Estação Santa Apolónia (☎218 88 40 25), on Av. Infante D. Henrique, east of the Alfama on the Rio Tejo, runs the international, northern, and eastern lines. Take bus #9, 39, 46, or 90 to Pr. dos Restauradores and Estação Rossio. To: **Coimbra** (2½hr., 7 per day, €8-13); **Madrid** (10hr., 10pm, €41); **Porto** (4½hr., 12 per day, €10-19).

Buses: Arco do Cego, Av. João Crisóstomo, around the block from the M: Saldanha. All "Saldanha" buses (#36, 44, 45) stop in the *praça* (€0.60). Fast **Rede Expressos** (☎213 54 54 39 or 310 31 11; www.rede-expressos.pt) go to many destinations, including: **Coimbra** (2½hr., 16 per day, €9); **Évora** (2hr., 13 per day, €8); **Lagos** (5hr., 9 per day, €15); **Porto** (4hr., 7 per day, €12), via **Leiria.**

Public Transportation: CARRIS (☎213 61 30 00; www.carris.pt) operates **buses, trams,** and **funiculars** (each €0.90); *passe turistico* (tourist pass) good for unlimited CARRIS travel. 1-day pass €2.30, 3-day pass €5.50, 4-day pass €9, 7-day pass €13. **Metro** (☎213 55 84 57; www.metrolisboa.pt) covers downtown and the modern business district. Individual tickets €0.55; book of 10 tickets €4.50. Trains run daily 6:30am-1am; some stations close earlier.

Taxis: Rádio Táxis de Lisboa (☎218 11 90 00), **Autocoope** (☎217 93 27 56), and **Teletáxis** (☎218 11 11 00) all line up along Av. da Liberdade and the Rossio.

■ ▪ 🛈 ORIENTATION AND PRACTICAL INFORMATION

The city center is the **Baixa,** the old business area, between the **Bairro Alto** and the **Alfama.** The Baixa's grid of mostly pedestrian streets is bordered to the north by the Rossio (a.k.a. Praça Dom Pedro IV), adjacent to Praça da Figueira and Praça dos Restauradores (at the tourist office and airport buses stop); **Avenida da Liberdade** runs north, uphill from Pr. dos Restauradores. At the Baixa's southern end is the **Praça do Comércio,** on the **Rio Tejo** (River Tagus). Along the river are the Expo '98 grounds, now called the **Parque das Nações** (Park of Nations), and the fast-growing **Alcântara** and **Docas** (docks) districts. **Alfama,** a labyrinth of narrow alleys and stairways beneath the Castelo de São Jorge, is the city's oldest district. Across the Baixa from Alfama is **Bairro Alto** and its upscale shopping district, the **Chiado,** which is traversed by R. do Carmo and R. Garrett, near much of the city's nightlife.

TOURIST, FINANCIAL, AND LOCAL SERVICES

Tourist Offices: Palácio da Foz, Pr. dos Restauradores (☎213 46 33 14). M: Restauradores. This is the mother of all Portuguese tourist offices; it houses information about the entire country. The **Welcome Center,** Pr. Comécio (☎210 31 28 10), is the office for the city of Lisbon. Both offices open daily 9am-8pm. Office at the **Aeroporto de Lisboa** (☎218 45 06 06) is just outside the baggage claim area. Open daily 6am-2am.

Embassies: Australia, Av. da Liberdade 200-2 (☎213 10 15 00; austemb@oninet.pt); **Canada,** Av. da Liberdade 198-200, 3rd fl. (☎213 16 46 00; lsbon-cs@dfait-maeci.gc.ca); **Ireland,** R. Imprensa à Estrela, 4th fl. (☎213 92 94 40; fax 97 73 63); **New Zealand** (consulate) R. do S. Felix 13-2 (☎213 50 96 90); **South Africa,** Av. Luis Bivar 10 (☎213 19 22 00; safrica@mail.eunet.pt); **UK,** R. São Bernardo 33 (☎213 92 40 00; www.uk-embassy.pt); **US,** Av. das Forças Armadas (☎217 27 33 00; www.american-embassy.pt).

American Express: Top Tours, Av. Duque de Loulé 108 (☎213 19 42 90). M: Marquês de Pombal. Exit the Metro stop and walk up Av. da Liberdade toward the Marquês de Pombal statue, then turn right; the office is 2 blocks up on the left side of the street. Handles all AmEx functions. English spoken. Open M-F 9:30am-1pm and 2:30-6:30pm.

Luggage Storage: Estação Rossio. Lockers €3 for 48hr. Open daily 8:30am-11:30pm. Also available at Estação Sta. Apolónia.

English-Language Bookstore: Livraria Británica, R. Luis Fernandes 14-16 (☎213 42 84 72), in the Bairro Alto. Open M-F 9:30am-7pm.

Laundromat: Lavatax, R. Francisco Sanches 65A (☎218 12 33 92). M: Arroios. Wash, dry, and fold €5.50 per 5kg. Open M-F 8:30am-1pm and 3-7pm, Sa 8:30am-1pm.

EMERGENCY AND COMMUNICATIONS

Emergency: ☎112. **Ambulance:** ☎219 42 11 11.

Police: R. Capelo 13 (☎213 46 61 41). English spoken.

Late-night Pharmacy: ☎118 (directory assistance). Rotates; check the list posted on the door of any pharmacy.

Medical Services: British Hospital, R. Saraiva de Carvalho 49 (☎213 95 50 67). **Cruz Vermelha Portuguesa,** R. Duarte Galvão 54 (☎217 71 40 00).

Internet Access: Web C@fe, R. Diário de Notícias 126 (☎213 42 11 81). €2 per 15min., €2.50 per 30min., €4 per hr. Open daily 4pm-2am. **Abracadabra,** Pr. Dom Pedro IV 66. €1 per 15min., €2 per 30min., €3 per hr. Open M-Sa 8am-8pm. **Ciber Chiado,** Largo Picadeiro 10 (☎213 22 57 64). Upstairs in the National Cultural Center building. Ring the bell to enter. €1.50 per 15min., €2 per 30min., €3 per 1hr., €4 per 2hr. Open M-F 4pm-midnight, Sa 8pm-midnight.

Post Office: Marked by red *Correios* signs. **Main office** (☎213 23 89 71), Pr. dos Restauradores. Open M-F 8am-10pm, Sa-Su 9am-6pm. **Branch office** (☎213 22 09 21) at Pr. Comércio. Open M-F 8:30am-6:30pm. Credit cards not accepted. **Postal Code:** 1100 for central Lisbon.

ACCOMMODATIONS

Most hotels are in the center of town on **Avenida da Liberdade,** while many convenient budget hostels are in the **Baixa** along the **Rossio** and on **Rua Prata, Rua Correeiros,** and **Rua Ouro.** Lodgings near the **Castelo de São Jorge** or in the **Bairro Alto** are quieter and closer to the sights. If central accommodations are full, head east to the hostels along **Avenida Almirante Reis.** At night, be careful in the Baixa, the Bairro Alto, and especially the Alfama; many streets are isolated and poorly lit.

Casa de Hóspedes Globo, R. Teixeira 37 (☎/fax 213 46 22 79), on a small street across from the Parque São Pedro de Alcântara at the top of the funicular. From the park entrance, cross the street and go one block on Trav. da Cara, then turn right onto R. Teixeira. A popular spot for young travelers. All rooms newly renovated with phones. Most with TV; all but two with bath. Laundry €10 per load. Singles €15, with bath €25; double with bath €25-35; triple with bath €40. ❷

Pensão Royal, R. do Crucifixo 50, 3rd fl. (☎218 86 95 06). M: Baixa/Chiado. Take a right out of the station on R. do Crucifixo; it's on the left before the intersection with R. São Nicolas. This new *pensão* offers airy rooms with hardwood floors, TVs, and bath. May-Oct. dorms €15; singles €20; doubles €30. Nov.-Apr. €5 less. ❷

Pensão Estação Central, Calçada da Carmo 17, 2nd-3rd fl. (☎213 42 33 08), a block from the central station, across the Largo Duque Cadaval. M: Rossio. Small, plain rooms in a central location. Rooms without full bath have shower. June-Sept. singles €15, with bath €20; doubles €30/€35. Oct.-May €5 less. ❷

PORTUGAL

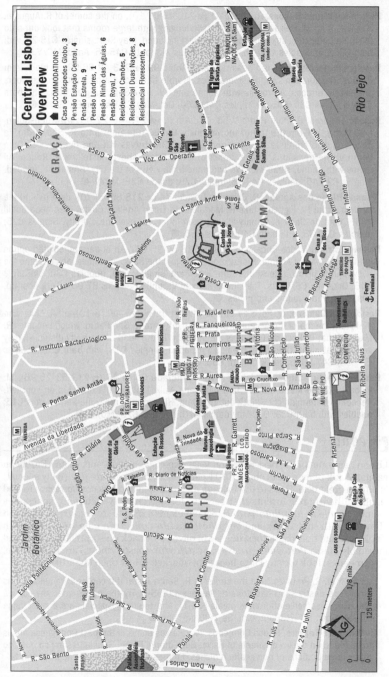

Central Lisbon Overview

▲ ACCOMMODATIONS
Casa de Hóspedes Globo, 3
Pensão Estação Central, 4
Pensão Estrela, 9
Pensão Londres, 1
Pensão Ninho das Águias, 6
Pensão Royal, 7
Residencial Camões, 5
Residencial Duas Nações, 8
Residencial Florescente, 2

Residencial Duas Nações, R. Vitória 41 (☎213 46 07 10), on the corner of R. Augusta, 3 blocks from M: Baixa-Chiado. Hotel-style lodging with large rooms that look out onto the main pedestrian street of Baixa. Breakfast included. May-Sept. singles €15-20, with bath €30-35; doubles €20-25/€40-45; triples with bath €45-55. AmEx/MC/V. ❷

Residencial Florescente, R. Portas de Santo Antão 99 (☎213 42 66 09), 1 block from Pr. dos Restauradores. M: Restauradores. Marble baths and rooms with French doors and small terraces. All rooms with phone and TV. June-Sept. singles €25, with bath €40; doubles €30/€45-60; triples €45/€60. Oct.-May €5 less. AmEx/MC/V. ❸

Pensão Londres, R. Dom Pedro V 53, 2nd-4th fl. (☎213 46 22 03; www.pensaolondres.com.pt). From the top of the Ascensor Glória, turn right onto R. São Pedro de Alcântara and continue past the park as the road curves left and becomes R. Dom Pedro V; the *pensão* is on the corner of R. da Rosa, above Pastelaria S. Roque. All rooms with phone, some with TVs and panoramic views of the city. Breakfast included. Singles €28-45; doubles €40-65; triples €76; quads €86. MC/V. ❸

Pensão Ninho das Águias, R. Costa do Castelo 74 (☎218 85 40 70), right behind the Castelo. From Pr. Figueira, take R. Madalena to Largo Adelino Costa, then head uphill to R. Costa do Castelo. Canary-filled garden looks out over the old city. Singles €25; doubles €30-38, with bath €40; triples €50. ❸

Pensão Estrela, R. dos Bacalhoeiros 8 (☎218 86 95 06). An under appreciated option in the lower part of Alfama. Breezy rooms with just the basic amenities look out onto the busy square below. Checkout 11am. June-Sept. singles €20; doubles €30; one triple €45. Oct.-May €5-7 less. The similar **Pensão Verandas** (☎218 87 05 19), a floor up, has comparable rooms and prices. ❷

Residencial Camões, Tr. Poço da Cidade 38, 1st fl. (☎213 47 75 10), off R. Misericórdia. From the top of the Ascensor Glória, turn left onto R. São Pedro, which becomes R. Misericórdia; Tr. Poço da Cidade is the 5th right. In the heart of the party district—it may get noisy at night. TV lounge. Breakfast included. Singles €18, with bath €30; doubles €37.50/€47.50; triples with bath €50. ❷

Pousada da Juventude de Lisboa (HI), R. Andrade Corvo 46 (☎213 53 26 96). M: Picoas. Exit the Metro station, turn right, and walk 1 block; the hostel is on your left. Reception 8am-midnight. Check-out 10:30am. HI card required. June-Sept. dorms €15; doubles with bath €33. Oct.-May dorms €10; doubles €25. MC/V. ❷

🔲 FOOD

Lisbon has some of the best wine and least expensive restaurants of any European capital. A full dinner costs about €9-11 per person; the *prato do dia* (daily special) is often a great deal. Head to the **Calçada de Santa Ana** and **Rua dos Correeiros** to find small, authentic restaurants that cater to locals. The city's culinary specialties include *amêjoas à bulhão pato* (steamed clams), *creme de mariscos* (seafood chowder with tomatoes), and *bacalhau cozido com grão e batatas* (cod with chick-peas and boiled potatoes, doused in olive oil). Snack on surprisingly filling and incredibly cheap Portuguese pastries; *pastelarias* (pastry shops) are everywhere. For groceries, look for any **Pingo Doce** supermarket. (Most open M-Sa 10am-7pm.)

Lua da Mel, R. Prata 242, on the corner of R. Santa Justa. If it can be caramelized, this diner-style pastry shop has done it. Pastries €0.55-1. Try the house specialty *Lua da Mel*. They also serve affordable meals (€5-7), and the daily specials are a great value (€4-5). Open M-F 7:30am-9pm, Sa 7:30am-7pm. ❶

Restaurante Tripeiro, R. dos Correeiros 70A, serves some of the best Portuguese meals to be found on the lower streets of Baixa. Busy during lunch. Specializes in fish but also offers large portions of non-seafood dishes. Entrees €5-8. Open M-Sa noon-10pm. ❷

Churrasqueira O Cofre, R. dos Bacalhoeiros 2C-D, at the foot of the Alfama near Pensão Estrela. A display case at the entrance shows everything available for grilling. Entrees €6-11. Open daily 9am-midnight, meals noon-4pm and 7-11:30pm. AmEx/MC/V. ❷

Sul, R. do Norte 13. Dark-wood paneling and candlelight give this restaurant and wine bar a romantic feel. Food tastes as good as it looks. Converts to a bar at 10pm. Spanish-themed entrees €7.50-13.50. Open Tu-Su noon-3pm and 7pm-1am. ❸

Restaurante Ali-a-Papa, R. da Atalaia 95. Serves generous helpings of traditional Moroccan food in a quiet atmosphere. Vegetarian options. Entrees €7.50-12. Open M-Sa 7-11pm. ❷

Restaurante Calcuta, R. do Norte 17, near Lg. Camões. Indian restaurant with wide selection of vegetarian options entrees (€5-7). Meat entrees €6-8.50. Fixed price *menú* €12.50. Open M-Sa noon-3pm and 6:30-11pm. ❷

A Brasileira, R. Garrett 120-122. Considered by many to be "the best cafe in Portugal," it has an after-dinner scene enjoyed by locals and tourists alike. Traditionally, a group of intellectuals gather at the first two tables. Mixed drinks €5. Restaurant downstairs; specialty is *bife à brasileira* (€11). Open daily 8am-2am. ❸

🞇 SIGHTS

THE BAIXA. Start at the heart of Lisbon, the **Rossio** (also known as the **Praça Dom Pedro IV**). Once a cattle market, the site of public executions, a bullfighting arena, and a carnival ground, the *praça* is now the domain of drink-sipping tourists and heart-stopping traffic, which whizzes around a statue of Dom Pedro IV. Past the train station, an obelisk and a sculpture of the "Spirit of Independence" in the **Praça dos Restauradores** commemorate Portugal's independence from Spain in 1640. The *praça* is the start of **Avenida da Liberdade,** Lisbon's most imposing, elegant promenade. Modeled after the wide boulevards of 19th-century Paris, this shady, mile-long thoroughfare ends at **Praça do Marquês do Pombal.** On the other side of the Rossio from Pr. dos Restauradores, the **Baixa**'s grid of pedestrian streets and wide mosaic sidewalks invites wandering. From the Baixa, all roads lead to **Praça do Comércio,** on the banks of the Rio Tejo, where several government ministries are housed.

BAIRRO ALTO. From the Baixa, walk uphill to the *bairro* or view the neighborhood from on high in the **Ascensor de Santa Justa,** a 1902 elevator in a Gothic wrought-iron tower. *(Elevator runs M-F 7am-11pm, Sa-Su 9am-11pm.)* **Pr. Camões,** which adjoins **Largo Chiado** at the top of R. Garrett, is a good place to rest and orient yourself while sightseeing. To reach R. Garrett, turn left from the Rossio and take R. do Carmo uphill; it's the first street on the right. Half-mad Maria I, desiring a male heir, made fervent religious vows promising God anything if she were granted a son. When a baby boy was finally born, she built the exquisitely ornate 🞖**Basílica da Estrêla.** *(On Pr. Estrêla. Take tram #28 from Pr. Comércio. Open daily 8am-12:30pm and 3-7:30pm. Free.)* For a perfect picnic, walk up R. Misericórdia to the shady **Parque de São Pedro de Alcântara.** The **Museu Nacional de Arte Antiga** hosts a large collection of Portuguese art as well as a survey of European painting dating back as far as the 12th century and ranging from Gothic primitives to 18th-century French masterpieces. *(R. das Janelas Verdes, Jardim 9 Abril. 30min. down Av. Infante Santo from the Ascensor de Santa Justa. Buses #40 and 60 stop to the right of the museum exit and head back to the Baixa. Open Tu 2-6pm, W-Su 10am-6pm. €3, students €1.50. Su before 2pm free.)*

ALFAMA. Lisbon's medieval quarter slopes in tiers from the **Castelo de São Jorge,** facing the Rio Tejo. Between the Alfama and the Baixa is the **Mouraria** (Moorish quarter), established after the Crusaders expelled the Moors in 1147. Walking is the best way to explore the neighborhood: from Pr. Comércio, follow R. Alfandega two blocks, climb up R. Madalena, turn right after the church on Largo Madalena,

THE LOCAL STORY

RUNNING FROM FAME

Let's Go met up with Ábilio Ferro at Ta Bar Es in Nazaré to talk about his experience as a musician in Portugal. Look for Ábilio's debut CD, scheduled for release in December 2002.

Q: What kind of music do you play?
A: All types of music—jazz, bossa nova, *fado*, blues, rock-n-roll. I'm 46 and I am still trying to discover myself. I have all kinds of influences and I am not sure which to follow.

Q: Where did you pick up these musical influence—here in Portugal?
A: Both here in Portugal, and when I turned 16 and sailed all over the world. I've been to 70 countries. When I went to Canada and the United States, I met a lot of good musicians. I've already played with Nick McGrain from Iron Maiden and with Nellie Furtado. I know all the star music artists here in Portugal. I've learned a lot, but my base is here. My friends like to hear me play. I've just been running away from fame.

Q: Where do you play?
A: Here in the bars and then I did a few tours through Europe, to the Azores, to Canada. Finally, I came back [to Portugal] four years ago and I've played all over the country. But now I need to rest my voice.

Q: How do you see yourself fitting into the live music scene here in Nazaré?
A: I see what the audience wants. If they want more *fado* or reggae, then I'll play more *fado* or more reggae. It's easy—I like all kinds of music.

walk down R. Santo António da Sé, and follow the tram tracks to the richly ornamented **Igreja de Santo António**. *(Open daily 8am-7pm. Mass daily 11am, 5, 7pm.)* Follow yellow signs to the 5th-century **⊠Castelo de São Jorge**, a Visigoth castle expanded by the Moors that offers a spectacular ocean view. *(Open daily Apr.-Sept. 9am-9pm; Oct.-Mar. 9am-6pm. Free.)*

SALDANHA. Lisbon's business center, the modern district of Saldanha has two excellent museums. The **⊠Museu Calouste Gulbenkian** houses oil tycoon Calouste Gulbenkian's collection, including an extensive array of ancient art as well as more modern European pieces. *(Av. Berna 45. M: S. Sebastião. Bus #18, 46, or 56. Open Tu-Su 10am-5pm. €3, students free.)* The adjacent **Museu do Centro de Arte Moderna** has a sizeable modern art collection and beautiful gardens. *(On R. Dr. Nicolau Bettencourt. Open Tu-Su 10am-5pm. €3, students free.)*

BELÉM. A pseudo-suburb of Lisbon, Belém showcases the opulence and extravagance of the Portuguese empire with well-maintained museums and historical sites. King Dom Manuel I established the **monastery** in 1502 to give thanks for Vasco da Gama's successful voyage to India. *(Take tram #15 from Pr. Comércio (15min.), bus #28 or 43 from Pr. Figueira (15min.), or the train from Estação Cais do Sodré (10min.). From the train station, cross the tracks and the street, then go left. The Mosteiro dos Jerónimos is to the right, through the public gardens. Open Tu-Su 10am-5pm. €3, students €1.50. Free Su 10am-2pm.)* Take the underpass beneath the highway to the **⊠Torre de Belém** (10min.), with views of Belém, the Tejo, and the Atlantic beyond. Surrounded by the ocean due to the receding shoreline, it's accessible only by bridge. *(Open Tu-Su 10am-6pm. €3, students €1.50.)*

⊠ PARQUE DAS NAÇÕES (PARK OF NATIONS). The government took a chance on the former Expo '98 grounds, spending millions to convert it into the Parque das Nações. The gamble paid off—the futuristic park is constantly packed. Take the Metro to Oriente and enter through the **Centro Vasco da Gama.** The biggest attraction is the **Pavilhão dos Oceanos,** the largest oceanarium in Europe. The 145m **Torre Vasco da Gama** offers spectacular views of the city. *(Shopping mall open daily 10am-midnight. Oceanarium open daily Apr.-Sept. 10am-7pm; Oct.-Mar. 10am-6pm. €9, under 18 €5. Torre open daily 10am-8pm. €2.50, under 18 €1.25.)*

🎵 ENTERTAINMENT

Agenda Cultural and *Follow Me Lisboa* have information on arts events and bullfights; get either for free at kiosks in the Rossio, on R. Portas de Santo Antão, and at the tourist office. Lisbon's trademark is

fado, an art combining singing and narrative poetry that expresses sorrowful *saudade* (nostalgia and yearning). The Bairro Alto has many *fado* joints off R. Misericórdia and on streets by the Museu de São Roque, but the prices alone may turn a knife in your heart. Various bars offer free performances. **Machado,** R. Norte 91, is one of the larger *fado* restaurants. (Entrees €20-68. Min. purchase €15. Open Tu-Su 8pm-3am; *fado* starts at 9:15pm. AmEx/MC/V.)

NIGHTLIFE

The **Bairro Alto** is the first place to go for nightlife, where a plethora of small bars and clubs fills the side streets. In particular, **Rua Norte, Rua Diário Notícias,** and **Rua Atalaia** have many small clubs packed into three short blocks, making club-hopping as easy as crossing the street. Most gay and lesbian clubs are found between Pr. Camões and Trav. da Queimada, as well as in the **Rato** area near the edge of Bairro Alto. **Avenida 24 de Julho** and the **Rua das Janelas Verdes** in the **Santos** area above have some of the most popular bars and clubs. Newer hot spots include the area along the river across from the **Santa Apolo'nia** train station. There's no reason to arrive before midnight; crowds flow in around 2am.

Lux/Fra'gil, Av. Infante D. Henrique A. In a class of its own, three years after its opening Lux continues to be the newest big thing in Lisbon. Take a taxi to the area across from the Sta. Apolo'nia train station to get to this imaginative mix of lights and boxes. Beer €1.50-2.50. Min. purchase €10. Open Tu-Sa 6pm-6am; arrive after 2am.

Litro e Meio (1.5 Lt.), R. das Janelas Verdes 27, in the Santos area above the clubs on Av. 24 de Julho. This unpretentious bar attracts a young crowd and plays house and Latin music. Most popular from 1-2:30am, before clubbing picks up on the street below. Beer €1.50, mixed drinks €3.50. Min. purchase €5. Open M-Sa 10pm-4am.

Resto, R. Costa do Castelo 7, in the Alfama, is located at the site of an old circus school. Huge outdoor patio has one of the best views of the city. Filled with a young crowd, especially 10pm-midnight. Live Portuguese guitar F-Su. *Caipirinha* €4. Beer €1.25. Open daily 7:30pm-2am.

Trumps, R. Imprensa Nacional 104B, in the Bairro Alto. Lisbon's biggest gay club features several bars in addition to a massive dance floor. Min. purchase €5. Open F-Sa 11:30pm-6:30am, Tu-Th and Su 11:30pm-4:30am.

Clandestino, R. da Barroca 99. Cavernous bar with messages sprawled by former patrons on its rock walls. Beer €2, mixed drinks €4. Open Tu-Su 10pm-2am.

A Capella, R. Atalaia 45. A spacious bar with gold walls and red velvet cushions. Popular in the late hours. Beer €3, mixed drinks €5. Open daily 9pm-2am.

DAYTRIPS FROM LISBON

ESTORIL AND CASCAIS. Glorious beaches draw sun-loving tourists and locals alike to Estoril and neighboring Cascais. For the beach-weary, the marvelous (and air-conditioned) **Casino Estoril,** Europe's largest casino, is a welcome relief. (☎214 66 77 00; www.casino-estoril.pt. No swimwear, tennis shoes, jeans, or shorts. Slots and game room 18+. Passport required. Open daily 3pm-3am.)

Trains from Lisbon's Estação do Sodré stop in Cascais via Estoril (30min., every 20min. 5:30am-2:30am, €1.10). Estoril and Cascais are only a 20min. stroll along the coast or Av. Marginal from each other. **Bus** #418 to Sintra departs from Av. Marginal, in front of the train station (35min., every hr. 6:10am-11:40pm, €2.30). From the station, cross Av. Marginal and head to the Estoril **tourist office,** which is left of the Casino on Arcadas do Parque, for a free map of both towns. (☎214 66 38 13.

Open M-Sa 9am-7pm, Su 10am-6pm.) Ask for help finding a room at the Cascais **tourist office,** Av. Dos Combatantes da Grande Guerra 25. From the Cascais train station, cross the square and take a right onto Av. Valbom. Look for a small sign at Av. Dos Combatantes. (☎214 86 82 04. Open M-Sa 9am-7pm, Su 10am-6pm.)

SINTRA. With fairy-tale castles, enchanting gardens, and spectacular mountain vistas, Sintra (pop. 20,000) is a favorite among tour groups and backpackers alike. Perched on the mountain overlooking the old town, the **Castelo dos Mouros** provides stunning views of the mountains and coast. Follow the blue signs 3km up the mountain or take bus #434 (15min., every 30min., daypass €3.60), which runs to the top from the tourist office. The awestruck are usually sun-struck; a bottle of water is recommended. (Open June-Sept. 9am-8pm; Oct.-May 9am-7pm. €3, seniors €1.) A mix of Moorish, Gothic, and Manueline styles, the **Palácio Nacional de Sintra,** in Pr. República, was once the summer residence of Moorish sultans and their harems. (☎219 10 68 40. Open Th-Tu 10am-5:30pm, closed bank holidays. Buy tickets by 5pm. €3, seniors €1.50.) Farther uphill is the **Palácio Nacional da Pena,** a Bavarian castle decorated with Arabic minarets, Gothic turrets, Manueline windows, and a Renaissance dome. (Open July-Sept. Tu-Su 10am-6:30pm; Oct.-June Tu-Su 10am-5pm. €5, seniors and students €1.50.)

Trains (☎219 23 26 05) arrive at Av. Dr. Miguel Bombarda from Lisbon's Estação Rossio (45min., every 15min. 6am-2am, €1.10). Stagecoach **buses** leave from outside the train station for Cascais (#417, 40min., every hr. 6:30am-7pm, €2.60) and Estoril (#418, 40min., every hr. 6am-9:40pm, €2). Down the street, Mafrense buses go to Ericeira (50min., every hr. 7:25am-8:25pm, €2). The **tourist office,** Sintra-Vila Pr. República 23, is in the historic center. From the bus station, turn left on Av. Bombarda, which becomes the winding Volta do Duche. Continue straight into the Praça da República; the Palácio Nacional de Sintra is ahead, and the tourist office is to the left. (☎219 23 11 57. Open June-Sept. daily 9am-8pm; Oct.-May 9am-7pm.) To reach the **Pousada da Juventude de Sintra (HI) ❶,** on Sta. Eufémia, take bus #434 from the train station to the Palácio da Pena. Look for signs leading through the palace garden to the hostel. (☎219 24 12 10. Reservations recommended. HI membership required. Dorms €8.50-10.50; doubles €20-24.)

ERICEIRA. Primarily a fishing village, Ericeira has become known for its spectacular beaches and surfable waves. The main beaches, **Praia do Sol** and **Praia do Norte,** crowd quickly; for something more secluded, stroll down the Largo da Feira toward Ribamar until you reach the stunning sand dunes of **Praia da Ribeira d'Ilhas.** If you stay, ask about rooms at the **tourist office,** R. Eduardo Burnay 46. (☎261 86 31 22. Open July-Sept. daily 9:30am-midnight; Oct.-June Su-M 9:30am-7pm, Sa 9:30-10pm.) Mafrense **buses** run from Lisbon's Campo Grande to Ericeira (1½hr., every hr. 6:30am-11:20pm, €3.80); get off at the Centro Rodoviario Municipal (Ericeira's bus station). Buses also go to Mafra (25min., every hr., €1.25).

MAFRA. The **Palácio Nacional de Mafra,** one of Portugal's most impressive sights, can be found in this sleepy town. The massive 2000-room palace, including a cathedral-sized church, a monastery, and a library, took 50,000 workers 13 years to complete. (Open W-M 10am-5:30pm; last entrance 4:30pm. Daily 45min. tours in English 11am and 2:30pm. €3, students and seniors €1.50, under 14 free.) Mafrense **buses** run from Lisbon's Campo Grande (1-1½hr., every hr. 5:30am-9:30pm, €2.75) and Ericeira (20min., every hr. 7:30am-midnight, €1.25), and stop in front of the palace. Don't take the **train** from Lisbon's Estação Sta. Apolónia unless you want a 2hr. walk to town.

CENTRAL PORTUGAL

Jagged cliffs and whitewashed fishing villages line the Costa de Prata of **Estremadura**, with beaches that rival even those in the Algarve. In the fertile region of the **Ribatejo** (Banks of the Tejo), lush greenery surrounds historic sights.

LEIRIA ☎244

Capital of the surrounding district and an important transport hub, prosperous and industrial Leiria fans out from a fertile valley, 22km from the coast. Chosen to host the Euro 2004 soccer finals, Leiria is preparing itself for the crowds that will flood the city. The city's most notable sight is its **Castelo de Leiria,** a granite fort built by Dom Afonso Henriques atop the crest of a volcanic hill after he snatched the town from the Moors. The terrace opens onto a panoramic view of the town and river. (Castle open Apr.-Sept. M-F 9am-6:30pm, Sa-Su 10am-6:30pm; Oct.-Mar. M-F 9am-5:30pm, Sa-Su 10am-5:30pm. €1.) Nearby **beaches,** including **Vieira, Pedrógão,** and **São Pedro de Muel,** are all accessible via buses.

Leiria makes a practical base for exploring the nearby region. **Trains** (☎244 88 20 27) run from the station 3km outside town to Coimbra (1½hr., 10 per day, €6) and Lisbon (2hr., 9 per day, €7). **Buses** (☎244 81 15 07), just off Pr. Paulo VI, next to the main park and close to the tourist office, run to: Batalha (20min., 9 per day, €1.50); Coimbra (1hr., 11 per day, €5.80); Lisbon (2hr., 11 per day, €7); Porto (3½hr., 10 per day, €9); Santarém (2hr., 5 per day, €4.50-8); and Tomar (1½hr.; M-F 7:15am and 5:45pm, Sa 6:15pm; €3-6). Buses also run between the train station and the **tourist office** (15min., every hr. 7am-7pm, €0.75), in the Jardim Luís de Camões. (☎244 82 37 73. Open May-Sept. daily 10am-1pm and 3-7pm; Oct.-Apr. 10am-1pm and 2-6pm.) If you're going to spend the night, go to **Pousada da Juventude de Leiria (HI) ❶,** on Largo Cândido dos Reis 9. (☎/fax 244 83 18 68. Dorms €8.50-10.50; doubles €21-27.) **Largo Cândido dos Reis** is lined with bars.

TOMAR ☎249

For centuries, the arcane Knights Templar plotted crusades from a celebrated convent-fortress high above this small town. The ■**Convento de Cristo** complex was the Knights' powerful and mysterious headquarters. The first structure was built in 1160. The **Claustro dos Felipes** is a Renaissance masterpiece. (☎249 31 34 81. Complex open June-Sept. daily 9am-6pm; Oct.-May 9am-5pm. €3, under 14 free.) **Trains** (☎249 31 28 15) run from Av. Combatentes da Grande Guerra, at the southern edge of town, to: Coimbra (2½hr., 6 per day, €5-6); Lisbon (2hr., 18 per day, €5-10); Porto (4½hr., 7 per day, €8-11); and Santarém (1hr., 12 per day, €2.60-4.20). Rodoviaria Tejo **buses** (☎249 31 27 38) leave from Av. Combatentes da Grande Guerra, by the train station, for: Coimbra (2½hr., 7am, €8.25); Leiria (1hr.; M-F 7:15am and 5:45pm, Sa 7am; €3-6); Lisbon (2hr., 4 per day, €6); Porto (4hr., 7am, €10.50); and Santarém (1hr., 9:15am and 6pm, €6). From the bus or train station, take a right onto Av. Combatentes da Grande Guerra and then a left onto Av. Torres Pinheiro and continue past the traffic circle on R. Everaro; the **tourist office** is on the left, just past the bridge. (☎249 32 24 27. Open July-Sept. daily 10am-8pm; Oct.-June 10am-6pm.) **Postal code:** 2300.

BATALHA ☎244

The centerpiece of Batalha is the gigantic ■**Mosteiro de Santa Maria da Vitória.** Built by Dom João I in 1385 to commemorate his victory over the Castilians, the complex of cloisters and chapels remains one of Portugal's greatest monuments. To get to the monastery, enter through the church. (Open Apr.-Sept. daily 9am-6pm; Oct.-Mar. 9am-5pm. €3, under 25 €1.50.) **Buses** run from the street across from the monastery to: Leiria (20min., 10 per day, €1.10); Lisbon (2hr., 6 per day, €6); and Tomar (1½hr.; 8am, noon, and 6pm; €2.60). The **tourist office**, on Pr. Mouzinho de Albuquerque along R. Nossa Senhora do Caminho, stands opposite the monastery. (☎244 76 51 80. Open May-Sept. daily 10am-1pm and 3-7pm; Oct.-Apr. 10am-1pm and 2-6pm.)

ÉVORA   ☎266

Designated a UNESCO World Heritage site, Évora is justly known as the "Museum City." Moorish arches line the winding streets of this picture-perfect town, which boasts a Roman temple, an imposing cathedral, and a 16th-century university.

🖃🔢 TRANSPORTATION AND PRACTICAL INFORMATION. Trains (☎266 70 21 25) run from Av. dos Combatentes de Grande Guerra to Lisbon (3hr., 5 per day, €4-6) and Porto (6½hr., 3 per day, €14). **Buses** (☎266 76 94 10) go from Av. Sebastião to Lisbon (2-2½hr., every 1-1½hr., €8) and Faro (5hr., 4 per day, €9.50). The **tourist office** is at Pr. Giraldo 65. (☎266 70 26 71. Open Apr.-Sept. M-F 9am-7pm, Sa-Su 9am-12:30pm and 2-5:30pm; Oct.-Mar. daily 9am-12:30pm and 2-5:30pm.) Free **Internet** access is available at **Instituto Portuguese da la Juventude**, R. República 105, but during the afternoon there's often a long line. (Open M-F 9am-11pm.) Alternatively, **Oficin@**, R. Moeda 27, is off Pr. Giraldo. (€2.50 per hr. Open Tu-F 8pm-3am, Sa 9pm-2am.) **Postal code:** 7000.

🔢🖸 ACCOMMODATIONS AND FOOD. *Pensões* cluster around **Praça Giraldo.** From the tourist office, cross Pr. Giraldo and take a right on R. República, then turn left on R. Miguel Bombarda to reach **Pousada da Juventude (HI) ❶**, R. Miguel Bombarda 40. (☎266 74 48 48; fax 74 48 43. Dorms €10-12.50; doubles with bath €25-30.) Or, take a right out of the tourist office and the first right onto R. Bernardo Mato to get to **Casa Palma ❷**, R. Bernardo Mato 29-A. (☎266 70 35 60. Singles €20, with bath €25; doubles €30/€40.) Many budget restaurants are near Pr. Giraldo, particularly along **Rua Mercadores**. Locals flock to **Adega do Neto ❶**, R. Mercadores 46, off Pr. Giraldo, for typical Alentejan dishes. (Entrees €3.50-5. Open M-Sa noon-3:30pm and 7-10pm.) From Pr. Giraldo, walk up R. 5 de Outubro and take a right onto R. Diogo Cão to reach the only real Italian restaurant in Évora, **Pane & Vino ❷**, Páteo do Salema. (Pizza €5-11, pasta €8-15. Open Tu-Su noon-3pm, 6:30-11pm.)

🖸🎵 SIGHTS AND ENTERTAINMENT. The city's most famous monument is the second-century **Roman temple,** on Largo Conde do Vila Flor. Facing the temple is the **Igreja de São João Evangelista;** its interior is covered with dazzling tiles. Ask to see the hidden chambers. (Open Tu-Su 10am-12:30pm and 2-6pm. €2.50.) From Pr. Giraldo, head up R. 5 de Outubro to the colossal 12th-century **cathedral;** the 12 apostles on the doorway are masterpieces of medieval Portuguese sculpture. The **Museu de Arte Sacra,** above the nave, has religious artifacts. (Cathedral open daily 9am-12:30pm and 2-5pm. Cloisters open daily 9am-noon and 2-4:30pm. Museum open Tu-Su 9am-noon and 2-4:30pm. Cathedral free. Cloisters and museum €2.50.) Attached to the pleasant **Igreja Real de São Francisco,** the bizarre **▧Capela dos Ossos** (Chapel of Bones) was built by three Franciscan monks using the bones of 5000 people. From Pr. Giraldo, follow R. República; the church is on the right and the chapel is around back to the right of the main entrance. (Open M-Sa 9am-1pm and 2:30-5:30pm, Su 10am-1pm. €1.) After sunset, head to **▧Jonas,** R. Serpa Pinta 67, to discover a warm, cavernous underground lounge and a mellow bar upstairs. (☎964 82 16 47. Open M-Sa 10:30am-3am.) A country fair accompanies the **Feira de São João** festival the last week of June.

ALGARVE

Nearly 3000 hours of sunshine per year have transformed the Algarve, a desert on the sea, into a popular vacation spot. In July and August, sun-seeking tourists mob the resorts, packing the bars and discos from sunset until way past dawn. In the off-season, the resorts become pleasantly de-populated.

LAGOS
☎282

As the town's countless international expats will attest, Lagos is a black hole: come for two days and you'll stay for two months. Lagos will keep you busy soaking in the view from the cliffs, the sun on the beach, and the drinks at the bars.

▐ ▌ TRANSPORTATION AND PRACTICAL INFORMATION

Running the length of the channel, **Avenida Descubrimentos** is the main road that carries traffic to and from Lagos. From the **train station,** walk through the pastel pink marina and cross over the channel on the pedestrian suspension bridge, then turn left onto Av. Descubrimentos. From the **bus station,** walk straight until you hit Av. Descubrimentos, then turn right. After 15m, take another right onto R. Porta de Portugal to reach **Praça Gil Eanes,** the center of the old town.

Trains: ☎282 76 29 87. Across the river (over the pedestrian suspension bridge) from the main part of town. To **Évora** (6hr., 8:20am and 5:15pm, €11) and **Lisbon** (4-4½hr., 5-6 per day, €13).

Buses: The **EVA** bus station (☎282 76 29 44), off Av. Descubrimentos, is across the channel from the train station. To: **Lisbon** (5hr., 12 per day, €14.50); **Sagres** (1hr., 17 per day, €2.40); **Sevilla,** Spain (5-6hr., 7:30am and 2pm, €15).

Tourist Office: Marques de Pombal Square (☎282 76 41 11), on the corner of R. Lima Leitão. Open July-Aug. M-Sa 10am-10pm; June and Sept. M-Sa 10am-8pm; Oct.-May M-F 10am-6pm.

Emergency: ☎112. **Police:** (☎282 76 29 30), R. General Alberto Silva.

Medical Services: Hospital (☎282 77 01 00), R. Castelo dos Governadores.

Internet Access: The Em@il Box (Ciaxa de Correieo), R. Cândido dos Reis 112 (☎282 76 89 50). €3.50 per hr. Open M-F 9:30am-8pm, Sa-Su 10am-3pm.

Post Office: R. Portas de Portugal (☎282 77 02 50), between Pr. Gil Eanes and the river. Open M-F 9am-6pm. **Postal Code:** 8600.

▐ ACCOMMODATIONS

In the summertime, *pensões* (and the youth hostel) fill up quickly and cost a bundle. Reserve rooms over a week in advance. Rooms in *casas particulares* run around €10-15 per person in summer; for reduced rates, try haggling with owners.

▨ **Pousada da Juventude de Lagos (HI),** R. Lançarote de Freitas 50 (☎282 76 19 70; www.hostalbooking.com), off R. 25 de Abril. Friendly staff and lodgers congregate in the courtyard. Breakfast included. In summer, book through the central **Movijovem** office (☎213 59 60 00). June 16-Sept. 15 dorms €15; doubles with bath €42. Sept. 16-June 15 dorms €10; doubles with bath €28. MC/V. ❶

▨ **Olinda Teresa Maria Quartos,** R. Lançarote de Freitas 37, 2nd fl. (☎282 08 23 29), across the street from the youth hostel. Offers doubles or dorm rooms with shared kitchen, terrace, and bath. If the owner is not in, check at the youth hostel. June 16-Sept. 15 dorms €15; doubles €24. Sept. 16-June 15 dorms €10; doubles €30. ❶

Residencial Rubi Mar, R. Barroca 70 (☎282 76 31 65; fax 76 77 49), off Pr. Gil Eanes toward Pr. Infante Dom Henrique. July-Oct. doubles €40, with bath €45; quads €75. Nov.-June doubles €28, with bath €33; quads €50. ❹

Residencial Lagosmar, R. Dr. Faria da Silva 13 (☎282 76 37 22), up from Pr. Gil Eanes. Friendly 24hr. reception. July-Aug. singles €60; doubles €70; extra bed €22. June and Sept. singles €35; doubles €40; extra bed €13. Nov.-Feb. singles €22; doubles €25; extra bed €9. Mar.-May and Oct. singles €30; doubles €35; extra bed €11. ❺

Residencial Caravela, R. 25 de Abril 8 (☎282 76 33 61), just up the street from Pr. Gil Eanes. Singles €24; doubles €33, with bath €36; triples €50. ❷

Camping Trindade (☎282 76 38 93), just outside of town. Follow Av. Descubrimentos toward Sagres. The way most Europeans experience the Algarve. €2.90 per person; €3.20 per tent, €3.50 per car. ❶

Camping Valverde (☎282 78 92 11), 6km outside Lagos and 1.5km west of Praia da Luz. Showers, grocery, and pool. €4.75 per person; €4.75 per tent, €4 per car. ❶

◖ FOOD

Peruse multilingual menus around **Praça Gil Eanes** and **Rua 25 de Abril.** For authentic Portuguese seafood, try **Praça Luis Camoes.** The morning **market,** on Av. Descubrimentos, 5min. from the town center, is cheap. **Supermercado São Toque,** R. Portas de Portugal 61, is opposite the post office. (Open July-Sept. M-F 9am-8pm, Sa 9am-7pm; Oct.-June M-F 9am-7:30pm, Sa 9am-7pm.) Hordes of backpackers enjoy €3.50 meals at ▨**Casa Rosa ❶,** R. Ferrador 22. (Open daily 6pm-midnight.) For Mediterranean and Thai cuisine, head to **Mediterraneo ❸,** R. Senhora da Graça 2. (Entrees €9-13.50.) Just off Pr. Gil Eanes, well-touristed **Snack-Bar Caravela ❷,** R. 25 de Abril 14, has the best pizza in town. (Pizzas and pasta €4.50-7. Open June-Sept. daily 9am-midnight; Oct.-Mar. 9am-10pm. AmEx/MC/V.)

◖▨ BEACHES AND NIGHTLIFE

Flat, smooth, sunbathing sand can be found at **Meia Praia,** across the river from town. Hop on the 30-second ferry near Pr. República (€0.50). For beautiful cliffs with less-crowded beaches and caves, follow Av. Descubrimentos toward Sagres to the **Praia de Pinhão** (20min.). A bit farther, **Praia Dona Ana** features the sculpted cliffs and grottos that grace most Algarve postcards.

The streets of Lagos pick up as soon as the sun dips down, and by midnight the city's walls are shaking. The area between **Praça Gil Eanes** and **Praça Luis de Camões** is filled with cafes. For late-night bars and clubs, try R. Cândido dos Reis, R. do Ferrador, and the intersection of R. 25 de Abril, R. Silva Lopes, and R. Soeiro da Costa. Staggered Happy Hours make drinking easy, even on the tightest of budgets. ▨**Eddie's,** R. 25 de Abril 99, is an easy-going bar popular with backpackers and seasonal workers. (Beer €2. Open M-Sa 4pm-2am, Su 8pm-2am.) **Taverna Velha (The Old Tavern),** R. Lançarote de Freitas 34, down the street from Pousada da Juventude, is the only air-conditioned bar in Lagos. (Beer €1.25-2.50. Open M-Sa 4pm-2am, Su 8pm-2am.) Fraternity posters and occasional streakers decorate **The Red Eye,** R. Cândido dos Reis 63. Mixed drinks €2.50-3.50. Open daily 8pm-2am.) **Joe's Garage,** R. 1 de Maio 78, is the rowdiest, and possibly raunchiest, bar in town. (Beer €2. 2-for-1 beers or drinks 10pm-midnight. Open daily 10pm-2am.)

◖ DAYTRIPS FROM LAGOS

SAGRES. Marooned atop a bleak desert plateau in Europe's southwesternmost corner, desolate Sagres and its cape were once considered the edge of the world. Near the town lurks the ▨**Fortaleza de Sagres,** the fortress where Prince Henry stroked his beard, decided to map the world, and founded his famous **school of navigation.** (Open May-Sept. daily 10am-8:30pm; Oct.-Apr. 10am-6:30pm. €3.) Six kilometers west lies the dramatic **Cabo de São Vicente,** where the second-most powerful lighthouse in Europe shines over 100km out to sea. To get there on weekdays, take the bus from the bus station on R. Comandante Matos near the tourist office (10min.; 11:15am, 12:30, 4:15pm; €1). Alternatively, hike 1hr. or bike past the several fortresses perched atop the cliffs. The most notable **beach** in the area is **Mareta,** at the bottom of the road from the town center. Just west of town, **Praia da Martinhal** and **Praia da Baleeira** have great windsurfing. The nearby coves of **Salema** and **Luz** are intimate and picturesque. At night, a young crowd fills lively **Rosa dos Ventos** in Pr. República. (Beer €1. Open Su-Tu and Th-Sa 10am-2am.)

EVA **buses** (☎282 76 29 44) run from Lagos (1hr., 17 per day, €2.80). The **tourist office,** on R. Comandante Matoso, is up the street from the bus stop. (☎282 62 48 73. Open Tu-Sa 9:30am-1pm and 2-5:30pm.)

PRAIA DA ROCHA. A short jaunt from Lagos, this grand **beach** is perhaps the very best the Algarve has to offer. With vast expanses of sand, surfable waves, rocky red cliffs, and plenty of secluded coves, Praia da Rocha has a well-deserved reputation and the crowds to match. From Lagos, take a bus to Portimão (40min., 14 per day, €1.80), then switch to the Praia da Rocha bus (10min., every 30min. 7:30am-8:30pm, €1.30). The **tourist office** is at the end of R. Tomás Cabreina. (☎282 41 91 32. Open May-Sept. daily 9:30am-7pm; Oct.-Apr. M-F 9:30am-12:30pm and 2-5:30pm, Sa-Su 9:30am-12:30pm.)

TAVIRA ☎281

Farmers tease police by riding their motor scooters over the Roman pedestrian bridge, but that's about as crazy as Tavira gets. For most visitors to this relaxing haven, speckled with white houses, palm trees, and Baroque churches, that's just fine. Steps from the central Pr. República lead up to the 16th-century **Igreja da Misericórdia.** (Open Tu-Th 9:30am-12:30pm and 2-5:30pm. Free.) Just beyond the church, the remains of the city's **Castelo Mouro** (Moorish Castle) sit next to **Santa Maria do Castelo.** (Castle open M-F 8am-5pm and Sa-Su 10am-5pm. Church open daily 9:30am-12:30pm and 2-5pm. Free.) Local beaches are accessible year-round by the bus to Pedras D'el Rei (10min., 8 per day, €0.90). To reach the golden shores of **Ilha da Tavira,** an island 2km away, take the ferry from the end of Estrada das 4 Aguas (round-trip €1.20).

Trains (☎281 32 23 54) leave Tavira for Faro (40min., 10-17 per day, €1.60) and Vila Real de Santo António (30min., 9-13 per day, €1.20). **EVA buses** (☎281 32 25 46) leave from the station upriver from Pr. República for Faro (1hr., 12-13 per day, €2.25). From the train station town is a short 5-10min. walk down Av. Dr. Teixeira de Azevedo, or you can catch the local **TUT bus** to the town center (10min., every 30min. 8am-8pm, €0.80). **Postal code:** 8800.

NORTHERN PORTUGAL

The Three Beiras region comprises the unspoiled Costa da Prata (Silver Coast), the plush greenery of the interior, and the rugged peaks of the Serra Estrela. Beyond trellised vineyards, *azulejo*-lined houses grace charming streets.

COIMBRA ☎239

Home to the country's only university from the mid-16th to the early 20th century, vibrant Coimbra continues to be a mecca for youth around the world.

🖭🛈 TRANSPORTATION AND PRACTICAL INFORMATION. Trains (☎239 83 49 98) from other regions stop only at **Estação Coimbra-B (Velha)**, 3km northwest of town, while regional trains stop at both Coimbra-B and **Estação Coimbra-A (Nova)**, two blocks from the lower town center. A train connects the two stations, departing after trains arrive (4min., €0.70). Trains run to Lisbon (3hr., 23 per day, €8-14) and Porto (2hr., 21 per day, €5-9.50). **Buses** (☎239 82 70 81) go from Av. Fernão Magalhães, past Coimbra-A on the university side of the river, to Lisbon (2½hr., 17 per day, €9) and Porto (1½hr., 10 per day, €7). From the bus station, turn right, follow the avenue to Coimbra-A, then walk to Largo Portagem to reach the **tourist office.** (☎239 85 59 30. Open M-F 9am-6pm, Sa-Su 10am-1pm and 2:30-5:30pm.) Check **email** at **Central Modem,** Escada de Quebra Costas, down the stairs from Lg. da Sé Velha. (€0.55 per 15min. Open M-F 10am-10pm.) **Postal code:** 3000.

🖭🛈 ACCOMMODATIONS AND FOOD. Directly across from the Igreja da Santa Cruz, **Pensão Santa Cruz ❷,** Pr. 8 de Maio 21, 3rd fl., has comfortable rooms, most with cable TV, some with bath. (☎/fax 239 82 61 97; www.pensaosantacruz.com. July-Sept. singles or doubles €20, with bath €30; triples €25/€35. Oct.-June €5 less.) For newly renovated rooms, try **Residencial Vitória ❷,** R. da Sota 11-19, across from Coimbra-A. (☎239 82 40 49; fax 84 28 97. Reception 24hr. Singles €15-25; doubles €20-35; triples €45. MC/V.) The best cuisine in Coimbra lies off Pr. 8 de Maio around **Rua Direita,** on the side streets between the river and Largo Portagem, and around **Praça República** in the university district. **Supermercado Minipreço,** R. António Granjo 6C, is in the lower town center. (Open M-Sa 8:30am-8pm, Su 9am-1pm and 3-7pm.)

🖭🛈 SIGHTS AND ENTERTAINMENT. Take in the old-town sights by climbing from the river up the narrow stone steps to the university. Begin your ascent at the **Arco de Almedina,** a remnant of the Moorish town wall, one block uphill from Largo Portagem. The looming 12th-century Romanesque **Sé Velha** (Old Cathedral) is at the top. (Open M-Th 10am-noon and 2-7:30pm, F-Sa 10am-1pm. Cloister €0.75.) Follow signs to the late 16th-century **Sé Nova** (New Cathedral), built by the Jesuits. (Open Tu-Sa 9am-noon and 2-6:30pm. Free.), just a few blocks from the 16th-century **University of Coimbra.** The **Porta Férrea** (Iron Gate), off R. São Pedro, opens onto the old university, whose buildings constituted Portugal's royal palace when Coimbra was the kingdom's capital. (Open May-Sept. daily 9am-7:30pm; Oct.-Apr. 9:30am-12:30pm and 2-5:30pm.) The stairs to the right lead to the **Sala dos Capelos,** which houses portraits of Portugal's kings, six of them Coimbra-born. (Open daily 9:30am-12:30pm and 2-5:30pm. €2.50.) The **university chapel** and the mind-boggling, entirely gilded 18th-century **Biblioteca Joanina** (University Library) lie past the Baroque clock tower. (Open May-Sept. daily 9am-7:30pm; Oct.-Apr. 9:30am-noon and 2-5:30pm. €2.50, students free. Ticket to all university sights €4; buy tickets in the main quad.) Cross the bridge in front of Largo Portagem to find the 14th-century **Convento de Santa Clara-a-Velha** and the 17th-century **Convento de Santa Clara-a-Nova.** (Interior closed until summer 2003 for massive renovation. Both open M-Sa 9am-noon and 2-6pm. Cloisters and sacristy €1.)

Nightlife in Coimbra gets highest honors. **Café Tropical,** Pr. República 35, is a great place to start. (Beer €0.70-1.25. Mixed drinks €3.50. Open M-Sa 9am-2am.) **Diligência Bar,** R. Nova 30, off R. Sofia, is known for its *fado.* (*Sangría* €9.20 per liter. Open M-Sa 6pm-2am, Su 7pm-2am.) **Hups!,** R. Castro Matoso 11, is one of the newest dance clubs in town (beer €1.50; open Tu-Su 10pm-5am), while **Via Latina,** R. Almeida Garrett 1, around the corner and uphill from Pr. República, is hot in all senses of the word (beer €1.50; open M-Sa 11pm-7am). **The English Bar,** R. Lourenço de Almeida Azevedo 24, is new and hip. (Beer €1.50-2. Mixed drinks

€3-4. Open M-Sa 10pm-4am.) Dance *and* check email at **@caffé,** Lg. da Sé Velha 4-8. (Open June to mid-Sept. M-Sa 11am-4am; mid-Sept. to May M-Sa 9pm-4am.) In early May, university graduates burn the narrow ribbons they got as first-years and get wide ones in return during Coimbra's week-long **Queima das Fitas.**

PORTO (OPORTO)   ☎ 22

Porto is famous for its namesake—strong, sugary port wine. Developed by English merchants in the early 18th century, the port industry is at the root of the city's successful economy. But there's more to Porto than just port; the country's second-largest city retains traditional charm with granite church towers, orange-tiled houses, and graceful bridges, and also hosts a sophisticated and modern lifestyle that won Porto its position as a Cultural Capital of Europe in 2001.

🖪🖪 TRANSPORTATION AND PRACTICAL INFORMATION. Most **trains** pass through Porto's main station, **Estação Campanhã** (☎225 36 41 41), on R. da Estação. Trains run to: Coimbra (2hr., 17 per day, €5.30); Lisbon (3½-4½hr., 14 per day, €11-19); and Madrid (13-14hr., 6:10pm, €48). **Estação São Bento** (☎222 00 27 22), Pr. Almeida Garrett, centrally located one block off Pr. Liberdade, is the terminus for trains with local and regional routes. Rede Expresso 366 **buses,** R. Alexandre Herculano 366 (☎222 05 24 59), in the Garagem Atlântico, has buses to Coimbra (1½hr., 11 per day, €7) and Lisbon (4hr., 12 per day, €12). REDM, R. Dr. Alfredo Magalhães 94 (☎222 00 31 52), two blocks from Pr. República, sends buses to Braga (1hr., 9-26 per day, €3.30). Buy tickets for the **intracity buses** and **trams** from small kiosks around the city, or at the **STCP office,** Pr. Almeida Garrett 27, downhill and across the street from Estação de São Bento (pre-purchased single ticket €0.40; day pass €2.50). The **tourist office,** R. Clube dos Fenianos 25, is off Pr. Liberdade. (☎223 39 34 72. Open July-Sept. daily 9am-7pm; Oct.-June M-F 9am-5:30pm, Sa-Su 9:30am-4:30pm.) Check **email** at **Portweb,** Pr. Gen. Humberto Delgado 291, by the tourist office. (10am-4pm €0.50 per hr., 4pm-2am €1.20 per hr. Open M-Sa 10am-2am, Su 3pm-2am.) The **post office** is on Pr. Gen. Humberto Delgado. (☎223 40 02 00. Open M-F 8:30am-9pm, Sa-Su 9am-6pm.) **Postal code:** 4000.

🖪🖪 ACCOMMODATIONS AND FOOD. For good accommodation deals, look west of **Avenida Aliados** or on **Rua Fernandes Tomás** and **Rua Formosa,** perpendicular to Av. dos Aliados. Popular with young travelers from around the world, **Pensão Duas Nações ❷** offers a variety of rooms at low rates. (☎222 08 96 21. Internet €0.50 per 15min. Reserve ahead. Singles €15; doubles €25-30; triples €30-35.) A few blocks away from the city center, **Pensão Portuguesa ❶,** Tr. Coronel Pacheco 11, has cheap rooms on a quiet street. (☎222 00 41 74. July-Aug. singles €12.50, with bath €15; doubles €15/€20. Sept.-June singles €10; doubles €13.) Take bus #35 from Estação Campanha to **Pousada de Juventude do Porto (HI) ❷,** R. Paulo da Gama 551, which is in a somewhat dodgy neighborhood; women should be cautious walking around at night. (☎226 17 72 57. Reception daily 8am-midnight. June-

---

THAT TOOK GUTS When native son Henry the Navigator geared up to conquer Cueta in the early 15th century, Porto's residents slaughtered their cattle, gave the meat to Prince Henry's fleet, and kept only the entrails. This dramatic generosity came in the wake of the Plague, when food supplies were crucial. The dish *tripàs a moda do Porto* commemorates their culinary sacrifice; to this day, the people of Porto are known as *tripeiros* (tripe-eaters). If you're feeling adventurous, try some of the tripe dishes, which locals—and few others—consider quite a delicacy.

Sept. dorms €15; doubles with bath €42. Oct.-May €12.50/€35.) Take bus #6, 50, 54, or 87 from Pr. Liberdade (only #50 and 54 run at night) to **camp** at **Prelada ❶**, on R. Monte dos Burgos, in Quinta da Prelada, 3km from the town center. (☎228 31 26 16. Reception 8am-11pm. €2.50-3.30 per person, per tent, or per car.) Look near the river in the **Ribeira** district on C. Ribeira, R. Reboleira, and R. Cima do Muro for great restaurants. The **⚑Majestic Café ❷**, R. de Santa Catarina 112, is the oldest, most famous cafe in Porto. (Open M-Sa 9:30am-midnight.) Across the street, **Confeitaria Império ❶**, R. de Santa Catarina 149-151, serves excellent pastries and inexpensive lunch specials. (Open M-Sa 7:30am-8:30pm.)

◖ 🎵 SIGHTS AND ENTERTAINMENT. Your first brush with Porto's rich stock of fine artwork may be the celebrated collection of *azulejos* (tiles) in the **São Bento train station.** Walk past the station and uphill on Av. Afonso Henriques to reach Porto's pride and joy, the 12th- to 13th-century Romanesque **cathedral.** (Open M-Sa 9am-12:30pm and 2:30-6pm, Su 2:30-6pm. Cloister €1.25.) From the station, follow signs downhill on R. Mouzinho da Silveira to R. Ferreira Borges and the **⚑Palácio da Bolsa** (Stock Exchange), the epitome of 19th-century elegance. The ornate **Sala Árabe** (Arabic Hall) took 18 years to decorate. (Open daily 9am-7pm. Tours every 30min., €4.) Next door, the Gothic **Igreja de São Francisco** glitters with an elaborately gilded wooden interior. Thousands of human bones are stored under the floor. (Open daily 9am-6pm. €2.50, students €1.25.) Up R. dos Clérigos from Pr. Liberdade rises the **Torre dos Clérigos** (Tower of Clerics), adjacent to the **Igreja dos Clérigos.** (Tower open June-July daily 10am-7pm; Aug. 10am-10pm; Sept.-May 10am-noon and 2-5pm. €1. Church open M-Th 10am-noon and 2-5pm, Sa 10am-noon and 2-8pm, Su 10am-1pm. Free.) From there, head up R. Restauração, turn right on R. Alberto Gouveia, and go left on R. Dom Manuel II to reach the **Museu Nacional Soares dos Reis,** R. Dom Manuel II 44. This former royal residence now houses an exhaustive collection of 19th-century Portuguese painting and sculpture. (Open Tu 2-6pm, W-Su 10am-6pm. €3, students €1.50.) Bus #78 from Av. dos Aliados runs several kilometers out of town to the **Museu de Arte Contemporânea,** which hosts contemporary art and an impressive park with sculpted gardens and fountains. (Museum open Tu-Th 10am-10pm, Sa-Su 10am-8pm. Park closes at sundown. €4, Su before 2pm free.) To get to Porto's rocky and polluted (but popular) **beach,** in the ritzy Foz district, take bus #1 from the São Bento train station or tram #1 from Igreja de São Francisco.

But we digress—back to the wine. Fine and bounteous port wines are available for tasting at 20-odd **port wine lodges,** usually *gratuito* (free). The lodges are all across the river in **Vila Nova da Gaia;** from the Ribeira district, cross the lower level of the large bridge. **Sandeman,** peopled by costumed guides, is a good place to start (entrance €2.50). **Ferreira,** one block up from the end of Av. Ramos Pinto, has a memorable atmosphere (entrance €2.50). **⚑Taylor's,** R. do Choupelo 250, has a terrace with views of the city and no entrance fee. (Most open daily 10am-6pm.)

BRAGA ☎253

Braga (pop. 160,000) originally served as the capital of a region founded by Celtic tribes in 300 BC. The city's beautiful gardens, plazas, museums, and markets earned it the nickname "Portuguese Rome." In Portugal's oldest **cathedral,** the treasury showcases the archdiocese's most precious paintings and relics, including a collection of *cofres cranianos* (brain boxes), one of which contains the 6th-century cortex of São Martinho Dume, Braga's first bishop. (Cathedral and treasury open June-Aug. daily 8:30am-6pm; Sept.-May 8:30am-5pm. Cathedral free. Treasury €2.) Braga's most famous landmark, **Igreja do Bom Jesús,** is actually 5km outside of town. To visit Bom Jesús, either take the 285m ride on the antique funicular (8am-8pm; €1), or walk 25-30min. up the granite paved pathway that forks into two zig-zagging 565-step stairways.

Buses (☎253 61 60 80) leave Central de Camionagem for: Coimbra (3hr., 6-9 per day, €8); Guimarães (1hr., every 30min., €2); Lisbon (5¼hr., 8-9 per day, €12); and Porto (1¾hr., every 45min., €3.80). The **tourist office**, Av. Central 1, is on the corner of Av. Liberdade in Pr. República. (☎253 26 25 50. Open July-Sept. M-F 9am-7pm, Sa-Su 9am-12:30pm and 2-5:30pm; Oct.-June closed Su.)

🖪 DAYTRIP FROM BRAGA: GUIMARÃES. Ask any Portugal native about the city of Guimarães (pop. 60,000), and they will tell you it was the birthplace of the nation. It is home to one of Portugal's most gorgeous palatial estates, the **🖪Paço dos Duques de Bragança** (Ducal Palace), which is modeled after the manor houses of northern Europe. Overlooking the city is the **Monte da Pena,** home to an excellent **campsite** as well as picnic areas, mini-golf, and cafes. To get there, take the **teleférico** from Lg. das Hortas. (☎253 51 50 85. Closed Oct.-May. Open Aug. daily 10am-8pm; June-July and Sept. M-F 11am-7pm, Sa-Su 10am-8pm. €1.50, round-trip €2.50.) The **tourist office** is on Alameda de São Dámaso 83, facing Pr. Toural. (☎253 41 24 50. Open June-Sept. M-Sa 9:30am-7pm; Oct.-May M-Sa 9:30am-6pm.) Guimarães is best reached by **bus** from Braga. REDM buses (☎253 51 62 29) run frequently between the cities until 8pm (1hr., €2).

VIANA DO CASTELO ☎258

Situated in the northwestern corner of the country, Viana do Castelo (pop. 20,000) is one of the loveliest coastal cities in all of Portugal. Visited mainly as a beach resort, Viana also has a lively historic district centered around the **🖪Praça da República.** Diagonally across the plaza, granite columns support the flowery facade of the **Igreja da Misericórdia.** Known for its *azulejo* interior, the **🖪Monte de Santa Luzia,** overlooking the city, is crowned by magnificent Celtic ruins and the **Templo de Santa Luzia,** an early 20th-century neo-Byzantine church. The view of Viana from the hill is fantastic. For more views of the harbor and ocean, visit the **Castelo de São Tiago da Barra,** built by Felipe I of Spain. Viana do Castelo and the surrounding coast feature excellent beaches. Most convenient are **Praia Norte,** at the end of Av. do Atlántico at the west end of town, and **Praia da Argaçosa,** on Rio Lima.

Trains (☎258 82 13 15) run from the top of Av. Combatentes da Grande Guerra to Porto (2hr., 13-14 per day, €4). **Buses** run to: Braga (1½hr., 4-8 per day, €3.50); Lisbon (5½hr., 2-3 per day, €18); and Porto (2hr., 4-9 per day, €3.50-5.25). The **tourist office,** R. do Hospital Velho, at the corner of Pr. Erva has a helpful English-speaking staff and offers maps and accommodation listings. (☎258 82 26 20. Open Aug. daily 9am-7pm; May-July and Sept. M-Sa 9am-1pm and 2:30-6pm, Su 9:30am-1pm; Oct.-Apr. M-Sa 9am-12:30pm and 2:30-5:30pm.) The **🖪Pousada de Juventude de Viana do Castelo (HI) ❶,** R. da Argaçosa (Azenhas D. Prior), is right on the marina, off Pr. de Galiza. (☎258 80 02 60; fax 82 08 70. Reception 8am-midnight. Checkout 10am. Reservations recommended. Mid-June to mid-Sept. dorms €12.50; doubles with bath €30. Mid-Sept.to mid-June dorms €10; doubles with bath €25.)

ROMANIA (ROMÂNIA)

Devastated by the lengthy reign of Nicolae Ceauşescu, Romania today suffers under the effects of a sluggish economy. Some Romanians are eager to move the country to Western European standards, while others are eager to simply move to Western Europe. Many travelers are deterred by Romania's largely undeserved reputation for poverty and crime, but those who do visit will discover a land of cosmopolitan cities, lovely medieval villages, and endless stretches of pristine countryside rich in history, rustic beauty, and hospitality.

FACTS AND FIGURES

Official Name: Romania.

Capital: Bucharest.

Major Cities: Bucharest, Cluj-Napoca, Braşov, Constanţa.

Population: 22,500,000.

Land Area: 230,340 sq. km.

Time Zone: GMT +2.

Languages: Romanian (official), Hungarian, German.

Religions: Romanian Orthodox (70%), Catholic (6%), Protestant (6%).

DISCOVER ROMANIA

Romania is blessed with snowy peaks, a superb stretch of Black Sea coast, and culturally rich cities—all at half the price of similar attractions in Western Europe. The vast and hectic capital, **Bucharest** (p. 826), has good museums, expanses of green parks, myriad historical monuments, and a hip night scene. For a hefty dose of Transylvanian vampire mythology, visit the legendary castle of Count Dracula at **Bran** (p. 832). Nearby **Braşov** (p. 831) provides access to the trails and slopes of the Transylvanian Alps. **Cluj-Napoca** (p. 830), Romania's cultural center and student capital, is the most diverse city in the country. For a holier take on Romania, visit the secluded **Bukovina Monasteries** (p. 833) near Gura Humorului.

ESSENTIALS

WHEN TO GO

As Romania experiences fairly extreme summers and winters, spring and fall are the best times to visit. Winters can be very cold, especially in the mountains, and there is often a lot of precipitation. The coasts are more moderate.

DOCUMENTS AND FORMALITIES

VISAS. Citizens of Australia, New Zealand, and South Africa need visas to enter Romania. Citizens of the EU (including Ireland and the UK) can stay without visas for 90 days. US citizens do not need visas for stays of up to 30 days. Americans staying longer than 30 days and others with visas who wish to stay longer than 90 days can obtain a visa **extension** at police headquarters in large cities or at Bucharest's passport office, Str. Luigi Cazzavillan 11. Apply early to allow the bureaucratic process to run its slow, frustrating course.

EMBASSIES. Foreign embassies in Romania are in Bucharest (p. 826). Romanian embassies abroad include: **Canada,** 655 Rideau St., Ottawa, ON K1N 6A3 (☎613-789-5345; romania@cyberus.ca); **Ireland,** 47 Ailesbury Rd., Ballsbridge,

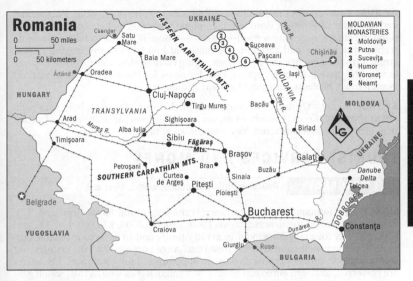

Romania map

0 ___ 50 miles
0 ___ 50 kilometers

UKRAINE
HUNGARY
TRANSYLVANIA
YUGOSLAVIA
BULGARIA
MOLDOVA
UKRAINE

Csenger, Satu Mare, Baia Mare, Ártánd, Oradea, Suceava, Pașcani, Chișinău, Iași, Cluj-Napoca, Tirgu Mureș, Bacău, Sighișoara, Arad, Mureș R., Alba Iulia, Birlad, Timișoara, Sibiu, Făgăraș Mts., Brașov, Galați, Petroșani, SOUTHERN CARPATHIAN MTS., Bran, Buzău, Danube Delta, Curtea de Argeș, Sinaia, Tulcea, Belgrade, Pitești, Ploiești, Bucharest, Craiova, Dunărea R., Constanța, Giurgiu, Ruse, Prut R., Siret R., MOLDAVIA, EASTERN CARPATHIAN MTS., DOBROGEA

MOLDAVIAN MONASTERIES
1 Moldovița
2 Putna
3 Sucevița
4 Humor
5 Voroneț
6 Neamț

ROMANIA

Dublin 4 (☎ 353 269 2852 or 353 269 2142; fax 353 269 2122); **South Africa,** 117 Charles St., Brooklyn, Pretoria; P.O. Box 11295, Brooklyn, 0181 (☎ 012 466 940; fax 012 466 947); **UK,** 4 Palace Green, Kensington, London W8 4QD (☎ 020 7937 9666; fax 020 7937 8069); and **US,** 1607 23rd St. NW, Washington, D.C. 20008 (☎ 202-332-4848; www.roembus.org).

TRANSPORTATION

BY PLANE. Numerous airlines fly into Bucharest; **TAROM** (Romanian Airlines), which is in the process of updating its aging fleet, flies direct from Bucharest to New York, Chicago, and major European cities. Bucharest's Otopeni International Airport (OTP) has improved its ground services but is still far from ideal.

BY TRAIN. Trains, a better option for international travel than buses, head daily to Western Europe via Budapest. **Interrail** is accepted, but **Eurail** is not. **CFR** (Che-Fe-Re) offices in larger towns sell international and domestic tickets up to 24hr. before departure. After that, only train stations sell tickets. The useful English timetable *Mersul Trenurilor* (L12,000) is available online at www.cfr.ro/IsaRR.htm. Schedule information is available at ☎ 221 in most cities. International trains (often blue) are usually indicated by "i" on timetables. *InterCity* trains ("IC" on timetables and at stations) stop only at major cities. *Rapid* trains (green) are the next fastest; *accelerat* trains (red) have four digits starting with "1" and are slower. Take the fastest train you can, which is usually *accelerat*. There is little difference between first class (*clasa întâi;* cars marked with a "1" on the side; 6 people per compartment) and second class (*clasa dova;* 8 people), except on *personal* trains (black), where first class is markedly better. On an **overnight train,** shell out for first class in a *vagon de dormit* (sleeping carriage). The best mode to exit the country is by direct train from Bucharest to the capital city of a neighboring country; the next best options are planes and buses.

BY BUS. Buses connect major cities in Romania to Athens, İstanbul, Prague, and various cities in Western Europe. Since plane and train tickets to Romania are often expensive, buses are a good—if slow—option. It is best to take a domestic train to the border and catch an international bus from there. Buying tickets straight from the carrier saves you from paying commission. Use the local bus system only if there is no other option; look for signs for the *autogară* (bus station) in each town. **Minibuses** are good for short distances.

BY THUMB. *Let's Go* does not recommend hitchhiking. If you do, hold your palm out as if waving. Know that drivers expect a payment similar to the price of a train ticket for the distance traveled. Never hitchhike at night.

TOURIST SERVICES AND MONEY

EMERGENCY	Police: ☎955. Ambulance: ☎961. Fire: ☎981.

MONEY. The Romanian unit of currency is the *leu*, plural **lei** (abbreviated "L"). Banknotes come in the denominations L500, L1000, L5000, L10,000, L50,000, and L100,000. Pay for everything in *lei* to avoid rip-offs and to save your reliable currency for emergencies and bribes. Private exchange bureaus litter the country, but few take credit cards or traveler's checks. Shop around for good rates. US dollars are preferred, although euros can usually be exchanged as well. ATMs, which generally accept MasterCard, and, less frequently Visa, exchange *lei* at reasonable rates. It is customary to give inexact change for purchases, generally rounding to the nearest L500; this usually suffices as a tip in restaurants.

BUSINESS HOURS. Posted hours are rarely definite, and many banks and businesses may be closed on Friday afternoons.

AUS$1 = L18,400		L10,000 = AUS$0.55
CDN$1 = L21,400		L10,000 = CDN$0.47
EUR€1 = L32,600		L10,000 = EUR€0.31
NZ$1 = L15,600		L10,000 = NZ$0.64
ZAR1 = L3200		L10,000 = ZAR3.17
UK£1 = L50,900		L10,000 = UK£0.20
US$1 = L33,200		L10,000 = US$0.30

COMMUNICATION

PHONE CODES	**Country code: 40. International dialing prefix: 00.** From outside Romania, dial int'l dialing prefix (see inside back cover) + 40 + city code + local number.

MAIL. Request *par avion* for airmail, which takes 2-3 weeks to reach international destinations. Mail can be received general delivery through *Poste Restante;* address mail to be held: Firstname SURNAME, Poste Restante, Str. Nicolae Iorga 1, Braşov 2200, ROMANIA.

TELEPHONES AND INTERNET. Nearly all public phones are orange and accept **phone cards,** although a few archaic blue phones take L500 coins. Cards (L50,000, L100,000, and L200,000) are available at telephone offices, major Bucharest Metro stops, and some post offices and kiosks. Rates per minute run: L10,000 to neighboring countries, L14,000 to most of Europe, and L18,000 to the US. Orange phones in major cities will operate in English when you press "i." Local calls cost L595 per minute and can be made from any phone; a busy signal may just indicate a connection problem. To make a phone call *prin comandă* (with the help of the operator) at the telephone office, write down the destination, duration, and phone number for your call. Pay up front, and ask for the rate per minute. For general information call ☎957; for the operator, call ☎930. **Internet cafes** are easy to find in most large cities; rates are around L10,000-Ll5,000 per hour.

LANGUAGES. Romanian is a Romance language; those familiar with French, Italian, Spanish, or Portuguese should be able to read signs. German and Hungarian are widely spoken in Transylvania. German and French are second languages for the older generation, English for the younger. For Romanian phrases, see p. 1063.

ACCOMMODATIONS AND CAMPING

ROMANIA	❶	❷	❸	❹	❺
ACCOMMODATIONS	under L350,000	L350,000-665,000	L665,000-1,000,000	L1,000,000-2,000,000	over L2,000,000

While some **hotels** charge foreigners 50-100% more than natives, lodging is still relatively cheap (€6-20). Youth hostels are usually nicer than one-star hotels, two-star establishments are decent, and three-star places are good but expensive. **Private accommodations** are generally the best option; be aware that renting a room "together" means sharing a bed. Rooms start from €5 per person, sometimes including breakfast and other amenities. Visit the room and fix a price before accepting. Many towns allow foreign students to stay in **university dorms** at low prices, but they may be hard to find if you don't speak Romanian. **Campgrounds** are crowded and often have intolerable bathrooms. Relatively cheap **bungalows** are often full in summer; reserve far in advance.

FOOD AND DRINK

ROMANIA	❶	❷	❸	❹	❺
FOOD	under L60,000	L60,000-100,000	L100,000-140,000	L140,000-180,000	over L180,000

Lunch usually starts with a soup, called *supă* or *ciorbă*, followed by a main dish (typically grilled meat) and dessert. Soups can be very tasty; try *ciorbă de perişoare* (vegetables and ground meatballs) or *supă cu găluşte* (fluffy dumplings). Pork comes in several cuts, of which *muşchi* and *cotlet* are the best quality. For dessert, *clătite* (crepes), *papanaşi* (doughnuts with jam and sour cream), and *tort* (creamy cakes) are all fantastic. Some restaurants charge by weight (usually 100g) rather than by portion. *Garnituri*, the extras that come with a meal, are usually charged separately, even down to that dollop of mustard. As a rule, you will pay for everything the waiter puts in front of you. "Fast food" means precooked and microwaved. Check expiration dates on everything you buy.

HEALTH AND SAFETY

Most public restrooms lack soap, towels, and toilet paper; carry a roll with you. *Farmacies* sometimes have what you need; *antinevralgic*, sometimes called "tylenol," is for headaches, *aspirină* or *piramidon* for colds and the flu, and *saprosan* for diarrhea. There are some American medical clinics in Bucharest with English-speaking doctors; pay in cash.

HOLIDAYS AND FESTIVALS

Holidays: New Year's (Jan. 1-2); Epiphany (Jan. 6); Easter (Apr. 20-21); Labor Day (May 1); National Unity Day (Dec. 1); Christmas (Dec. 25-26).

Festivals: Summer festivals abound in Transylvania. Sibiu's many festivals include the **International Theatre Festival** in early June. Sighişoara holds a huge **medieval festival** in the 2nd week of July, while Braşov hosts the **International Chamber Music Festival**.

BUCHAREST ☎ 021

Bucharest was once a fabled beauty on the Orient Express, but communist dictator Nicolae Ceauşescu replaced grand boulevards and Ottoman remnants with wide highways and concrete blocks during his 25 years in power. Although Bucharest is no longer the beautiful *Micul Paris* ("Little Paris") it once was, historic neighborhoods, secluded parks, and an intense club scene keep the capital lively.

╔ TRANSPORTATION

Flights: Otopeni Airport (OTP; ☎204 10 00), 18km from the city. Bus #783 to Otopeni leaves from Piaţa Unirii with stops in the other major *piaţele* of the city center. Buy **domestic tickets** at the **TAROM office**, Spl. Independenţei 7 (☎337 20 37, reservations ☎9361; open M-F 9am-7pm, Sa 9am-1pm).

Trains: Gara de Nord (☎223 08 80) is the main station. M3: Gara de Nord. L4000 to enter the station if you're not catching a train. To: **Budapest** (12-16hr., 7per day, L950,000); **Cluj-Napoca** (8-12hr., 4 per day, L248,000); **Iaşi** (6½hr., 4 per day, L248,000); **Sofia** (10-12hr., 3 per day, L750,000). Domestic tickets sold at **CFR**, Str. Domniţa Anastasia 10-14 (☎313 26 43, reservations ☎9522).

Buses: Filaret, Cuţitul de Argint 2 (☎335 11 40). M2: Tineretului. South of the Center. To Athens, your best bet is **Fotopoulos Express** (☎335 82 49). To İstanbul, catch a **Toros** (☎223 18 98) or a **Murat** (☎224 92 03) bus from outside Gara de Nord. To reach Western Europe, take **Double T,** Calea Victoriei 2 (☎313 36 42), affiliated with Eurail, or **Eurolines Touring,** Str. Ankara 6 (☎230 03 70). All international bus companies have offices near Piaţa Dorobanţilor.

Public Transportation: Buses, trolleys, and **trams** run until 11:30pm (L6000). Tickets sold at kiosks only; validate on board or face a fine. All **express buses** except #783 take only magnetic cards (L15,000 round-trip). Beware pickpockets during peak hours. The **Metro** offers reliable and less-crowded service to major points (5am-11:30pm). Magnetic cards L12,000 for 2 trips; L40,000 for 10 trips.

Taxis: Prof-Taxi (☎94 22), **H&V** (☎94 16), **Taxi 2000** (☎94 94). Ask the drivers to use the meter. Expect to pay L4000-5000 per km.

◆↔? ORIENTATION AND PRACTICAL INFORMATION

Bulevardul Nicolae Bălcescu runs north-south through the city's four main squares: **Piaţa Victoriei, Piaţa Romană, Piaţa Unirii,** and **Piaţa Universităţii.** The main train station, Gara de Nord, lies along the M3 Metro line. To reach the city center, take the M3 (dir.: Dristor) one stop to Piaţa Victoriei and change to the M2 line (dir.: Depoul); take this train one stop to Piaţa Romană, two stops to Piaţa Universităţii, or three stops to Piaţa Unirii. For a great guide to the city, get *Bucharest in Your Pocket* (L35,000), sold at many museums, bookstores, and some hotels.

Police: ☎955. **Ambulance:** ☎961. **Fire:** ☎981.

Tourist Information: Private tourist offices litter the city, but hotels and hostels are usually better sources of information.

Embassies and Consulates: Australia, Bd. Unirii 74, Et. 5 (☎320 98 26). M2: Piața Unirii, then bus #104, 123, or 124 to Lucian Blaga. Open M-Th 9:30am-12:30pm. **Canada,** Str. Nicolae Iorga 36 (☎307 50 00). M2: Piața Romană. Open M-Th 8am-5pm, F 8:30am-2pm. **Ireland,** Str. V. Lascăr 42-44 (☎210 89 48). M2: Piața Romană. Open M-F 10am-noon. **UK,** Str. Jules Michelet 24 (☎312 03 03). M2: Piața Romană. Open M-Th 8:30am-1pm and 2-5pm, F 8:30am-1:30pm. **US,** Str. Tudor Arghezi 7-9 (☎210 40 42, ext. 403 or 318; after hours 210 01 49). M2: Piața Universității. Citizens of **New Zealand** should contact the UK embassy. Citizens of **South Africa** should contact their embassy in Budapest (p. 523).

Currency Exchange: Exchange agencies are everywhere, but **ATMs** at major banks always give the best rates. Don't change money on the street; it's usually a scam.

American Express: Marshall Tourism, Bd. Magheru 43, 1st fl., #1 (☎212 97 87). M2: Piața Romană. Does not cash traveler's checks. Open M-F 9am-5pm, Sa 9am-1pm.

Luggage Storage: At Gara de Nord. Foreigners pay L25,000-L50,000. Open 24hr.

24hr. Pharmacy: Farmadex, Calea Moșilor 280 (☎211 95 60).

Internet Access: D&D Internet Cafe, Bd. Carol I 25, (☎313 10 48). M2: Piața Universității. With Hotel Intercontinental on your left, head down Bd. Carol I past Piața Rosetti. 6am-midnight L25,000 per hr., midnight-6am L15,000 per hr. Open 24hr.

Telephones: Telephone office, Calea Victoriei 35. M2: Piața Universității. Phone cards L100,000 or L200,000. Open 24hr.

Post Office: Str. Matei Millo 10 (☎315 90 30). M2: Piața Universității. Open M-F 7:30am-8pm, Sa 7:30am-2pm. **Poste Restante** nearby, next to Hotel Carpați. Address mail to be held: Firstname SURNAME, *Poste Restante,* Str. Matei Millo 10, Bucharest **70700** ROMANIA.

▐ ACCOMMODATIONS

Renting private rooms is not common. You won't go wrong with either of Bucharest's two youth hostels, but avoid "representatives" you meet at Gara de Nord.

▓ **Elvis's Villa,** Str. Avram Iancu 5 (☎315 52 73; www.elvisvilla.ro). M2: Piața Universității. Or, from Gara de Nord, take trolley bus #85 to the Calea Moșilor stop. Continue along Bd. Carol I into Piața Protopescu, turn right onto Str. Sfântul Ștefan and left onto Str. Avram Iancu. Brand-new hostel run by friendly Australians. A/C and fat mattresses. Laundry, Internet access, and breakfast included. US$12 per day; US$72 per week. ❷

▓ **Villa Helga Youth Hostel,** Str. Salcâmilor 2 (☎610 22 14). M2: Piața Romană. Or, take bus #86, 79, or 133 from Gara de Nord to Piața Gemeni. Continue 1 block on Bd. Dacia and turn right on Str. Viitorului. Romania's original hostel. Call ahead in summer. Breakfast and laundry included. US$10 per day; US$60 per week. ❶

Casa Victor, Str. Emanoil Porumbaru 44 (☎222 57 23). M2: Piața Aviatorilor. Lovely, quiet, four-star *pensiune.* Transportation to and from the airport or train station included (call ahead). Singles US$40-80; doubles US$80; mini-apartment US$90-100. ❹

◖ FOOD

Open-air markets sell produce, meat, and cheese—try the market at **Piața Gemeni,** near the corner of Bd. Dacia and Str. Vasile Lascăr. **La Mama ❷,** Str. Barbu Văcărescu 3, at M3: Ștefan cel Mare, serves traditional Romanian dishes for

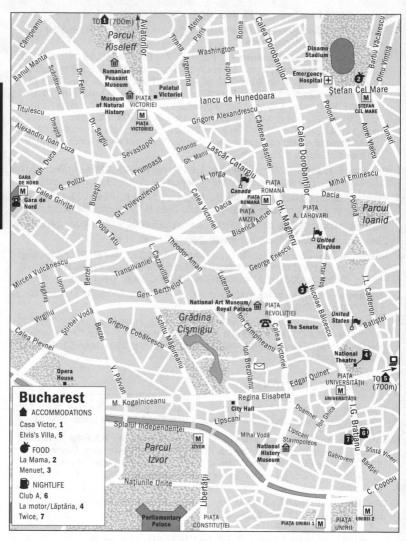

Bucharest

ACCOMMODATIONS
Casa Victor, **1**
Elvis's Villa, **5**

FOOD
La Mama, **2**
Menuet, **3**

NIGHTLIFE
Club A, **6**
La motor/Lăptăria, **4**
Twice, **7**

L70,000-95,000. (☎212 40 86. Reservations recommended. Open daily 10am-2am.)
Menuet ❸, Str. Nicolae Golescu 14, at M2: Piaţa Universităţii, offers elegant dining
on pan-European fare. (Main dishes L75,000-180,000. Open daily 12:30pm-1am.)

👁 SIGHTS

CIVIC CENTER. To create his ideal Socialist capital, Ceauşescu destroyed 5
sq. km of Bucharest's historical center, demolishing over 9000 19th-century
houses and displacing more than 40,000 Romanians. The **Civic Center** (Centru

Civic) lies at the end of the 6km-long Bd. Unirii, purposefully built 1m wider than the Champs-Elysées, after which it was modeled. Its centerpiece, the ◼**Parliamentary Palace** (Palatul Parlamentului), is the world's second-largest building (after the Pentagon in Washington, D.C.) and was built by 20,000 workers using wood and marble exclusively from Romania. *(M1 or 3: Izvor. Entrance (A3) off Calea Izvor, on the right side of the building from Bd. Unirii. Open daily 10am-4pm. Tours L100,000, students L30,000.)*

SIGHTS OF THE REVOLUTION. Bucharest is slowly putting the memory of its 1989 revolution behind it. Demonstrators were killed fighting Ceauşescu's forces at **Piata Universităţii** on December 21, 1989, the day before his fall. After Ceauşescu was deposed, students gathered in the small square now known as "Piaţa 22 Decembrie 1989," opposite Hotel Intercontinental, to protest the neo-communist government that succeeded him. In June, the government bussed in 10,000 Romanian miners to quash the protestors, killing 21 students. White crosses and plaques stand as memorials to those who died during the revolution of 1989. *(M2: Piaţa Universităţii; behind the fountain.)* With Hotel Intercontinental on your left, make a right onto Bd. Regina Elisabeta and then a right onto Calea Victoriei to reach **Piaţa Revoluţiei**, where the first shots of the revolution were fired.

MUSEUMS. The ◼**Village Museum** (Muzeul Satului), Şos. Kiseleff 28-30, is a unique open-air replica of a rural village. *(M2: Aviatorilor. Open Tu-Su 9am-8pm. L40,000, students L15,000.)* The **National Art Museum** (Muzeul Naţional de Artă), Calea Victoriei 49-53, in Piaţa Revoluţiei, has works by Monet, van Eyck, El Greco, and Romania's most famous painter, Nicolae Grigorescu. *(M2: Piaţa Universi-tăţii. Open May-Sept. W-Su 11am-7pm; Oct.-Apr. W-Su 10am-6pm. L80,000, students L40,000.)* The **National History Museum** (Muzeul Naţional de Istorie al României), Calea Victoriei 12, gives a thorough look at Romanian history. *(M2: Piaţa Universităţii. Open Apr.-Oct. 10am-6pm; Nov.-Mar. 9am-5pm. L15,000, students L6000.)* The **Museum of the Romanian Peasant** (Muzeul Ţăranului Român), Şos. Kiseleff 3, captures Romanian rural life. *(M2 or 3: Piaţa Victoriei. Open Tu-Su 10am-6pm. L30,000, students L5000.)*

OTHER SIGHTS. Several of modern Bucharest's most fashionable streets, including **Calea Victoriei**, **Şoseauna Kiseleff**, **Bulevardul Aviatorilor**, and **Bulevardul Magheru**, are sights in and of themselves. The sidestreets just off Piaţa Victoriei and Piaţa Dorobanţilor brim with villas and houses typical of beautiful 19th-century Buchar-est. The only remaining part of Bucharest's **old center** lies west of Bd. Brătianu and south of Bd. Regina Elisabetha, in the vicinity of Str. Lipscani and Str. Gabroveni.

🎵 🎭 ENTERTAINMENT AND NIGHTLIFE

Bucharest often hosts huge **rock festivals** (Michael Jackson once greeted scream-ing fans here with "Hello, Budapest!"). **Theater** and **opera** are cheap (L10,000-150,000); tickets go on sale at each theater's box office two Saturdays before per-formances. However, there are no shows June-Sept.

At night, pack a map and cab fare—streets are poorly lit and public transporta-tion stops at 11:30pm. **La motor/Lăptăria**, on top of the National Theater, has a lively terrace. *(M2: Piaţa Universitătii. Open daily 9am-2am.)* **Club A**, Str. Blănari 14, is a popular club. *(M2: Piaţa Universitătii. F-Sa men L50,000, women L20,000. Open daily 8pm-5am.)* **Twice**, Str. Sfânta Vineri 4, has two dance floors. *(M2: Piaţa Universitătii. F-Sa men L50,000. Open daily 9pm-5am.)* **Maxx**, Spl. Independenţei 290, an excellent *discotecă*, plays Romanian music. *(M3: Semănătoarea or Grozăveşti. Th-F L30,000, Sa L50,000. Open daily 10pm-late.)*

SINAIA
☎0244

Sinaia (sih-NYE-uh) first made its mark in the late 1880s as an alpine getaway for Romania's royal family. Although the construction of opulent ✦Peleş Castle began in 1873, it has central heating, electric lights, and an elevator. (Open W noon-5pm, Th-Su 9am-5pm. L70,000, students L30,000.) The equally striking ✦Pelişor Castle, built in the early 20th century, was designed by Ferdinand's wife, Maria, to fit modern progressive tastes. (Open W noon-5pm, Th-Su 9am-5pm. L50,000; students L20,000.) The nearby **Bucegi mountains** are good for hiking and hang-gliding in the summer and skiing in the winter. A *telecabina* (cable-car) to the mountains leaves from behind Hotel New Montana, Bd. Carol I 24. (Round-trip L90,000-130,000.)

Trains go to Bucharest (2hr., 20 per day, L120,000) and Braşov (1hr., 20 per day, L55,000). From the station, cross the street, climb two flights of stairs, bear right at the fork, and turn left onto Bd. Carol I, the main street. **Villa Retezat ❷**, Str. Kogalniceanu 64, has cozy rooms in a charming old house. From the train station, go left on Bd. Carol I, then right onto Str. Aosta; go left both times it forks, then go up the first staircase on the right. (☎31 47 47. Doubles L500,000.) **Liliana ❷**, Str. Mânăstirii 7, serves tasty international dishes. (Entrees L60,000-90,000. Open daily 8am-11pm.) There is an **open-air market** at Piaţa Unirii. (Open daily 7am-9pm.) Sheep cheese, a traditional local treat, can be found at **Piaţa Centrală** in the market; ask for *brânză de copac* (BRIN-zuh day co-PAHK). **Postal code:** 2180.

TRANSYLVANIA (TRANSILVANIA)

Transylvania's name evokes images of a dark land of black magic and vampires; such legends have their roots in the region's architecture, with buildings that are tilted, jagged, and more sternly Gothic than anywhere else in Europe. However, Transylvania is also filled with green hills and mountains descending gently from the Carpathians to the Hungarian Plain; some areas are largely untamed and allow for good hiking from Sinaia into the Făgăraş Mountains.

CLUJ-NAPOCA
☎0264

Cluj-Napoca is Transylvania's student center and unofficial capital. Colorful, relaxed, and relatively Western (with a sizable Hungarian minority), the city is a good starting point for a journey farther into Transylvania or north to Maramureş. The 80m Gothic steeple of the Catholic **Church of St. Michael** (Biserica Sf. Mihail) pierces the skyline in **Piaţa Unirii**. The **Franciscan Church** (Biserica Franciscanilor), founded on a Roman temple site, has a Baroque interior. (Open M-F 8am-5pm, Sa-Su 9am-3pm; services daily 9am and noon.) Take Bd. Ferdinand across the river, turn left on Str. Dragalina, and climb the stairs to your right to reach **Cetătuie Hill**, where a dazzling view awaits. To visit the serene **Botanical Gardens** (Grădină Botanica), return to Piaţa Unirii; with your back to the statue, take a right on Str. Napoca, then turn left on Str. Coh. Bilaşcu. (Open daily 9am-8pm. L15,000.)

Trains (☎43 20 01) run from Piaţa Mihai Viteazul to: Braşov (5-7hr., 5 per day, L205,000); Bucharest (8-13hr., 7 per day, L250,000); Iaşi (7hr., 4 per day, L250,000); Sibiu (4hr., 1 per day, L170,000); Timişoara (6hr., 4 per day, L215,000); and Budapest (6½-7hr., 2 per day, L835,000). **Local buses** and **trams** run 5am-11:15pm; buy tickets (2 trips L13,000) at **RATUC** kiosks. There are **ATMs** along Bd. Ferdinand and surrounding Piaţa Unirii. Check email at the **Kiro Internet Cafe**, Bd. Ferdinand 6, 3rd fl. (L5000-9000 per hr. Open 24hr.) **Hotel Vladeasa ❷**, Str. Regele Ferdinand 20, has a good location and clean, simple rooms. (☎19 44 29. Singles 550,000; doubles L800,000.) **Hotel Continental (HI) ❶**, Str. Napoca 1, in Piaţa Unirii, has both large, well-furnished three-star rooms and simpler one-star rooms. (☎19 14 41. One-star: singles US$9; doubles US$18; nonmembers add US$18. Three-star: singles US$48;

doubles US$62.) ▨**Restaurant Matei Corvin ❸**, Str. Matei Corvin 2, serves huge portions of Transylvanian food. (Main dishes L100,000-L140,000. Open M-Sa noon-10pm.) Kick back with students to enjoy the latest sounds in rock, jazz, and techno at **Music Pub**, Str. Horea 5. (Live music F-Sa 9 or 10pm. Open in summer daily 6pm-3am; off-season M-Sa 9am-4am, Su noon-4am.) **Postal code:** 3400.

⃰ DAYTRIP FROM CLUJ-NAPOCA: SIGHIŞOARA. Vlad Ţepeş, the model for Bram Stoker's *Dracula* (see **Bran**, p. 832) was born in enchanting Sighişoara (see-ghee-SHWAH-rah). Surrounded by mountains and crowning a green hill, its gilded steeples and old clock tower have survived centuries of attacks, fires, and floods. The **Citadel** (Cetate), built by the Saxons in 1191, is now a tiny medieval city-within-a-city. Enter through the **Clock Tower** (Turnul cu Ceas), off Str. O. Goga, passing through the museum and to the top for a great view. (Open in summer Tu-F 10am-6:30pm, Sa-M 10am-4:30pm; off-season Tu-F 9am-3:30pm, Sa-M 10am-3:30pm. L20,000, students L10,000.) The second weekend in July is the huge **medieval festival**, and a **Folk Art Festival** takes place the third week of August. **Trains** run to Bucharest (5hr., 8 per day, L186,000) and Cluj-Napoca (3½hr., 5 per day, L170,000). To reach the center, turn right on Str. Libertătii and the first left onto Str. Gării; veer left at the Russian cemetery, turn right, cross the footbridge over river Târnava Mare, and walk down Str. Morii. **Sighişoara Tour**, Str. Teculescu 1, has maps. From the train station, take a left on Str. 1 Decembrie 1918. (☎77 69 77. Open M-F 8am-3pm, Sa-Su 8-11am.) From the station, take a right to reach ▨**Elvis's Villa Hostel ❶**, Str. Libertatii 10. (☎77 25 46. Bike rental US$5. US$10.) ☎**0265.**

BRAŞOV ☎**0268**

Braşov is an ideal starting point for trips into the mountains. A *telecabina* (cable car) goes up **Muntele Tâmpa**; to reach it from **Piaţa Sfatului**, walk up **Strada Republicii** and turn right onto Str. M. Weiss, right on Str. Brediceanu, left onto steep Str. Suişul Castalului, and right on a paved road to climb two flights of stairs. (Runs Tu-F 9:30am-5pm, Sa-Su 9:30am-6pm. Round-trip L30,000). Trails on Aleea T. Brediceanu lead to the **Weaver's Bastion** and other medieval ruins. Braşov itself is a picturesque town with peaceful side-streets. Beyond the square along Str. Gh. Bariţiu looms Romania's most celebrated Gothic church, the Lutheran **Black Church** (Biserica Neagră), which was so named because it was charred by fire in 1689. (Open M-Sa 10am-5pm. L20,000, students L10,000.) Piaţa Sfatului, Str. Republicii, and **Piaţa Unirii** are nice areas to take a stroll.

Trains go to: Bucharest (3-4hr., 13 per day, L147,000); Cluj-Napoca (5-6hr., 5 per day, L203,000); Iaşi (11hr., 2 per day, L248,000); and Sibiu (4hr., 6 per day, L133,000). Buy tickets at **CFR**, Str. Republicii 53. (Open M-F 8am-7pm, Sa 9am-1pm.) From the station, take bus #4 (dir.: Piaţa Unirii) to Piaţa Sfatului (10min.); get off in front of the Black Church. Good maps are at kiosks on Str. Republicii. For a **private room**, expect to pay US$8-12. **Casa Beke ❷**, Str. Cerbului 32, rents rooms just a few blocks from the main square. Follow Str. Republicii to Piaţa Sfatului, turn left onto Str. Apollonia Hirscher, then take the second right on Str. Cerbului. (L330,000 per person.) **Elvis's Villa Hostel ❶**, Str. Democraţiei 2b, is plush and new. From Piaţa Unirii, walk up Sra. Bâlea and take the first right onto Str. Democraţiei. (☎47 89 30. Dorms US$8-12; singles US$25-28.) For Romanian and Mexican food as well as free shots of *pălinkă*, head to **Bella Musica ❶**, Str. G. Bariţu 2. (Main dishes L65,000-145,000. Open daily noon-11pm.) **Taverna ❷**, Str. Politehnicii 6, has an elegant atmosphere. (Entrees L60,000-200,000. Open daily noon-midnight.) The box office at Str. Republicii 4 sells tickets for **operas** and for the summer **International Chamber Music Festival**. (☎47 18 89. Open M-F 10am-5pm, Sa 10am-1pm.) **Postal code:** 2200.

ROMANIA

ROMANIA

📲 DAYTRIP FROM BRAŞOV: BRAN. Vlad Ţepeş Dracula, the model for the villain-hero of Bram Stoker's famed novel *Dracula*, once lived in Bran. The exploits of the real Vlad make those of his fictional counterpart pale in comparison. His father (also Vlad) was a member of the Order of the Dragon, a society that defended Catholicism from infidels, hence the name by which he ruled: Vlad Dracul ("Dragon"). As a local governor of the Wallachia region, Vlad Ţepeş protected the Bran pass from the Turks, and he became infamous for using a method that can only be described as horse-powered anal impalement. When the Turks invaded Wallachia in 1462, they were met by some 20,000 of their kinsmen impaled this way. Horrified, the Turks retreated. While Ţepeş may have been a guest at **Bran castle**, he did not actually live there—in fact, Stoker himself never even visited Romania. (Castle open Tu-Su 9am-5pm. L60,000, students L20,000.) From Braşov, take city bus #5 or 9 to Autogară 2 (officially Gară Bartolomeu) (45min., every 30min. 7am-6pm, L18,000), to reach Bran. Get off at the big souvenir market or at the "Cabana Bran Castle—500m" sign. Then take the main road back toward Braşov and take the first right to get to the castle.

SIBIU
☎0269

Sibiu (SEE-bee-oo), the ancient capital of Transylvania, is a city of medieval monuments and colorfully ornate houses. The nearby Făgăraş mountains offer some of the best hiking in Romania. Begin by taking the train from Sibiu to **Ucea** (1½hr., 4 per day, L25,000), where a bus connects to **Victoria** (25min., 7 per day, L12,000). From there, many itineraries are possible. The range can also be reached after a day's hike from the sleepy town of **Avrig** (1hr., 4 per day from Sibiu, L19,000). The very helpful *Crossing the Făgăraş Ridge from West to East* is sold in Libraria Friedrich Schiller in Sibiu (L45,000). Hiking season lasts from July to mid-September. Be prepared for cold temperatures year-round, and know that parts of the range can be very challenging. The mountain rescue team is **Salvamont** (☎21 64 77).

Trains from Sibiu run to: Braşov (3½hr., 7 per day, L133,000); Bucharest (6hr., 5 per day, L203,000); and Cluj-Napoca (4hr., 1 per day, L170,000). Buy tickets at **CFR**, Str. N. Balcescu 6. (Open M-F 7:30am-7:30pm.) **Buses** go to Bucharest (5hr., 4 per day, L180,000); and Cluj-Napoca (3½hr., 2 per day, L100,000). From the stations, take Str. General Magheru and turn right onto Str. Avram Iancu to reach **Piaţa Mare**, the main square. **◙Hotel Pensiune Leu ❶**, Str. Moş Ion Roată 6, has spotless rooms. From Str. Magheru, walk to the far side of Piaţa Mare and turn right. Go down the stairs past the Bruckenthal museum and turn left onto Str. Moş Ion Roată. (☎21 83 92. Singles L300,000; doubles L500,000.) To reach the **outdoor market,** follow the directions to Hotel Pensiune Leu, but walk straight instead of turning onto Str. Moş Ion Roată. (Open dawn-dusk.) **Crama Sibiul Vechi ❶**, Str. Papiu Ilarian 3, has good Romanian food. (Entrees L50,000-70,000. Open daily noon-midnight.) Sibiu has many **summer festivals,** including the International Theatre Festival in early June and the Medieval Festival in late August. **Postal code:** 2400.

TIMIŞOARA
☎0256

Timişoara, Romania's westernmost city, is one of the country's largest and liveliest. The city was the starting place for the 1989 revolution that overthrew the Communist regime; anti-Ceauşescu protestors gathered in **Piaţa Victoriei**. At one end of the square stands the **Metropolitan Cathedral,** designed in Moldavian folk style with a rainbow-tiled roof. (Open daily 6:30am-8pm.) Across the square is the **National Theater** (Teatrul Naţional) and the **Opera House** (Opera Timişoara); the opera box office is down the street, on Str. Mărăşeşti. (Open Sept.-May daily 10am-1pm and 5-7pm.) Nearby in Huniade Castle is the **Banat Museum** (Muzeul Banatului), which traces Timişoara's history. (Open Tu-Su 10am-4:30pm. L10,000, students L5000.)

Trains run from Timişoara Nord to: Bucharest (8hr., 7 per day, L300,000); Cluj-Napoca (7hr., 4 per day, L220,000); and Budapest (5hr., 2 per day, L300,000). Trams #1, 8, and 11, and **trolleybuses** #11 and 14 go to the city center (2 trips L14,000). **Libraria Mihai Eminescu,** in Piaţa Victoriei, sells maps. (L62,000. Open M-F 9am-7pm, Sa 9am-1pm.) **Hotel Cina Banatul ❷,** Str. Craiului 4, is clean and centrally located. (☎ 19 01 30. Singles L600,000; doubles L800,000.) There are many good restaurants in and around Piaţa Victoriei in the center of town. **Postal code:** 1900.

MOLDAVIA AND BUKOVINA

Eastern Romania, known as Moldavia (Moldova), extends from the Carpathians to the Prut River. Starker than Transylvania but more developed than Maramureş, Moldavia also boasts the distinctive painted monasteries of Bukovina (Bucovina).

IAŞI   ☎ 0232

Iaşi (YASH) rose to prominence in the 19th century as the home of the Junimea Society, a literary club whose members filled the city with Neoclassical architecture. Bd. Ştefan cel Mare leads south from the main square, **Piaţa Unirii,** past the gorgeous 1637 **Trei Ierarchi church,** whose walls display Moldavian and Turkish patterns in raised relief. The boulevard then continues to the massive, neo-Gothic **Palace of Culture** (Palatul Culturii), which contains historical, ethnographic, polytechnic, and art museums. (Open Tu-Su 10am-5pm. Each museum L15,000, students L10,000.) North of Piaţa Unirii, Bd. Copou leads from Piaţa Eminescu past some of the most beautiful buildings in Iaşi to **Copou Park,** Bd. Carol I. Inside the park is the **Eminescu Museum,** which exhibits some of the great Romanian poet's documents. (Open Tu-Su 10am-5pm. L10,000.)

Trains go from Str. Silvestru to: Braşov (6hr., 1 per day, L250,000); Bucharest (7½hr., 4 per day, L250,000); Cluj-Napoca (9hr., 4 per day, L250,000); Constanţa (8hr., 2 per day, L250,000); and Suceava (2hr., 4 per day, L135,000). **CFR,** Piaţa Unirii 9-11, sells train tickets. (☎ 14 52 69. Open M-F 8am-8pm.) The new station **Iaşi Vest,** Str. Moara de Foc 15, sends buses to Braşov (8hr., 1 per day, L230,000). **Libraria Junimea,** Piaţa Unirii 4, sells L25,000 maps. (Open M-F 9am-8pm, Sa 9am-3pm.) **Hotel Continental ❷,** Str. Cuza Vodă 4, has a good location and private baths. Coming from the train station, continue one intersection past Piaţa Unirii. (☎ 21 18 46. Singles L465,000;

YOUR OWN WAY

BLACK SEA COAST

Between the Danube and the Black Sea stretches a region of rocky hills and valleys filled with ancient ruins. The beautiful coast boasts popular resorts to the south, while the unspoiled regions in the north provide an escape from the crowds.

CONSTANŢA. Romania's second-largest city, the ancient port of Constanţa is a bustling cultural and commercial hub, full of ruins, museums, and monuments. Info: ☎ 0241 61 58 36.

BLACK SEA RESORTS. South of Constanţa, the coast is lined with sandy beaches and 1970s-revival tourist resorts, crowded with families, tourists, and young Romanians alike.

DANUBE DELTA. The tiny **Sfântu Gheorghe** fishing village serves as a base for this remote northern area where the mighty Danube empties into the sea. Here you will find a fantastic beach and thousands of plant and bird species, but few people.

TRANSPORTATION. Buses from Constanţa go to Tulcea (1½hr., 27 per day, L150,000), where **boats** depart for Sfântu Gheorghe (5hr.; leaves Tu-F 1:30pm, returns W-F and Su 6am; L130,000). **Trains** go to Constanţa from Bucharest (2½-4½hr., up to 15 per day, L220,000) and Iaşi (8hr., 2 per day, L250,000). **Buses** and **microbuses** head from the parking lot next to the Constanţa train station to the resorts. (20-40min., every 5-10min., L15,000-26,000.)

doubles L620,000-760,000.) **⬛Bolta Rece ❶**, Str. Rece 10, established in 1786, is one of Iaşi's best restaurants. Take Str. Cuza Vodă out of Piaţa Unirii and turn left on Str. Brătianu; at Bd. Independenţei, turn right, take an immediate left onto Str. M. Eminescu, then turn left onto Str. Rece. (Main dishes L20,000-75,000. Open daily 8am-midnight.) **Postal code:** 6600.

BUKOVINA MONASTERIES

Built 500 years ago by Moldavia's ruler, Ştefan cel Mare (Stephen the Great) and his successors, Bukovina's painted monasteries are hidden among green hills and farming villages. The exquisite structures mix Moldavian and Byzantine architecture with Romanian Christian images. Taking an organized tour from Gura Humorului or Suceava is often the best way to see the monasteries. Dress modestly.

GURA HUMORULUI   ☎0230

Within walking distance of the Humor and Voroneţ monasteries, small Gura Humorului is an ideal base. For information and **car tours,** visit the **⬛Dispecerat de Cazare,** at the end of Str. Câmpului on Str. Voroneţ; from the train station, head left off Ştefan cel Mare. The office also arranges villa rooms. (☎23 88 63. Open Mar.-Nov. 11am-9pm. Tours US$30-35 per car.) **Trains** come from: Bucharest (6hr., 1 per day, L248,100); Cluj-Napoca (5hr., 4 per day, L186,000); Iaşi (3hr., 4 per day, L152,000); and Suceava (1hr., 9 per day, L43,000). To reach the town center from the station, make a right onto Str. Ştefan cel Mare and continue over the bridge. **⬛Pensiunea Casa Ella ❶,** Str. Cetaţii 7, off Bd. Bucovina, offers soft beds and home-cooked meals. (☎23 29 61. Singles L350,000; doubles L400,000. Meals L60,000-100,000.) The more luxurious **Villa Fabian ❷** is across Str. Voroneţ from Dispecerat de Cazare. (☎23 23 87. Singles €13; doubles €25.) **Postal code:** 5900.

🖪 DAYTRIPS FROM GURA HUMORULUI: THE HUMOR, MOLDOVIŢA, AND VORONEŢ MONASTERIES. Bukovina's oldest frescoes are at **Humor,** which is known for a depiction of the life of the Virgin Mary on the south wall. The mural, based on a poem by the patriarch of Constantinople, shows Mary saving Constantinople from a Persian attack in 626. From Gura Humorului, **walk** right on Ştefan cel Mare from the train or bus station to the center of town. At the fork near a park on the right, take Str. Manasteria Humorului to the left and continue 6km to the monastery. (Open daily 8am-8pm. L30,000, students L20,000. Cameras L60,000.)

The largest monastery, **Moldoviţa,** has the best-preserved frescoes. Painted in 1537, the frescoes portray the Last Judgment, Jesse's Tree, and a monumental Siege of Constantinople. In the first room is a calendar depicting a saint for each day of the year. (Open daily 7am-9pm. L30,000, students L20,000. Cameras L60,000.) Take a **train** from Gura Humorului to Vama (20min., 5 per day) and continue to Vatra Moldoviţei (35min.).

The restoration of the 1488 **Voroneţ** has been delayed while preservationists attempt to reproduce its distinctive pigment, Voroneţ Blue. Its incredible frescoes include a depiction of the Last Judgment on the west wall, painted in five tiers and crossed by a river of fire from hell. Take a **bus** from Gura Humorului (15min.; mid-Sept. to mid-June 3 per day; L10,000). Or, walk left from the Gura Humorului train station, turn left again onto Cartierul Voroneţ, and continue 5km down the scenic road. (Open daily dawn-dusk. L30,000, students L25,000. Cameras L60,000.)

SUCEAVA   ☎0230

The capital of Moldavia under Ştefan cel Mare, Suceava has many noteworthy museums, as well as the grand 1388 **⬛Citadel of the Throne** (Cetatea de Scaun). Climb the ramparts for a spectacular view. Take a taxi (5min., L30,000) from the main square, Piața 22 Decembrie. (Open in summer daily 8am-8pm; off-season 9am-5pm. L10,000, students L5000.) At night, two of the citadel's terraces serve food and drinks, while the **Crama** disco thumps away under one of them. (Terraces open daily 8am-10:30pm. Disco open F-Su 10:30pm-late.)

Trains come from: Bucharest (6hr., 4 per day, L248,000); Cluj-Napoca (6hr., 4 per day, L250,000); Gura Humorului (1hr., 6 per day, L53,000); Iași (2hr., 5 per day, L31,000); and Putna (2hr., 5 per day, L31,000). Buy tickets at **CFR**, Str. N. Bălcescu 4. (☎21 43 35. Open M-F 7am-7pm.) **Buses** run from the intersection of Str. N. Bălcescu and Str. V. Alecsandri to: Bucharest (8hr., 2 per day, L200,000); Cluj-Napoca (7hr., 2 per day, L200,000); and Gura Humorului (1hr., 9 per day, L24,000). **Librăria Cipiran Porumbescu**, Aleea Ion Grămadă 5, sells English city-guides. **Hotel Suceava ❷**, Str. N Bălcescu 4, in Piața 22 Decembrie, has large rooms with private baths. (☎52 10 72. Singles L570,000; doubles L730,000.) **Postal code:** 5800.

🖅 DAYTRIP FROM SUCEAVA: PUTNA. Constructed around 1469, pure-white **Putna** was the first of 38 monasteries founded by Ștefan cel Mare, who built one church for each battle he won. He left the monastery's location up to God: climbing a nearby hill (now marked with a cross) to the left of the monastery, he shot an arrow into the air. A slice of the oak it struck is on display at the museum, along with manuscripts, icons, and tapestries. (Museum open daily 9am-8pm. L30,000, students L5000. No cameras.) The tomb of Ștefan cel Mare is in Putna's church. (Monastery and church open daily 6am-8pm. Free.) **Trains** from Suceava run a scenic route to Putna (2½hr.; 5 per day; L31,000). Exit the platform to the right, take a left at the first intersection, and keep walking.

RUSSIA (РОССИЯ)

More than a decade after the fall of the Soviet Union, vast Russia stumbles along with no clear direction; former Communists run the state, while impoverished pensioners long for a rose-tinted Soviet past. Heedless of the failing provinces, cosmopolitan Moscow gorges on hyper-capitalism, while majestic St. Petersburg struggles to remain one of Europe's major cultural centers. Although traveling here can be a bureaucratic nightmare, Russia is in many ways the ideal destination for a budget traveler—inexpensive and well served by public transportation, with hundreds of monasteries, kremlins, and churches.

FACTS AND FIGURES

Official Name: Russian Federation.

Capital: Moscow.

Major Cities: St. Petersburg, Ulan Ude, Vladivostok.

Population: 146,000,000.

Land Area: 17,075,200 sq. km.

Time Zone: GMT +3.

Language: Russian.

Religions: Unaffiliated (74%), Russian Orthodox (16%), Muslim (10%).

DISCOVER RUSSIA

Moscow (p. 840) is more than memories of revolution: the spires of St. Basil's are more brilliant in real life than in photos, and the collections of the Kremlin are mind-boggling. The cultural glory of **St. Petersburg** (p. 853) is reflected in Europe's largest art collection at the Hermitage, the opulence of the Summer and Winter Palaces, and one of the world's best ballet companies.

ESSENTIALS

WHEN TO GO

The best time to visit is May through September. Though cold, winter in Moscow and St. Petersburg can be picturesque, uncrowded, and romantic. Spring and fall are very slushy, and periodic snow flurries should be expected.

DOCUMENTS AND FORMALITIES

 BEFORE YOU GO. In August 1999, the US State Department issued a travel advisory regarding the bringing of Global Positioning Systems (GPS), cellular phones, and other radio transmission devices into Russia. Failure to register such devices can (and does) result in search, seizure, and arrest.

VISAS. Citizens of Australia, Canada, Ireland, New Zealand, South Africa, the UK, and the US all require a visa to enter Russia; you need an **invitation** stating your itinerary and dates of travel to get a visa. To obtain a visa, you may apply in person or by mail to a Russian embassy or consulate; travel agencies that advertise discounted tickets to Russia can often provide visas as well. **Visa assistance** (€30-45) is available at www.visatorussia.com. The following organizations can give invitations and/or visas for tourists:

Western Russia

Info Travel, 387 Harvard St., Brookline, MA 02146, (☎617-566-2197; info-study@aol.com). Invitations and visas to Russia start at €150.

Russia House provides invitations and visas for €225. In the **US:** 1800 Connecticut Ave. NW, Washington, D.C. 20009 (☎202-986-6010; lozansky@aol.com). In **Russia:** 44 Bolshaya Nikitskaya, Moscow 121854 (☎095 290 34 59; rushouse@clep.ru).

Host Families Association (HOFA), 5-25 Tavricheskaya ul., 193015 St. Petersburg, Russia (☎/fax 812 275 19 92; hofa@usa.net).

Red Bear Tours/Russian Passport, 401 St. Kilda Rd., Suite 11, Melbourne 3004, Australia (☎613 98 67 38 88; www.travelcentre.com.au).

Traveler's Guest House, Bolshaya Pereyaslavskaya 50, 10th fl., Moscow, Russia 129401 (Болшая Переславская; ☎095 971 40 59; tgh@startravel.ru).

Many hotels will **register** your visa for you on arrival, as should the organizations listed above. Some travel agencies in Moscow and St. Petersburg will also register your visa for approximately €30. As a last resort, you'll have to climb into the 7th circle of bureaucratic hell known as the central **OVIR** (ОВИР) office (in Moscow called UVIR—УВИР) to register.

EMBASSIES. All foreign embassies are in Moscow (p. 840); many consulates are also in St. Petersburg (p. 853). Russian embassies at home include: **Australia,** 78 Canberra Ave., Griffith ACT 2603 (☎06 295 90 33; fax 06 295 1847); **Canada,** 285 Charlotte St., Ottawa, ON K1N 8L5 (☎613-235-4341, visa information ☎613-236-7220; www.magna.ca/~rusemb); **Ireland,** 186 Orwell Rd., Rathgar, Dublin 14 (☎/fax 01 492 35 25; russiane@indigo.ie); **New Zealand,** 57 Messines Rd., Karori, Wellington (☎04 476 61 13, visa information ☎04 476 67 42; eor@netlink.co.nz); **South Africa,** Butano Building, 316 Brooke St., Menlo Park 0081, Pretoria; P.O. Box 6743, Pretoria 0001 (☎012 362 13 37; www.russianembassy.org.za); **UK,** 5 Kensington Palace Gardens, London W8 4QX (☎020 72 29 36 28, visa information ☎020 72 29 80 27; www.russialink.org.uk/embassy); and **US,** 2650 Wisconsin Ave. N.W., Washington, D.C. 20007 (☎202-298-5700; www.russianembassy.org).

TRANSPORTATION

BY PLANE. Most major international carriers fly into Sheremetyevo-2 (SVO) in Moscow or Pulkovo-2 (LED) in St. Petersburg. **Aeroflot** (www.aeroflot.org) is the most commonly used domestic airline.

BY TRAIN. If you take a train that passes through Belarus, you will need a €40 **transit visa.** For **domestic travel**, trains are best; weekend trains between Moscow and St. Petersburg sometimes sell out a week in advance, so buy your ticket well ahead of time if you have an important connection to make or if your visa is about to expire. When you plan ahead, you'll have four classes to choose from. The best is *lyuks* (люкс), which has two beds, while second-class *kupeyny* (купейний) has four bunks. The next class is *platskartny* (плацкартный), a car with 52 shorter, harder bunks. Aim for bunks 1-33; bunks 34-37 are next to the foul restrooms, and bunks 38-52 get horribly hot in the summer. **Women** traveling alone can try to buy out a *lyuks* compartment for security, or can travel *platskartny* and depend on the crowds to shame would-be harassers. Riding *platskartny* is also a good idea on the theft-ridden St. Petersburg-Moscow line, as you will be less conspicuous. *Elektrichka* (commuter rail; marked on signs as пригородные поезда; *prigorod-nye poezda*) has its own platforms; buy tickets at the *kassa*.

BY BUS. Buses, cheaper than trains, are better for shorter distances, but are often crowded and overbooked; don't hesitate to eject people who try to sit in your seat.

BY TAXI AND BY THUMB. In Russia, hailing a taxi is a lot like hitchhiking and should be treated with equal caution. Most drivers who stop will be private citizens. Those seeking a ride should stand off the curb and hold out a hand into the street, palm down; when a car stops, riders tell the driver the destination before getting in; he will either refuse the destination altogether or ask *skolko?* ("how much?"), leading to protracted negotiations. Non-Russian speakers will get ripped off unless they manage a firm agreement on the price—if the driver agrees without asking for a price, you must ask *skolko* yourself (sign language works too). Never get into a car that is already carrying a passenger.

TOURIST SERVICES AND MONEY

EMERGENCY | Police: ☎02. Ambulance: ☎03. Fire: ☎01.

TOURIST OFFICES. There are two types of Russian tourist office—those that only arrange tours and those that offer general travel services. Offices of the former type are often unhelpful or even rude, but those of the latter are often eager to assist, particularly with visa registration. Big hotels are often a good resource for maps and for other information.

MONEY. The **ruble** was revalued in 1998, losing three zeros; the old currency is gradually being phased out. You'll have no problem changing rubles back at the end of your trip (just keep exchange receipts), but don't exchange large sums at once, as the rate is unstable. Never exchange money on the street; find an *Obmen Valyuty* (Обмен Валюты; currency exchange) to exchange euros or US dollars for rubles. You must show your passport when you exchange money. **Banks** offer the best combination of good rates and security; main branches usually accept traveler's checks and give cash advances on credit cards, most often Visa. **ATMs** (банкомат; *bankomat*) linked to all major networks and credit cards can be found all over most cities. Banks, large restaurants, ATMs, and currency exchanges often accept major credit cards, especially Visa. Be aware that most establishments do not accept crumpled, torn, or written-on bills. Although in most places you must pay in rubles, it's wise to keep €20 on hand. A budget day will run you between €30-40. In St. Petersburg and Moscow, a 5-10% tip is becoming customary.

BUSINESS HOURS. Most establishments, even train ticket offices and "24hr. stores," close for a lunch break, and most also close at least 30 minutes earlier than posted—if they choose to open at all.

RUBLES		
AUS$1 = 17.5R		10R = AUS$0.57
CDN$1 = 20.3R		10R = CDN$0.49
EUR€1 = 31R		10R = EUR€0.32
NZ$1 = 14.9R		10R = NZ$0.67
ZAR1 = 3R		10R = ZAR3.33
UK£1 = 48.4R		10R = UK£0.21
US$1 = 31.6R		10R = US$0.32

COMMUNICATION

PHONE CODES	**Country code: 7. International dialing prefix: 810.** From outside Russia, dial int'l dialing prefix (see inside back cover) + 7 + city code + local number.

MAIL. Service is much more reliable for outgoing mail than for incoming. Letters to the US will arrive as soon as a week after mailing, although letters to other destinations take 2-3 weeks. Airmail is indicated by *avia* (авиа). Send your mail certified (заказное; 16R) to reduce the chance of it being lost. Regular letters to the US cost 7R; postcards cost 5R. *Poste Restante* is "Писмо До Востребования" (Pismo Do Vostrebovania); address mail to be held: SURNAME Firstname, 103 009 Москва, Писмо До востребования, RUSSIA.

TELEPHONES AND INTERNET. As the phone system charges very high rates, **email** is your best bet for keeping in touch. Internet cafes are most common in Moscow and St. Petersburg; rates are usually 30-60R per hr. Direct international calls can be made from telephone offices in St. Petersburg and Moscow; calls to Europe run €1-1.50 per min., to the US and Australia, about US$1.50-2.00. Old local telephones that use tokens are becoming obsolete; the new card phones, which often have instructions in English, are good for both local and intercity calls. **Phonecards** are sold at central telephone offices, Metro stations, and newspaper kiosks; at a telephone office or Metro station, the attendant will ask you, "На улицу?" (Na ulitsu; "On the street?") to distinguish between cards for the phones in the station or office and for outdoor public phones. For 5-digit numbers, insert a "2" between the dialing code and the phone number.

LANGUAGE. Familiarize yourself with the **Cyrillic alphabet** (see p. 1051); it will make getting around and getting by immeasurably easier. For some basic Russian words and phrases, see p. 1064.

ACCOMMODATIONS

RUSSIA	❶	❷	❸	❹	❺
ACCOMMODATIONS	under 600R	600-1400R	1401-1900R	1901-2400R	over 2400R

Homestays, arranged through a tourist office, are often the cheapest (50-100R per night) and best option in the country. Only Moscow and St. Petersburg have **hos-**

tels, which average around €18 per night. Reserve well in advance, especially in summer. Expect to pay 300-450R for a single in a budget **hotel.** There are several classes of rooms. *"Lux,"* usually two-room doubles with TV, phone, fridge, and bath, are the most expensive. *"Polu-lux"* rooms are singles or doubles with TV, phone, and bath. The lowest-priced rooms are *bez udobstv* (без удобств), which are individual rooms with a sink. Usually only cash is accepted as payment. In many hotels, hot water (and sometimes all water) is on for only a few hours each day. Reservations may help you get on the good side of hotel management, which can be suspicious of backpackers. **University dorms** offer cheap rooms, but don't expect sparkling bathrooms or reliable hot water. Some accept foreign students (about €5-10 per night); make arrangements through an institute from home.

FOOD AND DRINK

RUSSIA	❶	❷	❸	❹	❺
FOOD	under 50R	50-120R	121-300R	301-500R	over 500R

Russian dishes are often both delectable and disgusting; tasty *borscht* sometimes comes with *salo* (pig fat). The largest meal of the day, *obed* (обед; lunch), includes: *salat* (салат; salad), usually cucumbers and tomatoes or beets and potatoes with mayonnaise or sour cream; *sup* (суп; soup); and *kuritsa* (курица; chicken) or *myaso* (мясо; meat), often called *kotlyety* (котлеты) or *beefshteaks* (бифштекс). Ordering a few *zakuski* (закуски; small appetizers) instead of a main dish can save money. *Blini* (stuffed crepes), *shashlyki* (шашлыки; skewered meat), and *kvas* (квас), a dark-brown alcoholic drink, are sold on the streets.

HEALTH AND SAFETY

Water in much of Russia is drinkable in small doses, but not in Moscow and St. Petersburg; boil it to be safe. Russian bottled water is often mineral water—you may prefer to boil or filter your own, or buy imported bottled water. For medical emergencies, either leave the country or go to the **American Medical Centers** in Moscow or St. Petersburg, which have American doctors (see p. 844 and p. 854). Traveler's **health insurance** is essential (see p. 24). Reports of **crime** against foreigners are on the rise, particularly in Moscow and St. Petersburg. Although it is hard to look Russian (especially with a huge pack), try not to flaunt your true nationality. Reports of mafia warfare are scaring off tourists, but unless you bring a shop for them to blow up, you are unlikely to be a target. Due to the recent eruption of violence in the Northern Caucasus, avoid the Dagestan and Chechnya regions.

HOLIDAYS AND FESTIVALS

Holidays: New Year's (Jan. 1-2); Orthodox Christmas (Jan. 7); Defenders of the Motherland Day (Feb. 23); International Women's Day (Mar. 8); Labor Day (May 1-2); Orthodox Easter (May 5); Victory Day (May 9); Independence Day (June 12); Day of Accord and Reconciliation (Nov. 7); Constitution Day (Dec. 12).

Festivals: From June 21-July 11, when the sun barely touches the horizon, St. Petersburg and Moscow celebrate the **White Nights** with concerts and fireworks.

MOSCOW (MOCKBA) ☎ 8095

While St. Petersburg is Russia's "window on the West," Moscow is the window into the very heart of the nation and its current status. When Communism swept through Moscow, it leveled most of the capital's golden domes and left behind massive buildings, crumbling outskirts, and countless statues of Lenin. But things change quickly in this audacious city, and in the midst of its debauchery and corruption, Moscow is recreating itself using the same resourcefulness that helped it engineer—and then survive—the most ambitious social experiment in history.

■ TRANSPORTATION

Flights: International flights arrive at **Sheremetyevo-2** (SVO; Шереметьево-2; ☎578 90 05). Take the van under the "автолайн" sign in front of the station to M2: Rechnoy Vokzal (Речной Вокзал; 20min., every 10min. 7am-10pm, 15R). Or, take bus #851 or 551 to M2: Rechnoy Vokzal or bus #517 to M8: Planyornaya (Планёрная; 10R). Buses run 24hr., but the Metro closes at 1am. Purchase bus tickets at the kassa (касса) at **Tsentralny Aerovokzal** (Центральный Аэровокзал; Central Airport Station), Leningradsky pr. 37 corpus 6 (☎941 99 99), 2 stops on almost any tram or trolley from M2: Aeroport (the sign on front of bus should indicate Центральный Аэровокзал). **Taxis** to the center charge up to US$60; but bargaining can lower prices to $25. Go upstairs to the departures level to find cars that are returning to the city; you may be able to find $15-20 rides. Always agree on a price before getting into the car.

Trains: Buying tickets in Russia can be enormously frustrating. If you don't speak Russian, you may want to buy through **Intourist** or your hotel; you'll pay more, but you'll be spared the hassle of the *vokzal* (вокзал; station) experience. Buy tickets for the *elektrichka* (local trains) at the *prigorodniye kassa* (пригородная касса; local ticket booths) in each station. Tickets for longer trips can be purchased at the **Central Train Agency** (Центральное Железнодорожное Агенство; Tsentralnoe Zheleznodorozhnoe Agenstvo), to the right of Yaroslavsky Vokzal (see below). Schedules are posted on both sides of the hall. (☎266 93 33 or 266 83 33. *Kassa* open M-F 7am-9pm, Sa 7am-7pm, Su 7am-5pm.) There is 24hr. service at each station. Moscow's 8 train stations are on the Metro's circle line (M5).

Belorussky Vokzal (Белорусский), Tverskaya Zastara pl. 7 (Тверская Застара). To: Berlin (27hr., 1 per day, 3500R); Minsk (10hr., 3-4 per day, 750R); Prague (35hr., 1 per day, 2860R); Vilnius (16hr., 1-2 per day, 1950R); and Warsaw (21hr., 2 per day, 2520R).

Kazansky Vokzal (Казанский), Komsomolskaya pl. 2 (Комсомольская), opposite Leningradsky Vokzal, serves the east and southeast of Russia.

Kievsky Vokzal (Киевский), Kievskovo Vokzala pl. (Киевского Вокзала). To Kyiv (14hr., 4 per day, 950R); Lviv (26hr., 2 per day, 1100R); and Odessa (25-28hr., 1-2 per day, 1100R).

Kursky Vokzal (Курский), ul. Zemlyanoi Val 29/1 (Земляной), serves Sevastopol (26hr., 1-2 per day, 1100R) and the Caucasus.

Leningradsky Vokzal (Ленинградский), Komsomolskaya pl. 3. M1 and 5: Komsomolskaya. To: Helsinki (13hr. 1 per day, 2720R); St. Petersburg (8hr., 10-15 per day, 700R); and Tallinn (14hr., 1 per day, 1550R). Tickets to Helsinki are sold on the 2nd fl., at windows #19 and 20. (Open daily 10am-1pm and 2-10pm.)

Paveletsky Vokzal (Павлецкий), Paveletskaya pl. 1 (Павелецая), serves the Crimea and eastern Ukraine.

Rizhsky Vokzal (Рижский), Pr. Mira 79/3. To Rīga (16hr., 2 per day, 2050R) and Estonia.

Yaroslavsky Vokzal (Ярославский), Komsomolskaya pl. 5, begins the Trans-Siberian Railroad.

Public Transportation: The **Metro** (Метро) is large and efficient—a masterpiece of Stalinist urban planning. Trains run daily 6am-1am. Passages between lines or stations are indicated by signs of a man walking up stairs; street names are indicated on exit signs. A station serving more than 1 line may have more than 1 name. Buy token-cards (5R, 10 for 35R) from the *kassy* inside stations. Buy **bus** and **trolley** tickets from gray kiosks labeled "проездные билеты" or from the driver (4R). Punch your ticket when you get on, or risk a 10R fine.

Taxis: Avoid the labeled official taxis, which usually rip you off. It is common and cheaper to hail a private car on the street; just hold your arm out horizontally. Tell the driver your destination and agree on a price first (usually 50-100R across town), but never get into a car already carrying a passenger.

METRO MANIA. The Moscow Metro has one of the world's most notoriously confusing systems. To make navigation easier, *Let's Go* has created a numbering system for each Metro line that coordinates with the color Moscow Metro map at the beginning and end of this guide. When asking a Metro attendant about any of the lines, refer to the color or name, and not the number.

✦ ? ORIENTATION AND PRACTICAL INFORMATION

A series of concentric rings radiates outward from the **Kremlin** (Кремль; Kreml) and **Red Square** (Красная Площадь; Krasnaya ploshchad). The outermost **Moscow Ring Road** marks the city limits, but most sights lie within the **Sadovoe Koltso** (Садовое Кольцо; Garden Ring). Main streets include **Ulitsa Tverskaya** (Тверская), which extends north along the Metro's green line, and **Arbat** (Арбат) and **Novy Arbat** (Новый Арбат), which run west parallel to the blue lines. Familiarize yourself with the Cyrillic alphabet and orient yourself using the Metro. English and Cyrillic maps (20-50R) are at kiosks all over the city; there are also **color maps** in the back of this book. Be careful when crossing streets, as drivers are notoriously oblivious to pedestrians; use the underpasses *(perekhodi)* available at most intersections.

PAYING IN RUSSIA. Due to the fluctuating value of the Russian ruble, some establishments list their prices in US dollars. For this reason, some prices in this book may also appear in US dollars, but be prepared to pay in rubles.

TOURIST, FINANCIAL, AND LOCAL SERVICES

Tourist Office: Intourist, Milyutinsky per. 13 (Милютинскии; ☎924 31 01). M5: Turgenyevskaya. Open M-Sa 10am-7:30pm. Also at Teatralny pl. 3/5 (☎923 36 37). M6: Kuznetsky Most or M1: Lubyanka. Open M-F 10am-6:30pm.

Budget Travel: Student Travel Agency Russia (STAR), ul. Baltyskaya 9, 3rd fl. (Балтийская; ☎797 95 55; www.startravel.ru). M2: Sokol. ISICs, discount plane tickets, and hostel booking. Open M-F 10am-7pm, Sa 10am-4pm.

Embassies: Australia, Kropotkinsky per. 13 (Кропоткинский; ☎956 60 70; www.australianembassy.ru). M3: Smolenskaya. Open M-F 9am-12:30pm and 1:15-5pm. **Canada,** Starokonyushenny per. 23 (Староконюшенный; ☎956 66 66). M1: Kropotkinskaya or M: Arbatskaya. Open M-F 8:30am-1pm and 2-5pm. **Ireland,** Grokholsky per. 5 (Грохольский; ☎937 59 11). M5 and 6: Prospekt Mira. Open M-F 9:30am-1pm and 2:30-5:30pm. **New Zealand,** ul. Povarskaya 44 (Поварская; ☎956 35 79; www.nzembassy.msk.ru). M7: Barrikadnaya. Open daily 9am-5:30pm. **South Africa,** Bolshoy Strochenovsky per. 22/25 (Большой Строченовский; ☎230 68 69). Open M-F 8:30am-5pm. **UK,** Smolenskaya nab. 10 (Смоленская; ☎956 72 00). M3: Smolenskaya. Open M-F 9am-1pm and 2-5pm. **US,** Novinsky 19/23 (Новинский; ☎728 50 00; http://usembassy.state.gov/moscow). M7: Krasnopresnenskaya. Open M-F 9am-6pm. Consulate ☎728 55 88. Open M-F 9am-noon. Flash a US passport to cut long lines. American Citizen Services (ACS; ☎728 55 77; emergency ☎728 51 07) connects US citizens to various organizations.

Currency Exchange: *Moscow Express Directory,* free in most luxury hotels, lists places to buy and cash traveler's checks. Usually only main branches of large banks will change traveler's checks or issue cash advances. Nearly every bank and hotel has an **ATM;** avoid machines protruding from the sides of other buildings; they work erratically, and withdrawing cash on busy streets makes you a target for muggers.

RUSSIA

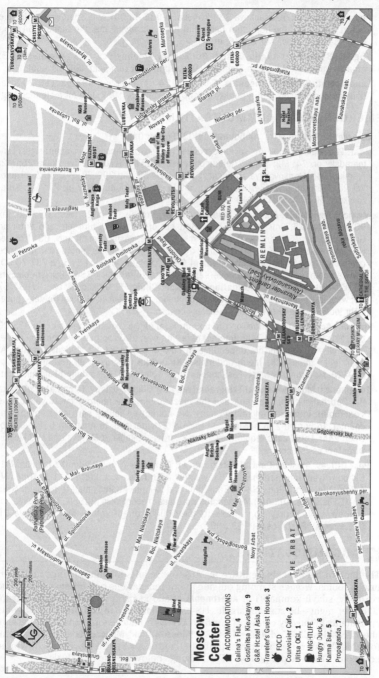

Moscow Center

▲ ACCOMMODATIONS
Galina's Flat, 4
Gostinitsa Kievskaya, 9
G&R Hostel Asia, 8
Traveler's Guest House, 3

♦ FOCD
Courvoisier Cafe, 2
Ulitsa OGI, 1

★ NIGHTLIFE
Hungry Duck, 6
Karma Bar, 5
Propaganda, 7

American Express: ul. Usacheva 33 (Усачева; ☎933 84 00). M1: Sportivnaya. Use the exit at the front of the train, turn right, and turn right again after the Global USA shop onto Usacheva. Open M-F 9am-6pm.

English Bookstore: Anglia British Bookshop, Khlebny per. 2/3 (Хлебный). M3: Arbatskaya. Open M-F 10am-7pm, Sa 10am-6pm, Su 11am-5pm. ISIC discount.

Laundromat: California Cleaners, Pokhodny 24 (Походный; ☎493 53 11). 20 locations around Moscow. 105R per kg; pick-up and delivery 105R, free for more than 8kg.

EMERGENCY AND COMMUNICATIONS

Emergency: Police: ☎02. **Ambulance:** ☎03. **Fire:** ☎01.

24hr. Pharmacies: Look for "круглосуточно" (*kruglosutochno;* always open) signs. Leningradsky pr. 74; M2: Sokol (Ленинградский; ☎151 45 70). Ul. Tverskaya 25; M2: Tverskaya or Mayakovskaya (Тверская; ☎299 24 59 and 299 79 69). Ul. Zemlyanoi Val 25; M5: Kurskaya (Земляной Вал; ☎917 12 85). Kutuzovsky pr. 24; M3: Kutuzovskaya (Кутузовский; ☎249 19 37).

Medical Assistance: American Medical Center, Prospekt Mira 26 (☎933 77 00; fax 933 77 01). M5: Prospekt Mira. Walk left out of the Metro, turn left, and enter on Grokholsky per. (Грохольский). Walk-in medical care; cash payment only. US$175 per visit. Membership US$50 per year; price doubles if you want bills sent to your insurance company. Open 24hr. **European Medical Clinic,** Spiridonievskiy Per. 5 (☎787 70 00; www.emcmos.ru). Comprehensive services. Consultations US$40-80, specialists US$60-200. Open 24hr. **International Medical Clinic,** 31 Grokholsky per. (☎937 57 60; www.internationalsos.com). See directions for the American Medical Center, above. 24hr. outpatient and emergency medical services.

Internet Access: Timeonline, on the bottom level of the Okhotny Ryad mall (☎363 00 60). M1: Okhotny Ryad. 24hr. Internet cafe with over 200 computers in the very center of the city. 30-60R per hr., depending on time of day; ask for a student discount. At night, enter through the Metro underpass. **Kukushka** (Кукушка), ul. Rozhdedestvenka 6/9/20. M: Kuznetsky Most. Fast connections. 60R per hr. Open daily 11am-midnight.

Telephones: Moscow Central Telegraph (see Post Offices, below). To **call abroad,** go to the 2nd hall with phones and use the *mezhdunarodnye telefony* (международные телефоны; international telephones). No collect or calling card calls; prepay at counter. To Europe 21R per min.; to the US 27R per min; to Australia 50R per min. Open 24hr. **Local calls** require new phone cards, available at Metro stops and kiosks. **Directory assistance:** ☎09.

Post Offices: Moscow Central Telegraph, ul. Tverskaya 7, uphill from the Kremlin. M1: Okhotny Ryad. **International mail** at window #23; **faxes** at windows #11-12. Open M-F 8am-2pm and 3-8pm, Sa-Su 7am-2pm and 3-7pm. Address mail to be held: SURNAME Firstname, **103 009** Москва, Писмо До востребования, RUSSIA. Pick up mail at window #24; if they don't have it, they might direct you to Myasnitskaya 26 (Мясницкая). **Postal code:** 103 009.

⌐ ACCOMMODATIONS

The lack of backpacking culture in Moscow results in slim pickings and overpriced rooms. Women standing outside major rail stations rent **private rooms** (сдаю комнату; sdayu komnatu) or **apartments** (сдаю квартиру; sdayu kvartiru) from 200R per night—be sure to haggle. US-based **Moscow Bed and Breakfast ❸** rents apartments in the city center. (US ☎603-585-3347; jkates@top.monad.net. Reserve ahead. Singles US$35; doubles US$52.) **"Moscow Rick" Moncher ❷** also offers comfortable, Westernized apartments in the center. (☎212 25 20; www.enjoymoscow.com. US$30-40 per person.) The lodgings below are the best deals.

Galina's Flat, ul. Chaplygina 8, #35 (Чаплыгина; ☎921 60 38; galinas.flat@mtu-net.ru). M1: Chistye Prudy. Take bul. Chistoprudny (Чистопрудный) past the statue of Griboedov and turn left onto Kharitonevsky per. (Харитоньевский), then take the 2nd right on Chaplygina. Go through the courtyard at house 8, curve around the building to the right, and enter by the "Уникум" sign. Homey apartment with cats. Hot showers. Kitchen facilities. Call ahead. Dorms US$8; doubles US$20; discounts for longer stays. Airport pickup US$25, drop-off US$20. ❶

Traveler's Guest House (TGH), ul. Bolshaya Pereyaslavskaya 50, 10th fl. (Болшая Переяславская; ☎971 40 59; tgh@startravel.ru). M5 and 6: Prospekt Mira (Проспект Мира). Exiting the Metro, turn left and walk 10min. along pr. Mira, take the 2nd right onto the unmarked *pereleuk* (little street) across from 61 pr. Mira, and turn left at the end onto ul. B. Pereyaslavskaya. Most budget travelers stay here, and the bulletin board serves as an open forum for travel advice. Clean, comfortable rooms. Internet 1R per min. Laundry 80R for 3kg. Check-out 11am. Airport pick-up and drop-off US$30. Russian visa invitations US$20 for TGH guests. Dorms US$18; singles US$36; doubles US$48, with bath US$54. 5% ISIC discount, 10% HI discount. MC/V. ❷

G&R Hostel Asia, ul. Zelenodolskaya 3/2 (Зеленодольская; ☎/fax 378 28 66; www.hostels.ru). M7: Ryazansky Prospekt (Рязанский Проспект). On the 15th fl. of the tall gray building with "Гостиница" in large letters on top, visible from either Metro exit. Clean rooms and helpful staff. Far from the center, but close to the Metro. Transport to or from the airport US$25. Dorms US$16; singles US$22, with bath US$30; doubles US$36/$44. HI discount US$1. MC/V. ❷

Gostinitsa Kievskaya (Гостиница Киевская), ul. Kievskaya 2 (☎240 14 44). M3 and 5: Kievskaya. Just outside the train station. Soviet-style rooms and soft beds. Singles 540R, with bath 740R; doubles 570R/820R; luxury suite 1100-1400R. ❶

🖪 FOOD

Eating out ranges from expensive to outrageous; kiosk fare is a cheap alternative. Restaurants serving local cuisine are often affordable, and many higher-priced places now offer business lunch specials (бизнес ланч; typically available noon-4pm; US$4-8). Russians tend to eat in late evening; avoid crowds by eating earlier.

RESTAURANTS

Courvoisier Cafe, Malaya Sukharevskaya 8, bldg. 1 (Сухаревская). M5: Sukharevskaya. With your back to Bolshaya Sukharevskaya pl., the cafe is down Malaya Sukharevskaya to the left. Great service and Russo-European flavors at this delightfully tasteful and inexpensive cafe. Soups 60-80R, *bliny* 40-60R, omelettes 40-100R, main dishes 220-350R. Breakfast 5-11:30am. Open 24hr. ❸

Ulitsa OGI (Улица ОГИ), Petrovka 26, str. 8. M7: Kuznetsky Most. Walk through the arch under the small blue 26 sign on Petrovka, to the right of the bank. The entrance is 150ft. down on the right, past the playground. A varied menu of classy, delicious Russian and European food. Salads 90-350R, business lunch 250R, main dishes 230-400R. Open daily 8am-11pm. ❸

Korchma Taras Bulba (Корчма Тарас Булба), ul. Sadovaya-Samotechnaya 13. M10: Tsvetnoi Bulvar. Exit left from the Metro and take Tsvetnoi Bulvar to Sadovaya-Samo-technaya. Authentic Ukrainian restaurant serves generous portions. Dumplings 109-165R, main dishes 140-300R. Open 24hr. ❸

Guria (Гуриа), Komsomolsky pr. 7/3 (Комсомольский). M1 and 5: Park Kultury; on the corner of ul. Frunze, opposite St. Nicholas of the Weavers. Tasty Georgian fare at some of the city's lowest prices. Most main dishes 40-90R. Open daily noon-midnight. ❷

RUSSIA

FROM THE ROAD

COPS AND ROBBERS

A word to the wise: register your visa within three days of arrival in every city you visit, especially Moscow. Hotels will usually register you automatically upon check-in, but a hostel can register you only if they issued your invitation. Your other options are visiting the OVIR office (if you don't mind waiting up to 2 months) or paying a hotel around €50 to do it for you. In Moscow, your best bet is **Visa House** (€30; ☎ 721 10 21; www.visahouse.com).

Why go to all this trouble? The Moscow *militsia* (police) loves to take advantage of naive travelers with unregistered visas, waiting around tourist sights in groups and demanding to see documents. You may stand out particularly if you are Asian, have darker skin, or look the least bit Chechen. When the police discover an unregistered visa, they give a long, imperious spiel about how they will take the traveler down to the police station, where he will spend a long time, pay a large fine, and be unpleasantly lectured by both the Russians and his own consulate.

In reality, the actual fine for an unregistered visa is often as low as 100R and is not such a big deal, but most foreigners don't know this. "This visa is not my problem; it is your problem," the crooked cop says in well-rehearsed English. "So what is it worth to you to fix?" They often extort up to 500R a pop. Resist the easy bribe; they'll give up once they realize they can't milk anything from you.

—Charles Black

MARKETS AND SUPERMARKETS

A visit to one of Moscow's many markets is worthwhile just for the sights: sides of beef, piles of peaches, jars of glowing honey, and huge pots of flowers. Impromptu markets, where produce is sold by the kilogram (bring your own bag), spring up around Metro stations (usually 10am-8pm); try Aeroport, Baumanskaya, Kievskayana, Kuznetsky Most, Turgenevskaya, and between Novoslobodskaya and Mendeleevskaya. **Eliseevsky Gastronom** (Елисеевский Гастроном), ul. Tverskaya 14 (M2: Tverskaya), is Moscow's most famous grocery store and is as much a feast for your eyes as it is a place to buy food. (Open M-Sa 8am-9pm, Su 10am-8pm.) There are other supermarkets all over; look for "продукты" (*produkty;* food products) signs. Wash fruit and vegetables with bottled or boiled water.

⊙ SIGHTS

Visitors can choose between 16th-century churches and Soviet-era museums, but there's little in between. Because St. Petersburg was the tsar's seat for 200 years, Moscow has no grand palaces, and while the city's art museums contain the very best Russian works, they have virtually no foreign pieces. Although the Soviet regime destroyed 80% of the city's pre-revolutionary splendor, there are still enough sights to occupy visitors for over a week.

RED SQUARE

The 700m-long Red Square (Красная площадь; Krasnaya Ploshchad) has been the site of everything from a giant farmer's market to public hangings, from Communist parades to a renegade Cessna landing. On one side is the **Kremlin,** home of the early tsars and the seat of the Communist Party for 70-odd years, the historical and religious heart of Russia; on the other is **GUM**, once a market and the world's largest purveyor of Soviet "consumer goods," now an upscale shopping mall. Also f lanking the square are **St. Basil's Cathedral,** the **State Historical Museum,** the **Lenin Mausoleum,** and the pink-and-green **Kazan Cathedral.**

ST. BASIL'S CATHEDRAL. (Собор Василия Блаженного; Sobor Vasiliya Blazhennovo.) There is no more familiar symbol of Moscow than the colorful onion domes of St. Basil's Cathedral. Commissioned by Ivan the Terrible to celebrate his 1552 victory over the Tatars in Kazan, it was completed in 1561. The cathedral bears the name of a holy fool, Vasily (Basil in English), who correctly predicted that Ivan would murder his own son. The labyrinthine interior—

unusual for Orthodox churches—is filled with both decorative and religious frescoes. *(M3: Ploshchad Revolutsii (Площадь Революции). Open daily 11am-7pm. 100R, students 50R. Buy tickets from the kassa to the left of entrance, then proceed upstairs.)*

LENIN'S TOMB. (Мавзолей В.И. Ленина; Mavzoley V.I. Lenina.) Lenin's likeness can be seen in bronze all over the city, but here he appears in the eerily luminescent flesh. In the glory days, this squat red structure was guarded fiercely, and the wait to get in took three hours. Today's line is still long, and the guards are still stone-faced, but the atmosphere is characterized by curiosity rather than reverence. Entrance to the mausoleum also gives access to the **Kremlin wall,** where Stalin, Brezhnev, Andropov, Gagarin, and John Reed (author of *Ten Days That Shook the World*) are buried. *(Open Tu-Th and Sa-Su 10am-1pm.)*

THE KREMLIN

The Kremlin (Кремль; Kreml) is the geographical and historical center of Moscow. Here, Ivan the Terrible reigned with his iron fist and Stalin ruled the lands behind the Iron Curtain. Napoleon simmered at this fortress while Moscow burned, and the USSR was dissolved here in 1991. The glory and the riches of the Russian Empire are all on display in the Kremlin's Armory and in its magnificent churches. Besides the sights listed below, the only other place in the triangular complex you are allowed to enter is the **Kremlin Palace of Congresses,** the white square monster built by Khrushchev in 1961 for Communist Party Congresses; today, it's a theater. English-speaking guides offer tours of the complex at typically outrageous prices; haggle away. *(Complex open F-W 10am-5pm. Buy tickets and enter at the midpoint of Alexander Gardens, on the west side of the Kremlin.)*

ARMORY MUSEUM AND DIAMOND FUND. (Оружейная и Выставка Алмазного Фонда; Oruzheynaya i Vystavka Almaznovo Fonda.) At the southwest corner of the Kremlin complex, the Armory Museum exemplifies the opulence of the Russian court. Among all the imperial thrones, coaches, and crowns are the legendary **Fabergé Eggs** in room 2, each revealing an intricate jewelled miniature. The Diamond Fund, in an annex of the Armory, has even more glitter, including a 190-carat diamond given to Catherine the Great by her lover Gregory Orlov. Soviet-era finds, including the world's largest chunks of platinum, are also on display. *(Armory open F-W 10-11:30am, noon-1:30pm, 2:30-4pm, and 4:30-6pm. 350R, students 175R, camera use 50R. Diamond Fund open F-W 10am-1pm and 2-6pm. 350R.)*

CATHEDRAL SQUARE. Russia's most famous golden domes can be seen in Cathedral Square. The church closest to the Armory is the **Annunciation Cathedral** (Благовещенский Собор; Blagoveshchensky Sobor), which guards luminous icons by Andrei Rublev and Theophanes the Greek. The square **Archangel Cathedral** (Архангельский Собор; Arkhangelsky Sobor), gleaming with vivid icons and metallic coffins, is the final resting place for many of the tsars who preceded Peter the Great, including Ivans III (the Great) and IV (the Terrible), as well as Mikhail Romanov. The 15th-century **Assumption Cathedral** (Успенский Собор; Uspensky Sobor), at the center of the square, was used by Napoleon as a stable in 1812. Nearby are the small **Patriarch's Palace** (Патриарший Дворец; Patriarshy Dvorets), which now houses a museum, and the even smaller **Church of the Deposition of the Robe.** To the right of Assumption Cathedral is the **Belltower of Ivan the Great** (Колокольня Ивана Великого; Kolokolnya Ivana Velikovo), now a display space for temporary exhibits. Directly behind the belltower is the **Tsar Bell** (Царь-колокол; Tsar-kolokol), the world's largest. It has never rung and probably never will—a 1737 fire caused an 11½-ton piece to break off. *(All cathedrals 200R, students 100R; after 4pm 90R. Camera use 50R, mandatory bag check 60R.)*

RUSSIA

NORTH OF RED SQUARE

The area just north of Red Square is a major cultural, shopping, and government center. To the West, teenagers loiter while tourists watch street performers at **Manezh Square** (Манежная площадь; Manezhnaya Ploshchad). The glass domes on the square provide sunlight to the ritzy **Okhotny Ryad underground mall**, which overflows with new trends and New Russians. (Open daily 11am-11pm. Enter directly from the square or through the Metro underpass.) More posh hotels, chic stores, and government buildings line **Tverskaya ulitsa** (Тверская), which runs northwest from Manezh Square. Some of Moscow's poshest residences line Tverskaya, the closest Moscow gets to a main thoroughfare. The famous **Moscow Hotel** (topped by a big white "Baltica" beer ad) overlooks the square and separates it from the older, smaller **Revolution Square** (Площадь Революции; Ploshchad Revolutsii). Both squares are bounded on the North by **Okhotny Ryad** (Охотный Ряд; Hunters' Row), where the **State Historical Museum** is located (see p. 850). Across Okhotny Ryad from the Moscow Hotel is the **Duma**, or lower house of Parliament, and across from Revolution Square is **Theatre Square** (Театральная площадь; Teatralnaya Ploshchad), home of the **Bolshoi** and **Maly Theatres** (see p. 851).

CHURCHES, MONASTERIES, AND SYNAGOGUES

CATHEDRAL OF CHRIST THE SAVIOR. (Храм Христа Спасителя; Khram Khrista Spasitelya.) The city's most controversial landmark is the enormous, gold-domed Cathedral of Christ the Savior. Stalin demolished Nicholas I's original cathedral on this site to make way for a gigantic Palace of the Soviets, but Khrushchev abandoned the project and built an outdoor pool instead. In 1995, after the heated pool's water vapors had damaged paintings in the nearby Pushkin Museum, mayor Yury Luzhkov and the Orthodox Church won the battle for the site and built the cathedral in a mere two years. As for where they got the money, let's just say it was a miracle. *(M1: Kropotkinskaya; between ul. Volkhonka (Волхонка) and the Moscow River. Open daily 10am-5pm. Service schedule varies. Free, but donations welcome.)*

NOVODEVICHY MONASTERY AND CEMETERY. (Новодевичий Монастырь.) Moscow's most famous monastery is hard to miss, thanks to its high brick walls, golden domes, and tourist buses. In the center of the convent, the **Smolensk Cathedral** (Смоленский Собор; Smolensky Sobor) shows off Russian icons and frescoes. As you exit the gates, turn right and follow the exterior wall back around to the **cemetery** (кладбище; kladbishche), a pilgrimage site that holds the graves of such famous figures as Bulgakov, Chekhov, Gogol, Mayakovsky, Shostakovich, and Stanislavsky. *(M1: Sportivnaya. Take the Metro exit that does not lead to the stadium, turn right, and walk several blocks. Open W-M 10am-5:30pm. Closed 1st M of every month. 40R, students 20R. Smolensk Cathedral and special exhibits each 93R, students 53R. Cemetery open in summer daily 9am-7pm, off-season 9am-6pm; 30R. Helpful English maps of cemetery 5R. Buy tickets at the small kiosk to the right of the entrance.)*

DANILOVSKY MONASTERY. (Даниловский.) The seat of the Patriarch, head of the Russian Orthodox Church, is at Danilovsky. An enormous mosaic of a stern-looking man, which watches over visitors, marks the Patriarch's office. The white exterior is complemented by stunning grounds and long-robed monks; unfortunately, visitors can enter only the church and the small museum, both to the left of the main entrance. *(M9: Tulskaya. From the square, follow the trolley tracks down Danilovsky val., away from the gray buildings. Open daily 6:30am-7pm. Services M-F 6, 7am, and 5pm, Sa-Su 6:30, 9am, and 5pm. Museum open W and Sa-Su 11am-1pm and 1:30-4pm. Free.)*

MOSCOW CHORAL SYNAGOGUE. Constructed in the 1870s, the synagogue is a break from the city's ubiquitous onion domes. Though it functioned during Soviet rule, all but the bravest Jews were deterred by KGB agents who photographed anyone who entered. Today, more than 200,000 Jews officially live in Moscow and services are increasingly well attended, but occasional graffiti serves as a sad reminder that anti-Semitism in Russia is not dead. *(Bolshoy Spasoglinishchevsky per. 10 (Большой Спасоглинищевский). M6 and 7: Kitai-Gorod. Go north on Solyansky Proezd (Солянский Проезд) and take the 1st left. Open daily 8am-9pm; services Su-Th 8:30am and 8pm, F 7:30pm, Shabbat services Sa 9 and 10am.)*

CHURCH OF ST. NICHOLAS OF THE WEAVERS. (Церковь Николы в Хамовниках; Tserkov Nikoly v Khamovnikakh.) The maroon-and-green trim of the Church of St. Nicholas of the Weavers gives it the appearance of a giant gingerbread house. Enter off ul. Lva Tolstovo (Лва Толстого) for the best view of the low ceilings and vivid interior. *(M1 and 5: Park Kultury. At the corner of Komsomolsky pr. and ul. Lva Tolstovo. Open daily 8am-8pm. Services M-Sa 8am and 5pm; Su 7, 10am, and 5pm.)*

AREAS FOR WALKING

THE ARBAT. Now a commercial pedestrian shopping arcade, the Arbat was once a showpiece of *glasnost* and a haven for political radicals, Hare Krishnas, street poets, and *metallisty* (heavy metal rockers). Some of the old flavor remains in the street performers and guitar-playing teenagers. Intersecting but nearly parallel to the Arbat runs the bigger, newer, and uglier **Novy Arbat,** lined with gray high-rises, foreign businesses, and massive Russian stores. *(M3: Arbatskaya or Smolenskaya.)*

MOSCOW METRO. (Московское Метро.) The beautiful Moscow Metro stations are each unique, and those inside the Circle Line have sculptures, stained glass, elaborate mosaics, and unusual chandeliers. Especially noteworthy stations include Kievskaya, Komsomolskaya, Mayakovskaya, Mendeleevskaya, Novoslobodskaya, Ploshchad Revolutsii, and Rimskaya. *(Open daily 6am-1am. 5R.)*

VICTORY PARK. (Парк Победы; Park Pobedy.) On the left past the **Triumphal Arch,** which celebrates the victories of 1812, is Victory Park, which was built as a lasting monument to World War II. It includes the gold-domed **Church of St. George the Victorious** (Храм Георгия Победоносного; Khram Georgiya Pobedonosnova) and the impressive **Museum of the Great Patriotic War** (Музей Отечественной Войны; Muzey Otechestvennoy Voyny). In the park behind the museum is the **Exposition of War Technology** (Експозиция Военной Техники; Ekspozitsiya Voyennoy Tekhniki), a large outdoor display of aircraft, tanks, and weaponry. *(M4: Kutuzovskaya. Museum and Exposition open Tu-Su 10am-5pm. 80R, students 40R. Exposition free.)*

KOLOMENSKOYE SUMMER RESIDENCE. (Коломенское.) The tsars' summer residence sits on a wooded slope above the Moskva River. The centerpieces of the grounds are the cone-shaped, 16th-century **Assumption Cathedral** (Успенский Собор; Uspensky Sobor) and the seven blue-and-gold cupolas of the nearby **Church of Our Lady of Kazan** (Церковь Казанской Богоматери; Tserkov Kazanskoy Bogomatyeri). The most notable of the park's several small museums is Peter the Great's 1702 log cabin. *(M2: Kolomenskaya; follow the exit signs to "к музею Коломенское." Turn right out of the Metro and walk down the tree-shaded path, through the small black gate, and uphill on the left-most path (10min). Grounds open Apr.-Oct. daily 7am-10pm, Oct.-Apr. 9am-9pm. Free. Museums open Tu-Su 10am-5:30pm. Each museum 60-70R, students 30-35R.)*

🏛 MUSEUMS

Moscow's museums remain patriotic and untouched by the West, and each is guarded by a team of loyal *babushki*. Large government museums and small galleries alike proudly display Russian art, and dozens of historical and literary museums are devoted to the nation's impressive past and its major figures. Most major art and literary museums are concentrated in the southern and western parts of central Moscow. Be prepared for inconvenience, though; most museums stop selling tickets up to an hour before closing time, many have Russian-only captions, and prices can get astronomically high.

⊠ STATE TRETYAKOV GALLERY. (Третьяковская Галерея; Tretyakovskaya Galereya.) A veritable treasure chest of 18th- to early 20th-century Russian art, the museum also displays a magnificent collection of icons, including works by Andrei Rublyov and Theophanes the Greek. *(Lavrushinsky per. 10 (Лаврушинский). M8: Tretyakovskaya. Turn left and then left again, then take an immediate right onto Bolshoy Tolmachevsky per. (Большой Толмачевский); after 2 blocks, turn right on Lavrushinsky per. Open Tu-Su 10am-7:30pm; kassa closes at 6:30pm. 225R, students 130R.)*

⊠ NEW TRETYAKOV GALLERY. (Государственная Третьяковская Галерея; Gosudarstvennaya Tretyakovskaya Galereya.) The new gallery picks up chronologically where the first Tretyakov leaves off, displaying the greatest Russian art of the 20th century. Behind the gallery and to the right is a graveyard for fallen statues, including decapitated Lenins and Stalins, as well as sculptures of Gandhi, Einstein, and Niels Bohr. From outside the gallery, you can (unfortunately) also get a great view of the metal statue of **Peter the Great** that towers over the Moscow River. Zurab Tsereteli, a favorite of mayor Yuri Luzhkov, built the statue in 1997 for Moscow's 850th anniversary, but Muscovites have despised the 100m-tall monstrosity from the start. *(Ul. Krymsky Val 10 (Крымский Вал). M5 and 6: Oktyabraskaya. Opposite Gorky Krymsky; shares a building with the Central House of Artists gallery. Walk toward the big intersection at Kaluzhskaya pl. and turn right onto ul. Krymsky. Open Tu-Su 10am-7:30pm; kassa closes at 6:30pm. 225R, students 130R.)*

PUSHKIN MUSEUM OF FINE ARTS. (Музей Изобразительных Искусств им. А.С. Пушкина; Muzey Izobrazitelnykh Iskusstv im. A.S. Pushkina.) The museum houses Moscow's most important collection of non-Russian art, with major Renaissance, Egyptian, and classical works as well as a superb pieces by Van Gogh, Chagall, and Picasso. *(Ul. Volkhonka 12 (Волхонка). M1: Kropotkinskaya. Open Tu-Su 10am-7pm; kassa closes at 6pm. 160R, students 60R.)*

STATE HISTORICAL MUSEUM. (Государственный Исторический Музей; Gosudarstvennyi Istoricheskii Muzey.) The comprehensive collection traces Russian history from the Neanderthals through Kyivan Rus to modern Russia. Highlights include ancient idols and jewelry, elaborate medieval icons, and paintings of various historical figures. *(Krasnaya pl. 1/2. M1: Okhotny Ryad. Entrance just inside the gate into Red Square, on the right. Open daily 11am-7pm; last entrance 6pm. Closed 1st M of the month. 150R, students 75R.)*

KGB MUSEUM. (Музей КГБ; Muzey KGB.) The museum displays Bond-esque devices and explains strategies of the Russian secret intelligence—the most feared in the world—from Ivan the Terrible to the present. The FSB (the new KGB) trains here. *(Ul. Bul. Lubyanka 12. M1: Lubyanka. The building behind the concrete behemoth that towers over the northeast side of the square. Pre-arranged tours only; Patriarshy Dom Tours (☎ 795 09 27) leads 2hr. group tours of the museum, from US$15.)*

CENTRAL MUSEUM OF THE ARMED FORCES OF THE USSR. (Центральный Музей Вооруженных Сил СССР; Tsentralny Muzey Vooruzhennykh Sil SSSR.) The museum exhibits a large collection of weapons, uniforms, and artwork from the time of Peter the Great to the debacle in Chechnya. Behind the museum is a large outdoor display of tanks and planes. *(Ul. Sovetskoy Armii 2 (Советской Армии). M5: Novoslobodskaya. Walk down ul. Seleznevskaya (Селезневская) to the square/rotary (10min.). Turn left just after the huge theater and bear right at the fork. Open W-Su 10am-5pm. 20R, students 10R.)*

HOMES OF THE LITERARY AND FAMOUS

■ **PUSHKIN LITERARY MUSEUM.** (Литературный Музей Пушкина; Literaturny Muzey Pushkina.) If you've never seen Pushkin-worship first-hand, this large collection of Pushkin memorabilia will either convert or frighten you. *(Ul. Prechistenka 12/2 (Пречистенка). Entrance on Khrushchevsky per. (Хрущевский). M1: Kropotkinskaya. Open Tu-Su 11am-7pm; kassa closes at 6pm. 25R, students 10R.)*

TOLSTOY MUSEUM. (Музей Толстого; Muzey Tolstovo.) This museum in the neighborhood of Tolstoy's first Moscow residence displays original texts, paintings, and letters related to his masterpieces. *(Ul. Prechistenka 11 (Пречистенка). M1: Kropotkinskaya. From the Metro, walk 3 blocks down Prechistenka. Open Tu-Su 11am-7pm; kassa closes at 6pm; closed last F of the month. 70R, students 30R.)*

MAYAKOVSKY MUSEUM. (Музей им. В. В. Маяковского; Muzey im V. V. Mayakovskovo.) Basically a walk-through work of Futurist art, the museum was created as a poetic reminder of Mayakovsky's ideas, life, and death. His papers and work are arranged in a four-story assemblage of skewed chairs, spilled paint, and chicken wire. *(Lubyansky pr. 3/6 (Лубянский). M1: Lubyanka. Behind a bust of Mayakovsky on ul. Myasnitskaya (Мясницкая). Open F-Tu 10am-6pm, Th 1-9pm. 60R.)*

GORKY MUSEUM-HOUSE. (Музей-дом Горкого; Muzey-dom Gorkovo.) The museum is a pilgrimage site as much for its Art Nouveau architecture as for its collection of Maxim Gorky's possessions. *(Ul. Malaya Nikitskaya 6/2 (Малая Никитская). M3: Arbatskaya; cross Novy Arbat, turn right on Merelyakovsky per. (Мереляковский), and cross the small park. The entrance is through a courtyard on ul. Spiridonovka (Спиридиновка). Open W and F noon-7pm, Th and Sa-Su 10am-5pm. Closed last Th of each month. Free, but donation requested.)*

⬛ ENTERTAINMENT

From September to June, Moscow boasts some of the world's best theater, ballet, and opera, along with excellent orchestral performances. Advance tickets are often very cheap (US$2-5), and can be purchased from the *kassa* inside each theater or from "Театры" kiosks throughout the city.

Bolshoi Teatr (Большой Театр; Big Theater), Teatralnaya pl. 1 (☎292 00 50; www.bolshoi.ru). M2: Teatralnaya. Home to both the opera and the world-renowned ballet companies. *Kassa* open F-W 11am-3pm and 4-7pm, Th 11am-3pm and 4-9pm. Performances daily Sept.-June at noon and 7pm. Tickets 20-3500R.

Maly Teatr (Малый Театр; Small Theater), Teatralnaya pl. 1/6 (☎923 26 21). M2: Teatralnaya. Just right of the Bolshoy. Different Russian productions nightly. *Kassa* open daily noon-3pm and 4-7pm. Daily performances at 7pm. Tickets from 20-300R.

Operetty Teatr (Оперетты Театр; Operetta Theater), ul. Bolshaya Dmitrovka 6 (Большая Дмитровка; ☎292 12 37; www.operetta.org.ru), to the left of the Bolshoy. M2: Teatralnaya. Shows M-Th 7pm, F-Su 6pm, and some daytime performances. *Kassa* open M-Th noon-3pm and 4-7pm, F-Su noon-3pm and 4-6pm. Tickets 30-300R.

Stanislavsky Theater, ul. Tverskaya 23 (Тверская; ☎299 72 24). M2: Tverskaya. Avant-garde productions Sept.-June. *Kassa* open daily noon-3pm and 4-7pm. From 80R.

⬛ NIGHTCLUBS AND BARS

Moscow's bacchanalian nightlife is the most varied, expensive, and dangerous in Eastern Europe. Many of the more interesting clubs enjoy flaunting their exclusiveness and their high cover charges, while more sedate, less-expensive venues

RUSSIA

**YOUR
OWN
WAY**

THE GOLDEN RING

North and east of Moscow lies the Golden Ring (Золотое Кольцо; Zolotoye Koltso), a slow-paced region that maintains a distinctly medieval atmosphere. Some of the most beautiful and best-loved churches and *kremlins* (fortresses) in Russia are here.

YAROSLAVL. Filled with wide, green boulevards, parks, and riverside walks, Yaroslavl combines provincial charm with capital-city comforts. Info: ☎(80852) 30 54 13.

SUZDAL. Unscathed by Soviet construction, Suzdal looks as it always has, with a splendid *kremlin*, lazy streams, quiet fields, and dirt roads. Info: ☎(809231) 209 37.

VLADIMIR. Once Russia's capital, Vladimir's white stone monuments and grand cathedrals are well preserved in spite of Soviet "progress." Info: ☎(80922) 32 42 63.

TRANSPORTATION. Trains leave from Moscow for Vladimir (3-4hr., 10-20 per day, 64-80R) and Yaroslavl (4½hr., 19 per day, 125R). **Buses** go from Moscow to Vladimir (3½hr., 18-20 per day, 57-63R) and also run between Vladimir and Suzdal (50min., 1-2 per hr., 13-16R); Vladimir and Yaroslavl (5-5½hr., 4 per week, 112-130R); and Suzdal and Yaroslavl (4hr., 8 per week, 109R). For information or rail tickets from Moscow, contact the **Central Train Agency** (☎266 93 33 or 266 83 33).

attract bohemians and absinthe-seeking students. Check the weekend editions of *The Moscow Times* or *The Moscow Tribune* for club reviews and music festival listings. The Friday pull-out section of *The Moscow Times*, the nightlife section of *The Exile* (www.exile.ru), and *The Beat* have weekly calendars and up-to-date restaurant, bar, and club reviews.

▓ Propaganda (Пропаганда), Bolshoy Zlatoustinsky per. 7 (Большой Златоустинский). M6 and 7: Kitai-Gorod. Dance to good house without feeling like you're in a meat market. Beer 70R. Cover F 70R, Sa 100R. Open daily from 12pm-6am.

Project OGI (Проект ОГИ), 8/12 Potapovsky per., bldg. 2 (Потаповский). M1: Chistye Prudy. Head down bul. Chistoprudny (Чистопрудный), take the 1st right, then the 1st left onto Potapovsky per. This club has cheap, exceptional food and wine and a unique, colorful atmosphere. Cover 100-150R. Open 24hr.

Doug and Marty's Boar House, Zemlyanoi val 26 (Земляной). M3: Kurskaya, opposite the train station. This American-style bar is packed with patrons on weekends. Happy Hour 6-9pm. 50% discount on food noon-9pm. Beer 90-145R. Cover: men 150R, women 75R. Open daily noon-6am.

Hungry Duck, Pushechnaya ul. 9 (Пушечная). M1: Kuznetsky Most. Enter the courtyard and follow the red neon arrows. One of the most infamous clubs in the world. A spectacle to behold: the crowd dances—and strips—on the table, the bar, and everywhere in between. Ladies, to avoid being stripped, don't stand too close to the bar. Beers 70-100R. Cover: men 100-200R, women free-50R. Open daily 8pm-6am.

Karma Bar, ul. Pushechnaya 3. M: Kuznetzky Most. Walk through the archway on your left and turn right onto ul. Pushechnaya. Spins crowd-pleasing dance music. Amazing club dancers. Su hip-hop night. Beer 100-140R, vodka 80-150R, cocktails 180R. Cover: men 150R, women 50R. Open W-Su 7pm-6am.

Crazy Milk, ul. Bolshaya Polyanka 54 (Большая Полянка). M5: Dobryninskaya. Cross ul. Zhitnaya (Житная) to your left and make another left on Bolshaya Polyanka. Elegant and eclectic decor. Buffalo wings 29R Su-Th 6pm-midnight. Happy Hour specials Su-Th 5-7pm; 2-for-1 drinks Su-W midnight-6am. Cuban cigars 320-520R. Ask for the cheaper patio menu. Beer US$3-5. Open daily noon-6am.

Hippopotamus (Гиппопотам), ul. Mantulinsky 5/1 (Мантулинский). M7: Ulitsa 1905 Goda. Cross the intersection and walk down Tryokhgorny Val, with McDonald's on your left. Go right onto Shmitovskiy per., take the 1st left onto ul. 1905 Goda, and turn right onto ul. Mantulinsky. Plays hip-hop, R&B, and soul. Various theme nights. Beer US$2.50-3, cocktails US$2.50-5. Cover men US$2-6, women free-US$3, W free. Open W-Su 10pm-6am.

◪ DAYTRIP FROM MOSCOW: SERGIEV POSAD

Russia's most famous pilgrimage point, Sergiev Posad (Сергиев Посад) attracts Orthodox believers to a mass of churches huddled around its main sight—**St. Sergius's Trinity Monastery** (Свято-Троицкая Сергиева Лавра; Svyato-Troitskaya Sergieva Lavra). After decades of state-propagated atheism, the stunning monastery, founded around 1340, is again a thriving religious center. The splendid **Assumption Cathedral** (Успенский Собор; Uspensky Sobor) was modeled after its namesake cathedral in Moscow's Kremlin. The magnificent frescoes of the **Refectory** (Трапезная; Trapeznaya) and the gilded Andrei Rublyov icons at **Trinity Cathedral** (Троицкий Собор; Troitsky Sobor) are equally colorful and captivating. (Monastery open daily 9am-6pm.) **Commuter trains** (elektrichki) run to Sergiev Posad from Moscow's Yaroslavsky Vokzal (1½hr., every 20-50min., round-trip 61R). To get to the monastery from the station, turn right and look for the domes, cross the street, and walk down the road until you see the city (10-15min.).

ST. PETERSBURG (САНКТ-ПЕТЕРБУРГ) ☎ 8812

The splendor of St. Petersburg's wide boulevards and bright facades is exactly what Peter the Great envisioned when he founded his "window on the West." However, St. Petersburg was also the birthplace of the 1917 revolution, which would turn Russia away from the Western world. The city has inspired Dostoevsky, Gogol, Tchaikovsky, and Stravinsky, while its cafes fostered the revolutionary dreams of Lenin and Trotsky. Sophisticated but affordable, St. Petersburg remains the majestic symbol of Peter's great Russian vision. This year, the city celebrates its 300th anniversary.

▐ TRANSPORTATION

Flights: The main airport, **Pulkovo** (LED; Пулково), has 2 terminals: Pulkovo-1 (☎ 104 38 22), for domestic, and Pulkovo-2 (☎ 104 34 44), for international flights. M2: Moskovskaya. From the Metro, take bus #39 to Pulkovo-1 (25min.) or bus #13 to Pulkovo-2 (20min.). Hostels can often arrange for a taxi (usually US$30-35).

Trains: Central Ticket Offices (Центральные Железнодорожные Кассы; Tsentralnye Zheleznodorozhnye Kassy), Canal Griboyedova 24 (Грибоедого). International tickets at windows #4-6. Long lines, few English-speaking tellers. Prices vary; go to the **Intourist** office at each of the stations to purchase tickets on the day of departure. Check your ticket to see from which station your train leaves. Open M-Sa 8am-8pm, Su 8am-6pm.

Finlyandsky Vokzal (Финляндский Вокзал). M1: Pl. Lenina. To **Helsinki** (6hr., 2 per day, 1375R).

Moskovsky Vokzal (Московский Вокзал). M1: Pl. Vosstaniya. To **Moscow** (5-8hr., 12-15 per day, 600-1200R). Anna Karenina threw herself under a train here.

Vitebsky Vokzal (Витебский Вокзал). M1: Pushkinskaya. To: **Kyiv** (25hr., 2 every 2 days, 506-637R); **Odessa** (36hr., 1 per day, 654R); **Rīga** (13hr., 1 per day, 887R); **Tallinn** (9hr., 1 per day, 350R); **Vilnius** (14hr., every 2 days, 647R).

Buses: nab. Obvodnovo Kanala 36 (Обводного Канала; ☎ 166 57 77). M4: Ligovsky pr. Take trolley #42 or tram #19, 25, 44, or 49 to the stop just across the canal. Facing the canal, turn right and walk 2 long blocks. The station is to the right, behind a derelict building. **Eurolines Agency** (Агенство Евролайнс; Agenstro Evrolains), ul. Shkapina 10 (Щкапина; ☎ 168 27 40), sends buses to Rīga, Tallinn, and Vilnius. M1: Baltiiskaya.

RUSSIA

Local Transportation: The efficient, cheap **Metro** (Метро) is always busy, especially 8-9am and 5-6pm. **Tokens** (жетон; *zheton*) cost 6R. For **buses, trams,** and **trolleys,** buy tickets (5R) from the driver. All open daily 6am-midnight.

Taxis: Marked cabs are 9R per km. For unofficial cabs, haggle over flat fares, which are usually cheaper. Safety is not guaranteed; never get into a car that already has more than one person in it.

■ ⁊ ORIENTATION AND PRACTICAL INFORMATION

The city center lies on mainland St. Petersburg between the south bank of the **Neva River** and the **Fontanka River.** The easiest way to get around the city is by using the Metro. Most major sights, including the Winter and Summer Palaces and the Hermitage, are on or near **Nevsky prospekt** (Невский Проспект), the city's main street; **Moscow Train Station** (Московский Вокзал; Moskovsky Vokzal) is near the midpoint. Trolleys #1, 5, and 22 run along Nevsky. On the north side of the Neva is the **Petrograd Side** archipelago, where the **Peter and Paul Fortress** stands.

Museums and sights often charge several times more for "foreigners" than for Russians. To avoid paying the higher price, hand the cashier the exact amount for a Russian ticket, and say *adeen* (one). Walk as if you know where you are going, and do not keep your map, camera, or *Let's Go* in plain view. Dress like a local, and try to speak Russian when you can.

TOURIST, FINANCIAL, AND LOCAL SERVICES

Tourist Office: Ost-West Contact Service, ul. Mayakovskogo 7 (Маяковского; ☎327 34 16; www.ostwest.com). Visa service. Open M-F 10am-6pm, Sa noon-6pm.

Budget Travel: Sindbad Travel (FIYTO), ul. 3-ya Sovetskaya 28 (Советская; ☎324 08 80; www.sindbad.ru). In the International Hostel. Arranges tickets, tours, and adventure trips. Student discounts on plane tickets. Open M-F 9:30am-8pm, Sa-Su 10am-5pm.

Adventure Travel: Wild Russia, Nevsky pr. 22/24 (☎325 93 30; www.wildrussia.spb.ru). Outdoor excursions around St. Petersburg (weekends US$40-100).

Consulates: Canada, Malodetskoselsky pr. 32 (Малодетскосельский; ☎325 84 48). M2: Frunzenskaya. Open M-F 9am-5pm. **UK,** pl. Proletarskoi Diktatury 5 (Пролетарской Диктатуры; ☎320 32 00; www.britain.spb.ru). M1: Chernyshevskaya. Open M-F 9am-5pm. **US,** ul. Furshtatskaya 15 (Фурштатская; ☎275 17 01; 24hr. emergency ☎274 86 92; acs_stpete@state.gov). M1: Chernyshevskaya. Open M-F 9am-5:30pm. Services for US citizens 9:30am-1:30pm. Citizens of **Australia** and **New Zealand** should contact their embassies in Moscow (p. 842) or the UK consulate in an emergency.

Currency Exchange: Look for "Обмен валюты" *(obmen valyuty)* signs everywhere. Avoid the black market. **Menatep Bank** (Менатеп; ☎312 26 92), Nevsky pr. 1, at the corner of Admiralteysky pr. M2: Nevsky Prospekt. Also cashes traveler's checks and offers Western Union services. Open daily 10:30am-1:30pm and 2:30-9pm.

ATMs: Bankomati (Банкомати) are increasing in number and can be found in many hotels, restaurants, and large banks around Nevsky pr. and Griboedov canal.

EMERGENCY AND COMMUNICATIONS

Police: ☎02. **Ambulance:** ☎03. **Fire:** ☎01. Multilingual police office for crimes against foreigners at ul. Zakharevskaya 19 (Захаревская; ☎278 30 14). M1: Chernyshevskaya. In the event of a crime, contact your consulate for help.

24hr. Pharmacy: Nevsky pr. 22. Stocks Western medicines and toiletries.

Medical Assistance: American Medical Center, ul. Serpukhovskaya 10 (Серпуховская; ☎326 17 30). M1: Tekhnologichesky Institut (Технологический Институт). 24hr.

Internet Access: Tetris Internet Cafe (Тетрис), Chernyakhovskovo 33 (Черняховского). M4: Ligovsky Prospekt. 30-60R per hr. Open daily 24hr., except 9-10am. **5.3 GHz Internet Club,** Nevsky pr. 63. M4: pl. Vosstanya. 65R per hr., computer rentals 190R per night. Open daily 9am-11pm.

Telephones: Central Telephone and Telegraph. Central office closed for repairs; branches include Nevsky pr. 27, Nevsky pr. 88, Nevsky pr. 107, and Kronversky pr. 21. Open daily 8am-10pm. **Intercity calls** can be made from pay phones that take phone cards (25 units cost 61R, 400 units 368R; 1 unit per min. for local calls, 48 per min. to the US). Cards sold at the telephone offices, Metro stations, and news kiosks.

Post Office: ul. Pochtamtskaya 9 (Почтамтская). From Nevsky pr., take ul. Malaya Morskaya (Малая Морская), which becomes ul. Pochtamtskaya. It's about 2 blocks past St. Isaac's Cathedral on the right. Open M-Sa 9am-8pm, Su 10am-6pm. Address mail to be held: SURNAME Firstname, **190 000** Санкт-Петербург, Главпочтамт, Писмо До Востребования, RUSSIA.

ACCOMMODATIONS

International Youth Hostel (HI), 3-ya Sovetskaya ul. 28 (☎329 80 18; ryh@ryh.ru). M1: Pl. Vosstaniya. Walk 3 blocks down Suvorovsky pr. (Суворовский), then turn right on Sovetskaya. Great location in a pleasant neighborhood. Breakfast included. Internet 1R per min. Laundry US$4 for 5kg. Check-out 11am. No curfew. Dorms US$19, with ISIC US$18, with HI US$17. ❶

Puppet Hostel (HI), ul. Nekrasova 12 (Некрасова; ☎272 54 01; fax 272 83 61; puppet@ryh.ru). M3: Mayakovskaya. Take the 2nd left on Nekrasova; the hostel is next to the Bolshoy Puppet Theater, on the 4th floor. Friendly, English-speaking staff and clean, simple rooms. Breakfast included. Check-out noon. No curfew. Dorms US$18; doubles US$40. US$1 HI/ISIC discount. Oct.-Apr. US$2 less. ❶

Hostel "Holiday" (HI), Nab. Arsenalnaya 9 (Арсенальная; ☎327 10 70; www.hostel.spb.ru). M1: Pl. Lenina. Exit at Finlyandsky Vokzal, turn left on ul. Komsomola (Комсомола), right on ul. Mikhailova (Михаилова). At the end of the street turn left onto Arsenalnaya. Breakfast included. Internet 150R per hr. Call ahead. May-Oct. 15 dorms US$14; singles US$37; doubles US$38. Oct. 16-Apr. dorms US$12; singles US$27; doubles US$30. US$1 HI/ISIC discount, US$2 after 5 days. ❷

Petrovsky Hostel, ul. Baltyskaya 26 (Балтийская; ☎ 252 75 63; fax 252 65 12). M1: Narvskaya. From the Metro, turn left on Stachek pr. (Стачек); turn left on ul. Baltyskaya at the large square. Although far from the center, it's clean and comfy. Kitchen. Dorms 200R; luxury rooms 400-800R. ❶

Hotel Olgino (Отель Ольгино), Primorskoye Shosse 18 (Приморское Шоссе; ☎238 36 71; fax 238 37 63). M4: Staraya Derevnya. From the Metro, take bus #110. Outside city limits, but quiet. Horseback riding 200R per hr., sauna 500R per hr. Restaurant and disco. Check-out noon. Call ahead. Parking 116R. Singles US$41; doubles US$49; luxury rooms US$58-70; camping US$8. ❸

FOOD

Russian food is not known for innovation; most menus offer the staples of pike, sturgeon, beef, and sausage. Markets stock a wide range of items; bargain and play hard to get. The **covered market,** Kuznechny per. 3 (Кузнечьный), just around the corner from M1: Vladimirskaya, and the **Maltsevsky Rynok** (Мальцевский Рынок), ul. Nekrasova 52 (M1: Pl. Vosstaniya), at the top of Ligovsky pr. (Лиговский), are the largest and most exciting. For **groceries,** try **24 Super Market,** corner of ul. Zhukovskovo and ul. Vosstanya. (M3: pl. Vosstanya. Open 24hr.)

RUSSIA

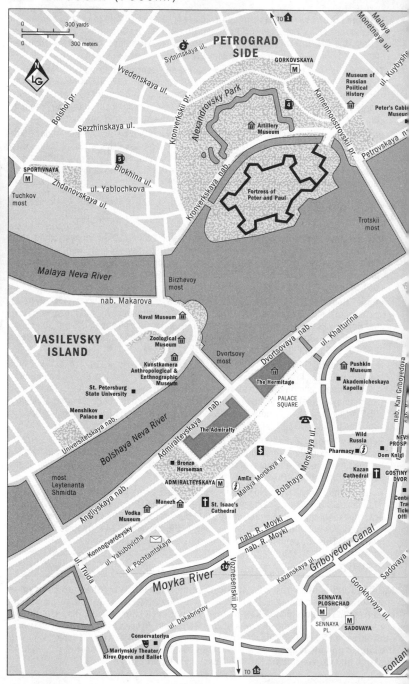

0   300 yards

0   300 meters

TO ①

PETROGRAD SIDE

Sytninskaya ul.

Vvedenskaya ul.

②

GORKOVSKAYA
Ⓜ

Museum of
Russian
Political
History

Peter's Cabin
Museum

Kronverkskii pr.

Alexandrovsky Park

Kamennoostrovskii pr.

Petrovskaya n

Bolshoi pr.

Sezzhinskaya ul.

④

Artillery
Museum

⑤

Blokhina ul.

SPORTIVNAYA
Ⓜ

Zhdanovskaya ul.

ul. Yablochkova

Fortress of
Peter and Paul

Tuchkov
most

Kronverkskaya nab.

Trotskii
most

Malaya Neva River

Birzhevoy
most

nab. Makarova

Naval Museum 🏛

**VASILEVSKY
ISLAND**

Zoological
Museum 🏛

Kunstkamera
Anthropological &
Enthnographic
Museum 🏛

St. Petersburg
State University ■

Menshikov
Palace ■

Universitetskaya nab.

Dvortsovy
most

Dvortsovaya nab.

ul. Khalturina

Pushkin
Museum 🏛

Akademicheskaya
Kapella ■

The Hermitage

PALACE
SQUARE

☎

nab. Kan Griboyedova

Wild
Russia
Pharmacy ■ ⓘ

NEVS
PROSP

Dom Knigi

Bolshaya Neva River

Admiralteyskaya nab.

The Admiralty

Bolshaya Morskaya ul.

$

Kazan
Cathedral 🛉

GOSTINY
DVOR

most
Leytenanta
Shmidta

Angliyskaya nab.

■ Bronze
Horseman

ADMIRALTEYSKAYA Ⓜ

AmEx

Malaya Morskaya ul.

Cent
Tra
Tick
Offi

Manezh 🏛

🛉 St. Isaac's
Cathedral

Vodka
Museum

Konnogvardeysky

ul. Yakubovicha

ul. Truda

ul. Pochtamtskaya

✉

nab. R. Moyki

nab. R. Moyki

Moyka River

ul. Dekabristov

Voznesenskii pr.

⑭

Kazanskaya ul.

Griboyedov Canal

Gorokhovaya ul.

Sadovaya

SENNAYA
PLOSHCHAD
Ⓜ

SENNAYA
PL.

Ⓜ
SADOVAYA

Conservatorlya
■

Marilynskly Theater/
Kirov Opera and Ballet

TO ⑮

Fontan

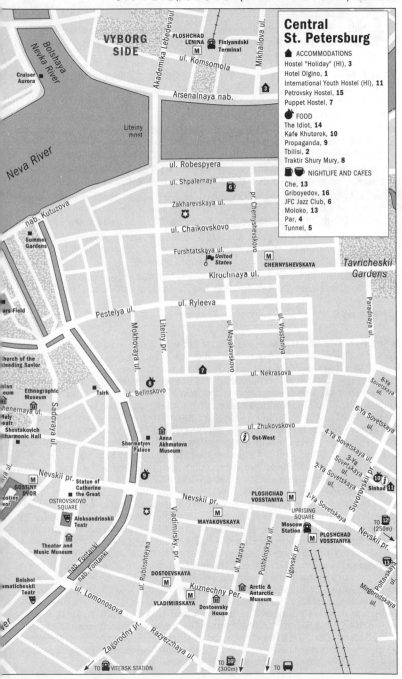

Central St. Petersburg

🏠 ACCOMMODATIONS
Hostel "Holiday" (HI), 3
Hotel Olgino, 1
International Youth Hostel (HI), 11
Petrovsky Hostel, 15
Puppet Hostel, 7

🍎 FOOD
The Idiot, 14
Kafe Khutorok, 10
Propaganda, 9
Tbilisi, 2
Traktir Shury Mury, 8

🍺☕ NIGHTLIFE AND CAFES
Che, 13
Griboyedov, 16
JFC Jazz Club, 6
Moloko, 13
Par, 4
Tunnel, 5

RUSSIA

VYBORG SIDE

Bolshaya Nevka River

Cruiser Aurora

Neva River

nab. Kutuzova

Summer Gardens

ars Field

hurch of the leeding Savior

sian eum
Ethnographic Museum

henernaya ul.
Maly eatr
Shostakovich ilharmonic Hall

Sadovaya ul.

GOSTINY DVOR
ostiny or

OSTROVSKOVO SQUARE

Aleksandrinskii Teatr

Theater and Music Museum

Bolshoi amaticheskii Teatr

ver

Akademika Lebedevai

PLOSHCHAD LENINA
Finlyandski Terminal

Mikhailova ul.

ul. Komsomola

Arsenalnaya nab.

Liteiny most

ul. Robespyera

ul. Shpalernaya

Zakharevskaya ul.

ul. Chaikovskovo

Furshtatskaya ul.
United States

Kirochnaya ul.

pr. Chernyshevskovo

CHERNYSHEVSKAYA

Tavricheskii Gardens

ul. Ryleeva

Pestelya ul.

Mokhovaya ul.

Liteiny pr.

ul. Mayakovskovo

ul. Vosstaniya

Paradnaya ul.

ul. Nekrasova

8-Ya Sovetskaya ul.

6-Ya Sovetskaya ul.

4-Ya Sovetskaya ul.

3-Ya Sovetskaya ul.

2-Ya Sovetskaya ul.

Suvorovskii pr.

Sinbad

1-Ya Sovetskaya

ul. Belinskovo

Tsirk

Shermetyev Palace

Anna Akhmatova Museum

ul. Zhukovskovo

Ost-West

Nevskii pr.
Statue of Catherine the Great

Nevskii pr.

PLOSHCHAD VOSSTANIYA

MAYAKOVSKAYA

Vladimirsky pr.

ul. Rubinshteyna

nab. Fontanki

ul. Lomonosova

DOSTOEVSKAYA

Kuznechny Per.

VLADIMIRSKAYA
Dostoevsky House

ul. Marata

Pushkinskaya ul.

Arctic & Antarctic Museum

UPRISING SQUARE

Moscow Station

PLOSHCHAD VOSSTANIYA

TO (250m)

Nevskii pr.

Ligovskii pr.

Mirgorodskaya ul.

Poltavskaya ul.

Zagorodny pr.

Razyezzhaya ul.

TO VITEBSK STATION

TO (300m)

TO

Note that there is no effective water purification system in St. Petersburg, making exposure to **giardia** very likely. Boil tap water or drink bottled water.

Traktir Shury Mury, ul. Belinskovo 8 (Белинсково). M2: Gostiny Dvor or M1: Vladimirskaya. Romantic country bistro serving delightful and inexpensive traditional dishes. Main dishes 100-250R. Wine 300-500R. ❸

Crocodile, 18 Galernaya ul. Take bus #27 to the 1st stop after St. Isaac's Square. Walk on Konnogvardeysky blvd. (Конногвардейский), take the first right onto per. Leonova, then right again onto Galernaya. Chill-out music and 25 kinds of whiskey; lounge around in the back room like a crocodile. Main dishes 120-300R, beer from 25R. ❸

Kafe Khutorok (Хуторок), 3-ya Sovetskaya ul. 24. M1: Pl. Vosstanya. Cafe serves home-style Russian food. Main dishes 75-140R. Alcohol 10-90R. Open daily 10am-11pm. ❷

The Idiot (Идиотъ), nab. Moyky 82 (Мойки). M2: Sennaya pl. Decadent expat hangout named for a Dostoyevsky novel. Vegetarian Russian cuisine and fun drinks. Main courses 150-300R. Happy Hour 6:30-7:30pm. Open daily 11am-1am. ❸

Propaganda, nab. Reki Fontanka 40. M2: Gostiny Dvor. Metallic, military bunker decor strikes a balance between hip and corny. Meat and seafood menu. Main dishes 225-400R. Open daily noon-5am. 20% discount from 1-5am. ❹

Tbilisi (Тбилиси), ul. Sytninskaya 10 (Сытнинская). M2: Gorkovskaya. Some of Russia's best Georgian cuisine. Entrees 40-260R. Live music. Open daily noon-11pm. ❸

⊙ SIGHTS

THE HERMITAGE. The State Hermitage Museum (Эрмитаж; Ermitazh) houses the world's largest art collection. The collection, which began with 255 paintings bought by Catherine the Great in 1764, now rivals the Louvre and the Prado in architectural, historical, and artistic significance. The **Winter Palace** (Зимний Дворец; Zimny Dvorets) began construction in 1762. The complex later expanded to include the Small Hermitage (Малый; Maly Ermitazh), the Large Hermitage (Большой; Bolshoy Ermitazh), the Hermitage Theater (Эрмитажный Театр; Ermitazhny Teatr), and the New Hermitage (Новый; Novy Ermitazh). The tsars lived with their collections in the complex until 1917, when the museum was nationalized. It is impossible to absorb the whole museum in a day or even in a week; only 5% of the three-million-piece collection is on display at a time. English floor plans are available at the information desk near the *kassa.*

Palace Square (Дворцовая Площадь; Dvortsovaya Ploshchad), the huge, wind-swept expanse in front of the Winter Palace, has witnessed many turning points in Russia's history. Catherine took the crown here after overthrowing Tsar Peter III, her husband; Nicholas II's guards fired into a crowd of peaceful demonstrators on "Bloody Sunday," which precipitated the 1905 revolution; and Lenin's Bolsheviks seized power from the provisional government during the storming of the Winter Palace in October 1917. The 700-ton **Alexander Column,** held in place by its massive weight alone, commemorates Russia's defeat of Napoleon in 1812. Across the bridge from the Hermitage, **Vasilevsky Island** splits the Neva in two; most of its sights lie on the eastern edge in the **Strelka** neighborhood. The area closest to the Hermitage, depicted on the 50R note, was a center for sea trade and now houses many of the city's best and strangest museums. *(Dvortsovaya nab. 34 (Дворцовая). M2: Nevsky Prospekt. Exiting the Metro, turn left and walk down Nevsky pr. to Admiralty. The Hermitage is to the right; enter on river side. Open Tu-Su 10:30am-6pm; cashier and upper floors close 1hr. earlier. 300R, students free. Cameras 100R. Long lines; come early.)*

ST. ISAAC'S CATHEDRAL. Glittering, intricately carved masterpieces of iconography await beneath the dome of **St. Isaac's Cathedral** (Исаакиевский Собор; Isaakievsky Sobor), a massive exemplar of 19th-century architecture. On a sunny day, the 100kg of pure gold that coat the dome shine for miles. The 360° view atop the **colonnade** is stunning. *(M2: Nevsky Prospekt. Exiting the Metro, turn left and walk almost to the end of Nevsky pr.; turn left onto Malaya Morskaya. Open daily 11am-7pm. 250R, students 125R. Colonnade open daily 11am-6pm. 100R, students 50R. Last entry 1hr. before closing. The kassa is to the right of the main entrance. Foreigners buy tickets inside.)*

PETER AND PAUL FORTRESS. Across the river from the Hermitage stand the walls and golden spire of the Peter and Paul Fortress (Петропавловская Крепость; Petropavlovskaya Krepost). Construction of the fortress, supervised by Peter the Great himself, began on May 27, 1703, which is considered the birthday of St. Petersburg. The fortress was intended as a defense against the Swedes, but was later used as a prison for political dissidents. Inside, the **Peter and Paul Cathedral** (Петропавловский Собор; Petropavlovsky Sobor) glows with rosy marble walls and a breathtaking Baroque partition covered with intricate iconography. The cathedral holds the remains of Peter the Great and his successors. Before the main vault sits the **Chapel of St. Catherine the Martyr.** The bodies of the last Romanovs—Tsar Nicholas II and his family, along with their faithful servants— were entombed here on July 17, 1998, the 80th anniversary of their murders at the hands of the Bolsheviks. Condemned prisoners awaited their common fate at **Trubetskoy Bastion** (Трубецкой Бастион), where Peter the Great held and tortured his first son, Aleksei. Dostoevsky, Gorky, Trotsky, and Lenin's older brother also spent time here. *(M2: Gorkovskaya. Exiting the Metro, turn right on Kamennoostrovsky pr. (Каменноостровский), the street in front of you (there is no sign). Continue to the river and cross the wooden bridge to the island fortress. Open M and Th-Su 10am-5pm, Tu 10am-4pm; closed last Tu of each month. Purchase a single ticket that covers most sights (120R, students 60R) at the kassa in the "boathouse" in the middle of the complex.)*

ALEKSANDR NEVSKY MONASTERY. A major pilgrimage site and peaceful strolling ground, Aleksandr Nevsky Monastery (Александро-невская Лавра; Aleksandro-Nevskaya Lavra) became one of four Orthodox monasteries to receive the highest monastic title of *lavra* in 1797. The **Artists' Necropolis** (Некрополь Мастеров Искусств; Nekropol Masterov Uskusstv) is the permanent resting place of Fyodor Dostoevsky and composers Tchaikovsky, Rimsky-Korsakov, and Mussorgsky. The nearby **Lazarus Cemetery** (Лазаревское Кладбище; Lazarevskoye Kladbishche), also known as the 18th-century Necropolis, is the city's oldest burial ground. The **Church of the Annunciation** (Благовещенская Церковь; Blagoveshchenskaya Tserkov), farther along the central stone path on the left, holds the remains of war heroes and is the original burial place of the Romanovs, who were moved to Peter and Paul Cathedral in 1998. The active **Holy Trinity Cathedral** (Свято-Троицкий Собор; Svyato-Troitsky Sobor), teeming with priests and devout *babushki*, is at the end of the path. *(M3, 4: Pl. Aleksandra Nevskovo. The 18th-century Necropolis lies behind and to the left of the entrance; the Artists' Necropolis is behind and to the right. Cemeteries open F-W 9:30am-5:30pm. 40R, students 20R. Dress modestly.)*

ALONG NEVSKY PROSPEKT. Many sights cluster around the western end of vibrant Nevsky pr., the city's 4.5km main thoroughfare. Unfortunately, there is no Metro station immediately nearby; one built, but after the station was completed, local residents refused to allow the construction of an entrance or exit connecting it to the surface. The **Admiralty** (Адмиралтий; Admiralteystvo) towers over the surrounding gardens and most of Nevsky pr. The golden spire of this former naval headquarters was painted black during World War II to disguise it from German artillery bombers. In the park to the left of the Admiralty is the

Bronze Horseman statue of Peter the Great, one of the most widely recognized symbols of the city; copies are all over Russia. *(M2: Nevsky. Exit the Metro and walk to the end of Nevsky pr. toward the golden spire.)* Walking back east on Nevsky pr., the enormous, Roman-style **Kazan Cathedral** (Казанский Собор; Kazansky Sobor) looms to the right. *(M2: Nevsky. Open daily 8:30am-7:30pm. Free.)* Half a block down, looking up Canal Griboyedova to the left, you can see the brilliantly colored ■**Church of the Savior on the Blood** (Спас На Крови; Spas Na Krovi), which sits on the site of the 1881 assassination of Tsar Aleksandr II. *(Open Th-Tu 11am-7pm; kassa closes at 6pm. 250R, students 150R.)* To the right is the 220-year-old **Merchants' Yard** (Гостиный Двор; Gostiny Dvor). *(M3: Gostiny Dvor. Open daily 10am-9pm.)* Nearby **Ostrovskovo Square** (Островского) houses the historic Aleksandrinsky Theater and an impressive monument to Catherine the Great. Much farther down Nevsky is **Ploshchad Vosstaniya** (Площадь Восстания; Uprising Square), where the bloodiest confrontations of the February Revolution of 1917 took place. *(M1: Ploshchad Vosstaniya.)*

SUMMER GARDENS AND PALACE. (Летний Сад и Дворец; Letny Sad i Dvorets.) The long, shady paths of the Summer Gardens are a romantic place to rest and cool off. In the northeast corner sits Peter's small **Summer Palace;** the decor reflects his European tastes, with everything from Spanish and Portuguese chairs to Dutch tile and German clocks. **Mars Field** (Марсово Поле; Marsovo Polye), a memorial to the victims of the Revolution and the Civil War (1917-19), extends next to the Summer Gardens. Don't walk on the grass; it covers a massive common grave. *(M2: Nevsky. Turn right at the Griboyedov Canal, pass the Church of the Bleeding Savior, cross the Moyka, and turn right onto ul. Pestelya (Пестеля). The palace and gardens are on your left, just after the next small canal. Garden open May-Oct. daily 10am-9:30pm; Nov.-Apr. 10am-8pm. May-Oct. 10R, students 7R, children 5R.; Nov.-Apr. free. Palace open May-Oct. W-M 11am-6pm; closed last M of the month. 75R, students 45R.)*

PISKARYOV MEMORIAL CEMETERY. (Пискарёвское Мемориальное Кладбище; Piskaryovskoye Memorialnoye Kladbishche.) Close to a million people died during the 900-day German siege of St. Petersburg during World War II; 490,000 of them are buried here at this remote, hauntingly tranquil cemetery. An eternal flame and grassy mounds are all that mark the dead. The inscription on the cemetery monument reads: "No one is forgotten; nothing is forgotten." *(M2: Ozerki (Озерки). Catch bus #123 outside the Metro. Ride 20 stops (35min.); the cemetery is on the left, marked by a low granite wall and 2 stone gatehouses. Open 24hr. Free.)*

MUSEUMS. The ■**Russian Museum** (Русский Музей; Russky Muzey) boasts the world's second largest collection of Russian art. *(M3: Gostiny Dvor. Down ul. Mikhailovskaya past the Grand Hotel Europe. Open M 10am-5pm, W-Su 10am-6pm; kassa closes 1hr. earlier. 240R, students 120R.)* The **Pushkin Museum** (Музей Пушкина; Muzey Pushkina) displays the personal effects of Russia's adored poet. *(M2: Nevsky Prospekt. Walk toward the Admiralty and turn right onto nab. Reki Moyki. Open W-M 10:30am-5pm. 28R, students 14R.)* **Dostoyevsky House** (Дом Достоевского; Dom Dostoyevskovo) is where the author wrote *The Brothers Karamazov.* *(M1: Vladmirskaya. On the corner of ul. Dostoevskovo, just past the market. Open Tu-Su 11am-6pm; kassa closes 5pm. 60R, students 30R.)* The **Museum of Russian Political History** (Музей Политической Истории России; Muzey Politicheskoy Istorii Rossii) has Soviet propaganda as well as artifacts from WWII. *(M2: Gorkovskaya. Go down Kamennoostrovsky toward the mosque and turn left on Kuybysheva. Open F-W 10am-6pm. 60R, students 30R.* The **Russian Vodka Museum** (Музей Водки; Muzey Vodki), Konnogvardeysky bul. 5, features exhibits on the history of vodka, and the cafe in the back sells vodka shots. *(Near St. Isaac's Cathedral; from the Manezh, walk toward the river and go right on Konnogvardeysky. Open daily 11am-11pm. 50R. Vodka shots 30-40R.)*

◑ ♫ FESTIVALS AND ENTERTAINMENT

St. Petersburg celebrates its 300th anniversary in 2003. Billions of rubles have gone into restoring major sights and planning glorious displays. In an effort to outshine Moscow's 850th anniversary in 1997, annual city festivals will be bigger than ever. The *St. Petersburg Times* (www.sptimes.ru) and the jubilee's official website (www.300.spb.ru) give details about shows and exhibits.

Tickets to world-class performances are often as little as 100R, although many of the renowned theaters are known to overcharge foreigners. Buying Russian tickets from scalpers will save you money, but you'll have to pose as a Russian to get in. The **Mariinsky Teatr** (Мариийнский), also known as the "Kirov," Teatralnaya pl. 1 (Театральная), M4: Sadovaya, where Tchaikovsky's *Nutcracker* and *Sleeping Beauty* premiered, is one of the most famous ballet halls in the world. Pavlova, Nureyev, Nizhinsky, and Baryshnikov all started here. In June, the theater hosts the **White Nights Festival.** Tickets go on sale 20 days in advance. (☎114 52 64. 1450-2320R for foreigners. *Kassa* open Tu-Su 11am-3pm and 4-7pm.) **Maly Teatr** (Малый Театр), also called the "Mussorgsky," pl. Iskusstv 1 (Искусств), is open July-Aug., when Mariinsky is closed. (☎595 43 05. Tickets 100-300R for Russians, 450R for foreigners. *Kassa* open M and W-Su 11am-7pm, Tu 11am-6pm. Bring your passport.) **Shostakovich Philharmonic Hall,** ul. Mikhailovskaya 2, opposite the Russian Museum, has both classical and modern concerts. (☎164 38 83. M3: Gostiny Dvor. Tickets from 150-750R. *Kassa* open daily 11am-3pm and 4-7:30pm.) **Aleksandrinsky Teatr** (Александринский Театр), pl. Ostrovskovo 2, attracts famous Russian actors and companies. (☎311 15 33. M3: Gostiny Dvor. Tickets 80-800R. *Kassa* open daily 11am-3pm and 4-7:15pm.)

◙ NIGHTLIFE

St. Petersburg's famed "White Nights" cast a pale glow on the night sky from mid-June to early July. In summer, lovers stroll under the illuminated heavens and watch the bridges over the Neva go up at 1:30am. Be careful when going home; cabs are usually a safe bet, but make sure your bridge isn't up: the bridges don't go back down until 4-5am, although some close briefly between 3 and 3:20am. Although expensive dance and strip clubs abound, you'll find better times hidden off the main drag. Check the Friday issue of *St. Petersburg Times* and *Pulse* for current events and special promotions.

■**Tunnel,** ul. Blokhina 16. M2: Gorkovskaya. Spacious techno club with the best sound system in the city. Beer and vodka 40R. Cover 100-200R. Open F-Sa midnight-9pm.

■**Par,** 5B Alexandrovsky Park. M2: Gorkovskaya. Exit the Metro and bear right, walking through the park toward Peter and Paul Fortress. Progressive club spinning underground house. Cover 100-200R. Open Th-Su from 11pm.

Moloko, Perekupnoy per. 12 (Перекупной). M3, 4: Pl. Aleksandra Nevskovo. A glitz-free rock club. Cover 50-100R. Open W-Su 7pm-midnight.

Griboyedov, ul. Voronezhskaya 2A (Воронежная). M4: Ligovsky prospekt. A former bomb shelter, now a popular club. Cover 60-130R. Open daily 6pm-6am.

JFC Jazz Club, Shpalernaya ul. 33 (Шпалерная). M1: Chernyshevskaya. Showcases exciting local jazz. Cover 50-100R. Open daily 7-11pm.

Che, ul. Poltavskaya 3. M1: pl. Vosstaniya. This cafe was named for a fiery revolutionary, but its vibe is calm and composed. Drinks 50-250R. Live music daily. Open 24hr.

RUSSIA

⚡ DAYTRIPS FROM ST. PETERSBURG

PETERHOF. The 300-year-old Peterhof (Петергоф) is the largest and the best-restored of the Russian palaces. It was burned to the ground during the Nazi retreat, but Soviet authorities provided the staggering sums needed to rebuild it. The gates open onto the **Lower Gardens,** a perfect place for a picnic along the shores of the Gulf of Finland. (Open May-Sept. daily 10:30am-6pm; Oct.-Apr. 9am-5pm. 160R, students 80R.) Wanting to create his own Versailles, Peter started building the first residence at the **Grand Palace** (Большой Дворец; Bolshoy Dvorets) in 1714; his daughter Empress Elizabeth and later Catherine the Great greatly expanded and remodeled it. (Open Tu-Su 10:30am-6pm; closed last Th of the month. 300R, students 150R.) The elegant, gravity-powered fountains of the **Grand Cascade** shoot from the palace into the Grand Canal. To enter the cozy but impressive stone grotto underneath the fountains, buy tickets just outside the palace. (Grotto open Tu-Su 11am-4:30pm. 100R, students 50R.) The Grand Palace was saved for special occasions—Peter actually lived at **Monplaisir.** (Open Th-Tu 10:30am-6pm; closed third Tu of the month. 190R, students 95R.) Next door is the **Catherine Building** (Екатерининский Корпус; Ekaterininsky Korpus), where Catherine the Great lay low while her husband was being overthrown on her orders. (Open M-W and F-Su 10:30am-6pm. 100R, students 50R.) Across the street from Peterhof, near the bus stop, is the church **Sobor Pervoverkhovikh of the Apostles of Peter and Paul.** Its soaring painted domes make this functioning church worth a quiet visit. (Services daily 9:30am and 5pm.)

Take the **train** from St. Petersburg's Baltysky station (Балтийский; M1: Baltiyskaya; 35min., every 10-50min., 24R). Tickets are sold at the office (Пригородная касса; *prigorodnaya kassa*) in the courtyard. Get off at Novy Peterhof. From the station, take any bus (6R; 10min.) or van (10-15R; 5min.) to Fontany (Фонтаны; fountains). Or, in summer, take the **hydrofoil** from the quay on Dvortsovaya nab. (Дворцовая) in front of the Hermitage (30min.; every 20-40min. 9:30am-6pm; 150-350R, students 120-200R.)

TSARSKOYE SELO (PUSHKIN). About 25km south of St. Petersburg, Tsarskoye Selo (Царское Село; Tsar's Village), also known as "Pushkin," surrounds **Catherine's Palace,** the opulent summer residence of Catherine the Great. The gorgeous azure, white, and gold Baroque palace was largely destroyed by the Nazis, but many of the salons have been restored to their former glory. (Open W-M 10am-6pm. 300R, students 150R.) The palace overlooks sprawling **parks** where Catherine once rambled with her dogs, who some believed she loved more than her own children. (Open May-Sept. daily 9am-11pm; Oct.-Apr. 10am-11pm. 60R, students 30R; free after 6pm.) In summer a ferry runs across the Great Pond to the **Island Pavilion.** (Ferry every 40min. noon-6pm. Round-trip 100R, students 50R. All buildings open May-Sept.) The **Cold Bath Pavilion,** which contains the exotic Agate Rooms, stands in front of the palace to the left. (Open W-Su 10am-5pm. 160R, students 80R.) Across the street from the palace, the **lycée** schooled a 12-year-old Pushkin. His classrooms and spartan dorm room can still be seen through hordes of awestruck Russians. (Open W-M 10:30am-5:30pm. 80R, students 16R.) The *elektrichka* runs from Vitebsky Station (M1: Pushkinskaya). All trains from platforms 1-3 go to Pushkin, the first stop that looks like a real station (30min.). From the station, take bus #371 or 382 to the end (10min., 4R). Finding the stop is tricky; watch for the palace through the trees to the right.

SLOVAK REPUBLIC (SLOVENSKA REPUBLIKA)

After centuries of nomadic invasions and Hungarian domination as well as 40 years of Soviet rule, the Slovak Republic has finally emerged as an independent nation. While still part of Czechoslovakia, the country rejected communism in the 1989 Velvet Revolution, then split from its Czech neighbor in 1993. The Slovak Republic is now stuck in a state of flux between industry and agriculture, with many rural Slovaks still sticking to their peasant traditions while their offspring flock to the city. Meanwhile, budget travelers are discovering its castle ruins and spectacular terrain, made even more attractive by the country's low prices.

FACTS AND FIGURES

Official Name: Slovak Republic.

Capital: Bratislava.

Population: 5,400,000.

Land Area: 48,845 sq. km.

Time Zone: GMT +1.

Languages: Slovak, Hungarian.

Religions: Roman Catholic (60%), atheist (10%), Protestant (8%), other (22%).

DISCOVER THE SLOVAK REPUBLIC

The Slovak Republic is an outdoor-lover's paradise. In the west, the relatively deserted **Low Tatras** near **Liptovský Mikuláš** (p. 871) offer everything from day hikes in the range's wooded foothills to overnight treks above the tree line. One of the best—and cheapest—mountain playlands in Europe, the snow-capped **High Tatras** near **Starý Smokovec** (p. 871) are filled with German and Slovak tourists. Farther south, **Slovenský Raj National Park** (p. 872) contains miles of ravine-crossing, cliff-climbing, and heart-stopping treks, as well as ice caves ripe for spelunking. The often-overlooked capital, **Bratislava** (p. 867), has its own man-made treasures, including a ruined castle towering over the Danube.

ESSENTIALS

WHEN TO GO

In general, the weather is best May through September, but rain is common any time of the year. Always pack warm clothing if you plan to travel into the mountains. August is the best time for hiking. Winters are very cold, damp, and snowy; November through February is the best time for skiing.

DOCUMENTS AND FORMALITIES

VISAS. Citizens of South Africa and the US can visit the Slovak Republic without a visa for up to 30 days; Australia, Canada, Ireland, and New Zealand 90 days; and the UK 180 days. To apply for a visa, contact an embassy or consulate in person or by mail; processing may take up to 30 days, and prices vary with exchange rate (30-day single-entry €28; 90-day multiple-entry €58; 180-day multiple-entry €79; 30-day transit €28). Travelers must also register their visa within three days of entering the country; most hotels do so automatically. If you intend to stay longer or get a visa extension, notify the Office of Border and Alien Police.

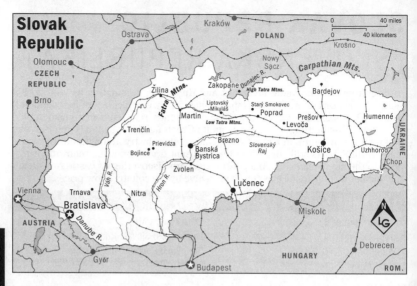

EMBASSIES. All foreign embassies are in Bratislava (see p. 868). Slovakian embassies at home include: **Australia,** 47 Culgoa Circuit, O'Malley, Canberra, ACT 2606 (☎06 290 1516; www.slovakemb-aust.org); **Canada,** 50 Rideau Terrace, Ottawa, ON K1M 2A1 (☎613-749-4442; www.slovakembassy.com); **Ireland,** 20 Clyde Rd., Ballsbridge, Dublin 4 (☎01 660 0012 or 660 0008); **South Africa,** 930 Arcadia St., Arcadia, Pretoria, P.O. Box 12736, Hatfield, 0028 (☎012 342 2051; fax 342 3688); **UK,** 25 Kensington Palace Gardens, London W8 4QY (☎020 7243 0803; www.slovakembassy.co.uk); and **US,** 2201 Wisconsin Ave. NW, Suite 250, Washington, D.C. 20007 (☎202-237-1054; fax 202-965-5166).

TRANSPORTATION

BY PLANE. Entering the country through Bratislava's international airport (BTS) can be inconvenient and expensive. Flying to Vienna and then taking a bus or train into the Slovak Republic is cheaper and takes about the same amount of time.

BY TRAIN. ŽSR (www.zsr.sk) is the national train company; **Cestovný poriadok** (58Sk), the master schedule, is available at every information desk, and is also printed on a large, round board in stations. **EastRail** is valid in the Slovak Republic, but **Eurail** is not. Tickets must be bought before boarding the train, except in the tiniest towns. Large stations have **BIJ-Wasteels** offices, which sell discounted tickets to those under 26. Fast *InterCity* and *EuroCity* trains are more expensive. If a boxed R appears on the timetable, a reservation (*miestenka;* 7Sk) is required; if you board without a reservation, expect to pay a fine. Reservations are also recommended for *expresný* (express) trains and first-class seats, but are not necessary for *rychlík* (fast), *spešný* (semi-fast), or *osobný* (local) trains. First and second class are both relatively comfortable.

BY BUS. In many hilly regions, ČSAD or SAD **buses** are the best—and sometimes only—option. Except for long trips, buy tickets on the bus. Schedule symbols include: **X,** weekdays only; **a,** Saturdays and Sundays only; **r** and **k,** excluding holidays. Numbers refer to the days of the week on which the bus runs—1 is Monday, 2 is Tuesday, and so forth. *"Premava"* means including and *"nepremava"* is except; following those words are often lists of dates (day, then month).

BY BIKE AND BY THUMB. The Slovaks love to ride **bikes**, especially in the Tatras, the western foothills, and Šariš. VKÚ publishes color maps of most regions (70-80Sk). *Let's Go* does not recommend **hitchhiking**, which is legal, but neither convenient nor common; if you hitch, write your destination on a sign.

TOURIST SERVICES AND MONEY

EMERGENCY	Police: ☎ 123. Ambulance: ☎ 233. Fire: ☎ 23.

TOURIST OFFICES. The main tourist offices form a loose conglomeration called **Asociácia Informačných Centier Slovenska (AICS);** look for the green logo. The offices, often with English-speaking staff, are invariably in or near the town's main square; for the nearest location, dial ☎ 186. The **Slovakotourist** travel agency can help arrange transportation and accommodations.

MONEY. One hundred *halér* make up one **Slovak koruna** (Sk). Inflation is currently around 8%. **Banks** are usually the best—and often the only—places to change money. **Všeobecná Úverová Banka (VÚB)**, which has offices in even the smallest towns, cashes American Express Traveler's Cheques for a 1% commission and often gives MasterCard cash advances. Many **Slovenská Sporiteľňa** bureaus handle Visa cash advances. There are 24hr. **ATMs** in all but the smallest towns. The most commonly accepted credit cards are MasterCard and Visa. Tipping is common in restaurants; as there are no exact rules, most people simply round up. Do not try to bargain in the Slovak Republic; it is especially rude when foreigners do so.

BUSINESS HOURS. Many banks close at 3:30pm, while shops are usually open 9am-6pm during the week and 9am-noon on Saturdays. Museums are usually closed on Monday.

SLOVAK KORUNA		
AUS$1 = 24.5SK	10SK = AUS$0.41
CDN$1 = 28.6SK	10SK = CDN$0.35
EUR€1 = 43.6SK	10SK = EUR€0.23
NZ$1 = 20.9SK	10SK = NZ$0.48
ZAR1 = 4.2SK	10SK = ZAR2.37
UK£1 = 68SK	10SK = UK£0.15
US$1 = 44.4SK	10SK = US$0.23

COMMUNICATION

PHONE CODE	Country code: 421. International dialing prefix: 00. From outside the Slovak Republic, dial int'l dialing prefix (see inside back cover) + 421 + city code + local number.

MAIL. The Slovak Republic has an efficient mail service. International mail takes two to three weeks, depending on the destination. Almost every post office *(pošta)* provides **Express Mail Services,** but use a *colnice* (customs office) to send packages abroad. When sending mail *Poste Restante*, put a "1" after the city name to indicate the main post office; address mail to be held: Firstname SURNAME, *Poste Restante*, Nám. SNP 35, 81000 Bratislava 1, SLOVAK REPUBLIC.

TELEPHONE AND INTERNET. Card phones are common and are much better than the coin-operated variety. Purchase cards at kiosks; buy the "GlobalPhone" card to make international calls. International direct access numbers include: **AT&T,** ☎ 00 42 70 01 01; **British Telecom,** ☎ 080 00 44 01; **Canada Direct,** ☎ 08 00 00 01 51; and **MCI,** ☎ 08 00 00 01 12. **Internet** access is common even in small towns; Internet cafes usually offer the cheapest and fastest connections (around 1Sk per min.).

LANGUAGES. Slovak, closely related to Czech, is a complex Slavic language. Attempts to speak it are appreciated. English is often spoken at tourist offices and by Bratislava's youth. Elsewhere, people are more likely to know German. Russian is often understood, but not always welcome.

ACCOMMODATIONS AND CAMPING

SLOVAK REPUBLIC	❶	❷	❸	❹	❺
ACCOMMODATIONS	under 400Sk	400-800Sk	801-1100Sk	1101-1800Sk	over 1800Sk

Foreigners often must pay up to twice as much as Slovaks for the same room. Finding cheap accommodations in Bratislava before the student dorms open in July is impossible, and without reservations, the outlook in Slovenský Raj and the Tatras can be bleak. In other regions, it's not difficult to find a bed as long as you call ahead. A tourist office or Slovakotourist agency can usually help. **Juniorhotels (HI),** though uncommon, are a step above the usual hostel. **Hotels** are rarely full, and prices fall dramatically outside Bratislava and the High Tatras. **Pensions** *(penzióny)* are smaller and less expensive than hotels. **Campgrounds** lurk on the outskirts of most towns, and many offer bungalows. Note that camping in national parks is illegal. In the mountains, **chaty** (mountain huts/cottages) range from a friendly bunk and outhouse for 200Sk per night to plush quarters for 400Sk.

FOOD AND DRINK

SLOVAK REPUBLIC	❶	❷	❸	❹	❺
FOOD	under 70Sk	70-200Sk	201-400Sk	401-700Sk	over 700Sk

The national dish, *bryndžové halušky*, is a plate of dumpling-like pasta smothered in a thick sauce of sheep or goat cheese, often flecked with bacon. *Knedliky* (dumplings) frequently accompany main dishes, but it is possible to opt for *zemiaky* (potatoes) or *hranolky* (fries) instead. Note that a *syrový burger* (cheeseburger) is made of only cheese, and hamburgers are made from ham. *Kolačky* (pastry) is baked with cheese, jam or poppy seeds, and honey. Enjoy flavorful wines at a *vináreň* (wine hall); the western Slovak Republic produces the celebrated full-bodied *Modra*. *Pivo* (beer) is served at a *pivnica* or *piváreň* (tavern). The favorite Slovak beer is *Zlatý Bažant*, a light, slightly bitter Tatran brew.

HEALTH AND SAFETY

Tap water varies in quality and appearance but is generally safe. UK citizens are entitled to free medical care in the Slovak Republic. *Drogerie* (drugstore) stock Western brand names: bandages are *obväz*, aspirin *aspirena*, tampons *tampony*, and condoms *kondómy*. The Slovak Republic is friendly toward **lone women travelers**, though they may encounter stares. **Minority** travelers with darker skin may be mistaken for the stigmatized Roma (Gypsies) and are thus advised to exercise caution. **Homosexuality** is legal, but is not always tolerated.

HOLIDAYS

Holidays: Independence Day (Jan. 1); Epiphany (Jan. 6); Good Friday (Apr. 18); Easter (Apr. 20); Labor Day (May 1); Sts. Cyril and Methodius Day (July 5); Anniversary of Slovak Uprising (Aug. 29); Constitution Day (Sept. 1); Our Lady of the Seven Sorrows (Sept. 15); All Saints' Day (Nov. 1); Christmas (Dec. 24-26).

BRATISLAVA   ☎ 02

Directly between Vienna and Budapest, Bratislava is often treated as a pit stop, but the Slovak capital will surprise those who take the time to discover it. The Old Town is filled with cobblestones, Baroque buildings, and cafes, while the outskirts are laced with vineyards and ruins. Since the split of Czechoslovakia in 1993, Bratislava has been forging ahead in both industry and the arts, and the city's progress shows no signs of stopping.

⌐ TRANSPORTATION

Trains: Bratislava Hlavná stanica (☎ 52 49 82 75). Some trains stop at other stations far from the center; when entering Bratislava by train, get off only at Hlavná stanica. To get downtown, take tram #1 to Poštová, or head straight past the waiting buses, turn right on Šancová, and left on Štefánikova. International tickets at counters #5-13. **Wasteels** (☎ 52 49 93 57; www.wasteels.host.sk) sells discounted tickets to those under 26. Open M-F 8:30am-4:30pm. To: **Berlin** (10hr.; 2 per day; 3136Sk, Wasteels 2470Sk); **Budapest** (2½-3hr.; 7 per day; 499Sk/446Sk); **Kraków** (8hr.; 1 per day; 1460Sk/971Sk); **Prague** (5hr., 7 per day, 415Sk); **Vienna** (1½hr.; 3 per day; 561Sk/490Sk); and **Warsaw** (8hr.; 1 per day; 1707Sk/1121Sk).

Buses: Mlynské nivy 31 (☎ 55 42 16 67). Take trolleybus #202 to the center, or turn right on Mlynské nivy and continue to Dunajská, which leads to Kamenné nám. (2km). To: **Berlin** (12hr., F 9pm, 1800Sk); **Budapest** (4hr., 1 per day, 480Sk); **Prague** (5hr., 7 per day, 320Sk); **Vienna** (1½hr., 7 per day, 350Sk); and **Warsaw** (13hr., F 9:20pm, 670sk). More reliable than trains for domestic transport. Check ticket for bus number *(č. aut.)* since several different buses may depart from the same stand.

Public Transportation: Tickets for daytime **trams** and **buses** (4am-11pm) are sold at kiosks and orange ticket machines in bus stations (12Sk for 10min., 14Sk for 30min., 20Sk for 1hr.). **Night buses**, marked with black and orange numbers in the 500s, require 2 tickets (every 1-2hr., midnight-4am). Stamp your ticket on board or face a 1200Sk fine. **Tourist passes** are sold at some kiosks: 75Sk for 1 day, 140Sk for 2 days, 170Sk for 3 days, 255Sk for 7 days.

Taxis: BP (☎ 169 99); **FunTaxi** (☎ 167 77); **Profi Taxi** (☎ 162 22).

Hitchhiking: Hitching is legal (except on major highways), but not recommended by *Let's Go*. Hitchers to **Vienna** usually cross Most SNP and walk down Viedenská cesta; this road also goes to **Hungary** via Győr, but fewer cars head in that direction. Hitchers to **Prague** take bus #21 to Patronka.

◼◪ ORIENTATION AND PRACTICAL INFORMATION

The **Dunaj** (Danube) runs through the city, which is a stone's throw from the borders of Austria and Hungary. The city center lies between **Námestie Slovenského Národného Povstania** (Nám. SNP; Slovak National Uprising Square) and the river. Suché mýto leads from Nám. SNP to **Kamenné námestie** (Stone Square).

Bratislava

🏠 ACCOMMODATIONS

Hotel Astra, **5**
Pension Gremium, **7**
Ubytovacie Zariadnie Zvárač, **1**

🍴 FOOD

1. Slovak Pub, **2**
Prašná Bašta, **4**
Prešporská Kúria, **6**

🍺 NIGHTLIFE

Dubliner Irish Pub, **8**
Kelt Bar and Grill, **9**
KGB, **3**

Tourist Office: Bratislavská Informačná Služba (BIS), Klobúčnicka 2 (☎161 86; www.bratislava.sk/bis), books rooms (singles 1000-1200Sk) for a 50Sk fee, sells maps (50Sk) and a pass to four major museums (75Sk), and gives tours. From Nám. SNP, take Uršsulínka. Open M-F 8am-7pm, Sa 9am-2pm.

Embassies: Canada (consulate), Mišíkova 28D (☎52 41 21 75; fax 52 41 21 76). Open M-F 8:30am-noon and 1:30-4pm. **Ireland,** Mostová 2 (☎54 43 57 15; fax 54 43 06 90). Open M-F 9am-noon. **South Africa,** Jančova 8 (☎531 15 82; embassy@sae.sk). Open M-F 8:30am-5pm. **UK,** Panská 16 (☎54 41 96 32; bebra@internet.sk). Open M-F 8:30am-12:30pm and 1:30-5pm. **US,** Hviezdoslavovo nám. 4 (☎54 43 08 61; emergency ☎(0903) 70 36 66; www.usis.sk). Open M-F 8am-4:30pm. Citizens of **Australia** and **New Zealand** should contact the UK embassy.

Currency Exchange: VÚB, Gorkého 7 (☎59 55 11 11). 1% commission on traveler's checks. MC/V cash advances. Open M-W and F 8am-5pm, Th 8am-noon. A **24hr. currency exchange** machine is outside Československá Obchodná Banka. There are 24hr. MC/V **ATMs** at the train station and throughout the center.

Emergency: Police: ☎158. **Ambulance:** ☎155. **Fire:** ☎150.

Pharmacy: Lekáreň Pod Manderlom, Nám. SNP 20 (☎54 43 29 52), on the corner of Štúrova and Laurinská. Open M-F 7:30am-7pm, Sa 8am-5pm, Su 9am-5pm. 24hr. emergency service; ring bell after hours.

Internet Access: On-Line Internet Café, Obchodná 2. 1Sk per min. Open M-F 9:30am-midnight, Sa 10am-midnight, Su 10am-11pm. **Internet Centrum,** Michaelská 2. 1Sk per min. Open M-Su 9am-midnight.

Post Office: Nám. SNP 34 (☎49 22 24 13). Open M-F 7am-8pm, Sa 7am-6pm, Su 9am-2pm. *Poste Restante* at counter #5; open M-F 7am-8pm, Sa 7am-2pm. Address mail to be held: Firstname SURNAME, Poste Restante, Nám. SNP 35, **81000** Bratislava 1, SLOVAK REPUBLIC.

ACCOMMODATIONS

Good off-season deals are hard to find. In July and August, several **university dorms** ❶ open as hostels; they are sometimes run-down but are quite cheap (from 150Sk; BIS, above, has a list). Pensions or **private rooms** ❷ (600-2500Sk; see BIS, above) are an inexpensive and comfortable alternative.

Ubytovacie Zariadenie Zvárač, Pionierska 17 (☎49 24 66 00; ubyt@cert.vuz.sk). Take tram #3 from the train station to Pionierska; backtrack and turn right at the intersection. Clean, modest dorm rooms. Check-out 10am. Ring the bell after midnight. Singles 560-750Sk; doubles 640-1000Sk. ❷

Hotel Astra, Prievozská 14/A (☎58 23 81 11, reservations ☎58 23 82 22; www.hotelastra.sk). Take trolley bus #201 from the train station or #202 from the bus station (dir.: Cilizská) to Mileticova. Comfortable, renovated rooms in a traditional communist-style building. Apartments have a kitchen corner and sitting room. Doubles 1000Sk; triples 1200Sk; apartment 2000-2500Sk. ❸

Pension Gremium, Gorkého 11 (☎54 13 10 26; cherrytour@mail.pvt.sk). Just off Hviezdoslavovo nám. Sparkling private showers. English-speaking reception. Check-out noon. Only 5 rooms, so call well in advance. Single 890Sk; doubles 1290-1590Sk. ❸

FOOD

The grocery store **Tesco Potraviny** is at Kamenné nám. 1. (Open M-F 8am-9pm, Sa 8am-7pm, Su 9am-7pm.) The square in front of Tesco is full of fast food stalls.

1. Slovak Pub, Obchodná 62. A well-priced selection of traditional soups (28Sk) and meals (50-120Sk). Open M-Th 10am-midnight, F-Sa 10am-2am, Su noon-midnight. ❷

Prešporská Kúria, Dunajská 21, has a bistro, cafeteria, and restaurant all in a small park close to Kamenné nám. Tasty pizzas 60-100Sk, cafeteria menu 50-100Sk. Bistro open M-F 8am-5pm, cafeteria and restaurant noon-9pm. ❶

Prašná Bašta, Zámočnícka 11. A largely 20-something crowd dines on the leafy terrace in the Old Town. Main dishes 100-185Sk. Open daily 11am-11pm. ❷

SIGHTS

NÁMESTIE SNP AND ENVIRONS. With the exception of Devín Castle, most of the city's major attractions are in **Old Bratislava** (Stará Bratislava). From Nám. SNP, which commemorates the bloody 1944 Slovak National Uprising against fascism, walk down Uršulínska to reach the Baroque **Primate's Palace** (Primaciálny Palác). Napoleon and Austrian Emperor Franz I signed the Peace of Pressburg in the palace's **Hall of Mirrors** (Zrkadlová Sieň) in 1805. *(Primaciálné nám. 1. Open Tu-Su 10am-5pm. 30Sk, students free.)* Turn left down Kostolná as you exit the palace to reach **Hlavné námestie.** On your left as you enter the square is the **Town History Museum** (Muzeum Histórie Mesta) which has an impressive

1:500 scale model of the Bratislava of 1945-1955. *(Open Tu-F 10am-5pm, Sa-Su 11am-6pm. 30Sk, students 10Sk.)* Continue to the opposite end of the square and take a left onto Rybárska Brana to **Hviezdoslavovo námestie,** where the gorgeous 1886 **Slovak National Theatre** (Slovenské Národné Divadlo) is located. *(See Entertainment, below.)* Go through the square and take Mostová; turn left at the Danube to reach the **Slovak National Gallery,** which displays artwork from the Gothic and Baroque periods as well as some modern sculptures. *(Rázusovo nábr. 2. www.sng.sk. Open Tu-Su 10am-6pm. 25Sk, students 20Sk.)* With the Danube on your left, continue to the gaudy neon-lit **Nový Most** (New Bridge), designed by the Communist government in the 1970s. Backtrack from the bridge and turn left on Rigoleho, continue straight onto Strakova (which becomes Ventúrska, then Michalská), and pass through **St. Michael's Tower** (Michalská Brána), Bratislava's last remaining medieval gateway. Keep going as Michalská becomes Županénám and take a left onto Kapucínska; take the pedestrian bridge over the highway to reach the **Museum of Jewish Culture** (Múzeum Zidovskej Kultúry). *(Židovská 17. Open Su-F 11am-5pm. 60Sk, students 40Sk.)*

CASTLES. Visible from much of the city, the four-towered **Bratislava Castle** (Bratislavský hrad) is the city's defining landmark. The castle burned in 1811 and was bombed during World War II; what's left today is a communist-era restoration. Its towers provide fantastic views of the Danube. To reach the castle, start beneath Nový Most and climb the stairs to Židovská; turn right on Zámocké schody and head uphill. The ruins of **Devín Castle** sit above the Danube and Morava Rivers, a stone's throw from Austria. Take bus #29 from below Nový Most to the last stop, 9km west of Bratislava. Originally a Celtic fortification, the castle was held by the Romans, Slavs, and Hungarians before it was destroyed by Napoleon's armies in 1809. A museum highlights the castle's history. *(Museum open July-Aug. Tu-F 10am-5pm, Sa-Su 10am-6pm; May-Oct. Tu-Su 10am-5pm. 40Sk, students 10Sk.)*

🎵 🍷 ENTERTAINMENT AND NIGHTLIFE

The regular theater season is September through June. BIS (see Tourist Office, p. 868) has the monthly *Kam v Bratislave,* which provides film, concert, and theater schedules (http://media.gratex.sk/kam/kamvba.htm). The ballets and operas at the **Slovak National Theatre,** Hviezdoslavovo nám. 1, draw crowds from neighboring Austria. (☎54 43 30 83; www.snd.sk. Open Sept.-June M-F 8am-5:30pm, Sa 9am-1pm. 100-200Sk.) The **Slovak Philharmonic** (Slovenská Filharmónia) plays regularly at Medená 3; the box office is around the corner at Palackého 2. (☎54 43 33 51; www.filharm.sk. Open Sept.-June M-Tu and Th-F 1-7pm, W 8am-2pm. 100-200Sk.)

By day, **Hlavné námestie** features souvenir stands and free outdoor concerts; by night, it fills with strolling couples and local teens warming up for an evening out. A small circular sign with a beer mug is all that marks **Krcma Gurmanov Bratislavy (KGB),** Obchodna 52, one of Bratislava's most popular pubs. It's no accident that the initials spell KGB—the decorations bring back the memories of years under communist rule. (Meals 25-125Sk; drinks 20-100Sk; beer 15-50Sk. Open M-Th 11am-1:30am, F 11am-3:30am, Sa 3:30pm-1:30am, Su 3:30-11pm.) A lively mix of tourists and locals fill **Kelt Bar and Grill,** Hviezdoslavovo nám. 26. (Drinks 50-100Sk; meals 50-150Sk. Open daily 11am-1am.) **Dubliner,** Sedlárska 6, mixes the best drinks in Bratislava. (Cocktails 120Sk; Guinness 45-85Sk; meals 50-225Sk. Open M-Sa 9am-1am, Su 11am-midnight.)

THE TATRA MOUNTAINS (TATRY)

The mesmerizing High Tatras, which span the border between the Slovak Republic and Poland, offer hundreds of hiking and skiing trails along the Carpathians' highest peaks (2650m). One of the most compact ranges in the world, the High Tatras feature sky-scraping hikes, glacial lakes, and deep snows. Cheap mountain railways and accommodations add to the allure for the budget hiker.

 The Tatras are a great place to hike, but many of the hikes are extremely demanding and require experience, even in summer. In winter, a guide is almost always necessary. For current conditions, check **www.tanap.sk.**

STARÝ SMOKOVEC. Spectacular trails run from Starý Smokovec, the High Tatras' most central resort. To reach **Hrebienok** (1285m), which leads to hiking country, ride the funicular (every 30-40min. 6:35am-7:45pm; round-trip 160Sk). Or, from the funicular station behind the train station, hike 35min. up the green trail. The green trail continues 20min. north from Hrebienok to the foaming **Cold Stream Waterfalls** (Volopáday studeného potoka). From the falls, take the red trail, which connects with the eastward blue trail to **Tatranská Lomnica** (1¾hr.). The hike to **Little Cold Valley** (Malá studená dolina) is also fairly relaxed; take the red trail (40min.) from Hrebicnok to **Zamkovského chata** (hut) ❶ (☎442 26 36; rooms 290Sk per person) and onto the green trail (2hr.) which climbs above the tree-line to a high lake and **Téryho chata** ❶ (☎442 52 45; rooms 280Sk per person).

TEŽ trains arrive from Poprad (30min., every hr., 16Sk). **Buses** to many Tatran resorts stop in a parking lot to the right of the train station. Head uphill on the road that runs just left of the train station, then veer left across the main road. The **Tatranská Informačná Kancelária**, in Dom Služieb, has weather information and sells hiking maps, including the essential **VKÚ sheet #113.** (Open July-Aug. M-F 8am-5:30pm, Sa-Su 8am-1pm; Sept.-June M-F 9am-4:30pm, Sa 8am-1pm.) Most budget accommodations are down the road in **Horný Smokovec.** From the station, turn right on the main road and walk 5min. to **Hotel Šport** ❷, which has a cafe, sauna, pool, and massage parlor. (☎442 23 61; fax 442 27 19. Reserve ahead. Singles 420Sk; doubles 705Sk; Sept.-June 295Sk/515Sk.) ☎**052.**

ŠTRBSKÉ PLESO. The 1975 "Interski" Championship was held at placid Štrbské Pleso (Štrbské Lake). Many beautiful **hikes** begin from the town, but just one lift runs in summer, hoisting visitors to **Chata pod Soliskom** (1840m), which overlooks the lake and the valleys behind Štrbské Pleso. (June 25-Sept. 9 8:30am-4pm; July-Aug. 115Sk, round-trip 180Sk; June and Sept. 80Sk/100Sk.) The challenging but rewarding yellow route heads from the east side of the lake (follow the signs to Hotel Patria) out along **Mlynická dolina** to mountain lakes and **Vodopády Skok** (Waterfalls). It then crosses **Bystré Sedlo** (Saddle; 2314m) and circles **Štrbské Solisko** (2302m) before returning to Štrbské Pleso (8-9hr.). **TEŽ trains** arrive from Starý Smokovec (30min., every 30min., 20Sk).

LIPTOVSKÝ MIKULÁŠ. Liptovský Mikuláš is a good springboard for hiking in the **Low Tatras** (Nízke Tatry). To scale **Mt. Ďumbier**, the region's tallest peak (2043m), catch an early bus from platform #11 at the bus station to Liptovský Ján (25min., every hr., 13Sk), then follow the blue trail up the Štiavnica River to the **Svidovské Sedlo** (5hr.). Next, bear left on the red trail to the ridge, which leads to the summit (45min.). Descend the ridge and follow the red sign to neighboring peak **Chopok** (2024m), the second-highest in the range. From Chopok, it's a winding walk down the blue trail to the **bus** stop behind the Hotel Grand at Otupné (1¾hr.). **Trains** from

Bratislava to Liptovský Mikuláš (4hr., 9 per day, 280Sk) are cheaper and more frequent than buses. Get to the town center by following Štefánikova toward the gas station at the far end of the lot, then turn right onto Hodžu. The **tourist office**, Nám. Mieru 1, in the Dom Služieb complex on the north side of town, books private rooms (180-400Sk) and sells dozens of hiking maps. (☎551 61 86; www.lmikulas.sk. Open June 15-Sept. 15 and Dec. 15-Mar. 31 M-F 8am-7pm, Sa 8am-2pm, Su noon-6pm; off-season reduced hours.) **Kriváň ❷**, Štúrova 5, is across from the tourist office. (☎552 24 14. Singles 480Sk; doubles 750Sk.) ☎**044.**

SLOVENSKÝ RAJ. Southeast of the Nizke Tatry is the less-touristed Slovenský Raj (Slovak Paradise) National Park, filled with forested hills, deep ravines, and fast-flowing streams. Get a copy of **VKÚ sheet #4** (85-140Sk) before entering the region. The **Dobšinská Ice Caves** (Dobšinská ľadová jaskyňa) form a 23km stretch of ice composed of 110,000 cubic meters of water still frozen from the last Ice Age. The 30min. tour covers 475m of the cave, passing hall after hall of frozen columns, gigantic ice wells, and hardened waterfalls. To get there from **Dedinky** (pop. 400), the largest town on Slovenský Raj's southern border, take the **train** for two stops (15min., 12:30 and 2:30pm, 11Sk). The road from the caves' train station leads 100m out to the main road. Turn left, and the cave parking lot is 250m ahead. From there, the blue trail (20min.) leads up a steep incline to the caves. (www.ssj.sk. Open July-Aug. Tu-Su 9am-4pm; mid-May to June and Sept. Tu-Su 9am-2pm. English tours 110Sk, students 90Sk. 20-person min.)

The **bus** to Poprad (dir.: Rožňava; 1hr., 6 per day, 37Sk) stops at a junction 2km south of Dedinky. Watch for the huge blue road signs at the intersection, just before the bus stop. From the intersection, walk down the road that the bus did *not* take, turn right at the next intersection, cross the dam after the train station, turn left, and walk 10min. to Dedinky. *Privat, ubytowanie,* or *zimmer* signs indicate **private rooms** (150-300Sk). **Hotel Priehrada ❶** rents tidy rooms. (☎798 12 12. 250Sk per person, with bath 300Sk. **Camping** 30Sk per person. Tents 30Sk.) ☎**053.**

SLOVENIA
(SLOVENIJA)

Slovenia, the most prosperous of Yugoslavia's breakaway republics, revels in its newfound independence and has quickly separated itself from its neighbors. With a hungry eye turned toward the West, Slovenia is now using liberal politics and a high GDP to gain entrance into coveted alliances like the EU and NATO. Fortunately, modernization has not adversely affected the tiny country's natural beauty and diversity: you can still have breakfast on an Alpine peak, lunch under the Mediterranean sun, and dine in a Pannonian vineyard, all in one day.

FACTS AND FIGURES

Official Name: Republic of Slovenia.
Capital: Ljubljana.
Population: 2,000,000.
Land Area: 20,253 sq. km.

Time Zone: GMT +1.
Language: Slovenian.
Religions: Roman Catholic (69%), atheist (4%), other (27%).

DISCOVER SLOVENIA

Any visit should start in youthful **Ljubljana** (p. 876), which has the majesty of the Habsburg cities and a cafe scene on par with Paris or Vienna. **Lake Bled** (p. 879) and **Lake Bohinj** (p. 879) in the Julian Alps are traversed by miles of hikes that range from casual to treacherous. In winter, the Alps allow for very snowy, steep, and relatively cheap skiing.

ESSENTIALS

WHEN TO GO

April through October is warm and dry—great beach weather—but tourists flood in from July to August, so earlier or later is the best time to visit. In the mountains, it can be chilly even in summer. Winters are cold and snowy, perfect for skiing.

DOCUMENTS AND FORMALITIES

VISAS. Australian, Canadian, Irish, New Zealand, UK, and US citizens can visit without visas for up to 90 days. South Africans need visas (3-month single-entry or 5-day transit €26; 3-month multiple-entry €52). Apply in your home country.

EMBASSIES. Foreign embassies are in Ljubljana (p. 876). Slovenian embassies at home include: **Australia,** Level 6, Advance Bank Center, 60 Marcus Clarke St. 2608, Canberra ACT 2601 (☎06 243 4830; http://slovenia.webone.com.au); **Canada,** 150 Metcalfe St., #2101, Ottawa, ON K2P 1P1 (☎613-565-5781; fax 613-565-5783); **New Zealand,** Eastern Hutt Rd., Pomare, Lower Hutt, Wellington (☎04 567 0027; fax 04 567 0024); **UK,** Cavendish Ct. 11-15, Wigmore St., London W1V 1AN (☎171 495 7775; fax 171 495 7776; www.embassy-slovenia.org.uk); **US,** 1525 New Hampshire Ave. NW, Washington, D.C. 20036 (☎202-667-5363; www.embassy.org/slovenia).

TRANSPORTATION

BY PLANE. Commercial flights arrive at the Ljubljana Airport (LJU). **British Airways** flies direct to Slovenia, and other major lines offer connections to Slovenia's national carrier, **Adria Airways** (☎ (386) 14 31 81 55; www.adria.si). Flying to Vienna and taking the train to Ljubljana is cheaper but more time-consuming.

BY TRAIN. Trains are cheap, clean, and reliable. First and second classes do not differ much; save your money and opt for the latter. For most international destinations, travelers under 26 can get a 20% discount; check at the Ljubljana station (look for the BIJ-Wasteels logo). Domestic tickets are 30% off for ISIC holders—ask for a *"popust"* (discount). *"Vlak"* means train, *"prihodi vlakov"* means arrivals, and *"odhodi vlakov"* means departures. Schedules usually list trains by direction; look for those that run *dnevno* (daily).

BY BUS. Slovenia's bus network is extensive. Though usually more expensive than trains, buses are often the only option in mountainous regions. Tickets are sold at the station or on board. Put your luggage in the passenger compartment if it's not too crowded; all large backpacks cost 220Sit extra.

BY BOAT, CAR, BIKE, OR THUMB. In the summer, a regular **hydrofoil** runs between Venice and Portorož. When not traveling by bus or train, most Slovenes transport themselves by **bike;** most towns have a rental office. For those traveling by car, the emergency number for the **Automobile Association of Slovenia** is ☎987. *Let's Go* does not recommend hitchhiking, which is uncommon in Slovenia.

TOURIST SERVICES AND MONEY

EMERGENCY	Police and Fire: ☎ 112. Ambulance: ☎ 113.

TOURIST OFFICES. The main tourist organization is **Kompas.** Tourist offices, which can usually help with accommodations, are located in most major cities and tourist spots. Staffs generally speak English, German, or, on the coast, Italian.

MONEY. The national currency is the **Slovenian tolar** (Sit). Inflation is currently around 6%, so expect some changes in prices. Rates vary, but tend to be better at **exchange offices;** post offices have the worst rates. **ATMs** are common. Major credit cards are not accepted consistently, but American Express Traveler's Cheques and Eurocheques often are. Tipping is not expected, but rounding up is appreciated; 10% is sufficient for good service. Bargaining is often considered offensive.

BUSINESS HOURS. Hours are generally Monday to Friday 8am-5pm and Saturday 8am-noon.

TOLARS		
	AUS$1 = 127SIT	100SIT = AUS$0.79
	CDN$1 = 148SIT	100SIT = CDN$0.68
	EUR€ = 226SIT	100SIT = EUR€0.44
	NZ$1 = 108SIT	100SIT = NZ$0.92
	ZAR1 = 22SIT	100SIT = ZAR4.48
	UK£1 = 352SIT	100SIT = UK£0.28
	US$1 = 230SIT	100SIT = US$0.44

COMMUNICATION

PHONE CODES	**Country code: 386. International dialing prefix: 00.** From outside Slovenia, dial int'l dialing prefix (see inside back cover) + 386 + city code + local number.

MAIL. Airmail (ask for *letalsko*) takes 1-2 weeks to reach North America, Australia, New Zealand, and South Africa. To the US, letters cost 105Sit and postcards cost 95Sit; to the UK, 100Sit/90Sit; to Australia and New Zealand, 110Sit/100Sit. For *Poste Restante*, address mail to be held: Firstname SURNAME, *Poste Restante*, Slovenska 32, 1000 Ljubljana, SLOVENIA.

TELEPHONES AND INTERNET. Slovenia is **changing** all of its numbers. Correct numbers may differ from those at the time of publication; however, changed numbers should direct you to the new number in English and Slovenian. All phones now take **phone cards,** which are sold at post offices, kiosks, and gas stations (750Sit per 50 impulses; 1 impulse yields 1½min. to the US). Most international telecommunications companies do not have international direct dialing numbers in Slovenia. Dial ☎ 115 for **collect calls** assisted by an English-speaking operator. Calling the US costs over US$6 per minute. If you must, try the phones at the post office and pay when you're finished. **Internet access** is very common throughout the country; rates are around 800-1200Sit per hr.

LANGUAGES. Slovene is a Slavic language using the Latin alphabet. Most young people speak some English, but the older generation (especially in the Alps) is more likely to understand German (in the north) or Italian (along the Adriatic). Serbian and Croatian are also commonly spoken.

ACCOMMODATIONS AND CAMPING

SLOVENIA	❶	❷	❸	❹	❺
ACCOMMODATIONS	under 1000Sit	1000-3500Sit	3500-5000Sit	5000-6000Sit	over 6000Sit

Pensions, the most common form of lodgings, usually have private singles as well as inexpensive triples and dorms. Youth **hostels** and student dormitories are cheap (2500-3000Sit), but generally open only in summer (June 25-Aug. 30). While hostels are often the cheapest and most fun option, **private rooms** are the only budget lodgings on the coast and at Lake Bohinj; inquire at the tourist office or look for *Zimmer frei* or *Sobe* signs. Prices vary according to location, but rarely exceed €30, and most rooms are very comfortable. **Campgrounds** can be crowded but are in excellent condition. Camp only in designated areas in order to avoid fines.

FOOD AND DRINK

SLOVENIA	❶	❷	❸	❹	❺
FOOD	under 400Sit	400-800Sit	800-1200Sit	1200-1600Sit	over 1600Sit

For homestyle cooking, try a *gostilna* or *gostisče* (both refer to a restaurant with a country flavor). Meals start with *jota*, a soup with potatoes, beans, and sauerkraut. *Svinjska pečenka* (roast pork) is tasty, but vegetarians should look for *štruklji*—large, slightly sweet dumplings. Pizzerias usually have meatless dishes. A favorite dessert is *potica*, a pastry with a rich filling (usually walnut). The country's wine-making tradition dates from antiquity. *Renski Rizling* and *Šipon* are popular whites, while *Cviček* and *Teran* are well-known reds. Good beers include *Lasko* and *Union*. For something stronger, try the fruit brandy *žganje*. The most enchanting alcoholic concoction is *Viljamovka*, distilled by monks who manage to fit a full pear inside the bottle.

HEALTH AND SAFETY

Tap water is safe to drink everywhere. **Medical facilities** are of high quality, and most have English-speaking doctors. UK citizens receive free medical care with a valid passport; other foreigners must pay cash. **Pharmacies** are also stocked to Western standards; ask for *obliž* (band-aids), *tamponi* (tampons), and *vložki* (sanitary pads). **Crime** is rare, and even in the largest cities, overly friendly drunks and bad drivers are the greatest public menace. There are few **minorities** in Slovenia; while incidents of discrimination are uncommon, minority travelers may encounter curious stares, especially in rural areas. **Homosexuality** is legal, but may elicit unsure or unfriendly reactions from the middle-aged and elderly or outside of urban areas.

HOLIDAYS AND FESTIVALS

Holidays: New Year's (Jan. 1-2); Culture Day (Prešeren Day; Feb. 8); Easter (Apr. 20-21); National Resistance Day (Apr. 27); Labor Day (May 1-2); Pentecost (June 8); National Day (June 25); Assumption (Aug. 15); Reformation Day (Oct. 31); Remembrance Day (Nov. 1); Christmas (Dec. 25); Independence Day (Dec. 26).

Festivals: The **International Summer Festival** (July-Sept.) in Ljubljana is an extravaganza of opera, theater, and classical music.

LJUBLJANA
☎061

Modern Ljubljana is reminiscent of 1920s Paris or 1990s Prague—hip in a way that doesn't focus on transient trends. Ljubljana is small yet cosmopolitan, easy to reach but free of tourists, and charming but not kitschy. Laid-back cafes, bars, and clubs line the Ljubljanica River. Near Ljubljana, the Škocjanske caves offer a glimpse of unspoiled natural beauty.

▊ TRANSPORTATION

Trains: Trg O.F. 6 (☎291 33 32). To: **Budapest** (9hr., 2 per day, 10,000Sit); **Trieste** (3hr., 2-3 per day, 4400Sit); **Venice** (6hr., 3 per day, 7027Sit); **Vienna** (5-6hr., 2 per day, 11,600Sit); and **Zagreb** (2hr., 5 per day, 2452Sit).

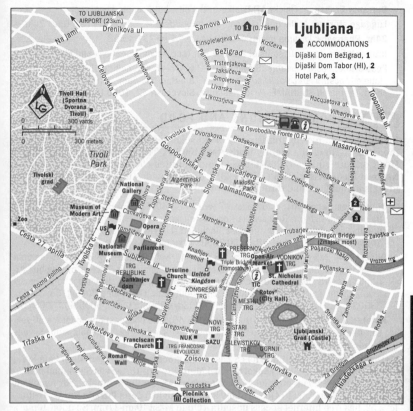

Ljubljana

🏠 ACCOMMODATIONS
Dijaški Dom Bežigrad, 1
Dijaški Dom Tabor (HI), 2
Hotel Park, 3

Buses: Trg O.F. 4 (☎ 090 42 30), by the train station. **Zagreb** (3hr., 2 per day, 2970Sit).

Public Transportation: Buses run until midnight. Drop 230Sit in change in the box beside the driver or buy 170Sit tokens *(žetoni)* at post offices and kiosks. Daily passes (660Sit) sold at **Ljubljanski potniški promet,** Trdinova 3 and Celovška 160.

🗺️🛈 ORIENTATION AND PRACTICAL INFORMATION

Train and **bus stations** are on **Trg Osvobodilne Fronte** (Trg O.F. or O.F. Square). Turn right as you exit the train station, then left on **Miklošiceva cesta** and follow it to **Prešernov Trg,** the main square. Cross the **Tromostovje** (Triple Bridge) over the **Ljubljanica River** to **Stare Miasto** (Old Town) at the base of the castle hill.

Tourist Office: Tourist Info Center (TIC), Stritarjeva 1, on the left at the corner of Stritarjeva and Adamič-Lundrovo nabr. English brochures and free maps. (☎306 12 15; tic@ljubljana-tourism.si; www.ljubljana.si. Open M-F 8am-8pm, Sa-Su 10am-6pm; Oct.-May M-F 8am-6pm, Sa-Su 10am-6pm. Also see www.ljubljanalife.com.)

Embassies and Consulates: Australia, Trg Republike 3 (☎425 42 52). Open M-F 9am-1pm. **Canada,** Miklošičeva 19 (☎430 35 70; fax 430 35 77). Open M-F 9am-1pm. **UK,** Trg Republike 3 (☎200 39 10; fax 425 01 74). Open M-F 9am-noon. **US,** Prešernova cesta (☎200 55 00; fax 200 55 55). Open M-F 8am-5pm.

Currency Exchange: Finicky **ATMs** all over the city, but accepted cards vary.

Luggage storage: At the train station; look for *garderoba*. 400Sit per day. Open 24hr.

24hr. Pharmacy: Lekarna miklošič, Miklošičeva 24 (☎231 45 58).

Internet: Free access upstairs of **Pizzeria Bar** (see Accommodations and Food, below).

Post Office: *Poste Restante*, Slovenska 32 (☎426 46 68) held for 1 month at counter labeled *"poštno ležeče pošiljke."* Open M-F 7am-8pm, Sa 7am-1pm. Address mail to be held: Firstname SURNAME, *Poste Restante*, Slovenska 32, **1000** Ljubljana, SLOVENIA.

▌◖ ACCOMMODATIONS AND FOOD

Ljubljana is not heavily touristed by backpackers, so it lacks true budget accommodations. There is a nightly **tourist tax** (160Sit). The tourist office (see above) finds private singles (3000-4500Sit) and doubles (5000-7500Sit). The **Slovene National Hostel Association** (PZS; ☎231 21 56) provides information about youth hostels in Ljubljana and throughout Slovenia.

> **Dijaški Dom Tabor (HI),** Vidovdanska 7 (☎234 88 40; fax 234 88 55). Go left from the train station, right on Resljeva, left on Komenskega, and left on Vidovdanska. Clean; popular with backpackers. Breakfast included. Luggage storage. Free Internet 6am-10pm. Open June 25-Aug. 28. 3200-3850Sit per person with student ID. ❷

> **Dijaški Dom Bežigrad,** Kardeljeva pl. 28 (☎534 28 67; fax 534 28 64). From the train station, cross the street and turn right; at the intersection with Slovenska, take bus #6 (Črnuče) or #8 (Ježica) and get off at Stadion (5min.), then walk 1 block to the crossroads. Clean, comfortable. Negotiable check-out 8am. Open June 20-Aug. 25. Singles 3300Sit, with shower 3800Sit; doubles 4400Sit/6600Sit; triples 6600Sit/7800Sit. ❷

> **Hotel Park,** Tabor 6 (☎433 13 06; fax 433 05 46). The cheapest option for the off-season backpacker, aside from private rooms. Clean, with knowledgeable staff. Singles 5254-9354Sit; doubles 7908-1170Sit. Students 10% discount. ❹

Maximarket on Trg Republike has a basement **grocery store.** (Open M-Th 9am-8pm, F 9am-10pm, Sa 8am-3pm.) **Sokol ❸,** Ciril Metodov Trg 18, serves Slovenian delicacies. (Open M-Sa 9am-midnight.) Visit **Samsara ❶,** Petkovško nabr., for excellent ice cream. (Open Apr. 15-Oct. 10 daily 9am-midnight.) **Cerin Pizzeria Bar ❷,** Trubarjeva 52, has free Internet access upstairs. (Open M-Sa 10am-11pm, Su noon-10pm.)

◉ ♫ SIGHTS AND ENTERTAINMENT

A good way to see the city is to meet in front of the *rotovž* (city hall), Mestni Trg 1, for the two-hour **walking tour** in English and Slovene. (June-Sept. daily 5pm; July-Aug. also Su 11am. 1200Sit, students 600Sit.) A short walk from the *rotovž* down Stritarjeva across **Tromostovje** (Triple Bridge), which majestically guards Stare Miasto, leads to the main square, **Prešernov Trg,** with its pink 17th-century **Franciscan Church** (Frančiškanska cerkev). Cross the bridge back to Stare Miasto and take a left; continue along the river, you'll see a big **outdoor fruit market** on the right (Open June-Aug. M-Sa 9am-6pm; Sept.-May M-Sa 9am-4pm) and Vodnikov Trg, where **Zmajski most** (Dragon Bridge) stretches back across the Ljubljanica. On the far side of Vodnikov Trg, the narrow path Studentovska leads uphill to **Ljubljana Castle** (Ljubljanski Grad), from which the view of Ljubljana is breathtaking. (Open 10am-dark; Oct.-May 10am-5pm. 700Sit, students 400Sit.) Cross the Dragon Bridge back to Resljeve cesta, turn left on Tubarjea cesta, continue to Prešernov trg, take a left onto Wolfova (which becomes Gosposka), then take a right onto Zoisova cesta and a left onto Emonska ul. Across a bridge is the **Plečnik Collection** (Plečnikova zbrika), Karunova 4, which shows the works of Ljubljana's most famous architect. (Open Tu and Th 10am-2pm. 600Sit, students 300Sit.) Walking back from the museum, take a left onto Zoistova and a right onto Slovenska. After the Ursuline

Church, take a left to find **Trg Republike,** home to the national Parliament, the large Maximarket, and *Cankarjev Dom,* the city's cultural center.

The **Ljubljana International Summer Festival** (June 14-Sept. 13) has musical, operatic, and theatrical performances. The cafe/bar **Kavarna Macek,** Krojaska 5, is the epicenter of the city's student nightlife. (Open Th-Sa 9am-12:30am; Happy Hour 4pm-7pm.) Popular **Oz,** Smartinska 152, a trendy disco and bar for those over 23, offers a varied music selection. (Open M-Tu 6pm-1am, W-Su 6pm-5am.)

◪ DAYTRIP FROM LJUBLJANA: ŠKOCJANSKE CAVES

Škocjanske is an amazing system of UNESCO-protected ◪**caverns** with limestone formations and a 120m gorge created by the Reca River. Be prepared; this physically demanding trip is for the truly adventurous. (☎ (057) 63 28 40; www.gov.si/parkskj. Tours June-Sept. daily 10am-5pm every hr.; Oct.-May 10am, 1, and 3pm. 1500Sit, students 700Sit.) **Trains** run from Ljubljana to Divača (1½hr., 10 per day, 1370Sit). Follow signs out of town to the ticket booth (40min.).

BLED   ☎ 04

Alpine hills, snow-covered peaks, a turquoise lake, and a stately castle make Bled one of Slovenia's most striking destinations. The **Church of the Assumption** (Cerkev Marijinega Vnebovzetja) stands on the **island** in the center of the lake. To get there, you can rent a boat (1700-2000Sit per hr.), hop on a gondola (round-trip 1800Sit), or even swim. High above the water perches the picture-perfect 16th-century **Bled Castle** (Blejski grad), which houses a museum detailing the history of the Bled region. (Open daily 8am-8pm. 700Sit, students 600Sit.) ◪**Blejski Vintgar,** a 1.6km gorge traced by the waterfalls and rapids of the Radovna River, carves through the rocks of the **Triglav National Park** (Triglavski Narodni). To see the 16m **Šum Waterfall,** go over the hill on Grajska cesta and turn right at the bottom. After 100m, turn left and follow the signs for Vintgar.

Trains (☎ 574 11 13) from Ljubljana arrive at the Lesce-Bled station, about 4km from Bled (1hr., 11 per day, 900 Sit). Frequent **local buses** (10min., 280Sit) shuttle to **Ljubljanska** (the main street) and then the bus station (☎ 574 11 14), cesta Svobode 4, which is closer to the hostel and castle. **Intercity buses** run directly from Ljubljana (1½hr., 1 per hr., 1200Sit). The **tourist office,** cesta Svobode 15, sells maps (1400Sit) of Bled and the local trails. (☎ 574 11 22. Open in summer daily 8am-8pm; winter M-Sa 8am-7pm, Su and holidays 11am-5pm.) To find **private rooms,** look for *Sobe* signs on Prešernova cesta and Ljubljanska. ◪**Bledec Youth Hostel (HI) ❸,** Grajska cesta 17, was just renovated. From the bus station, turn left and follow the street to the top, bearing left at the fork. (☎ 574 52 50. Reserve ahead July-Aug. Reception 24hr. HI 3750Sit; nonmembers add 1000Sit.) To get to **Camping Bled ❷,** Kidričeva 10c, from the bus station, walk downhill on cesta Svobode, then turn left and walk along the lake for 25min. (☎ 575 20 00; campingbled@s5.net. Reception 24hr. Open Apr.-Oct. 1100-1725Sit.) A **Mercator supermarket** is in the complex at Ljubljanska cesta 13. (Open M-Sa 7am-7pm, Su 8am-noon.) **Postal code:** 4260.

LAKE BOHINJ (BOHINJSKO JEZERO)   ☎ 04

Although only 30km southwest of Bled, Bohinjsko Jezero (BOH-heen-sko YEH-zeh-roh) feels worlds away. The three farming villages that border the lake, Ribčev Laz, Stara Fužina, and Ukranc, retain a traditional Slovene atmosphere. Surrounded by **Triglav National Park,** the glacial lake is Slovenia's center for alpine tourism. Hikes from the lake's shores range from casual to nearly impossible. Trails are marked with a white circle inside a red circle; look for the blaze on trees and rocks. Maps are available at the tourist office (see below). The most popular and accessible destination is **Savica Waterfall** (Slap Savica). Take a bus from Ribčev Laz to Bohinj-Zlatorog, get off at Hotel Zlatorog, and follow signs uphill (1hr. to trailhead at Koča pri Savici, then 20min. to waterfall).

S
L
O
V
E
N
I
A

The nearest town is **Bohinjska Bistrica,** 6km to the east. **Trains** from Ljubljana (2½hr., 8 per day, 1360Sit) pass through Jesenice. **Buses** from Ljubljana (2hr., every hr., 1620Sit) pass through Bled (35min., 680Sit) and Bohinjska Bistrica (10min., 300Sit) on their way to the lake; they stop at Hotel Jezero in Ribčev Laz or at Hotel Zlatorog in Ukanc, on the other side of the lake. The **tourist office,** Ribčev Laz 48, sells maps, arranges accommodations, and plans guided excursions. (☎572 33 70; tdbohinj@bohinj.si. Open July-Aug. daily 8am-8pm; Sept.-June M-Sa 8am-6pm, Su 9am-3pm.) To reach **AvtoCamp Zlatorog ❷,** Ukanc 2, take the bus to Hotel Zlatorog and backtrack a bit. (☎572 34 82. July-Aug. 1900Sit; May-June and Sept. 1300Sit. Tourist tax 154Sit per night.) The restaurant ◪**Gostišče Kramar ❸,** Stara Fužina 3, offers outstanding views of the lake. (Main dishes 900-1500Sit. Open M-F noon-8pm, Sa-Su 11am-9pm.) A **Mercator supermarket** is next to the tourist office. (Open M-F 7am-8pm, Sa 7am-5pm.) **Postal code:** 4265.

SPAIN (ESPAÑA)

Fiery flamenco dancers, noble bullfighters, and a rich history blending Christian and Islamic culture set Spain apart from the rest of Europe and draw almost 50 million tourists each year. The raging nightlife of Madrid, Barcelona, and the Balearic Islands has inspired the popular saying "Spain never sleeps," yet the afternoon siestas of Andalucía exemplify the country's laid-back, easy-going approach to life. Spain houses stunning Baroque, Mudejar, and Mozarabic cathedrals and palaces; hangs the works of Velasquez, Dali, and Picasso on its hallowed walls; and offers up a backyard of beauty with long sunny coastlines, snowy mountain peaks, and the dry, golden plains wandered by Don Quixote. You can do Spain in one week, one month, or one year. But you must do it at least once.

DISCOVER SPAIN

Begin in **Madrid** (p. 886), enjoying its unique blend of art, architecture, and cosmopolitan life; after days of soaking up art and nights of the dancing 'til dawn, take your bleary-eyed self to the austere palace of **El Escorial** (p. 898) and the

Spain

FACTS AND FIGURES

Official Name: Kingdom of Spain.

Capital: Madrid.

Major Cities: Barcelona, Valencia, Sevilla, Granada, and Madrid.

Population: 40 million.

Land Area: 499,542 sq. km.

Time Zone: 1hr. ahead of GMT.

Language: Spanish (Castilian); Catalan, Valencian, Basque, Galician dialects.

Religions: Roman Catholic (though it's no longer the official religion).

twisting streets of **Toledo** (p. 899), once home to El Greco. Head into the Don Quixote territory of central Spain, to the famed university town of **Salamanca** (p. 902), then to the heart of bullfights and flamenco in **Seville** (p. 910). Visit the stunning mosque in **Córdoba** (p. 906) and the world-famous Alhambra in **Granada** (p. 919). The ethereal beaches of the **Costa del Sol** stretch along the Mediterranean; delay your return to earth in posh **Marbella** (p. 919). Move up along the east coast to **Valencia** (p. 927) and indulge in *paella* and oranges. The gem of the northeast is **Barcelona** (p. 927). After a tour of bizarre Modernista architecture and even crazier nightlife, discover the enchanting seaside resort of **Tossa de Mar** (p. 945). Moving westward into Basque Country, **San Sebastián** (p. 950) entertains with beaches and fabulous *tapas* bars; **Bilbao** (p. 953), home of the incredible Guggenheim museum, is only a daytrip away. Finish up with the 24-hour party that is **Ibiza** (p. 956).

ESSENTIALS

WHEN TO GO

Summer is high season for the coastal and interior regions. In many parts of the country, high season includes Semana Santa (Holy Week; mid-April) and festival days. Tourism peaks in August; the coastal regions overflow while inland cities empty out, leaving behind closed offices, restaurants, and lodgings. Traveling in the off season has the advantage of noticeably lighter crowds and lower prices, but smaller towns virtually shut down, and tourist offices and sights cut their hours nearly everywhere.

DOCUMENTS AND FORMALITIES

VISAS. Citizens of Australia, Canada, the EU, New Zealand, South Africa, and the US do not need a visa for stays of up to 90 days.

EMBASSIES. Foreign embassies are in Madrid (p. 888); all countries have consulates in Barcelona (p. 929). Australia, UK, and US also have consulates in Seville (p. 910). Another Canadian consulate is in Málaga; UK consulates are also in Bilbao, Palma de Mallorca, Ibiza, Alicante, and Málaga; more US consulates are in Las Palmas and Valencia. For Spanish embassies at home, contact: **Australia,** 15 Arkana St., Yarralumla, ACT 2600. Mailing address: P.O. Box 9076, Deakin, ACT 2600 (☎(02) 62 73 35 55; www.embaspain.com); **Canada,** 74 Stanley Ave., Ottawa, ON K1M 1P4 (☎613-747-2252; www.docuweb.ca/SpainInCanada); **Ireland,** 17A Merlyn Park, Ballsbridge, Dublin 4 (☎(01) 269 1640); **South Africa,** 169 Pine St., Arcadia, P.O. Box 1633, Pretoria 0083 (☎(012) 344 3875); **UK,** 39 Chesham Pl., London SW1X 8SB (☎(207) 235 5555); and **US,** 2375 Pennsylvania Ave. NW, Washington, D.C. 20037 (☎202-738-2330; www.spainemb.org).

TRANSPORTATION

BY PLANE. Airports in Madrid and Barcelona handle most international flights; Seville also has a major international airport. **Iberia,** the national carrier, serves all domestic locations and all major international cities.

BY TRAIN. Spanish trains are clean, relatively punctual, and reasonably priced, but tend to bypass many small towns. Spain's national railway is **RENFE** (www.renfe.es). Avoid *transvía, semidirecto,* or *correo* trains—they are very slow. *Alta Velocidad Española* (AVE) trains are the fastest between Madrid, Córdoba, and Seville. *Talgos* are almost as fast; there are four lines from Madrid to Málaga, Algeciras, Cádiz, and Huelva. *Intercity* is cheaper, but still fairly fast. *Estrellas* are slow night trains with bunks. *Cercanías* (commuter trains) go from cities to suburbs and nearby towns.

There is absolutely no reason to buy a **Eurail** if you are planning on traveling only within Spain and Portugal. Trains are cheap, so a pass saves little money; moreover, buses are an easier and more efficient means of traveling around Spain. However, there are several **RailEurope** passes that cover travel within Spain. You must purchase railpasses at least 15 days before departure. (US ☎ 1-800-4EURAIL; www.raileurope.com.) **Spain Flexipass** offers three days of unlimited travel in a two-month period (first-class €211; 2nd-class €164). The **Iberic Railpass** is good for three days of unlimited first-class travel in Spain and Portugal (€217). The **Spain Rail 'n' Drive Pass** is good for three days of unlimited first-class train travel and two days of unlimited mileage in a rental car (€250-345).

BY BUS. In Spain, ignore romanticized visions of European train travel—buses are cheaper, run more frequently, and are faster than trains. Bus routes also provide the only public transportation to many isolated areas. Spain has numerous private companies; the lack of a centralized bus company may make itinerary planning an ordeal. **ALSA** (☎ 902 42 22 42; www.alsa.es), serves Madrid, Galicia, Asturias, and Castilla y León, as well as international destinations in Portugal, Morocco, France, Italy, and Poland. **Auto-Res/Cunisa, S.A.** (☎ 902 02 09 99; www.auto-res.net), serves Madrid, Castilla y León, Extremadura, Galicia, and Valencia.

BY CAR. Gas prices average €1.40-1.50 per liter. Speeders beware: police can "photograph" the speed and license plate of your car and issue a ticket without pulling you over. **Renting a car** in Spain is cheaper than in many other Western European countries. International rental companies offer services throughout the country, but you may want to check with **Atesa** (☎ 902 10 01 01; www.atesa.es), Spain's largest national rental agency. The Spanish automobile association is **Real Automóbil Club de España (RACE),** C. José Abascal 10, Madrid (☎ 915 94 74 75).

BY BIKE AND BY THUMB. With hilly terrain and extremely hot summer weather, biking is difficult. Renting a bike should be easy, especially in the flatter southern region. Hitchers report that Castilla, Andalucía, and Madrid offer little more than a long, hot wait. The Mediterranean Coast and the islands are much more promising, but *Let's Go* does not recommend hitchhiking.

TOURIST SERVICES AND MONEY

TOURIST OFFICES. The Spanish Tourist Office operates an extensive official website (www.tourspain.es) and has 29 offices abroad. Municipal tourist offices, called *oficinas de turismo,* are a good stop to make upon arrival in a town; they usually have free maps and region-specific advice for travelers.

EMERGENCY	Emergency: ☎112. **Local Police:** ☎092. **National Police:** ☎091. **Ambulance:** ☎124.

MONEY. Santander Central Hispano often provides good exchange rates. **Tipping** is not very common in Spain. In restaurants, all prices include service charge. Satisfied customers occasionally toss in some spare change—usually no more than 5%—but this is purely optional. Many people give train, airport, and hotel porters €1 per bag; taxi drivers sometimes get 5-10%. **Bargaining** is common only at flea markets and with street vendors.

Spain has a 7% **Value Added Tax,** known as IVA, on all restaurants and accommodations. The prices listed in *Let's Go* include IVA unless otherwise mentioned. Retail goods bear a much higher 16% IVA, although listed prices are usually inclusive. Non-EU citizens who have stayed in the EU fewer than 180 days can claim back the tax paid on purchases at the airport. Ask the shop where you made the purchase to supply you with a tax return form.

BUSINESS HOURS. Banking hours from June through September are generally Monday through Friday 9am to 2pm; from October to May, banks are also open Saturday 9am to 1pm. Some banks are also open in the afternoon. Most **shops** are open 9am to 6pm, although many in the south still close in the afternoon for siesta.

HEALTH AND SAFETY

While Spain is a relatively stable country, travelers should beware that there is some terrorist activity; the militant Basque separationist group **ETA** has carried out attacks on government officials and tourist destinations. Though the attacks are ongoing, the threat is relatively small. Travelers should be aware of current levels of tension in the region and exercise appropriate caution. Recreational **drugs** are illegal in Spain. Possession of small amounts of marijuana sometimes goes unpunished, but any attempt to buy or sell could land you in jail or with a heavy fine.

COMMUNICATION

PHONE CODES	**Country code: 34. International dialing prefix:** 00. From outside Spain, dial int'l dialing prefix (see inside back cover) + 34 + local number.

MAIL. Air mail (*por avión*) takes five to eight business days to reach the US or Canada; service is faster to the UK and Ireland and slower to Australia and New Zealand. Standard postage is €0.70 to North America. Surface mail (*por barco*), while less expensive than air mail, can take over a month, and packages take two to three months. Registered or express mail (*registrado* or *certificado*) is the most reliable way to send a letter or parcel home and takes four to seven business days. To send mail *Poste Restante* to Spain, address the letter as follows: SURNAME, First Name; Lista de Correos; City Name; Postal Code; SPAIN; AIR MAIL.

TELEPHONES. The central Spanish phone company is *Telefónica*. The best way to make local calls is with a phone card, issued in denominations of €6 and €12 and sold at tobacconists (*estancos* or *tabacos*) and most post offices. You can also ask tobacconists for calling cards known as *Phonepass*. (62min. to US €6, 212min. €12.) American Express and Diner's Club cards now work as phone card substitutes in most pay phones. The best way to call home is with an international calling card issued by your phone company.

EMAIL. Email is easily accessible within Spain and much quicker and more reliable than the regular mail system. An increasing number of bars offer Internet access for a fee of €1-4.50. Cybercafes are listed in most towns and all cities. In small towns, if Internet access is not listed, check the library or the tourist office. The website www.tangaworld.com lists nearly 200 cybercafes in Spain.

LANGUAGE. Catalán is spoken in Cataluña, Valencian in Valencia. The Basque language (Euskera) is common in north-central Spain, Galician (Gallego, related to Portuguese) in the once-Celtic northwest. Spanish (Castilian, or *castellano*) is spoken everywhere. For basic Spanish words and phrases, see p. 1065.

ACCOMMODATIONS AND CAMPING

SYMBOL	❶	❷	❸	❹	❺
ACCOMMODATIONS	under €15	€15-24	€25-34	€35-50	over €50

The cheapest and barest options are **casas de huéspedes** and **hospedajes,** while **pensiones** and **fondas** tend to be a bit nicer. All are basically just boarding houses. Higher up the ladder, **hostales** generally have sinks in bedrooms and provide sheets and lockers, while **hostal-residencias** are similar to hotels in overall quality. The government rates *hostales* on a two-star system; even establishments receiving one star are typically quite comfortable. The system also fixes *hostales* prices, posted in the lounge or main entrance. **Red Española de Albergues Juveniles (REAJ),** C. Galera 1a, Sevilla 41001 (☎954 216 803; www.reaj.com), the Spanish Hostelling International (HI) affiliate, runs 165 youth hostels year-round. Prices depend on location (typically some distance away from town center) and services offered, but are generally €9-15 for guests under 26 and higher for those 26 and over. Breakfast is usually included; lunch and dinner are occasionally offered at an additional charge. Hostels usually lock guests out around 11:30am and have curfews between midnight and 3am. As a rule, don't expect much privacy—rooms typically have four to 20 beds in them. To reserve a bed in high season (July-Aug. and during fiestas), call in advance. A national **Youth Hostel Card** is usually required. **Campgrounds** are generally the cheapest choice for two or more people. Most charge separate fees per person, per tent, and per car; others charge for a *parcela*—a small plot of land—plus per-person fees. Tourist offices provide information, including the *Guía de campings*.

FOOD AND DRINK

SYMBOL	❶	❷	❸	❹	❺
FOOD	under €6	€6-10	€11-15	€16-25	over €25

Spanish food has tended to receive less international attention than the country's beaches, bars, and discos. Taste often ranks above appearance, preparation is rarely complicated, and many of the best meals are served not in expensive restaurants but in private homes or streetside bars. All of this has begun to change as Spanish food becomes increasingly sophisticated and cosmopolitan, but fresh local ingredients are still an integral part of the cuisine; consequently, it varies according to each region's climate, geography, and history. Most experts, in fact, argue that one can speak of Spanish food only in local terms. Spaniards breakfast lightly and wait for a several-course lunch, served between 2 and 3pm. Supper, a light meal, begins at around 10pm. Some restaurants are "open" from 8am until 1 or 2am, but most serve meals only from 1 to 4pm and from 8pm until midnight.

Prices for a full meal start at about €4 in the cheapest *bar-restaurantes*. Many places offer a *plato combinado* (main course, side dishes, bread, and sometimes a beverage) or a *menú del día* (two or three set dishes, bread, beverage, and dessert) for roughly €5-9. If you ask for a *menú*, this is what you may receive; the word for menu is *carta*. *Tapas* (savory meats and vegetables cooked according to local recipes) are truly tasty. *Raciones* are large *tapas* served as entrees. *Bocadillos* are sandwiches on hunks of bread. Specialties include *tortilla de patata* (potato omelette), *jamón serrano* (smoked ham), *calamares fritos* (fried squid), *arroz* (rice), *chorizo* (spicy sausage), *gambas* (shrimp), *lomo* (pork), *paella* (steamed saffron rice with seafood, chicken, and vegetables), and *gazpacho* (cold tomato-based soup). Vegetarians should learn the phrase *"yo soy vegetariano"* (I am a vegetarian) and specify that means no *jamón* (ham) or *atún* (tuna). *Vino blanco* is white wine and *tinto* is red. Beer is *cerveza;* Mahou and Cruzcampo are the most common brands. *Sangría* is red wine, sugar, brandy, and fruit.

HOLIDAYS AND FESTIVALS

Holidays: New Year's Day (Jan. 1); Epiphany (Jan. 6); Maundy Thursday (Apr. 17); Good Friday (Apr. 18); Easter (Apr. 20); Labor Day (May 1); La Asunción (Aug. 15); National Day (Oct. 12); All Saints' Day (Nov. 1); Constitution Day (Dec. 6); Feast of the Immaculate Conception (Dec. 8); Christmas (Dec. 25).

Festivals: Just about everything closes down during festivals. Almost every town has several, and in total there are more than 3000. All of Spain celebrates **Carnaval** from Feb. 9 to 13; the biggest parties are in Cataluña and Cádiz. Valencia hosts the annual **Las Fallas** in mid-March. From April 13-20, the entire country honors the Holy Week, or **Semana Santa.** Sevilla's **Feria de Abril** takes place in late April. Pamplona's **San Fermines** (Running of the Bulls) will break out from July 6 to 14. For more fiesta info, see www.tourspain.es, www.SiSpain.org, or www.cyberspain.es.

MADRID ☎91

After Franco's death in 1975, young *madrileños* celebrated their liberation from totalitarian repression with raging, nocturnal parties in bars and on streets across the city. This partying became so widespread that it defined an era, and *la Movida* (the Movement), is recognized as a world-famous nightlife renaissance. While the newest generation is too young to recall the Franco years, it has kept the spirit of *la Movida* alive—neither cognizant of the city's historic landmarks nor preoccupied with the future—young people have taken over the streets, shed their parents' decorous reserve, and captured the present. Bright lights and a perpetual stream of cars and people blur the distinction between 4pm and 4am, and infinitely energized party-goers crowd bars and discos until dawn. Madrid's sights and culture equal its rival European capitals, and have twice the intensity.

▐▀ TRANSPORTATION

Flights: All flights land at **Aeropuerto Internacional de Barajas** (MAD), 20min. northeast of Madrid. The **Barajas metro line** connects the airport to all of Madrid (€0.95). Another option is the green **Bus-Aeropuerto #89** (look for EMT signs just outside the airport doors), which leaves from the national and international terminals and runs to the city center (every 12min. 4:45am-2am, €2.50). The bus stops underground beneath the Jardines del Descubrimiento in **Plaza de Colón.** Serving national and international destinations, **Iberia** is at Santa Cruz de Marcenado 2, M: San Bernardo. (Office ☎915 87 47 47. Open M-F 9:30am-2pm and 4-7pm. 24hr. reservations and info ☎902 40 05 00).

Trains: Two *Largo Recorrido* (long distance) **RENFE** stations, **Madrid-Chamartín** and **Madrid-Atocha**, connect Madrid to the rest of Europe. Call RENFE (☎913 28 90 20; www.renfe.es) for reservations and info. Try the **RENFE Main Office**, C. Alcalá 44, at Gran Vía (M: Banco de España) for schedules.

Estación Chamartín (24hr. info for international destinations ☎934 90 11 22; domestic ☎902 24 02 02, Spanish only), Agustín de Foxá. M: Chamartín. Bus #5 runs to and from Sol (45min.). Ticket windows open 8am-10:30pm. Most *cercanías* (local) trains stop at Atocha and Chamartín. To: **Barcelona** (7-10hr., 10 per day, €40-42); **Lisbon** (10hr., 10:45pm, €48); **Paris** (13hr., 7pm, €117).

Estación Atocha (☎913 28 90 20). M: Atocha-Renfe. Ticket windows open 7:15am-10pm. Trains to Andalucía, Castilla y León, Castilla-La Mancha, El Escorial, Extremadura, Sierra de Guadarrama, Toledo, and Valencia. AVE service (☎915 34 05 05) to **Córdoba** (1¾hr., 20 per day, €39-46) and **Sevilla** (2½hr., 20 per day, €53-62).

Intercity Buses: Numerous private companies, each with its own station and set of destinations, serve Madrid; many buses pass through the **Estación Sur de Autobuses.**

Estación Sur de Autobuses, C. Méndez Álvaro (☎914 68 42 00). M: Méndez Álvaro. Info booth open daily 7am-11pm. **Continental-Auto** (☎915 27 29 61) to **Toledo** (1½hr.; M-Sa every 30min. 6:30am-10pm, Su 8:30am-midnight; €3.75).

Empressa Larrea (☎915 30 48 00) to **Ávila** (2½hr.; M-F 8 per day, Sa-Su 4 per day; €6).

Estación Auto Res, Pl. Conde de Casal 6 (☎902 02 09 99). M: Conde de Casal. To: **Cuenca** (3hr.; M-F 8-10 per day 6:45am-10pm, Sa-Su 5-6 per day 8am-8pm; €8.50); **Salamanca** (3-3¼hr., 7 per day 8:30am-10pm, €10); **Trujillo** (3¼hr., 11-12 per day 8am-1am, €13); **Valencia** (5hr., 4 per day 1am-2pm, €19).

Estación La Sepulvedana, Po. Frontera 16 (☎915 30 48 00). M: Príncipe Pío (via extension from M: Ópera). To **Segovia** (1½hr., every 30min. 6:30am-10:15pm, €5).

Public Transportation: Metro: Madrid's metro puts most major subway systems to shame. Individual metro tickets cost €0.95, a **bonotransporte** (ticket of 10 rides for metro or bus system) is €5. Buy both at machines in any metro stop, *estanco* (tobacco shop), or newsstand. For more details, call **Metro info** (☎902 44 44 03; www.metro-madrid.es) or ask at a ticket booth. Keep your ticket; metro officials often board and ask to see them, and travelers without tickets get fined.

Intracity Buses: For general info, call **Empresa Municipal de Transportes** (☎914 06 88 10, Spanish only). 6am-11:30pm, €0.95. *Buho* (owl), the night bus service, runs every 20min. midnight-3am, every hr. 3-6am, and is the cheapest form of transportation for late-night revelers. Look for buses N1-20.

Taxis: Call ☎914 45 90 08, 914 47 51 80, or 913 71 21 31. A *libre* sign in the window or a green light indicates availability. Base fare €1.35, plus €0.63-0.81 per km.

◄▶ ORIENTATION AND PRACTICAL INFORMATION

Marking the epicenter of both Madrid and Spain, **"Kilometro 0"** in **Puerta del Sol** ("Sol" for short) is within walking distance of most sights. To the west is the **Plaza Mayor**, the **Palacio Real**, and the **Ópera** district. East of Sol lies **Huertas**, the heart of cafe, theater, and museum life, which is centered around Pl. Santa Ana and bordered by C. Alcalá to the north, Po. Prado to the east, and C. Atocha to the south. The area north of Sol is bordered by **Gran Vía**, which runs northwest to **Plaza de España**. North of Gran Vía are three club and bar-hopping districts, linked by Calle de Fuencarral: **Malasaña**, **Bilbao**, and **Chueca**. Modern Madrid is beyond Gran Vía and east of Malasaña and Chueca. East of Sol, the tree-lined thoroughfares **Paseo de la Castellana**, **Paseo de Recoletos**, and **Paseo del Prado** split Madrid in two, running from Atocha in the south to **Plaza Castilla** in the north, passing the Prado, the fountains of **Plaza Cibeles**, and **Plaza Colón**. Use the **color map** of Madrid's metro in the back of this book. Madrid is safer than its European counterparts, but Sol, Pl. España, Pl. Chueca, and Malasaña's Pl. Dos de Mayo are still intimidating late at night. As a general rule, travel in groups, avoid the parks and quiet streets after dark, and always watch for thieves and pickpockets in crowds.

TOURIST, FINANCIAL, AND LOCAL SERVICES

Tourist Offices: Municipal, Pl. Mayor 3 (☎/fax 913 66 54 77). M: Sol. Open M-Sa 10am-8pm, Su 10am-3pm. **Regional/Provincial Office of the Comunidad de Madrid,** Duque de Medinacelia 2 (☎914 29 49 51; www.comadrid.es/turismo). **Branches** at Estación Chamartín and the airport.

Websites: www.comadrid.es/turismo; www.tourspain.es; www.cronicamadrid.com; www.guiadelocio.com; www.madridman.com; www.red2000.com/spain/madrid.

Budget Travel: Viajes TIVE, C. Fernando el Católico 88 (☎915 43 74 12; fax 915 44 00 62). M: Moncloa. Exit the metro at C. Isaac Peral, walk straight down C. Arcipreste de Hita, and turn left on C. Fernando el Católico; it'll be on your left. Organizes group excursions and language classes. Lodgings and student residence info. ISIC €4.25, HI card €11. Open M-F 9am-2pm, Sa 9am-noon. Arrive early to avoid long lines.

Embassies: Australia, Pl. Descubridor Diego de Ordás 3 (☎914 41 60 25; www.embaustralia.es). **Canada,** C. Núñez de Balboa 35 (☎914 23 32 50; www.canada-es.org). **Ireland,** Po. Castellana 46, 4th fl. (☎914 36 40 93; fax 914 35 16 77). **New Zealand,** Pl. Lealtad 2, 3rd fl. (☎915 23 02 26; fax 915 23 01 71). **South Africa,** Claudio Coello 91, 6th fl. (☎914 36 37 80; fax 915 77 74 14). **UK,** C. Fernando el Santo 16 (☎917 00 82 00; fax 917 00 82 72). **US,** C. Serrano 75 (☎915 87 22 00; www.embusa.es).

Currency Exchange: In general, credit and ATM cards offer the best exchange rates. Avoid changing money at airport and train station counters; they tend to charge exorbitant commissions on horrible rates. **Banco Central Hispano** charges no commission on cash or traveler's checks up to €500. **Main branch,** Pl. Canalejas 1 (☎915 58 11 11). M: Sol. Follow C. San Jeronimo to Pl. Canalejas. Open Apr.-Sept. M-F 8:30am-2:30pm, Sa 8:30am-1pm; Oct.-Mar. M-Th 8:30am-4:30pm, F 8:30am-2pm, Sa 8:30am-1pm.

American Express: Pl. Cortés 2 (traveler services ☎913 22 54 40; currency exchange ☎917 43 77 83). M: Sevilla. From the metro stop, take a right on C. Alcala, another right down C. Cedacero, and a left on C. San Jerónimo; the office is on the left. Traveler services open M-F 9am-5:30pm, Sa 9am-noon; currency exchange M-F 9am-7:30pm, Sa 9am-2pm. 24hr. Express Cash machine outside.

Luggage Storage: Barajas Airport. Follow the signs to *consigna*. One day €3; 2-15 days €3-5 per day; after day 15, €0.60-1.25 per day. **Estación Chamartín** and **Estación Atocha.** Lockers €2.40-5 per day. Open daily 6:30am-10:15pm.

Bi-Gay-Lesbian Resources: Most establishments in the Chueca area carry a free guide to gay nightlife in Spain called **Shanguide. Colectivo de Gays y Lesbianas de Madrid (COGAM),** C. Fuencarral 37 (☎/fax 915 23 00 70). M: Gran Vía. Provides a wide range of services and activities, and an HIV support group (☎915 22 45 17; M-F 6-10pm). Reception daily M-Sa 5:30-9pm. Free counseling M-Th 7-9pm.

Laundromat: Lavandería, C. Cervantes 1. M: Puerta del Sol or Banco de España. From Pl. Santa Ana follow C. Prado, turn right on C. Leon, and then go left onto C. Cervantes. Wash €4, dry €1 for 9min. Open M-Sa 9am-8pm.

EMERGENCY AND COMMUNICATIONS

Emergency: All emergencies: ☎112. Medical: ☎061. National police: ☎091. Local police: ☎092.

Police: C. de los Madrazo 9 (☎915 41 71 60). M: Sevilla. From C. Arenal make a right onto C. Cedacneros and a left onto C. los Madrazo. To report crimes committed in the **metro,** go to the office in the Sol station (☎915 21 09 11). Open daily 8am-11pm.

Rape Hotline: ☎915 74 01 10. Open M-F 10am-2pm and 4-7pm.

Medical Services: Equipo Quirúrgico Municipal No. 1, C. Montesa 22 (☎915 88 51 00). M: Manuel Becerra. **Hospital Ramón y Cajal,** Ctra. Colmenar Viejo (☎913 36 80 00). Bus #135 from Pl. Castilla. For non-emergency concerns, **Anglo-American Medical Unit,** Conde de Aranda 1, 1st fl. (☎914 35 18 23), is quick and friendly.

Internet Access: New Internet cafes are surfacing everywhere. While the average is a reasonable €2 per hr., small shops in apartments charge even less; keep a lookout.

▓ **Easy Everything,** C. Montera 10 (☎915 23 29 44; www.easyeverything.com). M: Sol. From the Plaza del Sol, look for C. Montera, which goes toward Gran Vía. Open 24hr. a day, with literally hundreds of computers, fast connections, good music, and a cafe. Access from €0.50.

Conéctate, C. Hilarión Eslava 27 (☎915 44 54 65; www.conectate.es). M: Moncloa. Over 300 flatscreens and some of the lowest prices in Madrid. Open 24hr.

Yazzgo Internet, Gran Vía 84 & 69 (☎915 22 11 20; www.yazzgo.com). M: San Bernado or Pl. de España. Also locations at Puerta del Sol 6, Gran Vía 60, Estación Chamartín, and Estación Méndez Álvaro. A growing chain; check their website for new locations. Open daily 8:30am-10:30pm, except Gran Vía 69, open 8:30am-1am.

Post Office: Palacio de Comunicaciones, C. Alcala 51, on Pl. Cibeles (☎902 19 71 97). M: Banco de España. Windows open M-Sa 8:30am-9:30pm, Su 9am-2pm for stamp purchases, certified mail, telex, and fax service. **Poste Restante** (Lista de Correos) at windows 80-82; passport required. **Postal Code:** 28080.

▐▀ ACCOMMODATIONS AND CAMPING

Make reservations for summer visits. Expect to pay €17 to €50 per person, depending on location, amenities, and season. Tourist offices provide information about the 13 or so **campsites** within 50km of Madrid. **Centro,** the triangle between Puerta del Sol, Opera, and Plaza Mayor, is full of *hostales,* but you'll pay for the prime location. The cultural hotbed of **Huertas,** framed by C. San Jeronimo, C. las Huertas, and C. Atocha, is almost as central and more fun. Festive **Malasaña** and **Chueca,** bisected by C. Fuencarral, host cheap rooms in the heart of the action, but the sleep-deprived should beware; the party doesn't quiet down for rest. *Hostales,* like temptations, are everywhere among **Gran Vía's** sex shops and scam artists.

EL CENTRO: SOL, ÓPERA, AND PLAZA MAYOR

▓ **Hostal Paz,** C. Flora 4, 1st and 4th fl. (☎915 47 30 47). M: Ópera. Don't be deterred by the dark street, parallel to C. Arenal, off C. Donados or C. Hileras. Peaceful rooms with large windows are sheltered from street noise and lavished with amenities. Reservations advised. Singles €17; doubles €27-32; triples €40. MC/V. ❷

▓ **Hostal-Residencia Luz,** C. Fuentes 10, 3rd fl. (☎915 42 07 59 or 915 59 74 18; fax 915 42 07 59), off C. Arenal. M: Ópera. Neck and neck with Hostal Paz for the best digs in Madrid. Newly redecorated rooms with hardwood floors and elegant furniture ooze comfort. Singles €15; doubles €28-33; triples €33-39. ❷

Hostal-Residencia Rober, C. Arenal 26, 5th fl. (☎915 41 91 75). M: Ópera. Brilliant balcony views down Arenal. Singles with double bed and shower €25, with bath €33; doubles with bath €38; triples with bath €58. Discounts for longer stays. ❸

Hostal Valencia, Pl. Oriente 2, 3rd fl. (☎915 59 84 50). M: Ópera. Narrow glass elevator leads to elegant rooms. Singles €42; doubles €60; master suite €78. ❹

TO
MONCLOA
(800m)

TO
C. GALILEO
(650m)

PL. DOS
DE MAYO

NOVICIADO

C. Velarde

TRIBUNAL

C. L. Fernanda

C. de Tudor

VENTURA
RODRIGUEZ

C. Martin

C. la Princesa

C. de Conde Duque

Trv. Conde Duque

B. López García

C. de Limón

C. de Acuerdo

C. del Norte

C. de la Palma

C. San Vincente Ferrer

Cda. Alta San Pablo

ARGÜELLES

San
Marcos

C. S. Leonardo

C. San Bernardo

Porciado

C. Amaniel

C. Noviciado

C. Espíritu Santo

C. Ventura Rodriguez

C. de los Heroes

Museo
Cerralbo

Torre
de Madrid

C. la Princesa

C. los Reyes

C. Los Reyes

C. del Pez

C. Pozas

C. Tesoro

C. Marqués de Santa Ana

C. Jesús del Valle

C. Madera

C. Don Felipe

PL. DE SA
ILDEFONS

C. Colon

C. Ferraz

Plaza de
España

PLAZA DE
ESPAÑA

Edificio de
España

C. Gen. Mitre

C. A. Grilo

C. Andrés Borrego

C. Manzana

C. del Pez

MALASAÑA

C. Molino de

Jardines
Ferraz

Cadarso

C. Río

C. de Fomento

C. Reloj

C. Legantos

C. Isabel la Católica

C. Flor Baja

Av. Gran Vía

C. Parada

C. la Luna

C. S. Roque

Corrida Baja San Pablo

C. Ballesta

C. Puebla

C. Barco

C. Valverde

C. Onó

Cuesta San Vicente

C. Torija

C. Flor Alta

C. Libreros

C. de Silva

C. Miguel Moya

C. Tudesco

C. del Desengaño

PL. DE LA
MARINA ESPAÑOLA

PL. SANTO
DOMINGO

Jardines de
Sabatini

C. Encarnación

C. Guillermo Rolland

C. la Bola

SANTO
DOMINGO

C. Jacometrezo

CALLAO

PL. DEL
CALLAO

GRAN VÍA

PL. DE RI
DE SAN L

Convento de
la Encarnación

C. S. Alberto

C. Chinchilla

C. Salud

C. Tetuán

GRAN
VÍA

Museo de
Carruajes
Reales

Jardines
Cabo Noval

C. de Arrieta

Cuesta Santo Domingo

C. Campomanes

C. Carlos de Peral

C. Preciados

Convento de las
Descalzas Reales

C. del Carmen

C. Montera

PL. DEL
CARMEN

Palacio
Real

Teatro
Real

PL. DE
ORIENTE

Carlos III

PL. DE
ISABEL II

ÓPERA

C. Priora

C. Flora

PL. SAN
MARTÍN

PL.
DESCALZAS

C. San Martín

Museo de la
Academia de Bellas A
de San Ferna

PLAZA
ARMERÍA

C. Bailén

Jardines
Lepanto

C. Requena

C. Vergara

C. Amnistía

C. Unión

Independencia Espejo

Escalinata

C. Fuentes

C. las Hileras

C. Bordadores

C. Pasadizo de Sandines

C. Arenal

Maestro

C. Tetuán

SOL

C. Alcalá

PUERTA
DEL SOL

C. Espoz y Mina

C. de Victoria

Catedral de
Almudena

CENTRO

C. Mayor

Postas

Espateros

Correo

C. Carretas

C. Factor

C. Cruzada

C. Santiago de Lucía

C. Santiago

PL. DE
LA VILLA

Ayuntamiento

Torre
de los
Lujanes

Casa de los
Lujanes

Marqués Viudo Pontejos

Zaragoza

PLAZA
MAYOR

PL. SANTA
CRUZ

C. Bolsa

Santa Cruz

PL.
JACINTO
BENAVENTE

C. Atocha

C. Mayor

Casa de
Cisneros

C. de Sacramento

C. Toledo

C. Imperial

C. Salvador

C. Concepción Jerónima

C. S. Tomás

C. Villa

C. Segovia

Jardines de
las Vistillas

C. de Bailén

C. de Morería

C. Redondilla

C. Segovia

PL. DE LA
PAJA

Capilla
del Obispo

PL. DE
HUMILLADERO

Cava Baja

PL.
SEGOVIA
NUEVA

C. la Colegiata

PL. TIRSO
DE MOLINA

TIRSO DE
MOLINA

Conde Romanones

C. Duque de Cortezo

C. Relatores

C. Magda

C. de Cal

San Andrés

PUERTA
DE MOROS

PL. DE LA
CEBADA

Cava Alta

Catedral de
San Isidro

LA
LATINA

C. San Millán

Duque de Alba

C. Juanelo

C. Jesús y María

C. Calvario

C. Don Pedro

C. Maldonadas

PL. DE
CASCORRO

C. Encomienda

C. del Amparo

Car. S. Francisco

C. Angel

C. Tabernillas

C. Humilladero

C. la Cebada

C. Dos Hermanas

C. Abades

C. Oso

Mesón de Paredes

Caravaca

C. Rosario

C. Aguila

C. Mediodía

C. Toledo

C. Santa Ana

Ribera de Curtidores

Cabestreros

C. Sombrer

Gran Vía de S. Francisco

C. de Calatrava

C. Mira el Río Alta

El
Rastro

Embajadores

LA LATINA

C. la Ventosa

TO GLORIETA PUERTA
DE TOLEDO (190m)

C. la Arganzuela

C. Carnero

C. Tribu

SPAIN

Central Madrid

SERRANO Ⓜ

Jardines del Descubrimiento

C. Goya

PL. DE COLÓN

COLÓN Ⓜ

Centro Cultural

PL. DE LA VILLA DE PARIS

Biblioteca Nacional

Museo Arqueológico

C. de Serrano

C. Villanueva

PL. SALESAS

Teatro María Guerrero

C. de Recoletos

PL. DE LA INDEPENDENCIA

RETIRO Ⓜ

Palacio de Buenavista

Casa de América

Puerta de Alcalá

Av. Méjico

PL. DEL REY

PL. DE LA CIBELES

Main Post Office/Palacio de Comunicaciones

C. Alcalá

BANCO DE ESPAÑA Ⓜ

Las Calatravas

Círculo de Bellas Artes

Museo Naval

C. Montalbán

Bolsa de Madrid

SEVILLA Ⓜ

Palacio Miraflores

HUERTAS

PLAZA DE LA LEALTAD

Parlamento

Museo Thyssen-Bornemisza

PL. DE LAS CORTES

Ateneo

Teatro Español

Casa de Lope de Vega

PL. CÁNOVAS DEL CASTILLO

Museo del Prado

Real Academia de la Historia

Maestro Telleria

PL. PLATERÍA MARTINEZ

PL. DE MURILLO

ANTÓN MARTÍN Ⓜ

PL. DE SAN JUAN

Conservatorio Superior de Música

ATOCHA

PL. EMPERADOR CARLOS V

Centro de Arte Reina Sofia

Estación Atocha

0   200 yards
0   200 meters

Central Madrid

🏠 ACCOMMODATIONS
Hostal A. Nebrija, 6	A2
Hostal Armesto, 24	D4
Hostal Chelo, 11	D2
Hostal Gonzalo, 28	E5
Hostal Internacional, 21	D4
Hostal Lorenzo, 17	D3
Hostal Margarita, 7	B2
Hostal Palacios, 8	C2
Hostal Paz, 13	B3
Hostal-Residencia Carreras, 22	D4
Hostal-Residencia Domínguez, 5	D1
Hostal-Residencia Lido, 21	D4
Hostal-Residencia Luz, 19	B4
Hostal-Residencia Rober, 14	B3
Hostal Ribadavia, 8	C2
Hostal Triana, 16	C3
Hostal Valencia, 12	A3
Hostal Villar, 23	D4

🍴 FOOD
Al-Jaima, 10	D2
Ananias, 1	A1
Arepas con Todo, 4	D1
Casa Alberto, 26	D5
Cáscaras, 2	A1
Champagneria Gala, 29	E5
El Estragón Vegetariano, 25	A5
La Granja Restaurante Vegetariano, 3	C1
Inshala, 18	A4

⭐ NIGHTLIFE
Acuarela, 9	D2
El Café de Sheherezade, 27	D5
Kapital, 30	E6
Palacio Gaviria, 20	B4

HUERTAS

▨ **Hostal Gonzalo,** C. Cervantes 34, 3rd fl. (☎914 29 27 14; fax 914 20 20 07). M: Antón Martín. Off C. León, which is off C. Atocha. A budget traveler's dream: pristine baths, firm beds, TVs, and fans in the summer. Singles €35; doubles €43; triples €55. ❸

Hostal Internacional, C. Echegaray 5, 2nd fl. (☎914 29 62 09). M: Sol or Sevilla. Rooms are newly renovated. Nice common room. Singles €30; doubles €36. ❸

Hostal-Residencia Lido, C. Echegaray 5, 2nd fl. (☎914 29 62 07). M: Sol or Sevilla. Across the hall from Internacional, Lido recently finished a makeover, showcasing new rooms with comfy beds, TVs and complete baths. Singles €18; doubles €30. ❷

Hostal Villar, C. Príncipe 18, 1st-4th fl. (☎915 31 66 00; www.arrakis.es/~h-villar). M: Sol. From the metro, walk down C. San Jerónimo and turn right on C. Príncipe. A secluded feeling despite its busy location. Singles €20, with bath €23; doubles €27/€35; triples €37/€49. ❷

Hostal Armesto, C. San Agustín 6, 1st fl. (☎914 29 90 31). M: Antón Martín. In front of Pl. Cortés. This *hostal* offers exceptional hospitality and a quiet night's sleep. All rooms with private bath and A/C. Older crowd. Singles €39; doubles €45; triples €53. ❹

Hostal-Residencia Carreras, C. Príncipe 18, 3rd fl. (☎/fax 915 22 00 36). M: Sol or Sevilla. Off C. San Jerónimo, between Pl. Santa Ana and Canalejas. Ask for a room with a balcony—they tend to be larger. Singles €21, with bath €48; doubles €36/€42-48; triples €54/€60. ❷

GRAN VÍA

Hostal A. Nebrija, Gran Vía 67, 8th fl., elevator A (☎915 47 73 19). M: Pl. España. A grandson continues tradition with pleasant, spacious rooms offering magnificent views of the city landscape. Singles €26; doubles €36; triples €49. AmEx/MC/V. ❸

Hostal Margarita, Gran Vía 50, 5th fl. (☎/fax 915 47 35 49). M: Callao. Simple rooms with large windows, and TV; most with street views. Singles €25; doubles €36, with bath €38; triples with bath €48. MC/V. ❷

Hostal Triana, C. de la Salud 13, 1st fl. (☎915 32 68 12; www.hostaltriana.com). M: Callao or Gran Vía. From Gran Vía, turn onto C. Salud; the sign is quite visible. Catering to those seeking a little more comfort than the standard *hostal*. Reserve 2 weeks ahead. Singles €35; doubles €41. ❸

MALASAÑA AND CHUECA

▨ **Hostal-Residencia Domínguez,** C. Santa Brígida 1, 1st fl. (☎/fax 915 32 15 47). M: Tribunal. Go down C. Fuencarral toward Gran Vía, turn left on C. Santa Brígida, and climb up a flight. Hospitable young owner ready with tips on local nightlife. English spoken. Singles €21, with bath €30; doubles with bath and A/C €40. ❷

Hostal Chelo, C. Hortaleza 17, 3rd fl. (☎915 32 70 33; www.chelo.com). M: Gran Vía. Great location, hospitable staff. Rooms are spacious, with complete bath. Singles €30; doubles €36. ❸

Hostal Lorenzo, C. Clavel 8 (☎915 21 30 57; fax 915 32 79 78). M: Gran Vía. From the metro, walk up C. Clavel; it's on the corner of the plaza. New furniture and modern bathrooms. Reservations recommended. Singles €45; doubles €65-80. AmEx/MC/V. ❹

Hostal Palacios and **Hostal Ribadavia,** C. Fuencarral 25, 1st-3rd fl. (☎915 31 10 58 or ☎915 31 48 47). M: Gran Vía. Both run by the same cheerful family. Singles €20, with bath €27; doubles €28/€35; triples €45/€48. AmEx/MC/V. ❷

🗋 FOOD

In Madrid, it's not hard to fork it down without forking over too much. Most restaurants offer a *menú del día*, which includes bread, one drink, and one choice from each of the day's selection of appetizers, main courses, and desserts (€7-9). Many small eateries line **Calles Echegaray, Bentura de la Vega,** and **Manuel Fernández González** in Huertas; **Calle Agurrosa** at Lavapiés has some funky outdoor cafes, and there are good restaurants up the hill toward Huertas; and **Calle Fuencarral** in Gran Vía is lined with cheap eats. **Bilbao,** the area north of Glorieta de Bilbao, is the place to go for ethnically diverse culinary choices. Bars along **Calle Hartzenbusch** and **Calle Cisneros** offer cheap *tapas*. Keep in mind the following essential buzz words for quicker, cheaper *madrileño* fare: *bocadillo* (a sandwich on a long, hard roll, €2-2.75); *ración* (a large *tapa*, served with bread €1.85-3.75); and *empanada* (a puff pastry with meat fillings, €1.25-1.85). Vegetarians should check out the *Guía del Ocio,* which has a complete listing of Madrid's vegetarian havens under the section *"Otras Cocinas,"* or the website www.mundovegetariano.com. For **groceries, %Dia** and **Simago** are the cheapest supermarket chains. More expensive are **Mantequerías Leonesas, Expreso,** and **Jumbo.**

🏮 **Inshala,** C. Amnistia 10 (☎915 48 26 32). M: Ópera. Eccentric menu filled with delicious Spanish, Mexican, Japanese, Italian, and Moroccan dishes. Weekday lunch *menú* €7.25. Dinner *menú* €8-€15. Reservations strongly recommended for both lunch and dinner. Open M-Sa 2-6pm and 9pm-1am, Su 2-5pm. ❷

🏮 **Champagneria Gala,** C. Moratín 22 (☎91 429 25 62). Down the hill from C. Atocha on C. Moratín. The *paella* buck stops here, with decor as colorful and varied as its specialty. *Menú* €11. Reserve on weekends. Open daily 1:30-5pm and 9pm-12:30am. ❸

🏮 **El Estragón Vegetariano,** Pl. de la Paja 10 (☎91 365 89 82). M: La Latina. Perhaps the best medium-priced restaurant—of any kind—in Madrid, with vegetarian food that could turn the most die-hard carnivores into switch-hitters. Try the delicious *menú* (M-F €9; Sa-Su and evenings €18). Open daily 1:30-4:30pm and 8pm-1am. AmEx/MC/V. ❹

Cáscaras, C. Ventura Rodríguez 7 (☎915 42 83 36). M: Ventura Rodríguez. Facing the green outside the metro, take your first right off C. Princesa. Popular for *tapas, pinchos,* and ice-cold Mahou beer in the early afternoon and evening. Exotic vegetarian entrees €5-6. Open M-F 7am-1am, Sa-Su 10am-1am. AmEx/MC/V. ❷

Ananias, C. Galileo 9 (☎914 48 68 01). M: Argüelles. From C. Alberto Aguilera, take a left onto C. Galileo. Swirling waiters serve Castilian dishes with a flourish. Entrees €9-15. Open Su-Tu and Th-F 1-4pm and 9-11:30pm, Sa 9-11:30pm. AmEx/MC/V. ❸

Arepas con Todo, C. Hartzenbusch 19 (☎91 448 75 45), off C. Cardenal Cisneros, from C. Luchana. Hanging gourds and waitresses in festive dress fill this classic Colombian restaurant. A rotating *menú* (€10-12) for every night of the month, and 60 fixed dishes (€11-15). Only the live music acts repeat themselves. Open daily 2pm-1am. MC/V. ❸

Casa Alberto, C. Huertas 18 (☎914 29 93 56). M: Antón Martín. Interior dining room decorated with bullfighting and Cervantine relics; Cervantes wrote the second part of *El Quijote* here. The *tapas* are all original house recipes. Get the feel of their *gambas al ajillo* (shrimp with garlic and hot peppers; €7.50) or the filled *canapés* (€2). Sit-down dinner is a bit pricey. Open Tu-Sa noon-5:30pm and 8pm-1:30am. AmEx/MC/V. ❸

Al-Jaima, Cocina del Desierto, C. Barbieri 1 (☎915 23 11 42). M: Gran Vía or Chueca. Lebanese, Moroccan, and Egyptian food in intimate North African setting. Specialties include pastela, couscous, shish kebabs, and tayin. Meals €4-8. Dinner reservations recommended, sometimes required. Open daily 1:30-4pm and 9pm-midnight. ❷

SPAIN

La Granja Restaurante Vegetariano, C. San Andrés 11 (☎915 32 87 93), off Pl. 2 de Mayo. M: Tribunal or Bilbao. Dimmed yellow lights glow above intricately tiled walls in this Arab-themed restaurant. Lunchtime *menú* €7.25. Open W-M 1:30-4:30pm and 9pm-midnight. Closed Su in summer. ❷

Restaurante Casa Botin, C. de Cuchilleros 17 (☎913 66 42 17), off Pl. Mayor. The "oldest restaurant in the world," founded in 1725, serves filling Spanish dishes (€7-20). Reservations recommended. Lunch daily 1-4pm, dinner 8pm-midnight. ❸

La Finca de Susana, C. Arlaban 4 (☎913 69 35 57). M: Sevilla. Probably the most popular lunch place in Madrid; fine dining at an extremely low price (*menú* €6.50). Be prepared to wait in line for lunch. Open daily 1-4pm and 8-11:30pm. ❷

Pizzeria Vesuvio, C. Hortaleza 4. (☎915 21 51 71). M: Gran Vía. Mix and match pasta and sauce or try the 30+ combinations of personal pizzas. Delicious food and fast service. Counter seating only. Try the pasta fresca. Take-out available. Meals €3.30-€5. Open M-Sa 1-4pm and 8pm-midnight, F-Sa until 1am. ❶

Anatolia, C. de la Cruz 10. M: Sol. One of the many Turkish restaurants in Madrid that serves succulent Doner Kebabs (chicken or lamb gyro sandwiches). Tavuk Kebab with all the trimmings €3, other Turkish specialties €2.70-€4.50. Closed Su. ❶

Al Natural, C. Zorrilla 11 (☎913 69 47 09). M: Sevilla. From the metro stop, take a left off C. de Cedaceros; it's behind the Congress building. Vegetarian Mediterranean dishes (€8-12) served in a lively atmosphere. Open daily 1-4pm, M-Sa 7pm-midnight. ❷

🔵 SIGHTS

Madrid, as large as it may seem, is a walker's city. The word *paseo* refers to a major avenue, but literally means "a stroll." The municipal tourist office's *Plano de Transportes*—which marks monuments as well as bus and metro lines—is indispensable.

EL CENTRO: SOL, ÓPERA, AND PLAZA MAYOR

PUERTA DEL SOL. Kilómetro 0, the origin of six national highways, marks the center of the city (and the country) in the most chaotic of Madrid's plazas. Puerta del Sol (Gate of Sun) blazes with taxis, bars, and street performers. The statue **El Oso y el Madroño,** a bear and strawberry tree, is a popular meeting place. *(M: Sol.)*

PLAZA MAYOR. Juan de Herrera, architect of El Escorial, also designed this plaza. Its elegant arcades, spindly towers, and open verandas, erected for Felipe III in 1620, came to define "Madrid-style" architecture and inspired every peering *balcón* thereafter. Toward evening, Pl. Mayor awakens as *madrileños* resurface, tourists multiply, and cafe tables fill with lively patrons. Live flamenco performances are a common treat. *(M: Sol. From Pta. Sol, walk down C. Mayor. The plaza is on the left.)*

CATEDRAL DE SAN ISIDRO. Designed in the Jesuit Baroque style at the beginning of the 17th century, the cathedral received San Isidro's remains in 1769. During the Civil War, rioting workers burned the exterior and damaged much of the cathedral—only the primary nave and a few Baroque decorations remain from the original. *(M: Latina. From Pta. Sol, take C. Mayor to Pl. Mayor, cross the plaza, and exit onto C. Toledo. Open for mass only. Mass daily 9, 10, 11am, and noon.)*

PLAZA DE LA VILLA. Plaza de la Villa marks the heart of what was once old Madrid. Though only a few medieval buildings remain, the plaza still features a stunning courtyard (surrounding the statue of Don Alvara de Bazón), beautiful tile-work, and eclectic architecture. Across the plaza is the 17th-century **Ayuntamiento (Casa de la Villa),** designed in 1640 by Juan Gomez de Mora as both the mayor's home and the city jail. *(M: Sol. From Pta. Sol, go down C. Mayor, past Pl. Mayor.)*

AROUND THE PALACIO REAL. This amazingly luxurious palace was built for the first Bourbon King, Felipe V, to replace the Alcázar after it burned down. It took 40 years to build, and the decoration of its 2000 rooms with 20km of tapestry dragged on for a century. *(M: Sol. From Pta. Sol, take C. Mayor and turn right on C. Bailen. Open Apr.-Sept. M-Sa 9am-6pm, Su 9am-3pm; Oct.-Mar. M-Sa 9:30am-5pm, Su 9am-2pm. €6, students €3. Tours €6.90. W free for EU citizens.)* The palace faces **Plaza de Oriente**, a sculpture garden. Most of its statues were designed for the palace roof, but were placed in this shady plaza after the queen had a nightmare about the roof collapsing. *(From Pta. Sol, take C. Arenal to the plaza. Free.)* Next door to the palace is the **Cathedral de la Almudena**, begun in 1879 and finished a century later. The cathedral's modern interior stands in contrast to the gilded Palacio Real. *(M: Sol. From Pta. Sol, go down C. Mayor and it's just across C. Bailén. Open M-Sa 1-7pm. Closed during mass. Free.)*

HUERTAS, GRAN VÍA, MALASAÑA, CHUECA, AND ARGÜELLES

East of Pta. del Sol, **Huertas** reflects its literary ilk, from famed authors' houses to legendary cafes. The neighborhood was home to Cervantes, Góngora, Calderón, and Moratín, and enjoyed a fleeting return to literary prominence when Hemingway hung out here. *(M: Sol.)* **Gran Vía**, which stretches from Pl. de Callao to Pl. de España, is the busiest street in Madrid; massive skyscrapers, fast-food joints, and bustling stores grace this chaotic thoroughfare. *(M: Callao and Pl. España.)* **Malasaña** and **Chueca** lie at the core of Madrid's alternative scene; the area between C. de Fuencarral and C. de San Bernardo, north of Gran Vía, boasts avant-garde architecture, chic eateries, and the city's hippest fashion. Out of the way in **Argüelles**, Goya's frescoed dome in the beautiful **Ermita de San Antonio de la Florida** arches above his buried corpse. *(M: Príncipe Pío. From the metro, go left on C. de Buen Altamirano, walk through the park, and turn left on Po. Florida; the Ermita is at the end of the street. Open Tu-F 10am-2pm and 4-8pm, Sa-Su 10am-2pm. €1.80, students €0.90. W and Su free.)* The **Temple de Debod**, Spain's only Egyptian temple, was built by Pharaoh Zakheramon in the 4th century BC. *(M: Ventura Rodríguez. From the metro, walk down C. Ventura Rodríguez into the Parque de la Montaña; the temple is on the left. Open Tu-F 9:45am-1:15pm and 4:15-5:45pm; Sa-Su 10am-1:45pm. €1.80, students €0.90. W and Su free.)* The **Faro de Moncloa**, a 92m-tall metal tower, offers spectacular views of the city. *(Open M-Su 10am-1:45pm and 5-8:45pm. €1.50 to ascend the tower.)*

▓ RETIRO

Join an array of vendors, palm-readers, soccer players, and sunbathers in what Felipe IV once intended to be a hunting ground, a *buen retiro* (nice retreat). The finely landscaped 300-acre Parque del Buen Retiro is centered around a rectangular lake and a magnificent monument to King Alfonso XII. Dubbed **Estanque Grande**, this central location is popular among casual rowers. Built by Ricardo Velázquez to exhibit Filipino flowers, the exquisite steel-and-glass **Palacio de Cristal** hosts a variety of art shows. *(Open Apr.-Sept. M and W-Sa 11am-8pm, Su 11am-6pm; Oct.-Mar. M and W-Sa 10am-6pm, Su 10am-4pm. Closed Tu. Free.)* All artists should dream of having their art displayed in the **Palacio de Velázquez**, with its billowing ceilings, marble floors, and ideal lighting. Avoid venturing into the park alone after dark. *(Past the Estanque, turn left on Paseo del Venezuela. Open Apr.-Sept. M and W-Sa 11am-8pm, Su 11am-6pm; Oct.-Mar. M and W-Sa 10am-6pm, Su 10am-4pm. Closed Tu. Free.)*

EL PARDO

Built as a hunting lodge for Carlos I in 1547, El Pardo was enlarged by generations of Hapsburgs and Bourbons. El Pardo gained attention in 1940 when Franco made it his home; he resided here until his death in 1975. It is renowned for its collection of tapestries—several of which were designed by Goya—but the palace also holds paintings by Velázquez and Ribera. *(Take bus #601 (15min., €1) from the stop in front of the Ejército del Aire building. M: Moncloa. Open Apr.-Sept. M-F 10:30am-6pm, Su 9:30am-1:40pm; Oct.-Mar. M-F 10:30am-5pm, Su 10am-1:40pm. Compulsory 45min. guided tour in Spanish. €4.80, students €1.50. W free for EU citizens.)*

🏛 MUSEUMS

The worthwhile **Paseo del Arte** ticket grants admission to the Museo del Prado, Museo Thyssen-Bornemisza, and Centro de Arte Reina Sofía (€8).

🖾 **MUSEO DEL PRADO.** One of Europe's finest museums, the walls of the Prado are graced by Goya's "black paintings" and Velázquez's *Las Meninas*. As a result of the Spanish Hapsburgs' long reign over the Netherlands, the museum has an extraordinary collection of Flemish paintings by Van Dyck, van der Weyden, Albrecht Dürer, Pieter Brueghel the Elder, and Rubens. Other notable collections include works by: Titian, Raphael, Botticelli, Bosch, and El Greco. *(M: Banco de España. On Po. Prado at Pl. Cánovas del Castillo. http://museoprado.mcu.es. Open Tu-Sa 9am-7pm, Su 9am-2pm. €3, students €1.50; Sa 2:30-7pm, Su, and holidays free.)*

🖾 **MUSEO NACIONAL CENTRO DE ARTE REINA SOFÍA.** The centerpiece of this 20th-century collection is Picasso's masterwork *Guernica*, depicting the agony of the Nazi bombing of the Basque town of Guernica for the Fascists during the Spanish Civil War. Works by Miró, Julio González, Juan Gris, and Dalí illustrate the essential role of Spanish artists in Cubism and Surrealism. *(M: Atocha. C. Santa Isabel 52, opposite Estación Atocha at the south end of Po. Prado. Open M, W-Sa 10am-9pm, Su 10am-2:30pm. €3, students €1.50; Sa after 2:30pm, Su, and holidays free.)*

🖾 **MUSEO THYSSEN-BORNEMISZA .** This 18th-century palace houses a fabulous art collection accumulated by generations of the Austro-Hungarian magnates. The museum surveys it all, parading canvases and sculptures by many of the greats, including El Greco, Titian, Caravaggio, Picasso, Rothko, Hopper, Renoir, Klee, Chagall, and Dalí. To view the collection in chronological order, observing the evolution of styles and themes, begin on the top floor and work down. *(M: Banco de España. Bus #6, 14, 27, 37, or 45. On the corner of Po. Prado and C. San Jerónimo. www.museothyssen.org. Open Tu-Su 10am-7pm. Last entrance 6:30pm. €4.20, students with ISIC €2.40, under 12 free.)*

MUSEO DE AMÉRICA. This under appreciated museum documents the cultures of America's pre-Columbian civilizations and the legacy of the Spanish conquest. *(M: Moncloa. Av. Reyes Católicos 6, next to the Faro de Moncloa. Open Tu-Sa 10am-3pm, Su 10am-2:30pm. €3, students €1.50, Su free.)*

MUSEO DE LA REAL ACADEMIA DE BELLAS ARTES DE SAN FERNANDO. An excellent collection of the Old Masters, surpassed only by the Prado. *(M: Sol. C. Alcalá 13. Open Tu-F 9am-7pm, Sa-M 9am-2:30pm. €2.50, students €1.25, W free.)*

🎵 ENTERTAINMENT

🖾 **EL RASTRO (FLEA MARKET).** For hundreds of years, El Rastro has been a Sunday morning tradition. The market begins in La Latina at Pl. Cascorro off C. Toledo and ends at the bottom of C. Ribera de Curtidores. Get lost in the insanity and find anything from jewelry and jeans to antique tools and pet birds. El Rastro is open Sundays and holidays from 9am to 2pm.

CLASSIC CAFES. Spend an afternoon lingering over a *café con leche* and soak up Madrilenian culture in historic cafes. At ▨**Café Gijón,** Po. Recoletos 21 (*M: Colón*), a 115-year-old literati hangout; thought-provoking conversation makes good coffee well worth the price. (*Open daily 9am-1:30am.*) Or, gaze at the Palacio Real from the ritzy **Café de Oriente,** Pl. Oriente 2. (*M: Ópera. Open daily 8:30am-1:30am.*)

MUSIC AND FLAMENCO. Anyone interested in live entertainment should stop by the **Círculo de Bellas Artes,** C. Alcala 42 (*M: Sevilla or Banco de España.* ☎913 60 54 00; www.circulobellasartes.com). Their magazine, *Minerva,* is indispensable. Check the *Guía del Ocio* for information on the city-sponsored movies, plays, and concerts. **Flamenco** in Madrid is tourist-oriented and expensive. A few nightlife spots are authentic, but pricey. **Casa Patas,** C. Cañizares 10, is good quality for less than usual. (☎913 69 04 96; www.casapatas.com.) At **Corral de la Morería,** C. Morería 17, shows start at 9:45pm and last until 2am. (☎913 65 84 46. *M: Ópera. Cover €24, includes one drink.*)

SPORTS. Spanish sports fans go ballistic for **fútbol** (soccer to North Americans). Every Sunday and some Saturdays from September to June, one of two local teams plays at home. **Real Madrid** plays at Estadio Santiago Bernabéu, Po. Castellana 104. (☎914 57 11 12. *M: Lima.*) **Atlético de Madrid** plays at Estadio Vicente Calderón, C. Virgen del Puerto 67. (☎913 66 47 07. *M: Pirámides or Marqués de Vadillos. Tickets €18-42.*) **Corridas** (bullfights) are held during the Festival of San Isidro and every Sunday from March to October; they are less frequent the rest of the year. **Plaza de las Ventas,** C. Alcalá 237, east of Madrid, is Spain's largest bullfighting ring. (☎913 56 22 00. *M: Ventas. Tickets €5-92.*)

▨ NIGHTLIFE

Spaniards average one hour less sleep a night than other Europeans, and *madrileños* claim to need even less than that. Proud of their nocturnal offerings—they'll say with a straight face that Paris or New York bored them—they don't retire until they've "killed the night" and a good part of the morning. As the sun sets, *terrazas* and *chiringuitos* (outdoor cafes/bars) spill across sidewalks. *Madrileños* start in the *tapas* bars of **Huertas,** move to the youthful scene in **Malasaña,** and end at the crazed parties of **Chueca** or late-night clubs of **Gran Vía. Bilbao** and **Moncloa** are student-filled. Madrid's gay scene, centered on **Plaza Chueca,** is fantastic. Most clubs don't heat up until around 2am; don't be surprised by a line still

waiting outside at 5:30am. The *entrada* (cover) can be as high as €12, but usually includes a drink. Bouncers on power trips love to make examples; dress well to avoid being overcharged or denied. Women may not be charged at all.

▨ Palacio Gaviria, C. Arenal 9. M: Sol or Ópera. A grand red carpet leads to two huge ballrooms turned club spaces with dancers and blazing light shows; the most exceptional of Madrid's grandiose discotecas. Cover varies depending on the night (€7-15). Open M-Th 10:30pm-late, F-Sa 11:30pm-late, Su 9pm-late.

▨ Pasapoga, Gran Vía 37. M: Callao. Around the corner from Plaza de Callao. Gay nightlife explodes here on the weekends, especially on Saturdays. Beautiful interior, beautiful people. F-Sa are gay nights. Cover €15. Open daily midnight-late.

Suite, Virgen de los Peligros 4, off C. de Alcalá. M: Sevilla. Classy restaurant, bar, and club boasts *nouveau tapas* by day and sleek drinks (€6) by night. Mixed crowd, gay friendly. Open daily 11am-6pm and 8pm-3:30am.

Joy Madrid, C. Arenal 11. M: Sol or Ópera. Next to the Palacio Gaviria. Well-dressed crowd parties the night away to disco, techno, and R&B on a three-tiered dance floor. Cover Su-Th €12, F-Sa €15. Open daily 11:30pm-5:30am.

Cool, Isabela La Catolica 6. M: Santo Domingo. Heavenly drag performances and the occasional underwordly goth parties for a wild, mixed crowd. Drinks €5-8. Open F-Sa midnight-late. Su is the **Shangay Tea Dance,** primarily gay event; 9pm-late.

Acuarela, C. Gravina 10. M: Chueca. A welcome alternative to the club scene. Buddhas and candles surround antique furniture, inspiration for good conversation and a good buzz. Coffees and teas €3-5. Liqueur €4. Open M-Su 3pm-3am.

Why Not? C. San Bartolome 7. M: Chueca. Small, downstairs bar packed almost every night of the week with a wild, mixed crowd. Open daily 10pm-4am.

Kapital, C. Atocha, 125. M: Atocha. *Thumba la casa* (bring down the house) on 7 floors of *discoteca* insanity. Dress to impress the bouncer. Drinks €9. Cover €12, includes 1 drink. Open Th-Su midnight-6am, and Sa-Su also 5:30-11pm.

Cardamomo, C. Echegaray 15. M: Sevilla. Flamenco music spins all night. A local crowd dances flamenco occasionally; come W to see professionals. M bumps with Brazilian and other exotic beats. Open daily 9pm-4am.

Sugar Hill, C. Fundadores 7. M: Manuel Becerra or O'Donell. Named after the original, this is the only real hip-hop club in town. The dance floor doesn't really get packed until 3:30am. €9, includes 1 drink. Drinks €6. Open Sa only 12:45-5:30am.

El Café de Sheherezade, C. Santa María 18. M: Antón Martín. Surrounded by Middle Eastern music and decor, groups cluster around *pipas* (pipes; €7-10) that filter sweet smoke through whiskey or water. Open daily 7pm-5am.

▨ DAYTRIPS FROM MADRID

EL ESCORIAL. The **Monasterio de San Lorenzo del Escorial** was a gift from Felipe II to God, the people, and himself, commemorating his victory over the French at the battle of San Quintín in 1557. Near the town of **San Lorenzo,** El Escorial is filled_with artistic treasures, two palaces, two pantheons, a church, and a magnificent library. Don't come on Monday, when the complex and most of the town shut down. To avoid crowds, enter via the gate on C. Florida Blanca, on the west side. The adjacent **Museos de Arquitectura and Pintura** chronicle the construction of El Escorial and include masterpieces by Bosch, El Greco, Titian, Tintoretto, Velázquez, Zurbarán, and Van Dyck. The **Palacio Real,** lined with 16th-century *azulejos* (tiles), includes the majestic **Salón del Trono** (Throne Room), Felipe II's spartan 16th-century apartments, and the luxurious 18th-century rooms of Carlos III and Carlos IV. The macabre **Panteón Real** is filled with tombs of monarchs and glitters with gold-and-marble designs. (Complex ☎918 90 59 03. Open Apr.-Sept. Tu-Su 10am-6pm; Oct.-Mar. 10am 5pm. Last admission 1hr. before closing. Monastery €6, students and seniors €3.) **Autocares Herranz buses** arrive from Madrid's Moncloa Metro station (50min.; every 15min. M-F 7am-11:30pm, Sa 9am-10pm, Su 9am-11pm; last return 1hr. earlier; €3).

EL VALLE DE LOS CAÍDOS. In a valley of the Sierra de Guadarrama, Franco built the overpowering **Santa Cruz del Valle de los Caídos** (Valley of the Fallen) as a memorial to those who died in the Civil War. The massive granite cross was meant to honor only those who died "serving *Dios* and *España*," in other words, the fascist Nationalists. Thousands of non-fascists forced to build the monument died during its construction. Franco is buried beneath the high altar, but there is no mention of his tomb in tourist literature. It is accessible only via El Escorial. (Mass M-Sa 11am; Su 11am, 12:30, 1, and 5:30pm. Entrance gate open Tu-Su 10am-6pm; basilica open 10am-6:30pm. €5, seniors and students €2.50. EU citizens free W. Funicular to the cross €2.50.) **Autocares Herranz** runs one **bus** to the monument (leaves El Escorial from C. Juan de Toledo; 20min.; Tu-Su 3:15pm, return 5:30pm; round-trip plus admission €7).

CENTRAL SPAIN

In Castilla La Mancha, surrounding Madrid to the east and south, medieval cities and olive groves fill the land. To the west, Castilla y León's dramatic cathedrals stand testament to its glorious history. Farther west, bordering Portugal, stark Extremadura was birthplace to hundreds of world-famous explorers.

CASTILLA LA MANCHA

Although Castilla La Mancha is one of Spain's least-developed regions, you don't need Don Quixote's imagination to fall in love with this battered, windswept plateau; its austere beauty surfaces through its tumultuous history, gloomy medieval fortresses, and awesome crags.

TOLEDO ☎925

Cossío called Toledo "the most brilliant and evocative summary of Spain's history." Toledo (pop. 66,000) may today be marred by armies of tourists and caravans of kitsch, but this former capital of the Holy Roman, Visigoth, and Muslim empires remains a treasure trove of Spanish culture. The city's numerous churches, synagogues, and mosques share twisting alleyways, emblematic of a time when Spain's three religions coexisted peacefully.

◤◢ TRANSPORTATION AND PRACTICAL INFORMATION. Trains, Po. Rosa 2 (☎902 24 02 02), arrive from Madrid's Estación Atocha (1hr., 9-10 per day, €4.80). **Buses** (☎925 21 58 50) to Valencia depart 5min. from the city gate (5½hr., M-F 3pm, €17; buy ticket on the bus). Take bus #5 or 6 from the right of the train station to Pl. Zocodóver (€0.78), follow C. Armas downhill as it changes names and leads through the Puerta Nueva de Bisagra gates, and cross the intersection to reach the **tourist office.** (☎925 22 08 43. Open Tu-Su 10:30am-2:30pm and 4:30-7pm.) Surf the **Internet** at **Punto Com,** C. Armas 4, 2nd fl., in Pl. Zocodóver. (€0.90 per 15min., €1.50 per 30min. Open M-Sa 11:30am-10pm, Su 3:30-10pm.) **Postal code:** 45070.

SPAIN

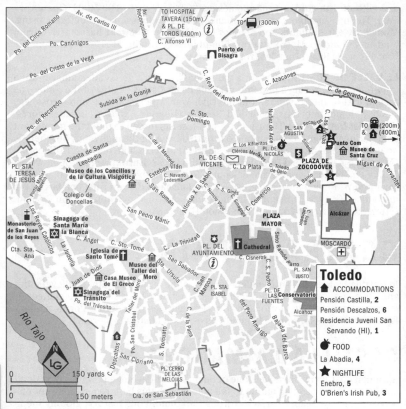

Toledo

🏠 ACCOMMODATIONS
Pensión Castilla, **2**
Pensión Descalzos, **6**
Residencia Juvenil San
  Servando (HI), **1**

🍴 FOOD
La Abadia, **4**

⭐ NIGHTLIFE
Enebro, **5**
O'Brien's Irish Pub, **3**

🏠🍴 **ACCOMMODATIONS AND FOOD.** The 🏠**Residencia Juvenil San Servando (HI) ❶**, on Castillo San Servando (10min.), uphill from the train station, sits inside a 14th-century castle. (☎925 22 45 54. Reception 7am-midnight. Dorms €8.50, over 26 €11. HI card required.) From Pl. Zocodóver, take C. Armas downhill, then the first left up C. Recoletos to get to **Pensión Castilla ❷**, C. Recoletos 6. (☎925 25 63 18. Singles €15; doubles with bath €25.) Down the steps off Po. del Tránsito, near the Sinagoga del Tránsito, you'll find the high-class **Pensión Descalzos ❻**, C. Descalzos 30. (☎925 22 28 88. Apr.-Oct. singles €24; doubles €39-44; Oct.-Mar. singles €23; doubles €34-39. MC/V.) Try Toledo's marzipan delights at the *pastelerías*, or have a square meal at **La Abadía ❹**, Pl. San Nicolás 3. (Lunch *menú* €8.30. Open M-Th 8am-midnight, F 8am-1:30am, Sa noon-2:30am, Su noon-midnight.)

🏛🎭 **SIGHTS AND NIGHTLIFE.** The vast collection of museums, churches, synagogues, and mosques lies within the city walls; despite well-marked streets, you'll probably get lost. Toledo's grandiose 🏛**cathedral,** southwest of Pl. Zocodóver at the Arco de Palacioz, boasts five naves, delicate stained glass, and unapologetic ostentation. (Open June-Aug. daily 10am-noon and 4-7pm; Sept.-May 10am-noon and 4-6pm.) Toledo's most formidable landmark, the 🏛**Alcázar,** Cuesta Carlos V 2, uphill from Pl. Zocodóver, has been a stronghold of Romans, Visigoths, Moors, and

Spaniards. Today, it houses a national military museum. (Open Tu-Su 9:30am-2pm. €2, W free.) El Greco spent most of his life in Toledo. Many of his works are displayed throughout town; his famous *El entierro del Conde de Orgaz (Burial of Count Orgaz)* is housed on the west side of town in the **Iglesia de Santo Tomé**, Pl. Conde. (Open Mar.-Oct. 15 daily 10am-6:45pm; Oct. 16-Feb. 10am-5:45pm. €1.20; under 18, students, and seniors €0.90.) Downhill and to the left lies the **Casa Museo de El Greco**, C. Samuel Levi 2, which houses 19 works by the master. (Open Tu-Sa 10am-2pm and 4-6pm, Su 10am-2pm. €1.20; under 18, students, and over 65 free. Sa-Su afternoons free.) The simple exterior of the 14th-century **Sinagoga del Tránsito**, on C. Samuel Levi, hides ornate Mudéjar plasterwork and an intricate wooden ceiling. (Open Tu-Sa 10am-1:45pm and 4-5:45pm, Su 10am-2pm. €2.40; under 18 and students €1.20; Sa after 4pm and Su free.) The 12th-century **Sinagoga de Santa María la Blanca**, down the street to the right, was built as a mosque and then used as the city's main synagogue until its conversion to a church in 1492. (Open June-Aug. daily, 10am-1:45pm and 3:30-6:45pm; Sept.-May until 5:45pm. €1.20; under 16, students, and seniors €0.90.) At the western edge of the city resides the Franciscan **Monasterio de San Juan de los Reyes**, commissioned by Isabel and Fernando. (Open Apr.-Sept. daily 10am-1:45pm and 3:30-6:45pm; Oct.-Mar. until 6pm. €1.20.)

For nightlife, head through the arch and to the left from Pl. Zocodóver to **Calle Santa Fé**, which brims with beer and local youth. **Trébol**, C. Sante Fe 1, has excellent *tapas*. (Open M-Sa 10am-3:30pm and 7pm-midnight, Su from 1pm.) **Enebro**, on small Pl. Santiago Balleros off C. Cervantes, serves free *tapas* in the evenings. (Open daily 11am-4pm and 7pm-2:30am.) For more upscale bars and clubs try **Calle Sillería** and **Calle Alfileritos**, west of Pl. Zocodóver. **O'Brien's Irish Pub**, C. Armas 12, is a favorite with 20-somethings. (Open M-Th noon-2:30am, Sa-Su noon-4am.)

CUENCA ☎969

Cuenca (pop. 50,000) is a hilltop city flanked by two rivers and the stunning rock formations they created. The enchanting **old city** safeguards most of Cuenca's unique charm, including the famed *casas colgadas* (hanging houses) that dangle high above the Río Huécar, on C. Obispo Vaero off Pl. Mayor. Cross the San Pablo bridge to **Hoz del Huécar** for a spectacular view of the *casas* and cliffs. Many of the *casas* house museums; on Pl. Ciudad de Ronda is the excellent **Museo de Arte Abstracto Español**. (Open Tu-F and holidays 11am-2pm and 4-6pm, Sa 11am-2pm and 4-8pm, Su 11am-2pm. €3, students and seniors €1.50.) In the Pl. Mayor sits the perfectly square **Cathedral de Cuenca**. (Open Tu-Sa 8:45am-2pm and 4-6pm (Oct.-July to 7pm), Su 9am-2pm. Mass daily 9:20am, Su also noon and 1pm.)

Trains (☎902 24 02 02) run to Madrid (2½-3hr., 5-6 per day, €8.60) and Valencia (3-4hr., 3-4 per day, €9.50). **Buses** (☎969 22 70 87) depart from C. Fermín Caballero for: Barcelona (3½hr., 1-2 per day, €27); Madrid (2½hr., 8-9 per day, €8.20-10.15); and Toledo (3hr., 1-2 per day, €9.75). To get to Pl. Mayor in the old city from either train station take a left on to C. Fermín Caballero, following it as it becomes C. Cervantes and C. José Cobo, then bear left through Pl. Hispanidad. The **tourist office** is in Pl. Mayor. (☎969 23 21 19. Open July-Sept. M-Sa 9am-9pm, Su 9am-2pm; Oct.-June M-Sa 9am-2pm and 4-6pm, Su 9am-2pm.) ◼**Hostal-Residencia Posada de San José ❷**, C. Julián Romero 4, a block up from the left side of the cathedral, has gorgeous views worth cashing an extra traveler's check. (☎969 21 13 00. Prices drop Sept.-June. Singles €18, with full bath €39; doubles €29/€57.) To reach **Pensión Tabanqueta ❸**, C. Trabuco 13, head up C. San Pedro from the cathedral past Pl. Trabuco. (☎969 21 12 90. Doubles €30; triples €45.) Budget eateries line **Calle Cervantes** and **Calle República Argentina**. Grab groceries at **%Día**, on Av. Castilla La Mancha. (Open M-Th 9:30am-2pm and 5:30-8:30pm, F-Sa 9am-2:30pm and 5:30-9pm.) **Postal Code:** 16004.

CASTILLA Y LEÓN

Castilla y León's cities rise like green oases from a desert of burnt sienna. The majestic Gothic cathedrals of Burgos and León, the slender Romanesque belfries along Camino de Santiago, the sandstone of Salamanca, and the city walls of Ávila have emblazoned themselves as regional and national images.

SALAMANCA   ☎923

For centuries, the gates of Salamanca have welcomed scholars, saints, rogues, and royals. The bustling city is famed for its golden sandstone architecture as well as its university—the oldest in Spain, and once one of the "four leading lights of the world" along with the universities of Bologna, Paris, and Oxford.

▐▌▐▌ TRANSPORTATION AND PRACTICAL INFORMATION. Trains run from Po. de la Estación (☎923 12 02 02) to Lisbon (6hr., 4:30am, €33) and Madrid (2½hr., 4 per day 7:45am-7:30pm, €13). **Buses** run from Av. Filiberto Villalobos 71-85 (☎923 23 67 17) to: León (2½hr.; M-F 3 per day 11am-6:30pm, Sa 11am, Su 10pm; €11); Madrid (3hr., M-Sa 15 per day, €10); and Segovia (3hr., 2 per day, €8). Visit the **tourist office** at Pl. Mayor 14. (☎923 21 83 42. Open M-Sa 9am-2pm and 4:30-6:30pm, Su 10am-2pm and 4:30-6:30pm.) Access the **Internet** at **Informática Abaco Bar,** C. Zamora 7. (Open M-F 9:30am-2am, Sa-Su 11am-2am. €1.20 per hr.)

▐▌▐▌ ACCOMMODATIONS AND FOOD. Reasonably priced *hostales* and *pensiones* cater to the floods of student visitors, especially off Pl. Mayor and C. Meléndez. **Pensión Las Vegas ❷,** C. Meléndez 13, 1st fl., has TVs and friendly owners. (☎923 21 87 49. Doubles €24; triples with bath €36. MC/V.) At **Pensión Villanueva ❶,** C. San Justo 8, 1st fl., Sra. Manuela shares local lore and gossip. Exit Pl. Mayor via Pl. Poeta Iglesias, cross the street, and take the first left. (☎923 26 88 33. Singles €12; doubles €24.) **Hostal Anaya ❷,** C. Jesús 18, is steps away from Pl. Mayor. (☎923 27 17 73. Singles €24; doubles €42; triples €54; quads €72.) Albetur buses shuttle **campers** from Gran Vía (every 30min.) to the first-class **Regio ❶,** 4km toward Madrid on Ctra. Salamanca. (☎923 13 88 88. €2.70 per person, €5.11 per tent, €2.70 per car.) Cafes and restaurants surround **Plaza Mayor;** full meals in cheaper back alley spots run about €8. **El Patio Chico ❷,** C. Meléndez 13, is crowded at lunch time, but the large and delicious portions are worth the wait. (*Menú* €11, entrees €4-8, *bocadillos* €2-3. Open daily 1-4pm and 8pm-midnight.) **Mesón Las Conchas ❸,** R. Mayor 16, is the quintessential *bar español*. (*Menú* €10.50, *raciones* €6-14. Open daily 1-4pm and 8pm-12am. MC/V.) **Champion,** C. Toro 64, has a downstairs supermarket. (Open M-Sa 9:15am-9:15pm.)

BULLBOARDS Gazing out the window of your preferred mode of transportation, you may notice rather unusual monuments along the highway: massive black paper silhouettes of solitary bulls. Once upon a time (in the 1980s) these cutouts were advertisements for Osborne Sherry. In the early 1990s, however, billboards were prohibited on national roads. A plan was drafted to take the bulls down, but Spaniards protested, as the lone bull towering along the roadside had become an important national symbol. After considerable clamoring and hoofing, the bulls were painted black and left to loom proudly against the horizon. The familiar shape now decorates t-shirts and pins in souvenir shops, but the real thing is still impressive.

◉ **SIGHTS.** The ◪**Plaza Mayor,** designed by Alberto Churriguera, has been called one of the most beautiful squares in Spain. Between its nearly 100 sandstone arches hang medallions with bas-reliefs of famous Spaniards, from El Cid to Franco. Walk down R. Mayor to Pl. San Isidro to reach the 15th-century **Casa de las Conchas** (House of Shells), one of Salamanca's most famous landmarks, adorned with over 300 rows of scallop shells chiseled in sandstone. Go down Patio de las Escuelas, off C. Libreros (which leads south from Pl. San Isidro), to enter the ◪**Universidad,** founded in 1218. The university's 16th-century entryway is one of the best examples of Spanish Plateresque, named for the delicate filigree work of *plateros* (silversmiths). Hidden in the sculptural work lies a tiny frog; according to legend, those who can spot the frog without assistance will be blessed with good luck and even marriage. Inside the Patio de Escuelas Menores, the University Museum contains the **Cielo de Salamanca,** a 15th-century fresco of the zodiac. (Open M-F 9:30am-1:30pm and 4-7:30pm, Sa 9:30am-1:30pm and 4-7pm, Su 10am-1:30pm. €2.40, students and seniors €1.20.) Continue down R. Mayor to Pl. Anaya to reach the *vieja* (old) and *nueva* (new) cathedrals. Begun in 1513 to accommodate the growing tide of Catholics, the spindly spired late-Gothic **Catedral Nueva** wasn't finished until 1733. The 1140 **Catedral Vieja** has a striking cupola with depictions of apocalyptic angels separating the sinners from the saved. The **museum** in the back houses a Mudéjar Salinas organ, one of the oldest organs in Europe. (*Nueva:* open Apr.-Sept. daily 9am-2pm and 4-8pm; Oct.-Mar. 9am-1pm and 4-6pm. Free. *Vieja:* cloister and museum open Apr.-Sept. daily 10am-1:30pm and 4-7:30pm. €3, students €2.25, children €1.50.) **Casa Lis Museo Art Nouveau Y Art Deco,** C. Gibraltar 14, behind the cathedrals, houses the oddities of Miguel de Lis's art nouveau and art deco collection. Exhibits range from elegant fans signed by noteworthies like Salvador Dalí to racy sculptures of animals and people in compromising positions. (Open Apr.-Oct. 15 Tu-F 11am-2pm and 5-9pm, Sa-Su 11am-9pm; Oct. 16-Mar. Tu-F 11am-2pm and 4-7pm, Sa-Su 11am-8pm. €2.10, students €1.50, children and Tu mornings free.)

◪◪ **ENTERTAINMENT AND NIGHTLIFE.** According to Salamantinos, Salamanca is the best place in Spain to party; they say there is one bar for every one hundred people living in the city. There are *chupiterias* (shot bars), *bares,* and *discotecas* on nearly every street, and while some close at 4am, others go all night. Nightlife centers on **Plaza Mayor** and spreads out to Gran Vía, C. Bordadores, and side streets. **Calle Prior** and **Rua Mayor** are also full of bars. Locals gather in the terrazas on **Plaza de la Fuente,** off Av. Alemania. Intense partying occurs off **Calle Varillas.** Begin at **El Ochavo,** Pl. San Juan Bautista 7, for *litros* of beer or *sangría* (€3 each). Students also pregame at **La Chupitería,** Pl. Monterrey (at the intersection of C. Prior and Bordadores), which serves inexpensive shots (€0.90 each) and slightly larger *chupas* (€1 each). Drink to modern funk and jazz at **Birdland,** C. Azafranal 57. At **Cum Laude,** C. Prior 5, the dance floor is a replica of the Pl. Mayor. Try **Camelot,** C. Bordadores 3, a monastery-turned-club. Swing to Top 40 songs at the popular **Café Moderno,** Gran Vía, 75. A mixed clientele grooves under black lights at **Submarino,** C. San Justo 27.

◪ **DAYTRIP FROM SALAMANCA: ZAMORA.** Perched atop a rocky cliff over the Rio Duero, Zamora (pop. 65,000) is an intriguing mix of the modern and medieval: 15th-century palaces harbor Internet cafes and luxury hotels. Zamora's foremost monument is its Romanesque **cathedral,** built between the 12th and 15th centuries. Highlights are its intricately carved choir stalls (complete with seated apostles laughing and singing) and the main altar, an ornate structure of marble, gold, and silver. Inside the cloister, the **Museo de la Cate-**

dral features the priceless 15th-century Black Tapestries, which tell the story of the Trojan War and Achilles's defeat. (Cathedral and museum open Tu-Su 10am-2pm and 5-8pm. Mass daily at 10am, also Sa 6pm and Su 1pm. Cathedral free, museum €1.80.) All in all, twelve handsome Romanesque churches remain within the walls of the old city, gleaming in the wake of recent restoration. Most visitors follow the **Romanesque Route,** a self-guided tour of all of the churches available from the **tourist office,** C. Santa Clara 20. (Open M-Sa 9am-2pm and 5-7pm.) The ■**Museo de Semana Santa,** in sleepy Pl. Santa María La Nueva 9, is a rare find. Hooded mannequins stand guard over elaborately sculpted floats, dating back to the early 17th century. (Open M-Sa 10am-2pm and 5-8pm, Su 10am-2pm. €2.70.) **Buses** depart from Salamanca, Av. Filiberto Villalobos 71-85 (☎923 23 67 17), to Zamora (1hr.; M-F 22 per day 6:40am-10:35pm, Sa 10 per day 7:45am-8:30pm; €3.50).

LEÓN ☎987

Formerly the center of Christian Spain, today León (pop. 300,000) is best known for its 13th-century Gothic ■**cathedral,** arguably the most beautiful in Spain. Its spectacular stained-glass windows have earned the city the nickname *La Ciudad Azul* (The Blue City) and alone warrant a trip to León. The cathedral's **museum** displays gruesome wonders, including a sculpture depicting the skinning of a saint. (Cathedral: open in summer daily 8:30am-2:30pm and 5-7pm; off-season 8:30am-1:30pm and 4-7pm. Free. Museum: open in summer daily 9:30am-1:30pm and 4-6:30pm; off-season M-F 9:30am-1pm and 4-6pm, Sa 9:30am-1:30pm. €3.50.) The **Basílica San Isidoro,** dedicated in the 11th century to San Isidoro of Sevilla, houses the bodies of countless royals in the impressive *Panteón Real.* From Pl. Santo Domingo, walk up C. Ramon y Cajal; the basilica is up the flight of stairs on the right just before C. La Torre. (Open M-Sa 9am-1:30pm and 4pm-6:30pm, Su 9am-1:30pm. €3.) For nearby bars, discos, and techno music, head to the *barrio húmedo* (drinker's neighborhood) around **Plaza de San Martín** and **Plaza Mayor.** After 2am, the crowds weave to **Calle Lancia** and **Calle Conde de Guillén,** both heavily populated with discos and bars.

Trains (☎ (902) 24 02 02) run from Av. Astorga 2 to Madrid (4½hr., M-Sa 7 per day 1am-6pm, €27.50). **Buses** (☎987 21 00 00) leave from Po. Ingeniero Sáenz de Miera for Madrid (4½hr.; M-F 12 per day 2:30am-10:30pm, Sa-Su 8 per day 2:30am-7:30pm; €16.10). Av. Palencia (a left out of the main entrance of the bus station or right out of the main entrance of the train station) leads across the river to **Plaza Glorieta Guzmán el Bueno,** where, after the rotary, it becomes **Avenida de Ordoño II** and leads to León's cathedral and the adjacent **tourist office,** Pl. Regla 3. (☎987 23 70 82. Open M-F 9am-2pm and 5-7pm, Sa-Su 10am-2pm and 5-8pm.) Many accommodations cluster on **Av. de Roma, Av. Ordoño II,** and **Avenida República Argentina,** which lead into the old town from Pl. Glorieta Guzmán el Bueno. **Hostal Orejas ❹,** C. Villafranca 6, 2nd fl., is just down Av. República Argentina from Pl. Glorieta Guzmán el Bueno. Each brand-new room comes with bath, shower, and cable TV. (☎987 25 29 09; janton@usarios.Retecal.es. Free Internet. Su-W singles €28, doubles €34; Th-Sa singles €39, doubles €47.) Inexpensive eateries fill the area near the cathedral and on the small streets off C. Ancha; also check **Plaza San Martín,** near Pl. Mayor.

▶ DAYTRIP FROM LEÓN: ASTORGA. Astorga's fanciful ■**Palacio Episcopal,** designed by Antoni Gaudí in the late-19th century, now houses the **Museo de los Caminos.** (☎987 61 88 82. Open M-Sa 10am-1:30pm and 4-7:30pm, Su 10am-1:30pm. €1.50.) Opposite the *palacio* is Astorga's cathedral and museum. (Both open daily 10am-2pm and 4-8pm. Cathedral free; museum €1.50.) Astorga is most easily reached by **bus** from Po. Ingeniero Saenz de Miera in León (45min.; M-F 16 per day 6:15am-9:30pm, Sa-Su 6-7 per day 8:30am-8:30pm; €2.58).

EXTREMADURA

Arid plains bake under the intense summer sun, relieved only by scattered patches of glowing sunflowers. This land of harsh beauty and cruel extremes hardened New World conquistadors such as Hernán Cortés and Francisco Pizarro.

TRUJILLO ☎927

The gem of Extremadura, hill-perched Trujillo (pop. 10,000) is an unspoiled joy. It's often called the "Cradle of Conquistadors" because the city produced over 600 explorers of the New World. Scattered with medieval palaces, Roman ruins, Arabic fortresses, and churches of all eras, Trujillo is a glorious hodge-podge of histories and cultures. Its most impressive monument is its tallest, a 10th-century **Moorish castle** that offers a panoramic view of surrounding plains. The **Plaza Mayor** was the inspiration for the Plaza de Armas in Cuzco, Perú, which was constructed after Francisco Pizarro defeated the Incas. Festooned with stork nests, **Iglesia de San Martín** dominates the northeastern corner of the plaza. (All churches open June-Sept. daily 10am-2pm and 5-8:30pm; Oct.-May 9:30am-2pm and 4:30-7:30pm. Each €1.20-1.25; all €4.20.)

Buses run to Madrid (2½hr., 12-14 per day, €13). To get to the Plaza Mayor, turn left up C. de las Cruces as you exit the station, right on C. de la Encarnación, then left on C. Chica; turn left on C. Virgen de la Guia and right on C. Burgos, continuing on to the Plaza (15min.). The **tourist office** is across the plaza and posts information in its windows when closed. (☎927 32 26 77. Open June-Sept. 9:30am-2pm and 4:30-7:30pm; Oct.-May 9:30am-2pm and 4-8pm.) **Pensión Boni ❶,** C. Mingo de Ramos 117, is off Pl. Mayor to the right of the church. (☎927 32 16 04. Singles €12; doubles €21, with bath €30.) Try **Hostal Trujillo ❷,** C. de Francisco Pizarro 4-6. From C. de las Cruces, turn right on C. de la Encarnación, then right again onto C. de Francisco Pizarro. (☎927 32 26 61. Singles €21; doubles €39.) The **Plaza Mayor** teems with tourist eateries. **Meson Alberca ❸,** C. Victoria 8, has an interior garden and an excellent three-course *menú* for €15. (Open Su-T and Th-Sa 11am-1am.)

SOUTHERN SPAIN (ANDALUCÍA)

Andalucía is all that you expect Spain to be—flamenco shows, bullfighting, tall pitchers of *sangría*, white-washed villages, and streets lined with orange trees. The Moors arrived in AD 711 and bequeathed the region with far more than the flamenco music and gypsy ballads proverbially associated with southern Spain, sparking the European Renaissance and reintroducing the wisdom of Classical Greece and the Near East. Under their rule, Sevilla and Granada reached the pinnacle of Islamic arts and Córdoba matured into the most culturally influential Islamic city. Despite (or perhaps because of) the poverty and high unemployment in their homeland, Andalucians have always maintained a passionate, unshakable dedication to living the good life. The never-ending *festivales, ferias*, and *carnavales* of Andalucía are world-famous for their extravagance.

CÓRDOBA
☎ 957

The light of the Dark Ages, Córdoba (pop. 310,000) was built on religious tolerance and intellectual achievement. Once the largest city in Western Europe, its prestigious university (founded in the 12th century) and paved streets welcomed Jews, Christians, and Arabs alike; the city's mosques, synagogues, and cathedrals stand testament to its incredible legacy of tolerance. Today, springtime festivals, flower-filled patios, and a steady nightlife make it one of Spain's most beloved cities.

⌐ TRANSPORTATION

Trains: Plaza de las Tres Culturas, Av. América (☎957 40 02 02). To: **Madrid** (AVE 2hr., 18 per day, €38-45); **Cádiz** (AVE 2¾hr., 2 per day, €22; regular 3-4hr., 5 per day, €15-22); **Málaga** (AVE 2¼hr., 6 per day, €12-13.50; regular 3hr., 9 per day, €10-18); and **Sevilla** (AVE 45min., 18 per day, €14.50-17.50).

Buses: Estación de Autobuses, Glorieta de las Tres Culturas (☎957 40 40 40) across from the train station. **Alsina Graells Sur** (☎957 27 81 00) covers most of Andalucía. To: **Cádiz** via Los Amarillos or Comes Sur (4-5hr., 2 per day, €17); **Granada** (3hr., 9 per day, €10); **Málaga** (3-3½hr., 5 per day, €10); and **Sevilla** (2hr., 10-12 per day, €8). **Bacoma** (☎957 45 65 14) runs to **Barcelona** (10hr., 1 per day, €51). **Secorbus** (☎(902) 22 92 92) sends exceptionally cheap buses to **Madrid** (4½hr., 6 per day, €10.50) and departs from C. de los Sastres in front of Hotel Meliá. **Empresa Rafael Ramírez** (☎957 42 21 77) runs buses to nearby towns and camping sites.

✴ ⏃ ORIENTATION AND PRACTICAL INFORMATION

Córdoba is split into two parts: the **old city** and the **new city**. The modern and commercial northern half extends from the train station on Avenida América down to **Plaza de las Tendillas,** the center of the city. The old section in the south is a medieval maze known as the **Judería** (Jewish quarter). The easiest way to reach the old city from the adjacent train and bus stations is to take bus #3 to **Campo Santo de los Mártires** (€0.80.) Or to walk (20min.), exit left from the station, cross the parking plaza and make a right onto Av. de los Mozarabes. When you reach the Roman columns, turn left and cross Gta. Sargentos Provisionales. Make a right on Paseo de la Victoria and continue until you reach Puerto Almodovar and the old city.

Tourist Offices: Oficina Municipal de Turismo y Congresos, Pl. Judá Leví (☎957 20 05 22), next to the youth hostel, has maps and free event brochures. Open M-F 8:30am-2:30pm. **Tourist Office of Andalucía,** C. Torrijos 10 (☎957 47 12 35), in the Junta de Andalucía, across from the Mezquita. From the train station, take bus #3 along the river until a stone arch appears on the right. Office is 1 block up C. Torrijos. General information on Andalucía. Open May-Sept. M-F 9:30am-8pm, Sa 10am-7pm, Su 10am-2pm; Oct.-Apr. M-Sa 9:30am-6pm, Su 10am-2pm.

Currency Exchange: CajaSur, Ronda de los Tejares 18-24 (☎957 21 42 42), across from the Corte Ingles. 10% commission, €4.50 minimum. Open M-F 8:30am-2:30pm.

Emergency: ☎092. **Police:** Av. Doctor Flemming 2 (☎957 59 45 80).

Córdoba

ACCOMMODATIONS
Camping Municipal, **1**
Hostal El Triunfo, **10**
Hostal La Calleja, **8**
Hostal Maestre, **3**
Hostal-Residencia Séneca, **6**
Hostal Rey Heredia, **7**
Residencia Juvenil
  Córdoba (HI), **9**

RESTAURANTS
El Churrasco Restaurante, **5**
El Picantón, **4**
Mesón San Basilio, **11**

NIGHTLIFE
Soul, **2**

Alonso el Sabio
C. Haza Tranco
C. Molinos Alta
Av. de las Ollerías
C. M. de la Misericordia
C. Moriscos
PL. DE COLON
C. Marroquíes
C. de Adare
PL. CONDE DE RIEGO
PL. STA. MARINA
C. del Zarco
Palacio del Marqués de Viana
Acera Aguirre
TO ▲ (2km), BARRIO EL BRILLANTE & CAFETERÍA TERRA (1.5km)
Isabel Losa
PL. D. GOME
PL. CAPUCHINAS
Cristo de los Faroles
Cahrera
R. Casas Deza
C. de las Imágenes
C. del Osario
Obispo Ffrero
Juan
Santa Marta
Rufo
Conde de Arenales
Pedro Fernández
C. Conde de Torres
C. Alfonso
C. San Pablo
Av. de América
F. de Córdoba
C. La Bodega
Av. del Gran Capitán
Av. de Cervantes
El Corte Inglés
Av. Ronda de los Tejares
C. los Reyes Católicos
Doce de Octubre
C. del Caño
Av. del Gran Capitán
C. Conde de Robledo
C. Cruz Conde
C. Conde de Gondomar
C. de Alfonso XIII
Ayuntamiento
TO UNIVERSIDAD DE CÓRDOBA (400m)
Medical Assistance (Casa de Socorro)
PL. DE S. IGNACIO DE LOYOLA
C. Góngora
C. Menéndez y Pelayo
C. Morería
Concepción
C. Claudio Marcelo
PL. TENDILLAS
C. Pedro López
Plaza de la Corredera
Av. de la República Argentina
JARDINES DE LA VICTORIA
Paseo de la Victoria
C. Eduardo Dato
Pérez de Castro
PL. SAN NICOLÁS
San Felipe
C. Sevilla
Málaga
PL. EMILIO LUQUE
El Corte Inglés
C. Jesús María
J. de Mena
R. Sánchez
Reloj
C. Ambrosio de Morales
Diario Córdoba
Fernando Colón
P. Muñoz
Pera
PL. CAÑAS
Guitiérrez de los Ríos
Lope de Hoces
PL. TRINIDAD
de la Teria
Telón Marín
Argote
PL. S. JUAN
R. Barroso
Juan Valera
C. de San Fernando
Maese Luis Tornillo
Candelaria
C. Lineros
Soclbus Bus Stop
Puerta de Almodóvar
C. Almanzor Romero
C. Buen Pastor
Blanco Belmonte
Museo Arqueológico
M. del Villar
PL. J. PÁEZ
Julio Romero
Museo de Bellas Artes
PL. DEL POTRO
C. Francisco
Museo Julio Romero de Torres
Statue of Maimónides
Casa Andalusí
Museo Taurino y de Arte Cordobés
Deanes
Céspedes
C. Judería
C. Cardenal Herrero
PL. BENAVENTE
Calleja de Flores
Conde de Luna
Encarnación
Cale de Díaz
Sta. Clara
C. Bataneros
C. Cabeza
Calderones
R. Barros
Posada del Potro
PL. MAIMÓNIDES Municipal
Córdoba Vision
PL. JUDA LEVI
Tourist Office of Andalucia
Museo Diocesano de Bellas Artes
Marquéz
C. Torrijos
Mezquita
C. Corregidor Luis de la Cerda
Ronda de Isasa
Río Guadalquivir
Old City Bus Stop
PL. CAMPO SANTO DE LOS MÁRTIRES
Amador de los Ríos
Palacio de Congresos
Puente Romano
Av. Conde Vallellano
C. San Basilio
C. Enmedio
C. Martín de Roa
Caballerizas Reales
Alcázar
Ancient Roman Mills
Av. de Alcázar
Av. del Corregidor
TO PUENTE SAN RAFAEL (10m)
Av. de la Confederación
Av. de Cádiz
Torre de la Calahorra
PL. STA. TERESA
C. del Santo Cristo

IU ■ ☐ (200m)

SPAIN

200 yards
200 meters

Medical Assistance: Emergencies ☎061. **Red Cross Hospital,** Paso de la Victoria (urgent ☎957 22 22 22, main line 957 42 06 66). M-F 9am-1:30pm and 4:30-5:30pm. **Ambulance:** urgent ☎902 505 061, main line ☎957 767 359.

24hr. Pharmacy: On a rotating basis. Refer to the list posted outside the pharmacy in Pl. Tendillas or the local newspaper.

Internet Access: e-Net, C. Garcia Lovera 10 (☎957 48 14 62). Leave Pl. Tendillas on C. Claudio Marcelo, take second left. €1.20 per hr. Open daily 9am-2pm and 5-10pm.

Post Office: C. Cruz Conde 15 (☎957 47 97 96), 2 blocks up from Pl. Tendillas. *Lista de Correos.* Open M-F 8:30am-8:30pm, Sa-Su 9:30am-2pm. **Postal Code:** 14070.

▐ ACCOMMODATIONS AND CAMPING

Most accommodations cluster around the whitewashed walls of the Judería, and in old Córdoba between Mezquita and C. San Fernando, a quieter and more residential area. Call up to several months ahead during *Semana Santa* and summer.

▨ **Residencia Juvenil Córdoba (HI),** Pl. Juda Leví (☎957 29 01 66; informacion@inturjoven.junta.andalucia.es), next to the municipal tourist office and a 2min. walk from the Mezquita. A backpacker's utopia. Internet €0.50 per 12min. 24hr. reception. Reservations recommended. €12.90 per person; ages 26 and up €17.25. ❶

Hostal El Triunfo, Corregidor Luis de la Cerda 79 (☎902 15 83 92; reservas@htriunfo.com), across from the southern side of La Mezquita. All rooms have A/C, phone, TV, bath, and a safe. Singles €25-38; doubles €44-57. ❸

Hostal-Residencia Séneca, C. Conde y Luque 7 (☎/fax 957 47 32 34). Follow C. Céspedes 2 blocks from the Mezquita. Breakfast included. Reservations recommended. Singles with sink €15-18, with bath €26-30; doubles €27-32, with bath €35-39. ❷

Hostal Rey Heredia, C. Rey Heredia 26 (☎957 47 41 82). From C. Cardenal Herrero on the northeast side of La Mezquita, take C. Encarnación to C. de Rey Heredia; turn right and the hostal will be half a block down on the right. Singles €12; doubles €24. ❶

Hostal Maestre, C. Romero Barros 4-5 (☎/fax 957 47 53 95), off C. de San Fernando. Immaculate and pleasantly decorated rooms. All with private bath, most with TVs. Singles €18; doubles €32; triples €38. AmEx/MC/V. ❷

Hostal La Calleja, Calleja de Rufino Blanco y Sánchez 6 (☎/fax 957 48 66 06), at the intersection of C. Calereros and C. Cardenal Gonzalez. Reception 24hr. Singles €17, with bath and TV €20; doubles €27/€29. ❷

Camping Municipal, Av. Brillante 50 (☎957 40 38 36). From the train station, turn left on Av. América, left on Av. Brillante, and walk uphill for about 20min; or, take bus #10 or 11 from Av. Cervantes. Pool, supermarket, restaurant, and laundry service. Camping equipment for rent. One person and tent €8; two people and tent €11.60. ❶

◖ FOOD

The Mezquita area attracts nearly as many high-priced eateries as tourists to fill them, but a five-minute walk in any direction yields local specialties at reasonable prices. Córdobans converge on the outdoor *terrazas* between **Calle Severo Ochoa** and **Calle Dr. Jimenez Diaz** for drinks and *tapas* before dinner. Cheap eateries cluster farther away from the Judería in **Barrio Cruz Conde,** around **Avenida Menéndez Pidal** and **Plaza Tendillas.** Regional specialties include *salmorejo* (a gazpacho-like cream soup) and *rabo de toro* (bull's tail simmered in tomato sauce). **El Corte Ingles,** Av. Ronda de los Tejeres 30, has a grocery store (open M-Sa 10am-10pm).

▨ **El Picantón,** C. F. Ruano 19, 1 block from the Puerta de Almodovar. Take ordinary *tapas*, pour on *salsa picante*, stick it in a roll, and you've got lunch (€1.50-2.25). There's nothing else as cheap or as filling. Open daily 10am-3:30pm and 8pm-midnight. ❶

El Churrasco Restaurante, C. Almanzor Romero 16. A complimentary aperitif and excellent service start the meal off right. Delicious dishes. *Menu* €22, meat and fish dishes €10-38. Open daily 1-4pm and 8:30-11:30pm. Closed in August. MC/V. ❹

Casa Dona Vicenta, C. Gonzalo Xicueuea de Quesada 17. Excellent food, great prices, and friendly service. Entrees €6-18. Open Tu-Su 9am 11pm. MC/V. ❸

Mesón San Basilio, C. San Basilio 19. The locals love it, and so will you. Dine on one of two floors surrounding a breezy patio or have a drink at the bar. Menú M-F €6, Sa-Su €9. Entrees €6-14. Open daily 1-4pm and 8pm-midnight. AmEx/MC/V. ❷

🔘 SIGHTS

Considered the most important Islamic monument in the Western world, Córdoba's famous ▨**Mezquita** was built in AD 784 to surpass all other mosques in size. Visitors enter through the **Patio de los Naranjos,** an arcaded courtyard featuring carefully spaced orange trees and fountains; inside the mosque, 850 pink-and-blue marble and alabaster columns support hundreds of striped arches. At the far end of the Mezquita lies the **Capilla Villaviciosa,** where Caliphal vaulting appeared for the first time. In the center, intricate marble Byzantine mosaics—a gift from Emperor Constantine VII—shimmer across the arches of the **Mihrab,** the dome where Muslims guarded the Qur'an. Although the town rallied violently against the proposed erection of a **cathedral** in the center of the mosque, after the Crusaders conquered Córdoba in 1236 the towering **Crucero** (transept) and **Coro** (choir dome) were built. (Open July-Oct. 10am-7pm; Apr.-June M-Sa 10am-7:30pm, Su and holidays 2-7:30pm; Nov.-Mar. 10am-6pm. €6.50, under 10 free.)

The **Judería** (Jewish quarter) is the historic area northwest of the Mezquita. Downhill from the Moorish arch, the small **Sinagoga,** on C. Judíos, is one of Spain's few remaining synagogues, a solemn reminder of the 1492 expulsion of the Jews. (Open M-Sa 10am-2pm and 2:30-5:30pm, Su 10am-1:30pm. €0.50, EU citizens free.) To the south, along the river, is the ▨**Alcázar,** constructed for Catholic monarchs in 1328 during the conquest of Granada. Fernando and Isabel bade Columbus *adios* here, and the building served as Inquisition headquarters. (Open July-Aug. Tu-Su 8:30am-2:30pm; May-June and Sept. Tu-Sa 10am-2pm and 5:30-7:30pm, Su 9:30am-2:30pm; Oct.-Apr. Tu-Sa 10am-2pm and 4:30-6:30pm, Su 9:30am-2:30pm.) The **Museo Taurino y de Arte Cordobés,** on Pl. Maimónides, highlights the history of the bullfight. (Open July-Aug. Tu-Sa 8:30am-2:30pm, Su 9:30am-2:30pm; Sept.-June Tu-Sa 10am-2pm and 5:30-7:30pm, Su 9:30am-2:30pm. €3, students €1.50; F free.) There is a **combined ticket** for the Alcázar, Museo Taurino y de Arte Cordobés, and the **Museo Julio Romero,** which displays Romero's sensual portraits of Córdoban women (€7, students €3.60.).

🎵 🔘 ENTERTAINMENT AND NIGHTLIFE

For the latest cultural events, pick up a free copy of the *Guía del Ocio* at the tourist office. Hordes of tourists flock to see the flamenco dancers at the **Tablao Cardenal,** C. Torrijos 10, facing the Mezquita. The price is high, but a bargain compared to similar shows in Sevilla and Madrid. (€18 includes 1 drink. Shows M-Sa 10:30pm.) **La Bulería,** C. Pedro López 3, is even less expensive. (€11 includes 1 drink. Daily, 10:30pm.) Close to town is ▨**Soul,** C. Alfonso XIII 3, a hip and relaxed bar with cozy tables and dreadlock-sporting bartenders. (Beer €1.20, mixed drinks €3.60. Open 9am-3am; closed July-Aug.) Starting in June, the **Barrio Brillante,** uphill from Av. de América, is packed with young, well-dressed *Córdobeses* hopping between packed outdoor bars and dance clubs. Bus #10 goes to Brillante from the train station until about 11pm, but the bars don't wake up until around 1am (most stay open until 4am); a lift from **Radio Taxi** (☎957 76 44 44) should cost €3-6. If you're walking, head up Av. Brillante, passing along the way **Pub BSO,** C. Llanos de Pretorio, and **Brujas Bar** is right around the corner. Once in Barrio Brillante, where C. Poeta Emilia Prados meets C. Poeta Juan Ramón Jiménez, stop at **Cafetería Terra** before hitting the bars. Along Av. Brillante run a string of popular nightclubs, including **Pub La Moncloa, Club Don Luis,** and **Club Kachoamba.** During the winter months, nightlife shifts to the pubs surrounding the Universidad de Córdoba, mostly on C. Antonio Maura and C. Camino de los Sastres.

Of Córdoba's festivals, floats, and parades, **Semana Santa** in early April is the most extravagant. During the **Festival de los Patios** in the first two weeks of May, the city erupts with classical music concerts, flamenco dances, and a city-wide patio decorating contest. Late May brings the **Feria de Nuestra Señora de la Salud** (*La Feria*), a week of colorful garb, live dancing, and nonstop drinking.

▐█ DAYTRIP FROM CÓRDOBA: MADINAT AL-ZAHRA

Built in the **Sierra Morena** mountain range by Abderramán III for his favorite wife, this 10th-century medina was considered one of the greatest palaces of its time. The site, long thought to be mythical, was discovered in the mid-19th century and excavated in the early 20th-century. Today it's one of Spain's most impressive archaeological finds. (Open May to mid-Sept. Tu-Sa 10am-8:30pm, Su 10am-2pm; mid-Sept. to Apr. Tu-Su 10am-2pm. €1.50, EU citizens free.) **Córdoba Vision,** Av. Doctor Flemming 10, offers transportation and a 2½hr. guided visit to the site in English. (☎957 76 02 41. €18.) Reaching Madinat Al-Zahra takes some effort if you don't go with an organized tour. The O-1 **bus** leaves every hour from Av. República Argentina in Córdoba for Cruce Medina Azahara; from there, walk 45min. to the palace. (☎957 25 57 00. €0.80.) A taxi from Córdoba should cost about €24.

SEVILLE (SEVILLA) ☎954

Site of a Roman acropolis, capital of the Moorish empire, focal point of the Spanish Renaissance, and guardian angel of traditional Andalusian culture, Sevilla never disappoints. Flamenco, *tapas*, and bullfighting are at their best here, and the city's cathedral is among the most impressive in Spain. But it's the city's infectious, vivacious spirit that defines Seville, and fittingly, the local *Semana Santa* and *Feria de Abril* celebrations are among the most extravagant in all of Europe.

▐▀ TRANSPORTATION

Flights: All flights arrive at **Aeropuerto San Pablo** (SVQ; ☎954 44 90 00), 12km out of town on Ctra. Madrid. A taxi ride to the town center costs about €13. **Los Amarillos** (☎954 98 91 84) runs a bus to the airport from outside the Hotel Alfonso XIII at the Pta. Jerez (1-2 per hr. 6:15am-11pm; €2.25).

Trains: Estación Santa Justa (☎954 41 41 11), on Av. Kansas City. Near Pl. Nueva is the **RENFE** office, C. Zaragoza 29 (☎954 54 02 02). Open M-F 9am-1:15pm and 4-7pm. **AVE** trains run to **Córdoba** (45min., 18-20 per day, €15-17) and **Madrid** (2½hr., 18-20 per day, €62). **Talgo** trains run to: **Barcelona** (12hr., 3 per day, €53); **Cádiz** (2hr., 7-12 per day, €8); **Córdoba** (1½hr., 6 per day, €8); **Granada** (3hr., 5 per day, €17); **Málaga** (2½hr., 4-7 per day, €14); **Valencia** (8½hr., 4 per day, €36).

Buses: The old bus station at Prado de San Sebastián, C. Manuel Vazquez Sagastizabal (☎954 41 71 11), mainly serves Andalucía:

Transportes Alsina Graells (☎954 41 88 11). To: **Córdoba** (2hr., 10-12 per day 7:30am-9:30pm, €8); **Granada** (3hr., 10 per day 8am-11pm, €16); **Málaga** (3hr., 11 per day 7am-12am, €13).

Transportes Comes (☎954 41 68 58). To **Cádiz** (1½hr., 11-13 per day 7am-10pm, €9) and **Jerez de la Frontera** (2hr., 6 per day 8:30am-10pm, €6).

Los Amarillos (☎954 98 91 84). To **Arcos de la Frontera** (2hr., 8am and 4:30pm, €6) and **Marbella** (3hr., 3 per day 8am-8pm, €7).

Enatcar-Bacoma (☎902 42 22 42). To **Barcelona** (12-17hr., 9:30am and 5:30pm, €61-73) and **Valencia** (9-11hr., 9:30am and 5:30pm, €40-47).

Socibus (☎954 90 11 60). To **Madrid** (6hr., 11 per day 9am-1am, €17).

Public Transportation: TUSSAM (☎900 71 01 71), the city bus network. Most lines run every 10min. (6am-11:15pm) and converge on Pl. Nueva, Pl. Encarnación, or in front of the cathedral. Night service departs from Pl. Nueva (every hr., midnight-2am). Fare €0.90, *bonobús* (10 rides) €4.50. Particularly useful are C3 and C4, which circle the center, and 34, which hits the youth hostel, university, cathedral, and Pl. Nueva.

Taxis: TeleTaxi (☎954 62 22 22). **Radio Taxi** (☎954 58 00 00). Base rate €2.15, Su 25% surcharge. Extra charge for luggage and night taxis.

✈🛈 ORIENTATION AND PRACTICAL INFORMATION

The **Río Guadalquivir** flows roughly north to south through the city. Most of the touristed areas of Seville, including the **Barrio de Santa Cruz** and **El Arenal**, are on the east bank. The **Barrio de Triana**, the **Barrio de Santa Cecilia, Los Remedios,** and the Expo '92 fairgrounds occupy the west bank. The cathedral, next to Barrio de Santa Cruz, is Seville's centerpiece. If you're disoriented, look for the conspicuous **Giralda** (the minaret-turned-belltower). **Avenida de la Constitución,** home of the tourist office, runs alongside the cathedral. **El Centro,** a busy commercial pedestrian zone, lies north of the cathedral, starting where Av. Constitución hits **Pl. Nueva,** site of the Ayuntamiento. **C. Tetuan,** a popular street for shopping, runs northward from Pl. Nueva through El Centro.

Tourist Offices: Centro de Información de Sevilla, Av. Constitución 21B (☎954 22 14 04; fax 22 97 53), 1 block from the cathedral. Open M-F 9am-7pm, Sa 10am-2pm and 3-7pm, Su 10am-2pm. **Info booths** at the train station and Pl. Nueva.

Currency Exchange: Santander Central Hispano, C. la Campaña 19 (☎902 24 24 24). Open M-F 8:30am-2pm, Sa 8:30am-1pm.

American Express: Pl. Nueva 7 (☎954 21 16 17). Open M-F 9:30am-1:30pm and 4:30-7:30pm, Sa 10am-1pm.

Luggage Storage: At Pr. San Sebastián bus station (€0.90 per bag per day; open 6:30am-10pm) and the train station (€3 per day).

Bi-Gay-Lesbian Resources: COLEGA (Colectiva de Lesbianas y Gays de Andalucía), (☎954 50 13 77; www.colegaweb.net). Pl. Encarnación 23, 2nd fl. Look for the sign in the window; the door is not marked. Open M-F 10am-2pm.

Laundromat: Lavandería Auto-servicio, C. Castelar 2 (☎954 21 05 35). Wash and dry €6. Open M-Sa 9:30am-1:30pm and 5-8:30pm.

Emergency: Medical: ☎061. **Police:** Po. Concordia (Local ☎092; national ☎091).

Late-Night Pharmacy: Rotates; check list posted at any pharmacy.

Medical Assistance: Red Cross: (☎913 354 545). **Ambulatorio Esperanza Macarena** (☎954 42 01 05). **Hospital Universitario Virgen Macarena** (☎954 24 81 81), Av. Dr. Fedriani. English spoken.

TO SAN LORENZO Y JESÚS DEL GRAN PODER (100m)

TO ALAMEDA DE HÉRCULES (150m)

C. Baños

C. Alfaqueque

C. Ríos Ramos

C. Mendaza

C. Gracia

C. San Vicente

C. Miguel Cid

C. A. Gordillo

C. Jesús de la Veracruz

PL. GAVIDIA

C. Jesús del Gran Poder

C. Trajano

C. Amor de Dios

C. Atienza

C. Jerónimo Hernández

C. Sor Ángela de la Cruz

C. Geronia

Palacio de las Dueñas

C. S. de la Palma

C. S. Felipe

C. Alfonso XII

El Corte Inglés

PL. DUQUE DE LA VICTORIA

C. la Campana

C. Martín Villa

C. Laraña

La Anunciación

PL. DE LA ENCARNACIÓN

Convento de Sta. Inés

PL. SAN PEDRO

Museo Provincial de Bellas Artes

C. Monsalves

C. Gravina

C. Bailén

Pedro del Toro

C. S. Pedro Mártir

San Roque

C. San Eloy

C. O'Donnell

C. Velázquez

C. las Sierpes

CENTRO

C. Cuna

C. Santa Ángela

C. Zuñiga

C. O. Zuñiga

PL. CRISTO DE BURGOS

C. Alhóndiga

PL. DE ARMAS

Marqués de Paradas

C. Trastamara

C. Albuera

C. Alfona

C. Reyes Católicos

C. Canalejas

C. Julio César

C. San Pablo

C. Moratín

C. Santos Patronos

C. Carlos Cañal

C. Murillo

Méndez Núñez

C. Rosario

C. Tetuán

C. Rioja

C. Granada

PL. DEL SALVADOR

El Salvador

PL. PESCADERÍA

C. Alfalfa

PL. ALFALFA

Capilla San José

Villegas

Fabiola

PL. DE ARMAS

Almansa

C. Gemil

C. Bilbao

PL. NUEVA

Ayuntamiento

C. S. Isidoro

Corral del Rey

C. Zaragoza

C. Madrid

PL. SAN FRANCISCO

C. Pajaritos

Monolitos Romanos

C.F. Rubio

C. Alfona

C. Padre Marchena

C. Castelar

C. Gamazo

C. Harinas

C. Jimios

Av. de la Constitución

C. Francos

C. Álvarez Quintero

C. Argote de Molina

C. Aire

C. Madre

C. Gemil

C. Adriano

Plaza de Toros de la Real Maestranza

C. Adriano

C. Antonia Díaz

C. Varflora

C. G. de Vinuesa

C. Alemanes

C. Placentines

Fernando

Abades

C. Museos

C. M. Reina

PTE. ISABEL II

P. Alcalde Marqués de Contadero

Paseo Cristóbal Colón

EL ARENAL

PL. DEL CABILDO

Cathedral

Palacio Arzobispal

PL. V. REYES

Convento Encarnación

Casa de Murillo

Hospital Venerables

PL. DOÑA ELVIRA

Alcázar

C. de Pureza

C. del Betis

Canal de Alfonso XIII

C. Dos de Mayo

C. Temprado

PL. TRIUNFO

Casa Lonja

Main Post Office

Hospital de la Caridad

Canadá

Capilla de los Marineros

Santa Ana

C. Pelay de Correa

C. del Betis

Teatro de la Maestranza

C. Santander

Junta de Andalucía

Librería Beta

PUERTA DE JEREZ

C. Almirante Lobo

San Fernando

Jardines Alcázar

TO (1500m)

TO (300m)

Av. de Roma

Av. de las Delicias

Palacio de San Telmo

Fábrica de Tabacos (Universidad Nueva)

Palos de la Frontera

Av. María Luisa

C. de la Rábida

C. Perú

United States

TO (50m)

TO (700m)

TO PARQUE DE MARÍA LUISA (300m) & MUSEO ARQUEOLÓGICO (800m)

Sevilla

🏠 **ACCOMMODATIONS**
Camping Sevilla, **24**
Hostal Goya, **16**
Hostal Lis, **3**
Hostal Lis II, **4**
Hostal Sánchez Sabariego, **9**
Hostal-Residencia Córdoba, **10**
Hostal Dulces Sueños, **15**
Pensión Vérgara, **17**
Sevilla Youth Hostal (HI), **23**

🍎 **FOOD**
Acropolis Taberna Griega, **21**
Café-Bar Campanario, **18**
Pizzeros Orsini & Angelo, **6**
Restaurante-Bar El Baratillo/
 Casa Chari, **20**
El Rinconcillo, **1**

⭐ **NIGHTLIFE**
Antique, **22**
El Capote, **12**
Isbiliyya, **11**
Palenque, **13**
Terraza Chile, **14**

● **SERVICES**
American Express, **8**
COLEGA, **2**
The E-mail Place, **5**
RENFE, **7**
Seville Internet Center, **19**

Internet Access: Seville Internet Center, C. Almirantazgo 2, 2nd fl., across from the cathedral. €3 per hr. Open M-F 9am-10pm, Sa-Su 10am-10pm. **CiberBoston,** C. San Fernando 23. €3 per hr. Open M-F 9am-1am, Sa-Su noon-midnight. **The Email Place,** C. Sierpes 54. €2.20 per hr. Open June-Sept. M-F 10am-10pm, Sa-Sa noon-8pm; Oct.-May M-F 9am-11pm, Sa-Su noon-9pm.

Post Office: Av. Constitución 32 (☎954 21 64 76), opposite the cathedral. *Lista de Correos* and fax. Open M-F 10am-8:30pm, Sa 9:30am-2pm. **Postal Code:** 41080.

▐▌ ACCOMMODATIONS

Rooms vanish and prices soar during *Semana Santa* and the *Feria de Abril;* reserve ahead. The narrow streets east of the cathedral around **Calle Santa María la Blanca** are full of cheap, centrally located hostels. Hostels by the **Plaza de Armas** bus station, mostly on C. Gravina, are convenient for visits to **El Centro** and the lively C. Betis on the west bank of the river.

▨ **Pensión Vergara,** C. Ximénez de Enciso 11, 2nd fl. (☎954 21 56 68), at C. Mesón del Moro. Beautiful rooms of varying size with lace bedspreads, antique-style furniture, and a sitting room with book swap. Singles, doubles, triples, and quads available; all have fans. Towels provided on request. €15-18 per person. ❷

▨ **Hostal Dulces-Sueños,** Santa Maria la Blanca 21 (☎954 41 93 83). Comfortable rooms, all with A/C. Singles €20; doubles €40, with bath €50; one triple with bath €60. ❷

▨ **Hostal Lis,** C. Escarpín 10 (☎954 21 30 88), in an alley near Pl. Encarnación. Nice-sized rooms with traditional Spanish tile. Owner is in the process of adding TV and A/C to all rooms, free Internet service, laundry service, and a rooftop terrace. Singles with shower €21; doubles with bath €42; triples with bath €63. MC/V. ❷

Hostal Sánchez Sabariego, C. Corral del Rey 23 (☎954 21 44 70). Comfortable rooms with unique furnishings. A/C upstairs, fans in all other rooms. Singles €15-30; doubles with bath €30-60; triples with bath €40-90. ❷

Hostal Lis II, C. Olavide 5 (☎954 56 02 28), off the busy shopping street San Eloy. Pleasant, good-sized rooms all with fans. Internet access. May 16-Mar.14 singles €19-22; doubles €32-35, with bath €35-42; triple with shower €45-51, with bath €48-55. Mar. 15-May 15 singles €39/€71; doubles €77/€90; triple €98. MC/V. ❷

Hostal Goya, C. Mateos Gago 31 (☎954 21 11 70; fax 56 29 88), 3 blocks from the cathedral. Spacious, sparkling rooms; A/C and shower. Doubles €51, with bath €57; triples €72/€80. MC/V. ❸

Hostal-Residencia Córdoba, C. Farnesio 12 (☎954 22 74 98), off C. Fabiola. Run by a friendly and helpful family, this *hostal* offers immaculate and spacious air-conditioned rooms. Curfew 3am. Singles €25, with shower €33; doubles €40/€51. ❷

Sevilla Youth Hostel (HI), C. Isaac Peral 2 (☎954 61 31 50; reservas@inturjoven.junta-andalucia.es). Take bus #34 across from the tourist office near the cathedral; the 5th stop is behind the hostel. Isolated and difficult to find. A/C. Many private baths. Breakfast included. Dorms Mar.-Oct. €13, over 26 €17; Nov.-Feb. €11, over 26 €15. ❶

Camping Sevilla, Ctra. Madrid-Cádiz km 534 (☎954 51 43 79), near the airport. From Pr. San Sebastián, take bus #70 (stops 800m away at Parque Alcosa). Hot showers, supermarket, and pool. €3 per person, €3 per car, €2.50 per tent. ❶

▐▌ FOOD

Seville, which claims to be the birthplace of *tapas*, keeps its cuisine light. *Tapas* bars cluster around **Plaza San Martín** and along **Calle San Jacinto.** Popular venues for *el tapeo* (*tapas*-barhopping) are **Barrio Santa Cruz** and **El Arenal.** Locals imbibe

Seville's own Cruzcampo beer, a light, smooth pilsner. **Mercado del Arenal,** near the bullring on C. Pastor y Leandro, has fresh meat and produce. (Open M-Sa 9am-2pm.) For a supermarket, try **%Día,** C. San Juan de Ávila, near El Corte Inglés. (Open M-F 9:30am-2pm and 6:30-9pm, Sa 9am-1pm.)

🔣 **Restaurante-Bar El Baratillo/Casa Chari,** C. Pavía 12 (☎954 22 96 51), on a tiny street off C. Dos de Mayo. Hospitable owner will help you practice your Spanish. Order at least an hour in advance for the *tour-de-force*: homemade *paella* (vegetarian options available) with a jar of wine, beer, or *sangría* (€18 for 2). *Menú* €4-9. Open M-F 10:30am-11pm, Sa noon-5pm; stays open later when busy. ❷

🔣 **Pizzeros Orsini & Angelo,** C. Luchana 2 (☎954 21 61 64), 2 blocks from Pl. del Salvador. Crisp and filling pizza served straight from the oven. Romantic outdoor seating in front of a Baroque church. Pizzas €3.60-7, pasta €5-7, salads €4-5, and Italian desserts €2.50. Open daily 1-4pm and 8pm-1am. ❷

Historico Horno, S.A., Av. de la Constitución 16 (☎954 22 18 19), across from the cathedral. Excellent pastries, cookies, and cakes. Open daily 7:30am-11pm. MC/V. ❷

Café-Bar Campanario, C. Mateos Gago 8 (☎954 56 41 89), half a block from the cathedral. Mixes the best (and strongest) jugs of *sangría* around (0.5L €7.25, 1L €10). *Tapas* €1.50-2, *raciones* €6-9. Open daily 11am-midnight. ❷

Acropolis Taberna Griega, C. Rosario Vega 10 (☎954 28 46 85), 2 blocks from the Pl. Cuba. This small restaurant serves delicious Greek food. Many vegetarian options. Entrees and appetizers €2.50-4. Open Aug.-June M 8:30-11:30pm, Tu-Sa 1:30-3:30pm and 8:30-11:30pm. MC/V. ❶

El Rinconcillo, C. Gerona 40 (☎954 22 31 83), behind the Church of Santa Catalina. Founded in 1670, this *bodega* continues to attract loyal patrons. *Tapas* €1-4, *raciones* €4-13. Open Th-Tu 1pm-2am. ❷

🅖 SIGHTS

🔣**THE CATHEDRAL.** To clear space for Seville's most impressive sight, Christians demolished an Almohad mosque in 1401, leaving only the **Patio de Los Naranjos** (orange trees) and the famed **La Giralda** minaret. That tower and its siblings in Marrakesh and Rabat are the oldest and largest surviving Almohad minarets. The **cathedral**—the third-largest in the world—took over 100 years to complete and is the largest Gothic edifice ever constructed. The **retablo mayor** (altarpiece) is a golden wall of intricately wrought disciples and saints. Circle the choir to view the **Sepulcro de Cristóbal Colón** (Columbus's tomb). His coffin-bearers represent the grateful kings of Castilla, León, Aragón, and Navarra. The cathedral's **Sacristía Mayor** museum holds Riberas, Murillos, and a glittering Corpus Christi icon. The neighboring **Sacristía de los Cálices** (or **de los Pintores**) displays canvases by Zurbarán and Goya. In the corner of the cathedral are the perfectly oval **cabildo** (chapter house) and **Sala de Las Columnas.** (☎954 21 49 71. Open M-Sa 9:30am-4:30pm, Su 2:30-7pm. Tickets sold until 1hr. before closing. €6, seniors and students €1.50. Su free. Mass held M-F 8:30, 9, 10am; Sa 8:30, 10am, 8pm; Su 8:30, 10, 11am, noon, 1pm.)

🔣**ALCÁZAR.** The imposing 9th-century walls of the Alcázar, which faces the cathedral next to Pl. Triunfo, date from the Moorish era, as does the exquisitely carved **Patio de las Muñecas** (Patio of the Dolls). Of the later Christian additions to the palace, the most exceptional is the **Patio de las Doncellas** (Maid's Court), which has ornate archways and complex tilework. The astonishing, golden-domed **Salón de los Embajadores** is where Fernando and Isabel supposedly welcomed Columbus back from America. (Pl. Triunfo 7. Open Tu-Sa 9:30am-7pm, Su 9:30am-5pm. €5; students, seniors, and under 16 free. Audio guides €3.)

MUSEO PROVINCIAL DE BELLAS ARTES. This museum contains Spain's finest collection of works by painters of the Seville school, notably Murillo, Valdés Leal, and Zurbarán, as well as El Greco and Dutch master Jan Breughel. The building itself is a work of art; take time to sit in its shady gardens. *(Pl. Museo 9, off C. Alfonso XII. Open Tu 3-8pm, W-Sa 9am-8pm, Su 9am-2pm. €1.50, EU citizens free.)*

PLAZA DE TOROS DE LA REAL MAESTRANZA. Home to one of the two great bullfighting schools (the other is in Ronda), Plaza de Toros de la Real Maestranza fills to capacity for weekly fights and the 13 *corridas* of the *Feria de Abril.* The museum inside has costumes, paintings, and antique posters. *(Open non-bullfight days 9:30am-2pm and 3-7pm, bullfight days 9:30am-3pm. Tours every 30min., €3.)*

BARRIO DE SANTA CRUZ. King Fernando III forced Jews fleeing Toledo to live in the Barrio de Santa Cruz, now a neighborhood of weaving alleys and courtyards. Beyond C. Lope de Rueda, off C. Ximénez de Enciso, is the **Plaza de Santa Cruz.** South of the plaza are the **Jardines de Murillo,** a shady expanse of shrubbery. Pl. Santa Cruz's church houses the grave of the artist Murillo, who died after falling from a scaffold while painting ceiling frescoes in a Cádiz church. Nearby, **Iglesia de Santa María la Blanca,** built in 1391, contains Murillo's *Last Supper. (Church open M-Sa 10-11am and 6:30-8pm, Su 9:30am-2pm and 6:30-8pm. Free.)*

LA MACARENA. This area northwest of El Centro is named for the Virgin of Seville. A stretch of 12th-century **murallas** (walls) runs between the Pta. Macarena and the Pta. Córdoba on the Ronda de Capuchinos. At the west end is the **Basílica Macarena,** whose venerated image of *La Virgen de la Macarena* is paraded through town during *Semana Santa.* A **treasury** within glitters with the virgin's jewels and other finery. *(Basilica open daily 9:30am-1pm and 5-9pm; free. Treasury open daily 9:30am-1pm and 5-8pm; €2.70.)* Toward the river is the **Iglesia de San Lorenzo y Jesús del Gran Poder,** with Montañés's remarkably lifelike sculpture *El Cristo del Gran Poder.* Worshipers kiss Jesus's ankle through an opening in the bulletproof glass for luck. *Semana Santa* culminates in a procession honoring the statue. *(Open Sa-Th 8am-1:45pm and 6-9pm, F 7:30-10pm. Free.)*

🎵 📷 ENTERTAINMENT AND FESTIVALS

The tourist office distributes *El Giraldillo,* a free monthly magazine with complete listings on music, art exhibits, theater, dance, fairs, and film. Get your

IN RECENT NEWS

DISCOVERING COLUMBUS

For well over a century, historians in both Spain and the Americas have been puzzled by the question: "Where is Columbus buried?"

Spain has always claimed that the remains of the celebrated discoverer of the New World—who sailed under the Spanish flag—are buried under a magnificent altar in the cathedral of Seville. However, authorities in Santo Domingo, in the Dominican Republic, hold that Columbus rests within a large cross on their island known as the *Faro a Colon* (Columbus lighthouse). Despite the lengthy duration of this argument, there has been no scientific evidence to substantiate either side's claims.

Two Spanish high school teachers want to change that. In what is perhaps the most controversial scientific, moral, and cultural debate currently being discussed in Spain, the proposal to exhume, and with the assistance of the Laboratory of Genetic Identification at the University of Granada, test the remains at both sites has excited many who wish to resolve this question once and for all.

But it has also alarmed many, particularly in the Spanish Roman Catholic church, who see it as a disturbance of religious grounds and an infringement of cultural patrimony.

For now, the issue remains unresolved. As Spain struggles to build its image as a progressive, modernized nation, it finds itself torn between scientific advancement and a strong history of tradition.

flamenco fix at **Los Gallos,** Pl. Santa Cruz 11, on the west edge of Barrio Santa Cruz. (Cover €27, includes 1 drink. Shows daily 9pm and 11:30pm.) If you're going to see a **bullfight** somewhere in Spain, Seville is probably the best place to do it; the bull-ring here is generally considered the most beautiful in the country. The cheapest place to buy bullfight tickets is at the ring on Po. Marqués de Contadero; or try the booths on C. Sierpes, C. Velázquez, or Pl. Toros (€18-75). Seville's world-famous ⊠**Semana Santa** (Holy Week) festival, during which penitents in hoods guide can-dle-lit processionals, lasts from Palm Sunday to Good Friday. In the last week of April, the city rewards itself for its Lenten piety with the **Feria de Abril.**

⬛ NIGHTLIFE

Seville's reputation for gaiety is tried and true—most clubs don't get going until well after midnight, and the real fun often starts after 3am. Popular bars can be found around **Calle Mateos Gago** near the cathedral, **Calle Adriano** by the bullring, and **Calle Betis** across the river in Triana.

⊠ **Terraza Chile,** Po. de las Delicias, at the intersection of Av. Uruguay and Av. Chile. Loud salsa and Spanish pop keep this small club packed and pounding through the early morning hours. Beer €2. Open summer, daily 9pm-6am.

⊠ **La Carbonería,** C. Levies 18, off C. Santa María La Blanca. Popular bar with free live fla-menco and a massive outdoor patio replete with banana trees, picnic tables, and gui-tar-strumming Romeos. Beer €2.50. Open M-Sa 8pm-3:30am, Su 8pm-2:30am.

⊠ **Isbiliyya,** Po. de Colon 2, across from Pte. Isabel II. Friendly mixed bar with outdoor seat-ing and a good dance floor. Beer €2-2.50. Open M-W 7pm-4am, Th-Su 7pm-5am.

Palenque, Av. Blas Pascal, on the grounds of Cartuja '93. Once a stadium-sized audito-rium, now the largest dance club in Seville. Beer €2, mixed drinks €4.20. Cover €6 for men, €4 for women. Open in summer Th-Sa midnight-7am.

El Capote, next to Pte. Isabel II, at the intersection of C. Arjona and C. Reyes Católicos. A hugely popular outdoor bar with live music performances throughout the summer. Open in summer daily 11pm-3am.

Antique, C. Materatico Rey Pastor. Decorated entirely in white, with swirling spotlights and Ottoman pavilions doubling as bars in the yard and patio. Plays mostly Spanish pop-house. No cover for women, men €7. Open Th-Sa midnight-7am.

⬛ DAYTRIPS FROM SEVILLE

CÁDIZ. Founded by the Phoenicians in 1100 BC, Cádiz (pop. 155,000) is thought to be the oldest inhabited city in Europe. **Carnaval** is perhaps Spain's most dazzling party (Feb. 27-Mar. 9, 2003), but year-round the city offers golden sand **beaches** that put its pebble-strewn eastern neighbors to shame. **Playa de la Caleta** is the most convenient, but better sand awaits in the new city; take bus #1 from Pl. España to Pl. Glorieta Ingeniero (€0.80) to reach ⊠**Playa de la Victoria,** which has earned the EU's *bandera azul* for cleanliness. Back in town, the gold-domed, 18th-century **cathedral** is considered the last great cathedral built by colonial riches. To get there from Pl. San Juan de Dios, follow C. Pelota. (Museum open Tu-F 10am-12:45pm and 4:30-6:45pm, Sa 10am-12:45pm. €3. Cathedral open W and F 7-8pm, Su 11am-1pm. Free.) From the train station, walk two blocks past the foun-tain, with the port on your right, and look left for **Plaza San Juan de Dios,** the town center. Transportes Generales Comes **buses** (☎956 22 78 11) arrive at Pl. Hispan-idad from Sevilla (2hr., 11 per day, €9). From the bus station, walk 5min. down Av.

Puerto with the port on your left; Pl. de San Juan de Dios will be after the park on your right. The **tourist office** is at #11. (☎/fax 956 24 10 01. Office open M-F 9am-2pm and 5-8pm. Kiosk in front of office open Sa-Su and holidays 10am-1pm and 5-7:30pm.) Most *hostales* huddle in Pl. San Juan de Dios, just behind it on C. Marqués de Cádiz, and around the harbor. **Quo Qádis ❶**, C. Diego Arias 1, one block from Pl. Falla, offers flamenco classes, planned excursions, and vegetarian dinners. (☎/fax 956 22 19 39. Dorms €6; singles €13; doubles €24.)

ARCOS DE LA FRONTERA. With castles and Roman ruins at every turn, Arcos (pop. 33,000) is in essence a historical monument. Wander the winding alleys, ruins, and hanging flowers of the **old quarter,** and marvel at the stunning view from ▨**Plaza Cabildo.** In the square is the **Iglesia de Santa María,** a mix of Baroque, Renaissance, and Gothic styles. To reach the old quarter from the bus station, exit left, turn left, and continue 20min. uphill on C. Muñoz Vásquez as it changes names. **Buses** (☎956 70 20 15), C. Corregidores, run to Cádiz (1½hr., 6 per day, €4.50) and Seville (2hr., 7am and 5pm, €6). The **tourist office** is on Pl. Cabildo. (☎956 70 22 64. Open Mar. 15-Oct. 15 M-Sa 10am-2pm and 4-8pm; Oct. 16-Mar. 14 M-Sa 10am-2pm and 3:30-7:30pm. **Hostal San Marcos ❷**, C. Marqués de Torresoto 6, past C. Dean Espinosa and Pl. Cabildo, is run by a friendly, young family and crowned by a scenic rooftop terrace. (☎956 70 07 21. Singles €25; doubles €36.) Restaurants huddle at the bottom end of **Calle Corredera,** while *tapas* nirvana can be found uphill in the old quarter.

RONDA. Most people's strongest impression of Ronda (pop. 38,000), the birthplace of modern bullfighting, is the stomach-churning ascent to get there. A precipitous gorge, carved by the Río Guadalevín, dips below the **Puente Nuevo,** opposite Pl. España. Bullfighting aficionados charge over to Ronda's **Plaza de Toros,** Spain's oldest bullring (est. 1785) and cradle of the modern *corrida.* For something just as bloody, visit the ▨**Museo del Bandolero,** C. Armiñán 59, dedicated to presenting "pillage, theft, and rebellion in Spain since Roman times." (☎952 87 77 85. Open in summer daily 10am-8:30pm; off-season 10am-6pm. €2.70.) **Buses** (☎952 18 70 61) go from Pl. Concepción García Redondo 2, near Av. Andalucía, to: Cádiz (4hr., 4 per day, €11); Málaga (2½hr., 5 per day, €8); Marbella (1½hr., 4 per day, €5); and Sevilla (2½hr., 3-5 per day, €9). The **tourist office** is at Pl. España 1. (☎952 87 12 72. Open M-F 9am-7pm, Sa-Su 10am-2pm.) The best budget deal in town is ▨**Hostal González ❶**, C. San Vincente de Paul 3. (☎952 87 14 45. Singles €10; doubles €16.) **Postal code:** 29400.

GIBRALTAR

| PHONE CODE | ☎350 from the UK or the US; ☎9567 from Spain. |

From the morning mist just off the southern shore of Spain emerges the Rock of Gibraltar. Bastion of empire, Jerusalem of Anglophilia, this rocky peninsula is among history's most contested plots of land. Ancient seafarers called "Gib" one of the Pillars of Hercules, believing it marked the end of the world. After numerous squabbles between Moors, Spaniards, and Turks, the English successfully stormed Gibraltar in 1704 and have remained in possession ever since.

▣▨ **TRANSPORTATION AND PRACTICAL INFORMATION. Buses** arrive in the Spanish border town of **La Línea** from: Algeciras (40min., every 30min., €1.50); Cádiz (3hr., 4 per day, €10); and Granada (5-6hr., 2 per day, €17). From the bus station, walk directly toward the Rock; the border is 5min. away. After bypassing the line of motorists, Spanish customs, and Gibraltar's passport control, catch bus #9 or 10 or walk across the airport tarmac and along the highway into town (20min.). Stay left on Av. Winston Churchill when the road forks at Corral Lane; Gibraltar's **Main Street**, a commercial strip lined with most services, begins at the far end of a square, past the Burger King on the left.

The **tourist office**, Duke of Kent House, Cathedral Sq., is across the park from the Gibraltar Museum. (☎ 450 00; tourism@gibraltar.gi. Open M-F 9am-5:30pm.) Although **euros** are accepted almost everywhere (except pay phones and public establishments), the **pound sterling (£)** is preferred. Merchants sometimes charge a higher price in euros than in the pound's exchange equivalent. Change is often given in English currency rather than euros. As of press date, **1£ = €1.58.**

◙ SIGHTS. About halfway up the Rock is the infamous **Apes' Den,** where barbary monkeys cavort on the sides of rocks, the tops of taxis, and the heads of tourists. At the northern tip of the Rock facing Spain are the **Great Siege Tunnels.** Originally used to fend off a combined Franco-Spanish siege at the end of the American Revolution, the underground tunnels were later expanded during World War II to span 33 miles. The eerie chambers of **St. Michael's Cave,** located 0.5km from the siege tunnels, were cut into the rock by thousands of years of water erosion. (Cable car to above sights every 10min. daily 9:30am-5:15pm. Combined admittance ticket, including one-way cable car ride, £7/€11, children £5/€8.15.)

⌐◘ ACCOMMODATIONS AND FOOD. Gibraltar is best done as a daytrip. The few accommodations in the area are often full, especially in the summer, and camping is illegal. **Emile Youth Hostel Gibraltar ❷,** Montague Bastian, off Line Wall Rd., has cramped bunkbeds in cheerfully painted rooms with clean communal bathrooms. (☎511 06. Breakfast included. Lock-out 10:30am-4:30pm. Dorms £12/€19; singles £15/€24; doubles £27/€44.) International restaurants are easy to find, but you may choke on the prices. **The Viceroy of India ❸** serves fabulous Indian food. (Entrees £4-10. Open M-F noon-3pm and 7-11pm, Sa 7-11pm. MC/V.) As a back-up, there's the **Checkout** supermarket on Main St., next to Marks & Spencer. (Open M-F 8:30am-8pm, Sa 10am-6pm, Su 1am-3pm. MC/V.)

ALGECIRAS
☎956

Hidden beyond Algeciras's seedy port is a more serene old neighborhood, worthy of a visit for those with a few hours to spare. However, for most itinerary-bound travelers, this is a city seen only in transit. RENFE **trains** (☎902 24 02 02) run from C. Juan de la Cierva to Granada (4hr., 3 per day, €15) and Ronda (1½hr., 4 per day, €6). Empresa Portillo **buses** (☎956 65 43 04) leave from Av. Virgen del Carmen 15 for: Córdoba (6hr., 3-4 per day, €18); Granada (5hr., 4 per day, €16); Málaga (3hr., 8-9 per day, €8.70); and Marbella (1hr., 8-9 per day, €5). Transportes Generales Comes (☎956 65 34 56) goes from C. San Bernardo 1 to Cádiz (2½hr., 6 per day, €8). La Línea runs to: Gibraltar (45min., every 30min. 7am-9:30pm, €1.50); Madrid (8hr., 4 per day, €22); and Sevilla (4hr., 4 per day, €14). To get to the **ferries** from the bus and train stations, follow C. San Bernardo to C. Juan de la Cierva and turn left at the end of the street; the port entrance will be on your right. (For times and prices to Morocco, see p. 705) The **tourist office** is on C. Juan de la Cierva. (☎956 57 26 36. Open M-F 9am-2pm.) Hostels cluster around **Calle José Santacana.** To get to **Hostal Rif ❶,** C. Rafael de Muro 11, follow C. Santacana into the market square, bear left around the kiosk, and continue one block up C. Rafael del Muro. (☎956 65 49 53. Singles €8; doubles €17.) **Postal code:** 11203.

COSTA DEL SOL

The Costa del Sol mixes natural beauty with chic promenades and swank hotels. While some spots have been over-developed and can be hard on the wallet, the coast's stunning natural beauty has been left untouched in lesser-known areas. Summer brings swarms of tourists, but nothing takes away from the main attraction: eight months of spring and four months of summer.

MARBELLA. Like your vacation spots shaken, not stirred? Scottish smoothie Sean Connery and a host of other jet-setters choose Marbella (pop. 100,000) as their vacation home. While there may be more yachts here than hostels, it's still possible to have a budgeted good time. The beaches beckon with 320 days of sunshine per year, but no visit would be complete without a stroll through the ▓**casco antiguo** (old town), a maze of cobblestone streets and white-washed facades trimmed with wild roses. City buses along Av. Richard Soriano (dir.: San Pedro; €0.90) run to chic and trendy **Puerto Banús,** where beautiful, clean beaches are buffered by white yachts. With 22km of **beach,** Marbella offers a variety of settings. Beaches to the east of the port are popular with British backpackers; those to the west attract a more posh crowd. The **Museo del Grabado Español Contemporáneo,** on C. Hospital Bazán, displays engravings by Miró, Picasso, Dalí, and Goya. (Open M 10am-2pm, Tu-Sa 10am-2pm and 6-9pm; €2.50.)

Accessible only by **bus,** the station atop Av. Trapiche (☎952 76 44 00) goes to: Algeciras (1½hr., 7 per day, €5); Cádiz (4hr., 6 per day, €14); Granada (4hr., 8 per day, €12); Madrid (7½hr., 10 per day, €19); Málaga (1½hr., every 30min., €4); and Sevilla (4hr., 2-3 per day, €13). The **tourist office** is on Pl. Naranjos. (☎952 82 35 50. Open June-Aug. M-F 9:30am-9pm, Sa 10am-2pm.) The area in the *casco antiguo* around Pl. Naranjos is packed with quick-filling hostels. **Hostal del Pilar ❶,** C. Mesoncillo 4, is off C. Peral. (☎952 82 99 36. Dorms €15-20; roof mattresses €12.) The excellent **Albergue Juvenil (HI) ❶,** Av. Trapiche 2, downhill from the bus station, feels more like a hotel than a hostel. (☎952 77 14 91. Dorms €10-13, over 26 €11-17.) A **24hr. minimarket** beckons from the corner of C. Pablo Casals and Av. Fontanilla. Nightlife in Marbella begins and ends late. The rowdiest corner of the *casco antiguo* is where C. Mesoncillo meets C. Peral. Loud music and cheery Spaniards spill from **El Güerto,** C. Peral 9, while a mixed crowd of backpackers and locals enjoy the **The Tavern,** C. Peral 7. (Both open at 8:30pm; El Güerto opens only on weekends.) A mellow ambience suffuses the ▓**Townhouse Bar,** C. Alamo, tucked down an alley off C. Nueva. Ask for a shot of apple pie. (Open daily from 10pm.) Many clubs and bars are located down by the port at the bottom of Av. Miguel Cano, including the waterfront **House of Silk** and the more grungy **Loco's;** both play dance hits. **Postal Code:** 29600.

GRANADA ☎958

Legend says that in 1492, when Moorish ruler Boabdil fled Granada, the last Muslim stronghold in Spain, his mother berated him for casting a longing look back at the Alhambra. "You do well to weep as a woman," she told him, "for what you could not defend as a man." A spectacular palace celebrated by poets and artists throughout the ages, the Alhambra continues to inspire melancholy in those who must leave its timeless beauty. The Albaicín, an enchanting maze of Moorish houses and twisting alleys, is Spain's best-preserved Arab quarter and the only part of the Muslim city to survive the *Reconquista.*

⌐ TRANSPORTATION

Trains: RENFE Station, Av. Andaluces (☎902 24 02 02). To: **Algeciras** (5-7hr., 3 per day 7:15am-5:50pm, €16); **Madrid** (5-6hr., 8am and 4:40pm, €26-32); **Sevilla** (4-5hr., 4 per day 8:18am-8:15pm, €16).

Buses: Major bus routes originate from the **bus station** on the outskirts of Granada on Ctra. Madrid, near C. Arzobispo Pedro de Castro. **Alsina Graells** (☎958 18 54 80) runs to **Córdoba** (3hr., 10 per day 7:30am-8pm, €10) and **Sevilla** (3hr., 9 per day 8am-3am, €15). **La Línea** runs to **Algeciras** (5hr., 6 per day 9am-8pm, €16) and **Madrid** (5hr., 14 per day 7am-1:30am, €12.50). **Bacoma** (☎958 15 75 57) goes to **Alicante** (6hr., 5 per day, €21), **Barcelona** (14hr., 3 per day, €50), and **Valencia** (8hr., 4 per day, €30). All Bacoma buses run 10:15am-1:45am.

Public Transportation: From the bus station take bus #10 to the youth hostel, C. de Ronda, C. Recogidas, or C. Acera de Darro or bus #3 to Av. Constitución, Gran Vía, or Pl. Isabel la Católica. From Pl. Nueva catch #30 to the Alhambra or #31 to the Albaicín. Rides €0.85, *bonobus* (10 tickets) €5. Free map at tourist office.

◼◪ ORIENTATION AND PRACTICAL INFORMATION

The geographic center is the small **Plaza de Isabel la Católica,** at the intersection of the city's two main arteries, **Calle de los Reyes Católicos** and **Gran Vía de Colón.** To reach Gran Vía and the **cathedral** from the train station, walk three blocks up Av. Andaluces and take bus #3-6, 9, or 11 from Av. Constitución; from the bus station, take bus #3. Two blocks uphill on C. Reyes Católicos sits **Plaza Nueva.** Downhill on C. Reyes Católicos lies Pl. Carmen, site of the **Ayuntamiento** and Puerta Real. The **Alhambra** commands the steep hill above Pl. Nueva.

Tourist Office: Oficina Provincial, Pl. Mariana Pineda 10 (☎958 24 71 28; www.dipgra.es). From Pta. Real, turn right onto C. Angel Ganivet, then take a right 2 blocks later to reach the plaza. Open M-F 9am-8pm, Sa 10am-7pm, Su 10am-4pm.

American Express: C. Reyes Católicos 31 (☎958 22 45 12), between Pl. Isabel la Católica and Pta. Real. Open M-F 9am-1:30pm and 2-9pm, Sa 10am-2pm and 3-7pm.

Luggage Storage: At the train and bus stations. €2.40. Open daily 4-9pm.

Laundromat: C. La Paz 19. From Pl. Trinidad, take C. Alhóndiga, turn right on C. La Paz, and walk 2 blocks. Wash €3, dry €0.90 per 15min. Open M-F 9:30am-2pm and 4:30-8:30pm, Sa 9am-2pm.

Emergency: ☎112. **Police:** C. Duquesa 21 (☎958 24 81 00). English spoken.

Medical Assistance: Clínica de San Cecilio, C. Dr. Oloriz 16 (☎958 28 02 00 or 27 20 00), on the road to Jaén. **Ambulance:** ☎958 28 44 50.

Internet Access: Net (☎958 22 69 19) has 3 locations: C. Santa Escolástica 13, up C. Pavaneras from Pl. Isabel la Católica; Pl. de los Girones 3; and C. Buensucesco 22, 1 block from Pl. Trinidad. €1.20 per hr. All open M-Sa 9am-1am, Su 3pm-1am.

Post Office: Pta. Real (☎958 22 48 35; fax 22 36 41), on the corner of Carrera del Darro and C. Angel Ganinet. **Lista de Correos** and **fax** service. Open M-F 8am-9pm, Sa 9:30am-2pm. Wires money M-F 8:30am-2:30pm. **Postal Code:** 18009.

⌐ ACCOMMODATIONS

Hostels line Cuesta de Gomérez, Plaza Trinidad, and Gran Vía. Call ahead during *Semana Santa.*

■ **Hostal Venecia,** Cuesta de Gomérez 2, 3rd fl. (☎958 22 39 87). Wake up to a soothing cup of tea, candles, and a hint of incense. Singles €14; doubles €26; triples €39; quads €52. ❶

■ **Hostal Residencia Britz,** Cuesta de Gomérez 1 (☎/fax 958 22 36 52), on the corner of Pl. Nueva. Large rooms with luxurious beds. Singles €18; doubles €27.50, with bath €38. Show the reception your copy of *Let's Go* for a 6% discount. MC/V. ❷

■ **Hospedaje Almohada,** C. Postigo de Zarate 4 (☎958 20 74 46). From Pl. Trinidad, follow C. Duquesa to C. Málaga and take a right; it's the red door with the small sign on your right. A successful experiment in communal living. Dorms €11; singles €13.50; doubles €24; triples €32.50. Discounts available for stays over 1 week. ❶

Hostal Antares, C. Cetti Meriém 10 (☎958 22 83 13), on the corner of C. Elvira, 1 block from Gran Vía and the cathedral. Singles €18; doubles €30-45; triples €31.50-63. ❷

Hostal Navarro-Ramos, Cuesta de Gomérez 21 (☎958 25 05 55), near the outer walls of the Alhambra. Memorabilia from Queen Elizabeth's silver jubilee cover the walls. Showers €0.90. Singles €10; doubles €16, with bath €27; triples with bath €36. ❶

Hostal-Residencia Lisboa, Pl. Carmen 29 (☎958 22 14 13 or 22 14 14; fax 22 14 87). Take C. Reyes Católicos from Pl. Isabel la Católica; Pl. Carmen is on the left. TVs and fans. Singles €16, with bath €24; doubles €24/€35; triples €32/€47. MC/V. ❷

Hostal Zurita, Pl. Trinidad 7 (☎958 27 50 20). Beautiful rooms, high-quality beds. Singles €15; doubles €27, with bath €33; triples €39/€45. ❷

◘ FOOD

Cheap North African cuisine can be found around the Albaicín, while more typical *menú* fare awaits in Pl. Nueva and Pl. Trinidad. The adventurous eat well in Granada—try *tortilla sacromonte* (omelette with calf's brains, bull testicles, ham, shrimp, and veggies). Feast on sumptuous seafood at **El Ladrillo II ❷,** C. Panaderos 13. (Entrees €6.60-12. Open daily 12:30pm-1:30am. MC/V.) **Naturi Albaicín ❷,** C. Calderería Nueva 10, serves excellent vegetarian cuisine in a serene Moroccan ambiance. (No alcohol served. *Menús* €5.70-6.90. Open Sa-Th 1-4pm and 7-11pm, F 7-11pm.) Get groceries at **Supermercado T. Mariscal,** C. Genil, next to El Corte Inglés. (Open M-F 9:30am-2pm and 5-9pm, Sa 9:30am-2pm.)

◎ SIGHTS

■ **THE ALHAMBRA.** From the streets of Granada, the Alhambra appears simple, blocky, faded—but up close, it's an elaborate and detailed piece of architecture, magically uniting water, light, wood, stucco, and ceramics to create a fortress-palace of rich aesthetics and symbolic grandeur. The age-old saying holds true: "If you have died without seeing the Alhambra, you have not lived." The first Nasrid King Alhamar built the fortress **Alcazaba,** the section of the complex with the oldest recorded history. A dark, spiraling staircase leads up to a 360° view of Granada and the mountains. Follow signs for the *Palacio Nazaries* to see the stunningly ornate **Alcázar,** a 14th-century royal palace full of dripping stalactite archways, multicolored tiles, and sculpted fountains. Fernando and Isabel restored the Alcázar after they drove the Moors from Spain, but two generations later, Emperor Carlos V demolished part of it to make way for his **Palacio de Carlos V;** although glaringly incongruous with such Moorish splendor, many consider it one of the most beautiful Renaissance buildings in Spain. Over a bridge are the vibrant blossoms, towering cypresses, and streaming waterways of ■**El Generalife,** the sultan's vacation retreat. *(Take C. Cuesta de Gomérez off Pl. Nueva (20min). Or take the cheap, quick Alhambra-Neptuno micro-*

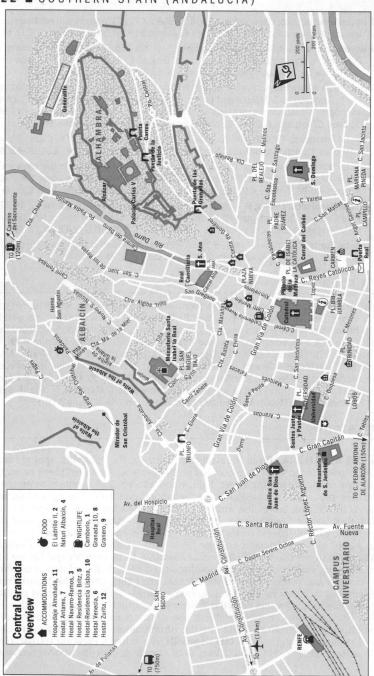

Central Granada Overview

▲ ACCOMMODATIONS
Hospedaje Almohada, 11
Hostal Antares, 7
Hostal Navarro-Ramos, 3
Hostal Residencia Britz, 5
Hostal-Residencia Lisboa, 10
Hostal Venecia, 6
Hostal Zurita, 12

◆ FOOD
El Ladrillo II, 2
Naturi Albaicín, 4

■ NIGHTLIFE
Camborio, 1
Granada 10, 8
Granero, 9

SPAIN

bus from Pl. Nueva (every 5min., €0.80). Open Apr.-Sept. daily 8:30am-8pm; Oct.-Mar. M-Sa 9am-5:45pm. Nighttime visits June-Sept. Tu, Th, and Sa 10-11:30pm; Oct.-May Sa 8-10pm. All visits €7. Limited visitors each day; get there early and stand in line. Alcázar entry only during the time specified on your ticket. It is possible to reserve tickets a few days in advance at banks for a €0.75 service charge.)

THE ALBAICÍN. A labyrinth of steep streets and narrow alleys, the Albaicín was the only Moorish neighborhood to escape the torches of the *Reconquista* and remains a quintessential part of Granada. After the fall of the Alhambra, a small Muslim population remained here until their expulsion in the 17th century. The abundance of North African cuisine and the recent construction of a mosque near Pl. San Nicolás attest to the persistence of Islamic influence in Andalucía. Spectacular sunsets over the surrounding mountains can be seen from C. Cruz de Quirós, above C. Elvira. Although generally safe, the Albaicín is disorienting and should be approached with caution at night. *(Bus #12 runs from beside the cathedral to C. Pagés at the top of the Albaicín.)*

OTHER SIGHTS. Downhill from the Alhambra's Arab splendor, the **Capilla Real,** Fernando and Isabel's private chapel, exemplifies Christian Granada. The sacristy shelters Isabel's private art collection, the first Christian banner to flutter in triumph over the Alhambra, and the glittering royal jewels. *(Both open daily M-Sa 10:30am-1pm and 2-7pm, Su 11am-1pm and 4-7pm. €2.50.)* Fernando and Isabel began the construction of the adjacent **cathedral** in 1523 upon the foundation of an Arab mosque. However, it wasn't completed until 1704. It was the first purely Renaissance cathedral in Spain, and its Corinthian pillars support an astonishing 45m vaulted nave. *(Open Apr.-Sept. M-Sa 10:45am-1:30pm and 4-7pm, Su 4-7pm; Oct.-Mar. M-Sa 10:30am-1:30pm and 3:30-6:30pm, Su 11am-1:30pm. €2.50.)*

🎵🎭 ENTERTAINMENT AND NIGHTLIFE

The *Guía del Ocio*, sold at newsstands (€0.85), lists clubs, pubs, and cafes. The tourist office also distributes a monthly guide, *Cultura en Granada*. The most boisterous nightspots belong to **Calle Pedro Antonio de Alarcón,** running from Pl. Albert Einstein to Ancha de Gràcia, while hip new bars and clubs line **Calle Elvira** from Cárcel to C. Cedrán. **Gay bars** cluster around Carrera del Darro; a complete list of gay clubs and bars is available at the tourist office. A smoky, intimate setting awaits at **Eshavira,** C. Postigo

IN RECENT NEWS

GITANO GENES

Ever since *Gitanos* (gypsies) arrived in Spain from India in the 15th century, they have faced discrimination, assimilation, and expulsion.

About 600,000 *Gitanos* (who are credited with the creation of flamenco) reside in Spain, nearly half of them in Andalucía. Most live in rural areas below the poverty line; an average *Gitano* is five times poorer than the rest of the population; school absenteeism is common, and the group's literacy rate is among the lowest in Spain. Unfortunately, slow transfer of funds for reform programs and a lack of cooperation among officials have largely stymied efforts to change the status quo.

The *Gitano* situation has improved only slightly since the 1978 constitution, which granted equal rights to the group. It's a sensitive issue because the government hopes to integrate *Gitanos* into modern Spanish life without compromising their traditions; a task that could prove difficult.

In 1999, a new parliamentary commission was created to address the issue, and results have been promising. *Gitanos* are pursuing vocational educations, and programs fostering better relations among all Spanish people has had some success.

However, a recent influx of immigrants from North Africa has negatively impacted the *Gitano:* these immigrants have adopted Spanish ways and risen up the socioeconomic ladder quickly, which has left many *Gitanos* feeling frustrated about their prospects for advancement.

de la Cuna, in an alley off C. Azacayes, between C. Elvira and Gran Vía; it's the place to go for flamenco and jazz. (☎958 29 08 29. 1 drink min.) Gypsies and highwaymen once roamed the caves of Sacromonte; now, scantily clad clubbers can also at **Camborio,** Camino del Sacromonte 48. (€4.20 cover F-Sa. Open Tu-Sa 11pm-dawn.) **Granero,** Pl. Luis Rosales. Isabel Católica, is a New-Age barn filled with grooving Spanish yuppies. (Open daily 10pm-dawn.) **Granada 10,** C. Carcel Baja 3, is a movie theater by evening and a raging dance club by night. (€6 cover Th-Sa includes 1 drink. Open daily.)

■ HIKING AND SKIING NEAR GRANADA: SIERRA NEVADA

The peaks of **Mulhacén** (3481m) and **Veleta** (3470m), Spain's highest, sparkle with snow and buzz with tourists for most of the year. **Ski** season runs from December to April. The rest of the year, tourists hike, parasail, and take jeep tours. Call **Cetursa** (☎958 24 91 11) for information on outdoor activities. The Autocares Bonal bus (☎958 27 31 00), between the bus station in Granada and Veleta, is a bargain (9am departure, 5pm return; €5.40).

EASTERN SPAIN (VALENCIA)

Valencia's rich soil and famous orange groves, fed by Moorish irrigation systems, have earned it the nickname *Huerta de España* (Spain's Orchard). Dunes, sandbars, jagged promontories, and lagoons mark the grand coastline, while lovely fountains and pools grace carefully landscaped public gardens in Valencian cities. The famed rice dish *paella* was born in this region.

ALICANTE (ALICANT)   ☎965

Sun-drenched Alicante has it all: relaxing beaches, fascinating historical sites, and an unbelievable collection of bars and port-side discos. High above the rows of bronzed beach-goers, the ancient *castillo*, spared by Franco, guards the tangle of streets in the cobblestone *casco antiguo*.

■ TRANSPORTATION AND PRACTICAL INFORMATION. RENFE **trains** (☎902 24 02 02) run from Estación Término on Av. Salamanca, at the end of Av. Estación, to: Barcelona (4½-6hr., 9 per day, €36-62); Madrid (4hr., 9 per day, €34-52); and Valencia (1½hr., 10 per day, €9-32). Trains from **Ferrocarriles de la Generalitat Valenciana,** Estació Marina, Av. Villajoyosa 2 (☎965 26 27 31), on Explanada d'Espanya, serve the Costa Blanca. **Buses** run from C. Portugal 17 (☎965 13 07 00), to: Barcelona (7hr., 11 per day, €28); Granada (6hr., 7 per day, €21); and Madrid (5hr., 9 per day, €20-30). The **tourist office** is on Rbla. de Méndez Nuñez 23. (☎965 20 00 00. Open June-Aug. M-F 10am-8pm; Sept.-May M-F 10am-7pm, Sa 10am-2pm and 3-7pm.) Use the **Internet** at **Yazzgo,** Explanada 3. (Open M-Sa 8am-11pm, Su 9am-11pm. €1.50-3 per hr.) **Postal code:** 03070.

■ ACCOMMODATIONS AND FOOD. The ◨**Habitaciones México ❶**, C. General Primo de Rivera 10, off the end of Av. Alfonso X El Sabio, has a friendly atmosphere and small, cozy rooms. (☎965 20 93 07. Free Internet. Singles €12-

15; doubles €27; triples €33.) **Hostal Les Monges Palace ❷,** C. San Augustín 4, behind the Ayuntamiento in the center of the historic district, is one of the most luxurious hostels in Spain. (☎965 21 50 46. Singles €18-30; doubles €33-78; triples €42-90.) Take bus #21 to **camp** at **Playa Mutxavista ❶.** (☎965 65 45 26. June-Sept. €4 per person, €11 per tent; Oct.-May €2 per person, €7.50 per tent.)Try the family-run *bar-restaurantes* in the *casco antiguo,* between the cathedral and the castle steps. ▧**Kebap ❷,** C. Italia 2, serves heaping entrees of Middle Eastern cuisine. (Open daily 1-4pm and 8pm-midnight.) Buy basics at **Supermarket Mercadona,** C. Alvarez Sereix 5, off Av. Federico Soto. (Open M-Sa 9am-9pm.)

◙ ▣ **SIGHTS AND ENTERTAINMENT.** The ancient Carthaginian **Castell de Santa Bárbara,** complete with drawbridges, dark passageways, and hidden tunnels, keeps silent guard over Alicante's beach. A paved road from the old section of Alicante leads to the top, but most people take the **elevator** from a hidden entrance at the end of the tunnel that begins on Av. Jovellanos, across the street from Playa Postiguet. (Castle open daily Apr.-Sept. 10am-7:30pm; Oct.-Mar. 9am-6:30pm. Free. Elevator €2.40.) Modernist art resides along with works by Miró, Picasso, Kandinsky, and Calder in the **Museu de Arte del Siglo XX La Asegurada,** Pl. Santa María 3, at the east end of C. Mayor. (Open mid-May to mid-Sept. M-F 10am-2pm and 5-9pm, Sa-Su 10:30am-2:30pm; mid-Sept. to mid-May M-F 10am-2pm and 4-8pm, Sa-Su 10:30am-2:30pm. Free.) Alicante's **Playa del Postiguet** attracts beach lovers, as do nearby **Playa de San Juan** (take TAM bus #21, 22, or 31) and **Playa del Mutxavista** (take TAM bus #21; all buses depart every 15min., €0.75). Most everyone begins the night bar-hopping in the *casco antiguo;* the complex of bars that overlook the water in Alicante's **main port** tend to fill up a little later. For an even crazier night, the **Trensnochador** night train (July-Aug. F-Sa every hr. 9pm-5am; Su-Th 4 per night 9pm-5am; round-trip €0.90-4.20) runs from Estació Marina to discotecas and other stops along the beach, where places are packed until dawn. Try **Pachá, KU, KM,** and **Space** (open nightly until 9am) at the Disco Benidorm stop. During the hedonistic **Festival de Sant Joan** (June 20-29), *fogueres* (symbolic or satiric effigies) are erected around the city and then burned in the streets.

VALENCIA   ☎ 963

Stylish, cosmopolitan, and business-oriented, Valencia is a striking contrast to the surrounding orchards and mountain ranges. Parks and gardens soothe the city's congested environment, and nearby beaches complement its frenetic pace.

▣ ▨ **TRANSPORTATION AND PRACTICAL INFORMATION. Trains** arrive at C. Xàtiva 24 (☎963 52 02 02). **RENFE** (24hr. ☎902 24 02 02) runs to: Alicante (2-3hr., 9 per day, €9-25); Barcelona (3hr., 12 per day, €31); and Madrid (3½hr., 9 per day, €28). **Buses** (☎963 49 72 22) go from Av. Menéndez Pidal 13 to: Alicante via the Costa Blanca (4½hr., 13 per day, €12); Barcelona (4½hr., 15 per day, €19); Madrid (4hr., 13 per day, €21); and Sevilla (11hr., 4 per day, €40). Bus #8 (€0.80) connects to Pl. Ayuntamiento and the train station. Transmediterránea **ferries** (☎902 45 46 45) sail to the Balearic Islands (see p. 955).

The main **tourist office,** C. Paz 46-48, has branches at the train station and Pl. Ayuntamiento. (☎963 98 64 22. Open M-F 10am-6pm, Sa 10am-2pm.) **Internet** access is at **Ono,** C. San Vicente 22, around the corner from Pl. Ayuntamiento. (☎963 28 19 02. €1.20 per hr. Open daily 9am-1am.) The **post office** is at Pl. Ayuntamiento 24. (Open M-F 8:30am-8:30pm, Sa 9:30am-2pm.) **Postal Code:** 46080.

SPAIN

⌐◨ ACCOMMODATIONS AND FOOD. The best lodgings are around **Plaza Ayuntamiento** and **Plaza Mercado.** The **Home Youth Hostel ❶,** C. Lonja 4, is directly behind the Lonja, on a side street off Pl. Dr. Collado. Brightly painted rooms, a spacious common living room, and a kitchen create a homey atmosphere for road-weary guests. (☎963 91 62 29; www.likeathome.net. Internet €0.50 per 15min. Laundry €4. Dorms €14; singles €21; doubles €30; triples €43; quads €54.) **Hostal Alicante ❷,** C. Ribera 8, is right on the pedestrian street off Pl. Ayuntamiento, as central as it gets. Its clean, well-lit rooms and firm beds are hugely popular with backpackers. (☎963 51 22 96. Singles €19, with bath €24; doubles €27/€36. MC/V.) To get to **Hostal Antigua Morellana ❸,** C. En Bou 2, walk past Pl. Dr. Collado; it's on the small streets behind the Lonja. Quiet and comfortable rooms with bath and A/C cater to an older crowd. (☎/fax 963 91 57 73. Singles €29; doubles €42.)

Paella is the most famous of Valencia's 200 rice dishes; try as many of them as you can before leaving. Buckets of fresh fish, meat, and fruit (including Valencia's famous oranges) are sold at the **Mercado Central,** on Pl. Mercado. (Open M-F 7am-3pm.) For groceries, stop by the basement of **El Corte Inglés,** C. Colon, or the fifth floor of the C. Pintor Sorilla building. (Open M-Sa 10am-10pm.)

◙ SIGHTS. Touring Valencia on foot is a good test of stamina. Most of the sights line Río Turia or cluster near Pl. Reina, which is linked to Pl. Ayuntamiento by C. San Vicente Mártir. EMT bus #5, dubbed the **Bus Turistic,** makes a loop around the old town sights (€0.80; 1-day pass €3). Head toward the beach along the riverbed off C. Alcalde Reig. or take bus #35 from Pl. Ayuntamiento to reach the modern, airy, and thoroughly fascinating **◪Ciudad de las artes y las ciencias.** This mini-city has created quite a stir; it's become the fourth biggest tourist destination in Spain. The complex is divided into four large attractions; only two of which are currently completed: **Palau de les Arts** and **L'Oceanografic** will not open until at least 2004. The **◪Museu de Les Ciencias Principe Felipe** is an interactive playground for science and technology fiends; **L'Hemisfèric** has an IMAX theater and planetarium. (www.cac.es. Museum open daily 10am-8pm. €6, M-F students €4.20. IMAX shows €6.60, M-F students €4.80.) The 13th-century **◪cathedral,** in Pl. Reina, was built on the site of an Arab mosque. The **Museo de la Catedral** squeezes a great many treasures into three tiny rooms. (Cathedral open in summer daily 8am-2pm and 5-8pm; in off-season closes earlier. Free. Tower open daily 10am-1pm and 4:30-7pm. €1.20. Museum open June-Sept. M-F 10am-1pm and 4:30-6pm, Sa-Su 10am-1pm; Oct.-May closes 1hr. earlier. €1.20.) Across the river, the **Museu Provincial de Belles Artes,** on C. Sant Pius V, displays superb 14th- to 16th-century Valencian art. Its collection includes El Greco's *San Juan Bautista*, Velázquez's self-portrait, and a slew of Goyas. (Open Tu-Sa 10am-2:15pm and 4-7:30pm, Su 10am-7:30pm. Free.) West across the old river, the **Instituto València de Arte Moderno (IVAM),** C. Guillem de Castro 118, has works by 20th-century sculptor Julio González. (Open Tu-Su 10am-7pm. €2.10, students €1, Su free.)

◪◪ ENTERTAINMENT AND NIGHTLIFE. The most popular **beaches** are **Las Arenas** and **Malvarrosa**—buses #20, 21, 22, and 23 all pass through. To get to the more attractive **Salér,** 14km from the center of town, take an Autobuses Buñol bus (☎963 49 14 25) from the corner of Gran Vía Germanias and C. Sueca (25min., every 30min. 7am-10pm, €0.90). Bars and pubs abound in the El Carme district. Follow C. Bolsería out of Pl. Mercado, bearing right at the fork, to guzzle *agua de Valencia* (orange juice, champagne, and vodka) in Pl. Tossal. The loud **Cafe Negrito,** Pl. del Negrito 1, off C. Caballeros, is wildly popular with locals. (Pitcher of *agua de Valencia* €6. Open daily 10pm-3am.) **Rumbo 144,** Av. Blasco Ibañez 144, plays a wide variety of music, from Spanish pop to house. (Cover €6-8. Open F-Su midnight-7am.) For more information, consult the *Qué y Dónde* weekly magazine (€0.90), available at newsstands, or the weekly entertainment supplement *La Cartelera* (€0.75). The most famed festival in Valencia is **Las Fallas** (Mar. 12-19), which culminates with the burning of gigantic (up to 30m) papier-maché effigies.

COSTA BLANCA

You could while away a lifetime touring the charming resort towns of the Costa Blanca. The "white coast" that extends through Dénia, Calpe, and Alicante derives its name from its fine white sands. ALSA **buses** (☎902 42 22 42) run from Valencia to: Alicante (4½hr., 13 per day, €12); Altea and Calpe (3-3½hr., 12 per day, €8); and Gandía (1hr., 13 per day, €5). From Alicante, buses run to Altea (1¼hr., 18 per day, €4) and Calpe (1½hr., 18 per day, €4). Going to **Calpe** (Calp) is like stepping into a Dalí landscape. The town cowers beneath the **Peñó d'Ifach** (327m), which drops straight to the sea, making it one of the most picturesque coastal settings in Spain. Peaceful **Gandía** has fine sand beaches. The **tourist office,** Marqués de Campo, is opposite the train station. (☎962 87 77 88. Open June-Aug. M-F 9:30am-1:30pm and 4:30-7:30pm, Sa 10am-1:30pm; Sept.-May M-F 9:30am-1:30pm and 4-7pm, Sa 10am-1pm.) Buses depart from outside the train station for **Platja de Piles** (M-Sa 4-5 per day, €0.75). To sleep at the fantastic **Alberg Mar i Vent (HI) ❶** in Platja, follow the signs down C. Dr. Fleming. The beach is out the back door. (☎962 83 17 48. 3-day max. stay, flexible if uncrowded. Sheets €1.80. Curfew Su-F 2am, Sa 4am. Closed Oct. 2002-Feb. 2003 for renovations. Dorms €7, over 26 €10.)

NORTHEAST SPAIN

Northeastern Spain encompasses the country's most avidly regionalistic areas and is home to some of its best cuisine. Cataluña is justly proud of its treasures, from mountains to beaches to hip Barcelona. However, Cataluña isn't the only reason to head northeast. The area is also home to the glorious mountains of the Pyrenees, the running bulls of Navarra, the industrious cities of Aragón, the beautiful coasts of Basque Country, and the crazy parties of the Balearic Islands.

CATALUÑA

From rocky Costa Brava to chic Barcelona, Cataluña is a vacation in itself. Graced with the nation's richest resources, it is one of Spain's most prosperous regions. Catalán is the region's official language (though most everyone is bilingual), and local cuisine is lauded throughout Spain.

BARCELONA ☎93

Barcelona loves to indulge in the fantastic. From the urban carnival that is Las Ramblas to buildings with no straight lines, from wild festivals to even wilder nightlife, the city pushes the limits of style and good taste in everything it does— and with amazing results. The center of the whimsical and daring *Modernisme* architectural movement, and once home to the most well-known Surrealist painters, even Barcelona's art is grounded in an alternate reality. In the quarter-century since Spain was freed from Franco's oppressive regime, Barcelona has led the autonomous region of Cataluña in a resurgence of a culture so esoteric and unique it is puzzling even to the rest of Spain. The result is a vanguard city where rooftops drip toward the sidewalk, serpentine park benches twist past fairy-tale houses, and and an unfinished cathedral captures imaginations around the world.

▐ TRANSPORTATION

Flights: El Prat de Llobregat Airport (BCN; ☎ 932 98 38 38), 12km southwest of Barcelona. To get to the central Pl. Catalunya, take the **Aerobus** (approx. 40min.; every 15min.; to Pl. Catalunya M-F 6am-midnight, Sa-Su 6:30am-midnight; to the airport M-F 5:30am-11:15pm, Sa-Su 6am-11:20pm; €3.30) or a RENFE **train** (40min.; every 30min.; from airport 6:10am-11:15pm, from Estació Barcelona-Sants 5:30am-11:20pm; €2.15).

Trains: Barcelona has 2 main train stations. For general info about trains and train stations, call ☎ 902 24 02 02. **Estació Barcelona-Sants**, in Pl. Països Catalans (M: Sants-Estació) is the main terminal for domestic and international traffic. **Estació França**, on Av. Marquès de l'Argentera. M: Barceloneta. Services regional destinations, including Girona Tarragona and Zaragoza, and some international arrivals.

Ferrocarrils de la Generalitat de Cataluña (FGC) (☎ 93 205 15 15; www.fgc.catalunya.net), has commuter trains with main stations at Pl. Catalunya and Pl. Espanya.

RENFE: (☎ 902 24 02 02, international ☎ 934 90 11 22; www.renfe.es). RENFE has extensive service in Spain and Europe. Popular connections include: **Bilbao** (8-9hr., 5 per day, €30-32); **Madrid** (7-8hr., 7 per day, €31-42); **San Sebastián** (8-9hr., 5 per day, €31); **Seville** (11-12hr., 6 per day, €47-51); **Valencia** (3-5hr., 15 per day, €28-32). International destinations include **Milan**, Italy (via Figueres and Nice) and **Montpellier**, France with connections to Geneva, Paris, and various stops along the French Riviera. 20% discount on round-trip tickets.

Buses: Most buses arrive at the **Barcelona Nord Estació d'Autobuses**, C. Ali-bei 80 (☎ 932 65 61 32). M: Arc de Triomf. **Sarfa** (☎ 902 30 20 25; www.sarfa.com) goes to: **Cadaqués** (2½hr., 11:15am and 8:25pm, €15); **Palafrugell** (2hr., 13 per day, €12); **Tossa del Mar** (1½hr., 10 per day, €7.50). **Linebús** (☎ 932 65 07 00) travels to **Paris** (13hr., M-Sa 8pm, €80), southern France, and Morocco. Discounts for travelers under 26 and over 60. **Alsa Enatcar** (☎ 902 42 22 42; www.alsa.es) goes to: **Alicante** (9hr., 3 per day, €33); **Madrid** (8hr., 13 per day, €22); **Naples** (24hr., 5:15pm, €113); **Valencia** (4hr., 16 per day, €21); **Zaragoza** (3½-4½hr., 20 per day, €18).

Ferries: Trasmediterránea (☎ 902 45 46 45), in Estació Marítima-Moll Barcelona, Moll de Sant Bertran. In the summer months only to: **Ibiza** (10-11hr., 1 per day M-Sa, €46); **Mahón** (10½hr., 1 per day starting mid-June, €46); **Palma** (3½hr., 1 per day, €63).

Public Transportation: ☎ 010. Pick up a *Guia d'Autobusos Urbans de Barcelona* for Metro and bus routes. **Buses** run 5am-10pm and cost €1 per ride. The **Metro** (☎ 934 86 07 52; www.tmb.net) runs M-Th 5am-midnight, F-Sa 5am-2am, Su and holidays 6am-midnight. Buy tickets at vending machines and ticket windows. Tickets cost €1 per *sencillo* (ride). A **T1 Pass** (€5.60) is valid for 10 rides on the bus or Metro; a **T-DIA** Card entitles you to unlimited bus and Metro travel for 1 (€4.20) or 3 days (€10.80).

Taxis: ☎ 933 30 03 00.

Car Rental: Avis/Auto Europe, Casanova 209 (☎ 932 09 95 33). Will rent to ages 21-25 for an additional fee of about €5 a day.

ORIENTATION

Barcelona's layout is simple. Imagine yourself perched on Columbus's head at the **Monument a Colom** (on Passeig de Colom, along the shore), viewing the city with the sea at your back. From the harbor, the city slopes upward to the mountains. From the Columbus monument, **Las Ramblas**, the main thoroughfare, runs from the harbor up to **Plaça de Catalunya** (M: Catalunya), the city's center. The **Ciutat Vella** (Old City) is the heavily touristed historical neighborhood, which centers around Las Ramblas and includes the Barri Gòtic, La Ribera, and El Raval. The **Barri Gòtic** is east of Las Ramblas (to the right, with your back to the sea), enclosed on the other side by **Vía Laietana.** East of Vía Laietana lies the maze-like neighborhood of **La Ribera,** which borders Parc de la Ciutadella and the Estació França train station. To the west of Las Ramblas (to the left, with your back to the sea) is **El Raval.** Beyond La Ribera, (farther east, outside the Ciutat Vella) is the **Poble Nou** neighborhood and the **Vila Olímpica,** with its twin towers (the tallest buildings in Barcelona) and an assortment of discos and restaurants. Beyond El Raval (to the west) rises **Montjuïc,** crammed with gardens, museums, the 1992 Olympic grounds, Montjuïc castle, and other attractions. Directly behind the Monument a Colom is the **Port Vell** (Old Port) development, where a wavy bridge leads across to the ultra-modern shopping and entertainment complexes **Moll d'Espanya** and **Maremagnum.** Beyond the Ciutat Vella is **l'Eixample,** the gridded neighborhood created during the expansion of the 1860s, which runs from Pl. Catalunya toward the mountains. **Gran Via de les Corts Catalanes** defines its lower edge, and the **Passeig de Gràcia,** l'Eixample's main street, bisects the neighborhood. **Avinguda Diagonal** marks the border between l'Eixample and the **Zona Alta** ("Uptown"), which includes Pedralbes, Gràcia, and other older neighborhoods in the foothills. The peak of **Tibidabo,** the northwest border of the city, offers the most comprehensive view of Barcelona.

 PRACTICAL INFORMATION

TOURIST AND FINANCIAL SERVICES

Tourist Info: (☎010, 906 30 12 82, or 933 04 34 21; www.barcelonaturisme.com). Barcelona has 4 main tourist offices and numerous mobile information stalls.

Informacio Turistica at Plaça Catalunya, Pl. Catalunya 17S. M: Catalunya. The biggest, best, and busiest tourist office. Open daily 9am-9pm.

Informacio Turista at Plaça Sant Jaume, Pl. Sant Jaume 1, off C. Ciutat. M: Jaume I. Open M-Sa 10am-8pm, Su 10am-2pm.

Oficina de Turisme de Catalunya, Pg. Gràcia 107 (☎932 38 40 00; www.gencat.es/probert). M: Diagonal. Open M-Sa 10am-7pm, Su 10am-2pm.

Estació Central de Barcelona-Sants, Pl. Països Cataláns, in the Barcelona-Sants train station. M: Sants-Estació. Open M-F 4:30am-midnight, Sa-Su 5am-midnight.

Aeroport El Prat de Llobregat, in the international terminal. Open daily 9am-9pm.

Budget Travel Offices: usit UNLIMITED, Ronda Universitat 16 (☎934 12 01 04; www.unlimted.es). Open M-F 10am-8:30pm and Sa 10am-1:30pm.

Consulates: Australia, Gran Vía Carlos III 98, 9th fl. (☎933 30 94 96); **Canada,** Elisenda de Pinos 8 (☎932 04 27 00); **New Zealand,** Traversa de Gràcia 64, 4th fl. (☎932 09 03 99); **South Africa,** Teodora Lamadrid 7-11 (☎934 18 64 45); **US,** Pg. Reina Elisenda 23 (☎932 80 22 27).

A   B   C

Universitat

URGEL

PL. DE LA
UNIVERSITAT

M UNIVERSITAT

Via de les Corts Catalanes

C. Comte D' Urgel

C. Sepulveda

C. Vilamroel

C. Casanova

R. de Sant Antoni

C. Muntaner

Ronda Universitat

C. Pelai

CATALUNYA

C. Floridablanca

C. Valldonzella

C. Tigre

C. Tallers

C. Paloma

Centro de Cultura
Contemporanea

Museu d'Art
Contemporani

C. Ferlandina

Tamarit

Ronda de Sant Antoni

C. La Riera Alta

C. Nou de Dulce

C. Sant Gil

C. Sant Vicenç

Lluna Lleo

C. Joaquim Costa

PL. DELS
ANGELS

C. Montalegre

C. Elisabets

C. Xucla

C. Sitges

C. Bonsuccés

Mercat de
Sant Antoni

Manso   M

SANT ANTONI

C. Sant Antoni Abat

C.l Peu de la Creu

C. Alta

C.ls Angels

C. Dr. Dou

Pintor Fortuny

C. Xucla

C. Portaferrissa

Las Ramblas

EL RAVAL

Roman
Ruins

C. la Cera

C. Vista Alegre

C. la Reina Amalia

Ronda de Sant Pau

C. L'Hospital

C. Baixa

C. d'en Roig

C. Egipciaques

C.l Carme

C. Floristes de la Rambla

Palau
de la Virreina

C. Rica

C. Patricol

C.l Pi

C. de L'Aurora

C. les Carretes

C. S. Pacia

C. la Rierta

C. la Cadena

C. Sant Rafael

C. d'en Robador

C. Junta de Comerç

C. L'Hospital

Mercat
Boqueria

C. Petxina

PL. DEL
PI

C. Casalas

LICEU   M

Santa Maria
del Pi

C. Leialtat

PL. J. Ma.
FOLCH i TORRES

C. Aldana

C. Sant Jeroni

C. Sta. Elena

C. Sant Josep Oriol

C. Espasa

C. Sant Pau

Gran Theatre
de Liceu

Las Ramblas

C. la Boqueria

Quintana

C. Ferran

C. Banys No

PARAL-LEL   M

C. de Sant Pau

Sant Pau

C. S. Ologuer

C. S. Ramón

C. la Unió

C. la Pen

C. Colom

PL.
REIAL

C. la Lleona

C. d'Agla

Central Barcelona

■ ACCOMMODATIONS

Albergue de Juventud Kabul, **18**	C5
Albergue Juvenil Palau (HI), **22**	D5
California Hotel, **16**	C4
Casa de Huéspedes Mari-Luz, **21**	D5
Hostal Avinyó, **23**	D5
Hostal Benidorm, **5**	C5
Hostal Campi, **9**	C3
Hostal Fernando, **15**	C4
Hostal Levante, **19**	D5
Hostal Opera, **3**	C4
Hostal Plaza, **6**	D2
Hostal-Residencia Rembrandt, **11**	C3
Mare Nostrum, **4**	C4
Pensión Dalí, **13**	C4
Pensión L'Isard, **1**	B1

C. Nou de la Rambla

Palau
Güell

Guardia

Lancaster

C. Escudellers

PL. DEL
TEATRE

Ptge. dels
Escudellers

C. Nou Sant Francesc

C. Ruff

C.ls Cdols

Av. de les Drassanes

C. Arc del Teatre

Santa Mònica

Ptge. de
Banys

C. L' Om

C. Cid

Montserrat

Museu
de Cera

C. Ample

PL. DUC DE
MEDINACELI

C. Portal Santa Madrona

Museu
Marítim
Drassanes

Las Ramblas

C. Josep Anselm Clavé

C. Parc

Pg. de Color

DRASSANES   M

Ronda del Litoral (expressway

MAREMAGNUM
(80m)

TO PL. PORTAL
■ Monument a Colom
DE LA PAU

SPAIN

D / PASSEIG DE GRACIA

E

F

Jardins de la
eina Victoria

Via de les Corts Catalanes

PL.
TETUÁN
M
TETUÁN

C. Pau

C. Roger

C. Bruc

Passeig de Gràcia

L'EIXAMPLE

Pg. de Sant Joan

CATALUNYA
M
PL.
ATALUNYA

Ronda de Sant Pere

CATALUNYA
M

URQUINAONA

PL.
D'URQUINAONA
M

● FOOD
Bar Ra, **2**   C3
Betawi, **8**   D3
Els Quatre Gats, **7**   D3
Irati, **12**   C4
Les Quinze Nits, **17**   C5
Los Caracoles, **20**   C5
Va de Vi, **24**   E5
Xampanyet, **25**   E5

● SERVICES

Pharmacy, **10**   C3
Tintorería Ferran (laundry), **14** C4

CATALUNYA

El Corte
Ingles

C. Fontanella

C. Estruc

C. de les Moles

C. les Jonqueres

Ronda de Sant Pere   C. d' Alí-Bei

TO ESTACIÓ NORD
VILLANOVA (300m)

santa Anna

C. Comtal

C. d'Ortigosa

C. Trafalgar

C. Méndez Núñez

C. Trafalgar

ARC DE
TRIOMF
M

Canuda

Portal de l'Àngel

C. Montsió

C. Durán i Bas

Via Laietana

C. Sant Pere Mes Alt

Palau de la
Música Catalana

C. d'en Morer

PL.
SANT
PERE

Pg. Lluís Companys

Arc de
Triomf

C. Boters

C. Dr. J. Pou

C. Sant Pere Mitjà

C. Sant Pere Mes Baix

C. Rec Comtal

C. Sagristans

PL.
NOVA Av. de la Catedral

PL.
ANTONI
MAURA

Av. de
Francesc Cambó

C. Avellà

C. Jaume Giralt

C. Fonollar

C. d'en Cortines

PL. DEL
COMERÇ

C. Portal Nou

Pg. Lluís Companys

Pàlla

PL. DE
LA SEU

Palau
Real

LA RIBERA

Catedral
de la
Santa Creu

Museu
Frederic Marès

Mercat Santa
Caterina

C. ls Carders

Pg. de Pujades

Cascada
Fountains

Palau
eneralitat

Museu d'Història
de la Ciutat

C. ls Assannadors

C. Tantarantana

Museu de
Zoologia

Museu
d'Art Modern

C. Bisbe

C. de la

PL. DE
L'ANGEL
M

C. ls Corders

C. ls Passadors

C. Comerç

Pg. de Picasso

PL. DE
SANT JAUME   C. Jaume I

C. Princesa

Museu Textil
i l'Indumentaria

C. Rec

C. Fussina

Museu de
Geologia

C. Llibreteria

JAUME I

Via Laietana

C. Argenteria

C. Banys Vells

Museu
Picasso

PL.
DE SANT
MIQUEL   Ajuntament

BARRI
GÒTIC

C. Ciutat

C. Manresa

C. la Nau

C. Mosques

C. Montcada

Antic
Mercat
del Born

Museu de
Geologia

antes

C. Regomir

C. ls Sots

Santa Maria
del Mar

Pg. del Born

Parc de la
Ciutadella

Comtessa

C. d'Atuall

C. Canvis Nous

C. Espaseria

C. Vidrieria

C. la Ribera

d'Avinyo
olen

C. Gignàs

C. la
Fusteria

C. Consolat de Mar

Av. Marquès de L'Argentera

TO ZOO
(50m)

C. Simó Oller

C. Mercè

PL. D'ANTONI
LOPEZ

Pg. d'Isabel II

PL. DEL
PALAU

Canvis Vells

Gobierno
Civil

Parc
Zoològic

nel)

Moll de la Fusta

TO MOLL
D'ESPANYA (50m)

BARCELONETA
M

Estació
de
França

Pg. Circumval·lació

Av. D'Icària

TO VILA
OLIMPICA
(800m)

S P A I N

Currency Exchange: ATMs give the best rates (with no commission); the next best rates are available at banks. General banking hours M-F 8:30am-2pm.

American Express, Pg. Gràcia 101 (☎933 01 11 66). M: Diagonal. Open M-F 9:30am-6pm, Sa 10am-noon. Also at Las Ramblas 74. Open daily 9am-8pm.

Luggage Storage: Estació Barcelona-Sants. M: Sants-Estació. Large lockers €4.50. Open daily 5:30am-11:00pm. **Estació França.** M: Barceloneta. Open daily 7am-10pm.

Department Store: El Corte Inglés, Pl. Catalunya 14 (☎933 06 38 00). M: Catalunya. Behemoth department store. **Free map** of Barcelona at the information desk. Also has English books, salon, cafeteria, supermarket, and the *oportunidades* discount department. Open M-Sa and first Su of every month 10am-10pm. **Branches:** Portal de l'Angel 19-2 (M: Catalunya); Av. Diagonal 471-473 (M: Hospital Clinic); Av. Diagonal 617 (M: Maria Cristina).

Laundromat: Tintorería Ferrán, C. Ferrán 11. M: Liceu. Open M-F 9am-8pm. **Tintorería San Pablo,** C. San Pau 105 (☎933 29 42 49). M: Paral·lel. Wash, dry, and fold €10; do-it-yourself €7.25. Open July-Sept. M-F 9am-2pm; Oct.-June M-F 9am-2pm and 4-8pm.

EMERGENCY AND COMMUNICATIONS

Emergency: ☎112. **Local police:** ☎092. **National police:** ☎091. **Medical:** ☎061.

Police: Las Ramblas 43 (☎933 44 13 00), across from Pl. Reial and next to C. Nou de La Rambla. M: Liceu. Multilingual officers. Open 24hr.

Late-Night Pharmacy: Rotates; check any pharmacy for the nearest on duty.

Hospital: Hospital Clinic, Villarroel 170 (☎932 27 54 00). M: Hospital Clinic. Main entrance at the intersection of C. Roselló and C. Casanova.

Internet Access: ▧ **easyEverything,** Las Ramblas 31. M: Liceu. About €1.20 per 40min. Open 24hr. Branch at Ronda Universitat 35, right next to Pl. Catalunya. **Bcnet (Internet Gallery Café),** Barra de Ferro 3, right down the street from the Picasso museum. M: Jaume I. €1.50 per 15min., €3.60 per hr.; 10hr. ticket €18. Open daily 10am-1am. **Cybermundo Internet Centre,** Bergara 3 and Balmes 8. M: Catalunya. Just off the Pl. Catalunya, behind the Triangle shopping mall. Allows uploading of disks. €1 per hr. **Workcenter,** Av. Diagonal 441. M: Hospital Clinic or Diagonal. Another branch is at C. Roger de Lluria 2. M: Urquinaona. €0.50 per 10min. Open 24hr.

Post Office: Pl. de Antoni López (☎902 197 197: general info). M: Jaume I or Barceloneta. Fax and **lista de correos.** Open M-F 8:30am-9:30pm. A little shop in the back of the post office building, across the street, wraps packages for mailing (about €2). Shop open M-Sa 9am-2pm and 5-8pm. **Postal Code:** 08003.

▌ ACCOMMODATIONS AND CAMPING

The area between Pl. Catalunya and the water—the **Barri Gòtic, El Raval,** and **La Ribera**—offers budget beds, but reservations are a must. Last-minute travelers can crash in **Gràcia** or **l'Eixample,** outer boroughs with more vacancies.

LOWER BARRI GÒTIC

▧ **Hostal Levante,** Baixada de San Miguel 2 (☎933 17 95 65; www.hostallevante.com). M: Liceu. The best deal in Barri Gòtic. Singles €27; doubles €46-52. MC/V. ❸

▧ **Hostal Fernando,** C. Ferran 31 (☎/fax 933 01 79 93; www.barcelona-on-line.es/fernando). M: Liceu. Fills from walk-in requests. Dorms with lockers. In summer dorms €17, with bath €18; doubles €40/€54; triples with bath €60. MC/V. ❷

Hostal Benidorm, Las Ramblas 37 (☎933 02 20 54). M: Drassanes. The best value on Las Ramblas, with phones and complete baths in each of the very clean rooms, balconies overlooking Las Ramblas, and excellent prices. Singles €25-29; doubles €33-45; triples €50-60; quads €65-70; quints €75. ❸

Casa de Huéspedes Mari-Luz, C. Palau 4 (☎/fax 933 17 34 63). M: Liceu. Tidy 4- to 6-person dorm rooms and a few comfortable doubles. Reservations require a credit card. In summer dorms €16; doubles €37. Off-season prices lower. MC/V. ❷

Hostal Avinyó, C. Avinyó 42 (☎933 18 79 45; www.hostalavinyo.com). M: Drassanes. Rooms with couches, high ceilings, fans, safes, and stained-glass windows. Singles €16; doubles €28, with bath €40; triples €42/€60. ❷

Albergue Juvenil Palau (HI), C. Palau 6 (☎934 12 50 80). M: Liceu. A tranquil refuge in the heart of the Barri Gòtic. Kitchen (open 7-10pm), dining room, and clean 3- to 8-person dorm rooms with lockers. Breakfast included. Showers available 8am-noon and 4-10pm. Sheets €1.50. Reception 7am-3am. Curfew 3am. No reservations. Dorms €13. Cash only. ❶

Albergue de Juventud Kabul, Pl. Reial 17 (☎933 18 51 90; www.kabul-hostel.com). M: Liceu. Legendary among backpackers; squeezes in up to 200 frat boys at a time. Key deposit €10. Laundry €2.50. No reservations. Dorms €20. ❷

California Hotel, C. Rauric 14 (☎933 17 77 66). M: Liceu. Enjoy one of the 31 clean, sparkling rooms, all with TV, phone, full bath, and A/C. Convenient location. Singles €47; doubles €76; triples €95. ❹

UPPER BARRI GÒTIC

Between C. Fontanella and C. Ferran, accommodations are pricier but more serene than in the lower Barri Gòtic. Early reservations are obligatory in summer. The nearest Metro stop is Catalunya, unless otherwise specified.

▨ **Hostal Plaza,** C. Fontanella 18 (☎/fax 933 01 01 39; www.plazahostal.com). Savvy, super-friendly Texan owners; fun, brightly painted rooms with wicker furniture; great location. Laundry €9. Singles €52, with bath €65; doubles €58/€67; triples €68/€86. 12% discount Nov. and Feb. AmEx/MC/V. ❺

Hostal Campi, C. Canuda 4 (☎/fax 933 01 35 45; hcampi@terra.es). The first left off Las Ramblas (bear right at the fork). A great bargain. Call ahead to reserve 9am-8pm. Prices vary, but generally doubles €40, with bath €48; triples €60. ❹

Hostal-Residencia Rembrandt, C. Portaferrissa 23 (☎/fax 933 18 10 11). M: Liceu. Ask for a room with a balcony. Fans €2 per night. Singles €25; doubles €42, with bath €50; triples €52/€60. ❸

Pensión Dalí, C. Boquería 12 (☎933 18 55 90; pensiondali@wanadoo.es). M: Liceu. Designed as a religious house by Domènech i Montaner, the architect of the Palau de la Música Catalana. All rooms have TVs. In the high season, doubles €45, with bath €51; triples with bath €69; quads with bath €83. AmEx/MC/V. ❹

Mare Nostrum, Las Ramblas 67 (☎933 18 53 40; fax 934 12 30 69). M: Liceu. The swankiest hostel on the strip. All rooms have A/C and satellite TV. Breakfast included. Doubles €57, with bath €67; triples €77/€87; quads €93/€107. ❺

EL RAVAL

Be careful in the areas nearer to the port and farther from Las Ramblas.

▨ **Pensión L'Isard,** C. Tallers 82 (☎933 02 51 83; fax 933 02 01 17). M: Universitat. A simple, elegant, clean find. Singles €19; doubles €33, with bath €42; triples €48. ❷

Hostal Opera, C. Sant Pau 20 (☎933 18 82 01). M: Liceu. Sunny rooms feel like new. All rooms come with bath, phone, and A/C. Singles €31; doubles €50. MC/V. ❸

L'EIXAMPLE

▨ **Pensión Fani,** València 278 (☎932 15 36 45). M: Catalunya. Oozes quirky charm. Rooms rented by month; single nights also available. Singles €276 per month; doubles €490 per month; triples €760 per month. One-night stay €20 per person. ❷

▨ **Hostal Ciudad Condal,** C. Mallorca 255 (☎932 15 10 40). M: Diagonal. Prices reflect the generous amenities and prime location. Singles €65; doubles €90. Prices often drop in winter. MC/V. ❺

▨ **Hostal Eden,** C. Balmes 55 (☎934 52 66 20; www.eden.iberica.com). M: Pg. Gràcia. Modern rooms are equipped with TVs and fans; most have big, new bathrooms. May-Oct. singles €29, with bath €39; doubles €39/€55. Nov.-Apr. singles €23/€32; doubles €29/€45. AmEx/MC/V. ❸

Hostal Qué Tal, C. Mallorca 290 (☎/fax 934 59 23 66; www.hotelsinbarcelona.net/hostalquetal), near C. Bruc. M: Pg. Gràcia or Verdaguer. This high-quality gay-and-lesbian friendly hostel has one of the best interiors of all the hostels in the city. Singles €35; doubles €55, with bath €66. ❹

GRÀCIA

Hostal Lesseps, C. Gran de Gràcia 239 (☎932 18 44 34). M: Lesseps. Spacious, classy rooms sport red velvet wallpaper. All 16 rooms have a TV and bath; 4 have A/C (€5.60 extra). Singles €34; doubles €52; triples €70; quads €90. MC/V. ❸

Pensión San Medín, C. Gran de Gràcia 125 (☎932 17 30 68; www.sanmedin.com). M: Fontana. Embroidered curtains and ornate tiling adorn this family-run pension. Common room with TV. Singles €30, with bath €39; doubles €48/€60. MC/V. ❸

Hostal Bonavista, C. Bonavista 21 (☎932 37 37 57). M: Diagonal. Well-kept rooms. TV lounge. Showers €1.50. No reservations. Singles €18; doubles €25, with bath €34. ❷

CAMPING

El Toro Bravo, Autovía de Castelldefells km 11 (☎936 37 34 62; www.eltorobravo.com). Take bus L95 (€1.50) from Pl. Catalunya to the campsite. Offers beach access, laundry facilities, currency exchange, 3 pools, 2 bars, a restaurant, and a supermarket. Possibility of long-term stays. Reception 8am-7pm. Open Sept.-June 14 only. €5 per person, €5 per site, €5 per car, €3.65 electricity charge. IVA tax not included. AmEx/MC/V. ❶

Filipinas, Autovía de Castelldefells km 12 (☎936 58 28 95), 1km down the road from El Toro Bravo, accessible by bus L95. Same prices and services as El Toro Bravo. ❶

🗋 FOOD

The *Guia del Ocio* (available at newsstands; www.guiadelociobcn.es) is an invaluable source of culinary suggestions. **Port Vell** and **Port Olímpic** are known for seafood. The restaurants on **Calle Aragó** by Pg. Gràcia have great lunchtime *menús*, and the **Passeig de Gràcia** has beautiful outdoor dining. Gràcia's **Plaça Sol** and La Ribera's **Santa Maria del Mar** are the best places to head for *tapas*. If you want to live cheap and do as Barceloneses do, buy your food fresh at a *mercat* (marketplace). For wholesale fruit, cheese, and wine, head to **La Boqueria** (Mercat de Sant Josep), outside M: Liceu. For groceries, try **Champion Supermarket,** Las Ramblas 11. (M: Liceu. Open M-Sa 10am-10pm.)

BARRI GÒTIC

■ **Les Quinze Nits,** Pl. Reial 6 (☎933 17 30 75). M: Liceu. One of the most popular restaurants in Barcelona, with nightly lines. Delicious Catalán entrees at unbelievable prices (€3-7). No reservations. Open daily 1-3:45pm and 8:30-11:30pm. MC/V. ❶

■ **Els Quatre Gats,** C. Montsió 3 (☎933 02 41 40). M: Catalunya. *Tapas* €2-4. Live piano and violin 9pm-1am. Open M-Sa 9am-2am, Su 5pm-2am. Closed Aug. AmEx/MC/V. ❷

Irati, C. Cardenal Casañas 17 (☎933 02 30 84). M: Liceu. An excellent Basque *tapas* bar. Keep your toothpicks to figure out your bill. Bartenders pour *sidra* (cider) behind their backs. Entrees €15-18. Open daily noon-1am. AmEx/MC/V. ❹

Los Caracoles, C. Escudellers 14 (☎933 01 20 41). M: Drassanes. Started as a snail shop in 1835; specialties include, of course, *caracoles* (snails; €7), half of a rabbit (€10), and chicken (€9). Open daily 1pm-midnight. AmEx/MC/V. ❷

Betawi, C. Montsió 6 (☎934 12 62 64). M: Catalunya. A peaceful Indonesian restaurant with food that verges on gourmet. *Menú* €8. Open M 1-4pm, Tu-Sa 1-4pm and 8-11pm. AmEx/MC/V. ❷

ELSEWHERE IN BARCELONA

■ **Xampanyet,** C. Montcado 22 (☎933 19 70 03). M: Jaume I. The house special *cava* is served at a colorful bar. Glasses €1. Bottles €5 and up. Open Tu-Sa noon-4pm and 7-11:30pm, Su 7-11:30pm. Closed Aug. MC/V. ❶

■ **Va de Vi,** C. Banys Vells 16 (☎933 19 29 00). M: Jaume I. Romantic, medieval wine bar in a 16th-century building. Wine €1.60-4 per glass, cheeses €3-7, *tapas* €3-5. Open Su-W 6pm-1am, Th 6pm-2am, F-Sa 6pm-3am. ❷

■ **Bar Ra,** Pl. Garduña (☎933 01 41 63). M: Liceu. A mix of traditional Spanish and trendy Californian cuisine. Dinner by reservation. Open M-Sa 1:30-4pm and 9:30pm-2am. ❷

El Racó d'en Baltá, C. Aribau 125 (☎934 53 10 44). M: Hospital Clínic. Offers creative Mediterranean dishes. Fish and meat entrees €10-16. Open M 9-10:45pm, Tu-Sa 1-3:45pm and 9-10:45pm. AmEx/MC/V. ❸

Thai Gardens, C. Diputació 273 (☎934 87 98 98). M: Catalunya. Extravagant decor. Weekday lunch *menú* €11. Pad thai €6. Entrees €9-13.50. Open Su-Th 1:30-4pm and 8:30pm-midnight, F-Sa 1:30-4pm and 8:30pm-1am. Wheelchair accessible. ❸

La Buena Tierra, C. Encarnació 56 (☎932 19 82 13). M: Joanic. Vegetarian delicacies with a Catalán twist. Get back to nature on the backyard terrace. Entrees €5-7. Open Tu-F 1-4pm and 8-11pm, F 1-4pm and 8pm-midnight, Su 1-4pm. ❷

🜨 SIGHTS

Barcelona is defined by its unique Modernist architecture. The tourist areas are **Las Ramblas,** a bustling avenue smack in the city center, and the **Barri Gòtic,** Barcelona's "old city." But don't neglect vibrant La Ribera and El Raval, the upscale avenues of l'Eixample, the panoramic city views from Montjuïc and Tibidabo, Gaudí's Park Güell, and the harborside Port Olímpic. The **Ruta del Modernisme** pass is the cheapest and most flexible option for those with a few days and an interest in seeing all the biggest sights. Passes (€3; students, over 65, and groups of 11 or more €2) are good for a month and give holders a 50% discount on entrance to Palau Güell, La Sagrada Família, Casa Milà, Palau de la Música Catalana, Casa-Museu Gaudí, Fundació Antoni Tàpies, the Museu d'Art Modern, the Museu de Zoologia, tours of El

Hospital de la Santa Creu i Sant Pau, tours of the facades of La Manzana de la Discòrdia (Casas Amatller, Lleó Morera, and Batlló), and other attractions. You can purchase passes at **Casa Amatller,** Pg. Gràcia 41. (☎934 88 01 39. M: Pg. de Gràcia.)

LAS RAMBLAS

Las Ramblas's pedestrian-only median strip is a veritable urban carnival, where street performers dance, fortune-tellers divine, human statues shift poses, and vendors sell birds—all, of course, for a small fee. The sights below are arranged beginning with Pl. Catalunya in the north, continuing to the port in the south.

UPPER LAS RAMBLAS. A port-ward journey begins at the **Font de Canaletes** (more a pump than a fountain), where visitors who wish to eventually return to Barcelona are supposed to sample the water. The upper part of Las Ramblas has been dubbed "Rambla de las Flores" for the numerous flower vendors that inhabit it. Halfway down Las Ramblas, **Joan Miró**'s pavement mosaic brightens up the street.

GRAN TEATRE DEL LICEU. Once one of Europe's leading stages, the Liceu has been ravaged by anarchists, bombs, and fires. It is adorned with palatial ornamentation, gold facades, sculptures, and grand side rooms—including a fantastic Spanish hall of mirrors. (Las Ramblas 51-59, by C. Sant Pau. Office open M-F 2-8:30pm and 1hr. before performances. ☎934 85 99 13. Guided tours M-F 10am, by reservation only. €5.)

MONUMENT A COLOM. Ruis i Taulet's Monument a Colom towers at the port end of Las Ramblas. Nineteenth-century *Renaixença* enthusiasts convinced themselves that Columbus was Catalán, from a town near Girona. The fact that Columbus points proudly toward Libya, not the Americas, doesn't help the claim; historians agree that Columbus was from Italy. Take the elevator to the top to enjoy a stunning view. (Portal de la Pau. M: Drassanes. Elevator open June-Sept. 9am-8:30pm; Oct.-Mar. M-F 10am-1:30pm and 3:30-6:30pm, Sa-Su 10am-6:30pm; Apr.-May 10am-2pm and 3:30-7:30pm, Sa-Su 10am-7:30pm. €1.80, children and those over 65 €1.20.)

BARRI GÒTIC

While the weathered, narrow streets of the Barri Gòtic, including **Carrer de la Pietat** and **Carrer del Paradis,** have preserved their medieval charm, the ever-growing tourist economy has infused the area with a new, multilingual liveliness.

ESGLÉSIA CATEDRAL DE LA SANTA CREU. This cathedral is one of Barcelona's most popular monuments. Beyond the choir are the altar with the bronze cross designed by Frederic Marès in 1976 and the sunken **Crypt of Santa Eulalia,** one of Barcelona's patron saints. The **cathedral museum** holds Bartolomé Bermejo's *Pietà.* Catch a performance of the **sardana** in front of the cathedral on Sunday after mass (at noon and 6:30pm). (M: Jaume I. In Pl. Seu, up C. Bisbe from Pl. St. Jaume. Cathedral open daily 8am-1:30pm and 4-7:30pm. Cloister open 9am-1:15pm and 4-7pm. Elevator to the roof open M-Sa 10:30am-12:30pm and 4:30-6pm; €1.35. Choir area open M-F 9am-1pm and 4-7pm, Sa-Su 9am-1pm; €0.90. English audioguide €1.)

PLAÇA DE SANT JAUME. Plaça de Sant Jaume has been Barcelona's political center since Roman times. Two of Cataluña's most important buildings have dominated the square since 1823: the **Palau de la Generalitat,** the headquarters of Cataluña's government, and the **Ajuntament,** the city hall. (Palau open the 2nd and 4th Su of every month 10:30am-1:30pm. Closed Aug. Mandatory tours in Catalán, Spanish, or English every 30min. starting at 10:30am. Free. Ajuntament open Su 10am-1:45pm. Free.)

LA RIBERA

This neighborhood has recently evolved into Barcelona's bohemian nucleus, with art galleries, chic eateries, and exclusive bars.

PALAU DE LA MÚSICA CATALANA. In 1891, the Orfeó Catalán choir society commissioned Modernist Luis Domènech i Montaner to design this must-see concert venue. The music hall glows with tall stained-glass windows, an ornate chandelier, marble reliefs, intricate woodwork, and ceramic mosaics. Concerts given at the Palau include all varieties of symphonic and choral music in addition to more modern pop, rock, and jazz. *(C. Sant Francese de Paula 2. ☎932 95 72 00. M: Jaume I. Mandatory tours in English every hr. Reserve 1 day in advance. Open daily Aug. 10am-6pm, Sept.-July 10am-3:30pm. €5, students and seniors €4. Check the Guía del Ocio for concert listings. Concert tickets €9-125. MC/V.)*

MUSEU PICASSO. The most-visited museum in Barcelona traces the development of Picasso as an artist, with the world's best collection of work from his formative period in Barcelona. *(C. Montcada 15-19. ☎933 19 63 10. M: Jaume I. Walk down C. Princesa from the Metro and turn right on C. Montcada. Open Tu-Sa 10am-8pm, Su 10am-3pm. €5, students and seniors €2.40, under 16 free. First Su of each month free.)*

SANTA MARIA DEL MAR. This architectural wonder was built in the 14th century in a quick 55 years. At a distance of 13m apart, the supporting columns span a width greater than any other medieval building in the world. It's a fascinating example of the limits of Gothic architecture—were it 2ft. taller, it would have collapsed from structural instability. *(Pl. Santa Maria 1. M: Jaume 1. ☎933 10 23 90. Open M-Sa 9am-1:30pm and 4:30-8pm, Su 9am-2pm and 5-8:30pm. Free.)*

PARC DE LA CIUTADELLA. Host of the 1888 Universal Exposition, the park harbors several museums, well-labeled horticulture, the wacky Cascada fountains, a pond, and a zoo. Buildings of note include Domènech i Montaner's Modernista **Castell dels Tres Dragons** (now the Museu de Zoología), the geological museum, and Josep Amergós's Hivernacle. **Floquet de Neu** (a.k.a. *Copito de Nieve*; Little Snowflake), the world's only known albino gorilla, lounges in the **Parc Zoològic,** on the end of the park closer to the sea. *(M: Ciutadella. Open May-Aug. 9:30am-7:30pm; Apr. and Sept. 10am-7pm; Mar. and Oct. 10am-6pm; Nov.-Feb. 10am-5pm. €10.)* In the center of the park, the **Museu d'Art Modern** houses a potpourri of works by 19th-century Catalán artists. *(Pl. D'Armes. Open Tu-Sa 10am-7pm, Su 10am-2:30pm. €3, students €2. Free entrance first Th of every month.)*

EL RAVAL

PALAU GÜELL. Gaudí's Palau Güell (1886)—the Modernist residence built for patron Eusebi Güell (of Park Güell fame)—has one of Barcelona's most spectacular interiors. Güell and Gaudí spared no expense. *(C. Nou de La Rambla 3-5. M: Liceu. Mandatory tour every 15min. Open Mar.-Oct. Su 10am-2pm, M-Sa 10am-8pm, last tour at 6:15pm; Nov.-Dec. M-Sa 10am-6pm. €3, students €1.50.)*

MUSEU D'ART CONTEMPORANI (MACBA). This monstrosity of a building was constructed with the idea that sparse decor would allow the art to speak for itself. The MACBA has received worldwide acclaim for its focus on avant-garde

MATING GAME Some call him Snowflake, but in his native Catalán he's Floquet de Neu, the world's only white gorilla in captivity. Taken from the forest in west Africa in the 60s, Floquet has been the toast of Barcelona ever since. With gorillas and other apes in endangered species status, zoos are making concerted efforts to aid breeding. Because of Floquet's dashing good looks, special measures are taken in his case—in an effort to breed another white gorilla, he has been encouraged to mate with his daughters. With over a dozen offspring to date, there's still no Floquet Jr.; Floquet de Neu may be the last of his kind, all the more reason for a pilgrimage to Barcelona.

art between the two world wars, as well as Surrealist and contemporary art. *(Pl. dels Angels 1. M: Catalunya. Open July-Sept. M, W, and F 11am-8pm; Th 11am-9:30pm; Sa 10am-8pm; Su 10am-3pm. Oct.-June M and W-F 11am-7:30pm, Sa 10am-8pm, Su 10am-3pm. €6, students €4, under 17 free.)*

L'EIXAMPLE

The Catalán Renaissance and the growth of Barcelona during the 19th century pushed the city past its medieval walls and into modernity. Ildefons Cerdà drew up a plan for a new neighborhood where people of all social classes could live side by side; however, l'Eixample (pronounced luh-SHOMP-luh) did not thrive as a utopian community but rather as a playground for the bourgeois.

■ **LA SAGRADA FAMÍLIA.** Although Antoni Gaudí's unfinished masterpiece is barely a shell of the intended finished product, La Sagrada Família is without a doubt the world's most visited construction site. Despite the fact that only eight of the church's eighteen planned towers have been completed (and those the shortest, at that) and the church still doesn't have an "interior," millions of people make the touristic pilgrimage to witness its work-in-progress majesty. Of the three proposed facades, only the Nativity Facade was finished under Gaudí. A furor has arisen over recent additions, especially sculptor Josep Subirachs's Cubist Passion Facade on C. Sardenya, which is criticized for being inconsistent with Gaudí's plans. *(C. Mallorca 401. M: Sagrada Família. Open Oct.-Mar. daily 9am-6pm, elevator open 9:30am-5:45pm; Apr.-Sept. 9am-8pm, elevator open 9:30am-7:45pm.* ■ *Guided tours Apr.-Sept. daily 11am, 1, 3, and 5:30pm; Oct. 11am, 1, and 3pm; Nov.-Mar. F-M 11am and 1pm. €3. Entrance €6, students and those with the Ruta pass €4. Cash only.)*

■ **LA MANZANA DE LA DISCÒRDIA.** A short walk from Pl. Catalunya, the odd-numbered side of Pg. Gràcia between C. Aragó and Consell de Cent is popularly known as *la manzana de la discòrdia* (block of discord), referring to the stylistic clashing of three buildings. Regrettably, the bottom two floors of **Casa Lleó i Morera**, by Domènech i Montaner, were destroyed to make room for a fancy store, but you can buy the **Ruta del Modernisme pass** (p. 935) there and take a tour of the upstairs, where sprouting flowers, stained glass, and legendary doorway sculptures adorn the interior. Puig i Cadafalch opted for a geometric, Moorish-influ-

FAR-OUT FACADE

Gaudí was a religious man, and his plans for La Sagrada Família called for elaborate and deliberate symbolism in almost every single decorative element of the church. The cypress tree on the **Nativity Facade,** according to one theory, symbolizes the stairway to heaven (cypress trees do not put down deeper roots with time, yet grow increasingly taller); the tree is crowned with the word "Tau," the Greek word for God. Similarly, the top of each of the eight finished towers carries the first letter of one of the names of the apostles (and the words "Hosanna" and "Excelsis" are written in a spiral up the sides of the towers). Inside, on the **Portal of the Rosary,** overt references to modern life lurk amongst more traditional religious imagery: the Temptation of Man is represented in one carving by the devil handing a bomb to a terrorist and in another by his waving a purse at a prostitute.

Subirachs, Gaudí's successor, continued the religious symbolism in his **Passion Facade.** To the left a snake lurks behind Judas, symbolizing the disciple's betrayal of Jesus. The 4x4 box of numbers contains 310 possible combinations of four numbers, each of which adds up to 33, the age at which Christ died. The faceless woman in the center of the facade, **Veronica,** represents the Biblical woman who witnessed the miraculous appearance of Christ's face on the cloth with which she wiped his face.

enced pattern on the facade of **Casa Amatller** at #41. Gaudí's balconies ripple like skulls, and tiles sparkle in blue-purple glory on **Casa Batlló** #43. The most popular interpretation of Casa Batlló is that the building represents Cataluña's patron Sant Jordi (St. George) slaying a dragon; the chimney plays the lance, the scaly roof is the dragon's back, and the bony balconies are the remains of his victims.

■**CASA MILÀ (LA PEDRERA).** Modernism buffs argue that the spectacular Casa Milà apartment building, an undulating mass of granite popularly known as *La Pedrera* (the Stone Quarry), is Gaudí's most refined work. Note the intricate ironwork around the balconies and the irregularity of the front gate's egg-shaped window panes. The roof sprouts chimneys that resemble armored soldiers, one of which is decorated with broken champagne bottles. Rooftop tours provide a closer look at these Prussian helmets. The winding brick attic has been transformed into the **Espai Gaudí,** a multimedia presentation of Gaudí's life and works. *(Pg. Gràcia 92. Open daily 10am-8pm. €6; students and over 65 €3, with Ruta del Modernisme pass €4.20. Free guided tours in English M-F 4pm, Sa-Su 11am.)*

WATERFRONT

■**L'AQUÀRIUM DE BARCELONA.** Barcelona's aquarium—the largest in Europe—is an aquatic wonder, featuring a large number of octopi and penguins. The highlight is an 80m glass tunnel through an ocean tank of sharks and sting rays, as well as one two-dimensional fish. *(Moll d'Espanya, next to Maremàgnum. M: Drassanes. Open July-Aug. daily 9:30am-11pm; Sept.-June 9:30am-9pm. €11, under 12 and seniors €8, students 10% off.)*

■**TORRE SAN SEBASTIÀ.** One of the easiest and best ways to view the city is on these cable cars, which span the entire Port Vell, connecting beachy Barceloneta with mountainous Montjuïc. The full ride, which takes about 10min. each way and makes an intermediate stop at the Jaume I tower near Colom, gives an aerial perspective of the entire city. *(Pg. Joan de Borbo. M: Barceloneta. In Port Vell, as you walk down Joan de Borbo and see the beaches to the left, stay right and look for the high tower. To Jaume round-trip €7.50; to Montjuïc one-way €7.50, round-trip €9.50. Open daily 11am-8pm).*

VILA OLÍMPICA. The Vila Olímpica, beyond the east side of the zoo, was built to house 15,000 athletes and entertain millions of tourists for the 1992 Summer Olympics. It's home to several public parks, a shopping center, and business offices. In the area called **Barceloneta,** beaches stretch out from the port. *(M: Ciutadella/Vila Olímpica. Walk along the waterfront on Ronda Litoral toward the two towers.)*

MONTJUÏC

Throughout Barcelona's history, whoever controlled Montjuïc (Hill of the Jews) controlled the city. Dozens of rulers have modified the **fortress,** built atop an ancient Jewish cemetery; Franco made it one of his "interrogation" headquarters, rededicating it to the city in 1960. A huge stone monument expresses Barcelona's (forced) gratitude for its return. The three statues in the monument symbolize the three seas surrounding Spain. *(M: Espanya, then catch bus #50 (every 10min.) at Av. Reina María Cristina.)*

■**CASTELL DE MONTJUÏC.** A visit to this historic fortress and its ■**Museum Militar** is a great way to get an overview of the city's layout and history. From the castle's exterior *mirador*, gaze over the city. Enjoy coffee at the cafe while cannons stare you down. *(From M: ParaHel, take the funicular (every 10min.) to Av. Miramar and then the Teleféric de Montjuïc cable car to the castle. Teleféric open M-Sa 11:15am-9pm. One-way €3.20, round-trip €4.50. Or, walk up the steep slope on C. Foc, next to the funicular station. Open Mar. 21-Nov. 14 Tu-Su 9:30am-7:30pm; Nov. 15-Mar. 20 Tu-Su 9:30am-5pm.)*

FONTS LUMINOSES. The Illuminated Fountains, dominated by the huge central **Font Mágica** (Magic Fountain), are visible from Pl. Espanya up Av. Reina María Cristina. During the summer, they are employed in a weekend music and laser show that illuminates the mountainside and the **Palau Nacional,** located behind the fountains. *(Shows June-Sept. Th-Su every 30min. 9:30pm-12:30am; Oct.-May F-Sa 7-8:30pm. Free.)* The **Museu Nacional d'Art de Cataluña,** behind the fountains, houses an impressive collection of paintings, including many of brutal martyrings. *(M: Espanya; walk up Av. Reina María Cristina to the escalators. Open Tu-Sa 10am-7pm, Su 10am-2:30pm. €4.80, €6 with temporary exhibits; students €3.30. Free first Th of every month.)*

■ **FUNDACIÓ MIRÓ.** Designed by Miró's friend Josep Luís Sert and tucked into the side of Montjuïc, the Fundació links interior and exterior spaces with massive windows and outdoor patios. Skylights illuminate an extensive collection of statues and paintings from Miró's career. His best-known pieces in the museum include *El Carnival de Arlequin, La Masia,* and *L'or de L'azuz.* Room 13 displays experimental work by young artists. The Fundació also sponsors music and film festivals. *(Av. Miramar 71-75. Take the funicular from M: ParaHel. Turn left out of the funicular station; the museum is a 5min. walk up on the right. Open July-Aug. Tu-W and F-Sa 10am-8pm, Th 10am-9:30pm, Su 10am-2:30pm; Oct.-June Tu-W and F-Sa 10am-7pm, Th 10am-9:30pm, Su 10am-2:30pm. €7.20, students and seniors €4.)*

GRÀCIA
Just beyond L'Eixample, this neighborhood charms and confuses with its narrow alleys and numerous plazas. In August, Gràcia hosts the **Fiesta Mejor.**

■ **PARK GÜELL.** This fantastic park was designed entirely by Gaudí but—in typical Gaudí fashion—was not completed until after his death. Gaudí intended Park Güell to be a garden city, and its dwarfish buildings and sparkling ceramic-mosaic stairways were designed to house the city's elite. Two mosaic staircases flank the park, leading to a towering Modernist pavilion that Gaudí originally designed as an open-air market. The longest park bench in the world, a multicolored serpentine wonder made of tile shards, decorates the top of the pavilion. In the midst of the park is the **Casa-Museu Gaudí.** *(Bus #24 from Pl. Catalunya stops at the upper entrance. Park free. Open May-Sept. daily 10am-9pm; Mar.-Apr. and Oct. 10am-7pm; Nov.-Feb. 10am-6pm.)*

CASA VICENS. One of Gaudí's earliest projects, Casa Vicens is decorated with cheerful ceramic tiles. The *casa* shows the influence of Arabic architecture and a rigidness that is uncharacteristic of Gaudí's later works. *(C. Carolines 24-26. M: Fontana. Walk down Gran de Gràcia and turn left onto C. Carolines.)*

PEDRALBES
■ **MUSEU DEL FÚTBOL CLUB BARCELONA.** A close second to the Picasso Museum as Barcelona's most-visited museum, the FCB museum merits all the attention it gets. Sports fans will appreciate the storied history of the team. The high point is the chance to enter the stadium and take in the enormity of Camp Nou. *(C. Aristides Maillol, next to the stadium. M: Collblanc. Enter through access gates 7 or 9. €5. Open M-Sa 10am-6:30pm, Su 10am-2pm.)*

🎵 🎭 ENTERTAINMENT AND FESTIVALS

For entertainment tips, pick up the *Guía del Ocio* (www.guiadelociobcn.es) at any newsstand. Most of Barcelona's galleries are in **La Ribera** around C. Montcada. Grab face paint to join F.C. Barcelona at the Nou Camp stadium for **fútbol.** (☎ 93 496 36 00. Box office C. Aristedes Maillol 12-18.) The ■**sardana,** Cataluña's regional dance, is a popular amusement; join the dance circle in front of the cathedral after mass on Sundays (noon and 6:30pm). Bullfights are held at the **Plaça de Toros Monumental,** on C. Castillejos 248. (☎ 93 245 58 04. Tickets €16-90.) The **Festa de Sant Jordi** (St. George; Apr. 24) celebrates Cataluña's patron saint with a feast. Men give women roses, and women give men books. On August 15-21, city folk jam at Gràcia's **Fiesta Mayor.** Lights blaze in the plazas and rock bands play all night. On September 11, the **Fiesta Nacional de Cataluña** brings traditional costumes, dancing, and Catalán flags hanging from balconies.

◙ NIGHTLIFE

The Barcelona evening begins at *bares-restaurantes* or *cervecerías*, moves to the *bares-musicales*, and ends after sunrise in discotecas. Consult the *Guía del Ocio* for information on movies, live concerts, bars, discos, and cultural events.

BARRI GÓTIC

Here, cookie-cutter *cervecerías* and *bar-restaurantes* can be found every five steps. The Barri Gótic is perfect for chit-chatting your night away, sipping *sangría*, or scoping out your next dance partner.

▨ **Schilling,** C. Ferran 23. M: Liceu. The fancy exterior conceals a surprisingly diverse bar. Mixed gay and straight crowd. Excellent *sangría* (pitcher €14). Mixed drinks €5. Beer €2. Open daily 10am-2:30am.

▨ **Jamboree,** Pl. Reial 17. M: Liceu. In the corner immediately to your right coming from Las Ramblas. What was once a convent now serves as one of the city's most popular live music venues. Daily jazz or blues performances. Cover M-F €6, Sa-Su €9-12; includes one drink. Open daily 11pm-1am. Upstairs, the attached club **Tarantos** hosts flamenco shows (€25). Open M-Sa 9:30pm-midnight.

Vildsvin, C. Ferran 38. M: Liceu. On your right as you go down C. Ferran from Las Ramblas. Oysters and international beers (€4-7.50) are the specialties. *Tapas* €3-5, desserts €3.50-10, entrees €8-26.50. Open 9am-2am, F-Sa 9am-3am.

El Bosq de les Fades, M: Drassanes. A fairy-tale world, complete with gnarly trees, waterfalls, gnomes, a small bridge, and plush side rooms. Open M-Th until 1:30am, F-Sa until 2:30am.

LA RIBERA

In La Ribera, crowds gather at *tapas* bars to soak up artsy flavor.

▨ **Plàstic Café,** Pg. del Born 19. M: Jaume I. Hyper-trendy bar. Beer €2.40-3, mixed drinks €3 and up. Open Su-Th 10pm-2:30am, F-Sa 10pm-3am.

El Copetin, Pg. del Born 19. M: Jaume I. Cuban rhythm infuses everything in this casual nightspot. Open Su-Th 6pm-2am, F-Sa 6pm-3am.

EL RAVAL

Though El Raval has traditionally been home to a local, unpretentious set of bars, this neighborhood to the west of Las Ramblas is rapidly becoming a hot spot for funky new lounge-style hangouts.

▨ **La Oveja Negra,** C. Sitges 5. M: Catalunya. The most touristed tavern in town. Open M-Th 9am-3am, F 9am-3:30am, Sa 5pm-3:30am, Su 5pm-3am.

(El Café que pone) Muebles Navarro, Riera Alta 4-6. Draws mature local crowd with a mellow ambience ideal for conversation. Beer and wine €2.50, mixed drinks €3.60-9. Open Tu-Th 6pm-2am, F-Sa 6pm-3am.

London Bar, C. Nou de la Rambla 34, off Las Ramblas. M: Liceu. Rub shoulders with unruly, fun-loving expats. Live music nightly. Beer €3, wine €2, absinthe €3. Open Su and Tu-Th, 7:30pm-4:30am, F-Sa 7:30pm-5am.

L'EIXAMPLE

L'Eixample has upscale bars and some of the best gay nightlife in Europe.

◪ **La Fira,** C. Provença 171. M: Hospital Clinic or FGC: Provença. A bar like no other, La Fira is a hodgepodge of fun-house and circus castaways. Bartenders pour drinks for a hip crowd dangling from carousel swings. DJs spin a mix of funk, disco, and oldies. Open M-Th 10pm-3am, F-Sa 10pm-4:30am, Su 6pm-1am.

◪ **Buenavista Salsoteca,** C. Rosselló 217. FGC: Provença. This over-the-top salsa club manages to attract a laid-back, mixed crowd. The dancers are not shy. Free salsa and merengue lessons W-Th at 10:30pm. F-Sa cover €9, includes 1 drink. Open W-Th 11pm-4am, F-Sa 11pm-5am, Su 8pm-1am.

Dietrich, C. Consell de Cent 255. M: Pg. Gràcia. A rather unflattering painting of Marlene Dietrich in the semi-nude greets a mostly gay crowd. Beer €3.50. Drinks €5-8. Open Su-Th 10:30pm-2:30am, F-Sa 10:30pm-3am.

Fuse, C. Roger de Llúria 40. M: Tetuán or Pg. Gràcia. A cutting-edge Japanese-Mediterranean restaurant, cocktail bar, dance club. Mixed gay and straight crowd. Beer €3, mixed drinks €6. Restaurant open M-Sa 8:30pm-1am. Bar open Th-Sa 1-3am. MC/V.

PORT OLÍMPIC

Tracing the coast and marked by a gigantic metallic fish structure, the Olympic Village brims with glitzy restaurants and throngs of European dance fiends. Nearly 20 bars and clubs occupy the strip. Revelry begins at midnight and winds down at 6am. From the Metro stop Ciutadella-Vila Olímpica, walk down C. Marina toward the twin towers.

Luna Mora, C. Ramón Trias Fargas, on the corner of Pg. Marítim. This planetarium-like disco with a more mature crowd is one of the best places for late-night dancing on the beach. The mostly local crowd doesn't arrive until 3am. Beer €5, mixed drinks €8. Cover €12. Open F midnight-6am, Sa midnight-6:30am.

El El, Pg. Marítim 36. Hidden behind the Greek restaurant Dionisos; enter from above. Colored strobe lights, fog machines, and techno beats entrance the wild crowd. Beer €4, mixed drinks €7. Cover (includes 2 drinks) Th-F and Su €12, Sa €15; free if you eat dinner at Dionisos. Open July-Aug. daily midnight-6am; Sept.-June Th-Su midnight-6am.

MAREMAGNUM

Like Dr. Jekyll, Barcelona's biggest mall has more than one personality. At midnight, the complex turns into a tri-level maze of clubs, complete with escalators to cut down on navigating effort. Each club plays its own music for international students, tourists, and the occasional Spaniard. This is not the most "authentic" experience in Barcelona, but it is an experience. No one charges cover; clubs make their money from exorbitant drink prices. Good luck catching a cab home.

MONTJUÏC

Lower Montjuïc is home to Barcelona's epic "disco theme park," **Poble Espanyol,** Av. Marqués de Comillas (☎ 933 22 03 26). Take a cab from M: Espanya and fall in love with the craziest disco experience in all of Barcelona. Some of the most popular (and surreal) discos include **La Terrrazza** (an outdoor madhouse; open Sept.-June Th-Su midnight-6am; July-Aug. Su only), **Torres de Ávila** (with speedy glass elevators; open Th-Sa midnight-6:30am), and **Tinta Roja** (for tango lovers; open July-Aug. Tu-Th 7pm-1:30am, F-Sa 8pm-3am; Sept.-June also Tu-Th). Dancing starts at around 1:30am and doesn't end until 9am.

WEST OF GRÀCIA

The area around C. de Marià Cubí has great nightlife, but you'll have to take a taxi. For more accessible fun in Gràcia, head to Pl. Sol.

Otto Zutz, C. Lincoln 15 (ozlistas@hotmail.com). FGC: Pl. Molina. Walk downhill on Via Augusta and take C. Lincoln when it splits off to the right. Groove to house, hip-hop, and funk while Japanimation lights up the top floor. Beer €5. Cover €15, includes 1 drink; email ahead for a discount. Open Tu-Sa midnight-6:30am.

D_Mer, C. Plató 13. FCG: Muntaner. Walk uphill on C. Muntaner 2 blocks and turn right on C. Plató. A blue-hued heaven for lesbians of all ages. A touch of class, a dash of whimsy, and a ton of fun. Cover €6, Includes 1 drink. Beer €3.50, mixed drinks €6. Open Th-Sa 11pm-3:30am.

Bar Fly, C. Plató 15. FGC: Muntaner. Same directions as D_Mer (see above). More popular in the winter. Grab a drink at one of the 2 bars, hit the red-tinted dance floor, or shoot some pool out back. Drinks €6. No cover. Open Th-Sa midnight-3:30am.

🔀 DAYTRIPS FROM BARCELONA

MONTSERRAT

An hour northwest of Barcelona, the mountain of Montserrat is where a wandering 9th-century mountaineer had a blinding vision of the Virgin Mary. In the 11th century, a monastery was founded to worship the Virgin, and the site has since evolved into a major pilgrimage center. The **monastery's** ornate **basilica** is above Pl. Creu. To the right of the main chapel is a route through the **side chapels** that leads to the 12th-century Romanesque **La Moreneta** (the black Virgin Mary), Montserrat's venerated icon. (Open July-Sept. daily 8-10:30am and noon-6:30pm; Nov.-June M-F 8-10:30am and noon-6:30pm, Sa-Su 8-10:30am and noon-6:30pm.) In Pl. Santa María, the **Museo de Montserrat** exhibits a sweeping range of art, from an Egyptian mummy to several Picassos. (Open July-Sept. M-F 10am-7pm, Sa-Su 9:30am-7pm; Nov.-June M-F 10am-6pm, Sa-Su 9:30am-6:30pm. €4.50, students and over 65 €3.50.) The **Santa Cova funicular** descends from Pl. Creu to paths that wind along to ancient hermitages. (Apr.-Oct. daily every 20min. 10am-6pm; Nov.-Mar. Sa-Su only, 10am-5pm. Round-trip €2.50.) Take the **St. Joan funicular** up for more inspirational views. (Apr.-Oct. daily every 20min. 10am-6pm; Nov.-Mar. M-F 11am-5pm, Sa-Su 10am-5pm. Round-trip €6.10; joint round-trip ticket with the Sta. Cova funicular €6.90, over 65 €6.20.) The dilapidated **St. Joan monastery** and **shrine** are only 20min. from the highest station. The real prize is **St. Jerónim** (1235m), about 2hr. from Pl. Creu (1hr. from the terminus of the St. Joan funicular); take the sharp left at the little old chapel (after 45min.).

FGC **trains** (☎932 05 15 15) to Montserrat leave from M: Espanya in Barcelona (1hr.; every hr. 8:35am-5:35pm; round-trip including cable car €11); get off at Aeri de Montserrat, not Olesa de Montserrat. From the base of the mountain, the Aeri cable car runs up to the monastery. (July-Aug. every 15min. daily 9:25am-6:35pm; Mar. and Oct. 9:25am-1:45pm and 2:20-6:45pm. €6, free with FCG. Schedules change frequently; call ☎938 77 77 01 to check.)

SITGES

Forty kilometers south of Barcelona, the resort town of Sitges is famed for its prime tanning grounds, lively cultural festivals, international gay community, and wired nightlife. Long considered a watered-down Ibiza, Sitges has better beaches than the notorious Balearic hotspot; you won't find much crazier beach-oriented nightlife on mainland Spain. The **beach** is 10min. from the train station via any street. In town, **Calle Parellades** is the main tourist drag. Late-night foolhardiness clusters around **Calle Primer de Maig,** which runs directly from the beach, and its continuation, **Calle Marques Montroig.** The wild things are at the "disco-beach" **Atlántida,** in Sector Terramar. Or dance at **Pachá,** on Pg. Sant Didac, in nearby Vallpineda. Buses run to the two discos from C. Primer de Maig (midnight-4am). During **Carnaval** (Feb. 27-Mar. 5 in 2003), Spaniards crash the town for a frenzy of dancing, costumes, and alcohol. The **tourist office,** on Pg. Vilafranca, is near the train station. From the station, turn right on C. Artur Carbonell and go downhill. (☎938 94 50 04. Open July-Aug. daily 9am-9pm; Sept.-June W-M 9am-2pm, and 4-6:30pm.) If you plan to stay the night, reserve early. **Hostal Parellades ❷,** C. Parellades 11, is close to the beach. (☎938 94 08 01. Singles €20; doubles €32, with bath €38; triples with bath €45.) Cercanías **trains** (☎93 490 02 02) link Sitges to Barcelona-Sants Station (40min., every 15-30min. 5:25am-11:50pm, €2.15).

GIRONA (GERONA)   ☎972

A world-class city patiently waiting for the world to notice it, Girona (pop. 70,500) is really two cities in one: a hushed medieval masterpiece on one riverbank and a thriving, modern metropolis on the other. Though founded by the Romans, the city owes more to the renowned *cabalistas de Girona,* who for centuries spread the teachings of Kabbalah (mystical Judaism) in the West. Still a cultural center and university town, Girona is a magnet for artists, intellectuals, and activists.

Most sights are in the old city, across the river from the train station. The **Riu Onyar** separates the new city from the old. The **Pont de Pedra** bridge connects the two banks and heads into the old quarter by way of C. Ciutadans, C. Peralta, and C. Força, which lead to the cathedral and ▧**El Call,** the medieval Jewish neighborhood. A thriving community in the Middle Ages, El Call was virtually wiped out by the 1492 Inquisition and mass expulsion and conversion. The entrance to **Centre Bonastruc Ça Porta,** the site of the last synagogue in Girona (today a museum), is off C. Força, about halfway up the hill. (Center and museum open May-Oct. M-Sa 10am-8pm, Su 10am-3pm; Nov.-April M-Sa 10am-6pm, Su 10am-3pm. Museum €2, students €1.) Uphill on C. Força and around the corner to the right, the Gothic **cathedral** rises a record-breaking 90 Rococo steps from the plaza below. The **Tesoro Capitular** within contains some of Girona's most precious possessions, including the **Tapis de la Creació,** a 15th-century tapestry depicting the creation story. (Both open Mar.-Sept. Tu-Sa 10am-2pm and 4-7pm, Su-M 10am-2pm; Oct.-Mar. Tu-Sa 10am-2pm and 4-6pm, Su-M 10am-2pm. Tesoro and cloister €3.) **La Rambla** and **Plaza de Independéncia** are the places to see and be seen in Girona. The expansive, impeccably designed **Parc de la Devesa** explodes with *carpas,* temporary outdoor bars. Bars in the old quarter draw crowds in the early evening. **Café la Llibreria,** C. Ciutadans 15, serves cocktails (€3.60) and *tapas* (€3) to intellectual types. (Open M-Sa 8:30am-1am, Su 8:30am-midnight. MC/V.)

RENFE **trains** (☎972 24 02 02) depart from Pl. de Espanya to **Barcelona** (1½hr., 6:10am and 9:25pm, €5) and **Figueres** (30-40min., 23 per day, €2). **Buses** (☎972 21 23 19) depart from just around the corner. The **tourist office,** Rambla de la Libertat 1, is directly on the other side. (☎972 22 65 75. Open in summer M-F 9am-3pm, Sa 9am-2pm; off-season M-F 9am-7pm, Sa 9am-2pm.) Most budget accommodations are in the old quarter and are well-kept and reasonably priced. The **Pensió Viladomat ❷,** C. Ciutadans 5, next to the hostel, has open, well-furnished rooms. (☎972 20 31 76. Singles €16; doubles €31, with bath €50.) Girona abounds with innovative cuisine; **Calle Cort Reial** is by far the best place to find good, cheap food. **La Crêperie Bretonne ❶,** C. Cort Reial 14, is potent proof of Girona's proximity to France. (☎97 221 81 20. Open Su 8pm-midnight, Tu-Sa 1-4pm and 8pm-midnight.) Pick up groceries at **Caprabo,** C. Sequia 10, a block from C. Nou off the Gran Via. (Open M-Sa 9am-9pm.) **Postal Code:** 17070.

THE COSTA BRAVA

The Costa Brava's jagged cliffs cut into the Mediterranean Sea from Barcelona to the French border. Though rugged by name, the Brave Coast is tamed in July and August by the planeloads of Europeans dumped onto its once-tranquil beaches.

TOSSA DE MAR. Falling in love in (and with) Tossa is easy. The pretty town (pop. 3800), 40km north of Barcelona, is packed with tourists every summer. But Tossa draws on its legacy as a 12th-century village, its cliff-studded landscape, its small coves, and its small-town charm to resist becoming the average resort. Inside the walled **Vila Vella** (Old Town), spiraling medieval alleys lead to a tiny plaza where the **Museu Municipal** displays 20s and 30s art. (☎972 34 07 09. Open June 16-Sept. 15 daily 10am-8pm; June 1-15 and Sept. 16-30 M-F 11am-1pm and 3-5pm, Sa-Su 11am-6pm; Oct. M-F 11am-1pm and 3-5pm, Sa-Su 11am-5pm. €3, students and seniors €1.80.) Sarfa **buses** run to Pl. de les Nacions Sense Estat, at Av. de Pelegrí, from Barcelona (1½hr., 18 per day 7:25am-8:10pm, €8) and Girona (1hr., 1-2 per day, €4). The **tourist office** shares the same building. (☎972 34 01 08. Open June 15-Sept. 15 M-Sa 9am-9pm, Su 10am-2pm and 5-8pm; Apr.-May and Oct. M-Sa 10am-2pm and 5-8pm, Su 10:30am-1:30pm; Mar. and Nov. M-Sa 10am-1pm and 5-7pm; Dec.-Feb. M-F 10am-1pm and 5-7pm, Sa 10am-1pm.) To get to **Fonda/Can Lluna ❶,** C. Roqueta 20, turn right off Pg. Mar onto C. Peixeteras, walk through C. Estalt, turn left at the end, and head straight. (☎972 34 03 65. Dorms €12-16.) **Pensión Pepi ❷,** C. Sant Miguel 10, offers cozy rooms with bath. (☎972 34 05 26. Singles €20; doubles €39) The old quarter has the best cuisine and ambience in Tossa. **Postal Code:** 17320.

FIGUERES. In 1974, Salvador Dalí chose his native, beachless Figueres (pop. 37,000), 36km north of Girona, as the site to build a museum to house his works, catapulting the city to instant fame. His personal tribute is undeniably a masterpiece—and the second most popular museum in Spain. The **Teatre-Museu Dalí** is in Pl. Gala. From the Rambla, take C. Girona, which becomes C. Jonquera, and climb the steps. The museum parades the artist's erotically nightmarish landscapes and bizarre installations. (☎972 67 75 00; www.salvador-dali.org. Open July-Sept. 9am-7:15pm; Oct.-June daily 10:30am-5:15pm. €9, students €6.50. Call ahead about night hours during the summer.) **Trains** (☎902 24 02 02) run to Barcelona (2hr., 23 per day, €8) and Girona (30min., 23 per day, €2.40). **Buses** (☎972 67 33 54) rum from Pl. Estació to: Barcelona (2¼hr., 2-6 per day, €13); Cadaqués (1¼hr.; July-Aug. 5 per day, Sept.-June 2-3 per day; €3.50); and Girona (1hr., 2-6 per day, €3.40). The **tourist office** is on Pl. Sol. (☎972 50 31 55. Open July-Aug. M-Sa 9am-8pm, Su 9am-3pm; Apr.-June and Oct. M-F 9am-3pm and 4:30-8pm, Sa 9:30am-1:30pm and 3:30-6:30pm; Sept. M-Sa 9am-8pm; Nov.-Mar. M-F 9am-3pm.) **Hostal La Barretina ❷,** C. Lasauca 13, is a lesson in luxury. (☎972 67 64 12. Singles €23; doubles €39.) **Postal Code:** 17600.

CADAQUÉS. The whitewashed houses and rocky beaches of Cadaqués (pop. 1800) have attracted artists, writers, and musicians—not to mention tourists—ever since Dalí built his summer home here. **Casa-Museu Salvador Dalí,** Port Lligat, Dalí's home until 1982, is complete with a lip-shaped sofa and pop-art miniature Alhambra. Follow the signs to Port Lligat (bear right with your back to the statue of liberty) and then to the Casa de Dalí. (☎972 25 10 15. Open June 15-Sept. 15 daily 10:30am-9pm; Sept. 16-Nov. and Mar. 15-June 14 Tu-Su 10:30am-6pm. Tours are the only way to see the house; make reservations 1-2 days in advance. Ticket office closes 45min. before closing. €8; students €5.) **Buses** arrive from Barcelona (2½hr., 11:15am and 4:15pm, €15); Figueres (1hr., 5-7 per day, €4); Girona (2hr., 1-

2 per day, €7). With your back to the Sarfa office at the bus stop, walk right along Av. Caritat Serinyana; the **tourist office,** C. Cotxe 2, is off Pl. Frederic Rahola, opposite the *passeig.* (☎972 25 83 15. Open July-Aug. M-Sa 9:30am-1:30pm and 4-8pm, Su 10:30am-1:30pm; Sept.-June M-Sa 9am-2pm and 4-7pm.) **Postal Code:** 17488.

THE PYRENEES ☎973

The jagged green mountains, Romanesque churches, and tranquil towns of the Pyrenees draw hikers and skiers in search of outdoor adventures. Spectacular views make driving through the countryside an incredible experience in and of itself. Without a car, transportation is tricky but feasible.

VAL D'ARAN. Some of the Catalán Pyrenees' most dazzling peaks cluster around Val d'Aran, in the northwest corner of Cataluña. The Val d'Aran is best known for its chic ski resorts: the Spanish royal family's favorite slopes are those of **Baquiera-Beret.** The **Albérja Era Garona (HI),** a few kilometers away in the lovely town of **Salardú,** is accessible by shuttle **bus** in high-season from Vielha. (☎973 64 52 71. Breakfast included. Sheets €2. Dorms €12-15, over 25 €17-19.) While you're in town, don't miss Salardú's impressive 12th-century **church,** where one of the valley's most coveted paintings—an image of Santo Christo with the mountains of Salardú in the background—hangs on the back wall. For skiing info, contact the **Oficeria de Baquiera-Beret** (☎973 64 44 55; fax 64 44 88).

The biggest town in the valley, **Vielha** (pop. 7000) welcomes hikers and skiers to its lively streets with every service the outdoorsy type might desire. It's only 12km from Baquiera-Beret; **shuttle buses** connect the two during July and August (schedules at the tourist office). **Alsina Graells buses** (☎973 27 14 70) also run to Barcelona (5½hr., 5:30am and 1:30pm, €23). The **tourist office,** C. Sarriulèra 8, is one block upstream from the *plaça.* (☎973 64 01 10; fax 64 03 72. Open daily 9am-9pm.) Several inexpensive *pensiones* cluster at the end of C. Reiau, off Pg. Libertat (which intersects Av. Casteiro at Pl. Sant Antoni); try **Casa Vicenta ❷** at C. Reiau 3. (☎973 64 08 19. Closed Oct.-Nov. Singles €22; doubles €38.)

PARQUE NACIONAL DE ORDESA. The beauty of Ordesa's Aragonese Pyrenees will enchant even the most seasoned traveler; its well-maintained trails cut across idyllic forests, jagged rock faces, snow-covered peaks, rushing rivers, and magnificent waterfalls. For more info about the park, pay a cyber visit to www.ordesa.net. The **Visitors Center** is on the left, 1.8km past the park entrance. (Open Apr. daily 9am-2pm and 3-6pm; May-Oct. 9am-2pm and 4:30-7pm.) The **Soaso Circle** is the most practical hike; frequent signposts clearly mark the 5hr. journey, which can be cut to a 2hr. loop. Enter the park through the village of **Torla,** where you can buy the indispensable *Editorial Alpina* guide (€7.50). La Oscense (☎974 35 50 60) sends a **bus** from Jaca to Sabiñánigo (20min., 2-3 per day, €1). Sabiñánigo is also easily accessible by **train;** all trains on the Zaragoza-Huesca-Jaca line stop here. From there, Compañía Hudebus (☎974 21 32 77) runs to Torla (55min., 1-2 per day, €2.40). During the high season, a bus shuttles between Torla and Ordesa (15min., 6am-6pm, €2). Off-season, you'll have to hike the 8km to the park entrance or catch a Bella Vista **taxi** (☎974 48 61 53 or 48 62 43; €12). To exit the park area, catch the bus as it passes through Torla at 3:30pm on its way back to Sabiñánigo. In the park, many *refugios* (mountain huts) allow overnight stays. The 120-bed **Refugio Góriz ❶** is a 4hr. hike from the parking lot. (☎974 34 12 01. €9 per person.) In Torla, ascend C. Francia one block to reach **Refugio L'Atalaya ❶,** C. a Ruata 45 (☎974 48 60 22), and **Refugio Briet ❶** (☎974 48 62 21), across the street. (Both €7-9 per person.) Outside Torla are **Camping Río Ara ❶** and **Camping San**

Anton ❶. (Ara ☎974 48 62 48, San Anton ☎974 48 60 63. Open Apr.-Oct. Both €3.50 per person, per tent, and per car.) Stock up at **Supermercado Torla,** on C. a Ruata. (Open May-Oct. daily 9am-2pm and 5-8pm; Nov.-Apr. closed Su.)

JACA. For centuries, pilgrims bound for Santiago would cross the Pyrenees into Spain, spend the night in Jaca (pop. 14,000), and be off the next morning. They had the right idea; use it as a launching pad for the Pyrenees. RENFE **trains** (☎974 36 13 32) run from C. Estación to Madrid (7hr., Su-F 1:45pm, €24) and Zaragoza (3hr., daily 7:30am and 6:45pm, €9). La Oscense **buses** (☎974 35 50 60) run to Pamplona (2hr., 1 per day, €6) and Zaragoza (2hr., 3-4 per day, €10). The **tourist office,** Av. Regimiento de Galicia 2, is off C. Mayor. (☎974 36 00 98. Open July-Aug. M-F 9am-2pm and 4:30-8pm, Sa 9am-1:30pm and 5-8pm, Su 10am-1:30pm; Sept.-June M-F 9am-1:30pm and 4:30-7pm, Sa 10am-1pm and 5-7pm.) From the bus station, cross the park and head right past the church to the next plaza to find **Hostal Paris ❷,** San Pedro 5, one of the best deals in town. (☎974 36 10 20. Singles €15-16; doubles €23-26; triples €32-35.) Or check out the hip *casa rural* **El Arco ❷,** C. San Nicolas 4. (☎974 36 44 48. €18 per person.)

NAVARRA

Bordered by Basque Country to the west and Aragón to the east, Navarra's villages—from the rustic Pyrenean pueblos on the French border to bustling Pamplona—are seldom visited apart from the festival of *San Fermines*, and greet non-bullrunning tourists with enthusiasm and open arms.

PAMPLONA (IRUÑA)   ☎948

While the lush parks, impressive museums, and medieval churches of Pamplona (pop. 200,000) await exploration, it's an annual, eight-minute event that draws visitors from around the world. Since the publication of Ernest Hemingway's *The Sun Also Rises*, hordes of travelers have come the week of July 6-14 to witness and experience *San Fermines*, the legendary "Running of the Bulls."

🖅🛂 TRANSPORTATION AND PRACTICAL INFORMATION. RENFE **trains** (☎902 24 02 02) run from off Av. San Jorge to Barcelona (6-8hr., 3-4 per day 12:25pm-12:55am, €27) and Madrid (5hr., 7:15am and 6:10pm, €34). **Buses** go from C. Conde Oliveto, at C. Yanguas y Miranda, to: Barcelona (5½hr.; 8:30am, 4:30pm and 12:45am; €19); Bilbao (2hr., 4-6 per day 7am-8pm, €10); Madrid (5hr., 4-7 per day 7am-6:30pm, €22); San Sebastián (1hr., 2-9 per day 7am-11pm, €5); and Zaragoza (2-3hr., 6-8 per day 7:15am-8:30pm, €11). From Pl. Castillo, take C. San Nicolás, turn right on C. San Miguel, and walk through Pl. San Francisco to get to the **tourist office,** C. Hilarión Eslava 1. (☎948 20 65 40; www.pamplona.net. Open during *San Fermines* daily 8am-8pm; July-Aug. M-Sa 10am-2pm and 4-7pm, Su 10am-2pm; Sept.-June M-F 10am-2pm and 4-7pm, Sa 10am-2pm.) During *San Fermines*, **store luggage** at the Escuelas de San Francisco, the big stone building at the end of Pl. San Francisco. (€2 per day. Open 24hr.) Check **Email** at **Kuria.Net,** C. Curia 15. (€3 per hr. Open 10am-10pm, Su 4:30-9:30pm; during *San Fermines* daily 9am-11pm.) **Postal code:** 31001.

🖬🖺 ACCOMMODATIONS AND FOOD. And now, a lesson in supply and demand: smart *san ferministas* take the bull by the horns and book their rooms up to a year (or at least two months) in advance to avoid paying rates up to four

FROM THE ROAD

OTRA VEZ?

Cheers and cries of *olé* floated through the window of my pension room in Pamplona's *casco antiguo*. At 6am any other day, this might have been a frustrating wake-up call, but not today. I was was already up. I checked my watch: July 7th. Two hours until the running of the bulls.

I stepped outside, clad in the requisite *San Fermines* garb—all white except the red *faja* encircling my waist and the red *pañuelo* around my neck. Thousands of eager spectators were already planted on, under, and between wooden fences lining the path to the *plaza del toros*. I ducked under one of the gates and made my way up the final stretch of the run, towards the bulls' holding pen. Fences to jump over, or, if need be, roll under, were nearby. Failing that, I told myself, the *capótico de San Fermín* (San Fermin's cape) would shield me; apparently, it's responsible for a few miraculous escapes each year. That morning, I had no idea how much I would need such protection.

Eight o'clock neared. Police passed, dragging runners out of the way; last-minute doubters scaled the sides of storefronts, clambering for the safety of a balcony; the mass slowly drifted away from the holding pen, deciding they'd start a bit closer to the finish line. I began to stampede-proof myself, slipping the loose end of my *faja* into a pocket and scuffing my tennis shoes as best I could to prevent slipping on the champagne- and urine-slicked cobblestone. Murmurs of anticipation resonated in the chilly morning air.

times higher than those listed here. Beware of hawkers at the train and bus stations—quality and prices vary tremendously. Check the newspaper *Diario de Navarra* for **casas particulares.** Many roomless folks are forced to fluff up their sweat-shirts and sleep on the lawns of the Ciudadela or on Pl. Fueros, Pl. Castillo, or the banks of the river. Be careful—if you can't store your backpack (storage fills fast), sleep on top of it. During the rest of the year, finding a room in Pamplona is no problem. Budget accommodations line C. San Nicolás and C. San Gregorio off Pl. Castillo. **Hotel Europa,** C. Espoz y Mina 11, off Pl. Castillo, offers bright, luxurious rooms away from the noise of C. San Nicolás. One good night's sleep is worth the price. Reservations are recommended, especially for *San Fermines.* (☎948 22 18 00. Year-round singles €70; doubles €80. MC/V.) To reach the impressive 18th century mansion of **Pensión Santa Cecilia,** C. Navarrería 17, follow C. Chapitela, take the first right on C. Mercaderes, and make a sharp left. (☎948 22 22 30. *San Fermines* dorms €45. Otherwise singles €15-20; doubles €20-30; triples €30-35. MC/V.) Show up early during the fiesta to get a room at **Fonda La Montañesa,** C. San Gregorio 2, which doesn't take reservations. (☎948 22 43 80. *San Fermines* dorms €40. Otherwise dorms €13.) To get to **Camping Ezcaba** in Eusa, take city bus line 4-1 from Pl. de las Merindades to the campground (4 per day, €0.70). (☎948 33 03 15. *San Fermines* €8.25 per person, per tent, or per car. Otherwise €3.50 per person, per tent or per car. AmEx/MC/V.) Look for food near Pensión Santa Cecilia, above **Plaza San Francisco,** and around **Paseo Ronda. Calles Navarrería** and **Paseo Sarasate** host *bocadillo* bars. **Vendi,** at C. Hilarión Eslava and C. Mayor, has **groceries.** (Open M-F 9am-2pm and 5:30-7:30pm, Sa 9am-2pm.)

🔲🔲 **SIGHTS AND NIGHTLIFE.** Pamplona's rich architectural legacy is reason enough to visit during the 51 other weeks of the year. The restored 14th-century Gothic **cathedral** is at the end of C. Navarrería. (Open M-F 10am-1:30pm and 4-7pm, Sa 10am-1:30pm. Guided tours €3.20.) Church lovers will also enjoy the 13th-century **Iglesia de San Saturnino,** near the Ayuntamiento, and **Iglesia de San Nicolás,** in Pl. San Nicolás. (Both open daily 9am-12:30pm and 6-8:30pm. Free.) The impressive walls of the pentagonal **Ciudadela** once humbled even Napoleon; today the Ciudadela hosts free exhibits and summer concerts. From C. Redín at the far end of the cathedral plaza, head left along the walls past the **Portal de Zumalacárregui** and along the Río Arga, and bear left through the **Parque de la Taconera.** (Open daily

7:30am-10pm; closed for *San Fermines*. Free.) The **Museo de Navarra** shelters beautifully preserved 4th- and 5th-century Roman mosaics and a nice collection of 14th- to 20th-century paintings, including Goya's portrait of the Marqués de San Adrián. (Open Tu-Sa 9:30am-2pm and 5-7pm, Su 11am-2pm; San Fermines Tu-Su 11am-2pm. €1.80, Sa afternoons and Su mornings free.) Throughout the year, **Plaza de Castillo** is the heart of the social scene. Hemingway's favorite haunt was the **Café-Bar Iruña**, immortalized in *The Sun Also Rises*. (*Menú* €10. Open M-Th 8am-11pm, F-Sa 9am-2am, Su 9am-11pm.) The young and the restless booze up at bars in the *casco antiguo*, around **Calles de Jarauta, San Nicolás**, and **San Gregorio**.

 Although Pamplona is usually very safe, crime skyrockets during *San Fermines*. Beware of assaults and muggings, do not walk alone at night, and take care in the *casco antiguo*.

■ **LOS SAN FERMINES (JULY 6-14).** Visitors overcrowd the city as Pamplona delivers an eight-day frenzy of parades, bullfights, parties, dancing, fireworks, concerts, and wine. Pamplonese, clad in white with red sashes and bandanas, literally throw themselves into the merry-making, displaying obscene levels of both physical stamina and tolerance for alcohol. The "Running of the Bulls," called the *encierro*, is the highlight of *San Fermines;* the first *encierro* of the festival takes place on July 7 at 8am and is repeated at 8am every day for the next seven days. Hundreds of bleary-eyed, hungover, hyper-adrenalized runners flee from large bulls as bystanders cheer from barricades, windows, balconies, and doorways. Both the bulls and the mob are dangerous; terrified runners react without concern for those around them. Hemingway had the right idea: don't run. Arrive at the bullring around 6:45am to watch the *encierro*. Tickets for the Grada section of the ring are available before 7am (€4). You can watch for free, but the free section is overcrowded, making it hard to see and breathe. If you want to participate in the bullring excitement, line up by the Pl. Toros well before 7:30am and run in *before* the bulls are in sight. **Be very careful; follow the tourist office's guidelines for running.** To watch a bullfight, wait in the line that forms at the bullring around 8pm (€15-70). As one fight ends, tickets go on sale for the next day. Once the running ends, insanity spills into the streets and gathers steam until nightfall, when it explodes with singing in bars, dancing in alleyways, spontaneous parades, and a no-holds-barred party in Pl. de Castillo, Europe's biggest open-air dance floor.

Seconds before the signal, a wave of about 50 men rushed toward me, clawing past my startled frame and diving in between the wooden fences. Not a moment later, two blasts shot through the air. I turned and ran.

About halfway through the seven-minute ordeal, I heard the trampling gait of a bull not far behind. Desparate to escape, I tore past the frightened mob in front of me, drilling through the clog of bodies any way I could. I'll admit it—I kicked, I grabbed, I spit, I punched. And so did anyone else who valued his health.

My mad scrambling was to no avail. The *toro* easily advanced alongside me. It jerked its body around and bucked back its head into my left hip, lifting me off the ground. Airborne, I felt something brush against my leg but was so busy readying for the fall that I didn't notice the horn shredding my left pant leg. As my knee hit the ground, I did my best sprinter-start away. The bull's hooves had slipped out from under him, tossing him sidelong to the ground. It wasn't until the next day, when I saw AP photographs of myself contending with the bull in the local and international newspapers, that I realized how much danger I'd been in.

My head ached, my lungs hurt, and the vinegary aftertaste of last night's *kalimotxo* burned my throat, but I had never felt better. I spotted another exhausted runner and gave him a victorious smile.

"Mañana," he wheezed. "Otra vez [again], eh?"

—Nate Gray

BASQUE COUNTRY (PAÍS VASCO)

Basque Country's varied landscape resembles a nation complete in itself, combining cosmopolitan cities, verdant hills, industrial wastelands, and quaint fishing villages. Many believe that the strongly nationalistic Basques are the native people of Iberia, as their culture and language cannot be traced to any known source.

SAN SEBASTIÁN (DONOSTIA)   ☎943

Glittering on the shores of the Cantabrian Sea, coolly elegant San Sebastián (pop. 180,000) is known for its world-famous beaches, bars, and scenery. Locals and travelers down *pintxos* (tapas) and drinks in the *parte vieja* (old city), which claims the most bars per square meter in the world. Residents and posters lend a constant reminder: you're not in Spain, you're in Basque Country.

☞ TRANSPORTATION

Trains: RENFE, Estación del Norte (☎902 24 02 02), on Po. Francia, on the east side of Puente María Cristina. Info office open daily 7am-11pm. To: **Barcelona** (9hr.; Su-F 10:45am and 10:55pm, Sa 10:45am; €30); **Madrid** (8hr., Su-F 10:30pm, €19-22); **Zaragoza** (4hr., daily 10:45am, €19).

Buses: PESA, Av. Sancho el Sabio 33 (☎902 10 12 10), to **Bilbao** (1¼hr., every 30min., €7.50). **Continental Auto,** Av. Sancho el Sabio 31 (☎943 46 90 74), to **Madrid** (6hr., 7-9 per day, €25). **La Roncalesa,** Po. Vizcaya 16 (☎943 46 10 64), to: **Pamplona** (1hr., 9 per day, €5.50). **Vibasa,** Po. Vizcaya 16 (☎943 45 75 00), to **Barcelona** (7hr., 3 per day, €22).

⚡ 🛈 ORIENTATION AND PRACTICAL INFORMATION

The **Río Urumea** splits San Sebastián. The city center, most monuments, and the two most popular beaches, Playa de la Concha and Playa de Ondaretta, line the peninsula on the west side of the river. The tip of the peninsula is called **Monte Urgull.** On the east side of the river, Playa de la Zurriola attracts a younger surfing and beach crowd. Inland lies the *parte vieja* (old city), San Sebastián's restaurant, nightlife, and budget accommodation nexus, where you'll find the most tourists. South of the *parte vieja*, at the base of the peninsula, is the commercial district. The **bus station** is south of the city on Pl. Pío XII, while the RENFE **train station, Barrio de Gros,** and Playa de la Zurriola are east of the city. The river is spanned by four bridges: Puentes Zurriola, Santa Catalina, María Cristina, and de Mundaiz (listed north to south). To get to the *parte vieja* from the train station, head straight to Puente María Cristina, cross the bridge, and turn right at the fountain. Continue four blocks north to Av. Libertad, then take a left and follow it to the port; the *parte vieja* fans out to the right and Playa de la Concha rests to the left.

Tourist Office: Municipa, Centro de Atracción y Turismo, C. Reina Regente 3 (☎943 48 11 66; fax 943 48 11 72), in front of the Puente Zurriola. From the train station, turn right immediately after crossing Puente María Cristina and continue until reaching Puente Zurriola; the office is on the left. From the bus station, start down Av. Sancho el Sabio. At Pl. Centenario, bear right onto C. Prim, follow the river until the third bridge (Puente Zurriola), and look for the plaza on your left. Open June-Sept. M-Sa 8am-8pm, Su 10am-2pm; Oct.-May M-Sa 9am-1:30pm and 3:30-7pm, Su 10am-2pm.

Hiking Information: Izadi (☎943 29 35 20), C. Usandizaga 18, off C. Libertad. Sells hiking guides. Open M-F 10am-1pm and 4-8pm, Sa 10am-1:30pm and 4:30-8pm.

> **SAY WHAT?** Linguists still cannot pinpoint the origin of *euskera*. Its commonalities with Caucasian and African dialects suggest that prehistoric Basques may have migrated from the Caucasus mountains through Africa. Referred to by other Spaniards as *la lengua del diablo* (the devil's tongue), *euskera* has come to symbolize cultural self-determination. Only half a million natives speak the language, chiefly in País Vasco and northern Navarra. During his regime, Franco banned *euskera* and forbade parents to give their children Basque names (like Iñaki or Estibaliz). Since his death, there has been a resurgence of everything from *euskera* TV shows to Basque schools, and the language is frequently used in the País Vasco.

Luggage Storage: At the **train station.** €3 per day; buy tokens at the ticket counter. Open daily 7am-11pm.

Laundromat: Lavomatique, C. Iñigo 14, off C. San Juan in the *parte vieja*. 4kg wash €3.75, dry €2.70. Soap €0.45. Open M-F 9:30am-2pm and 4-8pm, Sa-Su 10am-2pm.

Emergency: ☎112. **Municipal police:** C. Easo (☎943 45 00 00).

Medical Services: Casa de Socorro, Bengoetxea 4 (☎943 44 06 33).

Internet Access: Netline, C. Urdaneta 8 (☎943 44 50 76). €1.80 per 30min., €3 per hr., €18 for 10hr. ticket. Open M-Sa 10am-10pm.

Post Office: Po. De Francia 13 (☎943 44 68 26), near the RENFE station, just over the Santa Catalina bridge and to the right; look for the yellow trim on left side of the street. Open M-F 8:30am-8:30pm, Sa 9:30am-2pm. **Postal Code:** 20006.

ACCOMMODATIONS

Desperate backpackers will scrounge for rooms in July and August, particularly during *San Fermines* (July 6-14) and *Semana Grande* (starts Su the week of Aug. 15); September's film festival is just as booked. Budget options center in the *parte vieja* and by the cathedral. The tourist office has lists of accommodations and most hostel owners know of *casas particulares*.

PARTE VIEJA

▓ **Pensión Amaiur,** C. 31 de Agosto 44, 2nd fl. (☎943 42 96 54). From Alameda del Boulevard, follow C. San Jerónimo to its end, turn left, and look for the lower, obscured front. Nine beautiful rooms, five common bathrooms. July-Aug. and *Semana Santa* dorms €24; May-June and Oct. €18; Sept. and Nov.-Apr. €13. MC/V. ❷

Pensión Larrea, C. Narrica 21, 2nd fl. (☎943 42 26 94). Spend time with Mamá and Papá, as the friendly owners are often called, in this comfortable and welcoming *pensión*. July-Aug. singles €21; doubles €34; triples €45. Sept.-June €18/€30/€45. ❷

Pensión San Lorenzo, C. San Lorenzo 2 (☎943 42 55 16), off C. San Juan. Doubles with TV and refrigerators. July-Aug. doubles €45; June-Sept. €30-42; Oct.-May €24. ❷

Pensión Loinaz, C. San Lorenzo 17 (☎943 42 67 14), off C. San Juan. English-speaking owners. Common bathrooms. July-Aug. doubles €40; Sept.-June €25. ❷

Pensión Urgull, Esterlines 10 (☎943 43 00 47). Follow the winding staircase to the 3rd floor. Rooms have sinks. Prices are not set in stone, so bargain away. July-Aug. doubles €36-42; June and Sept. €24-27; Oct.-May €24-30. ❷

Pensión Boulevard, Alameda del Boulevard 24 (☎943 42 94 05). Spacious rooms, all with radios, some with balconies. 2 large shared baths for 8 rooms. July-Aug. doubles €50; June and Sept €36-42; Oct.-May €30. ❸

OUTSIDE PARTE VIEJA

Most of these places tend to be quieter but just as close to the port, beach, bus and train stations, and no more than 5min. from the old city.

Pensión La Perla, C. Loiola 10, 2nd fl. (☎943 42 81 23), on the street directly ahead of the cathedral. English spoken. Private baths and TVs. July-Sept. singles €30; doubles €46. Oct.-June €24/€32. ❸

Pensión Easo, C. San Bartolomé 24 (☎943 45 39 12). Head toward the beach on C. San Martín, turn left on C. Easo, and right on C. San Bartolomé. July-Sept. 15 singles €32.45, with bath €48; doubles €41/€60. June and Sept. 15-30 singles €27/€40; doubles €33/€45. Oct.-May singles €25/€33; doubles €30/€40. ❸

Pensión Urkia, C. Urbieta 12, 3rd fl. (☎943 42 44 36), located on C. Urbieta between C. Marcial and C. Arrasate. Borders the Mercado de San Martín. All rooms with bath. July-Sept. singles €30; doubles €39; triples €54. Oct.-June €24/€30/€40. ❸

Pensión Añorga, C. Easo 12 (☎943 46 79 45), at C. San Martín. Shares entryway with 2 other *pensiones.* Spacious rooms have wood floors and comfy beds. July-Aug. singles €25; doubles €32, with bath €43. Sept.-June singles €19; doubles €25/€32. ❷

Albergue Juvenil la Sirena (HI), Po. Igueldo 25 (☎943 31 02 68), a large, light-pink building 3min. from the beach at the far west end of the city. Bus #24 and #27 run from the train and bus stations to Av. Zumalacárregui; from there, take the street angling toward the mountain (Av. Brunet) and turn left at its end. Clean rooms, multilingual staff. HI members and ISIC-carriers only. Breakfast included. Sheets €2.50. Curfew Sept.-May Su-Th midnight, F-Sa 2am. €11-13, over 25 €13-15. MC/V. ❶

◨ FOOD

Pintxos (tapas; around €1.50 each), chased down with the fizzy regional white wine *txacoli,* are a religion here; bars in the old city spread an array of enticing tidbits on toothpicks or bread. The entire *parte vieja* seems to exist for no other purpose than to feed. The chef at ▧**Kursaal** ❷, Zurriola 1, is a legend among locals; enjoy an elegant lunch on the breezy, outdoor patio. (*Menú* €10-14.) **Casa Marita** ❷, C. Euskal Herria, off Po. Salamanca, uses only fresh, natural ingredients. (*Menú* €15, lasagna €7.50, smoked salmon €7. Open Th-Tu 8-11pm.) **Mercado de la Bretxa,** on Alameda del Boulevard at C. San Juan, sells fresh produce. (Open M-Sa 9am-9pm.) **Super Todo Todo,** on Alameda del Boulevard around the corner from the tourist office, also sells groceries. (Open M-Sa 8:30am-9pm, Su 10am-2pm.)

◉ ◨ SIGHTS AND BEACHES

San Sebastián's most attractive sight is the city itself, filled with green walks, grandiose buildings, and the placid bay. The views from ▧**Monte Igueldo,** west of the center, are the best in town: by day, the countryside meets the ocean in a line of white and blue, and by night the flood-lit **Isla Santa Clara** (island) seems to float on a ring of light. The walk up the mountain is not too strenuous, but the weary can take a funicular (round-trip €1.50). Across the bay from Monte Igueldo, the gravel paths on **Monte Urgull** wind through shady woods, monuments, and stunning vistas. The overgrown **Castillo de Santa Cruz de la Mota** tops the summit with 12 cannons, a chapel, and the statue of the *Sagrado Corazón de Jesús* blessing the city. (Open May-Sept. daily 8am-8pm; Oct.-Apr. 8am-6pm.) Directly below the hill, on Po. Nuevo in the *parte vieja,* the serene **Museo de San Telmo** resides in a Dominican monastery strewn with Basque funerary relics, and the main museum beyond the cloister displays a fascinating array of pre-historic Basque artifacts, a few dinosaur skeletons, and a piece of contemporary art. (Open Tu-Sa 10:30am-

8:30pm, Su 10:30am-2pm. Free.) The gorgeous **Playa de la Concha** curves from the port to the **Pico del Loro,** the beak-shaped promontory home to the Palacio de Miramar. The virtually flat beach disappears during high tide, which comes in a matter of minutes in the late afternoon. Sunbathing crowds jam onto the smaller and steeper **Playa de Ondarreta,** beyond Miramar, and surfers flock to **Playa de la Zurriola,** across the river from Mt. Urguel. Picnickers head for the alluring **Isla de Santa Clara** in the center of the bay, either by rented rowboat or public motorboat ferry (5min., June-Sept. every 30min., round-trip €1.95).

🎵 📷 ENTERTAINMENT AND NIGHTLIFE

For info on **theater** and special events, pick up the weekly *Kalea* (€1.40) from tobacco stands or newsstands. World-class jazz musicians arrive in Vitoria-Gasteiz the second or third week of July for the week-long **Festival de Jazz de Vitoria-Gasteiz** (☎945 14 19 19; www.jazzvitoria.com). Rockets mark the start of the **Fiesta de la Virgen Blanca** (Aug. 4-9) at 6pm on the 4th in Pl. Virgen Blanca. The *parte vieja* pulls out all the stops in July and August, particularly on **Calle Fermín Calbetón,** three blocks in from Alameda del Boulevard. During the year, when students outnumber backpackers, nightlife tends to move beyond the *parte vieja*. Keep an eye out for discount coupons on the street. A favorite pub among expats and young travelers, **The World's End,** Po. de Salamanca 14, is a block from the *parte vieja* toward the beach. (Open Su-Th 2pm-2:30am, F-Sa 2pm-3:30am.) **Zibbibo,** Plaza Sarriegi 8, is a hip club with a dance floor and a blend of hits and techno. (Open daily 2pm-4am.) **Bar Tas-Tas,** C. Fermín Calbetón 35, attracts backpackers. (Open daily 3pm-4am.) **Akerbeltz,** C. Koruko Andra Mari 10, is a sleek, cavernous bar. (Open M-Th 3pm-2:30am, F-Sa 3pm-3:30am.)

BILBAO (BILBO)   ☎944

Bilbao (pop. 370,000) is a city transformed; what was once all industry—bourgeois, business-minded, and ugly—is now new, avant-garde, and futuristic. 20th-century success showered the city with a new subway system, a stylish river-walk, and other additions all designed by renowned international architects. But above all else, it is the shining Guggenheim Museum that has most powerfully fueled Bilbao's rise to international prominence.

🚆 🛈 TRANSPORTATION AND PRACTIAL INFORMATION. Trains (☎944 23 86 23) arrive at the **Estación del Norte,** Pl. Circular 2, from: Barcelona (9-11hr., Su-F 10am and 10:45pm, €32); Madrid (6-8hr.; Su-F 4:30pm and 11pm, Sa 9:50am; €28-36); and Salamanca (5½hr., 2pm, €23). From Pl. Circular, head right around the station and cross the Puente del Arenal to reach Pl. Arriaga, the entrance to the *casco viejo*. Most **bus** companies leave from the **Termibús terminal,** C. Gurtubay 1 (☎944 39 52 05; M: San Mamés), on the west side of town, for: Barcelona (7¼hr., 4 per day, €34); Madrid (4-5hr.; M-F 10-18 per day, Su 2 per day; €22); Pamplona (2hr., 4-6 per day, €11); and San Sebastián (1¼hr., daily every hr., €7.50). The **tourist office** is on Pl. Arenal 1. (☎944 79 57 60; www.bilbao.net. Open M-F 9am-2pm and 4-7:30pm, Sa 9am-2pm, Su 10am-2pm.) Surf the **Internet** at **Ciberteca,** C. José Maria Escuza 23, on the corner of C. Simón Bolívar. (€0.60 per 10min., €2.10 per hr. Open M-Th 8am-10pm, F-Sa 8am-midnight, Su 10am-10pm.) **Postal code:** 48008.

🛏 🍴 ACCOMMODATIONS AND FOOD. During **Semana Grande** (August 17-25) rates are higher than those listed below. **Plaza Arriaga** and **Calle Arenal** have budget accommodations galore, while upscale hotels line the river or are in the new

city off **Gran Vía.** For large, lavish rooms with private bath and A/C, try **Hotel Arriaga ❹,** C. Ribera 3. (☎944 79 00 01; fax 944 79 05 16. Singles €39; doubles €60; triples €72. AmEx/V.) **Pensión Méndez ❷,** C. Santa María 13, 4th fl., is insulated from the raging nightlife below. From the Puente del Arenal, take C. Bidebbarrieta; after two blocks, take a right onto C. Perro, then turn right on C. Santa María. (☎944 16 03 64. Singles €25; doubles €33.) To get to **Pensión Ladero ❷,** C. Lotería 1, 4th fl., from the Puente del Arenal, take C. Corre; after three blocks, take a right onto C. Lotería. This *pensión* has modern common bathrooms and winter heating. (☎944 15 09 32. Singles €18; doubles €30.) **Mercado de la Ribera,** on the bank of the river at the bottom of the old city, is the biggest indoor **market** in Spain. (Open M-Th and Sa 8am-2:30pm; F 8am-2:30pm and 4:30-7:30pm.) Pick up groceries at **Champión,** Pl. Santos Juanes. (Open M-Sa 9am-9:30pm.) **Restaurante Vegetariano Garibolo ❷,** C. Fernández del Campo 7, serves delicious and creative vegetarian meals. (*Menú* €9.75. Open M-Sa 1-4pm. MC/V.) At **Restaurante Beroki ❸,** Pl. Circular 2, an elegant upstairs dining room is decorated with flowers and wine bottles. (Creamy chowder €8, entrees €9-15. Open Su-Th 1-4pm, F-Sa 1-4pm and 9-11:30pm.)

◙ ◘ SIGHTS AND ENTERTAINMENT. Frank O. Gehry's ▨**Guggenheim Museum Bilbao,** Av. Abandoibarra 2, can only be described as breathtaking. Lauded by the international press, it has catapulted Bilbao into cultural stardom. The building's undulating curves of glistening titanium, limestone, and glass resemble an iridescent scaly fish. The museum currently hosts rotating exhibits culled from the Guggenheim Foundation's collection. (☎944 35 90 00; www.guggenheim-bilbao.es. Handicapped accessible. Guided tours in English Tu-Su 11am, 12:30, 4:30, and 6:30pm. Sign up 30min. before tour at the info desk. Audio tour €3.60. Open July-Aug. daily 9am-9pm; Sept.-June Tu-Su 10am-8pm. €8.40, students €4.20, under 12 free.) The often overshadowed **Museo de Bellas Artes,** Pl. Museo 2, hordes an impressive collection of 12th- to 20th-century art. To get there, take C. Elcano to Pl. Museo, or bus #10 from Pte. Arenal. (Audioguides €2. Open Tu-Sa 10am-8pm, Su 10am-2pm. €4.50, students €3, under 12 free. W free.)

Revelers in the *casco viejo* spill into the streets, especially on **Calle Barrencalle** (Barrenkale). A young crowd jams at **Calle Licenciado Poza** on the west side of town. For a more mellow scene, people-watch at the elegant 19th-century **Café Boulevard,** C. Arenal 3. **The Cotton Club,** C. Gregorio de la Revilla 25, decorated with over 30,000 beer caps, draws a huge crowd on Friday and Saturday nights. (Open M-Th 4:30pm-3am, F 4:30pm-6am, Sa 6:30pm-6am, and Su 6:30pm-3am.) The massive blowout fiesta in honor of *Nuestra Señora de Begoña* takes place during **Semana Grande,** a nine-day party beginning the Sunday after August 15.

▨ DAYTRIP FROM BILBAO: GUERNICA (GERNIKA). On April 26, 1937, the Nazi "Condor Legion" released an estimated 29,000kg of explosives on Guernica, obliterating 70% of the city in three hours. The nearly 2000 people who were killed in the bombings were immortalized in Pablo Picasso's stark masterpiece *Guernica,* now in Madrid's Reina Sofía gallery (see p. 896). To reach the **tourist office,** C. Artekalea 8, from the train station, walk three blocks up C. Adolfo Urioste and turn right on C. Artekalea. At the first crosswalk on the road, take a right into the alleyway; the office will be on your right. (☎946 25 58 92; www.gernika-lumo.net. Open July-Sept. M-Sa 10am-7:30pm, Su 10am-2:30pm; Oct.-June M-Sa 10am-1:30pm and 4-7pm, Su 11am-2pm.) The office can direct you to several memorial sites, including the modest **Museo de la Paz de Gernika,** Pl. Foru 1, which features an exhibition chronicling the bombardment. **Trains** (☎902 543 210; www.euskotren.es) roll in from Bilbao (45min., every 45min., €2).

BALEARIC ISLANDS

Every year, discos, ancient history, and beaches—especially beaches—draw nearly two million of the hippest Europeans to the *Islas Baleares*.

⌐ TRANSPORTATION

Flights to the islands prove the easiest way to get there. Those under 26 often get discounts from **Iberia** (☎902 40 05 00; www.iberia.com), which flies to Palma de Mallorca and Ibiza from: Barcelona (40min., €60-120); Madrid (1hr., €150-180); and Valencia. **Air Europa** (☎902 24 00 42) and **SpanAir** (☎902 13 14 15; www.spanair.com) offer budget flights to and between the islands. Most cheap round-trip **charters** include a week's stay in a hotel; some companies called *mayoristas* sell leftover spots on package-tour flights as "seat-only" deals. Look for newspaper ads or inquire at travel agencies.

Ferries to the islands are less popular. **Trasmediterránea** (☎902 45 46 45; www.trasmediterranea.com) departs from Barcelona's Estació Marítima Moll and Valencia's Estació Marítima for Mallorca, Menorca, and Ibiza (€43-58). **Buquebus** (☎902 41 42 42) goes from Barcelona to Palma (4hr., 2 per day, €49). Book airplane or ferry tickets through a travel agency.

Between islands, **ferries** are the most cost-efficient way to travel. **Trasmediterránea** (see above) sails between Palma and Mahón (6½hr., Su only, €23) and between Palma and Ibiza (2½hr., 7am, €37). **Car** rental costs around €36 per day, **mopeds** €18, and **bikes** €6-10.

MALLORCA   ☎971

A favorite with Spain's royal family, Mallorca has been a popular member of the in-crowd since Roman times. Lemon groves and olive trees adorn the jagged cliffs of the northern coast, and lazy beaches sink into calm bays to the east. The capital of the Balearics, **Palma** (pop. 323,000) embraces conspicuous consumption and pleases with its well-preserved old quarter, colonial architecture, and local flavor.

The tourist office (see below) distributes a list of over 40 nearby **beaches,** many a mere bus ride away; one popular choice is **El Arenal** (Platja de Palma; bus #15), 11km southeast toward the airport. When the sun sets, **La Bodeguita del Medio,** C. Vallseca 18, keeps its crowd dancing to Cuban rhythms. (Open Th-Sa 8pm-3am, Su-W 8pm-1am.) Follow the Aussie accents down C. Apuntadores to the popular **Bar Latitude 39,** C. Felip Bauza 8, a self-proclaimed "yachtie" bar. (Open M-Sa 7pm-3am.) Palma's clubbers start their night in the *bares-musicales* lining the **Paseo Marítimo** strip such as salsa-happy **Made in Brasil,** Po. Marítimo 27 (open daily 8pm-4am) and dance-crazy **Salero,** Po. Marítimo 31 (open daily 8pm-6am). The bars and clubs around **El Arenal** overflow with fashion-conscious German disco-fiends, but braving them is well worth the price at **Riu Palace,** one block from the beach. (Cover €15, includes unlimited free drinks. Open M-Su 10pm-6:30am.) **Tito's Palace,** Po. Marítimo, is Palma's hippest disco. (Cover €15-18. Open daily 11pm-6am.)

From the airport, take bus #17 or 25 to **Plaza Espanya** (15min., every 20min., €1.80). To reach the **tourist office,** C. Sant Dominic 11, from Pl. Reina, take C. Conquistador to C. Sant Dominic. (☎971 72 40 90. Open M-F 9am-8pm, Sa 9am-1:30pm.) **Branches** are in Pl. Reina and the Pl. Espanya. Centrally located **Hostal Ritzi ❷,** C. Apuntadores 6, above "Big Byte" cyber cafe, has cheerful rooms overlooking an interior patio. (☎971 71 46 10. Laundry €7. Singles €23; doubles €34, with bath €49.) **Hostal Brondo ❷,** C. Can Brondo 1, off Pl. Rei Joan Carles I, is an old, converted house filled with character. (☎971 71 90 43. Reception M-Sa 9am-2pm and 6-8pm, Su 10am-1:30pm. Singles €21; doubles €33.) **Hostal Apuntadores ❶,**

C. Apuntadores 8, is in the middle of the action, less than a block from Pl. Reina. (☎971 71 34 91. Dorms €12; singles €18; doubles €30.) Truly budget eaters tend to head to the side streets off **Passeig Born,** to the cheap cafes along **Avenida Joan Miró,** or to the carbon-copy pizzerias along **Paseo Marítimo.** For groceries, try **Servicio y Precios,** on C. Felip Bauzà. (Open M-F 8:30am-8:30pm, Sa 9am-2pm.)

IBIZA

☎971

Perhaps nowhere on Earth does style rule over substance (or substances over style) more than on the island of Ibiza (pop. 84,000). Once a 60s hippie enclave, Ibiza has long forgotten her roots in a new-age decadence. None of Ibiza's beaches is within quick walking distance of **Eivissa (Ibiza City),** but **Platja de Talamanca, Platja des Duros, Platja d'en Bossa,** and **Platja Figueredes** are at most a 20min. bike ride away; buses also leave from Av. Isidor Macabich 20 for Platja d'en Bossa (every 30min., €0.75). One of the most beautiful beaches near Eivissa is **Playa de Las Salinas,** where the nude sunbathers are almost as perfect as the crystal-blue water and silky sand. The crowds return from the beaches by nightfall, arriving at the largest party on Earth. The bar scene centers around **Calle Barcelona,** while **Calle Virgen** is the center of gay nightlife. The island's **⚑discos** (virtually all a mixed gay/straight crowd) are world-famous. Refer to *Ministry in Ibiza* or *DJ,* free at many hostels, bars, and restaurants, for a full list of nightlife options. The **Discobus** runs to and from all the major hot spots (leaves Eivissa from A. Isidoro Macabich every hr. 12:30am-6:30am; €1.50; schedule available at tourist office and hotels). According to the Guinness Book of World Records, wild **⚑Privilege** is the world's largest club. The club can fit up to 30,000 bodies, has more than a few bars, and is the place to be Monday nights. (Cover €30-48, includes 1 drink. Open June-Sept. daily midnight-7am.) At **Amnesia,** on the road to San Antonio, you can forget who you are and who you came with. (Cream and MTV parties Th; foam parties W and Su. Open daily midnight-7am.) Elegant **Pachá,** on Pg. Perimitral, is a 15min. walk from the port or a 2min. cab ride. (Cover €30-42. Open daily midnight-7:30am.) Cap off your night in **Space,** which starts hopping around 8am, peaks mid-afternoon, and doesn't wind down until 5pm. (Cover €30 and up.)

The local paper *Diario de Ibiza* (www.diariodeibiza.es; €0.75) features an *Agenda* page with everything you need to know about Ibiza. The **tourist office,** C. Antoni Riquer 2, is on the water. (☎971 30 19 00; www.ibizaonline.com. Open M-F 9:30am-1:30pm and 5-8pm, Sa 10:30am-1pm.) Email friends about your crazy night while ⚑washing the beer out of your clothes at **Wash and Dry,** Av. España 53. (☎971 39 48 22. Wash and dry €4.20 each. Internet €5.40 per hr. Open M-F 10am-3pm and 5-10pm, Sa 10am-5pm.) The letters **"CH"** *(casa de huespedes)* mark many doorways; call the owners at the phone number on the door. **Hostal Residencia Sol y Brisa ❷,** Av. B. V. Ramón 15, parallel to Pg. Vara de Rey, has clean rooms, a central location, and a social atmosphere. (☎971 31 08 18; fax 30 30 32. Singles €21; doubles €36.) **Hostal La Marina ❸,** Puerto de Ibiza, C. Barcelona 7, is across from Estació Marítima, right in the middle of a raucous bar scene. (☎971 31 01 72. Singles €27-48; doubles €42-96.) **Hostal Residencia Ripoll ❸** is at C. Vicente Cuervo 14. (☎971 31 42 75. July-Sept. singles €27; doubles €39; 3-person apartments with TV, patio, and kitchen €72.) For a supermarket, try **Hiper Centro,** C. Ignacio Wallis, near C. Juan de Austria. (Open M-Sa 9am-2pm and 5-9pm.)

MENORCA

☎971

Menorca's 200km coastline of raw beaches, rustic landscapes, and well-preserved ancient monuments draws ecologists, photographers, and wealthy young families. Unfortunately, the island's unique qualities and ritzy patrons have resulted in elevated prices. Atop a steep bluff, **Mahón** (pop. 23,300) is the main gateway to the island. The more popular **beaches** outside Mahón are accessible by bus. Transportes Menorca **buses** (7 per day; €1.65) leave from C. Josep Quadrado for ▧**Platges de Son Bou,** which offers 4km of gorgeous beaches on the southern shore. Autocares Fornells buses (2-7 per day; €1.60) leave C. Vasallo in Mahón for the breathtaking views of sandy **Arenal d'en Castell,** while TMSA buses (7 per day; €1) go to touristy **Cala en Porter** and its whitewashed houses, orange stucco roofs, and red sidewalks. A 10min. walk away, the ▧ **Covas d'en Xoroi,** caves residing on cliffs high above the sea, are inhabited by a network of bars during the day, and a popular disco at night. (Bars open Apr.-Oct. daily 10:30am-9pm. Cover €3.50. Disco open daily 11pm-late. Cover €15.)

The **tourist office** is at Sa Rovellada de Dalt 24. (☎971 36 37 90. Open M-F 9am-1:30pm and 5-7pm, Sa 9am-1pm.) To get to **Hostal La Isla ❷,** C. Santa Catalina 4, take C. Concepció from Pl. Miranda. (☎/fax 971 36 64 92. Singles €15; doubles €30.) **Hostal Orsi ❷** is at C. Infanta 19; from Pl. s'Esplanada, take C. Moreres, which becomes C. Hannover; turn right at Pl. Constitució, and follow C. Nou through Pl. Reial. (☎971 36 47 51. Breakfast included. Singles €15-21; doubles €26-35.)

NORTHWESTERN SPAIN

Northwestern Spain is the country's best-kept secret; its seclusion is half its charm. Rainy **Galicia** hides mysterious Celtic ruins, and on the northern coast tiny **Asturias** allows access to the dramatic Picos de Europa mountain range.

GALICIA (GALIZA)

If, as the Galician saying goes, "rain is art," then there is no gallery more beautiful than the Northwest's misty skies. Often veiled in silvery drizzle, it is a province of fern-laden eucalyptus woods, slate-roofed fishing villages, and endless white beaches. Locals speak *gallego,* a linguistic hybrid of Castilian and Portuguese.

SANTIAGO DE COMPOSTELA ☎981

Santiago (pop. 130,000) has long drawn pilgrims eager to gaze at one of Christianity's holiest cities. The cathedral marks the end of the *Camino de Santiago,* a pilgrimage believed to halve one's time in purgatory. Today, sunburnt pilgrims, street musicians, and hordes of tourists fill the streets.

▞▞ **TRANSPORTATION AND PRACTICAL INFORMATION. Trains** (☎981 52 02 02) run from R. Hórreo to Madrid (8hr.; M-F 1:45 and 10:25pm, Sa 10:30pm, Su 9:45am, 1:45, and 10:30pm; €36). A schedule is printed daily in *El Correo Gallego.* To reach the city, take bus #6 to Pr. Galicia or walk up the stairs across the parking lot from the main entrance, cross the street, and bear right onto R. Hórreo, which leads to Pr. Galicia. **Buses** (☎981 58 77 00) run from R. de Rodríguez (20min. from downtown) for: Bilbao (11¼hr., 9am and 9:30pm, €39); Madrid (8-9hr., 4 per day, €31); and San Sebastián (13½hr., 8am and 5:30pm, €44). From the station, take bus #10 to Pr. Galicia. The **tourist office** is at R. Vilar 43. (☎981 58 40 81. Open M-F 10am-2pm and 4-7pm, Sa 11am-2pm and 5-7pm, Su 11am-2pm.) Check **email** at **Nova 50,** R. Nova 50. (€1.20 per hr. Open daily 9am-1am.) **Postal code:** 15701.

▞▞ **ACCOMMODATIONS AND FOOD.** Nearly every street in the old city houses at least one or two *pensiones.* The liveliest and most popular streets are **Rúa Vilar** and **Rúa Raíña.** ▧**Hospedaje Ramos ❶,** C. Raíña 18, 2nd fl., above O

Papa Una restaurant, is in the center of the *ciudad vieja*. (☎981 58 18 59. Singles €12; doubles €22.) **Hospedaje Santa Cruz ❷**, R. Vilar 42, 2nd fl., is close to a myriad of bars and restaurants. (☎981 58 28 15. Singles €15; doubles €25, with bath €30.) **Hostal Barbantes ❸**, R. Franco, lets big rooms, each with bath. (☎981 58 17 93. Singles €26; doubles €39.) **Hospedaja Fonseca ❶**, R. Fonseca 1, 2nd fl., offers colorful, sunny rooms to high-season travelers. (☎981 57 24 79. Open July-Sept. Singles, doubles, triples, and quads all €12 per person.) Take bus #6 or 9 to get to **Camping As Cancelas ❶**, R. 25 de Xullo 35, 2km from the cathedral on the northern edge of town. (☎981 58 02 66. €4 per person, €4 per car or per tent.) Bars and cafeterias line the streets, offering a variety of inexpensive *menús*; most restaurants are on R. Vilar, R. Franco, R. Nova, and R. Raíña. Santiago's **market**, between Pl. San Felix and Convento de San Augustín, is a sight of its own. (Open M-Sa 7:30am-2pm.) **Supermercado Lorenzo Froiz,** Pl. Toural, is one block into the old city from Pr. Galicia. (Open M-Sa 9am-3pm and 4:30-9pm, Sa 9am-3pm and 5-9pm.)

◎▨ SIGHTS AND NIGHTLIFE. Santiago's cathedral has four facades, each a masterpiece from a different era, with entrances opening to four different plazas: Praterías, Quintana, Obradoiro, and Inmaculada. The southern **Praza das Praterías** is the oldest of the facades; the Baroque **Obradoiro** encases the Maestro Mateo's **Pórtico de la Gloria,** considered the crowning achievement of Spanish Romanesque sculpture. The remains of **St. James** lie beneath the high altar in a silver coffer. Inside the **museum** are gorgeous 16th-century tapestries and two poignant statues of the pregnant Virgin Mary. (Cathedral open daily 7am-7pm. Museum open June-Sept. M-Sa 10am-1:30pm and 4-7:30pm, Su 10am-1:30pm; Oct.-Feb. M-Sa 11am-1pm and 4-6pm, Su 11am-1pm; Mar.-May M-Sa 10:30am-1:30pm and 4-6:30pm, Su 10:30am-1:30pm. Museum and cloisters €3.) Those curious about the Camino de Santiago can head to the **▨Museo das Peregrinacións,** Pl. San Miguel. (Open Tu-F 10am-10pm, Sa 10:30am-1:30pm and 5-8pm, Su 10:30am-1:30pm. €2.50; free most of the summer.) At night, crowds looking for post-pilgrimage consumption flood cellars throughout the city. To party with local students, take C. Montero Ríos to the bars and clubs off **Praza Roxa.** **▨Casa das Crechas,** Vía Sacra 3, just off Pl. Quintana, is a smoky pub with a witchcraft theme. (Beer €3. Open M-F noon-2am, Sa-Su noon-4am.) **Xavestre,** R. de San Paolo de Antaltares 31, is packed with 20-somethings. (Mixed drinks €5. Open daily 12pm-late.) Students dance the night away at **La Quintana Cafe,** Pr. Quintana 1. (Beer €3-5. Open daily from 11pm-late.)

▨ DAYTRIP FROM SANTIAGO: O CASTRO DE BAROÑA. South of the town of **Noia** is a little-known treasure of historical intrigue and mesmerizing natural beauty: the seaside remains of the 5th-century Celtic fortress of **▨O Castro de Baroña.** Its foundations dot the isthmus, ascending to a rocky promontory above the sea and then descending to a crescent **beach,** where clothing is optional. Castromil **buses** from Santiago to Muros stop in Noia (1hr.; M-F 15 per day, Sa 10 per day, Su 8 per day; €3) and Hefsel buses from Noia to Riveira stop at O Castro—tell the driver your destination (30min.; M-F 14 per day, Sa 7 per day, Su 11 per day; €1.50).

ASTURIAS

Spaniards call the tiny land of Asturias a *paraíso natural* (natural paradise). Surrounded by centuries of civilization, its impenetrable peaks and dense alpine forests have remained untouched. Unlike the rest of the country, travelers don't come here to see the sights; they come here to brave them.

PICOS DE EUROPA

This mountain range is home to **Picos de Europa National Park,** the largest national park in Europe. The most popular trails and peaks lie near the **Cares Gorge** (Garganta del Cares). For a list of mountain *refugios* (cabins with bunks but not blankets) and general park info, contact the **Picos de Europa National Park Visitors' Center** in Cangas de Onís. (☎/fax 985 84 86 14. Open daily 9am-2pm and 5-6:30pm.)

CANGAS DE ONÍS. During the summer months the streets of Cangas are packed with mountaineers and vacationing families looking to spelunk and hang-glide in the Picos de Europa National Park. Cangas itself is, if not particularly thrilling, a relaxing town rich in history. The **tourist office,** Jardines del Ayuntamiento 2, is just off Av. Covadonga across from the bus stop. (☎985 84 80 05. Open May-Sept. daily 10am-10pm; Oct.-Apr. 10am-2pm and 4-7pm.) **ALSA,** Av. Covadonga 18 (☎985 84 81 33), in the Picaro Inmobiliario building across from the tourist office, runs **buses** to Madrid (7hr., 2:35pm, €25) via Valladolid (5hr., €14).

SWEDEN (SVERIGE)

The Swedish concept of *lagom* ("moderation") implies that life should be lived somewhere between wealth and poverty, ecstasy and depression. In the 20th century, this ideal was translated into a successful experiment with egalitarian socialism that is still in place today. Described by its prime minister in 1928 as *folkhemmet* ("the people's home"), Sweden has a strong sense of national solidarity and a warm culture that is welcoming to travelers. An even greater draw for many visitors is the striking Scandinavian landscape, stretching from the mountainous Arctic reaches of northern Lapland to the flat farmland and white sand beaches of Skåne and Småland in the south. Dalarna, Värmland, and Norrland evoke images of quiet woods, folk music, and rustic Midsummer celebrations, while the capital city of Stockholm shines as a thoroughly cosmopolitan center.

FACTS AND FIGURES

Official Name: Kingdom of Sweden.

Capital: Stockholm.

Major Cities: Gothenburg, Malmö.

Population: 8,875,000.

Land Area: 410,930 sq. km.

Climate: Cold winter, cool summers.

Language: Swedish.

Religions: Lutheran (87%).

DISCOVER SWEDEN

The natural starting point for any tour of Sweden is the vibrant chain of islands that constitutes **Stockholm** (p. 964), arguably one of the most attractive capitals in Europe. Leave time to visit **Skärgård**, the city's lovely archipelago (p. 973), and the nearby university town of **Uppsala** (p. 973). The island of **Gotland** (p. 974), in the Baltic Sea, invites travelers to bike and camp amid its timeless landscape, medieval sites, and gorgeous beaches. On the west coast, Sweden's second-largest city, **Gothenburg** (p. 978), counterbalances the capital's fast-paced atmosphere with a laid-back attitude and elegant cafe culture. If you want to go farther north, consider a student flight or a night train to **Kiruna** in **Lapland** (p. 983), where you can explore Sami culture and vast stretches of Arctic wilderness, including the breathtaking mountain scenery of **Abisko National Park** (p. 984).

ESSENTIALS

WHEN TO GO

The best time to visit Sweden is in the summer, when daytime temperatures average 20°C (68°F) in the south and 16°C (61°F) in the north; nights can get chilly. Bring an umbrella for the frequent light rains. If you go in winter, bring heavy cold-weather gear; temperatures are frequently below -5°C (23°F). The midnight sun is best seen between early June and mid-July.

DOCUMENTS AND FORMALITIES

VISAS. South Africans need a visa for stays of any length. Citizens of Australia, Canada, the EU, New Zealand, and the US do not need a visa for stays of up to 90 days, but this three-month period begins upon entry into any Nordic

country; for more than 90 days in any combination of Denmark, Finland, Iceland, Norway, and/or Sweden, you will need a visa.

EMBASSIES. Foreign embassies in Sweden are in Stockholm (p. 964). Swedish embassies at home include: **Australia,** 5 Turrana St., Yarralumla, Canberra, ACT 2600 (☎62 70 27 00; www.embassyofsweden.org.au); **Canada,** 377 Dalhousie St., Ottawa, ON K1N 9N8 (☎613-241-8553; www.swedishembassy.ca); **Ireland,** 12-17 Dawson St., Dublin 2 (☎671 58 22; www.swedishembassy.ie); **New Zealand,** P.O. Box 12538, Wellington (☎04 499 98 95; sweden@xtra.co.nz); **South Africa,** P.O. Box 13477, Hatfield, 0028 (☎12 426 64 00; sweden@iafrica.com); **UK,** 11 Montagu Pl., London W1H 2AL (☎020 79 17 64 00; www.swedish-embassy.org.uk); and **US,** 1501 M St. NW, Washington, D.C. 20005 (☎202-467-2600; www.swedish-embassy.org).

SWEDEN

TRANSPORTATION

BY PLANE. Most international flights land in Stockholm, although domestic flights also connect to northern Sweden. **Scandinavian Airlines (SAS;** ☎ (08) 797 4000; www.scandinavian.net) offers youth fares (ages 12-25) on flights within Scandinavia (round-trip from 750kr; 50kr discount for Internet booking).

BY TRAIN. Statens Järnväger (SJ), the state railway company, runs reliable and frequent trains throughout the southern half of Sweden. Seat reservations (20-50kr) are required on some trains (indicated by an R, IN, or IC on the schedule) and are recommended on all other routes. Reservations are also mandatory on the new high-speed **X2000** trains (to Stockholm, Gothenburg, Malmö, and Mora); they are included in the normal ticket price but extra for railpass holders (reservations ☎ (020) 75 75 75). In southern Skåne, private **pågatågen** trains service Helsingborg, Lund, Malmö, and Ystad; **InterRail** and **ScanRail** passes are valid. Northern Sweden is served by two main rail routes: the coastal **Malmbanan** runs north from Stockholm through Boden, Umeå, and Kiruna to Narvik, Norway; from Midsummer (June 21-23) to early August, the privately run **Inlandsbanan** (☎ 63 19 44 09; www.inlandsbanan.se) travels a north-south inland route from Mora to Gällivare. The 35min. trip over the **Øresund bridge** connecting Malmö to Copenhagen is the fastest way to enter Sweden from continental Europe (see p. 976). Schedules for most trains can be found online at www.samtrafiken.se.

Eurail is valid on all trains in Sweden. The *buy-in-Scandinavia* **ScanRail Pass** allows five days within 15 (2040kr, under 26 1530kr) or unlimited travel on 21 consecutive days (3160kr/2370kr) throughout Scandinavia, and free or discounted ferry rides. Only three of those days can be used in the country of purchase, however, so the *buy-outside-Scandinavia* **ScanRail Pass** (see p. 59) is more economical for those not visiting Denmark, Finland, or Norway.

BY BUS. In the north, buses may be a better option than trains. **Swebus** (☎ (08) 655 90 00; www.swebus.se) is the main company; its **Swebus Express** (☎ (020) 64 06 40) serves southern Sweden only. **Bus Stop** (☎ (08) 440 85 70) reserves tickets for buses from Stockholm. Bus tickets are treated as an extension of the rail network and can be bought from state railways or on board. Express buses offer discounts for children, seniors, students, and youth. Bicycles are not allowed on buses.

BY FERRY. Ferries cross from Malmö (p. 976) to Copenhagen. Ystad (p. 977) sends boats to Bornholm and Poland. Ferries from Gothenburg (p. 978) serve Frederikshavn, Denmark; Kiel, Germany; and Newcastle, England. From Stockholm (p. 964), ferries run to the Åland Islands, Gotland, Turku, and Helsinki. North of Stockholm, **RG Line ferries** (☎ (090) 18 52 10) connect Umeå and Vaasa, Finland.

BY CAR. Swedish roads are remarkably uncrowded and in good condition. Unleaded gas costs an average of 10kr per liter. When gas stations are closed, look for pumps marked *sedel automat*, which operate after hours. Renting a car within Sweden averages 300-500kr per day, including VAT. Special discounts abound, particularly if you opt for a fly/drive package or if you rent for an extended period.

BY BIKE. Sweden is a biker's heaven; paths cover most of the country, particularly in the south, and the hostel-spotted **Sverigeleden bike route** makes a complete circuit through the country. Contact STF (see p. 963) for information.

TOURIST SERVICES AND MONEY

TOURIST OFFICES. Nearly every village and town has a tourist office. For more information before arriving in Sweden, contact the **Swedish Tourist Board:** 655 Third Ave., New York, NY 10017, USA (☎ 212-885-9700; www.gosweden.org).

EMERGENCY	Police, Ambulance, and Fire: ☎ 112.

MONEY. The unit of Swedish currency is the **krona,** divided into 100 *öre.* Bills come in denominations of 20kr, 50kr, 100kr, and 500kr; coins come in 1kr and 5kr, and 10 and 50 *öre.* Many post offices are also banks. Although a gratuity is usually added to the bill, tipping is becoming more common; a 10-15% tip is now considered standard, as is a few coins for good service. Tip 10% for taxis. The **value-added tax (VAT)** in Sweden is 25%; refunds can be had on purchases over 200kr (see p. 15).

SWEDISH KRONOR		
US$1 = 9.39KR	1KR = US$0.11
CDN$1 = 6.03KR	1KR = CDN$0.17
UK£1= 14.28KR	1KR = UK£0.07
AUS$1 = 5.11KR	1KR = AUS$0.20
NZ$1 = 4.40KR	1KR = NZ$0.23
ZAR1 = 1.15KR	1KR = ZAR0.87
EUR€1 = 9.12KR	1KR = EUR€0.11

BUSINESS HOURS. Banks are usually open Monday to Friday 10am-3pm (6pm in some large cities). Stores generally stay open Monday to Friday 10am-7pm, Saturday and Sunday noon-4pm. Museums open Tuesday to Sunday, anywhere from 10am-noon, and close 4-6pm. Some are open until 9pm on Tuesday or Wednesday.

COMMUNICATION

PHONE CODE	Country code: 46. International dialing prefix: 009. From outside Sweden, dial int'l dialing prefix (see inside back cover) + city code + local number.

TELEPHONES. Most payphones only accept *Telefonkort* (phone cards); buy them at newsstands and post offices in 30, 60, or 120 units (35kr, 60kr, and 100kr). International direct dial numbers include: **AT&T,** ☎ 020 79 56 11; **British Telecom,** ☎ 020 79 91 44; **Canada Direct,** ☎ 020 79 90 15; **Ireland Direct,** ☎ 020 79 93 53; **MCI,** ☎ 020 79 59 22; **Sprint,** ☎ 020 79 90 11; **Telecom New Zealand,** ☎ 020 79 90 64; **Telkom South Africa,** ☎ 020 79 90 27; and **Telstra Australia,** ☎ 020 79 90 61.

MAIL. Mailing a postcard or letter from Sweden to Australia, Canada, New Zealand, the US, and South Africa costs 10kr.

LANGUAGE. Almost all Swedes speak some English; most under 50 are fluent. For basic Swedish words and phrases, see p. 1066.

ACCOMMODATIONS AND CAMPING

SWEDEN	❶	❷	❸	❹	❺
ACCOMMODATIONS	under 150kr	150-225kr	225-350kr	350-500kr	over 500kr

Youth hostels *(vandrarhem)* in Sweden cost about 110-200kr per night. The 315 HI-affiliated hostels run by the **Svenska Turistföreningen (STF)** are invariably top-notch. Nonmembers pay 45kr extra per night. Most hostels have kitchens, laundry facilities, and common areas. To reserve ahead, call the hostel directly or contact the STF headquarters in Stockholm (☎ (08) 463 22 70); all sell **Hostelling International (HI)** membership cards (175kr) or offer guest cards. Tourist offices often book beds in hostels for no fee, and can help find **private rooms** (200-350kr). **Private hotels** are very good as well. More economical hotels are beginning to offer reduced-service rooms at prices competitive with hostels, especially for groups of three or more. STF also manages **mountain huts** in the northern wilds with 10-80 beds that cost 155-195kr in high season (nonmembers 200-240kr). Huts are popular; plan ahead. Many **campgrounds** (80-110kr per site) also offer *stugor* (cottages) for around 85-175kr per person. International Camping Cards are not valid in Sweden; **Swedish Camping Cards** are virtually mandatory. Year-long memberships (60kr per family) are available through **Sveriges Campingvärdars Riksförbund (SCR)**, Box 255, 451 17 Uddevalla (www.camping.se), or at any SCR campground. You may camp for free for one or two nights anywhere as long as you respect the flora, fauna, and the owner's privacy, and pick up all garbage. Pick up the brochure *Right (and Wrongs) of Public Access in Sweden* from STF or from tourist offices, or call the **Swedish Environmental Protection Agency** (☎ (08) 698 10 00).

FOOD AND DRINK

SWEDEN	❶	❷	❸	❹	❺
FOOD	under 50kr	50-75kr	75-125kr	125-200kr	over 200kr

Restaurants can be expensive in Sweden, but supermarkets, *saluhallen* (food halls), outdoor fruit and vegetable markets, and kebab stands (45-65kr) make budget eating relatively easy. Most restaurants offer affordable *dagens ratt* (55-70kr), daily lunch specials including salad, bread, an entree, and a drink. Breakfast usually consists of bread, coffee, and muesli with *filmjölk*, a fluid yogurt. Relatively light lunches at midday are usually followed by early-evening suppers. Traditional Swedish fare is based around meat and potatoes, but the country's growing diversity has made ethnic and vegetarian cuisine quite common, especially in cities. Other than the weak beer *lättöl* (under 3.5% alcohol), which can be bought at supermarkets and convenience stores for 8-12kr per 0.5L, alcoholic beverages can be purchased only at state-certified Systembolaget liquor stores and in licensed bars and restaurants. A real beer *(starköl)* costs 10-15kr in stores and 30-50kr per pint in city pubs. You must be 20 to buy alcohol. Although the drinking age is 18, bars and many nightclubs have age restrictions as high as 25.

HOLIDAYS AND FESTIVALS

Holidays: New Year's Day (Jan. 1); Epiphany (Jan. 5-6); Easter Sunday and Monday (Apr. 20-21); Valborg's Eve (Apr. 30); May Day (May 1); Ascension Day (May 29); National Day (June 6); Whit Sunday and Monday (June 11-12); Midsummer's Eve and Midsummer (June 21-23); All Saints' Eve and Day (Nov. 2-3); Christmas Eve and Day (Dec. 24-25); Boxing Day (Dec. 26); New Year's Eve (Dec. 31).

Festivals: Midsummer (June 21-23) incites family frolicking and bacchanalian dancing around Midsummer poles. July and August bring two special festivals, the *surströmming* (rotten herring) and crayfish parties.

STOCKHOLM ☎ 08

In recent decades, Stockholm has been seen as the model city of social democracy, a living example of that communal ideal. This heritage can be seen in Stockholm's high standard of living, its low crime rate, and its beautiful public spaces. With lush urban parkland, swimmable waterways, and a subway system decorated by world-class art, Stockholm may be the most pleasant city in Europe.

⌐ TRANSPORTATION

Flights: Arlanda Airport (ARN; ☎ 797 60 00), 45km north of the city. **Flygbussar** shuttles (☎ 686 37 87) run between Arlanda and the bus station (40min., every 10min. 4am-10pm, 80kr; SL and Stockholm Cards not valid), as do **Arlanda Express** trains (☎ (020) 22 22 24; 20min.; every 15min. 5am-midnight; 140kr, students 80kr). **Bus** #583 runs to T-bana: Märsta (10min., 35kr or 5 coupons; SL Card valid); T-Centralen is 40min. farther by T-bana. Public transportation takes longer but is far cheaper.

Trains: Centralstation (☎ (0771) 75 75 75). T-bana: T-Centralen. To **Copenhagen** (7-8hr.; 5-6 per day; 627kr, under 25 462kr) and **Oslo** (6hr.; 2 per day; 562kr/392kr). See p. 962 for info on reservations. **Lockers** 20-60kr per 24hr. **Showers** 25kr.

Buses: Cityterminalen, above Centralstation. **Terminal Service** (☎ 762 59 97) to: airport (80kr); Gotland ferries (70kr). **Biljettservice** (☎ 762 59 79) and **Bus Stop** (☎ 440 85 70) handle longer routes. To: **Copenhagen** (10hr., 3 per day, 380kr); **Gothenburg** (7hr.; 7 per day; 350kr, under 25 285kr); **Malmö** (8½hr.; 2 per day; 435kr/345kr).

Ferries: Silja Line, Kungsg. 2 (☎ 22 21 40), sails overnight to Finland: **Helsinki** (16hr., 1 per day, 446kr; book ahead); **Mariehamn** (5hr., 2 per day, 99kr); and **Turku (Åbo)** (12hr., 2 per day, 220-370kr). To get to the terminal, take T-bana to Gärdet and follow "Värtahamnen" signs, or take the Silja bus (20kr) from Cityterminalen. 50% ScanRail discount; free with Eurail. **Viking Line** sails to: **Helsinki** (15hr.; every day; 258-372kr, with ScanRail 135kr); **Mariehamn** (5½hr.; 1 per day; 104kr/52kr); and **Turku (Åbo)** (12hr.; 2 per day; 130-307kr/65-79kr). Viking Line terminal is at Stadsgården on Södermalm. T-bana: Slussen. See p. 974 for info on ferries to **Gotland**.

Public Transportation: SL office (☎ 600 10 00), Sergels Torg. T-bana: T-Centralen. Open M-F 7am-9pm, Sa-Su 8am-9pm. **Walk-In office** in Centralstation basement open M-Sa 6:30am-11:15pm, Su 7am-11:15pm. Most destinations cost 2 coupons (20kr, 1hr. unlimited bus/subway transfer). **Rabattkuponger**, books of 20 coupons (110kr), are sold at Pressbyrån news agents. The **SL Turistkort** (Tourist Card) is valid on buses, subways, commuter trains, trams, and Djurgården ferries (1-day 80kr; 3-day 150kr). The **Stockholmskortet** (Stockholm Card), available at Sweden House and Centralstation, also allows unlimited use of public transportation, as well as free admission to 70 museums and attractions (1-day 220kr, under 17 60kr; 2-day 380kr/120kr; 3-day 540kr). **Tunnelbana (T-bana;** subway) runs 5am-12:30am, nightbuses 12:30-5:30am.

Taxis: High fares. Many cabs have fixed prices; try to agree on a price beforehand. 435kr from airport to Centralstation. **Taxi Stockholm** (☎ 15 00 00); **Taxicard** (☎ 97 00 00).

Bike Rental: Sjöcaféet (☎ 660 57 57), on Djurgårdsbron. Bikes and rollerblades 250kr per day. Open daily 9am-9pm.

Hitchhiking: Waiting on highways is illegal in Sweden, and hitching is uncommon among travelers. Hitchers going south take the T-bana to the gas station on Kungens Kurva in Skärholmen; those going north take bus #52 to Sveaplan and stand on Sveav. at Norrtull. *Let's Go* does not recommend hitchhiking.

⬛✴ ⬛ ORIENTATION AND PRACTICAL INFORMATION

This compact city spans seven small islands (linked by bridges and the T-bana) at the junction of **Lake Mälaren** to the west and the **Baltic Sea** to the east. The large northern island is divided into two sections: **Norrmalm,** home to Centralstation and the shopping district on Drottningg., and **Östermalm,** which boasts the elegant **Strandvägen** waterfront and vibrant nightlife fanning out from **Stureplan.** The mainly residential western island, **Kungsholmen,** holds grassy beaches and the majestic Stadhuset (City Hall). The southern island of **Södermalm** retains an old

SWEDEN

Stockholm

ACCOMMODATIONS
City Backpackers' Vandrarhem, 4
Hostel af Chapman, 9
Långholmens Vandrarhem, 12
Mälarens, 11
Mitt i City, 2
Östra Real Vandrarhem, 3
Zinkensdamm Vandrarhem, 18

FOOD
Café Tabac, 10
Chokladkoppen/
Kaffekoppen, 8
Herman's, 14
Köfi, 6
STHLM, 5

NIGHTLIFE
Bröderna Olssons Garlic
and Shots, 17
Daily News Café, 7
Folkhemmet, 19
Kvarnen, 16
Mosebacke
Etablissement, 13
Snaps, 15
Tip Top, 1

T T-BANA STATIONS

600 yards
600 meters

neighborhood feel in the midst of a budding cafe culture. Nearby **Långholmen** is a nature preserve, as is much of the eastern island **Djurgården.** At the center of these five islands is **Gamla Stan** (Old Town). Gamla Stan's neighbor (via Norrmalm) is **Skeppsholmen,** an island of museums. The city's streets are easy to navigate: each begins with the number one at the end closest to the city palace in Gamla Stan; the lower the numbers, the closer you are to Gamla Stan.

Tourist Offices: Sweden House, Hamng. 27 (☎789 24 90; www.stockholmtown.com), in the northeast corner of Kungsträdgården. From Centralstation, walk up Klarabergsg. to Sergels Torg (the plaza with the 50 ft. glass tower) and bear right on Hamng. A vital resource for travelers. Friendly, multilingual agents. Sells the **SL** and **Stockholm Cards** (see Public Transportation, above). Arranges and sells tickets for theater, concerts, and excursions. Open June-Aug. M-F 8am-7pm, Sa-Su 9am-5pm; Sept.-May M-F 9am-6pm, Sa-Su 10am-3pm. The **HotellCentralen** at the train station (☎789 24 25; hotels@sto-info.se), books rooms (50kr). Open June-Aug. daily 8am-8pm; Sept.-May 9am-6pm.

Embassies: Australia, Sergels Torg 12, 11th fl. (☎613 29 00; www.austemb.se). **Canada,** Tegelbacken 4 (☎453 30 00; www.canadaemb.se). **Ireland,** Ostermalmsg. 97 (☎661 80 05; fax 660 13 53). **South Africa,** Linnég. 76 (☎24 39 50; www.southafricanemb.se). **UK,** Skarpög. 6-8 (☎671 30 00; www.britishembassy.com). **US,** Daghammarskjölds Väg 31 (☎783 53 00; www.usemb.se).

Currency Exchange: Forex in Centralstation (☎248 800; open daily 7am-9pm), Cityterminalen (☎21 42 80; open M-F 7am-10pm, Sa 8am-5pm), and Sweden House (☎20 03 89; open M-F 8am-7pm, Sa-Su 9am-5pm). 15-20kr commission.

American Express: Norrlandsg. 21 (☎411 05 40). T-bana: Östermalmstorg. No fee to cash AmEx Traveler's Cheques, 20kr for cash. Open M-F 9am-5pm, Sa 9am-1pm.

Gay and Lesbian Services: RFSL, Sveav. 57-59 (☎457 13 20; www.rfsl.se). T-bana: Rådmansg. Located above Tip Top, a popular gay club (see Nightlife). Open M-F 9am-5pm. Occasional evening activities; call for a schedule. *Queer Extra (QX)* and the **QueerMap,** available at Sweden House, give info about Stockholm's gay hot spots.

Emergency: Ambulance, fire, and **police:** ☎112.

Pharmacy: Look for the green and white "Apoteket" signs. **Apoteket C. W. Scheele,** Klarabergsg. 64, at the overpass over Vasag. T-bana: T-Centralen. Open 24hr.

Medical Assistance: ☎32 01 00.

Hospitals: Karolinska, ☎517 700 00. Sankt Göran, ☎587 100 00.

Internet Access: Stadsbiblioteket (library), Odeng. 59, in the annex. T-bana: Odenplan. 10min. free. Open M-Th 11am-7pm, F 9am-7pm, Sa-Su 11am-5pm. **Sweden House** (see above) provides free terminals. **Nine,** Odeng. 44. T-bana: Odenplan. Turn left on Odeng. 45kr per hr. Open M-Th 10am-1am, F-Sa 10am-midnight, Su 11am-1am.

Telephones: Buy phone cards at **Pressbyrån** stores, 30 (35kr), 60 (60kr), or 120 (100kr) units. **National directory assistance:** ☎079 75, 15kr per min.

Post Office: Main office in T-bana: T-Centralen (☎781 46 82). Open M-F 8am-6:30pm, Sa 11am-2pm. Address mail to be held: Firstname SURNAME, *Poste Restante*, **10110** Stockholm 1, Sweden. Also in Centralstation (☎781 24 25). Open M-F 7am-10pm, Sa-Su 10am-7pm.

▐▌ ACCOMMODATIONS AND CAMPING

Summer demands reservations, and many HI hostels limit stays to five nights. If you haven't booked ahead, arrive around 7am. Stockholm's several **boat-hostels (botels)** are a novel solution to space issues, but they can be cramped and noisy—request a room on the water side of the boat. Note that many independent (non-HI) hostels are hotel/hostels; specify if you want to stay in a dorm-style hostel, or risk paying hotel rates. **Campers** should bring insect repellent to ward off the infamous Swedish mosquitoes. If you don't have a **Swedish Camping Card** (see p. 963), either site below will sell you one for 90kr. Using an SL bus pass (or Stockholm Card) is the cheapest way to get to the more remote campsites.

City Backpackers' Vandrarhem, Upplandsg. 2A (☎20 69 20; www.citybackpackers.se). From Centralstation, go left on Vasag. and bear right on Upplandsg. Airy hostel, close to the station. Helpful staff and great amenities. Sauna 20kr. Internet access. Kitchen. Laundry 50kr. Reception 9am-noon and 2-7pm. Dorms 170-200kr; doubles 490kr. ❷

Hostel af Chapman/Skeppsholmens Vandrarhem (HI/STF), Flaggmansvägen 8, on Skeppsholmen (☎463 22 66; www.stfchapman.com). From T-Centralen, take bus #65 to the parking lot or walk 20min. along the waterfront over the Skeppsh. Olmsbron bridge. Modern on-shore hostel and unusually roomy 19th-century botel. Great view of Gamla Stan. Kitchen. Breakfast 55kr. Laundry 35kr. Reception 24hr. Lockout 11am-3pm. Botel curfew 2am. Dorms 150kr; botel doubles 180kr. Nonmembers add 45kr. ❶

Långholmens Vandrarhem (HI), Långholmsmuren 20, on Långholmen (☎668 05 10; vandrarhem@langholmen.com). T-bana: Hornstull. Walk north on Långholmsg., turn left onto Högalidsg., and turn right to cross to the island on Långholmsbron. After crossing, turn left and follow the yellow fence to the end; reception is on the right. Former prison cells in a peaceful lakeside hostel and hotel. Kitchen, cafe/pub, and laundry. Breakfast 65kr. Sheets 40kr. Reception 24hr. Check-out 10am. Book far in advance. Hostel rooms 165-190kr; nonmembers add 45kr. ❷

Zinkensdamm Vandrarhem (HI), Zinkens Väg 20, in Södermalm (☎616 81 00; www.zinkensdamm.com). T-bana: Zinkensdamm. Head south on Ringv. 3 blocks, then turn right and head down Zinkens Väg. Bright, inviting hostel and hotel next to a huge city park. Kitchen and laundry. Bike rental (20kr per hr., 100kr per day). Reception 24hr. Book at least a month in advance. 155kr, nonmembers 200kr. ❷

Hostel Mitt i City, Västmannag. 13 (☎21 76 30; www.stores.se/hostal.htm). T-bana: T-Centralen. Turn left up Vasag. and bear left on Västmannag. for 2 blocks. Reception on 5th fl. Sunny rooms a short walk from the station. Breakfast included. Sheets 50kr. Reception 24hr. Dorms 175kr; doubles 590kr; quads 900kr. ❷

Mälarens, Södermälarstrand, Kajplats 6 (☎644 43 85; www.rodabaten.nu). T-bana: Gamla Stan. Take Centralbron across the river and then walk 100m to the right along the shore. Small rooms, great maritime decor. Breakfast 55kr. Reception in cafe 8am-11pm. Dorms 185kr; singles 400kr; doubles 450kr; quads 860kr. ❷

Östra Real Vandrarhem (SVIF), Karlavägen 79, in Östermalm (☎664 11 14; realostra@hotmail.com). T-bana: Karlaplan. Exit toward Karlaplan, turn right, and then take the second right onto Karlavägen; the hostel is on the third block. Light-filled dorms and friendly common rooms. Kitchen. Sheets 45kr. Reception 8:30am-9pm. Curfew M-Th 1am, F-Sa 3am. Open mid-June to mid-Aug. 7- to 10-bed dorms 125kr; 4- to 6-bed dorms 150kr; doubles 450kr (sheets included). ❶

Ängby Camping, Blackebergsv. 24, on Lake Mälaren (☎37 04 20; www.angbycamping.se). T-bana: Ängbyplan. Go downstairs, turn left on Färjestadsvägen, and bear left at the fork; it's at the bottom of the road. Wooded campsite with swimming area, walking paths. Reception in summer 7am-11pm; off-season 8am-10pm. 115kr per couple with tent; 80kr per extra person. RVs 165kr, with electricity 190kr. Cabins 300-675kr. ❶

Bredäng Camping, Stora Sällskapets Väg, near Lake Mälaren (☎97 70 71; www.camping.se/plats/A04). T-bana: Bredäng. Turn left onto Stora Sällskapets Väg under tunnel and follow the street 700m, past Ålgrytevägen; hostel reception is on the left, camping reception on the right. Reception 7am-10pm. Open mid-Apr. to late Oct. Campground: single tents 85-95kr; group tents 165-180kr; 4-bed cottage 450kr; RV hookups 30kr. Hostel: singles 140kr; doubles 380kr; quads 500kr; cabins 630-830kr. ❶

🖸 FOOD

Your best budget bet is to fuel up on the all-you-can-eat breakfasts offered by most hostels, then track down lunch specials (*dagens rätt*; 45-80kr, usually 11:30am-3pm). Cafes line **Götgatan** and **Skånegatan** in Södermalm; many cheap eateries are on **Odengatan** in Vasastaden. **Birger Jarlsgatan** is great for people-watching, but its restaurants tend to be overpriced. **Grocery stores** are easy to find around any T-bana station. There's also a bustling **fruit market** at Hötorget (M-Sa 7am-6pm).

🖾 Café Tabac, Stora Nyg. 46. T-bana: Gamla Stan. Cafe by the waterfront with delicious salads (68-84kr) and huge panini sandwiches (46-60kr); small restaurant in back (entrees 100-190kr). ❷

Herman's, Fjällg. 23A, in Södermalm. T-bana: Slussen. Vegetarian buffet with sweeping views of the city over the water. Lunch 65kr; dinner 95kr. Open in summer daily 11am-11pm; off-season M-F 11am-9pm, Sa-Su noon-10pm. ❷

STHLM, Drottningg. 73c. 7 blocks north of T-Centralen. Urbane cafe on Vasastaden's main pedestrian avenue. Beautifully presented salads, pastas, and sandwiches (45-75kr), and tempting desserts. Open M-F 8am-8pm, Sa 10am-8pm, Su 10am-6pm. ❷

Kófi, Birger Jarlsg. 11. T-bana: Östermalmstorg. The most affordable cafe on chic Birger Jarlsg. Open in summer daily 7am-1am; off-season 7am-11pm. ❶

Chokladkoppen and **Kaffekoppen,** Stortorget 18-20. T-bana: Gamla Stan. Light meals (34kr-65kr) and generous desserts (from 34kr). Open in summer 9am-11pm; off-season Su-Th 9am-10pm. ❶

🖸 SIGHTS

Stockholm's bridges and frequent open spaces make it an extremely walkable city. Its parks—especially **Ekoparken,** the world's first urban national park—set it apart from all other European cities. The best way to get a taste of Stockholm's neighborhoods and rich street life is to explore by foot, hopping on the T-bana (sometimes called the longest art exhibit in the world) to get to more remote places.

GAMLA STAN. (Old Town.) At the center of Stockholm's islands is the city's medieval core, known for its winding streets and for **Kungliga Slottet** (Royal Palace), the winter home of the Swedish royal family and the site of the daily Changing of the Guard. *(30min.; M-Sa 12:15pm, Su 1:15pm.)* The palace houses the lavish **State Apartments** and, in an underground space formerly used as the royal wine cellars, the **Skattkammaren** (Royal Treasury) and the **armory.** Also in the palace complex are the **Gustav III Antikmuseum** (Museum of Antiquities) and the **Tre Kronor Museum,** which holds the excavated remains of the original 13th-century castle. *(www.royalcourt.se. Open mid-May to Aug. daily 10am-4pm; Sept.-Apr. Tu-Su noon-3pm. Each attraction 70kr, students 35kr; whole palace 110kr/65kr. English-language tours included.)* Behind the palace on **Stortorget** (Town Square) is the impressive **Storkykar** (Royal Chapel), site of royal weddings and the dramatic sculpture of Saint Göran slaying a dragon. Near the square are Gamla Stan's main pedestrian streets: **Västerlånggatan,** which can be a bit overrun with tourists, and nearby **Stora Nygatan** and **Österlånggatan,** which are quieter and good for window-shopping. *(T-bana: Gamla Stan, or take bus #46 or 55. Tours of Gamla Stan June-Aug. 2 per day. Meet at the Royal Opera House. 85kr.)*

KUNGSHOLMEN AND STADSHUSET. On the tip of Kungsholmen closest to Gamla Stan towers the regal **Stadshuset** (City Hall). Jutting above the skyline at 106m, the **Stadshustornet** (City Hall Tower) offers a stunning aerial view of downtown. The interior contains municipal chambers in the shape of Viking Ships; the **Blå Hallen** (Blue Hall, although it is not blue), where the Nobel Prize

SWEDEN

IN RECENT NEWS

WOMEN AND CHILDREN FIRST

Thanks to social democracy and a robust feminist movement, Sweden is the safest country on earth for children, according to U.N. studies, and the world leader in gender equality. "If women are ever to take their rightful place in society," Susan Faludi writes, "it seems likely that it will happen first in Sweden." Advancement in this arena is a significant national self-stereotype, a symbol of what distinguishes Swedes from others.

No other country has a higher percentage of women as parliamentarians, cabinet ministers, and professional and technical workers. More generally, Sweden leads the developed world in the proportion of women in the labor force. This is due both to job opportunities in the large public sector, and to quality public child-care institutions that make it easier for women to work outside the home.

Social democrats and women's movements have helped bring about four legislative milestones. First, a 1979 law prohibited corporal punishment, making Sweden the first nation in which parents were forbidden to strike their children. Second, the long-standing practice of nonmarital cohabitation, *sambo* ("living with"), has since 1988 entailed the same legal rights and responsibilities as marriage. Roughly one of four committed couples consists of unmarried partners—the highest rate in the industrialized world. Marrying for security is rare; the general-welfare society frees individuals to nurture genuine affection not based on economic need.

dinner is held; and the mosaic-tiled **Gyllene Salen** (Gold Room), where guests dance the night away after the ceremonies. *(Hantverkarg. 1. T-bana: T-Centralen. Walk toward the water and turn right on Stadshusbron. Mandatory tours June-Aug. daily 10, 11am, noon, and 2pm; Sept.-May 10am and noon. 50kr. Tower open daily May-Sept. 10am-4:30pm. 15kr.)*

BLASIEHOLMEN AND SKEPPSHOLMEN. On Blasieholmen, a short peninsula jutting out from Norrmalm, is the **Nationalmusem,** Stockholm's major art museum. It displays works by Rembrandt, Renoir, and Rodin as well as national artists such as Carl Larsson, Anders Zorn, and Eugen Jansson. *(www.nationalmuseum.se. T-bana: Kungsträdgården. The museum is on the left before Skeppsh. Olmsbron bridge. Open Tu 11am-8pm, W-Su 11am-5pm. 75kr, students 60kr, under 16 free. W reduced prices.)* The **Moderna Museet** and the **Arkitektur Museet,** across the bridge on Skeppsholmen, are closed for renovation through 2003. The museums' collections are being housed temporarily at various locations throughout the city. *(For details, see www.modernamuseet.se and www.arkitekturmuseet.se.)*

DJURGÅRDEN. Djurgården is a lush national park in the heart of the city, a perfect place for a long walk or a summer picnic. It is also home to **Skansen,** a popular open-air museum featuring 150 historical buildings, handicrafts, and a zoo. The homes, extracted from different periods of Swedish history, are inhabited by costumed actors. *(Bus #44 or 47 from Drottningg. and Klarabergsg. in Sergels Torg. Park and zoo open June-Aug. daily 10am-10pm; Sept.-Apr. 10am-4pm; May 10am-8pm. Historical buildings open May-Aug. daily 11am-5pm; Sept.-Apr. 11am-3pm. 60kr, 30kr in winter.)* Before the entrance to Skansen is the haunting ◙**Vasa Museet,** which houses a salvaged warship that sank on its 1628 maiden voyage before even leaving the harbor. *(Galärvarvet. Take bus #44, 47, or 69. Open June 10-Aug. 20 daily 9:30am-7pm; Aug. 21-June 9 Th-Tu 10am-5pm, W 10am-8pm. 70kr, students 40kr.)* Next door, the **Nordiska Museet** (Nordic Museum) presents an innovative exhibit on Swedish history and culture from the Viking age to the modern era. *(Djurgårdsvägen 6-16. Bus #44, 47, or 69. Open June 24-Aug. daily 10am-5pm; Jan.-June 23 Tu and Th-S 10am-5pm, W 10am-9pm. 60kr, students 30kr, under 18 free.)* On the far side of the island, **Prins Eugens Waldemarsudde,** former home of the full-time prince and part-time painter, contains its namesake's major works and personal collection. The seaside grounds also boast a beautiful sculpture garden. *(Prins Eugen Väg 6. Bus #47. Open May-Aug. Tu-Su 11am-5pm, Th until 8pm; Sept.-Apr. 11am-4pm. 60kr.)*

🎵 📷 ENTERTAINMENT AND FESTIVALS

Stockholm offers a number of venues for theater and music, many of which are small establishments that can be found by looking through *What's On*, available at the tourist office. There are also a number of larger, more widely known performance spots. The six stages of the national theater, **Dramaten**, Nybroplan (☎667 06 80), feature Swedish- and English-language performances of works by August Strindberg and other playwrights (50-260kr). The **Kulturhuset** (Culture House), an arts complex built in the 60s, provides "high culture" at publicly appealing prices (☎5083 1508). The **Operan**, Jakobs torg 2 (☎24 82 40) stages operas and ballets. (135-460kr. Student, obstructed-view, and rush-ticket discounts.) The **Konserthuset** at Hötorget (☎10 21 10) is home to the Stockholm Philharmonic (100-270kr, 15% student discount). Pop music venues include the **Globen** arena (☎600 34 00; 250-500kr), **Skansen** (☎5789 0005), and the stage at **Gröna Lund,** Djurgården's huge outdoor Tivoli amusement park (☎670 76 00; late Apr. to early Sept., at 7:30pm). In summer, **Kungsträdgården** (a large park bordered by Kungsträdgårdsg. and Västra Trädgårdsg.) hosts several free outdoor concerts; also look for signs about **Parkteatern,** a summer-long program of free theater, dance, and musical productions in different parks around the city. Check theater and concert listings in *Stockholm this Week* and *What's On*, and visit Sweden House or call BiljettDirekt (☎(07) 7170 7070) for tickets to events and performances.

Stockholm's festivals include the world-class **Jazz and Blues Festival** at Skansen (July; ☎747 92 36; www.stockholmjazz.com); **Strindberg Festival** (late Aug. or early Sept.; ☎34 14 01; www.strindberg.stockholm.se/festivalen); and the gay **Stockholm Pride** (late July or early Aug.; ☎33 59 55; www.stockholmpride.org).

📷 NIGHTLIFE

Stockholm proves that blondes have more fun, partying until 5am at the many nightclubs and bars around Stureplan in **Östermalm** (T-bana: Östermalmtorg). Be prepared for steep covers and long lines. **Södermalm** ("Söder"), across the river, is known for local flavor and a more mellow feel; most establishments close between 1 and 3am. Bars and cafes line **Götgatan** (T-bana: Slussen, Medborgplatsen, or Skanstull) and are appearing in **Vasastaden** (T-bana:

Third, in a 1995 policy without precedent elsewhere, Sweden began reserving a portion of parental leave for fathers. After the birth of a child, the parents receive 480 days of paid leave to divide between them, with two months set aside for each parent. A father who chooses not to participate forfeits part of the couple's parental benefit payment. This policy has resulted in Europe's highest rate of paternal participation in child-care.

The fourth legal innovation concerns prostitution: in 1999, Sweden became the first nation to criminalize the buyer, but not the seller, of sexual services. The law's authors noted their aim of prosecuting only those they considered the exploiters (normally men), not the exploited (normally women).

Swedish public schools inaugurated modern sex education in 1955—to the dismay of many other Europeans and Americans—and the society was known for sexual liberalism in the 1960s and 1970s. No longer: today's public debate emphasizes protecting people from sexual exploitation. The most celebrated Swedish film of 2002, "Lilja 4-ever," tells the story of a Russian girl forced into prostitution; plans are afoot to create an S.O.S. center, based in Stockholm, for women and girls threatened with violence anywhere in the world.

Sankt Eriksplan) and **Kungsholmen** (T-bana: Rådhuset). Stockholm's size and the excellent **night bus** service allow revelers to partake of any or all of these scenes in a single night. Alcohol is expensive at bars (35-55kr) but cheap (10-15kr per 0.5L) at **Systembolaget** state liquor stores. (Most open M-F 9am-5pm.) For information about Stockholm's **gay scene**, pick up *QX (Queer Extra)* or the Queer-Map, which have entertainment and nightlife listings.

▓ **Daily News Café,** Kungsträdgården, next to Sweden House. T-bana: T-Centralen. Delivers great live and house music to a slick but friendly clientele. Music changes nightly; call for a schedule (☎21 56 55). Cover 60-90kr. Open Su-Th 9pm-3am, F-Sa 9pm-5am.

Tip Top, Sveav. 57, next to RFSL. T-bana: Rådmansg. Walk one block left of the station. This trendy gay club's large dance floor draws a mixed crowd on the weekends. Beer 44kr, mixed drinks 68kr. Cover 70kr F-Sa after 9pm. Open M-Sa 5pm-3am.

Bröderna Olssons Garlic and Shots, Folkungag. 84 in Söder. T-bana: Medborgarplatsen. Walk 3 blocks up Folkungag. Quirky bar with an electric atmosphere. Trademark garlic-flavored beer 48kr. 101 unique shots (35kr each). Open daily 5pm-1am.

Snaps, Medborgarplatsen. T: Medborgarplatsen. The free-standing yellow house across from the station. Basement dance floor (jungle, reggae, and dance music). Beer 42kr, mixed drinks from 64kr. Women 23+, men 25+. Open in summer Tu-Sa 3pm-3am, Su-M 3pm-midnight; off-season M 3pm-midnight, Tu-W 3pm-2am, Th-Sa 3pm-3am.

Mosebacke Etablissement, Mosebacke Torg 3. T-bana: Slussen. Take the Katarina lift to the "Söder Heights." Eclectic array of live music and a summer terrace with a spectacular view. Cover 50-100kr. Beer 43kr, mixed drinks 62kr. 20+. In summer, terrace open daily 11am-1am, bar and club Th-Sa 8pm-1am; off-season bar and club 5pm-1am.

Folkhemmet, Renstiernas Gata 30. T-bana: Medborgarplatsen. Down-to-earth locals' bar. DJ every night from 8pm. Beer 39kr, mixed drinks 79kr. 21+. Open daily 5pm-1am.

Kvarnen, Tjärhovsg. 4. T-bana: Medborgarplatsen. A 200-year-old beer hall along with a new cocktail bar, **H2O,** and a basement dance club, **Eld.** 23+. Kvarnen and H2O: open M-F 11am-3am, Sa-Su 5pm-3am; H2O closed Su. Eld: W-Su 10pm-3am.

▨ DAYTRIPS FROM STOCKHOLM

Stockholm is situated in the center of an archipelago, where the mainland gradually crumbles into the Baltic. The islands in either direction—east toward the Baltic or west toward Lake Mälaren—are well worth exploration. Visit the **Excursion Shop** in Sweden House (p. 967) for more information. **Ferries** to the archipelago leave from in front of the Grand Hotel on the **Stromkajen** docks between Gamla Stan and Skeppsholmen (T-Bana: Jakobskyrka) or the **Nybrohamnen** docks (T-Bana: Östermalmstorg.; walk down Birger Jarlsg. toward the water).

LAKE MÄLAREN. The island of **Björkö** on Lake Mälaren is home to **Birka,** where the Vikings established the country's first city and where Christianity first reached Sweden in AD 829. The island now holds a Viking museum as well as fascinating excavation sites and burial mounds. A **ferry** departs Stockholm from the Stadshusbron docks next to the Stadshuset. (1¾hr.; May-Sept. 10am, July-Aug. also 2pm. Return from Björkö 3:30pm, July-Aug. also 6:30pm. 1hr. guided tour, museum admission, and round-trip ferry 200kr. 2pm ferry includes tour of excavation.)

The Swedish royal family's home, **Drottningholm Palace,** is only 1hr. away by ferry. The ghost of Lovisa Ulrika, Drottning (Queen) from 1720 to 1782, for whom the palace was a wedding gift, presides over the lush Baroque gardens and extravagant Rococo interiors. Catch the English-language tour of the palace's **theater.** (every hr.; 60kr, students 30kr). **Kina Slott,** Drottningholm's Chinese pavilion, was an 18th-century royal summer cottage. (Palace open May-Aug. daily 10am-4:30pm; Sept. noon-3:30pm. 50kr, students 25kr. Pavilion open May-Aug. daily 11am-

4:30pm; Apr. and Sept.-Oct. noon-3:30pm. 60kr/30kr.) Strömma Kanalbolaget **ferries** depart from Stadshusbron from May to early Sept. (M-F every hr., Sa-Su more frequently.) Or, take the **subway** to T-bana: Brommaplan, then take **bus** #301-323.

THE ARCHIPELAGO (SKÄRGÅRD). The wooded islands of the Stockholm archipelago grow rockier and increasingly dramatic closer to the Baltic. The archipelago is perfect for picnicking and hiking; the water is very cold but swimmable. The **Waxholmsbolaget ferry company** (☎679 58 30) serves even the tiniest islands and offers the 16-day **Båtluffarkortet card** (385kr), good for unlimited boat travel. The Excursion Shop at Sweden House (see p. 967) sells the ferry pass and has information on hostels and camping, as well as kayak and canoe rentals. Overnight stays in the area's 20 **hostels** must be booked months ahead, but the odd night may be available on short notice. There are **hostels ❶** on **Möja** in the outer archipelago (☎571 647 20) and **Vaxholm,** closer to Stockholm (☎541 322 40). Consult Sweden House for complete listings. Or, enjoy **free camping** courtesy of the law of public access (see p. 963) on almost any island except Sandhamn. (Some islands are also in military protection zones and are not open to foreigners.)

To fish or investigate the waterways by canoe or kayak, rent **boats** on Vaxholm (☎541 377 90) or Utö (☎501 576 68). **Vaxholm,** a fortress town founded in 1647, is small enough to explore by foot and is accessible by boat. (A ferry departs from Nybroplar in Stockholm at noon and returns at 4:30pm.) **Utö** has great bike paths; **bike rental** and ferry packages are available from Sweden House. **Sandhamn,** three hours from Stockholm, is ideal for swimming and **sailing.** The labyrinth north of Landsort on **Öja** is reputed to bring luck to fishermen. Take the *pendeltag* (commuter train) from Stockholm to Nynashamn, then ride bus #852 to Ankarudden and hop the ferry (55kr) to Landsort (2hr.).

UPPSALA. Uppsala, the most biker-friendly town in Sweden, houses the 20,000 students of Sweden's oldest university in a beautiful urban setting of grand churches and footbridges. The towers of Scandinavia's largest cathedral, the soaring **Domkyrka,** dominate the skyline. (Open daily 8am-6pm. Tours in English June 24-Aug. M-Sa 2pm. Free.) A walk through the center of town along the Fyrisån River is an excellent way to get a taste of the city's flourishing gardens and cafes. For an aerial view, walk away from the river on Drottningg. and take the path up to the **castle,** which also houses an art museum. (Open W-F noon-4pm, Sa-Su 11am-5pm.) The **Universitetsbiblioteket** (University Library), at the foot of the castle, has an exhibition hall and a popular cafe, a promising spot for meeting students. (Library open Aug. 19-June 15 M-F 9am-8pm, Sa 10am-5pm, Su 11am-4pm; June 16-Aug. 18 reduced hours. May 14-Sept. 16 20kr; Sept. 17-May 13 free.) The university museum, **Gustavianum,** across from the Domkyrka, houses scientific curiosities and the **Anatomical Theater,** the site of 18th-century public human dissections. (Open June 25-Aug. 25 11am-5pm; Aug. 26-June 24 Tu-Su 11am-4pm. 40kr, students 30kr.) Many claim that the haunting, quiet site of **Gamla Uppsala** (Old Uppsala), 4km north of the town center, was once occupied by a pagan temple. Today, little remains except huge burial mounds of monarchs and the **Gamla Uppsala Kyrka,** one of Sweden's oldest churches. (Open Apr.-Sept. daily 9am-6pm; Oct.-Mar. 9am-4pm. Free.) Near the mounds, a new museum, the **Gamla Uppsala Historiskt Centrum,** outlines the history of the mounds and their excavation. (Open May-Aug. 20 daily 10am-5pm; Aug. 21-Sept. 10am-4pm. 50kr, students 40kr, under 16 free.) Take bus #2, 20, 24, or 54 (16kr) north from Dragarbrunnsg. Further afield is **Skokloster,** a dazzling Baroque palace that is accessible by boat. (Open May-Aug. daily 11am-4pm. Entrance and tour 65kr, students 50kr. Boat departs Tu-Su 11:30am from Islandsbron on Östra Åg. and Munkg.; returns 5:15pm. Round-trip 115kr.) Uppsala's students drive a lively night scene. You'll find students lounging on terraces along the river and bars in and around **Stortorget.**

SWEDEN

Trains pull in from **Stockholm** (40min.; every 30min., less frequently on weekends; 70kr, under 25 55kr) after a stop at Arlanda Airport. To get from the station to the **tourist office**, Fyristorg 8, walk right on Kungsg., left on St. Persg., and across the bridge. (☎27 48 00. Open in summer M-F 10am-6pm, Sa 10am-3pm, Su noon-4pm; off-season closed Su.) Around the corner from the tourist office is **Internet Horna**, Drottning. 3, on the first floor of the city newspaper office. (20kr per 30min. Open M-F 9:30am-5:30pm, Sa 10:30am-2:30pm.) For renovated rooms in a lovely pastoral setting, try **Sunnersta Herrgård (HI) ❸**, Sunnerstav. 24, 6km south of town. Take bus #20, 25, 50, or 802 (20kr) from Dragarbrunnsg. to Herrgårdsv., cross the street, walk two blocks down the path behind the kiosk, and walk 50m left. (☎32 42 20. Breakfast 65kr. Reception June-Aug. M-F 8-10am and 5-9pm; Sept.-May M-F 7:30am-8pm, Sa-Su 7:30-10am. Singles 330kr; doubles 360kr; triples 540kr. Nonmembers 45kr extra per person.) **Fyrishov Camping ❶**, Idrottsg. 2, off Svartbäcksg., is 2km from the city center. Take bus #4 or 6 (bus #50 or 54 at night; 10min.) to Fyrishov. (☎27 49 60. Reception 7am-10pm. Tents 130kr; 4- to 5-bed huts 450-800kr. Swedish Camping Card required.) **Postal code:** 75101. ☎018.

GOTLAND

Gotland, Sweden's largest island, is 300km south of Stockholm. Famed for whitesand beaches, green meadows dotted with old stone churches, and its medieval capital of Visby, Gotland's timeless landscape is best seen at a leisurely pace.

⌗ TRANSPORTATION. Destination Gotland ferries (☎(0498) 20 10 20) sail to Visby from **Nynäshamn**, south of Stockholm (3-5hr.), and **Oskarshamn**, north of Kalmar (2½-4hr.). Fares are highest on weekends and from mid-June to Aug. and cheapest for early-morning and late-night departures. (June-Aug. 2-5 per day; Oct.-May 1-3 per day. 150-475kr, students 95-300kr; 40% ScanRail discount.) To get to Nynäshamn from **Stockholm**, take the *Batbussen* bus from Cityterminalen (1hr.; leaves 1¾hr. before ferry departures; 70kr, 95kr on bus) or the *pendeltag* from Centralstation (1hr., 60kr; SL passes and *rabattkuponger* valid). To get to Oskarshamn, hop on a bus (1¾hr., 69kr) or train from **Kalmar**. If you're planning your trip from Stockholm, **Gotland City**, Kungsg. 57A, books ferries and has tourist information. (☎(08) 406 15 00. Open June-Aug. M-F 9:30am-6pm, Sa 10am-2pm; Sept.-May M-F 9:30am-5pm.)

To explore the island, pick up a bus timetable at the ferry terminal or at the Visby **bus station**, outside the wall north of the city at Kung Magnusväg 1 (☎(0498) 21 41 12; 59kr, bikes 40kr extra). **Cycling** along Gotland's extensive paths and bikefriendly motorways is the best way to explore its flat terrain; bike rental shops are all over the island, especially in Visby and Klintehamn.

VISBY. This sleepy village looks straight out of a fairy tale, its medieval wall enclosing knotted cobblestone streets and crumbling churches. Visby awakens in August for **Medeltidsveckan**, a recreation of Visby's medieval past complete with costumes and tournaments (between the 31st and 32nd Sundays of the year).

Once you reach Gotland, exit the ferry terminal and walk 10min. to the left to get to the **tourist office**, Hamng. 4. (☎20 17 00. Open mid-June to mid-Aug. M-F 8am-7pm, Sa-Su 8am-6pm; May to mid-June M-F 8am-5pm, Sa-Su 10am-4pm; mid-Aug. to Apr. M-F 8am-4pm.) Dozens of **bike rental** shops surround the ferry terminal. **Gotlandsresor**, Färjeleden 3, 75m right of the ferry terminal, will help you book ferries, rent a bicycle, and find a room. (☎20 12 60; www.gotlandsresor.se. Open June-Aug. daily 6am-10pm, until 11:30pm when a late ferry comes in; Sept.-May 8am-6pm.) **Private rooms ❸** cost about 240-290kr for singles and 380-430kr for doubles. ◪**Visby Fängelse Vandrarhem ❷**, Skeppsbron 1, is 300m to the left as you exit the ferry terminal.

You'll recognize it by the barbed wire atop its yellow walls, the only remnants of the 19th-century prison that preceded this airy, whimsically decorated hostel. (☎20 60 50. Reception in summer M-F 11am-2pm and 5-6:30pm; off-season 11am-2pm. Call ahead if arriving at another time. Reserve ahead. Dorms 170-200kr; doubles, triples, and quads 200-275kr per person.) **Postal code:** 62101. ☎**0498.**

ELSEWHERE ON GOTLAND. Great daytrips from Visby during the high season include visits to the popular **Tofta** beach 15km south (bus #31, 30min.); the calcified cliffs of **Hoburgen,** at the island's southernmost tip (bus #11, 3hr.); and the mystical monoliths on **Fårö,** off the northern tip of the island (bus #23, 2hr.). The friendly **Fårögarden (STF) hostel ❶,** 17km north of the ferry terminal, is a warm retreat in Fårö's gorgeous countryside. Stay on the bus from the ferry terminal and ask to get off at the hostel. Guests can borrow bikes free of charge. (☎22 36 39. Open May-Aug. only. Reception 8am-noon and 5-7pm. Dorms 85kr; doubles and quads 130kr per person. Nonmembers 45kr extra.) **Gotlandsresor** (see above) has information on over 30 hostels, campgrounds, and bike rentals elsewhere on Gotland. You can also take advantage of the right of public access (see p. 963).

SOUTHERN SWEDEN

This mild region is graced with flat beaches, wide fields of waving grasses, and Swedish summer homes. **Halland** and the southwest **Småland** coastline, between Västervik and Kalmar, are especially popular.

KALMAR ☎0480

Across the footbridge from downtown Kalmar is the elegant 16th-century **Kalmar Slott,** which has evocative exhibits on castle life and a great art space. (Open daily July 10am-6pm; June and Aug. 10am-5pm; Apr.-May and Sept. 10am-4pm; Oct.-Mar. reduced hours. 70kr, students 40kr; Oct.-Mar. reduced prices.) The castle hosts an annual **Renaissance Festival** in late June and early July (☎45 06 62 for information and tickets). Adjoining the castle's seaside grounds is the tree-lined **Kyrkogarden** cemetery. The **Kalmar Konstmuseum,** down the street at Slottsvagan 1D, is a center for modern Swedish art and design. (Open F-W 11am-5pm, Th 11am-8pm. 40kr, students 30kr.) The **Läns Museum,** Skeppsbrog. 49, has relics from the wreckage of the 17th-century warship Kronan, which sank in a battle against the Danes. (Open mid-June to mid-Aug. daily 10am-6pm; mid-Aug. to mid-June Tu-F 10am-4pm, Sa-Su 11am-4pm. 50kr, students 25kr.)

Trains and buses arrive south of town, across the bay from the castle. **Buses** run directly to Stockholm (3 per day; 305kr, students 245kr). **Trains** go to: Gothenburg (2-5 per day; 395kr/275kr); Malmö (6 per day; 375kr/260kr); and Stockholm (2 per day; 475kr/335kr). To get from the train station to the **tourist office,** Larmg. 6, go right on Stationsg. and turn left on Ölandsg. (☎153 50. Open July M-F 9am-8pm, Sa-Su 10am-5pm; June and Aug. M-F 9am-7pm, Sa-Su 10am-4pm; Sept.-May M-F 9am-5pm.) To hike from the tourist office to the modern **Vandrarhem Svanen (HI) ❷,** Rappeg. 1, on the island of Ängö, go north on Larmg., turn right on Södra Kanalg., cross the bridge, and turn left on Ängöleden; it will be on the right. (☎129 28. Breakfast 55kr. Sheets 45kr. Laundry 25kr. Reception mid-June to mid-Aug. M-F 7am-10pm, Sa-Su 7:30am-9pm; mid-Aug. to mid-June M-F 7am-9pm, Sa-Su 7:30am-9pm. 160kr, nonmembers 205kr.) Seaside **Stensö Camping ❶** is 2km south of Kalmar; take bus #3. (☎888 03. Call ahead. Tents and RVs 105-135kr; electricity 30kr; cabins 400kr, 1900kr per week. Mid-Aug. to mid-June reduced prices.) **Larmtorget** is the best place to find cheap restaurants. **Postal code:** 39101.

⚑ DAYTRIPS FROM KALMAR: ÖLAND AND GLASRIKET. Visible from Kalmar's coast, the island of **Öland** stretches over 100km of green fields and white sand beaches. The royal family roosts here on holiday; Crown Princess Victoria's birthday, Victoriadagen (July 14), is celebrated island-wide. Commoners fill the **beaches** of Löttorp and Böda in the north and Grönhögen and Ottenby in the south. **Buses** #101 and 106 go from Kalmar's train station to Borgholm, the island's main town (45kr); bus #106 continues to Löttorp and Böda (77kr), while bus #103 goes to Grönhögen and Ottenby (53kr). Öland's **tourist office** (☎56 06 00) is outside Färjestaden; follow signs from the first bus stop after the bridge. ☎**0485.**

In nearby towns, collectively dubbed **Glasriket** (Kingdom of Crystal), artisans craft some of the world's most exquisite hand-blown glassworks. To visit workshops at **Orrefors** (☎(0481) 341 95) and **Kosta Böda** (☎(0478) 345 00), take bus #138 (1hr., 100kr). (Both open M-F 9am-6pm, Sa 10am-4pm, Su noon-4pm.)

MALMÖ
☎**040**

The former industrial town of Malmö is in the midst of a rebirth following the construction of the new Øresund bridge to Copenhagen. **Lilla Torg,** a small square neighboring **Stortorget,** is known as the best meeting-place in Sweden. **Möllevång-storget,** in the diverse neighborhood of **Möllevången,** has a lively open-air market, laid-back local bars, and lots of affordable ethnic restaurants. The **Form Design Center,** Lilla Torg 9, showcases the cutting edge of Swedish design. (☎664 51 50; www.scandinaviandesign.com. Open T-W and F 11am-5pm, Th 11am-6pm, Sa 10am-4pm, Su noon-4pm. Free.) The **Malmö Konsthall,** St. Johannesg. 7, exhibits challenging but accessible modern art. (☎34 12 94. Open Th-Tu 11am-5pm, W 11am-6pm. Free.) Surrounded by a beautiful park in Malmö's West End, **Malmöhus** castle houses the **Malmös Museer,** which documents the city's history. (☎34 44 37. Open June-Aug. 10am-4pm; Sept.-May noon-4pm. 40kr, students 20kr.) For a completely different cultural experience, walk along the **Ribersborg beach** to the **Kallbadhuset,** a naturist swimming bath and sauna, where locals are known to break through the ice to go swimming in winter; in summer, it hosts jazz and poetry evenings. (☎26 03 66. Open May-Aug. M-F 8:30am-7pm; Sept.-Apr. M-F noon-7pm, Sa-Su 9am-4pm. 35kr.)

The **train station** and **harbor** lie north of the Old Town. **Trains** arrive from: Copenhagen (35min.; every 20min.; 80kr, under 25 40kr); Gothenburg (3½hr.; every hr.; 390kr/275kr); and Stockholm (4½hr.; every hr.; 685kr/480kr). The **tourist office** in the train station books rooms for a 70kr fee. (Open June-Aug. M-F 9am-8pm, Sa-Su 10am-5pm; May and Sept. M-F 9am-6pm, Sa-Su 10am-3pm; Oct.-Apr. M-F 9am-6pm, Sa 10am-2pm.) **Cityroom** (☎79 59 94) also books rooms. **Vandrarhem Malmö (HI) ❷,** Backav. 18, is out of the way but well-kept. Roadside rooms are quite loud; ask for a room on the yard. From the train station or harbor, cross the canal and Norra Vallg. and take bus #21 to Vandrarhemmet. (☎822 20. Breakfast 50kr. Sheets 40kr. Kitchen. Reception May-Aug. 8-10am and 4-10pm; Sept.-Apr. 8-10am and 4-8pm. Dorms 130kr; singles 285kr; doubles 350kr; triples 450kr. Nonmembers add 45kr.) **Hotel Pallas ❹,** across from the train station at Norra Vallg. 74, is a bit pricier but has a great location. (☎611 50 77. Breakfast 30kr. Singles 355kr; doubles 395-475kr.) Nightlife resides in the bars on Lilla Torg and Möllevangstorget and the clubs around Stortorget. **Postal code:** 20110.

LUND
☎**046**

What Oxford and Cambridge are to England, Lund and Uppsala are to Sweden. Lund University's antagonism with its scholarly northern neighbor in Uppsala has inspired countless pranks, drag shows, and drinkfests in Lund's bright streets. The town's Romanesque cathedral, **St. Laurentius,** is an impressive 900-

year-old reminder of the time when Lund was the religious center of Scandinavia; its floor-to-ceiling 14th-century astronomical clock rings in the hour at noon and 3pm. To find the cathedral from the train station, walk straight across Bang. and Knut den Storestorg, then turn left on Kyrkog. (Open M-Sa 8am-6pm, Su 9am-6pm.) The University campus is a calm stroll across the park from the cathedral; find events information at **Student Info**, Sang. 2, in the student union. (☎38 49 49; af.lu.se. Open Sept.-May M-F 10am-4pm.) **Kulturen**, at the end of Sankt Anneg. on Tegnerplastén, is an engrossing open-air museum with 17th-and 18th-century homes, churches, and historical displays. (Open mid-Apr. to Sept. daily 11am-5pm; Oct. to mid-Apr. Tu-Su noon-4pm. 50kr.)

Lund is easily accessible from Malmö on most **SJ trains** and by local **pågatågen** (10min., 1-5 per hr., 34kr; railpasses valid). Trains also run to: Stockholm (4-6hr., every 1-2hr., 175-315kr); Gothenburg (3hr.; every hr.; 355kr, students 175kr); and Kalmar (3hr.; every 2hr.; 205kr, students 145kr). The **tourist office**, opposite the cathedral at Kyrkog. 11, books rooms (200kr) for a 50kr fee. (☎35 50 40. Open June-Aug. M-F 10am-6pm, Sa-Su 10am-2pm; May and Sept. M-Sa only; Oct.-Apr. M-F only.) The delightful but cramped **Hostel Tåget (HI) ❶**, Vävareg. 22, is housed in a 1940s train. Take the overpass to the park side of the station. (☎14 28 20. Breakfast 50kr, sheets 50kr. Reception Apr.-Oct. daily 8-10am and 5-8pm; Nov.-Mar. 8-10am and 5-7pm. Call ahead. 120kr, nonmembers 165kr.) To get to **Källby Camping ❶**, take bus #1 (dir.: Klostergården) 2km south of the city center. (☎35 51 88. Open mid-June to Aug. 45kr per tent, 160kr per rv.)

Budget food can be found on Stortorget and Stora Söderg. as well as at the open-air fruit and vegetable **market** at Mårtenstorget (7am-2pm) and the adjoining covered market, **Saluhallen** (M-F 9:30am-3pm, Sa 9am-3pm). **Cafe Ariman ❶**, Kungsg. 2B, right off Stortorget, is a student hangout with music on Friday and Saturday nights. (Sandwiches 32-40kr. Open M 11am-11pm, Tu-Th 11am-1am, F-Sa 11am-3am, Su noon-11pm.) Lund's active nightlife revolves around the student "nations"; stop by Student Info for tips on getting a guest pass. The best options that don't require a pass are **Stortorget**, Stortorget 1, a bar and nightclub (bar open Su-W 11:30am-midnight, Th 11:30am-1am, F-Sa 11:30am-2am; nightclub open Th-Sa 11pm-3am; 22+, 20+ with student ID), and **Palladium**, Stora Söderg. 13 (bar open Aug. to mid-June 11:30am-10pm; nightclub open Th-Sa 10pm-3am, 50kr cover). The multi-purpose bar and art-house theater **Mejeriet**, Stora Söderg. 64, is also popular with students (☎211 00 23 for info). **Postal code:** 22101.

YSTAD   ☎0411

Travelers passing through Ystad en route to Bornholm, Denmark (see p. 283) often miss out on the charms of this quiet town's rose-lined streets and half-timbered houses. South of **Stortorget**, the market square, lies the ancient monastery **Gråbrödraklostret** and its graceful, understated church. (Open M-F noon-5pm, Sa-Su noon-4pm. 20kr.) A pleasant trail runs by the waters of **Sandskogen**, the lovely beach just east of town. **Ales Stenar** (Ale's Stones), a mysterious Iron-Age stone formation outside the city, is accessible via bus #322 (30min., 3 per day, 23kr). Bornholms Trafikken (☎130 13) **ferries** leave from behind the train station for Bornholm (2½hr., 3 per day in summer, 150kr). Pol-Line ferries (☎55 69 00) sail for Świnoujście, Poland. **Trains** pull in from Malmö (45min., every hr., 70kr). The **tourist office** across from the station books rooms for a 30kr fee. (☎57 76 81. Open mid-June to mid-Aug. M-F 9am-7pm, Sa 10am-7pm, Su 11am-6pm; mid-Aug. to mid-June M-F 9am-5pm.) The train station houses the **Vandrarhemmet Stationen ❷**, a sunny hostel perfectly located for those stopping over in Ystad. (☎(070) 857 79 95. Sheets 60kr. Reception June-Aug. 9-10am and 5-7pm; Oct.-May 5-6pm. 180kr.) To get to the beachfront **Vandrarhem Kantarellen ❶**, turn right from the station and walk about 2km on Österleden, then turn right on Fritidsvägen (30min.). Or, take bus #572 (5min., 10kr) from the station. (☎665 66. Kitchen. Reception 9-10am and 4-8pm. Call ahead. 120kr, nonmembers 160kr.) **Sandskogens Camping ❶** is right next door. (☎192 70. 125kr.) Get groceries at **Saluhallen**, off the main square at the corner of Theatergrand and St. Västerg. (Open daily 8am-9pm.) **Postal code:** 27101.

GOTHENBURG (GÖTEBORG) ☎031

Sweden's industrial hub, Gothenburg (pop. 460,000) has a strong sense of identity and an atmosphere that is both laid-back and urbane. Gothenburg is known for its thriving arts scene, vibrant streets, beautiful parks, fabulous nightlife, and textured neighborhoods.

🖥🖫 TRANSPORTATION AND PRACTICAL INFORMATION. Trains go from Nordstaden to: Malmö (2¾-3¾hr.; 12 per day; 390-700kr, under 25 275-490kr); Oslo (4hr.; 3 per day; 362kr, under 25 255kr); and Stockholm (3-5½hr.; 15 per day; 545-1045kr, under 25 380-730kr). Stena Line **ferries** (☎704 00 00) sail to Frederikshavn, Denmark (2-3¼hr.; 8 per day; 125-150kr, 50% discount with ScanRail, Interrail, or Eurail) and Kiel, Germany (13½hr., daily, 870kr). DFDS Seaways (☎65 06 50) sends **ferries** to Newcastle, England (22-25hr.; 525-1175kr, under 26 25% discount). The **tourist office**, Kungsportsplatsen 2, books rooms (60kr fee) and sells the **Göteborg Pass,** which grants free public transit and admission to various attractions (1-day 175kr; 2-day 295kr). From the station, cross Drottningtorget and follow Östra Larmag. from the right of the Radisson. (☎61 25 00. Open late June to early Aug. daily 9am-8pm; early June and late Aug. M-F 9am-6pm, Sa-Su 10am-2pm; May M-F 9am-6pm; Sept.-Apr. M-F 9am-5pm, Sa 10am-2pm.) The stylish **stadsbibliotek** (city library), on Götaplatsen, provides free **Internet** access. (Open M-F 10am-8pm, Sa 11am-5pm.) **Postal code:** 40401.

🖥🖸 ACCOMMODATIONS AND FOOD. Gothenburg's hostels are mainly in the west end of the city. ▨**Masthuggsterrassen ❶**, Masthuggsterrassen 8, has a welcoming atmosphere and rooms with fantastic harbor views. Take tram #3, 9, or 11 to Masthuggstorget, cross the square diagonally onto Angra Långg., walk up the stairs, and follow the signs along the terrace. (☎42 48 20; fax 42 48 21. Breakfast 55kr. Sheets 55kr. Laundry 20kr. Kitchen. Reception 8-10am and 5-8pm. Dorms 150kr; doubles 380kr; quads 540kr.) Nearby **Stigbergsliden Vandrarhem (STF/HI) ❷**, Stigbergsliden 10, offers airy accommodations and rents bicycles (50kr per day). Take tram #3, 9, or 11 to Stigbergsliden and walk east down the hill. (☎24 16 20; www.hostel-gothenburg.com. Breakfast 40kr. Sheets 50kr. Laundry 40kr. Reception 8am-noon and 4-10pm. Dorms 115kr; singles 240kr; doubles 280kr. Nonmembers add 45kr per person.) The modern **Slottskogens Vandrarhem (STF/HI) ❶**, Vegag. 21, is near the huge Slottskogen park and the cafes and bars of Linnégatan. Take tram #1 or 2 (dir.: Frölunda) to Olivedalsg. and walk uphill to Vegag. (☎42 65 20; www.slottsskogenvh.se. Kitchen, sauna, and bike rental. Reception 8am-noon and 3-6pm. Dorms 100kr; singles 215kr. Nonmembers add 45kr.) The elegant **Hotel Flora ❹** is the best budget option in the center of town. Take tram #1, 7, or 9 from Centralstation. (☎13 86 16; www.hotelflora.nu. Breakfast included. Reception 24hr. Singles 415kr; doubles 575kr.) For simpler lodging, pitch your tent at **Kärralund Camping ❶**, Olbersg. Catch tram #5 to Welanderg., then go east on Olbersg., crossing the highway. (☎84 02 00; fax 84 05 00. Reception May-Aug. 7am-11pm; Sept.-Apr. reduced hours. Tents 60-120kr.)

Affordable restaurants and cafes are easy to find on Linnég., Viktoriag., and Vasag., and around Haga. ▨**Solrosen ❶**, Kaponjarg. 4a, a mellow vegetarian restaurant, is a neighborhood institution. (Salad bar 45kr, daily specials 65kr. Open M-F

11:30am-1am, Sa 2pm-1am. Kitchen closes at 9pm.) Cafes on Kungsportsavenyn
are abundant but pricey; try the popular **Eva's Paley ❷**, Kungsportsavenyn 39,
known for huge portions and great people-watching. (Lunch buffet 52kr. Happy
Hour F 4-7pm. Open M-Th 8am-11pm, F 8am-2:30am, Sa 10am-12:30pm, Su 10am-
11pm.) The **Saluhallen**, Kungstorget, is a covered market with a great selection of
groceries. (Open M-F 9am-6pm, Sa 9am-2pm.)

◙◪ SIGHTS AND NIGHTLIFE. To the south of Nordstaden, just across Drottningtorget and the Hamn canal from the train station, is the bustling shopping district of **Inom Vallgraven**. Tree-lined paths wind through **Tradgardsforeningens Park**.
The city's main drag, **Kungsportsavenyn** (known simply as **Avenyn**), stretches from
Kungsportsplatsen next to the tourist office all the way to **Götaplatsen**, site of Carl
Milles's famous **sculpture fountain** of Poseidon. The size of Poseidon's manhood
caused an uproar when the design was unveiled; it was later modified. On the
same square, the regal **Konstmuseet** houses a thoroughly engrossing collection of
Nordic art as well as the **Hasselblad Center**, an excellent photo exhibit. (Open Tu
and Th 11am-6pm, W 11am-9pm, F-Su 11am-5pm. 40kr, students 10kr.) The **Göteborgs Operan**, Lilla Bommen, an architectural marvel that mimics a ship at full
mast, is en route to the **Göteborg Maritime Centrum**, which features a large number
of docked ships and sailing vessels that you can board and tour. (Opera in session
during winter; purchase tickets at ☎13 13 00 or at the box office. Maritime center
open July-Aug. daily 10am-8pm; June and Sept. 10am-6pm; Oct.-Nov. and Mar.-May
10am-4pm. 60kr.) The **Stadsmuseet**, Norra Hamng. 12, houses exhibits on city history from the Vikings to city's post-industrial rebirth. (Open May-Aug. daily 10am-
5pm; Sept.-Apr. Tu and Th-Su 10am-5pm, W 10am-8pm. 40kr, students 10kr.)

One canal farther to the west lie two of Gothenburg's most appealing small
neighborhoods, the relatively untouristed **Linnéstan** and the **Haga** district, a formerly working-class neighborhood that is now lined with art galleries, antiquarian
bookstores, and cafes. Southwest of the Haga and Linnéstan, past the lush
Slottsskogsparken, a path leads up from Stigbergsliden to the hilltop **Masthuggskyr-
kan**, an intriguing brick church with a timber ceiling that suggests the inside of
Viking ship; the view of the city from here is gorgeous. A short trip from the mainland of Gothenburg, **Göteborgs Skärgård** is a summer paradise for beach-goers and
sailors. The secluded beach on **Vrångö** island in the archipelago makes a good daytrip; take tram #11 to Saltholmen, then catch a ferry (☎80 12 35).

Gothenburg has a thriving theater and classical music scene—pick up *What's
on in Göteborg* at the tourist office. Posh nightclubs line **Kungsportsavenyn**; especially popular are **Nivå**, **Madison Danceroom**, and **Valand**. ◙**Nefertiti**, Hvitfeldtsplat-
sen 6, is an intimate jazz bar that transforms into a popular dance club after 1am.
(Cover 70kr for club, 120kr for concerts. Open Th-Sa 9pm-4am.) Across the canal
on Nya Allén, striking **Tragar'n** has a classy dance floor and an outdoor bar. (21+.
Cover 80kr. Th 11pm-3am, F-Sa 11pm-5am.) **Icibar**, Viktoriag. 3, is a more relaxed
bar in Linnéstan. (Open F-Sa 8pm-3am, W-Th and Su 8pm-1am.)

◪ DAYTRIP FROM GOTHENBURG: VARBERG. Between Gothenburg and
Malmö beckon the expansive beaches of Varberg and its spectacular **fortress**.
(Tours mid-June to mid-Aug. every hr. 11am-4pm. 40kr.) South of town, the shal-
low bay of **Apelviken** offers some of the best surfing and windsurfing in northern
Europe. Follow the *Strandpromenaden* along the beach 2km south of town.
Surfer's Paradise, Söderg. 22, rents gear and gives tips. From the tourist office,
walk away from the train station on Västra Vallg., then turn left on Söderg. (☎67
70 55. Call ahead.) To explore the gorgeous beaches, rent **bikes** at BF Cykel, Östra
Langg. 47. From the tourist office, walk away from the water on Kyrkog. until you
reach Östra Langg. (90kr per day, 300kr per week. Open M-F 9:30am-6pm, Sa

9:30am-2pm.) **Trains** arrive from Gothenburg (1hr., 100-200kr) and Malmö (2½hr., 300-500kr). To get from the station to the **tourist office**, in Brunnsparken, walk four blocks right on Västra Vallg. (☎887 70. Open mid-June to mid-Aug. M-Sa 9am-7pm, Su 3-7pm; mid-Aug. to mid-June M-F 9am-6pm.) The tasteful and wonderfully situated ◪**Varbergs Fästning Vandrarhem ❷**, inside the fortress, has singles in a former prison and dorms in an old bakery. Book well in advance. (☎887 88. Breakfast 55kr. Sheets 55kr. Kitchen. Reception June-Aug. 8-10am and 5-9pm; Sept.-May 2-5pm. 165-185kr.) **Apelvikens Camping ❶** is on the beach. (☎141 78. Open late Mar. to Oct. 115-185kr.) **Postal code:** 43201. ☎**0340.**

DALARNA

Three hours west of Stockholm, Dalarna is the seat of Sweden's folk culture, home to its most spirited Midsummer celebrations and the birthplace of the national symbol, the Dala horse. Many urban Swedes spend their summer holidays soaking up the region's quiet beauty and reconnecting with their village roots.

MORA. An excellent base for exploring Dalarna, bright and compact Mora skirts the western shore of Lake Siljan. The 310km **Siljansleden bike trail** skirts the shore of Lake Siljan, and a 340km **walking trail** traverses pastures, forests, small lakes, and lovely mountain scenery. Both pass through Mora and Leksand; contact either tourist office for information about food and lodging and to pick up a map. The legendary red wooden **dalahäst** (Dala horses) are hand-made in **Nusnäs**, 10km east of Mora (bus #108; 15min., 15kr). The **Inlandsbanan** train route begins in Mora and runs to Östersund and Gällivare (see p. 962). The **tourist office**, which books 135-155kr rooms for a 25kr fee, is in Mora's train station. (☎59 20 20. Open mid-June to mid-Aug. M-F 9am-7pm, Sa-Su 10am-5pm; mid-Aug. to mid-June M-F 9am-5pm.) The Morastrand stop is closer to the town's sights than the station. The central, homey **Vandrarhem Mora (STF) ❶**, Fredsg. 6, is 500m from Morastrand; turn right on the main road and cross the street when you see Målkull Ann's Cafe, which operates as the hostel office after hours. (☎381 96. Breakfast 60kr. Sheets 60kr. Kitchen. Reception 8-10am and 5-7pm. Dorms 140kr; doubles 320kr. Nonmembers add 45kr.) Browse the bakeries on **Kyrkogatan.** The **ICA supermarket** is also on Kyrkog. (Open M-Sa 9am-8pm, Su 11am-8pm.) **Postal code:** 79201. ☎**0250.**

LEKSAND. Over 20,000 people flock to this town above Lake Siljan for Midsummer festivities that feature the tallest maypole in Sweden, folk music, and the **Siljansrodden**, a series of churchboat competitions that revives the tradition of rowing to church. The annual **Musik vid Siljan** festival in Leksand and Rättvik has classical, jazz, and folk music from around the world. (☎(0248) 102 90; www.siljan.se. First week in July. Tickets 60-400kr.) The **tourist office**, Stationsg. 14, inside the Leksand train station, has more details. (☎79 61 30; www.leksand.se. Open mid-June to mid-Aug. M-F 9am-7pm, Sa-Su 10am-5pm; mid-Aug. to mid-June 10am-5pm.) **Trains** run from Stockholm (3½hr., 3-7 per day), passing through Mora on the way. From Leksand's quay you can take breezy summer **cruises** on the *M/S Gustaf Wasa* a few times a day to Rättvik and Mora (☎(070) 542 10 25; 2-4hr., 80-250kr).

Accommodations are extremely hard to come by during Midsummer, but the tourist office can find you a private room for a 25kr fee. (Doubles from 275kr.) Camping options abound; check out www.leksand.se. The friendly **STF hostel (HI) ❶** is 2½km from the train station. Before 7pm, bus #58 comes from the bus station. (☎152 50. Sheets 45kr. Laundry 40kr. Kitchen. Bikes 60kr first day, 50kr additional days. Reception June-Aug. 8-10am and 5-8pm; Sept. and May 5-7pm; Oct.-Apr. 6-

SWEDEN

7pm. 110kr. Nonmembers add 45kr.) A 20min. walk along the road toward Tällberg brings you to **Leksands Camping Stugby ❶**. (☎/fax 803 13. 100kr per tent, off-season 85kr. 4-bed cabin 450kr. Electricity 35kr.) **ICA Supermarket** is at Leksandsv. 5. (Open M-Sa 9am-8pm, Su 10am-8pm.) **Postal code:** 79301. ☎0247.

ÖSTERSUND ☎063

Östersund is a natural stopover from Trondheim for travelers heading to or from Norway and a required one for those riding the length of the *Inlandsbanan*. The hilly lakeside town is perfect for boating and swimming in the summer and skiing in the winter. **Lake Storsjön** is home to a cousin of the Loch Ness monster, which is "spotted" every year by lucky eyewitnesses; the steamer **S/S Thomée** runs round-trip cruises and monster-spotting tours on the lake. (☎ 14 40 01. 65-95kr.) The local newspaper awards a 10,000kr prize for the best summer sighting, and the city is currently sponsoring a naming contest. Check out the harpoons of unsuccessful monster-hunters at the **Jamtli museum**, north of the city center on Kyrkg., which also features Sami photography, an open-air museum, and a perfectly preserved collection of Viking tapestries. Take bus #2 from the city center. (Open mid-June to Aug. daily 11am-5pm, 90kr; Sept. to mid-June Tu-Su 11am-5pm, 60kr.) Rent a **bike** at **Cykelogen**, Kyrkg. 45. (☎ 12 20 80; open M-F 10am-1pm and 2-6pm, Sa 10am-2pm; 100kr per day), and pedal over the footbridge to **Frösön Island**, once thought to be the home of Viking gods. The island's 11th-century **rune stone** and 13th-century **church** tell part of the story of how Christianity was brought to Sweden.

Trains run to Stockholm (6hr., 7-8 per day, 500kr) and Trondheim (5½hr., 2 per day, 300kr); from June 24 to August 3, the *Inlandsbanan* runs to Mora (7hr.; 3pm; 240kr, Interrail and ScanRail discount) and to Gällivare in Lapland (15hr.; 7:05am; 485kr, Interrail and ScanRail discount). The **tourist office,** Rådhusg. 44, books rooms for free. From the train station, walk up the hill on your left and continue down Prästg.; hang a right one block up Postgränd. (☎ 14 40 01. Open June 24-Aug. 8 M-Sa 9am-9pm, Su 9am-7pm; Aug. 9-June 23 reduced hours.) Wild strawberries grow on the thatched roofs of whimsical log cabins at the ◙**Frösötornets Härbärge hostel ❶**. Take bus #5 from the city center (last bus 10:20pm) to avoid most of the daunting climb. (☎51 57 67. **Internet** access. Reception 9am-9pm. Call ahead. Open May-Oct. only. Dorms 125kr.) Stock up at the supermarket **Hemköp** at Kyrkg. 56. (Open M-F 8am-8pm, Sa 9am-6pm, Su noon-4pm.) **Postal code:** 83101.

GULF OF BOTHNIA

The Gulf of Bothnia can be both gentle and dramatic, rural and sophisticated, lively and peacefully remote. Even in the most developed areas, like the bustling university town of Umeå, solitude is never out of reach.

ÖRNSKÖLDSVIK. Off the main train route is Örnsköldsvik (urn-SHULDS-vik; "Ö-vik" to locals), surrounded by hills and a harbor of tiny islands. Most visitors use the town as a base for superb **hiking**. The 127km **Höga Kusten Leden (High Coast Trail)** links Ö-vik with Hornoberget in the south and winds along the most beautiful, dramatic section of Sweden's Baltic coast. Pick up a trail guide and map (80kr) at the tourist office for information on transport links and huts along the way. Several **day hikes** are also nearby, including the easy **Yellow Trail** loop (6km). You'll find the trailhead on Hantverkareg.; from the tourist office, walk uphill on Nyg. and turn right on Hantverkareg. Throughout the island of **North Ulvön** are scenic hiking trails, the most rewarding of which leads to the peak of **Lotsberget Mountain**. The **M/S Otilia** sails from O-vik at 9:30am, arrives at Ulvön at noon, and departs for Ö-vik at 3pm (round-trip 110kr), stopping en route at the island of **Trysunda** (arrives 11am, departs 4pm; round-trip 70kr). Contact the tourist office for information about accommodations and camping. **Gene Fornby**, a 1500-year-old settlement 5km from Ö-vik, has been rebuilt to look as it did in AD 500; to reach it, take bus #21 to the Nybyggarevagen stop. (Open late June to early Aug. daily noon-5pm; tours at 12:30, 2, and 3:30pm. 50kr, children 30kr.) **Buses** run from Örnsköldsvik to Umeå (2hr., 7 per day; 102kr) and Östersund (4½hr., 1-3 per day, 240kr) in the north and Sundsvall (2hr., 6-7 per day, 133kr) in the south. The **tourist office**, Nyg. 18, books rooms and cottages for a 40kr fee. (☎125 37; fax 881 23. Open mid-June to mid-Aug. M-F 9am-7pm, Sa-Su 10am-3pm; mid-Aug. to mid-June M-F 10am-5pm.) To get there, walk up the steps behind the bus station, follow Fabriksg., and turn left on Nyg. The remote **STF Vandrarhem Örnsköldsvik (HI)** ❶, Högsnäsgården pl. 1980, is a gracious country house surrounded by wildflowers and distant mountains. The last bus to the hostel (#421; 25kr) leaves by 9pm on weekdays, earlier on weekends. (☎702 44. Reception in summer 9-10am and 5-7pm; off-season 9-10am. 120kr, nonmembers 155kr.) **Strand City Hotel** ❹, Nyg. 2, is downhill from the tourist office; it's a bit pricey for a no-frills hotel, but it's the most affordable option in the city center. (☎106 10. Breakfast included. Reception M-F 6am-9pm, Sa-Su 7am-6pm. In summer singles 450kr, off-season 650kr; doubles 550kr/900kr.) **Postal code:** 89101. ☎**0660.**

UMEÅ. Umeå (OOM-eh-oh), the largest city in northern Sweden, is a fast-growing university town surrounded by beautiful countryside. The 30km **Umeleden bike and car trail** snakes past old hydropower stations, ancient rock-carvings, an arboretum, and **Baggböle Herrgård**, a delightful cafe in a 19th-century mansion. (Open June-Aug. Tu-Su noon-7pm.) A bridge upriver allows for a more manageable 15km loop. **Cykel och Mopedhandlaren**, Kungsg. 101, rents and repairs **bikes**. (☎14 01 70. 70kr per day, 195kr per week. Open M-F 9:30am-5:30pm, Sa 10am-1pm.) The **Tavelsjöleden** (24km) and **Isälvsleden** (60km) trails are the best of the area's hikes; for information about lodging along the way, contact the tourist office (see below).

Regular trains do not run north from Umeå, but the private **Tågkompaniet** goes north to Kiruna and Narvik, Norway. The company honors some Sweden Rail passes; for information, call **Din resebyrå** (☎14 28 90), or stop by their office in the train station. **Trains** reach Umeå from Gothenburg (14½hr., 2 per day; 350kr) and Luleå (4½hr., 2 per day; 250kr). **Buses** operated by **Ybuss** (☎(0200) 33 44 44) run down the coast to Stockholm (10hr.; daily; 320kr, students 230kr), and **Norrlands Kusten** (☎(020) 51 15 13) sends buses north to Luleå (4hr., 240kr) and on to Kiruna (9½hr., 390kr). The bus terminal is across from the train station. **RG Line ferries** (☎18 52 00) to Vasa, Finland are available daily in summer and every other day in the off-season (4hr.; 360kr, students 270kr). The harbor is 20km south of Umeå; buses leave from the tourist office an hour before departure. To get to the **tourist office,** Renmarkstorget 15, which lists private rooms from 150kr, walk straight down Rådhusesplanaden from the train station and turn right on Skolg. (☎16 16 16; www.umea.se. Open mid-June to late Aug. M-F 8am-7pm, Sa 10am-4pm, Su noon-4pm; late Aug. to Sept. M-F 10am-5pm, Sa 10am-2pm; May to mid-June M-F 10am-6pm, Sa 10am-2pm; Oct.-Apr. M-F 10am-5pm.) The **Youth Hostel (HI)** ❶, V. Esplanaden 10, is to the left off Skolg. (☎77 16 50. Breakfast 50kr. Sheets 45kr. Reception M-F 8am-noon and 5-8pm, Sa-Su 8-10am and 5-8pm. Dorms 120kr, 140-155kr with bath; nonmembers add 45kr.) Take Holmsund bus #124 from Vasaplan to **Ljumvikens Camping** ❶; tell the bus driver your destination. (☎417 10. 75kr per tent.) The elegant **Rex** ❹, in the statehouse building on Rådhustorget, is worth the price. The cocktail bar hosts a disco on Friday and Saturday nights. (Entrees 100-180kr. Beer 45kr. Open M 11am-midnight, Tu-Th 11am-1am, F 11am-2am, Sa 1pm-2am. Restaurant closes at 10pm.) **Postal code:** 90101. ☎**090.**

LULEÅ. At the mouth of the **Lule Älv** lies the university town of Luleå (LOOL-eh-oh), just next to the UNESCO World Heritage church-town of **Gammelstad.** Going to church used to require a full day's travel in winter, so 15th-century farmers built hundreds of tiny cottages near the church to house their families on Sunday night. (Bus #32 in summer, #32 or 9 in the off-season; 23kr. Church open June-Aug. daily 9am-6pm, Sept.-May M-F 10am-2pm. In summer, tours every hr. 10am-4pm. Off-season, call Kyrktorget ☎29 35 81.) The mostly uninhabited **Luleå archipelago** awaits exploration by ferry, canoe, or kayak; contact the tourist office to book ferries to the various islands (200-400kr). In the town itself, **Storgatan** is full of cafes and bars that convert the laid-back daytime atmosphere into an energetic night scene. Chic **Magneto** picks up during the school year for afternoon jazz and club nights each Saturday. (50kr cover for club nights. Open M-Tu 11am-11pm, W-Th 11am-midnight, F-Sa 11am-3am.) **O'Leary's,** Skomakaresg. 22, right off the main street, is a laid-back bar with great local atmosphere. (Open M-Tu 5-10pm, W-Th 5pm-midnight, F-Sa 5pm-2am.) The **tourist office,** Storg. 43b, books **private rooms ❷** (120-450kr) for free. From the train station, cross Prästg. and follow it to the right, walk diagonally across the park, cross Hermalingsg., and tromp up Storg. (☎29 35 00. Open June to mid-Aug. M-F 9am-7pm, Sa-Su 10am-4pm; mid-Aug. to May M-F 10am-6pm, Sa 10am-2pm.) **EFS Sundet ❶** is the closest campground; take bus #6. (☎25 20 74. Reception 8am-9pm. Open June-Aug. 75kr per tent; 2-bed cabins 300kr.) **Postal code:** 97101. ☎**0920.**

LAPLAND (SÁPMI)

Lapland is where Sweden's ancestral past lives on, in the wild and striking landscape beyond the Arctic Circle. Its allure is in the swampy forests of the vast lowlands and in the humbling mountains that meet the Norwegian border. It is a region rich in the culture of the Sami, descendants of prehistoric Scandinavians who now use helicopters and snowmobiles to tend their herds of reindeer.

■ TRANSPORTATION. There are two **rail** routes to Lapland. The **coastal route** runs from Stockholm through Boden, Umeå, and Kiruna to Narvik, Norway, along the **Malmbanan.** From Midsummer (June 24) to early August, the privately run **Inlandsbanan** (p. 962) travels from Mora to Gällivare. A train leaves daily at 6:30am from the Morastrand train station in **Mora** and arrives at Östersund at 1:50pm (240kr); another train leaves Östersund daily at 7:05am and arrives in **Gällivare** at 10:10pm (485kr). **Tågkompaniet,** a private company that often provides the only train link between towns, does not maintain strict schedules. For information, contact **Din resebyrå** in Umeå (☎(090) 14 28 90) or **Centralens resebyrå** in Kiruna (☎(0980) 660 15). **Buses,** most of which do not accept railpasses, are the only transportation to smaller towns and are generally the best way to travel in the north. Call ☎(020) 47 00 47 for schedules.

■ TRAINS AND BUSES TO NORWAY AND FINLAND. Two trains per day travel the gorgeous route from Luleå to Narvik, Norway (6½hr.), stopping in Gällivare, Kiruna, and Abisko. Buses link Kiruna to Karesuando on the Finnish border (3¼hr., daily, 125kr), then continue to Skibotn in Norway or Kilpisjärvi and Muonio in Finland. Finland is also accessible by bus from Boden.

KIRUNA. The only large town in Swedish Lapland, Kiruna (pop. 23,000) is an industrial center in the middle of the wilderness, where traditional Sami culture exists beside cutting-edge research facilities. The world's largest underground **mine** (Kirunavaara) put Kiruna on the map and is still its main draw. (Mandatory tours depart from the tourist office June-Aug. every hr. 9am-4pm. 140kr.)

SWEDEN

THE BIG SPLURGE

THE ICEHOTEL

Jukkasjärvi, a town just outside Kiruna, is home to the remarkable **Icehotel,** a truly surreal structure that melts into the Torne River each spring and is redesigned by a team of ice-sculptors each winter. At -5° C, guests sleep on snowy beds covered in reindeer skins, bathe in the building's otherworldly light, and even say their wedding vows at the frozen altar of the Ice Church.

The hotel is open to the visiting public, drawing about 33,000 sightseers in addition to its 14,000 guests. In 2003, the Icehotel will stage Shakespearean performances in their brandnew **Ice Globe Theater,** a replica of the London original. The **Absolut Icebar** has earned acclaim as one of the world's most stunning bars, serving bilberry vodka in ice glasses to backpackers and notables alike.

The Icehotel invariably melts away each April, but many of its ice sculptures are displayed in a temperature-controlled warehouse until the hotel is shaped anew. While the hotel is open from December to April, there is no splurge in Sweden more worthwhile than a night in the Icehotel.

(☎ 668 99; www.icehotel.com. Non-guest visits 100kr, students and seniors 80kr. Rooms include breakfast and sauna. Dec. and Apr. singles 1780kr, doubles 1960kr; Jan.-Mar. singles 2320kr, doubles 2490kr. Year-round lodging in igloos and chalets from 300kr per person.)

ESRANGE, a space center and launchpad 40km outside Kiruna, studies the aurora borealis and the ozone layer. (4hr. tours depart from the tourist office June-Aug. M-F 9:30am. 190kr.) Kiruna is also a useful gateway to **⬛Abisko National Park,** among the most beautiful sections of Sweden. Abisko is the northern endpoint of the 450km **Kungsleden** (Royal Trail), the most beloved hiking trail in the country; contact **STF** for more information (Abisko ☎ 402 00; Stockholm ☎ (08) 463 22 00).

Buses run regularly to Kiruna from Luleå (230kr) and Jokkmokk (185kr). Tågkompaniet **trains** run south to Luleå and north to Abisko and Riksgränsen, Sweden, as well as Narvik, Norway. Regular **flights** to Stockholm depart from **Kiruna Flygplats.** (KRN; ☎ 28 48 10. 2-3 per day. 500kr, students 300kr, standby 250kr.) The **Kiruna-Lapland tourist office** is in the **Folk-shuset** in the town center. Walk straight from the train station, follow the footpath through the tunnel, and then walk up to the top of the hill. The agents book rooms for free, schedule tours, and arrange dog-sled excursions in winter. (☎ 188 80; www.lapp-land.se. Open June-Aug. M-F 8:30am-9pm, Sa-Su 8:30am-6pm; Sept.-May M-F 9am-5pm, Sa 10am-4pm.) The **Yellow House Hostel ❶,** Hantverkareg. 25, has a sauna and spacious rooms with kitchenettes. (☎ 137 50. Breakfast 50kr. Sheets 50kr. Dorms 120kr; singles 300kr; doubles 200kr.) From the tourist office, go up Hjalmer Lundbohmsv., turn right on Adolf Hedinsv., and turn left on Hantverkareg.; the hostel is 75m ahead on the left. **Postal code:** 98135. ☎ **0980.**

SWITZERLAND

(SCHWEIZ, SVIZZERA, SUISSE)

The unparalleled natural beauty of Switzerland entices all outdoor enthusiasts from all over the globe to romp in its Alpine playground. Three-fifths of the country is dominated by mountains: the Jura cover the northwest region bordering France, the Alps stretch gracefully across the entire lower half of Switzerland, and the eastern Rhaetian Alps border Austria. While the stereotypes of Switzerland as a "Big Money" banking and watch-making mecca are to some extent true, its energetic youth culture belies its staid reputation. Although the country is not known for being cheap, the best things—warm Swiss hospitality and sublime vistas—always come with no charge.

DISCOVER SWITZERLAND

Head directly for **Interlaken** (p. 999), a backpacker town brimming with paragliding, bungee jumping, canyoning, river rafting, kayaking, and other adventure opportunities. Most importantly, Interlaken provides easy access to the other wonders of the **Jungfrau Region.** Continue on to **Valais,** with hiking and year-round skiing in **Zermatt** (p. 1000). While many come to Switzerland to commune with nature, others come to commune with other backpackers: popular hotspots include **Montreux** (especially during the Jazz Festival; p. 1007), cosmopolitan **Geneva** (p. 1001), and cutting-edge, consumer-culture **Zurich** (p. 992). Finally, taste the *dolce vita* in Italian Switzerland with stops at **Lugano** (p. 1009) and **Locarno** (p. 1009).

ESSENTIALS

WHEN TO GO

November to March is ski season; prices in eastern Switzerland double and travelers need reservations months in advance. The situation is reversed in the summer, when the flatter, western half of Switzerland fills up. Sights and accommodations are cheaper and less crowded in the shoulder season (May-June and Sept.-Oct.); call ahead to check if the Alpine resort areas will be open then.

DOCUMENTS AND FORMALITIES

VISAS. Switzerland does not require visas for nationals of Australia, Canada, the EU, New Zealand, South Africa, or the US for stays shorter than three months.

EMBASSIES. Most foreign embassies are in **Bern** (p. 989). Swiss embassies at home include: **Australia,** 7 Melbourne Ave., Forrest, Canberra, ACT 2603 (☎(02) 62 73 39 77); **Canada,** 5 Marlborough Ave., Ottawa, Ontario KIN 8E6 (☎613-235-1837); **Ireland,** 6 Ailesbury Rd., Ballsbridge, Dublin 4 (☎(01) 218 63 82 or 218 63 83); **New Zealand,** 22 Panama St., Wellington (☎(04) 472 15 93 or 472 15 94); **South Africa,** P818 George Ave., Arcadia 0083, 0001 Pretoria (☎(012) 430 67 07); **UK,** 16-18 Montague Pl., London W1H 2BQ (☎(020) 76 16 60 00); and **US,** 2900 Cathedral Ave. NW, Washington, D.C. 20008-3499 (☎202-745-7900).

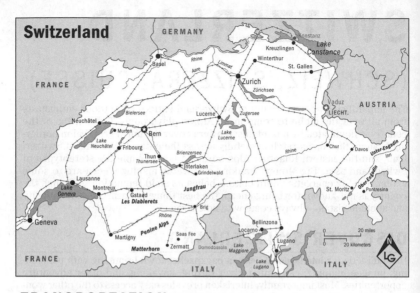

TRANSPORTATION

BY PLANE. Major international airports for overseas connections are in Bern (BRN), Geneva (GVA), and Zurich (ZRH). From the UK, **easyJet** (☎(0870) 600 00 00; www.easyjet.com) has flights from London to Geneva and Zurich (UK£47-136). From Ireland, **Aer Lingus** (☎(01) 886 88 88; www.aerlingus.ie) sells round-trip tickets from Dublin, Cork, Galway, Kerry, and Shannon to Zurich for €105-300.

BY TRAIN. Federal **(SBB, CFF)** and private railways connect most towns, with trains running frequently. **Eurail, Europass,** and **Interrail** passes are all valid on Switzerland's trains. The **SwissPass,** which is sold worldwide, offers five options for unlimited rail travel: 4, 8, 15, 21, or 30 consecutive days. In addition to rail travel, it entitles you to unlimited urban transportation in 36 cities and unlimited travel on certain private railways and lake steamers. (2nd-class 4-day pass US$160, 8-day US$225, 15-day US$270, 21-day US$315, 1-month US$350.) The **Swiss Flexipass** entitles you to any 3-8 days of unlimited rail travel within a 1-month period, with the same benefits as the SwissPass. (2nd-class 3-day pass US$156, 5-day US$184, 6-day US$240, 8-day US$282.)

BY BUS. PTT Post Buses, a barrage of government-run banana-colored coaches, connect rural villages and towns that trains don't service. **SwissPasses** are valid on many buses; **Eurail** passes are not. Even with the SwissPass, you might have to pay a bit extra (5-10SFr) if you're riding one of the direct, faster buses.

BY CAR. With armies of mechanized road crews ready to remove snow at a moment's notice, roads at altitudes of up to 1500m generally remain open throughout winter. The speed limit is 50kph in cities, 80kph on open roads, and 120kph on highways. Many small towns forbid cars to enter; some require special permits, or restrict driving hours. Call ☎140 for roadside assistance.

BY BIKE. Cycling, though strenuous, is a splendid way to see the country; most train stations rent bikes and allow you to return them at another station. The **Touring Club Suisse,** chemin de Blandonnet 4, Case Postale 820, 1214 Vernier (☎(022) 417 27 27; fax 417 20 20), is a good source of information, maps, brochures, and route descriptions.

TOURIST SERVICES AND MONEY

EMERGENCY	Police: ☎117. Ambulance: ☎144. Fire: ☎118.

TOURIST OFFICES. The **Swiss National Tourist Office,** marked by a standard blue "i" sign, is represented in nearly every town in Switzerland; most speak English. The tourist information website for Switzerland is www.myswitzerland.ch.

MONEY. The Swiss monetary unit is the **Swiss Franc (SFr),** divided into 100 *centimes* (called *Rappen* in German Switzerland). Coins come in 5, 10, 20, and 50 *centimes* and 1, 2, and 5SFr; bills come in 10, 20, 50, 100, 500, and 1000SFr. Switzerland is not the cheapest destination; if you stay in hostels and prepare your own food, expect to spend 45-100SFr per day. There is **no value-added tax (VAT),** although there are frequently tourist taxes of a few SFr for a night at a hostel. Gratuities are automatically factored into prices; however, it is considered polite to round up your bill 1-2SFr as a nod of approval for good service.

SWISS FRANC (SFR)		
	AUS$1 = 1.51SFR	1SFR = AUS$1.21
	CDN$1 = 0.97SFR	1SFR = CDN$1.03
	EUR€1 = 1.47SFR	1SFR = EUR€0.68
	NZ$1 = 0.71SFR	1SFR = NZ$1.41
	ZAR1 = 0.14SFR	1SFR = ZAR7.12
	US$1 = 1.51SFR	1SFR = US$0.66
	UK£1 = 2.41SFR	1SFR = UK£0.43

COMMUNICATION

PHONE CODES	**Country code:** 41. **International dialing prefix:** 00. From outside Switzerland, dial int'l dialing prefix (see Inside back cover) + 41 + city code + local number.

TELEPHONES. Whenever possible, use a calling card for international phone calls, as the long-distance rates for national phone services are often exorbitant. Most pay phones in Switzerland accept only prepaid phone cards. Phone cards are available at kiosks, post offices, or train stations. Direct dial access numbers include: **AT&T,** ☎0800 89 00 11; **British Telecom,** ☎0800 55 25 44; **Canada Direct,** ☎0800 55 83 30; **Ireland Direct,** ☎0800 40 00 00; **MCI,** ☎0800 89 02 22; **Sprint,** ☎0800 89 97 77; **Telecom New Zealand,** ☎0800 55 64 11; **Telkom South Africa,** ☎0800 55 85 35.

MAIL. **Airmail** from Switzerland averages 4-7 days to North America, although times are more unpredictable from smaller towns. Domestic letters take 1-3 days.

LANGUAGES. German, French, Italian, and Romansch are the national languages. Most urban Swiss speak English fluently. For basic German words and phrases, see p. 1057; for French, see p. 1056; for Italian, see p. 1060.

ACCOMMODATIONS AND CAMPING

SWITZERLAND	❶	❷	❸	❹	❺
ACCOMMODATIONS	under 16SFr	16-35SFr	36-60SFr	61-120SFr	over 120SFr

There are **hostels** (*Jugendherbergen* in German, *Auberges de Jeunesse* in French, *Ostelli* in Italian) in all big cities and in most small towns. *Schweizer Jugendherbergen* (**SJH,** or Swiss Youth Hostels; www.youthhostel.ch) runs HI hostels in Switzerland and has a website with contact information for member hostels. Hostel beds are usually 20-34SFr. Non-HI members can stay in any hostel but are usually charged a surcharge. The smaller, more informal **Swiss Backpackers (SB)** organization (www.backpacker.ch) has 28 hostels for the young, foreign traveler interested in socializing. Most Swiss **camping sites** are not isolated areas but large plots with many camper vans and cars. Most sites are open in the summer only. Prices average 6-9SFr per person and 4-10SFr per tent site. **Hotels** and **pensions** tend to charge at least 50-75SFr for a single room, 80-150SFr for a double. The cheapest have Gasthof, Gästehaus, or Hotel-Garni in the name. **Privatzimmer** (rooms in a family home) run about 25-60SFr per person. Breakfast is included at most hotels, pensions, and Privatzimmer.

FOOD AND DRINK

SWITZERLAND	❶	❷	❸	❹	❺
FOOD	under 9SFr	9-15SFr	16-24SFr	25-34SFr	over 35SFr

Switzerland is not for the lactose-intolerant. The Swiss are serious about dairy products, from rich and varied **cheeses** to decadent milk chocolate—even the major Swiss soft drink is a dairy-based beverage, *rivella*. Switzerland's hearty cooking will keep you warm through those frigid alpine winters but will make your cholesterol skyrocket. Bernese *Rösti*, a plateful of hash-brown potatoes (sometimes flavored with bacon or cheese), is prevalent in the German regions; cheese or meat *fondue* is popular in the French. Try Valaisian *raclette*, made by melting cheese over a fire then scraping it onto a baked potato and garnishing it with meat or vegetables. Supermarkets Migros and Co-op double as self-serve cafeterias; stop in for a cheap meal as well as groceries. Each canton has its own local beer—it's relatively cheap, often less expensive than Coca-Cola.

 HIKING AND SKIING. Nearly every town has **hiking trails;** consult the local tourist office. Lucerne, Interlaken, Grindelwald, and Zermatt offer particularly good hiking opportunities. Trails are usually marked with either red-white-red markers (only sturdy boots and hiking poles needed) or blue-white-blue markers (mountaineering equipment needed). **Skiing** in Switzerland is often less expensive than in North America if you avoid pricey resorts. **Ski passes** run 30-50SFr per day, 100-300SFr per week; a week of lift tickets, equipment rental, lessons, lodging, and *demi-pension* (breakfast plus one other meal) averages 475SFr. **Summer skiing** is less common than it once was but is still available in a few towns, such as Zermatt and Saas Fee.

HOLIDAYS AND FESTIVALS

Holidays: New Year's Day (Jan. 1-2); Good Friday (Apr. 18); Easter Monday (Apr. 20); Labor Day (May 1); Swiss National Day (Aug. 1); Christmas (Dec. 25-26).

Festivals: Two raucous festivals are the **Fasnacht** (Carnival, Mar.) in Basel and the **Escalade** (early Dec.) in Geneva. Music festivals occur throughout the summer, including the **Montreux Jazz Festival** (July) and **Open-Air St. Gallen** (late June).

GERMAN SWITZERLAND

The cantons in northwest Switzerland are gently beautiful, with excellent museums, a rich Humanist tradition, and charming old town centers. Previously thought of as a financial mecca, the region has begun to change its image with the growing popularity of Interlaken and the cultural attractions of Lucerne.

BERN ☎031

The city has been Switzerland's capital since 1848, but don't expect fast tracks and power politics—Bern prefers to focus on the lighter things in life, and the city has a decidedly relaxed atmosphere.

⌗ TRANSPORTATION. The **airport** (BRN; ☎960 21 11) is 20min. from the city; a bus departs from the train station 50min. before each flight (10min., 14SFr). **Trains** leave the station at Bahnhofpl., in front of the tourist office, for: Basel (1¼hr., every hr., 34SFr); Berlin (8hr., 3 per day, 245SFr); Geneva (2hr., every 30min., 47SFr); Interlaken (50min., every hr., 23SFr); Lausanne (1¼hr., every 30min., 32SFr); Lucerne (1½hr., every 30min., 32SFr); Vienna (11hr., 4 per day, 157SFr); and Zurich (1¼hr., every 30min., 45SFr). International fares are reduced 25% for ages 26 and under. **Bike rental** is available from the **Bernrollt Kiosk** outside the train station. (Free, but ID and 20SFr deposit required. Same-day return. Open May-Oct. 7:30am-9:30pm.)

⛿ PRACTICAL INFORMATION. Most of medieval Bern lies in front of the train station and along the Aare River. The **tourist office**, at the station, offers daily **city tours** (8-35SFr) in the summer by bus, on foot, or by raft. (Open June-Sept. daily 9am-8:30pm; Oct.-May M-Sa 9am-6:30pm, Su 10am-5pm.) Get online in the basement of **Jäggi Bücher**, Spitalg., on Bubenbergpl. 47-51 in the Loeb department store. Two computers have free **Internet access;** four terminals are 5SFr per 30min. The **post office**, Schanzenpost 1, is a block from the train station. (Open M-F 7:30am-6:30pm, Sa 8am-noon.) For **Poste Restante,** address mail to be held: Postlagernde Briefe für Firstname SURNAME, Schanzenpost **3000**, Bern 1, SWITZERLAND.

⌂⌂ ACCOMMODATIONS AND FOOD. From the train station, turn left on Spitalg., left on Kornhauspl., and right on Rathausg. to reach **Backpackers Bern/Hotel Glocke ❷**, Rathausg. 75. (☎311 37 71. Kitchen. Internet access. Laundry 3.80SFr. Reception June-Aug. 8-11am and 3-10pm; Sept.-May 8-11am and 3-8pm. Dorms 27-32SFr; singles 75SFr; doubles 120SFr, with bath 160SFr. Sept.-May 2-10SFr less. MC/V.) To reach the **Jugendherberge (HI) ❷**, Weiherg. 4, from the station, cross the tram lines and go down Christoffelg., take the stairs to the left of the park entrance gates, go down the steep slope, and turn left on

GRIN AND BEAR IT Legend has it that Duke Berchtold V of Zähringen, founder of Bern, wanted to name the city after the first animal he caught when hunting on the site. The animal was a you-know-what, and Bern (derived from *Bären*, or bears) was born. The *Bärengraben* themselves weren't built until the Bernese victory at the Battle of Nouana in 1513, when they dragged home a live bear as part of the war booty. A hut was erected for the beast in what is now *Bärenplatz* (Bear Square) and his descendants have been Bern's collective pets ever since.

Weiherg. (☎311 63 16. Breakfast included. Laundry 7SFr. 3-night max. stay. Reception June-Sept. daily 7-10am and 3pm-midnight; Oct.-May 7-10am and 5pm-midnight. Check-out 10am. Closed 2nd and 3rd weeks in Jan. Dorms 28SFr; overflow mattresses 20SFr. Nonmembers add 6SFr. MC/V.)

Almost every *platz* overflows with cafes and restaurants; the bigger ones tend to be pricier and more touristy. **Fruit and vegetable markets** sell fresh produce on Bärenpl. (May-Oct. daily 8am-6pm) and Bundespl. (every Tu and Sa). **Manora ❷**, Bubenbergpl. 5A, over the tramlines from the station, is a self-service chain with nutritious, cheap food. (Open M-Sa 6:30am-10:45pm, Su 8:30am-10:45pm.) **Migros Supermarket ❶**, Marktg. 46, also has a restaurant and take-away counters. (Open M 9am-6:30pm, Tu-W and F 8am-6:30pm, Th 8am-9pm, Sa 7am-4pm.)

◙ SIGHTS. The massive **Bundeshaus**, seat of the Swiss national government, dominates the Aare. (45min. tour every hr. M-Sa 9-11am and 2-4pm; free.) From the Bundeshaus, turn left off Kocherg. at Theaterpl. to reach the 13th-century **Zytglogge** (clock tower). At 4min. before the hour, figures on the tower creak to life, but it's more entertaining to watch the tourists scramble for their cameras. Continue down Kocherg. to the **Protestant Münster** (cathedral); which has a fantastic view from its 100m spire. (Open Easter-Oct. Tu-Sa 10am-5pm, Su 11:30am-5pm; Nov.-Easter Tu-F 10am-noon and 2-4pm, Sa 10am-noon and 2-5pm, Su 11am-2pm. Tower closes 30min. earlier. 3SFr.) Several steep walkways lead from the Bundeshaus to the **Aare River.** On hotter days, locals dive from the banks for a quick ride in the swift current; only experienced swimmers should join in. Across the Nydeggbr. lie the recently renovated **Bärengraben** (bear pits) Feed the bears for €3 and attempt to make up for the indignity of being on display for gawking crowds. (Open June-Sept. daily 9am-5:30pm; Oct.-May 10am-4pm.) The path up the hill to the left leads to the **◪Rosengarten** (Rose Garden), which has one of the best views of the *Altstadt.*

▥ MUSEUMS. The **Kunstmuseum**, Hodlerstr. 8-12, near the Lorrainebrücke, houses the world's largest Paul Klee collection and a smattering of other 20th-century art. (Open Tu 10am-9pm, W-Su 10am-5pm. 15SFr, students and seniors 10SFr, 7SFr/5SFr for Klee collection only.) The **Bernisches Historische Museum**, Helvetiapl. 5, is packed with anything and everything from Bern's history. (Open Tu and Th-Su 10am-5pm, W 10am-8pm. 13SFr, students 8SFr.) **Albert Einstein's House**, Kramg. 49, where he conceived the theory of relativity, is now filled with his photos and letters. (Open Feb.-Nov. Tu-F 10am-5pm, Sa 10am-4pm. 3SFr, students 2SFr.)

♫▣ ENTERTAINMENT AND NIGHTLIFE. Luminaries such as Bob Dylan and Björk have played at the **Gurten Festival** in July (www.gurtenfestival.ch); jazz-lovers flock to the **International Jazz Festival** (www.jazzfestivalbern.ch) in early May. The orange grove at Stadgärtnerei Elfnau (tram #19 to Elfnau) has free Sunday **concerts** in summer, and from mid-July to mid-August. **OrangeCinema** screens recently released films in the open air; tickets are available from the tourist office.

At night, the fashionable folk linger in the bars and cafes of the *Altstadt*, while a seedier crowd gathers under the gargoyles of the Lorrainebrücke. **Rablaus Bar,** Schmiedenpl. 3, is a popular nightspot. (Open M-W 5pm-1:30am, Th 5pm-2:30am, F-Sa 5pm-3:30am.) **Sous le Pont** is a den of alternative culture serving a colorful and diverse crowd; from Bollwerk, head left before Lorrainebrücke through the cement park. (Open Tu 11:30am-12:30am, W-F 11:30am-2:30pm and 6pm-12:30am, Sa 6pm-2:30am.) **Warning:** Avoid walking around the Parliament park and terraces at night. Like many cities, Bern has a drug community; it tends to congregate there.

BASEL (BÂLE)   ☎061

Situated on the Rhine near France and Germany, Basel is home to a large medieval quarter as well as one of the oldest universities in Switzerland—graduates include Erasmus and Nietzsche. Visitors encounter art from Roman times through the 20th century and are serenaded by musicians on every street corner.

▐▌ TRANSPORTATION AND PRACTICAL INFORMATION. Basel has three **train stations:** the French SNCF and Swiss SBB stations on Centralbahnpl., near the *Altstadt*; and the German DB station across the Rhine. **Trains** leave from the SBB for: Bern (1¼hr., every hr. 5:50am-11:50pm, 34SFr); Geneva (3hr., every hr. 6:20am-8:45pm, 71SFr); Lausanne (2½hr., every hr. 6am-10:30pm, 60SFr); and Zurich (1hr., every 15-30min. 4:40am-midnight, 30SFr). Make international connections at the SNCF or DB stations. To reach the **tourist office,** Schifflände 5, from the SBB station, take tram #1 to Schifflände; the office is on the river, near the Mittlere Rheinbrücke. (☎268 68 68. Open M-F 8:30am-6pm, Sa-Su 10am-4pm.) For **bi-gay-lesbian** information, stop by **Arcados,** Rheing. 69, at Clarapl. (☎681 31 32. Open Tu-F noon-7pm, Sa 11am-4pm.) To reach the **post office,** Rüdeng 1., take tram #1 or 8 to Marktpl. and backtrack one block, away from the river. (Open M-W and F 7:30am-6:30pm, Th 7:30am-8pm, Sa 8am-noon.) **Poste Restante:** Postlagernde Briefe für Firstname SURNAME, Rüdengasse, **CH-4001** Basel, Switzerland.

▐▐ ACCOMMODATIONS AND FOOD. Basel's shortcoming is its lack of cheap lodgings. Call ahead to ensure a spot at the only hostel in town, the **Jugendherberge (HI) ❷,** St. Alban-Kirchrain 10. Take tram #2 to Kunstmuseum; turn right on St. Alban-Vorstadt and follow the signs. (☎272 05 72. Breakfast included. Laundry 7SFr. Internet 10SFr per hr. Reception Mar.-Oct. 7-10am and 2-11pm; Nov.-Feb. 2-11pm. Check-out 10am. Mid-Feb. to Sept. dorms 29-31SFr; singles 79SFr; doubles 98SFr. Nov. to mid-Feb. 2.50SFr less. Nonmembers add 6SFr. AmEx/MC/V.) To reach **Hotel Steinenschanze ❹,** Steinengraben 69, from the SBB, turn left on Centralbahnstr. and follow signs for Heuwaage; go up the ramp under the bridge to Steinengraben and turn left. (☎272 53 53. Breakfast included. Reception 24hr. Singles 110-180SFr, with ISIC 60SFr per night for up to 3 nights; doubles with shower 160-250SFr, 100SFr. AmEx/MC/V.)

Barfüsserpl., Marktpl., and the streets connecting them are especially full of restaurants. **Wirtshaus zum Schnabel ❷,** Trillengässlein 2, serves tasty German fare. (Open M-Sa 9am-midnight. AmEx/MC/V.) Vegetarians can dine at **Restaurant Gleich ❸,** Leonhardsberg 1. (Open M-F 9am-9:30pm.) Groceries are available at **Migros supermarket,** in the SBB station. (Open M-F 6am-10pm, Sa-Su 7:30am-10pm.)

◙ SIGHTS. Groß-Basel (Greater Basel), and the train station are separated from **Klein-Basel** (Lesser Basel) by the Rhine. The very red **Rathaus** brightens Marktpl. in Groß-Basel with its blinding facade and gold and green statues. Behind the Marktpl. is the 775-year-old **Mittlere Rheinbrücke** (Middle Rhine Bridge), which connects the two halves of Basel. At the other end of Marktpl. is a spectacular **Jean Tinguely**

Fountain, also known as the **Fasnachtsbrunnen.** Behind Marktpl. stands the red sandstone **Münster,** where you can visit the tomb of Erasmus or climb the tower for a spectacular view of the city. (Open Easter-Oct. 15 M-F 10am-5pm, Sa 10am-4pm, Su 1-5pm; Oct. 16-Easter M-Sa 11am-4pm, Su 2-4pm. Free. Tower closes 30min. before the church. 3SFr.)

🏛 📠 **MUSEUMS AND ENTERTAINMENT.** Basel has over 30 museums; pick up the comprehensive museum guide at the tourist office. The **Basel Card,** available at the tourist office, provides admission to all museums as well as discounts around town. (24hr. card 25SFr, 48hr. card 33SFr, 72hr. card 45SFr.) The 📠**Kunstmuseum,** St. Alban-Graben 16, houses outstanding collections of old and new masters; admission also gives access to the **Museum für Gegenwartkunst** (Modern Art), St. Alban-Rheinweg 60. (Kunstmuseum open Tu and Th-Su 10am-5pm, W 10am-7pm. Gegenwartskunst open Tu-Su 11am-5pm. 10SFr, students 8SFr; first Su of every month free.) At 📠**Museum Jean Tinguely,** Grenzacherstr. 214a, everything rattles and shakes in homage to the Swiss sculptor's vision of metal and movement. Take tram #2 or 15 to Wettsteinpl. and then bus #31 or 36 to Museum Tinguely. (Open W-Su 11am-7pm. 7SFr, students 5SFr.) The **Fondation Beyeler,** Baselstr. 101, is one of Europe's finest private art collections, housing works by nearly every major artist. Take tram #6 to Fondation Beyeler. (Open daily 9am-8pm. M-F 16SFr, Sa-Su 20SFr; students 5SFr daily. 12SFr after 6pm daily.)

In a year-round party town, Basel's carnival, or **Fasnacht,** still manages to distinguish itself. The festivities commence the Monday before Lent with the *Morgestraich,* the 600-year-old, 72hr. parade beginning at 4am. The goal is to scare away winter—it rarely succeeds. During the rest of the year, head to **Barfüsserplatz** for an evening of bar-hopping. 📠**Atlantis,** Klosterberg 10, is a multi-level, sophisticated bar with reggae, jazz, and funk. (Open Tu-Th 11am-midnight, F 11:30am-4am, Sa 6pm-4am.) **Brauerei Fischerstube,** Rheing. 45, brews the delectably sharp 📠*Hell Spezial* ("light special") beer. (Open M-Th 10am-midnight, F-Sa 10am-1am, Su 5pm-midnight. Full dinner menu from 6pm.)

ZURICH (ZÜRICH)   ☎01

Zurich contains a disproportionate number of Switzerland's many banks, but there's more to Zurich than money. The city was once the focal point of the Reformation in German Switzerland, led by Ulrich Zwingli. In the 20th century, Zurich's Protestant asceticism succumbed to avant-garde artistic and philosophical radicalism: James Joyce toiled away at *Ulysses,* the quintessential modernist novel, in one corner of the city, while Russian exile Vladimir Lenin read Marx and dreamt of revolution in another; meanwhile, a group of raucous young artists calling themselves the Dadaists founded the Cabaret Voltaire. A walk through Zurich's *Altstadt* and student quarter will immerse you in the energetic youth counter-culture that spawned these subversive thinkers, only footsteps away from the rabid capitalism of the famous Bahnhofstraße shopping district.

📠 **TRANSPORTATION**

Flights: Kloten Airport (ZRH; ☎816 2500) is the main hub for **Swiss International Airlines** (☎(084) 885 20 00) with daily connections to Frankfurt, Paris, London, and New York. Trains to the *Hauptbahnhof* (main train station) leave every 10-20min. (5.40SFr).

Trains: From the **Hauptbahnhof** at Bahnhofpl. to: **Basel** (1¼hr., 1-3 per hr., 30SFr); **Bern** (1¼hr., 1-2 per hr., 45SFr); **Geneva** via Bern (3hr., every hr., 76SFr); **Lucerne** (1hr., 2 per hr., 19.80SFr); **Lugano** (3hr., 1-3 per hr., 60SFr); **Milan** (4½hr., every hr., 72SFr); **Munich** (4hr., 4 per day, 86SFr); **Paris** (6-8hr., 2 per day, 133SFr); **Salzburg** (6hr., 5 per day, 97SFr); **Vienna** (9hr., 4 per day, 124SFr). Discount for those under 26 on international trains.

Public Transportation: Public buses, trams, and trolleys run 5:30am-midnight. **Short rides** (under 5 stops) 2.10SFr (yellow button on ticket machine); **long rides** 3.60SFr (blue button). Buy tickets before boarding and validate in machine or face a fine. A **Tageskarte** (7.20SFr) is valid for 24hr. of unlimited public transport. **Nightbuses** run from the city center to outlying areas F-Sa at 1, 1:30, 2, and 3am.

Bike Rental: Globus (☎(079) 336 36 10); **Enge** (☎(079) 336 36 12); **Hauptbahnhof** (☎210 13 88), at the very end of track 18. All have **free** bike rental. Passport and 20SFr deposit required. Open daily 7:30am-9:30pm.

ORIENTATION AND PRACTICAL INFORMATION

The **Limmat River** splits the city down the middle. On the west side of the river are the **Hauptbahnhof** and **Bahnhofstraße.** Halfway down Bahnhofstr. lies **Paradeplatz,** the town center; **Bürkliplatz** is at the far end of Bahnhofstr. On the east side of the river is the University district, full of bars, restaurants, and hostels.

Tourist Offices: Main office (☎215 40 00), in the main station. The staff finds rooms after 10:30am. Open Apr.-Oct. M-Sa 8am-8:30pm, Su 8:30am-6:30pm; Nov.-Mar. M-F 8:30am-7pm, Sa-Su 8:30am-6:30pm.

Currency Exchange: At the main train station. Cash advances with MC/V and photo ID; 200SFr minimum. Open daily 6:30am-10pm. **Credit Suisse,** Bahnhofstr. 53. 2.50SFr commission. Open daily 6am-10pm.

Luggage Storage: At the Hauptbahnhof. Lockers 5-8SFr per day. Luggage watch 5SFr at the *Gepäck* counter. Open daily 6am-10:50pm.

Bi-Gay-Lesbian Resources: Homosexuelle Arbeitsgruppe Zürich (HAZ), Sihlquai 67, P.O. Box 7088, CH-8023 (☎271 22 50), offers meetings, a library, and the free newsletter *InfoSchwül.* Open Tu-F 7:30-11pm, Su noon-2pm and 6-11pm.

Laundromat: Speed Wash Self Service Wascherei, Müllerstr. 55. Wash and dry 5kg for 10.20SFr. Open M-Sa 7am-10pm, Su 10:30am-10pm.

Emergency: Police: ☎117. **Ambulance:** ☎144. **Fire:** ☎118.

Rape Crisis Line: ☎291 46 46.

24-Hour Pharmacy: Theaterstr. 14 (☎252 56 00), on Bellevuepl.

Internet Access: The **ETH Library,** Ramistr. 101, in the Hauptgebäude, has 3 free computers. Take tram #6, 9, or 10 to ETH, enter the main building, and take elevator to fl. H. Open M-F 8:30am-9pm, Sa 9am-2pm. **Telefon Corner,** downstairs in the station next to Marché Mövenpick. 6SFr per hr. Open daily 8am-10pm.

IN RECENT NEWS

RECLAIMING THE PAST

In the period between the two world wars, Switzerland, a stable country amid Europe in turmoil, was a logical safe destination for money. The Nazi era turned Europe upside down; a large number of accounts went untouched after the war ended. Unlike most countries, Switzerland did not have banking dormancy laws until 2001, meaning that the accounts remained untouched. Under increasing pressure, a tribunal was established in Zurich to deal with accounts left over from before 1945. Between 1998 and 2001, we arbitrated over 10,000 claims to nearly 2500 dormant accounts. The stimulus came from the fact that many accounts were owned by victims of the Holocaust and had found their rightful heirs.

The work was long and often emotionally draining. In my most rewarding case, I reunited cousins who had each thought they were their family's sole survivor. The claims were most often not about the money. Many claimants just wanted their relatives to be remembered. It was rewarding to receive thank you notes, even from those who had been denied. They were grateful simply because we listened to their stories. No amount of money can put the past right, but we have been able to restore money to entitled heirs, and, in all cases pay tribute to their memories.

—*Charles Ehrlich is a former Researcher-Writer for Let's Go: Spain and Portugal. As Senior Staff Attorney at the Claims Resolution Tribunal, he adjudicated claims to Nazi-era Swiss bank accounts.*

Zürich

⌂ ACCOMMODATIONS
Camping Seebucht, **12**
The City Backpacker/
Hotel Biber, **3**
Hotel Otter, **11**
Justinus Heim Zürich, **1**
Martahaus, **2**

🍎 FOOD
Bodega Española, **9**
Gran-Café, **6**
Hiltl, **4**
Restaurant Mère
Catherine, **10**

★ NIGHTLIFE
Cranberry, **7**
Double-U (W) Bar, **5**
Oepfelchammer, **8**

Schweizerisches
Landesmuseum
TO MUSEUM
FÜR GESTALLUNG
Museumstr.
Walchestr.
Neumühlequai
Stampfenbachstr.
Weinbergstr.
Auf der Mauer
Leonhardstr.
Sonneggstr.
Universitätstr.
TO 1 (1km)
Rämistr.
STA Travel
Tannenstr.
ETH Library
Universität Zürich
Museum of Classical Archaeology

Hauptbahnhof
BAHNHOFPL.
Bahnhofbr.
Co-op
Hirschengraben
Künstlerg.

Schützeng.
BEATENPL.
Beateng.
Werdmühlestr.
Mühlesteg
Bahnhofquai
Niederdorfstr.
Zähringerstr.
Limmatquai
Mühleg.
Zentralbibliothek

Uraniastr.
Rud. Brunr.
Preyerg.
Baderg.
Köngeng.
Graueg.
Hirscheng.
Roseng.
Weing.
Spitalg.
Spital
Brunng.
Froschaug.
ZÄHRINGERPL.
(PREDIGERPL.)
Seilergraben

Uraniastr.
Sihlstr.
Oetenbachg.
Rennweg
Fortuna G.
Lindenhofstr.
Schipfe
Stüssihofstatt
Rindermarkt
Theatre
Neumarkt

Sihlstr.
Füsslistr.
St. Annag.
Kuttelg.
Lindenhof Park
WEINPL.
Rathausbrücke
Marktg.
Spiegelg.
Untere Zäune

Nüschelerstr.
Pelikanstr.
Augustinerg.
Rathaus
Münsterg.
Obere Zäune

PELIKANPL.
St. Peterstr.
St. Peter's
In Gassen
Waag.
Limmatquai
Kirchg.
Schlosserg.
Trittlig.
Winkelwiese
Hirschengraben
Kunsthaus Zürich

Talstr.
Bäreng.
Talacker
MÜNSTERHOF
Poststr.
MÜNSTERHOF
Münsterbr.
Grossmünster
Frankleng.
Oberdorfstr.
Heimstr.

PARADEPL.
Fraumünster
Kappelerg.
Stadthausquai
SCHIFFPL.
Weiteg.
Krugg.
Torg.
Rämistr.

Bleicherweg
Talstr.
Börsenstr.
Fraumünsterstr.
Limmatquai
24hr. Pharmacy
BELLEVUEPL.
Freieckstr.
Stadelhoferstr.
St. Urban G.

Glärnischstr.
Clandenstr.
Dreikönigstr.
BÜRKLIPL.
Quaibr.
Limmat
Zürichsee

Beethovenstr.
0   200 yards
0   200 meters

Gotthardstr.
Stockerstr.
General Guisan quai
⚓ Ferry Terminal
Zürichsee

General Guisan
Goethestr.
Falken strasse
Seehofstr.

TO 12 (3km)

Post Office: Main office, Sihlpost, Kasernestr. 97, just behind the station. Open M-F 6:30am-10:30pm, Sa 6am-8pm. Address *Poste Restante* to: Firstname SURNAME, Sihlpost, Postlagernde Briefe, **CH-8021** Zürich, SWITZERLAND.

ACCOMMODATIONS AND CAMPING

Martahaus, Zähringerstr. 36 (☎251 45 50). From the station, cross Bahnhofbrücke and take the 2nd right after Limmatquai at the Seilgraben sign. Sparkling clean and in a great location. Breakfast and Internet access included. Reception 24hr. Partitioned dorms 37SFr; singles 75-80SFr; doubles 98-110SFr; triples 129SFr. AmEx/MC/V. ❸

The City Backpacker-Hotel Biber, Niederdorfstr. 5 (☎251 90 15). From the station, cross Bahnhofbrücke, turn right on Niederdorfstr. Tightly packed rooms are balanced by the great location. Internet 12SFr per hr. Kitchen available. Sheets 3SFr. Laundry 10SFr. Key deposit 20SFr or passport. Reception 8am-noon and 3-10pm. Check-out 10am. 4- to 6-bed dorms 29SFr; singles 65-66SFr; doubles 88-92SFr. MC/V. ❷

Justinus Heim Zürich, Freudenbergstr. 146 (☎361 38 06). Take tram #9 or 10 to Seilbahn Rigiblick, then take the hillside tram (by the Migros) uphill to the end. Quiet and spacious. Breakfast and kitchen access included. Reception daily 8am-noon and 5-9pm. Check-out 10am. Singles 50SFr, with shower 60SFr; doubles 80SFr/100SFr; triples 135SFr/165SFr; all rates reduced for multiple week stays. V. ❸

Hotel Otter, Oberdorfstr. 7 (☎251 22 07). Attracts an eclectic and artsy student crowd. All rooms have TV and phone. Breakfast included. Reception 8am-5pm. Check-out noon. Single 100SFr; doubles 130-160SFr. AmEx/MC/V. ❹

Camping Seebucht, Seestr. 559 (☎482 16 12). Take tram #11 to Bürklipl., then catch bus #161 or 165 to Stadtgrenze. Showers 2SFr. Reception M-Sa 7:30am-noon and 3-10pm, Su 8am-noon. Open May-Sept. 8SFr per person, 12SFr per tent. 1.50SFr tax. ❶

FOOD

Zurich's specialty is *Geschnetzeltes mit Rösti*, slivered veal in a cream sauce with hash-brown potatoes. The cheapest meals (around 6SFr) are along **Niederdorfstraße.** Try the **farmer's market,** Burklipl. (Tu and F 6-11am), or stop by the **Co-op Super-Center,** next to the train station, for groceries (open M-F 7am-8pm, Sa 7am-4pm). **Manor ❶,** off Bahnhofstr. 75 (corner of Uraniastr.) has a self-service restaurant with cheap meals on the 5th floor (open M-F 9am-8pm, Sa 9am-4pm). Check out *Swiss Backpacker News* (at the tourist office and Hotel Biber) for more information on budget meals in Zurich.

▧ **Bodega Española,** Münsterg. 15. Catalan delights such as potato tortilla dishes (15.50SFr) and *tapas* (4.80SFr). Open daily 10am-12:30am. AmEx/MC/V. ❷

Gran-Café, Limmatquai 66. Sit right by the Limmat and enjoy some of the tastiest meals around. Daily *menü* from 13.80SFr. Open M-Th 6am-11:30pm, F 6am-midnight, Sa 7am-midnight, Su 7:30am-11:30pm. AmEx/MC/V. ❸

CHOCOHOLICS The Swiss have long had a love affair with chocolate—milk chocolate was first concocted in here in 1876, and Nestlé, Lindt, and Toblerone all call Switzerland home. But has this seemingly innocuous romance turned into an obsession? In May 2001, the Swiss government introduced postage stamps that look and smell like squares of chocolate. (The original design called for chocolate-*flavored* stamps, but the idea was dropped for hygienic reasons.) The stamps are even packaged on paper designed to look like foil wrappers. Officially, they commemorate the centennial of Chocosulsse, the association of chocolate makers and importers, but it might just be evidence that the Swiss truly are addicted.

Hiltl, Sihlstr. 28. A surprisingly cheap vegetarian joint; salad or Indian buffet 4.60SFr per 100g. Open M-Sa 7am-11pm, Su 11am-11pm. ❶

Restaurant Mère Catherine, Nägelihof 3. Hidden in a small street near Großmünster, this yuppie restaurant offers delightful French dishes (from 21SFr) and an upscale ambience. Open daily 11am-midnight. AmEx/MC/V. ❹

ⓖ SIGHTS

IN THE ALTSTADT. Right off Paradepl. stands the 13th-century **Fraumünster;** although it's a Protestant church, Jewish artist Marc Chagall agreed to design the beautiful stained-glass windows in the late 1960s. *(Open May-Sept. 9am-6pm; Mar.-Apr. and Oct. 10am-5pm; Nov.-Feb. 10am-4pm.)* Next door, **St. Peter's Church** has the largest clock face in Europe. The twin towers of the nearby **Großmünster** have become a symbol of Zurich. Zwingli spearheaded the German-Swiss Reformation here—one of his Bibles lies in a case near the pulpit from which he preached. Venture downstairs to the 12th-century crypt to see Charlemagne's statue and sword, then climb the towers for a great view of Zurich. *(Church open Mar. 15 to Oct. 9am-6pm; Nov. to Mar. 14 10am-5pm. Tower open Mar.-Oct. daily 1:30-5pm; Nov.-Feb. Sa-Su 9:15am-5pm. Tower 2SFr.)*

MUSEUMS. The incredible ■**Kunsthaus Zürich,** Heimpl. 1, covers Western art since the 15th century. *(Take tram #3, 5, 8, or 9 to Kunsthaus. Multilingual audio tours available. Open Tu-Th 10am-9pm, F-Su 10am-5pm. 10SFr, students 6SFr; W free.)* ■**Museum Rietberg,** Gablerstr. 15, presents an exquisite collection of Asian, African, and other non-European art. *(Take tram #7 to Museum Rietberg. Open Tu and Th-Su 10am-5pm, W 10am-8pm. 6SFr, students 3SFr.)* The **Schweizerisches Landesmuseum,** Museumstr. 2, next to the main train station, encapsulates Swiss history; exhibits include 16th-century astrological instruments and Ulrich Zwingli's weapons from the fatal 1531 Battle of Kappel. *(Open Tu-Su 10:30am-5pm. 5SFr, students 3SFr.)* The museum at the **Lindt and Sprüngli Chocolate Factory,** Seestr. 204, has exhibits in German only, but the free chocolates transcend language barriers. *(Tram #1 or 8 to Kilburn. Open W-F 10am-noon and 1-4pm. Free.)*

ⓠ NIGHTLIFE

Niederdorfstraße is the epicenter of Zurich's nightlife, although women may not want to walk alone in this area at night; **Münstergasse** and **Limmatquai** are lined with cafes and bars. Pick up *ZüriTip* for more information. On Friday and Saturday nights in summer, **Hirschenplatz** (on Niederdorfstr.) hosts an assortment of impressive street performers. Locals and students guzzle beer (from 10SFr) on the terrace at **Double-U (W) Bar,** Niederdorfstr. 21. (Open M-Th 4pm-2am, F-Su until 4am.) **Oepfelchammer,** Rindermarkt 12, is a popular Swiss wine bar. (3-5SFr per glass. Open Tu-Sa 11am-12:30am.) **Cranberry,** Metzgerg. 3, is a gay-friendly bar right off Limmatquai. (Open Su-Tu 5pm-midnight, W-Th 5pm-1am, F-Sa 5pm-2am.)

ST. GALLEN ☎071

St. Gallen's main draw is the **Stiftsbibliothek** (Abbey Library), a baroque library designated as a World Heritage Treasure by UNESCO. Visitors marvel at the lavishly carved and polished shelves, rows of gilt-spined books, and ancient manuscripts. (☎227 34 16. Open M-Sa 10am-5pm, Su 10am-4pm; closed Nov.-Dec. 7SFr, students 5SFr.) Often overshadowed by the library, but no less beautiful, is the **Kathedrale St. Gallen,** which has enormous stained glass windows, intricately carved confessionals, and impressive murals. (☎227 33 88. Open daily 7am-6pm except during mass.) In late June, the **Open-Air St. Gallen Music Festival** features over 20 live bands. Past headliners have included the Red Hot Chili Peppers, B.B. King, and James Brown. (☎(087) 887 79 94; www.openairsg.ch. Tickets 104-134SFr.)

Trains roll to: Bern (2½hr., 5am-10:40pm, 63-65SFr); Geneva (4½hr., 5am-8:40pm, 94SFr); Munich (3hr., 4 per day 8:30am-6:30pm, 62SFr, under 26 51SFr); and Zurich (1hr., 5am-10:40pm, 26-34SFr). To get to the **tourist office**, Bahnhofpl. 1a, from the train station, cross the bus stop and pass the fountain on the left; it's on the right. (☎227 37 37. Open M-F 9am-6pm, Sa 9am-noon. City tours June-Sept. M, W, and F 2pm. 15SFr.) **Internet** access is available at **Media Lounge**, Katherineng. 10. (☎244 30 90. 2SFr per 10min. Open M-F 9am-9pm, sporadic hours Sa-Su.) The impeccably clean 🏠**Jugendherberge St. Gallen (HI) ❷**, Jüchstr. 25, has a TV room, library, and Internet access (1SFr per 4min.). From the Appenzeller/Trogener station next to the main station, take the orange train on track #12 (dir.: Trogen) to Schülerhaus; from the stop, walk uphill, turn left across the tracks, and head downhill. (☎245 47 77. Reception daily 7-10am and 5-10:30pm. Check-out 10am. Closed Dec.-Feb. Dorms 26SFr; singles 46SFr; doubles 72SFr; nonmembers add 6SFr. AmEx/MC/V.) Perched high above the hostel, **Restaurant Scheitlinsbüchel ❸**, Scheitlinsbüchelweg 10, offers a sublime view and traditional Swiss meals. (Open Tu-Su 9am-late.) The **Migros supermarket,** St. Leonhardstr., and adjoining buffet restaurant are one block behind the train station. (Open M-W and F 8am-6:30pm, Th 8am-9pm, Sa 8am-5pm.) **Postal code:** CH-9000.

LUCERNE (LUZERN)   ☎041

Lucerne is the Swiss traveler's dream come true. The small, cosmopolitan city is in a region full of outdoors possibilities. Sunrise over the famous **Mt. Pilatus** has hypnotized hikers and artists—including Twain, Wagner, and Goethe—for centuries.

🖥🚍 TRANSPORTATION AND PRACTICAL INFORMATION. Trains leave Bahnhofpl. for: Basel (1¼hr., 1-2 per hr. 4:40am-11:50pm, 29SFr); Bern (1½hr., 1-2 per hr. 4:40am-11:50pm, 30SFr); Geneva (3½hr., every hr. 4:40am-9:55pm, 64SFr); Interlaken (2hr., every hr. 6:30am-7:35pm, 26SFr); Lausanne (2½hr., every hr. 4:40am-9:55pm, 56SFr); Lugano (3hr., every hr. 6:40am-10:15pm, 56SFr); and Zurich (1hr., 2 per hr. 4:55am-11:10pm, 20SFr). **VBL buses** depart from in front of the station and provide extensive coverage of Lucerne (1 zone 2.40SFr, 2 zones 3.60SFr, 3 zones 5.60SFr; day pass 9SFr; Swiss Pass valid); **route maps** are available at the tourist office. The **tourist office,** in the station, has free city guides, makes hotel reservations and sells the **Visitor's Card.** (☎227 17 17. Open May-Oct. M-F 8:30am-7:30pm, Sa-Su 9am-7:30pm; Nov.-Apr. M-F 8:30am-6pm, Sa-Su 9am-6pm.) **C+A Clothing,** on Hertensteinstr. at the top of the *Altstadt*, has two free but busy **Internet** terminals. (Open M-W 9am-6:30pm, Th-F 9am-9pm, Sa 8:30am-4pm.) The **post office** is on the corner of Bahnhofstr. and Bahnhofpl. Address mail to be held: Postlagernde Briefe für Firstname SURNAME, Hauptpost, **CH-6000** Luzern 1. (Open M-F 7:30am-6:30pm, Sa 8am-noon.)

🛏🍴 ACCOMMODATIONS AND FOOD. Inexpensive beds are limited in Lucerne, so call ahead. To reach 🏠**Backpackers ❷**, Alpenquai 42, turn right from the station on Inseliquai and follow it until it turns into Alpenquai (20min.); the hostel is on the right (☎360 04 20. Laundry 8SFr. Internet 10SFr per hr. Reception daily 7:30-10am and 4-11pm. 2- to 4-bed dorms 27-33SFr.) Until 1998, **Hotel Löwengraben ❷**, Löwengraben 18, was a prison; now it's a trendy, clean hostel with a bar, a restaurant, and all-night dance parties for guests every summer Saturday. (☎417 12 12.

Breakfast 11SFr. Internet 15SFr per hr. 3- to 4-bed dorms 30SFr; double with shower 140-165SFr.) **Markets** along the river sell cheap fresh goods on Tuesday and Saturday mornings. Additionally, there's a **Migros supermarket** at the train station. (Open M-W and Sa 6:30am-8pm, Th-F 6:30am-9pm, Su 8am-8pm.)

■ ■ **SIGHTS AND NIGHTLIFE.** The *Altstadt*, across the river over Spreuer-brücke from the station, is famous for its frescoed houses; the best examples are those on Hirschenpl. The 660-year-old **Kapellbrücke,** a wooden-roofed bridge, runs from left of the train station to the *Altstadt* and is ornately decorated with Swiss historical scenes; further down the river, the **Spreuerbrücke** is decorated by Kaspar Meglinger's eerie *Totentanz* (Dance of Death) paintings. On the hills above the river, are the **Museggmauer** and its towers, all that remain of the medieval city's ramparts. Three of the towers are accessible to visitors and provide panoramas of the city; walk along St. Karliquai, head uphill to the right, and follow the brown castle signs. (Open daily 8am-7pm.) To the east is the magnificent **Löwen-denkmal** (Lion Monument), the dying lion of Lucerne, which is carved into a cliff on Denkmalstr. The **Picasso Museum,** Am Rhyn Haus, Furreng. 21, displays 200 intimate photographs of Picasso as well as a large collection of his unpublished works. From Schwanenpl., take Rathausquai to Furreng. (Open Apr.-Oct. daily 10am-6pm; Nov.-Mar. 11am-4pm. 8SFr, with guest card 7SFr, students 5SFr.) The ■**Verkehrshaus der Schweiz** (Swiss Transport Museum), Lidostr. 5, has interactive displays on all kinds of vehicles, but the real highlight is the warehouse of trains. Take bus #6, 8, or 24 to Verkehrshaus. (Open Apr.-Oct. daily 10am-6pm; Nov.-Mar. 10am-5pm. 21SFr, students 19SFr; with SwissPass 16SFr, with Eurail 14SFr.)

Lucerne's nightlife is more about lingering than club-hopping. **The Loft,** Halden-str. 21, is a smoky club playing hip-hop and house. (Open W-Th 10pm-3am and F-Su 9pm-4am. Cover 10-15SFr.) Lucerne attracts big names for its two jazz festivals: **Blue Balls Festival** (3rd week in July) and **Blues Festival** (2nd week in Nov.).

■ **DAYTRIPS FROM LUCERNE: MT. PILATUS AND RIGI KULM.** The view of the Alps from the top of **Mt. Pilatus** (2132m) is absolutely phenomenal. For the most memorable trip, catch a boat from Lucerne to Alpnachstad (1½hr.), ascend by the world's steepest **cogwheel train,** then descend by cable car to Krienz and take the bus back to Lucerne (entire trip 78.40SFr; with Eurail or SwissPass 40-43SFr). For less money and more exercise, take a train or boat to Hegiswil and hike up to Fräkmüntegg (3hr.), then get on the cable car at the halfway point (23SFr; 19SFr with Eurail or SwissPass). Across the sea from Pilatus soars the **Rigi Kulm,** which has a magnificent view of the lake and its neighbor. Ferries run from Lucerne to Vitznau, where you can catch a cogwheel train to the summit. You can also conquer Rigi on foot; it's 5hr. from Vitznau to the top, and anyone who tires out halfway can pick up the train at Rigi Kaltbad (3hr. up the hill) and ride the rest of the way. Return by train, take the cable car from Rigi Kaltbad to Weggis, and head back to Lucerne by boat (round-trip 87SFr; with Eurail or Swisspass 29SFr).

JUNGFRAU REGION

The Jungfrau area has attracted tourists for hundreds of years with glorious hiking trails and snow-capped peaks. From Interlaken, the valley splits at the foot of the Jungfrau: the eastern valley contains Grindelwald and the western valley holds many smaller towns. The two valleys are divided by an easily hikeable ridge.

INTERLAKEN ☎ 033

Interlaken lies between the Thunersee and the Brienzersee at the foot of the largest mountains in Switzerland. With easy access to these natural playgrounds, Interlaken has earned its rightful place as one of Switzerland's prime tourist attractions and as its top outdoor adventure spot.

🖥🔁 TRANSPORTATION AND PRACTICAL INFORMATION. The Westbahnhof (☎826 47 50) and Ostbahnhof (☎828 73 19) have **trains** to: Basel (5:30am-10:30pm, 56SFr); Bern (6:35am-10:30pm, 24SFr); Geneva (5:30am-9:30pm, 63SFr); Lucerne (5:30am-8:35pm, 26SFr); Lugano/Locarno (5:30am-4:35pm, 87SFr); and Zurich (5:30am-10:30pm, 62SFr). The Ostbahnhof also sends trains to Grindelwald (June-Sept. every 30min., Sept.-May every hr. 6:35am-10:35pm; 9.80SFr).

The **tourist office**, Höheweg 37, in the Hotel Metropole, offers free maps. (☎826 53 00. Open July-Aug. M-F 8am-6pm, Sa 8am-5pm, Su 10am-noon and 4-6pm; Sept.-June M-F 8am-noon and 1:30-6pm, Sa 9am-noon.) Rent **bikes** at either train station. (30SFr per day. Open daily 6am-7pm.) For **snow and weather information,** call ☎828 79 31. In case of emergency, call the **police** ☎117 or the **hospital** ☎826 26 26. **YESS** on Centralstr. has 5 terminals for **Internet access.** (4SFr per 20min. Open daily 11am-11pm.) **Postal Code:** CH-3800.

🔂🔃 ACCOMMODATIONS AND FOOD. 🔳**Backpackers Villa Sonnenhof ❷,** Alpenstr. 16, diagonally across the Höhenmatte from the tourist office, is friendly and low-key. (☎826 71 71. Internet 10SFr per hr. Mountain bikes 28SFr per day. Laundry 10SFr. Breakfast and lockers included. Reception 7:30-11am and 4-10pm. Check-out 9:30am. 4- to 7-bed dorms 29-32SFr; doubles 82-88SFr; triples 111-120SFr. 5SFr extra for balcony. AmEx/MC/V.) 🔳**Swiss Adventure Hostel ❷,** in the tiny town of Boltigen, provides access to all of Interlaken's activities with beds far from the craziness of the town. A free shuttle runs to and from Interlaken each day (40min.); call for times and availability. The adventure company run out of this hostel offers the same activities as the Interlaken companies, but with a more personal touch. (☎773 73 73. 4- to 10-bed dorms 20SFr; double with shower 70SFr; quad with shower 100SFr. Special deals if combined with adventure sports.) **Happy Inn,** Rosenstr. 17, lives up to its name with a friendly staff. From Westbahnhof, turn left towards the tourist office, then right on Rosenstr. at Centralpl. (☎822 32 25. Breakfast 8SFr. Reception 7am-6pm. Call early for rooms. Dorms 22SFr; singles 38SFr; doubles 76SFr.) Most hostels serve cheap food—**Migros supermarket ❶,** across from the Ostbahnhof or behind the Westbahnhof, and its restaurant is available. (Open M-Th 8am-7pm, F 8am-9pm, Sa 7:30am-5pm).

🔂🔃 OUTDOORS AND HIKING. Interlaken offers a wide range of adrenaline-pumping activities. **Alpin Raft** (☎823 41 00), the most established company in Interlaken, has qualified, personable guides and offers: paragliding (150SFr); canyoning (110-195SFr); river rafting (95-109SFr); skydiving (380SFr); bungee jumping (125-165SFr); and hang gliding (180SFr). All prices include transportation and lessons from any hostel in Interlaken. A number of horse and hiking tours, as well as rock-lessons, are also available upon request. **Outdoor Interlaken** (☎826 77 19) offers rock-climbing lessons (89SFr per half-day) and **white-water kayaking** tours (155SFr per half-day). The owner of **Skydiving Xdream,** Stefan Heuser, has been on the Swiss skydiving team for 17 years. (Skydiving 380SFr. ☎079 759 34 83. Open Apr.-Oct.)

Interlaken's most traversed trail climbs to the **Harder Kulm** (1310m). From the Ostbahnhof, head toward town, take the 1st road bridge right across the river, and follow the yellow signs that later give way to white-red-white markings on the

> Interlaken's adventure sports industry is thrilling, but accidents do happen. On July 27, 1999, 19 tourists were killed by a sudden flash flood while canyoning. Be aware that you participate in all adventure sports at your own risk.

rocks. From the top, signs lead back down to the Westbahnhof. A funicular runs from the trailhead near the Ostbahnhof to the top from May-October. (2½hr. up, 1½hr. down. May to mid-Oct. 13.40SFr, round-trip 21SFr; 25% Eurailpass and SwissPass discount.) For flatter **trails,** turn left from the train station and left before the bridge, then follow the canal over to the nature reserve on the shore of the Thunersee. The trail winds up the Lombach river and through pastures at the base of the Harder Kulm back toward town (3hr.).

GRINDELWALD   ☎036

Grindelwald, launching point to the only glaciers accessible by foot in the Bernese Oberland, crouches beneath the north face of the Eiger. The town has all kinds of hikes, from easy valley walks to challenging peaks for top climbers. The **Bergführerbüro** (Mountain Guides Office), 200m past the tourist office, sells hiking maps and coordinates glacier walks, ice climbing, and mountaineering. (☎853 52 00. Open June-Oct. M-Sa 9am-noon and 3-6pm, Su 4-6pm.) The **Lower Glacier** *(Untere Grindelwaldgletscher)* hike is moderately steep (5hr.). To reach the trailhead, walk up the main street away from the station and follow the signs downhill to Pfinstegg. Hikers can either walk the first forested section of the trail (1hr.), following signs up to Pfinstegg., or take a funicular to the Pfinstegg. hut (July to mid-Sept. 8am-7pm; mid-Sept. to June 8am-4pm; 9.80SFr). From the hut, signs lead up the glacier-filled valley to Stieregg., a hut that offers food.

The **Jungfraubahn** runs to Grindelwald from Interlaken's *Ostbahnhof* (40min., 6:35am-10:30pm, 9.80SFr). The **tourist office,** located in the Sport-Zentrum to the right of the station, provides chairlift information and a list of free guided excursions. (☎854 12 12. Open July-Aug. M-F 8am-7pm, Sa 8am-6pm, Su 9-11am and 3-5pm; Sept.-June M-F 8am-noon and 2-6pm, Sa 8am-noon and 2-5pm.) **Hotel Hirschen** ❹, to the right of the tourist office, offers clean, bright rooms with comfortable beds. (☎854 84 84. Breakfast included. Reception daily 8am-10pm. Singles 90-135SFr; doubles 150-220SFr.) To reach the **Jugendherberge (HI)** ❷, head left out of the train station for 400m, then cut uphill to the right just before Chalet Alpenblume and follow the steep trail all the way up the hill. (☎853 10 09. Breakfast and lockers included. Reception daily 7:30-10am and 3pm-midnight. Dorms 27.50-29.50SFr; doubles 69SFr, with toilet and shower 101SFr. Nonmembers add 6SFr. AmEx/MC.) **Tea Room Riggenburg** ❶, past the tourist office in the opposite direction from the station, offers soups, salads, lasagna, and fresh-baked desserts. (Open Tu-Sa 7am-10pm, Su 8am-6pm.) There's a **Co-op supermarket** on Hauptstr., across from the tourist office. (Open M-F 8am-6:30pm, Sa 8am-4pm.)

VALAIS

The Valais occupies the deep, wide, glacial gorge traced by the Rhône river. Though mountain resorts can be over-touristed, the region's spectacular peaks and the skiing, hiking, and climbing make fighting traffic worthwhile.

ZERMATT AND THE MATTERHORN   ☎027

The valley blocks out the great Alpine summits that ring Zermatt, allowing the **Matterhorn** (4478m) to rise alone above the town. Spectacular, well-marked ski paths are accessible to all visitors, including **Europe's longest run,** the 13km trail from

Klein Matterhorn to Zermatt. A one-day ski pass for any of the area's regions runs 60-77SFr. The **Zermatt Alpin Center,** which houses both the **Bergführerbüro** (Guide's Office; ☎966 24 60) and the **Skischulbüro** (Ski School Office; ☎966 24 66), is located past the post office from the station; the Bergführerbüro provides ski passes, four-day weather forecasts, and info on guided climbing. (Open July-Sept. M-F 8:30am-noon and 3:30-7pm, Sa 3:30-7pm, Su 10am-noon and 3:30-7pm; late Dec. to mid-May daily 5-7pm.) Rental prices for **skis** and **snowboards** are standardized throughout Zermatt (28-50SFr per day, 123-215SFr per week). Try **Slalom Sport,** on Kirchstr. (☎966 23 66; open M-Sa 8am-noon and 2-6:30pm), or **Bayard Sports,** directly across from the station (☎966 49 60; open daily 8am-noon and 2-7pm). **Freeride Film Factory** (☎213 38 07) offers custom **hiking, biking,** and **climbing** expeditions (160-250SFr) that come with a videotape of your trek.

To preserve the Alpine air, cars and buses are banned in Zermatt; the only way in is the hourly **BVZ** (Brig-Visp-Zermatt) rail line. Connect to Brig (1½hr.; 6am-9pm; 34SFr, round-trip 67SFr, and on to Lausanne 73SFr, round-trip 140SFr). The **tourist office,** on Bahnhofpl. in the station, sells a hiking map for 25.90SFr. (☎966 81 00. Open mid-June to mid-Oct. M-F 8:30am-6pm, Sa 8:30am-6:30pm, Su 9:30am-noon and 4-6:30pm; mid-Oct. to mid-Dec. and May to mid-June M-F 8:30am-noon and 1:30-6pm, Sa 8:30am-noon; mid-Dec. to Apr. 8:30am-noon and 1:30-6:30pm, Sa 8:30am-6:30pm, Su 9:30am-noon and 4-6:30pm.) **Hotel Bahnhof ❷,** on Bahnhofstr. to the left of the station, provides hotel housing at hostel rates. (☎967 24 06. Dorms 30SFr; singles 54-56SFr, with shower 64-68SFr; doubles 84-86SFr/94-96SFr. MC/V.) Treat yourself to Swiss fare for reasonable prices at **Walliserkanne ❸,** on Bahnhofstr. next to the post office. (Open 9am-midnight. AmEx/MC/V.) Pick up groceries at the **Co-op Center,** opposite the station. (Open M-F 8:15am-12:15pm and 1:45-6:30pm, Sa 8:15am-12:15pm and 1:45-6pm.) **Postal code:** CH-3920.

FRENCH SWITZERLAND

All around Lac Léman, hills sprinkled with villas and blanketed by patchwork vineyards seem tame and settled—until the haze clears. From behind the hills surge rough-hewn mountain peaks with the energizing promise of unpopulated wilderness and wide lonely expanses.

GENEVA (GENÈVE)   ☎022

A stay in Geneva will likely change your definition of diversity. As the most international city in Switzerland, Geneva is a brew of 178,000 unlikely neighbors: wealthy businessmen speed past dreadlocked skaters in the street while nuclear families stroll past hardworking artists squatting in abandoned factories. Part of Geneva's malleability comes from its strongly international component; only one-third of the city's residents are natives of the canton. Today, multinational organizations (including the Red Cross and the United Nations) continue to lend the city an international feel.

⊠ INTERCITY TRANSPORTATION

Flights: Cointrin Airport (GVA; ☎717 71 11, flight info ☎799 31 11) is a hub for **Swiss Airlines** (☎(0848) 85 20 00) and also serves **Air France** (☎827 87 87) and **British Airways** (☎(0848) 80 10 10). Several direct flights per day to Amsterdam, London, New York, Paris, and Rome. Bus #10 runs to the Gare Cornavin (15min., every 5-10min., 2.20SFr). The train provides a shorter trip (6min., every 10min., 4.80SFr).

Trains: Trains run approximately 4:30am-1am. **Gare Cornavin,** pl. Cornavin, is the main station. To: **Basel** (2¾hr., every hr., 63-71SFr); **Bern** (2hr., every hr., 47SFr); **Interlaken** (3hr., every hr., 63SFr); **Lausanne** (40min., every 20-30min., 19SFr); **Montreux** (1hr., 2 per hr., 29SFr); **Zurich** (3½hr., every hr., 76SFr). Ticket counter open M-F 8:30am-6:30pm, Sa 9am-5pm. **Gare des Eaux-Vives** (☎736 16 20), on av. de la Gare des Eaux-Vives (tram #12 to Amandoliers SNCF), connects to France's regional rail through **Annecy** (1½hr., 6 per day, 14SFr) or **Chamonix** (2½hr., 4 per day, 24SFr). Ticket office open M-F 9am-6pm, Sa 11am-5:45pm.

▐▌ LOCAL TRANSPORTATION

Carry your passport with you at all times; the French border is never more than a few minutes away and buses frequently cross it. Ticket purchasing is largely on the honor system, but you may be fined 60SFr for evading fares. Much of the city can be walked in good weather.

Public Transportation: Geneva has an efficient bus and tram network. **Transport Publics Genevois** (☎308 34 34), next to the tourist office in Gare Cornavin, provides *Le Réseau* (a free map of bus routes) and inexpensive timetables. Open M-Sa 7am-7pm, Su 10am-6pm. **Day passes** 6SFr-12SFr. Stamp multi-use tickets before boarding. Buses run roughly 5:30am-midnight; **Noctambus** (3SFr, 1:30-4:30am) runs when the others don't. SwissPass valid on all buses; Eurail not valid.

Taxis: Taxi-Phone (☎331 41 33). 6.80SFr plus 2.90SFr per km. Taxi from airport to city 30SFr, max. 4 passengers (15-20min.).

Bike Rental: Geneva has well-marked bike paths and special traffic lights for spoked traffic. For routes, get *Itineraires cyclables* or *Tours de ville avec les vélos de location* from the tourist office. Behind the station, **Genève Roule,** pl. Montbrillant 17 (☎740 13 43), has free bikes available (50SFr deposit; hefty fine if bike is lost or stolen). Slightly nicer neon bikes from 5SFr per day. Open daily 7:30am-9:30pm.

Hitchhiking: Those headed to Germany or northern Switzerland take bus #4 to Jardin Botanique. Those headed to France take bus #4 to Palettes, then line D to St. Julien. *Let's Go* does not recommend hitchhiking.

▟▐ ORIENTATION AND PRACTICAL INFORMATION

The labyrinthine cobbled streets and quiet squares of the historic *vieille ville*, around **Cathédrale de St-Pierre,** are the heart of Geneva. Across the **Rhône River** to the north, banks and five-star hotels gradually give way to lakeside promenades, **International Hill,** and rolling parks. Across the **Arve River** to the south lies the village of **Carouge,** home to student bars and clubs (take tram #12 or 13 to pl. du Marché).

TOURIST, FINANCIAL, AND LOCAL SERVICES

Tourist Offices: The **main office,** r. du Mont-Blanc 18 (☎909 70 00), in the Central Post Office Building. From Cornavin, walk 5min. toward the Pont du Mont-Blanc. Staff books hotel rooms for 5SFr, leads walking tours, and offers free city maps. Open July-Aug. daily 9am-6pm; Sept.-June M-Sa 9am-6pm. During the summer, head for **Centre d'Accueil et de Renseignements** (☎731 46 47), an office-in-a-bus parked in pl. Mont-Blanc, by the Metro Shopping entrance to Cornavin Station. Lists free performances and makes hotel reservations. Open mid-June to mid-Sept. daily 9am-9pm.

Consulates: Australia, chemin des Fins 2 (☎799 91 00). **Canada,** av. de l'Ariana 5 (☎919 92 00). **New Zealand,** chemin des Fins 2 (☎929 03 50). **South Africa,** r. de Rhône 65 (☎849 54 54). **UK,** r. de Vermont 37 (☎918 24 26). **US,** r. Versonnex 5 (☎798 16 05; recorded info ☎798 16 15).

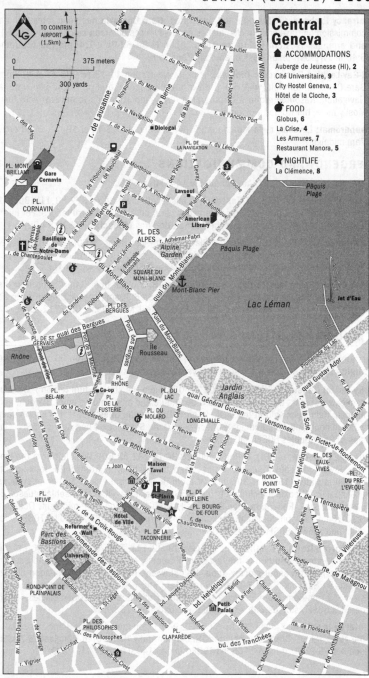

TO COINTRIN
AIRPORT ✈
(1.5km)

0   375 meters

0   300 yards

Central Geneva

🏠 ACCOMMODATIONS

Auberge de Jeunesse (HI), 2
Cité Universitaire, 9
City Hostel Geneva, 1
Hôtel de la Cloche, 3

🍴 FOOD

Globus, 6
La Crise, 4
Les Armures, 7
Restaurant Manora, 5

⭐ NIGHTLIFE

La Clémence, 8

SWITZERLAND

Currency Exchange: ATMs offer the best rates. **Gare Cornavin** has good rates with no commission on traveler's checks, makes cash advances on credit cards (min. 200SFr), and arranges Western Union transfers. Open M-Sa 6:50am-7:40pm, Su 6:50am-6:40pm. Western Union desk open daily 7am-7pm.

Bi-Gay-Lesbian Resources: Diologai, r. de la Navigation 11-13 (☎906 40 40). From Gare Cornavin, turn left, walk 5min. down r. de Lausanne, and turn right onto r. de la Navigation. Resource group with programs from support groups to outdoor activities. Mostly male, but women welcome.

Laundromat: Lavseul, r. de Monthoux 29. Wash 5SFr, dry 1SFr per 10min. Open daily 7am-midnight.

EMERGENCY AND COMMUNICATIONS

Emergency: Police: ☎117. **Ambulance:** ☎144. **Fire:** ☎118.

Medical Assistance: Hôpital Cantonal, r. Micheli-du-Crest 24 (☎372 33 11). Bus #1 or 5 or tram #12. Door #2 is for emergency care, door #3 for consultations. For information on walk-in clinics, contact the **Association des Médecins** (☎320 84 20).

Internet Access: Point 6, r. de Vieux-Billard 7a, off r. des Bains (☎800 26 00). 5SFr per hr. Open daily noon-midnight. **Connections Net World,** r. de Monthoux 58. 3SFr per 30min., 5SFr per hr. Copier available. Open M-Sa 9:30am-2:30am, Su 1pm-2am.

Post Office: Poste Centrale, r. de Mont-Blanc 18, a block from Gare Cornavin in the stately Hôtel des Postes. Open M-F 7:30am-6pm, Sa 8:30am-noon. Address mail to be held: *Poste Restante,* Firstname SURNAME, Genève 1 Mont-Blanc, **CH-1211,** Geneva.

▌ ACCOMMODATIONS

The indispensable *Info Jeunes,* free at the tourist office, lists about 50 options; the highlights are below. Even for short stays, reservations are a must.

City Hostel Geneva, r. Ferrier 2 (☎901 15 00). From the station, turn left on r. de Lausanne, walk 5min., then turn left onto r. de Prieuré and right onto r. Ferrier. TV room and kitchen. Heinekens sold at the desk. Internet 8SFr per hr. Sheets 3SFr. Reception daily 7:30am-noon and 1pm-midnight. Check-out 10am. Single-sex 4-bed dorms 25SFr; singles 55SFr; doubles 80SFr. MC/V. ❷

Auberge de Jeunesse (HI), r. Rothschild 28-30 (☎732 62 60). Walk left from the station down r. de Lausanne for 10min., then turn right on r. Rothschild. Restaurant, kitchen facilities (1SFr per 30min.), TV room, lockers, library, and 3 Internet stations (7SFr per hr.) Breakfast included. Laundry 6SFr. Special facilities for disabled guests. 6-night max. stay. Reception June-Sept. daily 6:30-10am and 2pm-midnight; Oct.-May 6:30-10am and 4pm-midnight. Lockout 10am-3pm. Dorms 25SFr; doubles 70SFr, with toilet and shower 80SFr; quads 110SFr. MC/V. ❷

Cité Universitaire, av. Miremont 46 (☎839 22 11). Take bus #3 (dir.: Crets-de-Champel) from the station to the last stop. TV rooms, restaurant, disco (Th and Sa, free to guests), and a small grocery shop. Hall showers. Reception M-F 8am-noon and 2-10pm, Sa 8am-noon and 6-10pm, Su 9-11am and 6-10pm. Check-out 10am. Dorm lockout 11am-6pm. Dorm curfew 11pm. Dorms (July-Sept. only) 20SFr; singles 49SFr; doubles 66SFr; studios with kitchenette and bathroom 75SFr. ❷

Hôtel de la Cloche, r. de la Cloche 6 (☎732 94 81), off quai du Mont-Blanc across from the Noga Hilton. Breakfast included. Reception daily 8am-10pm. Singles 65-70SFr; doubles 85-95SFr; triples 110SFr-140SFr; quads 140SFr. AmEx/MC/V. ❹

Camping Pointe-à-la-Bise, Chemin de la Bise (☎ 752 12 96). Take bus #8 to Rive, then bus E (north) to Bise and walk 10min. to the lake. Reception daily 8am-noon and 2-9pm. Open Apr.-Sept. 6.20SFr per person, 9SFr per tent space. No tents provided. Beds 15SFr. 4-person bungalows 60SFr. ❶

🍴 FOOD

You can find anything from sushi to *paella* in Geneva, but you may need a banker's salary to foot the bill. Do-it-yourselfers can pick up basics at *boulangeries*, *pâtisseries*, or at the ubiquitous supermarkets. Many supermarkets also have attached cafeterias; try the **Co-op** on the corner of r. du Commerce and r. du Rhône, in the Centre Rhône Fusterie. (Open M 9am-6:45pm; Tu-W and F 8:30am-6:45pm; Th 8:30am-8pm; Sa 8:30am-5pm.) There are cheap restaurants in the *vieille ville* near the cathedral. To the south, the village of Carouge is known for its cozy pizzerias and funky, chic brasseries. Around pl. du Cirque and plaine de Plainpalais, cheap, student-oriented tea rooms offer traditional fare at reasonable prices.

Le Rozzel, Grand-Rue 18. Take bus #5 to pl. Neuve, then walk up the hill past the cathedral on r. Jean-Calvin to Grand-Rue. Large dinner crepes (4-18SFr), dessert crepes (5-9SFr). Open M 7am-4pm, Tu-W 7am-7pm, Th-F 7am-10pm, Sa 9am-10pm. ❷

Restaurant Manora, r. de Cornavin 4, to the right of the station in the Placette department store. This huge self-serve restaurant has a varied and high-quality selection and free water (rare in Switzerland). Open M-Sa 7:30am-9:30pm, Su 9am-9:30pm. ❶

Les Armures, r. due Puits-St-Pierre 1, near the main entrance to the cathedral. Enjoy the elegance in the heart of the *Altstadt*. Fondue 24-26SFr. Pizza 14-17SFr. Open M-F 8am-midnight, Sa 11am-midnight, Su 11am-11pm. ❹

Globus, r. de Rhône 48, on pl. du Molard. Inexpensive gourmet delights, including fresh seafood. Open M-W and F 7:30am-6:45pm, Th 7:30am-8pm, Sa 8am-5:45pm. ❷

Chez Ma Cousine, r. de la Fontaine 6, in the *vieille ville*. Their specialty is chicken (13.90SFr). Open M-F 7am-midnight, Sa 11am-midnight, Su 11am-11pm. ❷

La Crise, r. de Chantepoulet 13. From the station, turn right on r. de Cornavin and left on r. de Chantepoulet. This small but popular snack bar dishes out tasty and veggie-friendly meals at reasonable prices. Open M-F 6am-3pm and 5-8pm, Sa 6am-3pm. ❷

👁 SIGHTS

The city's most interesting historical sites are in a dense, easily walkable space. The tourist office offers 2hr. **walking tours.** (Mid-June to Sept. M-Sa 10am; Oct.-May Sa 10am. 12SFr, students and seniors 8SFr.)

VIEILLE VILLE. From 1536 to 1564, Calvin preached at the **Cathédrale de St-Pierre.** The **north tower** provides a commanding view of the old town. *(Open June-Sept. daily 9am-7pm; Oct.-May M-Sa 10am-noon and 2-5pm, Su 11am-12:30pm and 1:30-5pm. Tower 3SFr.)* Ruins, including a Roman sanctuary and a 4th-century basilica, rest in an **archaeological site** below the cathedral. *(Open June-Sept. Tu-Sa 11am–5pm, Su 10am-5pm; Oct.-May Tu-Sa 2-5pm, Su 10am-noon and 2-5pm. 5SFr, students 3SFr.)* At the west end of the *vieille ville* sits the 14th-century **Maison Tavel,** which now houses a history museum. *(Open Tu-Su 10am-5pm. Free.)* Across the street is the **Hôtel de Ville** (town hall), where world leaders met on August 22, 1864, to sign the Geneva Convention that still governs war conduct today. The **Grand-Rue,** which begins at the Hôtel de Ville, is crammed with clustered medieval workshops and 18th-century mansions; plaques commemorate famous residents, including Jean-Jacques Rousseau, born at #40. Below the cathedral, along r. de la Croix-Rouge, the **Parc des Bastions** stretches from pl. Neuve to pl. des Philosophes and includes **Le Mur des Réformateurs (Reformers' Wall)**, a sprawling collection of bas-relief figures of the Reformers themselves. The park's center walkway leads to the ▨**Petit-Palais,** Terrasse St-Victor 2, a beautiful mansion containing art by Picasso, Renoir, Gauguin, and Chagall, as well as themed exhibitions. *(Bus #36 to Petit Palais or #1, 3, or 5 to Claparède. Open M-F 10am-6pm, Sa-Su 10am-5pm. 10SFr, students 5SFr.)*

WATERFRONT. As you descend from the cathedral to the lake, medieval lanes give way to wide quais and chic boutiques. Down quai Gustave Ardor, the **Jet d'Eau,** the world's highest fountain, spews a spectacular 7-ton plume of water 140m into the air. The **floral clock** in the nearby **Jardin Anglais** pays homage to Geneva's watch industry. It's probably Geneva's most overrated attraction and was once the most hazardous—the clock had to be cut back almost 1m because tourists, intent on taking the perfect photograph, repeatedly backed into oncoming traffic. On the north shore, the beach **Pâquis Plage,** quai du Mont-Blanc 30, is popular with locals. *(Open 9am-8:30pm. 2SFr.)*

INTERNATIONAL HILL. The International Red Cross building contains the moving ▨**International Red Cross and Red Crescent Museum,** Av. de la Paix 17. *(Bus #8 or F to Appia or bus V or Z to Ariana. Open W-M 10am-5pm. 10SFr, students 5SFr.)* The nearby European headquarters of the **United Nations** is in the same building that sheltered the now-defunct League of Nations. The constant traffic of international diplomats (often in handsome non-Western dress) provides more excitement than the dull guided tour. *(Open July-Aug. daily 10am-5pm; Apr.-June and Sept.-Oct. daily 10am-noon and 2-4pm; Nov.-Mar. M-F 10am-noon and 2-4pm. 8.50SFr, seniors and students 6.50SFr.)*

♪ ▨ ENTERTAINMENT AND NIGHTLIFE

Genève Agenda, available at the tourist office, is your guide to fun, with event listings ranging from major festivals to movies (be warned—a movie runs about 16SFr). In July and August, the **Cinelac** turns Genève Plage into an open-air cinema screening mostly American films. **Free jazz concerts** take place in July and August in Parc de la Grange. Geneva hosts the biggest celebration of **American Independence Day** outside the US (July 4), and the **Fêtes de Genève** in early August is filled with international music and fireworks. The best party is **L'Escalade** in early December, which lasts a full weekend and commemorates the dramatic repulsion of invading Savoyard troops.

Place Bourg-de-Four, in the *vieille ville* below the cathedral, attracts students and professionals to its charming terraces and old-world atmosphere. **Place du Molard,** on the right bank by the pont du Mont-Blanc, offers terrace cafes and big, loud bars and clubs. **Les Paquis,** near Gare Cornavin and pl. de la Navigation, is the city's red-light district, but it also has a wide array of rowdy, low-lit bars, many with an ethnic flavor. **Carouge,** across the river Arve, is a student-friendly locus of nightlife activity. Generations of students have eaten at the famous ▨**La Clémence,** pl. du Bourg-de-Four 20. (Open M-Th 7am-12:30am, F-Sa 7am-1:30am.)

LAUSANNE ☎021

Lausanne's unique museums, distinctive neighborhoods, and lazy waterfront make it well worth a stay. In the *vieille ville*, two flights of medieval stairs lead to the Gothic **Cathédrale.** (Open July to mid-Sept. M-F 7am-7pm, Sa-Su 8am-7pm; mid-Sept. to June closes 5:30pm.) Below the cathedral is the **Hôtel de Ville,** on pl. de la Palud, the meeting point for guided tours of the town. (Tours M-Sa 10am and 3pm. 10SFr, students free. English available.) The ▨**Collection de l'Art Brut,** av. Bergières 11, is filled with disturbing and beautiful sculptures, drawings, and paintings by artists on the fringe—including institutionalized schizophrenics, poor and uneducated peasants, and convicted criminals. Take bus #2 or 3 to Jomini. (Open July-Aug. daily 11am-6pm; Sept.-June Tu-F 11am-1pm and 2-6pm, Sa-Su 11am-6pm. 6SFr, students 4SFr.) The **Musée Olympique**, Quai d'Ouchy 1, is a high-tech temple to modern Olympians with an extensive video collection, allowing visitors to relive almost any Olympic moment. Take bus #2 to Ouchy. (Open May-Sept. daily 9am-6pm, Th until 8pm; Oct.-Apr. Tu-Su 9am-6pm, Th until 8pm. 14SFr, students 9SFr.) In Ouchy, several booths along quai de Belgique and pl. de la Navigation rent **pedal boats** (10SFr per 30min.) and offer water skiing or wake boarding on **Lake Léman** (30SFr per 15min.).

Trains leave from pl. de la Gare 9 for: Basel (2½hr., every hr. 5:25am-9:25pm, 68SFr); Geneva (50min., every 20min. 4:55am-12:45am, 19SFr); Montreux (20min., every 30min. 5:25am-2:25am, 10SFr); Paris (4hr., 4 per day 7:35am-5:50pm, 71SFr); and Zurich (2½hr., 3 per hr. 5:25am-10:25pm, 65SFr). The **tourist office** in the train station reserves rooms. (☎ 613 73 73. Open daily 9am-5pm.) ◙**Lausanne Guesthouse & Backpacker ❷**, Chemin des Epinettes 4, is conveniently located and has comfortable rooms. Head left and downhill out of the station on W. Fraise; take the first right on Chemin des Epinettes. (☎ 601 80 00. Sheets for dorms 5SFr. Laundry 5SFr. Reception daily 7am-noon and 3-10pm. 4-bed dorms 29SFr; singles 80SFr, with bathroom 88SFr; doubles 86SFr/98SFr. MC/V.) **Camping de Vidy ❶**, chemin du Camping 3, has a restaurant (open May-Sept. 7am-11pm) and supermarket. Take bus #2 (dir.: Bourdonnette) to Bois-de-Vaux, cross the street, follow chemin du Bois-de-Vaux past Jeunotel and under the overpass, and it's straight ahead across rte. de Vidy. (☎ 622 50 00. Showers included. Electricity 3-4SFr. Reception Sept.-June daily 8am-12:30pm and 5-8pm; July-Aug. 8am-9pm. Open year-round. 6.50SFr per person, students 6SFr. 8-12SFr per tent; 1- to 2-person bungalow 54SFr; 3- to 4-person bungalow 86SFr.) Restaurants, cafes, and bars cluster around **place St-François** and the *vieille ville*, while *boulangeries* sell cheap sandwiches on every street and grocery stores abound. **Manora ❶**, pl. St-François 17, beneath the Zürich Bank sign, offers fresh food and "the longest buffet in Lausanne." (Hot food 11am-10pm. Buffet 10:45am-10:30pm. Open daily 7am-10:30pm.)

MONTREUX ☎ 021

Montreux is postcard Switzerland at its swanky, genteel best. The crystal-blue water of Lac Léman (Lake Geneva) and the snow-capped Alps are a photographer's dream. The gloomy medieval fortress, the **Château de Chillon**, on a nearby island, is one of the most visited attractions in Switzerland. It features all the comforts of home—including prison cells, a torture chamber, and a weapons room. Take the CGN **ferry** (13.80SFr) or bus #1 (2.80SFr) to Chillon. (Open Apr.-Sept. daily 9am-6pm; Mar. and Oct. 9:30am-5pm; Nov.-Feb. 10am-4pm. 8.50SFr, students 6.50SFr.) The ◙**Montreux Jazz Festival,** world-famous for exceptional musical talent, pushes everything aside for 15 days starting the first Friday in July (www.montreuxjazz.com; tickets 39-69SFr). If you can't get tickets, come anyway for the **Jazz Off,** 500 hours of free, open-air concerts by new bands and musicians.

Trains leave the station, on av. des Alpes, for: Bern (1½hr., 2 per hr. 5:30am-11pm, 37SFr); Geneva (1hr., 2 per hr. 5:30am-11:30pm, 26SFr); and Lausanne (20min., 3-5 per hr. 5:25am-midnight, 9.80SFr). Descend the stairs opposite the station, head left on Grand Rue for 5-10min., and look to the right for the **tourist office,** on pl. du Débarcadère. (☎ 962 84 84. Open mid-June to mid-Sept. M-F 9:30am-6pm, Sa-Su 10am-5pm; mid-Sept. to mid-June M-F 8:30am-5pm, Sa-Su 10am-3pm.) Cheap rooms are scarce in Montreux and almost nonexistent during the jazz festival; book ahead. ◙**Riviera Lodge ❷**, pl. du Marché 5, in the neighboring town of

THE HIDDEN DEAL

THE SWISS ALP RETREAT

A gem unknown to most travelers, the town of **Gryon** provides a tranquil mountain setting within reach of the Dents du Midi and Les Diablerets glaciers. The real reason to visit Gryon, however, is the popular Swiss Alp Retreat, housed in Chalet Martin. Owners Robyn and Bertrand (and a friendly young staff) provide backpackers a temporary family and various activities to fill their days. New arrivals are immediately welcomed into the bohemian community. Happy to "take a vacation from their vacation," world travelers passing through Gryon have been know to stay long and return often.

Amenities include discounted ski rentals, Internet access (10SFr per hr.), DVD rental (4SFr), and large kitchen facilities. The hostel has daily sign-ups for paragliding, thermal baths, guided overnight hikes, cheese-farm tours, and various other excursions like trips to Montreux and Zermatt.

Gryon is accessible by cog railway from Bex (30min.; every hr., last train 8:20pm; 5.20SFr; Eurail and Swiss-Pass valid), which lies on the main rail line connecting Geneva, Lausanne, and Montreux. From the cog rail station in Gryon, follow the tracks uphill to find the hostel; you'll see backpackers signs to your left. (☎(024) 498 33 21. Laundry 3-5SFr. Check-in 9am-9pm. Call ahead. Dorms 18-25SFr; doubles 50-75SFr. Discounted prices for longer stays. Cash only; the closest ATM is a 45min. walk away.) ❷

Vevey, is the area's best budget accommodation. Take bus #1 to Vevey (20min.; every 10min.; 2.80SFr). From the bus stop, head away from the train station on the main road to the open square on the waterfront; the hostel is on the right. (☎923 80 40. Sheets 5SFr. Laundry 7SFr. Reception daily 8am-noon and 5-8pm. Call if arriving late. 4- to 8-bed dorms 24SFr; doubles 80SFr. MC/V.) For **Hôtel Pension Wilhelm** ❸, r. du Marché 13-15, take a left on av. des Alpes from the station, walk up 3min., and take a left on r. du Marché, uphill past the police station. (☎963 14 31. Breakfast included. Reception daily 7am-10pm. Closed Oct.-Feb. Singles 60SFr, with shower 70SFr; doubles 100SFr/120SFr.) Grand Rue and av. de Casino have reasonably priced markets. **Marché de Montreux**, pl. du Marché, is an outdoor food market. (F 7am-1pm.) There's a **Co-op supermarket** at Grand Rue 80. (Open M-F 8am-12:15pm and 2-6:30pm, Sa 8am-5pm.) **Postal Code:** CH-1820.

NEUCHÂTEL   ☎032

Alexandre Dumas once said that Neuchâtel appeared to be carved out of butter. He was referring to its yellow stone architecture, but his comment could easily be taken as a reference to the rich treats in its famous *pâtisseries*. The *vieille ville* is a block from **place Pury,** a major square centered on **place des Halles,** and the hub of every bus line. From pl. des Halles, turn left onto r. de Château and climb the stairs on your right to reach **Collégiale church** and **château** (church open Apr.-Sept. daily 9am-8pm; Oct.-Mar. 9am-6:30pm). You can enter the château only on free but dull guided tours. (Apr.-Sept. M-F every hr. 10am-noon and 2-4pm, Sa 10-11am and 2-4pm, Su 2-4pm.) The nearby **Prison Tower (Tour des Prisons),** on r. Jehanne-de-Hochberg, has a magnificent view. (Open Apr.-Sept. daily 8am-6pm. 1SFr.) The **Musée d'Histoire Naturelle,** off r. de l'Hôpital, is a more innovative version of the standard natural history museum. (Turn right from pl. des Halles onto Croix du Marché, which becomes r. de l'Hôpital. Open Tu-Su 10am-6pm. 6SFr, students 3SFr.) The **Musée d'Art et d'Histoire,** Esplanade Léopold-Robert 1, houses an eclectic collection of coins, weapons, and textiles. (Open Apr.-May daily 10am-6pm; June-Mar. Tu-Su 10am-6pm. 7SFr, students 4SFr; W free.)

Trains run to: Basel (1¾hr., every hr. 5:30am-10:20pm, 34SFr); Bern (45min., every hr. 5:15am-11:20am, 17.20SFr); and Geneva (1½hr., every hr. 5:55am-11:35pm, 40SFr). An underground tram runs from the station to the shore area, where you can catch bus #1 to pl. Pury and the **tourist office,** in the same building as the post office. (☎889 68 90. Open

M-F 9am-noon and 1:30-6pm, Sa 9am-noon.) To reach **Oasis Neuchâtel ❷**, r. du Suchiez 35, take bus #1 (dir.: Cormondrèche) to Vauseyon; continue walking in the same direction on the smaller uphill road, follow the bend, and look for the yellow happy face affixed to the hostel on the left about 100m up the hill. (☎ 731 31 90. Breakfast 7SFr. Reception daily 8-10am and 5-9pm. 4- to 6-bed dorms 30SFr; doubles 70SFr; 2-person garden teepee in summer 40SFr. V.) To find **Hotel des Arts ❹**, r. Pourtales 3, from the underground tram exit, walk a block towards the city center on a. du Premier Mars and turn left on r. Pourtales. (☎ 727 61 61. Breakfast included. Reception 24hr. Check-out noon. Singles 80SFr, with bath 98-130SFr; doubles 100SFr/140-176SFr.) **Migros**, r. de l'Hôpital 12, sells groceries. (Open M-W 8am-7pm, Th 8am-9pm, F-Sa 7:30am-7pm.)

ITALIAN SWITZERLAND

Ever since Switzerland won the Italian-speaking canton of Ticino (Tessin in German and French) from Italy in 1512, the region has been renowned for its mix of Swiss efficiency and Italian dolce vita—no wonder the rest of Switzerland vacations here among jasmine-laced villas painted the bright colors of Italian gelato.

LUGANO ☎ 091

Set in a valley between two mountains, Lugano draws plenty of visitors with its seamless blend of religious beauty, artistic flair, and natural spectacle. The frescoes of the 16th-century **Cattedrale San Lorenzo,** just south of the train station, are still vivid despite their advanced age. The most spectacular fresco in town, however, is the gargantuan *Crucifixion* in the **Chiesa Santa Maria degli Angiuli,** on the waterfront to the right of the tourist office. Armed with topographic maps and trail guides (sold at the tourist office), hikers can tackle the nearby mountains, **Monte Bré** (933m) and **Monte San Salvatore** (912m). Alpine guides at the **ASBEST Adventure Company,** V. Basilea 28 (☎ 966 11 14), offer everything from snowshoeing and skiing (full-day 90SFr) to paragliding (170SFr) and canyoning (from 90SFr).

   Trains leave P. della Stazione for: Locarno (1hr., every 30min. 5:30am-midnight, 16.60SFr); Milan (45min., every hr. 7am-9:45pm, 21SFr); and Zürich (3½hr., 1-2 per hr. 6am-8:35pm, 60SFr). To reach the **tourist office** from the station, cross the footbridge labeled Centro and head down Via Cattedrale, which passes through P. Cioccaro and then bears right as it becomes Vie Pessina; turn left on Via dei Pesci and continue through P. Riforma towards the Polizei Communale building. The office is across the street from the ferry launch. (Open July-Aug. M-Th 9am-7:30pm, F-Sa 9am-10pm, Su 10am-4pm; Apr.-May and Sept.-Oct. M-F 9am-7:30pm, Sa 9am-5:30pm, Su 10am-4pm; Nov.-Mar. M-F 9am-12:30pm and 1:30-5pm.) **Hotel Montarina ❷,** Via Montarina 1, is a palm-tree-enveloped hostel with a swimming pool, kitchen, and terrace. (☎ 966 72 72. Parking available. Breakfast 12SFr. Sheets 4SFr. Laundry 4SFr. Reception daily 8am-10pm. Call 2 weeks July-Aug. Open Mar.-Oct. Dorms 25SFr; singles 70-80SFr; doubles 100SFr, with bath 120SFr.) The **Migros ❶,** Via Pretoria 15, two blocks left from the post office, has a food court. (Open M-W and F 8am-6:30pm, Th 8am-9pm, Sa 7:30am-5pm.)

LOCARNO ☎ 091

A Swiss vacation spot, Locarno gets over 2200 hours of sunlight per year—the most of any place in Switzerland. For centuries, visitors have journeyed to Locarno solely to see the orange-yellow **Church of Madonna del Sasso** (Madonna of the Rock), founded in 1487. A 20min. walk up the smooth stones of the Via al Sasso leads to the top, passing life-size wooden niche statues along the way. Hundreds of silver heart-shaped medallions on the church walls commemorate acts of Mary's intervention in the lives of worshipers who have made pilgrimages here. (Grounds open 6:30am-7pm.) Each August, Locarno swells with pilgrims of a different sort; its world-famous **film festival** draws visitors from all over the globe.

Trains run frequently from P. Stazione to: Lucerne (2½hr., every 30min. 6am-9pm, 54SFr); Lugano (50min., every 30min. 5:30am-midnight, 16.60SFr); Milan via Bellinzona (2hr., every hr. 5am-9:25pm, 34SFr); and Zermatt (4hr., every hr. 7:50am-7pm, 84SFr; change trains in Domodossola, Italy). The **tourist office**, on P. Grande in the *Kursaal* (casino), makes hotel reservations. (☎791 00 91. Open M-F 9am-6pm, Sa 10am-5pm, Su 3-6pm.) ▨**Baracca Backpacker ❷,** in the nearby town of Aurigeno, is perhaps the best reason to come to Locarno. From the train station in Locarno, take bus #10 (dir.: Valle Maggia) to Ronchini. (25min., every hr. 7am-8:10pm and 11:35pm, 7.20SFr.) Cross the street, continue along the road, then turn left, following the hostel signs through the forest, across the big metal bridge, and into the town (15min.). Follow the road until the end and turn left; the hostel is beside the church. What this hostel lacks in size (only 10 beds) is made up for in comfort and local hiking, biking, and swimming information. (☎(079) 207 15 54. Kitchen access. Bike rental 10SFr per day. Reception daily 9-11am and 5-8pm. Open Apr.-Oct. Dorms 25SFr.) To reach **Pensione Città Vecchia ❷,** Via Toretta 13, turn right onto Via Toretta from P. Grande. (☎751 45 54. Breakfast included. Reception daily 8am-9pm. Check-in 1-6pm. Dorms 30SFr; doubles 80SFr; triples 111SFr; quads 140SFr.) **Ristorante Manor ❷,** 1 Via della Stazione, left of the station, provides meals for cheap. (Open M-Sa 7:30am-9pm, Su 8am-9pm; Mar.-Oct. open until 10pm.) Get **groceries,** at the **Aperto** in the station (open daily 6am-10pm). **Postal code:** CH-6900.

TURKEY
(TÜRKİYE)

The modern Republic of Turkey is one of the world's great paradoxes: it is neither Europe, Asia, nor the Middle East, but rather an awe-inspiring amalgam of the three. The empires that carved Asia Minor between them over the past 10,000 years—from the Hittites to the Assyrians, Romans, Byzantines, and Ottomans—each left their distinctive mark, layering history upon history: Urartrian fortresses tower over Armenian churches converted into Selçuk mosques. Though resolutely secular by government decree, every facet of Turkish life is graced by the religious traditions of a 99% Muslim population. The terrain ranges from the ribboned, white sand beaches of the Aegean Coast resort towns, across the great Anatolian plains to the harsh, forbidding peaks of Mt. Ararat in the East. Millionaire playboys pull up to the exclusive clubs of İstanbul in private yachts, while shepherds and farmers scratch out an often desperate living in the boiling lands of the southeast. Millions of tourists every year cram the Sultanahmet district of İstanbul, the glittering western coasts, and the ever-popular moonscapes of Cappadocia, while the rest of Anatolia remains a purist backpacker's paradise: pristine alpine meadows, cliffside monasteries, medieval churches, tiny fishing villages, and countless cups of çay offered by people who take pride in their tradition of hospitality.

FACTS AND FIGURES

Official Name: Turkey.
Capital: Ankara.
Major Cities: İstanbul, İzmir.
Population: 65,000,000.

Land Area: 770,760 sq. km.
Time Zone: GMT +2.
Languages: Turkish; also Kurdish, Arabic.
Religions: Sunni Muslim (98.8%).

DISCOVER TURKEY

Bargain at bazaars and wander through Ottoman palaces in **İstanbul** (p. 1016). Swing northeast to **Edirne** (p. 1026), home to the finest mosque in all of Turkey, before trekking down the sparkling **Aegean Coast.** From **Çanakkale** (p. 1029), make daytrips to the famed battlefield of **Gallipoli** (p. 1029) and the ruins of **Troy** (p. 1029), then head south to the incomparable remnants of **Ephesus** (p. 1032). After aphrodisiacal **Bodrum** (p. 1033), the "Bedroom of the Mediterranean," head inland to **Aphrodisias** (p. 1033) to visit some of antiquity's best temples. From there it's just a bit farther south to the **Mediterranean Coast,** where **Ölüdeniz** (p. 1035) shelters a secluded blue lagoon. Pass through **Kaş** to reach the eternal flame of **Olimpos** (p. 1036). Then hit the central **Cappadocia** region, known for its surreal rock formations and backpacker scene, and the underground cities of **Göreme** (p. 1038).

 Let's Go was unable to send a researcher to some areas of Turkey in 2002. Much of the information in this chapter was gathered in the summer of 2001; we recommend that you plan ahead and check with individual establishments so as not to be surprised by changes in prices, openings, etc.

TURKEY

ESSENTIALS

WHEN TO GO

Summer (especially July to August) is high tourist season. Late spring and early fall temperatures are far milder and prices may be 10% lower, but some facilities and sights close in the off-season. During Ramadan, the Islamic holy month, public eating, drinking, and smoking are generally taboo during daylight hours.

DOCUMENTS AND FORMALITIES

VISAS. As of June 2002, citizens of Australia, Canada, Ireland, the UK, and the US require a visa to enter Turkey. New Zealanders may stay for up to three months with a valid passport, South Africans for up to one month. Though visas can be obtained from a Turkish embassy or consulate in your home country, it is most convenient to get them upon arrival in Turkey, at the airport or border. A three-month visa costs AUS$30 for Australians, UK£10 for British citizens, IR£13 for Irish citizens, and US$45 for US citizens.

EMBASSIES. Foreign embassies are all in Ankara (p. 1037); consulates are in İstanbul (p. 1017). Turkish embassies at home include: **Australia,** 60 Mugga Way, Red Hill, Canberra ACT 2603 (☎02 62 95 02 27; turkembs@ozemail.com.au); **Canada,** 3 Crescent Rd. Rockcliffe, Ontario KIM ON1 (☎613-748-3737; turkish@magma.ca); **Ireland,** 11 Clyde Rd., Ballsbridge, Dublin 4 (☎01 668 52 40; turk@embiol.ie); **New Zealand,** 15-17 Murphy St., Level 8, Wellington (☎04 472 12 90; turkem@xtra.co.nz); **South Africa,** 1067 Church St., Hatfield, Pretoria 0028 (☎012 342 60 53; www.turkishembassy.co.za); **UK,** 43 Belgrave Sq., London SWIX 8PA (☎020 73 93 02 02; www.turkishembassy-london.com); and **US,** 2525 Massachusetts Ave. NW, Washington, D.C. 20008 (☎202-612-6700; www.turkey.org).

TRANSPORTATION

Road travel in Turkey is considered dangerous by European and US standards. Whether taking a bus or driving, travelers should educate themselves about road conditions. Travel only on reputable bus companies such as **Ulusoy, Varan,** and **Kamil Koç,** and avoid travel at night and in inclement weather.

BY PLANE. Turkish Airlines (THY; www.thy.com) connects over 30 Turkish cities; many European airlines fly into İstanbul, with some flights to Ankara and Antalya.

BY TRAIN. Trains link Turkey to Athens and Bucharest, but some lines may be suspended due to political crises in the Balkans. Trains are cheap, but they follow painfully slow, circuitous routes. **Eurail** is not valid; **Interrail** passes are. With a Eurail pass, take the train to Alexandroupolis, Greece, and ride the bus from there.

BY BUS. Frequent, modern, and cheap, buses connect all Turkish cities and are the best way to get around. In large cities, bus companies run free shuttles called *servis* from their town offices to the *otogar* (bus station), which is often quite a distance away. Buy tickets from local offices or purchase them directly at the station. Many lines grant students a 10% discount. **Fez Travel,** 15 Akbıyık Cad., Sultanahmet, İstanbul (☎(212) 516 90 24; www.feztravel.com) offers a hop-on, hop-off "backpacker bus" loop (June-Oct. €175, under 26 €168).

BY FERRY. For information on ferries connecting the Aegean Coast to Greece and Italy, see p. 1028. Boats also connect Greece to Turkey's Mediterranean Coast; see p. 1034. Domestic **Turkish Maritime Lines** (TML) ferries sail from İstanbul to İzmir

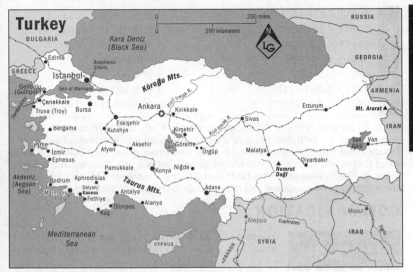

and the Black Sea Coast. Fares jump sharply in July and August, but student discounts are often available. Reserve ahead and check in at least two hours in advance. If you arrive in Turkey by boat, expect to pay a Turkish port tax (€11). Most countries also charge a port tax for exit.

BY DOLMUŞ AND BY CAR. Shared taxis known as *dolmuş* (usually minibuses) let passengers off at any point along a fixed route; they post their destination on the windshield and leave whenever they fill up. Sit first and pay later. The speed limit is 50kph (31mph) in cities, 90kph (55mph) on highways, and 130kph (80mph) on *oto yolu* (toll roads). You must have an International Driving Permit (IDP) to drive; *Let's Go* does not encourage driving. If you get in an accident, file a report with the traffic police (☎118). Contact the **Turkish Touring and Automobile Association** in the US (TTOK; ☎(212) 282 81 40) for more information.

BY MOPED AND BY THUMB. Mopeds are an easy, cheap way to tour coastal areas and the countryside. Expect to pay €20-35 per day; remember to bargain. Be sure to ask if the quoted price includes tax and insurance. *Let's Go* does not recommend **hitchhiking** in Turkey; lone women should never hitchhike. However, those who choose to accept the risks of hitchhiking generally pay half what the trip would cost by bus. The hitching signal is a waving hand or the standard thumb.

TOURIST SERVICES AND MONEY

EMERGENCY	Police: ☎110. Ambulance: ☎112. Fire: ☎155.

TOURIST OFFICES. Virtually every town has a tourist office. The website for Turkish tourism is www.turkey.org.

MONEY. Turkey's currency, the **lira (TL),** comes in denominations of 100,000TL; 250,000TL; 500,000TL; 1,000,000TL; 5,000,000TL; and 10,000,000TL. Coins are in values of 5000TL; 10,000TL; 25,000TL; 100,000TL; and 25,000TL. Because the *lira* suffers from sky-high inflation, *Let's Go* quotes prices in euros. (See p. 16 for conversion rates.) Tip taxi drivers, hotel porters, and waiters (leave it on the table)

TURKISH LIRA		
AUS$1 = 812,803TL		1,000,000 TL = AUS$1.22
CDN$1 = 934,055TL		1,000,000 TL = CDN$1.06
EUR€1 = 1,337,488TL		1,000,000 TL = EUR€0.74
NZ$1 = 688,792TL		1,000,000 TL = NZ$1.44
ZAR1= 145,262TL		1,000,000 TL = ZAR6.78
UK£1 = 2,085,421TL		1,000,000 TL = UK£0.47
US$1 = 1,432,000TL		1,000,000 TL = US$0.69

about €1 for good service. 15-20% tips are required only in ritzy restaurants, where service may be included *(servis dahil)*. **Bargaining** is common at markets, bazaars, and carpet shops. Allow the seller to name a price, then counter with a price that is less than what you intend to pay, but not less than half the seller's price. A 10-20% **value-added tax (VAT)** *(katma değer vergisi;* KDV) is included in the prices of most goods and can theoretically be reclaimed upon departure.

COMMUNICATION

PHONE CODE	**Country code: 90. International dialing prefix: 00.** From outside Turkey, dial int'l dialing prefix (see inside back cover) + 90 + city code + local number.

TELEPHONES. Make international calls at post offices. New phones accept phone cards *(telekart)*, available at the PTT, while old ones require tokens *(jeton)*. Card phones have English directions. For directory assistance, dial ☎118; for an international operator, dial ☎115. International direct dial numbers include: **AT&T,** ☎00 800 122 77; **British Telecom,** ☎00 800 89 09 00; **Canada Direct,** ☎00 800 166 77; **Ireland Direct,** ☎00 800 353 11 77; **MCI,** ☎00 800 111 77; **Sprint,** ☎00 800 144 77; and **Telkom South Africa,** ☎00 800 27 11 77.

MAIL. PTTs (Post, Telegraph, and Telephone offices) are well-marked by yellow signs. Some PTTs may charge a small sum for *Poste Restante.* Airmail from Turkey takes 1-2 weeks; mark cards and envelopes *"uçak ile"* and tell the vendor the destination: *Avustralya, Kanada, Büyük Bretanya* (Great Britain), *İrlanda, Yeni Zelanda* (New Zealand), *Güney Afrika* (South Africa), or *Amerika.*

LANGUAGE AND CUSTOMS. When a Turk raises his chin and clicks his tongue, he means *hayır* (no); this is sometimes accompanied by a shutting of the eyes or the raising of eyebrows. *Evet* (yes) may be signalled by a sharp downward nod. It is considered rude to point your finger or the sole of your shoe toward someone. Although public displays of affection are considered inappropriate, Turks often greet one another with a kiss on both cheeks. For Turkish basics, see p. 1066.

ACCOMMODATIONS AND CAMPING

TURKEY	❶	❷	❸	❹	❺
ACCOMMODATIONS	€1-10	€11-25	€26-50	€51-100	over €100

Clean, cheap accommodations are available nearly everywhere. Basic rooms cost €4-8 per person. **Pensions** *(pansiyon)*, by far the most common accommodations, are often private homes with rooms for travelers; don't expect toilet paper or towels. Most towns have a **hamam,** or bathhouse, where you can get a steam bath for €4; they schedule different times for men and women. **Camping** is popular, and cheap campgrounds are easy to find (around €2-4 per person). Official government campsites are open from April or May to October.

FOOD AND DRINK

TURKEY	❶	❷	❸	❹	❺
FOOD	€1-3	€4-8	€8-15	€15-40	over €40

Staples like *çorban salatası* (shepherd's salad), *mercimek çorbası* (lentil soup), rice pilaf, and *yoğurt* are not listed on *lokanta* (restaurant) menus, but are always available. *Et* is the word for meat: lamb is *kuzu*, veal is *dana eti*. Chicken, usually called *tavuk*, becomes *piliç* when roasted. *Kebap*, the most famous Turkish meat dish, may come on a skewer *(şiş)* or spit *(döner)*. *Köfte* are medallion-sized spiced meatballs. Turks eat a lot of seafood: *kalamar* (squid), *midye* (mussels), and *balık* (fish). Vegetarians will largely have to stick to *meze* (appetizers). *Dolma* are peppers, grape leaves, or eggplant stuffed with rice and served with or without meat. Turks drink *çay* (tea) hot, with sugar. *Kahve* (coffee) comes *sade* (unsweetened), *orta* (medium-sweet), and *şekerli* (sweet). Ice-cold *rakı*, an aniseed liquor, is the national drink. *Baklava*, a flaky pastry filled with nuts and soaked in honey, and *lokum*, Turkish delight, are the most famous Turkish sweets.

HEALTH AND SAFETY

The most significant health concerns are parasites and other gastrointestinal ailments. Never drink unbottled or unpurified water, and be wary of food from street vendors. Eat fruits with thick peels that can be removed. Always carry toilet paper; expect to encounter pit toilets. Signs in pharmacy windows indicate night-duty pharmacies *(nöbetçi)*. If you're caught doing **drugs** in Turkey (or are caught in the company of someone who is), you're screwed. Stories of dealer-informers and lengthy prison sentences are true; embassies are utterly helpless in all cases. Exporting antiques is punishable by imprisonment. Foreign **women,** especially those traveling alone, attract significant attention. Catcalls and other forms of verbal harassment are common; physical harassment is rare. One way of deflecting unwanted attention is showing displeasure by making a scene; try the expressions *"ayıp!"* ("shame!") or *"haydi git"* ("go away"). Holler *"eem-DAHT"* ("help") if the situation gets out of hand. Touristed areas may be more comfortable for women. Dress modestly, especially farther east. While Kurdish guerillas are no longer active in the southeast, political tensions remain in that region. Over the last two years, Chechen sympathizers have developed a strategy of taking hostages in luxury hotels; that said, violent acts of **terrorism** are not common. While neither of these circumstances is reason to curtail a visit, travelers should stay away from large crowds and all political demonstrations, and should stay abreast of recent developments. The US State Department issues travel warnings (www.state.gov).

HOLIDAYS

Holidays: New Year's Day (Jan. 1); National Sovereignty and Children's Day (Apr. 23); Atatürk Commemoration and Youth and Sports Day (May 19); Victory Day (Aug. 30); and Republic Day (Oct. 29). During the month of **Ramadan** (beginning Oct. 27), pious Muslims abstain from eating, drinking, smoking, and sex between dawn and dusk; businesses may have shorter hours, and public eating is inappropriate. **Eid al-Fitr** breaks the Ramadan fast. During the 3-day **Şeker Bayramı** (Sugar Holiday), which marks the end of Ramadan, bus and train tickets and hotel rooms may be scarce. **Kurban Bayramı** (Sacrifice Holiday), when animals are slaughtered and distributed to the poor, occurs a few months after Ramadan.

İSTANBUL

CITY CODES	☎212 (European side) and ☎216 (Asian side).

Straddling two continents and three millennia of history, İstanbul exists on an incomprehensible scale, set against a dense landscape of Ottoman mosques, Byzantine mosaics, and Roman masonry. The Bosphorus Straits have proven both a blessing and a curse, providing a strategic location that has attracted countless sieges. Having survived wars, natural disasters, and foreign occupations, İstanbul comprises a unique mix of civilizations that also shows through in religious practices and everyday customs. Conservative black-veiled women merge in the swelling crowds with younger women in Western dress, and major religious and historical sights double as the backdrops for Turkish pop videos. Explore the İstanbul beyond carpet salesmen and backpacker bars, and venture out into neighborhood produce markets and back-alley tea shops.

▛ TRANSPORTATION

Flights: Atatürk Havaalanı (IST), 30km from the city. The domestic and international terminals are connected by **bus** (every 20min. 6am-11pm). To reach **Sultanahmet,** take a Havaş **shuttle bus** from either terminal to Aksaray (every 30min., €7), then walk 1 block south to Millet Cad. and take an Eminönü-bound **tram** to the Sultanahmet stop. Or, take a **taxi** (€4) to the Yeşilköy train station and take the commuter rail *(tren)* to the end of the line in Sirkeci. A direct taxi to Sultanahmet costs €9. To reach **Taksim,** take the Havaş shuttle to the end of the line (every 30min., 6am-9pm, €5). To reach the airport, have a private service such as **Karasu** (☎638 66 01) or **Zorlu** (☎638 04 35) pick you up from your hostel (€5.50), or take the Havaş shuttle from the McDonald's in Taksim (45min., every 30min., €6.75).

Buses: Esenler Otobüs Terminal (☎658 00 36), in Esenler, 3km from central İstanbul. Serves intercity buses. To get there, take the tram to Yusufpaşa (1 stop past Aksaray; €0.50), walk 1min. to the Aksaray Metro station on broad Adnan Menderes Bul., and take the Metro to the *otogar* (15min., €0.40). Most companies have **courtesy buses** *(servis)* that run to the *otogar* from Eminönü, Taksim, and elsewhere in the city (free with bus ticket purchase). Various companies serve additional international destinations. The following have good reputations; be careful when choosing a company. Many find it easier to use a travel agency (see p. 1017).

> **Kamil Koç** (☎658 20 03). To **Ankara** (6hr.; every hr.; €22, students €20) and **Bursa** (4hr.; every 30min.; €9/€8.25).
>
> **Pamukkale** (☎/fax 658 22 22). To **Pamukkale** (10hr.; 7 per day; €21, students €19).
>
> **Parlak Tur** (☎658 17 55). To **Prague** (2 days; Sa 4pm; €100, students €95).
>
> **Ulusoy** (☎658 30 00; fax 658 30 10). To: **Athens** (21hr.; Th and Sa 1 per day; €60, students €51); **Bodrum** (13hr.; 3 per day; €31/€27); **İzmir** (9hr.; 4 per day; €28/€24).
>
> **Varan** (☎658 02 74). To **Ankara** (6hr.; 7 per day; €25, students €23) and **Bodrum** (14hr.; 2 per day; €31/€28.50).

Trains: Intercity buses are faster and cheaper in most cases. All trains to Anatolia leave from **Haydarpaşa Garı** (☎(216) 336 04 75), on the Asian side. Take the ferry (every 20min., €0.65) from Karaköy pier #7, halfway between Galata Bridge and the Karaköy tourist office. Rail tickets for Anatolia can be bought in advance at the **TCDD** office upstairs. To **Ankara** (6½-9½hr., 6 per day, €6-12). Europe-bound trains via Athens or Bucharest leave from **Sirkeci Garı** (☎(212) 527 00 50), in Eminönü, downhill from Sultanahmet toward the Golden Horn. Some lines may be suspended due to political crises in the Balkans. Call ahead for info and student fares. To: **Athens** (24hr., 1 per day, €60); **Bucharest** (17hr., 1 per day, €30); and **Budapest** (40hr., 1 per day, €90).

Ferries: Turkish Maritime Lines (☎ 249 92 22), near Karaköy pier #7, just left of the **Haydarpaşa** ferry terminal. Look for the building with the blue awning marked *Denizcilik İşletmeleri*. Ferries leave for **Bandırma**, with train connections to **İzmir** (combination ticket €10-25). Points on the Bosphorus are served by less frequent and more expensive day cruises. Local ferries run between Europe and Asia. Pick up a timetable (*feribot tarifesi;* €0.60) at any pier. Fast **seabus** catamarans also run along the ferry routes. Address any questions to **Seabus Information** (☎ (216) 362 04 44).

Public Transportation: Buses serve most stops every 10min. 5am-10:30pm, less frequently 10:30pm-midnight. Signs on the front indicate destination; on the right side, major stops. **Dolmuş** run during daylight hours and early evening and are found near most major bus hubs, including Aksaray and Eminönü. In neighborhoods far from the bustle of Taksim and Sultanahmet they serve as local group taxis; it's best to hail them on their way back into the center of İstanbul. A **tramvay** (tram) runs from Eminönü to Zeytinburnu (€0.50); follow the tracks back to Sultanahmet even if you don't actually take it. **AKBİL** is an **electronic ticket system** that works on municipal ferries, buses, trams, seabuses, and the subway (but not *dolmuş*). A deposit of €5 will get you a plastic tab that will save you 15-50% on fares; you can add money in 1,000,000TL increments. Add credit at any white IETT public bus booth with the "AKBİL *satılır*" sign (at bigger bus and tram stops); press your tab into the reader, remove it, insert a 1,000,000TL note, and press again. **Regular tickets** are not interchangeable. Tickets for trams and buses without ticket sellers are available from little white booths, while ferries and seabuses take *jeton* (tokens), available at ferry stops.

Taxis: Little yellow speed-demons. Taxi drivers are even more reckless than other İstanbul drivers. Scams are widespread. Be alert when catching a cab in Sultanahmet or Taksim. One light on the meter means day rate, while 2 mean night rate. Check change carefully. Rides within the city center shouldn't cost more than €5.

✈ 🛈 ORIENTATION AND PRACTICAL INFORMATION

The **Bosphorus Strait** (Boğaz) separates Asia from Europe. Turks call the western, European side of İstanbul **Avrupa** and the eastern, Asian side **Asya**. The **Golden Horn,** a river originating outside the city, splits Avrupa into northern and southern parts. Directions are usually specified by district (i.e. Kadıköy, Taksim, or Fatih). Most of the sights and tourist facilities are in **Sultanahmet**, south of the Golden Horn, toward the eastern end of the peninsula. The other half of "Europe" is focused on **Taksim Square,** the commercial and social center of the northern bank. Two main arteries radiate from the square: **İstiklâl Caddesi,** the main downtown shopping street, and the hotel-lined **Cumhuriyet Caddesi.** The Asian side of İstanbul is mostly residential but offers wandering at a relaxed pace, including the Kadıköy district.

TOURIST, FINANCIAL, AND LOCAL SERVICES

Tourist Office: 3 Divan Yolu (☎/fax 518 87 54), in Sultanahmet, in the white metal kiosk at the north end of the Hippodrome. Open daily 9am-5pm. **Branches** in the Sirkeci train station (☎ 511 58 11; open daily 8:30am-5:30pm) and in the Atatürk Airport (☎ 573 41 36; open 24hr.). In Taksim the main office (☎ 233 05 92; open daily 9am-5pm) is in the **Hilton Hotel Arcade** on Cumhuriyet Cad.

Travel Agencies: Tourist agencies line the beginning of Divan Yolu Cad. and Akbıyık Cad., the main backpacker drag in Sultanahmet. **7-Tur,** 37 Gümüşsuyu Cad., 2nd fl., is İstanbul's STA Travel equivalent and handles all STA ticket changes. ISICs available (€15). From Taksim Sq., walk downhill to the right of Atatürk Cultural Center. **Tur-Ista,** 16 Divan Yolu (☎ 527 70 85; fax 519 37 92), convenient for Sultanahmet, will arrange a free transport to the bus or train station if you buy a ticket through them.

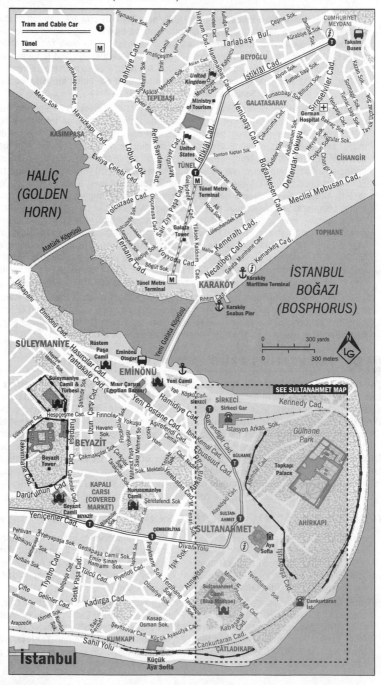

İstanbul

Consulates: Australia, 58 Tepecik Yolu, Etiler (☎(212) 257 70 50; fax 257 70 54). **Canada,** 107/3 Büyükdere Cad., Bengün Han, Gayrettepe (☎(212) 272 51 74; fax 272 34 27). **Ireland** (honorary), 25/A Cumhuriyet Cad., Mobil Altı, Elmadağ (☎(212) 246 60 25). **New Zealand,** Level 24, 100-102 Maya Akar Center, Büyükdere Cad., Esentepe (☎(212) 275 28 89; fax 275 50 08). **South Africa,** Serbetci ış Merkezi, 106/15 Büyükdere Cad., Esentepe (☎(212) 288 04 28; fax 275 76 42). **UK,** 34 Meşrutiyet Cad., PK33, Beyoğlu/Tepebaşı (☎(212) 293 75 40; fax 245 49 89). **US,** 104-108 Meşrutiyet Cad., Tepebaşı (☎(212) 251 36 02; fax 251 32 18).

Currency Exchange: Exchange shops open M-F 8:30am-noon and 1:30-5pm; most charge no commission. Banks exchange traveler's checks.

American Express: Türk Express, 47/1 Cumhuriyet Cad., 3rd fl. (☎235 95 00), uphill from Taksim Sq. Open M-F 9am-6pm. Their office in the Hilton Hotel lobby (☎230 15 15), Cumhuriyet Cad., helps when Türk Express is closed. Neither grants cash advances or accepts wired money. Open daily 8:30am-8:30pm. AmEx's agent is **Akbank,** with branches across the city. To get a cash advance on your card, you must have a personal check or know the account number and address of your bank. Attempt this service only after visiting an AmEx branch office.

Laundromats: Star Laundry, 18 Akbıyık Cad. (☎638 23 02), below Star Pension in Sultanahmet. Wash and dry €3 per 2kg. Open daily 8am-8pm.

EMERGENCY AND COMMUNICATIONS

Emergency: ☎155. **Tourist Police:** at the beginning of Yerebatan Cad. in Sultanahmet (24hr. ☎527 45 03 or ☎528 53 69; fax 512 76 76).

Medical Assistance: American Hospital, Admiral Bristol Hastanesi, 20 Güzelbahçe Sok., Nişantaşı (☎231 40 50). The **German Hospital,** 119 Sıraselviler Cad., Taksim (☎251 71 00) is more conveniently located for Sultanahmet hostelers.

Pharmacy: The Turkish word for pharmacy (or chemist) is *eczanesi.* **Çemberlitaş Eczanesi,** No. 46 Vezirhan Cad. (☎522 69 69), off Divan Yolu by the Çemberlitaş tram stop, is among the most helpful. Open M-Sa 7:30am-8pm.

Internet Access: The **Antique Internet Café,** 51 Kutlungun Sok., offers a fast connection—despite its name. €1.50 per hr. Open 24hr.

Post Office: The **PTT** (Post, Telegraph, and Telephone) office nearest Sultanahmet is the yellow booth opposite the entrance to Aya Sofia. **Main branch,** 25 Büyük Postane Sok, in Sirkeci. Stamp and **currency exchange** services open 8:30am-midnight. Phones open 24hr. Address mail to be held: Firstname SURNAME, *Poste Restante,* Merkez 3 Postane, PTT, Sirkeci, 25 Büyük Postane Sok., **5270050** İstanbul, TURKEY.

▟ ACCOMMODATIONS

Budget accommodations are mainly in **Sultanahmet,** bounded by Aya Sofia, the Blue Mosque, and Topkapı Palace. The **Taksim** district, home to many five-star hotels and a few budget lodgings, is less touristy. The sidestreets around **Sirkeci** train station and **Aksaray** offer tons of dirt-cheap hotels, but may not be the most pleasant places to stay. **Lâleli** is the center of prostitution in İstanbul and should be avoided. Rates can rise by 20% in July and August.

▧ **İstanbul Hostel,** 35 Kutlugün Sok. (☎516 93 80). From the path between the Aya Sofia and the Blue Mosque, walk south down Tevkifane Sok. to Kutlugün Sok; it's on the right. Spotless. Internet. Happy Hour 6:30-9:30pm. Dorms €7; doubles €16. ❶

▧ **Moonlight Pension,** 87 Akbıyık Cad. (☎517 54 29; moonlight@superonline.com). Clean rooms, a kind staff, and clear rooftop views away from the noisy backpacker scene. Laundry. Kitchen. Internet. Dorms €5; doubles €16; triples €21. ❶

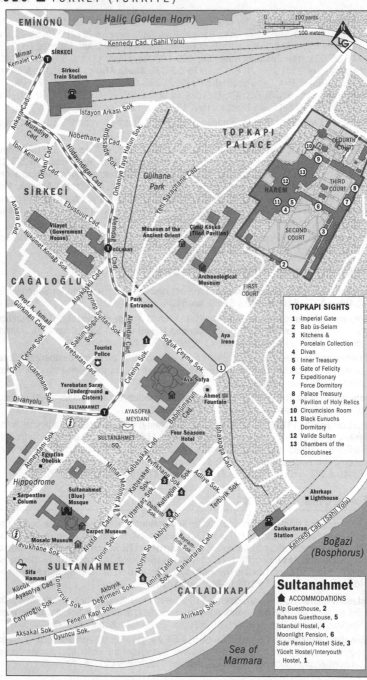

TOPKAPI SIGHTS
1 Imperial Gate
2 Bab üs-Selam
3 Kitchens &
  Porcelain Collection
4 Divan
5 Inner Treasury
6 Gate of Felicity
7 Expeditionary
  Force Dormitory
8 Palace Treasury
9 Pavilion of Holy Relics
10 Circumcision Room
11 Black Eunuchs
  Dormitory
12 Valide Sultan
13 Chambers of the
  Concubines

Sultanahmet

⌂ ACCOMMODATIONS

Alp Guesthouse, **2**
Bahaus Guesthouse, **5**
Istanbul Hostel, **4**
Moonlight Pension, **6**
Side Pension/Hotel Side, **3**
Yücelt Hostel/Interyouth
Hostel, **1**

Side Pension/Hotel Side, 20 Utangaç Sok. (☎517 65 90; www.sidehotel.com), near the entrance to the Four Seasons Hotel. Occupies the 2 wooden buildings by the corner of Tevkifane Sok. and Utangaç Sok. *Pension* singles €20; doubles €25; triples €35. Add €10 for bath. Hotel singles €40; doubles €50; triples €60. ❷

Seagull Pension, Küçük Ayasofya Cad., Aksakal Sok. 22 (☎517 11 42; seagullpension@hotmail.com). From Aya Sofya, head down the hill on Küçük Ayasofya Cad toward the Marmara. A block before Kennedy Cad and the sea; close to the train station. Internet. Dorms €5; singles €10; doubles €20-25. ❶

Alp Guesthouse, Akbıyık Cad., 4 Adliye Sok. (☎517 95 70; www.alpguesthouse.com). Head down Tevkifane Sok., turn left after the Four Seasons, and take the 1st right. Family-run hotel with spacious, spotless rooms and a Mediterranean feel. Free airport transport with 3-day stay. Free Internet. Singles €30; doubles €50; triples €60. ❸

Hotel Plaza, 19-21 Aslanyatağı Sok. (☎245 32 73), in Taksim. Down Arslanyata Sok., the small side street off Siraselviler. Bear left when Arslanyata turns right, and look for the big building in a courtyard. Quiet, classy rooms with Bosphorus views, sitting rooms, fridges, glass tables, and large windows. Breakfast included. Dorms €7; singles €20; doubles €40. ❶

Nayla Palace Pension, 22 Kutlugün Sok. (☎516 35 67; nayla@superonline.com). A homey atmosphere, quiet garden courtyard, and rooftop lounge. Breakfast included. Internet. Dorms €5; singles €15; doubles €25-30; triples €35. ❶

Yücelt Hostel/Interyouth Hostel, 6/1 Caferiye Cad. (☎513 61 50; www.yucelthostel.com). Massive 3-building complex has billiards, table tennis, Internet, travel library, book exchange, safes, luggage storage, and videos in the rooftop lounge. Laundry. Dorms €4-8; doubles €16-20. ❶

Bahaus Guesthouse, Akbıyık Cad., 11 Bayram Fırını Sok. (☎517 66 97). From the front of the Blue Mosque, head two blocks down Mimar Mehmet Ağa Cad. and turn left on Akbıyık Cad. Spare, standard rooms. Terrace has various musical instruments available. Breakfast included. Singles €20; doubles €30-35; triples €40. ❷

Hotel As, 26 Bekar Sok. (☎252 65 25; fax 245 00 99), off upper İstiklâl Cad, in Taksim. Unbeatable price and location. Tiny balconies overlook busy cafe alleys. All rooms with bath and phone. Singles €10; doubles €17; triples €21. ❶

🍴 FOOD

Sultanahmet's heavily advertised "Turkish" restaurants are easy to find, but much better meals can be found on **İstiklâl Caddesi** and around **Taksim.** Small Bosphorus towns such as **Arnavutköy** and **Sariyer** (on the European side) and **Çengelköy** (on the Asian side) are the best places for fresh fish. **Kanlıca,** on the Asian side, reputedly has the best yogurt. Covered boats in **Eminönü** and **Karaköy** fry up fish sandwiches on board (€1.50). Good *kebap* shops are everywhere, but quality tends to be better in more residential areas. **Ortaköy** is the place for baked potatoes stuffed with all kinds of fillings. Because of space considerations and cultural differences, there are very few supermarkets; luckily, **markets** all over the city sell cheese, bread, produce, and more at rock-bottom prices. Browse the fresh selection of produce in the city's **open-air markets;** the best is the daily one in **Beşiktaş,** near Barbaros Cad.

SULTANAHMET AND DİVAN YOLU

Doy-Doy, 13 Şifa Hamamı Sok. From the south end of the Hippodrome, walk down the hill around the Blue Mosque and look for the blue-and-yellow signs. The best of Sultanahmet's cheap eats. Tasty *kebap* and salads (under €4). Open daily 8:30am-late. ❶

Can Restaurant, 10 Divan Yolu. Across the street from the tourist information office at the north end of the Hippodrome. A no-nonsense, dirt-cheap cafeteria. Veggie combination plates from €1.75; meat dishes €2.50-5. Open daily 8am-9pm. ❶

Pudding Shop, 6 Divan Yolu. A pit stop on the hippie trail to the Far and Middle East during the 70s, it was the setting for the drug deal scene in *Midnight Express*. It is now a self-serve restaurant (dishes €1.50-2.50) and super dessert stop whose walls are lined with newspaper clippings and notes about its storied past. Continental breakfast €2. ❶

İSTİKLÂL CADDESİ AND TAKSİM

❦ **Hacı Abdullah,** 17 Sakizağacı Cad., down the street from Ağa Camii. This family style restaurant has been serving it up since 1888. Main dishes €3-6, delicious soups €1. Open daily noon-11pm. ❶

❦ **Naregatsi Cafe,** upstairs at the mouth of Sakizağacı Cad., across from the Ağa Camii. Gourmet cafe fare in a kitschy setting. Inflatable superheroes, live accordion, and cappuccino (€3.50). Open daily noon-11:30pm. ❷

Hacı Baba, 49 İstiklâl Cad., has perfected a wide range of Turkish standards in its nearly 80 years. The menu is extensive; pick something from the deli case in front or try the huge vegetarian *meze* selection. Main dishes €3.50-6.50. Open daily 10am-10pm. ❷

Şampiyon, Balık Pazarı. Down Sahne Sok., next to Çiçek Pasajı. Famous across Turkey for *kokoreç* (grilled tripe cooked with spices and tomatoes). For something quick, visit the stand out front for fresh mussels (€0.25 each). Open daily 8:30am-midnight. ❶

GOLDEN HORN

Cibalikapı Balikçisi Fish Restaurant, right along the Golden Horn in Fatih, serves fresh fish starting at €2.60 and veggies starting at €1.30. ❶

Tarihi Haliç Işkembecisi, along the Golden Horn. Their specialty is the *Işkembe Çorbası,* a bizarre but appetizing soup of butter, garlic, and shredded fish meat (€1.30). ❶

◎ SIGHTS

İstanbul hosts an incomparable array of world-famous churches, mosques, palaces, and museums. Most budget travelers spend a lot of time in **Sultanahmet,** the area around the Aya Sofia, south of and uphill from Sirkeci. Merchants crowd the district between the **Grand Bazaar,** east of the university, and the **Egyptian Bazaar,** just southeast of Eminönü.

AYA SOFIA (HAGIA SOPHIA)

Aya Sofia, built in just five years, opened in December of AD 537. Covering 7570 sq. m and rising 55.6m, it was then the biggest building in the world. Twenty years later, an earthquake brought the dome crashing to the ground. The new dome went up in AD 563. After falling to the Ottomans in 1453, Aya Sofia was converted into a mosque and remained one until Atatürk established it as a museum in 1932. Aya Sofia's austere interior makes it seem even bigger. The nave is overshadowed by the massive, gold-leaf mosaic dome. The **mihrab,** the calligraphy-adorned portal pointing toward Mecca, stands in the **apse,** which housed the altar during the mosque's Orthodox incarnation. The elaborate marble square in the floor marks the spot where Byzantine emperors were once crowned. The **minber,** the platform used to address the crowd during prayer, is atop the stairway to the right of the *mihrab*. At the back end of the **narthex,** a quiet hallway with lace-like column capitals at the north side of the building, is the famed **sweating pillar,** sheathed in bronze. The pillar has a hole where you can insert your finger to collect the odd drop of water, believed to possess healing powers. Be prepared to wait a while. The **gallery** contains Byzantine mosaics found beneath a thick layer of Ottoman plaster. *(Museum open Tu-Su 9:30am-4:30pm. Gallery open Tu-Su 9:30am-4pm. €6.50.)*

BLUE MOSQUE (SULTANAHMET CAMII)

Between the Hippodrome and Aya Sofia, the Blue Mosque, Sultan Ahmet's response to Aya Sofia in 1617, is named for its beautiful blue İznik tiles. Not as large as Aya Sofia, but still massive, the mosque's internal framework of iron bars enables the entire structure to bend in earthquakes (so far, it has withstood 20). Enter from the east side through the **courtyard.** The mosque's **six minarets** are the primary source of its fame; at the time, only the mosque at Mecca had six minarets, and the thought of equaling that sacred edifice was considered heretical. Sultan Ahmet circumvented this difficulty by financing the construction of a seventh minaret at Mecca. A small stone from the **Ka'aba** at Mecca is almost invisible from the tourists' area. *(Open Tu-Sa 8:30am-12:30pm, 2-4:45pm, and 5:45-6:30pm. Donation requested. Dress modestly—no shorts or tank tops, and women must wear head coverings. Speak quietly.)* The small, square, single-domed structure in front of the Blue Mosque, **Sultan Ahmet's Tomb** (Sultanahmet'in Türbesi), contains the sultan's remains as well as those of his wife and sons, Osman II and Murat IV. The holy relics include strands of Muhammed's beard. *(Open Tu-Su 9:30am-4:30pm. €1, students free.)*

THE HIPPODROME (AT MEYDANI)

Behind the Blue Mosque, the remains of this ancient Roman circus form a pleasant park whose tranquility defies its turbulent history. Built by the Roman Emperor Septimus Severus in AD 200, the Hippodrome was the site of chariot races and public executions. Constantine, the first Byzantine Emperor, enlarged the racetrack to 500m on each side. The tall, northernmost column with hieroglyphics is the **Egyptian Obelisk** (Dikili Taş), erected by the Pharaoh Thutmosis III in 1500 BC and brought from Egypt to Constantinople in the 4th century by Emperor Theodosius I. Farther south, the subterranean bronze stump is all that remains of the **Serpentine Column**, originally placed at the Oracle of Delphi. The southernmost column is the **Column of Constantine**, whose original gold-plated bronze tiling was looted by members of the Fourth Crusade during the sack of Constantinople. On the east side of the Hippodrome along Atmeydanı Sok. is the superb **Museum of Turkish and Islamic Art** (İbrahim Paşa Sarayı). The Ottoman calligraphy is particularly impressive. *(Museum open Tu-Su 9:30am-4:30pm. €2, students €1.20.)*

TOPKAPI PALACE (TOPKAPI SARAYI)

Main entrance on Babıhümayun Cad., off Aya Sofia square. Open Tu-Su 9am-4:30pm. €6.50. Harem open Tu-Su 9am-4pm; mandatory tours every 30min. €4.

Towering from the high ground at the tip of the old city, hidden behind walls up to 12m high, Topkapı Palace was the nerve center of the Ottoman Empire from the 15th to the 19th centuries. Topkapı offers unparalleled insight into the wealth, excess, cruelty, and artistic vitality that characterized the Ottoman Empire at its peak. Built by Mehmet the Conqueror between AD 1458 and 1465, the palace became an imperial residence under Süleyman the Magnificent. The palace is divided into a series of courts surrounded by palace walls.

FIRST AND SECOND COURTYARDS. The general public was permitted entrance via the **Imperial Gate** to the first courtyard, where they watched executions, traded, and viewed the nexus of the Empire's glory. At the end of the first courtyard, the capped conical towers of the **Gate of Greeting** (Bab-üs-Selam) mark the entrance to the second courtyard. To the right, beyond the colonnade, the **Imperial Kitchens** feature distinctive vaulted chimneys and house three collections of porcelain and silver. The last set of doors on the left of the narrow alley leads to the palace's world-famous **Chinese and Japanese porcelain collections.** Across the courtyard, where ostriches and eunuchs once roamed, lie the **Privy Chambers** (*Kubbealtı*), whose window grilles, awnings, walls, and ceilings are bathed in gold leaf. The

Council Chamber, the room closest to the Harem, retains its original classical Ottoman calligraphic decor. Abutting the Council Chamber is the plush Rococo room in which the **Grand Vizier** received foreign dignitaries. Next door and to the right is the **Inner Treasury,** which holds various cutting and bludgeoning instruments.

THIRD COURTYARD. The third courtyard, officially known as **Enderun** (inside), is accessible through the **Gate of Felicity.** The **School of Expeditionary Pages** holds a costume collection that traces the evolution of imperial costumes. Move along down the colonnade to the incredible **Palace Treasury,** which contains ornate gold objects, the legendary **Topkapı dagger** (essentially three giant emeralds with a knife sprouting out of them), and the 86-carat **Spoonmaker's Diamond.** Just on the other side of the courtyard is the **Pavilion of Holy Relics,** which houses the booty taken by Selim the Grim after the Ottoman capture of Egypt, as well as gifts sent by the governor of Mecca and Medina upon Selim's victory.

FOURTH COURTYARD. Three passages lead into the fourth courtyard. If Topkapı can be thought of as the brain of the Ottoman Empire, then the fourth courtyard certainly qualifies as the pleasure center, as it was among these pavilions, gardens, and fountains that the infamous merriments and sordid garden parties occurred. From the broad marble terrace at the west end, you can take in the uninterrupted vistas of the Sea of Marmara and the Bosphorus. The **Revan Pavilion,** the building farthest from the edge of the terrace, was built in 1635 to commemorate Sultan Murat IV's Revan campaign; at the other end of the portico is the **Circumcision Room,** an octagonal chamber that overhangs the edge of the pavilion, built by Ibrahim the Mad. At the other end of the terrace stands the **Bağdat Köşku,** Murat I's monument to his capture of Baghdad in 1638. An octagonal/cruciform base supports the dome; the interior sports an amazing radial symmetry.

HAREM. These 400-plus rooms housed the sultan, his immediate family, and a small army of servants, eunuchs, and general assistants. Because it was forbidden for men other than the sultan and his sons to live here, the Harem became a source of intrigue and the subject of endless gossip. The mandatory tour proceeds to the **Black Eunuchs' Dormitory** on the left, then into the women's section of the harem, beginning with the chambers of the **Valide Sultan,** the sultan's mother. If a concubine attracted the sultan's affections or if the sultan spent a night with her, she would be promoted to nicer quarters with the chance for further advancement; if she bore the sultan a son, she could become one of his eight wives.

OTHER SIGHTS

THE ARCHAEOLOGICAL MUSEUM COMPLEX. Mehmet the Conqueror built the **tiled pavilion** to view athletic competitions below; the display covers the spectrum of Ottoman tile-making, including some rare early İznik tiles. The smaller building adjacent to the tiled pavilion, the ▨**Museum of the Ancient Orient,** is rarely open; hidden inside is an excellent collection of stone artifacts from Anatolia, Mesopotamia, and Egypt dating from the first and 2nd millennia BC. The **Archaeology Museum** contains one of the world's great collections of Classical and Hellenistic art. *(About 100m downhill from the 1st courtyard of Topkapı Palace. When the palace is closed, enter the museums through Gülhane Park; a separate road next to the park ticket booths leads to the complex. Complex open Tu-Su 9:30am-5pm. €5.)*

GRAND BAZAAR (KAPALI ÇARŞISI). With over 4000 shops, several banks, mosques, police stations, and restaurants, this enormous "covered bazaar" could be a city in itself. It began in 1461 as a modest affair during the reign of Mehmet the Conqueror, but today it forms the entrance to the massive galleria that starts at Çemberlitaş and covers the hill down to Eminönü, ending at the **Egyptian Spice**

Bazaar (Mısır Çarşısı) and the Golden Horn waterfront. You'll get lost, so enjoy it. *(From Sultanahmet, follow the tram tracks toward Aksaray for 5min. until you see the Nuruosmanıye Camii on the right. Walk one block down Vezirhanı Cad., keeping the mosque on your left. Follow the crowds left into the bazaar. Open M-Sa 9am-7pm.)*

■ **UNDERGROUND CISTERN (YEREBATAN SARAYI).** This subterranean "palace" is actually a vast underground cavern whose shallow water eerily reflects the images of its 336 supporting columns, all illuminated by colored ambient lighting. Echoing sounds of dripping water and muted classical tunes accompany strolls across the elevated wooden walkways. Underground walkways linking it to Topkapı Palace were blocked to curb rampant trafficking in stolen goods and abducted women. *(With your back to Aya Sofia, the entrance is 175m away on the left side of Yerebatan Cad. Open daily 9:30am-5:30pm. €4, students €3.25.)*

SÜLEYMANİYE COMPLEX (SÜLEYMANİYE KÜLLİYESİ). To the north of İstanbul University sits the massive and elegant **Süleymaniye Camii,** one of architect Sinan's great masterpieces, part of a larger complex that includes tombs, an *imaret* (soup kitchen), and several *medreses* (Islamic schools). Walk along the Süleymaniye Camii's southwest side to the large arch just below the dome and enter the mosque's central courtyard through the smaller tourist entrance to the left of the main door. After removing your shoes (women should also put on a headscarf), proceed inside the vast and perfectly proportioned mosque. The stained-glass windows are the work of the master Sarhoş İbrahim (İbrahim the Drunkard). *(From the university, head out the northwest gate to Süleymaniye Cad. From Sultanahmet, either walk along the tramvay (15min.) or take it to the Üniversite stop, walk across the square, and take Besim Ömer Paşa Cad. past the walls of the university to Süleymaniye Cad. Mosque open Tu-Su 9:30am-4:30pm, except during prayers.)* Prof. Sıddık Sami Onar Sok. runs between the university and the mosque. Passing through the graveyard brings you to the superbly decorated **royal tombs** of Süleyman I and his wife, Haseki Hürrem. *(Open Tu-Su 9:30am-4:30pm. Donation requested.)*

PRINCE'S ISLANDS (ADALAR). The craggy Prince's Islands are known simply as the *Adalar* (islands). **Büyükada** is the largest and most enjoyable island, with pine forests, swimming spots, and peaceful walks. **Yöruk Ali** is the main beach and picnicking spot; you can also take the buggy to **Luna Park,** the local amusement park on the far side of the island (10-15min.; no more than €7.50). The main forms of transportation on the islands are walking, biking, and horse-and-buggy rides. The lovely ■**Ideal Aile Pansiyon,** 14 Kadıyoran Cad., is a big old house with huge rooms. *(☎382 68 57. €13 per person.)* **Ferries** depart from the north side of Eminönü or Kabataş; look for "Sirkeci Adalar" signs. *(3-4 per day, round-trip €2.)*

⌂ HAMAMS (TURKISH BATHS)

Women should request female washers. Self-service is always an option; signal your preference by showing the attendants your bar of soap and wash cloth.

■ **Çemberlitaş Hamamı,** 8 Verzirhan Cad. Near Çemberlitaş tram stop. Built by Sinan in 1584, this place has beautiful and clean marble interiors and good service. Vigorous "towel service" after bath requires a tip of €1.50-3. Bath with your own towel and soap €9; with a sudsy rubdown, massage, and wash €15 (tip included, but after you change the washers wait around for another €1-3). Open daily 6am-midnight.

Mihrimah Hamamı, next to Mihrimah Mosque on Fevzi Paşa Cad., about 50m from Edirnekapı. One of the better local baths: large, quiet, clean, cheap, and hot. Women's facilities are good, though smaller. Bath €3; massage €2.50. Men's section open daily 7am-midnight; women's section 8am-7pm.

TURKEY

Galatasaray Hamamı, at the end of Turanacıbaşı Sok., off İstiklâl Cad., on a side street across from the high school on Istiklâl; just uphill from Galatasaray. Bath and massage €15.50. Men's section open daily 7am-11pm; women's section 8am-8pm.

NIGHTLIFE

İstanbul's best clubs and bars are poorly advertised, so unplanned club-hopping usually proves fruitless. Small, relaxed **cafe-bars** serve tea in the afternoon and alcohol in the evening, often with a jazz soundtrack. Cavernous **rock bars** range from dark heavy-metal halls to mellow classic-rock hangouts. Convenient and cheap backpacker bars are concentrated in the **Sultanahmet** area. The hippest clubs and discos often move from unlisted locations in Taksim in the winter to unlisted summer locations throughout the city. The Beşiktaş end of **Ortaköy** is a maze of upscale hangouts; along the coastal road toward **Arnavutköy** are a string of open-air clubs (cover €18-45). Bouncers are highly selective, but wander between Ortaköy and **Bebek** and try your luck. Men heading out without female companions will have a tough time getting into some of the more upscale clubs and bars, which require every man to be accompanied by at least one woman. İstanbul night action is centered around **Taksim** and **İstiklâl Cad.** Sultanahmet's bars all lie within 100m of one another. Male-only *çay* houses, backgammon parlors, and dancing shows tend to be dingy and dangerous; *Let's Go* does not recommend these establishments. Team up with others and take cabs when out late, even in nicer areas. Cafe-bars and backpacker bars tend to be less threatening than rock bars or clubs.

▧ **Jazz Stop,** at the end of Büyük Parmakkapı Sok. in Taksim. Live music nightly 11pm. Beer €3. No cover June-Aug.; Sept.-May F-Sa €10. Open daily 11am-4am.

▧ **Riddim,** 6 Büyük Parmakkapı Sok., in Taksim, spins reggae, island, and African music all night long. Unaccompanied men turned away on weekends. Beer €2.50. Open F-Sa 8pm-4am, Su-Th 9pm-1:30am.

Cheers, Akbıyık Cad. The best music on a backpacker alley, with comfortable outdoor benches. Delicious fresh fruit soaking in bottled water and a friendly scene make this one of the best places to grab a beer in the area.

Traveler's Cafe and Bar, Akbıyık Cad., Trade adventures with the super-friendly staff. Also offers a *nargile* (water pipe) and a standard bar menu. Beer €1.80.

Madrid Bar, İpek Sok., off Küçük Parmakkapı Sok., which is off İstiklâl Cad. Surrealist Spanish paintings decorate this small, mellow spot, popular with Turkish students and young foreigners looking for the cheapest pints in Taksim (€1.25). Open 2pm-2am.

> **NIGHTLIFE SCAMS.** Though most tourists have no problem when out on the town, scams do exist. One involves Turkish men who befriend a male tourist, lead him to a bar where they are joined by women who order drinks and then leave, sticking the tourist with a big bill. Buying drinks for women can be a front for prostitution; that €50 "drink" might get you more than you bargained for. There have also been reports of tourists being given drugged drinks and then robbed. While a drink invitation is usually simply a gesture of hospitality, use your best judgement when accepting drinks from strangers.

EDIRNE   ☎ 284

In almost 2000 years of historical prominence, Edirne has experienced a mixed and fickle fate, ranging from imperial splendor to hostile occupation. It has been a Roman outpost, an Ottoman capital, and a modern Greek military possession. An easy *dolmuş* ride from the Greek (7km away) or Bulgarian (20km) border, Edirne once nourished the genius of Sinan, the quintessential Ottoman architect. His masterpiece, the ■Selimiye Camii, considered by many to be Turkey's finest mosque, presides over the city with 71m minarets, a 32m-wide dome, and 999 windows. Its vast, ornately decorated interior is even more impressive. Another Edirne must-see is the **Beyazıt Complex**, built in the late 1480s by the court architect of Beyazıt II. The centerpiece is the **Beyazıt Camii**, a beautiful, single-domed mosque surrounded by multi-domed buildings designed to be schools, storehouses, and asylums. For a long but pleasant walk to the complex, follow Horozlu Bayir Cad. from its origin near the Sokollu Hamamı across two bends of the river. Unfortunately, only the wing once used for medical purposes is open; it now houses Trakya University's **Museum of Health**. (Open Tu-Su 8:30am-5:30pm. €1.50.) Back in town, Sinan's 16th-century **Sokollu Hamamı**, (Sokollu Bath) beside the Üç Şerefeli Camii, has superior service and inspiring architecture. (☎225 21 93. €2.50, with massage €6.25. Open daily 7am-11pm for men; 9am-6pm for women.) Those less interested in cleanliness can get down and dirty with the competitors who don giant leather breeches, slather themselves in oil, and hit the mats for the **Kšrkpšnar Grease Wrestling Festival,** which comes to town in early July; call tourist office for details.

Numerous companies send **buses** from the *otogar*, 2km from the city center, to: Ankara (9hr., €20); Bursa (7hr., €16.50); İstanbul (2-3½hr., €5-8.25); and İzmir (9hr., €15.50). Before you buy a ticket, especially to İstanbul, be sure to shop around. Upon arrival, walk across the four-lane road opposite the *otogar* and hail one of the frequent *dolmuş* heading to town. The **tourist office,** 17 Talat Paşa Cad., 300m from the town center, has free maps. (☎213 92 08. Open June-Aug. M-F 8:30am-5:30pm and occasional weekend hours; Sept.-May M-F 8:30am-5:30pm.) Luxurious ■Efe Hotel ❷, 13 Maarif Cad., offers modern bathrooms, phones, and TV. (☎213 61 66; www.efehotel.com. Breakfast included. Singles €16.50; doubles €23; triples €27.) The basic **Hotel Aksaray ❶** is at the intersection of Maarif Cad. and Ali Paşa Ortakapı Cad. (☎225 39 01. Singles €5.50-12.50; doubles €11-16; triples €13.50-19.) Sip *çay* (€0.25-0.40) at **Şera Park Café,** on Selimiye Meydanı, in the park between Selimiye Camii and Eski Camii. **Postal code:** 22100.

BURSA   ☎224

In the shadow of the slopes of Mt. Uludağ, Bursa is both one of Turkey's holiest cities and a major industrial center. Surrounded by fertile plains and filled with vast gardens and parks, the city has been dubbed "Green Bursa." In addition, its fantastic early Islamic architecture is some of the most stunning in all of Turkey. Most of Bursa's sights lie roughly in a long row along Atatürk Cad. and its continuations. The immense **Ulu Cami** stands in the center of town on Atatürk Cad. The domes, arranged in four rows of five with a glass center, hover above a large fountain, one of the unique features of the mosque. From the statue of Atatürk, head east along Atatürk Cad., bear right, and continue along Yeşil Cad. following the "Yeşil" signs to reach the hilltop **Yeşil Türbe** (Green Tomb; open daily 8:30am-noon and 1-5:30pm) and the onion-shaped minaret caps of the 15th-century **Yeşil Camii** across the street. *Şehade* (royal sons) are buried in tombs surrounding the **Muradiye Camii,** a testament to the early Ottoman practice of fratricide. To reach the complex, catch a "Muradiye" *dolmuş* or bus from the Atatürk Cad.-Heykel area. (Open daily 8:30am-noon and 1-5:30pm. €0.60.) Bursa's fabled **mineral baths** are in the **Çekirge** ("Grasshopper") area west of the city. The shiny ■Eski Kaplıca ("old bath"), on Çekirge Cad., is one of the finest baths in the country, with ever-hotter pools and a great massage room. Take bus #40 or a Çekirge *dolmuş* and ask for Eski Kaplıca. (☎233 93 00. Men €4; women €3.30; scrub or massage €3.) On the road to Çekirge is the **Karagöz Sanat Evi,** with exhibitions on shadow theater from around the world. (Open M-Sa 11am-4pm. €1.50, students €0.80.) The master **puppeteer** R.

Sinasi Çelikkol gives performances every Wednesday and Saturday at 11am. A short trip away, **Mt. Uludağ** is a popular ski area during the winter and a picturesque picnic area in summer. From Bursa, take bus 3-C, 3-İ, or any with a "Teleferik" sign from Peron 1 on Atatürk Cad. (every 5-10min., €0.40). Alternatively, catch the *dolmuş* from behind Adliye and Heykel (€0.60).

In Bursa, Kamil Koç **buses** go from the terminal, 20km outside the city center, to: Ankara (5½hr., every hr., €6); Çeşme (8hr., 2 per day, €6.70); İstanbul (3½hr., very frequent, €5); İzmir (5hr., every hr., €5); and Kuşadası (7½hr., 4 per day, €6.60). Local bus #90/A goes downtown (€0.45). **Seabuses** (☎(226) 812 04 99) go between İstanbul and Yalova (30-40min., 14 per day, €2), from which buses connect to Bursa (1hr., every 30min., €2.50). To get to the **tourist office,** head to the Ulu Cami side of Atatürk Cad., walk past the fountain toward the Atatürk statue, and go down the stairs on the left. (☎220 18 48. Open M-Sa 8:30am-6pm; Oct.-Apr. M-Sa 8am-5pm.) **Elite Internet Cafe** is at 37 Yeşil Cad., before the overpass leading to the Emir Sultan Cami. (€1.30 per hr. Open daily 10am-1am.) Find the basic but friendly **Otel Güneş ❷** at 75 İnebey Cad. (☎222 14 04. Singles €5; doubles €7.50; triples €14.50; quads €20.) Walk along Atatürk Cad. with the mosque on your right and turn left after the Sümerbank, then right onto Veziri Cad. to reach **Otel Deniz ❶,** 19 Tahtakale Veziri Cad. (☎222 92 38. Shared bath and free laundry. Singles €4; doubles €8.) 🍴**Kebapçı İskender ❶** claims to have invented the unbeatable dish *İskender kebap* (lamb with tomato sauce, bread, and yogurt; €2.50); one branch is at 7 Ünlü Cad. and another by the Cultural Center on Atatürk Bul. (Open daily 11am-9pm.) **Postal code:** 16300.

✈ BORDER CROSSINGS: BULGARIA AND GREECE

By far the easiest way to cross into **Bulgaria** from Turkey is to take a direct bus from İstanbul. Or, for a more adventurous route, take a local bus (€1) to **Kapıkale,** the Turkish border town, 18km west of Edirne, where a *dolmuş* will drop you directly at the entrance (both €1). Although going on foot is possible (if the guards on duty allow it), the several (hot) kilometers between the two border towns makes walking impractical. On the other side, you have to catch a taxi from Andreevo to **Plovdiv,** the closest town with direct transport to Sofia.

The easiest way to cross into **Greece** is also a direct bus from İstanbul; the border crossing between **Pazarkule** and the Greek border (open 9am-noon) is inconvenient, but feasible. From Edirne, you can either take a taxi all the way to Pazarkule (15min., €6.25), or catch the local bus to **Karaağiç** (€0.50) and then walk the remaining 2km to Pazarkule. Although the 1km between the Turkish and Greek borders is a no-man's land (no one may walk through without a military escort), Greek taxis usually wait at the border to ferry travelers across the stretch to **Kastanies,** from which you can make bus and train connections to elsewhere in Greece.

AEGEAN COAST

With classical ruins and hidden beaches, Turkey's winding Aegean coastline has become popular with tourists. In Pergamon, Ephesus, and Pamukkale, ruins lie where they fell when earthquakes leveled them centuries ago—this area's 5000-year legacy isn't going anywhere.

🌙 FERRIES TO GREECE AND ITALY

From **Çeşme,** ferries run to **Chios, Greece** (1hr.; June Tu and Th-Sa, July-Aug. Tu-Su, Sept. 21-Oct. and May Tu and Th, Nov.-Apr. Th; €30, round-trip €40; €10 Greek port tax for stays longer than one day). From June to September, **Turkish**

Maritime Lines (☎(232) 712 10 91) runs ferries from **Çeşme** to **Brindisi, Italy** (34hr.; Tu 11am, F 11pm; €90-100). From **Kuşadası**, ferries head to **Samos, Greece** (1½hr.; in summer daily 8:30am and 4:30pm, off-season 2 per week; €30, including port tax). From Bodrum, **Bodrum Express Lines** (☎(252) 316 40 67) runs ferries to **Kos** (1½hr., May-Oct. 1 per day) as well as hydrofoils to **Kos** (20min.; 1 per day; €18, round-trip €28) and **Rhodes** (2¼hr.; 6 per week; €46, round-trip €57).

GELIBOLU (GALLIPOLI) AND ECEABAT ☎286

The strategic position of the Gallipoli Peninsula (Gelibolu in Turkish) on the Dardanelles made it the backdrop of a major World War I Allied offensive to take Constantinople and create a Balkan front. Eighty thousand Ottomans and more than 200,000 soldiers of the British Empire—Englishmen, Australians, New Zealanders, and Indians—lost their lives in the blood-soaked stalemate. This battle launched its hero **Atatürk** into his status as Turkey's founding father. It's best to visit the battlefields from nearby Eceabat or Çanakkale. ◪**TJ's Tours** (☎814 31 21; tjs_tours@excite.com) offers tours through TJ's Hostel in Eceabat and the Yellow Rose Pension in Çanakkale. **Hassle Free Travel Agency** (☎213 59 69; hasslefree@anzachouse.com), runs tours through Anzac House in Çanakkale.

Eceabat is cheaper and more convenient than Gelibolu Town as a base for exploring the Gelibolu battlefields. **Minibuses** run there (30min., every hr., €1). ◪**TJ's Hostel ❶**, Cumhuriyet Sok., to the right of the main square, has clean rooms. (☎814 10 65; fax 814 29 41. Dorms €4.50; singles €6; doubles €9.)

ÇANAKKALE ☎286

With cheap accommodations and good bus connections, Çanakkale (pop. 60,000) is a great base for exploring Gelibolu and Troy. The **Çimenlik Kalesi** (Grassy Castle), 200m from the harbor, combines a park and naval museum. (Open Tu-W and F-Su 9am-noon and 1:30-5pm. €0.50, students €0.20.) **Buses** arrive frequently from: Bursa (4½hr., €6.50); İstanbul (5hr., €10); and İzmir (5hr., €7). To get to the **tourist office**, 67 İskele Meydanı, go left from the bus station, take a right on Demircioğlu Cad., and follow the signs marked *Feribot* to the docks; it's on the left. (☎/fax 217 11 87.) **Yellow Rose Pension ❶** arranges tours of Gelibolu through TJ's Tours (above). Turn right at the clock tower, then take the second right. (☎217 33 43. Dorms €3; singles €6; doubles €11.) **Anzac House ❶**, 61 Cumhuriyet Meydanı, arranges tours of Gelibolu and Troy through the Hassle Free Tour Agency (above). Facing Cumhuriyet Meydani with your back to the ferry docks, it's immediately on your right. (☎213 59 69. Dorms €3; singles €7; doubles €11.50.)

◪ **DAYTRIP FROM ÇANAKKALE: TROY (TRUVA).** Troy, made famous by Homer, remained under a blanket of mythology until archaeologist Heinrich Schliemann uncovered the ancient city 32km south of Çanakkale—proving that the sto-

AHEAD OF HIS TIME
Statues all over Gelibolu celebrate the achievements of the town's local hero Piri Reis, a seaman and cartographer born in Gelibolu in 1470. As an admiral in the Ottoman Navy, he collected new charts and maps from the bazaars of his many ports-of-call. In 1513, he used his extensive library of charts to draw a map of the world. Reis's map resurfaced in 1929, when a group of historians discovered it while poking around in İstanbul's Topkapı Palace. They were astonished to discover that the 1513 map showed the coastal outlines of South and North America and included precise data on Antarctica, supposedly not discovered until 1818. Further studies of Reis's map have suggested that his reference charts may have been drawn from aerial pictures; the rivers, mountain ranges, islands, deserts, and plateaus are drawn with unusual accuracy.

ries about Helen and the wooden horse are more than myth. The ruins as they appear today, however, are a little underwhelming. Nine layers of Bronze Age fortifications are explained in the **Excavation House.** (Site and house open in summer daily 8am-7pm; off-season 8am-5pm. €3, students €1.50.) **TJ's Tours,** based in Eceabat (see Gelibolu), has excellent tours (€14). **Anzac House** (see above) leads tours from Çanakkale at 8:30am (€14); bring water. Or, visit the site by taking a **dolmuş** from the lot in Çanakkale (every hr., €0.75).

PERGAMON (BERGAMA) ☎ 232

The ruins of ancient Pergamon are scattered about the modern town of Bergama. From the river (near Pension Athena), cross the bridge, head diagonally to the right and uphill through the old town, and follow the paved road to the cluster of concrete buildings. Enter the compound and follow the path through the gymnasium and the Temple of Demeter to the main ruins of the **Acropolis** at the top of the hill. As you exit the lower city, the Hellenistic **theater,** which once seated 10,000, comes into view. Farther up, you can try to land three coins on top of the column inside the **wishing well** for good luck, or marvel at the newly restored **Temple of Trajan.** Follow the yellow signs from Atatürk Meydanı on the west side of town to reach the famed **Asclepion,** a healing center where the ancient doctor Galen, once worked. (Open daily 8am-6:30pm. €3, free with ISIC.) Near the river and the old part of Pergamon stand the remnants of **Kızıl Avlu** (Red Basilica), a pagan temple that became one of the Seven Churches of the Apocalypse mentioned in the Book of Revelations. **Buses** run to: Ankara (10hr., 9pm, €11.50); İstanbul (10hr., 10am and 9:15pm, €13); and İzmir (2hr., every 45min., €2.25). From the bus station, walk 1km right on İzmir Cad. and turn left on Cumhuriyet Meydanı to reach the **tourist office.** (☎631 28 51. Open daily M-F 8:30am-noon and 1-5:30pm.) **Pension Athena ❶,** on the road beyond İstiklâl Meydanı, boasts, "Not the best, but we're trying to get there." Charming honesty, but a bit of an undersell. (☎633 34 20. Laundry. **Internet.** €4.50-5.75 per person; 10% *Let's Go* discount.) **Postal code:** 35700.

İZMIR ☎ 232

İzmir (pop. 3 million), formerly **Smyrna** (reputed to be the birthplace of Homer), rose from the rubble of the 1922 Turkish War of Independence to become Turkey's third-largest city. Wide boulevards, plazas, and plenty of greenery line the waterfront, but inland İzmir is a bleak wasteland of factories. *Çay salonular* (teahouses), street vendors, and a full-fledged **bazaar** (open M-Sa 9am-8pm) line the streets of Anafartalar Cad. İzmir's **Archaeological Museum,** near Konak Sq., houses finds from Ephesus and other local sites. (Open Tu-Su 9am-5pm. €1.75, students €1.) Uphill from the archaeological museum, the **Ethnographical Museum** displays traditional folk art and Ottoman weaponry. (Open Tu-Su 9am-noon and 1-5pm. €0.75, students €0.40.) From mid-June to early August, the **International İzmir Festival** brings Turkish and international acts to İzmir, Çeşme, and Ephesus. (For tickets and info, call the numbers listed in the İzmir Festival brochure distributed at the tourist office, or visit www.izmirfestival.org. Tickets €8-38.) Budget hotels, cheap restaurants, bus company offices, and the **Basmane train station** are around **9 Eylül Meydanı,** a rotary at the center of the Basmane district. **Buses** run from **Yeni Garaj,** İzmir's new intercity bus station, to: Ankara (8hr., every hr., €9.25); Bodrum (4hr., every hr., €6); Bursa (5hr., 10 per day, €6.50); İstanbul (9hr., every hr., €13); Kuşadası (1hr., every hr., €2.25); and Marmaris (5hr., every hr., €6.50). Take city bus #50, 51, 53, 54, 60, 601, or 605 from the station (€0.50; buy tickets from the kiosk before boarding) and tell the driver you want "Basmane Meydanı," which is the same as 9 Eylül Meydanı. From there, walk down Gazi Bul. to the first main intersection, then turn right onto Gazi Osmanpaşa Bul.

The **tourist office** is on the right at 1/1D Gazi Osmanpaşa Bul., 30m past the Hilton Hotel toward the sea. (☎445 73 90. Open daily 8:30am-5:30pm.) **Lâleli Otel ❶**, 1368 Sok. #5-6, one block from 9 Eylül Meydanı, has spacious rooms with private baths. (☎484 09 01. €5.75 per person.) **Hotel Oba ❷**, 1369 Sok. #27, four blocks down 1369 Sok from 9 Eylül Meydanı, is pricier, but more comfortable. (☎441 96 05. Breakfast included. Singles €11.50.) **Postal code:** 35000.

TURKEY

🔁 DAYTRIP FROM IZMIR: SART (SARDIS). While small, Sart stands out as Turkey's best-restored archaeological site. The **old city** boasts a magnificent two-story **gymnasium**, a long-deserted **swimming pool**, a ruined **Palaestra**, and a gorgeous **synagogue**. The patterns of the synagogue's 3rd-century mosaic floors are strangely juxtaposed with Corinthian and Doric columns. (Open daily 8am-6pm. €1, students €0.50.) The amazing 4th-century BC **Temple of Artemis** was one of the largest temples of the ancient world. (Open daily 8am-5pm. €1, students €0.50.) Take a **bus** bound for Salihli from the upper floor of İzmir's Yeni Garaj (1½hr., every 30min., €1) and ask to be let off at Sart; you will be dropped near a yellow "Temple of Artemis" sign, by the shops scattered along the highway. The gymnasium, synagogue, and baths are about 50m ahead on the left. To catch a return bus to İzmir, follow the road across from the sign to the right as it splits, until you reach another highway. Flag a bus down at the pull-off on the far side (€1).

ÇEŞME   ☎ 223

A breezy seaside village an hour west of İzmir, Çeşme has gained popularity for its cool climate, crystal-clear waters, and proximity to the Greek island of Chios. With a long ribbon of clean white sand flanked by rolling dunes, **Altınkum Beach** is one of Turkey's finest. **Dolmuş** run to Altınkum from the lot in Çeşme, by the tourist office (15min., June-Sept. every 20min., €1). Çeşme's most impressive site is the **castle**, which houses a sparse **Archaeological Museum.** (Open Tu-Su 8am-noon and 1-6pm. €2.50.) **Buses** (☎712 64 99) run from the *otogar*, at the corner of A. Menderes Cad. and Çevre Yolu Cad., to: Ankara (10hr., 9:30pm, €12); İstanbul (11hr., 2 per day, €13); and İzmir (1½hr., every 20min., €2.50). Buy **ferry** tickets from **Ertürk Tourism and Travel Agency**, 6/7 Beyazıt Cad., next to the *kervansaray*. (☎712 67 68. Open in summer daily 8am-9pm; off-season 8am-6pm.) From the main gate of the *otogar*, follow Turgutozal Cad. down to the sea, turn right, and walk 300m to the main square in front of the castle. The **tourist office,** 8 İskele Meydanı, is across from the castle and *kervansaray*, near numerous budget accommodations. (☎/fax 712 66 53. Open in summer M-F 8:30am-5:30pm, Sa-Su 9am-5pm; off-season M-F 8:30am-5:30pm.) **Alim Pension ❶**, Tarini Turk Hamami Yani, is on the corner past the *kervansaray* and *hamam* as you walk on Alpaslan Cad. with the sea on your right (☎712 83 19. €4 per person.) Walking away from the sea, turn onto Mektep Sok off İnkılap Cad. and then right again onto Dellal Sok.; the refreshingly clean **Filiz Pension ❶** is at #16. (☎712 67 94. Doubles €8.) **Postal code:** 35930.

SELÇUK   ☎ 232

Selçuk is a convenient base from which to explore Ephesus and offers its own archaeological sites as well. The colossal **Basilica of Saint John** lies off Atatürk Cad. on the supposed site of St. John's grave. (Open daily 8am-7pm. €1.75.) The stunning 14th-century **İsa Bey Camii** is at the foot of the hill on which the Basilica of St. John and the Ayasoluk castle stand. (Open 10min. before and after prayer times.) A few hundred meters down Dr. Sabri Yayla Bulvarı as you walk away from town with the tourist office on your right, are the sad remains of the **Temple of Artemis,** one of the seven wonders of the ancient world. (Open daily 8:30am-5:30pm. Free.) The **Ephesus Museum** (Efes Müzesi), directly across from the tourist office, houses a world-class collection of recent finds from Ephesus. (Open daily 8:30am-noon and 1-7pm. €5.) **Trains** go to İzmir (1½hr., 7 per day, €1). **Buses** run from the *otogar*, at the corner of Şabahattın Dede Cad. and Atatürk Cad., to: Ankara (9hr., 3 per day, €11.25); Bodrum (3hr., every hr., €5); Fethiye (6hr., every 2hr., €7.25); İstanbul (10hr., 5 per day, €11.25); İzmir (1hr., every 30min., €1.50); and Marmaris (4hr., every hr., €5.75). **Minibuses** run to Kuşadası (20min., every 20min., €1). The **tourist office**, 35 Agora Çarşısı, Atatürk Mah., is on the southwest corner of Sabahattındede and Atatürk Cad. (☎892 63 28. Open Apr.-Dec. M-F 8am-noon and 1-5pm, Sa-Su 9am-5pm.) Guests at the ⊠**Artemis Guest House ❶**, Atatürk Mah., 1012 Sok. 2, will find clean rooms and an attentive staff. (☎892 19 82; enquiries@artemisguesthouse.com. €5.) The **All Blacks Hotel and Pension ❶**, has some of the nicest rooms in the budget circuit. (☎892 36 57; abnomads@egenet.com.tr. Singles €6.50; doubles €9.75.)

🖪 **DAYTRIP FROM SELÇUK: EPHESUS (EFES).** Ephesus has a concentration of Classical art and architecture surpassed only by Rome and Athens; its ruins rank first among Turkey's ancient sites in terms of sheer size and state of preservation. Guided tours are not necessary. (Site open 8am-6pm. €6.50 entrance fee.) On the left of the road to the lower entrance is the **Vedius Gymnasium,** built in AD 150; beyond the vegetation are the horseshoe-shaped remains of the city's **stadium.** Just inside the lower entrance, a dirt path leads to the right to the ruins of the **Church of the Seven Councils.** After the Ecumenical Council met here to question the Virgin Mary's divinity, the church became known as the **Church of the Virgin Mary.** A tree-lined path leads from the main entrance to the **Arcadiane,** Ephesus's main drag. **The Grand Theater** is a stunning, restored beast carved into the side of Mt. Pion. From the theater, walk along **Marble Way,** which has a metal inscription thought to be the world's oldest advertisement—it's for a brothel. The slight incline signals the beginning of the **Street of Curetes,** which leads to the **Library of Celsus,** the brothel, the 5th-century **Baths of Scholastica,** and the ruins of the **Temple of Hadrian.** Across from the temple are the newly excavated **Terrace Houses,** whose mosaics, frescoes, and peristyle architecture are believed to date back to the 6th century. (Open daily 8am-6:30pm. €5.75.) Farther up the hill on the left are the ruins of the exquisite **Fountain of Trajan.** The building on the left as you walk up the ramp is the **Prytaneion,** which was dedicated to the worship of Vesta and contained an eternal flame tended by the Vestal Virgins. The road that runs by the top entrance leads to the **House of the Virgin Mary** (8km, €15 taxi ride), where Mary lived after leaving Jerusalem. The easiest way to get to Ephesus from **Selçuk** is to take one of the free shuttles run by hotels. Or, from the Kuşadası *otogar*, take a **dolmuş** to Selçuk and ask to stop at Ephesus (30min., €1). From the Selçuk *otogar*, take a Pamucak-bound *dolmuş* (5min., every 15-20min., €0.75). **Taxis** run from Selçuk to the site (€4). It's also an easy **walk** from Selçuk (25min.).

PAMUKKALE ☎258

Pamukkale ("Cotton Castle"), formerly ancient Hierapolis (Holy City), has been drawing the weary and the curious to its thermal springs for more than 23 centuries. A favorite getaway spot for vacationing Romans almost two millennia ago, the warm **baths** at Pamukkale still bubble away. (Open 24hr. €3.20, students €0.80.) Don't leave town without a dip in the sacred fountain at the **Pamukkale Motel,** (☎272 20 24. Pool open daily 8am-8pm. €4 per 2hr.) Behind the motel, the enormous and well-preserved **Grand Theater** dominates the **ruins of Hierapolis.** The former city bath has been converted into an **Hierapolis Museum** housing finds unearthed by Italian archaeologists. (Open daily 9am-6pm. €1.20, students €0.40.) **Buses** to Pamukkale stop in the center of Pamukkale Köyü; some direct buses arrive from Kuşadası and pass through Selçuk (3½hr.; daily 9am, return 5pm; €6.50), but the usual route is through **Denizli**, where buses arrive from: Bodrum (5hr., 5 per day, €5.60); İstanbul (10hr., 6 per day, €14.40); İzmir (4hr., 30 per day, €4.80); Kuşadası (4hr., take any İzmir bus and get off at Selçuk for a *dolmuş*, €4); and Marmaris (4hr., 8 per day, €4.80). *Dolmuş* go between Denizli and Pamukkale (30min., every 15min., €0.40). Many accommodations, including those listed here, offer free pick-up from Denizli. The **tourist office** is at the top of the hill, within the site gates. (☎272 20 77. Open in summer daily 8am-noon and 1:30-6:30pm; off-season M-F 8am-noon and 1-5:30pm.) Just outside Cumhuriyet Meydanı, the backpacker-friendly **✍Meltem Motel ❶** is at 9 Kuzey Sok. (☎272 24 13; meltemmotel@superonline.com.tr. Dorms €3.20; singles €4.) The **Koray Hotel ❷**, 27 Fevzi Çakmak Cad., has a beautiful vined courtyard. (☎272 23 00. Singles €16; doubles €24.) Both hotels have swimming pools with local thermal water.

◪ DAYTRIP FROM PAMUKKALE: APHRODISIAS. Still under excavation, the ruins of Aphrodisias are expected to eclipse Ephesus in grandeur. Highlights include the soaring Ionic columns of the **Temple of Aphrodite,** one of the best-preserved **stadiums** ever excavated, and a new and well-funded **museum** near the site entrance that features a fabulous collection of Roman-era sculpture. (Site open in summer daily 8am-8pm; off-season 8am-5pm. Museum open daily 9am-6:30pm; in winter 9am-5pm. Each site €3.20, students €1.20.) **Buses** leave Pamukkale daily at 9:30am and depart Aphrodisias at 2:30pm (2hr., round-trip €10). Many hotels make additional trips if they have enough interested guests.

BODRUM   ☎252

Bodrum is known for nightlife, impressive ruins, and some of the best beaches in Turkey. Before it became the "Bedroom of the Mediterranean," the ancient city of **Halicarnassus** was known for **Herodotus,** the "father of history," and for the 4th-century BC funerary monument to King Mausolus, so magnificent that its **mausoleum** (from which we get the word) was declared one of the seven wonders of the ancient world. Unfortunately, most of the remains were destroyed, buried beneath modern Bodrum, incorporated into the Bodrum castle, or shipped to London's British Museum. Take Kulucii Sok. from behind the *otogar* and the mausoleum will be on your right. (Open Tu-Su 8am-noon and 1-5pm. Students €1.) Bodrum's formidable **castle,** built over the ruins of an ancient acropolis by crusaders from the Knights of St. John, now features a flock of peacocks, exhibits, the remains of a 4th-century BC Carian Princess, and the **Glass Hall,** home of the oldest shipwreck ever discovered. (Open Tu-F 10am-noon and 1-5pm. €5, students €2.50.) Nightlife abounds on **Cumhuriyet Caddesi,** the road that runs along the beach beyond the marina. The opulent **✍Halikarnas Disco,** on Z. Müren Cad., at the far end of Cumhuriyet Cad. from the marina, flashes strobes 1km from the center of town. (Cover €12. Beer €3.) The club **Hadi Gari,** Cumhuriyet Cad., by the castle, fuses elegance and funk. (Open midnight-4am.)

From the *otogar* on Cevat Şakir Cad., Pamukkale **buses** (☎316 663 26) go to: Bursa (10hr., 3 per day, €13); Fethiye (5hr., 4 per day, €7); İstanbul (12hr., 3 per day, €18); İzmir (4hr., every hr., €7.50); Kuşadası (2½hr., every hr., €6); Marmaris (3hr., every hr., €5); and Pamukkale (5hr., 3 per day, €7). **Dolmuş** go from the *otogar* to Marmaris (3hr., every hr., €5). **Turkish Airlines** (☎313 12 03) flies to İstanbul and Ankara (1hr., 5 per day, €98). **Bodrum Express Lines** (☎316 40 67) has offices in the *otogar* and past the castle on the left toward the sea. For information on **ferries** to Greece, see p. 1028. The **tourist office**, 48 Barış Meydanı, at the foot of the castle, has room listings. (☎316 10 91; fax 316 76 94. Open Apr.-Oct. daily 8:30am-5:00pm; Nov.-Mar. M-F 8am-noon and 1-5pm.) To get from the *otogar* to the peaceful **Emiko**

TURKEY

HOW TO DRINK RAKI The art of drinking *rakı*, Turkey's most famous and potent local drink, is a skill deeply ingrained for most Turks and pitifully elusive to most foreigners. Made with aniseed and white grapes, *rakı* contains 40% alcohol and smells strongly of licorice. The best *rakı*, coming from **Tekirdağ,** near İstanbul, is best complemented by white cheese, watermelon, or fish, which bring out the flavor while soothing the stomach from the fiery impact of the liquor. Though most commonly drunk mixed with cold water (which turns it a cloudy white), *rakı* is occasionally mixed with orange juice or *salgam,* a spicy turnip juice. However you take it, *rakı* is best drunk slowly—you'll learn to respect its kick—and in the company of good friends. Try drinking a spoonful of olive oil beforehand if you want to stay sober.

Pansiyon ❶, Atatürk Cad., 11 Uslu Sok., follow Cevat Şakir Cad. toward the castle, turn left on Atatürk Cad., and turn right after 50m down the sign-covered alley. (☎/fax 316 55 60. Breakfast €2. Kitchen. Singles €10; doubles €16.) **Otel Kilavuz ❷,** 50 Atatürk Cad., boasts a pool and bar. (☎316 38 92; fax 316 28 52. Singles €12; doubles €16.) On your right before the mosque lies **Zetas Saray Restaurant ❷,** which serves fine Turkish cuisine. (Meals €3-10. Open 9am-3am.) **Postal code:** 48400.

⚡ DAYTRIP FROM BODRUM: BODRUM PENINSULA. Bodrum's popularity among Turks stems largely from its location at the head of the **Bodrum Peninsula,** where traditional villages mingle with coastal vistas and dramatic crags. Explore the peninsula's greener northern coast or its drier, sandier southern stretch. Tour **boats** bound for **beaches** on the peninsula's southern coast skirt the front of the castle (daily 9am-noon, return 5-6pm; €10-12, including lunch). Check the tour schedule at the dock. Popular destinations include **Kara Ada** (Black Island), where orange clay from deep within a cave is said to restore youthful beauty, and **Deveplajı** (Camel Beach), where you can ride a camel (€4 per 10min.). The peninsula's northern end, calmer than the southern coast, has rocky beaches and deep water. **Dolmuş** depart frequently from Bodrum's *otogar* for the quiet shores, swimming docks, and clear water of **Gölköy** and **Türkbükü** (30min., €1); the sand paradise of **Yahşi,** Bodrum's longest beach (30min., every 10min., €0.80); the peaceful shore of **Bağla** (30min., every 30min., €1); and the sunken ruins of **Mindos,** near **Gümüşlük**'s beach (40min., €1.40).

MEDITERRANEAN COAST

At turns chic, garish, and remote, the Mediterranean coast stretches along lush national parks, sun-soaked beaches, and shady pine forests. By day, travelers take peaceful boat trips, hike among waterfalls, and explore submerged ruins; by night, they visit Ephesus, dance under the stars, and sleep in treehouses.

◀ FERRIES TO GREECE

From **Marmaris, catamarans** (1hr., May-Oct. 1 per day, round-trip €40), **hydrofoils** (1hr., May-Oct. 2 per day, €40-60), and **ferries** (2hr., when there are enough cars, round-trip €40 plus taxes) all go to **Rhodes.** Make reservations the day before at a travel agency; try **Yeşil Marmaris** (☎(252) 412 64 86).

DALYAN AND KAUNOS (CAUNOS) ☎252

The placid village of Dalyan seems to have grown out of the nearby breezy river. Carian **rock tombs** built into cliffs are visible from the harbor, and thick reed beds teem with wildlife just a few minutes away. Dalyan's sites are best seen on **boat**

tours that visit the ruins of ancient **Kaunos** (June-Oct. open daily 8am-7pm; Nov.-May daily 9am-5pm; €1.50); **İztuzu Beach**, where endangered loggerhead turtles lay their eggs by night (open daily 8am-8pm); and local **mud baths** and **thermal springs** (open daily 7am-7:30pm; €0.90). Boat tour offices are behind the turtle statue in town on Maraş Sok. (Tours €10, including lunch). The *dolmuş* from Ortaca stops in front of the mosque. Facing the PTT (post office), turn left and follow the road right, then go straight. City **buses** go to Ortaca (20min., every 15min., €0.40), where you can get a bus headed to Fethiye (1¼hr., €2.40) and Marmaris (1½hr., €2.40). A *dolmuş* also runs directly to Marmaris and Fethiye (3 per day, €1.80). With your back to the turtle statue, head into the passageway across from the statue to reach the **tourist office**. (☎284 42 35. Open in summer daily 8:30am-noon and 1-6pm; off-season 8:30am-noon and 1-5:30pm.) From the turtle statue, walk 75m down Maraş Sok., make the 2nd left on 10 Sok., and walk a block to find **Gül Motel Pension ❶**. (☎284 24 67. Singles €7; doubles €12.) You'll find plenty of pensions, restaurants, and some bars on Maraş Sok. **Postal code:** 48840.

FETHIYE   ☎252

Fethiye, on a harbor ringed by pine forests and mountains, is a backpacker base with unique hiking opportunities. Daytrips to **Saklikeut Gorge** allow you to wade in a river and scale waterfalls. (Entrance €0.60, students €0.30). The ghost town of **Kayaköy** offers many hikes; call the nearby Kayaköy Motel and Restaurant (☎ (258) 618 00 69) for trekking advice. The marvelous pebble beach and **Blue Lagoon** in **Ölüdeniz**—a peninsula of beach cradled in wooded hills and lapped by clear water—are an easy trip. Enter from Tabiat Park, on the right of the road. From the *dolmuş* station, it's a 20min. walk or a €3.50 taxi ride to the tip. (Park and lagoon open 8am-7pm. €0.75.) To reach Saklikeut, Kayaköy, or Ölüdeniz from Fethiye, take a *dolmuş* from the stop near the intersection of Hastane and Atatürk Cad., near the mosque (25-45min., every 10min., round-trip €2-3). Take a boat from the beach in Ölüdeniz (45min., 3 per day, €3) to reach the tiny, beautiful bay of **Butterfly Valley**, home to waterfalls and the nocturnal orange-and-black Jersey Tiger butterfly. Paths marked by blue dots wind their way up to two waterfalls (€1). **Fetur**, 50m past the tourist office on Fevzi Çakmak Cad., arranges daily tours. (☎614 20 34. Open daily 9am-5:30pm.)

Buses run frequently from Fethiye's *otogar* on Ölüdeniz Cad. Coastal road buses can drop off passengers anywhere, so there's no need to wait for a specific bus into town. If there are no shuttles to the center, take a *dolmuş* to the PTT in town (every 5min., €0.40). From there, walk down Atatürk Cad. through the harbor to the **tourist office**. (☎/fax 612 19 75. Open in summer daily 8:30am-5pm; off-season M-F 8:30am-5pm.) Call for free pickup from the *otogar* to **◪Ideal Pansiyon ❶**, Karagözler Zafer Cad. #1 (☎/fax 614 19 81. Breakfast included. Delicious dinner €3.50. Laundry. Dorms €6.50.) **Postal code:** 48300.

KAŞ   ☎242

Sandwiched between sea and mountains, cosmopolitan Kaş is hassle-free. Its pleasant streets are lined with cheap, hospitable lodgings, excellent restaurants, and laid-back bars. A peninsula curving around one side of the town's harbor creates a calm, rock-lined lagoon ideal for swimming in the cool turquoise water. The city also serves as a gateway to the backpacker haven of Olimpos (see below). The *otogar*, uphill on Atatürk Cad., sends **buses** to: Ankara (12hr., 8:30pm, €19); Antalya (3hr., every 30min., €5.40); Fethiye (2hr., 5 per day, €2.50); İstanbul (15hr., 6:30pm, €21); and İzmir (9hr., 2 per day, €12.50). The **tourist office,** 5 Cumhuriyet Meydanı, is to the left as you face the back of the Atatürk statue. (☎836 12 38. Open in summer daily 8am-noon and 1-7pm; off-season M-F 8am-5pm.) Budget

pensions line the sidestreets to the right of Atatürk Bul. (as you head from the *otogar* to the waterfront). A breezy rooftop terrace awaits at **Ateş Pension ❶**, Yeni Cami Cad. No. 3. (☎836 13 93; atespension@superonline.com. Breakfast included. Free **Internet**. Singles €7; doubles €14.) **Postal code:** 07580.

OLIMPOS   ☎242

Olimpos awes visitors with its scenery. Tall cliffs streaked mauve, red, and gray tower above acres of pine forest and orange orchards. **Roman and Byzantine ruins** lie hidden among the vines of a marshy jungle. Wander through to discover ancient temples and the crumbling walls of medieval castles. A pebble beach awaits at the end of the road. (Ruins and beach €5, students €2. Hold on to your ticket stub.) The town's other main attraction is ▨**Chimæra**, the perpetual flame springing from the mountainside 7km away. Mythology explains the flame as the breath of a mythical beast; geologists suggest natural methane gas. **Bus tours** leave Olimpos at 9pm (3hr., €3); ask at any hostel for details. To get to Olimpos from Kaş, take an Antalya-bound bus. **Buses** stop at a rest station on the main road. From there, *dolmuş* (15min., every hr., €1.25) take passengers into town. As Olimpos is classified as an archaeological site, the use of concrete is banned, so resourceful locals have constructed **treehouse pansiyons,** which line the dirt road to the beach and ruins. ▨**Bayram's Treehouse Pension ❶** is the ultimate black hole of chill, with colorful bungalows and a friendly staff. (☎892 12 43; bayrams1@turk.net. Breakfast and dinner included. **Internet** access. Arranges travel. Close to beach and ruins. Treehouses €7.50; pensions €11.) **Postal code:** 07350.

ANTALYA   ☎242

Antalya's concrete block buildings encircle *Kaleiçi* ("inside the fortress"), a crescent-shaped old city brimming with Ottoman houses, pensions, and restaurants. ▨**The Antalya Museum,** 2 Konyaaltı Bul., 2.5km from town, won the 1988 European Museum of the Year Award for its exhibits ranging from prehistoric times to the founding of the Turkish Republic. *Dolmuş* labeled "Konyaaltı/Liman" head along Cumhuriyet Bul., which changes its name to Konyaaltı Bul., stopping at the large "D" signs (€0.30). Get off at the yellow museum signs before heading downhill to the beach. The tram (€0.25) also runs from Kaleiçi to the museum. (Open in summer Tu-Su 9am-6pm; off-season 8am-5pm. €6, students €4.50.) **Lara** and **Konyaaltı** beaches are both accessible by *dolmuş* (to Lara from the Doğu Garaj, to Konyaaltı from Konyaaltı Bul.; €0.30). Every fall, the huge **Antalya Altın Portakal** ("Golden Orange") Film Festival features international and Turkish cinema.

   Flights from Antalya International Airport (AYT; domestic flights ☎330 30 30, international flights ☎330 36 00), 15km outside of town, leave for İstanbul (€61, students €51) and various foreign cities. Buses run between the Turkish Airlines THY office, next to the tourist office, and Antalya Airport (in summer 10 per day, €3). **Buses** leave from the orange *otogar*, 4km out of town at Anadolu Kavşağı, for: Bodrum (8hr., €15); Göreme (10hr., 2 per day, €16); İstanbul (12hr., €17); Kaş (3hr., every 30min., €4); and Olimpos (1¼hr., every 20min., €1.50). Gray buses (€0.40) run from outside the *otogar* to the city center, near Kaleiçi. The **tourist office,** on Cumhuriyet Cad., is to the left of the red minaret and past the military complex. (☎241 17 47. Open in summer M-F 8am-7pm, Sa-Su 9am-7pm; off-season M-F 8am-5pm, Sa-Su 10am-5pm.) Almost all of the 200 pensions and hotels within the ancient walls of Kaleiçi include breakfast private showers. **La Paloma Pansiyon ❷**, Kılıçarslan Mah., 60 Hesapçı Sok., offers gorgeous rooms. (☎244 79 24. Singles €20; doubles €35.) Backpackers hang out at **Sabah Pansiyon ❶**, Kaleiçi Kılıçarslan Mah., 60 Hesapçı Sok. (☎247 53 45. Singles €6; doubles €8-18; roof, couch, or floor €3. **Camping** €2.50-3.) **Postal code:** 07000.

CENTRAL TURKEY

Central Turkey is less heavily touristed than the Aegean and Mediterranean coasts. It offers cooler weather, a wealth of ancient ruins, and some of the country's most hospitable towns, from sophisticated Ankara to the surreal cities of Cappadocia.

ANKARA ☎312

Ankara is a new city with an ancient history. In 1923, after the Turkish War of Independence, Atatürk transformed the small town into an administrative metropolis. The city has vibrant nightlife, being the nation's premier college town.

▐▀▞ TRANSPORTATION AND PRACTICAL INFORMATION. Trains arrive at the *otogar*, 1.5km down Cumhuriyet Bul. from Ulus Square, from İstanbul (6½-9½hr., 7 per day, €4-35) and İzmir (15hr., 3 per day, €9). To get to the city center, follow the covered tunnel past the last platform into the Maltepe station of the east-west **Ankaray subway,** which stops in Kızılay and Ulus (5-ride pass €2.50, students €1.50). The **tourist office,** 121 Gazi Mustafa Kemal Bul., is directly outside the Maltepe subway stop. (☎231 55 72. Open daily 9am-5pm.) **Embassies** in Ankara include: **Australia,** 83 Nenehatun Cad., Gaziomanpaşa (☎446 11 80); **Canada,** 75 Nenehatun Cad. (☎436 12 75); **New Zealand,** 13/4 İran Cad., Kavaklıdere (☎467 90 56); **Northern Cyprus,** 20 Rabat Sok., Gaziosmanpaşa (☎446 29 20); **South Africa,** 27 Filistin Sok., Gaziomanpaşa (☎446 40 56); **UK,** 46A Şehit Ersan Cad., Çankaya (☎468 62 30); and **US,** 110 Atatürk Bul. (☎468 61 10). Check **email** at the ▧ **Internet Center Café,** 107 Atatürk Bul. (€1.25 per hr. Open daily 9am-11pm.) **Postal code:** 06443.

▛▘ ACCOMMODATIONS AND FOOD. Of the two main accommodation centers, **Ulus** is cheaper and closer to sights, but student-oriented **Kızılay** is cleaner. In Ulus, the best bet for quality and price is at **Otel Zümrüt ❶,** 16 Şehit Teğmen Kalmaz Cad. From the equestrian statue, go south on Atatürk Bul. and take the second left. (☎311 33 93. Singles €5-8; doubles €12-17; triples €17-21.) **Otel Hisar ❶,** Hisarparkı Cad., #6, is east of the statue, toward the citadel. (☎311 98 89. Singles €6.50; doubles €11.) To reach peaceful **Otel Ertan ❷,** 70 Selânik Cad. in Kızılay, head south on Atatürk Bul., take the fourth left after the McDonald's on Meşrutiyet Cad., and take the third right on Selânik Cad. (☎418 40 84. Singles €15.50; doubles €24.50.) The main culinary neighborhoods are **Gençlik Park** (cheap), **Kızılay** (mid-range), **Hisar** (formal), and **Kavaklıdere** (upscale). In Kızılay, ▧**Göksu Restaurant ❷,** 22A Bayındır Sok., has classy Turkish and European food. (Open daily noon-midnight.) Many other places dot Karanfil Sok. and Selânik Sok. Gima **supermarkets** are on Anafartalar Cad. in Ulus and Atatürk Bul. in Kızılay. Cheaper markets abound in Ulus.

◪▐ SIGHTS AND NIGHTLIFE. The award-winning **Museum of Anatolian Civilizations** (Anadolu Medeniyetleri Müzesi) lies at the foot of the citadel looming over the old town. The museum is in a restored 15th-century Ottoman covered bazaar and features a tightly organized collection of world-class artifacts. From the equestrian statue in Ulus, walk to the top of Hisarparkı Cad., turn right at the bottom of the Citadel steps, and follow the Citadel boundaries. (Open Tu-Su 8:30am-5:30pm. €3, students €2.) Don't miss Atatürk's mausoleum, **Anıt Kabir;** nearly 1km long, it houses Atatürk's sarcophagus and personal effects. Take the subway to Tandoğan and follow the signs; when you reach the unmarked entrance guarded by two soldiers, head 10min. uphill. (Open M 1:30-5pm, Tu-Su 9am-5pm. Free.) The immense **Kocatepe Mosque** looms east of Kızılay on Mithat Paşa Cad. Take the subway to Kızılay, then walk along Ziya Gökalp Cad. until you hit Mithat Paşa Cad (10min.). Completed in 1987, it's billed as a 16th-century mosque utilizing 20th-century technology, like glowing digital clocks that indicate prayer times. At night, enjoy live music in the bars of **Kızılay**; pub life centers on **İnkilâp Sokagi** and the livelier **Bayındır Sokagi**, to the left of Kızılay. **S.S.K. İşhanı**, on the corner of Ziya Gökalp Cad. and Selânik Cad., is packed with live music bars.

CAPPADOCIA

Cappadocia's unique landscape began to take shape 10 million years ago, when volcanic lava and ash hardened into a layer of soft rock called tufa. Rain, wind, and flooding from the Kızılırmak River shaped the tufa into cone-shaped monoliths called *peribaca* ("fairy chimneys"), grouped in cave-riddled valleys and along gorge ridges. Throughout Cappadocia, stairs, windows, and sentry holes have been carved into the already-eroded rock.

GÖREME   ☎384

Göreme is the capital of Cappadocia's backpacker scene. The city goes all out with its cave theme—most bars and discos are subterranean, and pensions often have "cave" rooms. Visitors have been known to extend their stays: a local saying goes, "Once you've tasted Göreme's water, you're bound to come back."

🖹🖹 TRANSPORTATION AND PRACTICAL INFORMATION. Buses leave via Nevşehir for: Ankara (4hr., 9 per day, €8); Bodrum (14hr., 3 per day, €20); Bursa (10hr., 2 per day, €16); İstanbul (11hr., 7 per day, €16); İzmir (12hr., 6 per day, €16); Marmaris (14hr., 5 per day, €20); Olimpos (12hr., 8 per day, €19); and Pamukkale (10hr., 4 per day, €14). The *otogar*, in the center of town, contains the town's only official **tourist office** (☎271 25 58), which has information on most of Göreme's lodgings. As you exit the station, the main road is directly in front of you. The **Post Office (PTT)**, which has the best exchange rate in town, is on the main road just after the turnoff for the Open-Air Museum. (Open daily 8:30am-12:30pm and 1:30-5:30pm.) **Postal code:** 50180.

🖸🖸 ACCOMMODATIONS AND FOOD. Kelebek Hotel ❶, just uphill from Tuna Caves, is clean and well-run, with spectacular views of surrounding valleys. (☎271 25 31; www.kelebekhotel.com. Dorms €4; fairy chimney rooms €12, with shower €18; deluxe suites €50.) To get to **Tuna Caves Pension ❶** from the *otogar*, take the first right after the ATM and follow signs. (☎271 26 81; tunacaves@hotmail.com. Dorms €4; singles €6; deluxe suites $23.) The **Special Cave Pension ❶** has the coziest caves in town, with clean private showers in every room. (☎271 23 47; cheilker@yahoo.com. €7 per person.) **Kookabura Pansiyon ❶** has stunning views and a cave bar with old Turkish flair. (☎271 25 49. Breakfast €3. Dorms €4; singles €5, with shower €7.) **🖹Sedef Restaurant ❶,** on the left as you head out of Göreme on Bilal Eroglu Cad., serves a bulging stuffed eggplant (€1.50) and has live music.

🖸🖸 SIGHTS AND HIKING. One of Cappadocia's biggest draws is its **Open-Air Museum,** 2km out of Göreme on the Ürgüp road, which contains seven Byzantine churches, a convent, and a kitchen. In the 4th century, St. Basil founded one of the first Christian monasteries here, setting down religious tenets that influenced the entire Western monastic movement. The churches are full of frescoes; spectacular scenes from Jesus's life within the **Karanlık Kilise** (Dark Church). Follow the canal downhill from the bus station. With the canal on your left, take a left at the first major intersection. (Open 8am-5pm. Museum €3. Dark Church €7.)

Cappadocia's breathtaking landscape is a **hiking** heaven. On the way, you can descend into **Kirmizi Vadi** (Rose Valley), where bizarre, multi-colored rock formations make for one of the area's better hikes. Although rewarding, the 10km valley can be disorienting. There are exits at 3km and 7km for those who wish to arrange return transportation. You'll end up in Çavuşin, where you can take the Avanos-Nevşehir **bus** or the Avanos-Zelve-Göreme-Ürgüp **dolmuş** back to Göreme (M-F every 30min. until 6pm, Sa-Su every hr.); or, take a **taxi** (€5). Other notable hikes include more challenging **Pigeon Valley** and smoldering **Love Valley.** Although most area hikes are moderate and safe, hiking with friends or guides are your best bets to stay safe, navigate trickier areas, and see all sights.

⚑ DAYTRIPS FROM GÖREME: UNDERGROUND CITIES AND ÇAVUŞIN.
Cappadocia contains almost 200 **underground cities; Kaymaklı** and **Derinkuyu** are the largest. The cities were carved from tufa with mind-boggling ingenuity. Beware of uncharted tunnels. All explorable areas are marked and lit (though flashlights are still handy); red arrows lead down, blue arrows lead up. (Cities open in summer daily 8am-5pm. €3.75.) From Göreme, **dolmuş** run to Nevşehir (€0.50) and go on to Kaymaklı (30min., €0.60) and Derinkuyu (45min., €0.80).

The nearby provincial village of **Çavuşin** (2km from Göreme) is home to Cappadocia's oldest church, the 5th-century **St. John the Baptist.** Or, head over to Zelve's **Open Air Museum** (open daily 8am-5:30pm; €4), where ruins of tufa villages make for hours of exploring, climbing, and burrowing; watch for gaps and holes underfoot. Both the Ürgüp-Avanos **dolmuş** and the Göreme-Avanos **bus** pass through Çavuşin. On foot, follow the main road past Çavuşin, take a right up the dirt road behind the pottery shop, and continue to climb for a magnificent ridge walk.

UKRAINE (УКРАЇНА)

Translated literally, "Ukraine" means "borderland," and the country has occupied this precarious position for most of its history. Vast and fertile, perpetually tempting to invaders, newly independent Ukraine is now caught between overbearing Russia on one side and a bloc of *nouveau riche* countries on the other. The country offers fascinating, uncrowded museums and theaters, wonderful castles, and the magnificent, spirited Black Sea coast. With no beaten path from which to stray, Ukraine rewards travelers with a challenging but unique experience.

FACTS AND FIGURES

Official Name: Ukraine.

Capital: Kyiv.

Major cities: Kyiv, Lviv, Odessa.

Population: 49,000,000 (73% Ukrainian, 22% Russian).

Land Area: 603,700 sq. km.

Time Zone: GMT +2.

Languages: Ukrainian, Russian, Tatar.

Religions: Ukrainian Orthodox (29%), Uniate (7%), Protestant (4%).

DISCOVER UKRAINE

Start any trip to Ukraine in **Kyiv** (p. 1044); once the seat of the Kyivan Rus dynasty, the modern city's park-covered environs and riverside vistas are a breathtaking backdrop to its incomparable mix of urban rush and provincial charm. The country's undiscovered jewel is **Lviv** (p. 1047), in western Ukraine. Khrushchev gave the **Crimea** (p. 1049) to Ukraine, and the Russians didn't object—unfortunately for them, they didn't realize how much sun and fun they were losing. Farther west is **Odessa** (p. 1048), a former USSR party town.

ESSENTIALS

WHEN TO GO

The best time to visit is between May and September, when it's warmer. Spring and early fall can be unpredictable; snow flurries are always possible. Winter is bitterly cold. Along the Black Sea, summers are hot and winters are mild.

DOCUMENTS AND FORMALITIES

VISAS. Travelers from Australia, Canada, Ireland, New Zealand, South Africa, the UK, and the US must have a visa. (Processing fee €45; single-entry €30; double-entry €60; multiple-entry €120; transit €15. Fees waived for American students with proper documents.) Citizens of Australia, New Zealand, and South Africa require an **invitation,** but citizens of Canada, the EU, and the US do not. See p. 836 for organizations that arrange invitations and visas. **International Management Services** also arrange invitations; fax the request a month in advance. (US ☎757-573-8362; fax 757-622-4693; Ukraine ☎/fax 044 516 2433; www.travel-ims.com.) When proceeding through **customs** you will be required to declare all valuables and foreign currency above €1000 (including traveler's checks). It is illegal to bring Ukrainian currency into Ukraine. Foreigners arriving at Kyiv's Borispol airport must buy a health insurance policy (€23 per week), which is essentially an entry tax and does not provide health care coverage.

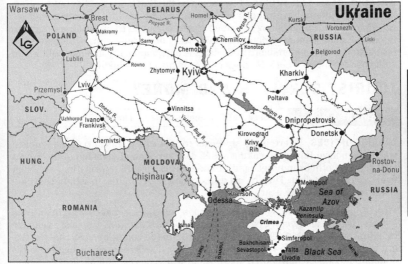

Ukraine

The **Office of Visas and Registration** (OVIR; ОВИР), in Kyiv at blv. Tarasa Shevchenka 34 (Тараса Шевченка; ☎(044) 224 9051), and in police stations in smaller cities, extend visas. Do not lose the paper given to you when entering the country to supplement your visa; it is required to leave the country.

EMBASSIES. All foreign embassies are in Kyiv (see p. 1045). Ukrainian embassies at home include: **Australia** (consulate), 902-912 Mt. Alexander Rd., Ground fl. #3, Essendon, Victoria 3040 (☎613-326-0135; fax 613-326-0139); **Canada,** 331 Metcalfe St., Ottawa, ON K2P 0J9 (☎613-230-2961; www.infoukes.com/ukremb); **South Africa,** 398 Marais Brooklyn, Pretoria; P.O. Box 57291, Arcadia, 0181 (☎012 461 946; fax 461 944); **UK,** 78 Kensington Park Rd., London W11 2PL (☎020 7727 6312; 020 7792 1708); **US,** 3350 M St. NW, Washington, D.C. 20007 (☎202-333-0606; www.ukremb.com).

TRANSPORTATION

BY PLANE. Ukraine International Airlines (US ☎800-876-0114; in Kyiv ☎(044) 461 5050 or 234 4528; www.ukraine-international.com) flies to Kyiv (KBP and IEV), Lviv (LWO), and Odessa (ODS) from a number of European capitals. Several other international carriers also fly to Kyiv, generally once or twice per week.

BY TRAIN. Trains run frequently from Ukraine's neighboring countries, and are the best way to travel. Be prepared for a two-hour stop at the border. On most trains within Ukraine there are three classes: *platzkart,* where you'll be crammed in with *babushki* and their baskets of strawberries; *coupé,* a more private 4-person compartment; and *SV,* or first-class, which is twice as roomy (and expensive) as *coupé.* Paying the extra two dollars for *coupé* can make a big difference. Arrive well before the train departs so you can show your ticket to cashiers or fellow passengers, look helpless, and ask "платформа?" (plaht-FORM-ah).

BY BUS. Buses cost about the same as trains, but are often much shabbier, except for modern AutoLux (АвтоЛюкс) buses. Schedules are generally reliable, but low demand can cause cancellations. Buy tickets at the *kassa* (box office); if they are sold out, go directly to the driver, who might find you an extra seat.

BY FERRY, TAXI, AND THUMB. Ferries across the Black Sea are limited to a few routes from Odessa, Sevastopol, and Yalta to İstanbul. In cities, private minibuses called *marshrutke* run along the same routes as public transportation; they are faster but slightly more expensive. **Taxi** drivers may try to gouge foreigners, so negotiate the price beforehand. **Hitchhiking** is uncommon; if you must, hold a sign with your destination. *Let's Go* does not recommend hitchhiking.

TOURIST SERVICES AND MONEY

EMERGENCY	Police: ☎02. Ambulance: ☎03. Fire: ☎01.

TOURIST OFFICES. There is no state-run tourist office. Local travel agencies, which often have English-speaking staffs, can be helpful. Remnants of the Soviet **Intourist** have offices in hotels and provide tourist-related information, although usually not in English. They're used to dealing with groups, to whom they sell "excursion" packages to nearby sights.

MONEY. The *karbovanets* (Krb; a.k.a. *kupon*) has been replaced with the **hryvnia** (гривна; hv; plural *hryvny*), each worth 100,000 *karbovantsi*. The best exchange rates are at **Obmin Valyut** (Обмін Валют) kiosks in the center of most cities. Western Union and ATMs are everywhere. Traveler's checks can be changed into US dollars for small commissions. Most banks will give Visa and MasterCard cash advances for a high commission. The lobbies of fancier hotels usually exchange US dollars at lousy rates. Private money changers lurk near legitimate kiosks, ready with brilliant schemes for ripping you off; do not exchange money with them—it's illegal. Although locals don't usually leave tips, most expats give 10%. Accommodations in Ukraine average €10-20; meals run €5-7.

HRYVNY		
AUS$1 = 2.94HV	1HV = AUS$0.34	
CDN$1 = 3.42HV	1HV = CDN$0.29	
EUR€1 = 5.24HV	1HV = EUR€0.19	
NZ$1 = 2.50HV	1HV = NZ$0.40	
ZAR1 = 0.50HV	1HV = ZAR2.00	
UK£1 = 8.25HV	1HV = UK£0.12	
US$1 = 5.33HV	1HV = US$0.19	

COMMUNICATION

PHONE CODE	**Country code: 380. International dialing prefix:** 810. From outside Ukraine, dial int'l dialing prefix (see inside back cover) + 380 + city code + local number.

MAIL. Mail is cheap and quite reliable (about 10 days to North America). The easiest way to mail letters is to buy pre-stamped envelopes at the post office. For *Poste Restante*, address envelope to be held: Firstname, SURNAME, До Запитание, Ul. Sadovaya 10, 270015 Odessa, UKRAINE.

TELEPHONES. The Ukrainian phone system is stumbling toward modernity. The easiest way to make international calls with a calling card or collect is with Utel (Ukraine Telephone). Buy a Utel phonecard (sold at most Utel phone locations), dial ☎8 and wait for another tone, then enter the international direct access number (counted as a local call): **AT&T,** ☎100 11; **British Telecom,** ☎10 04 41; **Canada**

Direct, ☎ 100 17; and **MCI,** ☎ 100 13. Or, call at the central telephone office; guess how long your call will take, pay at the counter, and they'll direct you to a booth. Dial ☎ 810, followed by country code, city code, and number. Calling is expensive: per minute charges are: to Eastern Europe €0.06, to Western Europe €1.50, to North America €2.50. For an English-language operator, dial ☎ 8 192.

LANGUAGES. It's extremely difficult to travel without knowing some Ukrainian or Russian. In Kyiv, Odessa, and the Crimea, Russian is more common than Ukrainian (although all official signs are in Ukrainian). In Transcarpathia, Ukrainian is preferred—people will speak Russian with you only if they know that you are not Russian. *Let's Go* uses Ukrainian names in Kyiv and Western Ukraine, and Russian in the Crimea and Odessa. For basic Russian phrases, see p. 1064.

ACCOMMODATIONS AND CAMPING

UKRAINE	❶	❷	❸	❹	❺
ACCOMMODATIONS	under 55hv	55-105hv	106-266hv	267-480hv	over 480hv

There are no youth hostels, and budget accommodations are usually in unrenovated Soviet-era buildings. Not all **hotels** accept foreigners, and those that do often charge them many times more than what a Ukrainian would pay. Although room prices in Kyiv are astronomical, singles run anywhere from 5hv to 90hv in the rest of the country. The phrase *samoe deshovoe miesto* (самое дешёвое место) means "the cheapest place." More expensive hotels aren't necessarily nicer; in some hotels, women lodging alone may be mistaken for prostitutes. Standard hotel rooms include a TV, phone, and a refrigerator. You will be given a *vizitka* (визитка; hotel card) to show to the hall monitor (дежурная; dezhurnaya) to get a key; surrender it on leaving the building. Valuables should never be left unattended; ask at the desk if there's a safe. Hot water is a rarity—ask before checking in. **Private rooms** can be arranged through overseas agencies or bargained for at the train station. Most cities have a **campground,** but camping outside of designated areas is illegal, and enforcement is merciless.

FOOD AND DRINK

UKRAINE	❶	❷	❸	❹	❺
FOOD	under 11hv	11-27hv	28-54hv	55-105hv	over 105hv

There are few choices between fancy restaurants and *stolovayas* (cafeterias), dying bastions of cheap, hot food. Stale *stolovaya* food can knock you out of commission for hours, but a good *stolovaya* meal is a triumph of the human spirit. Vegetarians can create their own meals from potatoes, mushrooms, and cabbage sold at markets; bring your own bag. State food stores are classified by content: *hastronom* (гастроном) sell packaged goods; *moloko* (молоко) milk products; *ovochi-frukty* (овочі-фрукты) fruits and vegetables; *myaso* (мясо) meat; *hlib* (хліб) bread; *kolbasy* (колбаси) sausage; and *ryba* (риба) fish. Tea is a popular national drink, as is the beer-like *kvas* (see below).

A TASTE OF KVAS When the sun is blazing, a true Ukrainian thirsts for **kvas** (квас). The taste depends on its container—in Kyiv, you'll see it served from siphons, in the provinces from rusty cisterns—but the tingling sensation always comes down to the sourdough solution on which *kvas* is based. Kyivans crave the beverage so much that even in the rain, citizens of all ages can be found huddled around taps.

HEALTH AND SAFETY

SAFETY. The risk of crime is actually about the same as in the rest of Eastern Europe, but it is always wise to register with your embassy once you get to Ukraine. While Ukraine is neither violent nor politically volatile, it is poor; keep a low profile and watch your belongings.

HEALTH. Water is bad and hard to find in bottled form; it's best to boil it or learn to love brushing your teeth with soda. Fruits and vegetables from open markets are generally safe, although storage conditions and pesticides make thorough washing imperative. Meat purchased at public markets should be checked very carefully and cooked thoroughly. Embassy officials say that Chernobyl-related radiation poses minimal risk to short-term travelers, but the region should be given a wide berth. Public toilets are disgusting; pay toilets are cleaner and sometimes have toilet paper, but bring your own anyway. Pharmacies are quite common and carry basic Western products.

HOLIDAYS AND FESTIVALS

Holidays: Orthodox Christmas (Jan. 7); International Women's Day (Mar. 8); Good Friday (Apr. 18); Easter (Apr. 20-21); Labor Day (May 1-2); Victory Day (May 9); Holy Trinity (June 15); Constitution Day (June 28); Independence Day (Aug. 24).

KYIV (КИЇВ)   ☎8044

Straddling the wide Dniepro river and layered with hills, Kyiv greets visitors with golden-domed churches, a sprawling old town, and winding streets. The cradle of Slavic-Orthodox culture, and once the USSR's third-largest city, Kyiv has been struggling to adjust to its new role as the capital of an independent and nationalist Ukraine. Although foreign tourists often pass it by for Moscow, the city is focused on improvement, and extensive reconstruction projects are in progress.

▐▀ TRANSPORTATION

Flights: Boryspil International Airport (КВР; Бориспіль; ☎296 72 43), 30km southeast. Private **Polit** buses (Полит; ☎296 73 67) go to Ploscha Peremohi every 30min.-1hr; buy tickets (8-10hv) on board. Or, take a taxi (70-100hv) to the center.

Trains: Kyiv-Passazhyrsky (Київ-Пассажирський), Vokzalna pl. (☎005). MR: Vokzalna. Info kiosk (довидка; dovidka) in the center of the main hall. (Open daily 6:30-11pm.) **Tickets** are sold at counters to the left and right of the main hall; a passport is required for ticket purchase. To: **Bratislava** (18hr., 1 per day, 329hv); **Budapest** (25hr., 1 per day, 419hv); **Minsk** (12-13hr., 1 per day, 84hv); **Moscow** (15-17hr., 4 per day, 156hv); **Prague** (34hr., 1 per day, 446hv); and **Warsaw** (15hr., 1 per day, 222hv).

Buses: Tsentralny Avtovokzal (Центральний Автовокзал), Moskovska pl. 3 (Московська; ☎250 99 86), is 10min. past Libidska, the last stop on the MG line. Go right and then left out of the Metro; take trolleybus #4 or walk 100m down the big highway and follow it to the right for 500m. To: **Lviv** (2 per day, 52hv); **Moscow** (21hr., 2 per day, 75hv); and **Odessa** (10hr., 4 per day, 57hv).

Public Transportation: The 3 intersecting lines of the **Metro**—blue (MB), green (MG), and red (MR)—are efficient but limited. Purchase blue tokens (0.50hv), good on all public transport, at the "каса" (kasa). "Вхід" (vkhid) indicates an entrance, "перехід" (perekhid) a walkway to another station, and "вихід у місто" (vykhid u misto) an exit onto the street. **Trolleys, buses,** and **marshrutki** (private vans numbered with bus routes) go where the Metro doesn't. Bus tickets are sold at kiosks; punch your ticket on board to avoid a 10hv fine. *Marshrutki* tickets (1hv) are sold on board.

▰▰ ORIENTATION AND PRACTICAL INFORMATION

Most attractions and services lie on the west bank of the Dniepro. Three Metro stops from the train station is the main avenue **vulitsa Khreshchatyk** (Хрещатик; on the MR line). The center of Kyiv is vul. Khreshchatyk's fountained **Maydan Nezalezhnosti** (Майдан Незалежності; Independence Plaza; on the MB line).

Tourist Office: Kyiv still lacks official tourist offices. There are travel agency representatives at the airport, and the Kyiv Business Directory (available in hotels) lists more agencies. Try **Yana Travel Group** (Яна), vul. Saksaganskoho 42 (Саксаганського; ☎246 62 13; www.travel.kiev.ua/yana). Open M-F 9am-5pm.

Embassies: Australia, vul. Kominternu 18/137 (Комінтерну; ☎235 75 86). Open M-Th 10am-1pm. **Canada,** vul. Yaroslaviv Val 31 (Ярославів Вал; ☎464 11 44; www.canadaeuropa.gc.ca/ukraine). Open M-Th 8:30am-noon. **Russia,** visa section at vul. Kotuzova 8v (Котузова; ☎296 45 04). Open M-Th 9am-1pm and 3-6pm, F 9am-1pm and 3-5pm. **UK,** vul. Desyatynna 6 (☎462 00 11; www.britemb-ukraine.net); visa section at vul. Sichnevoho Povstannya 6 (Січневого Повстання; ☎290 73 17). Open M-F 9am-1pm and 2-5pm. **US,** vul. Kotsyubinskoho 10 (Коцюбинського); consular section at vul. Pimonenka 6 (Пімоненка; ☎490 44 22, emergency ☎216 38 05; www.usinfo.usemb.kiev.ua). Open M-F 9-6pm. Call ahead to make an appointment.

Medical Assistance: Ambulance ☎03. The Kyiv Business Directory lists hospitals. The **American Medical Center,** vul. Berdicherska 1 (☎/fax 490 7600; patientservices@amc.corn.ua) staffs English-speaking doctors.

Internet Access: Cyber Cafe (Кібер Кафе), Prorizna 21 (www.cybercafe.com). Centrally located. 10hv per hr. Open daily 9am-11pm.

Telephones: Myzhmisky Perehovorny Punkt (Мижміський Переговорний Пункт), at the post office. **Telefon-Telefaks** (Телефон-Телефакс), around the corner (enter on vul. Khreshchatyk). Both open 24hr. **Public telephones** (Таксофон; Taksofon) work only with phone cards, available at the post office. **English operator** ☎8192.

Post Office: vul. Khreshchatyk 22, next to Maydan Nezalezhnosti. Address mail to be held: Firstname SURNAME, *Poste Restante*, **01001** Київ-1, Почтамт до Воетребовання, UKRAINE. Open M-Sa 8am-9pm, Su 9am-7pm.

▰▰ ACCOMMODATIONS AND FOOD

It can be hard to find a decent room for a reasonable price. The best values in town are the **private rooms** offered at the train station and sometimes outside of hotels. **Hotel Express ❷** (Експресс), blv. Shevchenka 38/40 (Шевченка), which has clean, inexpensive rooms, is straight up vul. Kominternu from the train station. (☎239 89 95. Singles US$24; doubles US$42.) **Grazhdanski Aviatski Institut Student Hotel ❶** (Гражданский Авіатский), vul. Nizhinska 29E (Ніжінська), is a good deal, but a trek. From behind MR: Vokzalna, turn right into the passageway to the trams. Take tram #1K or 1 to Harmatna (Гарматна). Backtrack and turn right onto vul. Nizhinska, cross at the first intersection with a trolleybus, then follow the stairs up into the complex. Walk diagonally, keeping the first building to your right; pass block "Д" on the right, and look for the Hotel NAU (Готел НАУ) sign above. (☎484 90 59. Check-out noon. Singles 35hv, with bath 98hv; doubles 160hv.)

UKRAINE

KYIV 3, NAZIS 0 After the Nazis invaded Kyiv and imprisoned thousands of Ukrainians in September 1941, a German soldier discovered that one prisoner was on the *Dynamo Kyiv* soccer team. The Nazi officers quickly rounded up the other players and arranged a "death match" between the Ukrainians and the German army team. Despite the weakened condition of the Dynamo's players, Ukraine won 3-0. Shortly thereafter, the entire team was thrown into a concentration camp, where most of them perished in front of a firing squad. Their memory—and Kyiv's pride—lives on in a monument overlooking Khreshchaty Park. Recent scholarship suggests, however, that the match never took place and was fiction created by Soviet propagandists.

Kyiv's *rynki* (markets) are a good budget food option; **Bessarabsky Rynok** (Бессарабский Ринок), at the intersection of vul. Khreshchatyk and blv. Shevchenka, has the best meat and produce. **Korchma pid Osokorom ❶** (Корчма під Осокором), vul. Mikhaylivsky 20b, is an intimate cafe with traditional food. (MB: Maydan Nezalezhnosti. Vodka 1.90hv; main dishes 5-8hv. Open daily 10am-10pm.) **Café Chicot ❸** (Кафе Шикот), vul. Ivana Franka 27, serves Ukrainian and European dishes. (MR: Universytet. Entrees 30-50hv.) **Tequila House ❹**, vul. Spasskaya 8, is a popular Tex-Mex restaurant. (Cocktails 29hv. Main dishes 50-80hv; 11am-3pm 20% off. Open daily 11am-1am.)

👁 SIGHTS

VULITSA KHRESHCHATYK AND ENVIRONS. Broad and commercial **vulitsa Khreshchatyk** (Хрещатик) begins at the intersection with blv. Tarasa Shevchenka and goes up to the recently redone **Independence Plaza** (Maydan Nezalezhnosti), filled with fountains and covering an underground shopping mall. *(MR: Khreshchatyk.)* Historical monuments celebrating Prince Volodymyr, who converted Kyivan Rus to Christianity, and the legendary soccer players who resisted the Nazis (see above) are found in **Khreshchaty Park**, past the silver **Arch of Brotherhood.**

VOLODYMYRSKA VULITSA: ST. SOPHIA TO GOLDEN GATE. The **St. Sophia Monastery** complex was the religious center of Kyivan Rus and is still the focal point of Ukrainian nationalism. The monastery's golden onion domes, decorated facades, and exquisite Byzantine icons make it one of the main attractions in Kyiv. *(MG: Zoloty Vorota or trolley #16 from Maydan Nezalezhnosti. Grounds open daily 10am-7:30pm. 1hv. Museums open F-Tu 10am-6pm, W 10am-5pm. 10hv, with camera 30hv.)* The **Golden Gate** (Золоти Ворота; Zoloty Vorota), once the entrance to the city, houses a small museum; next to it is a statue of Yaroslav the Wise. Several other small churches are scattered throughout the area.

ANDRIYIVSKY UZVIZ AND THE PODIL DISTRICT. Full of cafes, vendors, and galleries, the cobblestone **Andriyivsky uzviz** (Андріївскі узвіз; Andriyivsky path) can be reached by funicular (every 5min., daily 6:30am-11pm, 0.50hv) from the subway. *(MB: Poshtova. Alternatively, walk down from Mikhaylivska Square.)* The ☒**Museum of One Street** at Andriyivsky 2B creatively covers the history of Kyiv's most famous street. *(Open Tu-Sa noon-6pm. 3hv.)* Climb the gray steps at the corner of Desyatinna and Volodymyrska (Володимирска) to see the ruins of **Tithe Church** (Десятинна Церква; Desyatinna Tserkva), the oldest stone church of Kyivan Rus, and the **National Museum of Ukrainian History.** *(Open Th-Tu 10am-5pm. 4.20hv.)* Nearby is the impressive 18th-century **St. Andrew's Cathedral.** The path spills out into the church-filled **Podil** district, which was the center of Kyiv in the 10th and 11th centuries. Just east of the *ploscha*, the **Chernobyl Museum**, Provulok Khorevii 1, details the legacy of the nuclear disaster; ask to see the video of the explosion. *(Open M-F 10am-6pm; Sa 10am-5pm; closed last M of each month. 5hv.)*

KYIV-PECHERY MONASTERY. Kyiv's oldest and holiest religious site, the mysterious **Kyiv-Pechery Monastery** (Киево-Печерська Лавра; Kievo-Pecherska Lavra) deserves a full day of exploration. In addition to several museums, the complex houses the **Holy Trinity Gate Church,** the **Refectory Church,** and the fascinating ▓**caves** where saints and the monastery's monks lie mummified and entombed. Buy a candle to help you navigate the caves. *(MR: Arsenalna. Turn left as you exit; walk 10min. down vul. Sichnevoho Povstanyiya. Monastery open daily 9am-7pm. Museums open daily 10am-5pm. Monastery 16hv, students 8hv; museums 3hv/1hv. Caves open daily 8am-2pm. Dress modestly.)*

BABYN YAR. The monument at **Babyn Yar** is a moving tribute to the first victims of the Nazis in Ukraine. The statue, a group of interlocking figures falling to their deaths, is accompanied by a plaque stating that 100,000 Kyivans died at Babyn Yar; the current estimate of victims—mostly Jews—is twice that figure. *(MG: Dorohozhychy. In the park near the TV tower, at the intersection of vul. Oleny Telihy and vul. Melnykova.)*

🎵 🎭 ENTERTAINMENT AND NIGHTLIFE

Check the *Kyiv Post* (www.kyivpost.com) and *What's On* (www.whatsonkyiv.com) for entertainment listings and the latest nightspots. The **Shevchenko Opera and Ballet Theater,** vul. Volodymyrska, has several performances each week. (☎224 71 65. MR: Teatralna. Ticket office open daily 11am-3pm, Tu-Su also 4:30-7pm.) The **Dynamo Kyiv** soccer team (see p. 1046) plays from late spring to fall; buy tickets at the office in front of the stadium. (Tickets 5-20hv.) On hot summer days, escape to the **Hydropark** (Гідропарк), an amusement park and beach on an island on the Dniepro River. (MR: Hydropark.)

The pub **Golden Gate,** vul. Zolotovoritskaya, directly across from the Golden Gate entrance, is an expat favorite. (Local beer 8-12hv. Open daily 11am-late.) **Artclub 44,** in the basement of Khreshchatyk 44, has more than 150 kinds of whiskey. Enter the courtyard and through the unmarked door on the left. (Live jazz daily 10pm-midnight. Open daily 10am-2am.) **Cocktailbar "111,"** Peremohy pl. 1, in Hotel Lybid, has a revolving bar serving 111 classic cocktails. (Cover W-Su 20hv. Open daily 7am-2am.) Put on your fancy outfit and hop aboard **River Palace,** a nightclub, casino, and bar on a boat docked at the right bank of the Dnieper. (Cocktails 30-50hv; main dishes 70-200hv. Club cover 30-50hv. Open daily noon-6am.)

LVIV (ЛЬВІВ)   ☎80322

Divorced from Poland in 1945 after 600 years of ups and downs, Lviv is now tied to Kyiv even though the two cities speak different languages. Though often overlooked, energetic Lviv is much more affordable than Kyiv, and rewards visitors with its steeple-filled center, castle, museums, and theater.

📧 🛈 TRANSPORTATION AND PRACTICAL INFORMATION. Trains (☎748 20

68) go from pl. Vokzalna (Вокзальна) to: Bratislava (18hr., 1 per day, 215hv); Budapest (14hr., 1 per day, 250hv); Kraków (8hr., 1 per day, 136hv); Kyiv (11hr., 3 per day, 51hv); Moscow (29hr., 1 per day, 161hv); Odessa (14hr., 1 per day, 50hv); and Prague (21hr., 1 per day, 336hv). **Tickets** are sold at windows #20-25 on the top floor, and at Hnatyka 20 (Гнатюка). The main **bus station,** vul. Stryska 189 (Стрийська; ☎63 24 73), on the outskirts of town, sends buses to Kraków (8hr., 1 per day, 73hv) and Warsaw (10hr., 3 per day, 82hv). From the bus station, *marshrutka* #18 goes to the train station, where trams run to town. **Lviv Tourist Info Center** is in city hall *(ratusha),* pl. Rynok 1. (☎97 57 67; www.about.lviv.ua. Open M-F 9am-6pm.) **Internet Klub,** vul. Dudayeva, has 24hr. high-speed Internet access. (8am-midnight 4hv per hr., midnight-8am 2hv per hr.) **Postal code:** 79 000.

ACCOMMODATIONS AND FOOD. At the end of pr. Svobody is **Hotel Lviv** ❷, vul. Chornovola 7 (Чорновола). Take tram #6 from the train station to the Opera House; backtrack and turn right on Chornovola. (☎ 79 22 70. Singles 35hv, with bath 70hv; doubles 50hv/100hv.) Take tram #1 to Doroshenka (Дорошенка) to reach **Hotel George** ❸, pl. Mitskevycha 1, which is known for luxury suites, but also has budget options with common baths. (☎ 74 21 82. Singles 111hv, with bath 361hv; doubles 157/381hv.) **Ploschad Rynok** is the restaurant and cafe center of Lviv; the most convenient market, one block from Hotel George, is **Halytsky Rynok** (Галицький Ринок), behind the flower stands across from St. Andrew's Church. The trendiest place to have dessert, **Videnska Kavyarnya** ❸ (Віденська Кавярня), pr. Svobody 12., also serves great dinner and breakfast. (Breakfast 3-13hv; entrees 10-25hv; desserts 3-10hv. Open daily 9am-11pm.) Feast under ancient trees on the outdoor patio of **Kafe Kupol** ❸ (Кафе Купол), vul. Tchaikovskoho 37. From Hotel George, walk down pr. Shevchenko, take the second right, and continue to the hill. (Entrees 15-30hv. Open daily 11am-11pm.)

SIGHTS AND ENTERTAINMENT. Climb up to **High Castle Hill** (Высокий Замок; Vysoky Zamok), the former site of the Galician King's Palace, for a panoramic view of Lviv. Follow vul. Krivonoca (Кривоноса) from its intersection with Hotny and Halytskono, go until you pass #39, then take a left down the long dirt road to wind your way up around the hill counterclockwise. Return to the heart of the city and begin a walking tour from pr. Svobody, which is dominated by the dazzling exterior of the **Theater of Opera and Ballet** (Театра Опери а Балету; Teatr Opery a Baletu; ☎ 72 88 60. Tickets from 10hv.) The heart of the city is **ploschad Rynok**, the historic market square, surrounded by countless churches and richly decorated merchant homes dating from the 16th-18th centuries. The 19th-century **town hall** is topped with a trident-wielding Neptune statue. The **History Museum** (Історичний Музей; Istorychny Muzey) complex is at pl. Rynok #4, 6, and 24. The displays at #4 recount episodes of Lviv's history that were ignored under the Soviets; in WWII, Ukrainian citizens fought for the Nazis, then for Soviet Russia, and later faced oppression from both sides. King Jan III Sobieski lived at building #6 in the 17th century; museum #24 focuses on earlier Ukrainian history. (Open Th-Tu 10am-5pm. 0.50-1hv.) Walk up vul. Staroyevrejska (Old Jewish Road) to reach **Golden Rosa Synagogue.** For centuries, Lviv was an important center of Jewish culture, but now only ruins remain; Nazis destroyed the synagogue in 1942.

Cheap tickets for performances ranging from opera to experimental drama are available at each theater's *kasa* or at the *teatralny kasy* (театральни каси; ticket windows), pr. Svobody 37. (Open M-Sa 10am-1pm and 2-5pm.) Lviv is renowned for its cafe culture. ■**Club-Cafe Lyalka** (Клуб-Кафе Лялька), vul. Halytskoho 1 (Галицького), below the Puppet Theater (Театр Лялок; Teatr Lyalok), often has live music or art installations. (Wine 3hv; coffee 1.50hv. Cover 7-10hv. Open M-Th 11am-midnight, F-Su 11am-2am.) **Club-Cafe za Kulisamy** (Клуб-Кафе за Кулісами), vul. Tchaikovshoho 7, on the 2nd floor of the Philharmonic, is a small bar filled with enthusiastic students. (Open daily noon-midnight.)

ODESSA (ОДЕССА) ☎ 80482

Catherine the Great fortified Odessa with the limestone on which it stood, leaving behind the longest network of catacombs in the world. The city became a crucial port; luck and geography allowed it to prosper to the point of decadence. A haven for intellectuals, *mafiosi*, and a flood of summer cruise groups, Odessa can be pricey, but the city's ancient beauty makes it worth visiting.

TRANSPORTATION AND PRACTICAL INFORMATION.

Trains go from pl. Privokzalnaya 2 (Привокзальная), at the north end of ul. Pushkinskaya, to: Kyiv (12hr., 2 per day, 58hv); Moscow (26hr., 2-3 per day, 178hv); and St. Petersburg (35hr., 1 per day, 206hv). Trolley #1 goes to the main thoroughfare, ul. Deribasovskaya (Дерибасовская). To reach the bus station, take tram #5 from the train station to the last stop. **Buses** run from ul. Kolontayevskaya 58 (Колонтасвская) to Kyiv (12hr., 4 per day, 36hv) and Simferopol (8hr., 1 per day, 43hv). Buy tickets at least the night before. **Ferries** go from Morskoy Vokzal (Морской Вокзал; Sea Terminal), ul. Primorskaya 6 (Приморская) to Istanbul (1-2 days, 2 per week, US$80-90). **FGT Travel** (also called Fagot; Фагот), ul. Rishelievskaya 4, in the wax museum, runs tours and has lodging information. (☎37 52 01; museum@mail.od.ua. Open daily 8:30am-10pm.) **Postal code:** 65 000.

ACCOMMODATIONS AND FOOD.

Staying in **private rooms** is cheap (from US$5 per person). From the train station, take trams #3 or 12 to reach the downtown hotels, most near noisy pl. Grecheskaya (Греческая) and ul. Deribasovskaya. **Passazh ❷** (Пассаж), ul. Preobrazhenskaya 34, has small, pleasant rooms, but no hot water in the summer. (☎22 48 49. Reservations recommended. Singles 67-130hv; doubles 172hv; triples 220hv.) **Odessa State University Dormitory #8 ❶,** ul. Dovzhenko 9B (Довженко), rents spartan rooms in July and August. (Russian ☎63 04 67, English ☎23 84 77. Dorms 10hv.) **Spartak ❷** (Спартак), ul. Deribasovskaya 25, has old, clean rooms in a great location. (Singles 110hv; doubles 103-146hv; triples 132hv.) Odessa has good restaurants and cafes, especially along ul. Deribasovskaya. **Klarabara ❸** (Кларабара), ul. Preobrazhenskaya 28, is in the Gorsad. (Main dishes 26-39hv. Live jazz and blues F-Su 8-11pm. Open Su-Th 10am-midnight, F-Sa 10am-1am.) The **Privoz mega-market** (Привоз), Privoznaya ul., is across from the train station. (Open daily 8am-6pm.)

SIGHTS AND ENTERTAINMENT.

Street performers of all kinds gather on **ulitsa Deribasovskaya.** Turn right on Preobrazhenska, left on Sofiyevskaya (Софиевская), and walk up two blocks to reach the **Odessa Art Museum** (Одеський художеотвеный музей), ul. Sofiyevskaya 5a, where you can explore the grotto below. (Grotto tour with guide only; ☎23 84 62. Museum 2hv; grotto 2hv plus guide fee. Open W-M 10:30am-5pm; closed last F of the month.) Left off ul. Deribasovskaya onto ul. Yekaterinskaya, the

YOUR OWN WAY

THE CRIMEA

Since antiquity, the Crimea (Крым) has been a political hotbed and trading artery thanks to its key position on the rocky Black Sea Coast. Despite a flagging economy, visitors still flock to the region's rocky shores.

SIMFEROPOL. The transportation hub Simferopol (Симферополь) is a gateway to the dry cliffs of the ancient Tartar town of **Bakhchisarai.**

YALTA. Once the inspiration of Chekhov, Rachmaninov, and Tolstoy, Yalta (Ялта) is now thronged with crowds who come to enjoy its sanatoria and beautiful beaches. Info: ☎(80654) 32 81 40; http://co.net/travel.

LIVADIA. During the 1945 Yalta Conference, Churchill, Roosevelt, and Stalin actually met in Livadia (Ливадия), at the former summer palace of Tsar Nicholas II, which is open to visitors.

SEVASTOPOL. Suffering tragic losses in WWII, Sevastopol (Севастополь) rebuilt its elegant streets before ornament became taboo in Soviet cities. Info: ☎(80692) 16 55 00 81.

TRANSPORTATION. Trains go to Simferopol from: Kyiv (19hr., 6 per day, 78hv); and Odessa (14hr., 1 per day, 38hv.). **Buses** go from Simferopol (☎80652 005) to: Bakhchisarai (5 per day, 2.97hv); Sevastopol (2hr., 7 per day, 7.23hv); and Yalta (2hr., every 20min., 4hv). A **water shuttle** runs from Yalta to Livadia (15min., every 30min., 2.50hv).

statue of the **Duc de Richelieu**, the city's first governor, looks down the **Potemkin Stairs** (Потемкинская Лестница; Potomkinskaya Lestnitsa) toward the shiny port, **Morskoy Vokzal**. The **Literature Museum** (Литературный Музей; Literaturny muzey), Lanzheronovskaya 2 (Ланжероновская), provides a look at the city's intellectual and cultural heritage. (Open Tu-Su 10am-5pm. 9hv. English tour 54hv.) Turn right from the Literature Museum to reach **ulitsa Pushkinskaya**, Odessa's most beautiful street. The **Pushkin Museum and Memorial** (Литературно-мемориальный музей Пушкина; Literaturno-memorialny muzey Pushkina) at #13 is the former hotel where Pushkin during his brief exile (1823-1824) from St. Petersburg. (Open Tu-Su 10am-5pm. 9hv, students 6hv.) Directly underneath the city is Odessa's main quarry, the world's longest series of ▨**catacombs**. During the Nazi occupation, the resistance was based here; the city has set up an excellent subterranean **museum** in its honor. FGT (see above) gives tours in English. (75hv. Bring a sweater.) Most **beaches** are accessible either by public transportation or on foot. Tram #5 goes to: **Arkadiya** (Аркадия), the most popular on summer nights; **Lanzheron** (Ланжерон), the closest to central Odessa; and **Otrada** (Отрада). Trams #17 and 18 go to **Golden Shore** (Золотой Берег; Zolotoy Bereg), as well as the **Chayka** (Чайка) and **Kurortny** (Курортный) beaches.

The **Opera and Ballet Theater** (Театр Оперы и Балета; Teatr Opery i Baleta), at the end of ul. Rishelievskaya, has shows Tu-Su at 6pm and Sunday at noon. Buy tickets in advance from the ticket office to the right of the theater. (Open Tu-Su 10am-6pm. 15-30hv, major acts 100-600hv.) On **ulitsa Deribasovskaya**, restaurants, cafes, and bars stay open late, playing music ranging from Euro-techno to Slavic folk. The open-air discos in **Arkadiya** (tram #5 from pl. Grechskaya) attract dancing crowds as the summer nights grow warm.

LANGUAGE BASICS

CYRILLIC ALPHABET

CYRILLIC	ENGLISH	PRONOUNCE
А а	a	a as in garden
Б б	b	b as in burn
В в	v	v as in village
Г г	g	g as in good
Д д	d	d as in dog
Е е	ye or e	ye as in yellow
Ё ё	yo	yo as in your
Ж ж	zh	as in Persia
З з	z	z as in zany
И и	ee	ee as in seen
Й й	y	(see * below)
К к	k	k as in kitten
Л л	l	l as in lemon
М м	m	m as in meteor
Н н	n	n as in night
О о	o	o as in hole
П п	p	p as in Peter

CYRILLIC	ENGLISH	PRONOUNCE
Р р	r	r as in red
С с	s	s as in sun
Т т	t	t as in top
У у	oo	oo as in doodle
Ф ф	f	f as in fish
Х х	kh	as in chutzpah (hkh)
Ц ц	ts	ts as in Let's Go
Ч ч	ch	ch as in Chinese
Ш ш	sh	ch as in champagne
Щ щ	shch	as in Khrushchev
ъ	(hard)	(no sound)
ы	y	as in lit
ь	(soft)	(no sound)
Э э	eh	as in Alexander
Ю ю	yoo	You
Я я	yah	yah as in yahoo!

* Й creates dipthongs, altering the sounds of the vowels it follows: ОЙ is pronounced "oy" (boy), АЙ is pronounced "aye" (bye), ИЙ is pronounced "ee" (baby), and ЕЙ is pronounced "ehy" (bay).

The Cyrillic alphabet is used in Belarus, Bulgaria, Russia, and the Ukraine. A few languages have some transliteration or pronunciation quirks:

Belarus: Belarussian substitutes "i" for "и." The Cyrillic "г" is transliterated as "h" but is pronounced "g" (for example, "Hrodna" is pronounced "Grodno").

Bulgaria: Bulgarian transliterates "х" as "h," "щ" as "sht," and "ъ" as either "a" or "u" (pronounced like the "u" in "bug"). Let's Go transliterates this letter as a "u."

Ukraine: Ukrainian adds the "i" (pronounced "ee") and the "ï" (pronounced "yee")—the "и" is closest to the "i" in "sit." The rarely used "є" sounds like "ye" in "yep!" The "ґ" (hard "g"), and the "г," pronounced "g" in Russian, comes out like an "h."

GREEK ALPHABET

SYMBOL	LETTER	PRONOUNCE
α A	alpha	a as in father
β B	beta	v as in velvet
γ Γ	gamma	y as in yo or g as in go
δ Δ	delta	th as in there
ε E	epsilon	e as in jet
ζ Z	zeta	z as in zebra
η H	eta	ee as in queen
θ Θ	theta	th as in health
ι I	iota	ee as in tree
κ K	kappa	k as in cat
λ Λ	lambda	l as in land
μ M	mu	m as in moose

SYMBOL	LETTER	PRONOUNCE
ν N	nu	n as in net
ξ Ξ	ksi	x as in mix
o O	omicron	o as in row
π Π	pi	p as in peace
ρ P	rho	r as in roll
σ (ς) Σ	sigma	s as in sense
τ T	tau	t as in tent
υ Y	upsilon	ee as in green
φ (φ) Φ	phi	f as in fog
χ X	xi	ch (h) as in horse
ψ Ψ	psi	ps as in oops
ω Ω	omega	o as in row

LANGUAGE BASICS

BULGARIAN

For the Cyrillic alphabet, see p. 1051.

ENGLISH	BULGARIAN	PRONOUNCE
yes/no	Да/Не	dah/neh
please	Извинете	eez-vi-NEH-teh
thank you	Благодаря	blahg-oh-dahr-YAH
Hello	Добър ден	DOH-bur den
Goodbye	Добиждане	doh-VIZH-dan-eh
Sorry/excuse me	Извинете	iz-vi-NEE-tye
Help!	Помощ!	PO-mosht
police	полиция	pohl-EE-tsee-ya

ENGLISH	BULGARIAN	PRONOUNCE
ticket	билет	bi-LYET
train/bus	влак/автобус	vlahkahv-to-BOOS
departure	заминаващи	zaminavashti
grocery	бакалия	bah-kah-LIH-ya
hotel/hostel	хотел/общежитие	kho-tel/ob-shcheh-zhee-tee-yeh
pharmacy	аптека	ahp-TEH-kah
toilet	тоалетна	to-ah-LYET-na
exchange	обменно бюро	OB-myen-na byu-ROH

ENGLISH	BULGARIAN	PRONOUNCE
Where is...?	Къде е ...?	kuh-DEH eh
How do I get to...?	Как да стигна ...?	kak dah STEEG-na
How much does this cost?	Колко Струва ...?	KOHL-ko STROO-va
Do you have...?	Имате Ли ...?	EEH-mah-teh lee
Do you speak English?	Говорите ли Английски?	go-VO-rih-te li an-GLIS-keeh

CROATIAN

ENGLISH	CROATIAN	PRONOUNCE
yes/no	Da/Ne	da/neh
please	Molim	MO-leem
thank you	Hvala lijepa	HVAH-la leepa
Hello	Dobardan	Do-bar-DAHN
Goodbye	Bog	Bog
Sorry/excuse me	Oprostite	o-PRO-sti-teh
Help!	U pomoć!	OO pomoch
police	policija	po-LEE-tsee-ya
embassy	ambasadu	ahm-bah-sah-du

ENGLISH	CROATIAN	PRONOUNCE
one-way	u jednom smjeru	oo YEH-dnom smee-YEH-roo
round-trip	povratna karta	POV-rat-na KAR-ta
train/bus	vlak/autobus	vlahk/au-TOH-bus
taxi	taksi	tahksi
departure	odlažak	OD-lazh-ak
grocery	trgovina	TER-goh-vee-na
hotel	hotel	hoh-tel
pharmacy	ljekarna	lye-KHA-rna
bathroom	WC	vay-tsay

ENGLISH	CROATIAN	PRONOUNCE
Where is...?	Gdje je?	GDYE je
How do I get to...?	Kako mogu doći do ...?	KAH-ko MO-goo DO-chee do...
How much does this cost?	Koliko to košta?	KO-li-koh toh KOH-shta
Do you have...?	Imate li...?	EEM-a-teh lee
Do you speak English?	Govorite li engleski?	GO-vor-i-teh lee eng-LEH-ski

All letters are pronounced; "č" and "c" are both "ch"; "š" is "sh"; "ž" is "sh"; and "j" is equivalent to "y." The letter "r" is rolled except in the absence of a vowel.

CZECH

ENGLISH	CZECH	PRONOUNCE
yes/no	Ano/ne	AH-no/neh
please	Prosím	PROH-seem
thank you	Děkuji	DYEH-koo-yih
Hello	Dobrý den	DO-bree den
Goodbye	Nashedanou	NAH sleh-dah-noh-oo
Sorry/excuse me	Promiňte	PROH-mihn-teh
Help!	Pomoc!	POH-mots
police	policie	PO-lits-iye
passport	cestovní pas	TSE-stov-neeh
hotel	hotel	HOH-tel
single room	jednolůžkový pokoj	YED-noh-luu-zhko-veeh PO-koy
double room	dvoulůžkový pokoj	DVOU-luu-zhko-veeh PO-koy
with bath	s koupelnou	SKOH-pel-noh
with shower	se sprchou	SE SPR-khou
bathroom	WC	VEE-TSEE
open/closed	otevřeno/zavřeno	O-te-zheno/ZAV-rzhen-o
left/right	vlevo/vpravo	VLE-voh/VPRA-voh
straight	běžte rovně	BYEZH-teh ROHV-nye
center of town	centrum měšťá	MNEHST-skeh TSEN-troom
castle	hrad	KHRAD
church	kostel	KO-stel
square	náměstí	NAH-mye-stee

ENGLISH	CZECH	PRONOUNCE
departure	odjezd	OD-yezd
one-way	jen tam	yen tam
round-trip	zpáteční	SPAH-tech-nyee
reservation	místenka	mis-TEN-kah
ticket	lístek	LIS tek
train/bus	vlak/autobus	vlahk/OUT-oh-boos
station	nádraží	NA-drah-zhee
airport	letiště	LEH-tish-tyeh
taxi	taxi	TEHK-see
bank	banka	BAN-ka
exchange	směnárna	smyeh-NAR-na
grocery	potraviny	PO-tra-vee-nee
pharmacy	lékárna	LEE-khaar-nah
tourist office	turistické informace	TOO-rist-it-skeh IN-for-mat-tseh
post office	pošta	POSH-ta
vegetarian	vegetariánský	VEHG-eh-tah-rih-aan-skee-ee
kosher	košer	KOH-sher
nuts/milk	ořech/mléko	OH-rekch/MLEH-koh
menu	listek	LIS-tek
beer	pivo	PEE-voh
market	trh	TH-rh
bakery	pekařství	PE-karzh-stvee

ENGLISH	CZECH	PRONOUNCE
Where is...?	Kde je...?	k-DEH
How do I get to...?	Jak se dostanu do...?	YAK seh dohs-TAH-noo doh
How much does this cost?	Kolik to stojí?	KOH-lihk STOH-yee
Do you have...?	Máte...?	MAH-teh
Do you speak English?	Mluvíte anglicky?	MLOO-vit-eh ahng-GLIT-ski
I'd like to order...	Prosím...	PROH-seem

Every letter is pronounced, and stress is always placed on the first syllable. Letters with certain diacriticals (á, é, í, ó, ú, ů, ý) should be held longer. "C" is pronounced "ts"; "g" is always hard; "č" is pronounced "ch"; "ch" is considered one letter (alphabetized after h) and is pronounced like a gutteral "h"; "j" is pronounced "y"; "r" is slightly rolled; "ř" is "rzh"; "š" is "sh"; "w" is pronounced "v"; and "ž" is "zh." The letter "ě" sounds like "ye" or "nye" (e.g., "ně" is "nyeh," "mě" is "mnyeh").

DANISH

ENGLISH	DANISH	PRONOUNCE
yes/no	ano/ne	AH-no/neh
please	vær så venlig	vair soh VEN-li
thank you	tak	tack
Hello	Goddag	go-DAY
Goodbye	Farvel	fah-VEL
Sorry/excuse me	undskyld	UN-scoold
Help!	Hjælp!	yelp
police	politiet	por-lee-TEE-ehth
embassy	ambassade	ahm-ba-SA-theh

ENGLISH	DANISH	PRONOUNCE
ticket	billet	bill-ETT
train/bus	toget/bussen	TOE-et/BOO-sehn
airport	lufthavns	LAYFD-haown
departure	afgang	af-gahng
market	marked	mah-GEHTH
hotel/hostel	hotel/vandrerhjem	ho-TEL/VAN-drar-yem
pharmacy	apotek	ah-por-TIG
toilet	toilet	toy-LEHD
city center	centrum	SEHN-trum

ENGLISH	DANISH	PRONOUNCE
Where is...?	Hvor er...?	voa air
How do I get to...?	Hvordan kommer jeg til...?	vo-DAN KOM-ah yai tee
How much does this cost?	Hvad koster det?	va KOS-tor dey
I'd like a...	Jeg vil gerne have en...	yai vi GEHR-neh ha en
Do you speak English?	Taler du engelsk?	TAY-luh dou ENG-elsk

In Danish, stress is usually placed on the first syllable of the word. Unfortunately, there are no firm rules for pronouncing the alphabet. Danish is a North Germanic language and thus resembles Swedish, Norweigan, Faeroese, and Icelandic.

DUTCH

ENGLISH	DUTCH	PRONOUNCE
yes/no	ja/nee	ya/nay
please	alstublieft	AL-stoo-bleeft
thank you	dank u wel	dank oo vel
Hello	Hallo	hal-LO
Goodbye	Tot ziens	tot zeens
Sorry/excuse me	Neemt u mij niet/pardon	naymt oo mi neet/par-DON
Help!	Help!	help
police	politie	po-LEET-see
embassy	ambassade	am-bass-AH-duh

ENGLISH	DUTCH	PRONOUNCE
ticket	kaartje	KAHRT-yuh
train/bus	trein/bus	trin/boos
taxi	taxi	TAX-ee
departure	vertrek	ver-TREK
grocery	kruidenier	krow-duh-EER
hotel	hotel	ho-TEL
pharmacy	apotheek	ah-po-TAYK
bathroom	badkamer	BAT-kah-mer
narcotics	drugs	droogs

ENGLISH	DUTCH	PRONOUNCE
Where is...?	Waar is...?	vaar is
How do I get to...?	Hoe kom ik in...?	hoo kom ik in
How much does this cost?	Wat kost het?	vat kost het
Do you have...?	Heeft u...?	hayft oo
Do you speak English?	Sprekt u Engels?	spraykt oo EN-gels

In Dutch, "j" is pronounced like the "s" in treasure. A gutteral "g" sound is used for both "g" and "ch." The Dutch "ui" is pronounced "ow," and the dipthong "ij" is best approximated in English as "ah" followed by a long "e." There are two plural endings for nouns: -en (more common) and -s.

ESTONIAN

ENGLISH	ESTONIAN	PRONOUNCE
yes/no	jaa/ei	jah/ay
please	palun	PAH-loon
thank you	tänan	TA-nahn
Hello	tere	TEH-reh
Goodbye	head aega	heh-ahd EYE-gah
Sorry/excuse me	vabandage	vah-bahn-DAHG-eh
Help!	Appi!	APP-pi
police	politsei	POH-leet-say
passport	pass	pahs

ENGLISH	ESTONIAN	PRONOUNCE
ticket	pilet	PEE-leht
train/bus	rong/buss	rong/boos
taxi	takso	TAHK-sah
departs	väljub	VAL-yoob
grocery	toidupood	TOY-doo-POOD
hotel	hotellis	HAH-teh-lees
pharmacy	apteek	ahp-TEEK
toilet	tualett	twa-LET
bank	pank	pahnk

ENGLISH	ESTONIAN	PRONOUNCE
Where is...?	Kus on...?	koos õn
I'd like to go to...	Soovin minna...	sõõ-veen MEEN-nah
How much does this cost?	Kui palju?	kwee PAHL-yoo
Do you have...?	Kas teil on...?	kahs tayl õn
Do you speak English?	Kas te räägite inglise keelt?	kahs teh raa-GEE-teh een-GLEE-seh kehlt

The first syllable is always stressed. The letter "c" is pronounced "ts"; "j" is "y"; "š" is "sh"; "w" is "v"; "z" is either "z" or "ts"; and "ž" is "zh."

FINNISH

ENGLISH	FINNISH	PRONOUNCE
yes/no	kyllä/ei	EW-la/ay
please	pyydän	BU-dan
thank you	kiitos	KEE-tohss
Hello	hei	hey
Goodbye	näkemiin	NA-kay-meen
Sorry/excuse me	anteeksi	ON-take see
Help!	Apua!	AH-poo-ah
police	poliisi	PO-lee-see
embassy	suur lähetystöä	SOOHR LA-heh-tüs-ter-ah

ENGLISH	FINNISH	PRONOUNCE
ticket	lipun	LEE-pun
train/bus	juna/bussi	YU-nuh/BUS-si
boat	bussi	BOOS-see
departures	lähtevät	lah-teh-vaht
market	oria	TOH-ree-uh
hotel/hostel	hotelli/retkelly-maja	HO-tehl-lee/
pharmacy	apteekki	UHP-teehk-kee
bathroom	WC	VEE-see
telephone	puhelinta	POO-heh-lin-tuh

ENGLISH	FINNISH	PRONOUNCE
Where is...?	Missä on...?	MEESS-ah OWN
How do I get to...?	Miten minä pääsen...?	MEE-ten MEE-na PA-sen
How much does this cost?	Paljonko tämämaksaa?	PA-lee-onk-o teh-meh MOCK-sah
I'd like to buy...	Haluaisin ostaa...	HUH-loo-ay-sin OS-tuh
Do you speak English?	Puhutteko englantia?	POO-hoo-teh-kaw ENG-lan-ti-ah?

In Finnish, "x" may be written as "ks," and "z" may be written (and is pronounced) "ts." "V" and "w" are considered the same letter and are alphabetized under "v." Double consonants are held longer and split the word into two syllables.

FRENCH

ENGLISH	FRENCH	PRONOUNCE	ENGLISH	FRENCH	PRONOUNCE
yes/no	oui/non	wee/nohn	departure	le départ	DAY-part
please	S'il vous plaît.	see-voo-PLAY	one-way	le billet simple	BEE-AY-samp
thank you	Merci.	mehr-SEE	round-trip	le billet retour	BEE-AY-re-TOOR
Hello	Bonjour.	bohn-ZHOOR	reservation	le réservation	rez-er-va-SHE-on
Goodbye	Au revoir.	oh re-VWAHR	ticket	le billet	BEE-AY
Sorry/excuse me	Excusez-moi!	ex-KU-zay-MWAH	train/bus	le train/le bus	tran/boos
Help!	Au secours!	oh-sek-OOR	station	la gare	gar
police	la police	po-LEES	airport	l'aéroport	ler-O-port
embassy	l'ambassade	lam-bas-SADE	taxi	le taxi	tax-EE
passport	le passeport	pass-PORT	ferry	le bac	bak
hotel/hostel	l'hôtel	LO-tel	bank	la banque	bahnk
hostel	l'auberge de jeunesse	LO-berzh-de-zhun-ESS	exchange	l'échange	lay-SHAN-je
single room	une chambre simple	oon-SHAM-bra-samp	grocery	l'épicerie	lep-IZ-er-ie
double room	une chambre pour deux	oon-SHAM-bra-poor-do	pharmacy	la pharmacie	far-ma-SEE
with shower	avec la douche	a-VEK-la-DOO-sh	tourist office	le bureau de tourisme	byur-O-de-toor-EE-sm
bathroom	la salle de bain	SAL-de-BAN	town hall	l'hôtel de ville	LO-tel-de-vill
open/closed	ouvert/fermé	OO-vert/fer-MAY	vegetarian	le végétarien	ve-JAY-ter-REE-en
left/right	à gauche/ à droite	a-GOsh/a-dwat	vegan	le végétaliene	ve-JAY-tal-EE-en
straight	tout droit	TOOT-dwat	kosher/halal	kascher/halal	ka-SHER/ha-lal
turn	tournez	toor-NAY	nuts/milk	les cacahouètes/ le lait	CAK-a-hwets/ LAY
newsstand	le tabac	ta-BAK	change/coins	la monnaie	mon-AY
candy	le bonbon	bon-bon	tip	la service	ser-VEE-s
United States	les États-Unis	AY-tats-YOU-nee	waiter	le garçon	GAR-son
bicycle	la vélo	vay-LO	cigarette	la cigarette	SEE-gar-et
car	la voiture	vwa-TURE	condom	le préservatif	PRAY-ser-va-teef

ENGLISH	FRENCH	PRONOUNCE
Where is...?	Où se trouve...?	OOH-suh-troov
How do I get to...?	Comment peut on aller à...?	KOM-mo-put-on-a-LAY-a
How much does this cost?	Ça fait combien?	sa-FAY-com-BEE-en
Do you have...?	Avez vous...?	ah-VAY-VOO
Do you speak English?	Parlez-vous anglais?	par-LAY-VOO-an-GLAY
I'd like to order...	Je voudrais...	zhe-VOO-DRAY
I'm allergic to...	Je suis allergique à...	zhe-SWEE-al-er-ZHEEK-a
I love you.	Je t'aime.	zhe-TEM

Le is the masculine singular definite article (the); *la* the feminine; both are abbreviated to *l'* before a vowel, while *les* is the plural definite article for both genders. *Un* is the masculine singular indefinite article (a or an), *une* the feminine; while *des* is the plural indefinite article for both genders ("some").

GERMAN

ENGLISH	GERMAN	PRONOUNCE	ENGLISH	GERMAN	PRONOUNCE
yes/no	ja/nein	yah/nain	departure	Abfahrt	AHB-fart
please	bitte	BIH-tuh	one-way	einfache	AYHN-fah-kuh
thank you	danke	DAHNG-kuh	round-trip	rundreise	RUND-RY-suh
Hello	Hallo	HAH-lo	reservation	reservierung	reh-zer-VEER-ung
Goodbye	Auf Wiedersehen	owf VEE-der-zayn	ticket	Fahrkarte	FAR-kar-tuh
Sorry/excuse me	entschuldigung	ent-SHOOL-di-gung	train/bus	Zug/Bus	tsug/boos
Help!	Hilfe!	HIL-fuh	station	Bahnhof	BAHN-hohf
police	Polizei	poh-lit-ZAI	airport	Flughafen	FLOOG-hahf-en
embassy	Botschaft	BOT-shaft	taxi	Taxi	TAHK-see
passport	Reisepass	RY-zeh-pahss	ferry	Fährschiff	FAYHR-shif
hotel/hostel	Hotel/Jugendherberge	ho-TEL/YOO-gend-her-BER-guh	bank	Bank	bahnk
single room	Einzelzimmer	AIN-tsel-tsim-muh	exchange	wechseln	VEHK-zeln
double room	Doppelzimmer	DOP-pel-tsim-muh	grocery	Lebensmittelgeschäft	LAY-bens-mit-tel-guh-SHEFT
dorm	Schlafsaal	SHLAF-zahl	pharmacy	Apotheke	AH-po-TAY-kuh
with shower	mit Dusche	miht DOO-shuh	tourist office	Touristbüro	TOR-ist-byur-oh
bathroom	Badezimmer	BAH-deh-tsim-muh	city center	Altstadt	AHLT-shtat
open/closed	geöffnet/geschlossen	geh-ERF-net/geh-shlos-sen	vegetarian	vegetarier	veh-geh-TAYR-ee-er
left/right	links/rechts	links/rekts	vegan	veganer	VAY-gan-er
straight	geradeaus	geh-RAH-de-OWS	kosher/halal	koscher/halaal	KOH-shayr/hah-LAAL
(to) turn	drehen	DRAY-en	nuts/milk	Nüsse/Milch	NYOO-suh/milch
castle	Schloß	shloss	church	Kirche	KEER-shuh
square	Platz	plahtz	bridge	Brücke	BROOK-eh

ENGLISH	GERMAN	PRONOUNCE
Where is...?	Wo ist...?	vo Ist
How do I get to...?	Wie komme ich nach...?	vee KOM-muh ish NOCK
How much does that cost?	Wieviel kostet das?	VEE-feel KOS-tet das
Do you have...?	Haben Sie...?	HAB-en zee
Do you speak English?	Sprechen Sie English?	SHPREK-en zee EHNG-lish
I would like...	Ich möchte ...	ish MERK-tuh
I'm allergic to...	Ich bin zu ___ allergisch.	ish bihn tsoo ___ ah-LEHR-jish

Every letter is pronounced. Consonants are pronounced as in English with the following exceptions: "j" is pronounced as "y"; "qu" is pronounced "kv"; a single "s" is pronounced "z"; "v" is pronounced "f"; "w" is pronounced as "v"; and "z" is pronounced "ts." "Sch" is "sh"; "st" is "sht"; and "sp" is "shp." The "ch" sound, as in "ich" ("I") and "nicht" ("not"), is tricky; you can substitute a "sh." The letter ß (esstset) is a symbol for a double-S and is pronounced "ss."

GREEK

ENGLISH	GREEK	PRONOUNCE
yes/no	ναι/οχι	NEH/OH-hee
please	παρακαλω	pah-rah-kah-LO
thank you	ευχαριστω	ef-khah-ree-STO
Hello/Good-bye (polite)	Γεια σας	YAH-sas
Hello/Good-bye (familiar)	Γεια σου	YAH-soo
Sorry/excuse me	Συγνομη	sig-NO-mee
Help!	Βοητηεια!	vo-EE-thee-ah
Go away!	Φυγε!	FEEG-he
police	αστυνομεια	as-tee-no-MEE-a
doctor	ιατροσ	yah-TROS
embassy	πρεσβεια	prez-VEE-ah
passport	διαβατηριο	dhee-ah-vah-TEE-ree-o
hotel/hostel	ξενοδοχειο	kse-no-dho-HEE-o
single room	μονο δωματιο	mon-NO do-MA-shee-o
double room	διπλο δωματιο	dheep-LO do-MA-shee-o
room to let	δωματια	do-MA-shee-ah
with shower	υε ντουζ και τουαλεττα	me dous ke tou-ah-LET-ta
bathroom	τουαλεττα	tou-ah-LET-ta
open/closed	ανοικτο/κλειστο	ah-nee-KTO/klee-STO
left/right	αριστερα/δεξια	ah-rees-teh-RAH/dhek-see-AH
straight	ευθεια	ef-THEE-ah
turn	στριψτε	STREEP-ste

ENGLISH	GREEK	PRONOUNCE
departure	αναχωρηση	ah-nah-HO-ree-see
one-way ticket	μονο εισιτηιριο	mon-NO ee-see-TEE-ree-o
round-trip ticket	εισιτηιριο με επιστροψη	ee-see-TEE-ree-o me e-PEE-stro-FEE
reservation	κρατηση	KRA-tee-see
train/bus	τραινο/λεωφορειο	TREH-no/leh-o-fo-REE-o
station	σταθμοζ	stath-MOS
airport	αεροδρομειο	ah-e-ro-DHRO-mee-o
taxi	ταξι	tax-EE
ferry	πλοιο	PLEE-o
port	λιμανι	lee-MAH-nee
bank	τραπεζα	TRAH-peh-zah
exchange	ανταλλασσω	an-da-LAS-so
pharmacy	φαρμακειο	fahr-mah-KEE-o
tourist office	τουριστικο γραψειο	tou-ree-stee-KO graf-EE-o
market	αγορα	ah-go-RAH
restaurant	εστιατοριο	es-tee-ah-TO-ree-o
acropolis	ακροπολη	ah-KROP-o-lee
ruins	αρχαια	ar-HEE-ah
cathedral	μητροπολη	mee-TROP-o-lee
monastery	μοναστηρι	mon-ah-STEE-ree
vegetarian	χορτοψαγουζ	hor-to-FUH-gos
mineral water	μεταλλικο νερο	me-tal-lee-KO ne-RO

ENGLISH	GREEK	PRONOUNCE
Where is...?	Που ειναι...?	pou-EE-neh
How do I get to...?	Πως θα παω στο...?	pos tha PA-o sto
How much does this cost?	Ποσο κανει?	PO-so KAH-nee
Do you have...?	Εχετε...?	Eh-khe-teh
Do you speak English?	Μιλας αγγλικα?	mee-LAHS ahn-glee-KAH
I'd like to order...	Θα ηθελα...	tha EE-thel-ah
I don't eat dairy products.	Δεν τρωω γαλακτοκοηικα προιοντα.	dhen DRO-o gha-lak-to-ko-mee-kah pro-EEON-dah

For more information on pronouncing the Greek alphabet, see p. 1051.

LATVIAN (LETTISH)

ENGLISH	LATVIAN	PRONOUNCE
yes/no	Jā/nē	yah/ney
please	Lūdzu	LOOD-zuh
thank you	Paldies	PAHL-dee-yes
Hello	Labdien	LAHB-dyen
Goodbye	Uz redzēšanos	ooz RE-dzeh-shan-was
Sorry/excuse me	Atvainojiet	AHT-vah-een-wah-yet
Help!	Palīgā!	PAH-lee-gah
police	policiju	POH-lit-see-yuh
bathroom	tualete	TOOH-wa-let-eh

ENGLISH	LATVIAN	PRONOUNCE
ticket	biļeti	BIL-yeh-tih
train	vilciens	VIL-tsee-ehnz
bus	autobuss	OW-toh-buhs
taxi	taksometrs	TAK-soh-mehtrs
departure	atiet	AHT-yet
station	stacija	STAH-tsee-uh
grocery	pārtikas veikals	PAHR-tih-kas VEY-kalss
hotel	viesnīca	VEE-yes-nee-tsa
pharmacy	aptieka	UHP-tee-uh-kuh

ENGLISH	LATVIAN	PRONOUNCE
Where is...?	Kur ir...?	kuhr ihr
How much does this cost?	Cik maksā?	sikh MAHK-sah
Do you have...?	Vai jums ir...?	vai yoomss ir
Do you speak English?	Vai jūs runājat angliskl?	vai yoos ROO-nah-yat AN-glee-ski

In Latvian, the vowels "ā," "ē," "ī," and "ū" are lengthened. Palatalized consonants are pronounced as follows: "ğ" sounds like "j," "ķ" like "ty" as in "tune," "ļ" like "ly" as in "stallion," and "ņ" as in "petunia." The consonant "c" is pronounced "ts," "č" sounds like "ch," "š" is "sh," and "ž" is pronounced like the "s" in "leisure."

LITHUANIAN

ENGLISH	LITHUANIAN	PRONOUNCE
yes/no	Taip/ne	tye-p/neh
please	Prašau	prah-SHAU
thank you	Ačiū	AH-chyoo
Hello	Labas	LAH-bahss
Goodbye	Viso gero	VEE-soh GEH-roh
Sorry/excuse me	Atsiprašau	AHT-sih-prh-SHAU
Help!	Gelbėkite!	GYEL-behk-ite
police	policija	poh-LIH-tsih-yah

ENGLISH	LITHUANIAN	PRONOUNCE
train	traukinys	trow-kih-NEES
bus	autobusas	ow-TOH-boo-suhs
ticket	bilietas	BYEE-lyeh-tas
departure	išvyksta	ish-VEEK-stah
grocery	maisto prekės	MY-stoh PREH-kays
hotel	viešbutis	vyesh-BUH-tis
pharmacy	vaistinė	VY-stee-neh
bathroom	tualetas	TUH-wa-le-tuhs

ENGLISH	LITHUANIAN	PRONOUNCE
Where is...?	Kur yra...?	Koor ee-RAH
How much does this cost?	Kiek kainuoja?	KEE-yek KYE-new-oh-yah
Do you have...?	Ar turite..?	ahr TU-ryite
Do you speak English?	Ar kalbate angliškai?	AHR KULL-buh-teh AHN-gleesh-kye

In Lithuanian, "r" is always trilled. "C" is pronounced "ts," "č" is like ch, "š" is like "sh," and "ž" is pronounced like the "s" of "pleasure." Accent-markings on vowels lengthen the sound of the vowel.

NORWEGIAN

ENGLISH	NORWEGIAN	PRONOUNCE	ENGLISH	NORWEGIAN	PRONOUNCE
yes/no	ja/nei	yah/nay	ticket	billett	BEE-leht
please	vær så snill	va sho SNEEL	train/bus	toget/bussen	TOR-go/boosn
thank you	takk	tuhk	airport	lufthavn	LUFT-huhvn
Hello	Goddag	gud-DAHG	departures	avgang	av-gang
Goodbye	Ha det	HUH-deh	market	torget	TOHR-geh
Sorry/excuse me	Beklager, tilgi meg/unnskyld	BEH-KLAH-gehrr til-yee mai/UN-shül	hotel	hotell	hoo-TEHL
Help!	Hjelp!	yelp	pharmacy	apotek	uh-pu-TAYK
police	politi	pohl-ih-TEE	bathroom	do	doo
embassy	ambassade	uhm-buhs-SAH-do	city center	sentrum	SEHN-trum

ENGLISH	NORWEGIAN	PRONOUNCE
Where is...?	Hvor er...?	VOOR arr
How do I get to...?	Hvordan kommer jeg til...?	voor-duhn kom-morr yay til
How much is...?	Hvor mye koster det...?	vorr moo-yo KOS-TOR deh...?
Do you speak English?	Snakker du engelsk?	snu-ko du EHNG-olsk

Vowel length (long and short) can affect the meaning of the word; they are usually long when followed by one consonant and short when followed by two or more.

POLISH

ENGLISH	POLISH	PRONOUNCE	ENGLISH	POLISH	PRONOUNCE
yes/no	Tak/nie	tahk/nyeh	ticket	bilet	BEE-leht
please	Proszę	PROH-sheh	train	pociąg	POH-chawnk
thank you	Dziękuję	jen-KOO-yeh	bus	autobus	ow-TOH-booss
Hello	Cześć	cheshch	departure	odjazd	OHD-yazd
Goodbye	Do widzenia	doh veedz-EN-yah	grocery	sklep spożywczy	sklehp spoh-ZHIV-chih
Sorry/ excuse me	Przepraszam	psheh-PRAH-shahm	hostel	schronisko młodzieżowe	skh-rah-NIHS-kah mwa-jee-eh-SHAH-veh
Help!	Na pomoc!	nah POH-mots	pharmacy	apteka	ahp-TEH-ka
police	policja	poh-LEETS-yah	bathroom	toaleta	toh-uh-LEH-tuh

ENGLISH	POLISH	PRONOUNCE
Where is...?	Gdzie jest...?	g-JEH yest
How much does this cost?	Ile to kosztuje?	EE-leh toh kohsh-TOO-yeh
Do you have...?	Czy są...?	chih sawn
Do you (male/female) speak English?	Czy pan(i) mówi po angielsku?	chih PAHN(-ee) MOO-vee poh ahn-GYEL-skoo

The Polish "ł" is pronounced "w"; "ą" is a nasal "on"; "ę" is a nasal "en." "Ó" and "u" are both equivalent to "oo." "Ż" and "rz" are both like the "s" in "pleasure"; "w" is pronounced "v." "Sz" is pronouced "sh"; "cz" is "ch"; and both "ch" and "h" are like the English "h." "C" sounds like an English "ts"; "dż" is "dg" as in "fridge"; "dź" is "j" as in "jeep"; "ć" or "ci" is "chyi"; and "zi" or "z" is "zhy."

PORTUGUESE

ENGLISH	PORTUGUESE	PRONOUNCE	ENGLISH	PORTUGUESE	PRONOUNCE
yes/no	sim/não	seeng/now	ticket	bilhete	beel-YEHT
please	Por favor	pur fah-VOR	train/bus	comboio/auto-carro	kom-BOY-yoo/OW-to-KAH-roo
thank you	Obrigado (m)/Obrigada (f)	oh-bree-GAH-doo/dah	airport	aeroporto	aye-ro-POR-too
Hello	olá	oh-LAH	departure	partida	par-TEE-da
Goodbye	Adeus	ah-DAY-oosh	market	mercado	mer-KAH-doo
Sorry/excuse me	Desculpe	desh-KOOLP	hotel	pousada	poh-ZAH-dah
Help!	Socorro!	so-KO-ro!	pharmacy	farmácia	far-MAH-see-ah
police	polícia	po-LEE-see-ah	bathroom	banheiro	bahn-YAY-roo

ENGLISH	PORTUGUESE	PRONOUNCE
Where is...?	Onde é que é ...?	OHN-deh eh keh eh...?
How much does this cost?	Quanto custa?	KWAHN-too KOOSH-tah?
I want...	Quero...	KAY-roo...
Do you speak English?	Fala inglês?	FAH-lah een-GLAYSH?

Vowels with a *til* (ã, õ, etc.) or before "m" or "n" are pronounced with a nasal twang. At the end of a word, "o" is pronounced "oo" as in "room," and "e" is sometimes silent. "S" is pronounced "sh" or "zh" when it occurs before another consonant. "Ch" and "x" are pronounced "sh"; "j" and "g" (before e or i) are pronounced "zh." The combinations "nh" and "lh" are pronounced "ny" and "ly" respectively.

ROMANIAN

ENGLISH	ROMANIAN	PRONOUNCE	ENGLISH	ROMANIAN	PRONOUNCE
yes/no	Da/nu	dah/noo	ticket	bilet	bee-LET
please	Vă rog	vuh rohg	train	trenul	TRAY-null
thank you	Mulţumesc	mool-tsoo-MESK	bus	autobuz	ahu-toh-BOOZ
Hello	Bună ziua	BOO-nuh zee-wah	station	gară	GAH-ruh
Goodbye	La revedere	lah reh-veh-DEH-reh	departure	plecări	play-CUHR
Sorry	Îmi pare rău	im PA-reh rau	taxi	taxi	tak-SEE
excuse me	Scuzaţi-mă	skoo-ZAH-tz muh	hotel	hotel	ho-TELL
Help!	Ajutor!	AH-zhoot-or	bathroom	toaletă	toh-ahl-EH-tah
police	poliţie	poh-LEE-tsee	grocery	băcănie	bah-kah-NEE

ENGLISH	ROMANIAN	PRONOUNCE
Where is...?	Unde...?	OON-deh
How much does this cost?	Cît costă?	kiht KOH-stuh
Do you have...?	Aveţi...?	a-VETS
Do you speak English?	Vorbiţi englezeşte?	vor-BEETS ehng-leh-ZESH-te

Romanian resembles Italian with the additional vowel "ă," which is pronounced like "e" in "pet," and the interchangeable "â" and "î," which are like the "i" in "pill." Two consonants particular to Romanian are "ş" ("sh" in "shiver") and "ţ" ("ts" in "tsar"). At the end of a word, "i" is dropped, but softens the previous consonant.

RUSSIAN

For the Cyrillic alphabet, see p. 1051.

ENGLISH	RUSSIAN	PRONOUNCE
yes/no	Да/нет	Dah/Nyet
please	Пожалуйста	pa-ZHAL-u-sta
thank you	Спасибо	spa-SEE-bah
Hello	Добрый день	DOH-bri DEN
Goodbye	До свидания	da svee-DAHN-ya
Sorry/ excuse me	Извините	iz-vi-NEET-yeh
Help!	Помогите!	pah-mah-GI-tye
embassy	посольство	pah-SOHL'-stva
police	милиция	mee-LEE-tsi-ya
passport	паспорт	PAS-pahrt
hotel	гостиница	gahs-TEE-nee-tsah
single room	на одного	nah AHD-nah-voh
double room	двойная комната	dvai-NA-ya KOM-na-ta
dorm/hostel	общежитие	ob-she-ZHEE-tee-ye
with shower	с душом	s DOO-sham
bathroom	туалет	tu-a-LYET
left/right	налево/ направо	nah-LYEH-va/ nah-PRAH-va
straight	прямо	pr-YAH-moh
open/closed	открыт/ закрыт	ot-KRIHT/ za-KRIHT

ENGLISH	RUSSIAN	PRONOUNCE
train	поезд	PO-ist
bus	автобус	av-toh-BOOS
station	вокзал	VOK-zal
airport	аэропорт	a-ero-PORT
reservation	предваритель-ный заказ	pred-va-RI-tyel-nui za-KAZ
one-way	в один конец	v ah-DEEN kah-NYETS
round-trip	туда и обратно	too-DAH ee ah-BRAHT-nah
ticket	билет	bil-YET
departure	отъезд	at-YEZD
exchange	обмен валюты	ab-MYEN val-YU-tyi
bank	банк	bahnk
pharmacy	аптека	ahp-TYE-kah
grocery	гастроном	gah-stra-NOM
market	рынок	RYHN-nak
post office	лочта	POCH-ta
square	площадь	PLOSH-chad
vegetarian	вегетариан	veg-eh-tah-ri-AHN
kosher	кошер	koh-SHAIR
nuts/milk	орехи/молоко	oh-REKH-ee/ mah-lah-KOH

ENGLISH	RUSSIAN	PRONOUNCE
Where is...?	Где находится...?	gdyeh nah-KHOH-di-tsah
How do I get to...? **Is this the right train/bus to...?**	Как пройти...? Это поезд/автобус на...?	kak prai-TEE EH-tah PO-ist/av-toh-BOOS nah
Will you tell me when to get off?	Вы мне скажите, когда надо выйдти?	vui mnyeh skah-ZHIH-tyeh, kahg-DAH NAH-dah VYI-ti
How much does this cost? **Do you have...?**	Сколько это стоит? У вас есть...?	SKOHL'-ka E-ta STO-it oo vas YEST'
I don't understand.	Я не понимаю	ya ni pa-nee-MAH-yoo
Do you speak English?	Вы говорите по-английски?	vy ga-va-REE-tye pa an-GLEE-ski
I'd like to order...	Я хотел(а) бы	ya khah-TYEL(a) byi
I'm allergic to...	Я аллергический на...	ya al-ler-GEE-che-skee na

Take some time to familiarize yourself with the Cyrillic alphabet. It's not as difficult as it looks, and once you get the hang of the alphabet, you'll be able to sound through just about any Russian word.

SPANISH

ENGLISH	SPANISH	PRONOUNCE	ENGLISH	SPANISH	PRONOUNCE
yes/no	si/no	see/noh	departure	salida	sah-LEE-dah
please	por favor	pohr fah-VOHR	one-way	ida	EE-dah
thank you	gracias	GRAH-see-ahs	round-trip	ida y vuelta	EE-dah ee voo-EL-tah
Hello	Hola	OH-lah	reservation	reservación	res-er-vah-see-OHN
Goodbye	Adiós	ah-di-OHS	ticket	boleto	boh-LEH-toh
Sorry/excuse me	perdón	pehr-DOHN	train	tren	trehn
			bus	autobús	ow-toh-BOOS
Help!	¡Ayuda!	ay-YUH-duh	station	estación	es-tah-see-OHN
police	policía	poh-lee-SEE-ah	airport	aeropuerto	ay-roh-PWER-toh
embassy	embajada	em-bah-HA-dah	taxi	taxi	tahk-SEE
passport	pasaporte	pas-ah-POR-tay	ferry	transbordador	trahns-BOR-dah-dohr
hotel/hostel	hotel/hostal	oh-TEL/OH-stahl	bank	banco	BAHN-koh
single room	cuarto solo	KWAR-toh SOH-loh	exchange	intercambio	een-tehr-CAHM-bee-oh
double room	cuarto doble	KWAR-to DOH-blay	grocery	supermercado	soo-pehr-mer-CHAH-doh
dorm	dormitorio	dor-mlh-TOR-ee-oh	pharmacy	farmácia	far-MAH-see-ah
with shower	con ducha	kohn DOO-chah	tourist office	oficina de turismo	oh-fee-SEE-nah day toor-EEZ-moh
bathroom	baño	BAHN-yoh	market	mercado	mehr-KAH-doh
open	abierto(a)	ah-bee-AYR-toh	vegetarian	vegetariano(a)	vay-hay-tayr-ee-AH-no
closed	cerrado(a)	sehr-RAH-doh			
left	izquierda	EES-kee-AYR-da	vegan	vegetariano estricto	vay-hay-tayr-ee-AH-no AY-strik-toh
right	derecha	deh-RAY-chah			
straight	recto	REK-toh	kosher/halal	kosher/jalal	KOH-shayr/hahl-AHL
turn	dobla	DOH-blah	nuts/milk	nuezes/leche	noo-AYS-ays/LAY-chay
cathedral	catedral	kat-tay-DRAL	square	cuadrado	kwad-RAH-doh
monastery	monasterio	mon-ah-STAR-ee-oh	castle	castillo	kas-TEE-oh
beach	playa	PLAI-uh	church	iglesia	ee-GLAY-see-ah

ENGLISH	SPANISH	PRONOUNCE
Where is...?	Dónde está...?	DOHN-day eh-STA
How do I get to...?	Cómo voy a...?	COH-mo voy ah
How much does this cost?	Cuánto cuesta...?	KWAN-toh KWEHS-tah
Do you have...?	Usted tiene....?	ooh-STED tee-EN-ay
Do you speak English?	Habla inglés?	AH-blah een-GLAYS
I'd like to order...	Me gustaría...	may goos-tah-REE-ah
I'm allergic to...	Soy alérgico a...	soy ah-LEHR-hee-coh ah

Vowels are always pronounced in the same way: "a" ("ah" in father); "e" ("eh" in egg); "i" ("ee" in eat); "o" ("oh" in oat); "u" ("oo" in boot). The letter "j" is pronounced "h"; "ll" is pronounced "y", "ñ" is pronounced "ny"; and "rr" is a trilled "r." The letter "y" by itself is pronounced "ee," and "h" is always silent.

SWEDISH

ENGLISH	SWEDISH	PRONOUNCE
yes/no	ja/nej	yah/nay
please	tack	TOOHK
thank you	tack	toohk
Hello	Hej	hay
Goodbye	Adjö	uh-YEHR
Excuse me	Ursäkta mig	oo-SHEHK-tuh MAY
Help!	Hjälp!	yelp
police	polisen	poo-LEE-sehn
embassy	ambassad	uhm-buh-SAHD

ENGLISH	SWEDISH	PRONOUNCE
ticket	biljett	bil-YEHT
train/bus	går/tåget	gorr/TOR-geht
ferry	färjan	FAR-yuhn
departure	avgång	UHV-gong
market	torghandel	TOH-ree-HUHN-dehl
hotel	mitt hotell	mit hoo-TEHL
pharmacy	apotek	uh-poo-TEEK
toilet	toalett	too-uh-LEHT
post office	posten	POHS-tehn

ENGLISH	SWEDISH	PRONOUNCE
Where is...?	Var finns det...?	vahr FINS deh
How much does this cost?	Hur mycket kostar det?	hurr MUK-keh KOS-tuhr deh
I'd like to buy...	Jag skulle vilja ha...	yuh SKUH-leh vil-yuh HAH
Do you speak English?	Talar du engelska?	TA-luhr du EHNG-ehls-kuh

The letter "g" is pronounced "j" and "k" is pronounced "ch" in front of "e," "i," "y," "ä," and "ö"; "j" is always pronounced "y"; "tj" is "ch"; "sj" is like "sh." The stressed syllable can often change the meaning of words.

TURKISH

ENGLISH	TURKISH	PRONOUNCE
yes/no	evet/hayir	EH-veht/HA-yir
please	lütfen	lewt-FEHN
thank you	teşekkür ederim	teh-sheh-KUR eeh-DEH-rim
Hello	merhaba	MEHR-hah-bah
Goodbye	allahısmarladık	ah-lah-SMAR-lah-duk
Sorry/Excuse me	pardon	par-DOHN
Help!	yardım	yahr-DUM
police	polis	poh-LEES
embassy	elcilik	EHL-jee-leek

ENGLISH	TURKISH	PRONOUNCE
ticket	bilet	bee-LEHT
train/bus	tren/otobüs	tee-REHN/oh-toh-BEWS
taxi	taksi	TAHK-see
departure	hareket	hah-reh-KEHT
grocery	bakkal	bahk-KAHL
hotel/hostel	otel/pansyon	oh-TEHL/pahns/YOHN
pharmacy	eczâne	eh-zah-NEH
bathroom	banyo	BAHN-yoh
bank	banka	BAHN-kah

ENGLISH	TURKISH	PRONOUNCE
Where is...?	...nerede?	NEHR-deh
How much does this cost?	...ne kadar?	neh kah-DAHR
Do you have...?	...var mı?	VAHR muh
Do you speak English?	İngilizce konuşabilir misiniz?	een-gee-LEEZ-jeh koh-noo-shah-bee-LEER mih-sih-nihz

Letters are pronounced as in English with the following exceptions: the letter "â" is pronounced "ya"; "c" is "j"; "ç" is "ch"; "ı" is like "uh"; "i" is "ee"; "j" is "zh"; "ş" is "sh"; "u" is "oo"; and "û" is "ew." Stress usually falls on the last syllable.

GOT CHANGE FOR A EURO?
A Quick Guide to the New International Currency

Cleaning out one's pack at the end of a trip through Europe used to turn into a comparison between the small change picked up in each country—whose bills looked the most like Monopoly money, whose national engravings were the corniest, or who had the most uselessly small denominations. This game has become a fair bit less interesting, though, now that the euro has been put into circulation in 12 member states of the EU. The euro has been hailed as a turning point in the future of European prosperity, both a symbol of and a step toward a cohesive, long-lasting alliance of autonomous countries. Its introduction into everyday life on January 1, 2002, was all but flawless, silencing critics and, incidentally, making multi-country travel infinitely more convenient.

The transition to the euro has been a long, carefully planned process. The European Economic Community was founded in 1958; the first suggestion of a common currency was made 11 years later, in response to dangerously fluctuating exchange rates. The specific steps of the euro's introduction were outlined in 1989, culminating in fixed exchange rates in 1999 and the establishment of the euro as the sole currency of all 12 eurozone states in 2002. Design contests were held in the mid-1990s to determine the look of the currency, resulting in a comfortable mix of international unity and national representation. The face of each of the seven bills depicts an architectural period from Europe's history, progressing from a Roman facade on the 5 euro to a 20th-century office building on the 500 euro. The backside of each note bears a bridge from the same period, symbolizing connection and communication between the countries. After a bit of contention as to whose landmarks would grace the more valuable bills—and the discovery that the pontoon bridge on the five was actually in India—it was decided that the images would be stylized creations rather than existing structures. The eight coins, which range in value from one-cent pieces to one- and two-euro coins, bear maps of Europe on their faces; their tails, on the other hand, have been designed separately by each of the eurozone countries. As a result, distinct emblems of national pride are shared across borders, as images of the Grand Duke of Luxembourg are tendered in Ireland and coins bearing Finnish cloudberries circulate through German banks.

Although all 15 European Union countries meet or come close to eurozone's stringent financial criteria, only 12 countries joined in for the fledgling currency's debut. Denmark, Sweden, and the UK have all chosen to stay out of the eurozone indefinitely. Although national identity plays a role in their choices, economic factors may be more influential; the UK, for one, is wary of tying its strong economy to the fortunes of a dozen continental countries. Euro-skeptics forecasted a rough transition due to a number of possible hitches, such as hidden price increases due to retailers rounding prices up to the nearest euro and heavy counterfeiting while the general public was still unfamiliar with the security features of the new notes. Some went so far as to predict an anti-integrationist backlash that would jeopardize the EU as a whole.

In practice, however, the transition has been surprisingly smooth. Extensive preparation included massive public education efforts and the monstrous task of converting all printed signs and coin-operated machines to the euro. In many towns and cities, the first few days brought dozens of confusions and inconveniences, as stores ran out of change and consumers struggled to remember the relative value of the new denominations. Prices did jump slightly, but economists attribute the increases to higher food costs stemming from bad weather. On the whole, the European public was quickly satisfied with the transition. Although pockets of discontent remain strong in The Netherlands and in many rural areas, surveys by the European Commission in April 2002 found that 81% of people throughout the eurozone judged the changeover successful.

Tobie Whitman was a Researcher-Writer for Let's Go: London 1999 *and* 2001, *as well as* Let's Go: Britain & Ireland 1998. *After an internship with the EU, she entered the University of Cambridge to pursue a Master's Degree in European Studies.*

WITH OR WITHOUT EU
The Current Candidates for EU Enlargement

Thirteen countries have applied to join the 15-strong EU; ten of them may enter as early as January 1, 2004, uniting almost the entire continent into one big, happy, free-market economy. Yet despite real enthusiasm and a widespread sense of the importance of the project, enlargement does have its opponents. The countries that joined the original six-member EU in the past were relatively well-off at the time and came to the table in small, easy-to-digest bites rather than as a ten-course meal. It's proving difficult for the current members to contemplate dividing the spoils of the Union—agricultural subsidies, regional development funds, and chairs at the EU's tables of power—with their neighbors to the east and south. The candidate countries themselves are not without a number of concerns that make a match with the EU questionable.

The enlargement process began philosophically after the fall of the Berlin Wall but took a decade to pick up any real steam. The hot favorites from the beginning were the large countries closest to the EU—Poland, Hungary, and the former Czechoslovakia—but a little-known contender has taken the lead in the race to the finish line: Slovenia, which was nearly 100% EU-compliant at the end of 2002. The plucky little country is already looking and acting like the newest member of the club, with new international super-highways and a GDP per capita that's higher than any other applicant in Central or Eastern Europe—higher, even, than some of them combined. While Hungary and the Czech Republic have made great strides in the race, the Slovak Republic has fallen behind due to some messy domestic politics, and Poland has proven a bit stubborn; as the largest country likely to join the EU in this round of enlargement, Poland has been holding out in some negotiations in hope of a better accession package.

After a slow start, Lithuania and Latvia have made good progress toward readiness, but still lag behind their Baltic sister-state, Estonia. Yet despite booming growth and one of Europe's freest economies, Estonian public opinion regarding accession has been cooling off fast. The most recent Eurobarometer survey showed public support for EU membership at a mere 38%—compared to 85% in Romania and 70% in Hungary, for instance. Some of this is due to public exhaustion in the wake of the EU's much-delayed plans for their accession, but good old-fashioned scepticism plays a role as well. As one Estonian-on-the-street put it, "We just left a Union, and look where that one got us…"

Romania and Bulgaria are still a bit shy of EU criteria, and analysts say it will be 2010 before they make it to the finish line. Turkey, it seems, has limited prospects for the time being, producing a bit of a quandary over Cyprus. Although the island—divided since 1974 into Greek and Turkish zones of influence—is as prepared a candidate as Slovenia, its accession has become quite controversial. Greece insists that it will veto everyone if Cyprus doesn't join in the first wave, while Turkey has quietly threatened to do the same in the concurrent NATO enlargement if the EU doesn't consider its own application more seriously. The EU, for its part, has always felt that rapid accession may be the best—if not only—solution to the divided island's persistent ethnic problems.

Malta has come back in on the action, having defrosted its earlier application. While it had made headway in the last enlargement round, it pulled out of the race before it was over due to a lack of support at home. Norway, though having been officially accepted for membership, never took up the EU's offer, twice holding referenda in which the Norwegian public rejected membership. Referenda—as the Estonian opinion polls show—may prove to be enlargement's Achilles' heel. Indeed, this entire project hangs on the consent of, well… the Irish. Until Ireland ratifies the enlargement-centered Treaty of Nice from 2001, no new countries can be admitted to the EU.

And what of that most geographically and linguistically European of nations, Switzerland? Having voted to join the UN this year, some speculate that the EU may be nearing the Swiss horizon. If nothing else, Switzerland's accession would fill the lake-like gap in the map on the front of the €2 coin—although some wags point out that, with Norway still missing from the picture, Sweden and Finland give an altogether different kind of impression. Take a look for yourself the next time you have a jingle in your pocket...

Jeremy Faro is a former Senior Consultant at Interbrand and has worked in the past on Let's Go: Britain & Ireland. *He is currently a master's student in European Studies at Cambridge University.*

EUROPE IN BLACK AND WHITE
The Prevalence of Xenophobia in Modern Europe

In Europe as in America, cultural racism has long been a tale of bodies told as a story about minds—an evaluation of hair and skin behind claims about culture and language. This is evident to every child who, though born and raised in Europe, is perceived as an immigrant because she "looks Middle Eastern" or "looks African."

Anti-immigrant agitators have caused several recent electoral earthquakes. In 1999, the ultra-nationalist party of Jörg Haider shocked the European Union by attracting more than one-fourth of Austria's voters and becoming part of the country's governing coalition. Regimes in Italy, Portugal, and Denmark also depend on the extreme right to maintain parliamentary majorities. Osama bin Laden's September 11th gift to reactionary forces worldwide aided the Dutch Muslim-baiting party of the late Pim Fortuyn as well as France's Jean-Marie Le Pen, who was supported by 17% of the electorate in the first round of the 2002 presidential election.

Political entrepreneurs of the far right fan xenophobic fires by framing immigrants and native workers as rival claimants to material resources and social respect. In a western Europe of advanced general-welfare policies, resources for health-care, education, and housing, as well as unemployment benefits, have been squeezed during recent decades of retrenchment. Some politicians portray immigrants as getting something for nothing, receiving social support without having contributed to society. The immigrants themselves are in a catch-22: they are resented if they are unemployed (and thus seen as living off other people's taxes), but also if they find jobs (seen as taking them from natives).

Support for anti-immigrant parties comes largely from the working classes; bourgeois racism also exists, but wealthy citizens often value the inexpensive labor provided by immigrants even while looking down on them. Working-class opposition to immigration arises above all from the humiliations that workers have suffered. A man who welds fenders eight hours a day at a Renault factory, barely supporting his family in a dreary suburban flat—then finds himself unemployed when production is shifted abroad—is unlikely to welcome a Rwandan refugee, much less to empathize with her own biography of humiliations.

Immigration is also debated as part of Europe's ongoing cultural globalization. Multinational products perceived as American—from food to news to movies—have saturated the continent. Citizens of many countries (not least France) see this development as jeopardizing national integrity. Non-European immigrants may be framed as further eroding an imagined cultural homogeneity due to their different diets, clothing, religion, and language.

The more extreme right-wing politicians supplement economic and cultural discourses with imagery of bodily and sexual danger. As in racisms the world over, men of the disfavored groups are presented as violent, criminal, and predatory toward women—invaders, Le Pen once said, "who want to sleep in my bed, with my wife." In fact, it is the immigrants who are often the victims of crimes, committed largely by the underemployed sons of marginalized workers. Here racism is at its most obvious: those targeted may not be "foreign" at all, but native citizens who happen not to be white.

A politician who opposes anti-immigrant parties and the violence they sometimes condone faces a political obstacle course. How to protect asylum seekers arriving from a war-torn world while at the same time reassuring the public that the nation is strictly guarding its borders? How to reduce unemployment while also encouraging immigration of needed workers in such sectors as high technology and care of the expanding elderly population? How to balance respect for cultural and religious differences with the need to socialize new arrivals in the values and habits of the host society? In the hard-won answers to these questions lies the fate of the European Dream, a vision of an inclusive and egalitarian society extending across a continent.

Dr. Brian Palmer lectures on ethnography and ethics, and Kathleen Holbrook researches globalization and human values. They were voted Harvard's best young faculty member and teaching fellow, respectively, for a course which the New York Times nicknamed "Idealism 101."

INDEX

A

Å, NOR 770
Aachen, GER 448–449
Aalborg, DEN 288
Aalsmeer, NETH 735
Aberfoyle, BRI 209
Abisko, SWE 984
Accademia, ITA 657
accommodations 25–31
  bed and breakfasts 29
  camping 29
  guesthouses 26
  home exchange 29
  hostels 25
  hotels 26
  pensions 26
  RVs 31
  university dorms 29
  YMCAs 26
adventure tours 32
Aegean Coast, TUR 1028–1034
Aeolian Islands, ITA 672–673
Ærø, DEN 285–286
aerogrammes 32
Ærøskøbing, DEN 285
Agia Napa, CYP 241
AIDS 23
airplanes 43–53
  charter 50
  courier 49
  standby 50
Aix-en-Provence, FRA 373
Ajaccio, FRA 387
Akrotiri, GRE 510
alcohol 20
Ålesund, NOR 765
Algarve, POR 815–817
Algeciras, SPA 918
Alghero, ITA 674
Alhambra, SPA 921
Allinge, DEN 283
Alonnisos, GRE 506
The Alps, FRA 389–392
Alsace-Lorraine, FRA 398–402
alternatives to tourism 68–73
  au pair 71
  long-term work 70
  study abroad 68
  teaching 71
  volunteering 72–73
Amalfi, ITA 669
Ambleside, BRI 190
Amboise, FRA 361
American Express 16, 63
  mail 33
American Red Cross 21
Amsterdam, NETH 720–735
Ancona, ITA 663
Andalucía, SPA 905–924
Andorra 74–75
  Andorra La Vella 74–75
Angers, FRA 362
Ankara, TUR 1037–1038
Annecy, FRA 392
Antalya, TUR 1036
Antibes-Juan-les-Pins, FRA 378
Antwerp, BEL 125–126
Aphrodisias, TUR 1033
Apollonas, GRE 509
Aran Islands, IRE 575
Arcos de la Frontera, SPA 917
Ardennes, LUX 701–703
Areopolis, GRE 496
Argostoli, GRE 504
Århus, DEN 286
Arles, FRA 372
Arras, FRA 405
Asilah, MOR 709
Assisi, ITA 662
Astorga, SPA 904
Asturias, SPA 958
Athens, GRE 486–492
ATM cards 16
Atrani, ITA 669
au pair 71
Aurland, NOR 756
Auschwitz-Birkenau, POL 789
Austria 76–106
  Carinthia 93–94
  Dachstein Ice Caves 101
  Franz-Josefs-Höhe 101–102
  Graz 93–94
  Hallstatt 100–101
  Heiligenblut 102
  Hohe Tauern National Park 101–102
  Innsbruck 102–105
  Kärnten. See Carinthia
  Kitzbühel 106
  Krimml 102
  Lustschloß Hellbrunn 100
  Salzburg 95–100
  Salzburger Land 94–102
  Schloß Ambras 105–106
  Tirol. See Tyrol
  Tyrol 102–106
  Untersberg Peak 100
  Vienna 80–93
  Wien. See Vienna
Avignon, FRA 371

B

Bacharach, GER 458
Bachkovo Monastery, BUL 223
backpacks 31
Bakewell, BRI 187
Bakhchisarai, UKR 1049
Balchik, BUL 225
Bâle. See Basel
Balearic Islands, SPA 955–957
Balestrand, NOR 758
Ballintoy, NIRE 585
Balloch, BRI 209
Ballycastle, NIRE 585
Barcelona, SPA 927–943
Basel, SWI 991–992
Basque Country, SPA 950–954
Bastia, FRA 388
Batalha, POR 813
Bath, BRI 172–173
Bavaria, GER 464–480
Bay of Naples Islands, ITA 670–671
Bayern. See Bavaria
Bayeux, FRA 354
Bayonne, FRA 366
Beaune, FRA 398
bed and breakfasts 29
Belarus 107–110
  Minsk 109–110
  Mir Castle 110
Belarussian ruble 107

Belfast, NIRE 579–583
Belgium 111–128
  Antwerp 125–126
  Bruges 121–125
  Brussels 115–120
  Dinant 127
  Flanders 121–127
  Ghent 126–127
  Mechelen 121
  Namur 127
  Wallonie 127–128
  Waterloo 120
Bellaggio, ITA 633
Ben Nevis, BRI 211
Berchtesgaden, GER 475–476
Bergama, TUR 1030
Bergamo, ITA 641
Bergen, NOR 759–763
Berlin, GER 412–431
Bern, SWI 989–991
Berry-Limousin, FRA 397
Besançon, FRA 401
Biarritz, FRA 367
bicycles 65
Bilbao, SPA 953
Billund, DEN 288
Birmingham, BRI 180
bisexual travelers 37
Björkö, SWE 972
Black Forest, GER 463–464
Black Sea Coast, BUL 224–226
Black Sea Coast, ROM 833
Blarney, IRE 568
Bled, SLN 879
Blois, FRA 360
Blue Lagoon, ICE 547
boat. See ferry
Bodensee, GER 464
Bodrum, TUR 1033
Bohemia, CZR 247–264
Bologna, ITA 646–648
Bolzano, ITA 635
Bomarsund, FIN 310
Bonifacio, FRA 388
Bonn, GER 453–454
Bordeaux, FRA 365
borders 13
Borgo Verezzi, ITA 644
Bornholm, DEN 283
Borromean Islands, ITA 633
Bosnia and Herzegovina 129–134
  Sarajevo 131–134
Bosnian convertible mark 130

Boulogne-sur-Mer, FRA 405
Bourges, FRA 397
Bowness, BRI 190
Boyne Valley, IRE 564
Brač Island, CRO 235
Braga, POR 820
Bran, ROM 832
Braşov, ROM 831
Bratislava, SLK 867–870
Brecon Beacons National Park, BRI 193–194
Brecon, BRI 194
Brighton, BRI 169–170
Brijuni Archipelago, CRO 233
Briksdalsbreen, NOR 764
Britain 135–213
  Aberfoyle 209
  Ambleside 190
  Bakewell 187
  Balloch 209
  Bath 172–173
  Ben Nevis 211
  Birmingham 180
  Bowness 190
  Brecon 194
  Brecon Beacons National Park 193–194
  Brighton 169–170
  Caernarfon 196
  Cairngorm Mountains 210
  Callander 209
  Cambridge 181–183
  Canterbury 169
  Cardiff 192
  Castleton 187
  Cheltenham 179
  Chepstow 193
  Conwy 196
  The Cornish Coast 173–174
  The Cotswolds 179–180
  East Anglia and the Midlands 174–183
  Edale 187
  Edinburgh 197–204
  England 140–191
  Fort William 211
  Glasgow 205–208
  Glastonbury 173
  Grasmere 191
  Harlech 195
  Harris 212
  Hay-on-Wye 193
  The Inner Hebrides 211–212
  Inverness 210–211
  Isle of Skye 211–212

  Keswick 191
  Kyle of Lochalsh 211
  Kyleakin 211
  Lake District National Park 190–191
  Lewis 212
  Liverpool 184–186
  Llanberis 195
  Llyn Peninsula 196
  Loch Lomond 209
  Loch Ness 210–211
  London 140–168
  Manchester 183–184
  Moreton-in-Marsh 180
  Newcastle-Upon-Tyne 189
  Newquay 173
  Northern England 183–191
  The Outer Hebrides 212–213
  Oxford 175–178
  Peak District National Park 186–187
  Penzance 174
  Porthmadog 196
  Portree 212
  Portsmouth 170
  St. Andrews 204
  St. David's 194
  St. Ives 174
  Salisbury 171–172
  Scotland 196–213
  Sligachan 212
  Snowdonia National Park 194–195
  Southern England 168–174
  Stirling 208–209
  Stonehenge 172
  Stow-on-the-Wold 180
  Stratford-Upon-Avon 178–179
  Tintern 193
  The Trossachs 209–210
  Wales 191–196
  Winchester 170–171
  Winchombe 180
  Windermere 190
  Wye Valley 192–193
  York 187
British pound 553
Brno, CZR 265
Bruges, BEL 121–125
Brussels, BEL 115–120
Bucharest, ROM 826–829
Buchenwald, GER 439
Budapest, HUN 520–530
Bukovina, ROM 833–835

Bukovina Monasteries, ROM 834–835
Bulgaria 214–226
Bachkovo Monastery 223
Balchik 225
Black Sea Coast 224–226
Burgas 225
Koprivshtitsa 223
Nesebur 225
Plovdiv 223
Rila 222
Sofia 218–222
Sozopol 226
Varna 224
Veliko Tarnovo 224
Bulgarian lev 216
Burgas, BUL 225
Burgundy, FRA 397–398
The Burren, IRE 573–574
Bursa, TUR 1027
bus 61

C

Cadaqués, SPA 945
Cádiz, SPA 916
Caen, FRA 353
Caernarfon, BRI 196
Cagliari, ITA 674
Caherdaniel, IRE 571
Cahersiveen, IRE 570
Cairngorm Mountains, BRI 210
Calais, FRA 405
Callander, BRI 209
calling cards 34
The Camargue, FRA 372
Cambridge, BRI 181–183
Camogli, ITA 645
camping 29
equipment 30
RVs 31
Çanakkale, TUR 1029
Cannes, FRA 377
Canterbury, BRI 169
Cap Corse, FRA 389
Cap d'Ail, FRA 385
Cap Fréhel, FRA 358
Cape Clear Island, IRE 569
Cape Greco, CYP 242
Cappadocia, TUR 1038–1039
Capri, ITA 670
Carcassonne, FRA 369
Cardiff, BRI 192
Carinthia, AUS 93–94

cars
rental 62–64
See also driving
Cascades d'Ouzoud, MOR 715
Cascais, POR 811
Cashel, IRE 566
Castelnaud-La Chapelle, FRA 364
Castilla la Mancha, SPA 899–901
Castilla y León, SPA 902–905
Castleton, BRI 187
Cataluña, SPA 927–946
Causeway Coast, NIRE 585–586
Cauterets, FRA 368
Çavuşin, TUR 1039
CDC (Centers for Disease Control) 20
Çeşme, TUR 1031
České Budějovice, CZR 263
Český Krumlov, CZR 264
Český Ráj National Preserve, CZR 261
Chambord, FRA 361
Chamonix, FRA 391
Champagne and the North, FRA 402–406
Charlottenlund, DEN 282
Chartres, FRA 351
Chefchaouen, MOR 710
Cheltenham, BRI 179
Chepstow, BRI 193
Cherbourg, FRA 355
Cheverny, FRA 361
Chiemsee, GER 474–475
children and travel 39
Chios, GRE 513
cholera 22
chunnel 51
Cinque Terre, ITA 645
Cirrus 17
Clare Island, IRE 576
Clervaux, LUX 702
Clifden, IRE 575–576
climate 1
Cluj-Napoca, ROM 830
Coimbra, POR 817–819
Colleville-sur-Mer, FRA 355
Colmar, FRA 400
Cologne, GER 449–453
Como, ITA 633
Connemara National Park, IRE 576

Connemara, IRE 575–576
Constance, GER 464
Constanţa, ROM 833
convertible mark, Bosnian 130
Conwy, BRI 196
Copenhagen, DEN 273–280
Córdoba, SPA 906–910
Corfu, GRE 503–504
Corinth, GRE 497–498
Cork City, IRE 566–568
Corniches, FRA 384–385
The Cornish Coast, BRI 173–174
Corsica, FRA 386–389
Corte, FRA 389
Costa Blanca, SPA 927
Costa Brava, SPA 945–946
Costa del Sol, SPA 919
The Cotswolds, BRI 179–180
Council Travel 43
County Donegal, IRE 577–578
courier flights 49
credit cards 16
Crete, GRE 510–512
Crimea, UKR 1049
Croatia 227–239
Brač Island 235
Brijuni Archipelago 233
Dalmatian Coast 234–239
Dubrovnik 236–239
Gulf of Kvarner 232
Hvar Island 235
Istrian Peninsula 232
Korčula Island 236
Krk Island 235
Lopud Island 239
Mljet National Park 235
Plitvice Lakes National Park 232
Pula 232
Rab Island 233
Split 234
Trogir Island 234
Vis Island 235
Zagreb 231–232
Croatian kuna 229
Cuenca, SPA 901
Cushendall, NIRE 585
Cushendun, NIRE 585
customs 15
The Cyclades, GRE 507–510
Cyprus 240–242
Agia Napa 241
Cape Greco 242
Larnaka 241

Paphos 242
Platres 242
Troodos 242
Cyprus pound 240
Czech koruna 245
Czech Republic 243–267
  Bohemia 247–264
  Brno 265
  České Budějovice 263
  Český Krumlov 264
  Čcský Ráj National
    Preserve 261
  Hluboká nad Vltavou 264
  Karlovy Vary (Carlsbad)
    262
  Karlštejn 260
  Kutná Hora 261
  Mělník 261
  Moravia 265–267
  Moravský Kras 267
  Plzeň 263
  Prague 247–260
  Telč 266
  Terezín (Thereslenstadt)
    260

D

Dachau, GER 473–474
Dachstein Ice Caves, AUS
  101
Dalarna, SWE 980–981
Dalmatian Coast, CRO 234–
  239
Dalyan, TUR 1034
Danish kroner 271
Danube Bend, HUN 531–532
Danube Delta, ROM 833
D-Day Beaches, FRA 354–
  355
dehydration 21
Delft, NETH 739
Delos, GRE 507–508
Delphi, GRE 493
Denmark 268–290
  Aalborg 288
  Ærø 285–286
  Ærøskøbing 285
  Allinge 283
  Århus 286
  Billund 288
  Bornholm 283
  Charlottenlund 282
  Copenhagen 273–280
  Fredensborg 281
  Frederikshavn 288

Funen 284–285
Grenen 289
Helsingør 282
Hillerød 281
Hornbæk 282
Humlebæk 280
Jutland 286–290
Klampenborg 282
Kværndrup 284
Møn 282
Odense 284
Ribe 289
Rønne 283
Roskilde 281
Rungsted 280
Sandvig 283
Skagen 289
Svendborg 285
Tåsinge 285
Derry, NIRE 583–584
Derryveagh Mountains, IRE
  578
diarrhea 22
Diekirch, LUX 702
dietary concerns 40
Dijon, FRA 397
Dimitsana, GRE 495
Dinant, BEL 127
Dingle Peninsula, IRE 571–
  572
Dingle Town, IRE 571
dirham, Moroccan 706
disabled travelers 38
diseases
  food- and water-borne 22
  infectious 23
  insect-borne 22
  sexually transmitted 23
Dodoni, GRE 503
The Dolomites, ITA 634–635
Donegal Town, IRE 577
Doolin, IRE 573
dorms 29
Dresden, GER 432–436
driving
  laws and regulations 63
  permits 62
  precautions 64
Drøbak, NOR 755
drugs 20
Dublin, IRE 555–563
Dubrovnik, CRO 236–239
Dunlewy, IRE 578
Dunquin, IRE 571
Düsseldorf, GER 447–448

E

East Anglia and the
  Midlands, BRI 174–183
Eastern Aegean Islands,
  GRE 512–515
Eceabat, TUR 1029
Echternach, LUX 703
Edale, BRI 187
Edam, NETH 735
Edinburgh, BRI 197–204
Edirne, TUR 1026
Eftalou, GRE 513
Eger, HUN 533
Eidfjord, NOR 764
Eisenach, GER 439–440
elderly travelers 37
email 35
emergency medical services
  21
Emilia-Romagna, ITA 646–
  650
England, BRI 140–191
Ennis, IRE 573
Epernay, FRA 403
Ephesus, TUR 1032
Epidavros, GRE 497
Ericeira, POR 812
El Escorial, SPA 898
Essaouira, MOR 712–713
Estonia 291–299
  Estonian Islands 299
  Hiiumaa 299
  Pärnu 298
  Saaremaa 299
  Tallinn 294–297
  Tartu 298
Estonian Islands, EST 299
Estonian kroon 293
Estoril, POR 811
Esztergom, HUN 532
Ettelbrück, LUX 701
EU 15
Eurail 53, 56–59
euro 16
Euro Domino 60
Eurolines 62
European Union (EU) 15
Évora, POR 814
exhaustion, heat 21
Extremadura, SPA 905
Les-Eyzies-de-Tayac, FRA
  364
Eze, FRA 385

F

Făgăraş Mountains, ROM
  832
Fårö, SWE 975
Federal Express 32
Ferrara, ITA 649
ferry 64
Fethiye, TUR 1035
Fez, MOR 710–712
Figueres, SPA 945
Finale Ligure, ITA 644
Finland 300–316
  Bomarsund 310
  Hanko 309
  Helsinki 304–309
  Kuopio 315
  Lahti 310
  Naantali 312
  Oulo 315
  Pori 312
  Porvoo 309
  Punkaharju 314
  Rauma 312
  Rovaniemi 316
  Savonlinna 314
  Tampere 313–314
  Turku 310–312
Finse, NOR 756
Fira, GRE 510
Fiskardo, GRE 504
Fjærland, NOR 758
The Fjords, NOR 759–767
Flakstad, NOR 770
Flåm, NOR 756
Flanders, BEL 121–127
Florence, ITA 650–659
Fontainebleau, FRA 351
Foot and Mouth Disease 23
forint, Hungarian 518
Fort William, BRI 211
France 317–406
  Aix-en-Provence 373
  Ajaccio 387
  The Alps 389–392
  Alsace-Lorraine 398–402
  Amboise 361
  Angers 362
  Annecy 392
  Antibes-Juan-les-Pins 378
  Arles 372
  Arras 405
  Avignon 371
  Bastia 388
  Bayeux 354
  Bayonne 366

Beaune 398
Berry-Limousin 397
Besançon 401
Biarritz 367
Blois 360
Bonifacio 388
Bordeaux 365
Boulogne-sur-Mer 405
Bourges 397
Burgundy 397–398
Caen 353
Calais 405
The Camargue 372
Cannes 377
Cap Corse 389
Cap d'Ail 385
Cap Fréhel 358
Carcassone 369
Castelnaud-La Chapelle
  364
Cauterets 368
Chambord 361
Chamonix 391
Champagne and the North
  402–406
Chartres 351
Cherbourg 355
Cheverny 361
Colleville-sur-Mer 355
Colmar 400
Corniches 384–385
Corsica 386–389
Corte 389
D-Day Beaches 354–355
Dijon 397
Epernay 403
Les-Eyzies-de-Tayac 364
Eze 385
Fontainebleau 351
Franche-Comté 398–402
Fréjus 377
Giverny 352
Les Grands Lacs 404
Grenoble 390
Le Havre 353
Jura 401
Languedoc-Roussillon
  368–370
Lascaux 364
Lille 404
Loire Valley 359–363
Lourdes 367
Lyon 392–396
Marseilles 374–376
Monaco 385
Monte-Carlo 385
Montignac 364

Mont-St-Michel 355
Nancy 402
Nice 379–384
Nîmes 370
Normandy 352–355
Normandy Coast 353–354
Orléans 360
Paimpol 359
Paris 323–350
Pays Basque and Gascony
  366–368
Périgord and Aquitaine
  363–366
Périgueux 363
Pointe du Hoc 355
Pont du Gard 371
Pontarlier 401
Provence 370–376
Pyrenees 368
Reims 403
Rennes 355
Riviera 376–386
Rouen 352
La Route du Vin 399–401
St-Émilion 366
St-Jean-de-Luz 367
St-Jean-de-Port 366
St-Jean-Cap-Ferrat 385
St-Malo 357
St-Raphaël 377
St-Tropez 376
Ste-Mère-Eglise 354
Stes-Maries-de-la-Mer 373
Sarlat 363
Sélestat 400
Strasbourg 398
Toulouse 369
Tours 361
Troyes 403
Utah Beach 354
Versailles 350
Villefranche-sur-Mer 384
Vimy 405
Franche-Comté, FRA 398–
  402
francs, Swiss 987
Frankfurt am Main, GER
  454–457
Franz-Josefs-Höhe, AUS
  101–102
Frascati, ITA 618
Fraueninsel, GER 475
Fredensborg, DEN 281
Frederikshavn, DEN 288
Freiburg im Breisgau, GER
  463
Fréjus, FRA 377

French Riviera, FRA 376–386
Friedrichshafen, GER 464
Friuli-Venezia Giulia, ITA 631–632
frostbite 21
Funen, DEN 284–285
Füssen, GER 479

G

Galicia, SPA 957–958
Gallipoli, TUR 1029
Galway City, IRE 574–575
Garmisch-Partenkirchen, GER 474
gasoline. See petrol
gay travelers 37
Gdańsk, POL 796–799
Gdynia, POL 799
Gefyra, GRE 496–497
Geirangerfjord, NOR 765
Gelibolu, TUR 1029
general delivery 33
Geneva, SWI 1001–1006
Genève. See Geneva
Genoa, ITA 642
Germany 407–480
  Aachen 448–449
  Bacharach 458
  Bavaria 464–480
  Bayern. See Bavaria
  Berchtesgaden 475–476
  Berlin 412–431
  Black Forest 463–464
  Bodensee 464
  Bonn 453–454
  Buchenwald 439
  Chiemsee 474–475
  Cologne 449–453
  Constance 464
  Dachau 473–474
  Dresden 432–436
  Düsseldorf 447–448
  Eisenach 439–440
  Frankfurt am Main 454–457
  Fraueninsel 475
  Freiburg im Breisgau 463
  Friedrichshafen 464
  Füssen 479
  Garmisch-Partenkirchen 474
  Hamburg 441–445
  Hanover 440–441
  Heidelberg 459–462
  Herreninsel 475

Koblenz 458–459
Köln. See Cologne
Königsschlößer 479–480
Konstanz. See Constance
Leipzig 436–438
Lindau 464
Lübeck 446
Mainz 458
Meersburg 464
Meißen 436
München. See Munich
Munich 465–473
Nuremberg 477–478
Nürnberg. See Nuremberg
Passau 476
Potsdam 431
Prien am Chiemsee 474–475
Regensburg 476–477
Rheintal. See Rhine Valley
Rhine Valley 457–458
Romantic Road 478–480
Rostock 441
Rothenburg ob der Tauber 479
Royal Castles. See Königsschlößer
Sächsische Schweiz. See Saxon Switzerland
St. Märgen 463–464
St. Peter 463–464
Saxon Switzerland 435
Schleswig 446–447
Stuttgart 462–463
Triberg 464
Trier 459
Weimar 438–439
Wittenberg 438
Würzburg 478–479
Geysir, ICE 547
Ghent, BEL 126–127
Giant's Causeway, NIRE 586
giardiasis 22
Gibraltar, BRI 917
Girona, SPA 944
Giverny, FRA 352
Glasgow, BRI 205–208
Glasriket, SWE 976
Glastonbury, BRI 173
Glenariff, NIRE 584
Glenarm, NIRE 584
Glendalough, IRE 564
Glens of Antrim, NIRE 584–585
Glyfada, GRE 504
GO25 card 14
Golden Ring, RUS 852

Gothenburg, SWE 978–979
Gotland, SWE 974–975
Granada, SPA 919–924
Les Grands Lacs, FRA 404
Grasmere, BRI 191
Graz, AUS 93–94
Greece 481–515
  Akrotiri 510
  Alonnisos 506
  Apollonas 509
  Areopolis 496
  Argostoli 504
  Athens 486–492
  Chios 513
  Corfu 503–504
  Corinth 497–498
  Crete 510–512
  The Cyclades 507–510
  Delos 507–508
  Delphi 493
  Dimitsana 495
  Dodoni 503
  Eastern Aegean Islands 512–515
  Eftalou 513
  Epidavros 497
  Fira 510
  Fiskardo 504
  Gefyra 496–497
  Glyfada 504
  Hania 511
  Ioannina 502–503
  Ionian Islands 503–505
  Ios 509–510
  Iraklion 511
  Ithaka 504–505
  Kalamata 495
  Kalambaka 502
  Kephalonia 504
  Knossos 511
  Kos 514–515
  Lesvos 513–514
  Litohoro 501
  Meteora 502
  Methoni 495
  Molyvos 513
  Monemvasia 496–497
  Mount Olympus 501–502
  Mycenae 497
  Mykonos 507
  Mystras 496
  Mytilini 513
  Nafplion 497
  Naxos 509
  Oia 510
  Olympia 494
  Omalos 512

Paroikia 508
Paros 508
Patitiri 506
Patmos 515
Patras 493–494
Pelekas 504
The Peloponnese 493–498
Petra 513
Pylos 495
Pyrgi 513
Pythagorion 513
Rhodes 514
Samaria Gorge 511–512
Sami 504
Samos 512–513
Santorini 510
Sitia 512
Skiathos 505
Skopelos 506
Sparta 496
The Sporades 505–506
Stavros 505
Stemnitsa 495
Steni Vala 506
Taygetus Mountains 496
Temple of Poseidon 493
Thessaloniki 498–501
Tinos 508
Tripoli 494–495
Varia 513
Vathy 504
Vergina 501
Votsi 506
green card 63
Grenen, DEN 289
Grenoble, FRA 390
Grindelwald, SWI 1000
Groningen, NETH 742
Gryon, SWI 1008
Guernica, SPA 954
guesthouses 26
Guimarães, POR 821
Gulf of Bothnia, SWE 981–983
Gulf of Kvarner, CRO 232
Gura Humorului, ROM 834
Győr, HUN 535

H

The Hague, NETH 738
Hallstatt, AUS 100–101
Hamburg, GER 441–445
handicapped travelers 38
Hania, GRE 511
Hanko, FIN 309

Hanover, GER 440–441
Hardangerfjord, NOR 764
Harlech, BRI 195
Harris, BRI 212
Le Havre, FRA 353
Hay-on-Wye, BRI 193
health 20–23
heatstroke 21
Heidelberg, GER 459–462
Heiligenblut, AUS 102
Helsingør, DEN 282
Helsinki, FIN 304–309
hepatitis 22, 23
Herculaneum, ITA 668
Herreninsel, GER 475
HI hostels 26
Hierapolis. See Pamukkale
Hiiumaa, EST 299
hiking equipment 30
Hillerød, DEN 281
hitchhiking 66
HIV 23
Hluboká nad Vltavou, CZR 264
Hoburgen, SWE 975
Hoge Veluwe National Park, NETH 741
Hohe Tauern National Park, AUS 101–102
Holywood, NIRE 583
home exchange 29
Hornbæk, DEN 282
Hostelling International (HI) 26
hostels 25
hotels 26
Howth, IRE 563
hryvnia, Ukrainian 1042
Humlebæk, DEN 280
Hungarian forint 518
Hungary 516–537
  Budapest 520–530
  Danube Bend 531–532
  Eger 533
  Esztergom 532
  Győr 535
  Keszthely 537
  Lake Balaton 536–537
  Őrség 535–536
  Pannonhalma 536
  Pécs 532
  Siófok 536
  Southern Transdanubia 532–535
  Szentendre 531
  Szilvásvárad 534
  Tihany 536

Visegrád 531
Hvar Island, CRO 235
hypothermia 21

I

Iaşi, ROM 833–834
Ibiza, SPA 956
Iceland 538–549
  Blue Lagoon 547
  Geysir 547
  Þingvellir National Park 548
  Reykjavík 542–547
  Westman Islands 548
Icelandic króna 540
identification 14
immunizations 20
Inisheer, IRE 575
Inishmaan, IRE 575
Inishmore, IRE 575
Inishowen Peninsula, IRE 578
The Inner Hebrides, BRI 211–212
Innsbruck, AUS 102–105
insurance 24
Interlaken, SWI 999–1000
International Driving Permit (IDP) 62
International Insurance Certificate 63
International Student Identity Card (ISIC) 14, 43
International Teacher Identity Card (ITIC) 14
International Youth Travel Card (IYTC) 43
Internet
  cafes 35
  flight planning 44
  travel resources 41
Inverness, BRI 210–211
invitations 14
Ioannina, GRE 502–503
iodine tablets 22
Ionian Islands, GRE 503–505
Ios, GRE 509–510
Iraklion, GRE 511
Ireland 550–578
  Aran Islands 575
  Blarney 568
  Boyne Valley 564
  The Burren 573–574
  Caherdaniel 571
  Cahersiveen 570

Cape Clear Island 569
Cashel 566
Clare Island 576
Clifden 575–576
Connemara 575–576
Connemara National Park 576
Cork City 566–568
County Donegal 577–578
Derryveagh Mountains 578
Dingle Peninsula 571–572
Dingle Town 571
Donegal Town 577
Doolin 573
Dublin 555–563
Dunlewy 578
Dunquin 571
Ennis 573
Galway City 574–575
Glendalough 564
Holywood 583
Howth 563
Inisheer 575
Inishmaan 575
Inishmore 575
Inishowen Peninsula 578
Iveragh Peninsula 570
Kilkenny 565
Killarney 569–570
Kilronan 575
Kinvara 574
Letterfrack 576
Letterkenny 578
Limerick 572
Lisdoonvarna 573
Malin Head 578
Mizen Head Peninsula 569
Newgrange 564
Ring of Kerry 570–571
Rossaveal 575
Rosslare Harbour 564–565
Schull 569
Slea Head 571
Slieve League 577–578
Sligo 577
Tralee 572
Trim 564
Valentia Island 570
Waterford 565–566
Westport 576
Ischia, ITA 670
ISIC card 14
Isle of Skye, BRI 211–212
İstanbul, TUR 1016–1026
Istrian Peninsula, CRO 232
Italian Riviera, ITA 642–646
Italy 587–674

Riviera di Levante 645–646
Aeolian Islands 672–673
Alghero 674
Amalfi 669
Ancona 663
Assisi 662
Atrani 669
Bay of Naples Islands 670–671
Bellaggio 633
Bergamo 641
Bologna 646–648
Bolzano 635
Borgo Verezzi 644
Borromean Islands 633
Cagliari 674
Camogli 645
Capri 670
Cinque Terre 645
Como 633
The Dolomites 634–635
Emilia-Romagna 646–650
Ferrara 649
Finale Ligure 644
Florence 650–659
Frascati 618
Friuli-Venezia Giulia 631–632
Genoa 642
Herculaneum 668
Ischia 670
Italian Riviera 642–646
La Spezia 646
Lake Como 633
The Lake Country 633–634
Lake Garda 634
Lipari 672
Lombardy 635–642
Mantua 641
The Marches 663–664
Menaggio 633
Milan 635–640
Milazzo 672
Mt. Vesuvius 668
Naples 664–667
Oristano 674
Padua 629
Paestum 670
Palermo 671
Parma 648
Perugia 662
Piedmont 632–633
Pisa 661
Pompeii 668
Ponza 617
Portofino 645

Positano 669
Ravello 669
Ravenna 648
Riva del Garda 634
Rome 592–618
Salerno 670
San Gimignano 660
Santa Margherita Ligure 645
Sardinia 673–674
Sicily 671–672
Siena 659
The Sinis Peninsula 674
Sorrento 669
Stresa 633
Stromboli 673
Trent 634
Trieste 631
Turin 632
Tuscany 650–661
Umbria 662–663
Urbino 663
The Veneto 618–631
Venice 618–629
Verona 630
Vulcano 673
Ithaka, GRE 504–505
ITIC card 14
itineraries 6
Iveragh Peninsula, IRE 570
İzmir, TUR 1030

J

Jaca, SPA 947
Jostedalsbreen, NOR 764
Jukkasjärvi, SWE 984
Jungfrau Region, SWI 998–1000
Jura, FRA 401
Jūrmala, LAT 681
Jutland, DEN 286–290

K

Kaş, TUR 1035
Kalamata, GRE 495
Kalambaka, GRE 502
Kalmar, SWE 975
Karkonosze National Park, POL 793
Karlovy Vary (Carlsbad), CZR 262
Karlštejn, CZR 260
Kärnten. See Carinthia

Karpacz, POL 793
Kaunas, LIT 692
Kaunos, TUR 1034
Kephalonia, GRE 504
Keswick, BRI 191
Keszthely, HUN 537
Kilkenny, IRE 565
Killarney, IRE 569–570
Kilronan, IRE 575
Kinvara, IRE 574
Kiruna, SWE 983
Kitzbühel, AUS 106
Klaipėda, LIT 693
Klampenborg, DEN 282
Knossos, GRE 511
Koblenz, GER 458–459
Köln. See Cologne
Kołobrzeg, POL 795
Königsschlößer, GER 479–480
Konstanz, GER. See Constance, GER
Koprivshtitsa, BUL 223
Korčula Island, CRO 236
koruna, Czech 245
koruna, Slovak 865
Kos, GRE 514–515
kosher 40
Kraków, POL 784–789
Krimml, AUS 102
Kristiansand, NOR 767–769
Krk Island, CRO 235
króna, Icelandic 540
kroner, Danish 271
kroon, Estonian 293
kuna, Croatian 229
Kuopio, FIN 315
Kutná Hora, CZR 261
Kværndrup, DEN 284
Kyiv, UKR 1044–1047
Kyle of Lochalsh, BRI 211
Kyleakin, BRI 211

L

La Spezia, ITA 646
Lagos, POR 815–816
Lahti, FIN 310
Lake Balaton, HUN 536–537
Lake Bohinj, SLN 879
Lake Como, ITA 633
The Lake Country, ITA 633–634
Lake District National Park, BRI 190–191
Lake Garda, ITA 634

Lake Mälaren, SWE 972
Languedoc-Roussillon, FRA 368–370
Lapland, SWE 983–984
Larnaka, CYP 241
Lascaux, FRA 364
lat, Latvian 676
Latvia 675–682
Jūrmala 681
Rīga 677–681
Sigulda 682
Latvian lat 676
Lausanne, SWI 1006–1007
Leiden, NETH 737
Leipzig, GER 436–438
Leiria, POR 813
Leksand, SWE 980
León, SPA 904
lesbian travelers 37
Lesvos, GRE 513–514
Letterfrack, IRE 576
Letterkenny, IRE 578
leu, Romanian 824
lev, Bulgarian 216
Lewis, BRI 212
Liechtenstein 683–684
Malbun 684
Schaan 684
Triesenberg 684
Vaduz 683–684
Lille, FRA 404
Lillehammer, NOR 755
Limerick, IRE 572
Lindau, GER 464
Lipari, ITA 672
Liptovský Mikuláš, SLK 871
Lisbon, POR 804–811
Lisdoonvarna, IRE 573
Lisse, NETH 735
litas, Lithuanian 686
Lithuania 685–694
Kaunas 692
Klaipėda 693
Nida 693, 694
Palanga 693
Trakai 692
Vilnius 688–692
Lithuanian litas 686
Litohoro, GRE 501
Livadia, UKR 1049
Liverpool, BRI 184–186
Ljubljana, SLN 876–879
Llanberis, BRI 195
Llyn Peninsula, BRI 196
Locarno, SWI 1009–1010
Loch Lomond, BRI 209
Loch Ness, BRI 210–211

Łódź, Poland 795
Lofoten Islands, NOR 770–771
Loire Valley, FRA 359–363
Lom, NOR 758
Lombardy, ITA 635–642
London, BRI 140–168
Lopud Island, CRO 239
Lourdes, FRA 367
Lübeck, GER 446
Lublin, POL 791
Lucerne, SWI 997–998
Lugano, SWI 1009
Luleå, SWE 983
Lund, SWE 976
Lustschloß Hellbrunn, AUS 100
Luxembourg 695–703
Ardennes 701–703
Clervaux 702
Diekirch 702
Echternach 703
Ettelbrück 701
Luxembourg City 697–701
Vianden 701
Luxembourg City, LUX 697–701
Luzern. See Lucerne
Lviv, UKR 1047–1048
Lyon, FRA 392–396

M

Maastricht, NETH 741
Mad Cow Disease 22
Madinat Al-Zahra, SPA 910
Madrid, SPA 886–898
Mafra, POR 812
mail 32–33
Mainz, GER 458
Malbork, POL 799
Malbun, LIE 684
Malin Head, IRE 578
Mallorca, SPA 955
Malmö, SWE 976
Manchester, BRI 183–184
Mantua, ITA 641
Marbella, SPA 919
The Marches, ITA 663–664
Marrakesh, MOR 713–715
Marseilles, FRA 374–376
Matterhorn, SWI 1000
Mechelen, BEL 121
Medic Alert 21
Meersburg, GER 464
Meißen, GER 436

INDEX

Mělník, CZR 261
Menaggio, ITA 633
Menorca, SPA 956
Meteora, GRE 502
Methoni, GRE 495
Milan, ITA 635–640
Milazzo, ITA 672
minority travelers 39
Minsk, BLR 109–110
Mir Castle, BLR 110
Mizen Head Peninsula, IRE 569
Mljet National Park, CRO 235
Moldavia, ROM 833–835
Molyvos, GRE 513
Møn, DEN 282
Monaco, FRA 385
Monemvasia, GRE 496–497
Monte-Carlo, FRA 385
Montignac, FRA 364
Montreux, SWI 1007–1008
Mont-St-Michel, FRA 355
Montserrat, SPA 943
mopeds 65
Mora, SWE 980
Moravia, CZR 265–267
Moravský Kras, CZR 267
Moreton-in-Marsh, BRI 180
Moroccan dirham 706
Morocco 704–715
  Asilah 709
  Cascades d'Ouzoud 715
  Chefchaouen 710
  Essaouira 712–713
  Fez 710–712
  Marrakesh 713–715
  Tangier 707–709
Moscow, RUS 840–853
Moskenes, NOR 770
mosquitoes 22
motorcycles 65
Mount Olympus, GRE 501–502
Mt. Pilatus, SWI 998
Mt. Vesuvius, ITA 668
München. See Munich
Munich, GER 465–473
Mycenae, GRE 497
Mykonos, GRE 507
Mystras, GRE 496
Mytilini, GRE 513

N

Naantali, FIN 312

Nafplion, GRE 497
Namur, BEL 127
Nancy, FRA 402
Naples, ITA 664–667
Navarra, SPA 947–949
Naxos, GRE 509
Nesebur, BUL 225
The Netherlands 716–743
  Aalsmeer 735
  Amsterdam 720–735
  Delft 739
  Edam 735
  Groningen 742
  The Hague 738
  Hoge Veluwe National Park 741
  Leiden 737
  Lisse 735
  Maastricht 741
  Rotterdam 739
  Texel 743
  Utrecht 740
  Wadden Islands 743
Neuchâtel, SWI 1008–1009
Newcastle-Upon-Tyne, BRI 189
Newgrange, IRE 564
Newquay, BRI 173
Nice, FRA 379–384
Nida, LIT 693, 694
Nigardsbreen, NOR 757
Nîmes, FRA 370
Nordfjord, NOR 764
Normandy Coast, FRA 353–354
Normandy, FRA 352–355
Northern Ireland 579–586
  Ballintoy 585
  Ballycastle 585
  Belfast 579–583
  Causeway Coast 585–586
  Cushendall 585
  Cushendun 585
  Derry 583–584
  Giant's Causeway 586
  Glenariff 584
  Glenarm 584
  Glens of Antrim 584–585
Norway 744–771
  Å 770
  Ålesund 765
  Aurland 756
  Balestrand 758
  Bergen 759–763
  Briksdalsbreen 764
  Drøbak 755
  Eidfjord 764

Finse 756
Fjærland 758
The Fjords 759–767
Flakstad 770
Flåm 756
Geirangerfjord 765
Hardangerfjord 764
Jostedalsbreen 764
Kristiansand 767–769
Lillehammer 755
Lofoten Islands 770–771
Lom 758
Moskenes 770
Nigardsbreen 757
Nordfjord 764
Oslo 749–755
Oslo-Bergen Rail Line 756
Sogndal 757
Sognefjord 757
Stavanger 769
Stryn 764
Tromsø 771
Trondheim 766–767
Vestvågøy 770
Voss 757
Nuremberg, GER 477–478
Nürnberg. See Nuremberg
Nusnäs, SWE 980
Nynäshamn, SWE 974

O

O Castro de Baroña, SPA 958
Odense, DEN 284
Odessa, UKR 1048
Oia, GRE 510
Öland, SWE 976
Olimpos, TUR 1036
Ölüdeniz, TUR 1035
Olympia, GRE 494
Omalos, GRE 512
Oristano, ITA 674
Orléans, FRA 360
Örnsköldsvik, SWE 981
Őrség, HUN 535–536
Oskarshamn, SWE 974
Oslo, NOR 749–755
Oslo-Bergen Rail Line, NOR 756
Östersund, SWE 981
Oulo, FIN 315
The Outer Hebrides, BRI 212–213
Oxford, BRI 175–178

P

packing 24–25
  backpacks 31
Padua, ITA 629
Paestum, ITA 670
Paimpol, FRA 359
Palanga, LIT 693
Palermo, ITA 671
Pamplona, SPA 947
Pamukkale, TUR 1032
Pannonhalma, HUN 536
Paphos, CYP 242
Paris, FRA 323–350
Parma, ITA 648
Pärnu, EST 298
Paroikia, GRE 508
Paros, GRE 508
Parque Nacional de Ordesa, SPA 946
Passau, GER 476
passports 12–13
Patitiri, GRE 506
Patmos, GRE 515
Patras, GRE 493–494
Pays Basque and Gascony, FRA 366–368
Peak District National Park, BRI 186–187
Pécs, HUN 532
Pelekas, GRE 504
The Peloponnese, GRE 493–498
pensions 26
Penzance, BRI 174
Pergamon, TUR 1030
Périgord and Aquitaine, FRA 363–366
Périgueux, FRA 363
Perugia, ITA 662
Peterhof, RUS 862
Petra, GRE 513
petrol 63
phones. See telephones.
pickpockets 19
Picos de Europa, SPA 959
Piedmont, ITA 632–633
Þingvellir National Park, ICE 548
Pisa, ITA 661
Platres, CYP 242
Plitvice Lakes National Park, CRO 232
Plovdiv, BUL 223
Plzeň, CZR 263
Pointe du Hoc, FRA 355

Poland 772–800
Auschwitz-Birkenau 789
Częstochowa 784
Gdańsk 796–799
Gdynia 799
Karkonosze National Park 793
Karpacz 793
Kołobrzeg 795
Kraków 784–789
Łódź, Poland 795
Lublin 791
Malbork 799
Poznań 793
Sopot 799
Toruń 794
Tri-City Area 796–800
Warsaw 776–784
Wieliczka 790
Wrocław 792
Zakopane 791
Żelazowa Wola 784
Polish złoty 774
Pompeii, ITA 668
Pont du Gard, FRA 371
Pontarlier, FRA 401
Ponza, ITA 617
Pori, FIN 312
Porthmadog, BRI 196
Porto, POR 819–820
Portofino, ITA 645
Portree, BRI 212
Portsmouth, BRI 170
Portugal 801–821
Algarve 815–817
Batalha 813
Braga 820
Cascais 811
Coimbra 817–819
Ericeira 812
Estoril 811
Évora 814
Guimarães 821
Lagos 815–816
Leiria 813
Lisbon 804–811
Mafra 812
Porto 819–820
Praia da Rocha 817
Sagres 816
Sintra 812
Tavira 817
Tomar 813
Viana do Castelo 821
Porvoo, FIN 309
Positano, ITA 669
post. See mail

Poste Restante 33
Potsdam, GER 431
pound, British 553
pound, Cyprus 240
Poznań, POL 793
Prado, SPA 896
Prague, CZR 247–260
Praia da Rocha, POR 817
Prien am Chiemsee, GER 474–475
Provence, FRA 370–376
Pula, CRO 232
Punkaharju, FIN 314
Pylos, GRE 495
Pyrenees, FRA 368
Pyrenees, SPA 946–947
Pyrgi, GRE 513
Pythagorion, GRE 513

R

Rab Island, CRO 233
rail 53–61
  discounted tickets 61
railpasses
  Eurail 56–59
  Euro Domino 60
  national 60
  regional 59
Rauma, FIN 312
Ravello, ITA 669
Ravenna, ITA 648
Red Cross 21
Regensburg, GER 476–477
Reims, FRA 403
Rennes, FRA 355
rental cars 62
Reykjavík, ICE 542–547
Rheintal. See Rhine Valley
Rhine Valley, GER 457–458
Rhodes, GRE 514
Ribe, DEN 289
ride-sharing 67
Rīga, LAT 677–681
Rigi Kulm, SWI 998
Rila, BUL 222
Ring of Kerry, IRE 570–571
Riva del Garda, ITA 634
Riviera di Levante, ITA 645–646
Romania 822–835
Black Sea Coast 833
Brașov 831
Bran 832
Bucharest 826–829
Bukovina 833–835

Bukovina Monasteries 834–835
Cluj-Napoca 830
Constanţa 833
Danube Delta 833
Făgăraş Mountains 832
Gura Humorului 834
Iaşi 833–834
Moldavia 833–835
Sfântu Gheorghe 833
Sibiu 832
Sighişoara 831
Sinaia 830
Timişoara 832
Transylvania 830–832
Romanian leu 824
Romantic Road, GER 478–480
Rome, ITA 592–618
Ronda, SPA 917
Rønne, DEN 283
Roskilde, DEN 281
Rossaveal, IRE 575
Rosslare Harbour, IRE 564–565
Rostock, GER 441
Rothenburg ob der Tauber, GER 479
Rotterdam, NETH 739
Rouen, FRA 352
La Route du Vin, FRA 399–401
Rovaniemi, FIN 316
Royal Castles. See Königsschlößer
ruble, Belarussian 107
ruble, Russian 838
Rungsted, DEN 280
Russia 836–862
Golden Ring 852
Moscow 840–853
Peterhof 862
St. Petersburg 853–861
Sergiev Posad 853
Suzdal 852
Tsarskoye Selo 862
Vladimir 852
Yaroslavl 852
Russian ruble 838
RVs 31

S

Saaremaa, EST 299
Sächsische Schweiz. See Saxon Switzerland

safety 18–20
Sagres, POR 816
St. Andrews, BRI 204
St. David's, BRI 194
St-Émilion, FRA 366
St. Gallen, SWI 996–997
St. Ives, BRI 174
St-Jean-de-Luz, FRA 367
St-Jean-de-Port, FRA 366
St-Jean-Cap-Ferrat, FRA 385
St-Malo, FRA 357
St. Märgen, GER 463–464
St. Peter, GER 463–464
St. Petersburg, RUS 853–861
St-Raphaël, FRA 377
St-Tropez, FRA 376
Ste-Mère-Eglise, FRA 354
Stes-Maries-de-la-Mer, FRA 373
Salamanca, SPA 902
Salerno, ITA 670
Salisbury, BRI 171–172
Salzburg, AUS 95–100
Salzburger Land, AUS 94–102
Samaria Gorge, GRE 511–512
Sami, GRE 504
Samos, GRE 512–513
San Gimignano, ITA 660
San Sebastián, SPA 950–953
Sandvig, DEN 283
Santa Margherita Ligure, ITA 645
Santiago de Compostela, SPA 957–958
Santorini, GRE 510
Sarajevo, BOS 131–134
Sardinia, ITA 673–674
Sarlat, FRA 363
Sart, TUR 1031
Savonlinna, FIN 314
Saxon Switzerland, GER 435
Schaan, LIE 684
Schengen zone 13
Schleswig, GER 446–447
Schloß Ambras, AUS 105–106
Schull, IRE 569
Scotland, BRI 196–213
Selçuk, TUR 1031
Sélestat, FRA 400
senior citizen travelers 37
Sergiev Posad, RUS 853
Sevastopol, UKR 1049

Seville, SPA 910–916
sexually transmitted diseases 23
Sfântu Gheorghe, ROM 833
Sibiu, ROM 832
Sicily, ITA 671–672
Siena, ITA 659
Sierra Nevada, SPA 924
Sighişoara, ROM 831
Sigulda, LAT 682
Simferopol, UKR 1049
Sinaia, ROM 830
The Sinis Peninsula, ITA 674
Sintra, POR 812
Siófok, HUN 536
Sitges, SPA 943
Sitia, GRE 512
Skagen, DEN 289
Skärgård, SWE 973
Skiathos, GRE 505
Škocjanske Caves, SLN 879
Skopelos, GRE 506
Slea Head, IRE 571
Slieve League, IRE 577–578
Sligachan, BRI 212
Sligo, IRE 577
Slovak koruna 865
Slovak Republic 863–872
Bratislava 867–870
Liptovský Mikuláš 871
Slovenský Raj 872
Starý Smokovec 871
Štrbské Pleso 871
Tatra Mountains 871–872
Slovenia 873–880
Bled 879
Lake Bohinj 879
Ljubljana 876–879
Škocjanske Caves 879
Slovenian tolar 875
Slovenský Raj, SLK 872
Smyrna. See Izmir 1030
Snowdonia National Park, BRI 194–195
Sofia, BUL 218–222
Sogndal, NOR 757
Sognefjord, NOR 757
Sopot, POL 799
Sorrento, ITA 669
Southern Transdanubia, HUN 532–535
Sozopol, BUL 226
Spain 881–959
Algeciras 918
Andalucía 905–924
Arcos de la Frontera 917
Astorga 904

Asturias 958
Balearic Islands 955–957
Barcelona 927–943
Basque Country 950–954
Bilbao 953
Cadaqués 945
Cádiz 916
Castilla la Mancha 899–901
Castilla y León 902–905
Cataluña 927–946
Córdoba 906–910
Costa Blanca 927
Costa Brava 945–946
Costa del Sol 919
Cuenca 901
El Escorial 898
Extremadura 905
Figueres 945
Galicia 957–958
Gibraltar 917
Girona 944
Granada 919–924
Guernica 954
Ibiza 956
Jaca 947
León 904
Madinat Al-Zahra 910
Madrid 886–898
Mallorca 955
Marbella 919
Menorca 956
Montserrat 943
Navarra 947–949
O Castro de Baroña 958
Pamplona 947
Parque Nacional de Ordesa 946
Picos de Europa 959
Pyrenees 946–947
Ronda 917
Salamanca 902
San Sebastián 950–953
Santiago de Compostela 957–958
Seville 910–916
Sierra Nevada 924
Sitges 943
Toledo 899–901
Tossa de Mar 945
Trujillo 905
Val d'Aran 946
Valencia 925–927
Valle de los Caídos 899
Vielha 946
Zamora 903
Sparta, GRE 496

specific concerns
bisexual, gay, and lesbian travelers 37
children and travel 39
dietary concerns 40
disabled travelers 38
minority travelers 39
senior citizen travelers 37
women travelers 35
Split, CRO 234
The Sporades, GRE 505–506
STA Travel 43
standby flights 50
Starý Smokovec, SLK 871
Stavanger, NOR 769
Stavros, GRE 505
STDs 23
Stemnitsa, GRE 495
Steni Vala, GRE 506
Stirling, BRI 208–209
Stockholm, SWE 964–972
Stonehenge, BRI 172
Stow-on-the-Wold, BRI 180
Strasbourg, FRA 398
Stratford-Upon-Avon, BRI 178–179
Štrbské Pleso, SLK 871
Stresa, ITA 633
Stromboli, ITA 673
Stryn, NOR 764
study abroad 68–70
Stuttgart, GER 462–463
suggested itineraries 6
Suzdal, RUS 852
Svendborg, DEN 285
Sweden 960–984
Abisko 984
Björkö 972
Dalarna 980–981
Fårö 975
Glasriket 976
Gothenburg 978–979
Gotland 974–975
Gulf of Bothnia 981–983
Hoburgen 975
Jukkasjärvi 984
Kalmar 975
Kiruna 983
Lake Mälaren 972
Lapland 983–984
Leksand 980
Luleå 983
Lund 976
Malmö 976
Mora 980
Nusnäs 980
Nynäshamn 974

Öland 976
Örnsköldsvik 981
Oskarshamn 974
Östersund 981
Skärgård 973
Stockholm 964–972
Umeå 982
Uppsala 973
Varberg 979
Visby 974
Ystad 977
Swiss francs 987
Switzerland 985–1009
Bâle. See Basel
Basel 991–992
Bern 989–991
Geneva 1001–1006
Genève. See Geneva
Grindelwald 1000
Gryon 1008
Interlaken 999–1000
Jungfrau Region 998–1000
Lausanne 1006–1007
Locarno 1009–1010
Lucerne 997–998
Lugano 1009
Luzern. See Lucerne
Matterhorn 1000
Montreux 1007–1008
Mt. Pilatus 998
Neuchâtel 1008–1009
Rigi Kulm 998
St. Gallen 996–997
Valais 1000–1001
Zermatt 1000–1001
Zurich 992–996
Szentendre, HUN 531
Szilvásvárad, HUN 534

T

Tallinn, EST 294–297
Tampere, FIN 313–314
Tangier, MOR 707–709
Tartu, EST 298
Tåsinge, DEN 285
Tatra Mountains, SLK 871–872
Tavira, POR 817
taxes 15
Taygetus Mountains, GRE 496
teaching English 71
Telč, CZR 266
telephones 33
phone cards 34

Temple of Poseidon, GRE 493
Terezín (Theresienstadt), CZR 260
Texel, NETH 743
theft 19
Thessaloniki, GRE 498–501
Thomas Cook 16
ticks 22
Tihany, HUN 536
Timişoara, ROM 832
Tinos, GRE 508
Tintern, BRI 193
Tirol. See Tyrol
tolar, Slovenian 875
Toledo, SPA 899–901
Tomar, POR 813
Toruń, POL 794
Tossa de Mar, SPA 945
Toulouse, FRA 369
Tours, FRA 361
train. See rail
Trakai, LIT 692
Tralee, IRE 572
transportation 43–67
    airplanes 43–53
    bicycles 65
    bus 61
    cars 62
    ferry 64
    mopeds 65
    rail 53
Transylvania, ROM 830–832
travel advisories 19
travel agencies 43
traveler's checks 16
Trent, ITA 634
Triberg, GER 464
Tri-City Area, POL 796–800
Trier, GER 459
Triesenberg, LIE 684
Trieste, ITA 631
Trim, IRE 564
Tripoli, GRE 494–495
Trogir Island, CRO 234
Tromsø, NOR 771
Trondheim, NOR 766–767
Troodos, CYP 242
The Trossachs, BRI 209–210
Troy, TUR 1029
Troyes, FRA 403
Trujillo, SPA 905
Tsarskoye Selo, RUS 862
Turin, ITA 632
Turkey 1011–1039
    Aegean Coast 1028–1034
    Ankara 1037–1038

Antalya 1036
Aphrodisias 1033
Bergama 1030
Bodrum 1033
Bursa 1027
Çanakkale 1029
Cappadocia 1038–1039
Çavuşin 1039
Çeşme 1031
Dalyan 1034
Eceabat 1029
Edirne 1026
Ephesus 1032
Fethiye 1035
Gallipoli 1029
Gelibolu 1029
İstanbul 1016–1026
İzmir 1030
Kaş 1035
Kaunos 1034
Mediterranean Coast 1034–1036
Olimpos 1036
Ölüdeniz 1035
Pamukkale 1032
Pergamon 1030
Sart 1031
Selçuk 1031
Troy 1029
Turku, FIN 310–312
Tuscany, ITA 650–661
Tyrol, AUS 102–106

U

Ukraine 1040–1050
    Bakhchisarai 1049
    Crimea 1049
    Kyiv 1044–1047
    Livadia 1049
    Lviv 1047–1048
    Odessa 1048
    Sevastopol 1049
    Simferopol 1049
    Yalta 1049
Ukrainian hryvnia 1042
Umbria, ITA 662–663
Umeå, SWE 982
Untersberg Peak, AUS 100
Uppsala, SWE 973
Urbino, ITA 663
US State Department
    money transfer 17
    travel advisories 19
usit world 44
Utah Beach, FRA 354

Utrecht, NETH 740

V

vaccinations 20
Vaduz, LIE 683–684
Val d'Aran, SPA 946
Valais, SWI 1000–1001
Valencia, SPA 925–927
Valentia Island, IRE 570
Valle de los Caídos, SPA 899
valuables, protecting 19
value-added tax (VAT) 15
Varberg, SWE 979
Varia, GRE 513
Varna, BUL 224
Vathy, GRE 504
vegetarians and vegans 40
Veliko Tarnovo, BUL 224
Venice, ITA 618–629
Vergina, GRE 501
Verona, ITA 630
Versailles, FRA 350
Vestvågøy, NOR 770
Viana do Castelo, POR 821
Vianden, LUX 701
Vielha, SPA 946
Vienna, AUS 80–93
Villefranche-sur-Mer, FRA 384
Vilnius, LIT 688–692
Vimy, FRA 405
Vis Island, CRO 235
visas 13
    invitations 14
Visby, SWE 974
Visegrád, HUN 531
Vladimir, RUS 852
volunteering 72–73
Voss, NOR 757
Votsi, GRE 506
Vulcano, ITA 673

W

Wadden Islands, NETH 743
Wales, BRI 191–196
Wallonie, BEL 127–128
Warsaw, POL 776–784
Wasteels 44
water purification 22
Waterford, IRE 565–566
Waterloo, BEL 120
Weimar, GER 438–439
Western Union 17

Westman Islands, ICE 548
Westport, IRE 576
Wieliczka, POL 790
Wien, AUS 80
Winchester, BRI 170–171
Winchombe, BRI 180
Windermere, BRI 190
Wittenberg, GER 438
women travelers 35
women's health 23
working. See alternatives to
 tourism.
Wrocław, POL 792
Würzburg, GER 478–479
Wye Valley, BRI 192–193

Y

Yalta, UKR 1049
Yaroslavl, RUS 852
YMCAs 26
York, BRI 187
Ystad, SWE 977

Z

Zagreb, CRO 231–232
Zakopane, POL 791
Zamora, SPA 903
Żelazowa Wola, POL 784
Zermatt, SWI 1000–1001
złoty, Polish 774
Zurich, SWI 992–996

Book your air, hotel, and transportation all in one place.

Hotel or hostel? Cruise or canoe? Car? Plane? Camel?
Wherever you're going, visit Yahoo! Travel and get total control
over your arrangements. Even choose your seat assignment.
So. One hump or two? travel.yahoo.com

MAP INDEX

Amsterdam 724
Athens 487
Austria 76
Barcelona 930-931
Belfast 581
Belgium 112
Bergen 761
Berlin Overview 414-415
Berlin: East Center 419
Berlin: West Center 417
Bloomsbury 146
Bosnia and Herzegovina 130
Bratislava 868
Britain 136
Bruges 122
Brussels 116
Bucharest 828
Budapest 522
Bulgaria 215
Cambridge 182
Cologne 450
Copenhagen 274
Cordoba 907
Croatia 228
Cyprus 241
Czech Republic 244
Denmark 269
Dresden Neustadt 433
Dublin Center 559
Dubrovnik 237
Edinburgh 198
Estonia 291
Europe xiv-xv
Finland 301
Florence 652
France 319
Frankfurt 455
Geneva 1003

Germany 408
Glasgow 206
Granada 922
Greece 482
Hamburg 442
Heidelberg 460
Helsinki 305
Hungary 517
Iceland 539
Innsbruck 103
Ireland 551
Istanbul Overview 1018
Istanbul: Sultanahmet 1020
Italy 589
Krakow 787
Latvia 675
Liechtenstein 683
Lisbon 807
Lithuania 687
Ljubljana 877
London Center 142-143
Luxembourg 696
Luxembourg City 699
Lyon 393
Madrid Center 890-891
Milan 637
Morocco 705
Moscow Center 843
Munich 466
Naples Center 665
The Netherlands 717
Nice 380
Norway 745
Oslo 751
Oxford 176
Paris Center 326-327
Paris Nightlife 348-349
Poland 773

Portugal 802
Prague Center 248
Rail Planner 54-55
Reykjavik 543
Riga 680
Romania 823
Rome: Centro Storico &
   Trastevere 596-597
Rome: Termini &
   San Lorenzo 594
Russia 837
Salzburg 96
Sarajevo 132
Sevilla 912
Slovak Republic 864
Slovenia 874
Sofia 219
Spain 881
St. Petersburg 856-857
Stockholm 966
Sweden 961
Switzerland 986
Tallinn 295
Tangier 708
Thessaloniki 499
Toledo 900
Turkey 1013
Ukraine 1041
Venice Center 622
Venice Overview 620
Vienna Center 83
Vienna Overview 81
Vilnius 689
Warsaw 779
York 188
Zurich 994

MAP LEGEND

⊞ Hospital	✈ Airport	🏛 Museum
⊠ Police	🚌 Bus Station	♠ Hotel/Hostel
✉ Post Office	🚂 Train Station	⛺ Camping
ⓘ Tourist Office	Ⓜ METRO STATION	Food & Drink
$ Bank	⚓ Ferry Landing	Shopping
⚑ Embassy/Consulate	✝ Church	★ Entertainment
■ Site or Point of Interest	✡ Synagogue	Nightlife
☎ Telephone Office	Mosque	Cafe
Theater	Castle	Internet Café
Library	▲ Mountain	Pedestrian Zone

The Let's Go compass always points **NORTH**.